American Casebook Series

Hornbook Series and Basic Legal Texts

Nutshell Series

of

WEST PUBLISHING COMPANY

St. Paul, Minnesota 55102

ACCOUNTING

Fiflis and Kripke's Cases on Accounting for Business Lawyers, 687 pages, 1971.

ADMINISTRATIVE LAW

Davis' Basic Text on Administrative Law 3rd Ed., 617 pages, 1972.

Davis' Cases, Text and Problems on Administrative Law, 5th Ed., 650 pages, 1973.

Davis' Police Discretion, about 120 pages, 1975.

Gellhorn's Administrative Law in a Nutshell, 336 pages, 1972.

Mashaw and Merrill's Cases and Materials on Introduction to the American Public Law System, about 1080 pages, 1975.

Robinson and Gellhorn's Teaching Materials on The Administrative Process, 928 pages, 1974.

ADMIRALTY

Healy and Sharpe's Cases on Admiralty, 2nd Ed., 875 pages, 1974.

AGENCY

Seavey and Hall's Cases on Agency, 431 pages, 1956.

Seavey's Text on Agency, 329 pages, 1964.

See Agency-Partnership.

AGENCY–PARTNERSHIP

Henn's Cases on Agency, Partnership and Other Unincorporated Business Enterprises, 396 pages, 1972.

Seavey, Reuschlein & Hall's Cases on Agency and Partnership, 599 pages, 1962.

Steffen's Cases on Agency and Partnership, 3rd Ed., 733 pages, 1969.

ANTITRUST LAW

Oppenheim's Cases on Robinson-Patman Act, Pamphlet, 295 pages, 1967.

Oppenheim and Weston's Cases on Antitrust, 3rd Ed., 952 pages, 1968.

Oppenheim and Weston's Supplement, 1972.

Posner's Cases on Antitrust, 885 pages, 1974.

BANKRUPTCY

MacLachlan's Text on Bankruptcy, 500 pages, 1956.

Selected Bankruptcy Statutes, 486 pages, 1974.

Selected Commercial Statutes, 1016 pages, 1973.

See Creditors' Rights.

BUSINESS ORGANIZATIONS

See Agency-Partnership.

See Corporations.

BUSINESS PLANNING

Painter's Problems and Materials in Business Planning, about 890 pages, 1975.

Painter's Problems and Materials in Business Planning, 1975 Supplement.

CIVIL PROCEDURE

See Pleading and Procedure.

CLINICAL TEACHING

Cooper and Rabb's Fair Employment Litigation—Text and Materials for Student and Practitioner, about 550 pages, 1975.

Freeman and Weihofen's Cases on Clinical Law Training—Interviewing and Counseling, 506 pages, 1972.

See Office Practice.

COMMERCIAL PAPER

See Commercial Transactions.

See Negotiable Instruments.

LAW SCHOOL PUBLICATIONS — Continued

COMMERCIAL TRANSACTIONS

Murray's Problems and Materials on Commercial Law, about 400 pages, 1975.

Speidel, Summers and White's Teaching Materials on Commercial and Consumer Law, 2nd Ed., 1475 pages, 1974.

Stone's Uniform Commercial Code in a Nutshell, 507 pages, 1975.

White and Summers Text on the Uniform Commercial Code, 1054 pages, 1972.

Selected Commercial Statutes, 1016 pages, 1973.

See Negotiable Instruments.

See Sales.

COMMON LAW PLEADING

Koffler and Reppy's Text on Common Law Pleading, 663 pages, 1969.

McBaine's Cases, Introduction to Civil Procedure, 399 pages, 1950.

Shipman's Text on Common Law Pleading, 3rd Ed., 644 pages, 1923.

COMMUNITY PROPERTY

Burby's Cases on Community Property, 4th Ed., 342 pages, 1955.

Huie's Texas Cases on Marital Property Rights, 681 pages, 1966.

Verrall and Sammis' Cases on California Community Property, 2nd Ed., 398 pages, 1971.

CONFLICT OF LAWS

Cramton, Currie and Kay's Cases—Comments—Questions on Conflicts, 2nd Ed., about 940 pages, 1975.

Ehrenzweig's Text on Conflicts, 824 pages, 1962.

Ehrenzweig's Conflicts in a Nutshell, 3rd Ed., 432 pages, 1973.

Ehrenzweig and Louisell's Jurisdiction in a Nutshell, 3rd Ed., 291 pages, 1973.

Goodriche and Scoles' Text on Conflict of Laws, 4th Ed., 483 pages, 1964.

Scoles and Weintraub's Cases on Conflict of Laws, 2nd Ed., 966 pages, 1972.

CONSTITUTIONAL LAW

Engdahl's Constitutional Power in a Nutshell, 411 pages, 1974.

Ginsburg's Cases on Constitutional Aspects of Sex Based Discrimination, 129 pages, 1974.

Lockhart, Kamisar and Choper's Cases — Comments — Questions on Constitutional Law, 4th Ed., about 1500 pages, 1975.

Lockhart, Kamisar and Choper's Cases on The American Constitution, 4th Ed., about 1100 pages, 1975.

CONSTITUTIONAL LAW—Continued

Lockhart, Kamisar and Choper's Annual Supplement.

See Constitutional Rights and Liberties.

CONSTITUTIONAL RIGHTS & LIBERTIES

Lockhart, Kamisar and Choper's Cases on Constitutional Rights and Liberties, 4th Ed., about 1100 pages, 1975.

Lockhart, Kamisar and Choper's Annual Supplement.

CONSUMER CREDIT

Kripke's Cases on Consumer Credit, 454 pages, 1970.

Schrag's Cases on Consumer Credit, 2nd Ed., Pamphlet reprint from Cooper, et al. Law and Poverty, 2nd Ed., 197 pages, 1973.

CONTRACTS

Calamari & Perillo's Text on Contracts, 621 pages, 1970.

Corbin's Cases on Contracts, 3rd Ed., 1381 pages, 1947. 1953 Supplement, 36 pages.

Corbin's Text on Contracts, Student Edition, 1224 pages, 1952.

Freedman's Cases on Contracts, 658 pages, 1973.

Fuller and Eisenberg's Cases on Contracts, 1043 pages, 1972.

Jackson's Cases on Contract Law in a Modern Society, 1404 pages, 1973.

Reitz' Cases and Materials on Contracts as Basic Commercial Law, about 665 pages, 1975.

Schaber and Rohwer's Contracts in a Nutshell, about 300 pages, 1975.

Selected Commercial Statutes, 1016 pages, 1973.

Simpson's Cases on Contracts, 592 pages, 1956.

Simpson's Text on Contracts, 2nd Ed., 510 pages, 1965.

White and Summer's Text on the Uniform Commercial Code, 1054 pages, 1972.

COPYRIGHT

Nimmer's Cases on Copyright and Other Aspects of Law Pertaining to Literary, Musical and Artistic Works, 828 pages, 1971.

Nimmer's 1974 Supplement.

CORPORATIONS

Henn's Text on Corporations, 2nd Ed., 956 pages, 1970.

Henn's Cases on Corporations and Other Business Enterprises, 1279 pages, 1974.

Henn's Statutory Supplement to Cases on Corporations, 1974.

CORRECTIONS

Krantz' Cases on the Law of Corrections and Prisoners' Rights, 1130 pages, 1973.

Krantz' 1974 Supplement.

Model Rules and Regulations on Prisoners Rights and Responsibilities, 212 pages, 1973.

CREDIT TRANSACTIONS

See Mortgages.

CREDITORS' RIGHTS

Epstein's Teaching Materials on Debtor-Creditor Relations, 525 pages, 1973.

Epstein's Debtor-Creditor Relations in a Nutshell, 309 pages, 1973.

Riesenfeld's Cases and Materials on Creditors' Remedies and Debtors' Protection, 2nd Ed., about 760 pages, 1975.

Riesenfeld's Statutory Supplement, 1975.

Selected Bankruptcy Statutes, 486 pages, 1974.

CRIMINAL LAW

Dix and Sharlot's Cases on Criminal Law, 1360 pages, 1973.

Heyman and Kenety's A Homicide in the Family, 340 pages, 1975.

Johnson's Cases, Materials and Text on the Substantive Criminal Law in its Procedural Context, 878 pages, 1975.

LaFave and Scott's Text on Criminal Law, 763 pages, 1972.

Loewy's Criminal Law in a Nutshell, 282 pages, 1975.

Miller's Text on Criminal Law, 649 pages, 1934.

Stumberg's Texas Cases on Criminal Law, 505 pages, 1954.

Stumberg and Maloney's Texas Cases Supplement, 117 pages, 1965.

CRIMINAL PROCEDURE

Davis' Police Discretion, about 120 pages, 1975.

Federal Rules of Civil-Appellate-Criminal Procedure, Law School Edition, 346 pages, 1975.

Grano's Problems in Criminal Procedure, 171 pages, 1973.

Kamisar, LaFave and Israel's Cases on Modern Criminal Procedure, 4th Ed., 1572 pages, 1974.

Kamisar, LaFave and Israel's Cases on Basic Criminal Procedure, 4th Ed., 767 pages, 1974.

CRIMINAL PROCEDURE—Continued

Kamisar, LaFave, and Israel's Annual Criminal Procedure Supplement.

Israel's and LaFave's Criminal Procedure in a Nutshell, 2nd Ed., about 425 pages, 1975.

Uviller's Cases on The Processes of Criminal Justice-Adjudication, 991 pages, 1975.

Uviller's Cases on The Processes of Criminal Justice-Investigation, 744 pages, 1974.

Vorenberg's Cases and Materials on Criminal Law and Procedure, about 1,010 pages, 1975.

DAMAGES

Crane's Cases on Damages, 3rd Ed., 337 pages, 1955.

McCormick's Text on Damages, 811 pages, 1935.

See Remedies.

DECEDENTS ESTATES

See Wills, Intestate Succession, Trusts, Gifts and Future Interests.

DICTIONARIES

Black's, one volume.

Bouvier's, two volumes.

DOMESTIC RELATIONS

Clark's Cases on Domestic Relations, 2nd Ed., 918 pages, 1974.

Clark's Text on Domestic Relations, 754 pages, 1968.

Kay's Cases on Sex Based Discrimination in Family Law, 305 pages, 1974.

Paulsen's Cases on Family Law and Poverty, 2nd Ed., Pamphlet reprint from Cooper, et al. Law and Poverty, 2nd Ed., 200 pages, 1973.

See Juvenile Courts.

DRUG ABUSE

Uelman and Haddox Cases on Drug Abuse Law, 564 pages, 1974.

EDUCATION LAW

Morris' Cases on the Constitution and American Education, 833 pages, 1974.

ENVIRONMENTAL LAW

Currie's Cases and Materials on Pollution, about 640 pages, 1975.

Hanks, Tarlock and Hanks Cases on Environmental Law and Policy, 1242 pages, 1974.

EQUITY

Cook's Cases on Equity, 4th Ed., 1192 pp., 1948.

Dobbyn's Injunctions in a Nutshell, 264 pages, 1974.

McClintock's Text on Equity, 2nd Ed., 643 pages, 1948.

Van Hecke, Leavell and Nelson's Cases on Equitable Remedies and Restitution, 2nd Ed., 717 pages, 1973.

See Remedies.

ESTATE PLANNING

Lynn's Text on Introduction to Estate Planning, 274 pages, 1975.

EVIDENCE

Broun and Meisenholder's Problems in Evidence, 130 pages, 1973.

Cleary and Strong's Cases on Evidence, 2nd Ed., about 1065 pages, 1975.

McCormick, Elliott & Sutton's Cases on Evidence, 4th Ed., 1088 pages, 1971.

McCormick, Cleary, et al., Text on Evidence, 2nd Ed., 938 pages, 1972.

Rothstein's Evidence in a Nutshell, 406 pages, 1970.

FEDERAL ESTATE AND GIFT TAXATION

See Taxation.

FEDERAL INCOME TAXATION

See Taxation.

FEDERAL JURISDICTION AND PROCEDURE

Currie's Cases on Federal Courts, 2nd, 1040 pages, 1975.

Ehrenzweig and Louisell's Jurisdiction in a Nutshell, 3rd Ed., 291 pages, 1973.

Forrester, Currier and Moye's Cases on Federal Jurisdiction and Procedure, 2nd Ed., 933 pages, 1970.

Forrester, Currier and Moye's Supplement, 1973.

Merrill and Vetri's Problems in Federal Courts and Procedure, 460 pages, 1974.

Wright's Text on Federal Courts, 2nd Ed., 745 pages, 1970.

Wright's Supplement, 1972.

FUTURE INTERESTS

Gulliver's Cases on Future Interests, 624 pages, 1959.

Gulliver's Introduction to the Law of Future Interests, Pamphlet reprint from Gulliver's Cases, 87 pages, 1959.

Powell's Cases on Future Interests, 3rd Ed., 621 pages, 1961.

Simes' Text on Future Interests, 2nd Ed., 355 pages, 1966.

See Wills, Intestate Succession, Trusts, Gifts and Future Interests.

GRATUITOUS TRANSFERS

See Wills, Intestate Succession, Trusts, Gifts and Future Interests.

HOUSING AND URBAN DEVELOPMENT

Berger's Cases on Housing, 2nd Ed., Pamphlet reprint from Cooper, et al. Law and Poverty, 2nd Ed., 254 pages, 1973.

Krasnowiecki's Cases on Housing and Urban Development, 697 pages, 1969.

Krasnowiecki's Statutory Supplement 1969.

See Land Use.

INSURANCE

Keeton's Cases on Basic Insurance Law, 655 pages, 1960.

Keeton's Basic Text on Insurance Law, 712 pages, 1971.

Keeton's Case Supplement to Keeton's Basic Text, 398 pages, 1971.

Keeton's Programmed Problems in Insurance Law, 243 pages, 1972.

Keeton & Keeton's Compensation Systems, Pamphlet reprint from Keeton & Keeton's Cases on Torts, 85 pages, 1971.

Vance's Text on Insurance, 3rd Ed., 1290 pages, 1951.

INTERNATIONAL LAW

Friedmann, Lissitzyn and Pugh's Cases on International Law, 1,205 pages, 1969.

Friedmann, Lissitzyn and Pugh's Supplement, 1972.

INTRODUCTION TO LAW

Fryer and Orentlicher's Cases on Legal Method and Legal System, 1,043 pages, 1967.

Kempin's Historical Introduction to Anglo-American Law in a Nutshell, 2nd Ed., 280 pages, 1973.

Kimball's Historical Introduction to Legal System, 610 pages, 1966.

Kinyon's Introduction to Law Study and Law Examinations in a Nutshell, 389 pages, 1971.

Mashaw and Merrill's Cases and Materials on Introduction to the American Public Law System, about 1,060 pages, 1975.

Rombauer's Legal Problem Solving, 2nd Ed., 212 pages, 1973.

Smith's Cases on Development of Legal Institutions, 757 pages, 1965.

See Legal Method.

JUDICIAL ADMINISTRATION

Nelson's Cases on Judicial Administration and the Administration of Justice 1032 pages, 1974.

JURISPRUDENCE

Christie's Text and Readings on Jurisprudence—The Philosophy of Law, 1056 pages, 1973.

JUVENILE JUSTICE

Fox's Cases on Modern Juvenile Justice, 1012 pages, 1972.

Fox's The Law of Juvenile Courts in a Nutshell, 286 pages, 1971.

LABOR LAW

Oberer and Hanslowe's Cases on Labor Law, 1091 pages, 1972.

Oberer and Hanslowe's Statutory Supplement, 1972.

Oberer and Hanslowe's 1975 Case Supplement.

Sovern's Cases on Racial Discrimination in Employment, 2nd Ed., Pamphlet reprint from Cooper et al. Law and Poverty, 2nd Ed., 167 pages, 1973.

See Workmen's Compensation.

LAND USE

Beuscher and Wright's Cases on Land Use, 788 pages, 1969.

Hagman's Cases on Public Planning and Control of Urban and Land Development, 1208 pages, 1973.

Hagman's Text on Urban Planning and Land Development Control Law, 559 pages, 1971.

LEGAL BIBLIOGRAPHY

Cohen's Legal Research in a Nutshell, 2nd Ed., 259 pages, 1971.

How To Find The Law, with Special Chapters on Legal Writing, 6th Ed., 313 pages, 1965.

How To Find The Law Student Problem Book.

Rombauer's Legal Problem Solving, 2nd Ed., 212 pages, 1973.

LEGAL ETHICS

Mellinkoff's Text on The Conscience of a Lawyer, 304 pages, 1973.

Pirsig's Cases on Professional Responsibility, 2nd Ed., 447 pages, 1970.

Pirsig's 1974 Supplement.

LEGAL HISTORY

Kempin's Historical Introduction to Anglo-American Law in a Nutshell, 2nd Ed., 280 pages, 1973.

Kimball's Historical Introduction to Legal System, 610 pages, 1966.

Smith's Cases on Development of Legal Institutions, 757 pages, 1965.

LEGAL INTERVIEWING AND COUNSELING

See Clinical Teaching.

LEGAL METHOD—LEGAL SYSTEM

Fryer and Orentlicher's Cases on Legal Method and Legal System, 1043 pages, 1966.

See Introduction to Law.

LEGAL PROCESS

See Legal Method.

LEGAL PROFESSION

See Legal Ethics.

LEGAL WRITING STYLE

Weihofen's Text on Legal Writing Style, 323 pages, 1961.

See Legal Bibliography.

LEGISLATION

Davis' Legislative Law and Process in a Nutshell, about 390 pages, 1975.

Nutting, Elliott and Dickerson's Cases on Legislation, 4th Ed., 631 pages, 1969.

LOCAL GOVERNMENT LAW

Michelman and Sandalow's Cases on Government in Urban Areas, 1216 pages, 1970.

Michelman and Sandalow's 1972 Supplement.

Stason and Kauper's Cases on Municipal Corporations, 3rd Ed., 692 pages, 1959.

Valente's Cases on Local Government Law, 914 pages, 1975.

See Land Use.

MASS COMMUNICATION LAW

Gillmor and Barron's Cases on Mass Communication Law, 2nd Ed., 1007 pages, 1974.

MORTGAGES

Maxwell, Riesenfeld, Hetland and Warren's California Cases on Security Transactions in Land, 2nd Ed., about 600 pages, 1975.

Osborne's Cases on Secured Transactions, 559 pages, 1967.

Osborne's Text on Mortgages, 2nd Ed., 805 pages, 1970.

MUNICIPAL CORPORATIONS

See Local Government Law.

NATURAL RESOURCES

Trelease, Bloomenthal and Geraud's Cases on Natural Resources, 1131 pages, 1965.

NEGOTIABLE INSTRUMENTS

Nordstrom and Clovis' Problems on Commercial Paper, 458 pages, 1972.

Selected Commercial Statutes, 1016 pages, 1973.

NEGOTIABLE INSTRUMENTS—Cont'd

Weber's Commercial Paper in a Nutshell, 2nd Ed., 361 pages, 1975.
See Commercial Transactions.

OFFICE PRACTICE

Strong and Clark's Law Office Management, 424 pages, 1974.
See Clinical Teaching.

OIL AND GAS

Hemingway's Text on Oil and Gas, 486 pages, 1971.
Huie, Woodward and Smith's Cases on Oil and Gas, 2nd Ed., 955 pages, 1972.
See Natural Resources.

PARTNERSHIP

Crane and Bromberg's Text on Partnership, 695 pages, 1968.
See Agency-Partnership.

PATENTS

Choate's Cases on Patents, 1060 pages, 1973.

PERSONAL PROPERTY

Aigler, Smith and Tefft's Cases on Property, 2 Vols., 1339 pages, 1960.
Bigelow's Cases on Personal Property, 3rd Ed., 507 pages, 1942.
Fryer's Readings on Personal Property, 3rd Ed., 1184 pages, 1938.

PLEADING AND PROCEDURE

Cound, Friedenthal and Miller's Cases on Civil Procedure, 2nd Ed., 1186 pages, 1974.
Cound, Friedenthal and Miller's Cases on Pleading, Discovery and Joinder, 643 pages, 1968.
Cound, Friedenthal and Miller's Civil Procedure Supplement, 1974.
Ehrenzweig and Louisell's Jurisdiction in a Nutshell, 3rd Ed., 291 pages, 1973.
Federal Rules of Civil-Appellate-Criminal Procedure, Law School Edition, 346 pages, 1975.
Hodges, Jones and Elliott's Cases on Texas Trial and Appellate Procedure, 2d Ed., 623 pages, 1974.
Hodges, Jones, Elliott and Thode's Cases on Texas Judicial Process Prior to Trial, 935 pages, 1966.
Karlen, Meisenholder, Stevens and Vestal's Cases on Civil Procedure, about 900 pages, 1975.
Karlen and Joiner's Cases on Trials and Appeals, 536 pages, 1971.
Karlen's Procedure Before Trial in a Nutshell, 258 pages, 1972.
McBaine's Cases on Introduction to Civil Procedure, 399 pages, 1950.

PLEADING AND PROCEDURE—Cont'd

McCoid's Cases on Civil Procedure, 823 pages, 1974.
McElhaney's Trials, Problems and Materials on Effective Litigation, 457 pages, 1974.

POVERTY LAW

Cooper, Dodyk, Berger, Paulsen, Schrag and Sovern's Cases on Law and Poverty, 2nd Ed., 1208 pages, 1973.
Cooper and Dodyk's Cases on Income Maintenance, 2nd Ed., Pamphlet reprint from Cooper, et al. Law and Poverty, 2nd Ed., 449 pages, 1973.
LaFrance, Schroeder, Bennett and Boyd's Text on Law and the Poor, 558 pages, 1973.

REAL PROPERTY

Aigler, Smith & Tefft's Cases on Property, 2 Vols., 1339 pages, 1960.
Bernhardt's Real Property in a Nutshell, about 365 pages, 1975.
Browder, Cunningham & Julin's Cases on Basic Property Law, 2d Ed., 1397 pages, 1973.
Burby's Text on Real Property, 3rd Ed., 490 pages, 1965.
Donahue, Kauper and Martin's Cases on Property, 1501 pages, 1974.
Moynihan's Introduction to Real Property, 254 pages, 1962.
Phipps' Titles in a Nutshell—The Calculus of Interests, 277 pages, 1968.
Smith and Boyer's Survey of the Law of Property, 2nd Ed., 510 pages, 1971.
See Housing and Urban Development.

REMEDIES

Cribbet's Cases on Judicial Remedies, 762 pages, 1954.
Dobbs' Text, on Remedies, 1067 pages, 1973.
Dobbs' Problems in Remedies, 137 pages, 1974.
Dobbyn's Injunctions in a Nutshell, 264 pages, 1974.
Van Hecke, Leavell and Nelson's Cases on Equitable Remedies and Restitution, 2nd Ed., 717 pages, 1973.
Wright's Cases on Remedies, 498 pages, 1955.
York and Bauman's Cases on Remedies, 2nd Ed., 1381 pages, 1973.
See Equity.

RESTITUTION

See Equity.
See Remedies.

REVIEW MATERIALS

Ballantine's Problems.
Burby's Law Refreshers.
Smith Reviews.

SALES

Nordstrom's Text on Sales, 600 pages, 1970.

Nordstrom and Lattin's Problems on Sales and Secured Transactions, 809 pages, 1968.

Selected Commercial Statutes, 1016 pages, 1973.

See Commercial Transactions.

SECURED TRANSACTIONS

Henson's Text on Secured Transactions, 364 pages, 1973.

See Commercial Transactions.

See Sales.

SECURITIES REGULATIONS

Ratner's Materials on Securities Regulations, 893 pages, 1975.

Ratner's Statutory Supplement.

SEX BASED DISCRIMINATION

See Women and the Law.

SOCIAL LEGISLATION

See Workmen's Compensation.

SURETYSHIP AND GUARANTY

Osborne's Cases on Suretyship, 221 pages, 1966.

Simpson's Cases on Suretyship, 538 pages, 1942.

TAXATION

Chommie's Text on Federal Income Taxation, 2nd Ed., 1051 pages, 1973.

Chommie's Review of Federal Income Taxation, 90 pages, 1973.

Hellerstein's Cases on State and Local Taxation, 3rd Ed., 741 pages, 1969.

Kragen & McNulty's Cases on Federal Income Taxation, 2nd Ed., 1107 pages, 1974.

Lowndes, Kramer and McCord's Text on Federal Estate and Gift Taxes, 3rd Ed., 1099 pages, 1974.

McNulty's Federal Estate and Gift Taxation in a Nutshell, 343 pages, 1973.

McNulty's Federal Income Taxation in a Nutshell, 322 pages, 1972.

Rice's Problems in Federal Estate & Gift Taxation, 2nd Ed., 496 pages, 1972.

Rice's Problems in Federal Income Taxation, 2nd Ed., 589 pages, 1971.

Selected Federal Taxation Statutes and Regulations, about 1125 pages, 1975.

TORTS

Green, Pedrick, Rahl, Thode, Hawkins and Smith's Cases on Torts, 1311 pages, 1968.

Green, Pedrick, Rahl, Thode, Hawkins and Smith's Cases on Injuries to Relations, 466 pages, 1968.

TORTS—Continued

Keeton and Keeton's Cases on Torts, 1193 pages, 1971.

Keeton and Keeton's 1974 Supplement.

Noel and Phillips' Products Liability in a Nutshell, 365 pages, 1974.

Prosser's Text on Torts, 4th Ed., 1208 pages, 1971.

TRADE REGULATION

See Anti-Trust Law.

See Unfair Trade Practices.

TRIAL AND APPELLATE PRACTICE

See Pleading and Procedure.

TRUSTS

Bogert's Text on Trusts, 5th Ed., 726 pages, 1973.

Powell's Cases on Trusts and Wills, 639 pages, 1960.

See Wills, Intestate Succession, Trusts, Gifts and Future Interests.

UNFAIR TRADE PRACTICES

Oppenheim's Cases on Unfair Trade Practices, 3rd Ed., 1071 pages, 1974.

Oppenheim's Robinson-Patman Act Pamphlet, 258 pages, 1974.

WATER LAW

Trelease's Cases on Water Law, 2nd Ed., 863 pages, 1974.

WILLS

Atkinson's Text on Wills, 2nd Ed., 975 pages, 1953.

Mennell's Cases on California Decedents' Estates, 566 pages, 1973.

Turrentine's Cases on Wills, 2nd Ed., 483 pages, 1962.

See Wills, Intestate Succession, Trusts, Gifts and Future Interests.

WILLS, INTESTATE SUCCESSION, TRUSTS, GIFTS AND FUTURE INTERESTS

Gulliver, Clark, Lusky and Murphy's Cases on Gratuitous Transfers: Wills, Intestate Succession, Trusts, Gifts and Future Interests, 1017 pages, 1967.

WOMEN AND THE LAW

Davidson, Ginsburg and Kay's Cases on Sex Based Discrimination, 1031 pages, 1974.

WORKMEN'S COMPENSATION

Malone, Plant and Little's Cases on the Employment Relation, 1055 pages, 1974.

McCORMICK'S HANDBOOK

OF THE

LAW OF EVIDENCE

Second Edition

BY

EDWARD W. CLEARY,
General Editor
Professor of Law, Arizona State University

CONTRIBUTING AUTHORS

VAUGHN C. BALL
Professor of Law, University of Southern California

RALPH C. BARNHART
Dean and Professor of Law, University of Arkansas

KENNETH S. BROUN
Associate Professor of Law, University of North Carolina

GEORGE E. DIX
Professor of Law, University of Texas

ERNEST GELLHORN
Professor of Law, University of Virginia

ROBERT MEISENHOLDER
Professor of Law, University of Washington

E. F. ROBERTS
Professor of Law, The Cornell Law School

JOHN W. STRONG
Professor of Law, University of Oregon

ST. PAUL, MINN.
WEST PUBLISHING CO.
1972

McCormick et al. on Evid. 2nd Ed. HB
3rd Reprint—1975

PREFACE

The modesty with which Dean McCormick disclaimed "pretensions to completeness" in the original edition of this work has been belied by myriad citations over the years. Few legal texts have exerted greater influence on the growth and development of the law, and this influence seems not to have diminished with the passage of time. Nevertheless, despite the longevity of the original, changes in many areas of the law of evidence and the appearance of new ones combine to warrant a new edition.

The process of revision and updating has adhered to the original in organization and style. Some subjects, notably the constitutional aspects of evidence, have been completely rewritten in view of developments in the field. Others have required only updating of citations with little or no change of substance. And many fall between in varying degrees.

Aside from the enhanced incursion of constitutional principles into the realm of evidence, the most notable development in evidence since the appearance of the original edition no doubt is the accelerating pace of codification. If a pattern is visible in the nonconstitutional area, it is that cases increasingly should be decided on the basis of the evidence which is admitted rather than by what is excluded.

Citations of the American Law Institute Model Code of Evidence take the form MODEL CODE OF EVIDENCE, and the Uniform Rules of Evidence of the National Conference of Commissioners on Uniform State Laws appear as UNIFORM RULES. Citations of the Proposed Federal Rules of Evidence are to the Revised Draft of 1971, F.R.Ev. (R.D.1971), which appears in permanent form in 51 F.R.D. 315. Unless otherwise noted, citations to Wigmore are to the third edition (1940).

My colleagues in this undertaking are Professor Vaughn C. Ball of the University of Southern California, Dean Ralph C. Barnhart of the University of Arkansas, Associate Professor Kenneth S. Broun of the University of North Carolina, Professor George E. Dix of the University of Texas, Professor Ernest Gellhorn of the University of Virginia, Professor Robert Meisenholder of the University of Washington, Professor E. F. Roberts of Cornell Law School, and Professor John William Strong of the University of Oregon. The major effort has been theirs.

EDWARD W. CLEARY

Tempe, Arizona
March, 1972

*

IX

SUMMARY OF CONTENTS

TITLE 1. INTRODUCTION

TITLE 2. EXAMINATION OF WITNESSES

TITLE 3. ADMISSION AND EXCLUSION

TITLE 4. COMPETENCY

TITLE 5. PRIVILEGE: COMMON LAW AND STATUTORY

TITLE 6. PRIVILEGE: CONSTITUTIONAL

TITLE 7. RELEVANCY AND ITS COUNTERWEIGHTS: TIME, PREJUDICE, CONFUSION AND SURPRISE

SUMMARY OF CONTENTS

TABLE OF CONTENTS

TITLE 1. INTRODUCTION

CHAPTER 1. PREPARING AND PRESENTING THE EVIDENCE

TITLE 2. EXAMINATION OF WITNESSES

CHAPTER 2. THE FORM OF QUESTIONS ON DIRECT: THE JUDGE'S WITNESSES: REFRESHING MEMORY

CHAPTER 3. THE REQUIREMENT OF FIRSTHAND KNOWLEDGE: THE OPINION RULE: EXPERT TESTIMONY

TABLE OF CONTENTS

CHAPTER 4. CROSS–EXAMINATION AND SUBSEQUENT EXAMINATIONS

CHAPTER 5. IMPEACHMENT AND SUPPORT

TITLE 3. ADMISSION AND EXCLUSION

CHAPTER 6. THE PROCEDURE OF ADMITTING AND EXCLUDING EVIDENCE

TITLE 4. COMPETENCY

CHAPTER 7. THE COMPETENCY OF WITNESSES

TITLE 5. PRIVILEGE: COMMON LAW AND STATUTORY

CHAPTER 8. THE SCOPE AND EFFECT OF THE EVIDENTIARY PRIVILEGES

CHAPTER 9. THE PRIVILEGE FOR MARITAL COMMUNICATIONS

CHAPTER 10. THE CLIENT'S PRIVILEGE: COMMUNICATIONS BETWEEN CLIENT AND LAWYER

CHAPTER 11. THE PRIVILEGE FOR CONFIDENTIAL INFORMATION SECURED IN THE COURSE OF THE PHYSICIAN–PATIENT RELATIONSHIP

CHAPTER 12. PRIVILEGES FOR GOVERNMENTAL SECRETS

TITLE 6. PRIVILEGE: CONSTITUTIONAL

CHAPTER 13. THE PRIVILEGE AGAINST SELF-INCRIMINATION

TABLE OF CONTENTS

CHAPTER 14. CONFESSIONS

CHAPTER 15. THE PRIVILEGE IN REGARD TO IMPROPERLY OBTAINED EVIDENCE

TABLE OF CONTENTS

TITLE 7. RELEVANCY AND ITS COUNTERWEIGHTS: TIME, PREJUDICE, CONFUSION AND SURPRISE

CHAPTER 16. RELEVANCY

CHAPTER 17. CHARACTER AND HABIT

TABLE OF CONTENTS

CHAPTER 18. SIMILAR HAPPENINGS AND TRANSACTIONS

CHAPTER 19. INSURANCE AGAINST LIABILITY

CHAPTER 20. EXPERIMENTAL AND SCIENTIFIC EVIDENCE

TITLE 8. DEMONSTRATIVE EVIDENCE

CHAPTER 21. DEMONSTRATIVE EVIDENCE

TABLE OF CONTENTS

TITLE 9. WRITINGS

CHAPTER 22. AUTHENTICATION

CHAPTER 23. THE REQUIREMENT OF THE PRODUCTION OF THE ORIGINAL WRITING AS THE "BEST EVIDENCE"

TITLE 10. THE HEARSAY RULE AND ITS EXCEPTIONS

CHAPTER 24. THE HEARSAY RULE

TABLE OF CONTENTS

CHAPTER 25.   TESTIMONY TAKEN AT A FORMER HEARING OR IN ANOTHER ACTION

CHAPTER 26.   ADMISSIONS OF A PARTY–OPPONENT

TABLE OF CONTENTS

CHAPTER 27. DECLARATIONS AGAINST INTEREST

CHAPTER 28. DYING DECLARATIONS

CHAPTER 29. SPONTANEOUS DECLARATIONS

CHAPTER 30. RECORDS OF PAST RECOLLECTION

TABLE OF CONTENTS

TABLE OF CONTENTS

CHAPTER 34. THE PRESENT AND FUTURE OF RULES ABOUT HEARSAY

TITLE 11. JUDICIAL NOTICE

CHAPTER 35. JUDICIAL NOTICE

TITLE 12. BURDEN OF PROOF AND PRESUMPTIONS

CHAPTER 36. THE BURDENS OF PROOF AND PRESUMPTIONS

TITLE 13.   ADMINISTRATIVE EVIDENCE

CHAPTER 37.   ADMINISTRATIVE EVIDENCE

†

HANDBOOK

OF THE

LAW OF EVIDENCE

TITLE 1

INTRODUCTION

CHAPTER 1

PREPARING AND PRESENTING THE EVIDENCE

Sec.
1. Planning and Preparation of Proof as Important as the Rules of Evidence
2. Preparation for Trial on the Facts, Without Resort to the Aid of the Court
3. Invoking the Aid of the Court in Preparing for Trial: Discovery and Depositions; Requests for Admissions; Pretrial Conferences
4. The Order of Presenting Evidence at the Trial

1. Planning and Preparation of Proof as Important as the Rules of Evidence.

The law of Evidence is the system of rules and standards by which the admission of proof at the trial of a lawsuit is regulated. But it should be emphasized that this trial stage, when proof is offered and the rules of evidence come into play, is a late stage in a long process. Thus, every case which will be encountered, dealing with a dispute over a rule of evidence or its application, presents a situation in which the lawyers concerned have been required to shoulder many other tasks in the planning and production of testimony, and in anticipation of problems of presentation of proof at the trial under the law of evidence, long before any question of evidence law is presented to the court. As a reminder, some of these earlier stages in the problem of proof will be mentioned in this chapter.

2. Preparation for Trial on the Facts, Without Resort to the Aid of the Court.[1]

The client must be interviewed to ascertain the facts, and these interviews should include a tactful but searching cross-examination to overcome the client's natural tendency to confine the story to the facts favorable to himself.   The witnesses who have firsthand knowledge of the transaction in controversy must likewise be interviewed, and where possible, their written statements taken.   Apart

1. There is much dross in the professional writing on this subject, but also much of value. See the following trial practice pamphlets of the Practising Law Institute: Bodin, Marshalling the Evidence (1966); Frost and Ausubel, Preparation of a Negligence Case (1970); Dawson, Examinations Before Trial in State Courts (1953); Bodin, Final Preparation for Trial (1954). Stimulating general suggestions will be found in addresses such as Conboy, The Preparation of a Case for Trial, 11 A.B.A.J. 310 (1925); Buckner, The Trial of Cases, 15 A.B.A.J. 271, 273 (1929); Nizer, The Art of Jury Trial, 32 Corn.L.Q. 59 (1946). See also Wellman, Success

from the ordinary eyewitnesses, it is increasingly necessary to arrange for the employment of technical experts, such as physicians in personal injury cases, chemists and physicists in patent litigation, engineers and architects in controversies over construction contracts, psychiatrists in criminal cases, and handwriting experts in disputes over the genuineness of documents. To prepare himself to testify, and to give to counsel the information he will need to frame his questions at the trial, the expert must usually be furnished with a detailed request for an investigation and report upon specific questions.[2] Also, it will often be necessary to assemble available documentary evidence, such as contracts, letters, receipts, loose-leaf records, deeds, certified copies of conveyances, judgments, and decrees. Other physical evidence, such as the revolver of the attacker and the perforated coat of the victim in a murder case, or a sample of the goods in an action for breach of warranty, should be discovered and preserved for use at the trial. The lawyer, moreover, must be fertile in planning for the production of all those aids to the senses which quicken the jury's interest in and understanding of the testimony, such as photographs, motion picture films, X-ray photographs, plats, diagrams, and models. Where practicable, the task of proof should be lightened by securing written stipulations from opposing counsel of the existence of facts not in controversy, such as the execution of documents, or the ownership of a vehicle, or of premises, involved in the suit. If it is anticipated that the terms of a document in the possession of the adversary will need to be proved by use of a copy, written notice to produce the original at the trial must be given to opposing counsel.

Manifestly, all of this preparation must be planned, and the plan will develop as new information is disclosed, but as the trial approaches, a definite program must be formulated. Each fact involved in the claim or defence should be listed, with the witnesses and documents by which it will be proved.[3] This may well be supplemented by a list of the witnesses in the order in which they will be called, including the subjects upon which they will be examined. Finally, and most important, at the last minute before the witnesses are to go on the stand, the counsel who calls them must talk to each in order to ascertain what he is prepared to swear, to cause him to refresh his memory, if necessary, by reading his signed statement, and to warn him of the probable line of the adversary's cross-examination.

3. Invoking the Aid of the Court in Preparing for Trial: Discovery and Depositions; Requests for Admission; Pretrial Conferences.

The official discovery procedures in the various jurisdictions are treated at length in treatises and one-volume works concerning the subjects of civil and criminal procedure.[4] Consequently, only a very short and sum-

---

in Court (1941). For detailed practical suggestions, see Goldstein and Lake, Trial Technique (2d ed. 1969); Keeton, Trial Tactics and Methods (1954); Belli, Modern Trials (1954); Busch, Law and Tactics in Jury Trials, §§ 200–216 (1949). Hornaday, Some Suggestions on the Investigation of Facts, 15 Ind.L.J. 499 (1940), deals with the interviewing of witnesses. See also Bowman, How to Make an Investigation, 21 Okl.B.A.J. 1346 (1950), 19 Ins. Council J. 23 (1952).

2. See Carr, Pre-Trial Preparation of the Medical Evidence, 20 U.Kan.City L.Rev. 103 (1952); Investigating and Preparing the Medical Aspects of Personal Injury Actions, P.L.I. Forum Series (1957).

3. See Goldstein and Lake, Trial Technique § 2.48 (2d ed. 1969) (questionnaire to witness), 3.17 (diagram of case), 5.03 (trial brief).

4. For procedures in civil cases see Barron and Holtzoff, Federal Practice and Procedure (Wright ed.) (to appear in revised form by Wright and Miller); 4 Moore's Federal Practice; James, Civil Procedure Ch. 6 (1965); Wright, Federal Courts §§ 81–90 (2d ed. 1970). For procedures in criminal cases, see Wright, Federal Practice and Procedure Rules 15, 16 (1969); 8A Moore's Federal Practice Rules 15, 16.

mary review of these procedures is included here.

In addition to preparation for trial without the use of any official pretrial procedures, adequate preparation requires the use of official procedures that are made available once a lawsuit has been commenced. Since the pleadings in civil cases may be fairly general and need not outline the opponent's factual case in any detail in most jurisdictions,[5] the rules for civil cases in many states provide for fairly thorough discovery processes by which each party may discover the facts and possible evidence in the case, and at least ascertain in part what detailed fact issues may arise for trial, as well as the opponent's positions concerning factual matters.[6]

The most important discovery procedure in civil cases is undoubtedly the procedure by which each party may orally examine the other under oath and may likewise examine any persons who may possibly have any knowledge of the subject matter of the lawsuit. Over half the states have substantially copied the federal rules for this procedure.[7] Although an order for a commission authorizing an officer to preside at such an oral examination is required in some states, the procedure for taking oral depositions more often specifies only a notice to the person to be examined and a subpoena requiring him to appear at a certain time and place for the examination before a notary public, plus a notice of the examination to the opposing party, if he is not the person to be examined.[8] In many jurisdictions, following the lead of the federal discovery process for civil cases, the examination upon oral deposition may seek information "reasonably calculated to lead to the discovery of admissible evidence" even if the information will not be admissible at the trial.[9] In these jurisdictions, effective employment of the taking of oral depositions will enable a party to discover the evidence both for and against his positions concerning the facts.

In civil cases, written interrogatories may also be directed to the opponent in many states, and he will be required to answer them.[10] Usually these interrogatories are used hand in hand with the procedure of taking oral depositions. Further a party is often permitted to secure an order requiring the adversary to permit him to examine all papers and things—even real property—relating to the subject matter of the suit.[11] At least in personal injury suits, and sometimes in other suits in which the physical or mental condition of a party is in issue, an order for examination of the condition of the party may be secured in over half the states.[12] Further, although not strictly speaking a discovery device, a party may in many states send requests for admissions to his opponent who must either admit or deny the detailed requests.[13]

Finally, the pretrial hearing or conference is authorized for civil cases in many

5. See discussion in James, Civil Procedure §§ 2.9, 2.11 (1965). Furthermore, the rules governing amendments of the pleadings are very liberal, permitting amendment rather freely, even at the trial stage of the suit. Id. §§ 5.2–5.8.

6. The discovery processes summarized in this section also afford means to preserve evidence for the trial. See generally, Developments in the Law —Discovery, 74 Harv.L.Rev. 940 (1961).

7. Rules 26–37, Rules of Civil Procedure for the District Courts of the United States. At least 28 states have adopted the federal rules with variations. See review in Barron and Holtzoff, Federal Practice and Procedure (Wright ed.) §§ 9–10. Amendments to the federal rules, effective July 1, 1970, will undoubtedly be adopted in many of these states in the future.

8. Details in the Federal Rules of Civil Procedure are spelled out in Rule 30.

9. F.R.Civ.P. 26(b) (1). See detailed discussion in 4 Moore's Federal Practice ¶ 26.17.

10. F.R.Civ.P. 33. See general discussion in Wright, Federal Courts § 86 (2d ed. 1970).

11. F.R.Civ.P. 34.

12. F.R.Civ.P. 35.

13. This device is not usually available in states which have not adopted Rule 36, Federal Rules of Civil Procedure.

jurisdictions, although it has not necessarily been frequently used in all of them.[14] When the case is approaching the time for trial, usually two or three weeks before the date set, the judge summons the counsel for both sides, and sometimes the parties, and seeks to settle all preliminary questions of pleading, to ascertain the scope of the dispute, and to secure agreements as to the facts not really at issue. The federal rule [15] mentions, as among the objects of the hearing:

"(1) The simplification of the issues;

. . .

"(3) The possibility of obtaining admissions of fact and of documents which will avoid unnecessary proof;

"(4) The limitation of the number of expert witnesses;

"(5) The advisability of a preliminary reference of issues to a master for findings to be used as evidence when the trial is to be by jury" . . ..

Pretrial conference can serve as a vehicle for reaching agreement upon various factual issues, although it will not necessarily have that result.[16]

A final step that should be mentioned before concluding this summary of ways in which the aid of the court is invoked in civil cases in the preparation for trial on the facts, is the procurement of the issuance and service of writs of subpoena for the witnesses who are to be used at the trial. In the case of a document or other physical evidence held by another, the party who desires its production at the trial may secure a subpoena duces tecum addressed to the possessor commanding him to attend the trial as a witness and to bring with him the document or other object.

Finally, it should be mentioned that the use of some of the above-described discovery devices may result in testimony and other evidence which may be introduced into evidence at the trial. The testimony upon the taking of oral or written depositions may be introduced under varying circumstances. Under rules similar to the federal rules, the deposition testimony of an opposing party may be introduced virtually without any conditions.[17] The most common conditions for the introduction of deposition testimony of persons other than witnesses are the requirements expressed in the federal rules.[18]

The proper use of all these pretrial devices for trial preparation is, of course, in and of itself an important art.

---

14. For general discussion of pretrial conferences, see Kincaid, A Judge's Handbook of Pre-Trial Procedure, 17 F.R.D. 437 (1955).

15. F.R.Civ.P. 16. The history of pretrial conference is outlined in Sunderland, The Theory and Practice of Pre-Trial Procedure, 36 Mich.L.Rev. 215 (1937).

16. See study of the pretrial conference in Rosenberg, The Pretrial Conference and Effective Justice 23–71 (1964).

17. F.R.Civ.P. 32(a) (2).
"(2) The deposition of a party or of anyone who at the time of taking the deposition was an officer, director, or managing agent, or a person designated under Rule 30(b) (6) or 31(a) to testify on behalf of a public or private corporation, partnership or association or governmental agency which is a party may be used by an adverse party for any purpose."

18. Rule 32(a) (1), (3) provides that depositions may be used at the trial in accordance with the following provisions:
"(1) Any deposition may be used by any party for the purpose of contradicting or impeaching the testimony of deponent as a witness."
"(3) The deposition of a witness, whether or not a party, may be used by any party for any purpose if the court finds: (A) that the witness is dead; or (B) that the witness is at a greater distance than 100 miles from the place of trial or hearing, or is out of the United States, unless it appears that the absence of the witness was procured by the party offering the deposition; or (C) that the witness is unable to attend or testify because of age, illness, infirmity, or imprisonment; or (D) that the party offering the deposition has been unable to procure the attendance of the witness by subpoena; or (E) upon application and notice, that such exceptional circumstances exist as to make it desirable, in the interest of justice and with due regard to the importance of presenting the testimony of witnesses orally in open court, to allow the deposition to be used."

Discovery procedures available to a criminal defendant should also be mentioned. Only in recent times have rules or statutes been enacted to provide for any true discovery procedures for criminal defendants,[19] and these procedures are limited. The Crime Control Act of 1970 provides for taking depositions primarily for the preservation of the evidence of the witness (for future use as evidence) and not for the purpose of discovery of facts. For the first time depositions have been authorized on motion of the government.[20] A broad discovery provision concerning discovery and examination by defendant of reports, tests, grand jury testimony, books, papers, documents, tangible objects, and places is provided for by Rule 16 of the federal rules.[21] Only the most limited provision is made in the federal rules for discovery of matters of this kind by the government.[22]

In the various states, all manner of miscellaneous and limited provisions which might have some limited use for discovery of facts exist, but no detailed review will be attempted here.[23]

4. The Order of Presenting Evidence at the Trial.

Under the usual order of proceeding at the trial, the plaintiff, who has the burden of establishing his claim, will first introduce the evidence to prove the facts necessary to enable him to recover,[24] e. g., the making of the contract sued on, its breach, and the amount of damages. At this stage the plaintiff will bring forward successively all the witnesses on whom he will rely to establish these facts, together with the documents pertinent for this purpose, which will be offered when they have been authenticated by the testimony of the witnesses. During this stage each witness of the plaintiff will first be questioned by the plaintiff's counsel, upon direct examination, then cross-examined by opposing counsel, and these examinations may be followed by re-direct and re-cross examinations. When all of the plaintiff's witnesses to his main case have been subjected, each in turn, to this process of questioning and cross-questioning, the plaintiff signifies the completion of his case in chief by announcing that he rests.

Then the defendant presents the witnesses (and also the documents and other tangible evidence) in support of his case. At this stage the defendant will produce evidence not only in denial of the plaintiff's claim, such as evidence that a contract sued on was never actually agreed on, or in a negligence case that some bodily injury was not permanent

19. See discussion and cited articles in Wright, Federal Practice and Procedure: Criminal § 251. See also § 97, infra.

20. 18 U.S.C.A. § 3503. See Wright, Federal Practice and Procedure: Criminal § 241.

21. F.R.Crim.P. 16.

22. Present Rule 16 conditions limited government discovery rights to situations in which defendant has sought discovery under the rule.

23. See various state provisions cited in Advisory Committee Note for Rule 16, Preliminary Draft of Proposed Amendments to the Federal Rules of Criminal Procedure, January 31, 1970.

24. This is the usual order, since the plaintiff has the "burden of proof," in the sense of the duty of first proceeding with evidence to establish the facts pleaded in the complaint. But this burden of opening the evidence usually carries with it the compensating advantage called the "right to open and close," that is, the privilege of having the first and the last word in the argument to the jury. To get this advantage, the defendant will occasionally admit the plaintiff's cause of action, and rest solely on some affirmative defense in the answer, and thus assume the burden of proceeding with the evidence first, along with the right to open and close the argument. The order of presenting evidence and the right to open and close are clearly described in Abbott, Civil Jury Trials chs. V and VI, (5th ed. 1935). See also 6 Wigmore, Evidence § 1866 (a helpful chart showing the stages in presenting evidence, and in examining the individual witness), § 1867 (discussing the power of the trial judge to permit variations from the usual order). As will appear in Chapter 36 herein, the sufficiency of the proof to meet the requirements of claim or defense is often a turning point in the case.

as claimed by the plaintiff, but also in support of any affirmative defenses which the defendant has pleaded, such as the defense of fraud in the procurement of a contract sued on, or the making of a release of a personal injury claim. Here again each witness's story on direct examination is subject to be tested by cross-examination and supplemented on re-direct, etc., before he leaves the stand. When the defendant has thus completed the presentation of his proof of affirmative defenses, if any, and his evidence in denial of the plaintiff's claims, the defendant announces that he rests.

The plaintiff is now entitled to another turn at bat. He may now present his case in rebuttal. The plaintiff is not entitled to present at this stage witnesses who merely support the allegations of the complaint, but is confined to testimony which is directed to refuting the evidence of the defendant, unless the court in its discretion permits him to depart from the regular order of proof. The plaintiff's witnesses in rebuttal may be new ones, but he may often recall witnesses who testified for him on the case in chief, to answer some point first raised by the defendant's witnesses. In this, as in the other stages, the witness may not only be examined on direct, but cross-examined and re-examined. When the plaintiff's case in rebuttal is finished, he closes his case. If new points are brought out in the plaintiff's rebuttal evidence, the defendant may meet them by evidence in rejoinder, otherwise he closes his case at once. When both parties have announced that they have closed, the hearing on the facts comes to an end and the trial proceeds with the argument of counsel and the court's instructions to the jury.

To sum up: The stages of the hearing of the facts are

(1) the plaintiff's main case, or evidence in chief,

(2) the defendant's case or evidence in defense,

(3) the plaintiff's evidence in rebuttal, and

(4) the defendant's evidence in rejoinder.

In each of these stages, all of the witnesses to the facts appropriate at the particular period will be called by the party, and the examination of each witness may pass through these steps:

(1) the direct examination, conducted by the party who calls the witness,

(2) the cross-examination by the adversary,

(3) re-direct, and

(4) re-cross.[25]

25. In general, the order of presentation of evidence is similar in a criminal case.

TITLE 2

EXAMINATION OF WITNESSES

CHAPTER 2

THE FORM OF QUESTIONS ON DIRECT: THE JUDGE'S WITNESSES: REFRESHING MEMORY

5. The Form of Questions: (a) Questions Calling for a Free Narrative versus Specific Questions.

The art of direct examination of your own witness, and of telling a composite story from the mouths of your own witnesses, is far more important, though perhaps less difficult, than the art of cross-examination.[1] One of the problems of tactics is whether the information which a particular witness will give can best be elicited by a succession of questions about specific facts and happenings or will be brought out more effectively by a general question. In the latter case, the attention of the witness will be directed to the incident in litigation by asking him whether he was on the scene at the time and then requesting him to tell what he saw and heard on that occasion. This latter method, narrative testimony, may often be more effective. The narrative does not seem to come from the counsel, as it might when specific interrogation is employed. If the witness has a good memory, a good personality, and some effective-ness in speaking, his spontaneous statement of his own story may well be more interesting and impressive. Scientific tests give some indication that spontaneous narrative is more accurate (because less influenced by suggestion) while the fully interrogated testimony is, naturally, more complete in its representation of the facts.[2] Specific interrogation may be desirable to ensure the presentation of facts in proper order; to give the witness confidence in the courtroom; to supplement the testimony properly by visual aids, demonstrative evidence, and writings; to prevent dull testimony; and to accomplish a variety of other purposes.

If a witness is to be examined by the narrative method, counsel must plan to be ready to interrupt with specific questions, if necessary, or to supplement the narrative by specific questions which bring out omitted facts.

Under the prevailing view, there is no general rule of law requiring or preferring either form of questioning. Courts have empha-

---

1. See B. K. and W. F. Elliott, The Art of the Advocate Ch. VII (2d ed. 1911); Wellman, Day in Court Ch. 10 (1910), reprinted in Davenport, Voices in Court 86–98 (1958); Spellman, Direct Examination of Witnesses (1968).

2. Gardner, The Perception and Memory of Witnesses, 18 Corn.L.Q. 391, 404 (1923), citing Marston, Studies in Testimony, 15 J.Crim.Law and Criminology, 1–31 (1924); Wigmore, The Science of Judicial Proof § 264 (3d ed., 1937).

sized the danger that when asked to tell his story the witness will include hearsay or other incompetent testimony,[3] but a proper caution by court or counsel, on the adversary's request, will usually prevent this. True, if the improper statement comes out in the story, there is only the remedy of striking out that part of the evidence. There is also a danger that counsel may waive an objection if he does not interrupt promptly and move to strike. But the need for eliciting what the witness knows in the most vivid and accurate way is an interest to be balanced against the need of the adversary for a fair opportunity to object. The guiding principle is that the trial judge has a discretion, not reviewable except for abuse,[4] to control the form of examination,[5] to the end that the facts may be clearly and expeditiously presented; hence he may permit either of the methods discussed.[6] It is believed, however, that when-

ever circumstances make narrative testimony feasible, its use is likely to be in the interest of the examining party and of the accurate disclosure of the truth, and that the use of this method will seldom be curbed by enlightened judges, except, perhaps, in criminal trials when it may entail the risk that testimony will be given concerning a matter which is not constitutionally admissible.

6. The Form of Questions: (b) Leading Questions.

In the preceding section, the method of soliciting the free and unguided narrative of the witness on direct examination is compared with the method of drawing out testimony by specific questions. A danger of the latter method is that the witness may acquiesce in a false suggestion. The suggestion itself may plant the belief in its truth. Some studies have confirmed the convictions of judges that this danger is greater than one who has had no experience with trials would suppose.[7] And, regardless of his beliefs, a friendly or pliant witness may follow suggestions on direct examination. On the other hand, it can be urged that there is little reason for barring suggestive questions.[8] In many instances, at least, the objection is trivial.

A leading question then is one that suggests to the witness the answer desired by the examiner. A question may be leading because of its form, but often the mere form of a question does not indicate whether it is

---

3. State v. Allemand, 153 La. 741, 96 So. 552, 553 (1923) (better practice is to ask definite questions but here no prejudice); State v. Sullivan, 159 La. 589, 105 So. 631 (1925) (witness volunteered incompetent evidence in course of story which jury were instructed to disregard; no prejudice).

4. Pumphrey v. State, 84 Neb. 636, 122 N.W. 19, 21 (1909).

5. Ewing v. People, 87 Colo. 6, 284 Pac. 341 (1930); State v. Larsen, 42 Idaho 517, 246 Pac. 313, 314 (1926); Dec.Dig. Witnesses ⟨⇌226; Model Code of Evidence Rule 105 (1942).

6. Northern P. R. Co. v. Charless, 51 Fed. 562, 570 (9th Cir. 1892) reversed on other grounds, 162 U.S. 359 (leading case permitting free narrative in court's discretion); Mobile, J. & K. C. R. Co. v. Hawkins, 163 Ala. 565, 51 So. 37, 44 (1909); Temple v. State, 245 Ind. 21, 195 N.E.2d 850 (1964); People v. Belcher, 189 Cal.App. 404, 11 Cal.Rptr. 175 (1961); Kincaide v. Cavanagh, 198 Mass. 34, 84 N.E. 307 (1908) (within court's discretion to permit counsel to place statement of account before witness and ask her generally to explain each item); Hendricks v. St. Louis Transit Co., 124 Mo.App. 157, 101 S.W. 675, 676 (1907) (deposition); Pumphrey v. State, 84 Neb. 636, 122 N.W. 19, 21 (1909) (in court's discretion to require specific questions); Call v. Linn, 112 Ore. 1, 228 Pac. 127, 130 (1924) (question should have been limited to time and place, but since answer so limited no harm); Deams v. State, 159 Tex.Cr.R. 496, 265 S.W. 2d 96 (1954) (judge in discretion could require specific questions). See also Ward v. City of Pitts-

burgh, 353 Pa. 156, 44 A.2d 553 (1945), where it was held not improper for judge to permit witness, whose power of speech had been affected by a stroke, to give his testimony by a written statement, where he was present and could have been cross-examined.

7. Gardner, The Perception and Memory of Witnesses, 18 Corn.L.Q. 391, 405 (1933), citing statements of psychologists and judges. F.R.Ev. (R.D. 1971) 611(c) preserves the objection to leading questions, but more in terms of suggestion than mandate.

8. Cleary, Evidence as a Problem in Communicating, 5 Vand.L.Rev. 277, 287 (1952).

leading. The question which contains a phrase like "Did he not?" is obviously and invariably leading, but almost any other type of question may be leading or not, dependent upon the content and context. It is sometimes supposed that a question which can be answered yes or no is by that fact marked as leading, and the beginner finds it helpful to couch his inquiries in the form of a neutral alternative ("State whether or not . . .") to escape the charge of leading. But quite often the former kind of question will not be leading and equally often the latter kind will be.[9] The whole issue is whether an ordinary man would get the impression that the questioner desired one answer rather than another. The form of a question, or previous questioning, may indicate the desire, but the most important circumstance for consideration is the extent of the particularity of the question itself. If the question describes an incident in detail and asks if the incident happened, the natural inference is that the questioner expects an affirmative answer. Or if one alternative branch of a question is concrete and detailed and the other vague ("Was the sound like the scream of a woman in fear or was it otherwise?") the impression is that the first alternative is suggested. On the other hand, if a question is sufficiently neutral ("At what time did this occur?") or sufficiently balanced ("Was the water hot or cold?"), it is not leading.

As we have seen, the normal practice is for the careful lawyer to interview in advance all witnesses whom he expects to call for direct examination to prove his own case. This practice is entirely proper, but it does create a probability that the lawyer and the witness will have reached an *entente* which will make the witness especially susceptible to suggestions from the lawyer. On the other hand, normally when counsel cross-examines a witness called by the adversary, he has had no opportunity to talk to the witness previously, and in any event there is less likelihood of an understanding between them about the facts. Hence the practice: upon objection, the judge will ordinarily forbid leading questions on direct examination and will ordinarily permit them on cross-examination. But the entire matter of the allowability of leading questions is discretionary,[10] and the judge's action will not be reviewed unless it is charged that it amounted to, or contributed to, the denial of a fair trial.[11]

9. A question which may be answered yes or no is not on that account leading unless it suggests the answer wanted. Harward v. Harward, 173 Md. 339, 196 Atl. 318 (1938); State v. Scott, 20 Wash. 2d 696, 149 P.2d 152 (1944); Implement Dealers Mutual Ins. Co. v. Castleberry, 368 S.W.2d 249 (Tex.Civ.App.1963). And it has been said that prefacing a question by "whether or not" seldom removes its leading character. State v. Murphy, 216 S.C. 44, 56 S.E.2d 736 (1949). For illustrative cases, see 3 Wigmore, Evidence (Chadbourn rev.) §§ 769–772; Dec.Dig. Witnesses ☞240(3–5).

10. See, e. g., Stahl v. United States, 144 F.2d 909 (8th Cir. 1944); People v. Merritt, 367 Ill. 521, 12 N.E.2d 7 (1938); Commonwealth v. Sheppard, 313 Mass. 590, 48 N.E.2d 630 (1943); State v. Painter, 265 N.C. 277, 144 S.E.2d 6 (1965); Model Code of Evidence Rule 105(g) ("The judge . . . in his discretion determines . . . to what extent and in what circumstances a party calling a witness shall be permitted, and a party not calling him shall be forbidden, to put to the witness questions suggesting the desired answers."); Dec.Dig. Witnesses ☞240(2).

11. The formula has been stated in various terms. The abuse must be clear, United States v. Durham, 319 F.2d 590 (4th Cir. 1963), or palpable and prejudicial. Hawthorne v. Pope, 51 Ga.App. 498, 180 S.E. 920 (1935). Other formulas are also used. The trial judge's control is virtually absolute and will be reversed only for gross abuse of power resulting in miscarriage of justice. Usher v. Eckhardt, 176 Minn. 210, 222 N.W. 924 (1929). See Dec.Dig. Appeal and Error ☞971(5); Witnesses ☞240(2). Exaggerated use of leading questions that warp a case may be abuse. Straub v. Reading Co., 220 F.2d 177 (3d Cir. 1955).

Ordinarily, a successful objection to a leading question can be obviated by reframing the question even though theoretically prejudice might result because the suggestion has already been made. Allen v. Hartford Life Ins. Co., 72 Conn. 693, 45 Atl. 955, 956 (1900) (. . . "This result is an incident of that imperfection attaching to all that man does, and from which even judicial procedure cannot be kept free. The only remedy is a preventive one, and lies in the power of trial courts to regulate the conduct of counsel at the bar.").

When the normal assumption about the relation between the witness and the examining counsel or his client appears unfounded, the usual practice is reversed. If, on direct, the witness appears hostile to the examiner, or reluctant, or unwilling; the danger of suggestion disappears, and the judge will permit leading questions,[12] and conversely, if on cross-examination the witness appears to be biased in favor of the cross-examining party, counsel may be prohibited from leading.[13]

In various other situations, leading questions are permitted. They may be used to bring out preliminary matters, such as the name and occupation of the witness; or to elicit matters not substantially in dispute.[14] They may be employed to suggest a subject or topic, as distinguished from an answer.[15] Additional relaxations are grounded in necessity. Thus, the judge, when need appears, will ordinarily permit leading questions to children, or to witnesses so ignorant, timid, weak-minded, or deficient in the English language, that they cannot otherwise be brought to understand what information is sought.[16] It is recognized, especially as to children,[17] that in these cases the danger of false suggestion is at its highest, but it is better to face that danger than to abandon altogether the effort to bring out what the witness knows. Similarly, when a witness has been fully directed to the subject by nonleading questions without securing from him a complete account of what he is believed to know, his memory is said to be "exhausted" and the judge may permit the examiner to ask questions which by their particularity may revive his memory but which of necessity may thereby suggest the answer desired.[18]

In some jurisdictions, there is a long-standing practice that permits leading questions to

While the judge has undoubted authority to foreclose the witness from answering at all on the matter inquired into by the leading question, 3 Wigmore, Evidence (Chadbourn rev.) § 770, n. 4, and a fortiori to prevent counsel from returning to the matter except after an excursion into other matters sufficient to dissipate the effect of the leading question, the authority is seldom exercised.

12. People v. Gallery, 336 Ill. 580, 168 N.E. 650 (1929) (questions by prosecutor to unwilling state's witness; permissible to refresh memory, not to impeach); Bresch v. Wolf, 243 Mich. 638, 220 N.W. 737 (1928); McNeill v. Fidelity & Cas. Co. of New York, 336 Mo. 1142, 82 S.W.2d 582 (1935) (plaintiff's examination of witness employed in agency of defendant insurance company); Dec.Dig. Witnesses ☞244; Annot., 117 A.L.R. 328. In many jurisdictions, a rule or statute permits a party to call the adverse party and interrogate him by leading questions. See F.R.Civ.P. 43(b) (copied in many states); F.R.Ev. (R.D.1971) 611(c). See also § 38, infra.

13. Rush v. French, 1 Ariz. 99, 25 Pac. 816, 828 (1874) (court in discretion may forbid cross-examiner to lead if witness biased in his favor); Moody v. Rowell, 34 Mass. (17 Pick.) 490, 498 (1835); J. & B. Motors v. Margolis, 75 Ariz. 392, 257 P.2d 588 (1953) (cross-examination of officer of corporate party who was called to the stand by opponent); 3 Wigmore, Evidence (Chadbourn rev.) § 773.

14. Southern Ry. Co. v. Hall, 209 Ala. 237, 96 So. 73 (1923) (introductory questions identifying time and place of incident in suit). So also as to preliminary matters triable to the court in the absence of the jury. State v. Castelli, 92 Conn. 58, 101 Atl. 476, 479 (1917) (question whether threats were made or inducements given to secure confession); Dec.Dig. Witnesses ☞241.

15. People v. Hodge, 141 Mich. 312, 104 N.W. 599 (1905); Gerler v. Cooley, 41 Ill.App.2d 233, 190 N.E.2d 488 (1963); State v. Ward, 10 Utah 2d 34, 347 P.2d 865 (1958).

16. State v. Tenney, 137 Wash. 47, 241 Pac. 669 (1925) (child 12 years old, prosecuting witness in rape); Campion v. Lattimer, 70 Neb. 245, 97 N.W. 290 (1903) (ignorant, dull person); Preston v. Denkins, 94 Ariz. 214, 382 P.2d 686 (1963) (78 year old witness in poor health and with defective independent recall); Dec.Dig. Witnesses ☞243.

17. See Coon v. People, 99 Ill. 368, 370 (1879).

18. Gray v. Kelley, 190 Mass. 184, 76 N.E. 724 (1906); O'Hagan v. Dillon, 76 N.Y. 170, 173 (1879); Born v. Rosenow, 84 Wis. 620, 54 N.W. 1089 (1893); People v. Jones, 221 Cal.App.2d 619, 34 Cal.Rptr. 618 (1963); 3 Wigmore, Evidence (Chadbourn rev.) § 777; Dec.Dig. Witnesses ☞242. And where a hostile witness surprises the examiner by testimony contrary to his earlier statement before trial, the examiner may ask leading questions about the former statement, not to discredit but to refresh his recollection. People v. Gallery, 336 Ill. 580, 168 N.E. 650 (1929); Malone v. State, 192 Wis. 379, 212 N.W. 879 (1927); People v. Jehl, 150 Cal.App. 2d 665, 310 P.2d 495 (1957).

a witness who, for impeachment purposes, is to testify to a statement of a previous witness that is inconsistent with the testimony of that witness.[19] Necessity again is said to be the basis of the practice. It might otherwise be impossible to call attention to the subject of the testimony.[20] It has been argued, however, that the practice should not be followed.[21]

7. The Form of Questions: (c) Misleading and Argumentative Questions.

The examiner may not ask a question that merely invokes the witness's assent to the questioner's inferences from or interpretations of the facts proved or assumed. This kind of question is subject to objection as "argumentative"[22], but the trial court has a wide range of discretion in enforcing the rule, particularly on cross-examination, the more frequent occasion for such questions. A still more common vice is for the examiner to couch the question so that it assumes as true matters to which the witness has not testified, and which are in dispute between the parties.[23] The danger here is twofold. First, if the examiner is putting the question to a friendly witness, the recitation of the assumed fact may suggest the desired answer; and second, whether the witness is friendly or hostile, the answer is likely to be misleading. Oftentimes, the question will be so separate from the assumption that if the witness answers the question without mentioning the assumption, it is impossible to ascertain whether he ignored the assumption or affirmed it.

Occasionally questions are considered objectionable because they are too broad or too indefinite. Often this objection is in reality an objection of lack of relevancy.[24]

---

19. People v. Abair, 102 Cal.App.2d 765, 228 P.2d 336 (1951); Swanson v. McDonald, 58 S.D. 119, 235 N.W. 118 (1935) (citing authorities); Dec.Dig. Witnesses ⊂⊃391.

20. 3 Wigmore, Evidence (Chadbourn rev.) § 779. The practice is justified also as pinpointing the inquiry and thus avoiding the bringing out of incompetent matter which might result from general questions. Elgin, J. & E. Ry. Co. v. Lawlor, 132 Ill.App. 280 (1907), aff'd 229 Ill. 621, 82 N.E. 407.

21. See Swoboda v. Union P. R. Co., 87 Neb. 200, 127 N.W. 215, 220, 221 (1910), and Norton v. Parsons, 67 Vt. 526, 32 Atl. 481, 482 (1895), which recognize, but deprecate, the practice.

22. Questions held argumentative: Pettus v. Louisville & N. R. Co., 214 Ala. 187, 106 So. 807 (1926) ("If you had not been burning off the grass and weeds . . . on the right of way, it was still there?"); Johnson v. Wilmington City Ry. Co., 23 Del. 5, 76 Atl. 961 (1905) ("Was there any other force of any kind, other than the suction created by the rapidly moving car, that would cause the rope to become entangled in the gearing?"); White v. State, 22 Okl.Cr. 131, 210 Pac. 313 (1922) (in mayhem prosecution, question, "Isn't it a fact that [defendant's] mouth is so small that he could not reach up and get it wide enough open to get [complainant's] ear in there?", argumentative where both mouth and ear were visible to jury); C.J.S. Witnesses § 328b(5).

23. Questions held objectionable: Haithcock v. State, 23 Ala.App. 460, 126 So. 890 (1930) (questions on cross-examination of defendant's witness, as to how long defendant was making liquor); Price v. Rosenberg, 200 Mass. 36, 85 N.E. 887 (1908) (in action for price of goods, question to plaintiff as to how he knew that goods delivered were goods called for in contract, improper as assuming that the goods delivered were those called for); Reardon v. Boston Elev. Ry. Co., 311 Mass. 228, 40 N.E.2d 865 (1942) (question as to how many years water used to come through walls, bad as assuming that it had come through at all in the past); Central Radiator Co. v. Niagara Fire Ins. Co., 109 N.J.L. 48, 160 Atl. 342 (1932) (questions as to what the custom is, without any previous testimony that any custom about the matter exists); Kirschman v. Pitt Pub. Co., 318 Pa. 570, 178 Atl. 828 (1935) (affirmative answer to question assuming disputed fact is no evidence of the fact assumed); Cherry v. Hill, 283 Ala. 74, 214 So.2d 427 (1968) (question as to how long witness had seen pedestrians use a roadway assumed pedestrians had been using roadway); Dec.Dig. Witnesses ⊂⊃237; 3 Wigmore, Evidence (Chadbourn rev.) §§ 771, 780.

But the questioner may properly assume the truth of a disputed fact previously testified to by the same witness. State v. Marshall, 105 Iowa 38, 74 N.W. 763 (1898); Graham v. McReynolds, 90 Tenn. 673, 18 S.W. 272 (1891) (question by court).

24. See for example, People v. Williams, 200 Cal. App.2d 838, 19 Cal.Rptr. 743 (1962), and cases cited in Dec.Dig. Witnesses ⊂⊃236.

8. The Judge May Examine [25] and Call [26] Witnesses.

Under the Anglo-American adversary trial system, the parties and their counsel have the primary responsibility for finding, selecting, and presenting the evidence.[27] However, our system of party-investigation and party-presentation has some limitations. It is a means to the end of disclosing truth and administering justice; and for reaching this end the judge may exercise various powers.

Prominent among these powers is his power to call and question witnesses.

The judge in his discretion may examine any witness to bring out needed facts which have not been elicited by the parties.[28] Also, it is sometimes said that the judge may have a duty to question witnesses, although the exercise of such a duty does not appear to have been enforced by any appellate court decisions.[29]

In those states—the great majority—in which the judge does not have power to comment on the weight of the evidence, the judge's questioning in jury cases must be cautiously guarded so as not to constitute an implied comment.[30] Thus, if the judge uses leading questions, suggesting the desired answer, the questions may often strongly imply that the desired answer is the truth, and thus may offend the rule against comment.[31] Subject to the limitation that a leading question may constitute prohibited comment, it has been held that the policy against leading questions by counsel, namely, that of avoiding false testimony elicited by partisan suggestion,[32] has no application in general to judges,[33] whose office is to be impartial. This

---

25. 3 Wigmore, Evidence (Chadbourn rev.) § 784, 9 id. § 2484; C.J.S. Witnesses §§ 348–349; Annot., 84 A.L.R. 1172; Dec.Dig. Witnesses ⚓246.

26. 9 Wigmore, Evidence § 2484, n. 1; C.J.S. Witnesses § 350; Annot., 67 A.L.R.2d 538; Annot., 95 A.L.R.2d 390; Dec.Dig. Witnesses ⚓246(2).

27. The adversary system should be compared with the inquisitional system that prevails in some European countries where the judge has a wider responsibility for investigating the facts and presenting the proofs. See 9 Wigmore, Evidence § 2483. In the adversary system, the judge cannot exclude a party from examining witnesses called by the party and proceed to conduct the direct examination himself. Dreyer v. Ershowsky, 156 App.Div. 27, 140 N.Y.S. 819 (1913).

28. State v. Kirby, 273 N.C. 306, 160 S.E.2d 24 (1968); Griffin v. United States, 83 U.S.App.D.C. 20, 164 F.2d 903 (1947); State v. Keehn, 85 Kan. 765, 118 Pac. 851 (1911); McLaughlin v. Municipal Court, 308 Mass. 397, 32 N.E.2d 266, 271 (1941); State v. Riley, 28 N.J. 188, 145 A.2d 601 (1958) cert. denied 359 U.S. 313.

Jurors, with the judge's leave, may question the witnesses. White v. Little, 131 Okla. 132, 268 Pac. 221 (1928); Stamp v. Commonwealth, 200 Ky. 133, 253 S.W. 242 (1923); C.J.S. Witnesses § 351; Annot., 159 A.L.R. 347. See O'Nellion v. Haynes, 122 Cal.App. 329, 9 P.2d 853 (1932), where a juror asked the defendant "You carry liability insurance, don't you?" and was answered, "Yes," before objection could be made. The privilege of permitting jurors to ask questions of witnesses should be granted only when in sound discretion of court it appears that it will aid a juror in understanding a material issue involved, and ordinarily when some juror has indicated that he wishes the point clarified. State v. Anderson, 108 Utah 130, 158 P.2d 127 (1945). A judge's invitation to jurors to interrogate witnesses was condemned in State v. Martinez, 7 Utah 2d 387, 326 P.2d 102 (1958). If questions are allowed, a requirement that they be submitted to the judge in writing will facilitate consideration in the absence of the jury and avoid prejudice to an objecting party.

29. "He enjoys the prerogative, rising often to the standard of a duty, of eliciting those facts he deems necessary to the clear presentation of the issues. Pariser v. City of New York, 2 Cir., 146 F.2d 431." Clark, J., in United States v. Brandt, 196 F.2d 653, 655 (2d Cir. 1952); C.J.S. Witnesses § 348. F.R.Ev. (R.D.1971) 614(b) provides that the judge may interrogate witnesses.

30. People v. De Lordo, 350 Ill. 148, 182 N.E. 726, 730, 731 (1932); Risley v. Moberg, 69 Wash.2d 560, 419 P.2d 151 (1966); Annot., 84 A.L.R. 1181.

31. See, e. g., People v. Bowers, 79 Cal. 415, 21 Pac. 752 (1889); Frangos v. Edmunds, 179 Ore. 577, 173 P.2d 596 (1946); Anderson v. State, 83 Tex.Cr.R. 261, 202 S.W. 944 (1918); State v. Crotts, 22 Wash. 245, 60 Pac. 403 (1900).

32. See § 6, supra.

33. Commonwealth v. Galavan, 91 Mass. (9 Allen) 271 (1864); Connor v. Township of Brant, 31 Ont.L. Rep. 274 (1913). Instances wherein particular leading questions by the judge were held necessary and within his discretion: Stinson v. State, 125 Ark. 339, 189 S.W. 49 (1916) (carnal abuse, questions to victim); Driscoll v. People, 47 Mich. 413, 11 N.W. 221, 223 (1882); State v. Riley, 28 N.J. 188, 145 A.2d 601 (1958) cert. denied 359 U.S. 313.

reasoning seems somewhat questionable.[34] Also, questions which are aimed at discrediting or impeaching the witness, though allowable for counsel, when asked by the judge may often—not always—intimate the judge's belief that the witness has been lying, and thus be an implied comment on the weight of his testimony.[35]

In the federal courts and in the few states where the common law power to comment is retained, and in judge-tried cases in all jurisdictions, these restrictions on leading questions and impeaching questions are relaxed. Nevertheless, even then, the judge, though he has a wide power to examine witnesses, must avoid extreme exercises of the power to question, just as he must avoid extreme exercises of the power to comment. He must not assume the role of an advocate or of a prosecutor.[36] If his questions are too partisan or even if they are too extensive, he faces the risk that the appellate court will find that he has crossed the line between judging and advocacy.[37]

34. See remark in Commonwealth v. Berklowitz, 133 Pa.Super. 190, 2 A.2d 516 (1938).

35. State v. Allen, 100 Iowa 7, 69 N.W. 274 (1896) (error to ask defendant's witness if he had conversed with defendant's counsel before trial); State v. Drew, 213 S.W. 106 (Mo.1919) (questions indicating a purpose to discredit defendant and one of his witnesses). But it seems that not all questions bearing on credibility would show an adverse opinion, even though the answer might happen to be discrediting. Thus, neutral questions about knowledge or interest seemingly might be needed and desirable. See Cusmano v. United States, 13 F. 2d 451 (6th Cir. 1926) (questions disclosing witness's absence of knowledge, proper). See also Madison v. State, 200 Md. 1, 87 A.2d 593 (1958) (murder; judge's questioning of accused held not erroneous: "A judge's right to ask questions is not confined to questions which have no possible bearing on credibility."). Accordingly, the view of the court in State v. Perry, 231 N.C. 467, 57 S.E.2d 774 (1950), that "it is improper for a trial judge to ask questions for the purpose of impeaching" may need qualification.

36. United States v. Lee, 107 F.2d 522, 529 (7th Cir. 1939); State v. Winchester, 166 Kan. 512, 203 P.2d 229, 233 (1949).

37. See United States v. Brandt, 196 F.2d 653 (2d Cir. 1952) (conviction set aside where judge asked

Not only may the judge examine witnesses called by the parties, but in his discretion he may also, for the purpose of bringing out needed facts, call witnesses whom the parties might not have chosen to call.[38] The power to call witnesses is perhaps most often exercised when the prosecution expects that a necessary witness will be hostile and desires to escape the necessity of calling him and being cumbered by the traditional rule against impeaching one's own witness. The prosecutor may then invoke the judge's discretion to call the witness,[39] in which event either

more than 900 questions during eight-day trial and cross-examined accused and defense witnesses with apparent purpose of emphasizing inconsistencies in defense and discrediting defense witnesses; instructive opinion by Clark, J.); United States v. Fry, 304 F.2d 296 (7th Cir. 1962) (1,210 questions by judge); United States v. Hill, 332 F.2d 105 (7th Cir. 1964) (implication of incredulity by course of questioning); Taylor v. Taylor, 177 Minn. 428, 225 N.W. 287 (1929) (in judge-tried case judge by questioning took charge of party's case and became a partisan, but judgment not reversed).

38. Marin Water & Power Co. v. R. R. Comm., 171 Cal. 706, 154 Pac. 864, 867 (1916) (commission as a judicial tribunal may call witnesses); Merchants Bank v. Goodfellow, 44 Utah 349, 140 Pac. 759 (1914) (suit on bill of exchange, court called last endorser). See Annot., 67 A.L.R.2d 538; Annot., 95 A.L.R.2d 390; 51 Nw.U.L.Rev. 761 (1957). F.R. Ev. (R.D.1971) 614(a) provides that the judge may call witnesses.

There has been a suggestion that in some cases, in the interest of justice, the judge may have the duty as well as the power to call witnesses and hence may be reversed for a failure to do so. See Moore v. Sykes' Estate, 167 Miss. 212, 149 So. 789 (1933); Frankfurter, J., dissenting, in Johnson v. United States, 33 U.S. 46 (1948); 58 Yale L.J. 183 (1948). But efforts at reversal on this ground have been unavailing, e. g., Steinberg v. United States, 162 F.2d 120 (5th Cir. 1947); United States v. Lester, 248 F.2d 329 (2d Cir. 1957); State v. Hines, 270 Minn. 30, 133 N.W.2d 371 (1964); Halloran-Judge Trust Co. v. Carr, 62 Utah 10, 218 Pac. 138 (1923). And Wigmore denies the existence of a duty. 9 Wigmore, Evidence § 2484.

39. See, e. g., Young v. United States, 107 F.2d 490 (5th Cir. 1939) (sole surviving eyewitness of homicide who had made inconsistent statements to prosecution); People v. Shelton, 388 Ill. 56, 57 N.E. 2d 473 (1944) (rape of girl under age, court called joint indictee for whose integrity prosecution could not vouch); 3A Wigmore, Evidence (Chadbourn rev.) § 918; but the judge's discretion was limited to prosecution witnesses whose testimony relates

party may cross-examine and impeach him. Another use of the power, implemented by statute in some jurisdictions, is to mediate the battle of partisan expert witnesses employed by the parties, through the judge's resumption of his ancient power to call an expert of his own choosing, or one agreed upon by the parties, to give impartial testimony to aid him or the jury in resolving a scientific issue.[40] But the judge's power of calling witnesses in aid of justice is general and is not necessarily limited to meeting these particular needs.[41]

9. Refreshing Recollection.[42]

It is abundantly clear from everyday observation that the latent memory of an experience may be revived by an image seen, or a statement read or heard. This is a part of the group of phenomena which the classical psychologists have called the law of association. The recall of any part of a past experience tends to bring with it the other parts that were in the same field of awareness, and a new experience tends to stimulate the recall of other like experiences.[43] The effect of a reminder, encountered in reading a newspaper or in the conversation of a friend, which gives us the sensation of recognizing as familiar some happening which we had forgotten, and prompts our memory to bring back associated experiences, is a frequently encountered process.[44]

As we have seen,[45] the interviewing of witnesses by counsel who will examine them in court is a necessary step in preparing for trial. It is at this stage that the memory of the witness can best be refreshed about the facts of the case, by giving him the opportunity to read his own written statements previously made, or the letters, maps, or other documents in the case. It is only when this review of the data is insufficient to enable the

directly to the issues upon a showing that the state was unable to vouch for credibility in People v. Moriarity, 33 Ill.2d 606, 213 N.E.2d 516 (1966). In civil cases, the calling of witnesses by the judge for this purpose is said to be in his discretion. McBride v. Dexter, 250 Iowa 7, 92 N.W.2d 443 (1958). But the case authority in civil cases is relatively sparse. Denying the accused in criminal cases standing to invoke the judge's discretion may suggest constitutional problems.

The rule against impeaching one's own witness is on the decline. See § 38, supra.

40. See, e. g., Hunt v. State, 248 Ala. 217, 27 So.2d 186 (1946) (murder; experts on sanity, pursuant to statute); Citizens State Bank v. Castro, 105 Cal. App. 284, 287 Pac. 559 (1930) (handwriting expert, pursuant to statute); Christina v. Cusimano, 125 La. 1056, 52 So. 157, 158 (1910) (same, pursuant to statute; power recognized but here improperly exercised); Polulich v. J. G. Schmidt Tool, Etc. Co., 46 N.J.Super. 135, 134 A.2d 29 (1957) (workmen's compensation: deputy having power of judge may call impartial expert: extensive discussion); State v. Horne, 171 N.C. 787, 88 S.E. 433 (1916) (alienist in murder case: "expert witnesses . . . were originally regarded as amici curiae and were called generally by the court," citing 3 Chamberlayne, Evidence, §§ 2376, 2552); Scott v. Spanjer Bros., 298 F.2d 928 (2d Cir. 1962); Annot., 95 A.L.R.2d 390.

In some jurisdictions, a court rule or statute authorizes court appointment of expert witnesses. See discussion in § 17, infra.

41. If there is no statutory authority, there may be practical problems concerning costs and pretrial services of the expert.

42. 3 Wigmore, Evidence (Chadbourn rev.) §§ 758–765; Maguire and Quick, Testimony, Memory and Memoranda, 3 How.L.J. 1 (1957); Dec.Dig. Witnesses ⟜ 253–260; Annots., 125 A.L.R. 19, 82 A.L.R.2d 473; Note, 3 U.C.L.A.L.Rev. 616 (1956); C.J.S. Witnesses § 357.

43. These are the principles of contiguity and similarity. See Gardner, The Perception and Memory of Witnesses, 18 Corn.L.Q. 390, 392 (1933); Hutchins and Slesinger, Some Observations on the Law of Evidence—Memory, 41 Harv.L.Rev. 860 (1928); 2 Encyc.Brit. Association of Ideas (1948).

44. "In permitting a witness to refresh his recollection by consulting a memorandum, the courts are in accord with present psychological knowledge. A distinction is drawn, in the analysis of the memory process, between *recall*, which is the reproduction of what has been learned, and *recognition*, which is recall with a time-factor added, or an awareness that the recall relates to past experience. It is with recognition that the law is principally concerned in permitting a witness to revive his recollection. The psychological evidence is clear that in thus allowing to be brought to mind what has been forgotten, the law is following sound psychological procedure." Cairn, Law and the Social Sciences 200 (1935).

45. See § 2, supra.

witness to recall the facts while testifying that refreshing his memory on the stand is advisable. If it is matter which a jury would suppose he should remember unaided, the use of a crutch lessens their confidence in the testimony.

At trials, the practice has long been established that in interrogating a witness counsel may hand him a memorandum to inspect for the purpose of "refreshing his recollection," with the result that when he speaks from a memory thus revived, his testimony is what he says, not the writing.[46] This is the process of *refreshing recollection* in the strict and accurate sense. But when this simple but helpful expedient had become established, it was natural for counsel to seek to carry it a step further. If the witness, being shown the writing, states that his memory is not revived thereby and that he cannot testify from a refreshed recollection, he may indicate on looking at the writing, that he recognizes it as a memorandum made by him when the facts were fresh in his mind, and *therefore,* though he has no present memory of the transaction described, he is willing to testify that the facts were as recited in the memorandum. We now recognize this latter situation as quite a different process from the process of *refreshing recollection.* In the process of refreshing recollection, the witness testifies orally on his present refreshed memory; when his memory is not jogged, he merely relies upon his written recital of things remembered in the past.[47]

The procedure of tendering a memorandum to the witness is alike in both cases, and it was convenient to justify the extension by the old and approved phrase, "refreshing recollection." But the underlying justification in the newer situation is quite different. It rests on the reliability of a writing which the witness swears is a *record of his past recollection.* Appropriate safeguarding rules have been developed for this latter kind of memoranda, requiring that they must have been written by the witness or examined and found correct by him, and that they must have been prepared so promptly after the events recorded that the events must have been fresh in the mind of the witness when the record was made or examined and verified by him. In this volume these latter memoranda are considered separately, as a possible exception to the hearsay rule.[48]

Apparently, the earlier English cases of genuine refreshment of recollection imposed no restriction upon *the use of memoranda to refresh.*[49] The memoranda were not required to have been written by the witness or under his direction, or to have been made near in time to the event. In the later-developed practice of using records of *past recollection* restrictions of this kind, with good reason, were imposed. Since, however, the old name of "refreshing recollection" was given to both practices, it was natural that the restrictions developed for one kind of memoranda should be applied to the other.

Which is the wiser practice, the rule of the older cases, championed by Wigmore and by most present-day courts, to the effect that any memoranda, without restriction of authorship, time, or correctness, may be used when the purpose is to revive memory; or the rule requiring that the memorandum to refresh must meet the same tests as the record of past recollection? Even if the latter requirement is an historical or analytical blunder, it will be none the worse for that

---

46. Henry v. Lee, 2 Chitty 124 (1810), cited 3 Wigmore, Evidence (Chadbourn rev.) § 758.

47. See Jewett v. United States, 15 F.2d 955, 956 (9th Cir. 1926), and extended explanation in United States v. Riccardi, 174 F.2d 883 (3d Cir. 1949) cert. denied 337 U.S. 941.

48. See Ch. 30, infra. But if the memorandum was prepared by the witness it is also arguable that it is admissible as a non-hearsay statement. See § 251, infra.

49. Henry v. Lee, supra n. 46; Rex v. St. Martin's, 2 Ad. & El. 210, 111 Eng.Rep. 81 (K.B.1834).

if it is a safeguard needed in the search for truth.

It is true that any kind of stimulus, "a song, or a face, or a newspaper item," [50] may produce the "flash" of recognition, the feeling that "it all comes back to me now." But the genuineness of the feeling is no guaranty of the correctness of the image recalled. The danger that the mind will "remember" something that never happened is at least as great here as in the case of leading questions. "The problem is complicated by the deceptive certainty of the recognizer. This certainty is a direct function of the similarity of the material. As a result it has an eccentric relation to objective accuracy. . . . It will be objected that, although the foregoing criteria may be interesting as far as recognition is concerned, a present refreshed recollection is based only in part on recognition. Granting this inaccuracy, is there any proof that recall, stimulated by that recognition, and supposed to 'function independently thereof,' is also inaccurate? A recent experiment answers the objection decisively. In a class lecture the instructor made certain unequivocal statements about the results of a series of experiments. A well-meaning, but none too thoughtful, reporter on the local student paper printed an entirely erroneous account of the lecture. On the routine examination at the end of the week, after the usual questions, each student was asked to indicate on his paper whether or not he had read the press account. Most of those who had read it 'recognized' it as accurate, and on the examination paper remembered what they had erroneously recognized. Those who had not read the article reported the lecture with their customary accuracy." [51] "Imagination

and suggestion are twin artists ever ready to retouch the fading daguerrotype of memory." [52]

Thus, decisions which import into the realm of refreshing memory the requirements developed for memoranda of past recollection recorded, namely, the requirements that the witness must have made the writing or have recognized it as correct, and that the making or recognition must have occurred at the time of the event or while it was fresh in memory,[53] have a plausible basis in expediency.

Nevertheless, most courts today when faced with the clear distinction between the two uses of the memoranda, will adhere to the "classical" view that any memorandum or other object may be used as a stimulus to present memory, without restriction by rule as to authorship, guaranty of correctness, or time of making.[54] On balance, it would seem

50. See Jewett v. United States, supra, n. 47.

51. Hutchins and Slesinger, Some Observations on the Law of Evidence—Memory, 41 Harv.L.Rev. 860, 868, 869 (1928). See also the telling passage quoted from Bentham, 3 Wigmore, Evidence (Chadbourn rev.) § 758.

52. Gardner, The Perception and Memory of Witnesses, 18 Corn.L.Q. 390, 401 (1933).

53. See, e. g., Putnam v. United States, 162 U.S. 687, 695 (1896) (transcript of prior testimony by witness not allowed to be used to refresh, because not contemporaneous with events testified about); State v. Patton, 255 Mo. 245, 164 S.W. 223 (1914) (similar to last; "the ease with which, as Prof. Muensterberg tells us, the human mind is influenced by suggestion would seem to form an insuperable psychological objection to the use of data for this purpose, of the correctness of which the witness is ignorant"); NLRB v. Hudson Pulp and Paper Corp., 273 F.2d 660 (5th Cir. 1960) (affidavit used was too remote in time; alternate ground of decision).

These requirements would create special difficulties in respect to the use of a transcript of the witness's own prior testimony. Hale, The Use by a Witness of His Own Prior Testimony for the Purpose of Refreshing His Recollection, 15 St. Louis L.Rev. 137, 146 (1930). However, most cases involving transcripts have not imposed the requirements. Annot., 82 A.L.R.2d 473, 597–602. See Ch. 25, infra.

54. For rule that witness need not have made the memorandum, see Henowitz v. Rockville Savings Bank, 118 Conn. 527, 173 Atl. 221, 222 (1934) (photograph of stairway excluded from evidence because not fairly representative, allowed to be used to refresh); People v. Griswold, 405 Ill. 533, 92 N.E.2d 91 (1950) (memorandum of conversation not made by witness); Commonwealth v. McDermott, 255 Mass. 575, 152 N.E. 704 (1926) (any paper though not made by witness); Litchfield v. Paynes-

that this liberality of practice is the wiser solution because there are other sufficient safeguards to protect against abuse. The first safeguard is the power of control by the trial judge. It is a preliminary question for his decision whether the memorandum actually does refresh, and from the nature of the memorandum and the witness's testimony he may find that it does not.[55] Moreover, in the exercise of his discretion to control the manner of the examination,[56] as

in the case of leading questions, he may decline to permit the use of the aid to memory where he regards the danger of undue suggestion as outweighing the probable value.

The second safeguard is the rule which entitles the adverse party, when the witness seeks to resort to the memorandum, to inspect the memorandum so that he may object to its use if ground appears,[57] and to have the memorandum available for his reference in cross-examining the witness.[58] With the memorandum before him, the cross-examiner has a good opportunity to test the credibility of the witness's claim that his memory has been revived, and to search out any discrepancies between the writing and the testimony. This right to demand inspection has usually been limited to writings used by the witness on the stand,[59] but the reasons seem

ville, 258 Minn. 210, 103 N.W.2d 402 (1960); State v. Hale, 85 N.H. 403, 160 Atl. 95 (1932); Copeland Co. v. Davis, 125 S.C. 449, 119 S.E. 19 (1923); 3 Wigmore, Evidence (Chadbourn rev.) § 759; Annot., 82 A.L.R.2d 473. Compare People v. Betts, 272 App.Div. 737, 74 N.Y.S.2d 791 (1947), noted 23 N.Y. U.L.Q. 529, 34 Va.L.Rev. 607. There the court held that a policeman who had destroyed the notes taken by him during a conversation with accused, and also his transcript from those notes, to avoid their use on cross-examination, was improperly allowed to refresh his memory from another version of his transcript embodied in the complaint. Also, compare Gardner v. Hobbs, 69 Idaho 288, 206 P.2d 539 (1949); State v. Peacock, 236 N.C. 137, 72 S.E.2d 612 (1952).

That a memorandum need not be made at or near the time of the event recorded, see Commonwealth v. McDermott, 255 Mass. 575, 152 N.E. 704 (1926); Sagers v. International Smelting Co., 50 Utah 423, 168 Pac. 105 (1917); Litchfield v. Paynesville, 258 Minn. 210, 103 N.W.2d 402 (1960); Smith v. Bergmann, 377 S.W.2d 519 (Mo.App.1964) (memorandum prepared by witness the night before testifying); State v. Little, 57 Wash.2d 516, 358 P.2d 120 (1961).

That a witness need not vouch for the correctness of the memorandum is indicated by Williams v. Stroh Plumbing & Elec. Inc., 250 Iowa 599, 94 N.W.2d 750 (1959); United States v. McKeever, 169 F.Supp. 426 (D.C.N.Y.1958). But several opinions contain a contrary implication. Anderson v. State, 150 Neb. 116, 33 N.W.2d 362 (1948); Tebeau v. Baden Equipment & Const. Co., 295 S.W.2d 184 (Mo.App.1956). See also, Rasbury v. State, 303 P.2d 465 (Okl.Cr.1956).

55. The statement of the witness is not conclusive when the circumstances show that his memory is in fact not revived. Weigel v. Powers Elevator Co., 49 N.D. 867, 194 N.W. 113, 120 (1923). Compare an important case in which it was held that the memory of witnesses who testified while consulting a lengthy list of articles was actually refreshed. United States v. Riccardi, 174 F.2d 883 (3d Cir. 1949) (instructive opinion by Kalodner, J.).

56. The element of discretion is recognized in United States v. Lonardo, 67 F.2d 883 (3d Cir. 1933); Farmers Elev. Co. v. Great Northern R. Co., 131 Minn.

152, 154 N.W. 954 (1915); State v. Bradley, 361 Mo. 267, 234 S.W.2d 556 (1950); Myers v. Weger, 62 N.J.L. 432, 42 Atl. 280, 283 (1899); Dec.Dig. Witnesses ⊕255; C.J.S. Witnesses § 358; Model Code of Evidence Rule 105(i).

57. Morris v. United States, 149 Fed. 123, (5th Cir. 1907); Shell Oil Co. v. Pou, 204 So.2d 155 (Miss. 1967). See also State v. Gadwood, 342 Mo. 466, 116 S.W.2d 42, 51 (1938) (in trial judge's discretion whether inspection postponed to time of cross-examination); State v. Bean, 119 Vt. 184, 122 A.2d 744 (1956) (cites and applies State v. Gadwood).

58. Little v. United States, 93 F.2d 401 (8th Cir. 1937); People v. Gezzo, 307 N.Y. 385, 121 N.E.2d 380 (1954) (prejudicial error to refuse inspection); State v. Carter, 268 N.C. 648, 151 S.E.2d 602 (1966); Green v. State, 53 Tex.Cr.R. 490, 110 S.W. 920 (1908); Dec.Dig. Witnesses ⊕256; Annot., 125 A.L.R. 194; Annot., 82 A.L.R.2d 473, 557–562; 3 Wigmore, Evidence (Chadbourn rev.) § 762. Compare United States v. Socony Vacuum Oil Co., 310 U.S. 150, 233 (1940), in which it was held (reversing the Circuit Court of Appeals) that where a transcript of prior testimony was not shown to the witness, but the judge read from it to refresh the witness, the opposing counsel was not entitled of right to inspect it, but under these conditions the matter was in the judge's discretion.

59. Lennon v. United States, 20 F.2d 490 (8th Cir. 1927); Star Mfg. Co. v. Atlantic Coast Line R. Co., 222 N.C. 330, 23 S.E.2d 32 (1942); State v. Paschall, 182 Wash. 304, 47 P.2d 15 (1935) (transcript of prior testimony, in hands of state's counsel, in court) and cases collected in Annot., 125 A.L.R. 200; Annot., 82 A.L.R.2d 473, 562–569; C.J.S. Witnesses § 362.

equally applicable to writings used by the witness to refresh his memory before he testifies. Doubtless the courts have thought that to require inspection of such papers may unduly encourage prying into the opponent's file, but increasingly, the decisions reflect the view that there is a public interest in the full disclosure of the source of a witness's testimony.[60]

Not only may the adversary inspect the memoranda used to refresh memory, but he may submit them to the jury for their examination.[61] On the other hand, the party offering the witness may not do so unless the memoranda constitute independent evidence and are not barred by the hearsay rule.[62] The cardinal rule is that unless they may be introduced under the hearsay rule or one of its exceptions, they are not evidence, but only aids in the giving of evidence. Consequently, a copy may be used without accounting for the original.[63]

The line between using the writing as an aid to memory and basing one's testimony upon it as a correct record of past memory is sometimes shadowy. Must it be shown that the witness has no present recollection of the matters embodied in the memorandum before he can use it as an aid to memory? It is sometimes said that this must appear,[64] but it is believed that this requirement is unsound. The witness may believe that he remembers completely but on looking at the memorandum he would be caused to recall additional facts. As the Chinese proverb has it, "The palest ink is clearer than the best memory." On the other hand, there is here

---

60. Early cases are primarily criminal cases. The Alpha, 44 F.Supp. 809, 815 (E.D.Pa.1942) (not a criminal case); State v. Deslovers, 40 R.I. 89, 100 Atl. 64, 69 (1917), relying on 3 Wigmore, Evidence § 762. If the memorandum is not in court or immediately available, the court should have a discretion whether to require its production. Commonwealth v. Lannan, 95 Mass. (13 Allen) 563, 569 (1866).

Recent cases usually involve a demand by defendant in a criminal case to examine documents used by government witnesses to refresh their memories. State v. Mucci, 25 N.J. 423, 136 A.2d 761 (1957) (noteworthy opinion by Heher, J.); People v. Scott, 29 Ill.2d 97, 193 N.E.2d 814 (1963); State v. Bradshaw, 101 R.I. 233, 221 A.2d 815 (1966); Pruitt v. State, 172 Tex.Cr.R. 187, 355 S.W.2d 528 (1962); Petition of Massachusetts Trustees of Eastern G. & F. Ass'n, 200 F.Supp. 625 (D.C.Va.1962) (not a criminal case; court speaks of the "rule in admiralty").

In civil cases, the availability of broad discovery rules in many states, see § 3, supra, tends to minimize the instant problem, but does not eliminate it. In criminal cases, broad rules of discovery do not as yet exist to the same extent. See § 3, supra, § 97, infra. It might also be observed that the requirement that a criminal defendant be awarded the right to inspect reports of government agents, as established in Jencks v. United States, 353 U.S. 657 (1957), and now governed and restricted for the federal courts by the so-called Jencks Act, 18 U.S.C.A. § 3500, is not related to production for inspection when the reports are used to refresh memory. But in his opinion in United States v. Augenblick, 393 U.S. 348 (1969), Justice Douglas, referring to the *Jencks* case and the Jencks Act, observed their rules had never been applied to state criminal trials, but added, "It may be that denial of production of a Jencks Act type of a statement might be a denial of the Sixth Amendment right."

F.R.Ev. (R.D.1971) 612 provides for the production of writings used to refresh memory prior to taking the stand, in both civil and criminal cases. To the same effect is West's Ann.Cal.Evid.Code, § 771.

61. Smith v. Jackson, 113 Mich. 511, 71 N.W. 843 (1897); Annot., 125 A.L.R. 78. When so submitted by the adversary it would seem that he may place it in evidence, to let the jury compare it with the testimony. Riley v. Fletcher, 185 Ala. 570, 64 So. 85, 87 (1913); Annot., 82 A.L.R.2d 473, 518, 519; West's Ann.Cal.Evid.Code, § 771. But see, contra, Jurgiewicz v. Adams, 71 R.I. 239, 43 A.2d 310 (1945).

62. Luse v. United States, 49 F.2d 241 (9th Cir. 1931); Shear v. Rogoff, 288 Mass. 357, 193 N.E. 63 (1934); Miller v. Borough of Exeter, 366 Pa. 336, 77 A.2d 395 (1951); Dec.Dig. Witnesses ☞257; Annot., 125 A.L.R. 65; Annot., 82 A.L.R.2d 473, 517, 518.

63. Atlanta, & St. A. B. Ry. R. Co., v. Ewing, 112 Fla. 483, 150 So. 586 (1933); Commonwealth v. Levine, 280 Mass. 83, 181 N.E. 851 (1932); Dec.Dig. Witnesses ☞255(5); Annot., 125 A.L.R. 50; Annot., 82 A.L.R.2d 473, 505, 506. Compare Jewett v. United States, 15 F.2d 955 (9th Cir. 1927), where the court considered that the memory of the witness who testified from copied memoranda was not actually refreshed, and that it was error, therefore, to allow use of a copy.

64. People v. Kraus, 377 Ill. 539, 37 N.E.2d 182 (1941); Battle Creek Food Co. v. Kirkland, 298 Mich. 515, 299 N.W. 167 (1941) (dictum); Dec.Dig. Witnesses ☞254; C.J.S. Witnesses § 358; Annot., 125 A.L.R. 27; Annot., 82 A.L.R.2d 473.

the ever-present danger that a suggestible witness may think that he remembers a fact because he reads it. It seems eminently a matter for discretion, rather than rule. Similarly, it would seem that a witness may recognize from present memory the correctness of successive facts set out in a memorandum, but that he may be unable, despite this recognition, to detail those facts from memory without continuing to consult the writing. Accordingly, the statement that a witness once refreshed must speak independently of the writing [65] seems too inflexible, and it is believed that the matter is discretionary and that the trial judge may properly permit the witness to consult the memorandum as he speaks, especially where it is so lengthy and detailed that even a fresh memory would be unable to recite all the items unaided.[66]

65. Roll v. Dockery, 219 Ala. 374, 122 So. 630 (1929) (dictum); C.J.S. Witnesses § 358.

66. United States v. Riccardi, 174 F.2d 883 (3d Cir. 1949) (list of articles); Ward v. Morr Transfer & Storage Co., 119 Mo.App. 83, 95 S.W. 964 (1906) (itemized list of goods lost); World Fire & Marine Ins. Co. v. Edmondson, 244 Ala. 224, 12 So.2d 754 (1924) (similar); People v. Allen, 47 Cal.App.2d 735, 118 P.2d 927 (1941) (aged witness' prior testimony read to her and she assented to its correctness).

But the witness must swear that he is genuinely refreshed. Wolf v. Mallinckrodt Chem. Wks., 336 Mo. 746, 81 S.W.2d 323 (1935); Freeland v. Peltier, 44 S.W.2d 404 (Tex.Civ.App.1931). And he cannot be allowed to read the writing in the guise of refreshment, as a cloak for getting in evidence an inadmissible document. Freeland v. Peltier, supra; S. W. Bridges & Co. v. Candland, 88 Utah 373, 54 P.2d 842, 846, 847 (1936) (clear statement by Wolfe, J.). Of course when the writing is admissible as evidence in the case, it may be introduced and read by the witness. See Guiffre v. Carapezza, 298 Mass. 458, 11 N.E.2d 433 (1937).

CHAPTER 3

THE REQUIREMENT OF FIRSTHAND KNOWLEDGE: THE OPINION RULE: EXPERT TESTIMONY

10. The Requirement of Knowledge from Observation.[1]

The common law system of proof is exacting in its insistence upon the most reliable sources of information. This policy is apparent in the Opinion rule, the Hearsay rule and the Documentary Originals rule. One of the earliest and most pervasive manifestations of this attitude is the rule requiring that a witness who testifies to a fact which can be perceived by the senses must have had an opportunity to observe, and must have actually observed the fact.[2] The same requirement, in general, is imposed upon declarations coming in under exceptions to the hearsay rule, that is, the declarant must so far as appears have had an opportunity to observe the fact declared.[3]

This requirement may easily be confused with the hearsay rule which bars the repetition of out-of-court statements described as hearsay under that rule.[4] Technically, if the testimony of the witness on its face and in form purports to be testimony of observed facts, but the testimony is actually repetition of statements of others, the objection is that the witness lacks firsthand knowledge. If the

1. 2 Wigmore, Evidence §§ 650–670; C.J.S. Witnesses § 52; 58 Am.Jur. Witnesses §§ 113, 114; Dec.Dig. Witnesses ⊂⊃37.

2. Barnett v. Aetna Life Ins. Co., 139 F.2d 483 (3d Cir.1943); State v. Dixon, 420 S.W.2d 267 (Mo. 1967); State v. Johnson, 92 Idaho 533, 447 P.2d 10 (1968).

   See Uniform Rule 19: *"Prerequisites of Knowledge and Experience.* As a prerequisite for the testimony of a witness on a relevant or material matter, there must be evidence that he has personal knowledge thereof, or experience, training or education if such be required. Such evidence may be by the testimony of the witness himself. The judge may reject the testimony of a witness that he perceived a matter if he finds that no trier of fact could reasonably believe that the witness did perceive the matter. The judge may receive conditionally the testimony of the witness as to a relevant or material matter, subject to the evidence of knowledge, experience, training or education being later supplied in the course of the trial."

F.R.Ev. (R.D.1971) 602: "A witness may not testify to a matter unless evidence is introduced sufficient to support a finding that he has personal knowledge of the matter. Evidence, to prove personal knowledge may, but need not, consist of the testimony of the witness himself. This rule is subject to the provisions of Rule 703, relating to opinion testimony by expert witnesses."

3. 2 Wigmore, Evidence § 670, and see the discussion herein of the various exceptions. There are some instances, however, in which the requirement is not applied, e. g., admissions of a party-opponent, see § 263, infra. And where reputation is used as hearsay evidence of a fact (see § 324), while the witness who testifies to the reputation must know the reputation, the community-talk itself need not be shown to be based on knowledge, though the reputation is limited to that in the locality where people would presumably know the reputed fact.

4. See Ch. 24, infra.

form of the testimony indicates the witness is repeating out-of-court statements, the hearsay objection possibility is raised.[5] Often courts disregard this distinction.[6]

The burden of laying a foundation by showing that the witness had an adequate opportunity to observe is upon the party offering the testimony.[7] By failing to object the adversary waives the preliminary proof, but not the substance of the requirement, so that if it later appears that the witness lacked opportunity, or did not actually observe the fact, his testimony will be stricken.[8] If under the circumstances proved, reasonable men could differ as to whether the witness did or did not have adequate opportunity to observe, then the testimony of the witness should come in,

and the jury will appraise his opportunity to know in evaluating the testimony.[9]

In laying this foundation of knowledge, it is allowable for the examiner to elicit from the witness the particular circumstances which led him to notice or observe or remember the fact.[10]

While the law is exacting in demanding firsthand observation, it is not so impractical as to insist upon preciseness of attention by the witness in observing, or certainty of recollection in recounting the facts.[11] Accordingly, when a witness uses such expressions as "I think," "My impression is," or "In my opinion," this will be no ground of objection if it appears that he merely speaks from an inattentive observation, or an unsure mem-

---

5. Thus, the Advisory Committee's Note to F.R.Ev. (R.D.1971) 602 (see note 2, supra) states, "This rule does not govern the situation of a witness who testifies to a hearsay statement as such, if he has personal knowledge of the making of the statement. Rules 801 to 805 would be applicable. This rule would, however, prevent him from testifying to the subject matter of the hearsay statement, as he has no personal knowledge of it."

See Fox v. Allstate Ins. Co., 22 Utah 2d 383, 453 P.2d 701 (1969) (court states counsel's hearsay objection should have been objection based upon lack of knowledge).

6. Citizens' Bank & Trust Co. v. Rudebeck, 90 Wash. 612, 156 P. 831 (1916).

7. Cleveland, T. & V. Co. v. Marsh, 63 Oh.St. 236, 58 N.E. 821 (1900) (error to admit evidence, over objection without proof of knowledge); State v. Prescott, 70 R.I. 403, 40 A.2d 721 (1944) (no error to exclude evidence where foundation not laid). But the judge has a discretion to admit the evidence, deferring the proof of knowledge to a later stage. Sofas v. McKee, 100 Conn. 541, 124 Atl. 380 (1924).

8. City Nat. Bank v. Nelson, 218 Ala. 90, 117 So. 681, 61 A.L.R. 938, 944 (1928); State v. Dixon, note 2; Jamestown Plumbing & Heating Co. v. City of Jamestown, 164 N.W.2d 355 (N.D. 1969) (illustrates procedure). But it has been held that if there is no objection to the testimony of the witness on direct examination and no effort to show lack of knowledge in cross-examination, the presumption in the absence of anything to the contrary is that the witness is testifying of his own knowledge. Canal Ins. Co. v. Winge Bros., 97 Ga.App. 782, 104 S.E.2d 525 (1958).

9. Jack Cole, Inc. v. Walker, 240 Ala. 683, 200 So. 768 (1941) (opportunity in brief time to judge speed of truck); Senecal v. Drollette, 304 N.Y. 446, 108 N.E.2d 602 (1952) (error to exclude testimony of 12-year-old boys as to speed and make of automobile, based on brief glance); Humphries v. Louisiana Ry. & Irr. Co., 291 S.W. 1094 (Tex.Comm.App.1927) (speed of train); Uniform Rule 19, note 2, supra. But compare Davidson v. Beacon Hill Taxi Service, 278 Mass. 540, 180 N.E. 503 (1932), which seems to treat a similar question of opportunity to estimate speed as a preliminary question for the judge. Many decisions apparently assume the principle stated in the text without discussion.

10. Cole v. Lake Shore & M. S. Ry. Co., 105 Mich. 549, 63 N.W. 647 (1895) (witness could say that he remembered that the wind was so high because "we spoke about it"); Brown v. Chicago, B. & Q. R. Co., 88 Neb. 604, 130 N.W. 265 (1911) (witness may state that his attention was called to approaching vehicle by remark of his little boy); People v. Neely, 163 Cal.App.2d 289, 329 P.2d 357 (1958) (witness may state reason he had occasion to recall a particular time, but erroneous exclusion cured by cross-examination).

11. Ewing v. Russell, 81 S.D. 563, 137 N.W.2d 892 (1965) (testimony of condition of floor held admissible although witness also testified she "didn't pay any particular attention to the floor"); Eitel v. Times, Inc., 221 Ore. 585, 352 P.2d 485 (1960) (alleged insufficient inspection of wire did not make testimony of its source inadmissible); Harding v. State, 5 Md.App. 230, 246 A.2d 302 (1968) cert. denied 395 U.S. 949 (witness had told different stories prior to trial and had achieved her knowledge of testimony at trial after being hypnotized some time before trial).

ory,[12] though it will if the expressions are found to mean that he speaks from conjecture or from hearsay.[13]

One who has no knowledge of a fact except what another has told him cannot, of course, satisfy the present requirement of knowledge from observation. When the witness, however, bases his testimony partly upon first-hand knowledge and partly upon the accounts of others, the problem is one which calls for a practical compromise. Thus when he speaks of his own age,[14] or of his kinship with a relative,[15] the courts will allow the testimony. And in business or scientific matters when the witness testifies to facts that he knows partly at first hand and partly from reports, the judge, it seems, should admit or exclude according to his view of the need for and the reasonable reliability of the evidence.[16]

THE OPINION RULE [17]

11. The Evolution of the Rule Against Opinions: Opinions of Laymen.

The opinion rule, though it developed from practices and expressions of the English courts, seems to be emphasized more generally and enforced far more inflexibly here than in the mother country.[18] In the first place a rule against "opinions" may have had a different meaning for the English judge. We are told that in English usage of the 1700's and earlier, "opinion" had the primary meaning of "notion" or "persuasion of the mind without proof or certain knowledge." [19] It carried an implication of lack of grounds, which is absent from our present-day meaning of the term "opinion" in this country. We use the word as denoting a belief, inference, or conclusion without suggesting that it is well- or ill-founded.

---

12. Auerbach v. United States, 136 F.2d 882 (6th Cir. 1943) (witness testified to identity of man he saw, "to the best of my belief" but acknowledging he might be mistaken, allowed); People v. Palmer, 351 Ill. 319, 184 N.E. 205 (1932) ("I believe"); E. F. Enoch Co. v. Johnson, 183 Md. 326, 37 A.2d 901 (1944) ("It looked like that truck . . . swung in"); Tews v. Bamrick, 148 Neb. 59, 26 N.W.2d 499 (1947) ("I guess," as to speed of car); Covey v. State, 232 Ark. 79, 334 S.W.2d 648 (1960) ("Seems like he said something like . . ."); 2 Wigmore, Evidence § 658.

13. Lovejoy v. Howe, 55 Minn. 353, 57 N.W. 57 (1893) ("impression"); State v. Thorp, 72 N.C. 186 (1875) ("my best impression"); State v. Dixon, 420 S.W.2d 267 (Mo.1967) ("I think").

14. Antelope v. United States, 185 F.2d 174, (10th Cir. 1950) (statutory rape: victim may testify to her age and date of birth); State v. Olson, 260 Ia. 311, 149 N.W.2d 132 (1967) (extra-judicial statement of age). So as to the age of a near relative. Hancock v. Supreme Council, 69 N.J.L. 308, 55 Atl. 246 (1903) (elder brother).

15. Brown v. Mitchell, 88 Tex. 350, 31 S.W. 621, 623 (1895) (witness testified that he was son of decedent, based on fact that she called him son and on other facts); State v. Schut, 71 Wash.2d 400, 429 P.2d 126 (1967) (parentage of witness).

16. The evidence was admitted in Hunt v. Stimson, 23 F.2d 447 (6th Cir. 1928) (sales manager of lumber yard testified to amount of lumber on hand, based on his estimates from inspection and tallies made by other employees); Gresham v. Harcourt, 33 Tex.Civ.App. 196, 75 S.W. 808 (1903) (witness,

present when sheep were counted, testified to the number; she heard the two men who did the counting call out the numbers, and she at the time put them down in a book); Dick v. Puritan Pharmaceutical Co., 46 S.W.2d 941, 946 (Mo.App.1932) (owner-manager of business testified that samples and letters were mailed to his customers, though he did not personally mail them, but supervised the mailing); Schooler v. State, 175 S.W.2d 664 (Tex.Civ. App.1943) (geologist's testimony as to structure and oil prospects of land based on inspection and on reports of other geologists); Vogt v. Chicago, Milwaukee, St. Paul & Pacific R. Co., 35 Wis.2d 716, 151 N.W.2d 713 (1967) (wife permitted to testify to her husband's earnings although books were incomplete). Cases are collected and acutely discussed in Maguire and Hahesy, Basis for Expert Opinion, 5 Vand.L.Rev. 432 (1952). See also § 15, infra.

17. 7 Wigmore, Evidence §§ 1917–2028; Dec.Dig. Crim.Law ⬅448–494, Evidence ⬅470–574; 32 C.J.S. Evidence §§ 438–575; King and Pillinger, Opinion Evidence in Illinois (1942) (a work valuable in any jurisdiction for its original analysis and creative ideas).

18. See for example the brief treatment of opinion evidence in Phipson, Evidence ch. 36 (10th ed., 1963). See also Cowen and Carter, Essays on the Law of Evidence 163 (1956) ("In practice the English judges have paid little more than lip service to the rule.")

19. Samuel Johnson's Dictionary (1st ed., 1755) cited in King and Pillinger, op. cit. n. 17, at p. 8.

The requirement that witnesses must have personal knowledge, already discussed, was a very old rule, having its roots in medieval law,[20] which demanded that they speak only "what they see and hear." [21] The classic dictum of Coke in 1622, that "It is no satisfaction for a witness to say that he 'thinketh' or 'persuadeth himself'" [22] and Mansfield's statement in 1766, "It is mere opinion, which is not evidence" [23] are to be understood as condemning testimony when not based upon personal knowledge. Statements founded only on hearsay or conjecture would fall under this ban. But as Wigmore interprets the historical evidence, there was not until the 1800's any recognition of an opinion rule which would exclude inferences by witnesses possessing personal knowledge.[24]

By the middle of the 1800's [25] the disparagement of "mere opinion" in the sense of a notion or conjecture not rooted in observation had emerged into a much more questionable canon of exclusion. This is the doctrine that witnesses generally must give the "facts" and not their "inferences, conclusions, or opinions." [26]

This classic formula, based as it is on the assumption that "fact" and "opinion" stand in contrast and hence are readily distinguishable, has proven the clumsiest of all the tools furnished the judge for regulating the examination of witnesses. It is clumsy because its basic assumption is an illusion. The words of the witness cannot "give" or recreate the "facts," that is, the objective situations or happenings about which the witness is testifying. Drawings, maps, photographs, even motion pictures, would be only a remote and inaccurate portrayal of those "facts" and how much more distant approximations of reality are the word pictures of oral or written testimony. There is no conceivable statement however specific, detailed and "factual," that is not in some measure the product of inference and reflection as well as observation and memory. The difference between the statement, "He was driving on the left-hand side of the road" which would be classed as "fact" under the rule, and "He was driving

---

20. 9 Holdsworth, Hist.Eng.L. 211 (1926).

21. In 1349 it was held that witnesses were not challengeable "because the verdict will not be received from them, but from the jury; and the witnesses are to be sworn 'to say the truth,' without adding 'to the best of their knowledge,' for they should testify nothing but what they . . . know for certain, that is to say what they see and hear." Anon.Lib.Ass. 110, 11 (1349), quoted in Phipson, op. cit. at p. 475.

22. Adams v. Canon, Dyer 53b, quoted 7 Wigmore, Evidence § 1917, p. 2.

23. Carter v. Boehm, 3 Burr. 1905, 1918 (1766) quoted 7 Wigmore, Evidence § 1917, p. 7.

24. 7 Wigmore, Evidence § 1917; King and Pillinger, op. cit. n. 17, at p. 7. The latter work cites Peake on Evidence, an English work published in 1801 as the source of the first statement that witnesses generally must state "facts" rather than "opinion."

25. See, e. g., Donnell v. Jones, 13 Ala. 490, 511 (1848) (opinion of one acquainted with business whether levy of attachment had destroyed credit and forced business into assignment, excluded. "The general rule requires, that witnesses should depose only to facts, and such facts too as come within their knowledge. The expression of opinions, the belief of the witness, or deductions from the facts, however honestly made, are not proper evidence as coming from the witness; and when such deductions are made by the witness, the prerogative of the jury is invaded."); Hartford Protection Ins. Co. v. Harmer, 2 Oh.St. 452, 456 (1853). It is notable, however, that even in the 1850's, the

Illinois court states the matter thus hesitantly, "It is true, probably, that mere opinions, as opinions, when offered in evidence, should be confined to experts in the questions of skill or science as such, which are open to that kind of proof, and for want of better." Butler v. Mehrling, 15 Ill. 488, 491 (1854). And Greenleaf in the 6th edition of his treatise, issued in 1852, when he deals with opinions in § 440 cites no cases for his statement that "the opinions of witnesses are in general not evidence" but devotes his numerous citations in the main to cases where opinions were received.

26. Among the leading cases discussing and applying the rule, in addition to the cases in the next preceding note, are Baltimore & O. R. Co. v. Schultz, 43 Ohio 270, 1 N.E. 324 (1885) (opinion of observer that fence not fit to keep stock off, excluded); Graham v. Pennsylvania Co., 139 Pa. 149, 21 A. 151, 12 L.R.A. 293 (1891) (opinion of architect who had seen defendant's platform, for alighting passengers, that because of construction and lighting it was unsafe, excluded).

carelessly" which would be called "opinion" is merely a difference between a more concrete and specific form of descriptive statement and a less specific and concrete form. The difference between so-called "fact," then, and "opinion," is not a difference between opposites or contrasting absolutes, but a mere difference in degree with no recognizable line to mark the boundary.[27]

If trial judges are given the task of distinguishing on the spur of the moment between "fact" and "opinion", no two judges, acting independently, can be expected to reach the same results on the same questions. Of course, it is true that many recurring questions have been used and hence have been customarily classified as calling for "fact" or "opinion", but in a changing world there will constantly be presented a myriad of new statements to which the judge must apply the distinction. Thus, good sense demands that the trial judge be accorded a wide range of discretion in classifying evidence as "fact" or "opinion," as well as in admitting evidence even where found to constitute opinion. Various courts have expressed this viewpoint.[28]

The recognition of the impossibility of administering the opinion standard as a mandatory rule, however, came but slowly. The alleviation of the strictness of the standard was at first limited to cases of strict necessity.[29] This rule as stated in the cited case, which in form of statement excludes opinion except in the circumstances listed, doubtless remains as the "orthodox" view of many

ceived in any particular case, are matters resting largely in the administrative discretion of the court."); Central Railroad Co. of New Jersey v. Monahan, 11 F.2d 212 (2d Cir. 1926) ("But except in extreme cases, where we can see that harm is done, all such matters are in the discretion of the trial judge."); McDuffie v. Root, 300 Mich. 286, 1 N.W.2d 544 (1942); Dowling v. L. H. Shattuck, Inc., 91 N.H. 234, 17 A.2d 529, 532 (1941); Wilson v. Pennsylvania Railroad Co., 421 Pa. 419, 219 A.2d 666 (1966); Osborn v. Lesser, 201 Kan. 45, 439 P.2d 395 (1968) interpreting K.S.A. 60–456(a), i. e., Uniform Rule 56(1); and see other cases collected in C.J.S. Evidence § 449, p. 86.

There is some tendency to follow the notion that "it is more important to get to the truth of the matter than to quibble over impractical distinctions." See cases cited in C.J.S. Evidence § 546(1), notes 85, 86. And cases tend to illustrate the generality that matters which are usually stated in opinion form, and which are part of the common stock of knowledge, may be expressed in opinion form. See cases cited in C.J.S. Evidence § 546(2).

Nevertheless, surprisingly, a very large number of opinions of appellate courts dispose of objections to trial court rulings without mentioning the trial court's discretion.

27. For a masterly exposition of this view, see 7 Wigmore, Evidence § 1919. Another discussion, with vivid illustrative material, is King and Pillinger, Opinion Evidence in Illinois 1–6, 21–23 (1942).

28. Fred J. Keisel & Co. v. Sun Ins. Office, 88 F. 243, 249 (8th Cir. 1898) ("The trial court sees and hears each witness, and in doubtful cases is far better qualified than the court of appeals to determine whether a witness should be confined to the facts, or should be allowed to state his conclusions"); Farish v. Madison Distributing Co., Inc., 37 F.2d 455 (2d Cir. 1930); Dersis v. Dersis, 210 Ala. 308, 311, 98 So. 27 (1923) ("A certain discretion is rightly vested in the trial courts in directing the search for the truth by this class of evidence, and their action should not be disturbed unless it is apparent some right of a party has been invaded or suppressed. We think a man sitting up all night with a sick man, or one grievously wounded in the head may form an opinion whether he is conscious or unconscious, which may be given to the jury for what it is worth"); Grismore v. Consolidated Products, 232 Ia. 328, 5 N.W.2d 646 (1942) ("The courts and other authorities uniformly agree that the receipt of opinion evidence, whether lay or expert, and the extent to which it will be re-

29. See, e. g., the following passage from a leading case: "A few general propositions are submitted, which, it is believed, fairly reflect the current of authority on the subject of the admissibility of the opinions of witnesses as evidence. (1) That witnesses shall testify to facts and not opinions is the general rule. (2) Exceptions to this rule have been found to be, in some cases, necessary to the due administration of justice. (3) Witnesses shown to be learned, skilled, or experienced in a particular art, science, trade, or business may, in a proper case, give their opinions upon a given state of facts. This exception is limited to experts. (4) In matter more within the common observation and experience of men, non-experts may, in cases where it is not practicable to place before the jury all the primary facts upon which they are founded, state their opinions from such facts, where such opinions involve conclusions material to the subject of inquiry. (5) In such cases the witnesses are required, so far as may be, to state the primary facts which support their opinions." Baltimore & O. R. Co. v. Schultz, 43 Ohio 270, 1 N.E. 324, 331 (1885).

courts,[30] but the actual practice in the trial of cases is becoming, if indeed it has not always been, far more liberal than the older formulas, and might more accurately be reflected in a formula expressed by some courts that sanctions the admission of opinions on grounds of "expediency" or "convenience" rather than "necessity." The so-called "shorthand rendition" rule seems to incorporate this more liberal notion.[31] "Convenience" is the principle incorporated in progressive proposals for reform.[32]

30. See, e. g., Whitney v. Central Paper Stock Co., 446 S.W.2d 415 (Mo.App.1969) ("when it is impossible or extremely difficult for a witness to convey an actual and accurate meaning"; exclusion of opinion that wooden floor was "rotten" was held error); C.J.S. Evidence § 546(4), note 36. The standard is stated in varying terms. See, e. g., Beutenmuller v. Vess, 447 S.W.2d 519 (Mo.1969) (opinion may be stated when "facts and circumstances are such that they may not be readily and accurately described").

31. A long-established "exception" to the opinion-rule in some states is the practice of admitting "opinions" where they can be justified as "shorthand renditions" of a total situation, or as "statements of collective facts": Dulaney v. Burns, 218 Ala. 493, 513, 119 So. 21, 24 (1928) ("Did you ever say anything to influence him about not leaving anything to his kinfolks?"); Pollard v. Rogers, 234 Ala. 92, 173 So. 881 (1937) ("He looked like he was dying"; opinion has extensive discussion); City of Beaumont v. Kane, 33 S.W.2d 234, 241, 242 (Tex. Civ.App., 1930) ("The situation at the end of Pearl Street presented such an appearance that a stranger on a rainy night would be liable to drive off into the river."); Horn v. State, 12 Wyo. 80, 148, 73 P. 705, 721–723 (1903) (a witness who overheard, but did not see, defendant and another person in conversation was allowed to state whether defendant's admission of killing was "sincere" or "joshing"; an extremely picturesque case). See cases cited in C.J.S. Evidence § 546(3).

This so-called exception certainly seems to savor of a principle of mere convenience rather than of necessity, and also arguably incorporates the notion that witnesses may use more general statements when such statements state opinion that are commonly used in actual life. See note 28, supra.

32. Uniform Rule 56 maintains a general limitation upon opinion-evidence with a leeway, however, for liberal administration under subsec. (1) (b). Its provisions follow: "(1) If the witness is not testifying as an expert his testimony in the form of opinions or inferences is limited to such opinions or inferences as the judge finds (a) may be rationally based on the perception of the witness and (b) are

It is believed that the standard actually applied by many of the trial judges of today, though not often stated in opinions on appeal, includes the principle espoused by Wigmore, namely that opinions of laymen should be rejected only when they are superfluous in the sense that they will be of no value to the jury.[33] It seems fair to observe that the prevailing practice in respect to the admission of the opinions of non-expert witnesses may well be described, not as a rule excluding opinions, but as a rule of preference. The more concrete description is preferred to the more abstract. Moreover, it seems that the principal impact of the rule is upon the form of examination. The questions, while they cannot suggest the particular details desired, else they will be leading, must nevertheless call for the most specific account that the witness can give. For example, he must not be asked, "Did they agree?" but "What did they say?" When recognized as a matter of the form of the examination rather than the substance of the testimony—again, a difference of degree—the opinion rule, like other regulations of form, such as the control over leading questions and questions calling for a free narrative and over the order of proof is seen to fall naturally in the realm of discretion. Furthermore, it seems that this habit and tradition of Anglo-American lawyers to examine about specific details is a valuable heritage. The problem is to preserve this scientific habit of approach but yet to curb the time-wasting quibbling over trivial objections on the ground of "opinion" which may still be heard in those courts which attempt a literal application of the older formulas.

One solution is a rule giving the judge discretion to require the witness, before giving

helpful to a clear understanding of his testimony or to the determination of the fact in issue."

33. 7 Wigmore, Evidence § 1918. The test above is quoted in Allen v. Matson Navigation Co., 255 F.2d 273, 278 (9th Cir. 1958) (holding admissible testimony that floor was "slippery").

testimony in terms of inference or general description, first to state the concrete details on which the inference or description is founded, so far as feasible.[34] Many critics of the opinion rule would, however, simply eliminate the matter from the category of things governed by rules.[35] They would find a sufficient substitute in the natural desire of a lawyer to present his case in detail as being the most convincing technique and in the ability of the adversary on cross-examination to expose the non-existence or inconsistency of details not developed on direct.[36]

12. The Relativity of the Opinion Rule: Opinions on the Ultimate Issue.

As pointed out in the next preceding section, the terms "fact" and "opinion" denote merely a difference of degree of concreteness of description or a difference in nearness or remoteness of inference. The opinion rule operates to prefer the more concrete description to the less concrete, the direct form of statement to the inferential. But there is still another variable in the equation. The purpose of the testimony has had an effect on the degree of concreteness required. In the outer circle of collateral facts, near the rim of relevancy, evidence in general terms will be received with relative freedom, but as we come closer to the hub of the issue, the courts have been more careful to call for details in-

stead of inferences. This is clearly pointed out in the following passages:

"There are many degrees of generality of statement. In comparison with the next broader statement, each statement may be said (and is said) to be a statement of fact. Thus, in comparison with the statement 'X was not mentally competent to execute a will' the statement 'X was insane' is a statement of fact. In comparison with the statement 'X was insane' the statement 'X acted peculiarly' is a statement of fact. In comparison with the statement 'X acted peculiarly' the statement 'X had a vacant stare' is a statement of fact. . . ."[37]

. . . .

The trial judge may well be more liberal in the use of his discretion to admit opinions and inferences as to collateral matters and less liberal in order to see that the concrete details are brought out as to more crucial matters. Is it expedient to go further and to tie his hands by a rule forbidding opinion-evidence as to these "ultimate" matters?

Undoubtedly there is a kind of statement by the witness which amounts to no more than an expression of his general belief as to how the case should be decided or as to the amount of unliquidated damages which should be given. It is believed all courts would exclude such extreme expressions.[38] There is no necessity for this kind of evidence; to receive it would tend to suggest that the judge and jury may shift responsibility for decision to the witnesses; and in

---

34. Uniform Rule, Rule 57: "The judge may require that a witness before testifying in terms of opinion or inference be first examined concerning the data upon which the opinion or inference is founded." Much present case law requires that the witness state the facts relating to his opinion. See C.J.S. Evidence § 546(4).

35. See 7 Wigmore, Evidence § 1929 (The Future of the Opinion Rule); Bozeman, Suggested Reforms of the Opinion Rule, 13 Temple U.L.Q. 296 (1939).

36. The Revised Draft of Proposed Federal Rules of Evidence (1971) contains no requirement of preliminary disclosure of details by lay witnesses but does require in Rule 701 that their opinions be based on firsthand knowledge and be helpful to the trier of fact. Rule 403 allows exclusion of evidence on grounds of waste of time.

37. King and Pillinger, Opinion Evidence in Illinois 10 (1942).

38. See, e. g., Warren Petroleum Co. v. Thomasson, 268 F.2d 5 (5th Cir. 1959) (error to admit highway patrolman's statement after collision that owner of one of vehicles "should assume liability", quoting text above); Duncan v. Mack, 59 Ariz. 36, 122 P. 2d 215 (1942) (whether public convenience would be served by transfer of license); Grismore v. Consolidated Products, 232 Ia. 328, 5 N.W.2d 646, (1942) (opinions as to guilt, negligence, testamentary capacity, reasonable cause—dictum).

any event it is wholly without value to the trier of fact in reaching a decision.

But until about twenty-five years ago, a very substantial number of courts had gone far beyond this commonsense reluctance to listen to the witness's views as to how the judge and jury should exercise their functions and had announced the general doctrine that witnesses would not be permitted to give their opinions or conclusions upon an ultimate fact in issue.[39]

The reason was sometimes given that such testimony "usurps the function"[40] or "invades the province"[41] of the jury. Obviously these expressions were not intended to be taken literally, but merely to suggest the danger that the jury might forego independent analysis of the facts and bow too readily to the opinion of an expert or otherwise influential witness.

Although the rule had been followed in many states prior to 1942,[42] there has been a trend since then to abandon or reject it[43] with the result that now in a majority of state courts an expert may state his opinion upon an ultimate fact, provided that all other requirements for admission of expert opinion are met.[44] Some courts seem to have adopted the rule that opinions may be given on ultimate fact issues even in the case of opinions of laymen,[45] although the other general rules of admissibility for such opinions would often preclude opinions of laymen on ultimate facts in any event.[46]

Probably the extreme instances mentioned above, of opinions as to how the case should be decided and the like, should still be excluded as impolitic and superfluous, and it seems likely that under the most liberal rules judges would be prone to exclude them on the ground indicated in Rule 45 of the Model Code of Evidence, that their value is outweighed by a "substantial danger of undue prejudice, or of confusing the issues or of misleading the jury".[47]

This change in judicial opinion has resulted from the fact that the rule excluding opinion on ultimate facts in issue is unduly restrictive, pregnant with close questions of application and the possibility of misapplication,

39. United States v. Spaulding, 293 U.S. 498, 506 (1935); State v. Carr, 196 N.C. 129, 144 S.E. 698 (1928) and earlier cases collected in Dec.Dig. Evidence ⬯472 and 506, Criminal Law ⬯450; and see 7 N.C.L.Rev. 320 (1928), 16 id. 180 (1938); 26 Ia.L.Rev. 819 (1941).

40. Chicago & Alton R. Co. v. Springfield & N. W. R. Co., 67 Ill. 145 (1873).

41. De Groot v. Winter, 261 Mich. 660, 247 N.W. 69, 71 (1933). Michigan no longer follows the rule. See note 44, infra.

42. See sources cited in note 39, supra.

43. The trend appears to have begun with the leading case of Grismore v. Consolidated Products, 232 Ia. 328, 5 N.W.2d 646 (1942).

44. More recent cases include Rabata v. Dohner, 45 Wis.2d 111, 172 N.W.2d 409 (1969) (abandoning rule that expert opinions on ultimate facts must be based upon hypothetical questions); Redman v. Ford Motor Co., 253 S.C. 266, 170 S.E.2d 207 (1969) (stating that the matter is in the discretion of the trial judge); Grocc v. Fidelity General Ins. Co., 448 P.2d 554 (Ore.1968); Southern Pacific Co. v. Watkins, 83 Nev. 471, 435 P.2d 498 (1968); McKay Machine Co. v. Rodman, 11 Ohio St.2d 77, 228 N.E.2d 304 (1967); In re Baxter's Estate, 16 Utah 2d 284, 399 P.2d 442 (1965); Commonwealth, Dept. of Highways v. Widner, 388 S.W.2d 583 (Ky.1965); Dudek v. Popp, 373 Mich. 300, 129 N.W.2d 393 (1964). See review of the cases in Stoebuck, Opinions on Ultimate Facts: Status, Trends, and a Note of Caution, 41 Denver L.C.J. 226 (1964); C.J.S. Evidence § 446(b). See also note 45, infra.

45. Weber v. Chicago, R. I. & P. R. Co., 175 Ia. 358, 151 N.W. 852, 859, L.R.A.1918A, 626 (1915) (lay opinion testimony as to whether spikes holding rails had been pulled with a crowbar, admissible) cited and discussed in Grismore v. Consolidated Products, 232 Ia. 328, 5 N.W.2d 646, 662 (1942); Model Code of Evidence Rule 401, adopted as case law, Church v. West, 75 Wash.2d 502, 452 P.2d 265 (1969). See also West's Ann.Cal.Evid.Code § 805, "Testimony in the form of an opinion that is otherwise admissible is not objectionable because it embraces the ultimate issue to be decided by the trier of fact"; Uniform Rule 56(4) (similar); F.R.Ev. (R.D.1971) 704 (similar).

46. See § 11, supra.

47. Model Code of Evidence Rule 45. The Advisory Committee's Note for F.R.Ev. (R.D.1971) 704 suggests an opinion of this kind could be rejected under Rule 403, which provides for exclusion of evidence that wastes time.

and often unfairly obstructive to the presentation of a party's case, to say nothing concerning the illogic of the idea that these opinions usurp the function of the jury.[48]

In those jurisdictions in which the prohibitive rule is retained,[49] there remain difficult and confusing questions whether or not an opinion is an opinion concerning an ultimate fact. Usually, the process of breaking down general opinions concerning ultimate fact into more specific opinions is required in order to avoid opinions on ultimate facts,[50] but this process tends to result in inconsistent or unexplainable decisions.[51] This rule, involving the notion of "invasion of the province of the jury", is also easily confused with the rule that expert opinion should not be heard upon commonplace matters. In connection with this latter rule, courts have also often mentioned that this employment of experts invades the province of the jury.[52]

A very few courts have intimated that the form of the witness' testimony may be significant, in that a direct statement of the fact in issue may be inadmissible while a mere statement that it is the witness' opinion that the fact is so, or a statement in the subjunctive mood, would be allowable.[53] This has

been rightly called a mere quibble.[54] The two forms of statement are both mere expressions of belief and should be treated alike. The degree of positiveness should make no difference in admissibility.

Regardless of the rule concerning admissibility of opinion upon ultimate facts, courts do not permit opinion on a question of law,[55] unless the issue concerns a question of foreign law.[56] A court which does not ban opinion on the ultimate issue as such may nevertheless condemn a question phrased in terms of a legal criterion not adequately defined by the questioner so as to be correctly understood by laymen, the question being interpreted by the court as calling for a legal opinion. But

Co. of Statesville, Inc., 268 N.C. 489, 151 S.E.2d 71 (1966) (expert can testify what causes "would produce the result").

54. Annot., 78 A.L.R. 755, 758.

55. See the enlightening opinions by Smedley, C. in Federal Underwriters' Exchange v. Cost, 132 Tex. 299, 123 S.W.2d 332, 334, 335 (1938), and by Bliss, J. in Grismore v. Consolidated Products, 232 Iowa 328, 5 N.W.2d 646, €63 (1942). In the latter case the court said: "No witness should be permitted to give his opinion directly that a person is guilty or innocent, or is criminally responsible or irresponsible, or that a person was negligent or not negligent, or that he had capacity to execute a will, or deed, or like instrument, or, as held by us in Halligan v. Lone Tree Farmers Exchange, 230 Iowa 1277, 1283, 300 N.W. 551, respecting whether a county attorney had probable cause to believe the plaintiff was guilty of the crime charged. But the reason is that such matters are not subjects of opinion testimony. They are mixed questions of law and fact. When a standard, or a measure, or a capacity has been fixed by law, no witness whether expert or non-expert, nor however qualified, is permitted to express an opinion as to whether or not the person or the conduct, in question, measures up to that standard. On that question the court must instruct the jury as to the law, and the jury must draw its own conclusion from the evidence."

The general rule is illustrated by Briney v. Tri-State Mutual Grain Dealers Fire Ins. Co., 254 Iowa 673, 117 N.W.2d 889 (1962) (testimony concerning legal effect of relationship between independent adjusters and fire insurance companies who hired them); Hawkins v. Chandler, 88 Idaho 20, 396 P.2d 123 (1964) (testimony that the law did not require the use of flares but error held not prejudicial); see cases cited in C.J.S. Evidence § 453.

56. See § 335, infra.

48. See the discussion in Grismore v. Consolidated Products, 232 Ia. 328, 5 N.W.2d 646 (1942); 7 Wigmore Evidence §§ 1920, 1921.

49. See, e. g., State v. Gail, 373 P.2d 955 (Wyo. 1962); Barger v. Mizel, 424 P.2d 41 (Okla.1967) (stating the rule is applied generally in Oklahoma); Hubbard v. Quality Oil Co. of Statesville, Inc., 268 N.C. 489, 151 S.E.2d 71 (1966); Redman v. Community Hotel Corp., 138 W.Va. 456, 76 S.E.2d 759 (1953).

50. See, e. g., disagreement between court and counsel in Spiezio v. Commonwealth Edison Co., 91 Ill.App.2d 392, 235 N.E.2d 323 (1968).

51. See, e. g., discussion of earlier Ohio cases, Note, 20 U.Cin.L.Rev. 484 (1951), and earlier North Carolina cases in Note, 16 N.C.L.Rev. 180 (1938).

52. See § 13, infra. One court has held that the objection that a question invades the province of the jury is not a proper objection (and thus is apparently only a general objection). Hooten v. Dunbar, 347 S.W.2d 775 (Tex.Civ.App.1961).

53. Turnbow v. Hayes Freight Lines, 15 Ill.App.2d 57, 145 N.E.2d 377 (1957); Hubbard v. Quality Oil

it is often convenient or desirable to use questions that are not intended to call forth any legal conclusion but that are phrased in terms of some legal standard familiar to lawyers. There is thus a problem of interpretation of the questions.[57]

The problem has arisen often in relation to testimony on the issue of capacity to make a will. Thus, a court taking the view that there may be opinion upon an ultimate issue would approve a question, "Did X have mental capacity sufficient to understand the nature and effect of his will?"[58] but would frown on the question, "Did X have sufficient mental capacity to make a will?"[59] because the latter question may be incorrectly understood by the witness and the jury if they do not know the law's definition of "capacity to make a will." But a court which prohibits generally opinions on the ultimate issue would condemn both forms of questions,[60] or even one where the questioner breaks down "testamentary capacity" into its factual ele-

ments as legally defined.[61] Similar problems may arise in respect to such issues as undue influence, total and permanent disability, negligence and the like.

On the whole, it is thought that the danger that these questions phrased in terms of "legal conclusions" will be understood as calling for a conclusion or opinion of law is very slight, since they will seldom be asked except when the popular meaning is approximately the same as the legal meaning. In a jurisdiction where there is no general rule against opinions on the ultimate issue, it seems that a request by the adversary that the questioner define his terms should be the only recourse.[62]

13. Expert Witnesses:[63] Subjects of Expert Testimony: Qualifications.[64]

An observer is qualified to testify because he has firsthand knowledge of the situation or transaction at issue. The expert has something different to contribute. This is a power to draw inferences from the facts which a jury would not be competent to draw. To warrant the use of expert testimony, then, two elements are required. First, the subject of the inference must be so distinctively related to some science, profession, business or occupation as to be beyond the ken of the average layman.[65] Some courts emphasize

57. McClellan v. French, 246 Ark. 728, 439 S.W.2d 813 (1969) (held that witness, in testifying a doctor was not guilty of malpractice, used the term in its connotation "standard medical procedure in the community"); Groce v. Fidelity General Ins. Co., 448 P.2d 554 (Ore.1968) (no error in permitting witness to testify to "good faith" of insurer; (possibly dictum). But see Lindley v. Lindley, 384 S.W.2d 676 (Tex.1964) (doctor not permitted to testify that a person's belief was an "insane delusion" because his concept might be quite different from the legal concept).

58. See Scalf v. Collin County, 80 Tex. 514, 16 S.W. 314 (1891) (capacity to understand nature and effect of deed); McDaniel v. Willis, 157 S.W.2d 672 (Tex. Civ.App.1941, error ref'd) (opinion that testator mentally incapable of transacting business). See also, Slough, Testamentary Capacity: Evidentiary Aspects, 36 Texas L.Rev. 1, 5–16 (1957).

59. Brown v. Mitchell, 88 Tex. 350, 31 S.W. 621, 36 L.R.A. 64 (1895); and Carr v. Radkey, 393 S.W.2d 806 (Tex.1965).

60. See Baker v. Baker, 202 Ill. 595, 67 N.E. 410 (1903) ("whether he was able understandingly to execute a will"); Schneider v. Manning, 121 Ill. 376, 12 N.E. 267 (1887) ("Had he mental capacity to dispose of his property by will or deed?") and see King and Pillinger, Opinion Evidence in Illinois 225–228 (1942).

61. Baddeley v. Watkins, 293 Ill. 394, 127 N.E. 725 (1920); King and Pillinger, op. cit. 226.

62. This suggestion is cited in Groce v. Fidelity General Ins. Co., 448 P.2d 554 (Ore.1968). It is in effect rejected in Carr v. Radkey, 393 S.W.2d 806 (Tex.1965).

63. See Ladd, Expert Testimony, 5 Vand.L.Rev. 414 (1952); Voorhis, Expert Opinion Evidence, 13 N.Y. L.F. 651, 657 (1967); Smith v. Hobart Mfg. Co., 185 F.Supp. 751 (D.C.Pa.1960), for possibilities of abuse in using witnesses supposedly learned in one subject, or even in all subjects.

64. Dec.Dig. Crim.L. ☞477–481, Evidence ☞535–546; C.J.S. Evidence §§ 456–458; 7 Wigmore, Evidence §§ 1923, 1925.

65. Admissible: Manhattan Oil Co. v. Mosby, 72 F. 2d 840 (8th Cir. 1934) (effects of drinking salt water by cattle; how much weight cattle should gain on certain range); Bank of Vance v. Crowder, 194 N.C. 331, 139 S.E. 604 (1927) (explanation of entries

that the judge has discretion in administering this aspect of the rule,[66] and other courts will admit expert opinion concerning matters about which the jurors may have general knowledge if the expert opinion would still aid their understanding of the fact issue.[67] This latter approach emphasizes the true function of expert testimony. Second, the witness must have sufficient skill, knowledge, or experience in that field or calling as to make it appear that his opinion or inference will probably aid the trier in his search for truth.[68] The knowledge may in some fields

be derived from reading alone, in some from practice alone, or as is more commonly the case, from both.[69] While the court may rule that a certain subject of inquiry requires that a member of a given profession, as a doctor, an engineer or a chemist, be called, usually a specialist in a particular branch within the profession will not be required.[70] The practice, however, in respect to experts' qualifications has not for the most part crystallized in specific rules, but is recognized as a matter for the trial judge's discretion reviewable only for abuse.[71] Reversals for abuse are rare.

in books of bank cashier). Inadmissible: Collins v. Zedeker, 421 Pa. 52, 218 A.2d 776 (1966) (how fast does a person walk?); Webb v. Fuller Brush Co., 378 F.2d 500 (3d Cir. 1967) (whether warning should have been placed on the jar of facial cream); Cramer v. Theda Clark Memorial Hospital, 45 Wis.2d 147, 172 N.W.2d 427 (1970) (long discussion but dictum); Hill v. Lee, 209 Va. 569, 166 S.E.2d 274 (1969) (whether automobile would make tracks in soil); Dec.Dig. Evidence ⟨505–534.

66. Hanson v. Christensen, 275 Minn. 204, 145 N.W. 2d 868 (1966); Salem v. United States Lines Co., 370 U.S. 31 (1962) (dictum). See McCoid, Opinion Evidence and Expert Witnesses, 2 U.C.L.A.L.Rev. 356, 362–363 (1955).

67. Har-Pen Truck Lines, Inc. v. Mills, 378 F.2d 705 (5th Cir. 1967) (testimony of economics professor as to value of housewife's life); Swartley v. Seattle School District No. 1, 70 Wash.2d 17, 421 P.2d 1009 (1966) (quoting from earlier decision and Ladd, Expert and Other Opinion Testimony, 40 Minn. L.Rev. 437, 443 (1956), "If the issue involves a matter of common knowledge about which inexperienced persons are capable of forming a correct judgment, there is no need for expert opinion. There are many matters, however, about which the triers of fact may have a general knowledge, but the testimony of experts would still aid in their understanding of the issues."); Currier v. Grossman's of New Hampshire, Inc., 107 N.H. 159, 219 A.2d 273 (1966) (opinion of cause of accident admissible when it "might aid the jury"); Miller v. Pillsbury Co., 33 Ill.2d 514, 211 N.E.2d 733 (1965) ("the trend is to permit expert testimony in matters which are complicated and outside the knowledge of the average person, and even as to matters of common knowledge and understanding where difficult of comprehension and explanation"). F.R.Ev. (R.D.1971) 702 simply provides for admission of expert opinion if it assists the trier of fact to understand the evidence or to determine the fact in issue. Presumably, the judge would have a broad area of discretion under this rule.

68. Pennsylvania Threshermen, etc. Ins. Co. v. Messenger, 181 Md. 295, 29 A.2d 653 (1943) (pro-

fessor of science may give computation of distances); Bebont v. Kurn, 348 Mo. 501, 154 S.W.2d 120 (1941) (one with long experience in railroad work as brakeman and otherwise could testify as to distance required for stopping train, though he had never been engineer); State v. Killeen, 79 N.H. 201, 107 A. 601 (1919) (experienced clerk who checks delivery orders may give opinion as to signatures). Cases admitting psychologist's opinion concerning mental condition are cited in Annot., 78 A.L.R.2d 919.

69. Norfolk & Western Ry. Co. v. Anderson, 207 Va. 567, 151 S.E.2d 628 (1966) (one expert qualified by experience and one by experience and study as to cause of tomato crop damage); Smith v. Cedar Rapids Country Club, 255 Ia. 1199, 124 N.W.2d 557 (1964) (wax salesman qualified by reading and experience as to qualities of wax); Central Illinois Light Co. v. Porter, 96 Ill.App.2d 338, 239 N.E.2d 298 (1968) (conservation officer and duck hunter qualified to give opinion as to effect of transmission lines on duck hunting); Hanna v. Fletcher, 104 U.S.App.D.C. 246, 261 F.2d 75 (1958) (iron worker and instructor in iron work permitted to testify to standard for repair of iron handrail); Grohusky v. Atlas Assurance Co., 195 Kan. 626, 408 P.2d 697 (1965) (one experienced in insurance business, but with little or no formal education, could testify as to practices and procedures in the insurance business).

70. Parker v. Gunther, 122 Vt. 68, 164 A.2d 152 (1960) (general practitioner could testify as to brain damage); Seawell v. Brame, 258 N.C. 666, 129 S.E.2d 283 (1963) (general practitioner may testify injury caused or aggravated a neurosis, but testimony held inadmissible for other reasons); Wolfinger v. Frey, 223 Md. 184, 162 A.2d 745 (1960) (general practitioner may testify as to cause of kidney condition, citing many local cases); Dec.Dig. Evidence ⟨537.

71. Bronaugh v. Harding Hospital, Inc., 12 Ohio App. 2d 110, 231 N.E.2d 487 (1967) (patient who used bed was not permitted to testify as to his opinion concerning lack of use of rails); Oborski v. New

Finally, opinion evidence is not admissible if the court believes that the state of the pertinent art or scientific knowledge does not permit a reasonable opinion to be asserted even by an expert.[72] Nor will expert opinion be admitted if the court believes that an opinion based upon the facts in evidence cannot be reasonably grounded upon those facts.[73]

14. Grounds for Expert Opinion: Hypothetical Questions.[74]

The traditional view, still followed in most jurisdictions, has been that an expert may state an opinion based upon his firsthand knowledge [75] or based upon facts in the record at the time he states his opinion, or based partly on firsthand knowledge and partly on the facts of record. If the opinion is to be based on the facts of record, they may be in the expert's possession by virtue of his having been present at the taking of the testimony asserting those facts,[76] or they may be furnished to him prior to his statement of his opinion by including them in a hypothetical question that asks him to assume their truth

and state a requested opinion based upon them.[77] However, these methods of eliciting expert opinion have been subject to a great deal of criticism, and, in response, in a very few states the traditional requirements have been relaxed, permitting an expert to state his opinion without prior disclosure of the underlying data or facts by the use of a hypothetical question, or otherwise, and leaving the process of disclosure of those data or facts to the opponent in his cross-examination, if the opponent desires disclosure.[78] The traditional requirements, mentioned above, concerning eliciting the grounds for expert opinion are considered in this section, and the more recent rule, representing a much more liberal point of view, is discussed in Section 16.

If an expert witness has firsthand knowledge of material facts, he may describe what he has seen, and give his expert inferences therefrom. In this situation, it is unnecessary to couch questions eliciting the inferences in hypothetical form [79] and it would certainly weaken the effect of the testimony to do so. Before the expert testifies to the inferences on this basis, some courts require that he first specify the data gleaned from observation upon which he founds his inferences,[80] so that the jury may know the basis

---

Haven Gas Co., 151 Conn. 274, 197 A.2d 73 (1964); Moore, Kelly & Reddish, Inc. v. Shannondale, Inc., 152 W.Va. 549, 165 S.E.2d 113 (1968); Dec.Dig. Evidence ⟨⟩546.

72. See, e. g., Tonkovich v. Department of Labor & Industries, 1948, 31 Wash.2d 220, 195 P.2d 638 (1948) (court took viewpoint that the cause of cancer was unknown). See Chapter 20, infra, as to the admissibility of scientific evidence generally.

73. See, e. g., Huguley v. State, 39 Ala.App. 104, 96 So.2d 315 (1957) cert. denied 266 Ala. 697, 96 So. 2d 319 (1957) (speed deduced from impact); Flores v. Barlow, 354 S.W.2d 173 (Tex.Civ.App., 1962) (speed deduced from damaged condition of vehicles). But, for a variety of theories and results concerning the admission of opinions of speed based upon physical facts, see Annot., 29 A.L.R. 3d 248. For an interesting examination of the reliability of expert opinion of speeds based on various data, see, Cook, Speed Calculations and the Expert Witness, 42 Neb.L.Rev. 100 (1962).

74. 2 Wigmore, Evidence §§ 672–686; C.J.S. §§ 549–560; Dec.Dig.Crim.Law ⟨⟩482–489, Evidence ⟨⟩547–557; Note, 13 Wes.R.L.Rev. 755 (1962).

75. See n. 79, infra.

76. See n. 84, infra.

77. See n. 90, infra.

78. Rabata v. Dohner, 45 Wis.2d 111, 172 N.W.2d 409 (1969) (a landmark case); Kan.Code Civ.Proc. (K.S.A. 60–456, 60–547); N.J.R.Ev. 57, 58; McKinney's N.Y. CPLR Rule 4515. See § 16, infra.

79. Penn Fruit Co. v. Clark, 256 Md. 135, 259 A.2d 512 (1969) (physician questioned as to permanency of injury); Holecek v. Janke, 171 N.W.2d 94 (N.D. 1969); Walrod v. Matthews, 210 Va. 382, 171 S.E. 2d 180 (1969); Sherman v. City of Springfield, 77 Ill.App.2d 195, 222 N.E.2d 62 (1967); Hester v. Horton Motor Lines, 219 N.C. 743, 14 S.E.2d 794 (1941) (medical expert, cause of injury) and see, for form of question, Note, 20 N.C.L.Rev. 100 (1941); Annot., 82 A.L.R. 1338.

80. Raub v. Carpenter, 187 U.S. 159 (1902) (opinion as to sanity "from all you know about him yourself," properly excluded); State Highway Commission v. Barnes, 151 Mont. 300, 443 P.2d 16 (1967).

for his opinion. Other courts hold that he need not state the data before he states his opinion,[81] since the opponent is free to elicit the grounds for the opinion upon cross-examination. The wisest view may be to leave the matter to the trial court's discretion.[82]

When the expert has no firsthand knowledge of the situation at issue, and has made no investigation of the facts for himself, then traditionally the required method of securing the benefit of his scientific skill is to ask him to assume certain facts and then to give his opinions or inferences in view of the assumptions. These questions are known as hypothetical questions, and the rules regulating their form and content have perhaps been evolved more on the basis of theoretical logic than on the basis of practicalities.

In many jurisdictions, it seems permissible to have the expert witnesses in court during the taking of testimony, and then when the expert is himself called as a witness, to simplify the hypothetical question by asking the expert to assume the truth of the previous testimony, or some specified part of it and to state his opinion upon that assumption.[83] This practice has some advantages, and some limitations. Two obvious requirements are that the assumed facts must be clear to the jury and must not be conflicting. A question which asks the witness to assume the truth of one previous witness' testimony will usually meet these requirements,[84] but as the range of assumption is widened to cover the testimony

of several witnesses,[85] or all the testimony for one side [86] the risk of infraction is increased; and when it covers all the testimony in the case, the question would manifestly be approved only when the testimony on the issue is not conflicting and is brief and simple enough for the jury to recall its outlines without having them recited.[87] In framing these hypothetical questions in which the witness is asked to assume the truth of previous testimony, one difficulty may be overlooked. What if part of the previous testimony is itself the inference (as to the cause or the probable consequences of an injury, for example) of a previous expert? Of course, it will often be apparent that the witness is being asked only to accept the objective descriptions given by the previous experts, not their inferences or conclusions, and then there can be no objection,[88] and it might be arguable, that

---

81. Arkansas State Highway Com'n v. Johns, 236 Ark. 585, 367 S.W.2d 436 (1963); Commonwealth v. Johnson, 188 Mass. 382, 74 N.E. 939, 940 (1905) (dictum); Annot., 82 A.L.R. 1338, 1343; C.J.S. Evidence § 550, n. 38. And it has been held that if the facts are too voluminous they need not be stated. Grison Oil Corp. v. Corporation Com'n, 186 Okl. 548, 99 P.2d 134 (1940).

82. See People v. Youngs, 151 N.Y. 210, 218, 45 N.E. 460, 462 (1896).

83. See 2 Wigmore, Evidence § 681; Annot., 82 A.L.R. 1460.

84. Bosse v. Ideco Division of Dresser Industries, Inc., 412 F.2d 567 (10th Cir. 1969).

85. Damm v. State, 128 Md. 665, 97 A. 645 (1916) (abortion: opinion of doctor based on evidence of attending and examining doctors, approved); Cornell v. State, 104 Wis. 527, 80 N.W. 745 (1899) (murder: defense, insanity: opinion of doctor based on 40 or 50 pages of testimony of other witnesses, approved on ground testimony not conflicting, and whether too voluminous and complicated was in trial judge's discretion).

86. State v. Eggleston, 161 Wash. 486, 297 P. 162, 82 A.L.R. 1439, 1441 (1931) (murder: defense, insanity: "assuming all of the testimony given by the defendant's witnesses is true . . . what is your opinion as to whether the defendant was sane . . . ?" approved).

87. Rhea v. M-K Grocer Co., 236 Ark. 615, 370 S.W. 2d 33 (1963) (citing text); Shouse, Doolittle & Morelock v. Consol. Flour Mills Co., 132 Kan. 108, 294 P. 657 (1931) (opinion as to value of legal services, from all the testimony, disapproved, testimony conflicting); State v. Reilly, 25 N.D. 339, 141 N.W. 720, 734 (1913) (discussing the practice). But compare State v. Carroll, 52 Wyo. 29, 69 P.2d 542, 550–552 (1937) where the court suggests that more consideration should be given to the fact that the cross-examiner has a complete opportunity to clear up any ambiguity in the hypothesis flowing from the conflict in the testimony.

88. Sepich v. Department of Labor and Industries, 75 Wash.2d 312, 450 P.2d 940 (1969); Cody v. Toller Drug Co., 232 Iowa 475, 5 N.W.2d 824 (1942) (question which asked expert witness to assume truth of testimony of previous witness, a chemist, as to the results of tests made by him, proper).

since the expert in giving a private opinion would certainly take into account previously expressed opinions of other experts on the same question, he should be allowed to do so on the stand. But on the stand he is not asked merely to take them into account, but to assume them to be true, and if he does this his own opinion may then be but an academic echo. It is held that this kind of question, which asks the witness to assume the truth of testimony which itself includes expert opinions is improper.[89] It is apparent, however, that the line between observed "fact" and inferential "opinion" is here, as always, a shadowy one and the trial judge should be allowed a wide latitude in passing on this objection.

The type of hypothetical questions just discussed, namely those based on other testimony in the case, satisfy the requirement imposed upon all hypothetical questions, that the facts assumed must be supported by evidence in the case.[90] This requirement is based on the notion that if the answer is founded on premises of fact which the jury, for want of evidence, cannot find to be true, then they are equally disabled from using the answer as the basis for a finding. Direct testimony supporting the fact assumed is not required. It is sufficient if it is fairly inferable from circumstances proved.[91] Moreover,

the supporting evidence need not have been already adduced if the interrogating counsel gives assurance that it will be.[92] And of course, it is no objection that the supporting evidence is controverted.[93] The proponent is entitled to put his side of the case to the witness for his opinion.

There is a possible danger, however, that by omitting some of the facts, the proponent may present an unfair and inadequate picture to the expert, and that the jury may give undue weight to the answer, without considering its faulty basis. What safeguards should be supplied? Some courts have required that all facts material to the question should be embraced in the hypothesis,[94] but this view-

89. Zelenka v. Industrial Com'n, 165 Ohio St. 587, 138 N.E.2d 667 (1956); Cummings v. Jess Edwards, Inc., 445 S.W.2d 767 (Tex.Civ.App.1969); 6816.5 Acres of Land, etc. v. United States, 411 F.2d 834 (10th Cir. 1969); American Hoist and Derrick Co. v. Chicago, M., St. P. & P. R. Co., 414 F.2d 68 (6th Cir. 1969); Annot., 98 A.L.R. 1109; C.J.S. Evidence § 356. Whether opinion testimony is actually based upon other opinions may be a question in specific circumstances. Dennis v. Prisock, 221 So.2d 706 (Miss.1969) ("she was being treated by doctors in Jackson and I had correspondence with doctors in Jackson" did not indicate the opinion of the witness was based on opinions of others).

90. Barnett v. State Workmen's Compensation Com'r, 172 S.E.2d 698 (W.Va.1970); Nisbet v. Medaglia, 356 Mass. 580, 254 N.E.2d 782 (1970); C.J.S. Evidence § 552, n. 33.
Krewall, 450 P.2d 506 (Okl.1969); State ex rel.

91. Farmer's Co-op Exchange of Weatherford v.

McCormick et al on Evid. 2nd Ed. HB—3

Richardson v. Edgeworth, 214 So.2d 579 (Miss. 1968); Friedman v. General Motors Corp., 411 F. 2d 533 (3d Cir. 1969); Dec.Dig. Evidence ⬅553(3).

92. Gibson v. Healy Brothers & Co., 109 Ill.App.2d 342, 248 N.E.2d 771 (1969) (practice is to be discouraged but is within the sound discretion of the court). The rule was applied to cross-examination in Barretto v. Akau, 51 Haw. 383, 461, 463 P.2d 917 (1969) (cross-examination hypothetical to demonstrate alternative theories or contest a substantive element in the case).
It should be noted, however, that hypothetical questions may usually be put upon cross-examination to test the expert's knowledge and skill, even though the questions are not based upon evidence in the case. Randall v. Goodrich-Gamble Co., 244 Minn. 401, 70 N.W.2d 261 (1955); Seibert v. Ritchie, 173 Wash. 27, 21 P.2d 272 (1933); 2 Wigmore, Evidence § 684.

93. Rasmussen v. Thilges, 174 N.W.2d 384 (Ia.1970); Louisville & Nashville R. Co. v. Self, 45 Ala.App. 530, 233 So.2d 90 (1970); Kresha Const. Co. v. Kresha, 184 Neb. 188, 166 N.W.2d 589 (1969); Fidelity & Casualty Co. v. McKay, 73 F.2d 828 (5th Cir. 1934) (jury should be instructed to disregard answer if they find facts are not true); Martin v. Frear, 184 Neb. 266, 167 N.W. 2d 69 (1969) (facts conforming to examiner's theory may be included even if they are controverted).

94. Stumpf v. State Farm Mutual Auto. Ins. Co., 252 Md. 696, 251 A.2d 362 (1969) (question should contain a fair summary of the material facts in evidence essential to the formulation of a rational opinion concerning the matter to which it relates); Ames & Webb Inc. v. Commercial Laundry Co., Inc., 204 Va. 616, 133 S.E.2d 547 (1963) (question must embody all material facts which evidence tends to prove); Dec.Dig. Evidence ⬅553 (2).

point seems undesirable because it is likely to multiply disputes as to the sufficiency of the hypothesis, and may tend to cause counsel, out of abundance of caution, to propound questions so lengthy as to be wearisome and almost meaningless to the jury.[95] The more expedient and more widely prevailing view is that there is no rule requiring that all material facts be included.[96] The safeguards are that the adversary may on cross-examination supply omitted facts and ask the expert if his opinion would be modified by them,[97] and further that the trial judge if he deems the original question unfair may in his discretion require that the hypothesis be reframed to supply an adequate basis for a helpful answer.[98]

As indicated in Section 16, however, none of these traditional rules governing the requirements for hypothetical questions has furnished sufficient safeguards against evils arising from the use of these questions.

15. Expert's Opinion Based on Reports of Others.

We have seen that if an expert has first-hand knowledge of a situation, as in the situation in which a physician has examined and treated an injured person, he may give his inferences or opinions positively and directly, rather than in the muffled, abstract form of an answer based on a hypothesis. The question calling for the direct opinion is so much simpler and more effective that a party may desire to use it when the expert's acquaintance with the material facts is not derived from observation, but from statements made by third persons. Often these statements are of a highly reliable kind such as a report of an examination by another physician, or hospital charts and records showing the symptoms, treatment and progress of a patient. The majority view, however, is that a question is improper if it calls for the witness' opinion on the basis of reports that are not in evidence or are inadmissible as substantive evidence under the hearsay rule (without reciting their contents as hypotheses, to be supported by other evidence as to their truth).[99] The essential objection seems to be that the jury is asked to accept as evidence the witness' inference, based upon someone's hearsay assertion of a fact which is, presumably, not supported by any evidence at the trial and which therefore the jury has no basis for finding to be true. Moreover, want of the knowledge-qualification may be asserted. Should these objections still prevail when the witness is asked to give a similar direct (not hypothetical) opinion, on the basis not merely of reports of this kind, but of these reports supplemented by the witness' own observa-

---

Various courts have also held that undisputed material facts should not be ignored. Jackson v. Nelson, 382 F.2d 1016 (10th Cir. 1967); Christianson v. City of Chicago Heights, 103 Ill.App.2d 315, 243 N.E.2d 677 (1968).

95. See, e. g., Treadwell v. Nickel, 194 Cal. 243, 228 P. 25, 35 (1924) where the court refers to a question "contained in some 83 pages of typewritten transcript, and an objection involved in 14 pages more of the record."

96. Napier v. Greenzweig, 256 F. 196 (2d Cir. 1919); Virginia Beach Bus Line v. Campbell, 73 F.2d 97 (3d Cir. 1934) (reviewing prior decisions); United States v. Aspinwall, 96 F.2d 867 (4th Cir. 1938); Pickett v. Kyger, 151 Mont. 87, 439 P.2d 57 (1968); Gordon v. State Farm Life Ins. Co., 415 Pa. 256, 203 A.2d 320 (1964).

97. See authorities cited in n. 96, supra.

98. See authorities cited in n. 96, supra.

99. Equitable Life Assur. Soc. v. Kazee, 257 Ky. 803, 79 S.W.2d 208 (1935) (opinion based on X-ray picture and reports from others); Sykes v. Norfolk & Western R. Co., 200 Va. 559, 106 S.E.2d 746 (1959) (excluding opinion based upon a study on figures furnished by others and not under supervision of the expert or upon subject matter observed by him, a railroad crossing); Humble Oil & Refining Co. v. Church, 100 N.J.Super. 495, 242 A.2d 652 (1968) (dictum); Dec.Dig. Evidence ⚖555.

But see Arkansas State Highway Com'n v. Russell, 240 Ark. 21, 398 S.W.2d 201 (1966) (dictum: expert may testify to value of land although testimony is based wholly or partly upon hearsay); Ward v. Brown, 301 F.2d 445 (10th Cir. 1962); West's Ann.Cal.Evid.Code, § 801(b), n. 4, infra.

Of course, if the hearsay rule were relaxed, then much of such matter might be admitted as substantive evidence. See generally Ch. 24, infra.

tion of the person or situation in question? Probably many courts would apply the same reasoning, and exclude the evidence under a variety of circumstances,[1] but there is a strong trend toward a contrary view.[2] It is

1. Fidelity & Casualty Co. of New York v. Hendrix, 440 P.2d 735 (Okl.1968) (opinion based upon skid-marks and conversation with the driver); Wild v. Bass, 252 Miss. 615, 173 So.2d 647 (1965) (doctor may not base his opinion in part upon observation and in part upon history of patient related by patient's mother; see n. 2); Dec.Dig. Evidence ☞555, Crim.Law ☞486.

2. Schooler v. State, 175 S.W.2d 664 (Tex.Civ.App. 1943) (geologist testified to opinion as to prospects for oil in a certain region, based on his own inspection and upon geological reports); Sutherland v. McGregor, 383 S.W.2d 248 (Tex.Civ.App.1964) (opinion of petroleum engineer admissible though based partly on reports made by others); Sundquist v. Madison Rys. Co., 197 Wis. 83, 221 N.W. 392 (1928) (opinion of doctor who treated plaintiff, based in part upon reports of examinations made by hospital technicians); Taylor v. Monongahela Ry. Co., 155 F.Supp. 601 (D.C.Pa.1957) (physician, though not the treating doctor, permitted to testify on basis of history, laboratory reports, and witness' own examination, quoting from text above; see following paragraph); Jenkins v. United States, 113 U.S.App.D.C. 300, 307 F.2d 637 (1962) (psychiatrist's opinion, "better reasoned authorities admit testimony based, in part, upon reports of others which are not in evidence but which the expert customarily relies upon in the practice of his profession", citing text); Carrington v. Civil Aeronautics Board, 337 F.2d 913 (4th Cir. 1964) cert. denied 381 U.S. 927 (records used in part by psychiatrist); Masheter v. C. H. Hooker Trucking Co., 19 Ohio App.2d 169, 250 N.E.2d 621 (1969) (appraiser testified in part on basis of statements of others concerning profitability of operation of property); State Highway Commission v. Oswalt, 1 Ore. App. 449, 463 P.2d 602 (1970) (citing text); Trinity Universal Ins. Co. v. Town of Speedway, 137 Ind. App. 510, 210 N.E.2d 95 (1965) (estimate of cost of repair based in part upon reports of others; "an expert is competent to judge the reliability of statements made to him by other persons and taking these statements made to him by other persons together with his own first hand observations comprises a sufficient basis for a direct examination of his own professional opinion as to the cost of repairing the street"). See Moore v. Cataldo, 356 Mass. 325, 249 N.E.2d 578 (1969) (dictum taking view that under Finnegan v. Fall River Gas Works Co., 159 Mass. 311, 34 N.E. 523 (1893), opinion testimony might rest in part on hearsay). Actually, whether opinion can rest in part upon hearsay may well depend in part upon the nature of the subject matter of the opinion and the nature of the hearsay involved. The question of whether opinion may be based in part upon information

reasonable to assume that an expert in a science is competent to judge the reliability of statements made to him by other investi-

from others (that is not in evidence) has arisen most often in connection with the testimony of medical experts and property valuation experts. Most courts will permit the opinion of the medical expert who has treated the patient whose condition is the subject of his opinion, although the opinion is based in part upon history given by the patient. See, e. g., Dornberg v. St. Paul City R. Co., 253 Minn. 52, 91 N.W.2d 178 (1958); Annot., 51 A.L.R. 2d 1051, 1057. As to the admissibility of the history of the patient as substantive evidence, see §§ 292, 293, infra. Some courts also include within this rule information received from persons in the medical profession (or connected with it). See Carrington v. Civil Aeronautics Board, supra; Sundquist v. Madison Rys. Co., supra; Jenkins v. United States, supra (psychiatrist's opinion); Gray v. Bird, 380 S.W.2d 908 (Tex.Civ.App.1964) (psychiatrist's opinion). Some cases permit the treating medical expert to use in part a history furnished by a relative of the patient under particular circumstances. See Miller v. Watts, 436 S.W.2d 515 (Ky.1969) (history furnished by mother of infant patient); Gordon v. Engineering Constr. Co., 271 Minn. 186, 135 N.W.2d 202 (1965) (history of infant patient furnished by mother who was also an attending nurse). In the majority of jurisdictions the above extensions have not been established. See, e. g., Seawell v. Brame, 258 N.C. 666, 129 S.E.2d 283 (1963); cases reviewed in Comment, 35 So.Cal.L.Rev. 193 (1962), and Rheingold, The Basis of Medical Testimony, 15 Vand.L.Rev. 473 (1962).

On the other hand, the majority of courts have refused to permit opinion of so-called forensic medical experts, e. g., experts consulted only to prepare for trial, based in part on medical history related by the person examined or on information received from third persons. See Briney v. Williams, 143 Ind.App. 691, 242 N.E.2d 132 (1968) (opinion based on "subjective symptoms and statements of person who sought examination; otherwise patient's self-serving statements would be carried to jury and bolstered by the expert opinion); Goodrich v. Tinker, 437 S.W.2d 882 (Tex.Civ.App. 1969) (statements and subjective symptoms of patient); Brown v. Blauvelt, 152 Conn. 272, 205 A.2d 773 (1964); Annot., 51 A.L.R.2d 1051, 1065. Whether a medical expert is one in this latter category is sometimes a difficult problem and may not depend entirely upon whether treatment was prescribed. See, Goodrich v. Tinker, cited above. Some cases have attached weight to the time at which the expert was consulted. Annot., 51 A.L.R. 2d 1051, 1078.

For the wide variety of views upon all of the above, and related, matters see in general, Comment, 35 So.Calif.L.Rev. 193 (1962); Rheingold, The Basis of Medical Testimony, 15 Vand.L.Rev. 473 (1962). The variety of views is illustrated by a Washington decision that appears to hold that a forensic

gators or technicians.[3] He is just as competent indeed to do this as a judge and jury are to pass upon the credibility of an ordinary witness on the stand. If the statements, then, are attested by the expert as the basis for a judgment upon which he would act in the practice of his profession, it seems that they should ordinarily be a sufficient basis even standing alone for his direct expression of professional opinion on the stand, and this argument is reinforced when the opinion is founded not only upon reports but also in part upon the expert's firsthand observation. The data of observation will usually enable the expert to evaluate the reliability of the statement.[4]

medical expert's opinion concerning a plaintiff's condition must be based solely upon objective facts only if the opinion and supporting consultation was sought by the plaintiff. State v. Russell, 70 Wash.2d 552, 424 P.2d 639 (1967).

There is a pronounced trend to permit opinion of valuation experts based in part upon personal knowledge and in part upon information received from others. See, e. g., United States v. Sowards, 339 F.2d 401 (10th Cir. 1964); Masheter v. C. H. Hooker Trucking Co., supra; Warren v. Waterville Urban Renewal Authority, 235 A.2d 295 (Me.1967) cert. denied 390 U.S. 1006 (information concerning comparable sales of property); Annot., 12 A.L.R.3d 1064.

3. "In making a diagnosis for treatment, physicians must of necessity consider many things that do not appear in sworn proof on the trial of a lawsuit —things that mean much to the trained eye and touch of a skilled medical practitioner. This court has held that it will not close the doors of the courts to the light which is given by a diagnosis which all the rest of the world accepts and acts upon, even if the diagnosis is in part based upon facts which are not established by the sworn testimony in the case to be true." Stevens, J., in Sundquist v. Madison Rys. Co., cited n. 2, supra; see also, Jenkins v. United States, cited n. 2, supra; State Highway Commission v. Oswalt, cited n. 2, supra; Trinity Universal Ins. Co. v. Town of Speedway, cited n. 2 supra.

4. The text suggestion is in essence embodied in F.R.Ev. (R.D.1971) 703 ("facts or data . . . of a type reasonably relied upon by experts in the particular field in forming opinions or inferences upon the subject"); West's Ann.Cal.Evid.Code, § 801(b) ("matter . . . whether or not admissible, that is of a type that reasonably may be relied upon by an expert in forming an opinion upon the subject to which his testimony related").

In any event, opinions based upon hearsay should be less objectionable if they are opinions upon subject matters that have an indirect relation to the fact issues in the case, rather than opinions directly concerning the facts in issue.[5]

Of course, almost all expert opinion embodies hearsay indirectly, a matter which the courts often recognize and accept.[6]

16. Should the Hypothetical Question Be Retained?

The hypothetical question is an ingenious and logical device for enabling the jury to apply the expert's scientific knowledge to the facts of the case. Nevertheless, it is a failure in practice and an obstruction to the administration of justice. If we require that it recite all the relevant facts, it becomes intolerably wordy. If we allow, as most courts do, the interrogating counsel to select such of the material facts as he sees fit,[7] we tempt him to shape a one-sided hypothesis. Those expert witnesses who have given their views seem to agree that this partisan slanting of the hypothesis is the fatal weakness of the practice.[8] The legal writers who have studied

5. See, e. g., Town of Framingham v. Department of Public Utilities, 355 Mass. 138, 244 N.E.2d 281 (1969) (court approved expert's evaluation of studies on the effect of electromagnetic fields on human and animal systems).

6. See, e. g., Ryan v. Payne, 446 S.W.2d 273 (Ky. 1969) (acceptable that expert consulted skidmark distance tables prior to taking stand); Thompson v. Underwood, 407 F.2d 994 (6th Cir. 1969) (acceptable for medical expert to testify to partial permanent disability of about 37 percent, the expert having used a manual published by the American Medical Association, but having also reached his own independent opinion); 2 Wigmore, Evidence § 665(b).

7. See § 14, n. 96, supra.

8. See, e. g., White, Insanity and the Criminal Law 56 (1923) ("in a large experience, I have never known a hypothetical question, in a trial involving the mental condition of the defendant, which in my opinion offered a fair presentation of the case"); Hulbert, Psychiatric Testimony in Probate Proceedings, 2 Law & Contemp. Prob. 448, 455 (1935) ("But the present practice of misusing the hypothetical

the problem seem equally agreed in condemnation.[9] What is the remedy? It seems hardly practicable to require the trial judge to undertake such a preliminary study of the case as would be necessary to enable him to make the selection of the significant facts to be included. It would probably be feasible for the questions to be framed by both counsel in conference with the judge, either at a pretrial hearing or during the trial, with the jury excluded.[10] But this is wasteful of time and effort. The only remaining expedient is the one generally advocated, namely, that of dispensing with the requirement that the question be accompanied by a recital of an hypothesis, unless the proponent elects to use the hypothetical form, or unless the trial judge in his discretion requires it.[11] It will be for the cross-examiner to bring out if he

so desires, the bases for the expert's opinion.[12] Manifestly, this does not lessen the partisanship of the question or the answer, but it does greatly simplify the examination, and removes the occasion for imperiling the judgment by mistakes in the form of hypothetical questions. For these and other reasons, this general approach has been adopted recently by rule or statute in a few jurisdictions and more importantly in a landmark decision that should be followed in other jurisdictions in the absence of the adoption of a pertinent rule or statute.[13]

17. Proposals for Improvement of the Practice Relating to Expert Testimony.[14]

In common law countries we have the contentious, or adversary, system of trial, where

question as restatement of the case to re-impress the jury is bad strategy, though good tactics; bad strategy because it is so unfair, confusing and degrading that it does not clarify the issue nor help achieve justice"); Roberts, Some Observations on the Problems of the Forensic Psychiatrist, 1965 Wis.L.Rev. 240, 258 (1965).

9. See, e. g., 2 Wigmore, Evidence § 686 ("It is a strange irony that the hypothetical question, which is one of the truly scientific features of the rules of Evidence, should have become that feature which does most to disgust men of science with the law of Evidence."); Judge Learned Hand, New York Bar Association Lectures on Legal Topics, 1921–1922, ("the most horrific and grotesque wen on the fair face of justice"). See Rabata v. Dohner, 45 Wis.2d 111, 172 N.W.2d 409 (1969) stating in part, "moreover the members of this court, based upon their experience gleaned as practicing lawyers and trial judges, are satisfied that a mechanistic hypothetical question has the effect of boring and confusing the jury. Rather than inducing a clear expression of expert opinion and the basis for it, it inhibits the expert and forecloses him from explaining his reasoning in a manner that is intelligible to a jury."

10. See Hulbert, op. cit., n. 8, supra.

11. F.R.Ev. (R.D.1971) 705:
"The expert may testify in terms of opinion or inference and give his reasons therefor without prior disclosure of the underlying facts or data, unless the judge requires otherwise. The expert may in any event be required to disclose the underlying facts or data on cross-examination." See similar provisions in Uniform Rule 58 and Uniform Act on Expert Testimony, § 9. See also note 30, infra.

12. But for this procedure to work fairly, the cross-examiner must have advance knowledge for effective cross-examination, making desirable, if not necessary, the opportunity for advance discovery of experts to be used and substantial discovery of the facts they have at hand and their opinions. See, F.R.Civ.P. 26(b) (4); Advisory Committee's Note, F.R.Ev. (R.D.1971) 705 (text of rule at n. 11, supra); Rabata v. Dohner, 45 Wis.2d 111, 172 N.W. 2d 409, 420, n. 1 (1969).

13. Kan.Code Civ.Proc. (K.S.A. 60–458); N.J.R.Ev. 57, 58; McKinney's N.Y. CPLR § 4515; Mich. Gen.Court Rule 605.

In Rabata v. Dohner, 45 Wis.2d 111, 172 N.W.2d 409 (1969) the court quoted the entire text of this original section as well as other sources. It referred to Rule 409 of the Model Code of Evidence, and stated ". . . we accept that rule as one properly to be applied in trial matters, both civil and criminal, in the courts of Wisconsin and in the discretion of the trial judge. That rule provides: 'An expert witness may state his relevant inferences from matters perceived by him or from evidence introduced at the trial and seen or heard by him or from his special knowledge, skill, experience or training, whether or not any such inference embraces an ultimate issue to be decided by the trier of fact, and he may state his reasons for such inferences and need not, unless the judge so orders, first specify, as an hypothesis or otherwise, the data from which he draws them; but he may thereafter during his examination or cross-examination be required to specify those data.' "

14. Comprehensive discussions are to be found in 2 Wigmore, Evidence § 563; Second Annual Report, New York Law Revision Commission, 795–910 (1936); Expert Testimony (a series of several articles) 2 Law & Contemp.Prob. 401–527 (1935).

the opposing parties, and not the judge as in other systems, have the responsibility and initiative in finding and presenting proof.[15] Advantageous as this system is in many respects, its present application in the procurement and presentation of expert testimony is widely considered a sore spot in judicial administration.   There are two chief points of weakness in the use of experts. The first is the choice of experts by the party, who will naturally be interested in finding, not the best scientist, but the "best witness." As an English judge has said:

" . . .   the mode in which expert evidence is obtained is such as not to give the fair result of scientific opinion to the Court. A man may go, and does sometimes, to half-a-dozen experts . . . He takes their honest opinions, he finds three in his favor and three against him; he says to the three in his favor, 'will you be kind enough to give evidence?' and he pays the three against him their fees and leaves them alone; the other side does the same . . .   I am sorry to say the result is that the Court does not get that assistance from the experts which, if they were unbiased and fairly chosen, it would have a right to expect." [16]

The second weakness is that the adversary method of eliciting scientific testimony, by direct and cross-examination in open court, frequently upon hypothetical questions based on a partisan choice of data, is ill-suited to the dispassionate presentation of technical data, and results too often in over-emphasizing conflicts in scientific opinions which a jury is incapable of resolving.[17]

The remedy for the first weakness is not far to seek. It lies simply in using the trial judge's common law power to call experts. Cases are recorded as early as the 14th century—before witnesses were heard by juries —of the summoning of experts by the judges to aid them in determining scientific issues.[18] The existence of the judge's power to call witnesses generally and expert witnesses particularly seems fairly well recognized in this country.[19] It has been declared by rules and statutes in a substantial number of states empowering the trial judge to summon expert witnesses of his own choosing.[20] Some of these provisions apply to scientific issues in any case, civil or criminal,[21] some are limited to criminal cases [22] and some refer to issues of sanity in criminal cases.[23] The principle is implemented in the carefully drafted Model Expert Testimony Act approved in 1937 by the Commissioners on Uniform State Laws,[24] and embodied in abbrevi-

15. See Millar, Legal Procedure, 12 Encyc.Soc.Sc. 439, 450 (1934), and Millar, The Formative Principles of Primitive Procedure, 18 Ill.L.Rev. 1, 4 (1923), where the two principles of party-prosecution and judicial prosecution are contrasted, but it is pointed out that most systems of procedure make use of both principles in some degree.

16. Jessel, M. R., in Thorn v. Worthington Skating Rink Co., L.R. 6 Ch.D. 415, 416 (1876), note to Plimpton v. Spiller, 6 Ch.D. 412 (1877). See also similar criticisms by Grier, J., in Winans v. N. Y. & Erie R. R., 21 How. 88, 101 (U.S.1858); Henshaw, J., in In re Dolbeer's Estate, 149 Cal. 227, 243, 86 P. 695, 702 (1906) and Cartwright, C. J. in Opp v. Pryor, 294 Ill. 545, 128 N.E. 580 (1920).

17. See criticism cited in notes 14 and 16, supra.

18. Rosenthal, The Development of the Use of Expert Testimony, 2 Law & Contemp.Prob. 403, 406– 411 (1935).

19. See § 8, supra; Note, The Trial Judge's Use of his Power to Call Witnesses, 51 Nw.U.L.Rev. 761 (1957); Note, Judicial Authority to Call Expert Witnesses, 12 Rutgers L.Rev. 375 (1957); Annot., 95 A.L.R.2d 390.

20. See collection of statutes in 2 Wigmore, Evidence § 563.

21. See, e. g., West's Ann.Cal.Evid. Code, §§ 730– 733; Rhode Island Gen. Laws 1956, § 9–17–19.

22. See, e. g., Florida Stat.Ann. § 932.30 (felony trials); Wis.Stat.Ann. § 957.27.

23. See, e. g., Ohio R.C. § 2945.40; N.Dak.Cent. Code 29–20–03, 29–20–04, 29–20–05; Burns' Ann. Ind.Stat. § 957–27.

24. The Act is set out in 1937 Handbook, Nat'l Conf.Com'rs on Unif.State Laws 339–348 and in 9A Unif.L.Ann. 536. The Act was adopted in South Dakota, S.Dak.Comp.Laws, 1967, §§ 19–6–1 through 19–6–11.

ated form in the Uniform Rules of Evidence and the proposed federal rules of evidence.[25] The substance of these proposals should be adopted in every state.[26]

The further mechanism of establishing panels of impartial experts designated by groups in the appropriate fields, from which panel court-appointed experts would be selected, should also be considered along with the above-mentioned systems of court-ap-

pointed expert witnesses.[27] An American Bar Association committee has approved in principle this procedure for impartial medical expert witnesses.[28]

It is not only essential to reduce the partisan element in the selection of experts, but it is equally important that the contentious character of the presentation of the results of the expert's investigation be modified. Otherwise, the "battle of experts" might merely evolve into a battle of examiner and cross-examiner in the interrogation of the official expert at the trial. In some kinds of controversies a well-devised plan of scientific investigation and report may operate to reduce greatly the need for contested trials in court.[29] In the Uniform Act, it is provided that the court may require a conference of the experts, whether chosen by the court or the parties, so that they may as far as possible resolve together, in the light of the knowledge and observations of all of them, their

---

25. Uniform Rule 58.

F.R.Ev. (R.D.1971) 706 provides:

"**(a) Appointment.** The judge may on his own motion or on the motion of any party enter an order to show cause why expert witnesses should not be appointed, and may request the parties to submit nominations. The judge may appoint any expert witnesses agreed upon by the parties, and may appoint witnesses of his own selection. An expert witness shall not be appointed by the judge unless he consents to act. A witness so appointed shall be informed of his duties by the judge in writing, a copy of which shall be filed with the clerk, or at a conference in which the parties shall have opportunity to participate. A witness so appointed shall advise the parties of his findings, if any; his deposition may be taken by any party; and he may be called to testify by the court or any party. He shall be subject to cross-examination by each party, including a party calling him as a witness.

"**(b) Compensation.** Expert witnesses so appointed are entitled to reasonable compensation in whatever sum the judge may allow. The compensation thus fixed is payable from funds which may be provided by law in criminal cases and cases involving just compensation under the Fifth Amendment. In other civil cases the compensation shall be paid by the parties in such proportion and at such time as the judge directs, and thereafter charged in like manner as other costs.

"**(c) Disclosure of Appointment.** In the exercise of his discretion, the judge may authorize disclosure to the jury of the fact that the court appointed the expert witness.

"**(d) Parties' Experts of Own Selection.** Nothing in this rule limits the parties in calling expert witnesses of their own selection."

Rule 28 of the Federal Rules of Criminal Procedure is similar.

26. The system of impartial court-appointed experts has not escaped attorneys' criticism or expert's criticism. See Levy, Impartial Medical Testimony—Revisited, 34 Temple L.Q. 416 (1961); Diamond, The Fallacy of the Impartial Expert, 3 Archives of Criminal Psychodynamics 221 (1959), excerpts reprinted in Allen, Furster and Rubin, Readings in Law and Psychiatry 145 (1968).

27. Review and discussion of various plans is found in Myers, "The Battle of the Experts": A New Approach to an Old Problem in Medical Testimony, 44 Neb.L.Rev. 539 (1965); Van Dusen, A United States District Judge's View of the Impartial Medical Expert System, 32 F.R.D. 498 (1963); Impartial Medical Testimony Plans, Alleghany County Medical Society Medico-Legal Committee (1961). See also, Botein, The New York Medical Expert Testimony Project, 33 U.Det.L.J. 388 (1956).

A further, and perhaps more questionable suggestion is the plan for medical-malpractice panels, staffed by physicians and attorneys. A claim could be voluntarily submitted to the panel. If the panel found it meritorious, the panel would aid in securing medical testimony.

28. American Bar Association, Section of Judicial Administration, Committee on Impartial Medical Testimony, Report, 1956 (August); Handbook on the Improvement of the Administration of Justice, American Bar Association, 79–80 (5th ed. 1971).

29. In states where the statutes provide for the examination by psychiatrists of persons charged with serious crimes, the tendency has been for the prosecution, the defendant, and the court to acquiesce in the expert's conclusions in various situations. See Weihofen, An Alternative to the Battle of Experts: Hospital Examination of Criminal Defendants Before Trial, 2 Law & Contemp.Prob. 419, 422 (1935); Overholser, The History and Operation of the Briggs Law of Massachusetts, 2 id. 436, 444.

differences of view and their difficulties in interpreting the data. As a result, there will be possibilities of a complete agreement which may practically settle the issue for the parties. If not, it will at least make clear the area of agreement and may narrow the controversy within manageable limits. Two or more experts, it is provided, may join in a single report. At the trial, moreover, the individual report of the expert witness, or a joint report, may be read to the court and jury as a part of his testimony, and he may be cross-examined thereon. (In any event, each expert may be required to file a report which is subject to inspection.) As previously stated,[30] the Act dispenses with the requirement of the use of the hypothetical question.

There are other features of the common law procedure not dealt with in the Uniform Act which greatly hamper the effectiveness of expert testimony. Among these are, first, the unsuitability of the jury, a body of laymen usually required to be unanimous, as a tribunal for appraising scientific evidence; [31] second, the rules of privilege, especially the physician-patient privilege and the privilege against self-crimination; [32] and third, the occasional employment by the courts of standards of liability, which do not accord with the scientific standards which the experts are accustomed to use as criteria, as in the case of the "understanding of right and wrong" test of responsibility of insane persons.[33]

Finally, it should be borne in mind that the need for better employment by the courts of the resources of technicians and scientists goes beyond the use of expert witnesses. A judge has said:

> "The methods of courts might well be supplemented by the use of well tested examples of administrative tribunals, of expert investigators acting for the court—engineers, scientists, physicians, economic and social investigators, as needed—in addition to, not in substitute for, similar experts acting for the parties
>
> . . .
>
> "Why should not judge and jury in cases involving multitudinous scientific exhibits, or scientific questions, have the benefit of the assistance of those competent to organize such data and analyze such questions? Why should not courts have adequate fact finding facilities for all kinds of cases? Boards of directors do. Administrative tribunals do. The parties, and in a large sense the public, have an interest in the decision of cases on whole truth, not on partial understanding. The machinery and expert staffs developed by the interstate commerce commission, state public service commissions, and workmen's compensation boards have values for fact finding which may profitably be studied in reference to judicial reorganization . . . " [34]

The judicial tradition has known an abundance of procedures which are well adapted to the utilizing of the services and knowledge of experts. Perhaps pretrial conferences could be designed more specifically to deal with matters involving expert opinion. Most important is the power, often regulated by statute or rule, but in any event presumably one of the latent, "inherent" judicial pow-

---

30. See § 16, n. 11, supra.

31. Many related problems exist. For example, psychiatric expert testimony may well differ in that it may depend upon whether the expert is "dynamically" or "organically" or otherwise oriented. See Allen, Furster and Rubin, Readings in Law and Psychiatry 153 (1968).

32. See §§ 99 and 134, infra.

33. Weihofen, Insanity as a Defense in Criminal Law 64–68, 409–418 (1933). See also the body of literature which has grown up around Durham v. United States, 94 U.S.App.D.C. 228, 214 F.2d 862, 45 A.L.R.2d 1430 (1954).

34. Mr. Justice Harold M. Stephens, What Courts can Learn from Commissions, 21 A.B.A.J. 141, 142 (1933). Also, see generally, Ch. 37, infra.

ers,[35] of referring a question to a master, referee, auditor or similar officer, standing or special. The reference may contemplate merely an investigation and report, or a hearing followed by a report or a preliminary decision.[36] It has been urged that these traditional procedures be more widely used and more effectively prescribed by statute.[37] It is suggested likewise that the courts make wider use of the technical resources of the sister branch of the government, the administrative commissions.[38] It may be predicted that all of these opportunities of the courts for using expert knowledge less clumsily may eventually be employed more widely in the future. They would not merely be useful as aids to a more intelligent final trial of an issue in this context of employment of expert knowledge, but it is likely they would more and more often render trial unnecessary.

18. Application of the Opinion Rule to Out-of-Court Statements.

Does the opinion rule apply to statements made out of court, and offered in court under some exception to the hearsay rule? If we accept the traditional view [39] that the opinion rule is a categorical rule of exclusion, rejecting a certain definable type of evidence, it is natural to assume that if this kind of evidence is excluded when elicited from a witness on the stand, it should also be rejected when offered in the form of the repetition in court of what some narrator has said out of court. Consequently, many decisions have simply discussed the admissibility of opinions contained in hearsay declarations as if they had been given by a witness on the stand, and have rejected or admitted them accordingly,[40] although common sense doubtless has an unspoken influence toward a more liberal treatment of the out-of-court opinions. If on the other hand we adopt the view to which the courts seem now to be tending, namely, that the opinion rule is not an absolute rule of exclusion, but rather a relative rule for the examination of witnesses, preferring when it is feasible the more concrete form of examination to the more general and inferential,[41] then it becomes obvious that the opinion rule has no sensible application to statements made out of court. Sustaining an objection to counsel's question to a witness as calling for an "opinion" is usually not a serious matter since counsel can in most cases easily reframe the question to call for the more concrete statement. But to reject the statement of the out-of-court narrator of what he observed, as in a dying declaration, on the

---

35. See the statesmanlike opinion of Brandeis, J. in Ex parte Peterson, 253 U.S. 300, 312 (1919) (District Court may appoint auditor with provision that his report shall be used in evidence. "Courts have (at least in the absence of legislation to the contrary) inherent power to provide themselves with appropriate instruments required for the performance of their duties. Compare Stockbridge Iron Co. v. Cone Iron Works, 102 Mass. 80, 87–90. This power includes authority to appoint persons unconnected with the court to aid judges in the performance of specific judicial duties, as they may arise in the progress of a cause.")

A helpful discussion of the relative advantages and disadvantages of the use of adversary experts, masters, advisors, and court-appointed experts is found in Manual for Complex and Multidistrict Litigation, Appendix § 3.51 (1969).

At present, however, the power to appoint a master is restricted, or at least unexercised in many jurisdictions, or is conditioned by statutory or rule limitations. See, e. g., 5 Moore, Federal Practice § 53.05.

36. Beuscher, The Use of Experts by the Courts, 54 Harv.L.Rev. 1105, 1111–1120 (1941). A doctor has suggested that there should be a routine reference to a medical master of all personal injury and other cases having medical issues, for investigation and report. The report would be received as evidence at the trial. Koerner, Diagnosis and Treatment of Legal Congestion, 22 J.Am.Jud.Soc. 168 (1939).

37. Beuscher, op. cit., at p. 1126. There are, however, substantial general objections to the use of masters, and the like, even in a traditional way, in many types of cases.

38. Id. at 1123.

39. See § 11, supra.

40. E. g., Philpot v. Com., 195 Ky. 555, 242 S.W. 839 (1922); Pendleton v. Com., 131 Va. 676, 109 S.E. 201 (1929) (dying declaration); Cox v. Esso Shipping Co., 247 F.2d 629 (5th Cir. 1957).

41. See §§ 11, 12, supra.

ground that the statement is too general in form to meet the courtroom rules of interrogation mistakes the function of the opinion rule and may shut out altogether a valuable item of proof. Many of the cases, and Wigmore, have taken this view as to admissions,[42] and it is believed that it is in the process of prevailing as to the other classes of declara-

tions coming in under exceptions to the hearsay rule.[43]

Of course, the speciously similar question of the want of personal knowledge of the declarant should be distinguished. If it appears that the out-of-court declarant had not observed at first hand the fact declared, this goes not to form but to substance and is often fatal to admissibility if the statement is offered to prove the fact.[44]

---

42. Swain v. Oregon Motor Stages, 160 Ore. 1, 82 P.2d 1084 (1938) (statement by injured party after collision that he considered driver of other car to blame); Taylor v. Owen, 290 S.W.2d 771 (Tex. Civ.App.1956) (statement that other driver was not at fault); 4 Wigmore, Evidence § 1053(3); and see § 264, infra. Compare the similar problem presented in respect to evidence of inconsistent statements to impeach, see § 35, infra.

43. As to dying declarations see § 285, infra.

44. See §§ 285 and 300, infra. But the situation is to the contrary with respect to admissions, see § 264, infra and the entry of items in business records, see § 310, infra.

CHAPTER 4

CROSS–EXAMINATION AND SUBSEQUENT EXAMINATIONS

19. The Right of Cross-Examination:[1] Effect of Deprivation of Opportunity to Cross-Examine.

For two centuries, common law judges and lawyers have regarded the opportunity of cross-examination as an essential safeguard of the accuracy and completeness of testimony,[2] and they have insisted that the opportunity is a right[3] and not a mere privilege.[4]

This right is available, of course, at the taking of depositions, as well as on the examination of witnesses at the trial.[5] And the premise that the opportunity of cross-examination is an essential safeguard has been the principal justification for the exclusion generally of hearsay statements,[6] and for the admission as an exception to the hearsay rule of reported testimony taken at a former hearing when the present adversary was afforded the opportunity to cross-examine.[7] Finally, state constitutional provisions guaranteeing to the accused the right of confrontation have been interpreted as codifying this right of cross-

1. As to cross-examination generally, see 5 Wigmore, Evidence §§ 1390–1394, 6 id. §§ 1884–1894; Dec. Dig. Witnesses ☞266–284; C.J.S. Witnesses §§ 368–376; 58 Am.Jur. Witnesses §§ 609–673.

2. See 5 Wigmore, Evidence § 1367. See also Hungate v. Hudson, 353 Mo. 944, 185 S.W.2d 646, 157 A.L.R. 598 (1945).

3. Alford v. United States, 282 U.S. 687, 691 (1931). See n. 9, infra.

4. Resurrection Gold Min. Co. v. Fortune Gold Min. Co., 129 F. 668, 674 (8th Cir. 1904).

5. State ex rel. Bailes v. Guardian Realty Co., 237 Ala. 201, 186 So. 168 (1939). F.R.Civ.P. 30(c) recognizes the right at the taking of depositions.

6. See § 245, infra.

7. See §§ 254, 255, infra.

examination.[8] In fact, the right of confrontation required by the Sixth Amendment of the federal constitution in general guarantees the accused's right to the opportunity of cross-examination in criminal proceedings.[9]

What are the present consequences of a denial or failure of the right? There are several common situations.[10] First, a party testifying on his own behalf may unjustifiably refuse to answer questions necessary to a complete cross-examination. Here it is generally agreed that the adversary is entitled to have the direct testimony stricken out,[11] a result that seems warranted.

Second, a non-party witness may similarly refuse to be cross-examined, or to answer proper questions of the cross-examiner. Here the case is a little less clear, but the expressions of some judges and writers seem to sanction the same remedy of excluding the direct.[12] This minimizes the temptation for the party to procure the witness's refusal, a collusion which is often hard to prove and protects the right of cross-examination strictly. There is also some authority for the view that the matter should be left to the judge's discretion.[13] Finally, there is support for the notion that if the privilege against self-incrimination is invoked upon cross-examination to questions which go to the credibility of the witness and are otherwise immaterial, the testimony on direct examination should not be stricken, or at the least the judge should have an area of discretion in making his ruling on that matter.[14]

Third, the witness may become, or purport to become, sick or otherwise physically or mentally incapacitated, before cross-examination is begun or completed. Many of such cases arouse suspicion of simulation, particularly when the witness is a party, and consequently the party's direct examination will often be excluded.[15] In the case of the non-

---

8. State v. Crooker, 123 Me. 310, 122 A. 865, 33 A.L.R. 821 (1923) (confrontation right does not mean merely that accused shall see the witness, but the right to cross-examine) and see § 252, infra.

9. See for example, Smith v. State of Illinois, 390 U.S. 129 (1968); Douglas v. Alabama, 380 U.S. 415 (1965); Pointer v. Texas, 380 U.S. 400 (1965); Barber v. Page, 390 U.S. 719 (1968); California v. Green, 399 U.S. 149 (1970). See § 252, infra.

10. See the analyses of these problems in 5 Wigmore, Evidence § 1390, and in Degnan, Non-Rules Evidence Law: Cross-Examination, 6 Utah L.Rev. 323 (1959).

11. People v. McGowan, 80 Cal.App. 293, 251 P. 643 (1926) (direct testimony of accused to an alibi stricken when on cross-examination he refused to answer question as to name of person who was with him at the time); Aluminum Industries, Inc. v. Egan, 61 Ohio App. 111, 22 N.E.2d 459 (1938) (direct testimony of party-witness, refusing to answer pertinent cross-questions on unjustified ground of privilege). See also People v. Barthel, 231 Cal.App.2d 827, 42 Cal.Rptr. 290 (1965); In re Monaghan, 126 Vt. 53, 222 A.2d 665 (1966); C.J.S. Witnesses § 373; Dec.Dig. Witnesses ⟨284. Seemingly the cross-examiner could invoke the court's action to compel the witness to answer, if the privilege against self-incrimination has not been invoked or is not applicable, but is not required to do so.

12. State v. Davis, 236 Iowa 740, 19 N.W.2d 655 (1945) (but here held that full opportunity was later accorded); Hadra v. Utah Nat. Bank, 9 Utah 412, 414, 35 P. 508 (1894) (deposition properly excluded for witness's refusal to answer material cross-question); 5 Wigmore, Evidence § 1391; C.J.S. Witnesses § 373.

13. See Stephan v. United States, 133 F.2d 87 (6th Cir. 1943) (refusal to answer only a few of the cross-questions; judge in discretion properly refused to strike direct testimony); Moormeister v. Golding, 84 Utah 324, 27 P.2d 447 (1933) (whether deposition should be excluded for witness's failure to answer a question under notary's prompting, in judge's discretion). But in criminal cases, this rule raises constitutional questions. See text at n. 9, supra.

14. United States v. Cardillo, 316 F.2d 606 (2d Cir. 1963) cert. denied 375 U.S. 822, reh. denied 375 U.S. 926; Coil v. United States, 343 F.2d 573 (8 Cir., 1965) cert. denied 382 U.S. 821; United States v. Marcus, 401 F.2d 563 (2d Cir., 1968) cert. denied 393 U.S. 1023. But the thwarted cross-examination may be pertinent to material issues as well as to credibility as pointed out in Board of Trustees of Mt. San Antonio Jr. College Dist. v. Hartman, 246 Cal.App.2d 726, 55 Cal.Rptr. 144 (1967) (but error held not prejudicial).

15. See, e. g., Louisville & N. R. Co. v. Gregory, 284 Ky. 297, 144 S.W.2d 519 (1940) (plaintiff suing for personal injuries testified from a cot and on cross-examination professed to be unable to proceed; judge refused to strike direct but offered to let defendant use cross-examination taken at for-

party witness, the same result is usually reached,[16] but, at least in civil cases, it is arguable that this result should be qualified so that the judge is directed to exclude unless he is clearly convinced that the incapacity is genuine, in which event he should let the direct testimony stand. He should then be authorized to explain to the jury the weakness of such uncross-examined evidence.[17] Temporary incapacity may change this result, as indicated below.

The fourth situation is that of the death of the witness before the cross-examination. Here again it is usually said that the party thus deprived of cross-examination is entitled to have the direct testimony stricken,[18] unless, presumably, the death occurred during a postponement of the cross-examination consented to or procured by him.[19] In case of death there seems no adequate reason for excluding the direct testimony, except that exclusion may well be required if the witness is a state's witness in a criminal case. It has been suggested that exclusion of the direct should be discretionary [20] but no matter how

valuable cross-examination may be, common sense tells us that the half-loaf of direct testimony is better than no bread at all.[21] To let the direct testimony stand was the accepted practice in equity.[22] It is submitted that except for the testimony of the state's witnesses in criminal cases the judge should let the direct testimony stand but should be required on request to instruct the jury in weighing its value to consider the lack of opportunity to cross-examine.

The above results may be modified in certain situations. It has been held that where the incapacity is temporary the cross-examiner may not insist upon immediate exclusion of the direct testimony, but must be content with the offer of a later opportunity to cross-examine even when this makes it necessary for him to submit to a mistrial.[23]

It has been assumed in the preceding paragraphs that, though some cross-questions may have been answered, a failure to secure a complete cross-examination would be treated as if cross-examination had been wholly denied. It seems, however, that a cross-examination, though cut off before it is finished, may yet under the circumstances be found to have been so substantially complete as to satisfy the requirement of opportunity

---

mer trial, which the defendant declined to do; held error to refuse to strike).

16. Wray v. State, 154 Ala. 36, 45 So. 697 (1908); People v. Cole, 43 N.Y. 508, 512 (1871). But where the importance of the direct has been unusually emphasized by the proponent, the failure of cross-examination may require a mistrial. United States v. Malinsky, 153 F.Supp. 321 (S.D.N.Y. 1957).

17. This is suggested in Note, 27 Colum.L.Rev. 327 (1927). But it is doubtful that this procedure would be constitutional if the witness is one called by the state in a criminal case. See n. 9, supra.

18. Kemble v. Lyons, 184 Iowa 804, 169 N.W. 117 (1918); Sperry v. Moore's Estate, 42 Mich. 353, 4 N.W. 13 (1880) (death during continuance procured by direct examiner); State v. Bigham, 133 S.C. 491, 131 S.E. 603 (1926); In re Sweeney's Estate, 248 Wis. 607, 22 N.W.2d 657 (1946) (right of cross-examination specially reserved by judge); C.J.S. Witnesses § 373.

19. See 5 Wigmore, Evidence § 1390, n. 5. The cases cited there, however, are cases of disabilities other than death.

20. 5 Wigmore, Evidence § 1390, p. 110 ("But the true solution would be to avoid any inflexible

rule, and to leave it to the trial judge to admit the direct examination so far as the loss of cross-examination can be shown to him to be not in that instance a material loss") quoted approvingly in Kubin v. Chicago Title and Trust Co., 307 Ill.App. 12, 29 N.E.2d 859, 863 (1940) (ruling excluding direct examination affirmed in absence of showing of prejudice).

21. See Note, 27 Colum.L.Rev. 327 (1927) which points out that the testimony is more trustworthy than evidence admitted under many of the established hearsay exceptions.

22. See Scott v. McCann, 76 Md. 47, 24 A. 536 (1892).

23. Gale v. State, 135 Ga. 351, 69 S.E. 537 (1910) (where witness collapsed on defendant's cross-examination, no error in refusing to strike out the evidence when defendant declined to consent to mistrial).

to cross-examine.[24] It also appears that cross-examination may be regarded in the particular situation as having been sufficient as to part of the direct testimony to allow that part to stand though the rest must be stricken.[25]

Finally, the infringement of the right of cross-examination may come, not from the refusal or inability of the witness, but from the action of the judge. The judge, as we shall see, has wide discretionary control over the *extent* of cross-examination upon particular topics, but the denial of cross-examinations altogether, or its arbitrary curtailment upon a proper subject of cross-examination will be ground for reversal.[26]

20. Form of Interrogation.

In contrast with direct examination, cross-examination may usually be conducted by leading questions.[27] The cross-examiner's purpose in the main is to weaken the effect of the direct testimony, and furthermore, the witness is usually assumed to be a more or less uncooperative one. Consequently the danger of undue acquiescence in the examiner's suggestions is not ordinarily present. However, when it appears that the witness is biased in favor of the cross-examiner, and likely to be unduly yielding to the suggestions of leading questions the judge in many jurisdictions may restrain the asking of them,[28] and in those jurisdictions where the scope of cross-examination is limited, if the examiner goes beyond the proper field of cross-examination he may be required to refrain from leading the witness.[29] There are, on the other hand, a number of somewhat illogical decisions which permit leading questions on cross-examination even though the witness appears biased in favor of the cross-examiner.[30]

21. Scope of Cross-Examination: Restriction to Matters Opened up on Direct: The Various Rules.[31]

The practice varies widely in the different jurisdictions on the question whether the

---

24. Fuller v. Rice, 70 Mass. (4 Gray) 343 (1855). Again, the application of this principle to a state's witness in a criminal proceeding may be questionable. See n. 9, supra.

25. See Curtice v. West, 50 Hun. 47, 48, 2 N.Y.S. 507 (1888) and compare In re Mezger's Estate, 154 Misc. 633, 278 N.Y.S. 669 (1935). See also Jaiser v. Milligan, 120 F.Supp. 599 (D.C.Neb.1954) (a cross-examination begun but unfinished through no fault of the witness or her attorney is said to suffice if its purposes have been substantially accomplished). But see comment in n. 24, supra.

26. Alford v. United States, 282 U.S. 687 (1931) (refusal to permit cross-examination of government witness about his present residence, in custody of U.S. marshal, to show bias); Fahey v. Clark, 125 Conn. 44, 3 A.2d 313 (1938) (refusal to permit cross-examination of plaintiff about prior injury); People v. Crump, 5 Ill.2d 251, 125 N.E.2d 615 (1955) (refusal to permit cross-examination of accomplice witness to show that he was a drug addict or had used narcotics on day of crime).
In fact, the right of the criminal defendant in such a case in both state and federal courts is a federal constitutional right.
See § 29, infra.

27. Ewing v. United States, 135 F.2d 633 (D.C.Cir. 1943); In re Mitgang, 385 Ill. 311, 52 N.E.2d 807 (1944); 3 Wigmore, Evidence (Chadbourn rev.) § 773; Dec.Dig. Witnesses ☞282.

28. Moody v. Rowell, 34 Mass. 490, 498 (1835) ("So a judge may, in his discretion, prohibit certain leading questions from being put to an adversary's witness, where the witness shows a strong interest or bias in favor of the cross-examining party, and needs only an intimation, to say whatever is most favorable to that party."); 3 Wigmore, Evidence (Chadbourn rev.) § 773; Annot., 38 A.L.R.2d 952. See Tolomeo v. Harmony Short Line Motor Transport Co., 349 Pa. 420, 37 A.2d 511 (1944) (in collision case where plaintiff called defendant's bus driver to show defendant's ownership, court improperly permitted defendant to cross-examine driver by leading questions on negligence). But it is largely a matter of discretion. Lauchheimer & Sons v. Jacobs, 126 Ga. 261, 55 S.E. 55 (1906); Westland Housing Corp. v. Scott, 312 Mass. 375, 44 N.E.2d 959 (1942). Both are cases of a party called by his adversary and cross-examined by his own counsel.

29. People v. Melone, 71 Cal.App.2d 291, 162 P.2d 505 (1945).

30. Martyn v. Donlin, 151 Conn. 402, 198 A.2d 700 (1964) (defense counsel permitted to use leading questions on cross-examination of defendant who had been called by plaintiff as an adverse witness); Wilcox v. Erwin, 49 S.W.2d 677 (Mo.App. 1932) (similar case); Annot., 38 A.L.R.2d 952.

31. See 6 Wigmore, Evidence §§ 1886–1891; Dec. Dig. Witnesses ☞269; C.J.S. Witnesses §§ 393–397;

cross-examiner is confined in his questions to the subjects testified about in the direct examination, and if so to what extent.

The traditional rule of wide-open cross-examination. In England and in about one-fifth of the states, the simplest and freest practice prevails. In these jurisdictions, the cross-examiner is not limited to the topics which the direct examiner has chosen to open,[32] but is free to cross-examine about any subject relevant to any of the issues in the entire case, including facts relating solely to the cross-examiner's own case or affirmative defence.

Notes, 37 Colum.L.Rev. 1373 (1937), 24 Iowa L.Rev. 564 (1939).

32. Mayor and Corporation of Berwick-on-Tweed, v. Murray, 19 L.J.Ch. 281, 286 (V.C., 1850); Morgan v. Brydges, 2 Stark, 314, 171 Eng.Rep. 657 (N.P.1818) (witness called by plaintiff for formal proof, may be cross-examined by defendant, his employer, on the whole case); Riddle v. Dorough, 279 Ala. 527, 187 So.2d 568 (1966); Ariz. Rules of Civil Procedure, Rule 43(g), 16 Ariz.R.S. ("Any witness may be cross-examined on any matter material to the case"); Podol v. Jacobs, 65 Ariz. 50, 173 P.2d 758, 764 (1946) ("This now commits us to the English rule"); Ficken v. Atlanta, 114 Ga. 970, 41 S.E. 58 (1902); LSA–R.S. 15:280 (a witness who "has testified to any single fact . . . may be cross-examined upon the whole case"); King v. Atkins, 33 La.Ann. 1057, 1064 (1881); Falmouth v. Windham, 63 Me. 44 (1873); Moody v. Rowell, 34 Mass. 490 (1835) (leading case, opinion by Shaw, C. J.); Mask v. State, 32 Miss. 405 (1856); Saxon v. Harvey, 190 So.2d 901 (Miss.1966); State v. West, 349 Mo. 221, 161 S.W.2d 966 (1942) (citing statutes permitting cross-examination "on the entire case" except in case of cross-examination of the accused, or the spouse of accused, in a criminal case); State v. Huskins, 209 N.C. 727, 184 S.E. 480 (1936); State v. Howard, 35 S.C. 197, 14 S.E. 481 (1892); Sands v. Southern Ry. Co., 108 Tenn. 1, 64 S.W. 478 (1901); Pride v. Pride, 318 S.W.2d 715 (Tex.Civ.App.1958); Wentworth v. Crawford, 11 Tex. 127, 132 (1853); Boller v. Cofrances, 42 Wis.2d 170, 166 N.W.2d 129 (1969) (court states that it approves the English rule); and cases cited C.J.S. Witnesses § 393, note 86.

F.R.Ev. (R.D.1971) 611(b) provides:
"A witness may be cross-examined on any matter relevant to any issue in the case, including credibility. In the interests of justice, the judge may limit cross-examination with respect to matters not testified to on direct examination."

The "restrictive" rule, in various forms, limiting cross-examination to the scope of the direct. The Federal courts generally and the majority of the states have agreed in the view that the cross-examination must be limited to the matters testified to on the direct examination.[33] This doctrine can be employed narrowly to restrict the cross-questions to those relating only to the same acts or facts,[34] and, perhaps, those occurring or appearing at the same time and place. The doctrine has often been formulated in a way to suggest this meaning. Thus, the cross-examination has been said to be limited to "the same points" brought out on direct,[35] to the "matters testified to," [36] to the "subjects mentioned," [37] and the like. Slightly more expansive is the extension to "facts and circumstances connected with" the matters stated on di-

33. Among the leading cases which served to introduce this innovation upon common law practice were Ellmaker v. Buckley, 16 S. & R. 72, 77 (Pa. 1827), People v. Horton, 4 Mich. 67, 82 (1856), and Philadelphia & Trenton R. Co. v. Stimpson, 39 U.S. (14 Pet.) 448, 461 (1840) by Story, J.

34. See, e. g., State v. Guilfoyle, 109 Conn. 124, 145 A. 761 (1929) (doctor testified to general description of wound, cross-examination as to opinion whether wound caused by near or far shot properly excluded); Wheeler & Wilson Mfg. Co. v. Barrett, 172 Ill. 610, 50 N.E. 325 (1898) (plaintiff testified she bought and paid for sewing machine from defendant, cross-examination designed to show she took possession under written lease contract properly excluded); McNeely v. Conlon, 216 Iowa 796, 248 N.W. 17 (1933) (eye-witness described accident, prejudicial error to permit defendant on cross to elicit that witness just after and at scene said to defendant, "It was not your fault"); Nagel v. McDermott, 138 Wash. 536, 244 P. 977 (1926) (witness testified to location of bicycle in collision incident, but could not testify to speed of bicycle on cross-examination). But these cases are not necessarily consistent with others in the same jurisdictions. See, e. g., Iowa cases cited in n. 40, infra.

35. Carey v. City of Oakland, 44 Cal.App.2d 503, 112 P.2d 714 (1941).

36. McAden v. State, 155 Fla. 523, 21 So.2d 33 (1945); Nadeau v. Texas Co., 104 Mont. 558, 69 P. 2d 586 (1937).

37. State v. Bagley, 339 Mo. 215, 96 S.W.2d 331 (1936) (the English rule not followed in criminal cases as to a defendant or his spouse; V.A.M.S. (Mo.) §§ 491.070, 546.260).

rect,[38] but this still suggests the requirement of identity of transaction, and proximity in time and space. Seemingly a much wider extension is accomplished by another variation of the formula. This is the statement that the cross-examination is limited to the matters opened in direct and to facts tending "to explain, contradict, or discredit the testimony given in chief," [39] and even more widely, facts tending to rebut any "inference or deduction" from the matters testified on direct.[40] There is little consistency in the expression and the use of formulas, even in the same jurisdiction.[41] All express criteria are too vague to be employed with precision. Assuming that cross-examination is somehow to be limited to the subject matter of the direct examination, the subject matter of questions on direct examination can always be defined in particular instances with greater or lesser generality regardless of the general formulas.

All these limiting formulas have a common escape valve, namely, the notion that where part of a transaction, "res gestæ," contract, or conversation has been revealed on direct,

the remainder may be brought out on cross-examination.[42] The fact that this is substantially a mere statement of the converse of the limiting rule itself does not detract from its usefulness as an added tool for argument. Another escape valve for appeal purposes is the notion that the trial judge has a certain amount of discretion in ruling upon the scope of cross-examination.

The half-open door: cross-examination extends to any matters except cross-examiner's affirmative case. A third view as to the scope of cross-examination would take a middle course between the two extremes. Under this view, now mostly obsolete, the cross-examiner could question the witness about any matters relevant to any issue in the action, except facts relating only to the cross-examiner's own affirmative case, such as defendant's affirmative defences or cross-claims, or in case of a plaintiff, his new matter in reply.[43] This rather liberalized stand-

---

38. Story, J., in Philadelphia & Trenton R. Co. v. Stimpson, 39 U.S. (14 Pet.) 448, 461 (1840); Austin v. State, 14 Ark. 555, 563 (1854); Williams v. State, 32 Fla. 315, 317, 13 So. 834 (1893).

39. Krametbauer v. McDonald, 44 N.M. 473, 104 P.2d 900 (1940); Lewis v. State, 458 P.2d 309 (Okl. Cr.1969).

40. A case indicating this view is Conley v. Mervis, 324 Pa. 577, 188 A. 350, 108 A.L.R. 160 (1936) (suit for damages for injury caused by a truck; defendant denies ownership; plaintiff calls defendant as witness and proves on direct that defendant owned license plates on truck; held, error to refuse to permit defendant to be cross-examined by his own counsel to show the plates were taken from his place of business without his knowledge or consent; this was allowable to rebut the inference of ownership of the truck and agency of the driver which would be derived from ownership of the plates). So also Parente v. Dickinson, 391 Pa. 162, 137 A.2d 788 (1958); Crosby v. De Land District, 367 Ill. 462, 11 N.E.2d 937 (1937); State v. Harvey, 130 Iowa 394, 106 N.W. 938 (1906); Eno v. Adair County Mutual Ins. Ass'n, 229 Iowa 249, 294 N.W. 323 (1940); and cases cited in Annot., 108 A.L.R. 167.

41. See Note, 37 Colum.L.Rev. 1373 (1937).

42. Gilmer v. Higley, 110 U.S. 47 (1884) (transaction); Rosenberg v. Wittenborn, 178 Cal.App.2d 846, 3 Cal.Rptr. 459 (1960) (conversation); Ah Doon v. Smith, 25 Ore. 89, 34 P. 1093 (1893) (transaction); Johnson v. Cunningham, 104 Ill.App.2d 406, 244 N.E.2d 205 (1969) (conversations); Glenn v. Philadelphia & W. C. Traction Co., 206 Pa. 135, 139, 55 A. 860 (1903) (conversation); Smith v. Philadelphia Traction Co., 202 Pa. 54, 51 A. 345 (1902) ("res gestae"); Vingi v. Trillo, 77 R.I. 55, 73 A.2d 43 (1950) (conversation); Dec.Dig. Witnesses ⟨⟩268(3). But see In re Campbell's Will, 100 Vt. 395, 138 A. 725, 726 (1927) (will contest: proponents placed witness on stand who testified that Mrs. Campbell told her that instrument claimed to be a will was in trunk; contestants were allowed to bring out on cross-examination that Mrs. Campbell told her on same occasion that she wanted her husband to destroy the instrument; held, error, but harmless. "The fact that the proponents had, in effect, put in evidence a part of a statement of Mrs. Campbell, did not, of itself, entitle the contestants to put in all of that statement. The latter could give in evidence whatever Mrs. Campbell then said that tended to qualify, explain, or contradict what Mrs. Stevens had testified to, but no more.").

43. Legg v. Drake, 1 Ohio St. 286, 290 (1853) (party may cross-examine "as to all matters pertinent to the issue on the trial; limited, however, by the rule that a party cannot, before the time of opening his own case introduce his distinct grounds of defense

ard in some instances served as a half-way house, for a time, for courts which later turned to the "wide-open" practice.[44] It has the merit, as compared with the restrictive practice, of lessening dispute by widening the ambit of examination. Its present drawback is that it would often be difficult to determine, particularly under the liberal pleading rules of today, whether the matter inquired about does relate solely to the examiner's "distinct grounds of defense or avoidance." [45]

22. Cross-Examination to Impeach Not Limited to the Scope of the Direct.

One of the main functions of cross-examination is to afford an opportunity to elicit answers which will impeach the veracity, ca-

pacity to observe, impartiality, and consistency of the witness; and yet the direct can seldom be expected to touch explicitly on the points to which impeachment is directed. Accordingly, the rule prevails, even in jurisdictions adopting the most restrictive practice, that cross-examination to impeach is not, in general, limited to matters brought out in the direct examination.[46]

23. Practical Consequences of the Restrictive Rules: Effect on Order of Proof: Side-Effects.

It is sometimes asserted that the only "essential" difference between the "wide-open" and the restrictive rules as to scope of cross-examination is in the time or stage at which the witness may be called upon to testify to the facts inquired about.[47] Thus the difference between the rules would be primarily in their effect upon the order of proof.[48] Under the "wide-open" rule the witness may be questioned on the new matter on cross-examination, whereas under the restrictive rules the cross-examiner can merely postpone

---

or avoidance" by cross-examination); Smith v. State, 125 Ohio St. 695 (1932); Dietsch v. Mayberry, 70 Ohio App. 527, 47 N.E.2d 404 (1942). See also, discussion of "Michigan rule" to date of the article, Comment, 36 U. of Det.L.J. 162 (1958). The objection that the cross-examination elicits matter proper only to the cross-examiner's own case has often, in the past, been given as a ground of decision in states that follow the more restrictive practice limiting the cross to the scope of the direct. See n. 44, infra. But even under the more restrictive view, if the matter is opened in direct, it may be followed up in cross-examination, though this may happen to sustain the cross-examiner's affirmative claim or defense. Garlich v. Northern Pac. Ry. Co., 131 F. 837 (8th Cir. 1904); and cases cited in C.J.S. Witnesses § 397.

44. See, e. g., Chandler v. Allison, 10 Mich. 460, 476 (1862) where this standard is perhaps first adumbrated, when Campbell, J., in sustaining the propriety of cross-questions said, "They were designed to determine the real character of the transaction in issue. They did not relate to matter in avoidance of it. . . ." See also Rush v. French, 1 Ariz. 99, 139, 140, 25 P. 816, 828 (1874) (witness may be cross-examined "upon all matters pertinent to the case of the party calling him, except exclusively new matter; and nothing shall be deemed new matter except it be such as could not be given under a general denial"). Arizona now follows the "wide-open" practice, see cases cited in note 32, supra. See Silver v. London Assur. Corp., 61 Wash. 593, 112 P. 666 (1911) (apparently approving the "half-open door" rule). Washington now restricts cross-examination to the subject matter of the direct. Wilson v. Miller Flour Mills, 144 Wash. 60, 256 P. 777 (1927).

45. See discussion in Note, 37 Colum.L.Rev. 1373, 1382 (1937).

46. Chicago City Ry. Co. v. Carroll, 206 Ill. 318, 324, 68 N.E. 1087, 1089 (1903) (cross-question to doctor as to who paid him); Dickey v. Wagoner, 160 Kan. 216, 160 P.2d 698 (1945) (discretionary to permit impeaching cross-examination upon matters not touched in direct); State v. Elli, 267 Minn. 185, 125 N.W.2d 738 (1964) (question whether witness was an alibi witness in another case); Kennamer v. State, 59 Okl.Cr. 146, 57 P.2d 646, 659 (1936) (cross-examination about prior contradictory statements); Dayton v. Fenno, 99 Ore. 137, 195 P. 154 (1921) (rule stated, not applicable on the facts); Beck v. Hood, 185 Pa. 32, 38, 39 A. 842, 843 (1898) (that witness had talked at previous trial with foreman of jury); 6 Wigmore, Evidence § 1891; C.J.S. Witnesses §§ 484(2), 399a.

47. Valliant, J., in Ayers v. Wabash R. Co., 190 Mo. 228, 88 S.W. 608, 609 (1905); 6 Wigmore, Evidence § 1895.

48. F.R.Ev. (R.D.1971) 611(b), while adopting the wide-open rule of cross-examination, nevertheless authorizes the judge to limit inquiry with respect to matters not testified to on direct when the interests of justice require. As the Advisory Committee's Note points out, the purpose of the provision is to eliminate confusion, complication, or protraction of the case which application of the wide-open rule may appear to be developing in a given case.

the questions until his own next stage [49] of putting on proof, and then call the witness and prove the same facts.[50] This difference is, of course, a substantial difference, but in many instances a mere postponement of the questions will not necessarily be the result of a ruling excluding a cross-question as not in the scope of the direct. Unless the question is vital and he is fairly confident of a favorable answer, the cross-examiner will at the least take considerable risk if he calls the adversary's witness at a later stage as his own, and will often be motivated to abandon the inquiry. Getting concessions from the opponent's witness while his story is fresh is worth trying for. To call the perhaps unfriendly witness later when his first testimony is stale is usually a much less effective expedient. Also promotion of orderly presentation of proof, supposedly promoted by restrictive rules, may not be an effective reason in particular cases in which a party has injected an issue by one witness but not by a second witness who may not be cross-examined on the issue although he may have knowledge relevant to that issue.[51]

A ruling excluding questions as not within the scope of the direct is not the only consequence of the restrictive rule. There are many collateral effects. Thus the courts adopting the restrictive practice often say that if the cross-examiner, perhaps without objection, cross-examines on new matter he makes the witness his own.[52] This being so, he is normally forbidden to ask leading questions about the new matter,[53] and under the traditional rule against impeaching one's own witness [54] may be precluded from impeaching the witness as to those facts.[55] Furthermore, the application of the restrictive rule so as to exclude unfavorable testimony from the plaintiff's witness which could otherwise be elicited on cross-examination, may save the plaintiff from a directed verdict at the close of his case in chief.[56] This is usually a tactical advantage, affording the plaintiff a wider possibility for strengthening his case from his opponent's witnesses, even though the unfavorable testimony of the cross-examined witness may be later elicited by the defendant in the course of his own case in defense, and standing undisputed may thus ultimately result in a directed verdict, anyway. Finally, in one situation, the restrictive rule may become a rule of final exclusion, not a rule of postponement. This is the situation

49. Grievance Committee of Bar of Fairfield Co. v. Dacey, 154 Conn. 129, 222 A.2d 339 (1966). As to the order of proof, by stages, of the respective parties, see § 4, supra.

50. If party avails himself of the opportunity to call the witness at a later stage, he cannot complain on appeal of a restriction on cross-examination. Clucas v. Bank of Montclair, 110 N.J.L. 394, 166 A. 311, 315, 88 A.L.R. 302 (1933); and see State v. Savage, 36 Ore. 191, 61 P. 1128 (1900) (same questions asked on re-call).

51. This suggestion is made in Maguire, Weinstein, Chadbourn and Mansfield, Cases and Materials on Evidence 285, 286 (1965). The authors raise the question whether the scope of cross-examination should be determined by the posture of the whole case rather than by the scope of the direct examination of the second witness mentioned in the text.

52. Longini Shoe Mfg. Co. v. Ratcliff, 108 F.2d 253, 257 (C.C.P.A.1939); State v. Spurr, 100 W.Va. 121, 130 S.E. 81 (1925); 3A Wigmore, Evidence (Chadbourn rev.) § 914 (critical of rule).

53. People v. Court of Oyer and Terminer, 83 N.Y. 436, 459 (1881). But this result rests upon an assumption of a hard-and-fast rule that leading questions are always permissible in the proper field of cross-examination and never in the proper area of direct. 3A Wigmore, Evidence (Chadbourn rev.) § 915. The criterion is whether the witness is probably willing or unwilling to yield to suggestion, and as to this there is usually no difference in the attitudes of the witness, when the question is, or is not, within the scope of the direct. See § 6, supra.

54. This rule, however, has now been much liberalized in many jurisdictions. See § 38, infra.

55. Pollard v. State, 201 Ind. 180, 166 N.E. 654 (1929); 3 Wigmore, Evidence (Chadbourn rev.) § 914; Dec.Dig. Witnesses ☞325.

56. Seemingly this was the result in the trial court of the judge's ruling limiting the cross-examination, in Conley v. Mervis, described in § 21, n. 40, supra. See also Ah Doon v. Smith, 25 Ore. 89, 34 P. 1093 (1893) where the judge's ruling permitting the cross-examination as to alleged new matter exposed the plaintiff to a dismissal of the action at the close of his testimony.

where the witness has a privilege not to be called as a witness by the cross-examiner. Thus, the privilege of the accused, and of the spouse of the accused, not to be called by the state in a criminal case may prevent the prosecutor from eliciting the new facts at a later stage, if he cannot draw them out on cross-examination.[57]

24. The Scope of the Judge's Discretion Under the Wide-Open and Restrictive Rules.

When Gibson, C. J.[58] and Story, J.[59] introduced the innovation upon the orthodox "wide-open" cross-examination, by suggesting that questioning about new matter was not proper at the stage of cross-examination, they thought of their admonitions as relating solely to the order of proof. Traditionally the order of proof[60] and the conduct and extent of cross-examination[61] have been said to be specially subject to discretionary control by the trial judge.

Accordingly, the earlier cases[62] and many of the more recent cases[63] in jurisdictions adopting the restrictive rule in any of its forms, emphasize the power of the trial judge in his discretion to allow deviations. It has been said, indeed, that both the courts following the wide-open and those adopting the restrictive practice "recognize the discretionary power of the trial court to allow variations from the customary order and decline ordinarily to consider as an error any variation sanctioned by the trial court."[64] If this statement were fully true, the hazards of injustice at the trial, or of reversals on appeal, in the administration of either rule would not be substantial. But the statement probably paints too bright a picture.

In the states adopting "the scope of the direct" test, trial courts and lawyers tend to find it easier to administer the test as a rule than as a flexible standard of discretion. Also, appellate courts have reversed many cases for error in the application of the test, although there may be some trend to give a greater scope of power to the trial judge.[65]

In jurisdictions following the traditional wide-open view, there seems to have been little tendency to apply the general notion that the order of proof is discretionary. The tradition has not been shaped in terms of order of proof, but in the language of a right to

---

57. See §§ 25, 26, infra.

58. In Ellmaker v. Buckley, 16 Sarg. & Rawles 72, 77 (Pa.1827).

59. In Philadelphia & Trenton R. Co. v. Stimpson, 39 U.S. (14 Pet.) 448, 461 (1840).

60. See 6 Wigmore, Evidence §§ 1867, 1885, 1886.

61. See 3A Wigmore, Evidence (Chadbourn rev.) §§ 944, 983(2).

62. See, e. g., Chicago & R. I. Ry. Co. v. Northern Illinois C. & I. Co., 36 Ill. 60 (1864); Glenn v. Gleason, 61 Iowa 28, 32, 15 N.W. 659 (1883); Blake v. People, 73 N.Y. 586 (1878); Kaeppler v. Red River Nat. Bank, 8 N.D. 406, 410, 79 N.W. 869 (1899); Schnable v. Doughty, 3 Pa.St. 392, 395 (1846); State v. Bunker, 7 S.D. 639, 642, 65 N.W. 33 (1895); Lueck v. Heisler, 87 Wis. 644, 58 N.W. 1101 (1894).

63. See, e. g., United States v. Minuse, 142 F.2d 388, 389 (2d Cir. 1944); Goodbody v. Margiotti, 323 Pa. 529, 187 A. 425 (1936); State v. Brown, 174 Neb. 387, 118 N.W.2d 328 (1962); Marlow v. Davis, 227 Md. 204, 176 A.2d 215 (1961); State v. Pearson, 206 Minn. 477, 110 N.W.2d 206 (1961).

64. St. Louis, I. M. & S. Ry. Co. v. Raines, 90 Ark. 398, 119 S.W. 665, 668 (1909).

65. See Note, 37 Colum.L.Rev. 1373, 1381 (1937) giving the results of a study of 810 decisions, indicating many reversals. More recent examples, include Papa v. Youngstrom, 146 Conn. 37, 147 A.2d 494 (1958); Muscarello v. Peterson, 20 Ill.2d 548, 170 N.E.2d 564 (1960); State ex rel. Rich v. Bair, 83 Idaho 475, 365 P.2d 216 (1961); Shupe v. State, 238 Md. 307, 208 A.2d 590 (1965); Golden Gate Corp. v. Providence Redevelopment Agy., 260 A.2d 152 (R.I. 1970).

For cases emphasizing the discretion of the court, see the cases in note 63, supra, and cases cited C.J.S. Witnesses § 396.

Where the adverse party is called as an adverse witness by his opponent, there seems to be a particularly strong tendency to emphasize on a practical level the judge's discretion in limiting cross-examination. See City of Kotzebue v. Ipalook, 462 P.2d 75 (Alaska 1969) (restriction of cross-examination was harmless error when witness could be called as an adverse witness); Kline v. Kachmar, 360 Pa. 396, 61 A.2d 825 (1948); Lindsay v. Teamster's Union Local No. 74, 97 N.W.2d 686 (N.D. 1959).

cross-examine upon the whole case.[66] The situation which puts the most strain upon the wide-open rule is the one where a party, usually the plaintiff, finds himself compelled at the outset to call from the adversary's camp either the party himself or some ally or employee to prove up a formal fact not substantially in dispute. Shall the adversary be allowed to disrupt the proponent's case at this stage by cross-examining the willing witness about matters of defense unrelated to the direct examination? This is an appealing situation for the exercise of a discretion to vary from the wide-open practice and to require the cross-examiner to call the witness for these new matters when he puts on his own case. So far, however, as the decisions examined reveal, the power is not emphasized in the "wide-open" jurisdictions.[67]

25. Application of Wide-Open and Restrictive Rules to the Cross-Examination of Parties—(a) Civil Parties.[68]

In the cross-examination of party witnesses two situations are to be distinguished, namely, the hostile cross-examination by the adversary of a party who calls himself as a witness in his own behalf, and the friendly cross-examination by the counsel of a party who has been called as an adverse witness by his opponent. In the first situation, in jurisdictions following the restrictive rules it is usually held that while the range of discre-

tion to permit the relaxation of the restrictive practice is wider,[69] the general limitation to the "scope of the direct," based on the maintenance of the normal order of proof is still applicable.[70] A few courts, however, without much discussion of reasons have said that upon the hostile cross-examination of a party, the limitation to the scope of the direct will not be applied.[71] Of course, in the "wide-open" states the usual freedom from the restriction is accorded without question.

When a party calls the adverse party as a hostile witness, it is usually provided by statute or rule [72] that he may question him "as upon cross-examination," i. e., he may ask leading questions, and that he is not "bound" by the answers of the adverse witness, which means chiefly that he may impeach the testimony by showing inconsistent statements. When this examination, savoring so nearly of a cross-examination, is concluded, there is a view that gives no right to the party to be further examined immediately by his own

---

66. See Morgan v. Brydges, 2 Stark, 314, 171 Eng. Rep. 657 (N.P.1818) (witness called by plaintiff for formal proof, may be cross-examined by defendant, his employer, on the whole case); Cowart v. Strickland, 149 Ga. 397, 100 S.E. 447, 7 A.L.R. 1110, 1114 (1919) ("The rule in this state is that 'when a witness is called and examined, even to only a formal point, by one party, the other party has the right to cross-examine him as to all points.'")

However, the discretion of the court is emphasized in Boller v. Cofrances, 42 Wis.2d 170, 166 N.W.2d 129 (1969).

67. See § 25 infra.

68. 6 Wigmore, Evidence § 1890; C.J.S. Witnesses §§ 399, 400; Dec.Dig. Witnesses ⊂⊃275(5), 275(8).

69. California Fruit Canners' Ass'n v. Lilly, 184 F. 570, 572 (9th Cir. 1911); Tawzer v. McAdams, 134 Kan. 596, 7 P.2d 516 (1932); Ward v. Thompson, 146 Wis. 376, 131 N.W. 1006 (1911); Marlow v. Davis, 227 Md. 204, 176 A.2d 215 (1961).

70. See, e. g., Farmers' Fertilizer Co. v. Lillie, 18 F. 2d 197 (6th Cir. 1927) (applying restrictive rule without discussion); Grosse v. Grosse, 166 Neb. 55, 87 N.W.2d 900 (1958) (similar).

71. Felsenthal Co. v. Northern Assurance Co., 284 Ill. 343, 120 N.E. 268 (1918); Viens v. Lanctot, 120 Vt. 443, 144 A.2d 711 (1958); Ingles v. Stealey, 85 W.Va. 155, 158, 101 S.E. 167, 168 (1919); Geelen v. Pennsylvania Railroad Co., 400 Pa. 240, 161 A.2d 595 (1960).

72. See e. g., F.R.Civ.P. 43(b): *"Scope of Examination and Cross-Examination.* A party may interrogate any unwilling or hostile witness by leading questions. A party may call an adverse party or an officer, director, or managing agent of a public or private corporation or of a partnership or association which is an adverse party, and interrogate him by leading questions and contradict and impeach him in all respects as if he had been called by the adverse party, and the witness thus called may be contradicted and impeached by or on behalf of the adverse party also, and may be cross-examined by the adverse party only upon the subject matter of his examination in chief."

counsel, but gives the judge a discretion to permit it or to require that his examination be deferred until the witness-party's own "case" is put on.[73] Most states, however, permit the immediate further examination of the witness by his own counsel.[74] Presumably upon request the trial judge would forbid leading questions,[75] and there is no tendency here in the restrictive states to relax for this "cross-examination" of a friendly witness, the usual restrictions limiting the questions to the scope of the direct.[76]

26. Application of Wide-Open and Restrictive Rules to the Cross-Examination of Parties—(b) The Accused in a Criminal Case.[77]

As a means of implementing the prescribed *order* of producing evidence by the parties, the restrictive rules limiting cross-examination to the scope of the direct or to the proponent's case are arguably burdensome, but they are understandable. The cross-examiner who has been halted has at least a theoretical remedy. He may call the witness for questioning when he puts on his own next stage of evidence. However, when the restrictive practice is applied to the accused in a criminal case, as it is in jurisdictions that follow that practice generally,[78] the accused may carefully limit his direct examination to some single aspect of the case such as age, sanity, or alibi[79] and then invoke the court's ruling that the cross-examination be limited to the matter thus opened. This restrictive practice has been criticized.[80] Of course, there is no problem of the accused escaping searching inquiry on the whole case if the scope of cross-examination is "wide-open".[81]

Regardless of whether the result under the restrictive rule may be desirable, it may be that the scope of cross-examination of the accused in a criminal case is not controlled solely by evidence case law, and statutes or rules governing the matter.[82] The outer limits of

---

73. See, e. g., Davis v. Wright, 194 Ga. 1, 21 S.E.2d 88 (1942); Wyant v. Dunn, 140 Mont. 181, 368 P.2d 917 (1962).

74. See, e. g., Peters v. Shear, 351 Pa. 521, 41 A.2d 556 (1945); Van Hise v. Trino, 143 Colo. 179, 352 P.2d 284 (1960) (but refusal of right of further examination held not error when witness was called later and testified upon direct examination); Lindsay v. Teamsters Union, Local No. 74, 97 N.W. 2d 686 (N.D.1959) (similar).

75. Cunningham v. Security Title Ins. Co., 241 Cal. App.2d 626, 50 Cal.Rptr. 724 (1966); but in Brookbank v. Mathieu, 152 So.2d 526 (Fla.App.1963), the court holds that the examination may be by leading questions.

76. Simon v. Akin, 79 N.M. 689, 448 P.2d 795 (1969); Grievance Committee of Bar of Fairfield Co. v. Dacey, 154 Conn. 129, 222 A.2d 339 (1966); Frame v. Bauman, 202 Kan. 461, 449 P.2d 525 (1969).

77. 6 Wigmore, Evidence § 1890, 8 id. (McNaughton rev.) §§ 2276(d), 2278; Dec.Dig. Witnesses ⟲277 (4); C.J.S. Witnesses § 400; Carlson, Cross-Examination of the Accused, 52 Cornell L.Q. 705 (1967).

78. Tucker v. United States, 5 F.2d 818 (8th Cir. 1925); Enriquez v. United States, 293 F.2d 788 (9th Cir. 1961); State v. Ragona, 232 Iowa 700, 5 N.W.2d 907, 909 (1942); Erving v. State, 174 Neb. 90, 116 N.W.2d 7 (1962) cert. denied 375 U.S. 876.

79. Except, of course, that cross-examination to impeach is not confined to the scope of the direct (see § 22, supra). State v. Shipman, 354 Mo. 265, 189 S.W.2d 273 (1945) (may be cross-examined about prior convictions); State v. Allnutt, 156 N.W. 2d 266 (Iowa 1968). And defendants are prone on direct to testify to their past records, which may open the door even wider to cross-examination on misconduct than the ordinary rule of impeachment would allow. See, e. g., Ivey v. State, 132 Fla. 36, 180 So. 368 (1938); State v. Hargraves, 62 Idaho 8, 107 P.2d 854 (1941); State v. McDaniel, 272 N.C. 556, 158 S.E.2d 874 (1968) vacated and remanded for consideration of other issues, 392 U.S. 665, on remand, 274 N.C. 574, 164 S.E.2d 469 (1968).

80. 6 Wigmore, Evidence § 1890, note 2.

81. Clarke v. State, 78 Ala. 474, 480, 56 Am.Rep. 45 (1885) ("cross-examination relating to any matter connected with the transaction, or pertinent to the issue, and impeachment . . ."); State v. McGee, 55 S.C. 247, 33 S.E. 353 (1899); Brown v. State, 38 Tex.Cr.R. 597, 44 S.W. 176 (1898). In Missouri, however, where the wide-open practice prevails in civil cases (see § 21, note 32, supra) the legislature has enacted that the accused and his spouse shall be shielded from cross-examination except upon matters referred to in the examination in chief. V.A.M.S. § 546.260, construed in State v. Davit, 343 Mo. 1151, 125 S.W.2d 47 (1939). See also, State v. Harvey, 449 S.W.2d 649 (Mo.1970).

82. See language in Tucker v. United States, 5 F.2d 818 (8th Cir., 1925); Fitzpatrick v. United States, 178 U.S. 304 (1900); Brown v. United States, 356 U.S. 148 (1958); United States ex rel. Irwin v. Pate, 357 F.2d 911 (1966). But see Johnson v.

cross-examination may well be controlled, at least in the future, by constitutional doctrine concerning the extent to which the accused waives his privilege of self-incrimination by taking the stand and testifying.[83] Some judicial language suggests that under the Fifth Amendment of the United States Constitution the waiver should extend only to questioning concerning matters mentioned upon direct examination.[84] If this position ultimately prevails, state practice would be governed by the constitutional limits of waiver,[85] making "wide-open" cross-examination of criminal defendants, and perhaps even extremely liberal restrictive rules, unconstitutional.

27. Merits of the Systems of Wide-Open and Restricted Cross-Examination.[86]

The principal virtue claimed for the restrictive rules is that they tend to require the parties to present their *facts* in due order, first the facts on which the plaintiff has the burden, then those which the defendant must prove, and so on, following the prescribed stages.[87] Avoided is the danger, mentioned

in section 24, supra, that one party's plan of presenting *his* facts will be interrupted by the interjection on cross-examination of new and damaging matters which constitute his adversary's case. This interjection, if permitted, lessens the impact and persuasiveness of the proponent's facts. The nice case which he planned to lay out fact by fact has been muddled and complicated during its very presentation by new and doubt-raising facts drawn out in cross-examination of the proponent's own witnesses. The regular order of presenting the two parties' "cases" by separate stages is thus modified. The "case," formerly a single melody, becomes convertible to counterpoint.

It must be remembered, however, that like all rules of order, the common law order of proof by "cases" or stages, is to some extent arbitrary. Two witnesses cannot be allowed to speak at once, so some rules must be worked out as to who shall call the witnesses and in what order. A further rule, however, that a witness who knows many facts about the case shall be allowed to tell only certain ones at his first appearance, and as to others must be called later, seems even more artificial. The freer system under the wide-open practice, by which on the direct examination the regular order of proof of the "cases" of the respective parties is maintained, but under which the adversary is free to draw out all the damaging facts on cross-examination, has a natural order of its own. The procedure by which each witness successively may be caused to tell all he knows about the case, is a system which would be followed spontaneously in any informal investigation untrammeled by rules. It serves the convenience of witnesses and may appear to the jury as a natural way of developing the facts. Moreover, to the objection that diversion into new paths upon cross-examination lessens the unity and persuasiveness of the direct examiner's presentation of his case, we may raise the doubt whether the direct examiner is in

United States, 318 U.S. 189 (1943). See generally § 132, infra.

83. See discussion in Carlson, Cross-Examination of the Accused, 52 Cornell L.Q. 705 (1967).

84. See cases cited in note 82, supra.

85. The privilege against self-incrimination under the Constitution of the United States was extended to the states in Malloy v. Hogan, 378 U.S. 1 (1964).

86. See 6 Wigmore, Evidence §§ 1887, 1888 (marshaling arguments pro and con, including judicial views and favoring "wide-open" practice); Maguire, Evidence: Common Sense and Common Law, 45–49 (1947) (something for both sides). The compilers of the Model Code of Evidence made no clear choice. Rule 105(h) would leave to the judge's discretion "to what extent and in what circumstances a party cross-examining a witness may be forbidden to examine him concerning material matters not inquired about on a previous examination by the judge or by an adverse party".

The Proposed Federal Rules of Evidence, after initially favoring a restricted rule with discretion in the judge to depart from it, F.R.Ev. (P.D.1969) 6–11(b), later opted for a wide-open rule, also with discretion to depart from it, F.R.Ev. (R.D.1971) 611(b).

87. See § 4, supra.

justice entitled to the psychological advantage of presenting his facts in this falsely simple and one-sided way.[88] Is he in justice entitled to this clear impact on the jury's mind, to this favorable first impression which, though to be answered later, may be hard to dislodge?

Another factor is the consideration of economy of time and energy. Obviously, the wide-open rule presents little or no opportunity for dispute in its application.[89] The restrictive practice in all its forms, on the other hand, can be productive in the courtroom of bickering over the choice of the numerous variations of the "scope of the direct" criterion, and of their application to particular cross-questions. These controversies are often reventilated on appeal, and there may be the possibility of reversal for error.[90] Observance of these vague and ambiguous restrictions is a matter of constant and hampering concern to the cross-examiner. If these efforts, delays and misprisions were the necessary incidents to the guarding of substantive rights or the fundamentals of fair trial, they might be worth the cost. As the price of the choice of an obviously debatable regulation of the order of evidence, the sacrifice seems misguided. The American Bar Association's Committee for the Improvement of the Law of Evidence for the year 1937–38 said this:

" 'The rule limiting cross-examination to the precise subject of the direct examination is probably the most frequent rule (except the Opinion rule) leading in trial practice today to refined and technical quibbles which obstruct the progress of the trial, confuse the jury, and give rise

to appeal on technical grounds only. Some of the instances in which Supreme Courts have ordered new trials for the mere transgression of this rule about the order of evidence have been astounding.

" 'We recommend that the rule allowing questions upon any part of the issue known to the witness . . . be adopted. . . .' "[91]

There are thus strong reasons for the "wide-open" rule.

28. Cross-Examination About Witness's Inconsistent Past Writings: Must Examiner Show the Writing to the Witness Before Questioning About Its Contents?

A fatal weakness of liars is letter writing. Betraying letters are often inspired by mere boastfulness, sometimes by greed or other reasons. Properly used they have destroyed many a fraudulent witness.[92] An eminent trial lawyer makes these suggestions to the attacking cross-examiner:

" . . . There is an art in introducing the letter contradicting the witness' testimony. The novice will rush in. He will obtain the false statement and then quickly hurl the letter in the face of the witness. The witness, faced with it, very likely will seek to retrace his steps, and sometimes do it skillfully, and the effect is lost.

"The mature trial counsel will utilize the letter for all it is worth. Having obtained the denial which he wishes, he will, perhaps, pretend that he is disappointed. He will ask that same question a few moments

---

88. This query was first suggested by the late Professor Clarence Morris.

89. A glance at Dec.Dig. Witnesses ☞269 demonstrates the almost entire absence of appellate dispute over the application of the wide-open practice, and the large number of such questions from jurisdictions following the restrictive practice.

90. See § 24, n. 65, supra.

91. See 6 Wigmore, Evidence § 1888, p. 545, where the relevant part of the Committee's report is set out in full.

92. Probably the most famous instance is the demolition by Sir Charles Russell of the witness Richard Pigott before the Parnell Commission in 1888, described in ch. 20 of Wellman, The Art of Cross-Examination (4th ed. 1936), and set out in Busch, Law and Tactics in Jury Trials § 350 (1949). This and many other striking instances are detailed in 4 Wigmore, Evidence § 1260.

later, and again and again get a denial. And he will then phrase—and this requires preparation—he will then phrase a whole series of questions not directed at that particular point, but in which is incorporated the very fact which he is ready to contradict—each time getting closer and closer to the language in the written document which he possesses, until he has induced the witness to assert not once, but many times, the very fact from which ordinarily he might withdraw by saying it was a slip of the tongue. Each time he draws closer to the precise language which will contradict the witness, without making the witness aware of it, until finally, when the letter is sprung, the effect as compared with the other method is that, let us say, of atomic energy against a firecracker." [93]

However, there may be an obstacle in the way of this effective method. This is the rule in *Queen Caroline's Case*, pronounced by English judges in an advisory opinion in 1820.[94] The significant part of the opinion for present purposes is the pronouncement that the cross-examiner cannot ask the witness about any statements made by the witness in writing, or ask whether the witness has ever written a letter of a given purport, without *first* producing the writing or letter and exhibiting it to the witness, and permitting the witness to read the writing or such part of it as the cross-examiner seeks to ask him about. Thus, in vain is the potential trap laid before the eyes of the bird. While reading the letter the witness will be warned by what he sees not to deny it and can quickly weave a new web of explanation.

The rule that the writing must first be shown to the witness before he can be questioned about it was thought by the judges to be an application of the established practice requiring the production of the original document *when its contents are sought to be proved*.[95] This notion was a misconception in at least two respects. First, the cross-examiner is not seeking to prove *at this stage* the contents of the writing by the answers of the witness. On the contrary, his zealous hope is that the witness will deny the existence of the letter. Second, the original documents rule is a rule requiring the production of the document as proof of its contents to the judge and jury, not to the witness.[96] So obstructive did the powerful Victorian cross-examining barristers find the rule in the *Queen's Case* that they secured its abrogation by Parliament in 1854.[97]

When urged upon them, this practice requiring exhibition to the witness has been usually accepted without question by Ameri-

---

93. Nizer, The Art of Jury Trial, 32 Corn.L.Q. 59, 68 (1946). An instructive, similar suggestion as to the technique of "exposure by document" is found in Love, Documentary Evidence, 38 Ill.Bar J. 426, 429–30 (1950). See also 2 Belli, Modern Trials 1590–1592 (1954).

94. 2 B. & B. 284, 286–90, 129 Eng.Rep. 976, 11 Eng. Rul.C. 183 (1820). (The House of Lords put the question to the judges: "First, whether, in the courts below, a party on cross-examination would be allowed to represent in the statement of a question the contents of a letter, and to ask the witness whether the witness wrote a letter to any person with such contents, or contents to the like effect, *without having first shown* to the witness the letter, and having asked that witness whether the witness wrote that letter and his admitting that he wrote such letter? . . ." Abbott, C. J., for the judges, answered the first question in the negative).

95. This rule, also called the best evidence rule, is developed in Ch. 23, infra.

96. For these and other refutations of the theory of the *Queen's Case*, see the masterly discussion in 4 Wigmore Evidence § 1260.

97. St. 17 & 18 Vict. c. 125, § 24 ("A witness may be cross-examined as to previous statements made by him in writing or reduced into writing, relative to the subject-matter of the cause, without such writing being shown to him; but if it is intended to contradict such witness by the writing, his attention must, before such contradictory proof can be given, be called to those parts of the writing which are to be used for the purpose of so contradicting him; providing always that it shall be competent for the judge, at any time during the trial, to require the production of the writing for his inspection, and he may thereupon make such use of it for the purposes of the trial as he shall think fit").

can courts [98] and occasionally by legislators.[99] It is believed, however, that its actual invocation in trials is relatively infrequent in most states, and that the generality of judges and practitioners are unaware of this possible hidden rock in the path of the cross-examiner.

So far, the rule has been discussed as it works in the situation where the cross-examiner is seeking to uncover in a dramatic and devastating fashion the perjury of a calculating witness. In this situation, the rule seems to blunt one of counsel's sharpest weapons of exposure. But the weapon may be misdirected. Innocent and well-meaning witnesses write letters and forget their contents and later testify mistakenly to facts inconsistent with the assertions in the letters. Their forgetfulness may need to be revealed, and their present testimony thus discredited to that extent. Arguably, however, they should not be invited by subtle questioning to widen the gap between their present statements and their past writings, and then be devastated by a dramatic exposure. Under this viewpoint, the judge should be vested with the discretion whether to permit the questioning about the writing without requiring its exhibition to the witness.[1]

A somewhat different approach would abolish the rule of *Queen Caroline's Case,* and also recognize the difficulty of exercise of discretion by judge in this situation, by permitting the cross-examination without prior showing of the writing to the witness, and substituting the requirement that the writing be shown or disclosed to opposing counsel at his request as an assurance of good faith on the part of the cross-examiner.[2]

29. The Standard of Relevancy as Applied on Cross-Examination: [3] **Trial Judge's Discretion.** [4]

There are three main functions of cross-examination: (1) to shed light on the credibility of the direct testimony; (2) to bring out additional facts related to those elicited on direct,[5] and (3) in states following the "wide-open" rule,[6] to bring out additional facts which tend to elucidate any issue in the case.

---

98. See, e. g., Washington v. State, 269 Ala. 146, 112 So.2d 179 (1959) (cross-examination of accused as to statement signed by him; must be shown before questioning about contents); Glenn v. Gleason, 61 Iowa 28, 33, 15 N.W. 659 (1883) (whole letter must be read, relying on 1 Greenleaf on Evidence § 463, which popularized the rule in this country before judges here became aware that it had been abrogated in England); McDonald v. Bayha, 93 Minn. 139, 100 N.W. 679 (1904); Price v. Grieger, 244 Minn. 466, 70 N.W.2d 421 (1955) (cited with approval in Hillesheim v. Stippel, 283 Minn. 59, 166 N.W.2d 325 (1969); and cases collected 4 Wigmore, Evidence § 1263; Dec.Dig. Witnesses ⚖271(2) (4), 277(6); C.J.S. Witnesses § 391, notes 52, 53; 58 Am.Jur. Witnesses § 643.

The rule is often applied to cross-examination of parties about what they have written, see Washington v. State, supra, but if the original documents principle is the basis, it has no application, as a party's oral admission of what he has written is a recognized exception to that rule, see § 242, infra.

It is arguable that the rule is applicable to a signed deposition which may be looked on as a writing, and it is sometimes applied to them, though this seems an inconvenient practice. See 4 Wigmore, Evidence § 1262. But most courts have distinguished from depositions transcripts of oral testimony at a former trial, as to which the "show-me" rule is not applicable. Toohey v. Plummer, 69 Mich. 345, 349, 37 N.W. 297 (1888) (reporter's notes); Couch v. St. Louis Pub. Service Co., 173 S.W.2d 617, 622 (Mo.App.1943); Charles v. McPhee, 92 N.H. 111, 26 A.2d 30 (1942). Contra: Meadors v. Com., 281 Ky. 622, 136 S.W.2d 1066 (1940).

99. See, e. g., Ark.Stats. § 28–708; Georgia Code § 38–1803; Idaho Code § 9–1210; Montana R.C.M. 1947, § 93–1901–12; Oregon ORS 45.610. On the other hand, statutes in New Mexico, 1953 Comp. § 20–2–1, and in California, West's Ann.Evid.Code, § 769, have abrogated the rule.

1. Distinguish the situation in which, for purposes of impeachment, the prior inconsistent statement is sought to be proved in evidence, and conventional practice requires that he first be afforded an opportunity to deny or explain. See § 37, infra.

2. F.R.Ev. (R.D.1971) 613(a).

3. Dec.Dig. Witnesses ⚖270; 58 Am.Jur. Witnesses §§ 623–626; C.J.S. Witnesses §§ 377, 386.

4. Dec.Dig. Witnesses ⚖267; 58 Am.Jur. Witnesses §§ 623–626; C.J.S. Witnesses §§ 386, 404.

5. See § 21, supra.

6. See § 21, supra.

As to cross-examination designed to serve the second or third of these functions, there seems to be no reason why the usual standard of relevancy as applied to testimony offered on direct examination should not equally be applied to facts sought to be elicited on cross-examination.[7]

As to the first function, that of evaluating the credibility of the evidence given on direct, the purpose is contrastingly different. Here the test of relevancy is not whether the answer sought will elucidate any of the main issues, but whether it will to a useful extent aid the court or jury in appraising the credibility of the witness and assessing the probative value of the direct testimony. There are many recognized lines of questioning for this purpose, none of which is commonly relevant to the main issues. A familiar type is the question or series of questions, often used as preliminary questions on cross-examination, inquiring as to residence and occupation, designed to place the witness in his setting.[8]

A further common question is, "Have you talked to anyone about this case?"[9] Another is the testing or exploratory type of question. In asking this kind of question, the cross-examiner (who it will be remembered may not have the advantage of having previously interviewed the witness) will ask disarming questions often remote from the main inquiry, which are designed to test by experiment the ability of the witness to remember detailed facts of the nature of those which he recited on direct, or his ability accurately to perceive such facts, or his willingness and capacity to tell the truth generally, without distortion or exaggeration.[10] This is part of the

---

7. See, e. g., Moulton v. State, 88 Ala. 116, 6 So. 758, 759 (1889) (cross-examination must relate to facts in issue, except that irrelevant questions which tend to test credibility may sometimes be asked); Marut v. Costello, 34 Ill.2d 125, 214 N.E.2d 768 (1966).

8. A leading case is Alford v. United States, 282 U.S. 687 (1931) (abuse of discretion for the judge to refuse to allow cross-examination of government's witness respecting his residence where the accused suspected that witness was detained in custody of federal authorities; "Cross-examination of a witness is a matter of right . . . Its permissible purposes, among others, are that the witness may be identified with his community so that independent testimony may be sought and offered of his reputation for veracity in his own neighborhood . . . that the jury may interpret his testimony in the light reflected upon it by knowledge of his environment . . . .").

In Smith v. Illinois, 390 U.S. 129 (1968), the *Alford* case was carried further by holding that a criminal defendant was denied Sixth Amendment and Fourteenth Amendment rights under the United States Constitution when he was denied the right on cross-examination to ask the principal prosecution witness his correct name and address. The court quoted from Brookhart v. Janis, 384 U.S. 1, 3 (1966) to the effect that a denial of cross-examination "would be constitutional error of the first

magnitude and no amount of showing of want of prejudice would cure it." However, the exact scope of the decision is not presently certain. Where defendant was permitted full examination on the place of the witness in life, including the fact that he was staying in a motel at government expense, the court's sustaining an objection to a question as to his "present" address was upheld in United States v. Teller, 412 F.2d 374 (7th Cir. 1969) cert. denied 91 S.Ct. 1603. See also United States v. Lawler, 413 F.2d 622 (7th Cir. 1969) (inquiry barred as to where informer-witness was working at the time of trial); United States v. Lee, 413 F.2d 910 (7th Cir. 1969) cert. denied 396 U.S. 916 (cross-examination as to present address barred); United States v. Palermo, 410 F.2d 468 (7th Cir. 1969) (name and address need not be given if actual threat to life of witness is shown by prosecution to the judge in camera).

9. The question is usually approved. See cases cited in Annot., 35 A.L.R.2d 1045. In various cases, exclusion of similar questions has been deemed error. See, e. g., United States v. Standard Oil Co., 316 F.2d 884 (7th Cir. 1963). But see State v. Yost, 241 Ore. 362, 405 P.2d 851 (1965) (not error to exclude question asking witness with whom he had talked during recess when question did not shed some light on accuracy or credibility of the witness under all the circumstances).

10. Kervin v. State, 254 Ala. 449, 48 So.2d 204 (1950) (wide latitude to test recollection of witness is permitted subject to judge's discretion); People v. Sorge, 301 N.Y. 198, 93 N.E.2d 637 (1950) (proper for district attorney in cross-examining accused about other offenses, to persist after denial, "in the hope of inducing the witness to abandon his negative answers" and "on the chance that he may change his testimony") but see § 42, infra. See also Alford v. United States, 282 U.S. 687, 692 (1931) ("Counsel often cannot know in advance what pertinent facts may be elicited on cross-examination. For that reason it is necessarily ex-

tradition and of the art of cross-examination and many of the famous instances of dramatically devastating cross-examinations are of this type.[11] The courts recognize that a rule limiting questions to those relevant to the main issues would cripple the usefulness of this kind of examination.[12] A final instance of evaluative cross-examination is the direct attack by impeaching questions seeking to show such matters as bias, inconsistent statements, or conviction of crime.[13]

As to all the lines of inquiry mentioned in the next preceding paragraph, designed to shed light on the credibility of the witness and his direct testimony, the criteria of relevancy are vague, and the purpose of the cross-examiner is often experimental. Accordingly too tight a rein upon the cross-examiner may unduly curb the usefulness of the examination. On the other hand, dangers of undue prejudice [14] to the party or the witness and of waste of time from extended exploration are apparent. Consequently, the trial judge has a recognized discretionary power to control the extent of examination.[15] This exercise of discretion will only be reviewed for abuse resulting in substantial harm to the complaining party.[16] An examination of a large number of these cases leaves the impression that in practice abuse is more often found when complaint is made that the judge has unduly curbed the examination than when undue extension of the discretion to permit the questioning is charged.[17]

30. The Cross-Examiner's Art.

A cursory and general examination of the art of cross-examination, gleaned from the

P.2d 727 (1969) (abuse of discretion to permit question in regard to large telephone bill incurred by defendant-witness).

11. For instructive examples, see Wellman, The Art of Cross-Examination ch. 26 (4th ed. 1936) (by Littleton); Reed, Conduct of Law Suits §§ 423–439 (2d Ed. 1912); Kiendl, Some Aspects of Cross-Examination, 51 Case and Comment, No. 6, pp. 27–30 (1946); Busch, Law and Tactics in Jury Trials § 303 (1949); Belli, The Voice of Modern Trials Vol. III (long play recording); Heller, Do You Solemnly Swear? Part VI (1968).

ploratory; and the rule that the examiner must indicate the purpose of his inquiry does not, in general, apply.") Enlightening discussion of the technique of the "testing" cross-examination, with examples, is found in Busch, Law and Tactics in Jury Trials § 303 (1949); Lake, How to Cross-Examine Witnesses Successfully 137–151 (1957).

12. Accordingly, some opinions point out that the rules of relevancy are not applied with the same strictness on cross-examination as on direct: State v. Smith, 140 Me. 255, 37 A.2d 246 (1944); O'Sullivan v. Simpson, 123 Mont. 314, 212 P.2d 435 (1949); Grocers Supply Co. v. Stuckey, 152 S.W.2d 911 (Tex.Civ.App.1941, error refused) (on cross-examination any fact bearing on credit of witness is relevant).

13. See ch. 5, infra, dealing with impeachment of witnesses.

14. Lee Won Sing v. United States, 94 U.S.App.D.C. 310, 215 F.2d 680 (1954) (question on cross whether accused had paid his co-defendant $20,000 to plead guilty, asked without reasonable foundation, was improper and not adequately cured by instructions); State v. Lampshire, 74 Wash.2d 888, 447

15. Alford v. United States, 282 U.S. 687, 694 (1931) ("The extent of cross-examination with respect to an appropriate subject of inquiry is within the sound discretion of the trial court. It may exercise a reasonable judgment in determining when the subject is exhausted"; but here, excluding inquiry as to place of residence of witness held an abuse of discretion); Hider v. Gelbach, 135 F.2d 693 (4th Cir. 1943) (judge properly exercised discretion to curb repetitious cross-examination); Simpson v. State, 32 Wis.2d 195, 145 N.W.2d 206 (1966) cert. denied, 386 U.S. 965 (objections to various questions to expert were sustained); Casey v. United States, 413 F.2d 1303 (5th Cir. 1969) (court excluded questions implying United States gave covert support to defendant's enterprise); State v. Cummings, 445 S.W.2d 639 (Mo.1969) (court could exclude question to prosecuting witness concerning an insurance requirement that he make a criminal charge); Dec.Dig. Witnesses ⟨~267.

16. Bates v. Chilton County, 244 Ala. 297, 13 So.2d 186 (1943); Commonwealth v. Greenberg, 339 Mass. 557, 160 N.E.2d 181 (1959).

17. For notable and instructive instances of holdings of abuse in curbing the cross-examination of government witnesses by the accused, see Alford v. United States, 282 U.S. 687 (1931); District of Columbia v. Clawans, 300 U.S. 617 (1937). Many kinds of rulings have been held an abuse of discretion. See, e. g., People v. Mason, 28 Ill.2d 396, 192 N.E.2d 835 (1963) (limiting questions to show bias in an arguably close case on the question); United States v. Hogan, 232 F.2d 905 (3d Cir. 1956) (excluding cross-examination to the effect that witnesses had their sentences postponed, etc., because they had agreed to testify for the government and hoped for preferential treatment).

prolific writing on the subject,[18] may serve to aid the beginning advocate by bringing him some of the wisdom lawyers have learned from hard experience and may also serve to aid in considering the discussion in the next succeeding section, which attempts to appraise the significance of cross-examination.

Preparation is the key. Certainly, some lawyers seem to have a native talent for conducting effective cross-examination. A great Victorian advocate, Montagu Williams, seemed to share this view when he said, "I am by trade a reader of faces and minds." [19] Today, however, the stress is upon thorough preparation, not upon sudden sallies of inspiration.[20] Improvisation is often necessary

but its results are small compared to those from planned questions based on facts dug out before trial. The steps in preparation are explained in many of the works concerning the art of cross-examination.[21] Not all steps can be taken as to all adverse witnesses. Nor can every case bear the expense of thorough preparation. Nevertheless, preparation before trial is the only soil from which, in the day-to-day run of cases, successful cross-examination can grow.[22] At the trial, some lawyers recommend that notes in preparation for later questions should be made by an associate or by the client, rather than by the examiner. Oral suggestions to the examiner in court should be avoided.[23]

No cross-examination without a purpose. As we have seen, these purposes may be, first, to elicit new facts, qualifying the direct, or in some states bearing on any issue in the case; second, to test the story of the witness by exploring its details and implications, in the hope of disclosing inconsistencies or impossi-

18. For a hundred years, lawyers have been fascinated with the topic and have developed practical maxims and gathered dramatic instances. Important is Wigmore's section on the "Theory and Art" in his Treatise, § 1368. Most helpful and practical are the hints and examples in Busch, Law and Tactics in Jury Trials Ch. 15 (1949) and in Goldstein and Lane, Trial Technique, Ch. 19 (1969). See also Reed, Conduct of Lawsuits (2d ed. 1912); Elliott, The Work of the Advocate (2d ed. 1912); Wellman, The Art of Cross-Examination (4th ed. 1936); Stryker, The Art of Advocacy Chs. 4, 5 (1954); Friedman, Essentials of Cross-Examination (1968); Bodin, ed., Trial Techniques Library (1967); Harolds, Kelner and Fuchsberg, Examination of Witnesses (1965); Lake, How to Cross-Examine Witnesses Successfully (1957); Redfield, Cross-Examination and the Witness (1963); Wrottesley, The Examination of Witnesses in Court Ch. 3 (2d ed. 1926); and the ironic comments of Lord Darling in Scintillae Juris 61–70 (1914). Numerous readable articles include the following: Henderson, The High Art of Cross-Examination, 19 Case and Comment, 594 (1913); Steeves, The Art of Cross-Examination, 38 Can.Law Times 97, quoted in The Dangers of Cross-Examination, 86 Cent.L.J. 206 (1918); Ramage, A Few Rules for Cross-Examination, 91 Cent. L.J. 354 (1920); Nizer, The Art of Jury Trial, 32 Corn.L.Q. 59 (1946); Comisky, Observations on the Preparation and Conduct of Cross-Examination, 2 Prac.Law, 24 (1956); Von Moschzisker, Some Maxims for Cross-Examination, 3 id. 78 (1957); Hilton, Cross-Examination of a Handwriting Expert by Test Problem, 13 Rutgers L.Rev. 306 (1958).

19. Quoted Elliott, op. cit. 231.

20. See especially the works of Busch and Goldstein, and the article of Nizer, cited above, n. 18. Nizer says at p. 68: "Most lawyers who will tell you of brilliant cross-examination will not confess this: We are entranced by a brilliant flash of insight

which broke the witness, but the plain truth of the matter is, as brother to brother, that ninety-nine per cent of effective cross-examination is once more our old friend 'thorough preparation,' which places in your hands a written document with which to contradict the witness. That usually is the great gift of cross-examination."

21. See particularly, Busch, Law and Practice in Jury Trials §§ 286–290 (1949); Friedman, Essentials of Cross-Examinations 15–36 (1968).

22. That most of the famous, devastating cross-examinations were grounded in pre-trial preparation is illustrated by such celebrated instances as the cross-examination of Richard Pigott by Sir Charles Russell before the Parnell Commission, see Wigmore, op. cit. n. 18, supra, and Wellman, op. cit., ch. 22. It is even more clearly evident in that storehouse of great cross-examinations, Aron Steuer, Max D. Steuer, Trial Lawyer (1950), especially in the account of People v. Gardner in the second chapter.

23. Another phase of preparation that is often neglected is the cautioning of one's own witnesses about the probable line of cross-examinations, and especially warning them of such pitfall questions as "Whom have you talked to about this case?" and "When did you first know you would be called as a witness?" Goldstein and Lane, Trial Technique §§ 19.25, 19.30 (1969).

bilities; and third, to prove out of the mouth of the witness, impeaching facts known to the cross-examiner such as prior contradictory statements, bias and conviction of crime. In considering any of these objectives, but particularly the latter two, the cross-examiner must be conscious that the odds are slanted against him. An unfavorable answer is more damaging when elicited on cross-examination. It is hard for a cross-examiner to win his case on cross-examination; it is easy for him to lose it. Accordingly, if the witness has done no harm on direct examination, a cross-examination for the second or third purpose is usually ill-advised. There remains the witness whose direct testimony has been damaging, or even threatens to be destructive of the cross-examiner's case if the jury believes it. Cross-examination will usually be needed, and whether the object shall be a skirting reconnaissance distant from the crucial issues, or a frontal attack on the story or the credit of the witness, will depend on the availability of impeaching material disclosed by preparation and on a judgment of the risks and advantages of the holding defence or the counter-attack.[24]

A question directed to a crucial or critical fact on which the outcome of the case depends should seldom be asked an adverse witness unless the cross-examiner is reasonably confident the answer will be favorable. Similarly, broad questions which open the door for an eager witness to reinforce his direct testimony with corroborating circumstances, e. g., "How do you explain?" or "How did it happen?" are usually ill-advised.[25] If a discrepant fact has been drawn out on cross-examination, it is often better to wait and stress the inconsistency in argument than to press

the witness with it. It is the responsibility of the proponent's counsel to elicit an explanation, if any, on re-direct.

In conducting a testing or exploratory examination, for obvious reasons it is inadvisable to follow the order of the witness's direct testimony. "If the witness is falsifying, jump quickly with rapid-fire questions from one point of the narrative to the other, without time or opportunity for a connected narrative: backward, forward, forward, backward from the middle to the beginning, etc." [26]

Cross-examine for the jury, not for your client. It is often a temptation to the cross-examiner to display his wit and skill before his client, or to feed the vengeful feelings of the latter toward opposing witnesses by tripping and humiliating them upon cross-examination.[27] Frequently these small victories upon collateral inquiries are easy to secure. The odds between the experienced advocate and the witness, nervous in new surroundings, are not even. The cross-examiner needs constantly to remind himself that the jury is keenly aware of this inequality of position, and that each juror is prone to imagine himself in the shoes of the witness. Better results with the witness, and a better impression upon the jury will usually flow from tact and consideration than from bulldozing and ridicule. The cloak falls more easily in the sunshine than in the hurricane. In the rare case when the cross-examiner is convinced

---

24. See the enlightening discussion in Kiendl, Some Aspects of Cross-Examination, 51 Case and Comment, No. 6, p. 25 (1946), and generally, Lake, How to Cross-Examine Witnesses Successfully (1957).

25. Goldstein and Lane, Trial Technique § 19.18 (1969).

26. Ramage, A Few Rules for the Cross-Examination of Witnesses, 91 Cent.L.J. 354 (1920). For illustrative instances see Reed, Conduct of Lawsuits 307–312 (2d ed. 1912).

27. "The object of cross-examination is not to produce startling effects, but to elicit facts which will support the theory intended to be put forward. Sir William Follett asked the fewest questions of any counsel I ever knew; and I have heard many cross-examinations from others listened to with rapture from an admiring client, each question of which has been destruction to his case." Sergeant Ballantine's Experiences, 1st Am.ed., 106, quoted in Reed, Conduct of Lawsuits 278 (2d ed. 1912).

that a crucial witness is dishonest and that he can demonstrate it, the attack must be pressed home to the jugular. But the cross-examiner should always be mindful of his duty to use his skills and weapons justly and fairly, and also of the need so to conduct himself that the jury, with its latent sympathy for witnesses, will be impressed with his fairness.[28]

Make one or two big points; end on a high note. When the cross-examiner has led up to and secured an important admission, he should not dull the edge of the effect by too many explanatory details, nor risk a recantation by calling for a repetition. He should pass on to another important point if he has one, and end the examination when his last big point is made. "When you have struck oil stop boring." [29]

While the above generalities are worthwhile general guideposts, the cross-examiner must adapt his techniques to the specific situation he faces. Of course, different experts might well use different techniques in cross-examining the same witness at a particular trial.[30]

31. Cross-Examination Revalued

Early Victorian writers on advocacy exaggerated the strategic significance of cross-examination as affecting the outcome of trials. One of them wrote, "There is never a cause contested, the result of which is not mainly dependent upon the skill with which the ad-vocate conducts his cross-examination." [31] This stands in contrast with the view of Scarlett, a great "leader" of a later day, who said, "I learned by much experience that the most useful duty of an advocate is the examination of witnesses, and that much more mischief than benefit generally results from cross-examination. I therefore rarely allowed that duty to be performed by my colleagues. I cross-examined in general very little, and more with a view to enforce the facts I meant to rely upon than to affect the witness's credit,—for the most part a vain attempt." [32] Reed, who was one of our most sensible American writers on trial tactics, expresses the modern informed opinion when he says, "Sometimes a great speech bears down the adversary, and sometimes a searching cross-examination turns a witness inside out and shows him up to be a perjured villain. But ordinarily cases are not won by either speaking or cross-examining." [33] At the same time, most lawyers who write concerning the art of cross-examination still believe that failure to use this tool can lose a case.[34] To the advocate of today, it is often a means of gleaning additional facts but it is also still employed as a means of attack upon the credit of the direct testimony or the witness whenever possible.[35] Cross-examination of experts seems particularly important, in many instances. Thus while cross-examination does not loom large as a determinant of victory in

---

31. Quoted from Cox, The Advocate 434, in Reed, Conduct of Lawsuits 277 (2d ed. 1912).

28. These points are especially well made by Kiendl, op. cit., 51 Case & Comment, No. 6, pp. 24, 32 (1946). See also Goldstein and Lane, Trial Technique §§ 19.39–61 (1969).

29. Credited to Josh Billings in Steeves, The Dangers of Cross-Examination, 86 Cent.L.J. 206, 207 (1918). "If you have made a homerun do not run around the bases twice." Ramage, A Few Rules, 91 Cent.L.J. 354, 356 (1920). See also, Friedman, Essentials of Cross-Examination 119 (1968).

30. See, e. g., the cross-examination of the same witnesses by three different lawyers at a demonstration session in Examining the Medical Expert 143–148 (1969).

32. Memoir of Lord Abinger 75, quoted in Reed, op. cit. 278.

33. Reed, op. cit. 276.

34. "Failure to examine a witness's background, recollection, bias and knowledge of the subject still can and often does lose a case that should have been won." Friedman, Essentials of Cross-Examination 6 (1968).

35. "The type of cross-examination which is employed most frequently is that intended to discredit the direct testimony of the witness." Bodin, Principles of Cross-Examination, Trial Techniques Library 8 (1967).

many cases, it still may be an important ingredient in other cases.

In the appraisal of policies upon which the modernizing of the existing system of evidence rules must be based, it seems that a similar evaluation of cross-examination as an engine for discovering truth is called for. The present assumption is that the statement of a declarant or witness, if opportunity for cross-examination is not afforded, is so fatally lacking in reliability that it is not even worth hearing in a court of justice, and that the opportunity for cross-examination is indispensable. Now obviously cross-examination is a useful device to secure greater accuracy and completeness for the witness's testimony as a whole, and in the hands of a skillful advocate will often—not always—expose fraud or honest error in the witness. But it has its own hazards of producing errors.[36] It is, in truth, quite doubtful whether it is not the honest but weak or timid witness, rather than the rogue, who most often goes down under the fire of a cross-examina-

tion.[37] Certainly every witness in judicial proceedings should in fairness be made available for cross-examination by the opponent wherever possible. But the premise that where cross-examination is not possible, as in the case of out-of-court statements, or as in the case of a witness who dies before cross-examination, the statement or testimony should generally be excluded for that reason alone, seems ill-founded. Cross-examination, it is submitted, should be considered as useful but not indispensable as an agency of discovering truth, and absence of opportunity to cross-examine should only be one factor to be weighed in determining whether the statement or testimony should be received. Such an approach to hearsay problems might lead us to conclude that when opportunity to cross-examine a witness is permanently cut off without fault of either party, the direct testimony should nevertheless be received as suggested in a previous section.[38] It might lead us to further conclude that hearsay statements should be admitted if the statement was made by the declarant on personal knowledge and reported by the witness at first hand, and if the declarant is now dead or unavailable for cross-examination or, on the other hand, if the declarant is alive and still available for cross-examination.[39] Perhaps written statements should be admitted wherever production for cross-examination can fairly be dispensed with.[40]

It should be noted, however, that although these modern viewpoints are supportable, there remains a special problem concerning the criminal defendant's right of cross-examination under the Fifth, Sixth, and Fourteenth Amendments of the federal constitution and the scope of the right as it affects

---

36. For some accounts of staged experiments attempting to show some comparative results as to accuracy and completeness of free narrative, direct examination and cross-examination see Marston, Studies in Testimony, 15 J.Crim.Law & Criminology, 1 (1924); Cady, On the Psychology of Testimony, 35 Am.J.Psych. 10 (1924); Weld and Danzig, Study of Way in Which a Verdict is Reached by a Jury, 53 Am.J.Psych. 518 (1940) (effect of cross-examinations upon jurors during progress of simulated trial); Snee and Lush, Interaction of the Narrative and Interrogatory Methods of Obtaining Testimony, 11 Am.J.Psych. 229 (1941) and the conclusions thereon in Gardner, The Perception and Memory of Witnesses, 18 Corn.L.Q. 391, 404 (1933) and Burtt, Legal Psychology 147 (1931) ("It appears that when we really go after the observer in a rigorous fashion we tend to introduce some errors, perhaps through the mechanism of suggestion. . . .").

Some abuses of cross-examination are reflected in Erle Stanley Gardner, Confessions of a Cross-Examiner, 3 J.For.Sci. 374 (1958) (unfair questioning of a medical expert as to compensation). Hazards of inadequate mastery of the art of cross-examination which may add to production of error are pointed out in most of the references cited in note 18, supra.

37. Elliott, The Work of the Advocate 235 (2d ed. 1911).

38. Compare § 19, supra.

39. Compare Ch. 34, infra.

40. Compare Ch. 34, infra.

interrupted cross-examination and the scope of the hearsay rule.[41]

32. Redirect and Subsequent Examinations.[42]

One who calls a witness is normally required to elicit on his first examination, the direct, all that he wishes to prove by him. This norm of proving everything so far as feasible at the first opportunity is manifestly in the interest of fairness and expedition. Whether the cross-examiner is limited to answering the direct is, as we have seen, a matter as to which our jurisdictions are divided, with the greater number favoring the restrictive rule.[43] As to the redirect, however, and all subsequent examinations, there is no such division and the practice is uniform that the party's examination is normally limited to answering any new matter drawn out in the next previous examination of the adversary. It is true that the judge under his general discretionary power to vary the normal order of proof may permit the party to bring out on redirect examination some matter which is relevant to his case or defense and which through oversight he has failed to elicit on direct.[44] But the reply to new matter drawn out on cross-examination is the normal function of the redirect, and examination for this purpose is a matter of right,[45] though

its extent is subject to control in the judge's discretion.[46]

A skillful re-examiner may often draw the sting of a lethal cross-examination.[47] The reply on redirect may take the form of explanation, avoidance, or qualification of the new substantive facts or matters of impeachment elicited by the cross-examiner.[48] The approach direct, such as "What did you mean by"[49] or "What was your reason for"[50] a statement made by the witness on cross-examination, may often be proper, but a mere reiteration of assertions previously made on

---

41. See § 19, supra, and § 252, infra.

42. See 6 Wigmore, Evidence §§ 1896, 1897; Dec. Dig. Witnesses ☞285–291; C.J.S. Witnesses §§ 417–429.

43. See § 21, supra.

44. State v. Conner, 97 N.J.L. 423, 118 A. 211 (1922); State v. Bennett, 158 Me. 109, 179 A.2d 812 (1962); Fisher Body Division, General Motors Corp. v. Alston, 252 Md. 51, 249 A.2d 130 (1969); C.J.S. Witnesses § 419.

45. Villeneuve v. Manchester St. R. Co., 73 N.H. 250, 60 A. 748 (1905) (when inconsistent statement out of court proved on cross, witness and party have right that witness be permitted to explain on redirect); Gray v. Metropolitan St. R. Co., 165 N.Y. 457, 59 N.E. 262 (1901); Martin's Adm'r v. Richmond F. & P. R. Co., 101 Va. 406, 44 S.E. 695 (1903).

46. Southern Farm Bureau Casualty Ins. Co. v. Mitchell, 312 F.2d 485 (8th Cir. 1963) (court rejected redirect examination on a collateral matter); People v. Kynette, 15 Cal.2d 731, 104 P.2d 794 (1940); Commonwealth v. Galvin, 310 Mass. 733, 39 N.E.2d 656 (1942).

47. An interesting example is the examination by Sir Edward Carson quoted in 6 Wigmore, Evidence § 1896.

48. Johnson v. Minihan, 355 Mo. 1208, 200 S.W.2d 334 (1947) (collision case; plaintiff's witness, driver of car in which plaintiff was guest, admitted signing, without reading, damaging statements on cross-examination; abuse of discretion to deny redirect examination about fact that witness signed statement in order to secure settlement from defendant of witness's own claim); Long v. F. W. Woolworth Co., 232 Mo.App. 417, 109 S.W.2d 85 (1937) (proper to allow plaintiff, asked on cross if she had consulted doctor, to explain on redirect that she had not, because she could not pay); Crowell v. State, 147 Tex.Cr.R. 299, 180 S.W.2d 343 (1944) (in prosecution for keeping bawdy house, where deputy sheriff on cross-examination admitted he said he wanted to run defendant out of town, proper for him to explain on redirect that it was because of citizens' complaints against defendant); Hawkins v. United States, 417 F.2d 1271 (5th Cir. 1969) cert. denied 397 U.S. 914 (redirect concerning defendant's brutal treatment of witness was permitted to rebut attempted impeachment of witness on cross-examination, citing Beck v. United States, 317 F.2d 865 (5th Cir. 1963)); Abeyta v. People, 156 Colo. 440, 400 P.2d 431 (1965) (illustrating similar principle).

Whether a witness who admits a conviction on cross-examination is allowed on redirect to explain the circumstances of the conviction is the subject of conflicting decisions. See § 43, infra.

49. People v. Buchanan, 145 N.Y. 1, 39 N.E. 846, 853 (1895) (dictum); C.J.S. Witnesses § 421, note 61.

50. State v. Kaiser, 124 Mo. 651, 28 S.W. 182 (1894); C.J.S. Witnesses § 420, note 47.

the direct or cross-examination is not usually sanctioned,[51] although the judge has an area of discretion in this matter.

The rule of completeness,[52] which permits proof of the remainder of a transaction, conversation, or writing when a part thereof has been proven by the adversary,[53] so far as the remainder relates to the same subject-matter,[54] is often invoked by the re-examiner. Moreover, the principle of curative admissibility,[55] under which evidence that is irrelevant or otherwise incompetent may sometimes be allowed to be answered by the adversary, is likewise frequently resorted to by the examiner on redirect.[56]

Re-cross-examination, following the rule of first opportunity mentioned above, is normally confined to questions directed to the explanation or avoidance of new matter brought out on redirect.[57]

---

51. Moore-Handley Hardware Co. v. Williams, 238 Ala. 189, 189 So. 757 (1939) (question calling for summation of witness's theory of accident as already given on direct and cross, properly excluded in judge's discretion); Clayton v. Bellatti, 70 Ill. App.2d 367, 216 N.E.2d 686 (1966); Forslund v. Chicago Transit Authority, 9 Ill.App.2d 290, 132 N.E.2d 801 (1956). But where witness on cross-examination was confronted with her written statement contradicting her story on direct, it was held proper to ask her on redirect whether her testimony on direct was true. Grayson v. United States, 107 F.2d 367 (8th Cir. 1939).

52. See § 56, infra.

53. Mathis v. People, 167 Colo. 504, 448 P.2d 633 (1969); State v. Kendrick, 173 N.W.2d 560 (Iowa 1970).

54. White v. Com., 292 Ky. 416, 166 S.W.2d 873 (1942); State v. Williams, 448 S.W.2d 865 (Mo. 1970).

McCormick et al on Evid. 2nd Ed. HB—5

55. See § 57, infra.

56. Barrett v. United States, 82 F.2d 528 (7th Cir. 1936); United States v. Maggio, 126 F.2d 155 (3d Cir. 1942); Chamberlain v. State, 348 P.2d 280 (Wyo.1960). But the "open the gate" theory will not permit eliciting incompetent and prejudicial evidence on redirect, according to some cases. See, e. g., People v. Arends, 155 Cal.App.2d 496, 318 P.2d 532 (1958).

57. Where no new matter was opened on redirect the trial court's action in denying a recross was approved in Faulk v. State, 47 Ga.App. 804, 171 S.E. 570 (1933) and in Commonwealth v. Gordon, 598 Mass. 356, 254 N.E.2d 901 (1970). But a recross, though not in reply to new matter on redirect may be allowed in the court's discretion. Maryland Wrecking & Equipment Co. v. News Pub. Co., 148 Md. 560, 129 A. 836 (1925); Dege v. United States, 308 F.2d 534 (9th Cir. 1962) (matter referred to on cross-examination but not in redirect examination).

CHAPTER 5

IMPEACHMENT AND SUPPORT

33. Introductory: The Stages of Impeachment and the Lines of Attack.

There are five main lines of attack upon the credibility of a witness.[1] The first, and probably the most effective and most frequently employed, is an attack by proof that the witness on a previous occasion has made statements inconsistent with his present testimony. The second is an attack by a showing that the witness is biased on account of emotional influences such as kinship for one party or hostility to another, or motives of pecuniary interest, whether legitimate or corrupt. The third is an attack upon the character of the witness. The fourth is an attack by showing a defect of capacity in the witness to observe, remember or recount the matters testified about. The fifth is proof by other witnesses that material facts are otherwise than as testified to by the witness under attack.[2] Finally, it might be observed that lack of religious belief is not available as a basis of attack on credibility.

The process of impeachment may be employed in two different stages. First, the facts

---

1. The components of credibility, i. e., the factors which determine whether testimony is believable, are the perception, memory, and narration of the witness. Morgan, Hearsay Dangers and the Application of the Hearsay Concept, 62 Harv.L.Rev. 177 (1948); Strahorn, A Reconsideration of the Hearsay Rule and Admissions, 85 U.Pa.L.Rev. 484, 485 (1937). See also the usual jury instructions on credibility. Sometimes sincerity is also named, but in fact it seems to be but an aspect of the other three. While in theory the subject of impeachment might be organized according to these various "components," the rules have in fact grown up around particular techniques, without any particular consideration as to the particular component which may be under attack. As a result, the subject is here approached by examining the various techniques.

2. Of course, credibility may also be attacked by eliciting on cross-examination statements from the witness contradictory to his own statements on direct or in other parts of the cross-examination. The practice of asking exploratory or testing questions designed to elicit self-contradictions is described in §§ 29, 30, supra.

discrediting the witness or his testimony may be elicited from the witness himself upon cross-examination. Certain kinds of attack are limited to this stage; it is said, "you must take his answer." Second, in some situations, the facts discrediting the witness are proved by extrinsic evidence, that is, the assailant waits until the time for putting on his own case in rebuttal, and then proves by a second witness or by documentary evidence, the facts discrediting the testimony of the witness attacked.

There is a cardinal rule of impeachment. Never launch an attack which implies that the witness has lied deliberately, unless you are convinced that the attack is justifiable, and is essential to your case. An assault which fails often produces in the jury's mind an indignant sympathy for the intended victim.

It is believed that, in general, there is less practical emphasis upon impeachment of witnesses than formerly, and that the elaborate system of rules regulating the practice and scope of impeachment which has been developed in the past should be applied in the future with less strictness and should be simplified by confiding the control less to rules and more to judicial discretion.

34. Prior Inconsistent Statements:[3] Degree of Inconsistency Required.[4]

When a witness testifies to facts material in a case, the opponent may have available proof that the witness has previously made statements that are inconsistent with his present testimony. Under a modern view of the hearsay rule, these previous statements would be admissible as substantive evidence of the facts stated. This viewpoint is discussed in the chapter concerning hearsay.[5] However, under more traditional views of hearsay these previous statements will often be inadmissible as evidence of what they state because they constitute hearsay and are not within any exceptions to the hearsay rule.[6] Even though inadmissible hearsay as evidence of the facts stated, they are nevertheless admissible for the limited purpose of impeaching the witness.[7]

It is important to note that the treatment of inconsistent statements in this chapter is confined to the situation in which the statements are introduced for impeachment purposes and may not be used as substantive evidence (over proper objection of the opponent).[8] For this purpose, the making of the previous statements may be drawn out in cross-examination of the witness himself, or if on cross-examination the witness has denied making the statement, or has failed to remember it,[9] the making of the statement may be proved by another witness. This form of impeachment is sometimes loosely

---

3. 3A Wigmore, Evidence (Chadbourn rev.) §§ 1017–1046; Hale, Prior Inconsistent Statements, 10 So. Cal.L.Rev. 135 (1937); Dec.Dig. Witnesses ⬅379–397; C.J.S. Witnesses §§ 573–628; 58 Am.Jur. Witnesses §§ 767–781.

4. 3A Wigmore, Evidence (Chadbourn rev.) §§ 1040–1043; Dec.Dig. Witnesses ⬅386; C.J.S. Witnesses § 583.

5. See § 251, infra.

6. See generally Chapter 24, infra.

7. Any form of statement is acceptable. It may have been made orally, as testimony at another trial or by deposition, or in writing, as a letter, accident-report or witness-statement or affidavit, or in any other form. Conduct, likewise, evincing a belief inconsistent with the facts asserted on the stand is usable on the same principle. See, e. g., Missouri Pac. Transp. Co. v. Norwood, 192 Ark. 170, 90 S.W.2d 480 (1936) (assertion of negligence claim by witness admitted); State v. Fenix, 311 S.W.2d 61 (Mo.1958) (a purchase of property for particular purpose held consistent and inadmissible); Dec.Dig. Witnesses ⬅347. But settlements or offers to compromise are governed by other rules. See § 274, infra; Bratt v. Western Air Lines, 169 F.2d 214 (1948).

The use of unconstitutionally obtained evidence for purposes of impeachment is discussed in § 178, infra.

8. The use of prior inconsistent statements as substantive evidence is discussed in § 251, infra.

9. See § 37, infra.

called "contradiction". It is to be distinguished from the mere production of evidence as to material facts conflicting with the evidence of the assailed witness. The mere production of evidence that conflicts with the evidence of a witness is discussed in a later section.[10]

The theory of attack by prior inconsistent statements is not based on the assumption that the present testimony is false and the former statement true but rather upon the notion that talking one way on the stand and another way previously is blowing hot and cold, and raises a doubt as to the truthfulness of both statements.[11] More particularly the prior statement, assuming it is inadmissible as substantive evidence under the hearsay rule,[12] may be used in this context only as an aid in judging the credibility of the testimony with which the previous statement is inconsistent.[13] To create the above-mentioned doubt by introduction of the previous statement of the witness what degree of inconsistency between the testimony of the witness and his previous statement is required? The language of some of the cases seems overstrict in suggesting that a contradiction must be found,[14] and under the more widely accepted view any material variance between the testimony and the previous statement will suffice.[15] Accordingly, if the former statement fails to mention a material circumstance presently testified to, which it would have been natural to mention in the prior statement, the prior statement is sufficiently inconsistent.[16] Again, an earlier statement by the witness that he had no knowledge of facts now testified to, should be provable.[17] Seemingly the test should be, could the jury reasonably find that a witness who believed the truth of the facts testified to would have been unlikely to make a prior statement of this tenor?[18] Thus, if the previous statement is ambiguous and according to one meaning would be inconsistent with the testimony, it should be admitted for the jury's considera-

---

10. See § 47, infra.

11. Compare the discussion in 3A Wigmore, Evidence (Chadbourn rev.) § 1017.

12. See n. 6, supra.

13. See discussion in Chapter 24, infra.

14. See, e. g., Sanger v. Bacon, 180 Ind. 322, 328, 101 N.E. 1001, 1003 (1913) (must be contradictory construing the statement most favorably to the witness); State v. Bowen, 247 Mo. 584, 153 S.W. 1033, 1038 (1913) ("must be such as, either in their substance or their general drift, contradict"); and cases cited C.J.S. Witnesses § 583, n. 44.

15. Commonwealth v. West, 312 Mass. 438, 440, 45 N.E.2d 260 (1942) ("And it is not necessary that there should be a contradiction in plain terms. It is enough if the proffered testimony, taken as a whole, either by what it says or by what it omits to say, affords some indication that the fact was different from the testimony of the witness whom it is sought to contradict."); O'Neill v. Minneapolis St. Ry. Co., 213 Minn. 514, 7 N.W.2d 665, 669 (1942) ("Whether a prior statement does in fact impeach a witness does not depend upon the degree of inconsistency between his testimony and his prior statement. If there is any variance between them, the statement should be received and its effect upon the credibility of the witness should be left to the jury." Statement held not to meet the test.); Morgan v. Washington Trust Co., 249 A.2d 48 (R.I.1969).

16. Esderts v. Chicago Rock Island & Pacific Co., 76 Ill.App.2d 210, 222 N.E.2d 117 (1966) cert. denied 386 U.S. 993 ("If a witness fails to mention facts under circumstances which make it reasonably probable he would mention them if true, the omission may be shown as an indirect inconsistency."); Erickson v. Erickson & Co., 212 Minn. 119, 2 N.W. 2d 824 (1942) (workmen's compensation automobile accident claimant testified on stand that his trip was for two purposes, one individual, the other for the employer; held, his prior statements to adjuster mentioning only the individual purpose admissible to impeach). Contra: Hall v. Phillips Petroleum Co., 358 Mo. 313, 214 S.W.2d 438 (semble) (1948).

17. Hoagland v. Canfield, 160 F. 146, 171 (C.C.S.D. N.Y.1908); In re Olson's Estate, 54 S.D. 184, 223 N.W. 41 (1929); C.J.S. Witnesses § 583, n. 52. Similarly, it seems that a previous statement denying recollection of facts testified to should be provable. But see Lewis v. American Road Ins. Co., 199 Ga.App. 507, 167 S.E.2d 729 (1969) (witness refused to answer questions on prior deposition; inadmissible); Grunewald v. United States, 353 U.S. 391 (1957) (defendant's refusal to answer same questions before grand jury, on grounds the answers would tend to incriminate him, was inadmissible because refusal was not inconsistent under the circumstances).

18. The text is cited in Morgan v. Washington Trust Co., 249 A.2d 48 (R.I.1969).

tion.[19] In applying the criterion of material inconsistency reasonable judges will be likely to differ, and a fair range of discretion should be accorded to the trial judge. Moreover, it is to be hoped that instead of restricting the use of prior statements by a mechanical use of the test of inconsistency, the courts will lean toward receiving such statements in case of doubt, to aid in evaluating the testimony. The statements, indeed, having been made when memory was more recent and when less time for the play of influence has elapsed, are often inherently more trustworthy than the testimony itself.[20] A logical extension of this reasoning justifies the admission of prior testimony about an independent and unrelated event so similar to testimony now given as to arouse suspicion of fabrication.[21]

35. Prior Inconsistent Statements: Opinion in Form.[22]

If a witness, such as an expert, testifies in terms of opinion, of course all courts will permit impeachment by showing a previous expression by the witness of an inconsistent opinion.[23] More troublesome is the question which arises when the witness testifies to specific facts and then is sought to be impeached by prior inconsistent expressions of opinion. For example, in a collision case the plaintiff's witness testifies to particular facts inculpating the driver of a bus involved in the accident. The opponent proposes to show that the witness said just after seeing the collision, "The bus was not to blame." [24]

Should the opinion rule be applied to exclude such an impeaching statement? The early American tradition of a strict rule against opinions has been much relaxed in recent trial administration.[25] What was once supposed to be a difference in kind between fact and opinion is now regarded as a difference in degree only.[26] Wigmore considers that the rule goes no further than to exclude opinion as superfluous when more concrete statements could be resorted to.[27] Thus, the principal practical value of the opinion rule is as a regulation of trial practice requiring the examining counsel to bring out his facts by more specific questions if practicable, before resorting to more general ones. For this reason, it is a mistake of policy to apply it to any out-of-court statements whatsoever, since no such controls are possible.[28] Moreover,

19. State v. Kingsbury, 58 Me. 238, 242 (1870); Town of Concord v. Concord Bank, 16 N.H. 26, 32 (1844); C.J.S. Witnesses § 583, n. 53, 54. But there are contrary decisions. State v. Bush, 50 Idaho 166, 295 P. 432 (1930), and cases cited.

20. The text above is quoted in Commonwealth v. Jackson, 281 S.W.2d 891, 896 (Ky.1955). See the comment by Davis, J. for the court in Judson v. Fielding, 227 App.Div. 430, 237 N.Y.S. 348, 352 (1929): "In considering the evidence so sharply in dispute, the jury was entitled to know the contrary views the witness had expressed when the incident was fresh in his mind, uninfluenced by sympathy or other cause. Very often by calm reflection a witness may correct inaccurate observations or erroneous impressions hastily formed. But the jury should have all the facts in making an appraisement of the value and weight to be given the testimony."

See Ch. 24, infra.

21. People v. Rainford, 58 Ill.App.2d 312, 208 N.E.2d 314 (1965) (testimony of prosecuting witness in prior rape case was exactly the same in unlikely details as testimony of the witness in the instant prosecution against the same defendants for assault with intent to rape the witness in a different and independent incident).

22. Dec.Dig. Witnesses ☞384; C.J.S. Witnesses § 592. As noted in § 34, this section assumes that inconsistent statements are sought to be introduced (and can be introduced) only for impeachment purposes. 58 Am.Jur. Witnesses § 768; Annot., 66 A.L.R. 289, 158 A.L.R. 820.

23. Hutson v. State, 164 Tex.Civ.R. 24, 296 S.W.2d 245 (1956); McGrath v. Fash, 244 Mass. 327, 139 N.E. 303 (1923) (doctor who testified to moderate injuries, impeached by his statement after examining plaintiff that "this was the worst accident case he handled in the last ten years"); In re County Ditch, 150 Minn. 69, 184 N.W. 374 (1921) (value-witness impeached by his report on value as viewer); C.J.S. Witnesses § 581, n. 13.

24. Judson v. Fielding, 227 App.Div. 430, 237 N.Y.S. 348 (1929) (impeachment allowed).

25. See §§ 11, 12, 17, supra.

26. See §§ 11, 12, supra.

27. 7 Wigmore, Evidence § 1918.

28. See § 18, supra.

when the out-of-court statement is not offered at all as evidence of the fact asserted, but only to show the asserter's inconsistency, the whole purpose of the opinion rule, to improve the objectivity and hence reliability of testimonial assertions, is quite inapplicable. Hence, though many earlier decisions, influenced perhaps by a statement in Greenleaf [29] and a casual English holding at *nisi prius*,[30] and some later opinions, exclude impeaching statements in opinion form,[31] the trend of holdings and the majority view is in accord with the commonsense notion that if a substantial inconsistency appears the form of the impeaching statement is immaterial.[32]

36. Prior Inconsistent Statements: Subject Matter.

On cross-examination we have seen that strict rules of relevancy are relaxed,[33] and generally the trial judge in his discretion may permit the cross-examiner to inquire about any previous statements inconsistent with assertions, relevant or irrelevant, which the witness has testified to on direct or cross. At this stage, there is no strict requirement that the previous impeaching statements must not deal with "collateral" matters.[34] But as appears in the next paragraph, if the inquiry on cross-examination is as to inconsistent statements about "collateral" matters, the cross-examiner must "take the answer"—he cannot bring on other witnesses to prove the making of the alleged statement.[35]

At this latter stage, of extrinsic evidence, that is, the production of attacking witnesses, the range of impeachment by inconsistent statements is sharply narrowed for obvious reasons of economy of time and attention. The tag, "You cannot contradict as to collateral matters," applies, and here the meaning is that to impeach by extrinsic proof of prior inconsistent statements, the statements

---

29. Greenleaf, Evidence § 449 (3d ed.1846).

30. Elton v. Larkins, 5 Car. & P. 385, 172 Eng.Rep. 1020 (1832) (suit on marine policy; the broker who effected policy for the plaintiff, called as witness for defendants, testified to facts showing material concealment; plaintiff sought to show by extrinsic evidence after witness denied it, that witness had said that "the underwriters had not a leg to stand on," excluded by Tindal, C. J. as "only a contradiction on a matter of judgment").

31. See, e. g., City Bank v. Young, 43 N.H. 457, 460 (1862); Morton v. State, 43 Tex.Crim.R. 533, 67 S.W. 115 (1902), and see cases cited Annot., 158 A.L.R. 820, 821. See, also, Dorsten v. Lawrence, 20 Ohio App.2d 297, 253 N.E.2d 804 (1969); State v. Thompson, 71 S.D. 319, 24 N.W.2d 10 (1946); Hirsh v. Manley, 81 Ariz. 94, 300 P.2d 588 (1956) (rule applied where court thought the out-of-court opinion required expertise but witness had not been qualified as an expert); C.J.S. Witnesses § 592.

32. Tigh v. College Park Realty Co., 149 Mont. 358, 427 P.2d 57 (1967); and see the description of the trend and the collections of cases in Annot., 158 A.L.R. 821–824, and in Grady, The Admissibility of a Prior Statement of Opinion for Purposes of Impeachment, 41 Cornell L.Q. 224 (1956). See also C.J.S. Witnesses § 592.

33. See § 29, supra.

34. Howard v. City Fire Ins. Co., 4 Denio 502, 506 (S.Ct.N.Y.1847); Dane v. MacGregor, 94 N.H. 294, 52 A.2d 290 (1947); 3A Wigmore, Evidence (Chadbourn rev.) § 1023.

Since the matter is within the discretion of the trial court, his ruling will usually be upheld upon appeal. See, e. g., Lenske v. Knutsen, 410 F.2d 583 (9th Cir. 1969); State v. Brewster, 75 Wash.2d 137, 449 P.2d 685 (1969) (trial judge permitted questions concerning collateral matter); Wiesemann v. Pavlat, 413 S.W.2d 23 (Mo.App.1967). Nevertheless, if the matter is clearly material it has been held that the cross-examination must be permitted. State v. Thompson, 280 S.W.2d 838 (Mo.1955); Healy v. City of Chicago, 109 Ill.App.2d 6, 248 N.E.2d 679 (1969). If the matter is immaterial and prejudicial, the trial judge may be reversed, at least if no appropriate requested instruction is given. Kantor v. Ash, 215 Md. 285, 137 A.2d 661 (1958).

It might be noted that occasionally an opinion will contain a flat statement that cross-examination may not be had concerning an inconsistent statement on a matter that is collateral. Kantor v. Ash, supra; State v. Wilson, 158 Conn. 321, 260 A.2d 571 (1969).

35. That a denial on cross-examination of a statement relating to a "collateral" matter cannot be disputed by extrinsic evidence, see Montgomery v. Nance, 425 P.2d 470 (Okl.1967); State v. Mangrum, 98 Ariz. 279, 403 P.2d 925 (1965) (court states cross should have been permitted but the extrinsic evidence was inadmissible); cases cited in Dec.Dig. Witnesses ☞383; C.J.S. Witnesses § 611.

must have as their subject (1) facts relevant to the issues in the cause, or (2) facts which are themselves provable by extrinsic evidence to discredit the witness.[36] Facts showing bias

or interest,[37] and presumably facts showing that the witness had no opportunity to know the material matters testified to,[38] would fall in the second class.

A distinct but somewhat cognate notion is the view that if a party interrogates a witness about a fact which would be favorable to the examiner if true, and receives a reply which is merely negative in its effect on examiner's case, the examiner may not by extrinsic evidence prove that the first witness had earlier stated that the fact was true as desired by the inquirer.[39] An affirmative answer would have been material and subject to be impeached by an inconsistent statement, but a negative answer is not damaging to the examiner, but merely disappointing, and may not be thus impeached. In this situation the policy involved is not the saving of time and confusion, as before, but the protection

36. The classic statement of the test of "collateralness" is in the opinions in Attorney-General v. Hitchcock, 1 Exch. 91, 99, 154 Eng.Rep. 38 (1847). That case was an information under the revenue laws. A witness for the plaintiff was asked on cross-examination if he had not said he had been offered 20 pounds to testify by officers of the Crown, which he denied. Held, the defendant could not call a witness to testify that the first witness had made the alleged statement. Pollock, C. B. said: "A distinction should be observed between those matters which may be given in evidence by way of contradiction as directly affecting the story of the witness touching the issue before the jury, and those matters which affect the motives, temper, and character of the witness, not with respect to his credit, but with reference to his feelings towards one party or the other. It is certainly allowable to ask a witness in what manner he stands affected toward the opposite party in the cause . . . and whether he has not used expressions importing that he would be revenged on some one or that he would give such evidence as might dispose of the cause in one way or the other. If he denies that, you may give evidence as to what he said,—not with the view of having a direct effect on the issue, but to show what is the state of mind of that witness in order that the jury may exercise their opinion as to how far he is to be believed." It should be observed that the alleged statement was that the witness had been *offered* a bribe, not that he had accepted one. But query as to evidence of attempted bribery of a witness as an admission. See § 273, infra.

Another illuminating discussion is the opinion of Rutledge, J. in Ewing v. United States, 77 U.S. App.D.C. 14, 135 F.2d 633, 640–642 (1942). Here a witness for defendant accused of rape swore to facts which if believed made it impossible to believe complainant's story. Over the witness's denial, the government was (it was held) properly allowed to prove that the witness had said (1) I believe the defendant guilty but (2) he is facing the electric chair and I must be on his side. The court rejected the test of collateralness used in some cases (see, e. g., Butler v. State, 179 Miss. 865, 176 So. 589 (1937) whether the party would have been entitled to prove the matter "as part of his case," and approved Wigmore's statement of the test as follows: "Could the fact as to which the prior self-contradiction is predicated have been shown in evidence for any purpose independently of the self-contradiction?" 3A Wigmore, Evidence (Chadbourn rev.) § 1020. This seems to be equivalent to saying that the fact which is the subject of the previous statement must be (1) relevant to an issue, or (2) provable under impeachment practice by extrinsic evidence. Of course, the second

previous statement in the *Ewing* case is not a prior inconsistent statement but is a direct expression of bias, and provable as such for impeachment regardless of self-contradiction. Somewhat similar is State v. Sandros, 186 Wash. 438, 58 P.2d 362 (1936), where, despite his denials, the state was allowed to prove that defense witness, claimed to be an accomplice with accused in forging a will, had (1) said that he had carried the will in his pocket for three weeks (which was material as tending to show it could not have been made at the time it was dated) and (2) made efforts to persuade a person to testify falsely to the genuineness of the signature. The court approved the Wigmore test, as given above.

37. See, e. g., the *Ewing* and *Sandros* cases in the next preceding note.

38. See 3A Wigmore, Evidence (Chadbourn rev.) § 1022.

39. Miller v. Comm., 241 Ky. 818, 45 S.W.2d 461 (1932) (witness for defense who denied she heard defendant say he was going to kill deceased, improperly allowed to be impeached by proof that she had said she had heard such threats); Woodroffe v. Jones, 83 Me. 21, 21 A. 177 (1890) (suit by wife for sprained ankle due to defective sidewalk; defense, plaintiff negligent in wearing high-heeled shoes; husband, as witness, denied on cross-examination that he had spoken to his wife about her high heels; held proof by another witness that he had said "that he told his wife about wearing such high heeled boots" improperly admitted to impeach his denial which was merely negative and without probative significance).

of the other party against the hearsay use by the jury of the previous statement.[40]

37. Prior Inconsistent Statements: Requirement of Preliminary Questions on Cross-Examination as "Foundation" for Proof by Extrinsic Evidence.[41]

In 1820 in the answers of the judges in *Queen Caroline's Case*, it was announced: "If it be intended to bring the credit of a witness into question by proof of anything he may have said or declared touching the cause, the witness is first asked, upon cross-examination, whether or no he has said or declared that which is intended to be proved." [42] Thus was crystallized a practice which was previously occasional and discretionary. Only later and gradually was it almost universally accepted in this country.[43] The purposes of the requirement are (1) to avoid unfair surprise to the adversary, (2) to save time, as an admission by the witness may make the extrinsic proof unnecessary, and (3) to give the witness, in fairness to him, a chance to explain the discrepancy. On the other hand, the requirement may work unfairly for the impeacher. He may only learn of the inconsistent statement after he has cross-examined and after the witness by leaving the court has made it impracticable to recall him for further cross-examination to lay the foundation belatedly. It is moreover a requirement which can serve as a trap since it must be done in advance before the final impeachment is attempted and is supremely easy to overlook.

The requirement applies not only to oral inconsistent statements but also to those in writing. Its application to writings is discussed in an earlier section.[44]

To satisfy the requirement the cross-examiner will ask the witness whether he made the alleged statement, giving its substance, and naming the time, the place, and the person to whom made.[45] The purpose of this particularity is, of course, to refresh the memory of the witness as to the supposed statement by reminding him of the accompanying circumstances.[46]

If the witness denies the making of the statement, or fails to admit it, but says "I don't know" or "I don't remember" then the requirement of "laying the foundation" is satisfied and the cross-examiner, at his next stage of giving evidence, may prove the making of the alleged statement.[47] If, however,

---

40. Of course, if the inconsistent statements of the witness are not hearsay, either under the more traditional rule, or modern proposed rules, there would be no such hearsay use. See generally § 251, infra; § 34, supra.

41. 3A Wigmore, Evidence (Chadbourn rev.) §§ 1025–1039; Hale, Inconsistent Statements, 10 So. Cal.L.R. 135–147 (1937); Dec.Dig. Witnesses ⚬388, 389; C.J.S. Witnesses §§ 598–612; 58 Am.Jur. Witnesses §§ 776–780.

42. 2 Brod. & Bing. 284, 313, 129 Eng.Rep. 976 (1820).

43. 3A Wigmore, Evidence § 1026. A foundation question has not been required in Massachusetts unless a party is attempting to impeach his own witness. Allin v. Whittemore, 171 Mass. 259, 50 N.E. 618 (1898) is a leading case. See also Thompson v. J. P. Morin & Co., 80 N.H. 144, 114 A. 274 (1921) (citing earlier cases). See n. 64, infra, concerning the rule that the matter should be in the discretion of the trial judge.

44. See § 28, supra.

45. This is the usual formula. See, e. g., Angus v. Smith, Moo. & M. 473, 474, 173 Eng.Rep. 1228 (1829) ("you must ask him as to time, place, and person . . . it is not enough to ask him the general question whether he has ever said so and so"); Nichols v. Sefcik, 66 N.M. 449, 349 P.2d 678 (1960); Peyton v. State, 40 Ala.App. 556, 120 So.2d 415 (1959) cert. denied 270 Ala. 740, 120 So.2d 429 (1959) cert. denied, 364 U.S. 870. The use of leading questions in examining the impeaching witness is discussed in § 6 at n. 19, supra.

46. Since the purpose of the foundation question is to warn the witness sufficiently of the out-of-court statement so that he may remember it, the usual formula may be relaxed under circumstances in which it is indicated that the witness was sufficiently warned although the foundation question was not completely specific under the formula. State v. Caldwell, 251 La. 780, 206 So.2d 492 (1968) (time not exactly specified); cases cited in C.J.S. Witnesses § 605.

47. People v. Perri, 381 Ill. 244, 44 N.E.2d 857 (1942) (denial); Ream's Administrator v. Greer, 314

the witness unequivocally admits the making of the supposed statement, may the cross-examiner still choose to prove it again by another witness? Wigmore, with some support, suggests that he may,[48] but the prevailing view is to the contrary[49] and in the usual situation this seems the more expedient practice. It saves time and minimizes the calling of witnesses upon what is only a side issue; yet circumstances may be such, especially when the statement is in writing, that the judge's discretion to allow the impeachment to proceed should be recognized.[50]

The trial situation to which the requirement of the preliminary question typically applies, is of course the situation where the witness attacked is on the stand in the present trial. What if he is not present, but his testimony given in this or some other case, by deposition or at a trial, is used as evidence in the present trial? Will the impeachment by inconsistent statements be excluded unless the impeacher at the former hearing asked the preliminary question?[51] Most of the decisions forbid the impeachment for want of the "foundation" without making any distinctions.[52] It seems, however, that in the case of a deposition taken upon written interrogatories when the cross-questions must be propounded before the answers to the direct can usually be known, the foundation should not be required. Even more clearly it seems that when the inconsistent statement was made after the testimony was given, the foundation should be dispensed with.[53]

S.W.2d 511 (Ky.1958) (witness stated he did not recall "using those words"); State v. Miles, 73 Wash.2d 67, 436 P.2d 198 (1968) (witness stated she could not remember inconsistent statement); Dec.Dig. Witnesses ⊂⊃389; C.J.S. Witnesses §§ 610, 612.

48. 3A Evidence (Chadbourn rev.) § 1037, note 4. A case supporting this view is People v. Schainuck, 286 N.Y. 161, 36 N.E.2d 94 (1941) (arson: prosecution witness admitted on cross-examination that in investigation-hearing by Fire Marshal he said he knew nothing about cause of fire; held, error to refuse request of defense counsel to inspect hearing-record with a view to proving statements of witness). Several cases in Illinois support the view that the inconsistent statement is admissible; others seem contrary. See discussion in People v. Knowles, 91 Ill.App.2d 109, 234 N.E.2d 149 (1968).

49. Duran v. People, 162 Colo. 419, 427 P.2d 318 (1967) (writing); State v. Jackson, 248 La. 919, 183 So.2d 305 (1966) (writing; Art. 493 Code of Criminal Procedure applied); Alabama Electric Co-operative, Inc. v. Partridge, 284 Ala. 442, 225 So.2d 848 (1969) (writing); State v. Buffone, 65 Utah 92, 234 P. 539 (1925) (oral statements; "If the witness' attention is called to the conflicting statements he may admit them, and may perhaps make a satisfactory explanation why he made them. If he admits the statements, whether he explains them or not, that ends the inquiry"); and decisions collected in C.J.S. Witnesses § 610.

50. Gordon v. United States, 344 U.S. 414 (1953) (error to deny access to prior inconsistent written statements of government witness, despite his admission of inconsistency on cross-examination, since judge might nevertheless have admitted them "as a more reliable, complete and accurate source of information.").

51. The discussion assumes a jurisdiction in which a foundation question is otherwise required.

In the converse case when the witness now on the stand is sought to be impeached by inconsistent statements contained in previous testimony of the witness at a former hearing or trial, the need for the preliminary question, to give opportunity for explanation is usually conceded. See cases cited 3A Wigmore, Evidence (Chadbourn rev.) § 1035; Dec.Dig. Evidence ⊂⊃388(8); C.J.S. Witnesses § 604.

52. Mattox v. United States, 156 U.S. 237 (1895) (witness for government in murder case died after first trial, and his testimony was read at second trial: defendant offered evidence that after first trial witness said his testimony was secured by duress and was untrue; held, three judges dissenting, properly excluded for want of foundation); Doe v. Wilkinson, 35 Ala. 453 (1860) (written deposition); Gregory v. Cheatham, 36 Mo. 155, 161 (1865) (letter written after deposition taken); Nagi v. Detroit United Ry., 231 Mich. 452, 204 N.W. 126 (1925) (on motion for new trial, defendant offers evidence that witness for plaintiff, who committed suicide after the trial, wrote a letter confessing that plaintiff had paid him $500 for testifying falsely: held, excluded), and cases cited 3A Wigmore, Evidence (Chadbourn rev.) §§ 1031, 1032.

53. People v. Collup, 27 Cal.2d 829, 167 P.2d 714, 718 (1946) (prosecution for rape: testimony of state's witness, at preliminary hearing read at trial; held, error to exclude evidence of subsequent inconsistent statements of witness, now absent from state; "the goal of all judicial proceedings is to bring before the trier of fact all pertinent evidence. Hence the rule allowing the use of former testimony is a salutary expedient . . . But it is equally clear that by reason of the same principle the impeaching evidence should be admitted

A similar question arises with respect to the impeachment by inconsistent statements of declarants whose hearsay declarations have been admitted under exceptions to the hearsay rule. But here the declarant has never been on the stand, and thus the opportunity for the preliminary question has never been afforded. Accordingly the courts are generally agreed that inconsistent statements of the makers of dying declarations [54] and declarations against interest [55], and of attesting witnesses,[56] and presumably of the makers of other hearsay declarations,[57] may be proven to impeach, despite the want of a foundation.

If one of the parties to the suit takes the stand as a witness, and the adversary desires to use against him his prior statement inconsistent with his testimony, the statement is receivable in two aspects, first as the admission of an opposing party,[58] and second, as an inconsistent statement to impeach the witness. In the first aspect, it is relevant evidence upon the fact issues; in the second aspect, it is not.[59] If the inconsistent statement is offered as an admission, the requirement of the preliminary question is almost universally held inapplicable.[60] In the case of the party there is less danger of unfair surprise than in the case of the ordinary witness, and the party will have ample opportunity for denial or explanation after the inconsistent statement is proved. Occasionally, the courts inadvertently assume that the requirement applies to the party-witness.[61] Sometimes they impose it if the proponent offers the statement only for impeachment,[62] and in one state the judge has discretion to impose the requirement as prerequisite to proof of a party-witness's admission.[63] These niggling qualifications seem hardly worth their salt and in jurisdictions which otherwise require the foundation question the sensible practice is the simple one of dispensing with the "foundation" entirely in respect to parties' admissions.

When it is complied with, the preliminary question requirement conduces to fairness and economy of time. When it is overlooked by the impeacher, as it often is, then seemingly the judge should have a discretion to consider such factors as the lack of knowledge of the inconsistent statement on the part of the impeacher when he cross-examined, the importance or unimportance of the testimony under attack, and the practicability of recalling the witness for denial or explanation; and in the light of these circumstances,

for what it is worth"). See approving Note, 20 So.Calif.L.Rev. 102. See present West's Ann.Cal. Evid.Code, § 1202 providing that inconsistent statements of deponents in the same case, may be introduced, in effect without the use of a foundation question.

54. Carver v. United States, 164 U.S. 694 (1897) (two judges dissenting); State v. Debnam, 222 N.C. 266, 22 S.E.2d 562 (1942).

55. 3A Wigmore, Evidence (Chadbourn rev.) § 1033.

56. Mobley v. Lyon, 134 Ga. 125, 67 S.E. 668 (1910). Contra: Craig v. Wismar, 310 Ill. 262, 141 N.E. 766 (1923).

57. See Am-Cal Investment Co. v. Sharlyn Estates, Inc., 255 Cal.App.2d 526, 63 Cal.Rptr. 518 (1967) (inconsistent statement of declarant, whose out-of-court statements were erroneously admitted because they were hearsay, should have been admitted); West's Ann.Cal.Evid.Code, § 1202 (permits introduction of inconsistent statements of declarants whose declarations have been received in evidence as hearsay, in effect without foundation questions); F.R.Ev. (R.D.1971) 806 (similar).

58. See ch. 26, infra.

59. See discussion in § 34, supra.

60. Howe v. Messimer, 84 Mont. 304, 275 P. 281 (1929); McDaniel v. Farlow, 132 Neb. 273, 271 N.W. 905 (1937); Stillwell v. State Industrial Accident Commission, 243 Ore. 158, 411 P.2d 1015 (1966); State v. Hephner, 161 N.W.2d 714 (Iowa 1968); and cases cited 4 Wigmore, Evidence § 1051; Dec. Dig. Witnesses ⟾388(3); C.J.S. Witnesses § 604b.

61. See, e. g., Wiggins v. State, 27 Ala.App. 451, 173 So. 890 (1937); Finn v. Finn, 195 S.W.2d 679 (Tex. Civ.App.1946).

62. Washington & O. D. Ry. Co. v. Smith, 53 App. D.C. 184, 289 F. 582 (1923); Industrial Farm Home Gas Co. v. McDonald, 234 Ark. 744, 355 S.W.2d 174 (1962); C.J.S. Witnesses § 604b.

63. Giles v. Valentic, 355 Pa. 108, 49 A.2d 384 (1946).

to permit the impeachment without the foundation or to permit departure from the traditional time sequence if it seems fairer to do so.[64]

38. Prior Inconsistent Statements: Rule Against Impeaching One's Own Witness.[65]

The common law rule forbidding a party to impeach his own witness, which has been modified to an extent indicated later in this section, is of obscure origin but probably is a late manifestation of the evolution of the common law trial procedure from an inquisitorial to a contentious or adversary system.[66] The prohibition is general, applying to all forms of impeachment. It applies not only to attack by inconsistent statements but to attack on character, or by a showing of bias, interest or corruption. It does not, however, forbid the party to introduce other evidence to dispute the facts testified to by his witness.[67]

Among the reasons, or rationalizations, found for the rule are, first, that the party by calling the witness to testify vouches for his trustworthiness, and second, that the power to impeach is the power to coerce the witness to testify as desired, under the implied threat of blasting his character if he does not. The answer to the first reason is that, except in a few instances such as character witnesses or expert witnesses, the party has little or no choice of witnesses. He calls only those who happen to have observed the particular facts in controversy. The answers to the second reason are (a) that it applies only to two kinds of impeachment, the attack on character and the showing of corruption, and (b) that to forbid the attack by the calling party leaves the party at the mercy of the witness and his adversary. If the truth lies on the side of the calling party, but the witness's character is bad, the witness may be attacked by the adversary if he tells the truth; but if the witness tells a lie, the adversary will not attack him, and the calling party, under the rule, cannot. Certainly it seems that if the witness has been bribed to change his story, the calling party should be allowed to disclose this fact to the court.

The most important, because most effective, kind of impeachment, is by inconsistent statements and most of the cases applying the rule are of this type. It is hard to see any justification for prohibiting this sort of showing as to the reliability of a witness who has testified contrary to his previous position. Perhaps there is a fear that the previous

---

64. Model Code of Evidence Rule 106(2) leaves the enforcement of the requirement to the judge's discretion. Uniform Rule 22(b), West's Ann.Cal.Evid. Code, § 770, and N.J.Ev.Rule 22(b) likewise give the judge discretion. F.R.Ev. (R.D.1971) 613(b) provides that the witness must have an opportunity to explain or deny the inconsistent statement, although there is no particular requirement of time sequence, and the judge may dispense with the requirement.

It might be noted that in a very few jurisdictions in which a foundation question is required, it may be error for the cross-examiner to fail to produce extrinsic evidence of the inconsistent statement. People v. Williams, 105 Ill.App.2d 25, 245 N.E.2d 17 (1969) (error not reversible error under circumstances); State v. Yoakum, 37 Wash.2d 137, 222 P.2d 181 (1950) (where it was said that the effect of cross-examination was to place cross-examiner's statements as evidence before the jury). Probably this requirement does not exist in most jurisdictions. See F.R.Ev. (R.D.1971) 613(a), requiring disclosure of the statement to opposing counsel on request, when the witness is being examined upon it, as an assurance of good faith.

65. 3A Wigmore, Evidence (Chadbourn rev.) §§ 896–918; Ladd, Impeachment of One's Own Witness—New Developments, 4 U.Chi.L.Rev. 69 (1936); Hauser, Impeaching One's Own Witness, 11 Oh.St. L.J. 364 (1950); Comment, 49 Va.L.Rev. 996 (1963); Dec.Dig. Witnesses ⟜320–325; C.J.S. Witnesses §§ 477, 578.

66. Ladd, article cited in preceding note, at p. 70.

67. Vondrashek v. Dignan, 200 Minn. 530, 274 N.W. 609 (1937) (principle recognized, but court refused to apply it to permit party to contradict by other witnesses his own testimony that he was not drunk—a picturesque case of behind the scenes conflict between the party and his insurer); Duffy v. National Janitorial Services, Inc., 429 Pa. 334, 240 A.2d 527 (1968); and cases cited in Dec.Dig. Witnesses ⟜400–402, 320, 321, and C.J.S. Witnesses § 630.

statement will be considered by the jury as substantive evidence of the facts asserted if, as in many jurisdictions, the statement for that purpose will be hearsay.[68] Except in those few jurisdictions which have altogether abandoned it,[69] the common law rule against impeaching one's own witness persists for the most part with respect to attacks showing bias and attacks upon character.[70] On the other hand, it has been relaxed in a number of jurisdictions by statute or decision insofar as it prohibits impeachment by inconsistent statements. A provision in the draft of the Field Code of Civil Procedure in 1849 found fruit in the English Common Law Procedure Act of 1854, as follows (St. 17 & 18 Vict. c. 125, § 22): "[1] A party producing a witness shall not be allowed to impeach his credit by general evidence of bad character; [2] but he may, in case the witness shall in the opinion of the judge prove adverse, [3] contradict him by other evidence, [4] or by leave of the judge prove that he has made at other times a statement inconsistent with his present testimony." This statute has been copied in a few states.[71] Other states, following the example of Massachusetts in 1869 have adopted the English statute except for omitting the troublesome condition that the witness must have proved "adverse." [72] Some courts have reached a similar result by decision.[73]

These statutes and similar decisions open the door to the most important type of impeachment of one's own witness, namely, prior inconsistent statements. But whether the extension is derived from statute or decision, two troublesome qualifications have been imposed on the reform by most courts. The first is that the party seeking to impeach must show that he is surprised at the testimony of the witness.[74] The second is that he cannot impeach unless the witness' testimony is positively harmful to his cause, reaching further than a mere failure ("I do not remember," "I do not know") to give expected favorable testimony.[75] These limitations are explainable only as attempts to safeguard the hearsay policy by preventing the party from proving the witness' prior statements in situations where it appears that its

---

68. See § 251, infra.

69. See n. 76, infra.

70. See discussion in Comment, 49 Va.L.Rev. 996, 1009 (1963).

71. Fla.Stat.Ann. § 90.09; N.M.1953 Comp. § 20–2–4; Va.Code 1950, § 8–292; 12 Vt.Stat.Ann. § 1642; Hawaii Rev.L. § 222–25.

72. Alaska R.Civ.P. 43(g) (11) [a]; Ark.Stats. § 28–706; Idaho Code § 9–1207; Ind.Burns' Ann.St. § 2–1726; Ky.R.Civ.P. 43.07; Mont.Rev.Code § 93–1901–8; Or.Rev.Stat. § 45–590; Texas, Vernon's Ann.C.C.P. art. 38.28; Wyo.Stat.1957, § 1–143; N.Y. CPL 60.35; N.Y. CPLR 4514 (limited to writings); Wis.Stat.Ann. 885.35 (limited to criminal cases).

73. See, e. g., cases cited in n. 74, infra.

74. Young v. United States, 97 F.2d 200 (5th Cir. 1938) (error to admit prior statement where prosecutor knew before placing witnesses on the stand that they would recant); Missouri Pac. R. Co. v. Sullivan, 197 Ark. 360, 122 S.W.2d 947 (1938) (surprise; allowed; statute permitted inconsistent statement); State v. Schwartz, 266 Minn. 104, 122 N.W.2d 769 (1963) (surprise; allowed; no statute); Foremost Dairies, Inc. of the South v. Cutler, 212 So.2d 37 (Fla.App.1968) (statute permitted inconsistent statement if witness adverse); cases cited C.J.S. Witnesses § 578c. Surprise is required at least by two statutes, D.C. Code § 14–104; Ga.Code § 38–1801 (if "entrapped"). The concept of "surprise," moreover, varies in the various jurisdictions. Sometimes "actual" or genuine surprise is required; in other decisions, it is not. Compare Young v. United States, supra, with Wheeler v. United States, 93 U.S.App.D.C. 159, 211 F.2d 19 (1953) cert. denied 374 U.S. 1019, and see Comment, 49 Va.L.Rev. 996 (1963). A possible escape from the requirement can be had if the judge will "call" the witness as a court's witness. See § 8, supra.

75. Mitchell v. Swift & Co., 151 F.2d 770 (5th Cir. 1945); Roe v. State, 152 Tex.Cr.R. 119, 210 S.W.2d 817 (1948); Virginia Elec. & Power Co. v. Hall, 184 Va. 102, 34 S.E.2d 382 (1945); Wurm v. Pulice, 82 Idaho 359, 353 P.2d 1071 (1960) (statute permits impeachment by inconsistent statement); Commonwealth v. Strunk, 293 S.W.2d 629 (Ky.1956) (rule permits inconsistent statement; court states "where the witness testifies positively to the existence of a fact prejudicial to the party, or to a fact clearly favorable to the adverse party"); cases cited in C.J.S. Witnesses § 578c; and see Comment, 49 Va.L.Rev. 996 (1963).

only value to the proponent will be as substantive evidence of the facts asserted. The rule against such use of the statements, and the soundness of its policy, as well as growing authority to the contrary, is the theme of a subsequent section in Chapter 24.

The prohibitory rule itself has been abandoned in its entirety in a very few jurisdictions.[76] Abandonment is proposed in the Uniform Rules and the proposed Federal Evidence Rules.[77] While the power to attack the character of one's own witness may be of little practical value to the attacker, and is of little moment to the administration of justice, a rule against the showing of the prior statements of one's own witness, to aid in evaluating his testimony, is a serious obstruction to the ascertainment of truth.

Two principal matters concerning the common law rule where it persists even in a modified form should be mentioned. First, a principal means of escape from the prohibition, insofar as it prevents introduction of inconsistent statements, is by resort to questioning of the witness by the calling party about the previous statement not avowedly to discredit but to refresh his memory, or as it is sometimes more urgently phrased, "to awaken his conscience."[78]

Second, who is the party's own witness within the prohibitory rule? It is not the mere calling of the witness but the eliciting of his testimony that makes him the party's witness.[79] In the case of deposition testimony it is the introduction of the deposition in evidence, not the taking of the deposition, that constitutes the adoption of the witness as the party's own.[80] The calling and examining of an attesting witness,[81] or other witness required by law to be called,[82] is not adoption.[83] When a party calls an adverse party as a witness, the reasons for the prohibition, such as they are, seem inapplicable, and the Federal Rule [84] and a few other regulations,[85] expressly permit the calling party to impeach. In the absence of such a provision, many courts mechanically apply the prohibition.[86] When the same witness is

---

79. Fall Brook Coal Co. v. Hewson, 158 N.Y. 1, 65 N. E. 1095 (1899).

Moreover, in some jurisdictions restricting the cross-examination to the scope of the direct, if the cross-examiner elicits new matter he makes the witness his own as to such testimony. 3A Wigmore, Evidence (Chadbourn rev.) § 914; Dec.Dig. Witnesses ⊂⊃325.

80. F.R.Civ.P. 32(c), formerly Rule 26(f), adopted in many states; 3A Wigmore, Evidence (Chadbourn rev.) §§ 912, 913.

81. Whitman v. Morey, 63 N.H. 448, 456, 2 A. 899 (1886).

82. People v. Connor, 295 Mich. 1, 294 N.W. 74 (1940) (prosecutor can impeach witness endorsed on indictment and called by him at defendant's insistence).

83. 3A Wigmore, Evidence (Chadbourn rev.) § 917; Dec.Dig. Witnesses ⊂⊃322.

84. F.R.Civ.P. 43(b) and corresponding state rules.

A witness who was the managing agent of the opposite party may be examined by leading questions and impeached under the Federal Rule, though he is no longer such at the time of trial. Melton v. O. F. Shearer & Sons, Inc., 436 F.2d 22 (6th Cir. 1970). For the text of the rule see § 25, n. 72, supra.

85. See, e. g., N.H.Rev.Stat.Ann. 516:24; S.D. Comp.L.1967, § 15-6-43(b).

86. Price v. Cox, 242 Ala. 568, 7 So.2d 288 (1942) (can contradict but not impeach); Tullis v. Tullis, 235 Iowa 428, 16 N.W.2d 623 (1944) (same). See 3A Wigmore, Evidence (Chadbourn rev.) § 916; C.J.S. Witnesses § 477d; Dec.Dig. Witnesses ⊂⊃324. But see Wells v. Goforth, 443 S.W.2d 155 (Mo.1969) (rejecting former rule that adverse party witness cannot be impeached by inconsistent state-

---

76. West's Ann.Cal.Evid.Code, § 785; Kan.Code of Civ.P. § 60-420. See also United States v. Freeman, 302 F.2d 347 (2d Cir.1962). But cf. N.J.R.Ev. 20 which allows one generally to impeach his own witness, but not by prior inconsistent statements except in case of surprise.

77. Uniform Rule 63(1); F.R.Ev. (R.D.1971) 801(d) (2).

78. People v. Michaels, 335 Ill. 590, 167 N.E. 857 (1929). Or "for the purpose of probing his recollection, recalling to his mind the statements he has previously made and drawing out an explanation of his apparent inconsistency." Bullard v. Pearsall, 53 N.Y. 230, 231 (1873); Hicks v. Coleman, 240 S.C. 223, 125 S.E.2d 473 (1962). Or to show why the proponent called the witness. Meyerson v. State, 181 Md. 105, 28 A.2d 833 (1942).

called twice, first by A and then by B, the courts have been troubled.[87] The most practical solution would be to hold that the prohibitory rule does not apply at all, and both A and B may freely impeach. Next most sensible is to say, as some courts do, that either A or B may impeach, at least by inconsistent statements, as to the testimony elicited on the other's call of the witness.[88] Another view that the witness is the witness of A, and A at any event is precluded,[89] has less to commend it. Surely the worst solution is to hold, as some states do, that both parties have adopted the witness and neither may impeach.[90]

39. Previous Statements as Substantive Evidence of the Facts Stated.

As previously indicated,[91] inconsistent statements of a witness, and consistent statements for that matter, are treated in this chapter upon the assumption that they may be inadmissible as substantive evidence on the issues in the case under the traditional hearsay rule as administered in the majority of jurisdictions. Of course, under traditional hearsay rule exceptions, particular inconsistent or even consistent prior statements of a witness may be admissible as substantive relevant evidence as well as for impeachment

purposes.[92] However, under another view prior statements of a person who is available as a witness at the trial or testifies may be considered substantive evidence, not barred by hearsay rule, perhaps not even classed as hearsay, and not restricted to the purpose of impeachment. This latter viewpoint is discused in Chapter 24.

40. Bias.[93]

The law recognizes the slanting effect upon human testimony of the emotions or feelings of the witness toward the parties or the self-interest of the witness in the outcome of the case. Partiality, or any acts, relationships or motives reasonably likely to produce it, may be proved to impeach credibility. The kinds and sources of partiality are too infinitely varied to be here reviewed, but a few of the common instances may be mentioned. *Favor or friendly feeling toward a party* may be evidenced by family [94] or business relationship,[95] by employment by a party [96] or his

---

ment although statute permitted examination by cross-examination).

87. See decisions collected 3A Wigmore, Evidence (Chadbourn rev.) § 913; C.J.S. Witnesses § 477e.

88. See, e. g., People v. Van Dyke, 414 Ill. 251, 111 N.E.2d 165 (1953) cert. denied 345 U.S. 978, noted 1953 U.Ill.L.F. 296; Arnold v. Manzella, 186 S.W. 2d 882 (Mo.App.1945); Dec.Dig. Witnesses ⟜380 (9).

89. Smith v. Provident Savings Life Ins. Co., 65 F. 765, 772 (6th Cir. 1895) (contradiction); Hanrahan v. New York Edison Co., 238 N.Y. 194, 144 N.E. 499 (1924) (conviction); Johnson v. State, 178 So. 2d 724 (Fla.App.1965) (but rule not applied since A could impeach because of surprise); Dec.Dig. Witnesses ⟜380(9).

90. Re Campbell, 100 Vt. 395, 138 A. 725 (1927).

91. See § 34, supra.

92. See § 34, supra.

93. 3A Wigmore, Evidence (Chadbourn rev.) §§ 943–969; Hale, Bias as Affecting Credibility, 1 Hastings L.J. 1 (1949); Dec.Dig. Witnesses ⟜363–378; C.J.S. Witnesses §§ 538–572; 58 Am.Jur. Witnesses §§ 706–722.

94. Christie v. Eager, 129 Conn. 62, 26 A.2d 352 (1942) (in suit by guest against motorist, duty of jury in weighing testimony of motorist and wife to consider fact the plaintiff is brother of motorist's wife, and that insurance company is the real defendant); Williams v. State, 44 Ala.App. 503, 214 So.2d 712 (1968) (court should have permitted defendant to show that state's witness was "kin" to alleged victim of defendant); 3A Wigmore, Evidence (Chadbourn rev.) § 949; C.J.S. Witnesses § 550.

95. Curry v. Fleer, 157 N.C. 16, 72 S.E. 626 (1911) (that witness for party had sold his land to him at big price, admissible); Aetna Ins. Co. v. Paddock, 301 F.2d 807 (5th Cir. 1962) (that witness had borrowed money from party); C.J.S. Witnesses § 551.

96. Arnall Mills v. Smallwood, 68 F.2d 57 (5th Cir. 1933) (witnesses' employment by defendant may be considered on credibility but is not, by itself, sufficient ground for disregarding their testimony); Dec.Dig. Witnesses ⟜369; C.J.S. Witnesses § 551.

insurer,[97] or by sexual relations,[98] or by particular conduct or expressions by the witness evincing such feeling.[99] It is commonly held in collision cases that when a witness appears for defendant the fact that he has made a claim against the defendant and has been paid a sum in settlement tends to show bias in favor of defendant.[1] Similarly, *hostility* toward a party may be shown by the fact that the witness has had a fight or quarrel with him,[2] or has a law-suit pending against him,[3] or has contributed to the defense [4] or employed special counsel to aid in prosecuting the party.[5] In criminal cases, the feeling of the witness toward the victim sheds light on his feeling toward the charge.[6] *Self-interest* of the witness is manifest when he is himself a party,[7] or a surety on the debt sued on.[8] It may be shown likewise as reflecting on his interest that he is being paid by a party to give evidence, even though payment beyond regular witness fees may as in the case of an expert be entirely proper.[9] *Self-interest* may

97. It is usually held that the relevancy of the showing that the witness is an employee of defendant's liability insurer outweighs the danger of prejudice in disclosing the fact of insurance. Westgate Oil Co. v. McAbee, 181 Okl. 487, 74 P.2d 1150 (1937); Nunnellee v. Nunnellee, 415 S.W.2d 114 (Ky.1967); and see numerous decisions, pro and con, collected in Annot., 4 A.L.R.2d 779–781.

98. Parsley v. Com., 306 S.W.2d 284 (Ky.1957) (rape; held evidence that defendant's fiancee who testified for him was pregnant by him was admissible to show her interest, as defendant's conviction would prevent his rendering aid and comfort to her); Dec.Dig. Witnesses ☞370(4); C.J.S. Witnesses § 548.

99. State v. McKee, 131 Kan. 263, 291 P. 950 (1930) (witness for accused may be cross-examined as to furnishing appearance bond and advancing attorneys' fees for him); Junior Hall, Inc. v. Charm Fashion Center, Inc., 264 N.C. 81, 140 S.E.2d 772 (1965) (witness, a friend of plaintiff, could be asked whether she had appeared as witness for plaintiff in similar suit of plaintiff against a third person); 3A Wigmore, Evidence (Chadbourn rev.) § 950.

1. See § 274, n. 94.

2. Fields v. State, 46 Fla. 84, 35 So. 185, 186 (1903) (error to exclude cross-examination of state's witness as to "personal difficulty" with defendant); 3A Wigmore, Evidence (Chadbourn rev.) § 950.

In Jacek v. Bacote, 135 Conn. 702, 68 A.2d 144 (1949) a question asking whether witness was prejudiced against negroes, to which race defendant belonged, was held proper. See also United States v. Kartman, 417 F.2d 893 (9th Cir. 1969) (holding it was error to foreclose inquiry whether government witness had prejudice against persons who participated in anti-draft and anti-war demonstrations and hence against defendant); and cases cited in United States v. Kartman, supra.

3. State v. Michelski, 66 N.D. 760, 268 N.W. 713 (1936) (manslaughter by automobile; held defendant entitled to show that state's witnesses had civil actions against defendant arising from same collision, on far-fetched ground that conviction would be admissible to impeach defendant in civil actions); Blake v. State, 365 S.W.2d 795 (Tex.Cr.App.1963)

(case involving embezzlement). But, on similar facts, the evidence was excluded in State v. Lawson, 128 W.Va. 136, 36 S.E.2d 26 (1945) and this was held a proper exercise of discretion. Cases are collected in 3A Wigmore, Evidence (Chadbourn rev.) § 949, notes 5, 6; C.J.S. Witnesses § 546; Dec.Dig. Witnesses ☞370(3).

4. State v. Cerar, 60 Utah 208, 207 P. 597 (1922).

5. Brogden v. State, 33 Ala.App. 132, 31 So.2d 144 (1947); State v. Wray, 217 N.C. 167, 7 S.E.2d 468 (1940) (court assumes fact relevant on bias, but upholds exclusion as being discretionary and not shown prejudicial).

6. Richardson v. State, 91 Tex.Cr. 318, 239 S.W. 218 (1922) (witness for defense said deceased "was dead in hell, where he ought to be").

7. Accordingly, it is held in some jurisdictions that the court, on request, must charge that the jury in weighing the party's testimony is to bear in mind his interest in the outcome. Denver City Tramway Co. v. Norton, 141 F. 599, 608 (8th Cir. 1905); C.J.S. Witnesses §§ 542, 543.

8. Southern Ry. Co. v. Bunnell, 138 Ala. 247, 36 So. 380, 383 (1903) (question whether employee witness had given indemnity bond to employer defendant, proper).

9. Grutski v. Kline, 352 Pa. 401, 43 A.2d 142 (1945); 3A Wigmore, Evidence (Chadbourn rev.) § 961, n. 2. A medical witness may be asked if the payment of his fee depends on the outcome of the case. Most cases hold that the judge in his discretion may permit the opponent to bring out the amount of extra compensation the expert witness has received or will receive or expects to receive. Current v. Columbia Gas of Kentucky, 383 S.W.2d 139 (Ky. 1964) (judge limited attack to showing that witness was paid unspecified extra compensation; affirmed); cases cited in Annot., 33 A.L.R.2d 1170. In Reed v. Philadelphia Transp. Co., 171 Pa.Super 60, 90 A.2d 371 (1952) the judge sustained objection to the question, "How much do you expect to get paid for testifying here today?"; the ruling was held reversible error. A witness as to value may be asked how much he has received from the defendant city for similar testimony in the past year.

be shown also in a criminal case when the witness testifies for the state and it is shown that an indictment is pending against him,[10] or that he is an accomplice or co-indictee in the crime on trial.[11] Self-interest in an extreme form may be manifested in *corrupt* activity by the witness, such as seeking to bribe another witness,[12] or by taking or offering to take a bribe to testify falsely,[13] or by the making of other similar charges on other occasions without foundation.[14]

City of Chicago v. Van Schaack Bros. Chem. Works, 330 Ill. 264, 161 N.E. 486 (1928).

10. United States v. Padgent, 432 F.2d 701 (2d Cir. 1970) (error to refuse to allow defense to bring out that government witness had jumped bail and was not being prosecuted for that offense); People v. Dillwood, 106 Cal. 129, 39 P. 438 (1895) (pendency of charges against witness as motive for testifying favorably to prosecution); State v. Ponthier, 136 Mont. 198, 346 P.2d 974 (1959) (same, citing many authorities); 3A Wigmore, Evidence (Chadbourn rev.) § 967, n. 2.

The pressure to curry favor with the prosecutor is not present in a civil suit, and in a collision suit where plaintiff introduced as witness the driver of one of the cars, it was held error to permit the defendant to impeach him by showing that he had been indicted for driving while intoxicated on the occasion in question and that the indictment was pending because of its liability to misuse as evidence of his guilt. Holden v. Berberich, 351 Mo. 995, 174 S.W.2d 791, 149 A.L.R. 929 (1943), annotated on this point. But if it had appeared that plaintiff had instigated and was controlling the prosecution of the criminal case a different result might be warranted.

11. People v. Simard, 314 Mich. 624, 23 N.W.2d 106 (1946) (defendant should have been allowed to ask state's witness if she had not been arrested for participation in same crime); 3A Wigmore, Evidence (Chadbourn rev.) § 967.

12. People v. Alcalde, 24 Cal.2d 177, 148 P.2d 627 (1944); 3A Wigmore, Evidence (Chadbourn rev.) § 960. Or writing a letter designed to intimidate another witness into giving perjured testimony. State v. Moore, 180 Ore. 502, 176 P.2d 631 (1947).

13. See Martin v. Barnes, 7 Wis. 239, 241, 242 (1858) (bargain between doctor-witness and plaintiff that she should pretend to be injured from fall, and they should share recovery): 3A Wigmore, Evidence (Chadbourn rev.) § 961.

14. But the cases are conflicting. See 3A Wigmore, Evidence (Chadbourn rev.) § 963, note 2; Annot., 69 A.L.R.2d 593, 602. Among those supporting this kind of impeachment is People v. Evans, 72 Mich. 367, 40 N.W. 473 (1888) (rape upon daughter: other false charges by daughter against other men, al-

Preliminary question.[15] A majority of the courts impose the requirement of a foundation question as in the case of impeachment by prior inconsistent statements. Before the witness can be impeached by calling other witnesses to prove acts or declarations showing bias, the witness under attack must first have been asked about these facts on cross-examination.[16] A minority decline to impose this requirement.[17] Fairness to the witness is most often given as the reason for the requirement, but the saving of time by making unnecessary the extrinsic evidence seems even more important. Some courts, adhering to the analogy of inconsistent statements, make a difference between declarations and conduct evidencing bias, requiring the preliminary question as to the former and not as to the latter.[18] But as suggested in a leading English case, words and conduct are usually intermingled in proof of bias, and "nice and subtle distinctions" should be avoided in shaping this rule of trial practice.[19]

---

lowed). Such charges may also evidence mental abnormality, see § 45, infra. Compare cases involving the question whether a plaintiff may be cross-examined about the previous institution of other suits and claims to show "claim-mindedness." Mintz v. Premier Cab Ass'n, Inc., 75 U.S.App.D.C. 389, 127 F.2d 744 (1942) (yes); Cammarata v. Payton, 316 S.W.2d 474 (Mo.1958) (no).

15. 3A Wigmore, Evidence (Chadbourn rev.) § 964; Annot., 87 A.L.R.2d 407; Dec.Dig. Witnesses ⊜373; C.J.S. Witnesses § 566.

16. People v. Payton, 72 Ill.App.2d 240, 218 N.E.2d 518 (1966); State v. Shaw, 93 Ariz. 40, 378 P.2d 487 (1963); Annot., 87 A.L.R.2d 407, 431.

As in the case of inconsistent statements, the preliminary question as to declarations showing bias should call attention to time, place, and persons involved. See Wright v. State, 133 Ark. 16, 201 S.W. 1107 (1918); State v. Harmon, 21 Wash.2d 581, 152 P.2d 314 (1944); cases cited in Annot., 87 A.L.R.2d 407, 431.

17. Kidd v. People, 97 Colo. 480, 51 P.2d 1020 (1935) (witness' threat to "pin something on" another witness unless he testified for the state); People v. Michalow, 229 N.Y. 325, 128 N.E. 228 (1920); cases cited in Annot., 87 A.L.R.2d 407.

18. See cases cited in Annot., 87 A.L.R.2d 407, 418–420, 423–426.

19. See the excerpt from the opinion of Abbott, C. J. in the Queen's Case, 2 Brod. & B. 284, 129

Better require a "foundation" as to both or neither. It seems that jurisdictions recognizing the requirement should recognize also a discretion in the judge to dispense with it when mere matters of indisputable relationship, such as kinship, are concerned, or where the foundation was overlooked and it is not feasible to recall the witness, or where other exceptional circumstances make it unfair to insist on the prerequisite.

Cross-examination and extrinsic evidence; main circumstances. We have seen that in the majority of states the impeacher must inquire as to the facts of bias on cross-examination as the first step in impeachment. It seems arguable that if the witness fully admits the facts claimed to show bias, the impeacher should not be allowed to repeat the same attack by calling other witnesses to the admitted facts.[20] And it is held that when the main circumstances from which the bias proceeds have been proven, the trial judge has a discretion to determine how far the details, whether on cross-examination or by other witness, may be allowed to be brought out.[21] After all, impeachment is not a central matter, and the trial judge, though he may not deny a reasonable opportunity at either stage to prove the bias of the witness, has a

discretion to control the extent to which the proof may go.[22] He has the responsibility for seeing that the sideshow does not take over the circus. On the other hand, if the witness on cross-examination denies or does not fully admit the facts claimed to show bias, the attacker has the right to prove those facts by extrinsic evidence. In courtroom parlance, facts showing bias are not "collateral,"[23] and the cross-examiner is not required to "take the answer" of the witness,[24] but may call other witnesses to prove them.[25]

41. Character: In General.

The character of a witness for truthfulness or mendacity is relevant circumstantial evidence on the question of the truth of particular testimony of the witness. The discussion of the rules which have developed as to character-impeachment will reveal certain general questions of balancing policies. Among them are these: How far in any particular situation does the danger of unfair prejudice against the witness and the party calling him from this type of impeachment outweigh the probable value of the light shed on credibility? Again, should the field of character-impeachment be limited so far as practicable to attack on the particular character-trait of truthfulness or should it ex-

---

Eng.Rep. 976 (1820) as quoted in Annot., 16 A.L.R. 989.

20. This is the prevailing holding as to inconsistent statements, see § 37, supra, and similar reasons apply here, pro and con.

21. State v. Malmberg, 14 N.D. 523, 105 N.W. 614, 616 (1905) (village political rivalry; proof of main facts, matter of right; extent of proof of details, discretionary; here unduly curbed); Brink v. Stratton, 176 N.Y. 150, 68 N.E. 148 (1903) (similar); People v. Dye, 356 Mich. 271, 96 N.W.2d 788 (1959) (trial court permitted examination into details; approved); Dods v. Harrison, 51 Wash.2d 446, 319 P.2d 558 (1958) (trial court's refusal to permit examination as to details upheld); 3A Wigmore, Evidence (Chadbourn rev.) § 951, note 2; C.J.S. Witnesses § 556. A few courts have held that if the witness admits bias in general terms this precludes further inquiry. See, e. g., Walker v. State, 74 Ga.App. 48, 39 S.E.2d 75, 77 (1946); 3A Wigmore, Evidence (Chadbourn rev.) § 951, note 2.

22. Glass v. Bosworth, 113 Vt. 303, 34 A.2d 113 (1943) (wide scope on cross-examination, in court's discretion); People v. Lustig, 206 N.Y. 162, 99 N.E. 183, 186 (1912) (extent of testimony by other witnesses in court's discretion). See also Marcus v. City of Pittsburgh, 415 Pa. 252, 203 A.2d 317 (1964) (trial judge abused discretion by permitting examination which entered into prejudicial detail that was not impeaching).

23. State v. Day, 339 Mo. 74, 95 S.W.2d 1183, 1184 (1936); Smith v. Hockenberry, 146 Mich. 7, 109 N.W. 23, 24 (1906); cases cited in C.J.S. Witnesses § 559.

24. Smith v. United States, 283 F.2d 16 (6th Cir. 1960) cert. denied 365 U.S. 847 (dictum); 6 Wigmore, Evidence § 1005(b) (c). See references to "taking the answer" in § 47, infra and § 36, supra.

25. Smith v. Hornkohl, 166 Neb. 702, 90 N.W.2d 347 (1958) (dictum); 3A Wigmore, Evidence (Chadbourn rev.) § 943; C.J.S. Witnesses §§ 563, 565.

tend to "general" character for its undoubted though more remote bearing upon truthfulness, on the notion that the greater includes the less? [26]

It seems probable, moreover, that the tendency is to use this form of attack more and more sparingly. It was part of the melodrama of the pioneer trial to find "the villian of the piece." It fits less comfortably into the more businesslike atmosphere of the present courtroom. Moreover, as a method of advocacy, the danger to the attacker is great if the attack fails of its mark, or if it is pressed too far. Finally, judges and lawyers are more and more conscious of their duty of fairness to witnesses. The Code of Professional Responsibility of the American Bar Association states the matter thus:

"In appearing in his professional capacity before a tribunal, a lawyer shall not:

. . .

(2) Ask any question that he has no reasonable basis to believe is relevant to the case and that is intended to degrade a witness or other person. . . . " [27]

42. Character: Misconduct, for Which There Has Been No Criminal Conviction. [28]

The English common law tradition of "cross-examination to credit" permits counsel to inquire into the associations and personal history of the witness, including any particular misconduct which would tend to discredit his character, though it has not been the basis for conviction of crime. [29] (This is the kind of misconduct referred to in this section unless otherwise indicated.) Under the common law tradition the courts trusted to the disciplined discretion of the bar to avoid abuses. [30] In this country, there is a confusing variety of decisions, occasionally even in the same jurisdiction. At present, however, it can be said generally that the majority of courts limit cross-examination concerning acts of misconduct as an attack upon character to acts which have some relation to the credibility of the witness. [31] Some courts permit an attack upon character by fairly wide-open cross-examination upon acts of misconduct which show bad moral character and can have only an attenuated relation to credibility. [32] Finally, a substantial number of courts prohibit altogether cross-examination as to acts of misconduct

---

26. See the general discussion of relevancy and its counterweights in Ch. 16, infra, and of the relevancy of character evidence in various other situations in Ch. 17, infra.

27. American Bar Association, Code of Professional Responsibility, Disciplinary Rule 7–106(C) (2), p. 88 (1969). Compare the phrasing of the duty in West's Ann.Cal.Bus. and Prof.Code, § 6068: "To abstain from all offensive personality, and to advance no fact prejudicial to the honor or reputation of a party or witness, unless required by the justice of the cause with which he is charged."

28. 3A Wigmore, Evidence (Chadbourn rev.) §§ 981–987; Dec.Dig. Witnesses ☞344, 349; C.J.S. Witnesses §§ 491–531.

29. 3A Wigmore, Evidence (Chadbourn rev.) §§ 983–986; Phipson, Evidence §§ 541, 1551, 1552 (10th ed. 1963).

30. See quotations from Stephen and Birkenhead in 3A Wigmore, Evidence (Chadbourn rev.) § 983; and 13 Halsbury's Laws of England, Evidence § 836 (2d ed. 1934) ("There are, also, certain limits, which must be determined by the discretion of the judge to the questions which may be asked affecting a witness's credit . . .").

31. Vogel v. Sylvester, 148 Conn. 666, 174 A.2d 122 (1961); Schreiberg v. Southern Coatings & Chemical Co., 231 S.C. 69, 97 S.E.2d 214 (1957); C.J.S. Witnesses §§ 502–506, 515.

32. People v. Sorge, 301 N.Y. 198, 93 N.E.2d 637 (1950); State v. Jones, 215 Tenn. 206, 385 S.W.2d 80 (1964); C.J.S. Witnesses, § 515d. See Annot., 90 A.L.R. 870. Some decisions have admitted misconduct which either bears directly on veracity or indicates such moral depravity "as would likely render him insensible to the obligations of an oath." Coulston v. United States, 51 F.2d 178, 181 (10th Cir. 1931) (morphine transactions, excluded); Miller v. Territory, 149 F. 330, 338 (8th Cir. 1906). To meet this test the conduct need not be criminal. People v. Johnston, 228 N.Y. 332, 127 N.E. 186 (1920) (sending money to an accused prisoner for him to buy witnesses). The fact that the witness has been dishonorably discharged from the army was held so doubtful in its implications as to "moral character" as to warrant the judge, in discretion, to exclude the inquiry. Kelley v. State, 226 Ind. 148, 78 N.E.2d 547 (1948).

for impeachment purposes.[33] This latter view is arguably the fairest and most expedient practice because of the dangers otherwise of prejudice (particularly if the witness is a party), of distraction and confusion, of abuse by the asking of unfounded questions, and of the difficulties, as demonstrated in the cases on appeal, of ascertaining whether particular acts relate to character for truthfulness.[34]

The above-mentioned notions should be distinguished from the showing of conduct which indicates bias and prejudice and the showing of conduct as an admission.[35]

In this country, the danger of victimizing witnesses and of undue prejudice to the parties has led most of our courts which permit the showing of acts of misconduct under the rules mentioned above, to recognize that

cross-examination concerning acts of misconduct is subject to a discretionary control by the trial judge.[36] Some of the factors that may, it seems, sway discretion, are (1) whether the testimony of the witness under attack is crucial or unimportant, (2) the relevancy of the act of misconduct to truthfulness, depending upon the rule followed in the jurisdiction in that respect,[37] (3) the nearness or remoteness of the misconduct to the time of trial,[38] (4) whether the matter inquired into is such as to lead to time-consuming and distracting explanations on cross-examination or re-examination,[39] (5) whether there is undue humiliation of the witness and undue prejudice.

In the formative period of Evidence law, there came to be recognized, as a sort of vague corollary of the privilege against self-incrimination, a privilege of a witness not to answer questions calling for answers which would degrade or disgrace him, provided such questions were not material to the issues in the case.[40] The privilege, though sporadically recognized from time to time during the

33. Christie v. Brewer, 374 S.W.2d 908 (Tex.Civ. App.1964); Sparks v. State, 366 S.W.2d 591 (Tex. Cr.App.1963); Commonwealth v. Schaffner, 146 Mass. 512, 16 N.E. 280 (1888) (but see Campbell v. Ashler, 320 Mass. 475, 70 N.E.2d 302 (1946) (mentioning discretion); Berliner v. Schoenberg, 117 Pa.Super. 254, 178 A. 330 (1935); Commonwealth v. Ornato, 191 Pa.Super. 581, 159 A.2d 223 (1960), aff'd 400 Pa. 626, 163 A.2d 90 (1960) cert. denied 364 U.S. 912; Smith v. Abel, 211 Ore. 571, 316 P.2d 793 (1957) (citing ORS 45:600); State v. Albe, 10 Ariz.App. 545, 460 P.2d 651 (1969) (dictum); State v. Lampshire, 74 Wash.2d 888, 447 P.2d 727 (1969) (but the judge has discretion to permit cross-examination of prosecuting witness, in prosecution for carnal knowledge, as to other sexual acts); C.J.S. Witnesses § 515b. Statutes prohibit the showing of acts of misconduct for impeachment in some states. See, e. g., Idaho Code § 9–1302; West's Ann.Cal.Evid. Code § 787; N.J. R.Ev. 22.

34. Uniform Rule 22(d) provides that "evidence of specific instances of his conduct relevant only as tending to prove a trait of his character, shall be inadmissible." Another theory, akin to but distinguishable from misconduct as showing character, is the theory that on cross-examination the examiner is entitled to place the witness in his setting by showing his residence and occupation. See § 29, supra. As to whether this principle permits questions as to a disreputable occupation, see cases pro and con collected in Dec.Dig. Witnesses ☞344(4); Annot., 1 A.L.R. 1402.

35. See § 40, supra, re bias and §§ 269–275, infra, re admissions by conduct. Inconsistent conduct is yet another subject. See § 37, supra.

36. Lehr v. Rogers, 16 Mich.App. 585, 168 N.W.2d 636 (1969) (court excluded questions concerning stealing as cause for discharge of witness from prior employment and that witness lied in subsequent investigation; affirmed with remark evidence could have been admitted); People v. Sorge, 301 N.Y. 198, 93 N.E.2d 637 (1950) (in abortion prosecution, accused properly cross-examined as to previous abortions; manner and extent in judge's discretion); State v. Neal, 222 N.C. 546, 23 S.E.2d 911 (1943) (accused in murder case properly asked about previous cutting affrays, larceny, vagrancy, nuisance and violation of the prohibition law, in judge's "sound discretion"); C.J.S. Witnesses § 515j.

37. See n. 30, 31, supra.

38. Shailer v. Bullock, 78 Conn. 65, 61 A. 65, 67 (1905); C.J.S. Witnesses § 515g.

39. See Robinson v. Atterbury, 135 Conn. 517, 66 A.2d 593 (1949).

F.R.Ev. (R.D.1971) 608(b) allows cross-examination on specific misconduct if relevant to truthfulness, not outweighed by prejudice, and not harassing or unduly embarrassing.

40. See 3A Wigmore, Evidence (Chadbourn rev.) §§ 984, 986(3).

1800s,[41] has in the present century been generally abandoned,[42] except as it is encysted in the Codes of a few states.[43] The practical protection to the witness is not so effective as that given by courts which prohibit such cross-examination altogether, since the prohibitory rule will be invoked by counsel or by the court of its own motion, whereas the privilege must be claimed by the witness, and such a claim is almost as degrading as an affirmative answer.

In jurisdictions which permit character-impeachment by proof of misconduct for which no conviction has been had, an important curb is the accepted rule that proof is limited to what can be brought out on cross-examination. Thus, if the witness stands his ground and denies the alleged misconduct, the examiner must "take his answer," not that he may not further cross-examine to extract an admission,[44] but in the sense that he may not call other witnesses to prove the discrediting acts.[45]

A further important curb is the privilege against self-incrimination. While a witness who without objecting makes a partial disclosure of incriminating matter cannot then invoke the privilege when asked to make the disclosure complete,[46] it seems clear that the mere act of testifying cannot be regarded as a waiver of the privilege with respect to inquiry on cross-examination into criminal activities for the purpose of attacking his credibility.[47] While an accused, unlike an ordinary witness, has an option whether to testify at all, exacting such a waiver as the price of taking the stand leaves little of the right to testify in one's own behalf.[48]

43. Character: Conviction of Crime.[49]

At common law the conviction of a person of treason or any felony, or of a misdemeanor involving dishonesty *(crimen falsi)*, or the obstruction of justice, rendered the convicted person altogether incompetent as a witness.

41. See 3A Wigmore, Evidence (Chadbourn rev.) §§ 986(3) note 13, 987.

42. Among decisions rejecting the privilege are Wallace v. State, 41 Fla. 547, 26 So. 713, 722 (1899); State v. Pfefferle, 36 Kan. 90, 92, 12 P. 406, 408 (1886) (degrading character of question factor for judge's discretion); Carroll v. State, 32 Tex.Cr.R. 431, 24 S.W. 100 (1893); State v. Carter, 1 Ariz. App. 57, 399 P.2d 191 (1965) (subject to discretion of the court).

43. Georgia Code, §§ 38–1205, 38–1711 (facts "which shall tend to bring infamy or disgrace or public contempt upon himself or any member of his family"); Iowa, I.C.A. §§ 622.14, 622.15 (answers which would "expose him to public ignominy," with exceptions); Montana, R.C.M.1947, § 93–2101–2 (privilege not to give "an answer which will have a direct tendency to degrade his character, unless it be to the very fact in issue, or to a fact from which the fact in issue would be presumed" and must answer to a conviction for felony); Nebraska, R.S.1943, §§ 25–1210, 25–1214 (like Iowa, supra); Nevada, N.R.S. 48–130 (like Montana, supra); Oregon, ORS 44.070 (like Montana, supra); Utah, U.C.A.1953, 78–24–9 (like Montana, supra).

44. People v. Sorge, 301 N.Y. 198, 93 N.E.2d 637 (1950) (when witness denies, examiner in good faith may question further in hope of inducing witness to change answer).

45. State v. Bowman, 232 N.C. 374, 61 S.E.2d 107 (1950) (improper for state to attack credibility of

defendant's witness by calling other witnesses to testify to her acts of misconduct); Martinez v. Avila, 76 N.M. 372, 415 P.2d 59 (1966); C.J.S. Witnesses § 516; 3A Wigmore, Evidence (Chadbourn rev.) § 979.

46. For more detailed discussion, see § 140, infra.

47. Coil v. United States, 343 F.2d 573 (8th Cir. 1965) cert. denied 382 U.S. 821; F.R.Ev. (R.D. 1971) 608(b).

Statements in such cases as People v. Sorge, 301 N.Y. 198, 93 N.E.2d 637 (1950), that a witness, including the defendant in criminal cases, may be asked on cross-examination "about any vicious or criminal act in his life that has a bearing on his credibility" must be read against a surprising oversight of the constitutional limitation. When the question was raised in People v. Johnson, 228 N.Y. 332, 127 N.E. 186 (1920), the court conceded that the waiver resulting from an accused taking the stand did not extend to facts affecting credibility only.

48. F.R.Ev. (R.D.1971) 608(b) (no waiver). See Griffin v. California, 380 U.S. 609 (1965); Ferguson v. Georgia, 365 U.S. 570 (1961). Surely, today the right of an accused to testify in his own behalf must be of constitutional dimension.

49. 3A Wigmore, Evidence (Chadbourn rev.) §§ 980, 980a, 985–987; Ladd, Credibility Tests, 89 U.Pa. L.Rev. 166, 174 (1940); Dec.Dig. Witnesses ⟨=345; 98 C.J.S. Witnesses §§ 507, 515i(3) (c), 534e; 58 Am.Jur. Witnesses §§ 734–753.

These were said to be "infamous" crimes.[50] By statutes which are virtually universal in the common law world, this primitive absolutism has been abandoned and the disqualification for conviction of crime has been abrogated, and by specific provision or by decision has been reduced to a mere ground of impeachment of credibility. Just as the common law definition of disqualifying crimes was not very precise, so also the abrogating statutes are correspondingly indefinite,[51] and the resulting definitions of crimes for which a conviction[52] shall be ground of impeachment vary widely among the states.

A few jurisdictions seem to adhere to the loose common law definition, described above, of "infamous crimes."[53] The California Code[54] and some other codes[55] specify only "felonies," a limitation which is at least simple to apply. Similarly easy is the administration of a rule which includes "any felony or misdemeanor." This is the construction which some of the courts place upon statutes worded in terms of "crime" or "any crime."[56] But most courts have been unwilling to accept such simple mechanical tests, and have read into such general statutes the requirement that as to misdemeanors at least, the offense must be one involving "moral turpitude."[57] Thus does the serpent of uncertain-

50. Greenleaf, Evidence § 373 (1842); 2 Wigmore, Evidence § 520.

51. See, e. g., Connecticut, C.G.S.A. § 52–145: "No person shall be disqualified as a witness in any action by reason of his interest in the event of the same as a party or otherwise, or of his disbelief in the existence of a Supreme Being, or of his conviction of crime; but such interest or conviction may be shown for the purpose of affecting his credit"; Iowa, I.C.A. § 622.1: "Every human being of sufficient capacity to understand the obligation of an oath is a competent witness in all cases, except as otherwise declared"; § 622.2: "Facts which have heretofore caused the exclusion of testimony may still be shown for the purpose of lessening its credibility"; Minnesota, M.S.A. § 610.49: "Every person convicted of crime shall be a competent witness in any civil or criminal proceeding, but his conviction may be proved for the purpose of affecting the weight of his testimony, either by the record or by his cross-examination, upon which he shall answer any proper question relevant to that inquiry; and the party cross-examining shall not be concluded by his answer thereto", and other statutes collected in 2 Wigmore, Evidence § 488.

52. Conviction, of course, is the present requirement, and though it was once thought otherwise, there cannot be inquiry about an accusation, though official, such as an arrest, indictment, or information. Hurley v. State, 6 Md.App. 348, 251 A.2d 241 (1969) (charged with strong armed robbery; but error held not prejudicial); Commonwealth v. Ross, 434 Pa. 167, 252 A.2d 661 (1969) (arrest; opinion mentions exception as to indictment for same or closely related offense); Johnson v. State, 82 Nev. 338, 418 P.2d 495 (1966) (arrest; cross-examination at preliminary hearing); State v. Goodwin, 29 Wash.2d 276, 186 P.2d 935 (1947) (indictment); 3A Wigmore, Evidence (Chadbourn rev.) § 980a. Contra: People v. Brocato, 17 Mich. App. 277, 169 N.W.2d 483 (1969) (holding defendant as witness may not be so inquired into, but other witnesses of defendant may be in the discretion of

the judge); Annot., 20 A.L.R.2d 1421. In collision cases, proof is often sought to be made, under guise of impeachment, that one of the drivers has been arrested for negligent driving at the time of the collision. It may have a remote bearing upon bias, but its prejudicial use by the jury as hearsay evidence of guilt is an overweening danger, and the courts usually exclude it. See Holden v. Berberich, 351 Mo. 995, 174 S.W.2d 791 (1943) (cross-examination of driver as to indictment for driving while intoxicated at time of collision); Annot., 149 A.L.R. 935.

53. People v. Birdette, 22 Ill.2d 577, 177 N.E.2d 170 (1961) (does not include malicious mischief, petty larceny, possession of narcotics or disorderly conduct); see also Drazen v. New Haven Taxicab Co., 95 Conn. 500, 111 A. 861 (1920) (defining infamous crimes as those involving moral turpitude); Cousins v. State, 230 Md. 2, 185 A.2d 488 (1962) (discussing statute as to "infamous crimes"; pointing out convictions include those involving moral turpitude or having tendency to show witness should not be believed).

54. West's Ann.Cal.Evid.Code, § 788.

55. See Idaho I.C. § 9–1209.

56. State v. Hurt, 49 N.J. 114, 228 A.2d 673 (1967) ("crime" includes misdemeanors, regardless of moral turpitude); Sullivan v. State, 333 P.2d 591 (Okl.Cr.1958) ("conviction of crime" not limited to offenses involving moral turpitude).

57. Sims v. Callahan, 269 Ala. 216, 112 So.2d 776 (1959) (extensive review of prior Ala. law); State v. Jenness, 143 Me. 380, 62 A.2d 867 (1948) (Me. Rev.Stat. c. 113, § 127, "felony, any larceny or any other crime involving moral turpitude" does not extend to illegal possession and sale of liquor); Smith v. State, 346 S.W.2d 611 (Tex.Cr.App.1961) (conviction for selling and handling whiskey did not involve moral turpitude); Tasker v. Com., 202 Va. 1019, 121 S.E.2d 459 (1961) (misdemeanor did

ty crawl into the Eden of trial administration. Still more uncertain is the rule that gives the trial judge discretion on the basis of whether the particular conviction substantially affects the credibility of the witness.[58] Under the rule requiring moral turpitude, it seems questionable whether the creation of a detailed catalog [59] of crimes involving "moral turpitude" and its application at the trial and on appeal is not a waste of judicial energy in view of the size of the problem. Moreover, shifting the burden to the judge's discretion raises problems as to the adequacy of his information or basis upon which to exercise his discretion. A rule involving a clear and certain definition has advantages in administration. The proposal of the Uniform Rules to limit impeachment to conviction of crimes "involving dishonesty or false statement" [60] is a fairly definite but not arbitrary criterion.

Convictions in another state [61] or in the federal court [62] are usable to impeach. Though a judgment against a lawyer of suspension or disbarment for criminal misconduct is not technically a conviction, it has been held to be provable to impeach.[63] In statutes relating to proceedings in juvenile courts it is frequently provided that an adjudication of delinquency shall not be used in evidence against the child in any other court and shall not be deemed a "conviction." These statutes are usually construed as precluding the finding from being used as a conviction to impeach credibility.[64]

---

not involve moral turpitude); State v. Fournier, 123 Vt. 439, 193 A.2d 924 (1963) (2 Vt.Stat.Ann. § 1608 "conviction of a crime involving moral turpitude").

In actions for injuries incurred in highway accidents, attempts are often made to cross-examine the participants about previous convictions for traffic offenses, but it is usually held that these convictions do not show moral turpitude or affect veracity. Nesbit v. Cumberland Contracting Co., 196 Md. 36, 75 A.2d 339 (1950) (allowing plaintiff to be cross-examined about traffic offenses was improper, notwithstanding he had answered on cross-examination that he considered himself a good driver).

Convictions for violations of city ordinances cannot usually be used. See, e. g., Caldwell v. State, 282 Ala. 713, 213 So.2d 919 (1968). Contra: Scott v. State, 445 P.2d 39 (Alaska 1968) cert. denied 393 U.S. 1082 (violation of city ordinance is a "crime" as that term is used in governing rule).

58. Johnson v. State, 4 Md.App. 648, 244 A.2d 632 (1968); Taylor v. Walter, 15 Mich.App. 361, 166 N.W.2d 646 (1968) (unrelated misdemeanors in civil cases); Mullin v. Builders Develop. & Finance Serv., Inc., 62 Wash.2d 202, 381 P.2d 970 (1963) (in civil cases).

59. For an example, see Drazen v. New Haven Taxicab Co., 95 Conn. 500, 111 A. 861, 863 (1920).

60. Uniform Rule 21: "Evidence of the conviction of a witness for a crime not involving dishonesty or false statement shall be inadmissible for the purpose of impairing his credibility. . . ." F.R. Ev. (R.D.1971) 609(a) limits provable convictions to crimes "punishable by death or imprisonment

in excess of one year," or involving "dishonesty or false statement regardless of the punishment."

The proposition that at least some crimes are relevant to credibility is generally accepted. The reasons for limiting inquiry into specific instances of misconduct which have not resulted in a conviction, discussed in the preceding section, tend to disappear: danger of self-incrimination is usually absent; risks of confusion and surprise are lessened; and risk of prejudice to a party from proof of conviction of an ordinary witness is so slight as scarcely to arouse comment. The preliminary part of this present section is devoted to witnesses generally; the much more troublesome problems which arise when the witness is the accused in a criminal case are discussed in the text beginning at n. 87, infra.

61. City of Boston v. Santosuosso, 307 Mass. 302, 30 N.E.2d 278 (1940); State v. Velsir, 61 Wyo. 476, 159 P.2d 371 (1945).

62. See Burford v. Com., 179 Va. 752, 20 S.E.2d 509 (1942) where it was assumed that the federal conviction would be admissible if it met the Virginia standard of felony or misdemeanor affecting credibility. A state conviction may be proved in the federal court. United States v. Skidmore, 123 F.2d 604 (7th Cir. 1941) (semble).

Convictions under the laws of another jurisdiction are treated by analogy to local crimes. People v. Kirkpatrick, 413 Ill. 595, 110 N.E.2d 519 (1953) (federal conviction of transporting stolen car in interstate commerce analogous to receiving stolen property, not infamous under state law and hence error to admit).

63. Lansing v. Michigan Central Ry. Co., 143 Mich. 48, 106 N.W. 692 (1906); State v. Pearson, 39 N.J. Super. 50, 120 A.2d 468 (1956) (and cases cited therein).

64. People v. Peele, 12 N.Y.2d 890, 188 N.E.2d 265, 237 N.Y.S.2d 999 (1963); State v. Coffman, 360 Mo. 782, 230 S.W.2d 761 (1950); C.J.S. Witnesses § 510. But compare the views expressed in 3A Wigmore,

A pardon does not prevent the use of the conviction to impeach,[65] nor by the predominant view does the pendency of an appeal from the conviction,[66] but most courts hold that lapse of time may have this effect, and that a conviction too remote in time may be excluded by the judge if in his discretion he finds that under the circumstances it lacks probative value.[67] The authorities are divided respecting the use of a judgment based upon a plea of *nolo contendere*.[68]

The general rule in other situations is that proof of an official record must if feasible be made by the use of a certified or examined copy, in preference to oral testimony of its contents.[69] The rule was applied in England to proof of records of conviction, so as to preclude the cross-examiner from asking about convictions.[70] This practice still lingers in a few states,[71] but the inconvenience of the requirement, and the obvious reliability of the answer of a witness acknowledging his own conviction, have led most jurisdictions, by statute or decision, to permit the proof to be made either by production of the record or a copy, or by the oral statement of the convicted witness himself.[72] Here the cross-examiner need not "lay a foundation" for proof by copy or record,[73] nor is he bound to "take the answer" if the witness denies the conviction, but may prove it by the record.[74]

Evidence (Chadbourn rev.) §§ 924a, 980(7). He collects the statutes in § 196, note 5. In re Gault, 387 U.S. 1 (1967), fixing certain procedural requirements in juvenile cases, does not bear directly upon this subject. F.R.Ev. (R.D.1971) 609(d) provides for use of juvenile adjudications under some circumstances when the juvenile is not the accused. See Giles v. Maryland, 386 U.S. 66 (1967).

65. Richards v. United States, 89 U.S.App.D.C. 354, 192 F.2d 602 (1951) (one judge dissenting); Vedin v. McConnell, 22 F.2d 753 (9th Cir. 1927); C.J.S. Witnesses, § 508; Annot., 30 A.L.R.2d 893. Contra: West's Ann.Cal.Evid.Code, § 788. See also F.R.Ev. (R.D.1971) 609(c) (pardon, annulment, or certificate of rehabilitation prevents use of conviction, if procedure of issuance required substantial showing of rehabilitation or if issuance based upon innocence).

66. People v. Bey, 42 Ill.2d 139, 246 N.E.2d 287 (1969); Suggs v. State, 6 Md.App. 231, 250 A.2d 670 (1969), and the many cases cited therein. Contra: Campbell v. United States, 85 U.S.App.D.C. 133, 176 F.2d 45 (1949); cases cited in Suggs v. State, supra; C.J.S. Witnesses § 507f, and Annot., 16 A.L.R.3d 726.

67. Fire Ass'n of Philadelphia v. Weathered, 62 F.2d 78 (5th Cir. 1932) (court in discretion properly excluded convictions 30 and 50 years old); Lanier v. State, 43 Ala.App. 38, 179 So.2d 167 (1965) (not abuse of discretion to admit conviction 30 years before trial). Decisions are collected in C.J.S. Witnesses § 507d.

68. Commonwealth v. Snyder, 408 Pa. 253, 182 A.2d 495 (1962) cert. denied 371 U.S. 957 (admissible); Pfotzer v. Aqua Systems, Inc., 162 F.2d 779 (2d Cir. 1947) (admissible); Lacey v. People, 166 Colo. 152, 442 P.2d 402 (1968); West's Ann.Cal.Evid. Code, § 788. Contra: Clinkscales v. State, 104 Ga. App. 723, 123 S.E.2d 165 (1961) cert. denied 369 U.S. 888. Many jurisdictions do not recognize the plea. Attitudes toward it are mixed.

A conviction in a prosecution where accused was denied counsel has been held not usable for impeachment, Gilday v. Scafati, 428 F.2d 1027 (1st Cir. 1970) cert. denied 401 U.S. 222, but the decision must be read in light of the subsequent deci-

sion in Harris v. New York, 401 U.S. 222 (1971). See § 178, infra.

69. See, e. g., Jones v. Melindy, 62 Ark. 203, 208, 36 S.W. 22 (1896), and discussion § 240, infra, and 4 Wigmore, Evidence § 1269.

70. R. v. Castell Careinion, 8 East 77, 79, 103 Eng. Rep. 273 (K.B.1806).

71. People v. McCrimmon, 37 Ill.2d 40, 224 N.E.2d 822 (1967) cert. denied 389 U.S. 863 (1967), (to impeach defendant as a witness in a criminal case; dictum); Carrol v. Crawford, 218 Ga. 635, 129 S.E.2d 865 (1963); cases cited in C.J.S. Witnesses § 528b.(3). Arguably the practice lessens the adverse impact of the evidence when the witness is the accused in a criminal case and affords some amelioration of his unfortunate predicament.

72. Gaskill v. Gahman, 255 Iowa 891, 124 N.W.2d 533 (1963); State v. Wolfe, 343 S.W.2d 10 (Mo. 1961) cert. denied 366 U.S. 953. Authorities are collected in 4 Wigmore, Evidence § 1270, n. 5; C.J.S. Witnesses § 528b.(3), n. 23, 24. A few courts have permitted impeachment by showing of a verdict of guilty without judgment and a few have rejected such proof. Annot., 14 A.L.R.3d 1272.

73. Moe v. Blue Springs Truck Lines, Inc., 426 S.W. 2d 1 (Mo.1968); State v. Beard, 148 Wash. 701, 269 P. 1051 (1928).

74. See MacKnight v. United States, 263 F. 832 (1st Cir. 1920) (where witness denies he was same person who served term in penitentiary, impeacher may prove he was inmate by men who saw him there); Ivey v. State, 132 Fla. 36, 180 So. 368 (1938) (by statute). A few cases have raised the

How far may the cross-examiner go in his inquiries about convictions? He may ask about the name of the crime committed,[75] i. e. murder or embezzlement, and the punishment awarded.[76] It will certainly add to the pungency of the impeachment where the crime was an aggravated one if he may ask about the circumstances, for example, whether the murder victim was a baby, the niece of the witness.[77] And it has been suggested by a few courts that since proof by record is allowable, and the record would show some of these circumstances, the cross-examination should at least be permitted to touch all the facts that the record would.[78] On the whole, however, the more reasonable practice, mini-

mizing prejudice and distraction from the issues, is the generally prevailing one that beyond the name of the crime,[79] the time and place of conviction,[80] and the punishment; further details such as the name of the victim [81] and the aggravating circumstances may not be inquired into.[82]

It may be thought that if the impeacher is precluded from showing details and circumstances of aggravation, the witness should similarly be cut off from explaining or extenuating the conviction or denying his guilt. Certainly it is impractical and forbidden to retry the case on which the conviction was based. And many courts forbid any explanation, extenuation or denial of guilt even by the witness himself on redirect.[83] This rule

question whether there is error if the prosecutor fails to introduce the record after the witness upon cross-examination denies the existence of a conviction. The decisions seem inconclusive. See Annot., 3 A.L.R.3d 965. A suggested approach is to require the cross-examiner to satisfy the judge in the latter's discretion, as to the existence of grounds for making the inquiry, particularly with respect to an accused-witness, by making a preliminary inquiry out of the presence of the jury, or by assurances of counsel. See Michelson v. United States, 335 U.S. 469 (1948).

75. State v. Phillips, 102 Ariz. 377, 430 P.2d 139 (1967); People v. Terry, 57 Cal.2d 538, 21 Cal. Rptr. 185, 370 P.2d 985 (1962) cert. denied 375 U.S. 960 (dictum); Barnett v. State, 240 Ind. 129, 161 N.E.2d 444 (1959); C.J.S. Witnesses § 515, p. 436.

76. See, e. g., Reid v. State, 100 Tex.Cr. 512, 271 S.W. 625 (1925) (payment of fine as prostitute); Finch v. State, 103 Tex.Cr. 212, 280 S.W. 597 (1926) (permissible to ask if he has not served a term in penitentiary).

77. Choice v. State, 54 Tex.Cr. 517, 521, 114 S.W. 132, 133 (1908) (properly excluded).

78. See State v. Lindsey, 27 Wash.2d 186, 177 P.2d 387 (1947) (court upheld cross-examination to show nature of offense and punishment "for the reason that these matters were set forth in the judgment of conviction"); see also State v. Rodia, 132 N.J.L. 199, 39 A.2d 484 (1944). ("Were you ever convicted of the crime of atrocious assault and battery by cutting," approved over objection that "by cutting" was improper, on ground that the charge of cutting would have been shown by the record of conviction); State v. Garvin, 44 N.J. 268, 208 A.2d 402 (1965) ("the statute has been consistently construed to authorize proof by cross-examination of what the record for conviction disclosed", citing cases).

79. See note 75, supra.

80. Hadley v. State, 25 Ariz. 23, 212 P. 458, 462 (1923) ("Were you ever convicted of a felony in Oklahoma," approved).

81. Stevens v. State, 138 Tex.Cr. 59, 134 S.W.2d 246 (1939).

82. State v. Norgaard, 272 Minn. 48, 136 N.W.2d 628 (1965) (age of girl involved in conviction for assault with intent to rape; but error not prejudicial in this instance); Powers v. State, 156 Miss. 316, 126 So. 12 (1930) ("You are under suspended sentence for beating your wife and son?", improper; approved in dictum in Emily v. State, 191 So.2d 925 (Miss.1966)); White v. State, 202 Miss. 246, 30 So.2d 894 (1947) (inquiry whether conviction for wilful trespass followed a withdrawn plea of guilty of burglary, improper); State v. Mount, 73 N.J.L. 582, 64 A. 124 (1906) (error to inquire of accused about particulars of prior assault for which he was convicted, such as size of the man assaulted and weapon used); C.J.S. Witnesses §§ 507, 515b.-(3) (c). But according to some courts, if the witness testifies to matters pertaining to a conviction on direct examination, he may "open the door" to some cross-examination of the circumstances. See, e. g., State v. Rush, 248 Ore. 568, 436 P.2d 266 (1968) (dictum); State v. Wilson, 26 Wash.2d 468, 174 P.2d 553 (1946).

83. State v. Gregg, 230 S.C. 222, 95 S.E.2d 255 (1956) (defendant-witness not permitted to state mitigating details on redirect examination); Mayo v. State, 32 Ala.App. 264, 24 So.2d 769 (1946) (accused-witness not allowed to show he was given probation for offence for which convicted); Lamoureux v. New York, N. H. & H. R. Co., 169 Mass. 338, 47 N.E. 1009 (1897) (witness's extenuation properly excluded; leading opinion, by Holmes, J.); State v. Lapan, 101 Vt. 124, 141 A. 686 (1928) (extensive discussion, following preceding case).

is a logical consequence of the premise of conclusiveness of the judgment. It does not, however, satisfy our feeling that some reasonable outlet for the instinct of self-defense by one attacked should be conceded, if it can be done without too much damage to the business at hand. Accordingly a substantial number of courts, while not opening the door to a retrial of the conviction, do permit the witness himself to make a brief and general statement in explanation, mitigation, or denial of guilt,[84] or recognize a discretion in the trial judge to permit it.[85] Wigmore aptly terms it a "harmless charity to allow the witness to make such protestations on his own behalf as he may feel able to make with a due regard to the penalties of perjury."[86]

The sharpest and most prejudicial impact of the practice of impeachment by conviction (as is true also of cross-examination as to misconduct, see § 42, above) is upon one particular type of witness, namely, the accused in a criminal case who elects to take the stand. If the accused is forced to admit that he has a "record" of past convictions, particularly if the convictions are for crimes similar to the one on trial, there is an obvious danger that the jury, despite instructions, will give more heed to the past convictions as evidence that the accused is the kind of man who would commit the crime on charge, or even that he ought to be put away without too much concern with present guilt, than they will to the legitimate bearing of the past convictions on credibility.[87] The accused, who has a "record" but who thinks he has a defense to the present charge, is thus placed in a grievous dilemma. If he stays off the stand, his silence alone will prompt the jury to believe him guilty. If he elects to testify, his "record" becomes provable to impeach him, and this again is likely to doom his defense. Where does the balance of justice lie? Most prosecutors would argue with much force that it would be misleading to permit the accused to appear as a witness of blameless life, and this argument has prevailed widely. An intermediate view, between permitting convictions generally to be introduced and excluding all convictions of the accused to impeach him as a witness, is a proposal that the convictions be restricted to those supposedly bearing directly upon character for truthfulness.[88] Another intermediate view, but with the disadvantage of uncertainty, is a rule which would permit the introduction of prior convictions of the defendant-witness in the discretion of the judge, who is to balance in each instance the possible prejudice against the probative value of the conviction as to credibility.[89] In

---

84. United States v. Crisafi, 304 F.2d 803 (2d Cir. 1962) (plea of guilty to save 16 year old sister involved in the charges; error not prejudicial since counsel stated matter); Hopper v. State, 151 Ark. 290, 236 S.W. 595 (1922) (that he was only 19 and was persuaded by another to commit a robbery); Perry v. State, 146 Fla. 187, 200 So. 525 (1941) (witness may testify he has been paroled or pardoned); Perin v. Peuler, 373 Mich. 531, 130 N.W.2d 4 (1964) (dictum); 4 Wigmore, Evidence § 1117, note 3.

85. United States v. Boyer, 80 U.S.App.D.C. 202, 150 F.2d 595 (1945) (witness, in discretion, may be allowed to extenuate or to assert innocence; fine discussion by Edgerton, J.); Donnelly v. Donnelly, 156 Md. 81, 143 A. 648 (1928) (witness may not deny guilt, but judge in discretion may permit him to explain and extenuate); Commonwealth v. Ford, 199 Pa.Super. 102, 184 A.2d 401 (1962) (approving judge's discretion in excluding reputation testimony but allowing introduction of pardon); Annot., 166 A.L.R. 211.

86. 4 Evidence § 1117, p. 191.

87. Griswold, The Long View, 51 A.B.A.J. 1017, 1021 (1965); Schaefer, Police Interrogation and the Privilege Against Self-Incrimination, 61 Nw. U.L.Rev. 506, 512 (1966); McGowan, Impeachment of Criminal Defendants by Prior Convictions, 1970 Ariz.St.L.J. 1. Statistical support is indicated in Kalven and Zeisel, The American Jury 124, 126–130, 144–146, 160–162 (1966).

88. Uniform Rule 21 limits provable convictions with respect to witnesses generally to those for crimes involving dishonesty or false statement.

89. In Luck v. United States, 121 U.S.App.D.C. 151, 348 F.2d 763 (1965), the court found authority for such an approach in the provision then in D.C. Code § 14–305 that conviction "may" be given in evidence to impeach. Brown v. United States, 125 U.S.App.D.C. 220, 370 F.2d 242 (1966) and Gordon v. United States, 127 U.S.App.D.C. 343, 383 F.2d

Pennsylvania,[90] the accused who takes the stand is shielded, under certain circumstances, from cross-examination as to misconduct or conviction of crime when offered to impeach but not from proof of conviction by the record of conviction.[91] Finally, the Uniform Rule [92] provides that if the accused does not

offer evidence supporting his own credibility the prosecution shall not be allowed, on cross-examination or otherwise, to prove for impeachment purposes his conviction of crime. The variety of solutions, both actual and proposed, indicate the stubborn and troublesome nature of the problem.

The suggestion has been made that impeachment of the accused by showing of prior convictions is an unconstitutional procedure, but at present, this result is not established.[93]

44. Character: Impeachment by Proof of Opinion or Bad Reputation.[94]

In most jurisdictions the impeacher may attack the character of a witness by using the following question formula:

> "Do you know the general reputation at the present time of William Witness in the community in which he lives, for truth and veracity?"
>
> "Yes."
>
> "What is that reputation?"
>
> "It is bad."

This routine is the distillation of traditions which have become established in a majority of American courts. It is the result of choices between alternative solutions, some wise, some seemingly misguided.

Misguided it seems is the first choice of the majority doctrine that this attack on character for truth must be in the abstract, debilitated form of proof of reputation. By what

936 (1967) cert. denied 390 U.S. 1029, developed standards for the exercise of discretion, including the nature of the crime, nearness or remoteness in time, the subsequent career of the person, and whether the crime was similar to the one charged. F.R.Ev. (R.D.1971) gives the judge discretion to exclude for unfair prejudice, imposes a 10-year limit on convictions for impeachment, and excludes in the event a showing of rehabilitation is made. See n. 65, supra. D.C.Code § 14–305 now contains the substance of original F.R.Ev. (P.D.1969) 6–09. District of Columbia Court Reform and Criminal Procedure Act, P.L. 91–358, § 133. See Rauh and Silbert, Criminal Law and Procedure: D.C. Court Reform and Criminal Procedure Act of 1970, 20 Am.U.L.Rev. 252, 315–317 (1970–71); House Report 91–907, Conference Report 91–1303, D.C.Code Legis. & Adm. Serv., 91st Cong.2d Sess., at 458, 575.

90. 19 P.S. § 711, discussed in 1 Wigmore, Evidence § 194b.

In England the Criminal Evidence Act, 1898 (61 & 62 Vict. c. 36), subs. 1(f) provided: "A person charged and called as a witness in pursuance of this Act shall not be asked, and if asked shall not be required to answer, any question tending to show that he has committed or been convicted of or been charged with any offence other than that wherewith he is then charged, or is of bad character, unless—(i) the proof that he has committed or been convicted of such other offence is admissible evidence to show that he is guilty of the offence wherewith he is then charged; or (ii) he has personally or by his advocate asked questions of the witnesses for the prosecution with a view to establish his own good character, or has given evidence of his good character, or the nature or conduct of the defence is such as to involve imputations on the character of the prosecutor or the witnesses for the prosecution; or (iii) he has given evidence against any other person charged with the same offence." See analysis and discussion, 1 Wigmore, Evidence § 194a; Cross, Evidence ch. 15 (3d ed. 1967).

91. See discussion in Note, 66 Dick.L.Rev. 339 (1962).

92. Uniform Rule 21: ". . . . If the witness be the accused in a criminal proceeding, no evidence of his conviction of a crime shall be admissible for the sole purpose of impairing his credibility unless he has first introduced evidence admissible solely for the purpose of supporting his credibility."

93. See discussion in Note, 37 U.Cin.L.Rev. 168 (1968). Spencer v. Texas, 385 U.S. 554 (1967), sustaining the constitutionality of presenting evidence of prior convictions on an habitual criminal issue at the trial of the principal charge, may well be pertinent.

94. See 3A Wigmore, Evidence (Chadbourn rev.) §§ 920–930; Ladd, Techniques of Character Testimony, 24 Iowa L.Rev. 498 (1939); Dec.Dig. Witnesses ⬥333–343, 356–358; C.J.S. Witnesses §§ 491–501; 58 Am.Jur. Witnesses §§ 725–732.

is apparently a misreading of legal history,[95] the American courts have generally prohibited proof of character by having a witness describe his belief or opinion of the character of the second witness under attack when the belief or opinion is based upon experience with the witness under attack and upon observation of his conduct.[96] The limitation to reputation has been defended on the ground that to let in opinion from observation would provoke distracting side-issues over disputes about specific conduct of the witness attacked, since the impeaching witness may be cross-examined about the grounds of his opinion.[97] Furthermore, a difficult assessment of the impeaching witness might be necessary. These dangers undoubtedly exist, and the controversies would need to be held to reasonable

limits by the judge. However, the question is whether the choice of reputation instead of experience and observation has not eliminated most of the objectivity from the attempt to appraise character, and has not encouraged the parties to select those who will give voice, under the guise of an estimate of reputation, to prejudice and ill-will. The hand is the hand of Esau, but the voice is the voice of Jacob. And, in addition, reputation in modern, impersonal urban centers is often evanescent, fragile, or actually non-existent.

The courts also have faced here a further choice—a recurrent one in various phases of character-impeachment—namely, shall the inquiry be as to "general character," or as to other specific types of bad traits such as sexual immorality, or shall it be directed solely and specifically to the trait of veracity? Surely it is clear that in this elusive realm of reputation as to character it is best to reach for the highest degree of relevancy that is attainable. Fortunately the great majority of our courts have taken this view and have limited the inquiry to "reputation for truth and veracity." [98] Only a few open the door, in addition, to reputation for "general character" [99] or "general moral character" [1], and

95. See 7 Wigmore, Evidence §§ 1981, 1982, and further discussion infra, § 186.

96. Sisson v. State, 168 Ark. 783, 272 S.W. 674 (1925); Gifford v. People, 148 Ill. 173, 176, 35 N.E. 754 (dictum) (1893); State v. Steen, 185 N.C. 768, 117 S.E. 793 (1923); State v. Polhamus, 65 N.J.L. 387, 47 A. 470 (1900). See also, cases in which direct opinion was sought in connection with attempts to obtain reputation testimony. Parasco v. State, 168 Tex.Cr.R. 89, 323 S.W.2d 257 (1959) ("In your opinion is the testimony of . . . under oath worthy of belief?"; held error); People v. Wendt, 104 Ill.App.2d 192, 244 N.E.2d 384 (1969); State v. Swenson, 62 Wash.2d 259, 382 P.2d 614 (1963).

Many courts, however, perhaps conscious of the weakness of evidence limited strictly to reputation, have compromised by permitting the injection of personal opinion by such questions as these (after proving bad reputation): "From that reputation, would you believe him on oath?" Burke v. Zwick, 299 Ill.App. 558, 20 N.E.2d 912 (1939); United States v. Walker, 313 F.2d 236 (6th Cir. 1963). Or an even more curious straddle: "From your association with W. and from what you know about his reputation . . . do you believe him entitled to credit under oath?" See Bowles v. Katzman, 308 Ky. 490, 214 S.W.2d 1021 (1941).

97. See Willard Bartlett, J. in People v. Van Gaasbeck, 189 N.Y. 408, 82 N.E. 718, 721 (1907) (discussing the analogous problem as to character-evidence offered by the accused on the issue of guilt). The contrary argument of policy is powerfully presented in 7 Wigmore, Evidence § 1986. The current trend in favor of allowing proof in the form of opinion is apparent in F.R.Ev. (R.D.1971) 608(a).

98. McHargue v. Perkins, 295 S.W.2d 301 (Ky.1956) (applying Ky.C.R. 43.07); Hoffman v. State, 93 Md. 388, 49 A. 658 (1901) (reputation for veracity exclusively; see also Poff v. State, 3 Md.App. 289, 239 A.2d 121 (1968)); State v. Kahner, 217 Minn. 574, 15 N.W.2d 105 (1944) (reputation for truth but not "moral character"); Schueler v. Lynam, 80 Ohio App. 325, 75 N.E.2d 464 (1947) (confined to veracity, does not extend to "general moral character"); C.J.S. Witnesses § 497; 3A Wigmore, Evidence (Chadbourn rev.) § 923; Dec.Dig. Witnesses ⊂⇒342.

99. Grammer v. State, 239 Ala. 633, 196 So. 268, 272 (1940) (but reputation for specific traits of character is not permitted; see note 2, infra).

1. Indiana Burns' Ann.St. §§ 2–1724, 9–1608; State v. Teager, 222 Iowa 391, 269 N.W. 348 (1936) (under I.C.A. § 622.18, general moral character may be shown, but proponent not precluded from showing veracity-reputation); New Mexico 1953 Comp. § 20–2–4 ("general evidence of bad moral character not restricted to his reputation for truth and veracity"); C.J.S. Witnesses § 498.

fewer still permit proof of reputation for specific traits other than veracity.[2]

The crucial time when the character of the witness under attack has its influence on his truth-telling is the time when he testifies.[3] But obviously reputation takes time to form and is the resultant of earlier conduct and demeanor, so that it does not precisely reflect character at a later date. The practical solution is to do what most courts actually do, that is, (1) to permit the reputation-witness to testify about the impeachee's "present" reputation, as of the time of the trial, if he knows it,[4] and (2) to permit testimony as to reputation (which is usually a settled, continuing condition) as of any time before trial which the judge in his discretion finds is not too remote to be significant.[5]

As to place,[6] the traditional inquiry is as to general reputation for veracity "in the community where he lives." The object of this limitation of place is obviously to restrict evidence of repute, to reputation among the people who know him best.[7] The limitation was appropriate for the situation in England (and less so in America) before the Industrial Revolution, when most people lived either in small towns or in rural villages. But as an exclusive limitation it would not be appropriate in this country today, where a person may be little known in the suburb or city neighborhood where he lives, but well known in another locality where he spends his workdays or in several localities where he does business from time to time. Thus, today it is generally agreed that proof may be made not only of the reputation of the witness where he lives, but also of his repute, as long as it is "general" and established, in any substantial community of people among whom he is

---

2. Among decisions excluding the evidence are Pugh v. State, 42 Ala.App. 499, 500, 169 So.2d 27 (1964) (bad reputation for being a thief); State v. Mondrosch, 108 N.J.Super. 1, 259 A.2d 725 (1969) (reputation with regard to a propensity or an inclination to be accusatory in nature against others, applying Ev.Rules 22 and 47); State v. Albert, 241 Iowa 1000, 43 N.W.2d 703 (1950) (bad reputation for an honest, upright citizen and industrious man; dictum). Most of the cases admitting the evidence are cases of prosecutions for sexual offences where the reputation for chastity of the prosecutrix is assailed. Wheeler v. State, 148 Ga. 508, 97 S.E. 408 (1918). See C.J.S. Witnesses § 504. Contra: State v. Wolf, 40 Wash.2d 648, 245 P.2d 1009 (1952) (carnal knowledge; reputation for chastity). In this class of cases, it may be a psychological fact that the sexual experiences and propensities of the complainant do have great significance in respect to the probable truth in her complaints. See 3A Wigmore, Evidence (Chadbourn rev.) § 924a, citing the views of eminent psychiatrists as to the prevalence, and the abnormal motivations, of groundless complaints of sexual crime.

3. See United States v. Null, 415 F.2d 1178 (4th Cir. 1969) (when accused proves good character on issue of guilt, it is reputation at the time of act that counts, but if his credibility as a witness is in question, it is reputation at the time of trial that is proved).

Decisions as to time are collected in 3A Wigmore, Evidence (Chadbourn rev.) § 928; Dec.Dig. Witnesses ☞343; C.J.S. Witnesses § 500.

4. Carter v. State, 226 Ala. 96, 145 So. 814 (1933) (time to which the character relates is "the time of trial and prior thereto"); Goehring v. Comm., 370 S.W.2d 822 (Ky.1963) (time must be time of trial "and a reasonable period thereafter"; 9 months before trial was within a reasonable period). See

also, Frith v. Comm., 288 Ky. 188, 155 S.W.2d 851 (1941) (manslaughter: held impeachment by showing reputation for bad moral character as of time of trial ordinarily proper but error to admit where witness impeaching witness testifies bad reputation was due to the homicide).

5. Snow v. Grace, 29 Ark. 131, 136 (1874) (character seven years before properly received); Shuster v. State, 62 N.J.L. 521, 41 A. 701 (1898) (reputation 18 years before, properly excluded); State v. Thomas, 8 Wash.2d 573, 113 P.2d 73 (1941) (sodomy, evidence that prosecuting witness 13 years old had bad reputation for truth two years before trial, held, exclusion, in view of child's age, not abuse of discretion; careful opinion by Driver, J.).

6. See 3A Wigmore, Evidence (Chadbourn rev.) § 930; Dec.Dig. Witnesses ☞343; C.J.S. Witnesses §§ 500, 520; Annot., 112 A.L.R. 1020.

7. See Brill v. Muller Brothers, Inc., 40 Misc.2d 683, 243 N.Y.S.2d 905 (1962), rev'd because evidence rules inapplicable in arbitration proceeding 17 App.Div.2d 804, 232 N.Y.S.2d 806 (1962), aff'd 13 N.Y.2d 776, 192 N.E.2d 34, 242 N.Y.S.2d 69 (1963) cert. denied 376 U.S. 927 (trial court stated that reputation testimony cannot come from a stranger sent out by the adverse party to investigate the reputation).

well known,[8] such as the group with whom he works,[9] does business[10] or goes to school.[11] The trial judge has a reasonable need of discretion to determine whether the reputation sought to be proved among the group in question meets these standards.[12]

8. Craven v. State, 22 Ala.App. 39, 111 So. 767 (1927).

The question of place is often essentially a matter of the time when the reputation was acquired, discussed in the preceding paragraph. See, e. g., Lee v. State, 179 Miss. 122, 174 So. 85 (1937) (reputation in place where witness lived six months before trial, provable).

9. Hamilton v. State, 129 Fla. 219, 176 So. 89 (1937) (reputation could be proved by fellow-employees at hotel where accused worked); State v. Axilrod, 248 Minn. 204, 79 N.W.2d 677 (1956) cert. denied 353 U.S. 938 (not error to admit testimony confined primarily to community in which impeached witness worked).

10. Hubert v. Joslin, 285 Mich. 337, 280 N.W. 780 (1938) (reputation in locality 15 miles away from home, where he owned a farm, visited frequently and had many business dealings); State v. Henderson, 29 W.Va. 147, 1 S.E. 225, 240 (1886).

11. People v. Colantone, 243 N.Y. 134, 152 N.E. 700, 702 (1926) (error to exclude evidence of reputation of ex-soldier, by instructors at vocational school, members of his company in army, and member of disabled veterans' post of 250 men. "The determining factor is whether the community in which the defendant has lived his life is sufficiently large for the persons to become acquainted with his character and to form a general opinion of it. This we call general reputation. The cases are quite right which exclude evidence of reputation among such a small class of persons or business associates, as to make it, not a general reputation, but rather the evidence of individual and independent dealings."). Compare Williams v. United States, 168 U.S. 382 (1897), (error to permit evidence of reputation of immigration inspector "in the custom house"; evidence as to his reputation "among the limited number of people in a particular public building" was inadmissible); State v. Swenson, 62 Wash.2d 259, 382 P.2d 614 (1963) (error to permit showing of reputation in the church of which impeached witness was a member or among people of that church).

12. Ulrich v. Chicago, B. & Q. Ry. Co., 281 Mo. 697, 220 S.W. 682, 684 (1920) (judge did not abuse discretion in admitting evidence of plaintiff's reputation at time of trial in locality where he formerly lived and continued to do business).

45. Defects of Capacity: Sensory or Mental.[13]

Any deficiency of the senses, such as deafness, or color blindness or defect of other senses which would substantially lessen the ability to perceive the facts which the witness purports to have observed, should of course be provable to attack the credibility of the witness, either upon cross-examination or by producing other witnesses to prove the defect. Probably the limits and weaknesses of human powers of perception should be studied more widely by judges and lawyers in the interest of a more accurate and objective administration of justice.[14]

As to the mental qualities of intelligence and memory, a distinction must be made between attacks on competency[15] and attacks on credibility, the subject of this section. Sanity in any general sense is not the test of competency, and a so-called insane person may testify if he is able to report correctly the matters to which he testifies and if he understands the duty to speak the truth.[16] Manifestly, however, the fact of mental "abnormality" either at the time of observing the facts or at the time of testifying will be provable, on cross or by extrinsic evidence, as bearing on credibility.[17] The use of expert

13. See 3A Wigmore, Evidence (Chadbourn rev.) §§ 931–935, 989–995; C.J.S. Witnesses §§ 461, 470, 486, 487, 488; Annot., 20 A.L.R.3d 684.

14. See C. C. Moore, A Treatise on Facts (1908); Wigmore, Principles of Judicial Proof ch. 22 (3d ed. 1937); Gardner, The Perception and Memory of Witnesses, 18 Corn.L.Q. 391 (1933); E. Moore, Elements of Error in Testimony, 28 Ore.L.Rev. 293 (1943).

15. See § 62, infra.

16. State v. Schweider, 5 Wis.2d 627, 94 N.W.2d 154 (1959); People v. Dixon, 81 Ill.App.2d 330, 225 N.E.2d 445 (1967); Dec.Dig. Witnesses ⏤41; and § 62, infra.

17. State v. Vigliano, 50 N.J. 51, 232 A.2d 129 (1966) (error to sustain objection to cross-examination to show witness was committed to psychiatric ward during trial); State v. Miskell, 161 N.W.2d 732 (Iowa 1968) (permitting cross-examination showing witness had been adjudged senile); Commonwealth v. Towber, 190 Pa.Super. 93, 152 A.2d 917

opinion as extrinsic evidence in this situation is discussed in the last part of this section.

What of defects of mind within the range of normality, such as a slower than average mind or a poorer than usual memory? These qualities reveal themselves in a testing cross-examination by a skilled questioner.[18] May they be proved by other witnesses? The decisions are divided.[19] It seems eminently a case for discretion.[20] The trial judge would determine whether the crucial character of the testimony attacked and the evaluative light shed by the impeaching evidence overbalance the time and distraction involved in opening this side-dispute. The development of standardized tests for intelligence and their widening use in business, government and the armed forces, suggest that they may eventually come to serve as useful aids in the evaluation of testimony.[21]

Abnormality, we have seen, is a horse of a different color. It is a standard ground of impeachment.[22] One form of abnormality exists when one is under the influence of drugs or drink. If the witness was under the influence at the time of the happenings which he reports in his testimony or is so at the time he testifies, this condition is provable, on cross or by extrinsic evidence, to impeach.[23] Habitual addiction stands differently. It is generally held that the mere fact of chronic alcoholism is not provable on credibility.[24]

(1959) (admission of hospital record showing commitment for mental treatment improperly refused). Cases are collected in 3A Wigmore, Evidence (Chadbourn rev.) § 932, n. 1; Dec.Dig. Witnesses ⬠377; C.J.S. Witnesses § 461. See also cases cited in n. 33, infra. But see, Adams v. Ford Motor Co., 103 Ill.App.2d 356, 243 N.E.2d 843 (1968) (sustaining rejection of offer of records of prior commitments of witness to mental institution).

18. That a cross-examination to test intelligence is allowable, see dicta in Blanchard v. People, 70 Colo. 555, 203 P. 662 (1922) and Henry v. State, 6 Okl. Cr. 430, 119 P. 278 (1911).

19. Admissible: Isler v. Dewey, 75 N.C. 466 (1876) (evidence of impeaching witness that memory of impeached witness is weak); State v. Armstrong, 232 N.C. 727, 62 S.E.2d 50 (1950) (expert testimony that witness was a moron should not have been excluded). Excluded: Blanchard v. People, 70 Colo. 555, 203 P. 662 (1922) (forgery: witness for defendant testified that interlineation was made before instrument signed; held, error to permit witnesses to testify that he was of low intelligence); Fries v. Berberich, 177 S.W.2d 640 (Mo. App.1944) (expert testimony as to weak memory). Decisions are collected in 3A Wigmore, Evidence (Chadbourn rev.) § 935, note 1; Annot., 20 A.L.R.3d 684, 696–697.

20. See, e. g., Mangrum v. State, 227 Ark. 381, 299 S.W.2d 80 (1957) (trial court rejection of testimony of counselor where witness had been a pupil, showing intelligence test score and conclusion of counselor, was properly within range of the trial court's discretion). See also, Polson v. State, 246 Ind. 674, 207 N.E.2d 638 (1965) (rejection of cross-examination question whether witness was "a little behind in school" was proper exercise of discretion).

21. See Hutchins and Slesinger, The Competency of Witnesses, 37 Yale L.J. 1017, 1019 (1928); Gardner, op. cit., 18 Corn.L.Q. 391, 409 (1933); Redmount, The Psychological Bases of Evidence Practices: Intelligence, 42 Minn.L.Rev. 559 (1958).

22. See note 17, supra.

23. Drink. Walker's Trial, 23 How.St.Tr. 1157 (1794) ("Do you know whether he had drunk any [liquor]?" "He had had a little; he knew what he was saying and doing." "Just as much as he knows now?" "He was not half so much in liquor then as he is now."); Olstad v. Fahse, 204 Minn. 118, 282 N.W. 694 (1938) (that the witness had been drinking beer at the time of the accident, and was under influence; extrinsic evidence allowable); 3A Wigmore, Evidence (Chadbourn rev.) § 933; C.J.S. Witnesses § 461h. However, there is a variety of decisions whether or not particular evidence is admissible to prove intoxication at the time of the incident about which the witness testifies. See collection of cases in Annot., 8 A.L.R.3d 749.

Drugs. Wilson v. United States, 232 U.S. 563 (1914) (witness having admitted addiction, and that she had taken a dose in the morning before testifying, was asked how often she used it and whether she had with her the "implements"; held, proper, to show whether at the moment of testifying she was under its influence); State v. Smith, 103 Wash. 267, 174 P. 9 (1918) (in prosecution for selling morphine without a physician's prescription where evidence showed that prosecuting witness was under the influence of morphine at the time of the alleged sale, expert testimony as to the effect of morphine upon the mind and memory of its user was admissible); Annot., 52 A.L.R. 848; C.J.S. Witnesses § 470.

24. Springer v. Reimers, 4 Cal.App.3d 325, 84 Cal. Rptr. 486 (1970) (must be shown that intoxication occurred contemporaneously with events about which witness testifies); Indemnity Ins. Co. v. Marshall, 308 S.W.2d 174 (Tex.Civ.App.1958) (similar case); C.J.S. § 461h.; Annot., 8 A.L.R.3d 749. But it seems that where general moral character

On the other hand, as to drug addiction to which more social odium has been attached, many decisions allow it to be shown to impeach, even without evidence that it did in the particular case affect truth-telling,[25] although apparently more courts, absent a particular showing of effect on the witness's veracity, would exclude it.[26] In respect to both addictions the excluding courts seem to have the better of the arguments. It can scarcely be contended that there is enough scientific agreement to warrant judicial notice that addiction in and of itself usually affects credibility.[27] Certainly it is pregnant with prejudice. On the other hand, there is an increasing recognition among non-legal authorities that addiction may in various instances be linked with personality and other defects which do bear upon credibility.[28]

In recent decades with the growth in importance of psychiatry, the testimony of psychiatrists upon issues of sanity in cases of wills and crimes has become familiar to the legal profession. Naturally, the use of expert psychiatric testimony as to mental disorders and defects suggests itself as a potential aid in determining the credibility of crucial witnesses in any kind of litigation. In one type of case, namely that of sex offenses, the indispensable value of this kind of testimony has been urged by Wigmore,[29] and other commentators,[30] and it has been widely received by the courts.[31] An earlier leading case [32] ex-

may be shown to impeach (see § 44, supra), habitual drunkenness is let in. Willis v. Wabash Railroad Co., 284 S.W.2d 503 (Mo.1955) (permitted showing of incidents of drunkenness as immoral acts by cross-examination).

25. See, e. g., State v. Fong Loon, 29 Idaho 248, 158 P. 233 (1916); People v. Crump, 5 Ill.2d 251, 125 N.E.2d 615 (1955) (but in Illinois, cross-examiners must be prepared to make a showing concerning intended questions to bring out addiction; People v. Brown, 76 Ill.App.2d 362, 222 N.E.2d 227 (1966)); and see the valuable descriptions and analyses of the cases in Hale, Comment, 16 So.Calif.L.Rev. 333 (1943), and discussion and citations in 3A Wigmore, Evidence (Chadbourn rev.) § 934; Annot., 52 A.L.R.2d 848; C.J.S. Witnesses § 470; Note, 1966 Utah L.Rev. 742.

26. See e. g., Kelly v. Maryland Casualty Co., 45 F.2d 782 (W.D.Va.1929) (scholarly and comprehensive opinion by McDowell, J.), aff'd 45 F.2d 788 (4th Cir. 1930) without passing on this question, on the ground that the evidence offered did not show excessive use; People v. Smith, 4 Cal.App.3d 403, 84 Cal.Rptr. 412 (1970) (testimony as to narcotics addiction and its effects is not permitted unless it is followed by evidence that the witness attacked was under the influence at the trial, or at the time of the events to which he testifies, or that as a result his mental faculties were actually impaired); and see general references, next preceding note.

27. In the Kelly case, in the next preceding note, Judge McDowell marshals the medical opinions pro and con (45 F.2d 782, 784, 785). See also, the lengthy discussion in People v. Williams, cited below.

There is also disagreement whether expert opinion is admissible to show the effect of narcotic addiction upon credibility. People v. Williams, 6 N.Y.2d 18, 159 N.E.2d 549, 187 N.Y.S.2d 750 (1959), cert. denied 361 U.S. 920, reviewing authorities at length.

28. Comment, Testimonial Reliability of Drug Addicts, 35 N.Y.U.L.Rev. 259 (1960); Mack, Forensic Psychiatry and the Witness—A Survey, 7 Clev.-Mar.L.Rev. 302, 311 (1958).

29. 3A Evidence (Chadbourn rev.) § 934a.

30. Note, Psychiatric Aid in Evaluating Credibility of Rape-Complainant, 26 Ind.L.J. 98 (1950) (arguing with force and originality that clinical examination be required where no substantial confirmation of complainant's story: collection of references to psychiatric literature); Machtinger, Psychiatric Impeachment in Sex Cases, 39 J.Crim.L. 750 (1949). Note, Sex Offenses: Credibility of the Complaining Witness, 43 Iowa L.Rev. 650 (1958).

31. People v. Cowles, 246 Mich. 429, 224 N.W. 387 (1929) (evidence of doctors that the girl was a pathological liar and nymphomaniac received without objection); People v. Bastian, 330 Mich. 457, 47 N.W.2d 692 (1951); State v. Wesler, 137 N.J.L. 311, 59 A.2d 834 (1948) (testimony of doctors that girls are psychopaths and immoral and that psychopaths are prone to be untruthful did not require rejection of girls' stories); Miller v. State, 49 Okl.Cr. 133, 295 P. 403 (1930) (testimony of superintendent of insane hospital that girl, said to be nymphomaniac, was normal, admissible on credibility; Rice v. State, 195 Wis. 181, 217 N.W. 697 (1928) (indecent liberties with child; conviction set aside, relying on testimony of doctor that girl "had a mental condition calculated to induce unreal and phantom pictures in her mind").

32. State v. Driver, 88 W.Va. 479, 107 S.E. 189 (1921) (judge properly refused to appoint commission to examine complainant and report on her competency and credibility, also properly excluded testimony of experts who from observation in court would testify that girl was moron and prone to tell lies).

cluded the evidence, but failed to discriminate between the question of competency and that of credibility, and misconceived the attack as one on character rather than on mental capacity for truth-telling, as it was. This case would probably not be followed today. The special danger of sympathy swaying the judgment on credibility in sex cases points to the need for making possible expert opinion concerning the credibility of the prosecuting witness in such cases. However, various courts have tended to take the position that there is also a need to permit impeachment of principal witnesses in other cases by expert psychiatric opinion.[33] Undoubtedly, if there is ground for believing that a principal witness is subject to some mental abnormality that may affect his credibility, a need for employment of the resources of psychiatry exist.[34]

Doubtless most courts today would accept the principle that psychiatric evidence should be received, at least in the judge's discretion, when its value outweighs the cost in time, distraction, and expense and other disadvantages.[35] The value seems to depend first upon the importance of the appraised witness's testimony, and second upon the opportunity of the expert to form a reliable opinion. This first factor, the importance of the testimony, is a relevant factor at least from the standpoint of policy considerations relating to the feasibility and desirability of subjecting witnesses (even party-witnesses) to an ordeal of psychiatric attack which may or may not be justified. The above-mentioned second factor, opportunity to form a reliable opinion, raises difficulties. An opinion based solely upon a hypothetical question seems almost valueless here. Only slightly more reliable is an opinion derived from the subject's demeanor and his testimony in the courtroom. Most psychiatrists would say that a satisfactory opinion can only be formed after the witness has been subjected to a clinical examination.[36] A discretionary power has been recognized in a few instances, granting the judge the power to order an examination of a prosecuting witness, but the conditions for exercising that discretion are unclear.[37] It

33. United States v. Hiss, 88 F.Supp. 559 (D.C.N.Y. 1950) (expert permitted to testify to diagnosis formed from courtroom observation that the star witness for the government was a psychopathic personality with "a tendency towards making false accusations"); Ingalls v. Ingalls, 257 Ala. 521, 59 So.2d 898 (1952) (doctor's opinion based upon a previous examination should have been admitted); Ellarson v. Ellarson, 198 App.Div. 103, 190 N.Y.S. 6 (1921) (doctor's opinion based upon a previous examination); State v. Burno, 200 N.C. 267, 156 S.E. 781 (1931) (opinion of an examining doctor as to mental state of prosecuting witness in prosecution for assault with intent to kill held properly admitted); Taborsky v. State, 142 Conn. 619, 116 A.2d 433 (1955) (opinion of psychiatrist in prosecution for murder, regarding hallucinations, delusions, etc. of prosecuting witness, would be admissible in a new trial); Annot., 20 A.L.R.3d 684. However, a number of cases (primarily older cases) hold these opinions inadmissible. See, e. g., State v. Driver, n. 32, supra; Blanchard v. People, 70 Colo. 555, 203 P. 662 (1922); Thompson v. Standard Wholesale Phosphate & Acid Works, 178 Md. 305, 13 A.2d 328 (1940); Mell v. State, 133 Ark. 197, 202 S.W. 33 (1918). See criticism of the earlier cases in Weihofen, Testimonial Competence and Credibility, 34 Geo.Wash.L.Rev. 53, 68 (1965).

34. These are classified and described in comment, Psychiatric Evaluation of the Mentally Abnormal Witness, 59 Yale L.J. 1324, 1326 (1950); Weihofen, Testimonial Competence and Credibility, 34 Geo. Wash.L.Rev. 53 (1965). See suggestions for future studies in Juviler, Psychiatric Opinions as to Credibility of Witnesses: A Suggested Approach, 48 Calif.L.Rev. 648 (1960).

35. See discussion in People v. Williams, 6 N.Y.2d 18, 159 N.E.2d 549, 187 N.Y.S.2d 750 (1959) and Weihofen, Testimonial Competence and Credibility, 34 Geo.Wash.L.Rev. 53, 75–76 (1965). See also, Juviler, Psychiatric Opinions as to Credibility of Witnesses: A Suggested Approach, 48 Calif.L.Rev. 648 (1960).

36. Comment, 59 Yale L.J. 1324, at p. 1339 (1950); Note, 30 Neb.L.Rev. 513, 519 (1951); Weihofen, cited supra, n. 23. A slashing cross-examination of the psychiatrist witness in United States v. Hiss, n. 33, supra, illustrates the difficulties of reliance upon observance of courtroom demeanor and upon a reading of the record.

37. Most of the cases seem to recognize the discretion although rejecting a contention that failure of the trial court to order an examination was an abuse of discretion. Commonwealth v. Kosh, 305 Pa. 146, 157 A. 479 (1931); People v. Lewis, 25 Ill.2d 442, 185 N.E.2d 254 (1962); People v. Stice, 165 Cal.App.2d 287, 331 P.2d 468 (1958); State v.

seems the power to exercise discretion should exist in any type of case, to be exercised not only upon the bases of whether undue expenditure of time or expense and undue distraction will result, but also upon the bases of whether the witness is a key witness and whether there are substantial indications that the witness is suffering from mental abnormality at the time of trial or was so suffering at the time of the happening about which he testifies. Only if there is no power to order an examination should expert opinion on the bases of courtroom observation and reading of the record be considered.[38] Even then, permitting opinion based upon such material seems very questionable.[39]

46. "Lie-Detectors" and "Truth Serums."

These devices offer interesting possibilities for the appraisal of the credibility of testimony—possibilities which have been realized to some extent in out-of-court investigations, and which may in the future be somehow directly utilized by the courts. They are discussed in the chapter on experimental and scientific evidence.[40]

47. Impeachment by "Contradiction": Disproving the Facts Testified to by the First Witness.[41]

"Contradiction" may be explained as follows. Statements are elicited from Witness One, who has testified to a material story of an accident, crime, or other matters, to the effect that at the time he witnessed these matters the day was windy and cold and he, the witness, was wearing his green sweater. Let us suppose these latter statements about the day and the sweater to be "disproved." This may happen in several ways. Witness One on direct or cross-examination may acknowledge that he was in error. Or judicial notice may be taken that at the time and place it could not have been cold and windy, e. g., in Tucson in July. But commonly disproof or "contradiction" is attempted by calling Witness Two to testify to the contrary, i. e., that the day was warm and Witness One was in his shirt-sleeves. It is in this latter sense that the term "contradiction" is used in this section.[42]

What impeaching value does the contradiction have in the above situation? It merely

---

Cox, 352 S.W.2d 665 (Mo.1962); State v. Klueber, 81 S.D. 223, 132 N.W.2d 847 (1965); State v. Miller, 35 Wis.2d 454, 151 N.W.2d 157 (1967) (but court may not compel if witness refuses). In State v. Butler, 27 N.J. 560, 143 A.2d 530 (1958), the court stated that the state's witness should have been examined for competency and that evidence at the competency hearing would be admissible on the issue of credibility. On the other hand, for the view that the court has no power to order examination of witnesses, see State v. Walgraeve, 243 Ore. 328, 412 P.2d 23 (1966) reh. denied 243 Ore. 328, 413 P.2d 609 (1966).

38. See similar suggestion, Weihofen, Testimonial Competence and Credibility, 34 Geo.Wash.L.Rev. 53, 77–78 (1965).

39. Compare F.R.Ev. (R.D.1971) 608(a) and 706, which provide generally for attack upon credibility by opinion as to truthfulness and untruthfulness, and for court appointed experts.

40. See §§ 174, 175, infra. It might be noted that a ruling allowing the witness to state he had agreed to take a lie detector test (as a means of rehabilitating the witness) has been held error. Kaminski v. State, 63 So.2d 339 (Fla.App.1953), aff'd 72 So.2d 400 (Fla.1954), cert. denied 348 U.S.

832. See also Nichols v. State, 378 S.W.2d 335 (Tex.Cr.1964) (error to question witness on redirect whether he had taken a lie detector test); Mattox v. State, 240 Miss. 544, 128 So.2d 368 (1961) (testimony that test was given held inadmissible). In State v. Mottram, 158 Me. 325, 184 A.2d 225 (1962) results of lie detector test to impeach a witness were held inadmissible.

41. 3A Wigmore, Evidence (Chadbourn rev.) §§ 1000–1007; Dec.Dig. Witnesses ☞398–409; C.J.S. Witnesses §§ 629–644.

The extent to which evidence obtained in violation of a constitutional right may be used to impeach is treated in § 178, infra.

42. In the courtroom and in the cases "contradiction" is loosely extended to include impeachment by proof of a prior inconsistent statement of the first witness. See, e. g., Calley v. Boston & M. R. Co., 92 N.H. 455, 33 A.2d 227 (1943). Because of the requirement of a preliminary question, see § 37, supra, the proof by a second witness of the prior inconsistent statement usually entails a contradiction too, but it is the witness's inconsistency that is the heart of the attack.

tends to show—for Witness One may be right and Witness Two may be mistaken—that Witness One has erred or falsified as to certain particular facts, and therefore is capable of error or lying, and this should be considered negatively in weighing his other statements. But all human beings have this capacity and all testimony should be discounted to some extent for this weakness. It is true that the trial judge in his discretion may permit the cross-examiner to conduct a general test of the power of Witness One to observe, remember and recount facts unrelated to the case, to "test" or "explore" these capacities.[43] To permit a dispute, however, about such extraneous or "collateral" facts as the weather and the clothing of Witness One, that are material only for "testing" the witness, by allowing the attacker to call other witnesses to disprove them, is not practical. Dangers of surprise, of confusion of the jury's attention,[44] and of time-wasting [45] are apparent.

Therefore, the courts maintain the safeguarding rule that a witness may not be impeached by producing extrinsic evidence of "collateral" facts to "contradict" the first witness's assertions about those facts.[46] If the collateral fact sought to be contradicted is elicited on cross-examination, this safeguarding rule is often expressed by saying that the answer is conclusive or that the cross-examiner must "take the answer." [47] By the better view, if the "collateral" fact happens to have been drawn out on direct, the rule against contradiction should still be applied.[48] The danger of surprise is lessened, but waste of time and confusion of issues stand as objections.

What is to be regarded here as within this protean word of art, "collateral"? The inquiry is best answered by determining what facts are not within the term, and thus finding the escapes from the prohibition against contradicting upon collateral facts. The classical approach is that facts which would have been independently provable regardless of the contradiction are not "collateral." [49]

43. See § 29, supra.

44. ". . . Witnesses are not expected to come prepared to sustain all the statements they have made upon subjects not involved in the controversy, and because its admission would involve the trial of too many issues as to the truth of the statements the determination of which would at last have little effect upon the decision of the cause." Williams, J., in Gulf, C. & S. F. R. Co. v. Matthews, 100 Tex. 63, 93 S.W. 1068, 1070 (1906).

45. "If we lived for a thousand years, instead of about sixty or seventy, and every case were of sufficient importance, it might be possible and perhaps proper to throw a light on matters in which every possible question might be suggested, for the purpose of seeing by such means whether the whole was unfounded, or what portion of it was not, and to raise every possible inquiry as to the truth of the statements made. But I do not see how that could be; in fact, mankind find it to be impossible. Therefore, some line must be drawn." Rolfe, B. in Attorney General v. Hitchcock, 1 Exch. 104, 154 Eng.Rep. 38 (1847).

46. Gaddis v. State, 360 P.2d 522 (Okl.Cr.1961); Klein v. Keresey, 307 Mass. 51, 29 N.E.2d 703 (1940); C.J.S. Witnesses § 633, note 87.

The rule against impeaching on collateral matters may, however, on occasion yield to the theory that inadmissible evidence may be rebutted by evidence which otherwise would be inadmissible. See § 57, infra.

47. Howard v. State, 234 Md. 410, 199 A.2d 611 (1964); Latham v. State, 152 Neb. 113, 40 N.W.2d 522 (1949); C.J.S. Witnesses § 633, note 88.

48. Lambert v. Hamlin, 73 N.H. 138, 59 A. 941 (1905); State v. Price, 92 W.Va. 542, 115 S.E. 393, 405 (1922); 3A Wigmore, Evidence (Chadbourn rev.) § 1007. But many courts hold to the contrary. See, e. g., Howell v. State, 141 Ark. 487, 217 S.W. 457 (1920) (carnal knowledge; testimony of complainant on direct that she had never had intercourse with anyone but defendant should have been allowed to be contradicted, distinguishing situation where brought out on cross-examination) and cases cited Wigmore, ibid. and C.J.S. Witnesses § 633, n. 6. See § 57, infra.

49. State v. Kouzounas, 137 Me. 198, 17 A.2d 147 (1941); State v. Oswalt, 62 Wash.2d 118, 381 P.2d 617 (1963); 3A Wigmore, Evidence (Chadbourn rev.) § 1003; C.J.S. Witnesses § 633b.

The same test of "collateralness" of subject-matter is applied to impeachment by prior inconsistent

Two general kinds of facts meet the test. The first kind are facts that are relevant to the substantive issues in the case.[50] It may seem strained to label this proof of relevant facts with the terms, "contradiction" or "impeachment." But it does have the dual aspect of relevant proof and of reflecting on the credibility of contrary witnesses.[51] Here the "contradiction" theory has at least one practical consequence, namely, it permits contradicting proof, which without the contradiction would be confined to the case in chief, to be brought out in rebuttal.[52]

The second kind of facts meeting the above mentioned test for facts that are not collateral includes facts which would be independently provable by extrinsic evidence, apart from the contradiction, to impeach or disqualify the witness.[53] Among these are facts showing bias, interest,[54] conviction of crime,[55] and want of capacity or opportunity for knowledge. Facts showing misconduct of the witness (for which no conviction has been had) are not within this second kind of facts, but are collateral, and if denied on cross-examination cannot be proved to contradict.[56]

Finally, a third kind of fact must be considered. Suppose a witness has told a story of a transaction crucial to the controversy. To prove him wrong in some trivial detail of time, place or circumstance is "collateral." But to prove untrue some fact recited by the witness that if he were really there and saw what he claims to have seen, he could not have been mistaken about, is a convincing kind of impeachment that the courts must make place for, although the contradiction evidence is otherwise inadmissible because it is collateral under the tests mentioned above. To disprove such a fact is to pull out the linchpin of the story. So we may recognize this third type of allowable contradiction, namely, the contradiction of any part of the witness's account of the background and circumstances of a material transaction, which as a matter of human experience he would not have been mistaken about if his story were true.[57] This test is of necessity a vague

---

statements, see § 36, supra; 3A Wigmore, Evidence (Chadbourn rev.) § 1020.

50. Examples: Louisville Taxicab & Tr. Co. v. Tungent's Adm'r, 313 Ky. 1, 229 S.W.2d 985 (1950) (in action for death of one riding in truck struck by defendant's taxicab at street intersection, testimony as to decedent's and truck driver's drunkenness at time of collision was admissible as bearing on questions of negligence and credibility of driver, who testified that neither she nor decedent drank any liquor during morning before collision); Thompson v. Walsh, 203 Okl. 453, 223 P.2d 357 (1950) (in action for injury to and death of cattle from drinking salt water negligently permitted to escape from defendants' oil lease testimony that salt water was seen running from defendants' wells into creek on day before trial was permissible to impeach the testimony of a defendant that salt water never escaped from the lease into the creek).

51. Thus, the limitation upon impeaching one's own witness does not prevent a party from contradicting his own witness by adducing contrary proof as to a material fact. Talley v. Richart, 353 Mo. 912, 185 S.W.2d 23 (1945); Dec.Dig. Witnesses ⟨≈⟩400, and see § 38, supra.

52. People v. Jeffrey, 233 Cal.App.2d 279, 43 Cal. Rptr. 524 (1965); Hensley v. Comm., 264 Ky. 718, 95 S.W.2d 564 (1936) (wounding with intent to kill: where defendant said, on cross, that he did not remember whether he made a threat, evidence that he did threaten admissible, not only in chief, but in rebuttal, to contradict).

53. 3A Wigmore, Evidence (Chadbourn rev.) § 1005.

54. State v. Kouzcunas, 137 Me. 198, 17 A.2d 147 (1941) (accused in arson prosecution, who had been charged by witness with offering money to get him to change his testimony, denied on cross-examination that he visited lawyer with this witness; held, state may contradict this denial by evidence of lawyer that accused came to his office with witness). See § 40, supra.

55. Storer v. State, 84 Okl.Cr. 176, 180 P.2d 202 (1947). See § 43, supra.

56. People v. Rosenthal, 289 N.Y. 482, 46 N.E.2d 895 (1943) (accused was asked on cross-examination about other like crimes, and denied them, held state cannot produce other witnesses to contradict); State v. Broom, 222 N.C. 324, 22 S.E.2d 926 (1942) (similar); Commonwealth v. Boggio, 204 Pa.Super. 434, 205 A.2d 694 (1964) (party cannot contradict answer to question whether witness ever had intercourse with another man). See § 42, supra.

57. See, e. g., East Tennessee R. Co. v. Daniel, 91 Ga. 768, 18 S.E. 22 (1893) (witness of alleged killing of

one because it must meet an indefinite variety of situations, and consequently in its application a reasonable latitude of discretionary judgment must be accorded to the trial judge.[58]

Of course, the contradicting witness may simply state the facts as he asserts them, without reference to the prior testimony which is being contradicted. It seems, however, that where appropriate the contradiction may be more direct. Thus it would seem acceptable to recite in the question the pertinent part of the prior testimony of the first witness, and inquire, "What do you say as to the correctness of this statement?" [59]

48. Beliefs Concerning Religion.[60]

As indicated in a subsequent section,[61] the common law required as a qualification for taking the oath as a witness, the belief in a God who would punish untruth. This rule grew up in a climate of custom and assumptions which today seem primitive and archaic. It has quite generally been abandoned in most common law jurisdictions. General provisions like that in the Illinois constitution to the effect that "No person shall be denied any civil or political rights, privilege or capacity on account of his religious opinions" [62] have

---

mule at crossing accounted for his presence by saying he left home to get some tobacco, going to a certain store and getting the tobacco on credit, and on his way home he saw the accident; adversary offered evidence of store-keeper that witness did not buy tobacco at that time, held, erroneously excluded, "it was indirectly material because it contradicted the witness as to the train of events which led him to be present"); Stephens v. People, 19 N.Y. 549, 572 (1859) (murder by poisoning with arsenic; defendant's witnesses testified the arsenic was administered to rats in cellar where provisions kept; held proper for state to prove by another witness that no provisions were kept in cellar, "not strictly collateral"); Gulf C. & S. F. Ry. Co. v. Matthews, 100 Tex. 63, 93 S.W. 1068, 1070 (1906) (suit for death of M., run over by train; controverted issue was whether M. was sober and walking or drunk and lying on tracks; A., a hotel clerk, crucial witness for plaintiff, said M. left hotel early in morning, sober: foul play in the death of M. was publicly suspected; A. said on cross-examination that he had never mentioned M.'s presence and departure from hotel except a couple of times to one W.; defendant offered evidence that A. when he gave above testimony by deposition believed W. was dead, and produced W. and offered proof by him that A. had never told him about M.'s presence in the hotel; held exclusion of defendant's evidence was error. "Evidence therefore which bears upon the story of a witness with sufficient directness and force to give it appreciable value in determining whether or not that story is true cannot be said to be addressed to an irrelevant or collateral issue. . . . The effort of the defendant was . . . to maintain its contention that he had never told any one; and that fact being relevant, the defendant had the right, we think, to meet his apparent effort to break its force." Able opinion by Williams, J.); Shepherd v. Denver & R. G. R. Co., 45 Utah 295, 145 P. 296 (1915); Hartsfield v. Carolina Cas. Ins. Co., 451 P.2d 576 (Alaska 1969) (on issue whether insurance cancellation notice was sent to defendant by insurer, defendant denied receipt and also receipt of notices of cancellations of the insurance from two other sources. Evidence of the mailing by the two latter sources was held not collateral citing the *Matthews* case, supra, and the instant section); Commonwealth v. Jackson, 281 S.W.2d 891 (Ky. 1955) (cites this section 47 with approval in connection with proof of inconsistent statement). See also, Hutchins v. State, 172 Tex.Cr.R. 525, 360 S.W.2d 534 (1962).

58. The cases dealing with discretion in the field of contradiction seem to go further than the text.

Some imply that the trial judge has a discretion to decide what is and is not "collateral." Radio Cab, Inc. v. Houser, 128 F.2d 604 (D.C.Cir. 1942). Others suggest that even if "collateral" the judge has a discretion to permit the contradiction. Salem News Co. v. Caliga, 144 F. 965 (1st Cir. 1906); Todd v. Bradley, 99 Conn. 307, 122 A. 68 (1923); Lizotte v. Warren, 302 Mass. 317, 19 N.E.2d 60 (1939) (self-contradiction by party). See cases collected in C.J.S. Witnesses § 633a, n. 1.

59. See Uhlman v. Farm Stock & Home Co., 126 Minn. 239, 148 N.W. 102 (1914) and compare Scoggins v. Turner, 98 N.C. 135, 3 S.E. 719, 723 (1887). Cases are collected in C.J.S. Witnesses § 638.

60. See 2 Wigmore, Evidence § 518 (competency), 3A id. (Chadbourn rev.) § 936 (impeachment), 8 id. (McNaughton rev.) § 2213 (privilege), and the excellent comment by Chadbourn on State v. Beal, 199 N.C. 278, 154 S.E. 604, 1930, 9 N.C.L.Rev. 77 (1930); Annot., 95 A.L.R. 723; Swancara, Impeachment of Non-Religious Witnesses, 13 Rocky Mt.L. Rev. 336 (1941). Dec.Dig. Witnesses ☞340(2); C.J.S. Witnesses § 511.

61. See § 63, infra.

62. Quoted in Starks v. Schlensky, 128 Ill.App. 1, 4 (1906).

been construed in many states to abrogate the rule of incompetency to take the oath.[63]

The general tendency, as indicated in Sections 43 and 65, has been to convert the old grounds of incompetency to testify, such as interest and infamy, into grounds of impeaching credibility, and this principle of conversion is sometimes expressly enacted in constitutional provisions and in statutes.[64] Should the principle be applied so as to permit the credibility of a witness to be attacked by showing that he is an atheist or an agnostic and does not believe in Divine punishment for perjury? The greater number of courts that have answered the question at all have said no, either by interpreting general provisions [65] such as that quoted above from the Illinois constitution, or by mandate of specific constitutional or statutory language.[66] Thus many states recognize a privilege of the witness not to be examined about his own religious faith or beliefs, except so far as the judge in his discretion [67] finds that the relevance of the inquiry upon some substantive issue in the case outweighs the interest of privacy and the danger of prejudice.[68] A minority, either reasoning from the principle of conversion or following specific provisions, allows this ground of impeachment.[69] It is to

63. See the constitutional and statutory provisions, and decisions interpreting them, from twenty-four states, compiled in 70 C.J. 98, 99, note 76, and see § 63, infra. A compilation of specific references to the articles and sections of the constitutions dealing with Witnesses appears in 3 Constitutions, 1813 (1938) published by N. Y. State Const. Committee. Forty jurisdictions are listed as having abolished by statute or constitutional provision the requirement for witnesses of religious belief. Torpey, Judicial Doctrines of Religious Rights 278 (1948).

64. "N.M.Ann.Stat. § 2165 [now § 20–1–80] provides: 'Hereafter in the courts of this state no person [now added, "offered as a witness"] shall be disqualified to give evidence on account of any disqualification known to the common law, but all such common law disqualifications may be shown for the purpose of affecting the credibility of any such witness and for no other purpose. . . .' A legitimate construction would be that want of religious belief was not a testimonial disqualification and is thus not covered by the statute. However, the express wording of the following unfortunate statutes would have to be disregarded to prevent impeachment by religious belief: . . . Neb. Comp.Stat. (1922) § 8845; Iowa Code (1927) § 3637 [now § 622.2]; State v. Elliott, 45 Iowa 486 (1877); Searcy v. Miller, 57 Iowa 613, 10 N.W. 912 (1881)." Chadbourn, 9 N.C.L.Rev. 78, n. 5, cited in n. 60, supra.

65. See, e. g., McClellan v. Owens, 335 Mo. 884, 74 S.W.2d 570, 576 (1934) and cases from California, Illinois, Kansas, Kentucky, Louisiana, Maine, Michigan, Missouri, New Hampshire, New York, Pennsylvania and Texas in Annot., 95 A.L.R. 724. To like effect is Darby v. Ouseley, 1 H. & N. 1, 156 Eng.Rep. 1093 (1856).

66. A constitutional provision (Ariz.Const. Art. 2, § 12) forbids the questioning of a witness "touching his religious belief . . . to affect the weight of his testimony." This was held to forbid counsel, when a particular church is interested as a legatee in the outcome of the suit on trial, to ask a witness if he is a member of that church. Tucker v. Reil, 51 Ariz. 357, 77 P.2d 203 (1938). The decision seems not to be within the purpose of the provision. See State v. Estabrook, 162 Ore. 476, 91 P.2d 838 (1939) where a similar Oregon provision was held to forbid cross-examining a witness who has testified to the good reputation of the accused, as to whether she is a Christian Scientist and hence believes no evil of anyone.

67. Searcy v. Miller, 57 Iowa 613, 621, 10 N.W. 912, 916 (1881) ("He is not to be questioned as to his religious belief . . ."); Commonwealth v. Burke, 82 Mass. 33 (1860) (improper to question witness about his beliefs on voir dire or on cross-examination, despite statute permitting impeachment on this ground); Free v. Buckingham, 59 N.H. 219, 225 (1879) ("This is not because the inquiry might tend to disgrace him, but because it would be a personal scrutiny into the state of his faith and conscience, contrary to the spirit of our institutions"); 8 Wigmore, Evidence (McNaughton rev.) § 2213.

68. Examples of situations where relevancy did outweigh: McKim v. Philadelphia Transp. Co., 364 Pa. 237, 72 A.2d 122 (1950) (under statute recognizing privilege judge properly permitted cross-examination of personal injury plaintiffs to show they were ministers in Jehovah's Witnesses sect and what their duties were, on issue of damages); Ft. Worth & D. C. Ry. Co. v. Travis, 45 Tex.Civ.App. 117, 99 S.W. 1141 (1907) (personal injury plaintiff could be cross-examined as to her beliefs as Christian Scientist, as to suffering, and as to whether her faith caused her not to take medicine prescribed). But compare cases where inquiry into the plaintiff's faith as Christian Scientist was found not to be sufficiently relevant to the substantive issues. City of Montgomery v. Wyche, 169 Ala. 181, 53 So. 786 (1910); Adams v. Carlo, 101 S.W.2d 753 (Mo. App.1937).

69. Allen v. Guarante, 253 Mass. 152, 148 N.E. 461 (1925) and decisions cited from Georgia, Indiana,

be observed, however, that the common law analogy would not extend to permit inquiry into particular creeds, faiths or affiliations except as they shed light on the witness's belief in a God who will punish untruth.[70]

There is a strong reason why the legislatures and courts should, in addition to recognizing the privilege of a witness not to answer to his own religious beliefs, forbid the party to impeach by bringing other witnesses to attack the faith of the first one. This reason of course is that there is no basis for believing that the lack of faith in God's avenging wrath is today an indication of greater than average untruthfulness. Without that basis, the evidence of atheism is simply irrelevant upon the question of credibility.[71]

A Pennsylvania statute is a model of clarity and settles most of the questions left unsettled in other states: "No witness shall be questioned, in any judicial proceeding, concerning his religious belief; nor shall any evidence be heard upon the subject, for the purpose of affecting either his competency or credibility." [72]

Iowa, Massachusetts, Mississippi, and Ohio in Annot., 95 A.L.R. 726. Most of the cases, however, are old, and we may assume that the decent restraint of lawyers leaves this field of impeachment to lapse into dormancy.

70. "The credibility of witnesses can be affected only by evidence of their disbelief in the existence of God. . . . Adherence to any particular sect is no basis for argument in this respect." Allen v. Guarante, 253 Mass. 152, 148 N.E. 461, 462 (1925).

71. "Unorthodox religious convictions, even though they extend to the extremes of agnosticism and atheism, may quite often exist because of honest intellectual doubts. It is untenable to argue that there is a correlation between this kind of unorthodoxy and inveracity. That correlation which may exist between what Pope calls 'blind unbelief' and untruthfulness is so slight that the value of the evidence is outweighed by the possibilities for prejudice with which it is pregnant." Chadbourn, 9 N.C.L.Rev. 81, cited in n. 60, supra.

72. 28 P.S. § 313, quoted and interpreted in McKim v. Philadelphia Transp. Co., 364 Pa. 237, 72 A.2d 122 (1950). See also F.R.Ev. (R.D.1971) 610.

49. Supporting the Witness.

Impeachment is not a dispassionate study of the capacities and character of the witness, but is regarded in our tradition as an *attack* upon his credibility. Under our adversary system of trials the opponent must be given an opportunity to meet this attack by evidence sustaining or rehabilitating the witness. One general principle is that in the absence of an attack upon credibility no sustaining evidence is allowed.[73] A second truism is that

73. Woey Ho v. United States, 109 F. 888 (9th Cir. 1901) (petitioner resisting deportation properly refused permission to support her witnesses, who were Chinese, by evidence of their good character, there being no attack); State v. Harmon, 278 S.W. 733 (Mo., 1925) (testimony offered to support unimpeached character for truth of accused as witness, properly excluded); McPhearson v. State, 271 Ala. 533, 125 So.2d 709 (1960) (defendant properly refused permission to show good reputation of a defense witness for truth and veracity); State v. Parsons, 83 N.J.Super. 430, 200 A.2d 340 (1964) (state properly refused permission to support state's witness by showing he changed his story after being shown results of a polygraph test, thus anticipating an attack on the credibility of the state's witness); Martin v. Crow, 372 S.W.2d 724 (Tex. Civ.App.1963) (not error to refuse to permit plaintiff's witness to testify that he had no interest in the suit); Annot., 15 A.L.R. 1065, 33 id. 1220; C.J.S. Witnesses § 471.

The exclusion of character-support, in the absence of attack, is frequently explained as the corollary of a presumption that the character of the witness is good. See, e. g., Johnson v. State, 129 Wis. 146, 108 N.W. 55, 58 (1906). 4 Wigmore, Evidence § 1104 n. 1, says that the character is simply unknown.

It has been held that an act done by the witness which is consistent with his testimony about the main fact is admissible, even in the absence of attack, as corroborating the testimony. See the subtle and ingenious opinion of Allen, J., in State v. Slocinski, 89 N.H. 262, 197 A. 560 (1938) (witness to arson threat, allowed to testify that he reported the threat to the police and to his own lawyer, at the time it was made). Such evidence may often be justified as furnishing relevant corroboratory evidence. Mahoney v. Minsky, 39 N.J. 208, 188 A.2d 161 (1963) (testimony by witness that he made a cash payment of $2500 and cashed a check to obtain the cash amount; error to refuse admission of the check).

Nor can the party bolster his witness by proof, in the case in chief, that the witness has previously told the same story that he tells on the stand. Newton v. State, 147 Tex.Cr.R. 400, 180 S.W.2d 946 (1944) (prosecuting witness in attempted murder,

when there has been evidence of impeaching facts the proponent may bring contradictory evidence asserting the untruth of the alleged impeaching facts. Such a denial is always relevant and generally allowable.[74]

A discussion of rehabilitation and support of witnesses is more readily organized around the techniques employed than in terms of principle, just as was seen to be the case with respect to impeachment. The two most common specific methods that are attempted are (1) introduction of supportive evidence of good character of the witness attacked, and (2) introduction of consistent statements of the witness who has been attacked. The most common rehabilitation problem is whether these two types of rehabilitation evidence may be introduced in connection with the various methods of impeachment that have been attempted, as outlined in the previous sections of this chapter. The general test for solution is whether evidence of the good character of the witness or of his consistent statements is logically relevant to explain the impeaching fact. The rehabilitating facts must meet a particular method of impeachment with relative directness. The wall, attacked at one point, may not be fortified at another and distinct point.[75] Credibility is a side is-

where issue is identity of assailant, allowed to recite his report to guests of identity of telephone caller on night of attack, held error); State v. Herrera, 236 Ore. 1, 386 P.2d 448 (1963) (prosecution witness' prior consistent statement was admitted; error, however, was not reversible error because defendant later impeached the witness); 4 Wigmore, Evidence § 1124. This can be justified on grounds of saving of time, by avoiding a defense of the witness before a need for one appears. In addition, the prior statement may be inadmissible as proof on the issues because it is hearsay for that purpose. See § 251, infra. But when the principal fact to which this "bolstering" evidence is addressed is later denied by the adversary's witness (as in the *Newton* case cited above), does this furnish the "attack" and convert the present point into one of mere order of proof? Usually mere contradiction in relevant testimony is not an attack. See text at n. 83, infra.

74. Thus, evidence of bad character to impeach may be rebutted by evidence of good character. See, e. g., Prentiss v. Roberts, 49 Me. 127, 137 (1860); 4 Wigmore, Evidence § 1105; C.J.S. Witnesses § 534. Some courts at least permit a summary denial or explanation by the witness of guilt where he has been impeached by conviction. See § 43, notes 84, 85, supra; C.J.S. Witnesses § 534. Facts showing bias may of course be denied, 4 Wigmore, Evidence § 1119, or explained, People v. Burke, 52 Ill.App.2d 159, 201 N.E.2d 636 (1964). See also, Ryan v. Dwyer, 33 App.Div.2d 878, 307 N.Y.S.2d 565 (1969) (party calling witness may prove any fact tending to show absence of interest or bias of witness; here after a showing that witness settled a claim with plaintiff, arising out of the accident, a similar settlement with defendant may be proved). The making of an inconsistent statement may also be denied or explained. Tri-State Transfer Co. v. Nowotny, 198 Minn. 537, 270 N.W. 684 (1936) (rebutting witness may testify that complaint introduced as inconsistent statement of former witness, was not drawn by him but by attorney); Ryan v. Dwyer, cited supra (witness may explain inconsistent statement; dictum that he may deny making it).

75. The approach is illumined by the opinion of Holmes, J., in Gertz v. Fitchburg R. Co., 137 Mass. 77, 78 (1884). In holding that the plaintiff, impeached as a witness by conviction of crime, could give evidence of his good reputation for truth, he said: "We think that the evidence of his reputation for truth should have been admitted, and that the exception must be sustained. There is a clear distinction between this case and those in which such evidence has been held inadmissible, for instance, to rebut evidence of contradictory statements; Russell v. Coffin, 8 Pick. 143; Brown v. Mooers, 6 Gray 451; or where the witness is directly contradicted as to the principal fact by other witnesses. Atwood v. Dearborn, 1 Allen, 483.

"In such cases, it is true that the result sought to be reached is the same as in the present,—to induce the jury to disbelieve the witness. But the mode of reaching the result is different. For, while contradiction or proof of contradictory statements may very well have the incidental effect of impeaching the character for truth of the contradicted witness in the minds of the jury, the proof is not directed to that point. The purpose and only direct effect of the evidence are to show that the witness is not to be believed in this instance. But the reason why he is not to be believed is left untouched. That may be found in forgetfulness on the part of the witness, or in his having been deceived, or in any other possible cause. The disbelief sought to be produced is perfectly consistent with an admission of his general good character for truth, as well as for the other virtues; and until the character of a witness is assailed, it cannot be fortified by evidence.

"On the other hand, when it is proved that a witness has been convicted of a crime, the only ground for disbelieving him which such proof affords is the general readiness to do evil which the conviction may be supposed to show."

sue and the circle of relevancy in this context may well be drawn narrowly. How narrowly is a question of degree as to which reasonable courts differ, and a solution reached in a particular state soon becomes part of the local "cake of custom".

When may the party supporting the witness, who has been attacked by one of the impeachment methods discussed in this chapter, offer evidence of good character of the witness for truth? Certainly attacks by evidence of bad reputation,[76] conviction of crime,[77] or eliciting from the witness on cross-examination acknowledgment of misconduct which has not resulted in conviction,[78] will all open the door to character support. The evidence of good character for truth is logically relevant to meet these kinds of impeachment. Moreover, a slashing cross-examination may carry strong accusations of misconduct and bad character, which the witness's denial will not remove from the jury's mind. If the judge considers that fairness requires it, he may permit evidence of good character, a mild palliative for the rankle of insinuation by such cross-examination.[79]

Corrupt conduct of a witness of a sort to show bias should also seemingly be regarded as including an attack on veracity-character and thus warranting character support,[80] but impeachment for bias or interest by facts not involving corruption, such as proof of family relationship,[81] may not be met by proof of good character for truth.

Attempts to support the witness by showing his good character for truth have resulted in contradictory conclusions when the witness has been impeached by evidence of an inconsistent statement, or has been met by the adversary's evidence denying the facts to which the witness has so testified. If the witness has been impeached by the introduction of an inconsistent statement, the greater number of courts permit a showing of his good character for truth,[82] but if the adversary has merely introduced evidence denying the facts to which the witness testified, the greater number of courts will not permit a showing of the witness's good character for truth.[83]

76. See n. 74, supra.

77. See n. 75, supra. See likewise Derrick v. Wallace, 217 N.Y. 520, 112 N.E. 440 (1916); C.J.S. Witnesses § 534; 4 Wigmore, Evidence § 1106. But see Commonwealth v. Ford, 199 Pa.Super. 102, 184 A.2d 401 (1962) (affirming rejection of reputation evidence and stating matter was within the discretion of the trial judge); Lakes v. Buckeye State Mutual Ins. Ass'n, 110 Ohio App. 115, 168 N.E.2d 895 (1959) (possibly dictum).

78. First Nat. Bank v. Blakeman, 19 Okl. 106, 91 P. 868 (1907) ("when the witness has been impeached by evidence of particular acts of criminal or moral misconduct, either on cross-examination or by record of conviction," citing cases); 4 Wigmore, Evidence § 1106.

79. Harris v. State (1906) 49 Tex.Cr.R. 338, 94 S.W. 227 (most rigid cross-examination, in a manner tending to bring witness into disrepute before jury and indirectly attack his testimony). See also Commonwealth v. Ingraham, 73 Mass. (7 Gray) 46, 49 (1856) which sanctions proof of good character after a mere abortive attempt to prove the witness's bad character; C.J.S. Witnesses § 532. Mere inconsistencies in the testimony of the witness, exposed by cross-examination, were held insuffi-

cient to justify good character reputation evidence in Royal v. Cameron, 382 S.W.2d 335 (Tex.Civ.App. 1964).

80. People v. Ah Fat, 48 Cal. 61, 64 (1874) (evidence that state's witness had offered to identify killer "if there was any coin in it"). See also, Rodriguez v. State, 165 Tex.Cr.R. 179, 305 S.W.2d 350 (1957) (where attempt has been made to show corrupt motives of witness).

81. Lassiter v. State, 35 Ala.App. 323, 47 So.2d 230 (1950), Note, 3 Ala.L.Rev. 206 (1950).

82. Dickson v. Dinsmore, 219 Ala. 353, 122 So. 437 (1929); Turner v. State, 112 Tex.Cr. 245, 16 S.W.2d 127 (1929). Contra: State v. Hoffman, 134 Iowa 587, 112 N.W. 103 (1907). See 4 Wigmore, Evidence § 1108; C.J.S. Witnesses § 623; Annot., 6 A.L.R. 862.

83. Louisville & N. R. Co. v. McClish, 115 F. 268 (C.C.A.Tenn.1902, opinion by Day, J.) (witness who testified he saw decedent pass along railway track shortly before train passed, contradicted by witness who testified first witness was not at the scene but was in opera house at the time; held error to admit character-support, though contradiction "admits of no reconciliation . . . upon any theory of honest mistake or failure of memory"); Whaley v. State, 157 Fla. 593, 26 So.2d 656 (1946) (murder: material conflict between testimony of accused and of officers as to terms of al-

Convenient as automatic answers to these seemingly minor trial questions may be, surely it is unrealistic to handle them in this mechanical fashion. A more sensible view is the notion that the judge should consider in each case whether the particular impeachment for inconsistency and the conflict in testimony,[84] or either of them, amounts in net effect to an attack on character for truth and should exercise his discretion accordingly to admit or exclude the character-support.[85]

Turning to the attempts to rehabilitate or support a witness by introduction of a prior statement consistent with his present testimony after the credibility of the witness has been attacked in some way, a similar question arises. What kind of attack upon the witness opens the door to evidence of prior statements by the witness consistent with his present story [86] on the stand? When the attack takes the form of impeachment of character, by showing misconduct, convictions or bad reputation, it is generally agreed that there is no color for sustaining by consistent statements.[87] The defense does not meet the assault. Further, if the attacker has charged bias, interest, corrupt influence, contrivance to falsify, or want of capacity to observe or remember, the applicable principle is that the prior consistent statement has no relevancy to refute the charge unless the consistent statement was made before the source of the bias, interest, influence or incapacity originated.[88]

---

leged oral confession, does not warrant admission of defendant's good reputation for truth). Contra: Redd v. Ingram, 207 Va. 939, 154 S.E.2d 149 (1967). See 4 Wigmore, Evidence § 1109; C.J.S. Witnesses § 643. Wigmore, supra, suggests that the argument for supporting character here is weaker than in the case of impeachment for inconsistency. This may be so when viewed from the requirement of an attack on character, but from the view of the administration of justice can one imagine a greater need for the jury to know "what manner of man" the witness is than in these cases of irreconcilable conflicts? It is only a pity that the minority who admit character support, have nothing better to avail themselves of than the feeble aid of "reputation for truth." Surely it is here that progress is needed so that courts may use an observer's opinion from observation of the witness's character, see § 41, supra; results of deception-tests, see § 46, supra; and results of tests for capacity to perceive and remember, see § 45, supra.

84. In most cases both the inconsistency and the conflict are available. The proof by the second witness of an inconsistent statement by the first, after the witness has denied on cross-examination making the inconsistent statement, always involves a conflict, and in general whenever a witness is impeached for inconsistency his substantive story will be contradicted.

85. See the stress placed upon discretion by Sibley, J. in Outlaw v. United States, 81 F.2d 805, 808 (5th Cir. 1936) and by Burford, C. J. in First Nat. Bank v. Blakeman, 19 Okl. 106, 91 P. 868, 871 (1907).

86. It will be noted that when the sole purpose of introducing the prior statement is to support the credibility of the witness, it is not "substantive" evidence. Townsend v. United States, 106 F.2d 273 (3d Cir. 1939) (dictum); 4 Wigmore, Evidence § 1132.

Likewise, it is important to note that the instant discussion assumes that the prior consistent statements cannot be introduced as evidence on the issues in the case because they are inadmissible under the traditional hearsay rule and its exceptions. For explanation of the view that prior consistent statements are not hearsay, but are admissible as evidence on the issues, see § 251, infra.

87. Stanford v. State, 34 Tex.Cr.R. 89, 29 S.W. 271 (1895) (bad reputation); 4 Wigmore, Evidence § 1125; Annot., 75 A.L.R.2d 909, 927.

88. Excluded on this ground: Abernathy v. Emporia Mfg. Co., 122 Va. 406, 95 S.E. 418 (1918) (corrupt offer by witness to sell testimony; consistent statement not shown to have been before the corrupt intent arose, improperly received); Sesterhenn v. Saxe, 88 Ill.App.2d 2, 232 N.E.2d 277 (1967) (consistent statement held inadmissible when impeachment attempt went to showing bias and not a recent fabrication); People v. Gardineer, 2 Mich.App. 337, 139 N.W.2d 890 (1966) (statement after alleged bias held inadmissible). Admitted where statement was made before the alleged influence arose. People v. Kynette, 15 Cal.2d 731, 104 P.2d 794, (1940); Burns v. Clayton, 237 S.C. 316, 117 S.E. 2d 300 (1960) (consistent statement made by witness "prior to the existence of his relation to cause"; impeachment suggesting witness had been paid to testify falsely). See Annot., 140 A.L.R. 21, 80, 117–128; Annot., 75 A.L.R.2d 909, 937, 117–118.

If the witness's accuracy of memory is challenged, it seems clear common sense that a consistent statement made shortly after the event and before he had time to forget, should be received in support. ". . . The accuracy of memory is supported by proof that at or near the time when the facts deposed to have transpired, and were fresh in the mind of the witness, he gave the same version

There is much division of opinion on the question whether impeachment by inconsistent statements opens the door to support by proving consistent statements.[89] A few courts hold generally that the support is permissible.[90] This rule has the merit of easy application in the court room. Most courts, since the inconsistency remains despite all consistent statements, hold generally that it does not.[91] But certain exceptions should be recognized. If the attacked witness denies the making of the inconsistent statement then some courts consider that the evidence of consistent statements near the time of the alleged inconsistent one, is relevant to fortify his denial.[92] Again, if in the particular situation, the attack by inconsistent statement is accompanied by, or interpretable as, a charge of a plan or contrivance to give false testimony, then proof of a prior consistent statement *before* the plan or contrivance was

formed, tends strongly to disprove that the testimony was the result of contrivance. Here all courts agree.[93] It is for the judge to decide whether the impeachment amounts to a charge of contrivance,—ordinarily this is the most obvious implication—and it seems he is entitled to have an avowal one way or another from counsel. If it does not, then it may often amount to an imputation of inaccurate memory. If so the consistent statement made when the event was recent and memory fresh should be received in support.[94] Recognition of these exceptions would leave it still open to these courts to exclude most statements procured after the inconsistent statement, and thus to discourage pressure on witnesses to furnish successive counter-statements.[95]

---

of them that he testified to on the trial." Smith, C. J. in Jones v. Jones, 80 N.C. 246, 250 (1879). See also Cross v. State, 118 Md. 660, 86 A. 223, 227 (1912). But some courts seem to reject this view. Annot., 140 A.L.R. 21, 48; Annot., 75 A.L.R. 2d 909, 929.

89. See decisions collected in 4 Wigmore, Evidence § 1126; Annot., 140 A.L.R. 21, 49–77; Annot. 75 A.L.R.2d 909, 930–935; Dec.Dig. Witnesses ⟨⟩395, 414(2).

90. See, e. g., Cross v. State, 118 Md. 660, 86 A. 223 (1912); Stafford v. Lyon, 413 S.W.2d 495 (Mo. 1967); State v. Bethea, 186 N.C. 22, 118 S.E. 800 (1923) (allowable after any form of impeachment); Annot., 140 A.L.R. 21, 59; Annot., 75 A.L.R.2d 909, 933.

91. See, e. g., Ellicott v. Pearl, 35 U.S. (10 Pet.) 412, 439 (1836) (opinion by Story, J.); Commonwealth v. Jenkins, 76 Mass. (10 Gray) 485, 488 (1858).

92. Stewart v. People, 23 Mich. 63, 74 (1871) (opinion by Cooley, J.); Parker v. State, 183 Ind. 130, 108 N.E. 517 (1915) (rule recognized); Twardosky v. New England Tel. & Tel. Co., 95 N.H. 279, 62 A.2d 723 (1948); Donovan v. Moore McCormack Lines, 266 App.Div. 406, 42 N.Y.S.2d 441 (1943); Annot., 140 A.L.R. 21, 68; Annot., 75 A.L.R.2d 909, 938. Contra: Burks v. State, 78 Ark. 271, 93 S.W. 983 (1906). See also Commonwealth v. White, 340 Pa. 139, 16 A.2d 407 (1940), which suggests that where the witness denies the inconsistent statement the admission of the supporting statement is in the judge's discretion.

93. Coates v. People, 106 Colo. 483, 106 P.2d 354 (1940); State v. Galloway, 247 A.2d 104 (Me.1968); People v. Mirenda, 23 N.Y.2d 439, 245 N.E.2d 194, 297 N.Y.S.2d 532 (1969) (witness himself testified to consistent statement on redirect); People v. Singer, 300 N.Y. 120, 89 N.E.2d 710 (1949), noted 35 Cornell L.Q. 867. In the last case the court points out that though the common phrase is "recent" fabrication or contrivance, the "recent" is misleading. It is not required to be recent as regards the trial, but only that the contrivance be more recent than the consistent statement. See cases collected 4 Wigmore, Evidence § 1129; C.J.S. Witnesses § 624; Annot., 140 A.L.R. 21, 93–128; Annot., 75 A.L.R.2d 909, 939–946. Some decisions also mention that the consistent statement should have been made before the witness would foresee its effect upon the fact issue, see Annot., 75 A.L.R. 2d 909, 946, or before motive to falsify even if made before an inconsistent statement, Giordano v. Eastern Utilities, Inc., 9 App.Div.2d 947, 195 N.Y.S.2d 753 (1959).

Also, there is authority that if the inconsistent statement used to impeach is part of a statement, the remainder may be introduced to explain or negative the inconsistent part. Affronti v. United States, 145 F.2d 3 (8th Cir. 1944); C.J.S. Witnesses § 622.

94. See n. 88, supra.

95. These after-statements have usually been excluded. See, e. g., Weiler v. Weiler, 336 S.W.2d 454 (Tex.Civ.App.1960); United States v. Sherman, 171 F.2d 619 (2d Cir. 1948, opinion by L. Hand, J.); Crawford v. Nilan, 289 N.Y. 444, 46 N.E.2d 512 (1943) (consistent statement procured from witness on morning of trial, held improperly admitted); Sweazey v. Valley Transport, 6 Wash.2d 324, 107 P.2d 567 (1940). The last two cases exemplify the stresses of the race for statements in accident

The fact of a complaint of rape and in some instances the details of the complaint have been held admissible. Both the fact of complaint and, where allowed, the details of the complaint may be admissible on the theory of rehabilitating or bolstering the complaining witness,[96] but since this evidence may also come in as substantive evidence under some theories, the matter is dealt with later.[97] Likewise, prior consistent statements of identification may be admissible substantively or to rehabilitate, but because prior identifications may be admissible as substantive evidence and also involve constitutional requirements, the subject is also discussed elsewhere.[98]

50. Proposed Changes in Existing Law.

One who has read the description of the present practice of impeachment and support, in the preceding sections, will have marveled at the archaic and seemingly arbitrary character of many of the rules. He will also have observed with regret the laggard pace of the law in taking advantage of the techniques and knowledge which are afforded by the modern sciences of physiology and psychology in appraising the perception, memory and veracity of witnesses. Two principal retarding influences are apparent, namely, an undue distrust by the judges of the capacity of jurors, and an over-emphasis upon the adversary or contentious aspect of our trial tradition.

The drafters of the Proposed Rules of Evidence for the United States District Courts and Magistrates, in the proposed rules dealing with credibility, have greatly simplified and modernized the practice. The following changes, among others, are proposed:

1. Inconsistent and consistent statements used to impeach or rehabilitate are made admissible as substantive evidence.[99]

2. A party may impeach his own witness.[1]

3. Opinions, as well as reputation, concerning truthfulness of witnesses are admissible. Specific instances relevant to truthfulness may be inquired into.[2]

---

controversies. See Maguire, Evidence: Common Sense and Common Law 63 (1947). Pressures by investigators of defendants and insurance companies often secure from witnesses one-sided statements in defendants' favor, and if the witness's testimony diverges in plaintiff's favor, these come in as inconsistent statements. The obviously needed opportunity to counter these statements comes in the witness's opportunity to deny or explain on cross-examination and re-direct. In a New York case where the plaintiff raised doubts as to the accuracy of his signed inconsistent statement written by defendant's investigator and said that he "talked him into giving it," the court admitted the plaintiff's consistent statement made five days later to plaintiff's employer and not for the purpose of the action, as bearing on the issue as to the accuracy of the inconsistent statement. One judge dissented in a vigorous opinion. Donovan v. Moore-McCormack Lines, 266 App.Div. 406, 42 N.Y.S.2d 441 (1943).

96. See 4 Wigmore, Evidence §§ 1134–1140, 6 id. §§ 1760, 1761; Dec.Dig. Rape ⮞48; C.J.S. Rape § 53.

97. See § 297, n. 56–61, infra.

98. See §§ 176, 251, infra.

99. F.R.Ev. (R.D.1971) 801:
"(d) Statements Which Are Not Hearsay. A statement is not hearsay if
(1) *Prior Statement by Witness.* The declarant testifies at the trial or hearing and is subject to cross-examination concerning the statement, and the statement is (i) inconsistent with his testimony, or (ii) consistent with his testimony and is offered to rebut an express or implied charge against him of recent fabrication or improper influence or motive, or (iii) one of identification of a person made soon after perceiving him; . . . ."

1. F.R.Ev. (R.D.1971) 607:
"The credibility of a witness may be attacked by any party, including the party calling him."

2. F.R.Ev. (R.D.1971) 608:
"(a) Opinion and Reputation Evidence of Character. The credibility of a witness may be attacked or supported by evidence in the form of reputation or opinion, but subject to these limitations: (1) the evidence may refer only to character for truthfulness or untruthfulness, and (2), except with respect to an accused who testifies in his own behalf, evidence of truthful character is admissible only after the character of the witness for truthfulness has been attacked by opinion or reputation evidence or otherwise.
"(b) Specific Instances of Conduct. Specific instances of the conduct of a witness, for the purpose of attacking or supporting his credibility, other

4. With limitations, convictions of crime may still be proved.[3]

than conviction of crime as provided in Rule 609, may not be proved by extrinsic evidence. They may, however, if clearly probative of truthfulness or untruthfulness and not remote in time, be inquired into on cross-examination of the witness himself or on cross-examination of a witness who testifies to his character for truthfulness or untruthfulness.

"The giving of testimony, whether by an accused or by any other witness, does not operate as a waiver of his privilege against self-incrimination when examined with respect to matters which relate only to credibility."

3. F.R.Ev. (R.D.1971) 609:

"(a) General Rule. For the purpose of attacking the credibility of a witness, evidence that he has been convicted of a crime, except on a plea of *nolo contendere*, is admissible but only if the crime (1) was punishable by death or imprisonment in excess of one year under the law under which he was convicted or (2) involved dishonesty or false statement regardless of the punishment, unless (3), in either case, the judge determines that the probative value of the evidence of the crime is substantially outweighed by the danger of unfair prejudice.

"(b) Time Limit. Evidence of a conviction under this rule is not admissible if a period of more than 10 years has elapsed since the date of conviction or of the release of the witness from confinement, whichever is the later date.

5. Finally, proof of religious views is prohibited.[4]

The Uniform Rules of Evidence propose somewhat different reforms.[5]

"(c) Effect of Pardon, Annulment, or Certificate of Rehabilitation. Evidence of a conviction is not admissible under this rule if (1) the conviction has been the subject of a pardon, annulment, certificate of rehabilitation, or other equivalent procedure, and (2) the procedure under which the same was granted or issued required a substantial showing of rehabilitation or was based on innocence.

"(d) Juvenile Adjudications. Evidence of juvenile adjudications is generally not admissible under this rule. The judge may, however, allow evidence of a juvenile adjudication of a witness other than the accused if conviction of the offense would be admissible to attack the credibility of an adult and the judge is satisfied that admission in evidence is necessary for a fair determination of the issue of guilt or innocence.

"(e) Pendency of Appeal. The pendency of an appeal therefrom does not render evidence of a conviction inadmissible. Evidence of the pendency of an appeal is admissible."

4. F.R.Ev. (R.D.1971) 610:

"Evidence of the beliefs or opinions of a witness on matters of religion is inadmissible for the purpose of showing that by reason of their nature his credibility is impaired on enhanced."

5. Uniform Rules 20, 21, 22, 28. See also N.J.R.Ev., 20, 21, 22; Kan.Stat.Ann., 60–420, 421, 422.

TITLE 3

ADMISSION AND EXCLUSION

CHAPTER 6

THE PROCEDURE OF ADMITTING AND EXCLUDING EVIDENCE

51. Presentation of Evidence: Offer of Proof.

At the outset, it should be noted that our adversary system imposes on the parties the burden of presenting evidence at the trial pursuant to rules and practices that make it clear when proof has been presented so that it is officially introduced and thereupon can be considered by the trier of fact in the resolution of fact issues.[1] The rules of practice concerning presentation of evidence, offers of proof, and the taking of objections are thus slanted to secure this result.

The presentation of things such as writings, photographs, knives, guns, and all kinds of tangible things often proves troublesome to neophytes.[2] There are variations in local procedures, but the process may be shortly and generally described here.[3] The party wishing to introduce any sort of evidence of this type should first have the thing marked by the clerk for identification as an exhibit for the party.[4] Having had the thing marked by the clerk for identification as an exhibit, the proponent should "lay the foundation" for its introduction as an exhibit by having it appropriately identified or authenticated by the testimony of a witness who is qualified to identify or authenticate it.[5]

Next, the proposed exhibit should be submitted to the opposing attorney for his in-

---

1. The fact issues at the trial should be decided upon the facts "in the record", i. e., facts officially introduced in accordance with the rules of practice, and facts which the court may judicially notice. See Ch. 35, infra.

2. Introduction of depositions does not require the procedures described in the subsequent text.

3. The techniques for introducing things in evidence as exhibits are described and illustrated in detail in Goldstein and Lane, Trial Technique §§ 12.01–12.58 (2d ed. 1969); Keeton Trial Tactics and Methods 57–63 (1954); Virgie v. Stetson, 73 Me. 452, 461 (1882); C.J.S. Trial §§ 61–64.

4. The usual purpose of having the clerk mark proposed exhibits for identification is to make them part of the record in case they are refused as exhibits. See Duncan v. McTiernan, 151 Conn. 469, 199 A.2d 332 (1964) (stating that it is error for the trial court to refuse to permit a proposed exhibit to be marked for identification). Tags may be used for marking, if needed.

5. Certain items are "self authenticating". See generally, Authentication, Ch. 22, infra.

spection, at least upon his request, and then the proponent should present it to the judge, stating, e. g., "Plaintiff offers this (document or object, describing it), marked, 'Plaintiff's Exhibit No. 2' for identification, as Plaintiff's Exhibit No. 2." At this point, the opponent may make his objection to its receipt in evidence, and the judge will make his ruling upon the objection. Assuming the judge rules that the thing will be accepted in evidence, if it is a writing, it may be read to the jury by the counsel offering it or by the witness, or if it is a thing it may be shown, or passed, to the jury, in the discretion of the judge or in accordance with local custom or rules, for inspection by the jury.

Of course, the usual way of presenting oral testimony is to call the witness to the stand and ask him questions. Normally, (but not always) the opponent is required to object to testimony by objections to the questions of the examiner before the witness answers the questions.[6] Ordinarily, the admissibility of testimony is thus decided by the judge's sustaining or overruling objections to questions. If the court sustains an objection to a question, the witness is prevented from answering the question and from testifying to that extent.

In such case, for two reasons, the proponent of the question should ordinarily make "an offer of proof". The usual practice is for the proponent to state to the judge what the witness would say if he were permitted to answer the question and what he expects to prove by the answer to the question.[7] While a sec-

ondary reason for an offer of proof is that it permits the judge to consider further the claim for admissibility, the primary reason is to include the proposed answer and expected proof in the official record of the trial, so that in case of appeal upon the judge's ruling, the appellate court may understand the scope and effect of the question and proposed answer in considering whether the judge's ruling sustaining an objection was proper. The trial court will usually require this offer of proof to be made out of the hearing of the jury.[8] It is also important to note that upon cross-examination the requirement is relaxed.[9]

"(b) **Record of Offer and Ruling.** The judge may add any other or further statement which shows the character of the evidence, the form in which it was offered, the objection made, and the ruling thereon. He may direct the making of an offer in question and answer form.

"(c) **Hearing of Jury.** In jury cases, proceedings shall be conducted, to the extent practicable, so as to prevent inadmissible evidence from being suggested to the jury by any means, such as making statements or offers of proof or asking questions in the hearing of the jury."

The term "proffer" is sometimes used to describe an offer of proof.

For cases stating the requirement of an offer of proof, see Philadelphia Record Co. v. Sweet, 124 Pa.Super. 414, 188 A. 631 (1936) (reversible error to refuse counsel opportunity of making offer); In re Polly's Estate, 174 Neb. 222, 117 N.W.2d 375 (1962); D'Acchioli v. Cairo, 87 R.I. 345, 141 A.2d 269 (1958) (rule applied to trial without a jury). See generally, Dec.Dig. ⊂⊃44–49; C.J.S. Trial §§ 73–84; Annot., 89 A.L.R.2d 279. See also, n. 15, infra.

When an offer of proof is proper, the trial court must permit it to be made. See C.J.S. Trial § 73; Annot., 89 A.L.R.2d 279, 286–287.

On occasion, circumstances may call for the judge to exercise his discretion to allow or require an offer to be made by actually putting questions and having the witness answer. Thus doubts as to what the witness might in fact say are put to rest, a method of dealing with "optimistic" offers. Such an offer should, of course, be made out of the presence of the jury. In nonjury cases, offers in question and answer form may also serve to put an appellate court in possession of facts necessary for a final disposition of the case, rather than remanding, if it disagrees with a trial judge's exclusionary ruling. See 5 Moore's Federal Practice ¶ 43.11 (2d ed. 1968).

8. See cases cited in C.J.S. Trial § 84.

9. On cross-examination, the examining counsel is ordinarily assumed not to have had an advance

---

6. See § 52, infra.

7. F.R.Ev. (R.D.1971) 103:

"(a) **Effect of Erroneous Ruling.** Error may not be predicated upon a ruling which admits or excludes evidence unless a substantial right of the party is affected, and

. . .

(2) *Offer of Proof.* In case the ruling is one excluding evidence, the substance of the evidence was made known to the judge by offer or was apparent from the context within such questions were asked.

For the purpose of appeal, a question, in the context of the record, may itself so specifically indicate the purport of the expected answer that the appeal court will consider the propriety of the ruling upon the question without an offer of proof.[10] But when, as is more usual, an offer of proof is required before the appellate court will consider a ruling sustaining an objection to a question, the statement constituting the offer of proof must be reasonably specific [11] and must state the

purpose of the proof offered unless the purpose is apparent.[12] Where the offered testimony suggests a question as to its materiality or competency, the offer of proof must indicate the facts on which relevancy [13] or admissibility of the testimony depends.[14]

opportunity to know what the witness will answer, and the requirement of an offer will not usually be applied. Cohen v. Cohen, 196 Ga. 562, 27 S.E.2d 28, 30 (1943); Higgins v. Pratt, 316 Mass. 700, 56 N.E.2d 595 (1944); Calci v. Brown, 95 R.I. 216, 186 A.2d 234 (1962) (dictum). But even on cross-examination the court in its discretion may require counsel to hint his purpose far enough to show the materiality of the answer hoped for, or enough must be made to appear so that error will be indicated upon appeal. Fahey v. Clark, 125 Conn. 44, 3 A.2d 313 (1938) (court here required too strong an assurance); Lavieri v. Ulysses, 149 Conn. 396, 180 A.2d 632 (1962) (insufficient hint); Perry v. Carter, 332 Mass. 508, 125 N.E.2d 780 (1955) (error in exclusion of questions did not appear from questioning). And it has been held that the cross-examiner may make an offer of proof if he desires to do so. Abbadessa v. Tegu, 122 Vt. 338, 173 A.2d 153 (1961).

10. Hartnett v. Boston Store, 265 Ill. 331, 106 N.E. 837 (1914); Marshall v. Marshall, 71 Kan. 313, 80 P. 629, 630 (1905) (". . . the question itself may be, and often is, of such character that, in connection with the other proceedings, it clearly indicates the materiality of the answer sought, and renders superfluous any statement as to what it is expected to be," a dictum); Hartwig v. Olson, 158 N.W.2d 81 (Ia.1968) (dictum); Manning v. Redevelopment Agency of Newport, 103 R.I. 371, 238 A.2d 378 (1968) (court held answer to particular question was not apparent in part).

Obviously, the skillful trial lawyer will make an offer rather than gambling on a successful invocation of this approach, which is often the resort of those who forgot.

11. Kane v. Carper-Dover Merc. Co., 206 Ark. 674, 177 S.W.2d 41 (1944) ("we offer to prove . . . that C. D. is not the proper plaintiff for recovery or damage": too indefinite; must be so specific as to give the opportunity to court to rule on particular testimony); Douillard v. Woodd, 20 Cal.2d 665, 128 P.2d 6 (1942) (counsel for defendant offered to show by defendant and "by other witnesses" that the plaintiffs took positions inconsistent with asserted agreement, too general); Ostmo v. Tennyson, 70 N.D. 558, 296 N.W. 541 (1941) (must show what facts are sought to be introduced, so that court may see whether they have any bear-

ing); Albert Johann & Sons Co. v. Echols, 143 Ind. App. 122, 238 N.E.2d 685 (1968) (offer of proof far exceeded scope of question and contained conclusions of law and fact); Shoemaker v. Selnes, 220 Or. 573, 349 P.2d 473 (1960) (one offer so vague it could not be understood; second offer stated counsel "believed" witness would testify as specified).

Compare Moran v. Levin, 318 Mass. 770, 64 N.E.2d 360 (1945) (deceit for sale of dairy cows, one of which was alleged not to produce milk because diseased, plaintiff's offer to show by plaintiff and wife "certain representations made by defendant with reference to the condition, the health of these cows, as to whether they were milk producers" held, sufficient though a "summary" or "abstract" of the proposed evidence); Woods v. Woods, 177 Neb. 542, 129 N.W.2d 519 (1964) (offer need not state every detail of proposed testimony but is sufficient if it directs court's attention to material testimony).

12. Holman v. Kemp, 70 Minn. 422, 73 N.W. 186, 188 (1897) (counsel asked plaintiff if he did not drink a good deal before the accident, excluded; appellant claimed this was relevant to explain plaintiff's physical condition at time of trial; held, insufficient offer. "If such was the real purpose of the evidence, it was not apparent upon the record, and the trial court's attention should have been specifically called to the object of the evidence."); Davey Bros., Inc. v. Stop & Shop, Inc., 351 Mass. 59, 217 N.E.2d 751 (1966) (offer of proof failed to indicate purpose for which testimony would be relevant); and cases cited C.J.S. Trial § 76.

13. Braman v. Wiley, 119 F.2d 991 (7th Cir.Ind. 1941) (collision; there was evidence that defendant was drunk; defendant offered a witness to testify to a conversation with defendant soon after; on appeal defendant contended this was material to negative drunkenness; held, not relevant to the purpose stated); Taylor v. Henderson, 112 Vt. 107, 22 A.2d 318 (1941) (must point out evidentiary relation to the issue on which offered); Ex Parte Taylor, 322 S.W.2d 309 (Tex.Civ.App.1959) (statement that "the whole matter is relevant to this matter" held insufficient when judge inquired as to purpose of question); Fuchs v. Kupper, 22 Wis.2d 107, 125 N.W.2d 360 (1963) (question immaterial in absence of offer of proof of additional facts). Unless relevancy must have been apparent. Joslin v. Idaho Times Pub. Co., 60 Idaho 235, 91 P.2d 386 (1939); Creighton v. Elgin, 387 Ill. 592, 56 N.E.2d 825 (1944) (question itself showed purposes and materiality).

14. Smith v. Pine, 234 Iowa 256, 12 N.W.2d 236 (1943) (failure to state time of making of state-

If counsel specifies a purpose for which the proposed evidence is inadmissible and the judge excludes, counsel cannot complain of the ruling on appeal though it could have been rightly admitted for another purpose.[15]

If part of the evidence offered, as in the case of a deposition, a letter, or a conversation, is admissible and a part is not, it is incumbent on the offeror, not the judge, to select the admissible part. If counsel offers both good and bad together and the judge rejects the entire offer, the offeror may not complain on appeal.[16]

The method of offer of proof described above assumes there is a witness upon the stand who is being questioned.[17] Suppose, however, that there are several witnesses who are available, but not in court, to prove a line of facts, and the judge's rulings on the law have indicated that he will probably exclude this line of testimony, or the judge rules in advance that the line of testimony is inadmissible. Must the party produce each of these witnesses, question them, and on exclusion, state the purport of each expected answer? A few decisions have said that this procedure must be followed before an effective ruling can be secured.[18] Obviously it would often be a wasteful performance which witnesses, counsel and judge would desire to avoid. The better view is that it is not invariably essential, but that a sufficient offer of proof may be made without producing the witnesses, if it is sufficiently specific [19] and if there is nothing in the record to indicate a want of good faith or inability to produce the proof.[20]

ment offered as "res gestae"); Emery v. F. P. Asher, Jr. & Sons, 196 Md. 1, 75 A.2d 333 (1950) (collision: trial court properly refused to permit plaintiff to prove by expert witness the normal reaction time, the stopping distance on highway involved and other scientific deductions, where proffer did not take into consideration fact that accident occurred at night on highway with which plaintiff was unfamiliar, and that plaintiff did not know whether his headlights were depressed or shining full distance ahead); Deaton & Son v. Miller Well Servicing Co., 231 S.W.2d 944 (Tex. Civ.App.1950) (party offering evidence which would ordinarily be hearsay—here declarations of an agent—must show facts bringing it under some exception); Clements v. Jungert, 90 Idaho 143, 408 P.2d 810 (1965) (party offering evidence excluded as hearsay was required to show authority of declarer).

15. Dietrich v. Kettering, 212 Pa. 356, 61 A. 927 (1905); Davey Bros., Inc., v. Stop and Shop, Inc., n. 12, supra. Likewise, if a specific ground for admission is claimed in the offer of proof but is not applicable and the judge excludes the evidence, the proponent cannot complain if there was another ground for admission. Johnson v. Rockaway Bus Corp., 145 Conn. 204, 140 A.2d 708 (1958) (claim of admissibility as a declaration against interest precluded consideration on appeal of admissibility as an admission of a party); Watkins v. Watkins, 397 S.W.2d 603 (Mo.1966) (on cross-examination examiner made an offer of proof apparently on basis matter was relevant to issues; bearing on credibility not considered on appeal); C.J.S. Trial § 82; Annot., 89 A.L.R.2d 279, 306.

16. Sooner Pipe & Supply Corp. v. Rehm, 447 P.2d 758 (Okl.1968) (offer of incompetent evidence included); Morris v. E. I. DuPont de Nemours & Co., 346 Mo. 126, 139 S.W.2d 984 (1940) (motion picture, in part irrelevant); Williams v. Rhode Island Hospital Trust Co., 88 R.I. 23, 143 A.2d 324 (1958); C.J.S. Trial § 82; Annot., 89 A.L.R.2d 279, 306.

17. In the case of a single witness, an offer of proof is usually held ineffective when made before putting a question to the witness (to which objection may be taken) and some cases hold that a witness must ordinarily be placed on the stand and questioned in connection with the making of an offer of proof. See cases cited in Annot., 89 A.L.R.2d 279, 283–286.

18. Chicago City Ry. Co. v. Carroll, 206 Ill. 318, 68 N.E. 1087 (1903); Eschbach v. Hurtt, 47 Md. 61, 66 (1877) ("If the defendant had at the trial witnesses who could have proved . . . it was his duty to have called them or one of them to the stand and propounded appropriate questions. . . .").

19. It would seem wise to name the witness or witnesses and to indicate the particulars that each would prove.

20. Scotland County v. Hill, 112 U.S. 183, 186 (1884) ("If the trial court has doubts about the good faith of an offer of testimony, it can insist on the production of the witness, and upon some attempt to make the proof, before it rejects the offer; but if it does reject it, and allows a bill of exceptions which shows that the offer was actually made and refused, and there is nothing else in the record to indicate bad faith, an appellate court must assume that the proof could have been made. . . ."); Witt v. Voigt, 162 Wis. 568, 156 N.W. 954 (1916) (counsel said he had witnesses in court who would testify to certain facts, whereon court said such evidence would not be received, held a sufficient

52. Objections.[21]

If the administration of the exclusionary rules of evidence is to be fair and workable the judge must be informed promptly of contentions that evidence should be rejected, and the reasons therefor. The initiative is placed on the party, not on the judge. The general approach, accordingly, is that a failure to object to an offer of evidence at the time the offer is made, assigning the grounds, is a waiver upon appeal of any ground of complaint against its admission. *It is important to note, however, that this usual approach is modified by the doctrine of plain error, which is discussed at the end of this section.*

Time of Making: Motions to Strike. Consistently with the above approach, counsel is not allowed to gamble upon the possibility of a favorable answer,[22] but must object to the admission of evidence as soon as the ground for objection becomes apparent.[23] Usually, in the taking of testimony of a witness an objection is apparent as soon as the question is asked, since the question is likely to indicate that it calls for inadmissible evidence. Then counsel must, if opportunity affords, state his objection before the witness answers.[24] But sometimes an objection before an answer to a question is not feasible. A forward witness may answer before counsel has a chance to object.[25] A question which is not objectionable may be followed by an objectionable unresponsive answer.[26] Or, after the evidence is received, a ground of objection to the evidence may be disclosed for the first time in the later course of the trial.[27] In all these cases, an "after-objection" may be stated as soon as the ground appears. The proper technique, for such an objection is to phrase a motion to strike out the objectionable evidence, and to request an instruction to the jury to disregard the evidence. Counsel should use the term "motion to strike", as just indicated, but it seems that any phraseology which directs the judge's attention to

offer). For cases involving one witness, see Missouri Pac. Ry. Co. v. Castle, 172 F. 841 (8th Cir. 1909); Garvey v. Chicago Rys. Co., 339 Ill. 276, 171 N.E. 271, 274, 275 (1930) (offer of evidence on motion for new trial without producing witness held sufficient, distinguishing *Carroll* case in next preceding note). There are cases contra these latter cases. See n. 17, supra.

It has been held that an offer of proof is not necessary when the judge indicates, in consistently excluding a line of testimony while witnesses are examined, that he will exclude such testimony, and when he is advised of the facts the party was seeking to prove. See State v. Pigques, 310 S.W. 2d 942 (Mo.1958).

21. 1 Wigmore, Evidence § 18; Dec.Dig. Trial ⚏73–97; C.J.S. Trial §§ 113–132; 53 Am.Jur. Trial §§ 132–155.

22. Hastings v. Serleto, 61 Cal.App.2d 672, 143 P.2d 956 (1943); Kuiken v. Garrett, 243 Iowa 785, 51 N.W.2d 149 (1952).

23. Cheffer v. Eagle Discount Stamp Co., 348 Mo. 1023, 156 S.W.2d 591 (1941). In Thomson v. Wheeler Constr. Co., 385 P.2d 111 (Alaska, 1963) the court stated it strongly disapproved a stipulation by the parties that all relevant evidence be admitted without objection subject to objection and motion to strike at the termination of the trial.

24. Stark's Adm'x v. Herndon's Adm'r, 292 Ky. 469, 166 S.W.2d 828 (1942) (question asked by juror); Lineberry v. Robinett, 446 S.W.2d 481 (Mo. App.1969).

25. A motion to strike should be made. Wightman v. Campbell, 217 N.Y. 479, 112 N.E. 184 (1916) (but in the particular situation an objection sufficed); Sorenson v. Smith, 65 Ore. 78, 129 P. 757, 131 P. 1022 (1913).

26. Wallace v. American Toll Bridge Co., 124 Or. 179, 264 P. 351 (1928) (proper question improper answer, approved practice is motion tó strike); Brown v. Parker, 375 S.W.2d 594 (Mo.App.1964) (dictum).

The mere fact that the answer is unresponsive is not an objection available to the opponent. Hester v. Goldsbury, 64 Ill.App.2d 66, 212 N.E.2d 316 (1965) and cases cited therein; Isham v. Birkel, 184 Neb. 800, 172 N.W.2d 92 (1969) (exclusion by trial judge on objection of opponent held reversible error under particular circumstances). The objection is only available to the questioner, who may move to strike. Davidson v. State, 211 Ala. 471, 100 So. 641 (1924).

27. Manley v. Combs, 197 Ga. 768, 30 S.E.2d 485 (1944) (diagnosis testified to by doctor on direct, disclosed on cross-examination to have been possibly based on hearsay: held, objection at time of later disclosure insufficient, should have made motion to rule out the earlier testimony); Young v. Dueringer, 401 S.W.2d 165 (Mo.App.1966).

the grounds as soon as they appear, and asserts the objection, should be sufficient.[28]

In the taking and subsequent use at the trial of depositions on oral or written questions, the time when objections must be made to the questions and answers is a matter variously regulated by rules and statutes in the different jurisdictions.[29] Usually objections going to the "manner and form" of the questions or answers, such as objections to leading questions or disclaimers of unresponsive answers—sometimes opinions and secondary evidence are put in this class—, must be made at the time of taking the deposition and disposed of upon motion before the trial.[30] Objections going to the "substance," such as relevancy and hearsay, may usually be urged for the first time when the deposition is offered in evidence at the trial.[31]

If evidence was introduced at the first trial of a case, and an available objection was not made at the first trial, may the same evidence when tendered at a second trial of the same case be effectively objected to at the second trial for the first time? It is usually held that when the objection is to the competency of the witness under the Dead Man's Statute,[32] or is a claim of privilege for confidential communications,[33] the failure to object at the first trial operates as a waiver of the objection for the second trial. These holdings are justified by the dubious policy of the Dead Man's Acts, which leads the courts to say they should be strictly confined,[34] and by the fact that a confidential communication once made public has lost its secrecy forever. However, in the absence of special considerations such as these, it seems that an objection to admissibility of evidence,[35] or to the competency of a witness,[36] based on substance rather than form, should be assertable at the second trial though it was available and not asserted at the first. This conclusion assumes that the enforcement generally of the substantial rules of evidence and competency will make for the better administration of justice.

---

28. See Hackenson v. City of Waterbury, 124 Conn. 679, 2 A.2d 215 (1938) (where plaintiff-witness "jumped the gun" and answered a question before defendant objected, and court sustained the objection; held, sufficient to eliminate evidence from jury's consideration, though there was no motion to strike); Wightman v. Campbell, 217 N.Y. 479, 112 N.E. 184 (1916) (where first question in series in proving the making by witness of a survey of land was answered before objection, and objection then made "to all that proof," and overruled; held, objector has benefit of his exception without motion to strike).

As to the adequacy of instructions to disregard, see § 58, n. 64, and § 59, infra.

29. Decisions are collected in Dec.Dig. Depositions ⊨105–111, and C.J.S. Depositions §§ 101–105.

30. 1 Wigmore, Evidence § 18, notes 7–14; C.J.S. Depositions § 101.

A fair rule of thumb is to include in this category objections which probably could have been obviated by the examiner if raised at the time.

31. See references next preceding note. For details under the federal rules, see F.R.Civ.P. 30(c), 32(b), 32(d) (3).

32. Faden v. Midcap's Estate, 112 Colo. 573, 152 P.2d 682 (1944); Billingsley v. Gulick, 256 Mich. 606, 240 N.W. 46 (1932); Collins v. Collins' Estate, 104 Vt. 506, 162 A. 361 (1932); Annot., 79 A.L.R. 176; C.J.S. Witnesses § 249.

33. Green v. Crapo, 181 Mass. 55, 62 N.E. 956 (1902) (attorney-client; Holmes, C. J., "The privacy for the sake of which the privilege was created was gone by the appellant's own consent . . ."); Elliott v. Kansas City, 198 Mo. 593, 96 S.W. 1023 (1906) (patient's privilege); People v. Bloom, 193 N.Y. 1, 85 N.E. 824 (1908) (same). Contra: Maryland Casualty Co. v. Maloney, 119 Ark. 434, 178 S.W. 387 (1915). See Annot., 79 A.L.R. 176, 179; 1 Wigmore, Evidence § 18(3); F.R.Ev. (P.D.) 5–11.

But because the question of waiver of privilege was novel in the case of a privilege afforded newsmen, the court directed that the usual rule not be applied at a new trial which the court ordered in Brogan v. Passaic Daily News, 22 N.J. 139, 123 A.2d 473 (1956).

34. Lucas v. Hamilton Realty Corp., 70 App.D.C. 277, 105 F.2d 800 (1939); Dec.Dig. Witnesses ⊨126.

35. State v. Kelleher, 224 Mo. 145, 123 S.W. 551 (1909) (dying declaration not confined to facts attending the act of killing); Meekins v. Norfolk & S. R. Co., 136 N.C. 1, 48 S.E. 501 (1904) (hearsay).

36. Young v. State, 122 Ga. 725, 50 S.E. 996 (1905) (want of knowledge of nature and sanctity of oath by witness, child of 12 years).

General and Specific Objections.[37] The precept constantly urged in the opinions is that objections must be accompanied by a reasonably definite statement of the grounds,[38] that is to say, that objections must reasonably indicate the appropriate rules of evidence as reasons for the objections made. These objections are labeled specific objections in contrast to so-called general objections which assign no such grounds for the objection. The purposes of the requirement are that the judge may understand the question raised and that the adversary may have an opportunity to remedy the defect, if possible.[39] This precept does not *per se* ban the use of general objections (objections which state no grounds) at the trial, but rather it is one that is enforced to a certain extent on appeal. If the judge *over-rules* a general objection, the objecting party may not ordinarily complain of the ruling on appeal by urging a valid ground not mentioned when the objection was made.[40] However, there are three exceptional situations in which this rule on appeal will not be followed—in which the appeal court will consider whether a valid ground of objection resulted in an erroneous overruling although it was, of course, not stated by the general objection made to the trial judge. The

first is that, if the ground for exclusion should have been obvious to judge and opposing counsel without stating it, the want of specification of the ground is immaterial for purposes of complaining on appeal of the judge's action in overruling the general objection.[41] This exception is clear good sense. Second, it has also been said that if the evidence is not admissible for any purpose, the general objection may be sufficient to secure on appeal a review of the judge's action in overruling the objection.[42] But if the ground is not apparent, it seems there is still need for specification, for appeal purposes. Third, it has been suggested that if the omitted ground was one that could not have been obviated, the general objection may serve to secure consideration on appeal of an unstated specific ground for objection.[43] It is believed that

37. 1 Wigmore, Evidence § 18(c) (1) (2); Dec.Dig. Trial ☞81–84; C.J.S. Trial §§ 123–132; C.J.S. Criminal Law § 1036.

38. See, e. g., Craig v. Citizens Trust Co., 217 Ind. 434, 26 N.E.2d 1006 (1940); Fisher v. Suko, 98 N.W.2d 895 (N.D.1959) (objection held sufficient).

F.R.Ev. (R.D.1971) 103:

"**(a) Effect of Erroneous Ruling.** Error may not be predicated upon a ruling which admits or excludes evidence unless a substantial right of the party is affected, and

"*(1) Objection.* In case the ruling is one admitting evidence, a timely objection or motion to strike appears of record, stating the specific ground of objection, if the specific ground was not apparent from the context. . . ."

39. City of Yuma v. Evans, 85 Ariz. 229, 336 P.2d 135 (1959).

40. See, e. g., Reed v. Trainor, 142 Ind.App. 192, 233 N.E.2d 685 (1968) and see C.J.S. Appeal and Error §§ 247, 253; C.J.S. Trial § 124.

41. Styblo v. McNeil, 217 Ill.App. 316, 45 N.E.2d 1011 (1943) ("An objection, except where it is obvious, should be stated in such a manner as to inform the court of the point being urged"); Johnson v. Jackson, 43 Ill.App.2d 251, 193 N.E.2d 485 (1963) ("it is difficult to show that a particular defect cannot be cured or that the ground for objection is obvious"; held not obvious in this case); Floy v. Hibbard, 227 Iowa 149, 287 N.W. 829 (1939) (general objection sufficient, "where the grounds of the objection are discernible"); Hungate v. Hudson, 353 Mo. 944, 185 S.W.2d 646 (1945) (when evidence "self-evidently wholly incompetent" or obviously prejudicial, general objection of irrelevancy sufficient). See People v. Bob, 29 Cal.2d 321, 175 P.2d 12 (1946) where the evidence offered was hearsay but the opponent did not specifically make that objection; the court said that where it was obvious from the colloquy that an objection specifying hearsay would have been overruled, the lack of precision in the objection would not render it ineffective.

At the trial level, trial judges constantly act upon general objections, whose grounds are obvious, by sustaining them.

On appeal, however, reliance on this doctrine may indicate oversight in failing to "protect the record."

42. Granberry v. Gilbert, 276 Ala. 486, 163 So.2d 641 (1964) (if illegal for any purpose, and incurable by other evidence or by reframing question); Scally v. Flannery, 292 Ill.App. 349, 11 N.E.2d 123 (1937); State v. Rauscher Chevrolet Co., 291 S.W. 2d 89 (Mo.1956).

43. Floy v. Hibbard, 227 Iowa 149, 287 N.W. 829 (1939); Smith v. Fine, 351 Mo. 1179, 175 S.W.2d 761 (1943).

this exception overlooks the consideration that though the objection to the particular evidence could not have been obviated, yet if the ground of objection had been stated the judge and adverse counsel might have appreciated its force, and the offer might have been excluded or withdrawn, and the adversary might have introduced other evidence to fill the gap.[44]

As a result of the above-mentioned rules, a trial judge's action in overruling a general objection will usually be supported on appeal. And if the trial judge *sustains* a general objection, the upper court is again charitable toward his ruling. "When evidence is *excluded* upon a mere general objection, the ruling will be upheld, if any ground in fact existed for the exclusion. It will be assumed, in the absence of any request by the opposing party or the court to make the objection definite, that it was understood, and that the ruling was placed upon the right ground." [45]

Examples of general objections are "I object;" [46] or objections on the ground that the evidence is "inadmissible," [47] "illegal," [48] or "incompetent," [49] or is not proper testimony for the jury; [50] or an objection "on all the grounds ever known or heard of".[51] One of the most overworked forms is an objection on the ground that the evidence is "incompetent, irrelevant and immaterial." Its rhythm and alliteration have seduced some lawyers to employ it as a routine and meaningless ritual, a "vain repetition." Thus, courts frequently treat this form as equivalent merely to the general objection,[52] "I object." The word "incompetent" as applied to evidence means no more than inadmissible, and thus cannot be said to state a ground of objection. However, the terms, "irrelevant and immaterial," do state, though in general terms, a distinct and substantial ground for exclusion.[53] A requirement that the objector state specifically wherein the evidence, as applied to the particular issues, is irrelevant or immaterial, as the courts seem to demand, seems in many situations unduly burdensome. It would be far more practical to consider the irrelevancy objection in this general form as the equivalent of a specific objection with the qualification that if the judge has any doubt of relevancy, he may call upon the proponent to explain the purpose of the proof.[54]

---

44. See Campbell v. Paschall, 132 Tex. 226, 121 S.W. 2d 593 (1938).

45. Tooley v. Bacon, 70 N.Y. 34, 37 (1877). To like effect: Morgan Hill Paving Co. v. Pratt City Sav. Bank, 220 Ala. 686, 127 So. 502 (1930); General Acc. Fire & Life Assur. Corp. v. Camp, 348 S.W.2d 782 (Tex.Civ.App.1961); C.J.S. Trial § 124b; 1 Wigmore, Evidence § 18, note 26. If the offering counsel, however, requests of the objector and the judge the reason for objection, and the request is denied, when if the grounds had been furnished they could have been obviated, the ruling can be attacked. Colburn v. Chicago, St. Paul, M. & O. Ry. Co., 109 Wis. 377, 85 N.W. 354 (1901).

46. Gerald v. Caterers, Inc., 382 S.W.2d 740 (Mo. App.1964); C.J.S. Trial § 124c.

47. Fowler v. Wallace, 131 Ind. 347, 31 N.E. 53 (1892).

48. Johnston v. Johnston, 174 Ala. 220, 57 So. 450 (1912).

49. Minchen v. Hart, 72 F. 294 (8th Cir. 1896); C.J.S. Trial § 124c.

50. Itasca Lumber Co. v. Martin, 230 F. 584 (8th Cir. 1916).

51. Johnston v. Clements, 25 Kan. 376 (1881) (possibly a world's record). For additional examples of general objections, see C.J.S. Trial § 124.

52. Vogel v. Sylvester, 148 Conn. 666, 174 A.2d 122 (1961) (objection on basis of irrelevancy); Goldfoot v. Lofgren, 135 Ore. 533, 296 P. 843 (1931); Dec.Dig. Trial ☞83(2); C.J.S. Trial § 124c.

53. See ch. 16, infra.

54. Compare the practice, under a statute in Oklahoma (12 Okla.Stat.Ann. § 424) which makes an objection to evidence on the ground that it is incompetent, irrelevant, and immaterial cover all matters ordinarily embraced within those objections, and makes it unnecessary "to specify further the grounds of such objections or to state the specific reasons whereby the question is so objectionable," unless the court or opposing counsel inquire of the objector wherein the question is so objectionable, and thereupon the objector shall state specifically his reasons or grounds for such objection. McDonald v. Strawn, 78 Okl. 271, 190 P. 558, 562 (1920). See broader rule, Md. Rules of Proc. 522 d.1, "Unless requested by the court, it is not necessary to state the grounds for objections to evidence." See also Price v. Bates, 320 S.W.2d 786 (Ky.1959).

If relevancy is adequately challenged, it seems that it is not essential to specify in addition that the evidence is "prejudicial" in the sense of arousing undue hostility against the party.[55] Prejudice is a mere factor in weighing relevancy, i. e., in determining whether the evidence has sufficient probative value to outweigh its liabilities.

It is important to note that the above rules relate more directly to the creation of grounds for appealing a judge's ruling, but that, on the other hand, the trial judge may rule on objections with these rules for appeal purposes in mind. Thus, it is usually thought desirable for counsel to make specific objections at the trial, at least whenever counsel has some confidence concerning his grounds for objection.[56]

Objections should be specific not only with respect to the statement of grounds, but also with respect to a particular part of an offer, in view of another rule as to saving error for appeal. If evidence sought to be introduced consists of several statements or items tendered as a unit, e. g., a deposition, a letter, a conversation, a transcript of testimony or the like, and if the objection is to the whole of the evidence when parts are subject to the objection made and parts are not, the judge will not be put in error for overruling the objec-

tion.[57] It is not the judge's duty to sever the bad parts if some are good.[58] Obviously such a rule should not be administered rigidly by the appellate courts but with due concession, if need be, to the realities of the particular trial situation.

Even more clearly, if evidence offered is properly admissible on a particular issue, but not upon some other issue, or is admissible against one party but not against another,[59] an objector who asks that this evidence be excluded altogether, though he assigns grounds, cannot complain on appeal if his objection is overruled. He should have asked that the admission of the evidence be limited to the particular purpose or party.[60]

For appeal purposes, there is also some hazard in making a specific objection because the overruling of an objection, based on an untenable ground, will not be overturned on appeal if there was a tenable ground for exclusion which could have been urged.[61]

---

55. Hungate v. Hudson, 353 Mo. 944, 185 S.W.2d 646 (1945) and Luechtefeld v. Marglous, 151 S.W.2d 710, 713 (Mo., 1941), wherein the court said: "Of course a party objecting to evidence under the general assignment that it is irrelevant may on appeal show its prejudicial effect, though not specifically pointed out to the trial court, but such prejudice must be of the character naturally to be expected from the admission of such evidence." On the other hand, if evidence is relevant and admissible the mere objection that it is "prejudicial" is not operative. Isley v. Little, 219 Ga. 23, 131 S.E.2d 623 (1963).

The holding contrary to the text in McEwen v. Texas & P. Ry. Co., 92 S.W.2d 308 (Tex.Civ.App.1936) seems difficult to support.

56. Keeton, Trial Tactics and Methods 199–200 (1954).

57. Clayton v. Prudential Ins. Co. of America, 4 N.C.App. 43, 165 S.E.2d 763 (1969) (objection to letter as a whole was insufficient although part was inadmissible because hearsay and opinion); Jacobson v. Bryan, 244 Wis. 359, 12 N.W.2d 789 (1944) (traffic officer's report of accident partly based on personal knowledge, partly not; objection to whole report, insufficient); Dec.Dig. Trial ⟨key⟩85; C.J.S. Trial § 130.

58. Mucci v. LeMonte, 157 Conn. 566, 254 A.2d 879 (1969) (citing above text). And the judge may sustain the objection without error, since he has no duty to separate the good from the bad. See § 51, supra.

59. *Issues.* Finley v. Smith, 240 Ark. 323, 399 S.W. 2d 271 (1966); Curtin v. Benjamin, 305 Mass. 489, 26 N.E.2d 354 (1940); Dec.Dig. Trial ⟨key⟩86.

Parties. Solomon v. Dabrowski, 295 Mass. 358, 3 N.E.2d 744 (1936); Dec.Dig. Trial ⟨key⟩87. But see Scott v. State, 19 App.Div.2d 574, 240 N.Y.S.2d 279 (1963) (absent some signal that proof properly admissible against one party, but inadmissible against a second party, is to be received against the second party, counsel for second party "ought to be safe in believing that the judge will receive and consider the evidence only against the party in whose case it is admissible").

60. Finley v. Smith, next preceding note; Walls v. Clark, 252 Ore. 421, 449 P.2d 141 (1969) (parties).

61. Kroger Grocery & Baking Co. v. Harpole, 175 Miss. 227, 166 So. 335 (1936); People ex rel. Black-

Repetition of Objections. A offers testimony by one witness which his adversary, B, thinks is incompetent. He objects, and the objection is *sustained.* In such event, if A offers similar testimony by the same or another witness, B must of course repeat his objection if he is to complain of the later evidence.[62] Suppose, however, the first objection is *overruled.* Must B then repeat his objection when other like evidence similarly objectionable is offered? A few decisions intimate that he must,[63] a practice which places B in the invidious semblance of a contentious obstructor, and conduces to waste of time and fraying of patience. Most courts, however, hold that B is entitled to assume that the judge will continue to make the same ruling and that he need not repeat the objection.[64] It seems that the consequence of this view should be, that the first objection remains good and is not waived, and that in addition, the reach of this objection extends to all similar evidence subject to the same objection. It seems that in any jurisdiction where the practice in this respect is at all doubtful, it is a wise precaution for objecting

counsel to ask the judge to have the record show that it is understood that the objection goes to all other like evidence, and when later evidence is offered, to have it noted that the earlier objection applies.

The Exception.[65] Closely associated with the objection but distinct from it in the classic common law practice is the exception. Taking an exception includes two steps. After the judge's adverse ruling excluding his evidence or overruling his objection, the party's counsel says, "We except." This is a protest against the correctness of the ruling and a statement that the party does not acquiesce in it.[66] Following this protest the party aggrieved will request that "a bill of exception be allowed," and the terms of this may then be briefly agreed on between judge and counsel. This bill of exceptions will recite (1) the evidence admitted, when the ruling overrules the objection, or (2) the evidence expected or proffered, if the ruling excludes, (3) the objection, (4) the ruling, and (5) the fact that the protestation was made and the bill requested and allowed.[67] The bill of exceptions when finally signed by the judge becomes part of the record for the reviewing court by the terms of the ancient Statute of Westminster the Second.[68]

This procedure for exceptions is clumsy and burdensome. The policy of requiring counsel to protest against the court's rulings when the party's position is already clear from the

---

mon v. Brent, 97 Ill.App.2d 438, 240 N.E.2d 255 (1968); State v. Dietz, 115 N.W.2d 1 (N.D.1962).

However, if a specific objection is made on an untenable ground and sustained, it seems that if there were another valid ground for exclusion, the ruling should be upheld unless it appears that the **true** objection if stated could have been obviated, **or** if incurable the gap could have been filled by other testimony. Compare, however, Bloodgood v. Lynch, 293 N.Y. 308, 56 N.E.2d 718 (1944) where the court intimates that where the evidence is excluded on a specific objection, the appellate court will not consider the availability of a different ground.

62. Wagner v. Jones, 77 N.Y. 590 (semble) (1879); Frost v. Goddard, 25 Me. 414 (1845).

63. See, e. g., Shelton v. Southern Ry. Co., 193 N.C. 670, 139 S.E. 232 (1927).

64. Tucker v. Reil, 51 Ariz. 357, 77 P.2d 203 (1938); Louisville & N. R. Co. v. Rowland's Adm'r, 215 Ky. 663, 286 S.W. 929 (1926); West-Nesbitt, Inc. v. Randall, 126 Vt. 481, 236 A.2d 676 (1967); Dec. Dig. Trial ⊕79; C.J.S. Trial § 122; 53 Am.Jur. Trial § 146, and see an excellent discussion in Ladd, Common Mistakes in the Technique of Trial, 22 Iowa L.Rev. 609, 612–617 (1937).

65. 1 Wigmore, Evidence § 20; Dec.Dig. Trial ⊕99–105; C.J.S. Trial § 146; 53 Am.Jur. Trial §§ 154, 155.

66. The two functions of the exception are lucidly described by Harris, J., in State v. Laundy, 103 Ore. 443, 206 P. 290, 291 (1922).

67. Compare the requirements of the bill of exceptions under the Connecticut Practice Book of 1908, see Leahy v. Cheney, 90 Conn. 611, 98 A. 132 (1916) (a finding stating the objection, the exception, and the answer).

68. 1285, St. 13 Edw. I, Westminster Second, c. 31, quoted 1 Wigmore, Evidence § 20, note 1. The note also has references to the history of the early practice.

terms of his offer or objection is of dubious wisdom. Moreover, the modern practice of having a stenographer in attendance who records in his notes all of the matters embodied in the ancient bill of exceptions makes it unnecessary to halt the proceedings to recite the terms of a bill. Indeed, the practice of having court reporters dispenses with the need of separate bills of exception in the record or of any memorial (including the oral statement that the party "excepts") beyond the stenographer's transcript of the testimony, offers of proof, objections, and rulings. Accordingly, the Federal rules and the practice in many states have dispensed with exceptions,[69] and have provided that for all purposes formerly served thereby, "it is sufficient that a party, at the time the ruling or order of the court is made or sought, makes known to the court the action which he desires the court to take or his objection . . . and his grounds therefor." [70]

The Tactics of Objecting. Jurors want to know the facts and they may well look upon objections as attempts to hide the facts, and upon successful objections as the actual suppression of facts.[71] If this description of the jury's attitude is sound, certain consequences as to desirable tactics seem to follow.

No objections should be made unless there is reason to believe that the making of the objection will do more good than harm. If an objection has little chance of being sustained, at the trial or on appeal, it should usually not be made. It has also been pointed out that objections to leading questions, or to opinion evidence, frequently result in strengthening the examiner's case by requiring him to elicit his testimony in more concrete and convincing form.[72] In general, objections should be few and should be directed only to evidence which if admitted will be substantially harmful, and then only if the objector believes he can obtain a favorable ruling at the trial or upon appeal.[73]

Finally, since objections are usually made in the jury's presence, the manner of the objector and the terms of the objection are important. An objection should be stated so that it does not appear to rest merely upon some technical rule.[74] Thus, an objection to a copy under the best evidence rule should not be stated solely in terms of "secondary evidence" but should also be grounded upon the safer reliability of the original writing. The objection of "hearsay", for example, should be expanded by an explanation of the need, in justice and fairness, for producing the original informant so that the jury may see him, and his sources of knowledge may be explored.

Withdrawal of Evidence. If a party has introduced evidence which is not objected to and which turns out to be favorable to the adversary, it has sometimes been intimated that the offering party may withdraw the evidence as of right.[75] The accepted rule seems to be, however, that such a withdrawal is not of right. Rather, the adversary is entitled to have the benefit of the testimony as it bears in his favor,[76] unless the special situ-

---

69. Among the many states which have followed the federal lead are Arizona, Colorado, Missouri, Nevada, New Jersey, New Mexico, Texas and Washington.

70. F.R.Civ.P. 46; F.R.Crim.P. 51.

71. See general discussion in Keeton, Trial Tactics and Methods 158–163 (1954).

72. Ladd, Common Mistakes in the Technique of Trial, 22 Iowa L.Rev. 609, 617 (1937).

73. Goldstein and Lane, Trial Technique § 13.01 (2d ed. 1969).

74. See examples of objections in Busch, Law and Tactics in Jury Trials §§ 488, 492 (1949); Goldstein and Lane, Trial Technique ch. 13 (2d ed. 1969); Keeton, Trial Tactics and Methods 198–205 (1954).

75. See Young v. United States, 97 F.2d 200, 205 (5th Cir. 1938), and comment on this point in Note, 17 Tex.L.Rev. 373, 374 (1939).

76. Alabama Great Southern Ry. Co. v. Hardy, 131 Ga. 238, 62 S.E. 71 (1908) (enlightening discussion by Evans, P. J.); Page v. Payne, 293 Mo. 600, 240 S.W. 156 (1922) (defendant had no right to withdraw parts of documents introduced by him); Loo-

ation makes it fair for the judge in his discretion to permit the withdrawal.[77] On the other hand, if the evidence is admitted over the adversary's objection, and the proponent later decides to yield to the objection, and asks to withdraw the evidence, the court may revoke its ruling and permit the withdrawal.[78]

Plain Error Rule. All the rules concerning the necessity for objection to evidence in order to challenge its admissibility on appeal, as well as the rules concerning general and specific objections, discussed above, may be modified or disregarded under the so-called "plain error" rule.

It is said that if action at the trial is fundamental error or so taints a trial that the trial was unfair and biased, the error will be noticed although there was no objection.[79] This broad principle has sometimes been applied in the case of admission of evidence that would have been inadmissible had an objection been made.[80] The scope and definition

of fundamental error in this situation remains somewhat indefinite,[81] but the principle applies more often where important constitutional prohibitions were violated by admission of the evidence.[82]

The plain error rule is applicable in civil cases, but it seems to be rarely used.[83]

---

man Realty Corp. v. Broad Street Nat. Bank, 74 N.J.Super. 71, 180 A.2d 524 (1962) (no withdrawal unless evidence irrelevant or immaterial); 1 Wigmore, Evidence § 17c, Dec.Dig. Trial ☞58; C.J.S. Trial § 93.

77. Maas v. Laursen, 219 Minn. 461, 18 N.W.2d 233, 235 (1945) (discretionary, may be allowed if evidence irrelevant, or if favorable only to withdrawing party; court here did not err in denying withdrawal).

78. Alabama Great Southern Ry. Co. v. Hardy, 131 Ga. 238, 62 S.E. 71, 72 (1908); McCarty v. Bishop, 231 Mo.App. 604, 102 S.W.2d 126 (1937) (may be withdrawn in court's discretion, despite objection of opposing party).

79. See the many cases cited C.J.S. Appeal and Error § 245; C.J.S. Criminal Law §§ 1669, 1672.

F.R.Ev. (R.D.1971) 103(d): "Nothing in this rule [providing that error may not be predicated without objection, etc.] precludes taking notice of plain errors affecting substantial rights although they were not brought to the attention of the judge."

80. Payton v. United States, 96 U.S.App.D.C. 1, 222 F.2d 794 (1955) (confession not objected to); Bunter v. United States, 245 A.2d 839 (D.C.App.1968) (rule recognized but held inapplicable); United States ex rel. Gainer v. New Jersey, 278 F.Supp. 127 (D.C. N.J.1967) (failure to make issue properly of involuntary nature of confession); State v. Lampshire, 74 Wash.2d 888, 447 P.2d 727 (1969) (failure

to object to judge's comment on the evidence); C.J.S. Criminal Law § 1672.

81. Campbell, Extent to Which Courts of Review Will Consider Questions Not Properly Raised and Preserved, 7 Wis.L.Rev. 91, 160 (1932); Vestal, Sua Sponte Consideration in Appellate Review, 27 Fordham L.Rev. 477 (1958–59); Notes, 73 Dick L. Rev. 496 (1969), 64 Harv.L.Rev. 652 (1951), 43 Temp.L.Q. 228 (1970).

82. When constitutionally prohibited evidence is introduced against a defendant in a criminal case without timely objection, there is a serious question whether review of a conviction will be precluded in the United States Supreme Court. In Henry v. Mississippi, 379 U.S. 443 (1965), the court in a dictum stated that a state rule requiring immediate objection served a legitimate state interest [and thus might be ground for refusal to review], but remanded for a hearing of the question whether defendant deliberately bypassed his objection, in view of the possibility under Fay v. Noia, 372 U.S. 391 (1963), that petitioner might still pursue his remedy for the error in a habeas corpus proceeding in federal court, which he might do successfully if he had not deliberately bypassed his state procedural right. The response of state courts to this doctrine, in state court appellate review of claimed error in the admission of unconstitutional evidence which was not objected to, has been varied and inconsistent. See analysis of Pennsylvania cases in Comment, 43 Temp.L.Q. 228 (1970), pointing out treatment of the matter under the Pennsylvania doctrine concerning plain error. Many cases seem to apply the usual waiver rule. People v. Routt, 100 Ill.App. 388, 241 N.E.2d 206 (1968) (alleged failure to warn of *Miranda* rights; but alternate ground that evidence was admissible). But see statement in opinion in People v. Wilson, 20 Mich. App. 410, 174 N.W.2d 79 (1969) (alleged failure to warn of *Miranda* rights; failure to object did not waive constitutional right of defendant and admission of evidence was held reversible error). See cases cited in Dec.Dig. Criminal Law ☞698. The failure to object should seemingly be treated on appeal consistently with the rule to be used in habeas corpus and post-conviction remedies. See further § 183, infra. See § 180, infra, for necessity for motion to suppress illegally obtained evidence.

83. See cases cited in C.J.S. Appeal and Error §§ 289–291. See, e. g., Underwood v. Pennsylvania R. Co., 34 Ill.2d 367, 215 N.E.2d 236 (1966) (prejudicial questions objected to but no objections to many prejudicial remarks of counsel).

The rule that error in evidence rulings will not be grounds for reversal unless the error was prejudicial (except in some cases with respect to admission of evidence prohibited by constitutional rules) is a rule distinct from the above rules.[84]

53. Preliminary Questions of Fact Arising on Objections.[85]

The great body of the law of evidence consists of rules that operate to exclude relevant evidence.[86] Examples are the hearsay rule, the rule preferring original writings, and the various rules of privilege for confidential communications. These exclusionary rules are all "technical" in the sense that they have been developed by a special professional group, namely judges and lawyers, and in the further sense that for long-term ends they sometimes obstruct the ascertainment of truth in the particular case. Many if not most of these technical exclusionary rules, and the exceptions thereto, are in terms conditioned upon the existence of certain facts. Thus a copy of a writing will not be received unless the original is lost, destroyed, or oth-

erwise unavailable.[87] Suppose a copy is offered and there is conflicting evidence as to whether the original is destroyed or intact. The judge of course ascertains and announces the rule of evidence law setting up the criterion of admission or exclusion, but who is to decide whether the original is lost, destroyed or unavailable—the preliminary question of fact upon which hinges the *application* of the rule of evidence law?

Issues of fact are usually left to the jury, but there are strong reasons here for not doing so. If the special question of fact were submitted to the jury when objection was made, cumbersome and awkward problems about unanimity would be raised. If the judge admitted the evidence (the copy as above) to the jury and directed them to disregard it unless they found that the disputed fact existed, the aim of the exclusionary rule would likely be frustrated, for two reasons. First, the jury would often not be able to erase the evidence from their minds, if they found that the conditioning fact did not exist. They could not if they would. Second, the average jury would not be interested in performing this intellectual gymnastic of "disregarding" the evidence. They are intent mainly on reaching their verdict in a case in accord with what they believe to be true, rather than in enforcing the long-term policies of evidence law.

Accordingly, under the traditional view and the generally accepted principle the trial judge decides with finality those preliminary questions of fact upon which depends the admissibility of an item of evidence that is objected to under an exclusionary rule of evidence.[88] The same practice extends to the

---

84. The requirement that the ruling have been prejudicial is phrased in Uniform Rule 4, with respect to admission of evidence, "that the admitted evidence . . . probably had a substantial influence in bringing about the verdict or finding." Correspondingly, Uniform Rule 5 requires that erroneously excluded evidence "would probably have had a substantial influence in bringing about a different verdict or finding." Compare F.R.Ev. (R.D. 1971) 103(a): "Error may not be predicated upon a ruling which admits or excludes evidence unless a substantial right of the party is affected . . . ."
See also § 59, n. 80, infra.

85. 9 Wigmore, Evidence § 2550; Maguire, Evidence: Common Sense and Common Law 211–230 (1947); Maguire and Epstein, Preliminary Questions of Fact, 40 Harv.L.Rev. 392 (1927); Morgan, Functions of Judge and Jury in Preliminary Questions, 43 Harv.L.Rev. 165 (1929); Dec.Dig. Trial ☞138; Dec. Dig. Criminal Law ☞736; C.J.S. Trial § 207.

86. "And chiefly it [the law of evidence] determines as among probative matters . . . what classes of things shall not be received. This excluding function is the characteristic one in our law of evidence." Thayer, Preliminary Treatise on Evidence 264 (1898).

87. See § 230, infra.

88. The many different situations in which the principle has been applied include the following. Bartlett v. Smith, 11 M. & W. 483, 152 Eng.Rep. 895 (Exch., 1843) (question whether bill drawn in London or Dublin, on which depended its admissibility under the Stamp Act, should have been decided by judge instead of leaving to jury); Runels v. Lowell

determination of preliminary facts conditioning the application of the rules as to com-

> Sun Co., 318 Mass. 466, 62 N.E.2d 121 (1945) (declarations admissible against party only if made in course of conspiracy; held, existence of conspiracy question of fact for judge preliminary to admission of declaration, and his decision conclusive in absence of error of law); W. A. Manda, Inc. v. City of Orange, 82 N.J.L. 686, 82 A. 869 (1912) eminent domain: evidence of prices paid for other properties, admissible if substantially similar property, which is to be decided by judge); State v. Elder, 70 Wash.2d 414, 423 P.2d 533 (1967) (similar case); State v. Maynard, 184 N.C. 653, 113 S.E. 682 (1922) (admissibility in criminal case of former testimony of witness, held judge properly decided and refused to submit to jury, preliminary question whether witness absent by defendant's procurement); Blue v. City of Union, 159 Ore. 5, 75 P.2d 977 (1938) (whether offer to accept sum was intended as compromise was question of fact of intention, for the judge); Nielsen v. Dierking, 418 S.W.2d 146 (Mo.1967) (held judge on motion for new trial properly decided he had erred in admitting evidence of prior consistent statement to rehabilitate witness after finding on motion that as a matter of fact such statement had not been made before a prior inconsistent statement, a requirement under Missouri law); Weissman v. Department of Labor and Industries, 52 Wash.2d 477, 326 P.2d 743 (1958) (whether there is evidence in the record to support a hypothetical question is for the judge, not the jury; People v. Graziadio, 231 Cal.App.2d 525, 42 Cal.Rptr. 29 (1965) (trial judge properly decided preliminary fact question whether amount mentioned in conversation was offer of compromise or independent statement of value, but case law changed by later evidence code); Potter v. Baker, 162 Ohio St. 488, 124 N.E.2d 140 (1955) (accuracy of words testified to, nature of occurrence, etc., are preliminary questions for judge in decision concerning admissibility of spontaneous exclamations as exceptions to the hearsay rule). See Uniform Rule 8: "When the qualification of a person to be a witness, or the admissibility of evidence, or the existence of a privilege is stated in these rules to be subject to a condition, and the fulfillment of the condition is in issue, the issue is to be determined by the judge, and he shall indicate to the parties which one has the burden of producing evidence and the burden of proof of such issue as implied by the rule under which the question arises. The judge may hear and determine such matters out of the presence or hearing of the jury, except that on the admissibility of a confession the judge, if requested, shall hear and determine the question out of the presence and hearing of the jury. But this rule shall not be construed to limit the right of a party to introduce before the jury evidence relevant to weight or credibility." See also F.R.Ev. (R.D.1971) 104.

Whether former testimony meets preliminary fact requirements for admission (see Ch. 25, infra) is for the judge, not the jury. State v. Maynard, supra

petency [89] and privileges [90] of witnesses. On all these preliminary questions the judge, on request, will hold a hearing in which each side may produce evidence.[91]

> (court should determine whether witness absent by defendant's procurement; no error to refuse to submit question to jury); Dec.Dig. Criminal Law ☞736 (1). If reasonably supported by the evidence, his decision will not be reversed. Smith v. United States, 106 F.2d 726 (4th Cir. 1939) (sufficiency of showing of unavailability, where witness temporarily ill); People v. Centers, 56 Cal.App.2d 631, 133 P.2d 29 (1943) (sufficiency of showing of diligence in search for absent witness); New York Central R. Co. v. Pinnell, 112 Ind.App. 116, 40 N.E.2d 988 (1942) (similar to last case); See Ben Realty Co. v. Gothberg, 56 Wyo. 294, 109 P.2d 455, 462 (1941) (whether showing should be made that out-of-county witness was requested to attend trial). There will be reversal if his decision is not reasonably supported. Smith v. United States, 106 F.2d 726 (4th Cir. 1939); People v. Cavazos, 25 Cal. 198, 153 P.2d 177 (1944); New York Central R. Co. v. Pinnell, 112 Ind.App. 116, 40 N.E.2d 988 (1942); State v. Maynard, 184 N.C. 653, 113 S.E. 682 (1922).

See § 159, infra, for rules concerning the admission of confessions of a criminal defendant.

89. Bell v. State, 164 Ga. 292, 138 S.E. 238 (1927) (competency of nine-year-old boy as witness, for judge, error to submit to jury); Moosbrugger v. Swick, 86 N.J.L. 419, 92 Atl. 269 (1914) (whether assignor of claim sued on had assigned in good faith and hence escaped incompetency under Dead Man's Act, for judge); Meiselman v. Crown Heights Hospital, 285 N.Y. 389, 34 N.E.2d 367 (1941) (whether doctor qualifies as expert, for judge, reviewable only for serious mistake, error of law, or abuse of discretion; here error to exclude on ground that his training and practice were abroad).

90. Robinson v. United States, 144 F.2d 392 (6th Cir. 1944) (attorney-client communications); Phelps Dodge Corp. v. Guerrero, 273 Fed. 415 (9th Cir. 1921) (physician-patient privilege). The last case holds that the burden of proof of the facts of privilege is on the asserter of the privilege.

91. Should the exclusionary law of evidence, "the child of the jury system" in Thayer's phrase, be applied to this hearing before the judge? Sound sense backs the view that it should not, and that the judge should be empowered to hear any relevant evidence, such as affidavits or other reliable hearsay. Wigmore states this as the law, without citing supporting authority. 5 Evidence § 1385. English texts and scattered cases give some color to this view. Cross, Evidence 53 (3d ed. 1967) states there is no modern English authority. Occasional American judicial expressions in support of this view may be found, see, e. g., Schwimmer v. United States, 232 F.2d 855, 863 (8th Cir. 1956) cert. denied, 352 U.S. 833 (in passing on question

Such is the orthodox principle, but there are qualifications to be noted, and a distinction.

First, some courts, out of a supposed tenderness for persons accused of crime, in cases wherein dying declarations are offered in evidence have given to the jury some share in passing upon the preliminary question of the existence in the declarant of a settled, hopeless expectation of death.[92] It may be doubt-

ed whether this sharing with the jury of the responsibility of enforcing this condition has enured to the benefit of defendants.

Confessions are subject to special rules.[93]

A second group of cases has placed a strain upon the practice of giving decisive power to the judge over preliminary facts. These are the cases in which it happens that the preliminary fact-question on which competency of evidence or witness depends is also one of the ultimate disputed fact-issues which the jury would normally decide. Examples are the cases of prosecution for bigamy where the first marriage is disputed, the second wife

of waiver of attorney-client privilege, court "is not bound by the technical rules of evidence"); Healy v. Rennert, 9 N.Y.2d 202, 173 N.E.2d 777, 213 N.Y.S.2d 44 (1961) (hearsay rule did not exclude letter bearing on requirements for admission of prior testimony). It is adopted by E.R.Ev. (R.D. 1971) 104(a) (only the rules of privilege apply) and in N.J.R.Ev. 8(1). Some cases, however, tend to require the observance of jury trial rules of evidence. These are principally cases holding affidavits inadmissible. Valuenzuela v. State, 30 Ariz. 458, 248 Pac. 36 (1926); Becker v. Quigg, 54 Ill. 390 (1870); Poignand v. Smith, 25 Mass. (8 Pick.) 272, 277 (1829); Viles v. Moulton, 13 Vt. 510, 515 (1841). See, however, Lyons v. State, 76 Okl.Cr. 41, 133 P.2d 898 (1943) (doctor's certificate used). One realistic shortcut is generally allowed, in that the trial judge is permitted to consider as part of the evidence on the hearing, the testimony of the challenged witness. James v. Fairall, 168 Iowa 427, 434, 148 N.W. 1029 (1914) (interest). Or the hearsay declaration, the admissibility of which is being disputed. Armour & Co. v. Industrial Commission, 78 Colo. 569, 243 Pac. 546 (1926) (whether declaration by engineer, since deceased, as to fall was "spontaneous"; statement itself seemingly considered). Decisions admitting the declarations as spontaneous without direct proof of the shocking event are sometimes explainable on the ground that there is sufficient circumstantial evidence of the happening of the event. See, e. g., Insurance Co. v. Mosley, 8 Wall. 397, 19 L.Ed. 437 (1869). Other cases presenting the problem are Collins v. Equitable Life Ins. Co., 122 W.Va. 171, 8 S.E.2d 825 (1940) noted in 47 W.Va.L.Q. 340, 130 A.L.R. 287; Stewart v. Baltimore & Ohio R. Co., 137 F.2d 527 (2d Cir. 1943); Preferred Accident Ins. Co. of New York v. Combs, 76 F.2d 775 (8th Cir. 1935); Johnston v. W. S. Nott Co., 183 Minn. 309, 236 N.W. 466 (1931); National Life & Accident Ins. Co. v. Hedges, 233 Ky. 840, 27 S.W.2d 422 (1930); Industrial Commission v. Diveley, 88 Colo. 190, 192, 193, 294 Pac. 532 (1930). See § 297, n. 24, infra.

The best discussion of the topic is Maguire and Epstein, Rules of Evidence in Preliminary Controversies as to Admissibility, 36 Yale L.J. 1101 (1927).

92. One of the usual requirements for admission of dying declarations into evidence under an exception to the hearsay rule has been that the declarant

be conscious of impending death. See § 282, infra. Many courts would follow the practice that fact questions with respect to this requirement are preliminary fact questions for the judge. Comer v. State, 212 Ark. 66, 204 S.W.2d 875 (1947); Tillman v. State, 44 So.2d 644 (Fla.1950); People v. Hubbs, 401 Ill. 613, 83 N.E.2d 289, 297 (1949) (admissibility for court, weight for jury); State v. Rich, 231 N.C. 696, 58 S.E.2d 720 (1950); West's Ann. Cal.Evid.Code, § 405. Cases pro and con are collected in 5 Wigmore, Evidence § 1451, and in Dec.Dig., Homicide ☞218. But if the judge admits the declaration the jury in appraising its weight may consider, among other factors of credibility, whether they believe that the declaration was made under a sense of impending death. Comm. v. Knable, 369 Pa. 171, 85 A.2d 114 (1952) (semble). Hence they are entitled to hear the evidence as to the circumstances of the making of the declaration. Conway v. State, 177 Miss. 461, 171 So. 16 (1936); State v. Dotson, 96 W.Va. 596, 123 S.E. 463, 464 (1924).

Other courts have adopted the practice of admitting dying declarations if reasonable men could differ as to whether the declarant was conscious that death was at hand. Emmett v. State, 195 Ga. 517, 25 S.E.2d 9, 19 (1943); People v. Denton, 312 Mich. 32, 19 N.W.2d 476 (1945); Berry v. State, 143 Tex. Cr. 67, 157 S.W.2d 650 (1942). Still other courts seem to follow the practice of delegating to the judge the preliminary question of fact as to consciousness of impending death, but require him if he decides to admit the declaration, to direct the jury to disregard it if they find there was no such consciousness. See State v. Garver, 190 Or. 291, 225 P.2d 777, 780 (1950).

There are other variants. For example, it has been held by one court that in deciding the preliminary fact question the judge should decide all doubts in favor of admission of the evidence and submit the matter to the jury. State v. Proctor, 269 S.W. 2d 624 (Mo.1954).

93. See § 159, infra.

is offered as a state's witness, and the defendant objects under a statute disqualifying the wife to testify against her husband.[94] Another example is the situation where the plaintiff sues on a lost writing, and the defendant contends that it was not lost because it was never in existence. When the plaintiff offers as secondary evidence a copy of the alleged writing, logically it seems that to decide the preliminary question of loss, the judge would have to decide the ultimate issue of whether there was an original.[95] Some of the decisions even in these cases of coincidence with an ultimate issue, steadfastly adhere to the traditional view, that the judge decides finally the preliminary fact.[96] Others have adopted what is probably a more acceptable accommodation of powers of judge and jury. In these cases of coincidence they direct the judge, if he finds that the offering party has given evidence on the preliminary question from which a jury could reasonably find in his favor, to admit the offered evidence or witness.[97]

We have been discussing situations wherein *competency* of evidence or witnesses is in question, that is, situations in which relevant data is kept out under a "technical" exclusionary rule.[98] These *competency* cases are to be sharply marked off from another type of situation—the cases where the *relevancy*, *i. e.* probative value, of a fact offered in evi-

94. See, e. g., Matz v. United States, 81 U.S.App.D.C. 326, 158 F.2d 190 (1946) (for the judge to decide whether first marriage established).

95. Stowe v. Querner, L.R. 5 Exch. 155 (1870) (suit on insurance policy, defense: denial of issuance of policy; plaintiff offered a copy of the policy, with evidence that it was furnished by defendant's broker; defendant at that point requested a hearing on whether copy admissible and offered evidence that there was no policy; the trial judge refused, and admitted the copy; held, no error, "where the objection goes to show that the very substratum and foundation of the cause of action is wanting, the judge must not decide . . . but receive the copy and leave the main question to the jury.") See discussion of this case in Maguire, Evidence: Common Sense and Common Law 228–230 (1947).

96. Matz v. United States, note 94, supra; State v. Lee, 127 La. 1077, 54 So. 356 (1911) (murder by Mack Lee conceded, but defendant claims he is not Mack Lee; defense offers as a witness the wife of Mack Lee, who presumably would have testified defendant was not her husband; trial judge, after preliminary hearing rejected witness under statute forbidding wife to testify for husband, on the ground that he was satisfied that the accused was Mack Lee; held, no error, general rule applies).

97. Thus when declarations of one party to an alleged conspiracy, the existence of which is part of the issue, are offered against another, most cases hold that the judge should require prima facie proof only (not necessarily proof convincing to him) of the existence of common design. Connecticut Mutual Life Ins. Co. v. Hillmon, 188 U.S. 208, 217 (1903); Budd v. Morgan, 187 Cal. 741, 945–9, 203 P. 754 (1922); Cooke v. Weed, 90 Conn. 544, 97 A. 765 (1916); Rowley v. Braly, 286 S.W. 241 (Tex.Civ.App.1926); State v. Wappenstein, 67 Wash. 502, 507, 121 P. 989 (1912); see also, Carbo v. United States, 314 F.2d 718 (9th Cir. 1963) cert. denied 377 U.S. 953 (preliminary questions of foundation to admit co-conspirator's declarations are for the judge who must decide if prima facie case is made for admission; thereafter jury decides whether evidence, including the declarations, make case for conspiracy beyond a reasonable doubt). And when in a suit on a writing, the making of the writing is in issue, and the plaintiff offers secondary evidence of the terms of the writing, the plaintiff is usually required to produce prima facie proof only, not to convince the judge, of the execution of the original. Stowe v. Querner, note 95, supra; St. Croix Co. v. Seacoast Canning Co., 114 Me. 521, 96 A. 1059 (1916); Fauci v. Mulready, 337 Mass. 532, 150 N.E.2d 286 (1958). Various authorities are cited and discussed in Maguire and Epstein, Preliminary Questions, 40 Harv.L.Rev. 392, 415–420 (1927). Compare Smith v. Barrick, 151 Ohio St. 201, 85 N.E.2d 101 (1949) (competency of witness depended upon whether opponent was assignee of deceased person which involved ultimate issue of whether assignor owned bonds at time; held issue as to ownership must go to jury).

Where the declarations or the copy of a writing are thus admitted upon a mere prima facie showing of conspiracy or of execution of the writing, shall the judge instruct the jury to disregard the evidence unless they find that the conspiracy, or the writing, exists? The more logical and practical view is that he should not. See Rowley v. Braly, supra, and the incisive dicta of Learned Hand, J., in United States v. Dennis, 183 F.2d 201, 230, 231 (2d Cir. 1950). See also, Carbo v. United States, supra.

98. These rules "assume relevancy and then under special circumstances apply an extra safeguard to meet special dangers." 4 Wigmore, Evidence § 1171, quoted and discussed in Note, 21 Tex.L. Rev. 778, 779 (1943).

If the preliminary fact question is left to the jury in these cases, the exclusionary rule is likely to be disregarded.

dence depends on the existence of another conditioning fact.[99] Questions of authenticity of writings, that is, whether a writing, offered as the writing of A, was actually signed by him, are usually of this sort. So likewise are questions of the authority of an agent, when the acts of A are offered as proof of a tort or contract of B. When the conditioning fact determines merely the relevancy of the offered fact there is no need for any special safeguarding procedure, for relevancy is a mere matter of probative pertinence which the jury understands and is willing to observe. Accordingly, where the fact conditions relevancy merely, the judge will not permit the adversary to raise a preliminary dispute upon it, but will merely require the proponent to bring forward evidence from which the jury could find it to be true, after which the conditionally relevant fact will be admitted. At his next stage of proof, the adversary may bring disputing evidence, and the dispute will in the end be for the jury, not the judge, to resolve.[1]

99. The best discussion of this distinction, and of the cases applying and failing to apply it, is in Morgan, Functions of Judge and Jury in Preliminary Questions of Fact, 43 Harv.L.Rev. 164, especially 164–175 (1929).

Ordinarily, when there is an objection of relevancy, the judge will rule on the offered evidence, considering whether it is relevant under the usual tests for relevancy. See Mattero v. Silverman, 71 N.J.Super. 1, 176 A.2d 270 (1961). See the general treatment of authentication in Ch. 22, infra.

1. Patton v. Bank of Lafayette, 124 Ga. 965, 53 S. E. 664 (1906) (suit on note, execution denied; held, note admissible when evidence offered from which it could be found to be genuine); Coleman v. McIntosh, 184 Ky. 370, 211 S.W. 872 (1919) (breach of promise; defendant offered in evidence a purported letter from plaintiff to another man; plaintiff denied she wrote it and judge excluded; held, error, there being some evidence of genuineness, letter should have been admitted and authenticity left to jury); Winslow v. Bailey, 16 Me. 319 (1839) (defense to note on ground of fraudulent misrepresentation; defendant offered as evidence of the false statement, a certificate of a third person as to the amount of timber on a tract; held, judge properly ruled that he should not determine whether the certificate was used as an inducement to plaintiff, but should only require prima facie evidence of this, before admitting the certificate); Coghlan v. White, 236 Mass. 165, 128 N.E. 33 (1920)

54. Availability as Proof of Evidence Admitted Without Objection.

As indicated in section 52, a failure to make a sufficient objection to evidence which is incompetent waives any ground of complaint as to the admission of the evidence.[2] But it has another effect, equally important. If the evidence is received without objection, it becomes part of the evidence in the case, and is usable as proof to the extent of the rational persuasive power it may have.[3] The fact that it was inadmissible does not prevent its use as proof so far as it has probative value. The incompetent evidence, unobjected to, may be relied on in argument,[4] and alone or in part

(whether required statutory written notice was delivered to defendant was not for judge as fact preliminary to admitting notice in evidence, but for jury on conflicting testimony). But the distinction is one over which the courts occasionally stumble. Gila Valley, Globe & No. Ry. v. Hall, 232 U.S. 94 (1914) (there was issue whether plaintiff knew of defect in appliance; defendant offered evidence of remark about defect made when plaintiff less than 20 yards away: on objection judge excluded on ground not proved to have been heard by plaintiff: held, no error, preliminary question for judge); Dexter v. Thayer, 189 Mass. 114, 75 N.E. 223 (1905) (whether agreement between parties alleged to have been made for one by purported agent, was authorized, preliminary fact for judge); Dunklee v. Prior, 80 N.H. 270, 116 A. 138 (1922) (prior contradictory statement in writing, denied by witness, offered to impeach; trial judge finding on conflicting testimony of witness himself that it was not made by him, excluded it; held proper though judge might in his discretion have admitted it and left the question of its making to the jury; Brandon v. Peoples Natural Gas Co., 417 Pa. 128, 207 A.2d 843 (1965) (in ruling on post trial motion judge had discretion to regard evidence of gas leak around a gas meter subsequent to accident as not relevant and inadmissible without additional proof that there had been no change of condition to the subsequent time of leak). See also, F.R.Ev. (R.D. 1971) 104(b); West's Ann.Cal.Evid.Code, § 403; N.J.R.Ev. 8(2).

2. This statement is subject to the "plain error" rule. See § 52, supra.

3. McWilliams v. R & T Transport, Inc., 245 Ark. 882, 435 S.W.2d 98 (1968) (citing text; hearsay); Old v. Cooney Detective Agency, 215 Md. 517, 138 A.2d 889 (1958) (quoting text). Again the text is subject to the "plain error" rule. See § 52, supra.

4. Birmingham Elec. Co. v. Wildman, 119 Ala. 547, 24 So. 548 (1898); Chicago & E. I. Ry. Co. v. Mochell, 193 Ill. 208, 61 N.E. 1028 (1901).

may support a verdict or finding.[5] This principle is almost universally accepted,[6] and it applies to any ground of incompetency under the exclusionary rules. It is most often invoked in respect to hearsay,[7] but it has been applied to evidence vulnerable as secondary evidence of writings,[8] opinions,[9] evidence elicited from incompetent witnesses [10] or subject to a privilege,[11] or subject to objection because of the want of authentication of a writing,[12] of the lack-of-knowledge qualification of a witness,[13] or of the expertness qualification.[14] Relevancy and probative worth, however, stand on a different footing. If the evidence has no probative force, or insufficient probative value to sustain the proposition for which it is offered, the want of objection adds nothing to its worth [15] and it will not support a finding. It is still irrelevant or insufficient. However, the failure to object to evidence related to the controversy but not covered by the pleadings, may often amount to the informal framing of new issues.[16]

5. Indianapolis Blue Print & Mfg. Co. v. Kennedy, 215 Ind. 409, 19 N.E.2d 554 (1939); Department of Emp. Sec. v. Minnesota Drug Products, 258 Minn. 133, 104 N.W.2d 640 (1960) (dictum); Gregoire v. Insurance Co. of North America, 261 A.2d 25 (Vt. 1969); Dafoe v. Grantski, 143 Neb. 344, 9 N.W.2d 488 (1943) (hearsay standing alone may sustain a finding), and see decisions collected in Dec.Dig. ⊂⇒105; C.J.S. Trial §§ 150–156.
But see Pearson v. Stevens, 446 S.W.2d 381 (Tex. Civ.App.1969) (contra as to hearsay forming basis of finding of fact or judgment). See n. 6, infra.

6. See references in next preceding note. However, in Texas and Georgia, hearsay admitted without objection is said to have no probative force. See extensive discussion in Annot., 79 A.L.R.2d 890. This notion is also expressed in Wheelock Bros., Inc. v. Lindner Packing & Provision Co., 130 Colo. 122, 273 P.2d 730 (1954) (hearsay insufficient in determining whether plaintiff made a prima facie case).

7. Ventromile v. Malden Elec. Co., 317 Mass. 132, 57 N.E.2d 209 (1944) (statement of plaintiff after accident made in presence of defendant's employee); De Moulin v. Rotheli, 354 Mo. 425, 189 S.W.2d 562 (1945) (statement by manager of defendant's grocery store after plaintiff's fall); People v. McCoy, 101 Ill.App.2d 69, 242 N.E.2d 4 (1968) (unusual case in which prosecuting attorney took stand and presented state's case). See n. 6, supra, for contrary view. Annot., 79 A.L.R.2d 890, collects numerous cases.

8. Elster's Sales v. Longo, 4 Cal.App.3d 216, 84 Cal.Rptr. 83 (1970); Carter v. Commonwealth, 450 S.W.2d 257 (Ky.1970); Glover v. Mitchell, 319 Mass. 1, 64 N.E.2d 648 (1946) (federal price regulations); Dec.Dig. Trial ⊂⇒105(5).

9. Curtin v. Franchetti, 156 Conn. 387, 242 A.2d 725 (1968) (opinion as to ownership of property); Dieter v. Scott, 110 Vt. 376, 9 A.2d 95 (1939) (testimony of defendant that he acted as agent of lessee is a conclusion, but not objected to, it is entitled to consideration if not in conflict with underlying facts regarding the relationship); Dec.Dig. Trial ⊂⇒105(3). But the Georgia court weakens when the opinion is on the ultimate issue. Morgan v. Bell, 189 Ga. 432, 5 S.E.2d 897 (1940) (mental capacity to make will).

10. Walker v. Fields, 247 S.W. 272 (Tex.Com.App. 1923) (testimony of interested survivor, not objected to, "not without probative force"). Contra:

Brittain v. McKim, 204 Ark. 647, 164 S.W.2d 435 (1942) (result based on fact that incompetency rule was contained in the constitution), but disapproved in Starbird v. Cheatham, 243 Ark. 181, 419 S.W.2d 114 (1967).

11. Gruner v. Gruner, 165 S.W. 865 (Mo.App.1914) (marital communications).

12. Collins v. Streitz, 95 F.2d 430 (9th Cir. 1938); Elswick v. Charleston Transit Co., 128 W.Va. 241, 36 S.E.2d 419 (1946) (city ordinance: failure to object waives proof of existence and authenticity); Dec.Dig. Trial ⊂⇒105(4).

13. See Winsor v. Hawkins, 130 Conn. 669, 37 A.2d 222 (1944) (plaintiff's testimony, received without objection, that she had neuritis and water on the knee, though she probably had it second-hand from doctor, could be given such weight as it deserved).

14. McGuire v. Baird, 9 Cal.2d 353, 70 P.2d 915 (1937) (malpractice: defendant by not objecting admitted qualifications of plaintiff's doctor to testify to skill ordinarily exercised in that community); Woods v. Siegrist, 112 Colo. 257, 149 P.2d 241 (1944) (evidence of chiropractor-witness, whose qualifications were not objected to, sustains findings though contradicted by qualified neurologists); Jones v. Treegoob, 433 Pa. 225, 249 A.2d 352 (1969); Dec.Dig. Trial ⊂⇒105(3).

15. Danahy v. Cuneo, 130 Conn. 213, 33 A.2d 132 (1943); Craig v. Citizens' Trust Co., 217 Ind. 434, 26 N.E.2d 1006 (1940); DeLong v. Iowa State Highway Commission, 229 Iowa 700, 295 N.W. 91, 97 (1941) (but here the court goes on to adopt the untenable view that inadmissible hearsay, standing alone, can never have sufficient probative worth to support a finding).

16. Phillips v. New Amsterdam Cas. Co., 193 La. 314, 190 So. 565 (1939) (evidence in support of defense not pleaded "enlarges the pleadings and must be considered by court"). Many jurisdictions have adopted Rule 15(b) of the Rules of Civil Procedure for the United States District Courts or

When this is held to have been the result, the failure to object on the ground that the evidence is not material to any issue raised by the pleadings is waived,[17] and the evidence will support the proponent's side of the new informal issue.[18]

55. Waiver of Objection.

A failure to assert promptly and specifically an objection is a waiver.[19] What other conduct is a waiver?

Demand for inspection of a writing. One party, D, gives notice to his opponent, O, to produce a document, and O does produce it at the trial. Thereupon in open court D asks to inspect it, and is allowed to do so. The document if offered by O would be inadmissible, except for the notice, production, and inspection. Do these facts preclude D from objecting when the document is offered by O? England, Massachusetts, and a few other states say yes, D is precluded from objecting.[20] This result was based at first upon the notion that it would be unconscionable to permit the demanding party to examine the private papers of the producing party without being subjected to some corresponding risk on his own part.[21] A later case, however, has justified the result on the ground that the party who is called on in open court before a jury to produce a writing for inspection may be suspected of evasion or concealment unless he is given the privilege of introducing the writing.[22] Cases from other states recognize that the older policy against compelled disclosure to his adversary of relevant writings in possession of a party is now outmoded[23] and that the prevailing policy is just the opposite, namely, that of exerting pressure for full disclosure except for privileged matter. Accordingly, these states reject the rule,[24]

This viewpoint should apply in states which have adopted in substance the federal discovery rules. See also Dec.Dig. Evidence ☞368(14).

But the rule does not apply when the writing is used by one party to refresh the memory of his witness: the other party is entitled to inspect the writing without being penalized by being required to permit its introduction in evidence. Clearly the supposed reason of the rule does not apply. Nussenbaum v. Chambers & Chambers, 322 Mass. 419, 77 N.E.2d 780 (1948). See § 9, n. 57, supra.

21. Clark v. Fletcher, next preceding note, at p. 57, quoted 151 A.L.R. 1013.

22. Leonard v. Taylor, note 20, supra. This shifting of ground, however tenuous the new justification may seem, at least implies that the rule should be restricted to the limits of the new reason, namely, to jury trials where request for inspection is made in the jury's presence.

23. See the vigorous criticism of the rule in 7 Wigmore, Evidence § 2125.

24. Scully v. Morrison Hotel Corp., 118 Ill.App.2d 254, 254 N.E.2d 852 (1969) (rejecting "English" rule in Illinois); Merlino v. Mutual Service Cas. Ins. Co., 23 Wis.2d 571, 127 N.W.2d 741 (1964); Kane v. New Idea Realty Co., 104 Conn. 508, 133 A. 686 (1926) (party called on to produce may not require that demanding party promise to put writing in evidence, before surrendering it for inspection); Smith v. Rentz, 131 N.Y. 169, 30 N.E. 54, 56 (1892) ("The party who has in his possession books or papers which may be material to the case of his opponent has no moral right to conceal them from his adversary. . . . The party calling for books and papers would be subjected to great hazard if an inspection merely, without more, would make them evidence in the case. That rule tends rather

have similar statutes. Pursuant to this rule, pleadings are deemed amended when issues not raised by the pleadings are "tried by the express or implied consent of the parties". Pursuant to this rule, evidence not objected to can raise new issues. See Filliben v. Jackson, 247 A.2d 913 (Del. 1968) cert. denied 394 U.S. 906; Moore, Federal Practice ¶ 15.13 et seq.

17. Atlanta Enterprises v. James, 68 Ga.App. 773, 24 S.E.2d 130 (1943).

18. Wood v. Claxton, 199 Ga. 809, 35 S.E.2d 455 (1945) (can be considered by jury).

19. See § 52, supra.

20. Wharem v. Routledge, 5 Esp. 235, 170 Eng.Rep. 797 (Nisi Prius, 1805, Lord Ellenborough); Calvert v. Flower, 7 Car. & P. 386, 173 Eng.Rep. 172 (1836); United States Fidelity & Guaranty Co. v. Continental Baking Co., 172 Md. 24, 190 A. 768 (1937) (witness statement, but when admitted it only bears on credibility and does not "prove the fact"); Clark v. Fletcher, 83 Mass. (1 Allen) 53 (1861) (leading case); Leonard v. Taylor, 315 Mass. 580, 53 N.E.2d 705 (1944); Decker v. George W. Smith & Co., 88 N.J.L. 630, 96 A. 915 (1916), and cases cited in Annot., 151 A.L.R. 1006, 1012. However, as remarked in Zimmerman v. Zimmerman, 12 N.J.Super. 61, 79 A.2d 59 (1950), the spirit of the federal discovery rules adopted in New Jersey "seems to run counter" to the old practice as indicated in Decker v. George W. Smith & Co., supra.

and permit him to assert any pertinent objection if the producing party offers the writing. It should be emphasized that the older policy is inconsistent with the pretrial discovery policy of the federal civil discovery rules, which have been adopted in many states.[25]

Failure to object to earlier like evidence. A party has introduced evidence of particular facts without objection. Later he offers additional evidence, perhaps by other witnesses or writings, of the same facts or a part thereof. May the adversary now object, or has he waived his right by his earlier quiescence? It is often summarily stated in the opinions that he is precluded from objecting.[26] But in opinions where the question is carefully discussed it is usually concluded that the mere failure to object to other like evidence is not a waiver of objection to new incompetent evidence.[27] Of course, an overruling of this new

objection will frequently not be prejudicial, but that is a different question.[28] The practice of the best advocates of withholding objection unless it is clear that the evidence would be damaging is in the interest of dispatch of business and would be encouraged by the nonwaiver rule. On the other hand, when the evidence of the fact, admitted without objection, is extensive,[29] and the fact though incompetent has some probative value, the trial judge should be conceded a discretion to find that the objector's conduct has amounted to a waiver.

The Offering of Like Evidence by the Objector. If it happens that a party who has objected to evidence of a certain fact himself produces evidence from his own witness of the same fact, he has waived his objection.[30] However, when his objection is made and overruled he is required and entitled to treat this ruling as the "law of the trial" and to explain or rebut, if he can, the evidence which

to the suppression than the ascertainment of truth, and the opposite rule is, as it seems to us, better calculated to promote the ends of justice."); Summers v. McKim, 12 Serg. & R. (Pa.) 405, 411 (1825); Ellis v. Randle, 24 Tex.Civ.App. 475, 60 S.W. 462, 465 (1900).

25. See Zimmerman v. Zimmerman, n. 20, supra.

26. Star Realty v. Strahl, 261 Iowa 362, 154 N.W.2d 143 (1967); Rash v. Waterhouse, 124 Vt. 476, 207 A.2d 130 (1965); State v. Tranchell, 243 Ore. 215, 412 P.2d 520 (1966) (matter is in discretion of the court); Shelton v. Southern Ry. Co., 193 N.C. 670, 139 S.E. 232 (1927) (benefit of exception ordinarily lost if same evidence admitted earlier or later without objection—an arguendo statement); C.J.S. Trial § 115.

But no court would hold that because earlier evidence was subject to an objection under a particular exclusionary rule, e. g., hearsay, and was received without objection, that this would preclude the adversary to assert this ground of objection against new evidence. See, e. g., New York Life Ins. Co. v. Neasham, 250 F. 787 (9th Cir. 1918) (consent to use transcript of testimony of one witness at coroner's hearing, not waiver of right to object to transcript of testimony of another witness at same hearing).

27. Lowery v. Jones, 219 Ala. 201, 121 So. 704, 64 A.L.R. 553 (1929) ("If these [later] objections had been sustained, the force of the former testimony would probably have been weakened in the minds of the jury"); Slocinski v. Radwan, 83 N.H. 501, 144 A. 787 (1929); Bobereski v. Insurance Co. of Pa.,

105 Pa.Super. 585, 161 A. 412, 415 (1932) (". . . the fact that incompetent, irrelevant, and immaterial evidence may be introduced on a trial by one party, without objection from the other party, because he may deem it of no importance and harmless, does not prevent the latter from objecting to the further introduction and elaboration of such evidence when he is of opinion that it is both important and harmful. The principle of estoppel does not apply in such case."); McLane v. Paschal, 74 Tex. 27, 11 S.W. 837, 839 (1889).

28. As pointed out by Phillips, C. J. in Slayden v. Palmo, 103 Tex. 413, 194 S.W. 1103, 1104 (1917).

29. Of course, evidence and counterevidence may make the fact material, though not pleaded. See, e. g., Sweazey v. Valley Transport, 6 Wash.2d 324, 107 P.2d 567 (1940), and see § 54, supra.

30. Trouser Corp. v. Goodman & Theise, 153 F.2d 284 (3d Cir. 1946) (recognizing principle: but not clear here whether elicited in effort to rebut); Inter-City Trucking Co. v. Mason & Dixon Lines, 38 Tenn.App. 450, 276 S.W.2d 488 (1955); City of Houston v. McFadden, 420 S.W.2d 811 (Tex.Civ. App.1967); Ryder v. Board of Health, 273 Mass. 177, 173 N.E. 580 (1930); In re Forsythe's Estate, 221 Minn. 303, 22 N.W.2d 19 (1946) (other letter from same person giving similar but more prejudicial facts, a waiver); and cases in 1 Wigmore, Evidence § 18, note 35; C.J.S. Trial §§ 116, 661. See also, Russian v. Lipet, 103 R.I. 461, 238 A.2d 369 (1968) (elicited same testimony from same witness).

has come in over his protest. Consequently, it will not be a waiver if he cross-examines the adversary's witness about the matter,[31] even though the cross-examination entails a repetition of the fact,[32] or if he meets the testimony with other evidence which under the theory of the objection would be incompetent.[33] The closely related question of whether he may so meet the testimony by extrinsic evidence at all is considered in Sec. 57. Generally, he may do so.

Exclusion by Judge in Absence of Objection. A party's failure to object usually waives the objection and precludes the party from complaining if the evidence is let in.[34] But the failure by the party does not of itself preclude the trial judge from excluding the evidence on his own motion if the witness is disqualified for want of capacity or the evidence is incompetent, and he considers that the interests of justice require the exclusion of the testimony.[35] There is much evidence, however, such as reliable affidavits or copies of writings, which though incompetent under the technical exclusionary rules, may be valuable in the particular situation and which the trial judge in the absence of objection would not be justified in excluding. It is only when the evidence is irrelevant, unreliable, misleading, or prejudicial, as well as incompetent, that the judge should exercise his discretionary power to intervene. Privileged evidence, such as confidential communications between husband and wife, should be treated differently. The privileges protect the outside interests of the holders, not the interest of the parties in securing justice in the present litigation. Accordingly, in case privi-

---

31. Chester v. Shockley, 304 S.W.2d 831 (Mo.1957); Sayner v. Sholer, 77 N.M. 579, 425 P.2d 743 (1967); Haase v. Ryan, 100 Ohio App. 285, 136 N.E.2d 406, 410 (1955); Cathey v. Missouri, K. & T. Ry. Co. of Texas, 104 Tex. 39, 133 S.W. 417 (1911). There are some holdings to the contrary, see, e. g., Grain Dealers Mutual Ins. Co. v. Julian, 247 S.C. 89, 145 S.E.2d 685 (1965) (previous objection must be reserved).

Similarly, when the evidence objected to is elicited on cross-examination, the objector may seek to explain or refute on redirect without a waiver. Tucker v. Reil, 51 Ariz. 357, 369, 77 P.2d 203 (1938).

32. See, e. g., *Cathey* case in next preceding note. While calling for a repetition is a permissible part of a testing or exploratory cross-examination, as a tactical matter such repetition should be held to a minimum.

33. State v. Tiedemann, 139 Mont. 237, 362 P.2d 529 (1961); Glennon v. Great Atlantic & Pacific Tea Co., 87 R.I. 454, 143 A.2d 282 (1958); Salt Lake City v. Smith, 104 F. 457, 470 (8th Cir. 1900) (lucid discussion by Sanborn, J.); State v. Beckner, 194 Mo. 281, 91 S.W. 892, 896 (1906) (accused did not waive objection to evidence of his bad character by meeting it with evidence of good character).

34. See § 52, supra.

35. Barber v. State Highway Comm'n, 80 Wyo. 340, 342 P.2d 723 (1959); Bodholdt v. Garrett, 122 Cal.App. 566, 10 P.2d 533 (1932) (truck driver's unexcited statement that broken spring was cause of collision, excluded by judge: held, no error. "The court on its own motion in the interest of justice may exclude. . . ." Query, whether the ruling was in the interest of justice); South Atlantic S. S. Co. v. Munkacsy, 37 Del. 580, 187 A. 600 (1936) (suit by seaman for injury: opinion of boatswain as to safe character of work, excluded by judge; held, no error; "the trial judge is something more than a mere umpire"; careful exposition of judge's authority); City of Detroit v. Porath, 271 Mich. 42, 260 N.W. 114 (1935) (irrelevant picture); Electric Park Amusement Co. v. Psichos, 83 N.J.L. 262, 83 A. 766 (1912) (judge upheld in excluding opinion of expert of inadequate qualification, distinguishing case of disqualification for interest which parties may effectively waive; extensive discussion by Kalisch, J.); Wisniewski v. Weinstock, 130 N.J.L. 58, 31 A.2d 401 (1943) (truck driver's testimony as to speed from tire-tracks excluded for lack of qualification); Best v. Tavenner, 189 Ore. 46, 218 P.2d 471 (1950) (where witness died from stroke after direct testimony partly completed, judge had discretion to withdraw testimony from jury on own motion, or declare mistrial); King v. Baker, 109 Ga.App. 235, 136 S.E.2d 8 (1964) (judge excluded answer which was not responsive but was otherwise admissible). Cases are collected in Dec.Dig. Trial ☞105(6) and in C.J.S. Trial § 156.

It is even sometimes said that the judge at the close of the case may of his own motion withdraw incompetent evidence from the jury though not objected to when received. See, e. g., American Workmen v. Ledden, 196 Ark. 902, 120 S.W.2d 346 (1938). But an opposite result is advocated "to prevent unfairness, in that, if the counsel offering the testimony were made aware of the objection to the testimony at the time, he would have had an opportunity to cure it." Electric Park Amusement Co. v. Psichos, supra, 83 A. 766, 768.

leged matter is called for, and the holder is present, the judge may if necessary explain the privilege to the holder, but will not assert it of his own motion; but if the holder is absent the judge, in some jurisdictions, has a discretionary power to assert it in his behalf.[36]

56. The Effect of the Introduction of Part of a Writing or Conversation.[37]

Two important considerations come into play when a party offers in evidence a portion only of a writing, or of an oral statement or conversation. The first is the danger of admitting the portion only, thereby wresting a part of such a body of expressions out of its context. "The fool hath said in his heart, there is no God," [38] where the last phrase only is quoted, is an example of the possibilities of distortion.[39] This danger, moreover, is not completely averted by a later, separate, supplying of the relevant omitted parts. The distorted impression may sometimes linger, and work its influence at the subconscious level. Second is the opposing danger of requiring that the whole be offered, thereby wasting time and attention by cumbering the trial and the record, in the name of completeness, with passages and statements which have no bearing on the present controversy.

In the light of these alternatives, is a party who seeks to give in evidence part of a writing or statement required to offer it in entirety, or at least all of it that is relevant to the facts sought to be proved? The prevailing practice seems to permit the proponent to prove only such part as he desires.[40] It seems, however, that to guard against the danger of an ineradicable false first impression, the adversary should be permitted, at least within the court's discretion, to require the proponent to prove so much as pertains to the fact sought to be proved, that is, all that

---

36. People v. Atkinson, 40 Cal. 284 (1870) (where witness, an attorney, on examination was unable to say whether communications from client were public or private, judge, over defendant-client's objection admitted the evidence, held error, and by way of dictum that the court should have excluded on its own motion); Hodges v. Millikin, 1 Bland Ch. (Md.) 503, 509 (1828) ("and if the client be no party . . .   the lips of his attorney must remain closed and the Court cannot allow him to speak. . . ."). See Model Code of Evidence Rule 105(e) ("The judge . . . in his discretion determines . . .   (e) whether to exclude, of his own motion, evidence which would violate a privilege of a person who is neither a party nor the witness from whom the evidence is sought if the privilege has not been waived or otherwise terminated, or which would be excluded on appropriate objection by an adverse party"). The general subject of asserting privilege is discussed in § 73, infra.

37. 7 Wigmore, Evidence §§ 2094–2125; Dec.Dig. Evidence ☞155(8, 10); C.J.S. Evidence §§ 190, 774.

38. The oft-repeated, classic illustration, see 7 Wigmore, Evidence § 2094.

39. "The setting of a word or words gives character to them, and may wholly change their apparent meaning. A notable instance of such practice is that of the minister, displeased with the manner of hairdressing used by the women of his congregation, who preached from the text, '*Topknot come down!*' which was found to be the latter part of the scriptural injunction, 'Let them that are upon the *housetop not come down.*' " Lattimore, J., in

Weathered v. State, 129 Tex.Cr. 514, 89 S.W.2d 212, 214 (1935).

40. See, e. g., Gencarella v. Fyfe, 171 F.2d 419 (1st Cir. 1948) (plaintiff wished to introduce part of police officer's report of highway accident giving measurements of scene without introducing part reporting statements of by-standers as to who was to blame, held, error for trial judge to prevent him from introducing part, which was severable); Melnick v. Melnick, 154 Pa.Super. 481, 36 A.2d 235 (1944) (plaintiff could offer a part of the petition and admission in corresponding paragraph of answer without including other matters in that paragraph by way of avoidance or defense); and see People v. Adamson, 27 Cal.2d 478, 165 P.2d 3 (1946) (witness may testify to part of conversation where that is all he heard and it is intelligible); State Highway Dept. v. Thomas, 115 Ga.App. 372, 154 S.E.2d 812 (1967) (attorney could introduce part of a lease contract).

But see Flood v. Mitchell, 68 N.Y. 507, 511 (1877) (whole of instrument creating or transferring rights should be introduced). See also 7 Wigmore, Evidence § 2099. With respect to testimony given at a former trial, it is fairly common to require that the substance of all the testimony of the witness on the particular subject be given, though there are holdings to the contrary. 7 Wigmore, Evidence § 2098, n. 4, § 2099(4).

explains or is useful in interpreting the part proved.[41]

As to the adversary's other alternative the cases are much clearer and more consistent. He may wait until his own next stage of presenting proof, and then merely by reason of the fact that the first party has introduced a part, he has the right to introduce the remainder of the writing, statement, correspondence, former testimony, or conversation so far as it relates to the same subject matter and hence tends to explain and shed light on the meaning of the part already received.[42]

This right is subject to the qualification that where the remainder is incompetent, not merely as to form as in the case of secondary evidence or hearsay, but because of its prejudicial character then the trial judge should exclude if he finds that the danger of prejudice outweighs the explanatory value.[43]

57. Fighting Fire with Fire: Inadmissible Evidence as Opening the Door.[44]

One party offers evidence which is inadmissible. Because the adversary fails to object, or because he has no opportunity to do so, or because the judge erroneously overrules an objection, the incompetent evidence comes in. Is the adversary entitled to answer this evidence, by testimony in denial or explanation of the facts so proved? It has been stated that in some jurisdictions the adver-

---

41. F.R.Civ.P. 32(a) (4) contains the following practical and flexible rule for depositions: "If only part of a deposition is offered in evidence by a party, an adverse party may require him to introduce any other part which ought in fairness to be considered with the part introduced, and any party may introduce any other parts." The fairness concept originated in Ill.Sup.Ct.R. 212(c).

F.R.Ev. (R.D.1971) 107 treats writings in this manner but does not extend to conversations; in view of practical problems of determining readily and without undue consumption of time just what a conversation contained, full development is left to cross-examination or to the opponent's own case.

42. West's Ann.Cal.Evid.Code, § 356 provides, "Where part of an act, declaration, conversation, or writing is given in evidence by one party, the whole on the same subject may be inquired into by an adverse party; when a letter is read, the answer may be given; and when a detached act, declaration, conversation or writing is given in evidence, any other act, declaration, conversation, or writing which is necessary to make it understood may also be given in evidence".

The results indicated by this statute have been dictated by various similar statutes and by case law without benefit of statutes. See, e. g., Spani v. Whitney, 172 Neb. 550, 110 N.W.2d 103 (1961) (defendant brought out part of statement to police officer, whereupon plaintiff introduced the entire statement; similar statute not limited to impeachment situations and judge has an area of discretion); Dispenza v. Picha, 98 Ill.App.2d 110, 240 N.E.2d 325 (1968) (conversation); Stewart v. Sioux City & New Orleans Barge Lines, Inc., 431 S.W.2d 205 (Mo.1968) (plaintiff introduced hospital record insofar as it recorded various matters, some inadmissible; defendant could then introduce remainder containing diagnosis based on such matters. But the remaining portion sought to be introduced must be related to the use of the part initially introduced, if that use was a limited one. Rosener v. Larson, 255 Cal.App.2d 871, 63 Cal.Rptr. 782 (1968) (a limited use of a doctor's report not as evidence but as basis for an expert's opinion did not authorize introduction of another inadmissible portion containing conclusions); Camps v. New York City Transit Authority, 261 F.2d 320 (2d Cir. 1958) (use of initial part for impeachment).

It has sometimes been said that this type of "remainder" evidence is a mere aid in interpreting the evidence already received or in appraising credibility, and is not itself substantive evidence. People v. Schlessel, 196 N.Y. 476, 90 N.E. 44 (1909); 7 Wigmore, Evidence § 2113. But in another place, Wigmore has properly termed this "an artificial doctrine tending to a quibble." Student Textbook on Evidence 322 (1935). It is not the more usual rule. Statutes and cases permitting the remainder to be introduced to make the part already introduced "fully understood, to explain the same" are not usually to be understood in the above-mentioned limited sense. See Spani v. Whitney, supra.

43. Socony Vacuum Oil Co. v. Marvin, 313 Mich. 528, 21 N.W.2d 841 (1946) (when part of transcribed interview between plaintiff's investigator and defendant was introduced by plaintiff, defendant not entitled to offer remaining part stating his poor financial condition and that he was not insured); Jeddeloh v. Hockenhull, 219 Minn. 541, 18 N.W.2d 582 (1945) (where part of conversation after accident proved, door not opened to proof of part showing defendant insured); State v. Skaug, 63 Nev. 59, 161 P.2d 708 (1945) (separable part of confession showing commission of other unconnected crimes should have been excluded).

44. See 1 Wigmore, Evidence § 15 ("Curative Admissibility"); Note, 35 Mich.L.Rev. 636 (1937); Dec.Dig. Evidence ☞155(5); C.J.S. Evidence § 190a; 29 Am.Jur.2d Evidence § 267.

sary is not entitled to so meet the evidence, in others he may do so, and finally in some he may do so if he would be prejudiced by rejection of efforts to meet the evidence; but that in reaching these results many of the decisions seem merely to affirm the action of the trial court.[45] However, most of the courts seem to say generally that "one who induces a trial court to let down the bars to a field of inquiry that is not competent or relevant to the issues cannot complain if his adversary is also allowed to avail himself of the opening." [46]

Many of these pronouncements do not settle the questions as to how the trial judge should deal with the problem, or as to whether the adversary is entitled as of right to introduce the answering evidence. Because of the many variable factors affecting the solution in particular cases the decisions do not lend themselves easily to generalizations, but the following conclusions, having some support in the decisions, are submitted as reasonable:

(1) If the incompetent evidence sought to be answered is immaterial and not prejudice-arousing, the judge, to save time and to avoid distraction of attention from the issues, should refuse to hear answering evidence; but if he does hear it, under the prevailing view, the party opening the door has no standing to complain.[47]

(2) If the evidence, though inadmissible, is relevant to the issues and hence probably damaging to the adversary's case, or though irrelevant is prejudice-arousing to a material degree, and if the adversary has seasonably objected or moved to strike, then the adversary should be entitled to give answering evidence as of right.[48] By objecting he has done

---

45. 1 Wigmore, Evidence § 15.

46. St. Clair County v. Bukacek, 272 Ala. 323, 131 So.2d 683 (1961) (irrelevant evidence; "rule is that irrelevant, incomplete or illegal evidence may be admitted to rebut evidence of like character"); Hartman v. Maryland Casualty Co., 417 S.W.2d 640 (Tex.Civ.App.1967); Mobile & B. Ry. Co. v. Ladd, 92 Ala. 287, 9 So. 169 (1891) (meeting immaterial evidence that night was dark by evidence that moon was shining); Perkins v. Hayward, 124 Ind. 445, 24 N.E. 1033, 1034 (1890); Sisler v. Shafer, 43 W.Va. 769, 28 S.E. 721 (1897) ("strange cattle having wandered through a gap made by himself, he cannot complain"); Corley v. Andrews, 349 S.W.2d 395 (Mo.App.1961) (counter evidence was hearsay; "should have been allowed").

Some courts, however, have, at least occasionally, expressed the view that admission of incompetent evidence does "not open the door" to answering inadmissible evidence. People v. McDaniel, 59 Cal. App.2d 672, 140 P.2d 88 (1943); Savannah News-Press, Inc. v. Hartridge, 110 Ga.App. 203, 138 S.E.2d 173 (1964) (immaterial evidence; introduction did not entitle opponent to rebuttal evidence; "there can be no equation of errors in the trial of a case").

Other courts have stated that the admission of incompetent evidence "opens the door" only if the opponent is prejudiced unless he can meet the evidence. 1 Wigmore, Evidence § 15.

47. If the evidence sought to be answered is immaterial, the rule against contradicting on a collateral issue would generally indicate exclusion of evidence in answer to it. See § 47, supra. If, however, the opening-the-door theory prevails, then attention ought to be given to the nature of the original and rebutting evidence. Ordinarily no more of a problem may be presented than a possible harmless excursion into immateriality, as suggested in note 46, supra, but on occasion a relatively slight breach of materiality may be used as an excuse to violate fundamental exclusionary principles. Illustrative are the cases where an accused takes the stand and makes an overly-broad denial of guilt ("I never"). Numerous decisions allow the prosecutor to rebut by evidence of otherwise inadmissible other offenses. People v. Westek, 31 Cal.2d 469, 190 P.2d 9 (1948); State v. Barnett, 156 Kan. 746, 137 P.2d 133 (1943). In Walder v. United States, 347 U.S. 62 (1954) this principle was carried to the extreme of allowing the results of an unconstitutional search and seizure to be introduced. The case has been much criticized. See § 178, infra. If the statement is elicited on cross-examination, much authority refuses to allow it to be used as a door opener. State v. Goldsmith, 104 Ariz. 226, 450 P.2d 684 (1969); Dalton v. People, 224 Ill. 333, 79 N.E. 669 (1906); and Agnello v. United States, 269 U.S. 20 (1925) disallowed use of the results of an unconstitutional search and seizure under these circumstances. The preferable result would be disallowance of prejudicial answering evidence without regard to whether elicited on direct or cross. State v. Johnson, 94 Ariz. 303, 383 P.2d 862 (1963). Objection to the original immaterial evidence or an instruction to disregard it should protect the interests of the prosecution adequately.

48. Budd v. Meriden Elec. Co., 69 Conn. 272, 37 A. 683 (1897); Bremhorst v. Phillips Coal Co., 202 Iowa 1251, 211 N.W. 898, 904 (1927) ("It was the

his best to save the court from mistake, but his remedy by assigning error to the ruling is not an adequate one.[49] He needs a fair opportunity to win his case at the trial by refuting the damaging evidence. This situation should be distinguished from the question, considered in section 55, whether the prior objection is waived if the answering evidence is permitted.

(3) If again the first incompetent evidence is relevant, or though irrelevant is prejudice-arousing, but the adversary has failed to object or to move to strike out, where such an objection might apparently have avoided the harm, then the allowance of answering evidence should rest in the judge's discretion.[50] He should weigh the probable influence of the first evidence, the time and distraction incident to answering it, and the possibility and effectiveness of an instruction to the jury to disregard it. However, here various courts have indicated that introduction of the answering evidence is a matter of right.[51]

(4) In any event, if the incompetent evidence, or even the inquiry eliciting it, is so prejudice-arousing that an objection or motion to strike can not have erased the harm, then it seems that the adversary should be entitled to answer it as of right.[52]

It will be noted that the question discussed in this section as to rebutting incompetent evidence, is a different one from whether a party's introduction of evidence incompetent under some exclusionary rule (such as hearsay or secondary evidence of writings) gives license to the adversary to introduce other evidence which is incompetent under the same exclusionary rule but which bears on some different issue or is not relevant to the original incompetent evidence.[53] The doctrine of "opening the door" has not been extended to that extent.

58. Admissibility of Evidence Dependent on Proof of Other Facts: "Connecting Up." [54]

Very often the relevancy or admissibility of evidence of a particular fact hinges upon the proof of other facts. Thus, proof that a swaying automobile passed a given spot at

duty of the court to give both parties the benefit of the same rules of evidence."); Lake Roland Elec. Ry. Co. v. Weir, 86 Md. 273, 37 A. 714, 715 (1897) (a considered dictum); Mattechek v. Pugh, 153 Ore. 1, 55 P.2d 730, 168 A.L.R. 725 (1936). Contra: Buck v. St. Louis Union Trust Co., 267 Mo. 644, 185 S.W. 208, 213 (1916) (". . . his objection will save him on appeal and he needs no other protection", leading Missouri case). For other cases see Note, 35 Mich.L.Rev. 636, 637 (1937).

49. See Note, 35 Mich.L.Rev. 636, 637 (1937). Wigmore takes the opposite view. 1 Evidence § 15.

50. Grist v. Upjohn Co., 16 Mich.App. 452, 168 N.W. 2d 389 (1969) (permitting introduction of hearsay concerning same conversation was within the court's discretion); Crosby v. Keen, 200 Miss. 590, 28 So.2d 322 (1946); Biener v. St. Louis Pub. Service Co., 160 S.W.2d 780 (Mo.App.1942) (semble); Franklin Fire Ins. Co. v. Coleman, 87 S.W.2d 537 (Tex.Civ.App.1935) (suit on fire policy, defense, arson; defendant's witness volunteered statement that he arrested plaintiff after the fire; held, permitting defendant to show that complaint on which he was arrested was dismissed was discretionary).

51. Moschetti v. City of Tucson, 9 Ariz.App. 108, 449 P.2d 945 (1969); London v. Standard Oil Co. of California, 417 F.2d 820 (9th Cir. 1969); Sprenger v. Sprenger, 146 N.W.2d 36 (N.D.1966) (counter evidence objectionable under the best evidence

rule); Shoup v. Mannino, 188 Pa.Super. 457, 149 A.2d 678 (1959); Commonwealth v. Wakelin, 230 Mass. 567, 575, 576, 120 N.E. 209, 212, 213 (1918).

52. Thus, in State v. Witham, 72 Me. 531, 535 (1881) the birth of a child to an unmarried woman was improperly admitted as evidence of defendant's adultery, and counterevidence of other men's intercourse was received to rebut it. The court said: "The introduction of immaterial testimony to meet immaterial testimony on the other side is generally within the discretion of the presiding judge. But if one side introduces evidence irrelevant to the issue, which is prejudicial and harmful to the other party, then, although it come in without objection, the other party is entitled to introduce evidence which will directly and strictly contradict it."

53. The distinction is acutely discussed by Hughes, P. J. in Longmire v. Diagraph-Bradley Corp., 237 Mo.App. 553, 176 S.W.2d 635, 646 (1944), and applied in Daniels v. Dillinger, 445 S.W.2d 410 (Mo. App.1969).

54. 1 Wigmore, Evidence § 14, 6 id. § 1871; Note, 32 Ill.L.Rev. 882 (1938); Annot., 88 A.L.R.2d 12; Dec.Dig. Trial ⚲51, 79, 90; C.J.S. Trial § 85.

a certain time,[55] or that a conversation was had by the witness at a given time and place with an unidentified stranger,[56] will become relevant and significant only when the automobile is identified as the defendant's, or the stranger is shown to be the deceased for whose death the plaintiff is suing. So evidence of acts and declarations may not become material or admissible until shown to be those of an agent of the other party,[57] and a copy of a writing may not become competent evidence until the original is proven to be lost or destroyed.[58] Some of these missing facts may be thought of, in terms of the logic of pleading or argument, as preliminary to the fact offered, some as co-ordinate with it. It matters not. In either event, often only one fact can be proven at a time or by a given witness, and the order of convenience in calling witnesses or of clear presentation may not in a particular case be the order of logical statement.[59]

Who decides the order of facts? In the first instance, the offering counsel does so by making his offer. The court in its general discretionary supervision of the order of proof,[60] may, to avoid a danger of prejudice or confusion, require that the missing fact be proved first.[61] But he seldom does, and the every-

day method of handling the situation when the adversary objects to the relevancy or the competency of the offered fact is to permit it to come in conditionally, upon the assurance, express or implied, of the offering counsel that he will "connect up" the tendered evidence by proving, in the later progress of his case, the missing facts.[62]

In a long trial, however, where the witnesses are many and the facts complex, it is easy for the offering counsel to forget the need for making the required "connecting" proof, and for the judge and the adversary to fail to observe this gap in the evidence. Who invokes the condition subsequent, upon such a breach? The burden is placed upon the objecting party to renew the objection and invoke the condition.[63] By the majority view this is to be done by a motion to strike out the evidence conditionally received,[64] when

---

55. State v. Freeman, 93 Utah 125, 71 P.2d 196 (1937).

56. Atlanta & W. P. Ry. Co. v. Truitt, 65 Ga.App. 320, 16 S.E.2d 273 (1941).

57. Smith v. Ohio Millers' Mutual Fire Ins. Co., 320 Mo. 146, 6 S.W.2d 920 (1928).

58. See Ch. 23, infra.

59. See the remarks of Miller, J. in a conspiracy case: "The logical sequence of events—from agreement in a common purpose to perpetration of an act designed to carry it out—does not require that introduction of the evidence must follow that same rigorous sequence." McDonald v. United States, 77 U.S.App.D.C. 33, 133 F.2d 23 (1942).

60. Matz v. United States, 81 U.S.App.D.C. 326, 158 F.2d 190 (1946) (order of prosecution's evidence in a bigamy case); and see 6 Wigmore, Evidence §§ 1867, 1871.

61. Gerber v. Columbia Palace Corp., 183 A.2d 398 (D.C.Mun.App.1962) (judge ruled evidence inadmissible without proof of other facts).

62. For decisions approving the practice see, e. g., Wickman v. Bohle, 173 Md. 694, 196 A. 326 (1938); Innes v. Beauchene, 370 P.2d 174 (Alaska 1962).

63. Webb v. Biggers, 71 Ga.App. 90, 30 S.E.2d 59 (1944); Annot., 88 A.L.R.2d 12, 23–31; Dec.Dig. Trial ⊙79.

64. Little Klamath Water Ditch Co. v. Ream, 27 Ore. 129, 39 P. 998 (1895); State v. Freeman, 93 Utah 125, 71 P.2d 196 (1937) (motion to strike necessary; request for instruction to disregard, at close of case, insufficient: full discussion, one judge dissenting); Arnold v. Ellis, 5 Mich.App. 101, 145 N.W.2d 822 (1966) (in judge-tried case, judge could consider evidence when no motion to strike was made). But it has been said in one decision that in a jury case a motion for an instruction to disregard the evidence is the proper recourse. Kolka v. Jones, 6 N.D. 461, 71 N.W. 558, 564 (1897). See also, Caley v. Manicke, 29 Ill.App.2d 323, 173 N.E.2d 209 (1961) rev'd 24 Ill.2d 390, 182 N.E.2d 206 (dictum that failure to connect "at the very least would occasion an instruction to disregard"). As a practical matter, both a motion to strike and a request for an instruction should be made. Decisions are collected in 6 Wigmore, Evidence § 1871, note 6; Annot., 88 A.L.R.2d 12, 102.

Normally, it is assumed when evidence is improperly received, or is not "connected up," an instruction to disregard is a sufficient corrective. But the evidence may be so prejudicial that an instruction does not cure the harm. National Cash Register Co. v. Kay, 119 S.W.2d 437 (Mo.App.1938). "Human nature does not change merely because it is found in the jury box. The human mind is not a slate, from which can be wiped out, at the will and in-

the failure of condition becomes apparent. It seems that it does become apparent when the offering party completes the particular stage of his case in which the evidence was offered,[65] and that when he "rests" without making the missing proof, the adversary should then move to strike, failing which, he cannot later claim as of right to invoke the condition. Some weight should be given, however, to the duty assumed by the offering party in promising to furnish the connecting proof, and recognition of this can best be given by according the trial judge a discretion to allow the adversary to invoke the condition, if the continuing availability of the missing proof makes it fair to do so, at any time before the case is submitted to the jury or before final judgment in a judge-tried case.[66] Though some courts have considered the difference in form material, it seems that a motion to strike, a motion to withdraw the fact from the jury, or a request that the jury be instructed to disregard the evidence should each be regarded as a sufficient invocation of the condition.

To be distinguished from the practice described above of conditional admission pending further proof, is the practice of admitting evidence provisionally where objection is made, subject to a later ruling on the objection in the light of further consideration when the case has been more amply developed. Here again the objecting counsel, to preserve the objection must renew the objection before the case is concluded.[67] The practice seems appropriate enough in a judge-tried case [68] but where the trial is with a jury there is danger that letting the evidence in, even provisionally, may make an impression that a later ruling of exclusion may not erase [69]—a danger that here seems unnecessary to incur. Accordingly this practice, though doubtless in the realm of discretion, has been criticised.[70]

59. Evidence Admissible for One Purpose, Inadmissible for Another: "Limited Admissibility." [71]

An item of evidence may be logically relevant in several aspects, as leading to distinct inferences or as bearing upon different issues. For one of these purposes it may be competent, but for another incompetent. In this frequently arising situation, subject to the limitations outlined below, the normal practice is to admit the evidence.[72] The interest

struction of another, ideas and thoughts written thereon." People v. Deal, 357 Ill. 634, 192 N.E. 649, 652 (1934). See the discussion of the adequacy of curative and limiting instructions in § 59, infra.

65. In Keber v. American Stores Co., 116 N.J.L. 437, 184 A. 795 (1936) this was said to be the proper time and that an earlier motion was premature. See also Note, 32 Ill.L.Rev. 882, 883 (1938); Annot., 88 A.L.R.2d 12, 107.

66. See Note, 32 Ill.L.Rev. 882, 884 (1938).

67. McGee v. Maryland Casualty Co., 240 Miss. 447, 127 So.2d 656 (1961) (jury case). See cases collected in Annot., 88 A.L.R.2d 12, 109 et seq.

68. Its advantages are pointed out by Sanborn, Cir.J., in Builders' Steel Co. v. Commissioner, 179 F.2d 377, 379 (8th Cir. 1950).

69. McKee v. Bassick Mining Co., 8 Colo. 392, 8 P. 561 (1885). But though sometimes criticized this practice has been used in jury cases. See cases in Annot., 88 A.L.R.2d 12, 108–122; Dec.Dig. Trial ⟊51. It is forbidden by statute in Connecticut even in judge-tried cases. Conn.Gen.St.Ann. § 52–208, construed in Kovacs v. Szentes, 130 Conn. 229, 33 A.2d 124 (1943). See n. 64, supra, as to the effectiveness of instructions to disregard.

70. See, e. g., Missouri Pac. Transportation Co. v. Beard, 179 Miss. 764, 176 So. 156 (1937); Dec.Dig. Trial ⟊51; Annot., 88 A.L.R.2d 12, 121–122.

71. 1 Wigmore, Evidence § 13; Dec.Dig. Trial ⟊48; C.J.S. Trial §§ 87, 88.

72. Sprinkle v. Davis, 111 F.2d 925 (4th Cir. 1940) (suit for injury to highway workman, plaintiff, by defendant's automobile: court erred in excluding defendant's evidence that plaintiff had been compensated by Highway Department; not admissible on issue of liability or damages but admissible to show bias of witnesses who were highway employees); Williams v. Milner Hotels Co., 130 Conn. 507, 36 A.2d 20 (1944) (guest, suing hotel for having been bitten by rat while lying in bed, could prove that rat-holes in room were later closed by tin patches; inadmissible as admission of fault, admissible to show control, existence of rat-holes, and to corroborate guest's evidence); Low v. Honolulu Rapid Transit Co., 50 Hawaii 582, 445 P.2d 372 (1968); Stoeppelman v. Hays-Fendler Const. Co.,

of the adversary is to be protected, not by an objection to its admission,[73] but by a request at the time of the offer for an instruction that the jury is to consider the evidence only for the allowable purpose.[74] Such an instruction may not always be effective, but admission of the evidence with the limiting instruction is normally the best available reconciliation of the respective interests. It seems, however, that in situations, where the danger of the jury's misuse of the evidence for the incompetent purpose is great, and its value for the legitimate purpose is slight or the point for which it is competent can readily be proved by other evidence, the judge's power

to exclude the evidence altogether would be recognized.[75]

Similarly, evidence may frequently be competent as against one party, but not as against another, in which event the practice is to admit the evidence, with an instruction, if requested, that the jury are to consider it only as to the party against whom it is competent.[76]

However, limiting instructions are not sufficient to correct the constitutional error of admitting into evidence the confessions or admissions of a codefendant who does not take the stand when the confessions or admissions implicate the defendant. A violation of

---

437 S.W.2d 143 (Mo.App.1969) (evidence showing insurance existed properly admissible to show control exercised over property).

It seems, however, that the proponent, to complain of the judge's exclusion of evidence inadmissible in one aspect, must have stated the purpose for which it is competent. Archer v. Sibley, 201 Ala. 495, 78 So. 849 (1918). Unless the admissible purpose is plainly apparent. Kansas City Southern Ry. Co. v. Jones, 241 U.S. 181 (1916). The rule was applied where an admissible purpose and an inadmissible purpose were stated, in Richter's Bakery, Inc. v. Verden, 394 S.W.2d 230 (Tex.Civ. App.1965). See C.J.S. Trial § 87.

73. Scott v. Missouri Ins. Co., 361 Mo. 51, 233 S.W. 2d 660 (1950) (action on life policy; defendant offered report of its investigators on the death; plaintiff objected as hearsay, and judge excluded; held error to exclude, should have admitted to show good faith in denying liability with limiting instruction, if requested); Bialek v. Pittsburgh Brewing Co., 430 Pa. 176, 242 A.2d 231 (1968) (proper to admit evidence to show article was not defective with instruction indicating evidence should not be used for improper purpose of showing due care, which was not in issue).

74. Hatfield v. Levy Bros., 18 Cal.2d 798, 117 P.2d 841 (1941) (opponent, not having requested instruction, waived right thereto); Bouchard v. Bouchard, 313 Mass. 531, 48 N.E.2d 161 (1943); Rynar v. Lincoln Transit Co., 129 N.J.L. 525, 30 A.2d 406, 409 (1943) (". . . The party . . . may summon the court's assistance by request for charge or other appropriate means."); Sims v. Struthers, 267 Ala. 80, 100 So.2d 23 (1958) (admission not error when instruction was not requested on ground that the remedy was a request for an instruction); State ex rel. State Highway Comm'n v. Yackel, 445 S.W.2d 389 (Mo.App.1969) (if party feared improper use of the evidence, he should have requested an instruction).

75. See the persuasive statement to this effect, which may have been a dictum, by Olney, J. in Adkins v. Brett, 184 Cal. 252, 193 P. 251, 254 (1920) (in husband's action for alienation, evidence of wife's statement as to parties with and gifts from defendant, though would ordinarily be competent to show wife's feelings, might be excluded if danger great that jury would use it as evidence of defendant's conduct). See also Shepard v. United States, 290 U.S. 96, 103 (1933); State v. Goebel, 40 Wash.2d 18, 240 P.2d 251 (1952) (evidence of other crimes admissible for specific purpose should be excluded in discretion of the court if unduly prejudicial); Uniform Rule 45: ". . . The judge may in his discretion exclude evidence if he finds that its probative value is substantially outweighed by the risk that its admission will (a) necessitate undue consumption of time, or (b) create substantial danger of undue prejudice or of confusing the issues or of misleading the jury, or (c) unfairly and harmfully surprise a party who has not had reasonable opportunity to anticipate that such evidence would be offered." See also text at n. 79, infra, and § 58, n. 64, supra.

76. Grimm v. Gargis, 303 S.W.2d 43 (Mo.1957) (evidence properly admissible against one party with proper instruction); Chesapeake & O. Ry. Co. v. Boyd's Adm'r, 290 Ky. 9, 160 S.W.2d 342 (1942) (statement of engineer, codefendant, admissible against him, if not against railway; general objection without request to limit the evidence ineffective); Ft. Worth Hotel Co. v. Waggoman, 126 S.W.2d 578 (Tex.Civ.App.1939) (evidence admissible against one of defendants, joint tortfeasors, not subject to objection by other defendant; his only relief is a request to have it limited).

But if the evidence is offered generally and excluded there is no error. Hudson v. Smith, 391 S.W.2d 441 (Tex.Civ.App.1965), unless of course, undue prejudice results or a constitutional rule is involved. See n. 77, infra.

the Sixth Amendment right to confront witnesses results.[77] This rule is applicable in state courts.[78] The definite implication of the decision to this effect is that if evidence has multiple purposes, one purpose being in violation of a constitutional protection for a criminal defendant, the evidence is simply inadmissible.[79] However if the case against the defendant was so overwhelming, apart from a confession or an admission of a co-defendant, that its admission into evidence was harmless beyond a reasonable doubt, the Supreme Court will not require reversal.[80]

60. Admission and Exclusion of Evidence in Trials Without a Jury.

Thayer considers that our law of evidence is a "product of the jury system . . . where ordinary untrained citizens are acting as judges of fact." [81] It might have been more expedient if these rules had been, at least in the main, discarded in trials before judges.[82] Their professional experience in valuing evidence greatly lessens the need for exclusionary rules. But the traditional starting point is that in general the jury-trial system of evidence governs in trials before the judge as well.[83] Nevertheless, the feeling of the inexpediency of these restrictions as applied to judges has caused courts to say that the same strictness will not be observed in applying the rules of evidence in judge-trials as in trials before a jury.[84]

The most important influence in encouraging trial judges to take this attitude toward evidence rules in nonjury cases is a rule of presumption obtaining in most appellate courts. These courts have said that in reviewing a case tried without a jury the admission of incompetent evidence over objection will not ordinarily be a ground of reversal if there was competent evidence received sufficient to support the findings. The judge will be presumed to have disregarded the inadmissible and relied on the competent evidence.[85] If he errs, however, in the opposite direction, by excluding evidence which he ought to have received, his ruling will of course be subject to reversal [86] if it is substantially harmful to the losing party.

77. Bruton v. United States, 391 U.S. 123 (1968). See The Supreme Court, 1967 Term, 82 Harv.L.Rev. 95, 231–238 (1968); Note, 35 Mo.L.Rev. 125 (1970). The decision seems limited to erroneous admission of evidence contrary to constitutional prohibitions. It was held to have retroactive effect in Roberts v. Russell, 392 U.S. 293 (1968), reh. denied 393 U.S. 899.

78. Harrington v. California, 395 U.S. 250 (1969).

79. See The Supreme Court, 1967 Term, 82 Harv.L. Rev. 95, 234–236 (1968).

80. Harrington v. California, 395 U.S. 250 (1969); Chapman v. California, 386 U.S. 18, Comment, 83 Harv.L.Rev. 814 (1970). See § 183, infra.

81. Preliminary Treatise on Evidence 509 (1898).

82. See argument for special rules in judge-tried cases, Davis, An Approach to Rules of Evidence for Nonjury Cases, 50 A.B.A.J. 723 (1964), Hearsay in Nonjury Cases, 83 Harv.L.Rev. 1362 (1970).

83. See, e. g., Stewart v. Prudential Ins. Co., 147 Pa. Super. 296, 24 A.2d 83 (1942).

84. See e. g., Weisenborn v. Rutledge, 233 Mo.App. 464, 121 S.W.2d 309, 313 (1938); and numerous cases collected in Dec.Dig. Trial ☞377(1); C.J.S. Trial § 589.

85. Clark v. United States, 61 F.2d 695 (8th Cir. 1932) aff'd 289 U.S. 1; General Metals, Inc. v. Truitt Mfg. Co., 259 N.C. 709, 131 S.E.2d 360 (1963); Lenahan v. Leach, 245 Ore. 496, 422 P.2d 683 (1967); Gray v. Grayson, 76 N.M. 255, 414 P.2d 228 (1966) (but findings indicated evidence erroneously admitted did affect trial judge's decision; reversed); Dec.Dig. Appeal & Error ☞931(6); C.J.S. Appeal and Error § 1564e; Maguire and Epstein, Preliminary Questions of Fact, 36 Yale L.J. 1100, 1115 (1927). See general discussion of requirement that error be in fact prejudicial, § 52, n. 84, supra.

Kansas requires a motion to strike as well as an objection. State of Kansas ex rel. Glen Longier v. Reed, 190 Kan. 376, 375 P.2d 588 (1962).

Occasional decisions decline to apply the presumption when the evidence was objected to and the objection overruled. Farish v. Hawk, 241 Ala. 352, 2 So.2d 407 (1941) (equity case); (but cf. Bessemer Theatres v. City of Bessemer, 261 Ala. 632, 75 So. 2d 651 (1954) nonjury law case); Bellew v. Iowa State Highway Comm'n, 171 N.W.2d 284 (Iowa 1969) (prejudice presumed unless record affirmatively shows evidence was later discarded; record so indicated).

86. Examples of reversals where the exclusion was found prejudicial: Kelly v. Wasserman, 5 N.Y.2d

These contrasting attitudes of the appellate courts toward errors in receiving and those in excluding evidence seem to support the wisdom of the practice adopted by many experienced trial judges in nonjury cases of provisionally admitting all evidence which is objected to if he thinks its admissibility is debatable,[87] with the announcement that all questions of admissibility will be reserved until the evidence is all in. In considering the objections if renewed by motion to strike at the end of the case, he will lean toward admission rather than exclusion [88] and at the end will seek to find clearly admissible testimony on which to base his findings.[89] This practice will lessen the time spent in arguing objections and will ensure that the appellate court will have in the record the evidence that was rejected as well as that which was received. This will often help them to make an end of the case.[90] It will readily be seen, however, that this practice of hearing everything first and deciding upon its competency later creates an atmosphere which muffles the impact and de-emphasizes the importance of the exclusionary rules of evidence.

425, 158 N.E.2d 241, 185 N.Y.S.2d 538 (1959) (tried before referee); McCloskey v. Charleroi Mountain Club, 390 Pa. 212, 134 A.2d 873 (1957). See Dec. Dig. Appeal and Error ☞1056(5); C.J.S. Appeal and Error § 1746, notes 13, 14.

87. Builders Steel Co. v. Commissioner, 179 F.2d 377, 379 (8th Cir. 1950) (valuable discussion by Sanborn, J.); Powell v. Adams, 98 Mo. 598, 12 S.W. 295, 297 (1889); Degginger v. Martin, 48 Wash. 1, 92 P. 674 (1907); Simpson v. Vineyard, 324 S.W.2d 276 (Tex.Civ.App.1959); Holendyke v. Newton, 50 Wis. 635, 638, 7 N.W. 558 (1880) (referee or judge should be very careful in rejecting evidence, and where there is reasonable doubt, though he thinks it inadmissible, should receive it subject to objections); C.J.S. Trial § 589.

But occasionally appellate courts (misguidedly it is believed) disapprove. See Kovacs v. Szentes, 130 Conn. 229, 33 A.2d 124 (1943) (based on Conn.Gen. St.Ann. § 52–208 forbidding court to admit evidence subject to objection unless parties agree; "A judge has not such control over his mental faculties that he can definitely determine whether or not inadmissible evidence he has heard will affect his mind . . ."); Havas v. 105 Casino Corp., 82 Nev. 282, 417 P.2d 239 (1966) ("We disapprove the practice of trial courts holding in abeyance rulings on evidence. It precipitates all manners of difficulty."); Holcombe v. Hopkins, 314 Mass. 113, 49 N.E.2d 722 (1943) (semble); Dec.Dig. Trial ☞51, 379.

88. See *Powell, Degginger* and *Holendyke* cases in next preceding note.

89. As in Hatch v. Calkins, 21 Cal.App.2d 364, 122 P.2d 126 (1942) where the judge in his memorandum decision recited that his decision was based on the competent portion of certain affidavits.

90. As pointed out in the decisions cited in the first paragraph of note 87, supra.

TITLE 4

COMPETENCY

CHAPTER 7

THE COMPETENCY OF WITNESSES

61. In General.[1]

The common law rules of incompetency have been undergoing a process of piecemeal revision by statutes for over a century, so that today most of the former grounds for excluding a witness altogether have been converted into mere grounds of impeaching his credibility.

Since the disqualification of witnesses for incompetency is thus dwindling in importance, and since the statutory modifications vary substantially from state to state, a development of the law in the different jurisdictions is not justified. The common law grounds of incompetency and the general lines of statutory and rule change are summarized in the following sections.

---

1. The subject is covered in detail in 2 Wigmore, Evidence §§ 483–721. Its history is fully treated in 9 Holdsworth Hist.Eng.Law 177–197, 1926, and briefly sketched in Rowley, The Competency of Witnesses, 24 Iowa L.Rev. 482 (1939). A valuable summary is Fryer, Note on Disqualification of Witnesses, Selected Writings on Evidence and Trial 345 (1957).

The present rules regulating the competency of witnesses (as well as admissibility of evidence generally) in the Federal Courts are as follows:

F.R.Civ.P. 43(a): *"Form and Admissibility.* In all trials the testimony of witnesses shall be taken orally in open court, unless otherwise provided by these rules. All evidence shall be admitted which is admissible under the statutes of the United States, or under the rules of evidence heretofore applied in the courts of the United States on the hearing of suits in equity, or under the rules of evidence applied in the courts of general jurisdiction of the state in which the United States court is held. In any case, the statute or rule which favors the reception of the evidence governs and the evidence shall be presented according to the most convenient method prescribed in any of the statutes or rules to which reference is herein made. The competency of a witness to testify shall be determined in like manner."

F.R.Crim.P. 26: "In all trials the testimony of witnesses shall be taken orally in open court, unless otherwise provided by an act of Congress or by these rules. The admissibility of evidence and the competency and privileges of witnesses shall be governed, except when an act of Congress or these rules otherwise provide, by the principles of the common law as they may be interpreted by the courts of the United States in the light of reason and experience."

F.R.Ev. (R.D.1971) 601 would provide a new broad rule: "Every person is competent to be a witness except as otherwise provided in these rules." The only rules of incompetency specifically provided in the rules concern judges and jurors as witnesses. See Advisory Committee's Note.

62. Mental Incapacity [2] and Immaturity.[3]

There is no rule which excludes an insane person as such,[4] or a child of any specified age, from testifying,[5] but in each case the traditional test is whether the witness has intelligence enough to make it worthwhile to hear him at all and whether he feels a duty to tell the truth.[6] Is his capacity to observe, remember, and recount, such that he can probably bring added knowledge of the facts? The test is sometimes phrased in language as a requirement that the witness must have intelligence enough to "understand the nature and obligation of an oath." [7] This requirement is manifestly inappropriate. It confounds a religious standard with a mental standard, and if literally applied the most intelligent witness could hardly meet the standard, much less a child or an insane person.

The liberalization that has been accomplished in the practice has come by liberalization in judicial custom, as the statutes have seldom purported to change the common law standard. Disqualification for mental capacity or immaturity would doubtless have long since been abandoned, except for the presence of the jury as the trier of facts. The judges distrust a jury's ability to assay the words of a small child or of a deranged person. Conceding the jury's deficiencies, the remedy of excluding such a witness, who may be the only person available who knows the

2. 2 Wigmore, Evidence §§ 492–501; C.J.S. Witnesses § 57; Annot., 26 A.L.R. 1491, 148 A.L.R. 1140; Dec.Dig. Witnesses ⊂=39–41; Weihofen, Testimonial Competence and Credibility, 34 Geo. Wash.L.Rev. 53 (1965).

3. 2 Wigmore, Evidence §§ 505–509; C.J.S. Witnesses § 58; Annot., 81 A.L.R.2d 386; Dec.Dig. Witnesses ⊂=40, 45.

4. District of Columbia v. Arms, 107 U.S. 519 (1883) (feeble-minded man competent); People v. McCaughan, 49 Cal.2d 409, 317 P.2d 974 (1957); Truttmann v. Truttmann, 328 Ill. 338, 159 N.E. 775 (1927) (mental defective competent); People v. Lambersky, 410 Ill. 451, 102 N.E.2d 326 (1951); State v. Wildman, 145 Ohio St. 379, 61 N.E.2d 790 (1945) (imbecile girl competent); People v. Rensing, 14 N.Y.2d 210, 199 N.E.2d 489, 250 N.Y.S.2d 401 (1964).

5. Radiant Oil Co. v. Herring, 146 Fla. 154, 200 So. 376, 377 (1941) ("not an arbitrary age but the degree of intelligence . . . is the test . . ."); Rueger v. Hawks, 150 Neb. 834, 36 N.W.2d 236, 244 (1949) ("There is no precise age which determines the question of a child's competency"); Litzkuhn v. Clark, 85 Ariz. 355, 339 P.2d 389 (1959); Artesani v. Gritton, 252 N.C. 463, 113 S.E.2d 895 (1960) (error to exclude seven-year old child as witness solely "by reason of age"). The many statutes that refer to "children under ten years of age who appear incapable of receiving just impressions of the facts respecting which they are examined, or of relating them truly," do not change the rule stated in the text. See, e. g., Litzkuhn v. Clark, supra.

6. State v. Segerberg, 131 Conn. 546, 41 A.2d 101, 102 (1945) ("The principle . . . is that the child shall be sufficiently mature to receive correct impressions by her senses, to recollect and narrate intelligently and to appreciate the moral duty to tell the truth"); Burman v. Chicago Great Western Ry. Co., 340 Mo. 25, 100 S.W.2d 858 (1936) (child, 5 at time of injury, 8 at time of trial, competent though had been held incompetent at earlier trial); Collier v. State, 30 Wis.2d 101, 140 N.W.2d 252 (1966); State v. Smith, 16 Utah 2d 374, 401 P.2d 445 (1965).

The judge will ordinarily conduct an interrogation of the witness to ascertain and test his capacity. Commonwealth v. Tatisos, 238 Mass. 322, 130 N.E. 495 (1921); State v. Collier, 23 Wash.2d 678, 162 P.2d 267 (1945).

7. Examples of decisions in which the court recites this as one of the tests are Bielecki v. State, 140 Tex.Cr.R. 355, 145 S.W.2d 189 (1945), and Mullins v. Commonwealth, 174 Va. 472, 5 S.E.2d 499 (1939). See C.J.S. Witnesses § 63. The more modern approach is illustrated in Hill v. Skinner, 81 Ohio App. 375, 377, 79 N.E.2d 787, 789 (1947). There a child of four was held competent. He testified that if he didn't tell the truth God wouldn't love him. The court said: "The nature of his conception of the obligation to tell the truth is of little importance if he shows that he will fulfill the obligation to speak truthfully as a duty which he owes a Deity or something held in reverence or regard, and if he has the intellectual capacity to communicate his observations and experiences." Variation in the form of oath was authorized in State v. Collier, 23 Wash.2d 678, 162 P.2d 267 (1945) ("You are promising what you are going to say as a witness that you will tell the truth, all of the truth and nothing but the truth, so help you God. You promise that, do you?").

A useful precedent may be the Canada Evidence Act, R.S.C.1952, c. 307, s. 16, which provides that a child of tender years need not be given the oath if, in the opinion of the judge, the child is possessed of sufficient intelligence to justify the reception of his evidence and understands the duty of speaking the truth. See discussion in Bigelow, Witnesses of Tender Years, 9 Crim.L.Q. 298 (1967).

facts, seems inept and primitive. Though the tribunal is unskilled, and the testimony difficult to weigh, it is still better to let the evidence come in for what it is worth, with cautionary instructions.[8] As already indicated,[9] mental derangement, where it affects the ability of the witness to observe, remember, and recount, may always be proved to attack credibility.

63. Religious Belief.[10]

Belief in a divine being who, in this life or hereafter, will punish false swearing was a prerequisite at common law to the capacity to take the oath.[11] Members of many major religions could meet the test, but members of other religions, as well as atheists and agnostics, could not. This ground of incapacity has fortunately been abandoned in most state jurisdictions,[12] either by explicit state constitutional or statutory provisions,[13] or by expansive interpretation of state provisions forbidding deprivation of rights for religious beliefs,[14] or by changing the common law "in the light of reason and experience," [15] or because such a requirement "would be inconsistent with our law and with the spirit of our institutions." [16] In any event, this rule of incapacity appears to be prohibited in any state or federal court by the first and fourteenth amendments of the federal constitution.[17] A witness can object

8. The philosophy expressed in the text is reflected in F.R.Ev. (P.D.) 6–01.

9. See § 45, supra.

10. 2 Wigmore, Evidence § 518, 6 id. §§ 1816–1829; C.J.S. Witnesses § 62; Dec.Dig. Witnesses ⚮44, 227.

11. Attorney-General v. Bradlaugh, [1885], L.R. 2 Q.B.D. 697; 6 Wigmore, Evidence § 1817.

12. See the constitutional and statutory provisions listed and described in 6 Wigmore, Evidence § 1828, note 1.

13. E. g., Calif.Const.1879, art. I, § 4 ("No person shall be rendered incompetent to be a witness or juror on account of his opinions on matters of religious belief"); New York Const.1895, Art. I, § 3 (similar to last, as to witnesses); Texas Const. 1876, Art. I, § 5 ("No person shall be disqualified to give evidence in any of the courts of this state on account of his religious opinions or for want of any religious belief . . ."); Penn., 28 P.S. § 312 ("The capacity of any person who shall testify in any judicial proceeding shall be in no wise affected by his opinions on matters of religion.")

14. E. g., Hroneck v. People, 134 Ill. 139, 152, 24 N.E. 861, 865 (1890) (under Const. Art. 2, § 3, S.H.A.Ill., which provided that "no person shall be denied any civil or political right, privilege or capacity on account of his religious opinions" a wit-ness is qualified though he lacked the religious belief required at common law); and see State v. Levine, 109 N.J.L. 503, 162 Atl. 909 (1932), noted 33 Col.L.Rev. 539 (under Art. 1, § 5, N.J.Const. N.J. S.A., which provided that no person shall be denied enjoyment of civil rights because of religious principles, it was error to deny accused privilege of affirming as a witness on account of his want of religious belief, even though he was allowed to tell his story to the jury. But see State v. Walton, note 16, infra).

15. See Gillars v. United States, 87 U.S.App.D.C. 16, 182 F.2d 962, 969, 970 (1950). In that case it was held proper to allow a witness to "affirm" and testify though he did not believe in divine punishment for perjury and though D.C.Code, Title 14, § 101 provided that "all evidence shall be given under oath according to the forms of the common law," except that a witness with conscientious scruples against an oath may affirm. Fahy, J., said for the court: "The early common law rule, and therefore the rule which at an earlier period would have prevailed under the Code might well have rendered Schnell incompetent. But the Code must now be read with Rule 26 of the Federal Rules of Criminal Procedure, 18 U.S.C.A., which provides, inter alia: '. . . competency and privileges of witnesses shall be governed, except when an act of Congress or these rules otherwise provide, by the principles of the common law as they may be interpreted by the courts of the United States in the light of reason and experience.'
"A fair reading together of the Code and the Rule leads to the conclusion that the common law rule in the District of Columbia is to be interpreted now in the light of reason and experience. This brings into the area of competence witnesses who were under disability under the older criteria."
See also Flores v. State, 443 P.2d 73 (Alaska 1968) (holding that a witness who was sworn under the usual oath was competent although in cross-examination he stated he did not believe in God).

16. Gantz v. State, 18 Ga.App. 154, 88 S.E. 993, (1916) (cited in Pitts v. State, 219 Ga. 222, 132 S.E.2d 649 (1963)). But in State v. Walton, 72 N.J.Super. 527, 179 A.2d 78 (1962), the court discussed a New Jersey rule that no person other than a party can be a witness, unless he believes there is a God, without holding that the rule was ineffective.

17. The textual statement may be inferred from Torcaso v. Watkins, 367 U.S. 488 (1961) (belief in

to an oath directly or inferentially stating his belief in God, but it has been held that routinely swearing witnesses to tell the truth using the phrase, "so help me God," does not vitiate a trial, when the witnesses have not objected.[18] Probably the loser has no standing to object on appeal in such a case, but it is conceivable that in some circumstances he could make a strained argument that he has an interest and is affected. Inquiry into the religious opinions of the witness for impeachment purposes is discussed in another section.[19]

64. Conviction of Crime.[20]

The common law disqualified altogether the witness who had been convicted of treason, felony, or a crime involving fraud or deceit.[21] In England and in most of the states during the last hundred years, this disqualification has been swept away by legislation.[22] In 1917, the Supreme Court of the United States determined that "the dead hand of the common law rule" of disqualification should no longer be applied in criminal cases in the federal courts.[23] In a few states, however, it has been retained for conviction of perjury and subornation thereof.[24] These statutes are now of questionable validity un-

der a holding of the Supreme Court of the United States that declared unconstitutional Texas statutes which barred the persons charged or convicted as co-participants in the same crime from testifying for each other.[25]

65. Parties and Persons Interested: The Dead Man Statutes.[26]

By far the most drastic of the common law rules of incompetency was the rule that excluded the testimony of the parties to the lawsuit and of all persons having a direct pecuniary or proprietary interest in the outcome. In effect, this rule imposed a disability upon the party to testify in his own behalf and conferred upon him a privilege not to be used as a witness against himself by the adversary. The disability had the specious justification of preventing self-interested perjury; the privilege had not even a specious excuse. It is almost unbelievable that the rule could have continued in force in England until the middle of the 19th century, and in this country for a few decades longer. In England, the reform was sweeping, and no shred of disqualification in civil cases remains.

In this country, however, a compromise was forced upon the reformers. The objection was raised that in controversies over contracts or other transactions where one party to the transaction had died and the other survived, hardship and fraud would result if the surviving parties or interested persons were permitted to testify to the transactions. The survivor could testify though the adverse party's lips would be sealed in death. This is a seductive argument. It was accepted in nearly all the early statutes, at a time when the real dispute was

God, a Maryland constitutional test for public office, was held unconstitutional under the First and Fourteenth Amendments of the federal constitution).

18. State v. Albe, 10 Ariz.App. 545, 460 P.2d 651 (1969).

19. See § 48, supra.

20. 2 Wigmore, Evidence §§ 488, 519–524; C.J.S. Witnesses §§ 65–67; Dec.Dig. Witnesses ⊜48, 49.

21. 2 Wigmore, Evidence §§ 519, 520.

22. See the statutes collected in 2 Wigmore, Evidence § 488. Some of the cited statutes that retain vestiges of the common law rule have been amended since the collection was compiled.

23. Rosen v. United States, 245 U.S. 467 (1917). The disqualification is not recognized in F.R.Ev. (R.D.1971) (see Rule 601).

24. The majority of courts have denied disqualification by reason of a conviction in another state, although conviction in the forum would have resulted in disqualification. See Annot., 2 A.L.R.2d 579.

25. Washington v. Texas, 388 U.S. 14 (1967).

26. 2 Wigmore, Evidence §§ 488, 575–580; C.J.S. Witnesses §§ 132–251; Dec.Dig. Witnesses ⊜80–183½; Ray, Dead Man's Statutes, 24 Ohio St.L.J. 89 (1963).

whether the general disqualification should be abolished or retained, and the concession for survivors' cases undoubtedly seemed a minor one. But the concession has now become so ingrained a part of judicial and professional habits of thinking that it is hard to dislodge by argument.

Accordingly, statutes in many states now provide that the common law disqualification of parties and interested persons is abolished, except that they remain disqualified to testify concerning a transaction or communication with a person since deceased in a suit prosecuted or defended by the executor or administrator of the decedent.[27] However, it is often provided by the statute or by case law that the surviving party or interested person may testify if called by the adversary, i. e., by the executor or administrator, thus abrogating the privilege feature of the common law rule. The practical consequence of these statutes is that if a survivor has rendered services, furnished goods or lent money to a man whom he trusted, without an outside witness or admissible written evidence, he is helpless if the other dies and the representative of his estate declines to pay. The survivor's mouth may even be closed in an action arising from a fatal automobile collision,[28] or in a suit upon a note or an account which the survivor paid in cash without taking a receipt.

Most commentators agree that the expedient of refusing the listen to the survivor is, in the words of Bentham, a "blind and brainless" technique. In seeking to avoid injustice to one side, the statute-makers have ignored the equal possibility of creating injustice to the other. The temptation to the survivor to fabricate a claim or defense is obvious enough, so obvious indeed that any jury will realize that his story must be cautiously heard. A searching cross-examination will usually, in case of fraud, reveal discrepancies inherent in the "tangled web" of deception. In any event, the survivor's disqualification is more likely to balk the honest than the dishonest survivor. One who would not balk at perjury will hardly hesitate at suborning a third person, who would not be disqualified, to swear to the false story.

Slowly, the lawmakers are being brought to see the blindness of the traditional survivors' evidence acts, and liberalizing changes are being adopted. A few states have provided that the survivor may testify, but his testimony will not support a judgment, unless corroborated by other evidence.[29] Others authorize the trial judge to permit the survivor to testify when it appears that his testimony is necessary to prevent injustice.[30] Both of these solutions have reasonably apparent drawbacks [31] which are avoided by a third type of statute that sweeps away the disqualification entirely and permits the survivor to testify without restriction, but seeks to minimize the danger of injustice to the decedent's estate by admitting any writings of the deceased or evidence of oral statements made by him, bearing on the controversy,

---

27. This is the most common general form, but the variants are so numerous that no statute seems entirely typical. The cases interpreting one statute must be treated with great caution in the interpretation of another statute, and a great deal of confusing and conflicting interpretive case law exists. Some statutes apply to suits by or against other persons deriving interests from a deceased person, as well as to suits by or against guardians of incompetents. The variations in the statutes were summarized and graphically charted in Vanderbilt, Minimum Standards of Judicial Administration 334–341 (1949).

28. Annot., 80 A.L.R.2d 1296; Dec.Dig. Witnesses ☞159(3); Stout, Should the Dead Man's Statute Apply to Automobile Collisions, 38 Texas L.Rev. 14 (1959).

29. Statutes and cases are collected in Annot., 21 A.L.R.2d 1013.

30. See Mont.Rev.Code 1947, § 93–701–3; Ariz.Rev. Stat. § 12–2251.

31. See discussion in Ray, Dead Man's Statutes, 24 Ohio St.L.J. 89 (1963).

both of which would ordinarily be excluded as hearsay.[32]

The Model Code of Evidence, the Uniform Rules of Evidence, and the Revised Draft of Rules of Evidence for the United States District Courts and Magistrates propose to abandon the instant disqualification altogether. It should be noted that in addition all three proposals relax traditional hearsay restrictions generally.

Interest, then, as a disqualification in civil cases has been discarded, except for the fragmentary relic retained in the survivors' evidence statutes. The disqualification of parties defendant in criminal cases which at common law prevented the accused from being called as a witness by either side has been abrogated in England and in this country to the extent it disabled the defendant to testify in his own behalf, but it survives to the extent that the prosecution cannot call him. In this form, it is a rule of privilege, and constitutes one aspect of the privilege against self-incrimination, treated in a later section.[33]

While the disqualification of parties and persons interested in the result of the lawsuit has thus been almost entirely swept away, the fact of interest of the witness, whether as a party or otherwise, is by no means disregarded. It may be proved to impeach credibility,[34] and in most jurisdictions the court will instruct that a party's testimony may be weighed in the light of his interest.[35]

66. Husbands and Wives of Parties.[36]

Closely allied to the disqualification of parties, and even more arbitrary and misguided, was the early common law disqualification of the husband or wife of the party. This disqualification prevented the party's husband or wife from testifying either for or against the party in any case, civil or criminal.[37] Doubtless we should classify the disability of the husband or wife as a witness to testify *for* the party-spouse as a disqualification, based upon the supposed infirmity of interest, and the rule enabling the party-spouse to prevent the husband or wife from testifying *against* the party as a privilege.[38]

Of course, the common law rule has been modified. In the majority of jurisdictions statutes have made the husband or wife fully competent to testify for or against the party-spouse in civil cases.[39] In criminal cases, the disqualification of the husband or wife to testify for the accused spouse has been removed,

---

32. This solution was recommended by the American Bar Association in 1938, as follows: "That the rule excluding testimony of an interested party as to transactions with deceased persons, should be abrogated by the adoption of a statute like that of Connecticut, which removes the disqualification of the party as a witness and permits the introduction of declarations of the decedent, on a finding by the trial judge that they were made in good faith and on decedent's personal knowledge." As of 1949, six states, Connecticut, Louisiana, Massachusetts, Oregon, Rhode Island and South Dakota, had such statutes. Vanderbilt, 334, 338, supra, n. 27. New Hampshire also adopted the provision. For valuable discussion of the entire problem and the alternative solutions, see 2 Wigmore, Evidence § 578; Morgan and others, The Law of Evidence, Some Proposals for Its Reform, Ch. III (1927); Ladd, The Dead Man Statute, 26 Iowa L.Rev. 201 (1941); Ray, Dead Man's Statutes, 24 Ohio St.L.J. 89 (1963).

33. See §§ 116, 130, infra.

34. See § 40, supra.

35. See, e. g., Hancheft v. Haas, 219 Ill. 546, 76 N.E. 845 (1906); Lovely v. Grand Rapids & I. Ry. Co., 137 Mich. 653, 100 N.W. 894 (1904); State v. Turner, 320 S.W.2d 579 (Mo.1959); C.J.S. Trial § 276.

36. 2 Wigmore, Evidence §§ 488 (statutes), 600–620 (marital disqualification to testify for the spouse), 8 id. (McNaughton rev.), §§ 2227–2245 (privilege of party-spouse to prevent other spouse from testifying against the party); C.J.S. Witnesses §§ 75–104; Dec.Dig. Witnesses ☞51–65; Hutchins and Slesinger, Some Observations on the Law of Evidence: Family Relations, 13 Minn.L.Rev. 675 (1929); Note, 56 Nw.L.Rev. 208 (1961).

37. See authorities in next preceding note. See also survey of the law in the various American jurisdictions in Note, 38 Va.L.Rev. 359 (1952).

38. 8 Wigmore Evidence (McNaughton rev.) § 2227.

39. See statutes collected in 2 Wigmore, Evidence § 488, 8 id. (McNaughton rev.) § 2245, and summary of statutes in Note, 38 Va.L.Rev. 359 (1952).

but it is generally provided that the prosecution may not call the spouse, without the consent of the accused spouse, thus preserving for criminal cases the privilege of the accused to keep the spouse off the stand altogether.[40] In some jurisdictions either spouse may claim the privilege.[41] Finally, in other jurisdictions spouses may be called to the stand to testify just as any other witnesses.[42]

Even at common law the instant privilege was withheld from the husband in criminal prosecutions against him for wrongs directly against the person of the wife.[43] The statutes which retain the instant privilege usually broaden this exception to include prosecution of any "crime committed by one against the other" and various other miscellaneous exceptions.[44] There is some disagreement

concerning the time in which the instant privilege exists, but most courts regard the initial time at which it comes into being as the date of the creation of the marriage and the terminal date as the date of termination of marriage, as by divorce.[45]

Several procedural questions may arise. The holder of the privilege must be ascertained.[46] There is disagreement whether it is error for the prosecution to call the spouse to the stand in a criminal case thereby forcing the accused spouse to object in the presence of the jury.[47] Most courts protect the privilege by denying the right to comment upon its exercise.[48]

The privilege is often applied to extrajudicial statements of the spouse.[49]

The privilege has sometimes been defended on the ground that it protects family harmony. But family harmony is nearly always past saving when the spouse is willing to aid the prosecution. The privilege is an archaic survival of a mystical religious dogma [50] and

---

40. See sources cited in n. 39, supra. See also United States v. Mitchell, 137 F.2d 1006, 1008 (2d Cir. 1943) (dictum: ". . . clearly the better view is that the privilege is that of either spouse who chooses to claim it"). State v. Dunbar, 360 Mo. 788, 230 S.W.2d 845, 849 (1950) (prosecution of husband for shooting wife in arm, so that it had to be amputated; held under statute that wife though competent was not compellable to testify, reversing defendant's conviction because she was required to testify; this ignores the principle that a party cannot complain of the infringement of a witness's privilege, see § 73, infra).

41. See sources cited in n. 39, supra.

42. See sources cited in n. 39, supra.

43. 1 Blackstone, Commentaries 443 (1765); 8 Wigmore, Evidence (McNaughton rev.) § 2239.

44. 2 Wigmore, Evidence § 488, 8 id. (McNaughton rev.) §§ 2239, 2240. And the statutes frequently go further and expressly except particular crimes (aside from crimes against the person or property of the spouse) such as bigamy, adultery, rape, crimes against the children of either or both, and abandonment and support proceedings. Note, 38 Va.L.Rev. 359, 364, 365 (1952); 8 Wigmore, Evidence (McNaughton rev.) § 2240. Occasionally similar results are reached in the absence of express exceptions in the disqualifying statute. State v. Kollenborn, 304 S.W.2d 855 (Mo.1957) (in prosecution of husband for assault on their minor child, wife could testify for state). See also Wyatt v. United States, 362 U.S. 525 (1960) (transportation of wife for purpose of prostitution, in violation of Mann Act is crime against her and she can be compelled to testify).

45. 8 Wigmore, Evidence (McNaughton rev.) § 2237. See dictum in Pereira v. United States, 347 U.S. 1 (1953).

46. See sources cited in n. 39, supra; also § 73, infra.

47. State v. Tanner, 54 Wash.2d 535, 341 P.2d 869, (1959) (improper to force objection before jury, but case may be restricted to its facts); Hignett v. State, 168 Tex.Cr.R. 380, 328 S.W.2d 300 (1959) (requiring defendant to object in presence of jury is error); State v. Hixson, 237 Ore. 402, 391 P.2d 388 (1964) (contra; not error to call spouse to stand and request defendant's permission to examine her); Annot., 76 A.L.R.2d 920. F.R.Ev. (R.D.1971) 513(b) directs that claims of privilege be handled outside the presence of the jury to the extent practicable. See § 76, infra.

48. See cases cited at 8 Wigmore Evidence (McNaughton rev.) § 2243; F.R.Ev. (R.D.1971) 513(a).

49. See cases cited in 8 Wigmore, Evidence (McNaughton rev.) § 2232, but vicarious admissions and a few other exceptions are noted. A contrary decision is Eubanks v. State, 242 Miss. 372, 135 So.2d 183 (1961) (extra-judicial statement of wife admitted as part of the res gestae).

50. Coke, Commentary on Littleton 6b (1628), ". . . a wife cannot be produced either for or against her husband, *quia sunt duae animae in carne una*" ("for they are two souls in one flesh").

of a way of thinking about the marital relation that is today outmoded.[51] Nevertheless, the Supreme Court upheld the policy of the privilege in 1958,[52] and the proposed rules of evidence for the federal courts recognize it in criminal cases.[53]

Both the instant privilege, and the ancient disqualification, must be clearly distinguished from another privilege—the privilege against disclosure of confidential communications between husband and wife. It is discussed in another place.[54]

67. Incompetency of Husband and Wife to Give Testimony on Non-Access.[55]

In 1777, in an ejectment case where the issue of the legitimacy of the claimant was raised, Lord Mansfield delivered a pronouncement which apparently was new-minted doctrine, "that the declarations of a father or mother cannot be admitted to bastardize the issue born after marriage . . . it is a rule founded in decency, morality and policy, that they shall not be permitted to say after marriage that they have had no connection and therefore that the offspring is spurious. . . . " [56] This invention of the great jurist though justly criticised by Wigmore as inconsistent, obstructive and pharisaical,[57] was

followed by later English decisions [58] until abrogated by statute,[59] and has been generally accepted in this country.[60] A few courts have wisely rejected it by construing the general statutes abolishing the incompetency of parties and of spouses as abolishing this eccentric incompetency also,[61] but most courts have not yielded to this argument.[62] The points of controversy in the application of the rule are (a) whether it is limited strictly to evidence of non-access,[63] or whether it extends to other types of evidence showing that some one other than the husband is the

58. See, e. g., Russell v. Russell, [1924] App.C. 687 (H.L.)

59. St.1949, 12, 13, and 14 Geo. 6, ch. 100, Law Reform (Miscellaneous Provisions) Act, 1949, § 7 ("evidence of a husband or wife shall be admissible in any proceedings to prove that marital intercourse did or did not take place between them during any period . . . husband or wife shall not be compellable in any proceeding to give evidence of the matters aforesaid"). Similar provisions are contained in St. 1950, 14 Geo. 6, ch. 25, Matrimonial Causes Act, 1950, § 32.

60. See authorities cited in n. 1, above. The realistic opinion of Smith, C. J., writing for the court in Moore v. Smith, 178 Miss. 383, 172 So. 317 (1937), rejects outright the reasoning in Goodright v. Moss, supra, n. 56.

61. In re McNamara's Estate, 181 Cal. 82, 183 Pac. 552, 7 A.L.R. 313, 325 (1919); State v. Soyka, 181 Minn. 533, 233 N.W. 300 (1930); Loudon v. Loudon, 114 N.J.Eq. 242, 168 Atl. 840, 89 A.L.R. 904 (Ct. Errors & App. 1933) (extensive discussion by Perskie, J.); State v. Schimschal, 73 Wash.2d 141, 437 P.2d 169 (1968); Ventresco v. Bushey, 159 Me. 241, 191 A.2d 104 (1963) (overruling Hubert v. Cloutier, 135 Me. 230, 194 A. 303 (1937) and citing additional cases).

62. See, e. g., State v. Wade, 264 N.C. 144, 141 S.E.2d 34 (1965); State ex rel. Worley v. Lavender, 147 W.Va. 803, 131 S.E.2d 752 (1963).

Specific statutes, however, often limit or abrogate the rule in particular proceedings. See, e. g., the statutes described in Sayles v. Sayles, 323 Mass. 66, 80 N.E.2d 21, 22 (1948) (statutes permitting spouses testimony to non-access in prosecutions for non-support and in illegitimacy proceedings).

63. As held in Hall v. State, 176 Md. 488, 5 A.2d 916 (1939) but possibly the Lord Mansfield rule, abolished in part by the legislature, should be considered ineffective, Shelly v. Smith, 249 Md. 619, 241 A.2d 682 (1968); Commonwealth v. Gantz, 128 Pa.Super. 97, 193 Atl. 72 (1937); Commonwealth v. Ludlow, 206 Pa.Super. 464, 214 A.2d 282 (1966).

51. See Hutchins and Slesinger, Some Observations on the Law of Evidence: Family Relations, 13 Minn.L.Rev. 675, 678 (1929), but compare Note, 17 U.Chi.L.Rev. 525, 530 (1950). See also the criticisms of the privilege collected in 8 Wigmore, Evidence (McNaughton rev.) § 2228, ranging from the philippic by Jeremy Bentham in 1827 to the recommendation for its abolition by the Committee on the Improvement of the Law of Evidence of the American Bar Association in 1937.

52. Hawkins v. United States, 358 U.S. 74 (1958).

53. F.R.Ev. (R.D.1971) 505.

54. See Ch. 9, infra.

55. 7 Wigmore, Evidence §§ 2063, 2064; C.J.S. Witnesses § 90; Dec.Dig. Witnesses ☞57; Annot., 60 A.L.R. 380, 68 id. 421, 89 id. 911.

56. Goodright v. Moss, 2 Cowp. 291, 98 Eng.Rep. 1257 (1777).

57. 7 Evidence § 2064.

father,[64] (b) whether the rule is limited to proceedings wherein legitimacy is in issue [65] or extends to suits for divorce where the question is adultery rather than the legitimacy of the child,[66] and (c) whether it is confined to prohibiting the testimony of husband and wife on the stand,[67] or extends to excluding evidence of the previous admissions or declarations of the spouse.[68] In view of the impolicy of the rule it is believed that in all these instances the more restrictive application is to be preferred.

68. Judges [69] and Jurors.[70]

A judicial officer called to the stand in a case in which he is not sitting as a judge is not disqualified by his office from testifying.[71] But when a judge is called as a witness in a trial before him, his role as witness is manifestly inconsistent with his customary role of impartiality in the adversary system of trial.[72] Nevertheless, under the older view he was in general regarded as a competent witness,[73] though he might have a discretion to decline to testify.[74] This view is preserved in some state statutes.[75] A second view is that the judge is disqualified from testifying to material, disputed facts, but may testify to matters merely formal and undisputed.[76] This distinction is not easy to draw, and formal matters nearly always can be proved by other witnesses. Accordingly the third view, for which support is growing, that a judge is incompetent to testify in a case which he is trying,[77] seems the most expedient one.

---

64. As in Grates v. Garcia, 20 N.M. 158, 148 Pac. 493 (1915); Esparza v. Esparza, 382 S.W.2d 162 (Tex.Civ.App.1964).

65. The reasoning, if not the holding, in Sayles v. Sayles, 323 Mass. 66, 80 N.E.2d 21 (1948), supports the view that a suit for divorce for adultery is not within the rule. Biggs v. Biggs, 253 N.C. 10, 116 S.E.2d 178 (1960), seems a holding to that effect.

66. As in Gonzalez v. Gonzalez, 177 S.W.2d 328 (Tex.Civ.App.1943).

67. As held in Sayles v. Sayles, 323 Mass. 66, 80 N.E.2d 21 (1948).

68. As in Zakrzewski v. Zakrzewski, 237 Mich. 459, 212 N.W. 80 (1927) (wife's admission that child not her husband's excluded under the rule); Schmidt v. State, 110 Neb. 504, 194 N.W. 679, 681 (1923) (wife's declarations); West v. Redmond, 171 N.C. 742, 88 S.E. 341 (1916). See Annot., 31 A.L.R. 2d 989, 1024.

69. 6 Wigmore, Evidence § 1909; C.J.S. Witnesses § 105; 58 Am.Jur. Witnesses, § 150; Dec.Dig. Witnesses ☜68–70; Annot., 157 A.L.R. 315.

70. 6 Wigmore, Evidence § 1910; 8 id. §§ 2345–2356; C.J.S. Witnesses § 108; C.J.S. New Trial § 169; 58 Am.Jur. Witnesses, § 151; Dec.Dig. Witnesses ☜73, New Trial ☜141–143.

71. Thus, it is not uncommon for judges to testify about matters occurring in former trials in which they presided. See, e. g., Woodward v. City of Waterbury, 113 Conn. 457, 155 Atl. 825 (1931); State v. Hindman, 159 Ind. 586, 65 N.E. 911 (1903). They should be competent witnesses in subsequent habeas corpus proceedings. See Leighton v. Henderson, 220 Tenn. 91, 414 S.W.2d 419 (1967); Report of the Special Committee on the Propriety of Judges Appearing as Witnesses, 36 A.B.A.J. 630 (1950).

72. "The two characters are inconsistent with each other and their being united in one person is incompatible with the fair and safe administration of justice." Parker, J., in Morss v. Morss, 11 Barb. (N.Y.) 510, 511 (1851).

73. See examples in the English practice in the 1600s and 1700s, described in 6 Wigmore, Evidence § 1909, note 1.

74. See O'Neill & Hearne v. Bray's Adm'x, 262 Ky. 377, 90 S.W.2d 353 (1936); O'Neal v. State, 106 Tex.Cr. 158, 291 S.W. 892 (1927).

75. See similar statutes described in 6 Wigmore, Evidence § 1909. The Tennessee statute is applied in State ex rel. Phillips v. Henderson, 220 Tenn. 701, 423 S.W.2d 489 (1968).

Under the view that a judge is competent as a witness, he should give his evidence under the procedures which apply to other witnesses, Great Liberty Life Ins. Co. v. Flint, 336 S.W.2d 434 (Tex. Civ.App.1960).

76. See, e. g., Wingate v. Mach, 117 Fla. 104, 157 So. 421 (1934) (testimony as to formal matter did not constitute the judge a "material" witness under disqualifying statute); State ex rel. Smith v. Wilcoxen, 312 P.2d 187 (Okl.Cr.1957) (judge not competent to testify to material facts and if he is to be called he should disqualify himself). This view seems to be advocated by Wigmore. See Evidence § 1909, p. 592. A similar line is drawn in Model Code of Evidence R. 302 ("If the judge testifies concerning a disputed material matter, he shall not continue as a judge in the action against . . . objection . . ."). Compare 28 U.S. C.A. § 455, as amended June 25, 1948 ("Any justice or judge of the United States shall disqualify himself in any case in which . . . he is or has been a material witness. . . .").

77. See the general statements of the rule of disqualification, or of the impropriety of testimony

A somewhat similar danger to the impartial position of the tribunal is present when a juror sitting in the case is called as a witness, and thus it may well be that he should be held incompetent.[78] But the traditional common law and present-day practice holds him competent generally to testify.[79] There is one limitation upon this competency, namely, the doctrine that a juror is incompetent to testify in impeachment of his verdict.[80] In that form the doctrine has been much criticized, but retains currency in the decisions.[81] Though arbitrary in its limits, in that it disqualifies jurors but not officers and eavesdroppers who may gain knowledge of misconduct,[82] it does serve to protect in some measure the finality of verdicts, and it is this policy that has doubtless led to its survival. Other courts would abandon the rule of disqualification, and would permit jurors to testify to misconduct and irregularities which are ground for new trial.[83] For protection of finality they would trust to a doctrine which excludes, as immaterial, evidence as to the expressions and arguments of the jurors in their deliberations and evidence as to their own motives, beliefs, mistakes and mental operations generally, in ar-

---

by the judge, in State v. Sandquist, 146 Minn. 322, 178 N.W. 883, 885 (1920); Brashier v. State, 197 Miss. 237, 20 So.2d 65, 157 A.L.R. 311, 313 (1944); Maitland v. Zanga, 14 Wash. 92, 44 Pac. 117 (1896); State v. Eubanks, 232 La. 289, 94 So.2d 262 (1957) rev'd on other grounds 356 U.S. 584. See Report of the Special Committee on the Propriety of Judges Appearing as Witnesses, 36 A.B.A.J. 630, 633 (1950) ("The modern rule is that a judge is not a competent witness in a case in which he is presiding, unless there is a statute permitting it.") See also Uniform Rule 41; F.R.Ev. (R.D.1971) 605; West's Ann.Cal.Evid.Code, § 703.

Nevertheless, even though the judge may be incompetent, his testimony, if not harmful, may not be ground for reversal. See, e. g., McCaffrey v. State, 105 Ohio St. 508, 138 N.E. 61, 63 (1922), and cases cited in Annot., 157 A.L.R. 315, 319, 320.

78. This view is embodied in Uniform Rule 42, and in F.R.Ev. (R.D.1971) 606. See also West's Ann. Cal.Evid.Code, § 704.

79. Statutes have frequently so provided. See, e. g., State v. Cavanaugh, 98 Iowa 688, 68 N.W. 452 (1896) (juror may testify, under I.C.A. § 780.17). Of course instances in which jurors will be called as ordinary witnesses are rare because of the procedures for selection of the jurors.

80. Like the rule forbidding parents to bastardize their issue, see § 67, supra, this dogma was an innovation introduced by Lord Mansfield. The parent case was Vaise v. Delaval, 1 T.R. 11, 99 Eng. Rep. 944 (K.B. 1785). There affidavits of jurymen that their verdict was based on chance was rejected and Lord Mansfield said: "The Court cannot receive such an affidavit from any of the jurymen themselves, in all of whom such conduct is a very high misdemeanor; but in every such case the Court must derive their knowledge from some other source, such as some person having seen the transaction through a window or by some such other means". The weaknesses of this position are pointed out in 8 Wigmore, Evidence (McNaughton rev.) §§ 2352, 2353.

81. See, e. g., McDonald v. Pless, 238 U.S. 264 (1915) (affidavits as to quotient verdict excluded); Hoff-

man v. City of St. Paul, 187 Minn. 320, 245 N.W. 373 (1932) (same) and cases collected in 8 Wigmore, Evidence (McNaughton rev.) § 2354 and in Dec.Dig. New Trial ⚭142, 143.

The various problems are analyzed and the lines of decision indicated in an extensive comment, Impeachment of Jury Verdicts, 25 U.Chi.L.Rev. 360 (1958).

Some courts which follow the dogma of the juror's incompetency to impeach his verdict limit the disqualification to testimony about matters occurring within the jury room, and allow the juror to testify to irregularities occurring outside. Pierce v. Brennan, 83 Minn. 422, 86 N.W. 417 (1901) (jurors' affidavits as to their privately viewing the scene); and see Welshire v. Bruaw, 331 Pa. 392, 200 Atl. 67 (1938) (while jurors cannot testify to misconduct among themselves in jury room, can testify as to misconduct there of outsiders—here a drunken tipstaff puts pressure on them for a verdict by remarks in jury room). The disqualification to "impeach" the verdict does not preclude the juror from testifying in support of the verdict, when it is attacked by testimony of outsiders. Morakes v. State, 201 Ga. 425, 40 S.E.2d 120, 127 (1946); Iverson v. Prudential Ins. Co., 126 N.J.L. 280, 19 A.2d 214 (Ct.E. & A.1941).

82. Reich v. Thompson, 346 Mo. 577, 142 S.W.2d 486, 129 A.L.R. 795, 802, 803 (1940), annotated on this point. In the cited case testimony of the clerk, who overheard from adjoining room statements made in the jury room, was held admissible.

83. Some leading opinions favoring this view: Whyte, J., in Crawford v. State, 10 Tenn. (2 Yerg.) 60, 67 (1821); Cole, J., in Wright v. Illinois & Miss. Telegraph Co., 20 Iowa 195, 210 (1866); Brewer, J., in Perry v. Bailey, 12 Kan. 539, 544 (1874); State v. Kociolek, 20 N.J. 92, 118 A.2d 12 (1955). For other decisions and statutes in the various jurisdictions, see 8 Wigmore, Evidence (McNaughton rev.) § 2354, note 2; Annot., 48 A.L.R.2d 971. The view is embodied in F.R.Ev. (R.D.1971) 606(b).

riving at their verdict.[84] To be distinguished from these rules of incompetency and exclusion, is the doctrine which has the support of Wigmore [85] and of some judicial expressions,[86] to the effect that each juror has a privilege against the disclosure in court of his communications to the other jurors during their retirement.

69. Firsthand Knowledge and Expertness.

Two other rules, already considered, may be related to the subject of competency of witnesses. These rules are the requirement that a witness testifying to objective facts must have had means of knowing them from observation,[87] and the rule that one who would testify to his inference or opinion in matters requiring special training or experience to understand, must be qualified as an expert in the field.[88] It should be noted that unlike most of the other rules of competency, which go to the capacity of the witness to speak at all, these last are directed to his capacity to speak to a particular matter.

70. The Procedure of Disqualification.[89]

Under the earlier common law practice, the witness was not sworn until he was placed upon the stand to begin his testimony. Before the oath was administered the adversary had an opportunity to object to his competency and the judge or counsel would then examine the witness touching upon his qualifications, before he was sworn as a witness. This was known as a voir dire examination. The practice in many courts requires that when the witness is first called to the stand to testify, the opponent must then challenge his competency, if grounds of challenge are

---

84. See, e. g., Davis v. United States, 47 F.2d 1071 (5th Cir.1931) (testimony of some jurors that defendant's failure to take stand was discussed as indicating guilt and that this was given weight, excluded); Caldwell v. E. F. Spears & Sons, 186 Ky. 64, 216 S.W. 83 (1919) (that jury misunderstood instructions); Collings v. Northwestern Hospital, 202 Minn. 139, 277 N.W. 910 (1938) (same as last); State v. Best, 111 N.C. 638, 15 S.E. 930 (1892) (affidavit of five jurors that they assented to verdict of guilty on belief that recommendation to mercy would save accused from death penalty). Such matters are said to "inhere in the verdict." Schindler v. Mulhair, 132 Neb. 809, 273 N.W. 217 (1937). Grenz v. Werre, 129 N.W.2d 681 (N.D. 1964). Decisions are collected in 8 Wigmore, Evidence (McNaughton rev.) § 2349; Dec.Dig. New Trial ☞143(4, 5).

While these expressions and mental operations are thus no ground of attack upon the verdict, it seems that when an allowable attack is made for misconduct, such as an unauthorized view, evidence of the jurors as to whether the misconduct actually influenced their finding (and this evidence would usually support the verdict) might be received. Caldwell v. Yeatman, 91 N.H. 150, 15 A.2d 252 (1940) (semble). But some decisions are to the contrary. People v. Stokes, 103 Cal. 193, 37 Pac. 207, 209 (dictum) (1894); City of Houston v. Quinones, 142 Tex. 282, 177 S.W.2d 259 (1944). See Annot., 58 A.L.R.2d 556. But as to the influence on the jurors of erroneous instructions, improper arguments of counsel, etc., as distinguished from misconduct of the jurors, the considerations may well be different and the test may be, not were the jurors influenced, but was the instruction or the argument calculated to mislead. See, e. g., People v. Duzan, 272 Ill. 478, 112 N.E. 315 (1916) (error in refusing instruction, jurors' evidence that they did not notice that instruction was marked refused, rejected); 8 Wigmore, Evidence (McNaughton rev.) § 2349.

85. 8 Evidence (McNaughton rev.) § 2346.

86. In Clark v. United States, 289 U.S. 1 (1933), on appeal from a conviction of a juror for contempt in giving false answers, Cardozo, J., for the court said: "The books suggest a doctrine that the arguments and votes of jurors, the media concludendi, are secrets, protected from disclosure unless the privilege is waived. . . . Freedom of debate might be stifled and independence of thought checked if jurors were made to feel that their arguments and ballots were to be freely published to the world. The force of these considerations is not to be gainsaid. . . . Assuming that there is a privilege which protects from impertinent exposure the arguments and ballots of a juror while considering his verdict, we think the privilege does not apply where the relation giving birth to it has been fraudulently begun or fraudulently continued." The privilege was held inapplicable because of such fraudulent conduct.

87. See § 10, supra.

88. See § 13, supra.

89. 2 Wigmore, Evidence §§ 483–487; C.J.S. Witnesses §§ 115–119; Dec.Dig. Witnesses ☞76–79, 121–124, 180–183.

then known to him.[90] On the other hand, if it is error for the accused to call a spouse to the stand and require the accused spouse to object before the jury, as it is in some courts,[91] prior voir dire examination without the presence of the jury is required. In some courts, voir dire examination may also be required of proposed infant witnesses and in some circumstances of proposed witnesses who are allegedly incompetent.[92] If grounds of incompetency are not known when the witness takes the stand but are disclosed in his testimony, the challenge may then be made.[93] If the challenge goes to incompetency generally, as for mental incapacity, the burden rests on the objector to show by examination of the challenged witness, or by other evidence, that the disqualification exists.[94] With respect to knowledge or expertness, on the other hand, the offering party must first prove, usually by questioning the witness himself, that he is qualified.

If the question of fact is disputed or doubtful on the evidence, the trial judge sitting with a jury does not submit this question of fact to the jury. As with all similar issues of fact arising in the determination of the admissibility of evidence [95] the judge himself decides the preliminary issue and sustains or rejects accordingly the challenge to the witness or the objection to evidence.[96]

71. Probable Future of the Rules of Competency.

The rules which disqualify witnesses who have knowledge of relevant facts and mental capacity to convey that knowledge are serious obstructions to the ascertainment of truth. For a century the course of legal evolution has been in the direction of sweeping away these obstructions. Rule 101 of the Model Code of Evidence provides: "Every person is qualified to be a witness as to any material matter unless the judge finds that (a) the proposed witness is incapable of expressing himself concerning the matter so as to be understood by the judge and jury either directly or through interpretation by one who can understand him, or (b) the proposed witness is incapable of understanding the duty of a witness to tell the truth." Similarly, broad proposed rules of evidence for the United States courts provide only for rules of competency with respect to personal knowledge and for judges and jurors.[97]

---

90. 2 Wigmore, Evidence § 586.

Observe the parallel treatment of objections to evidence, § 52, supra.

91. See § 66, supra, § 76, infra.

92. Saucier v. State, 156 Tex.Cr.R. 301, 235 S.W.2d 903 (Tex.Civ.App.1951) cert. denied 341 U.S. 949, reh. denied 342 U.S. 843 (challenge to mental competency of witness); State v. Morrison, 43 Wash.2d 23, 259 P.2d 1105 (1953) (challenge to mental incompetency of a witness, dictum that examination "might well have been in the absence of the jury"). It often seems assumed that the examination may be or should be held in the presence of the jury presumably because it can affect credibility in any event.

93. Nunn v. Slemmons' Adm'r, 298 Ky. 315, 182 S.W.2d 888 (1944).

94. State v. Barker, 294 Mo. 303, 242 S.W. 405 (1922); Batterton v. State, 52 Tex.Cr. 381, 107 S.W. 826 (1908); 2 Wigmore, Evidence §§ 484, 497.

95. See § 53, supra.

96. De Silvey v. State, 245 Ala. 163, 16 So.2d 183 (1944); State v. Teager, 222 Iowa 391, 269 N.W. 348 (1936); 2 Wigmore, Evidence § 487; Dec.Dig. Witnesses ☞79(1).

97. F.R.Ev. (R.D.1971) 601–606.

TITLE 5

PRIVILEGE: COMMON LAW AND STATUTORY

CHAPTER 8

THE SCOPE AND EFFECT OF THE EVIDENTIARY PRIVILEGES

72. Distinction between Rules of Privilege and Rules of Incompetency—[1] (a) Difference in Purpose.

In our offhand thinking about evidential privileges as distinguished from rules of exclusion, we are apt to assume that the difference is that a privilege may be claimed or waived at someone's election, whereas a rule of exclusion operates automatically to keep evidence out. A moment's reflection will cause us to abandon this view. We would recall that the rule of exclusion, no less than the privilege, will also be waived ordinarily, if it is not promptly claimed,[2] and only in rare instances will the trial judge of his own motion interpose to enforce the rule.

If we call to mind the subjects of the two groups of rules, the underlying distinction becomes apparent. Among the most prominent of the rules of exclusion are the hearsay rule, the opinion rule, the rule rejecting proof of bad character as evidence of crime, and the rule excluding secondary evidence until the original document is shown to be unavailable. On the other hand the privileges which come most familiarly to mind are the one which protects a witness against self-crimination, and those which give their shield to con-

---

1. As to the basis of privileges see 8 Wigmore, Evidence (McNaughton rev.) §§ 2192, 2197, and 2285 and the opinion by Learned Hand, Circuit Judge, in McMann v. Securities and Exchange Commission, 87 F.2d 377, 378 (1937), in which he says in denying the claim of a customer to a privilege against disclosure of his broker's records relating to his trading account: "The suppression of truth is a grievous necessity at best, more especially when as here the inquiry concerns the public interest; it can be justified at all only when the opposed private interest is supreme." See also Donnelly, The Law of Evidence: Privacy and Disclosure, 14 La.L.Rev. 361 (1954); Barnhart, Theory of Testimonial Competency and Privilege, 4 Ark.L. Rev. 377 (1950); Falknor, Extrinsic Policies Affecting Admissibility, 10 Rutgers L.Rev. 574 (1956). See also Quick, Privileges under the Uniform Rules, 26 U.Cin.L.Rev. 537 (1958); Louisell and Crippin, Evidentiary Privileges [under the Uniform Rules], 40 Minn.L.Rev. 413 (1956); Note, Privileged Communications—Some Recent Developments, 5 Vand. L.Rev. 590 (1952).

For particular aspects, see Weinstein, Recognition in the United States of the Privileges of Another Jurisdiction, 56 Colum.L.Rev. 535 (1956), The Uniformity—Conformity Dilemma Facing Draftsmen of Federal Rules of Evidence, 69 Colum.L.Rev. 353 (1969); Advisory Committee's Note, F.R.Ev. (R.D.) 501, 437 F.2d No. 3, p. 42; Note, Congressional Investigations and the Privileges of Confidential Communications, 45 Calif.L.Rev. 347 (1957).

As to availability of the common law privileges in administrative hearings, see Ch. 37, infra.

2. Diaz v. United States, 223 U.S. 442 (1911) (hearsay); Hill v. Baylor, 23 Tex. 261 (1859) (objections to evidence not taken at trial cannot be urged on appeal); 1 Wigmore, Evidence, § 18, n. 1, and see §§ 52, 55, supra.

fidential communications between husband and wife, attorney and client, and in many jurisdictions to those between priest and penitent, and physician and patient.

Manifestly the first group have as their common purpose to facilitate the ascertainment of the facts by guarding against evidence which is unreliable or is calculated to prejudice or mislead. Equally obviously, the second group of rules is devised for no such end. They do not in any wise aid the ascertainment of truth, but rather they shut out the light. Their sole warrant is the protection of interests and relationships which, rightly or wrongly, are regarded as of sufficient social importance to justify some incidental sacrifice of sources of facts needed in the administration of justice.[3]

We may doubt today whether these aims and interests, the encouragement of full and free disclosure between the husband and the wife, and by the client to the attorney, by the penitent to the confessor, and by the patient to the doctor, and the liberty of silence about one's misdeeds, really need this sort of protection bought at such a price. There can be little doubt, however, that the rules extending such protection stand apart from the rules which segregate and exclude classes of evidence as unreliable or prejudicial.

73. Distinction between Rules of Privilege and Rules of Incompetency—(b) Who May Assert?[4]

This difference in foundation between the two groups of rules manifests itself in an-

other line of cleavage. The rule of exclusion or preference, being designed to make the trial more efficient as a vehicle of fact disclosure, may be invoked, as of right, only by the person whose interest in having the verdict follow the facts is at stake in the trial. Thus, when evidence condemned by one of these rules is offered, only the adverse party may object, unless the judge elects to interpose. But by contrast, if the evidence is privileged, the right to object does not attach to the opposing party as such, but to the person vested with the outside interest or relationship fostered by the particular privilege.[5] True, other persons present at the trial, including the adverse party,[6] may call to the court's attention the existence of the privilege, or the judge may choose to intervene of his own accord to protect it, but this is regarded as having been done on behalf of the owner of the privilege.[7]

The right to complain on appeal is a more crucial test. If the court erroneously recognizes an asserted privilege and excludes proffered testimony on this ground, of course the adverse party has been injured in his capacity as litigant and may complain on appeal. But if a claim of privilege is wrongly denied, and the privileged testimony erroneously let in, the distinction which we have suggested between privilege and a rule of exclusion

---

3. The same discrimination may be made between privileges of witnesses not to testify, such as the privilege of the wife not to testify against the husband, or the privilege of the accused not to be called as a witness, and the rules declaring witnesses incompetent, as for mental incapacity, or as being an interested survivor in litigation with an estate of a decedent. The present discussion, however, is chiefly confined to privileges attaching to evidence by reason of its subject matter.

4. See Notes, 34 Ky.L.J. 213 (1946), 20 U.Cin.L.Rev. 76 (1951); Annot., 2 A.L.R.2d 645; 58 Am.Jur. Witnesses § 368; Dec.Dig. Witnesses ☞217.

5. State v. Knight, 204 Iowa 819, 216 N.W. 104 (1927) (self-disgracing testimony); Ingersoll v. McWillie, 87 Tex. 647, 30 S.W. 869 (1895) (self-crimination); 8 Wigmore, Evidence (McNaughton rev.) § 2196. See also San Francisco v. Superior Court, 37 Cal.2d 227, 231 P.2d 26, 25 A.L.R.2d 1418 (1951) (only patient, not physician, may claim).

6. Dalton v. People, 68 Colo. 44, 189 Pac. 37 (1920) (wife's privilege asserted by prosecution); O'Brien v. New England Mutual Life Ins. Co., 109 Kan. 138, 197 Pac. 1100 (1921) (absent client's privilege asserted, apparently by lawyer-witness or by adverse party); Comment, 30 Colum.L.Rev. 686, 690 (1930).

7. Ex parte Lipscomb, 111 Tex. 409, 415, 239 S.W. 1101 (1922) (attorney-client privilege).

Compare the provisions under recently adopted statutes and rules cited in the sections dealing with particular privileges.

would seem to be material. If the adverse party to the suit is likewise the owner of the privilege, then, while it may be argued that the party's interest *as a litigant* has not been infringed,[8] most courts decline to draw so sharp a line, and permit him to complain of the error.[9]

Where, however, the owner of the privilege is not a party to the suit, it is somewhat difficult to see why this invasion of a third person's interest should be ground of complaint for the objecting party, whose only grievance can be that the overriding of the outsider's rights has resulted in a fuller fact-disclosure than the party desires. It has not been thought necessary to afford this extreme sanction in order to prevent a breakdown in their protection.[10] In at least two classes of privileges, the privileges against self-incrimination[11] and against the use of evidence secured by unlawful search or seizure,[12] this distinction has been clearly perceived and the party is quite consistently denied any ground for reversal, despite the constitutional bases of the two privileges. The results in cases of erroneous denials of other privileges are more checkered; a considerable number of the older cases seem to allow the party to take advantage of the

error on appeal.[13] Uniform Rule 43 is clear-cut: "A party may predicate error on a ruling disallowing a claim of privilege only if he is the holder of the privilege."

74.   Privilege or Rule of Exclusion?

The great constitutional protections which have evolved around self-incrimination, confessions, and unlawfully obtained evidence are considered elsewhere.[14] They are generally classified as privileges.

Another group of situations, exemplified by the rules excluding offers of compromise[15] and remedial measures following an injury,[16] has something of a dual aspect. In one aspect, they involve problems of relevancy and thus share the character of exclusionary rules, generally assertable only by a party to the litigation. In another aspect, they serve to encourage or discourage certain

---

8.   8 Wigmore, Evidence (McNaughton rev.) § 2196.

9.   People v. Werner, 225 Mich. 18, 195 N.W. 697 (1923) (privilege not to have husband testify); Garrett v. State, 118 Neb. 373, 224 N.W. 860 (1929) (same); People v. Brown, 72 N.Y. 571, 28 Am.Rep. 183 (1878) (self-disgracing testimony); Ex parte Lipscomb, 111 Tex. 409, 239 S.W. 1101 (1922) (where attorney refuses to testify as to communications with client, in a suit to which the client is a party, the attorney when committed for contempt cannot test by habeas corpus the propriety of the denial of the privilege; appeal by the client is the proper remedy); Comment, 30 Colum.L.Rev. 686, 693, n. 41 (1930).

10.   But see the vigorous expression of an opposing view by the dissenting judges in State v. Snook, 94 N.J.Law 271, 109 Atl. 289, 290 (1920).

11.   See § 120, infra.

12.   See § 179, infra.

13.   Many of the cases are explainable by the fact that the question of the party's standing to raise the point was not noticed, e. g., Bell v. State, 88 Tex.Crim.Rep. 64, 224 S.W. 1108 (1920) (marital communications; witness' privilege denied; defendant allowed to assign as ground of error on appeal). In other cases the court assumes that the evidence usually classified as privileged is "unlawful" or incompetent, e. g., State v. Jolly, 20 N.C. 108, 32 Am.Dec. 656 (1838) (privilege against disclosure of facts learned by spouse confidentially). A few opinions in cases permitting the party to complain place it expressly on ground of public policy. State v. Barrows, 52 Conn. 323 (1884) (client's privilege); Bacon v. Frisbie, 80 N.Y. 394, 36 Am.Rep. 627 (1880) (client's privilege). The more recent cases where the point is considered seem to be coming around, under the influence of the Wigmore treatise (§ 2196) to the contrary holding. Martin v. State, 203 Miss. 187, 33 So.2d 825, 2 A.L.R.2d 640 (1948) (marital communications); Luick v. Arends, 21 N.D. 614, 132 N.W. 353, 362 (1911) (marital communications); Coles v. Harsch, 129 Ore. 11, 276 Pac. 248, 255 (1929) (marital communications); State v. Snook, 93 N.J. Law 29, 107 Atl. 62 (Sup.Ct.1919), aff'd by equally divided court, 94 N.J.Law 271, 109 Atl. 289 (1920) (client's privilege). See Comment, 30 Colum.L.Rev. 686, 694, n. 44 (1930); Annot., 2 A.L.R.2d 645.

14.   Ch. 13, infra (self-incrimination), Ch. 14, infra (confessions), Ch. 15, infra (unlawfully obtained evidence).

15.   See § 274, infra.

16.   See § 275, infra.

kinds of conduct and thus show a functional relationship to privilege. The fact is, however, that this encouragement or discouragement comes into operation only by virtue of admitting or excluding the evidence in litigation to which the affected person is a party. For example, the rule excluding evidence of offers of compromise is designed to encourage compromise; admitting the evidence in a case where the offeror is not a party will in no wise serve to discourage compromises. Thus the "privilege," if one chooses to call it such, is assertable only by a party, and whether it is classed as privilege or rule of exclusion is attended by no practical consequences.

75. Limitations on the Effectiveness of Privileges— (a) Risk of Eavesdropping and of Interception of Letters.

On some points, the older decisions reveal a surprising unwillingness to extend to a privilege the full measure of protection which one would expect. This distortion probably results from straining toward conflicting ends, the end of truth and the end of furthering the outside interest. The reluctance is manifested in the cases holding that an eavesdropper might testify to privileged confidential communications,[17] and that a letter, confidential and privileged, was not protected if it was purloined or intercepted before reaching the addressee, or otherwise secured without the addressee's connivance.[18] Perhaps

these incidental hazards may have been thought so remote as not to be likely to discourage disclosure; simple eavesdropping could be guarded against by taking simple precautions.

With the advent of more sophisticated techniques for invading privacy in general and intercepting confidential communications in particular, the picture changed and a very different concept of the eavesdropper emerged.[19] As a consequence statutes began to appear prohibiting wiretapping and electronic surveillance, and denying admissibility

---

17. This seems to have been the holding even when the overhearing was not due to carelessness on the part of the confidants. Commonwealth v. Griffin, 110 Mass. 181 (1872) (conversation in jail of husband and wife, overheard by officers in concealment); Commonwealth v. Wakelin, 230 Mass. 567, 120 N.E. 209 (1918) (dictograph hidden in cell of husband and wife); Clark v. State, 159 Tex.Cr.R. 187, 261 S.W.2d 339 (1953) (conversation of accused with attorney over long distance telephone reported by operator who eavesdropped in violation of company rule); Annot., 33 L.R.A.,N.S., 477, 485, 63 A.L.R. 107; 58 Am.Jur. 216; Dec.Dig. Witnesses ⬅206.

18. Intercepted letters, admitted: Hammons v. State, 73 Ark. 495, 84 S.W. 718, 68 L.R.A. 234 (1905);

People v. Dunnigan, 163 Mich. 349, 128 N.W. 180, 31 L.R.A.,N.S., 940 (1910); Commonwealth v. Smith, 270 Pa. 583, 113 Atl. 844 (1921). Testimony of person who saw letters without recipient's connivance, admitted: Harris v. State, 72 Tex.Cr.R. 117, 161 S.W. 125 (1913). But a conflicting view excludes the letters, whether secured with or without the addressee's consent. McKie v. State, 165 Ga. 210, 140 S.E. 625 (1927) (letters of wife to husband, produced at trial of wife for husband's murder, by temporary administrator appointed during trial to secure the letter from husband's deposit box offered by state, held inadmissible. "If the privilege cannot be destroyed by collusion between a spouse and a third party, it should not be permitted to be destroyed by some one surreptitiously and wrongfully obtaining letters from the possession of the spouse to whom they were written. The purpose of the law in excluding communications between husband and wife is to produce perfect trust and confidence between them, which cannot be secured if the communications can be disclosed either by the party to whom they were made or by third parties who surreptitiously or otherwise obtain the letters containing them from the spouse to whom they were addressed." Id. at 218, 140 S.E. at 629. In the opinion in the last-named case the authorities are collected and discussed. See also 8 Wigmore, Evidence (McNaughton rev.) §§ 2325, 2326, 2329; 58 Am.Jur., Witnesses § 366.

19. See, e. g., Lanza v. New York State Legislative Committee, 3 N.Y.2d 92, 143 N.E.2d 772, 164 N.Y.S. 2d 9; 3 N.Y.2d 877, 145 N.E.2d 178, 166 N.Y.S.2d 500 (1957) (client consults attorney confidentially in "counsel room" of jail; conversation was recorded by secret concealed electronic device; client seeks injunction against use of this recording by Committee; held, the statute codifying attorney-client privilege when neither the attorney or client is sought to be examined, does not give right to prevent disclosure by another person of the privileged communication; injunction denied); noted, 42 Minn.L.Rev. 664, 37 Neb.L.Rev. 472, 106 U.Pa.L. Rev. 307, 36 Texas L.Rev. 505, 32 N.Y.U.L.Rev. 1309.

to evidence obtained in violation.[20] These provisions are, of course, in addition to such protection as may rest on constitutional grounds. Moreover, statutes and rules defining privileges began to include provisions entitling the holder to prevent anyone from disclosing a privileged confidential communication.[21]

76. Limitations on the Effectiveness of Privileges—(b) Adverse Arguments and Inferences from Claiming the Privileges.

The underlying conflict comes most clearly in view in the decisions relating to the allowability of an adverse inference from the assertion of privilege. Plainly, the inference may not ordinarily be made against a party when a witness for that party claims a privilege personal to the witness, for this is not a matter under the party's control.[22] But where the party himself suppresses evidence by invoking a privilege given to him by the law, should an adverse inference be sanctioned? The question may arise in various forms, for example, whether an inquiry of the witness, or of the party, calling for information obviously privileged, may be pressed for the pointed purpose of forcing the party to make an explicit claim of the privilege in the jury's hearing, or again, whether the inference may be drawn in argument, and finally, whether the judge in the instructions may mention the inference as a permissible one.

Under familiar principles an unfavorable inference may be drawn against a party not only for destroying evidence, but for the mere failure to produce witnesses or documents within his control.[23] No showing of wrong or fraud seems to be required as a foundation for the inference that the evidence if produced would have been unfavorable. Why should not this same conclusion be drawn from the party's active interposing of a privilege to keep out the evidence? A leading case for the affirmative is Phillips v. Chase,[24] where the court said:

"It is a rule of law that the objection of a party to evidence as incompetent and immaterial, and insistence upon his right to have his case tried according to the rules of law, cannot be made a subject of comment in argument.[25] . . . On the other hand, if evidence is material and competent except for a personal privilege of one of the parties to have it excluded under the law, his claim of the privilege may be referred to in argument and considered by the jury, as indicating his opinion that the evidence, if received, would be prejudicial to him."

An oft-quoted statement by Lord Chelmsford gives the contrary view:

"The exclusion of such evidence is for the general interest of the community, and therefore to say that when a party refuses to permit professional confidence to be broken, everything must be taken most strongly against him, what is it but to deny him the protection which, for public purposes, the law affords him, and utterly to take away a privilege which

---

20. See, e. g., West's Ann.Cal.Penal Code, §§ 631(c), 632(d); Ill.Rev.Stat. c. 38, § 14–5 (1971 supp.) So strictly drawn is the Illinois statute that a specific exemption was included in order to allow the hard-of-hearing to wear hearing aids.

See the discussion of proceedings to which the Fourth Amendment applies in § 167, infra, and of eavesdropping in § 174, infra.

21. E. g., with respect to the attorney-client privilege, West's Ann.Cal.Evid.Code, § 954; F.R.Ev. (R.D.1971) 503(b).

22. See § 73, supra, and more particularly as to self-incrimination § 120, infra.

23. See § 272, infra.

24. 201 Mass. 444, 480, 87 N.E. 755, 758 (1909), writ of error dism'd 216 U.S. 616 (1910).

25. See also 5 Busch, Law and Tactics in Jury Trials § 658 (1963).

can thus only be asserted to his prejudice?" [25.5]

The first of these arguments is based upon an unfounded distinction between incompetent and privileged evidence, namely, a supposition that the privilege can be waived and the incompetency cannot.[26] As we have seen, both may be waived with equal facility. As to the second, it may be an overstatement to say that permitting the inference "utterly takes away" the privilege. A privilege has its most substantial practical benefit when it enables a party to exclude from the record a witness, document, or line of proof which is essential to the adversary's case, lacking which he cannot get to the jury at all on a vital issue. The inference does not supply the lack of proof.[27] In other situations, the benefit accruing from a successful claim of privilege will depend upon circumstances. It is evident, however, that in a case which does survive a motion for a directed verdict or its equivalent, allowing comment upon the exercise of a privilege or requiring it to be claimed in the presence of the jury tends greatly to diminish its value. In Griffin v. California [28] the Supreme Court held that allowing comment [29] upon the failure of an accused to take the stand violated his privilege against self-incrimination "by making its assertion costly." Whether one is prepared to extend this protection to all privileges probably depends upon his attitude towards privileges in general and towards the

particular privilege involved. The cases, rather naturally, are in dispute.[30] It is submitted that the best solution is to recognize only privileges which are soundly based in policy and to accord those privileges the fullest protection. Thus comment, whether by judge or by counsel, or its equivalent of requiring the claim to be made in the presence of the jury, and the drawing of inferences from the claim, all would be foreclosed.[31]

77. New Statutory Privileges: The Future of Privilege.

The development of judge-made privileges virtually halted a century ago.[32] In more recent times the attitude of commentators, whether from the bench, the bar, or the schools, has tended to view privileges from the standpoint of the hindrance to litigation resulting from their recognition. In this regard, the granting of a claim of privilege can serve only to "shut out the light" so far as the party seeking to bring the privileged matter into the lawsuit is concerned.[33] The commentators generally advocated a narrowing of the field of privilege. Beginning in 1939 a group of distinguished scholars and judges undertook preparation of a Model Code of Evidence under the auspices of the American Law Institute with a view "not to its Restate-

---

30. For cases see Annots., 144 A.L.R. 1007 (requiring claim to be made or asking party if he will waive, in presence of jury), 76 A.L.R.2d 920 (calling of spouse of accused by prosecution), 32 A.L.R. 3d 906 (comment in argument on exercise of privilege), 34 A.L.R.3d 775 (comment by judge in summing up or instructing).

31. See Uniform Rule 39; West's Ann.Cal.Evid. Code, § 913; N.J.Ev.Rule 39; F.R.Ev. (R.D.1971) 513.

32. Exceptions are noteworthy. See, e. g., Mullen v. United States, 105 U.S.App.D.C. 25, 263 F.2d 275 (1958) (privilege recognized for confessional-type statement to clergyman without assistance of any statute). A carefully worked out proposal for a parent-child privilege, Coburn, Child-Parent Communications: Spare the Privilege and Spoil the Child, 74 Dick.L.Rev. 599 (1970), suggests only enactment of a statute as the means of effecting the privilege.

33. See § 72, supra.

25.5 Wentworth v. Lloyd, 10 H.L.Cas. 589, 591 (1864).

26. See § 72, supra. In fact both can be waived, and if the ability of the opponent to waive is the basis for allowing the argument, then the statement at note 25 would be incorrect (which it is not).

27. See § 272, infra.

28. 380 U.S. 609 (1965).

29. The comment assumed the form both of a jury instruction and argument by the prosecutor, but the Court indicated that either alone would be a violation.

ment but to its revision." [34] The draftsmen of the Model Code clearly favored limiting the scope of some, if not all, of the privileges,[35] but when the proposed draft was submitted to the American Law Institute for final approval concessions had to be made and in the form approved the generally recognized common law and statutory privileges had been largely retained though "with important modifications." [36] The Model Code did not gain acceptance as a statement of the law by legislatures or courts and the National Conference of Commissioners on Uniform State Laws undertook a statement that it was hoped would be more acceptable. This work resulted in the Uniform Rules of Evidence, approved by the American Bar Association in its meeting in August, 1953.[37] While the approach of the draftsmen of the Uniform Rules was also generally unsympathetic to the recognized privileges and favored limiting their operation in litigation, the Rules as finally adopted continued the privileges in large measure as they had been enforced by the courts.[38] The Uniform Rules of Evidence have therefore had little effect upon the law of privilege.

The privileges have survived largely unaffected by these winnowings of the law by eminent scholars and jurists who saw them as suppressing the truth, for it is evident that for many people, judges, lawyers and laymen, the protection of confidential communications from enforced disclosure has been thought to represent rights of privacy and security too important to relinquish to the convenience of litigants.[39] Growing concern in recent times with the increase in official prying and snooping into the lives of private individuals has reinforced support for the traditional privileges and no doubt aided in the creation of new ones.[40]

---

34. See Introduction, Model Code of Evidence, American Law Institute (1942), p. ix.

35. American Law Institute Proceedings 187 (1941–1942).

36. Model Code of Evidence, Foreword, 17 (1942).

37. See Uniform Rules of Evidence, Prefatory Note.

38. Uniform Rules of Evidence, Rules 23 to 39 and Comments.

39. "It has always been recognized in this country, and it is well to remember, that few if any of the rights of the people guarded by fundamental law are of greater importance to their happiness and safety than the right to be exempt from all unauthorized, arbitrary or unreasonable inquiries and disclosures in respect of their personal and private affairs." Butler, J. in Sinclair v. United States, 279 U.S. 263, 292 (1929).

See also the additional statement of Edgerton, J. in Mullen v. United States, 105 U.S.App.D.C. 25, 263 F.2d 275, 281 (1958); "I think a communication made in reasonable confidence that it will not be disclosed, and in such circumstances that disclosure is shocking to the moral sense of the community, should not be disclosed in judicial proceeding, whether the trusted person is or is not a wife, husband, doctor, lawyer, or minister. As Mr. Justice Holmes said of wire-tapping, 'We have to choose, and for my part I think it a less evil that some criminals should escape than that the Government should play an ignoble part.' Olmstead v. United States, 277 U.S. 438, 470, 48 S.Ct. 564, 72 L.Ed. 944 (dissenting opinion)."

See Barnhart, Privilege in the Uniform Rules of Evidence, 24 Ohio St.L.J. 131 (1963); Louisell, Confidentiality, Conformity and Confusion: Privileges in Federal Court Today, 31 Tulane L.R. 101 (1956).

40. "We are rapidly entering the age of no privacy, where everyone is open to surveillance at all times; where there are no secrets from government. The aggressive breaches of privacy by the Government increase by geometric proportions. Wiretapping and 'bugging' run rampant, without effective judicial or legislative control.

"Secret observation booths in government offices and closed television circuits in industry, extending even to rest rooms, are common. Offices, conference rooms, hotel rooms, and even bedrooms (see Irvine v. California, 347 U.S. 128) are 'bugged' for the convenience of government. Peepholes in men's rooms are there to catch homosexuals. See Smayda v. United States, 352 F.2d 251. Personality tests seek to ferret out a man's innermost thoughts on family life, religion, racial attitudes, national origin, politics, atheism, ideology, sex, and the like. Federal agents are often 'wired' so that their conversations are either recorded on their persons (Lopez v. United States, 373 U.S. 427) or transmitted to tape recorders some blocks away. The Food and Drug Administration recently put a spy in a church organization. Revenue agents have gone in the disguise of Coast Guard officers. They have broken and entered homes to obtain evidence.

This desire for reinforcement of traditional privileges is illustrated by the privilege for communications between penitent and priest. All but four of the fifty states now have the privilege by statute, over twenty of them having enacted statutes within the past fifteen years.[41] A number of statutes, particularly those more recently enacted, do not confine the privilege to communications made as a matter of "enjoined religious discipline" as do statutes of some states and as does Rule 29 of the Uniform Rules, but extend the privilege to information confidentially communicated to a clergyman in circumstances that disclosure would violate a sacred or moral trust.[42]

The same rationale which supports the right of privacy for communications to a priest or clergyman by persons deeply troubled, likewise supports recent statutory privileges for communications to psychotherapists.[43]

"Polygraph tests of government employees and of employees in industry are rampart. The dossiers on all citizens mount in number and increase in size. Now they are being put on computers so that by pressing one button all the miserable, the sick, the suspect, the unpopular, the offbeat people of the Nation can be identified.

"These examples and many others demonstrate an alarming trend whereby the privacy and dignity of our citizens is being whittled away by sometimes imperceptible steps. Taken individually, each step may be of little consequence. But when viewed as a whole, there begins to emerge a society quite unlike any we have seen—a society in which government may intrude into the secret regions of man's life at will." Justice Douglas, dissenting in Osborn v. United States, 385 U.S. 323, 341 (1966) (footnotes omitted).

The newer statutory privileges are discussed in 8 Wigmore, Evidence (McNaughton rev.) § 2286; Vanderbilt, Minimum Standards of Judicial Administration 344–348 (1949); Note, 5 Vand.L.Rev. 590, 601 (1952). See the discussions of eavesdropping and related techniques in § 75 supra and §§ 167, 174, infra.

41. Wigmore considered that the privilege never became established as part of the common law, but that there were adequate reasons of policy for its recognition. 8 Wigmore, Evidence (McNaughton rev.) §§ 2394–2396. But see Mullen v. United States, 105 U.S.App.D.C. 25, 263 F.2d 275 (1958). The statutes are listed in Wigmore, § 2395. All the states except Alabama, Connecticut, Mississippi and New Hampshire have enacted statutes recognizing the privilege. C.J.S. Witnesses § 263. The privilege is codified in Uniform Rule 29, as follows: "(1) As used in this rule, (a) 'priest' means a priest, clergyman, minister of the gospel or other officer of a church or of a religious denomination or organization, who in the course of its discipline or practice is authorized or accustomed to hear, and has a duty to keep secret, penitential communications made by members of his church, denomination or organization; (b) 'penitent' means a member of a church or religious denomination or organization who has made a penitential communication to a priest thereof; (c) 'penitential communication' means a confession of culpable conduct made secretly and in confidence by a penitent to a priest in the course of discipline or practice of the church or religious denomination or organization of which the penitent is a member.

"(2) A person, whether or not a party, has a privilege to refuse to disclose, and to prevent a witness from disclosing a communication if he claims the privilege and the judge finds that (a) the communication was a penitential communication and (b) the witness is the penitent or the priest, and (c) the claimant is the penitent, or the priest making the claim on behalf of an absent penitent."

The comment to Rule 29 states "The privilege is intentionally limited to communications by communicants within the sanctity and under the necessity of their own disciplinary requirements. Any broader treatment would open the door to abuse and would clearly not be in the public interest."

42. For example the Texas statute provides:

"Art. 3715a. Clergyman-penitent privilege

No ordained minister, priest, rabbi or duly accredited Christian Science practitioner of an established church or religious organization shall be required to testify in any action, suit, or proceeding, concerning any information which may have been confidentially communicated to him in his professional capacity under such circumstances that to disclose the information would violate a sacred or moral trust, when the giving of such testimony is objected to by the communicant; provided, however, that the presiding judge in any trial may compel such disclosure if in his opinion the same is necessary to a proper administration of justice."

As to the penitent-priest privilege generally, see the excellent discussion with a listing of state statutes in Reese, Confidential Communications to the Clergy, 24 Ohio St.L.J. 55 (1963); see also Stoyles, The Dilemma of the Constitutionality of the Priest-Penitent Privilege, 29 U.Pitt.L.Rev. 27 (1967); Note, 46 N.C.L.Rev. 427 (1968).

43. See Slovenko, Psychiatry and a Second Look at the Medical Privilege, 6 Wayne L.Rev. 175 (1960); Note, Confidential Communications to a Psychotherapist: A New Testimonial Privilege, 47 Nw.U.L.Rev. 384 (1952); Report No. 45. Group for the Advancement of Psychiatry 92 (1960). See also F.R.Ev. (R.D.1971) 504. See infra, § 102, n. 41.

A fairly widespread privilege is given by statute to journalists to withhold sources of information.[44] Communications to accountants are made privileged in about an equal number of states.[45] Their underpinnings may be less substantial.

Unfortunately the justifiable demands of privacy and confidence have on more than one occasion been diverted to serve the purposes of politically powerful groups seeking the convenience and prestige of a professionally-based privilege.[46] Whether in a given situation a privilege is justified calls for a balancing of values not likely to be achieved by those interested in the result.

Whether a proliferation of privileges is an appropriate method of securing the legitimate interests of privacy and confidentiality may be questioned. Privilege paints with a broad brush. Reconciling interests in privacy and confidentiality with the needs of litigants is not readily achieved in terms of broad categories; it calls for the finer touch of the specific solution. A tool already at hand, though perhaps largely unrecognized, consists of recognizing standing on the part of the possessor of information to question the legitimacy of need for it in litigation, i. e., to raise issues of relevancy in the broad sense.[47] The suggested approach is essentially that taken by the Ninth Circuit Court of Appeals in balancing governmental need against considerations of freedom of the press under the particular facts in determining whether a journalist need appear and disclose his sources of information before a grand jury.[48] A similar thread runs through the Federal Rules of Civil Procedure limitation of discovery to matter "relevant to the subject matter involved in the pending action." [49] Relevancy itself, of course, contemplates a

44. The statutes are cited and analyzed in 8 Wigmore, Evidence (McNaughton rev.) § 2286, note 21, and in Notes 36 Va.L.Rev. 61 (1950) (excellent study of the history of the privilege, with conclusion adverse to the policy of the statutes); Beaver, The Newsman's Code, the Claim of Privilege and Everyman's Right to Evidence, 47 Ore.L.Rev. 243 (1968); 35 Neb.L.Rev. 562 (1956); 54 Nw.U.L.Rev. 243 (1959) (proposes statute conferring the privilege, "unless disclosure be essential to prevent injustice or to protect the public interest"); 32 Temp. L.Q. 432 (1959) (proposes a qualified, discretionary privilege).

Efforts to construct a journalist privilege under the aegis of the First Amendment have generally failed. Garland v. Torre, 259 F.2d 545 (2d Cir. 1958) cert. denied 358 U.S. 910; In re Goodfader's Appeal, 45 Haw. 317, 367 P.2d 472 (1961); In re Pappas, 266 N.E.2d 297 (Mass.1971); State v. Buchanan, 250 Ore. 244, 436 P.2d 729 (1968) cert. denied 392 U.S. 905; State v. Knops, 49 Wis.2d 647, 183 N.W.2d 93 (1971). But see Caldwell v. United States, 434 F.2d 1081 (9th Cir. 1970); Note, Reporters and Their Sources: The Constitutional Right to a Confidential Relationship, 80 Yale L.J. 317 (1970).

45. To date fifteen states and Puerto Rico have conferred this privilege by statute. Statutes are cited and summarized in 8 Wigmore, Evidence (McNaughton rev.) § 2286, note 22. See Notes 46 N.C. L.Rev. 419 (1968); 5 Vand.L.Rev. 590, 603 (1952), 32 Tex.L.Rev. 453 (1954), 6 Drake L.Rev. 92 (1957).

Statutes creating a privilege for confidential communications to confidential stenographers and clerks are collected in Wigmore, Evidence (McNaughton rev.) § 2286. See also note, 96 A.L.R. 2d 159 (1964).

46. See, e. g., § 105, infra.

47. See, e. g., Herron v. Blackford, 264 F.2d 723, 725 (5th Cir. 1959) ("the right of the citizen to be let alone, and to hold his writings inviolate from alien eyes in the absence of evidence that the material sought is relevant;" attempt to subpoena records of nonparty corporation). See also In re Lifschutz, 2 Cal.3d 415, 425, 85 Cal.Rptr. 829, 835, 467 P.2d 557 (1970) (psychiatrist claiming privilege in own right; state may require businessman "to disclose communications, confidential or otherwise relevant to pending litigation"; "the incidental infringement of the psychotherapist's economic interest in such practice [confidentiality] does not succumb to constitutional challenge so long as the circumstances of disclosure are properly confined to serve a legitimate governmental interest.")

The standing of governmental agencies to raise relevancy questions respecting data sought from their files is treated in § 107, n. 12, infra.

48. Caldwell v. United States, 434 F.2d 1081 (9th Cir. 1970).

49. F.R.Civ.P. 26(b) (1). The subsequent reference to "admissible evidence" at the end of the paragraph in the rule should be read subject to this limitation.

process of weighing,[50] and inevitably the judge must be accorded a substantial measure of discretion.

50.   See § 185, infra.

In this manner, perhaps an increased involvement of judges in the general area of privacy and confidentiality may be in the making.

CHAPTER 9

THE PRIVILEGE FOR MARITAL COMMUNICATIONS [1]

78. History and Background and Kindred Rules.[2]

We are dealing here with a late offshoot of an ancient tree. The older branches are discussed in another chapter.[3] Those earlier rules, to be sharply distinguished from the present doctrine, are first, the rule that the spouse of a party or person interested is disqualified from testifying for the other spouse, and second, the privilege of a party against having the party's husband or wife called as an adverse witness. These two former rules forbid the calling of the spouse as a witness at all, for or against the party, regardless of the actual testimony to be elicited, whereas the privilege presently discussed is limited to a certain class of testimony, namely communications between the spouses or more broadly in some states, information gained on account of the marital relation.

The movement for procedural reform in England in the first half of the 1800s found expression in the evidence field in the agitation for the break up of the system of disqualification of parties and spouses. One of the auxiliary reasons which had been given to justify the disqualification of spouses was that of preserving marital confidences.[4] As to the disqualification of spouses the reform was largely accomplished by the Evidence Amendment Act, 1853. On the eve of this legislation, Greenleaf writing in this country in 1842, clearly announced the existence of a distinct privilege for marital communications, and this pronouncement was echoed in England by Best in 1849,[5] though seemingly there was little or no support for such a view in the English decisions.[6] Moreover, the Second Report of 1853 of the Commissioners on Common Law Procedure, after rejecting the arguments for the outmoded rules of disqualification, calls attention to the

---

1. 8 Wigmore, Evidence (McNaughton rev.) §§ 2332–2341; Dec.Dig. Witnesses ☞187–195; C.J.S. Witnesses §§ 266–275; 58 Am.Jur. Witnesses §§ 375–400.

2. 8 Wigmore, Evidence (McNaughton rev.) § 2332–2334.

3. See § 66, supra.

4. See 8 Wigmore, Evidence (McNaughton rev.) § 2333; Taylor, Evidence, 899 (1848) (recounting this as a reason given but rejecting it as "too large"), quoted Shenton v. Tyler, L.R.1939 Ch.D. 620, 634.

5. See the citations to these early editions of Greenleaf and Best in Shenton v. Tyler, L.R. 1939 Ch. D. 620, 633, 634.

6. The English decisions before 1853 are carefully dissected in the opinion of Greene, M.R. in Shenton v. Tyler, supra, n. 5.

special danger of "alarm and unhappiness occasioned to society by . . . compelling the public disclosure of confidential communications between husband and wife . . . ." and declares that "[a]ll communications between them should be held to be privileged." [7]

However, though the policy supporting a privilege for marital communications had thus been distinctly pointed out, there had been little occasion for its judicial recognition, since the wider disqualifications of the spouses of parties left small possibility for the question of the existence of such a privilege to arise.[8]

Nevertheless, the English Act of 1853, mentioned above, after it abolished the disqualification of husbands and wives of the parties, enacted that "no husband shall be compellable to disclose any communication made to him by his wife during the marriage, and no wife shall be compellable to disclose any communication made to her by her husband during the marriage." [9] Moreover, nearly all of the states in this country, while making spouses competent to testify have included provisions disabling them from testifying to communications between them.[10]

7. See quotation from this report, 8 Wigmore, Evidence (McNaughton rev.) § 2332.

8. See 8 Wigmore, Evidence (McNaughton rev.) § 2333.

9. St. 16 & 17 Vict. c. 83, § 3.

10. See, for example:
West's Ann.Cal.Evid.Code, Art. 5.
"§ 980. **Privilege for confidential marital communications.** Subject to Section 912 [waiver] and except as otherwise provided in this article, a spouse (or his guardian or conservator when he has a guardian or conservator), whether or not a party, has a privilege during the marital relationship and afterwards to refuse to disclose, and to prevent another from disclosing, a communication if he claims the privilege and the communication was made in confidence between him and the other spouse while they were husband and wife.
"§ 981. **Exception: Crime or fraud.** There is no privilege under this article if the communication was made, in whole or in part, to enable or aid

In the light of this history the Court of Appeal in England has denied that there was

anyone to commit or plan to commit a crime or a fraud.
"§ 982. **Exception: Commitment or similar proceeding.** There is no privilege under this article in a proceeding to commit either spouse or otherwise place him or his property, or both, under the control of another because of his alleged mental or physical condition.
"§ 983. **Exception: Proceeding to establish competence.** There is no privilege under this article in a proceeding brought by or on behalf of either spouse to establish his competence.
"§ 984. **Exception: Proceeding between spouses.** There is no privilege under this article in:
    (a) A proceeding brought by or on behalf of one spouse against the other spouse.
    (b) A proceeding between a surviving spouse and a person who claims through the deceased spouse, regardless of whether such claim is by testate or intestate succession or by inter vivos transaction.
"§ 985. **Exception: Certain criminal proceedings.** There is no privilege under this article in a criminal proceeding in which one spouse is charged with:
    (a) A crime committed at any time against the person or property of the other spouse or of a child of either.
    (b) A crime committed at any time against the person or property of a third person committed in the course of committing a crime against the person or property of the other spouse.
    (c) Bigamy or adultery.
    (d) A crime defined by Section 270 or 270a of the Penal Code. [Nonsupport of child or wife.]
"§ 986. **Exception: Juvenile court proceeding.** There is no privilege under this article in a proceeding under the Juvenile Court Law. . . .
"§ 987. **Exception: Communication offered by spouse who is criminal defendant.** There is no privilege under this article in a criminal proceeding in which the communication is offered in evidence by a defendant who is one of the spouses between whom the communication was made."

N.Y. CPLR § 4502.
"(b) **Confidential communication privileged.** A husband or wife shall not be required, or, without consent of the other if living, allowed, to disclose a confidential communication made by one to the other during marriage."

12 Okl.St.Ann. § 385. "The following persons shall be incompetent to testify: . . .
"3. Husband or wife, for or against each other, except concerning transactions in which one acted as the agent of the other, or in an action growing out of personal injuries to either spouse, or when they are joint parties and have a joint interest in the action; but in no case shall either be permitted to testify concerning any communication made by one to the other during the marriage, whether called while that relation subsisted, or afterwards."
Statutes on this topic are compiled in 2 Wigmore, Evidence § 488. See generally, Comment, The

any common law privilege for marital communications.[11] In this country, however, the courts have frequently said that the statutes protecting marital communications from disclosure are declaratory of the common law.[12] This approach may well be justifiable even if no common law decision can be found sanctioning the privilege in advance of a statute. The principle upon which the privilege is founded was clearly recognized, as we have seen, by leading law writers before the statutes. The statutes all derive from a common source in this previously recognized principle, and in this country they have usually been treated despite minor variations in phrasing as expressions of a common policy. This attitude probably makes for a broader and juster development and application of the privilege than would an attitude of concentration on local variations of phraseology with little regard to the conclusions of other courts under cognate statutes.

79. What is Privileged? Communications Only, or Acts and Facts? [13]

Greenleaf arguing in 1842 for a privilege distinct from marital incompetency, and furnishing the inspiration for the later statutes by which the privilege was formally enacted,

Husband-Wife Privileges of Testimonial Non-Disclosure, The Privilege for Confidential Communications, 56 Nw.U.L.Rev. 208, 216 (1961).

11. Shenton v. Tyler, L.R. 1939 Ch.D. 620, and see Notes, 55 Law Q.Rev. 329, Holdsworth, 56 id. 137. In this case the court held that the English statute, cited note 9, supra, providing that "husbands" and "wives" shall not be compellable to testify to communication, did not apply to exempt a surviving widow from interrogation as to conversations with her husband claimed to have created a secret trust in favor of the plaintiff, a third person.

12. Hopkins v. Grimshaw, 165 U.S. 342 (1897); Hagerman v. Wigent, 108 Mich. 192, 194, 65 N.W. 756 (1896); Gjesdahl v. Harmon, 175 Minn. 414, 221 N.W. 639, 641 (1928); 70 C.J. 379, note 90(b); C.J.S. Witnesses § 266.

13. 8 Wigmore, Evidence (McNaughton rev.) § 2337; Annot., 10 A.L.R.2d 1389; Notes, 35 Corn.L.Q. 187 (1949), 57 J.Crim.L. & Cr. 205 (1956), 34 Minn.L. Rev. 257 (1950), 3 Vand.L.Rev. 656 (1950), 35 Va. L.Rev. 1111 (1949).

spoke only of "communications" and "conversations."[14] Those later statutes themselves (except one or two [15]) sanctioned the privilege for "communications" and for nothing beyond.[16] Accordingly it would seem that the privilege should be limited to *expressions* intended by one spouse to convey a meaning or message to the other. These expressions may be by words, oral, written or in sign-language, or by expressive acts, as where the husband opens a trunk before his wife and points out objects therein to her. Moreover, the protection of the privilege will shield against indirect disclosure of the communication,[17] as where a husband is asked for his wife's whereabouts which he learned only from her secret communication.[18] It seems,

14. See § 78, supra.

15. Ohio R.C. § 2317.02 ("communication made by one to the other, or an act done by either in the presence of the other, during coverture unless . . . in the known presence or hearing of a third person competent to be a witness"); Tenn. Code Ann. § 24–103 (". . . neither husband nor wife shall testify to any matter that occurred between them by virtue of or in consequence of the marital relation").

16. See the statutes compiled in 2 Wigmore, Evidence § 488; also those quoted in § 78, n. 10, supra.

17. See by analogy Quarfot v. Security Nat. Bank & Trust Co., 189 Minn. 451, 453, 249 N.W. 668 (1933) (in action against executor to recover note alleged to constitute gift, plaintiff's testimony stating reason why he left note in decedent's possession held inadmissible as conclusion and as concerning conversation with deceased; M.S.A. § 595.04. In Sampson v. Sampson, 223 Mass. 451, 112 N.E. 84 (1916), a proceeding to vacate a divorce for fraud of the husband, the wife testified, without objection, that as a result of a talk with the husband she did nothing about the pending divorce suit of her husband. The court held (1) that the fact of a communication is not privileged, and (2) that the trial judge could properly find from this testimony that the husband made fraudulent representations. It seems that this result can best be justified on the ground of waiver, or of absence of privilege for fraudulent statements.

18. Blau v. United States, 340 U.S. 332 (1951) (witness's wife was hiding out to avoid service of subpœna in connection with Communist investigation; held, since witness got his knowledge of his wife's whereabouts from what she "secretly told" him, he could refuse to disclose). But the mere fact that a transaction involving marital property happened

nevertheless, that logic and policy should cause the courts to halt with communications as the furthest boundary of the privilege, and a substantial number have held steadfast at this line.[19]

An equal or greater number of courts, however, have construed their statutes which say "communications" to extend the privilege to acts, facts, conditions and transactions not amounting to communications at all. One group seems to announce the principle that acts done privately in the wife's presence amount to "communications."[20] Another

would go even further and say that any information secured by the wife as a result of the marital relation and which would not have been known in the absence of such relation is protected.[21] Some at least of this latter group would hold that information secured by one spouse through observation during the marriage as to the health,[22] or intoxication, habitual or at a particular time,[23] or the mental condition[24] of the other spouse, would be protected by the privilege.

All extensions beyond communications seem unjustified. The acts thus protected are frequently acts done in furtherance of a crime or fraud,[25] and thus under the principle developed for the cognate privilege for at-

---

during the marriage is insufficient to show that the husband's knowledge was derived from communications made by his wife. Petition of Fuller, 63 Nev. 26, 159 P.2d 579 (1945).

19. Pereira v. United States, 347 U.S. 1 (1954); United States v. Mitchell, 137 F.2d 1006 (2d Cir. 1943) (prosecution for transporting wife in interstate commerce for purpose of prostitution; held, wife's testimony as to husband's act of taking money from her not privileged); Posner v. New York Life Ins. Co., 56 Ariz. 202, 106 P.2d 488 (1940) (former husband's testimony that he purchased insulin for plaintiff and saw her make tests of her urine, not privileged); Tanzola v. De Rita, 45 Cal.2d 1, 285 P.2d 897 (1955), note, 34 Tex.L.Rev. 474 (where husband placed check on desk of wife, who was his office assistant and who deposited it in his personal account, according to custom, the husband's act was not "communicative"); Shanklin v. McCracken, 140 Mo. 348, 41 S.W. 898 (1897) (widow may testify she saw deeds delivered to her husband); Note, 35 Corn.L.Q. 187, 189 n. 27 (1949).

20. People v. Daghita, 299 N.Y. 194, 86 N.E.2d 172, 10 A.L.R.2d 1385 (1949) (husband charged with theft, wife's testimony as to the husband's acts in her presence of bringing in the loot and hiding it under the bed and in the basement held violation of statutory privilege for "confidential communication"); Menefee v. Comm., 189 Va. 900, 55 S.E.2d 9 (1949) noted 34 Minn.L.Rev. 257 (wife's testimony as to husband's leaving home before robbery, as to time of returning, as to his placing pistol on mantle-piece, and as to her driving with him near where stolen safe was hid, held privileged as "communication privately made"). Perhaps the reductio ad absurdum of the "acts" cases is State v. Robbins, 35 Wash.2d 389, 213 P.2d 310 (1950). There the husband was charged with automobile theft, and evidence of his former wife that when she was presenting application for license for the stolen car at the office her husband was waiting outside in an automobile was a "communication" and privileged. The court said, "It is obvious that he would not have waited in the automobile had

he not relied on the confidence between them by reason of the marital relation."

In People v. Melski, 10 N.Y.2d 78, 217 N.Y.S.2d 65, 176 N.E.2d 81 (1961) the New York Court of Appeals held by a four to three decision that there was no privilege for the wife's observation of her husband, the defendant, and several of his friends in defendant's kitchen with stolen guns. The dissent asserted that the presence of the third persons did not destroy confidentiality but was "part of the very fact confidentially communicated."

21. Prudential Ins. Co. v. Pierce's Adm'x, 270 Ky. 216, 109 S.W.2d 616 (1917) (formula held to apply to knowledge gleaned by the wife from the entry of husband's birth in his family Bible); State v. Americk, 42 Wash.2d 504, 256 P.2d 278 (1953) (but formula held not to require exclusion of testimony of ex-wife that husband had beaten her while they were married).

22. Griffith v. Griffith, 162 Ill. 368, 44 N.E. 820 (1896) (impotence); Willey v. Howell, 168 Ky. 466, 182 S.W. 619 (1916) (venereal disease). But it has been held that testimony as to the general condition of health, accessible to other persons, would not be privileged. Supreme Lodge v. Jones, 113 Ill.App. 241 (1903), and see Annot., 10 A.L.R.2d 1397–1400.

23. Monaghan v. Green, 265 Ill. 233, 106 N.E. 792 (1914). Contra: In re Van Alstine's Estate, 26 Utah 193, 72 Pac. 942 (1903) (privilege does not cover testimony as to facts learned from observation). See Annot., 10 A.L.R.2d 1389, 1400.

24. McFadden v. Welch, 177 Miss. 451, 170 So. 903 (1936). Contra: Lanham v. Lanham, 62 Tex.Civ. App. 431, 146 S.W. 635 (1912) (husband's demeanor in wife's presence on train); Annot., 10 A.L.R.2d 1389, 1401.

25. See, e. g., the cases cited in note 20, supra.

torney-client communications,[26] should not be protected from disclosure even by direct communication. Moreover, the confidence which the court relies on in these cases is more often a general family confidence, which is concededly unprivileged, not specifically a confidence reposed in the wife alone. The attitude of the courts in these cases seems in effect a reaching back toward the old common law principle of preserving family harmony by disqualifying a spouse from testifying for or against the other. A different attitude it is believed would be wiser, namely, that of accepting the view that all privileges, in general, and this privilege for marital confidences in particular, are inept and clumsy devices to promote the policies they profess to serve, but are extremely effective as stumbling blocks to obstruct the attainment of justice. Accordingly the movement should be toward restriction, and not toward expansion, of these mechanisms for concealment of relevant facts.

80. The Communication Must Be Confidential.[27]

Most statutes expressly limit the privileges to "confidential communications."[28] However, even where the words used are "any communication" or simply "communica-

tions," the notion that the privilege is born of the "common law" and the fact that the pre-statutory descriptions of the privilege had clearly based it upon the policy of protecting confidences,[29] have actuated most courts to read into such statutes the requirement of confidentiality.[30] Communications in private between husband and wife are assumed to be confidential unless the subject of message or the circumstances show to the contrary.[31] They are confidential if expressly made so, or if the subject is such that the communicating spouse would probably desire that the matter be kept secret, either because its disclosure would be embarrassing or for some other reason.[32] If a third person (other than

26. See § 95, infra. The application of this limitation, so clearly justified in policy, is suggested in Fraser v. United States, 145 F.2d 139, 143, 144 (6th Cir. 1944) cert. denied 324 U.S. 849 (citing cases); People v. Coleman, [1945] Irish Rep. 237, 247; C.J.S. Witnesses § 269; and is embodied in Uniform Rule 28(2): "Neither spouse may claim such privilege (a) in an action by one spouse against the other spouse, or . . . (e) if the judge finds that sufficient evidence, aside from the communication, has been introduced to warrant a finding that the communication was made, in whole or in part, to enable or aid anyone to commit or to plan to commit a crime or a tort." See also West's Ann.Cal.Evid.Code, § 981, quoted supra § 78, n. 10.

27. 8 Wigmore, Evidence (McNaughton rev.) § 2336; Dec.Dig. Witnesses ⚎192, 193; C.J.S. Witnesses § 268.

28. See statutes compiled in 2 Wigmore, Evidence § 488. See also California and New York provisions, supra, § 78, n. 10.

29. See § 78, supra.

30. New York Life Ins. Co. v. Mason, 272 Fed. 28 (10th Cir. 1921) ("any communications" in R.C.M. 1947, § 93–701–3 should be interpreted as limited to confidential statements); Shepherd v. Pacific Mut. Life Ins. Co., 230 Iowa 1304, 300 N.W. 556 (1941); Thayer v. Thayer, 188 Mich. 261, 154 N.W. 32, 35 (1915). Contra: Pugsley v. Smyth, 98 Ore. 448, 194 Pac. 686 (1921) (reviewing statutes and decisions in various states). See, generally, C.J.S. Witnesses § 268.

31. Blau v. United States, 340 U.S. 332 (1951); West's Ann.Cal.Evid.Code § 917.

32. For general discussions, see e. g., Parkhurst v. Berdell, 110 N.Y. 386, 393, 18 N.E. 123, 127 (1888) ("such communications as are expressly made confidential, or such as are of a confidential nature, or induced by the marital relation"); Mitchell v. Mitchell, 80 Tex. 101, 15 S.W. 705 (1891) ("determined by the subject-matter of the communication or the circumstances under which it was made or both").

Threats of bodily harm, though in secret, being a violation of marital duty, should not, it seems, be privileged. People v. Zabijak, 285 Mich. 164, 280 N.W. 149 (1938). Contra: O'Neil v. O'Neil, 264 S.W. 61 (Mo.App.1924) (private threats privileged, unless accompanied by violence). In a New York suit for separation, the husband defended on grounds of cruelty and testified that the wife said she had committed adultery with another man and they were going away. Two judges thought the communication not privileged because not prompted by confidentiality of marriage relation; three judge concurred in result but on grounds of an exception for wrongs by one spouse against the other; two dissented. Poppe v. Poppe, 3 N.Y.2d 312, 144 N.E.2d 72, 165 N.Y.S.2d 99 (1957), 58 Colum. L.Rev. 126 (1958), § 84, n. 76, infra.

a child of the family) is present to the knowledge of the communicating spouse, this stretches the web of confidence beyond the marital pair, and the communication is unprivileged.[33] If children of the family are present this likewise deprives the conversation of protection unless the children are too young to understand what is said.[34] The fact that the communication relates to business transactions tends to show that it was not intended as confidential.[35] Examples are statements about business agreements between the spouses,[36] or about business matters transacted by one spouse as agent for the other,[37] or about property [38] or convey-

---

Where the husband left a note for the wife, at their home, written on a large cardboard, the message was held not to be confidential. Yoder v. United States, 80 F.2d 665 (10th Cir. 1935).

Letters written by husband in jail awaiting trial which were handed to the sheriff for delivery to the wife and were not folded, sealed or otherwise arranged to suggest confidentiality were ruled not privileged in Guyette v. State, 84 Nev. 160, 438 P.2d 244 (1968).

33. Pereira v. United States, 347 U.S. 1 (1954) ("The presence of a third party negatives the presumption of privacy."); United States v. Mitchell, 137 F.2d 1006 (1943) (threats against wife in presence of others); Shepherd v. Pacific Mut. Life Ins. Co., 230 Iowa 1304, 300 N.W. 556 (1941) (negotiations between husband, wife, and her father); Gutridge v. State, 236 Md. 514, 204 A.2d 557 (1964) (defendant in jail sent oral message to wife by a trusty); State v. Fiddler, 57 Wash.2d 815, 360 P.2d 155 (1961) (husband sent letters to illiterate wife knowing someone would have to read them to her); People v. Ressler, 17 N.Y.2d 174, 269 N.Y.S.2d 414, 216 N.E.2d 582 (1966) (conversation between husband and wife in presence of victim of homicide before he was slain by husband); Dec.Dig. Witnesses ⊛193; C.J.S. Witnesses § 271.

A letter from a husband to his wife, dictated by him to a stenographer, has been held not privileged. "Normally husband and wife may conveniently communicate without stenographic aid, and the privilege of holding their confidences immune from proof in court may be reasonably enjoyed and preserved without embracing within it the testimony of third persons to whom such communications have been voluntarily revealed. . . . The privilege suppresses relevant testimony, and should be allowed only when it is plain that marital confidence cannot otherwise reasonably be preserved. Nothing in this case suggests any such necessity." Wolfle v. United States, 291 U.S. 7, 16, 17 (1934) (Stone, J.)

34. Freeman v. Freeman, 238 Mass. 150, 130 N.E. 220 (1921) (in presence of children, the oldest nine years old, held, for the judge to determine whether old enough to pay attention and understand); Hicks v. Hicks, 271 N.C. 204, 155 S.E.2d 799 (1967) (presence of 8 year old daughter did not destroy privilege.); Fuller v. Fuller, 100 W.Va. 309, 130 S.E. 270 (1925) (in presence of 13 year old daughter, not privileged); C.J.S. Witnesses § 271.

35. "So, too, it cannot be that the rule of privilege must be held to extend so far as to exclude all communications between husband and wife having reference to business relations existing either as between them directly, or as between them—one or both—and others. Certainly as to business relations existing between husband and wife directly, there can be no adverse consideration of public policy. Quite to the contrary, public policy, as reflected by statute and by our decisions, permits of such relations to the fullest extent. And it would be shocking to say that a contract thus made, or rights or liabilities thus accruing, could not be enforced because, forsooth, a communication between the parties having relation thereto, and essential to proof, was privileged. The cases are almost unanimously against such a conclusion." Bishop, J. in Sexton v. Sexton, 129 Iowa 487, 105 N.W. 314, 316 (1905). See C.J.S. Witnesses § 269d, p. 772; Annot., 4 A.L.R.2d 835.

36. Appeal of Spitz, 56 Conn. 184, 14 A. 776 (1887) (claim of wife against insolvent estate of husband: held, wife's testimony as to husband's promises and representations which induced her to advance money, not privileged; "they were no more privileged than a promissory note would have been, if he had made his contract in that form"); Brooks v. Brooks, 357 Mo. 343, 208 S.W.2d 279, 4 A.L.R.2d 826, 832 (1948) (wife sues husband for proceeds of joint adventure. "In actions between a husband and wife involving property rights the rule excluding relevant conversations . . . yields to the necessity of the situation for the prevention of injustice. . . ."); Bietman v. Hopkins, 109 Ind. 177, 9 N.E. 720 (1887) (in suit by husband's creditor to set aside husband's deed to wife, plaintiff objects to wife's testimony that deed given to repay advances—seemingly could be based on ground that the plaintiff is not the holder of the privilege); Ward v. Oliver, 129 Mich. 300, 88 N.W. 631 (1902) (similar to last).

37. Schmied v. Frank, 86 Ind. 250, 257 (1882) (wife's testimony that she authorized husband to buy note as her agent, not privileged: such authority "is intended to be known and would be worthless unless known"); Lurty's Curator v. Lurty, 107 Va. 466, 59 S.E. 405 (1907) (husband's account of money due wife on sale of their joint property not privileged). See such statutes as Oklahoma, quoted § 78, n. 10, supra.

38. Hagerman v. Wigent, 108 Mich. 192, 65 N.W. 756 (1896) (wife's delivery of mortgage to husband with instructions to give to plaintiff after wife's

ances.[39]　Usually such statements relate to facts which are intended later to become publicly known.　To cloak them with privilege when the transactions come into litigation would be productive of special inconvenience and injustice.

81. The Time of Making the Communication;[40] Marital Status.

The privilege is created to encourage marital confidences and is limited to them.　Consequently, communications between the husband and wife before they were married,[41] or after their divorce[42] are not privileged.　A bigamous marriage will not sustain the privilege.[43]　A communication made during a purported marriage, later annulled for fraud, by the victim of the fraud, has, however, been held to be privileged.[44]　What of husband and wife living apart?　It has been said that the privilege "should not apply when the parties are living in separation and especially, as in this case, so living under articles of separation, and the one making the communication is actively hostile to the other."[45]　In other circumstances when the separation has not been sanctioned by contract or decree and the communication has been made in hope of reconciliation, it might well be found to be a privileged confidence.[46]

82. Hazards of Disclosure to Third Persons Against the Will of the Communicating Spouse.[47]

The weight of decision seems to support the view that the privilege does not protect against the testimony of third persons who have overheard (either accidentally or by eavesdropping) an oral communication between husband and wife,[48] or who have secured possession or learned the contents of a letter from one spouse to another by interception,[49] or through loss or misdelivery by the custodian.[50]　There is one important

---

death, not privileged, as it was expected to be disclosed); Parkhurst v. Berdell, 110 N.Y. 386, 18 N.E. 123 (1888) (husband's conversation with wife as to securities in his hands belonging to third person, not privileged; "they were ordinary conversations, relating to matters of business, which there is no reason to suppose he would have been unwilling to hold in the presence of any person").

39.　Eddy v. Bosley, 34 Tex.Civ.App. 116, 78 S.W. 565 (1903) (communication by husband to second wife preceding his deed to her advising her of the interest of his children in the property will be received to show notice to her; claim of privilege overruled on ground that the conveyance "if accomplished would operate as a fraud" upon the children).

40.　C.J.S. Witnesses § 267.

41.　United States v. Mitchell, 137 F.2d 1006 (2d Cir. 1943); Forshay v. Johnston, 144 Neb. 525, 13 N.W. 2d 873 (1944) (agreement establishing a common law marriage not a "communication between husband and wife"); Dec.Dig. Witnesses ☞194.

42.　Yoder v. United States, 80 F.2d 665 (10th Cir. 1935).

43.　People v. Mabry, 71 Cal.2d 430, 78 Cal.Rptr. 655, 455 P.2d 759 (1969); People v. Keller, 165 Cal. App.2d 419, 332 P.2d 174 (1958).

44.　People v. Godines, 17 Cal.App.2d 721, 62 P.2d 787 (1936) noted 25 Calif.L.Rev. 619 (1937).

45.　Holyoke v. Holyoke's Estate, 110 Me. 469, 87 Atl. 40 (1913).　See also McEntire v. McEntire, 107 Ohio St. 510, 140 N.E. 328 (1923) (communications about property settlement between spouses who had been separated under oral agreement for several months), and cases cited C.J.S. Witnesses § 267.

46.　This seems to be assumed without discussion in McCoy v. Justice, 199 N.C. 637, 155 S.E. 452 (1930).

47.　8 Wigmore, Evidence (McNaughton rev.) § 2339; Annot., 63 A.L.R. 107; C.J.S. Witnesses §§ 270, 271.

48.　Commonwealth v. Everson, 123 Ky. 330, 96 S.W. 460 (1906) (eavesdropper); Nash v. Fidelity Phenix Fire Ins. Co., 106 W.Va. 672, 146 S.E. 726, 63 A.L.R. 101, 104 (1929) (same).　But see notes 58 and 59, infra.

49.　Batchelor v. State, 217 Ark. 340, 230 S.W.2d 23 (1950) (letter to wife intercepted by jailer); Connella v. Terr., 16 Okl. 365, 86 Pac. 72 (1906) (letter from defendant to his wife, sent by messenger; letter came in hands of sheriff); People v. Dunnigan, 163 Mich. 349, 128 N.W. 180 (1910) (spy entering prisoner's cell ostensibly to cut his hair promises to take letter to wife but gives it to sheriff).

50.　Hammons v. State, 73 Ark. 495, 84 S.W. 718 (1905) (letter to wife from defendant in jail delivered by messenger to wife's father: two judges dissenting); O'Toole v. Ohio German Fire Ins. Co., 159 Mich. 187, 123 N.W. 795 (1909) (letter from wife to husband, dropped and lost by husband).

qualification which many if not most of the cases announce, namely that the privilege will not be lost if the eavesdropping,[51] or the delivery or disclosure of the letter [52] be due to the betrayal or connivance of the spouse to whom the message is directed. Just as that spouse would not be permitted, against the will of the communicating spouse, to betray the confidence by testifying in court to the message, so he or she may not effectively destroy the privilege by out-of-court betrayal.

The first mentioned doctrine that the eavesdropper, or the interceptor of the letter, may testify to the confidential message is sometimes supported on the ground that the particular statute is phrased in terms of incompetency of the spouses to testify to the communication, and should not be extended to disqualify third persons.[53] Perhaps it may

be better sustained on the more general view that since the privilege has as its only effect the suppression of relevant evidence, its scope should be confined as narrowly as is consistent with reasonable protection of marital communications.

In this latter view, it seems, since the communicating spouse can ordinarily take effective precautions against overhearing, he should bear the risk of a failure to use such precautions.[54] Moreover, if he sends a messenger with a letter, he should ordinarily assume the risk that the chosen emissary may lose or misdeliver the message.[55] But if a prisoner in jail speaks to his wife with all the secrecy that his poor cell affords, it seems unduly harsh to forfeit the privilege if by an electronic device or by eavesdroppers in the next cell his confidences are overheard.[56] He has done what he could. Similarly, it seems that when one sends a written message to his wife by an agent there are no practical precautions that sender or agent can use against forcible seizure, and if the letter is so taken it should still be privileged.[57] As has been observed elsewhere, the development of so-

51. Hunter v. Hunter, 169 Pa.Super. 498, 83 A.2d 401 (1951) (husband suing wife for divorce offers wire-recordings of their conversation in bed: the wire-recorder having been set up by plaintiff's son, with plaintiff's connivance without wife's knowledge, held privileged), Notes, 1 Buff.L.Rev. 314, 50 Mich.L.Rev. 933.

52. Wilkerson v. State, 91 Ga. 729, 17 S.E. 990 (1893) (letter from husband to wife delivered by her to paramour, inadmissible against husband); Scott v. Comm., 94 Ky. 511, 23 S.W. 219 (1893) (letter to wife voluntarily surrendered by her); McCoy v. Justice, 199 N.C. 637, 155 S.E. 452 (1930) (husband's letters disclosed by wife to third persons).

Nevertheless, there are a substantial number of cases which disregard this element of betrayal and hold the privilege not applicable. See, e. g., People v. Swaile, 12 Cal.App. 192, 107 Pac. 134 (1909) (prisoner sends wife letter by police officer: she gives it back to officer at his request); State v. Sysinger, 25 S.D. 110, 125 N.W. 879 (1910) (prisoner's letter to wife, delivered by her to State's attorney); Annot., 63 A.L.R. 107, 124.

53. See, e. g., Commonwealth v. Wakelin, 230 Mass. 567, 120 N.E. 209, 212 (1918); Connella v. Terr., 16 Okl. 365, 86 Pac. 72, 75 (1906).

In Rumping v. Director of Public Prosecutions, H.L. (1962) 3 All E.R. 256 (1962) the accused, a mate on a Dutch ship, wrote a letter to his wife amounting to a confession of murder, handed the letter in a sealed envelope to a member of the ship's crew to post when the ship reached a port outside England. When the accused was arrested the man gave the letter to the captain who turned it over to the police. The House of Lords held the letter admis-

sible on the ground that the Criminal Evidence Act, 1898, does not recognize a privilege for confidential communications in providing that: "No husband shall be compellable to disclose any communication made to him by his wife during the marriage, and no wife shall be compellable to disclose any communication made to her by her husband during the marriage."

54. Commonwealth v. Everson, 123 Ky. 330, 96 S.W. 460, 461 (1906) (likened to attorney-client privilege as to which "it has been said that if persons wish the communications they have with their attorneys to be kept secret, they should be careful not to talk in the hearing of others"); 8 Wigmore, Evidence (McNaughton rev.) §§ 2339(1), 2326.

55. See *Hammons* and *O'Toole* cases, supra note 50.

56. Cf. Commonwealth v. Wakelin, 230 Mass. 567, 120 N.E. 209 (1918) (dictograph planted in cell where husband and wife were held).

57. See Ward v. State, 70 Ark. 204, 66 S.W. 926 (1902) (letter to wife and enclosure to third person given by husband in jail to wife and seized from her by officers, held, the former privileged, the latter not).

phisticated eavesdropping techniques has led to curbs upon their use and upon the admissibility of evidence obtained thereby.[58] It has also led to including in rules governing privileged communications provisions against disclosure by third persons.[59]

If the spouse to whom the letter is addressed dies and it is found among the effects of the deceased, may the personal representative be required or permitted to produce it in court? Here is no connivance or betrayal by the deceased spouse, and on the other hand this is not a disclosure against which the sender could effectively guard. If the privilege is to be held, as most courts do,[60] to survive the death of one of the spouses, it seems that only a court which strictly limits the effect of the statute to restraining the spouses themselves from testifying, could justify a denial of the privilege in this situation.[61]

83. Who Is the Holder of the Privilege? Enforcement and Waiver.

Greenleaf in 1842 in foreshadowing the protection of marital communications, wrote of the projected rule as a "privilege" based on "public policy." Many legislatures, however, when they came to write the privilege into law phrased the rule simply as a survival in this special case of the ancient incompetency of the spouses, which the same statutes undertook to abolish or restrict. So it is often provided that the spouses are "incompetent" to testify to marital communications. Consequently, the courts frequently overlook this "common law" background[62] of privilege, and permit any party to the action to claim the benefit of the rule by objection. Doubtless counsel often fail to point out that privilege, not incompetency, is the proper classification, and that the distinctive feature of privilege is that it can only be claimed by the holder or beneficiary of the privilege, not by a party as such.[63] The latter principle is clearly correct.[64]

Who is the holder? Wigmore's argument, that the policy of encouraging freedom of communication points to the communicating spouse as the holder,[65] seems convincing. Under this view, in the case of a unilateral oral message or statement, of a husband to his wife, only the husband could assert the privilege, where the sole purpose is to show the expressions and attitude of the husband. If

---

58. See § 75, supra, and §§ 167, 174, infra.

59. West's Ann.Cal.Evid.Code, § 980, quoted § 78, n. 10, supra.

60. See § 85, infra.

61. Privilege applied. Bowman v. Patrick, 32 Fed. 368 (C.C.Mo.1887) (forcible opinion by Miller, J.); McKie v. State, 165 Ga. 210, 140 S.E. 625 (1927) (trial of wife for murder of husband; wife's letter to husband, produced by his temporary administrator, held improperly admitted, two judges dissenting), noted critically, 37 Yale L.J. 669. Privilege denied. Dickerson v. United States, 65 F.2d 824 (1st Cir. 1933) (trial of husband for murder of wife; letter to wife found by third person among her effects, held admissible).

62. See § 78, supra.

63. See § 73, supra.

64. Luick v. Arends, 21 N.D. 614, 132 N.W. 353, 362, 363 (1911) (statutory phrase, "nor can either be . . . without consent of the other examined as to any communication" creates a privilege, not a disqualification, which only a spouse can assert, and the defendant in the alienation suit here, cannot assert the privilege or complain on appeal of its denial); Coles v. Harsch, 129 Ore. 11, 276 Pac. 248, 253–255 (1929) (alienation action, plaintiff's wife having later married defendant; defendant, not being the holder of the privilege, could not object at the trial or on appeal to plaintiff's disclosure of marital communications); Patterson v. Skoglund, 181 Ore. 167, 180 P.2d 108 (1947) (only husband or wife, not the defendant, can assert the privilege).

65. 8 Wigmore, Evidence (McNaughton rev.) § 2340 (1). This view is approved in Fraser v. United States, 145 F.2d 139 (6th Cir. 1944) cert. denied 324 U.S. 849. But see Hagedorn v. Hagedorn, 211 N.C. 175, 189 S.E. 507 (1937) which construed a statute which said that no spouse "shall be compellable" to disclose communications to mean that either could disclose, though the other objects. See critical Note, 15 N.C.L. Rev. 282 (1937). Uniform Rule 28 vests the privilege in the communicating spouse, but West's Ann.Cal.Evid.Code § 980, quoted supra, § 78, n. 10, makes both spouses holders.

the object, however, were to show the wife's adoption of the husband's statement by her silence, then the husband's statement and her conduct both became her communication and she can claim the privilege. Similarly, if a conversation or an exchange of correspondence between them is offered to show the collective expressions of them both, either it seems could claim privilege as to the entire exchange.

A failure by the holder to assert the privilege by objection, or a voluntary revelation by the holder of the communication,[66] or of a material part, is a waiver. The judge, however, may in some jurisdictions in his discretion protect the privilege [67] if the holder is not present to assert it, and objection by a party not the holder may serve the purpose of invoking this discretion, though the party may not complain [68] if the judge fails to protect this privilege, belonging to the absent spouse.

84. Controversies in Which the Privilege Is Inapplicable.[69]

The common law privilege against adverse testimony of a spouse was subject to an exception in cases of prosecution of the husband for offenses against the wife, at least those of violence.[70] When nineteenth century statutes in this country limited and regulated this privilege and the incompetency of spouses as witnesses and defined the new statutory privilege for confidential communications the common law exception above mentioned was usually incorporated and extended, and frequently other exceptions were added. Under these statutes [71] it is not always clear how far the exceptions are intended to apply only to the provisions limiting the competency of the spouses as witnesses, or whether they apply also to the privilege for confidential communications. Frequently, however, in the absence of a contrary decision, it is at least arguable that the exception does have this latter application, and in some instances this intent is clearly expressed. Any other result would, in principle, indeed be difficult to justify.

The types of controversies in which the marital communication privilege is made inapplicable vary, of course, from state to state. They may be derived from express provision, from statutory implication, or from decisions based upon common law doctrine.[72] They may be grouped as follows: [73]

1. Prosecutions for crimes committed by one spouse against the other or against the

---

66. Pendleton v. Pendleton, 103 Ohio App. 345, 145 N.E.2d 485 (1957) (privilege may be waived, and once waived may not later be asserted in the same cause); Patterson v. Skoglund, note 64, supra; Uniform Rule 37; West's Ann.Cal.Evid.Code § 912(a). It is suggested in Fraser v. United States, 145 F.2d 139, 144 (6th Cir. 1945) cert. denied 324 U.S. 849, that when the husband claims the privilege on the stand, but answers when ordered by the court to do so, this is a waiver, but this conclusion seems questionable.

67. Coles v. Harsch, 129 Or. 11, 276 Pac. 248, 255 (1929); Model Code of Evidence Rule 105(e).

68. See decisions cited note 64, supra.

69. 8 Wigmore, Evidence (McNaughton rev.) § 2338; C.J.S. Witnesses § 273; 58 Am.Jur. Witnesses §§ 396, 398; Model Code of Evidence Rule 216.

70. See § 66, supra, and 8 Wigmore, Evidence (McNaughton rev.) § 2239.

71. See the compilation of statutes in 2 Wigmore, Evidence § 488.

72. See e. g., United States v. Walker, 176 F.2d 564, 568 (2d Cir. 1949) (L. Hand, C. J.: "We do not forget that a wife from the earliest times was competent to testify against her husband, when the crime was an offense against her person. . . . The same exception probably extends to the privilege against the admission of confidential communications"); People v. McCormack, 278 App.Div. 191, 104 N.Y.S.2d 139, 143 (1951) (common law exception for testimony as to assaults on wife is to be read into statute creating privilege, though exception not mentioned).

73. Compare Uniform Rule 28(2): "Neither spouse may claim such privilege (a) in an action by one spouse against the other spouse, or (b) in an action for damages for the alienation of the affections of the other, or for criminal conversation with the other, or (c) in a criminal action in which one of them is charged with a crime against the person or property of the other or of a

children of either. Besides statutes in general terms, particular crimes, most frequently family desertion and pandering, are often specified, and as to these latter the withdrawal of the privilege for communications is usually explicit.

2. Actions by one of the spouses against an outsider for an intentional injury to the marital relation. Thus far this exception has been applied, sometimes under statutes, sometimes as a continuation of common law tradition, chiefly in actions for alienation of affection or for criminal conversation.[74] It is usually applied to admit declarations expressive of the state of affection of the alienated spouse.[75]

3. Actions by one spouse against the other. Some of the statutes are in this broader form. Some apply only to particular kinds of actions between them, of which divorce suits are most often specified. This exception for controversies between the spouses,[76] which should extend to controversies between the representatives of the spouses, seems

worthy of universal acceptance. In the analogous case of clients who jointly consult an attorney, the clients are held to have no privilege for such consultation in controversies between themselves.[77] So here it seems that husband and wife, while they would desire that their confidences be shielded from the outside world, would ordinarily anticipate that if a controversy between themselves should arise in which their mutual conversations would shed light on the merits, the interests of both would be served by full disclosure.[78]

4. A criminal prosecution against one of the spouses in which a declaration of the other spouse made confidentially to the accused would tend to justify or reduce the grade of the offense.[79]

85. If the Communication Was Made During the Marriage, Does Death or Divorce End the Privilege? [80]

The incompetency of husband or wife to testify for the other, and the privilege of each spouse against adverse testimony are terminated when the marriage ends by death or divorce.[81] The privilege for confidential communications of the spouses, however, was

---

child of either, or a crime against the person or property of a third person committed in the course of committing a crime against the other, or bigamy or adultery, or desertion of the other or of a child of either, or (d) in a criminal action in which the accused offers evidence of a communication between him and his spouse. . . ."
See also the exceptions in the California statute quoted § 78, n. 10, supra.

74. Stocker v. Stocker, 112 Neb. 565, 199 N.W. 849, 36 A.L.R. 1063 (1924); Hafer v. Lemon, 182 Okl. 578, 79 P.2d 216 (1938). Contra: Gjesdal v. Harmon, 175 Minn. 414, 221 N.W. 639 (1928); McKinnon v. Chenoweth, 176 Ore. 74, 155 P.2d 944 (1945). Cases are collected in Annot., 36 A.L.R. 1068.

75. Annot., 36 A.L.R. 1068, 1070.

76. See statutes in 2 Wigmore, Evidence § 488. And see Poppe v. Poppe, 3 N.Y.2d 312, 165 N.Y.S. 2d 99, 144 N.E.2d 72, 76 (1957), noted 58 Colum.L. Rev. 126 (1958), where, absent an explicit statutory exception, an exception was recognized in a separation suit for the wife's declaration that she had committed adultery and "they thought they would go away together," which was relied on as an act of cruelty by the defending husband. See also the reference to this case in § 80, note 32, supra. Cf. Oliver v. Oliver, 325 S.W.2d 33 (Mo.App.1959) (divorce action; communications held privileged).

77. See § 91, infra.

78. However, in *Poppe*, supra n. 76, the dissenting judges thought this the kind of free communication encouraged by the law.

79. Texas Vernon's Ann.C.C.P. art. 38.11 recognizes an exception, "where one or the other is on trial for an offense and a declaration or communication made by the wife to the husband or by the husband to the wife goes to extenuate or justify the offense." Wigmore argues for such an exception. Evidence, § 2338(4). And he calls attention to the "cruel absurdity" of excluding the communication in these circumstances in Steeley v. State, 17 Okl.Cr. 252, 187 Pac. 820 (1920) (defendant charged with murder of wife's paramour could not testify to wife's communications to him disclosing deceased's conduct in debauching her) and other cases cited. This view is adopted in Model Code of Evidence Rule 216(d) and Comment.

80. 8 Wigmore, Evidence (McNaughton rev.) § 2341; C.J.S. Witnesses § 275; 58 Am.Jur. Witnesses § 379; Dec.Dig. Witnesses ⟨key⟩195.

81. See § 66, supra.

based (in the mind of its chief sponsor, Greenleaf) upon the policy of encouraging confidences and its sponsor thought that encouragement required not merely temporary but permanent secrecy.[82] The courts in this country have accepted this need for permanent protection [83]—though it may be an unrealistic assumption—and about one-half of our statutes codifying the privilege explicitly provide that it continues after death or divorce.[84] It is probably in these cases where the marital tie has been severed, that the supposed policy of the privilege has the most remote and tenuous relevance, and the possibilities of injustice in its application are most apparent. Wigmore points out that in this area, "there must arise occasional instances of hardship where ample flexibility should be allowed in the relaxation of the rule." [85]

In the famous English case of Shenton v. Tyler,[86] the court was faced with one of those instances of hardship. The plaintiff sued a widow and alleged that her deceased husband had made an oral secret trust, known to the widow, for the benefit of plaintiff, and sought to interrogate the widow. The widow relied on sec. 3 of the Evidence Amendment Act, 1853, as follows: " . . . no wife shall be compellable to disclose any communication made to her during the marriage." The court rejected the Greenleaf theory of a common law privilege for communications surviving the end of the marriage, and was "unable to find any warrant for extending the words of the section by construction so as to include widowers and widows and divorced persons." [87] However debatable may be the court's position that there was no common law privilege for marital communications,[88] it seems clear that the actual holding that the privilege for communications ends when the marriage ends is preferable in policy to the contrary result reached under American statutes and decisions.

86.   Policy and Future of the Privilege.[89]

The most substantial argument that present day judges and writers advance in support of the privilege is that the privilege against courtroom disclosure is needed for the encouragement of marital confidences, which confidences in turn promote harmony between husband and wife. Freedom of marital confidences to a reasonable extent at least is desirable, but this freedom is generally a result rather than a cause of marital harmony. The main answer to the argument of policy, however, is that the contingency of courtroom disclosure would almost never (even though the privilege did not exist) be in the minds of the parties in consid-

82. "The happiness of the married state requires that there should be the most unlimited confidence between husband and wife; and this confidence the law secures by providing that it shall be kept forever inviolable; that nothing shall be extracted from the bosom of the wife which was confided there by the husband. Therefore, after the parties are separated, whether it be by divorce or by the death of the husband, the wife is still precluded from disclosing any conversations with him . . . .." 1 Greenleaf, Evidence 296 (13th ed. 1876).

83. Rance v. Hutchinson, 131 Fla. 460, 179 So. 777 (1938) (divorced wife of decedent may not testify to communications between herself and husband during marriage, about conveyance by spouses to husband in trust for children); In re Osbon's Estate, 205 Minn. 419, 286 N.W. 306 (1939) (in will contest, trial judge properly refused to permit divorced wife of testator to testify to their conversations during marriage); Pace v. State, 61 Tex.Cr. 436, 135 S.W. 379 (1911) (confession of husband to wife that he killed a man).

84. See the compilation of statutes in 2 Wigmore, Evidence § 488.

85. 8 Wigmore, Evidence (McNaughton rev.) § 2341.

86. L.R. [1939] Ch.Div. 620 (C.A.).

87. L.R. [1939] Ch.Div. 620, 652 (by Luxmoore, L.J.).

88. See § 78, supra.

89. 8 Wigmore, Evidence (McNaughton rev.) § 2332; C.J.S. Witnesses § 266; 58 Am.Jur. Witnesses § 375; Dec.Dig., Witnesses ☞188(1). The foregoing give the supporting arguments of policy. Two law review articles criticize with much penetration the soundness of these reasons. Hutchins and Slesinger, Some Observations on the Law of Evidence: Family Relations, 13 Minn.L.Rev. 675, 682 (1929); Hines, Privileged Testimony of Husband and Wife in California, 19 Calif.L.Rev. 390, 410–414 (1931).

ering how far they should go in their secret conversations. What encourages them to fullest frankness is not the assurance of courtroom privilege, but the trust they place in the loyalty and discretion of each other. If the secrets are not told outside the courtroom there will be little danger of their being elicited in court. In the lives of most people appearance in court as a party or a witness is an exceedingly rare and unusual event, and the anticipation of it is not one of those factors which materially influence in daily life the degree of fullness of marital disclosures.[90] Accordingly, we must conclude that, while the danger of injustice from suppression of relevant proof is clear and certain,[91] the probable benefits of the rule of privilege in encouraging marital confidences and wedded harmony, is at best doubtful and marginal.

Probably the policy of encouraging confidences is not the prime influence in creating and maintaining the privilege. It is really a much more natural and less devious matter. It is a matter of emotion and sentiment. All of us have a feeling of indelicacy and want of decorum in prying into the secrets of husband and wife. It is important to recognize that this is the real source of the privilege. When we do, we realize at once that this motive of delicacy, while worthy and desirable, will not stand in the balance with the need for disclosure in court of the facts upon which a man's life, liberty, or estate may depend.

This feeling of disproportion between the interest of delicacy and the interest of justice has doubtless swayed the courts in limiting the privilege in groups of cases where injustice in its application was most apparent,[92] in the illogical permission to the third party intercepting or overhearing the message to make disclosure,[93] and in the oft-repeated admonition that the scope of the privilege should, in case of doubt, be strictly confined.[94] Seemingly all of these limiting prac-

---

90. ". . . Very few people ever get into court, and practically no one outside the legal profession knows anything about the rules regarding privileged communications between spouses. As far as the writers are aware (though research might lead to another conclusion) marital harmony among lawyers who know about privileged communications is not vastly superior to that of other professional groups." Hutchins and Slesinger, op. cit., p. 682.

F.R.Ev. (R.D.1971) 505, does not include a privilege for confidential communications. The Advisory Committee's Note to this proposed rule states with respect to the privilege:

"The rule recognizes no privilege for confidential communications. The traditional justifications for privileges not to testify against a spouse and not to be testified against by one's spouse have been the prevention of marital dissension and the repugnancy of requiring a person to condemn or be condemned by his spouse. 8 Wigmore §§ 2228, 2241 (McNaughton rev. 1961). These considerations bear no relevancy to marital communications. Nor can it be assumed that marital conduct will be affected by a privilege for confidential communications of whose existence the parties in all likelihood are unaware. The other communication privileges, by way of contrast, have as one party a professional person who can be expected to inform the other of the existence of the privilege. Moreover, the relationships from which those privileges arise are essentially and almost exclusively verbal in nature, quite unlike marriage. See Hutchins and Slesinger, Some Observations on the Law of Evidence: Family Relations, 13 Minn.L. Rev. 675 (1929). Cf. McCormick § 90; 8 Wigmore § 2337 (McNaughton rev. 1961)."

91. Examples of cases where the possibilities of injustice seem conspicuous are In re DeNeef, 42 Cal. App.2d 691, 109 P.2d 741 (1941) (wife sues on life insurance policy taken out in her favor by deceased husband. Defense: fraudulent representations by husband as to his health. Held, wife cannot be interrogated as husband's statements to her as to his physical condition. "We are not concerned with the reason for the rule or its effect on the administration of justice"); McKie v. State, 165 Ga. 210, 140 S.E. 625 (1927) (wife's conviction for murder of husband because of admission of wife's letters to husband, found in his effects after he was killed); Todd v. Barbee, 271 Ky. 381, 111 S.W.2d 1041 (1938) (excluding husband's testimony that he gave wife money to pay rent) and People v. Daghita, 299 N.Y. 194, 86 N.E.2d 172 (1949) (error to allow wife to testify in prosecution of husband for grand larceny, that she saw him bringing stolen property into their home and hiding it under his bed).

92. See § 84, supra.

93. See § 82, supra.

94. " 'The policy of the law is to require the disclosure of all information by witnesses in order that

tices are paths leading to and converging in a wider solution. This solution is to recognize, by statute, rule of court or decision, that the privilege is not an absolute but a qualified one, which must yield if the trial judge finds that the evidence of the communication is re-

quired in the due administration of justice.[95] The judge could then protect the marital confidence when it should be protected, namely, when the material fact sought to be established by the communication is not substantially controverted and may be proven with reasonable convenience by other evidence.

justice may prevail. The granting of a privilege from such disclosure constitutes an exception to that general rule.' People ex rel. Mooney v. Sheriff of New York County, 269 N.Y. 291, 295, 199 N.E. 415, 416, 102 A.L.R. 769. 'The suppression of truth is a grievous necessity at best.' McMann v. Securities and Exchange Commission, 2 Cir., 87 F.2d 377, 378. And apropos of the particular question of privilege before us, we have it on the authority

of Wolfle v. United States, 291 U.S. 7, at pages 14, 17, that:

'. . . The privilege suppresses relevant testimony and should be allowed only when it is plain that marital confidence cannot otherwise reasonably be preserved.' " People v. McCormack, 278 App.D. 191, 104 N.Y.S.2d 139, 144 (1951).

95. See § 77, supra, as to a similar possible approach in other situations.

CHAPTER 10

THE CLIENT'S PRIVILEGE: COMMUNICATIONS BETWEEN CLIENT AND LAWYER

87. Background and Policy of the Privilege.

The notion that the loyalty owed by the lawyer to his client disables him from being a witness in his client's case is deep-rooted in Roman law.[1] This Roman tradition may or may not have been influential in shaping the early English doctrine of which we find the first traces in Elizabeth's time, that the oath and honor of the barrister and the attorney protect them from being required to disclose, upon examination in court, the secrets of the client.[2] But by the eighteenth century in England the emphasis upon the code of honor had lessened and the need of the ascertainment of truth for the ends of justice loomed larger than the pledge of secrecy. So a new justification for the lawyer's exemption from disclosing his client's secrets was found. This was the theory that claims and disputes which may lead to litigation can most justly and expeditiously be handled by practised experts, namely lawyers, and that such experts can act effectively only if they are fully advised of the facts by the parties whom they represent.[3] Such full disclosure will be promoted if the client knows that what he tells his lawyer cannot, over his objection, be extorted in court from the lawyer's lips.

The proposition is that the detriment to justice from a power to shut off inquiry to pertinent facts in court, will be outweighed by the benefits to justice (not to the client) from a franker disclosure in the lawyer's office. Wigmore who supports the privilege, acknowledges that "Its benefits are all indi-

1. See Radin, The Privilege of Confidential Communication between Lawyer and Client, 16 Calif. L.Rev. 487, 488 (1928).

2. 8 Wigmore, Evidence (McNaughton rev.) § 2290 (history of the privilege).

3. ". . . An increase of legal business, and the inabilities of parties to transact that business themselves, made it necessary for them to employ . . . other persons who might transact that business for them; that this necessity introduced with it the necessity of what the law hath very justly established, an inviolable secrecy to be observed by attornies, in order to render it safe for clients to

175

rect and speculative; its obstruction is plain and concrete." [4]

The tendency of the client in giving his story to his counsel to omit all that he suspects will make against him, is matter of everyday professional observation. It makes it necessary for the prudent lawyer to cross-examine his client searchingly about possible unfavorable facts. Perhaps in criminal cases the accused if he knew the lawyer could be compelled to repeat the facts disclosed might be induced by fear of this to withhold an acknowledgement of guilt. He knows that the prosecution cannot compel him, the accused, to testify. And in civil cases, before the mid-nineteenth century statutes making parties compellable to testify, the party might have feared to give damaging facts to his counsel if the latter could have been called to disclose these admissions in court. Now, however, when the party knows that he himself can be called as a witness by the adversary, the danger from disclosure to counsel is less important.

Perhaps we need not yield fully to the force of Bentham's slashing argument that the privilege is not needed by the innocent party with a righteous cause or defense, and that the guilty should not be given its aid in concerting a false one.[5] Wigmore in answer points out that in lawsuits all is not black and white but a client's case may be one where there is no clear preponderance of morals and justice on either side, and he may mistakenly think a fact fatal to his cause,

when it is not, and thus be impelled, if there were no privilege, to forego resort to counsel for advice in a fair claim.[6] Yet it must be acknowledged that the existence of the privilege may often instead of avoiding litigation upon unfounded claims, actually encourage such litigation. A rascally client consults one lawyer who tells him that certain facts disclosed are fatal to his case. The client then goes to another attorney and tells the story differently, so that a claim may be supported—a course which in the absence of the privilege would be much more dangerous.[7]

If one were legislating for a new commonwealth, without history or customs, it might be hard to maintain that a privilege for lawyer-client communications would facilitate more than it would obstruct the administration of justice. But we are not writing on a blank slate. Our adversary system of litigation casts the lawyer in the role of fighter for the party whom he represents. A strong sentiment of loyalty attaches to the relationship, and this sentiment would be outraged by an attempt to change our customs so as to make the lawyer amenable to routine examination upon the client's confidential disclosures regarding professional business. Loyalty and sentiment are silken threads, but they are hard to break. Accordingly, confined as we are by this "cake of custom," it is unlikely that enough energy could now be generated to abolish the privilege, particularly since its obstructive effect has been substantially lessened by the development of liberal doctrines as to waiver and as to denial of the privilege in case of consultation for unlawful ends. Nevertheless, some progress toward liberalization of the practice, some better reconciliation of the conflicting pulls of sentiment and delicacy on the one hand

communicate to their attornies all proper instructions. . . ." Mounteney, B. in Annesley v. Earl of Anglesea, 17 How.St.Tr. 1225 (1743) quoted in 8 Wigmore, Evidence § 2291 (McNaughton rev.) (policy of the privilege).

4. 8 Wigmore, Evidence (McNaughton rev.) § 2291, p. 554. For an opposing view see Barnhart, Privilege in the Uniform Rules of Evidence, 24 Ohio St.L.J. 131 (1963).

5. See Bentham, Rationale of Judicial Evidence (1827), 7 The Works of Jeremy Bentham 473, 474, 475, 477, 479 (Bowring ed. 1842), passages quoted Wigmore, op. cit., § 2291.

6. 8 Wigmore, Evidence (McNaughton rev.) § 2291, p. 552.

7. Radin, op cit., 16 Calif.L.Rev. at 490. See also Morgan, Foreword, Model Code of Evidence 26, 27 (1942).

and of the need, on the other, for full ascertainment of the crucial facts by a tribunal of justice, seems possible. It has been suggested that

1. The lawyer's duty to maintain out of court the secrecy of his client's confidential disclosures be retained intact. This assurance furnishes to most clients having a good faith claim or defense all the security (and hence encouragement to full disclosure) for which they would feel any need.[8]

2. The present privilege against disclosure of such communications in judicial proceedings, should be made subject to the exception that the trial judge may require a particular disclosure if he finds that it is necessary in the administration of justice.[9] Notwithstanding such a change, the present reluctance of lawyers to call an opposing counsel for routine examination on his client's case would continue as a restraining influence. The duty to the client of secrecy would still be recognized and protected in the ordinary course, but the lawyer's duty as an officer of the court to lend his aid in the last resort to prevent a miscarriage of justice would be given the primacy which a true balancing of the two interests would seem to demand.

8. Canon 4 of the Code of Professional Responsibility of the American Bar Association reads: "A lawyer should preserve the confidences and secrets of a client."

9. Compare Gen.Stats.N.C. 1969, § 8–53, which after directing that physicians shall not be required to disclose information acquired in attending a patient, adds "Provided, that the court, either at the trial or prior thereto, may compel such disclosure, if in his opinion the same is necessary to a proper administration of justice." See also the court's language regarding the attorney-client privilege in Jackson v. Pillsbury, 380 Ill. 554, 44 N.E.2d 537, 547 (1942): "The resulting injury to the relation by the disclosure of the communications must be greater than the benefit thereby gained for the correct disposal of the litigation." For a suggestion that the probable and desirable course of evolution for all the privileges is the path from rule to discretion, see McCormick, The Scope of Privilege in the Law of Evidence, 16 Tex.L.Rev. 447, 469 (1938).

A clear statement of the scope of the privilege as now generally accepted is embodied in the Uniform Rules.[10]

10. Uniform Rule 26: "(1) *General Rule.* Subject to Rule 37 [as to waiver] and except as otherwise provided by Paragraph 2 of this rule communications found by the judge to have been between lawyer and his client in the course of that relationship and in professional confidence, are privileged, and a client has a privilege (a) if he is the witness to refuse to disclose any such communication, and (b) to prevent his lawyer from disclosing it, and (c) to prevent any other witness from disclosing such communication if it came to the knowledge of such witness (i) in the course of its transmittal between the client and the lawyer, or (ii) in a manner not reasonably to be anticipated by the client, or (iii) as a result of a breach of the lawyer-client relationship. The privilege may be claimed by the client in person or by his lawyer, or if incompetent, by his guardian, or if deceased, by his personal representative. The privilege available to a corporation or association terminates upon dissolution.

"(2) *Exceptions.* Such privileges shall not extend (a) to a communication if the judge finds that sufficient evidence, aside from the communication, has been introduced to warrant a finding that the legal service was sought or obtained in order to enable or aid the client to commit or plan to commit a crime or a tort, or (b) to a communication relevant to an issue between parties all of whom claim through the client, regardless of whether the respective claims are by testate or intestate succession or by *inter vivos* transaction, or (c) to a communication relevant to an issue of breach of duty by the lawyer to his client, or by the client to his lawyer, or (d) to a communication relevant to an issue concerning an attested document of which the lawyer is an attesting witness, or (e) to a communication relevant to a matter of common interest between two or more clients if made by any of them to a lawyer whom they have retained in common when offered in an action between any of such clients.

"(3) *Definitions.* As used in this rule (a) 'Client' means a person or corporation or other association that, directly or through an authorized representative, consults a lawyer or the lawyer's representative for the purpose of retaining the lawyer or securing legal service or advice from him in his professional capacity; and includes an incompetent whose guardian so consults the lawyer or the lawyer's representative in behalf of the incompetent, (b) 'communication' includes advice given by the lawyer in the course of representing the client and includes disclosures of the client to a representative, associate or employee of the lawyer incidental to the professional relationship, (c) 'lawyer' means a person authorized, or reasonably believed by the client to be authorized to practice law in any state or nation the law of which recognizes a privilege against disclosure of confidential communications between client and lawyer."

The application of the privilege for the benefit of a corporate client, as distinguished from a natural person, was never questioned until a federal district court in 1962 held that a corporation is not entitled to claim the privilege.[11] The decision attracted wide attention and much comment, most of which was adverse, until reversed on appeal.[12] There seems to be little reason to believe that the issue will arise soon again.[13]

When the client is a corporation, questions arise as to who "speaks" for it for purposes of the privilege. Should a communication from any employee suffice? Or should the privilege apply only to communications from members of the "control group", i. e. those authorized to seek and act upon legal advice?[14] Or should some intermediate position be taken?[15] Lower level employees can scarcely be said to speak for the corpo-

11. Radiant Burners, Inc. v. American Gas Ass'n, 207 F.Supp. 771 (N.D.Ill.1962).

12. Radiant Burners, Inc. v. American Gas Ass'n, 320 F.2d 314, 98 A.L.R.2d 228 and note, (7th Cir. 1963) cert. denied 375 U.S. 921. The case is remarkable for the number of amici curiae briefs urging reversal including briefs from the Chicago Bar Ass'n., the Illinois State Bar Ass'n. and the American Bar Ass'n.

For comment on the District Court decision, see 76 Harvard L.Rev. 655 (1963), 52 Ill.B.J. 666 (1963), 61 Mich.L.Rev. 603 (1963), 57 Nw.U.L.Rev. 596 (1962).

On the privilege as applied to corporations generally, see Simon, The Attorney-Client Privilege as Applied to Corporations, 65 Yale L.J. 953 (1956).

13. F.R.Ev. (R.D.1971) 503(a) defines a client within the lawyer-client privilege as follows:

"(1) A "client" is a person, public officer, or corporation, association, or other organization or entity, either public or private, who is rendered professional legal services by a lawyer, or who consults a lawyer with a view to obtaining professional legal services from him."

14. An affirmative answer is given in City of Philadelphia v. Westinghouse Elec. Corp., 210 F.Supp. 483 (E.D.Pa.1962); Day v. Illinois Power Co., 50 Ill.App.2d 52, 199 N.E.2d 802 (1964); F.R.Ev. (R.D. 1971) 503(a) (3). These authorities proceed on the theory that the purpose and spirit of the privilege is served by including communications from members of the control group and do not require going below them and including lesser employees. See Note, 70 Harv.L.Rev. 424 (1970); cf. Note, 69 Mich. L.Rev. 360 (1970).

15. A leading case, D. I. Chadbourne, Inc. v. Superior Court, 36 Cal.Rptr. 468, 60 Cal.2d 723, 388 P.2d 700 (1964) (statement of corporate employee delivered to corporation's insurance carrier held not privileged), has suggested the following approach:

"But reason dictates that the corporation not be given greater privileges than are enjoyed by a natural person merely because it must utilize a person in order to speak. If we apply to corporations the same reasoning as has been applied in regard to natural persons in reference to privilege, and if we adapt those rules to fit the corporate concept, certain principles emerge clear. These basic principles may be stated as follows:

"1. When the employee of a defendant corporation is also a defendant in his own right (or is a person who may be charged with liability), his statement regarding the facts with which he or his employer may be charged, obtained by a representative of the employer and delivered to an attorney who represents (or will represent) either or both of them, is entitled to the attorney-client privilege on the same basis as it would be entitled thereto if the employer-employee relationship did not exist;

"2. When such an employee is not a co-defendant (or person who may be charged with liability), his communication should not be so privileged unless, under all of the circumstances of the case, he is the natural person to be speaking for the corporation; that is to say, that the privilege will not attach in such case unless the communication constitutes information which emanates from the corporation (as distinct from the nonlitigant employee), and the communicating employee is such a person who would ordinarily be utilized for communication to the corporation's attorney;

"3. When an employee has been a witness to matters which require communication to the corporate employer's attorney, and the employee has no connection with those matters other than as a witness, he is an independent witness; and the fact that the employer requires him to make a statement for transmittal to the latter's attorney does not alter his status or make his statement subject to the attorney-client privilege;

"4. Where the employee's connection with the matter grows out of his employment to the extent that his report or statement is required in the ordinary course of the corporation's business, the employee is no longer an independent witness, and his statement or report is that of the employer;

"5. If, in the case of the employee last mentioned, the employer requires (by standing rule or otherwise) that the employee make a report, the privilege of that report is to be determined by the employer's purpose in requiring the same; that is to say, if the employer directs the making of the report for confidential transmittal to its attorney, the communication may be privileged;

"6. When the corporate employer has more than one purpose in directing such an employee to make

ration, and their status realistically seems to be simply that of any witness who possesses information. At the other extreme, no one would deny the privilege in the case of mem-

such report or statement, the dominant purpose will control, unless the secondary use is such that confidentiality has been waived;

"7. If otherwise privileged under the rules stated above, a communication does not lose its privilege merely because it was obtained, with the knowledge and consent of the employer, by an agent of the employer acting under such agency;

"8. For such purpose an insurance company with which the employer carries indemnity insurance, and its duly appointed agents, are agents of the employer corporation; but the extent to which this doctrine may be carried, and the number of hands through which the communication may travel without losing confidentiality must always depend on reason and the particular facts of the case;

"9. And in all corporate employer-employee situations it must be borne in mind that it is the intent of the person from whom the information emanates that originally governs its confidentiality (and hence its privilege); thus where the employee who has not been expressly directed by his employer to make a statement, does not know that his statement is sought on a confidential basis (or knowing that fact does not intend it to be confidential), the intent of the party receiving and transmitting that statement cannot control the question of privilege;

"10. Similarly, where the corporate employer directs the employee, at the request of its insurance carrier, to make such a statement, the intent of the employer controls; and unless the insurance carrier (or its agent) has advised the employer that the employee's statement is to be obtained and used in such manner, it cannot be said that the corporation intended the statement to be made as a confidential communication from client to attorney;

"11. Finally, no greater liberality should be applied to the facts which determine privilege in the case of a corporation than would be applied in the case of a natural person (or association of persons), except as may be necessary to allow the corporation to speak."

See also Harper & Row Publishers, Inc. v. Decker, 423 F.2d 487 (7th Cir. 1970) (communication by employee privileged if made at direction of employer and dealt with his duties), aff'd by vote of 4 to 4 without opinion, 400 U.S. 955. Cf. Rucker v. Wabash R. Co., 418 F.2d 146 (7th Cir. 1969) (train crew not "of such rank as to qualify as representative of the corporate client" in report of grade-crossing accident). Harper & Row has been characterized as failing to reflect the purposes of the privilege. Note, 84 Harv.L.Rev. 424 (1970).

As to investigative reports, see § 96, n. 67, infra.

bers of the control group. The area of controversy lies between.

88. The Professional Relationship.

The privilege for communications of a client with his lawyer hinges upon the client's belief that he is consulting a lawyer in that capacity and his manifested intention to seek professional legal advice.[16] It is sufficient if he reasonably believes that the person consulted is a lawyer, though in fact he is not.[17] Communications in the course of preliminary discussion with a view to employing the lawyer are privileged though the employment is in the upshot not accepted.[18] The burden of proof (presumably in both senses) rests on the person asserting the privilege to show that the consultation was a professional one.[19] Payment or agreement to pay a fee, however, is not essential.[20] But where one

16. See Note, Nature of Professional Relationship Required under Privilege Rule, 24 Iowa L.Rev. 538 (1939).

17. People v. Barker, 60 Mich. 277, 27 N.W. 539 (1886) (confession to detective pretending to be an attorney).

A student in a law office would not come within the privilege except as he might be acting as a clerk or agent for the lawyer. Wartell v. Novograd, 48 R.I. 296, 137 A. 776 (1927).

18. In re Dupont's Estate, 60 Cal.App.2d 276, 140 P.2d 866 (1943) (preliminary negotiations fall within language of Code Civ.Proc. § 1881, subd. 2 [now West's Ann.], conferring privilege to communications, "in the course of professional employment", "no person could ever safely consult an attorney for the first time . . . if the privilege depended on the chance of whether the attorney after hearing the statement of the facts decided to accept the employment or decline it"); Denver Tramway Co. v. Owens, 20 Colo. 107, 36 P. 848 (1894); Keir v. State, 152 Fla. 389, 11 So.2d 886 (1943) (letters); Taylor v. Sheldon, 172 Ohio St. 118, 173 N.E.2d 892 (1961); In re Graf's Estate, 119 N.W.2d 478 (N.D.1963); Of course, statements made after the employment is declined are not privileged. McGrede v. Rembert N. Bank, 147 S.W.2d 580 (Tex.Civ.App.1941) (citing authorities).

19. McGrede v. Rembert N. Bank, 147 S.W.2d 580 (Tex.Civ.App.1941); McKnew v. Superior Court, 23 Cal.2d 58, 142 P.2d 1 (1943).

20. Matters v. State, 120 Neb. 404, 232 N.W. 781 (1930) (citing authorities); Hodge v. Garten, 116 W.Va. 564, 182 S.E. 582 (1935); C.J.S. Witnesses § 277, n. 41, and cases cited.

consults an attorney not as a lawyer but as a friend [21] or as a business adviser [22] or banker,[23] or negotiator,[24] or as an accountant,[25] or where the communication is to the attorney acting as a "mere scrivener" [26] or as an

attesting witness to a will or deed,[27] or as an executor [28] or as agent,[29] the consultation is not professional nor the statement privileged. The privilege does not extend to communi-

---

21. Modern Woodmen v. Watkins, 132 F.2d 352, (5th Cir. 1942) (disclosure of suicidal intent); Solon v. Lichtenstein, 39 Cal.2d 75, 244 P.2d 907 (1952); Lifsey v. Mims, 193 Ga. 780, 20 S.E.2d 32 (1942) (lawyer drawing deed as a "friendly act"); In re Conner's Estate, 33 N.W.2d 866 (1948) (modified on other grounds, 240 Iowa 479, 36 N.W. 2d 833 (1949) (divulging grandson's illegitimacy, to secure friend's help in telling boy).

22. Lowy v. C. I. R., 262 F.2d 809, (2d Cir. 1959); United States v. United Shoe Machinery Corp., 89 F.Supp. 357 (1950) (a communication soliciting business advice, not privileged, and attorney-client privilege does not extend to attorneys employed in a department of corporation which functions as a business branch, but does exist between corporation and attorneys in its legal department who perform substantially the same service as outside counsel; United States v. Vehicular Parking, 52 F.Supp. 751, (D.Del.1943) (business advice and directions by attorney who was promoter, director and manager of corporation concerned); Clayton v. Canida, 223 S.W.2d 264 (Tex.Civ.App.1949) (attorney acting as accountant, income tax return). As to the position of "house counsel" in respect to the privilege, see the able article, Simon, The Attorney Client Privilege as Applied to Corporations, 65 Yale L.J. 953, 969–978 (1956).

23. Belcher v. Somerville, 413 S.W.2d 620 (Ky.1967).

24. Myles v. Rieser Co. Inc. v. Loew's Inc., 194 Misc. 119, 81 N.Y.S.2d 861 (1948) (attorneys acting both as lawyers and as negotiators; communications in latter capacity not privileged); Henson v. State, 97 Okl.Cr. 240, 261 P.2d 916 (1953) (communication between defendant and attorney sharing office and secretary with defendant's attorney, not privileged and no attorney-client relationship existed where defendant knew attorney represented another and attorney tried to settle differences between his client and defendant).

25. Olender v. United States, 210 F.2d 795 (9th Cir. 1954) (attorney engaged as an accountant to prepare financial statement and income tax returns).

26. The phrase is often used as a justification for denying the privilege, see e. g., Benson v. Custer, 236 Iowa 345, 17 N.W.2d 889 (1945); Sparks v. Sparks, 51 Kan. 195, 201, 32 P. 892 (1893). The distinction is usually drawn between instances where the lawyer is employed merely to draft the document and cases where his advice is sought as to terms and effect. Mueller v. Batcheler, 131 Iowa 650, 652, 109 N.W. 186, 187 (1906) (conveyances); Dickerson v. Dickerson, 322 Ill. 492, 153 N.E. 740 (1926) (deed); Cranston v. Stewart, 184 Kan. 99, 334 P.2d 337 (1959); Wilcox v. Coons, 359

Mo. 52, 220 S.W.2d 15 (1949); Shelley v. Landry, 97 N.H. 27, 79 A.2d 626 (1951). Usually it will be found that an attorney asked to draw a will, is not a mere scrivener, but is acting professionally. Booher v. Brown, 173 Ore. 464, 146 P.2d 71 (1944). And the strict view of privilege in respect to the employment of lawyers as conveyancers seems somewhat inconsistent with the bar's present-day emphasis upon the importance of this as a lawyer's function. See Houck, Real Estate Instruments and the Bar, 5 Law & Contemp.Prob. 66 (1938).

27. Jones v. Smith, 266 Ga. 162, 56 S.E.2d 462 (1949) (lawyer may testify as to client's mental condition, his knowledge of the contents and other pertinent facts attending execution of contract, prepared and attested to by him); In re Heiler's Estate, 288 Mich. 49, 284 N.W. 641 (1939) (lawyer attesting will could testify to what he learned in his capacity as witness); Larson v. Dahlstrom, 214 Minn. 304, 8 N.W.2d 48 (1943) (lawyer attesting deed could testify to statements made by client at time of execution as bearing on mental condition); Anderson v. Thomas, 108 Utah 252, 159 P.2d 142 (1945) (deed; attesting lawyer may testify to conversations at time of execution).

28. Peyton v. Werhane, 126 Conn. 382, 11 A.2d 800 (1940).

29. United States v. Bartone, 400 F.2d 459, (6th Cir. 1969) cert. denied 393 U.S. 1027 (services consisted of tracing funds); Banks v. United States, 204 F.2d 666 (8th Cir. 1953) (attorney acting also in capacity of agent in negotiations with Internal Revenue Officer); Pollock v. United States, 202 F.2d 281 (5th Cir. 1953) (money deposited with attorney to be applied on purchase of real estate); Hansen v. Janitschek, 31 N.J. 545, 158 A. 2d 329 (1960) (attorney-client relationship held not to exist where attorney employed solely to assist in obtaining loan). See also Zenith Radio Corp. v. Radio Corp. of America, 121 F.Supp. 792 (D.Del.1954) critically noted 23 Geo.Wash.L.Rev. 786 (1955) (attorney-employee of corporate patent department would be regarded as "acting as a lawyer" within discovery rule when preponderantly engaged in giving legal advice but not when largely concerned with technical aspects of a business or engineering character). In Sperti Products, Inc. v. Coca-Cola Co., 262 F.Supp. 148 (D.Del.1966) the same court held that the rule of Zenith did not extend to take communications between clients and outside attorneys who represent them before the Patent Office from out the privilege. The Court cited Chore-Time Equipment, Inc. v. Big Dutchman, Inc., 255 F.Supp. 1020 (W.D.Mich. 1966) (communications between outside patent attorney and client privileged).

For cases on the above as well as related categories, see C.J.S. Witnesses § 280.

cations between a client and administrative practitioners who are not attorneys,[30] although the privilege may apply when the same services are performed by lawyers.[31]

Ordinarily an attorney can lawfully hold himself out as qualified to practice only in the state in which he is licensed, and consultation elsewhere on a continuing basis would ordinarily not be privileged,[32] but exceptionally by custom he might lawfully be consulted elsewhere in respect to isolated transactions.[33]

Traditionally, the relationship sought to be fostered by the privilege has been that between the lawyer and a private client, but more recently the privilege has been held to extend to communications to an attorney representing the state.[34] However, disclosures to the public prosecuting attorney by an informer are not within the attorney-client privilege,[35] but an analogous policy of protecting the giving of such information has led to the recognition of a privilege against the disclosure of the identity of the informer, unless the trial judge finds that such disclosure is necessary in the interests of justice.[36] Communications to an attorney appointed by the court to serve the interest of a party are of course within the privilege.[37] A communication by a lawyer to a member of the Board of Governors of the state bar association, revealing a fraudulent conspiracy in which he had been engaged and expressing his desire to resign from the practice of law was held not privileged.[38]

Wigmore argued for a privilege analogous to the lawyer-client privilege for "confessions or similar confidences" made privately by persons implicated in a wrong or crime to the judge of a court.[39] As to judges generally there seems little justification for such a

30. U. S. v. Zakutansky, 401 F.2d 68 (7th Cir. 1968), cert. denied 393 U.S. 1021 (work papers used by accountant in preparing tax return); Falsone v. United States, 205 F.2d 734 (5th Cir. 1953) (certified public accountant having the same rights as an enrolled attorney under Treasury Department regulations); United States v. United Shoe Machinery Corp., 89 F.Supp. 357 (1950) (patent solicitors not members of bar employed in corporation's patent department); Kent Jewelry Corp. v. Kiefer, 113 N.Y.S.2d 12 (Sup.1952) (patent agent authorized to practice before the United States Patent Office).

31. United States v. Summe, 208 F.Supp. 925 (D.C. Ky.1962) (lawyer employed to fill out tax return); Ellis-Foster Co. v. Union Carbide & Carbon Corp., 159 F.Supp. 917 (D.C.N.J.1958), reversed on other grounds in 284 F.2d 917 (3d Cir. 1962) (patent office proceedings conducted by lawyer). See Petersen, Attorney-Client Privilege in Internal Revenue Service Investigations, 54 Minn.L.Rev. 67 (1969).

32. United States v. United Shoe Machinery Corp., 89 F.Supp. 357 (D.Mass.1950).

33. Zenith Radio Corp. v. Radio Corp. of America, 121 F.Supp. 792, 794 (D.Del.1954) ("Bar membership should properly be of the court for the area wherein the services are rendered, but this is not a sine qua non, e. g., visiting counsel, long distance services by correspondence, pro hac vice services, 'house counsel' who practice law only for the corporate client and its affiliates and not for the public generally, for which local authorities do not insist on admission to the local bar."); Georgia Pac. Plywood Co. v. United States Plywood Corp., 18 F.R.D. 463 (S.D.N.Y.1956) (where house counsel of corporation not licensed in state where suit pending was actively engaged in legal service to corporation in multi-state litigation communications with him relating to legal service were privileged); Paper Converting Machine Co. v. F. M. C. Corp., 215 F.Supp. 249 (E.D.Wis.1963) (patent counsel member of Ohio bar but not of California bar where employed, communications held privileged).

34. People v. Glen Arms Estate, Inc., 41 Cal.Rptr. 303, 230 Cal.App.2d 841 (1965); Hartford Accident & Indemnity Co. v. Cutter, 108 N.H. 112, 229 A.2d 173 (1967); Riddle Spring Realty Co. v. State, 107 N.H. 271, 220 A.2d 751 (1966) (appraisals and reports confidentially made at request of attorney for state held privileged).

35. Fite v. Bennett, 142 Ga. 660, 83 S.E. 515 (1914); Cole v. Andrews, 74 Minn. 93, 76 N.W. 962 (1898); Application of Heller, 184 Misc. 75, 53 N.Y.S.2d 86 (1945).

36. Wilson v. United States, 59 F.2d 390, (3d Cir. 1932); 8 Wigmore, Evidence (McNaughton rev.) §§ 2374, 2375.

37. Jayne v. Bateman, 191 Okl. 272, 129 P.2d 188 (1942) (lawyer appointed as guardian ad litem of incompetent party apparently expected to act as attorney also).

38. Steiner v. United States, 134 F.2d 931 (5th Cir. 1943).

39. 8 Wigmore, Evidence (McNaughton rev.) § 2376.

privilege if the policy-motive is the furtherance of the administration of justice by encouraging a full disclosure.[40]   Unlike the
lawyer the judge needs no private disclosures
in advance of trial to enable him to perform
his functions.   In fact such revelations would
ordinarily embarrass rather than aid him in
carrying out his duties as a trial judge.[41]   The
famous case of Lindsey v. People,[42] however,
raised the question whether the judge of a
juvenile court does not stand in a special
position with regard to confidential disclosures by children who come before him.   The
majority of the court held that when a boy
under promise of secrecy confessed to the
judge that he had fired the shot that killed
his father the judge was compellable, on the
trial of the boy's mother for murder, to divulge the confession.   The court pointed out
that a parent who had received such a confidence would be compellable to disclose.   In
the case of this particular court the need for
encouraging confidences is clear, but in most
cases the most effective encouragement will
come from the confidence-inspiring personality of the judge, even without the aid of
assurances of secrecy.[43]   The court's conclu-

sion that the need for secrecy for this type
of disclosure does not outweigh the sacrifice
to the administration of justice from the suppression of the evidence seems justifiable.

89.   Subject-Matter of the Privilege—(a) Communications.

The modern justification of the privilege,
namely, that of encouraging full disclosure
by the client for the furtherance of the administration of justice,[44] arguably gives no
foundation for extending the privilege beyond communications of the client or his
agents [45] to the lawyer or his clerk.[46]   Accordingly it may be claimed that, in keeping
with the policy of restricting rather than extending privileges which shut out relevant
evidence,[47] the courts should in states where
the question is open confine the privilege to
those communications.   There are statutes [48]

---

40.   Authority is scanty.   People v. Pratt, 133 Mich.
125, 94 N.W. 752, 67 L.R.A. 923 (1903) tends to
support the privilege.   Of opposite tendency are
People v. Sharac, 209 Mich. 249, 176 N.W. 431
(1920); Agnew v. Agnew, 52 S.D. 472, 218 N.W.
633 (1928), and Lindsey v. People, cited in n. 43,
infra.

41.   Prichard v. United States, 181 F.2d 326 (6th Cir.
1950), aff'd 339 U.S. 974 (communications between
judge and attorney seeking legal advice concerning
his conduct which was to be investigated by a
grand jury called by the judge to investigate election frauds, not privileged and attorney-client relationship did not arise).

42.   66 Colo. 343, 181 P. 531, 16 A.L.R. 768 (1919)
(three judges dissenting), discussed in 33 Harv.L.
Rev. 88, 35 id. 693, 29 Yale L.J. 356, 4 Minn.L.Rev.
227; State v. Bixby, 27 Wash.2d 144, 177 P.2d 689
(1947).

43.   The special nature of juvenile court proceedings
with respect to the need for confidentiality of reports and records is recognized by modern juvenile
court statutes.   See statutes set out in 8 Wigmore,
Evidence § 2376 n. 3 (McNaughton rev.).

Cases recognizing the application of the informer's
privilege for information given to judges (see cases
pro and con collected in Annot., 59 A.L.R. 1555) are
to be distinguished.

44.   See § 87, supra.

45.   Anderson v. Bank of British Columbia [1876]
L.R. 2, Ch. D. 644 (Ct.App.); Wheeler v. Le Mar-
chant [1881] L.R. 17 Ch. D. 675 (Ct.App.);   State
v. 62.96247 Acres of Land in New Castle County,
193 A.2d 799 (Del.Super.1963) (expert appraiser
employed by client who aided attorney in preparation of case barred by privilege from testifying
for opponents); Annot., 139 A.L.R. 1250; Note,
1943 Wis.L.Rev. 424.

46.   United States v. Kovel, 296 F.2d 918 (2d Cir.
1961) (statements to accountant in employ of attorney);   State v. Krich, 123 N.J.L. 519, 9 A.2d 803
(1939) (communication to attorney's secretary);
Wigmore, Evidence (McNaughton rev.) § 2301;
Annot., 53 A.L.R. 369.

47.   See §§ 77, 86, supra.

48.   See, e. g., the Arkansas, California, Indiana,
Kentucky, Missouri and Ohio statutes set out in
8 Wigmore, Evidence (McNaughton rev.) § 2292 n.
2.

F.R.Ev. (R.D.1971) 503:
"(b) General Rule of Privilege.   A client has a privilege to refuse to disclose and to prevent any other
person from disclosing confidential communications made for the purpose of facilitating the rendition of professional legal services to the client,
(1) between himself or his representative and his
lawyer or his lawyer's representative, or (2) be-

and decisions [49] however which extend the protection to communications by the lawyer to the client. If offered to show circumstantially the client's own communications,[50] or as an admission of the client by his failure to object, there is reason, particularly in the former instance, for considering them as being in effect communications of the client, and extending the shield.[51] And in fact they seem unlikely to be offered on any other theory.

tween his lawyer and the lawyer's representative, or (3) by him or his lawyer to a lawyer representing another in a matter of common interest, or (4) between representatives of the client or between the client and a representative of the client."

49. Schwimmer v. United States, 232 F.2d 855 (8th Cir. 1956); United States v. United Shoe Machinery Corp., 89 F.Supp. 357 (1950); Sovereign Camp W. O. W. v. Ward, 196 Ala. 327, 71 So. 404 (1916); Missouri, K. and T. Ry. Co. v. Williams, 43 Tex. Civ.App. 549, 96 S.W. 1087 (1906).

50. As would have been the effect in the cases cited in the next previous note.

51. A defamatory statement made by the lawyer in declining employment and sought to be proved solely as a basis for an action against the lawyer for slander was held privileged in Minter v. Priest, [1929] 1 K.B. 655. It is criticized as unwarranted by the policy of the privilege in a Note, 43 Harv. L.Rev. 134.

Communications upon their respective clients' business between counsel defending them against a common charge have been said to be within the privilege. Continental Oil Co. v. United States, 330 F.2d 347, 9 A.L.R.3d 1413 (9th Cir. 1964) (exchange of confidential memoranda between counsel for several clients summoned before grand jury investigating antitrust violations); In re Felton, 60 Idaho 540, 94 P.2d 166 (1939); C.J.S. Witnesses § 276e; Annot., 9 A.L.R.3d 1420.

F.R.Ev. (R.D.1971) 503(b) (3), dealing with "pooled information" cases, is set forth in note 48, supra.

See also Missouri, K. & T. Ry. Co. v. Williams, 43 Tex.Civ.App. 549, 96 S.W. 1087 (1906) (general counsel of railway writes to local attorney). United States v. United Shoe Machinery Corp., 89 F. Supp. 357 (privilege extends to communications to and from corporation's outside counsel or general counsel and staff and employees in its patent department); Gen. Acc. Fire & Life Assur. Corp. v. Mitchell, 259 P.2d 862 (Colorado, 1953) (order for production of all correspondence between home office and local counsel and local agents and all telegrams and written memoranda between home office, its attorneys and agents and insured, should have been denied on ground of privilege).

Some statutes likewise draw the curtain over matters of which the attorney has gained knowledge while acting as such, but from sources other than the client.[52] This seemingly carries the obstructive effect of the privilege far beyond any justification in present-day policy, and is probably a carry-over from the days when the privilege was thought of as primarily for the protection of the honor of the profession. However, the matter is not free from difficulty. A confidential communication may be made by acts as well as by words, as if the client rolled up his sleeve to show the lawyer a hidden scar, or opened the drawer of his desk to show a revolver there. Certainly the fact that the client made the communication and its contents as a communication would be privileged against disclosure by either client or attorney.[53] Also the facts communicated would

52. See, e. g., the Alabama, Georgia, and Louisiana statutes quoted in 8 Wigmore, Evidence (McNaughton rev.) § 2292, n. 2, and Vernon's Texas Ann.C.C.P. art. 713.

53. City and County of San Francisco v. Superior Ct., 37 Cal.2d 227, 231 P.2d 26 (1951); State v. Douglass, 20 W.Va. 770 (1882) (counsel's testimony that he received pistol from client, privileged).

"The rule of privileged communications arose in order that a party might with safety completely inform his attorney as to the matters in which he is employed to the end that the attorney might act with full understanding of them. The limits of the rule, however, are well defined, and as its tendency is to stifle a full disclosure of the truth, courts have been careful to confine it within its legitimate scope, and so it has been held that the rule does not apply to the discovery of facts within the knowledge of an attorney which were not communicated by a client, though he became acquainted with such facts while engaged as attorney for the client. Crosby v. Berger, 11 Paige (N.Y.) 377, 42 Am.Dec. 177." Tutson v. Holland, 50 F.2d 338, 340 (D.C.Cir.1931). See also Hawley v. Hawley, 114 F.2d 745 (D.C.Cir.1940) (attorney's knowledge of client's handwriting, though gained while in employ, not privileged); Kerr v. Hofer, 347 Pa. 356, 32 A.2d 402 (1943) (information about accident obtained by lawyer, not from client, not privileged); Burton v. McLaughlin, 117 Utah 483, 217 P.2d 566 (1950) (facts observed by attorney as to services rendered client when attorney visited client in his home to draw up will and on subse-

be privileged against disclosure by the attorney, since a contrary ruling would in effect, disclose the communication, provided in the latter case the facts would not have been apparent to the lawyer in the absence of any effort by the client to reveal them.[54] But the facts would not be privileged against disclosure by the client, since he knew them already and no disclosure of the communication results. The difficulty arises when one assisting the lawyer, e. g., an examining physician, learns and communicates to the lawyer matters not known to the client. The privilege seems to apply with respect to the communication itself. If the physician is considered as aligned with the client, his knowledge would be that of the client and not privileged; but if aligned with the lawyer, the privilege seems to apply, as held in the leading case.[55]

The application of the privilege to writings presents practical problems requiring discriminating analysis. A professional communication in writing, as a letter from client to lawyer for example, will of course be privileged.[56] These written privileged communications are steadily to be distinguished from preexisting documents or writings, such as deeds, wills, and warehouse receipts, not in themselves constituting communications between client and lawyer. As to these pre-existing documents two notions come into play. First, the client may make communications about the document by words or by acts, such as sending the document to the lawyer for perusal or handing to him and calling attention to its terms. These communications, and the knowledge of the terms and appearance of the documents which the lawyer gains thereby are privileged from disclosure by testimony in court.[57] Second, on a different footing entirely stands the question, shall a lawyer who has been entrusted with the possession of a document by his client be subject to an order of court requiring him to produce the document at the trial or in pretrial discovery proceedings whether for inspection or for use in evidence? The policy of encouraging full disclosure does of course apply to encouraging the client to apprise his lawyer of the terms of all relevant docu-

quent visits as a friend); and see C.J.S. Witnesses § 283e.

54. Clark v. Skinner, 334 Mo. 1190, 70 S.W.2d 1094 (1934) (attorney's knowledge of client's mental capacity and of want of any undue influence and that deeds were delivered, not privileged); State v. Fitzgerald, 68 Vt. 125, 34 A. 429 (1896) (attorney's testimony to client's intoxication, observable by all, not privileged); 8 Wigmore, Evidence (McNaughton rev.) § 2306.

Of course, where the client calls in the attorney as a witness to a transaction with a third person, though the client desires that the attorney keep secret the details of the transaction, there is no privilege. McKnew v. Superior Court, 23 Cal.2d 58, 142 P.2d 1 (1943) (attorney asked by client to witness client's making deposit of money in bank, so that attorney could verify deposit to enable client to secure credit, with understanding attorney not to reveal name of bank, held no privilege for latter fact); Note, 17 So.Calif.L.Rev. 410.

55. City and County of San Francisco v. Superior Court, n. 54, supra. Unless this is regarded as privileged, F.R.Civ.P. 26(b) (4) (B) seems to permit discovery in such case if hardship is shown. Distinguish the situation of the expert who examines for the purpose of testifying, thus contemplating disclosure and eliminating the privilege. See § 91, n. 77, infra.

56. Peyton v. Werhane, 126 Conn. 382, 11 A.2d 800 (1940).

An interesting case presented the question whether confidential letters of the client were usable, not as evidence of their contents but as specimens for comparison by expert witnesses with an anonymous letter charged to have been written by the client. People v. Smith, 318 Ill. 114, 149 N.E. 3 (1925) (not privileged against use for this purpose).

57. Wheatley v. Williams, 1 M. & W. 533, 150 Eng. Rep. 546 (Exch.1836) (attorney not required to testify whether paper shown him by client bore a stamp); Arbuckle v. Templeton, 65 Vt. 205, 25 A. 1095 (1892) (whether note exhibited to lawyer by client bore an endorsement); C.J.S. Witnesses § 283l.

But the act of the execution of a document by the client in the lawyer's presence is not ordinarily intended as a confidential communication and thus is usually not privileged. Chapman v. Peebles, 84 Ala. 283, 4 So. 273 (1888). A fortiori, when the attorney signs as a witness and takes the acknowledgment of the client as a notary. McCaw v. Hartman, 190 Okl. 264, 122 P.2d 999 (1942).

ments, and the disclosure itself and the lawyer's knowledge gained thereby as we have seen is privileged. It is true also that placing the documents in the lawyer's hands is the most convenient means of disclosure. But the next step, that of adding to the privilege for communications a privilege against production of the pre-existing documents themselves, when they would be subject to production if still in the possession of the client, would be an intolerable obstruction to justice. To prevent the court's gaining access to a relevant document a party would only have to send it to his lawyer. So here the principle is controlling: if a document would be subject to an order for production if it were in the hands of the client it will be equally subject to such an order if it is in the hands of his attorney.[58] An opposite conclusion would serve the policy of encouraging the client to make full disclosure to his lawyer right enough, but reasonable encouragement is given by the privilege for communications about documents, and the price of an additional privilege would be intolerably high. There are other doctrines which may impel a court to recognize a privilege against production of a pre-existing document,[59] but not the doctrine of privilege for lawyer-client communications.

90. Subject-Matter of the Privilege—(b) Fact of Employment and Identity of the Client.

When a client consults an attorney for a legitimate purpose, he will seldom, but may occasionally, desire to keep secret the very fact of consultation or employment of the lawyer. Nevertheless, consultation and employment are something more than a mere private or personal engagement. They are the calling into play of the services of an officer licensed by the state to act in certain ways in furtherance of the administration of justice, and vested with powers of giving advice on the law, of drafting documents, and of filing pleadings and motions and appearing in court for his client, which are limited to this class of officers.

Does the privilege for confidential communications, extend to the fact of consulting or employing such an officer, when intended to be confidential? The weight of authority denies the privilege for the fact of consultation or employment,[60] including the component facts of the identity of the client,[61] such identifying facts about him as his

---

58. Falsone v. U. S., 205 F.2d 734 (5th Cir. 1953); Sovereign Camp v. Reed, 208 Ala. 457, 94 So. 910 (1922); Andrews v. Railway Co., 14 Ind. 169, 174 (1860); Palatini v. Sarian, 15 N.J.Super. 34, 83 A.2d 24 (1951); Pearson v. Yoder, 39 Okl. 105, 134 Pac. 421, 48 L.R.A.,N.S., 334 (1913); 8 Wigmore, Evidence (McNaughton rev.) § 2307.

And as a necessary incident the attorney may be required to testify whether he has possession of such a document of the client. Guiterman, Rosenfield & Co. v. Culbreth, 219 Ala. 382, 122 So. 619 (1929).

In State ex rel. Sowers v. Olwell, 64 Wash.2d 828, 394 P.2d 681, 16 A.L.R.3d 1021 (1964), a knife presumably obtained by the attorney from his client was held not within the privilege, but the prosecution was barred from disclosing its source; the privilege against self-incrimination was held not claimable by the attorney for the client.

59. See § 96, infra.

60. Behrens v. Hironimus, 170 F.2d 627 (4th Cir. 1948). See authorities collected in 8 Wigmore, Evidence (McNaughton rev.) § 2313; C.J.S. Witnesses § 283e; Annot., 16 A.L.R.3d 1047.

61. Behrens v. Hironimus, 170 F.2d 627 (4th Cir. 1948); Tomlinson v. United States, 68 App.D.C. 106, 93 F.2d 652, 114 A.L.R. 1315 (1937) (robbery: one of the defendants, a lawyer, testified on direct, that a codefendant was brought into his office by "a client," held, he was properly required on cross-examination to identify the client); Mauch v. Commissioner of Internal Revenue, 113 F.2d 555 (3d Cir. 1940) (attorney who claimed bank deposits in his name were for clients required to disclose their identity); United States v. Pape, 144 F.2d 778 (2d Cir. 1944) (prosecution for violation of White Slave Traffic Act; lawyer-witness properly allowed to be asked by prosecution whether accused employed him to represent the woman whom he was charged with transporting and himself; Learned Hand, Cir. J., dissenting); In re Richardson, 31 N.J. 391, 157 A.2d 695 (1960) (attorney-client relation does not privilege lawyer from disclosing the identity of the person who retained him, or of the person who paid his fee; able opinion by Jacobs, J., citing prior decisions); People ex rel.

address [62] and occupation,[63] the identity of the lawyer,[64] and the scope or object of the employment.[65]

Vogelstein v. Warden of County Jail, 150 Misc. 714, 270 N.Y.S. 362 (S.Ct.Sp.T.1934, affirmed without opinion, 242 App.Div. 611, 271 N.Y.S. 1059) (attorney who entered appearance for fifteen defendants charged with violation of gambling laws, required in grand jury investigation to testify as to whether one person, the man behind the scene, had not employed him to act for all these defendants; opinion by Shientag, J., is the best on the question); In re Illidge, 162 Ore. 303, 91 P.2d 1100 (1939) (attorney accused in disbarment proceedings properly compelled to testify as to identity and residence of client for whom he had entered appearance as counsel in a lawsuit).

Contra: Ex parte McDonough, 170 Calif. 230, 149 P. 566, L.R.A.1916C, 593, Ann.C.1916E, 327 (facts similar to People v. Warden, supra; court reviews the authorities elaborately; dissenting opinion by Lawlor, J.); cases cited in note 68, infra; comment 28 U.Chi.L.Rev. 533 (1961).

62. United States v. Lee, 107 F. 702 (E.D.N.Y. 1901); Falkenhainer v. Falkenhainer, 198 Misc. 29, 97 N.Y.S.2d 467 (1950); Dike v. Dike, 75 Wash.2d 1, 448 P.2d 490 (1968) (whereabouts of client who had possession of child in violation of custody order); Annot., 114 A.L.R. 1328.

63. Tomlinson v. United States, supra n. 61.

64. Goddard v. United States, 131 F.2d 220 (5th Cir. 1942).

65. Upon an issue as to whether some act done by the attorney was authorized, the attorney may testify as to the terms of employment. Pacific Tel. & Tel. Co. v. Fink, 141 Cal.App.2d 332, 296 P. 2d 843 (1956) (authority to enter into stipulation under which default judgment was taken); Sachs v. Title Ins. & Trust Co., 305 Ky. 153, 202 S.W.2d 384 (1947) (on question whether defendant in prior judgment was before court attorney who appeared for her can testify to employment to defend suit); Kentucky-Virginia Stages v. Tackett, 298 Ky. 78, 182 S.W.2d 226 (1944) (whether one of attorneys in instant case was authorized to file motion for new trial); Coley v. Hall, 206 Ark. 419, 175 S.W. 2d 979 (1943) (client claimed attorney who filed suit was unauthorized); Falkenhainer v. Falkenhainer, 198 Misc. 29, 97 N.Y.S.2d 467 (1950).

It may be, however, that when the object of the employment is not directly in issue but only circumstantially relevant, the testimony would be limited to a more general statement of purpose. See Chirac v. Reinicker, 11 Wheat. (U.S.) 280 (1826) (in action for mesne profits, court intimated that attorneys could be asked whether they appeared in former ejectment suit for one of present defendants, but questioned whether they could be asked if they were employed by him to conduct the suit for him as landlord of the premises); Stephens v. Mattox, 37 Ga. 289 (1867) (similar; whether em-

Some reasons have been advanced which are sufficient for the particular situation but which should not be understood as limitations on the doctrine. Among these are: (1) that the fact of employment is not a confidential communication,—but we have seen that it may be the product of such a communication; (2) "the mere fact of the engagement of counsel is out of the rule [of privilege] because the privilege and duty of being silent do not arise until that fact is ascertained"; [66] (3) that a party to legal proceedings is entitled to know the identity of his adversary who is putting in motion or staying the machinery of the court,[67] and to know the authority of counsel appearing in adverse interest; but the rule should not be limited to employment in litigation,[68] and is

ployed by plaintiff to sue for him individually or in his right as administrator).

66. Shientag, J. in People v. Warden, 270 N.Y.S. at 369, cited note 2, supra. But the party propounding the question as to the identity of the client may state and assume that the relationship exists, so that there is no need to establish it. In re Shawmut Mining Co., 94 App.Div. 156, 87 N.Y.S. 1059, 1062 (1904).

67. "Every litigant is in justice entitled to know the identity of his opponents." 8 Wigmore, Evidence (McNaughton rev.) § 2313.

68. Compare Neugass v. Terminal Cab Corp., 139 Misc.Rep. 699, 249 N.Y.S. 631, 634 (1931) (action by occupant of taxicab injured in collision with another taxicab; plaintiff seeks order requiring attorney for owner of taxicab in which he was riding to disclose name of owner of other cab, for whom he was also acting as attorney for casualty company; motion denied. "His client is not seeking to use the courts, and his address cannot be disclosed on that theory. . . .").

See also N. L. R. B. v. Harvey, 264 F.Supp. 770 (W.D. Va.1966) on remand from 349 F.2d 990, 16 A.L.R. 3d 1035 (4th Cir. 1965) (identity of client held within privilege in National Labor Relations Board proceedings where an attorney not connected with the case under investigation employed a private investigator to keep a union organizer under surveillance at request of a client who was a business competitor of the employer in the N. L. R. B. proceeding); Tillotson v. Boughner, 350 F.2d 663 (7th Cir. 1965) and Baird v. Koerner, 279 F.2d 623, 95 A.L.R.2d 303; (9th Cir. 1960) noted in 49 Calif.L. Rev. 382, 388 (1961) 39 Tex.L.Rev. 512 (1961) 47 Va.L.Rev. 126 (1961) (in both these cases identity of clients was held within the privilege where

carried further by the next theory; (4) that the fact of employment should be disclosed where the employment is for a purpose of performing acts which would affect the rights of third persons;[69] this would seem to cover most employments but it is questionable whether even this should be imposed as a limitation. Finally, it has been suggested, (5) that where the fact of employment is relevant for other purposes it may be shown, but not where it is offered as evidence of an acknowledgment of guilt or of an admission of liability of the client.[70] This limitation would negative much of the effect of the rule of disclosure, and it is not generally accepted.[71]

The rule exempting the fact of employment, and the component facts such as the identity of the client, from the curtain of the privilege, seems to be based upon a judicial consideration of the balance of conflicting policies.[72] One who reviews the cases in this area will be struck with the prevailing flavor of chicanery and sharp practice pervading most of the attempts to suppress the proof of professional employment, and the broader solution of a general rule of disclosure seems the one most consonant with the preservation of the high repute of the lawyer's calling.[73] Cases may arise, however, where protection of the client's identity is conceivably in the public interest.[74]

91. The Confidential Character of the Communications: Presence of Third Persons and Agents: Joint Consultations and Employments: Controversies Between Client and Attorney.

It is of the essence of the privilege that it is limited to those communications which the client either expressly made confidential or which he could reasonably assume under the circumstances would be understood by the attorney as so intended. This common law requirement seems to be read into those statutes which codify the privilege without mentioning the confidentiality requirement.[75] A mere showing that

anonymous checks were delivered by attorneys to Internal Revenue Service on behalf of unidentified taxpayers). In these cases it may well be questioned whether the attorney was not in fact merely purveying anonymity, scarcely a professional legal service. This suspicion is enhanced by *Baird's* reliance upon a California Bar ethics opinion stating that an attorney retained to collect a reward for a watch, without disclosing the client's identity could not disclose her identity when a warrant was issued for his arrest for theft. A strange activity for a lawyer! Cf. Hughes v. Meade, 453 S.W.2d 538 (Ky.1970) (lawyer employed to return stolen property could not withhold identity of client because not rendering legal service), noted 59 Ky.L. J. 229 (1970).

69. In re Shawmut Mining Co., 94 App.Div. 156, 87 N.Y.S. 1059, 1063 (1904).

70. Ex parte McDonough, supra n. 61, 149 P. at p. 568; In re Shawmut Mining Co., supra n. 69.

71. See, e. g., United States v. Pape, In re Illidge, and People v. Warden, supra n. 61 and cases cited in Annot., 16 A.L.R.3d 1047–1068.

72. See discussion of Clark, Circ. J., in Mauch v. Commissioner of Internal Revenue, 113 F.2d 555, 556 (3d Cir. 1940).

73. "The conclusion reached would seem to be inevitable, if we are to maintain the honor of the profession, and make an officer of the court an agency to advance the ends of justice, rather than to be used as an instrument to subvert them. The identity of an employer or client who retains a lawyer to act for him or for others in a civil or criminal proceeding should not be veiled in mystery. The dangers of disclosure are shadowy and remote; the evils of concealment are patent and overwhelming. As between the two social policies competing for supremacy, the choice is clear. Disclosure should be made if we are to maintain confidence in the bar and in the administration of justice." Shientag, J. in People v. Warden, supra n. 61, 270 N.Y.S. at p. 371.

74. In re Kaplan, 8 N.Y.2d 214, 168 N.E.2d 660, 203 N.Y.S.2d 836 (1960) (client's communication to attorney for purpose of disclosing wrongdoing by others communicated by attorney to public officials held to justify protection of identity of client) noted in 10 Buffalo L.Rev. 364 (1961), 46 Iowa L.Rev. 904 (1961), 59 Mich.L.Rev. 791 (1961), 12 Syracuse L. Rev. 408 (1961). Cf. Hughes v. Meade, supra, n. 68.

75. See, e. g., the Alabama, Arkansas, Georgia, Minnesota, Missouri, Nebraska, Ohio, Oklahoma, Tennessee, Wisconsin, and West Virginia statutes, privileging "communications" generally, quoted in 8 Wigmore, Evidence (McNaughton rev.) § 2292, note 2.

the communication was from client to attorney does not suffice, but the circumstances indicating the intention of secrecy must appear.[76] Wherever the matters communicated to the attorney are intended by the client to be made public or revealed to third persons, obviously the element of confidentiality is wanting.[77] Similarly, if the same statements have been made by the client to third persons on other occasions this is persuasive that like communications to the lawyer were not intended as confidential.[78]

Questions as to the effect of the presence of persons other than the client and the lawyer often arise. At the extremes answers would be clear. Presumably the presence of a casual disinterested third person within hearing to the client's knowledge would demonstrate that the communication was not intended to be confidential.[79] On the other hand if the help of an interpreter is necessary to enable the client to consult the lawyer his presence would not deprive the communication of its confidential and privileged character.[80] Moreover, in cases where the client has one of his agents attend the conference,[81] or the lawyer calls in his clerk [82] or

76. Gardner v. Irvin, L.R.Exch.Div. 49, 53 (1878); Hiltpold v. Stern, 82 A.2d 123, 26 A.L.R.2d 852 (D.C.Mun.App.1951).

77. United States v. Tellier, 255 F.2d 441 (2d Cir. 1958), 37 Texas L.Rev. 337 (attorney's advice to client where client expected attorney to prepare letter to third person setting forth his objections); Wilcoxon v. United States, 231 F.2d 384 (10th Cir. 1956) cert. denied 351 U.S. 943 (private directions by client to attorney on preliminary hearing that he should propound certain questions to witness, not privileged); Himmelfarb v. United States, 175 F.2d 924 (9th Cir. 1949) cert. denied 338 U.S. 860 (disclosures to accountant by attorney, impliedly authorized by client under special circumstances of previous meetings with accountant concerning income taxes and client's knowledge of accountant's employment with attorney); Hill v. Hill, 106 Colo. 492, 107 P.2d 597 (1940) (letters by wife to attorney giving data on alimony in arrears, with intention that he should present the information to delinquent husband); Spencer v. Burns, 413 Ill. 420, 108 N.E.2d 413 (1952) (statement of true marital status made by client for purpose of transmission to seller and examiner of title to property client wished to purchase); Clayton v. Canida, 223 S.W.2d 264 (Tex.Civ.App.1949) (information given to attorney for use in preparing income tax return for transmittal to Internal Revenue Department); Anderson v. Thomas, 108 Utah 252, 159 P.2d 142 (1945) (suit to cancel deed of deceased for mental incapacity, testimony of attorney that deceased asked him to arrange for bank not to cash his checks without attorney's approval, not privileged. Good discussion of confidentiality-requirement by Wolfe, J.).

78. Solon v. Lichtenstein, 39 Cal.2d 75, 244 P.2d 907 (1952); Bryan v. Barnett, 205 Ga. 94, 52 S.E.2d 613 (1949); Travelers Indemnity Co. v. Cochrane, 155 Ohio St. 305, 98 N.E.2d 840 (1951).

79. Mason v. Mason, 231 S.W. 971 (Mo.1921); Re Quick's Estate, 161 Wash. 537, 297 P. 198 (1931), and cases collected in 8 Wigmore, Evidence (McNaughton rev.) § 2311, note 6; C.J.S. Witnesses § 290; Note, Privilege as Affected by the Presence of Third Parties, 36 Mich.L.Rev. 641 (1938). See also cases collected in Annot., 96 A.L.R.2d 125.

In the case of persons overhearing without the knowledge of the client, it seems that the more reasonable view if there is to be any privilege at all, would protect the client against disclosure, unless he has failed to use ordinary precautions against overhearing, but the cases permit the eavesdropper to speak. Van Horn v. Commonwealth, 239 Ky. 833, 40 S.W.2d 372 (1931), and see Perry v. State, 4 Idaho 224, 38 P. 655 (1894) (court mentions want of precaution); Schwartz v. Wenger, 267 Minn. 40, 124 N.W.2d 489 (1963) (conversation between client and attorney in public corridor of courthouse overheard by third person, held not privileged). But cf. F.R.Ev. (R.D.1971) 503(b) which allows the client to prevent disclosure by third persons who overhear communications intended to be confidential.

80. Du Barre v. Linette, Peake 108, 170 Eng.Rep. 96 (N.P.1791); State v. Loponio, 85 N.J.L. 357, 88 A. 1045 (1913).

In United States v. Kovel, 296 F.2d 918 (2d Cir. 1961), the court relied upon the analogy of an interpreter, in applying the privilege to an accountant employed by the lawyer to assist in the litigation.

81. In re Busse's Estate, 332 Ill.App. 258, 75 N.E. 36, 38 (1947) (client's agent who was nurse and business caretaker present at conference with attorney); Foley v. Poschke, 137 Ohio St. 593, 31 N.E.2d 845 (1941) (detective employed by divorce plaintiff to investigate husband's conduct present at conference with lawyer).

Of course, the presence of additional counsel to participate in the consultation does not detract from confidentiality. Dickerson v. Dickerson, 322 Ill. 492, 153 N.E. 740 (1926).

82. Sibley v. Wopple, 16 N.Y. 180 (1857); Hunt v. Taylor, 22 Vt. 556 (1850); Annot., 96 A.L.R.2d 125, 133.

confidential secretary,[83] the presence of these intermediaries will be assumed not to militate against the confidential nature of the consultation, and presumably this would not be made to depend upon whether the presence of the agent, clerk or secretary was in the particular instance reasonably necessary to the matter in hand.[84] It is the way business is generally done and that is enough. As to relatives and friends of the client, the results of the cases are not consistent,[85] but

it seems that here not only might it be asked whether the client reasonably understood the conference to be confidential but also whether the presence of the relative or friend was reasonably necessary for the protection of the client's interests in the particular circumstances.[86]

When two or more persons, each having an interest in some problem or situation, jointly consult an attorney, their confidential communications with the attorney, though known to each other, will of course be privileged in a controversy of either or both of the clients with the outside world, that is, with parties claiming adversely to both or either of those within the original charmed circle.[87] But it will often happen that the two original clients will fall out among themselves and become engaged in a controversy in which the communications at their joint consultation with the lawyer may be vitally material. In such a controversy it is clear that the privilege is inapplicable. In the first place the policy of encouraging disclo-

A substantial number of state statutes provide that communications to the employees of the attorney are privileged. See statutes collected and quoted, 8 Wigmore, Evidence (McNaughton rev.) § 2292, note 2. And disclosures to a physician employed by the client's attorney to examine the client have been held subject to the attorney-client privilege. City & County of San Francisco v. Superior Court, 37 Cal.2d 227, 231 P.2d 26 (1951); Annot., 96 A.L.R. 2d 159, 160.

A law student in the office is not within the rule, unless he acts as clerk. Wartell v. Navograd, 48 R.I. 296, 137 A. 776, 53 A.L.R. 365 (1927).

83. Taylor v. Taylor, 179 Ga. 691, 693, 177 S.E. 582 (1934) ("Under modern practice of law the business of an attorney in most offices cannot be conducted without such an assistant"; Ga.Code, § 38–419, however, expressly extended privilege to communications to attorney "or his clerk"). A Texas case would seemingly give the privilege only when the secretary or stenographer is the medium of communication. Otherwise, the court suggests "it could as well be claimed that the rule would extend to the employee, who swept the attorney's floor." Morton v. Smith, 44 S.W. 683, 684 (Tex. Civ.App.1898) (stenograher allowed to testify to statements made by client to attorney).

84. But compare Morton v. Smith, supra, and Himmelfarb v. United States, 175 F.2d 924 (9th Cir. 1949) (testimony of accountant employed as attorney's agent, not privileged where his presence at conference with client was not indispensably necessary to communication between attorney and client). Cf. United States v. Kovel, n. 80, supra.

85. Cafritz v. Koslow, 167 F.2d 749 (D.C.Cir. 1948) (sister accompanies brother, client, to attorney's office; "There was no identity of interest between [brother and sister] nor can it be said that [sister] stood in relation of agent to [brother]"); Baldwin v. Commissioner of Internal Revenue, 125 F.2d 812, (9th Cir. 1942) (son accompanied mother to conferences with her attorney over proposed transfer of some of her property to son, held presence of son did not destroy privilege but chiefly on ground that it was joint consultation in which son was interested); Smith v. State, 204 Ga. 184, 47 S.E. 579 (1948) (murder prosecution, evidence of what was said in conference with attorney by wife of

defendant, when deceased was present, held privileged, without discussion); Bowers v. State, 29 Ohio St. 542, 546 (1876) (prosecution for seduction of girl under eighteen; girl's statements at conference with attorney consulted about bastardy proceedings against defendant held privileged despite presence of girl's mother).

86. Compare the remarks of the court in Bowers v. State, in the preceding note: "We think it is only a dictate of decency and propriety to regard the mother in such a case as being present and acting in the character of confidential agent of her daughter. The daughter's youth and supposed modesty would render the participation of her mother appropriate and necessary." 29 Ohio St. at 546.

87. People v. Abair, 102 Cal.App.2d 765, 228 P.2d 336 (1951); In re Selser, 27 N.J.Super. 259, 99 A.2d 313 (1953); State v. Archuleta, 29 N.M. 25, 217 Pac. 619 (1923) and cases cited in Annot., 141 A.L.R. 562 (communication privileged as against the state in a criminal case, although parties fall out and one acts as witness against others); Minard v. Stillman, 31 Ore. 164, 49 Pac. 976 (1897); Vance v. State, 190 Tenn. 521, 230 S.W.2d 987, cert. den. 339 U.S. 988 (communications at conference between codefendants and their separate counsel in preparation of joint defense, privileged as against the state in a criminal case, but not privileged where one defendant makes no defense).

sure by holding out the promise of protection seems inapposite, since as between themselves neither would know whether he would be more helped or handicapped, if in any dispute between them, both could invoke the shield of secrecy.   And secondly, it is said that they had obviously no intention of keeping these secrets from each other, and hence as between themselves it was not intended to be confidential.   In any event, it is a qualification of frequent application [88] and of even wider potentiality, not always recognized. Thus, in the situation mentioned in the previous paragraph where a client calls into the conference with the attorney one of the client's agents, and matters are discussed which bear on the agent's rights against the client, it would seem that in a subsequent controversy between client and agent, the limitation on the privilege accepted in the joint consultation cases should furnish a controlling analogy.[89]

One step beyond the joint consultation where communications by two clients are made directly in each other's hearing is the situation where two parties separately interested in some contract or undertaking as in the case of borrower and lender or insurer and insured, engage the same attorney to represent their respective interests, and each communicates separately with the attorney about some phase of the common transaction.   Here again it seems that the communicating client, knowing that the attorney represents the other party also, would not ordinarily intend that the facts communicated should be kept secret from him.[90]   Accordingly, the doctrine of limited confidentiality has been applied to communications by the insured under a liability insurance policy to the attorney employed by the insurance company to represent both the company and the insured.   A confidential statement made by the insured to the attorney, or to the insurer for the use of the attorney, would thus be privileged if sought to be introduced at the trial of the injured person's action against the insured,[91] but not in a controversy be-

---

88.   Grand Trunk Western R. Co. v. H. W. Nelson Co., 116 F.2d 823, reh. denied 118 F.2d 252 (6th Cir. 1941); Re Bauer, 79 Cal. 304, 21 Pac. 759 (1889); Luthy v. Seaburn, 242 Iowa 184, 46 N.W.2d 44 (1951); Thompson v. Cashman, 181 Mass. 36, 62 N.E. 976 (1902); Wahl v. Cunningham, 320 Mo. 57, 6 S.W.2d 576, 67 A.L.R. 489 (1928); Jenkins v. Jenkins, 151 Neb. 113, 36 N.W.2d 635 (1949); Hurlburt v. Hurlburt, 128 N.Y. 420, 28 N.E. 651, 26 Am.St.Rep. 482 (1891); Emley v. Selepchak, 76 Ohio App. 257, 63 N.E.2d 919 (1945); and cases cited in 8 Wigmore, Evidence (McNaughton rev.) § 2312; Annot., 141 A.L.R. 553.

It has been held that the beneficiary of a contract made by the jointly consulting clients at the conference or discussed thereat, stands in the shoes of the parties and is entitled to disclosure.   Allen v. Ross, 199 Wis. 162, 225 N.W. 831, A.L.R. 180 (1929).   So also as to personal representatives and others in privity.   Hurlburt v. Hurlburt, supra (action by administrator of one client against administratrix of the other).   Query as to judgment creditors, but seemingly they should be in like case. Annot., 141 A.L.R. 558.

The analogy to two persons consulting the same lawyer on a common matter has been invoked to deny a claim of privilege by management in stockholder's derivative suits with respect to communications between management and corporate counsel prior to the litigation.   Garner v. Wolfinbarger, 430 F.2d 1093 (5th Cir. 1970); Pattie Lea, Inc. v. District Court, 161 Colo. 493, 423 P.2d 27 (1967) (accountant privilege).   Cf. Note, 69 Colum.L.Rev. 309 (1969).

89.   But in the only cases encountered in which this situation was presented the analogy was not discussed and the privilege was sustained against the agent.   In re Busse's Estate and Foley v. Poschke, cited and described in note 81, supra.   The Busse case is criticized on this point in Note, 61 Harv. L.Rev. 717, and on another point in Note, 15 U. Chi.L.Rev. 989.

90.   See, e. g., Gottwald v. Mettinger, 257 App.Div. 107, 12 N.Y.2d 241 (1939) (in suit on bond where attorney originally represented borrower and lender in arranging loan, statement of borrower to attorney of amount owed, not privileged.)

91.   Vann v. State, 85 So.2d 133, (Fla.1956) (where policy required insurer to defend insured through its attorney, communications between the insured and insurer intended for the use of attorney, are privileged; In re Klemann, 132 Ohio St. 187, 5 N.E. 2d 492 (1936) (in suit of injured person, written statement made by insured to insurance company for transmittal to attorney held privileged).

tween the insured, or one claiming under him, and the company itself over the company's liability under the policy.[92]

The weight of authority seems to support the view that when client and attorney become embroiled in a controversy between themselves, as in an action by the attorney for compensation or by the client for damages for the attorney's negligence, the seal is removed from the attorney's lips.[93]

Though sometimes rested upon other grounds [94] it seems that here again the notion that as between the participants in the conference the intention was to disclose and not to withhold the matters communicated offers a plausible reason.[95] As to what is a controversy between lawyer and client the decisions do not limit their holdings to litigations between them, but have said that whenever the client, even in litigation between third persons, makes an imputation against the good faith of his attorney in respect to his professional services, the curtain of privilege drops so far as necessary to enable the lawyer to defend his conduct.[96] Perhaps the whole doctrine that in controversies between attorney and client the privilege is relaxed, may best be based upon the ground of practical necessity that if effective legal service is to be encouraged the privilege must not stand in the way of the lawyer's just enforcement of his rights to be paid a fee and to protect his reputation. The only question about such a principle is whether in all cases the privilege ought not to be subject to the same qualification, that it should yield when the evidence sought is necessary to the attainment of justice.

But see Jacobi v. Podevels, 23 Wis.2d 152, 127 N.W.2d 73 (1964) (statement by insured to adjuster for his insurer before commencement of action, not privileged).

92. Henke v. Iowa Home Mutual Casualty Co., 249 Iowa 614, 87 N.W.2d 920 (1958), 44 Iowa L.Rev. 215 (action by insured against insurer for negligent failure to settle claims against insured); Klefbeck v. Dous, 302 Mass. 383, 19 N.E.2d 308 (1939) (suit by injured party after judgment to subject policy to payment of judgment, defended by insurer on ground automobile not legally registered in state of issuance; held, plaintiff, claiming under insured, entitled to use letter of attorney, acting for both, to insurer); Travelers Indemnity Co. v. Cochrane, 155 Ohio St. 305, 98 N.E.2d 840 (1951); Shafer v. Utica Mut. Ins. Co., 248 App.Div. 279, 289 N.Y.S. 577 (1936) (action by injured party after judgment to subject policy to payment of judgment contested by company on ground of failure of insured to cooperate; held, company entitled to prove statements of insured to joint attorney); Liberty Mutual Ins. Co. v. Engels, 41 Misc.2d 49, 244 N.Y.S.2d 983 (1963); Hoffman v. Labutzke, 233 Wis. 365, 289 N.W. 652 (1940) (on motion to set aside verdict against automobile liability insurer for damages to injured party, on ground of non-cooperation by insured, statement of insured to joint attorney not privileged); Annot., 22 A.L.R.2d 659, 662.

93. Sokol v. Mortimer, 81 Ill.App.2d 55, 225 N.E.2d 496 (1967) (attorney's suit for fee); Mave v. Baird, 12 Ind. 318 (1859) (suit by client for negligence); Weinshenk v. Sullivan, 100 S.W.2d 66 (Mo.App. 1937) (attorney's suit for compensation); Stern v. Daniel, 47 Wash. 96, 91 P. 552 (1907) (lawyer's suit for fee; client's letters to lawyer not privileged though it discloses client's improper conduct. "They would have been privileged, no doubt as between either of the parties to this suit and third parties; but as between the attorney and client the rule of privilege will not be enforced where the client charges mismanagement of his cause by the attorney, as was the case here, and where it would be a manifest injustice to allow the client to take advantage of the rule of privilege to the prejudice of the attorney, or when it would be carried to the extent of depriving the attorney of the means of obtaining or defending his own rights."); State v. Markey, 259 Wis. 527, 49 N.W.2d 437 (1951).

94. As that a contract for compensation is not a communication from the client, and is "collateral" to the professional relation. Strickland v. Capital City Mills, 74 S.C. 16, 54 S.E. 220, 7 L.R.A.,N.S., 426 (1906); Baskerville v. Baskerville, 246 Minn. 496, 75 N.W.2d 762 (1956).

When the client claims that the attorney has given incompetent advice the lawyer may testify as to the advice given. Leverich v. Leverich, 340 Mich. 133, 64 N.W.2d 567 (1954); Chase v. Chase, 78 R.I. 278, 81 A.2d 686 (1951).

95. Minard v. Stillman, 31 Ore. 164, 49 Pac. 976 (1897); see 8 Wigmore, Evidence (McNaughton rev.) § 2312(2).

96. United States v. Monti, 100 F.Supp. 209 (E.D. N.Y.1951); Pierce v. Norton, 82 Conn. 441, 74 Atl. 686 (1909); Hyde v. State, 70 Ga.App. 823, 29 S.E. 2d 820 (1944); Moore v. State, 231 Ind. 690, 111 N.E.2d 47 (1953); Doll v. Loesel, 288 Pa. 527, 136 Atl. 796 (1927); Chase v. Chase, 78 R.I. 278, 81 A. 2d 686 (1951).

92.　The Client as the Holder of the Privilege: Who May Assert, and Who Complain on Appeal of Its Denial? [97]

A rule regulating the *competency* of evidence or of witnesses—a so-called "exclusionary" rule—is normally founded on the policy of safeguarding the fact-finding process against error, and it is assertable by the party against whom the evidence is offered. The earmarks of a *privilege*, as we have seen, are first, that it is not designed to protect the fact-finding process but is intended to protect some "outside" interest, other than the ascertainment of truth at the trial, and second, it cannot be asserted by the adverse party as such, but only by the person whose interest the particular rule of privilege is intended to safeguard.[98] While once it was conceived that the privilege was set up to protect the lawyer's honor, we know that today it is agreed that the basic policy of the rule is that of encouraging clients to lay the facts fully before their counsel. They will be encouraged by a privilege which they themselves have the power to invoke. To extend any benefit or advantage to someone as attorney, or as party to a suit, or to people generally, will be to suppress relevant evidence without promoting the purpose of the privilege.

Accordingly it is now generally agreed that the privilege is the client's and his alone.[99] It is thought that this would be rec-

ognized even in those states which, before modern notions of privilege and policy were adequately worked out, codified the rule in terms of inadmissibility of evidence of communications, or of incompetency of the attorney to testify thereto.[1] These statutes are generally held not to be intended to modify the common law doctrines.[2]

It is not surprising that the courts, often faced with statutes drafted in terms of obsolete theories, and reaching these points rarely and usually incidentally, have not worked out a consistent pattern of consequences of this accepted view that the rule is one of privilege and that the privilege is the client's. It is believed that the applications suggested below are well grounded in reason and are supported by some authority, whether of text or decision.

First, it is clear that the client may assert the privilege even though he is not a party to the cause wherein the privileged testimony is sought to be elicited.[3] Second, if he is present

---

Foster v. Hall, 12 Pick. (Mass.) 89 (1931); Russell v. Second National Bank, 136 N.J.L. 270, 55 A.2d 211 (1947); Ex parte Lipscomb, 111 Tex. 409, 239 S.W. 1101 (1922).

1. See the statutes collected and quoted in 8 Wigmore, Evidence (McNaughton rev.) § 2292, n. 2.

2. See e. g. In re Young's Estate, 33 Utah 382, 94 P. 731, 732 (1908) where the court said: "Subdivision 2 of section 3414, Rev.St.1898, so far as material to the present inquiry, provides as follows: 'An attorney cannot, without the consent of his client, be examined as to any communication made by the client to him, or his advice given therein in the course of professional employment.' It will be observed that, under the foregoing provision, the privilege therein given, as at common law, is purely personal, and belongs to the client. If the client waives the privilege, neither the attorney nor any one else may invoke it. It is likewise apparent that the privilege given by the statute is simply declaratory of that existing at common law. Without this statute, therefore, in view of section 2488, Rev.St.1898, in which the common law of England is adopted, the privilege would exist and be in force in this state. The mere fact that the common-law privilege is declared in statutory form does not extend the scope of its operation."

3. See Ex parte Martin, 141 Ohio St. 87, 47 N.E.2d 388 (1943) (client who was a witness whose testi-

---

97. See 8 Wigmore, Evidence (McNaughton rev.) § 2321; Note, Persons Entitled to Waive or Claim Privileges, 30 Colum.L.Rev. 686 (1930); 58 Am.Jur. Witnesses § 519.

98. See the discussion in §§ 72, 73, supra, of the distinction between competency and privilege.

Of course, a party may be the holder of a privilege.

99. Among the many cases where this is recognized are Minter v. Priest, [1930] A.C. 558, 579 (By Lord Atkin: "But the right to have such communications so protected is the right of the client only. In this sense it is a 'privilege', the privilege of the client"); Abbott v. Superior Court, 78 Cal.App.2d 19, 177 P.2d 317 (1947) (where client has no privilege because of his illegal purpose, attorney has none);

at the hearing whether as party, witness, or bystander he must assert the privilege personally or by attorney, or it will be waived.[4] Third, in some jurisdictions, if he is not present at the taking of testimony, nor a party to the proceedings, the privilege may be called to the court's attention by anyone present, such as the attorney [5] for the absent client, or a party in the case,[6] or the court of its own motion may protect the privilege.[7] Fourth: While if an asserted privilege is erroneously sustained, the aggrieved party may of course complain on appeal of the exclusion of the testimony, the erroneous denial of the privilege can only be complained of by the client whose privilege has been infringed.

This opens the door to appellate review by the client if he is also a party and suffers adverse judgment.[8] If he is not a party, the losing party in the cause, by the better view is without recourse.[9] Relevant, competent testimony has come in, and the privilege was not created for his benefit. But the witness, whether he is the client or his attorney, may refuse to answer and suffer an adjudication of contempt and may, in some jurisdictions at least, secure review on habeas corpus if the privilege was erroneously denied.[10] This remedy, however, is calculated to interrupt and often disrupt progress of the cause on trial. Does a lawyer on the witness stand who is asked to make disclosures which he thinks may constitute an infringement of his client's privilege, owe a duty to refuse to answer and if necessary to test the judge's ruling on habeas corpus or appeal from a judgment of contempt? It seems clear that, unless in a case of flagrant disregard of the law by the judge, the lawyer's duty is merely to present his view that the testimony is

mony by deposition was sought, allowed to test question of privilege).

4. Steen v. First National Bank, 298 F. 36 (8th Cir. 1924) (client's testimony on preliminary hearing to conversation with lawyer, a waiver); Hill v. Hill, 106 Colo. 492, 107 P.2d 597 (1940) (client as witness asked for production of documents to refresh her memory, waiver of privilege, if any, for documents).

5. Republic Gear Co. v. Borg-Warner Corp., 381 F. 2d 551 (2d Cir. 1967) (opinion by Waterman, J., "Not only may an attorney invoke the privilege in his client's behalf when the client is not a party to the proceeding in which disclosure is sought, (citations omitted) but he should do so, for he is 'duty-bound to raise the claim in any proceeding in order to procommunications made in confidence.' . . ."); Chicago Great Western Ry. Co. v. McCaffrey, 178 Iowa 1147, 160 N.W. 818 (1917) (attorney for railway, party to present suit, asked to produce correspondence with client properly claimed privilege).

F.R.Ev. (R.D.1971) 503(c) provides: "The person who was the lawyer at the time of the communication may claim the privilege but only on behalf of the client. His authority to do so is presumed in the absence of evidence to the contrary." West's Ann. Cal.Evid.Code, §§ 954, 956 require the lawyer to claim the privilege unless instructed otherwise by the holder.

6. O'Brien v. New England Mutual Life Ins. Co., 109 Kan. 138, 197 P. 1100 (1921) (absent client's privilege asserted, apparently by lawyer-witness or by party).

7. Tingley v. State, 16 Okl.Cr. 639, 184 P. 599 (1919). And the judge may advise the witness of the privilege. See State v. Madden, 161 Minn. 132, 134, 201 N.W. 297, 298 (1924).
See also § 73, supra.

8. Ex parte Lipscomb, 111 Tex. 409, 239 S.W. 1101, 1105 (1922) (attorney for one of the parties when required by judge to testify to transaction with client, refused and sought to raise question of privilege on habeas corpus; held, writ denied because of client's adequate remedy by appeal).

9. Schaibly v. Vinton, 338 Mich. 191, 61 N.W.2d 122 (1953); Dowie's Estate, 135 Pa. 210, 19 A. 936, (1890).

10. Ex parte Martin, 141 Ohio St. 87, 47 N.E.2d 388 (1943); Elliott v. United States, 23 App.D.C. 456 (1904); C.J.S. Habeas Corpus § 37, note 77. But not if the client is a party and so has an adequate remedy by appeal. Ex parte Lipscomb, note 8 supra.

Appeal from the judgment of contempt is ordinarily available as a means of reviewing the ruling, and enforcement of the judgment will be stayed pending review. But see Dike v. Dike, 75 Wash.2d 1, 448 P.2d 490 (1968), noted in 45 Wash.Law Rev. 181 (1970) in which the trial judge had the lawyer handcuffed, removed to the county jail, fingerprinted, "mugged", and held until released on $5,000 bail. The court on appeal vacated the contempt order, while ruling at the same time that the order to disclose was not erroneous.

See also note, The Attorney Client Privilege: The Remedy of Contempt, 1968 Wis.Law Rev. 1193.

privileged, and if the judge rules otherwise, to submit to his decision.[11]

93. Waiver.[12]

Since as we have seen, it is the client who is the holder of the privilege, the power to waive it is his, and he alone, or his attorney or agent acting with his authority, may [13] exercise this power. Waiver includes, as Wigmore points out, not merely words or conduct expressing an intention to relinquish a known right, but conduct, such as a partial disclosure, which would make it unfair for the client to insist on the privilege thereafter.[14]

Of course, if the holder of the privilege fails to claim his privilege by objecting to disclosure by himself or another witness when he has an opportunity to do so, he waives his privilege as to the communications so disclosed.[15]

By the prevailing view, which seems correct, the mere voluntary taking the stand by the client as a witness in a suit to which he is party and testifying to facts which were the subject of consultation with his counsel is no waiver of the privilege for secrecy of the communications to his lawyer.[16] It is the communication which is privileged, not the facts. If on direct examination, however, he testifies to the privileged communications, in part, this is a waiver as to the re-

---

11. Compare the remarks of Shaw, C. J., in Foster v. Hall, 12 Pick. (Mass.) 89, (1831): "Mr. Robinson [an attorney-witness] very properly submitted it to the court to determine, on the facts disclosed, whether he should answer, or not, having no wish either to volunteer or withhold his testimony. The rule in such case is, that the privilege of confidence is the privilege of the client, and not of the attorney, and, therefore, whether the facts shall be disclosed or not, must depend on the just application of the rule of law, and not upon the will of the witness."

A.B.A. Code of Professional Responsibility, Disciplinary Rule 4–101(C): "A lawyer may reveal . . . (2) Confidences or secrets when . . . required by law or court order."

12. See 8 Wigmore, Evidence (McNaughton rev.) §§ 2327–2329; Note, Waiver of Attorney-Client Privilege, 16 Minn.L.Rev. 818 (1932); Dec.Dig. Witnesses ⚷219(3); 58 Am.Jur. Witnesses §§ 522–530.

13. Lietz v. Primock, 84 Ariz. 273, 327 P.2d 288, 67 A.L.R.2d 1262 (1958) (guardian ad litem, in controversy with attorney); Annot., 67 A.L.R.2d 1268; Wilcox v. Coons, 359 Mo. 52, 220 S.W.2d 15 (1949) (either personal representative or devisee of deceased may waive); In re Selser, 27 N.J.Super. 257, 99 A.2d 313 (1951) (personal representative of deceased client); Yancy v. Erman, 99 N.E.2d 524 (Ohio App.1951) (guardian of an incompetent client may waive his privilege), noted in 36 Minn. L.Rev. 408 (1952).

14. 8 Wigmore, Evidence (McNaughton rev.) § 2327.
Traditionally, waiver is described as intentional relinquishment of a known right. Johnson v. Zerbst, 304 U.S. 458, 464 (1938). However, voluntary disclosure, regardless of knowledge of the existence of the privilege, deprives a subsequent claim of privilege based on confidentiality of any significance.

15. Steen v. First National Bank, 298 F. 36 (6th Cir. 1924); Hurley v. McMillan, 268 S.W.2d 229 (Tex. Civ.App.1954); C.J.S. Witnesses, § 310, note 76. But see People v. Kor, 129 Cal.App.2d 436, 277 P.2d 94 (1955) (failure of one of defendants, who jointly consulted a lawyer, to claim his privilege when examined about disclosures to attorney, does not waive his right to claim privilege against examination of attorney about the same disclosures). The decision is criticized, it seems soundly, in Note 2 U.C.L.A.L.Rev. 573.

16. Magida v. Continental Can Co., 12 F.R.D. 74 (1951); Bigler v. Reyher, 43 Ind. 112 (1873); Barker v. Kuhn, 38 Iowa 392 (1874); State v. White, 19 Kan. 445, 27 Am.Rep. 137 (1877); Shelly v. Landry, 97 N.H. 27, 79 A.2d 626 (1951). An early Massachusetts decision is to the contrary. Woburn v. Henshaw, 101 Mass. 193, 200 (1869). But there is some inconsistency in later opinions, see Spalding, The Uncertain State of the Law as to Waiver of Professional Confidences, 20 Mass. L.Q. 16 (May, 1935). So also decisions under statutes, in Ohio and Oregon. Spitzer v. Stillings, 109 Ohio 297, 142 N.E. 365 (1924) (in civil cases, under R.C. § 2317.02; Note, 33 Yale Law J. 782; Sitton v. Peyree, 117 Ore. 107, 241 Pac. 62, (1925) (under ORS 44–040); Annot., 51 A.L.R.2d 521.

The accused in a criminal case by taking the stand waives his privilege against self-incrimination, at least pro tanto, see § 132, infra, but not his privilege for communications with his attorney, unless he voluntarily gives evidence; respecting the privileged matter. People v. Shapiro, 308 N.Y. 453, 126 N.E.2d 559, 51 A.L.R.2d 515 (1955); Jones v. Jones, 208 Misc. 721, 144 N.Y.S.2d 820 (1955); Note, 41 Iowa L.Rev. 457.

mainder of the privileged consultation or consultations about the same subject.[17]

What if the client is asked on cross-examination about the communications with his lawyer, and he responds without asserting his claim of privilege? Is this a waiver? Unless there are some circumstances which show that the client was surprised or misled, it seems that the usual rule that the client's failure to claim the privilege when to his knowledge testimony infringing it is offered,[18] would apply here,[19] and that the decisions treating such testimony on cross-examination as being involuntary and not constituting a waiver [20] are hardly supportable.

How far does the client waive by calling the attorney as a witness? If the client elicits testimony from the lawyer-witness as to privileged communications this obviously would waive as to all consultations relating to the same subject,[21] just as the client's own testimony would.[22] It would seem also that by calling the lawyer as a witness he opens the door for the adversary to impeach him by showing his interest.[23] And it seems reasonable to contend as Wigmore does [24] that if the client uses the lawyer to prove matter which he would only have learned in the course of his employment this again should be considered a waiver as to related privileged communications.[25] But merely to call the lawyer to testify to facts known by him apart from his employment should not be deemed a waiver of the privilege. That would

17. General Accident, Fire & Life Assurance Corp. v. Savage, 35 F.2d 587 (8th Cir. 1929); Steen v. First National Bank, 298 Fed. 36 (8th Cir. 1924); Kelly v. Cummens, 143 Iowa 148, 121 N.W. 540, 20 Ann.Cas. 1283 (1909); Chase v. Chase, 78 R.I. 278, 81 A.2d 686 (1951); Rodriguez v. State, 130 Tex.Cr.R. 438, 94 S.W.2d 476 (1936). Similarly, if the party-client introduces part of his correspondence with his attorney, the production of all the correspondence could be demanded. Kunglig Jarnvagsstyrelson v. Dexter & Carpenter, 32 F.2d 195 (2d Cir. 1929). But the waiver extends only to so much of the privileged communications as relates to the matter testified to. People v. Gerold, 265 Ill. 448, 107 N.E. 165, Ann.C.1916A, 636. Testimony by the client in a prior suit may constitute a waiver of the privilege. Agnew v. Superior Court, 156 Cal.App.2d 838, 841, 320 P.2d 158 (1958). See also the decisions cited in note 27, infra.

18. See, e. g., Rock v. Keller, 312 Mo. 458, 278 S.W. 759 (1926); Weisser v. Preszler, 62 N.D. 75, 241 N.W. 505 (1932).

19. General Accident, Fire & Life Assurance Corp. v. Savage, 35 F.2d 587, 592 (8th Cir. 1929); Steen v. First National Bank, 298 F. 36, 43 (6th Cir. 1924) (persuasive opinion by Sanborn, Cir. C. J.); Raleigh and C. Ry. Co. v. Jones, 104 S.C. 332, 88 S.E. 896, 898 (1916) (failure to object on cross-examination entitles other party to call attorney); Pinson v. Campbell, 124 Mo.App. 260, 101 S.W. 621 (1907) (similar). It is clear, of course, that the party-witness may claim the privilege during the cross-examination. Ex parte Bryant, 106 Ore. 359, 210 P. 454 (1922).

20. Seaboard Air Line Ry. Co. v. Parker, 65 Fla. 543, 62 So. 589 (1913); Lauer v. Banning, 140 Iowa 319, 118 N.W. 446, 450 (1908), on later appeal, 152 Iowa 99, 131 N.W. 783 (1911); Foley v. Poschke, 66 Ohio App. 227, 32 N.E.2d 858, 861 (1940), affirmed 137 Ohio St. 593, 31 N.E.2d 845

(1941); State v. James, 34 S.C. 49, 12 S.E. 657 (1891). In none of these opinions is there any discussion of why the usual rule of waiver from failure to object does not apply. In most of them, however, the testimony on cross-examination consisted of a denial of having made to the attorney the statement inquired about, and it is arguable that a layman might not realize when he anticipated making such an answer, that there was any occasion to claim privilege.

21. Brooks v. Holden, 175 Mass. 137, 55 N.E. 802 (1900); 8 Wigmore, Evidence (McNaughton rev.) § 2327.

22. See cases cited note 17, supra.

23. Conyer v. Burckhalter, 275 S.W. 606 (Tex.Civ. App., 1925) (error to exclude cross-examination as to attorney's fee-interest in outcome of suit); Moats v. Rymer, 18 W.Va. 642, 41 Am.Rep. 703 (1881).

24. See reference, note 21, supra.

25. This view seems supported by the result in Jones v. Marble Co., 137 N.C. 237, 49 S.E. 94 (1904) (action for attorney's fees; defendant called attorney formerly associated with plaintiff in employment for which fee is claimed, to testify that fee claimed is excessive; held, this waived defendant's right to object to plaintiff's introducing letter from witness during pendency of employment which would otherwise have been privileged).

But there is authority for the view that if the lawyer's testimony does not relate to the privileged communications themselves, there is no waiver. Drayton v. Industrial Life & Health Ins. Co., 205 S.C. 98, 31 S.E.2d 148 (1944).

attach too harsh a condition on the exercise of the privilege.[26] Unless the lawyer-witness is acting as counsel in the case on trial, there is no violation of the Code of Professional Responsibility,[27] and if he is, it recognizes that his testifying may be essential to the ends of justice. Moreover, these are matters usually governed not by the client but by the lawyer, to whom the ethical mandate is addressed.

26. See 8 Wigmore, Evidence (McNaughton rev.) § 2327; Note, 16 Minn.L.Rev. 818, 827 (1932). But see Martin v. Shaen, 22 Wash.2d 508, 156 P.2d 681, 685 (1945) (where attorney-executor testified that he received a certain deed from the deceased client, and the court said that when he "voluntarily took the stand and testified upon a vital issue in the case, he waived the privilege of withholding his testimony as to all matters relevant to that issue" including communications between lawyer and client at the time the deed was placed in the lawyer's hands.)

27. A.B.A.Code of Professional Responsibility:

"CANON 5

"A Lawyer Should Exercise Independent Professional Judgment on Behalf of a Client

"ETHICAL CONSIDERATIONS

"**EC 5–9** Occasionally a lawyer is called upon to decide in a particular case whether he will be a witness or an advocate. If a lawyer is both counsel and witness, he becomes more easily impeachable for interest and thus may be a less effective witness. Conversely, the opposing counsel may be handicapped in challenging the credibility of the lawyer when the lawyer also appears as an advocate in the case. An advocate who becomes a witness is in the unseemly and ineffective position of arguing his own credibility. The roles of an advocate and of a witness are inconsistent; the function of an advocate is to advance or argue the cause of another, while that of a witness is to state facts objectively.

"**EC 5–10** Problems incident to the lawyer-witness relationship arise at different stages; they relate either to whether a lawyer should accept employment or should withdraw from employment. Regardless of when the problem arises, his decision is to be governed by the same basic considerations. It is not objectionable for a lawyer who is a potential witness to be an advocate if it is unlikely that he will be called as a witness because his testimony would be merely cumulative or if his testimony will relate only to an uncontested issue. In the exceptional situation where it will be manifestly unfair to the client for the lawyer to refuse employment or to withdraw when he will likely be a witness on a contested issue, he may serve as advocate even though he may be a witness. In making such

When at an earlier trial or stage of the case the privilege has been waived and testimony as to the privileged communications elicited without objection, the prevailing view is that this is a waiver also for any subsequent hear-

decision, he should determine the personal or financial sacrifice of the client that may result from his refusal of employment or withdrawal therefrom, the materiality of his testimony, and the effectiveness of his representation in view of his personal involvement. In weighing these factors, it should be clear that refusal or withdrawal will impose an unreasonable hardship upon the client before the lawyer accepts or continues the employment. Where the question arises, doubts should be resolved in favor of the lawyer testifying and against his becoming or continuing as an advocate.

"DISCIPLINARY RULES

"**DR 5–101** Refusing Employment When the Interests of the Lawyer May Impair His Independent Professional Judgment.

"(B) A lawyer shall not accept employment in contemplated or pending litigation if he knows or it is obvious that he or a lawyer in his firm ought to be called as a witness, except that he may undertake the employment and he or a lawyer in his firm may testify:
  (1) If the testimony will relate solely to an uncontested matter.
  (2) If the testimony will relate solely to a matter of formality and there is no reason to believe that substantial evidence will be offered in opposition to the testimony.
  (3) If the testimony will relate solely to the nature and value of legal services rendered in the case by the lawyer or his firm to the client.
  (4) As to any matter, if refusal would work a substantial hardship on the client because of the distinctive value of the lawyer or his firm as counsel in the particular case.

"**DR 5–102** Withdrawal as Counsel When the Lawyer Becomes a Witness.

"(A) If, after undertaking employment in contemplated or pending litigation, a lawyer learns or it is obvious that he or a lawyer in his firm ought to be called as a witness on behalf of his client, he shall withdraw from the conduct of the trial and his firm, if any, shall not continue representation in the trial, except that he may continue the representation and he or a lawyer in his firm may testify in the circumstances enumerated in DR 5–101(B)(1) through (4).

"(B) If, after undertaking employment in contemplated or pending litigation, a lawyer learns or it is obvious that he or a lawyer in his firm may be called as a witness other than on behalf of his client, he may continue the representation until it is apparent that his testimony is or may be prejudicial to his client."

ing of the same case.[28] In the words of Holmes, J., "the privacy for the sake of which the privilege was created was gone by the appellant's own consent, and the privilege does not remain in such circumstances for the mere sake of giving the client an additional weapon to use or not at his choice."[29] The same reasons seem to apply where the waiver was thus publicly made up on the trial of one case, and the privilege later sought to be asserted on the hearing of another cause.[30] How far does this argument of once published, permanently waived, apply to out-of-court disclosures made by the client or with his consent? Authority is scanty, but it seems that if the client makes public disclosure, this should clearly be a waiver,[31] and even where privately revealed to a third person,[32] or authorized to be revealed[33] it

should have the same effect, by analogy to the cases which deny privilege when a third person is present at the consultation. The Uniform Rule[34] accepts this view for all privileges, with a comment stating that the principle is generally recognized for confidential communications.

The question as to who may waive the privilege after the death of the client will be considered in the next section.

94. The Effect of the Death of the Client.[35]

The accepted theory is that the protection afforded by the privilege will in general survive the death of the client.[36] But under various qualifying theories the operation of the privilege has in effect been nullified in the class of cases where it would most often be asserted after death, namely, cases involving the validity or interpretation of a will, or other dispute between parties claiming by succession from the testator at his death. This result has been reached by different routes. Sometimes the testator will be found to have waived the privilege in his lifetime,

28. Green v. Crapo, 181 Mass. 55, 62 N.E. 956, 959 (1902) (waiver at probate court hearing, effective at subsequent hearing on appeal); In re Whiting, 110 Me. 232, 85 A. 79 (1913) (similar); 8 Wigmore, Evidence (McNaughton rev.) § 2328; Note, 16 Minn. L.Rev. 818, 829 (1932). See also discussions of the question as applied to waiver of objections generally by waiver at an earlier trial: 58 Am.Jur. Witnesses § 373; Annot., 79 A.L.R. 176.

29. Green v. Crapo, supra, 62 N.E. 956, 959.

30. Thus in Steen v. First National Bank, 298 F. 36 (6th Cir. 1924) it was held that a failure to object to questions to the client's representative about privileged matter at the preliminary hearing in a criminal prosecution, prevented assertion of the privilege at the trial of an action for malicious prosecution. Compare Alden v. Stromsem, 347 Ill. App. 439, 106 N.E.2d 837 (1952) (in suit for engineering fees, communications disclosed by both parties at previous trial for attorney fees, not privileged). But see Matison v. Matison, 95 N.Y.S.2d 837, aff'd on appeal 97 N.Y.S.2d 550 (1950) (in action by third party, communications between attorney and client were privileged, though attorney had testified thereto in previous action by him for attorney fees).

31. In re Burnette, 73 Kan. 609, 85 P. 575, 583 (1906) (procured stranger to read, published contents in newspaper interview, and spread substance on record of a court in a pleading).

32. Holland v. State, 17 Ala.App. 503, 86 So. 118 (1920) (oral disclosure by defendant to witness of advice given him by lawyers); and see Seeger v. Odell, 64 Cal.App.2d 397, 148 P.2d 901, 906 (1944).

33. Phillips v. Chase, 201 Mass. 444, 87 N.E. 755, 131 Am.St.Rep. 406 (1909) (deceased client had

requested attorney to communicate facts disclosed to him, to her brothers after her death.); Halloran v. Tousignant, 230 Minn. 399, 41 N.W.2d 874 (1950) (arrangement of insurance carriers to exchange statements of their insured, as waiver of privilege). As to latter case, however, compare § 89, n. 19, supra.

34. Uniform Rule 37: "A person who would otherwise have a privilege to refuse to disclose or to prevent another from disclosing a specified matter has no such privilege with respect to that matter if the judge finds that he or any other person while the holder of the privilege has (a) contracted with anyone not to claim the privilege or, (b) without coercion and with knowledge of his privilege, made disclosure of any part of the matter or consented to such a disclosure made by any one."

35. See 8 Wigmore, Evidence (McNaughton rev.) §§ 2314, 2329; Model Code of Evidence Rule 213(2); Annot., 64 A.L.R. 184, 66 A.L.R.2d 1302; 58 Am. Jur. Witnesses § 505.

36. In re Busse's Estate, 332 Ill.App. 258, 75 N.E.2d 36 (1947); Martin v. Shaen, 22 Wash.2d 505, 156 P.2d 681 (1945); 8 Wigmore, Evidence (McNaugton rev.) § 2323.

as by directing the attorney to act as an attesting witness.[37] Wigmore argues, as to the will contests, that communications of the client with his lawyer as to the making of a will are intended to be confidential in his lifetime but that this is a "temporary confidentiality" not intended to require secrecy after his death [38] and this view finds approval in some decisions.[39] Other courts say simply that where all the parties claim under the client the privilege does not apply.[40] The distinc-

tion is taken that when the contest is between a "stranger" and the heirs or personal representatives of the deceased client, the heirs or representatives can claim privilege,[41] and they can waive it.[42] Even if the privilege were assumed to be applicable in will contests, it could perhaps be argued that since those claiming under the will and those claiming by intestate succession both equally claim under the client, each should have the power to waive.[43]

This doctrine that the privilege is ineffective, on whatever ground, when both litigants claim under the deceased client has been applied to suits by the heirs or representatives to set aside a conveyance by the deceased for mental incapacity [44] and to suits for the enforcement of a contract made by the deceased to make a will in favor of plain-

---

37. In re Landauer's Estate, 261 Wis. 314, 52 N.W. 2d 890, reh. denied 53 N.W.2d 627 (1952); Annot., 64 A.L.R. 192, 66 A.L.R.2d 1310. See § 91, n. 77, supra.

38. 8 Wigmore, Evidence (McNaughton rev.) § 2314.

39. See, e. g., Dickerson v. Dickerson, 322 Ill. 492, 153 N.E. 740 (1926) (communications between client and attorneys concerning deed, intended to be confidential during client's lifetime only); Hecht's Admr. v. Hecht, 272 Ky. 400, 114 S.W.2d 499 (1938) (death removes the pledge of secrecy); Snow v. Gould, 74 Me. 540, 543 (1883); In re Graf's Estate, 119 N.W.2d 478 (N.D.1963).

40. Russell v. Jackson, 9 Hare 387, 392, 68 Eng.Rep. 558, 560 (V.C.1851) ("The disclosure in [testamentary] cases can affect no right or interest of the client. The apprehension of it can present no impediment to the full statement of his case to his solicitor. . . . In the cases of testamentary dispositions the very foundation on which the rule proceeds seems to be wanting . . ."); Glover v. Patten, 165 U.S. 394, 406 (1897) (bill by devisees to construe will and to charge estate with claims); Clark v. Turner, 183 F.2d 141 (D.C. Cir. 150) (in suit to establish lost will, testimony as to existence of will); Olsson v. Pierson, 237 Iowa 1342, 25 N.W. 2d 357 (1946) (suit to set aside conveyance of deceased for constructive fraud and mental incapacity); In Re Kemp's Will, 236 N.C. 680, 73 S.E. 2d 906 (1953) (will contest—mental capacity); Gaines v. Gaines, 207 Okl. 619, 251 P.2d 1044 (1953) (in action to construe written assignment of deceased, testimony of attorney and his stenographer as to statements of deceased concerning his intentions); Pierce v. Farrar, 60 Tex.Civ.App. 12, 126 S.W. 932 (1910) (will contest, undue influence); In re Young's Estate, 33 Utah 382, 94 Pac. 731, 17 L.R.A.,N.S., 108 (1908) (will contest, undue influence); Re Healy, 94 Vt. 128, 109 Atl. 19 (1920) (will contest, mental capacity); Annot., 64 A.L.R. 185–189, 66 A.L.R.2d 1395, 1396. Contra: In re Coon's Estate, 154 Neb. 690, 48 N.W.2d 778 (1951). See also Uniform Rule 26(2) (b), which provides that the privilege shall not extend "to a communication relevant to an issue between parties all of whom claim through the client, regardless of whether the respective claims are by testate or

intestate succession or by intervivos transaction." This last liberal criterion is in effect rejected in two recent cases. De Loach v. Myers, 215 Ga. 255, 109 S.E.2d 777 (1959) (action to enforce alleged contract to make a will in plaintiff's favor; held, decedent's instructions to attorney to draw will which was never executed, privileged); In re Creekmore's Estate, 1 N.Y.2d 284, 152 N.Y.S.2d 449, 135 N.E. 2d 193 (1956) (proceeding involving question whether decedent had intended to create joint accounts when she signed joint deposit slips; held, decedent's attorney precluded from testifying as to legal advice he gave her).

41. Doyle v. Reeves, 112 Conn. 521, 152 A. 882 (1931) (claim of servant against estate for value of services to deceased); In re Busse's Estate, 332 Ill.App. 258, 75 N.E.2d 36 (1947) (similar); Runnels v. Allen's Adm'r, 169 S.W.2d 73 (Mo.App.1943) (similar); In re Smith's Estate, 263 Wis. 441, 57 N.W.2d 727 (1953); Annot., 64 A.L.R. 191, 66 A.L.R. 2d 1307. In Doyle v. Reeves, supra, the plaintiff seems to have relied on a promise by decedent to make provision in his will for payment for the services.

42. Phillips v. Chase, 201 Mass. 444, 87 N.E. 755 (1909) (in controversy with stranger, either personal representative or heir may waive—dictum).

43. See Wilcox v. Coons, 359 Mo. 52, 220 S.W.2d 15 (1949) (privilege of deceased client accrues to his personal representatives and may be waived either by his grantees under deed or his devisees under will.) See also Walton v. Van Camp, 283 S.W.2d 493 (Mo.1955).

44. Olsson v. Pierson, 237 Iowa 1342, 25 N.W.2d 357 (1946).

tiff.[45] The cases encountered where the party is held to be a "stranger" and hence not entitled to invoke this doctrine are cases where the party asserts against the estate a claim of a promise by the deceased to pay, or make provision in his will for payment, for services rendered.[46] It may well be questioned whether the deceased would have been more likely to desire that his attorney's lips be sealed after his death in the determination of such claims than in the case of a controversy over the validity of the will. The attorney's offered testimony would seem to be of more than average reliability. If such testimony supporting the claim is true, presumably the deceased would have wanted to promote, rather than obstruct the success of the claim. It would be only a short step forward for the courts to apply here the notion that the privilege is "personal" to client, and to hold that in all cases death terminates the privilege. This could not in any substantial degree lessen the encouragement for free disclosure which is the purpose of the privilege.

95. Consultation in Furtherance of Crime or Fraud.[47]

Since the policy of the privilege is that of promoting the administration of justice, it would be a perversion of the privilege to extend it to the client who seeks advice to aid him in carrying out an illegal or fraudulent scheme. Advice given for those purposes would not be a professional service but participation in a conspiracy. Accordingly, it is settled under modern authority that the privilege does not extend to communications between attorney and client where the client's purpose is the furtherance of a future intended crime or fraud.[48] Advice secured in

sufficient evidence, aside from the communication, has been introduced to warrant a finding that the legal service was sought or obtained in order to enable or aid the client to commit or plan to commit a crime or a tort. . . ."

48. Queen v. Cox, 14 Q.B.D. 153 (C.C.R.1884) (prosecution for conspiracy to defraud judgment creditor by transfer of debtor's property; communications between debtor and solicitor in respect to preventing collection of judgment by transfer of assets, not privileged); United States v. Bob, 106 F.2d 37, 125 A.L.R. 502 (2d Cir. 1939) (conspiracy for fraudulent sale of mining stock through use of mails); Fidelity-Phenix Fire Ins. Co. of New York v. Hamilton, 340 S.W.2d 218 (Ky.1960) (communication tending to show fraudulent claim under fire insurance policy) noted in 21 Md.L.Rev. 270 (1960); Standard Fire Ins. Co. v. Smithhart, 183 Ky. 679, 211 S.W. 441, 5 A.L.R. 972 (1919) (communications by insured in fire policy tending to show arson and fraudulent claim); Gebhardt v. United Rys. Co. 220 S.W. 677, 679, 9 A.L.R. 1076 (Mo.1920) (client asserting personal injury on street car, discloses to attorney that she was not on car; "The law does not make a law office a nest of vipers in which to hatch out frauds and perjuries"); Ott v. State, 87 Tex.Cr. 382, 222 S.W. 261 (1920) (husband consults attorney as to what punishment would probably be incurred if he killed his wife).

A leading case recognizes the rule, but places a seemingly unjustifiable restriction upon it in holding that the client may assert the privilege when he is sued or prosecuted for a different crime from the one involved in the consultation. Alexander v. United States, 138 U.S. 353 (1891) (client on trial for murder of his partner; error to admit communications to lawyer asserted to show plan to convert murder-victim's property). This restriction was called a "dictum" and rejected in In re Sawyer's Petition, 229 F.2d 805 (7th Cir. 1956), noted approvingly, 45 Calif.L.Rev. 75.

If the client consults the lawyer about a proposed course of action, about the legality of which he is doubtful and is advised that it would be unlawful and then desists, it can not be said that the consultation was in furtherance of wrong. Cummings v. Commonwealth, 221 Ky. 301, 298 S.W. 943 (1927). But a case which on this ground holds

45. Eicholtz v. Grunewald, 313 Mich. 666, 21 N.W. 2d 914 (1946) (suit by children to enforce contract of parents to make mutual wills and to set aside conveyance by father); Cummings v. Sherman, 16 Wash.2d 88, 132 P.2d 998 (1943) (similar); Allen v. Ross, 199 Wis. 162, 225 N.W. 831, 64 A.L.R. 180 (1929) (similar). But see, In re Smith's Estate, McGlone v. Fairchild, 263 Wis. 441, 57 N.W.2d 727 (1953) (in suit against estate based upon breach of contract by testatrix in making her last will, attorney's testimony privileged on ground that claimants were not claiming through testatrix but asserting adverse claim against the estate).

46. See the cases cited in note 41, supra.

47. 8 Wigmore, Evidence (McNaughton rev.) §§ 2298, 2299; Gardner, The Crime or Fraud Exception to the Attorney-Client Privilege, 47 A.B.A.J. 708 (1961); Dec.Dig. Witnesses ⊂⇒201(2); C.J.S. Witnesses § 285; 58 Am.Jur. Witnesses §§ 516, 517; Annot., 125 A.L.R. 508.

Uniform Rule 26(2): "Such privileges shall not extend (a) to a communication if the judge finds that

aid of a legitimate defense by the client against a charge of past crimes or past misconduct, even though he is guilty, stands on a different footing and such consultations are privileged.[49] If the privilege is to be denied on the ground of unlawful purpose, the client's guilty intention is controlling, though the attorney may have acted innocently and in good faith.[50]

Must the judge, before denying the claim of privilege on this ground find as a fact, after a preliminary hearing if contested, that the consultation was in furtherance of crime or fraud? This would be the normal procedure in passing on a preliminary fact, on which the admissibility of evidence depends, but here this procedure would facilitate too far the use of the privilege as a cloak for crime. As a solution, some courts have cast the balance in favor of disclosure by requiring only that the one who seeks to avoid the privilege bring forward evidence from which the existence of an unlawful purpose could reasonably be found.[51] Even this limitation seems needless when, as is commonly the case, the examining counsel, has sufficient information to focus the inquiry by specific questions, thus avoiding any broad exploration of what transpired between attorney and client.[52]

Questions arise fairly frequently under this limitation upon the privilege in the situ-

---

privileged a consultation about the effect of altering a deed in the client's favor, where the deed was later actually altered by someone, seems a misapplication. Williams v. Williams, 108 S.W.2d 297 (Tex.Civ.App.1937). The client could hardly have supposed that such an alteration could be innocent and the inquiry is itself strong circumstantial evidence that the client participated in the alteration.

In order to protect the client who acts upon professional advice in committing what later is ruled to be a crime or fraud, F.R.Ev. (R.D.1971) 503(d) (1) applies the furtherance of crime or fraud exception only when the client knew or reasonably should have known the act to be a crime or fraud.

49. "The privileged communications may be a shield of defense as to crimes already committed, but it cannot be used as a sword or weapon of offense to enable persons to carry out contemplated crimes against society." Gebhardt v. United Rys. Co., 220 S.W. 677, 699, 9 A.L.R. 1076 (Mo.1920). Clark v. State, 261 S.W.2d 339 (Tex.Cr.1953), cert. den. 346 U.S. 855; State ex rel. Sowers v. Olwell, 64 Wash.2d 828, 394 P.2d 681, 16 A.L.R.3d 1021 (1964) (knife obtained by attorney as result of confidential communication from client held not privileged from production but prosecution barred from disclosing source); Annot., 16 A.L.R.3d 1029.

50. Queen v. Cox, 14 Q.B.D. 153 (C.C.R.1884); In re Selser, 15 N.J. 393, 105 A.2d 395 (1954), noted in 24 Fordham L.Rev. 290 (1955), 30 N.Y.U.L.Rev. 1251 (1955); Orman v. State, 22 Tex.App. 604, 3 S.W. 468 (1886); Annot., 125 A.L.R. at 520. A converse question is raised in State v. Clark, next preceding note. The accused called his lawyer and told him that he had just killed his former wife. Though seemingly the call was for counsel in his defence, the lawyer volunteered advice that he should get rid of the fatal weapon. Apparently this advice was taken, as the weapon was not found. The court held that "the conversation was admissible as not within the realm of legitimate professional counsel and employment" (p. 347).

51. O'Rourke v. Darbishire, [1920] App.C. 581, 604, 614, 622 (H.L.) (evidence and not mere pleading of fraud required); Clark v. United States, 289 U.S. 1 (1933) ("There must be a showing of a prima facie case sufficient to satisfy the judge that the light should be let in"); United States v. Bob, 106 F.2d 37, 125 A.L.R. 502, 506 (2d Cir. 1939) cert. denied 308 U.S. 589; Pollock v. United States, 202 F.2d 281 (5th Cir. 1953), cert. denied 345 U.S. 993 (communication not privileged, where communication was made in furtherance of crime of which client was charged and evidence had been introduced giving color to the charge); United States v. Weinberg, 226 F.2d 161 (3d Cir. 1955); United States v. Summe, 208 F.Supp. 925 (E.D.Ky.1962); In re Selser, 15 N.J. 393, 105 A.2d 395 (1954), noted 24 Fordham L.Rev. 290 (1955), 30 N.Y.U.L.Rev. 1251 (1955); Uniform Rule 26(2), quoted note 47, supra.

The case most often relied upon to support the requirement of a preliminary prima facie showing, Clark v. United States, supra, actually involved the privilege of a petit juror, not that of attorney-client.

Of course, the inference of the client's wrongful intent will often be a circumstantial one. See, e. g., Sawyer v. Stanley, 241 Ala. 39, 1 So.2d 21 (1941) where a will was contested for forgery and evidence of an attorney was admitted that the purported beneficiary asked him whether decedent had left a will, without disclosing existence of purported will.

52. Thus in cases of fraudulent suits, where successive attorneys have been consulted, it seems common for the first attorney to furnish complete information to the defense. See cases cited note 53, infra, and A.B.A. Code of Professional Responsibility, Disciplinary Rule 4–101(C) (3).

ation where a client has first consulted one attorney about a claim, and then employs other counsel and brings suit. At the trial the defense seeks to have the first attorney testify to disclosures by the client which reveal that the claim was fabricated or fraudulent. This of course may be done,[53] but if the statements to the first attorney would merely reveal variances from the client's later statements or testimony, not sufficient to evidence fraud or perjury, the privilege would stand.[54]

It has been questioned whether the traditional statement of the area of the limitation, that is, in cases of communications in aid of crime or fraud is not itself too limited. Wigmore argues that the privilege should not be accorded to communications in furtherance of any deliberate scheme to deprive another of his rights by tortious or unlawful conduct.[55] Stricter requirements such as that the intended crime be *malum in se* or that it involve "moral turpitude", suggested in some of the older decisions,[56] seem out of place here where the only sanction proposed is that of opening the door to evidence concededly relevant upon the issue on trial.

96. Protective Rules Relating to Materials Collected for Use of Counsel in Preparation for Trial: Reports of Employees, Witness-Statements, Experts' Reports, and the Like.

A heavy emphasis on the responsibility of counsel for the management of the client's litigation is a characteristic feature of the adversary or contentious system of procedure of the Anglo-American tradition. The privilege against disclosure in court of confidential communications between lawyer and client as we have seen, is supported in modern times upon the policy of encouraging free disclosure by the client in the attorney's office to enable the lawyer to discharge that responsibility.[57] The need for this encouragement is understood by lawyers because the problem of the guarded half-truths of the reticent client is familiar to them in their day-to-day work.

Closely allied to this felt need of promoting a policy of free disclosure by the client to enable the lawyer to do the work of managing his affairs most effectively in the interests of justice, is a feeling by lawyers of a need for privacy in their work and for freedom from interference in the task of preparing the client's case for trial. Certainly if the adversary were free at any time to inspect all of the correspondence, memoranda, reports, exhibits, trial briefs, drafts of proposed pleadings, and plans for presentation of proofs, which constitute the lawyer's file in the case, the attorney's present freedom to collect for study all the data, favorable and unfavorable, and to record his tentative impressions before maturing his conclusions, would be cramped and hindered.

The natural jealousy of the lawyer for the privacy of his file, and the courts' desire to protect the effectiveness of the lawyer's work

53. In re Koellen's Estate, Willie v. Lampe, 167 Kan. 676, 208 P.2d 595 (1949) (client admitted to first lawyer that he had forged will which he later sought to probate, not privileged); Standard Fire Ins. Co. v. Smithhart, 183 Ky. 679, 211 S.W. 441, 5 A.L.R. 972 (1919) (client sought first lawyer to sue on fire policy, disclosing that she had connived in burning her house; not privileged); Gebhardt v. United Rys. Co., 220 S.W. 677, 9 A.L.R. 1076 (Mo.1920) (fabricated personal injury claim: no privilege).

54. Nadler v. Warner Co., 321 Pa. 139, 184 A. 3 (1936); (offer to show statement of personal injury claimant, merely inconsistent with present position but not claimed to show fraud, rejected); Thomas v. Jones, 105 W.Va. 46, 141 S.E. 434 (1928) (inconsistency not such as to show fraud).

55. 8 Wigmore, Evidence (McNaughton rev.) § 2298, p. 577.

The Uniform Rule, quoted note 47, supra, specifies "a crime or a tort." West's Ann.Cal.Evid.Code, § 956 and F.R.Ev. (R.D.1971) 503(d) (1), however, substitute "fraud" in lieu of "tort," in view of the technical nature of many torts.

56. Bank of Utica v. Mersereau, 3 Barb.Ch. 528, 598 (1848) (limited to felony or malum in se); Hughes v. Boone, 102 N.C. 137, 9 S.E. 286, 292 (1889) (similar dictum).

57. See § 87, supra.

as the manager of litigation, have found expression, not only as we have seen in the evidential privilege for confidential lawyer-client communications, but in rules and practices about the various forms of pretrial discovery.[58] Thus, under the chancery practice of discovery, the adversary was not required to disclose, apart from his own testimony, the evidence which he would use, or the names of the witnesses he would call in support of his own case.[59] The same restriction has often been embodied in, or read into, the statutory discovery systems.[60]

Counterbalancing this need for privacy in preparation, of course, is the very need from which the discovery devices spring, namely, the need to make available to each party the widest possible sources of proof as early as may be so as to avoid surprise and facilitate preparation.[61] The present trend is manifestly in the direction of the wider recognition of this latter need, and the taboo against the "fishing expedition"[62] is yielding to a realization that the ends of justice require a wider availability than in the past of the various

devices for discovery,[63] such as interrogatories to the adverse party, demands for admissions, oral and written depositions of parties and witnesses, and orders for production and inspection of writings, and the like. In this country, the greatest influence in this development is the example of the liberal discovery procedures provided in the Federal rules.[64] How far has the interest in privacy of preparation been submerged by the tide flowing toward a wider scope of discovery?

In the first place, of course, it is recognized that if the traditional privilege for attorney-client communications applies to a particular writing which may be found in a lawyer's file, the privilege exempts it from pretrial discovery proceedings,[65] such as orders for production or questioning about its contents in the taking of depositions. On the other hand, if the writing has been in the possession of the client or his agents and was there subject to discovery, it seems axiomatic that the client cannot secure any exemption for the document by sending it to an attorney to be placed in his files.[66]

How do these distinctions apply to a report made by an agent to the client of the results of investigation by himself or another agent of facts pertinent to some matter which later becomes the subject of litigation,[67] such as a business dispute or a personal injury. It is usually held that an agent's report to

---

58. For general discussions of discovery, see James, Civil Procedure, ch. 6 (1965); Note, Developments in the Law—Discovery, 74 Harv.L.Rev. 940 (1961).

59. 6 Wigmore, Evidence § 1856. As to the application of the restriction in the United States, and the departures from it in some states, see Ragland, Discovery Before Trial, ch. 15, May a Party be Required to Disclose Evidence of his own Case? (1932); Dec.Dig. Discovery ⊜8. For a criticism of the requirement, see Sunderland, Scope and Method of Discovery Before Trial, 42 Yale L.J. 862, 866 (1933).

60. 6 Wigmore, Evidence §§ 1856a, 1856b; Ragland, supra, n. 59.

61. 2 Moore, Federal Practice ¶ 26.01 (2d ed. 1970); Wright, Law of Federal Courts § 81 (2d ed. 1970); Goodrich, Circ.J. in Hickman v. Taylor, 153 F.2d 212, 217 (3d Cir. 1945) aff'd 329 U.S. 495. Equally important is the need to supplement the inadequacy of the pleadings as a vehicle for disclosing what points are really in dispute. Moore, section cited above; Wright, supra, § 68; Sunderland, The Theory and Practice of Pre-trial Procedure, 36 Mich.L.Rev. 215, 216 (1937).

62. See Sunderland, Foreword, Ragland, Discovery Before Trial, p. iii (1932).

63. See F.R.Civ.P. 26–37.

64. Wright, Law of Federal Courts 354 (2d ed. 1970).

65. Leonia Amusement Corp. v. Loew's Inc., 13 F.R.D. 438 (S.D.N.Y.1952) (communications from attorney to client, privileged); Wise v. Western Union Telegraph Co., 178 Atl. 640 (Del.Super.1935); Ragland, Discovery Before Trial 146 (1932); Dec. Dig. Discovery ⊜90; 17 Am.Jur. Discovery § 28. F.R.Civ.P. 26(b) (1) specifically exempts privileged matters from discovery.

66. Cranston v. Stewart, 184 Kan. 99, 334 P.2d 337 (1959). See § 89, supra.

67. See Simon, Attorney-Client Privilege as Applied to Corporations, 65 Yale L.J. 953 (1956) (extensive discussion of discoverability of agent's reports to corporate employer made for use in litigation).

his principal though made in confidence is not privileged as such,[68] and looked on as a mere preexisting document it would not become privileged when sent by the client-principal to his lawyer for his information when suit is brought or threatened.[69] The problem frequently arises in connection with proceedings for discovery of accident reports by employees, with lists of eyewitnesses, and in connection with signed statements of witnesses attached to such reports or secured separately by investigators employed in the client's claim department or by an insurance company with whom the client carries insurance against liability.[70]

Whether a communication by the client's agent, on behalf of the client, to the latter's attorney would be privileged, has been discussed elsewhere.[71] If the employee is one who can be said to "speak" for the employer, it is an easy step to treat as privileged a report secured by the employer from his employee for the purpose of submitting it to counsel in connection with an actual or anticipated claim or suit. Numerous decisions treat these special reports as exempt from discovery under the privilege for attorney-client communications.[72] If the employee does not speak for the employer, his report is no different from that of any other witness; it may be exempt from discovery as work product, but it is not privileged. Routine reports of employees made in the regular course

of business, before suit is brought or threatened, have usually, though not always, been treated as preexisting documents which not being privileged in the client's hands do not become so when delivered into the possession of his attorney.[73] It must be admitted, how-

---

68. Southwark & V. Water Co. v. Quick, 3 Q.B.D. 315, 9 Eng.Rul.Cas. 587 (C.A.1878); Schmitt v. Emery, 211 Minn. 547, 2 N.W.2d 413, 416, 139 A.L. R. 1242 (1942); Annot., 146 A.L.R. 977, 978.

It should be borne in mind that the problem here is one of privilege, not of admissibility in evidence. As to the latter, see § 267, infra.

69. See § 89, supra.

70. Cases involving the claim of privilege for such reports and statements are collected in Note 26 Minn.L.Rev. 744 (1942); Annot., 22 A.L.R.2d 659.

71. See § 87, nn. 14 and 15, supra.

72. Lafone v. Falkland Islands Co., 4 K. & J. 34, 70 Eng.Rep. 14 (V.C.1857) (agent's report secured for purpose of communication to attorney); Cossey v.

London, Brighton & South Coast R. Co., L.R. 5 C.P. 146 (1870) (medical officer's report made after claim and with a view to litigation); Skinner v. Great Northern R. Co., L.R. 9 Exch. 298 (1874) (similar to last); Adams Steamship Co. v. London Assurance Co. [1914] 3 K.B. 1256 (special reports by agents of marine insurance to salvage association in anticipation of litigation); Schmitt v. Emery, 211 Minn. 547, 2 N.W.2d 413, 139 A.L.R. 1242, annotated (1942) and noted 26 Minn.L.Rev. 744 (statement from bus driver, codefendant with bus company in personal injury action, obtained by bus company's claim agent and delivered by him to attorney for both defendants; privilege asserted by bus company discussed and sustained, but apparently privilege was also asserted by driver, as to whom it was more clearly sustainable); Davenport Co. v. Penn. R. Co., 166 Pa. 480, 31 Atl. 245 (1895) (report of local agent of railway to superior officer relating to shipment of fruit for which claim of damage had been made, for express purpose of submission to counsel); Note, 146 A.L.R. 977, 987; Simon, The Attorney-Client Privilege as Applied to Corporations, 65 Yale L.J. 953, 960 (1956); 8 Wigmore, Evidence (McNaughton rev.) § 2318.

73. Woolley v. North London R. Co., L.R. 4 C.P. 602 (1869) (court allowed inspection of reports of accident by guard of train, an inspector, and the locomotive superintendent to the general manager; significant question was not time of reports nor whether confidential, but whether made in ordinary course of duty); Anderson v. Bank of British Columbia, L.R. 2 Ch.Div. 644 (C.A.1876) (letter from manager of branch bank to head office in response to telegram, reporting on transfer of funds from one account to another, written before suit filed though litigation then probable, not privileged against production, since there was no suggestion in the telegram that the report was for submission to counsel); Hurley v. Connecticut Co., 118 Conn. 276, 172 A. 86 (1934) (motorman's report of accident subject to inspection; mere fact that it was made for preparation against possibility of litigation not sufficient for privilege); Wise v. Western Union Telegraph Co., 178 A. 640 (Del. Super.1935) (report from one branch office to another, at latter's request, upon complaint of patron that forged telegram transmitted in his name; held not privileged from discovery in absence of clear showing that document was prepared with bona fide intention of laying before attorney); Linton v. Lehigh Valley R. Co., 25 App.Div.2d 334, 269 N.Y.S. 2d 490 (1966) (reports of members of train crew discoverable); Robertson v. Commonwealth, 181 Va. 520, 25 S.E.2d 352, 146 A.L.R. 966 (1943) (motorman's report of accident made in course of

ever, that these classifications are not quite mutually exclusive and that some cases will fall in a doubtful borderland.[74] And the law is in the making on the question whether a report of accident or other casualty by a policy-holder or his agents to a company insuring the policy-holder against liability, is to be treated as privileged when the insurance company passes it on to the attorney who will represent both the company and the insured.[75] Probably the insurance company may reasonably be treated as an intermediary to secure legal representation for the insured,

by whom the confidential communications can be transmitted as through a trusted agent. A report to a liability insurer can have no purpose other than use in potential litigation.[76]

The discussion thus far has centered upon the extent to which the attorney-client privilege, just as any other privilege, can be invoked as a bar to discovery. Another, and much more frequently encountered limitation upon discovery of materials contained in the files of counsel, is furnished by the so-called "work-product" doctrine, exempting trial preparations, in varying degrees, from discovery.[77] In the leading case of Hickman v.

---

ordinary duty before suit brought or threatened required to be produced at trial by counsel from his files); 8 Wigmore, Evidence (McNaughton rev.) § 2318; Annot., 146 A.L.R. 977, 980.

In Ohio, however, and perhaps in some other states, an accident report, made in ordinary course but in anticipation of the possibility of litigation, is when transmitted to counsel, privileged from discovery. Ex parte Schoepf, 74 Ohio St. 1, 77 N.E. 276, 6 L.R.A.,N.S., 325 (1906); In re Hyde, 149 Ohio St. 407, 79 N.E.2d 224 (1948) (but other routine records, such as names of operators of cars, and times of operation, not privileged).

74. See, e. g., The Hopper No. 13, [1925] Prob. 52 (shipmaster's report required by general rule, of a collision, on a printed form headed "confidential report . . . in view of anticipated litigation," sent to solicitors; held, privileged); Jessup v. Superior Court, 151 Cal.App.2d 102, 311 P.2d 177 (1957) (father of boy drowned in municipal pool not entitled to inspect report of investigation made for use of city attorney for defense purposes, where that was dominant purpose though it might also be used for study in accident prevention). Note, Attorney-Client Privilege for Documents Originating with Client's Agent, 88 U.Pa.L.Rev. 467, 469 (1940).

Resolving the question according to the dominant purpose of the report, as in Holm v. Superior Court, 42 Cal.2d 500, 267 P.2d 1025, 268 P.2d 722 (1954), will often pose difficulties of practical application. Perhaps the best solution is to apply the privilege only to reports having no purpose except use in litigation. Note, 21 U.Chi.L.Rev. 752 (1954).

75. Privilege denied: Virginia-Carolina Chem. Co. v. Knight, 106 Va. 674, 680, 56 S.E. 725, 727 (1907); Brown v. Meyer, 137 Kan. 553, 21 P.2d 368 (1933). Privilege accorded: People v. Ryan, 30 Ill.2d 456, 197 N.E.2d 15 (1964); In re Klemann, 132 Ohio St. 187, 5 N.E.2d 492, 108 A.L.R. 505 (1936); New York Casualty Co. v. Superior Court, 30 Cal.App.2d 130, 85 P.2d 965 (1938). Notes, 48 Mich.L.Rev. 364 (1950), 26 Minn.L.Rev. 744, 745 (1941), 88 U.Pa. L.Rev. 467, 470 (1940); Annot., 22 A.L.R.2d 659.

76. The case for applying the privilege is particularly appealing when the report contains incriminating statements, as in People v. Ryan, supra, n. 75. If the attorney-client privilege is denied, the insured is confronted with an unhappy choice between breaching the clause of his policy requiring him to co-operate in the defense of claims and waiving his privilege against self-incrimination.

77. The general provisions governing discovery under the Federal Rules of Civil Procedure are set out in Rule 26 as amended 1970. The methods and scope of discovery are set out in Rule 26(a) and (b) as follows:

"(a) **Discovery Methods.** Parties may obtain discovery by one or more of the following methods: depositions upon oral examination or written questions; written interrogatories; production of documents or things or permission to enter upon land or other property, for inspection and other purposes; physical and mental examinations; and requests for admission. Unless the court orders otherwise under subdivision (c) of this rule, the frequency of use of these methods is not limited.

"(b) **Scope of Discovery.** Unless otherwise limited by order of the court in accordance with these rules, the scope of discovery is as follows:

"(1) *In General.* Parties may obtain discovery regarding any matter, not privileged, which is relevant to the subject matter involved in the pending action, whether it relates to the claim or defense of the party seeking discovery or to the claim or defense of any other party, including the existence, description, nature, custody, condition and location of any books, documents, or other tangible things and the identity and location of persons having knowledge of any discoverable matter. It is not ground for objection that the information sought will be inadmissible at the trial if the information sought appears reasonably calculated to lead to the discovery of admissible evidence."

Rule 26(c) provides that upon proper showing the court may make any order which justice requires

Taylor,[78] suit was brought for the death of a member of the crew of a tug, who with four others was drowned when the tug sank in the course of towing a car-float across the Delaware River. About three weeks later a public hearing was held by the United States Steamboat Inspectors, at which the four surviving crew members were examined, and their testimony was made available to the parties interested. A few days later, before suit was brought, an attorney employed by the tug owners to defend against possible suits, interviewed the four survivors and took their signed statements, and likewise interviewed other persons believed to have information about the accident, and in some cases made memoranda (apparently not signed by the informants) of what they told him. After suit brought in the Federal court, the plaintiff filed interrogatories asking for copies of any written statements taken by the defendant and for disclosure of the terms of any oral statements or of any memoranda relating to the accident. The defendants and their counsel declined to furnish the information on the ground that it called "for privileged matter obtained in preparation for litigation" and was "an attempt to obtain indirectly counsel's private files." The trial judge ordered the production of the written statements, the disclosure by counsel of relevant facts learned from oral statements, and the submission of his memoranda to the court to determine which of them might be revealed to the plaintiff. The counsel persisted in refusal, was adjudged in contempt [79] and

an appeal was taken from this judgment. In the Court of Appeals, the judgment was reversed on the ground that the information sought was part of the "work product of the lawyer" and hence within the exemption in the Rules for "privileged" matter.[80]

The Supreme Court heard the case on certiorari, discussed extensively the questions involved and affirmed the decision, but with a somewhat different *rationale*. Restricting the exception in the Rules [81] for "privileged" matter to the traditional privileges of which the only one here relevant was that for attorney-client communications, they held that the information called for was not within the "privilege." But, as reflected in the following passages from the court's opinion, it seems to have recognized what might be termed a qualified privilege for some of the materials constituting the lawyer's preparation for trial. The court said: "Proper preparation of a client's case demands that he [the lawyer] assemble information, sift what he considers to be the relevant from the irrelevant facts, prepare his legal theories and plan his strategy without undue and needless interference. . . . This work is reflected, of course, in interviews, statements, memoranda, correspondence, briefs, mental impressions, personal beliefs, and countless other tangible and intangible ways—aptly though roughly termed by the Circuit Court of Appeals in this case as the 'work product of the lawyer.' Were such materials open to opposing counsel on mere demand, much of what is now put down in writing would remain unwritten. An attorney's thought, heretofore inviolate, would not be his own. Inefficiency, unfairness and sharp practices would inevitably develop in the giving of legal advice and in the prepara-

---

to protect a party or person from "annoyance, embarassment, oppression, or undue burden or expense".

78. 329 U.S. 495 (1947).

79. 4 F.R.D. 479 (1945).

While the reports of the decisions in the case as it progressed through the courts convey the impression that the attorney, Mr. Fortenbaugh, and his clients the defendants were jailed for contempt, the contrary was the case; enforcement of the contempt judgment was stayed throughout, from the time of its entry until ultimate disposition of

the proceeding. Fortenbaugh, Hickman versus Taylor Revisited, 13 Defense L.J. 1, 13 (1964).

80. 153 F.2d 221 (3d Cir. 1945, enlightening opinion by Goodrich, Circ.J.).

81. Rule 26(b) and Rule 34.

tion of cases for trial. The effect on the legal profession would be demoralizing. And the interests of the clients and the cause of justice would be poorly served.

"We do not mean to say that all written materials obtained or prepared by an adversary's counsel with an eye toward litigation are necessarily free from discovery in all cases. Where relevant and non-privileged facts remain hidden in an attorney's file and where production of those facts is essential to the preparation of one's case, discovery may properly be had. Such written statements and documents might, under certain circumstances, be admissible in evidence or give clues as to the existence or location of relevant facts. Or they might be useful for purposes of impeachment or corroboration. And production might be justified where the witnesses are no longer available or can be reached only with difficulty. . . . But the general policy against invading the privacy of an attorney's course of preparation is so well recognized and so essential to an orderly working of our system of legal procedure that a burden rests on the one who would invade that privacy to establish adequate reasons to justify production through a subpoena or court order. That burden, we believe, is necessarily implicit in the rules as now constituted." [82]

Applying these standards, the court concluded that since there was no showing by the plaintiff of necessity for the written statements, the witnesses so far as appears being still available to plaintiff for interviewing, there was no ground for the exercise of discretion to order production, and as to the oral statements, the court said, ". . . we do not believe that any showing of necessity can be made under the circumstances of this case so as to justify production. Under ordinary conditions, forcing an attorney to repeat or write out all that witnesses have told him and to deliver the account to his adversary gives rise to grave dangers of inaccuracy and untrustworthiness. No legitimate purpose is served by such production. The practice forces the attorney to testify as to what he remembers or what he saw fit to write down regarding witnesses' remarks. Such testimony could not qualify as evidence; and to use it for impeachment or corroborative purposes would make the attorney much less an officer of the court and much more an ordinary witness. The standards of the profession would thereby suffer." [83]

While the *Hickman* case was pending the Advisory Committee on Federal Rules submitted a proposed amendment to then Rule 30(b) which foreshadowed the approach adopted in the opinion and which went further in specifying the types of material which would be exempt, from discovery as part of the preparation for trial.[84] The court, evidently preferring to lead the way by its own decision to a case-by-case development of the

---

82. 329 U.S. 495 at 511, 512.
The result was squeezed into the framework of the Rules by finding, with respect to the written statements, that good cause, then required for production of writings under Rule 34, was absent, and, with respect to the oral statements, good cause for denying their discovery, under then Rule 30(b), was present. See, Cleary, Hickman v. Jencks: Jurisprudence of the Adversary System, 14 Vand. L.Rev. 865 (1961).

83. 329 U.S. 495 at 512, 513. See note, Developments in the Law—Discovery, 74 Harv.L.Rev. 940, 1027 (1961).

84. "The court shall not order the production or inspection of any writing obtained or prepared by the adverse party, his attorney, surety, indemnitor, or agent in anticipation of litigation or in preparation for trial unless satisfied that denial of production or inspection will unfairly prejudice the party seeking the production or inspection in preparing his claim or defense or will cause him undue hardship or injustice. The court shall not order the production or inspection of any part of the writing that reflects an attorney's mental impressions, conclusions, opinions, or legal theories or except as provided in Rule 35, the conclusion of an expert." Report of Proposed Amendments to Rules of Civil Procedure for District Courts of the United States, Rule 30(b) (1946) 5 F.R.D. 433, 456–457. See also Discovery Procedure Symposium, (1946) 5 F.R.D. 403; Note, 31 Minn.L.Rev. 712, 735, 736 (1947).

practice, failed to adopt the proposed amendment. Subsequent proposals by the Committee for amendment of the discovery rules similarly failed of acceptance by the court.[85]

The courts were therefore confronted with the task of applying the standards of the *Hickman* case under rules which contained no specific provision for trial preparation materials. Moreover, confusion resulted from the application of the "good cause" requirement of then Rule 34, which was applicable to discovery of documents and things generally whether or not trial preparation was involved,[86] and the requirement laid down in *Hickman* of a showing of "necessity or justification" or that "denial . . . would unduly prejudice the preparation of petitioner's case," or "cause hardship or injustice,"[87] where discovery was sought of materials obtained or prepared for litigation.

Some twenty years after the *Hickman* decision a preliminary draft of proposed amendments to the Federal Rules of Civil Procedure relating to depositions and discovery was submitted to the bench and bar, and with some changes these amendments were subsequently adopted by the Supreme Court of the United States in 1970.[88] These amendments were prepared after an intensive study of the operation of pre-trial discovery under the Federal Rules of Civil Procedure from the time of their adoption in 1938.[89]

The Rules as amended eliminate the requirement of "good cause" from Rule 34[90] but require a showing of need for the discovery of trial preparation materials other than discovery of his own statement by a party or witness.[91]

Professor Rosenberg's account of the Project for Effective Justice study, 45 F.R.D. 479 (1969).

90. Rule 34 as amended (1970).

91. Rule 26(b) now contains the following provisions with respect to preparation materials:

"(3) *Trial Preparation: Materials.* Subject to the provisions of subdivision (b) (4) of this rule, a party may obtain discovery of documents and tangible things otherwise discoverable under subdivision (b) (1) of this rule and prepared in anticipation of litigation or for trial by or for another party or by or for that other party's representative (including his attorney, consultant, surety, indemnitor, insurer, or agent) only upon a showing that the party seeking discovery has substantial need of the materials in the preparation of his case and that he is unable without undue hardship to obtain the substantial equivalent of the materials by other means. In ordering discovery of such materials when the required showing has been made, the court shall protect against disclosure of the mental impressions, conclusions, opinions, or legal theories of an attorney or other representative of a party concerning the litigation.

"A party may obtain without the required showing a statement concerning the action or its subject matter previously made by that party. Upon request, a person not a party may obtain without the required showing a statement concerning the action or its subject matter previously made by that person. If the request is refused, the person may move for a court order. The provisions of Rule 37(a) (4) apply to the award of expenses incurred in relation to the motion. For purposes of this paragraph, a statement previously made is (A) a written statement signed or otherwise adopted or approved by the person making it, or (B) a stenographic, mechanical, electrical, or other recording, or a transcription thereof, which is a substantially verbatim recital of an oral statement by the person making it and contemporaneously recorded.

"(4) *Trial Preparation: Experts.* Discovery of facts known and opinions held by experts, otherwise discoverable under the provisions of subdivision (b) (1) of this rule and acquired or developed in anticipation of litigation or for trial, may be obtained only as follows:

"(A) (i) A party may through interrogatories require any other party to identify each person whom the other party expects to call as an expert witness at trial, to state the subject matter on which the expert is expected to testify, and to state the substance of the facts and opinions to which the expert is expected to testify and a summary of the

85. See Tolman, Discovery under the Federal Rules, 58 Colum.L.Rev. 498, 509–513 (1958).

86. Rule 34 as amended (1970) eliminates the requirement of good cause. See note 90, infra.

87. 329 U.S. 495 at 509–510.

88. The amended Rules are set out in 48 F.R.D. 457 (1970).

See Cooper, Work Product of the Rulesmakers, 53 Minn. Law Rev. 1269 (1969).

89. An Advisory Committee on Civil Rules named by the Court drafted the proposed amendments following a field study of discovery practice by the Project for Effective Justice of Columbia Law School. See the Advisory Committee's Explanatory Statement Concerning Amendments of the Discovery Rules, 48 F.R.D. 487 (1970). See also

The amended Rules dealing with trial preparation materials include the specific provision that "In ordering discovery of such materials when the required showing has been made, the court shall protect against disclosure of the mental impressions, conclusions, opinions, or legal theories of an attorney or other representative of a party concerning the litigation.[92]

Prior to the amendments the courts divided upon whether the "work-product" rule extended only to that procured by lawyers.[93] This question was resolved in the amended Rules by the provision including "attorney, consultant, surety, indemnitor, insurer or agent" within the definition of the representative of the party by whom the work-product may be prepared.[94]

The term "good cause" is not used in the amended Rules as a condition precedent to discovery. Instead discovery of trial-preparation materials may be had upon a showing of the elements entitling the party to discovery, substantial need of the materials in preparation of his case, and that he is unable without undue hardship to obtain the substantial equivalent of the materials by other means.[95] As noted by the Advisory Committee these are factors noted in the *Hickman* case, and required by the decisions since *Hickman*.[96] Accordingly the showing required generally under the amended Rules is essentially that required by many of the decisions under the old rules.[97] However, a party

grounds for each opinion. (ii) Upon motion, the court may order further discovery by other means, subject to such restrictions as to scope and such provisions, pursuant to subdivision (b) (4) (C) of this rule, concerning fees and expenses as the court may deem appropriate.

"(B) A party may discover facts known or opinions held by an expert who has been retained or specially employed by another party in anticipation of litigation or preparation for trial and who is not expected to be called as a witness at trial, only as provided in Rule 35(b) or upon a showing of exceptional circumstances under which it is impracticable for the party seeking discovery to obtain facts or opinions on the same subject by other means.

"(C) Unless manifest injustice would result, (i) the court shall require that the party seeking discovery pay the expert a reasonable fee for time spent in responding to discovery under subdivisions (b) (4) (A) (ii) and (b) (4) (B) of this rule; and (ii) with respect to discovery obtained under subdivision (b) (4) (A) (ii) of this rule the court may require, and with respect to discovery obtained under subdivision (b) (4) (B) of this rule the court shall require, the party seeking discovery to pay the other party a fair portion of the fees and expenses reasonably incurred by the latter party in obtaining facts and opinions from the expert."

92. Rule 26(b) (3).

93. See Advisory Committee's Note, 48 F.R.D. 487, 501 (1970). See also 4 Moore Fed.Practice, ¶ 26.23 (8.1) (2d ed., 1966).

94. Rule 26(b) (3).

95. Rule 26(b) (3).

96. See Advisory Committee's Note, 48 F.R.D. 487, 500–501 (1970).

97. Some of the decisions discussing and applying the "good cause" requirement under the old rules: Martin v. Capital Transit Co., 170 F.2d 811 (D.C. Cir. 1948) (employee's report of accident, motion for discovery denied; movant must show in motion and affidavit grounds of "good cause"); Newell v. Capital Transit Co., 7 F.R.D. 732, 11 Fed. Rules Serv. 34.411 Case 2 (D.C.1948) (plaintiff's motion for discovery of witness-statements taken by defendant's investigators; fact that plaintiff unconscious after accident and his lawyers unable to locate witnesses is good cause); Lauritzen v. Atlantic Greyhound Corp., 8 F.R.D. 237, 11 Fed. Rules Serv. 34.411 case 6 (E.D.Tenn., 1948) (plaintiffs sue for death of son in bus accident and seek discovery, list of witnesses and statements, sufficient); Lindsay v. Prince, 8 F.R.D. 233, 11 Fed. Rules Serv. 34.411 case 5 (N.D.Ohio 1948) (defendant in personal injury, sued belatedly after plaintiff had sued other person, was not present at accident and made no investigation, sufficient); Haase v. Chapman, 308 F.Supp. 399 (W.D.Mo.1969) (where judgment debtor might have been engaged in fraudulent transactions involving corporation, calculated to conceal assets subject to execution good cause existed for broad discovery of records of corporation by judgment creditor); Merrin Jewelry Co. v. St. Paul Fire & Marine Ins. Co., 49 F.R.D. 54 (1969) (uniqueness of documents established the required good cause for discoverability); Talbott Construction Co. v. United States, 49 F.R.D. 68 (1969) (good cause as required by the rule for production of documents implies greater showing of need than relevance and materiality); Shultz v. Midtown, 49 F.R.D. 94 (1969) (before a court may grant an order requiring production of documents, it must be satisfied not only as to presence of relevancy and absence of privilege, the normal requisite for discovery, but also to presence of good cause for moving party's request).

may in any event obtain his own statement without any showing.[98] Also, a nonparty may obtain his own statement without any showing,[99] suggesting a ready means of circumventing the limitations upon discovery of his statement in the case of a cooperative witness. A further new provision of the rules relating to depositions and discovery permits, in proper circumstances, discovery of facts and opinions of experts whom the party expects to call as trial witnesses or who have been retained but not expected to be called as witnesses.[1]

97. Discovery in Criminal Cases: Required Production of Statements by Government Witnesses.

Increasing activity in the area of pretrial discovery in criminal cases seems to follow naturally from the general acceptance of pretrial discovery in civil cases.[2] Current proposals to broaden the scope of discovery under the Federal Rules of Criminal Procedure[3] and proposed Minimum Standards for Criminal Justice Relating to Discovery and Procedure Before Trial of the American Bar Association[4] are indicative of the developments in the field. These proposals would give greater discovery to both the prosecution and the defense. Both include work-product safeguards based upon the same considerations relative to preservation of the adversary process that were paramount in Hickman v. Taylor.[5]

Recent cases, state and federal, have come to the view that when statements of prosecuting witnesses contradicting their testimony are shown to be in the hands of the government the defendant is entitled to demand their production at the trial.[6] But

98. Rule 26(b) (3).

99. Id.

1. Rule 26(b) (4).

See Advisory Committee's Note, 48 F.R.D. 487, 503–505; Friedenthal, Discovery and Use of an Adverse Party's Expert Information, 14 Stan.L.Rev. 455 (1962); Long, Discovery and Experts Under the Federal Rules of Civil Procedure, 38 F.R.D. 111 (1965).

Under some circumstances, where the expert is retained, not to testify but to assist in the management of the litigation as "associate counsel," the attorney-client privilege may be applicable. See § 89, n. 56. To that extent, the privilege may operate as a limitation upon the discovery provided in Rule 26(b) (4).

2. Generally, see Fletcher, Pretrial Discovery in State Criminal Cases, 12 Stan.L.Rev. 293 (1960); Goldstein, The State and the Accused: Balance of Advantage in Criminal Procedure, 69 Yale L.J. 1149 (1960); Louisell, Criminal Discovery: Dilemma Real or Apparent? 49 Calif.L.Rev. 56 (1961); Traynor, Ground Lost and Found in Criminal Discovery, 39 N.Y.U.L.Rev. 228 (1964); Notes, 1955 U.Ill.L.F. 158, 59 W.Va.L.Rev. 221 (1957), 60 Yale L.J. 626 (1951); 6 Wigmore, Evidence §§ 1850–1855b, 1859g, 1863; Dec.Dig. Criminal Law ⌐627½.

Present Federal Criminal Rule 16(a) contains provisions for discovery by the defendant of his own statement, the results of examinations and experiments, and his own testimony before a grand jury. Subdivision (b) provides for discovery of other items "upon a showing of materiality to the preparation of his defense and that the request is reasonable." Subdivision (c) provides for limited discovery by the government if discovery has been granted the defendant.

3. See Proposed Amendments to Criminal Rules, 48 F.R.D. 553 (1970). Discovery for defendant would be expanded to include statements of codefendants, defendant's prior criminal record, and government witnesses. Discovery for the government would not be conditional upon the granting of discovery to the accused, although constitutional doubts led to the submission of an alternative draft retaining the requirement. Expanded discovery for the government would include examinations, tests, and lists of witnesses.

Constitutional problems in allowing discovery against an accused are considered in § 133, infra.

4. A.B.A. Project on Minimum Standards for Criminal Justice, Standards Relating to Discovery and Procedure Before Trial (1970).

5. Proposed Rule 16(a) (2) is substantially unchanged from the present Rule 16(b).

Standard 2.6(a) of the Standards, supra, n. 4 provides:

"(a) *Work product*. Disclosure shall not be required of legal research or of records, correspondence, reports or memoranda to the extent that they contain the opinions, theories or conclusions of the prosecuting attorney or members of his legal staff."

6. Gordon v. United States, 344 U.S. 414 (1953); People v. Riser, 47 Cal.2d 566, 305 P.2d 1, 13 (1957), cert. denied 353 U.S. 930.

when in the famous *Jencks* case [7] the Supreme Court held that the trial court had erroneously denied inspection of the reports of two undercover agents who were government witnesses, and held that it was not required that the defendant show that the reports were inconsistent with the witnesses' testimony, so long as they are shown to relate to the same subject, the holding was condemned in the dissent as affording the criminal "a Roman holiday for rummaging through confidential information [in government files] as well as vital national secrets." [8]

This was echoed in widespread protests by the press, the Department of Justice, and by members of the Congress, which found reflection in the so-called Jencks Act of 1959.[9]

Despite this background of protest, the Act is for the most part a codification of the holdings in the decision which was so vehemently attacked. Thus, after making clear that pretrial production of statements by government witnesses is not to be required,[10] it provides that after a government witness has testified on direct, "the court shall, on motion of the defendant, order the United States to produce any statement" of the witness in its possession, "which relates to the subject matter as to which the witness has testified." [11] It does, however, modify somewhat the practice embodied in the *Jencks* decision in respect to the trial judge's determination of a disputed issue as to whether the statement relates to the subject matter of the testimony,[12] and as to the remedy against the

---

7. Jencks v. United States, 353 U.S. 657 (1957) (prosecution for filing false non-Communist affidavit).

8. 353 U.S. at 681, 682.

9. 18 U.S.C.A. § 3500, which reads:

"(a) In any criminal prosecution brought by the United States, no statement or report in the possession of the United States which was made by a Government witness or prospective Government witness (other than the defendant) to an agent of the Government shall be the subject of subpoena, discovery, or inspection until said witness has testified on direct examination in the trial of the case.

"(b) After a witness, called by the United States has testified on direct examination, the court shall, on motion of the defendant, order the United States to produce any statement (as hereinafter defined) of the witness in the possession of the United States which relates to the subject matter as to which the witness has testified. If the entire contents of any such statement relate to the subject matter of the testimony of the witness, the court shall order it to be delivered directly to the defendant for his examination and use.

"(c) If the United States claims that any statement ordered to be produced under this section contains matter which does not relate to the subject matter of the testimony of the witness, the court shall order the United States to deliver such statement for inspection of the court in camera. Upon such delivery the court shall excise the portions of such statement which do not relate to the subject matter of the testimony of the witness. With such material excised, the court shall then direct delivery of such statement to the defendant for his use. If, pursuant to such procedure, any portion of such statement is withheld from the defendant, and the defendant objects to such withholding, and the trial is continued to an adjudication of the

guilt of the defendant, the entire text of such statement shall be preserved by the United States and, in the event the defendant appeals, shall be made available to the appellate court for the purpose of determining the correctness of the ruling of the trial judge. Whenever any statement is delivered to a defendant pursuant to this action, the court in its discretion, upon application of said defendant, may recess proceedings in the trial for such time as it may determine to be reasonably required for the examination of such statement by said defendant in his preparation for its use in the trial.

"(d) If the United States elects not to comply with an order of the court under paragraph (b) or (c) hereof to deliver to the defendant any such statement, or such portion thereof as the court may direct, the court shall strike from the record the testimony of the witness, and the trial shall proceed unless the court in its discretion, shall determine that the interests of justice require that a mistrial be declared.

"(e) The term 'statement,' as used in sub-sections (b), (c), and (d) of this section in relation to any witness called by the United States, means—(1) a written statement made by such witness and signed or otherwise adopted or approved by him; (2) a stenographic, mechanical, electrical, or other recording, or a transcription thereof, which is a substantially verbatim recital of an oral statement made by said witness and recorded contemporaneously with the making of such oral statement; or (3) a statement, however taken or recorded, or a transcription thereof, if any, made by said witness to a grand jury."

10. See statute, note 9, supra, subsec. (a).

11. Statute, note 9, supra, subsec. (b).

12. Statute, note 9, supra, subsec. (c).

government for failure to comply with the order to produce.[13] Finally, the statute adopts a restrictive definition of "statement," limiting it to signed or adopted statements or "substantially verbatim" transcriptions.[14]

Recent Supreme Court decisions have answered some questions as to the meaning and effect of the Act. Thus in Palermo v. United States [15] it was held that the Act is the exclusive source of authority to require production of statements of government witnesses, and thus a "summary" of what the witness said, not being within the statutory definition of a "statement" cannot be ordered to be produced. In Campbell v. United States,[16] an "interview report" of an F.B.I. agent compiled from notes made during the interview of the witness was producible under the Jencks Act where the agent read his notes back to the witness who indicated that they were accurate. Again, in Rosenberg v. United States [17] it was held that a letter written by a government witness to the F.B.I. stating that she feared that her memory of the events as to which she later testified "had dimmed" and "she would have to reread . . . [her] original statement" sufficiently related to the subject matter of her testimony, so that its production should

have been ordered, but that in view of the circumstances the error was harmless. However, in Pittsburgh Plate Glass Co. v. United States [18] the court decided that requests for production of statements of government witnesses embodied in grand jury minutes are not governed by the Jencks Act but by Rule 6(e) of the Federal Rules of Criminal Procedure which commits the matter to the discretion of the trial judge. The *Jencks* decision and the Act based upon it represent on balance the recognition of a just and humane practice of discovery in criminal cases. Their importance is evidenced by the profusion of able comments upon the legislation,[19] and it may be predicted that the decision and the Act will have a liberalizing influence upon the state practice of discovery in criminal cases.[20]

---

13. Statute, note 9, supra, subsec. (d).

14. Statute, note 9, supra, subsec. (e).

15. 360 U.S. 343 (1959).

16. 373 U.S. 487 (1963).

17. 360 U.S. 367 (1959).

18. 360 U.S. 395 (1959), but see further in § 113, infra.

19. See, e. g., The Supreme Court, 1958 Term, Criminal Discovery, 73 Harv.L.Rev. 179–186 (1959); Note, Jencks Legislation: Problems in Prospect, 67 Yale L.J. 674 (1958); Forgotson, Accused's Federal Discovery Right, 38 Texas L.Rev. 596 (1960); Note, The Aftermath of the Jencks Case, 11 Stan.L.Rev. 297 (1959).

20. See, e. g., People v. Chapman, 52 Cal.2d 95, 338 P.2d 428 (1959) (in order to secure production of statement of prosecuting witness, defendant not required to show inconsistent with testimony, relying on *Jencks* decision and repudiating implications of earlier California opinions); People v. Wolff, 19 Ill.2d 318, 167 N.E.2d 197 (1960) cert. denied 364 U.S. 874 (adheres to federal rule as evolved by decision and legislation).

For a comparison with Hickman v. Taylor, see Cleary, Hickman v. Jencks: Jurisprudence of the Adversary System, 14 Vand.L.Rev. 865 (1961).

CHAPTER 11

THE PRIVILEGE FOR CONFIDENTIAL INFORMATION SECURED IN THE COURSE OF THE PHYSICIAN– PATIENT RELATIONSHIP

98. The Statement of the Rule and Its Purpose.[1]

The common law knew no privilege for confidential information imparted to a doctor. When a physician raised the question before Lord Mansfield whether he was required to disclose professional confidences, the great Chief Justice drew the line clear: "If a surgeon was voluntarily to reveal these secrets, to be sure, he would be guilty of a breach of honor and of great indiscretion; but to give that information in a court of justice, which by the law of the land he is bound to do, will never be imputed to him as any indiscretion whatever." [2]

The pioneer departure from the common law rule was the New York provision of 1828 which in its original form was as follows: "No person authorized to practice physic or surgery shall be allowed to disclose any information which he may have acquired in attending any patient, in a professional character, and which information was necessary to enable him to prescribe for such patient as a physician, or to do any act for him as a surgeon." [3]

Another early act which has been widely copied is the following provision of the California Code of Civil Procedure of 1872, § 1881, par. 4, "A licensed physician or surgeon cannot, without the consent of his patient, be examined in a civil action as to any information acquired in attending the patient which was necessary to enable him to prescribe or act for the patient." These two ground-breaking statutes indicate the general scope and purport of this legislative privilege which in some form has been enacted in over two-thirds of the states.[4] No more than a dozen states maintain the common law posi-

---

1. See, in general, the able treatise, De Witt, Privileged Communications Between Physician and Patient (1958); 8 Wigmore, Evidence (McNaughton rev.) §§ 2380–2391; Model Code of Evidence Rules 220–223 and commentary; Uniform Rule 27; C.J.S. Witnesses §§ 293–301; Dec.Dig. Witnesses ⊂⇒208–214, 217, 219(4–6), 220–223. See also Hammelmann, Professional Privilege: A Comparative Study, 28 Can.Bar Rev. 750 (1950); Freedman, Medical Privilege, 32 id. 1 (1954); Note, The Physician-Patient Privilege, 58 W.Va.L.Rev. 76 (1955).

2. The Duchess of Kingston's Trial, 20 How.St.Trials 573 (1776).

3. N.Y.Rev.Stats. 1829, vol. II, Part III, c. 7, Tit. 3, art. eight, § 73.

4. The statutes are compiled and quoted in 8 Wigmore, Evidence (McNaughton rev.) § 2380, note 5, and in De Witt, op. cit. n. 1, supra, appendix.

tion denying any privilege for information disclosed to medical practitioners.[5]

It seems that the only purpose that could possibly justify the suppression in a law suit of material facts learned by the physician is the encouragement of freedom of disclosure by the patient so as to aid in the effective treatment of disease and injury.[6] To attain this objective, the immediate effect of the privilege is to protect the patient against the embarrassment and invasion of privacy which disclosure would entail.[7] But if this were the only interest involved it is hard to suppose that the desire for privacy would outweigh the need for complete presentation of the facts in the interest of justice. A fuller discussion of the policy of the privilege is reserved for a later section.[8]

99. Relation of Physician and Patient.

The first requisite for the privilege is that the patient must have consulted the physician [9] for treatment or for diagnosis looking toward treatment.[10] If consulted for treatment it is immaterial by whom the doctor is

5. Chafee, Is Justice Served by Closing the Doctor's Mouth, 52 Yale L.J. 607 (1943) listed seventeen states as follows: Alabama, Connecticut, Delaware, Florida, Georgia, Illinois, Maine, Maryland, Massachusetts, New Hampshire, New Jersey, Rhode Island, South Carolina, Tennessee, Texas, Vermont, and Virginia. Recently Illinois, Maine, New Hampshire, New Jersey and Virginia have enacted statutes creating a general privilege for communications between doctor and patient.

6. Thus the New York Commissioners on Revision in justifying the new privilege said, "unless such consultations are privileged men will be incidentally punished by being obliged to suffer the consequences of injuries without relief from the medical art." N.Y.Rev.Stats.2d ed. vol. III, p. 737 (1836). See also Metropolitan Life Ins. Co. v. Ryan, 237 Mo.App. 464, 172 S.W.2d 269, 272 (1943) (to encourage free disclosure); Yow v. Pittman, 241 N.C. 69, 84 S.E.2d 297 (1954).

7. This is stated as the aim of the privilege in Falkinburg v. Prudential Ins. Co., 132 Neb. 831, 273 N.W. 478 (1937) (to enable patient to secure medical service without fear of betrayal); Woernle v. Electromatic Typewriters, 271 N.Y. 228, 2 N.E.2d 638 (1936) (to prevent physician from disclosing matters which might humiliate the patient).

8. See § 105, below.

9. The statutes usually specify "physician" or "physician or surgeon," and sometimes require that they be "licensed" or "authorized." Accordingly, the decisions usually deny the privilege for communications to other practitioners, such as dentists, Gulf, Mobile & N. Ry. Co. v. Willis, 171 Miss. 732, 157 So. 899 (1934); druggists, Green v. Superior Court In and For San Joaquin County, 220 Cal.App.2d 121, 33 Cal.Rptr. 604 (1963); Brown v. Hannibal & St. J. Ry. Co., 66 Mo. 588, 597 (1877); chiropractors, S. H. Kress & Co. v. Sharp, 156 Miss. 693, 126 So. 650, 68 A.L.R. 167, 173 (1930) (dictum). See Annot., 68 A.L.R. 176; C.J.S. Witnesses § 294. An intern may be a "physician" though not yet licensed to practice. Franklin Life Ins. Co. v. William J. Champion & Co., 353 F.2d 919 (6th Cir. 1965) cert. denied 384 U.S. 928; Eureka-Maryland Assur. Co. v. Gray, 74 App.D.C. 191, 121 F.2d 104 (1941). As to nurses, assistants and technicians see § 101, infra.

Psychotherapists: On account of the special therapeutic need for assurance to the patient of protection against disclosures it is cogently argued (on the basis of a Circuit Court decision in Chicago) that even in states not having the physician-patient privilege generally, a privilege should be recognized, by statute or decision, for confidential disclosures to psychiatrists, qualified psychologists trained in the treatment of mental disorders, and (in the court's discretion) general practitioners consulted for diagnosis or treatment of mental disease. Note, Communications to a Psychotherapist, 47 Nw.U.L.Rev. 384, in Selected Writings on Evidence and Trial 254 (Fryer ed. 1957). See also Taylor v. United States, 95 U.S.App.D.C. 373, 222 F.2d 398, 401 (1955) and see Slovenko, Psychiatry and a Second Look at the Medical Privilege, 6 Wayne L.Rev. 175 (1960). He writes (pp. 199, 201) "A privilege of those receiving psychotherapy is necessary if the psychiatric profession is to fulfill its medical responsibility to its patients. . . . It is interesting to note that recently seven states (Ark., Calif., Ga., Ky., N.Y., Tenn., and Wash.), three of them not having a medical privilege (Cf. Ky.Rev.Stat. § 213.200), have passed legislation granting to the certified or licensed psychologist *qua* psychologist an absolute privilege as in the lawyer-client relationship. There exists the anomaly in some of these states of giving the privilege to client-psychologist communications while denying it to a psychiatrist's patient."

The privilege has fairly generally been included as a provision in statutes licensing the practice of psychology.

For privileged aspects of hospital records, see § 313 at n. 10, infra.

10. City and County of San Francisco v. Superior Court, 37 Cal.2d 227, 231 P.2d 26 (1951); Burgdorf v. Keeven, 351 Mo. 1003, 174 S.W.2d 816 (1943); People v. Austin, 199 N.Y. 446, 93 N.E. 57 (1910); City of Racine v. Woiteshek, 251 Wis. 404, 29 N.W.2d 752 (1947); Dec.Dig. Witnesses ⚷210. The examination contemplated reme-

employed.[11] Usually, however, when the doctor is employed by one other than the patient, treatment will not be the purpose and the privilege will not attach. Thus, when a participant at the request of a public officer is subjected to a blood test for intoxication,[12] or when a doctor is appointed by the court [13] or the prosecutor [14] to make a physical or mental [15] examination, or is employed for this purpose by the opposing party,[16] or is selected by a life insurance company to make an examination of an applicant for a policy [17] or even when the doctor is employed by plaintiff's own lawyers in a personal injury case to examine plaintiff solely to aid in preparation for trial,[18] the information secured is not within the present privilege. But when the patient's doctor calls in a consultant physician to aid in diagnosis or treatment, the disclosures are privileged.[19]

dial measures if possible, in Bassil v. Ford Motor Co., 278 Mich. 173, 270 N.W. 258, 107 A.L.R. 1491, 1493 (1936) (husband and wife consult doctor to ascertain why child was not born of their union). Information gained by a physician during a period of social relations before the subject became a patient is not privileged. Ranger, Inc. v. Equitable Life Assur. Soc., 196 F.2d 968 (6th Cir. 1952).

11. Russell v. Penn Mutual Life Ins. Co., 70 Ohio App. 113, 41 N.E.2d 251 (1941) (doctors who attended insured, apparently employed by life insurance company). See also Malone v. Industrial Comm., 140 Ohio St. 292, 43 N.E.2d 266 (1942) (privilege for communications to plant physician to whom employee was taken while in semi-conscious condition for examination and treatment). And when a patient goes, or is taken unconscious, to a hospital for care or treatment, the hospital doctors who are charged with the duties of examination, diagnosis, care or treatment are within the purview of the privilege statute. Smart v. Kansas City, 208 Mo. 162, 105 S.W. 709 (1907); Note, 72 U.S.L.Rev. 619 (1938); Annot., 22 A.L.R. 1217. Where the defendant, after being involved in a fatal automobile accident was taken to the county hospital by police after his arrest for examination, statements given by him to hospital physician as to his medical history of epilepsy were, under the circumstances, communications for the purpose of treatment and were privileged. People v. Decina, 2 N.Y.2d 133, 157 N.Y.S.2d 558, 138 N.E.2d 799 (1956), extensively noted in 43 Cornell L.Q. 295. So also if the doctor, though employed by the defendant, examines the plaintiff in the hospital under circumstances causing the patient to believe that the examination is part of the hospital's care. Ballard v. Yellow Cab Co., 20 Wash.2d 67, 145 P.2d 1019 (1944).

12. The decisions are conflicting. Not privileged: Hanlon v. Woodhouse, 113 Colo. 504, 160 P.2d 998 (1945); De Witt, Privileged Communication Between Physician and Patient 114 (1958). Privileged: Alder v. State, 239 Ind. 68, 154 N.E.2d 716 (1958).

13. People v. English, 31 Ill.2d 301, 201 N.E.2d 455 (1955) (under Sexually Dangerous Persons Act, Ill.Rev.Stat.1969 c. 38 §§ 105–1.01 to 105.12.); Keeton v. State, 175 Miss. 631, 167 So. 68 (1936) (to ascertain sanity of accused); Smiecek v. State, 243 Wis. 439, 10 N.W.2d 161 (1943) (same).

14. People v. Austin, 199 N.Y. 446, 93 N.E. 57 (1910) (sanity); Leard v. State, 30 Okl.Cr. 191, 235 Pac. 243 (1925).

15. When the purpose of the examination is solely to ascertain the person's mental condition, the physician-patient relationship is not created, and there is no privilege on that score for the person's disclosures. People v. Sliney, 137 N.Y. 570, 33 N.E. 150, 154 (1893); State v. Fouquette, 67 Nev. 505, 221 P.2d 404 (1950); State v. Riggle, 76 Wyo. 1, 298 P.2d 349 (1956); Simecek v. State, 243 Wis. 439, 10 N.W.2d 161 (1943); Dec.Dig. Witnesses ⚲209. But where the purpose of the committal to the hospital includes treatment as well as diagnosis, the disclosures will be protected. Taylor v. United States, 95 U.S.App.D.C. 373, 222 F.2d 398, 401, 402 (1955); Notes, 54 Mich.L.Rev. 423, 40 Minn.L.Rev. 621, 1955 Wash.U.L.Q. 405, Selected Writings on Evidence and Trial 258 (Fryer ed. 1957). And where the appointed panel includes the defendant's own psychiatrist who shared with the others his information gained in previous treatment, their testimony as to their findings is privileged. People v. Wasker, 353 Mich. 447, 91 N.W.2d 866 (1958).

As to whether an order for mental examination of an accused violates the privilege against self-incrimination, see § 134, infra.

16. Heath v. Broadway & S. A. Ry. Co., 8 N.Y.S. 863 (Super.Ct.Gen.T., 1890) But when the patient supposes that the doctor is a hospital specialist acting on his behalf, the privilege has been held to apply. Arizona & N. M. Ry. Co. v. Clark, 207 F. 817 (9th Cir. 1913).

17. McGinty v. Brotherhood of Railway Trainmen, 166 Wis. 83, 164 N.W. 249 (1917); 70 C.J. 441, n. 94. And so of an examination by employer's physician of an applicant for employment. Montzoukos v. Mutual Ben. Health & Accident Ins. Co., 69 Utah 309, 254 Pac. 1005 (1927).

18. City and County of San Francisco v. Superior Court, 37 Cal.2d 227, 231 P.2d 26 (1951) (but held that the communications were privileged under the attorney-client privilege), noted 25 So.Cal.L. Rev. 237, 13 U.Pitt.L.Rev. 428.

19. Leonczak v. Minneapolis, St. P. & S. S. M. Ry. Co., 161 Minn. 304, 201 N.W. 551 (1924); C.J.S. Witnesses § 294, n. 34.

If the patient's purpose in the consultation is an unlawful one, as to secure an illegal abortion,[20] to obtain narcotics in violation of law,[21] or as a fugitive from justice to have his appearance disguised by plastic surgery,[22] the law withholds the shield of privilege.

It has been held that where a doctor has attended a mother in her confinement and the newborn child, the child is a patient and can claim privilege against the doctor's disclosure of facts as to the apparent maturity of the child at birth.[23]

After the death of the patient the relation is ended and the object of the privilege can no longer be furthered. Accordingly, it seems the better view that facts discovered in an autopsy examination are not privileged.[24]

100. Subject Matter of the Privilege: Information Acquired in Attending the Patient and Necessary for Prescribing.

Although a considerable number of the statutes speak of "communications," most of them follow the lead of the pioneer New York and California provisions [25] in extending the privilege to all "information," secured by the doctor through his observation or examination [26] or by explicit communication from the patient, so far as "necessary to enable him to prescribe or act for the patient." [27]

While the information secured by the physician may be privileged the fact that he has been consulted by the patient and has treated

20. Seifert v. State, 160 Ind. 464, 67 N.E. 100 (1903); Sticha v. Benzick, 156 Minn. 52, 194 N.W. 752, 753 (1923).

21. The rule is codified in Uniform Narcotic Drug Act (1932, as amended 1958), § 17, par. 2, which provides that information given to a doctor "in an effort unlawfully to procure a narcotic drug, or unlawfully to procure the administration of any such drug" shall not be privileged.

22. Compare Model Code of Evidence Rule 222: "No person has a privilege under Rule 221 if the judge finds that sufficient evidence, aside from the communication, has been introduced to warrant a finding that the services of the physician were sought or obtained to enable or aid anyone to commit or to plan to commit a crime or a tort, or to escape detection or apprehension after the commission of a crime or a tort."

23. Jones v. Jones, 208 Misc. 721, 144 N.Y.S.2d 820 (S.Ct.Sp.T.1955); Notes, 28 Rocky Mt.L.Rev. 425, 7 Syracuse L.Rev. 347.

24. Eureka-Maryland Assur. Co. v. Gray, 74 App. D.C. 191, 121 F.2d 104, (1941); Ferguson v. Quaker City Life Ins. Co., 146 A.2d 580 (D.C.Mun.App. 1958); Cross v. Equitable Life Assur. Soc., 228 Iowa 800, 293 N.W. 464 (1940). Decisions pro and con are cited in 8 Wigmore, Evidence (McNaughton rev.) § 2382, note 11, and Note, 12 Minn.L. Rev. 390 (1928).

25. See § 98, supra.

26. This result is reached in states which have "communication" statutes, e. g., Heuston v. Simpson, 115 Ind. 62, 17 N.E. 261 (1888) (knowledge gained from words or by observation); Burns v. Waterloo, 187 Iowa 922, 173 N.W. 16 (1919) (intoxication, observed by doctor); McKee v. New Idea, 44 N.E.2d 697 (Ohio App.1942) (submission to examination is "communication"). And of course is also reached in the states having "information" statutes. Smoot v. Kansas City, 194 Mo. 513, 92 S.W. 363, 367 (1906) (information acquired from inspection, examination or observation, after the patient has submitted to examination); Hansen v. Sandvik, 128 Wash. 60, 222 Pac. 205 (X-ray photograph taken by attending doctor, privileged). Probably information which is apparent to everyone should not be regarded as privileged. People v. De France, 104 Mich. 563, 570, 62 N.W. 709, 711 (1895).

27. Instances of disclosures not necessary for treatment: Cook v. People, 60 Colo. 263, 153 Pac. 214 (1915) (defendant refused to allow physician to remove bullet from wound or tell how it was received); Meyers v. State, 192 Ind. 592, 137 N.E. 547, 24 A.L.R. 1196 (1922) (patient's threats, overheard by doctor, to kill his wife); Griffith v. Continental Casualty Co., 299 Mo. 426, 253 S.W. 1043 (1923) (patient's statement that life not worth living, might as well jump in river); see C.J.S. Witnesses § 295. It may well be debatable in a particular case whether the patient's statement as to how an accident happened, for which he is being treated, is information necessary for the treatment. See Raymond v. Burlington, C. R. & N. Ry. Co., 65 Iowa 152, 21 N.W. 495 (1884) (privileged); Green v. Metropolitan St. Ry. Co., 171 N.Y. 201, 63 N.E. 958 (1902) (not privileged: three judges dissenting). And whether the privilege attaches to the doctor's observation, when called to treat one injured by a collision or assault, that the patient shows signs of liquor, has been made to turn on this question. State v. Aguirre, 167 Kan. 266, 206 P.2d 118 (1949) (not privileged); Perry v. Hannagan, 257 Mich. 120, 241 N.W. 232, 79 A.L.R. 1127 (1932) (same: two judges dissenting). But other decisions sustaining the privilege without discussing the question of "necessity" are cited in Annot., 79 A.L.R. 1131.

him,[28] and the number and dates of his visits,[29] are not within the shelter of the privilege.

The extent to which the privilege attaches to the information embodied in hospital records is discussed in the chapter on Business Records.[30]

101.   The Confidential Character of the Disclosure: Presence of Third Persons and Members of Family: Information Revealed to Nurses and Attendants: Public Records.

We have seen that the statutes existing in many states codifying the privileges for marital communications and those between attorney and client usually omitted the requirement that to be privileged such communications must have been made in confidence. Nevertheless, the courts have read this limitation into these statutes, assuming that the legislatures must have intended this common law requirement to continue.[31]   The statutes giving the patient's privilege for information gained in professional consultations again omit the adjective "confidential." [32]   Should it nonetheless be read in, not as a continuation of a common law requirement, but as an interpretative gloss, spelled out from policy and analogy?   Certainly the policy arguments are strong.   First, the policy of holding all privileges within reasonable bounds since they cut off access to sources of truth. Second, the argument that the purpose of encouraging those who would otherwise be reluctant, to disclose necessary facts to their doctors, will be adequately served by extending a privilege for only such disclosures as the patient wishes to keep secret.

This principle of confidentiality [33] is supported by those decisions which hold that if a casual third person is present with the acquiescence of the patient at the consultation, the disclosures made in his presence are not privileged,[34] and thus the stranger, the patient and the doctor may be required to divulge them in court.

Under this view, however, if the third person is present as a needed and customary participant in the consultation, the circle of confidence may be reasonably extended to include him and the privilege will be maintained.   Thus the presence of one sustaining a close family relationship to the patient should not curtail the privilege.[35]   And the nurse present as the doctor's assistant during

---

28.   In re Albert Lindley Lee Memorial Hospital, 209 F.2d 122 (2d Cir. 1953) (names of patients not privileged in investigation of doctor's income tax liability), noted 67 Harv.L.Rev. 1272; Cross v. Equitable Life Assur. Soc., 228 Iowa 806, 293 N.W. 464 (1940).

29.   Padovani v. Liggett & Myers Tobacco Co., 23 F.R.D. 255 (E.D.N.Y.1959) ("The mere *facts* that on certain occasions the plaintiff submitted himself for diagnosis and treatment, as well as the dates of same, the names and addresses of the physicians, whether or not diagnoses were reduced to writing, and related matters, are subject to disclosure so long as the subject communicated is not stated."); Polish Roman Catholic Union v. Palen, 302 Mich. 557, 5 N.W.2d 463 (1942); Jenkins v. Metropolitan Life Ins. Co., 171 Ohio St. 557, 173 N.E.2d 122 (1961); In re Judicial Inquiry, 8 App.Div.2d 842, 190 N.Y.S.2d 406 (1959).

30.   See § 313, infra.

31.   See §§ 80, 91, supra.

32.   See § 98, supra.

33.   See 8 Wigmore, Evidence (McNaughton rev.) § 2381; C.J.S. Witnesses § 296; Dec.Dig. Witnesses ⊂⇒213.

34.   Horowitz v. Sacks, 89 Cal.App. 336, 265 Pac. 281 (1928) (several members of family present); In re Swartz, 79 Okl. 191, 192 Pac. 203, 16 A.L.R. 450, 453 (1920) (citing authorities); Note, 16 Neb.L.Bull. 206 (1937), Annot., 96 A.L.R. 1419; C.J.S. Witnesses § 299.

35.   Bassil v. Ford Motor Co., 278 Mich. 173, 270 N.W. 258, 107 A.L.R. 1491, 1493 (1936) (husband and wife consult doctor about their childlessness: but the principle of joint consultation could have been relied on); Denaro v. Prudential Ins. Co., 154 App.Div. 840, 139 N.Y.S. 758, 761 (1913) ("when a physician enters a house for the purpose of attending a patient, he is called upon to make inquiries, not alone of the sick person, but of those who are about him and who are familiar with the facts, and communications necessary for the proper performance of the duties of a physician are not public, because made in the presence of his immediate family or those who are present because of the illness of the person").

the consultation or examination, or the technician who makes tests or X-ray photographs under the doctor's direction, will be looked on as the doctor's agent in whose keeping the information will remain privileged.[36] What if the patient is taken in custody by an officer to the hospital, where he is examined and treated by a doctor and makes disclosures, willy nilly in the hearing range of the officer. Are these disclosures "confidential"? [37]

Many courts on the other hand do not analyze the problems in terms of whether the communications or disclosures were confidential and professional, but rather in terms of what persons are intended to be silenced as witnesses. This seems to be sticking in the bark of the statute, rather than looking at its purpose. Thus, these courts if casual third persons were present at the consultation will still close the mouth of the doctor but allow the visitor to speak.[38] And if nurses or other attendants or technicians gain information necessary to treatment they will be allowed by these courts to speak (unless the privilege statute specifically names them) but the physician may not.[39]

When the attending physician is required by law to make a certificate of death to the public authority, giving his opinion as to the cause, the certificate should be provable as a public record, despite the privilege. The duty to make a public report overrides the general duty of secrecy, and in view of the availability of the record to the public, the protection of the information from general knowledge, as contemplated by the privilege, cannot be attained. Accordingly, under the

---

36. Ostrowski v. Mockridge, 242 Minn. 265, 65 N.W. 2d 185 (1954) (nurse assisting doctor at examination; decisions cited and analyzed); Mississippi Power & Lt. Co. v. Jordan, 164 Miss. 174, 143 So. 483 (1932) (knowledge gained by nurse in assisting doctor to treat patient privileged); Culver v. Union Pac. Ry. Co., 112 Neb. 441, 199 N.W. 794, 797 (1924) (question to nurse as to doctor's taking blood specimen from patient in her presence and directing her to send the specimen for a test, and the results thereof privileged, as she acted as agent of doctor); State v. Bryant, 5 N.C.App. 21, 167 S.E.2d 841 (1969); and cases cited in Note, 22 Marq.L.Rev. 22 (1938), Annot., 47 A.L.R.2d 742.

A few courts will deny the privilege even when the nurse is acting as the doctor's assistant, see, e. g., Weis v. Weis, 147 Ohio St. 416, 72 N.E.2d 245, 169 A.L.R. 668 (1947). And if the nurse or technician acts independently of any physician, there is no privilege unless a statute so provides. See Block v. People, 125 Colo. 36, 240 P.2d 512 (1952) (blood test taken by technician), and on the topic generally see Dec.Dig. Witnesses ⊂⊃209; Annot., 47 A.L.R.2d 742.

The patient-privilege statutes in a few states, e. g., Arkansas and New York, specifically include information given to nurses within the scope of the privilege. See 8 Wigmore, Evidence (McNaughton rev.) § 2380, note 5.

For privileged aspects of hospital records, see § 313 at n. 10, infra.

37. A leading New York decision holds that despite the presence of a police guard, the question is whether under all the circumstances the disclosures were intended to be confidential. People v. Decina, 2 N.Y.2d 133, 157 N.Y.S.2d 558, 138 N.E.2d 799 (1956). But another court assumed that the presence of officers who had custody of the patient would like the presence of casual third persons render the disclosure nonconfidential. State v. Thomas, 78 Ariz. 52, 275 P.2d 408 (1954).

38. Iwerks v. People, 108 Colo. 556, 120 P.2d 961 (1942) (deputy sheriff present at doctor's examination of injured prisoner may testify as to what examination disclosed and prisoner's statements to doctor); Springer v. Byram, 137 Ind. 15, 36 N.E. 361, 363 (1894) (ambulance drivers could testify to accident victim's statements to doctor); Indiana Union Tr. Co. v. Thomas, 44 Ind.App. 468, 88 N.E. 356, 359 (1909) (patient privileged not to disclose communications with doctor, though in presence of daughter and friend); Leeds v. Prudential Ins. Co., 128 Neb. 395, 258 N.W. 672, 96 A.L.R. 1414, 1418 (1935) (bringing friend to consultation does not waive privilege); Annot., 96 A.L.R. 1419; C.J.S. Witnesses § 299.

And, as in the case of the other privileges for confidential communications, the eavesdropper is permitted to testify to what he overhears. Ryan v. Industrial Com'n, 72 N.E.2d 907 (Ohio App.1946) (dictum).

39. Collins v. Howard, 156 F.Supp. 322 (S.D.Ga. 1957); First Trust Co. v. Kansas City Life Ins. Co., 79 F.2d 48, 52 (8th Cir. 1935) (nurse and dietician could testify as to information gained in carrying out doctors' instructions for care of patient); Weis v. Weis, 147 Ohio St. 416, 72 N.E.2d 245, 169 A.L.R. 668 (1947) (similar to last); Prudential Ins. Co. v. Kozlowski, 226 Wis. 641, 276 N.W. 300 (1937) (testimony of nurse and X-ray operator received); Note, 22 Marq.L.Rev. 211 (1938); Annot., 47 A.L.R. 2d 742.

prevailing view, the privilege does not attach.[40]

102.   Rule of Privilege, Not Incompetency: Privilege Belongs to the Patient, Not to an Objecting Party as Such: Effect of the Patient's Death.

As has been pointed out in the discussion of privileges generally,[41] the rule which excludes disclosures to physicians is not a rule of incompetency of evidence serving the end of protecting the adverse party against unreliable or prejudicial testimony. It is a rule of privilege protecting the extrinsic interest of the patient and designed to promote health, not truth. It encourages free disclosure in the sickroom by preventing disclosure in the courtroom. The patient is the person to be encouraged and he is the holder of the privilege.[42]

Consequently, he alone during his lifetime has the right to claim or to waive the privilege. If he is in a position to claim it and does not, it is waived [43] and no one else may assert

it.[44] If he is not present and so far as known is unaware of the proposed disclosure, the judge in his discretion according to some authority may enforce the privilege of his own motion.[45] Accordingly, if the judge at the suggestion of a party or counsel or the physician-witness, enforces the privilege, this is not to be understood as the assertion of a right by the party or counsel or witness but as an informal invocation of discretion. The adverse party as such has no interest to protect if he is not the patient, and thus cannot object as of right,[46] and should have no right to complain on appeal if the patient's privilege is erroneously denied.[47]

The whole supposition of the patient-privilege legislation, that the patient's fear of revelation in court of the information he gives the doctor will be such as to discourage

---

40.   Polish Roman Catholic Union v. Palen, 302 Mich. 557, 5 N.W.2d 463 (1942); Randolph v. Supreme Liberty Life Ins. Co., 359 Mo. 251, 221 S.W.2d 155 (1949); Perry v. Industrial Commission, 160 Ohio St. 520, 117 N.E.2d 34 (1954); and cases cited 8 Wigmore, Evidence (McNaughton rev.) § 2385a. Contra: Davis v. Supreme Lodge, 165 N.Y. 159, 58 N.E. 891 (1900) (two judges dissenting). Compare the similar question about the records of public hospitals, discussed in 8 Wigmore, Evidence (McNaughton rev.) § 2382(3), and see § 313, infra.

41.   See § 72, supra.

42.   Metropolitan Life Ins. Co. v. Kaufman, 104 Colo. 13, 87 P.2d 758 (1939) (physician compelled to give testimony where privilege had been waived by patient. "Privileged communications are personal to the patient only."); Maas v. Laursen, 219 Minn. 461, 18 N.W.2d 233, 158 A.L.R. 213 (1945) (dictum, privilege belongs to patient and can be waived only by him); 8 Wigmore, Evidence (McNaughton rev.) § 2386; Dec.Dig. Witnesses ⚖217.

43.   People v. Bloom, 193 N.Y. 1, 85 N.E. 824 (1908) (patient who fails to claim privilege against testimony of his physicians, at first trial, a civil case, waives permanently and cannot object to similar testimony at his later trial for perjury).

44.   See State v. Thomas, 1 Wash.2d 298, 95 P.2d 1036 (1939) (defendant charged with carnal knowledge of child, could not object to physician's testimony where child and mother did not; but here physician made examination at instance of county and doctor-patient relation probably did not exist). A similar holding on similar facts is State v. Fackrell, 44 Wash.2d 874, 271 P.2d 679, 681 (1954).

45.   Model Code of Evidence Rule 105, "The judge . . . in his discretion determines . . . (e) whether to exclude, of his own motion, evidence which would violate a privilege of a person who is neither a party nor the witness from whom the evidence is sought if the privilege has not been waived or otherwise terminated. . . ."

West's Ann.Cal.Evid.Code, §§ 994, 995 require the physician to claim the privilege unless otherwise instructed by the patient.

46.   Thus, after the death of the patient, in a suit on an insurance policy, the insurer cannot assert the privilege. Olson v. Court of Honor, 100 Minn. 117, 110 N.W. 374, 377 (1907); Hier v. Farmers Mut. Fire Ins. Co., 104 Mont. 471, 67 P.2d 831, 110 A.L.R. 1051 (1937). Contra: Westover v. Aetna Life Ins. Co., 99 N.Y. 56, 1 N.E. 104 (1885). See Annot., 2 A.L.R.2d 645, 658.

47.   See Vance v. State, 143 Miss. 121, 108 So. 433, 45 A.L.R. 1348 (1926). In that case the defendant charged with murder objected to the testimony of the physician who examined the victim, and this was overruled. Ethridge, J. held that "if it was error to admit the evidence it is error of which he [the accused] cannot complain." Two judges concurred in affirmance on another ground. Three judges dissented.

free disclosure, is highly speculative. To think that he is likely to be influenced by fear that such revelations may occur after his death seems particularly fanciful. A rule that the privilege terminated with the patient's death would have reached a common-sense result which would have substantially lessened the obstructive effect of the privilege. The courts, however have not taken this tack but hold that the privilege continues after death.[48] Nevertheless, in contests of the survivors in interest with third parties, e. g., actions to recover property claimed to belong to the deceased, actions for the death of the deceased, or actions upon life insurance policies, the personal representative, heir or next of kin, or the beneficiary in the policy may waive the privilege,[49] and by the same token, the adverse party may not effectively assert the privilege.[50] In contests over the validity of a will, where both sides—the executor on the one hand and the heirs or next of kin on the other—claim under and not ad-

versely to the decedent, the assumption should prevail that the decedent would desire that the validity of his will should be determined in the fullest light of the facts.[51] Accordingly in this situation either the executor or the contestants may effectively waive the privilege without the concurrence of the other.[52]

103. What Constitutes a Waiver of the Privilege?

The physician-patient statutes, though commonly phrased in terms of incompetency, are nevertheless held to create merely a privilege for the benefit of the patient, which he may waive.[53]

Generally [54] it is agreed that a contractual stipulation waiving the privilege, such as is

48. Bassil v. Ford Motor Co., 278 Mich. 173, 270 N.W. 258, 107 A.L.R. 1491 (1936).

Acc. West's Ann.Cal.Evid.Code, § 996.

49. Aetna Life Ins. Co. v. McAdoo, 106 F.2d 618 (8th Cir. 1939) (beneficiary under life policy); Harvey v. Silber, 300 Mich. 510, 2 N.W.2d 483 (1942) (administrator suing for death due to defendants' alleged malpractice); Industrial Com'n v. Warnke, 131 Ohio St. 140, 2 N.E.2d 248 (1936) (widow suing for compensation for death of husband); Colwell v. Dyer, 35 N.E.2d 789, (Ohio App. 1941) (administrator, plaintiff in death action); Weis v. Weis, 147 Ohio St. 416, 72 N.E.2d 245, 169 A.L.R. 668 (1947) (contestee in will contest waives privilege when he calls attending doctor to testify to privileged matter—but here not privileged). A statute in Ohio codifying this result is discussed in Ball, Legislative Note, 14 Ohio St.L.J. 432 (1953). See also the valuable Note, Waiver of Privilege in Will Contest, 39 Minn.L.Rev. 800 (1955).

50. Wimberley v. State, 217 Ark. 130, 228 S.W.2d 991 (1950); Jasper v. State, 269 P.2d 375 (Okl.Cr. 1954); Dec.Dig. Witnesses ⊂⊃217, and see cases cited note 46, supra. An early New York case, however, holds that any party may raise the objection, and it remains for the patient to waive. Westover v. Aetna Life Ins. Co., 99 N.Y. 56, 1 N.E. 104, 105, 106 (1885). This position seems insupportable.

51. "If he did not have testamentary capacity, then the paper was not his will, and it is not the policy of the law to maintain such an instrument. It is undoubtedly the policy of the law to uphold the testamentary disposition of property, but not until it is ascertained whether such a disposition has been made. . . . And no one can be said to represent the deceased in that contest, for he could only be interested in having the truth ascertained, and his estate can only be protected by establishing or defeating the instrument as the truth so ascertained may require. The testimony of the attending physician is usually reliable, and often controlling, and to place it at the disposal of one party to such a proceeding and withhold it from the other would be manifestly partial and unjust." Ladd, J., in Winters v. Winters, 102 Iowa 53, 71 N.W. 184, 185 (1897).

52. Hyatt v. Wroten, 184 Ark. 847, 43 S.W.2d 726 (1931) (heirs); Marker v. McCue, 50 Idaho 462, 297 Pac. 401 (1931) (executor); Winters v. Winters, supra (heir); Gorman v. Hickey, 145 Kan. 54, 64 P.2d 587 (1937) (heir contesting the will could waive though executor opposed the waiver); Annot., 97 A.L.R.2d 393. It seems that suits attacking conveyances made by the deceased on grounds of incapacity are within the same principle. See Calhoun v. Jacobs, 79 App.D.C. 29, 141 F.2d 729 (1944) (heir may waive, despite grantee's invocation of the privilege); Schornick v. Schornick, 25 Ariz. 563, 220 Pac. 397, 31 A.L.R. 159 (1923) (same).

Acc., West's Ann.Cal.Evid.Code, § 1003.

53. Stayner v. Nye, 227 Ind. 231, 85 N.E.2d 496 (1949).

54. In Michigan such an agreement to waive is held invalid as against public policy. Gilchrist v. Mys-

frequently included in applications for life or health insurance, or in the policies themselves, is valid and effectual.[55]

How far does the patient's testifying waive the privilege? Doubtless, if the patient on direct examination testifies to,[56] or adduces other evidence of,[57] the communications exchanged or the information furnished to the doctor consulted this would waive in respect to such consultations. When, however, the patient in his direct testimony does not reveal any privileged matter respecting the consultation, but testifies only to his physical or mental condition, existing at the time of such consultation, then one view is that, "where the patient tenders to the jury the issue as to his physical condition, it must in fairness and justice be held that he has himself waived the obligation of secrecy." [58] This view has the great merit of curtailing the scope of an obstructive privilege, but there is some logic in the position of the larger number of courts which hold that the patient's testimony as to his condition without disclosure of privileged matter is not a waiver.[59] If the patient reveals privileged matter on cross-examination, without claiming the privilege, this is usually held not to be a

---

tic Workers of the World, 196 Mich. 247, 248, 163 N.W. 10, 11 (1917). A New York statute which provided that a waiver "must be made in open court, on the trial of the action or proceeding, and a paper executed by a party prior to the trial . . . shall be insufficient," is no longer in effect. N.Y.C.P.L.R. 4504.

55. New York Life Ins. Co. v. Taylor, 79 U.S.App. D.C. 66, 147 F.2d 297 (1945); Murphy v. Mut. L. Ins. Co., 62 Idaho 362, 112 P.2d 993, 994 (1941); Templeton v. Mut. Life Ins. Co., 177 Okl. 94, 57 P.2d 841 (1936); 1 Wigmore, Evidence § 7a; Note, 16 N.C.L.Rev. 53 (1938); Annot., 54 A.L.R. 412; Dec.Dig. Witnesses ⚲219(6). But occasionally a court by an eccentric interpretation may emasculate the waiver. Noble v. United Ben. Life Ins. Co., 230 Iowa 471, 297 N.W. 881 (1941) (consent to doctor's furnishing to insurer information gained in attending patient is not waiver of privilege as to doctor's testimony in court.)

56. Nolan v. Glynn, 163 Iowa 146, 142 N.W. 1029 (1913) (plaintiff in breach of promise case testifying as to consultation of doctor about pregnancy and abortion, waived as to such consultation, but not as to earlier, distinct ones); Epstein v. Pennsylvania R. Co., 250 Mo. 1, 156 S.W. 699 (1913) (". . . since plaintiff had himself voluntarily gone upon the stand, and in his case in chief, as a witness for himself, laid bare for lucre's sake all of the secrets of his sickroom, since he had told and retold what Dr. Elston, his physician, said to him, and what he said to Elston, since he had told the precise nature of his alleged hurts as he said Elston found them, and since he had also voluntarily related the treatment professionally given to him by Elston, he waived the competency of other physicians, also there present, having knowledge of the identical facts."); Annot., 114 A.L.R. 798, 802.

57. Buckminster's Estate v. Commissioner of Internal Revenue, 147 F.2d 331 (2d Cir. 1944) (executrix introducing statements and diagnosis of physician who attended decedent waived privilege).

58. Andrews, J. in Hethier v. Johns, 233 N.Y. 370, 135 N.E. 603 (1922). To like effect see O'Brien v. Gen. Accident, etc. Corp., 42 F.2d 48, 53 (8th Cir. 1930) (under 1925 amendment to Nebraska privilege statute, beneficiary waives "by offering any testimony touching the physical or mental condition of the insured"); Moreno v. New Guadalupe Mining Co., 35 Cal.App. 744, 170 Pac. 1088 (1918); Freisen v. Reimer, 124 Neb. 620, 247 N.W. 561 (1933) (under specific provision of Nebraska statute); 8 Wigmore, Evidence (McNaughton rev.) § 2389(2).

59. Arizona & N. M. Ry. Co. v. Clark, 235 U.S. 669 (1915) (plaintiff testified as to his injury and called nurse as witness, held no waiver under Arizona statute which provides that it is waiver if patient testifies as "to such communications," Hughes and Day, J.J., dissenting); Webb v. Quincy City Lines, Inc., 73 Ill.App.2d 405, 219 N.E.2d 165 (1966) (communications to psychiatrist concerning pain and suffering as result of injuries from automobile accident; held no waiver of privilege by bringing suit for damages); Harpman v. Devine, 133 Ohio St. 1, 10 N.E.2d 776, 114 A.L.R. 789 (1937) (two judges dissenting), critically noted 51 Harv.L.Rev. 931; Hudson v. Blanchard, 294 P.2d 554 (Okla.1956), critically noted 11 Okla.L.Rev. 450; Clawson v. Walgreen Drug Co., 108 Utah 577, 162 P.2d 759 (1945) (no waiver when patient testified concerning nature and extent of injury, but did not give evidence of what doctors told him nor of details of treatment); Noelle v. Hoquiam Lumber & Shingle Co., 47 Wash. 519, 92 Pac. 372 (1907) (forceful dissent by Root, J., joined by Hadley, C.J.); Green v. Nebagamain, 113 Wis. 508, 89 N.W. 520 (1902), and cases cited in Annot., 114 A.L.R. 798; Dec.Dig. Witnesses ⚲219(5).

See Bond v. Independent Order of Foresters, 69 Wash. 2d 879, 421 P.2d 351 (1966) (holding that pretrial deposition given by plaintiff testifying as to the nature and extent of her injuries did not constitute a waiver of the privilege).

waiver of the privilege enabling the adversary to make further inquiry of the doctors, on the ground that such revelations were not "voluntary." [60] The counter-argument, that the failure to assert the privilege should be a complete waiver, seems persuasive.

If the patient examines a physician as to matters disclosed in a consultation, or course of treatment, of course this is a waiver and opens the door to the opponent to examine him about any other matters then disclosed.[61] And if several doctors participated jointly in the same consultation or course of treatment the calling of one to disclose part of the shared information waives objection to the adversary's calling any other of the joint consultants to testify about the consultation, treatment or the results thereof.[62] Liberal courts go further and hold that calling by the patient of one doctor and eliciting privileged matter from him opens the door to the opponent's calling other doctors consulted by the patient at other times to bring out any facts relevant to the issue on which the privileged proof was adduced.[63] It is not con-

sonant with justice and fairness to permit the patient to reveal his secrets to several doctors and then when his condition comes in issue to limit the witnesses to the consultants favorable to his claims.[64] But a substantial number of courts balk at this step.[65]

A failure by a patient to object to the testimony of one of his physicians called by the adversary seems generally to be given the same effect, in respect to waiver, that the particular court would give to the patient's

stand to prove that he has had disability from tuberculosis since time of claim; held this warrants defendant in proving by another doctor that plaintiff had same disease several years before, in support of its plea of misrepresentation); Hogue v. Massa, 80 S.D. 319, 123 N.W.2d 131, 5 A.L.R.3d 1236 (1963) (malpractice action; held there was no waiver of privilege as to physician who treated the patient after his treatment by the defendant physicians with whom there had been no consultation); McUne v. Fuqua, 42 Wash.2d 65, 253 P.2d 632 (1953) (lucid discussion by Hamley, J.); and cases cited in Annot., 5 A.L.R.3d 1244; Note, 1955 Wash.U.L.Q. 405, 409–412.

Compare the provision in Rule 35(b) (2) of the Federal Rules of Civil Procedure to the effect that if a person who has been examined by a physician under order of court, requests and obtains a copy of the doctor's report, he "waives any privilege he may have . . . regarding the testimony of every other person who has examined or may thereafter examine him in respect of the same mental or physical condition."

64. "A litigant should not be allowed to pick and choose in binding and loosing; he may bind or he may loose. . . . He may choose a serviceable and mellow one out of a number of physicians to fasten liability upon the defendant, and then, presto! change! exclude the testimony of those not so mellow and serviceable, to whom he has voluntarily given the same information and the same means of getting at a conclusion on the matter already uncovered by professional testimony to the jury. There is no reason in such condition of things, and where reason ends the law ends." Lamm, J. in Smart v. Kansas City, 208 Mo. 162, 105 S.W. 709, 722 (1907).

60. Johnson v. Kinney, 232 Iowa 1016, 7 N.W.2d 188, 144 A.L.R. 997 (1943); Hemminghaus v. Ferguson, 358 Mo. 476, 215 S.W.2d 481 (1948) overruled on another aspect of waiver of the privilege in State ex rel. McNutt v. Keet, 432 S.W.2d 597 (Mo.1968) (see note 70, infra) (deposition of adverse party taken under the rules for cross-examination). Harpman v. Devine, 133 Ohio St. 1, 10 N.E.2d 776, 114 A.L.R. 789 (1937) and cases cited in Annot., 114 A.L.R. 798, 806.

61. Maas v. Laursen, 219 Minn. 461, 18 N.W.2d 233, 158 A.L.R. 215 (1945); Demonbrunn v. McHaffie, 348 Mo. 1120, 156 S.W.2d 923 (1942).

62. Doll v. Scandrett, 201 Minn. 319, 276 N.W. 281 (1937) (three judges dissenting), noted 22 Minn.L. Rev. 580; Morris v. New York, O. & W. R. Co., 148 N.Y. 88, 42 N.E. 410 (1895). Contra: Jones v. Caldwell, 20 Idaho 5, 116 Pac. 110 (1911). See Annot., 5 A.L.R.3d 1244.

63. Weissman v. Wells, 306 Mo. 82, 267 S.W. 400 (1924) (personal injury plaintiff who claimed nervous state due to injury, by calling doctor to testify to her condition after injury waived objection to defendant's proving by other doctor her same condition before injury); Steinberg v. New York Life Ins. Co., 263 N.Y. 45, 188 N.E. 152 (1933) (plaintiff suing on disability policy puts doctor on

65. No waiver as to doctors consulted separately. Mays v. New Amsterdam Cas. Co., 40 App.D.C. 249, 46 L.R.A.,N.S., 1108, 1112 (1913); Acme-Evans Co. v. Schnepf, 214 Ind. 394, 14 N.E.2d 561 (1938); Johnson v. Kinney, 232 Iowa 1016, 7 N.W.2d 188, 144 A.L.R. 997 (1942); United States Nat. Life & Cas. Co., 148 Okl. 274, 298 Pac. 619 (1931) and cases cited in Annot., 5 A.L.R.3d 1244; 58 Am. Jur. Witnesses § 458; Dec.Dig. Witnesses ☞219(5).

calling and examination of the doctor as his own witness.[66]

A shrinking from the embarrassment which comes from exposure of bodily disease or abnormality is human and natural. It is arguable that legal protection from exposure is justified to encourage frankness in consulting physicians. But it is neither human, natural, nor understandable to claim protection from exposure by asserting a privilege for communications to doctors, at the very same time when the patient is parading before the public the mental or physical condition as to which he consulted the doctor, by bringing an action for damages arising from that same condition.[67] This in the oft-repeated phrase is to make the privilege not a shield only, but a sword. Consequently, the California statute provides that there is no physician patient-privilege "as to a communication relevant to an issue concerning the condition of the patient" if the issue has been tendered by the patient or any party claiming through or under him or for his wrongful death.[68] Until recently a majority of the courts unaided by statute have been unwilling to take this step.[69] There is indication of a breakthrough and courts in at least two jurisdictions have held that the commencement of an action involving the physical condition of the plaintiff operates as a waiver of the privilege though no provision for waiver is set out by statute.[70] The question arises oftentimes when the defense seeks to take the physician's pretrial deposition and some courts hold that where the trial cannot proceed without waiver of the privilege by the plaintiff the action will be stayed until such time as the plaintiff would permit pretrial examination of the doctor. This in effect requires waiver of the privilege to be accelerated.[71] As Chief Justice Lamm said in respect to another phase of waiver of the patient's privilege, "The scandals in beating down the truth arising from a too harsh and literal interpretation of this law (if unaided and unrelieved by waiver) every one of us knows by experience and observation in the courtroom." [72]

If a testator by his request procures an attending doctor to subscribe his will as an attesting witness this is a waiver of the privi-

---

66. See, e. g., Captron v. Douglass, 193 N.Y. 11, 85 N.E. 827 (1908) (malpractice; failure of plaintiff to object to testimony of one of two doctors who treated him after defendant did, was waiver as to other also).

67. "The patient-litigant exception precludes one who has placed in issue his physical condition from invoking the privilege on the ground that disclosure of his condition would cause him humiliation. He cannot have his cake and eat it too." City and County of San Francisco v. Superior Court, 37 Cal. 2d 227, 231 P.2d 26, 28, 25 A.L.R.2d 1418 (1951) (by Traynor, J.).

68. West's Ann.Cal.Evid.Code, § 996.

69. Federal Mining & Smelting Co. v. Dalo, 252 Fed. 356, 359 (10th Cir. 1918); Smart v. Kansas City, 208 Mo. 162, 105 S.W. 709, 714, but see dissent by Lamm, J. at 722 (1907); Bond v. Independent Order of Foresters, 69 Wash.2d 879, 421 P.2d 351 (1966).

70. Mathis v. Hilderbrand, 416 P.2d 8, 21 A.L.R.3d 907 (Alaska 1966) (holding that the plaintiff by bringing a personal injury action waived the privilege to the extent that the attending physicians could be required to testify on pretrial depositions with respect to the injuries sued upon); State ex rel. McNutt v. Keet, 432 S.W.2d 597 (Mo.1968) opinion by Seiler, J., "We therefore hold that once the matter of plaintiff's physical condition is in issue under the pleadings, plaintiff will be considered to have waived the privilege under § 491.-060(5) so far as information from doctors or medical and hospital records bearing on that issue is concerned."); Note, 51 Minn.L.Rev. 575 (1967); Annot., 21 A.L.R.3d 912 (1968).

71. Mariner v. Great Lakes Dredge & Dock Co., 202 F.Supp. 430 (N.D.Ohio 1962); Awtry v. United States, 27 F.R.D. 399 (S.D.N.Y.1961); Kriger v. Holland Furnace Co., 12 App.Div.2d 44, 208 N.Y.S. 2d 285 (1960).

72. Epstein v. Pennsylvania R. Co., 250 Mo. 1, 156 S.W. 699, 711 (1913).

The principle is approved in Randa v. Bear, 50 Wash. 2d 415, 312 P.2d 640 (1957) (filing of cross-complaint on medical service contract waived privilege). Analogous is the holding that when an accused places his sanity in issue he waives the privilege as to doctors who have examined him as to sanity. State v. Cochran, 356 Mo. 778, 203 S.W.2d 707 (1947).

lege as to all facts affecting the validity of the will.[73]

104.   Kinds of Proceedings Exempted from the Application of the Privilege.[74]

Unless the statute creating the privilege limits its application the privilege generally applies to criminal as well as civil proceedings.[75] However, criminal prosecutions generally [76] and workmen's compensation proceedings [77] are frequently withdrawn by statute from the operation of the privilege. Other types of controversies in which the privilege is occasionally withheld or curtailed in the statutes are actions for malpractice,[78]

prosecutions for homicide,[79] assault with a deadly weapon,[80] lunacy proceedings [81] and will contests.[82] Whenever the issue turns upon the diagnosis and treatment of attending physicians and their assistants, then the application of the privilege closes the main source of knowledge and can end only in frustration and injustice. Thus, in New York City the City Council under statutory authority provided for a Committee with subpoena powers to investigate charges of maladministration of Lincoln Hospital. The Committee called upon the Commissioner of Hospitals to produce the records of treatment of certain patients. It was held, however, that the privilege forbade such production.[83] Here it seems strongly arguable that the very policy of promoting better medical care, which is the purpose of the privilege, should lead the court to open the door for this investigation.[84]

105.   The Policy and Future of the Privilege.[85]

Some statements of Buller, J., in 1792 in a case involving the application of the attor-

---

73. In re Mullin's Estate, 110 Cal. 252, 42 P. 645 (1895); Stormon v. Weiss, 65 N.W.2d 475, 512 (N.D.1954); 8 Wigmore, Evidence (McNaughton rev.) § 2390(1).

74. C.J.S. Witnesses § 301; 58 Am.Jur. Witnesses, §§ 432–434; Dec.Dig. Witnesses ⊂═208(2).

75. 8 Wigmore, Evidence (McNaughton rev.) § 2385; C.J.S. Witnesses § 301; Annot., 7 A.L.R.3d 1458. But see Moosa v. Abdalla, 248 La. 344, 178 So.2d 273 (1965) holding that under the Louisiana statute, Annotated R.S. 15:476, the privilege applies in criminal but not in civil cases.

76. The original California Code provision, C.C.P. § 1881, par. 4, was limited to "a civil action," and this limitation has been followed by many states which have taken over that code, e. g., Idaho, Oregon, South Dakota and Washington. The present California Code provides there is no physician-patient privilege in a criminal proceeding. West's Ann.Cal.Evid.Code § 998. Pennsylvania has a similar limitation. See the statutes as compiled in 8 Wigmore, Evidence (McNaughton rev.) § 2380, note 5. Most states apart from specific provision seem to deny the accused the power to assert the privilege as to information given by the victim of a crime to a physician. Annot., 2 A.L.R. 2d 645.

77. More than half the states which have the privilege provide that it shall not apply in Workmen's Compensation proceedings. See the statutes compiled in 8 Wigmore, Evidence (McNaughton rev.) § 2380, note 6.

78. As in West's Ann.Cal.Evid.Code, § 1001. See 8 Wigmore, Evidence (McNaughton rev.) § 2380, note 5. And even in the absence of specific provision, it is sometimes held that in such a suit the defendant, despite the privilege, must be permitted to testify to the facts necessary to his defence. Cramer v. Hurt, 154 Mo. 112, 55 S.W. 258 (1900). See § 91, supra.

79. As in the District of Columbia and in Wisconsin. See statutes compiled in 8 Wigmore, Evidence (McNaughton rev.) § 2380, note 5.

80. State v. Antill, 176 Ohio St. 61, 197 N.E.2d 548 (1961) (holding that it was proper for the physician who treated the victim of the assault to testify to the nature of the wound since the physician was required by statute to report the details to law-enforcement authorities and the only purpose served by sustaining the privilege would be to obstruct the course of justice).

81. As in West's Ann.Cal.Evid.Code, § 1004.

82. As in West's Ann.Cal.Evid.Code, §§ 1000, 1003. And see § 102, supra.

83. New York City Council v. Goldwater, 284 N.Y. 296, 31 N.E.2d 31, 133 A.L.R. 728 (1940) (two judges dissenting).

84. See Note, 26 Corn.L.Q. 482, 484. For other notes, see 4 U.Detroit L.J. 173, 54 Harv.L.Rev. 705, 16 Ind.L.J. 592, 39 Mich.L.Rev. 1258, 89 U.Pa.L.Rev. 961. See also Annot., 133 A.L.R. 732.

85. There is a wealth of cogent discussion of the policy of the privilege. All that I have seen are adverse. Wigmore's scalpel cuts deepest. 8 Evidence (McNaughton rev.) § 2380a. Other excellent

ney-client privilege seem to have furnished the inspiration for the pioneer New York statute of 1828 on the doctor-patient privilege. He said: "The privilege is confined to the cases of counsel, solicitor, and attorney. . . . It is indeed hard in many cases to compel a friend to disclose a confidential conversation; and I should be glad if by law such evidence could be excluded. It is a subject of just indignation where persons are anxious to reveal what has been communicated to them in a confidential manner. . . . There are cases to which it is much to be lamented that the law of privilege is not extended; those in which medical persons are obliged to disclose the information which they acquire by attending in their professional characters."[86]

These comments reveal attitudes which have been influential ever since in the spread of statutes enacting the doctor-patient privilege. One attitude is the shrinking from forcing anyone to tell in court what he has learned in confidence. It is well understood today, however, that no such sweeping curtain for disclosure of confidences in the courtroom could be justified. Another is the complete failure to consider the other side of the shield, namely, the loss which comes from depriving the courts of any reliable source of facts necessary for the right decision of cases.

Perhaps the main burden of Justice Buller's remarks, however, is the suggestion that since the client's disclosures to the lawyer are privileged, the patient's disclosures to the doctor should have the same protection. This analogy has probably been more potent than any other argument, particularly with the lawyers in the legislatures. They would be reluctant to deny to the medical profession a recognition which the courts have themselves provided for the legal profession. Manifestly, however, the soundness of the privilege may not be judged as a matter of rivalry of professions, but by the criterion of the public interest. It has been persuasively urged that the same need for the protection of the patient's confidences as in the case of the client's communications does not exist.[87] As the client considers what he shall reveal to his lawyer he will often have

---

discussions: De Witt, Privileged Communications Between Physician and Patient, Ch. IV (1958); Chafee, Is Justice Served by Closing the Doctor's Mouth?, 52 Yale L.J. 607 (1943); Purrington, An Abused Privilege, 6 Colum.L.Rev. 388 (1906) (historical, comparative, critical); Notes, 33 Ill.L.Rev. 483 (1939), 12 Minn.L.Rev. 390 (1928). See also for worthwhile treatments: Welch, Another Anomaly—the Patient's Privilege, 13 Miss.L.J. 137 (1941) (emphasis on local decisions); Curd, Privileged Communications between Doctor and Patient —an Anomaly, 44 W.Va.L.Q. 165 (1938); Long, Physician-Patient Privilege Obstructs Justice, 25 Ins.Counsel J. 224 (1958).

86. Wilson v. Rastall, 4 Term Rep. 753, 759, 100 Eng. Rep. 1287 (K.B.1792).

The Revisers who drafted the New York statute, supported it in their report as follows: "In 4 Term, Rep. 580, Buller, J. (to whom no one will attribute a disposition to relax the rules of evidence), said it was 'much to be lamented' that the information specified in this section was not privileged. Mr. Phillips expresses the same sentiment in his treatise on evidence, p. 104. The ground on which communications to counsel are privileged, is the supposed necessity of a full knowledge of the facts, to advise correctly, and to prepare for the proper defense for prosecution of a suit. But surely the necessity of consulting a medical adviser, when life itself may be in jeopardy, is still stronger. And unless such consultations are privileged, men will be incidentally punished by being obliged to suffer the consequences of injuries without relief from the medical art and without conviction of any offense. Besides, in such cases, during the struggle between legal duty on the one hand, and professional honor on the other, the latter, aided by a strong sense of the injustice and inhumanity of

the rule, will in most cases furnish a temptation to the perversion or concealment of truth, too strong for human resistance. In every view that can be taken of the policy, justice or humanity of the rule, as it exists, its relaxation seems highly expedient. It is believed that the proposition in the section is so guarded, that it cannot be abused by applying it to cases not intended to be privileged." Original Reports of Revisers, vol. 5, p. 34, quoted Purrington, op. cit., 6 Colum.L.Rev. 392, 393.

87. See especially the discussions of Wigmore and Chafee, cited in note 85, supra. Compare, however, recent suggestions, supported by a trial court decision, that confidences to a psychiatrist stand on a special footing and should be privileged even

in mind the possibility of the exposure of his statements in court, for the lawyer's office is the very anteroom to the courthouse. The patient, on the other hand, in most instances, in consulting his doctor will have his thoughts centered on his illness or injury and his hopes for betterment or cure, and the thought of some later disclosure of his confidences in the courtroom would not usually be a substantial factor in curbing his freedom of communication with his doctor. Accordingly, the justification in the need for encouraging the frank disclosure of information to the doctor seems to have slight relevancy to the actual play of forces upon the average patient.

Doubtless the willingness of the doctors to advocate the adoption of privilege statutes is in large part due to their esteem for the tradition, dignity and honor of the profession. The tradition of respect for the confidences of the patient is an ancient and honorable one. But the Hippocratic oath does not enjoin absolute secrecy on all occasions,[88] and doubtless the modern oaths of secrecy could well be understood as being subject to justified departure for the saving of life or in conformity with the requirements of law in the interest of justice. Actually, this practice of the physician in his everyday walks of abstaining from gossiping about his patients, of which the doctor's honor, and not the law, is the guardian, is a far more important factor in inspiring frankness in the patient than any courtroom privilege can be.[89]

Nor does the privilege in fact usually operate to protect against public exposure of humiliating facts. Usually the facts are not shameful, save as they may disclose falsehood in the patient's claims, and the various contentions as to what the facts are, are fully and publicly made known in the pleadings, the opening statements and the other testimony.[90]

If actually the chief effect of the privilege is to enable the patient to tell on the witness-stand a story of his ailment, injury or state of health, without contradiction from his physician whose testimony would prove the first story to be untrue, does such a privilege, and such enforced silence, promote the honor and dignity of the medical profession?

In a rare case, one will read between the lines a situation in which a doctor, after examining or treating a patient, will for mercenary motives betray his secrets before litigation to the defendant who has injured the patient, or to a life insurance company against whom the patient's family has a claim. Such rare cases, however, lend little support to the privilege. Despite his disloyalty the testimony of such a doctor may be

though a general patient's privilege is not recognized. Notes, Guttmacher and Weihofen, 28 Ind. L.J. 32 (1952), 47 Nw.U.L.Rev. 384 (1952); F.R.Ev. (R.D.1971) 504 and Advisory Committee's Note.

88. See Purrington, op. cit., 6 Colum.L.Rev. at 395, and see the discussion of the scope and effect of this oath in Morrison v. Malmquist, 62 So.2d 415 (Fla.1953) and in the able article, Dewitt, Medical Ethics and the Law, 5 West Reserve L.Rev. 5, 7 (1953).

89. Purrington calls attention to art. 378 of the French Code Pénal which makes the doctor's dis-

closure of a medical secret, *except under compulsion of law*, punishable by fine and imprisonment, and he adds this comment: "Litigation is too uncommon an incident in the life of the average man for the anticipation of it to prove a deterrent. Gossip, on the other hand, and the desire to publish scientific, or pseudo-scientific papers are constant temptations to violation of confidence. Yet the physician is left free under our law to prattle at will of his patient's condition and affairs, subject in remote contingencies to a civil action for damages, and is forbidden to speak of them only when the interests of justice demand disclosure of that truth which the patient, it may be, is suppressing or misrepresenting in court." 6 Colum.L.Rev. at pp. 394, 396, 397.

90. See 8 Wigmore, Evidence (McNaughton rev.) § 2380a, p. 830, where he says: "From asthma to broken ribs, from ague to tetanus, the facts of the disease are not only disclosable without shame, but are in fact often publicly known and knowable by everyone—except the appointed investigators of truth."

true, and a judge or jury when his motives have been exposed will not be inclined to give undue weight to his story.

It may happen, also, that the privilege will occasionally work in the interest of justice by defeating a life insurance company's defense of misrepresentation by the patient in answering questions as to the past state of his health. Such answers may be of trivial significance and may have been made in good faith. While the privilege which keeps the insured's physician from testifying may happen to obstruct such an unjust defense, the more effective remedy is an enlightened doctrine as to the materiality of the representation, or the requirement of a comprehensive incontestable clause of reasonably short duration.[91]

So much for the benefits which the privilege is supposed to furnish. After the description in the preceding sections of the actual working of the statutes, no detailed recital of the evil results of the privilege is needed. They may be summed up in general terms:

1. The suppression of what is ordinarily the best source of proof, namely, the physician who examined and treated the patient, upon what is usually a crucial issue, namely, the physical or mental condition of the patient.

2. The one-sided view of the facts upon which the court must act when it hears the story of the patient and some doctors selected by him but allows the patient to close the mouth of another doctor whom he has consulted, who would contradict them.

3. The complexities and perplexities which result from a statute which runs against the grain of justice, truth and fair dealing. These perplexities inevitably produce a spate of conflicting and confusing appellate decisions, and encrust the statutes with numerous amendments, reaching for but never attaining the reconciliation of the privilege with the needs of justice.

A palliative for these injustices is the application of the practice of strictly interpreting the statutes creating the privilege [92] rather than the contrary rule of liberally interpreting them, which some courts have espoused.[93]

Among the more sweeping remedies for the evils of the privilege the following should be considered.

First, the adoption of the provisions of the Uniform Rules of Evidence [94] which seem to

---

91. See 8 Wigmore, Evidence (McNaughton rev.) § 2389(b).

92. Rhodes v. Metropolitan Life Ins. Co., 172 F.2d 183 (5th Cir. 1949); Stayner v. Nye, 227 Ind. 231, 85 N.E.2d 496 (1949); Leusink v. O'Donnell, 255 Wis. 627, 39 N.W.2d 675 (1949); Dec.Dig. Witnesses ☞208(1).

93. Howard v. Porter, 240 Iowa 153, 35 N.W.2d 837 (1949); People v. Shapiro, 308 N.Y. 453, 126 N.E.2d 559 (1955).

94. Uniform Rule 27: "(1) As used in this rule, (a) 'patient' means a person who, for the sole purpose of securing preventive, palliative, or curative treatment, or a diagnosis preliminary to such treatment, of his physical or mental condition consults a physician, or submits to an examination by a physician; (b) 'physician' means a person authorized or reasonably believed by the patient to be authorized, to practice medicine in the state or jurisdiction in which the consultation or examination takes place; (c) 'holder of the privilege' means the patient while alive and not under guardianship or the guardian of the person of an incompetent patient, or the personal representative of a deceased patient; (d) 'confidential communication between physician and patient' means such information transmitted between physician and patient, including information obtained by an examination of the patient, as is transmitted in confidence and by a means which, so far as the patient is aware, discloses the information to no third persons other than those reasonably necessary for the transmission of the information or the accomplishment of the purpose for which it is transmitted.

"(2) Except as provided by paragraphs (3), (4), (5) and (6) of this rule, a person, whether or not a party, has a privilege in a civil action or in a prosecution for a misdemeanor to refuse to disclose, and to prevent a witness from disclosing, a communication, if he claims the privilege and the judge finds that (a) the communication was a confidential communication between patient and

eliminate the principal abuses of the privilege. This would be a great advance upon most

of the existing statutes but these provisions are detailed and complex calling for much judicial labor in their interpretation, and the drafters being human have not been able to foresee and provide against all the possibilities of injustice. The large number of exceptions now found in the more carefully drafted contemporary statutes raises serious doubt as to the scope and validity of what is left of the privilege.[95]

Second, the modification of the privilege-statute by adding a clause, as in the North Carolina Code, "Provided, that the court, either at the trial or prior thereto . . . may compel such disclosure, when, in his opinion, the same is necessary to a proper administration of justice."[96] A clear-eyed and courageous judiciary, trial and appellate,

physician, and (b) the patient or the physician reasonably believed the communication to be necessary or helpful to enable the physician to make a diagnosis of the condition of the patient or to prescribe or render treatment therefor, and (c) the witness (i) is the holder of the privilege or (ii) at the time of the communication was the physician or a person to whom disclosure was made because reasonably necessary for the transmission of the communication or for the accomplishment of the purpose for which it was transmitted or (iii) is any other person who obtained knowledge or possession of the communication as the result of an intentional breach of the physician's duty of nondisclosure by the physician or his agent or servant and (d) the claimant is the holder of the privilege or a person authorized to claim the privilege for him.

"(3) There is no privilege under this rule as to any relevant communication between the patient and his physician (a) upon an issue of the patient's condition in an action to commit him or otherwise place him under the control of another or others because of alleged mental incompetence, or in an action in which the patient seeks to establish his competence or in an action to recover damages on account of conduct of the patient which constitutes a criminal offence other than a misdemeanor, or (b) upon an issue as to the validity of a document as a will of the patient, or (c) upon an issue between parties claiming by testate or intestate succession from a deceased patient.

"(4) There is no privilege under this rule in an action in which the condition of the patient is an element or factor of the claim or defense of the patient or of any party claiming through or under the patient or claiming as a beneficiary of the patient through a contract to which the patient is or was a party.

"(5) There is no privilege under this rule as to information which the physician or the patient is required to report to a public official or as to information required to be recorded in a public office, unless the statute requiring the report or record specifically provides that the information shall not be disclosed.

"(6) No person has a privilege under this rule if the judge finds that sufficient evidence, aside from the communication has been introduced to warrant a finding that the services of the physician were sought or obtained to enable or aid anyone to commit or to plan to commit a crime or a tort, or to escape detection or apprehension after the commission of a crime or a tort.

"(7) A privilege under this rule as to a communication is terminated if the judge finds that any person while a holder of the privilege has caused the physician or any agent or servant of the physician to testify in any action to any matter of which the physician or his agent or servant gained knowledge through the communication."

These provisions are the same as Model Code of Evidence, Rules 220–223.

95. The California privilege, for example is subject to 12 exceptions: personal injury cases, services in aid of a crime or tort, criminal proceedings, damage actions for criminal conduct of the patient, will contests, malpractice cases, disputes as to intention of patient as to writing affecting property, validity of same, commitment proceedings, restoration proceedings, certain required reports, proceedings to terminate a license or privilege. West's Ann.Cal.Evid.Code §§ 996–1007. Not much except the smile is left for the doctor.

96. N.C.G.S. § 8–53 (1969 amendment). Such a proviso was recommended for enactment by other states by Committee on the Improvement of the Law of Evidence of the American Bar Association for 1937–38. 8 Wigmore, Evidence (McNaughton rev.) § 2380a, n. 4.

See Sims v. Charlotte Liberty Mutual Ins. Co., 257 N.C. 32, 125 S.E.2d 326 (1962) where Moore, J., in a perceptive opinion observed with respect to the application of G.S. § 8–53, "It seems to us that the privilege statute, when strictly applied without the exercise of discretion on the part of the judge, is more often unjust than just . . . Our Legislature intended the statute to be a shield and not a sword. It was careful to make provision to avoid injustice and suppression of truth by putting it in the power of the trial judge to compel disclosure. Judges should not hesitate to require the disclosure where it appears to them to be necessary in order that the truth be known and justice be done. The Supreme Court cannot exercise such authority and discretion, nor can it repeal or amend the statute by judicial decree. If the spirit and purpose of the law is to be carried out, it must be at the superior court level."

The Sims case is noted in 41 N.C.L.Rev. 621 (1963).

with an appreciation of the need for truth and a fear of its suppression, could draw the danger of injustice from the privilege, under this provision. A judiciary with the sentimental attitude of Buller, J., would administer the mixture as before.

Third, the retention or the reestablishment of the common law practice which makes accessible to the court the facts which the physician learns from consultation and examination. More than a century of experience with the statutes has demonstrated that the privilege in the main operates not as the shield of privacy but as the protector of fraud. Consequently the abandonment of the privilege seems the best solution.[97]

97. This is the course adopted by the draftsmen of the proposed Rules of Evidence for the United States District Courts and Magistrates. Rule 504 of the proposed rules provides for a psycho-therapist-patient privilege but the proposed rules contain no provision for a general physician-patient privilege. See Advisory Committee's Note, F.R. Ev. (R.D.1971) 504.

PRIVILEGES FOR GOVERNMENTAL SECRETS

106. Other Principles Distinguished.

In discussing the evidential privileges and rules of exclusion in respect to the production and admission of writings and information in the possession of government officers, it is well to mark off at the outset some other principles which may hinder the litigant seeking facts from the government, but which are beyond our present inquiry. Among them are these: (a) questions of substantive privilege of government officers from liability for their acts and words,[1] (b) questions as to the general exemption of the chief executive and other high officers from judicial process to enforce their appearance or attendance or to compel them to give evidence,[2] and (c) questions as to the irremovability of official records.[3]

1. See, e. g., Spalding v. Vilas, 161 U.S. 483 (1896) (exemption of Postmaster General from civil liability for official statement); Prosser, Torts (4th ed.) § 132; 8 Wigmore, Evidence (McNaughton rev.) § 2368.

2. See 8 Wigmore, Evidence (McNaughton rev.) §§ 2369–2371; Bishop, The Executive's Right of Privacy: An Unresolved Constitutional Question, 66 Yale L.J. 477 (1957); Hardin, Executive Privilege in the Federal Courts, 71 Yale L.J. 879 (1962); Hennings et al., Symposium, 19 Fed.Bar J. 1 (1959); Taubeneck and Sexton, Executive Privilege and the Court's Right to Know, 48 Geo.L.J. 486 (1960).

3. See, e. g., Dunham v. Chicago, 55 Ill. 357 (1870) (court will not order removal where certified cop-

107. The Common Law Privileges for Military or Diplomatic Secrets and Other Facts the Disclosure of Which Would be Contrary to the Public Interest.[4]

Since the turn of the century the activities of government have multiplied in number and widened in scope, and the need of litigants for the disclosure and proof of documents and other information in the possession of government officials has correspondingly increased. When this need is asserted

ies will serve as well); 8 Wigmore, Evidence (McNaughton rev.) § 2373.

4. 8 Wigmore, Evidence (McNaughton rev.) §§ 2378, 2378a, 2379; 4 Moore's Federal Practice ¶ 26.61 (1970); Sanford, Evidentiary Privileges Against the Production of Data within the Control of Executive Departments, 3 Vand.L.Rev. 73 (1949); Berger and Krash, Government Immunity from Discovery, 59 Yale L.J. 1451 (1950); Bishop, The Executive's Right of Privacy: An Unresolved Constitutional Question, 66 Yale L.J. 477 (1957); Carrow, Governmental Nondisclosure in Judicial Proceedings, 107 U.Pa.L.Rev. 166 (1958); Hardin, Executive Privilege in the Federal Courts, 71 Yale L.J. 879 (1962); Gromley, Discovery Against the Government of Military and Other Confidential Matters, 43 Ky.L.J. 343 (1955); Hennings et al., Symposium, 19 Fed.Bar J. 1 (1959); Mitchell, Governmental Secrecy in Theory and Practice, 58 Colum.L.Rev. 199 (1958); Rogers, Constitutional Law: The Papers of the Executive Branch, 44 A.B.A.J. 941 (1958); Taubeneck and Sexton, Executive Privilege and the Court's Right to Know, 48 Geo.L.J. 486 (1960); Zagel, State Secrets Privilege, 50 Minn.L.Rev. 875 (1966).

and opposed, the resultant question requires a delicate and judicious balancing of the public interest in the secrecy of "classified" official information against the public interest in the protection of the claim of the individual to due process of law in the redress of grievances.[5]

It is generally conceded that a privilege and a rule of exclusion should apply in the case of writings and information constituting military or diplomatic secrets of state.[6]

Wigmore seems to regard it as doubtful whether the denial of disclosure should go further than this,[7] but state statutes in this country sometimes state the privilege in broader terms,[8] and the English decisions

---

5. "Besides, the public good is in nothing more essentially interested, than in the protection of every individual's private rights, as modelled by the municipal law." 1 Blackstone, Commentaries *139 (1765), referred to in Pound, Administrative Discretion and Civil Liberties in England, 56 Harv.L. Rev. 806, 814 (1943).

6. 8 Wigmore, Evidence (McNaughton rev.) § 2378 (2). Examples of decisions in which the existence of a privilege for military or diplomatic secrets was affirmed or assumed: Aaron Burr's Trial, Robertson's Rep. I, 121, 127, 186, 255, II, 536 (1807) described and quoted from in 8 Wigmore, Evidence (3d ed. 1940) § 2379, p. 799 (subpena duces tecum issued by Marshall, C. J., to President Jefferson to produce correspondence with General Wilkinson, over objection of government that it involved relations with France and Spain; C. J. Marshall: "There is certainly nothing before the Court which shows that the letter in question contains any matter the disclosure of which would endanger the public safety; . . . if it does contain any matter which it would be imprudent to disclose, which it is not the wish of the Executive to disclose, such matter, if it be not immediately and essentially applicable to the point, will of course be suppressed. . . ."); Totten v. United States, 92 U.S. 105 (1875) (action by former spy, after Civil War, for services during war under contract with President; held, action denied since its maintenance will endanger secrecy of such employments); Firth Sterling Steel Co. v. Bethlehem Steel Co., 199 Fed. 353 (E.D.Pa.1912) (copies of drawings of armor-piercing projectiles made by Navy and classed as secret, excluded by court on objection, though witness did not claim privilege, recognizing "rule of public policy forbidding the disclosure of military secrets.")

In United States v. Reynolds, 345 U.S. 1 (1953), Vinson, C. J., for the court, after referring to "the privilege against revealing military secrets, a privilege which is well established in the law of evidence," said: "Judicial experience with the privilege which protects military and state secrets has been limited in this country. English experience has been more extensive, but still relatively slight compared with other evidentiary privileges. Nevertheless, the principles which control the applica-

tion of the privilege emerge quite clearly from the available precedents. The privilege belongs to the Government and must be asserted by it; it can neither be claimed nor waived by a private party. It is not to be lightly invoked. There must be a formal claim of privilege, lodged by the head of the department which has control over the matter, after actual personal consideration by that officer."

See also Machin v. Zuckert, 114 U.S.App.D.C. 335, 316 F.2d 336 (1963) cert. denied 375 U.S. 896 (investigative reports of Department of Air Force concerning aircraft accident held privileged in suit between private litigants where disclosure would hamper efficient operation of important program and perhaps impair national security by weakening a branch of the military).

F.R.Ev. (R.D.1971) 509, Military and State Secrets: **"(a) General Rule of Privilege.** The government has a privilege to refuse to give evidence and to prevent any person from giving evidence upon a showing of reasonable likelihood of danger that disclosure of the evidence will be detrimental or injurious to the national defense or the international relations of the United States.

"(b) Procedure. The privilege may be claimed only by the chief officer of the department of government administering the subject matter which the evidence concerns. The required showing may be made in whole or in part in the form of a written statement. The judge may hear the matter in chambers, but all counsel are entitled to inspect the claim and showing and to be heard thereon. The judge may take any protective measure which the interests of the government and the furtherance of justice may require.

"(c) Notice to Government. If the circumstances of the case indicate a substantial possibility that a claim of privilege would be appropriate but has not been made because of oversight or lack of knowledge, the judge shall give or cause notice to be given to the officer entitled to claim the privilege and shall stay further proceedings a reasonable time to afford opportunity to assert a claim of privilege.

"(d) Effect of Sustaining Claim. If a claim of privilege is sustained in a proceeding to which the government is a party and it appears that another party is thereby deprived of material evidence, the judge shall make any further orders which the interests of justice require, including striking the testimony of a witness, declaring a mistrial, finding against the government upon an issue as to which the evidence is relevant, or dismissing the action."

7. See 8 Wigmore, Evidence (McNaughton rev.) § 2378, n. 7.

8. West's Ann.Cal.Evid.Code, § 1040: **"Privilege for official information.** (a) As used in this section,

seem to have accepted the wide generalization that official documents and facts will be privileged whenever their disclosure would be injurious to the public interest.[9] Whether this wider principle is justified in point of policy is open to serious question. Situations where a true need for protection against disclosure exists are often covered by such standard privileges as attorney-client or in particular cases by specific statutory privileges.[10] In addition, the often unrealized standing of governmental agencies to raise questions of relevancy in the broad sense affords insulation against forcing truly unwarranted disclosure.[11] The difficulty of obtaining governmental information is a mat-

ter of common knowledge,[12] and the creation of an added obstacle in the form of a privilege so broad in terms and uncertain of application can scarcely be defended.

108.   Privileges Against Disclosure Created by Federal Statutes and Departmental Regulations.[13]

The so-called Federal Housekeeping Act, prior to its amendment in 1958 provided that "The head of each department is authorized to prescribe regulations, not inconsistent with law, for the government of his department, the conduct of its officers and clerks, the distribution and performance of its business, and the custody, use, and preservation of the records, papers, and property appertaining to it."[14] The phrase relating to the "custody, use and preservation of the records, papers," etc., was early assumed by administrators to authorize regulations requiring the subordinate officers, who are actually in possession of most of such papers and records, to decline to produce them when served with a subpoena issued by a court. Examples of these regulations are cited below.[15] Usually they provided that upon an application to the head of the department or a rule served upon him by the court, he may grant or refuse the request for production. The Supreme Court of the United States had consistently upheld the validity of such regulations insofar as they purported to empower a subordinate officer having custody of the paper to refuse to produce it in court upon subpoena or to tes-

'official information' means information acquired in confidence by a public employee in the course of his duty and not open, or officially disclosed, to the public prior to the time the claim of privilege is made.

"(b) A public entity has a privilege to refuse to disclose official information, and to prevent another from disclosing such information, if the privilege is claimed by a person authorized by the public entity to do so and:

(1) Disclosure is forbidden by an act of the Congress of the United States or a statute of this state; or

(2) Disclosure of the information is against the public interest because there is a necessity for preserving the confidentiality of the information that outweighs the necessity for disclosure in the interest of justice; but no privilege may be claimed under this paragraph if any person authorized to do so has consented that the information be disclosed in the proceeding. In determining whether disclosure of the information is against the public interest, the interest of the public entity as a party in the outcome of the proceeding may not be considered."

For additional statutes, see 8 Wigmore, Evidence (McNaughton rev.) § 2378, n. 9. See also Dec.Dig. Witnesses ☞216; Annot., 165 A.L.R. 1302, 1311.

9. The opinion of Viscount Simon, L.Ch., for the House of Lords in Duncan v. Cammell, Laird & Co., [1942] App.C. 624 accepts this principle and reviews the supporting precedents.

10. See § 112, infra.

11. Boeing Airplane Co. v. Coggeshall, 108 U.S.App. D.C. 106, 280 F.2d 654 (1960) (Renegotiation Board); Freeman v. Seligson, 132 U.S.App.D.C. 56, 405 F. 2d 1326 (1968) (Secretary of Agriculture); General Services Administration v. Benson, 415 F.2d 878 (9th Cir.1969).

12. See § 108, infra.

13. See § 107, n. 4, supra; Annot., 165 A.L.R. 1302, 1338; Dec.Dig. Federal Civil Procedure ☞1593.

14. 5 U.S.C.A. § 22 (1958), R.S. § 161 (1875).

15. See, e. g., the regulations of the Attorney General set out in United States v. Ragen, 340 U.S. 462 (1951), those of the Treasury summarized in Fowkes v. Dravo Corp., 5 F.R.D. 51 (E.D.Pa.1945), and those of the Department of Labor set out in Walling v. Richmond Screw Anchor Co., 4 F.R.D. 265, 268 (E.D.N.Y.1943).

tify as to its contents.[16] While the cases upholding the Act did not hold that it created a statutory privilege, the practical effect was that private litigants were unable to obtain needed information. It is true that the litigant might apply for production to the head of the department, but this recourse would often fail, and the resort to legal process against the head involved practical difficulties such as the territorial limits upon the service of subpoena, and the probable assertion of privilege upon the taking of his deposition.[17] The intent of the Congress not to create a statutory privilege out of the housekeeping provisions of the Act was made clear when the following provision was added in 1958: "This section does not authorize withholding information from the public or limiting the availability of records to the public." [18] This intent has had judicial confirmation in decisions holding that the Housekeeping Act does not entitle an executive officer to erect a privilege with respect to the official conduct of subordinates,[19] or agency records.[20]

Another effort by Congress to strike a workable balance between the right of the individual citizen to information and the need of the government to keep information in confidence without permitting indiscriminate secrecy, was the enactment of the so-called Freedom of Information Act as an amendment to the Administrative Procedure Act. Of particular importance is the provision giving an aggrieved person the right to file an action in the district where he resides or has his principal place of business, or where the agency records are situated. Previously if the responsible official was beyond the jurisdiction of the trial court disclosure practically could not be compelled even though authority for withholding was lacking.[21] While this Act is directed toward availability of information for the public in general and the news media in particular its pertinence in clearing the way for discovery in litigation

---

16. Boske v. Comingore, 177 U.S. 459 (1900) (statute conferring rulemaking power on heads of departments valid under the "necessary and proper" clause and Treasury regulation prohibiting production of records by collector of internal revenue valid; collector punished for contempt by state court for nonproduction discharged on habeas corpus); United States v. Ragen, 340 U.S. 462 (1951) (similar regulations of Attorney General approved, following above decision, in its application to subordinate officers; "When one considers the variety of information contained in the files of any government department and the possibilities of harm from unrestricted disclosure in court, the usefulness, indeed the necessity, of centralizing determination as to whether subpoenas duces tecum will be willingly obeyed or challenged is obvious.").

17. See Notes, 47 Nw.U.L.Rev. 519, 523 (1952), 69 Yale L.J. 452 (1960).

18. Pub.L. 85–619, 72 Stat. 547 (1958). The Act in its present form now reads: "The head of an Executive department or military department may prescribe regulations for the government of his department, the conduct of its employees, the distribution and performance of its business, and the custody, use, and preservation of its records, papers, and property. This section does not authorize withholding information from the public or limiting the availability of records to the public." 5 U.S.C.A. § 301 (1966).
See Note, 69 Yale L.J. 452 (1960).

19. NLRB v. Capitol Fish Co., 294 F.2d 868 (5th Cir. 1961).

20. Olson Rug Co. v. N. L. R. B., 291 F.2d 655 (7th Cir. 1961); Sperandeo v. Milk Drivers and Dairy Employees Local Union, 334 F.2d 381 (10th Cir. 1964); Rosee v. Board of Trade of the City of Chicago, 35 F.R.D. 512 (N.D.Ill.1964) (reports of commodity transactions held not privileged from disclosure under Commodity Exchange Act authorizing the Secretary of Agriculture to make investigations and to "publish from time to time, in his discretion, the result of such investigation and such statistical information gathered therefrom as he may deem of interest to the public, except data and information which would separately disclose the business transactions of any person and trade secrets or names of customers . . .." The Court pointed out that where Congress has intended to prohibit the use of government-held data in judicial proceedings it has not talked in terms of "publish" or "publication" but has expressed the prohibition explicitly, citing examples of such statutes).

21. 5 U.S.C.A. § 552. The Act reads:
"(a) (3) * * * [E]ach agency, on request for identifiable records made in accordance with published rules stating the time, place, fees to the extent authorized by statute, and procedure to be

is apparent.[22] In this connection, certain observations should be made. Any person is

> followed, shall make the records promptly available to any person. On complaint, the district court of the United States in the district in which the complainant resides, or has his principal place of business, or in which the agency records are situated, has jurisdiction to enjoin the agency from withholding agency records and to order the production of any agency records improperly withheld from the complainant. In such a case the court shall determine the matter de novo and the burden is on the agency to sustain its action. In the event of noncompliance with the order of the court, the district court may punish for contempt the responsible employee, and in the case of a uniformed service, the responsible member. Except as to causes the court considers of greater importance, proceedings before the district court, as authorized by this paragraph, take precedence on the docket over all other causes and shall be assigned for hearing and trial at the earliest practicable date and expedited in every way.

"(b) This section does not apply to matters that are—
(1) specifically required by Executive order to be kept secret in the interest of the national defense or foreign policy;
(2) related solely to the internal personnel rules and practices of an agency;
(3) specifically exempted from disclosure by statute;
(4) trade secrets and commercial or financial information obtained from a person and privileged or confidential;
(5) inter-agency or intra-agency memorandums or letters which would not be available by law to a party other than an agency in litigation with the agency;
(6) personnel and medical files and similar files the disclosure of which would constitute a clearly unwarranted invasion of personal privacy;
(7) investigatory files compiled for law enforcement purposes except to the extent available by law to a party other than an agency;
(8) contained in or related to examination, operating, or condition reports prepared by, on behalf of, or for the use of an agency responsible for the regulation or supervision of financial institutions; or
(9) geological and geophysical information and data, including maps, concerning wells.
"(c) This section does not authorize withholding of information or limit the availability of records to the public, except as specifically stated in this section. This section is not authority to withhold information from Congress."

The legislative history of this act appears in the House Report No. 1497, U.S.Code Congressional and Administrative News, 89th Congress—Second Session, Vol. 2, p. 2418.

22. For an instance of resort to the Freedom of Information Act as a means of obtaining information

eligible to proceed under the Act; no standing or showing of need for the desired information is exacted. As a result, the justifications for shutting off information under the Act are in some instances of lesser dimension than would warrant withholding information from a litigant with a genuine need for it in litigation.[23] Accordingly, the Act, in excepting certain matters from its disclosure provisions, does not purport to make them privileged in the evidentiary sense, although it does represent a significant Congressional expression of what areas are sensitive and does overlap evidentiary privilege in several instances.[24]

109. Effect of the Presence of the Government as a Litigant.

To the extent that the Freedom of Information Act is available as a means for obtaining government records and information for use in evidence, as discussed in the preceding section, no distinction is made between situations where the litigation is between parties other than the government and those where the government is a party. However, when procedures other than under the Act are resorted to, the difference may be substantial.

When the government is not a party and successfully resists disclosure sought by a party, the result is simply that the evidence is unavailable, as though a witness had died, and the case will proceed accordingly, with no consequences save those resulting from the loss of the evidence. But when the government is a party, whether by resorting to the courts as plaintiff in civil or criminal proceedings or by virtue of consent-

for use in litigation, see General Services Administration v. Benson, 415 F.2d 878 (9th Cir. 1969).

23. E. g., personnel or medical files under § 552(b) (6), quoted n. 21, supra.

24. E. g., matters of national defense or foreign policy and trade secrets, under § 552(b) (1) and (4), quoted n. 21, supra.

ing to be sued as defendant,[25] it is in court as a litigant, with important consequences. By invoking the court's aid by bringing suit, the government seems clearly to waive any claim of executive immunity in that the court can deny use of its facilities unless the government submits to making disclosure.[26] Accordingly in a criminal prosecution, the court may give the government the choice of making disclosure of matters of significance to the defense or suffering dismissal of the proceeding; any executive immunity is waived, and the government cannot as litigant invoke an evidentiary privilege, e. g., for military secrets, while at the same time seeking to proceed affirmatively with respect to its subject matter.[27] Nor may the government as plaintiff in a civil action proceed affirmatively against a defendant while at the same time seeking under the guise of privilege to deprive the defendant of evidence useful to the defense of the action.[28] On the other hand, when the government is defendant, as under the Tort Claims Act, an adverse finding cannot be rendered against it as the price of asserting an evidentiary privilege. This is not one of the terms upon which Congress has consented that the United States be subjected to liability.[29]

110. The Scope of the Judge's Function in Determining the Validity of the Claim of Privilege.[30]

When the head of department has made a claim of privilege for documents or information under his control as being military or diplomatic secrets is this claim conclusive upon the judge? Is he entitled to ascertain the content of the information withheld, and to apply for himself the standard of danger to the public interest? A decision of the House of Lords in 1942 limits the judge's function to ascertaining whether the claim is made by the proper officer in proper form. If he decides that it is, the claim is conclusive.[31] An earlier decision of the Privy Council had held that when the executive claim was made, the judge might nevertheless have the power to inspect the papers withheld and to decide

---

25. E. g., under the Tort Claims Act, 28 U.S.C.A. § 2674.

26. Thus it may fairly be said, "The Government as a litigant is, of course, subject to the rules of discovery." United States v. Procter & Gamble Co., 356 U.S. 677, 681 (1958). See also Bank Line, Ltd. v. United States, 163 F.2d 133 (2d Cir. 1947). The fact that enforcement measures may be designed to avoid confronting the embarrassing question whether a cabinet member may be committed for contempt makes them no less enforcement measures.

27. United States v. Andolschek, 142 F.2d 503, 506 (2d Cir. 1944) (in prosecution of inspectors of Alcohol Tax Unit for illegal dealings with permittees, error to sustain government's claim of privilege for reports of inspectors to their superiors as to these dealings; L. Hand, J.: "While we must accept it as lawful for a department of the government to suppress documents, even when they will help determine controversies between third persons, we cannot agree that this should include their suppression in a criminal prosecution, founded upon those very dealings to which the documents relate, and whose criminality they will, or may, tend to exculpate."); United States v. Grayson, 166 F.2d 863, 870 (2d Cir. 1948) (prosecution for fraudulent use of mails and violation of Securities Act, held error to exclude as confidential pertinent documents in possession of Securities and Exchange Commission). See also Reynolds v. United States, 345 U.S. 1, 12 (1953).

28. In United States v. Cotton Valley Operators Committee, 9 F.R.D. 719 (W.D.La.1949), a civil antitrust action, the Government failed to comply with the order to produce certain reports and correspondence and the action was dismissed. The judgment was affirmed by an equally divided court in 339 U.S. 940. See also United States v. Procter & Gamble Co., supra, n. 26.

29. If the matter arises in connection with efforts to obtain discovery, as in United States v. Reynolds, 345 U.S. 1 (1953), then it is significant that F.R. Civ.P. 26(b) (1) exempts from discovery matters which are privileged under the rules of evidence. If the matter arises on trial, see F.R.Ev. (R.D.1971) 513, which prohibits the drawing of an adverse inference from a claim of privilege.

30. 8 Wigmore, Evidence (McNaughton rev.) §§ 2378, 2379; Notes, 18 U.Chi.L.Rev. 122 (1950), 41 J. Crim.L. 330 (1950) 47 Nw.U.L.Rev. 259, 268 (1952), 47 Nw.U.L.Rev. 519, 527 (1952), 29 N.Y.U.L.Rev. 194 (1954).

31. Duncan v. Cammel, Laird & Co., [1942] App.C. 624. The holding is vigorously criticized in Note, 69 L.Q.Rev. 449 (1953).

whether disclosure would be injurious to the public.[32] The cases may be distinguished, in that the first mentioned was between private suitors and involved secret naval plans and the other was an action against the state and related to reports about wheat in a public warehouse, but the underlying question as to the scope of power remains.

When the privilege relates to official papers and information sought by the citizen as a means of proof in the assertion of his claims, and the disclosure is opposed as harmful to general security, the question is one of balancing conflicting policies. The head of an executive department can appraise the public interest of secrecy as well (or perhaps in some cases better) than the judge, but his official habit and leaning tend to sway him toward a minimizing of the interest of the individual. Under the normal administrative routine the question will come to him with recommendations from cautious subordinates against disclosure and in the press of business the chief is likely to approve the recommendation about such a seemingly minor matter without much independent consideration.[33] The determination of questions of fact and the applications of legal standards thereto in passing upon the admissibility of evidence and the validity of claims of evidential privilege are traditionally the responsibility of the judge.[34] As a public functionary he has respect for the executive's scruples against disclosure and at the same time his duties require him constantly to appraise private interests and to reconcile them with conflicting public policies; he may thus seem better qualified than the executive to weigh both interests understandingly and to strike a wise balance. What, however, of the danger that the judge by inquiring into the contents of the papers or the facts, in passing upon the validity of the claim of privilege, may effect a disclosure which even if the privilege is ultimately sustained will destroy the secrecy sought to be protected? Even where the general responsibility for inquiry is recognized, there is room for flexibility. In wartime the statement by the defence department of a military need for secrecy would seldom be questioned.[35] In some circumstances, as where the Navy's plans for construction of a submarine are sought,[36] the information "on its face" could be found to be a secret of state without further inquiry.

---

32. Robinson v. State of South Australia, [1931] App.C. 704.

33. See the graphic comments of Wigmore to like effect. 8 Evidence (McNaughton rev.) § 2378, n. 7.

In speaking of the grounds which should influence the executive, Simons, L. Ch., said in Duncan v. Cammel, Laird & Co., [1942] App.C. 624, 642: "It would not be a good ground that, if they were produced, the consequences might involve the department or the government in parliamentary discussion or in public criticism, or might necessitate the attendance as witnesses or otherwise of officials who have pressing duties elsewhere. Neither would it be a good ground that production might tend to expose a want of efficiency in the administration or tend to lay the department open to claims for compensation. In a word, it is not enough that the minister of the department does not want to have the documents produced. The minister, in deciding whether it is his duty to object, should bear these considerations in mind, for he ought not to take the responsibility of withholding production except in cases where the public interest would otherwise be damnified, for example, where disclosure would be injurious to national defence, or to good diplomatic relations, or where the practice of keeping a class of documents secret is necessary for the proper functioning of the public service." And in Robinson v. State of South Australia, [1931] App.C. 704, 715, the court declared that "the fact that production of the documents might in the particular litigation prejudice the Crown's own case" is not a legitimate reason for claiming privilege.

An instance of the operation of the privilege is Machin v. Zuckert, 114 U.S.App.D.C. 335, 316 F.2d 336 (1963) in which the court allowed in part a claim of privilege for military secrets by the Secretary of the Air Force but also rejected it in part and ordered the furnishing of information for use in private litigation. The Secretary made no claim of executive immunity.

34. See § 53, supra.

35. Compare the comments of C. E. Clark, J., in Bank Line, Ltd. v. United States, 163 F.2d 133, 139 (2d Cir. 1947).

36. As in Duncan v. Cammel, Laird & Co., [1942] App.C. 624.

In other cases, judges have directed that the information, or so much as is necessary, be disclosed privately to the judge alone, as a basis for his determining the claim of privilege.[37] However, in United States v. Reynolds,[38] involving a claim of privilege for military secrets, the Supreme Court while asserting a role for the judge in determining the claim of privilege, cautioned against destroying in the process the secrecy which the privilege was designed to protect. An analogy to the process of passing upon claims of self-incrimination was suggested:[39] "It may be possible to satisfy the court, from all the circumstances of the case, that there is a reasonable danger that compulsion of the evidence will expose military matters which, in the interest of national security, should not be divulged. When this is the case, the occasion for the privilege is appropriate, and the court should not jeopardize the security which the privilege is meant to protect by insisting upon an examination of the evidence, even by the judge alone, in chambers. . . . In each case, the showing of necessity which is made will determine how far the court should probe in satisfying that the occasion for invoking the privilege is appropriate."[40]

111.　The Privilege Against the Disclosure of the Identity of an Informer.[41]

Informers are shy and timorous folk, whether they are undercover agents of the police or merely citizens stepping forward with information about violations of law, and if their names were subject to be readily revealed, this enormously important aid to law enforcement would be almost cut off. On this ground of policy, a privilege is recognized in respect to disclosure of the identity of an informer,[42] who has given information about supposed crimes to a prosecuting or

---

37. As in Evans v. United States, 10 F.R.D. 255, 257, 258 (W.D.La.1950) ("It is not the exclusive right of any such agency of the Government to decide for itself the privileged nature of any such documents, but the Court is the one to judge of this when such contention is made. This can be done by presenting to the Judge, without disclosure in the first instance to the other side, whatever is claimed to have that status.")

38. 345 U.S. 1 (1953).

39. Id, at 10.

40. See also F.R.Ev. (R.D.1971) 509, quoted § 107, n. 3, supra.

41. 8 Wigmore, Evidence (McNaughton rev.) § 2374; Annot., 76 A.L.R.2d 262 (1961). 1 L.Ed.2d 1998;

56 Am.Jur. Witnesses § 534; C.J.S. Witnesses § 264, p. 751; Dec.Dig. Witnesses ⊝216. See also Comments, An Informer's Tale: Its Use in Judicial and Administrative Proceedings, 63 Yale L.J. 206 (1953) (a valuable critique); Three Non-Personal Privileges, 29 N.Y.U.L.Rev. 194, 200 (1954). The policy of the privilege seems drawn in question by the vigorous language of Mr. Justice Douglas's dissent in United States v. Nugent, 346 U.S. 1, 13 (1953) where the court held that one who claimed draft exemption was not entitled, in an advisory hearing in the Department of Justice, to see the F.B.I. reports containing information received from informers.

42. Marks v. Beyfus, 25 Q.D.Div. 494 (Ct.App.1890) (action for malicious prosecution; plaintiff sought to elicit from Director of Public Prosecutions, the name and statement of informers—who were presumably the present defendants—but the witness declined unless the judge was of opinion that he should disclose, but the judge declined to order him to answer; on plaintiff's appeal, held, no error —not a matter of discretion, but judge should exclude under the rule of policy, except where the evidence is needed to establish the innocence of an accused); Worthington v. Scribner, 109 Mass. 487, 12 Am.Rep. 736 (1872) (action for false charges made to U. S. Treasury that plaintiff was an imposter; interrogatories to the defendant as to his giving this information; held defendant privileged not to answer); Dellastatious v. Boyce, 152 Va. 368, 147 S.E. 267 (1929) (action for damages for trespass on premises and false arrest against prohibition inspector and special deputies in execution of warrant; error in requiring officer to disclose from whom he secured information on which warrant was issued).

Uniform Rule 36: "A witness has a privilege to refuse to disclose the identity of a person who has furnished information purporting to disclose a violation of a provision of the laws of this State or of the United States to a representative of the State or the United States or a governmental division thereof, charged with the duty of enforcing that provision, and evidence thereof is inadmissible, unless the judge finds that (a) the identity of the person furnishing the information has already been otherwise disclosed or (b) disclosure of his identity is essential to assure a fair determination of the issues."

See also F.R.Ev. (R.D.1971) 510.

investigating officer or to someone for the purpose of its being relayed to such an officer.[43] The privilege runs to the government or state, and may be invoked by its officers who as witnesses or otherwise are called on for the information, [44] and runs also, according to some authority, to one charged with being an informer,[45] and when neither the government nor the informer is represented at the trial, in some jurisdictions the judge as in other cases of privilege [46] may invoke it for the absent holder.[47] It is disputed whether the privilege is confined to disclosure of identity [48] or extends also to the contents of the communication.[49] Seldom will the contents of the statement be competent if the name is undisclosed, but it is believed that the policy of the privilege does not apply to shielding the purport of the communication from disclosure. Of course, if revealing the contents will in the circumstances probably reveal the identity of the informer, the privilege should attach.

The privilege has two important qualifications, one obvious and the other not so obvious but just. The first is that when the identity has already become known to "those

---

43. See Hardy's Trial, 24 How.St.Tr. 99 (1794), quoted 8 Wigmore, Evidence (3d ed. 1940) § 2374, p. 751 (Erle, L.C.J.: "I cannot satisfy myself that there is any substantial difference between the case of this man's going to a justice of the peace . . . or to some other person who communicated with a justice. . . .").

While traditionally thought of in respect to information about crimes, an increasing body of authority recognizes that similar considerations may be present in cases of informing of other kinds of law violation and that the privilege should prevail there also. Mitchell v. Roma, 265 F.2d 633 (3d Cir. 1959) (violations of Fair Labor Standards Act); Wirtz v. Continental Finance & Loan Co., 326 F.2d 561 (5th Cir. 1964) (same, dictum); F.R.Ev. (R.D. 1971) 510(a).

44. This is probably the most frequent source of objection, see e. g., Marks v. Beyfus, note 42, above; Wilson v. United States, 59 F.2d 390 (3d Cir. 1932) (on petition to suppress evidence secured on liquor raid; deputy prohibition commissioner refused to answer question as to source of information on raid and was committed for contempt; held, the court should have sustained his claim of privilege); Bocchicchio v. Curtis Pub. Co., 203 F.Supp. 403 (E.D.Pa.1962) (local police officer not represented by counsel successful in claiming the privilege when called as witness in civil libel action).

45. See, e. g., cases wherein the claim of privilege was successfully made by the alleged informer or on his behalf; Worthington v. Scribner, note 42, supra; Wells v. Toogood, 165 Mich. 677, 131 N.W. 124 (1911) (action for slander against alleged informer; when officer was asked as to complaint of theft made to him by defendant, defendant's counsel objected).

Compare: "What is usually referred to as the informer's privilege is in reality the Government's privilege to withhold from disclosure the identity of persons who furnish information of violations of law to officers charged with enforcement of that law. [Citations omitted.] The purpose of the privilege is the furtherance and protection of the public interest in effective law enforcement. The privilege recognizes the obligation of citizens to communicate their knowledge of the commission of crimes to law-enforcement officials and, by preserving their anonymity, encourages them to perform that obligation." Burton, J., in Roviaro v. United States, 353 U.S. 53, 59 (1957).

F.R.Ev. (R.D.1971) 510 allows the privilege to be claimed only by the government or state or subdivision or representative thereof.

46. See § 73, supra.

47. See the statement of Bowen, L. J., in Marks v. Beyfus, described note 42, supra: ". . . the privilege does not depend upon the witness claiming it when asked the question; but the judge should refuse to allow the question as soon as it is asked." (p. 500). The Uniform Rule (note 1, above) describes the doctrine as a rule of inadmissibility as well as privilege, but since no element of unreliability or prejudice is involved it may be preferable to class it as a privilege throughout.

48. This is the view of 8 Wigmore, Evidence (McNaughton rev.) § 2374, p. 765) and the form in which the doctrine is stated in many of the leading opinions, see, e. g., Marks v. Beyfus, Worthington v. Scribner, both cited in note 42, above, and Scher v. United States, 305 U.S. 251, 254 (1938) (". . . public policy forbids disclosure of an informer's identity"). See also Bowman Dairy Co. v. United States, 341 U.S. 214, 221 (1951), where in an antitrust prosecution it was held that the government could be required to produce complaints and statements received from third persons, but that the court must be "solicitous to protect against disclosures of the identity of informants. . . ."

49. Numerous opinions state the doctrine as including the contents of the statement but usually in situations where the wider coverage is not material. See, e. g., Michael v. Matson, 81 Kan. 360, 105 Pac. 537 (1909) and Wells v. Toogood, note 45, supra.

who would have cause to resent the communication," the privilege ceases.[50]   The second is that when the privilege is asserted by the state in a criminal prosecution, and the evidence of the identity of the informer becomes important to the establishment of the defence, the court will require the disclosure,[51] and if it is still withheld, that the

prosecution be dismissed.[52]   The view that the latter qualification may have less basis in civil than in criminal actions seems correct.[53]

112.   Statutory Privileges for Certain Reports of Individuals to Government Agencies: Accident Reports, Tax Returns, etc.[54]

A policy faintly similar to that which has prompted the common law privilege for the identity of informers may be thought to have some application to all reports required by law to be made by individuals to government agencies, giving information needed in the administration of their public functions. If the statements may be used against the reporters, they may in some degree be discouraged from making full and true reports. On the other hand, these reports often deal with facts highly material in litigation, and an early report to government may be reli-

50.   The quoted language is from Roviaro v. United States, 353 U.S. 53, 60 (1957).   The limitation is appropriate since many disclosures, e. g. to other law enforcing agencies, obviously should not effect a waiver.

In Westinghouse Elec. Corp. v. City of Burlington, 122 U.S.App.D.C. 65, 351 F.2d 762 (1965) the filing of a civil antitrust action was held to have eliminated any privilege with respect to complaints by plaintiffs to the Attorney General.   The complaints were material to a defense of statute of limitations.   See also, on remand, City of Burlington v. Westinghouse Elec. Co., 246 F.Supp. 839 (D.D.C.1965).

51.   In Roviaro v. United States, 353 U.S. 53 (1957), a narcotics conviction was reversed for refusal to require disclosure of an informer's identity.   The informer was in fact far more than an informer; he was present at the transportation and participated in the sale, on both of which counts accused was charged.   The Court pointed out that the "informer" might have testified to an entrapment, thrown doubt on the identity of the accused or the package, testified as to accused's lack of knowledge of the contents, or contradicted the government's version of an important conversation.   Merely being an informer does not insulate against disclosure when the informer's activities go beyond informing.   This sort of going-beyond seems more likely to occur when the offense is of a continuing type, e. g., narcotics sales, rather than a single nonrepetitive crime such as murder.

The much litigated question whether the prosecution must disclose his identity when information from an informer has been relied upon to establish probable cause, and the lawfulness of a search and seizure is in question, was answered in the negative in McCray v. Illinois, 386 U.S. 300 (1967).   Neither due process nor right of confrontation was violated, said the Court.   Justice Douglas, in dissent, suggested that the result was to entrust the Fourth Amendment exclusively to the police.

See § 172, n. 52, infra.   A possible middle ground is the practice of making the disclosure to the judge *in camera.*   United States v. Jackson. 384 F.2d 825 (3d Cir. 1967); Stelloh v. Liban, 21 Wis.2d 119, 124 N.W.2d 101 (1963); F.R.Ev. (R.D.1971) 510(c) (3).

When the informer testifies, should disclosure of his status be required as a possible indication of bias? A negative answer was given in Attorney General v. Briant, 15 M. & W. 159, 153 Eng.Rep. 808 (Exch. 1846).   The result is difficult to defend.   Compare

Harris v. United States, 371 F.2d 365 (9th Cir. 1967) (trial judge allowed protracted inquiry).

52.   "It is a sound rule to keep secret information furnished to the state of violations of its laws, but this commendable public policy must yield to a higher, or at least an equal, right accorded to an accused to have a court investigate the facts material to his offense in a criminal prosecution, and sometimes the departments of government will be put to a choice of either foregoing a criminal prosecution or disclosing the source of material information necessary to the conduct of orderly judicial procedure."   United States v. Keown, 19 F.Supp. 639, 646 (W.D.Ky.1937).

A like choice is put to the state in respect to neighboring privileges.   Centoamore v. State, 105 Neb. 452, 181 N.W. 182 (1920) (asserted privilege—see 8 Wigmore, Evidence (McNaughton rev.) § 2375— for confidential communications to public prosecutor;   where necessary to defence, must be disclosed); United States v. Krulewitch, 145 F.2d 76 (2d Cir. 1944) (same as last); United States v. Andolschek, 142 F.2d 503, 506 (2d Cir. 1944) (privilege for government documents may not be insisted on if government chooses to prosecute for transaction to which those documents relate).

53.   Stelloh v. Liban, 21 Wis.2d 119, 124 N.W.2d 101 (1963).

54.   8 Wigmore, Evidence (McNaughton rev.) § 2377; Annot., 165 A.L.R. 1302; Note, The Required Report Privileges, 56 Nw.U.L.Rev. 283 (1961);   58 Am.Jur. Witnesses §§ 533, 536; Dec.Dig. Witnesses ⬅216.

able and pressingly needed for ascertainment of the facts. The latter interest has prevailed with the courts, and in the absence of a statutory provision creating the privilege there is no privilege for these reports.[55] Nevertheless, in legislative halls when bills requiring such reports are proposed the need for encouraging frank and full reports looms large to the proponents, but the judges and lawyers who would urge the need for truth in litigation are not alerted to oppose the privilege. Accordingly, there has been incorporated in a very large number of statutes requiring various kinds of reports a privilege for the reporter against their use in court. Probably the most frequent of these statutory privileges are those for reports of accidents on the highways [56] and industrial accidents [57] and for returns of property [58] and income [59] for taxation.

113. The Secrecy of Grand Jury Proceedings: (a) Votes and Expressions of Grand Jurors: (b) Testimony of Witnesses.

The taking of evidence by grand jurors and their deliberations have traditionally been

---

55. Peden v. Peden's Adm'r, 121 Va. 147, 92 S.E. 984, 2 A.L.R. 1414 (1917) (report of property for taxation) and see Panik v. Didra, 370 Pa. 488, 88 A.2d 730 (1952) (report of accident required by city ordinance not privileged in absence of provision for privilege). Compare, however, Gerry v. Worcester Consol. St. Ry. Co., described in note 57, infra.

Required reports may, of course, raise problems of self-incrimination. See § 142, infra. The privileges discussed in the present section may to some degree represent an effort to meet that problem.

56. An extensive opinion discussing some of the problems arising under the statutory privilege for highway accident reports, quoting from the statutes and citing cases from various states, is that of Knutson, J., in Rockwood v. Pierce, 235 Minn. 519, 51 N.W.2d 670 (1952) (oral admissions made by defendant to highway patrolman as basis for latter's official report, which would be privileged under M.S.A. § 169.09, subd. 13, are not privileged). The case is noted in 36 Minn.L.Rev. 540. See also Notes, 44 Iowa L.Rev. 210 (1958), 11 Wyo.L.J. 99 (1957). The statutes and cases are collected in Annot., 165 A.L.R. 1302, 1315, and in 8 Wigmore, Evidence (McNaughton rev.) § 2377, note 8.

57. Louisville & N. Ry. Co. v. Stephens, 298 Ky. 328, 182 S.W.2d 447 (1944) (action for death: error to admit reports made by railway to Interstate Commerce Commission, which are privileged under provisions of Boiler Inspection Act, 45 U.S.C.A. §§ 33, 41); Gerry v. Worcester Consol. St. Ry. Co., 248 Mass. 559, 143 N.E. 694, 697 (1924) (death injury; report of injury erroneously received as admission in view of St.1913, c. 746, providing that reports to Industrial Accident Board "shall be kept available by the said Board, and shall be furnished in request to the State Board of Labor and Indus-

---

tries for its own use": "In giving this information to the Industrial Accident Board, the defendant's report was in the nature of a privileged communication; and although not expressly privileged by the words of the statute, it was not intended that these reports should be availed of in an action at law arising out of the subject-matter of the suit."); Winningham v. Travelers' Ins. Co., 93 F.2d 520 (5th Cir. 1937) (physician's report of injury made for employer to Industrial Accident Board inadmissible against employer under Tex.Vernon's Ann.Civ.St. art. 8309, § 5).

58. Brackett v. Comm., 223 Mass. 119, 111 N.E. 1036 (1916) (corporation tax return); Williams v. Brown, 137 Mich. 569, 100 N.W. 786 (1904) (error to permit discrediting plaintiff, who had testified to value of property, by producing his statements while listing property for taxes, in view of statute limiting use of such statements); Re Manufacturers Trust Co., 269 App.Div. 108, 53 N.Y.S.2d 923 (1945) (corporation's franchise tax return; interpreting statute forbidding divulging of tax information).

59. Provisions for secrecy of state income tax returns are construed in In re Valecia Condensed Milk Co., 240 Fed. 310 (7th Cir. 1917) (St.Wis.1915, § 1087 m 24 forbidding divulgence by state officer validly requires him to refuse production though ordered by subpena of Federal court) and in Oklahoma Tax Com'n v. Clendinning, 193 Okl. 271, 143 P.2d 143, 151 A.L.R. 1035 (1943), annotated on this topic (construing sec. 1454, Uniform State Tax Procedure Act, 68 O.S. 1951 [now 68 Okl.St.Ann. § 205]).

The Internal Revenue Code of 1954 (26 U.S.C.A.) provides, in Sec. 6103: "(1) Returns made with respect to taxes imposed by chapters 1, 2, 3, and 6 upon which the tax has been determined by the Secretary or his delegate shall constitute public records; but, except as hereinafter provided in this section, they shall be open to inspection only upon order of the President and under rules and regulations prescribed by the Secretary or his delegate and approved by the President."

Other subsections of Sec. 6103 provide for inspection by state officers, inspection of corporate returns by shareholders, and inspection by Committees of Congress. The regulations relating to inspection of returns appear in Code of Fed.Regs., Title 26, secs. 301.6103(a)–1 to 301.6103(f)–1. Sec. 301.6103(a)–1(c) (1) (ii) provides that the return of an individual may be inspected by him, his attorney in fact, or his personal representatives, heirs, etc. Sec. 301.6103(a)–1(h) deals with the furnish-

shrouded in secrecy.[60] The ancient oath administered to the grand jurors bound them to keep secret "the King's counsel, your fellows' and your own." [61]

Several objectives are commonly suggested as being promoted by the policy of secrecy: to guard the independence of action and freedom of deliberation of the accusatory body, to protect the reputations of those investigated but not indicted, to prevent the forewarning and flight of those accused before publication of the indictment, and to encourage free disclosure by witnesses. The procedure for attaining them assumes two forms, somewhat loosely described as "privilege." The first is a privilege against disclosure of the grand jurors' communications to each other during their deliberations and of their individual votes.[62] The propriety of such a measure as an assurance of free and independent deliberation can scarcely be doubted, though it may be of slight practical importance in view of the infrequency with which these communications and votes will be relevant to any material inquiry.[63] The second of these privileges involves disclosure of the testimony given by witnesses before the grand jury, and as an area of substantial controversy deserves thoughtful scrutiny.

While the grand jury in its origins may in considerable measure have been an instrument of and subservient to the crown, its position as an important bulwark of the rights of English citizens was established by the end of the 17th century.[64] This latter

ing of the original returns or copies for use in litigation. Sec. 301.6301(a)–2 provides that a copy of a return may be furnished to any person who is entitled to inspect it.

". . . (3) Whenever a return is open to the inspection of any person, a certified copy thereof shall, upon request, be furnished to such person under rules and regulations prescribed by the Secretary or his delegate. The Secretary or his delegate may prescribe a reasonable fee for furnishing such copy." See also Sec. 7213(a) as to unauthorized disclosure.

A litigant may, by the weight of authority, be compelled to produce his own retained copy of his federal income tax return or to obtain a copy from Internal Revenue Service for that purpose. Rhodes v. Edwards, 178 Neb. 757, 135 N.W.2d 453 (1965); Kine v. Forman, 205 Pa.Super. 305, 209 A.2d 1 (1965); Notes, 18 U.Pitt.L.Rev. 149 (1956), 10 Vand. L.Rev. 150 (1956); Annot., 70 A.L.R.2d 244.

60. Calkins, Grand Jury Secrecy, 63 Mich.L.Rev. 455 (1965); Comment, Secrecy in Grand Jury Proceedings, 38 Fordham L.Rev. 307 (1969); 8 Wigmore, Evidence (McNaughton rev.) § 2360; C.J.S. Grand Juries § 43; 38 Am.Jur.2d Grand Jury §§ 39–41; Dec.Dig. Grand Jury ⚿41; Annot., 127 A.L.R. 272.

61. For a modern counterpart, see F.R.Crim.P. 6(e): "Disclosure of matters occurring before the grand jury other than its deliberations and the vote of any juror may be made to the attorneys for the government for use in the performance of their duties. Otherwise a juror, attorney, interpreter, stenographer, operator of a recording device, or any typist who transcribes recorded testimony may disclose matters occurring before the grand jury only when so directed by the court preliminarily to or in connection with a judicial proceeding or when permitted by the court at the request of the defendant upon a showing that grounds may exist for a motion to dismiss the indictment because of matters occurring before the grand jury. No obligation of secrecy may be imposed upon any person except in accordance with this rule. The court may direct that an indictment shall be kept secret until the defendant is in custody or has given bail, and in that event the clerk shall seal the indictment and no person shall disclose the finding of the indictment except when necessary for the issuance and execution of a warrant or summons."

62. Wm. J. Burns Internat. Detective Agency v. Holt, 138 Minn. 165, 164 N.W. 590 (1917) (action to recover for detective services allegedly rendered at request of grand jurors; conversations among members, during deliberations, about employing detectives, excluded); Opinion of the Justices, 96 N.H. 530, 73 A.2d 433 (1950) (power of legislative investigating committee does not extend to inquiring into grand jurors' votes and opinions); F.R.Crim.P. 6(e), supra, n. 2; 8 Wigmore, Evidence (McNaughton rev.) § 2361. But the privilege does not extend to deliberations in the course of preparing a report which was outside the lawful functions of the grand jury. Bennett v. Stockwell, 197 Mich. 50, 163 N.W. 482 (1917).

63. 8 Wigmore, Evidence (McNaughton rev.) §§ 2361, 2364. But see Wm. J. Burns Internat. Detective Agency v. Holt, supra, n. 62.

64. 1 Holdsworth, A History of English Law 321–323 (7th ed. 1956); Younger, The People's Panel 2 (1963); Goldstein, The State and the Accused: Balance of Advantage in Criminal Procedure, 69 Yale L.J. 1148, 1170 (1960). The key case, Earl of Shaftesbury's Trial, 8 How.St.Tr. 759 (1681), is quoted in 8 Wigmore, Evidence (McNaughton rev.) § 2360, p. 729.

aspect is evident in the provision of the Fifth Amendment of the Constitution of the United States requiring presentment or indictment as a precondition of prosecution for a capital or infamous crime. During this period the grand jury's independence of incursion by both prosecution and defense appears to have been well recognized, and prosecutors were admitted to its councils only by suffrance.[65] However, the decline in the feeling of need for the grand jury as a protector of individual liberties which caused its abolition in England [66] seems in this country to have led in this country to a return of the grand jury, in its accusatorial capacity, to the role of subordinate arm of the prosecution, operating to a degree as rubber stamp but on occasion as a powerful instrumentality of discovery. Thus we find statutes and rules providing for the presence of prosecuting attorneys and stenographers except when the grand jury is deliberating or voting.[67] No serious question is raised today with respect to the prosecution's entitlement to a transcript of testimony given before the grand jury,[68] but attitudes differ widely concerning the right of the accused to a copy. In several states his right is immediate and absolute.[69] In many,

however, the right is limited in varying degrees though perhaps expanding.[70] The attitude of the Supreme Court of the United States with regard to the matter has been described as "curiously ambivalent." [71] The reasoning and possible constitutional foundation underlying the *Jencks* decision and statute, allowing a defendant access to statements of government witnesses after they have testified on direct,[72] would seem to apply with equal force to grand jury minutes, yet the argument was rejected in favor of a troublesome requirement of showing "a particularized need." [73] The conclusion is a difficult one to accept, and indications are evident of a federal trend in favor of granting disclosure to the defendant at least with respect to his own testimony and the testimony of government witnesses after they have testified on direct.[74] No infringement of the objectives of secrecy mentioned at the beginning of this section can result from this measure of disclosure, and it would seem to constitute the least acceptable minimum for both state and federal courts.[75]

65. Younger, op. cit., supra, n. 64, p. 77; People v. Klaw, 53 Misc. 158, 104 N.Y.S. 482 (1907).

66. Administration of Justice Act of 1933, 23 & 24 Geo. 5, c. 36.

67. E. g., F.R.Crim.P. 6(d): "Attorneys for the government, the witness under examination, interpreters when needed and, for the purpose of taking the evidence, a stenographer or operator of a recording device may be present while the grand jury is in session, but no person other than the jurors may be present while the grand jury is deliberating or voting."

68. See, e. g., F.R.Crim.P. 6(e), supra, n. 2.

Illustrative instances of prosecution use of transcript or testimony of grand jurors themselves are: People v. Goldberg, 302 Ill. 559, 135 N.E. 84 (1922) (impeachment of defense witness); United States v. Socony-Vacuum Oil Co., 310 U.S. 150, 233 (1940) (refreshing recollection of government witness); Izer v. State, 77 Md. 110, 26 Atl. 282 (1893) (proving perjury before grand jury).

69. West's Ann.Cal.Penal Code, § 938.1; Iowa Code Ann. § 772.4; Ky.R.Crim. 5.16; Minn.Stat.Ann. § 628.04; 22 Okl.St.Ann. § 340.

70. Compare Annot., 20 A.L.R.3d 7, and A.B.A. Project on Minimum Standards for Criminal Justice, Standards Relating to Discovery and Procedure Before Trial 64–66 (1970).

71. Sherry, Grand Jury Minutes: The Unreasonable Rule of Secrecy, 48 Va.L.Rev. 668, 670 (1962). Federal cases are collected in Annot., 3 A.L.R.Fed. 29.

72. See § 97, supra.

73. Pittsburgh Plate Glass Co. v. United States, 360 U.S. 395 (1959), rehearing denied 361 U.S. 855 (trial judge did not err in denying production of minutes of grand jury in absence of a showing of "a particularized need" which outweighed the policy of secrecy. The Court held that disclosure on cross-examination that a trial witness had testified on the same general subject matter before the grand jury "—and nothing more—" did not entitle the defense to production of the grand jury minutes as a matter of absolute right).

74. Dennis v. United States, 384 U.S. 855 (1966); United States v. Youngblood, 379 F.2d 365 (2d Cir. 1967), noted 81 Harv.L.Rev. 712; Cargill v. United States, 381 F.2d 849 (10th Cir. 1967) cert. denied 389 U.S. 1041; Comment, Secrecy in Federal Grand Jury Proceedings, 38 Fordham L.Rev. 307 (1969).

75. A.B.A. Project on Minimum Standards for Criminal Justice, Standards Relating to Discovery

Despite the stringent language of the federal rule imposing secrecy on grand jury proceedings,[76] witnesses are pointedly omitted from the enumeration of persons bound by its provisions,[77] and the rule seems to place no obstacle in the way of the practice of "debriefing" witnesses after they have given testimony.[78] That the judge has authority to

administer an oath of secrecy to witnesses may remain a possibility [79] but the practice would indeed appear to be a dubious one save under the most exceptional circumstances.

---

and Procedure Before Trial 52, 64–66, and Supp. 2 (1970), sensibly suggests that these items be furnished in advance, in order to expedite the trial, but carefully steers around the question whether the proceedings should be required to be recorded. Negative answers on the latter point are found in United States v. Harper, 432 F.2d 100 (5th Cir. 1970) and United States v. Kind, 433 F.2d 339 (4th Cir. 1970); affirmative answers are found in some state statutes and others are silent on the matter.

76. F.R.Crim.P. 6(e), quoted supra, n. 61.

77. Original Committee Note to F.R.Crim.P. 6(e) par. 2.

78. 8 Moore's Federal Practice ¶ 6.05 (Cipes ed. 1970); Wright, Federal Practice and Procedure: Criminal § 106. Local statutes should be checked with respect to state practice.

79. See cases cited in 38 Am.Jur.2d Grand Jury § 40, and C.J.S. Grand Juries § 43(a). Goodman v. United States, 108 F.2d 516, 127 A.L.R. 265 (9th Cir. 1939), in which a daughter called as a witness before a grand jury investigating the activities of her employer father was held properly required to take an oath of secrecy, was decided prior to the adoption of the Federal Rules of Criminal Procedure.

TITLE 6

PRIVILEGE: CONSTITUTIONAL

CHAPTER 13

THE PRIVILEGE AGAINST SELF-INCRIMINATION

114. The History of the Privilege: (a) Origin of the Common Law Privilege.[1]

Because of relatively widespread doubt as to the wisdom of the privilege against self-incrimination,[2] the origin and development of the rule have been of special interest to legal scholars. Unfortunately important aspects of the matter are still clouded with doubt. What is known suggests that the privilege had its roots in opposition to the use of the *ex officio* oath by the English ecclesiastical courts and that its development was intimately intertwined with the political and religious disputes of early England. The most significant ambiguity is whether the privilege as finally applied in the common law courts after 1700 represented a logical extension of principle underlying earlier opposition to the procedures of ecclesiastical courts, or rather, whether it represented condemnation by association of a procedure not inherently inconsistent with prevailing values.

1. See generally 8 Wigmore, Evidence (McNaughton rev.) § 2250; Levy, Origins of the Fifth Amendment (1968); M. Maguire, Attack of the Common Lawyers on the Oath Ex Officio, in Essays in History and Political Theory in Honor of Charles H. McIlwain (1936); Corwin, The Supreme Court's Construction of the Self-Incrimination Clause, 29 Mich.L.Rev. 1 (1930); Morgan, The Privilege Against Self-Incrimination, 34 Minn.L.Rev. 1 (1949); Pittman, The Colonial and Constitutional History of the Privilege Against Self-Incrimination in America, 21 Va.L.Rev. 763 (1935); Riesenfeld, Law-Making and Legislative Precedent in American Legal History, 33 Minn.L.Rev. 103 (1949).

2. Riesenfeld asserts that the maxim, *No man shall be compelled to accuse himself*, can be traced to a statement of St. Chrysostomous in his commentary to St. Paul's Epistle to the Hebrews. The statement translates as "I don't tell you to display that [your sin] before the public like a decoration, nor to accuse yourself in front of others." The maxim also appeared in early canonist writings and was incorporated into Gratian's Decretum, a restatement of earlier canon law, as "I do not tell you to incriminate yourself publicly or to accuse yourself in front of others." Riesenfeld, supra note 1, at 118. But see Corwin, supra note 1, at 3, who challenges the assertion that the maxim was derived from canon law.

Prior to the early 1200's, trials in the ecclesiastical courts had been by ordeal or compurgation oath, the formal swearing by the party and his oath helpers. Under the influence of Pope Innocent III, however, there was introduced into the ecclesiastical courts the "jusjurandum de veritate dicenda" or inquisitorial oath.[3] Unlike the procedure used in the administration of the compurgation oath, the inquisitorial oath involved active interrogation of the accused by the judge in addition to the accused's uncomfortable consciousness of his oath to reveal the entire truth of the matter under inquiry. There was some formal limitation upon the power of the ecclesiastical courts to use this new device. An accused could not be put to his oath in the absence of some presentation, which could take the form of formal accusation by one who thereby became a party to the resulting proceeding, denunciation to the court by one unwilling to become a party, or the accused's "popular reputation" as guilty of the subject of the inquiry.[4] The extent to which these restrictions were observed in practice is open to doubt. Mary Hume Maquire asserts that "in England *ex officio* procedure as practiced recognized little necessity of presentment by 'common report' or 'violent suspicion.' The judge *ex officio*, i. e., by virtue of his office as judge, summoned the party into court, and instituted action."[5] In practice then, an individual could be called before the court and made to respond to a broad inquiry into his affairs without regard to the nature or strength of the accusations against him.

The precise nature of the early opposition to the practices of the ecclesiastical courts is in dispute. Wigmore argues that the first three centuries of opposition were based

3. 8 Wigmore, Evidence (McNaughton rev.) § 2250, p. 273.

4. Maguire, supra note 1, at 203.

5. Id. at 203.

solely upon a desire to limit the potentially expansive jurisdiction of the ecclesiastical courts.[6] Maguire, on the other hand, asserts that in addition to the jealousy of jurisdiction there was "steady and growing opposition to the administration of the oath itself as 'repugnant to the ancient customs of our Realm' and contrary to the spirit of the common law." [7]

In any case, opposition to the oath became much greater when the procedure was adopted by two new courts and used for essentially political purposes.[8] In 1487 the Court of the Star Chamber was authorized to pursue its broad political mandate by means of the oath.[9] The Star Chamber was not even subjected to the requirement of presentation that theoretically provided protection from broad "fishing inquisitions" by the ecclesiastical courts. About one hundred years later the same procedure was authorized for the Court of the High Commission in Causes Ecclesiastical, established to maintain conformity to the recently established church.[10] The freewheeling methods of these politically-minded courts—including the use of torture [11]—undoubtedly stimulated a great deal

of additional opposition to the oath procedures.

Required self-incrimination and the use of the oath were not confined to the ecclesiastical courts and the courts of High Commission and Star Chamber. In criminal trials the accused was expected to take an active part in the proceedings, often to his own detriment.[12] He was examined before trial by justices of the peace, and the results of this examination were preserved for use by the judge at trial. Only in limited classes of cases was the examination under oath. This was not out of tenderness for the accused, but rather because it was believed that administering an oath would unwisely permit the accused to place before the jury an influential denial of guilt made under oath.[13] When formally accused, the defendant was required to plead and submit to trial; failure to do so sometimes resulted in extreme forms of torture. Once trial had begun, the accused was subject to vigorous interrogation.[14] He was again not placed under oath, but this again was because permitting him to take the oath would make available too easy a means of avoiding liability. Responding to Wigmore's suggestion that there was no opposition to inquisitorial procedures in the common law courts,[15] Maguire cites a series of petitions sent to the Crown in the mid 1300's from Commons, urging the king to prohibit in the King's Council the use of the oath procedure found objectionable in the ecclesiastical courts.[16] It is not clear, however, whether the basis for this complaint was the use of the oath procedure itself or

6. 8 Wigmore, Evidence (McNaughton rev.) § 2250, p. 278.

7. Maguire, supra note 1, at 205.

8. The power of the ecclesiastical courts to use the *ex officio* oath was severely limited in the early 1600's due in large part to the efforts of Sir Edward Coke who became Chief Justice of the Common Pleas in 1606. As early as 1607 Coke held that the ecclesiastical courts had the power to administer the *ex officio* oath to laymen only in cases relating to wills or marriages (causes testamentary or matrimonial) and to ecclesiastics only in regard to matters not punishable at common law. Corwin, supra note 1, at 6–8; 8 Wigmore, Evidence (McNaughton rev.) § 2250, p. 280.

9. 3 Hen. VII c. 1; 8 Wigmore, Evidence (McNaughton rev.) § 2250, p. 278.

10. 1 Eliz. I, ch. 1; Maguire, supra note 1, at 213–16.

11. Pittman, supra note 1, at 773, citing Jardine, Use of Criminal Torture in Criminal Law of England 13 (1837).

12. Morgan, supra note 1, at 12–23; 8 Wigmore, Evidence (McNaughton rev.) § 2250, p. 285–86.

13. 8 Wigmore, Evidence (McNaughton rev.) § 2250, p. 285.

14. Stephen, I History of the Criminal Law of England 325–26 (1883).

15. 8 Wigmore, Evidence (McNaughton rev.) § 2250, p. 285.

16. Maguire, supra n. 1, at 207–08.

the abuse of it by putting individuals to their oaths in the absence of a presentation.

Whatever its nature, opposition to the procedures of the High Commission and the Star Chamber was greatly stimulated by the efforts of John ("Freeborn John") Lilburn,[17] a vocal opponent of the Stuarts (although he later collided with the Parliament's government). Arrested upon a charge before the Star Chamber involving the printing or importing of heretical and seditious books, Lilburn denied these charges under the Attorney-General's interrogation. When asked about other matters, however, he refused to respond. For his failure to take a legal oath, he was whipped and pilloried. Undaunted, Lilburn applied to Parliament. In 1641 Commons voted that the sentence was illegal and voted reparation; in 1645, the House of Lords concurred that the sentence was illegal and must be vacated. Broader legislative relief preceded Lilburn's, when in 1641 the Long Parliament passed a bill to abolish the Courts of High Commission and Star Chamber and to prohibit the administration of an *ex officio* oath requiring an answer to "things penal."[18] It is possible, however, that this did not prevent the ecclesiastical courts from using the oath procedure upon proper presentment or in penal matters lying within the ecclesiastical jurisdiction.[19]

After 1641, the common law courts began to apply to their own procedure some of the restrictions that had been urged for their ecclesiastical counterparts. The reform, however, affected only the trial procedure; the practice of pre-trial examination (and use of the results at trial) remained unmodified until 1848. But there is general agreement that by 1700 extraction of an answer in any procedure in matters of criminality or forfeiture was improper.[20]

It is difficult to draw many helpful conclusions from the historical origin of the privilege. Wigmore accepts Bentham's suggestion that the privilege as ultimately applied in the common law courts was essentially a matter of overkill.[21] After early opposition to the scope of the jurisdiction of the ecclesiastical courts, Bentham asserts, attention was turned to their abuse of the oath whereby an individual was put to his oath without proper presentment. This procedure, pursuant to which an individual was required to respond accurately and fully to broad questions concerning his activities, was sometimes accompanied by torture and became the vehicle for effectuating the policies of foreign popes, bigoted prelates suppressing religious diversity, and dictatorial kings. Because of strong emotional feeling against the abuse of the procedure, the common law courts unnecessarily and illogically (according to Bentham) accepted the proposition that not only was it improper to compel an individual to respond to interrogation when no charge had been made against him, but also that it was inherently improper to compel him to respond at all. Wigmore and Bentham find no basis for the latter proposition in the history of opposition to the oath procedure. But perhaps this is too narrow a reading of the historical material. Even if the initial objection was only to the impropriety of putting individuals to their oath without presentation, this policy suggests at least limited objection to the use of information extracted from the mouth of the accused as the basis for a criminal prosecution. This

---

17. 8 Wigmore, Evidence (McNaughton rev.) § 2250, p. 282–83 summarizes the trial, which is reported at 3 How.St.Tr. 1315 (1637).

18. 8 Wigmore, Evidence (McNaughton rev.) § 2250, pp. 282–84.

19. Id. at 284.

20. Id. at 290–91.

21. Id., at 292, citing J. Bentham, Rationale of Judicial Evidence, in 7 The Works of Jeremy Bentham 456, 462 (Bowring ed. 1843). This view was also accepted in the first edition of this text. McCormick, Evidence 255 (1954).

early suspicion of compulsory self-incrimination—even if it extended only to situations where compulsion was exerted before an accusation had been made by some other method—is in no way inconsistent with later condemnation of the practice in broader circumstances. In fact both seem to be based upon a feeling that compelling an individual to provide the basis for his own penal liability should be limited because the position in which it places the individual—making a choice between violating a solemn oath and incurring penal liability—weighs against important policies of individual freedom and dignity. At first, there may have been agreement that the need to secure sufficient evidence for conviction from one whom there was significant reason to believe was guilty outweighed the invasion of personal dignity. But the decision of the common law courts in the later 1600's that even this did not outweigh the policy can certainly be viewed as consistent with and a logical extension of the opposition to the procedures of the ecclesiastical courts and the courts of Star Chamber and High Commission.

115. The History of the Privilege: (b) Development of the Privilege in America.[22]

There is also significant disagreement over the development of the privilege in America. Wigmore asserts that the privilege "remained an unknown doctrine" in the colony of Massachusetts for a generation after 1641.[23] Pittman, however, concludes that significant post-1640 opposition to testimonial compulsion developed in the New England colonies as well as in England and for largely the same reasons.[24] According to him, the New

England magistrates, claiming divine authority, were opposed by the Puritans, who sought removal of the right to compel self-incriminating testimony because they saw it as a means of enforcing compliance with an established church.

There is some evidence of the privilege in early colonial America.[25] Pittman concludes that the privilege in regard to an accused was fairly well established in the New England colonies before 1650 and in Virginia soon after.[26] In any case, it was inserted in the constitutions or bills of rights of seven American states before 1789,[27] and has since spread to all state constitutions except those of Iowa and New Jersey. In both of the latter states, however, it was accepted as a matter of nonconstitutional law.[28]

There is also dispute over the source of the provision in the fifth amendment to the federal constitution.[29] The first two editions of Wigmore's treatise argued that "the real explanation of the colonial convention's insistence upon it would seem to be found in the agitation then going on in France against the inquisitorial feature of the Ordinance of 1670."[30] Pittman, however, argued that the stream of influence was in fact running towards France from the American colonies at this time and that the colonies' own experience with high-handed prerogative courts provided the incentive for the

22. See generally 8 Wigmore, Evidence (McNaughton rev.) § 2250(4); Levy, Origins of the Fifth Amendment 333–404 (1968).

23. 8 Wigmore, Evidence (McNaughton rev.) § 2250, p. 293.

24. Pittman, The Colonial and Constitutional History of the Privilege Against Self-Incrimination in America, 21 Va.L.Rev. 763, 775 (1935).

25. Id. at 776–79.

26. Id. at 781.

27. Virginia (1776), Pennsylvania (1776), Maryland (1776), North Carolina (1776), Vermont (1777), Massachusetts (1780), and New Hampshire (1784). Pittman, supra n. 24, at 765.

28. Pittman, supra n. 24, at 763, n. 1.

29. See generally Levy, Origins of the Fifth Amendment 405–432 (1968); Mayers, The Federal Witness' Privilege Against Self-Incrimination: Constitutional or Common Law? 4 Am.J. Legal History 107, 108–20 (1960).

30. See 8 Wigmore, Evidence (McNaughton rev.) § 2250, p. 261, n. 1(4).

drive to insert the privilege into the Bill of Rights.[31] Wigmore's treatise now agrees.[32] In addition, Pittman suggests, American statesmen recognized that in the new nation there existed conflicts of interest and authority much the same as underlay the conflict between the Church and the Crown in England. The Fifth Amendment privilege, he concluded, not only was an answer to numerous instances of colonial misrule but was a shield against "the evils that lurk[ed] in the shadows of a new and untried sovereignty." [33]

116. The History of the Privilege: (c) Development of the Two Branches of the Privilege—The Privilege of an Accused in a Criminal Proceeding and the Privilege of a Witness.[34]

Historically, the privilege developed from objections to the procedure whereby the ecclesiastical courts were able to compel one against whom no charge had been made to respond in incriminating fashion to broad questions posed to him. Nevertheless, when the common law courts began to apply the privilege in their own proceedings, it soon became clear that the privilege could be invoked not only by a defendant in a criminal prosecution but also by a witness whose conviction could not procedurally be a consequence of the proceeding.[35] There is no historical indication that this was recognized as an important step in the growth of the privilege. Whatever the rationale of the English

courts for refusing to restrict the privilege to one himself on trial for a criminal offense, it was not discussed in the written decisions.

The early state constitutional provisions as well as the Fifth Amendment language permit a construction that prohibits only compulsion to cause an individual to give oral testimony in a criminal proceeding in which he is a defendant. Several authorities have argued that this was their original meaning.[36] This position is strengthened by the fact that early American cases upholding a witness's refusal to answer relied not on existing state constitutional provisions but rather on the existence of the common law privilege which clearly encompassed a witness in a criminal or civil proceeding.[37]

In any case, the Fifth Amendment privilege was not formally broadened beyond the apparent initial intent of the state provisions until a century after its adoption. In Counselman v. Hitchcock,[38] decided in 1892, the Supreme Court rejected the government's contention that the constitutional privilege extended a narrower privilege than the common law and that under the Fifth Amendment a witness could invoke the protection only when called upon to testify in a criminal case in which he was the accused. The precise holding was relatively narrow—that one called before a grand jury could invoke the privilege because the grand jury proceeding was a "criminal case" within the meaning of the amendment [39] —but the language portended a broader expansion of the privilege.[40]

---

31. Pittman, supra n. 24, at 765.

32. 8 Wigmore, Evidence (McNaughton rev.) § 2250, p. 294.

33. Pittman, supra n. 24, at 789.

34. See generally 8 Wigmore, Evidence (McNaughton rev.) § 2250, p. 290, § 2252, pp. 325–27; Levy, Origins of the Fifth Amendment 313 (1968).

35. 8 Wigmore, Evidence (McNaughton rev.) § 2250, p. 290. Levy, Origins of the Fifth Amendment 313 (1968) reported that the privilege had been extended to witnesses in the trial of King Charles in 1649.

36. Corwin, The Supreme Court's Interpretation of the Self-Incrimination Clause, 29 Mich.L.Rev. 1, 2 (1930); Mayers, The Federal Witness' Privilege Against Self-Incrimination: Constitutional or Common-Law, 4 Am.J. Legal History 107 (1960).

37. Mayers, supra n. 36, at 124.

38. 142 U.S. 547 (1892).

39. Id. at 563.

40. "It is impossible that the meaning of the constitutional provision can only be, that a person shall not be compelled to be a witness against himself. It would doubtless cover such cases; but it

Thirty years later, in holding the privilege available to a bankrupt sought to be examined concerning his estate, the Court could say with confidence:

> "The Government insists, broadly, that the constitutional privilege against self-incrimination does not apply in any civil proceeding. The contrary must be accepted as settled. The privilege is not ordinarily dependent upon the nature of the proceeding in which the testimony is sought or is to be used. It applies alike to civil and criminal proceedings, wherever the answer might tend to subject to criminal responsibility him who gives it. The privilege protects a mere witness as fully as it does one who is also a party defendant.[41]"

It is now generally accepted that the state constitutional provisions as well as that of the Fifth Amendment may be invoked by one whose testimony is sought in a proceeding other than a criminal prosecution in which he is the defendant.[42] In view of the application of the federal privilege to the states,[43] however, it is now the scope of the federal privilege which is of primary importance. It is also clear that the right of one not a defendant in a criminal case to decline to provide information tending to show that he has committed a criminal offense is merely one aspect of the broad privilege against self-incrimination. But there are significantly different problems raised when the privilege is invoked by one not a defendant in a criminal prosecution. There is, therefore, analytical

value in considering separately the two aspects of "branches" of the privilege: the privilege of the accused in a criminal proceeding, and the privilege of one not an accused (usually referred to as the privilege of a witness).

117. The History of the Privilege: (d) Application of the Fifth Amendment Privilege to the States.

In a long series of early decisions the United States Supreme Court made clear that it did not regard the Fifth Amendment's privilege against compulsory self-incrimination as binding on the states by reason of the due process clause of the Fourteenth Amendment.[44] Malloy v. Hogan,[45] decided in 1964, reversed this line of cases, thereby shifting the emphasis of any examination of the privilege from the state rules to the federal constitution.

Mr. Justice Brennan, speaking for the Court, justified the shift with two basic arguments. First, he relied heavily upon the line of Supreme Court decisions holding use of coerced confessions in state criminal prosecu-

---

is not limited to them. The object was to insure that a person should not be compelled, when acting as a witness to any investigation, to give testimony which might tend to show that he himself had committed a crime. The privilege is limited to criminal matters, but it is as broad as the mischief against which it seeks to guard." Id. at 562.

41. McCarthy v. Arndstein, 266 U.S. 34, 40 (1924).

42. 8 Wigmore, Evidence § 2252, pp. 326–27.

43. § 117, infra.

44. "Salutary as the principle may seem to the great majority, it cannot be ranked with the right to hearing before condemnation, the immunity from arbitrary power not acting by general laws, and the inviolability of private property. The wisdom of the exemption has never been universally assented to since the days of Bentham; many doubt it today, and it is best defended not as an unchangeable principle of universal justice but as a law proved by experience to be expedient. See Wigmore, § 2251. It has no place in the jurisprudence of civilized and free countries outside the domain of the common law, and it is nowhere observed among our own people in the search for truth outside the administration of the law. . . There seems to be no reason whatever . . . for straining the meaning of due process of law to include this privilege within it . . . ." Twining v. New Jersey, 211 U.S. 78, 113 (1908). See also Cohen v. Hurley, 366 U.S. 117 (1961); Snyder v. Commonwealth of Massachusetts, 291 U.S. 97 (1934).

45. 378 U.S. 1 (1964), noted in The Supreme Court, 1963 Term, 78 Harv.L.Rev. 223 (1964), 10 N.Y.L. Forum 602, 43 Texas L.Rev. 239, 18 Vand.L.Rev. 744.

tions a denial of due process of law.[46] Despite the Court's initial position that the coerced confession rule did not rest upon the Fifth Amendment privilege,[47] the line of cases, as the Court read them in *Malloy,* soon abandoned that position and came to accept fully the underlying federal standard governing admissibility which in turn was based upon the Fifth Amendment privilege. Speaking of this shift in the coerced confession cases, Mr. Justice Brennan concluded:

> "The shift reflects recognition that the American system of criminal prosecution is accusatorial, not inquisitorial, and that the Fifth Amendment privilege is its essential mainstay. . . . Governments, state and federal, are thus constitutionally compelled to establish guilt by evidence independently and freely secured, and may not by coercion prove a charge against an accused out of his own mouth. Since the Fourteenth Amendment prohibits the states from inducing a person to confess through 'sympathy falsely aroused' . . . or other like inducement far short of 'compulsion by torture' . . . it follows *a fortiori* that it also forbids the States to resort to imprisonment, as here, to compel him to answer questions that might incriminate him. The Fourteenth Amendment secures against state invasion the same privilege that the Fifth Amendment guarantees against federal infringement—the right of a person to remain silent unless he chooses to speak in the unfettered exercise of his own will, and to suffer no penalty . . . for such silence.[48] "

The Court also relied upon Mapp v. Ohio,[49] holding that the Fourteenth Amendment required that states in a criminal prosecution exclude evidence obtained by means of a search and seizure unreasonable within the meaning of the Fourth Amendment. The exclusionary rule applied to the states in *Mapp,* Mr. Justice Brennan declared, rested on the Fifth Amendment privilege against self-incrimination as well as the Fourth Amendment right to be free from unreasonable searches and seizures.[50] *Mapp,* then, to a limited extent had already applied the Fifth Amendment privilege to the states.

Not only is the Fifth Amendment privilege binding upon the states under *Malloy,* but the Court also made clear that its application in state courts must be consistent with federal constitutional standards. Rejecting the contention that the availability of the federal privilege to a witness in a state proceeding should be determined according to a less stringent standard than is applicable in a federal proceeding, the Court responded, "It would be incongruous to have different standards determine the validity of a claim of privilege based on the same feared prosecution, depending on whether the claim was asserted in a state or federal court. Therefore, the same standards must determine whether an accused's silence in either a federal or state proceeding is justified." [51]

---

46. Malloy v. Hogan, 378 U.S. 1, 6–8 (1964).

47. Brown v. Mississippi, 297 U.S. 278, 285 (1936). See the discussion of the relationship of the privilege to the rule prohibiting use of coerced confessions in § 148, infra.

48. Malloy v. Hogan, 378 U.S. 1, 7–8 (1964).

49. 367 U.S. 643 (1961).

50. Malloy v. Hogan, 378 U.S. 1, 8–9 (1964). Heavy reliance was placed upon the analysis in Boyd v. United States, 116 U.S. 616 (1886); see § 126, infra.

51. Malloy v. Hogan, 378 U.S. 1, 9–14 (1964). Mr. Justice White, joined by Mr. Justice Stewart, dissented on the ground that even applying the federal standard, Malloy had not properly invoked the privilege. Mr. Justice Harlan, joined by Mr. Justice Clark, agreed with Mr. Justice Stewart: "The Court's reference to a federal standard is, to put it bluntly, simply an excuse for the Court to substitute its own superficial assessment of the facts and state law for the careful and better informed conclusions of the state courts." Id. at 33 (Mr. Justice Harlan, dissenting).

As a result of *Malloy,* any examination of the current scope of the privilege against compulsory self-incrimination must emphasize the federal decisions in the area. *Malloy* makes clear not only that the states are bound by the privilege as embodied in the Fifth Amendment and federal decisions developing the "federal standard" for its application, but in addition that the federal courts will not be reluctant to examine thoroughly and review the application of the privilege and the federal standards to specific factual situations by the states.

118. The Policy Foundations of the Modern Privilege.[52]

It has been argued that whatever its propriety in the days of the Court of the Star Chamber, the privilege against compulsory self-incrimination is no longer a justifiable limitation upon the right of the state to demand cooperation in its investigations.[53] Opponents of the privilege make several points. First, dangers of the nature and scope of those against which the privilege historically protected—physical torture as a means of compelling responses to general inquiries—no longer exist.[54] Second, the privilege deprives the state of access to a valuable source of reliable information, the subject of the investigation himself, and therefore purchases whatever values it attains at too great a cost to the inquiry for truth. The subject is an especially valuable source of information when the alleged crime is one of the sophisticated "white collar" offenses, and in such situations the privilege may deny the prosecution access to the *only* available information.[55] Third, the privilege may as a practical matter be impossible to implement effectively. Although the law may extend the theoretical right to remain silent at no or minimal cost, in fact it is inevitable that inferences will be drawn from silence and that the inferences will be acted upon. Since these inferences are drawn from inherently ambiguous silence, they are less reliable than inferences from other sources, including compelled self-incriminatory testimony. The result is that one who chooses to invoke the privilege is not protected, but rather is subjected to potential prejudice in a manner ill designed to promote his own best interests.

Proponents of the privilege argue that the historical danger underlying the privilege still exists; the use of physical torture to compel incriminating admissions is not unknown today.[56] But in any case, the increased sensitivity of society might well find incarceration for contempt for refusal to testify as abhorrent as physical torture was regarded in the fifteenth century. Thus the historical basis for the privilege—or its modern equivalent—still provides a justification for its continued existence.

In addition, however, the privilege has come to serve functions other than its historical function of preventing the application of physical force to extract admissions of guilt of otherwise unprovable offenses.[57]

---

52. See generally 8 Wigmore, Evidence (McNaughton rev.) § 2251; Clapp, Privilege Against Self-Incrimination, 10 Rutgers L.Rev. 541 (1956).

53. E. g., Carman, A Plea for Withdrawal of Constitutional Privilege from the Criminal, 22 Minn.L. Rev. 200 (1937); Pound, Legal Interrogation of Persons Accused or Suspected of Crime, 24 J.Crim. L., C. & P.S. 1014 (1934); Terry, Constitutional Provisions Against Forcing Self-Incrimination, 15 Yale L.J. 127 (1905); Wigmore, Nemo Tenetur Seipsum Prodere, 5 Harv.L.Rev. 71, 85–87 (1891).

54. Critics have been especially eager to point out that there is little danger of physical abuse in the course of the formal trial, during which the privilege clearly applies, and that the privilege traditionally extended little aid to those in police custody, where the danger of physical abuse is much greater. E. g., American Law Institute, Model Code of Evidence, Comment on Rule 201(1) (1942). This argument is of somewhat less weight now that the privilege is applicable to police interrogation. See § 125, infra.

55. See Terry, supra note 53.

56. E. g., Beecher v. Alabama, 389 U.S. 35 (1967) (defendant threatened by police with firearms in effort to secure confession).

57. See Murphy v. Waterfront Com'n, 378 U.S. 52, 55 (1964).

These functions may justify its present existence without regard to its effectiveness in fulfilling its traditional role. In several ways, for example, the privilege serves the function of protecting the innocent from unjustified conviction.[58] One who is under the strain of actual or potential accusation, although innocent, might be unduly prejudiced by his own testimony for reasons unrelated to its accuracy. For example, he may have physical traits or mannerisms that would cause an adverse reaction from the trier of fact. Or, he might, under the strain of interrogation, become confused and thereby give an erroneous impression of guilt. Thus the privilege affords such an individual the opportunity to avoid discussing an incriminating situation and the danger of creating an unreliable but prejudicial impression of guilt.[59] In addition, the privilege is one part —but an important part—of our accusatorial system which requires that no criminal punishment be imposed unless guilt is established by a large quantum of especially reliable evidence. By denying the prosecution access to what is regarded as an inherently suspect type of proof—the self-incriminating admissions of the accused—the privilege forces the prosecution to establish its case on the basis of more reliable evidence,[60] thus creating an

additional assurance that every person convicted is in fact guilty as charged.

The privilege also, and perhaps most importantly, serves the function of assuring that even guilty individuals are treated in a manner consistent with basic respect for human dignity. Wholly apart from its function in assuring the accuracy of the guilt-determining process, the privilege demands that even those guilty of an offense not be compelled beyond a certain extent to participate in the establishment of their own guilt.[61] This is based upon the feeling that to require participation would be simply too great a violation of the dignity of the individual, whether or not he is guilty of a criminal offense. In part, this seems to be based upon the conclusion that compulsory incrimination faces a guilty person with a dilemma too cruel to be justifiable. To place an individual in a position in which his natural instincts and personal interests dictate that he should lie and then to punish him for lying, or for refusing to lie or violate his natural instincts, is an intolerable invasion of his personal dignity. In many cases, Judge Frank has argued, "the state would be forcing him to commit a crime and then punishing him for it."[62]

Apart from its value to individuals, whether innocent or guilty, the privilege also serves broader functions. It encourages respect for and protects the dignity of the judicial system. By removing a significant incentive for perjury, encouraging witnesses to come forward by removing the danger that they will be compelled to incriminate themselves, and forcing prosecutors to rely upon evidence

58. Griswold, The Fifth Amendment Today 20–21 (1955). Dean Griswold later, however, suggested that it had been a mistake to defend the privilege on the ground that it is "basically designed to protect those innocent of crime, at least in any numerical sense." Griswold, The Right to be Let Alone, 55 Nw.U.L.Rev. 216, 223 (1960).

59. See Wilson v. United States, 149 U.S. 60, 66 (1893).

60. The classic statement of this position was reported by Sir James FitzJames Stephen and attributed by him to an experienced Indian civil officer. Explaining why prisoners were sometimes tortured, the officer stated:
"There is a great deal of laziness in it. It is far pleasanter to sit comfortably in the shade rubbing red pepper into a poor devil's eyes than to go about in the hot sun hunting up evidence." Stephen, A History of the Criminal Law of England 442 n. 1 (1883).

61. "[W]e do not make even the most hardened criminal sign his own death warrant, or dig his grave, or pull the lever that springs the trap on which he stands. We have through the course of history developed a considerable feeling of the dignity and intrinsic importance of the individual man. Even the evil man is a human being." Griswold, The Fifth Amendment Today 7 (1955).

62. United States v. Grunewald, 233 F.2d 556, 591 (2d Cir. 1956) (Frank J. dissenting), rev'd 353 U.S. 391 (1957).

more reliable than incriminating admissions of the accused, the privilege enhances the judicial process's access to reliable information on which to make its decisions.[63] By tending to equalize the position of the lone suspect who is confronted with the huge investigatory and prosecutorial apparatus of the state, the privilege helps to make the criminal trial more nearly a contest between equals, thereby maximizing the opportunity for full development of the facts and an accurate resolution of the cases within the framework of the adversary system. By preventing the prosecution from degenerating into scenes which much of the population would find offensive, the privilege maintains public respect for the entire judicial process.[64]

Finally, the privilege deprives the state of a weapon which is particularly subject to abuse in especially sensitive areas.[65] Compelled self-incrimination, as history demonstrates, can serve as a valuable tool for suppressing dissent, opposition to the existing political authorities, and freedom of thought and opinion. In view of the difficulty—and perhaps impossibility—of making the right to compel incriminating answers available only in those situations in which no danger is posed to these areas of broad social concern, denying this right to the state in all situations is justified.

The privilege obviously reflects a large number of values, and consequently it is reasonable that its effect differs with the extent to which various values are affected by specific situations. This is most apparent in the difference between the privilege of an accused and that of one not an accused. Although many of the values served by the privilege are furthered by extending it to one who is not, when called upon to testify, himself on trial, the fact that the state's objective is not to secure this individual's conviction somewhat reduces the incentive for abuse of the interrogative process as applied to him. It is therefore appropriate to limit somewhat the impact of the privilege in this situation. This is accomplished by requiring one not a witness to submit to interrogation and to assert the privilege only in response to specific questions. The development of the privilege in other aspects is showing the same flexibility. For example, the privilege has been extended to one under police interrogation despite ambiguity as to the extent to which police agencies may require or encourage an incriminating response. Moreover, the subject of interrogation is protected by other factors, such as the right to counsel and the rule requiring the exclusion of nonvoluntary statements he may make. In this context the privilege apparently does not always shield the accused from all interrogation, although it requires that any questioning be conducted under circumstances designed to assure an effective right to assert the privilege in response to specific questions should the subject choose to do so.

The continued vitality and general acceptance of the privilege depend upon the maintenance of sufficient flexibility to adjust the privilege to different times and different contexts. The privilege as it exists today is a far different rule from that imposed upon the ecclesiastical courts in the seventeenth century, and it serves significantly different functions. Even today, the privilege of a member of a partnership engaging in a regulated business activity is far different from the privilege of a defendant on trial for robbery, and far different policy factors are involved in the two situations. If the privi-

---

63. Meltzer, Required Records, the McCarran Act, and the Privilege Against Self-Incrimination, 18 U.Chi.L.Rev. 687, 701 (1951) suggests that reliable self-incriminating testimony cannot be compelled, so that "unwillingness to command the impossible" is the most intelligible basis for the privilege in most situations.

64. E. g., Stephen, 1 A History of the Criminal Law of England 441 (1883).

65. Griswold, The Right to be Let Alone, 55 Nw.U.L. Rev. 216, 223 (1960).

lege is to remain viable it must retain such flexibility, and it must reflect an appropriate balance among the wide variety of policy factors as they are affected by the specific context in which it is invoked.

119. The Procedural Manner of Effectuating the Privilege.

The privilege against self-incrimination may be asserted in a variety of ways. The first, of course, is a blanket refusal to submit to interrogation which might lead to incrimination, as in the case of an accused in a criminal proceeding who is entitled to decline to take the witness stand at all. Second, an individual who is faced with a specific inquiry may decline to respond. Thus a witness who has taken the stand may decline to respond to specific questions on the basis that to do so would constitute self-incrimination. Third, one who has been subjected to what he views as a violation of his privilege may question the propriety of official use of the result of that activity. A criminal defendant, to put the most obvious case, may object to the introduction in evidence against him of his testimony in a prior proceeding given in response to judicial compulsion. Finally, the privilege may be asserted as a substantive defense to a criminal charge on the basis that compliance with the requirements of the law would have constituted self-incrimination. Thus the privilege may be raised as a defense in a prosecution for failure to obtain a gambling stamp on the grounds that compliance with the stamp requirement would have required that the defendant incriminate himself.

These various aspects are discussed in the sections which follow.

120. The Personal Nature of the Privilege.[66]

The case law makes frequent reference to the personal nature of the privilege, but these often offhand comments are somewhat misleading. It is clear that a criminal defendant cannot invoke the privilege of witnesses,[67] codefendants or even co-conspirators.[68] Nor can he successfully complain that their privilege was violated. It is also clear that an attorney cannot invoke the privilege of his client for his own protection.[69] For example, an attorney called as a witness before a grand jury cannot refuse to respond to a question on the ground that the answer would incriminate his client.[70] He can, however, as agent for his client invoke the privilege of his client for the protection of the client.[71] Thus an attorney who appears before a court as counsel for his client may at that time object to a proposed order on the basis that it would compel his client to incriminate himself (or, alternatively, he may waive his client's privilege).[72]

In light of the general agreement on the personal nature of the privilege, it is surpris-

---

(1948); C.J.S. Witnesses § 451 (1957); Dec.Dig. Witnesses ⊙306. See also Annot., 37 A.L.R.3d 1373.

67. State v. Dickens, 66 Wash.2d 58, 401 P.2d 321 (1965).

68. Poole v. United States, 329 F.2d 720 (9th Cir. 1964).

69. United States v. Goldfarb, 328 F.2d 280 (6th Cir. 1964).

70. Id. at 282.

71. Farmer v. State, 5 Md.App. 546, 248 A.2d 809 (1968); People v. Myers, 35 Ill.2d 311, 220 N.E.2d 297 (1966) (attorney in possession of client's letters could invoke client's privilege in response to subpoena duces tecum). Contra, Sears, Roebuck & Co. v. American Plumbing & Supply Co. 19 F.R. D. 334, 341 (E.D.Wis.1956) (dictum); State v. Manning, 134 N.W.2d 91 (N.D.1965) (trial court properly overruled objection by defendant's counsel that question asked of defendant during cross-examination might tend to convict of a collateral crime; waiver also used as alternative basis of holding). Defendant's counsel, of course, cannot invoke the privilege for a witness. State v. Evans, 249 La. 861, 192 So.2d 103 (1966). See the discussions in Brody v. United States, 243 F.2d 378, 387 n. 5 (1st Cir. 1957); United States v. Judson, 322 F.2d 460, 463–68 (9th Cir. 1963).

72. Brody v. United States, 243 F.2d 378, 387 (1st Cir. 1957).

66. See generally 8 Wigmore, Evidence (McNaughton rev.) § 2270(1); 58 Am.Jur. Witnesses § 48

ing to find a series of cases finding reversible error in the prosecution's calling a witness who invokes his own privilege and the action of the trial court in permitting the jury to draw from this invocation an inference that the answer would have tended to prove the defendant's guilt as well as that of the witness.[73]   If these decisions base the granting of relief on appeal upon an infringement of the witness privilege, they are on questionable grounds given the personal nature of the privilege.   The decisions are, however, supportable on other bases.   If the defendant has not taken the stand himself, arguably permitting the prosecution to emphasize the witness's invocation of the privilege draws the jury's attention to the defendant's failure to testify and thus endangers the privilege of the accused.[74]   Or, it is arguable that there is so great a danger that the jury will give undue weight to the inference of guilt that might be drawn from the witness's invocation of the privilege that this danger of abuse of the evidence outweighs its probative value.   But at least one court has enforced a general prohibition against drawing inferences from a witness' invocation of the privilege "although logically [such inferences] are very persuasive."[75]   The United States Supreme Court has suggested that this type of situation might amount to reversible error for either of two reasons:

"First, some courts have indicated that error may be based upon a concept of prosecutorial misconduct, when the Government makes a conscious and flagrant attempt to build its case out of inference arising from use of the testimonial privilege. . . .   A second theory seems to rest upon the conclusion that, in the circumstances of a given case, inferences from a witness' refusal to answer added critical weight to the prosecution's case in a form not subject to cross-examination, and thus unfairly prejudiced the defendant."[76]

Whether or not calling a witness who invokes his privilege constitutes reversible error depends, then, upon whether, under the circumstances, the interests involved have been significantly endangered.[77]

---

73.   State v. Boscia, 93 N.J.Super. 586, 226 A.2d 643 (1967) (reversible error to permit prosecutor to show for impeachment that defense's witness had invoked the privilege before grand jury); State v. Johnson, 243 Ore. 532, 413 P.2d 383 (1966) (error for prosecution to call codefendant to stand for purpose of requiring him to invoke privilege before jury); De Gesualdo v. People, 147 Colo. 426, 364 P.2d 374 (1961).   The error has been held correctable by proper instruction. United States v. Amadio, 215 F.2d 605 (7th Cir. 1954), rev'd on other grounds 348 U.S. 892; Commonwealth v. Granito, 326 Mass. 494, 95 N.E.2d 539 (1950).   Grunewald v. United States, 353 U.S. 391 (1957), cited in some of the decisions, is not helpful.   Since it held that a defendant should not have been cross-examined at trial on his earlier invocation of the privilege before a grand jury, it involved the significantly different matter of inferences to be drawn from the silence of the defendant himself.   See generally Annot., 86 A.L.R.2d 1443.

74.   See § 121, infra.

75.   United States v. Maloney, 262 F.2d 535, 537 (2d Cir. 1959).

76.   Namet v. United States, 373 U.S. 179, 186–87 (1963).

77.   Namet v. United States, 373 U.S. 179 (1963) (no reversible error in view of lack of prosecutorial misconduct and the fact that the bulk of the witness' testimony occurred before the privilege was invoked); United States v. Sing Kee, 250 F.2d 236, 239 (2d Cir. 1957), cert. denied 355 U.S. 954 ("in the setting of this case . . . the relevance of the witness' grand jury claim of privilege outweighed the danger that the jury might draw from it any impermissible inferences regarding the defendant's guilt"); Commonwealth v. Granito, 326 Mass. 494, 95 N.E.2d 539 (1950) (emphasis on prosecutor's ignorance that witness would invoke the privilege when called).

Invocation of the privilege by less than all codefendants presents special problems.   In De Luna v. United States, 308 F.2d 140 (5th Cir. 1962) one of two codefendants tried together did not take the stand to refute the version of the offense testified to by the other defendant.   This failure to take the stand was commented upon by counsel for the testifying defendant.   Although reversing the conviction of the nontestifying defendant on the basis of the comment, the court suggested in dictum that the comment had been a proper exercise of the testifying defendant's right to con-

121. General Scope of the Privilege: (a) What is Protected Against.[78]

The danger against which the privilege expressly protects its holders is that of incrimination. Despite vigorous objection, it has uniformly been held that the privilege does not protect against the disgrace and practical excommunication from society resulting from disclosure of matters which, under the circumstances, could not give rise to criminal liability.[79] It is only the danger of formal imposition of *legal criminal liability* against which the privilege protects. It is not clear, however, which incidents of a criminal proceeding constitute "incrimination" within the meaning of the privilege. No serious question exists as to one who has not yet been tried; the danger of trial, conviction, and imprisonment is clearly within the scope of the privilege. Nor is there any doubt that when the danger of such proceedings has been removed by passage of the period of limitations,[80] pardon,[81] prior conviction or acquittal,[82] or a grant of immunity[83] that no danger within the scope of the privilege exists. Problems arise, however, when attempts are made to compel testimony of individuals convicted but not sentenced or who have been

frontation. "[His attorneys] should be free to draw all rational inferences from the failure of a co-defendant to testify, just as an attorney is free to comment on the effect of any interested party's failure to produce material evidence in his possession or to call witnesses who have knowledge of pertinent facts." Id. at 143. The decision is critically discussed in Comment, Exercise of the Privilege Against Self-Incrimination by Witnesses and Codefendants: The Effect Upon the Accused, 33 U. Chi.L.Rev. 151, 161–65 (1965). Compare United States v. McKinney, 379 F.2d 259, 265 (6th Cir. 1967) ("such comment [by counsel for a testifying defendant] . . . would not be permissible"). The danger that the jury considering the nontestifying defendant's guilt will rely upon an improper inference in finding the nontestifying defendant guilty can, of course, be prevented by granting separate trials. See United States v. Echeles, 352 F.2d 892 (7th Cir. 1965). But this does not address itself to the propriety of reliance by the testifying defendant upon the silence of his codefendant. The Fifth Circuit has limited the application of the De Luna rule: "The *De Luna* rule applies only when it is counsel's *duty* to make a comment, and a mere desire to do so will not support an incursion of a defendant's carefully protected right to silence. Clearly, a duty arises only when the arguments of the codefendants are antagonistic." Gurleski v. United States, 405 F.2d 253, 265 (5th Cir. 1968). Cf. United States v. Caci, 401 F.2d 664 (2d Cir. 1968) cert. denied 394 U.S. 917. But what of the situation where no incursion upon a co-defendants "carefully protected right to silence" is involved? This would seem to be a question of probative value rather than of privilege. Since there is no danger that the inference will be used to the prejudice of the nontestifying defendant and no danger is posed to the rights of the testifying defendant, the issue would seem to be whether the inference is sufficiently reliable to permit its use by the jury.

Several courts have suggested an investigation in open court but without the jury present to determine the facts on which to balance the value and danger of permitting the witness to be interrogated before the jury. Commonwealth v. Douglas, 354 Mass. 212, 236 N.E.2d 865 (1968); State v. Nelson, 72 Wash.2d 269, 432 P.2d 857 (1967). Perhaps even if the inference is generally too unreliable to permit, when it is sought by a defendant clothed with the traditional protections of an accused the balance falls in favor of permitting him to invoke the inference for whatever value it might possess.

78. See generally 8 Wigmore, Evidence (McNaughton rev.) §§ 2254, 2255, 2256, 2257; 58 Am.Jur. Witnesses §§ 43, 45 (1948); C.J.S. Witnesses §§ 437, 438, 439, 444, 445, 446.

79. See the dissent of Mr. Justice Douglas in Ullmann v. United States, 350 U.S. 422, 440 (1956), arguing on historical grounds that the privilege was intended to protect against infamy which "was historically considered to be punishment as effective as fine and imprisonment." Id. at 451. Reasoning that the essence of infamy was the impact of public opinion, he concludes that the privilege should protect against the impact of public opinion even in the absence of any governmental action. Id. at 451–454. See also Brown v. Walker, 161 U.S. 591, 628 (1896) (Field, J., dissenting); United States v. James, 60 F. 257 (N.D.Ill.1894).

80. Markey v. Lee, 224 So.2d 789 (Fla.App.1969). But see Commonwealth v. Lenart, 430 Pa. 144, 242 A.2d 259 (1968) (running of the period of limitations would not justify contempt citation for refusal to testify because it constituted only a bar to conviction rather than prosecution and the interrogation might reveal crimes not barred by statute of limitation).

81. Moore v. Backus, 78 F.2d 571 (7th Cir. 1935) cert. denied 296 U.S. 640.

82. Ex parte Critchlow, 11 Cal.2d 751, 81 P.2d 966 (1938); People ex rel Gross v. Sheriff, 277 App. Div. 546, 101 N.Y.S.2d 271 (1950), aff'd 302 N.Y. 173, 96 N.E.2d 763 (1951).

83. See § 143, infra.

sentenced but still have the opportunity for reversal on appeal and a subsequent new trial. Generally, those courts that have expressly considered the matter have held that the privilege protects against use of compelled testimony in setting sentence and in use on a new trial, and therefore an individual may not be compelled to respond to questions until after sentencing and the time for appeal as of right has expired.[84] This is consistent with the policy of the privilege. Insofar as the privilege seeks to remove the incentive for the state to coerce testimonial responses from subjects of a criminal investigation, it makes little sense to conclude that coercion applied not for the purpose of attaching initial criminal liability but rather for imposing greater punishment or re-imposing liability after reversal of an improperly obtained conviction is not within the purpose. Somewhat more difficult is the matter of availability of review by a court whose jurisdiction is discretionary[85] and subsequent collateral attack. In theory, of course, the same arguments are applicable as support application of the privilege during the availability of review as of right. As a practical matter, however, the best solution would seem to treat the relatively limited period of availability of discretionary review the same as the period during which appeal as of right is available, but to consider the possibility of successful collateral attack and new trial as raising the question of whether the potential use of the responses in a new trial constitutes a "real and appreciable" danger.[86] In the absence of some specific showing that collateral attack is likely to be successful, the danger would probably not be "real and appreciable."

The privilege by its terms protects against only those disclosures or the use of disclosures which lead to "incrimination." There has never been any serious doubt that the danger of incurring ordinary civil liability for compensatory damages did not bring a situation within the privilege.[87] In Boyd v.

---

84. Mills v. United States, 281 F.2d 736 (4th Cir. 1960) (time for appeal had not run and trial judge had indicated he would take into account in sentencing any incriminating statements); State v. Tyson, 43 N.J. 411, 204 A.2d 864 (1964) cert. denied 380 U.S. 987 (privilege can be invoked before sentence is imposed); State v. Johnson, 77 Idaho 1, 287 P.2d 425 (1955) cert. denied 350 U.S. 1007 (witness with appeal pending properly permitted to invoke the privilege because of danger of use of testimony at new trial); People v. Den Uyl, 318 Mich. 645, 29 N.W.2d 284 (1947) (witness with appeal apparently pending properly permitted to invoke the privilege). Contra, Knox v. State, 234 Md. 203, 198 A.2d 285 (1964) (defendant not yet sentenced could not invoke privilege); Oliver v. State, 456 P.2d 431 (Nev.1969). It has been held that the privilege cannot be invoked when the danger is only revocation of probation. Holdren v. People, 168 Colo. 474, 452 P.2d 28 (1969). Cf. Powell v. Wainwright, 403 F.2d 33 (5th Cir. 1968); State v. Brusenhan, 78 N.M. 764, 438 P.2d 174 (1968). United States v. Gernie, 252 F.2d 664 (2d Cir. 1958) cert. denied 356 U.S. 968, often cited, involved a witness who had been convicted, but the case did not specifically discuss the effect of availability of appeal. Frank v. United States, 120 U.S.App.D.C. 392, 347 F.2d 486 (1965) cert. dismissed 382 U.S. 923, held that under a federal immunity statute a defendant who is forced to respond to incriminating questions while his appeal is pending is entitled to reversal; to affirm would be to subject him to a "penalty". Contra, State v. Simon, 132 W.Va. 322, 52 S.E.2d 725 (1949) (under state law). People v. Fine, 19 N.Y.S.2d 275, 173 Misc. 1010 (1940) held that compelled testimony before sentencing did not render the defendant immune to sentencing. In United States v. Worchester, 190 F.Supp. 548 (D.Mass.1961) the court held it could properly make responding to interrogation a condition of probation. See generally 21 Am.Jur.2d Criminal Law § 359; Annot., 9 A.L.R.3d 990.

85. In re Bando, 20 F.R.D. 610 (D.N.Y.1957), rev'd on other grounds sub nom. United States v. Miranti, 253 F.2d 135 (2d Cir. 1958) (pendency of application for certiorari to Supreme Court of United States to review conviction did not provide a basis for invoking the privilege).

86. See § 123, infra.

87. Laska v. Laska, 3 App.Div.2d 638, 158 N.Y.S.2d 63 (1956) (potential use in annulment action not sufficient); People ex rel Elkin v. Rimicci, 97 Ill. App.2d 470, 240 N.E.2d 195 (1968) (defendant in bastardy proceeding properly called to stand). In Allred v. Graves, 261 N.C. 31, 134 S.E.2d 186 (1964), noted in 50 Iowa L.Rev. 325 (1964), 42 N.C.L.Rev. 918 (1964), 17 Stan.L.Rev. 327 (1965), it was held that the defendant in a tort action could decline to answer any questions propounded in pretrial discovery that would necessarily tend to subject him to punitive damages. The court argued that

United States [88] the Supreme Court held that "proceedings instituted for the purpose of declaring the forfeiture of a man's property by reason of offenses committed by him, though they may be civil in form, are in their nature criminal." This has given rise to a wide division in the cases as to the applicability of the privilege when the end result of possible legal proceedings is the creation of liability to pay money other than compensatory damages or surrender other rights.[89] One suggested

criterion for distinguishing those situations in which the privilege was inapplicable relied upon the motive with which the liability was imposed: "If the object of the penalty is primarily to punish the wrongdoer, the action is criminal. If . . . its primary objective is to protect the public and to effectuate a public policy sought to be accomplished by the Act, it is remedial and is a civil action." [90] This seems inadequate. But to distinguish among equal impacts on the basis of the objective with which the liability is imposed seems inconsistent with the purpose of the privilege. Perhaps a more satisfactory solution would be to apply the privilege to those situations in which the liability imposed results in a direct public benefit. Thus imposition of general tort liability would not give rise to a privilege situation, but one would be created when the liability is one which furthers a general public interest, such as liability for triple damages under the antitrust laws. When there is a substantial public interest involved, there is sufficient reason to fear that the dispute will be so affected with policy factors weighted in favor of the party seeking to impose liability that extension of the privilege is justified as a means of balancing. Whenever public agencies are directly involved in imposing the liability, the arguments for extending the privilege are even stronger. Not only is the "public interest" present and aligned against the subject, but it actively participates in the impo-

punitive damages were not compensatory but were awarded as punishment and a warning to other potential wrongdoers. The possibility of civil arrest and imprisonment for failure to pay the judgment were also considered in reaching the conclusion that the punitive damages constituted a "penalty" within the meaning of the privileges. Cf. Comment, Criminal Safeguards and the Punitive Damages Defendant, 34 U.Chi.L.Rev. 408, 430–33 (1967) (extension of privilege to defendants in civil litigation involving potential punitive damages unjustified) In United States v. Detroit Vital Foods, Inc., 407 F.2d 570 (6th Cir. 1969) cert. denied 395 U.S. 935, rev'd 397 U.S. 1, evidence was used in a criminal prosecution which had been obtained by the government by means of interrogatories in a civil action to condemn food as misbranded. The convictions of the individual defendants were reversed on the grounds that the penalty in the civil case was within the protection of the privilege or, in the alternative, that to impose such a forfeiture as a condition of invoking the privilege would be to impose an improper burden on its exercise.

88. 116 U.S. 616 (1886).

89. The privilege apparently does not protect against deportation. United States ex rel. Bilokumsky v. Tod, 263 U.S. 149, 155 (1923) (dictum) (alleged alien might have been compelled to testify as to whether or not he was an alien, since deportation proceeding in which this was at issue was not a criminal proceeding and the response was not otherwise incriminating); United States v. Costello, 144 F.Supp. 779 (S.D.N.Y.1956), noted in 10 Vand.L. Rev. 854 (1957), aff'd 275 F.2d 355 (2d Cir. 1960) (defendant in deportation proceeding had no privilege to refuse to take the stand); United States v. Matles, 247 F.2d 378 (2d Cir. 1957), rev'd on other grounds, 356 U.S. 256 (1958). Where the proceeding is pursuant to a regulatory scheme, the privilege has been held not to protect against the outcome. Amato v. Porter, 157 F.2d 719 (10th Cir. 1946) cert. denied 329 U.S. 812 (privilege does not protect against triple damage recovery for violation of price fixing statute); Oleksiw v. Weidiner, 2 Ohio St.2d 147, 207 N.E.2d 375 (1965) (privilege does not protect against forfeiture of medical license); Lowe v. Texas Department of Public

Safety, 423 S.W.2d 952 (Tex.Civ.App.1968) (suspension of driver's license not "penalty, forfeiture or escheat" within meaning of state constitutional privilege); In re Colacasides, 6 Mich.App. 298, 148 N.W.2d 898 (1967) (immunity need not protect against use of compelled testimony in proceeding to revoke license to run restaurant and dispense alcoholic beverages).

90. Amato v. Porter, 157 F.2d 719, 721 (10th Cir. 1946) cert. denied 329 U.S. 812. As to the triple damage award which might result from the proceeding at issue, the court found that the purpose of the potential award was to secure compliance with measures designed to protect the economy from maladjustment during wartime and the privilege was consequently inapplicable.

sition of liability. This creates the very situation in which the privilege was designed to operate.

When the result of the proceeding is a deprivation of liberty rather than an impingement upon property rights, there has also been ambiguity as to the applicability of the privilege. Rejecting earlier lower court cases holding contrary, the Supreme Court in In re Gault [91] held the privilege applicable in juvenile court proceedings. Although it is possible that the Court was influenced by the possibility that the juvenile proceedings might subsequently involve a waiver to adult court (and the possibility of a criminal conviction), its language suggests that it regarded juvenile incarceration as sufficiently similar to a criminal penalty to justify application of the privilege.[92] Subsequent to *Gault,* it has been held by state tribunals that the privilege protects against deprivations of liberty as the result of sex psychopath proceedings [93] and narcotics addiction commitment.[94] In People ex rel. Keith v. Keith,[95] however, the Illinois Supreme Court held that the privilege did not protect against nonvoluntary hospitalization because of mental illness. Although recognizing the respondent's right to decline to testify concern-

ing matters which might give rise to criminal liability, with respect to matters that did not come within that category it concluded that "the fact that [the testimony] revealed a mental condition which required confinement for treatment does not bring it within the privilege." [96] *Gault,* however, seems to make quite clear that the existence of a beneficent motive to "treat" rather than "punish" does not mean that the deprivation of liberty imposed is beyond the protection of the privilege. Psychiatric hospitalization, like other systems involving detention, represents a combination of treatment and protective motivations. It would seem most consistent with recent development of the privilege to make it available to protect against any deprivation of liberty, without qualification.

Two related matters must be distinguished from the issue as to the dangers against which the privilege protects. First is the ancient privilege against compelled answers to matters not material to the issues which would disgrace or degrade (although not incriminate) the witness.[97] This privilege has been abandoned in England [98] and in most American states, except in a few where it is embodied in statute.[99] The policy underlying this privilege is probably better served by the rules relating to the permissible scope

91. 387 U.S. 1 (1967).

92. "[J]uvenile proceedings to determine 'delinquency', which may lead to commitment to a state institution, must be regarded as 'criminal' for purposes of the privilege against self incrimination. To hold otherwise would be to disregard substance because of the 'civil' label-of-convenience which has been attached to juvenile proceedings. . . . [O]ur Constitution guarantees that no person shall be 'compelled' to be a witness against himself when he is threatened with a deprivation of his liberty. . . ."
Id. at 149–50. See Annot., 43 A.L.R.2d 1128, 1133.

93. Sevigny v. Burns, 108 N.H. 95, 227 A.2d 775 (1967).

94. In re James, 54 Misc.2d 514, 283 N.Y.S.2d 126 (1967), rev'd 29 App.Div.2d 72, 285 N.Y.S.2d 793, rev'd 22 N.Y.2d 545, 293 N.Y.S.2d 531, 240 N.E.2d 29 (1968).

95. 38 Ill.2d 405, 231 N.E.2d 387 (1967).

96. Id. at 408, 231 N.E.2d at 390.

97. 3A Wigmore, Evidence (Chadbourn rev.) § 984; C.J.S. Witnesses § 445; Dec.Dig. Witnesses ☞296.

98. 3A Wigmore, Evidence (Chadbourn rev.) § 984.

99. E. g., Utah Code Ann. § 78–24–9 (1953):
"A witness . . . need not . . . give an answer which will have a direct tendency to degrade his character, unless it is to the very fact in issue or to a fact from which the fact in issue would be presumed. But a witness must answer as to the fact of his previous conviction of felony."
See In re Peterson, 15 Utah 2d 27, 386 P.2d 726 (1963) (witness need not answer whether he and defendant in homicide prosecution had homosexual relations; although the answer might tend to establish a motive, such motive would not be a "fact in issue" or "a fact from which the fact in issue would be presumed").

of cross-examination as to collateral misconduct of a witness and extrinsic proof of such misconduct.[1]

The second matter is the extent to which substantive disadvantages may be imposed upon an individual because of his invocation of the privilege.[2] In a series of decisions, the United States Supreme Court has held that a teacher may not be discharged solely because he invoked the privilege before a congressional committee,[3] that an attorney could not be disbarred because he refused, in reliance on the privilege, to produce documents during a judicial investigation into his alleged professional misconduct,[4] and that a police officer could not be dismissed for refusing to sign a general waiver of immunity during an investigation regarding the "fixing" of traffic tickets.[5] In each case the question was not whether the individual would be subjected to incrimination in violation of the privilege, but rather whether, as a consequence of his invoking the privilege, the state could act against him in other ways. The opinion in the last case makes clear that the Court distinguishes between potential incrimination as that term was defined above and collateral results of invoking the privilege. If the individual might be subjected to incrimination, there is no room for flexibility; the privilege requires that he be extended the right to remain silent or, if compelled to speak, to complete immunity from the incrimination. On the other hand, if as a result of availing himself of this right certain nonincriminating consequences might result, the danger posed to

the privilege by these consequences must be balanced against the governmental interest in both compelling the testimony and imposing the consequences. Thus the police officer in the last case could have been discharged if "he had refused to answer questions specifically, directly and narrowly related to the performance of his official duties, without being required to waive his immunity with respect to the use of his answers or the fruits thereof in a criminal prosecution of himself."[6] In this situation, the danger posed to the interests protected by the privilege would be outweighed by the governmental interest in maintaining the integrity of its police forces. But where the government had broadened its inquiry far beyond the scope necessary to effectuate this interest, the increased danger to the privilege tipped the balance the other way.

Aside from the United States Supreme Court decisions, courts have been rather generally unwilling to disapprove burdens placed upon those invoking the privilege.[7] This has been particularly true in regard to disabilities imposed upon civil litigants who invoke their privileges. In Nuckols v. Nuckols,[8] for example, the husband in a divorce suit filed a counterclaim asking that a decree of divorce be entered in his favor. Relying on the privilege, he refused to respond to questions regarding his relationship with the alleged "other woman." On appeal, judgment for

---

1. See § 42, supra.

2. 8 Wigmore, Evidence (McNaughton rev.) § 2272 (2).

3. Slochower v. Board of Higher Education, 350 U.S. 551 (1956).

4. Spevack v. Klein, 385 U.S. 511 (1967). For a critical appraisal of the decision, see Cole, Bar Discipline and Spevack v. Klein, 53 A.B.A.J. 819 (1967).

5. Gardner v. Broderick, 392 U.S. 273 (1968).

6. Id. at 278.

7. E. g., Duratron Corp. v. Republic Stuyvesant Corp., 95 N.J.Super. 527, 231 A.2d 854 (1967) (inference from invocation of the privilege may be drawn for purposes of establishing civil liability for damages).

8. 189 So.2d 832 (Fla.App.1966). See generally Annot., 4 A.L.R.3d 545 (penalties in civil action for asserting privilege); § 76, supra.

F.R.Ev. (R.D.1971) 513(a) provides with respect to privileges generally:

"Comment or Inference Not Permitted. The claim of a privilege, whether in the present proceeding or upon a prior occasion, is not a proper subject of comment by judge or counsel. No inference may be drawn therefrom."

him was reversed with directions to the trial court to strike the counterclaim if he continued to refuse to respond. In view of Supreme Court development of limitations on burdens, however, it seems clear that now the traditional view that disadvantages incurred in civil litigation because of an invocation of the privilege are valid must give way to a weighing of the policy factors in each instance in which a disadvantage is incurred. Only if the need for and value of the advantage given the other party sufficiently outweigh the danger posed to the free exercise of the privilege should the imposition of such a disadvantage be upheld against constitutional attack.[9]

122. General Scope of the Privilege: (b) Incrimination Under the Laws of Another Sovereign.[10]

The situations in which the danger of incrimination under the laws of another sovereign may be presented can be divided as follows: (a) a witness in either state or federal court claims danger of incrimination under the laws of a foreign country;[11] (b) a witness in a state court claims danger of incrimination under the laws of another state;[12] (c) a witness in a state court claims danger of incrimination under the federal laws;[13] (d) a witness in a federal court claims danger of incrimination under state laws.[14] Traditionally, most courts took the position that the privilege protected against only incrimination under the laws of sovereign which was attempting to compel the incriminating information.[15] In part, the basis for this conclusion seems to have been that courts regarded the danger of prosecution by another sovereignty as so unlikely as to not deserve protection under the privilege.[16] It has also been argued, however, that the purpose of the privilege is to prevent a sovereign from enlisting an accused's aid in achieving his own conviction and that this is not violated if the revelations compelled are of interest only to another sovereign. Thus the motive of the inquiring sovereign to inflict brutality is absent, and the dangers which the privileges guards against are not present.[17]

9. The so-called "good account" statutes, which require one observed in suspicious circumstances to give an inquiring police officer an explanation for his actions, pose a related problem. Insofar as the failure to speak serves as the basis for arrest the privilege is endangered. But see People v. Weger, 251 Cal.App.2d 584, 59 Cal.Rptr. 661 (1967) cert. denied 389 U.S. 1047 (use of mere silence in response to inquiries does not endanger the privilege). Such statutes have been saved by interpreting the criminal offense so that the failure to give an account of one's actions is not an element, but that providing an opportunity to explain the situation is a prerequisite to prosecution. State v. Zito, 54 N.J. 206, 254 A.2d 769 (1969).

10. See generally 8 Wigmore, Evidence (McNaughton rev.) § 2258; Annot., 59 A.L.R. 895; Annot., 82 A.L.R. 1380; Dec.Dig. Witnesses ⬛297(14).

11. In re Parker, 411 F.2d 1067 (10th Cir. 1969) vacated as moot 397 U.S. 96; Republic of Greece v. Koukouras, 264 Mass. 318, 162 N.E. 345 (1928).

12. State ex rel. Doran v. Doran, 215 La. 151, 39 So.2d 894 (1949) (claim of privilege sustained because prosecution in another state "is not only impending but an actual fact"); State v. Wood, 99 Vt. 490, 134 A. 697 (1926) ("the only danger to be considered is such as arose within this jurisdiction"); In re Werner, 167 App.Div. 384, 152 N.Y.S. 862 (1915) (witness failed to show any real and substantial danger of use in prosecution under laws of another state).

13. Jack v. Kansas, 199 U.S. 372 (1905) (no "real danger" of federal prosecution or use of evidence by federal authorities, so action by state in compelling testimony not violation of due process clause of Fourteenth Amendment); Commonwealth v. Rhine, 303 S.W.2d 301 (Ky.1957) (state constitutional privilege protects against incrimination under federal as well as state law); People v. Den Uyl, 318 Mich. 645, 29 N.W.2d 284 (1947) (state constitutional privilege, to be effective, must prohibit the compulsion of testimony which might be used in pending federal prosecution); Ex parte Copeland, 91 Tex.Cr.R. 549, 240 S.W. 314 (1922) (no real danger of use).

14. Brown v. Walker, 161 U.S. 591 (1896); Hale v. Henkel, 201 U.S. 43 (1906).

15. See cases cited in notes 11, 12 and 13, supra.

16. Brown v. Walker, 161 U.S. 591, 608 (1896); In re Werner, 167 A.D. 384, 152 N.Y.S. 862 (1915).

17. 8 Wigmore, Evidence (McNaughton rev.) § 2258, at 345; McNaughton, Self-Incrimination Under

This position was undermined, however, by the Supreme Court of the United States in Murphy v. Waterfront Commission.[18] Murphy and several others had been subpoenaed to testify before the Waterfront Commission regarding a work stoppage at certain New Jersey piers. Despite a grant of immunity to prosecution under New Jersey and New York law, they refused to testify on the ground that their responses might tend to incriminate them under federal law. Reversing the New Jersey Supreme Court, the United States Supreme Court held that the federal constitutional privilege protects a state witness from prosecution under federal as well as state law.[19] Emphasis was placed on the practical dangers in a time of "cooperative federalism" of actual use of testimony procured by a state in federal prosecutions.[20] The argument that a sovereign's grant of immunity removed the motive for it to engage in brutality was rejected as resting on too narrow a view of the interests the privilege is designed to protect.[21] As a means of effectuating the holding, the Court continued, it would direct as an exercise of its supervisory powers over lower federal courts that evidence obtained as the result of revelations compelled by a state under a grant of immunity from its own prosecutions would be inadmissible in federal trial.[22] Moreover, a defendant need only show initially that he has testified to matters related to the federal prosecution; the burden then shifts to the federal prosecution to establish an independent source for the offered proof and therefore it was not tainted by the state action.[23] In dictum, the Court also indicated that the privilege would protect a federal witness against incrimination under state as well as federal law.[24]

Murphy does not necessarily solve the problems raised in situations (a) and (b) at the beginning of this section. But the decision has destroyed the theoretical basis, weak as it was, for the traditional view that in those situations the privilege was inapplicable. It is likely in both that the Court would now hold that the privilege applied, except perhaps in the event of a showing that the danger of incrimination was so minimal as to be inapplicable to a specific set of facts.[25] One problem of implementation exists in regard to situation (b). States, of course, lack the authority to grant immunity to prosecution by another state. Moreover, the implementation device used by the Court in *Murphy* was expressly designated an exercise of the Court's supervisory power rather than a holding of constitutional dimensions; thus it does not apply to the states. Nevertheless, it is likely that the same result would be achieved should one state attempt to make use of evidence compelled by another under a grant of immunity by holding that the revelations were involuntary and thus subject to exclusion under

---

Foreign Law, 45 Va.L.Rev. 1299 (1959). Compare Grant, Federalism and Self-Incrimination, 4 U.C. L.A.L.Rev. 549 (1957).

18. 378 U.S. 52 (1964), noted in The Supreme Court, 1963 Term, 78 Harv.L.Rev. 143, 227 (1964), 31 Brooklyn L.Rev. 157 (1964), 10 N.Y.L. Forum 627 (1964).

19. Murphy v. Waterfront Com'n, 378 U.S. 52, 77–78 (1969).

20. Id. at 55–56.

21. Id. at 56 n. 5.

22. Id. at 79; Application of Longo, 280 F.Supp. 185 (S.D.N.Y.1967) (witness before state grand jury could be compelled to testify because *Murphy* protected against use in federal prosecution).

23. Id. at 79 n.18.

24. Id. at 78.

25. But see In re Parker, 411 F.2d 1067 (10th Cir. 1969) vacated as moot 397 U.S. 96. A witness before a grand jury refused to answer questions despite a grant of immunity on the ground that the answers would furnish a link in the chain of evidence necessary to prosecute her for an extraditable Canadian crime. Although the Court of Appeals suggested that it regarded the probability that the answers would actually increase the danger of incrimination as minimal, it affirmed the witness's contempt citation on the ground that despite *Murphy* the federal constitutional privilege did not protect against incrimination under Canadian law.

the constitutional rule prohibiting the states from using involuntary confessions.[26]

123.   General Scope of the Privilege: (c) Requirement that the Danger of Incrimination be "Real and Appreciable." [27]

Early in the development of the federal constitutional privilege it was established that the danger of incrimination must be "real and appreciable." A danger "imaginary and unsubstantial" would not be sufficient.[28] This is apparently still the formal requirement.[29] Much reliance in the cases has been placed on the English decision in Queen v. Boyes.[30] A witness asserted the danger of parliamentary impeachment as a basis for invoking the privilege. Rejecting this, the court held:

> "[T]he danger to be apprehended must be real and appreciable, with reference to the ordinary operation of the law in the ordinary course of things—not a danger of an imaginary and unsubstantial character, having reference to some extraordinary and barely possible contingency, so improbable that no reasonable man would suffer it to influence his conduct." [31]

This formula was invoked by the United States Supreme Court in several early cases as a basis for holding the privilege inapplicable [32] and there is some indication that it may currently be used by some lower courts in an attempt to minimize the impact of recent United States Supreme Court decisions expanding the privilege.[33] A recent Pennsylvania case,[34] however, is illustrative of the now prevailing general judicial attitude that almost any conceivable danger is "real and appreciable". The defendant, an unmarried woman, refused to testify before a grand jury concerning an abortion allegedly performed upon her, asserting the danger of criminal prosecution on the basis of the sexual intercourse giving rise to the child. Upholding her claim, the Pennsylvania Supreme Court commented:

> "[U]nless unusual circumstances exist as e. g., rape, common sense dictates that an unmarried female who admits an abortion has been performed upon her acknowledges and admits she has committed fornication. This, in itself, was sufficiently reasonable cause to give the appellant apprehension of the danger of prosecution. Remote though it may be, it still existed." [35]

---

26.   Cf. Garrity v. New Jersey, 385 U.S. 493 (1967). Zicarelli v. New Jersey State Commission of Investigation, 55 N.J. 249, 261 A.2d 129 (1970) reads *Murphy* as indicating that the Fifth Amendment will provide protection against use of compelled testimony by a sister state.

27.   See generally Dec.Dig. Witnesses ⇐297.

28.   Brown v. Walker, 161 U.S. 591 (1896).

29.   Marchetti v. United States, 390 U.S. 39, 48 (1968).

30.   1 B. & S. 311, 121 Eng.Rep. 730 (K.B.1861).

31.   Id. at 330, 121 Eng.Rep. at 738.

32.   Brown v. Walker, 161 U.S. 591 (1896) (possibility of conviction under laws of another sovereign a danger of an imaginary and unsubstantial character); Rogers v. United States, 340 U.S. 367,

374–75 (1951) (after witness had admitted holding office of treasurer of Communist Party, disclosure of acquaintance with her successor presents no more than a mere imaginary possibility of increasing the danger of prosecution).

33.   United States v. Della Rocca, 388 F.2d 525 (2d Cir. 1968) vacated and remanded for further consideration 390 U.S. 745 (mere danger of state prosecution on the basis of possession of sub-machine gun does not excuse compliance with National Firearms Act); United States v. Walden, 411 F.2d 1109, 112–13 (4th Cir. 1969) (absent proof of cooperation between state and federal law enforcement agencies concerned with production of alcohol, danger of state prosecution does not constitute basis for failure to comply with federal liquor laws). See also note 35, infra.

34.   Commonwealth v. Carrera, 424 Pa. 551, 227 A.2d 627 (1967).

35.   Id. at 554, 227 A.2d at 629. See also United States v. Miranti, 253 F.2d 135 (2d Cir. 1958) (although it was "unlikely" that defendants who had already been put in jeopardy for conspiracy to commit certain crimes would subsequently be prosecuted for the substantive offenses, the possibility was sufficient to support invocation of the privi-

124. General Scope of the Privilege: (d) Requirement that the Activity Sought to be Compelled be "Testimonial." [36]

It is arguable from the policies underlying the privilege that it ought to protect against any compelled cooperation of an accused in the procedure invoked by the state to punish him. Insofar as the privilege rests upon the inviolability of certain aspects of the human personality, it would be entirely consistent to hold that the privilege protects against any infringements of those aspects. The Supreme Court of the United States has, however, made clear that the scope of the privilege does not coincide with the "complex of values it helps to protect." [37] As early as 1910, the Court held that accused's privilege was not violated when he was compelled to put on a blouse for purposes of determining whether it fitted him. [38] "[T]he prohibition . . .", declared the Court, "is a prohibition of the use of physical or moral compulsion to exact communications from him . . ." [39]

Assuming that the privilege does not prevent compelling the accused's active cooperation in noncommunicative activity, however, the scope of the protection afforded is still not clear.

There are three potential formulations of the criterion to be used to determine whether a given activity is "communicative" and therefore within the scope of the protection of the privilege. First, the term might be limited to words spoken by the subject. This is the position urged by Wigmore. [40] Second, the test might readily be expanded to cover any activity performed for the purpose of communicating. In addition to spoken words, then, the privilege would cover gestures and other activities intended by the actor to communicate thoughts to another. Finally, the privilege's protection might be expanded to cover any activities of the subject which, if used to prove guilt, require reliance upon the accuracy of the accused's participation. [41] For example, taking the accused's fingerprints and relying on them in court would involve no such element. But in-court identification based upon the witness's hearing the accused speak during a police lineup would involve this element, as the reliability of the identification is dependent upon the accused having spoken during the lineup in a normal way or in the way in which he spoke at the time he was initially observed (or in which he would have spoken

---

lege); United States ex rel. Berberian v. Cliff, 300 F.Supp. 8, 12–13 (E.D.Pa.1969) (liability of unmarried woman who testifies regarding abortion to fornication prosecution supports invocation of the privilege).

But compare California v. Byers, 402 U.S. 424 (1971), upholding a statute requiring the driver of a motor vehicle involved in an accident to stop and give his name and address. Emphasizing that driving a motor vehicle is not inherently illegal and that accidents may occur without creating criminal liability on the part of the drivers involved, the plurality opinion, joined in by four justices, concluded that "disclosures with respect to automobile accidents simply do not entail the kind of substantial risk of self-incrimination" required.

36. See generally 8 Wigmore, Evidence (McNaughton rev.) §§ 2263–2265; Maguire, Evidence of Guilt § 2.04 (1959); Dann, The Fifth Amendment Privilege Against Self-Incrimination: Extorting Physical Evidence From A Suspect, 43 So.Cal.L.Rev. 597 (1970); 21 Am.Jur.2d Criminal Law §§ 360–69; 58 Am.Jur. Witnesses § 50; C.J.S. Witnesses § 447; Dec.Dig. Criminal Law ⮑393(1), 393(3), 393(4), Witnesses ⮑298½.

37. Schmerber v. California, 384 U.S. 757, 762 (1966).

38. Holt v. United States, 218 U.S. 245 (1910).

39. Id. at 252–53.

40. 8 Wigmore, Evidence (McNaughton rev.) § 2263, pp. 378–79. See the plurality opinion in California v. Byers, 402 U.S. 424 (1971) (joined in by four justices), upholding a statute requiring the driver of a motor vehicle involved in an accident to stop and furnish his name and address. "The act of stopping," Chief Justice Burger declared, "is no more testimonial—indeed less so in some respects—than requiring a person in custody to stand or walk in a police lineup, to speak prescribed words, to give samples of handwriting, fingerprints or blood." A majority of the Court, however, agreed that this action was "testimonial" within Fifth Amendment meaning.

41. See Maguire, Evidence of Guilt 31 (1966).

had he been the one observed) by the witness.[42]

The leading case on the nature of the activity protected by the privilege is Schmerber v. California.[43] Explaining that the privilege "protects an accused only from being compelled to testify against himself, or otherwise provide the state with evidence of a testimonial or communicative nature," [44] the Court held that blood extracted from a non-consenting suspect, "although an incriminating product of compulsion, was neither [his] testimony nor evidence relating to some communicative act or writing by [him. Thus] it was not inadmissible on privilege grounds." [45] Although it did not define precisely what was meant by evidence of a "testimonial or communicative nature", the Court expressly disclaimed adopting Wigmore's view as to the scope of the privilege.[46]

Subsequent cases from both the Supreme Court and lower tribunals suggest that the middle alternative has found widest acceptance. The tendency has been to uphold any requirement that the accused engage in nonverbal activity. Among those activities that have been held beyond the protection of the privilege have been participation in a lineup,[47] seizure of marked money or other physical evidence from an accused,[48] fingerprints taken from the accused,[49] photographs taken

of the accused while in custody,[50] and requiring the accused to remove clothing [51] or a toupee [52] for identification purposes. The fact that activities may involve the active cooperation of the accused in such a manner that their reliability depends upon the accuracy of his cooperation has not brought them within the privilege. Thus requiring the accused to provide a handwriting example [53] or to speak at a lineup [54] does not violate the privilege nor does requiring a suspect believed to be intoxicated to perform a balance test.[55] It is arguable that these activities involve the very dangers against which the privilege is intended to protect. When the activity is simple and such that the manner of its performance cannot reasonably be expected to affect the outcome of the investigatory procedure, there is little danger that the accused will be subjected to more than a minimal amount of coercion. This measure of coercion may be justified by the high reliability of the resulting evidence. Where, however, it is necessary to achieve the "accurate" cooperation of the accused,

42. Cf. State v. Jones, 188 Wash. 275, 62 P.2d 44 (1936) (defendant required to pronounce certain words for purposes of proving that his pronunciation of them at an earlier time was caused by intoxication rather than a speech defect or characteristic).

43. 384 U.S. 757 (1966).

44. Id. at 761.

45. Id. at 765.

46. Id. at 763, n. 7.

47. United States v. Wade, 388 U.S. 218, 221–23 (1967).

48. United States v. Vickers, 387 F.2d 703 (4th Cir. 1967) cert. denied 392 U.S. 912.

49. State v. Stuard, 104 Ariz. 305, 452 P.2d 98 (1969) (permissible to take defendant's fingerprints in open court and compare them with those of a prior offender); Washington v. State, 434 S.W.2d 138 (Tex.Cr.App.1968).

50. State v. Strickland, 5 N.C.App. 338, 168 S.E.2d 697, rev'd on other grounds 276 N.C. 253, 173 S.E. 2d 129 (1969) (motion picture of accused after arrest properly admitted to illustrate police officer's testimony that accused was intoxicated).

51. Vincent v. State, 256 A.2d 268 (Del.1969) (proper to require accused to remove shirt to permit inspection of scratches).

52. People v. Collins, 16 Mich.App. 667, 168 N.W.2d 624 (1969) (accused properly required to remove toupee at preliminary hearing).

53. Gilbert v. California, 388 U.S. 263, 265–67 (1967); United States ex rel. Harris v. Hendrick, 300 F. Supp. 554 (E.D.Pa.1969); People v. Brashier, 271 Cal.App.2d 298, 76 Cal.Rptr. 581 (1969). The conduct in this and the next note is fairly classed as nonverbal, since it is the appearance and sound of the words which is significant, not their content.

54. United States v. Wade, 388 U.S. 218, 222–23 (1967).

55. State v. Faidley, 202 Kan. 517, 450 P.2d 20 (1969).

the situation becomes more analogous to a request for a satisfactory verbal answer; thus the danger of coercion being applied until satisfactory cooperation is achieved becomes greater. In addition, if the reliability of the proof depends upon the cooperation of a pressured suspect, the proof becomes subject to the same objections of unreliability as are leveled against verbal statements obtained under threat of legal coercion. Moreover, coercion applied not simply to permit the performance of a relatively simple procedure such as a blood test but rather to require the accused affirmatively to construct the basis for solidifying the case against him comes much closer to requiring the condemned to spring his own trap, thus violating the sense of decency underlying the privilege.

Justice Traynor of the California Supreme Court addressed himself to one aspect of this matter in a case involving voice identification based upon the witness's having listened to the accused speak under police demand.[56] Although admitting that the accused's statement did involve a "testimonial element," the court held the potential unreliability "insignificant" in view of the minimal necessity for reliance on the veracity of the accused. "The difficulty of deceit and the practical impossibility of knowing attempt at false self-incrimination, through a voice impersonation of a guilty party," concluded the court, "lead us to reject this factor." [57] In view of the added factors of the motive for extensive coercion provided and the active nature of the cooperation involved, however, the better view would seem to be that the privilege protects against compulsion to en-

gage in those activities whose value as evidence to prove guilt is in any way related to the reliability of the accused's cooperation.[58]

125. General Scope of the Privilege: (e) Requirement that Compulsion be "Legal Compulsion",[59] and the Privilege in the Police Station.

Traditionally the privilege has been considered applicable only in situations in which the coercion exerted upon the holder was "legal compulsion," that is, compulsion authorized by law.[60] Most common was the threat of punishment for contempt based upon refusal to respond, clearly a type of coercion which, in a proper case, a court may impose. When the coercion was illegal—as when force was used to obtain a confession—the situation was considered more properly handled under the coerced confession rule.[61] The most significant result of this was that it was sometimes—but not uniformly—held that since the police had no legally recognized right to exert coercion upon an individual, the privilege had no application to what occurred during police investigation.[62]

---

56. People v. Ellis, 65 Cal.2d 529, 55 Cal.Rptr. 385, 421 P.2d 393 (1966).

57. Id. at 534 n. 4, 55 Cal.Rptr. at 387 n. 4, 421 P.2d at 395 n. 4. Contra, State v. Taylor, 213 S.C. 330, 49 S.E.2d 289 (1948) (requiring defendant to speak for voice identification violated privilege). See generally Annot., 16 A.L.R. 1322.

58. If compelling a person to submit to procedures not requiring testimonial activity on his part does not violate the privilege, use in evidence of his refusal to participate in such a procedure or his evasive conduct prior to a procedure might nevertheless violate the privilege. See generally, Comment, Admissibility of Testimonial By-Products of a Physical Test, 24 U.Miami L.Rev. 50 (1969). It is generally held, however, that no violation of the privilege occurs since the results of the test would be admissible. E. g., People v. Sudduth, 65 Cal.2d 543, 55 Cal.Rptr. 393, 421 P.2d 401 (1966) cert. denied 389 U.S. 850 (1967).

59. See generally 8 Wigmore, Evidence (McNaughton rev.) § 2252, pp. 327–29.

60. Id.

61. See § 147, infra.

62. 8 Wigmore, Evidence (McNaughton rev.) § 2252, p. 327, n. 27. Compare Abston v. State, 139 Tex. Cr.R. 416, 141 S.W.2d 337 (1940) and People v. Simmons, 28 Cal.2d 699, 172 P.2d 18 (1947), with Owens v. Commonwealth, 186 Va. 689, 43 S.E.2d 895 (1947). See generally, Note, The Privilege Against Self-Incrimination: Does it Exist in the Police Station? 5 Stan.L.Rev. 459 (1953).

In Miranda v. Arizona,[63] however, the United States Supreme Court held the privilege applicable to police interrogations. "We are satisfied," the Court concluded, "that all the principles embodied in the privilege apply to informal compulsion exerted by law-enforcement officers during in-custody interrogation." [64] This result is defensible on at least two grounds. First, because of the ambiguity in the law as to the powers appropriately exercised by the police, it is unclear to what extent they may legally subject a suspect to an interrogation procedure which does not involve physical torture but is conducted in such a way that it "carries its own badge of intimidation." Thus it is impossible to determine whether or not the police may properly use procedures which might be labeled coercion. Second, the privilege probably provides a better vehicle for setting forth a relatively detailed set of guidelines governing the constitutional limits upon what may be done during police interrogation than does the voluntariness rule. The latter has traditionally developed on a case-to-case basis with each decision turning on the specific facts involved; this has not lent itself to establishing detailed rules essential to effective judicial control of police interrogation. The specific rules applicable to police interrogation are examined in detail in Chapter 13.

126. The Privilege as Related to Documents and Tangible Items: (a) Compulsory Production.[65]

The extent to which the privilege limits the right of the state to obtain written material for use in a criminal conviction and the means by which it may do this has caused a significant amount of confusion in the cases. In Boyd v. United States,[66] the Supreme Court of the United States held that compelling the defendant in a forfeiture proceeding to produce invoices for use as proof of the quantity and value of glass allegedly improperly imported was a violation of the defendant's Fourth and Fifth Amendment rights. Much of the subsequent difficulty has arisen out of later readings of the Court's broad language in that case. After citing with approval Lord Camden's discussion in Entick v. Carrington and Three Other King's Messengers,[67] the Court declared:

> "[A]ny forcible and compulsory extortion of a man's own testimony or of his private papers to be used as evidence to convict him of a crime or to forfeit his goods, is within the condemnation of that judgment. In this regard the Fourth and Fifth Amendments run almost into each other. . . . ."

> "[W]e have been unable to perceive that the seizure of a man's private books and papers to be used in evidence against him is substantially different from compelling him to be a witness against himself." [68]

Later, in Gouled v. United States,[69] the Court held that the seizure of papers of evidentiary value only, without a warrant, constituted a violation of the Fourth Amendment and their admission in evidence violated both the Fourth and Fifth Amendments. Recently, however, the Court seems to have adopted the general view [70] that the privilege pro-

---

63.   384 U.S. 436 (1966).

64.   Id. at 461. Heavy reliance was placed on Bram v. United States, 168 U.S. 532 (1897), which many had regarded as settling the issue in favor of the applicability of the privilege.

65.   See generally 8 Wigmore, Evidence (McNaughton rev.) § 2294; 21 Am.Jur.2d Criminal Law § 355; 58 Am.Jur. Witnesses §§ 69–78; C.J.S. Witnesses § 448; Dec.Dig Witnesses ⟨key⟩298.

66.   116 U.S. 616 (1886).

67.   10 How.St.Tr. 1029 (1765).

68.   Boyd v. United States, 116 U.S. 616, 630, 633 (1886.)

69.   255 U.S. 298 (1921).

70.   E. g., People v. Defore, 242 N.Y. 13, 27, 150 N.E. 585, 590 (1926) (Cardozo, J.): "A defendant is 'protected from producing his documents in response to a subpoena duces tecum, for his produc-

tects only against a custodian of papers sought for use against him being compelled in response to a subpoena *duces tecum* to produce those papers.[71] This rule is defended on the theory that one who produces documents (or other matter) described in a subpoena *duces tecum* represents, by his production, that the documents produced are in fact the documents described in the subpoena. This representation is a testimonial activity and within the protection of the privilege.[72] Thus the privilege does not establish any right not to have the papers seized or used in evidence, but only the right not to testify as to the nature or description of the papers. It follows, of course, that the custodian at the time of seizure cannot be called to authenticate the document (assuming they have been appropriately obtained, as by seizure during a search conducted pursuant to a warrant) when they are offered against him.[73]

tion of them in court would be his voucher of their genuineness.' There would then be 'testimonial compulsion.' "

71. Curcio v. United States, 354 U.S. 118, 125 (1957): "The custodian's act of producing books or records in response to a subpoena *duces tecum* is itself a representation that the documents produced are those demanded by the subpoena."

72. But note the different considerations involved when a subpoena is served on custodians of the records of an association; see § 129, infra.

73. Insofar as the basis for the rule is the testimonial representation that the documents produced are those demanded, there seems no reason to restrict the rule to documents or written materials. The representation that a physical item produced in response to a demand is in fact the item demanded would seem to be equally offensive. This does not seem to have been discussed in the cases, however. See the discussion of the limits imposed upon pretrial discovery in criminal cases by the privilege in § 133, infra.

Allowing the prosecution to obtain the evidence by process and to use it at trial but without disclosure of its source seems not to have been considered as a possible means of avoiding the self-incrimination problem. See State ex rel. Sowers v. Olwell, 64 Wash.2d 828, 394 P.2d 681, 16 A.L.R.3d 1021 (1964), supra, § 89, n. 59, in which this approach was used to avoid disclosure of the communicative aspects of the client's giving his attorney a knife,

127. The Privilege as Related to Documents and Tangible Items: (b) Limits on Seizure and Use of "Private Papers": "Mere Evidence".

Support has been advanced in the cases for the view that some limitation upon the right of the state to seize and use private documents of an accused arises from the privilege against self-incrimination, taken either alone [74] or in conjunction with other consti-

while still allowing the prosecution access to the knife.

Distinguish the problem of immunity of "mere evidence" from seizure. See § 127, infra.

74. E. g., Frankfurter, J., in Davis v. United States, 328 U.S. 582, 595 (1946), observed that "private papers of an accused cannot be seized even though legal process because their use would violate the prohibition of the Fifth Amendment against self-incrimination." See also Brock v. United States, 223 F.2d 681, 686 (5th Cir. 1955) ("Private papers of evidentiary value alone are not admissible in evidence as against the Fifth Amendment, even where the Fourth Amendment has not been violated."); Westside Ford v. United States, 206 F.2d 627, 633, n. 3 (9th Cir. 1953) ("where the documents are relevant to an inquiry conducted for a lawfully authorized purpose . . . the Fourth Amendment is no bar to their inspection, whether they be of a quasi-public character or purely private. In such a case, the only valid ground of objection is the self-incrimination privilege. . . .); People v. Ellis, 65 Cal.2d 529, 535, 55 Cal.Rptr. 385, 388, 421 P.2d 393, 396 (1966) ("A related view of the individual interests protected by the privilege focuses on the right of privacy . . . . The Fifth Amendment right of privacy protects at least uncommunicated thoughts and has been extended to preclude compelled production of private papers and documents."). Cf. United States v. Boyette, 299 F.2d 92, 94–95 (4th Cir. 1962); People v. Thayer, 63 Cal.2d 635, 642–43, 47 Cal.Rptr. 780, 784–85, 408 P.2d 108, 112–13 (1966) cert. denied 384 U.S. 908. People v. Jones, 38 Ill.2d 427, 231 N.E.2d 580, 585 (1967) ("[an automobile registration card is not] a 'private paper' which may not be used in evidence under the Fifth Amendment.").

In Hill v. Philpott, 445 F.2d 144 (7th Cir. 1971) the seizure of thirty five cardboard cartons of a doctor's patient records from his office pursuant to a warrant was held over dissent to violate the Fifth Amendment. The distinction between obtaining the papers by seizure rather than process was described as "more shadow than substance." The dissent argued that even if a protected class of private papers existed, the records at issue in the case did not come within it because they were kept for business reasons and with the assistance of employees. Compare United States v. Scharfman,

tutional provisions.[75] This view was generally expressed in connection with discussion of the "mere evidence" rule, to the effect that items solely of "evidential" value were exempt from seizure and use in evidence.[76] The exemption did not extend to the instrumentalities or the fruits of the crime, nor did it extend to contraband. Enforcement of the rule was most enthusiastic when the item involved was a personal document, such as a diary.[77] Beyond that, application became uncertain and difficult.[78] For example, what might be mere evidence in one situation could be an instrumentality in another.[79] The most important objection to the "mere evidence" rule, however, was the inappropriateness of its reliance on the Fifth Amendment. Since, as pointed out elsewhere,[80] the Fifth Amendment applies only in those situations in which coercion might be applied for the purpose of compelling the subject to do something in response, the values here—and which the privilege resolves, rightly or wrongly—are significantly different from the values involved in determining whether once an individual has done something, such as transcribing his thoughts on paper, he should be entitled to preserve that past act free from official scrutiny. His initial activity may or may not have been testimonial, depending upon whether he intended that the transcription serve the function of communicating his thoughts to another individual, but in any event authorizing the use of such transcriptions would not encourage police to exert the types of coercion that the privilege historically protected against, because by definition these transcriptions would have been made before the opportunity for coercion existed.

In Warden, Maryland Penitentiary v. Hayden,[81] the Supreme Court announced its abandonment of the mere evidence rule. The language of the Court, however, left open the question "whether there are items of evidential value whose very nature precludes them from being the object of a reasonable search and seizure." [82] This question is more appropriately treated as a matter of the application of the Fourth Amendment.[83]

128. The Privilege as Related to Corporations, Associations, and Their Agents: (a) The Privilege of the Organization.[84]

It has long been clear that the privilege is not available to a corporation.[85] Two prin-

---

448 F.2d 1352 (2d Cir. 1971) (seizure of memo book containing handwritten entries not unreasonable in Fourth Amendment terms although compulsory production of the item would have been prohibited by the Fifth Amendment).

75. Usually the Fourth Amendment is the other provision invoked. Boyd v. United States, 116 U.S. 616 (1886); Gouled v. United States, 255 U.S. 298, 309 (1921).

76. See generally Shellow, The Continued Vitality of the Gouled Rule: The Search For and Seizure of Evidence, 48 Marq.L.Rev. 172 (1964); Note, Evidentiary Searches: The Rule and the Reason, 54 Geo.L.J. 593 (1966); Comment, Limitations on Seizure of "Evidentiary" Objects, A Rule in Search of a Reason, 20 U.Chi.L.Rev. 319 (1953).

77. See, e. g., United States v. Stern, 225 F.Supp. 187 (S.D.N.Y.1964) (personal diary improperly seized).

78. Shellow, supra note 76, at 179, suggests that "while the courts speak in broad terms of evidentiary materials being immune from seizure, the rule is applied only to private documents."

79. Compare Matthews v. Correa, 135 F.2d 534 (2d Cir. 1943) (address book a fruit of the crime of concealing certain property from the trustee in bankruptcy) with United States v. Lerner, 100 F. Supp. 765 (N.D.Cal.1951) (address book merely evidence of crime of harboring a fugitive). The underlying problem was the absence of clear definitions of the various categories, i. e., contraband, fruits, and instrumentalities. See Note, supra, n. 76, at 606–621; Comment, supra n. 76, at 320–22.

80. See § 118, supra.

81. 387 U.S. 294 (1967).

82. Id. at 303.

83. See § 170, at n. 86, infra.

84. See generally 8 Wigmore, Evidence (McNaughton rev.) §§ 2259a, 2259b; 58 Am.Jur. Witnesses § 47; C.J.S. Witnesses § 431; Dec.Dig. Witnesses ⊂⇒306.

85. E. g., George Campbell Painting Corp. v. Reid, 392 U.S. 286 (1968); United States v. White, 322 U.S. 694 (1944); Hale v. Henkel, 201 U.S. 43 (1906).

cipal factors underlie this rule. First, the policy of the privilege is the prevention of inappropriate force against the individual to force him to engage in incriminating testimonial activity. A corporation as a fictional entity cannot be subjected to the type of abuse that the privilege is intended to protect against.[86] Second, the privilege if applied would undoubtedly buy the protection of individuals involved at significant cost to efficient and successful criminal prosecution. Corporations exercise a great deal of economic power, and the state has a strong interest in a continuing ability effectively to regulate them by application of criminal sanctions.[87] In addition, the greatest portion of effective evidence that can be obtained for use against a corporation is contained in its official records and documents, items which might well become practically unavailable should the privilege be extended to them.[88] The rule, then, represents a policy judgment that there is little danger to the values the privilege protects against in compelling a corporation to incriminate itself, and that extending the privilege to it would impose too significant a limitation upon the ability of the state effectively to regulate powerful entities.

In United States v. White [89] the Court extended this exclusion to a labor union, setting out the appropriate test for determining the availability of the privilege to an association as follows:

"The test is . . . whether one can fairly say under all the circumstances that a particular type of organization has a character so impersonal in the scope of its membership and activities that it cannot be said to embody or represent the purely private or personal interests of its constituents, but rather to embody their common or group interests only. If so, the privilege cannot be invoked on behalf of the organization or its representatives in their official capacity.[90] "

The labor union at issue was found to meet the test. Emphasis was placed on a number of its characteristics: (a) its existence was not dependent upon the life of any individual members; (b) formal rules defined the relationship between member and organization, and were sometimes judicially enforced; (c) the undertakings of the organization were numerous and did not amount to the private undertakings of the members; (d) officers might perform only acts authorized by the organization and did not have authority to act for the members in matters affecting only the member's individual rights; (e) the union owned separate real and personal property; (f) books, records and funds of the organization were kept apart from the private records and personal funds of the members; (g) under only very limited circumstances were the members criminally liable for the actions of the union or its officer; (h) the law granted numerous rights to unions as institutions functioning separate and apart from their members.[91]

The Supreme Court's language was somewhat ambiguous as to whether, if an organization did not meet the exclusionary test of *White,* the privilege would be available to the association itself, its representatives in their official capacity, or both. It seems, however,

---

86. For example, the corporation cannot experience the subjective pain that makes physical torture abhorrent.

87. In addition, the argument was made in Hale v. Henkel, 201 U.S. 43, 74–75 (1906) that unlike the individual citizen, a corporation is the creature of the state and derives its rights from the state.

88. Hale v. Henkel, 201 U.S. 43, 74–75 (1906).

89. 322 U.S. 694 (1944).

Fiebach, The Constitutional Right of Associations to Assert the Privilege Against Self-Incrimination, 112 U.Pa.L.Rev. 394 (1964).

90. 322 U.S. at 699.

91. Id. at 701–04.

that if the association were not such as to meet the *White* test, its member or representative would be entitled to invoke his own privilege in regard to matters related to the association. Thus, in In re Subpoena Duces Tecum [92] a subpoena had been issued to one of six partners requiring him to produce certain specific records and communications. The court, ruling on a motion to quash the subpoena, held that the partner served had not by entering the partnership lost his personal right to invoke the privilege in regard to "his" records, defined as including all the records of the partnership. This is consistent with the result in another of the few cases dealing with the problem which held that one partner to whom a subpoena for partnership records was directed could not invoke the privilege on the basis that production would incriminate another partner.[93] The applicable privilege was regarded as the one held by the individual to whom the subpoena was directed.

Although there is relatively little case law, it does appear that associations of limited number of individuals, such as small partnerships, may come without the *White* test. This is consistent with the underlying policy of the privilege. Members of a small partnership may well use the partnership merely as means of convenience for accomplishing tasks that are essentially personal. On the other hand, it is clear that a partnership may be of sufficient size and function as to be, for purposes of the privilege, no different from a corporation. The question would seem to require case-by-case resolution.[94]

129. The Privilege as Related to Corporations, Associations, and Their Agents: (b) Availability of the Privilege to Agents.[95]

It is clear from the discussion above that an agent of an organization cannot invoke the privilege by asserting that the organization will be exposed to criminal liability. But what of the assertion that the agent himself will be subjected to prosecution? May, for example, an officer of a corporation decline to produce the corporation's documents in response to a subpoena *duces tecum* on the ground that the documents tend to incriminate him and that to require him to "testify" as to their genuineness by producing them would violate his personal privilege? This has been answered by the Supreme Court in the negative. In Wilson v. United States,[96] the Court held that corporate records were analogous to public records and maintained subject to the right of the state to inspect them. A corporate agent, then, by voluntarily accepting their custody is held to have accepted also the obligation to permit their inspection upon demand.[97] The decisions rest basically upon a policy determination that to extend the privilege to this situation would impede, if not wholly defeat, the power of the state to regulate corporations. It rests not upon a conscious and intentional waiver of the privilege by a corporate officer but rather upon the policy decision that the privilege is inapplicable in this situation without regard to the intent of the agent.

This holding has been carried to the logical next step, and a former corporate officer who has possession of books of a defunct corporation cannot assert the privilege in response to a demand for their production.[98]

---

92. 81 F.Supp. 418 (N.D.Cal.1948).

93. United States v. Onassis, 133 F.Supp. 327 (S.D. N.Y.1955). See also United States v. Cogan, 257 F.Supp. 170 (S.D.N.Y.1966); United States v. Lawn, 115 F.Supp. 674 (S.D.N.Y.1953).

94. The sole stockholder of a corporation was held not entitled to assert the privilege to prevent production of the corporate records. Wild v. Brewer, 329 F.2d 924 (9th Cir. 1964).

95. See generally 8 Wigmore, Evidence (McNaughton rev.) § 2259b.

96. 221 U.S. 361 (1911). See also Essgee Co. v. United States, 262 U.S. 151 (1923).

97. Wilson v. United States, 221 U.S. 361, 384–85 (1911).

98. Wheeler v. United States, 226 U.S. 478 (1913); Grant v. United States, 227 U.S. 74 (1913).

Moreover, an agent who may be required to produce documents may also be required to identify and authenticate them, as this involves little if any additional danger of incrimination.[99]

If taken somewhat further, this line of reasoning would lead to the conclusion that an agent of an organization may be required to testify concerning activities of the corporation and his own activities as agent of the corporation despite any danger of his own incrimination. If the public interest in the regulation of powerful associations demands that their officers be denied the privilege in regard to production of corporate records, does it not also dictate that they should be denied the privilege in regard to activities carried on as agent of the organization? In Curcio v. United States,[100] however, the Supreme Court rejected this view. Curcio, secretary-treasurer of a union local, had been subpoenaed to testify before a grand jury and produce certain union documents. He appeared but responded that the documents sought were no longer in his possession. In response to questions designed to elicit from him the whereabouts of the books and their possessor, he invoked the privilege. Reversing Curcio's conviction for contempt, the Supreme Court held that the privilege had no exception covering the situation. No hint was found in the prior decisions that a custodian of corporate documents forfeits his own constitutional privileges to this extent by assuming the duties of his office. Testimony which only served to authenticate the documents produced was characterized as merely "auxiliary to the production" of the documents and as subjecting the custodian who has produced the documents to little, if any, further danger of incrimination.[1]

The distinction is unquestionably a somewhat arbitrary one, but not necesarily inappropriate. Assuming that the public interest demands that the state be permitted some access to information regarding organization activities, the distinction between authentication of documents and testimony regarding documents not produced seems mechanically the easiest place to draw the line. Care must be taken, however, to recognize that the line is being drawn on this policy basis, and that the distinction is not that between production, in part a physical activity, and testifying, an oral activity.

130. The Privilege of an Accused in a Criminal Proceeding: (a) Definition of An Accused in a Criminal Proceeding.[2]

The privilege confers a significantly different right upon one who is the accused in a criminal proceeding as compared to one who is simply a witness in a criminal or other proceeding. Basically, the right of an accused is the right not only to avoid giving incriminating responses to inquiries put to him but also to be free from the inquiries themselves. Thus the privilege of an accused allows him not only to refuse to respond to questions directed at his alleged participation in the offense but also entitles him not even to be called as a witness at his own trial.[3] Because of this significant difference in the

---

99. United States v. Austin-Bagley Corp., 31 F.2d 229 (2d Cir. 1929), discussed with approval in Curcio v. United States, 354 U.S. 118, 125 (1957). See also Pulford v. United States, 155 F.2d 944 (6th Cir. 1946); Lumber Products Ass'n v. United States, 144 F.2d 546 (9th Cir. 1944), rev'd on other grounds, sub. nom. United Brotherhood of Carpenters & Joiners v. United States, 330 U.S. 395 (1947); Carolene Products Co. v. United States, 140 F.2d 61 (4th Cir. 1944), aff'd 323 U.S. 18; United States v. Illinois Alcohol Co., 45 F.2d 145 (2d Cir. 1930).

100. 354 U.S. 118 (1957).

1. Id. at 125.

2. See generally 58 Am.Jur. Witnesses § 44; C.J.S. Witnesses § 441.

3. United States v. Echeles, 352 F.2d 892 (7th Cir. 1965) cert. denied 382 U.S. 955 (one defendant may not call another defendant to stand); United States v. Housing Foundation of America, Inc., 176 F.2d 665 (3d Cir. 1949); 8 Wigmore, Evidence (McNaughton rev.) § 2268.

application of the privilege to the two situations, it becomes important to define an accused in a criminal proceeding.

The traditional view has been that an individual does not become an accused until the criminal process has been formally brought to bear upon him. Thus at such proceedings as a grand jury investigation,[4] a coroner's inquest,[5] and a preliminary hearing,[6] all theoretically designed to determine whether formal criminal processes should be invoked, no one has a right to refuse all cooperation in the inquiry.[7] The matter is often intertwined with related but separable questions, such as whether a witness in such a situation has been adequately informed of his right to decline to answer if that answer would tend to incriminate [8] and whether he has a right to counsel under the circumstances.[9]

The basis for the traditional position has been somewhat shaken by the Supreme Court's decisions culminating in Miranda v. Arizona.[10] Under the rules announced in

---

4. See United States v. Winter, 348 F.2d 204, 207–208 (2d Cir. 1965) (and cases cited therein); United States v. Cleary, 265 F.2d 459 (2d Cir. 1959); United States v. Price, 163 F. 904 (S.D.N.Y.1908), aff'd 216 U.S. 488; Ex parte Barnes, 73 Tex.Cr. 583, 166 S.W. 728 (1914); In re Lemon, 15 Cal.App.2d 82, 59 P.2d 213 (1936). New York, however, has held that under the state constitutional privilege a prospective defendant or one who is "a target of an investigation" has a right not to be examined before a grand jury. If he is called before the grand jury, he is entitled to the dismissal of any resulting indictment. People v. Laino, 10 N.Y.2d 161, 218 N.Y.S.2d 647, 176 N.E.2d 571 (1961), appeal dismissed and cert. denied 374 U.S. 104; People v. Steuding, 6 N.Y.2d 214, 189 N.Y.S.2d 166, 160 N.E.2d 468 (1959). He may, however, be prosecuted for perjury or other misconduct before the grand jury. People v. Ianniello, 21 N.Y.2d 418, 288 N.Y.S.2d 462, 235 N.E.2d 439 (1968) cert. denied 393 U.S. 827. See generally Annot., 38 A.L.R.2d 225. Compare People v. La Bello, 24 N.Y.2d 598, 301 N.Y.S.2d 544, 249 N.E.2d 412 (1969), holding that since the indictment had been based on the testimony of a subsequent witness and the defendants were protected from the use of any testimony given before the grand jury, they were not entitled to dismissal of the indictment by reason of having been called before the body. See also Jones v. United States, 119 U.S.App.D.C. 284, 342 F.2d 863 (1964) (four of eleven judges arguing that privilege bars prosecution from calling before a grand jury a defendant already bound over for trial); State v. Ruggeri, 19 Utah 2d 216, 429 P.2d 969 (1967) (improper to call subject of investigation without warning him that he was the subject of the inquiry; suggestion that it would be improper to call him at all when the purpose was to elicit an incriminating admission). For a general discussion, see Comment, The California Grand Jury—Two Current Problems, 52 Cal.L.Rev. 116, 125–28 (1964).

5. In Dykes v. State, 232 Miss. 379, 99 So.2d 602 (1957) the accused had testified before a coroner's inquest. The trial court did not admit this testimony at trial but also denied the defendant's plea of complete immunity. The Mississippi Supreme Court held that the testimony before the inquest was voluntary and that the accused had apparently waived his limited right to decline to answer specific questions.

6. The constitutional position of a prisoner at a preliminary is not clear. Most states specifically confer at least a limited right not to be called, either by statute or practice. E. g., West's Ann. Cal.Penal Code, § 866.5 (1956) ("The defendant may not be examined at the examination, unless he is represented by counsel, or unless he waives his right to counsel after being advised at such examination of his right to aid counsel.") But see N.C.Gen.Stat. § 15–80 (1953) (magistrate directed to examine prisoner in relation to offense charged; examination not to be under oath and prisoner to be informed of right not to answer); State v. Parker, 132 N.C. 1014, 43 S.E. 830 (1903). See generally Kauper, Judicial Examination of the Accused—A Remedy for the Third Degree, 30 Mich.L.Rev. 1224, 1236–38 (1931). There is a lack of case law on the role played by the privilege in this situation. See Wood v. United States, 75 U.S.App.D.C. 274, 128 F.2d 265, 270–71 (1942) ("The court has the power to examine the accused and others. . . . It cannot be . . . that the court's power to examine the accused, though conferred by statute, means authority to compel him to answer . . ."); State v. Zappia, 8 Ariz.App. 549, 448 P.2d 119 (1968) (right at preliminary to decline to take stand one of statutory origin). See generally Annot., 38 A.L.R.2d 225, 237; People v. Jackson, 23 Ill.2d 263, 178 N.E.2d 310 (1961) (apparently approving of calling the accused to the stand at the preliminary but insisting that he be adequately informed of his right to refuse to respond to incriminating questions).

7. This was the view taken in the first edition of this text. McCormick, Evidence, § 122, pp. 258–59 (1954). Cf. Annot., 5 A.L.R.2d 1404, 1425 (admissibility of statement or testimony of accused at preliminary).

8. See § 153, infra.

9. Id.

10. 384 U.S. 436 (1966).

Miranda, if the subject of custodial interrogation indicates "in any manner" that he wishes to remain silent, the interrogation must cease.[11] If the subject's attorney is present, however, the Court noted that "there may be some circumstances in which further questioning would be permissible," apparently those in which it could be ascertained that any incriminating responses elicited were free of any compulsion and constituted a free and voluntary waiver of the privilege.[12] Thus a suspect has at least a limited right to be free from interrogation even before the formal criminal process has been put into operation.

The extent to which a person who is the subject of investigatory procedures—most importantly the grand jury—is to be accorded the privilege of an accused depends in large part upon which function of the privilege of an accused is emphasized. In part, an accused is spared the necessity of having to submit at trial to questions and to invoke the privilege in regard to each in order to avoid emphasizing to the trier of fact the invocation of the privilege. This minimizes the possibility that an adverse inference will be drawn from the invocation of the privilege. If this function is emphasized, the privilege should not apply to grand jury and similar proceedings. Since guilt is not at issue, there is no danger that requiring the subject specifically to invoke the privilege in response to particular questions will lead to inferring guilt from his invocation of the privilege. But, on the other hand, an accused is undoubtedly also accorded the prerogative of declining to submit to interrogation to remove any vestiges of—and any incentive for —the abuses of interrogation against which the privilege has historically protected those who invoke it. The opportunity to interrogate, of course, also creates an incentive to make maximum use of that opportunity by techniques which may approach coercion or trickery. An accused subjected to such interrogation may well loose the ability intelligently to invoke the privilege that is essential to its effective operation. If this function of the privilege is emphasized, the privilege of an accused should be extended to the subject of grand jury and similar investigatory proceedings.[13]

Against these dangers to the interests protected by the privilege must be weighed the interests of the public in the efficient conduct of investigations. To extend the privilege of an accused to the subjects of the proceedings preliminary to formal trial may severely limit the effectiveness of these proceedings in accomplishing their investigatory and screening functions. Moreover, it may not be necessary to expand the privilege to this extent to achieve the desired objectives. It is arguable that if the right to counsel was clearly extended to those appearing in investigatory procedures and the subjects' right to be fully apprised of their rights and the factual situation was made clear, their rights would be sufficiently protected without undue infringement upon public interests by extending to them only the privilege of a witness.[14]

13. People v. Laino, 10 N.Y.2d 161, 218 N.Y.S.2d 647, 176 N.E.2d 571 (1961) appeal dismissed and cert. denied 374 U.S. 104, provides a concrete example of the dangers involved in refusing to permit a witness called by the grand jury to decline to submit to interrogation. Laino had been called before a grand jury investigating official misconduct in the purchase by the city of supplies from him. At the outset, Laino made clear that he desired to invoke the privilege; it later became clear that his records and transactions revealed failure accurately to report earnings for tax purposes. Despite his obvious desire to invoke the privilege, however, he failed to do so for reasons not entirely clear; probably either he erroneously felt that he had been granted immunity, or he felt that he had already sufficiently invoked it.

14. In Bacon v. State, 222 Ga. 151, 149 S.E.2d 111 (1966) it was held that a pretrial proceeding to determine the accused's competency to stand trial was a "civil proceeding" and thus the accused could

11. Id. at 444–45.

12. Id. at 474, n. 44.

A distinction can probably be drawn between those situations in which the objective is a general investigatory one and those in which it is merely the accumulation of evidence to convict one as to whom the decision to prosecute has already been made. In regard to the former, reliance upon the right of counsel and the privilege as accorded a witness represents the most appropriate balance of the conflicting values. As to the latter, the situation seems sufficiently akin to the formal trial itself to require that the subject be accorded the privilege of an accused, that is, the right to decline to be subjected to formal interrogation at all. Under some circumstances, coroner's inquests, police investigations, and grand jury proceedings would come within the former. Under other circumstances—when the decision to prosecute had already been made, for example—these same proceedings would come within the latter category. The preliminary examination, however, would almost inevitably come within the latter, and in these proceedings the subject should therefore be extended the accused's privilege to decline to be subjected to formal questioning.

131. The Privilege of an Accused in a Criminal Proceeding: (b) Comment on Failure to Testify and Other Forms of "Coercion." [15]

Because the scope of the privilege is, once the subject is identified as an accused, apparently so clear, it might be anticipated that what constitutes coercion would not constitute a troublesome question. Yet this has not been the case. In Griffin v. California,[16] the Supreme Court held that the federal constitutional privilege was violated by a prosecutor's argument which urged and a jury instruction which authorized the jury to draw an inference of guilt from a defendant's failure to testify when his testimony could have reasonably been expected to deny or explain matters proved by the prosecution. This, the Court concluded, constituted a penalty for exercising the privilege and a remnant of the inquisitorial system of criminal justice which the privilege prohibits.[17] "What the jury may infer given no help from the court is one thing," noted the Court. "What they may infer when the court solemnizes the silence of the accused into evidence against him is quite another." [18] Comment or argument by the prosecutor regarding the accused's failure to testify is equally improper.[19]

The issues arising out of the "no comment" rule can be grouped into four categories: (a) claims that the trier of fact has drawn and relied upon an inference of guilt from the failure to testify, (b) procedural situations which place a nontestifying accused at a significant disadvantage, (c) instructions serving significant policy functions but which incidentally may call attention to the accused's failure to testify, and (d) miscellaneous situations in which comments by the trial judge or counsel may have directed attention to the accused's silence.

---

be called to the stand and required to submit to cross-examination. This seems appropriate. The function of the competency determination is not one of substantive guilt, but one merely to determine the feasibility of proceeding.

15. See generally 8 Wigmore, Evidence (McNaughton rev.) § 2272; 21 Am.Jur.2d Criminal Law § 356; Am.Jur. Witnesses § 56; C.J.S. Criminal Law § 993(c); Dec.Dig. Criminal Law ☜656(7).

16. 380 U.S. 609 (1965). The decision invalidated a provision of the California constitution allowing comment. The great weight of authority in the states, by statute or decision, was already opposed to allowing comment. Id., 611, n. 3.

17. Id. at 614.

18. Id. The Court had held in Wilson v. United States, 149 U.S. 60 (1893) that comment was improper in a federal trial, although the stated basis of the decision was statutory rather than constitutional.

19. Id., 615; People v. Modesto, 59 Cal.Rptr. 124, 427 P.2d 788 (1967) cert. denied 389 U.S. 1009 (comment held error but not basis for reversal). See generally Dec.Dig. Criminal Law ☜721.

The few cases in the first category affirm that it is impermissible for a finder of fact to draw from the assertion of the privilege an inference of guilt. Nevertheless, they find in the offhand comments of the trial judge after trial to the court insufficient evidence that the judge attached enough weight to the defendant's failure to testify to justify reversal.[20] This is probably appropriate. Reconstructing by an appellate court the mental processes of a trial judge sitting as finder of facts is a difficult enough task in itself. It is doubtful whether it can be performed reliably by use of the judge's informal remarks.

The cases in the second category involve several situations. Two seem fairly well settled. A defendant may testify at a hearing on the admissibility of evidence or any other preliminary matter out of the presence of the jury without jeopardizing his ability to assert the privilege at trial. Testimony given at such a hearing may not be introduced against him at trial, nor may its scope be commented upon,[21] although it may be admissible for the limited purpose of impeachment should he take the stand at the trial in chief.[22] This rule seems to be based as much on a desire to obtain an adequate factual basis on which to administer the numerous exclusionary rules as by a desire to protect the accused's ability to exercise his privilege against self-incrimination.

Unitary trial procedures under which the jury deciding the issue of guilt or innocence also determines, without a separate hearing, the punishment for the offense have also been questioned on similar grounds. The argument is that an accused must, in order to put his personal plea for mitigation before the jury, abandon his privilege by taking the stand at the trial on the merits. The Supreme Court, however, upheld the unitary procedure in death penalty cases, finding nothing in "the history, policies, or precedents relating to the privilege" requiring that a defendant be accorded the opportunity to present personal testimony limited to the issue of punishment.[23] Lower courts have

---

20. In People v. Padilla, 240 Cal.App.2d 114, 49 Cal. Rptr. 340, 342 (1966) the trial judge commented, "There are five different factors that persuade me that the defendant should be found guilty. . . . In addition to all this, which is most convincing, I am impressed by the defendant not taking the stand and indicating that the matter [narcotics] is not his." See also Bowen v. State, 5 Md.App. 713, 249 A.2d 499, 502 (1969) (trial judge commented that had defendant taken the stand, "I might have been able to have elicited some information from you that might have persuaded me to have acquitted. . . .").

21. Simmons v. United States, 390 U.S. 377 (1968); Calloway v. Wainwright, 409 F.2d 59 (5th Cir. 1969) cert. denied 395 U.S. 909 (state trial court had ruled confession voluntary and submitted it to jury; defendant took the stand to testify as to its nonvoluntariness; court of appeals held that accused's privilege was violated by prosecutor's comment on accused's failure to testify before jury as to anything other than voluntariness of confession); United States v. Nielsen, 392 F.2d 849 (7th Cir. 1968) (right to testify on motion regarding statements made during interrogation); Bailey v. United States, 128 U.S.App.D.C. 354, 389 F.2d 305 (1967) (right to testify on motion regarding items seized in search made pursuant to ar-

rest); People v. Walker, 374 Mich. 331, 132 N.W.2d 87 (1965); State ex rel. Rasmussen v. Tahash, 272 Minn. 539, 141 N.W.2d 3 (1965); State v. Thundershield, 160 N.W.2d 408 (S.D.1968). Contra, State v. Goins, 232 La. 238, 94 So.2d 244 (1957).

Despite the absence of case law to this effect, it seems clear that the right to testify only as to a preliminary matter is not restricted to those matters related to constitutional exclusionary rules. Cf. State v. Agresta, 5 Conn.Cir. 242, 250 A.2d 346 (1968) (defendants who took the stand at preliminary hearing on motion to substitute one privately retained attorney for another were improperly examined on other matters). Thus a defendant could take the stand to testify regarding a nonconstitutional issue of the admissibility of evidence, such as the loss of the original document when a copy is offered, without affecting his ability to rely on his privilege during the trial on the merits.

22. Woody v. United States, 126 U.S.App.D.C. 353, 379 F.2d 130 (1967) cert. denied 389 U.S. 961; Gordon v. United States, 127 U.S.App.D.C. 343, 383 F.2d 936, 941 (1967) cert. denied 390 U.S. 1029; Lyter v. State, 2 Md.App. 654, 236 A.2d 432 (1967); F.R.Ev. (R.D.1971) 104(d). Cf. § 178, infra.

23. McGautha v. California, 402 U.S. 183 (1971). For lower court decisions reaching the same result, see Segura v. Patterson, 402 F.2d 249 (10th Cir.

also uniformly rejected arguments made in other contexts that the privilege is infringed because certain evidence which has been received will unduely prejudice the defendant unless he waives his privilege and testifies.[24] Both of these problems would be better analyzed under a broad due process approach rather than as potentially improper burdens upon the exercise of the privilege against self-incrimination. Clearly any evidence introduced by the prosecution and relevant to guilt creates pressure on a defendant to waive the privilege and testify, if his testimony might tend to exculpate him. The pressure to testify, however, is only one of numerous policy factors involved, and analysis under a privilege-burden approach tends to overemphasize this single factor.

The third category consists primarily of cases challenging the instruction that unexplained possession of stolen property permits the inference that the possessor committed the crime by which the property was taken from its owner. Almost without exception, the courts have sustained the validity of this and similar rules and instructions permitting the jury to draw the inference.[25] Similar re-

sults have been reached in related situations.[26]

The final category consists of a wide variety of cases in which, often during the heat of trial, statements have been made which arguably direct attention to the accused's failure to testify in his own behalf. Although appellate courts have voiced dismay at the situations, reversible error has

Asey, 85 Ill.App.2d 210, 229 N.E.2d 368 (1967); Anglin v. State, 244 Md. 652, 224 A.2d 668 (1966) cert. denied 386 U.S. 947; Commonwealth v. Wilbur, 353 Mass. 376, 231 N.E.2d 919 (1967) cert. denied 390 U.S. 1010; Schnepp v. State, 82 Nev. 257, 415 P.2d 619 (1966) cert. denied 385 U.S. 939. But cf. Robinson v. United States, 401 F.2d 523 (5th Cir. 1968). See generally 24 U.Miami L.Rev. 200 (1969).

In United States v. Gainey, 380 U.S. 63 (1965), the Court upheld the validity of a statute directing that presence at the site of a still is sufficient evidence to authorize conviction of carrying on an unlawful distilling operation, "unless the defendant explains such presence to the satisfaction of the jury . . . ." The quoted language, said the Court, referred to the evidence as a whole and not merely to testimony of the defendant himself.

26. State v. McRae, 4 Ohio App.2d 217, 211 N.E.2d 875 (1965) (during deliberations jury asked if the state could have caused the defendant to testify, court responded by citing to state constitutional privilege; codefendant testified; court instructed jury to consider his testimony in light of his interest in the outcome of the case).

A special problem is raised when the court instructs the jury that the defendant is entitled not to testify and to be free of any inference that might be drawn from such failure and the accused has not requested these instructions (and perhaps affirmatively resisted them). Several courts have held that to give such instructions when they have not been requested is reversible error, reasoning that the effect is to simply call the jury's attention to the accused's failure to testify and thus violating the *Griffin* rule. State v. Zaragosa, 6 Ariz.App. 80, 430 P.2d 426 (1967); Russell v. State, 240 Ark. 97, 398 S.W.2d 213 (1966), reversing Thompson v. State, 205 Ark. 1040, 172 S.W.2d 234 (1943); People v. Molano, 253 Cal.App.2d 841, 61 Cal.Rptr. 821 (1967). The general rule, however, seems to be that although it may be "better practice" not to give such instructions in the absence of a specific request, the giving of the instructions is not reversible error. United States v. Woodmansee, 354 F.2d 235 (2d Cir. 1965); United States v. Garguilo, 310 F.2d 249 (2d Cir. 1962); State v. McAlvain, 104 Ariz. 445, 454 P.2d 987 (1969). See generally Annot., 18 A.L.R.3d 1335.

1969); Segura v. People of the State of Colo., 163 Colo. 491, 431 P.2d 768 (1967); Johnson v. Commonwealth, 208 Va. 481, 158 S.E.2d 725 (1968). Cf. United States v. Curry, 358 F.2d 904 (2d Cir. 1966) cert. denied 385 U.S. 873. See 25 Wash. & Lee L.Rev. 287 (1968).

24. United States ex rel. Hill v. Pinto, 394 F.2d 470 (3d Cir. 1968); Harrison v. United States, 128 U.S.App.D.C. 245, 387 F.2d 203 (1967) (no violation of privilege in receipt at third trial of testimony given in second trial, even though defendants took stand at second trial only after introduction of post-arrest statements later held improperly received), rev'd 392 U.S. 219 (on the ground that the testimony was the "fruit" of the inadmissible statements); Birnbaum v. United States, 356 F.2d 856 (8th Cir. 1966); United States ex rel. Powell v. Commonwealth, 294 F.Supp. 849 (E.D.Pa.1968); United States v. Grunewald, 164 F.Supp. 644 (S.D.N.Y.1958).

25. State v. Young, 217 So.2d 567 (Fla.1968), reversing 203 So.2d 650 (Fla.App.1968); Shaw v. State, 209 So.2d 477 (Fla.App.1968); People v.

seldom been found,[27] apparently on the basis that the situations involved no conscious misconduct and the absence of any comment, and the minimal extent to which the situation focused attention upon the accused's invocation of the privilege.

132. The Privilege of an Accused in a Criminal Proceeding: (c) Waiver of the Privilege by Voluntary Testimony.[28]

Probably because of the absolute nature of the privilege of an accused, courts have been willing to find broad waivers of the privilege in the decisions of accused persons to testify in their own behalf. The Supreme Court has rejected the argument that an accused should, like an ordinary witness, be held to have waived the privilege only when testimony which was itself incriminating was given:

> "[The accused] has the choice, after weighing the advantages of the privilege against self-incrimination against the advantages of putting forward his version of the facts and his reliability as a witness, not to testify at all. He cannot reasonably claim that the Fifth Amendment gives him not only this choice but, if he elects to testify, an immunity from cross examination on the matters he has himself put in dispute. It would make of the Fifth Amendment not only a humane safeguard against judicially coerced self-disclosure but a positive invitation to mutilate the truth a party offers to tell.[29]"

It has generally been held that when an accused testifies [30] he becomes liable to cross

---

27. People v. Gomez, 252 Cal.App.2d 844, 60 Cal. Rptr. 881 (1967) (defendant cried out in open court that a witness was "telling lies" and court responded that defendant "could have taken the stand and testified. He elected not to do so. Therefore, he must remain silent." Any error held corrected by instructions to jury.); Hand v. State, 188 So.2d 364 (Fla.App.1966), rev'd on other grounds, 199 So.2d 100 (Fla.1967) (court asked, "Does the defense have any testimony?); Harvey v. State, 187 So.2d 59 (Fla.App.1966) cert. denied 386 U.S. 923 (court instructed jury, "You are not to discuss this case . . . until you have heard all the evidence that is to be introduced by both the State and by the defendants."); Pennington v. State, 117 Ga.App. 701, 161 S.E.2d 327 (1968) cert. denied 393 U.S. 1108 (after defendant's unsworn statement, prosecutor asked, "Do we get to cross-examine?" and court responded in the negative); Walton v. Commonwealth, 439 S.W.2d 953 (Ky. App.1969) (court directed defense to "call your first witness." and defense responded that it would offer no testimony); State v. Heissler, 324 S.W.2d 714 (Mo.1959) (jury instructed concerning alibi, including statement that the defendant "says he was not present"; "says" held to mean "claims" or "said by counsel in opening statement"). But see Davis v. United States, 357 F.2d 438 (5th Cir. 1966) cert. denied 385 U.S. 927 (reversing on the ground that trial judge sustained objections to defense counsel's cross-examination of witness with comment that counsel could put his own people on the stand); People v. Rial, 25 A.D.2d 28, 266 N.Y.S.2d 426 (1966) (reversible error found in prosecutor's argument, "Did you hear any evidence that [defendant] called [decedent] . . . ." when defendant was the logical source of such testimony, and in instructions that jury could draw inferences from "the failure of either party to call any witness who might reasonably be expected to throw light on the situation"). Cf. Ramer v. United States, 390 F.2d 564, 577 (9th Cir. 1968) cert. denied 393 U.S. 870.

Cases are Collected in Annot., 14 A.L.R.3d 723.

28. See generally 8 Wigmore, Evidence (McNaughton rev.) §§ 2276(b), 2277; Carlson, Cross-Examination of the Accused, 52 Cornell L.Q. 705 (1967); 21 Am.Jur.2d Criminal Law § 358; 58 Am.Jur. Witnesses §§ 95–101; C.J.S. Witnesses §§ 888, 889; Dec.Dig. Witnesses ☞301, 305(2).

29. Brown v. United States, 356 U.S. 148, 155–56 (1958).

30. In *Brown* the Court was careful to state that it was the testimony and not the action in taking the stand that constituted the waiver. Id. at 156–57. There is, however, some question as to what constitutes "testimony." In United States ex rel. Lewis v. Yeager, 285 F.Supp. 780 (D.N.J.1968), aff'd 411 F.2d 414 (3d Cir. 1969) the court held that when counsel had required the accused to stand close to a witness for purposes of demonstrating the similarity between the witness and the accused, this constituted an attempt to refute prosecution testimony and an instruction permitting an inference from the accused's silence was not constitutional error. Compare United States v. Curtiss, 330 F.2d 278 (2d Cir. 1964) (arguments and summation of an accused acting as his own counsel did not justify comment). In jurisdictions permitting an accused to make an unsworn statement before the jury, this does not justify cross-examination without his consent. E. g., Shoffeitt v. State, 107 Ga.App. 217, 129 S.E.2d 572 (1963).

examination under whatever rules would be applicable to any other witness, and by testifying he waives his privilege to that extent.[31] Not only may he be questioned concerning all facts relevant to the matters he has testified to on direct examination but he is also subject to searching cross-examination for impeachment purposes.[32] Except with re-

Where the accused acts as his own counsel his testimony does not constitute a waiver unless the court has fully informed him of his rights under the privilege. People v. Glaser, 238 Cal.App.2d 819, 48 Cal.Rptr. 427 (1966) cert. denied 385 U.S. 880; Cochran v. State, 117 So.2d 544 (Fla.App. 1960).

31. Brown v. United States, 356 U.S. 148 (1958); Johnson v. United States, 318 U.S. 189 (1943); Raffel v. United States, 271 U.S. 494 (1926); Fitzpatrick v. United States, 178 U.S. 304 (1900); Gandy v. United States, 386 F.2d 516 (5th Cir. 1967) cert. denied 390 U.S. 1004; Smith v. United States, 358 F.2d 683 (3d Cir. 1966); United States v. Walker, 313 F.2d 236 (6th Cir. 1963); Black v. State, 440 S.W.2d 668 (Tex.Cr.App.1969); State v. Schroeder, 201 Kan. 811, 443 P.2d 284 (1968). Of course, no waiver can be found if the accused was unaware of the privilege. Cf., Annot., 79 A.L.R. 2d 643 (duty of court to inform unrepresented defendant of privilege).

32. United States v. Greenberg, 268 F.2d 120 (2d Cir. 1959); Reilly v. State, 212 So.2d 796 (Fla.App. 1968); Dorroh v. State, 229 Miss. 315, 90 So.2d 653 (1956); State v. Dean, 400 S.W.2d 413 (Mo. 1966). For a discussion of the general scope of cross-examination, see §§ 21, 22, supra. There are few cases finding error in the scope of the prosecution's examination of the accused. Tucker v. United States, 5 F.2d 818 (8th Cir. 1925) enforced the federal rule on cross-examination as applied to an accused. The accused, charged with use of the mails to defraud, took the stand and testified as to the details of his promotional scheme, obviously for the purposes of refuting the allegation of a fraudulent intent. On cross-examination the prosecution elicited from the accused testimony concerning his participation in placing a newspaper advertisement, which had been alleged to establish use of the mails. On appeal it was held that the testimony as to the scheme did not waive the privilege in regard to the placing of the advertisement, which was characterized as relating to a different element of the offense. Other cases reversing seem to be based upon a rule of evidence rather than upon a careful definition of the privilege itself. State v. Frese, 256 Iowa 289, 127 N.W.2d 83 (1964) (defendant, taking the stand in trial for rape, asked about the whereabouts of his three alleged companions, who were imprisoned); State v. Leuty, 247 Iowa 251, 73 N.W.2d 64 (1955) (defendant, in trial for incest, asked about illicit re-

spect to impeachment, it is not a basis for restricting cross-examination that the response may be incriminating in regard to an offense other than the one for which the accused is presently being tried.[33] He may not only be compelled to respond to questions but he may be forced to produce demonstrative evidence or documents [34] or give handwriting exemplars.[35]

The traditional formulation of the scope of the waiver creates significant problems, especially after Malloy v. Hogan.[36] Traditionally the federal courts have been regarded as restricting cross-examination to matters testified to on direct, while a number of states have adopted the "Massachusetts" or "English" rule which permits cross-examination on all phases of the case.[37] Moreover, it is clear that under any formula-

lationship with another woman). See also People v. Butler, 65 Cal.2d 569, 55 Cal.Rptr. 511, 421 P.2d 703 (1967) (dictum) (at trial on guilt, accused may not be cross-examined concerning circumstances of prior offenses, punishment imposed or conduct during incarceration, although these would be properly subjects of inquiry at the penalty trial). Cf. State v. Hines, 270 Minn. 30, 133 N.W.2d 371 (1964).

33. Johnson v. United States, 318 U.S. 189 (1943); Carpenter v. United States, 264 F.2d 565, 569–70 (4th Cir. 1959); People v. De Georgio, 185 Cal.App. 2d 413, 8 Cal.Rptr. 295 (1960); State v. Manning, 134 N.W.2d 91 (N.D.1965). See § 42, supra, as to claiming the privilege on cross-examination directed to impeachment. See § 140, infra, with respect to waiver by witnesses generally through disclosure of incriminating matters without claiming the privilege.

34. State v. Taylor, 99 Ariz. 85, 407 P.2d 59 (1965) cert. denied 384 U.S. 979, discusses and cites the cases and adopts the view of the "numerical majority and better reasoned cases" that physical acts or exhibitions may be required.

35. United States v. Doremus, 414 F.2d 252 (6th Cir. 1969) (defendant required on cross-examination to write in presence of jury the exact words written on a form he had allegedly forged during alleged impersonation of a United States marshal).

36. 378 U.S. 1 (1964). See § 117, supra. Note, 45 N.C.L.Rev. 1030 (1967) discusses whether as a result of the general rule, the federal rule regarding scope of cross-examination is constitutionally binding on the states.

37. See § 21, supra.

tion of the rule regarding scope of cross-examination the trial judge exercises a great deal of discretionary control. If the scope of the waiver depends upon the permissible scope of cross-examination, this means that the waiver varies in scope from jurisdiction to jurisdiction, in addition to being subject to significant discretionary control by the trial judge. This merely emphasizes the inadequacies of using the permissible scope of cross-examination as a measure of the extent of the waiver.[38] Clearly the two matters are not identical, and fundamentally different factors are involved in each. The scope of cross-examination is essentially a matter of control over the order of production of evidence; the primary policy being served is the orderly conduct of the trial. The waiver of the privilege, however, involves the extent to which an accused must forfeit the protection of the privilege to place his own version of the facts before the trier of fact. An ordinary witness usually has no interest which deserves legal protection in restricting cross-examination; the accused, however, has the interests recognized by the privilege. The balance in regard to the scope of waiver should be struck independent of the scope of cross-examination of the ordinary witness.

Similar reasoning leads to rejection of the position that the accused, by testifying with respect to one count, waives his privilege with respect to all other counts of a multiple-count indictment. In People v. Perez,[39] the accused was tried on a four count indictment; counts one and two charged separate robberies and counts 3 and 4 related to a third incident in which two individuals were robbed. Perez testified to an alibi as to the times of the offenses charged in counts 1 and 2; he did not refer on direct examination to the robberies charged in counts 3 and 4. The prosecutor commented on the accused's failure to deny the robberies charged in counts 3 and 4, and the trial court instructed the jury that they could draw an adverse inference from the accused's failure to explain or deny facts within his knowledge. Over dissent, it was held that cross-examination as to these robberies would have been proper and therefore the comment and instruction were not error. Measuring the extent of waiver in this fashion by reference to the rules of joinder of counts, again involves resort to values unrelated to the privilege, just as when the extent of waiver is measured by the permissible scope of cross-examination of witnesses generally.

Two possible standards suggest themselves for measuring the extent of waiver by an accused who elects to take the stand and testify only as to certain aspects of an offense with which he is charged. One is that he waives as to all aspects of that offense.[40] It has the advantage of simplicity and ease of application but may run counter to the basic purposes of the rule. The privilege is not merely against taking the stand, and hence readily said to be waived *in toto* by taking the stand, but against self-incrimination. A rule of blanket waiver would not only discourage accused persons from testifying at all but would in effect make them prosecution witnesses,

---

38. The draftsmen of the proposed Federal Rules of Evidence expressly disclaimed any intent to affect the scope of waiver of the privilege by defining the scope of cross-examination of a witness. F.R.Ev. (R.D.1971) 611(b), Advisory Committee's Note.

39. 65 Cal.2d 615, 55 Cal.Rptr. 909, 422 P.2d 597 (1967) cert. dismissed 395 U.S. 208. See Comment, Joinder of Counts As A Violation of an Accused's Right to Remain Silent, 41 Temp.L.Q. 458 (1968). Ordinarily, of course, the problem could be avoided by a timely motion for severance. Cross v. United States, 118 U.S.App.D.C. 324, 335 F.2d 987 (1964); United States v. Baker, 262 F.Supp. 657, 687 (D.D.C. 1966). Thus in most cases the issue can be avoid-

ed; when it does not appear until trial, the trial judge still has a "continuing duty at all stages of the trial [to grant severance] if prejudice does appear." Schaffer v. United States, 362 U.S. 511, 516 (1960).

40. See 8 Wigmore, Evidence (McNaughton rev.) § 2276.

confronting them with the "cruel trilemma of self-accusation, perjury or contempt." [41]

A preferable standard may be that an accused who testifies forfeits his privilege only insofar as forfeiture is necessary to enable the prosecution reasonably to subject his testimony on direct examination to scrutiny regarding its truth. This would avoid an accused putting an entirely one-sided version of his facts before a jury. But it would also avoid sacrificing the privilege to any greater extent than the basis for sacrificing it at all requires. Under this approach, an accused could testify as to some but less than all matters at issue and be subjected to cross-examination as to those matters as to which he did not testify (assuming that such cross-examination would be additionally incriminating) only if this was reasonably necessary to an evaluation of his testimony on direct.[42] This approach would not unduly burden the prosecution. The prosecution has no legitimate justification for demanding forfeiture of the privilege beyond that necessary to assure that the accused, by testifying, has not placed the state at an unfair disadvantage.

The waiver has traditionally been regarded as effective throughout in the proceeding in which the accused testifies. During that proceeding the privilege does not reattach if the accused physically leaves the witness stand, and he can be recalled and required to testify again if this is otherwise procedurally proper.[43] On the other hand, testifying in one proceeding does not affect the right to invoke the privilege in a separate and independent proceeding. For example, an accused who testifies may not be questioned concerning an invocation of the privilege in preliminary proceedings or in an earlier trial.[44] Nor is an accused who testifies at one trial precluded from invoking the privilege during a second trial of the same charge.[45] Unlike the privilege of the witness, the privilege of the accused has not given rise to many questions concerning the prospective scope of a waiver.[46] Thus, although there may be some question concerning the position of a witness,[47] it is unlikely that an accused waives

41. The quotation is from Murphy v. Waterfront Com'n, 378 U.S. 52, 55 (1964). The analysis is found in People v. Schader, 71 Cal.2d 761, 80 Cal. Rptr. 1, 457 P.2d 841 (1969), oddly enough by the same court which decided People v. Perez, supra, n. 39.

42. The formula is supported by Tucker v. United States, 5 F.2d 818 (8th Cir. 1925); People v. Schader, supra, n. 41.

43. State v. Coty, 229 A.2d 205 (Me.1967); People v. Barboza, 213 Cal.App.2d 441, 28 Cal.Rptr. 805 (1963).

44. Raffel v. United States, 271 U.S. 494 (1926) held that a waiver had a retroactive effect and permitted investigation of prior instances of invoking the privilege. See May v. State, 211 So.2d 845 (Miss.1968) holding that a testifying accused was properly asked at trial about his silence before arresting officers. But in Grunewald v. United States, 353 U.S. 391 (1957) the Court held, pursuant to its supervisory power, that the action of the accused in testifying at trial did not permit comment upon his earlier refusal to testify before a grand jury; the Court characterized the issue as an "evidentiary matter" with "grave constitutional overtones." Id. at 423. And in Stewart v. United States, 366 U.S. 1 (1961) the government conceded that under Grunewald it was error for the prosecution to ask the accused whether he had taken the stand at an earlier trial for the same offense. Although the Supreme Court has not expressly so indicated, this would seem to be a rule of constitutional dimensions. United States v. Hoffa, 349 F.2d 20, 44 (6th Cir. 1965). See also Fagundes v. United States, 340 F.2d 673, 677 (1st Cir. 1965) (error to permit evidence of refusal to talk with officers at time of arrest); Jones v. State, 200 So.2d 574 (Fla.App.1967); People v. Jordan, 7 Mich.App. 28, 151 N.W.2d 242 (1967) (asking accused if he had taken the stand at the preliminary hearing was constitutional error); State v. Boscia, 93 N.J.Super. 586, 226 A.2d 643 (1967) (error to permit use of accused's refusal to respond when called before grand jury); Commonwealth v. Burkett, 211 Pa. Super. 299, 235 A.2d 161 (1967); Dean v. Commonwealth, 209 Va. 666, 166 S.E.2d 228 (1969) (error to ask accused whether he had invoked privilege in trial of codefendant).

45. Cf. United States v. Miranti, 253 F.2d 135 (2d Cir. 1958).

46. State v. Grady, 153 Conn. 26, 211 A.2d 674 (1965) (defendant who took stand during trial of first part of indictment did not waive privilege with regard to trial on second portion of indictment charging habitual criminality).

47. See § 140, infra.

his right to invoke the privilege at trial by voluntarily testifying before a grand jury. Such a distinction between the accused and a witness is difficult to justify on theoretical grounds and, if made, must rest primarily on the proposition that the interests protected by the privilege are placed in greater danger when the holder is himself on trial and so the waiver doctrine will be correspondingly restricted in its application to this situation.

133. Special Problems: (a) Limits on Pretrial Discovery by the Prosecution Imposed by the Privilege.[48]

The increasing liberality with which discovery is granted to defendants in criminal cases [49] has brought a demand that discovery be made a "two-way" street. Attempts to require a defendant to open his case to the prosecution, however, raise problems of potential conflict with the accused's Fifth Amendment privilege.

Arguably, requiring the accused to cooperate in any way in the preparation of the case against him violates the privilege. This broad contention has been generally rejected in accordance with the view that the activity compelled be "testimonial" before the privilege comes into play.[50] However, as has been seen, compelled production of existing items constitutes an implied representation that the material produced is that demanded, and

is testimonial in character.[51] Now if the prosecution seeks not only the production of specifically described material of which it is aware but by a broader demand seeks also to use the knowledge of the defendant to determine the existence of material it suspects might exist, the accused is being compelled to respond in terms of disclosing whether the requested material exists. This involves a significantly greater testimonial aspect than the implied representation inherent in mere production. It is this latter aspect of prosecutorial discovery that raises the most serious issue under the privilege.

The leading case is Jones v. Superior Court of Nevada County,[52] decided by the California Supreme Court in 1962. Jones, charged with rape, moved for a continuance on the ground that he needed additional time to obtain medical evidence of his alleged impotence caused by injuries suffered in 1953 and 1954. The prosecution then moved for discovery of (1) names and addresses of all physicians who would be subpoenaed to testify in regard to those injuries, (2) names and addresses of all physicians who had treated Jones prior to trial, (3) all reports bearing on the injuries and the alleged impotence, and (4) X rays taken of Jones following the injuries. If the case involved only the implied representation inherent in production, the court commented, then the infringement upon the privilege might be trivial; but the case involved additionally an attempt to require the accused also to inform the prosecution whether certain evidence existed as well as to produce it if it did exist. Given this more serious danger to the privilege, the court, through Justice Roger Traynor, held that discovery could be granted only as to names and addresses of witnesses Jones intended to call at trial and reports and X rays

---

48. See generally, Smith and McCollom, Counter-Discovery in Criminal Cases: Fifth Amendment Privilege Abridged, 54 A.B.A.J. 256 (1968); Wilder, Prosecution Discovery and the Privilege Against Self-Incrimination, 6 Am.Crim.L.Q. 3 (1967); Louisell, Criminal Discovery and Self-Incrimination: Roger Traynor Confronts the Dilemma, 53 Cal.L.Rev. 89 (1965); Comment, Discovery in Federal Criminal Cases—Rule 16 and the Privilege Against Self-Incrimination, 35 Fordham L.Rev. 315 (1966); Dec.Dig. Criminal Law ⚲627.5(3).

49. See generally Traynor, Ground Lost and Found in Criminal Discovery, 39 N.Y.U.L.Rev. 228 (1964); see also § 97, supra, for discussion of discovery from the prosecution.

50. See § 124, supra.

51. See § 126, supra.

52. 58 Cal.2d 56, 22 Cal.Rptr. 879, 372 P.2d 919 (1962), noted in 76 Harv.L.Rev. 838 (1963).

he intended to introduce at trial to support his "affirmative defense" [53] of impotence. Requiring Jones to turn over this information to the prosecution, reasoned the court, would have only the effect of depriving Jones of the procedural advantage of surprise at trial; he would in no way be coerced into revealing anything he would not otherwise eventually reveal. To go further, however, would be to permit the prosecution to compel Jones to reveal his knowledge of possible witnesses, reports, and X rays in violation of his privilege.[54]

Several other judicial decisions have approved orders granting discovery to prosecutors,[55] but undoubtedly the most significant development in this area was the 1966 amendment to Rule 16 of the Federal Rules of Criminal Procedure.[56] Under the amended rule a district court may grant a defendant discovery of statements or confessions made by the defendant,[57] results of examinations and tests made by the prosecution,[58] and the testimony of the defendant before the grand jury.[59] In addition, upon a showing of materiality to the preparation of the defense and the reasonableness of the request, discovery may be granted as to "books, papers, documents, tangible objects, buildings or places." [60] If, however, discovery is granted as to examinations or reports or "books, papers, documents, tangible objects, buildings or places," the court may, upon a showing of materiality and reasonableness, condition such discovery upon the defendant's permitting prosecution discovery of "scientific or medical reports, books, papers, documents, tangible objects" which are in the defendant's possession and which he intends to produce at trial.[61] Discovery on behalf of the prosecution may be granted only if the defendant successfully requests discovery on his

---

53. Although the court characterized the proof of impotence as an "affirmative defense," it clearly was not such within either traditional definitions or California law. It served—if proved—to create a "reasonable doubt" as to whether the accused committed the act required for liability and clearly was evidence in disproof. By characterizing it, perhaps the court was attempting to restrict prosecutorial discovery to situations in which the accused, by his defense tactics, undertakes to raise an issue other than those generally raised by the charge. But see McGuire v. Superior Court, 274 Cal.App.2d 583, 79 Cal.Rptr. 155, 161 (1969) ("affirmative defense" means "evidence which is offered . . . to prove the nonexistence of a fact which is essential to the proof of the *corpus delicti* . . . or evidence which shows that the defendant is not the perpetrator of the crime. . . . ").

54. There were two dissents. Justice Peters argued that "compelling the accused to give testimony prior to the establishment of a prima facie case against him is . . . a 'flagrant, shocking and prejudicial invasion of [his] constitutional rights . . . .'", 58 Cal.2d at 63–64, 22 Cal.Rptr. at 883, 372 P.2d at 923 (Peters, J., concurring and dissenting). Justice Dooling argued that so significant a curtailment of the rights of an accused, even if constitutionally permissible, should be imposed by the legislature. 58 Cal.2d at 69, 22 Cal.Rptr. at 887, 372 P.2d at 927 (Dooling, J., dissenting).

55. People v. Pike, 71 Cal.2d 595, 78 Cal.Rptr. 672, 455 P.2d 776 (1969) (not error to require defense to produce names, addresses and expected testimony of witnesses); People v. Sanders, 110 Ill.App. 2d 85, 249 N.E.2d 124 (1969) (order requiring defense to produce typewritten statement of defense witness for impeachment purposes did not violate privilege); People v. Damon, 24 N.Y.2d 256, 299 N.Y.S.2d 830, 247 N.E.2d 651 (1969) (order requiring defense to provide prosecution with prior state-

ments of witnesses who apparently already had testified was not in violation of the defendant's privilege); State v. Grove, 65 Wash.2d 525, 398 P. 2d 170 (1967) (discovery by prosecution of letter written by defendant to wife permitted).

56. F.R.Crim.P. 16: "(c) Discovery by the Government. If the court grants [the defendant's request for discovery of anything other than the defendant's statement or testimony before the grand jury] . . . it may, upon motion of the government, condition its order by requiring that the defendant permit the government to inspect and copy or photograph scientific or medical reports, books, papers, documents, tangible objects, or copies or portions thereof, which the defendant intends to produce at the trial and which are within his possession, custody or control, upon a showing of materiality to the preparation of the government's case and that the request is reasonable. . . ."

57. F.R.Crim.P. 16(a) (1).

58. F.R.Crim.P. 16(a) (2).

59. F.R.Crim.P. 16(a) (3).

60. F.R.Crim.P. 16(b).

61. F.R.Crim.P. 16(c).

own behalf; thus a defendant may avoid having to disclose those things covered by Rule 16 by not himself invoking the right to discovery.

The final scope of Rule 16 obviously represents a compromise which the draftsmen considered was demanded by Fifth Amendment considerations. The limitation of prosecution discovery to items intended to be produced at trial was an attempt to avoid conflict with the privilege by the approach adopted in *Jones*. Nevertheless, both Mr. Justice Douglas and Mr. Justice Black indicated in their dissents from the transmittal of the proposed 1966 amendments to Congress the constitutional problem posed by the provisions for prosecution discovery.[62]

At least two theories are advanced to reconcile prosecutorial discovery with the privilege. First, it does not infringe the privilege at all when, as *Jones* argued, there is compulsion to produce only what would ultimately be produced in any event. Thus discovery to this extent might be upheld on the same analysis as statutes requiring advance notice of a defendant's intent to assert at trial an alibi[63] or an insanity defense.[64]

This rationale has been criticized, however, on the ground that requiring the defendant to reveal information before he is tactically ready to do so substantially impairs his ability successfully to defend himself.[65] A second basis on which discovery from the accused might be upheld is that despite the fact that it infringes the privilege, the infringement is justifiable upon a "waiver" theory. Arguably a defendant, by demanding and obtaining discovery, waives to some extent his right to shroud his own case in secrecy. Insofar as the privilege is a constitutional one, however, this argument is difficult to sustain.[66] More appropriate would be a frank recognition that prosecutorial discovery constitutes an infringement of interests generally protected by the privilege but that this infringement is justified by the public interest in accurate resolution of factual issues at trial if it is limited in scope and if the infringement is balanced by liberal discovery rights granted to the accused.[67]

---

62. Amendments to the Rules of Civil Procedure for the United States District Courts, 383 U.S. 1032 (Black, J., dissenting); Amendments to Rules of Criminal Procedure for the United States District Courts, 383 U.S. 1089, 1090–92 (Douglas, J., dissenting in part). See United States v. Fratello, 44 F.R.D. 444 (S.D.N.Y.1968), greatly restricting discovery under the rule.

63. A 1963 study indicated that 14 states required a defendant to give advance notice of intent to assert an alibi and to furnish specific information as to the place where he claims to have been at the time of the crime. Seven require a list of witnesses who will be called to support the defense. Note, 76 Harv.L.Rev. 838, 838–39 (1963). The Florida requirement was upheld against constitutional attack in Williams v. Florida, 399 U.S. 916 (1970).

64. E. g., Ariz.Rules Crim.Proc. 192(A); Mich.Stat. Ann. § 28.1043 (1954). 13 Vt.Stat.Ann. § 6561 (1958) was upheld against a general constitutional attack in State v. Rickert, 124 Vt. 380, 205 A.2d 547 (1964).

65. Smith and McCollom, Counter-Discovery in Criminal Cases; Fifth Amendment Privilege Abridged, 54 A.B.A.J. 256 (1968).

A further question may be raised whether an advance decision may be made with assurance as to whether a particular witness will be called or evidence introduced at trial.

66. See Amendments to the Rules of Criminal Procedure for the United States District Courts, 383 U.S. 1089, 1091–92 (Douglas, J., dissenting in part). The Advisory Committee on Criminal Rules, noting "some uncertainty" regarding the constitutional validity of compulsory discovery by the defendant, has proposed two alternative drafts of an amended Rule 16. One would make the prosecution's right of discovery conditional upon a prior request by the defendant for discovery of similar evidence from the prosecution, and the other would make the prosecutor's right to discovery independent of any discovery by the defendant. Proposed Amendments to the Federal Rules of Criminal Procedure, Rule 16, Discovery and Inspection (1970). The latter, the committee concluded, is the more desirable approach. Id. at 44.

67. See also § 126, n. 73, supra, for a further possible solution.

134. Special Problems: (b) Psychiatric Examinations and the Privilege of the Accused.[68]

The increased emphasis upon the condition of mind of the accused both at the time of the alleged offense and at the time of trial has given rise to numerous statutory authorizations for compulsory psychiatric examination of the accused in a criminal proceeding.[69] These are authorized for two purposes: (a) to investigate the present condition of mind of an accused for purposes of determining his capacity to stand trial or otherwise proceed in the criminal system and (b) to obtain evidence regarding the condition of mind of the accused at the time of the offense, for purposes of determining whether he comes within the definition of those not criminally liable for their acts by reason of insanity. In practice, a single psychiatric examination may well serve both purposes.[70] In any case, however, compelling an accused to submit to such examinations raises potential problems in regard to the privilege. For analytical purposes it is helpful to distinguish three ways in which the privilege might be endangered in this situation.

First, it is arguable that merely requiring an accused to submit to an examination violates the privilege. Generally courts have upheld examinations if the accused was protected from later use of incriminating statements,[71] but this dismisses a potentially troublesome matter without adequate consideration. Insofar as the privilege of an accused protects him from interrogation as well as from being required to respond,[72] requiring an accused to participate in a psychiatric examination by submitting to questions seems inconsistent with the privilege. However, it is by no means clear that at early stages of criminal proceedings the privilege has this broad effect, as evidenced by the police interrogation, grand jury, and preliminary hearing situations.[73] Moreover, it is arguable that by asserting incompetency to stand trial or nonliability by reason of insanity the accused has, to a limited extent

68. See generally, Danforth, Death Knell for Pre-Trial Examinations? Privilege Against Self-Incrimination, 19 Rutgers L.Rev. 489 (1965); Note, Pre-Trial Mental Examination and Commitment; Some Procedural Problems in the District of Columbia, 51 Geo.L.J. 143, 145–56 (1962); Note, Requiring a Criminal Defendant to Submit to a Government Psychiatric Examination: An Invasion of the Privilege Against Self-Incrimination, 83 Harv.L.Rev. 648 (1970); Comment, Pre-Trial Mental Examinations in Maine: Are They Mechanisms for Compelling Self-Incrimination? 18 Maine L. Rev. 96 (1966); Note, Mental Examinations of Defendants Who Plead Insanity: Problems of Self-Incrimination, 40 Temple L.Q. 366 (1967); Comment, Compulsory Mental Examinations and the Privilege Against Self-Incrimination, 1964 Wis.L. Rev. 671; Annot., 32 A.L.R.2d 434. For a discussion of the related problem of a defendant's right to counsel at a pretrial psychiatric examination, see § 176 at n. 65, infra.

69. The statutes are collected in Danforth, Death Knell for Pre-Trial Examinations? Privilege Against Self-Incrimination, 19 Rutgers L.Rev. 489, 490 n. 4 (1965).

70. See Lewin, Incompetency to Stand Trial: Legal and Ethical Aspects of an Abused Doctrine, 1969 Law & Soc. Order 233, 269–74, describing the use of the competency examination to obtain expert assistance on the insanity defense.

71. Hunt v. State, 248 Ala. 217, 27 So.2d 186 (1946) (since court order did not require defendant to respond, no coercion involved); State v. Genna, 163 La. 702, 112 So. 655 (1927); State v. Eastwood, 73 Vt. 205, 50 Atl. 1077 (1901). French v. District Court, 153 Colo. 10, 384 P.2d 268 (1963), a frequently cited case, held that the trial court had erred in striking the insanity defense of an accused who refused to cooperate with psychiatric examiners. Although the court's language is broad ["A person accused of a crime who enters a plea of not guilty by reason of insanity, cannot be compelled to carry on conversations against his will under the penalty of forfeiture of the defense for failure to respond to questions or for a refusal to 'cooperate' with persons appointed to examine him." 384 P.2d at 270], the decision was based on the possibility that statements elicited during the examination might be admitted in a trial at which the commission of the acts was at issue.

18 U.S.C.A. § 4244 provides that no statement made by accused at an examination to determine competency to stand trial is admissible on the issue of guilt.

72. Cf. § 153, infra.

73. See § 130, supra.

at least, waived his right to rely on the privilege in regard to those matters.[74] Insofar as the prosecution is constitutionally precluded from convicting an accused who is incompetent to stand trial [75] or who was insane at the time of the crime,[76] it is doubtful whether a significant burden may be placed upon an accused who raises these matters. On the other hand, courts have uniformly rejected the argument that the privilege simply prohibits compelling an accused to submit to an examination.

A distinction can be drawn between an examination conducted for purposes of determining competency to stand trial and for marshalling evidence to prove mental status at the time of the acts. The former is arguably without the protection of the privilege, since the proceeding pursuant to which the examination is conducted cannot terminate in criminal conviction but merely in a factual determination whether it is appropriate to proceed with the inquiry into guilt or innocence. If this kind of investigation can be separated from the trial itself, the competency investigation can be accurately characterized as not involving a danger of incrimination and thus not giving rise to privilege status.[77] It is, however, true that as a result of an examination conducted pursuant to such an inquiry an accused may be found competent to stand trial and, upon trial, found guilty; "but for" the finding of competency, he would not have been found criminally liable. Moveover, in practice an examination for competency purposes is likely to be used on the insanity issue at trial; the theoretical separation discussed in the paragraph which follows may not be applied in practice.

Second, the psychiatric examination situation may run afoul of the privilege by virtue of the use at trial of the accused's statements for purposes of proving that the accused performed the acts necessary for criminal liability. Courts have agreed that this use is improper, although there is not unanimity on the appropriate protection to which an accused is entitled. There seems to be little dispute that during the examination an accused may properly decline to answer in such a manner as to make such statements available to the prosecution. Some courts have held that protective instructions, directing the jury to consider [78] the statements only as going to mental condition, are adequate in the event that the statements are made and come out during the trial testimony of the examiner.[79] The Wisconsin

---

74. Pope v. United States, 372 F.2d 710, 721 (8th Cir. 1967) vacated on other grounds 392 U.S. 651; State v. Swinburne, 324 S.W.2d 746 (Mo.1959). Cf. State v. Cerar, 60 Utah 208, 207 Pac. 597 (1922). State v. Obstein, 52 N.J. 516, 247 A.2d 5 (1968) holds that the privilege is violated by an order compelling a defendant to undergo examination when the defendant has raised no issue as to his mental state. This suggests that the court's earlier analysis in State v. Whitlow, 45 N.J. 3, 210 A.2d 763 (1965) rested in part at least on a waiver theory. See also United States v. Baird, 414 F.2d 700 (2d Cir. 1969), rejecting the *pro tanto waiver* theory of *Pope* in favor of a holding that a defendant's offer of expert opinion based upon his statements to the expert estopped him from objecting to an examination by a government expert for an analogous purpose and the introduction of the expert's testimony by the prosecution.

75. It is clear that due process prohibits the trial of an incompetent defendant. Pate v. Robinson, 383 U.S. 375 (1966).

76. The extent to which a state is constitutionally compelled to excuse an "insane" defendant from criminal liability is unclear. Compare Leland v. Oregon, 343 U.S. 790 (1952) and Powell v. Texas, 392 U.S. 514 (1968).

77. Commonwealth v. Anderson, 211 Pa.Super. 349, 236 A.2d 558 (1967) (competency determination "not criminal in nature"); People v. Esposito, 287 N.Y. 389, 39 N.E.2d 925, 929 (1942).

78. Statements made during examinations but found to be "voluntary" have been admitted. People v. Spencer, 60 Cal.2d 64, 31 Cal.Rptr. 782, 383 P.2d 134 (1963) cert. denied 377 U.S. 1007; Hall v. State, 209 Ark. 180, 189 S.W.2d 917 (1945).

79. In re Spencer, 63 Cal.2d 400, 46 Cal.Rptr. 753, 406 P.2d 33 (1965); State v. Whitlow, 45 N.J. 3, 210 A.2d 763 (1965). But see State v. Olson, 274 Minn. 225, 230, 143 N.W.2d 69, 72 (1966).

Supreme Court has gone further and, after holding that an accused could be required to give testimonial responses during a pre-trial psychiatric examination, declared that if it appears that any incriminating statements were in fact made the accused is entitled to a bifurcated trial in which the jury would decide the question of commission of the acts necessary to liability before it would hear evidence relating to mental condition.[80]

The third manner in which the privilege may be infringed in the psychiatric examination situation is the coercion and use of the accused's statements for purposes of establishing "sanity." The decisions generally assume, without satisfactory analysis, that the privilege does not prohibit reliance on the accused's statements by an expert witness in forming an opinion of sanity and testifying to it.[81] Nor does the privilege prohibit elicitation from the witness of the substance of such statements and reliance upon them by the trier of fact in determining the issue of sanity. Insofar as this conclusion rests upon an assumption that this use does not involve the danger of incrimination, it seems to have little support in the substantive criminal law which makes mental state as much a necessary element of liability as the proscribed act or omission. Perhaps the rule can be justified on a waiver theory, although the constitutional validity of requiring a waiver of the privilege as a condition of raising the issue of sanity is questionable. Finally, the holdings may be justified on the basis that the statements of the accused are nei-

ther elicited nor used in a "testimonial" manner,[82] although this analysis stretches the rationale for the "testimonial" limitation to its maximum.[83] Arguably the statements sought from the accused are not sought for their substantive truth but rather as "verbal acts" permitting a skilled clinician to draw from them inferences regarding the accused's state of mind. This is consistent with the "phenomenological" clinical approach of many psychological examiners in which the subject's perceptions rather than the objective accuracy of those perceptions are the working matter of the inquiry. Yet whether this analysis can pass muster is doubtful. Although this use may be made of the statements, substantive reliance may well also be placed upon the accused's own statements regarding his conscious thoughts at the time of the acts. Moreover, while a sophisticated clinical worker may adopt a phenomenological approach, whether a lay jury, even if carefully instructed, could be relied upon to consider the statements in this manner, is open to serious question.

Much analytical and practical confusion could be avoided if the relationship of the privilege to psychiatric examinations were recognized as requiring a specific exception to the protection afforded by the privilege. A limited exception, permitting the accused's statements to be elicited and used for purposes of determining his mental status at the time of trial and at the time of the alleged acts, would seem to be justified on a

---

80. State ex rel. LaFollette v. Raskin, 34 Wis.2d 607, 150 N.W.2d 318 (1968), noted in 19 Case W.Res. L.Rev. 382 (1968).

81. See, e. g., Parkin v. State, 238 So.2d 817, 821 (Fla.1970) ("Self-incrimination is not directly an issue in cases such as this, simply because the question to be resolved is not guilt or innocence, but the presence or absence of mental illness."); Jessner v. State, 202 Wis. 184, 231 N.W. 634 (1930), noted in 6 Wis.L.Rev. 184 (1931). Cf. United States v. Albright, 388 F.2d 719, 725 (4th Cir. 1968).

82. Note, Mental Examination of Defendants Who Plead Insanity: Problems of Self-Incrimination, 40 Temple L.Q. 366, 374–75 (1967); State v. Phillips, 245 Ore. 466, 422 P.2d 670 (1967); State v. Grayson, 239 N.C. 453, 80 S.E.2d 387 (1954).

83. Thornton v. Corcoran, 132 U.S.App.D.C. 232, 407 F.2d 695, 700 (1969): "[The argument that no evidence of a testimonial nature is extracted] can hardly do service in the context of a psychiatric examination . . . where the words of the accused are critically important in determining his mental condition."

policy basis.[84] The difficulties of the factual inquiry necessitated by the rule requiring competency to stand trial and the insanity defense, plus the limitations of psychological knowledge and techniques, dictate that if the law is to extend to the accused the opportunities to raise these matters that it may reasonably require in return that the accused assist in the difficult factual investigation, even at the expense of some interests protected by the privilege. Safeguards against abuse of the procedure, such as a bifurcated trial procedure in which the trier of fact would hear no admissions of the accused made during the examination as to the act until it had resolved the factual issue of whether the accused had in fact performed the actions necessary to liability, could reasonably be required.[85] This approach would focus attention on the underlying conflict of interests and would avoid the largely useless extended discussions found in many of the cases.[86]

84. See United States v. Albright, 388 F.2d 719, 724 (4th Cir. 1968), emphasizing the statutory right of an indigent defendant in federal court to state-provided psychiatric assistance and concluding that the maintenance of a "fair state-individual balance" required that the prosecution be permitted to examine the accused. See also Parkin v. State, 238 So.2d 817 (Fla.1970).

Judicial supervision of the examination would tend to diminish frustration of the basic values protected by the privilege.

85. See text at note 80, supra. In State v. Whitlow, 45 N.J. 3, 210 A.2d 763 (1965) the court went further and directed that during the compulsory psychiatric interview inquiry be made into the circumstances of the alleged offense only if an adequate psychiatric opinion could not be formed without the inquiry.

86. The problem of compelling compliance with a prosecution examiner is, of course, a difficult one. Compare French v. District Court, 153 Colo. 10, 384 P.2d 268 (1963) (trial court erred in striking the insanity defense of a defendant who refused to cooperate with examiners) with Parkin v. State, 238 So.2d 817 (Fla.1970) cert. denied 401 U.S. 974 (trial court did not err in ordering accused to cooperate in examination under treat of exclusion of evidence related to insanity defense).

135. The Privilege of a Witness: (a) Proceedings in Which the Privilege May be Invoked.[87]

The privilege of one not an accused is a privilege to be free from legal coercion imposed to compel an incriminating response to questions which may be put to the individual. Thus it is clear that the privilege extends to a party or witness in civil litigation,[88] not only during trial but in pretrial discovery proceedings,[89] a witness in a criminal proceeding,[90] a witness in a grand jury proceeding [91] or a legislative investigation,[92] and one who is subjected to police interrogation [93] or questioning by an administrative official or board.[94] When the coercion applied to com-

87. See generally 8 Wigmore, Evidence (McNaughton rev.) § 2252; 58 Am.Jur. Witnesses §§ 44, 45; C.J.S. Witnesses § 433; Dec.Dig. Witnesses ⊄293, 293½.

88. McCarthy v. Arndstein, 266 U.S. 34 (1924) (bankruptcy); Kendall v. Gore Properties, 98 U.S. App.D.C. 378, 236 F.2d 673 (1956); In re Sterling-Harris Ford, Inc., 315 F.2d 277 (7th Cir. 1963); Application of Leavitt, 174 Cal.App.2d 535, 345 P.2d 75 (1959).

89. Bradley v. O'Hare, 2 App.Div.2d 436, 156 N.Y.S. 2d 533 (1956) (refusal to respond to pre-trial order regarding production of books); Allred v. Graves, 261 N.C. 31, 134 S.E.2d 186 (1964).

90. See § 116, supra.

91. United States v. Pile, 256 F.2d 954 (7th Cir. 1958); Commonwealth v. Rhine, 303 S.W.2d 301 (Ky. 1957). See generally, Annot., 38 A.L.R.2d 225.

92. Quinn v. United States, 349 U.S. 155 (1955) (privilege invoked before subcommittee of House of Representative Committee on Unamerican Activities); United States v. Di Carlo, 102 F.Supp. 597 (N.D.Ohio, 1952); State v. Spindel, 24 N.J. 395, 132 A.2d 291 (1957) (answer elicited by Joint Legislative Committee to Study Wiretapping and the Unauthorized Recording of Speech not admissible in criminal proceeding). See Note, Applicability of Privilege Against Self-Incrimination to Legislative Investigations, 49 Colum.L.Rev. 87 (1949); Dec.Dig. Witnesses ⊄297(7).

93. Miranda v. Arizona, 384 U.S. 436 (1966).

94. In re Groban's Petition, 352 U.S. 330 (1957) (state fire marshal's investigation); Smith v. United States, 337 U.S. 137 (1949) (testimony given before an examiner of the Office of Price Administration under subpoena); Chapman v. Division of Employment Security of Department of Labor, 104 So.2d 201 (La.App.1958) (proceeding for un-

pel a response is not sanctioned by law, the privilege—which is a legal rule—is probably not applicable. The matter is relatively academic, as when the coercion being applied is extra-legal the availability or nonavailability of a legal privilege is unlikely to affect the subject of the coercion. But from an analytic sense, it is more appropriate to deal with these situations as questions of admissibility under the "voluntariness" rule.[95]

136. The Privilege of a Witness: (b) Manner of Invoking the Privilege.[96]

The privilege of one not an accused is a privilege to decline to respond to inquiries, not a prohibition against inquiries designed to elicit responses incriminating in nature. Because of this difference in the nature of the privilege of one not an accused, the manner of invoking it correspondingly differs from the manner of invoking the privilege of an accused. Thus by universal holding, one not an accused must submit to inquiry (including being sworn, if the inquiry is one conducted under oath) and may invoke the privilege only after the potentially incriminating question has been put. Moreover, invoking the privilege does not end the inquiry and the subject may be required to invoke it as to any or all of an extended line of questions.[97]

The rationale for requiring a witness to submit to questioning and to assert the privilege if he desires to invoke it is that the na-

ture of the privilege so requires. Since the privilege is applicable only if the specific response would come within the scope of protection and the witness is not the ultimate arbiter of whether this is the situation,[98] a decision on the propriety of invoking it cannot be made unless the question has been put and the witness has asserted his basis for refusal to answer. Of course, this procedure endangers to some extent the values which the privilege is designed to protect. Subjecting a witness to a series of questions to which he must respond by invoking the privilege is somewhat akin to the interrogation which the privilege has historically sought to protect against. Requiring that the witness make a question-by-question judgment on the legal necessity of responding creates a danger that the privilege will not be invoked because of confusion or exhaustion rather than the knowing and intentional decision not to invoke it required for a waiver of a constitutional right. Against these dangers, however, must be weighed the public interest in obtaining as much information as possible without directly infringing on the witness's protected rights. Moreover, where the purpose of the inquiry is not the taking of action against the subject of the inquiry, the danger of improper use of the inquiry is reduced. On balance, therefore, the policy factors support the imposition of a more stringent and complex procedure upon one not an accused who wishes to invoke the privilege.

137. The Privilege of a Witness: (c) Right to Counsel and to be Informed Regarding the Privilege.[99]

As one who is not the accused in a criminal proceeding is not entitled to be free from potentially self-incriminating interrogation, it might be expected that safeguards would be

---

employment compensation); Oleshko v. New York State Liquor Authority, 29 A.D.2d 84, 285 N.Y.S. 2d 696 (1967), aff'd, 21 N.Y.2d 788, 288 N.Y.S.2d 474, 235 N.E.2d 447 (1968).

95. See § 147, infra.

96. See generally 8 Wigmore, Evidence (McNaughton rev.) § 2268; 58 Am.Jur. Witnesses § 79; C.J.S. Witnesses § 452; Dec.Dig. Witnesses ☞307.

97. United States v. Luxenberg, 374 F.2d 241 (6th Cir. 1967); United States v. Harmon, 339 F.2d 354 (6th Cir. 1964) cert. denied 380 U.S. 944; People v. Austin, 159 Colo. 445, 412 P.2d 425 (1966); Shifflett v. State, 245 Md. 169, 225 A.2d 440 (1967); Royal v. State, 236 Md. 443, 204 A.2d 500 (1964); Hinds v. John Hancock Mutual Life Ins. Co., 155 Me. 349, 155 A.2d 721 (1959).

98. See § 139, infra.

99. See generally 8 Wigmore, Evidence (McNaughton rev.) § 2269; 58 Am.Jur. Witnesses § 80; C.J.S. Witnesses § 449; Dec.Dig. Witnesses ☞302.

erected to assure that during such interrogation the privilege was not endangered. This, however, has not been true. In what has traditionally been the leading case, In re Groban,[1] owners of premises destroyed by fire refused to appear as witnesses at a fire marshall's investigation unless their counsel was permitted to be present during the interrogation. The Supreme Court, over the vigorous dissent of four justices, affirmed the contempt incarceration of the witnesses in broad language:

> "Appellants here are witnesses from whom information was sought as to the cause of the fire. A witness before a grand jury cannot insist, as a matter of constitutional right, on being represented by his counsel, nor can a witness before other investigatory bodies. There is no more reason to allow the presence of counsel before a Fire Marshall trying in the public interest to determine the cause of a fire.[2]"

Thus the traditional position has been that one appearing as a witness, although he is entitled to invoke the privilege, is not entitled to a warning of the potentially incriminating nature of his statements, of his right to invoke the privilege, to the presence of counsel,[3] or even to consult with counsel who remains outside the room in which the testimony is taken when the proceeding, as a grand jury situation, is in secret.[4]

This approach by the courts quite clearly creates significant dangers to the privilege of the witness, especially when he appears before an investigatory body, such as a grand jury, that could conceivably have his criminal conviction as its objective. Not only is the witness subject to techniques of interrogation that may wear down his willingness to continue to invoke the privilege[5] but he may also fail because of ignorance or misunderstanding properly to invoke the privilege.[6] Moreover, the recognition of the danger posed to the privilege during police interrogation and the stringent protection afforded the subject of those proceedings[7] undermines the basic assumption of Groban that an "investigatory" proceeding is distinguishable from an accusatorial proceeding. Arguably the danger is even greater in nonpolice situations; unlike the police, grand juries and many administrative agencies can invoke legal coercion to compel answers to questions, thus recreating the very setting in which the privilege historically developed. In recognition of these dangers, the case law regarding the rights of a witness called to appear before a grand jury is beginning to recognize that certain procedural protections are essential, although there is as yet little indication that witnesses have the right to the continual presence and advice of counsel while testifying. When the witness is called not for general information purposes but because the investigation has to some extent focused upon him as a potential defendant, the case law suggests that he is entitled to a warning of

1. 352 U.S. 330 (1957).

2. Id. at 332–33. Justice Black, joined by Justice Warren, Douglas, and Brennan, dissented, emphasizing the danger posed to the privilege by a secret inquisition and the danger that without counsel a witness may be "coerced, tricked or confused . . . into making statements which may be untrue or may hide the truth by creating misleading impressions." Id. at 341.

3. United States v. Levinson, 405 F.2d 971 (6th Cir. 1968) cert. denied 395 U.S. 906; United States v. Corallo, 281 F.Supp. 24 (S.D.N.Y. 1968); State v. Stallings, 154 Conn. 272, 224 A.2d 718 (1966). It has also been held by several courts that the Miranda warnings are not required. United States v. DiMichele, 375 F.2d 959 (3d Cir. 1967) cert. denied 389 U.S. 838; State ex rel. Lowe v. Nelson, 202 So.2d 232 (Fla.App.1967) aff'd 210 So.2d 197 (Fla. 1968). Cf. In re Weiss, 279 F.Supp. 857 (S.D.N.Y. 1967).

4. Martin v. State, 208 So.2d 630 (Fla.App.1968).

5. See State v. Von Reeden, 9 Ariz.App. 190, 450 P.2d 702 (1969).

6. See People v. Laino, 10 N.Y.2d 161, 176 N.E.2d 571, 218 N.Y.S.2d 647 (1961) appeal dismissed 374 U.S. 104.

7. See §§ 151–153, infra.

the nature of the interrogation, an explanation of his rights, and the advice of counsel.[8] This "focusing" test seems to be a reasonable compromise between according all witnesses full procedural protection despite the lack of any indication of the need for protection and accepting the fiction that the rights of a witness in what is labeled an investigatory proceeding are not significantly endangered so as to require protection.[9]

Where the witness appears not in an investigatory proceeding in regard to which he is a potential subject but rather in litigation to which he is not a party, the danger posed to his privilege is arguably less and the cases indicate a more relaxed attitude toward requiring that he be fully informed of his rights. Since in most cases the purpose of compelling testimony will not be the conviction of the witness but rather the accurate resolution of factual issues in which he has no direct stake, there is less incentive to apply to him the type of pressure against which the privilege guards. Apparently for this reason, the case law speaks of the trial court's discretion to inform the witness of his privilege when he takes the stand or when the danger of incrimination becomes apparent.[10] The trend, insofar as one is discernable, is towards imposing a duty on the trial court to advise the witness of the potentially incriminating nature of his answers and of his right to decline to answer them; [11] in view of the personal nature of the privilege, however, violation of this duty is no basis for complaint by either party to the case.[12]

8. Jones v. United States, 119 U.S.App.D.C. 284, 342 F.2d 863 (1964) (taking of uncounseled defendant who had already been bound over for trial by magistrate before grand jury condemned in exercise of supervisory power); Mattox v. Carson, 295 F. Supp. 1054 (M.D.Fla.1969) rev'd on other grounds 424 F.2d 202 (*Miranda* warnings essential, and waivers signed without advice of right to be advised by counsel are invalid); United States v. Fruchtman, 282 F.Supp. 534 (N.D.Ohio 1968) (witness, because of intensity and nature of interrogation, was "virtually in the position of a defendant" and therefore entitled to suppression of evidence received in absence of warnings); Sheridan v. Garrison, 273 F.Supp. 673 (E.D.La.1967) rev'd on other grounds 415 F.2d 699 (*Miranda* fully applicable, and it is not sufficient simply to have counsel waiting outside grand jury room); State v. De Cola, 33 N.J. 335, 164 A.2d 729 (1960) (witness whose criminal liability is the object of a grand jury inquiry must be informed of his privilege to withhold evidence tending to his own incrimination); People v. Ianniello, 21 N.Y.2d 418, 288 N.Y.S.2d 462, 235 N.E. 2d 439 (1968) cert. denied 393 U.S. 827 (witness should be given opportunity to consult with counsel); State v. Ruggerie, 19 Utah 2d 216, 429 P.2d 969 (1967) (one being investigated by grand jury cannot be interrogated without advising him of his rights). See generally Dec.Dig. Grand Jury ⊕35, 37; Mechbesher, Right to Counsel Before a Grand Jury, 41 F.R.D. 189 (1967); Annot., 5 A.L.R.2d 1407.

9. The remedy for the violation of rights before the grand jury would seem to be the suppression of the evidence obtained by violation of those rights rather than barring of the prosecution or even quashing of the indictment. United States v. Blue, 384 U.S. 251 (1966). This has been characterized as leaving one improperly interrogated "without an effective remedy." 8 Cipes, Moore's Federal Practice ¶ 6.6[1], p. 6–32 (1965).

10. E. g., Commonwealth v. Slaney, 345 Mass. 135, 185 N.E.2d 919 (1962) (judge has discretion *sua sponte* to advise witness of privilege when reasonable ground to apprehend danger appears, and practice of exercising discretion is "commendable"); State v. Ceaser, 249 La. 435, 187 So.2d 432 (1966) (witness, who had privately retained counsel not present at trial, did not have right to be advised by trial judge at trial of codefendant that he had a right to consult with an attorney before testifying). The appellate cases suggest that while practice varies trial judges liberally exercise the discretion in favor of witnesses. People v. Cooper, 268 Cal.App.2d 34, 73 Cal.Rptr. 608 (1968) (appointment of attorney to advise 15 year old companion of defendant who had been called as defense witness not abuse of discretion); Forrester v. State, 224 Md. 337, 167 A.2d 878 (1961) (judge agreed to inform witness of privilege if any question asked might tend to incriminate her).

11. Salgado v. Gardner, 265 F.Supp. 894 (D.Puerto Rico 1967) (social security examiner had duty to advise claimant as to incriminating nature of statements and her right to decline to answer when he became aware of nature of answers); Commonwealth ex rel. Esterline v. Esterline, 181 Pa.Super. 532, 124 A.2d 133 (1956).

12. Informing the witness of his rights in the presence of the jury, of course, creates a danger that the jury will impermissably infer from the situation that the testimony not given would have been unfavorable to one party to the litigation. See § 120, supra; State v. Cassatly, 93 N.J.Super. 111, 225 A.2d 141 (1966) (informing witnesses not improper in view of curative instructions).

138. The Privilege of a Witness: (d) Definition of Incriminatory Response.[13]

The requirement that a demanded response be "incriminatory" has not been construed strictly by the courts. The statements demanded, for example, need not be such as would themselves support a criminal conviction, and it is sufficient if they would furnish a link in the chain of circumstantial evidence necessary for conviction.[14] Moreover, it is not necessary that the witness anticipate that the responses themselves be used as evidence even in this limited fashion. It is enough if the responses would provide a lead to a source of evidence which might be used.[15] This attitude, of course, is consistent with the proposition that the answer need only have a *tendency* to incriminate. It is also sufficient, though the response itself creates no significant danger of incrimination, that it may operate as a waiver of the privilege in regard to further questions which may create such a danger; [16] the questions asked cannot be considered in isolation and must be viewed together with other aspects of the inquiry.[17]

The scope of what is incriminating as thus evolved is illustrated by Malloy v. Hogan.[18] Malloy, convicted in 1959 of a gambling charge, was required to appear before a grand jury investigating gambling activities. When asked about the activities out of which his prior conviction had grown, he claimed his privilege. The Connecticut state courts overruled this claim on the ground that he was adequately protected by the double jeopardy rule and a one-year statute of limitations. The Supreme Court reversed on the ground that the prosecution desired ultimately to elicit from Malloy the names of those engaged with him in the illegal venture which formed the basis for the 1959 conviction. Under these circumstances, the court held, Malloy might fear that if these individuals were still engaged in illegal activities, the disclosures called for by the questions might furnish a link in a chain of evidence connecting him with more recent crimes for which he still might be prosecuted.[19]

139. The Privilege of a Witness: (e) Determination Whether a Specific Response Would be Incriminatory.[20]

Determining whether a specific demanded response would be incriminatory and thus within the protection of the privilege presents a more difficult problem than the general definition of incriminating responses. In some cases, of course, the matter is clear, as the question on its face calls for an incriminating response.[21] The difficulty centers around questions which are on their face innocent, as, for example, the question, "Do you know John Bergoti?" [22] When a witness invokes the privilege in response to such a question, these questions are raised: (a) who decides whether the response is incrim-

---

13. See generally 8 Wigmore, Evidence (McNaughton rev.) § 2260; 58 Am.Jur. Witnesses § 57; C.J.S. Witnesses § 436; Dec.Dig. Witnesses ⚹297(1), (2).

14. Blau v. United States, 340 U.S. 159, 161 (1950).

15. Counselman v. Hitchcock, 142 U.S. 547, 564 (1892) ([the defect in the immunity statute at issue was that] "it could not, and would not, prevent the use of his testimony to search out other testimony to be used in evidence . . ."); Hashagen v. United States, 283 F.2d 345, 348 (9th Cir. 1960); In re Levinson, 219 F.Supp. 589 (S.D.Cal.1963).

16. Malloy v. Hogan, 378 U.S. 1, 14 (1964).

17. United States v. Gordon, 236 F.2d 916 (2d Cir. 1956).

18. 378 U.S. 1 (1964).

19. Id. at 13.

20. See generally 8 Wigmore, Evidence (McNaughton rev.) § 2260; 58 Am.Jur. Witnesses §§ 81, 82; C.J.S. Witnesses §§ 453, 454; Annot., 88 A.L.R.2d 463; Annot., 51 A.L.R.2d 1178. Cf. Annot., 19 A.L.R.2d 388 (right to invoke privilege in regard to relationship to organization); Dec.Dig. Witnesses ⚹297(10), 307, 308.

21. "Did you bribe Officer Smith?" would be such a question. In re Boiardo, 34 N.J. 599, 170 A.2d 816 (1961).

22. See Malloy v. Hogan, 378 U.S. 1, 11–14 (1964).

inatory; (b) by what criterion is the propriety of the witness's invocation of the privilege determined; and (c) procedurally, who bears the burden of proof and the burden of making a factual record on which the issue is determined?

As to the first, the cases accept the proposition that the witness himself is not the final arbiter of whether his invocation is proper. Rather, the court itself has the obligation to determine whether the refusal to answer is in fact justifiable under the privilege.[23] Indeed, a contrary view would subordinate the effective operation of the judicial system to the desires of witnesses. The significance of this position, however, is clearly related to the second and third issues, as the effectiveness of granting the court authority to decide the matter depends in practice upon the criterion by which it decides the matter and the extent to which it can obtain a factual basis on which to make the decision.

As to the second question, the traditional statement of the criterion has been that "the Court must see, from the circumstances of the case, and the nature of the evidence which the witness is called to give, that there is reasonable ground to apprehend danger to the witness from his being compelled to answer."[24] Under this test, it seems that the court must find reasonable ground to believe that the witness is criminally liable and reasonable ground to believe that the response would at least lead to a link in the chain of evidence necessary for conviction. Thus a finding that the danger of a criminal prosecution is not "real and appreciable" requires the conclusion that invoking the privilege to

protect against the danger is improper. Moreover, a trial judge is not limited to the record in the case in which the privilege is invoked, but may consider newspaper reports,[25] other proceedings[26] and general knowledge concerning the activities of human beings.[27]

On the third question, the traditional view has been that the witness, in order to avoid liability for contempt on the basis of his refusal to answer,[28] may be required to provide sufficient information on which the court may find that a real danger of incrimination exists.[29] This limited requirement of disclosure as a condition of invoking the privilege clearly poses some danger to the interests the privilege is designed to protect. The classic defense of it was stated by Judge Learned Hand: "The . . . questions were on their face innocent, and it lay upon the defendant to show that the answers might criminate him. . . . Obviously a witness may not be compelled to do more than show that the answer is likely to be danger-

22. Hoffman v. United States, 341 U.S. 479, 486 (1951); Hashagen v. United States, 283 F.2d 345 (9th Cir. 1960); In re Newton, 12 Ohio App.2d 191, 231 N.E.2d 880 (1967); In re Petty, 18 Utah 2d 320, 422 P.2d 659 (1967).

24. Mason v. United States, 244 U.S. 362, 365 (1917). The phrase was initially used by Cockburn, C. J. in The Queen v. Boyes, 1 B. & S. 311, 330, 121 Eng.Rep. 730, 738 (Q.B.1861).

25. Hoffman v. United States, 341 U.S. 479 (1951); In re Portell, 245 F.2d 183 (7th Cir. 1957).

26. In Young v. Knight, 329 S.W.2d 195 (Ky.1959) the court relied upon the witness's earlier statement before a grand jury to hold that her testimony would show only presence at the scene of the crime, a circumstance that would not give rise to criminal liability. See also Hoffman v. United States, 341 U.S. 479 (1951) (judge who had impaneled grand jury should have considered the grand jury's purpose as set out in his charge to them.)

27. Hoffman v. United States, 341 U.S. 479 (1951) (judge should have considered that the chief occupation of some individuals involves evasion of federal laws).

28. See note 32, infra.

29. Presta v. Owsley, 345 S.W.2d 649 (Mo.App.1961) (witness has burden of proof of issue of incriminatory nature of answer); In re Boyd, 36 N.J. 285, 176 A.2d 793 (1963) ("naked assertion of possible incrimination by a mere statement of the abstract proposition" did not prevent contempt citation); In re Boiardo, 34 N.J. 599, 170 A.2d 816 (1961) ("except where the question itself contains the threat . . . a refusal to answer must be supplemented by a statement of the area of nature of the criminal exposure which is feared").

ous to him, else he would be forced to disclose those very facts which the privilege protects. Logically, indeed, he is boxed in a paradox, for he must prove the criminatory character of what it is his privilege to protect because it is criminatory. The only practicable solution is to be content with the door's being set a little ajar, and while at times this no doubt partially destroys the privilege . . . nothing better is available." [30] Unless a minimum disclosure of the circumstances is compelled, the argument is, the court cannot exercise its function of determining the appropriateness of the witness's invocation of the privilege. For example, a witness subpoenaed to produce certain records of a travel agency can be required to testify as to whether the agency is a partnership because this information is essential to determining the propriety of the attempt to invoke the privilege.[31] The dilemma of a witness is best illustrated by those cases in which a witness believes that an accurate response would be inconsistent with earlier testimony and tend to bring about a perjury prosecution based upon the earlier statement. To require any explanation, of course, would alert authorities to the possibility of perjury and perhaps stimulate an investigation that would lead to prosecution and conviction. The solution adopted by one court—to require the witness to answer but to exclude the answers from any subsequent perjury prosecution—not only leaves the door a little ajar but may substantially destroy the protection of the privilege.[32]

These traditional formulations of answers to the second and third questions respecting the determination of the propriety of a witness's invocation of the privilege have been severely shaken, however, and it is doubtful whether they accurately state existing law. The leading case is Hoffman v. United States,[33] in which the petitioner, subpoenaed before a federal grand jury, declined to answer any questions regarding recent contacts with one William Weisberg, a witness who had not responded to a subpoena issued by the grand jury. The Court of Appeals held that there had been an insufficient showing of the relationship between possible responses and criminal liability; the Supreme Court reversed. "To sustain the privilege," the Court stated, "it need only be evident from the implications of the question, in the setting in which it was asked, that a responsive answer to the question or an explanation of why it cannot be answered might be dangerous because injurious disclosure could result." [34] After examining the circumstances which the trial judge should have considered—including the purpose of the grand jury investigation, Hoffman's admitted long acquaintance with Weisberg, general knowledge that the chief occupation of some individuals is criminal activity and that one person with a criminal record (which Hoffman had) called before a grand jury might be hiding another person

---

30. United States v. Weisman, 111 F.2d 260, 261–62 (2d Cir. 1940) (Hand, J.).

31. Nitti v. United States, 336 F.2d 576 (10th Cir. 1964).

32. In re Boiardo, 34 N.J. 599, 170 A.2d 816 (1961); State v. De Cola, 33 N.J. 335, 164 A.2d 729 (1960). The court has indicated it would apply the same approach to other situations in which the witness refused to explain his basis for claiming the privilege, i. e., require him to answer but require the exclusion of his responses from any criminal prosecution that might result. In re Boyd, 36 N.J. 285, 176 A.2d 793 (1962).

See the discussion of immunity statutes, § 143, infra.

33. 341 U.S. 479 (1951). The suggestion that *Hoffman* indicated a liberalization of the definition of incriminating response is strengthened by the Court's subsequent per curiam reversals of several other decisions of the courts of appeal. Simpson v. United States, 355 U.S. 7 (1957), rev'g Wollam v. United States, 244 F.2d 212 (9th Cir. 1957), MacKenzie v. United States, 244 F.2d 712 (9th Cir. 1957), and Simpson v. United States, 241 F.2d 222 (9th Cir. 1957); Singleton v. United States, 343 U.S. 944, rev'g 193 F.2d 464 (3d Cir. 1952). See the discussion in Shendal v. United States, 312 F. 2d 564 (9th Cir. 1963).

34. Hoffman v. United States, 341 U.S. 479, 486–87 (1951).

also called—the Court concluded that "in this setting it was not *'perfectly clear*, from a careful consideration of all the circumstances in the case, that the witness is mistaken, and that the answer[s] *cannot possibly* have such tendency' to incriminate." [35] The Court's first statement seems consistent with traditional doctrine—unless the court can conclude that further inquiry would create a danger of injurious disclosure it cannot sustain the claim of privilege, and if this conclusion cannot be drawn from circumstances already available for scrutiny the witness has the obligation to bring the necessary circumstances to the attention of the court. The second statement, on the other hand, indicates that the court may not refuse to sustain the privilege unless it can conclude that the witness's invocation is improper; this, of course, reallocates the burden and suggests that, in the absence of a sufficient factual basis for the conclusion, the claim of privilege must be allowed.

A number of courts have adopted the approach suggested by the second statement in *Hoffman*.[36] Perhaps the question is at least partly academic; there are unlikely to be many situations in which there are no circumstances from which the court can draw its conclusions, so the burden of producing a minimal factual showing may be unimportant. Given an adequate opportunity to deal with the circumstances, however, the trend seems to be towards accepting the more important suggestion of the second statement in *Hoffman* that the privilege when claimed by a witness must be sustained unless a finding of fact can be made that it is "perfectly clear" that the requested response "cannot possibly" have a tendency to incriminate.

If taken to the extreme, this approach is unacceptable. In the sterile situation in which an ordinary witness simply invokes the privilege, serious impairment of the judi-

---

35. Id. at 488. The phrase was taken from the following passage in Temple v. Commonwealth, 75 Va. 892, 898 (1881):

"[W]here the witness on oath declares his belief that the answer to the question would criminate, or tend to criminate him, the court cannot compel him to answer, unless it is *perfectly clear*, from a careful consideration of all the circumstances in the case, that the witness is mistaken, and that the answer *cannot possibly* have such tendency."

36. In re U. S. Hoffman Can Corp., 373 F.2d 622 (3d Cir. 1967); United States v. Chandler, 380 F.2d 993 (2d Cir. 1967); American Cyanamid Co. v. Sharff, 309 F.2d 790, 794 (3d Cir. 1962); United States v. Gordon, 236 F.2d 916 (2d Cir. 1956); Application of Leavitt, 174 Cal.App.2d 535, 345 P.2d 75 (1959); Reynolds v. Pope, 28 Conn.Sup. 59, 249 A.2d 260 (1968); People v. Joseph, 14 Mich.App. 494, 165 N.W.2d 633 (1968), aff'd in part, rev'd in part 384 Mich. 24, 179 N.W.2d 383 ("it must be perfectly clear that the questions asked could not possibly have elicited testimony incriminating to the witness"); Murphy v. Commonwealth, 354 Mass. 81, 235 N.E.2d 552 (1968) (record inadequate to support conclusion that answers could not possibly lead to injurious disclosures); Commonwealth v. Baker, 348 Mass. 60, 201 N.E.2d 829 (1964), overruling Sandrelli v. Commonwealth, 342 Mass. 129, 172 N.E.2d 449 (1961) to the extent that it might require a lesser proof; Layman v. Webb, 350 P.2d 323 (Okl.Cr.1960); Commonwealth v. Hawthorne, 428 Pa. 260, 236 A.2d 519 (1968); Commonwealth v. Carrera, 424 Pa. 551, 227 A.2d 627 (1967); Hummell v. Superior Court, 100 R.I. 54, 211 A.2d 272 (1965) ("In our opinion [*Hoffman*] makes clear the duty of the court to refrain from placing upon the witness the burden of establishing the incriminating nature of responses to the questions by making disclosures that in themselves would be incriminating"). Compare Gambale v. Commonwealth, 355 Mass. 394, 245 N.E.2d 246 (1969) cert. denied 396 U.S. 881 (employee of club who was present at stabbing and admitted striking victim could be compelled to testify to what he observed at the scene of the stabbing, because "the questions . . . were not accusatory and did not implicate him as a participant" and "mere presence at [the scene of the crime] . . . is not enough to allow a claim of privilege."). In regard to a subpoena *duces tecum*, see United States v. Cogan, 257 F.Supp. 170 (S.D.N.Y.1966). The Third Circuit set out a somewhat different test in United States v. Coffey, 198 F.2d 438, 440 (3d Cir. 1952), when it indicated that it is enough to justify sustaining a claim of the privilege "(1) that the trial court be shown by argument how conceivably a prosecutor . . . might proceed step by step to link the witness with some crime . . ., and (2) that this suggested course and scheme of linkage not seem incredible in the circumstances of the particular case." In this view, the burden on the witness invoking the privilege seems to be one of argument rather than factual proof.

cial process would result from requiring the court, on this basis alone, to forego his testimony unless the party seeking the evidence establishes with perfect clarity the impossibility of any tendency to incriminate. On the other hand, where circumstances cast some doubt upon this impossibility, it would seem proper to sustain the privilege in the absence of a reliable factual basis excluding the danger. Perhaps the best approach would be to require the court to make the factual finding suggested by the second statement in *Hoffman* once there is some indication that a danger exists. In most cases, the nature of the question and the circumstances would be sufficient to raise this indication. Only where no reasonable man would see any possibility that the response would tend to incriminate would the witness be required to answer in the absence of his production of circumstances indicating a danger of incrimination. Whenever this indication exists, the burden would be on anyone seeking the testimony to establish with perfect clarity that the response would not possibly have a tendency to incriminate. This rule has been applied when one seeking the testimony of a reluctant witness argues that the statute of limitations has run.[37] On appeal, of course, any finding of this kind would call for at least the support in the record required for any other factual finding related to important constitutional rights.[38]

140. The Privilege of a Witness: (f) "Waiver" by Disclosure of Incriminating Facts.[39]

The accused in a criminal proceeding by the mere act of testifying forfeits his privilege to a significant extent.[40] This rule obviously cannot hold true in regard to one not an accused, as such a person has no privilege to decline to testify and therefore would be in effect precluded from ever invoking the privilege. On the other hand, after a witness has revealed a certain amount of information, requiring him to make further disclosure may not significantly endanger the interests which the privilege protects. When, however, does the witness reach the point at which he may no longer invoke the privilege?

The leading case is Rogers v. United States[41] in which petitioner had testified before a grand jury to having held the office of Treasurer of the Communist Party and to having had possession of its membership lists and books until January of 1948, at which time she turned them over to another. When asked the identity of the person to whom she turned them over, she declined to answer. Affirming a sentence for contempt, the Supreme Court found that in view of her prior testimony, petitioner was not justified in declining to reveal the name of the person to whom the documents had been given, relying upon the well-accepted rule that where incriminating facts have been revealed without claiming the privilege, the privilege cannot be invoked to avoid disclosure of the de-

37. United States v. Goodman, 289 F.2d 256 (4th Cir. 1961) (remanding to give government opportunity to prove that no prosecution was begun within the period); O'Neil v. O'Neil, 55 App.D.C. 40, 299 F. 914 (1924); Husband v. Wife, 201 A.2d 171 (Del.Super.Ct.1964); Lamson v. Boyden, 160 Ill. 613, 43 N.E. 781 (1896).

38. Murphy v. Commonwealth, 354 Mass. 81, 235 N.E.2d 552 (1968). Arguably a different approach should be taken when one party appeals on the basis of an allegedly erroneous grant of the privilege. Because of the personal nature of the privilege, neither party has basis for complaint when the privilege is erroneously denied a witness, § 120, supra, although this is not always recognized. E. g., State v. McLaughlin, 73 Wash.2d 247, 437 P.2d 902 (1968). In accordance with regular rules of ap-

pellate review, it would seem appropriate to require the complaining party to carry the burden of establishing the impropriety of the trial court's granting of the claim as well as the prejudicial nature of this action to his own cause.

39. See generally 8 Wigmore, Evidence (McNaughton rev.) § 2276(b) (1); Note, Waiver of the Privilege Against Self-Incrimination, 14 Stan L.Rev. 811 (1962); 58 Am.Jur. Witnesses §§ 95, 99, 100; C.J.S. Witnesses § 456; Dec.Dig. Witnesses ⊕305(1).

40. See § 132, supra.

41. 340 U.S. 367 (1951).

tails. But this holding, the Court made clear, did not rest upon a "waiver" as the term is generally used. Although the initial incriminating testimony may be accurately labeled a waiver, the duty to fully disclose details rests not upon an intentional relinquishment of a known right not to do so, but rather upon the circumstance that, in view of the testimony already given pursuant to a waiver,[42] the further information demanded would not be additionally incriminating within the meaning of the privilege. Thus, as to each "detail" requested, the court must address itself not to the witness's intent to relinquish the right to decline to testify concerning it but rather to the question whether, in view of the testimony already given, the disclosure of the detail demanded presents "a reasonable danger of further incrimination in light of all the circumstances, including any previous disclosures."[43]

Following the *Rogers* test and the generally liberalized approach of the Supreme Court towards the privilege, lower courts have tended to find relatively few situations in which a witness may be compelled to continue with his testimony.[44] This trend has

been reinforced by holdings that a person who testifies does not subject himself to a duty to respond to questions as to separate crimes unrelated to his direct, sought only for purposes of impeachment.[45]

A special problem arises when a witness whose testimony is potentially damaging to a criminal defendant invokes the privilege on cross-examination. In such a situation, severe danger is posed to the defendant's Sixth Amendment right to effective confrontation of witnesses presented against him.[46] The defendant's remedy depends upon the extent to which the inability to test the witness's testimony is affected.[47] If the invocation of

---

256 F.2d 654 (8th Cir. 1958) (testimony by witness that "I am not guilty of a crime so far as I know" did not forfeit right to decline to testify as to details of transaction allegedly giving rise to offense). Compare People v. Esse, 8 Mich.App. 362, 154 N.W.2d 545 (1967) (accomplice not on trial who testified to being with the accused at the scene of the crime at the time it was committed should not have been permitted to decline to answer further question); In re Sugar Creek Local School District, 185 N.E.2d 809 (Ohio Common Pleas 1962) (when witness testifies that he voted and it is shown that his vote was illegal, he may not invoke the privilege as a basis for declining to testify for whom he voted).

45. See § 42, n. 32, supra.

46. Pointer v. Texas, 380 U.S. 400 (1965) (admission into evidence at trial of transcript of testimony taken at a preliminary hearing at which the accused lacked counsel and therefore was unable effectively to cross-examine constituted a denial of right to confrontation).

Other aspects of claims of the privilege by witnesses are discussed in § 120, supra.

47. For full discussions of this matter, see Coil v. United States, 343 F.2d 573 (8th Cir. 1965) cert. denied 382 U.S. 821; United States v. Cardillo, 316 F.2d 606 (2d Cir. 1963) cert. denied 375 U.S. 822. See also Fountain v. United States, 384 F.2d 624, 628 (5th Cir. 1967) cert. denied 390 U.S. 1005 ("The distinction is generally drawn between invoking the privilege as to 'collateral matters', not requiring the striking of direct testimony, and invoking it as to 'direct' matters. . . . But the line between 'direct' and 'collateral' is not clear, and the question in each case must finally be whether defendant's inability to make the inquiry created a substantial danger of prejudice by depriving him of the ability to test the truth of the witness's direct testimony."); Smith v. United States, 331 F.2d 265 (8th Cir. 1964) cert. denied 379 U.S. 824.

---

42. The initial testimony, of course, must be a voluntary and knowing relinquishment of the right to decline to testify. United States v. Lyon, 397 F.2d 505 (7th Cir. 1968) cert. denied 393 U.S. 846 (testimony given under mistaken impression that immunity had been granted was not "waiver"); Gallegos v. People, 157 Colo. 484, 403 P.2d 864, 870 (1965) cert. denied 383 U.S. 971 (dictum) ("waiver" requires knowledge of testimonial privilege and willingness to testify notwithstanding its protection).

43. Rogers v. United States, 340 U.S. 367, 374 (1951).

44. Shendal v. United States, 312 F.2d 564 (9th Cir. 1963) (witness who testified that he made a "collection" for gamblers did not thereby lose right to decline to reveal amount of money or to whom payment was made, as to do so "might provide a link not already provided"); Hashagen v. United States, 283 F.2d 345 (9th Cir. 1960) (witness who testified to having received jewelry from one Packer could decline to testify as to her ownership of it or whether she had seen it before, but could be required to respond to whether a specific other witness was Packer); Isaacs v. United States,

the privilege leaves a significant portion of the witness's testimony insulated from cross-examination, thereby creating a substantial danger of prejudice, the defendant is entitled at least to have the untested portion of the testimony struck. Where the restriction of cross examination does not have as serious an effect, the matter may be cured by instruction to the jury, cautioning them to consider the testimony in light of its insulation from cross-examination.

Waiver of the privilege by one not an accused extends, as does the waiver of the privilege of an accused, throughout the proceeding in which it is made but not beyond to a separate and independent proceeding. In regard to the privilege of the witness, however, there is more ambiguity as to what constitutes a separate and independent proceeding, primarily in regard to grand jury proceedings. Traditionally the grand jury proceeding has been regarded as an informing and accusing process in contrast to the judicial trial on the merits, with the result that a witness who has testified to certain matters before the grand jury could decline to testify to them at the trial.[48] The current validity of this rule has been thrown into doubt, however, by a recent decision of the Court of Appeals of the District of Columbia holding that "where a nonindicted witness has waived his Fifth Amendment privilege by testifying before a grand jury voluntarily and with knowledge of his privilege, his waiver extends to a subsequent trial based on an indictment returned by the grand jury that heard his testimony." [49] This holding was supported with several arguments: (a) requiring the second testimony would pose no danger of additional "legal detriment"; (b) permitting a witness to invoke the privilege might place an undue burden on the prosecution, which may have based its entire preparation on the witness's apparent willingness to testify; and (c) the privilege of a witness is similar to the physician-patient privilege or the husband-wife privilege, and ceases to serve its function when the privileged information has been revealed by the holder of the privilege. All three arguments are subject to question. While in theory a witness may be subjected to no additional legal detriment, there is a reasonable possibility that in the process of rigorous examination and cross-examination he may make further damaging admissions because of confusion or excitement. As a practical matter, extending the waiver to trial testimony creates a danger of greater legal detriment. Moreover, if the waiver is given this additional scope, the result may be to discourage witnesses from waiving the privilege before the grand jury, thus depriving the prosecution not only of trial testimony but of the investigation assistance that grand jury testimony provides. Finally, the privilege against self-incrimination is not analogous to the privileges protecting certain confidential communications. The purpose of the latter is to preserve socially desirable relationships by assuring those entering into the relationships of the right to exercise the option of maintaining secrecy in the relationships. The

48. In re Neff, 206 F.2d 149 (3d Cir. 1953) (testimony before grand jury does not constitute waiver of privilege at trial because grand jury proceeding is an "informing or accusing" process rather than a judicial trial, and therefore a separate proceeding); United States v. Malone, 111 F.Supp. 37 (N.D.Cal.1953); Galloway v. Commonwealth, 374 S.W.2d 835 (Ky. 1964). Cf. Commonwealth v. Fisher, 189 Pa.Super. 13, 149 A.2d 666 (1959) rev'd on other grounds 398 Pa. 237, 157 A.2d 207 (1960) (statement to investigating officers did not deprive witness of right to decline to testify as to same facts at trial); United States v. Miranti, 253 F.2d 135 (2d Cir. 1958) (defendant's second appearance before same grand jury was not the "same proceeding" as first appearance, where the appearances were a year apart and the defendant had, in the interim, been convicted for offenses related to disclosures during the first appearance). See Annot., 36 A.L.R.2d 1403. Cf. Annot., 72 A.L.R.2d 830 (waiver by testimony in civil proceeding).

49. Ellis v. United States, 135 U.S.App.D.C. 35, 416 F.2d 791, 805 (1969).

privilege against compulsory self-incrimination seeks to preserve no such relationship but rather protects against procedures which pose dangers of abuse and violation of human dignity. Where the state seeks information and the subject resists with vigor which might reasonably be expected of one fearing criminal conviction, these dangers exist, whether or not there has been a prior disclosure. Nor does the rationale of the "waiver" rule dictate this extension. Underlying the rule is the policy against permitting a trier of fact to consider testimony not subjected to the normal devices used to assure accuracy. Where the witness is being compelled to testify before a different trier of fact concerned with a different determination, there has not been the one-sided presentation that justifies compelling further disclosure. In view of the dangers posed to the interests protected by the privilege and the lack of a justification for expanding the waiver rule to cover this situation, disclosure of information before a grand jury should not constitute a forfeiture of the right to invoke the privilege as to the same testimony at the trial.

141. Agreement to Waive the Privilege.[50]

It is clear from the previous discussion that an accused forfeits his privilege to a significant extent by testifying in his own behalf [51] and that one not an accused by testifying to incriminating matters loses the right under certain circumstances to decline to elaborate on those or related matters.[52] But may one agree in advance to forego the protection of the privilege and later be held to that promise? Few discussions of the matter are satisfactorily conclusive, but the Supreme

Court has recently drastically reduced the potential effectiveness of any such contractual commitment.

Wigmore [53] takes the position that a contract, either expressed or implied, to waive the privilege is if otherwise enforcible binding upon the party who agrees to waive his privilege. While the contract will not be specifically enforced (i.e., the party will not be held in contempt for refusal to testify) unless there is also a fiduciary duty or some other important public policy involved,[54] it will be given effect in determining rights between the parties to the agreement.[55] Little authority is cited, although Wigmore's position is more lenient than that of the Uniform Rules, which state that one who would otherwise have a privilege "has no such privilege" if he has contracted with anyone not to claim it.[56]

The effectiveness of any agreement of this nature respecting a constitutional privilege was minimized by the Supreme Court in Stev-

---

50. See generally 8 Wigmore, Evidence (McNaughton rev.) § 2275(a); Boudin, The Constitutional Privilege in Operation, 12 Lawyers Guild Rev. 128, 139–40 (1952).

51. § 132, supra.

52. § 140, supra.

53. 8 Wigmore, Evidence (McNaughton rev.) § 2275 (a).

54. Probably the leading case for this proposition is United States v. Field, 193 F.2d 92 (2d Cir. 1952) cert. dismissed 342 U.S. 908. Appellants were trustees of a bail fund which had furnished bail for the unsuccessful petitioners in Dennis v. United States, 341 U.S. 494 (1950). When four of the petitioners did not appear to commence service of their sentence, their bail was declared forfeited, and the trustees were examined by the court and by a grand jury, during which they invoked their privilege in response to questions relevant to the whereabouts of the fugitives. In affirming contempt convictions, the Second Circuit reasoned that by assuming the position of bondsmen, the trustees had lost the right to invoke the privilege in regard to these matters. The Court seems to find an implied term of the bail contract with this effect. Boudin, supra n. 50, severely criticizes the holding.

55. E. g., Hickman v. London Assurance Corp., 184 Cal. 524, 195 P. 45 (1920) (judgment ordered for insurer in action on a contract of insurance which provided for the insured to submit to examination under oath, on the ground that the privilege did not prevent the enforcement of the insured's contract).

56. Uniform Rule 37. Similar language appears in N.J.Stat.Ann. 2A:84A 31.

ens v. Marks.[57] Petitioner, a New York police officer, had, under threat of discharge from his employment, signed a waiver which the Court interpreted as purporting to have the effect of depriving him of his privilege as well as any immunity to which he might be entitled under New York law.[58] Reversing petitioner's contempt conviction for refusal to testify, the Court assumed the waiver valid but held that no justification appeared for denying the petitioner the right to withdraw it. Therefore, his effort to withdraw it [59] and rely on his privilege was effective. After *Stevens*, the value of a contract analysis in this context seems minimal. *Stevens* makes clear that even if valid the agreement can generally be revoked and thus it is not necessary to reach the question of specific enforceability. Insofar as the impact of such an agreement would be to place the waiving party at some other disadvantage vis-à-vis the state, the matter would seem to be more appropriately handled as raising the issue of whether an impermissible burden had been imposed on the exercise of the privilege.[60] Insofar as the exercise of the privilege constitutes a breach of an agreement between two (or more) entirely private parties, the matter would seem to remain essentially private and any burden imposed on the party waiving the privilege would not be a state-imposed disadvantage.[61] It would, therefore, be beyond the scope of the protection afforded by the privilege.

142.   The "Required Records" Exception.[62]

Access to carefully compiled records of regulated businesses and individuals is important to the success of many governmental regulatory schemes, schemes which are enforced in part at least by criminal sanctions imposed upon those who fail to comply. This need raises problems under the privilege. First, if a person is required to transcribe or otherwise maintain records which might subsequently be used to incriminate him, the requirement that the records be kept is quite arguably a compelling of testimonial activity in violation of the privilege.[63] Second, insofar as the government may compel one who has such records to produce them, the implied representations of the act of production may constitute a representation that the records produced are those demanded and thus may come within the privilege.[64] The required records exception to the privilege addresses itself to these issues: to what extent may the government require one to compile, maintain, and produce or permit inspection of records regarding one's activities, and then use these records or information obtained by their use in a criminal prosecution?

The leading case for the government's right to require, compel production of, and

---

57.   383 U.S. 234 (1966).

58.   Mr. Justice Harlan argued in dissent that the waiver signed by the petitioner was only a waiver of immunity rights under New York law and did not purport to deprive him of his federal constitutional privilege. Id. at 247 (Mr. Justice Harlan, dissenting). If this is an accurate characterization petitioner's privilege was legally intact but he could not testify (to save his employment) and escape prosecution by virtue of the state immunity statutes. The majority, however, cites convincingly from the record as proof that all concerned considered the effect of the document as a forfeiture of the privilege. Id. at 237–38.

59.   The Court left open the possibility that withdrawal of a waiver might in some circumstances cause sufficient administrative inconvenience as to constitute "justification." Id. at 244 n. 10.

60.   See § 121, supra.

61.   Conceivably a private agreement could impose a disadvantage of such a significant nature that judicial enforcement of it would be state action. Cf. Shelley v. Kraemer, 334 U.S. 1 (1948).

62.   See generally 8 Wigmore, Evidence (McNaughton rev.) §§ 2259c, 2259d; Meltzer, Required Records, the McCarran Act and the Privilege Against Self-Incrimination, 18 U.Chi.L.Rev. 687, 708 (1951); Comment, Required Information and the Privilege Against Self-Incrimination, 65 Colum.L.Rev. 681 (1965); 58 Am.Jur. Witnesses § 73; C.J.S. Witnesses § 448, p. 282; Dec.Dig. Criminal Law ⊂⊃393 (1).

63.   See § 124, supra.

64.   See § 126, supra.

use records of this description in criminal prosecutions is Shapiro v. United States.[65] Petitioner, a wholesale fresh produce dealer, was subject to the wartime Emergency Price Control Act of 1942.[66] Regulations promulgated under the Act required that anyone subject to the Act "preserve for examination by the Office of Price Administration all his records, including invoices, sales tickets, cash receipts, or other written evidences of sale or delivery . . ." and that he keep records of the kind he customarily had kept. In response to a subpoena *duces tecum*, petitioner produced the materials required by the Act. When he was subsequently prosecuted for violation of the Act he asserted as a plea in bar that the compulsory production of the materials had given him immunity, or, if no such immunity had been granted, that the statute under which he was prosecuted was unconstitutional. In rejecting his argument, the Court held that production of the material in issue could constitutionally be required of petitioner by the government without granting him immunity from prosecution or from its use. Although acknowledging limits on the government's right to require the keeping of records which must be made available to government investigators, the Court declared that "no serious misgivings that those bounds have been overstepped would appear to be evoked when there is a sufficient relationship between the activity sought to be regulated and the public concern. . . ."[67]

The bounds of this right remained substantially unexplored[68] until 1965 when the Court held in Albertson v. Subversive Activities Control Board[69] that officers of the Communist Party could not be required to file a registration statement for the party as required by the Subversive Activities Control Act of 1950. Three years later, in a trilogy of cases—Marchetti v. United States,[70] Grosso v. United States,[71] and Haynes v. United States[72]—the Court held that individuals could not be required to register or to pay the occupational tax as required by the federal wagering tax statutes[73] nor could they be required to register a regulated firearm as required by federal statute.[74] In distinguishing the required record doctrine and *Shapiro* the Court explained the limits of the required records rule as follows:

> "The premises of the doctrine, as it is described in *Shapiro*, are evidently three: first, the purposes of the United States' inquiry must be essentially regulatory; second, information is to be obtained by requiring the preservation of records of a kind which the regulated party has customarily kept; and third, the records themselves must have assumed 'public aspects' which render them at least analogous to public documents."[75]

Court had held the federal wagering tax provisions valid under constitutional attack on the basis that they required only disclosure of future criminal activities and that the privilege provided no protection against compelled disclosures relating to future acts. This rationale was also used in Lewis v. United States, 348 U.S. 419 (1955). In Marchetti v. United States, 390 U.S. 39, 52–53 (1968) the Court commented that this analysis had overlooked significant hazards of incrimination as to past acts and, in any case, had hinged upon an "excessively narrow view of the scope of the constitutional privilege."

---

65. 335 U.S. 1 (1948).

66. Ch. 26, 56 Stat. 23.

67. Shapiro v. United States, 335 U.S. 1, 32 (1948).

68. In United States v. Sullivan, 274 U.S. 259 (1927) the Court had held that the privilege did not entitle the petitioner to decline to file an income tax return, although it suggested that the privilege might have been invoked to sustain a refusal to respond to specific portions of the return. In United States v. Kahriger, 345 U.S. 22 (1953) the

69. 382 U.S. 70 (1965).

70. 390 U.S. 39 (1968).

71. 390 U.S. 62 (1968).

72. 390 U.S. 85 (1968).

73. Marchetti v. United States, 390 U.S. 39 (1968); Grosso v. United States, 390 U.S. 62 (1968).

74. Haynes v. United States, 390 U.S. 85 (1968).

75. Grosso v. United States, 390 U.S. 62, 67–68 (1968).

The federal wagering tax provisions and the firearm registration requirements, like the registration requirements in *Albertson*, were not essentially regulatory but rather concerned an area "permeated with criminal statutes" and were directed at "a highly selective group inherently suspect of criminal activities."[76] The records concerned in the wagering tax provisions, moreover, lacked any aspects making them analogous to public documents, and the information which the statute required be provided was unrelated to any records of the kind the individual customarily kept; thus the second and third requirement were also not met.[77]

An amended version of the National Firearms Act was, however, upheld in United States v. Freed.[78] Under the amended version, all possessors of firearms rather than principally those engaged in unlawful activities were required to comply. In addition, only one who lawfully made, manufactured, or imported firearms was required to register them prior to their transfer; the transferee had no such obligation, although the application for registration was required to include the transferee's photograph and fingerprints. (The statute also prohibited the receipt or possession of a firearm by one to whom the firearm was not registered under the act.) Finally, the federal statute specifically prohibited direct or indirect use of information or evidence provided in compli-

ance with the act in any criminal prosecution involving a violation of the law occurring prior to or concurrently with the filing of the information or the compiling of the records containing such information. The Solicitor General of the United States represented to the Supreme Court of the United States that as a matter of practice no information filed was disclosed to any law enforcement agency except as necessary to an investigation or prosecution under the act. Responding to the argument that the transferee's required cooperation in providing a photograph and fingerprints to be included in the application for registration would be compelled self-incrimination, the Court responded that in light of the prohibition against use of the information and the administrative practice of nondisclosure, the danger of incrimination was merely "trifling or imaginary."[79] Moreover, commented Mr. Justice Douglas for the Court, the self-incrimination clause could not be given as expansive an interpretation as would be required to establish a periphery which protects a person against not only past or present transgressions but also a career of crime about to be launched.[80]

A variety of rationales have been suggested for the "required records" exception, but none provides a satisfactory method of measuring its scope. Relying on the rule that a document, entry or writing which is part of the state's official records is available for inspection and use without regard to tendency to incriminate its custodian,[81] it has been suggested that a public property right attaches to records which are part of a regulatory scheme and that this property right in the public creates the public right to access and use.[82] This reasoning, however, begs the

---

76. Compare Galvan v. Superior Court, 70 Cal.2d 851, 866–69, 76 Cal.Rptr. 642, 652–54, 452 P.2d 930, 940–41 (1969), upholding a general gun registration ordinance. *Haynes* was distinguished on the basis that the statute involved there was not directed to the public at large as was the ordinance upheld in *Galvan*. If the statute is one of general regulatory purpose, not directed at a group inherently suspect of criminal activities, the *Marchetti* rule provides a defense only to those as to whom the statute creates a substantial hazard of self-incrimination.

77. In Leary v. United States, 395 U.S. 6 (1969) the Court held invalid the transfer tax provisions of the Marijuana Tax Act on the same grounds.

78. 401 U.S. 601 (1971).

79. Id. at 606.

80. Id. at 606–07.

81. 8 Wigmore, Evidence (McNaughton rev.) § 2259 (1).

82. Comment, Required Information and the Privilege Against Self-Incrimination, 65 Colum.L.Rev. 681, 685–86 (1968), reading *Shapiro* as suggesting

question—to what extent may and should the law attach such a property right? Another analysis suggests that since the state may prohibit the regulated activity it has the power to condition its performance upon forfeiture or "implied waiver" of the privilege.[83] This analysis, rejected in *Marchetti*,[84] does not explain application of the exception to businesses whose prohibition might well be beyond the legislative power in any reasonably conceivable situation and, like the "property right" analysis, begs the underlying question. The best approach seems simply in recognizing the doctrine as a limitation on the privilege based upon the public need for information in limited circumstances to make effective public regulation of certain activities. Thus in a specific case the question becomes whether there is a sufficient public interest to outweigh the strong policy in favor of maintaining the protection of the privilege. Following the Court's analysis of *Shapiro*, this should include: (a) a consideration of the importance of effective regulation of the underlying activity; (b) the availability of methods other than compulsory self-incrimination as a means of making this regulation effective; (c) the burden placed on the

party by the requirement, as, for example, whether he is required to perform extensive activities to collect the information that he would not otherwise perform, or whether the requirement is simply that he grant access to information that he would otherwise keep for his own use; (d) the extent to which the records are simply a convenient method of collecting essentially public information (such as the sales of a business) as opposed to requiring that the individual record and submit to public authorities information of a personal nature that would not otherwise be disclosed; (e) the extent to which the information revealed would be of value to the government for purposes other than the criminal prosecution of the individual to reveal it; and (f) the existence and effectiveness of any limitations upon the access of prosecuting agencies to the information.[85]

143. Removing the Danger of Incrimination: Immunity and Immunity Statutes.[86]

Since criminal liability for an act is a matter of legal mandate rather than an inherent

this analysis and citing Boyd v. United States, 116 U.S. 616 (1886) as precedent.

83. McCormick, Evidence § 134, pp. 282–83 (1954); Lewis v. United States, 348 U.S. 419 (1955).

84. Marchetti v. United States, 390 U.S. 39, 51–52 (1968). The argument was made in *Lewis* that since the petitioner had no constitutional right to gamble he had no right to gamble free of the duty to incriminate himself for doing so. He was put to the choice of either not gambling or gambling and forfeiting the privilege. The Court in *Marchetti* responded:
"We find this reasoning no longer persuasive. The question is not whether petitioner has a 'right' to violate state law, but whether, having done so, he may be compelled to give evidence against himself. The constitutional privilege was intended to shield the guilty and imprudent as well as the innocent and foresighted; if such an inference of antecedent choice were alone enough to abrogate the privilege's protection, it would be excluded from the situations in which it has historically been guaranteed, and withheld from those who most require it." Id. at 51.

85. In California v. Byers, 402 U.S. 424 (1971) the Supreme Court upheld the constitutionality of a statute requiring drivers of vehicles involved in accidents to stop and leave their names and addresses. The plurality opinion, joined in by four justices, held that in view of the nature of the group at which the requirement was aimed (not one composed of those "inherently suspect of criminal activities"), there was no substantial danger of incrimination. In the alternative, the opinion suggested that the activity involved was not "testimonial". Mr. Justice Harlan, whose concurrence established a majority, disagreed with the grounds relied upon by the plurality. Where self-reporting is used as a means of achieving regulatory goals, he concluded, "we must deal in degrees." "Considering the noncriminal governmental purpose in securing the information, the necessity for self-reporting as a means of securing the information, and the nature of the disclosures involved," the privilege against self-incrimination was not infringed and no immunity need be afforded the driver who complies with the statutory requirement. In view of the strong arguments that can be made against the reasoning of the plurality opinion (see Mr. Justice Brennan's dissent), Mr. Justice Harlan's analysis seems more satisfactory and consistent with Fifth Amendment policies.

86. See generally 8 Wigmore, Evidence (McNaughton rev.) §§ 2281–84; Note, Federal Immunity Stat-

characteristic of the act itself, it follows that the liability may also be removed by legal action. Removing liability removes the danger against which the privilege protects and makes the privilege unavailable. Thus if no conviction is possible because of a prior conviction [87] or acquittal,[88] passage of the period of limitations,[89] or executive pardon,[90] the privilege cannot be invoked. The same holds true if the one from whom testimony is sought is effectively granted legal immunity from any danger arising from his testimony which is within the protection of the privilege.[91]

Although in some jurisdictions prosecuting attorneys have been found to have inherent power to confer immunity,[92] in most juris-

dictions their ability to do so depends upon specific legislative authorization.[93] Legislative activity in this area, however, has been piecemeal and the statutory provisions for conferring immunity are consequently varied and often confusing. Most jurisdictions have a number of different provisions each relating to a single crime or a limited category of crimes difficult to prove unless a participant "turns State's evidence"; these provisions often differ in phraseology and substance within a jurisdiction.[94] Some states and the United States, however, have enacted general immunity statutes [95] and the Model State Witness Immunity Act [96] has been available as a

utes: Problems and Proposals, 37 Geo.Wash.L.Rev. 1276 (1969); Comment, The Federal Witness Immunity Act in Theory and Practice: Treading the Constitutional Tightrope, 72 Yale L.J. 1568 (1963); 58 Am.Jur. Witnesses §§ 84–93; Annot., 13 A.L.R. 2d 1439; C.J.S. Witnesses § 439; Dec.Dig. Witnesses ⬗303, 304.

87. E. g., Rhea v. State, 226 Ark. 581, 291 S.W.2d 505 (1956).

88. See § 121, supra, at n. 82.

89. Id. at n. 80.

90. Id. at n. 81.

91. It has been argued that immunity statutes cannot confer adequate immunity because the witness may despite the immunity be subjected to prosecution and required to assert a plea in bar or obtain a favorable ruling on a motion to quash. Brown v. Walker, 161 U.S. 591, 621–22 (1896) (Mr. Justice Shiras, dissenting). This view has found little support.

92. The Texas courts have found inherent power. Ex parte Copeland, 91 Tex.Cr.R. 549, 240 S.W. 314 (1922); Ex parte Muncy, 72 Tex.Cr.R. 541, 163 S.W. 29 (1914). Other courts have found less formal ways of avoiding the undesirable consequences which might flow from a promise of immunity without legislative authorization. Lowe v. State, 111 Md. 1, 73 A. 637 (1909) suggested that although an unauthorized promise of immunity from a prosecutor could not be pleaded in bar, the trial court should upon a showing of the promise continue the case to give the prosecutor an opportunity to file a *nolle prosequi* or to give the defendant an opportunity to apply for a pardon. The Illinois Supreme Court arrived at an interesting compromise. A defendant who testified pursuant to an unauthorized promise of immunity from the prosecutor was held entitled to a discharge in a subsequent prosecution brought in vio-

lation of the promise. People v. Bogolowski, 326 Ill. 253, 157 N.E. 181 (1927). But the court refused to give such a promise full logical effect, and a witness who refused to testify after receiving a prosecutor's promise of immunity could not be held in contempt. People v. Rockola, 339 Ill. 474, 171 N.E. 559 (1930). The actual reason underlying the decision probably was a reluctance in effect to confer a pardoning power upon prosecutors without judicial supervision.

93. See the discussion in Apodaca v. Viramontes, 53 N.M. 514, 212 P.2d 425 (1925). See generally Annot., 13 A.L.R.2d 1439.

94. Statutes are collected in 8 Wigmore, Evidence (McNaughton rev.) § 2281 n. 11.

95. West's Ann.Cal.Penal Code, §§ 1324, 1324.1; New York Penal Law of 1909 § 2447. (The New York statute was repealed in 1967 with the anticipation that the matter would be covered in the Code of Criminal Procedure. See McKinney's New York Criminal Procedure Law 50.10, 50.20 (1969).)

Title II of the Organized Crime Control Act of 1970 repealed more than fifty specific federal immunity statutes and substituted a general immunity statute, 84 Stat. 922 (codified as 18 U.S.C.A. §§ 6001–6005). See McClellan, The Organized Crime Control Act (S. 30) or Its Critics: Which Threatens Civil Liberties? 46 Notre Dame Law. 55, 82–86 (1970).

96. The text of the Model Act, omitting formal parts, is as follows:

"§ 1. Compelling Evidence in Criminal Proceedings; Immunity. In any criminal proceeding before a court or grand jury, [or examining Magistrate] if a person refuses to answer a question or produce evidence of any other kind on the ground that he may be incriminated thereby, and if the prosecuting attorney, in writing [and with the approval of the Attorney General], requests the court to order that person to answer the question or produce the

guide for those jurisdictions that choose this course, although the act is now somewhat outmoded.[97]

The constitutionally required scope of the immunity which must be conferred to render the privilege inoperative was not directly dealt with by the Supreme Court until 1964. In 1892 the Court had struck down a federal immunity statute on the ground that it did not protect the witness from "the use of his testimony to search out other testimony to be used in evidence against him." [98] The Court's dictum—"[W]e are clearly of the opinion that no statute which leaves the party or witness subject to prosecution after he answers the criminating questions put to him can have the effect of supplanting the privilege conferred by the Constitution of the United States"—[99] has been read as requiring that "transactional immunity" be conferred, that is, that the witness must be protected against prosecution based upon any transaction as to which he testified under compulsion.[1] It was not sufficient, under this view, that the witness was protected against the use of the testimony or its fruits. He must be protected against prosecution. Although the

Court's language referred to the federal privilege which was not held binding upon the states until much later, many state courts adopted the "transactional immunity" approach and much state as well as federal immunity legislation was drawn to confer this broad freedom from subsequent prosecution. The position has merit. That a witness is entitled to protection against indirect as well as direct use of his testimony has been generally accepted. Insofar as any lesser protection would require a defendant to prove that evidence offered by the prosecution was obtained by indirect use of his compelled testimony, it might well face him with an impossible task. Thus in practice a witness granted immunity only from the use of his testimony might well lack full protection by virtue of his inability to prove a causal relationship.

But in Murphy v. Waterfront Commission of New York Harbor,[2] the Court made clear that in some circumstances, at least, the federal constitutional privilege does not require the granting of transactional immunity. After concluding that a state could not compel a witness to give testimony if that testimony might give rise to a federal prosecution, the Court held only that the Federal Government "must be prohibited from making any . ., . use [in a criminal prosecution] of [state] compelled testimony and its fruits." [3] As to the problem of proving the causal relationship between the testimony and offered proof, the Court held that a defendant need only establish that he has testified under a state grant of immunity to matters related to the federal prosecution. Federal prosecutors then have the burden of showing that offered evidence is not "tainted"; this can be done by establishing that they had an "independent, legitimate" source for the evidence.[4]

---

evidence the court after notice to the witness and hearing shall so order [, unless it finds that to do so would be clearly contrary to the public interest,] and that person shall comply with the order. After complying, and if, but for this section, he would have been privileged to withhold the answer given or the evidence produced by him, that person shall not be prosecuted or subjected to penalty or forfeiture for or on account of any transaction, matter or thing concerning which, in accordance with the order, he gave answer or produced evidence. But he may nevertheless be prosecuted or subjected to penalty or forfeiture for any perjury, false swearing or contempt committed in answering, or failing to answer, or in producing, or failing to produce, evidence in accordance with the order."

97. See text at n. 5, infra.

98. Counselman v. Hitchcock, 142 U.S. 547, 564 (1892).

99. Id. at 586.

1. E. g., People v. Walker, 28 Ill.2d 585, 192 N.E.2d 819 (1963) (dictum); State ex rel. North v. Kirtley, 327 S.W.2d 166 (Mo. 1959). See generally Annot., 53 A.L.R.2d 1030.

2. 378 U.S. 52 (1964).

3. Id. at 79.

4. Id. at 79 n. 18.

Murphy involved only the scope of immunity necessary when the jurisdiction seeking to prosecute is not the jurisdiction which compelled the testimony. Although the reasoning of *Murphy* could be applied when the prosecuting jurisdiction is also the compelling jurisdiction, three justices of the Supreme Court of the United States have indicated that they would distinguish such a case from *Murphy* and require that transactional immunity be granted when the prosecuting and compelling jurisdictions were the same.[5] The arguments in support of this position [6] are essentially those in support of transactional immunity generally with several added factors. Where only one jurisdiction is involved, there is a greater likelihood that criminal prosecution will follow a grant of use immunity; this raises in more cases, then, the danger that one granted use immunity will not in fact be able successfully to establish a causal relationship between his testimony and offered evidence and consequently will not be able fully to assert his immunity. Moreover, where only a single jurisdiction is involved no need exists to permit use immunity as a means of preventing one jurisdiction from defeating another's interest in prosecuting a particular individual for a particular crime. Thus not only do the arguments in favor of transactional immunity apply more strongly in a one-jurisdiction situation, but one of the primary objections to transactional immunity in the multiple jurisdiction situation does not apply.[7]

If, however, *Murphy* means that use immunity is sufficient in single jurisdiction as well as multiple jurisdiction situations, it has rendered much existing immunity legislation (including the Model State Witness Immunity Act) [8] unnecessarily (although perhaps not undesirably) broad. This might be accommodated by judicial construction. The New York Court of Appeals apparently adopted the position that the state's immunity statute, although it used transactional immunity phraseology, was intended to confer only that immunity constitutionally required.[9] Reading *Murphy* as requiring only use immunity in the single jurisdiction situation, the court read the statute as granting only use immunity,[10] although it subsequently reversed this position.[11]

Although procedures for bringing immunity into effect depend upon the specific statute involved, the better drafted statutes have in common several important requirements that must be complied with in order to divest the witness of his privilege: [12]

(1) The witness must be faced with an attempt by the state to use its power of testimonial inquiry. Thus the witness's position must be such that if he wrongfully refused to answer he would be subject to legal sanctions.

---

5. Piccirillo v. New York, 400 U.S. 548, (1971) (Douglas, J., with Marshall, J., concurring, and Brennan, J., with Marshall, J. concurring, dissenting from dismissal of the writ of certiorari as improvidently granted).

6. See Piccirillo v. New York, 400 U.S. 548 (1971) (Brennan, J., dissenting).

7. The issue is likely to be resolved soon. See Zicarelli v. New Jersey State Commission of Investigation, 55 N.J. 249, 261 A.2d 129 (1970), probable jurisdiction noted limited to specific questions, 401 U.S. 933 (1971) and Illinois Investigating Crime Commission v. Sarno, 45 Ill.2d 473, 259

N.E.2d 267 (1970) cert. granted limited to specific questions, 401 U.S. 935 (1971).

8. See n. 96, supra.

9. People v. La Bello, 24 N.Y.2d 598, 301 N.Y.S.2d 544, 249 N.E.2d 412 (1969).

10. Id. The same conclusion was reached by the California Supreme Court. Byers v. Justice Court, 71 Cal.2d 1039, 80 Cal.Rptr. 553, 458 P.2d 465 (1969), rev'd on other grounds, 402 U.S. 424, 39 U.S. Law Week 4579 (1971).

11. Gold v. Menna, 25 N.Y.2d 475, 307 N.Y.S.2d 33, 255 N.E.2d 235 (1969).

12. See generally 8 Wigmore, Evidence § 2282. In the Model Act, note 11, supra, and some statutes the procedure is carefully defined. E. g., West's Ann.Cal.Penal Code, § 1324. In others, all or some of these requirements may be read in. Special difficulties are raised by the "automatic" immunity statutes; see note 14, infra.

(2) The witness must invoke the privilege.[13] If the witness is willing to testify without the grant of immunity, there would be little reason for the state to grant immunity and much reason not to do so. It is often required, therefore, that before immunity can be conferred the questions must be put to the witness and he must decline to answer them, relying on his privilege.

(3) The application for immunity must be made by the prosecution authorities. The decision to seek immunity in return for testimony involves a determination that the value of the testimony would ultimately be greater than the value of the right to prosecute the witness or to use any testimony that he might be persuaded to give without the immunity. This is essentially a matter within the province of prosecution authorities, and many statutes make explicit their option to decide whether to attempt to forfeit possible actions against the witness.

(4) The grant must be approved by the court, which under the Model Act and some statutes may decline to approve it if to do so would be clearly to the contrary of the public interest. This requirement serves the purpose of formalizing the "agreement" and making it a matter of formal court record. It also provides the witness with notice that immunity has been granted and that he may no longer rely on the privilege. In addition, however, many statutes appear to be based on the policy that there should be some check on the prosecutor's power to forfeit the state's right to proceed against individuals who may well be guilty of criminal offenses.

No such carefully defined procedure is defined in many of the statutes, especially the so-called "automatic" immunity statutes which by their terms provide only that in a given situation a witness shall not be excused from testifying and then direct that the witness is to be protected from prosecution or the use of his testimony.[14] Nevertheless, a witness may not be held in contempt for failure to testify under even these automatic statutes unless "it has been demonstrated to him that an immunity, as broad in scope as the privilege it replaces, is available and applicable to him."[15] It is reasonable that this

13. See Annot., 145 A.L.R. 1416. But see United States v. Monia, 317 U.S. 424 (1943) (since statute would appear to layman to grant immunity to one who simply testifies on request, there is no need for witness specifically to claim privilege).

14. See Marcus v. United States, 310 F.2d 143 (3d Cir. 1962) ("The immunity conferred by [47 U.S. C.A. § 409(1)] is the automatic statutory consequence of compulsory testimony."). The immunity conferred under these statutes has been held to extend only to matters which the testimony concerned "in a substantial way." Heike v. United States, 227 U.S. 131 (1913). The danger of the automatic immunity acts is that a government official may find after an investigation that by calling witnesses he has unintentionally conferred immunity upon them. United States v. Weber, 255 F.Supp. 40 (D.N.J.1965), aff'd sub nom. United States v. Fisher, 384 U.S. 212 (1966); United States v. Niarchos, 125 F.Supp. 214 (D.D.C.1954) (immunity conferred without regard to prosecutor's intent to confer immunity when subject matter of inquiry was "substantially related" to offenses); State ex rel. Lurie v. Rosier, 226 So.2d 825 (Fla. App.1969). See generally Wexler, Automatic Witness Immunity Statutes and the Inadvertent Frustration of Criminal Prosecutions: A Call for Congressional Action, 55 Geo.L.J. 656 (1967), urging that the statutes be amended so that no immunity is conferred unless the witness specifically claims immunity and is nevertheless required to answer. The new general federal immunity provision (see n. 95, supra) provides for immunity only when "a witness refuses, on the basis of his privilege against self-incrimination, to testify or provide other information" and an order is communicated to him ordering him to testify or to provide such information. 18 U.S.C.A. § 6002.

15. Stevens v. Marks, 383 U.S. 234, 246 (1966), relying on Raley v. Ohio, 360 U.S. 423 (1959). In Raley petitioners had been called to testify before a state commission. They had been expressly told that the privilege applied, and had declined to answer questions. Later, they were prosecuted under a statute making it a criminal offense to refuse to testify "when lawfully required" to do so; an automatic immunity statute, the state argued, made their reliance on the privilege improper. In view of commands that were not only vague and contra-

demonstration must include a representation by the court that in fact the statutory requirements have been complied with and the immunity has been validly conferred.

It is generally held that the immunity conferred does not include immunity for crimes committed in the giving of the testimony. Thus one who is granted immunity is not immune from a prosecution for perjury based upon false testimony given under immunity.[16] An interesting situation arises if immunity is granted and the testimony given turns out not to be incriminating. If the statutory immunity is transactional, has the state forfeited its right to proceed against the witness? It is generally concluded, on the basis of scant authority, that the answer is negative,[17] on the assumption that the legislature did not intend to confer immunity without

obtaining an equivalent benefit, and if no benefit accrues because the testimony was such that the state was entitled to have it without the grant of immunity, the immunity is of no effect.

Some statutes by their terms apply only to witnesses called on behalf of the prosecution in a criminal trial,[18] and statutes whose wording might permit another construction have been interpreted to authorize immunity only for prosecution witnesses.[19] In practice, since the prosecution often has a veto power over the application, immunity is granted under other statutes primarily for purposes of building up the prosecution's case. But what of the defendant whose case would be assisted if a key witness were granted immunity and required to testify in his behalf?[20] It is certainly arguable that without the right to have immunity granted a defendant lacks "compulsory process for obtaining witnesses in his favor" as guaranteed by the Sixth Amendment. Moreover, the imbalance created by the availability of this power to the prosecution but not to the defense may well constitute a deprivation of due process of law.[21]

dictory but "actively misleading," the Court held, the convictions could not be sustained. Cf. United States v. Monia, 317 U.S. 424 (1943) (in view of statutory language, a witness need not specifically assert the privilege when subpoenaed to testify in order to obtain immunity granted under statute). It follows that while a court may save a statute which compels self-incrimination by judicially creating a grant of immunity, Murphy v. Waterfront Commission of New York Harbor, 378 U.S. 52 (1964) (right to have compelled testimony and fruits excluded in federal courts saves state immunity legislation); Byers v. Justice Court of Mendocino County, 71 Cal.2d 1039, 80 Cal.Rptr. 553, 458 P.2d 465 (1969), a witness cannot be punished for failure to comply with the compulsion unless he is made aware of the immunity and given a chance to answer. Murphy v. Waterfront Commission of New York Harbor, supra, at 79–80.

16. Glickstein v. United States, 222 U.S. 139 (1911) (witness may be prosecuted for perjury committed while testifying pursuant to statute directing that "no testimony given [under immunity] . . . shall be offered in evidence against him in any criminal proceeding", and the witness's allegedly perjurious testimony may be admitted in evidence in the perjury prosecution); Washburn v. State, 167 Tex.Cr.R. 125, 318 S.W.2d 627 (1959) cert. denied 359 U.S. 965 (witness granted immunity was nevertheless subject to penalties for perjury and therefore competent).

17.   8 Wigmore, Evidence § 2282, pp. 512–13, relying on Carchidi v. State, 187 Wis. 438, 204 N.W. 473 (1925).

18. E. g., Idaho Code Ann. § 18–1308 (1948) (witnesses testifying in bribery prosecution "at the instance of the state").

19. State v. Perry, 246 Iowa 861, 69 N.W.2d 412 (1955). Cf. Smith v. United States, 58 F.2d 735 (5th Cir. 1932) (witness for state in prosecution of federal agent which had been removed to federal court and was defended by United States Attorney could not be granted immunity under federal statute upon application of state prosecutor).

20. Cf. State v. Shaw, 6 Ariz.App. 33, 429 P.2d 667 (1967), finding no error in the refusal on the part of the prosecution to grant immunity to a witness. The record established, however, that the anticipated testimony would not have established a defense.

21. See J. Maguire, Evidence of Guilt § 2.081 (1959). Wigmore argues that an opposite result would permit an offender to secure immunity by contriving with a defendant to be called as a witness. 8 Wigmore, Evidence § 2282, p. 519. But a requirement that the court approve any grant of immunity would sufficiently minimize this danger.

CHAPTER 14

CONFESSIONS

144. The Definition of "Confession." [1]

During the long history of concern over the use of "confessions" in criminal prosecutions, a significant amount of litigation has involved the question whether various statements were "confessions." Contrary to what might seem the simplest solution—that all out-of-court statements by a defendant offered against him at trial are "confessions" —much effort has been spent subdividing these statements into different categories, and especially distinguishing "confessions" from "admissions." The task has been undertaken primarily by courts seeking to avoid the application of stringent rules governing use of "confessions" to all statements made by an accused and offered at trial.[2] In view of the decreasing differences in the rules applicable to confessions and other statements, the labeling process has become of minimal importance. For federal constitutional purposes, it is probably meaningless.[3]

1. See generally, 3 Wigmore, Evidence (Chadbourn rev.) § 821; J. Maguire, Evidence of Guilt § 3.03 (1959); Developments in the Law—Confessions, 79 Harv.L.Rev. 935, 1031–32 (1966); 29 Am.Jur.2d Criminal Law § 523; C.J.S. Criminal Law § 816.

2. E. g., People v. Stanton, 16 Ill.2d 459, 158 N.E.2d 47 (1959) (statement was not a confession and therefore not within statute requiring that copy of any confession and names and addresses of those present when it was given be furnished to defendant).

3. See e. g., Miranda v. Arizona, 384 U.S. 436, 476–77 (1966) (*Miranda* rights must be accorded one who makes an admission or exculpatory statement); Opper v. United States, 348 U.S. 84, 90–92 (1954) (corroboration rule applies to admissions and exculpatory statements as well as to confessions). But see People v. Williams, 71 Cal.2d 614, 79 Cal. Rptr. 65, 456 P.2d 633 (1969) (erroneous introduc-

Courts which still distinguish between confessions and admissions generally define a confession as a statement admitting or acknowledging all facts necessary for conviction of the crime.[4] An admission, on the other hand, is an acknowledgment of a fact or facts tending to prove guilt which falls short of an acknowledgment of all essential elements of the crime.[5] For example, in a recent case [6] the defendant had been convicted of assault with a deadly weapon upon a police officer. At trial a deputy sheriff testified: "I asked him if he had shot at the deputies. He stated that he had." As the crime with which he had been charged required awareness of the victim's identity as a peace officer engaged in the performance of his duties, the out-of-court statement was held to be only an admission because it did not expressly or impliedly concede that the defendant had been aware of the victims' official character at the time he fired the shot.

An admission need not, of course, be an acknowledgment of a fact *essential* to the establishment of guilt. It is sufficient if it is an acknowledgment of a fact which, if true, tends to prove guilt or if the mere making of the assertion (without regard to its truth) tends to prove guilt. For example, in a conspiracy trial [7] evidence was introduced that one defendant had denied knowing the other defendants on a given date. This was an admission because the assertion, when considered with other proof which tended to show

it was erroneous, indicated consciousness of guilt and therefore permitted an inference of actual guilt. An admission need not consist of spoken words. Acts which tend to prove consciousness of guilt are "implied admissions" of guilt and subject to the same treatment as verbal admissions.[8] So-called "tacit admissions"—failure on the part of an accused to react as an innocent individual to statements made in his presence—are sufficiently important to be given special treatment.[9]

A final category of out-of-court statements by an accused that is often distinguished is that of exculpatory statements, i. e., assertions which were intended, at the time made, to exculpate rather than incriminate the speaker.[10] As is the case with many admissions, an exculpatory statement is frequently offered as proving consciousness of guilt,[11] although it may also be used to prove guilt circumstantially in other ways.

145. Theory of Admissibility of Confessions.[12]

As the definitions of confessions, admissions, and exculpatory statements make clear, all are out-of-court statements of the accused and therefore potentially subject to

---

tion of a confession requires reversal, but erroneous introduction of an admission requires reversal only if error was prejudicial).

4. Gladden v. Unsworth, 396 F.2d 373, 375 n. 2 (9th Cir. 1968); People v. Fitzgerald, 56 Cal.2d 855, 861, 17 Cal.Rptr. 129, 132, 366 P.2d 481, 484 (1961); Brown v. State, 111 So.2d 296 (Fla.App.1959); People v. Stanton, 16 Ill.2d 459, 158 N.E.2d 47 (1959).

5. See cases cited in note 4, supra.

6. In re Cline, 255 Cal.App.2d 115, 63 Cal.Rptr. 233 (1967).

7. Williamson v. United States, 310 F.2d 192, 199 (9th Cir. 1962).

8. See People v. Cramer, 67 Cal.2d 126, 60 Cal.Rptr. 230, 429 P.2d 582 (1967).

9. See § 161, infra.

10. State v. Cobb, 2 Ariz.App. 71, 73, 406 P.2d 421, 423 (1965): "An 'exculpatory statement' is a statement which tends to justify, excuse or clear the defendant from alleged fault or guilt. Some authorities consider it as a form of an admission against interest, while others consider it in a separate category."

11. Wilson v. United States, 162 U.S. 613, 620–21 (1896); Fox v. United States, 381 F.2d 125 (9th Cir. 1967); People v. Player, 161 Cal.App.2d 360, 327 P.2d 83 (1958); State v. Bridges, 349 S.W.2d 214 (Mo. 1961).

12. See generally 3 Wigmore, Evidence (Chadbourn rev.) § 816; Developments in the Law—Confessions, 79 Harv.L.Rev. 935, 951–54 (1966); 29 Am. Jur.2d Criminal Law § 526; C.J.S. Criminal Law § 817(1).

objection on the basis of the hearsay rule.[13] Whether considered not to be hearsay, or hearsay but the subject of an exception, there seems to be general agreement that the prosecution may introduce in a criminal trial any relevant out-of-court statement of the defendant.[14] If the statement is classed as hearsay but the subject of an exception, certain difficulties may be advanced, both theoretical and practical. If not classed as hearsay, these difficulties may no longer relate to theory, but they by no means disappear as practical problems.

Wigmore [15] and Morgan [16] group together in one exception to the hearsay rule statements made by a criminal defendant and parties to civil litigation. The exception is based, in their view upon the assumption that the major justification for excluding hearsay is the unavailability of the declarant for cross-examination. Since both criminal defendants and parties to civil litigation are available for explanation, the argument goes, the

rationale for the rule does not apply. There are several weaknesses in this explanation. First, historically these out-of-court statements were admissible before a party to a civil suit or an accused in a criminal proceeding became a competent witness.[17] Thus the rule would have preceded its justification. Second, it is clear that the Fifth Amendment privilege against compulsory self-incrimination recognizes a right on the part of a criminal defendant to decline to submit to either direct or cross-examination at trial. Justification of an exception to the hearsay rule on the availability of the opportunity to waive this right may be inconsistent with the solicitude with which the privilege has recently been treated.[18]

The hearsay exception for declarations against interest has also been offered as a basis for the rule regarding out-of-court statements of an accused.[19] This too is subject to question. That a declaration is, at the time made, against the penal interests of the declarant has not generally been considered sufficient to bring it within this exception.[20]

13. While traditionally considered as hearsay but the subject of an exception, substantial authority supports the position that the out-of-court statements of an accused are, like other admissions of a party-opponent, not hearsay. State v. Willis, 71 Conn. 293, 296, 41 Atl. 820, 823–24 (1898):
"[Out of court statements of an accused offered against him] are not admitted as testimony of the declarant in respect to any facts in issue. For that purpose they are open to the objections to hearsay evidence. They are admitted because conduct of a party to the proceeding, in respect to the matter in dispute, whether by acts, speech, or writing, which is clearly inconsistent with the truth of his contention, is a fact relevant to the issue."
See generally § 262, infra.

14. Lewis v. State, 458 P.2d 309, 312 (Okl.Cr.1969): "[A]ny statement made by a defendant which is in the nature of an admission or from which inference of guilt may be drawn, is admissible as direct and original evidence."

15. 3 Wigmore, Evidence (Chadbourn rev.) § 816: "[T]he ground for receiving admissions in general . . . suffices also for confessions."

16. Morgan, Admissions as an Exception to the Hearsay Rule, 30 Yale L.J. 355 (1921). J. Maguire, Evidence of Guilt, § 1.02 (1959) considers a confession "a specialized sort of admission."

17. Wigmore points out that extra-judicial confessions were received (without even any voluntariness consideration) during 1500's and 1600's. 3 Wigmore, Evidence (Chadbourn rev.) § 818. The rule that parties to a criminal or civil case were incompetent as witnesses, however, survived until mid-19th century. § 65, supra.

18. See §§ 130–132, supra.

19. Developments in the Law—Confessions, 79 Harv.L.Rev. 935, 953 (1966); 29 Am.Jur.2d Criminal Law § 526. In Hopt v. Utah, 110 U.S. 574, 584–85 (1884) Mr. Justice Harlan stated: "A confession if freely and voluntarily made, is evidence of the most satisfactory character. Such a confession, said Eyre, C.B., 1 Leach, 263, 'is deserving of the highest credit, because it is presumed to flow from the strongest sense of guilt, and, therefore, it is admitted as proof of the crime to which it refers.' . . . [T]he presumption upon which weight is given to such evidence [is] . . . that one who is innocent will not imperil his safety or prejudice his interests by an untrue statement . . . .'"

20. Morgan, Admissions as an Exception to the Hearsay Rule, 30 Yale L.J. 355, 359 (1921) concluded that admissions were received whether or not they were, at the time when made, against the

Moreover, it is clear that the rule is broad enough to include statements which were not against even the penal interests of the declarant at the time they were made and thus do not come within the reason asserted for the exception. While it is arguable that confessions, if carefully defined, will always come within the meaning of a declaration against penal interest and thus have some assurance of reliability, the same cannot be said of admissions or exculpatory statements.[21] Perhaps if an individual admits all elements of an offense he can reasonably be presumed to have been aware of the danger of criminal liability and to have spoken only for a reason of sufficient importance to assure that his statement is reliable. But an isolated acknowledgment of a fact which later becomes important in determining criminal liability certainly cannot be regarded in the same manner. Exculpatory statements, of course, are by their nature diametrically the opposite of the declaration against interest and arguably are often made under conditions involving strong pressures for unreliability. When offered to prove consciousness of guilt, however, they may not in theory come within the hearsay objection, as they are offered not to prove the truth of the matters asserted in them but to prove circumstantially a state of mind.[22] Nevertheless, it is arguable that they are generally made under conditions so conducive to unreliability that even this distinction should not save them from exclusion.

Basic differences between civil and criminal liability and their attendant circumstances of enforcement have led to the evolution of a substantially different set of rules to govern the admissibility of the out-of-court statements of an accused. The doubts expressed in the foregoing discussion have played an important part in formulating these rules and the procedures for applying them.

146. Bases for Exclusion of Confessions.

Despite the broad admissibility generally of out-of-court statements of an opposing party, a number of increasingly restrictive rules of evidence and procedure relating to such statements by an accused have developed. The result is that admissibility is becoming increasingly restricted. The most important limitations are the requirements that a confession be voluntary,[23] that it be obtained without violation of the accused's rights to remain silent and to representation by counsel,[24] and that if it is obtained during a period of custody of the accused, the custody not be violative of certain rules.[25] The ability of the prosecution effectively to utilize out-of-court statements of an accused is also restricted by the corroboration requirement[26] and the necessity for an independent hearing on admissibility.[27] These limiting rules to some extent serve the purpose of guarding against unreliable evidence, but

---

interest of the declarant, and that courts do not insist that admissions meet the requirements for declarations against interest. Wigmore finds the declaration against interest theory "not necessary to lean upon," and acknowledges that it does not explain why confessions of a *third* person are generally not admissible because of the hearsay rule. 3 Wigmore, Evidence (Chadbourn rev.) § 816 n. 1.

The current trend is to consider a penal interest sufficient to satisfy the exception. See § 278, infra.

21. Cf. Jones v. United States, 111 U.S.App.D.C. 276, 296 F.2d 398 (1962). Exculpatory out-of-court statements by the accused, if offered by the accused to prove innocence, are not admissible. Piassick v. United States, 253 F.2d 658 (5th Cir. (1958). "Evidence which is excluded under the so-called 'self-serving' doctrine is the extrajudicial declarations of a party which are offered in his own behalf as evidence of the truth of the facts declared. Actually such statements are excluded not because they are self-serving but because they are obnoxious to the hearsay rule." Commonwealth v. Fatalo, 345 Mass. 85, 185 N.E.2d 754, 755 (1962).

22. See §§ 249, 250, supra.

23. §§ 147–150, infra.

24. §§ 151–154, infra.

25. §§ 155–156, infra.

26. § 158, infra.

27. § 159, infra.

their primary purpose is the protection of interests other than the accurate resolution of factual issues presented by the case in which the confession is offered. Thus, they may properly be classified as rules of privilege rather than of incompetency.

147. The Requirement of Voluntariness: (a) The Common Law Rule.

Before the mid 1700's out-of-court statements of an accused were admissible against him at his trial without regard to the manner in which they had been obtained.[28] A plea of guilty on arraignment, however, was required not to "proceed from fear, menace, or duress." [29] The distinction, according to Wigmore, was justified on the ground that the plea was a conviction in itself and properly subjected to such scrutiny, an inquiry not justified when what was involved was only one piece of the evidence upon which a verdict would be returned.[30] There is little evidence of the manner by which the voluntariness requirement was extended from pleas to extrajudicial statements of the accused, but in 1775 Lord Mansfield commented offhandedly that "the instance has frequently happened, of persons having made confessions under threats or promises; the consequence has frequently been, that such examinations and confessions have not been made use of against them on their trial." [31] The early discussions make quite clear that the rationale for the rule was the purported lack of reliability of statements motivated not by guilt but by the desire to avoid pain or to secure some favor.[32]

Until the development of the due process rule, the common law requirement of voluntariness constituted the primary limitation on the use of an accused's statements. It prohibited the use of statements obtained by application of physical force or the threats of physical force and also statements obtained in response to promises of leniency. Although the common law requirement still exists, it has been overshadowed by the development of the federal constitutional requirement. For all practical purposes, then, the voluntariness requirement has become one of federal constitutional law, and although it is administered by state courts as well as by federal tribunals, state court administration has been significantly affected by the availability—and frequent exercise—of review by the federal courts.

148. The Requirement of Voluntariness: (b) Development of the Due Process Requirement.[33]

In 1936, with Brown v. Mississippi,[34] voluntariness became a requirement of due process of law protected against state infringement by the Fourteenth Amendment. Although *Brown* held as violative of that amendment a conviction resting "solely" upon a confession extorted by brutality and violence, it soon became clear that due process was violated by the mere use in a prosecution of a nonvoluntary confession.[35]

are or are not entitled to credit. . . . [A] confession forced from the mind by flattery of hope, or by the torture of fear, comes in so questionable a shape when it is to be considered as the evidence of guilt, that no credit ought to be given to it . . . .." See generally 3 Wigmore, Evidence (Chadbourn rev.) § 822.

33. See generally, Ritz, Twenty-Five Years of State Criminal Confession Cases in the U. S. Supreme Court, 19 Wash. & Lee L.Rev. 35 (1962). For a table summary of Supreme Court state confession cases through 1962, see Way, The Supreme Court and State Coerced Confessions, 12 J. Public Law 53, 54 (1963).

34. 297 U.S. 278 (1936).

35. In Payne v. Arkansas, 356 U.S. 560 (1958) the Court made clear that admission of a coerced

28. 3 Wigmore, Evidence (Chadbourn rev.) § 818.

29. Id.

30. Id.

31. Rudd's Case, 1 Leach Cr.C. 115, 118 (1775). See generally 3 Wigmore, Evidence (Chadbourn rev.) § 819.

32. The King v. Warickshall, 168 Eng.Rep. 234, 234–35, 1 Leach Cr. Cases 263, 263–64 (K.B. 1783): "Confessions are received in evidence, or rejected as inadmissible, under a consideration whether they

The theoretical basis for this holding is somewhat ambiguous. Although in *Brown* the Court stated that the privilege against self-incrimination was not involved,[36] it has subsequently characterized the due process voluntariness standard as "the same general

confession vitiated a conviction despite sufficient evidence other than the confession to support the conviction. See also Lynumn v. Illinois, 372 U.S. 528 (1963). In Chapman v. California, 386 U.S. 18 (1967) the Court suggested that the right not to have a coerced confession used in evidence may be "so basic to a fair trial" that its violation could never be harmless error. Id. at 23. This has been interpreted as requiring a rule of "automatic reversal" in coerced confession cases, i. e., the conviction must be reversed without regard to the prejudicial effect of the statement in the particular case. E. g., McKinley v. State, 37 Wis.2d 26, 154 N.W.2d 344 (1967) (reversal required even though involuntary confession was merely cumulative of substance of earlier voluntary confession). A distinction has been drawn between "confessions" and "admissions" to reach the result that receipt of an inadmissible confession requires automatic reversal but receipt of an inadmissible admission permits an inquiry into its prejudicial effect. E. g., People v. Williams, 71 Cal.2d 614, 79 Cal.Rptr. 65, 456 P.2d 633 (1969).

Although there are decisions to the contrary, e. g., Commonwealth v. Vivian, 426 Pa. 192, 231 A.2d 301 (1967), the general view has been that confessions which are voluntary but inadmissible by virtue of noncompliance with other requirements (such as the right to counsel) do not invoke an automatic reversal rule but must be analyzed under the federal standard set out in Chapman v. California, 386 U.S. 18 (1967). Thus an appellate court may find use of constitutionally-inadmissible evidence harmless error only if it is convinced beyond a reasonable doubt that the evidence did not contribute to the verdict. Id. at 24.

In applying this analysis, lower courts have viewed several factors as tending to permit a finding of harmless error: (1) exculpatory nature of the statement or its use to attack credibility rather than to prove guilt directly, People v. Williams, 71 Cal.2d 614, 79 Cal.Rptr. 65, 456 P.2d 633 (1969) (receipt of exculpatory admission harmless error since it tended only to impeach defendant's credibility which "was not determinative of his defense" and to establish facts already established by other evidence); Herhal v. State, 243 A.2d 703 (Del.1968) (erroneous admission of "wholly exculpatory" statement harmless); State v. Martin, 433 S.W.2d 565 (Mo.1968) (exculpatory statements made without *Miranda* warnings denying knowledge concerning marijuana thrown from car was harmless because it did not detract from version of facts given by defendant at trial); (2) other admissions by accused which make inadmissible statement cumulative, Sweeny v. United States, 408 F.2d 121 (9th Cir. 1969) (alternative holding) (receipt of confession of knowing possession of marijuana harmless because defendant, in testifying in support of entrapment defense, admitted same facts);

People v. Haston, 69 Cal.2d 233, 70 Cal.Rptr. 419, 444 P.2d 91 (1968) (receipt of confession to prior crime harmless error as prosecution also proved plea of guilty to that crime); People v. Jacobson, 63 Cal.2d 319, 46 Cal.Rptr. 515, 405 P.2d 555 (1965) (introduction of inadmissible confession harmless error when there was properly received an equally or more damaging earlier admission); State v. Warner, 237 A.2d 150 (Me.1967) (reference to silence in response to questions not prejudicial when defendant thereafter gave admissible incriminating responses to similar questions); State v. Sneed, 78 N.M. 615, 435 P.2d 768 (1967) (alternative holding) (statements were not prejudicial as they were substantially the same as defendant's trial testimony); (3) tendency of statements to prove only a fact not seriously in issue, People v. Morse, 70 Cal.2d 711, 76 Cal.Rptr. 391, 452 P.2d 607 (1969) (receipt of proof that defendant told psychiatrist that he had garrotted another inmate was harmless as there was no dispute that defendant had caused the death and there was "a great amount of persuasive evidence" of premeditation and malice); Blatch v. State, 216 So.2d 261 (Fla. App.1968) (alternative holding) (receipt of confession harmless error because defense never contested the assertion that defendant had killed the victim); (4) the ambiguity of the statement insofar as it might prove guilt, State v. Galasso, 217 So.2d 326 (Fla.1968) (proof that during search of defendant's room one defendant said, in response to query as to who owned envelope, "Some man. Don't say anything." was harmless because it was only "an inconclusive and insubstantial colloquy" with an unclear meaning); (5) the availability of overwhelming and reliable evidence of guilt, Guyette v. State, 84 Nev. 160, 438 P.2d 244 (1968) (receipt of statement was harmless error because of compliance by police with legal rule then applicable and "the most damaging" statements were volunteered rather than in response to interrogation); Hayes v. State, 39 Wis.2d 125, 158 N.W.2d 545 (1968) (receipt of defendant's exculpatory admissions was harmless in view of the physical evidence and testimony of fourteen witnesses which presented "an overwhelming picture of defendant's guilt"). See also Commonwealth v. Robinson, 430 Pa. 188, 242 A.2d 266 (1968) (receipt of statement in trial on degree of murder after plea of guilty was harmless because court found lower degree). See generally Note, Criminal Procedure—Self-Incrimination—Harmless Error—Application of the Harmless Error Doctrine to Violations of Miranda: The California Experience, 69 Mich.L.Rev. 941 (1971); Comment, A Comment on Application of the Harmless Constitutional Error Rule to "Confession" Cases, 1968 Utah L.Rev. 144; 65 Mich.L.Rev. 563 (1967); Dec.Dig. Criminal Law ☞1169(12).

36. Brown v. Mississippi, 297 U.S. 278, 285 (1936).

standard which [is] applied in federal prosecutions—a standard grounded in the policies of the privilege against self-incrimination." [37] Probably the most candid explanation of the rule was made in Blackburn v. Alabama,[38] in which the Court stated that "a complex of values underlies the stricture against use by the state of confessions which, by way of convenient shorthand, this Court terms involuntary." [39] Included in this "complex of values" underlying the *Brown* holding are undoubtedly the following:

(1) Protection of particular defendants against use of unreliable confessions.[40] In part, the voluntariness requirement still reflects the concern of the common law rule that a confession obtained in the absence of free choice is unreliable and therefore unworthy of consideration on the issue of guilt or innocence. This, however, has become only a minor aspect of the voluntariness requirement.[41] Moreover, while trustworthi-

ness may be a factor supporting the voluntariness requirement, the trustworthiness of a particular statement may not be considered in determining its admissibility.[42]

(2) The privilege against compulsory self-incrimination and the values underlying this rule.[43] While in theory police investigators probably have no legally enforceable right to require answers to questions, police interrogation might well convey the impression to a subject that his interrogators had the right or at least the power to compel responses. As a practical matter, then, the values underlying the privilege are endangered by pretrial interrogation. It is clear that this concern was a factor in the promulgation and development of the due process voluntariness requirement. Until Malloy v. Hogan,[44] of course, the federal self-incrimination privilege was not binding on the states; thus prior to *Malloy* the voluntariness rule as an aspect of Fourteenth Amendment due process served as a vehicle for federal relief in those cases in which the values protected

---

37. Davis v. North Carolina, 384 U.S. 737, 740 (1966).

38. 361 U.S. 199 (1960).

39. Id. at 207.

40. In *Brown* itself the defendant urged that the confession was false as well as coerced, and the Court in reversing emphasized that since the confession was the sole evidence supporting the jury verdict the trial had been "a mere pretense." Brown v. Mississippi, 297 U.S. 278, 286–87 (1936).

41. Lisenba v. California, 314 U.S. 219 (1941) is often pinpointed as the turning point in the Court's emphasis. In *Lisenba* the Court made clear that the due process requirement, unlike the common law voluntariness requirement, did not rest solely upon the need to exclude unreliable evidence but also had as its aim the prevention of fundamental unfairness in the use of evidence. Id. at 236. Following *Lisenba*, the Court began to place increasing emphasis on "fundamental unfairness" and less on the danger of unreliability.

That the danger of unreliability plays only a minimal role is also suggested by the rule that the involuntariness (or what would be involuntariness if a statement of the accused was at issue) of a witness's statement goes not to its admissibility but only to its weight. See People v. Chandler, 262 Cal.App.2d 350, 68 Cal.Rptr. 645 (1968) cert. denied 393 U.S. 1043 (any promises of leniency or immunity or any psychological coercion of the witness would affect only the weight, not the ad-

missibility of his testimony); Veney v. State, 251 Md. 159, 246 A.2d 608 (1968) cert. denied 394 U.S. 948 (admission by witnesses that the reason they testified was that the prosecutor had indicated he "might be disposed to drop indictments against them" did not affect admissibility of their testimony); People v. Bradford, 10 Mich.App. 696, 160 N.W.2d 373 (1968), noted in 58 Geo.L.J. 621 (1970) (witness who had been subjected to physical abuse during police interrogation was nevertheless properly permitted to testify, since coercion merely went to weight of testimony).

42. Haynes v. State of Washington, 373 U.S. 503 (1963) (error to suggest to jury that if confession was involuntary it might nevertheless be considered if corroborated by other evidence); Rogers v. Richmond, 365 U.S. 534, 543 (1961) (determination of admissibility of confession impermissibly "was answered by reference to a legal standard which took into account the circumstance of probable truth or falsity."); Hutcherson v. United States, 122 U.S.App.D.C. 51, 351 F.2d 748 (1965) (finding of voluntariness reversed on the ground that the trial judge's comments showed he was influenced in his decision on voluntariness by the apparent truth of the confession).

43. Davis v. North Carolina, 384 U.S. 737, 740 (1966).

44. 378 U.S. 1 (1964).

by the privilege were violated in an especially significant manner.

(3) Discouragement of police practices that are generally likely to result in unreliable evidence.[45] In addition to the unreliability of particular confessions challenged under the voluntariness requirement, the rule is in part based upon the assumption that as a general matter there is sufficient probability that an involuntary confession will be unreliable that the exclusion of the entire category is justified. Thus the rule serves the purpose of excluding a category of evidence which, as a whole, is sufficiently subject to question on reliability grounds to justify its exclusion.

(4) Discouragement of police practices which are unacceptable on grounds other than the unreliability of the resulting evidence.[46] Analogous to the policy basis of the privilege against self-incrimination, there is undoubtedly a feeling underlying the voluntariness requirement that the methods used to obtain nonvoluntary confessions are unacceptable without regard to the reliability of the resulting evidence. Here, as in the case of that privilege, the conclusion rests in large part upon acceptance of the propositions that even one guilty of an offense against society has a right to be treated in a manner consistent with his inherent dignity as a human being, and that the use of certain investigating tactics is inconsistent with this dignity.

(5) The preservation of the trial rights of an accused.[47] Because of the heavy weight which a trier of fact is likely to give to a statement of the defendant, the introduction of a confession makes the other aspects of a trial in court superfluous, and the real trial, for all practical purposes, occurs when the confession is obtained. Thus the decision to confess before trial amounts in effect to a waiver of the right to require the state at trial to meet its heavy burden of proof. Yet the imposition of this burden of proof upon the prosecution serves valuable social purposes, not only in assuring the guilt of particular defendants but also in minimizing the availability of the criminal process for political and other irregular purposes. The social interest in making the trial a truly adversary proceeding at which the state prove guilt beyond a reasonable doubt is served by a policy which minimizes the opportunity for the state to bypass this requirement by use of a statement obtained during pretrial investigation.

149. The Requirement of Voluntariness: (c) The Due Process Standard.[48]

Although the basic statement of the voluntariness requirement has not varied significantly since *Brown*, the application of the standard—and thus its operational definition—have changed significantly. The first cas-

---

Rev. 313, 320–27 (1964); Lisenba v. California, 314 U.S. 219 (1941).

45. The distinction between the inquiry whether a particular confession is unreliable and that which poses the question as "the likelihood, objectively considered, that the interrogation methods employed . . . create a substantial risk that a person subjected to them will falsely confess— whether or not this particular defendant did?" is discussed in Kamisar, What Is An Involuntary Confession? 17 Rutgers L.Rev. 728, 753–59 (1963)

46. See generally Paulsen, The Fourteenth Amendment and the Third Degree, 6 Stan.L.Rev. 411 (1954).

47. See generally Comment, The Coerced Confession Cases in Search of a Rationale, 31 U.Chi.L.

48. See generally 3 Wigmore, Evidence (Chadbourn rev.) §§ 824–855a; Kamisar, What is an "Involuntary" Confession? Some Comments on Inbau and Reid's Criminal Interrogation and Confessions, 17 Rutgers L.Rev. 728 (1963); King, Developing a Future Constitutional Standard for Confessions, 8 Wayne L.Rev. 481 (1962); Paulsen, The Fourteenth Amendment and The Third Degree, 6 Stan.L.Rev. 411 (1954); Ritz, Twenty-Five Years of State Criminal Confession Cases in the U. S. Supreme Court, 19 Wash. & Lee L.Rev. 35 (1962); Developments in the Law—Confessions, 79 Harv.L.Rev. 938, 966–84 (1966); Comment, Federal Constitutional Limitations on the Use of Coerced Confessions in the State Courts, 50 J.Crim.L.C. & P.S. 265 (1959); Comment, The Coerced Confession Cases in Search of a Rationale, 31 U.Chi.L.Rev. 313 (1964); 29 Am.Jur.2d Evidence, §§ 529, 543–54; C.J.S. Criminal Law § 817(2); Dec.Dig. Criminal Law 406(3), 412.1(1)–(4).

es following *Brown* involved extreme physical coercion, but in Ashcraft v. Tennessee [49] the Court made clear that the psychological as well as the physical impact of interrogation techniques might render a statement non-voluntary even in the absence of physical abuse. In 1961 Mr. Justice Frankfurter summarized the due process standard as follows:

> "The ultimate test . . . [is] voluntariness. Is the confession the product of an essentially free and unconstrained choice by its maker? If it is, if he has willed to confess, it may be used against him. If it is not, if his will has been overborne and his capacity for self-determination critically impaired, the use of his confession offends due process.

> ". . . The line of distinction is that at which governing self direction is lost and compulsion, of whatever nature or however infused, propels or helps to propel the confession.[50] "

The determination of voluntariness is not to turn on limited factual inquiries but depends rather on the "totality of the circumstances" under which the statement was obtained.[51]

The simplicity of statement of the rule is misleading. Its actual complexity is a reflection of the variety of values and purposes which it serves.

The cases may be divided into two categories,[52] although some decisions—especially recent ones—tend to combine the characteristics of both.[53] The first includes those

in which the totality of the circumstances is found to have been "inherently coercive." The confession is held inadmissible upon the basis of the situation alone, without inquiry as to whether the will of the particular subject was in fact overborne or whether he might, by virtue of extraordinary stamina or some other subjective characteristic, have maintained his capacity for self determination despite the objective intensity of the pressure upon him. Ashcraft v. Tennessee [54] is regarded as the first of the Supreme Court cases to apply the "inherently coercive" analysis. In *Ashcraft*, the police, despite the absence of "one single tangible clue pointing to his guilt," had interrogated Ashcraft for thirty-six hours. During this period he had been held incommunicado and without sleep or rest; the interrogation was conducted by relays of "officers, experienced investigators, and highly trained lawyers" who questioned him "without respite." This set of facts, held the Supreme Court, rendered the confession obtained at the end of the thirty-six hour period, "inherently coercive." "[A] situation such as that here shown . . .," the Court explained, "is so inherently coercive that its very existence is irreconcilable with the possession of mental freedom by a lone suspect against whom its full coercive force is brought to bear." [55] No inquiry was made as to Ashcraft's subjective response to the interrogation or his motive for confessing. In a number of other cases the Court has conducted equally "objective" inquiries. In several the Court regarded extended periods of incommunicado interrogation as justification for

---

49.　322 U.S. 143 (1944).

50.　Culombe v. Connecticut, 367 U.S. 568, 602 (1961).

51.　E. g., Clewis v. Texas, 386 U.S. 707 (1967); Greenwald v. Wisconsin, 390 U.S. 519 (1968).

52.　See generally Paulsen, The Fourteenth Amendment and the Third Degree, 6 Stan.L.Rev. 411 (1954); Developments in the Law—Confessions, 79 Harv.L.Rev. 938, 969–84 (1966).

53.　E. g., Greenwald v. Wisconsin, 390 U.S. 519 (1968) (per curiam). The factors considered—failure to provide counsel or to warn, lack of food and medication, length of interrogation—suggest

a subjective analysis and did not seem to be as basic as those which have given rise to findings of "inherent coercion". Yet in reversing, the Supreme Court did not deal expressly with the state court's finding that despite these factors the statement was the product of the defendant's free and deliberate choice. Greenwald v. State, 35 Wis.2d 146, 150 N.W.2d 507 (1967).

54.　322 U.S. 143 (1944).

55.　Id. at 154.

finding inherent involuntariness.[56] But in Haynes v. Washington [57] the Court seems to have applied the same approach to a much less aggravated set of facts. Haynes, who had prior experience with police procedures, was arrested at 9 p.m. for the robbery of a service station. On route to the police station he orally admitted the offense. He was then interrogated from about 10 to 10:30 p.m. and required to participate in a lineup. When he asked to call his wife, he was told that he could do so only if he confessed. The next morning he was interrogated from 9:30 to 11:00 a.m. during which time a statement was taken. This was signed when he was taken to the prosecutor's office. Not until 4 p.m. that afternoon was he taken before a magistrate. Emphasizing the "express threat of continued incommunicado detention," the Court held that "given the unfair and inherently coercive context in which made, [the choice to confess] cannot be said to be the voluntary product of a free and unconstrained will . . . ." [58] A similar approach was taken in the later case of Brooks v. Florida.[59] Brooks had confessed to participation in a prison riot after his 15th day of a 35 day "sentence" to a punishment cell, in which he was held naked and incommunicado and fed only a "restricted diet." Rather than discussing the impact of the conditions upon Brooks, however, the Court simply held that the "stark facts belie any contention that the confession . . . was not tainted by the 14 days he spent in such an oppressive hole." [60]

These cases are best viewed as serving the purpose of penalizing law enforcement actions which offend basic standards of fairness and decency. While they parade under the rubric of "voluntariness," their primary purpose is not the protection of the individual rights of the litigating defendant but rather the broader objective of discouraging disapproved police tactics. The increasing strictness, apparent from a comparison of *Ashcraft* with *Brooks*, simply reflects a growing sensitivity to violations of human dignity. Yet few if any objective standards for police conduct can be drawn from the cases. The best that can be gathered is a series of characteristics which seem to suggest that the police procedure involved is sufficiently worthy of condemnation to be labeled "inherently coercive." These include the following: (a) length of interrogation, including the failure to present the subject before a judicial officer within the required period of time; [61] (b) willingness to permit the subject access to family, friends and counsel, especially when such individuals affirmatively seek to contact the subject; [62] (c) physical abuse, or the threat of such abuse; [63] (d) the objectives of the interrogators (whether to obtain the suspect's version of the situation or to elicit a confession to a preconceived police version); [64] (e) the justification for belief by the police that the subject was guilty of the offense; [65] (f) whether the interrogators informed the subject of his legal rights; [66] and

---

56. Watts v. Indiana, 338 U.S. 49 (1949) (5 days of interrogation); Turner v. Pennsylvania, 338 U.S. 62 (1949) (5 days of interrogation). Cf. Harris v. South Carolina, 338 U.S. 68 (1949) (5 days of interrogation, but some emphasis on the subject's illiteracy).

57. 373 U.S. 503 (1963).

58. Id. at 514.

59. 389 U.S. 413 (1967).

60. Id. at 414–15.

61. E. g., cases cited in note 56, supra.

62. Darwin v. Connecticut, 391 U.S. 346 (1968) (lawyer tried to contact client who was subjected to 30 to 48 hours of incommunicado interrogation).

63. Beecher v. Alabama, 389 U.S. 35 (1967) (one officer pressed loaded gun to subject's face while another pointed a rifle against the side of his head, and first officer asked whether subject had raped and killed a white woman).

64. Clewis v. State of Texas, 386 U.S. 707 (1967) (interrogation "specifically designed" to elicit admission of police version of "truth").

65. Ashcraft v. Tennessee, 322 U.S. 143 (1944).

66. Darwin v. Connecticut, 391 U.S. 346 (1968); Greenwald v. Wisconsin, 390 U.S. 519 (1968); Davis v. North Carolina, 384 U.S. 737 (1966).

(g) the physical conditions under which the subject is held or the interrogation conducted.[67] It is impossible, however, to discern any pattern or single criterion which would permit prediction whether any given situation containing some combination of these factors would be "inherently coercive" within the meaning of the cases.

In contrast to the "inherently coercive" cases are those in which the Court considered not only the interrogation situation but also the subjective response of the subject. These cases pose the ultimate issue as whether the subject's confession was in fact the result of "free and uncontained choice" or rather of interrogation practices which overbore his capacity for self determination. While many cases are not devoid of improper law enforcement activity and judicial comment upon it, they pose the essential issue not of the impropriety of this activity but rather of the subjective response of the subject to the totality of the circumstances. In addition to the characteristics of interrogation listed above (which tend to show the extent of coercion applied by the specific interrogation techniques at issue) the Court in these cases has considered in addition two subjective characteristics of the subject: (a) the individual's appreciation of his legal right to refuse to respond to interrogation,[68] and (b) the individual's ability to resist external pressures upon him to not invoke the legal right.

In evaluating these characteristics, the Court has considered the following factors:

Age, sex, and race: Evidence of inability to resist external pressure has been found in youth,[69] female sex,[70] and membership in minority races,[71] apparently on the theory that these characteristics decrease the subject's ability to resist pressure in the situation.

Physical disability: Emphasis is given to any physical illness [72] or injury [73] which the subject might have, on the assumption that such physical discomfort makes resistance to interrogation more difficult and increases a subject's willingness to confess as a means of avoiding the additional unpleasantness of the interrogation.

Psychological abnormality: Mental deficiency [74] or mental illness [75] of the subject is a factor suggesting less power to resist interrogation. This holds equally true if the psychological abnormality is the result of medication, even if the interrogators were unaware of the impact of the medication.[76]

---

67. Brooks v. Florida, 389 U.S. 413 (1967) (subject confined for fourteen days prior to interrogation in a "punishment cell" with no external windows, no bed or furnishings except a hole flush with the floor which served as a commode); Payne v. Arkansas, 356 U.S. 560 (1958) (deliberate starvation); Davis v. North Carolina, 384 U.S. 737 (1966) ("extremely limited" diet); Greenwald v. Wisconsin, 390 U.S. 519 (1968) (placed overnight in a cell with only a plank for a bed, and no offer of food during approximately twelve hours of custody); Sims v. Georgia, 389 U.S. 404 (1967) (no food during eight hours of custody).

68. See generally King, Developing a Future Constitutional Standard for Confessions, 8 Wayne L.Rev. 481 (1962).

69. Gallegos v. Colorado, 370 U.S. 49 (1962) (fourteen year old boy "cannot be compared with an adult in full possession of his senses and knowledgeable of the consequences of his admissions").

70. Lynumn v. Illinois, 372 U.S. 528 (1963) (woman without experience with the criminal law).

71. Beecher v. Alabama, 389 U.S. 35 (1967) (Negro suspected of raping and killing a white woman).

72. Greenwald v. Wisconsin, 390 U.S. 519 (1968) (high blood pressure).

73. Beecher v. Alabama, 389 U.S. 35 (1967) (subject had been shot in leg during apprehension).

74. Culombe v. Connecticut, 367 U.S. 568 (1961) (mental defective of moron class). See generally Annot., 69 A.L.R.2d 348 (1960); Dec.Dig. Criminal Law ☞525.

75. Fikes v. Alabama, 352 U.S. 191 (1957) (evidence that subject was "a schizophrenic and highly suggestible").

76. Townsend v. Sain, 372 U.S. 293 (1963) (allegation that confession was the result of drug with "truth serum" qualities gave rise to a right to an evidentiary hearing in a federal habeas corpus proceeding even if interrogators were unaware of this quality of the drug, which had been administered to alleviate narcotic withdrawal symptoms). See generally Annot., 69 A.L.R.2d 384 (1960).

Intoxication: Intoxication voluntarily induced, i.e., caused by the voluntary consumption of beverages or drugs known to be intoxicating, has traditionally been regarded as affecting only the credibility of the confession unless the subject was, at the time he made the statement, intoxicated to a state of "mania" or to the point at which he was unable to understand the meaning of his statements.[77] In view of the development of the due process standard, however, it seems constitutionally necessary to consider voluntary intoxication merely as one factor of the totality of circumstances from which it must be determined whether the confession was the product of the subject's free choice. This view has been taken by several courts,[78] although others still adhere to the traditional "mania" standard.[79]

Educational level: The educational level of the subject has also been considered,[80] apparently on the theory that a person with a greater education is more likely to have a full appreciation of his legal rights and the manner by which these can be asserted than one without the benefit of extended formal education.

Experience with police procedure: Just as one with extensive prior contact with the police is less likely to be found to have involuntarily confessed,[81] one with no experience is regarded as more likely to have given in to the pressures of interrogation.[82] This is apparently on the assumption that experience with police procedures broadens one's knowledge of his rights and perhaps confirms the legal theory that police interrogators have no power to compel responses; whether this is realistic might well be subject to question in specific cases.

Whether the subject was informed by his interrogators of his rights: Although this factor has far greater significance following the *Escobedo-Miranda* cases,[83] the Court in determining voluntariness has frequently emphasized the factor whether the subject was informed by his interrogators of his right to remain silent and, when applicable, his right to counsel.[84] In part this factor serves

---

77. State v. Smith, 342 S.W.2d 940 (Mo.1961); State v. Logner, 266 N.C. 238, 145 S.E.2d 867 (1966) cert. denied 384 U.S. 1013. See generally Annot., 69 A.L.R.2d 362 (1960); Dec.Dig. Criminal Law ⊂⃝526.

78. Logner v. North Carolina, 260 F.Supp. 970 (M.D. N.C.1966) (use of confession in state prosecution violated due process because at time confession was made defendant was so intoxicated that "his capacity for self-determination was critically impaired" and affected his judgment); In re Cameron, 68 Cal.2d 487, 67 Cal.Rptr. 529, 439 P.2d 633 (1968) (intoxication considered with all other factors in applying totality of circumstances test); Wiggins v. State, 235 Md. 97, 200 A.2d 683 (1964) cert. denied 379 U.S. 861 (trial court determination that despite withdrawal symptoms confession was "voluntary" affirmed).

79. State v. Clark, 102 Ariz. 550, 434 P.2d 636 (1967) (exculpatory statements made while intoxicated admissible because subject not intoxicated "to such an extent that he was unable to understand the meaning of his statements"); Peters v. Commonwealth, 403 S.W.2d 686 (Ky.1966); State v. Manuel, 253 La. 195, 217 So.2d 369 (1969) (intoxication must "negate the defendant's comprehension and render him unconscious of what he is saying" to make confession inadmissible); State v. Williams, 208 So.2d 172 (Miss.1968) (confession inadmissible because defendant was "in an acute, rampant state of intoxication equivalent to mania"). In People v. Schompert, 19 N.Y.2d 300, 279 N.Y.S.2d 515, 226 N.E.2d 305 (1967), the New York Court of Appeals defended the application of the traditional test on the ground that the due process standard was intended to discourage improper police activities. Where there were no such improper official activities, the court asserted, the state was free to

apply its own test of trustworthiness. This is an oversimplification of the federal rule which clearly serves purposes other than the deterrence of improper police activities; see § 148, supra.

80. Greenwald v. Wisconsin, 390 U.S. 519 (1968) (confession of defendant with only ninth-grade education found involuntary).

81. Crooker v. California, 357 U.S. 433 (1958) (confession of "a college graduate who had attended the first year of law school" held voluntary).

82. Lynumn v. Illinois, 372 U.S. 528 (1963) (confession of woman with no prior experience with criminal law held involuntary).

83. See § 151, infra.

84. See cases cited in note 66, supra. Compare Frazier v. Cupp, 394 U.S. 731 (1969) (affirming finding of voluntariness with emphasis upon warnings given by police).

as a means of determining whether the subject was fully aware of his rights. In addition, however, affirmative action on the part of the interrogators in this respect indicates their awareness of the rights of the suspect and at least suggests the possibility of the inference that they did not intend to violate them.

In view of the number and breadth of the factors considered, it might well be argued that no incriminating statement is ever truly voluntary, i.e., that any choice to participate in one's own conviction is not a rational one and thus not the result of free and unconstrained choice. It is clear that if the statement is the result of significant deviation from the psychological norm it is involuntary within the meaning of the due process requirement. But the cases also suggest that the statement is voluntary if it is the result of relatively normal psychological pressures which may override rational self-interest narrowly defined as avoidance of criminal conviction. Speaking for the District of Columbia Circuit, Judge Leventhal summarized the matter:

> "The make-up of free man includes his mechanisms for self-preservation, to refrain from speech that may endanger him. If he does speak out his statement is admissible as the reflection of his free will if his self-preservation mechanism, and its impetus to silence, is overridden by pressures within his own personality, by his own conscience, religious feelings, sense of duty, etc. But his statement does not reflect his own free will or intellect if his statement is attributable in critical measure to the fact that his self-protective mechanism is negated or overridden by external force or fraud, a condition of insanity, the compulsion of drugs.[85]"

150. The Requirement of Voluntariness: (d) Promise of Benefits,[86] Deceit,[87] and the Bargaining Process.

The voluntariness standard, as generally articulated, requires that a statement "must not be extracted by any sort of threats or violence, nor obtained by any direct or implied promises, however slight, nor by the exertion of any improper influence."[88] The preceding section dealt with actual or threatened coercion, albeit in some cases sophisticated types of coercion. But it is clear that the voluntariness requirement goes further: it prohibits "direct and implied promises, however slight" as well as "any improper influences." When these requirements are applied to the pretrial bargaining process the ambiguities of the voluntariness requirement become most obvious.

It is arguable that a statement cannot be the result of free and rational choice unless the accused made it with full awareness of the facts and with full appreciation of the legal significance of those facts. Thus the voluntariness inquiry might be whether the accused had an adequate understanding of his tactical position and whether he was completely free to act as his best interests under the circumstances indicated. It would not be necessary, of course, that he actually act in a manner which minimized the probabilities of his conviction or the penalty he would receive; subjective relief from guilt might well be a factor which an accused could reasonably consider of maximum importance. But under this view it would be necessary that he have the *opportunity* to weigh against this subjective relief the significance of a

---

85. Pea v. United States, 130 U.S.App.D.C. 66, 397 F.2d 627, 634 (1967).

86. See generally, 3 Wigmore, Evidence (Chadbourn rev.) §§ 834–40; Dec.Dig. Criminal Law ⟜520.

87. See generally, 3 Wigmore, Evidence (Chadbourn rev.) § 841; Annot., 99 A.L.R.2d 772, Dec. Dig. Criminal Law ⟜523.

88. Malloy v. Hogan, 378 U.S. 1, 7 (1964), citing Bram v. United States, 168 U.S. 532, 542 (1897).

decision to confess in terms of his legal position.

The case law, however, does not assure an accused of any such opportunity. Except for a few early cases,[89] there are almost no decisions holding that even intentional misrepresentation by interrogators of the accused's factual situation makes a resulting confession involuntary.[90] This approach received at least tacit approval from the Supreme Court in Frazier v. Cupp.[91] Frazier was being interrogated concerning a homicide. The officers falsely informed him that his cousin, Rawls, with whom Frazier stated he had been on the night of the homicide,

had been brought in and had confessed. Although Frazier was still reluctant to talk, he nevertheless began to confess after an officer sympathetically suggested that the victim had begun the fatal altercation by making homosexual advances. "The fact that the police misrepresented the statement that Rawls made is," held the Court, "while relevant, insufficient in our view to make this otherwise voluntary confession inadmissible."[92]

Claims of involuntariness based on indications by interrogators that the accused will benefit by confessing have been received by the courts with more sympathy, but the cases are in almost hopeless confusion. Much of the difficulty arises from failure to reconcile the voluntariness requirement with the plea bargaining process and especially the role of the police in that practice. Thus while the cases agree that a mere exhortation to tell the truth will not invalidate a subsequent statement,[93] general suggestions that the accused will fare better in later proceedings if he confesses have been held to affect confessions fatally.[94] Other courts, however,

---

89. E. g., People v. McCullough, 81 Mich. 25, 45 N.W. 515 (1890) (accused told by police that the deceased was killed by a stone which the accused had thrown, although the police had no proof of this; resulting confession inadmissible); Cook v. State, 32 Tex.Cr. 27, 22 S.W. 23 (1893) (accused was sent false message that he had been seen stealing the goods and would be prosecuted unless he "settled"; resulting confession inadmissible).

90. United States ex rel. Caminito v. Murphy, 222 F.2d 698 (2d Cir. 1955) (police masqueraded as witnesses and purported to identify accused; confession not inadmissible on this basis alone); United States ex rel. Kern v. Maroney, 275 F.Supp. 435 (W.D.Pa.1967) (withholding information that victim of assault had died did not invalidate confession); Commonwealth v. Baity, 428 Pa. 306, 237 A.2d 172 (1968) (defendant confessed after being falsely told that accomplice had confessed and identified him as "triggerman"; confession admissible); People v. Boone, 22 N.Y.2d 476, 293 N.Y.S. 2d 287, 239 N.E.2d 885 (1968) cert. denied 393 U.S. 991 (accused falsely told that accomplice had confessed and identified accused as the killer; confession admissible); People v. McQueen, 18 N.Y.2d 337, 274 N.Y.S.2d 886, 221 N.E.2d 550 (1966) (accused told that she might as well confess because victim, who had in fact died, would "be likely to" identify her; held admissible); People v. Everett, 10 N.Y.2d 500, 225 N.Y.S.2d 193, 180 N.E.2d 556 (1962) (accused confessed after being told that deceased victim was not badly hurt and had identified him; held admissible). But see Macon v. Commonwealth, 187 Va. 363, 46 S.E.2d 396 (1948) (accused, a woman, "deliberately entrapped into secluded spot" by police and led to believe that confession would enable her to raise defense of self-defense and that it was the only way to avoid conviction on a murder charge; confession held inadmissible).

91. 394 U.S. 731 (1969).

92. Id. at 739. But cf. Leyra v. Denno, 347 U.S. 556 (1954), holding involuntary a statement obtained by a psychiatrist with "considerable knowledge" of hypnosis who was represented to the defendant as a general practitioner brought to relieve his acutely painful sinus attack. *Leyra*, however, apparently turned not so much upon the deception as upon the doctor's skillful techniques and the defendant's physical and emotional exhaustion. Id. at 561.

A statement made to one in the employment of police under the mistaken impression that the listener can be trusted not to reveal the statement is not "involuntary" on that basis, even if affirmative deception was practiced to hide the listener's status. United States v. White, 401 U.S. 745, (1971); Hoffa v. United States, 385 U.S. 293 (1966).

93. Crooker v. California, 357 U.S. 433, 437 (1958); Merchant v. State, 217 Md. 61, 141 A.2d 487 (1958).

94. Statements were held inadmissible in the following cases: Womack v. State, 281 Ala. 499, 205 So.2d 579 (1967) (interrogator told accused it would "go lighter on him" if he confessed); State v. Mullin, 249 Iowa 10, 85 N.W.2d 598 (1957) ("more mercy is going to be granted to you by the authorities that will handle the prosecution"); Lyter v. State, 2 Md.App. 654, 236 A.2d 432 (1968) (in-

have held otherwise.[95] Statements made in response to promises not to prosecute have been held involuntary,[96] as have those made after a promise to see that other charges would be dropped.[97] Specific misrepresentation to the effect that a confession would reduce susceptibility to punishment has been held to invalidate a statement,[98] but promises to help the accused gain release on bail have been held not to have this effect.[99]

Attempts to reconcile the cases involving the suggestion of advantage from confessing have been largely unsuccessful. The California Supreme Court attempted to distinguish between informing an accused of the results that "flow naturally from the truth" and representations of more lenient treatment.[1] Yet this distinction ignores the strong likelihood that an accused who fully cooperates with prosecuting authorities will in fact fare better than one who insists on putting the state to its proof. Other cases suggest the distinction between those practices which are reasonably likely to induce an untrue statement and those which are not.[2] The due process standard seems to make this line an impermissible one to draw.[3] Moreover, it does not explain the results in the cases. An experienced and well advised accused might conclude on the basis of false information that he was likely to be convicted although innocent and that his tactical advantage would consequently be best served by confessing falsely and otherwise cooperating. But this danger has impressed almost no courts.

terrogator told accused of several prior instances where defendants who confessed to him had received lighter sentences and that he "knew" the judges and lawyers); State v. Fox, 274 N.C. 277, 163 S.E.2d 492 (1968) (accused told that it would be better for him in court if he confessed and that he might be charged with a lesser offense); State v. Fuqua, 269 N.C. 223, 152 S.E.2d 68 (1967) (interrogator told accused that "if he wanted to talk to me then I would be able to testify that he talked to me and was cooperative"); Dorsciak v. Gladden, 246 Ore. 233, 425 P.2d 177 (1967) (interrogator told accused judge "would be easier on him").

95. In the following cases the statements were held admissible: Hargett v. State, 235 Ark. 189, 357 S.W.2d 533 (1962) (interrogator told accused he would "help him all I could" if he confessed); Brooks v. State, 229 A.2d 833 (Del.1967) (officers stated that they would see what they could do to help the accused, but that they could not promise him anything); People v. McGuire, 39 Ill.2d 244, 234 N.E.2d 772 (1968) cert. denied 393 U.S. 884 (deputy sheriff told accused that it would be better for him if he confessed); People v. Hartgraves, 31 Ill.2d 375, 202 N.E.2d 33 (1964) cert. denied 380 U.S. 961 ("It would go easier in court for you if you made a statement.").

96. State v. Ely, 237 Ore. 329, 390 P.2d 348 (1964) (defendant, accused of child molesting, led to believe that his confession would be used to keep him from teaching but that there would be no criminal prosecution); Fisher v. State, 379 S.W.2d 900 (Tex.Cr.App.1964) (accused's statement to victim would be involuntary if it were established on remand that victim had promised no legal action if the accused cooperated).

97. Williams v. United States, 328 F.2d 669 (5th Cir. 1964) (postal inspector promised to try to get state charges dropped). Grades v. Boles, 398 F.2d 409 (4th Cir. 1968) (accused, not represented by counsel, misunderstood prosecutor's statement as containing an unconditional promise that all other charges would be dropped).

98. United States ex rel. Everett v. Murphy, 329 F.2d 68 (2d Cir. 1964) cert. denied 377 U.S. 967 (police "falsely" promised assistance on a far less serious charge than they knew would be brought); State v. Castonguay, 240 A.2d 747 (Me.1968) (defendant revealed location of crime when, in federal prosecution, sentencing judge indicated that unless defendant did so, judge would "reconsider" sentence tentatively arrived at; defendant's admissions inadmissible in subsequent state prosecution); State v. Nelson, 63 N.M. 428, 321 P.2d 202 (1958) (police chief erroneously told accused that under state law one who confessed to murder could not be executed for the crime). Compare Milton v. Cochran, 147 So.2d 137 (Fla.1962) cert. denied 375 U.S. 869 (statement given after accused was told that only by confessing could he avoid death penalty held admissible).

99. United States v. Ferrara, 377 F.2d 16 (2d Cir. 1967) cert. denied 389 U.S. 908; Fernandez-Delgado v. United States, 368 F.2d 34 (9th Cir. 1966).

1. People v. Hill, 66 Cal.2d 536, 58 Cal.Rptr. 340, 426 P.2d 908 (1967) cert. denied 389 U.S. 993, 390 U.S. 911.

2. E. g., People v. Ragen, 262 Cal.App.2d 392, 68 Cal. Rptr. 700, 703 (1968); State v. Hofer, 238 Iowa 820, 28 N.W.2d 475 (1947); Commonwealth v. Johnson, 372 Pa. 266, 93 A.2d 691 (1953).

3. See § 148, supra.

Similar confusion exists as to discussions between an accused and his interrogators in regard to "collateral benefits" of a confession, i.e., benefits not directly concerned with his immediate criminal liability.[4] For example, in Lynumn v. Illinois[5] the Supreme Court held a confession involuntary on the basis that the accused, a woman, had been told that if she cooperated "it would go easier on her," but if she was convicted without cooperation her children might be taken from her. Ten years earlier, however, the Court considered a case[6] in which the accused confessed after receiving assurances that his father would be released from custody and his brother would not be considered to have violated parole. These factors, Mr. Justice Jackson implied, not only did not suggest involuntariness but tended to support a find-

ing of voluntariness: "[T]he spectacle of Cooper naming his own terms for [his] confession, deciding for himself with whom he would negotiate, getting what he wanted as a consideration for telling what he knew, reduces to absurdity his present claim that he was coerced into confession."[7]

151. The Right to Remain Silent and to Counsel: (a) Evolution of *Miranda*.[8]

Prior to 1964, the refusal of police or other interrogators to permit the subject of interrogation to consult with counsel, even in the face of a specific request to see a particular available lawyer, was regarded as only part of the "totality of circumstances" determining the voluntariness of a statement.[9] In Massiah v. United States,[10] however, the Supreme Court held that the Sixth Amendment's guarantee that "in all criminal prosecutions the accused shall enjoy the right . . . to have Assistance of Counsel for his defense" required the exclusion of incriminating statements elicited by government agents from the accused after he had been indicted and in the absence of counsel. Within a year it was made clear that this rule was equally binding on the states.[11]

Soon after *Massiah* came Malloy v. Hogan,[12] holding the Fifth Amendment's privilege against compulsory self-incrimination binding on the states as well as the federal

---

4. The following cases found statements involuntary: State v. McFall, 103 Ariz. 234, 439 P.2d 805 (1968) (interrogators told accused, who was a narcotics user, that his request for some of the drugs he had when arrested would be "considered" after the interrogation); United States ex rel. Williams v. Fay, 323 F.2d 65 (2d Cir. 1963) cert. denied 376 U.S. 915 (accused told he could see mother and chaplain if he confessed after eighteen hours of interrogation); Kier v. State, 213 Md.App. 556, 132 A.2d 494 (1957) (accused told that if he confessed it would be unnecessary to perform medical examination of his genitalia). The following cases held that the statements were voluntary: United States v. Ferrara, 377 F.2d 16 (2d Cir. 1967) cert. denied 389 U.S. 908 (federal agent's statement to experienced criminal that if he cooperated "I felt sure he would get out on reduced bail" was "not the kind of inducement or promise that would, by itself, make the confession involuntary"); Fernandez-Delgado v. United States, 368 F.2d 34 (9th Cir. 1966) (agent said he would help defendant get out on bail and any assistance would be brought to attention of prosecuting attorney); People v. Kendrick, 56 Cal.2d 71, 14 Cal.Rptr. 13, 363 P.2d 13 (1961) (accused was told that officer would take up the matter of release of accused's friends with someone "higher," and if there was a murder charge against them "he would see that it was lifted"); Beaver v. State, 220 Tenn. 133, 414 S.W.2d 841 (1967) (accused confessed after conversation with private individual which led him to believe that by confessing we would assure that reward would go to his common law wife).

5. 372 U.S. 528 (1963).

6. Stein v. New York, 346 U.S. 156 (1953).

7. Id. at 186.

8. See generally, Elsen and Rosett, Protection for the Suspect Under Miranda v. Arizona, 67 Colum.L. Rev. 645 (1967); Kamisar, A Dissent From the Miranda Dissents: Some Comments on the "New" Fifth Amendment and the Old "Voluntariness" Test, 65 Mich.L.Rev. 59 (1966); Developments in the Law—Confessions, 79 Harv.L.Rev. 938, 966–1023 (1966).

9. Crooker v. California, 357 U.S. 433 (1958); Cicenia v. La Gay, 357 U.S. 504 (1958).

10. 377 U.S. 201 (1964).

11. State v. McLeod, 173 Ohio St. 520, 184 N.E.2d 101 (1962), remanded 378 U.S. 582 (1964), on remand 1 Ohio St.2d 60, 203 N.E.2d 349 (1964), rev'd 381 U.S. 356 (1965).

12. 378 U.S. 1 (1964).

government. Immediately following *Malloy* the Court decided Escobedo v. Illinois,[13] ruling that Danny Escobedo's Sixth Amendment right to counsel had been violated when police obtained a statement implicating him in a homicide despite Escobedo's specific request to see his attorney who was unsuccessfully attempting to obtain police permission to consult with his client. Escobedo himself was told by the officers that his lawyer did not want to see him. "We hold," concluded the Court, "that where, as here, the investigation is no longer a general inquiry into an unsolved crime but has begun to focus on a particular suspect, the suspect has been taken into police custody, the police carry out a process of interrogation that lends itself to eliciting incriminating statements, the suspect has requested and been denied an opportunity to consult with his lawyer, and the police have not effectively warned him of his constitutional right to remain silent, the accused has been denied 'the Assistance of Counsel' . . . and that no statement elicited by the police during the interrogation may be used against him at a criminal trial." [14]

The next year, 1966, lightning struck. In an opinion actually disposing of four cases [15] but known generally as Miranda v. Arizona,[16] the Court abandoned the emphasis in *Escobedo* upon the factors in the particular case

and established broad universally applicable guidelines relating to the right to remain silent and to counsel in police interrogations, whether state or federal. After examining contemporary interrogation techniques, the Court concluded that "without proper safeguards the process of in-custody interrogation . . . contains inherently compelling pressures which work to undermine the individual's will to resist and to compel him to speak where he would not otherwise do so freely." [17] Finding the traditional voluntariness requirement inadequate to protect the endangered Fifth Amendment right in this context, the Court turned to the right to counsel as a method of protecting the privilege. Noting that even advice given by an attorney prior to questioning may be swiftly overcome by secret interrogation, the Court concluded that effective protection of the privilege in the interrogation situation required that an accused be extended not only the right to consult with counsel before interrogation but also to have counsel present during any questioning if the accused so desires. To fully implement this right the Court made clear that it would require that each subject of interrogation be given the "*Miranda* warnings":

> "[W]hen an individual is taken into custody or otherwise deprived of his freedom by the authorities in any significant way and is subjected to questioning . . . unless other fully effective means are adopted to notify the person of his right of silence and to assure that the exercise of the right will be scrupulously honored, the following measures are required. He must be warned prior to any questioning that he has the right to remain silent, that anything he says can be used against him in a court of law, that he has the right to the presence of an attorney, and that if

---

13. 378 U.S. 478 (1964). Escobedo can be read as merely an application of the "critical stage" test, i. e., counsel is required at all pretrial stages of the prosecution that, under the particular facts, are "critical." See, e. g., White v. Maryland, 373 U.S. 59 (1963); Hamilton v. Alabama, 368 U.S. 52 (1961). Given the investigation that the Illinois officials choose to pursue, the interrogation became a critical stage and Escobedo was entitled to representation during it.

14. Escobedo v. Illinois, 378 U.S. 478, 490–91 (1964).

15. In addition to Miranda v. Arizona (No. 759), these included Vignera v. New York (No. 760), Westover v. United States (No. 761), and California v. Stewart (No. 584).

16. 384 U.S. 436 (1966).

17. Id. at 467.

he cannot afford an attorney one will be appointed for him prior to any questioning if he desires. . . . After such warnings have been given, . . . the individual may knowingly and intelligently waive these rights and agree to answer questions or make a statement. But unless and until such warnings and waiver are demonstrated by the prosecution at trial, no evidence obtained as a result of interrogation can be used against him.[18]"

If, after the warnings have been given, the subject indicates "in any manner" that he wishes to remain silent, the interrogation must stop. If he states that he desires an attorney, the interrogation must cease until an attorney is provided and the accused has been given an opportunity to consult with him.[19] If the accused has an attorney *and* indicates a desire to remain silent, "there may be some circumstances in which further questioning would be permissible." Statements made under such circumstances, if free of "overbearing" and "the compelling influence of the interrogation process," would amount to a waiver of the privilege against compulsory self-incrimination insofar as those particular statements are concerned.[20] Prior warning and waiver of the underlying rights were clearly made essential to the admissibility of any admission or exculpatory statement as well as to full "confessions." [21]

Despite the relatively rapid development of the right to counsel during police interrogations from *Massiah* through *Miranda*, there was nevertheless a significant period of time during which the applicable rule was unclear. This ambiguity was resolved in

Johnson v. New Jersey [22] in which the Court held that both *Escodebo* and *Miranda* were to be applied only to those cases in which the trial had begun after the date of the Supreme Court decision. Thus *Escobedo* applies only to those cases tried between June 22, 1964 and June 13, 1966, and *Miranda* applies only after the 1966 date. Neither case applies to those cases tried before June 22, 1964, although the Court made clear that the failure to extend the rights established in those cases could be considered as part of the totality of circumstances determinative of voluntariness.

The shift in emphasis in *Miranda* from the subjective inquiry of the traditional voluntariness test to the objective *Miranda* requirements was probably due to several factors. One was almost certainly the administrative inadequacies of the voluntariness criterion. While the requirement that a statement be "voluntary" was easily stated, its application to particular sets of facts left a great deal of room for flexibility. This flexibility was used by lower tribunals—especially state courts—when unsympathetic with the requirement itself, to apply it in a manner inconsistent with the Supreme Court's objectives. The result was administrative overburdening, both of the lower federal courts called upon in post-conviction proceedings to review state court determinations of voluntariness,[23] and of the Supreme Court, which had assumed a willingness to evaluate for itself the voluntariness of nu-

---

18. Id. at 478–79.

19. Id. at 473–74.

20. Id. at 474, n. 44.

21. Id. at 476–77.

Admissibility for impeachment is discussed in § 178, infra.

22. 384 U.S. 719 (1966).

23. See Brown v. Allen, 344 U.S. 443 (1953). The burden on the lower federal courts was increased by the discussion of the duty and authority of a federal court to conduct evidentiary hearings of its own in Townsend v. Sain, 372 U.S. 293 (1963) and the decision that exhaustion of state remedies was not a prerequisite to federal habeas corpus in Fay v. Noia, 372 U.S. 391 (1963). See generally, Badger, A Judicial Cul-de-sac: Federal Habeas Corpus for State Prisoners, 50 A.B.A.J. 629 (1964); Bator, Finality in Criminal Law and Federal Habeas Corpus for State Prisoners, 76 Harv.L.Rev. 441 (1963).

merous statements despite a "factual" finding by lower courts on that issue.[24] The desire to relieve the federal judiciary from the burdensome task of case-by-case review of the subjective issue of voluntariness by substituting to some extent the objective requirements of *Miranda* was probably a major factor in stimulating the *Miranda* decision. In addition, however, the Court apparently felt that as the threats to the interests protected by the voluntariness requirement became more sophisticated and subtle, the voluntariness criterion became inadequate to protect those interests.[25] *Miranda,* then, represents a decision to protect those interests by replacing after-the-fact judicial scrutiny with the assistance of on-the-scene counsel.

This is not to say that the traditional voluntariness doctrine has passed into complete insignificance. *Miranda* does, however, indicate a shift in emphasis from that standard to compliance with the objective rules set out in the Court's opinion. The exact future role of the voluntariness requirement will have to await further developments. Uncertainty as to the function of the voluntariness test as well as the current significance of *Miranda* is further highlighted by legislative action purporting to supplant the *Miranda* requirements with a voluntariness test in which noncompliance with the *Miranda* rights would be merely factors to be taken into account in determining voluntariness. This legislation is discussed below.[26]

152. The Rights to Remain Silent and to Counsel: (b) "Custodial Interrogation".[27]

The requirements of *Miranda* apply only when the subject "is taken into custody" and is "questioned." Determining when these two conditions exist presents two of the major problem areas of the rights.

In *Miranda* itself the Court declared that "by custodial interrogation, we mean questioning initiated by law enforcement officers after a person has been taken into custody or otherwise deprived of his freedom of action in any significant way." [28] This statement was confused, however, by a footnote comment that "this is what we meant in *Escobedo* when we spoke of an investigation which had focused on an accused." [29] Some guidance as to the meaning of "custody" is available in two post-*Miranda* Supreme Court

---

24. In Chambers v. Florida, 309 U.S. 227, 229 (1940) the Court made clear that it was not bound by a state court finding of voluntariness and that it "must determine independently whether petitioners' confessions were . . . obtained [by means proscribed by the due process clause of the Fourteenth Amendment], by review of the facts upon which that issue necessarily terms. But although the Court has spoken of its duty to make an independent determination of the ultimate issue of voluntariness, Davis v. North Carolina, 384 U.S. 737, 741–42 (1966) and its "established practice" of determining voluntariness from "an independent examination of the whole record", Clewis v. Texas, 386 U.S. 707, 708 (1967), it has also indicated that "the determination of the trial judge or of the jury will ordinarily be taken to resolve evidentiary conflicts and may be entitled to some weight even with respect to the ultimate conclusion on the crucial issue of voluntariness." Haynes v. Washington, 373 U.S. 503, 515 (1963). In almost all cases in which a petitioner has raised a question of fact other than the "ultimate" one of voluntariness, the Court has avoided the need to resolve evidentiary conflicts by finding involuntariness on those facts undisputed by the parties. E. g., Brooks v. Florida, 389 U.S. 413 (1967); Beecher v. Alabama, 389 U.S. 35 (1967); Clewis v. Texas, 386 U.S. 707 (1967); Ashcraft v. Tennessee, 322 U.S. 143 (1944). See generally, Berman, Supreme Court Review of State Court "Findings of Fact" In Certain Criminal Cases: The Fact-Law Dichotomy in a Narrow Area, 23 So.Cal.L.Rev. 334, 335–40 (1950); Note, 38 Mich.L.Rev. 858 (1940).

25. "In these cases, we might not find the defendants' statements to have been involuntary in traditional terms. . . . [Nevertheless] unless adequate protective devices are employed to dispel the compulsion inherent in custodial surroundings, no statement obtained from the defendant can truly be the product of his free choice." Miranda v. Arizona, 384 U.S. 436, 457–58 (1966).

26. See § 163, infra.

27. Cf. Graham, What is "Custodial Interrogation?": California's Anticipatory Application of Miranda v. Arizona, 14 U.C.L.A.L.Rev. 59 (1966).

28. Miranda v. Arizona, 384 U.S. 436, 444 (1966).

29. Id. at 444, n. 4.

decisions. In Mathis v. United States,[30] the Court held that an Internal Revenue agent should have given the *Miranda* warning to the subject of a "routine tax investigation" who, at the time of the interview, was serving a state sentence in a state jail. In Orozco v. Texas,[31] four police officers were admitted to the accused's bedroom by an unidentified woman at 4 a. m. The accused, who was in bed, was asked if he had been at a certain restaurant (at which a shooting had occurred) the prior evening and whether he owned a gun. When he admitted owning a gun, he was asked where it was. Relying on the testimony of one of the officers to the effect that the accused had not been free to leave but was "under arrest" (although no formal arrest had been made), the Court held *Miranda* applicable. Mr. Justice White, joined by Mr. Justice Stewart, dissented, arguing that interrogation of the type at issue in *Orozco* did not present the dangers of station house interrogation in which *Miranda* was aimed. Interrogations in a home or on the street, argued White, are unlikely to be prolonged, carried out in isolation, or often productive of physical or psychological coercion. Thus they do not pose a sufficient threat to the privilege to justify imposing upon them the same requirements as are imposed upon station house interrogations.

Despite the Court's suggestion, there may be a significant difference between when an investigation focuses on a particular subject and when that subject is deprived of his freedom of action in any particular way. For example, in State v. Lipker[32] the accused was a plumber who was working in a home. When the daughter of the home owner complained that the accused had molested her, police were called and proceeded to question the accused concerning the allegations. Clearly the investigation had "focused" on the accused, yet it was held (apparently on the basis that no attempt had been made to restrict the accused's ability to leave) that the accused was not "in custody" within the meaning of *Miranda*.

The appropriate definition of "custody" might well turn on what function of the *Miranda* rule is emphasized. If emphasis is placed upon controlling police activity that endangers the privilege against compelled self-incrimination, custody should be defined as a situation in which police action (or inaction) [33] has in fact restricted the ability of the subject to leave the scene of the interrogation and thereby terminate the questioning. On the other hand, if emphasis is placed on the actual impact of the situation in the case at issue, "custody" would appropriately be defined as a situation in which the subject apprehends (perhaps subject to a requirement of reasonableness) that he is not free to terminate the interview upon his decision to do so. In the former, the focus is upon the objective nature of the police activity; in the latter it is upon the impact of the overall situation on the subjective state of mind of the accused. Evidence that the police investigation had focused on the particular subject would be relevant but not conclusive in either case. Evidence that the subject believed the investigation had focused on him, however, would be significant evidence tending to show that he inferred from this and other factors that he was not in fact free to terminate the interview. The post-*Miranda* lower

---

30. 391 U.S. 1 (1968).

31. 394 U.S. 324 (1969).

32. 16 Ohio App.2d 21, 241 N.E.2d 171 (1968).

33. See People v. Tanner, 31 App.Div.2d 148, 295 N.Y.S.2d 709 (1968), in which the hospitalized accused, who was incapable of physical movement, was held "in custody" because the police activity adequately demonstrated that they were merely taking advantage of the situation and would have restricted the accused's movement had this been necessary. See also Mulligan v. State, 6 Md.App. 600, 252 A.2d 476 (1969) (appellant was "in custody" when he agreed to go to police station but police testified that he would have been required to go had he not agreed to do so).

court cases are inconclusive but as a whole tend to emphasize actual restriction of liberty.[34]

A statement obtained without giving the *Miranda* warnings and according the defendant the prescribed rights is inadmissible only if it is the result of "questioning" or "interrogation." Thus there is no bar to officers simply listening to "volunteered" incriminating statements, nor need they interrupt an accused who begins to make such a statement and inform him of his rights.[35] Where the

police action is merely routine gathering of information to be used for standard administrative purposes, the warnings have not been required because the police action was neither intended nor reasonably likely to elicit incriminating information.[36] With this exception, the courts have had little difficulty characterizing police activity as "interrogation" when a statement is responsive to police inquiries which on their face call for an answer. But police action short of questioning in this manner may also stimulate an incriminating statement. For example, in one case a sheriff went to the accused's apartment and told the accused he had heard that the accused had some information on a recent burglary. The accused responded, "Hell, here it is; you might as well take it," and immediately made a full confession. This, however, was held not to be the result of questioning.[37] Nor does simply placing the accused under arrest constitute questioning.[38] Where, however, the accused was told, "You look down in the dumps . . . If you want to talk, talk," the resulting statement was held the product of interrogation.[39] In a somewhat more troublesome case,[40] the accused was given his *Miranda* warning and indicated that although he would make a statement he wished first to talk with a lawyer. The officer nevertheless read him a ballistics report. Upon hearing it, the accused began to cry and confessed. Over vigorous dissent,

34. Seagroves v. State, 282 Ala. 354, 211 So.2d 486 (1968) (minor in custody as runaway held "in custody"); Steigler v. Superior Court, 252 A. 2d 300 (Del.1969) cert. denied 395 U.S. 940 (interview at neighbor's home involved no deprivation of liberty); Myers v. State 3 Md.App. 534, 240 A.2d 288 (1968) (accused was "in custody" when officers told him they wanted to talk with him, the accused got into the officers' car, and the car moved towards police headquarters); State v. Evans, 439 S.W.2d 170 (Mo.1969) (questioning at hospital by officer who took accused there without formally arresting him was custodial because officer "was not going to let him get away"); Commonwealth v. Simala, 434 Pa. 219, 252 A.2d 575 (1969) (custody for parole violation was "custody" for purposes of *Miranda*). But see People v. Shipp, 96 Ill.App.2d 364, 239 N.E.2d 296 (1968) (high school student called to principal's office for questioning concerning false fire alarm was not "in custody"); Beason v. State, 453 P.2d 283 (Okl. Cr.1969) (accused was not in custody when sheriff went to accused's place of employment and told accused that he wanted to talk, accused asked if he was under arrest, and sheriff responded, "Not at this time"); Commonwealth v. Frye, 433 Pa. 473, 252 A.2d 580 (1969) cert. denied 396 U.S. 932 (accused who accompanied victim to hospital in police ambulance, giving police the impression he was the victim's brother, and on whom the investigation had not focused was not "in custody").

See Model Code of Pre-Arraignment Procedure, § 2.01(2) (Tent.Draft No. 2, 1969), which requires that an officer who merely requests a person to furnish information or to cooperate in an investigation warn the person that he has no legal obligation to respond if the officer suspects or has reasonable cause to suspect that the person may have committed a crime. If the noncustodial investigation takes place in a police station or "similar place," the person must also be informed of his right to communicate with counsel, friends, or relatives and that these persons may have access to him. This seems a reasonable compromise of the non-custodial investigatory situation.

35. United States v. Godfrey, 409 F.2d 1338 (10th Cir. 1969).

36. People v. Hernandez, 263 Cal.App.2d 242, 69 Cal.Rptr. 448 (1968) (booking officer asked defendant's birth date); State v. Rassmussen, 92 Idaho 731, 449 P.2d 837 (1969) (booking officer asked defendant's occupation and he responded, "pimp"); Clarke v. State, 3 Md.App. 447, 240 A.2d 291 (1968) (police officer asked where defendant was employed).

37. Hammond v. State, 244 Ark. 1113, 428 S.W.2d 639 (1968).

38. Smith v. State, 456 P.2d 626 (Okl.Cr.1969).

39. Commonwealth v. Simala, 434 Pa. 219, 252 A.2d 575 (1969).

40. Combs v. Commonwealth, 438 S.W.2d 82 (Ky. 1969).

the confession was held admissible as not being the product of "interrogation."

Probably the most appropriate approach to defining "interrogation" is to include within it any police action that is either calculated or reasonably likely to evoke an incriminating testimonial response from the accused. If the sheriff's confrontation with the accused in the first case, for example, was intended to do no more than follow up a lead that the defendant had general information, it would probably not amount to interrogation. But the addition of other facts might change the picture. If, for example, the information had in fact been that the defendant was involved in the burglaries, it could be found that the confrontation was intended to elicit an incriminating response. In the case of the ballistics report, it would be difficult to conceive of a motive other than to impress upon the accused the hopelessness of his situation and thereby to encourage him to confess immediately. Moreover, activity of this nature is reasonably likely to evoke such a response and therefore constitutes "questioning" without regard to the officer's subjective purpose.

The problems of defining custody and interrogation converge in the inquiry as to the applicability of *Miranda* to police field investigations. In *Miranda* the court stated that "general on-the-scene questioning as to facts surrounding a crime or other general questioning of citizens in the fact-finding process is not affected by our holding. . . . In such situations the compelling atmosphere inherent in the process of in-custody interrogation is not necessarily present." [41] But the extent of this exception is not at all clear. Generally, the decisions have supported the right of officers to ask questions in the field without first administering the *Miranda* warning; the fact that there has been at least a limited restriction of freedom of movement is usually ignored. [42] These decisions have undoubtedly been influenced by the mechanical difficulty or practical impossibility of actually providing counsel for the subject of a field investigation. In many cases, if the subject requests counsel, an attorney could simply not be provided, so the actual effect of extending *Miranda* to these situations would be to permit the subject to prevent interrogation.

Several situations might be distinguished. (1) Interrogation for purposes of determining whether any action is indicated in a suspicious circumstance. When police inquire only as to the nature of an apparently suspicious situation, there is generally no accusatorial focus of attention, although the inquiry may be for the purpose of determining whether to proceed on the basis of suspicious focus. For example, in State v. Twitty, [43] officers observed a car driving on school property without lights at 4 a. m. A chair protruded from the trunk. The car was stopped and the occupants asked where the chair had come from, but no warning was given. Where the inquiry, as here, is designed not to determine whether to proceed against a specific individual but rather to determine whether there is justification for police action at all, there would seem to be insufficient reason for requiring the warning. (2) Routine "administrative" interrogation. This arises often in cases involving ownership of automobiles. Routine police work frequently involves requiring a driver who is being interviewed for some unrelated reason to respond to questions directed at ownership of the vehicle he is driving. In view of the routine and relatively administrative nature of this inquiry, it alone should not require

---

41. Miranda v. Arizona, 384 U.S. 436, 477–78 (1966).

42. See cases cited in note 45, infra.

43. 18 Ohio App.2d 15, 246 N.E.2d 556 (1969). See also State v. Dubany, 184 Neb. 337, 167 N.W.2d 556 (1969) (officer investigating automobile apparently stuck in ditch made general inquiries).

the warnings.[44]   (3) Field interrogation of one "suspected" of a known crime for purposes of determining his potential participation.[45]   In this situation, the officer has established the need for police action and his attention has been focused on a particular individual who he believes may be criminally liable, and the danger of compelled self-incrimination outweighs opposing interests. The inquiry is no longer a general factual investigation; its purpose is to establish a particular suspect's relationship to the offense. In many cases, if a satisfactory exculpatory response is not obtained further custody and interrogation will take place, and this is often known to the subject.   Since the interrogator is unlikely to be able to exercise coercion of any sustained sort in the field a part of the underlying rationale for warning does not exist.   But the emotional impact of the confrontation is likely to be such that the subject will not be in a position to make a "knowing and intelligent" decision as to whether to make a statement that may later turn out to have tremendously important significance for him.   Moreover, application of the re-

quirement would probably not significantly affect police efficiency in the field and therefore the protection can be afforded at little cost.[46]

The difficulty of determining when one of the first two situations becomes one of the third is illustrated by the facts of Allen v. United States.[47]   An officer observed a station wagon being driven slowly without lights at 3:30 a. m.   When it turned into an alley, he signaled for it to stop.   Upon approaching it he observed a man in the rear whose face was beaten and bleeding.   His general inquiries of both the driver and the beaten man brought no helpful response.   When asked whether he had been beaten and, if so, by whom, the injured passenger mumbled unintelligibly and pointed to the driver.   The officer then turned to the driver and asked whether he had beaten the victim.   The driver, Allen, responded that he had.   In this situation it was appropriate for the officer to make general inquiries about the situation without observing *Miranda*.   But when he ceased a general factual investigation and sought to determine whether Allen himself had committed the crime which he by this time believed had been committed, he probably stepped over the line.   There is little doubt that "custody" existed; had Allen begun to walk away, the officer would have restrained him. The officer's inquiry was clearly "interrogation." [48]   The inquiry could easily have been

---

44. See State v. Bradford, 434 S.W.2d 497 (Mo. 1968) (officer approached car with out-of-state plates parked at closed shopping center at about 3 a. m. "to determine what the occupants were doing" and questioned them concerning ownership of car).

45. Most cases have upheld the officer's right to make extensive inquiries without first providing the warning.   E. g., Arnold v. United States, 382 F.2d 4 (9th Cir. 1967) (bank employee pointed out defendant as "possible suspect" in robbery that had just occurred; court upheld admission of defendant's response to officer's inquiries, emphasizing that the questions were limited to inviting an exculpatory explanation of defendant's presence at the scene of the crime); People v. Quicke, 71 Cal. 2d 502, 78 Cal.Rptr. 683, 455 P.2d 787 (1969) (officer, who came upon a car containing the body of a girl and defendant sleeping on top of the body, arrested defendant, and then asked him "What happened?"); State v. Caha, 184 Neb. 70, 165 N.W.2d 362 (1969) (officer "interviewed" in the police car the owner of a car meeting the description given by a rape victim of her assailant's car; the court suggested, without citing support in the record, that no restraint existed).

46. Reiss and Black, Interrogation and the Criminal Process, 374 Annals 47 (1967) concluded that admissions during field interrogation were "substantially more frequent" than admissions following subsequent interrogation.   But they also found that when an arrest was made the officers always had a basis for it apart from the results of a field interrogation.   "[I]ntroduction of *Miranda*-type warnings into field settings would have relatively little effect on the liability of suspects to criminal charges . . . ." they concluded.   Id. at 56.

47. 129 U.S.App.D.C. 61, 390 F.2d 476 (1968), supplemented 131 U.S.App.D.C. 358, 404 F.2d 1335.

48. See Agius v. United States, 413 F.2d 915 (5th Cir. 1969).   F. B. I. agents approached defendant

phrased so as to obtain the general information necessary to decide whether to conduct a further investigation without inquiring into the specific guilt of Allen. Moreover, while sustained interrogation could not have occurred in the alley, Allen could reasonably fear that he could be subjected to coercive techniques of short duration in this isolated spot early in the morning. Thus both the letter and spirit of *Miranda* suggest its applicability to such a situation,[49] although the court did not so hold in this case.

153. The Rights to Remain Silent and to Counsel: (c) Effective Application of the Rights.[50]

In the limited period since *Miranda* a number of troublesome ambiguities have arisen as to the scope of the required warning and of the substantive rights which must be afforded an accused if he chooses to invoke them.

Required Warning. Although there is no specifically prescribed language, the warning must clearly and effectively advise the accused of his privilege against self-incrimination, the potential use in court of any statement he might make, and his right to counsel.[51] Thus the warning is defective if it does not apprise the accused of his right to an appointed attorney if he is unable to retain counsel [52] and if it does not make clear that he has the right to the presence of an attorney during interrogation as well as the right to consult with counsel prior to interrogation.[53] The *Miranda* opinion itself is not clear whether an accused must be told that all interrogation must stop if he indicates a desire to remain silent, but the American Law Institute's Model Code of Pre-Arraignment Procedure's warning includes a statement that the accused "will not be questioned unless he wishes." [54]

---

who physically resembled a subject in a savings and loan robbery. The agents noticed a toy gun in his car, and questioned him about it without administering the full *Miranda* warning. In holding the defendant's response to the questions inadmissible, the court assumed that the questioning was "noncustodial and investigatory." Discovery of the gun, however, changed the nature of the investigation and required that the full *Miranda* rights be accorded at that time.

49. The Reporters of the A.L.I.'s Model Code of Pre-Arraignment Procedure conclude that *Orozco* "almost compel[s] the conclusion that legislation authorizing a stop without a full Miranda warning would be unconstitutional." As a matter of practicality, however, they assert that in the field interrogation situation the full warning would appear "burdensome and bizarre" to the officer and is likely to be ineffective since it refers largely to contingent future events, that is, it concerns provision of counsel which mechanically cannot take place unless the subject is detained for a longer period and in a location where such arrangements could be made. They propose a modified warning that the subject need not say anything and anything he says may be used in evidence against him. Model Code of Pre-Arraignment Procedure, Note on Section 2.02 (Tent.Draft No. 2, 1969).

50. See generally Elsen and Rosett, Protection for the Suspect Under Miranda v. Arizona, 67 Colum. L.Rev. 645 (1967).

51. Commonwealth v. Fisher, 354 Mass. 549, 238 N.E.2d 525, 528 (1968) (sufficient if rights were "understandably communicated" to accused). Some courts have examined the effectiveness of the language used with a great deal of care. See State v. Evans, 439 S.W.2d 170 (Mo.1969) ("if you don't have an attorney or can't afford one I'll get one for you" defective as it was subject to the interpretation that the lawyer provided would be one personally selected by the officer).

52. Story v. State, 452 P.2d 822 (Okl.Cr.1969).

53. Windsor v. United States, 389 F.2d 530 (5th Cir. 1968); State v. Evans, 439 S.W.2d 170 (Mo. 1969); Cardwell v. Commonwealth, 209 Va. 68, 161 S.E.2d 787 (1968). But see State v. Williams, 2 Ore.App. 367, 458 P.2d 699 (1969) (right to an attorney "before you say anything to anyone" adequate but not favored). Failure to include this part of the warning may not be prejudicial, however. See Square v. State, 283 Ala. 548, 219 So.2d 377 (1969), distinguishing McCants v. State, 282 Ala. 397, 211 So.2d 877 (1968) on the ground that absence of a statement as to the right to an appointed lawyer is not prejudicial where the accused already had retained counsel. See also Commonwealth v. Yount, 435 Pa. 276, 256 A.2d 464 (1969) (statement inadmissible because record failed to show that police had "that degree of certainty concerning appellant's ability to retain counsel so as to obviate the need for telling him that free counsel was available if necessary").

54. Model Code of Pre-Arraignment Procedure § 3.08(1) (d) (iii) (Tent.Draft No. 2, 1969).

The warning must be given before any interrogation. Thus it has been held improper to ask an accused about a specific crime and only when he indicates a desire to make a "clean sweep" to give him the warning.[55] A more difficult question is posed by the situations in which the interrogation is interrupted and then resumed or in which several successive interrogation sessions are conducted. Whether the initial warning is sufficient or whether another warning need be given when interrogation is resumed or again begun is unclear. In Miller v. United States,[56] for example, the accused was arrested at 11:10 a. m., effectively warned, and interrogated. At 12:45 p. m. he was taken to another location (a Federal office) and, after about one-half hour of additional interrogation which was not preceded by another warning, signed a statement. In holding the signed statement admissible, the court concluded that while the warning need not be repeated each time interrogation is interrupted, no general rule could be formulated. "In each case, the ultimate question is: Did the defendant, with a full knowledge of his legal rights, knowingly and intelligently relinquish them?"[57] Emphasizing that both interrogations were conducted by the same officers and that the substance of the written statement was almost identical to the oral statement given during the earlier interrogation, the court held that an effective relinquishment had occurred. This approach seems reasonable. If the length and nature of the break between interrogation sessions are such that they are reasonably likely to decrease the subject's appreciation of the warning, a second warning should be given. But when the break is of only short duration and neither intended nor objectively likely to affect the accused's awareness or attitudes, no objective would be served by requiring another warning.

Respecting Rights Once Invoked. If, after the warning, the subject invokes either his right to terminate the interrogation or his right to representation, several problems are posed. If he desires and is provided counsel, not only must counsel be permitted to attend any subsequent interrogation but a reasonably private opportunity to consult must be provided. Thus, when despite counsel's request for private consultation police officers remained within five to eight feet of the suspect and counsel in a twenty-by-twelve-foot room, it was held that the right to counsel had been denied.[58]

If the accused obtains counsel, either by private retention or appointment, is it permissible for interrogation to be carried on other than in counsel's presence under any circumstances? The New York Court of Appeals has held that "once an attorney enters the proceeding, the police may not question the defendant in the absence of counsel unless there is an affirmative waiver, *in the presence of the attorney,* of the defendant's right to counsel."[59] Other courts, however, have

55. State v. Johnson, 106 N.J.Super. 295, 255 A.2d 777 (1969), rev'd 55 N.J. 331, 261 A.2d 662.

56. 396 F.2d 492 (8th Cir. 1968), cert. denied 393 U.S. 1031.

57. Id. at 496.

58. Fowler v. State, 6 Md.App. 651, 253 A.2d 409 (1969).

59. People v. Arthur, 22 N.Y.2d 325, 329, 292 N.Y.S.2d 663, 666, 239 N.E.2d 537, 539 (1968). See also People v. Vella, 21 N.Y.2d 249, 287 N.Y.S.2d 369, 234 N.E.2d 422 (1967); People v. Isby, 267 Cal.App.2d 484, 73 Cal.Rptr. 294 (1968). After the information has been filed or the indictment returned, of course, the *Massiah* requirement becomes applicable. Some courts have interpreted *Massiah* as imposing a stricter requirement than *Miranda* applies to the early investigatorial stages. See State v. Isby, supra. See generally Annot., 90 A.L.R.2d 732. Such a holding raises the next question: If an accused requests counsel, is he subsequently precluded from making a statement until he has discussed the matter with counsel? See State v. McKnight, 52 N.J. 35, 243 A.2d 240 (1968) in which at 9:00 a. m. the accused executed a form application for assigned counsel, at 4:15 p. m. counsel was assigned, and at 4:30 p. m. the accused confessed in an interview with the prosecutor which was requested by the accused. Neither

held that an accused who is represented by counsel may nevertheless waive his right to have counsel present during interrogations without discussing the waiver with his counsel or without counsel's presence during the waiver.[60] The New York rule seems more appropriate. While it is in theory possible for an accused to form the mental state required for waiver without consultation with an attorney who is already in the case, the danger of interrogators using this as a means of encouraging waivers for impermissible purposes seems sufficient to justify a general rule requiring that if an accused is represented by counsel, he may not thereafter be interrogated without counsel's presence unless he waives this right after consultation with counsel and in counsel's presence.

When the accused invokes his rights following the warning, under what circumstances, if any, may he subsequently be interrogated? If he invokes his right to counsel, it seems clear that no interrogation can take place at least until that right has been fully accorded the accused. But a different situation is presented when the accused, without asserting his right to counsel, invokes his privilege against self-incrimination. Although the court in *Miranda* stated with apparent clarity that "any statement taken after the person invokes his privilege cannot be other than the product of compul-

sion, subtle or otherwise," [61] this may be regarded as an oversimplification. Two general situations can be distinguished. The first arises when an accused is informed of his right almost immediately after his arrest and indicates at this point that he desires to remain silent. It is arguable that this decision is so intimately connected with the emotional impact of the arrest that it should not preclude the police from again putting the choice, to talk or not, to the subject once the situation has "settled." Thus in a California case [62] an accused was arrested at 2:40 a. m. and, when informed of his rights, responded that "he would rather not talk about it." At 11:15 a. m. the next morning the accused was again fully warned of his rights and nevertheless confessed. Holding that the interrogation was not barred by the statement made after arrest, the court reasoned that approaching the subject the next morning was not "compulsion, subtle or otherwise," within the meaning of *Miranda*. The result seems sound on policy grounds. The officer making the arrest might well be ill-equipped to conduct a thorough interview should the accused desire to waive his rights. Thus the function of an arrest warning should be primarily to acquaint the accused with his rights until it is administratively feasible to put to him a choice under circumstances in which he can be expected to make a more reasoned decision and in which the police are in a position to follow through effectively should he decide to waive his rights.

A different situation is presented when the accused is confronted by interrogators in a context and at a time when the interrogators could reasonably be expected to give the accused a full choice and, if he chose to speak, fully follow up on the matter at that time. Under these circumstances, there seems to be

---

the accused nor the prosecutor was aware that counsel had actually been appointed, "[A] request for counsel," the court held, "does not *per se* disable an accused from thereafter waiving counsel."

60. Coughlan v. United States, 391 F.2d 371 (9th Cir. 1968) cert. denied 393 U.S. 870 (holding admissible, over a vigorous dissent, a statement taken during an interview conducted three days after counsel was appointed during the initial appearance before the U. S. Commissioner); Morris v. Cupp, 297 F.Supp. 234 (D.Or.1968) (after counsel was appointed at accused's request, accused summoned officers and proposed a "deal"; statement taken after warning but without presence of counsel held admissible); People v. Chambers, 276 Cal.App.2d 89, 80 Cal.Rptr. 672 (1969); Gunter v. State, 421 S.W.2d 657 (Tex.Cr.R.1967).

61. Miranda v. Arizona, 384 U.S. 436, 474 (1966).

62. People v. Duran, 269 Cal.App.2d 112, 74 Cal. Rptr. 459 (1969).

no justification whatsoever for further interrogation immediately following the invocation of the privilege. For example, in People v. Fioritto [63] the accused declined to sign a waiver of his rights after being fully warned. Nevertheless, he was "almost immediately thereafter" confronted with his accomplices who had already confessed. After this confrontation he was again warned and then confessed. His statement was properly held inadmissible. But if an accused invokes his privilege and, thereafter, new developments in the investigation are such that it would be reasonable to believe that the accused might want to reconsider his tactical decision in light of these developments, it would seem unreasonable to preclude the police from presenting this opportunity to him if it was done in a manner carefully designed to avoid "coercion." A contrary rule would be unrealistic and inconsistent with a practical view of the privilege. While the accused may well be better off under some circumstances in declining to make a statement, it cannot be doubted that under others it is to his tactical advantage to cooperate with prosecuting officials. Giving a refusal to cooperate, made under one set of facts, the effect of precluding the tender of an opportunity to decide to cooperate under a "new" set of facts would hardly work to the best interests of the accused. While there is undoubtedly a danger of abuse of the right to confront an accused again with the opportunity to confess, the possibility of benefit from it seems to outweigh the danger, if the right is carefully circumscribed. When, however, there has been no change in circumstances other than the passage of time, the question is more difficult.[64] Less justification exists for permitting further interrogation, and the danger increases that the right may be used for subtle purely coercive purposes. The objectives of *Miranda* would better be served by requiring the police to show changed circumstances to justify further interrogation once an accused has indicated a desire to remain silent.

154. The Rights to Remain Silent and to Counsel: (d) Waiver of the Rights.[65]

Miranda encompasses, of course, not merely the right to a warning but the underlying substantive rights to decline to incriminate oneself under police interrogation and to the presence of an attorney during such questioning. Although the Court recognized that these rights could be waived, it enunciated a strict policy in regard to waivers:

"If the interrogation continues without the presence of an attorney, and a statement is taken, a heavy burden rests on the government to demonstrate that the defendant knowingly and intelligently waived his privilege against self-incrimination and his right to retained or appointed counsel. . . . This Court has always set high standards of proof for the waiver of constitutional rights, . . . and we re-assert these standards as applied to in-custody interrogation. . . . An express statement that the individual is willing to make a statement and does not want an attorney followed closely by a statement could constitute a waiver. But a valid waiver will not be presumed simply from the silence of the accused after warnings are given or simply from the fact that a confession was in fact eventually obtained." [66]

---

63. 68 Cal.2d 714, 68 Cal.Rptr. 817, 441 P.2d 625 (1968).

64. See State v. Bishop, 272 N.C. 283, 158 S.E.2d 511 (1968), in which resuming interrogation the following day was held not to involve the vice of "continued, incessant harassment by interrogation"

which *Miranda* protects against. See also State v. Godfrey, 182 Neb. 451, 155 N.W.2d 438 (1968) cert. denied 392 U.S. 937.

65. See generally Dec.Dig. Criminal Law ⬳412.2 (5).

66. Miranda v. Arizona, 384 U.S. 436, 475 (1966).

To some extent the availability of waiver, at least under the conditions outlined in *Miranda*, appears inconsistent with the underlying purpose of the decision itself. In view of the complexities of interrogation situations, it is arguable that an accused cannot make what realistically could be called a meaningful waiver of his right to representation without consultation with counsel to determine the potential value to him of representation. Nevertheless, the language of the decision strongly suggests the validity of waivers made without consultation and lower courts have found them relatively freely.

Thus if the prosecution established that the interrogator informed the subject of his rights in language that would convey the understanding of them to a reasonable man and that the subject made a written or oral statement that he did in fact understand the rights, did not desire the presence of an attorney, and did want to make a statement, it has, in the absence of other evidence, made a sufficient showing of waiver.[67] A number of courts have held, however, that such an express statement by the subject is not essential and that waiver may also be established by evidence showing knowledge of the rights and willingness to make a statement.[68] While a showing that the required warning was given and the subject nevertheless made a statement is not, as the language of *Miranda* makes clear, sufficient, this showing when added to other evidence tending to prove knowledge and a voluntary decision to forego the exercise of the rights has been found adequate. Thus in Commonwealth v.

Fisher[69] the state was held to have sustained its burden when, in addition to showing the warning and an incriminating statement it proved that the subject signed a written waiver in regard to a polygraph test, declined an offer of a telephone to call an attorney with whom he was acquainted, and expressed a willingness to continue the interrogation. Other facts that have been held relevant include a request (which was granted) to make a telephone call,[70] "poise and cunning" displayed in the commission of the crime (which suggests that the subject was not "unnerved" by his arrest and interrogation),[71] and affirmative action in stopping the interrogation or declining to respond to some but not all the questions asked.[72] The latter, the court commented, "is persuasive evidence of [the subject's] continuing ability to make a free and rational choice, and lends strong support to the conclusion that any other rights he declined to exercise during the interrogation were knowingly and intelligently waived."[73]

On the other hand, even an express waiver may be ineffective if it is established that it was not in fact "knowingly and intelligently" as well as voluntarily made. This is a subjective inquiry, analogous to the inquiry whether a statement is "voluntary" within the meaning of the traditional voluntariness requirement,[74] and most of the same factors would seem to be relevant. Thus in United States v. Barber[75] the court refused to give

---

67. Holbrook v. United States, 406 F.2d 44 (10th Cir. 1969) (written waiver); United States v. Theriault, 268 F.Supp. 314 (W.D.Ark.1967) cert. denied 393 U.S. 1100.

68. United States v. Hayes, 385 F.2d 375 (4th Cir. 1967) cert. denied 390 U.S. 1006; Hill v. State, 223 So.2d 548 (Fla.App.1969); Miller v. State, 251 Md. 362, 247 A.2d 530 (1968); Gonzales v. State, 429 S.W.2d 882 (Tex.Cr.R.1968); State v. Adams, 76 Wash.2d 650, 458 P.2d 558 (1969).

69. 354 Mass. 549, 238 N.E.2d 525 (1968).

70. United States v. Hayes, 385 F.2d 375 (4th Cir. 1967) cert. denied 390 U.S. 1006.

71. United States v. Hayes, 385 F.2d 375 (4th Cir. 1967) cert. denied 390 U.S. 1006.

72. State v. Adams, 76 Wash.2d 650, 458 P.2d 558 (1969).

73. Id. at 571.

74. See § 149, infra. See also People v. Stephen, 23 N.Y.2d 611, 298 N.Y.S.2d 489, 246 N.E.2d 344 (1969), holding that while a minor can waive his *Miranda* rights, age is a factor to be used in determining whether the rights were understood.

75. 291 F.Supp. 38 (D.Neb.1968).

effect to a signed waiver executed after full *Miranda* warning where it was established that the subject, a woman, was "emotionally distraught" and feeling the effects of alcohol intoxication, had earlier requested an attorney but later abandoned that request, had undergone two interrogation sessions before the one during which she made the statement, had "discussed" certain inducements to confess with the interrogators, and feared for the safety of her children from her accomplice who was still at large. The subjective mental state necessary for waiver, however, appears to be limited to an intellectual understanding of the abstract rights involved and a freedom from external pressure in regard to whether or not to exercise them. Thus a waiver may be knowing and intelligent even if the subject fails to appreciate the value of legal advice in the specific situation in which he has been placed.[76] It seems for example, that an accused who desired to make what seemed to him to be a purely exculpatory statement could effectively waive his rights despite his lack of understanding that such a statement might well subsequently become an important piece of evidence against him.

155. Confessions Obtained During Improper Detention: (a) Failure to Comply with Requirement of Prompt Presentation Before a Magistrate—The *McNabb-Mallory* Rule.[77]

Rule 5(a) of the Federal Rules of Criminal Procedure directs that an arrested person be taken "without unnecessary delay" before the nearest available United States commissioner or officer empowered to commit persons charged with federal offenses.[78] As of 1966, twenty states had statutes with almost identical wording requiring prompt presentation before a state magistrate, nine had equivalent statutes using different language, and five states had specific time periods within which such presentation was required.[79] At the presentation, the magistrate informs the accused of his right to remain silent, asks him whether he desires a preliminary hearing to determine the sufficiency of the evidence to hold him for trial, and (if the accused is bailable) admits him to bail. If the accused indicates a desire for a preliminary hearing, the proceeding is often continued to permit both sides to prepare. Despite the statutory provisions, however, the cases indicate that with relative frequency arrested persons are not presented within the required time. What is the effect of such a failure upon an incriminating statement obtained from the accused?

In McNabb v. United States [80] the Supreme Court held that statements elicited during a period in which federal officers had failed to comply with a statutory directive that arrested persons be presented before a magistrate were inadmissible at the subsequent federal trial. This holding, the Court made clear, was not of constitutional dimensions but was rather an exercise of the Court's

---

76. See the extensive discussion in State v. McKnight, 52 N.J. 35, 243 A.2d 240 (1968), concluding that voluntariness in this context is not the same as is required for a waiver of counsel at trial or for a plea of guilty, and requires only an awareness of the rights to remain silent and to counsel.

77. See generally, Hogan and Snee, The McNabb-Mallory Rule: Its Rise, Rationale and Rescue, 47 Geo.L.J. 1 (1958); Rothblatt and Rothblatt, Police Interrogation: The Right to Counsel and to Prompt Arraignment, 27 Brooklyn L.Rev. 24 (1960); Note, Prearraignment Interrogation and the McNabb-

Mallory Miasma: A Proposed Amendment to the Federal Rules of Criminal Procedure, 68 Yale L.J. 1003 (1959); Dec.Dig. Criminal Law ☞519(8).

78. "Magistrate" is substituted in place of "commissioner or other officer" in Proposed Amendments to Federal Rules of Criminal Procedure, Rule 5a (January, 1970).

The federal requirement originally appeared in statutory form. See Advisory Committee's Note, 18 U.S.C.A. Rule 5(a).

79. The statutes are categorized and cited in A Model Code of Pre-Arraignment Procedure Appendix IV (Tent.Draft No. 1, 1966).

80. 318 U.S. 332 (1942).

supervisory power over lower federal courts. The rule, then still in the form of a statute, reflected Congressional desire to prevent secret interrogations and the resultant pressure to confess; to do other than to hold statements obtained in violation of the statute inadmissible would be to stultify Congressional policy. The substance of the statute was incorporated into the Federal Rules of Criminal Procedure, and after their effective date in 1946 the Court applied the same exclusionary rule to statements obtained during a period of custody in violation of Rule 5(a)'s requirement of presentation without "unnecessary delay." [81]

"Unnecessary delay" as used in Rule 5(a), however, is far from self-defining. In view of the general attitude that interrogation is essential to effective law enforcement, it is arguable that delay for purposes of interrogation might be "necessary," at least under certain circumstances. The Court addressed itself to the issue in Mallory v. United States.[82] Mallory was arrested for rape at about 2:30 p. m.; police evidence pointed strongly to him and his two nephews, but provided no indication as to which of the three was in fact the sole assailant. No attempt was made to present Mallory before a commissioner (although one was readily available) until after he had confessed under relatively steady interrogation. This, however, did not occur until about 10:00 p. m., and no commissioner was available at that time. Mallory was presented the next morning. Holding that the delay for purposes of interrogation was unreasonable within the meaning of Rule 5(a), the Court indicated that the Federal Rules of Criminal Procedure contemplated only "the ordinary administrative steps" between arrest and presentation. While an arrested person might be "booked," "he is not to be taken to police headquarters

in order to carry out a process of interrogation that lends itself, even if not so designed, to eliciting damaging statements to support the arrest and ultimately his guilt." The duty of presentation does not, however, call for "mechanical or automatic" obedience. Delay to confirm an exculpatory story volunteered by the person arrested might be proper "where the story . . . is susceptible of quick verification through third parties" but it must not be "of a nature to give the opportunity for the extraction of a confession." [83]

If the Court in *Mallory* meant that no delay which has as its purpose interrogation intended or likely to elicit incriminating statements is "reasonable" within the meaning of the federal rule, the lower federal courts have not enthusiastically or even accurately enforced it to this end. Thus it has been held that limited delay necessitated by the mechanical difficulties of placing the accused before a magistrate is permissible [84] and the accused may be interrogated during that delay.[85] If the arrested person tells a readily-verifiable story which, if true, would exculpate him, a limited delay for the purposes of checking that story is also permissible.[86] More important, several cases have held that

---

83. Id. at 454–455. The time does not begin to run, of course, until there has been an "arrest." When a defendant has been taken into custody or when custody becomes an arrest often presents a difficult problem. E. g., Gray v. United States, 394 F.2d 96 (9th Cir. 1967).

84. Nez v. United States, 365 F.2d 286 (10th Cir. 1966) (overnight delay while waiting for commissioner to return was permissible when next nearest commissioner was two hundred miles away); Golliher v. United States, 362 F.2d 594 (8th Cir. 1966) (Monday presentation of defendant arrested on Sunday permissible given arrest in "rural Nebraska community").

85. United States v. Curry, 358 F.2d 904 (2d Cir. 1966) cert. denied 385 U.S. 873.

86. United States v. Ferguer, 192 F.Supp. 377 (N.D. Iowa 1961) (when defendant properly arrested for car theft, permissible to detain without presentation to check out his explanation as to reason for possession).

---

81. Upshaw v. United States, 335 U.S. 410 (1948).

82. 354 U.S. 449 (1957).

limited delay for "investigatory interrogation" is permissible,[87] as is delay for the purposes of reducing an oral statement to writing.[88] If the delay and the interrogation do not create a danger of coercive incommunicado interrogation, these courts have reasoned, the underlying rationale of *McNabb* and *Mallory* does not apply. But these results are difficult to square with the language used by the Court in *Mallory*.

When statements received in state courts have been challenged on the ground that they were obtained during a delay in presentation in violation of state presentation requirements, both the Supreme Court and other tribunals have characterized the *McNabb-Mallory* rule as an exercise of the Supreme Court's supervisory power rather than a holding of constitutional dimensions, and

therefore not binding on the states.[89] Failure to present an accused before a magistrate, however, has generally been emphasized as a significant factor in determining voluntariness.[90] State courts have frequently rejected arguments that they should, as a matter of state law, adopt an equivalent rule excluding from state trials statements obtained during a failure to comply with state requirements of prompt presentation.[91] The sole exception is Wisconsin, which has in dictum accepted the *McNabb-Mallory* approach,[92] although it has not found occasion to apply it.[93]

Controversy concerning the *McNabb-Mallory* rule has centered less on the propriety of the prompt presentation requirement than on the appropriateness of the remedy for

87. United States v. Braverman, 376 F.2d 249 (2d Cir. 1967) cert. denied 389 U.S. 885 (delay of 29 minutes for investigatory questioning permissible); United States v. Vita, 294 F.2d 524, (2d Cir. 1961) cert. denied 369 U.S. 823; United States v. Ladson, 294 F.2d 535 (2d Cir. 1961) (one hour delay for interrogation not unreasonable in view of prior oral admissions). Cf. cases holding that delay for purposes of non-interrogation investigation is permissible: United States v. Quarles, 387 F.2d 551 (4th Cir. 1967) cert. denied 391 U.S. 922 (two hour delay for lineup does not require exclusion of identification); Caldwell v. United States, 338 F.2d 385 (8th Cir. 1964) cert. denied 380 U.S. 984 (delay from 3 p. m. to 11 a. m. next day for lineup permissible). Some panels of the District of Columbia Circuit, however, have interpreted the requirement much more strictly. E. g., Greenwell v. United States, 119 U.S.App.D.C. 43, 336 F.2d 962 (1964) cert. denied 380 U.S. 923 (any delay for production of evidence is unreasonable); Naples v. United States, 127 U.S.App.D.C. 249, 382 F.2d 465 (1967) (delay for 5 to 35 minutes of questioning by officer who did not believe defendant could be convicted on the evidence available unreasonable). But even within the circuit there is significant disagreement. Compare the views of Judge Bazelon (delay of five minutes for questioning for the purpose of evidence is unreasonable) with that of Judge McGowan (same interrogation impermissible only because of failure to give proper warnings) in Alston v. United States, 121 U.S.App.D.C. 66, 348 F.2d 72 (1965).

88. United States v. Curry, 358 F.2d 904 (2d Cir. 1965) cert. denied 385 U.S. 873; Walton v. United States, 334 F.2d 343 (10th Cir. 1964) cert. denied 379 U.S. 991.

89. Culombe v. Connecticut, 367 U.S. 568, 600–02 (1961); Payne v. Arkansas, 356 U.S. 560, 567 (1958); Fikes v. Alabama, 352 U.S. 191, 194 n. 2. (1957); Young v. Wainwright, 326 F.2d 255 (5th Cir. 1964); Dowlut v. State, 250 Ind. 86, 235 N.E. 2d 173 (1968) (holding a statement involuntary and emphasizing delay in presentation).

90. See cases cited in note 89, supra.

91. State v. Jordan, 83 Ariz. 248, 320 P.2d 446 (1958); Heard v. State, 244 Ark. 44, 424 S.W.2d 179 (1968); Rogers v. Superior Court, 46 Cal.2d 3, 291 P.2d 929 (1955); People v. Mallett, 244 N.E.2d 129 (Ill.1969); People v. Carter, 39 Ill.2d 31, 233 N.E.2d 393 (1968); Smith v. State, 252 Ind. 425, 249 N.E.2d 493 (1969); State v. Hodge, 252 Iowa 449, 105 N.W.2d 613 (1961); People v. Farmer, 380 Mich. 198, 156 N.W.2d 504 (1968). See Annot., 19 A.L.R.2d 1331.

92. Phillips v. State, 29 Wis.2d 521, 139 N.W.2d 41 (1966) (dictum) (any confession obtained during a delay other than a limited delay for the purpose of determining whether to release or charge is inadmissible).

93. Liphford v. State, 43 Wis.2d 367, 168 N.W.2d 549 (1969) (10 a. m. presentation of defendant arrested at 12:30 a. m. permissible, as magistrate did not begin to hear cases until 9 a. m.); State v. Herrington, 41 Wis.2d 757, 165 N.W.2d 120 (1969) (8:45 p. m. presentation of defendant arrested at 11 a. m. permissible, since detention was for a proper purpose, apparently investigation rather than to coerce a statement); Reimers v. State, 31 Wis.2d 457, 143 N.W.2d 525 (1966) cert. denied 385 U.S. 980 (10 a. m. Tuesday presentation of a defendant arrested at midnight Saturday permissible, as no magistrate was available on Sunday or Monday, since Monday was Veterans Day).

violation of that requirement. State courts that have rejected the rule have nevertheless emphasized their support of the requirement of prompt presentation. Where a statement meets the traditional voluntariness test, these courts have concluded that the potential deterrent impact upon police activity of excluding such confessions is outweighed by the cost in terms of losing reliable proof of guilt and requiring retrial (or release) of quite clearly guilty defendants. But the reluctance of the state courts to adopt the rule and the reluctance of many lower federal courts to enforce the federal rule enthusiastically is also due in part to what is seen as the unrealistic nature of the "prompt presentation" requirements. If the requirements are read literally, as Rule 5(a) apparently was read in *Mallory*, they prohibit virtually all in-custody interrogation. Upon arrest, police are required to present the accused before a magistrate who then admits him to bail, thereby making him unavailable for interrogation.

In 1968 the federal exclusionary rule was altered by Congressional action.[94] Under the new statutory provision, a confession (a) which is found by the trial judge to have been made voluntarily, (b) whose probative value is left to be determined by the jury, and (c) which was made within six hours of "arrest or other detention" is not to be inadmissible solely because of delay in bringing the defendant before a judicial officer. Moreover, the six-hour limitation does not apply if a delay of more than six hours is found "reasonable considering the means of transportation and the distance traveled to the nearest available" judicial officer. The constitutional validity of this attempted modification of the *McNabb-Mallory* rule is subject to question. Although the Court has not yet so held, the requirement of prompt

presentation may be of constitutional dimensions. There are at least two possible constitutional issues. Subjecting a defendant to possible detention and the other inconveniences of being put to trial without opportunity for judicial evaluation of the justification for this might amount to a denial of due process of law. Or, to the extent that deprivation of liberty is involved, the action might constitute an unreasonable seizure of the person in violation of the Fourth Amendment.[95] But in practice the *McNabb-Mallory* rule does not serve to enforce the right to a probable cause determination (which is seldom made during the first appearance of an arrested person before the judicial officer) as much as the right of one arrested to be informed of his rights by a judicial officer and to be admitted to bail. If a federal constitutional right to bail exists, it may require prompt presentation to render it effective.[96] Not only the scope but the very existence of such a right are, however, not clear. Moreover, the right to remain silent may not require a prompt *judicial* warning. The *Miranda* requirements arguably greatly reduce the importance of such a judicial warning, although it can be argued that warnings by those engaged in the interrogation process should be relied upon only as a stopgap measure until potentially more effective warnings can be given by an impartial judicial officer.

94. Pub.L. 90–351, Title II, § 701(a), 82 Stat. 210 (1968), codified as 18 U.S.C.A. § 3501(c).

95. The language of the Fourth Amendment—"The right of the people to be secure in their persons . . . against unreasonable searches and seizures, shall not be violated . . .." permits such an interpretation. For a general discussion of the limits imposed by the Fourth Amendment on seizures of the person, see § 173, infra. Cf. Ford v. United States, 122 U.S.App.D.C. 259, 352 F.2d 927 (1965), especially the concurring opinion of J. Skelly Wright, J.

96. The relationship of prompt presentation to the rights to bail, counsel, and the privilege against self-incrimination is discussed in Note, Prearraignment Interrogation and the McNabb-Mallory Miasma: A Proposed Amendment to the Federal Rules of Criminal Procedure, 68 Yale L.J. 1003, 1035–37 (1959).

Even if the right to prompt presentation is a constitutional one, restriction of the drastic exclusionary remedy of *McNabb-Mallory* to those cases in which the delay unreasonably exceeds six hours may be a permissible limitation on the manner of enforcing the right. Or, if there is a constitutional right to prompt presentation it may well be less strict than the *Mallory* interpretation of Rule 5(a)'s "without unnecessary delay" language. Thus the right might be defined so as to permit limited interrogation before presentation to a judicial officer, at which point admission to bail may end the opportunity for interrogation. Either approach could save the Congressional modification of the *McNabb-Mallory* rule despite a holding that the underlying right to prompt presentation is constitutional.

156. Confessions Obtained During Improper Detention: (b) Custody Following an Illegal Arrest.[97]

Traditionally a statement obtained during custody following an unjustified arrest has not been regarded as inadmissible by virtue of the illegality of the detention alone, although the illegality of the arrest has been one of the factors considered in determining the voluntariness of the statement.[98] Wong Sun v. United States,[99] however, casts significant doubt on the validity of this position and suggests that the Fourth Amendment requirement that a seizure of the person be "reasonable" provides the basis for excluding statements obtained after an unreasonable arrest or other detention.

In *Wong Sun,* federal narcotics officers had approached the laundry of James Wah Toy at 6 a.m. When Toy responded to their knock, the agents forced open the door and followed Toy as he fled to the area in the rear of the laundry where he and his family lived. Toy reached into a drawer. An agent pulled his gun, arrested Toy, and handcuffed him. When told that he had been named as a source of narcotics, Toy admitted possessing narcotics and told the agents he had obtained them from Yee. Yee was taken into custody. Toy later implicated Wong Sun, who was also arrested. All three were released on their own recognizances. Several days later Wong Sun voluntarily came to the office of the Bureau of Narcotics for interrogation. During that interrogation he made certain incriminating statements. Wong Sun's statement as well as the statement by Toy were admitted against their makers at trial.

On appeal, the Supreme Court held that both arrests were without probable cause and therefore violative of the Fourth Amendment. As to Toy's statement, the Court held that "verbal evidence which derives so immediately from an unlawful entry and an unauthorized arrest . . . is no less the 'fruit' of official illegality than the more common tangible fruits of the unwarranted intrusion" and thus inadmissible. Rejecting the government's argument that despite the illegality of the police action the statements were admissible because they resulted not from that action but from "an intervening independent act of a free will," the Court responded that an inference that the statements were, under the circumstances, an exercise of free will would be unreasonable[1] and suggested in a footnote that even if such an inference were proper the statements

---

97. See generally, Herman, The Supreme Court and Restrictions on Police Interrogation, 25 Ohio St. L.J. 449, 458–62 (1964); Pitler, "The Fruit of the Poisonous Tree" Revisited and Shepardized, 56 Cal. L.Rev. 579, 594–604 (1968); Note, Admissibility of Confessions Made Subsequent to An Illegal Arrest: Wong Sun v. United States Revisited, 61 J.Crim.L., C. & P.S. 207 (1970); Note, Criminal Procedure-Fourth Amendment Vitality of Wong Sun, 19 Rutgers L.Rev. 140 (1964); Note, 48 Minn.L.Rev. 792 (1964).

98. E. g., Dailey v. United States, 261 F.2d 870 (5th Cir. 1958).

99. 371 U.S. 471 (1963).

1. Id. at 485–486.

might nevertheless be inadmissible.[2] Wong Sun's statement, on the other hand, was held to have been admitted properly. Since the illegal custody had terminated and the statement was obtained several days later during interrogation to which Wong Sun had consented, the Court held, the statement was not the fruit of the arrest because "the connection between the arrest and the statement had 'become so attenuated as to dissipate the taint'." [3]

Despite some suggestions to the contrary,[4] it seems settled that *Wong Sun* rested on a constitutional basis rather than on the Court's supervisory power and therefore is binding on the states as well as the federal government.[5] The decision in *Wong Sun* left open a number of questions: Was Toy's statement inadmissible solely because it was made during custodial interrogation following an arrest made on less than probable cause, or did the aggravating circumstances—the invasion of the home, the display of the gun, and the handcuffing of the subject—contribute to the result? What, short of the intervening days of freedom, could attenuate the taint of an illegal arrest? Would the according of full *Miranda* rights have that result? Would presentation before a magistrate? Lower state and federal courts have not

agreed on the significance of *Wong Sun*. Some have read the case as merely reaffirming the traditional voluntary requirement and directing no change in the test to be applied to statements made during illegal custody.[6] At least one court has gone to the other extreme and read the case as requiring the exclusion of statements made during custody effected without probable cause for that reason alone.[7] Probably the majority, however, take an intermediate position patterned after the approach of the Connecticut Supreme Court in State v. Traub,[8] decided on remand from the Supreme Court of the United States:

> "Where . . . an arrest and detention are illegal, a confession made during such detention cannot be admitted in evidence unless and until the state proves that the confession was truly voluntary, and in making such proof, any element of coercion due to the arrest or detention itself will be a necessary ingredient. But even though . . . a confession made during an illegal detention is properly found to have been truly voluntary, nevertheless, if the illegal detention was an operative factor in causing or bringing about the confession, then the confession will be considered as the fruit of the illegal detention and will be inadmissible. It is this causation factor which *Wong Sun* added to the . . . voluntariness requirement. . . . [I]f the confession is truly voluntary and the causation factor of the illegal detention is so weak, or has been so attenuated, as not to have been an operative factor

2. Id. at 486 n. 12. Referring to the *McNabb* rule, the Court commented, "Even in the absence of such oppressive circumstances, and where an exclusionary rule rests principally on nonconstitutional grounds, we have sometimes refused to differentiate between voluntary and involuntary declarations."

3. Id. at 491.

4. Thompson v. Pepersack, 270 F.Supp. 793 (D.Md. 1967).

5. Traub v. Connecticut, 374 U.S. 493 (1963), remanding "for further consideration in light of Wong Sun" State v. Traub, 150 Conn. 169, 187 A.2d 230 (1962) (holding in part that "the existence of an unlawful arrest and detention does not automatically render inadmissible confessions made after the arrest or during the period of detention"); Collins v. Beto, 348 F.2d 823, 826 (5th Cir. 1965) (Tuttle, C. J.); Commonwealth v. Bishop, 425 Pa. 175, 228 A.2d 661 (1967) cert. denied, 389 U.S. 875.

6. Hollingsworth v. United States, 321 F.2d 342, 350–51 (10th Cir. 1963); People v. Nicholls, 42 Ill. 2d 91, 245 N.E.2d 771 (1969) cert. denied 396 U.S. 1016; People v. Harris, 105 Ill.App.2d 305, 245 N.E.2d 80 (1969); Prescoe v. State, 231 Md. 486, 191 A.2d 226 (1963).

7. Gatlin v. United States, 117 U.S.App.D.C. 123, 326 F.2d 666 (1966). See also State v. Mercurio, 96 R.I. 464, 194 A.2d 574 (1963) (dicta).

8. 151 Conn. 246, 196 A.2d 755 (1963) cert. denied, 377 U.S. 960 (Douglas, J., dissenting).

in causing or bringing about the confession, then the connection between any illegality of detention and the confession may be found so lacking in force or intensity that the confession would not be the fruit of the illegal detention.[9]"

Simply a "but for" relationship is not enough to establish this causal relationship,[10] but courts have had difficulty in articulating what more is required. Most have retreated to such vague formulations as a requirement that the decision to make the statement be "free of any element of coerciveness due to the unlawful arrest."[11] Cases in which statements have been held inadmissible have generally involved more than detention on less than probable cause.[12] Cases holding statements admissible have emphasized the absence of oppressive circumstances accompanying the arrest,[13] the passage of time between the arrest and the statement,[14] intervening appearances before a magistrate,[15]

and release on bail or on the defendant's own recognizance.[16]

The appropriate criterion for determining whether a sufficient relationship exists between an unjustified arrest and detention depends in part upon which of the potential functions of the *Wong Sun* holding is to be emphasized. If the purpose of the rule is to deter improper police practices, the required causal relationship should be broadly defined,[17] perhaps even to the extent to making a "but for" relationship sufficient. It is arguable that no such "but for" relationship existed between Wong Sun's arrest and his statement; if his appearance for interrogation was indeed voluntary, it could as well have proceeded as it did even if the officers had not previously arrested and released him. On the other hand, when the statement is made during custody caused by the illegal arrest, it would be doubtful under a "but for" criterion that the chain of causation could be broken. Certainly merely complying with *Miranda* should not be held to break the chain of causation. It is not impossible, however, to conceive of a set of facts in which it would be appropriate to find that had the officers stopped short of taking the accused into custody but merely confronted him with questions, the statement would nevertheless have been made.

But if the purpose of the rule is not the deterrence of improper police activity but rather the protection of the accused's freedom to determine whether to incriminate himself a narrower test of causation would appear appropriate. Especially when other procedural safeguards have been afforded the arrested person, it might not be unrealistic

---

9. Id. at 249, 196 A.2d at 757.

10. Commonwealth v. Bishop, 425 Pa. 175, 228 A.2d 661 (1967) cert. denied 389 U.S. 875.

11. Id.

12. Allen v. Cupp, 298 F.Supp. 432 (D.Ore.1969) rev'd 426 F.2d 756 (9th Cir.) (traffic arrest used as subterfuge to detain accused for thirty hours for felony investigation; confession held to be result of this invalid arrest); United States v. Sims, 231 F.Supp. 251 (D.Md.1964) (agents obtained access to accused's hotel room and waited there to arrest him; court emphasized unjustified breaking-in to effect the arrest); State v. Jones, 248 Ore. 428, 435 P.2d 317 (1967) (arrest made after breaking into motel room and involved physical violence after which accused, a girl, was rendered hysterical).

13. Thomas v. United States, 377 F.2d 118 (5th Cir. 1967) cert. denied 389 U.S. 917.

14. Thomas v. United States, 377 F.2d 118 (5th Cir. 1967) cert. denied 389 U.S. 917 (approximately three hours); Thompson v. Pepersack, 270 F.Supp. 793, 799 (D.Md.1967) (11 hours); Commonwealth v. Bishop, 425 Pa. 175, 228 A.2d 661 (1967) cert. denied 389 U.S. 875 (4 hours); Pearson v. State, 414 S.W.2d 675 (Tex.Cr.R.1967) (2 days).

15. Pearson v. State, 414 S.W.2d 675 (Tex.Cr.R.1967) (accused taken before a magistrate and warned of his rights 23 minutes after arrest).

16. Thomas v. United States, 377 F.2d 118 (5th Cir. 1967) cert. denied 389 U.S. 917 (defendant offered to confess before appearance, was released on own recognizance and then went directly to the agent's office to give a statement).

17. See Collins v. Beto, 348 F.2d 823, 835 (5th Cir. 1965) (Friendly, J., concurring).

to conclude that the illegal nature of the arrest had little or no impact upon his subjective state of mind and therefore ought not to render a voluntary confession inadmissible. The lower courts seem to be leaning towards this approach, although their verbal formulations are far from clear.

157. "Fruits" of an Inadmissible Confession.[18]

At early common law the inadmissibility of a statement did not affect the admissibility of other evidence obtained by use of that statement.[19] For example, if an accused were coerced into confessing to a murder and also into revealing the location of the fatal weapon, the weapon, if located, could be used although the statements as to guilt and as to the location of the weapon would be inadmissible by virtue of the voluntariness requirement. The rationale was that the confession was excluded because of its untrustworthiness, but if the other evidence was itself of sufficient probative value the reason for excluding the confession did not extend to its fruits.[20]

As the bases for excluding confessions extended beyond their purported unreliability, the justification for distinguishing between inadmissible confessions and their fruits became less clear. Especially insofar as the policy underlying an exclusionary requirement was the discouragement of certain practices, the policy was best served by requiring the exclusion of the fruits as well as the confession itself. Although there is

some suggestion to the contrary,[21] it appears that the policies underlying the rules requiring the exclusion of confessions under certain circumstances are sufficiently analogous to the policies underlying the rules requiring the exclusion of unconstitutionally obtained evidence to justify applying the same tests of exclusion to the "fruits" of both.[22] Thus the question whether the fruits of an inadmissible confession are admissible should be analyzed in the same manner as whether the fruits of unreasonably seized evidence should be excluded.[23]

A special problem that arises frequently in the confession cases is the effect of an inadmissible statement upon other statements taken from the accused later during the investigation.[24] No court has asserted that subsequent statements are inadmissible simply by virtue of the fact that an earlier inadmissible statement was taken.[25] Most

---

18. See generally, 3 Wigmore, Evidence (Chadbourn rev.) § 859; George, The Fruits of Miranda; Scope of the Exclusionary Rule, 39 U.Colo.L.Rev. 478 (1967); Note, 50 Calif.L.Rev. 723 (1962); Note, Miranda's Effect on the Admissibility of Evidence Obtained by Aid of an Involuntary Confession, 6 Washburn L.J. 133 (1966); Dec.Dig. Criminal Law ⚖537. See also the discussion of the admissibility of evidence related to items improperly obtained in § 177, infra.

19. 3 Wigmore, Evidence (Chadbourn rev.) § 859.

20. Id.

21. State v. Brauner, 239 La. 651, 119 So.2d 497 (1960) (accused, promised leniency, confessed to possession of narcotics and obtained the narcotics for officers; confession held inadmissible but receipt of narcotics in evidence upheld). Cf. Smith v. United States, 117 U.S.App.D.C. 1, 324 F.2d 879 (1963), noted in 50 Va.L.Rev. 187 (1964) (testimony of witness admissible despite showing that he was located by means of confession which was inadmissible under *McNabb-Mallory* rule); Brown v. United States, 126 U.S.App.D.C. 134, 375 F.2d 310 (1966) cert. denied 388 U.S. 915 (following *Smith*); Killough v. United States, 119 U.S.App.D.C. 10, 336 F.2d 929 (1964) (opinion of Washington, J.).

22. Gladden v. Holland, 366 F.2d 580 (9th Cir. 1966); People v. Ditson, 57 Cal.2d 415, 20 Cal.Rptr. 165, 369 P.2d 714 (1962) appeal dismissed 371 U.S. 937.

23. See § 177, infra.

24. See generally, 29 Am.Jur.2d Evidence § 537; C.J.S. Criminal Law § 817(1); Dec.Dig. Criminal Law ⚖519(2).

25. But see the suggestion of Mr. Justice Jackson: "[A]fter an accused has once let the cat out of the bag by confessing, no matter what the inducement, he is never thereafter free of the psychological and practical disadvantages of having confessed. He can never get the cat back in the bag. The secret is out for good. In such a sense, a later confession always may be looked upon as fruit of the first." United States v. Bayer, 331 U.S. 532, 540 (1947). "But," Mr. Justice Jackson continued, "this Court has never gone so far as to hold that

state courts, however, apply a presumption that the influences which caused an earlier statement to be involuntary continue and affect any subsequent statement in the same way.[26] Thus in order to secure admission of the later statement, the prosecution must establish that the earlier coercive influences were no longer operative or that they did not have a sufficient impact upon the accused at the time of the later statement to render it involuntary. The United States Supreme Court has not held that any special presumption applies to the successive confession situation, but it has regarded earlier involuntary confessions as an important factor in determining the voluntariness of later statements.[27] The inquiry focuses on whether, after the involuntary confession, there was a sufficient break in the stream of events to permit the accused to revitalize his capacity for self-determination.[28] Passage of time is an important factor, although it is not conclusive. In Beecher v. Alabama,[29] for example, the accused confessed under gunpoint at the time of arrest. This was given significant weight in holding involuntary a statement given by the accused five days later after being informed of his rights to remain silent and to representation by counsel, in view of the fact that during the five days the accused had been in custody in a prison infirmary undergoing treatment for a bullet wound in his leg.

When the earlier confession is inadmissible not by virtue of involuntariness but because of a failure on the part of interrogating officers to comply with warning or other requirements, the courts have taken a somewhat less stringent view. Some have held that the presumption that attaches to a statement following a nonvoluntary confession should not apply,[30] although others have implied otherwise.[31] Nevertheless, the cases suggest a greater willingness to ignore an earlier inadmissible confession when a second has been obtained after full *Miranda* rights have been observed than to ignore an earlier involuntary confession. This seems appropriate in view of the different emphasis of the two requirements. Under the voluntariness rule the determining factor is often the subjective reaction of the accused to the situation; the *Miranda* test is objective. When the criterion is objective, the determination whether the impact of the failure to observe the right has been dissipated is not easy to make.[32] Arguably it would make

making a confession under circumstances which preclude its use, perpetually disables the confessor from making a usable one after those conditions have been removed." Id. at 540–41.

26. Payne v. State, 231 Ark. 727, 332 S.W.2d 233 (1960); People v. Sanchez, 70 Cal.2d 562, 75 Cal. Rptr. 642, 451 P.2d 74 (1969) cert. dismissed 394 U.S. 1025; Armstrong v. State, 214 So.2d 589 (Miss.1968) cert. denied 395 U.S. 965; State v. Fox, 274 N.C. 277, 163 S.E.2d 492 (1968). But see Commonwealth v. White, 353 Mass. 409, 232 N.E.2d 335 (1967) cert. denied, 391 U.S. 968 ("Rather than any automatic presumption of illegality in the case of consecutive confessions where an earlier confession is invalid, the test is whether the later confession is voluntary."); People v. Stephen J. B., 23 N.Y.2d 611, 298 N.Y.S.2d 489, 246 N.E.2d 344 (1969).

27. E. g., Darwin v. Connecticut, 391 U.S. 346 (1968); Beecher v. Alabama, 389 U.S. 35 (1967); Clewis v. Texas, 386 U.S. 707 (1967). See also Myers v. Frye, 401 F.2d 18 (7th Cir. 1968).

28. See cases cited in note 27, supra.

29. 389 U.S. 35 (1967).

30. State v. Outten, 206 So.2d 392 (Fla.1968) (dictum); Commonwealth v. White, 353 Mass. 409, 232 N.E.2d 335 (1967) cert. denied 391 U.S. 968; People v. Stephen, J. B., 23 N.Y.2d 611, 298 N.Y.S.2d 489, 246 N.E.2d 344 (1969).

31. State v. Lekas, 201 Kan. 579, 442 P.2d 11, 18–19 (1968) ("where a confession is illegally obtained in violation of the mandate of Miranda, subsequent confessions, however or by whom abstracted, are likewise inadmissible unless the state convincingly demonstrates the absence of connection with the prior illegal confession"); Commonwealth v. Banks, 429 Pa. 53, 239 A.2d 416 (1968) (if first statement was obtained in violation of *Escobedo*, second statement must be shown not to have been exploitation of original illegality and to have been obtained under circumstances sufficiently distinguishing it to purge it of the original taint.).

32. The same difficulties arise in determining whether a confession given after presentation before a

sense to conclude that a *Miranda* warning could not have the necessary impact in the second confession situation unless the accused was aware that his earlier statement was inadmissible and that he was in a position to make a *de novo* choice as to whether to maintain silence.[33] But the cases suggest that a second confession obtained after full *Miranda* rights have been accorded is admissible in the absence of any proof that this action was affected by an earlier statement taken in violation of those same rights.[34]

U. S. commissioner is fatally related to a statement obtained during a delay in violation Rule 5(a) of the Federal Rules of Criminal Procedure. Compare Jackson v. United States, 106 U.S.App. D.C. 396, 273 F.2d 521 (1959) (signing of statement based on oral admission made during improper pre-presentation interrogation "cannot in any way be considered an independent act based upon proper counsel or as occurring after time for deliberate reflection") and Killough v. United States, 114 U.S.App.D.C. 305, 315 F.2d 241 (1962) with Goldsmith v. United States, 107 U.S.App.D.C. 305, 277 F.2d 335 (1960) (effect of pre-presentation statement dissipated by presentation and advice of own counsel).

33. Cf. Williams v. United States, 328 F.2d 669 (5th Cir. 1964) (when an invalid confession was obtained by inducements, "there was a burden on the government, before the acceptance of further oral admission or confession from the accused, to inform them that the original written confessions would not be . . . used against them.")

34. See cases cited in note 31, supra. See also United States v. Knight, 395 F.2d 971 (2d Cir. 1968) cert. denied 395 U.S. 930. But see Evans v. United States, 375 F.2d 355 (8th Cir. 1967) rev'd on other grounds sub nom. Bruton v. United States, 391 U.S. 123 (1968); Martin v. State, 440 S.W.2d 624 (Tenn.App.1968).

The impact of an inadmissible confession upon a subsequent plea of guilty presents a special problem. On one hand, application of traditional fruits doctrine would seem to invalidate the plea if there was a causal relationship between the confession and the plea. But on the other hand, the availability of counsel at the pleading stage suggests that defendants have at least the opportunity to challenge the admissibility of such a confession, and a plea entered under these conditions should not therefore be regarded as the fruit of the confession. In McMann v. Richardson, 397 U.S. 759 (1970) the Court held that an allegation that a plea of guilty was entered because of a prior coerced confession did not state a basis for a claim that the conviction based on the plea violated federal constitutional rights, even if supplemented by a claim

158. Procedural Safeguards Against Unreliable Confessions: (a) The Requirement of Corroboration.[35]

Early doubts as to the evidentary value of confessions gave rise to a requirement that in order for a conviction based upon a confession to be sustained, the confession must have been corroborated.[36] Although initially developed in cases involving violent crimes, the requirement is now imposed in all criminal cases[37] and, in the federal courts at least, applies to admissions and exculpatory statements[38] as well as confessions. Much confusion has been caused by failure to differentiate carefully between two different formulations of the requirement. The first requires only that in addition to the confession the prosecution introduce independent evidence which tends to establish the reliability of the confession. The second —the requirement of independent proof of the *corpus delicti*—requires that the corroborating evidence tend to prove the commission of the crime. The second formulation is sometimes phrased as a requirement that

that counsel misjudged the admissibility of the confession in advising the defendant. Apparently a subsequent plea under these circumstances is invalid only if the same factors rendering the confession inadmissible are determined to be of such a nature or have such an enduring effect as directly to affect the plea. See Parker v. North Carolina, 397 U.S. 790, 796 (1970).

35. See generally, 7 Wigmore, Evidence §§ 2070–2075; Margolis, Corpus Delicti: State of the Disunion, 2 Suffolk U.L.Rev. 44 (1968); Developments in the Law—Confessions, 79 Harv.L.Rev. 938, 1072–1084 (1966); Note, Proof of the Corpus Delicti Aliunde the Defendant's Confession, 103 U.Pa.L. Rev. 638 (1955); 30 Am.Jur.2d Evidence §§ 1136–1139; Annot., 45 A.L.R.2d 1316; C.J.S. Criminal Law § 839; Dec.Dig. Criminal Law ☞533–35.

36. 7 Wigmore, Evidence §§ 2070–71, discusses the historical background.

37. E. g., Thomas v. United States, 370 F.2d 621 (9th Cir. 1967) (federal Juvenile Delinquency Act); Yarbrough v. United States, 309 F.2d 936 (10th Cir. 1962) (interstate transportation of arms and ammunition).

38. Opper v. United States, 348 U.S. 84, 90–92 (1954).

independent proof of the *corpus delicti* be received before a confession is admissible.[39] Because of the trial court's discretion over the order of proof, however, it is for practical purposes not a condition of admissibility but rather, like the first approach,[40] a formulation of the required proof to take the case to the trier of fact or to sustain a finding of guilt.[41]

The vast majority of American jurisdictions have adopted the second approach.[42]

This, of course, requires that *corpus delicti* be defined. Literally, the phrase means the "body of the crime." To establish guilt, it is generally necessary for the prosecution to show that (a) the injury or harm specified in the crime occurred, (b) this injury or harm was caused by someone's criminal activity, and (c) the defendant was the guilty party. To sustain a conviction, the requirement of independent proof of the *corpus delicti* demands only that the prosecution have introduced independent evidence tending to show (a) and (b).[43] It is not necessary that the independent proof tend to connect the defendant with the crime.[44] Nor need the independent proof establish these elements beyond a reasonable doubt. Jurisdictions differ widely in their formulations of the amount of proof required. Some require only "slight" evidence,[45] others a "substantial" amount,[46] and some phrase the requirement as one of a "prima facie showing." [47] Once the required showing has been made, however, the confession may be considered together with the independent proof in determining whether the state has sus-

---

39. E. g., State v. Weis, 92 Ariz. 254, 260, 375 P.2d 735, 739 (1962) ("before . . . statements are admissible there must be independent evidence tending to prove corpus delicti").

40. Moll v. United States, 413 F.2d 1233 (5th Cir. 1969).

41. State v. Hernandez, 83 Ariz. 279, 320 P.2d 467 (1958) (failure to object to statements on ground that insufficient proof of *corpus delicti* had been produced did not waive the right to demand such proof because the statements would become admissible if the proof were ultimately submitted. "Whether [the statement] should be allowed at the particular time is merely a matter of the order of proof and not of its admissibility."); Murphy v. State, 221 Tenn. 351, 426 S.W.2d 509 (1968) (admission of confession prior to independent proof of the *corpus delicti* is harmless error if proof is later introduced).

42. Robinson v. State, 45 Ala.App. 74, 224 So.2d 675 (1969); Bivens v. State, 242 Ark. 362, 413 S.W.2d 653 (1967) (pursuant to statute); Self v. People, 167 Colo. 456, 448 P.2d 619 (1968); Ferguson v. Commonwealth, 401 S.W.2d 225 (Ky.1966) cert. denied 385 U.S. 938; Miller v. State, 251 Md. 362, 247 A.2d 530 (1968); People v. Barron, 381 Mich. 421, 163 N.W.2d 219 (1968); State v. Bass, 253 N.C. 318, 116 S.E.2d 772 (1960); State v. Breen, 250 Ore. 474, 443 P.2d 624 (1968) (pursuant to statute); State v. Lung, 70 Wash.2d 365, 423 P.2d 72 (1967). Massachusetts seems to be the only state expressly rejecting any corroboration requirement at all. See Commonwealth v. Machado, 339 Mass. 713, 162 N.E.2d 71 (1959), citing with approval Commonwealth v. Kimball, 321 Mass. 290, 73 N.E.2d 468 (1947) in which the court refused to adopt any quantitative rule regarding the proof necessary to support a conviction. Wisconsin, sometimes described as rejecting any such requirement, seem to have adopted the federal "trustworthiness" approach, as has New Jersey. State v. Portee, 46 N.J. 239, 216 A.2d 227 (1966); Holt v. State, 17 Wis.2d 468, 117 N.W.2d 626 (1963). Kansas has

abandoned whatever implication there was in State v. Cardwell, 90 Kan. 606, 135 P. 597 (1913) that the corroborating evidence need not tend to prove the *corpus delicti*, but makes clear that the *corpus delicti* may be proved by circumstantial evidence. State v. Long, 189 Kan. 273, 369 P.2d 247 (1962).

43. E. g., Mosley v. State, 246 Ark. 352, 438 S.W.2d 311 (1969) (sufficient to corroborate rape confession if independent evidence tends to prove that a rape was committed; it need not tend to connect defendant with the offense).

44. Id.

45. Self v. People, 167 Colo. 456, 448 P.2d 619 (1968); State v. Urie, 92 Idaho 71, 437 P.2d 24 (1968).

46. Miller v. State, 251 Md. 362, 247 A.2d 530 (1968).

47. State v. Hamilton, 1 N.C.App. 99, 160 S.E.2d 79 (1968); State v. Lung, 70 Wash.2d 365, 423 P.2d 72 (1967).

tained its burden of proving elements (a) and (b) as well as element (c).[48]

Two examples may make the independent proof of the corpus delicti formulation clearer. In People v. Perfecto [49] the defendant's confession to a rape was held to have been adequately corroborated by the following: (1) testimony of a witness that the defendant left his room, the lights in the victim's room went off and the door shook, the defendant emerged from the room a short time later, the defendant returned to his room holding a handkerchief over his face, and there were scratches on the victim's face, (2) proof of a red smear on the wall in the victim's room and papers scattered on the floor, and (3) testimony that the victim was bruised and sustained a broken collar bone and that blood flowed from her as she was lifted onto a stretcher. On the other hand, in Barry v. State [50] the defendant's confession to murder by burning with fire was found insufficiently corroborated by proof of the finding of the victim's body, that the cause of death was burning by fire, that defendant had roomed at the same rooming house as the victim, and that defendant had been seen in the neighborhood on the date of the fire. The independent proof, held the court, did not tend to show that the fire was of incendiary origin.

The federal courts have adopted an approach that differs from the requirement of independent proof of the *corpus delicti* in its formulation if not in the ultimate effect.[51]

Although the Supreme Court has indicated that corroborating proof serves the dual purposes of assuring the reliability of the statement and establishing independently the necessary elements of guilt, the criterion for determining whether there has been adequate corroboration is not the tendency to establish the *corpus delicti*. Rather, there need only be "substantial independent evidence which would tend to establish the trustworthiness of the statement." [52] Where several facts in the proof of an offense are established by admissions of the accused, corroboration is necessary in regard to all of these.[53] But this corroboration may take the form of independent evidence tending to prove that particular fact as well as evidence tending to prove the commission of the crime. Smith v. United States [54] provides an example. Smith was convicted of income tax evasion, and on appeal argued the insufficiency of the proof as to his net worth at the beginning of the period during which he allegedly willfully understated his income. His admission had been used to establish this opening net worth; the issue was whether this admission had been adequately corroborated. Although proof of net worth at this time was not even an element of the offense (it was only one item offered to prove understatement of income which, together with willfulness, constituted the offense), the Court held that nevertheless it was incumbent upon the prosecution to establish it by more than an uncorroborated admission of the accused. This, however, could be accomplished in two ways. First, the government could substantiate the opening net worth figure directly, which was found to have been adequately done by the introduction of the defendant's prior tax returns. Second, the government could intro-

---

48. People v. Perfecto, 26 Ill.2d 228, 186 N.E.2d 258 (1962); State v. O'Neal, 436 S.W.2d 241 (Mo.1968).

49. 26 Ill.2d 228, 186 N.E.2d 258 (1962).

50. 166 Tex.Cr.R. 372, 314 S.W.2d 90 (1958). For other cases in which a conviction was reversed on the grounds of insufficient corroboration of a confession, see Owen v. People, 155 Colo. 19, 392 P.2d 163 (1964); People v. Hubbard, 38 Ill.2d 104, 230 N.E.2d 220 (1967); Williams v. State, 214 Md. 143, 132 A.2d 605 (1957).

51. See Note, Proof of the Corpus Delicti Aliunde the **Defendant's Confession,** 103 U.Pa.L.Rev. 638, 666–67 (1955).

52. Opper v. United States, 348 U.S. 84, 93 (1954).

53. Smith v. United States, 348 U.S. 147, 156 (1954).

54. 348 U.S. 147 (1954).

duce evidence tending to establish the crime of tax evasion itself without using the net worth figure, which was found to have been done by showing expenditures, savings, and investments exceeding income during the period. This evidence tended to show that the defendant was understating his income, although it might not, without evidence of lack of assets at the beginning of the period, be sufficient alone to sustain a finding of guilt. Thus while the admission could have been corroborated by proof tending to establish the *corpus delicti* (the willful understatement of income), it could also be sufficiently corroborated by evidence tending to show the accuracy of the limited fact admitted i. e., net worth at the beginning of the period, which was not a part of the *corpus delicti*.

The lower federal courts have, with occasional departures,[55] phrased the requirement as only that the corroborating evidence established the trustworthiness of the confession and have not required that the proof tend to establish the *corpus delicti*.[56] It is doubtful whether this makes much practical difference.[57] Proof tending to establish the *corpus delicti* is likely also to confirm the trustworthiness of the confession, and in view of the liberality with which most courts

find sufficient corroboration of the *corpus delicti* it is likely that in most cases the trustworthiness of the confession is sufficiently established by proof which tends to establish the *corpus delicti*.

In view of the numerous safeguards against unreliable confessions developed after the corroboration rule, it has been questioned whether the corroboration rule still serves a useful purpose.[58] Perhaps the purpose of the rule—especially the *corpus delicti* formulation—would be better served by a more thorough review of the evidence to determine whether, in view of any factors that might tend to show the unreliability of the statements, the evidence as a whole is sufficient to sustain the verdict. As a practical matter the corroboration requirement seems in many cases to serve as a vehicle for what is really an appellate court judgment that the total proof is of insufficient probative value.[59] But in view of the difficulty of establishing subtle psychological factors that might influence the decision to confess, a general requirement that the prosecution corroborate the reliability of the statement does not seem unwise.

159. Procedural Safeguards Against Unreliable Confessions: (b) The Requirement of a Separate Determination of Admissibility:[60] Burden of Proof.

Procedures for determining the voluntariness of an offered statement by the defendant have fallen historically into three categories:[61] (1) The New York procedure,[62]

---

55. Zamora v. United States, 369 F.2d 855 (10th Cir. 1966) cert. denied 386 U.S. 913; Palacios v. Government of Guam, 325 F.2d 543 (9th Cir. 1963) (corroborating proof must tend to connect defendant with the offense); Yarbrough v. United States, 309 F.2d 936 (10th Cir. 1962) (proof of possession of car bearing out-of-state plates and postcard bearing picture of Utah motel was not sufficient corroboration of confession to interstate transportation of arms and ammunition; suggestion that proof must tend to establish corpus delicti). Cf. Hicks v. United States, 127 U.S.App.D.C. 209, 382 F.2d 158, 163, n. 6 (1967).

56. E. g., Moll v. United States, 413 F.2d 1233 (5th Cir. 1969); Mapys v. United States, 409 F.2d 964 (10th Cir. 1969); Mossbrook v. United States, 409 F.2d 503 (9th Cir. 1969); Smoot v. United States, 114 U.S.App.D.C. 154, 312 F.2d 881 (1962).

57. Sée generally Ackroud, Corroboration of Confessions in Federal and Military Trials, 8 Vill.L.Rev. 64 (1962).

58. Developments in the Law—Confessions, 79 Harv. L.Rev. 938, 1084 (1966) ("serious consideration should be given to elimination of the corpus delicti requirement").

59. E. g., People v. Hubbard, 38 Ill.2d 104, 230 N.E.2d 220 (1967) (testimony of complaining witness was "so weak as to defy belief" and thus insufficient to corroborate confession to rape).

60. See generally, 29 Am.Jur.2d Evidence, §§ 582–90; C.J.S. Criminal Law § 838; Annot., 1 A.L.R.3d 1252; Dec.Dig. Criminal Law ☜531–532.

61. See Meltzer, Involuntary Confessions: The Allocation of Responsibility Between Judge and Jury,

62. See note 62 on page 350.

under which the trial judge makes a preliminary determination of voluntariness and excludes the statement only if no question is presented as to its voluntariness. If the evidence presents a fair question as to voluntariness, or as to any factual matters relevant to the voluntariness issue, the statement is submitted to the jury with directions to determine voluntariness and to consider the statement only if it is found voluntary. (2) The "orthodox" rule,[63] under which the trial judge resolves any factual disputes necessary to determination of the voluntariness issue and also makes the sole formal determination of voluntariness. (3) The Massachusetts procedure,[64] in which the trial judge makes a full determination of voluntariness and submits the confession to the jury only if the statement is found voluntary. The jury, however, is instructed that it may also consider voluntariness and should not consider the statement if it finds it involuntary.

Whatever the theoretical value of the rights accorded one who has made incriminating statements, their practical value may well depend upon the procedural devices available to enforce them. Especially in regard to the right to have incriminating statements excluded, the procedural right to a separate determination of admissibility may be of equal importance to the right itself.

In Jackson v. Denno [65] the New York procedure was held to violate the due process clause of the Fourteenth Amendment because it did not provide a reliable determination of voluntariness and consequently did not adequately protect the accused's right to be free of a conviction based upon a coerced confession. The Court emphasized three dangers which existed under the New York procedure: (1) the jury may consider the confession true and this may distort its assessments of the factual questions upon which the voluntariness decision must be made; (2) especially when a trustworthy confession is involved, the jury may lack sympathy with the policy underlying the voluntariness requirement and decline to enforce the exclusionary rule; (3) even if it should determine that the confession is inadmissible, it may not as a practical matter be able to consider the issue of guilt or innocence without reference to the statement.[66] The same fatal defects were found in an almost identical procedure whereby the prosecution was required to make only "a prima facie case that the alleged confession was voluntary" and the ultimate determination of voluntariness was then submitted to the jury.[67] This does not necessarily mean, however, that the only constitutionally permissible procedure is for the trial judge, out of the presence of the jury,[68] to take evidence relating to voluntariness and make the ultimate decision as to that matter, the so-called "orthodox" rule. In a footnote in *Jackson* the Supreme Court indicated it was raising no question concerning the validity of the Massachusetts procedure.[69] "Given the integrity of the preliminary proceedings

21 U.Chi.L.Rev. 317, 319–25 (1954). The Appendix to Opinion of the Court and the Appendices to Opinion of Mr. Justice Black in Jackson v. Denno, 378 U.S. 368 (1964) discuss the approaches taken by various jurisdictions. In many jurisdictions it is unclear from the appellate case law which rule is followed; in some the approach is some combination of the basic alternatives. Jackson v. Denno, 378 U.S. 368, 378 n. 9 (1964).

62. See Stein v. New York, 346 U.S. 156 (1953) in which the constitutionality of the procedure was upheld.

63. See the cases listed in Appendix A to Opinion of Mr. Justice Black, Jackson v. Denno, 378 U.S. 368, 411–14 (1964).

64. Commonwealth v. Preece, 140 Mass. 276, 277, 5 N.E. 494, 495 (1885).

65. 378 U.S. 368 (1964).

66. Id. at 382–84.

67. Sims v. Georgia, 385 U.S. 538 (1967).

68. For a discussion of the cases considering the extent of prejudice caused by the jury's presence during the court's consideration of voluntariness, see Annot., 19 L.Ed.2d 1313.

69. Jackson v. Denno, 378 U.S. 368, 378 n. 8 (1964).

before the judge," the Court concluded, the Massachusetts procedure does not pose the hazards to the rights of the defendant that are created by the New York procedure.[70] Whether the procedure used is the orthodox or Massachusetts approach, it is necessary that it appear on the record "with unmistakable clarity" that the trial judge resolved the factual issue in favor of voluntariness, although formal findings of fact or a written opinion are not essential.[71]

The Supreme Court opinions leave several issues unresolved regarding constitutionally-required procedure for determining the voluntariness of an offered defendant. First, it is not clear what the constitutional requirements are in cases tried not to a jury but to the judge. In theory, of course, it can be argued that the trial judge, unlike the lay juror, possesses the ability to separate analytically the truth or reliability of the confession from its admissibility and should not be presumed to lack either sympathy for the voluntariness rule or the ability dispassionately to apply it despite his personal views. This position was sustained by the New York Court of Appeals.[72] But several courts have taken the opposite approach.[73] At a minimum, *Jackson* seems to require that when trial is to the court without a jury and a statement's voluntariness is challenged, the determination of voluntariness be made apart from the trial on guilt or innocence and the record contain a specific finding of voluntariness made before the beginning of evidence on the guilty issue. The better practice would seem to be the safer one, i. e., holding the voluntariness hearing before a judge other than the trial judge.[74]

Jackson also does not address itself to the allocation or nature of the burden of proof on the issue of voluntariness. There is general agreement that the prosecution bears the burden of proof.[75] Following *Jackson,* however, courts varied on the nature of that burden. The trend seemed towards requiring proof of voluntariness beyond a reasonable doubt,[76] although some courts adhered to the preponderance of the evidence [77] or some other formulation.[78] The matter was resolved in Lego v. Twomey [79] in which the Supreme Court held, by a four-to-three margin, that

---

70. Id.

71. Sims v. Georgia, 385 U.S. 538, 544 (1967); Javor v. United States, 403 F.2d 507 (9th Cir. 1968) (record considered as a whole did not show whether or not judge resolved factual issue of whether defendants were under the influence of LSD at the time of the statements); Smith v. Texas, 395 F.2d 958 (5th Cir. 1968) (where transcript did not show ruling on voluntariness, it was not sufficient that trial judge later testified that he had in fact made an unannounced decision on voluntariness).

72. People v. Brown, 24 N.Y.2d 168, 247 N.E.2d 153, 299 N.Y.S.2d 190 (1969), noted in 38 Fordham L.Rev. 120 (1969).

73. United States ex rel. Spears v. Rundle, 268 F. Supp. 691, 695–96 (E.D.Pa.1967) aff'd 405 F.2d 1037 (3d Cir. 1969); United States ex rel. Owens v. Cavell, 254 F.Supp. 154 (M.D.Pa.1966).

74. See United States ex rel. Owens v. Cavell, 254 F.Supp. 154 (M.D.Pa.1966).

75. 3 Wigmore, Evidence (Chadbourn rev.) § 860.

76. Pea v. United States, 130 U.S.App.D.C. 66, 397 F.2d 627 (1968) (en banc) (imposing beyond a reasonable doubt burden pursuant to the court's supervisory powers); Mullins v. United States, 382 F.2d 258 (4th Cir. 1967); United States v. Inman, 352 F.2d 954 (4th Cir. 1965); United States v. Schipani, 289 F.Supp. 43, 59 (E.D.N.Y.1968); State v. Alexander, 252 La. 564, 211 So.2d 650 (1968); State v. Scott, 243 La. 1, 141 So.2d 389 (1962); People v. Huntley, 15 N.Y.2d 72, 255 N.Y.S.2d 838, 204 N.E.2d 179 (1965).

77. People v. Jackson, 41 Ill.2d 102, 242 N.E.2d 160 (1968) (rejecting the "beyond a reasonable doubt" standard in favor of "the preponderance of the evidence.").

78. Bush v. State, 282 Ala. 134, 209 So.2d 416 (1968) (evidence must rebut the presumption of involuntariness); State v. Milow, 199 Kan. 576, 433 P.2d 538 (1967) (voluntariness must be made to "clearly appear"); State v. Foster, 183 Neb. 247, 159 N.W.2d 561 (1968) (proof must exclude any other reasonable hypothesis). Cf. Bradley v. Commonwealth, 439 S.W.2d 61 (Ky.1969) (under Massachusetts rule, jury is to be instructed that to consider the statement they must find beyond a reasonable doubt that it was voluntary; no indication of standard to be used by judge in his preliminary determination).

79. 92 S.Ct. 619 (1972).

voluntariness need as a constitutional matter only be established by a preponderance of the evidence. Arguments that a higher standard was required by the due process right to have guilt established beyond a reasonable doubt [80] and by the need to give adequate protection to the values served by the exclusionary rules were rejected. Viewing the voluntariness hearing as unrelated to the reliability of jury verdicts, the Court found the right to proof of guilt beyond a reasonable doubt inapplicable. And, the Court concluded, it had not been established that the values underlying the exclusionary rules had or would suffer by reason of a preponderance of the evidence standard.

Although *Jackson* dealt with a statement challenged on ground of involuntariness, it has been generally assumed that the requirement of a judicial evaluation of admissibility also applies to the determination of the admissibility of statements challenged on other grounds.[81] This, of course, is consistent with the traditional allocation of functions between judge and jury. And although Lego v. Twomey [82] presented only the issue of the burden of proof on voluntariness, it almost necessarily follows that the burden of proof as to admissibility need be no higher than a preponderance of the evidence when some other basis for exclusion is being considered.

160. Judicial Confessions and Guilty Pleas.[83]

Although most of the confession discussion revolves around statements made by accuseds to investigatory personnel during the pre-

trial stages of a criminal case, it sometimes occurs that a criminal defendant will, during the course of a judicial proceeding, make incriminating statements. These "judicial confessions" are, in general, treated no differently from nonjudicial confessions, and are admissible if the tests applicable to nonjudicial confessions are met.[84] Most significant, of course, is the right to representation by counsel.[85] This right applies whether the judicial confession takes the form of testimony in a prior trial in the same case,[86] testimony at the preliminary hearing in the case at hand,[87] or a plea of guilty.[88]

80. See In re Winship, 397 U.S. 358 (1970).

81. E. g., Auger v. Swenson, 302 F.Supp. 1131, 1141 W.D.Mo.1969) (hearing must be held on *Miranda* issue).

82. See text at n. 79, supra.

83. See generally, 29 Am.Jur.2d Evidence §§ 527, 528; C.J.S. Criminal Law § 830; Dec.Dig. Criminal Law ⮌519(5).

84. E. g., Brumit v. State, 220 So.2d 659 (Fla.App.) appeal dismissed 225 So.2d 908 (Fla.1969); State v. Snell, 177 Neb. 396, 128 N.W.2d 823 (1964).

85. Cf. White v. Maryland, 373 U.S. 59 (1963), in which the Court held that a preliminary hearing at which a plea of guilty could be entered was a critical stage in the proceeding and an accused was constitutionally entitled to representation by state-appointed counsel. Although the plea was not binding, it was admissible against the defendant at a trial on a subsequent plea of not guilty. See also Arsenault v. Massachusetts, 393 U.S. 5 (1968).

86. Brumit v. State, 220 So.2d 659 (Fla.App.) appeal dismissed 225 So.2d 908 (Fla.1969).

87. State v. Thomas, 78 Ariz. 52, 275 P.2d 408 (1954) aff'd, 356 U.S. 390 (1958) (testimony at preliminary distinguished from plea of guilty, which cannot be entered at that time); People v. Jackson, 23 Ill.2d 263, 178 N.E.2d 310 (1961) (confession at preliminary not admissible without proof that defendant was given advice as to his rights or that he otherwise was aware of them); State v. Jenkins, 56 N.M. 12, 239 P.2d 711 (1952).

88. State v. Snell, 177 Neb. 396, 128 N.W.2d 823 (1964) (plea of guilty at arraignment for another offense admissible only if defendant was extended right to state-appointed counsel).

A guilty plea entered in accordance with applicable procedural requirements and then withdrawn by leave of the court is, of course, generally inadmissible for reasons unrelated to the subject matter of this chapter; see § 265, infra. The troublesome questions concerning the validity of a guilty plea when the conviction based upon it is challenged are also beyond the scope of this discussion. See North Carolina v. Alford, 400 U.S. 25 (1970) (plea entered by defendant who denied his factual guilt not involuntary for that reason); Brady v. United States, 397 U.S. 742 (1970) (plea entered to avoid possible death penalty upon conviction for higher offense not involuntary for that reason); Boykin v. Alabama, 395 U.S. 238 (1969) (failure of record

161. "Tacit" or "Adoptive" Confessions in Criminal Cases.[89]

Pursuant to the general rule regarding adoptive admissions,[90] evidence has generally been held admissible that an accusatory statement was made in the presence and hearing of an accused and that his response was such as to justify the inference that he agreed with or "adopted" the accusation.[91] The response may be simple silence, or it may be an "equivocal" response, i. e., one that does not clearly challenge the accuracy of the accusation.[92] The response may also consist of conduct from which the accused's belief in the truth of the assertion can be inferred.[93] Underlying the rule is the assumption that human nature prompts an innocent man to deny false accusations and consequently a failure to deny a particular accusation tends to prove belief in the truth of the accusation.[94] Although this underlying assumption is subject to question insofar as the rule is applicable to both civil and criminal cases, the use of the "tacit confession" rule in criminal cases raises some special problems.

For a variety of reasons, a number of exceptions to the tacit confession rule have received general acceptance by courts. When the accusation has been made during a judicial proceeding, the accused's failure to deny it is inadmissible.[95] Although there is some suggestion that this is based upon Fifth Amendment considerations,[96] most courts have reached this result by reasoning that such accusations, in view of the circumstances, do not naturally call for denial and therefore the failure to deny lacks probative value.[97] When, on the other hand, the accusation and failure to deny occur before trial and not in connection with any criminal investigation, virtually all jurisdictions apply the rule and admit the accusation and response, subject to restrictions designed to assure probative value.[98] When the accusation was made in the course of a criminal investigation, courts have divided on the applicability of the rule. Some jurisdictions simply require close scrutiny of these tacit confessions, with the fact that the accused may have been under arrest at the time considered as only one of the factors to be used in determining whether the evidence is of sufficient probative value.[99] Others, however, have adopted the *"per se"* or Massachusetts rule, under

in state conviction affirmatively to show voluntary waiver of right to plead not guilty invalidated conviction based on plea); McCarthy v. United States, 394 U.S. 459 (1969) (failure of federal trial court to comply with F.R.Crim.P. 11 invalidated conviction based on plea).

89. See generally, 3A Wigmore, Evidence (Chadbourn rev.) § 821, n. 3; 4 id. §§ 1071, 1072; Developments in the Law—Confessions, 79 Harv.L.Rev. 938, 1036–44 (1966); Note, Tacit Criminal Admissions, 112 U.Pa.L.Rev. 210 (1963); 29 Am.Jur.2d Evidence §§ 638–45; C.J.S. Criminal Law § 734(1); Annots., 77 A.L.R.2d 463, 115 A.L.R. 1510, 80 A.L.R. 1235; Dec.Dig. Criminal Law ⊙⇒407–408.

90. See §§ 269, 270, infra.

91. The leading cases are Sparf v. United States, 156 U.S. 51 (1895) and Commonwealth v. Kenney, 53 Mass. (12 Metc.) 235 (1847).

92. An example would be, "Be certain," in response to an assertion. See People v. Stella, 344 Ill. 589, 176 N.E. 909 (1931).

93. State v. Lounsbery, 74 Wash.2d 659, 445 P.2d 1017 (1968) (defendant visited psychologist after wife accused him of sexually molesting his stepdaughter).

94. People v. Simmons, 28 Cal.2d 699, 172 P.2d 18 (1946); State v. Brown, 16 Utah 2d 57, 395 P.2d 727 (1964).

95. Pickens v. State, 111 Ga.App. 574, 142 S.E.2d 427 (1965) (proceedings before a magistrate); Commonwealth v. Zorambo, 205 Pa. 109, 54 A. 716 (1903); Jones v. State, 184 Tenn. 128, 196 S.W.2d 491 (1946).

96. Parrott v. State, 125 Tenn. 1, 139 S.W. 1056 (1911).

97. Pickens v. State, 111 Ga.App. 574, 142 S.E.2d 427 (1965) (no duty to respond in judicial proceeding); Diamond v. State, 195 Ind. 285, 144 N.E. 466 (1924) (dictum) (accused could not speak out with propriety and would not be expected to do so at a judicial proceeding).

98. See § 270, infra.

99. Dickerson v. United States, 62 App.D.C. 191, 65 F.2d 824 (1933); State v. Picciotti, 12 N.J. 205, 96 A.2d 406 (1953).

which the fact of arrest alone is sufficient to render any subsequent "tacit confession" inadmissible.[1] Their decisions reflect not only doubt as to the accuracy of the inference of guilt under such circumstances but also the fear of police abuse of the rule. The Report of the New Jersey Supreme Court Committee on Evidence concluded:

> "[T]he [tacit confession] rule has been subject to considerable abuse in certain jurisdictions. For example, it has become the practice of some police to make wholesale accusations against one who may not even yet be formally an accused, or against one who is in jail. If the unfortunate 'declarant' abides by the maxim that 'silence is golden' and holds his tongue, he may find police accusations brought into court against him as . . . evidence. . . ."[2]

A footnote statement in *Miranda* strongly suggests that in regard to tacit confessions during a criminal investigation a somewhat expanded form of the *per se* rule is constitutionally required. "In accord with our decision today," the Court stated, "it is impermissible to penalize an individual for exercising his Fifth Amendment privilege when he is under police custodial interrogation. The prosecution may not, therefore, use at trial the fact that he stood mute or claimed his privilege in the face of accusation."[3] This leaves little doubt that silence or a claim of the privilege made in response to a police accusation during custodial interrogation is inadmissible, and the decisions following *Mir-*

anda have so interpreted it.[4] There are a number of areas, however, in regard to which the constitutional requirements are not so clear.

First, to what extent may the prosecution resort to the tacit confession rule when, during permissible custodial interrogation, the accused responds to an accusation with an equivocal reply?[5] For example, X, after having been given the *Miranda* warning, waives his rights. When he is then confronted with damaging evidence and the police accusation of his guilt, he responds, "Are you sure you checked carefully?"

Second, what is the requirement when there is "custody" but not "police interrogation"? Suppose X has been taken into custody for the murder of Y. X is sitting in the police station prior to booking, and Y's widow passes by. She sees X, becomes hysterical, and shouts, "Why did you have to kill my husband?" X says nothing and stares at his feet. In this situation custody clearly exists but (assuming that the police had no part in arranging the confrontation between X and Y's widow) there might well not be "interrogation."

Third, what is the requirement when there is no custody?[6] Suppose a patrol officer

---

1. State v. Bates, 140 Conn. 326, 99 A.2d 133 (1953); Commonwealth v. McDermott, 123 Mass. 440, 25 Am.Dec. 120 (1877); People v. Rutigliano, 261 N.Y. 103, 184 N.E. 689 (1933).

2. New Jersey Supreme Court Committee on Evidence, Report 164 (1963).

3. Miranda v. Arizona, 384 U.S. 436, 468 n. 37 (1966). The statement is clearly dictum since none of the cases involved a tacit confession.

4. United States v. Brinson, 411 F.2d 1057 (6th Cir. 1969); Fowle v. United States, 410 F.2d 48 (9th Cir. 1969); Galasso v. State, 217 So.2d 326 (Fla. 1968); State v. Rice, 37 Wis.2d 392, 155 N.W.2d 116 (1967) cert. denied 393 U.S. 878 (*Miranda* required change in Wisconsin rule but need not be applied retroactively).

As *Brinson* and *Fowle*, supra, point out, quoting McCarthy v. United States, 25 F.2d 298, 299 (6th Cir. 1928), if the rule were otherwise, a warning would be required to say, "If you say anything it will be used against you; if you do not say anything, that will be used against you."

5. See Commonwealth v. Jefferson, 430 Pa. 532, 243 A.2d 412 (1968), holding that an equivocal reply to the reading of a codefendant's confession was admissible because it did not involve the same dangers to the privilege as would be created by admitting evidence of silence.

6. State v. McAlvain, 104 Ariz. 445, 454 P.2d 987 (1969) (police officer stopped car in which defend-

comes upon a crowd gathered at a street corner. He pushes his way through, asking "What's going on here?" One member of the crowd, pointing to X, says, "He shot this man?" X says nothing.

Finally, what, if any, is the constitutional limit on the use of tacit confessions made in circumstances unrelated to any official criminal investigation?[7] For example, X and Y meet Z at a tavern. Z asks X how he can afford the new clothing he appears to be wearing. X responds that he and Y recently knocked over a supermarket and made an excellent haul. Y does not say anything.

Both the traditional voluntariness requirement and the expanded rights to remain silent and to representation might be applicable. When there is proof of circumstances that might have caused an affirmative admission to be involuntary, the question posed is analogous to those generally raised by the voluntariness of confession cases: did the silence represent surrender of the will to these pressures? It is conceivable that pressures not strong enough to cause an accused to admit something affirmatively might nevertheless be strong enough to cause him not affirmatively to deny an accusation. Thus the voluntariness requirement might provide a limitation on the admissibility of the silence in any of the five situations above. If there is no evidence of such circumstances, however, the question posed becomes more difficult: must the silence, to be "voluntary," represent a conscious desire to communicate agreement with the assertion, or is it only necessary that the silence not be the result of external pressures? The spirit of the voluntariness requirement suggests the former. If this is the case, it is arguable that the inquiry into the motive of silence, since silence is inaction, is so difficult that no accurate results can be expected. And in that event, either the voluntariness requirement must be abandoned in this context or the danger of involuntariness must be regarded as sufficiently high to exclude all silences on this ground. In view of the high probability that silence is, in these situations, in fact motivated by a desire not to communicate any reaction to the assertion (and thus in effect to assert the privilege against compelled self-incrimination), a blanket rule of exclusion might well be most appropriate. Moreover, if the subject's silence is admissible against him and he is aware of this, the rule of admissibility itself arguably constitutes compulsion to respond in a potentially self-incriminating manner. This additional danger to the privilege also argues in favor of non-admissibility of silence.

Equivocal responses present a similar problem. Because of their affirmative nature, they arguably provide a somewhat better subject for factual inquiry into motive. Moreover, it cannot be said that an affirmative response—though equivocal—represents a desire not to communicate any reaction whatsoever to an assertion. On the other hand, an equivocal response may represent an at-

---

ant and companion were riding, companion asked officer to arrest defendant because defendant had just beaten him, and defendant remained silent; accusation and silence held admissible); Ryan v. State, 451 P.2d 383 (Okl.Cr.1969) (statement made by defendant's companion in defendant's presence after a police officer had entered the room but before he had arrested defendant; held admissible).

7. The post-*Miranda* cases have upheld the admissibility of tacit confessions made under these circumstances. State v. Saiz, 103 Ariz. 567, 447 P.2d 541 (1968) (statements by accomplices made in defendant's presence admissible); People v. Tolbert, 70 Cal.2d 790, 76 Cal.Rptr. 445, 452 P.2d 661 (1969) (when cousin asked defendant whether gun found in bathroom was his and whether he had put it there, and defendant responded, "Forget about it," questions and equivocal response were admissible); State v. McClain, 254 La. 56, 222 So.2d 855 (1969) (defendant's accomplice stated in presence of defendant that money came from a particular store that had been robbed, and defendant did not deny it); State v. Thomas, 440 S.W.2d 467 (Mo. 1969) (statement made in kitchen and in defendant's presence by associate that defendant and associate had robbed cab driver was admissible together with defendant's silence).

tempt to prevent an unfavorable inference from being drawn from silence, and thus be based upon a belief that invoking the privilege against compelled self-incrimination by simple silence is not an available alternative. Under such circumstances, of course, the policy of the privilege argues strongly in favor of rejecting evidence of equivocal responses. In addition, since an equivocal response is used as evidence of the motive for failure expressly to deny the accusation, it is arguable that the ultimate factual inquiry is little more subject to reliable resolution than in the case of simple silence. In view of the low probative value of both silence and equivocal responses, and the dangers posed by both to the privilege against self-incrimination, it might be well to find in the voluntariness requirement a blanket exclusionary requirement covering both. The cases, however, have not done so.

As to the application of the rights developed in *Miranda,* the determining factor should be the probability that the response represents a desire not to communicate incriminating information. *Miranda* represents a judgment that in the custodial interrogation situation the probability is sufficiently high that silence represents a desire not to communicate incriminating information that it is not permissible to inquire in specific cases whether that was the motive or whether the silence represented a voluntary decision to waive the privilege against self-incrimination and to communicate agreement with the accusation. Since an equivocal response provides no direct evidence of the speaker's motives for not disagreeing with the accusation, it should be treated no differently from silence. This, of course, would not affect the admissibility of an equivocal response (assuming other requirements are met) for purposes other than proving a tacit confession.

It is arguable that in any situation in which the accused is aware of the presence of an official investigator, the probability that failure to deny an accusation represents a desire to protect himself from incrimination is sufficiently high to require exclusion of the response under *Miranda.* In the third situation described above, for example, there is a high probability that X failed to respond to the statement of the member of the crowd because of his desire to avoid cooperating with the officer in establishing X's own criminal liability. Thus to permit the response to be used as proof of guilt would be to attach a significant burden on the exercise of the privilege.

When, as in situation four above, the accused was not aware of an official investigation at the time of his response, the problem is more difficult. It is conceivable that Y's failure to respond was motivated by his desire not to communicate to Z any direct admission of guilt because of a fear that it might ultimately be used to convict him. On the other hand, the probabilities of this being the motive are much less than when a police officer is present. Perhaps the best approach would be to require for the admissibility of such a tacit admission a preliminary finding by the trial judge that there is no reasonable possibility that the accused's silence or equivocal response was motived by a desire to minimize the danger of criminal conviction.

162. Statements Given to Private Individuals.[8]

Because of the official nature of most criminal investigations, concern over the admissibility of statements by accused persons has usually revolved around statements given

---

8. See generally, Note, Criminal Law—Admissibility of Confessions or Admissions of Accused Obtained During Custodial Interrogation by Non-police Personnel: Are the Miranda Warnings Required? 40 Miss.L.J. 139 (1968); Note, Confessions Obtained Through Interrogation Conducted by Private Persons, Investigators and Security Agents, 4 Willamette L.J. 262 (1966).

to "persons in authority," i. e., members of official law enforcement agencies such as police officers and prosecuting attorneys. Statements are also, however occasionally made to private individuals, and judicial treatment of these statements has differed significantly from that accorded statements made to those with public authority.

It is now generally accepted that the voluntariness requirement applies to statements made to private individuals as well as those made to public officials.[9] Nevertheless, courts have exhibited a tendency to scrutinize with greater care statements to public officials, apparently on the assumption that public office carries with it the ability to use public authority and that consequently the danger that an accused person's will has been overborne is greater if his interrogator was one in a position of authority.[10]

Early indications that inducements would render a confession involuntary only if made by one in a position of authority have given way to a recognition that the essential inquiry is whether the inducements, whatever their source, did in fact cause the statement.[11] The position of the interrogator is relevant insofar as suggestions of leniency by one in authority are more likely to be relied upon by the accused and thus are more likely in fact to have caused him to make a statement. But it is now perfectly clear that a suggestion of leniency by a private person,

such as the victim of the offense, may cause a resulting statement to be involuntary.[12]

In regard to the rights to remain silent and to representation by counsel, however, the courts have taken a different tack. It is generally accepted that a statement made to a private individual is not inadmissible by virtue of the private individual's failure to warn the accused in terms of the *Miranda* requirements.[13] This holds true even if the private individuals are members of a private security guard force and the interrogation procedure is identical with that carried out by official police investigators.[14] The reasoning underlying this result is that the purpose of the *Miranda* requirement is to assure that public criminal investigations are conducted within certain limits and that, how-

---

9. State v. Christopher, 10 Ariz.App. 169, 457 P.2d 356 (1969); State v. Ely, 237 Ore. 329, 390 P.2d 348 (1964); McElroy v. State, 204 So.2d 463 (Miss. 1967).

10. See State v. Christopher, 10 Ariz.App. 169, 457 P.2d 356 (1969) (statements made to private persons need not "meet the same stringent [voluntariness] test as those made to police officials").

11. See the traditional statement of the rule in State v. Tharp, 334 Mo. 46, 64 S.W.2d 249, 254 (1933): "a confession, to be inadmissible, must be made to an officer of the law in consequence of improper influences exerted by him. . . ." A confession by a servant to his master was also viewed with this suspicion. 2 Anderson, Wharton's Criminal Evidence § 391 (12th Ed. 1955).

12. Porter v. State, 206 Ark. 758, 177 S.W.2d 408 (1944) (owner of stolen property told defendant that if she confessed "it might make it lighter on her"); State v. Green, 128 Ore. 49, 273 P. 381 (1929) (when inducements were held out by one not in a position of authority, statement is involuntary if they did in fact have the effect of inducing the statement); Agee v. State, 185 So.2d 671 (Miss. 1966) (confession rendered involuntary where teacher told defendant that "it would be lighter on him if he told the truth"); Fisher v. State, 379 S.W. 2d 900 (Tex.Cr.R.1964) (when confession may have been induced by the promise of some benefits to defendant, court should look at actual relationship between subject and one making representations to determine whether defendant did actually believe as a result of the representations that his position would be bettered by a confession).

13. State v. Lombardo, 104 Ariz. 598, 457 P.2d 275 (1969) (state security agents were acting in private capacity and thus not required to give *Miranda* warnings); People v. Crabtree, 239 Cal.App.2d 789, 49 Cal.Rptr. 285 (1966) (*Escobedo* not applicable to admissions made during interrogation by private security guards); State v. Little, 201 Kan. 94, 439 P.2d 387 (1968) (shop owner, in presence of police officer, asked defendant if she had given him a forged check); State v. Rodgers, 251 La. 953, 207 So.2d 755 (1968) (defendant, under arrest, drove own car to police station and made statements to private individual who accompanied him); McElroy v. State, 204 So.2d 463 (Miss.1967); Schaumberg v. State, 432 P.2d 500 (Nev.1967) (admissions made by club employee to two supervisors while in room guarded by security guard); People v. Frank, 52 Misc.2d 266, 275 N.Y.S.2d 570 (1966).

14. See cases cited in note 13, supra.

ever reprehensible private deviations from these limits may be, they are not a sufficient basis for excluding the evidence obtained.

The propriety of these different approaches is subject to question. The attitudinal difference in the scrutiny of statements made to public and private individuals under the voluntariness test apparently rests on the assumption that what appears to be publicly sanctioned pressure is more likely to influence an accused than factors which are clearly perceived to be only the work of a private individual. It is true that one privately pressured might find strength to resist in the theoretical availability of eventual relief in the form of intervention by public authority, a factor greatly diminished in significance when the source of the pressure is itself public authority. On the other hand, it is undoubtedly true that in many cases private investigations will merge into public prosecutions with as much ease as if they were public investigations *ab initio*, and the subjects of the private prosecution perceive no difference between the investigation of which they are the subject and official police investigations. This, together with the lack of any official disciplinary apparatus with authority over private investigations, suggests that both should be approached with the same attitude.

Much the same can be said in regard to the applicability of the rights to silence and counsel. Much of the earlier reluctance to extend these rights to police investigations stemmed from the uncertainty as to the authority of police agencies to interrogate and encourage answers to even nonincriminating questions. *Miranda* did not resolve the ambiguity but acknowledged the practical pressure (whatever the abstract legal validity of its source) on the subject of such an investigation to surrender his right to decline to incriminate himself. There can be little doubt that private interrogations can contain

the same "inherent coercion" as those conducted by police agencies. The purpose of *Miranda* then, would be well served by applying its requirements to private investigators.

163. The Future of the Law of Confessions.

What of the future? That there is significant popular disagreement with the course of the law governing the admissibility of confessions cannot be doubted. This was graphically demonstrated when Congress, in 1968, provided by statute that voluntariness was to be the sole test of admissibility of self-incriminating statements offered in criminal prosecutions brought by the United States.[15] Time elapsing between arrest and presentation before a magistrate (the *McNabb-Mallory* Rule), and the absence of warning regarding the right to remain silent and the right to counsel, as well as absence of the assistance of counsel itself (the *Miranda* requirements) are to be considered in determining voluntariness but "need not be conclusive." The constitutionality of this legislation is, of course, open to question.[16] Insofar as the rights to prompt presentation, to full information regarding the right to remain silent and to counsel, and the right, to counsel itself, are of constitutional dimensions and the exclusionary remedy for their violation is the sole constitutionally-permissible means of enforcing the underlying right, *McNabb-Mallory* and *Miranda* are beyond the

---

15. Omnibus Crime Control and Safe Streets Act of 1968, 82 Stat. 197, Title II, § 701(a), now 18 U.S. C.A. § 3501.

16. The issue is discussed in Comment, Police Interrogation of Suspects: The Court Versus the Congress, 57 Calif.L.Rev. 740 (1969) and Recent Statute, 82 Harv.L.Rev. 1392 (1969). Perhaps the most promising argument favoring constitutionality is that a well-administered voluntariness test which strongly emphasized the actual impact of absence of counsel and failure fully to inform the suspect of his rights would qualify as a method "fully as effective" as the *Miranda* safeguards in protecting the rights of accused persons. See Miranda v. Arizona, 384 U.S. 436, 490 (1966).

power of legislative abrogation. But whatever the constitutional validity of this specific legislation, its passage indicates a strong public feeling that all is not right in the law of confessions.

Prediction, of course, is difficult, but it is likely that the future of the legal rules regarding the evidentiary use of statements of an accused is linked with—although not identical to—the future of police interrogation. That the two are not necessarily identical is clear from the fact that police interrogation serves important functions other than the collection of incriminating evidence for future use against the subject. Thus interrogation may be to "clear" other crimes for which prosecution is not necessarily desired, or to secure information for further investigation regarding the offense for which sufficient evidence for prosecution is already available. This interrogation might involve inquiry concerning the identity and location of accomplices or the fruits of the crime.[17]

Prediction is made especially difficult by the lack of clear definition of the policy objectives of the law relating to confessions. The gross dangers with which the early cases were concerned—physical brutality and false confessions—still undoubtedly exist to some extent, but *Miranda* makes clear that the Court's concern had shifted in some measure, at least, to subtle influences beyond the scope of the traditional voluntariness requirement. The model towards which the law of confessions had seemed to be moving was that an individual's decision to communicate to others information which is incriminating would be an informed tactical choice.[18] Under such a model, a defendant's pretrial testimonial activity would not be usable unless his statement was the result of a decision that to make such a statement was in his tactical best interests and was made with full knowledge of the legal and factual situation. Such a rule would give full effect to the policy that disputed issues should be resolved by appraisal of evidence introduced at trial. Use of statements by an accused, which creates a strong danger that the jury will overestimate their probative value and consequently not scrutinize other evidence, would be permitted only if the accused had, with full awareness of the situation, intentionally waived his right to an evaluation of such other evidence. This model would also emphasize the conception of fairness which holds that an accused should be under minimal pressure to participate in the process of his own conviction. Whether such a model is a realistic policy objective, however, is subject to doubt. It is inevitable that the decision to confess will be influenced by a number of external factors other than the individual's interest in minimizing the probability of criminal conviction and the unpleasant consequences of conviction. These external factors may in many cases be beyond the power of the law to affect significantly. In addition, the psychology of confession is by no means clear, although there is strong suggestion that the traditional legal assumptions may be oversimplifications.[19]

---

17. See Note, Interrogation in New Haven: The Impact of Miranda, 76 Yale L.J. 1519, 1593–97 (1967).

18. Cf. King, Developing a Future Constitutional Standard for Confessions, 8 Wayne L.Rev. 481 (1962).

19. Psychoanalytic theory, for example, suggests that psychic conflicts may create an unconscious striving for punishment. This striving may cause an individual to commit an offense and thus incur punishment. It may also cause him to admit to an offense which he may or may not have committed because this tends also to result in punishment. Cf. Reik, The Compulsion to Confess, 254–79 (1959). Confessions which are the product of these unconscious strivings present a substantial danger of inaccuracy, of course. But even if no danger of inaccuracy exists, it is doubtful whether an acknowledgment of guilt so significantly related to unconscious strivings could be accurately characterized as voluntary as that term is defined in the case law.

Other nonpsychoanalytic theorists have concluded that the psychological effects of interrogation techniques are far more complex than the traditional assumption that they merely create conscious guilt

In addition to the ambiguity of the policy objectives and the inherent difficulties of implementing the more ambitious possibilities, there are a number of other factors that cannot be ignored in evaluating or predicting the future of the law of confessions. First is the value of interrogation and resulting statements in the solving of crimes and the conviction of offenders and the impact of various restrictions upon the availability of interrogation and its fruits. Estimates as to both matters vary widely.[20] Second is the effectiveness of the exclusionary rule as a means of achieving the objective. Insofar as the source of concern is the interrogation process itself, it is arguable that the exclusion of resulting statements is a relatively inefficient method of controlling police practices, especially in those cases where the police objective is not to secure evidence for use against the subject of the interrogation.[21] Third is the matter of administrative feasibility. Given the im-

possibility of Supreme Court consideration of every case raising confession issues, the value of a rule which can be accurately interpreted and applied to specific factual situations by lower courts is obvious. But some inquiries may be so inherently difficult of precise definition that lower courts cannot discern from the general standard much that is particularly helpful in resolving specific later cases. The frequency with which the Supreme Court has reviewed lower court determinations of voluntariness suggests that this may have been the case with the voluntariness standard.

There are several alternative approaches that might be taken in response to concern regarding interrogation of criminal suspects and the use of resulting incriminating statements.

Limited Pre-Judicial Appearance Interrogation with Safeguards to Protect the Right of the Subject.

Miranda v. Arizona represents a recognition of the propriety of police custodial interrogation prior to (or at least independent of) presentation of the arrested person before a magistrate but under circumstances in which the threatened interests of the subject are protected by specific safeguards. The principal safeguard upon which reliance is placed is representation by counsel rather than case-by-case scrutiny by courts for other violations of the subject's rights. This approach has the value of administrative simplicity. Admissibility turns not on subjective state of mind but upon relatively easy-to-determine objective factors. The effectiveness of this device is subject to question, however, although empirical data is woefully inadequate.[22] What evidence there is suggests that

---

which is manifested in an admission. See Driver, Confessions and the Social Psychology of Coercion, 82 Harv.L.Rev. 42 (1968) (interrogation tactics are designed to create anxiety in the subject, which may cause him to change his stated beliefs); Foster, Confessions and the Station House Syndrome, 18 De Paul L. Rev. 683 (1969) (interrogation may lead to "a trance-like state of heightened suggestibility" during which the subject may make unreliable admissions).

20. For example, a New York judge has asserted that confessions constitute part of the evidence in less than ten percent of indictments. Sobel, The Exclusionary Rules in the Law of Confessions: A Legal Perspective—A Practical Perspective. N.Y. L.J., Nov. 22, 1965, p. 1, col. 4. In response, the District Attorney of New York County asserted that in 68 percent of pending homicide cases he planned to offer confessions in evidence and that in 27 percent an indictment could not have been obtained without a confession. N. Y. Times, Dec. 2, 1965, p. 1, col. 1. For a general discussion of the need for factual data on police interrogation, see Model Code of Pre-Arraignment Procedure Part II (Study Draft No. 1, 1968).

21. E. g., Wait, Police Regulation by Rules of Evidence, 42 Mich.L.Rev. 679, 685 (1944) (asserting that exclusion encourages police tactics that make the police action an end in itself, such as raids involving the destruction of the raided premises but resulting in no arrests). See generally § 149, supra.

22. The empirical evidence is well summarized in A Model Code of Pre-Arraignment Procedure 107–49 (Study Draft No. 1, 1968). The leading published studies are Note, Interrogation in New Haven: The Impact of Miranda, 76 Yale L.J. 1519 (1967); Seeburger and Wettick, Miranda in Pitts-

expansion of the right to counsel has minimal impact upon the interrogation situation insofar as it might be expected to result in more frequent exercise of the right to remain silent or more knowledgeable exercise of that right.[23] Moreover, this approach does not attack directly some potentially improper police tactics (such as trickery and deceit) or ignorance on the part of subjects as to the legal and factual matters essential to meaningful exercise of the right to remain silent. Reliance is placed rather on the assumption that with the aid of counsel a suspect will be able to avoid being unfairly prejudiced by such matters, a questionable assumption. In addition, the relatively broad waiver exception provides a vehicle by which *Miranda* may be rendered a mere formality. But if waiver is given a restrictive definition and a relatively informed state of mind is required for a valid waiver, the result might be to require the same case-by-case scrutiny upon which the voluntariness test floundered.

Other safeguards could be used, of course. For example, requiring police to maintain detailed records of a subject's treatment (including sound or visual tapes of interrogation) might provide a means more accurately later to reconstruct the circumstances surrounding an in-custody statement. Limitations on the period during which an individual is subject to interrogation might minimize the potentially coercive influence of in-custody interrogation upon him. But none of these attacks directly the danger of ignorance, either police-induced or otherwise.

Judicially Supervised Interrogation.

The major alternative to restricted prejudicial presentation police interrogation is interrogation under judicial supervision. Although proposals of this kind are not new,[24] they have recently been given impetus by the American Law Institute's consideration[25] and, in Britain, by the recommendation of the Justice Committee on Evidence.[26] These proposals, while they undoubtedly have value as a device for minimizing improper police tactics during the actual interrogation, do not attack the more subtle forms of ignorance against which the policy underlying the law of confessions seems to be moving. They also assume the existence of applicable standards as to what is and what is not permissible during the interrogation. In short, the primary and immediate problem is not the enforcement of standards upon police agencies but rather the formulation of standards in the first place. Until the standards are clear, it is doubtful whether close judicial supervision would serve a useful purpose.

24. E. g., Kauper, Judicial Examination of the Accused—A Remedy for the Third Degree, 30 Mich. L.Rev. 1224 (1932).

25. See Model B in A Model Code of Pre-Arraignment Procedure 43 (Study Draft No. 1, 1968.)

26. Justice Committee on Evidence, British Report on Interrogation of Suspects, 1 Crim.L.Rptr. 3155 (1967). British police interrogation is carried out under restrictions imposed by the Judges' Rules. [1964] 1 All E.R. 237. These rules require that a suspect be informed of his right to remain silent when the officer has evidence which would afford reasonable grounds for suspecting that the subject has committed an offense. "Only in exceptional cases" is questioning to continue after the accused has been charged or informed that he may be prosecuted. It has been asserted that the protection theoretically offered by these rules is ineffective because many subjects are either ignorant of their rights or pressured to waive them and the rules are not directly enforced by an exclusionary rule. (Exclusion is required only if the resulting statements fail to meet a voluntariness test.) See Glasbeck and Prentice, The Criminal Suspect's Illusory Right of Silence in the British Commonwealth, 53 Cornell L.Rev. 473 (1968). Despite this, however, the Justice Committee on Evidence found that police complained of having their hands tied and their investigations hampered; the solution, the Committee felt, was a system of judicially-supervised interrogation.

burg—A Statistical Study, 29 U.Pitts.L.Rev. 1 (1967); Medalie, Leitz and Alexander, Custodial Police Interrogation in Our Nation's Capitol; The Attempt to Implement Miranda, 66 Mich.L.Rev. 1347 (1968). See also Leiken, Police Interrogation in Colorado: The Implementation of Miranda, 47 Denver L.J. 1 (1970).

23. See generally the studies cited in note 22, supra.

Police Interrogation After Presentation to a Judicial Officer.

A compromise between the two approaches described above would prohibit police interrogation prior to presentation of the arrested person before a magistrate, but would authorize the judicial officer to remand the arrested person to police custody for a limited period of interrogation.[27] This would minimize the danger of more extensive use interrogation against those available for it by virtue of inability to secure release on bail. The magistrate's involvement would permit interrogation to be limited to cases where a judicial determination had been made that a justification for questioning existed, and would make it easier to impose and enforce limits on the duration and techniques of the questioning. It would also provide the opportunity for the warnings to be given by an individual with less incentive to minimize their effectiveness and might provide a less coercive forum for the making of the waiver decision. On the other hand, the necessity of obtaining judicial approval for interrogation and the delay involved might greatly decrease the value of interrogation in many investigations. Moreover, the routine giving of the warning by a judicial officer may be no more effective than the administration of the same warnings by a police officer, and the safeguards theoretically available under such a procedure could easily become illusory if the process degenerated into mere formal compliance with the procedural requirements.

No Use of Incriminating Statements Obtained by Interrogation.

A final alternative would completely bar the use of self-incriminating confessions obtained by interrogations. Insofar as the law of confessions seeks to prevent the imposi-

tion of unfair pressure upon a suspect, this may be the only adequate solution. Driver, for example, argues on the basis of an examination of interrogation techniques that the "subtle forces" involved in interrogation permissible under *Miranda* "appear at least equal to physical duress in influencing behavior." [28] These forces, he feels, are inherent in interrogation and thus could only be rendered ineffectual by abolishing interrogation. Without more adequate empirical knowledge regarding the value of self-incriminating statements in obtaining convictions, the cost of such a rule must remain speculative. No secular jurisdictions have adopted such a rule, although Jewish law rejects all confessions, whether voluntary or not.[29]

The most likely future course of the American law of confessions is continued reliance upon the right to the presence of counsel as the basic means of safeguarding against abuses of the interrogation procedure, together with development of more sophisticated rules within the voluntariness requirement regarding the use of specific interrogation techniques (such as deceit) and the admissibility of statements given under ignorance of the full factual or legal situation. The Court, after unsatisfactory experience with the voluntariness rule and case-by-case review of its application, seems committed to the extension of the adversary process to the interrogation room as the principal means of combating abuse of police questioning. There nevertheless remain problems of ignorance and de-

---

27. See Models C and D in A Model Code of Pre-Arraignment Procedure 78 et seq. (Study Draft No. 1, 1968).

28. Driver, Confessions and the Social Psychology of Coercion, 82 Harv.L.Rev. 42 (1968).

29. See Lamm, The 5th Amendment and Its Equivalent in Jewish Law, 17 Decalogue J. 9 (1967). The Halakhic principle, Lamm argues, is based upon a desire to safeguard against the "minority" of cases in which the confessor's psychological aberrations manifest themselves as completely fabricated confessions or exaggerations of the real facts. See also Horowitz, The Spirit of Jewish Law 641 (1963).

ceit which must be resolved, probably by development of the voluntariness requirement.[30]

The future of the exclusionary sanction as a means of implementing the standards governing interrogation is open to more question. The 1968 federal legislation [31] indicates legislative concern with the exclusionary remedy, and Harris v. New York,[32] approving the use of statements obtained in violation of *Miranda* for impeachment purposes, suggests that the Supreme Court is having second thoughts concerning the matter. It is not unlikely that the future will see a reduced willingness to invoke the exclusionary sanction. This might conceivably involve even a return to voluntariness as the standard of admissibility, with such circumstances as denial of the right to counsel as merely one factor tending to establish involuntariness.[33]

---

30. These objectives could also be reached by the development of the waiver requirements under *Miranda.* But in view of the objective orientation of the *Miranda* requirements, the voluntariness requirement would be a more appropriate doctrinal vehicle.

31. See text at note 15, supra.

32. 401 U.S. 222 (1971); see generally § 178, supra.

33. This result might be accomplished by sustaining the constitutional validity of the 1968 federal legislation. See note 16, supra.

CHAPTER 15

THE PRIVILEGE IN REGARD TO IMPROPERLY OBTAINED EVIDENCE

164. Introduction.

Probably the most important recent development in the law of evidence as applied to criminal litigation has been the increased use of the exclusionary sanction as a means of discouraging and disclaiming certain activities by which evidence is sometimes obtained. Rules of exclusion have been applied to evidence obtained in violation of a defendant's Fifth and Fourteenth Amendment right to due process of law,[1] his Fifth Amendment privilege against compelled self-incrimination, his Fourth Amendment right to be free from unreasonable searches and seizures,[2] his Sixth Amendment right to be represented by counsel,[3] as well as evidence related to a few

exclusion of capsules of morphine which defendant had vomited). Compare Breithaupt v. Abram, 352 U.S. 432 (1957) (taking blood from an unconscious subject was not within *Rochin*); Schmerber v. California, 384 U.S. 757 (1966) (taking blood sample from a conscious and verbally objecting defendant who did not physically resist was not within *Rochin*).

1. Rochin v. California, 342 U.S. 165 (1952) (forcing an emetic into defendant's stomach through his nose despite his physical resistance required

2. See §§ 165–178, infra.

3. See § 176, infra.

364

rules not of established constitutional dimensions.[4] The exclusion of evidence obtained in violation of a subject's Fifth Amendment privilege has been discussed in Chapter 13, and the exclusionary rules relating to confessions have been discussed in Chapter 14. The exclusionary rule based upon the general right to due process of law has probably been superseded by subsequent developments and is no longer independently important.[5] This chapter deals with the remaining exclusionary rules based upon the rights of one accused of a crime. These rules may be classified as privileges rather than as rules of incompetency, as they are designed to protect interests deemed of great social importance rather than to guard against evidence which is unreliable or calculated to prejudice or mislead the trier of fact.

165. Development of the Federal Fourth Amendment Exclusionary Rule.[6]

At common law and during the early years of American constitutional law it was almost universally accepted that the admissibility of evidence was unaffected by any impropriety that might have occurred in its procurance.[7] This position was based upon judicial unwillingness to forego the use of evidence of undoubted probative value and a reluctance to interject into trials the collateral but often complex issue of the propriety of the means by which offered evidence had been obtained.

In 1914, however the Supreme Court of the United States held that evidence obtained pursuant to a violation of the Fourth Amendment's prohibition against unreasonable searches and seizures could not be admitted in federal criminal trials.[8] If the evidence could be used, "the protection of the Fourth Amendment declaring [the] . . . right to be secure against such searches and seizures is of no value, and . . . might as well be stricken from the Constitution." Moreover, "to sanction such [use] . . . would be to affirm by judicial decision a manifest neglect if not an open defiance of the . . . Constitution. . . ." Until 1960, however, the Court refused to apply this exclusionary rule to the states. In Wolf v. Colorado,[9] decided in 1949, the Court left no doubt that the Fourth Amendment's bar against arbitrary intrusion by the police was implicit in "the concept of ordered liberty" and thus binding upon the states through the Due Process Clause of the Fourteenth Amendment.[10] But the Court refused to take the next step and hold that the exclusionary remedy was also binding on the states by reason of the Due Process Clause. Although the exclusionary rule appeared to be the most potent means of making effective the Constitutional protections, the Court rea-

---

4. See § 155, supra [*McNabb-Mallory*] and § 174, infra [wiretapping]. Generally, however, the mere fact that evidence was obtained in a manner which violated state law does not require exclusion of the evidence. E. g., United States v. Scolnick, 392 F.2d 320 (3d Cir. 1968) cert. denied 392 U.S. 931 (evidence obtained by search of safe deposit box pursuant to warrant was not subject to suppression because search violated state statutory requirement that search of safe deposit box be made no less than forty-eight hours after notice to the holders).

5. Rochin v. California, 342 U.S. 165 (1952) (see note 1, supra) was decided before Mapp v. Ohio, 367 U.S. 643 (1961) required the exclusion in state courts of evidence obtained in violation of an accused's Fourth Amendment rights. See § 165, infra. It is likely that *Rochin* represented the Court's unwillingness to permit a state to use the results of a particularly aggravated violation of Fourth Amendment rights and its reluctance to adopt the broad rule later applied in *Mapp*. After *Mapp*, any action which would bring *Rochin* into play would also constitute a violation of the subject's Fourth Amendment rights and thus be subject to exclusion under *Mapp*.

6. See generally 8 Wigmore, Evidence (McNaughton rev.) § 2184(a); 29 Am.Jur.2d Evidence §§ 411–12; C.J.S. Evidence § 187.

7. 8 Wigmore, Evidence (McNaughton rev.) § 2183.

8. Weeks v. United States, 232 U.S. 383 (1914).

9. 338 U.S. 25 (1949).

10. Id. at 27–28. See also Irvine v. California, 347 U.S. 128, 135 (1954).

soned, the states could appropriately rely upon other methods "which, if consistently enforced, would be equally effective." [11] Despite the lack of a federal constitutional mandate, however, by 1960 twenty-six of the states had adopted, as a matter of state law, rules requiring the exclusion of at least some improperly obtained evidence.[12]

In 1961 the Court reconsidered its position regarding the binding effect upon the states of the exclusionary rule, and in Mapp v. Ohio [13] held that the Fourth and Fourteenth Amendments required the exclusion in state courts of evidence obtained in violation of the prohibition against unreasonable searches and seizures. The decision was based upon the Court's conclusion that the factual underpinnings of the earlier cases had been destroyed. In view of the increasing number of states accepting the exclusionary rule as a matter of state law, it could no longer be said that the states as a whole held a view contrary to that of the federal courts.[14] Moreover, experience established that alternative methods of protecting the Fourth Amendment right to be free from unreasonable searches and seizures had been "worthless and futile." [15] Thus, the Court concluded, the exclusionary rule was "an essential part" of the Fourth and Fourteenth Amendments and consequently "all evidence obtained by searches and seizures in violation of the Constitution is, by that same authority, inadmissible in a state court." [16]

166. Policy Basis for the Fourth Amendment Exclusionary Rule.[17]

Mapp makes clear that the principal purpose of the exclusionary rule is the protection of rights by removing the incentive for their violation—the purpose of "policing the police." [18] Substantial question has been raised, however, whether the exclusionary rule is suited to accomplish this objective and, if so, whether it accomplishes it at too great a cost.

First, it has been argued that the exclusionary rule is not an effective means of controlling police conduct.[19] By its very nature, it can be effective only when police conduct has as its objective the gathering of evidence to be used in prosecution.[20] Thus it provides

---

11. Wolf v. Colorado, 338 U.S. 25, 31 (1949).

12. See Table 1 in Appendix to Opinion of the Court, Elkins v. United States, 364 U.S. 206, 224–25 (1960).

13. 367 U.S. 643 (1961).

14. Id. at 651.

15. Id. at 651–53. Emphasis was placed upon the thoughtful rejection of the traditional position by the California Supreme Court in People v. Cahan, 44 Cal.2d 434, 282 P.2d 905 (1955).

16. Mapp v. Ohio, 367 U.S. 643, 655 (1961). In Linkletter v. Walker, 381 U.S. 618 (1965) the *Mapp* rule was held retroactive only to the extent that it

applied to state court convictions which had not become final on the date Mapp v. Ohio was decided (June 19, 1961).

17. See generally, 8 Wigmore, Evidence (McNaughton rev.) § 2183; J. Maguire, Evidence of Guilt § 5.02 (1959); Skolnick, Justice Without Trial 211–19 (1966); LaFave, Improving Police Performance Through the Exclusionary Rule, 30 Mo.L.Rev. 391 (1965); LaFave and Remington, Controlling the Police: The Judge's Role in Making and Reviewing Law Enforcement Decisions, 63 Mich.L.Rev. 987 (1965); Oaks, Studying the Exclusionary Rule in Search and Seizure, 37 U.Chi.L.Rev. 665 (1970); Paulsen, The Exclusionary Rule and Misconduct by the Police, 52 J.Crim.L., C. & P. S. 255 (1961); Plumb, Illegal Enforcement of the Law, 24 Cornell L.Q. 337, 369–93 (1939); Waite, Judges and the Crime Burden, 54 Mich.L.Rev. 169 (1955); Comment, Search and Seizure in Illinois: Enforcement of the Constitutional Right of Privacy, 47 Nw.U.L. Rev. 493 (1952).

18. Mapp v. Ohio, 367 U.S. 643, 656 (1961): "Only last year the Court itself recognized that the purpose of the exclusionary rule 'is to deter—to compel respect for the constitutional guaranty in the only effectively available way—by removing the incentive to disregard it.' Elkins v. United States, [364 U.S. 206] 217." Any doubt was removed in Linkletter v. Walker, 381 U.S. 618 (1965) when the Court, in declining to make the rule of *Mapp* retroactive, relied heavily upon the "policing the police" purpose of the rule and the conclusion that retroactive application would not serve this purpose. Id. at 637.

19. E. g., LaFave and Remington, supra note 17.

20. Barrett, Personal Rights, Property Rights, and the Fourth Amendment, 1960 Supreme Ct.Rev. 54–55.

no deterrent to improper police conduct in the numerous instances in which the police objective is other than prosecution.[21] Moreover, insofar as nonprosecution tactics (such as harassment) are available as a means of circumventing the sanction, the exclusionary rule may encourage police reliance upon those informal practices rather than formal criminal prosecution.[22] Even in regard to cases in which conviction is an objective, however, the rule is arguably ill-suited to its purpose. Police officers may simply lack adequate knowledge of the underlying requirements.[23] This may be because of inadequate communications between the courts and police officers or it may be because the underlying requirements, developed pursuant to the case method, are elusive.[24] Even if officers have the knowledge necessary to conform, they may find it unnecessary to do so. Objections may be raised successfully in so few cases as to make noncompliance worth the risk in many situations. Or the officer, believing that the end justifies the means, may find it possible to misrepresent in court the circumstances attending procurance and thus avoid exclusion of the resulting evidence.[25]

Assuming that the exclusionary rule is nevertheless reasonably effective in controlling certain police practices, it is argued that this control is achieved at too great a cost.[26] Exclusion of evidence that is often highly probative may result in the release of defendants known to constitute a threat to society. Moreover, this result can be required by the misconduct of a single officer, thus giving each officer involved in an investigation the power to confer immunity upon the subject by acting improperly. Such a "fox hunting" approach to the establishment of criminal guilt—in which the emphasis is not upon the result but rather on compliance with rules of the game during the chase [27]—is inconsistent with the social interest in the conviction of those posing a danger to the public.[28] In addition, it is argued that the forums in which particular cases are resolved are ill-suited to the full development of facts and arguments favorable to the police, with the result that particular cases are decided and general rules are formulated with inadequate understanding of the real problems facing the police. The exclusionary rule thus encourages the formulation and enforcement of rules that do not represent a well-considered balance between individual and social interests.

Finally, it is suggested that reliance on the exclusionary rule is particularly unjustified in view of the more attractive alternative means available to protect individual rights against police infringement.[29] Civil liability under either state or federal law provides a

---

21. See LaFave, supra note 17, at 421–55, acknowledging that the exclusionary rule is obviously not alone to blame for such improper police activity.

22. Waite, supra note 17, at 196.

23. LaFave, supra note 17, at 402–03 notes that officers seldom have opportunity to develop a comprehensive understanding of rulings on motions to suppress made in local courts.

24. The case method, of course, is better suited to resolution of individual disputes than easy prediction of the outcome of future litigation. Moreover, inconsistent rulings on the local level may rob the rule of whatever predictability it might otherwise provide. LaFave, supra note 17, at 403–15. See generally, Murphy, The Problem of Compliance By Police Departments, 44 Tex.L.Rev. 939 (1966).

25. For a study of pre- and post-*Mapp* cases in a single court suggesting that the exclusionary requirement caused police misrepresentation regarding many challenged investigations, see The Effect of Mapp v. Ohio on Police Search-and-Seizure Practices in Narcotics Cases, 4 Colum.J.Law and Social Prob. 87 (1968).

26. See Waite, supra note 17.

27. See Paulsen, supra note 17, at 257.

28. "[A]re we justified in providing an additional remedy, above those ordinarily granted to individuals who have been wronged, a remedy useful only to a law-violator?" Waite, supra note 17, at 376.

29. Waite, supra note 17, at 385–393. Oaks, Studying the Exclusionary Rule in Search and Seizure, 37 U.Chi.L.Rev. 665, 756–57 (1970) concludes after exhaustive study that the exclusionary rule should be replaced by "an effective tort remedy against the offending officer or his employer."

means of redress for a victim of police misconduct that does not infringe upon society's interest in convicting him if he is in fact guilty. Criminal prosecution of misbehaving officers provides the same deterrent effect from a public source. Civilian Review Boards or similar external agencies provide another means of controlling improper police conduct without infringing upon the underlying social interest in protection. Perhaps most important, a general policy of recognizing police discretionary authority and encouraging the formulation of internal police standards and enforcement procedures may be the most efficient overall method of affecting day-to-day police activity.[30]

In response to these attacks upon the exclusionary rule, its supporters urge that whatever its defects, it is probably more effective than any of the alternatives. Other remedies are, as a practical matter, of little or no value in controlling improper police activity.[31] In part this is because the exclusionary rule often makes immunity from conviction the reward for successfully challenging improper police activity and therefore provides a stronger incentive to challenge that activity than the alternatives; thus the deterrence of the activities is maximized. Counting the release of guilty defendants as a "cost" of the rule, it is argued, is improper, because under the rules agreed upon society has no "right" to expect their conviction; thus their non-punishment is not properly labeled a cost of the remedy for which those rules provide.

Moreover, many of the so-called "costs" can be minimized by the development of sophisticated ancillary rules. Thus the limits upon what constitutes the inadmissible fruits of improper police conduct [32] may curb the power of a single officer to confer immunity from conviction. Provision for pretrial appeal by the prosecution from unfavorable rulings on motions to suppress [33] provides the vehicle for placing before appellate courts a more balanced selection of cases, thus encouraging a less defense-oriented body of case law developing the underlying rights.

Finally, it is urged that the rule is supportable by policies other than the necessity of controlling the police. By providing one whose rights have been violated by the investigatory apparatus of the criminal system with a remedy against that system itself, the exclusionary rule provides the most appropriate remedy. Whatever its long-run effect on police conduct, then, the exclusionary rule is justifiable on the ground that it appropriately vindicates a personal wrong. Perhaps more important, however, is the "moral position." By refusing to accept and consider evidence tainted by improper activity, the courts publicly reaffirm their own respect for the underlying rules. This bolsters the position of the courts in public opinion and by maintaining public respect for the criminal system arguably contributes as much to encouraging obedience to legal rules as would be accomplished by the punishment of those the exclusionary rule requires be released.[34]

---

30. See generally Task Force on the Police, The President's Commission on Law Enforcement and Administration of Justice, Task Force Report: The Police 28–30 (1967).

31. See generally Foote, Tort Remedies for Police Violation of Individual Rights, 39 Minn.L.Rev. 493 (1955). But see Waite, supra note 17, at 385–393, urging that these remedies be improved. For an empirical study suggesting the ineffectiveness of criminal prohibitions against police misconduct, see Schwartz, Complaints Against the Police: Experience of the Community Rights Division of the Philadelphia District Attorney's Office, 118 U.Pa.L.Rev. 1023 (1970).

32. See § 177, infra.

33. See § 181, infra.

34. The Supreme Court itself has recognized the limitations of the exclusionary rule. Terry v. Ohio, 392 U.S. 1, 13–15 (1968). "[A] rigid and unthinking application of the exclusionary rule, in futile protest against practices which it can never be used effectively to control, may exact a high toll in human injury and frustration of efforts to prevent crime." Id. at 15. Although it cautioned that the limitations must constantly be considered in deciding specific cases under the rule and empha-

167. Scope of the Fourth Amendment Exclusionary Rule: (a) Proceedings to Which the Rule is Applicable.[35]

The exclusionary rule is most frequently invoked as a means of effecting the exclusion of evidence in criminal proceedings, i.e., litigation in which the state seeks to obtain a criminal conviction of the defendant.[36] But

sized that its interpretations of the rule should not discourage employment of more appropriate remedies, the Court nevertheless concluded that when improper police conduct is identified, "it must be condemned by the judiciary and its fruits must be excluded from evidence in criminal trials." Id.

35. See generally, De Revil, Applicability of the Fourth Amendment in Civil Cases, 1963 Duke L.J. 472; Comment, The Applicability of the Exclusionary Rule to Civil Cases, 19 Baylor L.Rev. 263 (1967); Note, Evidence: Exclusion of Evidence Obtained by an Unreasonable Search in a Civil Action, 48 Cornell L.Q. 345 (1963); Note, Admissibility of Illegally Obtained Evidence in Noncriminal Proceedings, 22 U.Fla.L.Rev. 38 (1969); Note, Constitutional Exclusion of Evidence in Civil Litigation, 55 Va.L.Rev. 1484 (1969); Note, The Extent of the Exclusionary Rule, 9 Wm. & Mary L. Rev. 193 (1967); 29 Am.Jur.2d Evidence § 410; Annot., 5 A.L.R.3rd 670; C.J.S. Evidence § 187; Dec.Dig. Evidence ⟜154.

36. Although the applicability of the exclusionary rule to the formal trial stage of a criminal proceeding is beyond doubt, some question remains whether it applies to proceedings prior to or after formal trial. The rule probably has no effect upon grand jury proceedings. The Supreme Court has held that an indictment is not defective because the grand jury returning it considered hearsay, Costello v. United States, 350 U.S. 359 (1956), or evidence obtained in violation of the defendant's privilege against self-incrimination, Lawn v. United States, 355 U.S. 339 (1958). From these related situations, the conclusion has been drawn that consideration of illegally seized evidence also does not affect the validity of an indictment. Truchinski v. United States, 393 F.2d 627 (8th Cir. 1968) cert. denied 393 U.S. 831. But apart from this issue—whether consideration of illegally seized evidence vitiates an indictment—it has been argued that the Fourth Amendment extends no right to have the evidence excluded from the grand jury. Excluding the evidence at this point would arguably not significantly advance the deterrent purpose of the rule. Moreover, an accused has no practical opportunity to object to the offer of the evidence and, in the absence of a presiding judge, no opportunity to obtain a determination of admissibility save by possible anticipation of need for a motion to suppress. See generally West v. United States, 359 F.2d 50 (8th Cir. 1966) cert. denied 385 U.S. 867.

it need not necessarily be confined to that kind of proceedings. Insofar as the purpose

The general rule seems to be that the exclusionary rule does not apply to preliminary hearings. E. g., State v. Earley, 192 Kan. 167, 386 P.2d 189 (1963); Proposed Amendments to F.R.Crim.P. (P.D.), Rule 5.1 (January, 1970). See generally Comment, Preliminary Examination—Evidence and Due Process, 15 Kan.L.Rev. 374, 383–86 (1967). Also see Giordenello v. United States, 357 U.S. 480, 484 (1958) (by waiving his preliminary examination, a defendant did not forfeit his right to challenge the admissibility of evidence at trial because the U. S. Commissioner had no authority to adjudicate the admissibility of evidence at trial). There is some express authority to the contrary. Pinizzotto v. Superior Court, 257 Cal.App.2d 582, 65 Cal.Rptr. 74 (1968); and see Goldsmith v. Sheriff, 85 Nev. 295, 454 P.2d 86 (1969) (normal rules of competency and admissibility apply at preliminary hearings). Also, in a number of cases, appellate courts have declined to hold that the admissibility of evidence offered at the preliminary need not be determined and have found challenged proof admissible, thereby suggesting that the exclusionary rule applies. Martinez v. State, 90 Idaho 229, 409 P.2d 426 (1965) (statement admissible without prior showing of voluntariness because it is "admission" rather than "confession"); People ex rel. Ruppert v. Hoy, 50 Misc.2d 326, 270 N.Y.S.2d 647, aff'd 25 App. Div.2d 884, 270 N.Y.S.2d 975 (1966) (challenged statement was voluntary); State ex rel. Wojtycski v. Hanley, 248 Wis. 108, 20 N.W.2d 719 (1945) (challenged evidence had not been illegally seized). See also Brisk v. State, 44 Wis.2d 584, 172 N.W.2d 199 (1969) (court relates without comment dispute at preliminary concerning voluntariness of confession but notes that failure of magistrate to exclude it did not affect defendant's right to contest its admissibility at trial).

At the other end of the criminal process, the few cases on the subject are split on the applicability of the exclusionary rule after conviction. Compare Verdugo v. United States, 402 F.2d 599, 609–613 (9th Cir. 1968) (where use of illegally seized evidence at sentencing would provide a substantial incentive for unconstitutional searches and seizures, the evidence must be disregarded in sentencing) with Von Pickrell v. People, 163 Colo. 591, 431 P.2d 1003 (1967) (illegally seized evidence could be used in sentencing) and United States v. Schipani, 315 F.Supp. 253 (E.D.N.Y.), aff'd 435 F.2d 26 (2d Cir. 1970) cert. denied 401 U.S. 983, noted in 40 U.Cinn.L.Rev. 172 (1971) and 71 Colum.L.Rev. 1102 (1971) (evidence obtained in violation of Fourth Amendment can be used at sentencing because need for it outweighs deterrent effect of exclusion). See also In re Martinez, 1 Cal.3d 641, 83 Cal.Rptr. 382, 463 P.2d 734 (1970), holding, over dissent, that the exclusionary rule is not applicable to parole revocation proceedings. The incremental deterrent effect of extending the rule to those proceedings, Mr. Justice Tobriner argued for the court, would be outweighed by the "social consequences"

of the rule is to discourage invasions of constitutionally protected rights, this purpose would arguably be served by excluding the fruits of these invasions from noncriminal litigation as well.

The case law suggests that two factors are influential in determining whether an attempt to invoke the exclusionary rule in noncriminal litigation will succeed: the status of the person who committed the act which is claimed to violate an underlying constitutional right, and the nature of the litigation. When the evidence was obtained by government officials and is offered by the government in a "quasi-criminal" action, the cases have applied the rule. Thus the rule has been successfully invoked in forfeiture proceedings,[37] liquor license cancellations,[38] "civil" narcotics commitment procedures,[39] proceed-

ings to remove a judge from office,[40] a proceeding before the Federal Trade Commission for an order requiring the respondent to cease and desist from violations of the Robinson-Patman Act,[41] and even in a treble damage action brought by a state under the federal antitrust laws.[42] In such cases, the state is seeking to use the evidence for a general state purpose analogous to the objective sought by criminal conviction. If the state may not make use of evidence to achieve its objective through criminal prosecution it may not use it to achieve the same objective by means of other procedural routes.

When the evidence was improperly obtained by government agents but is offered by a private individual in litigation in which the government has no direct interest, there is little case law.[43] Insofar as the exclusionary rule rests upon the need to deter improper police activities, it would seem that exclusion is not justified. The prospective unavailability of the evidence to a private litigant is unlikely to be a significant factor in determining police conduct. On the other hand, insofar as the rule rests upon the unwillingness of courts to condone improper official activity, exclusion is arguably justified.

In cases in which the evidence was obtained by a private individual and offered by him

---

of so extending it. The same result was reached in United States ex rel. Sperling v. Fitzpatrick, 426 F.2d 1161 (2d Cir. 1970), noted in 45 N.Y.U.L.Rev. 1111 (1970), although each of the three judges wrote a separate opinion on the issue.

37. One 1958 Plymouth Sedan v. Pennsylvania, 380 U.S. 693 (1965) (state proceeding to declare forfeiture of automobile on the basis of its use to transport liquor not bearing state tax seals was "quasi-criminal in nature" because "its object, like a criminal proceeding, is to penalize for the commission of an offense against the law). Where the items seized are contraband *per se*, i. e., objects which cannot legally be possessed, they need not be returned to one from whose possession they have been seized, even if the seizure was clearly improper. To require return would clearly "frustrate the express public purpose against the possession of such objects." 380 U.S. at 699. See also United States v. Jeffers, 342 U.S. 48, 52–54 (1951). Apparently in the case of contraband *per se*, the need to respect a strong policy of prohibiting possession overrides the policy of prohibiting the state from using the fruits of improper activity as a means of discouraging the activity.

38. La Penta v. New York State Liquor Authority, 30 A.D.2d 1033, 294 N.Y.S.2d 947 (1968), aff'd 24 N.Y.2d 647, 301 N.Y.S.2d 584, 249 N.E.2d 440 (1969) (describing such procedures as "penal in nature although criminal in form").

39. People v. Moore, 69 Cal.2d 674, 72 Cal.Rptr. 800, 446 P.2d 800 (1968) (to permit use of the evidence would permit the state to profit from its own wrong, as civil commitment procedures serve a protective as well as a rehabilitative function).

40. Sarisohn v. Appellate Division of the Supreme Court, 21 N.Y.2d 36, 286 N.Y.S.2d 255, 233 N.E.2d 276 (1967).

41. Knoll Associates, Inc. v. FTC, 397 F.2d 530 (7th Cir. 1968).

42. State of Iowa v. Union Asphalt & Roadoils, Inc., 281 F.Supp. 391 (S.D.Iowa, 1968), aff'd sub nom. Standard Oil Co. v. Iowa, 408 F.2d 1171, 409 F.2d 1239 (8th Cir. 1969). The court declined comment on whether it would reach the same result if the plaintiff has not been the State of Iowa, although it characterized treble damage actions as "quasi-criminal".

43. See Lebel v. Swincicki, 354 Mich.2d 427, 93 N.W.2d 281 (1958) (blood taken from the defendant by state police in violation of the state constitution was inadmissible in action for damages brought by the administrator of a victim of the accident, by virtue of the state exclusionary rule).

in litigation in which the government has no direct interest, the cases are few but divided. The leading case for exclusion, Williams v. Williams,[44] involved evidence offered by a husband in a divorce proceedings; the evidence had been obtained by the husband in an unauthorized entry into the wife's automobile. In holding the evidence inadmissible, the court emphasized that no individual should have greater rights than the government to invade the rights of others, and to accept the evidence would be to recognize a greater right in the husband. The case law finding the evidence admissible tends to rely upon the factor that the seizure was by a private individual rather than the nature of the proceeding in which the proof is offered.[45] The most appropriate position is probably that when the evidence seized by a private individual would be inadmissible if offered by the government in a criminal proceeding, it should also be inadmissible if offered by the individual in noncriminal litigation. If the underlying right is protected against invasion by private individuals as well as public officials, exclusion in noncriminal actions would clearly serve the purpose of discouraging private invasions of the rights.[46]

168. Scope of the Fourth Amendment Exclusionary Rule: (b) Evidence Obtained by Private Individuals.[47]

Closely related to the question of the kinds of proceedings to which the exclusionary rule is applicable is the question of the impact upon its application of the status of the person whose improper acts are offered as the basis for excluding the evidence. The leading case is undoubtedly the 1921 Supreme Court decision in Burdeau v. McDowell.[48] McDowell moved for the suppression of material in the possession of an Assistant to the Attorney General which, the trial court found, had been stolen from him by certain private individuals. Reversing the trial court's order suppressing the material and ordering it returned to McDowell, the Supreme Court reasoned that the history and origin of the Fourth Amendment indicated that it was intended only as a restraint on "the activities of sovereign authority". Consequently the protection of the security of the individual's possession of property against invasion other than by governmental agencies was not within the amendment's protection. Since no

44. 8 Ohio Misc.2d 156, 221 N.E.2d 622 (1966). See also Del Presto, 92 N.J.Super. 305, 223 A.2d 217 (Superior Ct.1966) (evidence obtained by wife and private investigators pursuant to illegal entry inadmissible in divorce proceedings), rev'd 97 N.J.Super. 446, 235 A.2d 240 (App.Div.1967) (on ground that no violation of husband's rights had occurred and declining to reach issue of admissibility of improperly seized evidence in divorce proceeding).

45. Sackler v. Sackler, 15 N.Y.2d 40, 255 N.Y.S.2d 83, 203 N.E.2d 481 (1964) (5–2) (evidence obtained by husband and private detective admissible in divorce proceeding because Fourth Amendment does not apply to private searches); Commonwealth ex rel. Young v. Young, 213 Pa.Super. 515, 247 A.2d 659 (1968), allocatur refused, (testimony related to illegal entry by husband and private detective admissible in divorce case because private citizens not subject to same constitutional limitations as governmental officials). See § 168, infra.

46. Objection might be raised to a purported lack of state action when the evidence has been obtained by a private individual and is offered in litigation in which the state has no direct interest. Thus the overall procedure, whatever its defects, would not involve a state deprivation of liberty or property without due process of law within the meaning of the Fourteenth Amendment. Use of the evidence in private litigation leading to a judgment which is enforceable by the courts, however, is probably sufficient governmental involvement to constitute "state action". See Shelley v. Kraemer, 334 U.S. 1 (1948) (judicial enforcement of racially restrictive covenant is state action).

47. See generally, Comment, Unreasonable Private Searches and Seizures and the Exclusionary Rule, 16 Am.U.L.Rev. 403 (1967); 12 U.C.L.A.L.Rev. 232 (1964); Comment, Private Party Searches and Seizures—A Province of the Fifth Amendment, 3 U. San Francisco L.Rev. 159 (1968); Note, A Comment on the Exclusion of Evidence Wrongfully Obtained by Private Individuals, 1966 Utah L.Rev. 271; Note, Mapp v. Ohio and Exclusion of Evidence Illegally Obtained by Private Parties, 72 Yale L.J. 1062 (1963); 29 Am.Jur.2d Evidence § 417; Annot., 50 A.L.R.2d 531, 570–77; C.J.S. Searches & Seizures § 5(c); Dec. Dig. Searches & Seizures ⊗7(4).

48. 256 U.S. 465 (1921).

official of the federal government had anything to do with the wrongful seizure of the property at issue, there was no invasion of the security afforded by the Fourth Amendment and therefore no right to suppression. Mr. Justice Brandeis, with Mr. Justice Holmes concurring, dissented, arguing that regardless of whether federal officials had participated in the seizure of the property from McDowell the federal court now had the opportunity to restore the property to him. To fail to do so, Brandeis argued, would be to resort for law enforcement to means "which shock the common man's sense of decency and fair play" and which would have the effect of decreasing respect for law.

The validity of *Burdeau* has been somewhat shaken by Elkins v. United States,[49] in which the Court struck down the "silver platter" doctrine. Under the "silver platter" rule, evidence obtained improperly by state officials could nevertheless be used by federal prosecutors, on the reasoning that no federal official had participated in the underlying violation of the defendant's rights. If, under *Elkins*, federal courts could no longer use evidence improperly obtained by state officials who would be free to use it in state courts, does it not follow that use of evidence obtained by private individuals would be improper? This argument, however, ignores the fact that under the silver platter doctrine there was no doubt that the evidence was obtained pursuant to a violation of Fourth Amendment rights. The question was one of remedy. When the evidence has been obtained by a private individual, however, the problem is not one of remedy but rather whether there has been an invasion of rights which are protected by the amendment. Despite *Elkins*, both federal and state courts have almost uniformly held that evidence obtained by private individuals pursuant to activities which, if performed by governmental

agents, would constitute a violation of Fourth Amendment rights, is nevertheless admissible.[50]

This rule, however, is subject to the exception that exclusion is required when the pri-

49.   364 U.S. 206 (1960).

50.   Barnes v. United States, 373 F.2d 517 (5th Cir. 1967) (search of travel case by motel owner "did not involve governmental action" and was therefore not illegal within the meaning of the Fourth Amendment); Walker v. State, 244 Ark. 1150, 429 S.W.2d 121 (1968) (taking of blood sample by laboratory technician was not within Fourth Amendment prohibition); State v. Holliday, 169 N.W.2d 768 (Iowa 1969) (attaching of device to accused's telephone by officer of telephone company did not violate Fourth Amendment); State v. Brown, 391 S.W.2d 903 (Mo. 1965); People v. Zalduondo, 58 Misc.2d 326, 295 N.Y.S.2d 301 (1968) (evidence obtained by employer's search of employee's car not subject to suppression); State v. Bryan, 1 Ore.App. 15, 457 P.2d 661 (1969); Harmon v. Commonwealth, 209 Va. 574, 166 S.E.2d 232 (1969). But see Williams v. Williams, 8 Ohio Misc. 156, 221 N.E.2d 622 (1966) (evidence obtained by husband pursuant to illegal entry of wife's car inadmissible in divorce proceedings, because no private individual has greater power than the government to invade the rights of others). For a discussion of the present validity of *Burdeau*, see United States v. McGuire, 381 F.2d 306, 313 n. 5 (2d Cir. 1967) cert. denied 389 U.S. 1053.

Prior to Mapp v. Ohio, several state courts which were committed to the exclusion of evidence wrongfully obtained by officers of that state held that they would not exclude evidence improperly obtained by officers of a sister state. Young v. Commonwealth, 313 S.W.2d 580 (Ky.1958); People v. Winterheld, 359 Mich. 467, 102 N.W.2d 201 (1960). Since *Mapp*'s imposition of the exclusionary rule on the states, it seems clear that a state may not regard officers of another state as "private" individuals and decline to exclude evidence seized by them. See State v. Krogness, 238 Ore. 135, 388 P.2d 120 (1963) cert. denied 377 U.S. 992.

Evidence seized by agents of a foreign government pursuant to activities that would make it inadmissible had it been seized by American officers has been held admissible, however, on the theory that the Fourth Amendment is not designed to control the activities of agents of foreign governments. Stonehill v. United States, 405 F.2d 738 (9th Cir. 1968) cert. denied 395 U.S. 960 (evidence seized in raids which were found to have violated the Philippine Constitution and, if conducted by United States agents, would have violated United States Constitution); Brulay v. United States, 383 F.2d 345 (9th Cir. 1967) cert. denied 389 U.S. 986 (evidence seized by Mexican officials). See generally Note, Searches South of the Border: Admission of Evidence Seized by Foreign Officials, 53 Cornell L.Rev. 886 (1968).

vate individual is acting as an agent of governmental officials. The mere presence of police officers at the scene of a private search may not be enough to constitute the private individual an agent of the officers.[51] Where police participated in the planning and execution of an arrest by agents of a credit card company, however, this was sufficient to taint the agents' subsequent search at the scene of the arrest with governmental authority.[52] In United States v. Small,[53] the court found no violation of the accused's right in a routine search of lockers in a terminal by an employee of the locker company, but held that when, at the request of police, he changed the lock on a locker rented by the accused, the employee became an agent of the police. This exception has recently been expanded by a federal appellate court to require exclusion when (a) the evidence had been improperly obtained by a private individual for the purpose of assisting the government in a pending proceeding, and (b) the

evidence was accepted with knowledge of the unlawful manner in which it was received.[54]

As a matter of policy, is the *Burdeau* rule still acceptable? Certainly the protection of personal security from invasion by governmental sources is a far different matter from protection of the same security from private sources.[55] Because of the greater resources of public law enforcement agencies and their routine enforcement practices, public officers are more likely than private individuals to endanger private rights and more likely to have the ability successfully to invade them. Federalism arguably suggests that protection from private wrongs remain a matter of state law, and that the Fourth Amendment protection be confined to public invasions of private rights. Even if it is agreed, however, that the Fourth Amendment protects against private invasions, it is not clear that an exclusionary rule would be justified as a constitutionally-required remedy. Perhaps the exclusion of the fruits of private invasions would be significantly less effective in deterring invasions by private individuals, who unlike public officials, are not likely to have evidentiary use as their objective or who are less likely to be aware of the exclusionary penalty. Moreover, it may not be clear that other remedies are as ineffective in deterring private invasions of personal rights as they are in deterring official invasions. Tort remedies, for example, might well be more suc-

---

51. Del Presto v. Del Presto, 97 N.J.Super. 446, 235 A.2d 240 (App.Div.1968). The officers had been called when a husband and several detectives sought to break into the apartment of the wife's paramour. The officers apparently identified themselves to all involved, did not participate in the forcing of the door, and only entered the apartment upon the invitation of the paramour. See also Wright v. United States, 224 A.2d 475 (D.C.App.1966) (gun seized by private security officer who had been told by police not to seize it was not subject to suppression).

There is some suggestion that not all employees of governmental agencies are agents of the state for purposes of Fourth Amendment analysis. See In re Donaldson, 269 Cal.App.2d 509, 75 Cal.Rptr. 220 (1969) (high school vice principal acting within scope of his authority in making search was not an agent of the state for Fourth Amendment purposes). This result is difficult to justify. While the Fourth Amendment requirements in a noncriminal investigation may differ from the provision's requirements in a standard criminal investigation, it is clear that the fact that an employee's formal duties do not include criminal investigations does not prevent his actions from violating Fourth Amendment interests. Camara v. Municipal Court of San Francisco, 387 U.S. 523 (1967).

52. Stapleton v. Superior Court, 70 Cal.2d 97, 73 Cal.Rptr. 575, 447 P.2d 967 (1968).

53. 297 F.Supp. 582 (D.Mass.1969).

54. Knoll Associates, Inc. v. FTC, 397 F.2d 530 (7th Cir. 1968), noted in 44 N.Y.U.L.Rev. 206 (1969). It has been suggested that this is not inconsistent with *Burdeau*, as *Knoll* involved affirmative government action, i. e., knowing use. NLRB v. South Bay Daily Breeze, 415 F.2d 360, 363 (9th Cir. 1969). Although *Burdeau* did not involve affirmative use which might be interpreted as expressing "approval" of the private wrong, this was because the issue arose on a pretrial motion. Certainly use of the evidence with knowledge of the means by which it had been taken from the accused was anticipated in *Burdeau*, and the Court did not in any manner indicate disapproval.

55. See Note, Mapp v. Ohio and Exclusion of Evidence Illegally Obtained by Private Parties, 72 Yale L.J. 1062, 1069–72 (1963).

cessful when the defendant is a private individual rather than a police officer. Nor is it clear that the overall problem of private invasions of personal rights is of sufficient seriousness to justify requiring an exclusionary rule as a matter of constitutional law.

On the other hand, the cost of applying the exclusionary rule would probably be minimal (since relatively few private invasions probably occur), so it should not be necessary that the underlying problem be as serious as would be required were the remedy more costly. In addition, an exclusionary rule in this context is arguably required for reasons independent of its effectiveness in deterring the underlying invasion of the personal rights. Reliance by courts on evidence obtained by these means may well violate a public "sense of fairness", thereby decreasing respect for the judicial system and ultimately working to its disadvantage. There may be inherent unfairness in the use of evidence obtained in such a manner to the detriment of the one whose rights were violated in its seizure, without regard to the effectiveness of exclusion on the protection of these rights in the future.

On balance, the factors seem to favor the imposition of the exclusionary rule. Although the situation is distinguishable from that in *Mapp,* the distinction is not of sufficient breadth to justify a drastic difference in the treatment of the resulting evidence. While the need to protect personal security from private as well as public invasion is certainly an important factor, the controlling matter is the unfairness of the use of the evidence and the degrading of the judicial system that must necessarily accompany that use.

169. Evidence Obtained Pursuant to Unreasonable Searches and Seizures: (a) Definition of Searches and Seizures.

The Fourth Amendment, by its terms, protects against "searches and seizures." No question of reasonableness is raised, therefore, unless the challenged situation involves either a search or a seizure as those terms are defined in the amendment. In view of the wide variety of factual situations to which the amendment now pertains, it is possible that no meaningful generally applicable definition of these terms is possible.[56] Nevertheless, conceptual and analytical clarity suggests that an attempt is worthwhile.

The terms of the amendment must be defined in light of the underlying purpose of the provision. In Katz v. United States[57] the Supreme Court made clear that in general terms the amendment protects reliance upon reasonable expectations of privacy. The terms, then, must be defined in light of this underlying purpose. These definitions should be limited to defining the interest protected and its invasion and should not address themselves to the question whether the invasion is justified. The latter inquiry is more appropriately made pursuant to the determination whether a particular search or seizure is "reasonable" within the meaning of the amendment.

A search involves two elements, one mental and the other physical. The mental element is an intent to seize the object of the search.[58]

---

56. But see the definitions in A Model Code of Pre-Arraignment Procedure §§ 1.01(1), (2) (Tent. Draft No. 3, 1970).

57. 389 U.S. 347 (1967). The development of the concept of search in the area of electronic surveillance is discussed in detail in § 174, infra.

58. Cf. Weeks v. United States, 232 U.S. 383, 397 (1914) ("a search ordinarily implies a quest by an officer of the law"); Haerr v. United States, 240 F.2d 533 (5th Cir. 1957).

The seizure intended need not be the most significant seizure of the items that is physically possible. An officer who glances through a car window intends to observe whatever is in the vehicle and thus intends seizure in this limited fashion, although he may not at the time intend to exert physical control. (His actions may not violate any reasonable expectation of privacy, of course, and thus not fall within the definition of search for that reason; see text at n. 59, infra.)

The physical element is some action taken to effectuate the seizure in a manner which violates someone's reasonable expectation of privacy in regard to the object.[59] A seizure, on the other hand, is the exertion of domination over the object.[60] What constitutes a search or a seizure will depend upon the nature of the object and the circumstances. If the object is a tangible item, for example, domination may involve exerting physical control over it. But if the item is reasonably regarded as inaccessible to visual observation, action taken with the intent of observing it is a "search" and the observation a "seizure."[61] If the object is a sound (such as a conversation), merely hearing it may constitute a seizure of it.

These definitions are consistent with—and help define precisely—the often-invoked "plain view" doctrine. Under the "plain view" rule, observations made of items or actions which are open to general observation are not made pursuant to a search.[62] But as the definition of search makes clear, whether an item is in "plain view" depends upon whether under the circumstances there is a reasonable expectation that it will be free from the type of activity used to make the observation.[63] This also explains the "open fields" doctrine, under which no violation of Fourth Amendment rights occurs, even if officers commit a technical trespass upon land, when there was no invasion of the buildings or their immediate appurtenances forming

---

But cf. Wyman v. James, 400 U.S. 309 (1971), in which the majority holds that a "home visit" to a welfare recipient by a caseworker is not a search in the Fourth Amendment meaning of the term. Some reliance is put upon the fact that the recipient may prevent the visit by refusing permission, although this results in termination of assistance. Three justices dissented, and another declined to join in that portion of the majority opinion which held that the visit did not involve a search.

59. This formulation seems more satisfactory than the traditional language, "a prying into hidden places for that which is concealed." People v. Sylvester, 43 Ill.2d 325, 253 N.E.2d 429 (1969); People v. West, 144 Cal.App.2d 214, 300 P.2d 729 (1956).

60. The older cases suggest that a "forceful dispossession" is necessary. E. g., Weeks v. United States, 232 U.S. 383, 397 (1914). Although a search may be followed by voluntary relinquishment of privacy by the holder of that privacy, it is conceptually sounder to regard the exertion of domination over the object with the permission of another as a seizure consented to by the person rather than as no seizure at all.

61. See Bielicki v. Superior Court, 57 Cal.2d 602, 21 Cal.Rptr. 552, 371 P.2d 288 (1962) (evidence obtained by observing men's toilet through a hole in the roof not admissible); Britt v. Superior Court, 58 Cal.2d 469, 24 Cal.Rptr. 849, 374 P.2d 817 (1962) (observations of homosexual acts in men's room through ceiling vent not admissible even though one entering men's room might have observed acts). Contra, in prosecution for an offense committed in Yosemite National Park, Smayda v. United States, 352 F.2d 251 (9th Cir. 1965).

62. Burton v. United States, 414 F.2d 261 (5th Cir. 1969) (observation of gun as it was thrown from automobile was not pursuant to a search); Coates v. United States, 134 U.S.App.D.C. 97, 413 F.2d 371 (1969) (observation of wallet through car window was not made pursuant to search); City of Decatur v. Kushmer, 43 Ill.2d 334, 253 N.E.2d 425 (1969) (observations and photographs of unenclosed yard which could be observed from the sidewalk, street, and rear alley were not made pursuant to a search, even if officers trespassed by entering yard).

The apparent effect of the "plain view" doctrine of removing seizures from the warrant requirement—a distinguishable matter—is discussed in § 171, infra.

63. See Ponce v. Craven, 409 F.2d 621 (9th Cir. 1969) (occupants of motel room did not have reasonable expectation of privacy in regard to their conversations because they had left bathroom window open and conversations in the room could be overheard by one on public parking lot outside window); United States v. Richardson, 388 F.2d 842 (6th Cir. 1968) (examination of defendant's hands with ultraviolet light was not a search); State v. Purvis, 249 Ore. 404, 438 P.2d 1002 (1968) (over dissent) (defendant had no right of privacy in regard to marijuana butt which he had deposited in hotel ashtray after ashtray had been removed from room by maid, although his privacy interest in the room would have made a quest for the butt a search if it had been made before the ashtray had been removed). One who leaves items in an automobile at night in such a manner that they can be seen from outside by one who shines a flashlight into the car apparently has no reasonable expectation that the items will be free of official observation. Compare Lucas v. United States, 256 A.2d 574 (D.C.App.1969); State v. Daniels, 252 S.C. 591, 167 S.E.2d 621 (1969).

the curtilage.[64] No reasonable expectation of privacy exists as to activities carried on or items located at a point which can be observed from the open fields.

Careful definition of searches and seizures is of particular importance because it focuses attention on the need to examine separately different stages of what might appear to be a single process. For example, in State v. Elkins[65] the defendant was arrested for drunkenness. An examination of his shirt pocket by the arresting officer disclosed an unlabeled bottle containing several kinds of capsules and pills. The officer took possession of the bottle and caused the pills and capsules to be subjected to chemical analysis. Some of them were found to be methodone. Evaluating this factual situation under the Fourth Amendment requires that the situation be considered step-by-step: the officer's action in taking the defendant into custody (a "seizure" of his person), the examination of the defendant's shirt pocket (a search), the action of the officer in taking possession of the bottle and its contents (a seizure), and the chemical analysis of the contents of the bottle (a search). The reasonableness of each step must be tested individually.[66] For example, in the absence of some basis for believing that the pills were contraband, fruits of a crime, or evidence of criminal activity,

the chemical analysis may have been unreasonable in Fourth Amendment terms although the seizure of the bottle and its contents may have been entirely appropriate. In any case, the examination of the pills is an invasion of privacy separate and distinct from either the search of defendant's person or the seizure of the bottle containing the pills. Careful definition of search and seizure in each fact situation is the best method of avoiding confusion of these issues.[67]

170. Evidence Obtained Pursuant to Unreasonable Searches and Seizures: (b) The Substantive Requirement of Reasonableness.

The Fourth Amendment imposes two distinct limitations upon invasions of personal privacy. One, the "substantive" limitation, concerns the evidentiary basis which must exist before the invasion is permissible. The second, the "procedural" limitation, involves the procedure by which that evidentiary basis must be established. This procedural limitation, which usually takes the form of requiring that a warrant be obtained, is discussed in the next section.[68] The present section discusses only the substantive requirement.

The first portion of the Fourth Amendment [69] declares, "The right of the people to

---

64. Hester v. United States, 265 U.S. 57 (1924); United States v. Hollon, 420 F.2d 302 (5th Cir. 1969).

65. 245 Ore. 279, 422 P.2d 250 (1966).

66. It is possible to read the language of the Fourth Amendment—"The right of the people to be secure . . . against unreasonable *searches and seizures*, shall not be violated . . . ."—as directing that protection only be extended against invasions of privacy involving both a search *and* a seizure. There is no reason, however, so to read the words. Either a search *or* a seizure may, depending upon the situation, constitute a much greater infringement upon the interest of privacy than another situation involving both activities. It seems clear that a search alone or a seizure alone can violate the Fourth Amendment. Therefore, the reasonableness of each search and each seizure must be tested individually.

67. But cf. United States v. Van Leeuwen, 397 U.S. 249 (1970). A package mailed under suspicious circumstances was detained while an investigation was conducted. After one and one-half hours, probable cause existed to believe that the package was part of an illicit project; 29 hours after the mailing the package was opened pursuant to a warrant. In upholding the action, however, the Court suggested that the initial detention for one and one-half hours was not a "seizure" within the meaning of the Fourth Amendment: "No interest protected by the Fourth Amendment was invaded by forwarding the packages the following day rather than the day when they were deposited." Yet other language suggests that the Court may have regarded the detention of the packages as a seizure, albeit a reasonable one.

68. See § 171, infra.

69. "The right of the people to be secure in their persons, houses, papers, and effects, against unreasonable searches and seizures, shall not be violated, and no Warrants shall issue, but upon prob-

be secure in their persons, houses, papers, and effects, against unreasonable searches and seizures shall not be violated . . . .". The second portion directs that "no Warrants shall issue, but upon probable cause, supported by Oath or affirmation." It is arguable that the second clause provides the standard by which the ambiguous phrase "unreasonable searches and seizures" of the first clause should be construed. Thus a search or seizure would be "reasonable" only if made upon "probable cause, supported by Oath or affirmation."[70] This is not the construction, however, and the result seems appropriate. "Probable cause" is little more definte than "reasonableness," so such an interpretation would be of little help in defining the applicable standard. Moreover, a requirement that all activities which fall within the scope of searches or seizures be judged by the same evidentiary standard would deprive the law of the flexibility essential to realistic accommodation of essential law enforcement investigatory techniques. It seems reasonable, for example, that a suspect should not be taken into custody for the purpose of putting him to formal trial on the same evidentiary basis as would justify temporarily detaining him on the street for the limited purpose of determining whether there is need further to investigate his apparently suspicious actions.

The Fourth Amendment, then, cannot be said to contain any single precise substantive evidentiary standard. This has been recognized by the Supreme Court, although early Fourth Amendment cases suggest that the Court did not at that time acknowledge that the amendment contained this degree of flex-

ibility. Probable cause was first developed as the standard to be applied in determining whether a warrant authorizing a search had been appropriately issued [71] and in determining whether a search made without a warrant had been proper.[72] The same standard was then used to determine the constitutionality of an arrest [73] with little attention being given to whether specific deprivations of personal liberty were in fact "arrests" as that term might be narrowly defined.[74] "Probable cause" in these contexts requires facts and circumstances within the person's knowledge or of which he has reasonably trustworthy information which are sufficient to warrant a man of reasonable caution in believing the ultimate facts whose evidentiary basis is at issue.[75] Thus the requirement directs an evaluation of the quality as well as the quantity of the information relied upon. The probable cause requirement is to be administered not as a technicality but as a factual and practical consideration of everyday life upon which reasonable and prudent men, not legal technicians, act.[76] The issue arises in such a wide variety of situations, however, that the formulation of any more precise standard than is contained in the preceding phrases is probably impossible.[77]

---

71. E. g., Giordenello v. United States, 357 U.S. 480 (1958).

72. E. g., Carroll v. United States, 267 U.S. 132 (1925); Brinegar v. United States, 338 U.S. 160 (1949).

73. Johnson v. United States, 333 U.S. 10 (1948); Draper v. United States, 358 U.S. 307 (1959); Ker v. California, 374 U.S. 23 (1963).

74. E. g., Beck v. Ohio, 379 U.S. 89 (1964) (investigatory stop of automobile followed by arrest, but no consideration of the point at which the arrest occurred).

75. Carroll v. United States, 267 U.S. 132, 162 (1925); Draper v. United States, 358 U.S. 307 (1959).

76. Brinegar v. United States, 338 U.S. 160, 175 (1949).

77. "*Mapp* did not attempt the impossible task of laying down a 'fixed formula' for the application in specific cases of the constitutional prohibition against unreasonable searches and seizures; it

able cause, supported by Oath or affirmation, and particularly describing the place to be searched, and the persons or things to be seized." U.S.Const. Amend. IV.

70. See generally Landynsky, Search and Seizure and the Supreme Court 42–47 (1966) for a discussion of the wording of the amendment.

One particular situation in which the Court has attempted to formulate more precise guidelines is that in which the evidence offered is information obtained from an informer.[78] In Spinelli v. United States [79] the following allegations were made in support of an application for a search warrant: (a) on four of five days of surveillance, the subject had gone from Illinois into St. Louis, Missouri between 11 a.m. and 12:15 p.m. and had parked his car near a given apartment house; (b) on one of these days, he had been followed further and seen to enter a particular apartment; (c) a check with the telephone company revealed that the apartment was not listed in the subject's name and contained two telephones with particular numbers; (d) the subject was "known to . . . federal law enforcement agents as a bookmaker, an associate of bookmakers, a gambler, and an associate of gamblers."; (e) a "confidential reliable informant" had informed the F.B.I. that the subject was operating a handbook and was accepting wagers over telephones with two specific numbers (which were identical to those which the telephone company indicated were in the apartment). At issue was whether this constituted "probable cause" to believe that there were items on the premises subject to seizure (which, for all practical purposes, depended upon whether there was probable cause to believe that a gambling business was being conducted on the premises).

The appropriate analysis, held the Court, proceeded as follows:

(1) Did the "tip" alone constitute probable cause? Under Aguilar v. Texas,[80] a tip must be accompanied by (a) "some of the underlying circumstances on which the informant based his conclusions," and (b) some basis for concluding either that the informer was "credible" or that his information in this particular instance was "reliable." If the tip contained sufficiently detailed information, however, the detail itself may be a basis for inferring that the informant obtained his information in a reliable way. Corroboration of some of the information given might also provide the basis for such an inference.

(2) If the "tip" was not sufficient in itself, when considered with other information, it might together with that information have constituted probable cause.

Turning to the facts before it, the Court indicated that there was no proof other than the agent's mere assertion that the informer was reliable. Nor was there sufficient detail in the information or adequate corroboration to overcome this. As a "benchmark" of what constituted sufficient detail and corroboration, the Court cited Draper v. United States.[81] In *Draper*, the informer had reported that the subject had gone to Chicago the day before and would return to Denver by train with three ounces of heroin on one of two specified mornings. He had described in detail the clothes that the subject would be wearing, the bag he would be carrying, and his manner of walking. When police officers met the train from Denver on the second of the two specified mornings, they observed a man disembark whose clothing, luggage, and walk corresponded to the informer's description. The detail of the information itself,

recognized that we would be 'met with recurring questions of the reasonableness of searches' . . . ." Ker v. California, 374 U.S. 23, 31–32 (1963).

78. See generally, Note, The Informer's Tip as Probable Cause for Search or Arrest, 54 Cornell L.Rev. 958 (1969). In fact, the analysis of these cases is probably applicable far beyond situations involving what in common language is an "informer." The principle of the approach seems to apply to any situation in which the basis offered includes information as to which the person who must have probable cause does not have direct knowledge.

79. 393 U.S. 410 (1969).

80. 378 U.S. 108 (1964).

81. 358 U.S. 307 (1959).

the Court suggested, was such that a finder of fact could conclude that the tip itself met the probable cause requirements. But once the information was corroborated by the officers' observation, "it was perfectly clear that probable cause had been established."

The Court also held that the tip in *Spinelli* when considered together with the other evidence did not constitute probable cause. The assertion of F.B.I. suspicion that the subject was a gambler was only a "simple assertion" and, as such, must be given *no* weight. The results of the surveillance "contain no suggestion of criminal conduct when taken by themselves—and they are not endowed with an aura of suspicion by virtue of an informer's tip."

Spinelli illustrates the difficulty of articulating a precise standard for determining reasonableness or probable cause even in limited contexts. The Court did not explain why the detail of the *Spinelli* tip—the specific telephone numbers used—did not provide as adequate a basis for inferring that the informer had obtained his information in a reliable way as the detail in *Draper*. Except for the specification that the subject would have three ounces of heroin, the detail of the *Draper* tip in no way related to the facts really at issue; in contrast, the detail in *Spinelli* related to items which were believed to be the instruments of the crime. Nor did the Court explain why the corroboration in *Spinelli*— that the subject did indeed have access to two phones with the same numbers as were specified in the tip—was not as legally effective as the corroboration in *Draper*, which went only to purely collateral matters such as clothing. The Court also failed to provide a satisfactory criterion for determining what additional evidence would have been necessary to push the facts of *Spinelli* over the line drawn by the *Draper* benchmark. The Court's attempt to distinguish *Spinelli* from *Draper* suggests the futility of any effort to define "probable cause" precisely, even in a limited situation.[82]

82. The unsatisfactory nature of the analysis is also suggested by the Court's 4–1–3–1 division. Four members joined in Mr. Justice Harlan's opinion for the court; Mr. Justice White concurred, indicating doubt as to Mr. Justice Harlan's interpretation of *Draper* but agreeing with his refusal to extend it to the facts of *Spinelli*. Three members dissented, arguing that the affidavit was sufficient to sustain a determination of probable cause, and one member of the court did not participate in the decision.

The ambiguity of the situation was made obvious by the divisions of the Court in United States v. Harris, 403 U.S. 573 (1971). The affidavit offered as supporting a search warrant, given by a federal tax investigator, contained the affiant's statement that the subject of the search "had a reputation with me for over four years as being a trafficker of nontaxpaid distilled spirits, and over this period I have received numerous information from all types of persons as to his activities," and that at an unidentified time during this four year period, another police officer had located "a sizable stash of illicit whiskey" in an abandoned house "under [the subject's] control." The affiant also stated that an unidentified informant had in a sworn statement reported purchasing illicit whiskey from the subject at the address searched within the last two weeks. No averment of the informant's prior reliability was made, although the affiant stated that "I have interviewed this person, [and] found this person to be a prudent person . . . ." A majority of the Supreme Court upheld the warrant and search. Chief Justice Berger, speaking for the court, rejected the assertions that under *Spinelli* an averment of prior reliability of the informant was necessary and that an law enforcement-affiant's simple assertion of knowledge of the suspect's reputation could not be considered. Jones v. United States, 362 U.S. 257 (1962) was suggested as a "suitable benchmark" for determining the quantum of information necessary to support a belief that an unidentified informant's information is truthful, apparently to replace the emphasis on Draper v. United States, 358 U.S. 307 (1959) in *Spinelli*. Mr. Justices Black and Blackmun joined this portion of the opinion. Mr. Justices Stewart and White joined other portions of the Chief Justice's opinion holding in more general terms that the affidavit was adequate, especially in light of the fact that the informer's tip constituted a potentially incriminating admission. Mr. Justices Black, and Blackmun in concurring opinions, indicated their willingness expressly to overrule *Spinelli*. Mr. Justice Harlan (author of the majority opinion in *Spinelli*), joined by Justices Douglas, Brennan and Marshall, dissented, arguing that the affidavit failed to set forth sufficient underlying facts supporting the affiant's conclusion that the informer was reliable and that consideration of the affiant's assertion that he had received information from others that the subject was trafficking in il-

As the reach of the Fourth Amendment has expanded, probable cause has become a much more flexible standard than was first supposed. In Camara v. Municipal Court,[83] the Court considered the evidentiary standard applicable when a warrant was sought for inspection of premises under a housing code inspection program. Directly involved, then, was the Fourth Amendment directive that "no warrants shall issue, but upon probable cause." But the Court rejected the argument that in this context probable cause had the same meaning as that given it when the search was pursuant to the enforcement of the criminal law, i.e., that there must be probable cause to believe that the particular dwelling contains violations. "Probable cause," the Court held, is merely one aspect of reasonableness. "Unfortunately, there can be no ready test for determining reasonableness other than by balancing the need to search against the invasion which the search entails." Weighing the need for routine periodic inspections as a means of enforcing compliance with municipal codes, the public interest in assuring compliance with those codes, and the long history of judicial and public acceptance of liberal standards in this area against the relatively limited invasion of the subject's privacy involved, the Court concluded that " 'probable cause' to issue a warrant to inspect must exist if reasonable legislative or administrative standards for conducting an area inspection are satisfied with respect to a particular dwelling." Passage of time, the nature of the building, and the condition of the area may all be influential, but specific knowledge regarding the particular dwelling is unnecessary. Responding to the assertion that this emasculated the Fourth Amendment protection, the Court asserted, "[R]easonableness is still the ultimate standard. If a valid public interest justifies the intrusion contemplated, then there is probable cause to issue a suitably restricted search warrant." [84]

It necessarily follows that if the substantive standard of probable cause required for warrants may differ with the situation, the substantive standard applicable in situations where no warrant is necessary may also vary from situation to situation. As is discussed below,[85] the Court has already committed itself to such an approach when dealing with the constitutional limitations upon the basis required for depriving a person of his liberty pursuant to a criminal investigation. In other situations to which the Fourth Amendment is applicable, however, it is equally clear that the evidentiary basis constitutionally necessary for a contemplated invasion of privacy depends upon a balance between the public interest in the invasion—the public interest in the objective and the need for the invasion as a means of achieving that objective—and the seriousness of the violation of personal privacy involved. The seriousness of the invasion also depends upon the circumstances but clearly involves the purpose of the invasion as well as its extent and duration.

This raises the final question whether there are expectations of privacy which are completely immune from invasion by virtue of the Fourth Amendment. Prior to Warden, Maryland Penitentiary v. Hayden [86] formal

---

licit liquor was "flatly inconsistent" with *Spinelli.* Noting the absence of corroboration and precise detail of the information and rejecting the adequacy of other indicia of accuracy relied upon by the majority, the dissenters argued that the information submitted to the magistrate was insufficient to support a finding by the magistrate of probable cause.

83.　387 U.S. 523 (1967).

84.　387 U.S. at 538–539. See Comment, Constitutional Law—Administrative Searches and the Fourth Amendment: The Definition of "Probable Cause" in Camara v. Municipal Court of the City and County of San Francisco, 36 U.Mo.K.C.L.Rev. 111 (1968).

85.　See § 173, infra.

86.　387 U.S. 294 (1967).

Fourth Amendment doctrine held that "mere evidence," i.e., items not contraband, fruits or instrumentalities of the crime, or weapons by which an escape might be effected, were not subject to seizure.[87] This limitation upon the seizure power rested upon the assumption that the right to search for and seize property depended upon the state's assertion of a claim to possession of the property superior to that of others and that the mere desire to use property to secure the conviction of one accused of a crime was not an interest superior to other ownership or possessory rights.[88] This general limitation, upon items subject to seizure, often circumvented by lower courts,[89] was disclaimed in *Hayden*. It is now generally regarded as settled that not only may "mere evidence" be seized but also that a search may be conducted solely for those items. *Hayden* does not, however, foreclose the possibility that a more limited category of items might be immune from seizure: "This case . . . does not require that we consider whether there are items of evidential value whose very nature precludes them from being the object of a reasonable search and seizure."[90]

In some situations the importance of the individual's interest in privacy and the minimal public interest in its invasion might lead to the conclusion that under no circumstances can that privacy be invaded. Perhaps the most likely area for application of such a limitation is that of private papers. The Advisory Committee to the American Law Institute's Model Code of Pre-Arraignment Procedure recommended that personal diaries,

letters, and other private writings or recordings be regarded as immune from search or seizure unless they served "a substantial purpose in furtherance of a criminal enterprise."[91] Seizure of these documents constitutes an unusually serious invasion of personal privacy, it can be argued, and since they are of evidentiary value only the public interest in their seizure is minimal. In addition, since the use of documents of these kinds would involve proving a testimonial utterance, the privilege against compelled self-incrimination may offer some support against permitting their seizure.[92] Case law support for any such immunity from seizure is virtually nonexistent,[93] however, and it is probable that the Fourth Amendment does not im-

87. The "leading case" was Gouled v. United States, 255 U.S. 298 (1921).

88. Warden v. Hayden, 387 U.S. 294, 303–304 (1967).

89. Probably the most frequently used vehicle was a broad definition of "instrumentalities and means by which the crime was committed." See Comment, Limitations on Seizures of "Evidentiary" Objects, A Rule in Search of a Reason, 20 U.Chi. L.Rev. 319, 320–22 (1953).

90. Warden v. Hayden, 387 U.S. 294, 303 (1967).

91. A Model Code of Pre-Arraignment Procedure § SS 1.03(2) (Tent.Draft No. 3, 1970). An exception to the immunity is made for handwriting samples and other material of evidentiary value for reasons other than the testimonial content. A requirement that the writing or recording have been "made solely for personal use or communication to a person occupying a family, personal, or confidential relationship other than a relationship in criminal enterprise" was added in the next draft. A Model Code of Pre-Arraignment Procedure § SS 1.03(2) (Tent.Draft No. 4, 1971). See also Taylor, Two Studies in Constitutional Interpretation 68–71 (1969).

92. See generally § 127, supra, for a discussion of the direct applicability of the Fifth Amendment to this situation.

93. See United States v. Scharfman, 448 F.2d 1352 (2d Cir. 1971) (seizure of memo book containing handwritten entries not unreasonable in Fourth Amendment terms although compulsory production of it would have been prohibited by the Fifth Amendment privilege against compelled self-incrimination); United States v. Bennett, 409 F.2d 888 (2d Cir. 1969) cert. denied 396 U.S. 852 (Friendly, J.) (personal letter was not immune from seizure). Compare the discussion in the cases that "private papers" are immune from seizure by virtue of the Fifth Amendment privilege to be free from compelled self-incrimination in § 127, supra. See also Comment, Protection of the Right of Privacy of One's Personal Papers, 1970 L. & Soc.Order 269. The admissibility of a diary was raised in Hill v. California, 401 U.S. 797, 805–06 (1971), but the matter was not resolved because it had not been raised in the state courts. But see Hill v. Philpott, 445 F.2d 144 (7th Cir. 1971), discussed at § 127 n. 74, supra.

pose any such absolute restrictions on the right of the state to invade personal privacy.[94]

171. Evidence Obtained Pursuant to Unreasonable Searches and Seizures: (c) The Procedural Requirement of a Search Warrant, and Its Exceptions.[95]

General Requirement of a Warrant. The language of the Fourth Amendment itself is ambiguous as to the methods to be employed to assure that the right of the people to be secure against unreasonable searches and seizures is not violated. Although the second clause specifies a warrant procedure, the relationship between the clauses is such that it is not clear whether the framers intended that a warrant be required for all or most searches or seizures, or whether a search made upon a proper evidentiary basis might be "reasonable" despite the absence of a search warrant.[96] Early Supreme Court cases vacillated,[97] but the Court has now committed itself to the position that the Fourth Amendment directs heavy reliance upon the search warrant procedure as a means of protecting the right to be free from unreasonable searches and seizures.[98] Searches, at least, must be made pursuant to a warrant unless the situation falls within one of the exceptions in which the exigencies of the situation justify a warrantless search.

Whether this heavy reliance upon the search warrant procedure is justified is subject to question. If the procedure functioned as it is theoretically designed to function, of course, the magistrate would provide additional assurance that contemplated invasions of Fourth Amendment rights are justified. Mr. Justice Jackson concisely explained the theory:

> "The point of the Fourth Amendment, which often is not grasped by zealous officers, is not that it denies law enforcement the support of the usual inferences which reasonable men draw from evidence. Its protection consists in requiring that those inferences be drawn by a neutral and detached magistrate instead of being judged by the officer engaged in the often competitive enterprise of ferreting out crime. . . . When the right of privacy must reasonably yield to the right of search is, as a rule, to be decided by a judicial officer, not by a

---

94. Judge Friendly has suggested that the reasonableness requirement may make a search for personal documents impermissible under certain circumstances. For example, an inability to predict where in a personal diary seizable information will be found might mean that no search of the diary may be conducted for it. "Reasonableness" must take into account the seriousness of the invasion of privacy involved in permitting an inspection of an entire diary as a means of searching for a particular passage which, if found, would be subject to seizure. United States v. Bennett, 409 F.2d 888, 897 (2d Cir. 1969) cert. denied 396 U.S. 852.

95. See generally, Taylor, Two Studies in Constitutional Interpretation 21–50 (1969); Note, The Right of the People to be Secure: The Developing Role of the Search Warrant, 42 N.Y.U.L.Rev. 1119 (1967). Cf. Burnett, Search Warrants: Impact and Application of Chimel and Spinelli and Related Problems, 29 Fed.B.J. 170 (1970).

96. See generally, Landynski, Search and Seizure and the Supreme Court 42–44 (1966). Landynski suggests that the first clause of the amendment might be read as suggesting that some searches might be "reasonable" (and thus permissible) even if carried out without the warrant discussed in the second clause. He argues, however, that the history of the amendment shows that the first clause was intended to do no more than to recognize an existing right. It thus was not intended itself to perform a substantive function, either that of defining "unreasonable" searches or that of authorizing warrantless but still reasonable searches.

97. In Trupiano v. United States, 334 U.S. 699 (1948) agents raided a still, arresting the operator and seizing the equipment. The Court found the seizure to be "unreasonable," observing "It is a cardinal rule that, in seizing goods and articles, law enforcement agents must secure and use search warrants wherever reasonably practicable." Id. at 705. But in other cases the Court sustained as "incident to arrest" searches that were little less aggravated than that condemned in *Trupiano*. See Harris v. United States, 331 U.S. 145 (1947); United States v. Rabinowitz, 339 U.S. 56 (1950).

98. Chimel v. California, 395 U.S. 752, 762 (1969); Terry v. Ohio, 392 U.S. 1, 20 (1968); Schmerber v. California, 384 U.S. 757, 770 (1966).

policeman or government enforcement agent." [99]

In fact, however, this protection may be illusory, because the magistrates may not actively review the evidence or may lack the ability effectively to evaluate its sufficiency. The proceeding is *ex parte*; there is no adversary interchange to stimulate the decision making process. Magistrates may have no legal training and thus lack the ability to deal realistically with the difficult task of judging evidentiary sufficiency. If, as is sometimes the case, the magistrate is himself a former law enforcement officer, he may be less impartial than the theory supposes. Nevertheless, the field research of the American Bar Foundation suggests that in regard to applications for search warrants magistrates do perform a relatively active function.[1] Thus the warrant procedure may be more effective than its detractors have suggested.

Exceptions to the Warrant Requirement. Despite the general requirement of a warrant, warrantless searches or seizures have been upheld in several categories of situations. Searches incident to detentions of the person are discussed separately;[2] the other exceptions may be categorized as follows:

Border searches.[3] Since 1789 customs officials have been authorized by statute to stop and examine vehicles, persons, or baggage entering the United States.[4] The official need only "suspect" that the search will reveal items subject to duty or which are being brought into the country illegally, says the statute, unless the subject of the proposed search is a trunk or envelope, in which case "reasonable cause to suspect" is required. The Supreme Court has never directly ruled on the validity of this exception to both the substantive and procedural requirements of the Fourth Amendment,[5] although it has acknowledged its validity in dictum.[6] The justification urged for the border search exception to general warrant requirements is the strong national interest in enforcement of regulations regarding entry and duties, together with the impracticability of imposing either a substantive requirement of probable cause or a procedural warrant requirement. Whether these factors justify making the Fourth Amendment almost completely inapplicable, however, is subject to question.[7]

---

99. Johnson v. United States, 333 U.S. 10, 13–14 (1948) (Mr. Justice Jackson).

1. "With rare exceptions, magistrates do read and carefully consider the evidence presented by law enforcement officers requesting a search warrant, and they frequently require the prosecuting attorney to endorse the affidavit and recommend the issuance of the search warrant . . . . [I]n the search warrant case the magistrate often . . . reviews the evidence himself rather than relying totally on the police and prosecutor . . . ." Tiffany, McIntyre and Rotenberg, Detection of Crime 119 (1967).

This view is reinforced by the upgrading of magistrates in the federal system by the Federal Magistrates Act of 1968 (28 U.S.C.A. §§ 631–639).

2. See § 173, infra.

3. See generally, Note, At the Border of Reasonableness: Searches by Customs Officials, 53 Cornell L.Rev. 871 (1968); Comment, Intrusive Border Searches—Is Judicial Control Desirable?, 115 U.Pa. L.Rev. 276 (1966); Note, Border Searches and the Fourth Amendment, 77 Yale L.J. 1007 (1968).

4. 19 U.S.C.A. § 482. Insofar as mere suspicion is sufficient for a search, the border search is an exception to the substantive requirement that a reasonable basis exist for the belief that the search is justified as well as the procedural requirement that a judicial officer determine whether the basis is in fact reasonable.

5. For a listing of cases in which discretionary review was denied, see Note, At the Border of Reasonableness: Searches by Customs Officials, 53 Cornell L.Rev. 871, 872 n. 12 (1968). The Court has accepted a case, however, in which it is likely to deal with the matter directly. United States v. Johnson, 425 F.2d 630 (9th Cir. 1970) cert. granted, 400 U.S. 990, restored for reargument, 403 U.S. 956 (1971).

6. Carroll v. United States, 267 U.S. 132, 153–154 (1925).

7. The case law reveals several limiting rules. If, for example, entry is complete the search is not within the exception. See Marsh v. United States, 344 F.2d 317 (5th Cir. 1965) (search sixty-three miles from border might be a "hybrid" search, partially a border search and partially a normal search). If the search is one that involves an extraordinary invasion of privacy, such as a body

Searches of moving or movable vehicles. In two early decisions,[8] the Court upheld searches of automobiles which were, when observed, traveling on the highway and as to which there was probable cause to believe that they contained contraband subject to seizure. The rationale for the exception was twofold: Since the subject of the search was not a dwelling but rather a means of transportation, the demands of the Fourth Amendment were somewhat less stringent.[9] And because of the mobility of the vehicle, it would be able to leave the jurisdiction before an officer could return with a warrant; hence requiring a warrant would be impracticable.[10]

This exception was apparently expanded in Chambers v. Maroney.[11] Chambers and three companions were arrested while in an automobile; probable cause existed to believe that they had been involved in the robbery of a service station and that the weapon used in the crime and the fruits of the robbery were in the vehicle. The car was taken to the police station and searched; no search warrant was obtained. A gun and the fruits of the robbery were found. Arguing that the warrantless search was unreasonable, Chambers contended that the vehicle had become immobile by virtue of the arrest of the occupants and the action of the officers in driving it to the station and the exception for moving vehicles therefore did not apply. This argument was rejected. The Court reasoned that the remaining mobility of the vehicle even after the occupants' arrest demanded that the officers have either the power to immobilize it completely until a search warrant could be obtained or the right to search without a warrant. Which course of action would infringe less upon the Fourth Amendment interests of the subjects would depend upon the particular circumstances involved. For constitutional purposes, the Court concluded, either course of action was permissible.

The impact of *Chambers* upon the *Carroll* exception was considered in Coolidge v. New Hamshire.[11.5] Officers investigating a homicide proceeded to Coolidge's home to arrest him and to search his automobile pursuant to what was later held an invalid search warrant. After arresting Coolidge, the officers required his wife to leave the premises and towed the car to the police station about two and one-half hours after the arrest. It was searched two days later, again eleven months later, and finally a third time fourteen months after the arrest. Vacuum sweepings obtained during these searches were received at Coolidge's trial. Rejecting the state's attempt to justify the search as a valid warrantless search under *Chambers,* Mr. Justice Stewart, speaking for four members of the Court, limited the exception to those situations in which specific exigent circumstances make obtaining a warrant for the search of a vehicle impracticable.[11.10] *Chambers* was distinguished as involving only the issue of whether a warrantless search which might legitimately be made under *Carroll* on the open highway might be postponed and later made at the police station.[11.15] Under this reading, *Chambers* did not address itself to

---

cavity search, the evidentiary standard may be higher. See Rivas v. United States, 368 F.2d 703 (9th Cir. 1966) (body cavity search for narcotics requires "a clear indication" or "a plain suggestion" of possession of narcotics, which is a higher standard than the generally applicable requirement of "mere suspicion"); 18 DePaul L.Rev. 800 (1969).

8. Carroll v. United States, 267 U.S. 132 (1925); Brinegar v. United States, 338 U.S. 160 (1949).

9. Carroll v. United States, 267 U.S. 132, 153 (1925). Probable cause to believe the vehicle contains items subject to seizure must nevertheless exist. Ortiz v. United States, 317 F.2d 277 (5th Cir. 1963) (observation of car backing without lights from an unlighted filling station did not constitute adequate basis for warrantless search of car).

10. Carroll v. United States, 267 U.S. 132 (1925).

11. 399 U.S. 42 (1970), reh. denied 400 U.S. 856. See generally, Annot., 26 L.Ed.2d 893 (warrantless searches of automobile).

11.5 403 U.S. 443 (1971).

11.10 Id. at 458–464.

11.15 Id. at 463.

the underlying question of whether a warrantless search may be made at all. Rejecting the assertion that the mobility of a motor vehicle justified a broader exception to the warrant requirement, Mr. Justice Stewart found no distinction between automobiles and the large number of other physical objects capable of rapid removal.[11.20] Thus, given the fact that neither Coolidge nor his wife had access to the vehicle, (and apparently the lack of proof that anyone else had a motive to interfere with the vehicle), Mr. Justice Stewart held *Carroll* inapplicable. Mr. Justice Harlan, fifth of the five-man majority, declined to join in that portion of Mr. Justice Stewart's opinion specifically limiting *Chambers* but joined in the result and in that portion of Mr. Justice Stewart's opinion defending the general proposition that no warrantless search is reasonable in the absence of a showing of exigent circumstances.[11.25] Mr. Justice Black, joined by Mr. Justice Blackmun, dissented, arguing that *Chambers* explicitly rejected the reasoning used by Mr. Justice Stewart to distinguish it and held that the immediate search as well as the delayed one were "reasonable" in Fourth Amendment terms.[11.30] Mr. Justice White, joined by the Chief Justice, although carefully labeling his discussion of *Chambers* as dictum, apparently agreed with Mr. Justice Stewart's interpretation of *Chambers*.[11.35] He also read *Chambers,* however, as requiring "some expedition" in completing the search and releasing the vehicle unless there was some independent basis for justifying retention.[11.40] Thus *Chambers,* even as read by Mr. Justice Stew-

art, could not support the two later searches of the vehicle.

The scope of this exception remains unclear. A broad reading of *Chambers*—that "movable" vehicles, since they may be detained until a warrant is obtained may also be searched without a warrant—seems indefensible. Clearly the interests underlying the Fourth Amendment would be best served by extending to one whose interest in privacy is at stake the right to choose between an immediate warrantless search and requiring the police to submit the justification offered for the search to a magistrate. On the other hand, the suggestion in Mr. Justice Stewart's opinion in *Coolidge* that "no constitutional significance" should be attached to the special mobility of an automobile seems little more reasonable. Unlike other removable items, a vehicle often has an inherent and highly effective means of removal. The best solution would be to abolish the so-called moving or movable vehicle exception and treat such cases as merely one aspect of the "exigent circumstances" exception.[11.45] The mobility of the vehicle under the circumstances and the likelihood that someone will in fact take advantage of this likelihood thus become facts tending to establish the existence of exigent circumstances justifying a warrantless search.

Searches of items in official custody. An exception of uncertain scope was established by Cooper v. California.[12] Cooper's car had been seized and forfeiture proceedings under state law begun on the ground that the vehicle had been used to transport narcotics. One week after the car had been taken into police custody, a warrantless search of it was made. Upholding the search, the Supreme Court emphasized that the police had the

---

11.20   Id. at 461 n. 18.

11.25   Id. at 491 (Mr. Justice Harlan, concurring).

11.30   Id. at 504 (Mr. Justice Black, concurring and dissenting).

11.35   Id. at 524 (Mr. Justice White, concurring and dissenting).

11.40   Id. at 523 (Mr. Justice White, concurring and dissenting).

11.45   See text at note 27, infra.

12.   386 U.S. 58 (1967), noted in The Supreme Court, 1966 Term, 81 Harv.L.Rev. 69, 119–121 (1967); 52 Minn.L.Rev. 533 (1967).

duty to retain the car until the forfeiture proceeding was completed and that the search had been "closely related to the reason [Cooper] was arrested, the reason his car had been impounded, and the reason it was being retained." [13]   In Dyke v. Taylor Implement Manufacturing Co.,[14] the Court found *Cooper* inapplicable to a situation in which a search was conducted of an arrested person's car which had been brought to the police station following his arrest apparently merely as a convenience to him.   Distinguishing *Cooper,* the Court emphasized that in *Dyke* there was no evidence that the police had impounded or held the car or that they were authorized to do so, nor did it appear that the search was intended to implement the purpose for which the defendant had been taken into custody.[15] Lower court interpretations of *Cooper* have varied widely.[16]   It seems clear that the Court meant to go beyond authorizing a mere "inventory search" administratively necessary in regard to items as to which official agencies take even temporary custody.[17]   The most reasonable interpretation of the *Cooper* exception would limit it to situations in which the item is in official custody pursuant to formal seizure of a type which confers upon the custodian a right of more than a temporary nature to retain possession against other claimants.[18]   In addition, the purpose and scope of the search must be related to the justification for the seizure and retention.[19]   If so limited, the exception is justifiable on the ground that the additional invasion of privacy caused by the search is too small to justify imposing the search warrant requirement.   If the exception is limited to items in this type of custody, the rights of persons related to the item have already been so significantly infringed that to extend the right to search as suggested would not constitute a significant incremental invasion of their privacy. Searches of items in other types of official custody, or searches unrelated to the justification for the custody, constitute a much more significant added invasion of privacy

13.   Cooper v. California, 386 U.S. 58 (1967).

14.   391 U.S. 216 (1968).

15.   Id. at 220–221.

16.   Some courts have read *Cooper* as broadening the right to search subsequent to arrest.   Moreno-Vallejo v. United States, 414 F.2d 901 (5th Cir. 1969) (*Cooper* used to uphold a search of a car in which defendant was arrested, when car was moved twenty two miles to enable officers to search under better lighting conditions).   Others have read it as directing that searches—especially those subsequent to arrest—be tested under a broad and general "reasonableness" test.   E. g., Williams v. United States, 412 F.2d 729, 733 (5th Cir. 1969).   In light of Chimel v. United States, 395 U.S. 752 (1969) (see § 173, infra) and Dyke v. Taylor Implement Mfg. Co., 391 U.S. 216 (1968) (see text at note 14, supra) both readings seem inaccurate.   In regard to automobiles, the recent expansion of the exception for vehicles (see text at note 11, supra) moots the issue in regard to many vehicle situations.   The problem remains important, however, in regard to other property which comes into police possession.   E. g., State v. Elkins, 245 Ore. 279, 422 P.2d 250 (1966) (chemical analysis of capsules and pills found in pocket of person arrested for drunkenness discussed § 169 text n. 65, supra).

17.   E. g., United States v. Graham, 391 F.2d 439 (6th Cir. 1968) (an article taken from an arrested person for safekeeping while he is in custody may be examined for a serial number to identify it without a search warrant).   See generally, Stroud, The Inventory Search and the Fourth Amendment, 4 Ind.L.Forum 471 (1971).

18.   Thus one court has held that an arrested person's clothing, placed in a "property bag," was not subject to warrantless search three days after his arrest.   The custody was not sufficient to bring *Cooper* into play.   Brett v. United States, 412 F.2d 401, 406 (5th Cir. 1969).   The right to seize and retain a stolen vehicle for—or as agent of—the owner has been held to bring the *Cooper* exception into play.   E. g., United States v. Kucinich, 404 F.2d 262, 266 (6th Cir. 1968); Schoepflin v. United States, 391 F.2d 390 (9th Cir. 1968).

19.   Emphasis should be placed on the justification for the seizure and retention rather than upon the basis for any arrest that may have occurred at the time of the seizure.   Insofar as the arrest confers a right to conduct a warrantless search, it should be analyzed under the exception for searches incident to arrest and not confused with the *Cooper* exception.   Some courts seem to have confused the exceptions.   E. g., Wright v. United States, 131 U.S.App.D.C. 279, 404 F.2d 1256, 1285 n. 5 (1968); Morris v. Boles, 386 F.2d 395 (4th Cir. 1967).

and pose a greater danger of abuse. In those situations, the search warrant requirement should be applied.

Search pursuant to "hot pursuit" of a dangerous suspect. In Warden v. Hayden,[20] officers were informed by witnesses that an armed robber had entered a particular house. The officers entered the house and searched for the robber, ultimately finding him. Holding that the entry and search without a search warrant were permissible, the Court emphasized the "reasonableness" of a search for the robber and the weapons he had used (and might use against pursuing officers). "The Fourth Amendment does not require police officers to delay in the course of an investigation if to do so would gravely endanger their lives or the lives of others. Speed here was essential, and only a thorough search of the house for persons and weapons could have insured that Hayden was the only man present and that the police had control of all weapons which could be used against them or to effect an escape." [21] The Court carefully indicated that it was not justifying the search as incident to the arrest of Hayden and that the right to search in "hot pursuit" included the right to search beyond the area that could be searched incident to arrest.

Searches for persons as to whom there are grounds for arrest. Despite showing of opportunity to obtain a warrant, numerous courts have upheld the right of police officers to enter premises without a warrant (either a search warrant or a warrant for arrest) to effect a valid arrest if they have reasonable grounds to believe that the person sought is on the premises.[22] This blanket exception to the warrant requirement is diffi-

cult to justify. Although in some circumstances immediate entry is undoubtedly necessary to prevent the subject from fleeing, in others it seems equally clear that little would be sacrificed by requiring a warrant. Courts have somewhat ameliorated the potential impact of this exception by demanding compliance with statutory requirements that before breaking and entering to effect an arrest the officers announce their purpose and authority and demand voluntary admittance.[23] There

20. 387 U.S. 294 (1967).

21. Id. at 299.

22. E. g., United States v. Latimer, 415 F.2d 1288 (6th Cir. 1969); People v. Sprovieri, 43 Ill.2d 223, 252 N.E.2d 531 (1969).

23. Sabbath v. United States, 391 U.S. 585 (1968); Miller v. United States, 357 U.S. 301 (1958) (federal statute requiring prior announcement before breaking to execute warrant also applied to entry to effect arrest without a warrant); People v. Benjamin, 71 Cal.2d 296, 78 Cal.Rptr. 510, 455 P.2d 438 (1969). "Substantial compliance" with the requirement is sufficient. People v. Cockrell, 63 Cal. 2d 659, 408 P.2d 116, 47 Cal.Rptr. 788 (1965) (statute was substantially complied with when officers identified themselves but did not announce their purpose, because in view of marijuana sale a few minutes earlier the purpose was reasonably apparent.) If the requirement has not been complied with, however, evidence seized in a search pursuant to the arrest is inadmissible on the theory that the arrest is invalid and therefore cannot be used to justify a search. Sabbath v. United States, 391 U.S. 585 (1968); Miller v. United States, 357 U.S. 301 (1958); People v. Benjamin, 71 Cal.2d 296, 78 Cal.Rptr. 510, 455 P.2d 438 (1969) (police officer who "yelled 'Police Officer'" and forced entry did not comply substantially with statute). Failure to comply with the requirements is excused if announcement would endanger the arresting officers or third persons, the success of the arrest attempt, or evidence within the control of the subject. Gilbert v. United States, 366 F.2d 923 (9th Cir. 1966) cert. denied 388 U.S. 922 (announcement not required because of possible presence of armed murderer in apartment and danger that announcement would have alerted him, thereby increasing officers' peril); People v. Wojciechowski, 31 App.Div.2d 658, 296 N.Y.S.2d 524 (1968) (officer's belief that complainant was in apartment with suspect and that suspect had threatened complainant's life justified entry without announcement of purpose); People v. Maddox, 46 Cal.2d 301, 294 P.2d 6 (1956) cert. denied 352 U.S. 858 (good faith conclusion that compliance would allow subject to escape justifies noncompliance); People v. Newell, 272 Cal. App.2d 638, 77 Cal.Rptr. 771 (1969) (reasonable and good faith belief that subjects had specifically resolved to dispose of narcotics in the event of police intrusion justified unannounced entry).

Recent legislation applicable to the District of Columbia has codified the general requirement and the standard exceptions. District of Columbia Court Reform and Criminal Procedure Act of 1970,

is some suggestion that this requirement is of constitutional dimensions.[24] In addition, the Supreme Court has indicated that in aggravated circumstances warrantless searches incident to an attempt to arrest raise a "grave constitutional question." [25] This caution, in light of the Court's recent emphasis upon the warrant requirement, suggests that when the

exigencies of the situation do not make it unreasonable a warrant is required for searches for one sought to be arrested.[26]

"Emergency" situations or exigent circumstances. This exception covers situations in which warrantless activity is essential to the preservation of the items subject to seizure or to prevent immediately threatening harm to persons or property. In Schmerber v. California,[27] the Court upheld the right of an officer to conduct a blood test upon probable cause to believe that the subject was driving while intoxicated. In response to the argument that the officer was required first to obtain a search warrant, the Court noted that speed in performing the test was essential as the alcohol would be rapidly eliminated from the blood stream by normal body functions. Since the officer was confronted with a situation in which he might reasonably have believed that the delay necessary to obtain a warrant would have threatened the destruction of the evidence sought, he properly acted without a warrant. This exception extends to any situation in which there is a reasonable apprehension that obtaining a search warrant would endanger the success of the search.[28] It also provides a basis for

subchapter VI, § 23—591, 84 Stat. 473. Under this legislation, however, forcible entry without prior announcement can be made without a specific authorization on the warrant only if the circumstances justifying such entry were unknown to the officer at the time of application for the warrant. If they are known to him at that time, they must be submitted to the magistrate and he must authorize such entry.

See generally Sonnenreich and Ebner, No-Knock and Nonsense, An Alleged Constitutional Problem, 44 St. John's L.Rev. 626 (1970); Comment, Unannounced Entry to Search: The Law and the "No-Knock" Bill (S. 3246), 1970 Wash.U.L.Q. 205 (1970). See also Note, No-Knock and the Constitution: The District of Columbia Court Reform and Criminal Procedure Act of 1970 [A Critique and Proposed Alternatives], 55 Minn.L.Rev. 871 (1971).

24. In Ker v. California, 374 U.S. 23 (1963) officers entered without prior announcement, but the Court found that the officers' belief that appellant possessed narcotics which could be easily destroyed and that he was expecting police officers justified, under state law, the failure to comply with the state statutory requirement of prior announcement. Under these circumstances, the Court concluded, the method of entry was not "unreasonable" under Fourth and Fourteenth Amendment standards. This suggestion that the requirement of prior announcement is of constitutional dimensions is further supported by the Court's dictum in Sabbath v. United States, 391 U.S. 585, 591 n. 8 (1968). See generally Blakey, The Rule of Announcement and Unlawful Entry: Miller v. United States and Ker v. California, 112 U.Pa.L.Rev. 499 (1964).

25. In Jones v. United States, 357 U.S. 493, 499–500 (1958) the government argued that a 9:00 p. m. entry and search of Jones' home was justified on the ground that the officers had probable cause to believe that Jones was in the house committing felonies in relation to the production of illicit alcohol. Before holding that the issue was not raised (because the proof showed that the entry had been for purposes of search rather than arrest), the Court commented that "these contentions . . . would confront us with a grave constitutional question, namely, whether the forceful night-time entry into a dwelling to arrest a person reasonably believed therein, upon probable cause that he has committed a felony, under circumstances where no reason appears why an arrest warrant could not have been sought, is consistent with the Fourth Amendment."

26. Whether an arrest warrant alone would be sufficient is doubtful. Issuance of such a warrant provides no more than a magistrate's determination of probable cause for arrest. It does not provide a determination of justification for invasion of particular premises, that is, probable cause to believe the subject is in the premises sought to be searched. It has been suggested, however, that a magistrate might add to a normal arrest warrant an authorization to search specific places for the subject. See Dorman v. United States, 140 U.S. App.D.C. 313, 435 F.2d 385, 396 (1970) (en banc). And insofar as the amount and quality of evidence connecting the subject to the offense are relevant to the existence of sufficient exigent circumstances to excuse the failure to obtain a search warrant, the existence of an arrest warrant may tend towards justifying a warrantless search. See Dorman v. United States, supra, at 395–396.

27. 384 U.S. 757 (1966).

28. Kimbrough v. Beto, 412 F.2d 981 (5th Cir. 1969) (officers arriving at scene of automobile accident had right to "check" contents of pickup truck with

police emergency action when there is evidence of the need for immediate preventive action, the "cry for help" cases. For example, in State v. Hunt [29] a domestic employee reported to law enforcement officers that she had found her employers' five year old daughter tied to a furnace room with her head under a hot water heater and with her face bloody. Holding that the responding officer was justified in insisting that he accompany the mother to the furnace room, the court declared that the officer "had not only the lawful *right,* but the lawful duty to enter the premises, investigate, and take the child into custody if necessary, with or without the search warrant . . . ." [30]

Seizures: The "Plain View" Doctrine. The Fourth Amendment by its express terms protects against unreasonable searches *and seizures.* Under current interpretation the applicability of the warrant requirement to seizures differs significantly from its applicability to searches. Traditionally, seizures of the person have not been required to comply with the warrant requirement; this is discussed elsewhere.[30.5] For present purposes the issue is whether the general Fourth Amendment requirement that, except where exigent circumstances dictate otherwise, a warrant be obtained applies to the seizure of physical objects. The question may arise in a number of contexts. An officer making a valid search incident to arrest (or other appropriate warrantless search) may observe an item which he has probable cause to believe is subject to seizure because it is contraband, fruit of a crime, or has evidentiary value. May he seize it, or must he first obtain a warrant? An officer serving a search warrant authorizing a search of specified premises and the seizure of certain items comes upon other items that he has probable cause to believe are subject to seizure. May he seize them? An officer during routine patrol (i. e., conducting no specific search) comes across such items. May he seize them without a warrant?

In Marron v. United States [31] the petitioner's premises had been searched pursuant to a warrant authorizing seizure of intoxicating liquors and articles for their manufacture. While searching the premises, the officers came across a ledger showing inventories and expenses as well as bills for services relating to the premises. These were also seized. Holding that the seizure could not be justified under the search warrant, the Supreme Court declared that "the requirement that warrants shall particularly describe the things to be seized makes general searches under them impossible and prevents the seizure of one thing under a warrant describing another." [32] The items were held admissible, however, as having been seized in a valid search incident to the arrest of one found on the premises. The lower courts have seldom read *Marron* as holding that, during a search authorized by a warrant, items as to which there is probable cause to believe are subject to seizure but which are not described in the warrant are not subject to seizure. Some have simply stated that probable cause is sufficient, whatever the nature of the undescribed items.[33] Others have suggested somewhat more limited authority: undescribed items may be seized if they bear a reasonable rela-

---

unconscious occupant to determine occupant's identity and to safeguard his possessions); Boyden v. United States, 363 F.2d 551 (6th Cir. 1966) cert. denied 385 U.S. 978 (search without warrant of car damaged in accident was proper because leaking gasoline and hot engine created a danger of fire and of destruction of the contents of the car). See Note, Police Practices and the Threatened Destruction of Tangible Evidence, 84 Harv.L.Rev. 1465 (1971).

29. 2 Ariz.App. 6, 406 P.2d 208 (1965).

30. Id. at 12, 406 P.2d at 214.

30.5 See § 173, infra.

31. 275 U.S. 192 (1927).

32. Id. at 196.

33. E. g., State v. Yates, 202 Kan. 406, 449 P.2d 575 (1969) (stolen goods other than those listed in warrant could be seized).

tionship to the purpose of the search.[34] Following abandonment of the "mere evidence" rule in Warden v. Hayden,[35] some courts have read *Marron* as holding that the items there involved were not subject to seizure because they were only of evidentiary value.[36] Under such a reading, *Marron* is clearly of no current importance.

The entire matter received extensive consideration in Coolidge v. New Hampshire.[36.5]

Officers with invalid arrest and search warrants arrived at Coolidge's house to arrest him and search his automobile. The automobile was standing in the driveway when the officers arrived. Coolidge was arrested in his house, and the car was towed to the police station where it was searched two days later, eleven months later, and finally fourteen months later. Vacuum sweepings from all three searches of the car were introduced at Coolidge's trial. In defending the use of the sweepings, the state argued that the warrantless seizure of the vehicle was proper because there was probable cause to believe that it was an instrumentality of the crime and was in "plain view." In evaluating this argument, eight of nine members of the Supreme Court apparently accepted the basic proposition that if no unreasonable search was involved the warrant requirement did not demand that no seizure occur until the justification offered for its seizure was submitted to a magistrate and the magistrate determined the existence of probable cause to believe that the car was an instrument of the crime. If an object is in "plain view," it may be seized without a warrant, providing there is probable cause to believe it is subject to seizure. Mr. Justice Stewart, speaking for four members of the court, articulated two limitations upon the doctrine.[36.10] First, where the seizure would require some invasion of privacy in addition to merely exerting domination over the thing to be seized, absent exigent circumstances a warrant must be obtained. Thus, if an illicit still is on premises in "plain view," *entry* for purposes of seizure must be pursuant to a warrant unless exigent circumstances justify a warrantless entry.[36.15] Second, the discovery of the items

---

34. E. g., Mesmer v. United States, 405 F.2d 316 (10th Cir. 1969) (seizure of containers in which stolen stamps were found and other items which had disappeared along with the stamps at the time of the robbery was proper in search pursuant to warrant authorizing only seizure of stamps, because the additional items "bore a reasonable relationship to the purpose of the search"; United States v. Baldwin, 46 F.R.D. 63 (S.D.N.Y.1969) (*Marron* rule has exceptions for items "closely related" to those described, items the possession of which is a crime, and items which show that a different offense is being committed in the presence of the searching officers). United States v. Nolan, 416 F.2d 588 (10th Cir. 1969) suggests that instrumentalities and means of committing the offense to which the search relates may be seized even if not named in the warrant. In State v. Jones, 202 Kan. 31, 446 P.2d 851 (1968) the court apparently applied a "physical proximity" test, holding that the seizure of a handkerchief in a search pursuant to a warrant authorizing seizure of a pistol was proper because the handkerchief was "lying in close proximity" to the pistol.

35. 387 U.S. 294 (1967). See § 127 at n. 81, § 170 at n. 86, supra.

36. Compare United States ex rel. Nickens v. LaVallee, 391 F.2d 123 (2d Cir. 1968) (*Marron* still valid after *Hayden* and therefore seizure of newspaper clippings was improper when made during search pursuant to warrant authorizing search for and seizure of paraphernalia used by locksmith) and People v. Baker, 23 N.Y.2d 307, 296 N.Y.S.2d 745, 244 N.E.2d 232 (1968) (despite *Hayden*, seizure of sweater corresponding to that worn by assailant was improper under *Marron* as search was conducted pursuant to warrant authorizing only seizure of a knife) with Morales v. State, 44 Wis.2d 96, 170 N.W.2d 684 (1969) (*Marron* was overruled by *Hayden*, and therefore seizure of telephone bills and other documents during search pursuant to warrant authorizing search for and seizure of narcotics paraphernalia was proper). Some post-*Hayden* cases have sustained seizures of nondescribed items simply citing *Hayden*. State v. Jones, 202 Kan. 31, 446 P.2d 851 (1968); State v. Gray, 152 Mont. 145, 447 P.2d 475 (1968).

36.5 403 U.S. 443 (1971).

36.10 Id. at 468–473.

36.15. Mr. Justice Stewart expresses this by the statement, "[P]lain view alone is never enough to justify the warrantless seizure of evidence." Id. at 468. But his discussion makes clear that plain view plus circumstances making necessary no invasion

in plain view must be inadvertent. If discovery is anticipated, seizure may be made only with a warrant, even if the item appears in plain view to an officer in a place where he has a right to be. Four members of the court indicated an unwillingness to impose a requirement of inadvertency.[36.20] Mr. Justice Harlan, the fifth member of the majority, concurred in the result of Mr. Justice Stewart's opinion and in that portion of the opinion defending in general terms the result reached on the plain view issue; he did not, however, join in that portion of the opinion expressly setting out the scope of and limitations upon the doctrine.[36.25] The law seems clear, then, that where only a seizure is involved the warrant requirement is not applicable. To what extent this is modified by a requirement that discovery of the item seized be inadvertent is unsettled.

The underlying immunization of seizures from the warrant requirement is open to challenge. Mr. Justice Stewart argued in *Coolidge* that given the initial invasion of privacy (i. e., the "search"), the incremental invasion of privacy involved in a seizure is insignificant or at least outweighed by the inconvenience and danger to law enforcement personnel and the risk of destruction of the items which would be imposed by application of the warrant requirement.[37] But perhaps this underestimates the infringement of privacy which may be involved in a seizure. For example, entry onto premises by a police officer is certainly a significant invasion of privacy. But it is not clear that his action in seizing an automobile and exerting dominion over it for a significant period of time is not of nearly equal impact upon the underlying right of privacy. Why the subject should have the protection of the warrant requirement against one but not the other is less than obvious. If, of course, the officers have a reasonable apprehension that to delay seizure would endanger either the car or themselves, application of the general "exigent circumstances" exception would permit warrantless seizure. But it is not clear that such exigent circumstances would so routinely appear as to justify dispensing generally with the warrant requirement.

Procedural Implications of the Warrant Requirement. The policy objectives of the warrant rule are reflected in several requirements for a valid warrant procedure. Underlying the basic requirement, of course, is the policy of requiring that the decision whether the evidentiary basis for the proposed invasion of privacy be made not by the individual actively involved in the investigation but rather by a detached magistrate.[38] This judicial officer, the requirement assumes, will be better able dispassionately to weigh the evidence available and more accurately determine whether the evidentiary standard has been met. Thus it is essential to the warrant procedure that the judicial officer be presented with sufficiently detailed information that he make this de novo determination for himself rather than merely rubber-stamp the applicant's decision. In Aguilar v. Texas [39] the Court held that the Fourth Amend-

---

of privacy other than the seizure itself would, in his view, support a warrantless seizure.

36.20 Coolidge v. New Hampshire, 403 U.S. 443, 505–510 (1971) (Mr. Justice Black, joined by Mr. Justice Blackmun, concurring and dissenting); id. at 513–521 (Mr. Justice White, joined by Chief Justice Burger, concurring and dissenting).

36.25 Id. at 491 (Mr. Justice Harlan, concurring).

37. Id. at 467: "As against the minor peril to Fourth Amendment protections, there is a major gain in effective law enforcement." See also id. at 515–516 (Mr. Justice White, concurring and dissenting).

38. Thus a search warrant issued by a Justice of the Peace who was also the Attorney General of the state, actively in charge of the investigation, and was later to be chief prosecutor at the trial was not issued by the neutral and detached magistrate required by the Fourth Amendment. Coolidge v. New Hampshire, 403 U.S. 443 (1971). See also State ex rel. White v. Simpson, 28 Wis.2d 590, 137 N.W.2d 391 (1965).

39. 378 U.S. 108 (1964).

ment requires that the magistrate be given sufficient information to enable him to judge for himself the persuasiveness of the facts relied upon to establish probable cause. An affidavit that the applicant believes the facts upon the basis of reliable information, of course, does not meet this standard.[40]

The search warrant, when issued, must describe with particularity both the place to be searched and the things to be seized.[41] In the absence of such particularity, the warrant becomes merely a judicial authorization for the type of general search against which the Fourth Amendment was directed. Thus in Stanford v. Texas,[42] the Court considered insufficiently precise a warrant that described the items to be seized as "books, records, pamphlets, cards, receipts, lists, memoranda, pictures, recordings and other written instruments concerning the Communist Party of Texas, and the operations of the Communist Party in Texas." Although the Court suggested that somewhat less particularity might be sufficient if the subject of the proposed seizure was not material potentially subject to First Amendment protection, it is nevertheless clear that the preciseness required is such as to minimize the discretion of the officer executing the warrant.[43] When, however, the nature of the circumstances makes exact description of individual items impossible, a description of a generic class of items is sufficient. Thus a warrant authorizing the seizure of "gambling paraphernalia, including but not limited to dice, crap tables, wires, magnets . . ." has been held sufficient.[44]

172. Evidence Obtained Pursuant to Unreasonable Searches and Seizures: (d) Attack Upon Allegations Offered in Support of an Application for a Search Warrant.[45]

When an application for a search warrant is made to a judicial officer, he must be presented with evidence from which he can judge for himself the persuasiveness of the facts relied upon to justify the issuance of the warrant. Only if he himself finds that the facts alleged possess sufficient persuasiveness to meet the applicable evidentiary standard is he to issue the warrant.[46] At a subsequent hearing on the validity of action taken pursuant to the warrant, the search or seizure conducted pursuant to it can be challenged on the grounds that the allegations were insufficient on their face to support a finding that the evidentiary standard was met,[47] that the action taken was beyond the scope of the warrant,[48] or that the warrant was improperly executed.[49]

A less settled matter is presented by the assertion, that although the allegations made in the application justify on their face a finding that the evidentiary standard was met, in fact the allegations were inaccurate and the

---

40. Id. See generally, the discussion of Spinelli v. United States, 393 U.S. 410 (1969) at § 170, n. 79, supra.

41. See generally, Mascolo, Specificity Requirements for Warrants under the Fourth Amendment: Defining the Zone of Privacy, 73 Dick.L.Rev. 1 (1968).

42. 379 U.S. 476 (1965).

43. Id. at 486.

44. James v. United States, 416 F.2d 467 (5th Cir. 1969).

45. See generally, Kipperman, Inaccurate Search Warrant Affidavits as a Ground for Suppressing Evidence, 84 Harv.L.Rev. 825 (1971); Note, Testing the Factual Basis for a Search Warrant, 67 Colum.L.Rev. 1529 (1967); 41 Notre Dame Law. 822 (1966); Annot., 5 A.L.R.2d 394.

46. See § 170, supra.

47. E. g., Spinelli v. United States, 393 U.S. 410 (1969).

48. E. g., Haley v. State, 7 Md.App. 18, 253 A.2d 424 (1969) (search of automobile parked in driveway was beyond the scope authorized by a warrant authorizing the search of premises and persons found therein); State v. Fox, 283 Minn. 176, 168 N.W.2d 260 (1969) (search of defendant who was on described premises was not within scope of search permitted by warrant authorizing search of premises.)

49. E. g., Tyler v. State, 45 Ala.App. 155, 227 So.2d 442 (1969) (state failed to meet its burden of proving that warrant expressly limited to execution during the daytime was in fact executed during the daytime).

real facts would not have supported issuance of the warrant. The Supreme Court has admitted that it has never passed upon the extent to which a warrant is subject to such attack,[50] and lower court decisions are in conflict.[51] The issue can be broken down into several subquestions: Under what, if any, circumstances may a warrant be so attacked? Need a defendant make any preliminary showing to put the accuracy of allegations in issue? Once the accuracy of the assertions is at issue, who bears the burden of proof?

The answer to the first subquestion requires a careful definition of the concept of probable cause and other Fourth Amendment evidentiary standards. It seems generally agreed that these standards are not ultimate evaluations but merely minimal evidentiary requirements.[52] The applicant for a warrant does not assert the truth of his ultimate allegation but only that he has sufficient basis for believing it is true. If, despite the existence of sufficient evidence to believe the ultimate allegation true, it nevertheless is later proven false, this does not mean that the evidentiary standard was not met at the time of the application. Thus a subsequent attack on a warrant cannot properly be addressed to the ultimate issue, i.e., whether the defendant did commit a crime. Rather, it must be addressed to whether, at the time of the issuance of the warrant, there was sufficient evidence before the magistrate to support a conclusion on the ultimate issue, i.e., whether there was probable cause to believe a crime was committed and that the defendant committed it. If the affiant either intentionally or inadvertently misrepresented the factual basis for believing the evidentiary standard was met, the defendant should be permitted to prove the actual basis upon which the affiant relied and have the validity of the warrant tested on that basis. A defendant is entitled to a judicial evaluation of the evidence actually relied upon. For example, in United States v. Roth[53] the defendant was permitted to challenge the issuance of a search warrant by showing that although in his affidavit the officer had alleged that an informant had told him that electric blenders of a given brand were on the described premises, in fact the informer had merely said that products of that brand were on the premises. The latter, the court concluded, would have been insufficient on which to issue a warrant. If, however, the alleged inaccuracy is not in the affiant's statement of the information he had but in the information itself, the inaccuracy is significant only insofar as it tends to show that a reasonable man should not have credited the informa-

---

50. Rugendorf v. United States, 376 U.S. 528, 531–532 (1964).

51. The recent cases tend to permit the challenge. E. g., United States ex rel. Pugh v. Pate, 401 F.2d 6 (7th Cir. 1968) cert. denied 394 U.S. 999 (defendant permitted to show that affiant had signed false name); United States v. Roth, 391 F.2d 507 (7th Cir. 1967); United States v. Gillette, 383 F.2d 843 (2d Cir. 1967) (dictum not foreclosing the attack); United States v. Freeman, 358 F.2d 459, 463 n. 4 (2d Cir. 1966) cert. denied 385 U.S. 882 (dictum suggesting that defendant "may be able" to challenge the veracity of allegations); King v. United States, 282 F.2d 398 (4th Cir. 1960) (defendant permitted to show that affiant had misrepresented identity); People v. Alfinito, 16 N.Y.2d 181, 264 N.Y.S.2d 243, 211 N.E.2d 644 (1965). Contra, Kenney v. United States, 81 U.S.App.D.C. 259, 157 F.2d 442 (1946); United States v. Gianaris, 25 F.R.D. 194 (D.D.C.1960); United States v. Brunett, 53 F.2d 219 (W.D.Mo.1931); People v. Nelson, 171 Cal.App.2d 356, 340 P.2d 718 (1959); Baker v. State, 448 P.2d 282 (Okl.Cr.1968); Gaddis v. State, 447 P.2d 42 (Okl.Cr.1968); O'Brien v. State, 205 Tenn. 405, 326 S.W.2d 759 (1959).

52. This view supports the holding in McCray v. Illinois, 386 U.S. 300 (1967) that in a hearing on a motion to suppress, raising the validity of McCray's arrest without a warrant, the Illinois court did not err in refusing to require police officers to divulge the name of their informer. The Court's distinction between the situation at issue and the case in which the informer is sought in relation to the issue of guilt or innocence amounts to a recognition that if the arresting officers relied upon reasonably credible information from an informer reasonably considered reliable the informer's actual accuracy is of minimal importance. See § 170 at n. 78, supra.

53. 391 F.2d 507 (7th Cir. 1967).

tion. For example, in United States v. Ramos,[54] the defendant attempted to establish that the informant had relied upon hearsay in concluding that there were narcotics in the defendant's apartment. This, the court held, was irrelevant to the point at issue, i.e., whether the affiant had adequate basis for believing the informant.[55] Thus a warrant is properly subjected to such an attack only on the ground that the affiant misstated the basis for his conclusion that the evidentiary standard was met.[56]

Since it seems clear that a warrant may, to this limited extent, be attacked on the basis that the allegations made in the application were factually erroneous, it might be appropriate to take precautions against challenges to admissibility becoming routinely *de novo* evaluations of the factual accuracy of the allegations. The best method of accomplishing this end would be a requirement that the accuracy of the factual allegations not be placed in issue until the defendant offers some evidence of infirmities which, if

present, would justify a reexamination of the issuing officer's conclusion that the evidentiary basis was established.[57] Closely related to this is the burden of proof. The administrative necessity of discouraging nonmeritorious challenges to warrants strongly argues in favor of placing the burden on the attacking party to establish the inaccuracy of the challenged allegations.[58] This placement would seem to be a reasonable balance between the need to give finality to the decision made at the issuance of the warrant and the right of those whose privacy has been invaded to a judicial evaluation of the proof actually existing to justify the invasion.

173. Evidence Obtained Pursuant to Unreasonable Searches and Seizures: (e) Evidence Related to Seizures of the Person.[59]

It is clear that the Fourth Amendment protects against unreasonable seizures of the person as well as seizures of property and possessions.[60] It follows that evidence may be inadmissible under the exclusionary rule because of its relationship to an unreasonable seizure of the person. The matter is complicated, however, because one exception to the rule requiring warrants for a search has been that a limited search without a search warrant may be conducted "pursuant

54. 380 F.2d 717 (2d Cir. 1967).

55. See also United States v. Brunett, 53 F.2d 219, 225 (D.Mo.1931) ("a subsequent showing of its falsity cannot have the effect of retrospectively invalidating a warrant valid when issued"); Proposed Amendments to Federal Rules of Criminal Procedure, Rule 4 (January, 1970) (probable cause may be based in whole or in part on hearsay). Contra, United States v. Henderson, 17 F.R.D. 1 (D.D.C.1954) (affiant's honest but mistaken belief that defendant had a previous record for violation of the lottery laws required reexamination of existence of probable cause without regard to that belief).

56. Kipperman, Inaccurate Search Warrant Affidavits as a Ground for Suppressing Evidence, 84 Harv. L.Rev. 825 (1971) suggests an analysis in terms of permitting attacks that would further the exclusionary rule's purpose of preventing improper police activity. Thus he would permit attack on the ground of any intentional misstatement in the affidavit, whether it was material to probable cause or not, but on the basis of a negligent misstatement only if the misstatement was material to probable cause. No attack at all would be permitted upon the basis of "innocent representations," including statements of reasonable (but ultimately erroneous) reliance upon an untruthful source.

57. Cf. United States v. Gillette, 383 F.2d 843 (2d Cir. 1967) (no hearing on defendant's challenge to allegations in affidavit was necessary because defendant alleged nothing raising a factual issue); United States v. Halsey, 257 F.Supp. 1002, 1005 (S.D.N.Y.1966), aff'd Crim. No. 31369 (2d Cir., June 12, 1967) (alternative holding) (until defendant "has at least made some initial showing of some potential infirmities", allegations should be accepted at their face value).

58. See People v. Alfinito, 16 N.Y.2d 181, 264 N.Y.S. 2d 243, 211 N.E.2d 644 (1967) (although a defendant may attack allegations as "perjurious", the attacker bears the burden of proof and any "fair doubt" is to be resolved in favor of the accuracy of the allegations). See also 51 Cornell L.Q. 822 (1966).

59. See generally, Leagre, The Fourth Amendment and the Law of Arrest, 54 J.Crim.L., C. & P.S. 393 (1963).

60. Terry v. Ohio, 392 U.S. 1, 16 (1968).

to" an arrest or other seizure of the person. Thus evidence may be inadmissible because obtained pursuant to an unreasonable seizure of the person, but evidence otherwise inadmissible because obtained pursuant to a search without a search warrant may be rendered admissible by the fact that the search was incidental to a reasonable seizure of the person. In both situations the initial question is the "reasonableness" under Fourth Amendment standards of the seizure of the person.

For reasons not entirely clear, "reasonableness" in this area has not traditionally involved the requirement that, except where the situation in one in which obtaining a warrant is impracticable, a warrant must be obtained before the seizure is made.[61] Courts have, however, announced a preference for arrests made pursuant to an arrest warrant.[62] Consequently the prosecution bears the burden of establishing the validity of an arrest without a warrant but not one pursuant to a warrant, and a magistrate's determination that probable cause exists will be less closely scrutinized than an equivalent determination by an officer arresting without a warrant.[63] But apart from this attitudinal difference, the Fourth Amendment requirement in this context has furnished the standard for measuring both the evidentiary basis necessary for the particular type of seizure and the scope of any investigatorial activity sought to be justified as incidental to the seizure.

The two issues are clearly related. Analysis of the Supreme Court's opinions indicates that the substantive evidentiary standard

---

61. See Ford v. United States, 122 U.S.App.D.C. 259, 352 F.2d 927 (1965) (en banc) for a discussion. See also Odom v. United States, 403 F.2d 45 (5th Cir. 1968); State v. Brown, 250 La. 1125, 202 So. 2d 274 (1967). A number of recent cases have stressed that under the facts presented obtaining a warrant would have been impracticable rather than relying entirely upon a blanket exception from the warrant requirement for arrests. Churder v. United States, 387 F.2d 825, 830 (8th Cir. 1968); Garcia v. United States, 381 F.2d 778 (9th Cir. 1967) cert. denied 390 U.S. 1015; King v. Pinto, 376 F.2d 593 (3d Cir. 1967); People v. Livingston, 252 Cal.App.2d 630, 60 Cal.Rptr. 728 (1967).

The exception seems in part to represent judicial and legislative reading of the amendment as embodying the common law practice. See Landynski, Search and Seizure and the Supreme Court 45 (1966). In Ford v. United States, 122 U.S.App.D.C. 259, 352 F.2d 927 (1965) the court emphasized that the requirement of prompt presentation of an arrested person before a magistrate tends to accomplish more effectively the protections which the warrant requirement might provide. Of course, returns to a judicial officer are regularly required in the search warrant situation in addition to the pre-search evaluation of the evidentiary basis for the proposed search. See also United States v. Hall, 348 F.2d 837, 841 (2d Cir. 1965) cert. denied 382 U.S. 947: "One reason underlying the distinction may be that a person, save possibly when asleep at home during the night, always has the same potential mobility as do objects which are in a moving vehicle or, because of their small size and the proximity of someone with adequate motive, are in danger of being removed or destroyed, and are thus subject to search and seizure on probable cause without a search warrant."

On a less theoretical level, empirical research has suggested that in practice when warrants are used for arrest there is minimal judicial evaluation of the sufficiency of the evidence offered, significantly less than is the case when search warrants are issued. LaFave, Arrest: The Decision to Take Into Custody 15–16, 34 (1965); Tiffany, McIntyre, and Rotenberg, Detection of Crime 119 (1967). Part of the confusion can be traced to the fact that in practice issuance of the warrant often represents not a decision to take into custody (the defendant has already been arrested without a warrant), but rather a decision on the part of the prosecutor to press formal charges. See Miller, Prosecution: The Decision to Charge a Suspect with a Crime 25 (1969).

62. "While an arrest pursuant to a warrant is prima facie evidence of probable cause, . . . the prosecutor should be forced to come forward with evidence of probable cause in the absence of a warrant." Rogers v. United States, 330 F.2d 535, 542–43 (5th Cir. 1964) cert. denied 379 U.S. 916. In regard to the attitudinal difference, see Beck v. Ohio, 379 U.S. 89, 96 (1964) ("An arrest without a warrant bypasses the safeguards provided by an objective predetermination of probable cause, and substitutes instead the far less reliable procedure of an after-the-event justification for the arrest . . ., too likely to be subtly influenced by the familiar shortcomings of hindsight judgment."); Churder v. United States, 387 F.2d 825, 830 (8th Cir. 1968).

63. E. g., Rouse v. United States, 123 U.S.App.D.C. 348, 359 F.2d 1014, 1016 (1966).

applicable to each category of seizures of the person depends upon a balance between the need for efficient law enforcement on one hand and "the nature and quality of the intrusion on individual rights" which seizures of that category involve on the other. The scope of a search which may be justified as incidental to a seizure of the person is limited by the circumstances which rendered the search permissible in the first place, which may in turn be greatly affected by the nature and purpose of the seizure. This approach has been taken by the Supreme Court in two areas—arrest and frisk of one reasonably believed to be dangerous—and undoubtedly will be applied to other seizures of the person.

"Arrest," for purposes of the matters discussed in this section, has traditionally been defined as a seizure of the person for the purpose of subjecting him to formal prosecution for crime.[64] In regard to arrest, courts have frequently asserted that the validity of the seizure depends upon state law.[65] This position, however, is subject to qualification to the extent that minimum requirements of reasonableness are imposed by the Fourth Amendment. Thus "probable cause" is required—facts and circumstances sufficient to warrant a prudent man in believing that the person had committed or is committing an offense.[66] A reasonable search without a

warrant may be conducted as an incident to an arrest.[67] The search may be made for the purpose of removing possible weapons which the arrested person might use to resist or escape and to seize evidence which the arrested person might otherwise conceal or destroy.[68] The right to search, however, is limited by these purposes. Hence the search must be contemporaneous with the arrest. If, for example, a person is arrested in his automobile and then taken to jail, a search of his automobile after he has been "booked" cannot be justified as incidental to the arrest.[69] The scope of the search is also limited by its purpose. After a long period of vacillation,[70] the Supreme Court held in Chimel v. California [71] that the scope of a search incident to arrest was limited to the arrestee's "person and the area 'within his immediate control'—construing that phrase to mean the area from within which he might gain possession of a weapon or destructible evidence." [72]

In Terry v. Ohio,[73] the Court applied a similar analysis to the right of a police officer to conduct a "frisk" for weapons. Rejecting the argument that this was constitutionally permissible only upon probable cause, the Court held that the action was justified if a reasonable man in the position of the officer

---

64. Terry v. Ohio, 392 U.S. 1., 16 (1968); State v. Smolen, 4 Conn.Cir. 385, 232 A.2d 339 (1967) cert. denied 389 U.S. 1044 (arrest is a detention in order that the subject answer an alleged crime); State v. Murray, 106 N.H. 71, 205 A.2d 29 (1964); Smith v. State, 229 So.2d 551 (Miss.1969).

65. Montgomery v. United States, 403 F.2d 605 (8th Cir. 1968) (in absence of applicable federal statute, validity of arrest for federal crime depends upon law of state in which made); State v. Fair, 45 N.J. 77, 211 A.2d 359 (1965) (lawfulness of arrest for state crime depends upon state law).

66. Beck v. Ohio, 379 U.S. 89, 91 (1964) (constitutional validity of arrest turns upon whether, at the time the arrest was made, the officers had probable cause to believe the subject had committed or was committing an offense).

67. Chimel v. California, 395 U.S. 752 (1969); Harris v. United States, 331 U.S. 145 (1947); United States v. Rabinowitz, 339 U.S. 56 (1950).

68. Chimel v. California, 395 U.S. 752 (1969).

69. Preston v. United States, 376 U.S. 364 (1964).

70. The broadest authorizations were contained in Harris v. United States, 331 U.S. 145, (1947) (search of entire four room apartment upheld as incidental to an arrest in the living room); United States v. Rabinowitz, 339 U.S. 56 (1950) (hour and a half search of entire one-room office, including desk, safe and file cabinets, held incident to arrest in that office). A much more restrictive approach was taken in the intervening decision of Trupiano v. United States, 334 U.S. 699 (1948).

71. 395 U.S. 752 (1969).

72. Id. at 763. See Note, Search and Seizure Since Chimel v. California, 55 Minn.L.Rev. 1011 (1971).

73. 392 U.S. 1 (1968).

would believe that it was necessary to the preservation of his safety or that of others.[74] Any need to obtain or prevent the destruction of evidence could not, then, serve as a justification for such a search.[75] The scope of this "frisk" must be limited by its purpose. Thus it must involve only what is minimally necessary to discover whether the subject is armed and to disarm him should weapons be discovered.[76] For example, in Sibron v. New York [77] the officer had, with no initial exploration for weapons, thrust his hand into the subject's pocket and seized a packet of narcotics. "The search," held the Court, "was not reasonably limited in scope to the accomplishment of the only goal which might conceivably have justified its inception—the protection of the officer by disarming a potentially dangerous man." [78]

In Davis v. Mississippi [79] the Court suggested that the same analysis would be applied to a seizure of the person for the purpose of subjecting him to fingerprinting. It was "arguable," Mr. Justice Brennan commented for the Court, that detention for fingerprinting would be permissible on less than probable cause. Fingerprinting is a "reliable and effective crime-solving tool." Moreover, detention for such a purpose, if pursuant to a narrowly circumscribed procedure, would constitute a much less serious intrusion upon personal privacy than many other seizures of the person. No invasion of the privacy of the subject's personal life or thoughts need be involved, repeated detentions for this purpose (raising the danger

of harassment) were not a significant danger and the detention could be arranged at a time which caused minimal inconvenience for the subject. Most important, the Court observed that "the general requirement that the authorization of a judicial officer be obtained in advance of detention would not seem to admit of any exception in the fingerprinting context," [80] thus suggesting that since meeting the warrant requirement would not be impracticable it was constitutionally necessary.

In Terry v. Ohio [81] the Court expressly declined to evaluate the constitutional propriety of seizures of the person for field interrogation or other investigatory purposes.[82] Lower courts, however, have consistently upheld brief detention of "suspicious" persons on less than probable cause for purposes of obtaining information regarding their activities.[83]

---

74. Id. at 27.

75. Id. at 29.

76. Id.

77. 392 U.S. 40 (1968).

78. Id. at 65. See People v. Mosher, 1 Cal.3d 379, 82 Cal.Rptr. 379, 461 P.2d 659 (1969) (officer frisking defendant reasonably believed hard object felt in pocket was knife, so its seizure was proper, even though it was in fact a wristwatch).

79. 394 U.S. 721 (1969).

80. Id. at 728.

81. 392 U.S. 1 (1968).

82. Id. at 19 n. 16. These detentions are distinguishable from arrests both in purpose and form. An investigatorial detention is made for the purpose of gathering further information on which to base the decision whether to hold the subject formally to answer for a crime. It is necessarily of limited duration, and the collateral effects (such as the scope of any incidental search) are clearly limited. See generally, Comment, Constitutional Limitations on Pre-Arrest Investigations, 15 U.C.L. A.L.Rev. 1031 (1968).

83. United States v. Fallis, 414 F.2d 772 (9th Cir. 1969) (officer properly stopped car of subject meeting description of robber for "cursory inquiry"); People v. Reulman, 62 Cal.2d 92, 41 Cal. Rptr. 290, 396 P.2d 706 (1964); Barnes v. State, 85 Nev. 69, 450 P.2d 150 (1969); Tierney v. State, 7 Md.App. 56, 253 A.2d 528 (1969); State v. Goings, 184 Neb. 81, 165 N.W.2d 366 (1969). Where, however, objective basis for even limited investigational detention is lacking, courts have held the seizure unreasonable. E. g., United States v. Hostetter, 295 F.Supp. 1312 (D.Del.1969) (facts that subject was a stranger, shabbily dressed, and was walking slowly in the rain at a late hour did not, especially where no reports of thefts in the area had been received, justify stopping subject and searching suitcase); Irwin v. Superior Court, 1 Cal.3d 423, 82 Cal.Rptr. 484, 462 P.2d 12 (1969) (that subject was standing next to baggage with tag containing next sequential number to bag in which narcotics had been found did not justify investigatorial detention). Where investigatorial

This result is consistent with the Court's other decisions. Nevertheless, it is important specifically to articulate the evidentiary basis upon which such actions can constitutionally be taken and the extent of the seizure that can be made so that the Fourth Amendment continues to provide some protection in this area. The tentative draft of the American Law Institute's Model Code of Pre-Arraignment Procedure proposes to authorize investigatory stops if the officer "reasonably suspects" that the subject has just committed or is about to commit a felony or a misdemeanor involving danger of forcible injury to persons or loss of property.[84] The detention is to last no longer than is reasonably necessary to determine whether further action (such as arrest) is proper, but in no case longer than twenty minutes.[85] Other restrictions designed to minimize the impact upon the subject are also imposed: deadly force may not be used to enforce the right to stop,[86] only a frisk for weapons may be conducted pursuant to it,[87] a full warning must precede any questioning,[88] and a record is to be kept of the circumstances and purposes of the stop.[89] It is arguable that a more stringent evidentiary standard that "reasonable suspicion" would be theoretically desirable. But as a practical matter it is probably impossible to draft and accurately enforce a more precise standard than one which requires suspicion based upon some objec-

tive basis. In view of the protection afforded the subject, such a stop would not seem to involve an unreasonable seizure of the person within the meaning of the Fourth Amendment.

174. Evidence Obtained Pursuant to Unreasonable Searches and Seizures: (f) Electronic Surveillance.[90]

With the development of sophisticated mechanical extensions of an investigator's sensory organs [91] has come a multitude of problems that have not fit easily within traditional Fourth Amendment analysis. The traditional approach was established in 1928 when, in Olmstead v. United States,[92] the Supreme Court held that the Fourth Amendment did not forbid wiretapping unless it was accomplished by unlawful trespass upon the premises of the person challenging the practice. Spoken words, as intangibles, were held beyond the protection of the Fourth Amendment, which was viewed as protecting only "material things"; thus no violation of a Fourth Amendment right occurred unless unlawful entry into the premises was made.[93] This "trespass test" was subsequently employed, although in somewhat diluted form in the later cases, in other electronic surveillance situations to find that use of a detectaphone placed against the wall of a next-door office

---

detention is permissible, the scope of a warrantless search which may be justified as pursuant to it is limited. E. g., Commonwealth v. Lehan, 347 Mass. 197, 196 N.E.2d 840 (1964) (although officer could detain for limited inquiry one who appeared suspicious, this did not justify search of packages he was carrying).

84. A Model Code of Pre-Arraignment Procedure § 2.02(1) (b), (c) (Tent. Draft No. 2, 1969).

85. Id. at § 2.02.

86. Id. at § 2.02(3).

87. Id. at § 2.02(4).

88. Id. at § 2.02(5).

89. Id. at § 2.02(7).

90. See generally, American Bar Association Project on Minimum Standards for Criminal Justice, Standards Relating to Electronic Surveillance (1968); Scoular, Wiretapping and Eavesdropping Constitutional Development From Olmstead to Katz, 12 St.L.U.L.J. 513 (1968); Comment, Eavesdropping, Informers, and the Right of Privacy: A Judicial Tightrope, 52 Cornell L.Rev. 975 (1967); Comment, The Fourth Amendment and Electronic Eavesdropping: Katz v. United States, 5 Houston L.Rev. 990 (1968); Comment, Electronic Surveillance by Law Enforcement Officers, 64 Nw.U.L. Rev. 63 (1969); 29 Am.Jur.2d Evidence §§ 428–35; Annot., 97 A.L.R.2d 1283; C.J.S. Criminal Law §§ 657(21)–(24).

91. See Westin, Privacy and Freedom (1967); Dash, Knowlton and Schwartz, The Eavesdroppers (1959).

92. 277 U.S. 438 (1928).

93. 277 U.S. at 464.

did not violate the Fourth Amendment [94] and that no trespass—and consequently no Fourth Amendment violation—occurred when a government agent carrying a microphone or a recording device was invited into the suspect's premises (without knowledge of the device) and either broadcast the conversation to others stationed outside or recorded it for subsequent replaying.[95] On the other hand, when a "spike" microphone was driven into a party wall until it made physical contact with the heating duct serving the next-door room, an "unauthorized physical penetration into the premises" occurred and the "Fourth Amendment was violated by use of the device to overhear conversations next door.[96] The Federal Communications Act of 1934,[97] however, prohibited intercepting and divulging the contents of telephone communications, and the Supreme Court held that conversations obtained pursuant to a violation of this statute were inadmissible in federal courts.[98] This conclusion was based upon legislative purpose and intent and did not purport to be a constitutionally based exclusionary rule.[99]

Katz v. United States,[1] decided in 1967, was a major turning point. After concluding that the "trespass" doctrine of *Olmstead* had been so eroded by later opinions that it could no longer be regarded as controlling,[2] the Court held that the petitioner's Fourth Amendment rights had been violated when FBI agents attached an electronic listening device to the outside of a public telephone booth and used it to overhear and record phone calls made by the petitioner from the booth. "Words," then, were subject to seizure within the meaning of the Fourth Amendment. The government's activities, the Court held, "violated the privacy upon which [the petitioner] justifiably relied while using the telephone booth and thus constituted a 'search and seizure' within the meaning of the Fourth Amendment." [3] Under the circumstances, the agents' failure to obtain court authorization made their activity unreasonable within the meaning of the amendment and required the exclusion of the products.

Katz substituted for the traditional "trespass" test a new approach for determining when use of electronic surveillance violates Fourth Amendment rights. Two elements are necessary for a violation. First, the subject

---

94. Goldman v. United States, 316 U.S. 129 (1942).

95. On Lee v. United States, 343 U.S. 747 (1952); Lopez v. United States, 373 U.S. 427 (1963). See note 4, infra.

96. Silverman v. United States, 365 U.S. 505, 509 (1961).

97. 47 U.S.C.A. § 605. See generally, Annot., 20 L. Ed.2d 1717.

98. Nardone v. United States, 302 U.S. 379 (1937); Nardone v. United States, 308 U.S. 338 (1939). This ruling was, however, subject to the "consent" exception. In Rathbun v. United States, 355 U.S. 107 (1957) the Court held that when one party to a telephone conversation consented to a third party overhearing the conversation there was no "interception" within the meaning of the Act.

99. See Schwartz v. Texas, 344 U.S. 199 (1952) (exclusionary rule of *Nardone* cases did not extend to states). *Schwartz* has been overruled in light of Mapp v. Ohio, 367 U.S. 643 (1961). Lee v. Florida, 392 U.S. 378 (1968).

1. 389 U.S. 347 (1967).

2. In holding that the use of a "spike mike" constituted a violation of the Fourth Amendment, the Court in Silverman v. United States, 365 U.S. 505, 511–12 (1961) made clear that its decision did not turn upon whether or not there had been a technical trespass under the local property law relating to party walls. Rather, the decision was based upon "the reality of an actual intrusion into a constitutionally protected area."

In *Katz* the parties vigorously disputed whether the telephone booth was a "constitutionally protected area" within the meaning of the liberalized trespass rule of *Silverman*. But the Court rejected this analysis: "[T]his effort to decide whether or not a given 'area', viewed in the abstract, is 'constitutionally protected' deflects attention from the problem presented by this case. For the Fourth Amendment protects people, not places. What a person knowingly exposes to the public, even in his own home or office, is not a subject of Fourth Amendment protection. . . . But what he seeks to preserve as private, even in an area accessible to the public, may be constitutionally protected." Katz v. United States, 389 U.S. 347, 351–352 (1967).

3. Katz v. United States, 389 U.S. 347, 353 (1967).

must in fact have relied upon the circumstances to maintain the privacy of his activity. Second, the reliance must have been "justified". This second element involves an objective test of reasonableness. If, for example, Katz had relied upon a telephone booth with glass walls to preserve his physical movements from observation, his reliance would almost certainly have been unreasonable and thus without constitutional protection. On the other hand, the fact that he could not reasonably expect to be free from visual observation does not mean that he could not reasonably expect to be free from auditory observation. Although *Katz* dealt with the use of only one means of electronic surveillance (a listening device), there is no reason why the analysis of the case should not be extended to any activity which results in surveillance of any sort.[4]

The potential problems of discovering a relationship between electronic surveillance and the government's proof in any particular case were greatly reduced by Alderman v. United States.[5] Rejecting the government's contention that the government should be required only to permit *in camera* inspection by the trial judge of its records of any surveillance of the accused (and to turn over to the accused only records found by the judge to be "arguably relevant"), the Court held that an accused himself was entitled to access to the records of any surveillance which he had standing to challenge. Whether he is entitled to more than these records and the opportunity to cross examine the appropriate officials in regard to the records and the case made against him is to be left to the discretion of the trial judge. Although recognizing that this created a risk of costly disclosure of a large amount of material, the Court noted that the accused and his counsel could be placed under enforceable orders against unwarranted disclosure of the contents.

Searches conducted pursuant to electronic surveillance are, like other searches, subject to the Fourth Amendment's warrant requirement. But electronic surveillance differs significantly from the traditional police practices which have been subject to the warrant requirement. It may consequently be necessary somewhat to modify the warrant requirement in this area. The Supreme Court discussed the matter in Berger v. New York,[6] involving the installation pursuant to a state court order of a recording device in an office of a suspect. The order considered in *Berger* was held not to meet Fourth Amendment requirements for several reasons: (1) it did not specify (and the investigators were not required to establish) what specific crimes had been or were being committed, whose conversations were to be overheard, or the specific conversations sought to be overheard; (2) it authorized surveillance over a two-month period of time, thus in effect authorizing a

---

4. The federal Courts of Appeal have divided on the impact of *Katz* upon the "bugged agent" situation, in which surveillance is accomplished by having an agent record or broadcast conversations with the subject. Compare Koran v. United States, 408 F.2d 1321 (5th Cir. 1968) (*Katz* does not mean that such a surveillance is a search) with United States v. White, 405 F.2d 838 (7th Cir. 1969) (one can justifiably rely on those with whom one speaks not being equipped with mechanical devices, and therefore such action is a search within the meaning of the Fourth Amendment's warrant requirement). See 14 Vill.L.Rev. 758 (1969). In United States v. White, 401 U.S. 745 (1971), the Court, with four dissenters, held that "if the conduct and revelations of an agent without electronic equipment do not invade the defendant's constitutionally justifiable expectations of privacy, neither does a simultaneous recording of the same conversations made by the agent or by others from transmissions received from the agent to whom the defendant is talking and whose trustworthiness the defendant necessarily risks." 401 U.S. at 751. *Katz,* then, has not impaired the validity of Lopez v. United States, 373 U.S. 427 (1963) (agent could properly record conversation with electronic equipment concealed on his person) or On Lee v. United States, 343 U.S. 747 (1952) (agent could properly carry equipment which transmitted conversations to others located elsewhere).

5. 394 U.S. 165 (1969).

6. 388 U.S. 41 (1967).

series of surveillances; (3) no requirement that the surveillance be terminated once the described conversations were overheard was imposed; and (4) no provision was made for notice to the person subjected to the surveillance, either before or after the invasion of his privacy, a return on the order, or for any showing of special facts justifying this omission. Consequently, the procedure under which the order was issued failed to provide the judicial supervision which the warrant requirement demands.

The problem of fitting the warrant procedure to electronic surveillance practices was attacked directly in the Omnibus Crime Control and Safe Streets Act of 1968.[7] This statute prohibits any person from intercepting or attempting to intercept by the use of any electronic, mechanical, or other device any wire or oral communication except pursuant to a court order.[8] Oral communication is defined as "any oral communication uttered by a person exhibiting an expectation that such communication is not subject to interception under circumstances justifying such expectation." A specific procedure is established for the issuance of orders by federal courts on the application of federal prosecuting authorities, and provision is made for state prosecutors to follow similar procedures in state courts.[9] The most important of the procedural protections provided by the procedure are as follows:

1. The application for the order must contain extensive information regarding prior applications involving the same persons, facilities, or places;

2. Application may be made only pursuant to an investigation for relatively serious offenses (in the case of states, offenses punishable by one year or more of imprisonment);

3. Prior to issuing an order, the judge must determine that (a) probable cause exists to believe that the individual is committing, has committed, or is about to com-

7. Ch. 119, Title III, 82 Stat. 197, 211, now 18 U.S. C.A. § 2510 et seq. See generally Schwartz, The Legitimation of Electronics Eavesdropping: The Politics of "Law and Order", 67 Mich.L.Rev. 455 (1969). Under Lee v. Florida, 392 U.S. 378 (1968), evidence obtained in violation of the Federal Communications Act of 1934 is inadmissible in state courts as well as federal courts. Until the Omnibus Crime Control and Safe Streets Act of 1968, the Federal Communications Act of 1934 contained no exception or provision for legalized wiretapping. 47 U.S.C.A. § 605. The 1968 legislation, however, amended it to provide an exception for interceptions authorized by the Omnibus Crime Control and Safe Streets Act. 47 U.S.C.A. § 605 (1970 supp.). Among the analyses of the Act are Comment, Electronic Surveillance by Law Enforcement Officers, 64 Nw.U.L.Rev. 63, 69–86 (1969); Note, Wiretapping and Electronic Surveillance—Title III of the Crime Control Act of 1968, 23 Rutgers L.Rev. 319 (1969); Note, Eavesdropping Provisions of the Omnibus Crime Control and Safe Streets Act of 1968: How Do They Stand in Light of Recent Supreme Court Decision? 3 Valpariaso L.Rev. 89 (1968).

8. 18 U.S.C.A. § 2511. Special provision is made for interception without court order in "emergency" situations involving danger to the national security or "conspiratorial activities characteristic of organized crime" if no court order could be obtained. Application for a court order, however, must be made within 48 hours. 18 U.S.C.A. § 2518 (7). There is also a broad national emergency exemption. 18 U.S.C.A. § 2511(3) provides that neither the Crime Control Act nor the Communications Act of 1934 limits "the constitutional power of the President to take such measure as he deems necessary" to protect the nation from foreign threats or "to protect the United States against the overthrow of the Government by force or other unlawful means, or against any other clear and present danger to the structure or existence of the Government." These exceptions may be broader than constitutional requirements permit. See the analyses cited in note 7, supra. Specific exception is made for "a person acting under color of law" to intercept a communication "where such person is party to the communication or one of the parties to the communication has given prior consent to such interception." 18 U.S.C.A. § 2511(2) (c). This corresponds to the similar provision in the Federal Communications Act of 1934; see note 98, supra.

9. The state judge may grant the order in conformity with the applicable state statute *and* the procedure established for issuance of such orders in federal court. 18 U.S.C.A. § 2516(2) (1970 supp.). For a study of the impact of the federal statute upon the existing legislation of a specific state, see Comment, Electronic Surveillance in California: A Study in State Legislative Control, 57 Cal.L.Rev. 1182 (1969).

mit a designated crime, (b) probable cause exists to believe that particular communications concerning that offense will be obtained through the desired interception, (c) normal investigation procedures have either been tried and failed or are likely to fail or to be too dangerous if tried, and (d) probable cause exists to believe the facilities or place to be used are to be used in connection with the offense or leased by, listed in the name of, or are commonly used by the suspect;

4. The order must specify the nature, location, and owner of the facilities to be intercepted, a particular description of the communications sought, and the period during which interception is authorized;

5. The order may be only for as long as is necessary to achieve the objective of the interception, and no longer than thirty days. Requests for extensions are in effect to be *de novo* applications;

6. Interceptions are to be recorded if possible, and records of interceptions as well as of applications and orders are to be sealed and kept for at least ten years;

7. Within at least ninety days of the termination of the interception, the persons named in the application are to be notified of the application and whether or not communications were actually intercepted. Ten days prior to any use in court, the parties in the proceeding are to be given information regarding the manner in which the interception order was obtained;

8. Even when a communication has been validly intercepted, the contents remain privileged except to the extent disclosure is specifically authorized.[10] Knowledge of the contents or evidence derived from such knowledge may be used by an offi-

cer "to the extent such use is appropriate to the proper performance of his official duties" and may be disclosed only to other officers only if such disclosure is within the performance of the duties of the disclosing officer. Disclosure is also authorized during testimony under oath during grand jury and criminal proceedings.

Despite these factors, the statute presents significant constitutional issues. For example, the requirement that only the "type" of conversation sought be described[11] may not meet the requirement of specificity. Although it must be found that normal investigative procedures would not be adequate,[12] this may not cure the *Berger* objection to failure to require advance notice, or in the alternative, a showing of exigencies making the giving of notice impracticable. The notice served after the termination of an interception may be delayed ninety days or, upon a showing of unspecified "good cause," may be delayed longer.[13] This delay may make the notice inadequate. Notice need not be served upon all who might arguably have standing to challenge the results of the surveillance,[14] and the notice provision may be inadequate on this basis.

Moreover, the statute purports to encompass only electronic surveillance of the spoken word, and does not address itself to other forms of surveillance which unquestionably come within Fourth Amendment boundaries. While this does not mean that it is inadequate in regard to the subject matter

10. 18 U.S.C.A. § 2517.

11. 18 U.S.C.A. § 2518(4) (c). And see § 170, n. 94, supra.

12. 18 U.S.C.A. § 2518(3) (c).

13. 18 U.S.C.A. § 2518 (8) (d).

14. 18 U.S.C.A. § 2518(8) (d) provides for service "on the persons named in the order or the application, and such other parties to intercepted communications as the judge may determine in his discretion that is in the interest of justice." The exceptions to the statute's requirements are also of doubtful validity; see note 8, supra.

covered, it does suggest that legislative action in regard to other forms of investigatorial activity has been lacking. Perhaps experience with the eavesdropping provisions will provide a basis on which more adequately to attack the overall problem of surveillance.

175. Evidence Obtained Pursuant to Unreasonable Searches and Seizures: (g) Consent as a Waiver of Fourth Amendment Protection.[15]

Both the substantive and procedural limitations imposed by the Fourth Amendment can be waived. If a subject consents to an invasion of privacy, this has traditionally been considered a waiver, and evidence obtained pursuant to the invasion is admissible without regard to whether the invasion meets the requirements of the Fourth Amendment. The courts have been hostile to these waivers, however, and this hostility has been formalized in the rules that the state bears the burden of proving the existence of voluntary consent [16] and that acquiescence in the desire of law enforcement personnel to search will not be presumed and must be affirmatively demonstrated.[17]

The consent must be voluntary. In most contexts this has meant that it must not be simple submission to what is considered the authority or the power of the state to search. Thus a showing that a request to search was accompanied by a showing of force tends to establish that any subsequent consent was merely submission to the apparent inevitability of the search.[18] Or, if an officer relies upon a search warrant in obtaining entry to premises, he cannot later abandon reliance upon the warrant and successfully assert that there was consent to the search.[19] While valid consent may be given by one who is in police custody, the fact of custody militates against a finding of voluntariness.[20] A recent cataloguing of the factors that bear on the voluntariness of consent proceeded as follows:

> "Among the factors that may be considered in determining the effectiveness and validity of a consent to search are whether at the time when it was given the defendant was under arrest . . . ; whether he was overpowered by arresting officers, handcuffed, or similarly subject to physical restrictions . . . ; whether the keys to the premises searched had already been seized by the police from the defendant . . . ; whether

---

15. See generally Israel, Recent Developments in the Law of Search and Seizure 129–54, in Criminal Law and the Constitution (Institute of Continuing Legal Education, 1968); Note, Consent Searches: A Reappraisal After Miranda v. Arizona, 67 Colum. L.Rev. 130 (1967); Comment, Consent Search: Waiver of Fourth Amendment Rights, 12 St.L.U. L.J. 297 (1968); Note, Effective Consent to Search and Seizure, 113 U.Pa.L.Rev. 260 (1964); Note, Third Party Consent to Search and Seizure, 1967 Wash.U.L.Q. 12; Dec.Dig. Search and Seizure ☜7 (27)–(28).

16. United States v. Boukater, 409 F.2d 537, 539 (5th Cir. 1969) ("a voluntary consent to search cannot be lightly inferred but must be proved by clear and convincing evidence"); United States v. Como, 340 F.2d 891 (2d Cir. 1965).

17. United States v. White, 405 F.2d 838, 845 (7th Cir. 1969) rev'd on other grounds, 401 U.S. 745 (1971).

18. United States v. Dorman, 294 F.Supp. 1221, 1223 (D.D.C.1967) ("no valid consent can be found when police armed with shotguns present themselves at the door of a house or apartment late at night and state that they want to arrest the householder's son"); People v. Haskell, 41 Ill.2d 25, 241 N.E.2d 430 (1968) (nineteen year old wife of defendant "ordered" to get gun by police officers who told her that they had been sent to pick it up).

19. Bumper v. North Carolina, 391 U.S. 543 (1968). Consents given soon after incriminating and unlawful searches are also almost automatically involuntary. United States ex rel. Metze v. New York, 303 F.Supp. 1359 (S.D.N.Y.1969); People v. Superior Court, 71 Cal.2d 265, 78 Cal.Rptr. 210, 455 P.2d 146 (1969); People v. Johnson, 68 Cal.2d 629, 68 Cal.Rptr. 441, 440 P.2d 921 (1968).

20. Porter v. Ashmore, 298 F.Supp. 951, 956 (D.S. C.1969) rev'd on other grounds 421 F.2d 1186 (4th Cir.) (when defendant is in custody, government's burden becomes greater).

the defendant employed evasive conduct or attempted to mislead the police . . . ; and whether he denied guilt or the presence of any incriminatory objects in his premises . . . .

"The presence of some or all of the aforementioned factors is not controlling, since . . . each case 'must stand or fall on its own special facts,' . . . . Although the defendant need not express a 'positive desire' to have the search conducted in order to render his consent a voluntary waiver, . . . it must amount to more than mere submission or acquiscence in the nature of resignation to constitute a valid waiver.[21]"

What—if any—knowledge is necessary for consent poses a more difficult question. Since consent is essentially testimonial, it has been argued that Miranda v. Arizona [22] is applicable and no consent is valid unless the subject is warned and accorded his right to counsel.[23] But there seems to be agreement that the subject need not be specifically told of his right to decline to consent to a search, especially if he is not in formal custody at the time the consent is requested.[24] The failure

to advise of rights may affect the voluntariness of any consent, however.[25] It is difficult to reconcile with Miranda the absence of a requirement that the subject be fully informed of his Fourth Amendment rights (including his right not to consent) before a valid consent may be obtained. While it might be urged that Fourth Amendment rights are not as important as Fifth Amendment rights and therefore do not require the same solicitude, little basis exists for the differentiation. In fact, it is arguable that the nature of Fourth Amendment rights suggests that custody of the subject ought not to be a condition precedent to the obligation there to warn. The dangers created by custodial interrogation arise primarily because of the custody; noncustodial interrogation creates significantly less danger to the underlying rights of the subject. The extent to which a search or seizure endangers the analogous underlying rights of the subject, however, is generally unrelated to the custody of the subject. For example, the extent to which a search of a dwelling endangers the Fourth Amendment rights of the owner has little relationship to whether he is in custody. Given this difference, it seems inappropriate to extend the analogy of Miranda so as to require a warning of Fourth Amendment rights only when the subject is in custody.

More difficult problems are raised by searches conducted under consent related to misrepresentations made by the searching officers. In Gouled v. United States [26] a busi-

21. United States v. Lewis, 274 F.Supp. 184, 187–88 (S.D.N.Y.1967) (citations omitted).

22. 384 U.S. 436 (1966). See § 151, supra.

23. Virgin Islands v. Berne, 412 F.2d 1055 (3d Cir. 1969) cert. denied 396 U.S. 937; United States v. Pelensky, 300 F.Supp. 976 (D.Vt.1969). The argument for such a requirement is made in Note, Consent Searches: A Reappraisal After Miranda v. Arizona, 67 Colum.L.Rev. 130, 134–46 (1967).

24. United States ex rel. Combs v. La Vallee, 417 F.2d 523 (2d Cir. 1969); Byrd v. Lane, 398 F.2d 750, 754–55 (7th Cir. 1968) cert. denied 393 U.S. 1020; Gorman v. United States, 380 F.2d 158, 164 (1st Cir. 1967); Porter v. Ashmore, 298 F.Supp. 951 (D.C.S.C.1969) rev'd on other grounds 421 F.2d 1186 (4th Cir.); People v. Ledferd, 38 Ill.2d 607, 232 N.E.2d 684 (1967); State v. McCarty, 199 Kan. 116, 427 P.2d 616 (1967) vacated and remanded on other grounds 392 U.S. 308. But see United States v. Nikrasch, 367 F.2d 740, 744 (7th Cir. 1966); United States v. Moderacki, 280 F.Supp. 633, 636 (D.Del.1968); United States v. Blalock, 255 F.Supp. 268 (E.D.Pa.1966).

25. United States v. Miller, 395 F.2d 116 (7th Cir. 1968) cert. denied 393 U.S. 846 (fact that agent told defendant that he did not have to show items to officers considered in finding consent valid); People v. Superior Court, 71 Cal.2d 265, 78 Cal. Rptr. 210, 455 P.2d 146 (1969) (failure to warn of right to decline to consent considered in finding consent invalid). But cf. United States v. Curiale, 414 F.2d 744 (2nd Cir. 1969) (agent who indicated that if defendant did not consent he would obtain a warrant had no duty to disclose to defendant that basis for obtaining a warrant did not exist).

26. 255 U.S. 298 (1921).

ness associate acting as an agent of the police obtained entry into Gouled's office by representing that he was paying a social call. When Gouled left the office, the associate searched it and obtained certain papers which he turned over to authorities. Despite Gouled's consent to the entry of the associate, the Supreme Court held that the papers had been seized in violation of the Fourth Amendment. But the Court has reached a different result where the government agent deceives the subject as to his identity or purpose but searches no further than the subject, relying upon the deception, consents. In Hoffa v. United States,[27] involving an associate of the subject who turned informer but concealed this, the Court suggested that such a consent induced by deception involved "no interest legitimately protected by the Fourth Amendment."[28] Citing a dissent in an earlier case, the Court stated "The risk of being . . . deceived as to the identity of one with whom one deals is probably inherent in the conditions of human society. It is the kind of risk we necessarily assume whenever we speak."[29] Thus the current state of the law apparently makes deception irrelevant to the validity of consent to search, although where deception has been used there may be a tendency strictly to construe and enforce the scope, in physical terms, of the consent.[30]

This view was sharply attacked by Mr. Justice Douglas, who suggested that the distinction between consent limited in terms of the physical scope of the search and that limited in terms of the nature of the person who may enter was unnecessary: "There is no reason why an owner's Fourth Amendment rights cannot include the right to open up his house to limited classes of people."[31] Nor, he concluded, was such a distinction desirable on Fourth Amendment grounds:

> "[W]hen a homeowner invites a friend or business acquaintance into his home, he opens his house to a friend or acquaintance, not a government spy. . . .
>
> [A] person may take the risk that a friend will turn on him and report him to the police. But this is far different from the Government's 'planting' a friend in a person's entourage so that he can secure incriminating evidence. In the one case, the Government has merely been the willing recipient of information supplied by a fickle friend. In the other, the Government has actively encouraged and participated in a breach of privacy by sending in an undercover agent. . . .

27. 385 U.S. 293 (1966).

28. Id. at 302.

29. Id. at 303, citing Lopez v. United States, 373 U.S. 427, 465 (1963) (Brennan, J., dissenting). For similar results, see United States v. White, 401 U.S. 745 (1971); Lewis v. United States, 385 U.S. 206 (1966); Osborn v. United States, 385 U.S. 323 (1966); Lopez v. United States, 373 U.S. 427 (1963).

30. See Graves v. Beto, 424 F.2d 524 (5th Cir. 1970) cert. denied 400 U.S. 960. A blood sample was obtained by police who represented that it would be tested for alcohol content but who actually intended to test it for type and match it with a sample of blood found at the scene of a rape. The consent was held ineffective in regard to the test for the type. Compare Commonwealth v. Brown, 437 Pa. 1, 261 A.2d 879 (1970) and Brown v. Brier-

ley, 438 F.2d 954 (3d Cir. 1971), in which a suspect gave police officers a gun to sell for him. The officers did in fact sell it, then "borrowed" it from the purchaser to run ballistics tests on it. No violation of the suspect's Fourth Amendment rights was found by either the state or federal courts. But here, the suspect had consented to complete surrender of all rights in and over the gun, i. e., to its sale, and the additional "search" of the ballistics test was not made until after his rights had been terminated in full compliance with his directive. See also People v. Stuller, 10 Cal.App.3d 582, 596–597, 89 Cal.Rptr. 158, 167–168 (1970) (police use in rape investigation of fingerprints submitted by suspect in compliance with ordinance requiring bartenders to be fingerprinted was not violation of Fourth Amendment, since there was no misrepresentation by police and suspect voluntarily complied with ordinance knowing that he was a suspect in the investigation).

31. Osborn v. United States, 385 U.S. 323, 346 (1966) (Douglas, J., dissenting).

[T]he Government unlawfully enters a man's home when its agent . . . gets in by trickery or fraud." [32]

Perhaps the most difficult problems arise when the consent offered is not that of the aggrieved person but that of a third person. A third person with an interest in the premises but no immediate right to possession generally cannot give valid consent to a search of the premises. Thus in Chapman v. United States [33] a nonresident landlord was held unable to consent to the search of the leased premises, even though he had reserved the right to enter for limited reasons. In Stoner v. California [34] a hotel manager was held unable to consent to the search of a guest's room. Where there is joint possession, however, it has generally been held that each party may give consent valid against the other for search of those portions of the premises jointly occupied. A wife, for example, (with joint and equal right to possession) may consent to a search of the premises, and this consent circumvents the Fourth Amendment right of the husband.[35] A grandfather could consent to the search of his grandson's room since, although the grandson customarily slept there, he did not have exclusive possession and other family members also used it.[36] But several courts have either rejected[37] or greatly restricted[38] the "third party consent" rule, arguing that only the individual whose privacy is invaded has constitutional authority to consent. This position seems too inflexible. The extent to which one reasonably expects privacy from governmental invasion depends in large part upon whether others have the opportunity to authorize such an intrusion. When an area, for example, is subject to the control of several individuals, the reasonable expectation of privacy on the part of each may be sub-

---

32. Id. at 347–48. See also The Supreme Court, 1966 Term, 81 Harv.L.Rev. 112, 191–96 (1967).

33. 365 U.S. 610 (1961).

34. 376 U.S. 483 (1964).

35. People v. Haskell, 41 Ill.2d 25, 241 N.E.2d 430 (1968); Commonwealth ex rel. Cabey v. Rundle, 432 Pa. 466, 248 A.2d 197 (1968) (vigorous dissent by Roberts, J., arguing that Katz v. United States, 389 U.S. 347 (1967) requires a contrary result); Burge v. State, 443 S.W.2d 720 (Tex.Cr.App.1969) cert. denied 396 U.S. 934. Contra, Cofer v. United States, 37 F.2d 677 (5th Cir. 1930); Simmons v. State, 94 Okl.Cr. 18, 229 P.2d 615 (1951). See Gurleski v. United States, 405 F.2d 253 (5th Cir. 1968) cert. denied 395 U.S. 977 (*Cofer* rule would not be extended to cover a mistress).

For a general discussion of consent by family members, see 28 Wash. and Lee L.Rev. 207 (1971).

It has been held that a joint occupant who is away from the premises cannot authorize a search over the objection of another joint occupant who is present. Duke v. Superior Court, 1 Cal.3d 314, 82 Cal.Rptr. 348, 461 P.2d 628 (1969); Tompkins v. Superior Court, 59 Cal.2d 65, 27 Cal.Rptr. 889, 378 P.2d 113 (1963).

36. Rivers v. State, 226 So.2d 337 (Fla.1969). People v. Gorg, 45 Cal.2d 776, 291 P.2d 469 (1955) is generally credited with formulating the "apparent authority" approach relied upon by courts in California and some other jurisdictions. As summarized in People v. Hopper, 268 Cal.App.2d 774, 75 Cal.Rptr. 253, 256 (1969), the "apparent authority" rule holds that "[t]he Fourth Amendment is not violated by a warrantless entry and search of a dwelling if made with the consent of a third party whom the police reasonably and in good faith believe has authority to consent." It has been suggested that this approach—which apparently substitutes apparent for actual authority to consent and emphasizes the good faith of the officers—was rejected by Stoner v. California, 376 U.S. 483 (1964), but the California Supreme Court had read *Stoner* as merely enforcing the already existing requirement that the belief rest upon reasonable grounds. People v. Hill, 69 Cal.2d 550, 72 Cal. Rptr. 641, 446 P.2d 521 (1968). See also State v. Kearney, 75 Wash.2d 168, 449 P.2d 400 (1969) (consent of one "having apparent possession of the premises" conferred authority to search). But see People v. Miller, 40 Ill.2d 154, 238 N.E.2d 407 (1968) (apparent authority of owner of house in which defendant was arrested to consent to search of car in garage was not sufficient to sustain consent, when it was established that the car belonged not to the owner of the house but to the defendant).

37. State v. Matias, 51 Haw. 62, 451 P.2d 257 (1969) (right of overnight guest to privacy in apartment could not be waived by host, so search of apartment was unreasonable).

38. People v. Smith, 19 Mich.App. 359, 172 N.W.2d 902 (1969) (owner and occupier may not consent to search of premises if search constitutes an invasion of privacy of another person upon whom the investigation has focused); People v. Overall, 7 Mich.App. 153, 151 N.W.2d 225 (1967) (same).

ject to the reasonable possibility that the others will authorize official intrusion into the area.

Special problems of consent are raised when there is a bailment involved. Generally, courts have held that one who entrusts his property to another assumes the risk that the other will consent to a search of it.[39] In Frazier v. Cupp,[40] for example, petitioner Frazier had left some clothing in a duffel bag which he used jointly with his cousin Rawls. The bag was left in Rawls' home. Rawls was arrested and consented to a search of the bag; Frazier's clothing was seized in this search. In response to Frazier's argument that Rawls had actual permission to use only one compartment of the bag and thus did not have authority to consent to a search of the remainder, the Court declared, "Petitioner, in allowing Rawls to use the bag and in leaving it in his house must be taken to have assumed the risk that Rawls would allow someone else to look inside."[41]

Searches of regulated business premises also present special consent problems. In Davis v. United States[42] the Supreme Court indicated that it would less readily find a lack of voluntariness in the consent to a limited search of business premises for records which

by law the proprietor was required to submit for inspection. But statutory schemes regulating various commercial enterprises often provide for warrantless inspections and apparently dispense with any evidentiary requirement for such inspections.[43] Searches pursuant to these authorizations have repeatedly been upheld as "reasonable" searches within the meaning of the Fourth Amendment and as otherwise valid.[44] Some doubt was cast upon these holdings, however, by Camara v. Municipal Court[45] and See v. Seattle.[46] After holding in Camara that administrative searches of private premises were subject to the warrant requirement, the Court in See applied the same restriction to commercial structures. But Mr. Justice White, speaking for the Court in See, emphasized that the opinion should not be read as questioning "such accepted regulatory techniques as licensing programs which require inspections prior to operating a business or market-

39. United States v. Eldridge, 302 F.2d 463 (4th Cir. 1962) (friend who had borrowed car had authority to consent to its search); State v. Clift, 202 Kan. 512, 449 P.2d 1006 (1969) cert. denied 396 U.S. 910 (host could consent to seizure of clothing left in closet by guest who had left state); State v. Ray, 274 N.C. 556, 164 S.E.2d 457 (1968) (guest could consent to search of suitcase of guest who had slept on couch for several nights). But see United States v. Brown, 300 F.Supp. 1285 (D.N.H. 1969) (search, with friends' permission, of attache case which defendant had left with friends with whom he had stayed several nights was impermissible); United States v. Small, 297 F.Supp. 582 (D.Mass.1969) (lessee of locker consented to inspection by lessor but did not consent to search by police).

40. 394 U.S. 731 (1969).

41. Id. at 740.

42. 328 U.S. 582 (1946).

43. E. g., Ariz.Rev.Stat. § 3–710(G), (H), authorizing an inspector to "enter and inspect" any place handling eggs and to "take for inspection representative samples of . . . invoices, eggs, and cases or containers" for the purpose of determining whether regulations covering the production and marketing of eggs have been violated. But see Colonnade Catering Corp. v. United States, 397 U.S. 72 (1970) holding that the provision in 26 U.S.C.A. § 7342 (1965) for a fine for refusing to permit a federal officer to inspect premises used for the sale of liquor evinces a Congressional purpose not to authorize forceful entry of areas subject to inspection.

44. Hughes v. Johnson, 305 F.2d 67 (9th Cir. 1962) (warrantless search for and seizure of records and wild fowl permissible pursuant to statutory regulation of establishments processing migratory birds); State v. Zurawski, 89 N.J.Super. 488, 215 A.2d 564 (1965) aff'd 47 N.J. 160, 219 A.2d 614 (1966) (per curiam); Oklahoma Alcohol Beverage Control Board v. McCulley, 377 P.2d 568 (Okl.1962); Hines v. State, 362 S.W.2d 652 (Tex.Cr.App.1962). The authority was carried to the extreme in Peeples v. United States, 341 F.2d 60 (5th Cir. 1965) cert. denied 380 U.S. 988, upholding a warrantless search of a home because federal agents had "ample evidence" that distilling subject to regulation was being conducted on the premises.

45. 387 U.S. 523 (1967).

46. 387 U.S. 541 (1967).

ing a product. Any constitutional challenges to such programs can only be resolved   . . on a case-by-case basis under the general Fourth Amendment standard of reasonableness." [47]   Post-*See* cases, although relatively few in number, have agreed that restricted warrantless searches pursuant to regulatory schemes are still reasonable within Fourth Amendment standards.[48]

176. Evidence Obtained Pursuant to Denial of the Right to Counsel: Lineups and Similar Situations.

Evidence fatally related to denials of the Sixth Amendment's right to representation of counsel [49] is inadmissible, although the exclusionary sanction in this context rests upon the underlying Sixth Amendment right rather than the Fourth Amendment exclusionary rule applied to the states in Mapp v. Ohio.[50] Thus proof of a prior conviction, even though otherwise admissible, is subject to exclusion if the accused was denied the right to counsel during proceedings related to that conviction.[51] The most significant impact of the Sixth Amendment exclusionary rule, however, has come about by virtue of the extension of the right to counsel in the pretrial situation. Testimonial admissions made by an accused during custodial interrogation are inadmissible if full Fifth and Sixth Amendment rights were not accorded; this is discussed in detail elsewhere.[52] Apart from the interrogation process, the major area that has been affected by the expanding Sixth Amendment has been activities related to witnesses whose eyewitness identification testimony will later be used in court.

In United States v. Wade [53] the Court held that an accused was entitled to the right to counsel at a "lineup" during which witnesses to the crime—and potential prosecution witnesses at trial—were asked to identify the accused. Emphasizing the inherent unreliability of eyewitness identification and the potential for improper influence of identification in the lineup procedure, the Court held that counsel's assistance at the lineup was "necessary to preserve the defendant's basic right to a fair trial as affected by his right meaningfully to cross-examine the witnesses against him and to have effective assistance of counsel at the trial itself." [54] The underlying danger, of course, is that the line-

47. Id. at 546.

48. Colonnade Catering Corp. v. United States, 410 F.2d 197 (2d Cir. 1969) rev'd on other grounds, 397 U.S. 72 (1969) (reversing district court holding that *Camara* and *See* invalidated warrantless inspections of liquor dealers under the authority of 26 U.S.C.A. § 5146(b)); United States v. Sessions, 283 F.Supp. 746 (N.D.Ga.1968); Hutchins v. State, 426 S.W.2d 235 (Tex.Cr.App.1968) (summarily upholding warrantless search of club serving liquor with no discussion of *See*).

49. "In all criminal prosecutions, the accused shall enjoy the right   . . to have the Assistance of Counsel for his defence." U.S.C.A.Const. Amend. VI. Until Gideon v. Wainwright, 372 U.S. 335 (1963), failure to appoint counsel violated an accused's federal constitutional right only if the absence of counsel, under the particular circumstances involved, resulted in a conviction lacking in fundamental fairness. Betts v. Brady, 316 U.S. 455 (1942). In *Gideon*, however, the Court made clear that for serious offenses the federal constitution requires that trial counsel be made available to all criminal defendants financially unable to obtain counsel.

50. See § 165, supra.

51. Burgett v. Texas, 389 U.S. 109, 115 (1967):
"To permit a conviction obtained in violation of Gideon v. Wainwright to be used against a person either to support guilt or to enhance punishment for another offense . . . is to erode the principle of that case. Worse yet, since the defect in the prior conviction was denial of the right to counsel, the accused in effect suffers anew from the deprivation of that Sixth Amendment right."
See generally, Note, The Evidentiary Use of Constitutionally Defective Prior Convictions, 68 Colum. L.Rev. 1168 (1968).

52. See § 151, supra.

53. 388 U.S. 218 (1967). See generally, 63 Nw.U.L. Rev. 251 (1968); Comment, The Right to Counsel at Lineups: Wade and Gilbert in the Lower Courts, 36 U.Chi.L.Rev. 830 (1969); Comment, Lawyers and Lineups, 77 Yale L.J. 390 (1967).

54. United States v. Wade, 388 U.S. 218, 227 (1967).

up will function either consciously or unconsciously as a suggestion to the witness that the accused was the perpetrator of the offense. If this occurs, later identification at trial (as well as any identification during the lineup) will rest not upon the witness's recollection of what occurred at the time he observed the crime but rather upon "suggestions" that the accused committed the offense and thus "must be" the person observed. In the event that an identification witness at trial observed the accused at a lineup during which the accused was not represented by counsel, the eyewitness's testimony must be excluded [55] unless the trial court finds that it has an "independent" source, i.e., that it was not fatally related to the lineup and its deprivation of the right to counsel.[56]

Wade raises a number of difficult problems. One is the appropriate role of coun-

sel.[57] Is he to be merely an observer, whose presence is required so that he will have the information necessary effectively to point out to the trial jury any factors in the lineup that should be considered in weighing the probative value of the witnesses's trial testimony? If so, it is arguable that counsel is ill-equipped to perform this function. In the event that the facts at the lineup are put in issue, he would then be required to testify himself, an awkward position for an attorney who is also presenting the case. In the event that he observes conditions which might adversely affect the witnesses' trial testimony, does he have any authority to have them corrected? If he observes them but fails to bring them to the attention of the police until after the witnesses' testimony has been "tainted," has he waived any of his client's rights?

A second difficulty is the "independent source" test. In *Wade* the Court suggested that among the factors to be considered in determining whether specific trial testimony was affected by a defective pre-trial lineup are "the prior opportunity to observe the alleged criminal act, the existence of any discrepancy between any pre-lineup description and the defendant's actual description, any identification prior to lineup of another per-

---

55. It follows, of course, that testimony of other persons concerning any identification which the witness made at the lineup (i. e., "He said, 'That's the man.' "), though otherwise admissible to bolster the in-court identification, is likewise inadmissible.

56. United States v. Wade, 388 U.S. 218, 239–42 (1967). The *Wade* right to exclusion of eyewitness identification sufficiently related to a lineup conducted in violation of the right to counsel must be distinguished from the general due process right to the exclusion of evidence so unreliable that its introduction offends basic concepts of fairness. In Foster v. California, 394 U.S. 440 (1969) a witness was shown the defendant in a lineup with two dissimilar other individuals. The witness then spoke with the defendant personally and without other suspects being present. A week later—when the witness was still "not sure"—he was shown the defendant again in a second lineup. The defendant was the only person in the second lineup who had also appeared in the first. Although *Wade* was inapplicable as the lineups were held before the decision in that case, the Court nevertheless reversed, holding that the procedures involved employed were so defective that the identification of the defendant by the witness at trial and the testimony regarding the earlier identifications at the lineups was "constitutionally inadmissible as a matter of law." But see Stovall v. Denno, 388 U.S. 293 (1967) in which use of an identification by a witness who, while hospitalized by the assailant, identified the defendant when he was shown to her alone and while handcuffed to police officers was held not to offend due process. See generally Annot., 39 A.L.R.3d 791.

57. Polsky, Davis, and Uviller, The Role of the Defense Lawyer at a Line-up in Light of the Wade, Gilbert, and Stovall Decisions, 4 Crim.L.Bull. 273 (1968) (panel discussion); Comment, Right to Counsel at Police Identification Proceedings: A Program in Effective Implementation of An Expanding Constitution, 29 U.Pitt.L.Rev. 65 (1967).

Note the following from the A.B.A. Code of Professional Responsibility (1969):

EC 5–9 ". . . The roles of an advocate and of a witness are inconsistent; the function of an advocate is to advance or argue the cause of another, while that of a witness is to state facts objectively."

DR 5–102A "If, after undertaking employment in contemplated litigation, a lawyer learns or it is obvious that he . . . ought to be called as a witness on behalf of his client, he shall withdraw from the conduct of the trial . . . ."

son, the identification by picture of the defendant prior to the lineup, failure to identify the defendant on a prior occasion, and the lapse of time between the alleged act and the lineup identification." [58] Perhaps, as Mr. Justice Black suggested, what the decision required is "practically impossible," [59] or, as Mr. Justice White argued, it imposes an "impossible burden" on the prosecution and thus amounts to a rule of *per se* exclusion. [60]

Finally, the scope of the underlying right to counsel is not at all clear. Primarily at issue is the extent of its applicability to other procedures that may affect a witness's subsequent trial testimony. The Court has held that taking handwriting exemplars from an accused who had not been accorded representation did not affect the admissibility of the exemplar. [61] If the handwriting exemplar is unrepresentative, the accused could easily provide counsel with others and the inaccuracy could be brought out through the trial adversary process; thus there is only "minimal risk" that the absence of counsel at the initial taking of the exemplar might derogate from the accused's right to fair trial. Similar reasoning was used to support a holding that one from whom a blood sample was taken need not be accorded the right to counsel. [62] The lower courts have split as to the applicability of *Wade* to "alley confrontations" or "on-the-scene" identifications, [63] in

which officers during a field investigation present a subject to the victim or a witness. The possibility of suggestion, of course, is present, and since only a single subject is usually presented the danger of improper suggestion probably exceeds that inherent in the lineup. On the other hand, it would be impossible to provide representation at these confrontations, so the application of the right to counsel would, as a practical matter, amount to a constitutional prohibition of the practice. Moreover, it is arguable that the function of the attorney under *Wade* is simply to act as an observer and since field confrontations are performed under essentially similar circumstances there is less need for an observer who could later document exceptionally suggestive aspects of a particular situation. [64]

The application of the right to counsel to other pretrial matters is not clear. Perhaps the most perplexing issue involves attempts to expand the right to include representation during pretrial psychiatric ex-

---

58. United States v. Wade, 388 U.S. 218, 241 (1967).

59. Id. at 248 (Mr. Justice Black, dissenting in part and concurring in part).

60. Id. at 251. (Mr. Justice White, dissenting in part and concurring in part).

61. Gilbert v. California, 388 U.S. 263, 266–67 (1967).

62. Schmerber v. California, 384 U.S. 757 (1966).

63. Russell v. United States, 133 U.S.App.D.C. 77, 408 F.2d 1280 (1969) cert. denied 395 U.S. 928 (concluding, "with some hesitation", that *Wade* does not apply to an immediate on-the-scene confrontation at 5 a. m.); United States v. Davis, 399 F.2d

948 (2d Cir. 1968) cert. denied 393 U.S. 987. But see Rivers v. United States, 400 F.2d 935 (5th Cir. 1968) (identification by witness made at hospital while victim was being placed in ambulance violated *Wade* right to counsel); United States v. Kinnard, 294 F.Supp. 286 (D.D.C.1968). See generally, LaFave, "Street Encounters" and the Constitution; Terry, Sibron, Peters, and Beyond, 67 Mich.L.Rev. 39, 115–22 (1968); 1969 Law & Soc. Order 104; Comment, Right to Counsel At Scene-of-the-Crime Identifications, 117 U.Pa.L.Rev. 916 (1969) (suggesting that such confrontations should be permissible if conducted in the field, within thirty minutes of the crime, and within a reasonably restricted distance of the scene of the crime); 14 Vill.L.Rev. 535 (1969).

64. The same reasons argue in favor of not applying any similar rule to a procedure in which a victim or witness is shown photographs in an attempt to identify the perpetrator of a crime for apprehension. See Simmons v. United States, 390 U.S. 377 (1968) ("convictions based on eyewitness identification at trial following a pretrial identification by photograph will be set aside on that ground only if the photographic identification procedure was so impermissibly suggestive as to give rise to a very substantial likelihood of irreparable misidentification").

aminations.[65] Although a trial court's refusal to allow an attorney to be present during an examination of the defendant by state psychiatrists has been affirmed on appeal,[66] the United States Court of Appeals for the District of Columbia has recently described a defendant's assertion that under *Wade* he was entitled to counsel during all or part of the psychiatric evaluation proceeding as "anything but frivolous."[67] Here, as in the lineup situation, much of the difficulty revolves around the uncertainty as to the proper role of the attorney. If he is to function as an active participant, there is probably no substitute for a full right to counsel. Yet such activity on his part is likely to be regarded as disruptive of the procedure. On the other hand, if he is to function merely as an observer, perhaps the same function could be performed in a less disruptive (and costly) manner by providing counsel with full access to the medical files or even by recording the sessions for his later perusal.[68]

177. Evidence Fatally Related to Improper Activity: The "Fruit of the Poisonous Tree" Doctrine.[69]

While it is clear that evidence procured directly by improper activity, such as a physical item seized in an unreasonable search, is subject to the exclusionary sanction, improper activity may have a much less direct relationship to evidence offered at trial. Where only an indirect relationship exists, determining whether exclusion is required may be a difficult matter.

In Silverthorne Lumber Co. v. United States,[70] federal officers had improperly seized certain books and papers. The defendant secured a court order directing their return, but not before the officers had photographed them. At trial, the prosecution used the photographs to obtain a subpoena directing the production of the documents. The Supreme Court held that this use of the photographs was improper. "The essence of a provision forbidding the acquisition of evidence in a certain way," the Court declared, "is that not merely evidence so acquired shall not be used before the Court but that it shall not be used at all."[71] If, the Court continued, knowledge of the facts is gained from an independent source, i.e., a source other than the improper activity, the facts may be proved.[72] For example, had the government been able to prove the existence of the documents desired by means other than the observations of them made pursuant to their illegal

65. See Note, The Staff Conference Proceeding at a Pretrial Insanity Examination—Another Critical Stage, 15 Howard L.J. 294 (1969).

66. United States v. Baird, 414 F.2d 700 (2d Cir. 1969) cert. denied 396 U.S. 1005; State v. Whitlow, 45 N.J. 3, 210 A.2d 763 (1965). Cf. People v. DiPiazza, 24 N.Y.2d 342, 300 N.Y.S.2d 545, 248 N.E. 2d 412 (1969). But where a defendant has been subjected to an examination without notice to the defendant's attorney and without court approval, several decisions have found a violation of the right to counsel. Schantz v. Eyman, 418 F.2d 11 (9th Cir. 1969) cert. denied 397 U.S. 1021; People v. Abdul Karim Al-Kanani, 26 N.Y.2d 473, 311 N.Y.S.2d 846, 260 N.E.2d 496 (1970).

67. Thornton v. Corcoran, 132 U.S.App.D.C. 232, 407 F.2d 695, 702 (1969). After extensive discussion of the issue, the court determined that the petitioner's application for a writ of mandamus was not an appropriate vehicle for resolution of the issue. Id. at 703.

68. See Thornton v. Corcoran, 132 U.S.App.D.C. 232, 407 F.2d 695, 702–03 (1969). In United States v. Baird, 414 F.2d 700 (2d Cir.1969) cert. denied 396 U.S. 1005, the prosecution was ordered to give defense counsel a copy of any report of the examination by the psychiatrist, although defense counsel's requests for an order permitting him to be present or that a stenographer transcribe the interview were denied.

69. See generally, R. Maguire, How to Unpoison the Fruit—The Fourth Amendment and the Exclusionary Rule, 55 J.Crim.L., C & P.S. 307 (1964); Pitler, "The Fruit of the Poisonous Tree" Revisited and Shepardized, 56 Cal.L.Rev. 579 (1968); Comment, Fruit of the Poisonous Tree—A Plea for Relevant Criteria, 115 U.Pa.L.Rev. 1136 (1967); Dec.Dig. Crim. Law ⬤394.1(3). The impact of an inadmissible confession upon other evidence is discussed in § 157, supra.

70. 251 U.S. 385 (1920).

71. Id. at 392.

72. Id.

seizure, the proof of their existence would have had an "independent source" and would therefore be permissible.

In Nardone v. United States [73] the Court qualified the basic rule of Silverthorne by suggesting that, although there might be a causal connection between the "poisoned tree" or the initial improper activity and evidence offered at trial, the connection "may have become so attenuated as to dissipate the taint." [74] It did not, however, address itself to the question what attenuation would be sufficient to dissipate the taint of the initial illegality until Wong Sun v. United States: [75]

> "We need not hold that all evidence is 'fruit of the poisonous tree' simply because it would not have come to light but for the illegal actions of the police. Rather, the more apt question in such a case is 'whether, granting establishment of the primary illegality, the evidence to which instant objection is made has been come at by exploitation of that illegality or instead by means sufficiently distinguishable to be purged of the primary taint.'"

The issue was again presented in Harrison v. United States.[76] At Harrison's second trial for felony murder [77] the prosecution introduced three confessions of the defendant. The defendant then took the stand and gave his version of the crime, which placed him at the scene of the crime with the murder weapon but attributed his presence to a lawful purpose and the discharge of the gun to accidental causes. Harrison was convicted, but on appeal the conviction was reversed on the ground that the confessions were erroneous-

ly admitted.[78] At the third trial, the prosecution introduced Harrison's testimony at the second trial. The Supreme Court reversed, holding that the trial testimony was the fruit of the inadmissible confessions and therefore subject to exclusion. Responding to the argument that the tactical decision to testify attenuated the taint, the Court simply replied that "the question is not *whether* [Harrison] made a knowing decision to testify, but *why*." [79] If he decided to testify "in order to overcome the impact of confessions illegally obtained," the testimony was tainted by the same illegality as the initial confessions. It was not necessary that Harrison have established that his trial testimony was as a matter of fact impelled by the use of the inadmissible confessions. "Having . . . [used] the petitioner's unlawfully obtained confessions against him, the Government must show that its illegal action did not induce his testimony." [80]

Mr. Justice White, in a vigorous dissent,[81] argued that the majority adopted "an overly simple and mechanical notion of 'fruits.'" A more appropriate approach, he asserted, would extend the impact of the exclusionary rule by finding a lack of attenuation only if to do so would further the underlying purpose of the exclusionary rule, that is, the deterrence of improper law enforcement activity. At no point did the majority address itself to this question. Had they done so, Mr. Justice White concluded, they would have found the exclusion of Harrison's testimony unjustifiable. Police could not reasonably be expected to anticipate that a confession wrongfully

---

73. 308 U.S. 338 (1939).

74. Id. at 341.

75. 371 U.S. 471, 487–88 (1963).

76. 392 U.S. 219 (1968).

77. His first trial had ended in conviction, but this had been reversed on appeal.

78. Two of the confessions were found to have been obtained in violation of the *Mallory* rule. The third was held inadmissible because at the time it was obtained Harrison was within the original and exclusive jurisdiction of the juvenile court.

79. Harrison v. United States, 392 U.S. 219, 223 (1968).

80. Id. at 225.

81. Id. at 228 (Mr. Justice White, dissenting).

obtained would ever induce a defendant to take the witness stand and make damaging admissions. Thus to hold that their wrongful action called for excluding not only the confession directly resulting but the unforeseeable trial testimony would serve little if any of the underlying deterrent objective of the rule.[82]

The application of the "fruits" doctrine by the lower federal and state courts has been somewhat confusing. As a *sine qua non*, the courts have required a factual causal relationship.[83] Thus where the challenged evidence is discovered before the police activity becomes illegal, it is not causally related to the subsequent illegality.[84] Fine questions of causation are presented in the cases in which it is argued that an incriminating statement was made because of prior illegal activity. The courts have generally treated this as a factual question to be resolved on a case-by-case basis.[85] The most difficult problems are presented when illegal activity early in an investigation does not lead directly to subsequently discovered evidence but arguably stimulated the entire investigatorial process which led to the discovery. Where the facts indicate that the subsequent investigation would have been carried on even had the initial illegality not borne fruit, the courts find no causal relationship.[86] But, as Judge Weinstein recently declared in a thorough examination of the problem, if evidence illegally obtained "leads the government to substantially intensify an investigation", all subsequently discovered evidence is tainted by the initial illegality.[87]

82. Id. at 233–34.

83. In United States v. Carino, 417 F.2d 117 (2d Cir. 1969) officers were told that defendant was a possible suspect in an assault. Looking for powder used in the assault, an illegal search was conducted of his car. A gun was found and replaced under the seat; the car was placed under surveillance. One Novak came to the car and put the gun in a sack; when the officers appeared, he fled but was apprehended and the gun (which he discarded upon being caught) was seized. Holding that all the evidence, including the gun, was admissible, the court found that the seizure of the gun was not causally related to the finding of it during the illegal search but rather would have occurred the same way had the illegal search never been made. See also State v. Darwin, 155 Conn. 124, 230 A.2d 573 (1967) rev'd on other grounds 391 U.S. 346 (results of test for blood made on car seat cushion not inadmissible although earlier test had been made during illegal seizure of the car, because second test would have been made even if first had not been).

84. Smith v. United States, 402 F.2d 771 (9th Cir. 1968) (testimony as to articles seen prior to arrest was not fatally related to any defect in subsequent detention); State v. Warner, 237 A.2d 150 (Me. 1967) (officer's examination of suppressed photographs of automobile did not require suppression of his testimony based on earlier firsthand observation of the vehicle); State v. Beasley, 183 Neb. 681, 163 N.W.2d 783 (1969) (testimony of witness that at the time of robbery defendant was carrying suitcase was not fatally related to later illegal seizure of suitcase which required its suppression).

85. Some courts are willing to infer a causal relationship between an illegal activity known to the defendant and an incriminating statement from little more than those facts. Amador-Gonzalez v. United States, 391 F.2d 308 (5th Cir. 1968) (confession made within a few hours of illegal seizure of heroin "appears to have been a direct result of the discovery of the narcotics" and thus inadmissible); People v. Hendricks, 25 N.Y.2d 129, 303 N.Y.S.2d 33, 250 N.E.2d 323 (1969) (from showing that defendant, who had not incriminated himself, had "immediately responded" to questions with incriminating answers after being confronted with illegally seized incriminating evidence, "it is clear that the admissions are tainted by the primary illegality). But see Ashby v. State, 228 So.2d 400 (Fla.App.1969) (must consider all the circumstances to determine whether confession is related to illegal search rather than rely merely upon a showing of an admission after confrontation with the results of the search). See also People v. Faris, 63 Cal. 2d 541, 47 Cal.Rptr. 370, 407 P.2d 282 (1965).

86. In Durham v. United States, 403 F.2d 190 (9th Cir. 1968) federal officers had conducted an illegal search of defendant which revealed he had no wallet. Two days later, they asked defendant's employer if he had seen defendant's wallet; the employer replied that he had found it, and turned it over to the officers. Counterfeit money was discovered in it. Noting that in the interim another person had volunteered the information that defendant had been seen with a wallet, the court held that the visit to and questioning of the employer were part of a continuing investigation and the finding of the wallet was not fatally related to the illegal search of the defendant.

87. United States v. Schipani, 289 F.Supp. 43, 62 (E.D.N.Y.1968) aff'd 414 F.2d 1262 (2d Cir. 1969).

The Supreme Court has made clear that the existence of a causal relationship does not in every case compel exclusion. The most frequently invoked exception is that which holds that if it can be established that the alleged fruits would have been discovered even had the illegality not occurred, the actual causal relationship between the illegality and the evidence is not determinative.[88] There is no "but for" causal relationship. This approach, of course, presents a difficult factual issue to resolve, but courts have been relatively willing to find that particular evidence would have been discovered had the initial illegality never occurred. Despite the clear indication in *Harrison* that the prosecution bears the burden of establishing the absence of a fatal link between police illegality and offered evidence,[89] some lower courts have been quite willing to assume the absence of causal relationship from a lack of evidence that it exists.[90] Also some sug-

gestion is found that evidence of minimal importance in the investigation may be admissible despite a causal relationship. For example, when information received by means of an illegal wiretap was not used to establish probable cause for arrest but merely to locate the defendant for purposes of effecting the arrest, evidence discovered during a search incidental to an arrest was ruled not the fruit of the initial illegality.[91]

Assuming the existence of a sufficient "but for" causal relationship and the absence of a *"de minimis"* factor, what will so "attenuate" the relationship as to dissipate that taint? The principal factor seems to be an independent intervening act of the subject of the illegality or a third party. The Cali-

But compare Lockridge v. Superior Court, 3 Cal.3d 166, 474 P.2d 683, 89 Cal.Rptr. 731 (1970) cert. denied 402 U.S. 910, noted in 20 Buff.L.Rev. 696 (1971), holding over dissent that victims' identification of the defendant was admissible although an illegal search led police investigators to the inactive file on the victims' robbery. The court indicated that the underlying purpose of the exclusionary rule would not be served by suppression because the fruit of the illegal search was "mere happenstance" and there was no evidence that the police would not have come across the file anyway.

88. Cook v. State, 8 Md.App. 243, 259 A.2d 326 (1969) (gun seized in search of car admissible despite fact that defendant had told police officer before *Miranda* warnings that gun was in car, since evidence was sufficient for trial court to find that officer would have searched car anyway); Duckett v. State, 3 Md.App. 563, 240 A.2d 332 (1968) (evidence found at scene of rape admissible although police were led to scene by inadmissible statement of defendant, "since the victim herself could have undoubtedly identified the scene of the crime"); Pfeifer v. State, 460 P.2d 125 (Okl.Cr.1969) (evidence regarding cattle located by means of information obtained in search incident to improper arrest admissible because they would have been located despite the arrest).

89. See text at note 80, supra.

90. This resolution of the question is especially evident in those cases in which a witness' testimony

is challenged on the ground that he was located by means of unlawfully obtained evidence. Apparently on the assumption that the witness might voluntarily have come forward or have been discovered in routine further investigations, a number of courts have refused to exclude the witness' testimony upon a showing that police learned of his identity by means of illegal evidence. People v. Tucker, 19 Mich.App. 320, 172 N.W.2d 712 (1969) (the witness "might well have come forward voluntarily with his testimony"); People v. Stadd, 32 A.D.2d 940, 303 N.Y.S.2d 699 (1969) (although witness' identity was learned as a result of defendant's reference to her in his inadmissible statement, there was no evidence that defendant's statement was instrumental in inducing her to testify or in affecting the substance of her testimony); People v. Dannic, 30 App.Div.2d 679, 292 N.Y.S.2d 257 (1968); Pfeifer v. States, 460 P.2d 125 (Okl.Cr. 1969); Santiago v. State, 444 S.W.2d 758 (Tex.Cr. App.1969) (the witness would have been discovered in the normal course of investigation). See generally, McLindon v. United States, 117 U.S.App.D.C. 283, 329 F.2d 238, 251 n. 2 (1964). But compare the more stringent approach taken by the Illinois Supreme Court. People v. Albea, 2 Ill.2d 317, 118 N.E.2d 277 (1954) (witness discovered as the result of an illegal search was not competent to testify); People v. Martin, 382 Ill. 192, 46 N.E.2d 997 (1942).

91. Commonwealth v. Glavin, 354 Mass. 69, 235 N.E.2d 547 (1968). Other decisions seems defensible only on the basis that whatever stimulation the results of the illegal activity contributed to the investigation was *de minimis*. United States v. Hoffman, 385 F.2d 501 (7th Cir. 1967) cert. denied 390 U.S. 1031 (in-court identification by witnesses who had seen "mug shots" taken during illegal arrest was not "significantly affected" by having seen the photographs).

fornia Supreme Court has held this aspect essential to attenuation. "That degree of attenuation which suffices to remove the taint from evidence obtained as a result of unlawful police conduct requires at least an intervening independent act by the defendant or a third party which breaks the causal chain linking the illegality and evidence in such a way that the evidence is not in fact obtained 'by exploitation of that illegality.' " [92] Proof of such an intervening act is a difficult matter. In Wong Sun v. United States,[93] Wong Sun had been taken into custody under circumstances which the Court found to constitute an improper arrest. He was, however, released on his own recognizance. He returned "voluntarily" several days later for interrogation. During that interrogation he made incriminating oral statements. On this evidence, the Court held that the connection between the arrest and the oral statements had become sufficiently attenuated to dissipate the taint.[94] There is no indication that a "but for" causal relationship did not exist. Rather, the Court apparently concluded that Wong Sun's decision to submit to interrogation and to answer was a sufficient intervening independent act to deprive the prior arrest of its legal effect on the resulting statements despite any "but for" causal relationship. It is not clear what actions short of the period of freedom in *Wong Sun* will support a finding of a sufficiently voluntary intervening exercise of the will to dissipate the taint. Despite indications to the contrary,[95] the giving of the *Miranda* warning to one who has been confronted with the incriminating fruits of an illegal search has been held not in itself to justify a finding that a subsequent incriminating admission was not fatally related to the search.[96] Perhaps a formal appearance before a magistrate would attenuate the connection between any prior illegality and subsequent statements to remove the taint; the magistrate may be regarded as sufficiently independent that his warning can be assumed to have removed the coercive effect of prior illegality.

The lower courts have been unwilling to impose upon the prosecution the burden of demonstrating the absence of a "but for" causal relationship between police illegality and evidence offered at trial. The burden may be impossible to meet in most circumstances. Also, the lower courts have been unable to formulate a satisfactory definition of the degree of attenuation required to remove the taint of illegality when such a "but for" causal relationship does exist. The functional approach urged by Mr. Justice White in his *Harrison* dissent, which would find attenuation if the deterrent value to improper police misconduct was nonexistent or outweighed by the cost of excluding relevant evidence, is attractive from a theoretical point of view. It does, however, require a sophisticated balance that may be impracticable to achieve in individual cases. Perhaps the best solution would consist of extending the taint of illegal conduct to any evidence the obtaining of which was affected by the illegality. Only if the impact of the illegality was *de minimis* would an "in fact" causal relationship not require exclusion. This rule would be easier of application than the alternatives, and would maximize the deterrent objective of the exclusionary rule. In some situations the particular increase in the deterrent function might be outweighed

---

92. People v. Sesslin, 68 Cal.2d 418, 428, 67 Cal. Rptr. 409, 416, 439 P.2d 321, 328 (1968) cert. denied 393 U.S. 1080.

93. 371 U.S. 471 (1963).

94. Id. at 491.

95. See Collins v. Beto, 348 F.2d 823 (5th Cir. 1965), excluding the statement but suggesting that the result might have been different had defendant been effectively afforded the assistance of counsel before he made the statement.

96. People v. Johnson, 70 Cal.2d 541, 75 Cal.Rptr. 401, 450 P.2d 865 (1969) cert. denied 395 U.S. 969.

by the cost of excluding relevant evidence, but in the long run it is likely that the overall cost would be justified.

178.   Use of Otherwise Inadmissible Evidence for Impeachment Purposes.[97]

While the exclusionary rule, where applicable, bars the use of tainted evidence in proving facts directly in issue, an exception of uncertain scope grew up under the protection of Walder v. United States.[98] Walder, at his trial on several counts charging narcotics violations, took the stand. He denied the alleged transactions and attributed the testimony of the prosecution witnesses to personal animosity. Then, responding to questions from his own attorney, Walder testified that he had never improperly sold, possessed, or otherwise had anything to do with narcotics. On cross-examination, he was asked whether two years earlier narcotics had been taken from him at his home. In fact, he had then been charged with possession of heroin, but the charge had been dismissed after the trial court suppressed the single grain of heroin he was alleged to have possessed, on the basis that it had been unlawfully seized. Walder, however, denied that the heroin had in fact been taken from him, and the government offered the testimony of an agent that a capsule of heroin had in fact been taken from Walder. This testimony was admitted, but the jury was instructed to consider it only for the purpose of determining Walder's credibility and not for the purpose of deciding his guilt.

On appeal the Supreme Court affirmed. Noting that Walder had gone far beyond denying the crimes with which he had been charged and had "made the sweeping claim that he had never dealt in or possessed any narcotics", the Court found no justification "for letting the defendant affirmatively resort to perjurious testimony in reliance on the Government's disability to challenge his credibility." [99] So to extend the exclusionary rule, Mr. Justice Frankfurter said for the Court, "would be a perversion of the Fourth Amendment."

Following *Walder*, lower courts developed an exception to the exclusionary rule applicable when a defendant testified at trial [1] and made affirmative assertions [2] regarding matters collateral to the issue of guilt of the crime charged.[3] Under these circumstances,

---

97. See generally, Cole, Impeaching with Unconstitutionally Obtained Evidence: Some Reflections on the Palatable Fruit of the Poisonous Tree, 18 DePaul L.Rev. 25 (1968); Comment, The Collateral Use Doctrine: From Walder to Miranda, 62 Nw. U.L.Rev. 912 (1968); Comment, The Impeachment Exception to the Exclusionary Rules, 34 U.Chi.L. Rev. 939 (1967). Cf. Annot., 80 A.L.R.2d 478 (1968).

Impeachment by contradiction is treated generally in § 47, supra; inadmissible evidence as "opening the door" is discussed in § 57, supra.

98. 347 U.S. 62 (1954).

99. Id. at 65.

1. Comment, The Collateral Use Doctrine: From Walder to Miranda, 62 Nw.U.L.Rev. 912, 921 (1968).

2. In *Walder*, the Court distinguished Agnello v. United States, 269 U.S. 20 (1925) in which inadmissible evidence was held improperly used to impeach a defendant's negative response to the question of whether he had ever seen narcotics before, asked on *cross-examination*. Walder v. United States, 347 U.S. 62, 66 (1954).

3. In *Walder*, Mr. Justice Frankfurter emphasized that every defendant is guaranteed by the Constitution the "fullest opportunity" to meet accusations against him and therefore must be free to deny "all elements of the case against him" without surrendering his right to have improperly seized evidence excluded. Walder v. United States, 347 U.S. 62, 65 (1954). How far a testifying defendant could go without rendering otherwise inadmissible evidence admissible for impeachment purposes presented a troublesome problem. Compare United States v. Curry, 358 F.2d 904 (2d Cir. 1966) cert. denied 385 U.S. 873 (testimony by defendant that he participated in the planning of the robbery but not in its preparation was on a "collateral" matter and brought *Walder* into operation) with Johnson v. United States, 120 U.S.App.D.C. 69, 344 F.2d 163 (1964) (testimony by defendant as to his version of skirmish which led to criminal charges did not bring *Walder* into operation). Tate v. United States, 109 U.S.App.D.C. 13, 283 F.2d 377, 380 (1960) suggested that *Walder* would be brought into operation only if the defendant's testimony involved unlawful prior acts, and Bailey v. United States, 117 U.S.App.D.C. 241, 328 F.2d 542, 543

evidence obtained in violation of Fourth Amendment rights and statements illegally obtained were admissible to impeach the defendant. Miranda v. Arizona,[4] however, contained language suggesting that statements obtained in violation of the requirements of that case were inadmissible for *all* purposes.[5] A number of courts have read this as holding the *Walder* exception inapplicable to statements obtained in violation of *Miranda*.[6] The awkwardness of distinguishing between evidence obtained in violation of Fifth and Sixth Amendment rights and that obtained in violation of other constitutional rights

suggested that *Miranda* had overruled *Walder*.

Harris v. New York [7] made clear that this was not the case. Harris, charged with two sales of narcotics to a police undercover agent, took the stand in his own behalf. He denied having participated in the first transaction at all, and testified that in the second he sold the officer bags containing only baking powder. On cross-examination, a statement obtained by police from Harris in admitted violation of *Miranda* was used for impeachment purposes. The substance of the statement was that on both occasions Harris had acted as a middleman for the police agent and had purchased narcotics for him. The United States Supreme Court affirmed, declaring that "the shield provided by *Miranda* cannot be perverted into a license to use perjury by way of a defense, free from the risk of confrontation with prior inconsistent utterances." Acknowledging that Harris was impeached as to testimony "bearing more directly on the crimes charged" than Walder had been, the majority held that this did not require a result different from that reached in *Walder*. Responding to the argument that permitting such use of otherwise inadmissible statements would impair the effectiveness of the exclusionary rule as a deterrent to police misconduct, the Court termed the assertion as "speculative" and stated that "sufficient deterrence flows when the evidence in question is made unavailable to the prosecution in its case in chief."

Mr. Justice Brennan, dissenting,[8] expressed concern that the majority holding

(1964) cert. denied 377 U.S. 972 suggested that *Walder* was applicable only if the testimony concerned a "major" rather than a "minor" point. In Inge v. United States, 123 U.S.App.D.C. 6, 356 F.2d 345, 349–50 (1966) the Court of Appeals for the District of Columbia adopted a functional approach under which *Walder* was applicable only if the situation was such that the truth of the impeaching statement did not itself tend to establish guilt. Several courts rejected any attempt to make the application of *Walder* depend upon the nature of the defendant's testimony, terming such attempts "virtually unworkable." Groshart v. United States, 392 F.2d 172, 179 (9th Cir. 1968); State v. Brewton, 247 Or. 241, 422 P.2d 581 (1967) cert. denied 387 U.S. 943.

4. 384 U.S. 436 (1966).

5. "[S]tatements merely intended to be exculpatory by the defendant are often used to impeach his testimony at trial or to demonstrate untruths in the statement given under interrogation and thus to prove guilt by implication. These statements are incriminating in any meaningful sense of the word and may not be used without the full warnings and effective waiver required for any other statement." Miranda v. Arizona, 384 U.S. 436, 477 (1966).

6. Proctor v. United States, 131 U.S.App.D.C. 241, 404 F.2d 819, 821 (1968); United States v. Fox, 403 F.2d 97, 102–03 (2d Cir. 1968) (*Walder* does not apply to statements unconstitutionally obtained); Groshart v. United States, 392 F.2d 172, 178 (9th Cir. 1968); State v. Galasco, 217 So.2d 326 (Fla. 1968) (statement taken in violation of *Miranda* inadmissible for impeachment, but on facts admission was harmless error). Cf. Agius v. United States, 413 F.2d 915 (5th Cir. 1969) (continued vitality of *Walder* as applied to statements is "extremely questionable"). Contra, State v. Butler, 19 Ohio St.2d 55, 249 N.E.2d 818 (1969). But cf. People v. Kulis, 18 N.Y.2d 318, 274 N.Y.S.2d 873, 221 N.E.2d 541 (1966) (statement taken in violation of *Escobedo* admissible for impeachment purposes).

7. 401 U.S. 222 (1971). See Dershowitz and Ely, Harris v. New York: Some Anxious Observations on the Candor and Logic of the Emerging Nixon Majority, 80 Yale L.J. 1198 (1971); Note, Impeachment by Unconstitutionally Obtained Evidence: The Rule of Harris v. New York, 1971 Wash.U.L.Q. 441.

8. Justices Douglas and Marshall joined this opinion, and Mr. Justice Black dissented without opinion, creating a 5–4 division.

would "seriously undermine" the objective of deterring improper police behavior, would jeopardize the values underlying the privilege against compelled self-incrimination, and would endanger governmental stability by placing courts in the position of aiding and abetting the lawbreaking police officer. Most important, however, he argued that permitting such use of inadmissible statements constituted an infringement upon the defendant's constitutional right to decide whether or not to testify in his own behalf, a right which under Griffin v. California [9] must remain "unfettered."

The impact of *Harris* is likely to be significant. First, it establishes that the *Walder* exception is alive and well in regard to statements obtained in violation of *Miranda* rights. It is virtually certain that the same result would be reached if the evidence at issue has been obtained in violation of Fourth Amendment rights. Only where there is reason to doubt the reliability of the evidence—as in the case of the traditional involuntary confession [10]—is the Court likely to hold the evidence inadmisisble for *all* purposes. Second, *Harris* broadens the *Walder* exception by virtually eliminating the requirement that the defendant have opened up a "collateral" matter.[11] Harris' testimony amounted to little more than a denial of guilt of the specific offenses charged by denying participation in the transaction or by denying that the substance sold was that charged. Apparently all that will now be required is that the defendant testify and that the otherwise inadmissible evidence be relevant to his credibility.

In the long run, the *Harris* decision seems unfortunate. Assuming that the exclusionary rule has some effect in preventing police misconduct, permitting such use would seem to significantly impair that impact. In addition—and more importantly—the decision imposes an unreasonable burden upon the accused's right to testify in his own behalf. Although, as the majority pointed out, a criminal defendant who seeks to testify cannot demand immunity from all impeachment, the propriety of permitting impeachment of a specific kind must be a matter of balancing the value of the impeaching evidence against the costs of its admission. Given the suspicion which a violation of constitutional rights casts upon the reliability of a statement, the probative value of the statement would seem generally to be outweighed by the costs of burdening a defendant's decision to testify, of diluting the deterrent impact of the exclusionary rule, and of aligning the courts with the lawless police interrogator. Even where the evidence is not testimonial (and the suggestions of unreliability are thus removed from consideration), the factors still seem to weigh in favor of exclusion.[12]

179. Enforcement of the Right to Exclusion: (a) Standing to Object.[13]

Insofar as the purpose of an exclusionary rule is to prevent improper investigatory

---

9. 380 U.S. 609 (1965), prohibiting comment upon an accused's failure to testify in his own behalf at trial; see § 131, supra.

10. Cf. People v. Underwood, 61 Cal.2d 113, 37 Cal. Rptr. 313, 389 P.2d 937 (1964) (involuntary confession not admissible for impeachment purposes). See generally, Annot., 89 A.L.R.2d 478 (1963).

11. See note 3, supra.

12. The views here expressed are not inconsistent with allowing testimony given by an accused in support of a motion to suppress to be used as a prior inconsistent statement to impeach contradictory testimony given by him at the trial. See F. R. Ev. (R.D.1971) 104(d); § 179, n. 31, infra; § 131, n. 21, supra.

13. See generally, Grove, Suppression of Illegally Obtained Evidence: The Standing Requirement on Its Last Legs, 18 Catholic U.L.Rev. 150 (1968); White and Greenspan, Standing to Object to Search and Seizure, 118 U.Pa.L.Rev. 333 (1970); Note, Search and Seizure: Admissibility of Illegally Acquired Evidence Against Third Parties, 66 Colum. L.Rev. 400 (1966); Comment, Standing to Object to an Unreasonable Search and Seizure, 34 U.Chi. L.Rev. 342 (1967); Note, Standing and the Fourth Amendment, 38 U.Cinn.L.Rev. 691 (1969); Note,

tactics by eliminating the incentive for them, it would seem that any defendant should be able to invoke it to prevent the use against him of evidence improperly obtained. This, however, is not the case. In Jones v. United States [14] the Supreme Court made clear that a defendant may obtain suppression of relevant but improperly obtained evidence only if he establishes that he himself was a victim of the improper activity which forms the basis for the challenge to the evidence. Only then does he have "standing" to challenge the admissibility of the evidence.

Despite widespread criticism of the standing requirement by commentators,[15] the Court reaffirmed the requirement in 1969 in Alderman v. United States.[16] Fourth Amendment rights, Mr. Justice White asserted, are personal rights which cannot be asserted vicariously. "There is no necessity to exclude evidence against one defendant in order to protect the rights of another." Turning to the argument that permitting one defendant to obtain the exclusion of evidence on the ground that it has been obtained in violation of the rights of another would further the "police-the-police" purpose of the exclusionary rule, the Court engaged in a balancing test. Weighing the marginal increase in the effectiveness of the exclusionary rule anticipated from the abandonment of the standing requirement against the cost in terms of the suppression of reliable evidence, the Court indicated that the former did not justify the latter. Consequently the Court declined the petitioners' invitation to abrogate the standing requirement even to the limited extent of permitting one defendant or conspirator to assert a right to exclusion based upon the violation of a codefendant's or co-conspirator's Fourth Amendment rights.

The task of defining when a defendant seeking suppression has established that he was a victim of the improper activity involved in the obtaining of the challenged evidence is more difficult than might be supposed. The situations can be grouped into several categories:

Interest in the premises searched. A defendant may by virtue of his legal interest in the premises invaded or by virtue of his presence on those premises at the time of the invasion establish standing to challenge evidence obtained as the result of the invasion.[17]

In *Alderman* the Court indicated that a homeowner whose home was illegally searched during his absence would have standing to challenge evidence obtained pursuant to the search.[18] It therefore follows that one has standing to challenge the fruits of eaves-

Standing to Object to an Unlawful Search and Seizure, 1965 Wash.U.L.Q. 488; 29 Am.Jur.2d Evidence §§ 418–24; Annot., 86 A.L.R.2d 984, 992 (transiently occupied hotel rooms); Annot., 78 A.L.R.2d 246; Annot., 50 A.L.R.2d 531, 577–83; Annot., 4 L.Ed.2d 1999; Dec.Dig. Criminal Law ☞394.5(2), Search & Seizure ☞7(26).

14. 362 U.S. 257 (1960).

15. E. g., Comment, Standing to Object to an Unreasonable Search and Seizure, 34 U.Chi.L.Rev. 342, 350 (1967), arguing that the standing requirement rested heavily upon the Court's view that underlying the exclusionary rule was a Fifth Amendment personal right to avoid contributing to one's own incrimination. Thus when, in Linkletter v. Walker, 381 U.S. 618 (1965), the Court abandoned the personal incrimination theory in favor of a general deterrence rationale for the rule, the basis for the standing limitation disappeared. This argument— that the "right" involved is not a personal right but a general right to be free from the danger of unreasonable searches—was rejected in Alderman v. United States, 394 U.S. 165, 174 (1969).

16. 394 U.S. 165 (1969).

17. If there is sufficient interest in the premises to confer standing, it is of no consequence that the person challenging the suit may lack an interest in the material seized. Thus if a union official has standing to challenge a search of his office, he may challenge the introduction against him of papers belonging to the union and seized in the search. Mancusi v. DeForte, 392 U.S. 364, 367 n. 4 (1968).

18. Alderman v. United States, 394 U.S. 165, 177 n. 10 (1969). For an early discussion, see Edwards, Standing to Suppress Unreasonably Seized Evidence, 47 Nw.U.L.Rev. 471 (1952).

dropping which results in the overhearing of conversations occurring on one's premises, whether he is himself a participant in those conversations or even present when they take place. Nor is ownership essential. A lessee, for example, has a sufficient interest in the leased premises to confer standing to challenge their invasion.[19] One who rents a hotel room for a limited period of time is, during this period, no different from the owner.[20]

One need not, however, have a legal interest in the premises to bring this rule into play. In *Jones*, the Court rejected the government's invitation to distinguish between those with dominion of the premises sufficient to create standing and those, such as "mere guests and invitees," with some right of use but with too tenuous an interest to confer standing. Finding it "unnecessary and ill-advised to import such subtle distinctions into the law of searches and seizures", the Court held that presence on the premises with the permission of the owner or lessee at the time of the invasion was sufficient to confer standing.[21]

The search may, of course, be so limited in scope that even one rightfully on the premises within the meaning of *Jones* may lack standing. Thus in United States v. Humphrey[22] a car containing a driver and several passengers was stopped and the driver searched. Although the passengers were rightfully within the car, they were held to lack standing to challenge the search of the driver. On the other hand, standing cannot be defeated by waiting until a person rightfully on the premises leaves. In Spinelli v. United States,[23] officers waited until Spinelli left an apartment to execute a search warrant. When he entered the hallway, he was arrested and the search conducted. Nevertheless, he was found to have standing under *Jones* to challenge the search of the apartment on the basis of his presence. "It cannot matter", the court held, "that the agents preferred to delay the arrest until petitioner stepped into the hallway. . . . ."[24]

Ownership or right to possession of the items seized. The assertion of rights in the items seized will give rise to standing to challenge their search or seizure.[25] If, however, a defendant has retained ownership but relinquished possession to another, the other person may have the power to consent to a search which reveals the item; if the item has been revealed without an illegal search, its seizure may be entirely proper.[26]

---

19. Jones v. United States, 362 U.S. 257 (1960).

20. United States v. Jeffers, 342 U.S. 48 (1951) (defendant had standing to object to search of hotel room rented by third person when third person had permitted him to use it). But a search of a hotel room after the guest has vacated is not subject to the guest's challenge. Abel v. United States, 362 U.S. 217, 241 (1960).

21. A person on the premises unlawfully or without the consent of the owner may not have standing. See Johnson v. Smith, 414 F.2d 645 (5th Cir. 1969) (one defendant went to codefendant's apartment for first time and upon finding no one there entered; he "was not a guest or invitee, was not domiciled there, nor was he rightfully there with [his codefendant's] knowledge or consent" and therefore lacked standing to challenge a search of the apartment made while he was present).

22. 409 F.2d 1055 (10th Cir. 1969).

23. 393 U.S. 410 (1969).

24. Id. at 412 n. 2. But see Craft v. United States, 403 F.2d 360, 363 (9th Cir. 1968) (defendant, who got out of car before it arrived at customs inspection station, lacked standing to challenge search of car at station).

25. United States v. Eldridge, 302 F.2d 463 (4th Cir. 1962) (ownership of car gave defendant standing to challenge its search, even though he had loaned it to another person who was in possession at the time of the search); Schwimmer v. United States, 232 F.2d 855, 860 (8th Cir. 1956) cert. denied 352 U.S. 833 (owner of books and papers in possession of third party had standing to move to quash subpoenas directing third party to produce them, on ground that compelled production would be an unreasonable search and seizure). Cf. Harlow v. United States, 301 F.2d 361 (5th Cir. 1962) cert. denied 371 U.S. 814 (author of letter seized had standing to challenge its seizure).

26. See § 169, supra.

"Automatic" standing to avoid the necessity of a damaging admission. In *Jones,* petitioner had been charged with two offenses involving narcotics. Both could be established solely through proof of possession of the narcotics whose suppression was sought. Considering the nature of the charges, he argued, the standing requirement posed him with a dilemma. On the one hand, if at the hearing on the motion to suppress he testified that he had a sufficient interest in either the premises searched or the narcotics seized to create standing, this testimony might be admissible at trial against him. On the other hand if he took inconsistent positions with regard to his connection with the premises and the narcotics at the hearing on the motion and the trial itself, he might well perjure himself. To hold Jones to the normal standing requirement, the Court concluded, would be to permit the government to have the advantage of contradictory positions—denying standing because of the lack of interest in the narcotics, but securing conviction on the basis of the existence of an interest. To avoid this dilemma, an "automatic standing" rule was created: "In cases where the indictment itself charges possession, the defendant in a very real sense is revealed as a 'person aggrieved by an unlawful search and seizure' " and therefore is automatically granted standing to challenge the admissibility of those items he is charged with having possessed.[27] It is clear that this aspect of standing applies not only to charges of possession of contraband *per se,* but also to items whose possession is not inherently illegal but is so under the circumstances charged.[28] It is less

clear, however, whether this exception applies to items merely the fruit of a crime.[29] Mere possession of the items may not be sufficient for conviction, but it may be of significant evidentiary value. The same, of course, may be said of any items of evidentiary value, but there is general agreement that as to those items there is no "automatic standing" rule.[30] The matter may be academic, however. Given the Supreme Court's subsequent holding that testimony on a hearing at a motion to suppress is not admissible at the trial on the merits,[31] the dilemma posed by all the automatic standing cases is much less aggravated than it was formerly. Except insofar as it removes the incentive for a defendant to perjure himself, the automatic standing rule is now unnecessary. A defendant's interest in being able to assert inconsistent positions is significantly different from his interest in being able to assert his right to the exclusion of illegally seized evidence without fear of jeopardizing his right to put the prosecution to its proof on the issue of guilt. The former seems insufficient to support an exception to an otherwise justifiable rule.

Standing based upon a reasonable expectation of privacy. In Mancusi v. DeForte [32] the Supreme Court indicated that the standing touchstone may be undergoing further evolution. DeForte, a union official, shared

27. Jones v. United States, 362 U.S. 257, 264 (1960).

28. Niro v. United States, 388 F.2d 535 (1st Cir. 1968) (defendant charged with knowing possession of stolen goods that had been transported in interstate commerce entitled to automatic standing); Simpson v. United States, 346 F.2d 291 (10th Cir. 1965) (automatic standing rule applied to one charged with unlawful possession of an automobile transported in interstate commerce).

29. See People v. Cefaro, 21 N.Y.2d 252, 287 N.Y.S. 2d 371, 234 N.E.2d 423 (1967) (standing denied to defendants not present in one defendant's room when it was searched and fruits of crime found, although unexplained possession of stolen goods is sufficient evidence to support conviction of theft offenses which were charged). See White and Greenspan, Standing to Object to Search and Seizure, 118 U.Pa.L.Rev. 333, 340–42 (1970).

30. E. g., Stassi v. United States, 410 F.2d 946, 952 (5th Cir. 1969); Ramirez v. United States, 294 F.2d 277 (9th Cir. 1961).

31. Simmons v. United States, 390 U.S. 377 (1968). The question remains whether the testimony may be used for impeachment purposes. See § 131, n. 21, § 178, n. 12, supra.

32. 392 U.S. 364 (1968).

a large office with several other union officials. At a time when DeForte was present and protesting, state officials conducted a warrantless search of the office and seized certain union records. These records were admitted in DeForte's subsequent prosecution. Although DeForte was, at the time of the search, legitimately on the premises and therefore apparently had standing under *Jones*, the Court used a different rationale to justify its holding that standing existed. Citing Katz v. United States [33] for the proposition that the protection of the Fourth Amendment "depends not upon a property right in the invaded place but upon whether the area was one in which there was a reasonable expectation of freedom from governmental intrusion," the Court posed the "crucial issue" as "whether, in light of all the circumstances, DeForte's office was such a place." [34] Since DeForte could reasonably have expected that only the other union officers with whom he shared the office and their business guests would enter and that the records would not be examined without the permission of union officials, the office met the standard. Then, referring back to *Jones*, the Court suggested that the basis for that decision had been that Jones also had an equivalent expectation of privacy.

DeForte is a logical and necessary development of Fourth Amendment doctrine. If standing requires a violation of Fourth Amendment rights, and if the question whether a violation has occurred depends upon whether a reasonable expectation of privacy was violated, it necessarily follows that standing depends upon violation of a reasonable expectation of privacy. This emphasis upon expectations of privacy may portend an expansion of Fourth Amendment protection. *DeForte* merely makes clear

that the standing requirement poses no barrier to relief for one whose own Fourth Amendment rights have been violated. [35]

Several alternatives have been suggested to the existing approach to the standing question. One, adopted only in California, [36] is the complete abandonment of a standing requirement. A second [37] would grant wide

33. 389 U.S. 347 (1967).

34. Mancusi v. DeForte, 392 U.S. 364, 368 (1968).

35. McDonald v. United States, 335 U.S. 451 (1948) adds a confusing note. McDonald and his codefendant, Washington, were in a room which McDonald had rented in a private home. At a time when both McDonald and Washington were in the room, police illegally entered and seized items used in a gambling operation. After holding that the items should have been suppressed as to McDonald, the Court noted that apart from these items there was "little or no" evidence against Washington. Then, assuming that no privacy interest of Washington was invaded, the Court held that the denial of McDonald's motion was also prejudicial to Washington. If the property had been returned to McDonald, the majority reasoned, "it would not have been available for use at the trial." This, of course, suggests that a codefendant without standing may nevertheless complain of a denial of his codefendant's motion, thus avoiding the natural result of his own lack of standing to move for suppression. In commenting on *McDonald* in *Alderman*, Mr. Justice Harlan pointed out that two of the five justices of the majority joined in an opinion holding that Washington had standing because of his presence on the premises. "It is not at all clear that the McDonald opinion," he concluded, "would automatically extend standing to a codefendant." Alderman v. United States, 394 U.S. 165, 173, n. 7 (1969).

36. People v. Martin, 45 Cal.2d 755, 290 P.2d 855 (1955). In People v. Varnum, 66 Cal.2d 808, 427 P. 2d 772, 59 Cal.Rptr. 108 (1967) appeal dismissed and cert. denied 390 U.S. 529, the California Supreme Court refused to abandon a standing requirement to challenge evidence obtained in violation of Escobedo v. Illinois, 378 U.S. 478 (1964). See 81 Harv.L.Rev. 707 (1968); Note, Standing to Object to the Admission of Evidence Obtained in Violation of Another's Fifth and Sixth Amendment Rights: People v. Varnum, 15 U.C.L.A.L.Rev. 1060 (1968). See also State v. Isaacs, 24 Ohio App.2d 115, 265 N.E.2d 327 (1970), granting standing to the defendant to raise the denial of the right to counsel at the pretrial identification of the individual the defendant was charged with having aided and abetted in a robbery. The court relied heavily upon a purported rule that only evidence which would have been admissible against the principal may be admitted to prove the principal's guilt at the trial of the aider and abettor.

37. Note, Standing and the Fourth Amendment, 38 U.Cinn.L.Rev. 691, 701–02 (1969).

discretion to a trial judge but direct him to find standing if permitting the specific defendant to challenge the activity would significantly further the policy objective of deterring improper activity. The focus of the inquiry would be upon the issue whether it was foreseeable at the time of the activity that the party now seeking standing would be implicated. If this was foreseeable, granting the party standing would serve to discourage such activity. If this was not foreseeable, however, imposing the exclusionary penalty could not be expected to serve the deterrent function. A third alternative would grant standing to anyone who could establish that he was one against whom the activity was directed.[38] Thus if his conviction was among the conscious police objectives he could be said to have been the victim of the activity. This rule would not attempt to stimulate police awareness of who might be affected by the activity, but would limit itself to depriving the police of the right to use the evidence against those they actually intended to use it against.

The first alternative, of course, is subject to the objection that the value of whatever increased deterrence of improper police activity might result would not be offset by the cost in terms of the exclusion of relevant evidence. The second and third are subject to the same objection, although the cost under either would probably be somewhat less than in the case of the first. Both the second and the third would require relatively complex factual inquiries that might be too difficult to make reliably or at least too time consuming to be justifiable.[39] The third alternative might be preferable to the second

on the ground that the police should not be penalized for what they did not intend, even if they should have foreseen the result. This approach, of course, assumes that imposing the exclusionary penalty either would not be effective in causing the police to anticipate more carefully what the results of proposed conduct would be, or at least would accomplish this only at too great a cost in terms of relevant evidence.

180. Enforcement of the Right to Exclusion: (b) Time at Which Objection Must be Raised.[40]

Objections to the admissibility of evidence generally need not be made until the evidence is offered at trial by the objector's opponent.[41] Objections based upon the manner in which the offered proof was obtained, however, often raise questions of fact and law that may exceed in complexity and time consumption the determination of guilt or innocence. Consequently, most jurisdictions have developed by court rule, decision, or statute, requirements that, when practicable, objections of this nature be raised prior to trial.[42] This procedure permits the resolu-

---

38. Alderman v. United States, 394 U.S. 165, 208–09 (1969) (Mr. Justice Fortas, dissenting). The suggestion is supported in White and Greenspan, Standing to Object to Search and Seizure, 118 U.Pa.L.Rev. 333, 349–356 (1970).

39. See Alderman v. United States, 394 U.S. 165, 188, n. 1 (1969) (Mr. Justice Harlan, concurring).

40. See generally Annot., 50 A.L.R.2d 531, 583–92; Dec.Dig. Criminal Law ⊂⇒394.6(3).

41. See § 52, supra.

42. F.R.Crim.P. 41(e); State v. Wallace, 254 La. 477, 224 So.2d 461 (1969) (statutory requirement that motion be made three judicial days before trial); Commonwealth v. Cooper, 356 Mass. 74, 248 N.E. 2d 253 (1969) (rules of trial courts require that motion be made within ten days of entry of plea of not guilty); Commonwealth v. Pinno, 433 Pa. 1, 248 A.2d 26 (1968) (rules require motion not later than five days before trial); State v. Haynes, 233 Ore. 292, 377 P.2d 166 (1962) (case law requires motion prior to trial); State v. Duckett, 73 Wash.2d 692, 440 P.2d 485 (1968) (case law requires motion to be made within a reasonable time before case is called for trial). Even if a pretrial motion is not required, objections may not be saved until after the prosecution has completed its entire case. E. g., Veales v. State, 374 P.2d 792 (Okl.Cr.1962). Some jurisdictions impose no pretrial motion requirement, Bosley v. State, 414 S.W.2d 468 (Tex. Cr.App.1967) cert. denied 389 U.S. 876, although pretrial motions may be described as the "better practice", State v. Kananen, 97 Ariz. 233, 399 P.2d 426 (1965).

tion of the admissibility question at a separate hearing and allows the guilt trial to proceed uninterrupted by complex collateral investigations.

Although rules differ among jurisdictions, most conform approximately to Rule 41(e) of the Federal Rules of Criminal Procedure, which the Supreme Court has described as "carrying out an important social policy and not a narrow, finicky procedural requirement."[43] Rule 41(e) requires that a motion to suppress evidence obtained by an unlawful search and seizure[44] be made before trial unless the defendant was not aware of the grounds for the motion or opportunity to make the motion did not exist. The trial court may, however, in its discretion entertain an untimely motion. An untimely motion has been entertained under this discretionary authority when an unusual series of burglaries and a fire in counsel's office prevented timely presentation of a motion,[45] when defendant established that during a search of his room he was kept in the hall and consequently did not know that any items were seized,[46] and for no stated reason whatsoever.[47] On the other hand, it has been held that the mere fact that trial counsel

was not retained until shortly before trial does not require that he be permitted to make untimely objections, when defendant was represented by competent counsel before trial counsel took over the case.[48] A primary factor in determining whether to permit trial objection when neither of the specific exceptions of Rule 41(e) can be invoked is the extent to which permitting the objection would disrupt the trial. Thus objection might properly be heard if during the course of the trial on the merits facts are developed which show the impropriety of the means by which the evidence is obtained.[49] When facts of this kind are already before the court ruling on the motion, a determination of the validity of an objection requires little interruption of the trial and the rationale for the rule requiring prehearing objection does not apply. A court may even hear an untimely motion, consider the cost of disposing of it on the merits, and, if it determines that such a disposition would be too costly, find it untimely and decline to rule on the merits.[50]

As the grounds for objections to evidence increase, pretrial resolution of them raises a

---

43. Jones v. United States, 362 U.S. 257, 264 (1960).

44. The rule does not, by its terms, apply to confessions allegedly obtained in violation of rights of the accused. It has been held, however, that the pretrial motion procedure is available to test the admissibility of a confession. Smith v. Katzenbach, 122 U.S.App.D.C. 113, 351 F.2d 810, 814–15 (1965). The proposed amendments to the Federal Rules of Criminal Procedure would require that objections to confessions be raised before trial. Committee on Rules of Practice and Procedure of the Judicial Conference of the United States, Preliminary Draft of Proposed Amendments to the Federal Rules of Criminal Procedure for the United States District Courts, Advisory Committee's Note to Rule 10, p. 30 (1970).

45. United States v. Valdes, 280 F.Supp. 172 (S.D. N.Y.1968) aff'd 417 F.2d 335 (2d Cir. 1969).

46. People v. Thomas, 88 Ill.App.2d 71, 232 N.E.2d 259 (1967).

47. United States v. Adams, 289 F.Supp. 838 (D.D.C. 1968).

48. United States v. Bennett, 409 F.2d 888, 901 (2d Cir. 1969) cert. denied 396 U.S. 852. The motion to suppress cannot be used to make items unavailable to the government for a purpose not directly related to the criminal prosecution. United States v. McDonough, 265 F.Supp. 368 (W.D.Pa.1967) (motion made after plea of guilty and sentence for the purpose of preventing the use of material by the Internal Revenue Service in determining tax liability was improper); Von Pickrell v. People, 163 Colo. 591, 431 P.2d 1003 (1967) (motion made after plea of guilty to prevent use of material at sentencing hearing not proper). But a pre-indictment motion to suppress may be used to prevent the prosecution from presenting the evidence to a grand jury, even though an indictment returned by the grand jury would probably not be subject to attack on the grounds that it was based on improperly seized evidence. 8A Cipes, Moore's Federal Practice ¶ 41.08[1] (1969).

49. Amos v. United States, 255 U.S. 313 (1921).

50. United States v. Maloney, 402 F.2d 448 (1st Cir. 1968) cert. denied 394 U.S. 947.

problem that weighs against the interests promoted by the requirement of pretrial objection. Pretrial hearings on objections to prosecution evidence may turn out to have been an unjustified expenditure of time if defense objections are vague or groundless or if the prosecution decides not to offer the challenged evidence. The problem is especially troublesome when the subject of the objection is not physical items to which the accused may have a right of physical possession, but rather the testimony of witnesses or tangible proof to which the police are entitled to possession. In the latter situation, the disposition of the motion does not serve the function of returning the property, a function that is not dependent upon the prosecution's use or nonuse of the evidence in securing a conviction. Consequently, several courts have found motions to suppress "premature" when they involved potential evidence as to which the defendant had no right to possession and when there was no indication that the government intended to offer the challenged evidence at trial.[51]

---

51. United States v. Talbert, 271 F.Supp. 312 (S.D. N.Y.1967) (motion to suppress written statements premature in view of no showing of prosecution's intent to offer them in evidence); United States v. Dubin, 42 F.R.D. 434 (S.D.N.Y.1967) (post-indictment motion to suppress statements premature since no showing of intent to use them at trial). But see People v. Bryant, 87 Ill.App.2d 238, 231 N.E.2d 4 (1967) (pretrial motion to suppress statement not premature). Other courts have directed that the prosecution inform the defendant prior to trial of its intent to offer a confession or evidence obtained as a result of search and seizure, State ex rel. Rasmussen v. Tahash, 272 Minn. 539, 141 N.W.2d 3 (1965), or suggested that this be done. State ex rel. Goodchild v. Burke, 27 Wis.2d 244, 133 N.W.2d 753 (1965) cert. denied 384 U.S. 1017 (1966). The proposed amendments to the Federal Rules of Criminal Procedure would give defendant the right to request notice of the government's intent to introduce any evidence of which the defendant is entitled to discovery. Committee on Rules of Practice and Procedure of the Judicial Conference of the United States, Preliminary Draft of Proposed Amendments to the Federal Rules of Criminal Procedure for the United States District Courts, Rule 12(d) (2) (1970).

181. Enforcement of the Right to Exclusion: (c) Appellate Review of Trial Court Decisions on Admissibility.

Several procedural aspects of the exclusionary rule have given rise to criticism that the rule encourages development of a one-sided body of appellate case law and unnecessary litigation. Both criticisms are aimed primarily at traditional limitations upon the ability of both prosecution and defendant to obtain adequate appellate consideration of trial court rulings on motions to suppress.

The prosecution's right to appeal in criminal cases is, of course, greatly limited by the constitutional prohibition against double jeopardy. Consequently, the normal method of obtaining appellate review of decisions on admissibility—urging it as reversible error on appeal from the final outcome of the case —is unavailable to the government in a criminal case. The prosecution has also traditionally been unable to appeal from a ruling on a pretrial motion to suppress.[52] The Supreme Court, for example, has held that in the absence of specific statutory authorization, an order granting a motion to suppress is not appealable by the government even if the effect of the order was to require dismissal of the indictment.[53] These rulings serve purposes of economy; if a defendant will be found innocent, extensive pretrial appellate litigation concerning the admissibility of evidence will have been a waste of judicial time. But there are also significant counter-

---

52. Allen, The Exclusionary Rule in the American Law of Search and Seizure, 52 J.Crim.L.C. & P.S. 246, 249 (1961). Review may be available by means of the extraordinary writs. See State v. Coyle, 181 So.2d 671 (Fla.1966) (where trial court's order granting motion to suppress was "a departure from essential requirements of law" and state had no right of appeal, the writ of certiorari was available to quash the order). Cf. West's Ann.Cal. Penal Code, § 1538.5(o) (prosecution can obtain appellate review of suppression by petition for writ of mandamus or prohibition).

53. Carroll v. United States, 354 U.S. 394 (1957). Statutory authority was subsequently enacted. See text at n. 58, infra.

vailing considerations. As a result of limited prosecution access to appellate courts, rulings favorable to defendants are relatively immune from appellate scrutiny and a cautious trial judge can avoid appellate reversal by ordering suppression.[54] More important, however, this situation means that appellate courts receive only those cases which defendants seek to appeal. This category of cases is likely to contain a disproportionate number of cases involving improper police activity, thus providing appellate courts with a one-sided view of police practices. As a result, it has been argued that the appellate courts are ill suited to undertake an orderly development of rules regulating police activities.[55]

Increasingly this situation has been attacked by legislation and court rule conferring upon the prosecution the right to obtain pretrial appellate review of trial court rulings on motions to suppress. Some, e. g., the Illinois rule, authorize review of "an order or judgment . . . suppressing evidence." [56] Others, such as the New York provision, limit the state's right to appeal to situations in which the ruling significantly affects the prosecution's ability to proceed.[57] The federal statute requires that the prosecutor certify to the trial court that the appeal is not being taken for purpose of delay and that the suppressed evidence is "a substantial proof of the charge pending against the defendant." [58]

For the same reasons of economy of judicial time, defendants' ability to obtain appellate review of orders overruling their motions to suppress is generally limited to appeal from a resulting conviction. Under federal procedure, for example, an order denying a motion to suppress is interlocutory and thus unappealable if there was outstanding at the time of the motion "a complaint, or a detention or release on bail following arrest, or an arraignment, information or indictment." [59] Only if the motion for the suppression and return of property allegedly improperly seized is made solely for the return of property and is in no way tied to a criminal prosecution *in esse* against the moving party is the motion independent and the ruling on it thus appealable.[60] This limitation has several potential results that might outweigh the saving of time. First, a defendant who desires appellate review of the ruling on his motion must plead not guilty and go through trial, because his plea of guilty would result in waiver of his right to complain about the failure to suppress evidence.[61] Thus the traditional approach encourages full trials for defendants who, if they could fully litigate the propriety of the law enforcement activity involved in their apprehension, would plead guilty and avoid the time and expense of trial on the merits. Second, the limitation deprives appellate courts of another category of cases, thereby decreasing the representative nature of those cases brought before the appellate courts. Cases in which the defendant was acquitted despite the fa-

---

54. If the state is authorized to cross-appeal in the event that the defendant appeals from a conviction, a ruling favorable to the defendant might receive appellate review in this manner. See, e. g., Wis. Stat.Ann. 958.12(2) (1958) (authorizing state to cross-appeal).

55. LaFave, Search and Seizure: "The Course of True Law . . . Has Not . . . Run Smooth", 1966 U.Ill.L.Forum 255, 387.

56. Ill.Sup.Ct.Rule 604(a) (1).

57. McKinney's N.Y. CPL 450.50 requires that the prosecution append to its notice of appeal from an adverse ruling on a pretrial motion regarding evidence a statement that the deprivation of the evidence "has rendered the sum of the proof available . . . either (a) insufficient as a matter of law, or (b) so weak in its entirety that any reasonable possibility of prosecuting such charge or prospective charge to a conviction has been effectively destroyed."

58. 18 U.S.C.A. § 3731 (1969).

59. DiBella v. United States, 369 U.S. 121 (1962).

60. Id.

61. See generally Annot., 20 A.L.R.3d 724 (effect of plea of guilty on illegal search and seizure).

vorable ruling on the motion to suppress might contain a disproportionate number of cases in which the prosecution's case was weak and in which there consequently might have been a motive for investigatorial activity exceeding the bounds of propriety.

Several responses might be made to the problem. Interlocutory appeals from rulings on motions to dismiss might be generally permitted. This would permit the parties to litigate fully the admissibility of evidence and, once this has been decided, to begin the plea bargaining process with maximum awareness of the strength of their own and others' positions. Or, specific provision might be made for preserving a defendant's right to contest rulings on pretrial motions to suppress despite a plea of guilty. The New York Criminal Procedure Law, for example, provides that the order denying the motion to suppress is reviewable on appeal from a judgment of conviction notwithstanding the fact that the judgment rests upon a plea of guilty.[62] This provision, of course, assures that there will be no more than a single appeal in each case. But it also requires that the plea bargaining be performed in mere speculation of the appellate court's disposition of the ruling. Speculation whether the ruling on the motion to suppress might be reversed on appeal adds an undesirable element to the negotiations that would not be present were the parties able to resolve the admissibility question with finality before the plea. But permitting these appeals would provide the opportunity for two appeals in each case: one from the ruling on the motion to suppress, and the other from conviction and sentence. This is unlikely to prove burdensome, however, when the resolution of the suppression issue is followed by a guilty plea; appeals from conviction and sentence are likely to be few in view of the extremely limited issues that might be raised. A larger percentage of dual appeal cases can be expected from those situations in which the motion to suppress is followed by a trial on the merits, but in view of the small percentage of cases ever going to trial this would be a relatively minor problem.[63]

182. Enforcement of the Right to Exclusion: (d) Federal Injunctive Relief Against Use of Evidence in State Courts.[64]

On the assumption that federal tribunals are more likely than their state counterparts to look favorably upon a request for the suppression of evidence, defendants in state criminal cases have sometimes sought federal injunctive relief against anticipated use in a state proceeding of evidence subject to suppression. With a few exceptions, these attempts have been unsuccessful.

In 1951, the Supreme Court approved dismissal of a request to enjoin use in a state prosecution of evidence seized by state officers pursuant to an entry allegedly in violation of the Fourth Amendment.[65] At the

---

62. McKinney's N.Y. CPL Art. 710. See also West's Ann.Cal.Penal Code, § 1538.5(m). In view of the state statute, a defendant who pleads guilty following an unfavorable ruling on his motion to suppress does not thereby waive his *federal* right to the exclusion of unlawfully seized evidence. Nor does he waive his right to a federal forum. Thus one who has pleaded guilty may have access to the federal courts on habeas corpus without concern that his guilty plea constitutes a waiver for that purpose. United States ex rel. Rogers v. Warden, 381 F.2d 209 (2d Cir. 1967).

63. Only about nineteen percent of those convicted of major crimes demanded trials; the remainder have been convicted upon pleas of guilty. The President's Commission on Law Enforcement and Administration of Justice, The Challenge of Crime in a Free Society 262–63 (1967). Some of this nineteen percent are cases in which trial was demanded simply as a means of preserving the appealability of the ruling on the motion to suppress. Requiring pre-plea resolution of this matter would probably reduce the percentage of cases in which trial was demanded.

64. See generally, The Supreme Court, 1962 Term, 77 Harv.L.Rev. 62, 149–52 (1963); 48 Minn.L.Rev. 349 (1963); 29 Am.Jur.2d Evidence § 427; Annot., 6 L.Ed.2d 1118.

65. Stefanelli v. Minard, 342 U.S. 117 (1951).

time, use of the evidence would not have constituted a deprivation of due process [66] and the decision seemed to rest largely upon that ground. Five years later, however, in Rea v. United States,[67] the Court seemed to waver. Marijuana had been obtained from the defendant in a search conducted pursuant to a warrant issued by a United States commissioner. In a federal prosecution, the drugs were suppressed on the ground that the warrant had been issued in violation of Rule 41(c) of the Federal Rules of Criminal Procedure. A federal agent then swore out a complaint in a New Mexico state court, and defendant was arrested and held for trial. Defendant applied to the federal district court for an injunction ordering the federal agents not to testify in the state prosecution and directing the destruction or transfer of the drugs. This relief was denied. The Supreme Court reversed, but indicated that it was deciding no constitutional issue and merely using its supervisory power to enforce the Federal Rules of Criminal Procedure in regard to a federal officer who owed them obedience.

In 1961, shortly before Mapp v. Ohio,[68] the Court was again faced with a request to enjoin testimony by federal agents in a state court. In Wilson v. Schnettler,[69] the Court affirmed denial of injunctive relief, emphasizing that although the evidence was alleged to have been seized pursuant to an arrest made without a warrant, there was no allegation that the arrest had been made without probable cause. Heavy reliance was also placed on considerations of comity, the traditional reluctance of federal courts to interfere with pending state criminal prosecutions, and the absence of any allegation that

no adequate remedy existed in state procedure. Rea was distinguished on the ground that in Rea a federal court had issued a suppression order directing that the challenged evidence "shall not be admissible in evidence at any hearing or trial." The injunction in Rea, the Court asserted, had been issued only to prevent a federal officer from circumventing a federal court order.

The issue was raised again in 1963—after Mapp—in Cleary v. Bolger.[70] Federal customs agents had taken Bolger into custody, conducted an unlawful search of his home and seized evidence from it, and obtained a confession from him during detention which violated Federal Rule 5(a). Cleary, an investigator for the state Waterfront Commission, had not been present during the search. He had, however, been present by invitation of the federal agents at the interrogation and overheard the confession, although he had not actively participated in the interrogation. When state criminal and administrative proceedings were begun, Bolger requested federal injunctive relief directing that Cleary and the federal officers not testify in the state proceedings as to the confession and the search. The relief was granted; only Cleary appealed. The decision was upheld by the Second Circuit on appeal.[71] The Supreme Court reversed, emphasizing traditional reluctance to interfere with pending criminal prosecutions and considerations of comity. Rea was distinguished as involving a federal official, and the Court rejected the argument that relief against Cleary was necessary to make effective the relief granted as to the federal agents. "We need not decide," the Court commented, "whether petitioner's status as a state official might be ignored had it been shown that he had misconducted himself in this affair, that he had been utilized by the federal officers as a

---

66. Mapp v. Ohio, 367 U.S. 643 (1961) was not decided until 10 years later. See § 165, supra.

67. 350 U.S. 214 (1956).

68. 367 U.S. 643 (1961).

69. 365 U.S. 381 (1961).

70. 371 U.S. 392 (1963).

71. 293 F.2d 368 (2d Cir. 1961).

means of shielding their own alleged illegal conduct, or that he had received the evidence in direct violation of the federal court order." [72] The Court specifically declined to decide whether, if the state courts should find the evidence to have been seized only in violation of the Federal Rules of Criminal Procedure and not of the United States Constitution, admission of the evidence would constitute grounds for relief on appeal to the Supreme Court. Three members of the Court dissented, arguing that relief was essential as a means of enforcing Rule 5(a).

The cases leave no doubt that the exclusionary rule of *Mapp* will not ordinarily be enforced by federal injunction. *Rea* seems still valid insofar as it authorized federal injunctive relief against a federal agent's active participation in a state criminal prosecution in violation of a specific federal court order. The major ambiguity is the extent to which an individual not a federal officer may be enjoined as a means of enforcing federal exclusionary rules not of constitutional origin. In part this ambiguity is caused by uncertainty as to the underlying right. Under what circumstances may a state prosecution make use of evidence obtained pursuant to a violation of federal nonconstitutional standards? Is exclusion required only if a state officer actively participated in the conduct violating the federal rules or if he was used by federal officials as a means of circumventing the exclusionary penalty applicable in federal court to their misconduct? Perhaps the need to maintain respect for the federal limitations justifies requiring nonuse of the results even in state courts. But this objective might be sufficiently served by requiring exclusion only if it can be shown that either the state or the federal agents sought specifically to avoid the federal exclusionary remedy. On the other hand, it is arguable that when the rule is only of su-

pervisory status the need to assure its observation is not strong enough to justify interfering with the right of the states to determine their own rules of admissibility.

Assuming the existence of a right not to have the evidence used, the propriety of injunctive relief does not necessarily follow. If post-conviction federal relief is available, the same policies that justify denying pretrial federal injunctive relief would seem to apply. Mr. Justice Douglas, in his dissent in *Bolger,* reads the majority opinion as strongly suggesting that post-conviction review of state court ruling on a claim to exclusion based upon a violation of the federal rule is unavailable.[73] If this is the case, pretrial injunctive relief might be the only effective opportunity to assert the right in a federal forum, and federal injunctive relief would seem to be proper. But this seems too broad a reading of the language used in *Bolger.* If the right to exclusion exists, it is enforcible by virtue of post-conviction appeal to the Supreme Court from the state appellate system or habeas corpus relief after appeal opportunities have been exhausted. There is no satisfactory basis on which to distinguish this situation from others in which states are required as a matter of federal law to exclude certain evidence.

183. Admission of Improperly Obtained Evidence as "Harmless Error".[74]

In all American jurisdictions appellate review is subject to rules that a judgment may

---

72. Cleary v. Bolger, 371 U.S. 392, 399–400 (1961).

73. Id. at 404 (Mr. Justice Douglas, dissenting). Apparently the underlying fear is that the admission of such evidence, even if erroneous, would not give rise to appellate jurisdiction in the United States Supreme Court. See 28 U.S.C.A. § 1257.

74. See generally, Mause, Harmless Constitutional Error: The Implications of Chapman v. California, 53 Minn.L.Rev. 519 (1969); Thompson, Unconstitutional Search and Seizure and the Myth of Harmless Error, 42 Notre Dame Lawyer 457 (1967); Note, Harmless Constitutional Error: A Reappraisal, 83 Harv.L.Rev. 814 (1970); Note, Harmless Constitutional Error, 20 Stan.L.Rev. 83 (1967); Note, Harmless Constitutional Error, 30 U.Pitt.L.

be affirmed under certain circumstances despite errors in the conduct of the trial.[75] All these rules represent a judgment that time-consuming retrial is not justified if error has not affected the rights of the parties. These rules, of constitutional, statutory, or judicial origin, employ a variety of standards for determining whether a particular error is "harmless" but all require finally the resolution of whether the error significantly affected the interests of the complaining party. Mapp v. Ohio [76] raised the question whether states could apply their own harmless error rule in determining whether the admission of evidence which violated federal standards required reversal of judgments of conviction, or, if the state rule was not determinative, what standard must be applied.

The Supreme Court addressed itself to the problem in 1967 [77] in Chapman v. California.[78] The petitioners in *Chapman* had been convicted of murder in a trial at which the prosecuting attorney had commented at length to the jury concerning the petitioners' failure to testify in their own behalf. This procedure, of course, constituted a violation of Griffin v. California.[79] The California Supreme Court had concluded that the error was harmless within the meaning of the California constitutional directive that errors are to be deemed harmless unless "the court shall be of the opinion that the error . . . has resulted in a miscarriage of justice." [80] The Supreme Court reversed, holding that whether the violation of a federal right in a trial requires reversal is a matter of federal rather than state law.[81] Turning to the applicable federal standard, the Court rejected petitioners' contention that a rule of automatic reversal was applicable to all federal constitutional errors. It acknowledged, however, that "there are some constitutional rights so basic to a fair trial that their infraction can never be treated as harmless error." [82] But *Griffin's* prohibition against comment upon a defendant's invocation of his privilege against compulsory self-incrimination was not one of those basic rights and therefore could be tested under a harmless error rule. That rule requires that "before a federal constitutional error can be held harmless, the court must be able to declare a belief that it was harmless beyond a reasonable doubt." [83] With little further explanation, the Court held that the comment in *Chapman* had not been proved harmless, and reversed.

Although there are probably types of evidence whose admission requires automatic

---

Rev. 553 (1969); 5 Am.Jur.2d Appeal and Error §§ 776–819; Annot., 30 A.L.R.3d 128; C.J.S. Criminal Law §§ 1887–1912; Dec.Dig. Criminal Law 1163(3). For a broad discussion of harmless error, see Traynor, The Riddle of Harmless Error (1970).

75. Note, Harmless Constitutional Error: A Reappraisal, 83 Harv.L.Rev. 814 (1970).

76. 367 U.S. 643 (1961).

77. In Fahy v. Connecticut, 375 U.S. 85 (1963) the state courts had held that the admission of evidence seized in violation of the federal constitution was harmless error. Finding that the record made clear that the admission of the evidence was prejudicial to the accused, the Court specifically declined to decide whether erroneous admission of evidence obtained by illegal search and seizure could ever be harmless. Id. at 91–92.

78. 386 U.S. 18 (1967).

79. 380 U.S. 609 (1965). See § 131, supra.

80. West's Ann.Cal.Const. Art. 6, § 13.

81. For an examination of the potential bases for such a holding, see Mause, Harmless Constitutional Error: Implications of Chapman v. California, 53 Minn.L.Rev. 519, 533–37 (1969).

82. Chapman v. California, 386 U.S. 18, 23 (1967). The Court cited Payne v. Arkansas, 356 U.S. 560 (1958) (coerced confession), Gideon v. Wainwright, 372 U.S. 335 (1963) (denial of the right to representation by counsel at trial), and Tumey v. Ohio, 273 U.S. 510 (1927) (right to be tried by an impartial judge). See also Burgett v. Texas, 389 U.S. 109, 115 (1967) in which the Court described the admission into evidence of a prior conviction obtained pursuant to the denial of the *Gideon* right to representation as "inherently prejudicial". Compare Coleman v. Alabama, 399 U.S. 1 (1970) (remanded for determination whether denial of right to counsel at preliminary hearing was harmless error under *Chapman*).

83. Chapman v. California, 386 U.S. 18, 24 (1967).

reversal,[84] it is unlikely that improperly obtained evidence is one of them.[85] Insofar as the exclusionary rule is based upon unfairness to the accused inherent in the use of such evidence or the impact upon the judiciary of the implicit approval of the method used in obtaining the evidence by its receipt into evidence, a strong case for an automatic reversal rule can be made. But the same considerations of economy and the need for finality of judicial action that underlie the application of the harmless error rule in non-constitutional cases also apply to situations in which the error alleged is of constitutional dimensions. Insofar as the purpose of the exclusionary rules is to deter improper behavior on the part of investigators and prosecutors, the small addition to deterrent value that would be achieved by denying the prosecution the opportunity to bring itself within a stringent harmless error rule would not significantly further that objective. The Supreme Court's analyses in several cases involving the improper receipt of constitutionally inadmissible evidence also suggest that improperly obtained evidence is subject to a harmless error rule.[86]

The specific criterion for determining whether the admission of improperly obtained evidence constitutes harmless error is somewhat unclear.[87] *Chapman* holds only that the error to be harmless must not have contributed to the conviction.[88] There seem to be two principal interpretations of this criterion. One would hold that an error "contributed to" the conviction within the meaning of *Chapman* if it played any part in the jury's determination.[89] It has been argued, however, that such a standard, in view of the difficulty of establishing the actual factors considered by the triers of fact and the burden of proof resting upon the prosecution, would amount to an automatic reversal rule.[90] The other interpretation would have the harmless nature depend upon two factors: (a) the probative value of the inadmissible evidence, considered in light of (b) the amount and probative value of the other evidence in the record tending to sustain the finding of guilt. Only if (b), when compared to (a), is "overwhelming" can a court conclude that the admission of (a) was harmless beyond a reasonable doubt.[91]

---

84. See note 82, supra.

85. Note, Harmless Constitutional Error, 20 Stan.L. Rev. 83, 93–94 (1967).

86. In Bumper v. North Carolina, 391 U.S. 543 (1968) an illegally seized rifle which was received during trial on a rape charge was held "plainly damaging evidence" which required reversal. Mr. Justice Black argued in dissent that "overwhelming evidence" aside from the rifle demonstrated the petitioner's guilt beyond all shadow of doubt and thus reversal was not justified. Id. at 557–61 (Black, J., dissenting). The majority, however, emphasized the potential weaknesses in the prosecution's case: the two witnesses had first identified someone other than the petitioner as the guilty party, and identified the petitioner by his voice only after they were made aware that he was regarded as the "prime suspect" Id. at 550, n. 16. See also Mr. Justice Harlan's concurring discussion. Id. at 553–54 (Harlan, J., concurring). Cf. United States v. Lookretis, 390 U.S. 338 (1968), vacating and remanding 385 F.2d 487 (7th Cir. 1967) (vacating holding that admission of disclosures required by federal wagering tax statute did not prejudice defendant where it was merely cumula-

tive of other competent evidence); Biggers v. Tennessee, 390 U.S. 404, 408–09 (1968) (introduction of identification testimony obtained after police emphasized the suggestion that petitioner committed the crime was not harmless error because it was the only evidence of identification).

87. The issue, of course, is the same that is raised when nonconstitutional errors are asserted. See generally, Gibbs, Prejudicial Error: Admission and Exclusions of Evidence in the Federal Courts, 3 Vill.L.Rev. 48 (1957).

F.R.Crim.P. 52(a): "Any error, defect, irregularity or variance which does not affect substantial rights shall be disregarded."

88. Chapman v. California, 386 U.S. 18, 24 (1967).

89. Note, Harmless Constitutional Error, 83 Harv.L. Rev. 814, 819 (1970).

90. Id.

91. This interpretation seems most consistent with the application of the harmless error rule in cases involving comment upon an accused's failure to testify. Fontaine v. California, 390 U.S. 593 (1968) (state failed to meet its burden of proving error was harmless in narcotics case when the agent who allegedly bought narcotics from the defend-

In Harrington v. California,[92] the only post-*Chapman* case in which the Supreme Court approved a finding of harmless constitutional error, the Court seems to have adopted the "overwhelming evidence" standard. Harrington had been tried with three codefendants for attempted robbery and first degree murder. Confessions of all three codefendants which referred to Harrington (although not by name) were introduced with instructions that they be considered as evidence only against their maker. Only one codefendant took the stand, thereby providing Harrington with an opportunity to cross-examine him. The introduction of the confessions of the other defendants thus constituted a violation of Bruton v. United States.[93] The Supreme Court, however, affirmed the state court's determination that the introduction of the confessions had been harmless error. The confessions merely placed Harrington at the scene of the crime, the Court pointed out, and thus were cumulative of other evidence, including Harrington's own statement. The evidence tending to show that Harrington had a gun and had been an active participant in the robbery came from persons other than the codefendants. The case against Harrington was not "woven from circumstantial evidence" but rather was "so overwhelming" that unless no violation of *Bruton* could constitute harmless error the conviction must be allowed to stand.

ant did not testify and the prosecution's case was built of circumstantial evidence); Anderson v. Nelson, 390 U.S. 523, 523–24 (1968) (comment on failure to testify "cannot be labeled harmless where such comment is extensive, where an inference of guilt from silence is stressed to the jury as a basis of conviction, and where there is evidence that could have supported acquittal").

92.   395 U.S. 250 (1969).

93.   391 U.S. 123 (1968).

TITLE 7

RELEVANCY AND ITS COUNTERWEIGHTS: TIME, PREJUDICE, CONFUSION AND SURPRISE

CHAPTER 16

RELEVANCY

184.   Relevance as the Presupposition of Admissibility.

Relevance, as we shall see, is probative worth, and common sense would suggest that if there is to be any practice of excluding evidence which is offered, the first ground of exclusion should be the want of probative value. Correspondingly, in the search for the truth of the issue, reason would suggest that if evidence is logically probative, it should be received unless there is some distinct ground for refusing to hear it. Thayer, by recognizing and announcing these simple truths, placed the Anglo-American system of evidence rules in a new and just perspective. He said:

> "Observe, at this point, one or two fundamental conceptions. There is a principle—not so much a rule of evidence as a presupposition involved in the very conception of a rational system of evidence, as contrasted with the old formal and mechanical systems—which forbids receiving anything irrelevant, not logically probative.   .   .   .
>
> "There is another precept which should be laid down as preliminary, in stating the law of evidence; namely, that unless excluded by some rule or principle of law, all that is logically pro-

bative is admissible. This general admissibility, however, of what is logically probative is not, like the former principle, a necessary presupposition in a rational system of evidence; there are many exceptions to it.   .   .   .

> "In stating thus our two large, fundamental conceptions, we must not fall into the error of supposing that relevancy, logical connection, real or supposed, is the only test of admissibility; for so we should drop out of sight the chief part of the law of evidence. When we have said (1) that, without any exception, nothing which is not, or is not supposed to be, logically relevant is admissible; and (2) that, subject to many exceptions and qualifications, whatever is logically relevant is admissible; it is obvious that, in reality, there are tests of admissibility other than logical relevancy. Some things are rejected as being of too slight a significance, or as having too conjectural and remote a connection; others, as being dangerous, in their effect on the jury, and likely to be misused or overestimated by that body; others, as being impolitic, or unsafe on public grounds; others, on the bare ground of precedent. It is this sort of thing, as I said before,—the rejection on

one or another practical ground, of what is really probative,—which is the characteristic thing in the law of evidence; stamping it as the child of the jury system." [1]

185. The Meaning of Relevancy.[2]

In the courtroom the terms relevancy and materiality are often used interchangeably, but materiality in its more precise meaning looks to the relation between the propositions for which the evidence is offered and the issues in the case.[3] If the evidence is offered to prove a proposition which is not a matter in issue or probative of a matter in issue, the evidence is properly said to be immaterial. As to what is "in issue", that is, within the range of the litigated controversy, we look mainly to the pleadings, read in the light of the rules of pleading and controlled by the substantive law. Thus, in an action on a bond where the only plea is

a denial of execution, evidence offered by the defendant of a release would be immaterial,[4] and in a suit for workmen's compensation, evidence of contributory negligence would be immaterial, whether pleaded or not, since the statute abrogates it as a defense. But matters in the range of dispute may extend somewhat beyond the issues defined in the pleadings. Thus, under flexible modern systems of procedure issues not raised by the pleadings may be tried by express or implied consent of the parties.[5] In addition, the parties may draw in dispute the credibility of the witnesses and, within limits, produce evidence assailing and supporting their credibility.[6] Moreover, we must recognize that a considerable leeway is allowed even on direct examination for proof of facts which are not really offered as bearing on the dispute, however defined, but merely as details which fill in the background of the narrative and give it interest, color, and lifelikeness.[7]

We begin, then, with the notion of materiality, the inclusion of certain questions or

---

1. Thayer, Preliminary Treatise on Evidence 264–266 (1898). Some of the many opinions adopting this approach are: Sears v. Southern Pac. Co., 313 F.2d 498 (9th Cir. 1963); Cherry v. Hill, 283 Ala. 74, 214 So.2d 427 (1968); Love v. Wolf, 226 Cal. App.2d 378, 38 Cal.Rptr. 183 (1964); Kramer v. John Hancock Mut. Life Ins. Co., 336 Mass. 465, 146 N.E.2d 357 (1957). See also 1 Wigmore, Evidence §§ 9, 10; Uniform Rule 7(f); F.R.Ev. (R.D. 1971) 402.

2. A most illuminating discussion, to which the text is much indebted, is James, Relevancy, Probability and the Law, 29 Calif.L.Rev. 689 (1941). Also valuable is Trautman, Logical or Legal Relevancy—a Conflict in Theory, 5 Vand.L.Rev. 385 (1952). The major contributions in this country are Thayer, Preliminary Treatise on Evidence, 263–276, 515–518 (1898) and 1 Wigmore, Evidence § 12 (Distinctions between Relevancy and Admissibility); §§ 25, 26 (Circumstantial and Testimonial Evidence); §§ 27–29a (General Considerations Affecting Relevancy); §§ 31, 32 (Required Degree of Probability of Proposed Inference); §§ 38–42 (General Theory of Circumstantial Evidence). See also Phipson, Evidence, Ch. V (8th ed. 1942); Dec.Dig. Criminal Law, ☞338, Evidence, ☞99, 100, 114–117, 143–147.

3. Azimow's Estate v. Azimow, 141 Ind.App. 529, 230 N.E.2d 450 (1967): "Whereas materiality deals with the relationship between the issues of the case and the fact which the evidence tends to prove, relevancy deals with the requirement that the evidence must logically tend to prove a material fact."

4. See James, op. cit., 29 Calif.L.Rev. 689, 690, 691. See also 1 Wigmore, Evidence § 2; Model Code of Evidence Rule 1(8) (" 'Material matter' means a matter the existence or non-existence of which is provable in the action."), and comment.

5. See, e. g., F.R.Civ.P. 15(b) ("When issues not raised by the pleadings are tried by express or implied consent of the parties, they shall be treated in all respects as if they had been raised in the pleadings. Such amendment of the pleadings as may be necessary to cause them to conform to the evidence and to raise these issues may be made upon motion of any party at any time, even after judgment; but failure so to amend does not affect the result of the trial of these issues. . . .").

6. See Ch. 5, Impeachment, herein.

7. "Background" evidence, of facts not strictly "in dispute," is widely received to aid understanding. Maps and photographs are examples; once authenticated, they are universally admitted notwithstanding they tend to prove many undisputed facts along with disputed ones. Donley v. Christopher, 320 F.2d 24 (10th Cir. 1963). This penumbra, extending what is "provable" beyond what is "in issue," has led to other formulations of materiality. See F.R.Ev. (R.D.1971) 401 ("any fact that is of consequence to the determination of the action"), and Note.

propositions within the range of allowable proof in the lawsuit. Relevancy, in legal usage, embraces this test and something more. Relevancy in logic is the tendency of evidence to establish a proposition which it is offered to prove.[8] Relevancy, as employed by judges and lawyers, however, is the tendency of the evidence to establish a material proposition.[9] Thus, as James points out, "evidence may be excluded as 'irrelevant' for either of these two quite distinct reasons: because it is not probative of the proposition at which it is directed, or because that proposition is not provable in the case."[10] Our discussion, however, will henceforth leave materiality aside as mainly a matter of substantive law and of pleading rules, and center on the other aspect, the test of the probative quality of the evidence.

The characterization of evidence as "direct" or "circumstantial"[11] points to the kind of inference which is sought to be drawn from the evidence to the truth of the proposition for which it is offered. If a witness testifies that he saw A stab B with a knife, and this testimony is offered to prove the stabbing, the inference sought is merely from the fact that the witness made the statement, and the assumption that witnesses are worthy of belief, to the truth of the asserted fact. This is direct evidence.[12] When, however, the evidence is offered also for some further proposition based upon some inference other than merely the inference from assertion to the truth of the fact asserted, then the evidence is circumstantial evidence of this further fact-to-be-inferred. Thus in the case mentioned if the stabbing were proved and the culprit in doubt, testimony that A fled from the scene, offered to show his probable guilt, would be direct evidence of the flight but circumstantial evidence of his murderous act.[13] Similarly, testimony of a witness that he recognized A as one present on the scene would be direct evidence of the facts asserted, but testimony that he saw someone who was disguised and masked, but had a voice and a limp like A's, would be circumstantial evidence that the person seen was A.[14] Evidence offered for the "di-

---

8. Text writers and judges occasionally use the term in this sense. "The guiding principle is well stated in Stephen's Digest of the Law of Evidence (Chap. 1, p. 36), in these words: 'The word "relevant" means that any two facts to which it is applied are so related to each other, that according to the common course of events one either taken by itself or in connection with other facts proves or renders probable the past, present, or future existence or non-existence of the other.'" Baldwin, J., in Plumb v. Curtis, 66 Conn. 154, 166, 33 Atl. 998, 1000 (1895). See also United States v. Craft, 407 F.2d 1065 (6th Cir. 1969); Henninger v. Southern Pac. Co., 250 Cal.App.2d 872, 59 Cal.Rptr. 76 (1967).

9. "In legal usage, relevancy means the logical relationship between proposed evidence and a fact to be established, the tendency to establish a material proposition." State v. Wilson, 173 N.W.2d 563 (Iowa 1970). See also State v. Witham, 72 Me. 531 (1881); Words and Phrases, Relevancy, Relevant (1952); Uniform Rule 1(2): "'Relevant evidence' means evidence having any tendency in reason to prove any material fact." Cf. F.R.Ev. (R.D.1971) 401: "'Relevant evidence' means evidence having any tendency to make the existence of any fact that is of consequence to the determination of the action more probable or less probable than it would be without the evidence."

10. Op. cit., n. 2, supra 29 Calif.L.Rev. at 691.

11. For discussion of the meaning of these terms, see 1 Wigmore, Evidence § 25 (preferring "testi- monial," instead of "direct"). Judicial definitions are collected in 7 Words and Phrases 225.

12. It also embraces objects or documents offered in evidence to show their existence, characteristics or contents, or a view of some scene by the court. Here again the proof by perception depends upon the truthfulness of the identifying testimony of the authenticating witness.

13. ". . . Circumstantial evidence is direct evidence as to the facts deposed to but indirect as to the factum probandum." Brown v. State, 126 Tex. Cr. 449, 72 S.W.2d 269, 270 (1934); or, as it is sometimes put, "circumstantial evidence is merely direct evidence indirectly employed," Perry's Adm'x v. Inter-Southern Life Ins. Co., 248 Ky. 491, 58 S.W.2d 906 (1933).

14. Compare Welch v. State, 143 Tex.Cr.R. 529, 154 S.W.2d 248 (1941). For other situations illustrating the distinction, and judicial discussions, see United Textile Workers Local 120 v. Newberry Mills, Inc., 238 F.Supp. 366 (W.D.S.C.1965); Jennings v. Farmers Mut. Ins. Ass'n, 260 Iowa 279, 149

rect" inference merely, the truth of the fact asserted, has its own questions of probative value, but these are approached by the common law in terms of the qualification of witnesses, not in terms of relevancy.[15] In our usage questions of relevancy arise only in respect to circumstantial evidence.

Under our system, molded by the tradition of jury trial and of predominantly oral proof, a party offers his evidence not in mass, but item by item. The problem of relevancy may arise as to each fact proposed to be elicited by successive questions of counsel, or by successive offers of writings or other objects. Items are normally offered and admitted or rejected as units,[16] though of course the judge will consider any proof already made by the proponent as indicating the bearing of the item offered, and may in his discretion ask the proponent what additional circumstances he expects to prove. But when it is offered and judged singly and in isolation, as it frequently is, it cannot be expected by itself to furnish conclusive proof of the ultimate fact to be inferred.[17] Thus the common argument of the objector that the inference for which the fact is offered "does not necessarily follow" is untenable, as it supposes a standard of conclusiveness which probably no aggregation of circumstantial evidence, and certainly no single item thereof, could ever meet. This same practice of determining the admissibility of items of evidence singly as they are offered leads to another distinction, often stressed in judicial opinions. This is the distinction between relevancy and sufficiency. The test of relevancy, which is to be applied by the trial judge in determining whether a particular item or group of items of evidence is to be admitted is a different and less stringent one than the standard used at a later stage in deciding whether all the evidence of the party on an issue is sufficient to permit the issue to go to the jury.[18] A brick is not a wall.

What is the standard of relevance or probative quality which evidence must meet if it is to be admitted? We have said that it must "tend to establish" the inference for which it is offered.[19] How strong must this

---

N.W.2d 298 (1967); People v. Bretagna, 298 N.Y. 323, 83 N.E.2d 537 (1949); Wilkerson v. Clark, 264 N.C. 439, 141 S.E.2d 884 (1965).
As to the relative probative values of these two kinds of evidence, see 1 Wigmore, Evidence § 26.

15. This is pointed out in 2 Wigmore, Evidence § 475.

16. And consequently "an offer of proof cannot be denied as remote or speculative because it does not cover every fact necessary to prove the issue. If it be an appropriate link in the chain of proof, that is enough." McCandless v. United States, 298 U.S. 342 (1936) (proceedings for condemnation of ranch; as bearing on value as potential sugar-plantation, owner offered evidence that water was available at a distance; held, exclusion was not sustainable on theory that proponent did not also offer to show the probable cost of bringing the water to the land and the amount of probable enhancement); Townsend v. State, 86 Ga.App. 459, 71 S.E.2d 738 (1952) ("The case cannot be made out all at once; and evidence which tends to establish the issue in controversy is admissible. This is so, though it may be that no particular fact is sufficient, standing alone, to prove the issue in controversy."); People v. Scott, 29 Ill.2d 97, 193 N.E.2d 814 (1963). See the discussion of conditional relevancy herein, § 58, supra; 6 Wigmore, Evidence § 1871.

17. Thus, in a prosecution for possessing unstamped distilled spirits, the court in considering the relevancy of evidence that the defendant had previously had unstamped spirits in the same place said: "Its relevancy did not, and indeed could not, demand that it be conclusive; most convictions result from the cumulation of bits of proof which, taken singly, would not be enough in the mind of a fair minded person. All that is necessary, and all that is possible, is that each bit may have enough rational connection with the issue to be considered a factor contributing to an answer. Wigmore § 12." Learned Hand, Circ. J., in United States v. Pugliese, 153 F.2d 497, 500 (2d Cir. 1946). To like effect are State v. Sack, 210 Ore. 552, 300 P.2d 427 (1956) appeal dismissed and cert. denied 353 U.S. 962; Tyrrell v. Prudential Ins. Co., 109 Vt. 6, 192 Atl. 184, 115 A.L.R. 392 (1937).

18. Hardwick v. Price, 114 Ga.App. 817, 152 S.E.2d 905 (1966); State v. Giles, 253 La. 533, 218 So.2d 585 (1969); Superior Ice & Coal Co. v. Belger Cartage Service, 337 S.W.2d 897 (Mo.1960); State v. Gersvold, 66 Wash.2d 900, 406 P.2d 318 (1965); C.J.S. Evidence § 160; 1 Wigmore, Evidence § 29.

19. This tendency is the relationship, referred to earlier, between the evidence and the fact it is

tendency be? Some courts have announced tests, variously phrased, which seem to require that the evidence offered must render the inference for which it is offered more probable than the other possible inferences or hypotheses,[20] that is, the chances must appear to preponderate that the inference claimed is the true one. It is believed, however, that while this might be a reasonable standard by which to judge the sufficiency of all of a party's proof to enable him to get to the jury on the issue, it makes too heavy a demand upon a given item of proof at the admissibility stage, when we are gathering our bits of information piece by piece. And, in fact, most circumstantial evidence commonly received does not meet so stringent a test. Thus, when a violent death is shown and A is charged with the homicide, evidence that A as beneficiary in a policy on the life of the victim had a motive for the slaying will be admitted.[21] Yet if we state our reasoning in deductive form,[22] one of the assumptions which would be necessary to support admission under this test would be the proposition that when a homicide is proved, and a person is shown to have had a motive for the killing, it is more probable than not that this person was the killer. Few would contend that human experience would support this proposition. Similarly with evidence that A had an opportunity to commit the killing,[23] or that he expressed an intention to do so shortly before the death.[24] Though motive, opportunity, and design may well be thought when aggregated to make A's guilt more probable than not, singly they each manifestly fall short of establishing so high a probability. It is believed that a more modest standard better reflects the actual practice of the courts, and that the most acceptable test of relevancy is the question, does the evidence offered render the desired inference *more probable than it would be without the evidence?*[25] There are other formulas of relevancy found in the opinions which though expressed in more general

offered to prove. Although often spoken of as logical or reasonable, it is clearly not limited to formal logic, or to rigorous reasoning. Courts frequently stress that it may be measured by experience or common sense. See United States v. Craft, 407 F.2d 1065 (6th Cir. 1969); Hadley v. Baltimore & Ohio R. R., 120 F.2d 993 (3d Cir. 1941); Wadsworth v. State, 201 So.2d 836 (Fla. App.1967); Marut v. Costello, 34 Ill.2d 125, 214 N.E.2d 768 (1965); Glens Falls Ins. Co. v. Ogden, 310 S.W.2d 547 (Ky. 1958).

20. See, e. g., Engel v. United Traction Co., 203 N.Y. 321, 323, 96 N.E. 731 (1911) (injury to plaintiff in collision with electric car; admission of evidence that motorman was later discharged for "a piece of foolishness," ground for reversal. "A fact is admissible as the basis of an inference only when the desired inference is a probable or natural explanation of the fact and a more probable and natural one than the other explanations, if any.") See also Standafer v. First Nat. Bank, 236 Minn. 123, 52 N.W.2d 718 (1952); People v. Nitzberg, 287 N.Y. 183, 187, 38 N.E.2d 490, 138 A.L.R. 1253 (1941) (". . . a fact is relevant to another fact when the existence of the one renders the existence of the other highly probable, according to the common course of events").

21. See, generally as to relevance of facts showing motive as evidence of an act, 2 Wigmore, Evidence §§ 385, 390, 391.

22. The value of testing arguments on the relevancy of particular items of circumstantial evidence by stating them in deductive syllogistic form is shown, with enlightening illustrations, in James, op. cit., 29 Calif.L.Rev. 694–700.

23. 1 Wigmore, Evidence § 131.

24. 1 Wigmore, Evidence §§ 102, 103.

25. Thus, in the leading case of Mutual Life Insurance Co. v. Hillmon, 145 U.S. 285 (1892), the court in discussing the admissibility of certain letters of one Walters expressing an intention of going with Hillmon on a trip to Kansas, said: "The letters in question were competent, not as narratives of facts communicated to the writer by others, nor yet as proof that he actually went away from Wichita, but as evidence that, shortly before the time when other evidence tended to show that he went away, he had the intention of going, and of going with Hillmon, which made it more probable both that he did go and that he went with Hillmon than if there had been no proof of such intention." This test is ably advocated in James, op. cit., 29 Calif.L.Rev. at 699; and is adopted in People v. Warner, 270 Cal.App.2d 900, 76 Cal.Rptr. 160 (1969); Hagopian v. Fuchs, 66 N.J.Super. 374, 169 A.2d 172 (1961); F.R.Ev. (R.D.1971) 401. See Sears v. Southern Pac. Co., 313 F.2d 498, 503 n. 5 (9th Cir. 1963).

terms seem consistent with the test suggested.[26] It may be asked, how does the judge know whether the evidence does make more probable the truth of the fact to be inferred? Is an attempted escape by a prisoner charged with two serious but factually unconnected crimes relevant to show consciousness of guilt of crime number one?[27] There are no statistics for attempts at escape by those conscious of guilt and those not so conscious which will shed light on the probability of the inference. Nor are there any statistics regarding consciousness of guilt of the one crime or the other, or both, as a causative factor. The answer must filter through the judge's experience, his judgment, and his knowledge of human conduct and motivation. He must ask himself, could a reasonable juror believe that the attempt makes it more probable that accused was conscious of guilt of the crime being tried, than it would be in

the absence of the attempt; and if the answer is yes, the evidence is relevant.[28]

Relevant evidence, then, is evidence that in some degree advances the inquiry, and thus has probative value,[29] and is prima facie admissible. But relevance is not always enough. There may remain the question, is its value worth what it costs? There are several counterbalancing factors which may

26. "In determining the question of remoteness the test seems to be that if the offered evidence is so remote in time as to be irrelevant and have no probative value at all, it should not be admitted. On the other hand, if the evidence is relevant and has some degree of probative value, however small, it is admissible, and its weight is for the jury." Mason v. Stengell, 441 S.W.2d 412 (Ky.1969).

"Evidence tending to prove a material fact is admissible, even though its tendency in that direction may be exceedingly slight." Thomas v. State, 251 Ind. 76, 238 N.E.2d 20 (1968).

"Justice and common sense, fused by enlightened reasoning, engender a legal philosophy embodying the abolition of all obstacles having a tendency to deprive the jury of any facts, however remotely relevant or from whatever source, which gravitate toward assisting them in arriving at a correct solution of the factual equation before them. Intellectual productiveness is not increased, nor is the truth maintained by withhholding circumstances which may shed some helpful light." Miller v. Trans Oil Co., 18 N.J. 407, 113 A.2d 777 (1955).

"Any fact that makes more probable or less probable, where the probabilities are in question, renders such fact relevant." Smith v. Young, 109 Ohio App. 463, 168 N.E.2d 3 (1958).

27. Compare People v. Yazum, 13 N.Y.2d 302, 246 N.Y.S.2d 626, 196 N.E.2d 263 (1963) (relevant), and State v. Piche, 71 Wash.2d 583, 430 P.2d 522 (1967) cert. denied 390 U.S. 912 (relevant), with State v. Crawford, 59 Utah 39, 201 P. 1030 (1921) (irrelevant).

28. "The court's function is, in the usual simple case, only to decide whether a reasonable man might have his assessment of the probabilities of a material proposition changed by the piece of evidence sought to be admitted. If it may affect that evaluation it is relevant and, subject to certain other rules, admissible." United States v. Schipani, 289 F.Supp. 43, 56; 293 F.Supp. 156 (E.D.N.Y. 1968), aff'd 414 F.2d 1262 (2d Cir. 1969).

"The proper test for the admissibility of evidence ought to be, we think, whether it has a tendency to affect belief in the mind of a reasonably cautious person, who should receive and weigh it with judicial fairness." Stewart v. People, 23 Mich. 63 (1871), quoted in United States v. Craft, 407 F.2d 1065 (6th Cir. 1965).

An important function of scientific evidence is to supply the link which in other instances is furnished by "common sense" or experience. Strong, Questions Affecting the Admissibility of Scientific Evidence, 1970 U.Ill.L.Forum 1, 2:

"Scientific evidence may play a part in this process of conclusion drawing in two ways. First, science may serve to supply the trier of fact with specific propositions which neither the trier of fact nor the witnesses could obtain through the use of unaided or uninformed sensory perception. . . .

"The second possible function of scientific evidence is to supply the trier of fact with general propositions not the product of common experience, which may then be applied to specific scientific or nonscientific data that has been introduced in the case. This will allow the trier to draw conclusions from that data which would otherwise have been either impossible to reach, or at least impossible to reach with the same degree of certainty. Scientific evidence serving this second function is usually supplied through the medium of expert testimony, the expert witness being asked either to supply the general proposition itself or to apply it to an assumed set of data and state a conclusion. The state of technology being what it is, however, the role of the expert as applier of general propositions may occasionally be preempted by a scientific device which not only collects specific data but interprets it in light of some general scientific principle, as is true of radar devices for detection of automobile speed."

29. Stauffer v. McCrory Stores Corp., 155 F.Supp. 710 (W.D.Pa.1957); People v. Curtis, 232 Cal.App. 2d 859, 43 Cal.Rptr. 286 (1965).

move the court to exclude relevant evidence if they outweigh its probative value.[30] In

order of their importance, they are these. First, the danger that the facts offered may unduly arouse the jury's emotions of prejudice, hostility or sympathy.[31] Second, the probability that the proof and the answering evidence that it provokes may create a side issue that will unduly distract the jury from the main issues.[32] Third, the likelihood that

---

30. Uniform Rule 45: "Except as in these rules otherwise provided, the judge may in his discretion exclude evidence if he finds that its probative value is substantially outweighed by the risk that its admission will (a) necessitate undue consumption of time, or (b) create substantial danger of undue prejudice or of confusing the issues or of misleading the jury, or (c) unfairly and harmfully surprise a party who has not had reasonable opportunity to anticipate that such evidence would be offered." Cf. F.R.Ev. (R.D.1971) 403.

Similar general formulations can be found in United States v. Kearney, 136 U.S.App.D.C. 328, 420 F.2d 170 (1969) (citing the corresponding Model Code of Evidence Rule 303); United States v. Krulewitch, 145 F.2d 76 (2d Cir. 1944); State v. Slauson, 249 Iowa 755, 88 N.W.2d 806 (1958) (citing the Uniform Rule); Gatzke v. Terminal R. R. Ass'n, 321 S.W.2d 462 (Mo.1959); Coleman v. Dennis, 1 Wash.App. 299, 461 P.2d 552 (1969). The factors of confusion, surprise and prejudice are discussed in 1 Wigmore, Evidence § 29a. It is sometimes said that the process of balancing probative value against prejudice applies to circumstantial evidence only, Bunten v. Davis, 82 N.H. 304, 133 Atl. 16, 45 A.L.R. 1409 (1926); State v. Whitener, 228 S.C. 244, 89 S.E.2d 701 (1955). The value of direct evidence is not easily overbalanced, but the recognised power of the court to prevent excessive cumulation of witnesses shows that the general rule, at least in some of its aspects, is applicable to direct as well as to circumstantial proof. Cases are collected in the annotations on limitation of witnesses in 5 A.L.R.3d 169, 328.

In appraising the probative worth of the offered evidence, before determining whether it is outweighed by the countervailing dangers, the distance in time of the facts offered will often cause the court to discount its value. This factor is frequently termed "remoteness." See, e. g., International Shoe Mach. Corp. v. United Shoe Mach. Corp., 315 F.2d 449 (2d Cir. 1963); Dec.Dig. Evidence ☞145. Obviously, not the passage of time alone, but the weakening of inferences through the likelihood of supervening factors must be the basis of this discounting. City of Phoenix v. Boggs, 1 Ariz.App. 370, 403 P.2d 305 (1965); Brower v. Quick, 249 Iowa 569, 88 N.W.2d 120 (1958); Sherburne v. Meade, 303 Mass. 356, 21 N.E.2d 946 (1939).

A final factor which some opinions say the judge should consider in assessing the value of the offered evidence is one not related to its probative force. This is: the availability of other evidence of the same fact, which evidence does not carry the same dangers with it. In this sense, two pieces of evidence with the same probative force may have different "values." Frank v. United States, 104 U.S.App.D.C. 384, 262 F.2d 695 (1958) (" 'Although sensational and shocking evidence may be relevant, it has an objectionable tendency to prejudice the jury. It is, therefore, incompetent

unless the exigencies of p oof make it necessary or important that the case be proved that way.' United States v. 88 Cases, More or Less, Containing Bireley's Orange Beverage, 3d Cir., 187 F.2d 967, 975.")

31. State v. Flett, 234 Ore. 124, 380 P.2d 634, 94 A.L.R.2d 1082 (1963) (". . . its tendency to prove the issue in dispute must be weighed against the tendency of the offered evidence to produce passion and prejudice out of proportion to its probative value." Murder case; to show ill will between defendant and her husband, the victim, evidence of defendant's acts of marital infidelity within days before killing were properly admitted, but value of evidence of such acts done months before was so outweighed by danger of unfair prejudice as to require exclusion); Lyda v. United States, 321 F.2d 788 (9th Cir. 1963); Daniels v. Dillinger, 445 S.W.2d 410 (Mo.App.1969); C.J.S. Evidence § 159 n. 21.

It should be emphasized that prejudice, in this context, means more than simply damage to the opponent's cause. A party's case is always damaged by evidence that the facts are contrary to his contentions; but that cannot be ground for exclusion. What is meant here is an undue tendency to move the tribunal to decide on an improper basis, commonly, though not always, an emotional one. In the pungent phrase of Sloan, J., in State v. Rollo, 221 Ore. 428, 438, 351 P.2d 422, 426 (1960), the party "is entitled to hit as hard as he can above, but not below, the belt." See F.R.Ev. (R.D. 1971) 403 and Note. Since this competition between proper and improper bases for decision is involved, it is natural that what one court calls "unfair prejudice," another may refer to as "confusion of issues," or "distraction of the jury from the issue it should determine."

32. Herman Schwabe, Inc. v. United Shoe Mach. Corp., 297 F.2d 906, 912 (2d Cir. 1962) (voluminous tabulations, charts, and graphs, accompanying economist's opinion as to damages, held properly excluded on grounds of speculativeness and confusion: "It might indeed have been possible for a judge, with days in which to study the exhibits of plaintiff's expert, to come up with some rational computation of damages, on a theory wholly different from what the expert advocated, that would satisfy the Supreme Court's modest requirements in this area; it would be foolhardy to expect a jury to do so. 'When the risk of confusion is so great as to upset the balance of advantage, the evidence

the evidence offered and the counter proof will consume an undue amount of time.[33] Fourth, the danger of unfair surprise to the opponent when, having no reasonable ground to anticipate this development of the proof, he would be unprepared to meet it.[34] Often, of course, several of these dangers such as distraction and time consumption, or prejudice and surprise, emerge from a particular offer of evidence. This balancing of intangibles—probative values against probative dangers—is so much a matter where wise judges in particular situations may differ that a leeway of discretion is generally recognized.[35] In some areas, such as proof of character, the situations have been so constantly repeated that the leeway of discretion has hardened into rules discussed in the next chapter.[36] Some others where the element of discretion remains prominent are developed in a later chapter.[37]

Judges and textwriters have sometimes described the process of excluding evidence

---

goes out,' Shepard v. United States, 290 U.S. 96, 104, 54 S.Ct. 22, 26, 78 L.Ed. 196 (1933)."); Veer v. Hagemann, 334 Ill. 23, 28, 165 N.E. 175 (1929) ("Where the confusion of issues will not be compensated by the assistance of useful evidence it is proper to exclude the evidence offered."); Sellers v. State, 41 Ala.App. 612, 145 So.2d 853 (1962); Brooks v. Daley, 242 Md. 185, 218 A.2d 184 (1966); McCaffrey v. Schwartz, 285 Pa. 561, 132 Atl. 810 (1926); C.J.S. Evidence § 159, at 436 n. 18.

In measuring the danger of confusion of issues, as well as the danger of unfair prejudice, a factor which the judge may use to discount the danger is the efficacy of an instruction to the jury as to the proper use of the evidence. See § 59, supra; 1 Wigmore, Evidence § 13.

33. " . . . [S]o far as the introduction of collateral issues goes, that objection is a purely practical one—a concession to the shortness of life." Holmes, J., in Reeve v. Dennett, 145 Mass. 23, 11 N.E. 938, 943 (1887). See also Dankert v. Lamb Finance Co., 146 Cal.App.2d 499, 304 P.2d 199 (1956); Jones v. Boeing Co., 153 N.W.2d 897 (N.D. 1967).

34. Mention of this factor is usually coupled with mention of the other dangers. Stoelting v. Hauck, 32 N.J. 87, 159 A.2d 385 (1960); Thompson v. American Steel & Wire Co., 317 Pa. 7, 175 Atl. 541 (1934); Sanitary Groc. Co. v. Steinbrecher, 183 Va. 495, 32 S.E.2d 685 (1945). It was Wigmore's view that the common law did not, in general, consider surprise a ground for exclusion, 7 Wigmore, Evidence §§ 1845, 1849. Although included as a ground for rejection in the Uniform Rule, it has been eliminated from West's Ann. California Evidence Code § 352, New Jersey Rule 4, and the proposed Federal Rules of Evidence, on the basis that the appropriate remedy is a continuance, rather than rejection. F.R.Civ.P. 15(b) seems already to have adopted this position. Notice in advance avoids the ground of objection, and is required by some of the rules of pleading and discovery; but the cases cited above, suggesting that surprise alone may be ground of exclusion, should be distinguished from those in which evidence is excluded in enforcement of a rule of pleading or discovery, with which the proponent has previously failed to comply. See 7 Wigmore, Evidence § 1848.

35. State v. Anderson, 253 S.C. 168, 169 S.E.2d 706, 712 (1969), cert. denied 396 U.S. 948, 397 U.S. 958, reh. denied 397 U.S. 1031 (" . . . many hundreds of potential relevancy issues passed before the trial judge. It is neither desirable nor possible for this court to lay down any general rule that will serve as a solution for every issue, for it is a different question of experience and common sense in each instance . . . . The precedents in the area of relevancy are of very limited value, and the trial judge must have wide discretion on the innumerable questions of relevancy before him. His decision should be reversed only for abuse of that discretion."); Thompson v. American Steel & Wire Co., 317 Pa. 7, 11, 175 Atl. 541 (1934) ("He is constantly faced with questions on evidence in their special relation to the issue to be tried. He must deal with such questions in the light of the purposes of the ultimate inquiry and does so in the exercise of what is known as judicial discretion . . . . His conclusion or decision on such points will not be interfered with on appeal save for manifest abuse of power."); United States v. Ravich, 421 F.2d 1196 (2d Cir. 1970); Nonni v. Commonwealth, 356 Mass. 264, 249 N.E.2d 644 (1969) (condemnation proceeding in which one sale of other property was admitted as comparable and another excluded as noncomparable, both rulings being upheld as within the judge's discretion); C.J.S. Evidence §§ 435, 436. For discriminating discussions of the scope of discretion and the need for such leeway, see McElroy, Some Observations Concerning the Discretions Reposed in Trial Judges, Model Code of Evidence 356 (1942); James, op. cit., 29 Calif.L.Rev. 704; Trautman, Logical or Legal Relevancy, 5 Vand.L.Rev. 385, 392–394 (1952). Compare, F.R.Ev. (R.D.1971) 403, which makes exclusion mandatory when probative value is "substantially outweighed" by the danger of unfair prejudice, confusion of issues, or misleading the jury, but discretionary in the case of the other dangers.

36. Ch. 17, infra.

37. Ch. 18, infra.

having probative value, by reason of these counter factors of prejudice, confusion, time-consumption and surprise, as the application of a standard of "legal relevancy." [38] This same term, "legal relevancy," is used to describe the aggregate of rules which have been produced, as indicated above, by the use as precedents of discretionary rulings on the balance of value against dangers. [39] Again, "legal relevancy" has been taken as a standard requiring a "plus value"—more than a bare minimum of probative worth [40]—a standard which is doubtless implicit in the balancing process. It seems better to discard the term "legal relevancy" altogether. [41] Its use tends to emphasize conformity to precedent in an area where the need for discretionary responsibility for weighing of value against dangers in the particular case should be stressed. Moreover, to maintain a single standard of "relevancy," by the application of the test suggested herein, will make for clearer thinking in an area where confusion and uncertainty have been rife.

38. "All evidence must be logically relevant. . . . The fact, however, that it is logically relevant, does not insure admissibility. It must also be legally relevant. A fact which, in connection with other facts, renders probable the existence of a fact in issue, may still be rejected, if in the opinion of the judge and under the circumstances of the case it is considered essentially misleading or too remote." Hoag v. Wright, 34 App.Div. 260, 54 N.Y.S. 658, 662 (1898). To like effect is Cotton v. United States, 361 F.2d 673 (8th Cir. 1966).

39. Thus, in State v. LaPage, 57 N.H. 245, 288 (1876) in holding inadmissible evidence of another crime relevant only as showing a propensity to that kind of crime, the court said: ". . . [A]lthough undoubtedly the relevancy of testimony is originally a matter of logic and common-sense, still there are many instances in which the evidence of particular facts as bearing upon particular issues has been so often the subject of discussion in courts of law, and so often ruled upon, that the united logic of a great many judges and lawyers may be said to furnish evidence of the sense common to a great many individuals, and, therefore, the best evidence of what may be properly called common-sense, and thus to acquire the authority of law. It is for this reason that the subject of relevancy of testimony has become, to so great an extent, a matter of precedent and authority, and that we may with entire propriety speak of its legal relevancy." See also 1 Wigmore, Evidence § 12.

40. Frank R. Jelleff, Inc. v. Braden, 98 U.S.App.D.C. 180, 233 F.2d 671, 679 (1956). (" 'Each single piece of evidence must have a plus value', something more than a minimum of probative value."); Hebert v. Boston & M. R. R., 90 N.H. 324, 8 A.2d 744 (1939) (a questionable holding that direct evidence should have been rejected because unworthy of belief; cf. Wilson v. Manchester Sav. Bank, 95 N.H. 113, 58 A.2d 745 (1948); 1 Wigmore, Evidence § 28.

41. This seems to have been Thayer's view. Preliminary Treatise on Evidence 265 (1898) ("The law furnishes no test of relevance"). See the persuasive argument for abjuring "legal relevancy" in James, op. cit., 29 Calif.L.Rev. 693, 694, 702–704.

CHAPTER 17

CHARACTER AND HABIT

186. Character: In General.[1]

A conspicuous instance in which rules of admissibility have been molded by the effort to balance probative values against countervailing dangers of prejudice, distraction, etc., is the area of rules about the admissibility of evidence of character. The result is a complex of interwoven doctrines and distinctions which are not always easy to keep steadily in sight in the process of planning the proofs and putting on the evidence. It should be noticed at the outset that two considerations are paramount in the analysis and decision of problems of proof in this field.

The first is the *purpose* for which the evidence of character is offered: The two usual alternative purposes are these: (a) to prove the character of a person where the question of what that character is or was, is one of the ultimate issues in the case,[2] and (b) to prove the character of a man as circumstantial evidence of what his acts (and sometimes his accompanying state of mind) probably were.[3] In the one case the search for character is crucial and essential. In the other it represents only one of the types of proof usually available to prove conduct, and a type which is of somewhat inferior persuasive force. This consideration, then, of the pur-

1. 1 Wigmore, Evidence §§ 52–80; Ladd, Techniques and Theory of Character Testimony, 24 Iowa L.Rev. 498 (1939); Hale, Character Evidence, 22 S.Calif. L.Rev. 341 (1949); Udall, Character Proof, 18 U.Cin.L.Rev. 283 (1949); Slough, Relevancy Unraveled—Character and Habit, 5 Kan.L.Rev. 404 (1957); Falknor, Extrinsic Policies Affecting Admissibility, 10 Rutgers L.Rev. 574, 584 (1956); Notes: 20 Ga.B.J. 107 (1957); 13 Temple U.L.Q. 109 (1938); Dec.Dig. Evidence ☞106, 152, 155(2), Criminal Law ☞369–381; C.J.S. Evidence §§ 432–437; C.J.S. Criminal Law §§ 676–681.

2. 1 Wigmore, Evidence §§ 70–81.

3. 1 Wigmore, Evidence §§ 55–69.

pose of the character-proof bears upon the probative weight of the evidence and on the need for its use.

The second consideration is the *manner* of proof, i. e., the distinction between different types of proof which may be offered as evidence of character. These types are (a) testimony as to the conduct of the person in question as reflecting his character,[4] and (b) testimony of a witness as to his opinion of the person's character based on observation,[5] and (c) testimony as to his reputation.[6] These are listed in the order of their pungency and persuasiveness. In the same order, they differ in their tendency to arouse undue prejudice, to confuse and distract, to engender time-consuming side issues and to create a risk of unfair surprise. Modern common law doctrine makes the neutral and unexciting reputation evidence the preferred type, which will usually be accepted where character evidence can come in at all, whereas the other two, when they are received at all, are received only in limited and defined situations.

187. Character in Issue.[7]

A person's possession of a particular character trait may be an operative fact which under the substantive law determines the legal rights and liabilities of the parties. When this is so, and when that character-trait has been put in issue by the pleadings, the fact of character must of course be open to proof, and the courts have usually held that it may be proved by evidence of specific acts.[8] While this is the method most likely

4. 1 Wigmore, Evidence §§ 191–213.

5. 7 Wigmore, Evidence §§ 1980–1986.

6. 5 Wigmore, Evidence §§ 1608–1621.

7. 1 Wigmore, Evidence §§ 70, 81, 202–213.

8. Thus, in defamation when the slander charged bad character, and the defendant pleads truth, character is in issue and specific instances may be shown, subject usually to the proviso that notice of them is given in the plea. See Moore v. Davis, 27

to create prejudice and hostility, it is also the most decisive revelation of character, which is here the center of inquiry. We are willing to incur a hazard of prejudice and even surprise, which we are not when

S.W.2d 153 (Tex.Com.App.1930) (libel charging plaintiff with unfitness as judge: evidence of subsequent acts showing unfitness proper); Talmadge v. Baker, 22 Wis. 65 (1868) (slander: "he is in the habit of picking up things"; evidence of particular thefts wrongly excluded); 1 Wigmore, Evidence § 207. To be distinguished is the situation where reputation itself (not character) comes into issue, when defendant seeks to show that plaintiff's reputation was bad, in mitigation of damages. This in most jurisdictions is allowed. See 1 Wigmore, Evidence §§ 70–74.

So in a prosecution for seduction when the statute requires that the victim must have been "of previously chaste character," her previous use of indecent language and telling of obscene stories were receivable, State v. Wilcoxen, 200 Iowa 1250, 206 N.W. 260 (1925), as are previous acts of intercourse with others, Burrow v. State, 166 Ark. 138, 265 S.W. 642 (1924). But the issue may be regarded as one merely of physical virginity, not of chaste disposition. People v. Kehoe, 123 Cal. 224, 55 P. 911 (1898) (unchastity must be shown by acts of intercourse, not mere indecencies); 1 Wigmore, Evidence § 205.

When an employer's liability to a servant hinged upon negligent failure to select a competent fellow-servant, character was in issue and acts showing incompetence were received. Morrow v. St. Paul City Ry. Co., 74 Minn. 480, 77 N.W. 303 (1898). Contra: Hatt v. Nay, 144 Mass. 186, 10 N.E. 807 (1887). But a single instance might not be sufficient. Holland v. Southern Pac. Co., 100 Cal. 240, 34 Pac. 666 (1893). Cases are collected in 1 Wigmore, Evidence § 208.

More important today are the situations where the owner of a motor vehicle or any dangerous object is charged with liability for the acts of a person using it on grounds of negligent entrustment of the vehicle or object to an incompetent or unfit person. Here again the character of the custodian is in issue and his acts come in to show it. Clark v. Stewart, 126 Ohio St. 263, 185 N.E. 71 (1933) (acts of recklessness of defendant's son received, though defendant admitted that his son, the driver, was acting as agent in the course of father's business); Guedon v. Rooney, 160 Ore. 621, 87 P.2d 209, 120 A.L.R. 1298 (1939), annotated on this point; Ozan Lbr. Co. v. McNeely, 214 Ark. 657, 217 S.W. 2d 341, 8 A.L.R.2d 261 (1949), annotated on negligence in employing an incompetent contractor; Woods, Negligent Entrustment, 20 Ark.L.Rev. 101 (1966); Snowhite v. State, 243 Md. 291, 221 A.2d 342, 19 A.L.R.2d 1155 (1968), annotated on negligent entrustment to intoxicated or intemperate driver.

character is sought to be shown by specific acts on other occasions, only for a remoter and often doubtful inference as to the person's *acts* which are the subject of suit.

Moreover, in some of these situations wherein character for care or competence is at issue, the courts have reversed the usual preference for reputation as the vehicle of proof of character and have held that reputation is not even admissible as evidence of character, and that specific acts must be adduced if character is to be shown, though reputation may then come in as evidence that such character was known to the defendant.[9]

Similarly, in these cases where character is part of the ultimate issue, and where as we have seen it may be proven by the person's acts, the argument is strong for the allowability of opinion evidence as to character from one who has observed the man and his conduct. It is surely a proper case for opinion, since an impression from facts too detailed to recite may be valuable to the trier of fact. The fact that specific acts may be inquired into upon cross-examination, and thus the trier's attention be unduly distracted, is hardly an objection since the door has already been opened to specific acts as evidence of character in issue. This argument for opinion evidence has prevailed with many courts when the character involved is for care, competence, skill, or sanity—the non-moral traits.[10] As to traits of *moral* character, peacefulness, honesty and the like, presumably most courts would frown on opinion evidence, even when character is in issue, in view of the current questionable tradition against opinions where the character of a witness[11] or of an accused is in question.[12]

The Uniform Rule goes further and in keeping with its purpose of liberalizing and simplifying the rules in this area it would admit all three types of evidence to show character when character is in issue.[13]

188. Character as Circumstantial Evidence of Conduct and State of Mind:[14] (a) General Rule of Exclusion.

It will always be relevant, if we have the task of proving that A committed a certain act, and possibly of proving also his guilty or innocent state of mind, to show that A is the kind of man (in his disposition, tendencies, character) who is likely to act in that fashion with the intent charged. A thief will often steal but an honest man usually will not. And the law in two important instances at least, namely in its permission to an accused to prove his good character[15] and in its practice of witness impeachment,[16] sanc-

9. Young v. Fresno Flume & Irrigation Co., 24 Cal. App. 286, 141 Pac. 29, 32 (1914) (employer's liability to servant based on unfitness of fellow servant); Guedon v. Rooney, 160 Ore. 621, 87 P.2d 209, 217, 120 A.L.R. 1298 (1939), annotated on this question (negligent entrustment of automobile to unfit driver).

10. Marine Towing Co. v. Fairbanks Morse & Co., 225 F.Supp. 467 (E.D.Pa.1963) (skill of engine repair crew); Lewis v. Emery, 108 Mich. 641, 66 N.W. 569 (1896) (competency of fellow servant). Contra: Purkey v. Southern Coal & Transportation Co., 57 W.Va. 595, 50 S.E. 755 (1905) (competency of fellow servant). Cases are collected in 7 Wigmore, Evidence § 1984.

11. See §§ 41–44, supra.

12. See § 191, infra; Re Monaghan, 126 Vt. 53, 222 A.2d 665 (1966) (application to take bar examination; opinion as to moral character in issue not admissible), but see Wilson v. Wilson, 128 Mont. 511, 278 P.2d 219 (1954) (opinion as to fitness of parent to have child custody admissible in custody proceeding).

13. Uniform Rule 46: "When a person's character or a trait of his character is in issue, it may be proved by testimony in the form of opinion, evidence of reputation, or evidence of specific instances of the person's conduct, subject, however, to the limitations of Rules 47 [see § 188, n. 17 infra] and 48 [see § 189 n. 20, infra.]" To like effect is F.R.Ev.(R.D.1971) 405, which makes it clear however that to be in issue character must be an element of a claim or defense.

14. See 1 Wigmore, Evidence §§ 54–68; Dec.Dig. Evidence ☞106; C.J.S. Evidence §§ 423–432.

15. See § 191, infra.

16. See §§ 41–44, 49, supra.

tions this use of character. But in what are probably the greater number of cases when character could be offered for this purpose, the law sets its face against it. So while what we have called the exceptions could be stated as the rule,[17] it is believed that it is more accurate and illuminating to say that the approach in this area is that evidence of character in any form, whether reputation, opinion from observation, or specific acts, will not generally be received to prove that the person whose character is sought to be shown, engaged in certain conduct, or did so with a given intent, on a particular occasion.[18] To this rule, as we have said, there are important exceptions which will be developed in later sections. The reason for the general rule is that character when used for this purpose is not essential as it is when character is the issue, and generally it comes with too much dangerous baggage of prejudice, distraction from the issues, time consumption, and hazard of surprise.[19]

189. Character to Evidence Conduct—(b) Application of Rule of Exclusion to Evidence of Character for Care: Previous Accidents: "Accident Proneness."

The rule excluding character as evidence of acts has long been applied with relative consistency in negligence cases. Where a negligent act by the defendant or his servant is in issue, most courts will reject proof of the actor's reputation for care or negligence [20] or opinion testimony from observation of his character in this respect.[21] A minority of courts, however, have admitted such proof for this purpose, when there are no eyewitnesses available who saw the happening.[22] If these courts go so far in reject-

---

17. It is so stated in Uniform Rule 47: "Subject to Rule 48, [see § 189 n. 20, infra] when a trait of a person's character is relevant as tending to prove his conduct on a specified occasion, such trait may be proved in the same manner as provided by Rule 46, except that (a) evidence of specific instances of conduct other than evidence of conviction of a crime which tends to prove the trait to be bad shall be inadmissible, and (b) in a criminal action evidence of a trait of an accused's character as tending to prove his guilt or innocence of the offense charged, (i) may not be excluded by the judge under Rule 45 if offered by the accused to prove his innocence, and (ii) if offered by the prosecution to prove his guilt, may be admitted only after the accused has introduced evidence of his good character."

18. This generalization in the texts is usually stated as the rule for civil cases. See 1 Wigmore, Evidence § 64. The doctrine is here stated more broadly, since even in criminal cases the permission to the accused to use character as evidence of innocence seems better understood as an exception rather than the rule. The matter is dealt with in this manner in F.R.Ev. (R.D.1971) 404. See also, Rich v. Cooper, 234 Ore. 300, 380 P.2d 613 (1963) (general rule of exclusion, with exceptions).

19. See § 185, supra.

20. Denbigh v. Oregon-Washington R. & Navigation Co., 23 Idaho 663, 132 Pac. 112 (1913) (judge rightly excluded evidence that engineer "was known as a prudent and careful engineer"); Phinney v. Detroit United Ry. Co., 232 Mich. 399, 205 N.W. 124 (1925) (testimony of conductor that motorman had a reputation for recklessness inadmissible); Baltimore & O. R. Co. v. Colvin, 118 Pa.St. 230, 12 Atl. 337 (1888) (error to receive evidence of reputation of flagman for carelessness); 1 Wigmore, Evidence § 65; Uniform Rule 48: "Evidence of a trait of a person's character with respect to care or skill is inadmissible as tending to prove the quality of his conduct on a specified occasion."; F.R.Ev.(R.D.1971) 404.

21. Harriman v. Pullman Palace-Car Co., 85 Fed. 553 (8th Cir. 1898) (action for negligent act of porter, injuring plaintiff: error to admit evidence for defendant that porter "was usually careful, competent, courteous and attentive"); Williams v. Slusser, 104 Ga.App. 412, 121 S.E.2d 796 (1961) (opinion from knowing driver that he "drove in a careful manner," inadmissible); Louisville & N. R. Co. v. Adams' Adm'r, 205 Ky. 203, 265 S.W. 623 (1924) (death at a crossing: error to receive testimony that decedent was careful driver); 1 Wigmore, Evidence § 65. But a history of being careful about a particular danger may come in as being nearer to habit than to character. Hussey v. Boston & M. R. Co., 82 N.H. 236, 133 Atl. 9 (1926) (death of a lineman; no witnesses; evidence of his "habitual care in the presence of charged wires" proper). As to evidence of habit, see § 195, infra.

22. Hawbaker v. Danner, 226 F.2d 843 (7th Cir. 1956); Anderson v. Glass, 19 Ill.App.2d 414, 153 N.E.2d 863 (1958); Barana v. James A. Hannah, Inc., 12 Ill.App.2d 364, 140 N.E.2d 301 (1956). Some courts speak of their "no eyewitness" rule as applying to habit evidence, Missouri-Kansas-Texas R. v. McFerrin, 156 Tex. 69, 291 S.W.2d 931 (1956); see § 195, infra.

ing the policy of exclusion—and this policy is obviously open to reasonable debate—it is arguable that they should go further still and admit the evidence of character when there are eyewitnesses but their evidence is conflicting. There is almost as much need for evidence of character in such case, it seems, as when eyewitnesses are wanting.[23]

The rule of exclusion is even more uniformly applied, as would be expected, when evidence of negligent conduct of the party or his agent on other occasions is sought to be proved and its only substantial relevance is as showing a propensity for negligent acts and thus enhancing the probability of negligence on the occasion in suit.[24] This is the

most pungent way of showing a negligent disposition but its probative force has traditionally been thought too slight, where conduct is the issue, to overbear the dangers of prejudice, distraction by side issues, and unfair surprise.[25]

Articles [26] call attention to the theory developed in recent scientific studies of accidents that a limited group of persons have a special predisposition for accidents. They are "accident prone." In the case of drivers, inadequate training, defective vision, and certain mental attitudes and emotional traits may be identified as characteristic of the members of this group.[27] The writers of the articles suggest that the findings in respect to "accident proneness" invite a reconsideration of the rule forbidding the use of character for negligence and history of accidents as evidence of negligent acts on the occasion in suit.[28] They would advocate, apparently, that on the issue of negligence, proof of accident proneness by expert opinion, based on clinical tests and interviews and on the past accident record, be received. However, they also point out that these studies have not yet disclosed any connection between accident

---

23. A case taking this view, in a state which had applied the "no eyewitness rule" to habit evidence, is Glatt v. Feist, 156 N.W.2d 819, 825 (N.D. 1968) (habit evidence allowed when testimony of eye witnesses was in conflict).

24. Barnes v. Norfolk S. Ry., 333 F.2d 192 (4th Cir. 1964) (prior injuries to plaintiff excluded); Nesbit v. Cumberland Contracting Co., 196 Md. 36, 75 A.2d 339 (1950) (plaintiff sues for injuries sustained when he drove his car into a pile of dirt and rocks left on highway by defendant; on cross-examination plaintiff was asked if he considered himself a good driver and he answered "Yes"; then, over objection, he was asked about and admitted convictions for driving without license and reckless driver, held, error, convictions for traffic offenses not admissible to impeach—compare § 43, herein—and it was calculated to be used to show reckless character to show negligence on this occasion, an inadmissible inference); Brownhill v. Kivlin, 317 Mass. 168, 57 N.E.2d 539 (1944) (action for negligent burning of garage brought against administratrix of deceased, who was burned to death in same fire; plaintiff charged that deceased, whose body was in rear part of car, had caused fire by careless smoking; held proper to exclude evidence that on three previous occasions deceased had caused fires by going to sleep while smoking; but is not the propensity here so specific as to amount to a habit? See § 195, infra); Ryan v. International Harvester Co., 204 Minn. 177, 283 N.W. 129 (1938) (collision: defendant's question to his driver seeking to show that he had never previously had a collision, properly excluded); Matta v. Welcher, 387 S.W.2d 265 (Mo.App.1965) (contributory negligence not provable by prior negligent acts); Grenadier v. Surface Transportation Co., 271 App.Div. 130, 66 N.Y.S.2d 130 (1946) (injury from bus accident, error to permit plaintiff to cross-examine driver about prior accidents); 1 Wigmore, Evidence § 199.

But the previous accident or negligent act may have some other and weightier relevancy than merely showing character or disposition, and thus escape the present objection. Dallas Ry. & Term. Co. v. Farnsworth, 148 Tex. 584, 227 S.W.2d 1017 (1950) (action for injury alleged to be due to abrupt starting of street car when plaintiff alighted; held, plaintiff's testimony that previously on same trip motorman started car abruptly admissible as tending to show that motorman was nervous and in a hurry).

25. See 1 Wigmore, Evidence § 199.

26. Maloney and Rish, The Accident-Prone Driver, 14 U.Fla.L.Rev. 364 (1962); James and Dickinson, Accident Proneness and Accident Law, 63 Yale L.J. 769 (1950).

27. Maloney and Rish, op. cit., 14 U.Fla.L.Rev. 367–374; James and Dickinson, op. cit., 63 Yale L.J. 772–775.

28. James and Dickinson, op. cit., 63 Yale L.J. 793; cf. Maloney and Rish, op. cit., 14 U.Fla.L.Rev. 376–378.

proneness and fault or carelessness [29] and thus they have seemingly not yet gone far enough to persuade the courts to abandon the present evidentiary rule.[30] Nevertheless, the policy basis of the prohibitory rule, both as applied to character evidence based on reputation or individual opinion, and even as applied to proof of past accidents where they arc not isolated but repeated, is so doubtful that the courts may profitably be alert to the future developments of these scientific studies, in appraising the desirability of maintaining the legal barriers.

190. Character to Evidence Conduct—(c) Application of Rule of Exclusion to Forbid the Prosecution to Introduce Evidence Initially of Bad Character of Accused: Other Crimes.

The disfavor for receiving proof of the character of a person as evidence that on a particular occasion he acted in keeping with his disposition is strongly felt when the state seeks to show that the accused is a bad man and thus more likely to have committed the crime. The long-established rule, accordingly, forbids the prosecution, unless and until the accused gives evidence of his good character, to introduce initially evidence of the bad character of the accused.[31] It is not irrelevant, but in the setting of jury trial the danger of prejudice outweighs the probative value.

This danger is at its highest when character is shown by other criminal acts, and

the rule about the proof of other crimes is but an application of the wider prohibition against the initial introduction by the prosecution of evidence of bad character. The rule is that the prosecution may not introduce evidence of other criminal acts of the accused unless the evidence is substantially relevant for some other purpose than to show a probability that he committed the crime on trial because he is a man of criminal character.[32] There are numerous other purposes

---

29. James and Dickinson, op. cit., 63 Yale L.J. 775; but see Maloney and Rish, op. cit., 14 U.Fla.L.Rev. 377, 379.

30. Thornburg v. Perleberg, 158 N.W.2d 188 (N.D. 1968) (evidence of accident proneness inadmissible on issue of negligence).

31. United States v. Harris, 331 F.2d 185 (4th Cir. 1964) (reputation); Bedsole v. State, 274 Ala. 603, 150 So.2d 696 (1963) (reputation and prior convictions); State v. McCorvey, 262 Minn. 361, 114 N.W.2d 703 (1962) (reputation); Jones v. LaCrosse, 180 Va. 406, 23 S.E.2d 142 (1942) (character for drunkenness); 1 Wigmore, Evidence §§ 55, 57; Dec.Dig. Crim.Law ⊕376.

32. For a similar formulation see Model Code of Evidence Rule 311: ". . . evidence that a person committed a crime or civil wrong on a specified occasion is inadmissible as tending to prove that he committed a crime or civil wrong on another occasion if, but only if, the evidence is relevant solely as tending to prove his disposition to commit such a crime or civil wrong or to commit crimes or civil wrongs generally.", approved in Swann v. United States, 195 F.2d 689, 690 (4th Cir. 1952) and in State v. Scott, 111 Utah 9, 175 P.2d 1016, 1022 (1947). See also Lovely v. United States, 169 F.2d 386, 388, 389 (4th Cir. 1948); Gorski v. State, 1 Md.App. 200, 228 A.2d 835 (1967).

See also Uniform Rule 55: "Subject to Rule 47 [see § 188, n. 17] evidence that a person committed a crime or civil wrong on a specified occasion, is inadmissible to prove his disposition to commit crime or civil wrong as the basis for an inference that he committed another crime or civil wrong on another specified occasion but, subject to Rules 45 [see § 185, n. 30] and 48 [see § 189, n. 20], such evidence is admissible when relevant to prove some other material fact including absence of mistake or accident, motive, opportunity, intent, preparation, plan, knowledge or identity." To similar effect is F.R.Ev. (R.D.1971) 404(b).

A frequent form of statement is a general rule that evidence of other crimes is inadmissible except when offered for certain particular named purposes. See, e. g., People v. Molineux, 168 N.Y. 264, 61 N.E. 286, 293, 294 (1901): "The general rule of evidence applicable to criminal trials is that the state cannot prove against a defendant any crime not alleged in the indictment, either as a foundation for a separate punishment, or as aiding the proofs that he is guilty of the crime charged. . . . The exceptions to the rule cannot be stated with categorical precision. Generally speaking, evidence of other crimes is competent to prove the specific crime charged when it tends to establish (1) motive; (2) intent; (3) the absence of mistake or accident; (4) a common scheme or plan embracing the commission of two or more crimes so related to each other that proof of one tends to establish the others; (5) the identity of the person charged with the commission of the crime on trial." In that case, a prosecution for murder by

for which evidence of other criminal acts may be offered, and when so offered the rule of exclusion is simply inapplicable. Some of these purposes are listed below but warning must be given that the list is not complete, for the range of relevancy outside the ban is almost infinite; and further that the purposes are not mutually exclusive, for a particular line of proof may fall within several of them. Neither are they strictly coordinate. Some are phrased in terms of the immediate inferences sought to be drawn, such as plan or motive, others in terms of the ultimate fact, such as knowledge, intent, or identity which the prosecution seeks to establish.[33] The list follows.

(1) To complete the story of the crime on trial by proving its immediate context of happenings near in time and place.[34] This is often characterized as proving a part of the "same transaction" or the "res gestae."

(2) To prove the existence of a larger continuing plan, scheme, or conspiracy, of which the present crime on trial is a part.[35]

---

poisoning, the evidence was held not to fit any of these exceptions.

A similar statement of the rule has sometimes been embodied in statutes. See, e. g., La.Stat.Ann. 15:445, 446 (1967), discussed in Howerton, Evidence of Other Crimes, 11 La.L.Rev. 223 (1951); Mich. Comp.Laws Ann. § 768.27 (1968); Ohio Rev.Code Ann. § 2945.59 (1954), discussed in Notes, 5 Ohio St.L.J. 232 (1939) and 15 W.Res.L.Rev. 772 (1964). A critical discussion of such statutes is Stone, Exclusion of Similar Fact Evidence: England, 46 Harv.L.Rev. 954 (1933); America, 51 Harv.L.Rev. 988 (1938).

For general discussions, see 1 Wigmore, Evidence §§ 192–194; 1 Wharton, Criminal Evidence §§ 232–248 (12th ed. 1955); Slough and Knightly, Other Vices, Other Crimes, 41 Iowa L.Rev. 325 (1956); Lacy, Evidence of Crimes Not Charged, 31 Ore.L. Rev. 267 (1952). More localized treatments: Thomas, Looking Logically at Evidence of Other Crimes in Oklahoma, 15 Okla.L.Rev. 431 (1962); C. J. Morgan, Other Offenses, 3 Vand.L.Rev. 779 (1950); Comment, 7 U.C.L.A.L.Rev. 463 (1960); Notes, 18 Brooklyn L.Rev. 80 (1951), 35 Calif.L.Rev. 131 (1947), 37 Minn.L.Rev. 608 (1953), 28 N.C.L.Rev. 124 (1949), 54 W.Va.L.Rev. 142 (1952). Annot., 63 A.L.R. 602 (identity), 105 A.L.R. 1288 (stolen property); 20 A.L.R.2d 1012 (bribery), 34 A.L.R. 2d 777 (forgery), 40 A.L.R.2d 817 (illegal liquor sales); 42 A.L.R.2d 854 (robbery); 64 A.L.R.2d 823 (gambling); 77 A.L.R.2d 841 (sex offenses), 78 A.L.R.2d 1359 (false pretenses), 87 A.L.R.2d 891 (arson), 93 A.L.R.2d 1097 (narcotic sales). Cases, as the sands of the sea, are collected in Dec.Dig. Criminal Law ⊙365, 369–374; C.J.S. Criminal Law §§ 663–665, 682–691.

The spirit of the rule condemns not only evidence of other crimes not independently relevant, but also questions which, though negatively answered, carry with them the insinuation that the accused committed the other crimes. State v. Haney, 219 Minn. 518, 18 N.W.2d 315 (1945). Dealing with other such insinuations: Barnes v. United States, 124 U.S.App.D.C. 318, 365 F.2d 509 (1966); Boggs v. State, 268 Ala. 358, 106 So.2d 263 (1958); State v. Jacobs, 94 Ariz. 211, 382 P.2d 683 (1963).

33. "Motive, intent, absence of mistake, plan and identity are not really all on the same plane. Intent, absence of mistake, and identity are facts in issue—*facta probanda*. Motive, plan, or scheme are *facta probantia*, and may tend to show any *facta probanda*." Stone, op. cit., 51 Harv.L.Rev. 988, 1026n.

34. State v. Villavicencio, 95 Ariz. 199, 388 P.2d 245 (1964) (sales of narcotics to A and B at same time and place; evidence of sale to A admissible in prosecution for the sale to B; "This principle that the complete story of the crime may be shown even though it reveals other crimes has often been termed 'res gestae.' . . . [W]e choose to refer to this as the 'complete story' principle, rather than 'res gestae.' "); State v. Klotter, 274 Minn. 58, 142 N.W.2d 568 (1968) (burglary of sporting goods store; evidence of burglary of home of friend of defendant's family, 5 miles away on same night admissible, where guns from both burglaries found in defendant's possession; "connected closely enough in time, place and manner"); State v. Hendrix, 310 S.W.2d 852 (Mo.1958) (prosecution of convict for damaging penitentiary building by sawing bars on window; evidence of attempted escape of defendant and others, which was the purpose of the sawing, admissible as "circumstantial evidence of guilt"); People v. De Pompeis, 410 Ill. 587, 102 N.E.2d 813 (1952); Marshall v. State, 227 Ind. 1, 83 N.E.2d 763 (1949).

35. Makin v. Attorney General of New South Wales, [1894] App.C. 57 (Privy Council) (murder of an infant left with defendants for their care, with an inadequate premium; evidence that the bodies of ten other babies were found buried in the gardens of three houses formerly occupied by the accused, properly received, on question whether adoption bona fide and deaths accidental); Leonard v. United States, 324 F.2d 911 (9th Cir. 1963) (defendant obtained Treasury checks payable to others, induced A to forge payees' endorsements, then induced B to obtain false credentials, cash checks and split proceeds with defendant; all admissible to show scheme); State v. Toshishige Yoshimo, 45 Hawaii 206, 364 P.2d 638 (1961) (defendant and

This will be relevant as showing motive, and hence the doing of the criminal act, the identity of the actor, and his intention, where any of these is in dispute.

(3) To prove other like crimes by the accused so nearly identical in method as to earmark them as the handiwork of the accused.[36] Here much more is demanded than the mere repeated commission of crimes of the same class, such as repeated burglaries or thefts. The device used must be so un-

usual and distinctive as to be like a signature.[37]

(4) To show a passion or propensity for illicit sexual relations with the particular person concerned in the crime on trial.[38] Other like sexual crimes with other persons do not qualify for this purpose.[39] It has been argued that certain unnatural sex crimes are in themselves so unusual and distinctive that previous such acts by the accused with anyone are strongly probative of like acts upon the occasion involved in the charge,[40] but

---

others robbed A and obtained from him name and address of B as holder of another sum of money, proceeded to B's house and assaulted and robbed B; evidence of first robbery admissible in prosecution for second); State v. Long, 195 Ore. 81, 244 P.2d 1033 (1952) (that defendant after killing owner of truck, for which he is now on trial, in use of truck next day for robbery shot F.B.I. man while leaving scene of robbery properly proved as part of planned course of action); Haley v. State, 84 Tex.Cr. 629, 209 S.W. 675 (1919) (murder: that defendant desiring to continue illicit relations with wife of deceased, formed a plan to kill his own wife and deceased, provable but state's evidence here of his poisoning his wife not sufficiently cogent to be received).

36. R. v. George Joseph Smith (1915), reported in Notable British Trials (1922), and described in Marjoribanks, For the Defence: The Life of Edward Marshall Hall 321 (1937) (the famous "brides of the bath" case; defendant accused of murdering his wife, who left her property to him by will, by drowning her in the bathtub: defendant leaves their boardinghouse on a pretended errand, and then on his return purports to discover his wife drowning in the tub and so reports to the landlady; held proper to show that he had previously married several wives, who left him their property and were discovered by him drowned in the bath); People v. Peete, 28 Cal.2d 306, 169 P.2d 924 (1946) (where defendant had been previously convicted of killing another who was killed by means of a bullet from behind, severing the spinal cord at the neck, and deceased in present prosecution was shot from behind at close range in an attempt to sever the spinal cord, evidence of the prior homicide was admissible as tending to identify defendant as the murderer.); and see Note, 35 Colum.L.Rev. 131 (1935) which at p. 136 examines the distinction between this and purpose (2), above; Whiteman v. State, 119 Ohio St. 285, 164 N.E. 51, 63 A.L.R. 595 (1928) (robbery; evidence of other robberies committed by defendants according to same peculiar plan, as used in the robbery now on trial, that is, by using uniforms, impersonating officers, and stopping cars, thus "earmarking" the crimes as committed by the same persons).

37. See, e. g., State v. Sauter, 125 Mont. 109, 232 P.2d 731, 732 (1951) (forcible rape by defendant and S in automobile after picking victim up in barroom; held, error to admit evidence of rapes accomplished after similar pickups of other victims; "too common . . . to have much evidentiary value in showing a systematic scheme or plan"; two judges dissenting). A discussion of what is and is not sufficient is in People v. Haston, 69 Cal.2d 233, 70 Cal.Rptr. 419, 444 P.2d 91 (1968).

38. Woods v. State, 250 Ind. 132, 235 N.E.2d 479 (1968) (rape and incest; other like acts on victim admissible to show "depraved sexual instinct"); State v. Schut, 71 Wash.2d 400, 429 P.2d 126 (1967) (incest; prior acts with victim admissible to show a lustful inclination toward the offended female). See Annot., 77 A.L.R.2d 841; Notes, 2 Ala.L.Rev. 108 (1949), 96 U.Pa.L.Rev. 872 (1948), 98 U.Pa.L.Rev. 116 (1949), 23 Temp.L.Q. 133 (1949), 25 Tex.L.Rev. 421 (1947), 9 Wash. & Lee L.Rev. 86 (1952).

39. Landon v. State, 77 Okl.Cr. 190, 140 P.2d 242 (1943) (statutory rape on daughter: other offenses with another daughter on other occasions excluded); State v. Pace, 187 Ore. 498, 212 P.2d 755 (1949) (statutory rape); State v. Williams, 36 Utah 273, 103 Pac. 250 (1909) (statutory rape). But though not receivable to show propensity the evidence may come in on other theories. Landon v. State, supra ("res gestae"); Comm. v. Ransom, 169 Pa. Super. 306, 82 A.2d 547 (1951), affirmed on lower court's opinion, 369 Pa. 153, 85 A.2d 125 (1952) (charge of robbery and rape; other attempts at forcing intercourse on others during previous two days and up to two hours before offense admitted to show design or intent).

40. A few decisions have admitted the evidence seemingly on the theory, in part at least, of showing a special propensity. See, e. g., State v. Edwards, 224 N.C. 527, 31 S.E.2d 516 (1944) (incest); State v. Jackson, 82 Ohio App. 318, 81 N.E.2d 546 (1948) (incest). See also Comm. v. Kline, 361 Pa. 434, 65 A.2d 348 (1949) (statutory rape on daughter: State allowed to prove that defendant indecently exposed himself to a neighbor woman,

the danger of prejudice is likewise enhanced here, and most courts have in the past excluded such acts with other persons for this purpose. More recent cases show signs of lowering this particular barrier to admission.[41]

(5) To show, by similar acts or incidents, that the act on trial was not inadvertent, accidental, unintentional,[42] or without guilty knowledge.[43]

(6) To establish motive.[44] This in turn may serve as evidence of the identity of the

as showing he was an exhibitionist and thus had a moral trait consistent with the crime on trial).

41. Commentators assert that recently the limitations on proof of other offenses are being reduced in prosecutions for sex crimes, either directly, on the basis of the argument described in the text, or by forcing the evidence into the exceptions relating to design or intention. See Cleary and Strong, Cases on Evidence 225 n. 1 (1969); Gregg, Other Acts of Sexual Misbehavior, 6 Ariz.L.Rev. 212 (1965); Trautman, Logical or Legal Relevancy, 5 Vand.L.Rev. 385, 406 (1951); Comments, 78 Harv.L.Rev. 426, 435 (1964); 70 Yale L.J. 763 (1961); Annot., 77 A.L.R.2d 841 (1961). See Wollaston v. State, 358 P.2d 1111 (Okl.Crim.1961). Examples of cases rejecting evidence of acts on persons other than the present victim: State v. Searle, 125 Mont. 467, 239 P.2d 995 (1952) (sodomy); State v. Start, 65 Ore. 178, 132 Pac. 512 (1913).

42. United States v. Ross, 321 F.2d 61 (2d Cir. 1963) cert. denied 375 U.S. 894 (securities fraud; where defendant claimed he was an unwitting tool of his employer, proper for prosecution to show on cross-examination that he had long drifted among firms engaged in selling worthless securities by similar methods); People v. Williams, 6 Cal.2d 500, 58 P.2d 917 (1936) (larceny of coin-purse; state's theory and evidence were that defendant posing as customer standing near owner of bag, took purse from bag while owner was shopping; defendant claimed to have picked the purse from the floor, thinking it lost; held, evidence of detectives that they had seen defendant take another purse from another woman's bag in same manner, admissible); State v. Lapage, 57 N.H. 245, 294 (1876) (Cushing, C. J.; "Another class of cases consists of those in which it becomes necessary to show that the act for which the prisoner was indicted was not accidental,—e. g., where the prisoner had shot the same person twice within a short time, or where the same person had fired a rick of grain twice, or where several deaths by poison had taken place in the same family, or where the children of the same mother had mysteriously died. In such cases it might well happen that a man should shoot another accidentally, but that he should do it twice within a short time would be very unlikely. So, it might easily happen that a man using a gun might fire a rick of barley once by accident, but

that he should do it several times in succession would be very improbable. So, a person might die of accidental poisoning, but that several persons should so die in the same family at different times would be very unlikely."); 2 Wigmore, Evidence § 302. The similarity of the other acts need not be as great as under purpose (3) in the text above, nor is a connection by common plan as in purpose (2) demanded. The trial judge has a range of discretion in determining whether the probative value justifies admission. United States v. Feldman, 136 F.2d 394 (2d Cir. 1943). Subsequent as well as prior acts have been held admissible for this purpose. Schmeller v. United States, 143 F.2d 544 (6th Cir. 1944); State v. Addison, 249 Iowa 905, 87 N.W.2d 916 (1958). However, when the act charged is not equivocal, but the criminal intent is a necessary conclusion from the act, this theory of other acts as showing intent may not be availed of. People v. Lonsdale, 122 Mich. 388, 81 N.W. 277 (1899) (abortion where there was no room for inference of accident or that operation was performed to save life); State v. Barker, 249 S.W. 75, 77 (Mo.1923) (automobile theft); 1 Wharton, Criminal Evidence § 237 (12th ed. 1955).

43. United States v. Brand, 79 F.2d 605 (2d Cir. 1935), cert. denied 296 U.S. 655 (knowingly transporting stolen car in interstate commerce; evidence of previous sale of a stolen car); People v. Marino, 271 N.Y. 317, 3 N.E.2d 439, 105 A.L.R. 1283 (1936) (similar); 2 Wigmore, Evidence §§ 301, 310, 324; Dec.Dig. Criminal Law ⊙370. See also; State v. Haddad, 221 La. 337, 59 So.2d 411 (1952); McKusick, Other Crimes to Show Guilty Knowledge and Intent, 24 Iowa L.Rev. 471 (1939), and the references in note 32, supra.

44. State v. Simborski, 120 Conn. 624, 182 Atl. 221 (1936) (murder of officer who was seeking to arrest defendant; fact that defendant had committed two burglaries a short time before, admissible to show motive and as res gestae); People v. Odum, 27 Ill.2d 237, 188 N.E.2d 720 (1963) (murder; evidence that victim's name had been indorsed as witness on indictment against defendant for another crime, admissible to show motive, although conviction here reversed for other error); Gibbs v. State, 201 Tenn. 491, 300 S.W.2d 890 (1957) (defendant killed A, then killed Mrs. A when she discovered this, then killed A's daughter when she discovered Mrs. A's body; in trial for murder of Mrs. A, evidence as to the other killings admissible to show motive and as "inseparable components of a completed crime;" the killing of A's daughter, however, clearly belongs under (9) infra, as an admission of guilt by conduct, where the prosecution is for the killing of Mrs. A); State v. Simborski, 120 Conn. 624, 182 Atl. 221 (1936) (murder of an officer who was seeking to arrest defendant; fact that defendant had committed two burglaries a short time previously on the same

doer of the crime on charge, or of deliberateness, malice, or a specific intent constituting an element of the crime.

(7) To show, by immediate inference, malice, deliberation, ill will or the specific intent required for a particular crime.[45]

(8) To prove identity. This is accepted as one of the ultimate purposes for which evidence of other criminal conduct will be received.[46] It is believed, however, that a need

for proving identity is not ordinarily of itself a ticket of admission, but that the evidence will usually follow, as an intermediate channel, some one or more of the other theories here listed. Probably the second (larger plan), the third (distinctive device) and the sixth (motive) are most often resorted to for this purpose.[47]

(9) Evidence of criminal acts of accused, constituting admissions by conduct, intended to obstruct justice or avoid punishment for the present crime.[48]

(10) To impeach the accused when he takes the stand as a witness, by proof of his convictions of crime.[49]

Some general observations may be added. In the first place, it is clear that the other crime, when it is found to be independently relevant and admissible, need not be established beyond a reasonable doubt, either as to its commission or as to defendant's connection therewith,[50] but for the jury to be

morning admissible to show motive, and as res gestae); State v. Long, 195 Ore. 81, 244 P.2d 1033 (1952) (murder of owner of truck: that defendant a short time afterward used the truck to commit robbery admitted); Comm. v. Heller, 269 Pa. 467, 87 A.2d 287 (1952) (murder of wife: evidence of illicit relations with sister-in-law and attempt to procure her to get divorce admissible); State v. Gaines, 144 Wash. 446, 258 Pac. 508 (1927) (murder of daughter; evidence of incestuous relations between defendant and deceased and that daughter was threatening to end the relation). See also comment, 14 Wash.L.Rev. 147 (1939); 2 Wigmore, Evidence § 390, especially note 2; Dec.Dig. Criminal Law ⚮371(12).

45. Copeland v. United States, 152 F.2d 769 (D.C. Cir. 1945) (murder in first degree; that defendant after shooting deceased pursued and shot sister of deceased, proper to show first act done, not accidentally or in self-defense but with deliberate intent to kill); Patterson v. United States, 361 F.2d 632 (8th Cir. 1966); Dunson v. State, 202 Ga. 515, 43 S.E.2d 504, 508 (1947) (wife-murder: previous acts of violence to wife, to show malice); Clark v. State, 151 Tex.Cr.R. 383, 208 S.W.2d 637 (1948) (murder, by beating, of five year old stepson: previous whippings, to show malice); State v. Stationak, 1 Wash.App. 558, 463 P.2d 260 (1969). 2 Wigmore, Evidence §§ 363–365; 1 Wharton, Criminal Evidence §§ 237, 238 (12th ed. 1955); Dec.Dig. Criminal Law ⚮371.

46. People v. McMonigle, 29 Cal.2d 730, 177 P.2d 745 (1947) (murder of girl enticed by accused into his automobile; evidence that a naval T shirt, similar to that worn by murderer, was stolen by accused some weeks before, properly received to show plan to entice, and identity); Hawkins v. State, 199 So.2d 276 (Fla.1967); State v. King, 111 Kan. 140, 206 Pac. 883, 22 A.L.R. 1006 (1922) (murder; victim, an employee of defendant, disappeared, after which accused was in possession of his effects; ten years later victim's body found burned in defendant's premises; held, finding of other bodies on same premises of persons who had disappeared and whose effects were in defendant's possession, admissible to identify accused as murderer); Helton v. Comm., 244 S.W.2d 762 (Ky.1951) (assault committed as member of mob

of miners; accused denied being present; "other incidents" on same morning presumably involving accused, admissible to show larger plan, motive and identity); State v. Bock, 229 Minn. 449, 39 N.W.2d 887 (1949) (attempt to pass forged check, by making small purchase and getting cash for balance; evidence of similar subsequent passing of other checks at other stores, under similar plan, admissible in discretion to identify person who attempted to pass check in question here; but error to exclude evidence of accused that some other person passed these other checks) and cases collected 1 Wharton, Criminal Evidence § 235 (12th ed. 1955); C.J.S. Criminal Law § 684.

47. See decisions cited under these headings, above and cases in next preceding note.

48. People v. Gambino, 12 Ill.2d 29, 145 N.E.2d 42 (1957) cert. denied 356 U.S. 904 (escape and attempted escape while awaiting trial); People v. Spaulding, 309 Ill. 292, 141 N.E. 196 (1923) (killing of only eyewitness to crime); State v. Brown, 231 Ore. 297, 372 P.2d 779 (1962) (stealing cars to escape); Gibbs v. State, 201 Tenn. 491, 300 S.W.2d 890 (1957), discussed in note 44, supra. See generally § 273, infra.

49. See § 43, supra. As to the provability of criminal conduct for which there has been no conviction, see § 42, supra.

50. People v. Lisenba, 14 Cal.2d 403, 429, 94 P.2d 569, 583 (1939), noted in 13 S.Calif.L.Rev. 511

entitled to consider it there must of course be substantial evidence of these facts,[51] and some courts have used the formula that it must be "clear and convincing." [52] And it is believed that before the evidence is admitted at all, this factor of the substantial or unconvincing quality of the proof should be weighed in the balance.

Two considerations, one substantive and the other procedural, affect the ease or difficulty of securing admission of proof of other crimes. The first is that the courts are stricter in applying their standards of relevancy when the ultimate purpose of the state is to prove identity, or the doing by the accused of the criminal act charged than they are when the evidence is offered on the ultimate issue of knowledge, intent or other state of mind.[53] The second is that when the

crime charged involves the element of knowledge, intent, or the like, the state will often be permitted to show other crimes in rebuttal, after the issue has been sharpened by the defendant's giving evidence of accident or mistake, more readily than it would as part of its case in chief at a time when the court may be in doubt that any real dispute will appear on the issue.[54]

There is an important consideration in the practice as to the admission of evidence of

---

(1940); State v. Carvelo, 45 Hawaii 16, 361 P.2d 45 (1961); People v. Allen, 351 Mich. 535, 88 N.W. 2d 433 (1958); Scott v. State, 107 Ohio St. 475, 141 N.E. 19 (1914); Annot., 3 A.L.R. 784; 1 Wharton, Criminal Evidence § 247 (12th ed. 1955).

51. People v. Albertson, 23 Cal.2d 550, 557–581, 596–599, 145 P.2d 7, 22 (1944) (citing cases) and authorities cited in the next preceding note.

52. Tucker v. State, 82 Nev. 127, 412 P.2d 970 (1966) ("plain, clear, and convincing"); Wrather v. State, 179 Tenn. 666, 678, 169 S.W.2d 854, 858 (1943). See also State v. Porter, 229 Iowa 282, 294 N.W. 898 (1940) (must be clearly shown).

53. United States v. Fierson, 419 F.2d 1020 (7th Cir. 1970) (mere formal issue is not sufficient); Jones v. Com., 303 Ky. 666, 198 S.W.2d 969, 970, 971 (1947) ("The application of the rule of admissibility is more liberal in the matter of establishing guilty knowledge or intent where intent is a material ingredient of the offense charged, for a series of similar offenses tends to show the party knew or intended to do what he was doing on the particular occasion. Where the purpose is to identify the defendant, the circumstances may govern the degree of liberality or strictness. . . . where it is a question of the particular individual committing the particular offense, as it was here, the latitude is much smaller."); and see People v. Molineux, 168 N.Y. 264, 313, 61 N.E. 286, 302 (1901) ("As to identity: Another exception to the general rule is that, when the evidence of an extraneous crime tends to identify the person who committed it as the same person who committed the crime charged in the indictment, it is admissible. There are not many reported cases in which

this exception seems to have been affirmatively applied. A far larger number of cases, while distinctly recognizing its existence, have held it inapplicable to the particular facts then before the court.").

54. See, e. g., People v. Knight, 92 Cal.App. 143, 216 Pac. 96 (1923) (lewd acts with children; defendant testifies that he committed the acts but with no lewd intent; held no error to receive evidence of similar acts with other children: "defendant opened the door"); State v. Gilligan, 92 Conn. 526, 103 Atl. 649 (1918) (murder by keeper of old folks' home of one of the inmates: receiving evidence of other poisonings where state's evidence did not suggest possibility of accident, held error, "without prejudice to its possible admission in rebuttal"). The remarks of Lord Sumner in Thompson v. The King, [1918] App.C. 221, 232 are pertinent: "Before an issue can be said to be raised, which would permit the introduction of such evidence so obviously prejudicial to the accused, it must have been raised in substance if not in so many words, and the issue so raised must be one to which the prejudicial evidence is relevant. The mere theory that a plea of not guilty puts everything material in issue is not enough for this purpose. The prosecution cannot credit the accused with fancy defences in order to rebut them at the outset with some damning piece of prejudice."

The issues may be sharpened in advance by the raising of special defenses, such as alibi, People v. Horton, 78 Ill.App.2d 421, 223 N.E.2d 202 (1966); insanity, Mears v. State, 83 Nev. 3, 422 P.2d 230 (1967) cert. denied 389 U.S. 888, reh. denied 389 U.S. 945; or entrapment, State v. Carrillo, 80 N.M. 697, 460 P.2d 62 (1969) cert. denied, 80 N.M. 708, 460 P.2d 73. As to entrapment, a *contra* holding is People v. Benford, 53 Cal.2d 1, 345 P.2d 928 (1959).

Compare the situation where the defendant or his lawyer for him imprudently makes claim to an unblemished character or record. Holding that this opens the door to evidence of other crimes: People v. Westek, 31 Cal.2d 469, 190 P.2d 9, 13, 18 (1948); Molton v. People, 118 Colo. 147, 193 P.2d 271, 272 (1948); but see Keene v. Comm., 307 Ky. 308, 210 S.W.2d 926 (1908).

other crimes which is little discussed in the opinions. This is the question of rule versus discretion. Most of the opinions ignore the problem and proceed on the assumption that the decision turns solely upon the ascertainment and application of a rule. If the situation fits one of the classes wherein the evidence has been recognized as having independent relevancy, then the evidence is received, otherwise not. This mechanical way of handling these questions has the advantage of calling on the judge for a minimum of personal judgment. But problems of lessening the dangers of prejudice without too much sacrifice of relevant evidence can seldom if ever be satisfactorily solved by mechanical rules. And so here there is danger that if the judges, trial and appellate, content themselves with merely determining whether the particular evidence of other crimes does or does not fit in one of the approved classes, they may lose sight of the underlying policy of protecting the accused against unfair prejudice. The policy may evaporate through the interstices of the classification.

Accordingly, some of the wiser opinions (especially recent ones) recognize that the problem is not merely one of pigeonholing, but one of balancing,[55] on the one side, the actual need for the other-crimes evidence in the light of the issues and the other evidence available to the prosecution,[56] the convincingness of the evidence that the other crimes were committed and that the accused was the actor, and the strength or weakness of the other-crimes evidence in supporting the issue, and on the other, the degree to which the jury will probably be roused by the evidence to overmastering hostility.

Such a balancing calls for a large measure of individual judgment about the relative gravity of imponderables. Accordingly, some opinions stress the element of discretion.[57] It should be recognized, however, that this is not a discretion to depart from the principle that evidence of other crimes, having no substantial relevancy except to ground the inference that accused is a bad man and hence probably committed this crime, must be excluded. The leeway of discretion lies rather in the opposite direction, empowering the judge to exclude the other-crimes evidence, even when it has substantial independent relevancy, if in his judgment its probative value for this purpose is outweighed by the

55. United States v. Phillips, 401 F.2d 301 (7th Cir. 1969); United States v. Bradwell, 388 F.2d 619 (2d Cir. 1968) cert. denied 393 U.S. 867; Fierson v. United States, 419 F.2d 1020 (7th Cir. 1970); People v. Shaw, 9 Mich.App. 558, 157 N.W.2d 811 (1968); People v. McKinney, 24 N.Y.2d 180, 299 N.Y.S.2d 401, 247 N.E.2d 244 (1969); Whitty v. State, 34 Wis.2d 278, 149 N.W.2d 557 (1968) cert. denied 390 U.S. 959; Quarles v. Com., 245 S.W.2d 947, 948 (Ky.1951) (". . . evidence of an independent offense is inadmissible even though it may have some tendency to prove the commission of the crime charged, because the probative value of the evidence is greatly outweighed by its prejudicial effect. This is especially so where the evidence is of an isolated, wholly disconnected offense. But the balance of scales is believed to be the other way where there is a close relationship to the offense charged.").

56. The importance of this is clearly pointed out by Beach, J., in State v. Gilligan, 92 Conn. 526, 103 Atl. 649, 652, 653 (1918). See also the remarks of Olney, J., in Adkins v. Brett, 184 Cal. 252, 193 Pac. 251, 254 (1920). In discussing a question of the admission of a declaration, competent for one purpose, incompetent for another, he said: "The matter is largely one of discretion on the part of the trial judge. If the point to prove which the evidence is competent can just as well be proven by other evidence, or if it is of but slight weight or importance upon that point, the trial judge might well be justified in excluding it entirely, because of its prejudicial and dangerous character as to other points." See also, Tucker v. State, 82 Nev. 127, 412 P.2d 970 (1966).

Another factor mentioned as entitled to consideration is surprise. People v. Kelley, 66 Cal.2d 232, 57 Cal.Rptr. 363, 424 P.2d 947 (1967). The remedy here would seem to be notice, as required in State v. Spreigl, 272 Minn. 488, 139 N.W.2d 167 (1965); cf. State v. Boyce, 284 Minn. 242, 170 N.W.2d 104 (1969).

57. United States v. Gardin, 382 F.2d 601 (2d Cir. 1967); Neff v. United States, 105 F.2d 688 (8th Cir. 1939); People v. Shaw, 9 Mich.App. 558, 157 N.W.2d 811 (1968).

danger that it will stir such passion in the jury as to sweep them beyond a rational consideration of guilt or innocence of the crime on trial.[58] Discretion implies not only leeway but responsibility. A decision clearly wrong on this question of balancing probative value against danger of prejudice will be corrected on appeal as an abuse of discretion.[59]

191.   Character to Evidence Conduct—(d) The Exception to the General Rule of Exclusion Permitting the Accused to Produce Evidence of his Good Character: [60] Cross-Examination and Rebuttal by State.

The prosecution, as we have seen in the preceding section, is generally forbidden to initiate evidence of the bad character of the defendant when offered merely to show that he is a bad man and hence more likely to commit a crime. The objection is not that the evidence is not relevant for this purpose, but that its value is overbalanced by the danger of undue prejudice which the evidence would arouse. When the table is turned, and the accused himself offers evidence of his good character to show that he was unlikely to have committed the crime, the relevancy remains. The basic premise is the one by which we order our daily lives, that people generally act in keeping with their character. But the danger of prejudice now is almost wholly lacking.[61] So it is generally agreed that the accused in all criminal cases [62] may produce evidence of his good character as substantive evidence of his innocence. In courtroom parlance this is often termed "placing his character in issue," but the phrase is misleading. Character is almost never one of the ultimate issues or operative facts determining guilt or innocence.

58. State v. Goebel, 36 Wash.2d 367, 218 P.2d 300, 306 (1950) (Hill, J.: " . . . this class of evidence, where not essential to the establishment of the state's case, should not be admitted, even though falling within the generally recognized exceptions to the rule of exclusion, when the trial court is convinced that its effect would be to generate heat instead of diffusing light, or, as is said in one of the law review articles above referred to, where the minute peg of relevancy will be entirely obscured by the dirty linen hung upon it. This is a situation where the policy of protecting a defendant from undue prejudice conflicts with the rule of logical relevance, and a proper determination as to which should prevail rests in the sound discretion of the trial court, and not merely on whether the evidence comes within certain categories which constitute exceptions to the rule of exclusion."); People v. McKinney, 24 N.Y.2d 180, 299 N.Y.S.2d 401, 247 N.E.2d 244 (1969), and the cases cited in notes 55–57, supra.

59. See, e. g., Noor Mohamed v. The King, [1949] App.C. 182, 192, 193 (Privy Council) (murder by poisoning wife; death by poison of previous wife admitted; held, while judge had discretion to balance relevancy against prejudice, here erroneously exercised), critically noted, 12 Mod.L.Rev. 232; State v. Gilligan, 92 Conn. 526, 103 Atl. 649, 653 (1918) (murder by poisoning: other deaths by poisoning admitted and conviction reversed on this ground; "Courts are not infrequently required in criminal cases to pass upon preliminary questions of fact in order to determine the admissibility of evidence, and no doubt courts are vested with considerable discretionary powers in passing upon such preliminary questions . . . we think it would be an abuse of discretion to permit proof of similar but unconnected poisonings in a case where the state's evidence had already gone so far toward eliminating accident or mistake as to leave no reasonable doubt, in the absence of rebutting evidence, that the poison, if administered by the accused, must have been knowingly administered."); and cases in next preceding note.

60. See 1 Wigmore, Evidence §§ 55–60, 3A id. (Chadbourn rev.) § 925; 1 Wharton, Criminal Evidence §§ 221–231 (12th ed. 1955); Udall, Character Proof in the Law of Evidence, 18 Univ.Cin.L.Rev. 283, 299 (1949); C.J.S. Criminal Law §§ 676–679; Dec. Dig. Criminal Law ⚖️377–381.

61. There may be some danger that the jury will be induced by the evidence of good character to outstep their function by pardoning a man whom they believe to be guilty, but this kind of equitable dispensing power is one that the community while it does not explicitly sanction, probably does not disapprove.

62. It is said that the practice of permitting evidence of good character was introduced in the reign of Charles II, and was then confined to capital cases. Reddick v. State, 25 Fla. 112, 433, 5 So. 704 (1889). And later the evidence was limited to cases where under the other testimony guilt was in doubt. Daniels v. State, 2 Pen.(Del.) 586, 48 Atl. 196 (1901). But these limitations are now abandoned, and the character evidence itself may be relied on by the accused to engender the doubt. See the above cases and 1 Wharton, Criminal Evidence § 221 (12th ed. 1955).

It is merely circumstantial evidence bearing on the probability that the accused did or did not commit the act charged with the required guilty intent.[63] What the accused does, then, and what he has the exclusive power to do, is to initiate, and thus open the door to, circumstantial evidence of character.

Character for what? A few courts permit proof of "general good character"[64] but the prevailing and more practical view limits the inquiry to the trait or traits involved in the crime on trial[65]—honesty in theft cases, peaceableness in murder, and the like.[66]

By a rule of relatively recent origin and doubtful expediency,[67] the only way in which character for this purpose can be proved is by evidence of reputation.[68] This excludes evidence of specific acts or blameless life and rules out opinion evidence as to the character of the accused for the trait in question

63. See, e. g., Commonwealth v. Beal, 314 Mass. 210, 50 N.E.2d 14 (1943) (defendant may prove good character for purpose of establishing the improbability of his having done the wrong imputed to him); State v. Micci, 46 N.J.Super. 454, 134 A.2d 805 (1957); Morrison v. State, 217 Tenn. 374, 397 S.W.2d 826 (1965).

64. Thus in North Carolina the inquiry seems to be limited to "general character." State v. Sentelle, 212 N.C. 386, 193 S.E. 405 (1937) (driving while intoxicated: inquiry as to reputation for sobriety improper: must ask as to general character, but witness may then volunteer as to respect in which character good or bad!); State v. McKissick, 271 N.C. 500, 157 S.E.2d 112 (1967). See also United States v. Latin, 139 F.2d 569 (2d Cir. 1943) (setting up unregistered still: defendant entitled to prove good reputation as to "moral character"); State v. Quinn, 344 Mo. 1072, 130 S.W.2d 511 (1939) (when offense is only malum prohibitum, proper to prove trait of law-abiding citizenship).

65. Hawley v. United States, 133 F.2d 966 (10th Cir. 1943); State v. Howland, 157 Kan. 11, 138 P.2d 424 (1943) (rape: defendant not entitled to prove good reputation for veracity); People v. Van Gaasbeck, 189 N.Y. 408, 82 N.E. 718, (1907); 1 Wigmore, Evidence § 59; Dec.Dig. Criminal Law ☞ 377; C.J.S. Criminal Law § 677(5).

66. It is easy to confound the situation where the character is "put in issue" by proof of good reputation as evidence of innocence, and the distinct situation, with different rules, of the taking the stand by the accused as a witness. In the latter case, the prosecution may impeach his credibility by evidence of the bad reputation of the accused. Then the trait involved is veracity, and it is veracity-character at the time he testifies that we are interested in. Opinion may also be allowed. See § 44, supra. Moreover, the accused cannot support his veracity-character as a witness until the prosecution has first attacked it. People v. Jinkins, 82 Ill.App.2d 150, 225 N.E.2d 657 (1967); State v. Howland, 157 Kan. 11, 138 P.2d 424 (1943) (prose-

cution for statutory rape, defendant offered evidence of good reputation for veracity: held properly excluded, (1) as substantive evidence because not the trait involved in the crime, (2) as supporting credibility because state had not attacked his veracity-character); People v. Trahos, 251 Mich. 592, 232 N.W. 357 (1930) (receiving stolen goods: defendant's evidence of good reputation for veracity can only be considered on his credibility not as evidence of innocence); State v. Colson, 193 N.C. 236, 136 S.E. 730 (1927) (defendant testified but did not give evidence of good character: the state produced evidence of his bad character, held, this evidence could only be considered on his credibility, not as evidence of guilt). Cf. F.R.Ev. (R.D.1971) 608 allowing witness-accused to introduce evidence of good character for veracity though not attacked. See 3A Wigmore, Evidence (Chadbourn rev.) § 925. The distinction is discussed also in Carnley v. United States, 274 F.2d 68 (5th Cir. 1960) (error to exclude defendant's offer of character evidence directed to trait involved in crime; not cured by admission of evidence as to his truthfulness and veracity).

67. See 7 Wigmore, Evidence §§ 1981, 1986, for a discussion of the history and policy of the rule.

68. Blakely v. State, 30 Ala.App. 397, 6 So.2d 603 (1942); Berger v. State, 179 Md. 410, 20 A.2d 146, (1941); State v. Dancer, 116 N.J.Law 487, 184 Atl. 800 (1936); People v. Van Gaasbeck, 189 N.Y. 408, 82 N.E. 718 (1907). Dec.Dig. Criminal Law ☞379; C.J.S. Criminal Law § 678. A witness who testifies that he lives in the community where the accused resides, but that he has never heard the defendant's character in respect to the particular trait discussed is qualified to testify to his good reputation in that respect. People v. Van Gaasbeck, supra; Annot. Negative Proof of Good Character, 67 A.L.R. 1210.
A few states cling to the earlier tradition and permit the accused to produce not only reputation evidence, but testimony of those who know his good character from observation of his conduct. State v. Blake, 157 Conn. 99, 249 A.2d 232 (1968) (dictum); State v. Ferguson, 222 Iowa 1148, 270 N.W. 874 (1937); State v. Hartung, 239 Iowa 414, 30 N.W.2d 491 (1948); Sabo v. State, 119 Ohio St. 231, 163 N.E. 28, 31 (1928). It would be permitted under Model Code of Evidence, Rule 306(2) (a), under Uniform Rule 46, 47, and under F.R.Ev. (R.D. 1971) 404, 405. Military service records have generally been excluded. Annot., 9 A.L.R.2d 606. Sometimes the reason is said to be the rule now under discussion; sometimes the hearsay rule or irrelevancy to a particular character trait is cited.

based on the witness' knowledge and observation. Reputation evidence, though muted and colorless, is thought to have the advantage of avoiding distracting side issues as to particular acts and incidents in the past life of the accused.[69] The same advantage is, however, also possessed by opinions, and exclusion of this latter type of convincing evidence is difficult to justify.

It is character at the time of the alleged crime that bears most nearly on the inference of innocence or guilt, and the reputation evidence must be confined to reputation at that time or a reasonable time before.[70] The reputation traditionally was said to be limited to that which obtained in the community where the accused lived,[71] but this should be extended to embrace any considerable group with whom he constantly associated in his business, work, or other continued activity, and who might reasonably be

thought to have a collective opinion about him.[72]

It is a merciful dispensation to the accused of hitherto blameless life to allow him to open this door of character. To those with spotted records, however, it is a far more dangerous move to open this door than might at first glance be assumed. In the first place, the witness who has testified to the good reputation of the accused for the particular trait, may be cross-examined as to his means of knowledge of community opinion, not only generally, but specifically as to whether he "has heard" that the defendant has committed particular criminal acts inconsistent with the reputation vouched for on direct.[73]

---

69. "If a witness is to be permitted to testify to the character of an accused person, basing his testimony solely on his own knowledge and observation, he cannot logically be prohibited from stating the particular incidents affecting the defendant and the particular actions of the defendant which have led him to his favorable conclusion. In most instances it would be utterly impossible for the prosecution to ascertain whether occurrences narrated by the witness as constituting the foundation of his conclusion were or were not true. They might be utterly false, and yet incapable of disproof at the time of trial. Furthermore, even if evidence were accessible to controvert the specific statements of the witness in this respect, its admission would lead to the introduction into the case of innumerable collateral issues which could not be tried out without introducing the utmost complication and confusion into the trial, tending to distract the minds of the jurymen and befog the chief issue in litigation." Willard Bartlett, J., in People v. Van Gaasbeck, 189 N.Y. 408, 82 N.E. 718, 721 (1907); State v. Latham, 190 Kan. 411, 375 P.2d 788 (1962), cert. denied, 373 U.S. 919. Cf. § 44, supra.

70. People v. Willy, 301 Ill. 307, 133 N.E. 859, 864 (1922); Comm. v. White, 271 Pa. 584, 115 Atl. 870 (1922) (remoteness of earlier reputation in judge's discretion); Strader v. State, 208 Tenn. 192, 344 S.W.2d 546, 87 A.L.R.2d 963 (1961) (annotated on this point); C.J.S. Criminal Law § 677(2).

71. See, e. g., Baugh v. State, 218 Ala. 87, 117 So. 426 (1928).

72. Hamilton v. State, 129 Fla. 219, 176 So. 89, 112 A.L.R. 1013 (1937) (admitting reputation in locality where accused worked as a hotel employee); State v. Jackson, 373 S.W.2d 4 (Mo.1963); Jordan v. State, 163 Tex.Cr.R. 287, 290 S.W.2d 666 (1956); Annot., 112 A.L.R. 1020 reviews the cases pro and con. See also C.J.S. Criminal Law § 677(3).

For similar considerations with respect to character for veracity of a witness, see § 44, supra.

73. Vinson v. State, 247 Ala. 22, 22 So.2d 300 (1945); Carnley v. State, 143 Fla. 756, 197 So. 441 (1940); Commonwealth v. Becker, 326 Pa. 105, 191 Atl. 351 (1937); Garza v. State, 129 Tex.Cr.R. 443, 88 S.W. 2d 113 (1936) and cases cited 3A Wigmore, Evidence (Chadbourn rev.) § 988; Dec.Dig. Witnesses ⊷274; Annot., 71 A.L.R. 1504, 47 A.L.R.2d 1258. Of course, the inquiry must relate to crimes or misconduct relevant to the trait vouched for on direct. United States v. Wooden, 137 U.S.App.D.C. 1, 420 F.2d 251 (1969) (honesty, peace and quiet; cross-examination as to drunkenness not proper); Albertson v. Com., 312 Ky. 68, 226 S.W.2d 523 (1950) (peace and quiet: cross-examination as to illegal liquor traffic excluded); Kennedy v. State, 150 Tex.Cr. 215, 200 S.W.2d 400 (1947) (peace, quiet, law-abidingness, veracity; illicit relations with woman excluded).

But there are indications in at least three states of a practice forbidding questions which specify particular acts or rumors thereof. See Viliborghi v. State, 45 Ariz. 275, 285, 43 P.2d 210, 215 (1935) (". . . the questions must not be in such form as to imply specific acts of misconduct of the party, but should be confined to the source of his knowledge of the reputation and what he has heard from such sources."); People v. Page, 365 Ill. 524, 6 N.E.2d 845 (1937), and comment 25 Ill.Bar J. 335 (1937). Compare People v. Stanton, 1 Ill.2d 444, 115 N.E.2d 630 (1953) and People v. Greeley, 14

Logically, the courts hold that the witness may not be asked "if he knows" that the accused has committed such other crimes.[74]

As to indictments or other official charges, verdicts, convictions, or repeated arrests, or sentences for crime, it would seem allowable to ask the witness if he "knows" of these,[75] but some decisions require the "have you heard" form of inquiry as to these matters also.[76]

The rule permitting the cross-examiner to ask the character witness whether he "has heard" or knows of other particular crimes of accused involving the same trait is pregnant with possibilities of destructive prejudice.[77] The mere asking by a respected of-

Ill.2d 428, 152 N.E.2d 825 (1958), both approving majority rule in dicta; State v. Robinson, 226 N.C. 95, 36 S.E.2d 655 (1946).

74. Wilcox v. United States, 387 F.2d 60 (5th Cir. 1967); Stewart v. United States, 70 App.D.C. 101, 104 F.2d 234, 235 (1939) (". . . the witness on cross-examination should be asked only—'Have you heard?'—not—'Do you know?' "); Commonwealth v. Thomas, 282 Pa. 20, 127 Atl. 427 (1925); Couch v. State, 135 Tex.Cr. 479, 121 S.W.2d 367 (1938); Annot., 71 A.L.R. 1504, 47 A.L.R.2d 1258. Nevertheless, testimony of good reputation by a witness who knows of criminal acts has a whited sepulchre quality, and a few courts permit him to be asked, "Do you know?" State v. Shull, 151 Ore. 224, 282 Pac. 237, 71 A.L.R. 1498 (1929); State v. Duree, 52 Wash.2d 324, 324 P.2d 1074 (1958).

It seems, however, that personal knowledge by the witness of criminal public acts of accused presents different considerations. The impeachment chain from such a question takes the following form: The crimes occurred, they caused community talk, but witness has (a) not heard it (thus discounting his familiarity with defendant's reputation) or (b) heard it, but is either misrepresenting or is applying a low standard of "goodness." Since a finding that the crime occurred is the starting point, the method trenches close to the widely condemned one of proving the other crime extrinsically in order to show bad reputation as a logical result. So far as defendant is concerned, there is the same danger that the jury, finding the prior crime, will short cut the reputation process and use it more directly to convict in the case on trial. See the discussion of Jackson, J. in Michelson v. United States, 335 U.S. 469, 477–487 (1948), especially 481 n. 18. If what the community has said is the question, the parties should be required to begin there, rather than at crimes of defendant as causes of such sayings.

Note that, if opinion is allowed to prove defendant's character, the matter stands otherwise. Opinion is a generalization from observation of defendant's actions; and the witness may in good faith be asked what acts he knows, either to weaken the base of his opinion, or to show his standard of "goodness." See proposed F.R.Ev. (R.D.1971) 405, allowing use of both reputation and opinion, and expressly allowing the reputation witness to be cross-examined as to his knowledge of specific acts (public or not), as well as on what he has heard, on the ground that "these distinctions are of slight, if any, practical significance," and should be eliminated as a factor in formulating questions. Compare People v. Hurd, 5 Cal.App.3d 865, 85 Cal.Rptr. 718 (1970) (no error in cross-examination of opinion witness in "have you heard" form instead of "do you know", because the basis of his opinion was a mixture of personal acquaintance and reputation), with State v. Keul, 233 Iowa 852, 5 N.W.2d 849

(1942) (in state allowing both opinion and reputation evidence, error to cross-examine reputation witness about personal knowledge of defendant's acts.) Certainly the distinction is often blurred in practice; see State v. Cyr, 40 Wash.2d 840, 246 P.2d 480 (1952), where the court stated it was applying a rule allowing reputation witnesses to be cross-examined about knowledge of accused's conduct, but the questions were as to knowledge of arrests, convictions and sentences; and see the cautious statements of the annotator in 47 A.L.R. 2d 1258, 1330.

75. State v. Jacobs, 195 La. 281, 196 So. 347 (1940) (arrest); State v. Carroll, 188 S.W.2d 22 (Mo.1945) (arrests or accusations); Lyons v. State, 76 Okl. Cr. 41, 133 P.2d 898 (1943) (charges). All these are statements, made in the community, and a witness who "knows" of them is one who has heard (or read) the statements. To require him to have heard from still a third person that they were made, is to require that he receive the statement as hearsay upon hearsay. See, however, Commonwealth v. Jenkins, 413 Pa. 606, 198 A.2d 497 (1964) imposing just such a requirement, and indicating that evidence of a witness that he had heard of charges against defendant by being a spectator at a hearing in connection therewith should be excluded. See also, Wilcox v. United States, 387 F.2d 60 (5th Cir. 1967), reversing for asking witness whether he "knew" of arrests and convictions of defendant; People v. Neal, 85 Cal.App.2d 765, 194 P.2d 57 (1948) (same).

76. Roberson v. United States, 237 F.2d 536 (5th Cir. 1956) (arrests, convictions, sentences); Wright v. State, 247 Ala. 180, 23 So.2d 519 (1945) (served time in penitentiary for assault to murder); Parrish v. State, 163 Tex.Cr.R. 252, 290 S.W.2d 245 (1956) (arrest).

77. The considerations of fairness and policy which make for and against the prevailing practice were ably marshaled and evaluated in the opinions of Jackson, J., for the court and Rutledge, J., dissenting, in Michelson v. United States, 335 U.S. 469 (1948), noted in 34 Iowa L.Rev. 700 (1949), 40 J.

ficial of such a question, however, answered, may well suggest to the jury that the imputation is true. The courts agree that propounding such a question in bad faith may be ground of reversal.[78] But establishing bad faith may be a hopeless task.[79] It has been persuasively suggested that this danger of false suggestion and the hazard that the consideration of the case on trial will be overwhelmed by the importation of other misdoings of the accused, should be avoided by limiting the cross-examination to a general one on opportunities for knowledge of reputation excluding altogether any inquiries about other crimes or rumors thereof.[80] Such a rule, it seems, would tend to give too free a license to the parade of false or biassed character witness. Yet the asserted dangers of the prevailing practice are real and a curb is needed. The trial judge, it is believed, should be required, before permitting the prosecuting counsel to cross-examine the character witness on rumors of misconduct of the accused, or upon arrests, charges or convictions, to request the prosecutor to give his professional statement to the judge (in the absence of the jury) that he has reasonable ground to believe, and does believe, that the crimes or misconduct, which are imputed by the rumors, or which are the subject of the arrests or charges, were actually committed by the accused, and that the judgments of conviction inquired about were actually pronounced. Reasonable grounds would require, it is suggested, that the prosecutor's assurance be based on the statements of witnesses, believed to be credible, who purport to have firsthand knowledge.[81]

The other available counterthrust of the prosecution to the defendant's proof of good

Crim.L.C. & P.S. 58 (1949), 47 Mich.L.Rev. 843 (1949), 22 So.Cal.L.Rev. 489 (1949) and other reviews. The trial, held in 1947, was for bribery of a revenue agent. The accused, on direct examination, acknowledged a conviction for a trademark violation in 1927. He produced witnesses of his good reputation for honesty, truthfulness and veracity, some of whom testified that they had known him for thirty years. On cross-examination they were asked, "Did you ever hear that on Oct. 11, 1920, the defendant . . . was arrested for receiving stolen goods?" They answered, no. The prosecutor assured the court, in private, of the truth of the fact of such arrest, which was not questioned, and the judge explained to the jury the limited purpose of the question. The court affirmed. Jackson, J., for the court concludes: "We concur in the general opinion of courts, textwriters and the profession that much of this law is archaic, paradoxical and full of compromises and compensations by which an irrational advantage to one side is offset by a poorly reasoned counter-privilege to the other. But somehow it has proved a workable even if clumsy system when moderated by discretionary controls in the hands of a wise and strong trial court. To pull one misshapen stone out of the grotesque structure is more likely simply to upset its present balance between adverse interests than to establish a rational edifice."

78. See statements to this effect in State v. Keul, 233 Iowa 852, 5 N.W.2d 849 (1942); Commonwealth v. Selkow, 206 Pa.Super. 273, 212 A.2d 919 (1965); and cases cited in 47 A.L.R.2d 1258, 1320. But actual reversals on this ground have been rare.

79. In the absence of a showing to the contrary, earlier cases presumed that the prosecutor acted in good faith. People v. Burke, 18 Cal.App. 72, 122 Pac. 435 (1912). Trial judges sometimes assumed that they were helpless when defendant objected on the ground of bad faith. See State v. McDonald, 231 S.W. 927, 930 (Mo.1921). But as Wigmore pointed out in criticizing the holding, the judge could have questioned the prosecutor, in the absence of the jury, as to whether he had credible grounds for asking the question. 3A Wigmore, Evidence (Chadbourn rev.) § 988.

80. See the dissenting opinion of Rutledge, J., in Michelson v. United States, 335 U.S. 469, 496 (1948), where he says: "My own preference and, I think, the only fair rule would be to foreclose the entire line of inquiry concerning specific incidents in the defendant's past, both on cross-examination and on new evidence in rebuttal. This would leave room for proper rebuttal without turning the defendant's trial for a specific offense into one for all his previous misconduct, criminal or other, and would put the prosecution on the same plane with the defendant in relation to the use of character evidence. This, it seems to me, is the only fair way to handle the matter."

81. More recent cases in several jurisdictions have approved, recommended, or required this or a similar practice. Michelson v. United States, 335 U.S. 469 (1948); People v. Yoshio Futamata, 140 Colo. 233, 343 P.2d 1058 (1959); State v. Hinton, 206 Kan. 500, 479 P.2d 910 (1971); People v. Dorrikas, 354 Mich. 303, 92 N.W.2d 305 (1958); State v. Steensen 35 N.J.Super. 103, 113 A.2d 203 (1955); Miller v. State, 418 P.2d 220 (Okl.Cr.1966). These cases discuss the details of the procedure.

reputation is not so deadly. This is the power of the state to produce witnesses in rebuttal who will swear to his bad reputation,[82] limited of course to the trait or traits opened by the defendant [83] and to the period before the offense and not too remote.[84] Just as in the case of the reputation witnesses of the accused, the witnesses for the prosecution are limited on direct to assertions about the reputation and may not testify to particular acts [85] or rumors thereof.[86] Should the state be allowed to prove at this stage, in rebuttal of good character, judgments of conviction for crimes involving the same trait in or near the community where the accused lived, and within a reasonable time before the commission of the crime on trial? The cases are divided, with the majority rejecting the evidence.[87] But such convictions would bear

strongly on character and community and individual estimates of it, are provable with entire certainty, and while they carry a danger of prejudice, it is avoidable by the accused, who need not inject the issue of character. The argument here against the use of convictions is far less strong than against the use of convictions to impeach the accused when he takes the stand as a witness.[88] If he stays off the stand, the jury despite instructions will usually assume his guilt, but no such assumption is likely to be made from his failure to open the door of reputation. Moreover, since the prosecution may advert to the matter on cross-examination,[89] the matter may be academic.

192. Character to Evidence Conduct—(e) Exception to General Rule of Exclusion, Under Minority View, for Proof of Party's Character in Civil Cases Where Crime Is in Issue.[90]

The common law relaxed its ban upon evidence of character to show conduct to the extent of permitting the accused to open the door by producing evidence of his good character.[91] This was a special dispensation to criminal defendants whose life or liberty were at hazard. Should the same dispensation be accorded to the party in a civil action who has been charged by his adversary's pleading or proof with a criminal offence involving moral turpitude? The peril of judg-

---

82. See cases collected in 3A Wigmore, Evidence (Chadbourn rev.) § 988; C.J.S. Criminal Law §§ 677, 678; Dec.Dig. Criminal Law ⊙—378–380.

If opinion evidence is admissible for the accused, it is, of course, also admissible in rebuttal for the prosecution. F.R.Ev. (R.D.1971) 404(a), 405(a).

83. Salgado v. United States, 278 F.2d 830 (1st Cir. 1960) (dictum); 1 Wigmore, Evidence § 59, n. 1.

84. State v. Van Osten, 68 R.I. 175, 26 A.2d 858 (1942).

85. United States v. Beno, 324 F.2d 582 (2d Cir. 1963); Helms v. State, 254 Ala. 14, 47 So.2d 276 (1950) (wife murder, error to allow state in rebuttal of good reputation, to prove that accused had been placed under peace bond); Mimbs v. State, 189 Ga. 189, 5 S.E.2d 770 (1939) (murder; error to prove a previous fight); Woods v. State, 233 Ind. 320, 119 N.E.2d 558 (1954) (statutory rape, prior attempt); State v. Miller, 60 Idaho 79, 88 P.2d 526 (1939) (drunken driving; previous intoxication); Dec.Dig. Criminal Law ⊙—380.

86. Of course, the accused might cross-examine the state's bad-reputation witnesses as to whether they "have heard" comment on praiseworthy actions of the accused, but manifestly the browsing here is not as rich as in the prosecution's "have you heard" cross-examination.

87. Eley v. United States, 117 F.2d 526 (6th Cir. 1941); State v. Myrick, 181 Kan. 1056, 317 P.2d 485 (1957); Lewellen v. State, 172 Tex.Cr.R. 622, 361 S.W.2d 880 (1962); Zirkle v. Commonwealth, 189 Va. 862, 55 S.E.2d 24 (1949). Since the conviction evidences a specific act, the cases cited in note 85, supra, lend support to the majority view. Some states have made such convictions admissible

by statute to rebut defendant's good-character evidence, N.Y. CPLR 60.40(2) (McKinney's); Ohio Rev. Code Ann. § 2945.56 (Page 1954), and some cases have adopted the same rule in analogy to the procedure in impeaching the character of witnesses, Smith v. State, 11 Ga.App. 89, 74 S.E.2d 711 (1912); Giles v. State, 71 Ga.App. 736, 32 S.E.2d 111 (1944).

88. See § 43, supra.

89. See n. 75, supra.

90. 1 Wigmore, Evidence § 64; Annot., Evidence of character on issue of fraud in civil action, 78 A.L.R. 643; Note, 13 Tex.L.Rev. 531, 1935; Annot., Character in action for assault, 154 A.L.R. 121, 1 A.L.R. 3d 571; C.J.S. Evidence § 426; Dec.Dig. Evidence ⊙—106.

91. See § 191, supra.

ment here is less, and most courts have declined to pay the price in consumption of time and distraction from the issue which the concession entails.[92] A growing minority, however, has been impressed with the serious consequences to the party's standing, reputation, and relationships which such a charge, even in a civil action, may bring in its train,[93] and has followed the criminal analogy, by permitting the party to introduce evidence of his good reputation for the trait involved in the charge.[94] The balance of expediency is a close one.

Civil actions for assault and battery seem often to be treated as in a class by themselves.[95] When the issue is merely whether the defendant committed the act charged, then the courts would presumably admit or exclude defendant's evidence of good reputation according to their alignment with the majority or minority view on the general question, as discussed above. But when the defendant pleads self-defence, he may show the plaintiff's reputation for turbulence if he

92. Bosworth v. Bosworth, 131 Conn. 389, 40 A.2d 186 (1944) (error in wife's action of divorce for cruelty to permit her to prove defendant had been divorced by former wife for cruelty); Johnson v. Richards, 50 Idaho 150, 294 Pac. 507 (1930) (suit against defendant for alienation of affection, and adultery alleged in aggravation of damages, defendant denies adultery and seeks to prove reputation for chastity); Lakes v. Buckeye State Mut. Ins. Assn., 110 Ohio App. 115, 168 N.E.2d 895 (1959) defense of wilful misrepresentation to suit on fire policy; plaintiff's good character inadmissible); Greenberg v. Aetna Ins. Co., 427 Pa. 494, 235 A.2d 582 (1967) (suit on fire policy; defendant charges plaintiff with setting fire; held, plaintiff's evidence of good reputation rightly excluded); Kornec v. Mike Horse Mining, etc. Co., 120 Mont. 1, 180 P.2d 252 (1947) (action for assault; defendant's good reputation for peacefulness excluded); Baker v. First National Bank of Santa Rosa, 176 Okl. 70, 54 P.2d 355 (1936) (replevin: issue, whether defendants took stolen bonds with knowledge or in good faith).

93. See, e. g., Start, J., in Hein v. Holdridge, 78 Minn. 468, 81 N.W. 522, 523 (1900), admitting evidence of good reputation in an action for seduction: " . . . such evidence ought to be received in a civil action when it is of a character to bring it within all of the reasons for admitting such evidence in criminal cases. Civil actions for an indecent assault, for seduction, and kindred cases, are of this character; for such cases are not infrequently mere speculative and blackmailing schemes. The consequences to the defendant of a verdict against him in such a case are most serious, for the issue as to him involves his fortune, his honor, his family. From the very nature of the charge, it often happens that an innocent man can only meet the issue by a denial of the charge, and proof of his previous good character."

94. United States v. Genovese, 133 F.Supp. 820 (D.N.J.1955) (cancellation of naturalization for fraudulent answers; defendant's good character admissible as in criminal cases) (dictum); Dalton v. Jackson, 66 Ga.App. 625, 18 S.E.2d 791 (1942) (dam-

ages for rape; defendant's good character admissible); Waggoman v. Ft. Worth Well Machinery & Supply, Co., 124 Tex. 325, 76 S.W.2d 1005, 1006 (1934) (plaintiff sued for false imprisonment and to cancel a note for duress; counterclaim charging plaintiff with embezzlement; held plaintiff properly permitted to introduce evidence of his good character for honesty and veracity; holding seemingly is erroneous as to latter trait); Hess v. Marinari, 81 W.Va. 500, 94 S.E. 968 (1918) (assault; with claim for punitive damages; such claim requires finding of criminal intent, and defendant entitled as in criminal case entitled to show his good character for peace). Compare, however, Skidmore v. Star Ins. Co., 126 W.Va. 307, 27 S.E.2d 845 (1943), which approves the majority rule rejecting evidence of character to show conduct in civil cases, and distinguishes the *Hess* case on the inadequate ground that criminal intent was there material. See also as to West Virginia law, Mourikas v. Vardianos, 169 F.2d 53 (4th Cir. 1948), noted 22 So.Cal.L.Rev. 486 (1949), 51 W.Va.L.Rev. 273 (1949). Some courts have extended this principle to include charges of fraud, regardless of criminality. Rogers v. Atlantic Life Ins. Co., 135 S.C. 89, 133 S.E. 215 (1926) (whether deceased made false and fraudulent statements in application for life insurance; his good reputation for honesty provable by beneficiary); Continental Nat. Bank v. First Nat. Bank, 108 Tenn. 374, 68 S.W. 497 (1902) (suit charging that defendant bank induced plaintiff bank to lend money on certain paper by false representations pursuant to a fraudulent conspiracy in which one Duncan, a nonparty to the suit, was involved; held, proper to admit testimony as to the good character of Duncan for honor and integrity, since his honor was assailed though he was not a party to the suit). Contra: Grant v. Pendley, 39 S.W.2d 596, 78 A.L.R. 638 (Tex.Com. App.1931) (pleading charging party with procuring deed by fraud not ground for permitting party to introduce evidence of his good reputation for honesty and veracity; Beach v. Richtmyer, 275 A.D. 466, 90 N.Y.S.2d 332 (1949) (character of nonparty not admissible on claim that he was in effect charged with larceny).

95. See the extensive collection of decisions in Annot., 154 A.L.R. 121, 1 A.L.R.3d 571.

proves it was known to him, on the issue of reasonable apprehension.[96] Similarly, when on a plea of self-defence or otherwise there is an issue as to who committed the first act of aggression, most courts (regardless of their alignment on the general question) seem to admit evidence of the good or bad reputation of both plaintiff and defendant for peacefulness as shedding light on their probable acts.[97] This cannot be justified, as is sometimes attempted, on the ground that character is here "in issue"—the issue is clearly one of conduct—but probably there is in these cases a special need even beyond that in most cases of charges of crime in civil actions, for knowing the dispositions of the parties.

193.   Character to Evidence Conduct—(f) Exception to General Rule of Exclusion Admitting Evidence as to Character of Deceased in Homicide on Issue of Aggression in Self-Defence.[98]

When the accused has produced evidence that the deceased attacked him, thus grounding a claim of self-defence, this when met by counter-evidence raises an issue of conduct: was the deceased or the accused the first aggressor?   It is almost universally held that when such evidence has been produced the accused may introduce testimony of the reputation of the deceased for turbulence and violence.[99]   It is equally well settled of course that the prosecution may meet this by rebutting testimony of his good reputation for peacefulness.[1]   It is generally agreed also that the prosecution may not enter such proof as part of its main case.[2]   The conflict arises as to the condition under which the state may offer such proof in rebuttal.   By one view, it is allowed only when the accused directly opens the character-door by adducing evidence of bad character or reputation for violence.[3]   This has the advantage of permitting the accused to give evidence of self-defence and still keep out altogether this "collateral" evidence of character, in keeping with the general tradition against using evidence of character to show conduct. It restricts the opportunity for the appeal to pity and vengeance implicit in the praise of the character of the deceased. It has, moreover, an attractive consonance with the rule as to the exclusive privilege of the accused to put his own character "in issue." On the oth-

96.   Dingle v. Hickman, 32 Del. 49, 119 Atl. 311 (1922); Linkhart v. Savely, 190 Ore. 484, 227 P.2d 187 (1950); Martin v. Estrella, 266 A.2d 41 (R.I. 1970) (dictum); Annot., 154 A.L.R. 121, 1 A.L.R.3d 571.

97.   Cain v. Skillin, 219 Ala. 228, 121 So. 521, 64 A.L.R. 1022 (1929) (defendant entitled to show plaintiff's character for turbulence though defendant did not know of it); Linkhart v. Savely, 190 Ore. 484, 227 P.2d 187 (1950) (same); Bugg v. Brown, 251 Md. 99, 246 A.2d 235 (1968) (court, though adhering to majority view on general question of proof of reputation in civil cases, holds that reputation of both parties is "in issue," when dispute as to who was first aggressor); Annot., 1 A.L.R.3d 571, 601.

98.   1 Wigmore, Evidence § 63; 1 Wharton, Criminal Evidence § 228 (12th ed. 1955); C.J.S. Homicide § 272; 40 Am.Jur.2d Homicide, §§ 301–309; Dec.Dig. Homicide ☞188; Annot., 64 A.L.R. 1029; 1 A.L.R. 3d 571.

99.   State v. Wilson, 235 Iowa 538, 17 N.W.2d 138 (1945); Freeman v. State, 204 So.2d 842 (Miss. 1967); Annot., 1 A.L.R.3d 571, 601.

There is another use of testimony of the reputation for violence of the deceased, which does not transgress the policy against evidence of character to show conduct. This is the use of the reputation of deceased for violence, when the reputation is proved to be known to the accused, as evidence of the defendant's reasonable apprehension of immediate danger.   State v. Blair, 305 S.W.2d 435 (Mo. 1957); 2 Wigmore, Evidence § 246; Dec.Dig. Homicide ☞188(2); Annot., 1 A.L.R.3d 571, 596.

1.   State v. Brock, 56 N.M. 328, 244 P.2d 131, 34 A. L.R.2d 447 (1952).

2.   Miller v. State, 63 Okl.Cr. 64, 72 P.2d 520 (1937); Arthur v. State, 170 Tex.Cr.R. 161, 339 S.W.2d 538 (1960); 40 Am.Jur.2d Homicide § 308.

3.   People v. Hoffman, 195 Cal. 295, 311, 232 P. 974, 980 (1925); Richardson v. State, 123 Miss. 232, 85 So. 186 (1920); State v. Champion, 222 N.C. 160, 22 S.E.2d 232 (1942) (dictum); Lee v. Com., 188 Va. 360, 49 S.E.2d 608 (1948) (but here the state's own witnesses testified that the deceased was the first aggressor), noted 3 Ark.L.Rev. 464 (1949); 6 Wash. & Lee L.Rev. 224 (1948); Annot., 34 A.L.R.2d 451, 457.

er hand, when the crucial question as to who was the first attacker, on which the just decision of the murder charge may depend, is in doubt, the character of the dead man for peace or violence has a revealing significance which may well be thought to outweigh the possibility of prejudice, here so much less than in the case of an attack on the character of the accused. Accordingly, Wigmore and a group of courts have favored the view that whenever the accused claims self-defence and offers evidence that the deceased was the first aggressor, the state in rebuttal may produce evidence of the peaceful character of the deceased.[4]

194. Character to Evidence Conduct—(g) Exception to General Rule of Exclusion, in the Practice of Admitting Evidence of Character to Impeach a Witness.

The familiar practice of allowing proof of bad character of a witness for veracity, by the testimony of reputation-witnesses and by evidence of conviction of crime seems to constitute another exception to the traditional policy against using evidence of character to show conduct, here to show that the witness may have testified to an untruth. The scope of this exception is discussed in the chapter on impeachment.[5]

195. Habit and Custom as Evidence of Conduct on a Particular Occasion.[6]

Character and habit are close akin. Character is a generalized description of one's dis-

position, or of one's disposition in respect to a general trait, such as honesty, temperance, or peacefulness.[7] "Habit," in modern usage, both lay and psychological, is more specific.[8] It describes one's regular response to a repeated specific situation. If we speak of character for care, we think of the person's tendency to act prudently in all the varying situations of life, in business, family life, in handling automobiles and in walking across the street. A habit, on the other hand, is the person's regular practice of meeting a particular kind of situation with a specific type of conduct, such as the habit of going down a particular stairway two stairs at a time, or of giving the hand signal for a left turn, or of alighting from railway cars while

---

6. 1 Wigmore, Evidence §§ 92–97; 29 Am.Jur.2d Evidence §§ 303, 316, 317; Lewan, Rationale of Habit Evidence, 16 Syracuse L.Rev. 39 (1964); Falknor, "Customary" Negligence, 12 Wash.L.Rev. 35 (1937); Notes, 25 Boston U.L.Rev. 64 (1945), 33 Boston U.L.Rev. 205 (1953), 14 Detroit L.J. 32 (1951); Annot. 15 A.L.R. 125, 18 A.L.R. 1109, 46 A.L.R.2d 103, 28 A.L.R.3d 1293; Dec.Dig. Evidence ⬡138, 139.

Uniform Rules 49, 50: "Evidence of habit or custom is relevant to an issue of behavior on a specified occasion, but is admissible on that issue only as tending to prove that the behavior on such occasion conformed to the habit or custom. . . . Testimony in the form of opinion is admissible on the issue of habit or custom. Evidence of specific instances of behavior is admissible to prove habit or custom if the evidence is of a sufficient number of instances to warrant a finding of such habit or custom." Cf. Model Code of Evidence, Rule 307; F.R.Ev. (R.D.1971) 406.

7. See § 186, supra.

8. "[A] particular practice or usage: *the habit of shaking hands.* . . . an acquired behavior pattern regularly followed until it has become almost involuntary: *the habit of looking both ways before crossing the street.*" Random House International Dictionary, Habit, 635 (1969); "In psychology, a customary or automatic way of acting, usually as a result of frequent usage rather than of inborn origin." 10 Encyc. Brittanica, Habit, 1092 (1968). See Wigmore, Science of Judicial Proof 127, 128 (3d ed. 1937).

At least some measure of the disagreement in the cases with respect to the admissibility of habit evidence arises from uncertainty as to how often the conduct must be repeated and the degree to which it must be consistent in order to qualify as habit. See Lewan, Rationale of Habit Evidence, 16 Syracuse L.Rev. 39, 49 (1964).

---

4. Sweazy v. State, 210 Ind. 674, 5 N.E.2d 511 (1937); State v. Holbrook, 98 Ore. 43, 192 P. 640 (1920); 1 Wigmore, Evidence § 63, note 2. Some decisions reach like results by holding that in the particular case the threats or acts of aggression of deceased proved by accused were such as to constitute an attack on his character for peacefulness. State v. Rutledge, 243 Iowa 179, 47 N.W.2d 251 (1951); State v. Brock, 56 N.M. 338, 244 P.2d 131, 34 A.L.R.2d 447 (1952) (annotated on this and other character points). But to draw a line between those acts of aggression sufficient to raise the issue of self-defence which are and those which are not attacks on character, seems unrealistic.

5. See §§ 41–44, supra.

they are moving. The doing of the habitual acts may become semi-automatic.

Character may be thought of as the sum of one's habits though doubtless it is more than this. But unquestionably the uniformity of one's response to habit is far greater than the consistency with which one's conduct conforms to character or disposition. Even though character comes in only exceptionally as evidence of an act,[9] surely any sensible man in investigating whether X did a particular act would be greatly helped in his inquiry by evidence as to whether he was in the habit of doing it. We are shocked, then, to read such judicial pronouncements as the following: "For the purpose of proving that one has or has not done a particular act, it is not competent to show that he has or has not been in the habit of doing other similar acts."[10] But surely, if "habit" is used in the sense we have suggested above, expediency and sound reason would lead to the opposite approach, namely that evidence that an act was habitually done by X under like circumstances will be received as evidence that it was done by X on the particular occasion.[11] Nevertheless, the judge should possess the discretion usual in this field of circumstantial evidence to exclude if the habit is not sufficiently regular and uniform, or the circumstances sufficiently similar, to outweigh the danger, if any, of prejudice or confusion.[12]

The reluctance of some courts to accept this view of the general admissibility of habit to show an act,[13] and the doctrine of other courts that evidence of habit will be received only when there are no eyewitnesses,[14] are

---

9. See §§ 188–194, supra.

10. Knowlton, J., in Commonwealth v. Nagle, 157 Mass. 554, 32 N.E. 861 (1893). See also Cincinnati, N. O. & T. P. R. v. Hare's Adm'x, 297 Ky. 5, 178 S.W.2d 835 (1944) (". . . evidence of his practices or customs in relation to similar instances is not admissible. Likewise, of his habits generally in that relation. It is immaterial what the person may have done upon previous occasions or under like circumstances.")

11. Howard v. Capital Transit Co., 97 F.Supp. 578 (D.D.C.1951), aff'd 90 U.S.App.D.C. 359, 196 F.2d 593 (1952) (decedent's habit or custom of using defendant's busses to return from work admissible to show he was a passenger on night in question); Whittemore v. Lockheed Aircraft Corp., 65 Cal.App. 2d 737, 151 P.2d 670 (1944) (practice of pilot to fly plane to destination when he used left-hand seat); State v. Wadsworth, 210 So.2d 4 (Fla.1968) (prior intemperate habits admissible to corroborate evidence of drunkenness at time in question); Fissette v. Boston & Maine R., 98 N.H. 136, 96 A.2d 303 (1953) (decedent's habit as to looking and listening at railroad crossing); Glatt v. Feist, 156 N.W.2d 819, 28 A.L.R.3d 1278 (N.D.1968) (annotated on this

point) (plaintiff's habit of crossing outside crosswalk at particular place admissible to show where she crossed on occasion in question); Bown v. City of Tacoma, 175 Wash. 414, 27 P.2d 711 (1933) (plaintiff's habit of riding on cars in alley where accident occurred); Uniform Rule 50; F.R.Ev. (R.D. 1971) 406.

12. See § 185, supra; Levin v. United States, 119 U.S.App.D.C. 156, 338 F.2d 265 (1964) cert. denied 379 U.S. 999.

13. See, e. g., Commonwealth v. Nagle, and Cincinnati, N. O. & T. P. R. v. Hare's Adm'x, supra n. 10; Zucker v. Whitridge, 205 N.Y. 62, 98 N.E. 209 (1912) (fatal crossing accident, with several eyewitnesses; on issue of contributory negligence plaintiff introduced testimony that deceased when about to cross railway tracks "usually looked to right and left of him and put a restraining hand on my arm before crossing"; held, reversible error, probative value does not outweigh danger of "collateral issues," expenditure of time and confusion; "we are not now called upon to decide whether [such] evidence . . . is competent when there is no eye-witness. . . ."); Fenton v. Aleshire, 238 Ore. 24, 393 P.2d 217 (1964); Snell, Eying the Iowa No Eyewitness Rule, 43 Iowa L.Rev. 57 (1957); Note, 33 Boston U.L.Rev. 205 (1953); Annot., 15 A.L.R. 125, 18 A.L.R. 1109, 28 A.L.R.3d 1293.

14. In a number of states, an exception to the rule excluding character evidence on the issue of particular negligent conduct, is made where there are no eyewitnesses. See Annot., 28 A.L.R.3d 1293. Where a habit of specific conduct is concerned, the requirement that there be no eyewitnesses seems unwise, and the tendency has been to remove it, Glatt v. Feist, 156 N.W.2d 819, 28 A.L.R.3d 1278 (N.D. 1968) (where eyewitnesses disagreed, evidence of plaintiff's habit of jaywalking at particular spot admissible); F.R.Ev. (R.D.1971) 406 (expressly removing requirement) West's Ann.Cal.Evid.Code, § 1105, Comment (removing requirement by implication); Note, 10 Vand.L.Rev. 447 (1957). The need for the evidence seems as great where the eyewitnesses disagree, or for some other reason the issue of fact is doubtful, as where the absence of eyewitnesses produces the difficulty.

probably due to a failure to draw a clear line between character and habit. This is contributed to by the popular custom of describing character in terms of "habits," such as "habits of care" [15] or "habits of intemperance." [16] In consequence these courts mistakenly apply to evidence of specific habit, the restrictions developed for the far less probative and more prejudicial evidence of character.

On the other hand evidence of the "custom" of a business organization or establishment, if reasonably regular and uniform, is usually received much more willingly by the courts,[17] perhaps because there is here no temptation to confuse this with evidence of character. Thus, it is usually held that when a letter has been written and signed in the course of business and placed in the regular place for mailing, evidence of the custom of the establishment as to the mailing of such letters is receivable as evidence that it was duly mailed.[18]

15. The use of such expressions has served to obscure the distinction between character and specific habit, so that judges of distinction have occasionally treated evidence of a particular habit to show a particular act in accord, as if it had no greater relevance than general character for care. See, e. g., Cincinatti, N. O. & T. P. R. v. Hare's Adm'x, 297 Ky. 5, 178 S.W.2d 835 (1944) (custom to look both ways, shift to lower gear and slow down at specific crossing); Fenton v. Aleshire, 238 Ore. 24, 393 P.2d 217 (1964) (habit of using cross-walk at specific crossing). A case on the border between habit and isolated acts of carelessness is Brownhill v. Kivlin, 317 Mass. 168, 57 N.E.2d 539, 1944 (negligent burning of garage, defendant's previous acts of carelessness in smoking excluded); Note, 25 Boston U.L.Rev. 64 (1945).

16. The phrase may denote a general disposition for excessive drinking, or may amount to a specific habit of drinking a certain number of glasses of whiskey every day on going home from work, and according to medical beliefs such addiction may amount to a specific abnormality or disease. The probative force of such "habits" to prove drunkenness on a particular occasion depends on the degree of regularity of the practice and its coincidence with the occasion. On the other hand, "habits" of sobriety may well point to unvarying temperance or abstention and would seem to be highly probative on the question of sobriety on the particular occasion. See Annot., 46 A.L.R.2d 103. In addition, the judge should weigh the possibility of unfair prejudice which proof of a "habit of being drunk" may carry with it. Evidence of a habit of drinking has sometimes been considered probative enough to be admissible, when there is other evidence, but not sufficient standing alone to be admissible to show a drunken condition at a particular time. See State v. Wadsworth, 210 So.2d 4 (Fla.1968). Conflicting cases are collected in 1 Wigmore, Evidence § 96. Cf. F.R.Ev. (R.D.1971) 406, expressly eliminating any requirement of corroboration as a condition of admissibility.

17. United States v. Oddo, 314 F.2d 115 (2d Cir. 1963) cert. denied 375 U.S. 833 (customary practices of Immigration and Naturalization Service); Eaton v. Bass, 214 F.2d 896 (6th Cir. 1954) (custom of inspecting trucks); Russell v. Pitts, 105 Ga.App. 147, 123 S.E.2d 708 (1961) (customary sterilization procedures in medical center); Commonwealth v. Torrealba, 316 Mass. 24, 54 N.E.2d 939 (1944) (custom of store to give sales slip with each purchase received as evidence that goods found in defendant's possession, with no record of sale, were stolen); Lundquist v. Jennison, 66 Mont. 516, 214 Pac. 67 (1923) (breach of warranty of seed wheat; defendant denied selling seed wheat; proof that defendant was engaged in business of selling seed wheat generally received as evidence of sale to plaintiff); Buxton v. Langan, 90 N.H. 13, 3 A.2d 647 (1939) (rule or practice of defendant's shop for employees to test brakes before renting out car); and cases cited 1 Wigmore, Evidence § 93, note; Dec.Dig. Evidence ⬤139.

Model Code of Evidence Rule 307 defined the terms as follows: "(1) Habit means a course of behavior of a person regularly repeated in like circumstances. Custom means a course of behavior of a group of persons regularly repeated in like circumstances." But the distinction in terminology is not always made. Also, if habit is the sole category applicable to individuals, and is limited to automatic, "almost involuntary" conduct, much probative evidence may be excluded for want of a name. An individual may have a regular, voluntary, intentional, practice, equivalent in probative force to the custom of an organization made up of more than one person. Compare the cases in note 11, supra, with Levin v. United States, 119 U.S.App.D.C. 156, 338 F.2d 265 (1964) cert. denied 379 U.S. 999 (individual's religious practice; "Certainly the very volitional basis of the activity raises serious questions as to its invariable nature, and hence its probative value."). Cf. F.R.Ev. (R.D.1971) 406.

18. This is assumed in the cases and the issue centers upon whether such evidence is sufficient. Some courts, possibly the majority, say that it is not, and that the employee who did the mailing must be produced, though he can only rely, for his testimony that it was mailed, upon the custom, or that some other evidence that the custom was followed in this instance must be produced. Di Rosa v. Bosworth, 225 So.2d 42 (La.App.) writ refused 254 La. 843, 227 So.2d 591 (1969); Crissey

Proof of the existence of the person's habit or of the custom of the business may be made by testimony of a witness to his conclusion that there was such a habit or practice.[19] It also may be made by evidence of specific instances,[20] though these latter would be sub-ject to the judge's discretion to require that the instances be not too few or too many, and that the time be near and the circumstances be sufficiently similar.[21]

v. State Highway Comm'n, 147 Mont. 374, 413 P.2d 308 (1966); Note, 47 Mich.L.Rev. 420 (1948); Annot., 25 A.L.R. 9, 86 A.L.R. 541; C.J.S. Evidence § 136(c). But probably the more reasonable view is that the evidence is sufficient. United States v. Vandersee, 279 F.2d 176 (3d Cir. 1960); Mohr v. Universal C. I. T. Credit Corp., 216 Md. 197, 140 A.2d 49 (1958); Start v. Shell Oil Co., 202 Or. 99, 273 P.2d 225 (1954). See Slough, Relevancy Unraveled, 5 Kan.L.Rev. 404, 409 (1957); also F.R.Ev. (R.D.1971) 406 (expressly removing the requirement of corroboration).

19. This is the method usually employed. See cases cited in notes 11 and 17, supra; 1 Wigmore, Evidence § 93, 2 id. § 375; Uniform Rule 50; F.R.Ev. (R.D.1971) 406.

20. Whittemore v. Lockheed Aircraft Corp., 65 Cal. App.2d 737, 151 P.2d 670 (1944) (evidence that on all four occasions when W flew plane he occupied

McCormick et al on Evid. 2nd Ed. HB—30

left-hand seat admissible as evidence of his probable conduct on particular occasion); Petricevich v. Salmon River Canal Co., 92 Idaho 865, 452 P.2d 362 (1969) (dictum); Reagan v. Manchester St. Ry. Co., 72 N.H. 298, 56 Atl. 314 (1903) (testimony of defendant's motorman that he had gone through place of collision "a good many times" at 20 miles an hour competent as tending to show that defendant habitually ran its cars at high speed). 2 Wigmore, Evidence §§ 375, 376; Uniform Rule 50; F.R.Ev. (R.D.1971) 406.

But the line is close between particular instances to show habit or custom, and particular instances to show character for negligence which on an issue of conduct would not be allowed. See § 189, supra.

21. Petricevich v. Salmon River Canal Co., 92 Idaho 865, 452 P.2d 362 (1969) (number of instances and similarity of circumstances not sufficient); Lewan, Rationale of Habit Evidence, 16 Syracuse L.Rev. 39 (1964); Model Code of Evidence Rule 307, Comment and Illustrations (approving proof of "many" instances through a single witness).

CHAPTER 18

SIMILAR HAPPENINGS AND TRANSACTIONS

196. Similar Previous Claims, Suits or Defences of a Present Party, Offered against Him.[1]

In this area the need for the exposure of fraudulent claims comes in conflict with the need for the protection of innocent litigants from unfair prejudice. At two extremes the practice is fairly well agreed on. Thus, when it is sought to be shown merely that the plaintiff is a chronic litigant, or a chronic personal injury litigant, the courts consider that the slight probative value is overborne by the danger of prejudice, and they exclude the evidence.[2] At the other extreme, if it is proved not merely that the party has made previous claims or brought suits but that the former claims were similar to the present claim and were false and fraudulent, then the strong relevance of these facts to evidence the falsity of the present claim is apparent and most courts admit them.[3]

The intermediate situation is the difficult one. The evidence offered is that the present party, now suing for a loss claimed to be accidental, such as a loss of property by fire, or personal injury in a collision, has made repeated previous claims of similar losses. Here the relevance is based on the premise that under the doctrine of chances repeated injuries of the same kind are unlikely to happen to one person by accident.[4] On the other hand this kind of evidence is prejudice-

---

1. 3A Wigmore, Evidence (Chadbourn rev.) § 963.

2. Testa v. Moore-McCormack Lines, Inc., 229 F. Supp. 154 (S.D.N.Y.1964) (claim for slip on grease; prior claim for slip on grease inadmissible); Lowenthal v. Mortimer, 125 Cal.App.2d 636, 270 P.2d 942 (1954) (15 prior unrelated lawsuits inadmissible); Palmer v. Manhattan R., 133 N.Y. 261, 30 N.E. 1001 (1892) (slander and false imprisonment; evidence that plaintiff was "an habitual litigant" properly excluded); Knight v. Hasler, 24 Wis.2d 128, 128 N.W.2d 407 (1964) (similar). Contra, Mintz v. Premier Cab Ass'n, 75 U.S.App.D.C. 389, 127 F.2d 744 (1942) (cross-examination of plaintiff about 2 prior personal injury claims proper; whether plaintiff was "merely unlucky" or was "claim-minded" was for jury); Annot., 69 A.L.R.2d 593. Evidence of prior injury or claim therefor, offered to show that a subsequent accident did not cause the injury is, of course, distinguishable from the topic here considered.

3. Sessner v. Com., 268 Ky. 127, 103 S.W.2d 647 (1937) (disbarment for asserting fictitious claims, evidence of other unfounded claims allowed to show system and plan); Fairfield Packing Co. v. Southern Mut. F. Ins. Co., 193 Pa. 184, 44 Atl. 317 (1899) (action on fire policy; evidence that employee of and witness for plaintiff made intentional false statement in another proof of loss for same fire, allowed).

As to admissibility of other claims of sexual misconduct made by a prosecutrix, see People v. Scholl, 225 Cal.App.2d 558, 37 Cal.Rptr. 475 (1964) (sex offense against child; error to exclude evidence of similar charges by child against other men); State v. Nab, 245 Ore. 454, 421 P.2d 388 (1966) (statutory rape; similar ruling); Annot., 6 A.L.R. 1051, 1055 (civil cases), 75 A.L.R.2d 508 (criminal cases); 3A Wigmore, Evidence (Chadbourn rev.) § 963 n. 2. Psychiatric examination of the complaining witness has often been proposed for this type of case; the holdings have been that it is at most discretionary with the trial judge. See Annot., 18 A.L.R.3d 1433; 3A Wigmore, Evidence (Chadbourn rev.) § 924a.

4. In Mintz v. Premier Cab Ass'n, 75 U.S.App.D.C. 389, 127 F.2d 744 (1942), where plaintiff sued for injury in a taxicab collision, it was held proper to allow cross-examination of plaintiff about two

arousing and standing alone would seldom be sufficient to support a finding of fraud. It seems that the judge, balancing in his discretion probative value against prejudice, should

admit the evidence only when the proponent has produced or will produce other evidence of fraud.[5]

We have been discussing the problem in terms of the discrediting by circumstantial evidence of the verity of a party's claim or defence. Similar facts and inferences may be used in attacking the veracity of witnesses.[6] Moreover, it should be noticed that,

claims for personal injury within two years before this one, and to allow counsel to argue that this showed she was "claim-minded." The court said: "Fortuitous events of a given sort are less likely to happen repeatedly than once. . . . Negligent injury is not unusual, but it is unusual for one person, not engaged in hazardous activities, to suffer it repeatedly within a short period and at the hands of different persons. The court's rulings were therefore right. That all three of appellant's stories may have been true affects the weight of the evidence, not its admissibility. It was for the jury to decide from all the evidence, and from its observation of appellant on the stand, whether she was merely unlucky or was 'claim-minded.' "

In San Antonio Traction Co. v. Cox, 184 S.W. 722 (Tex.Civ.App.1916) the court conceded the force of the argument from probabilities, but held the evidence inadmissible. There the plaintiff sued for injury due to the sudden start of the car from which he was alighting. The defendant offered evidence that 17 claims for similar injuries in alighting from cars had been made by other members of the plaintiff's family! The court held that this was rightly rejected and said: "The evidence fails to connect plaintiff with the other claims, except in one instance in which he was with a cousin when he had his fall, and also witnessed the release executed by him to the company. We fail to find in the testimony given or excluded that evidence of concerted action such as is required to constitute a conspiracy. It is just as probable, if not more so, that each incident stood alone as that a conspiracy existed, and it is mere guesswork to say that any of the parties conspired together."

It should be pointed out that the relevancy premise is not itself free of difficulties. The low probability that a series of similar injuries will happen to the same person does not, of itself, lower the probability that a particular one occurred. If the doctrine of chances is appealed to, it would illustrate the preceding sentence this way: The probability that 10 fair coins tossed at once produced 10 heads is only $\frac{1}{1024}$, but that probability is derived from, and does not lower at all, the probability (of $\frac{1}{2}$) that a particular one of the coins came up heads. The use of this type of illustration has precedent. See Weiss v. United States, 122 F.2d 675, 684 (5 Cir.) cert. denied 314 U.S. 687, reh. denied 314 U.S. 716 (1941). Sometimes the argument takes the form: this highly unlikely series did occur—therefore claimant's own conduct is in some way a cause; but this seems to be a species of character evidence, which is forbidden. A more appealing form of the argument would seem to be: the proportion of "claim-minded" persons (including both mistaken and insincere claimants) is greater in the group of claimants making repeated

claims than in the group of claimants as a whole. The showing that plaintiff is in the repeater group therefore increases the probability that he is claim-minded. Since the actual proportions are unknown, it is not possible to say what this increase is, or what the *a posteriori* probability is. (*Mintz*, supra, suggests that a series of three similar claims within 2 years, plus claimant's demeanor, could support a finding that she was "claim-minded," thus leaving uncertain the effect of the series alone.) See also San Antonio Traction Co. v. Cox, supra; United States v. Hutul, 416 F.2d 607 (7th Cir. 1969) cert. denied 396 U.S. 1012, reh. denied 397 U.S. 1081 (1970); Monaghan, The Liability Claim Racket, 3 Law & Cont.Prob. 491 (1936).

5.   See Concordia Fire Ins. Co. v. Wise, 114 Okla. 254, 246 Pac. 595, 46 A.L.R. 456 (1926) (action on fire policy, frequent previous fires and collection of insurance, excluded especially since it did not appear that any of the properties were over-insured); Keiter v. Miller, 111 Pa.Super. 594, 170 Atl. 364 (1934) (in action on alleged contract to pay for board and lodging furnished defendant's minor son, where defense was that boy was to be cared for in return for his companionship, permitting cross-examination of defendant as to whether he raised same defense respecting other children cared for by strangers held error). See also Shannon v. Murphy, 49 Haw. 661, 426 P.2d 816 (1967). Cf. Terpstra v. Niagara Fire Ins. Co., 26 N.Y.2d 70, 308 N.Y.S.2d 378, 256 N.E.2d 536 (1970) (suit on fire policy; 3 prior fires and collection of insurance admissible as furnishing plaintiff with a motive to set instant fire to get money).

6.   See citations and discussion in notes 3 and 4, supra. When the claimant testifies, the impeaching argument seems to take this form: This witness has asserted (by his complaints) that a series of similar injuries happened to him. It was, *a priori*, highly unlikely that such a series occurred, and therefore likely that as to some of the injuries his assertions that they occurred were false. This should be considered when deciding what weight to give his testimony that the injury in suit did occur. This brings the case closer to, although not within, the rule discussed in note 3, supra, which requires additional proof of the falsity of the prior claims. Where probabilities are involved, the assertion as to each of several injuries that it more probably happened than not, is not equivalent to the assertion that all of them more probably hap-

in keeping with the customary relaxation of the standard of relevancy on cross-examination,[7] it is generally easier to secure the courts' approval of this sort of evidence when sought to be elicited on cross-examination of a party, than when offered by the proponent through the testimony of his own witnesses.

197. Other Misrepresentations and Fraudulent Devices.[8]

The policy against proving other misconduct of a party for the sole purpose of evidencing his character or disposition as raising the inference that he was probably guilty of the misconduct charged in the suit,[9] finds expression in civil as well as in criminal cases. Where redress for fraud or misrepresentation is sought, three alternative theories may be available to support the admission of evidence of other misrepresentations or fraudulent conduct by the party.

1. When under the applicable substantive law, knowledge or intent by the party is an essential ingredient for liability, then if it be proved that the party has made other misrepresentations, of similar purport, and false in fact, this tends to show that the representations in suit were made with *knowledge* of their falsity and with *intent* to deceive.[10]

This inference does not require that the other representations should have been identical in purport nor made under precisely like circumstances. Only a reasonable approximation in purport, time and circumstance is needed to ground the inference of knowledge or intent.

2. If the actual making of the misrepresentations charged in the suit is at issue, then to show the party's *conduct* in making the representations or committing the other acts of fraud as alleged, it is competent to prove other representations closely similar in purport or other fraudulent acts, when they may be found to be parts of a larger or continuing *plan* or *design*, of which the acts or misrepresentations in suit may also be found to be an intended part or object.[11] Similarly,

same misrepresentation to a third person in exchange with him, admissible to show plan and knowledge); Fulwider v. Woods, 461 S.W.2d 581 (Ark.1971) (similar); State v. Easter, 174 Neb. 412, 118 N.W.2d 515 (1962) (false pretenses; evidence of similar false pretenses admissible to show intent); 2 Wigmore, Evidence § 321 n. 1; Annots., 34 A.L.R.2d 777, 78 A.L.R.2d 1359.

But the evidence cannot come in on this theory if liability attaches from mere misrepresentation without regard to knowledge and intent. Johnson v. Gulick, 46 Neb. 817, 65 N.W. 883 (1896); Stowe v. Wooten, 62 S.W.2d 67 (1933); Standard Mfg. Co. v. Slot, 121 Wis. 14, 98 N.W. 923 (1904). The other representations must be shown to be false. Boyer v. United States, 76 U.S.App.D.C. 397, 132 F.2d 12, 13 (1942). Seemingly, if intent rather than knowledge is sought to be shown, acts subsequent as well as before the conduct in suit, may be considered. Johnson v. State, 75 Ark. 427, 88 S.W. 905 (1905); Early v. Eley, 243 N.C. 695, 91 S.E.2d 919 (1956) (fraud in stock sale; evidence that defendants subsequently purchased stocks like those sold to plaintiffs, and suffered loss, to show lack of intent); 2 Wigmore, Evidence § 316.

11. Mudsill Mining Co. Ltd. v. Watrous, 61 Fed. 163, 179 (6th Cir. 1894) (rescission for fraud in sale of silver mine through device of "salting" ore with powdered silver; salting of ore by defendant to secure favorable reports in course of previous negotiations for sale of mine to others admissible to show that silver was introduced into the ore by salting, and that it was defendant who did the salting on this occasion); Kindred v. State, 258 N.E.2d 411 (Ind.1970) (forgery; prior similar forgery admissible "to prove the defendant guilty of the crime charged."); Albrecht v. Rathai, 150 Minn. 256, 185 N.W. 259, 261 (1921) (". . . the

pened than not. Of course, this argument can be recast in the form mentioned in note 4; the proportion of claimants whose testimony is mistaken or insincere is greater among "repeaters" than among claimants in general. Showing that claimant is in the repeater class increases the chance that his testimony is mistaken or insincere, to the extent of this change in proportion (the extent of the change, and the *a posteriori* probability are, of course, not known).

7. See § 29, supra, and the discussion in n. 6, supra, suggesting that an additional explanation is possible where the complainant testifies.

8. 2 Wigmore, Evidence §§ 301–304, 321; Dec.Dig. Evidence ⊙⇒135.

9. See §§ 188, 190, supra.

10. United States v. Marine, 413 F.2d 214 (7th Cir. 1969), cert. denied 396 U.S. 1001 (mail fraud; other fraudulent sales admissible to show knowledge and intent); Olympic Land Co. v. Smithart, 1 Ariz.App. 175, 400 P.2d 846 (1965) (fraud in land exchange;

it would seem that if the identity of the perpetrator of the fraud in suit were in doubt, then other fraudulent acts of the party so like the conduct in suit as to earmark them as the product of the same mind and hand, would be received to show that he was the perpetrator.[12]

3. The courts have not generally gone so far, but it is believed that the admission of evidence of previous similar misrepresentations to show the making of the present representations should, in civil cases at least, be extended to cover the situation where there is testimony asserting the making of the misrepresentation at issue, and testimony denying it. Here it seems that evidence in reply of other like misrepresentations by the party (whether or not part of a plan or scheme) will be of much value to the trier upon the disputed question and that this need outweighs the danger of prejudice. While this evidence standing alone would not of course be sufficient to establish the issue, it can be of great value in resolving the conflict.

198. Other Contracts.[13]

Evidence of other contractual transactions between the same parties is readily received when relevant to show the probable meaning they attached to the terms of the contract in litigation.[14] Likewise, when the authority of an agent is in question, other similar transactions carried on by him in behalf of the alleged principal are freely admitted.[15]

However, when evidence of other contracts is offered as evidence on the issue of the terms or making of the contract in suit, the courts have shown a surprisingly stiff attitude, beguiled perhaps by the mystical influence of the *res inter alios acta* phrase or misled by a confusion of the requirements of sufficiency and relevancy.[16] When the evidence offered is of other contracts between the same parties, they have been willing to acknowledge that other similar contracts showing a custom, habit or continuing course of dealing between the same parties may be received as evidence of the terms of the present bargain.[17] Many courts, however, draw

---

other similar frauds shown may be of such a character as to show a series of connected fraudulent doings, a general scheme to defraud, broad enough to include that under consideration, and of which it is a part, so as to make them competent as substantive proof of it."); State v. Granville, 1 Wash. App. 976, 465 P.2d 693 (1970) (forgery; other forged checks found on defendant admissible as "direct evidence of the crime charged."); 2 Wigmore, Evidence § 304.

Courts often seem to overlook the availability of this theory of admissibility and by their strictness in limiting admissibility to the purpose of showing knowledge and intent seem unduly to hamper the investigation of fraud. See the forceful comment, 24 Tex.L.Rev. 351 (1946). Some of the confusion may be due to the different senses in which "intent" is used. Sometimes the act is assumed done by a particular person, and the issue is his purpose (intent to defraud). At other times the intention (plan; design) of X to do an act is offered as evidence that later X did it. The evidence permitted may vary accordingly. See Weiss v. United States, 122 F.2d 675 (5th Cir. 1941) cert. denied 314 U.S. 687, reh. denied 314 U.S. 716; C.J.S. Evidence § 580.

12. See § 190, supra.

13. 2 Wigmore, Evidence § 377; Dec.Dig. Evidence ⚖129(6).

14. See, e. g., Bourne v. Gatliff, 11 C. & F. 45, 49, 70, 8 Eng.Rep. 1019 (H.L.1844) (to ascertain meaning of bill of lading provision as to delivery of goods to owner previous transactions may be looked to); Hartford Steam Boiler Insp. & Ins. Co. v. Schwartzman Packing Co., 423 F.2d 1170 (10th Cir. 1970) (prior pattern of use of contracts by parties admissible to show meaning they attached to contract definitions and exclusions); Korner Roofing & Sheet Metal Co. v. Smylie Bros., Inc., 118 Ohio App. 461, 188 N.E.2d 802 (1963) (semble); see Uniform Commercial Code § 1–205 (course of dealing between parties).

15. Parker v. Jones, 221 Ark. 378, 253 S.W.2d 342 (1952) (prior instances of treating A as agent admissible to show authority to make timber contract); Goodwin & McDowell Motor Co. v. St. Clair Auto F. Co., 253 S.W.2d 543 (Mo.App.1952) (prior contracts for repairs made by A, recognized as binding by defendant, admissible to show A's authority to make such contracts).

16. See § 185, supra.

17. Conderback, Inc., v. Standard Oil Co., 239 Cal. App.2d 664, 48 Cal.Rptr. 901 (1966) (whether con-

a line here and hold that a party's other contracts with third persons offered as evidence of the terms of the disputed contract are inadmissible.[18]

This is too inflexible and bars out information valuable to the trier. Contracts of a party with third persons may show the party's customary practice and course of dealing and thus be highly probative as bearing on the terms of his present agreement.[19]

Even short of such extensive acts, when a business man has once adopted a particular mode of handling a bargaining topic, such as warranty, discount or the like, in a certain kind of transactions, it is often easier for him to follow the same solution in respect to the same feature of a new contract, than it is to work out a new one.

No strict rules or limits of admissibility are appropriate. There is no danger of unfair prejudice here. Seemingly, the courts should admit the evidence of other contracts in all cases where the testimony as to the terms of the present bargain is conflicting, and where the judge in his discretion finds that the probative value of the other transactions outweighs the risk of waste of time and confusion of issues.[20]

---

tract was firm-price or open-end; "Evidence of other similar contracts between the same parties establishing a custom, habit or continuous course of business dealing is admissible as showing that on a particular occasion the thing was done as usual."); Karp v. Coolview of Wisconsin, Inc., 25 Wis.2d 299, 130 N.W.2d 790 (1964) (prior extensions of credit to corporation by travel agent admissible on issue whether extension was to corporation or to individuals connected with corporation, in instant case). But an isolated previous instance, unaccompanied by any offer to prove additional instances going to show a continued course of dealing would presumably be rejected. See Roney v. Clearfield County Grange Mut. Fire Ins. Co., 332 Pa. 447, 3 A.2d 365 (1939).

18. McKee v. State, 172 Cal.App.2d 560, 342 P.2d 951 (1959) (evidence, offered by State, of series of cash sales not admissible to show its practice of making such sales rather than scrip sales; "What the State may have contracted for with others would not prove the nature of its contract with appellant."); Turpin v. Branaman, 190 Va. 818, 58 S.E. 2d 63 (1950) (whether defendant bought apples from plaintiffs on oral contract or was acting as broker; defendant's offer to show his practice was to execute written contracts when buying for himself, and oral ones when acting as broker, held properly rejected as irrelevant). The cases show some tendency to reject the evidence when the party offers his own practice, and to receive it when the party offers his opponent's practice. McKee v. State, supra, explains this on the basis that the second case is an example of the receipt of an "admission" of a party-opponent. The distinction is unsound. To reach the point the practice must be classified as an assertion, which other courts have not done; and to the extent that hearsay components relating to intention are involved, the exception for declarations of present mental state appears to suffice when the party offers his own practice (absent a finding by the judge of lack of sincerity). See Uniform Rule 63(12).

19. Joseph v. Krull Wholesale Drug Co., 147 F.Supp. 250 (D.Pa.1956), aff'd, 245 F.2d 231 (3d Cir. 1957) (whether officer's contract was for definite term; corporation's offer to show practice of making officers' contracts terminable at will properly re-

ceived); Moody v. Peirano, 4 Cal.App. 411, 88 Pac. 380 (1907) (suit for breach of warranty of wheat, sold as "White Australian"; defendant denies warranty; held, proper for judge in discretion to permit plaintiff to prove that defendant had sold other wheat from same shipment to third persons as "White Australian"); Re Isom's Estate, 193 Kan. 357, 394 P.2d 21 (1964) (oral contract to make will; prior similar contracts of decedent with others, offered by plaintiff, admissible to show existence of contract in suit); Magnet Cove Barium Corp. v. Brown, 419 S.W.2d 697 (Tex.Civ.App.1967) (reformation of deed; offer by plaintiff to show prior leases and deeds taken by defendant from others, all reserving oil and gas rights, admissible to show defendant's pattern of reservation, alleged to have been intended in instant deed); Super Tire Market, Inc. v. Rollins, 18 Utah 2d 122, 417 P.2d 132 (1966) (whether warranty on tires was given; seller's evidence of its policy not to give warranty admissible).

20. In Moody v. Peirano, described in the next preceding note, the court said: "The number and frequency of the sales in which the warranty had been made, and their proximity in time to the sale made to the plaintiff, would be circumstances addressed to the discretion of the court in determining the relevancy of the testimony; and, unless it should clearly appear therefrom that the court had abused its discretion, its action in admitting the evidence could not be regarded as error. These circumstances would also be addressed to the jury in determining the inference to be drawn from the testimony, or the strength of the probability in support of which it was introduced. The weight or conclusiveness to be given by the jury is entirely distinct from the question of the relevancy of the

199. Other Sales of Similar Property as Evidence of Value.[21]

In the case of ordinary personal property, where market value is sought, of course the most obvious resort is to evidence of what other similar property, whether wheat, shoes, horses, or what not, currently sold for on the market at that place. Not only may evidence of witnesses who know of such sales at firsthand be received for this purpose,[22] but price lists and market reports contained in newspapers, though they would be hearsay, if offered to show the actual sales recited,[23] and would be excluded by some courts on that ground, should be admitted either as a hearsay exception or as circumstantial evidence of what traders would have paid for such property, where the lists and reports are identified by witnesses as lists and reports actually relied upon by traders in buying and selling.[24]

Where the property, such as a pedigreed bull or a Rembrandt etching, is not of a standardized sort, one encounters difficulties as to whether any other like article sold is sufficiently similar for its price to be indicative.

Any tract of land is considered unique, and consequently it is in cases of land valuation, and especially in condemnation cases, that the question of admissibility of evidence of prices paid on other sales is most frequently discussed. A few states have been unwilling to admit the evidence save in exceptional circumstances.[25] This seems to put too heavy a strain on opinion evidence and the general knowledge of the jurors, and the view of the majority of courts which admits the evidence,[26] within safeguarding limits,[27] is preferable. These safeguards are the following: The sales of the other tracts must have been sufficiently near in time, and the other land must be located sufficiently near the land to be valued, and must be sufficiently alike in respect to character, situation, usability,

testimony." See also Wilkinson v. Dilenbeck, 184 Iowa 81, 168 N.W. 115, 116 (1918) where the trial judge's action in excluding testimony as to defendant's promises to other persons was sustained and the court said: "There is some force in the suggestion that such testimony had a tendency to corroborate the claims of the various plaintiffs, and that some latitude along that line could have been permitted. Some discretion, however, must be permitted to the trial court as to how far it will permit a digression from the main issue to collateral ones which bear only on the question of corroboration."

21. 2 Wigmore, Evidence §§ 463, 464; 29 Am.Jur.2d Evidence §§ 387–403; C.J.S. Evidence § 593; 5 Nichols, Eminent Domain §§ 21.1–22.2 (3d ed. 1969); Sengstock and McAuliffe, The Price of Eminent Domain, 44 J.Urban L. 185 (1967); Dec. Dig. Evidence ⚖142; Annots., 118 A.L.R. 870, 155 A.L.R. 262, 7 A.L.R.2d 781, 39 A.L.R.2d 209, 55 A.L.R.2d 791, 79 A.L.R.2d 677, 746, 85 A.L.R.2d 110, 12 A.L.R.3d 1064.

22. See Goralnik Hat Co. v. Delohery Hat Co., 98 Conn. 560, 120 Atl. 283 (1923); Harlan & Hollingsworth Corp. v. McBride, 6 Terry 85, 69 A.2d 9 (1949).

23. Doherty v. Harris, 230 Mass. 341, 119 N.E. 863 (1918); 6 Wigmore, Evidence § 1704.

24. F.R.Ev. (R.D.1971) 803(17); 6 Wigmore, Evidence § 1702; Freidman Iron & Supply Co. v. J. B. Beaird Co., 222 La. 627, 63 So.2d 144 (1952); Curtis v. Schwartzman Packing Co., 61 N.M. 305, 299 P.2d 776 (1956) (auto dealers' "Blue Book"); City Nat.

Bank v. Kiel, 348 S.W.2d 260 (Tex.Civ.App.1961) (traders' price reports); Annot., 43 A.L.R. 1192. See also, Uniform Commercial Code, § 2–723 (proof of market price of goods).

25. Petition of Mackie, 3 Mich.App. 415, 142 N.W.2d 907 (1966); State v. Winiecki, 263 Minn. 86, 115 N.W.2d 724 (1962). This minority view, usually called the "Pennsylvania rule" despite its modification by statute in that state, is said to be dying out; see Sengstock and McAuliffe, The Price of Eminent Domain, 44 J.Urban L. 185, 194; Redfield v. Iowa State Highway Comm'n, 251 Iowa 332, 99 N.W.2d 413, 85 A.L.R.2d 96 (1959). California, which appeared to leave the minority view in County of Los Angeles v. Faus, 48 Cal.2d 672, 312 P.2d 680 (1957), has retained a form of it by statute, for condemnation cases. West's Ann.Cal.Evid.Code § 813; Sacramento and S. J. D. Dist. v. W. P. Roduner Cattle & Farming Co., 268 Cal.App.2d 199, 73 Cal.Rptr. 733 (1968).

26. See, e. g., City of Paducah v. Allen, 111 Ky. 361, 63 S.W. 981 (1901) ("truly, here is where 'money talks.' "); Gregori v. City of Springfield, 348 Mass. 395, 204 N.E.2d 113 (1965) (the majority rule takes its name from the decisions in this state); and the many cases cited in Annot., 118 A.L.R. 870, 85 A.L.R.2d 110.

27. See cases under note 28, infra.

and improvements, to make it clear that the two tracts are comparable in value and that the price realized for the other land may fairly be considered as shedding light on the value of the land in question.[28] Manifestly, the trial judge in applying so vague a standard must be granted a wide discretion.[29]

Since the market value sought is the estimate of what a willing seller would have paid a willing buyer, prices on other sales of a forced character are generally inadmissible.[30] This excludes awards in condemnation of other land,[31] and many courts would automatically exclude evidence offered by the condemner of prices it has paid to other owners, on the theory that the threat, express or implied, of condemnation makes the sale too compulsive to be a fair indication of value.[32]

On the other hand this compulsion is not like a forced sale under execution. The owner here may have his land taken but he knows that he will be entitled to a judicial award of its market value. So, under what seems the better view, the evidence of the price paid should come in if the offeror of the evidence can satisfy the judge that the price paid was sufficiently voluntary to be a reasonable index of value.[33] In any event, the sale must be genuine, and the price must be actually paid or substantially secured.[34]

For prices on other lands to be admitted, they must be sale prices, and not mere offers.[35] These would often be of great sig-

28. The factors are discussed in Fairfield Gardens, Inc., v. United States, 306 F.2d 167 (9th Cir. 1962) (properly excluded as dissimilar); Illinois Bldg. Authority v. Dembinsky, 101 Ill.App.2d 59, 242 N.E.2d 67 (1968) (admissible as similar); Iowa Development Co. v. State Highway Com'n, 252 Iowa 978, 108 N.W.2d 487 (1961) (some tracts too dissimilar); and see the cases in Annot., 85 A.L.R.2d 110, 130. The property being valued has of course, the advantage of location-similarity; as to prior sales of it, see Annot., 55 A.L.R.2d 791. The proponent has the burden of showing similarity as a foundation for the evidence of other sales. Arkansas State Highway Com'n v. Witkowski, 236 Ark. 66, 364 S.W.2d 309 (1963); Kamrowski v. State, 37 Wis.2d 195, 155 N.W.2d 125 (1967) (requirement of similarity is more strict when sale is used as substantive evidence of value than where it is base for expert's opinion; here properly excluded for either purpose).

29. United States v. 55.22 Acres of Land, 411 F.2d 432 (9th Cir. 1969); State v. Wood, 22 Utah 2d 317, 452 P.2d 872 (1969); Annot., 85 A.L.R.2d 110, 126.

30. Knabe v. State, 285 Ala. 321, 231 So.2d 887 (1970); Waldenmaier v. State, 33 App.Div.2d 75, 305 N.Y.S.2d 381 (1970); Annot., 118 A.L.R. 870, 890, 85 A.L.R.2d 110, 157.

31. Whewell v. Ives, 155 Conn. 602, 236 A.2d 92 (1967); City of Chicago v. Lehmann, 262 Ill. 468, 104 N.E. 829, 831 (1914); Nantahala Power & Light Co. v. Sloan, 227 N.C. 151, 41 S.E.2d 361 (1947).

32. Bridges v. Alaska Housing Authority, 375 P.2d 696 (Alaska 1962); Annot., 118 A.L.R. 870, 893, 85 A.L.R.2d 110, 163. The decisions include in the

rule sales to a different party having the power of condemnation; and the majority would exclude the evidence even when offered by the condemnee, of prices paid by the condemnor (as admissions). Alaska State Housing Authority v. Du Pont, 439 P.2d 427 (Alas.1968); Stewart v. Commonwealth, 337 S.W.2d 880 (Ky.1960). Contra, State v. Cannon, 159 So.2d 49 (La.App.1963). Clearly, compulsion may be operating on either side in a given case; see 5 Nichols, Eminent Domain § 21.33 (3d ed. 1969); 1 Orgel, Valuation Under Eminent Domain § 147 (2d ed. 1953).

33. Transwestern Pipeline Co. v. O'Brien, 418 F.2d 15 (5th Cir. 1969); Commonwealth, Dept. of Highways v. McGeorge, 369 S.W.2d 126 (Ky.1963); Curley v. Jersey City, 83 N.J.L. 760, 85 A. 197, 43 L.R.A.,N.S., 985 (1912); Annot., 85 A.L.R.2d 110, 163.

34. See Macnaughtan v. Commonwealth, 220 Mass. 550, 108 N.E. 357 (1915) (option and sale admitted to be for purpose of influencing legislation, properly excluded); Muccino v. Baltimore & O. R. Co., 33 Ohio App. 102, 168 N.E. 752 (1929), and comment 39 Yale L.J. 748 (1929); Redfield v. Iowa State Highway Com'n, 251 Iowa 332, 99 N.W.2d 413, 85 A.L.R.2d 96 (1959) (speculative term contract).

As to the "cash or equivalent" rule, see Surfside of Brevard v. United States, 414 F.2d 915 (5th Cir. 1969); State v. Clevenger, 384 S.W.2d 207 (Tex.Civ. App.1964); 1 Orgel, Valuation Under Eminent Domain § 140 (2d ed. 1953); 5 Nichols, Eminent Domain § 21.5 (3d ed. 1969).

35. The rule applies to offers and options to buy or to sell, and to the land in question as well as comparable land: United States v. Smith, 355 F.2d 807 (5th Cir. 1966); State ex rel. Price v. Parcel No. 1, 243 A.2d 709 (Del.1968); State v. Lincoln Memory Gardens, Inc., 242 Ind. 206, 177 N.E.2d 655 (1961); State v. Morehouse Holding Co., 225 Ore. 62, 357 P.2d 266 (1960); Annot., 7 A.L.R.2d 781. Contra, where sales are lacking: City of Chi-

nificance, but the effort to determine their genuineness would lead to collateral disputes and waste of time at the trial. However, if one of the parties to the present action has himself offered to buy or sell the land in question, or other similar neighboring land, evidence of this offer may be offered against (not for) him as an admission.[36]

200. Other Accidents and Injuries in Negligence and Products Liability Cases.[37]

Proof of other similar accidents and injuries, offered for various purposes in negligence and products liability cases, is another kind of evidence which may present for consideration the counterpulls of the probative value of and need for the evidence on the one hand, and on the other the danger of unfair prejudice, undue consumption of time, and distraction of the jury's attention from the issues.[38] A few courts, influenced by an early Massachusetts decision,[39] adopted a more or

less inflexible rule of exclusion.[40] Most courts, however, wisely confide in the trial judge's discretion,[41] reviewable only for abuse, the responsibility for determining the balance of advantage and of admitting or excluding the evidence. Even in these liberal jurisdictions, most trial judges will scrutinize cautiously offers of evidence of other accidents, and counsel for proponent must be prepared to overcome opposition and to convince the judge of the preponderant value and need for the proof. The prospects for success will be much affected by the purpose for which the proof is offered, which in turn determines whether, and how strictly, the requirement of proof of similarity of conditions will be applied. Among the purposes for which the evidence may be tendered are the following:

1. To prove the existence of a particular physical condition, situation or defect. A fireman injured by coal falling from the tender, alleged that this was due to the fact that a bolt was missing from a hinge on the tender gate. To show this fact, he was allowed to prove a later collapse of the gate and the

---

cago v. Lehmann, 262 Ill. 468, 104 N.E. 829 (1914); Hardaway v. Des Moines, 166 N.W.2d 578 (Iowa 1969) (if proper foundation shown; dictum).

36. Offers by owner to sell, admissible against him: Springer v. City of Chicago, 135 Ill. 552, 26 N.E. 514, 12 L.R.A. 609, 613 (1891); Mark v. City of Indianapolis, 247 Ind. 511, 219 N.E.2d 434 (1966); Durika v. School Dist. of Derry Tp., 415 Pa. 480, 203 A.2d 474 (1964); unless too remote in time to be relevant, Lewisburg & N. R. Co. v. Hinds, 134 Tenn. 293, 183 S.W. 985, L.R.A.1916E, 420 (1916); likewise with options given by the owner, Humble Oil & Ref. Co. v. De Loache, 297 F.Supp. 647 (D.S. C.1969) (admissible against but not in behalf of owner).

37. 2 Wigmore, Evidence §§ 252, 457, 458; Morris, Proof of Safety History in Negligence Cases, 61 Harv.L.Rev. 205 (1948) (a penetrating and practical discussion on which the present treatment is based); C.J.S. Negligence § 234; 29 Am.Jur.2d Evidence §§ 305–313; Dec.Dig. Negligence ☞125; Notes, 2 U.Chi.L.Rev. 647 (1935), 20 Iowa L.Rev. 846 (1935) 28 Tex.L.Rev. 76 (1950) (crossing accidents); Annot., 31 A.L.R.2d 214, 70 A.L.R.2d 167 (comprehensive). As to products liability cases, see 1 Frumer and Friedman, Products Liability § 12.01 (1968); 1 Hursh, Products Liability §§ 116–119 (1961).

38. See § 185, supra.

39. Collins v. Inhabitants of Dorchester, 60 Mass. (6 Cush.) 396 (1850).

40. See, e. g., Fox Tucson Theaters Corp. v. Lindsay, 47 Ariz. 388, 56 P.2d 183 (1936); Diamond Rubber Co. v. Harryman, 41 Colo. 415, 92 Pac. 922, 924 (1907); Hudson v. Chicago & N. W. Ry. Co., 59 Iowa 581, 13 N.W. 735 (1882); Bremner v. Newcastle, 83 Me. 415, 22 Atl. 382 (1891). But this influence is now nearly gone. See, e. g., Buchanan v. Green, 73 Ariz. 159, 238 P.2d 1107 (1951); Lindquist v. Des Moines Union R. Co., 239 Iowa 356, 30 N.W.2d 120 (1947); Locke, Inc. v. Sonnenleiter, 208 Md. 443, 118 A.2d 509 (1955); Robitaille v. Netoco Community Theatres, 305 Mass. 265, 25 N.E.2d 749, 128 A.L.R. 592, 594 (1949); Freed v. Simon, 370 Mich. 473, 122 N.W.2d 813 (1963); Toftoy v. Ocean Shores Properties, Inc., 71 Wash.2d 833, 431 P.2d 212 (1967); Annot., 70 A.L.R.2d 167.

41. Cases stressing this trial court discretion are Jones & Laughlin Steel Corp. v. Matherne, 348 F.2d 394 (5th Cir. 1965) (admission upheld); Kopfinger v. Grand Central Public Market, 60 Cal.2d 852, 37 Cal.Rptr. 65, 389 P.2d 529 (1964) (exclusion upheld); Blood v. Allied Stores Corp., 62 Wash.2d 187, 381 P.2d 742 (1963); 2 Wigmore, Evidence § 444. The discretion is of course not unlimited. Chambers v. Loftin, 67 So.2d 220 (Fla.1953) (exclusion reversed); Robitaille v. Netoco Community Theatres, next preceding note (admission reversed).

replacement of the bolt.[42] But this is a sensational way of proving it, and unless the fact is substantially disputed, the judge might not find sufficient need for the evidence.

2. To show that the plaintiff's injury was caused by the alleged defective or dangerous condition or situation.[43] For this purpose the

other accidents may have occurred after, as well as before, the injury sued for.[44] Ordinarily the need is plainer here than in the next previous situation, since the issue of cause is usually in genuine dispute and the inference of causation is an elusive one as to which circumstantial evidence is appropriate. It must appear that conditions of the other accident and of the present one were similar.[45]

The next two theories are the ones most frequently invoked.

3. To show that the situation as of the time of the accident sued for was dangerous.[46] This points to a quality of the objective situation, namely, its capacity to produce or cause harm. This is the chief battleground over the admissibility of other accidents. If it is material to establish that the situation was hazardous, the fact that it has produced harm on other occasions is a natural and convincing way of showing it. Other methods such as expert testimony as to danger, which is likely to evoke an objection as being an impermissible opinion [47] or reliance

42. Gulf, C. & S. F. Ry. Co. v. Brooks, 73 S.W. 571, (Tex.Civ.App.1903). See also Jones & Laughlin Steel Corp. v. Matherne, next preceding note (defect in clamp); Parker v. Bamberger, 100 Utah 361, 116 P.2d 425 (1941) (defect in signal device—this problem is annotated in 46 A.L.R.2d 935); Denison v. Wiese, 251 Iowa 770, 102 N.W.2d 671 (1960) (loose seats on bar stools). Many of the products liability cases fit into this category: Vlahovich v. Betts Machine Co., 45 Ill.2d 506, 260 N.E.2d 230 (1970) (plastic truck-light lens; evidence of shattering of other lenses admissible); Styers v. Winston Coca-Cola Bottling Co., 239 N.C. 504, 80 S.E.2d 253 (1954) (exploding bottle; other explosions received). See also, Gober v. Revlon, Inc., 317 F.2d 47 (5th Cir. 1963) (allergic reactions of others than plaintiff to defendant's nail polish admissible to show nature of product and to negative unusualness of plaintiff); Albers Mill. Co. v. Carney, 341 S.W.2d 117 (Mo.1960) (alleged illness of turkeys due to moldy feed; receipt of moldy feed by others from same lot and illness of their turkeys admissible to show moldiness and causation).

43. See the cases in note 42, supra; Gearhardt v. American Reinforced Paper Co., 244 F.2d 920 (7th Cir. 1957) (cause of fire damage to plaintiff's building; evidence of results of defendant's prior burning of debris under same conditions admissible); Johnston v. Yolo County, 274 Cal.App.2d 46, 79 Cal.Rptr. 33 (1969) (faulty curve design in road); Gorman v. County of Sacramento, 92 Cal.App. 656, 268 Pac. 1083 (1928) (prior accidents to show boy rode bicycle off bridge by reason of absence of guard rails); Carter v. Yardley & Co., 319 Mass. 92, 64 N.E.2d 693, 164 A.L.R. 559 (1946) (in action to recover for a burn sustained as result of using perfume manufactured by defendant, testimony of other witnesses that same perfume irritated their skin was competent to show probability that injury to plaintiff was caused by some harmful ingredient in perfume other than by her own peculiar susceptibility and to authorize inference that skin of plaintiff and the witnesses was normal.); Poston v. Clarkson Constr. Co., 401 S.W.2d 522 (Mo.App. 1966) (blast damage to houses situated similarly to plaintiff's, admissible to show blast was cause of plaintiff's damage; see Annot., 45 A.L.R.2d 1121. The other accident may also help to show notice. Young v. Bank of America, 95 Cal.App.2d 725, 214 P.2d 106, 16 A.L.R.2d 1155 (1950) (injury to infant from defect in check on swinging door). And danger. Ringelheim v. Fidelity Trust Co., 330 Pa. 69, 198 Atl. 628 (1938) (fall on floor due to ex-

cess of floor polish, other falls show cause and dangerous character of place); Safeway Stores Inc. v. Bozeman, 394 S.W.2d 532 (Tex.Civ.App.1965) (same; also shows notice).

44. Ringelheim v. Fidelity Trust Co., supra.

45. Gober v. Revlon, Inc., supra, note 42; Ringelheim v. Fidelity Trust Co., supra, n. 43; Smith v. City of Rock Island, 22 Ill.App.2d 389, 161 N.E.2d 369 (1959) (absence of common causal feature; evidence inadmissible on causation or lack thereof); Di Frischia v. New York Central R. R. Co., 307 F.2d 473 (5th Cir. 1962) (similar).

46. Kanelos v. Kettler, 132 U.S.App.D.C. 133, 406 F.2d 951 (1967); Gulf Hills Dude Ranch v. Brinson, 191 So.2d 856 (Miss.1966); Turner v. City of Tacoma, 72 Wash.2d 1029, 435 P.2d 927 (1967); Annot., 70 A.L.R.2d 167, and see the cases in the preceding notes.

Other accidents after, as well as before, may be relevant for this purpose. Kanelos v. Kettler, supra; Taylor v. Northern States Power Co., 192 Minn. 415, 256 N.W. 674 (1934) (fall on wet, slippery linoleum floor).

47. See § 12, supra.

on a description of the situation plus the jury's general knowledge of its dangerous quality,[48] may be inadequate in particular cases. The requirement of similarity of conditions is probably at its strictest here.[49]

4. To prove that the defendant knew of the danger, or ought in the exercise of reasonable care to have learned of it.[50] If the defendant's duty to maintain a safe place were absolute this theory would not be available. Usually, however, his liability is restricted to a duty merely to use reasonable care to maintain safe conditions including the duty to inspect when due care so requires. An injury occurring from a newly arising peril before the owner has learned of or had a reasonable opportunity to appreciate the danger, would not be actionable. This restriction on liability widens the scope of evidence by offering an additional theory for receiving proof of other accidents and injuries. Here, of course, is one instance where the other happening must have occurred before the injury sued for. When possible the proponent will prove directly that the defendant had knowledge of the other accidents, but often the nature, frequency,[51] or notoriety[52] of the happenings will afford circumstantial evidence that the defendant was apprised of them, or that the danger had existed so long that the defendant by due inspection should have learned of it. Since all that is required here is that the previous injury should be such as to attract the defendant's attention to the dangerous situation which resulted in the litigated accident, the strictness of the requirement of similarity of conditions imposed when the purpose is to show causation or danger is here much relaxed.[53] The warn-

---

48. Where the situation clearly speaks for itself, evidence of other accidents has been held unnecessary and inadmissible. City of Birmingham v. McKinnon, 200 Ala. 11, 75 So. 487 (1917) (stake and wire about two feet above sidewalk certainly and obviously dangerous).

49. Examples of cases where the requirement was held not satisfied: Rexall Drug Co. v. Nihill, 276 F.2d 637 (9th Cir. 1960) (alleged baldness from home permanent wave solution, evidence of use by others inadmissible where result was dissimilar to plaintiff's); Horn v. Chicago, Rock I. & P. R. Co., 187 Kan. 423, 357 P.2d 815 (1960) (crossing accident, evidence of other accidents inadmissible as dissimilar); Royal Mink Ranch v. Ralston Purina Co., 18 Mich.App. 695, 172 N.W.2d 43 (1969) (evidence as to effect of feed on other mink inadmissible, where different mix from different supplier was used); Perry v. City of Oklahoma City, 470 P.2d 974 (Okl. 1970); and cases in Annot., 70 A.L.R.2d 167, 205.

50. See, e. g., Hecht Co. v. Jacobsen, 86 U.S.App. D.C. 81, 180 F.2d 13 (1950) (accident to child on escalator; accident to another child seven years before on a similar model escalator but on a different floor, received); Slow Development Co. v. Coulter, 88 Ariz. 122, 353 P.2d 890 (1960) (fall on hotel floor; prior falls at other locations but with same floor condition admissible); New York Central R. Co. v. Sarich, 133 Ind.App. 516, 180 N.E.2d 388 (1962) (collision with unmarked viaduct; prior collisions admissible); and cases cited in 2 Wigmore, Evidence § 252, and in Annot., 70 A.L.R.2d 167, 179.

51. Moore v. Bloomington D. & C. Ry. Co., 295 Ill. 63, 67, 128 N.E. 721, 722 (1920).

52. Lombar v. East Tawas, 86 Mich. 14, 20, 48 N.W. 947, 948 (1891).

53. Evans v. Pennsylvania R. R. Co., 255 F.2d 205 (3d Cir. 1958) (crossing accident; prior accidents with reversed direction of car or train, admissible); McCormick v. Great Western Power Co., 214 Cal. 658, 8 P.2d 145 (1932) (plaintiffs sued for shocks received from defendant's high tension wires while installing iron work on fifth floor of building under construction; evidence that other workmen had been injured by defendant's wires during construction of a nearby building received); Taylor v. Stafford, 196 Ill. 288, 63 N.E. 624 (1902) (the plaintiff claimed injuries from stumbling on a stake protruding between the planks of a sidewalk; the court held that evidence that there were other stakes protruding along the same block was held properly received, "not to prove negligence," but to show a general unsafe condition of the sidewalk "from which notice may fairly be inferred"); Blanco v. J. C. Penney Co., 251 Md. 707, 248 A.2d 645 (1968). The distinction, however, is occasionally overlooked. See Thompson v. Buffums, Inc., 17 Cal.App.2d 401, 62 P.2d 171 (1936). In that case the plaintiff was injured while walking down the stairs at defendant's store. She caught her shoe in a defective safety tread on the tenth step. Plaintiff, cross-examining the defendant's superintendent asked him, "Have any other women fallen on these particular stairs." Excluded. This ruling was sustained on appeal, on the ground that the inquiry was not limited to the tenth step; cf. Laird v. T. W. Mather, Inc., 51 Cal.2d 210, 331 P.2d 617 (1958).

ing radius of the happening is wider than its relevance for these other purposes.

5. When the defendant by pleading, opening statement, or by the testimony of his witnesses has asserted that the injury sued for could not have been caused by the defendant's conduct as alleged, then the plaintiff may show other similar happenings to rebut the claim of impossibility.[54]

Absence of other accidents or injuries.[55] It would seem that if other accidents and injuries are admissible where circumstances are similar, in the judge's discretion, to show such matters as the existence of a particular defect or condition, or that the injury sued for was caused in a certain way, or that a situation is dangerous, or that defendant knew or should have known of the danger, then logically it would follow that proof of the absence of accidents during a period of similar exposure and experience, would generally be receivable to show the nonexistence of these facts.

It is true that frequently the proof of absence of accidents does not have as much persuasive force, to show a safe situation, as the proof of another accident may in establishing danger, but that, it seems, is a matter of weight merely. Particular decisions excluding evidence of this kind of "safety history" may sometimes be justified on the ground that the persons passing in safety do not appear to have been exposed to the same test and use as occurred at the time of the injury sued for.[56] However, specific proof to that effect should not be required when the experience sought to be proved is so extensive as to justify the inference that it included an adequate number of situations like the one in suit.[57]

There are nevertheless a considerable number of decisions laying down a general rule against proof of absence of other accidents. A few of these are by courts aligned with the minority group denying admission generally

---

54. Texas & N. O. Ry. Co. v. Glass, 107 S.W.2d 924 (Tex.Civ.App.1937) (suit for destruction of barn by sparks from locomotive; testimony by defendant's experts that defendant's oil-burning locomotives are so constructed as not to emit sparks; held, plaintiff may rebut by evidence as to other fires set by such locomotives). An analogous problem is presented in such cases as Auzene v. Gulf Public Service Co., 188 So. 512 (La.App.1939). The plaintiff sued for injury from the explosion of a Coca-Cola bottle. The defendant's witnesses testified that its method of bottling was such that explosions could not occur. The plaintiff offered evidence of other instances of explosions, and it was held that the evidence was competent. In the product liability cases, plaintiff is often rebutting a claim that he became ill from another cause, or is supersensitive. See note 43, supra. Cases are collected in Dec.Dig. Negligence ⊂⇒125, Food ⊂⇒25(i).

55. C.J.S. Negligence § 234(8); 29 Am.Jur.2d Evidence §§ 310–314; Annot., 31 A.L.R.2d 190; Dec. Dig. Negligence ⊂⇒125.

56. See, e. g., Taylor v. Town of Monroe, 43 Conn. 36 (1875) (action for injury to plaintiff, who was driving buggy, when horse ran away and overturned buggy at bridge; plaintiff charged that highway was unduly raised and the railing was defective; held, no error to exclude evidence that in ordinary use of this highway there had been no accidents: absence of accidents would be relevant only if similar experience with runaway horses had been shown); Wray v. Fairfield Amusements Co., 126 Conn. 221, 10 A.2d 600 (1940) (suit for accident to passenger in roller coaster, held, where injury alleged to be due to defective strap on seat, error to admit evidence generally of absence of accidents to other passengers; should have been limited to experience of passengers riding in the particular seat of the particular car).

57. Stark v. Allis Chalmers & Northwest Roads, Inc., 2 Wash.App. 399, 467 P.2d 854 (1970) (death alleged due to defect in tractor-loader design; evidence that no similar accident had occurred to 10,000 of these tractors admissible); Erickson v. Walgreen Drug Co., 120 Utah 31, 232 P.2d 210 (1951) (suit for injury from fall on terrazzo floor in entranceway, rendered slippery by rain; error to exclude evidence that no complaint or report about anyone slipping had been received during 15 years though 4000 to 5000 persons entered the store every day); Stein v. Trans World Airlines, 25 App.Div.2d 732, 268 N.Y.S.2d 752 (1966) (fall in air terminal; error to exclude evidence that many thousands had used same area without tripping); and see cases in Annot., 31 A.L.R.2d 190.

As to the hearsay question see § 250, infra.

to proof of other accidents.[58] But some are by courts which by rule or discretion would admit proof of other accidents.[59] This paradoxical position has sometimes been defended as being justified on grounds of auxiliary policy.[60] It is believed, however, that this justification cannot be sustained. There is here no danger of arousing the prejudice of the jury, as the proof of another accident may do. Moreover, the danger of spending undue time and incurring confusion by raising "collateral issues," conjured up in some of the opinions,[61] seems not at all borne out by experience in jurisdictions where the evidence is allowed. The defendant will seldom open this door if there is any practical possibility that the plaintiff may dispute the fact. The trend of recent decision seems to favor admissibility, and it is believed that evidence of absence of other accidents may be relevant to show, (1) the nonexistence of

the defect or condition alleged,[62] (2) that the injury was not caused by the defect or condition charged,[63] (3) that the situation was

---

58. See, e. g., Sanitary Grocery Co., Inc. v. Steinbrecher, 183 Va. 495, 32 S.E.2d 685 (1945) (action by customer for injury from sharp corner of shelving; evidence that 1000 customers had used store daily for eleven months without injury irrelevant).

59. See, e. g., St. Gregory's Church v. O'Connor, 13 Ariz.App. 421, 477 P.2d 540 (1971) (alleged defective construction of step); Blackwell v. J. J. Newberry Co., 156 S.W.2d 14 (Mo.App.1941) (injury to customer from small concealed stepladder in aisle).

60. See the interesting opinion of Anderson, J., in Blackwell v. J. J. Newberry Co., supra, n. 59, and the further explanation in Vinyard v. Vinyard Funeral Home, Inc., 435 S.W.2d 392 (Mo.App.1968).

61. See Gilbert v. Bluhm, 291 S.W.2d 125 (Mo.1956); Temperance Hall Ass'n v. Giles, 33 N.J.L. 260, 265 (1869) ("The offer was to show that ten thousand persons passed these premises in each year since the hall was erected, without accident. The admission of this evidence would carry with it the right to cross examine as to the circumstances under which each individual of the multitude passed, and the degree of caution and circumspection used by each; and, also, the right to introduce evidence of the dangers encountered, and by the exercise of superior vigilance, avoided by each one of these individuals, together with evidence that some one or more of them had met with accidents at the place; in turn opening the way for evidence as to the degree of care exercised by such as had not been so fortunate as to escape. . . . .").

62. Becker v. American Air Lines, Inc., 200 F.Supp. 243 (S.D.N.Y.1961) (alleged malfunction of altimeter; safety history as to both malfunction and proper functioning admissible); Frank R. Jelleff, Inc., v. Braden, 98 U.S.App.D.C. 180, 233 F.2d 671 (1956) (flammability of fabric; rejection of absence of complaints not abuse of discretion; discusses the function of the rule in warranty cases); Birmingham Union Ry. Co. v. Alexander, 93 Ala. 133, 9 So. 525, 527 (1891) (action against streetrailway for injury due to insufficient surfacing and ballasting of its track; "It would therefore have been competent for the plaintiff to prove that other similar casualties had happened at that crossing as tending to show a defective condition of the track. On like considerations the defendant should be allowed the benefit of proof that the track, as it was at the time, was constantly crossed by other persons, under similar conditions, without inconvenience, hindrance, or peril, as evidence tending to show the absence of the alleged defect, or that it was not the cause to which the injury complained of be imputed. The negative proof in the one case, equally with the affirmative proof in the other, serves to furnish the means of applying to the matter the practical test of common experience."); Menard v. Cashman, 93 N.H. 273, 41 A.2d 222 (1945) (in action against owner of building for personal injuries sustained in fall on stairway, evidence that other persons had descended stairs without falling was admissible, as tending to show that stairway was in suitable condition.). Rathbun v. Humphrey Co., 94 Ohio App. 429, 113 N.E.2d 877 (1953) (location of amusement ride near trees; evidence of use by thousands of others without complaint of being struck admissible). The contrary holding in Johnson v. Kansas City Pub. Service Co., 360 Mo. 429, 228 S.W.2d 796 (1950) seems hard to sustain in justice or common sense. There a passenger in a streetcar sued for injury said to be due to tripping over loose metal strip in vestibule. Defendant's witnesses swore that there was no such loose strip. The court held that evidence that over 750 passengers had used the vestibule in the 24-hour period without tripping was properly rejected.

Cases on this and the remaining points are collected in Annot., 31 A.L.R.2d 190.

63. Birmingham Union Ry. Co. v. Alexander, supra, n. 62; Lawler v. Skelton, 241 Miss. 274, 130 So.2d 565 (1961) (illness from aerial spraying of insecticide; evidence of noninjury from such spraying on other persons admissible to show lack of causation). For other uses of history to show causation, see Taylor v. B. Heller & Co., 364 F.2d 608 (6th Cir. 1966); General Motors Corp. v. Dodson, 47 Tenn.App. 438, 338 S.W.2d 655 (1960).

not dangerous,[64] or (4) want of knowledge of, or of ground to realize, the danger.[65]

64. Zheutlin v. Sperry & Hutchison Co., 149 Conn. 364, 179 A.2d 829 (1962) (fall over curb; evidence that 50,000 others had used curb safely under similar conditions admissible); Nubbe v. Hardy Continental Hotel System, 225 Minn. 496, 31 N.W.2d 332 (1948) (action for injury due to fall on stairs; error to exclude evidence of defendant's manager that he had not had any reports of other accidents; admissible to show not dangerous, and that defendant was not chargeable with knowledge); Stein v. Trans World Airlines, 25 App.Div.2d 732, 268 N.Y.S.2d 752 (1966) (similar).

65. Nubbe v. Hardy Continental Hotel System, supra, n. 64. The purposes are often overlapping, and not all opinions spell them out separately. See Borrelli v. Top Value Enterprises, Inc., 356 Mass. 110, 248 N.E.2d 510 (Mass.1969) (electric shock from carpet sweeper, evidence of lack of complaints admitted; Mobberly v. Sears Roebuck & Co., 4 Ohio App.2d 126, 211 N.E.2d 839 (1965) (collapse of portable grain elevator; safety history admissible).

CHAPTER 19

INSURANCE AGAINST LIABILITY

Sec.
201.   Insurance Against Liability

201.   Insurance Against Liability.[1]

This area is one of the controversial corners of evidence law. The practice bears the marks of the pressures and counterpressures of opposing special interests, and the present evidential rule may eventually disappear as common law principles of negligence liability are displaced by new legislative systems of apportionment of risk for highway accidents.[2]

The starting point is the accepted doctrine that the fact that defendant is protected by a policy of insurance against liability up to a given amount is not relevant as evidence of negligence.[3] The financial protection may somewhat diminish the normal incentive to be careful, but this is of slight effect since the motive of regard for personal safety is usually present and is a much stronger incentive, and in any event it is overborne by the counter argument that the fact of insurance marks the defendant as one of the insured class, who may be assumed to be the more prudent and careful group as compared to the uninsured class.

Upon this principle of irrelevancy to show negligence—perhaps a rather inadequate foundation—has been built a general rule that evidence of the fact of such insurance is inadmissible[4] unless it falls within some one of a group of exceptional situations.[5] In

---

1.   2 Wigmore, Evidence § 282a; 29 Am.Jur.2d Evidence §§ 404–407; C.J.S. Trial §§ 53–54; Annot., 4 A.L.R.2d 761; Phillips, Mention of Insurance During Trial, 1961 Tr.Law.Guide 247; Black, Admissibility of Evidence that Defendant Has or Has Not Liability Insurance, 38 W.Va.L.Q. 362 (1932); Dec. Dig. Trial ☞108½, 127. Localized treatments: Walker, Insurance in Damage Actions, 11 S.Cal.L. Rev. 407 (1938); Gusmano, Admissibility in New York of Evidence that Defendant Is Insured, 14 St. John's L.Rev. 319 (1940); Roach, Evidence of Liability Insurance in Texas, 29 Tex.L.Rev. 949 (1951); Notes, 22 Ga.B.J. 96 (1959), 16 Syracuse L. Rev. 92 (1964), 70 Dick.L.Rev. 64 (1965).

Analogous problems arise as to disclosure of insurance held by plaintiffs. See McDonald v. Alamo Motor Lines, 22 S.W.2d 1023 (Tex.Civ.App.1949); Note, 2 Baylor L.Rev. 462 (1950). See Annot., 77 A.L.R.2d 1154.

2.   Discussions and proposals on this subject have reached a new peak since publication of such works as Conard, et al., Automobile Accident Costs and Payments (1964), and Keeton and O'Connell, Basic Protection for the Traffic Victim (1965). The following recent symposia can serve as no more than an introduction to the problem and the now voluminous literature: Automobile Compensation Plans, 51 Judicature 149 (1967); Changes for Automobile Claims, 1967 U.Ill.L.F. 361; Safety, 33 Law and Contemp.Prob. 429 (1968); Insurance, 57 Ky.L.J. 627 (1969); Automobile Liability Reparations Systems, 30 Gavel 3 (1969); The Automobile Insurance Problem, 6 Trial 8 (1970).

3.   See, e. g., Brown v. Walter, 62 F.2d 798, 800 (2d Cir. 1933); Sutton v. Bell, 79 N.J.Law 507, 77 Atl. 42 (1910); Barrett v. Bonham Oil & Cotton Co., 57 S.W. 602 (Tex.Civ.App.1900). Uniform Rule 54: "Evidence that a person was, at the time a harm was suffered by another, insured wholly or partially against loss arising from liability for that harm is inadmissible as tending to prove negligence or other wrongdoing."; F.R.Ev. (R.D.1971) 411.

Compare People v. Steele, 179 Misc. 587, 37 N.Y.S.2d 199 (1942) (prosecution for leaving the scene of an accident; error to exclude evidence that defendant carried liability insurance, as tending to establish lack of motive).

4.   Instances of reversals for admission of the evidence are Finch v. Conley, 422 S.W.2d 128 (Ky. 1967); Bischoff v. Koenig, 100 N.W.2d 159 (N.D. 1959); J. C. Penney Co. v. Barrientez, 411 P.2d 841 (Okl.1966); Hope Windows, Inc. v. Snyder, 208 Va. 489, 158 S.E.2d 722 (1968); Ellison v. Wood & Bush Co., 153 W.Va. 506, 170 S.E.2d 321 (1969).

5.   For a listing and discussion of these situations, see Rapoport, Proper Disclosure During Trial that Defendant is Insured, 26 Corn.L.Q. 137 (1940). See also Annot., 4 A.L.R.2d 761, 775–786; Notes, 70 Dick.L.Rev. 64 (1965), 16 Syracuse L.Rev. 92 (1964); F.R.Ev. (R.D.1971) 411.

these situations presumably the trial judge's discretionary power to exclude could still be invoked if he should consider that the need for and value of the evidence were outweighed by its likelihood of misuse by the jury.[6] What are these exceptions?

First, the fact of insurance may be relevant upon some other issue, such as agency [7] or ownership [8] or control [9] of the vehicle or instrumentality involved.

Second, the fact of insurance may be relevant as bearing upon the credibility of a witness.[10]

Third, the admission of a party bearing on negligence or damages may include a reference to the fact of insurance which cannot be severed without substantially lessening the evidential value of the admission.[11]

Fourth, the fact of insurance may be elicited unintentionally by examining counsel, when the witness makes an unexpected or unresponsive reference to insurance.[12] The witness often is unaware of the conspiracy of silence about insurance and makes with utmost naturalness a reference to this all-

6. Gerry v. Neugebauer, 83 N.H. 23, 136 Atl. 751 (1927) (plaintiff in cross-examining defendant's witness, having brought out that he was interviewed by defendant's counsel, sought to elicit that witness had also been interviewed by insurance adjuster; held, while proper to impeach, yet defendant was entitled to trial judge's discretionary ruling as to whether the answer would do more harm than good; excellent discussion by Snow, J.); Garfield v. Russell, 251 Cal.App. 275, 59 Cal.Rptr. 379 (1967); see § 185, supra.

7. Cherry v. Stockton, 75 N.M. 488, 406 P.2d 358 (1965) (employer-employee relationship disputed); Biggins v. Wagner, 60 S.D. 581, 245 N.W. 385, 85 A.L.R. 385 (1932) (whether truck-driver-owner was employee or independent contractor).

8. Barnett v. Butler, 112 So.2d 907 (Fla.App.1959) (ownership of automobile in dispute); Layton v. Cregan & Mallory Co., 263 Mich. 30, 248 N.W. 539 (1933) (where ownership of colliding automobile denied, plaintiff entitled to discovery of policy, which would be admissible on this issue).

9. Pinckard v. Dunnavant, 281 Ala. 533, 206 So.2d 340 (1968) (issue of management and maintenance of premises); Perkins v. Rice, 187 Mass. 28, 72 N.E. 323 (1904) (defendant admitted ownership of premises but denied that he had control of elevator).

10. O'Donnell v. Bachelor, 429 Pa. 498, 240 A.2d 484 (1968) (error to exclude evidence that investigator-witness was employed by defendant's insurer. "Once a witness commits himself to the ocean of a legal controversy, he must, under cross-examination, disclose the flag under which he sails." To which a dissent replied that revelation is thus being required of "not only the flag, but the seamstress who sewed it."—a reference to the rule of some states that this impeachment should be limited to showing that the witness was employed "on behalf of the defendant," see Hopper v. Comfort Coal-Lumber Co., 276 App.Div. 1014, 95 N.Y.S.2d 318 (1950); Pickett v. Kolb, 250 Ind. 449, 237 N.E.2d 105 (1968) (error to exclude evidence that defendant's insurer paid inspector-witness); Vindicator Consol. Gold Min. Co. v. Firstbrook, 36 Colo. 498,

86 P. 313 (1906); Dempsey v. Goldstein Bros. Amusement Co., 231 Mass. 461, 121 N.E. 429 (1919); Aguilera v. Reynolds Well Service, 234 S.W.2d 282 (Tex.Civ.App.1950). But the judge has a leeway of discretion, Gibson v. Grey Motor Co., 147 Minn. 134, 179 N.W. 729, 730 (1920); Dempsey v. Goldstein Bros. Amusement Co., supra (as to extent); Gerry v. Neugebauer, note 6, supra.

When plaintiff's witness is impeached by a prior inconsistent written statement, the majority of cases hold (if witness disputes its correctness) that plaintiff may show that the writing was prepared for the witness to sign, by an adjuster for the defendant's insurer. Roland v. Beckham, 408 S.W.2d 628 (Ky.1966); Brave v. Blakely, 250 S.C. 353, 157 S.E.2d 726 (1967). Contra, Texas Co. v. Betterton, 126 Tex 359, 88 S.W.2d 1039 (1936).

11. If the reference to insurance is severable from the defendant's admission, this should be done, Schlenker v. Egloff, 133 Cal.App. 393, 24 P.2d 224 (1933); Cameron v. Columbia Builders, Inc., 212 Or. 388, 320 P.2d 251 (1958); Connor v. McGill, 127 Vt. 19, 238 A.2d 777 (1968). But where the insurance reference is an "integral part" of the admission, the whole will be received, Reid v. Owens, 98 Utah 50, 93 P.2d 680, 684, 685, 126 A.L.R. 55 (1939) ("My boy was careless . . . We have taken out insurance to protect him," properly received. The reference to insurance was "itself freighted with admission"); Young v. Carter, 121 Ga.App. 191, 173 S.E.2d 259 (1970) (defendant's admission "that it was his fault—that his insurance company would take care of it for her" held admissible and therefore properly mentioned in plaintiff's opening statement); Herschensohn v. Weisman, 80 N.H. 557, 119 A. 705, 28 A.L.R. 514 (1923) (defendant, warned to be careful or he would kill somebody, said: "Don't worry, I carry insurance for that," admissible); Taylor v. Owen, 290 S.W.2d 771 (Tex.Civ.App.1956). Cases are collected in Annot., 4 A.L.R.2d 761, 781, 782.

12. Muehlebach v. Mercer Mortuary & Chapel, Inc., 93 Ariz. 60, 378 P.2d 741 (1963); Carver v. Lavigne, 160 Me. 414, 205 A.2d 159 (1964); Blake v. Roy Webster Orchards, 249 Ore. 348, 437 P.2d 757 (1968); Annot., 4 A.L.R.2d 761, 784–786.

pervading fact. The reference will be stricken on request but is usually not a ground for mistrial or reversal.

There is a fifth situation which though not an exception to the rule excluding evidence of insurance actually results in bringing before the jurors at the outset a strong intimation that the defendant is actually insured. This is the practice which obtains in most of the states of permitting the plaintiff's counsel in examining the prospective jurors upon their qualifications, to question them about their possible interest in or employment by a liability insurance company, where it appears that defendant is protected by insurance.[13]

Under the pressure of the enactment of more and more stringent financial responsibility laws, the practice of securing insurance protection against liability is rapidly becoming almost universal. By 1959, in 28 states, an average of over 83 percent of motorists had liability coverage.[14] In New York, where

the insurance is required, the coverage by 1956 was reported to exceed 96 percent.[15] When the rule against the disclosure of insurance originated doubtless the existence of such protection for defendants was exceptional and a "hush, hush" policy could be effective. But when we consider the ways in which the fact of insurance may be properly disclosed in evidence or suggested at the beginning of the trial upon the examination of jurors, and the fact that insurance has become usual rather than exceptional, it seems likely today that in nearly all cases the jury will either be informed of the fact of insurance or will consciously assume that the defendant is so protected.[16] The rule against the introduction of evidence of insurance thus becomes a hollow shell, except as it incidentally protects the defendant against improper argument that the jury should be influenced in their finding of liability or damages by the fact of insurance.

May the defendant give evidence that he is not protected by insurance? In view of the premise on which the rule prohibiting evi-

13. Although a few cases condemn this practice as more harmful than helpful, see Langley v. Turner's Express, Inc., 375 F.2d 296, 297 (4th Cir. 1967), almost all jurisdictions allow it in some form. In these latter states, many refinements exist as to consultation with the court in advance (in the absence of the jury panel) to establish a foundation of good faith belief that an insurer is interested, or that some venireman has an insurance connection; and as to the questions that may be asked. General discussions are: 21 Appleman, Ins.Law and Prac. §§ 12813–12818 (1962); Phillips, Mention of Insurance During Trial, 1961 Tr.Law. Guide 247; Annot., 4 A.L.R.2d 761, 792; Note, 50 Minn.L.Rev. 1088 (1966); Dec.Dig. Trial ⟨∞⟩108½. Localized treatments: Vetter, Voir Dire II: Liability Insurance, 29 Mo.L.Rev. 305 (1964); Comments, 17 Clev.-Mar.L.Rev. 504 (1968) (federal courts), 15 De Paul L.Rev. 148 (1965), 30 Ohio St. L.J. 432 (1965); Note, 13 Okla.L.Rev. 99 (1960).

It has been suggested that this information could be gained without prejudice by examining the entire venire at the time they are first assembled before drawing a panel for any particular case. Comment, 52 Harv.L.Rev. 166 (1938). Or by the use of a questionnaire. Comments, 15 De Paul L.Rev. 148 (1965), 28 Miss.L.J. 65 (1956); Note, 43 Mich.L. Rev. 621 (1944).

14. Ames, The Auto Accident Commission Proposal, 14 U.Fla.L.Rev. 398, 400 (1962). New York and

Massachusetts, which have compulsory insurance, were not included.

15. Coverly, New Provision for Protection From Injuries Inflicted by an Uninsured Automobile, 1956 Ins.L.J. 19.

16. With increasing frequency, judges assert that the jurors assume defendant is insured. See Brown v. Walter, 62 F.2d 798, 800 (2d Cir. 1933); Muehlebach v. Mercer Mortuary & Chapel, Inc., 93 Ariz. 60, 378 P.2d 741 (1963); Causey v. Cornelius, 164 Cal.App.2d 269, 330 P.2d 468, 472 (1958); Pinkerton v. Oak Park Nat. Bank, 16 Ill.App.2d 91, 147 N.E.2d 390, 394 (1958); Odegard v. Connolly, 211 Minn. 342, 1 N.W.2d 137, 139 (1941); Runnacles v. Doddrell, 59 N.J.Super. 363, 157 A.2d 836, 838 (1960); Hall, P. J., concurring in Young v. Carter, 121 Ga.App. 191, 173 S.E.2d 259 (1970) ("Any juror who doesn't know there is insurance in the case by this time [after voir dire] should probably be excused by virtue of the fact he or she is an idiot."); Bliss, C. J., in Connelly v. Nolte, 237 Iowa 114, 21 N.W.2d 311, 320 (1946) (". . . [The juror] doesn't require a brick house to fall on him to give him an idea."). Broeder, Voir Dire, 38 S.Cal.L.Rev. 503, 525 (1965) suggests that jurors do think there is insurance, but that voir dire is a minor reason for their doing so.

dence of insurance is based that there is danger that the fact will be used prejudicially by the jury, and in view of the inevitable assumption by jurors today that a defendant is probably insured, fairness seems to demand that a defendant be permitted to avoid the danger by showing that he is not insured. The courts, however, have considered that the balance lies the other way, and have excluded the evidence, as "a form of the inadmissible plea of poverty," [17] except in cases where the plaintiff has injected the suggestion that the defendant is insured.[18]

A re-examination of the soundness and expediency of the general rule forbidding disclosure of the fact of insurance seems desirable. That such fact is irrelevant to show negligence is as we have suggested hardly a sufficient foundation for the rule. The conspiracy of silence is hard to maintain. The truth will out, and the results are extensive arguments on appeal upon elusive questions of prejudice and good faith, and a considerable number of reversals and retrials. The heart of the policy of nondisclosure is really surrendered when the jurors are allowed to be examined upon their connection with insurance companies.

The courts have recently shown some tendency to relax their former stiffness in enforcing the rule by reversals.[19] It is submitted that they might well go further and consider whether evidence of the fact of insurance, though irrelevant on negligence, should not come in pursuant to another long-established policy. This is the principle that every litigant is entitled to know the identity of the party with whom he is contesting [20] and the court is entitled to know the parties that are using its officers and facilities. The company which under its policy is given the exclusive right to employ counsel, defend the suit and control the decision as to settling or contesting the action, is surely a party in all but name. The jury as a part of the tribunal is entitled to the knowledge of the existence of this masked but controlling party.[21] It will then make some assumptions as to the capacity of the insurance company to pay. These are no different from similar assumptions as to the capacity to pay of other corporations who may be parties of record before them. The corrective is not a futile effort at concealment, but an open assumption by the court of its function of explaining to the jury its duty of deciding according to the facts and the substantive law, rather than upon sympathy and ability to pay. The legislatures of Louisiana and Wisconsin have implemented the same policy by statutes

---

17. Piechuck v. Maguziak, 82 N.H. 429, 135 Atl. 534 (1926). Accord: Rojas v. Buocolo, 142 Tex. 152, 177 S.W.2d 962 (1944) (question by juror to one of several defendants); King v. Starr, 43 Wash.2d 115, 260 P.2d 351 (1953). See cases cited in Annot., 4 A.L.R.2d 761, 773; Note, 5 Standford L.Rev. 143 (1952).

18. Smith v. Raup, 296 Ill.App. 171, 15 N.E.2d 936 (1938); Whitman v. Carver, 337 Mo. 1247, 88 S.W. 2d 885 (1935). When plaintiff mistakenly questions the jurors on their interest in insurance companies, the defendant may prove that he is not insured. Stehouwer v. Lewis, 249 Mich. 76, 227 N.W. 759, 74 A.L.R. 844 (1929); Vick v. Moe, 74 S.D. 144, 49 N.W.2d 463 (1951); see also, Heiskell v. H. C. Enterprise, Inc., 244 Ark. 857, 429 S.W.2d 71 (1968); Potter v. Finan, 6 Mich.App. 696, 150 N.W. 2d 539 (1967). Where some defendants are insured and some not, and the jurors have been questioned about insurance, it seems that those not insured should be allowed to show this, but the court held to the contrary in Clayton v. Wells, 324 Mo. 1176, 26 S.W.2d 969 (1930).

19. See statement in Annot., 4 A.L.R.2d 761, 764; and the cases cited in note 16, supra.

20. 8 Wigmore, Evidence (McNaughton rev.) § 2313, and see § 94, herein; Annot., 13 A.L.R.2d 882 (discovery of coverage, amount, and insurer); F.R.Civ. P. 26(b) (2).

21. See the similar reasoning of Eberly, J., in Jessup v. Davis, 115 Neb. 1, 211 N.W. 190, 56 A.L.R. 1403 (1926) which sustained the right of plaintiff to elicit from the defendant on cross-examination the fact of insurance. Three judges dissented, however, and the holding was later overruled in Fielding v. Publix Cars, Inc., 130 Neb. 576, 265 N.W. 726, 105 A.L.R. 1306 (1936). See Beghtol, Present Rule as to Disclosure of Insurance, 15 Neb.L.B. 327 (1937).

which permit the insurance company to be named as a party defendant.[22]

22. La.R.S. 22:655; Wis.St.1953, §§ 85.93, 260.11. These statutes are set out in part in Annot., 4 A.L. R.2d 761, 767. See also Notes, Statutes Permitting Joinder of Insurance Companies, 20 Corn.L.Q. 110, 113 (1934), Joinder under Compulsory Insurance Laws, 39 Ill.L.Rev. 81 (1944). A number of states have interpreted their compulsory insurance laws as permitting direct action against the insurer, 8 Appleman, Ins.Law and Prac., §§ 4831–4838 (1962).

In Shingelton v. Bussey, 223 So.2d 713 (Fla.1969), the Florida court held an automobile liability insurer properly joined with insured as a codefendant, despite a no-action clause in the policy, on the doctrine of third-party beneficiary and the provisions of its joinder rule. Of the risks of prejudice, the court said: ". . . [W]e do think the stage has been reached where juries are more mature. Accordingly a candid admission at trial of the existence of insurance coverage, the policy limits of same, and an otherwise aboveboard revelation of the interest of an insurer in the outcome of a recovery action against insured should be more beneficial to insurers in terms of diminishing their overall policy judgment payments than the questionable 'ostrich head in the sand' approach which may often mislead juries to think insurance coverage is greater than it is." (223 So.2d 713, 718). In Beta Eta House Corp. v. Gregory, 237 So.2d 163 (Fla.1970), the court approved extension of the joinder ruling to other forms of liability insurance, but over a vigorous dissent, retreated from the disclosure-at-trial position to the extent of stating that the trial of the liability claim should normally be conducted without mention of insurance.

CHAPTER 20

EXPERIMENTAL AND SCIENTIFIC EVIDENCE

202. Experimental Evidence.[1]

Testing the truth of hypotheses by the use of controlled experiments is one of the key techniques of modern scientific method.[2] The courts in their task of investigating facts make extensive use of this technique, but under conditions which prevent them from exploiting the process to the full limits of its usefulness. The legal doctrines relating to experimental evidence are simple and the principal task of the lawyer is to recognize the opportunities for their use, to seize these opportunities boldly, and when experiments are employed to plan them inventively and correctly,[3] so that the results derived will be convincing to judge and jury. We are dealing here with experiments carried out before trial and presented at the trial through descriptions given by witnesses of the experiment and its results. Experiments conducted in the courtroom itself during the trial are discussed in the chapter on Demonstrative Evidence.[4]

The opportunities are of limitless variety. Some of the types of experiments most frequently encountered are these: tests of the composition and properties of substances;[5]

1. 2 Wigmore, Evidence §§ 445–460; C.J.S. Evidence §§ 586–591; C.J.S. Criminal Law § 645; 3 Am. Jur. Trials § 427; 29 Am.Jur.2d Evidence §§ 818–833; Dec.Dig. Evidence ⊙150, Criminal Law ⊙388; Note, 34 Ill.L.Rev. 206 (1939).

2. See Conant, On Understanding Science 104 (1946); Cohen, Reason and Nature 82 (1931).

3. Successful examples are seen in such cases as People v. Miller, 245 Cal.App.2d 112, 53 Cal.Rptr. 720 (1966) cert. denied 392 U.S. 616 (murder; state claimed victim was drugged and left unconscious in car which was set afire; defense claimed accidental crash with resulting fire; state introduced results of experiments to (1) show nail found in tire would cause leak rather than blowout, (2) show how much force was required to disconnect plastic flex fuel line, (3) show that fire started inside

passenger compartment could spread to underbody and to engine compartment); Torgeson v. Missouri-Kansas-Texas R. Co., 124 Kan. 798, 262 P. 564, 55 A.L.R. 1335 (1928) (witnesses described tests they had made as to the safest way of approaching a particular crossing in an automobile, comparing these methods: (1) merely stopping to look; (2) stopping and going to the track to look; (3) stopping and going to the point whence one could see farthest down the track.); Larson v. Meyer, 161 N.W.2d 165 (N.D.1968) (showing whether tractor could pull milk tank without raising front of tractor off the ground). See also a case described in Note, 34 Ill.L.Rev. 206, 210 (1939) where the services of a "magician" were ingeniously and effectively employed.

4. See § 215, infra.

5. Odell v. Frueh, 146 Cal.App.2d 504, 304 P.2d 45, 76 A.L.R.2d 345 (1956) (annotated extensively on this class of test); Dritt v. Morris, 235 Ark. 40, 357 S.W.2d 13 (1962) (slipperiness of floor); Beres-

testing firearms to show the patterns of powder and shot made upon the object at different distances; [6] experiments by human beings in the holding of firearms to determine whether a given gunshot wound could have been self-inflicted; [7] tests of the visibility of objects or persons at a given distance; [8] tests of audibility; [9] and tests of the speed of locomotives and motor vehicles and of the effectiveness of their brakes and headlights.[10] Some specialized tests and experi-

ments, such as lie-detector tests, blood tests for paternity and intoxication, and firearms identification are briefly discussed later in the present chapter.[11]

Here again, as in the problems presented in the preceding chapters of this title, the question is one of weighing the probative value of the evidence of experiments against the dangers of misleading the jury (who may attach exaggerated significance to the tests), unfair surprise, and, occasionally, undue consumption of time.[12] The danger of arousing hostility or prejudice is seldom present in respect to this type of evidence. Usually the best gauge of the probative value of experiments is the extent to which the conditions of the experiment were identical with or similar to those obtaining in respect to the litigated happening.[13] Accordingly, counsel in planning experiments must seek to make the conditions as nearly identical as may be, and in presenting the evidence he must be prepared to lay the foundation by preliminary proof of similarity of conditions.[14] Though

---

ford v. Pacific Gas & Elec. Co., 45 Cal.2d 738, 290 P.2d 498, 54 A.L.R.2d 910 (1955) (effects of electricity; annotated on this point); Kotiadis v. Gristede Bros., Inc., 20 App.Div.2d 689, 246 N.Y.S. 2d 662 (1964) (cause of explosion); and see Annot., 76 A.L.R.2d 402 (explosion experiments); People v. Carter, 48 Cal.2d 737, 312 P.2d 665 (1957) (to determine source of spattered blood from pattern); Alonzo v. State, 283 Ala. 607, 219 So.2d 858 (1969) (electronic test of tape to discover any alteration).

6. State v. Atwood, 250 N.C. 141, 108 S.E.2d 219, 86 A.L.R.2d 602 (1959) (annotated on this point); State v. Baublits, 324 Mo. 1199, 27 S.W.2d 16 (1930) trajectory tests).

7. Downing v. Metropolitan Life Ins. Co., 314 Ill. App. 222, 41 N.E.2d 297 (1942) (admitted); Epperson v. Comm., 227 Ky. 404, 13 S.W.2d 247 (1929) (excluded because tests made with body of deceased do not show what she could have done when living).

8. Patton v. Smith, 119 Ga.App. 664, 168 S.E.2d 627 (1969); Hurly v. Star Transfer Co., 14 Mont. 176, 376 P.2d 504 (1962); Carpenter v. Kurn, 348 Mo. 1132, 157 S.W.2d 213 (1941) (tests for ascertaining distance one standing on tracks could tell that a person sitting and dressed like deceased was human being). In a similar case, the court held that the fact that the persons making the tests knew beforehand that the object was a human being, whereas the engineer running the train did not, weakened the value of test, but did not require its exclusion. Norfolk & W. Ry. Co. v. Henderson, 132 Va. 297, 111 S.E. 277 (1922). But this is a weakness which in the interest of justice should be avoided in the planning of such visibility tests. See also, Annot., 78 A.L.R.2d 152.

9. Drake v. Tims, 287 P.2d 215 (Okla.1955) (distance ambulance siren could be heard; rejected for lack of similarity of conditions).

10. People v. Crawford, 41 Cal.App.2d 198, 106 P.2d 219 (1940) (facts closely resemble those in James M. Cain's novel, The Postman Always Rings Twice); Stevens v. People, 97 Colo. 559, 51 P.2d 1022 (1935) (experiment to show whether headlight would illuminate oncoming car when passing at particular place); Publix Cab Co. v. Colorado Nat. Bank, 139 Colo. 205, 338 P.2d 702, 78 A.L.R.2d 198

(1959) (annotated on speed and control experiments); Smith v. State Roads Com'n, 240 Md. 525, 214 A.2d 792 (1965) (control test, rejected for lack of similarity).

11. See §§ 206–211, infra.

12. Quinn v. McPherson, 73 Wash.2d 194, 437 P.2d 393 (1968); 2 Wigmore, Evidence § 443.

13. The requirement of similarity is constantly repeated. See, e. g., Love v. State, 457 P.2d 622 (Alas. 1969) (experiment to determine how vessel would drift in specific waters; inadmissible for lack of similarity); Smith v. State Roads Com'n, 240 Md. 525, 214 A.2d 792 (1965) (auto swerve test; decedent ran into roadside pole on damp night while intoxicated and driving 1948 pickup truck at unknown speed in unknown lane; test was conducted by sober police officer driving police car at 30–35 m. p. h. near center line on dry day; "Except for the fact that Officer Borgman's experiment was performed at the same curve, there are no circumstances or conditions which are the same."); Fort Worth and Denver Ry. Co. v. Williams, 375 S.W.2d 279 (Tex.1964) (visibility test); C.J.S. Evidence § 590.

14. The burden is on the proponent. Robinson v. Morrison, 272 Ala. 552, 133 So.2d 230 (1961) (visibility); McGough v. Hendrickson, 58 Cal.App.2d 60, 136 P.2d 110 (1943) (experiment to show visibility

the similarity formula is sometimes over-rigidly applied, most courts will recognize that the requirement is a relative one,[15] so that where a high degree of similarity is not attainable, the court might still conclude that the results of the experiment are of substantial enlightening value to the jury and admit the evidence.[16] Manifestly, if the trial judge is to be given responsibility for exercising such an indefinable value-judgment he must be accorded a reasonable leeway of discretion reviewable only for abuse.[17]

Moreover, the experiment may be offered for a purpose that does not depend for its persuasiveness upon identity or similarity of all conditions. Thus if one party contends that it is impossible *under any conditions* for a given result to follow certain acts or omissions, the other party may prove by experiment that on a particular occasion the consequence has actually occurred. Of course he is not hampered by a "similar-conditions" requirement.[18] He has only to meet the terms of the challenge. Similarly, the proponent may offer to prove that the agency for which he is responsible was not the cause of the injurious result. An experiment showing that the same result has happened *under different conditions,* and in the absence of that agency, has some logical value to increase the probability of the proponent's contention.[19] It

of pedestrian on highway; burden to show similarity as to time of day and season of year not satisfied); Hightower v. Alley, 132 Mont. 349, 318 P.2d 243 (1957) (time required to walk a given distance; similarity not shown); Enghlin v. Pittsburgh County Ry., 169 Okla. 106, 36 P.2d 32, 37, 94 A.L.R. 1180 (1934) (experiment with same streetcar, same place to show maximum speed, burden satisfied).

15. Lever Bros. Co. v. Atlas Assur. Co., 131 F.2d 770, 777 (7th Cir. 1942) (admissible if some valid points of similarity); Hansen v. Howard O. Miller, Inc., 93 Idaho 314, 460 P.2d 739 (1969) (braking experiment held properly admitted despite difference in make, year, weight and tire size of auto).

16. Hansen v. Howard O. Miller, Inc., supra, n. 15; Downing v. Metropolitan Life Ins. Co., 314 Ill.App. 222, 41 N.E.2d 297 (1942) (experiment by other men to determine whether deceased could have shot himself); Erickson's Dairy Products Co. v. Northwest Baker Ice Mach. Co., 165 Ore. 553, 109 P.2d 53 (1941) (action for causing fire in building by failing to protect wall during welding operations; experiment by welding near a piece of wallboard, properly received over objection board different from wall itself; "After all, we must assume that the jury was composed of men and women of ordinary sense and intelligence who would take into consideration the dissimilarity of which plaintiff complains."). Compare Lincoln Taxi Co. v. Rice, 251 S.W.2d 867 (Ky.1952), where the court announced a similar liberal criterion, but held that the experiment in question did not meet it.

7. Ramseyer v. General Motors Corp., 417 F.2d 859 (8th Cir. 1969); Hullum v. St. Louis Southwestern Ry., 384 S.W.2d 163 (Tex.Civ.App.1965) cert. denied 382 U.S. 906, reh. denied 382 U.S. 949; C.J.S. Evidence § 586; C.J.S. Criminal Law § 645 (1). Nearly all the cases state this to be the test, whether the trial court's action is being approved or disapproved.

18. Chambers v. Silver, 103 Cal.App.2d 633, 230 P. 2d 146 (1951) (where collision occurred when defendant's automobile veered onto wrong side of road and his sole defense, in suit for injuries to plaintiffs, was that main leaf in spring at front wheel had broken when wheel crossed two-inch deposit of soil on road and vehicle had thereby been rendered impossible to control, and mechanic testified for defendant that it was physically impossible to drive automobile with this type suspension in such condition, it was prejudicial error to refuse plaintiffs' rebuttal evidence as to an experiment in which automobile with same suspension system was driven without loss of control over 2 x 4 boards at a speed of 45 to 50 miles per hour.); Horn v. Elgin Warehouse Co., 96 Ore. 403, 190 Pac. 151 (1920) (plaintiff sued seller of wheat for breach of his warranty that it was Red Chaff wheat, plaintiff alleging it was not Red Chaff wheat; defendant allowed to prove that witnesses had planted same wheat and it produced Red Chaff wheat, without any showing of similarity of conditions.)

Of course, if the conditions prevailing at the time of the experiment are more unfavorable to the proponent than the conditions of the crucial happening this satisfies the requirement. People v. Spencer, 58 Cal.App. 197, 208 Pac. 380, 393 (1922); State Forester v. Umpqua River Nav. Co., 478 P.2d 631 (Ore.1970).

19. Lincoln v. Taunton Copper Mfg. Co., 91 Mass. 181, 191 (1864) (action for injury to plaintiff's land by contamination with copper from defendant's mill; plaintiff's expert having testified that he has obtained copper from grasses on plaintiff's land, defendants may introduce similar testimony that copper exists and has been obtained in grasses not exposed to contamination from defendant's mill); Coon v. Utah Constr. Co., 119 Utah 446, 228 P.2d 997 (1951) (alleged damage to house from trucks; tests showing defendant's trucks caused

seems also that experiments designed to show the general traits and capacities of materials involved in the controversy are often admitted in evidence without confining the experiments to the conditions surrounding the litigated situation. Most of these analyses are referred to as "tests" rather than "experiments," and the only question is one of authentication i. e., of tracing the material, unaltered in aspects relating to the purpose, into the test process. Further, where proponent makes no claim to have reenacted or simulated the whole or a substantial part of the original happening, recent decisions have distinguished these limited-purpose experiments, and have adapted the similarity requirement accordingly.[20] The question, as always, is whether the evidence will assist the jury without confusing them.

It seems that in respect to certain types of cases and issues, the use of experimental

evidence has far greater possibilities for aiding the court in the true determination of facts than have as yet been realized. This seems to be due to the failure of courts and lawyers to recognize that the adversary system of party-presentation of evidence must continually be modified, to keep it in step with the march of justice. Consideration might be given to allowing the judge to exclude any experiment from use in evidence unless reasonable *notice* has been given the adversary with an opportunity to make suggestions as to planning and to be present at the experiment.[21] Also worthy of consideration is appointment by the court of an *impartial* person to conduct or supervise an experiment.[22] If the parties can agree on such

no greater vibrations in the house than other traffic, admitted); 2 Wigmore, Evidence § 448.

20. Johnson v. Chicago & N. W. Ry. Co., 9 Ill.App. 2d 340, 132 N.E.2d 678 (1956) (auto-train collision; testimony as to obstruction by buildings of line of sight at various points admissible: "Here there was no attempt to duplicate the conditions and re-enact the occurrence. All that is involved is a showing as to how the visibility down the right-of-way is affected by permanent objects obstructing the view at various places."); Current v. Columbia Gas of Ky., 383 S.W.2d 139 (Ky.1964) (injury from carbon monoxide; tests run on heaters admitted without showing they were in same condition as when accident occurred: ". . . the matter of the relative conditions of the appliances at the time of the test and time of accident were made plain to the jury. It was not claimed for the tests that they showed the operating efficiency of the appliances as they were at the time of the accident. Rather, it was the operation of the space heater under one condition, which in our minds entitled appellants to go to the jury."); Council v. Duprel, 250 Miss. 269, 165 So.2d 134 (1964) (damage from crop spraying; "The experiment was not an effort to duplicate the conditions existing on the appellants' farm as to rainfall, soil condition, method of cultivation, time of fruitation or plant characteristics. The experiment's purpose was to establish the fact that 2–4D is far more destructive to cotton than 2–4-5T."); see also Miller's Nat. Ins. Co. v. Witchita Flour Milling Co., 257 F.2d 93, 76 A.L.R.2d 385 (10th Cir. 1958) (movies of demonstration of physics principles).

21. Under present practice, absence of notice and opportunity to be present are not a ground of rejection, but may be argued on the weight. Burg v. Chicago, R. I. & P. Ry. Co., 90 Iowa 106, 57 N.W. 680, 683 (1894) (evidence of tests made by defendant railway using locomotive and train, of visibility of person on track, and of stopping power of brakes); Larson v. Meyer, 161 N.W.2d 165 (N.D. 1968); Sinclair Oil & Gas Co. v. Albright, 161 Okl. 272, 18 P.2d 540, 543 (1933) (experiment as to effect of horse's drinking polluted water); Byers v. Nashville C. & St. L. Ry. Co., 94 Tenn. 345, 29 S.W. 128 (1895) (error to reject experiment like that in the *Burg* case, supra, for lack of notice); C.J.S. Evidence § 587.

Clearly no hard-and-fast rule can be made. Not every test of a substance should be classified as an experiment for purposes of notice; only experiments initiated post litem motam, with the object of using them in the litigation would be covered, and so on. The aims of the rule would be to encourage joint experiments by changing the existing case law to make rejection on this ground possible in appropriate circumstances; and to make more experiments admissible and useful, by improving their design and obviating objections which can be met if raised ahead of time.

Under the proposed practice, a pretrial hearing or conference such as is provided for under Rule 16 of the Federal Rules of Civil Procedure (or some earlier time) would be an appropriate occasion for giving notice of a proposed experiment and for negotiation about its planning.

22. Compare Rules of the Supreme Court (England), Order 40, r. 1 and r. 3: "1.—(1) In any cause or matter which is to be tried without a jury and in which any question for an expert witness arises the Court may at any time, on the application of any party, appoint an independent expert, or, if

a person the judge would be required to appoint him. A test thus conducted would in many cases be so conclusive a settlement of the controlling issue that a trial, being a foregone conclusion, would be avoided. In any case evidence of the results of such a test would give to the tribunal the benefit of the scientific method of controlled experiment far more completely than does our present system of secret one-sided experiments.

203. Some Problems in the Use of Scientific Techniques and Devices as Sources of Proof: [23] In General.

In a work of this scope we cannot cover the vast and growing body of experience in the various fields of scientific proof. The topic alone of medical science as a source of

more than one such question arises, two or more such experts, to inquire and report upon any question of fact or opinion not involving questions of law or of construction . . . .

"3. If the court expert is of the opinion that an experiment or test of any kind (other than one of a trifling character) is necessary to enable him to make a satisfactory report he shall inform the parties or their solicitors and shall, if possible, make an arrangement with them as to the expenses involved, the persons to attend and other relevant matters; and if the parties are unable to agree on any of those matters it shall be settled by the Court." 1 Supreme Court Practice 1970, p. 548. See, in this connection, Foster v. Agri-Chem, Inc., 235 Ore. 570, 385 P.2d 184 (1963) (experiments made by scientists unconnected with the litigation; "No decisions have been found pointing up this distinction. However, because this evidence is free from the taint of interest or bias that might accompany the usual 'experimental' evidence, we believe greater latitude should be shown in admitting such evidence.").

See also §§ 8, 17, supra, as to common law powers and statutory and rule provisions for appointment of expert witnesses by the court, in this country.

23. Richardson, Modern Scientific Evidence, Ch. 1 (1961); Boyd, Judicial Recognition of Scientific Evidence in Criminal Cases, 8 Utah L.Rev. 313 (1963); Kirk, The Interrelationship of Science and Law, 13 Buffalo L.Rev. 393 (1964); Korn, Law, Fact and Science in the Courts, 66 Colum.L.Rev. 1080 (1966); Ormrod, Scientific Evidence in Court, 1968 Crim.L.Rev. 240; Parker, Scientific Proof, 32 Rev.Jur.U.P.R. 201 (1963); Strong, Questions Affecting the Admissibility of Scientific Evidence, 1970 U.Ill.L.F. 1; Symposium, Medical and Scientific Evidence, 13 N.Y.L.F. 606 (1968).

legal evidence is the subject of many comprehensive textbooks and of an extensive body of articles.[24] Moreover, the rushing stream of new scientific techniques and devices soon renders obsolete any attempt at comprehensive description. Only a very limited sampling of a few of the areas, which have been the subject of wide discussion by the judges and commentators, will here be attempted.

Scientific evidence may enter into a case as a means of obtaining specific data [25] or as a means of evaluating the significance of data.[26] The decisions of many courts show a tendency to class some evidence as scientific and to apply special rules to its admission or exclusion. To the extent that expert witnesses testify as to matters of science, these requirements apply to their testimony.

How courts decide what evidence is to be chosen for this treatment, and the content of these special rules themselves, have never been precisely stated. In many instances, accidents of history must be assigned a major role. For centuries, "science" was treated as co-extensive with its Latin root, which encompassed all knowledge; and it was only in the middle of the 1800's that the term "scientist" began to be used to mark off from philosophers, scholars, and intellectuals in general, those who sought by the methods of observation, hypothesis, deduction, and experimental verification to find and ex-

24. To the point where there are now books and articles on how to find the books and articles; see, e. g., Brittain, A Bibliography of Medico-Legal Works in English (1962); Curran, Medical Literature for Lawyers, 47 Va.L.Rev. 666 (1961); Gilmer, Lawyers in Medical Bookland, 1970 U.Ill.L.F. 115.

25. E. g., data not visible to the eye without the use of a microscope. 2 Wigmore, Evidence § 417b.

26. James, Relevancy, Probability and the Law, 29 Calif.L.Rev. 689, 696, n. 15 (1941), divides the propositions upon which relevancy depends into those based on "the practical experience of the judge and jurors as men" and "generalizations of science."

plain empirical regularities in nature.[27] The problem could scarcely arise in its present form before that time. Even as late as 1892, in rejecting the testimony of the precursor of what would now be called a firearms identification expert, the court used the traditional test of admissibility of expert opinion, and simply decided that the witness possessed no special skill which would give added assistance to the jury: "These are all matters of common knowledge, and the jury was as competent to pass upon them as the witness." [28]

So far as it can be dated, the notion of a special rule of admissibility for scientific evidence seems to have arisen in 1923. The court [29] which first faced the question of admissibility of the results of a "lie-detector" examination (offered by the defendant in a criminal case) noted that the defendant's brief had relied upon the usual rule governing expert testimony, that when the question involved does not lie within the range of common experience or common knowledge, "then the opinions of witnesses skilled in that particular science, art or trade to which the question relates are admissible in evidence." The court said:

> "Just when a scientific principle crosses the line between the experimental and demonstrable stages is difficult to define. Somewhere in this twilight zone the evidential force of the principle must be recognized, and while courts will go a long way in admitting expert testimony deduced from a well-recognized scientific principle or discovery, the thing from which the deduction is made must be sufficiently established to have gained general acceptance in the particular field to which it belongs.[30] "

No authority was cited. The court's prior discussion had indicated that the "thing from which the deduction is made" might be either the general proposition that there is a connection between conscious insincerity and changes in blood pressure, or some proposition relating to the ability of an expert to interpret such data. The court concluded that "the systolic blood pressure deception test" had not yet gained the required standing and scientific recognition among authorities in the fields of physiology and psychology. This type of evidence and several others [31] have been rejected by the same court and many others ever since.

27. 14 International Encyclopedia of the Social Sciences 107 (1968), citing Ross, "Scientist," the Story of a Word, 18 Ann. of Sci. 65 (1962).

28. People v. Mitchell, 94 Cal. 550, 29 P. 1106 (1892); see People v. Weber, 149 Cal. 325, 86 P. 671 (1906); People v. Berkman, 307 Ill. 492, 139 N.E. 91 (1923) ("the statement that one can know that a certain bullet was fired out of a 32-caliber revolver, when there are hundreds and perhaps thousands rifled in precisely the same manner and of precisely the same character, is preposterous."); cf. People v. Fisher, 340 Ill. 216, 172 N.E. 743 (1930). Firearms identification seems to have crossed the line of admissibility partly through adoption of the comparison microscope and other instrumentation which rendered impossible the contention that the jury could observe the data for themselves. The new field of "accident reconstruction" is encountering a similar kind of "growing-problem."

29. Frye v. United States, 54 U.S.App.D.C. 46, 293 Fed. 1013 (1923). Wicker, The Polygraphic Truth Test and the Law of Evidence, 22 Tenn.L.Rev. 711, 715 (1953) states that Frye was exonerated some years after his conviction, when another person confessed to the murder.

30. Supra, n. 29, at 1014.

31. Among them the "truth-serum" tests and opinions based on hypnosis, discussed in succeeding sections. Blood-typing tests nearly failed to meet the new standard in one jurisdiction; see State v. Damm, 62 S.D. 123, 252 N.W. 7 (1933) (modern medical science not shown to be sufficiently agreed on "the transmissibility of blood characteristics"); on rehearing 64 S.D. 309, 266 N.W. 667 (1936) (science found unanimously agreed); cf. Huntingdon v. Crowley, 64 Cal.2d 647, 414 P.2d 382, 51 Cal.Rptr. 254 (1966) (Kell-Cellano test properly excluded as not sufficiently accepted; the hurdle here seems to have been the difficulty of performing the test, rather than the law of heredity).

The recently developed "voiceprint" is an interesting example of the differences produced by differing rules concerning admissibility of evidence labeled "scientific." In essence, the method is one for identifying a human voice by examination of spectrographic representations of it. See Kersta,

The difficulty of determining how to distinguish scientific evidence from other expert testimony, of deciding what is the particular field of science to which the evidence belongs, and of settling what is general acceptance, has led to an application of the new test which is highly selective, although not enlightening as to its details.[32] Recent cases

seem tacitly to have ignored it, and returned to the former test for admissibility of expert testimony. In one outstanding example,[33] defendant was charged with murder of his wife by injection of a lethal dose of an anesthetic called succinylcholine chloride. Up to the time of the trial, the medical profession generally believed that there was no way to detect in a corpse the presence of this compound or its components. One of the state's toxicologists developed, specifically for use in the case, a test for one component

Speaker Recognition and Identification by Voiceprints, 40 Conn.B.J. 586 (1966); Kamine, The Voiceprint technique, 6 San Diego L.Rev. 213 (1969); Hennessey and Romig, A Review of The Experiments Involving Voiceprint Identification, 16 J.For. Sci. 183 (1971). The skill of the examiner in interpretation is of course the critical factor, even if every voice is treated as unique. In People v. King, 266 Cal.App.2d 437, 72 Cal.Rptr. 478 (1966) and State v. Cary, 99 N.J.Super. 323, 239 A.2d 680 (1968), the *Frye* standard was applied and the evidence held inadmissible; in United States v. Wright, 17 U.S.C.M.A. 183, 37 C.M.R. 447 (1967), the usual test for expert testimony was applied and the evidence held admissible. In State ex rel. Trimble v. Hedman, 192 N.W.2d 432 (Minn.1971), a habeas corpus case, the evidence was held admissible to corroborate identification by ear alone, and for impeachment purposes. See also, People v. Straehle (N.Y.Sup.Ct.1966), admitting the evidence, discussed in Note, 13 N.Y.L.F. 677, 747 (1968). The *King* opinion discusses at length the question whether the expert witness to the voiceprints possessed the necessary qualifications in speech fields, in addition to acoustical and audio engineering, and might, even without the *Frye* test, have held his expertise insufficient.

32. For discussions of the selective application of the *Frye* principle and efforts to explain it, see Boyce, Judicial Recognition of Scientific Evidence in Criminal Cases, 8 Utah L.Rev. 313 (1964); Strong, Questions Affecting the Admissibility of Scientific Evidence, 1970 U.Ill.L.F. 1.

Two additional points may be noticed. First, the courts, when undertaking to pass on the question whether the evidence has sufficient probative value to assist the jury, mix that question with the one of effect on the jury, and seemingly require that the probative value be as great as the courts decide the jury will think it to be. In the case of matters labelled "lie-detector," "truth-serum," "voiceprint," or "mathematical certainty," the courts seem to conclude that the jury will consider the tests infallible, and so require that they be shown to be infallible before they are admitted. See Lindsey v. United States, 16 Alas. 268, 237 F.2d 893 (1956) ("In order to accept the Government's view, we must be able to say affirmatively that the sodium-pentothal interview is a test of truthfulness that is not only trustworthy, but reliably so in all cases."); People v. Forte, 279 N.Y. 204, 18 N.E.2d 31 (1938) ("Can [the lie detector] be depended upon to operate with complete success on persons of varying emotional stability?"); Peo-

ple v. Davis, 343 Mich. 348, 72 N.W.2d 269 (1955) (lie-detector; 75 to 90 per cent accuracy held insufficient). Once a requirement of infallibility of the total test has been set up, there is scarcely any need to refer the matter to the scientific community to find out whether a test administered by humans is generally accepted by scientists as infallible. Second, if "generally accepted as reliable" is left undefined, it is likely to be discovered that the phrase means different things, to the courts which invented the phrase and to the scientists appealed to. See, e. g., Kirk, The Interrelationship of Science and Law, 13 Buffalo L.Rev. 393 (1964); Fong, Criminalistics and the Prosecutor, in The Prosecutor's Sourcebook §§ 14.1–14.19 (George and Cohen eds. 1969); Hearings Before a Subcommittee of the House Committee on Government Operations, Use of Polygraphs as "Lie-Detectors" by the Federal Government, 88th Cong., 2d Sess., Part 3 at 292–93, 304, 310–313 (1964); cf. 2 Kennelly, Litigation and Trial of Aircrash Cases Ch. 3, at 13 (1968). To refer a question of courtroom admissibility to "science," only to find that the question is "unscientific," could create an impasse from which the law might need a long time to escape. *Hearings*, supra, at 337 (Testimony of Dr. Lacey): "The phrase is constantly being used, 'Is the lie detector valid?' . . . This is not a question that the scientist would ask."; cf., id., at 302 (Testimony of Dr. Orne); id. at 304 (Testimony of Dr. Lacey).

33. Coppolino v. State, 223 So.2d 68 (Fla.App.1969); appeals dismissed, 234 So.2d 120 (Fla.1969) cert. denied, 399 U.S. 927 (1970). Other examples are State v. Olivas, 77 Ariz. 118, 267 P.2d 893 (1954) (breath test; "where there is lack of unanimity in the medical profession whether intoxication can be tested by breath, the scientific disagreement affects only the weight and not the admissibility of evidence."); People v. Bobczyk, 343 Ill.App. 504, 99 N.E.2d 567 (1957) (same); People v. Williams, 164 Cal.App.2d Supp. 858, 331 P.2d 251 (1958) (Nalline test for recent narcotics use admissible despite concession that medical profession did not know of and therefore had not generally accepted it; "It has been generally accepted by those who would be expected to be familiar with its use. In this age of specialization more should not be required.").

(succinic acid) and found it in the body in abnormal amounts. The court, although stating that the new rule was being applied, held that on the conflicting testimony of the parties' experts as to the possibility of such a test and the reliability of its results, the trial judge had not abused his discretion in admitting the evidence.

The practice approved in the last mentioned case is the one which should be followed in respect to expert testimony and scientific evidence generally. "General scientific acceptance" is a proper condition for taking judicial notice of scientific facts, but not a criterion for the admissibility of scientific evidence. Any relevant conclusions which are supported by a qualified expert witness [34] should be received unless there are other reasons for exclusion. Particularly, probative value may be overborne by the familiar dangers of prejudicing or misleading the jury, and undue consumption of time.[35] If the courts used this approach, instead of repeating a supposed requirement of "general acceptance" not elsewhere imposed, they would arrive at a practical way of utilizing the results of scientific advances.

Among the weaknesses of our judicial process in the area of scientific proof are (1) the selection of experts by the parties, so that the experts chosen are often biased and are sometimes not highly qualified, as where a general practitioner is called upon a question of mental disorder, and (2) the difficulty for the jury of deciding between experts who disagree.

Many of the devices described herein, such as the lie detector, the truth serum and the blood tests, when administered without consent, raise questions of the privilege against self-incrimination, which have been discussed in the chapter relating to that privilege.[36] The widespread use of the polygraph in industry and government has also raised some issues of privacy, not related directly to admissibility in court.[37]

204. The Theory of Probabilities as Applied to Questions of Identification.[38]

Scientific proof has as one of its chief areas of operation the field of identification. This includes the identification of persons, through fingerprints, photographs and measurements, or by testimony describing a highwayman, whose identity is disputed. It likewise includes the search for the authorship of a document by means of identifying the handwriting of the writer or identifying the characteristics of the typewriter used from the peculiarities of the typescript. Similar-

---

34. Whether an expert is properly qualified may be, in view of the amount of specialization and overlapping of fields of expertise, an occasionally difficult question. It seems unlikely to be as difficult as the question of when and to what the "general scientific acceptance" test should be applied, with the added question of what that test is.

35. See § 185, supra. See also the illuminating discussion of these balancing considerations of auxiliary policy and of probative value, as applied to "lie-detector" evidence, in Trautman, Logical or Legal Relevancy, 5 Vand.L.Rev. 385, 395 (1952).

36. See §§ 124, 133, 134, supra.

37. See Hearings Before a Subcommittee of the House Committee on Government Operations, supra note 32; Burkey, Privacy, Property and the Polygraph, 18 Lab.L.J. 80 (1967); Falick, Lie Detectors and the Right to Privacy, 40 N.Y.S.B.J. 102 (1968); Notes, 15 Buffalo L.Rev. 655 (1966), 33 Geo. Wash.L.Rev. 932 (1965).

38. Goode, Probability and the Weighing of Evidence (1950); Wigmore, The Science of Judicial Proof § 154 (3d ed. 1937); Houts, From Evidence to Proof 132–134 (1956); Nagel, The Meaning of Probability, in 2 The World of Mathematics 1398 (Newman ed. 1956); Broun and Kelly, Playing the Percentages and The Law of Evidence, 1970 U.Ill. L.F. 23; Cullison, Identification by Probabilities and Trial by Arithmetic, 6 Houston L.Rev. 471 (1969); Finklestein and Fairlie, A Bayesian Approach to Identification Evidence, 83 Harv.L.Rev. 489 (1970); Kingston and Kirk, Use of Statistics in Criminalistics, 55 J.Crim.L.C. & P.S. 514 (1964); Liddle, Mathematical and Statistical Probability as a Test of Circumstantial Evidence, 19 Case W.Res. L.Rev. 254 (1968); Stoebuck, Relevancy and Probability, 51 Iowa L.Rev. 849 (1966); Tribe, Trial by Mathematics, 84 Harv.L.Rev. 329 (1971); Note, 1967 Duke L.J. 665. The modern criminalist prefers the term "individualization" to identification, for the question here discussed.

ly, a revolver used in a murder may be identified by tracing the marks found on the fatal bullet or the empty cartridge left at the scene of the killing. These and many other techniques of identification have been developed and refined by scientists and technicians in university and police laboratories and by independent scientific specialists, particularly since the turn of the century. Probably the extent of their accomplishments in making it possible to furnish evidence of identification has not been appreciated by most people who have not studied the results of their work, or learned of it through the perusal of detective fiction.

It has long been recognized by the courts that the jury deciding questions of identification operates on the basis not of unattainable absolute certainty, but of probability.[39] In criminal cases, where the state's burden is proof "beyond a reasonable doubt," the temptation to try to quantify the probative force of some concatenation of circumstantial evidence has historically been overwhelming. For long, such efforts were confined to the arguments of counsel, where the only limit is the broad latitude allowed to the assumptions, deductions, and rhetorical flourishes of the advocate; and no questions of admissibility of evidence were raised.[40]

With the development, especially in the nineteenth century, of a calculus of probabilities and its widespread use (and misuse), efforts to quantify the probative force of particular evidence took the form of sporadic but increasing attempts: (1) to introduce as part of the opinion testimony of an expert an explanation of the strength of his conclusion, based on the calculus; and (2) to introduce testimony by an expert explaining the calculus to the jury, and performing illustrative calculations for their use. Although the two were not always kept distinct, in the one, the expert was explaining to the jury how he had thought in combining data and arriving at his conclusion and his degree of confidence in it; in the other, he was putting forward a way in which the jurors themselves could think in arriving at their conclusion and degree of confidence in it. Both these methods raised questions of admissibility of his testimony.

No sophisticated discussion of probability [41] or of the calculus is necessary to describe these problems, because the cases in which they arose involved only a very simple fragment of it, known as the "product rule" or "calculus of compound probabilities". That rule states (in part) that if two or more events are mutually independent, the probability of their co-occurrence is equal to the product of their individual probabilities.[42] For example, if the probability of ob-

39. Cook v. Michael, 214 Ore. 513, 330 P.2d 1026 (1958); Morgan, Some Problems of Proof 81 (1956); McBaine, Burden of Proof: Degrees of Belief, 32 Calif.L.Rev. 242 (1944); Morgan, Instructing the Jury Upon Presumptions and Burden of Proof, 47 Harv.L.Rev. 59, 66 (1933); Annot., 93 A.L.R. 155. The recognition is not unanimous; see Lampe v. Franklin Am. Trust Co., 339 Mo. 361, 384, 96 S.W. 2d 710, 723 (1936); Frazier v. Frazier, 228 S.C. 149, 168, 89 S.E.2d 225, 235 (1955).

40. See, as only one of many possible examples, the summation of the celebrated Robert G. Ingersoll in the Davis will case, Hicks, Famous Jury Speeches 216–29 (1925). Col. Ingersoll concluded this part of his interpretation of the traces on the document: "Take up your table of logarithms and figure away until you are blind, and such an accident could not happen in as many thousand, billion, trillion, quintillion years as you can express by figures." (The jury hung, and the case was compromised).

41. The term itself is used with various meanings. See Nagel, The Meaning of Probability, in 2 The World of Mathematics 1398 (Newman ed. 1956). In the text of this section we speak of the probability of an event or events, because it is customary; strictly speaking, probability is a quality which attaches to propositions about events. Nagel, op. cit. supra, at 1406: "Thus when we seem to talk about the probability of an event we are simply talking inaccurately although conveniently about the probability of a proposition stating the occurrence of that event."

42. Mutual independence is essential to this simple version of the rule. It means that the probability of B is unaffected by the occurrence of A, and vice versa. This product rule was developed to solve questions involving games of chance, such as the

taining a head in a toss of coin A is one-half, and of obtaining a head in a toss of coin B is one-half, then when they are tossed independently and simultaneously, the probability of obtaining two heads is the product of these individual probabilities, or one-fourth. On the frequency theory of probability, which is usually appealed to (expressly or tacitly) in the cases, this means that in the long run, approximately one-fourth of the simultaneous tosses will produce two heads.

Given similar assumptions, the probability of the co-occurrence of any number of events can be calculated, with an ease which must be a partial explanation of the popularity of this form of the product rule in efforts to quantify the probative force of circumstantial evidence.

In a leading case,[43] for example, there was evidence from which the jury might have found that the couple committing a robbery and the couple on trial possessed, at the time in question, the characteristics listed below. The prosecution asked a college mathematics teacher to assume the individual probabilities shown below for them, to assume that they were mutually independent, and then to explain and apply the product rule.[44]

Characteristic	Individual Probability
A. Partly yellow automobile	1/10
B. Man with mustache	1/4
C. Girl with ponytail	1/10
D. Girl with blond hair	1/3
E. Negro man with beard	1/10
F. Interracial couple in car	1/1000

The expert did so, and gave 1/12,000,000 as the probability of the concurrence in a single couple (called by one critic a "magic couple"), of all of the characteristics. In argument, the prosecutor treated this as being the probability that a couple other than the defendants had committed the crime, leaving a probability of 11,999,999/12,000,-000 that the couple on trial were guilty.[45]

All the reported cases on this subject have exhibited some or all of the characteristics of this case, and analysis of it will indicate the problems involved. In reversing the conviction for admission of this testimony and for permitting the argument based on it, the

coin-tossing experiment which follows; and the assumption of independence was justified by long experience of such games. In the court cases being discussed, independence has usually been assumed by the offeror without noticing it, or explained as assumed because nothing was known to the contrary.

Notice that "A and B are mutually independent" means that in lawyer's terms A and B are "irrelevant" to one another; and that courts seem to make such an assumption in their rulings that evidence A, offered to prove fact B, is inadmissible unless A appears to be relevant to B. Absent any information as to the dependence of B on A, the courts exclude A as irrelevant, thus producing results which agree at all points with those produced by assuming A and B are independent when nothing to the contrary is known.

43. People v. Collins, 68 Cal.2d 319, 438 P.2d 33, 66 Cal.Rptr. 497, 36 A.L.R.3d 1176 (1968) (annotated briefly on this point). The case has generated substantial commentary, most of which reviews the earlier cases. See, e. g., Broun and Kelly, Playing the Percentages and the Law of Evidence, 1970 Ill. L.F. 23; Cullison, Identification by Probabilities and Trial by Arithmetic, 6 Houston L.Rev. 471 (1969); Finklestein and Fairley, A Bayesian Approach to Identification Evidence, 83 Harv.L.Rev. 489 (1970); Kingston, Probability and Legal Proceedings, 57 J.Crim.L.C. & P.S. 93 (1966); Liddle, Mathematical and Statistical Probability as a Test of Circumstantial Evidence, 19 Case W.Res.L.Rev. 254 (1968); Stoebuck, Relevancy and Probability,

51 Iowa L.Rev. 849 (1966); Tribe, Trial by Mathematics, 84 Harv.L.Rev. 329 (1971); Note, 50 Minn. L.Rev. 745 (1966).

44. There was some question as to whether these were the only factors and individual probabilities discussed, but the prosecutor settled on these in argument, and a table of these was displayed in the trial court.

45. At one point the prosecutor after stating that his estimates were conservative, urged that "the chance of anyone else besides these defendants being there, . . . having every similarity, . . . is somewhat like one in a billion."

The "magic couple" designation is used by Cullison, op. cit. supra, n. 43.

court pointed to the following grounds of objection:

(1) There was no foundation in the record, statistical or otherwise, for the choice of any of the individual probabilities assumed.[46]

(2) There was no basis for the assumption that the individual probabilities were mutually independent. On the contrary, some of the characteristics were so defined that they clearly included and were therefore interdependent with parts of the rest.[47]

(3) There was an error in the transfer of meaning by which the prosecutor took the probability of the concurrence of all the characteristics and treated it as the probability that the criminals and the defendants were different couples, thus claiming odds of almost 12 million to one that they were the same magic couple and therefore guilty.[48]

(4) In addition, the court pointed out that the prosecution's calculations began by hypothesizing that the couple committing the crime actually had all of the characteristics, a proposition to which it said no quantified probability could be assigned, thus facing the jury with the task of combining the prosecution's numbers with other, non-numerical probabilities.[49] In general, and apart from the actual errors in the technique, the court stated that the jury and the defense were not able to cope with the "mystique of the mathematical demonstration." Early in the opinion, it had said that "Mathematics, a veritable sorcerer in our computerized society, while assisting the trier of fact in the search for truth, must not cast a spell over him." Although the court treated the task of combining numerical and nonnumerical probabil-

---

46. The prosecutor's insistence that his estimates were "conservative" seems not to have reached the point of a request that the court take judicial notice, or allow jury notice, that the actual probabilities, whatever they might be, were at least as low as his estimates. The opinion does not consider whether this could ever be done. See § 332, infra.

47. The court noted that Negroes with beards and men with mustaches obviously overlapped, and inspection of the list shows that many of the others are interconnected by definition, especially F., which carried much of the result.

48. This error, and the one of assuming independence, have had a large vogue and great durability. What the prosecutor attempted was precisely described, with approval, in the first edition of the present work. It was not stated, however, whether it should be employed in argument only, or whether an expert giving testimony should be included. See also, Wigmore, The Science of Judicial Proof at 270 (3d ed. 1937); Osborn, Problems of Proof, 439–445 (1926). The passage from Osborn begins: "Even if this person is looked for in a city containing six millions of people, it can be shown how he can be identified with reasonable accuracy. For purposes of illustration *let it be assumed that these people are all available for examination.*" (Emphasis supplied). It is also assumed that the criminal comes from the six millions; and then suggested that if enough permanent characteristics of the criminal are known, and the entire population examined, we may eliminate all but one candidate. This method resolves all problems of dependence,

probability estimates, sample size, etc., by determining the entire matter by visual inspection. The procedure he approves for use when the entire population of interest is not available for examination would seem to be that used by the prosecutor in the *Collins* case. See Osborn, Questioned Documents 225–236, 596–599 (2d ed. 1929).

49. The court apparently assumed that jurors would not or could not attach any quantities to their own estimates of probabilities, or employ concepts such as "greater than" and "less than." Other courts have shown a preference for non-numerical estimates. See the history of Bertram v. Wunning, 385 S.W.2d 803 (Mo.App.1965); 417 S.W.2d 120 (Mo.App.1967), in which the court held insufficient a physician's statement that there was a 90 percent probability that an accident caused a hernia, and then approved "to a reasonable medical certainty" given at a subsequent trial. His response on cross-examination the second time, that "To me [90 percent is] reasonable medical certainty," was said to go to weight, not sufficiency.

Compare Simon, Judges' Translations of Burdens of Proof into Statements of Probability, 13 Trial Lawyer's Guide 29 (1969), stating that a sample of trial judges were almost unanimously opposed to instructions on the burdens in numerical terms. (Such instructions would of course, apply to every juror, and to his final conclusion). Suggestions as to how experts could help jurors become "more Bayesian" are made in the Finklestein and Fairley, A Bayesian Approach to Identity Evidence, 83 Harv.L.Rev. 489 (1970), and criticized in Tribe, Trial by Mathematics, 84 Harv.L.Rev. 1329 (1971); Broun and Kelly, Playing the Percentages and the Law of Evidence, 1970 U.Ill.L.F. 23.

ities as extremely difficult for the average juror (and defense counsel), it can hardly have meant it was impossible in every case. The facts which experts are asked to treat as true in a hypothetical question are frequently themselves in great doubt; and to hold that they must be conclusively established before the expert can quote any numbers himself would be to upset many decided cases.[50] The fourth objection must be treated as applicable only in very limited circumstances.

Most of the prior cases, in rejecting such testimony, had relied on the first reason stated above.[51] The second and third points represent a new and further analysis of the problem. Clearly, if the individual events are not independent, the form of the product rule which the state used was not applicable and produced incorrect results. A different form, requiring knowledge of the amount of dependence, would be required.[52]

50. See, for instance, People v. Trujillo, 32 Cal.2d 105, 194 P.2d 681 (1948) and People v. Jordan, 45 Cal.2d 697, 290 P.2d 484 (1955); which the *Collins* opinion expressly left undisturbed. Although the *Jordan* opinion mentions no numerical estimates, Houts, From Evidence to Proof 134 (1956) asserts that odds of one in 1,280,000,000 were quoted. See also Moore v. Tremelling, 78 F.2d 821 (9th Cir. 1935); Davis v. St. Louis S. W. Ry., 106 F. Supp. 547 (W.D.La.1962); Arthurs v. National Postal Transp. Ass'n, 49 Wash.2d 570, 304 P.2d 685 (1956); Anton v. Chicago, M. & St. P. Ry., 92 Wash. 305, 159 P. 115 (1916).

51. People v. Risley, 214 N.Y. 75, 108 N.E. 200 (1915) was a prosecution for offering in evidence a typewritten document, knowing that it had been fraudulently altered by the insertion of two words. At the trial the state offered as an expert witness a professor of mathematics, who testified about the probability against the appearance of seven particular identifying traits which appeared in the typing of the inserted words, all of which corresponded to defects in a typewriter possessed by the accused. He likewise testified that multiplying these separate odds, "the probability of these defects being reproduced by the work of a typewriter other than the machine of defendant, was one in four thousand million." The conviction was reversed for the admission of this evidence. The holding may be justified on the ground of the lack of qualification of the witness to testify to the underlying facts as to the odds against the appearance of each particular defect. As to argument on the matter, see the following remarks of Seabury, J., dissenting: "Common sense at once recognizes how remote is the probability that all of these defects should recur in these six identical letters in any other typewriter. Indeed, if the district attorney, basing his argument upon matters of common knowledge and the general perception of all men, had pointed out that there was not one chance in four thousand millions that these identical defects would be found in these identical six letters of another typewriter, he would, I think, have been within his rights. Substantially the same statement did not become prejudicial because it is made by one learned in the higher mathematics."

The question of independence was ignored throughout. The court further held that evidence of probability could be used, in any form, only when future events were in issue, a distinction patently untenable, and not adopted in the other cases. See Ball, The Moment of Truth: Probability Theory and Standards of Proof, 14 Vand.L.Rev. 807, 815 (1961); Tribe, Trial By Mathematics, 84 Harv.L.Rev. 1329, 1344 (1971). In State v. Sneed, 76 N.M. 349, 414 P.2d 858 (1966), noted extensively in 1967 Duke L.J. 665, the slight statistical evidence of individual probabilities was held inadequate (independence was not discussed); and a similar result was reached in Miller v. State, 240 Ark. 340, 399 S.W.2d 268 (1966).

52. This form requires us to know (or assume) the conditional probability of each individual event, given the occurrence of one or more of the other events, thus expressing the amount of dependence. For three events, A, B, and C, to compute the probability of the co-occurrence of all of them, the probability of A is multiplied by the probability of B given A, and this result is multiplied by the probability of C given A and B. The complexity of the inquiry when the number of events is considerable is obvious. So far as statistical inquiry is concerned, it may be easier to investigate the probability of the compound event ABC directly, than to bother with attempting to find each of the needed conditional probabilities. So long as the conditional probabilities are unknown, the most that can be said is that the probability of ABC cannot be greater than the smallest of the individual probabilities of its components, a rather unrewarding result (it would have left the *Collins* prosecutor with an estimate that there were no more than 12,000 magic couples). As indicated, the popularity of the simple product rule may lie in its (often tacit and unwarranted) assumption of independence, which means assuming that the probability of each individual event is unaffected by the occurrence or non-occurrence of any or all of the others. To use the "magic couple" setting, the prosecution assumed that the probability that a person was a Negro man with a beard would be unaffected by a prior determination that he was a man with a mustache. In frequency terms, this assumed that the proportion of Negro men with

As to the third point, although the prosecution was not clear about it, one way of looking at its calculations is to treat them (as the court did) as producing a number representing a "mathematical expectation," i. e., as the expected number of magic couples (one) in a supposed random sample of 12,000,000 couples if, as to each couple, the individual probabilities of possessing characteristics were as the prosecution assumed. On a frequency basis, this "expectation" is the *average* number of magic couples per sample that would be found in a long series of such samples containing 12,000,000 couples each.[53] Some samples would contain no magic couples, some one, some two, some three, and so on.[54] The prosecution was required to assume that the jury would find that its hypothetical population contained one magic couple (the criminals); so that in assessing the probability of identity, the proportion of samples which would contain no magic couple must be eliminated from consideration, and only the probabilities of other numbers of such couples must be compared. In its appendix containing this discussion, the court showed that in a sample of 12,000,000 couples, which contains one magic couple, the probability that it also contains more than one is about 41 percent.[55]

---

beards among men with mustaches was the same as the proportion of Negro men with beards among men without mustaches.

53. For discussions of the question involved in this concept, see Broun and Kelly, note 43, supra, at 43; Finklestein and Fairley, note 43, supra, at 493; Tribe, note 43, supra, at 1337. No sampling was ever done, and the state's idea of allowing for error in all its estimates was to invite the jury to substitute other individual probabilities. The question was, however: what was the margin of error in the prosecutor's final conclusion that there was only one magic couple in the supposed 12 millions of couples? The court's approach to that question is the one discussed, but any approach would have to concede some probability that the "expectation" of one couple per 12 million was imprecise, and therefore some probability that in fact the body of people involved contained some other number of magic couples. A juror who substituted his own individual estimates and applied the product rule to produce a compound probability of one magic couple per 600,000 couples was entitled to return with it to the prosecution's concession that the population involved was 12 million couples, and estimate the number of magic couples in it as 20; with obvious effects on his view of identity. See Broun and Kelly, op. cit. supra, at 44. But a juror who did not take this last step might, on the prosecution's argument, have thought that the difference between 600,000 to one and 12 million to one was not important for action purposes; see note 45, supra.

54. Using an approximation due to Poisson, which is close when the sample is very large and the probability of the occurrence of a "magic couple" very small, we can determine that when the average number of such couples in samples of 12 million is one, almost 37 percent of the samples will have no magic couple, almost 37 percent will have only one, about 18 percent will have two, six percent will have three, less than two percent will have four, and the rest more than four. See Cullison, Identification by Probabilities and Trial By Arithmetic, 6 Houston L.Rev. 471 (1969). These can then be treated (as the court did) as the probabilities that there were those numbers of couples.

55. To use the numbers of the preceding note, we are comparing the probabilities given, after dropping the 37 percent of samples containing no magic couple. We then have, of the remaining 63 percent, 37 percent probability of only one couple, and 26 percent probability of more than one, and $^{26}\!/_{63}$ is 41 percent, agreeing with the court's result.

The analysis in the court's opinion reached so far beyond anything determinable in the prosecutor's evidence and argument as to make the matter academic; but it may be noted that the court may have overstated its own argument here. If, as the court assumed *arguendo*, the criminals came from the 12 million sample, were correctly seen by the witnesses to be a magic couple, and then faded back into the sample, and if the police, by a random search of the sample, produced a magic couple, the situation seems to be as follows: If there were only one magic couple, the police produced the criminals; but if there were more, the probability that they had the right couple was not zero, as the court seems to assume. If there were two, then given the assumptions there was a probability of ½ that the police had the right one, if three, then ⅓, and so on. (This ignores, of course, the idea that the criminals might hide and the other couples not, and all the other factors likely to make the search not truly random). The matter, using Poisson's approximation, becomes an exercise in conditional probabilities, in which the probability that the sample contained one couple can be multiplied by the probability that the police were right, given that there was only one, and so on. See note 52, supra. The overall chance that the police had the right couple then would be viewed as about 77 percent, rather than the court's 59. No doubt it would have considered this still insufficient to sup-

Conceding that the appropriate sample size (the number of couples that might have committed the crime) was unknown, the court suggested strongly that it might never be knowable,[56] and used, as the prosecution seemed willing to use the 12 millions. It treated the probability of identity as 59 percent,[57] and held that to be an inadequate foundation for an argument in favor of conviction. In their distorted form, and with their lack of foundation, the testimony of the expert and the associated argument were held to be reversible error.

The case is notable as the first to deal explicitly with the questions of independence and sample size, and to detect the fallacy of confusing the probability of concurrence of the identifying marks with the probability of mistaken identification.

In areas in which statistical studies of samples can be made, criminalistics experts have made efforts to obtain counts of frequency of occurrence of particular characteristics, to support their estimates of the probabilities of individual characteristics.[58]

In the reported cases, little account of sampling error seems to have been taken, and in almost all, no investigation of the dependence conditions has been made. Likewise, almost all of them seem to present the error of substituting the alleged small probability of co-occurrence of the set of characteristics into the place of the probability that the persons or things are nonidentical.[59]

In the frequent cases where the expert has the two sets of characteristics in hand for comparison, such as cloth fibers, paint chips, hairs, or sweepings, a different problem enters the picture. In a recent murder case,[60] the expert had particles from the victim's clothing and from the defendant's car and clothing before him, seeking evidence of cross-transfer between them. He scanned the particles visually and selected an unstated number of pairs as similar. Of these

port an argument for conviction, a view shared by the trial judges in Simon, op. cit., supra note 49.

56. The court's whole enterprise depends critically upon this point, since with the probability of occurrence of a magic couple fixed, the chance that more than one will be found in a smaller sample falls off considerably. If the sample could be limited to 1,200,000 couples, then the Poisson approximation would yield odds of about 90 to 5, or a probability of 95 percent that there was only one magic couple; and the chance that the police had the right one would be about 97 percent (given all the assumptions mentioned). For more extended discussion of the arithmetic see Cullison, Identification by Probabilities and Trial by Arithmetic, 6 Houston L.Rev. 471 (1969); Kingston, Probability and Legal Proceedings, 57 J.Crim.L.C. & P.S. 93 (1966) (a different approximation); Note, 50 Minn.L.Rev. 745 (1966).

57. Strictly, 59 percent was the probability of nonduplication, rather than identity; see note 55, supra.

58. As examples, see Biassotti, Characteristics of Fired Bullets, 4 J.For.Sci. 34 (1959); Burd and Kirk, Clothing Fibers as Evidence, 32 J.Crim.L.C. & P.S. 353 (1942); Kingston and Kirk, The Use of Statistics in Criminalistics, 55 J.Crim.L.C. & P.S. 514 (1964). Many of the early gathering efforts re-

sponded to the doctrine of the early cases, treating the problem as one of building a base for estimates of individual probabilities and assuming that the "product rule" would do the rest. Recent work shows realization of the dimensions of the problem, see Kirk and Kingston, Evidence Evaluation and Problems in General Criminalistics, 9 J.For.Sci. 434 (1964), and comment, 59 Calif.L.Rev. 997 (1971), reinforcing the insight shown in Leibniz's letter to Bernoulli in 1703: "The calculation of probabilities is of the utmost value, but in statistical inquiries there is need not so much of mathematical subtlety as of a precise statement of all the circumstances." Quoted in Keynes, A Treatise on Probability 368 (Torchbook ed. 1962).

59. Counsel, and legal writers, must share some of the blame for this; see the remark of the eminent statistician Dr. W. Edwards Deming: "When a lawyer acts as his own statistician, the performance is about what you would expect from a statistician who acts as his own lawyer," quoted in Carter, Flora, Van Bowen, and Myers, Statistics and The Virginia Blood Test Statute, 56 Va.L.Rev. 349, 357 (1970). We should be used to such strictures by now; Dr. Harvey, the great British scientist, said of Bacon's *Novum Organum* that "he wrote on science like a Lord-chancellor." Quoted in Pierce, Essays in the Philosophy of Science 4 (Tomas ed. 1957). And, it can be added, when a criminalist acts as his own statistician, the results are not guaranteed. Kirk and Kingston, Evidence Evaluation and Problems in General Criminalistics, 9 J.For.Sci. 434 (1964).

60. State v. Coolidge, 109 N.H. 403, 260 A.2d 547 (1969) reversed on other grounds, Coolidge v. New Hampshire, 403 U.S. 443 (1971).

he selected 40 pairs for further testing, and found 27 matches, or pairs which were similar in all respects tested. He testified that he concluded that the pairs were mutually independent; [61] and using statistics gathered on other sweepings which indicated that the probability of finding a match in pairs coming from different sources [62] was 1/10, he used the product rule to conclude that the probability of the pairs coming from different sources was 1 over 10 to the 27th power. No point was made of the fact that given his original hypotheses, the probability of finding 27 *or more* matches, not exactly 27, is the one to be sought, nor that the expected number of matches depends upon the number of candidates for a match that are examined.[63] To use the setting of the "magic couple" case, the likelihood that different couples will possess a specified number of characteristics in common depends not only on the frequency of occurrence of the individual characteristics and upon their degree of mutual independence, but upon the number of couples in which the pair is sought, and the number of characteristics searched.

These questions have implications far beyond the cases in which they have been raised.[64] It is clear that in identification questions, the place of probability theory, or of statistical inference, as the basis of the opinions of experts themselves, or as a course of education for jurors in how to think in the jury room, will not be settled for some time to come.[65]

---

61. On cross-examination he conceded that the pairs "may not have been wholly independent." In this state of the testimony the court held that the concession went to the weight rather than the admissibility of his opinion. This seems correct, since any empirical determination of independence would have to contain some margin of error.

62. An advance over inquiries solely into the frequency of occurrence of characteristics. Nothing is said in the opinion about the frequency of matches when the particles are known to be from the same source; it would seem to be these two distributions that need to be compared, not only as to average number of matches, but as to their dispersions around those averages, to obtain an estimate of the likelihood that the case was one of common source or different source. See Biassotti, Characteristics of Fired Bullets, 4 J.For.Sci. 34 (1959), for an experiment comparing the percentage and numbers of certain kinds of matching lines for known same-gun and different-gun situations, but not evaluating the dispersions.

63. For discussion of these points see Broun and Kelly, Playing the Percentages and the Law of Evidence, 1970 U.Ill.L.F. 23, 47; Tribe, Trial by Mathematics, 84 Harv.L.Rev. 1329, 1342 n. 40 (1971), both suggesting considerable reductions in the estimate for the probability of different source (one leaving it 32 times as large as the other). Broun and Kelly compute that if 300 pairs were searched, the expected number of matches would be about 30. Neither article considers the effect of the possibility that the expert determined his original probabilities by searching unit quantities of particles, using the very same selecting and testing process that he used in the case.

An interesting example of this selection process is described in The Howland Will Case, 4 Am.L.Rev.

625 (1870), where one party, using 100 signatures of President John Quincy Adams, found about 20 which "covered" more closely than the alleged traced forgery and the exemplar in issue. See also, the discussion of the *Dreyfus* case in Tribe, supra, at 1332.

64. Although they seem to have refrained (except in the Howland Will Case, supra, note 63, and People v. Risley, supra, note 51) from testifying to numbers it is obvious that in documents examination, ballistics, and fingerprint cases, for example, the experts draw their conclusions of same source and different source from the similarities and dissimilarities they observe, and that they must be influenced by experience of the rarity or otherwise of the characteristics they examine. It is also clear that some of them have made calculations using the product rule. See Osborn, Questioned Documents 225–236, 596–599 (2d ed. 1929); Cherrill, Fingerprints Never Lie 40, 89 (1954).

Osterburg, An Inquiry into the Nature of Proof, 9 J.For.Sci. 413, 420–26 (1964) presents results of a survey indicating that experience does not produce very close agreement among fingerprint experts as to the rarity of particular print characteristics; their views as to independence were not surveyed.

65. In the short run, the chief use may be to attempt to deflate some of the astronomical figures previously used, and to expose on cross-examination whether any errors underlie a seemingly innocuous general conclusion. What can be done with more careful statistical work remains to be seen. Surely the identification of criminals, as in *Collins*, on the basis of beards, mustaches and hair styles, would not seem the most promising field of statistical inquiry.

One area in which the independence or otherwise of various characteristics and the frequencies of oc-

It should be re-emphasized, however, that none of these difficulties touches the relevancy of traces or characteristics as evidence of identity. Each characteristic possessed in common, so long as it is not universal and not completely dependent upon some other one also used, eliminates some possibilities otherwise open, and thus raises by some amount the probability of identity. The statistical arguments rage only over attempts to say through experts, by how much (numerically) that probability is raised, and where it stands when the evidence is weighed. Nor do these cases mean that evidence may not be introduced which shows a characteristic to be rare, or that counsel may not appeal in argument to the jury's general experience and urge conclusions on them, so long as he does not try to place a scientific seal of approval on results not shown to be scientifically based.

currence have been extensively investigated, is that of inherited factors of human blood. It seems likely that in blood-typing cases, some limit could be set on the "population" involved, which could lead to useful evaluations of weight of this evidence; not by comparing a known person against a "random man," but by helping to decide the likelihood that any other such person exists in that limited population. Mere comparison with a random man is relevant to identity, but it will not alone give the weight, or probability of identity, as all the commentators on the *Collins* case have agreed. See n. 53, supra, pointing out that a juror using the methods offered by the prosecutor could decide that the defendants were 600,000 times more likely to be the criminals than a random couple would be, and yet correctly estimate the probability of identity at only $\frac{1}{20}$. Unfortunately, even in the blood-type field, the distinction is not always observed. See Sussman, Blood Grouping Tests 83 (1968); Note, 3 U.S.F.L.Rev. 297, 302–303 (1969). Compare the more careful Dodd, The Scope of Blood Grouping Tests, 9 Med.Sci. & Law 56, 58–59 (1969). After working out an interesting comparison in which the putative father, through independent assortment of his known genes, had a probability of 0.5 to the 4th power of contributing the needed blood factors, while a random man had a probability of 0.21 x 0.46 x 0.41 x 0.58 x 0.05 of performing the same feat, the author states: "The balance of probabilities works out 60 to 1 in favor of a sperm from Mr. R;" but adds, "It is very important to realize that the mathematical probability based on these calculations is not, in the strict sense, the probability of paternity

205. Questioned Documents.[66]

The process of identifying by witnesses the authorship of a letter, deed or other writing may be carried through at various levels. At one level the proponent has the simple task of prima facie authentication of the writing as the writing of X, to secure its admission. Here all you need is someone who has enough knowledge of the general character of X's manner of writing to be able to say, "This looks like X's handwriting." If he has seen X write, or has corresponded with him and claims to know his writing, that is enough.[67]

of the alleged father. It is rather the chance the named man has of producing a sperm with the requisite characters compared with the chance of obtaining a suitable sperm from the random population . . ." Even this last depends on how large that population is. On the other hand, Mr. R. should not be cavalierly dismissed from consideration simply because he can perform the needed genetic feat only 6 percent of the time. If we can reduce the possible fathers to Mr. R. and one other (Mr. S., an otherwise equally likely candidate about whose blood nothing specific is ascertainable), the 60 to 1 odds would apply, and we might reasonably conclude (98 percent probability) that this case was one of the concededly rare occasions on which Mr. R. succeeded, because "not R." means Mr. S. Indeed, so long as the list of possible fathers is held below 61, we can use the theorem of Rev. Bayes, which is applicable here, to estimate that it is more probable than not that Mr. R. is the father on this set of facts. There may be, as with the clothing particles in *Coolidge*, a question of the number of attempts, a matter not discussed by Dodd. Bayes's Theorem is discussed at length in Finklestein and Fairley, op. cit. supra, n. 43.

66. 7 Wigmore, Evidence §§ 1991–2028; Baker, Law of Disputed and Forged Documents (1955); Conway, Evidential Documents (1959); Harrison, Suspect Documents (1958); Hilton, Scientific Examination of Questioned Documents (1956); A. S. Osborn, Questioned Documents (2d ed. 1929); A. S. and A. D. Osborn, Questioned Documents Problems (1944); Baxter, The Use and Abuse of Documents, 9 Med.Sci. & Law 39 (1969); Dec.Dig. Criminal Law ⚖=452(4), 458, 478(2), 491, 494, Evidence, ⚖=474(14), 480, 511, 561–567, 568(3). An extensive Questioned Documents Bibliography is contained in 20 Am.Jur. Proof of Facts 335–373.

67. Butler v. State, 38 Ala.App. 527, 93 So.2d 441 (1956), cert. denied 265 Ala. 694, 93 So.2d 445 (1957) ("looks to be"); see § 221, supra. The unreliability of this kind of testimony in distinguishing genuine from simulated handwriting is interest-

The second stage is the situation where there is a real dispute as to the genuineness of the writing, but the parties either because the amount involved is small or because they are ignorant of the power and resources of professional document examiners of the highest class, content themselves with secondary experts, such as a bank cashier,[68] or a long-time principal of a business college and teacher of handwriting.[69] It has been said that these may qualify by study without practice or by practice without study.[70] The sideline or part-time expert is of course much superior to the layman who has only a general acquaintance with the person's style of writing. The secondary expert by comparing the questioned writing with samples of genuine writings [71] before the jury may give substan-

tial assistance in reaching a just result. Nevertheless the gulf between the "second best" handwriting expert and the professional document examiner of good standing [72] is so wide that when the client's purse and the amount at stake will justify it, the conscientious and well-informed lawyer will insist on submitting the facts to such an examiner for his opinion, before accepting responsibility for trying the issue.

At this third level where one of the parties has the benefit of the testimony of a full-time accredited examiner of documents, the scientific method, in the investigation of the facts, in the preparation of the exhibits for analysis and comparison, and in the explanation of the reasons for the conclusion, is seen at its best. The many standard works on document examination [73] discuss, with illustrations, the various aspects of examination: the circumstances surrounding the writing and the writer or alleged writer (including his mental and physical characteristics); writing skill; systems of penmanship; speed, freedom and regularity of movement; letter sizes, proportion, and arrangement; strokes and pressure; number of lifts; characteristics of copying and tracing; and characteristics of use of particular writing instruments. Analysis of ink, paper, and subject matter may show the age of the document

---

ingly demonstrated in these articles: Inbau, Lay Witness Identification of Handwriting (An Experiment), 34 Ill.L.Rev. 433 (1939); Hilton, The Detection of Forgery, 30 J.Crim.L. & Criminology 568 (1939).

68. State v. Wickett, 230 Iowa 1182, 300 N.W. 268 (1941); Continental Royalty Co. v. Marshall, 239 S.W.2d 837 (Tex.Civ.App.1951).

69. First Galesburg Nat. Bank v. Federal Reserve Bank, 295 Ill.App. 524, 15 N.E.2d 337 (1938); and see the discussion of the requirements in Lewis v. State, 469 P.2d 689 (Alaska 1970) (rejection of defendant's expert reversed).

70. Fenias v. Reichenstein, 124 N.J.L. 196, 11 A.2d 10 (1940) (commissioner of registration and his assistants who were shown to have compared thousands of signatures each year and to have had experience in comparing voters' signatures were competent to testify concerning genuineness of signatures on petition).

71. The use of specimens of genuine handwriting for comparison with the disputed document is, of course, almost essential for the formation and explanation of an opinion as to genuineness. To avoid "collateral issues" the earlier practice required that the specimens be limited to writings already in the case (e. g., signatures to pleadings or bonds) or those admitted by the adversary to be genuine. This has been liberalized in England and most states, by statute or decision, to permit the use of specimens proved to the judge's satisfaction to be genuine. United States v. Garelle, 438 F.2d 366 (2d Cir. 1970); French v. United States, 232 F.2d 736 (5th Cir. 1956); In re McGowan's Will, 235 N.C. 404, 70 S.E.2d 189 (1952); 7 Wigmore, Evidence §§ 2015–16; Bohn, Admissibility of Standard Writings, 10 J.For.Sci. 441 (1965); Annot.,

41 A.L.R.2d 578, 72 A.L.R.2d 1274; Dec.Dig. Criminal Law 491, Evidence ☞197, 564. The texts of many of the statutory provisions are set out in Baker, Law of Disputed and Forged Documents § 69 (1955). F.R.Ev. (R.D.1971) 901(b) (3) adopts the same standard as for authentication generally.

72. A Kentucky judge marked the difference when in describing the experts called by one party, he said, " . . . one has made the study of handwriting his vocation while to the others it is but an avocation, to one it is his work to the others it is a diversion, one makes it his business the others make it a sideline." Drury, C., in Polley v. Cline's Ex'r, 263 Ky. 659, 93 S.W.2d 363, 368 (1936).

73. E. g., Conway, Evidential Documents (1959); Harrison, Suspect Documents (1958); Hilton, Scientific Examination of Questioned Documents (1956); Osborn, Questioned Documents (2d ed. 1929).

and help to identify illegible writings and fraudulent erasures and alterations.[74]

Similar, and often more easily and certainly demonstrable, is the identification of the authorship of typewritten documents.[75] The make and age of the machine, the kind of paper, ribbon and ink used, may usually be readily identified. Then the particular machine used will be searched for, and then the person who operated it. As to the former, among the factors of individuality are the relation of each letter to the neighboring letters, its position in relation to the line of writing, the comparative weight of impression of the different sides of the letter, and finally defects or scars in the various letters. Due to the wear and imperfections of machine tools, no two machine products, such as a rifle barrel, a bolt or a pin will be precisely alike under the microscope, and accordingly, no two typefaces of different typewriters are exactly alike even when new. Wear and tear in use produce further marks of individuality in each typeface. As to the writer himself, he may be known by his habits of touch, spacing, speed, arrangement, punctuation and by vagaries in spelling and the like, as shown by comparison with samples of his writing.

The chief instruments of investigation are the microscope and the camera,[76] though these may be supplemented by chemical and other tests. In reaching his conclusions the examiner will prepare photographs, photomicrographs, or enlarged photographs of the disputed document and of the genuine writings used for comparison. For more graphic comparison, the corresponding parts of the disputed or genuine writings may be cut out and placed alongside each other in a detailed exhibit of comparative features. This kind of exhibit may be displayed by the expert witness to the court and jury as illustrative of his testimony.[77] They are usually essential to a convincing demonstration.

The professional examiner possessed of genuine qualifications will not claim more power than he has, i.e., if given adequate standards and adequate time and facilities for comparing these with the disputed writing, he can tell the false from the true. The secondary expert, whether honest or dishonest, may claim to be able to distinguish them on momentary inspection. It seems that any one who claims to be an expert should be subject to a testing of his claim on cross-examination by presenting him with

74. Note 73, supra; Hilton, Progress Challenges the Documents Examiner, 55 A.B.A.J. 753 (1969); Annot., 34 A.L.R.2d 619, 653, 11 A.L.R.3d 1015.

75. See Baker, op. cit., ch. 22; Conway, op. cit., 109–138; Harrison, op. cit., ch. 8; Hilton, op. cit., chs. 11, 12; A. S. Osborn, Questioned Documents, ch. 32 (2d ed. 1929); A. S. Osborn and A. D. Osborn, Questioned Document Problems, chs. 18, 19 (1944).

Some cases of questioned typewritten documents: Schertzinger v. Williams, 198 Cal.App.2d 242, 17 Cal.Rptr. 719 (1962) (documents compared by court); Harlan v. Blume, 190 S.W.2d 273 (Mo.App. 1945) (trial judge ordered photographs of disputed letters to be made, and apparently called a typewriter salesman and repairman to testify as to differences); In re Bundy's Estate, 153 Ore. 234, 56 P. 2d 313, 106 A.L.R. 714 (1936) (will contest; typewritten will, which daughter contended was typed in office of testator's lawyer was shown by expert to have been typed on daughter's own machine: good discussion by Rossman, J.); In re Cravens' Estate, 206 Okl. 174, 242 P.2d 135 (1952) (will contest; expert document examiner convinced court, contrary to testimony of attesters, that alterations were typed by different person from one who typed original will; court stresses need for expert in disputes over typewritten documents, and the feasibility of identifying writer of such a document) and see cases in Annot., 106 A.L.R. 721.

76. See 1 Scott, Photographic Evidence §§ 471–556 (2d ed. 1969), an invaluable treatise, graphically illustrated, written by a lawyer who is also a document examiner. For a case in which various techniques were applied, see Glass v. State, 361 P.2d 230 (Okla.Cr.1961).

77. State v. Thompson, 254 Iowa 331, 117 N.W.2d 514 (1962) (enlargement from microfilm); Republic Nat. Life Ins. Co. v. Chilcoat, 368 P.2d 821 (Okla. 1962) (enlarged photostat of check); Adams v. Ristine, 138 Va. 273, 122 S.E. 126, 31 A.L.R. 1413 (1924) (annotated; includes display of enlarged and "side-by-side" comparison photographs); Annot., 72 A.L.R.2d 308, 316.

true and fabricated writings and asking him to distinguish.[78] Since in fairness he may properly request time for examination and testing, the judge should have a discretion to say whether under the circumstances the test is worth the time it will take.

"When the half-gods go, the gods arrive." With the growing realization by lawyers of the scientific advances in the process of document identification, the courts are coming to give freer play to qualified examiners to give fully their reasons for their conclusions,[79] and to recognize that the reasoning in a particular case may amount to a demonstration so certain and convincing that it may overcome direct testimony of purported eyewitnesses to the contrary.[80]

---

78. The rulings have not been uniform, partly through confusion with the rule as to exemplars. See 7 Wigmore, Evidence § 2015; Hilton, Cross-Examination of Handwriting Expert by Test Problem, 13 Rutgers L.Rev. 306 (1958).

79. In re Varney, 22 F.2d 231, 236, 237 (E.D.Ky.1927); Venuto v. Lizzo, 148 App.Div. 164, 132 N.Y.S. 1066, (1911); State v. Young, 210 N.C. 452, 187 S.E. 561 (1936) (conviction reversed for judge's refusal to allow expert to give his reasons completely). The expert's opinion is valuable only as it is based upon satisfactory reasons. Greenstreet v. Greenstreet, 65 Idaho 36, 139 P.2d 239, 243 (1943); Nelson v. Nelson, 249 Iowa 638, 87 N.W.2d 767 (1958). In re Barrie, 393 Ill. 111, 65 N.E.2d 433 (1946) is a case where the court considered minutely the reasons given by the expert in the light of its inspection of the writing and declared them unfounded.

80. Cases emphasizing the possibility that expert testimony to forgery may outweigh eyewitness testimony to genuineness, at least when supported by circumstances: Boyd v. Gosser, 78 Fla. 64, 82 So. 758, 6 A.L.R. 500 (1918) (annotated; a striking fact case); cf. In re Krugle's Estate, 134 So.2d 860 (Fla. App.1961); Hoover v. Hoover, 238 Iowa 88, 26 N.W.2d 98 (1947); Reffert v. Hughes, 396 S.W.2d 786 (Ky.1965); Estate of Simon, 381 Pa. 284, 113 A.2d 266 (1955); In re Young's Estate, 347 Pa. 457, 32 A.2d 901, 154 A.L.R. 643 (1945) (annotated on this point); Adams v. Ristine, 138 Va. 273, 122 S.E. 126, 31 A.L.R. 1413 (1924). Contrast the cases where the direct testimony prevailed, such as Fraser v. Lewis, 187 So.2d 684 (Fla.App.1966); First Nat. Bank of Chicago v. Rovell, 51 Ill.App.2d 282, 201 N.E.2d 140 (1964); Wrights Ex'r. v. Simpson, 232 Ky. 148, 22 S.W.2d 583 (1929).

---

206. Miscellaneous Tests and Techniques Employed in Investigation.[81]

Many of the methods of identification and investigation employed in police laboratories have become widely known, such as fingerprinting,[82] examination of questioned writings,[83] identification of firearms by microscopic study of bullets and cartridges,[84] and chemical analysis of poisons and narcotics.[85]

---

81. The literature in this case has grown so large that specialized, rather than general works are the rule. Some broad efforts are: Richardson, Modern Scientific Evidence (1961); Scientific and Medical Evidence (symposium), 13 N.Y.L.F. 607 (1967). In the criminal investigation field, see Prosecutor's Sourcebook (George and Cohen eds. 1969) chs. 15, 16; Gross, Criminal Investigation (5th Jackson ed. 1962); Jones, Scientific Investigation and Physical Evidence (1959); O'Hara, Fundamentals of Criminal Investigation (1956); Turner, Investigating the Criminal Case, 1 Am.Jur.Trials 357, 359 (1964) and Investigating Particular Crimes, 2 Am.Jur. Trials 172 (1964); Jones, Locating and Preparing Evidence in Criminal Cases, 1 Am.Jur. Trials 555 (1964). For the civil case, descriptions of tests and techniques can be found in such works as Magarick, Investigating Particular Civil Cases, 2 Am.Jur. Trials 165 (1964); Accident Reconstruction (Reed and Needham eds. 1966); Lacy, Scientific Accident Reconstruction (1964); 1 Krumer and Friedman, Products Liability § 12 (1966); 2 Kreindler, Aviation Accident Law, chs. 24, 39 (1963); Goodman, Automobile Design Liability (1970). A work with applicability to both criminal and civil cases is Baker, Traffic Investigator's Manual (3d ed. 1957); and see Greenwald, Scientific Evidence in Traffic Cases, 59 Crim.L.C. & P.S. 57 (1968).

82. And other body prints. See 5 Am.Jur. Proof of Facts 77 (1960); Moenssens, Admissibility of Fingerprint Evidence, 40 Chi-Kent L.Rev. 85 (1963); Annot., 28 A.L.R. 1115, 72 A.L.R.2d 1267. For works of popularization, see Bloch, Fingerprinting (1969); Cherrill, Fingerprints Never Lie (1954).

Similar in their uses are other forms of tracks. See Annot., 23 A.L.R.2d 112 (tire tracks), 35 A.L.R.2d 856 (shoe prints); 1 Am.Jur. Trials 616 (1964) (tool marks).

One form of "print" which has so far failed to find unanimous acceptance in the courts is the "voice-print," discussed in § 203, supra.

83. See the preceding section.

84. See Mathews, Firearms Identification (1962); Davis, Firearms Identification (1958); Annot., 26 A.L.R.2d 892.

85. See, e. g., 13 Am.Jur. Proof of Facts 391 (1963) (tests for narcotic drugs); Freimuth, Toxicology in Medicolegal Investigations, 1969 Leg.Med.Annual 187.

Others less familiar may be important resources of the police in the search for the criminal or the proof of his guilt, such as tests of the hand of a suspect to determine whether he has shot a firearm;[86] microscopic,[87] spectrographic,[88] and neutron activation analysis[89] of hair, fibers, seminal stains, minute particles of glass, dust, dirt, seeds, scrapings, and fragments of paper, wood, and metal; and other traces.[90] The possibilities of detection and proof which may be achieved by the expert and imaginative use of these scientific techniques are revealed by many reported cases; and it is likely that many in which the most effective work was done did not reach the appellate courts.[91]

In recent years there has been increasing adaptation of the scientific techniques for use in civil cases. The question of uniquely identifying a person may not loom so large in such cases; but the determination of what events occurred, and their causes, effects, and other characteristics has left much room for scientific assistance of every description.[92]

86. Harrison and Gilroy, Firearm Discharge Residues, 4 J.For.Sci. 184 (1959). Older tests have been found insufficient for admissibility: Brooke v. State, 139 Colo. 388, 339 P.2d 993 (1959); Clarke v. State, 218 Tenn. 259, 402 S.W.2d 863 (1966) cert. denied 385 U.S. 942; Turkel and Lipman, Unreliability of Dermal Nitrate Test for Gunpowder, 46 J.Crim.L.C. & P.S. 281 (1955).

87. O'Neill, Police Microanalysis, 25 J.Crim.L. 674, 835 (1934–35).

88. 1 Am.Jur.Trials 506 (1964); Wilson, Spectrographic Analysis 25 J.Crim.L. 160 (1934).

89. On this new method, see Watkins and Watkins, Neutron Activation Analysis, 15 Am.Jur. Proof of Facts 115 (1964); Comment, 59 Calif.L.Rev. 997 (1971); United States v. Stifel, 433 F.2d 431 (5th Cir.1970) cert. denied, 401 U.S. 994 (1971).

90. See 1 Am.Jur. Trials 555, 687 (1964), in which Jones considers 40 trace categories.

91. People v. Nelson, 127 Ill.App.2d 238, 262 N.E.2d 225 (1970) (blood stains, chemical properties of putty, optical properties and refractive index of glass fragments to identify defendant); Ferrell v. Comm., 177 Va. 861, 14 S.E.2d 293 (1941) (murderer identified and convicted upon testimony of F. B. I. operative who compared plaster cast of heel-print with defendant's rubber heel, and testified to the methods used in identifying a shotgun shell found at the scene as having been fired from defendant's gun); State v. Clark, 156 Wash. 543, 287 Pac. 18 (1930) (assault on child by person who lay in wait under the shelter of a blind made of fir branches cut from surrounding trees; the cut sections of branches were examined under microscope and knife-markings on them corresponded identically with those made on similar wood cut by the knife found on accused; Magnuson v. State, 187 Wis. 122, 203 N.W. 749 (1925) (murder by time bomb sent in package by mail at Christmas time; investigation and proof covered handwriting and

spelling peculiarities of inscription on wrapper, analysis of glue, ink, wood and metal fragments by specialists to whom the materials were submitted by prosecutor; the case is a model of scientific investigation, and as the court says: " . . . it discloses what may be done by a diligent prosecuting officer who has an intelligent comprehension of the things that are necessary to establish guilt in a case of this importance."). See also Wigmore, Science of Judicial Proof § 158 (3d ed. 1937); and the illustrations given in the works cited in n. 81, supra.

92. Illustrative cases are: Bitton v. Int'l Transp., Inc., 437 F.2d 817 (9th Cir. 1970) (cause of gouge in highway—organic chemist with training in physics and geology); Barnes v. Omark Industries, Inc., 369 F.2d 4 (8th Cir. 1966) (nail fired by powder-actuated tool—engineers and ballistics expert); Skalon v. Manning, Maxwell & Moore, Inc., 127 Ill.App.2d 145, 262 N.E.2d 146 (1970) (failure of hook and hoist—mechanical engineer); Geismar v. General Gas Corp., 182 So.2d 769 (La.App.1966) (butane explosion—petroleum gas experts); Thornton v. First Nat'l Stores, Inc., 340 Mass. 222, 163 N.E.2d 264 (1960) (amount of rock salt required to melt ice under given conditions—chemist); Humble Oil & Ref. Co. v. Pittman, 210 Miss. 314, 49 So.2d 408 (1951) (damage by blasting—physicist and geologist); Hayes Creek Country Club v. Central Pa. Quarry Stripping and Constr. Co., 407 Pa. 464, 181 A.2d 301 (1962) (capacity of pipes to vent water—hydraulics engineer); Bolstad v. Egleson, 326 S.W.2d 506 (Tex.Civ.App.1959) (auto accident—accident analyst); Wilson v. Wright, 52 Wash.2d 805, 329 P.2d 461 (1958) (metal fatigue—metallurgist); Schwalbach v. Antigo Elec. & Gas, Inc., 27 Wis.2d 651, 135 N.W.2d 263 (1965) (gas explosion—mechanical engineer and designer of regulators). See 2 Am.Jur. Trials 585, 614 (1964) for additional illustrations.

One difficulty facing the lawyer in the civil case is determining the need for and value of a scientific expert, and locating him. On this question, the "how-to" books have labored manfully to fill the gap. See Kirk, Locating Scientific and Technical Experts, 2 Am.Jur. Trials 293 (1964); Gair, Selecting and Preparing the Expert Witness, 2 Am.Jur. Trials 585 (1964); Goodman, Automobile Design Liability (1970) Pt. 6; Davies, Finding an Expert Witness in the Sciences, 13 Clev.Mar.L.Rev. 309 (1964). Bibliographies and directories can be found in many of the works cited in n. 81 at the beginning of this section.

207. Detection of Deception: The Lie Detector.[93]

In most persons, as has always been popularly believed, lying and consciousness of guilt are accompanied by emotion or excitement that expresses itself in bodily changes, —the blush, the gasp, the quickened heartbeat, the clenched hand, the sweaty palm, the dry mouth. The skilled cross-examiner may face the witness with his lies and involve him in a knot of new ones, so that these visible signs of lying become apparent to the jury. This is part of the demeanor of the witness that the jury is told they may observe and consider upon credibility.[94]

Signs of internal stress accompanying deception are not always visible, and efforts have long been made to discover them in other ways.[95] In the present century techniques for measuring and recording some of these bodily changes with instruments were developed and the appliance now commonly used is called a polygraph.[96] By sensors connected to the person being questioned, a record is made on a moving chart of three channels of information: blood pressure and pulse, respiration, and galvanic skin reflex, or electrodermal response (connected with sweat-gland activity). Since unobserved muscular movement or pressure may affect blood pressure, means of detecting and recording these is added to some polygraphs.

The interrogation will first allow time for allowing the subject to quiet down, and for recording his individual general level of bodily activity. Then key questions relating to the crime or other happening (Did you rob the supermarket?) will be interpersed with neutral or irrelevant questions (Is today Wednesday?), so that the bodily reactions accompanying the two kinds of questions, and their answers, may be compared.[97]

It seems to be conceded that the instrument does measure the information channels

93. The following is a selection of more recent items from a voluminous legal literature. Many refer to the earlier (and to the nonlegal) sources. Reid and Inbau, Truth and Deception (1966); 3A Wigmore, Evidence § 999 (Chadbourn rev.); Academy Lectures on Lie Detection (Leonard ed. 1958); Use of Polygraphs as "Lie-Detectors" by the Federal Government, Hearings Before a Subcommittee of the House Committee on Government Operations, 88th Cong., 2d Sess., Pts. 1–5 (1964); Burack, Theory, Method and Limitations of the Lie-Detector, 46 J.Crim.L.C. & P.S. 414 (1955); Burkey, The Case Against the Polygraph, 51 A.B. A.J. 855 (1965); Herman, The Use of Hypno-Induced Statements in Criminal Cases, 25 Ohio St. L.J. 1 (1964) (includes the polygraph); Highleyman, The Deceptive Certainty of the "Lie Detector," 10 Hasting L.J. 47 (1958); Koffler, The Lie Detector, 3 N.Y.L.F. 123 (1957); Laymon, Lie Detectors, 10 S.D.L.Rev. 1 (1965); Levin, Lie Detectors Can Lie, 15 Lab.L.J. 708 (1964); Levitt, Scientific Evaluation of the Lie Detector, 40 Iowa L.Rev. 440 (1955); Skolnick, Scientific Theory and Scientific Evidence: An Analysis of Lie Detection, 70 Yale L.J. 694 (1961); Symposium, The Polygraphic Truth Test, 22 Tenn.L.Rev. 711 (1953); Notes, 21 Fla.L.Rev. 541 (1969), 2 Natural Resources J. 162 (1962), 13 N.Y.L.F. 679, 686 (1968), 20 S.C.L.Rev. 804 (1968), 4 Suffolk L.Rev. 111 (1969); Annot., 23 A.L.R.2d 1306, 95 A.L.R.2d 819.

94. See 3A Wigmore, Evidence § 946 (Chadbourn rev.); Dec.Dig. Witnesses ☞315, Illinois Pattern Instructions 2.01.

95. A description of some ancient methods, having a kernel of psycho-physiological basis, is given in

Langley, The Polygraph Lie Detector, 16 Ala. Lawyer 209–210 (1955).

In earlier days, our courts admitted evidence of the refusal of an accused to submit to a superstitious test of guilt, on the theory that a jury could find that he believed (however erroneously) in its efficacy; and that his refusal was an implied admission. See State v. Wisdom, 119 Mo. 539, 24 S.W. 1047 (1894); 2 Wigmore, Evidence § 276(3). A modern court's view of the same question as applied to the refusal of a witness to submit to a lie-detector test is State v. Mottram, 158 Me. 325, 184 A.2d 225 (1962) (inadmissible absent showing as to reason for refusal; earlier cases not discussed). Other cases ignore this possibility and treat the matter as turning on whether the test result would be admissible. Aetna Ins. Co. v. Barnett Bros., Inc., 289 F.2d 30 (8th Cir. 1961) (witness; inadmissible).

96. For a history and details of the instrument, see Reid and Inbau, Truth and Deception 1–10 (1966).

97. The drafting of the questions, conduct of the interrogation, and interpretation of the results is discussed in Reid and Inbau, n. 96, supra. It is, of course, much more complex than the text description here. A description of the polygraph examination given to Jack Ruby during the investigation of the assassination of President Kennedy is set forth in *Hearings*, supra, note 93, Pt. 5, at 561.

it is designed to monitor, namely the physiological changes.[98] However, such changes can accompany internal stress having as its cause something other than conscious insincerity. The interpretation by the polograph examiner, not only of the charts, but of the questions and answers they accompany, and the total interview situation, is the critical factor in arriving at any opinion that when giving particular answers the subject was making a conscious effort to deceive.[99] Clearly, nothing in the entire technique can show the underlying empirical truth in the sense of the facts occurring in the past; but only whether the person examined himself believed his answers.[1]

The interpreter, like the diagnostician, must, of course, possess the "feel" or intuition, which comes from training and experience, in order to reach accurate results; and this means that the results depend on his qualifications and his skill in drawing the necessary inferences.[2]

No one could reasonably contend that the lie-detector test should be conducted in the courtroom at the trial.[3] The conditions are too exciting, and the judge and jury are not competent to interpret the results. The issue then is, shall the examiner who conducted the test be permitted to give his testimony presenting the chart and explaining his conclusion as to whether the subject believed he was telling the truth or was consciously

---

98. Improvements in instrumentation seem to be possible; see *Hearings*, supra, note 1, Pt. 3, at 356–364; Reid and Inbau, supra, n. 93, at 264–274.

99. Even the production of the emotional stress indications recorded on the chart depends, to an undefined extent, on conditioning the person being examined to believe that the test will detect lying. This is recommended to be done by reiteration, Reid and Inbau, Truth and Deception 13, 26, 38 (1966), and even by a trick redolent of the parlor magician. Id. at 27, n. 36 and at 35. This is the card "test", in which the subject is instructed to lie about his chosen card, and the lie is "detected." This result is insured because "The cards are arranged and shown to the subject in such a way that the examiner will immediately know which card has been picked by the subject. The reasons for this are: (1) The card test record itself may not actually disclose the card lie; . . .". Compare the discussion of superstitious tests, n. 95, supra; and see Lee, The Instrumental Detection of Deception 222 (1953).

1. *Hearings*, supra, n. 98, at 290: "We have examined people in mental hospitals. If the patient said he was Napoleon, and if he believed this, the lie detector response indicated that he was telling the truth. All that the lie detector showed is that he believed what he was saying."; State v. Galloway, 167 N.W.2d 89 (Iowa 1969) (polygraph expert should not be allowed to phrase opinion in terms of "involved in the shooting").

The tendency of some polygraph examiners to use terms like "guilty" or "involved in," is sometimes due, apparently, to imprecision in language. In other cases, it may represent a different inference. One method used to differentiate stress-indications which are relevant to the investigation from those resulting from other causes, is to ask the examinee about some detail of the crime which investiga-

tion has shown would be unlikely to be known to an innocent and uninvolved person. Reid and Inbau, Truth and Deception §§ 37–40 (1966) ("which could not have been known by an innocent person or by anyone who had not been informed previously"). The ability of the subject to recognize and react especially to this detail, among a number which would all seem equally important to the uninformed, may lead the examiner to a conclusion not merely of an attempt to deceive, but of "possession of guilty knowledge," or "involvement in the crime," or even simply "guilt." While this is (justifiably) treated as more than simply insincerity, the inference is a commonsense one when all the evidence is presented, and there is no reason to allow the whole chain of conclusions to be enfolded in expertise. The expert opinion consists of the determination that this knowledge was shown, rather than what its possession proves.

2. As late as 1964, an authority in the field estimated that only about 20 percent of the persons operating as polygraph examiners were adequately qualified. *Hearings*, n. 93, supra at 8 (testimony of Prof. Inbau); cf. Bennett, A Penal Administrator Views the Polygraph, 24 Fed.Probation 40 (Dec. 1960) (six to twelve in the United States qualified). A few states have by statute provided for licensing and some standardization of qualifications of polygraph examiners. See *Hearings*, n. 93, supra, Pt. 1, at 123–132 (statutes from Illinois, Kentucky, New Mexico).

3. In State v. Cole, 354 Mo. 181, 188 S.W.2d 43 (1945) the accused requested the trial judge that a lie-detector might be used in examining the witnesses in court including the accused himself. In sustaining the denial of the request the court said, "Such dramatics before the jury would distract them and impede the trial."

lying in his answers to the crucial questions?

Since the first appellate decision [4] held in 1923 that a requirement of general scientific acceptance should be applied to such evidence, and that it had not been met, the appellate courts have ruled generally that the opinion and supporting data of the polygraph examiner are inadmissible when offered by either party, either as substantive evidence or as relating to the credibility of a witness.[5] Further, they have held that evidence that the test was administered or of the willingness or unwillingness of a witness or a party to submit to the test, is inadmissible.[6] Whether the original decision be properly construed as merely a refusal to take some sort of judicial notice or not, many of the subsequent cases have treated the precedent as if it had taken judicial notice of a proposition rendering the test results inadmissible, without regard to the foundation testimony offered in the particular case.[7]

In the numerous opinions and the large commentary, the principles underlying the

test, the qualifications and procedures of the polygraph operator, and the considerable statistics developed concerning the technique, have been subjected to a more searching and critical analysis than that accorded to any other form of evidence considered in this chapter.[8] Neither the concessions of critics that its accuracy in the detection of insincerity is of the order of 70 percent or more,[9] nor

---

4. Frye v. United States, 54 U.S.App.D.C. 46, 293 Fed. 1013 (1923), discussed in detail in § 203, supra.

5. United States v. Tremont, 351 F.2d 144 (6th Cir. 1965); Marks v. United States, 260 F.2d 377 (10th Cir. 1958) cert. denied 358 U.S. 929; People v. Sinclair, 21 Mich.App. 255, 175 N.W.2d 893 (1970); State v. Royster, 57 N.J. 472, 273 A.2d 574 (1971); People v. Leone, 25 N.Y.2d 511, 307 N.Y.S.2d 430, 255 N.E.2d 696 (1969); Commonwealth v. Johnson, 441 Pa. 237, 272 A.2d 467 (1971); 3A Wigmore, Evidence § 999, n. 2 (Chadbourn rev.); Annot., 23 A.L.R.2d 1306.

6. McCain v. Sheridan, 160 Cal.App.2d 174, 324 P.2d 923 (1958); State v. Carnegie, 158 Conn. 264, 259 A.2d 628 (1969); State v. Perry, 274 Minn. 1, 142 N.W.2d 573 (1966); Mattox v. State, 240 Miss. 544, 128 So.2d 368 (1961); State v. Smith, 113 Ohio App. 461, 178 N.E.2d 605 (1960); State v. Parsons, 83 N.J.Super. 430, 200 A.2d 340 (1964); Annot., 95 A.L.R.2d 819.

7. For two strenuous but unsuccessful efforts to lay the necessary foundation, see People v. Davis, 343 Mich. 348, 72 N.W.2d 269 (1955); People v. Leone, 25 N.Y.2d 511, 307 N.Y.S.2d 430, 255 N.E.2d 696 (1969). In a large number of the cases, no evidentiary foundation was offered, thus reducing the matter to a question of judicial notice.

8. Discussions of the accuracy question are contained in almost every reference cited in n. 93 supra. Additional statistics are contained in *Hearings*, n. 93, supra, Pt. 2, at 269–273; Pt. 3, at 434, 438–443. Some descriptions of experiments are given in Levitt, Scientific Evaluation of the Lie Detector, 40 Iowa L.Rev. 440 (1955). They indicate that the early experimenters addressed what seems to be the important question, which is not merely whether the expert can detect deception more often than not, but whether he can do so better than a trier can without his assistance. The fact that no statistics are extant on the ability of a jury to detect insincerity makes it difficult to assess what this gap might be, even if the accuracy of the polygraph technique were completely known. This lack has not kept courts and commentators from making estimates about it; see, e. g. State v. Lowry, 163 Kan. 622, 185 P.2d 147 (1947); People v. Aragon, 154 Cal.App.2d 646, 316 P.2d 370 (1957).

Reports of two recent experiments are contained in Blum and Osterloh, Polygraph Examination of Police Informants, 59 J.Crim.L.C. & P.S. 133 (1968); Heckel, et al., Polygraphic Reactivity Variations, 53 J.Crim.L.C. & P.S. 380 (1962). Cureton, A Consensus as to the Validity of Polygraph Procedures, 22 Tenn.L.Rev. 728 (1953) was an attempt to answer the "general acceptance" question as of that time.

9. Burkey, Privacy, Property and the Polygraph, 18 Lab.L.J. 80 (1967). Supporters would put it much higher; see Reid and Inbau, Truth and Deception 234 (1966); Horvath and Reid, Reliability of Polygraph Examiner Diagnosis of Truth and Deception, 62 J.Crim.L.C. & P.S. 276 (1971); Arther, The Lie Detector—Is It of Any Value? 24 Fed.Prob. 36 (Dec.1960). There are questions not only of what is to be considered verification of an opinion arrived at, but of where to put cases in which no opinion can be arrived at; and even the word "reliable" means different things to a lawyer and a scientist. Numbers around 80 percent accuracy tend to recur in these discussions and statistics. See, e. g. *Hearings*, supra, n. 93, Pt. 2, at 281 (random sample of 100 cases from Office of Naval Intelligence indicating 79 percent independent verification, or 83 percent if no-opinion cases eliminated); Pt. 3 at 359 (average operator in one psychology laboratory attains accuracy of about 80 percent); Pt. 3 at

the widespread use of and reliance upon it in police investigation, business, industry, and government,[10] nor the persistent efforts of trial courts to make some use of the evidence,[11] have made any inroads on that position.

As suggested in a previous section, the explanation can scarcely be found in any serious contention that even the opinion of a qualified expert in the field throws no light on the question of whether relevant statements made by a party or witness were sincere or not. The exclusion seems to rest more upon a judicial estimate of the weight that the trier of fact will give to the opinion, and a demand that the opinion be almost infallible because the trier will think it so.[12]

The one avenue of admissibility that has not been completely closed is that of stipula-

tion by the parties. From an early case [13] allowing the use of the test evidence on this basis, there has developed a growing minority view that the results may be received if the parties enter into an adequate stipulation to that effect.[14] The experience gained in this way, especially on the question whether triers are actually unable to evaluate this type of evidence, may make possible a more informed conclusion on the larger question of general admissibility of polygraph results.

208. Statements Made While Under the Influence of Drugs or Hypnosis.[15]

Another possible method by which the truthfulness of the story of a witness may be

---

429 (with highly competent and well-trained operators, approximately 80 percent accuracy).

10. The routine use of the lie detector in business, industry, and government raises additional questions of privacy and prediction of future conduct which have aroused much opposition and led to some statutory restrictions. See Reid and Inbau, Truth and Deception 259–264 (1966) (listing Alaska, California, Hawaii, Massachusetts, Oregon, Rhode Island, and Washington); Burkey, Privacy, Property and the Polygraph, supra, n. 9; Notes, 15 Buffalo L.Rev. 655 (1965), 33 Geo.Wash.L.Rev. 932 (1965).

11. See Pfaff, The Polygraph: An Invaluable Judicial Aid, 50 A.B.A.J. 1130 (1964); Arther and Reid, Utilizing the Lie Detector Technique to Determine the Truth in Paternity Cases, 45 J.Crim. L.C. & P.S. 213 (1954). The effort has been curbed, by statute in Illinois; see People v. Nimmer, 25 Ill.2d 319, 185 N.E.2d 249 (1962); Reid and Inbau supra, n. 9, at 243–44.

12. See § 203; People v. Leone, 25 N.Y.2d 511, 307 N.Y.S.2d 430, 255 N.E.2d 696 (1969) ("We are all aware of the tremendous weight which such tests would necessarily have in the minds of a jury.") The minds of trial judges are assessed in the same way; see, e. g. People v. Sinclair, 21 Mich.App. 255, 175 N.W.2d 893 (1970) (error for trial judge to consider on motion for new trial). Judicial reluctance radically to revamp the legal factfinding process, especially by entrusting key participation to persons not under effective judicial control, is no doubt also a factor.

13. People v. Houser, 85 Cal.App.2d 686, 193 P.2d 937 (1948). Cases indicating if not holding, to the contrary, are Le Fevre v. State, 242 Wis. 416, 8 N.W.2d 288 (1943); State v. Trimble, 68 N.M. 406, 362 P.2d 788 (1961); Stone v. Earp, 331 Mich. 606, 50 N.W.2d 172 (1951); Pulakis v. State, 476 P.2d 474 (Alaska 1970).

14. Herman v. Eagle Star Ins. Co., 283 F.Supp. 33 (C.D.Cal.1966), affirmed 396 F.2d 427 (9th Cir. 1968) (appellate opinion states reliability not passed on); State v. Valdez, 91 Ariz. 274, 371 P.2d 894 (1962) ("its results are probative enough to warrant admissibility upon stipulation"; thorough discussion of features of an acceptable stipulation and use to be made of the evidence); People v. Davis, 270 Cal.App.2d 841, 76 Cal.Rptr. 242 (1969); State v. Brown, 177 So.2d 532 (Fla.App.1965); The Florida Bar v. Rayman, 238 So.2d 594, 596 (Fla.1970) (dictum); State v. McNamara, 252 Iowa 19, 104 N.W.2d 568, (1960); State v. Fields, 434 S.W.2d 507 (Mo.1968) (scientific acceptance expressly not decided); State v. Rowley, 15 Utah 2d 4, 386 P.2d 126 (1963); Notes, 21 Fla.L.Rev. 541 (1969), 34 Mo.L.Rev. 592 (1969), 16 N.Y.L.F. 646 (1969).

15. 3A Wigmore, Evidence § 998 (Chadbourn rev.) (citing much of the periodical literature); Bryan, Legal Aspects of Hypnosis (1962); Despres, Legal Aspects of Drug-Induced Statements, 14 U.Chi.L. Rev. 600 (1947); Dession, Freedman, Donnelly, and Redlich, Drug-Induced Revelation and Criminal Investigation, 62 Yale L.J. 315 (1953); Gall, The Case Against Narco-Interrogation, 7 J.For.Sci. 29 (1962); Geis, In Scopolamine Veritas, 50 J.Crim. L.C. & P.S. 347 (1959); Hanscom, Narco-Interrogation, 3 J.For.Med. 9 (1956); Herman, Use of Hypno-Induced Statements in Criminal Cases, 25 Ohio St.L.J. 1 (1964); McDonald, Truth Serum, 46 J.Crim.L.C. & P.S. 259 (1955); Moenssens, Narco-Analysis in Law Enforcement, 52 J.Crim.L.C. & P.S. 453 (1961); Polen, Admissibility of Truth

tested is the inducing of a mental state in which his normal power of "censorship" is removed, and in which it becomes difficult or impossible for him to suppress his thoughts or devise a falsehood. That alcohol has an influence in this direction is attested by the old maxim, *in vino veritas*. A physician administering the "twilight sleep" drug, scopolamine, to a woman in childbirth discovered that at a certain stage of anaesthesia the subject answered questions with childlike honesty.[16] Similar effects are produced by the injection of barbiturates, such as sodium amytal and sodium pentothal, which were widely used in World War II and the Korean conflict in the treatment of mental strains and neuroses produced by combat conditions. All these drugs have been extensively employed in the investigation of crime and in the securing of confessions, and in attempts to test the guilt or innocence of convicts. If the drug were administered without the consent of the subject, it is clear that a confession so induced would be excluded as "involuntary."[17] If it is claimed that the subject

consented to the use of the drug and the interrogation, then the admissibility of the confession, it seems, would depend upon whether the judge found that he had a reasonable capacity to understand and speak the truth when he confessed and had waived any rights and privileges involved.[18]

It is not significant that the drug may have been administered and the questions asked by persons unfamiliar with hyoscine's properties as a 'truth serum,' if these properties exist." 372 U.S. 293 at 307. The trustworthiness of the statements is also of no significance in this context: "whether scopolamine produces true confessions or false confessions, if it in fact caused Townsend to make statements, those statements were constitutionally inadmissible." Id., at 308 n. 5. See also, Beecher v. Alabama, 389 U.S. 35 (1967); People v. Dacy, 5 Cal.App.3d 216, 85 Cal.Rptr. 57 (1970); Reddish v. State, 167 So.2d 858 (Fla.1964).

18. All these findings present difficulties. Whether the basis for admitting confessions in evidence is a hearsay exception based on realization of truthfulness or a nonhearsay byproduct of the adversary system, see § 145, supra, the effect of the drug on the premise is uncertain. See authorities cited in n. 15, supra. Also unclear is what (if anything) would constitute a valid advance waiver. It would surely be necessary that defendant understand: not only that the drug would be administered and that he would be interrogated, but also the drug's possible effects, and that while under its influence his power to exercise his normal rationality and will, or to seek, understand, or follow the advice of a lawyer, for example, might be eliminated. No case has reached this waiver question, apparently because the first admissibility question has so far been answered negatively. However, in People v. Horton, 30 App.Div.2d 709, 290 N.Y.S.2d 767 (1968) cert. denied 394 U.S. 991, defendant, knowing he was a prime suspect in the inquiry into a murder, procured his own commitment to a mental hospital for the express purpose of submitting to questioning under sodium amytal about the matter. In two drug interviews, he made no admissions; but being unable to remember this, consulted another patient for advice, and confessed to him and later to the prosecutor. The two confessions were used at trial. In rejecting a post-conviction claim that the confessions were involuntary because of fear resulting from the effects of the tests, the court, after noting that statements made under the influence of drugs were inadmissible, said: "in any event if his self-commitment to the hospital, and his express consent to undergo sodium amytal tests for the purpose of eliciting the truth, were in all respects voluntary, the effects and results of the test would have to be found within the intent and contemplation of his consent. . . . While the confession may have

Serum Tests in Courts, 35 Temp.L.Q. 401 (1962); Silving, Testing the Unconscious in Criminal Cases, 69 Harv.L.Rev. 683 (1956); Teitlebaum, Admissibility of Hypnotically Adduced Evidence, 8 St. Louis U.L.J. 205 (1963); Notes, 21 U.Fla.L.Rev. 541, 550 (1969), 31 Neb.L.Rev. 575 (1952), 52 Nw.U.L.Rev. 666 (1957), 8 Utah L.Rev. 78 (1962), 14 Vand.L.Rev. 1509 (1961); Annot., 23 A.L.R.2d 1306, 1310, 69 A.L.R.2d 384, 1 A.L.R.3d 1205.

16. See the article by Dr. R. H. House, the original experimenter in this field, The Use of Scopolamine in Criminology, 18 Tex.St.Med.J. 259, 261 (1927), quoted in Despres, op. cit., 14 U.Chi.L.Rev. 602; Geis, In Scopolamine Veritas, 50 J.Crim.L.C. & P.S. 347 (1959).

17. Townsend v. Sain, 372 U.S. 293 (1963) (drug identical with scopolamine); People v. Heirens, 4 Ill.2d 131, 122 N.E.2d 231 (1954) (dictum); Annot., 69 A.L.R.2d 384, 1 A.L.R.3d 1205; see also Jackson v. Denno, 378 U.S. 368 (1964) (scopolamine); Pea v. United States, 130 U.S.App.D.C. 66, 397 F.2d 627 (1968) (dictum).

In the *Townsend* case, supra, the court said: "It is difficult to imagine a situation in which the confession would be less the product of a free intellect, less voluntary, than when brought about by a drug having the effect of a truth serum.

The primary problem of admissibility, both in substantive use of statements made during narco-interrogation, and in use of expert opinion as to credibility based thereon, has been the recurrent one of reliability and sufficiency of scientific acceptance. Here, exclusion of the statements finds more support than does admission among the professional experimenters with narcoanalysis.[19] Just as the ancient *in vino veritas* has no clause insuring *nil nisi veritas,* so "truth serum" is not only not a serum, but persons do not tell only truth under its influence. Many are capable of telling less, and others much more, including the products of fancy and suggestion. It is not clear, apparently, whether all these are sincerely believed by the patient at the time. If they are, the task of the expert, since he cannot himself know the truth of the critical events, is to sort out sincere statements based on recall from sincere statements based on something else.[20]

This combination of truth and other matter may offer leads for further investigation, or material for psychiatric diagnosis and treatment, all of which may produce admissible evidence.[21] But the statements made during the interview, when offered by the defendant in a criminal case, have been uniformly rejected on the basis of the hearsay rule, lack of scientific acceptance of the underlying premise, or absence of necessary scientific foundation in the particular case.[22]

with her without having personally experienced them"); Merritt v. Commonwealth, 386 S.W.2d 727 (Ky.1965) ("was telling the truth when he said he did not commit the robbery"); Commonwealth v. Butler, 213 Pa.Super. 388, 247 A.2d 794 (1968) ("probably telling the truth"). The description of the testimony is that given by the court in each case. In all these cases use of the declarations given by the subject was in effect disapproved. It should be remembered that although the courts discuss reliability in general terms, the test, as in the case of polygraph results should be not whether the expert can achieve perfect success, or no success at all, but whether he can achieve such success as to make his opinion helpful to the jury, without being outweighed by countervailing considerations.

been triggered by the tests, the tests, if consented to were not 'poisonous' in the first instance and never became so." See also, People v. Esposito, 287 N.Y. 389, 39 N.E.2d 925 (1942); Gall, The Case Against Narco-Interrogation, 7 J.For.Sci. 29, 44–52 (1962); Silving, Testing the Unconscious in Criminal Cases, 69 Harv.L.Rev. 683 (1956); Notes, 21 U.Fla.L.Rev. 541, 556 (1969), 13 N.Y. L.F. 677, 700 (1968).

19. Despres, Legal Aspects of Drug-Induced Statements, 14 U.Chi.L.Rev. 600, 606 (1947); Dession, Freedman, Donnelly, and Redlich, Drug-Induced Revelation and Criminal Investigation, 62 Yale L.J. 315, 318–19 (1953); Gagnieur, The Judicial Use of Psychonarcosis in France, 40 J.Crim.L.C. & P.S. 370 (1949); Gall, The Case Against Narco-Interrogation, 7 J.For.Sci. 29, 31 (1962); Moenssens, Narco-Analysis in Law Enforcement, 52 J.Crim. L.C. & P.S. 453, 456 (1961); McDonald, Truth Serum, 46 J.Crim.L.C. & P.S. 259 (1955).

20. "The authorities agree that the subject pours out both fact and fancy. Dr. Lorenz observes: 'Much care must be exercised by the experimenter to evaluate the results. He must discriminate, *if possible,* what is the product of fantasy and what of fact.'" Despres, op. cit., 14 U.Chi.L.Rev. 605.

The task seems to have been undertaken by the experts testifying in such cases as Lindsey v. United States, 16 Alas. 268, 237 F.2d 893 (1956) ("could not have gained the information she related concerning appellant's alleged sexual relations

21. Sallee v. Ashlock, 438 S.W.2d 538 (Ky.1969) (defendant in wrongful death case who had suffered brain concussion, impeached with earlier statements showing no memory of accident, held properly rehabilitated by evidence of narcoanalysis and treatment curing his amnesia); Freeman v. New York Central R.R. Co., 112 Ohio App. 395, 174 N.E.2d 550 (1960) (similar; admission by trial court not discussed); Lemmon v. Denver & Rio Grande R.R. Co., 9 Utah 2d 195, 341 P.2d 215 (1959) (similar; expert testimony to treatment and some discussion of sodium amytal interview allowed). Compare People v. Harper, 111 Ill.App.2d 204, 250 N.E.2d 5 (1969) (trial court's order suppressing evidence of "facts" given by rape victim solely through truth serum or hypnosis upheld; opinion not clear as to what was suppressed); People v. Cullen, 37 Cal.2d 614, 234 P.2d 1 (1951) (defendant's motion for appointment of psychiatrist to give him narcoanalysis denied); People v. Brownsky, 35 Misc.2d 134, 228 N.Y.S.2d 476 (1962) (same). In People v. McCracken, 39 Cal.2d 336, 246 P.2d 913 (1952) defendant's request to testify under "truth" drugs was held properly denied.

22. People v. McNichol, 100 Cal.App.2d 554, 224 P.2d 21 (1950); People v. Myers, 35 Ill.2d 311, 220 N.E.2d 297 (1966), cert. denied 385 U.S. 1019; Orange v. Commonwealth, 191 Va. 423, 61 S.E.2d 267 (1950); State v. White, 60 Wash.2d 551, 374 P.2d 942 (1962); Annot., 23 A.L.R.2d 1306, 1310.

Efforts to use the statements in support of the credit of a witness have met the same fate.[23] There seems no reason to expect a different result in civil cases.

The accepted uses of narcoanalysis in the psychiatric field itself rest on a different base. Clearly the medical expert evaluates the drug interview in some way; but whether the patient's statements are all "true" in the empirical sense is said to be of lessened importance, since the goal is to obtain insight into the patient's personality and mental condition.[24]

The questions then arise whether the expert, having used narcoanalysis as one of his examination tools, may testify to his opinion on sanity, or on the competence or credit of a witness. As to sanity, and presumably as to competence to be a witness, the tendency of the courts is to allow the expert opinion, but to curb the introduction of the statements made during the drug interview, even when offered only as the partial basis of the opinion.[25] As to credibility, admissibility involves

the general and unsettled issue as to use of expert opinion on this subject, whatever the basis of the opinion; and the courts have generally ruled out the evidence.[26]

Declarations made under hypnosis have been treated judicially in a manner similar to drug-induced statements. The hypnotized person is ultrasuggestible, and this manifestly endangers the reliability of his statements. The courts have recognized to some extent the usefulness of hypnosis, as an investigative technique and in diagnosis and therapy.[27] However, they have rejected confessions induced thereby, statements made under hypnosis when offered by the subject in his own behalf, and opinion as to mental state based on hypnotic examination.[28]

23. Lindsey v. United States, 16 Alas. 268, 237 F.2d 893 (1956) (statutory rape; reversible error to allow rehabilitation of prosecutrix by admitting tape recording of her statements under sodium pentothal); Knight v. State, 97 So.2d 115 (Fla. 1957).

24. Curran, Expert Psychiatric Evidence of Personality Traits, 103 U.Pa.L.Rev. 999, 1014 (1955); Dession, Freedman, Donnelly, and Redlich, Drug-Induced Revelation and Criminal Investigation, 62 Yale L.J. 315, 316, 322–323 (1953).

25. In the more recent cases the decisions go both ways, and the admissibility of the opinion is not always expressly distinguished from the admissibility of the statements made in the interview. People v. Cartier, 51 Cal.2d 590, 335 P.2d 114 (1959) (opinion of sanity and analysis of interview); People v. Jones, 42 Cal.2d 219, 266 P.2d 38 (1954) (opinion defendant not a psychopath); People v. Myers, 35 Ill.2d 311, 220 N.E.2d 297 (1966) cert. denied 385 U.S. 1019 (opinion as to sanity proper, answers at interview excluded); State v. White, 60 Wash.2d 551, 374 P.2d 942 (1962) (similar). Contra, State v. Sinnott, 24 N.J. 408, 132 A.2d 298 (1957) (sexual propensities); People v. Ford, 304 N.Y. 679, 107 N.E.2d 595 (1952) (sanity).

26. See the cases cited in n. 20, supra; State v. Lindemuth, 56 N.M. 257, 243 P.2d 325 (1952).

27. Harding v. Maryland, 5 Md.App. 230, 246 A.2d 302 (1968) cert. denied 395 U.S. 949 (rape; prosecutrix's testimony from recollection restored by treatment including hypnotism, and expert testimony as to treatment, admissible); Cornell v. Superior Court, 52 Cal.2d 99, 338 P.2d 447 (1959) (mandamus granted to allow defendant to have himself examined under hypnosis). Contra, State ex rel. Sheppard v. Koblentz, 174 Ohio St. 120, 187 N.E.2d 40 (1962).

28. Rex v. Booher, [1928] 4 Dom.L.Rep. 795 (nisi prius: judge, not satisfied that confession not secured by hypnotism or mental suggestion, excludes it), noted in 42 Harv.L.Rev. 704 (1929); Leyra v. Denno, 347 U.S. 556 (1954) (involuntary confession to psychiatrist with suggestion of hypnosis; subsequent confession held influenced); People v. Busch, 56 Cal.2d 868, 16 Cal.Rptr. 898, 366 P.2d 314 (1961) (opinion as to mental state rejected for unreliability and lack of qualification of expert); State v. Pusch, 77 N.D. 860, 46 N.W.2d 508 (1950) (opinion that defendant's denial was truthful and answers in hypnosis interview, inadmissible); Annot., 23 A.L.R.2d 1306, 1310.
In the unreported trial court case of State v. Nebb (C.P. Franklin Cty., Ohio 1962), defendant's testimony in open court was interrupted while he was examined under hypnosis by agreement of counsel, in the absence of the jury. At the conclusion of the examination, the state reduced the charge and a plea of guilty was accepted. The case is discussed in Herman, Use of Hypno-Induced Statements in Criminal Cases, 25 Ohio St.L.J. 1 (1964); Teitlebaum, Admissibility of Hypnotically Adduced Evidence, 8 St. Louis U.L.J. 205 (1963).

209. Chemical Tests for Drunkenness.[29]

In this field the courts, despite formidable conflicts in expert opinion, have been persuaded rather quickly to use the results of scientific experimentation, aided in recent years by broad statutes.

The present discussion will be limited to the questions of the admissibility of the various chemical tests as dependent upon their reliability, on the assumption that the tests are administered without objection, and leaving for separate treatment the questions of privilege which arise when the tests are administered involuntarily.[30] Presumably, it is the amount of alcohol in the brain that determines the extent of intoxication. However, since (except in case of autopsy after death) the brain tissue cannot be taken for analysis, resort must be had to other substances. Of these, the blood undoubtedly affords upon analysis the most satisfactory and reliable results, and the admission of blood tests when supported by adequate preliminary proof has been generally approved.[31] Resort is also had to tests of the urine [32] and of the breath.[33]

Dissenting scientists have objected to all these tests upon the ground, among others, of the existence of wide individual variations in sensitivity or tolerance to alcohol.[34] But the weight of medical and scientific opinion seems to favor the view that experience has demonstrated that the results of the tests are of great practical value in determining whether the persons tested are under the influence of alcohol.[35]

The subjects of standards of proof and testing are now largely controlled by statute in 49 states and the District of Columbia.[36] In the process, most of the original questions as to the general reliability of the tests and the relation between blood-alcohol levels and driver impairment have been answered, expressly or impliedly, by the legislatures.

The Uniform Vehicle Code,[37] as revised to 1968, furnishes a typical set of modern provisions, subject to local variations. It provides that in the trial of a civil or criminal proceeding involving driving or control of a vehicle while under the influence of intoxicating liquor, evidence of the operator's blood content at the time, as shown by chemical test of his blood, urine, breath, or other bodily substance, is admissible and gives rise to the following presumptions: If there was

---

29. Erwin, Defense of Drunk Driving Cases (2d ed. 1966) (very thorough coverage from defense viewpoint); Donigan, Chemical Tests and the Law (Fisher ed. 1957); Drunk Driving Cases: Prosecution and Defense (Freeman ed. 1970); Watts, Tests for Intoxication, 45 N.C.L.Rev. 34 (1966) (good coverage); Slough and Wilson, Legal By-Products of Chemical Testing for Intoxication, 11 Clev.Mar. L.Rev. 1 (1962); Annot., 127 A.L.R. 1513, 159 A.L.R. 209, 46 A.L.R.2d 1169, 77 A.L.R.2d 971, 16 A.L.R.3d 748; Dec.Dig. Crim.Law ☞388.

30. See § 124, supra (self-incrimination aspect); § 171, supra (whether search warrant required).

31. E. g., Lawrence v. Los Angeles, 53 Cal.App.2d 6, 127 P.2d 931 (1942); Commonwealth v. Capalbo, 308 Mass. 376, 32 N.E.2d 225 (1941); Kuroske v. Aetna Life Ins. Co., 234 Wis. 394, 291 N.W. 384, 127 A.L.R. 1505 (1940) (annotated on this point); Donigan, Chemical Tests and the Law (Fisher ed. 1957).

32. State v. Duguid, 50 Ariz. 276, 72 P.2d 435 (1937).

33. Toms v. State, 239 P.2d 812 (Okl.Cr.1952).

34. Erwin, Defending Drunk Driving Cases (2d ed. 1966) which discusses this matter generally in Ch. 14, and more specifically in connection with each test; Rabinowitch, Medico-Legal Aspects of Chemical Tests, 39 J.Crim.L. 225 (1948) (able and extensive canvassing of the numerous scientific factors of error); Note, 13 N.Y.L.F. 679, 760 (1968).

35. Erwin, Defending Drunk Driving Cases §§ 15.01, 16.02, 22.01, 22.02 (2d ed. 1966).

36. Erwin, Defending Drunk Driving Cases (Supp. 1970), containing a compendium of the state statutes; Donigan, Chemical Test Law (Fisher ed. 1957); 8 Wigmore, Evidence (McNaughton rev.) § 2265 n. 6 (listing statutes); Uniform Chemical Test for Intoxication Act; Uniform Motor Vehicle Code § 11–902 (rev.1968). In about half the states, test procedures are prescribed either by statute or by a state health agency under statutory authority.

37. § 11–902.

0.05 percent or less, by weight, of blood alcohol, it shall be presumed that he was not under the influence; more than 0.05 percent and less than 0.10 percent is relevant but not presumptive; and 0.10 percent or more is presumptive evidence that he was under the influence.[38] Analyses valid under the statute can be performed only by methods prescribed by the state health department, and only by a permittee of the department. Blood, for direct blood tests, may be withdrawn only by a physician, registered nurse, or other qualified person.

In the absence of the presumptive provision, it was customary for an expert, interpreting the test results, to explain the relationship between blood-alcohol and driver condition, and this could still be of importance in the intermediate range.[39]

There is usually some delay in making the test after the collision or other crucial happening, but the courts have been willing to accept expert testimony estimating the alcohol concentration at the earlier time, based on the average rate of clearance from the bodies of humans in general.[40] Indeed, where

the test has shown a particular blood alcohol content, the courts have expressly or tacitly assumed the proposition that the person's blood-alcohol was at least as high at the time of the accident as at the time of the subsequent test, absent further drinking in the interval.[41]

The breath test has the advantage of convenience. It does not require a physician or medical technician to extract a sample, as does the blood test. It may be administered by a trained policeman. Moreover, it is least likely to arouse objection, and thus to raise doubtful questions of privilege. Its reliability as an index of the alcoholic content of the blood, however, is less than that of direct blood tests, due in part to use of an average figure for the ratio of breath-alcohol to blood-alcohol and to problems in calculating the amount of alveolar air in a mixed sample.[42] On the other hand, there is substantial scientific support for the reasonable reliability of

---

38. The older provision, and the Uniform Chemical Test for Intoxication Act, followed in many states, had fixed 0.15 percent for the presumption of intoxication. On recommendations of the National Safety Council and the American Medical Association based on further researches, the figure was changed in 1962 to 0.10 percent, and 21 states have already followed suit. Erwin, Defending Drunk Driving Cases (Supp.1970).

39. See, e. g., Mattingly v. Eisenberg, 79 Ariz. 135, 285 P.2d 174 (1955); Betsill v. State, 98 Ga.App. 695, 106 S.E.2d 323 (1958).

40. Mitchell v. State, 166 Tex.Cr.R. 197, 312 S. W.2d 245 (1958); See also Toms v. State, 239 P.2d 812, 820 (Okl.Cr.1952) (urine and breath tests taken 1½ hours after collision held not too remote; expert testified that a human body will burn about "⅓ of an ounce of alcohol an hour, or about .015% of blood alcohol per hour"). For criticism of these holdings on the basis of individual variations, see Erwin, Defense of Drunk Driving Cases § 14.06 (2d ed. 1966). Some statutes expressly limit the time within which admissible tests can be made; see N.Y.Veh. & Traf.Law § 1194.

41. This is correct if no part of the "absorption time" is included, and is therefore seldom contested. See State v. Olivas, 77 Ariz. 118, 267 P.2d 893 (1954); Commonwealth v. Hartmann, 383 Pa. 461, 119 A.2d 211 (1956). City of West Allis v. Rainey, 36 Wis.2d 489, 153 N.W.2d 514 (1967) (construing a statute providing that if the test, made within two hours of the accident, showed specific levels, the presumptions were applicable, held that the statute itself actually evaluated the results, and that the only expert testimony required was that relating to proper conduct of the test). For cases tacitly assuming the proposition in the text, see Webb v. Stone, 445 S.W.2d 842 (Ky.1969); Benner v. B. F. Goodrich Co., 150 Mont. 97, 430 P.2d 648 (1967); Davis v. State, 165 Tex.Cr.R. 622, 310 S.W.2d 73 (1958), cert. denied 357 U.S. 923.

Prior to these statutes and holdings, it had been estimated that the requirement for expert testimony as to the effects of given alcohol levels, and to present the calculation of retrograde extrapolations was the major expert witness area in criminal cases. Watts, Tests for Intoxication, 45 N.C. L.Rev. 34, 78–79 (1966).

42. Rabinowitch, Medicolegal Aspects of Alcoholic Intoxication Tests, 39 J.Crim.L. 225 (1948); Harger, "Chemical" Tests for Intoxication, 39 J.Crim.L. 402 (1948).

these tests.[43] The legislatures in adopting the statutes already described, have taken the decision in favor of admissibility.[44]

The party offering the results of any of these chemical tests must first lay a foundation by producing expert witnesses who will explain the way in which the test is conducted, identify it as approved under the statute, and vouch for its correct administration in the particular case.[45]

Under the more modern statutes, the questions of relevancy, and to a large extent of weight, of the evidence, have thus been legislatively resolved. The presumptions have been upheld by the courts, subject to the reduced effect given these provisions in criminal cases;[46] and the prescription for test procedures adopted by the state health agency has been taken as acceptance of the general reliability of such procedures in showing blood-alcohol content.[47]

It is important to remember that none of these tests is conclusive, that it is always open to the opponent to adduce countervailing evidence of his sobriety. Likewise, it is important to remember that the tests are not the sole evidence admissible on either side of the issue. Field sobriety tests, especially in the form recommended by the National Safety Council,[48] sound motion pictures [49] and videotape recordings, may all supplement the tests in producing a reliable judgment on the issue of intoxication.

43. Ladd and Gibson, Legal Medical Aspects of the Blood Test for Intoxication, 24 Iowa L.Rev. 191, 199, 200 (1939).

44. Previously, the cases had divided, with a majority admitting the evidence. Admissible: People v. Bobczyk, 343 Ill.App. 544, 99 N.E.2d 567 (1951); Toms v. State, 239 P.2d 812 (Okl.Cr.1952); McKay v. State, 155 Tex.Cr. 416, 235 S.W.2d 173 (1951) (conflict in scientific opinions goes only to the weight of the evidence). Contra: People v. Morse, 325 Mich. 270, 38 N.W.2d 322 (1949) (one doctor and two policemen with brief training in the use of the test gave evidence in support; five doctors testified that they are not reliable, one saying "You have got a continuous series of errors, some for and some against so that the thing works like a slot-machine"; held, error to admit the test results, which had not yet gained general scientific recognition).

45. And deal with the extrapolation backward to the time of the transaction at issue, if that point is involved; see Commonwealth v. Hartmann, 383 Pa. 461, 119 A.2d 211 (1956).

Illustrative cases as to the foundation requirements: People v. Lyall, 372 Mich. 607, 127 N.W.2d 345 (1964) (identification of blood sample as defendant's); Bean v. Riddle, 423 S.W.2d 709 (Mo.1968) (same); Benner v. B. F. Goodrich Co., 150 Mont. 97, 430 P.2d 648 (1967) (test procedure); People v. Donaldson, 36 App.Div. 37, 319 N.Y.S.2d 172 (1971) (qualifications of tester); State v. Magoon, 264 A.2d 779 (Vt.1970) (qualifications of tester); KYHL v. Commonwealth, 205 Va. 240, 135 S.E. 2d 768 (1964) (noncompliance with statutory procedure); State v. Rines, 269 A.2d 9 (Me.1970) (manufacturer's label and certificate sufficient to prove nature of preservative chemicals in blood sample collecting kit; random sampling would be required of chemicals used in testing if variations would affect blood-alcohol result); Annot., 77 A.L. R.2d 971.

46. State v. Childress, 78 Ariz. 1, 274 P.2d 333, 46 A.L.R.2d 1169 (1954) (annotated on this point); State v. Protokowicz, 55 N.J.Super. 598, 151 A.2d 396 (1959); State v. Johnson, 42 N.J. 146, 199 A.2d 809 (1964) (presumption makes prima facie case for prosecution); State v. Cooke, 270 N.C. 644, 155 S.E.2d 165 (1967) (similar). See also Webb v. Stone, 445 S.W.2d 842 (Ky.1969) (noticing relevancy in civil case on basis of presumption statute applicable to criminal case); Annot., 16 A.L.R.3d 748. See §§ 344, 346, infra, as to effect of presumptions generally in criminal cases.

47. Even without such a statute, courts have judicially noticed the general reliability of particular forms of testing apparatus; People v. Donaldson, 36 App.Div. 37, 319 N.Y.S.2d 172 (1971) (breathalyzer); State v. Miller, 64 N.J.Super. 262, 165 A.2d 829 (1960) (drunkometer). Each has its own advantages and sources of error. For descriptions and evaluation of the machines see Ervin, Defense of Drunk Driving Cases (2d ed. 1966); Watts, Tests for Intoxication, 45 N.C.L.Rev. 34 (1966).

48. Ideally observations should be in the form of a clinical examination by a physician, but as a regular routine this is not feasible. For a description of the Safety Council's Alcohol Influence Report Form and the tests, see Watts, Tests for Intoxication, 45 N.C.L.Rev. 34, 44 (1966) (includes sources of error).

49. See Drunk Driving Cases: Prosecution and Defense 561 (Freeman ed. 1970).

210. Speed Detection and Recording Devices.[50]

The necessity for control of traffic speeds to maintain highway safety, and the uncertainties connected with opinion testimony to speeds, have led to the development of numerous devices aimed at detecting the speeds of vehicles and affording evidence thereof. From the acceptance of stopwatch evidence in an English speeding case in the early 1900's [51] to the present radar speedmeter and vascar, the history is one of increasing reliance on scientific devices of various kinds for this purpose.[52]

The instrument now in most widespread use is the radar speedmeter. Unlike military radar (named from Radio Detection and Ranging), which operates on a pulse system, the speedmeter transmits a continuous beam of microwaves of known frequency down the highway. An oncoming (or receding) auto reflects these waves; they are received, and the difference in frequency between the transmitted and received signals is measured. Due to the motion of the target, the received frequency will be higher in the case of an approaching car, and lower in the case of a receding one; and in both cases the difference is proportional to speed (this is the "Doppler shift").[53] A chart records the indications in miles per hour. Like all scientific instruments, it has its own sources of error;[54] but expert testimony in many cases indicates that when properly placed and in good working order it measures and records the speed of the target within about 2 miles per hour.

In the early cases involving the radar speedmeter, testimony was required not only to show that the target car had been identi-

---

50. 2 Wigmore, Evidence §§ 417b, 665a (1970 Supp.); Fisher, Legal Aspects of Speed Measurement Devices (1967); 11 Am.Jur. Proof of Facts 17 (Supp. 1970); McCarter, Legal Aspects of Police Radar, 16 Clev.-Mar.L.Rev. 455 (1966); Greenwald, Scientific Evidence in Traffic Cases, 59 J.Crim.L.C. & P.S. 57 (1968); Kopper, Scientific Reliability of Radar Speedmeters, 33 N.C.L.Rev. 343 (1955); Baer, Radar Goes to Court, 33 N.C.L.Rev. 355 (1955); Carosell and Coombs, Radar Evidence in the Courts, 32 Dicta 323 (Sept.-Oct. 1955); Russell, Radar Speedmeters in Court, 6 Law Notes 69 (1970); O'Brien, Radar Speed Detection in Illinois, 56 Ill.B.J. 296 (1967); Comment, 23 Tenn.L.Rev. 784 (1954); Notes, 35 Albany L.Rev. 562, 570–81 (1971), 9 Ariz.L.Rev. 106 (1967), 39 Iowa L.Rev. 511 (1954), 38 Marq.L.Rev. 129 (1955), 33 N.C. L.Rev. 385 (1955), 10 Rutgers L.Rev. 454 (1955), 28 Tul.L.Rev. 398 (1954), 7 Vand.L.Rev. 411 (1954); Annot., 49 A.L.R.2d 469, 27 A.L.R.3d 1442. As to the tachograph and aircraft flight recorder, see 20 Am.Jur. Proof of Facts 567 (1968); Conrad, The Tachograph as Evidence of Speed, 8 Wayne L.Rev. 287 (1962); Speiser, Airplane Flight Recorders, 2 Forum 97 (1967); Annot., 73 A.L.R.2d 1025.

51. See Fisher, Vehicle Traffic Law 240 (1961). An earlier case in which the constable used a watch with a second hand to clock a motorist, is Gorham v. Brice, 18 T.L.R. 424 (Div.Ct.1902) (defendant's complaint that lack of showing of accuracy of watch rendered evidence inadmissible, rejected). In the recent trend to use of aircraft to observe traffic on the highways, there has been a return to the stopwatch method. State v. Cook, 194 Kan. 495, 399 P.2d 835 (1965); State v. Peters, 9 Ohio App.2d 343, 224 N.E.2d 916, 27 A.L.R.3d 1442 (1967) (annotated on this point); Myren, Measurement of Motor Vehicle Ground Speed from Aircraft, 52 J.Crim.L.C. & P.S. 213 (1961); Note, 14 Hastings L.J. 427 (1963).

52. In Commonwealth v. Buxton, 205 Mass. 49, 91 N.E. 128 (1910) the court accepted evidence based

on a camera which took successive pictures of receding cars at set times; speed was calculated from the reduction in size of the pictured car. Speedometer readings taken in the "chase car" or motorcycle have long been admitted, Spokane v. Knight, 96 Wash. 403, 165 P. 105 (1917); and a number of other electrical or mechanical recording instruments have been used. City of Webster Groves v. Quick, 323 S.W.2d 386 (Mo. App.1959) (electric timer, sometimes named "Prather device" or "speed watch"); People v. Pett, 13 Misc.2d 975, 178 N.Y.S.2d 550 (Police J.Ct. Nassau Cty. 1958) ("Foto-patrol" device).

53. For a description of the device, including explanation of the Doppler-shift principle, see State v. Tomanelli, 153 Conn. 365, 216 A.2d 625 (1966); East Cleveland v. Ferell, 168 Ohio St. 298, 154 N.E. 2d 630 (1958); Kopper, The Scientific Reliability of Radar Speedmeters, 33 N.C.L.Rev. 343 (1955); McCarter, Legal Aspects of Police Radar, 16 Clev.-Mar.L.Rev. 455 (1966).

54. For discussion of these, from a critical standpoint, see Carosell and Coombs, Radar Evidence in the Courts, 32 Dicta 323 (Sept.-Oct. 1955).

fied [55] and measured by a qualified operator, and that his device was operating properly; but also to explain and assert the scientific acceptance of the Doppler-shift principle itself, and the manner of its application in the speedmeter.[56] Within a few years, however, the courts began to take judicial notice of the underlying scientific principles and of the general capability of the device to measure speed accurately, thus dispensing with expert testimony on those subjects.[57] In a number of states, statutes were enacted which expressly or implicitly performed the function of judicial notice.[58]

As regards evidence of accuracy of the particular instrument at the time the speed measurement was made, the decisions have diverged. They range from holdings that in the absence of evidence of tests on the particular speedmeter, in place, and close to the time of the measurement, the results are not admissible,[59] to holdings that lack of evidence of testing goes only to the weight and not to the admissibility of the results.[60]

Where test evidence is a prerequisite for admissibility or for sufficiency to support a finding, the decisions as to what tests are sufficient also show variations. The on-site test means are: (1) use of tuning forks, intended to produce frequencies which will cause the machine, if accurate, to read particular speeds (marked on the forks); (2) use of a signal generator within the machine for the same purpose; and (3) a "run-through," in which another police car closes on the site, holding a given speedometer reading, and is measured by the speedmeter. Naturally, the question has been raised whether evidence must be adduced of the accuracy of any or all of these testing means. The courts have recognized that to avoid an infinite regress of tests, there must be a "point of faith." [61] They seem to be arriving at the position that use of some one or some combination of the three methods constitutes sufficient testing for admissibility of the speed readings. Further, the more recent decisions, sometimes aided by statute, hold that evidence of radar speedmeter measurements, made as described, is sufficient to support a finding of speed in accordance with them, even when the burden is that of proof beyond reasonable doubt.[62]

55.　Honeycutt v. Commonwealth, 408 S.W.2d 421 (Ky.1966) (one vehicle of several held sufficiently identified); Commonwealth v. Bartley, 411 Pa. 286, 191 A.2d 673 (1963) (one vehicle of five in line sufficiently identified); Note, 13 N.Y.L.F. 677, 774 (1968).

56.　People v. Beck, 205 Misc. 757, 130 N.Y.S.2d 354 (Sup.Ct.1954); People v. Offerman, 204 Misc. 769, 125 N.Y.S.2d 179 (Sup.Ct.1953); Hardaway v. State, 202 Tenn. 94, 302 S.W.2d 351 (1957) (dictum).

57.　State v. Dantonio, 18 N.J. 570, 115 A.2d 35, 49 A.L.R.2d 460 (1955), noted 38 Marq.L.Rev. 129 (1955) and 10 Rutgers L.Rev. 454 (1955) is the leading case. Other cases taking judicial notice: United States v. Dreos, 156 F.Supp. 200 (D.Md. 1957) (applying Maryland law); Everight v. Little Rock, 230 Ark. 695, 326 S.W.2d 796 (1959); State v. Tomanelli, 153 Conn. 365, 216 A.2d 625 (1966); East Cleveland v. Ferell, 168 Ohio St. 298, 154 N.E.2d 630 (1958).

58.　Fisher Legal Aspects of Speed Measurement Devices 69–75 (1967) sets out these provisions, in force in about a dozen states.

59.　St. Louis v. Boecker, 370 S.W.2d 731 (Mo.App. 1963); Royals v. Commonwealth, 198 Va. 876, 96 S.E.2d 812 (1957). Fisher, Legal Aspects of Speed Measurement Devices 70, 73 (1967) shows statutes in some states dealing expressly with tests of the device for accuracy less stringently than do the cases requiring testing; see also Commonwealth v. Perdok, 411 Pa. 301, 192 A.2d 221 (1963).

60.　People v. Dusing, 5 N.Y.2d 126, 181 N.Y.S.2d 493, 155 N.E.2d 393 (1959); People v. Abdallah, 82 Ill.App.2d 312, 226 N.E.2d 408 (1967) (dictum); State v. Dantonio, 18 N.J. 570, 115 A.2d 35, 49 A.L.R.2d 460 (1955) (dictum).

61.　State v. Graham, 322 S.W.2d 188, 197 (Mo.App. 1959); State v. Snyder, 184 Neb. 465, 168 N.W.2d 530 (1969); People v. Lynch, 61 Misc.2d 117, 304 N.Y.S.2d 985 (Cty.Ct. 1969).

62.　People v. Stankovich, 119 Ill.App.2d 187, 255 N.E.2d 461 (1970) (single tuning fork); Kansas City v. Hill, 442 S.W.2d 89 (Mo.App.1969) (2 tuning forks); Peterson v. State, 163 Neb. 669, 80 N.W.2d 688 (1957) (run-through); People v. Lynch, 61 Misc.2d 117, 304 N.Y.S.2d 985 (Cty.Ct. 1969) (internal tone test and tuning forks); see Fisher

The newest speed detection and recording device to come before the courts is "Vascar" (Visual Average Speed Computer and Recorder), which can be contained and operated within the moving chase car. In effect, the machine and its operator clock the time the target takes to cover a premeasured distance, and the average speed is electronically computed, displayed, and recorded.[63] If its use expands, it can be expected that admissibility problems will follow the pattern experienced with the radar speedmeter: a period in which complete expert explanation is required, followed (if successful) by judicial notice of the underlying principles and general reliability of the system.

A speed detector and recorder not so closely tied to police work is the tachograph. As its name implies, it is a combination of tachometer and moving recording chart (or a clock with a paper recording dial) which furnishes over time the speed and mileage of the vehicle to which it is attached.[64] It is widely used on trains, trucks, and busses; and the information thus afforded has been admitted in civil and criminal cases, on a showing of its accuracy and evidence correlating it with the necessary features of the transaction at issue.[65]

The most advanced of the instruments here being discussed is the aircraft flight recorder, required by federal regulation in jet, propjet, and many other large aircraft.[66] It measures and records time, airspeed, magnetic heading, altitude, and vertical acceleration ("g" force), and will be expanded to provide information about aircraft attitude (orientation) and about the control and other systems. The aircraft flight recorder came into use to aid in the investigation of crashes following high speed, high altitude flight. In many instances, unfortunately, all the occupants are dead, and no evidence of value as to what happened immediately before the crash is obtainable from ground observers. In such cases, the physical evidence from the wreckage and the information from the flight recorder and the cockpit recorder may be the only means of determining the cause of the accident, and are of great value.

Admissibility of the flight recorder "foil" (chart) depends upon evidence of authenticity, and expert testimony to explain its workings and interpret the record, which would not otherwise be intelligible.[67]

Legal Aspects of Speed Measurement Devices 70–75 (1967) listing statutes making the measurements prima facie evidence of speed.

63. People v. Persons, 60 Misc.2d 803, 303 N.Y.S.2d 728 (Ct.Spec.Sess. 1969); Russell, Radar Speedmeters in Court, 6 Law Notes 69 (1970).

64. For descriptions of the tachograph, see Conrad, The Tachograph as Evidence of Speed, 8 Wayne L.Rev. 287 (1962); 3 Am.Jur. Trials 427, 479 (1965) (train speed tape).

65. Hall v. Dexter Gas Co., 277 Ala. 360, 170 So.2d 796 (1965) (truck tachograph disc sufficiently authenticated); Thompson v. Chicago & E. Ill. R. R. Co., 32 Ill.App.2d 397, 178 N.E.2d 151 (1961) (train speed tape, sufficient foundation evidence); Texas & N. O. R. R. Co. v. Lemke, 365 S.W.2d 148 (Tex.

1963) (train speed tape not sufficiently correlated with points on ground); Annot., 73 A.L.R.2d 1025.

66. 14 C.F.R. § 121.343 (1971). For descriptions and discussion, see Speiser, Airplane Flight Recorders, 2 Forum 97 (Jan. 1967); 20 Am.Jur. Proof of Facts 567 (1968); 1 Kennelly Litigation and Trial of Air Crash Cases 113–116 (1968); Note, 13 N.Y.L.F. 677, 769 (1968).

In addition to the flight recorder, 14 C.F.R. 121.359 (1971) requires a cockpit recorder, which provides information on conversations among the flight crew, and messages over the craft's communications and "public address" systems; see LeRoy v. Sabena Belgian World Airlines, 344 F.2d 246 (2d Cir. 1965), cert. denied 382 U.S. 878; Brown v. Civil Aeronautics Bd., 324 F.2d 523 (6th Cir. 1963).

67. See the works cited in the preceding note. Such testimony by federal investigators of the crash is limited; see 14 C.F.R. § 435.4 (1971).

211. Blood tests for Identification [68] and to Determine Paternity.[69]

In the investigation of crime it is often important to know whether a particular stain is blood or not, and if it is, whether it is human blood. Laboratory techniques are available by which these questions can usually be answered. When the substance is found to be human blood, then the search for the person from whom the blood came may be carried a step further by employing the methods of the rapidly developing technique of blood group testing. Under the first of the standard classifications, the following groups were recognized:

"Group O, in which you will find approximately 45% of the population;

"Group A, in which you will find approximately 42% of the population; and

"Group B, in which you will find approximatey 10% of the population, and

"Group AB, in which you will find the remaining 3%." [70]

In a leading case, the accused was charged with rape, and evidence was received to the effect that blood found on the coat of accused was of type O, and that the blood of the alleged victim was of the same type. As stated above, 45% of the population have blood of this type. The court overruled an objection to this evidence on the ground of remoteness and said: "The objection of remoteness goes to the weight of the evidence rather than to its admissibility. To exclude evidence merely because it tends to establish a possibility, rather than a probability, would produce curious results not heretofore thought of. In this case the fact that the accused was somewhere near the scene of the crime would not, in itself, establish a probability that he was guilty, but only a possibility, yet such evidence is clearly admissible as a link in the chain." [71]

The ABO system has an additional value in identification problems because of the existence of the "secretor property." It has been found that about 80 percent of the population produces in bodily secretions (saliva, sweat, semen, nasal and bronchial secretions, gastric juice, urine, tissue fluids) a substance which makes it possible to determine the secretor's blood group in the ABO system. The secretor property is itself gene-determined and inheritable.[72] The perpetrator of a crime (or any participant in any event) may leave, instead of his blood, one of these traces of his blood group behind, which may be used in

---

68. Gross, Criminal Investigation 103–106 (Jackson 5th ed. 1962); Jones, Scientific Investigation and Physical Evidence, ch. XI (1959); Sussman, Blood Grouping Tests 104 (1968).

69. 1 Wigmore, Evidence § 1652; Andresen, Human Blood Groups (1952); Schatkin, Disputed Paternity Proceedings (4th ed. 1967); Sussman, Blood Grouping Tests (1968). The law reviews present a rich array of articles from which the following list is only a selection: Krause, Scientific Evidence and the Ascertainment of Paternity, 5 Fam.L.Q. 252 (1971); Ross, The Value of Blood Tests as Evidence, 71 Harv.L.Rev. 466 (1958); Greene, "Blood Will Tell," 1 Mercer L.Rev. 266 (1950); Denton, Blood Groups and Disputed Parentage, 27 Can.B.Rev. 537 (1949); Littell and Sturgeon, Defects in Discovering and Testing Procedures, 5 U.C.L.A.L.Rev. 629 (1958); Whitlach and Marsters, Contribution of Blood Tests, 14 W.Res.L.Rev. 115 (1962); Notes, 3 U.San F.L.Rev. 297 (1969), 39 U.M.K.C.L.Rev. 121 (1970), 22 Md.L.Rev. 333 (1962); Annot., 163 A.L.R. 939, 46 A.L.R.2d 1000.

70. Quoted from the testimony of Dr. Freimuth in the opinion in Shanks v. State, 185 Md. 437, 45 A.

2d 85, 163 A.L.R. 931, 934 (1945). These frequencies vary somewhat according to race.

71. Shanks v. State, 185 Md. 437, 45 A.2d 85, 163 A.L.R. 931, 937 (1945). Cases of similar facts and like holding are United States v. Kearney, 136 U.S. App.D.C. 328, 420 F.2d 170 (1969); State v. Beard, 16 N.J. 50, 106 A.2d 265 (1954); State v. Jacobs, 6 N.C.App. 751, 171 S.E.2d 21 (1969). Contra, People v. Robinson, 27 N.Y.S.2d 864, 317 N.Y.S.2d 19, 265 N.E.2d 543 (1970) (dictum) (proof that defendant had type A blood and that semen found in body of decedent came from a man with type A blood "was of no probative value in the case against defendant in view of the large proportion of the general population having blood of this type, and, therefore, should not have been admitted.", an example of confusing the relevancy of evidence with its weight). See Annot., 46 A.L.R.2d 1000, 1025. One case holds that the evidence is conditionally relevant, Commonwealth v. Mussoline, 429 Pa. 464, 240 A.2d 549 (1968).

72. Andresen, Human Blood Groups, ch. VI (1952); Sussman, Blood Grouping Tests 25 (1968).

evidence in the same manner as a grouping determined directly from the blood.[73]

The classification of blood types mentioned in the preceding paragraphs was the outgrowth of the pioneer work of Landsteiner in 1900 in the recognition of blood groups, for which he was awarded the Nobel Prize, and the later demonstration by other workers that these blood characteristics are inheritable. Landsteiner discovered that when the red corpuscles from one person's blood were mixed with the serum from the blood of others the red corpuscles would sometimes gather into clumps, or agglutinate. Experimenting with the mixing of sera from the blood of various persons with the red corpuscles in the blood of others, and the consequent agglutination or failure to agglutinate, it was possible to differentiate the blood-types according to the presence or not of certain agglutinogens. These are acted upon by correspondingly classified substances (anti-A and anti-B) in the sera to produce this clumping of corpuscles. Thus if a person's blood possesses only the agglutinogen A, he is classed in group A; if only B, in that group; if both A and B, in group AB; and if it possesses neither then in group O. From the studies of scores of thousands of tests of the blood of parents and children, the two following laws were derived: (1) group A or B cannot exist in the blood of a child unless it exists in the blood of one or both parents, and (2) a parent of group AB cannot have offspring of group O, and a group O parent cannot have a child of group AB.[74]

The practical workings of these laws may be represented by the following table: [75]

Child	Known Parent	Unknown Parent Must Be	Unknown Parent Cannot Be
O	O	O, A, B	AB
	A	O, A, B	AB
	B	O, A, B	AB
	AB	Impossible for parent to be AB when child is in O	
A	O	A, AB	B, O
	A	O, AB, A, B	Exclusion impossible
	B	A, AB	B, O
	AB	O, AB, A, B	Exclusion impossible
B	O	B, AB	A, O
	A	B, AB	A, O
	B	O, AB, A, B	Exclusion impossible
	AB	O, AB, A, B	Exclusion impossible
AB	O	Impossible for parent to be O when child is in AB	
	A	B, AB	A, O
	B	A, AB	B, O
	AB	A, AB, B	O

It was computed that under the ABO classification the chances were about one in six [76] that a test of the blood of one falsely charged with the parenthood of a child would show his innocence rather than merely proving inconclusive.

In 1927 two additional inheritable qualities of the red blood cells were discovered by Landsteiner and Levine. These characteristics were termed M and N, and their recognition enables the analyst to classify blood as M, N, or MN. Every human being must belong to one of these types. Many thousands of tests have established these conclu-

73. Cases in which evidence of blood grouping by means of the secretor property was involved are People v. Kemp, 55 Cal.2d 458, 11 Cal.Rptr. 361, 359 P.2d 913 (1961) (admitted); People v. Robinson, note 71, supra.

74. Andresen, Human Blood Groups, ch. II (1952); Sussman, Blood Grouping Tests 34 (1968). In this and the other blood group types, spontaneous changes in type (due to mutation or disease) are not impossible, but their occurrence undetected is considered so unlikely as to be negligible. Sussman, op. cit. 13.

75. Copied by permission from Greene, op. cit., 1 Mercer L.Rev. 268.

76. Denton, op. cit., 27 Can.Bar Rev. 545; see the later discussion in Sussman, op. cit., placing the chance at one in five.

sions,[77] which parallel the law of inheritance for the A–B–O system: (1) Type M or N cannot exist in the blood of a child unless it exists in the blood of one or both parents, and (2) a parent of type M cannot have a child of type N, and a parent of type N cannot have a child of type M.

As a result, a table similar to the preceding one can be constructed to show the possibilities:

Child	Known Parent	Unknown Parent Must Be	Unknown Parent Cannot Be
M	M	M, MN	N
	N	Impossible for parent to be N when child is M	
	MN	M, MN	N
N	M	Impossible for parent to be M when child is N	
	N	N, MN	M
	MN	N, MN	M
MN	M	N, MN	M
	N	M, MN	N
	MN	M, N, MN	Exclusion impossible

The MN series is independent of the ABO groupings, and the addition of the new classification raised the chances of the falsely accused father of demonstrating his exclusion to one in three.[78]

In 1940 Weiner, a student of Landsteiner, announced the discovery of the rhesus blood factor, which provides a new and additional basis for classification of inherited qualities of the blood.[79] The discovery was made by immunizing rabbits and guinea pigs with blood from the rhesus monkey and mixing the anti-serums thus procured with the human blood to be tested. The anti-rhesus serum from animals enables the analyst to classify all human blood as Rh positive and Rh negative, and by further experimentation with anti-sera prepared by immunizing human volunteers, many additional types of agglutinogens based on the rhesus factor have been identified. Again, laws of exclusion, based on the genetic principles applied in the ABO and MN series, have been formulated and verified by extensive experimentation. It is estimated that the discovery of this new series of blood characteristics increases the chances of the alleged father falsely accused of proving his exclusion to better than even odds, i. e., he can do so in about 51% of the cases.[80]

A table of the possible and impossible parentages, based on the Rh–Hr groups would be too long and complicated for explication here, but is available in the standard works on the subject.[81]

These three systems which we have described do not exhaust the story, although they give some indication of the features of those so far recommended by the American Medical Association for general medico-legal application.[82] In addition to subdivisions of type A, and the addition of a type S to the M–N system, many other factors have been identified in recent years.[83] Indeed, Land-

77.   Andresen, op. cit., 40; Sussman, op. cit., 43.

78.   Denton, op. cit., 27 Can.Bar Rev. 545; Sussman, op. cit. 9.

79.   Sussman, op. cit., 51, 52.

80.   Sussman, op. cit. 9.

81.   See, e. g., Schatkin, Disputed Paternity Proceedings 136–147 (4th ed. 1967); Sussman, op. cit. 68; Whitlatch and Marsters, Contribution of Blood Tests, 14 W.Res.L.Rev. 115 (1962).

82.   Sussman, op. cit. 8 (1968); and the reports cited in Krause, Scientific Evidence and the Ascertainment of Paternity, 5 Fam.L.Q. 233, 261 (1971).

83.   See Sussman, op. cit. 23, 75–82 (1968), listing the Kk, P, Lu, Fy, Jk, Di, Vel, I, and Yt [a] systems; Kirk and Grunbaum, Individuality of Blood and Its Forensic Significance, 1969 Leg.Med. Annual 287. In Groulx v. Groulx, 98 N.H. 481, 103 A.2d 188, 46 A.L.R.2d 994 (1956), the court received and acted on evidence based on the S factor; in Huntingdon v. Crowley, 64 Cal.2d 647, 51 Cal.Rptr. 254, 414 P.2d 382 (1966), exclusion of evidence based on the Kk system was upheld on the ground that the

steiner's prophecy that except for identical twins no two persons would be found to have the same blood characteristics may come true.

How far are these contributions to scientific proof available to the courts and how effectively have they been used?

Frequently the parties will agree to the taking of the tests, and thus the test results will be available. Often, however, one party will refuse consent and an application will be made by the other for an order for the administration of the tests. A substantial number of states have statutes empowering the court to make such an order [84] and others have held that it is within the "inherent" power,[85] on the analogy to the similar power to order an examination of the plaintiff in an action for personal injury. In view of the trifling nature of the invasion involved and the magnitude of the interests at stake, it

has properly been held not to violate common law or constitutional privileges of bodily privacy under due process clauses,[86] nor under the sounder view should it be thought within the purview of the self-incrimination privilege.[87] The rule or statute may be mandatory [88] or discretionary,[89] but if discretionary, surely the range of reasons for refusal should be narrowly limited.[90]

When an adequate foundation of expert testimony, vouching the reliability of the technique and the correctness of its application in the particular case, has been laid, evidence of the results of the tests when they are interpreted by the experts as excluding the possibility that the person charged is the father, would now generally be received.[91]

system had not been sufficiently established to have gained "general acceptance in the particular field." In the future there may be many added blood cell or plasma systems. Sussman, op. cit. ch. 8 (1968); Note, U.S.F.L.Rev. 297, 314 (1969); and see Stocker v. Stocker, [1966] 1 W.L. 190 (P.) (admitting and acting on evidence of exclusion based on haptoglobin tests).

84. Yantis, Blood Test Exclusions as Decisive Evidence, 24 Rocky Mt.L.Rev. 237 (1952) listed eight at that time. Since then many more states have addressed themselves to the blood test-paternity problem; see 1 Wigmore, Evidence § 1652 n. 2; Annot., 46 A.L.R.2d 1000, 1007. The widespread adoption by the states of discovery procedures after the federal model has doubtless greatly expanded the list. In Beach v. Beach, 72 U.S.App. D.C. 318, 114 F.2d 479, 131 A.L.R. 804 (1940) it was held that Rule 35(a) of the Federal Rules of Civil Procedure providing for ordering a physical or mental examination of a party is broad enough to authorize an order for blood tests of wife, child and husband in an action by the wife for maintenance; the present version of the rule expressly covers blood-group tests of "a party, or of a person in the custody or under the control of a party." See Note, 45 Iowa L.Rev. 375 (1958).

85. State ex rel. Evertson v. Cornett, 391 P.2d 277 (Okl.1964); State v. Damm, 64 S.D. 309, 266 N.W. 667, 104 A.L.R. 441 (1936), a celebrated case of conversion on rehearing, and see other holdings pro and con cited in Annot., 163 A.L.R. 944, 945, and 46 A.L.R.2d 1000, 1005.

86. Et Min Ng v. Brownell, 258 F.2d 304 (9th Cir. 1958); Cortese v. Cortese, 10 N.J.Super. 152, 76 Atl.2d 717, 719 (1950) (cogent opinion by Brennan, J.A.D.) disapproving Bednarik v. Bednarik, 18 N.J.Misc. 633, 16 A.2d 80 (Ch.1940); Annot., 46 A.L.R.2d 1000, 1016. The *Brownell* case, supra, involved a nationality question. Although the text discussion in this section focusses on paternity proceedings, the grouping technique is useful in other matters where parenthood is in question, including kidnapping cases, alleged interchange of children in hospitals, and the like. See Sussman, op. cit., ch. 6.

87. See § 124, supra.

88. E. g., Uniform Act on Blood Tests to Determine Paternity § 1; and the Ohio provision relied on in State v. Stevens, 22 Ohio St.2d 4, 257 N.E.2d 396 (1970). Strong arguments have been advanced for mandatory tests in this type of case, see Sussman, op. cit., 89, 90, 101; Krause, Scientific Evidence and the Ascertainment of Paternity, 5 Fam.L.Q. 252, 268–9 (1971).

89. As in F.R.Civ.P. 35(a).

90. Thus, in Cortese v. Cortese, 10 N.J.Super. 152, 76 A.2d 717, 720 (1950) the court, recognizing a discretion, held that the refusal in that case was unfounded, and said that in the absence of substantial reasons to the contrary, "we think the demonstrated utility of this tool of evidence should move trial courts in civil actions to employ it freely."; and see the cases pro and con cited in Annot., 46 A.L.R.2d 1000, 1008.

91. See 1 Wigmore, Evidence § 165a, n. 2 (listing statutes); Houghton v. Houghton, 179 Neb. 275, 137 N.W.2d 861 (1965); see also Beach v. Beach, 72 U.S.App.D.C. 318, 114 F.2d 479, 480, 481, 131 A.L.R. 804 (1940) and State v. Damm, 64 S.D. 309, 266 N.W. 667, 104 A.L.R. 441 (1936) in both of

When the child is born of a married mother during wedlock, results of the blood tests may be offered to show that the husband was not the father. In many jurisdictions the rule has been that the presumption of legitimacy can be rebutted only by showing certain particular facts, such as that the husband had no opportunity of access, or that he was impotent, or that the child was of another race.[92] Shall the new source of uniquely reliable scientific proof be availed of to rebut the presumption? Should the social policy of fastening upon the husband the responsibility for children born during the marriage prevail at this point over the policy that a man shall not be answerable for a child that is clearly not his? To hold that the presumption is so far conclusive that rebuttal by blood tests is not allowable[93] would often give an escape from responsibility to the true father, and the cases admitting the tests in rebuttal[94] reflect the more expedient view.

When the scientists unanimously report that the tests have been accurately administered and adequately checked, and that they show that the man charged could not have been the father, should this be accepted as true? When plaintiff in a notorious California case claimed that Charles Chaplin was the father of her little girl, blood tests were made by physicians, chosen one by the child's guardian, one by the defendant, and a third by the other two. These three physicians reported the results: Charles Chaplin, Group O, the mother, Group A, the child, Group B. He *could not* have been the father. But the plaintiff testified (over Chaplin's denial) to intercourse with him at the appropriate season. The court said this made a conflict, which was properly submitted to the jury, and the jury having found for the mother, the verdict stood.[95] It seems, however, that if the scientific evaluation of this test is accepted, the situation is one where the courts might well apply the familiar doctrine that where the testimony of a witness is contradicted by incontrovertible physical facts the testimony of the witness cannot be accepted, it being either mistaken or false, and a verdict based on it will not be sustained. A case[96] in Maine blazed the trail for this view. In a bastardy proceeding the defendant admitted intercourse and the plaintiff girl, when asked if she had accused anyone else, said, "There is no other one to accuse." The court ordered a blood test by three physicians, one being the principal expert in that region. Eleven tests produced identical results. They excluded the possibility that defendant was the father. The

which the power of the court to order the tests was affirmed, and the admissibility of the evidence was discussed. Cases are collected in Annot., 163 A.L.R. 950–958, 46 A.L.R.2d 1000.

92. See 9 Wigmore, Evidence § 2527; 10 Am.Jur.2d Bastards §§ 10–32; Annot., 57 A.L.R.2d 736, 32 A.L.R.3d 1303.

93. As in West's Ann.Cal.Evid.Code, § 621 (issue of wife cohabiting with her husband who is not impotent); see the construction of this substantive law rule in Jackson v. Jackson, 671 Cal.2d 245, 60 Cal.Rptr. 649, 430 P.2d 289 (1967), noted 8 Santa Clara L. 248 (1968), 20 Stan.L.Rev. 754 (1968) (presumption conclusive if conception occurs during cohabitation and biological parentage is then irrelevant; but blood tests may show with other proof that conception did not so occur); Williams v. Williams, 230 La. 1, 87 So.2d 707 (1956), discussed in Pascal, Who is the Papa? 18 La.L.Rev. 685 (1958); Rasco v. Rasco, 447 S.W.2d 10 (Mo.App. 1969), noted 39 U.M.K.C.L.Rev. 121 (1970).

94. Beck v. Beck, 153 Colo. 90, 384 P.2d 731 (1963) (alleged father entitled to have tests made and exclusion received in evidence over contention that presumption rendered it incompetent; directed verdict for defendant affirmed); Crouse v. Crouse, 51 Misc.2d 649, 273 N.Y.S.2d 595 (Fam.Ct.1966) (similar; blood grouping tests performed in the courtroom by Dr. Alexander S. Weiner, a pioneer in the field); Cortese v. Cortese, 10 N.J.Super. 152, 76 A.

2d 717, (1950) (presumption cannot justify refusal to order tests).

95. Berry v. Chaplin, 74 Cal.App.2d 652, 169 P.2d 442 (1946, hearing den.) By the adoption of statutes resembling Uniform Act on Blood Tests to Determine Paternity §§ 4, 5, 6 or by decision, this view is dying out when the proper administration of the tests is established.

96. Jordan v. Mace, 144 Me. 351, 69 A.2d 670 (1949).

jury, as usual, found the defendant *was* the father, probably on the doctrine of assumption of risk. The Supreme Judicial Court set aside the verdict, saying: "The skill and accuracy with which the blood grouping tests were here conducted were clearly and convincingly demonstrated by the testimony of disinterested witnesses. . . . The statement by the complainant, 'There is no other one to accuse,' even if interpreted as a denial of intercourse with any man other than the respondent, is not sufficient to overcome the overwhelming effect of this positive testimony by disinterested witnesses." [97] It seems that the certain reliability of blood tests, carefully and expertly performed and adequately checked, to show nonpaternity is now so universally accepted by scientists that the courts should take judicial notice thereof [98] and could wisely accord them conclusive effect.[99]

The statutes usually provide that the results of the test when they *exclude* paternity of the person charged shall be received.[1] The decisions, with or without the aid of statute, have denied admission when the tests show that the person charged *could* have been the father and they are offered as evidence of his paternity.[2] These decisions are understandable as manifestations of a desire to move slowly in the judicial use of these new tests, and particularly to avoid such use of the tests in evidence as might lead juries to give them exaggerated weight in establishing paternity. Nevertheless, it may be doubted whether the wholesale exclusion of the tests when they show that the person charged belongs to one of the groups to which the father must have belonged, is a wise practice. The question is one of identity. Every identifying mark of the father, however common the trait, (so long as not universal) such as height, weight, color of hair, is relevant, and it is from the accumulation of identifying traits that circumstantial proof of identity gains its persuasive power.[3] The tests may show that the unknown father must have belonged to groups O, A, B, which make up 97% of the population.[4] To prove that the person charged belongs to one of these groups certainly has only a minimum of identifying value, which in a jury case could be outweighed by the danger of misleading. On the other hand,

---

97. Other cases where the court has set aside verdicts or findings which were contrary to the test results or approved treating results as conclusive: Retzer v. Retzer, 161 A.2d 469 (D.C.Mun.App.1960); Commonwealth v. D'Avella, 339 Mass. 642, 162 N.E.2d 19 (1959); Houghton v. Houghton, 179 Neb. 275, 137 N.W.2d 861 (1965); see discussion in Anonymous v. Anonymous, 1 App.Div.2d 312, 150 N.Y.S.2d 344 (1956); Annot., 46 A.L.R.2d 1000, 1028. A like decision is Ross v. Marx, 21 N.J.Super. 95, 90 A.2d 545, 546 (Co.Ct.1952), where the court said, "For a court to declare that these tests are not conclusive would be as unrealistic as it would be for a court to declare that the world is flat." The Uniform Act on Blood Tests to Determine Paternity § 4 gives conclusiveness to the tests excluding paternity, when the experts agree.

98. In Cortese v. Cortese, 10 N.J.Super. 152, 76 A.2d 717, 720 (1950), the court said, "It is plain we should hold, as we do, that this unanimity of respected authorities justifies our taking judicial notice of the general recognition of the accuracy and value of the tests when properly performed by persons skilled in giving them."; Annot., 46 A.L.R.2d 1000, 1018. See § 331, infra.

99. See authorities cited n. 92, supra. It should be stressed that the judicial notice does not cover the question of proper administration of the particular test. The problem of competency of the experts and technicians and the care used in testing has been a very troublesome problem. See Krause, Scientific Evidence and the Ascertainment of Paternity, 5 Fam.L.Q. 252, 265 (1971); Anony-

mous v. Anonymous, 10 Ariz.App. 496, 460 P.2d 32 (1969).

1. Uniform Act on Blood Tests to Determine Paternity § 4.

2. People v. Nichols, 341 Mich. 311, 67 N.W.2d 230 (1954); State v. Morris, 156 Ohio St. 333, 102 N.E. 2d 450 (1951) (statute permitting results of tests to be received "in cases where exclusion is established" requires that tests which merely show a possibility be excluded); Annot., 46 A.L.R.2d 1000, 1022.

3. See the illuminating opinion of Marbury, C. J. in Shanks v. State, 185 Md. 437, 45 A.2d 85, 163 A.L.R. 931, 936–939 (1945).

4. See list of percentages of population in each group in the first paragraph of this section.

the tests may reveal that the father must have belonged to groups B or AB, which together make up only 13% of the population. To prove then that the person accused belongs to this small minority class, has high identifying significance which would be substantially corroborative of other evidence that he was the father. This probative value is clearly recognized in the closely analogous cases where the blood found at the scene of a crime, or on the clothes of the accused or his victim, is classified as to blood groups and used as evidence of identity.[5] Accordingly, the Uniform Act embodies a compromise, as follows: "If the court finds that the conclusions of all the experts, as disclosed by the evidence based upon the tests, are that the alleged father is not the father of the child, the question of paternity shall be resolved accordingly. If the experts disagree in their findings or conclusions, the question shall be submitted upon all the evidence. If the experts conclude that the blood tests show the possibility of the alleged father's paternity, admission of this evidence is within the discretion of the court, depending upon the infrequency of the blood type."[6] In view of the probability that the development of new, additional tests may further narrow the groups in which the potential father must fall, the practice suggested in the Uniform Act seems an expedient solution.

---

5. See opening paragraphs of this section. In particular cases, with rare blood constellations, parent and child may have in common factors found in only one person per million; see Note, 3 U.S. F.L.Rev. 297 (1969). In the identity cases the blood-test evidence will ordinarily be farther removed from the center of the case and correspondingly less likely to result in undue prejudice.

6. Uniform Act on Blood Tests to Determine Paternity, § 4. Many states, in adopting the Act, have omitted this provision, but not all; see Harris, The Un-Uniform Act on Blood Tests, 9 Vill.L.Rev. 59 (1963).

TITLE 8

DEMONSTRATIVE EVIDENCE

CHAPTER 21

DEMONSTRATIVE EVIDENCE

212. Demonstrative Evidence in General.[1]

There is a type of evidence which consists of things, e. g., weapons, whiskey bottles, writings,[2] and wearing apparel, as distinguished from the assertions of witnesses (or hearsay declarants) about things. Most broadly viewed, this type of evidence includes all phenomena which can convey a relevant firsthand sense impression to the trier of fact,[3] as opposed to those which serve merely to report the secondhand sense impressions of others. Thus, for example, demeanor evidence, i. e. the bearing, expression, and manner of a witness while testifying,[4] is an instance of the type of evidence here considered, but the statements which he utters are not.

Evidence from which the trier of fact may derive a relevant firsthand sense impression is almost unlimited in its variety. As a result, the problem of satisfactorily labeling and classifying has proved a difficult one,[5] and it will be seen variously referred to as real, autoptic, demonstrative, tangible, and objective. For present purposes, the term "demonstrative" will be used to refer to the generic class, though it should be noted that some courts employ this term in a more limited sense.[6]

Since "seeing is believing," and demonstrative evidence appeals directly to the senses of the trier of fact,[7] it is today universally felt that this kind of evidence possesses an immediacy and reality which endow it with par-

---

1. See 4 Wigmore, Evidence §§ 1150–1169; C.J.S. Evidence §§ 601–622; Dec.Dig. Evidence ⬤188–195, Criminal Law ⬤404(1–4), Trial ⬤28 and 375.

2. Writings, except insofar as they contain statements which the writing is offered to prove, are examples of the present subject. They have, however, developed rules of their own which are treated independently. See, Ch. 22 (authentication) and Ch. 23 (documentary originals).

3. Schertzinger v. Williams, 198 Cal.App.2d 242, 17 Cal.Rptr. 719 (1961).

4. While demeanor evidence is analytically a type of demonstrative evidence, it is inseparably related to oral testimony and is thus treated elsewhere. See § 245, text at notes, 30–35, infra.

5. See, Michael and Adler, Real Proof, 5 Vand.L.Rev. 344 (1952); Nokes, Real Evidence, 65 L.Q.Rev. 57 (1949); Patterson, Types of Evidence, 19 Vand.L. Rev. 1 (1965); 4 Wigmore, Evidence § 1150.

6. I. e., as contrasted with "real" evidence. See discussion at n. 24, infra.

7. While the great bulk of demonstrative evidence is directed to the sense of sight, each of the other senses may on occasion be appealed to. See, e. g., Ragusa v. American Metal Works, Inc., 97 So.2d 683 (La.App.1957) (hearing); People v. Kinney, 124 Mich. 486, 83 N.W. 147 (1900) (taste); McAndrews v. Leonard, 99 Vt. 512, 134 A. 710 (1926) (touch); Western Cottonoil Co. v. Adkisson, 276 S.W.2d 411 (Tex.Civ.App.1955) (smell).

ticularly persuasive effect.[8] Largely as a result of this potential, the use of demonstrative evidence of all types has increased dramatically during recent years, and the trend seems certain to continue in the immediate future. At the same time, demonstrative evidence remains the exception rather than the rule, and its use raises certain problems for a juridical system the mechanics of which are essentially geared to the reception of *viva voce* testimony by witnesses. Some of these problems are so commonly raised by the offer of demonstrative evidence, and are so frequently made the bases of objections to its admission, that they deserve preliminary note.[9]

It has already been noted that evidence from which the trier of fact may derive his own perceptions, rather than evidence consisting of the reported perceptions of others, possesses unusual force. Largely for this reason, demonstrative evidence is frequently objected to as "prejudicial," by which is usually meant that the capacity of the evidence to inspire emotions such as, e.g., sympathy or repugnance, outweighs its probative value for the issues in litigation.[10] Again, even if no essentially emotional response is likely to result, demonstrative evidence may convey an impression of objective reality to the trier. Thus, the courts are frequently sensitive to the objection that the evidence is "misleading," and zealous to insure that there is no misleading differential between objective things offered at trial and the same or different objective things as they existed at the time of the events or occurrences in litigation.[11]

Further, and apart from its bearing on the issues of the case, demonstrative evidence as a class presents certain essentially logistical difficulties for the courts. Since the courts are basically structured, architecturally and otherwise, to receive the testimony of witnesses, the presentation of demonstrative evidence may require that the court physically move to receive it, or that unwieldy objects or paraphernalia be introduced into the courtroom, actions which may occasion delay and confusion.[12] Finally, while oral testimony is easily incorporated into a paper record for purposes of appellate review, demonstrative evidence will sometimes be insusceptible to similar preservation and transmission.[13]

The cogency and force of the foregoing objections to the introduction of demonstrative evidence will obviously vary greatly with the nature of the particular item offered, and the purpose and need for its introduction in the particular case. Since the types of demon-

---

8. Of the many articles emphasizing the point, the following may be cited: Belli, Demonstrative Evidence and the Adequate Award, 22 Miss.L.J. 284 (1951); Dooley, Demonstrative Evidence—Nothing New, 42 Ill.B.J. 136 (1953); Hinshaw, Use and Abuse of Demonstrative Evidence: The Art of Jury Persuasion, 40 A.B.A.J. 479 (1954); Hare, Demonstrative Evidence, 27 Ala.Law. 193 (1966); Kilroy, Seeing Is Believing, 8 Kan.L.Rev. 445 (1960); Knepper, Exhibits and Demonstrative Evidence, 30 Ins.L.J. 133 (1963); Lay, Use of Real Evidence, 37 Neb.L.Rev. 501 (1958); Perlman, Demonstrative Evidence, 33 Ky.S.B.J. 5 (1969); Spangenburg, The Use of Demonstrative Evidence, 21 Ohio St.L.J. 178 (1960).

9. For an extended treatment of the objections commonly raised to demonstrative evidence, see Cady, Objections to Demonstrative Evidence, 32 Mo.L. Rev. 333 (1967).

10. For types of demonstrative evidence to which this objection is frequently raised, see n. 22, and § 215, infra.

11. See discussion at n. 25, infra.

12. See, e. g., § 214 (motion pictures) and § 216, infra.

13. E. g., Supreme Court of Indiana, Rule 2–8 provides as follows:

"Exhibits—Physical Objects. Physical objects (except papers, maps, pictures and like materials) which, because of their nature cannot be incorporated in a transcript, shall not be sent to this Court on appeal, but shall remain in the custody of the trial court until the appeal is terminated. However, such objects shall be briefly named and identified in the transcript following the exhibit number therein, and a photograph thereof may be inserted in the transcript. Counsel may at their option bring such physical objects, properly identified by the court reporter taking the testimony in the trial court, to the Court on appeal in support of oral argument on appeal . . . ."

strative evidence and the purposes for which it is sought to be introduced are extremely varied, it is generally viewed as appropriate to accord the trial judge broad discretion in ruling upon the admissibility of many types of demonstrative evidence.[14]

Despite its great variety, certain classifications of demonstrative evidence appear both valid and useful. First, like other evidence, it may be either direct or circumstantial. If a material issue in the case is whether an object does or does not possess a perceptible feature, characteristic, or quality, the most satisfactory method of demonstrating the truth of the matter will ordinarily be to produce the object so that the trier of fact may perceive the quality, or its absence, for himself. Thus, where a party seeks damages for the loss of a limb or for an injury leaving a disfiguring scar, exhibition of the person will constitute direct evidence of a material fact.[15] Similarly, exhibition of the chattel purchased in an action for breach of warranty will, at least if the quality or characteristic warranted is a perceivable one, constitute direct evidence on the issue of condition.[16] In these cases no process of inference, at least in the ordinary sense, is required.[17] Similarly, exhibition of a person to establish such facts as race[18] and age[19]

may perhaps also be considered examples of demonstrative evidence of a direct sort, though the immediate perceptibility of these qualities may on occasion be subject to more doubt.

Demonstrative evidence may also be offered for its circumstantial value, i.e., as the basis for an inference beyond those facts which are perceivable. Such is the case when the exhibition of a person is made for the purpose of demonstrating his relationship to another, as in a filiation proceeding.[20] Even more clearly is the use of demonstrative evidence circumstantial when articles of clothing worn at the time of his arrest by the defendant in a robbery prosecution are exhibited to the jury to demonstrate their conformity with the descriptions of the robber given by witnesses.[21]

The practical significance of the foregoing distinction lies in the fact that direct evidence, because of its eminently satisfactory character, will always be admitted unless the situation involves some overriding contrary consideration of prejudice or physical difficulty.[22] When circumstantial evidence is

---

14. E. g., the types of demonstrative evidence discussed in §§ 213–216, infra.

15. See Calumet Paving Co. v. Butkus, 113 Ind.App. 232, 47 N.E.2d 829 (1943) (exhibition of plaintiff's shoulder most satisfactory evidence of injury); Hendricks v. Sanford, 216 Ore. 149, 337 P.2d 974 (1959) (exhibition "completely relevant" to show declivity in plaintiff's back).

16. See, e. g., Woodward & Lothrop v. Heed, 44 A.2d 369 (D.C.Mun.App.1945) (breach of implied warranty on fur coat; "When the issue of fact is the condition of . . . an article, the introduction in evidence of the thing itself, to enable a jury to observe its condition, is competent and persuasive evidence.")

17. 4 Wigmore, Evidence § 1150.

18. See, e. g., White v. Holderby, 192 F.2d 722 (5th Cir. 1951).

19. See, e. g., United States ex rel. Fong On v. Day, 54 F.2d 990, 991 (2d Cir. 1932) ("it can hardly be

doubted that [the jury] are at liberty to use their senses and draw an inference as to the person's age from his physical appearance"); State v. Dorathy, 132 Me. 291, 170 A.2d 506 (1934). But cf. Watson v. State, 236 Ind. 329, 140 N.E.2d 109 (1957) (appearance of defendant not alone sufficient to support finding as to age), noted in 15 Wash. & L.L. Rev. 290 (1958).

20. Many states hold that the trial court may, in its discretion, permit a child to be exhibited in a filiation proceeding for the purpose of showing a resemblance to the putative father. See, e. g., Judway v. Kovacs, 4 Conn.Cir. 713, 239 A.2d 556 (1967) (dictum); Lohsen v. Lawson, 106 Vt. 481, 174 A. 861 (1934). The practice is by no means universally accepted. See Annot., 40 A.L.R. 111, 95 A.L.R. 314; Dec.Dig. Bastards ⊂⇒63.

21. See, e. g., Caldwell v. United States, 338 F.2d 385 (8th Cir. 1964); Vanleeward v. State, 220 Ga. 135, 137 S.E.2d 452 (1964).

22. Rich v. Ellerman & Bucknall S. S. Co., 278 F.2d 704, 708 (2d Cir. 1960) ("Autoptic proference is always proper, unless reasons of policy apply to exclude it;" error to exclude photos of plaintiff's injuries). Thus, though it is commonly recognized

involved, however, in the present context as elsewhere, the trial judge will generally be viewed as possessing a broader discretionary power to weigh the probative value of the evidence against whatever prejudice, confusion, surprise and waste of time are entailed, and to determine admissibility accordingly.[23]

Again, demonstrative evidence may be classified as to whether the item offered did or did not play an actual and direct part in the incident or transaction giving rise to the trial. Objects offered as having played such a direct role, e.g., the alleged weapon in a murder prosecution, are commonly called "real" or "original" evidence and are to be distinguished from evidence which played no such part but is offered for illustrative or other purposes.[24] It will be readily apparent that when real evidence is offered an adequate foundation for admission will require testimony first that the object offered is *the* object which was involved in the incident, and further that the condition of the object is substantially unchanged.[25] If the offered item possesses characteristics which are fairly unique and readily identifiable, and if the substance of which the item is composed is relatively impervious to change, the trial court is viewed as having broad discretion to admit merely on the basis of testimony that the item is the one in question and is in a substantially unchanged condition.[26] On the other hand, if the offered evidence is of such a nature as not to be readily identifiable, or to be susceptible to alteration by tampering or contamination, sound exercise of the trial court's discretion may require a substantially more elaborate foundation.[27] A foun-

that gruesome and shocking demonstrative evidence may prejudice and inflame the jury, the gruesome nature of an item of direct evidence is today seldom viewed as warranting exclusion. 4 Wigmore, Evidence §§ 1157, 1158; Dec.Dig. Crim.Law ⚖404, Evidence ⚖188. There are many criminal cases in which gruesome photographs of the victim have been offered, and if materiality has appeared the courts have been inclined either to view probative value as outweighing prejudice, or to decline to view prejudice as a relevant factor. People v. Kemp, 55 Cal.2d 458, 359 P.2d 913, 11 Cal.Rptr. 361 (1969); State v. Bucanis, 26 N.J. 45, 138 A.2d 739 (1958) (conviction upheld though pictures were "more harmful than illuminating"); Wilson v. State, 247 Ind. 680, 221 N.E.2d 347 (1966) (gruesomeness not considered when evidence relevant). See also Shaffer, Judges, Repulsive Evidence and the Ability to Respond, 43 N.D.Law 503 (1968); Annots., 159 A.L.R. 1413, 73 A.L.R.2d 769; Notes, 22 Ga.B.J. 384 (1960), 8 D.P.L.Rev. 418 (1959), 3 Vill.L.Rev. 568 (1958). Of course, where materiality is entirely lacking, the admission of prejudicial demonstrative evidence is improper. See, e. g., State v. Bischert, 131 Mont. 152, 308 P.2d 969 (1957).

Many older decisions hold preservation of decency in the courtroom to be a policy warranting exclusion of some autoptic evidence. See, e. g., Garvick v. Burlington, C. R. & N. Ry. Co., 124 Iowa 691, 100 N.W. 498 (1904); Guhl v. Whitcomb, 109 Wis. 69, 85 N.W. 142 (1901). Most modern authority, however, reverses the priorities. See, e. g., Jensen v. South Adams County Water and San. Dist., 149 Colo. 102, 368 P.2d 209 (1962); Sullivan v. Minneapolis, St. P. & S. S. M. Ry. Co., 55 N.D. 353, 213 N.W. 841 (1927).

23. See, e. g., Bertram v. Harris, 423 P.2d 909 (Alas. 1967) (whiskey bottle found in defendant's car after accident; within trial court's discretion to exclude when fact testified to).

24. Smith v. Ohio Oil Co., 10 Ill.App.2d 67, 134 N.E. 2d 526 (1956).

25. See, e. g., Witt Ice & Gas Co. v. Bedway, 72 Ariz. 152, 231 P.2d 952 (1951); Gutman v. Industrial Com'n, 71 Ohio App. 383, 50 N.E.2d 187 (1942) (no testimony that steering wheel offered was from car in question); Semet v. Andorra Nurseries, Inc., 421 Pa. 484, 219 A.2d 357 (1966) (no testimony that photo offered was of the same ladder from which plaintiff fell). See also 7 Wigmore, Evidence § 2129.

26. See, e. g., Walker v. Firestone Tire & Rub. Co., 412 F.2d 60 (2d Cir. 1969) (tire rim and tire; admission discretionary where exhibit not easily alterable); State v. Coleman, 441 S.W.2d 46 (Mo.1969) (exhibit properly admitted upon identification without tracing chain of custody); American Reciprocal Insurers v. Bessonette, 241 Ore. 500, 405 P.2d 529 (1965) (water pipe, admission discretionary where nature and environment of exhibit did not raise substantial doubts of authenticity or unchanged condition). If the object offered is not claimed to possess any unique trait material to the suit, strict proof of identity is sometimes foregone. See, e. g., Isaacs v. National Bank of Commerce, 50 Wash.2d 548, 313 P.2d 684 (1957); see also Comment, Preconditions for Admission of Demonstrative Evidence, 61 Nw.U.L.Rev. 472 (1966).

27. See State v. Myers, 351 Mo. 332, 172 S.W.2d 946 (1943); State v. Boehme, 71 Wash.2d 621, 430 P.2d 527 (1967); Comment, Preconditions for Admission of Demonstrative Evidence, 61 Nw.U.L.Rev. 472 (1966). Chemical specimens are frequently recognized as raising possibilities of mistaken ex-

dation of the latter sort will commonly entail testimonially tracing the "chain of custody" of the item with sufficient completeness to render it improbable that the original item has either been exchanged with another or been contaminated or tampered with.[28]

Real evidence consisting of samples drawn from a larger mass are also generally held admissible, subject to the foregoing requirements pertaining to real evidence generally, and subject to the further requirement that the sample be established to be accurately representative of the mass.[29]

Demonstrative evidence, however, is by no means limited to items which may properly be classed as "real" or "original" evidence. It is today increasingly common to encounter the offer of tangible items which are not contended themselves to have played any part in the history of the case, but which are instead tendered for the purpose of rendering other evidence more comprehensible to the trier of fact.[30] Examples of types of items frequently offered for purposes of illustration and clari-

fication include models, maps, photographs, charts, and drawings.[31] If an article is offered for these purposes, rather than as real or original evidence, its specific identity or source is generally of no significance whatever.[32] Instead, the theory justifying admission of these exhibits requires only that the item be sufficiently explanatory or illustrative of relevant testimony in the case to be of potential help to the trier of fact.[33] Whether the admission of a particular exhibit will in fact be helpful, or will instead tend to confuse or mislead the trier, is a matter commonly viewed to be within the sound discretion of the trial court.[34]

213. Maps, Models, and Duplicates.[35]

Among the most frequently utilized types of illustrative evidence are maps, sketches,

---

change, tampering and contamination. See, e. g., Novak v. District of Columbia, 82 U.S.App.D.C. 95, 160 F.2d 588 (1947); Annot., 21 A.L.R.2d 1216. The various business records statutes, however, have proved of great utility in securing admission of regularly marked and labeled specimens. See, e. g., Gass v. United States, 135 U.S.App.D.C. 11, 416 F.2d 767 (1969).

28. See Erickson v. North Dakota Workmen's Comp. Bureau, 123 N.W.2d 292 (N.D.1963); see also, Gallego v. United States, 276 F.2d 914 (9th Cir. 1960) (narcotics, tracing sufficient to justify exercise of trial court's discretion in admitting); People v. Malone, 4 N.Y.2d 8, 197 N.E.2d 189 (1964) (tracing sufficient). It has sometimes been suggested that stringent tracing requirements, arguably appropriate in criminal prosecutions, should be relaxed in civil cases. See Woolley v. Hafner's Wagon Wheel, Inc., 22 Ill.2d 413, 176 N.E.2d 757 (1961) rev'g 27 Ill.App.2d 1, 169 N.E.2d 119 (1960), noted in 110 U.Pa.L.Rev. 895 (1962).

29. Kunzman v. Cherokee Silo Co., 253 Iowa 885, 114 N.W.2d 534 (1962); Annot., 95 A.L.R.2d 681.

30. Smith v. Ohio Oil Co., 10 Ill.App.2d 67, 134 N.E.2d 526 (1956) (holding skeleton properly admitted to illustrate medical testimony and distinguishing between "real" and "demonstrative" evidence).

31. 3 Wigmore, Evidence (Chadbourn rev.) § 790. But a map or photograph can easily figure in the history of a case and thus constitute real evidence. Goldner and Mrovka, Demonstrative Evidence and Audio-Visual Aids at Trial, 8 U.Fla.L.Rev. 185, 187 (1955).

32. See, e. g., Cohen v. Kindlon, 366 F.2d 762 (2d Cir. 1966) (failure to establish authorship of sketch used for illustration held "of no consequence"); Intermill v. Heumesser, 154 Colo. 496, 391 P.2d 684 (1964) (admission of X rays of unidentified person testified to be "normal" upheld and "encouraged"). But an occasional trial judge will be found confusing illustrative exhibits with real evidence and rejecting the former. See, e. g., Hernke v. Northern Ins. Co., 20 Wis.2d 352, 122 N.W.2d 395 (1963).

33. See, e. g., Slow Development Co. v. Coulter, 88 Ariz. 122, 353 P.2d 890 (1960) (charts, etc., admissible to illustrate anything witness allowed to describe); McKee v. Chase, 73 Idaho 491, 253 P.2d 787 (1953) (excellent statement of theory of admission); Kroeger v. Safranek, 161 Neb. 182, 72 N.W. 2d 831 (1955). See also Dec.Dig. Witnesses ⊂⊃252. A number of courts, while allowing illustrative exhibits, assert they are not "substantive" evidence. See, e. g., State v. Gardner, 228 N.C. 567, 46 S.E.2d 824 (1948). The practical consequences of the latter view are discussed in §§ 213, 216, infra.

34. See, e. g., Smith v. Ohio Oil Co., 10 Ill.App.2d 67, 134 N.E.2d 526 (1956); Commonwealth, Dept. of Highways v. Garland, 394 S.W.2d 450 (Ky.1965) (exclusion of photos held abuse of discretion); State v. Ray, 43 N.J. 19, 202 A.2d 425 (1964) (sound discretion would permit helpful charts; dictum).

35. 3 Wigmore, Evidence (Chadbourn rev.) §§ 790, 791; Dec.Dig. Evidence ⊂⊃194 (duplicates, models

diagrams,[36] models and duplicates.[37] Unlike real evidence, the availability of which will frequently depend upon circumstances beyond counsel's control, opportunities for the use of the types of demonstrative evidence here considered are limited only by counsel's ability to recognize them. The potential of these aids for giving clarity and interest to spoken statements seems sure to guarantee their continued and expanded use in the future.[38]

While all jurisdictions allow the use of demonstrative items to illustrate and explain oral testimony, there is considerable diversity of judicial opinion concerning the precise evidentiary status of articles used for this purpose.[39] Even in the majority of jurisdictions where there is no apparent bar to, or restriction upon, their full admission, it is not uncommon for maps, models, etc., to be displayed and referred to without being formal-

ly offered or admitted into evidence.[40] While no absolute prohibition would appear to be justified concerning such informal use of illustrative items, numerous appellate courts have commented upon the difficulties created on appeal when crucial testimony has been given in the form of indecipherable references to an object not available to the reviewing court.[41] By the more common, and clearly preferable practice, illustrative objects will be identified by the witness as substantially correct representations and will be formally introduced as part of the witness' testimony, in which they are incorporated by reference.[42]

Illustrative exhibits may often properly and satisfactorily be used in lieu of real evidence. As previously noted, articles actually involved in a transaction or occurrence may have become lost or be unavailable, or witnesses may be unable to testify that the article present in court is the identical one they have previously observed. Where only the generic characteristics of the item are significant no objection would appear to exist to the introduction of a substantially similar "duplicate."[43] While the matter is general-

---

and casts), 358 (maps, plats and diagrams), Criminal Law ⊜404(1)–(2), Trial ⊜39, Witnesses ⊜252.

36. Cases involving maps, sketches and diagrams are collected in Annot., 9 A.L.R.2d 1044.

37. Cases involving models and duplicates in various contexts are collected in Annots., 69 A.L.R.2d 424 (models of sites in civil actions); 23 A.L.R.3d 825 (models of property taken by eminent domain); 58 A.L.R.2d 689 (models and charts of human anatomy in civil cases); 93 A.L.R.2d 1097 (similar, criminal cases).

38. See authorities cited § 212, n. 8, supra.

39. A majority of jurisdictions appear to view maps, models, etc., used to illustrate testimony as fully admissible. See Annots., 9 A.L.R.2d 1044, 69 A.L.R. 2d 424. However, the following variegated positions are to be noted: Crocker v. Lee, 261 Ala. 439, 74 So.2d 429 (1954) ("The use of a map . . . for illustration must be distinguished from its admission in evidence"); State v. Peters, 44 Hawaii 1, 352 P.2d 329 (1959) ("irregular" to admit sketch used for illustration); Baker v. Zimmerman, 179 Iowa 272, 161 N.W. 479 (1917) (whether illustrative item formally admitted "insignificant," but it should not be taken to jury room); McCormick v. Smith, 246 N.C. 425, 98 S.E.2d 448 (1957) (map not "substantive evidence" but properly used to aid description); Chambers v. Robert, 160 N.E.2d 673 (Ohio App.1959) (stating illustrative sketch should not be admitted and opponent is entitled, on demand, to an instruction that item is illustrative).

McCormick et al on Evid. 2nd Ed. HB—34

40. See, e. g., Maxwell v. State, 236 Ark. 694, 370 S.W.2d 113 (1963); Grantham v. Herod, 320 S.W.2d 536 (Mo.1959); Traders & Gen. Ins. Co. v. Stone, 258 S.W.2d 409 (Tex.Civ.App.1953) (model spine and nerve charts used but not offered; no error). But compare Handford v. Cole, 402 P.2d 209 (Wyo. 1965) (error to allow reference to drawings before formally identified and introduced).

41. See, e. g., Radetsky v. Leonard, 145 Colo. 358, 358 P.2d 1014 (1961); Meglemry v. Bruner, 344 S.W. 2d 808 (Ky.1961); State ex rel. State Highway Com'n v. Hill, 373 S.W.2d 666 (Mo.1963) (remanding for new trial because of obscurity of record).

42. See Handford v. Cole, 402 P.2d 209 (Wyo.1965). Correspondingly, the blackboard as a device for illustrating testimony and argument has been replaced by an easel with a large pad of paper on which drawings may be made and the sheets included in the record on review when appropriate.

43. See, e. g., People v. Jordan, 188 Cal.App.2d 456, 10 Cal.Rptr. 495 (1961) (where real evidence unavailable, similar object may be admitted); Sherman v. City of Springfield, 77 Ill.App.2d 195, 222

ly viewed as within the discretion of the trial court,[44] it has been suggested that it would constitute reversible error to exclude a duplicate testified to be identical to the object involved in the occurrence.[45] On the other hand, if there is an absence of testimony that the object to be illustrated ever existed the introduction of a "duplicate" may foster a mistaken impression of certainty and thus merit exclusion.[46]

Models, maps, sketches, and diagrams (as distinguished from duplicates) are by their nature generally not confusable with real evidence, and are admissible simply on the basis of testimony that they are substantially accurate representations of what the witness is endeavoring to describe.[47] Some discretionary control in the trial court is generally deemed appropriate, however, since exhibits

of this kind, due to inaccuracies, variations of scale, etc., may on occasion be more misleading than helpful.[48] Nevertheless, when the trial court has exercised its discretion to admit, it will only rarely be found in error, at least if potentially misleading inaccuracies have been pointed out by witnesses for the proponent, or could have been exposed upon cross-examination.[49]

214. Photographs,[50] Movies,[51] and Sound Recordings.[52]

The principle upon which photographs are most commonly admitted into evidence is the same as that underlying the admission of illustrative drawings, maps and diagrams. Under this theory, a photograph is viewed merely as a graphic portrayal of oral testimony, and becomes admissible only when a witness has testified that it is a correct and accurate representation of relevant facts personally observed by the witness.[53] Accordingly, un-

N.E.2d 62 (1966) (error to exclude accurate duplicate where original unobtainable). Similar results have been reached by admitting objects as real evidence on the basis of equivocal "identifications". See, e. g., Crosby v. State, 2 Md.App. 578, 236 A.2d 33 (1967) (unique gun "looking like" that used admitted); Isaacs v. National Bank of Commerce, 50 Wash.2d 548, 313 P.2d 684 (1957) (hose "believed" to be the hose in question admitted). But compare Alston v. Shiver, 105 So.2d 785 (Fla.1958) (error to admit axe handle 3 feet long to illustrate one 2 feet long).

44. See, e. g., State v. McClain, 404 S.W.2d 186 (Mo.1966). An even more permissive view is suggested by Finch v. W. R. Roach Co., 295 Mich. 589, 295 N.W. 324 (1940) (duplicate admissible if proponent introduces testimony from which similarity might be found).

45. Cincinnati, N. O. & T. P. Ry. Co. v. Duvall, 263 Ky. 387, 92 S.W.2d 363 (1936) (error to exclude model of car step proved to be exact duplicate); Rich v. Cooper, 234 Ore. 300, 380 P.2d 613 (1963) (error to exclude exact duplicates; dictum).

46. See Young v. Price, 50 Haw. 430, 442 P.2d 67 (1968) (comprehensive discussion of problem).

47. See, e. g., Grayson v. Williams, 256 F.2d 61 (10th Cir. 1958) (plat admissible where substantially accurate but not exact); United States v. D'Antonio, 324 F.2d 667 (3d Cir. 1963) (blackboard sketch not to scale admissible) cert. denied 376 U.S. 909; City of Tucson v. LaForge, 8 Ariz.App. 413, 446 P.2d 692 (1968) (model; semble). But cf. Swiney v. State Highway Dept., 116 Ga.App. 667, 158 S.E.2d 321 (1967) (no error to exclude map not established as accurate).

48. San Mateo County v. Christen, 22 Cal.App.2d 375, 71 P.2d 88 (1937) (engineer's model excluded; "while models may frequently be of great assistance . . . even when constructed to scale they may frequently, because of the great disparity in size . . . also be very misleading, and trial courts must be allowed wide discretion . . .").

49. See, e. g., Grandquest v. Williams, 273 Ala. 140, 135 So.2d 391 (1961) (not error to admit sketch and toy autos not to scale where witness pointed out inaccuracies and could have been further cross-examined); Arkansas State Highway Comm'n v. Rhodes, 240 Ark. 565, 401 S.W.2d 558 (1966) (inaccuracies not misleading where explained); Mississippi Road Supply Co. v. Baker, 199 So.2d 820 (Miss.1967) (cross-examination as to inaccuracies allowed, no chance of misleading).

50. 3 Wigmore, Evidence (Chadbourn rev.) §§ 790–798; Scott, Photographic Evidence (2d ed. 1967); C.J.S. Evidence §§ 709–716; Dec.Dig. Evidence ⊕359(1), 380.

51. 3 Wigmore, Evidence (Chadbourn rev.) § 798(a); Dec.Dig. Evidence ⊕359(6); Paradis, The Celluloid Witness, 37 U.Colo.L.Rev. 235 (1965).

52. Dec.Dig. Evidence ⊕359(5), 380.

53. 3 Wigmore, Evidence (Chadbourn rev.) § 790, at 218: " . . . the mere picture . . . cannot be received except as a non-verbal expression of the *testimony of some witness* competent to speak

der this theory, the witness who lays the foundation need not be the photographer nor need he know anything of the time, conditions, or mechanisms of the taking.[54] Instead he need only know about the facts represented or the scene or objects photographed, and once this knowledge is shown he can say whether the photograph correctly and accurately portrays these facts.[54] Once the photograph is thus verified it is admissible as a graphic portrayal of the verifying witness'

testimony into which it is incorporated by reference.[55]

The foregoing doctrine concerning the basis on which photographs are admitted is clearly a viable one and has undoubtedly served to facilitate the introduction of the general run of photographs. Unfortunately, however, some courts have tended to carry the implications of the theory to unwonted lengths, admitting photographs as "illustrative" evidence but denying them "substantive" effect.[56] It is believed that this distinction is essentially groundless,[57] and fails to warrant the practical consequences which are sometimes seen to flow from it.[58]

The products of certain applications of the photographic process do not readily lend themselves to admission in evidence on the foregoing theory.[59] X-ray photographs are

to the facts represented." State v. Smith, 27 N.J. 433, 142 A.2d 890, 899 (1958) ("Fundamentally, photographs are deemed to be pictorial communications of a qualified witness.") In the effort to establish photographs as accurately illustrative of the data observed by the witness, it is sometimes forgotten that the data itself must be relevant. Knihal v. State, 150 Neb. 771, 36 N.W.2d 109, 9 A.L.R.2d 891 (1949) (holding photos improperly received where foundation established only that photo correctly portrayed objects photographed but did not establish what objects were.); Beattie v. Traynor, 114 Vt. 495, 49 A.2d 200, 204 (1946) ("A photograph . . . is merely a witness' pictured expression of the data observed by him . . . and its admission, when properly verified, rests on the relevancy of the fact pictured."). Kleveland v. United States, 345 F.2d 134 (2d Cir. 1965) (improper to exclude photo not seen taken by witness); Kortz v. Guardian Life Ins. Co., 144 F.2d 676 (9th Cir. 1944) (proper foundation may be laid either by photographer or another qualified person.); Adams v. City of San Jose, 164 Cal.App.2d 665, 330 P.2d 840 (1958).

54. Kooyumjian v. Stevens, 10 Ill.App.2d 378, 135 N.E.2d 146, 151 (1956) ("The witness need not be the photographer, nor need he know anything of the time or condition of the taking, but he must have personal knowledge of the scene or object in question and testify that is correctly portrayed by the photograph.") Even if the photograph is defective, or is taken after the scene or object in question has undergone changes, it may still come in if substantially correct and potentially helpful to the jury. Driver v. Worth Const. Co., 264 S.W.2d 174 (Tex.Civ.App.1954) rev'd on other grounds, 154 Tex. 66, 273 S.W.2d 603 (subsequent photo of scene admissible despite changed conditions); Owens v. Anderson, 58 Wash.2d 448, 364 P.2d 14 (1961) (slight changes in scene went to weight). But seriously defective photography or radically altered conditions may work exclusion. Stormont v. New York Cent. R. R. Co., 1 Ohio App.2d 414, 205 N.E.2d 74, n. 1 (1964) (improper to admit photos so poor as to distort conditions); Jones v. Talbot, 87 Idaho 498, 394 P.2d 316 (1964) (drastically altered conditions; photos properly excluded).

55. Finch v. W. R. Roach Co., 295 Mich. 589, 295 N.W. 324, 326 (1940).

56. See, e. g., Foster v. Bilbruck, 20 Ill.App.2d 173, 155 N.E.2d 366 (1959) (stating that photos stand on same footing as maps and models, and are not themselves evidence); State v. Bass, 249 N.C. 209, 105 S.E.2d 645 (1958) (citing many North Carolina precedents drawing the distinction.)

57. See Gardner, The Camera Goes to Court, 24 N.C.L.Rev. 233, 245 (1956) (cogent criticism of the distinction). Some courts explicitly reject the distinction, State v. Goyet, 120 Vt. 12, 132 A.2d 623, 631 (1957) (". . . a photograph is admissible in evidence, not merely as a map or diagram representing things to which a witness testifies, but as direct evidence of things which have not been directly described by a witness as having come from his observation."); a majority of courts simply seems to ignore it. See cases cited 3 Wigmore, Evidence (Chadbourn rev.) § 792, note 1; Dec.Dig. Evidence ⊂⊃359.

58. In those jurisdictions in which a photograph is considered merely illustrative, the adverse party may be entitled to an instruction that the photo is not substantive evidence. See Honeycutt v. Cherokee Brick Co., 196 N.C. 556, 146 S.E. 227 (1929); Hunt v. Wooten, 238 N.C. 42, 76 S.E.2d 326 (1953). Or, like other "illustrative" evidence, the jury may not be permitted to take the photo to the jury room. See cases cited supra, § 213, n. 39; and see generally § 217, infra.

59. Comment, Photographic Evidence—Is There a Recognized Basis for Admissibility? 8 Hast.L.J. 310 (1957) (noting that scenes photographed by infrared flash or by electronically triggered sur-

a common example, and are of course constantly admitted, despite the fact that no witness has actually viewed the objects portrayed.[60] The foundation typically required for X rays is calculated to demonstrate that a reliable scientific process was correctly utilized to obtain the product offered in evidence. Some few courts have explicitly recognized what the general treatment of X rays would imply, i. e., that the validity of the photographic process, together with adequate proof of its proper utilization, constitutes a valid alternative ground for the admission of photographic evidence.[61] More widespread recognition of this alternative basis of admissibility may perhaps be anticipated.[62]

The interest and vividness of photographs may be heightened by utilization of various techniques of photography, such as having the photographs taken in color, or having them enlarged so that pertinent facts may be more readily observed. While the use of these techniques clearly increases the number of factors subject to distortion, the basic standard governing admission of photos generally remains applicable.[63] Thus color and enlarged photographs have generally been viewed as admissible provided the photo represents the scene depicted with substantial accuracy.[64]

A somewhat more troublesome problem is presented by posed or artificially reconstructed scenes, in which people, automobiles, and other objects are placed so as to conform to the descriptions of the original crime or collision given by the witnesses.[65] When the posed photographs go no further than to por-

veillance cameras are not seen by any potential witness.) For additional illustrations of photographic evidence presenting difficulties under ordinary theory, see People v. Bowley, 59 Cal.2d 855, 382 P.2d 591, 31 Cal.Rptr. 471 (1963). And see 3 Wigmore, Evidence (Chadbourn rev.) § 790, p. 219.

60. See 3 Wigmore, Evidence (Chadbourn rev.) § 795; Dec.Dig. Evidence ⚷380.

61. People v. Bowley, 59 Cal.2d 855, 382 P.2d 591, 595, 31 Cal.Rptr. 471 (1963) ("We hold . . . that a photograph may, in a proper case, be admitted into evidence not merely as illustrated testimony of a human witness but as probative evidence in itself of what it shows."); People v. Doggett, 83 Cal.App.2d 405, 188 P.2d 792 (1948) (photos of defendants committing crime against nature; no other witnesses but photos admitted on basis of testimony by expert photographer that they were not composites or otherwise altered); State v. Matheson, 130 Iowa 440, 103 N.W. 137, 138 (1905) (". . . the court takes judicial notice of the fact that by the ordinary photographic process a representation can be secured, sufficiently truthful and reliable to be considered as evidence with reference to objects which are in a condition to be thus photographed without regard to whether they have been actually observed by any witness or not.").

62. Adoption of the alternative theory of admissibility would adequately solve a dilemma such as that faced by the court in United States v. Hobbs, 403 F.2d 977 (6th Cir. 1968) (photos of bank robbery by surveillance camera held properly admitted without positive identification by witness of individuals photographed; orthodox theory strained). Compare Mikus v. United States, 433 F.2d 719 (2d Cir. 1970) (bank teller testified that film by surveillance camera correctly represented daytime robbery at which she was present; held sufficient). See United States v. Cairns, 434 F.2d 643 (9th Cir. 1970) (proper to use expert testimony to establish identity of person in surveillance photograph and accused in photograph taken of him shortly before trial).

63. See, e. g., Johnson v. Clement F. Sculley Const. Co., 255 Minn. 41, 95 N.W.2d 409 (1959) (color photos of personal injury admissible if accurate); Commonwealth Dept. of Highways v. Williams, 317 S.W.2d 482 (Ky.1958) (semble); State v. Clark, 99 Ore. 629, 196 Pac. 360 (1921) (enlargements held admissible if not misleading; excellent older opinion). Nor does the presence of both factors together necessitate exclusion. See Commonwealth v. Makarewicz, 333 Mass. 575, 132 N.E.2d 294 (1955) (enlarged color photos held properly admitted).

64. See Annot., 53 A.L.R.2d 1102 (collecting cases on color photos); 72 A.L.R.2d 308 (enlargements). The following cases suggest that some failure to achieve exact reproduction is permissible: Green v. City and County of Denver, 111 Colo. 390, 142 P.2d 277 (1943) (color photos held admissible to show condition of putrid meat despite underexposure which made meat appear darker than it was.); State v. Smith, 27 N.J. 433, 142 A.2d 890 (1958) (color transparencies showing "bloody areas" admissible in trial court's discretion though witness testified pictures might "exaggerate on the red side").

65. Cases involving posed photos are collected in Annots., 27 A.L.R. 913, 19 A.L.R.2d 877. See also, Dec.Dig. Criminal Law ⚷438(k).

tray the positions of persons and objects as reflected in the undisputed testimony, their admission has long been generally approved.[66] Frequently, however, a posed photograph will portray only the version of the facts supported by the testimony of the proponent's witness. The dangers inherent in this situation, i. e., the tendency of the photographs unduly to emphasize certain testimony and the possibility that the jury may confuse parties' own reconstruction with objective fact, have led many courts to exclude photographs of this type.[67] The orthodox theory of photos as merely illustrated testimony, however, can be viewed to support the admission of any photo reflecting a state of facts testified to by a witness and the current trend would appear to be to permit even photos of disputed reconstructions in some instances.[68]

Motion pictures, when they were first sought to be introduced in evidence, were frequently objected to and sometimes excluded on the theory that they afforded manifold opportunities for fabrication and distortion.[69]

Even those older decisions which upheld the admission of motion pictures appear to have done so on the basis of elaborate foundation testimony detailing the methods of taking, processing, and projecting the film.[70] More recently, however, it appears to have become generally recognized that, as with the still photograph, the reliability and accuracy of the motion picture need not necessarily rest upon the validity of the process used in its creation, but rather may be established by testimony that the motion picture accurately reproduces phenomena actually perceived by the witness.[71] Under this theory, though the requisite foundation may, and usually will, be laid by the photographer, it may also be provided by any witness who perceived the events filmed.[72] Of course, if the foundation testimony reveals the film to be distorted in some material particular, exclusion is the proper result.[73]

Judicial discretion in the admission or exclusion of motion pictures is constantly em-

66. See, e. g., Langley v. State, 90 Okl.Cr. 310, 213 P.2d 886 (1950) (photos found illustrative of factual circumstances rather than party theory held properly admitted); Pollack v. State, 215 Wis. 200, 253 N.W. 560 (1934) (murder; photos of defendants in positions which they indicated they occupied at time of shooting). See also Note, 7 W. & M.L.Rev. 137 (1966) (collecting cases involving posed photos).

67. See, e. g., Martin v. State, 217 Miss. 506, 64 So.2d 629 (1953) (photos inadmissible where positions of persons shown was in dispute); Lynch v. Missouri-K.-T. R. Co., 333 Mo. 89, 61 S.W.2d 918 (1933).

68. See, e. g., Tumey v. Richardson, 437 S.W.2d 201 (Ky.1969) (photos of posed accident scene admissible despite conflict in testimony as to material particulars). A number of courts have recently adopted the intermediate position that photos of partisan reconstruction are admissible if a pressing necessity is shown. See, e. g., State v. Oldham, 92 Idaho 124, 438 P.2d 275 (1968); State v. Ray, 43 N.J. 19, 202 A.2d 425 (1964). See also, Note, 47 Ky.L.J. 117 (1958) (arguing for freer admission of posed photos).

69. See, e. g., Gibson v. Gunn, 206 App.Div. 464, 202 N.Y.S. 19 (1923); Massachusetts Bonding &

Ins. Co. v. Worthy, 9 S.W.2d 388 (Tex.Civ.App. 1928) ("It is common knowledge that pictures showing a person in action may be made very deceptive . . ."; not error to exclude).

70. See, e. g., McGoorty v. Benhart, 305 Ill.App. 458, 27 N.E.2d 289 (1940) (motion pictures of malingerer admitted after laying of elaborate foundation).

71. See, e. g., Long v. General Electric Co., 213 Ga. 809, 102 S.E.2d 9 (1958) (motion picture held admissible on basis of foundation testimony by witness-photographer that it portrayed what he saw); Haley v. Hockey, 199 Misc. 512, 103 N.Y.S.2d 717 (Sup.Ct.1950) (movie admissible upon identification of persons and actions filmed). See also, International Union v. Russell, 264 Ala. 456, 88 So.2d 175 (1956) aff'd, 356 U.S. 634 (1958); Annots., 62 A.L.R. 2d 686, 9 A.L.R.2d 921.

72. The witness through whom the foundation for introduction of motion pictures, as distinguished from stills, is laid must have been present when the pictures were taken. See Hare, Demonstrative Evidence, 27 Ala.Law 193 (1966).

73. Powell v. Industrial Com'n, 4 Ariz.App. 172, 418 P.2d 602 (1966) (films misrepresenting speed of actions portrayed inadmissible), vac. on other grounds 102 Ariz. 11, 423 P.2d 348 (1967); Utley v. Heckinger, 235 Ark. 780, 362 S.W.2d 13 (1962) (preferable not to have shown portion of film which accelerated portrayed action).

phasized in the decisions,[74] and is perhaps largely attributable to the fact that the presentation of this kind of evidence will involve considerable expenditure of time and inconvenience. At the same time, however, when motion pictures are offered which reproduce the actual facts or original events in controversy, such as films of an allegedly incapacitated plaintiff shoveling snow or playing baseball,[75] or post-arrest films of an allegedly intoxicated driver,[76] the cogency of the evidence is such that the taking of considerable time and trouble to view the evidence would appear amply warranted.[77]

The extreme vividness and persuasiveness of motion pictures, however, is a two-edged sword. If the film does not portray original facts in controversy, but rather represents a staged reproduction of one party's version of those facts, the danger that the jury may confuse art with reality is particularly great. Further, the vivid impressions on the trier of fact created by the viewing of motion pictures will be particularly difficult to limit or, if the film is subsequently deemed to be inadmissible, to expunge by judicial instruction.

The latter difficulty may be largely eliminated by a preliminary viewing of the film by the trial court in chambers, and the decided cases suggest that this expedient is widely employed.[78] The former difficulty, while not so easily met, may be of less significance today than formerly, due to a higher level of jury sophistication concerning motion pictures.[79]

Sound recordings will sometimes be offered as an integral part of a motion picture, but a recording alone may of course also be probative of relevant facts. When a sound recording consists of spoken words, questions concerning the "best evidence" rule and the rule of completeness may be raised.[80] But sound recordings may also be offered as reproducing relevant nonverbal sounds, and when this is the purpose the considerations potentially affecting admissibility are substantially similar to those relating to motion pictures. Thus, the recording will generally be admitted if a witness testifies that the recording as played is an accurate reproduction of relevant sounds previously audited by the witness.[81]

---

74. See, e. g., Luther v. Maple, 250 F.2d 916 (8th Cir. 1958) (no abuse of discretion despite appellate court's belief that admission had been unwise); International Union v. Russell, 264 Ala. 456, 88 So.2d 175 (1956) aff'd 356 U.S. 634 (question within discretion of trial court, reviewable only for gross abuse).

75. See, e. g., Heiman v. Market St. Ry. Co., 21 Cal. App.2d 311, 69 P.2d 178 (1937); McGoorty v. Benhart, 305 Ill.App. 458, 27 N.E.2d 289 (1940); Lamburt v. Wolf's, Inc., 132 So.2d 522 (La.App.1961).

76. See, e. g., Lanford v. People, 159 Colo. 136, 409 P.2d 829 (1966) (motion picture of alleged drunk driver admissible though film disclosed defendant's declination to take sobriety test; extensive review of pertinent authorities). See also, Commonwealth v. Roller, 100 Pa.Super. 125 (1930) (sound motion picture of defendant's confession).

77. Barham v. Nowell, 243 Miss. 441, 138 So.2d 493 (1962) (error to exclude motion pictures which in trial court's opinion were not "clear"); Wren v. St. Louis Public Service Co., 333 S.W.2d 92 (Mo. 1960) (containing suggestion that if cogent motion pictures could not be satisfactorily viewed in courtroom, court should move to see them).

78. See, e. g., Wren v. St. Louis Pub. Serv. Co., supra note 77. Additional cases are collected in Paradis, The Celluloid Witness, 37 U.Colo.L.Rev. 235, 246 at n. 52 (1965).

79. See, e. g., Greeneich v. Southern Pac. Co., 189 Cal.App.2d 100, 11 Cal.Rptr. 235 (1961), criticized in 47 Iowa L.Rev. 1138 (1963); Streit v. Kestel, 108 Ohio App. 241, 161 N.E.2d 409 (1949) (films of staged reenactment admissible in discretion of trial court where substantial similarity of conditions shown); Paradis, op. cit. n. 78, supra, at p. 267.

80. See Ch. 23, infra; § 56, supra.

81. See, e. g., Wilms v. Hand, 101 Cal.App.2d 811, 226 P.2d 728 (1951) (recordings of dog noises emanating from veterinary establishment and alleged to be a nuisance); Ragusa v. American Metal Works, 97 So.2d 683 (La.App.1957) (recordings of factory noises; semble). Cases dealing with the admissibility of sound recordings are collected in Annot., 58 A.L.R.2d 1024; Dec.Dig., Evidence ⊛358(5).

215. Bodily Demonstrations; Experiments in Court.

The exhibition of a wound or physical injury, e. g., the injury sustained by a plaintiff in a personal injury action, will frequently be the best and most direct evidence of a material fact.[82] Not surprisingly, therefore, exhibitions of physical injuries to the jury are commonly allowed.[83] In most jurisdictions the matter is viewed as subject to the discretion of the trial court,[84] but has sometimes been said to be a matter of right on the part of the injured party.[85] Further, in those jurisdictions which hold the matter to be discretionary, a trial court is rarely reversed for permitting a bodily exhibition. Thus, when the exhibition is permitted no abuse of discretion is generally found present even though the injury displayed was particularly shocking,[86] or even where the injury's nature or existence need not have been proved because admitted.[87]

Judicial opinion has been somewhat more divided concerning the propriety of going beyond the mere exhibition of an injury or physical condition by having the injured person perform actions or submit to manipulation by a physician.[88] The dangers inherent in demonstrations of this latter type include undue emotional response on the part of the jury and the fact that manifestations of pain and impairment of function are easily feigned and difficult to test by cross-examination.[89] Nevertheless, this matter too is commonly left to the discretion of the trial courts, and that discretion is frequently exercised in favor of permitting the demonstration.[90] Occasional cases have, however,

---

82. See, e. g., Calumet Paving Co. v. Butkus, 113 Ind.App. 232, 47 N.E.2d 829 (1943) ("There is no other class of evidence more satisfactory or convincing . . . than the production and inspection of the very object or person whose condition is being investigated . . ."); Chicago, R. I. & G. Ry. Co. v. DeBord, 62 Tex.Civ.App. 302, 132 S.W. 845 (1910) (exhibition of injuries proper; "evidence of a very high degree.") The significance of the exhibition, however, will vary with the issue to be proved. See Radosh v. Shipstad, 17 A.D.2d 660, 230 N.Y.S.2d 295 (1962) (exhibition of professional ice-skater in costume improper in breach of contract suit where issue was whether skater's weight at a prior time justified suspension.)

83. See Annot., 66 A.L.R.2d 1334; Dec.Dig. Evidence ⚷192, Trial ⚷27.

84. See, e. g., Spaak v. Chicago & N. W. Ry. Co., 231 F.2d 279 (7th Cir. 1956) (exhibition of injured foot; discretion of trial court not abused); Darling v. Charleston Comm. Mem. Hosp., 50 Ill.App.2d 253, 200 N.E.2d 149, 185 (1964) aff'd 33 Ill.2d 326, 211 N.E.2d 253 (1965) cert. den. 383 U.S. 946 ("Permitting the plaintiff to exhibit the stump of his amputated leg is within the discretion of the court, and only if there be an abuse of discretion . . . would such be reversible error"; no abuse found).

85. Olson v. Tyner, 219 Iowa 251, 257 N.W. 538 (1934) (plaintiff stripped to the waist to display shriveled left arm dangling "as though suspended by a string"; " . . . appellee had the right to exhibit to the jury his arm to show the condition he was in"); Missouri, K. & T. R. Co. v. O'Hare, 39 S.W.2d 939, 941 (Tex.Civ.App.1931) (" . . . we think appellee had the right if he desired, to exhibit his injured arm to the jury;" but propriety of repeated exhibitions questioned.).

86. See, e. g., Slattery v. Marra Bros., 186 F.2d 134, 138 (2d Cir. 1951) (" . . . ordinarily it would seem that the very hideousness of the deformity was a part of the suffering of the victim, and could not rationally be excluded in assessment of his damages."); Beal v. Southern Union Gas Co., 66 N.M. 424, 349 P.2d 337 (1960) (not abuse of discretion in allowing plaintiff whose eyes, nose and ears were burned out to display injuries); Shell Petroleum v. Perrin, 179 Okl. 142, 64 P.2d 309 (1936) (not error to permit mother of little girl suing for injury to eye to remove girl's glass eye before the jury).

87. See, e. g., Stegall v. Carlson, 6 Ill.App.2d 388, 128 N.E.2d 352 (1955) (exhibition proper even where fact and nature of injury not disputed); Chicago, B. & O. R. Co. v. Krayenbuhl, 70 Neb. 766, 98 N.W. 44 (1904) (rejecting contention that injury may not be displayed where admitted.) But compare Harper v. Bolton, 239 S.C. 541, 124 S.E. 2d 54 (1962) (finding abuse in admission of plaintiff's removed and preserved eye where loss of eye was admitted).

88. See cases collected Annot., 66 A.L.R.2d 1382; Dec.Dig. Evidence ⚷192.

89. The possible objections to the practice are enumerated in an excellent older opinion, Clark v. Brooklyn Heights R. Co., 177 N.Y. 359, 69 N.E. 647 (1904) (criticizing demonstration, but holding matter discretionary).

90. See, e. g., Happy v. Walz, 224 S.W.2d 380 (Mo. App.1951) (manipulation of feet and legs by doctor); Wilson & Co. v. Campbell, 195 Okl. 323, 157 P.2d 465 (1945) (going beyond mere exhibition requires

held the allowance of a particular demonstration to be an abuse of trial court discretion, a fact which may suggest that the tactic is a somewhat hazardous one for the party utilizing it.[91]

Whether demonstrations in the form of experiments in court are to be permitted is also largely subject to the discretion of the trial judge.[92] Unlike experiments performed out of court, the results of which are generally communicated testimonially, in-court experimentation may involve considerable confusion and delay, and the trial judge is viewed as in the best position to judge whether the game is worth the candle.[93]

Simple demonstrations by a witness are usually permitted, and may be strikingly effective in adding vividness to the spoken word.[94]

In addition to the limitations arising from the desirability of orderly and expeditious proceedings, in-court experiments are held to the same basic requirement of similarity of conditions which is applicable to experimental evidence generally.[95] This requirement may be particularly difficult to meet under courtroom conditions, and many proposed courtroom experiments have been held properly excluded on this ground.[96] Never-

---

discretionary control by trial court; no abuse to allow cross-plaintiff to demonstrate numbness of injured leg by use of pins); Green v. Boney, 233 S.C. 49, 103 S.E.2d 732 (1958) (no abuse of discretion to permit plaintiff, once sworn, to demonstrate limp to jury.) It may be noted that testimony as to pain and impairment of use is also subject to fabrication.

91. See, e. g., Willis v. Browning, 161 Mo.App. 461, 143 S.W. 516 (1912) (permitting plaintiff to show how she could walk without crutches held reversible error; court distinguishes mere exhibition of injury); Peters v. Hockley, 152 Ore. 434, 53 P.2d 1059 (1936) (abuse of discretion to permit demonstration calculated to make plaintiff cry out in pain.) It would appear that screaming by the party being manipulated, though sometimes viewed as not prejudicial, is a factor likely to lead to reversal. See cases cited Annot., 66 A.L.R.2d 1382.

92. See, e. g., Lynch v. Missouri-K.-T. Ry. Co., 333 Mo. 89, 61 S.W.2d 918 (1933) (admission of experimental evidence, whether experiment performed in or out of court, said to be "peculiarly within the discretion of the trial judge.") See also, Rex v. Duncan, [1944] 1 K.B. 713, Ct.Crim.App. (spiritualist medium, prosecuted under witchcraft statute, refused permission to summon departed spirits to courtroom); Coca Cola Co. v. Langston, 198 Ark. 59, 127 S.W.2d 263 (1939) (witness offered to swallow teaspoon of ground glass; refusal to permit discretionary); Raymond v. J. R. Watkins Co., 88 F.Supp. 932 (D.Minn.1950), rev'd on other grounds 184 F.2d 925 (breach of implied warranty on shampoo; discretion whether to allow defendant to shampoo another person in court exercised against experiment); Otte v. Taylor, 180 Neb. 795, 146 N.W.2d 78 (1966) (physician allowed to swallow nembutal tablets at beginning of testimony and to testify an hour later he was not drowsy; discretion to permit upheld).

93. See Otte v. Taylor, op. cit. supra n. 92; Hassebroek v. Norman, 236 Ore. 209, 387 P.2d 824 (1963)

(trial court refused to permit demonstration of child's toy which had injured plaintiff; "A request for a courtroom demonstration creates a problem peculiarly directed to the trial judge.")

94. See, e. g., Hamilton v. Pepsi Cola Bottling Co., 132 A.2d 500 (Mun.Ct.App.D.C., 1957) (no abuse in permitting demonstration that pop bottles could be unsealed and resealed without detection); Backstrom v. New York Life Ins. Co., 194 Minn. 67, 259 N.W. 681 (1935) (issue as to suicide or accidental shooting; witness who discovered body allowed to demonstrate its position by lying on the floor.); Geisel v. Maintl, 427 S.W.2d 525 (Mo.1968) (suit for personal injuries allegedly due to wobbly handrail; jurors held properly allowed to pull on scale previously used in out-of-court experiment to "see how much 25 pounds is.")

95. See § 202, supra.

96. See, e. g., Burriss v. Texaco, Inc., 361 F.2d 169 (4th Cir. 1966) (within trial court's discretion to refuse to permit re-enactment of fire on model of railroad yard where model was not to scale); Whitehurst v. Revlon, Inc., 307 F.Supp. 918 (E.D. Va.1969) (experiment to show inflammability of nail polish disallowed; conditions in court dissimilar to those of plaintiff's home); Pond v. Anderson, 241 Iowa 1038, 44 N.W.2d 372 (1952) (witness testified she overheard other end of a telephone call taken by her husband; not abuse of discretion to disallow experiment whether witness could overhear remote end of call to phone on judge's desk since conditions dissimilar); Beasley v. Ford Motor Co., 237 S.C. 506, 117 S.E.2d 863 (1961) (proper to refuse experiment to show gasoline in contact with hot metal surface will not ignite; "A hot plate in the hands of the witness would hardly be comparable to the hot automobile motor . . . ."). But experiments may sometimes illustrate a material fact even where similarity of conditions is lacking. See Davis v. Walter, 259 Iowa 837, 146 N.W.2d 247 (1966) (demonstration of operation of hazard lights proper in discretion of trial court simply to show mode of operation).

theless, the well-planned courtroom experiment may provide extremely striking and persuasive evidence, and the opportunities for utilizing such experiments should not be overlooked.

216. Views.[97]

The courts, like the prophet, have sensibly recognized that if a thing cannot be brought to the observer, the observer must go to the thing. Venturing forth to observe places or objects which are material to litigation but which cannot feasibly be brought, or satisfactorily reproduced, within the courtroom, is termed a "view." While statutes or court rules concerning views are in effect in nearly all states,[98] it is frequently said that even without express statutory authorization there is an inherent power in the trial judge to order a view by the jury[99] or, in a judge-tried case, to take a view himself.[1] This power extends to views of personalty[2] as well as realty, and to criminal[3] as well as civil cases.

Since a view is often time-consuming and disruptive of the ordinary course of a trial, the trial judge is in most instances vested with a wide leeway of discretion to grant or refuse a view.[4] It is to be noted, however, that in a number of states statutes provide that in certain types of cases, notably eminent domain, either party is entitled to a view upon request as a matter of right.[5] Where the grant of a view is discretionary with the trial court, as is usually the case, factors which are commonly stated to be appropriate for consideration by the court in determining whether to grant a view include the importance to the issue of the information to be gained by the view[6] the extent to which this information has or could have been secured from maps, photographs, or diagrams,[7] and the extent to which the place or object to be viewed has changed in appearance since the controversy arose.[8]

---

97. 4 Wigmore, Evidence §§ 1162–1169; Dec.Dig. Trial ☞28, Criminal Law ☞641.

98. See the rules and statutes collected in 4 Wigmore, Evidence § 1163, notes 7, 8.

99. Basham v. Owensboro City R. Co., 169 Ky. 155, 183 S.W. 492 (1916); State v. Black, 193 Ore. 295, 236 P.2d 326 (1951) (inherent power of trial court to order view of stolen cattle unaffected by statute expressly sanctioning only views of realty); State v. Coburn, 82 Idaho 437, 354 P.2d 751 (1960) (view of automobiles, semble). Compare Steward v. State, 75 Nev. 498, 346 P.2d 1083 (1959) (holding a truck to be a "place" within meaning of statute authorizing views of places).

1. Bobrick v. Taylor, 467 P.2d 822 (Colo.1970); In re Digbie's Estate, 79 N.E.2d 159 (Ohio App.1948).

2. See, e. g., cases cited note 99, supra. Even views of persons have sometimes been allowed. Nizer v. Phelps, 252 Md. 185, 249 A.2d 112 (1969) (view of personal injury victim in nursing home held permissible). Compare, however, Knight v. Landis, 11 Ga.App. 536, 75 S.E. 834 (1912) (holding views of personalty impermissible as a matter of "adopted common law," though stating that "no valid distinction" exists between views of realty and personalty).

3. Schonfeld v. United States, 277 Fed. 934 (2d Cir. 1921); State v. O'Day, 188 La. 169, 175 So. 838 (1937) (trial court had power to order view in

criminal case despite absence of statutory authorization).

4. Nearly every opinion stresses the discretion of the trial court. See, e. g., Hodge v. United States, 75 U.S.App.D.C. 332, 126 F.2d 849 (1942) (denial upheld as discretionary); Zipp v. Gasen's Drug Stores, Inc., 449 S.W.2d 612 (Mo.1970) (denial of view discretionary even where view would have been "helpful"); Bizich v. Sears, Roebuck & Co., 391 Pa. 640, 139 A.2d 663 (1958) (grant upheld); Dec.Dig. Trial ☞28(2). The trial judge's discretion extends to denying a view even though requested by both parties. Illinois Basin Oil Ass'n v. Lynn, 425 S.W.2d 555 (Ky.1968); Floyd v. Williams, 198 Miss. 350, 22 So.2d 365 (1945).

5. E. g., Fla.Stat.Ann. § 73.10(5) (1961); Ill.Rev.Stat. 1969, c. 47, § 9.

6. See, e. g., Eizerman v. Behn, 9 Ill.App.2d 263, 132 N.E.2d 788 (1956) (denial of view of washing machine upheld; present condition of washer of little significance where issue was condition at earlier time).

7. See, e. g., Peake v. Omaha Cold Storage Co., 158 Neb. 676, 64 N.W.2d 470 (1954) (numerous maps and pictures in evidence; denial of view upheld as discretionary); State v. Holden, 75 Wash.2d 413, 451 P.2d 666 (1969) (semble). See also Zipp v. Gasen's Drug Store, Inc., 449 S.W.2d 612 (Mo.1970) (other evidence, including photographs, precluded "right" to have view).

8. See, e. g., Wimberly v. City of Paterson, 75 N.J. Super. 584, 183 A.2d 691 (1962) (denial of view

The appropriate procedures to be followed in connection with views are widely regulated by statute. At common law, and generally in civil cases today, the presence of the trial judge at a view is not required,[9] the more common practice being for the jury to be conducted to the scene by "showers," expressly commissioned for the purpose.[10] Attendance at the view by the parties and their counsel is generally permitted though subject to the discretion of the trial judge.[11] In criminal cases, the rights of the defendant to have the judge present at the view, and to be present himself, are frequently provided for by statute.[12] Moreover, when testimony is taken at the view, or the view itself is deemed to constitute evidence, the right of the defend-

ant to be present in all probability possesses a constitutional underpinning.[13]

Statutory and constitutional considerations aside, the advisability of trial court attendance at views is strongly suggested by the numerous cases in which unauthorized comments, obviously hearsay,[14] have been made to the jury, or other improper events have occurred during the course of the view.[15] Presence of the trial judge would seem to afford the best guarantee available against the occurrence of events of this nature. On the other hand, where the trial judge is present to rule on admissibility, and provision for preparation of a proper record is made, there would appear no inherent vice in receiving testimony or allowing demonstrations or experiments during a view.[16] These practices,

---

not abuse of discretion where conditions changed and scene fully described by witnesses); Burke v. Thomas, 313 P.2d 1082 (Okl.1957) (denial proper within trial court's discretion where seasonal change of foliage had drastically altered scene.) See also Annot., 85 A.L.R.2d 512, collecting cases concerning effect of changed conditions upon propriety of granting view.

9. See, e. g., Sims Motor Transp. Lines, Inc. v. Foster, 293 S.W.2d 226 (Ky.1956) (attendance of trial judge at view in civil case discretionary); Yeary v. Holbrook, 171 Va. 266, 198 S.E. 441 (1938) (similar holding; excellent review of earlier authorities concerning views).

10. On occasion, the trial judge will act as shower, Yeary v. Holbrook, 171 Va. 266, 198 S.W. 441 (1938), or appoint counsel for the parties to act as showers, Snyder v. Commonwealth of Massachusetts, 291 U.S. 97 (1934).

11. See, e. g., Sims Motor Transp. Lines, Inc. v. Foster, supra n. 9.

12. As to the trial judge's obligation to attend a view in criminal cases, see, McCollum v. State, 74 So.2d 74 (Fla.1954) (holding local statute made trial judge's attendance mandatory; extensive review of authorities); State v. Rohrich, 135 N.W.2d 175 (N.D.1965) (semble). See also, Annot., 47 A.L.R.2d 1227 (necessity for presence of trial judge at view by jury in criminal case.)

Many states accord the defendant the right to be present at a view in a criminal case. See, e. g., State v. MacDonald, 229 A.2d 321 (Me.1967); Noell v. Commonwealth, 135 Va. 600, 115 S.E. 679 (1923). Others hold the matter to be discretionary. Commonwealth v. Belenski, 276 Mass. 35, 176 N.E. 501 (1931).

13. In Snyder v. Commonwealth of Massachusetts, 291 U.S. 97 (1934) the Supreme Court held, four justices dissenting, that due process had not been denied a defendant who was refused the opportunity to be present at a view, even if it were assumed that the right of confrontation guaranteed by the Sixth Amendment is "reinforced" by the Fourteenth. Thus, even though the confrontation clause has now been held operative against the states by virtue of the Fourteenth Amendment, Pointer v. Texas, 380 U.S. 400 (1965), the defendant appears to have no federally guaranteed right to attend a view in every instance. The Court, however, carefully limited its holding in Snyder to the facts of that case. These included the fact that a view is not deemed evidence in Massachusetts, that no oral testimony was taken at the view, and that the judge, court reporter, and also defendant's counsel were present. Compare State v. Garden, 267 Minn. 97, 125 N.W.2d 591 (1963) (holding defendant's constitutional rights violated by a view by jury in custody of sheriff, at which neither judge, court reporter nor defendant was present; "the substance of defendant's right is to know what transpired during the viewing.") See also Annots., 30 A.L.R. 1358; 90 id. 597.

14. 4 Wigmore, Evidence § 1167.

15. See, e. g., Scott v. Tubbs, 43 Colo. 221, 95 Pac. 540 (1908) (new trial required where petitioner entertained jury in saloon following view); Juett v. Calhoun, 405 S.W.2d 946 (Ky.1966) (error to allow jurors and party to ride together to view unaccompanied by officer.) Cases are collected in Annot., 45 A.L.R.2d 1128.

16. See, e. g., State v. O'Day, 188 La. 169, 175 So. 838, 841 (1937) ("It would seem that it would be better to explain the locus by testimony on the

however, have often been looked upon with disfavor by appellate courts,[17] and some jurisdictions appear to hold reception of testimony or experiments during a view improper under any circumstances.[18]

Closely related to the above questions is the troublesome problem of what evidentiary status a view possesses. A large number of jurisdictions, probably a majority, holds that a view is not itself evidence, but is only to assist the trier of fact in understanding and evaluating the evidence.[19] This doctrine undoubtedly rests in large part upon the consideration that facts garnered by the jury from a view are difficult or impossible to embody in the written record, thus rendering review of questions concerning weight or sufficiency of the evidence impracticable.[20] At the same time, however, this doctrine ignores the fact that many other varieties of demon-strative evidence are to some extent subject to the same difficulty, and further that it is unreasonable to assume that jurors, however they may be instructed, will apply the metaphysical distinction suggested and ignore the evidence of their own senses when it conflicts with the testimony of the witnesses. Commentators have uniformly condemned the downgrading of views to non-evidentiary status,[21] and a substantial number of courts holds a view to be evidence like any other.[22] The latter position appears to be the preferable one, at least when modified by the caveat that where the question is one of sufficiency, a view alone cannot logically be considered to constitute sufficient evidence of a fact the establishment of which ordinarily requires the introduction of expert testimony.

217. Exhibits in the Jury Room.[23]

Under modern American practice it is common to allow many types of tangible exhibits to be taken by the jury for consideration during the deliberations,[24] provided that the exhibits have been formally admitted into evidence.[25] The question whether a particular

---

scene . . ."); Tarr v. Keller Lumber & Const. Co., 106 W.Va. 99, 144 S.E. 881 (1928). For an excellent discussion of the question, generally favoring allowance of testimony and experiments at views, see Wendorf, Some Views on Jury Views, 15 Baylor L.Rev. 379, 394 (1963).

17. See, e. g., Yeary v. Holbrook, 171 Va. 266, 198 S.E. 441 (1938) (stating, "We do not approve the use of witnesses on a view . . . ," but finding no reversible error under circumstances.)

18. See, e. g., State v. Delaney, 15 Utah 2d 338, 393 P.2d 379 (1964) (statute authorizing views held not to authorize taking of testimony thereon); Brooks v. Gilbert, 250 Iowa 1164, 98 N.W.2d 309 (1960) ("recreation" of accident on view "never" permissible). A number of courts have found experiments during views involving the participation of jurors particularly offensive. See Cole v. McGhie, 59 Wash.2d 436, 367 P.2d 844 (1962) (citing numerous cases.)

19. See, e. g., Ernst v. Broughton, 213 Or. 253, 324 P.2d 241 (1959); Doherty v. Providence Journal Co., 94 R.I. 392, 181 A.2d 105 (1962); Kearns v. Hall, 197 Va. 736, 91 S.E.2d 648 (1956).

20. As to the ability of the trial judge to direct a verdict or grant a new trial for insufficiency of evidence where a view has been had, see Keeney v. Ciborowski, 304 Mass. 371, 24 N.E.2d 17 (1940). Compare Beatty v. Depue, 78 S.D. 395, 103 N.W.2d 187 (1960) (holding view does not constitute evidence, but that reviewing court should consider fact view was taken in ruling upon sufficiency of evidence).

21. Hardman, The Evidentiary Effect of a View: Stare Decisis or Stare Dictis, 53 U.W.Va.L.Rev. 103 (1951); Hardman, The Evidentiary Effect of a View—Another Word, 58 U.W.Va.L.Rev. 69 (1956); Wendorf, Some Views on Jury Views, 15 Baylor L.Rev. 379 (1963).

22. See, e. g., Neel v. Mannings, Inc., 19 Cal.2d 647, 122 P.2d 576 (1942) (view was "independent" evidence); Chouinard v. Shaw, 99 N.H. 26, 104 A.2d 522 (1954) (jury, as "sensible" persons, expected to consider view along with other evidence); Moore, Kelly & Reddish, Inc. v. Shannondale, Inc., 152 W.Va. 549, 165 S.E.2d 113 (1968).

Some courts have finessed the problems of sufficiency-evaluation attendant upon holding a view evidence by holding also that a verdict or finding must be supported by evidence apart from the view. See In re State Highway Running Through Sec. 2, Tp. 12, Cass County, 129 Neb. 822, 263 N.W. 148 (1935).

23. 6 Wigmore, Evidence § 1913; Dec.Dig. Trial ⟐307, Criminal Law ⟐858.

24. See Dec.Dig. Trial ⟐307, Criminal Law ⟐858.

25. It is uniformly viewed as improper to permit the jury to take with it items not admitted. See,

exhibit may be taken by the jury is widely viewed as subject to discretionary control by the trial judge,[26] but in some jurisdictions jury access to at least certain types of exhibits is apparently made mandatory either by judicial holding or legislative enactment.[27]

The current practice extends, unlike that at common law,[28] to written exhibits generally except for those which are testimonial in nature, such as depositions, dying declarations in writing, etc.[29] The reason underlying this latter exception is that writings which are merely testimony in a different form should not, by being allowed to the jury, be unduly emphasized over other purely oral testimony in the case.[30] As an exception to the exception, however, written or recorded confessions in criminal cases, despite their obvious testimonial character, are in many jurisdictions allowed to be taken by the jury,[31] apparently on the theory that their centrality in the case warrants whatever emphasis may result.

The practice of allowing nontestimonial written evidence generally to be taken by the jury would appear to be supported by many of the same considerations which underlie the so-called "Best Evidence Rule." [32] Legal rights and liabilities are frequently a function of particular words and figures, and may be drastically affected by seemingly minor variations in phraseology.[33] Thus crucial documents, such as deeds, contracts, or ledger sheets may frequently be of vital help to the jury.[34] On the other hand, where a writing

---

e. g., Osborne v. United States, 351 F.2d 111 (8th Cir. 1965); People v. Holcomb, 370 Ill. 299, 18 N.E. 2d 878 (1938). However, it would appear that most courts hold that the unadmitted exhibit must have been of a potentially prejudicial nature to warrant reversal. See Lyon v. Bush, 49 Haw. 116, 412 P.2d 662 (1966) (jury use of unadmitted charts and tables showing damages not shown prejudicial); Dallago v. United States, 138 U.S. App.D.C. 276, 427 F.2d 546 (1969) (unexplained presence of prejudicial record in jury room held reversible error).

26. See, e. g., People v. Allen, 17 Ill.2d 55, 160 N.E. 2d 818 (1959) (matter largely discretionary); Pakul v. Montgomery Ward Co., 282 Minn. 360, 166 N.W. 2d 65 (1969) (within trial court's discretion to withhold exhibits from jury); Durdella v. Trenton-Philadelphia Coach Co., 349 Pa. 482, 37 A.2d 481 (1944) (sending documentary exhibits with jury largely discretionary).

27. See, e. g., Texas Employers Ins. Ass'n v. Applegate, 205 S.W.2d 412 (Tex.Civ.App.1947) (statute held to require trial judge, upon written motion of one party, to send written exhibits to jury room). See also McCaffrey v. Glendale Acres, Inc., 250 Ore. 140, 440 P.2d 219 (1968) (exhibits are part of evidence and "should" go to jury room; dictum). But in some jurisdictions, statutes apparently mandatory in terms have been construed not to preempt exercise of trial judge discretion. See Mongar v. Barnard, 248 Iowa 899, 82 N.W.2d 765 (1957).

28. For explanation of the now obsolete common law practice limiting writings which could be taken to those under seal, see People v. Bartone, 12 Misc. 2d 926, 172 N.Y.S.2d 976 (1958).

29. See, e. g., Whitehead v. Seymour, 120 Ga.App. 25, 169 S.E.2d 369 (1969) (improper to allow depositions and answers to interrogatories to go to jury room, but rule does not apply to writings within Best Evidence rule); State v. Solomon, 96 Utah 500, 87 P.2d 807 (1939) (transcript of testimony at prior trial should not be sent to jury room; "The law does not permit depositions or witnesses to go to the jury room. Why should a witness be allowed to go there in the form of written testimony?").

30. Thus exhibits which, though tangible, are merely embodiments of oral testimony are said properly kept from the jury. See, e. g., Gallagher v. Viking Supply Corp., 3 Ariz.App. 55, 411 P.2d 814 (1966) (proper to refuse to send chart which illustrated testimony to jury room); Dibert v. Ross Pattern & Foundry Devel. Co., 105 Ohio App. 264, 152 N.E. 2d 369 (1958) (practice of sending exhibit marked by witness to jury room not approved). It may also be noted that the same principle underlies the frequently encountered prohibition against note-taking by jurors. See Annot., 14 A.L.R.3d 831.

31. See, e. g., People v. Caldwell, 39 Ill.2d 346, 236 N.E.2d 706 (1968) (citing numerous authorities favoring practice.) But compare State v. Lord, 42 N.M. 638, 84 P.2d 80 (1938) (holding confession not authorized to be sent to jury room under local statute).

32. Whitehead v. Seymour, 120 Ga.App. 25, 169 S.E.2d 369 (1969) (indicating writings subject to the Best Evidence rule are appropriate for jury examination).

See generally Chapter 23, infra.

33. See Morgan, Basic Problems of Evidence 385 (1962).

34. See State of N. J. v. Clawans, 38 N.J. 162, 183 A.2d 77 (1962) (subornation of perjury; sworn statement in conflict with later testimony properly allowed in jury room).

is of only minor relevance, despatch to the jury may induce an emphasis upon it out of proportion to its intrinsic worth.[35]

The case for allowing the jury to take with it tangibles other than writings is somewhat weaker, at least if in-court examination of the tangible by the jury has been had. As noted in an earlier section, demonstrative evidence has peculiar force which arguably does not stand in need of yet additional augmentation.[36] Further, the relevant characteristics of many tangible exhibits are sufficiently gross as not to require the close perusal appropriate to writings, while at the other end of the spectrum there appears some anomaly in allowing independent jury inspection of tangibles the relevant features of which are so fine as to require expert exposition and interpretation.[37] Nevertheless, the sending of tangible exhibits to the jury room is today probably so well established as to be practically irreversible.

The major problem stemming from relatively free jury access to tangible exhibits other than writings is that of controlling jury use of them for purposes of experimentation. The general limitations upon the introduc-

tion of evidence of experiments obviously become largely meaningless if the jury is allowed to conduct experiments of its own devising in the jury room. In attempting to distinguish between proper and improper jury use of tangible exhibits, the most commonly drawn distinction is between experiments which constitute merely a closer scrutiny of the exhibit and experiments which go "beyond the lines of the evidence" introduced in court and thus constitute the introduction of new evidence in the jury room.[38] The decisions reached under the aegis of this rubric are perhaps not totally reconcilable.[39] Most courts, however, emphasize the immunity of jury-conducted experiments from adversary scrutiny as their preeminently objectionable feature.[40] Thus it would seem correct to say that jury experimentation is improper if reasonable grounds existed for an adversary attack on the experiment by the complaining party and, in addition, if nothing transpiring during the in-court proceed-

35. The problem seems one best left to trial judge discretion as is done in many jurisdictions. See Durdella v. Trenton-Philadelphia Coach Co., 349 Pa. 482, 37 A.2d 481 (1944) (contradictory statement containing only minor discrepancies properly withheld in trial judge's discretion); Wilson v. Pennsylvania R. R. Co., 421 Pa. 419, 219 A.2d 666 (1966) (sending impeaching writing to jury room within trial court's discretion).

36. Some courts, however, have viewed the persuasive character of demonstrative evidence as *supporting* jury access to it! See People v. Williams, 187 Cal.App.2d 355, 9 Cal.Rptr. 722 (1960) (no error to permit gruesome photos of victim to go to jury room where photos showed "more persuasively" than testimony what happened).

37. The view here suggested appears to find support in scattered decisions. See, e. g., People v. McElroy, 63 Ill.App.2d 403, 211 N.E.2d 444 (1965) (proper exercise of discretion to refuse to allow handwriting exemplars introduced and passed among jury to go to jury room; comparison properly to be made during reception of evidence).

38. See, e. g., Imperial Meat Co. v. United States, 316 F.2d 435 (10th Cir. 1963); Higgins v. Los Angeles Gas & Elec. Co., 159 Cal. 651, 115 P. 313 (1911).

39. Compare, e. g., the following holdings: Wilson v. United States, 116 Fed. 484 (9th Cir. 1902) (prosecution for smuggling of opium "prepared for smoking;" whether opium so prepared was required to be proved by prosecution and could not be left to be ascertained by jury experiment in which opium was burned); United States v. Beach, 296 F.2d 153 (4th Cir. 1961) (improper for jury to experiment with adding machines to determine noise level, that fact bearing upon credibility of witness in case); Ingram v. State, 363 S.W.2d 284 (Tex.Cr.App.1963) (not error for jury to open and mix Copenhagen snuff with water to ascertain whether it smelled like rum as testified by witness); Taylor v. Commonwealth, 90 Va. 109, 17 S.E. 812 (1893) (holding that where defendant introduced evidence that the firing pin of his rifle did not make marks on cartridge cases similar to those of murder weapon, jury properly disassembled defendant's rifle to detect tampering with firing pin). Cases involving experimentation by the jury outside the courtroom are collected in Annot., 95 A.L.R.2d 351.

40. For able judicial statements to this effect, see United States v. Beach, 296 F.2d 153 (4th Cir. 1961); Higgins v. Los Angeles Gas & Elec. Co., 159 Cal. 651, 115 P. 313 (1911).

ings rendered such an attack inappropriate. Specifically, experiments which are merely reruns of in-court experiments, or which use techniques of examination not markedly different from those employed during trial are not generally held to fall within the proscribed class.[41] On the other hand, jury experiments utilizing techniques or equipment substantially different from any employed in court tend to be held error, at least where counsel has not specifically acquiesced in the experiment, such as by arguing that the jury should be allowed certain tools.[42]

---

41. See, e. g., Taylor v. Reo Motors, Inc., 275 F.2d 699 (10th Cir. 1960) (not improper for jury to dismantle and reassemble heat exchanger in jury room where essentially similar operation had been performed by experts in court); People v. Thorngate, 10 Mich.App. 317, 159 N.W.2d 373 (1968) (proper for jury to examine exhibits with magnifying glass); Layton v. Palmer, 309 S.W.2d 561 (Mo.1958) (semble); State v. Zobel, 81 S.D. 260, 134 N.W.2d 101 (1965) (within trial court's discretion to allow jury to have viewer with which to look at colored slides projected in court).

42. See, e. g., United States v. Beach, 296 F.2d 153 (4th Cir. 1961) (experiment with adding machine to ascertain level of noise produced held improper; court notes possible objections relating to accuracy to which experiment was subject); Jensen v. Dikel, 244 Minn. 71, 69 N.W.2d 108 (1955) (error for court to furnish tools for jury experiment in absence of express consent of parties); King v. Railway Express Agency, Inc., 94 N.W.2d 657 (N.D.1959) (introduction of ruler and string into jury room for purpose of experiment without consent of parties constituted error.)

For a suggestion of the possible problems involved in establishing that an improper jury experiment has in fact been performed, see State v. James, 70 Wash.2d 624, 424 P.2d 1005 (1967).

TITLE 9

WRITINGS

CHAPTER 22

AUTHENTICATION *

218. General Theory: No Assumption of Authenticity.

The concept of authentication, although continually used by the courts without apparent difficulty, seems almost to defy precise definition. Some writers have construed the term very broadly, as does Wigmore when he states that "when a claim or offer involves impliedly or expressly any element of *personal connection with a corporeal object*, that connection must be made to appear . . . ." [1] So defined, "authentication" is not only a necessary preliminary to the introduction of most writings in evidence, but also to the introduction of various other sorts of tangibles. For example, an article of clothing found at the scene of a crime can hardly constitute relevant evidence against the defendant unless his ownership or previous possession of the article is shown. Since au-thentication of tangibles other than writings,[2] has been treated elsewhere, however, the term authentication will here be used in the limited sense of proof of authorship of, or other connection with, writings.

It is clear that the relevancy of a writing to a particular issue raised in litigation will frequently be logically dependent upon the existence of some connection between that writing and a particular individual.[3] If Y sues X for libel and attempts to introduce into evidence a writing containing libelous statements concerning Y, it will readily appear that the writing is relevant only if some connection between the writing and X exists, as where X authored or published it. The real question, however, is not whether such a connection is logically necessary for relevancy, but rather what standards are to be applied in determining whether the connection has been made to appear.

---

* 7 Wigmore, Evidence §§ 2128–2169; Tracy, The Introduction of Documentary Evidence, 24 Iowa L. Rev. 436 (1939); Dec.Dig. Evidence ⚷369–382, Criminal Law ⚷444, 445; C.J.S. Evidence §§ 733–752; Uniform Rules 67–69, 71.

1. 7 Wigmore, Evidence § 2129 at 564.

2. See § 212, supra.

3. See, e. g., Palfy v. Rice, 473 P.2d 606 (Alas.1970) (authentication necessary to establish relevancy of document.) See also the discussion of conditional relevancy, § 53 at n. 99, and § 58, supra.

In the everyday affairs of business and social life, it is the custom to look merely at the writing itself for evidence as to its source. Thus, if the writing bears a signature purporting to be that of X, or recites that it was made by him, we assume, nothing to the contrary appearing, that it is exactly what it purports to be, the work of X. At this point, however, the law of evidence has long differed from the commonsense assumption upon which each of us conducts his own affairs, adopting instead the position that the purported signature or recital of authorship on the face of a writing will *not* be accepted as sufficient preliminary proof of authenticity to secure the admission of the writing in evidence.[4] The same attitude has traditionally extended as well to the authority of agents, with the result that if an instrument recites that it is signed by A as agent for P, not only must additional proof be given that A actually did the signing, but also of the fact that he was P's agent and authorized to sign.[5]

The principal justification urged for this judicial agnosticism toward the authorship of documents is that it constitutes a necessary check on the perpetration of fraud. Thus it is quite conceivable that the libelous writing previously adduced by way of example is not the work of X but of some third person who, for reasons of his own, wishes to embroil Y in difficulties,[6] or to libel X without suffering any adverse consequences. It is also possible that X has himself fabricated the writing to provide himself with a cause of action.

Another possibility against which traditional authentication is sometimes suggested to guard is that of mistaken attribution of a writing to one who fortuitously happens to possess the same name, etc., as the author.

On the other side of the coin, requiring proof of what may correctly be assumed true in 99 out of 100 cases is at best time-consuming and expensive. At the worst, the requirement will occasionally be seen to produce results which are virtually indefensible.[7]

---

4. McGowan v. Armour, 248 F. 676 (8th Cir. 1918) (letter bearing purported writer's signature, found in addressee's pocket, excluded); Continental Baking Co. v. Katz, 68 Cal.2d 512, 439 P.2d 889, 67 Cal.Rptr. 761, 897 (1968) ("We understand that in some legal systems it is assumed that documents are what they purport to be unless shown to be otherwise. With us it is the other way around. Generally speaking, documents must be authenticated in some fashion before they are admissible . . . ."); City of Randleman v. Hinshaw, 2 N.C. App. 381, 163 S.E.2d 95 (1968) (authentication of writing necessary to admission); Beltran v. State, 144 Tex.Cr.R. 338, 163 S.W.2d 211 (1942) (written confession purporting to be signed by accused); 7 Wigmore, Evidence § 2130, note 1; Dec.Dig. Evidence ☞370(1).

5. Grey v. First Nat. Bank, 393 F.2d 371 (5th Cir. 1968); Lee v. Melvin, 40 So.2d 837 (Fla.1949); Wiseth v. Traill County Telephone Co., 70 N.D. 44, 291 N.W. 689 (1940); Dec.Dig. Evidence ☞370(5).

Some of the difficulties of proof raised by this rule are in some jurisdictions resolved by statutes providing for the admissibility of instruments bearing what purports to be a corporate seal and further creating a presumption that any person whose name appears on such a sealed writing had authority to execute the instrument for the corporation. E. g., West's Ann.Cal.Corp.Code § 833; N.C.

Gen.Stat. § 355.36(c) (1955). Without benefit of statutes, some courts have been willing to accept the former proposition but not the latter. Robertson v. Burstein, 105 N.J.L. 375, 146 Atl. 355 (1929).

6. See Hughes v. Samuels Bros., 179 Iowa 1077, 159 N.W. 589 (1917) (undertaker mailed business card of competitor to man whose wife was seriously ill).

7. See, e. g., Mancari v. Frank P. Smith, Inc., 72 U.S. App.D.C. 398, 114 F.2d 834 (1940), noted 26 Iowa L.Rev. 134, 15 So.Calif.L.Rev. 115 (plaintiff sued as a result of mention of his name in a widely distributed circular which purported to be issued by a manufacturer and a local retailer of shoes. Held, Judge Rutledge dissenting, that the trial court properly directed a verdict for defendant on the ground that the terms of the circular did not make a prima facie case of defendant's authorship); Keegan v. Green Giant Co., 150 Me. 283, 110 A.2d 599 (1954), noted 103 U.Pa.L.Rev. 1095, 29 Temp. L.Q. 109 (plaintiff sued for personal injuries resulting from eating peas from a can labeled with the name of the defendant. Held, over a strong dissenting opinion, that the trial court properly refused to admit the label as evidence of defendant's connection with the peas, and properly directed a verdict for defendant.) Compare State v. Rines, 269 A.2d 9 (Me.1970).

Thus, while traditional requirements of authentication admittedly furnish some slight obstacles to the perpetration of fraud or occurrence of mistake in the presentation of writings, it has frequently been questioned whether these benefits are not outweighed by the time, expense, and occasional untoward results entailed by the traditional negative attitude toward authenticity of writings.[8]

219. Authentication by Direct Proof: (a) In General.

The simplest form of direct testimony authenticating a writing as that of X, is the production of a witness who swears that he saw X sign the offered writing.[9] Other examples would be the testimony of X himself, the signer, acknowledging execution, or the admission of authenticity by an adverse party in the present action, either made out of court and reported by another witness or shown by the party's own letter or other writing, or in the form of the party's testimony on the stand.[10] It is generally held that business records may be authenticated [11] by the evidence of one familiar with the books of the concern, such as a custodian or supervisor, who has not made the record or seen it

made, that the offered writing is actually part of the records of the business.[12]

220. Authentication by Direct Proof: (b) Requirement of Production of Attesting Witnesses.[13]

Our rules about the production of subscribing witnesses are survivals of archaic law. They have their origins in Germanic practice earlier than jury trial, when pre-appointed transaction-witnesses were the only kind of witnesses that could be summoned or heard in court. When jury trial came in, the attesting witnesses at first were summoned along with the jurors themselves, and this practice seems to have lingered until the middle fifteen hundreds.[14] The rule in its modern common law form requires, when a document signed by subscribing witnesses is sought to be authenticated by witnesses, that an attesting witness must first be called,[15]

---

8. See the quotation from Jeremy Bentham in 7 Wigmore, Evidence § 2148, p. 606; Broun, Authentication and Content of Writings, 1969 L. & Soc.O. 611; Erich, Unnecessary Difficulties of Proof, 32 Yale L.J. 436 (1923); Strong, Liberalizing the Authentication of Private Writings, 52 Cornell L. Q. 284 (1967).

9. Manifestly this is a sufficient authentication. Cottingham v. Doyle, 122 Mont. 301, 202 P.2d 533 (1949); Lancaster v. Marshall, 69 R.I. 422, 34 A.2d 718 (1943); Durham v. State, 422 P.2d 691 (Wyo. 1967). Connections other than by signing may be similarly established. See United States v. Rizzo, 418 F.2d 71 (7th Cir. 1969) (cards mailed to promote business of house of ill fame admissible where witness testified she had helped prepare "similar" cards for defendants).

10. See Ch. 26, infra.

11. Merely supplying the requirement that the books be identified as such, though other foundation proof may be required before the records will be accepted as evidence of the facts recorded under the hearsay exception for Business Records. See §§ 307–311, infra.

12. Rice v. United States, 411 F.2d 485 (8th Cir. 1969) (prosecution for theft of articles in interstate commerce, baggage tags showing destination properly admitted as business record on foundation testimony of company official who had not prepared tags); Miller v. State, 224 A.2d 592 (Del.1966) (church records; current pastor not preparing entries in question); Hood v. Commonwealth Trust & Sav. Bank, 376 Ill. 413, 34 N.E.2d 414 (1941) (cashier could "identify" bank's books though some entries made before he was employed); State v. Smith, 55 Wash.2d 482, 348 P.2d 417 (1960) (records identified, and mode of preparation established, by one not the custodian or keeper).

13. 4 Wigmore, Evidence §§ 1287–1321; Dec.Dig. Evidence ⟂374; C.J.S. Evidence § 739.

14. Thayer, Preliminary Treatise on Evidence 502 (1898), quoted in 4 Wigmore, Evidence § 1287.

15. If there are several attesters only one must be called. Sowell v. Bank of Brewton, 119 Ala. 92, 24 So. 585 (1898) (note); Shirley v. Fearne, 33 Miss. 653, 69 Am.Dec. 375 (1857) (deed with two attesters, though only one required by law.) But the Chancery rule in England required the calling or accounting for all attesters, and a number of American jurisdictions continue to impose the requirement in will cases. In re Coons' Estate, 154 Neb. 690, 48 N.W.2d 778 (1951); Swindoll v. Jones, 41 Tenn.App. 89, 292 S.W.2d 531 (Tenn.App.1955). Cases concerning the requirement in will cases are collected in Dec.Dig. Wills ⟂303(4). For a collection of statutes affecting the question, see 4 Wigmore, Evidence § 1304.

or all attesters must be shown to be unavailable,[16] before other witnesses can be called to authenticate it.[17]

The requirement has no application where the foundation for introducing the document is the opponent's judicial admission [18] of its genuineness,[19] either by stipulation of the parties in writing or in open court, or under modern rules and statutes by the opponent's failure to deny the genuineness of the writing.[20] Though it has been suggested that extra-judicial admissions also, if in writing, might properly be held to dispense with the production of attesters, such American authority as exists seems to deny that extra-judicial admissions of any sort have this effect.[21]

The requirement is that the attesting witnesses be called before other authenticating witnesses are heard, but it is not required that the attesters give favorable testimony establishing the writing. So even if they profess want of memory [22] or even deny that

they attested,[23] the writing may be established by other proof, and conversely if they support the writing, other proof may establish that it is not authentic.[24] Moreover, since the party calling the attester is required by law to do so, the prohibition upon impeaching one's own witness is held inapplicable.[25]

This requirement of calling particular persons, or accounting for them, to authenticate the writing is often inconvenient, and of doubtful expediency, and various exceptions have been carved out by the courts, as for ancient documents,[26] writings only "collaterally" involved in the suit,[27] and for certified copies of recorded conveyances, where the original is not required to be produced.[28] A more sweeping reform, generally effected by statute but on occasion by judicial deci-

---

16. Howard v. Russell, 104 Ga. 230, 30 S.E. 802 (1898) (semble: deed). But seemingly if there are more attesters than the law requires only the number required must be accounted for. Snider v. Burks, 84 Ala. 57, 4 So. 225, 226 (1888) (three witnesses to a will, only two accounted for, sufficient). And if the attesting witnesses' identities cannot be ascertained, even proof of unavailability may be held unnecessary. Skaling v. Remick, 97 N.H. 106, 82 A.2d 81 (1951). Statutes defining "unavailability" are collected in 4 Wigmore, Evidence § 1310.

17. For a summary statement of the rule, see 4 Wigmore, Evidence § 1289.

18. As to meaning, see § 265.

19. Jones v. Henry, 84 N.C. 320, 323 (1881) (stipulation of record, "defendants admit execution of bond" dispenses with producing attester); 4 Wigmore, Evidence § 1296.

20. See § 228, supra.

21. 4 Wigmore, Evidence § 1300.

22. Abbott v. Abbott, 41 Mich. 540, 2 N.W. 810 (1879) (excellent older opinion); In Matter of Katz' Will, 277 N.Y. 470, 14 N.E.2d 797 (1938) (will may be established in direct opposition to testimony of subscribing witnesses); In re Ellis' Will, 235 N.C. 27, 69 S.E.2d 25 (1952); In re Estate of Farnsworth, 176 N.W.2d 247 (S.D.1970) (failure of attesting wit-

nesses to recall execution does not preclude valid testamentary disposition).

23. Wheat v. Wheat, 156 Conn. 575, 244 A.2d 359 (1968); In re Lyons' Estate, 166 Ohio St. 207, 141 N.E.2d 151 (1957).

24. In re O'Connor's Estate, 105 Neb. 88, 179 N.W. 401, 12 A.L.R. 199 (1920).

25. Amerine v. Amerine, 177 Kan. 481, 280 P.2d 601 (1955); In re Warren's Estate, 138 Ore. 283, 4 P.2d 635, 79 A.L.R. 389 (1931).

26. Smythe v. Inhabitants of New Providence Township, 263 F. 481, 484 (3d Cir. 1920) ("the subscribing witnesses are presumed to be dead").

27. Steiner v. Tranum, 98 Ala. 315, 13 So. 365 (1893) (trover for horse: note given by plaintiff as evidence of his purchase, held "collateral"); Lugosch v. Public Service Ry. Co., 96 N.J.Eq. 472, 126 A. 170 (Ch.1924) (writing offered to impeach, "collateral"). Compare Snead v. Stephens, 242 Ala. 76, 5 So.2d 740 (1941) where it was held that in a suit for destruction of plaintiff's mortgage lien on cotton by defendant's resale of the cotton, the mortgage itself was not collateral. The reversal of the judgment for plaintiff because of his failure to produce the subscribing witness to a writing the genuineness of which was not actually in doubt, illustrates the profitless aridity of the requirement.

28. Powers v. Russell, 13 Pick. (Mass.) 69, 75 (1832); 4 Wigmore, Evidence § 1318. Seemingly some courts would admit the original recorded deed, without calling subscribers under statutes providing that they "prove themselves." See Foxworth v. Brown, 120 Ala. 59, 24 So. 1, 4 (1898) and § 228, infra.

sion, has been to dispense with the requirement of calling attesting witnesses except when the writing to be offered is one required by law to be attested.[29]

221. Authentication by Direct Proof: (c) Proof of Handwriting.[30]

A witness is placed on the stand. "Will you state whether you are acquainted with the handwriting of X?" "I am." "Will you look at this letter (or this signature) and tell me whether it is in the handwriting of X?" "It is." These or similar questions and answers are part of the familiar routine of authenticating writings, a routine which might be supposed to possess a rationale until note is taken of the qualifications typically required to be shown as part of his testimony by the witness through whom such a foundation is laid. These qualifications are minimal to say the least. Thus it is generally held that anyone familiar with the handwriting of a given person may supply authenticating testimony in the form of his opinion that a writing or signature is in the handwriting of that person.[31] Adequate familiarity may be present if the witness has seen the person write,[32] or if he has seen writings *purporting* to be those of the person in question under circumstances indicating their genuineness. Examples of the latter situation include instances where the witness has had an exchange of correspondence with the person,[33] or has seen writings which the person has asserted are his own,[34] or has been present in an office or other place where genuine writings of a particular person in the ordinary course of business would naturally be seen.[35] Similarly, specimens of

29. See, e. g., NYCPLR 4537. Various statutes of similar import are collected in 4 Wigmore, Evidence § 1290. The same rule appears in some jurisdictions to have been adopted by judicial decision. See Auto Owners Finance Co., Inc. v. Rock, 121 Vt. 194, 151 A.2d 292 (1959). Compare the even less restrictive provision of Uniform Rule 71 which provides: "Where the execution of an attested writing is in issue, whether or not attestation is a statutory requisite of its effective execution, no attester is a necessary witness even though all attesters are available unless the statute requiring attestation specifically provides otherwise." To the same effect is West's Ann.Cal.Evid.Code, § 1412.

30. See Berman, A Connecticut Commentary on Authenticating Private Documents, 28 Conn.B.J. 173 (1954) (good local treatment); Tracy, Documentary Evidence, 24 Iowa L.Rev. 436 (1939); Dec.Dig. Evidence ☞378(4). See also 20 Am.Jur. Proof of Facts 335 (bibliography).

31. See, e. g., Bennett v. Cox, 167 Ga. 843, 146 S.E. 835 (1929) (authenticating witness need not be expert if familiar with handwriting of person in question); Apple v. Commonwealth, 296 S.W.2d 717 (Ky. 1956) (lay witness' testimony of familiarity and identity warranted admission); Noyes v. Noyes, 224 Mass. 125, 112 N.E. 850 (1916) ("anybody familiar with a person's handwriting" may authenticate).

32. Auto Owners Finance Co. Inc. v. Rock, 121 Vt. 194, 151 A.2d 292 (1959). A single observation is frequently held sufficient. See State v. Bond, 12 Idaho 424, 86 P. 43 (1906); State v. Freshwater, 30 Utah 442, 85 P. 447 (1906). Further, the observation need not have been recent. See In re Diggins' Estate, 68 Vt. 198, 34 A. 696 (1896) (one observation, 20 years previously, apparently held sufficient.) But a few states apply more rigorous standards. Compare Storm v. Hansen, 41 N.J.Super. 249, 124 A.2d 601 (1956) (lay identification "weak and unsatisfactory" at best; substantial familiarity required).

33. Paccon, Inc. v. United States, 185 Ct.Cl. 24, 399 F.2d 62 (1968) (witness qualified to authenticate where he had seen 100 other documents purportedly signed by person over course of contract); Phoenix State Bank & Trust Co. v. Whitcomb, 121 Conn. 32, 183 A. 5 (1935) (witness shown to have had business dealings with purported author); Poole v. Beller, 104 W.Va. 547, 140 S.E. 534 (1927) (correspondence between members of family).

34. Hershberger v. Hershberger, 345 Pa. 439, 29 A. 2d 95 (1942) (witnesses had charged account of person with checks purporting to have been drawn by him, and he had not questioned them).

35. Hamilton v. Smith, 74 Conn. 374, 50 A. 884 (1902) (engineer who had frequently worked with maps signed by former town surveyor could authenticate latter's signature); Kinney v. Youngblood, 216 Ga. 354, 116 S.E.2d 608 (1960) (witness who had lived in apartment in defendant's home for three years and testified she knew his signature); Priest v. Poleshuck, 29 N.J.Super. 401, 102 A.2d 636 (1954) (bookkeeper competent to authenticate signature of employee); In re McDowell's Will, 230 N.C. 259, 52 S.E.2d 807 (1949) (granddaughter's identification of signature as that of grandfather with whom she lived held sufficient without testimony that witness "knew" handwriting of grandfather).

the handwriting of the person, themselves authenticated as genuine, may be produced for comparison with the writing sought to be proved, and submitted to the jury for their inference that the offered writing is genuine.[36]

Demonstration is available, if demonstration is thought to be needed, that evidence of the foregoing varieties is essentially meaningless in cases where the authenticity is actually disputed.[37] If a writing is in fact questioned no person not trained in the science and art of document examination is truly competent to distinguish a skilled forgery from a genuine writing. Certainly it is incredible that an unskilled layman who saw the person write once a decade before could make such a differentiation. In the event of an actual controversy over genuineness, both logic and good advocacy demand a more scientific approach and resolution of the issue mainly upon the testimony of bona fide handwriting experts.[38]

The minimal qualifications required of the ordinary witness authenticating a writing by identification of handwriting are defensible only on the basis that no more than one in a hundred writings is questioned. The current permissive standards allow the admission of the general run of authentic documents with a minimum of time, trouble, and expense. The latter argument, however, may prove too much since even greater sav-

ings in these commodities might safely be achieved by simply presuming the authenticity of writings for purposes of admissibility in the absence of proof raising a question as to genuineness.[39]

222. Authentication by Circumstantial Evidence: (a) Generally.

As has been seen there are various ways in which writings may be authenticated by direct evidence. Nevertheless, it will frequently occur that no direct evidence of authenticity of any type exists or can be found. Resort must then be had to circumstantial proof and it is clear that authentication by circumstantial evidence is uniformly recognized as permissible.[40] Certain configurations of circumstantial evidence have in fact been so frequently held to authenticate particular types of writings that they have come to be recognized as distinct rules, e. g., the ancient documents rule, the reply doctrine, etc. These more or less formalized rules are treated in succeeding sections.[41]

It is important to bear in mind, however, that authentication by circumstantial evidence is not limited to situations which fall within one of these recurrent patterns. Rather, proof of any circumstances which will support a finding that the writing is genuine will suffice to authenticate the writing.[42]

---

36. Brandon v. Collins, 267 F.2d 731 (2d Cir. 1959) (judge as trier of fact compared authenticated specimens and offered document); United States v. Cashio, 420 F.2d 1132 (5th Cir. 1970) (comparison by jury); Flickema v. Henry Kraker Co., 252 Mich. 406, 233 N.W. 362 (1930). See also Forte v. Schiebe, 145 Cal.App.2d 296, 302 P.2d 336 (1963) (similar procedure followed with respect to typewritten instrument.)

37. See the interesting article, Inbau, Lay Witness Identification of Handwriting (An Experiment), 34 Ill.L.Rev. 433 (1939); Hilton, The Detection of Forgery, 30 J.Crim.L. & Criminology 568 (1939).

38. See § 205, supra.

39. Broun, Authentication and Contents of Writings, 1969 Law & Soc.Or. 611; Levin, Authentication and Content of Writings, 10 Rut.L.Rev. 632 (1956); Strong, Liberalizing the Authentication of Private Writings, 52 Cornell L.Q. 284 (1967).

40. See, e. g., Champion v. Champion, 368 Mich. 84, 117 N.W.2d 107 (1962) (authentication on basis of circumstantial evidence upheld); Harlow v. Commonwealth, 204 Va. 385, 131 S.E.2d 293 (1963) (acknowledging permissibility of circumstantial evidence to authenticate, but holding specific evidence offered insufficient).

41. See §§ 223–226, infra.

42. See, e. g., McFarland v. McFarland, 176 Pa. Super. 342, 107 A.2d 615 (1954) (successful authentication by writing style).

223. Authentication by Circumstantial Evidence: (b) Ancient Documents.[43]

A writing which has been in existence for a number of years will frequently be difficult to authenticate by direct evidence. Where the maker of an instrument, those who witnessed the making, and even those familiar with the maker's handwriting have over the course of years died or become unavailable, the need to resort to authentication by circumstantial evidence is apparent.[44] The circumstances which may, in a given case, raise an inference of the genuineness of an aged writing are of course quite varied, and any combination of circumstances sufficient to support a finding of genuineness will be appropriate authentication.[45] Facts which may be suggested as indicative of genuineness include unsuspicious appearance, emergence from natural custody, prompt recording, and, in the case of a deed or will, possession taken under the instrument. Age itself may be viewed as giving rise to some inference of genuineness in that an instrument is unlikely to be forged for fruition at a time in the distant future.

The frequent necessity of authenticating ancient writings by circumstantial evidence [46] plus the consideration that certain of the above facts probative of authenticity are commonly found associated with genuine older writings have led the courts to develop a rule of thumb for dealing with the question.[47] Under this rule a writing is sufficiently authenticated as an ancient document if the party who offers it satisfies the judge that the writing is thirty years old,[48] that it is unsuspicious in appearance,[49] and further

---

43. 7 Wigmore, Evidence §§ 2137–2146; Dec.Dig. Evidence ☞372; C.J.S. Evidence §§ 743–752.

44. When possible, of course, the authenticity of ancient documents may be proved by direct evidence. Kanimaya v. Choctaw Lumber Co., 147 Okl. 90, 294 Pac. 817 (1930).

45. See Gaskins v. Guthrie, 162 Ga. 103, 132 S.E. 764 (1926) (showing of particular fact not essential, if totality of circumstances afford finding of genuineness.)

46. Wynne v. Tyrwhitt, [1821] 4 Barn. & Ald. 376, 106 Eng.Rep. 975 (rule founded on great difficulty of proving handwriting after lapse of time.) See also 7 Wigmore, Evidence § 2137.

47. See, e. g., Steele v. Fowler, 111 Ind.App. 364, 41 N.E.2d 678 (1942) ("When a document appears to be at least 30 years old and is found in proper custody, and is unblemished by alterations and otherwise free from suspicion, it is admissible without proof of execution."); Boucher v. Wallis, 236 S.W. 2d 519 (Tex.Civ.App.1951) (semble). The same rule is codified by Uniform Rule 67: "Authentication of a writing is required before it may be received in evidence. Authentication may be by evidence sufficient to sustain a finding of its authenticity or by any other means provided by law. If the judge finds that a writing (a) is at least thirty years old at the time it is offered, and (b) is in such condition as to create no suspicion concerning its authenticity, and (c) at the time of its discovery was in a place in which such a document, if authentic, would be likely to be found, it is sufficiently authenticated."

48. The selection of 30 years is justified by Wigmore as being the normal period beyond which direct evidence of authenticity becomes practically unavailable. This justification however, would appear to support 30 years as a rough standard only and to fall short of warranting such quibbles as whether the period should be measured from execution to filing of action or introduction of evidence. See Reuter v. Stuckart, 181 Ill. 529, 54 N.E. 1014 (1899) (execution to introduction proper measure). Viewing the rule positively, existence for a substantial period of time less than 30 years might be viewed as raising an inference of genuineness, and to warrant flexible application of the rule. See Lee Pong Tai v. Acheson, 104 F.Supp. 503 (E.D.Pa. 1952) (26-year-old document admitted); Neustadt v. Coline Oil Co., 141 Okl. 113, 284 Pac. 52 (1929) cert. denied 282 U.S. 799 (19 year-old document admitted under circumstances.)

Age of a writing may be proved circumstantially by appearance and contents, Commonwealth ex rel. Ferguson v. Ball, 277 Pa. 301, 121 A. 191, 29 A.L.R. 626 (1923). The purported date of the document, while providing some evidence of age, is obviously not conclusive. In re McGary's Estate, 127 Colo. 495, 258 P.2d 770 (1953).

The required age is reduced to 20 years in Ore.Rev. Stat. 41.360(34); F.R.Ev. (R.D.1971) 901(b) (8).

49. Stewart Oil Co. v. Sohio Petroleum Co., 202 F. Supp. 952 (D.C.Ill.1962) aff'd 315 F.2d 759 (alleged ancient document rejected as smacking of fraud); Apo v. Dillingham Investment Corp., 50 Haw. 369, 440 P.2d 965 (1968) (misspelling of grantor's name and other irregularities; deeds excluded as suspicious); Muehrcke v. Behrens, 43 Wis.2d 1, 169 N.W.2d 86 (1969) ("When the instrument shows an alteration on its face it is the obligation of the

proves that the writing is produced from a place of custody natural for such a document.[50] In addition to the foregoing requirements, some jurisdictions, if the writing is a dispositive one such as a deed or a will, impose the additional condition that possession must have been taken under the instrument.[51] The documents which may be authenticated under the rule here described, however, are not limited to dispositive instruments, and the rule has been applied to allow authentication of a wide variety of writings.[52]

In the case of a writing which purports to be executed by an agent, executor, or other person acting under power or authority from another, proof of the facts which authenticate the writing as an ancient document gives rise to a presumption that the person signing was duly authorized.[53]

It should be borne in mind that, despite the utility of the rule here discussed, it is merely a rule of authentication, the satisfaction of which does not necessarily guarantee the admission of the writing authenticated. Thus, it is sometimes forgotten that a writing may be proved perfectly genuine and yet remain inadmissible as being, e. g., hearsay or secondary evidence.[54] This source of confusion is compounded by a partial overlap between the requirements of the present rule and those of the distinct doctrine which holds that recitals in certain types of ancient instruments may be received as evidence of the facts recited.[55] The latter doctrine, however, constitutes an exception to the rule against hearsay and is quite distinct from the present rule concerning authentication. It is discussed in another place.[56]

---

party offering it to explain the alteration".); Roberts v. Waddell, 94 S.W.2d 211 (Tex.Civ.App.1936) (purported deed rejected because of mutilation and other reasons).

50. Sage v. Dayton Coal & Iron Co., 148 Tenn. 1, 251 S.W. 780 (1922) (careful preservation of instrument by one interested in subject matter raises inference of genuineness.) Proper custody would appear to extend to cover possession by any person so connected with the document that he might reasonably be found in possession of it without fraud. Ward v. Cameron, 76 S.W. 240 (Tex.Civ.App.1903).

51. The concept underlying the possession requirement has more recently been reflected in statutory enactments creating *presumptions* of authenticity of aged documents which, in addition to the usual requirements for authentication, have been "acted upon" as genuine by persons having an interest in the matter. West's Ann.Cal.Evid.Code, § 643; Ore. Rev.Stat. 41.360(34). The strengthened inference of genuineness arising from the added circumstance of action on the instrument probably warrants treatment as a presumption. But such statutes need not be construed as rendering the raising of a presumption essential to admission, since the mere inference of authenticity should suffice for this purpose. See Devereau v. Frazier Mountain Park & Fisheries Co., 248 Cal.App.2d 323, 56 Cal.Rptr. 345 (1967) (suggesting the conclusion here recommended on the basis of an arguably unnecessary flexible reading of the statute).

52. See, e. g., Kirkpatrick v. Tapo Oil Co., 144 Cal. App.2d 404, 301 P.2d 274 (1956) (ledger entries); Steele v. Fowler, 111 Ind.App. 364, 41 N.E.2d 678 (1942) (plat of town); Sinkora v. Wlach, 239 Iowa 1392, 35 N.W.2d 40 (1948) (foreign passports admitted; foreign church records of birth excluded); Trustees v. Farmers & Citizens Savings Bank Co., 66 Abs. 332, 113 N.E.2d 409 (Ohio App.1953) (old newspaper).

53. Wilson v. Snow, 228 U.S. 217 (1913) (deed of executrix; ". . . the ancient deed proves itself, whether it purports to have been signed by the grantor in his own right, as agent under power of attorney or—the original records having been lost—by an administrator under a power of sale given by order of court, not produced but recited in the deed itself"); Baumgarten v. Frost, 143 Tex. 533, 186 S.W.2d 982, 159 A.L.R. 428 (1945) (presumption recognized, but here receiver's assignment could not be presumed authorized where court's records intact and failed to show confirmation).

54. Town of Ninety-Six v. Southern Ry. Co., 267 F. 2d 579 (4th Cir. 1959) ("The fact that an instrument is an ancient document does not affect its admissibility in evidence further than to dispense with proof of its genuineness"; ancient letter excluded as inadmissible hearsay); King v. Schultz, 141 Mont. 94, 375 P.2d 108 (1962) (". . . ancient document rule does not change the basis for admission of evidence other than as to genuineness . . .").

55. The two doctrines are contrasted in Town of Ninety-Six v. Southern Ry. Co., supra, n. 54. Numerous cases noting the distinction in connection with old maps and plats are found in Annot., 46 A.L.R.2d 1318 (admissibility of ancient maps and the like under the ancient document rule).

56. See § 323, infra.

The preferable and majority view is that satisfaction of the ancient document requirements will serve to authenticate an ancient copy of an original writing.[57] And a fresh certified copy of an instrument of record for thirty years will prove the ancient writing,[58] though perhaps with the additional qualification that before the copy can come in, the original documents rule must be satisfied by showing the unavailability of the original.[59] Admission of a writing as an ancient document does, however, dispense with the production of attesting witnesses.[60]

224. Authentication by Circumstantial Evidence: (c) Custody.[61]

If a writing purports to be an official report or record and is proved to have come from the proper public office where such official papers are kept, it is generally agreed that this authenticates the offered document as genuine.[62] This result is founded on the probability that the officers in custody of such records will carry out their public duty to receive or record only genuine official papers and reports. Similarly, where a public office is the depository for private papers, such as wills, conveyances, or income tax returns, the proof that such a purporting deed, bill of sale, tax return or the like has come from the proper custody is usually accepted as sufficient authentication.[63] This again can be sustained on the same principle if it appears that the official custodian had a public duty to verify the genuineness of the papers offered for record or deposit and to accept only the genuine.

As is true with ancient documents, the question of the authenticity of official records should not be confused with the ultimate admissibility of such records. It is quite possible for a public record to be perfectly genuine, and yet remain inadmissible for some distinguishable reason, e. g., that it is excludable hearsay.[64]

Some question exists whether the rule which accepts, as prima facie genuine, documents which are shown to emerge from official custody should be extended beyond the field of public duty and recognized as to writ-

---

57. See, e. g., Schell v. City of Jefferson, 357 Mo. 1020, 212 S.W.2d 430 (1948) (ancient copy of city plat, original not available, held improperly excluded, one judge dissenting); and see 7 Wigmore, Evidence § 2143 (supporting majority position and collecting older authorities). But some jurisdictions hold that the rule does not apply to copies. See Anderson v. Anderson, 150 Neb. 879, 36 N.W.2d 287 (1949) ("the rule applies only to original instruments . . ."); Solomon v. Beck, 387 S.W.2d 911 (Tex.Civ.App.1965) (examined copy of ancient instrument not admissible under rule).

58. See Hodge v. Palms, 117 F. 396 (6th Cir. 1902); Solomon v. Beck, supra n. 57. The certified copy of the long-recorded writing obviously has a stronger claim to admissibility than the ancient unrecorded copy. See 7 Wigmore, Evidence § 2143.

59. Sudduth v. Central of Ga. Ry. Co., 201 Ala. 560, 77 So. 350 (1917); Woods v. Bonner, 89 Tenn. 411, 18 S.W. 67 (1890); Emory v. Bailey, 111 Tex. 337, 234 S.W. 660, 662 (1921) ("on filing proper affidavit of loss," under statute). See § 240, infra.

60. See § 220, supra.

61. 7 Wigmore, Evidence §§ 2158–2160; Dec.Dig. Evidence ☞366, Criminal Law ☞444.

62. United States v. Ward, 173 F.2d 628 (2d Cir. 1949) (records from files of Selective Service, identified by custodian); Tameling v. Commissioner, 43 F.2d 814 (2d Cir. 1930) (official assessment role shown to emanate from official custody admissible without further authentication); State v. Miller, 79 N.M. 117, 440 P.2d 792 (1968) (fingerprint record from F.B.I. file; stating rule in terms of above text).

63. Brooks v. Texas Gen. Indem. Co., 251 F.2d 15 (5th Cir. 1958) (application for benefits produced from files of Veteran's Administration); Sternberg Dredging Co. v. Moran Towing & Trans. Co., 196 F.2d 1002 (2d Cir. 1952) (letter report filed in compliance with statutory requirement and produced from official custody held improperly excluded; opinion by L. Hand, J.); Wausau Sulphate Fibre Co. v. Commissioner, 61 F.2d 879 (7th Cir., 1932) (waiver bearing purported signature of taxpayer, from Bureau's files); Halko v. State, 209 A.2d 895 (Del.1965) (application for driver's license produced from official files admissible under local statutes).

64. See, e. g., Matthews v. United States, 217 F.2d 409 (5th Cir. 1954) (statutorily required reports of sugar sales produced from government files properly identified but held inadmissible as hearsay).

ings found in private custody. Since the circumstances of private custody are infinitely more varied than those of public custody, a new rule in an already rule-ridden area seems inadvisable. No such rule, in fact, is needed, provided that, in their discretion, courts recognize that proof of private custody, together with other circumstances, is frequently strong circumstantial evidence of authenticity.[65]

225. Authentication by Circumstantial Evidence: (d) Knowledge: Reply Letters and Telegrams.[66]

When a letter, signed with the purported signature of X, is received "out of the blue," with no previous correspondence, the traditional "show me" skepticism of the common law trial practice [67] prevails, and the purported signature is not accepted as authentication,[68] unless authenticity is confirmed by additional facts.[69]

One circumstance recognized as sufficient is the fact that the letter discloses knowledge that only the purported signer would be likely to have.[70] Moreover, a convenient practice recognizes that if a letter has been written to X, and the letter now offered in evidence purports to be written by X and purports to be a reply to the first letter (that is either refers to it, or is responsive to its terms) and has been received without unusual delay, these facts authenticate it as a reply letter.[71] This result may be rested up-

---

65. Proof of private custody has frequently been so viewed. See, e. g., Reeves v. Warden, Maryland Penitentiary, 346 F.2d 915, 926, n. 29 (3d Cir., 1965) (incriminating note, discovered under petitioner's underclothing in bureau used exclusively by petitioner in petitioner's bedroom, which detailed activities of petitioner would have been admissible as against relevancy objection; dictum); United States v. Imperial Chem. Ind., 100 F.Supp. 504 (S.D.N.Y., 1951), supplemented 105 F.Supp. 215 (unsigned documents from corporate defendant's files admissible against corporation as authentic declarations of corporate agents; possibility of spurious or forged documents in files rejected as highly improbable. Cf. People v. Manganaro, 218 N.Y. 9, 112 N.E. 436 (1916).

66. 7 Wigmore, Evidence §§ 2148, 2153–2154; C J.S. Evidence § 706b; Dec.Dig. Evidence ⊕378, Criminal Law ⊕444.

67. See § 218, supra.

68. Early v. State, 42 Ala.App. 200, 158 So.2d 495 (1963); Continental Baking Co. v. Katz, 68 Cal.2d 512, 67 Cal.Rptr. 761, 439 P.2d 889 (1968); State v. Golden, 67 Idaho 497, 186 P.2d 485 (1947). See also Harlow v. Commonwealth, 204 Va. 385, 131 S.E.2d 293 (1963) (unsigned telegram inadmissible without proof of authorship).

69. See, e. g., Greenbaum v. United States, 80 F.2d 113 (9th Cir. 1935) (letter purporting to be signed for corporation by agent held authenticated by proof that person signing was agent of corporation

and city of posting was the place of business of company); Fuller v. State, 437 P.2d 772 (Alas. 1968) (telegram admissible where proved to have had been paid for by occupant of room, and defendant was shown to have been occupant); Cotton States Mut. Ins. Co. v. Clark, 114 Ga.App. 439, 151 S.E.2d 780 (1966) (surrounding circumstances, including facts that letter was on defendant's letterhead and contract was on defendant's form, sufficient for authentication).

70. United States v. Sutton, 138 U.S.App.D.C. 208, 426 F.2d 1202 (1969) (notes suggesting defendant's plan for murder-suicide held authenticated where subsequent events observed by eyewitnesses followed note's predictions); State v. Milum, 202 Kan. 196, 447 P.2d 801, 803 (1968) ("Proof of the genuineness of a letter may be established when the contents themselves reveal knowledge peculiarly referable to a certain person . . ."); Champion v. Champion, 368 Mich. 84, 117 N.W.2d 107 (1962) (knowledge of recipient's itinerary on European tour and of letters received at other points held circumstances indicating authenticity); State ex rel. Kunz v. Woodmansee, 156 Ore. 607, 69 P.2d 298 (1937) (series of letters showing intimate knowledge of details of life of alleged writer); State v. Huffman, 141 W.Va. 55, 87 S.E.2d 541 (1955) (notes allegedly from defendant to prosecuting witness held authenticated by internal evidence including use of correct initials of sender and sendee and reference to facts then exclusively within knowledge of the two); Annot., 9 A.L.R. 984. After a letter is written a statement about its contents may identify the declarant as the writer. See Deaderick v. Deaderick, 182 Ga. 96, 185 S.E. 89 (1936).

71. Winel v. United States, 365 F.2d 646, 648 (8th Cir. 1966) (". . . one of the principal situations where the authenticity of a letter is provable by circumstantial evidence arising out of the letter's context . . . is where it can be shown that the letter was sent in reply to a previous communication."); Purer & Co. v. Aktiebolaget Addo, 410 F.2d 871 (9th Cir. 1969) cert. denied 396 U.S. 834; Namerdy v. Generalcar, 217 A.2d 109 (D.C.App. 1966); Whelton v. Daly, 93 N.H. 150, 37 A.2d 1

on the knowledge-principle, mentioned above. In view of the regularity of the mails the first letter would almost invariably come exclusively into the hands of X, or those authorized to act for him, who would alone know of the terms of the letter. It is supported also by the fact that in common experience we know that reply letters do come from the person addressed in the first letter.

These same arguments apply to reply telegrams, but with a reduced degree of certainty. Some of the employees of the telegraph company, as well as the addressee, know the contents of the first telegram. Moreover, the instances of misdelivery of telegrams may be more numerous relatively than misdeliveries of letters. These considerations have led some courts to reject for reply telegrams this theory of authentication.[72] The contrary view, that the inference of authenticity of the reply telegram is substantial and sufficient,[73] seems more reasonable and expedient.

When the reply letter purports to be signed by an agent or other representative of X, the addressee of the first letter, the authority of the signing representative is presumed.[74]

The first step in authentication of the reply letter is to prove that the first letter was dated and was duly mailed at a given time and place addressed to X.[75] Seemingly oral testimony to these facts should suffice as to the first letter if the reply letter refers to it by date.[76] If, however, the reply letter only refers to it by reciting or responding to its terms, then since the terms of the first letter become important,[77] probably it would be necessary to satisfy the Best Evidence Rule. If X, as usually would be the case, is the party-opponent, and has the first letter in his hands, it would be necessary to give him notice to produce it, before a copy could be used to prove its terms.[78]

226. Authentication by Circumstantial Evidence: (e) Telephone Messages and Other Oral Communications.[79]

Modern technology makes commonplace the receipt of oral communications from persons who are heard but not seen. The problems of authentication raised by these communications are substantively analogous to the problems of authenticating writings. Thus, if the witness has received, e. g., a telephone call out of the blue from one who iden-

---

(1944) (Page, J.: "It is a fair inference, considering the habitual accuracy of the mails, that the letter addressed to B reached the real B, and that an answer referring to the contents of A's letter and coming back in due course of mail, leaves only a negligible chance that any other than B has become acquainted with the contents of A's letter so as to forge a reply."); Conner v. Zanuzoski, 36 Wash. 2d 458, 218 P.2d 879 (1950).

72. Smith v. Easton, 54 Md. 138, 146, 39 Am.St.Rep. 355 (1880); Howley v. Whipple, 48 N.H. 487, 488 (1869).

73. House Grain Co. v. Finerman & Sons, 116 Cal. App.2d 485, 253 P.2d 1034 (1953) (reply telegram held "self-authenticating); Peterman v. Vermont Sav. Bank, 181 La. 403, 159 So. 598 (1935); Annot. 5 A.L.R.3d 1018. The same principle, of course, should serve to authenticate telegrams in response to letters and vice versa. See Menefee v. Bering Mfg. Co., 166 S.W. 365 (Tex.Civ.App.1914) (telegram received in response to letter admitted).

74. Reliance Life Ins. Co. v. Russell, 208 Ala. 559, 94 So. 748 (1922) (to rebut presumption of genuineness of reply letter not sufficient to show that

purported sender did not sign it but must show that he did not authorize another to sign for him); Capitol City Supply Co. v. Beury, 69 W.Va. 612, 72 S.E. 657 (1911) (similar to last); Anstine v. McWilliams, 24 Wash.2d 230, 163 P.2d 816 (1945) (authority of purported agent, signing for principal presumed; full discussion and citations); Dec.Dig. Evidence ⊆378(3).

75. Consolidated Grocery Co. v. Hammond, 99 C.C. A. 195, 175 F. 641 (5th Cir. 1910) (statement in purported reply letter referring to previous letter does not suffice); Kvale v. Keane, 39 N.D. 560, 168 N.W. 74 (1918) (must make preliminary proof that first letter was duly addressed, stamped and posted).

76. See § 233, infra.

77. See § 233, infra.

78. See § 239, supra.

79. 7 Wigmore, Evidence § 2155; Notes, 11 N.C.L. Rev. 344 (1933), 26 Wash.U.L.Q. 433 (1941); Annots., 71 A.L.R. 5, 105 A.L.R. 326; Dec.Dig. Evidence ⊆148; 29 Am.Jur.2d Evidence §§ 380–386; C.J.S. Evidence § 188.

tified him as "X", this is not sufficient authentication of the call as in fact coming from X.[80] The requisite additional proof may take the form of testimony by the witness that he is familiar with X's voice and that the caller was X.[81] Or authentication may be accomplished by circumstantial evidence pointing to X's identity as the caller,[82] such as if the communication received reveals that the speaker had knowledge of facts that only X would be likely to know.[83] These same modes

of authentication are also recognized where communications have been received or recorded by modern devices other than the telephone.[84]

A somewhat easier problem is presented when the witness testifies that he himself placed a telephone call to a number listed to X, and that the person answering identified himself as X. In such a situation the accuracy of the telephone system, the probable absence of motive to falsify and the lack of opportunity for premeditated fraud all tend to support the conclusion that the self-identification of the speaker is reliable. Thus most courts today view proof of proper placing of a call plus self-identification of the speaker as sufficient proof of authenticity to admit the substance of the call.[85] Moreover, it is likewise held that where it is shown that the witness has called the listed number of a business establishment and spoken with someone purporting to speak for the concern, with

80. Price v. State, 208 Ga. 695, 69 S.E.2d 253 (1952) (identity of communicator not established); Texas Candy & Nut Co. v. Horton, 235 S.W.2d 518, 521 (Civ.App.Tex.1950) ("When the party called over a telephone depends entirely upon the word of the party calling as to his identity, the conversation is . . . inadmissible.").

81. People v. Ostrand, 35 Ill.2d 520, 221 N.E.2d 499 (1966) (identification of caller's voice held sufficient authentication); Chartrand v. Registrar of Motor Vehicles, 345 Mass. 321, 187 N.E.2d 135 (1963) (exclusion of phone conversation held error where witness not a party to call identified voice). The familiarity with a voice necessary to authenticate by voice identification may be acquired subsequent to the call, State v. Porter, 251 S.C. 393, 162 S.E.2d 843 (1968); Massey v. State, 160 Tex.Cr.R. 49, 266 S.W.2d 880 (1954) (identification of voice sufficient where witness met caller for first time one year after call). But see Hires v. Price, 75 Ill.App.2d 202, 220 N.E.2d 327 (1966) (familiarity acquired by listening to alleged caller during trial recess insufficient.) See also Note, The Reliability of the Identification of the Human Voice, 33 J.Crim.L. 487 (1943).

82. Carbo v. United States, 314 F.2d 718 (9th Cir. 1963) (call held authenticated by circumstantial evidence where testimony showed one conspirator had stated that call would be made and another had inquired when recipient could be reached by phone); Robinson v. Branch Brook Manor Apartments, 101 N.J.Super. 117, 243 A.2d 284 (1968) ("preferred rule" today allows authentication by circumstantial evidence, including events occurring both before and after call).

83. United States v. LoBue, 180 F.Supp. 955 (S.D. N.Y.1960) (call held authenticated by caller's knowledge of facts subsequently confirmed); Gutowsky v. Halliburton Oil Well Cementing Co., 287 P.2d 204 (Okla.1955) (identity of caller held sufficiently established by apparent knowledge of subject matter of conversation). But compare Smithers v. Light, 305 Pa. 141, 157 A. 489 (1931) (caller purporting to be customer X of brokerage house orders sale of designated stocks held by broker; authentication held insufficient without adverting to knowledge factor).

84. Radio: LeRoy v. Sabena Belgian World Airlines, 344 F.2d 266 (2d Cir. 1965) (radio transmission from airliner prior to crash held authenticated by equivocal voice identification plus circumstantial evidence); United States v. Sansone, 231 F.2d 887 (2d Cir. 1956) (incriminating comments of defendant transmitted over concealed transmitter held authenticated by voice identification plus long range visual identification). Recordings: United States v. Madda, 345 F.2d 400 (7th Cir. 1965) (tape recording of bribe attempt upon party to conversation's testimony identifying voices and asserting recording to be accurate reflection of conversation); In re Roth's Estate, 15 Ohio Op.2d 234, 170 N.E.2d 313 (1960) (recording of bedside conversation with decedent; semble); Annot., 58 A.L.R.2d 1008.

85. Palos v. United States, 416 F.2d 438 (5th Cir. 1969) (government informer shown to have dialed listed number, asked for defendant and received answer, "This is he"; sufficient to authenticate); United States v. Benjamin, 328 F.2d 854 (2d Cir. 1964) (applying rule that proper dialing plus self-identification of party call constitute prima facie authentication); Everette v. D. O. Briggs Lumber Co., 250 N.C. 688, 110 S.E.2d 288 (1959) (semble, and holding in addition that voice familiarity acquired through such calls may be relied upon to authenticate subsequent calls); F.R.Ev. (R.D.1971) 901(b) (6). See, however, the dictum to the contrary in Colbert v. Dallas Joint Stock Land Bank, 136 Tex. 268, 150 S.W.2d 771 (1941).

respect to matters within its ordinary course of business, it is presumed that the speaker was authorized to speak for the employer.[86]

227. Functions of Judge and Jury in Authentication.[87]

If direct testimony of the authorship of a writing or of an oral statement is given, this is sufficient authentication and the judge has no problem on that score.[88] The writing or statement comes in, if not otherwise objectionable. When the authenticating evidence is circumstantial, however, the question whether reasonable men could find its authorship as claimed by the proponent, may be a delicate and balanced one, as to which the judge must be accorded some latitude of judgment.[89] Accordingly, it is often said to be a matter of discretion.[90] It must be no-

ticed, however, that authenticity is not to be classed as one of those preliminary questions of fact conditioning admissibility under technical evidentiary rules of competency or privilege. As to these latter, the trial judge will permit the adversary to introduce controverting proof on the preliminary issue in support of his objection, and the judge will decide this issue, without submission to the jury, as a basis for his ruling on admissibility.[91] On the other hand, the authenticity of a writing or statement is not a question of the application of a technical rule of evidence. It goes to genuineness and conditional relevance, as the jury can readily understand.[92] Thus, if a prima facie showing is made, the writing or statement comes in, and the ultimate question of authenticity is left to the jury.[93]

228. Escapes from the Requirement of Producing Evidence of Authenticity: Modern Theory and Practice.

As the foregoing sections clearly imply, the authentication of writings and other communications by formal proof may prove troublesome, time consuming, and expensive even in cases where no legitimate doubt concerning genuineness would appear to exist. The ultimate explanation for the continuing insistence upon the furnishing of such proof, justifiable only upon assumptions which accord very little with common sense, is of course obscure. It may be speculated, however that in part the explanation is to be found in various procedural devices which afford escape from authentication requirements. Use of these devices will avert some of the impatience which might otherwise be engendered by formal authentication require-

---

86. Crist v. Pennsylvania R. Co., 96 F.Supp. 243, 245 (W.D.Pa.1951) (". . . one who answers a telephone call from the place of business of the person called for, and undertakes to respond as his agent, is presumed to have authority to speak for him in respect to the general business there carried on and conducted."); Thruway Service City, Inc. v. Townsend, 116 Ga.App. 379, 157 S.E.2d 564 (1967) (admissions of fault by persons answering at defendant's phone admissible); Ratliff v. City of Great Falls, 132 Mont. 89, 314 P.2d 880 (1957) (presumption of authority in absence of affirmative proof of wrong connection or officious intermeddler). The rule applies even lacking any indication of the identity of the answerer. Lynn v. Farm Bureau Mut. Auto Ins. Co., 264 F.2d 921 (4th Cir. 1959). While the probabilities of the situation alone adequately support the rule, it is sometimes said to rest upon the agency principle of apparent authority. Sauber v. Northland Ins. Co., 251 Minn. 237, 87 N.W.2d 591 (1958). This latter justification, however, may possibly generate unfortunate limitations on the rule.

87. Dec.Dig. Evidence ☞382; C.J.S. Evidence §§ 624, 625.

88. See §§ 219–221, supra.

89. See §§ 222–226, supra.

90. United States v. Sutton, 138 U.S.App.D.C. 208, 426 F.2d 1202 (1969) (determination of admissibility by trial court held largely discretionary); State v. Milum, 202 Kan. 196, 447 P.2d 801 (1968) (semble); Lundgren v. Union Indem. Co., 171 Minn. 122, 213 N.W. 553 (1927) (exclusion of telegrams, where more convincing evidence of authenticity available, not abuse of discretion).

91. See § 53, supra.

92. For a learned discussion of the distinction, see United States v. Schipani, 289 F.Supp. 43 (S.D. N.Y.1969) (Weinstein, J.).

93. See, e. g., United States v. Tellier, 255 F.2d 441 (2d Cir. 1958) (issue of authenticity for jury to determine once prima facie showing has been made).

ments. The legislatures, too, have frequently nibbled at the problem by enacting statutes relieving the rigors of authentication in what would otherwise be particularly troublesome contexts. Among these "escapes from authentication," the following are particularly noteworthy.

Requests for Admission. Under the practice in the Federal courts as provided by Rules 36 and 37(c) of the Federal Rules of Civil Procedure, and under analogous rules or statutes in many states,[94] a party may serve upon an adversary a written request for admission of the genuineness of any relevant document described in the request. If the adversary unreasonably fails within a specified time to serve an answer or objection, genuineness is admitted. If genuineness is denied and the requesting party thereafter proves the genuineness of the document at trial, the latter may apply for an order of court requiring the adversary to pay him the reasonable costs of making the authenticating proof.[95]

Securing Admission at Pretrial Conference. Under Rule 16 in the Federal courts and under analogous rules and statutes in many states,[96] it is provided that a pretrial conference of the attorneys may be called by the court to consider among other things, "the possibility of obtaining admissions of fact and of documents which will avoid un-

necessary proof." [97] Of course, similar stipulations often are secured in informal negotiation between counsel, but a skilful judge may create at a pretrial conference an atmosphere of mutual concession unusually favorable for such admissions.[98] This function of the pretrial practice has been considered one of its most successful features.[99]

Statutes and Rules Requiring Special or Sworn Denial of Genuineness of Writing. A common provision of practice acts and rules of procedure requires that when an action is brought upon a written instrument, such as a note or contract, copied in the complaint, the genuineness of the writing will be deemed admitted unless a sworn denial be included in the answer.[1] A useful and somewhat analogous provision is contained in the Illinois Practice Rules, enabling a party who seeks to put in evidence a public record to serve a copy on the opposing party and thus to secure its admission in evidence unless the adversary denies its accuracy by affidavit filed and served within 14 days.[2]

Writings Which "Prove Themselves": Acknowledged Documents, Certified Copies, and Law Books Which Purport to be Printed by Authority. There are certain kinds of writings which are said to "prove themselves" or to be "self-identifying." In consequence one of these may be tendered to the court and, even without the shepherding angel of an authenticating witness, will be accepted in evidence for what it purports to be. This convenient result is reached in two stages. First, by statutes which often provide that certain classes of writings, usually in some manner purporting to be vouched for by an

---

94. For a catalog of states adopting discovery provisions identical or analogous to the various Federal Rules, see Silverstein, Adoption of the Federal Rules in State Practice, 11 Kan.L.Rev. 213 (1962).

95. Under a 1970 amendment to Federal Rule 36, the requesting party may now move prior to trial for a determination of the sufficiency of answers or objections to his requests for admissions. If the court determines that the answer does not comply with the rule, it may order that the matter is admitted or that a new answer be served. This amendment should serve to render avoiding the admission of facts not genuinely disputed more difficult than previously.

96. Wright, The Law of Federal Courts 399 (2d ed. 1970).

97. F.R.Civ.P. 16(3).

98. James, Civil Procedure 224–5 (1965).

99. Clark, Objectives of Pre-Trial Procedure, 17 Ohio St.L.J. 163 (1956).

1. See, e. g., West's Ann.Cal.Code Civ.Proc. § 447; Ariz.R.Civ.Pro. 9(i)6.

2. Ill.Rev.Stat.1969, c. 11A § 216(d).

official, shall be received in evidence "without further proof." This helpful attribute is most commonly given by these statutes to (1) deeds, conveyances or other instruments, which have been acknowledged by the signers before a notary public,[3] (2) certified copies of public records,[4] and (3) books of statutes which purport to be printed by public authority.[5]

But in the first two of these classes of writings, which can qualify only when the acknowledgment is certified by a notary or the copy certified by the official who has custody of the record, how is the court to know without proof that the signature or seal appearing on the writing is actually that of the official whose name and title are recited? This second step is supplied by the traditional doctrines which recognize the seal or signature of certain types of officers, including the keeper of the seal of state, judicial officers, and notaries public, as being of themselves sufficient evidence of the genuineness of the certificate.[6] Moreover in many state codes particular provisions supplement or clarify tradition by specifying that the seals or signatures of certain classes of officialdom shall have this self-authenticating effect.[7]

Proposed Federal Rules of Evidence. The concept of self-authentication, previously recognized by statute in the case of the certain relatively limited classes of writings noted above, is given an expanded ambit of operation by Proposed Rules of Evidence for United States District Courts and Magistrates. Proposed Rule 902 accords prima facie authenticity not only to those types of writings such as acknowledged writings and public records which have commonly enjoyed such treatment by statute but also to various other types of writings not previously so favored. Among these new classes of self-authenticating writings are included books, pamphlets and other publications issued by public authority, newspapers and periodicals, and trade inscriptions and labels indicating ownership, control or origin.[8] Presumptive authenticity,

---

3. See, e. g., West's Ann.Cal.Evid.Code, § 1451 ("A certificate of the acknowledgment of a writing other than a will, or a certificate of the proof of such a writing, is prima facie evidence of the facts recited in the certificate and the genuineness of the signature of each person by whom the writing purports to have been signed, if the certificate meets [designated statutory requirements]."; Ky.Rev.Stat. 422.100 (1962) ("All instruments of writing required by law to be notarized, that are notarized, shall be received as evidence without further authentication."); F.R.Ev.(R.D.1971) 902(8). Statutes of this general variety are collected in 5 Wigmore, Evidence § 1676 and are discussed in Tracy, Introduction of Documentary Evidence, 24 Iowa L.Rev. 436, 439 (1939).

4. See, e. g., Colo.Rev.Stat. 35–1–3 (1963) ("Copies of all documents, writs, proceedings, instruments, papers and writings duly filed or deposited in the office of any county judge, county clerk, or county treasurer, and transcripts from books of record or proceedings kept by any such official, with the seal of his office affixed, shall be prima facie evidence in all cases."); 12 Okl.St.Ann. § 486 (1961); F.R. Ev. (R.D.1971) 902(4). The doctrine and statutes are discussed in 5 Wigmore, Evidence § 1677. Dec. Dig. Evidence ⟨key⟩338–349 collects cases.

5. See the Uniform Proof of Statutes Act, adopted or adapted in 23 states and territories, which provides that "printed books or pamphlets purporting on their face to be the session or other statutes of any of the United States, or the territories thereof, or of any foreign jurisdiction, and to have been printed and published by the authority of any such state, territory or foreign jurisdiction or proved to be commonly recognized in its courts shall be received in the courts of this state as prima facie evidence of such statutes." This and other like Acts are compiled in 5 Wigmore, Evidence § 1684. Their most frequent and useful employment is in the proof of statutes of sister states and of foreign countries, see § 335, infra.

6. The history and theory of the subject are reviewed and the decisions and statutes collected in 7 Wigmore, Evidence §§ 2161–2168.

7. See, e. g., the Uniform Acknowledgment Act, which attributes self-authenticating effect to acknowledgments taken by officers of the state in which the document is offered, and officers of the United States acting outside the country. Other statutes are collected in 7 Wigmore, Evidence §§ 2162, 2167.

8. F.R.Ev. (R.D.1971) 902. In State v. Rines, 269 A.2d 9 (Me.1970) the court relied upon the proposed rule in holding that the manufacturer's certificate made a sufficient prima facie case of the

as envisioned by the proposed rule, does not preclude evidentiary challenge of the genuineness of the offered writing, but simply serves to obviate the necessity of preliminary authentication by the proponent to secure admission. This commonsense approach is long overdue and might well be extended to apply to all writings purporting to have a connection with the party against whom offered.[9] The suggestion rests not only upon the proposition that the overwhelming majority of such writings will be genuine, but in addition on the superior position of the adversary to demonstrate through evidence that the purported connection of a writing with him is attributable to fraud or mistake.[10]

contents of swab and tubes in a kit designed to draw and preserve blood for a blood-alcohol test. Compare Keegan v. Green Giant Co., supra, § 218, n. 7.

9. Broun, Authentication and Contents of Writings, 1969 Law & Soc. Order 611; Strong, Liberalizing the Authentication of Private Writings, 52 Cornell L.Q. 284 (1967).

10. Strong, Liberalizing the Authentication of Private Writings, supra, note 9.

CHAPTER 23

THE REQUIREMENT OF THE PRODUCTION OF THE ORIGINAL WRITING AS THE "BEST EVIDENCE"

229. The "Best Evidence" Rule.

Thayer [1] tells us that the first appearance of the "best evidence" phrase, is a statement in 1700 by Holt, C. J. (in a case in which he admitted evidence questioned as secondary) to the effect that "the best proof that the nature of the thing will afford is only required." [2] This statement given as a reason for receiving evidence, that it is the best which can be had—a highly liberalizing principle—not surprisingly gives birth to a converse and narrowing doctrine that a man must produce the best evidence that is available—second-best will not do. And so before 1726 we find Baron Gilbert in one of the earliest treatises on Evidence saying, "the first and most signal rule in relation to evidence is this, that a man must have the utmost evidence the nature of the fact is capable of . . ." [3] Blackstone continues the same broad generalizing and combines both the positive and negative aspects of the "best evidence" idea when he says, ". . . the best evidence the nature of the case will admit of shall always be required, if possible to be had; but if not possible then the best evidence that can be had shall be allowed." [4] Greenleaf in this country in 1842 was still repeating these wide abstractions. [5]

Thayer, however, writing in 1898, points out that these broad principles, though they had some influence in shaping specific evi-

---

1. Thayer, Preliminary Treatise on Evidence at the Common Law 489 (1898).

2. Ford v. Hopkins, 1 Salk. 283, 91 Eng.Rep. 250 (1700).

3. Gilbert, Evidence (2d ed.) 4, 15–17, quoted Thayer, op. cit. 490.

4. 3 Blackstone, Commentaries 368, quoted Thayer op. cit. 491.

5. 1 Greenleaf, Evidence Part 2, ch. 4, secs. 82–97 (1842), quoted and analyzed in Thayer, op. cit., 484–487.

dence rules in the 1700s, were never received as adequate or accurate statements of governing rules, and that actually "the chief illustration of the Best Evidence principle, the doctrine that if you would prove the contents of a writing, you must produce the writing itself" is an ancient rule far older than any notion about the "best" evidence.[6] While some modern opinions still refer to the "best evidence" notion as if it were today a general governing legal principle [7] most would adopt the view of modern textwriters [8] that there is no such general rule.[9] The only actual rule that the "best evidence" phrase denotes today is the rule requiring the production of the original writing.[10]

6. Thayer, op. cit. 497–506.

7. See, e. g., Callahan v. Booth, 275 Ala. 275, 154 So.2d 32 (1963) (no error to reject as not best evidence oral testimony as to physical facts shown on photograph of car); Padgett v. Brezner, 359 S.W.2d 416, 422 (Mo.App.1962) (". . . the best evidence of which the case in its nature is susceptible and which is in the power of the party to produce, or is capable of being produced must always be produced in proof of every disputed fact;" rule applied to writing but said also to control operation of hearsay rule); Simon v. Hendricks, 330 P.2d 186 (Okl.1958) (holding it a violation of best evidence rule to allow doctor to testify to facts shown an X ray without introduction of X ray itself).

8. See 4 Wigmore, Evidence § 1174. See also J. Maguire, Evidence: Common Sense and Common Law 32 (1947); 2 Morgan, Basic Problems of Evidence 332 (1954); Comment, 14 Ark.L.Rev. 153 (1959) (pointing out a consistent broader application essentially impracticable).

9. See, e. g., Chandler v. United States, 318 F.2d 356 (10th Cir. 1963) (rule held not to require production of whiskey bottles alleged not to have carried federal revenue stamps); Meyer v. State, 218 Ark. 440, 236 S.W.2d 996 (1951) ("The best evidence rule deals with writings alone . . .;" rule held not to require production of piece of bologna); State ex rel. Alderson v. Halbert, 137 W.Va. 883, 74 S.E. 2d 772 (1953) (semble).

10. As a moral argument, however, which may be marshaled on many evidence questions, the idea still has appeal. ". . . The fact that any given way of proof is all that a man has must be a strong argument for receiving it if it be in a fair degree probative; and the fact that a man does not produce the best evidence in his power must always afford strong ground of suspicion." Thayer, op. cit. 507. The "best evidence" notion has sometimes

230. Original Document Rule.[11]

The specific context in which it is generally agreed that the best evidence principle is applicable today should be definitely stated and its limits clearly defined. The rule is this: in proving the terms of a writing, where the terms are material, the original writing must be produced unless it is shown to be unavailable for some reason other than the serious fault of the proponent. The discussion in the following sections is directed to adding content to this basic framework.

been given as a reason for admitting hearsay evidence when it is the most reliable which can be procured. See, e. g., Edwards v. Swilley, 196 Ark. 633, 118 S.W.2d 584 (1938). Contra: Fordson Coal Co. v. Vanover, 291 Ky. 447, 164 S.W.2d 966 (1942). The effect of failure to call witnesses or to produce evidence is discussed in § 272, infra.

11. 4 Wigmore, Evidence §§ 1177–1282; Dec.Dig. Crim. Law ☜398–403, Evidence ☜157–187; 32A C.J.S. Evidence, §§ 776–850; 29 Am.Jur.2d Evidence §§ 448–492. See also Model Code of Evidence Rule 602, and the comments thereon in Rogers, The Best Evidence Rule, 1945 Wis.L.Rev. 278. Uniform Rule 70, is as follows: "(1) As tending to prove the content of a writing, no evidence other than the writing itself is admissible, except as otherwise provided in these rules, unless the judge finds (a) that the writing is lost or has been destroyed without fraudulent intent on the part of the proponent, or (b) that the writing is outside the reach of the court's process and not procurable by the proponent, or (c) that the opponent, at a time when the writing was under his control has been notified, expressly or by implication from the pleadings, that it would be needed at the hearing, and on request at the hearing has failed to produce it, or (d) that the writing is not closely related to the controlling issues and it would be inexpedient to require its production, or (e) that the writing is an official record, or is a writing affecting property authorized to be recorded and actually recorded in the public records as described in Rule 63, exception (19).

"(2) If the judge makes one of the findings specified in the preceding paragraph, secondary evidence of the content of the writing is admissible. Evidence offered by the opponent tending to prove (a) that the asserted writing never existed, or (b) that a writing produced at the trial is the asserted writing, or (c) that the secondary evidence does not correctly reflect the content of the asserted writings, is irrelevant and inadmissible upon the question of admissibility of the secondary evidence but is relevant and admissible upon the issues of the existence and content of the asserted writing to be determined by the trier of fact."

231. The Reasons for the Rule.

Since its inception in the early 18th century, various rationales have been asserted to underlie the "best evidence rule." Many older writers have asserted that the rule is essentially directed to the prevention of fraud.[12] Wigmore, however, vigorously attacked this thesis on the analytical ground that it does not square with certain recognized applications and non-applications of the rule.[13] Most modern commentators follow his lead in asserting that the basic premise justifying the rule is the central position which the written word occupies in the law.[14] Because of this centrality, presenting to a court the exact words of a writing is of more than average importance, particularly in the case of operative or dispositive instruments such as deeds, wills or contracts, where a slight variation of words may mean a great difference in rights. In addition, it is to be considered (1) that there is substantial hazard of inaccuracy in many commonly utilized methods making copies of writings, and (2) oral testimony purporting to give from memory the terms of a writing is probably subject to a greater risk of error than oral testimony concerning other situations generally. The danger of mistransmitting critical facts which accompanies the use of written copies or recollection, but which is largely avoided when an original writing is present-

ed to prove its terms, justifies preference for original documents.

At the same time, however, it would appear a mistake totally to disregard all other justifications for the rule. It has long been observed that the opportunity to inspect original writings may be of substantial importance in the detection of fraud.[15] At least a few modern courts and commentators appear to regard the prevention of fraud as an ancillary justification of the rule.[16] Unless this view is accepted it is difficult to explain the rule's frequent application to copies produced by modern techniques which virtually eliminate the possibility of unintentional mistransmission.

Finally, one leading recent opinion[17] intimates that the rule should be viewed to protect not only against mistaken or fraudulent mistransmissions but also against intentional or unintentional misleading through introduction of selected portions of a comprehensive set of writings to which the opponent has no access. This seems to engraft upon the best evidence rule an aspect of completeness not heretofore observed.

Whatever rationale is viewed to support the rule, it will be observed that the advent of modern discovery and related procedures under which original documents may be ex-

---

12. 1 Greenleaf, Evidence 93 (1842); 1 Starkie, Evidence 387 (5th Am. ed. 1834); 1 Taylor, Evidence § 391 (1887).

13. 4 Wigmore, Evidence § 1180.

The inconsistencies noted by Wigmore are three: (1) that the rule is properly applicable even where the court may be satisfied that the proponent of secondary evidence is in utmost good faith; (2) that the rule is similarly applicable where possession by a third party should logically remove any suspicion of fraudulent suppression by the proponent, and (3) that were inference of fraud the foundation of the rule it should also apply to objects as well as writings, which it is at least generally agreed it does not.

14. See, e. g., Morgan, Basic Problems of Evidence 385 (1962).

15. Thus Quintilian, writing circa A.D. 88, is quoted by Osborn as stating:

"It is therefore necessary to examine all the writings related to a case; it is not sufficient to inspect them; they must be read through; for very frequently they are either not at all such as they were asserted to be, or they contain less than was stated, or they are mixed with matters that may injure the client's cause, or they say too much and lose all credit from appearing to be exaggerated. We may often, too, find a thread broken, or wax disturbed, or signatures without attestation . . . . ." Osborn, Questioned Documents, XVI (2d ed. 1929).

16. See, e. g., United States v. Manton, 107 F.2d 834 (2d Cir. 1939); Rogers, The Best Evidence Rule, 20 Wis.L.Rev. 278 (1945).

17. Toho Bussan Kaisha, Ltd. v. American President Lines, Ltd., 265 F.2d 418, 76 A.L.R.2d 1344 (2d Cir. 1959).

amined before trial rather than at it, have substantially reduced the need for the rule. Nevertheless, it has been pointed out that at present limitations on the availability of these alternatives leaves the original documents rule a continuing and important sphere of operations.[18]

232. What are Writings? Application to Objects Inscribed and Uninscribed.[19]

A rule which permitted the judge to insist that all evidence must pass his scrutiny as being the "best" or most reliable means of proving the fact would be a sore incumbrance upon the parties, who in our system have the responsibility of proof. In fact, as we have seen, no such general scrutiny is sanctioned, but only as to "writings" is a demand for the "best," the original, made.[20] This limitation on the ambit of the rule rests largely on the practical realization that writings exhibit a fineness of detail, lacking in chattels generally, which will often be of critical importance. Prevention of loss of this fine detail through mistransmission is a basic objective of the rule requiring production of documentary originals.

But while writings may be generally distinguished from other chattels with respect to the amount and importance of the detail they exhibit, chattels bearing more or less detailed inscriptions are far from uncommon. Thus, when an object such as a policeman's badge, a flag, or a tombstone bears a number or legend the terms of which are relevant the problem is raised as to whether the object shall be treated as a chattel or a writing. It is here clearly unwise to adapt a purely semantic approach and to classify the object according to whether its written component

predominates sufficiently to alter the label attached to it in common parlance.[21] At the same time, however, it would seem also unnecessary to classify as writings, as do the Uniform Rules,[22] any object which carries an inscription of any sort whatsoever. In the final analysis, it is perhaps impossible to improve upon Wigmore's suggestion,[23] followed by a number of courts,[24] that the judge shall have discretion to apply the present rule to inscribed chattels or not in light of such factors as the need for precise information as to the exact inscription, the ease or difficulty of production, and the simplicity or complexity of the inscription.

Within this general framework of discretion, certain types of chattels warrant specific mention. Thus, sound recordings, where their content is sought to be proved,[25] so clearly involve the identical considerations applicable to writings as to warrant in-

---

18. Cleary and Strong, The Best Evidence Rule: An Evaluation in Context, 51 Iowa L.Rev. 825 (1966).

19. 4 Wigmore, Evidence § 1182, Dec.Dig. Evidence ☞170, Criminal Law ☞400(1).

20. See § 229, supra.

21. See Comment, A Critical Appraisal of the Application of the Best Evidence Rule, 21 Rut.L.Rev. 526, 538 (1967).

22. Uniform Rule 1(13): " 'Writing' means handwriting, typewriting, printing, photostating, photographing and every other means of recording upon any tangible thing any form of communication or representation, including letters, words, pictures, sounds or symbols, or combinations thereof." Application of the rule has not, traditionally, been so broad. See, e. g., Streeter v. State, 60 Ga.App. 190, 3 S.E.2d 235 (1939) (witness allowed to testify that numbers of stolen automobile tires were on list found in defendant's possession); Quillen v. Commonwealth, 284 Ky. 792, 145 S.W.2d 1048 (1940) (testimony as to license number without production of plate).

23. 4 Wigmore, Evidence § 1182.

24. See, e. g., State v. Lewark, 106 Kan. 184, 186 P. 1002 (1920) (receiving stolen automobile: judge in discretion properly permitted testimony that engine number appeared to be altered, without requiring production of automobile); Quillen v. Comm., 284 Ky. 792, 145 S.W.2d 1048 (1940) (theft of automobile, testimony as to license number properly allowed without producing plate, where number not disputed); Mattson v. Minn. & N. W. R. Co., 98 Minn. 296, 108 N.W. 517 (1906) (wrappers on dynamite, not shown to be detachable; proper exercise of discretion to allow description without production).

25. For a discussion of those instances in which content is sought to be proved, see § 233, infra.

clusion within the present rule.[26] Pictures and photographs, on the other hand, in those relatively rare instances in which their contents are sought to be proved,[27] would generally seem to invite the contrary classification since representations of objects generally cannot logically be said to exhibit less intricacy of detail than do objects.[28] It should be noted, however, that X rays have frequently been held to be within the rule.[29]

233. What Constitutes Proving the Terms.

It is apparent that this danger of mistransmission of the contents of the writing, which is the principal reason for the rule, is only important when evidence other than the writing itself is offered for the purpose of proving its terms. Consequently, evidence

that a certain document is in existence [30] or as to its execution [31] or delivery [32] is not within the rule and may be given without producing the document.[33]

In what instances, then, can it be said that the terms of a writing are sought to be proved, rather than merely its identity, or existence? First, there are certain writings which the substantive law, e. g., the Statute of Frauds, the parole evidence rule, endow with a degree of either indispensability or primacy.[34] Transactions to which substantive rules of this character apply tend naturally to be viewed as written transactions, and writings embodying such transactions, e. g., deeds, contracts, judgments, etc., are universally considered to be within the present rule when actually involved in the litigation. Contrasted with the above described types of writings are those, essentially unlimited in variety, which the substantive law does not regard as essential or primary repositories of the facts recorded. Writings of this latter sort may be said merely to happen to record the facts of essentially non-

---

26. See Forrester v. State, 224 Md. 337, 167 A.2d 878 (1961) (rule applied to exclude testimony concerning conversation which had been recorded, but which witness had not overheard; recording in such case treated like writing. But, under the currently prevailing theory described in § 233, infra, the rule does not apply to recordings the "contents" of which are not sought to be shown. See, e. g., People v. Swayze, 220 Cal.App.2d 476, 34 Cal.Rptr. 5 (1963) (rule not applicable to require recording of conversation actually overheard by officer offering to testify).

27. The usual theory on which photographs and representations are admitted does not require proof of the "contents" of the picture. See § 214, supra. But contents will be seen to be involved in copyright and defamation cases where the picture is the allegedly offending article, or where a photograph is tendered as having evidentiary value apart from merely "illustrating" the testimony of a witness.

28. See, e. g., Lucas v. Williams [1892] 2 Q.B. 113 (C.A.) (original of painting not required in action for infringing copyright by selling photos of it). Decisions considering the question of the application of the present rule to motion pictures are collected in Annot., 62 A.L.R.2d 658.

29. See, e. g., Cellamare v. Third Ave. Transit Corp., 273 App.Div. 260, 77 N.Y.S.2d 91 (1948) (rule applicable to X ray); Simon v. Hendricks, 330 P.2d 186 (Okl.1958) (expert not permitted to testify to contents of X ray).

30. Fish v. Fleishman, 87 Idaho 126, 391 P.2d 344 (1964) (check stub to show existence of check); Mickle v. Blackmon, 252 S.C. 202, 166 S.E.2d 173 (1969) (existence of scientific writings properly established through testimony).

31. Redwine v. King, 366 P.2d 921 (Okl.1961) (proof that lease had been executed not requiring production of lease).

32. Higgins v. Arizona Sav. & Loan Ass'n, 90 Ariz. 55, 365 P.2d 476 (1961) (oral testimony receivable to show handwritten notes had been sent, rather than their contents).

33. See Dec.Dig. Evidence ☞159, 161(1). This sort of evidence will usually entail a more or less general description of a writing not considered to be proof of its terms. See, e. g., Hardy v. Hardy, 221 Ga. 176, 144 S.E.2d 172 (1965) (description of notes including testimony of dates and amounts held not proof of terms); Chambless v. State, 94 Okl.Cr. 140, 231 P.2d 711 (1951) (officers could testify that there was a federal liquor license on defendant's premises, but could not give "contents"). The problem will be seen to be very similar to that described above, § 232, supra.

34. See 4 Wigmore, Evidence § 1242.

written transactions.[35] Testimony descriptive of nonwritten transactions is not generally considered to be within the scope of the present rule and may be given without producing or explaining the absence of a writing recording the facts.[36] Thus, evidence of a payment may be given without production of the receipt,[37] or evidence of a marriage without production of the marriage certificate.[38]

While, however, many facts may be proved without resort to writings which record them, the party attempting to prove a fact may choose to show the contents of a writing for the purpose. Thus, for example, a writing may contain a recital of fact which is admissible under an exception to the hearsay rule. Here the recited fact might possibly be established without the writing, but if the contents are relied upon for the purpose the present rule applies and oral testimony as to its contents will be rejected unless the original writing is shown to be unavailable.[39]

Where the written record is complicated or voluminous, and is produced or made available to the opposing party, an expert who has examined it may testify as to his calculations, summaries, and conclusions in order to aid the court or jury to understand the writing.[40]

Certain criticisms may be leveled at the commonly applied distinction between facts the legal efficacy of which is affected by recordation, and facts which are legally effective whether or not contained in a writing. Thus, it has been suggested, that in modern law there are few if any instances in which a writing is anything more than a recordation of some nonwritten fact. For example, a written contract, it may be contended, merely records the operative legal fact, which is the agreement of the parties.[41] Moreover, the distinction has proved a difficult one to apply, and does not adequately serve to reconcile various common applications and nonapplications of the rule. Thus it is commonly held that oral evidence of a witness's prior testimony is receivable even though that testimony is embodied in a transcript.[42] But

---

35. Lund v. Starz, 355 Mich. 497, 94 N.W.2d 912 (1959) ("where the matter to be proved is a substantive fact which exists independently of any writing, although evidenced thereby, and which can be as fully and satisfactorily established by parole as by written evidence, then both classes of evidence are primary . . .").

36. Sayen v. Rydzewski, 387 F.2d 815 (7th Cir. 1967) (amount of income allowed to be proved without records); Allen v. W. H. O. Alfalfa Mill Co., 272 F.2d 98 (10th Cir. 1959) (costs of production); Herzig v. Swift & Co., 146 F.2d 444 (2d Cir. 1945) (earnings provable without records); Lin Mfg. Co. v. Courson, 246 Ark. 5, 436 S.W.2d 472 (1969) (company policy provable without production of written statement thereof); People v. Kulwin, 102 Cal.App.2d 104, 226 P.2d 672 (1951) (policeman who overheard conversation between defendants can testify thereto without producing sound-recording); Mars v. Meadville Tel. Co., 344 Pa. 29, 23 A.2d 856 (1942) (earnings).

37. Kendall v. Hargrave, 142 Colo. 120, 349 P.2d 993 (1960); Gonzalez v. Hoffman, 9 Mich.App. 522, 157 N.W.2d 475 (1968).

38. Lopez v. Missouri K. & T. Ry. Co. of Texas, 222 S.W. 695 (Tex.Civ.App.1920) (foreign marriage).

39. Mitchell v. Emblade, 80 Ariz. 398, 298 P.2d 1034 (1956) (error to allow witness with no knowledge of independent fact to testify as to what records showed).

40. Harris v. United States, 356 F.2d 582 (5th Cir. 1966) (summarization by expert of records available for inspection held proper); State v. Schrader, 64 N.M. 100, 324 P.2d 1025 (1958) (summary testimony admissible where records available for inspection but not introduced); Aldridge v. Burchfiel, 421 P.2d 655 (Okl.1966). But compare Bolling Co. v. Barrington Co., 398 S.W.2d 28 (Mo.App.1965) (summaries inadmissible where records not introduced and unavailable through absence from jurisdiction).

F.R.Ev. (R.D.1971) 1006:

"The contents of voluminous writings, recordings, or photographs which cannot conveniently be examined in court may be presented in the form of a chart, summary, or calculation. The originals, or duplicates, shall be made available for examination or copying, or both, by other parties at a reasonable time and place. The judge may order that they be produced in court."

41. See the dissenting opinion of Prettyman, J., in Meyers v. United States, 84 U.S.App.D.C. 101, 171 F.2d 800 (1948) cert. denied 336 U.S. 912.

42. See, e. g., Meyers v. United States, supra, note 41; State v. Bixby, 27 Wash.2d 144, 177 P.2d 689 (1947). But compare, Benge v. Commonwealth, 298

when a confession has been both orally made and reduced to writing, numerous courts require the writing.[43] Dying declarations both spoken and reduced to writing have produced a similar contrariety of opinion.[44]

Perhaps the most satisfactory solution to the problem would be to abandon the distinction between transactions essentially written and nonwritten and allow the application of the rule to turn upon the trial judge's determination of such factors as the centrality of the writing to the litigation, the importance of bringing the precise words of the writing before the trier, and the danger of mistransmission or imposition in the absence of the original. The result would simply be to merge the present confusing and confused doctrine with the collateral documents exception discussed below,[45] or at least to enlarge the scope of the latter.

234. Writings Involved Only Collaterally.[46]

At nearly every turn in human affairs some writing—a letter, a bill of sale, a newspaper, a deed—plays a part. Consequently any narration by a witness is likely to include many references to transactions consisting partly of written communications or other writings. A witness to a confession, for example, identifies the date as being the day after the crime because he read of the crime in the newspaper that day, or a witness may state that he was unable to procure a certain article because it was patented. It is apparent that it is impracticable to forbid such references except upon condition that the writings (e. g., the newspaper, and the patent) be produced in court. Recognition of an exception exempting "collateral writings" from the operation of the basic rule has followed as a necessary concession to expedition of trials and clearness of narration, interests which outweigh, in the case of merely incidental references to documents, the need for perfect exactitude in the presentation of these documents' contents.

While writings are frequently held to be collateral within the meaning of the present exception,[47] the purposes for which references to documents may be made by witnesses are so variegated that the concept of collateralness defies precise definition. Three principal factors, however, should, and generally do, play a role in making the determi-

Ky. 562, 183 S.W.2d 631 (1944). Cases are collected in Annot., 11 A.L.R.2d 30.

43. See 4 Wigmore, Evidence § 1332.

44. See Annot., 112 A.L.R. 43.

45. See § 234, infra. Such a merger has been previously suggested. Comment, The Best Evidence Rule—The Rule in Oregon, 41 Ore.L.Rev. 138 (1962). See also Comment, The Best Evidence Rule—A Rule Requiring the Production of A Writing to Prove the Writing's Contents, 14 Ark.L.Rev. 153 (1960) (noting that the two rules are inseparably commingled).

46. 4 Wigmore, Evidence § 1254; Dec.Dig. Evidence ☞171, Criminal Law ☞401; C.J.S. Evidence § 781; Annot., 1 A.L.R. 1143. See also Note, Secondary Evidence of Collateral Writings, 11 N.C.L.Rev. 342 (1933).

47. See, e. g., Lin Mfg. Co. v. Courson, 246 Ark. 5, 436 S.W.2d 472 (1969) (evidence of local companies' policies against hiring persons with back trouble allowed on damage without production of written policy statements; result also justified on ground that policy not a written fact, see § 233, supra); Farr v. Zoning Board of Appeals, 139 Conn. 577, 95 A.2d 792 (1953) (parties allowed to establish standing as aggrieved property owners without producing documents of title); Wilkins v. Hester, 119 Ga. App. 389, 167 S.E.2d 167 (1969) (witness testifying to value of car allowed to establish status as used car dealer without production of license, even though license was "best evidence"); Wilson Trans. Co. v. Owens-Illinois Glass Co., 125 N.J.L. 636, 17 A.2d 581 (1941) (plaintiff seeking to show damages due to defendant's breach of contract by proving sale of trucks acquired to haul defendant's goods not required to produce documentary proof of ownership); State v. Vaughan, 243 Ind. 221, 184 N.E.2d 143 (1962) (testimonial reference to ownership of properties surrounding tract condemned permissible as collateral fact); Van Valkenberg v. Venters, 200 Okl. 504, 197 P.2d 284 (1948) (oral evidence of ownership by plaintiff admissible in forcible detainer proceedings); Lamas v. State, 365 S.W.2d 163 (Tex.Cr.App.1963) (proof of public officer's status does not require production of commission where suit not between officer and public). See also, Annot., 1 A.L.R. 1143 (admissibility of parole evidence to prove title involved only collaterally).

nation of collateralness. These are: the centrality of the writing to the principal issues of the litigation; [48] the complexity of the relevant features of the writing; [49] and the existence of genuine dispute as to the contents of the writing.[50] Evaluation and weighting of these factors in the particular instance may perhaps best be left to the discretion of the trial judge, and as elsewhere in the application of this essentially administrative rule, exercise of that discretion should be reviewed only for grave abuse.[51]

235. Which is the "Writing Itself" That Must be Produced? [52] Telegrams,[53] Counterparts.[54]

What should be the application of the basic rule where two documents, X and Y, exist,

X having been created first and Y being some variety of reproduction of X? Copies, of course, are frequent and in most cases the document first prepared will be the one whose initial production is required by the rule. But the problem is not always so simple. For example, X may be a telegram written by the sender and handed to the company for transmission; or X may be a libelous handwritten letter given to a stenographer for copying and sending, and Y the letter actually received by the addressee; or X may be a ledger sheet in the creditor's books and Y the account rendered made up therefrom and sent to the debtor.

In any of the above cases, if a party in court offers document Y in evidence, what determines whether the document is "the writing itself" offered to prove its own terms, or merely a "copy" offered to establish the terms of X? The answer here clearly does not depend upon the chronology of creation or the ordinary semantic usage which would denominate Y as a "copy." [55] Instead it will depend upon the substantive law of contracts, defamation, property and the like. The question to be asked, then, is whether, under the substantive law, the creation, publication or other use of Y may be viewed as affecting the rights of the parties in a way material to the litigation. If the answer to this question is affirmative, the fact that Y happens to be a copy of another writing is completely immaterial.[56] Decisions illustra-

---

48. A few courts have gone so far as to classify as collateral all writings which do not form the foundation of the cause of action or defense. See, e. g., Freeman v. Commercial Union Assur. Co., 317 S.W.2d 563 (Tex.Civ.App.1958); Doman v. Baltimore & O. R. Co., 125 W.Va. 8, 22 S.E.2d 703 (1942); C.J.S. Evidence § 781. This rule would appear unduly embrasive as excluding from the operation of the general rule all nonwritten facts and even many written facts which, though not the basis of the action, possess substantial evidentiary significance. See, e. g., State v. Anderson, 5 N.C.App. 614, 169 S.E.2d 38 (1969) (production of threatening note handed prosecuting witness during perpetration of alleged attempted rape held not excused as collateral fact).

Cf. F.R.Ev. (R.D. 1971) 1004:
"The original is not required, and other evidence of the contents of a writing, recording, or photograph is admissible if—

. . . . .

"**(4) Collateral Matters.** The writing, recording, or photograph is not closely related to a controlling issue."

49. Testimony as to the nature of inscribed chattels is thus sometimes admitted as evidence of collateral facts. See § 232, supra.

50. See, e. g., Farr v. Zoning Board of Appeals, 139 Conn. 577, 95 A.2d 792 (1953) (citing absence of evidentiary challenge of status of plaintiffs as property owners as one basis for failing to require documentary evidence of title).

51. Compare 4 Wigmore, Evidence § 1253.

52. 4 Wigmore, Evidence § 1232.

53. 4 Wigmore, Evidence § 1236; Dec.Dig. Evidence ☞168, 183(14); C.J.S. Evidence §§ 792, 814.

54. 4 Wigmore, Evidence § 1233; Dec.Dig. Evidence ☞186(6); C.J.S. Evidence § 821.

55. 4 Wigmore, Evidence §§ 1232, 1235(2) and (3); Comment, The Best Evidence Rule—A Rule Requiring the Production of a Writing to Prove the Writing's Contents, 14 Ark.L.Rev. 153, 160 (1960).

56. McDonald v. Hanks, 52 Tex.Civ.App. 140, 113 S.W. 604, 607 (1908), where the court said: "If a writer desiring to preserve a copy of a letter, writes at the same time two copies exactly alike, one of which he proposes to send and the other to keep, it is a matter of indifference which copy he sends, but the one sent becomes the original and the other a copy, no matter by what force of evidence it is shown to be an absolutely accurate copy." See also Illinois Tuberculosis Ass'n v. Springfield Marine Bank, 282 Ill.App. 14 (1935)

tive of instances in which the terms of "copies" are the facts sought to be proved are cited below.[57]

It will also frequently occur that a written transaction, such as a contract or deed, will be evidenced by several counterparts or identical copies, each of which is signed by the parties or, at any rate, intended to be equally effective as embodying the transaction.[58] Such multiple counterparts are frequently termed "duplicate (or triplicate, etc.) originals". Each of these counterparts is admissible as an "original" without producing or

accounting for the others,[59] but before secondary evidence may be resorted to, all of the counterparts must be shown to be unavailable.[60]

236. Mechanical Reproductions: Letter-Press Copies: Carbons: Photo-Reproductions: Printed and Multigraph Copies.[61]

The treatment of copies under the rule requiring the production of the original document can only properly be understood when viewed in light of the technological history of copying itself. In its earliest stages, the rule appears to have developed against a background of copying performed by individuals of the Bob Cratchit sort, transcribing manually not always under the best of conditions. Errors under such circumstances were routinely to be expected. Only marginally greater reliability was to be found in the so-called letter-press. Here the original was written or typed in copying ink or with copying pencil. Presumably influenced by the infirmities present in such modes of copying, the courts generally declined to accept subsequently created copies as equivalent to originals.[62]

(bank mailed carbon of statement to customer; held, original).

57. Montgomery v. United States, 219 Fed. 162 (8th Cir. 1915) (in prosecution for Mann Act violation, writing delivered by defendant to telegraph company held original; "In suits between the immediate parties to telegrams, the telegram received is often the original. In suits against the telegraph company for damages for failure to send a telegram correctly or at all, the original would be the telegram sent") (dictum); Carpenter v. Dressler, 76 Ark. 400, 89 S.W. 89 (1905) (executed deed rather than public transcript of grant held the orginal under then existing state substantive law); Fuchs & Lang Mfg. Co. v. Kittredge & Co., 242 Ill. 88, 89 N.E. 723 (1909) (blueprint from which machine had been assembled, rather than drawing of which blueprint was a copy, held original when offered to show operation of machine); Prussing v. Jackson, 208 Ill. 85, 69 N.E. 771 (1904) (libel action against writer of letter printed in newspaper; letter rather than printed matter held original); State v. Calongne, 111 Kan. 332, 206 P. 1112 (1922) (prosecution for fraud defended on ground facts represented were believed by defendant to be true; telegrams received by defendant purporting to detail financial status of corporation held originals); In re Stringer's Estate, 80 Wyo. 389, 343 P.2d 508 (1959) (where testator actually executed only a "copy" of will, copy held the original dispositive instrument).

58. Courts have differed considerably with respect to what may constitute a duplicate original. Compare Tampa Shipbuilding & Eng. Co. v. General Const. Co., 43 F.2d 309 (5th Cir. 1930) ("Duplicates exist only when the two instruments have both been recognized and established by the parties concerned as evidence of their act, as where the parties to the sale sign a memorandum with carbon copy and each keeps one") with Parr Const. Co. v. Pomer, 217 Md. 539, 144 A.2d 69 (1958) (holding an ordinary unsigned retained copy is a duplicate), commented upon in Note, 20 Md.L.Rev. 50 (1960). Compare F.R.Ev. (R.D.1971) 1001 which avoids the

internally contradictory phrase "duplicate originals." See also § 236, infra.

59. Fistere, Inc., v. Helz, 226 A.2d 578, 579 (D.C. App.1967) ("When a document is executed in duplicate or multiplicate form, each of the parts is deemed an original and may be used without accounting for any other part"); Schroer v. Schroer, 248 S.W.2d 617 (Mo.1952) (duplicate deposit slip stamped and delivered to depositor held admissible as duplicate original); Cross v. Everybodys, 357 S.W.2d 156 (Tex.Civ.App.1962) (production of one duplicate original satisfies best evidence rule).

60. Norris v. Billingsley, 48 Fla. 102, 37 So. 564 (1904); American Empire Life Ins. Co. v. Long, 344 S.W.2d 513 (Tex.Civ.App.1961) (photostatic copy of newspaper admissible; showing that no original copy of newspaper available).

61. 4 Wigmore, Evidence § 1234; Dec.Dig. Evidence ⚓174(1), 186(6); C.J.S. Evidence §§ 815, 816, 821; Annots., 65 A.L.R.2d 342 (carbons), 76 A.L.R.2d 1356 (photographic copies).

62. See Philipson v. Chase, 2 Camp. 110, 170 Eng. Rep. 1097 (K.B.1809) (book entry on attorney's bill not admissible); Nodin v. Murray, 3 Camp. 228, 170 Eng.Rep. 1363 (1812) (deficiencies of letter-

The advent of carbon paper, however, made possible the creation of copies of substantially greater reliability and legibility. Here, since the copy is made by the same stroke of the pen or pencil as the original, there was an apparent factual distinction between these copies and copies produced subsequent to the original by the older methods.[63] It moreover became common, as it is today, to create multiple counterparts of a contract or transaction through the use of carbon paper, with each copy duly signed either through the same medium or individually. What makes such writings counterparts, of course, is the signing with intent to render each co-equal with the others, and the doctrine of counterparts can therefore hardly apply to a retained carbon copy which is not intended as a communication at all.[64] However, the fact that many true counterparts are made by the use of carbons coupled with the notion that writings generated simultaneously by the same stroke are in some way superior, has caused a great number of courts to treat all carbons as if they were duplicate originals, i. e., as admissible without accounting for the original.[65]

More comprehensibly, there is warrant for believing that the courts will accept as primary evidence of the contents of a given book or a given issue of a newspaper any other book or newspaper printed from the same sets of fixed type, or the same plates or mats. A like result should be reached as to all copies run off from the same mat by the multigraph, lithoprint or other duplicating process.[66]

In the present day, copying by various photographic and other processes has become commonplace, replacing the carbon for many purposes. Various types of photographic copying, of course, produce facsimiles of an extremely high degree of verisimilitude, and thus might have been expected, as have carbons, to win recognition as duplicate originals. In fact, an early judicial step in this direction was taken in a celebrated federal court of appeals decision [67] which held that "recordak" photographs of checks which had been paid, preserved by a bank as part of its regular records were admissible under the Federal Business Records Act. Subsequently, a uniform act was prepared under which photographic copies, regularly kept, of business and public records are admissible without accounting for the original.[68] This act has been widely adopted.[69] In the cases, however, in which photo-

---

press copy noted by Lord Ellenborough); Federal Union Sur. Co. v. Indiana Lumber & Mfg. Co., 176 Ind. 328, 95 N.E. 1104 (1911).

63. Many of the early cases dealing with carbons emphasizes the simultaneous nature of the duplicate's creation. See, e. g., International Harvester Co. v. Elfstrom, 101 Minn. 263, 112 N.W. 252 (1907).

64. Lockwood v. L. & L. Freight Lines, 126 Fla. 474, 171 So. 236 (1936).

65. Carmichael Tile Co. v. McClelland, 213 Ga. 656, 100 S.E.2d 902 (1957) (retained carbon copy of letter admissible though unsigned); Eastover Co. v. All Metal Fabricators, Inc., 221 Md. 428, 158 A.2d 89 (1960) (fact that offered bills were carbons "of no importance"); State v. Stockton, 38 Tenn. App. 90, 270 S.W.2d 586 (1954) (carbon copies of records or reports created simultaneously admissible as duplicate originals, no indication of signing or other manifestation of intent). Contra: Lockwood v. L. & L. Freight Lines, 126 Fla. 474, 171 So. 236 (1936) (carbon is duplicate only when intended to stand equal); Shirer v. O. W. S. & Associates, 253 S.C. 232, 169 S.E.2d 621 (1969) (semble;

general rule of carbons as duplicates distinguished and rejected). See also, Annot., 65 A.L.R.2d 342; Notes, 20 Md.L.Rev. 50 (1960), 19 Ohio St.L.J. 520 (1958), 3 Vill.L.Rev. 217 (1958).

66. See Rex v. Watson, 2 Stark. 116, 171 Eng.Rep. 591 (N.P.1817) (to prove contents of printed placard which had been posted, other placards from same printing admitted); Redding v. Snyder, 352 Mich. 241, 89 N.W.2d 471 (1958) (copy of printed instruction pamphlet admitted).

67. United States v. Manton, 107 F.2d 834 (2d Cir. 1938).

68. Uniform Photographic Copies of Business and Public Records as Evidence Act, 9A U.L.A. 584.

69. The uniform act has been adopted in 38 states. 9A U.L.A. 117 (1967 Supp.) Following preparation of the uniform act, its substance was expressly incorporated into the Federal Business Records Act,

graphs of writings have been offered to show the terms of the original, without the aid of specific statutes, they have been almost uniformly treated as secondary evidence, inadmissible unless the original is accounted for.[70]

The resulting state of authority, favorable to carbons but unfavorable to at least equally reliable photographic reproductions, appears inexplicable on any basis other than that the courts, having fixed upon simultaneous creation as the characteristic distinguishing of carbons from copies produced by earlier methods have on the whole been insufficiently flexible to modify that concept in the face of newer technological methods which fortuitously do not exhibit that characteristic. Insofar as the primary purpose of the original documents requirements is directed at securing accurate information from the contents of material writings, free of the infirmities of memory and the mistakes of hand-copying, we may well conclude that each of these forms of mechanical copying is sufficient to fulfill the policy. Insistence upon the original, or accounting for it, places costs, burdens of planning and hazards of mistake upon the litigants. These may be worth imposing where the alternative is accepting memory or hand-copies. They are probably not worth imposing when risks of inaccuracy are reduced to a minimum by the offer of a mechanically produced copy.

At the same time, however, if the original documents requirement is conceded to be supported by the ancillary purpose of fraud prevention, it will be seen that even copies produced by photographic processes are not totally as desirable as the original writing. Many indicia of putative fraud such as watermarks, types of paper and inks, etc., will not be discernable on a photographic copy. The most reasonable accommodation of the purposes of the basic rule to modern copying to date would appear to be that of the Proposed Federal Rules of Evidence.[71] Under Proposed Federal Rule 1001(d) copies produced by photography or by chemical reproduction are classed as "duplicates," and, under Rule 1003 are declared admissible as originals unless a genuine question is raised as to the authenticity of the original or it appears under the circumstances that it would be unfair to admit the duplicate in lieu of the original.[72]

An even more recent challenge to the flexibility of the rule requiring documentary originals has appeared in the form of machine readable records stored on punch cards or magnetic tape. Obviously, where records are originally deposited in such media nothing akin to a conventional documentary original will be created. To the credit of the courts, records there stored have generally fared well in the face of objection predicated on the original document rule, and machine printouts of such records have been admitted in several cases.[73]

---

28 U.S.C.A. § 1732(b), added by Act Aug. 28, 1951, c. 351, §§ 1, 3, 65 Stat. 206; Aug. 30, 1961, Pub.L. 87–183, 75 Stat. 413.

70. See, e. g., Cox v. State, 93 Ga.App. 533, 92 S.E. 2d 260 (1956) (photostatic copy secondary evidence); Benefield v. State, 355 P.2d 874 (Okl.Cr. 1960) (photostat held admissible under the uniform act; court noting by way of dictum that common law rule was contrary). See also, Annots. 76 A.L. R.2d 1356, 142 A.L.R. 1270 and Note, Photographic Copies of Business and Public Records, 34 Iowa L. Rev. 83 (1948).

71. F.R.Ev. (R.D.1971) 1001, 1003. See also the discussion of the proposed rules in Broun, Authentication and Content of Writings, 1969 Law & Soc. Ord. 611, 613. The proposed rule is supported by the reasoning in the following cases: Johns v. United States, 323 F.2d 421 (5th Cir. 1963); Sauget v. Johnston, 315 F.2d 816 (9th Cir. 1963).

72. As to circumstances which might warrant discretionary exclusion under the rule, compare Toho Bussan Kaisha, Ltd. v. American President Lines, Inc., 265 F.2d 418 (2d Cir. 1959) (photostats of portions of original records in Japan prepared for litigation excluded).

73. United States v. De Georgia, 420 F.2d 889 (9th Cir. 1969) (negative information obtained from computer of business corporation admitted on basis of foundation testimony establishing mode of recorda-

237. Excuses for Nonproduction of the Original Writing: (a) Loss or Destruction.[74]

The production-of-documents rule is principally aimed, not at securing a writing at all hazards and in every instance, but at securing the best *obtainable* evidence of its contents.[75] Thus, if as a practical matter the document cannot be produced because it has been lost or destroyed, the production of the original is excused and other evidence of its contents becomes admissible.[76] Failure to recognize this qualification of the basic rule would in many instances mean a return to the bygone and unlamented days in which to lose one's paper was to lose one's right. Recognition of the same qualification also squares with the ancillary purpose of the basic rule to protect against the perpetration of fraud, since proof that failure to produce the original is due to inability to do so tends logically to dispel the otherwise possible inference that the failure stems from design.

Loss or destruction may sometimes be provable by direct evidence but more often the only available evidence will be circumstantial, usually taking the form that appropriate search for the document has been made without discovering it. It would appear that where loss or destruction is sought to be proved by circumstantial evidence of

unavailing search, the declarations of a former custodian as to loss or destruction may be admitted to show the nature and results of the search,[77] though if offered as direct evidence of loss or destruction itself such declarations would be incompetent as hearsay.[78].

Where loss or destruction is sought to be shown circumstantially by proof of unsuccessful search, it is obvious that the adequacy of the showing will be largely dependent upon the thoroughness and appropriateness of the search. It was laid down in certain early decisions that when the writing is last known to have been in a particular place or in the hands of a particular person, then that place must be searched or the person produced,[79] and statements to the same effect are to be found in modern decisions.[80] It is believed, however, that these statements are best considered as general guides or cautions, rather than strict and unvarying rules. Virtually all jurisdictions view the trial judge as possessing some degree of discretion in determining the preliminary question as to whether it is feasible to produce the original document.[81] Such discretion is particularly ap-

---

tion and company's reliance thereon); King v. State ex rel. Murdock Acceptance Corp., 222 So.2d 393 (Miss.1969) (computer printouts admissible as "shop books" in absence of modern business records statute); Transport Indem. Co. v. Seib, 178 Neb. 253, 132 N.W.2d 871 (1965) (business entries made into computer in ordinary course of business held admissible in form of computer printout). See also, Note, 55 Cornell L.J. 1033 (1970); Annot., 11 A.L.R.3d 1377.

74. 4 Wigmore, Evidence §§ 1193–1198; Dec.Dig. Evidence ☞178; C.J.S. Evidence §§ 823, 824.

75. Fauci v. Mulready, 337 Mass. 532, 150 N.E.2d 286 (1958) (common law "best evidence" rule preferential rather than exclusionary).

76. See Sellmayer Packing Co. v. Commissioner, 146 F.2d 707 (4th Cir. 1944); Stipe v. First Nat. Bank, 208 Ore. 251, 301 P.2d 175 (1956); Hayes v. Bouligny, 420 S.W.2d 800 (Tex.Civ.App.1967).

77. Massie v. Hutcheson, 296 S.W. 939 (Tex.Civ. App., 1927), error refused (testimony that deceased grantee said: "Ashes tell no story" when questioned concerning deed, held admissible over objection that it was hearsay). See Interstate Investment Co. v. Bailey (Ky.1906) 93 S.W. 578, 580 ("What Elijah Davis learned that Stidham said about the loss of the paper may not have been evidence of its loss . . . yet it was evidence of his good faith in not prosecuting the inquiry further.") 4 Wigmore, Evidence § 1196(3).

78. Moore v. State, 179 Miss. 268, 175 So. 183 (1937) (testimony that addressee of letter said she had destroyed it properly excluded as hearsay, but error to admit secondary evidence of letter's contents).

79. Cook v. Hunt, 24 Ill. 535 (1860); Vandergriff v. Piercy, 59 Tex. 371 (1883).

80. See, e. g., Ragen v. Bennigsen, 10 Ill.App.2d 356, 135 N.E.2d 128 (1956).

81. See, e. g., Kramar v. Hackett, 316 Mich. 31, 24 N.W.2d 544 (1946) (question of loss one for trial judge); Barranco v. Kostens, 189 Md. 94, 54 A.2d 326 (1947) (sufficiency of search for lost deed for

propriate since the character of the search required to show probability of loss or destruction will, as a practical matter, depend on the circumstances of each case. Factors such as the relative importance of the document and the lapse of time since it was last seen have been seen to bear upon the extent of search required before loss or destruction may be inferred.[82] The only general requirement, however, should be that all reasonable avenues of search should be explored to the extent that reasonable diligence under the circumstances would dictate.[83]

If the original document has been destroyed by the person who offers evidence of its

contents, the evidence is not admissible unless, by showing that the destruction was accidental or was done in good faith, without intention to prevent its use as evidence, he rebuts to the satisfaction of the trial judge, any inference of fraud.[84]

238. Excuses for Nonproduction of the Original Writing: (b) Possession by a Third Person.[85]

When the writing is in the hands of a third person who is within the geographical limits of the trial court's subpoena power, the safest course is have a writ of subpoena duces tecum served on the possessor summoning him to bring the writing to court at the trial,[86] though some decisions will excuse resort to subpoena if the possessor is privileged not to produce it,[87] and others suggest that proof of

---

judge, reviewable only for abuse of discretion); Stipe v. First Nat. Bank, 208 Or. 251, 301 P.2d 175 (1956) (no absolute rule governing sufficiency of search; matter absolutely within discretion of trial judge); Vaught v. Nationwide Mut. Ins. Co., 250 S.C. 65, 156 S.E.2d 627 (1967) (trial court has discretion, though not absolute, to determine sufficiency of search).

82. See, e. g., Gathercole v. Miall, 15 M. & W. 319, 153 Eng.Rep. 872 (Exch. 1846); United States v. Ross, 321 F.2d 61 (2d Cir. 1963) cert. denied 375 U.S. 894 (insignificant paper prepared three years before trial; much less search required where subject is a useless paper which may reasonably be supposed lost); Agee v. Messer-Moore Ins. & Real Estate Co., 165 Ala. 291, 51 So. 829 (1910) (search required varies with value and importance of document).

83. Rash v. Peoples Deposit Bank & Trust Co., 91 F.Supp. 825 (E.D.Ky.1950) (no fixed degree of diligence required in search, but rather such search as nature of the case suggests); Pendley v. Murphy, 112 Ga.App. 33, 143 S.E.2d 674 (1965) (proponent must exhaust those sources which are suggested by facts of case); Chagnon Lumber Co. v. Patenaude, 103 N.H. 448, 174 A.2d 415 (1961) (every case of loss must be determined on its own facts). Of course, testimony by the last custodian, or lack of it, is properly viewed as a significant circumstance. See, e. g., Sylvania Elec. Prod. Inc. v. Flanagan, 352 F.2d 1005 (1st Cir. 1956) (each case of loss to be determined on its own circumstances; however, foundation insufficient where proponent never denied records were in existence and in fact testified he had some at home); In re 716 Third Ave. Holding Corp., 255 F.Supp. 268 (S.D. N.Y.1964) rev'd on other grounds 2d Cir., 340 F.2d 42 (testimony by president of corporation that corporation records had disappeared held insufficient proof of loss without showing of search); Wiggins v. Stapleton Baptist Church, 282 Ala. 255, 210 So.2d 814 (1968).

84. Reynolds v. Denver & Rio Grande W. Ry. Co., 174 F.2d 673 (10th Cir. 1949) (secondary evidence admissible if no "fraud or bad faith" in destruction); McDonald v. United States, 89 F.2d 128 (8th Cir. 1937) (government not precluded in kidnapping case from giving evidence of numbers on ransom bills by fact that subordinate official had improperly had bills destroyed); In re Rasnick, 77 N.J.Super. 380, 186 A.2d 527 (1962) (secondary evidence allowed where proponent had voluntarily destroyed original in a fit of rage where trial court found destruction free from suspicion under circumstances); Schroedl v. McTague, 256 Iowa 772, 129 N.W.2d 19 (1964) (semble; excellent discussion and criticism of strict prohibition against offer of secondary evidence by destroyer of original). For an example of the stricter view, see Booher v. Brown, 173 Ore. 464, 146 P.2d 71 (1944) (offering party must be "without neglect or fault").

85. 4 Wigmore, Evidence §§ 1211–1213; Dec.Dig. Evidence ⊂⊃179(3); C.J.S. Evidence §§ 830, 831.

86. Many decisions require this. See, e. g., Security Trust Co. v. Robb, 142 Fed. 78 (3d Cir. 1906); Pendley v. Murphy, 112 Ga.App. 33, 143 S.E.2d 674 (1965) (error to admit secondary evidence where no subpoena duces tecum issued to last known custodian); Schall v. Northland Motor Car. Co., 123 Minn. 214, 143 N.W. 357 (1913) (in possession of trustee in bankruptcy; "he is subject to subpena the same as other citizens"). If the possessor disobeys the summons, the party's production of the original should, of course, be excused.

87. See, e. g., People v. Powell, 71 Cal.App. 500, 236 P. 311 (1925) (letters tending to incriminate possessors).

a hostile or unwilling attitude on his part will be a sufficient excuse.[88]

If the writing is in the possession of a third person out of the state or out of the reach of the court's process, a showing of this fact alone will suffice, in the view of many courts, to excuse production of the writing.[89] This practice has the merit of being an easy rule of thumb to apply, but the basic policy of the original document requirement would tend to support the view of a substantially equal number of courts that a further showing must be made. These latter courts require that, before secondary evidence is used, the proponent must show either that he has made reasonable but unavailing efforts to secure the original from its possessor,[90] or circumstances which persuade the court that such efforts, had they been made, would have been fruitless.[91]

239. Excuses for Nonproduction of the Original Writing: (c) Failure of Adversary Having Possession to Produce after Notice.[92]

A frequently used method of showing that it is impracticable for the proponent to produce the original writing is to prove, first, that the original is in the hands of his adversary or under his control,[93] and second,

---

88. See, e. g., Mahanay v. Lynde, 48 Cal.App.2d 79, 119 P.2d 430 (1941) (adversary's mother got possession of paper and refused to give it back); Ragley-McWilliams Lumber Co. v. Hare, 130 S.W. 864, 868 (Tex.Civ.App.1910) (family Bible of third person, which plaintiffs tried to and were unable to obtain).

89. E. g., Hartzell v. United States, 72 F.2d 569 (8th Cir. 1934); Waters v. Mines, 260 Ala. 652, 72 So.2d 69 (1954); Moss v. State, 208 Ark. 137, 185 S.W.2d 92 (1945); Silvey v. Wynn, 102 Ga. App. 283, 115 S.E.2d 774 (1960); Flaharty v. Reed, 170 Kan. 215, 225 P.2d 98 (1950); Thurman v. St. Louis Public Service Co., 308 S.W.2d 680 (Mo.1957); Haire v. State, 118 Tex.Cr.R. 16, 39 S.W.2d 70 (1931).

90. E. g., Londoner v. Stewart, 3 Colo. 47, 50 (1876); McDonald v. Erbes, 231 Ill. 295, 83 N.E. 162 (1907); Sherman v. Sherman, 290 Ky. 237, 160 S.W.2d 637 (1942); Summons v. State, 156 Md. 390, 144 A. 501 (1929); Gasser v. Great Northern Ins. Co., 145 Minn. 205, 176 N.W. 484 (1920) (sufficiency of efforts a matter for judge's discretion); Mahoney-Jones Co. v. Osborne, 189 N.C. 445, 127 S.E. 533 (1925); Pringey v. Guss, 16 Okl. 82, 83, 86 P. 292, 8 Ann.Cas. 412 (1906); Bruger v. Princeton & S. etc. Ins. Co., 129 Wis. 281, 109 N.W. 95 (1906).

In the *McDonald, Sherman, Summons* and *Bruger* cases, supra, it is suggested that in some circumstances due diligence may require the proponent to take the deposition of the out-of-state possessor of the writing. Deposing the out-of-state holder, however, in addition to being inconvenient and expensive, will often be ineffective to obtain documents in the holder's possession. See Orton v. Poe, 19 Conn.Supp. 145, 110 A.2d 623 (Super.Ct.

1954) (statute authorizing issuance of state subpenas to procure depositions needed in out-of-state litigation construed not to authorize subpenas duces tecum). The problems incident to obtaining documents held by third persons outside the jurisdiction are fully reviewed in Cleary and Strong, The Best Evidence Rule: An Evaluation in Context, 51 Iowa L.Rev. 825 (1966). The uncertainties of the available techniques are such that resort to them should seemingly not ordinarily be required.

91. Missouri, K. & T. Ry. Co. v. Dilworth, 95 Tex. 327, 67 S.W. 88, 89 (1902) (waybill in hands of carrier outside the state, which they probably would not part with); Bruger v. Princeton & S., etc., Ins. Co., 129 Wis. 281, 109 N.W. 95, 97 (1906) ("unless it is clear that they would have been fruitless").

On this ground, efforts to secure public records in another state or country, which are not allowed to be removed under their law or practice, would not be required to be shown before using a copy. Sansoni v. Selvaggi, 121 N.J.L. 274, 2 A.2d 355 (1938) (postal savings passbook impounded by post-office in Italy); De la Garza v. McManus, 44 S.W. 704 (Tex.Civ.App.1898) (deed in archives in Mexico, presumably not removable, provable by examined copy). As to domestic public records, see § 240, herein.

92. 4 Wigmore, Evidence §§ 1202–1210; Dec.Dig. Evidence ⊂⊃179(2), 184, 185(1–12), Criminal Law ⊂⊃402(2); C.J.S. Evidence §§ 832–834, 843–848; 29 Am.Jur.2d Evidence §§ 467–469.

93. American Fire & Cas. Co. v. Kaplan, 183 A.2d 914 (D.C.Mun.App.1962); Jones v. Texas Dept. of Pub. Safety, 392 S.W.2d 176 (Tex.Civ.App.1965); Threatt v. Threatt, 212 Miss. 555, 54 So.2d 907 (1951) (notice to defendant provided sufficient foundation where original shown to be in possession of defendant's father).

Proof of possession by the opponent without proof of notice is generally insufficient. Padgett v. Brezner, 359 S.W.2d 416 (Mo.App.1962) (mere possession by adversary did not afford basis for admitting secondary evidence); In re Estate of Reuss, 422 Pa. 58, 220 A.2d 822 (1966) (copy of letter excluded where no demand made for original in hands of opponent). But compare Transamerica Ins. Co. v. Bloomfield, 401 F.2d 357 (6th Cir. 1968) (not error

that the proponent has notified him to produce it at the trial and he has failed to do so. Observe that the notice is without compulsive force,[94] and is designed merely to account for nonproduction of the writing by the proponent, and thus to enable him to use secondary evidence of the writing's terms. If the proponent actually needs the production of the original itself he will resort to subpoena duces tecum or under modern rules the motion for an order to produce. But when the notice is offered as an excuse for resorting to secondary evidence the adversary cannot fairly complain that he was only given opportunity, not compelled, to make the writing available.

An oral notice may be sufficient,[95] but the safest and almost universal practice is to give written notice beforehand to the party or his attorney, describing the particular documents, and then to call upon the adversary orally at the trial for the writings requested.[96] It is held that the nature of the complaint or of the defense may constitute a sufficient implied notice that the pleader is charging the adversary with possession of the original and that he considers its production essential.[97] As to the time of serving

notice it is sufficient if it allows the adversary a fair opportunity under the existing circumstances to produce the writing at the trial.[98] Accordingly, if it appears at the trial itself that the adversary has the original paper in the courtroom, an immediate notice then and there is timely.[99]

Some exceptions, under which notice is unnecessary before using secondary evidence of a writing in the adversary's possession, have been recognized. The first is well sustained in reason. It dispenses with the need for notice when the adversary has wrongfully obtained or fraudulently suppressed the writing.[1] The others seem more questionable. There is a traditional exception that no notice is required to produce a writing which is itself a notice.[2] This is understandable in

---

to admit copies of corporate records, apparently without notice, where opponent "was familiar with . . . books and could produce them himself if he so desired); Gardner v. Bernard, 401 S.W.2d 415 (Mo.1966) (semble).

94. Bova v. Roanoke Oil Co., 180 Va. 332, 23 S.E.2d 347, 144 A.L.R. 364 (1942). The failure to produce, however, might have another tactical consequence, namely, that of giving rise to an inference adverse to the party so failing. Missouri K. & T. R. Co. v. Elliott, 102 Fed. 96, 102 (8th Cir. 1900). See § 272, infra.

By contrast, production following notice may in some states lead to the tactical advantage of procuring admission of otherwise inadmissible material. See § 55, supra.

95. Especially when given in open court during the trial. Kerr v. McGuire, 28 N.Y. 446, 453 (1863). But see note 98, infra.

96. For details of the practice, see 4 Wigmore, Evidence § 1208.

97. How v. Hall, 14 East 274, 104 Eng.Rep. 606 (K.B. 1811) (trover for bond); Stipe v. First Nat. Bank,

208 Ore. 251, 301 P.2d 175 (1956) (copy of document attached to pleading is sufficient notice to other party to produce); Harris v. State, 150 Tex. Cr.R. 137, 199 S.W.2d 522 (1947) (notice held afforded by content of indictment for forgery). Similarly, a defensive pleading charging plaintiff with possession of a document necessary to the defense may serve as notice. J. L. Owens v. Bemis, 22 N.D. 159, 133 N.W. 59 (1911).

98. Beard v. Southern R. Co., 143 N.C. 136, 55 S.E. 505 (1906) (notice during trial not timely when adversary would have to go to his home in another town to get the writing). See also Waddell v. Trowbridge, 94 W.Va. 482, 119 S.E. 290 (1923) (notice to produce given at the trial timely as to one document, not as to another).

99. Brownlee v. Hot Shoppes, Inc., 23 App.Div.2d 848, 259 N.Y.S.2d 271 (1965) (held error to refuse secondary evidence where plaintiff during trial demanded the original which he asserted was in the courtroom in defendant's possession and defendant did not deny the allegation); Williams v. Metropolitan Life Ins. Co., 202 S.C. 384, 25 S.E.2d 243 (1943) (no previous notice required where paper called for is in court).

1. This exception is frequently recognized by statute. See, e. g., Ore.Rev.Stat. 41.610 (no notice required where document "wrongfully obtained or withheld by the adverse party). See also Cheatham v. Riddle, 8 Tex. 162 (1852) (party's principal "had gotten possession of the instrument and fled the country with it"); 4 Wigmore, Evidence § 1207.

2. Ore.Rev.Stat. 41.610 (notice unnecessary where the writing is itself a notice); Colling v. Treweek, 6 B. & C. 394, 108 Eng.Rep. 497 (1827); Eisenhart v. Slaymaker, 14 Serg. & R. 153 (Pa.1826) ("otherwise

respect to giving notice to produce a notice to produce, which would lead to an endless succession of notices, but there seems little justification for extending the exception, as the cases do, to notices generally. Finally an exception is made by the majority view for writings in the hands of the accused in a criminal prosecution. Under this view, secondary evidence may be received without notice to the accused to produce.[3] The logic of deriving this position, as seems to have been done, from the privilege against self-incrimination is dubious. For while a demand upon the accused to produce which is delivered before the jury clearly has a tendency to coerce the defendant and thus cheapen the privilege,[4] there is no logical necessity that the demand be so delivered.[5] Since the object of notice is to protect against imposition upon the opponent, and since this object may be achieved in the case of the criminal defendant by notice before trial, the minority view under which the prosecution must give notice as a necessary precondition to the use

. . . a fresh necessity would be constantly arising, *ad infinitum*, to prove notice of the preceding notice; so that the party would at every step be receding instead of advancing.")

3. See, e. g., Lisansky v. United States, 31 F.2d 846 (4th Cir. 1929); Dean v. State, 240 Ala. 8, 197 So. 53 (1940); State v. Pascarelli, 2 Conn.Cir. 305, 198 A.2d 239 (1963); and cases collected in Annot., 67 A.L.R. 77.

4. Notice delivered before the jury has frequently been held a violation of the privilege. See, e. g., McKnight v. United States, 115 Fed. 972 (6th Cir. 1902); Commonwealth v. Valeroso, 273 Pa. 213, 116 A. 828 (1922); Powell v. Commonwealth, 167 Va. 558, 189 S.E. 433 (1937); and cases collected in 110 A.L.R. 101.

As to compelling production generally by an accused, see § 126, supra.

5. Thus courts following the minority view discussed below commonly require that the notice be outside the jury's presence. See, e. g., State v. Hollingsworth, 191 N.C. 595, 132 S.E. 667 (1926) (accused should be given notice outside jury's presence). More questionable is the position that demand before the jury is improper but may be cured by jury instruction. See State v. Haye, 72 Wash.2d 461, 433 P.2d 884 (1968).

of secondary evidence [6] seems the fairer and more reasonable stand.[7]

240. Excuses for Nonproduction of the Original Writing: (d) Public Records.[8]

If the contents of the judgment of a court or of an executive proclamation are to be proved, shall the proponent be required to produce the original writing? The accepted view is that, in general, public and judicial records and public documents are required by law to be retained by the official custodian in the public office designated for their custody, and courts will not require them to be removed.[9] To require removal

6. "The object of the notice is not to compel the party to produce the paper, for no such power is assumed, either directly or indirectly, by placing him under a disadvantage if he does not produce it. Its object is to enable the prisoner to protect himself against the falsity of the secondary evidence." State v. Kimbrough, 13 N.C. (2 Dev.L.) 431 (1830).

7. See, e. g., Rex v. Ellicombe, 5 Car. & P. 522, 172 Eng.Rep. 1681 (1933); Kirk v. State, 227 So.2d 40 (Fla.App.1969); cases collected Annot., 67 A.L.R. 77.

8. 4 Wigmore, Evidence §§ 1215–1222; Dec.Dig. Evidence ⟲177, Criminal Law ⟲444.

9. Doe v. Roberts, 13 M. & W. 520, 530, 153 Eng. Rep. 217 (Exch.1844) ("When directed to be kept in any particular custody, and so deposited they are provable by examined copies . . . on the ground of the great inconvenience of removing them"); State v. Black, 31 N.J.Super. 418, 422, 107 A.2d 33, 35 (1954) ("It is firmly established in this State that a public document may be proved by producing the original . . . and on grounds of public convenience a well-known rule of the common law allows proof of such document by duly authenticated copies whenever the original would be admissible, a public document being for this purpose, a document, either judicial or nonjudicial, which is public in its nature and which the public had the right to inspect.").

Statutory treatment of the question is common. See, e. g., Ore.Rev.Stat. 41.640: "(1) There shall be no evidence of the contents of a writing, other than the writing itself, except . . . (c) when the original is a record or other document in the custody of a public officer . . . (2) In the cases mentioned in paragraph (c) . . . a copy or reproduction of the original shall be produced."

If, however, the original record of which proof is to be made is a record of the very court which is trying the present case, then it seems, since the original writing can be produced without violating

would be inconvenient for the public who might desire to consult the records and would entail a risk of loss of or damage to the official documents. Accordingly, statutes and rules have provided for the issuance of certified copies and for their admission in evidence in lieu of the original.[10] In addition, examined copies, authenticated by a witness who has compared it with the original record, are usually receivable.[11]

241. Preferences Among Copies and Between Copies and Oral Testimony.[12]

The basic policy of the original document requirement is that of specially safeguarding the accuracy of the presentation in court of the terms of a writing. If the original is unavailable does the same policy require a preference among the secondary methods of proving the terms? Some means of proof are clearly more reliable than others. In order of reliability the list might go something like this: (1) a mechanically produced copy, such as a photograph, a carbon, a letter-press copy, etc.,[13] (2) a firsthand copy by one who was looking at the original while he copied (immediate copy, sworn copy), (3) a copy, however made, which has been compared by a witness with the original and found correct (examined copy), (4) a secondhand or mediate copy, i. e., a copy of a firsthand copy, (5) oral testimony as to the terms of the writing, with memory aided by a previously made memorandum, and (6) oral testimony from unaided memory. There are many additional variations.

There is one rule of preference that is reasonable and is generally agreed on by the courts, namely, that for judicial and other public records, a certified, sworn or examined copy is preferred,[14] and other evidence of the terms of the record cannot be resorted to unless the proponent has no such copy available,

the rule and policy against removal, production should be required, if formal proof is to be made. Roby v. Title Guarantee & Trust Co., 166 Ill. 336, 46 N.E. 1110 (1896); 4 Wigmore, Evidence § 1215(b). But judicial notice would be simpler, see § 330, infra.

10. See, e. g., F.R.Civ.P. 44(a) which provides in part as follows: "An official record or an entry therein, when admissible for any purpose, may be evidenced by an official publication thereof or by a copy attested by the officer having the legal custody of the record, or by his deputy, and accompanied with a certificate that such officer has the custody . . . ." F.R.Ev. (R.D.1971) 1005 provides a model treatment of the problem succinctly: "The contents of an official record, or of a document authorized to be recorded or filed and actually recorded or filed, including data compilation in any form, if otherwise admissible, may be proved by copy, certified as correct in accordance with Rule 902 [see §§ 319, 320, infra] or testified to be correct by a witness who has compared it with the original. If a copy which complies with the foregoing cannot be obtained by the exercise of reasonable diligence, then other evidence of the contents may be given."

11. See Doe v. Roberts, quoted supra note 9 and F.R.Ev. (R.D.1971) 1005 quoted supra note 10. Nor have certified copies traditionally been preferred to examined copies. See Smithers v. Lowrance, 100 Tex. 77, 93 S.W. 1064 (1906); 4 Wigmore, Evidence § 1273(1).

12. 4 Wigmore, Evidence §§ 1265–1280; Byrdseye, Degrees of Secondary Evidence, 6 Wash.L.Rev. 21 (1931); Notes, 30 So.Cal.L.Rev. 355 (1957), 38 Mich. L.Rev. 864 (1940); Dec.Dig. Evidence ☜186; C.J.S. Evidence § 784.

13. See § 236, supra.

14. Jones v. Melindy, 62 Ark. 203, 36 S.W. 22 (1881) (proof of record of mortgage through testimony of custodian disallowed; use of examined or certified copy required); Whittier v. Leifert, 72 N.D. 528, 9 N.W.2d 402 (1943) (rule stated; dictum); 4 Wigmore, Evidence § 1269.

The requirement is relaxed in most jurisdictions, by statute or decision, to allow a witness to be asked upon cross-examination as to his conviction of crime. Bosarge v. State, 273 Ala. 329, 139 So.2d 302 (1962) (best evidence rule did not require certified copy of records where accused had already testified to convictions); Gaskill v. Gahman, 255 Iowa 891, 124 N.W.2d 533 (1963) (proof of witness' prior conviction may, under statute, be made by his own testimony or proof of record); Clemens v. Conrad, 19 Mich. 170, 175 (1869) ("The danger that he will falsely testify to a conviction that never took place or that he may be mistaken about it, is so slight, that it may almost be looked upon as imaginary"). But compare People v. Moses, 11 Ill.2d 84, 143 N.E.2d 1 (1957) (where witness is accused, conviction must be proved by introduction of record). See Dec.Dig. Witnesses ☜350, 359. Impeachment by proof of conviction is treated generally in § 43, supra.

and the original record has been lost or destroyed so that a copy cannot now be made.[15]

As to writings other than public records, there are two general approaches to the problem. First there is the view, fathered by some of the English decisions and espoused by a minority of the American cases, that "there are no degrees of substantive evidence." [16] This position has the virtues of simplicity and easiness of application. In addition, it may be observed that failure to apply the basic rule as between varieties of secondary evidence leaves unimpaired a substantial practical motivation to produce more satisfactory secondary evidence where it appears to exist. This practical motivation, of course, stems from apprehension of the adverse inference which may be drawn from failure to produce more satisfactory secondary evidence indicated to exist and not shown to be unavailable. These considerations have led the draftsmen of most modern codes of evidence to adopt the so-called "English" view.[17]

The second view is followed by a majority of the states which have passed on the question. Here a distinction is recognized between types of secondary evidence, with a written copy being preferred to oral testimony,[18] and, under circumstances varying from state to state, an immediate copy being preferred to a more remote one.[19] This view is justifiable chiefly on the ground that there is some incongruity in pursuing the policy of obtaining the terms of writings with fullest accuracy, by structuring a highly technical rule to that end, only to abandon it upon the unavailability of the original. In formulating this general approach of discrimination among types of secondary evidence, the courts following the American rule have sought to avoid a position which would require the proponent to produce or account for all possible copies that may have existed. A reasonable standard is suggested by an early New York judge, who said:

"I do not mean to contend that there are any arbitrary or inflexible degrees of secondary evidence, rendering it necessary for a party, who is driven to that description of proof, to show affirmatively, in every instance that there is no higher degree within his power, than the one he offers; but I

for original] may read a counterpart or if there is no counterpart an examined copy, or if there should not be an examined copy, he may give parole evidence of its contents."); Murphy v. Nielsen, 132 Cal.App.2d 396, 282 P.2d 126 (1955) (held error to receive parole where copies shown to exist; holding now codified by West's Ann.Cal.Evid. Code, § 1505); Cummings v. Pennsylvania Fire Ins. Co., 153 Iowa 579, 134 N.W. 79 (1911); Baroda State Bank v. Peck, 235 Mich. 542, 209 N.W. 827 (1926) (application of American rule affirmed by equally divided appellate court; full discussion). See also the law review treatments cited supra, note 16.

19. When the original is a public record and hence not producible, a certified or examined copy may be obtained at any time, and a copy of a copy would everywhere be excluded. Lasater v. Van Hook, 77 Tex. 650, 655, 14 S.W. 270 (1890) (deed record; examined copy of a certified copy excluded). When the original is unavailable and there is no copy of record, then under the majority view the proponent would be required to produce an immediate copy, if available, before using a copy of a copy. Schley v. Lyon, 6 Ga. 530, 538 (1949); State v. Cohen, 108 Iowa 208, 78 N.W. 857 (1899). Contra, under the minority, "no degrees" doctrine: Goodrich v. Weston, 102 Mass. 362 (1869).

The various situations are distinguished and the decisions collected in 4 Wigmore, Evidence § 1275.

---

15. People v. Cotton, 250 Ill. 338, 95 N.E. 283 (1911).

16. Doe d. Gilbert v. Ross, 7 M. & W. 102, 151 Eng. Rep. 696 (Exch.1840) (shorthand notes of counsel's statement at former trial of contents of settlement allowed, although attested copy requiring but not bearing a stamp was in existence); Beaty v. Southern Ry. Co., 80 S.C. 527, 61 S.E. 1006 (1908) ("there is no division of degrees of proof in case of the loss of an instrument"); Rick Furniture Co. v. Smith, 202 S.W. 99 (Tex.Civ.App.1918). Cases subscribing to the English view are collected in Byrdseye, Degrees of Secondary Evidence, 6 Wash. L.Rev. 21 (1931); Note, 38 Mich.L.Rev. 864 (1940).

17. Model Code of Evidence Rule 602 (1942); Uniform Rule 70; F.R.Ev. (R.D.1971) 1004. But compare, Report of New Jersey Supreme Court Committee on Evidence 232 (1963); West's Ann.Cal. Evid.Code § 1505.

18. Riggs v. Tayloe, 22 U.S. (9 Wheat.) 483, 486, 6 L.Ed. 140 (1824) (original contract destroyed, oral testimony permitted; "the party [after accounting

think it may be safely said, that where it appears in the very offer, or from the nature of the case itself, or from the circumstances attending the offer, that the party has better and more reliable evidence at hand, and equally within his power, he shall not be permitted to resort to the inferior degree first"[20]

242. Adversary's Admission as to the Terms of a Writing.[21]

Many American courts have followed the lead of Baron Parke's decision in Slatterie v. Pooley[22] and have held admissions by a party opponent admissible to prove the terms of a writing.[23] Upon reflection, however, it will be seen that Baron Parke's decision squares rather poorly with the primary modern day policy in favor of obtaining the contents of writings with accuracy.[24] The evidence determined admissible in Slatterie v. Pooley was actually at two removes from the writing itself, being witness' report of the defendant's comment. Perhaps the policy of holding admissible any admission which a party-opponent chooses to make will suffice to justify the first step, but the second frequently raises the possibility of erroneous transmission without corresponding justification. Accordingly, some American decisions have re-

jected testimony relating oral admissions concerning contents of writings.[25]

It will be observed, however, that the second possibility of mistransmission noted above is effectively eliminated where no testimonial report of the admission is required. Thus, the desirable solution, towards which it is believed the decisions may be drifting, is to receive admissions to evidence of a document's terms (1) when the admission itself is in writing and is produced in evidence,[26] or (2) when the party himself, on the stand in this or some other trial or hearing, makes the admission about the contents of the writing or concedes that he made such an admission on a former occasion.[27] Oral testimony by a witness that he heard the party's admission as to the terms of the writing, despite the authority of Slatterie v. Pooley, should be excluded.[28]

243. Review of Rulings Admitting Secondary Evidence.

It will be seen from the earlier sections of this chapter that the requirement of the pro-

20. Slossen, J. in Healy v. Gilman, 1 Bosw. (14 N.Y.Super.) 235 at 242 (1857), quoted in Note, 38 Mich.L.Rev. 864, 874 (1940).

21. 4 Wigmore, Evidence §§ 1255–1257; Dec.Dig. Evidence ☞172; C.J.S. Evidence § 788; Notes, 20 Md.L.Rev. 50 (1960), 17 Tex.L.Rev. 371 (1939).

22. 6 M. & W. 665, 151 Eng.Rep. 579 (Exch.1840).

23. In the following cases testimony of a third person as to a party's oral admission was received: Dunbar v. United States, 156 U.S. 185 (1895) (oral admission that telegram received was identical to one sent by party); Metropolitan Life Ins. Co. v. Hogan, 63 F.2d 654 (7th Cir. 1933) (oral admission by agent of nature of paper received from beneficiary); Morey v. Hoyt, 62 Conn. 542, 26 A. 127 (1893) (reviewing older authorities and approving Slatterie v. Pooley).

24. See 1 Jones, Evidence § 261 (5th ed. 1958); F.R. Ev. (R.D.1971) 1007, Advisory Committee's Note.

25. E. g., Grimes v. Fall, 15 Cal. 63 (1860) (oral testimony that party admitted that he was assignee under what court assumed to be written assignment, held inadmissible); Prussing v. Jackson, 208 Ill. 85, 69 N.E. 771 (1904) (stating that verbal admissions as to content of writings would, if admitted, abrogate basic rule).

26. Written admissions were held receivable in Clarke v. Warwick C. M. Co., 174 Mass. 434, 54 N.E. 887 (1899); Swing v. Cloquet Lumber Co., 121 Minn. 221, 141 N.W. 117 (1913) ("The rule is sound in principle, at least where the admissions are in writing"); Taylor v. Peck, 21 Grat., (62 Va.) 11 (1871). Even more clearly should a written pleading containing the admission be sufficient. Coca-Cola Bottling Co. v. International Filter Co., 62 Ind.App. 421, 113 N.E. 17 (1916).

27. Admissions on the witness stand have frequently been viewed as sufficient though the distinction between in and out-of-court admissions is not generally made: Barnett v. Wilson, 132 Ala. 375, 31 So. 521 (1902); Parr Const. Co. v. Pomer, 217 Md. 539, 144 A.2d 69 (1958); Gardner v. City of Columbia Police Dept., 216 S.C. 219, 57 S.E.2d 308 (1950). Contra, Prussing v. Jackson, supra, note 25.

28. See F.R.Ev. (R.D.1971) 1007.

duction of original writings, with the several excuses for nonproduction and the exceptions to the requirement itself, make up a fairly complex set of regulations for administration by the trial judge. Mistakes in the application of these rules are, understandably, not infrequent. The purpose of this system of rules, on the other hand, is simple and practical. That purpose is to secure the most reliable information as to the contents of documents, when those terms are disputed. A mystical ideal of seeking "the best evidence" or the "original document," as an end in itself is no longer the goal. Consequently when an attack is made, on motion for new trial or on appeal, upon the judge's admission of secondary evidence, it seems that the reviewing tribunal, should ordinarily make inquiry of the complaining counsel, "Does the party whom you represent actually dispute the accuracy of the evidence received as to the material terms of the writing?" If the counsel cannot assure the court that such a good faith dispute exists, it seems clear that any departure from the regulations in respect to secondary evidence must be classed as harmless error.[29]

29. Myrick v. United States, 332 F.2d 279 (5th Cir. 1964) (not error to admit photostatic copies of checks in absence of suggestion to trial judge that they were incorrect); Johns v. United States, 323 F.2d 421 (5th Cir. 1963) (not error to admit admittedly accurate copy of wire recording); Sauget v. Johnston, 315 F.2d 816 (9th Cir. 1963) (not error to admit copy when opponent had original agreement and on appeal made no claim of any discrepancy).

Compare, National Fire Ins. Co. v. Evertson, 153 Neb. 854, 46 N.W.2d 489 (1951) where the possibility of this approach was overlooked. There a judgment was reversed, partly on the ground that a material written settlement was proved only by a carbon copy. On the motion for new trial the winning plaintiff produced the original writing which corresponded with the carbon, but the court on appeal said that the judgment could not be "propped up" in that way.

TITLE 10

THE HEARSAY RULE AND ITS EXCEPTIONS

CHAPTER 24

THE HEARSAY RULE

244. The History of the Rule Against Hearsay.[1]

Ask the man on the street what he knows about the law of evidence. Usually the only doctrine he will be able to mention is the one called by the old English word hearsay. In an oft-quoted passage, Wigmore calls it "that most characteristic rule of the Anglo-American Law of Evidence—a rule which may be esteemed, next to jury trial, the greatest contribution of that eminently practical legal system to the world's methods of procedure."[2] How did this rule come about?

The development of the jury was, no doubt, an important factor. It will be remembered that the jury in its earlier forms was in the nature of a committee or special commission of qualified persons in the neighborhood to report on facts or issues in dispute. So far as necessary its members conducted its investigations informally among those who had special knowledge of the facts. Attesting witnesses to writings were summoned with the jurors and apparently participated in their deliberations,[3] but the practice of calling witnesses to appear in court and testify publicly about the facts to the jury, is a late development in jury trial. Though something like the jury existed at least as early as the 1100's,[4] this practice of hearing witnesses in court does not become frequent until the later 1400's. The changeover to the present conception that the normal source of proof is not the private knowledge or investigation of the jurors, but the testimony of witnesses in open court is a matter of gradual evolution thereafter. Finally, in the early 1500's it

---

1. The fullest and best account is in 5 Wigmore, Evidence § 1364, and the brief discussion here is based upon that. Following Wigmore's account, but with a slightly variant interpretation of the facts is 9 Holdsworth's History of English Law 214–219 (1926). The story of the development of jury trial and of the emergence of the practice of producing witnesses in court to testify before the jury is recounted in Thayer, Preliminary Treatise on Evidence, chs. 2–4, esp. ch. 3 (1898). See also Plucknett, A Concise History of the Common Law 120–130 (5th ed. 1956).

2. 5 Wigmore, Evidence p. 27.

3. Thayer, Preliminary Treatise on Evidence 97 (1898).

4. Thayer, op.cit. at pp. 53–65.

has become, though not yet the exclusive source of proof, the normal and principal one.[5]

It is not until this period of the gradual emergence of the witness testifying publicly in court that the consciousness of need for exclusionary rules of evidence begins to appear. It had indeed been required even of the early witnesses to writings that they could speak only of "what they saw and heard"[6] and this requirement would naturally be applied to the new class of testifying witnesses. But when the witness has heard at firsthand the statement of X out of court that he has seen and heard a blow with a sword, or witnessed a trespass on land, as evidence of the blow or the trespass, a new question is presented. Certainly it would seem that the earlier requirement of knowledge must have predisposed the judges to skepticism about the value of hearsay.[7]

Accordingly, it is the value of hearsay, its sufficiency as proof, that is the subject of discussion in this gestation period. In Continental Europe there had already developed a system of evaluating witnesses and their proofs quantitatively, based on a requirement of two witnesses, or their fractional equivalents, as "full proof."[8] In this system, Wigmore says, at this period there were rules "declaring (for example) one witness upon personal knowledge to be equal to two or three going upon hearsay."[9] And so through the reigns of the Tudors and the Stuarts there is a gradually increasing drumfire of criticism and objections by parties and counsel against evidence of oral hearsay declarations. While the evidence was constantly admitted, the confidence in its reliability was increasingly undermined.[10] It was derided as "a tale of a tale"[11] or "a story out of another man's mouth."[12] Parallel with this increasingly discredited use of casual oral hearsay was a similar development in respect to transcribed statements made under oath before a judge or judicial officer, not subject to cross-examination by the party against whom it is offered.[13] In criminal cases in the 1500's and down to the middle 1600's the main reliance of the prosecution was the use of such "depositions" to make out its case.[14] As oral hearsay was becoming discredited, uneasiness about the use of "depositions" began to take shape, first in the form of a limitation that they could only be used when the witness could not be produced at the trial.[15] It will be noted that the want of oath and the unreliability of the report of the oral statement cannot be urged against such evidence but only the want of cross-examination and observation of demeanor.

It was in the first decade after the Restoration that the century or so of criticism of hearsay had its final effect in decisions rejecting its use, first as to oral hearsay and then as to depositions. Wigmore finds that the period between 1675 and 1690 is the time of crystallization of the rule against hearsay.[16] For a time the rule was qualified by the notion that hearsay while not independ-

5.   5 Wigmore, Evidence § 1364 p. 12.

6.   Thayer, op.cit. at pp. 101, 519; 9 Holdsworth, History of English Law 211 (1926).

7.   See Thayer, op.cit. at pp. 518, 519; 9 Holdsworth, History of English Law 215 (1926).

8.   See the highly interesting description of this system and its origins in canon law theories built on Biblical texts, and its rejection in the common law courts, in 7 Wigmore, Evidence § 2032. See also 9 Holdsworth, op.cit. at pp. 203–211, and 5 Ency.Soc.Sc. title Evidence 638 (1931).

9.   5 Wigmore, Evidence § 1364, p. 14, n. 25.

10.   5 Wigmore, Evidence § 1364, pp. 15, 16.

11.   Colledge's Trial, 8 How.St.Tr. 549, 663 (1681) (counsel for prosecution warning his own witness), cited in 5 Wigmore, Evidence § 1364, p. 17.

12.   Gascoigne's Trial, 7 How.St.Tr. 959, 1019 (1680) (warning by judge, but evidence finally admitted) cited in 5 Wigmore, Evidence § 1364, p. 16.

13.   5 Wigmore, Evidence § 1364, pp. 19–26.

14.   9 Holdsworth, History of English Law 218 (1926).

15.   5 Wigmore, Evidence § 1364, p. 21.

16.   5 Wigmore, Evidence § 1364, p. 16.

ently admissible, could come in as confirmatory of other evidence, and this qualification survived down to the end of the 1700's in the limited form of admitting a witness's prior consistent statements out of court to corroborate his testimony.[17]

Whether the rule against hearsay was, with the rest of the English law of evidence, in fact "the child of the jury"[18] or the product of the adversary system[19] may be of no great contemporary significance. The important thing is that the rule against hearsay taking form at the end of the seventeenth century was neither a matter of "immemorial usage" nor an inheritance from Magna Charta but, in the long view of English legal history, was a late development of the common law.

245. The Reasons for the Exclusion of Hearsay.[20]

Holdsworth thinks that the immediate influences leading to the crystallization of the rule against hearsay, at the particular time in the late 1600's when this occurred, were first, a strong dictum by Coke in his Third Institute denouncing "the strange conceit that one may be an accuser by hearsay,"[21] and sec-

ond, the rejection of the attempt to naturalize in English law the requirement of two witnesses[22] and the consequent urge to provide some compensating safeguard.[23] As we have seen in the next preceding section, a century of increasing protests against the use of hearsay had preceded the establishment of the rule, but most of the specific weaknesses of hearsay, which were the underlying reasons for the adoption of the rule, and which have explained its survival, were not clearly pointed out until after the beginning of the 1700's when the newly established rule came to be rationalized by the judges and the text writers.

The factors upon which the credibility of testimony depends are the perception, memory, and narration of the witness. Did the witness perceive accurately? Has he retained an accurate impression of what he perceived? Is his language such as to convey that impression correctly?[24] While some writers add sincerity as a fourth factor, it seems rather to be only an aspect of the three mentioned above. Regardless of whether the witness lies deliberately or makes an honest mistake, his credibility is impaired.

In order to encourage witnesses to put forth their best efforts and to expose inaccuracies which might be present with respect to any of the foregoing factors, the Anglo-American tradition evolved three conditions under which witnesses ordinarily will be required to testify: oath, personal presence at the trial, and cross-examination.[25]

---

17. 5 Wigmore, Evidence § 1364, pp. 17, 18.

18. Thayer, Preliminary Treatise on Evidence 47, also 2–4, 180 (1898).

19. Morgan, The Jury and the Exclusionary Rules of Evidence, 4 U.Chi.L.Rev. 247, 258 (1937), Hearsay Dangers and the Application of the Hearsay Concept, 62 Harv.L.Rev. 177 (1948), also in Selected Writings on Evidence and Trial 764, 766–768 (Fryer ed. 1957).

20. See 5 Wigmore, Evidence § 1362; Maguire, The Hearsay System: Around and Through the Thicket, 14 Vand.L.Rev. 741, 743–749 (1961); Morgan, Hearsay Dangers and the Application of the Hearsay Concept, 62 Harv.L.Rev. 177 (1948), also in Selected Writings on Evidence and Trial 764 (Fryer ed. 1957); Introductory Note: The Hearsay Problem, F.R.Ev. (R.D.1971) p. 94.

21. Coke thus condemned the holding in Thomas's case, Dyer 99b (1553) to the effect that under a statute of Edward VI requiring two witnesses in treason if one accuser speaks from his own knowledge, "and he relate it to another, the other may well be an accuser." Coke Third Inst. 25 (1641).

22. See § 244, note 9, supra.

23. 9 Holdsworth, History of English Law 217, 218 (1926).

24. 2 Wigmore, Evidence § 478; Morgan, Hearsay Dangers and the Application of the Hearsay Concept, 62 Harv.L.Rev. 177 (1948), in Selected Writings on Evidence and Trial 764 (Fryer ed. 1957); Strahorn, A Reconsideration of the Hearsay Rule and Admissions, 85 U.Pa.L.Rev. 484 (1937), in Selected Writings on Evidence and Trial 756 (Fryer ed. 1957).

25. Strahorn, supra n. 24.

The rule against hearsay is designed to insure compliance with these ideal conditions, and when one of them is absent the hearsay objection becomes pertinent.

Oath. Among the earliest of the criticisms of hearsay, and one often repeated in judicial opinions down to the present, is the objection that the out-of-court declarant who made the hearsay statement commonly speaks or writes without the solemnity of the oath administered to witnesses in a court of law.[26] The oath may be important in two aspects. As a ceremonial and religious symbol it may induce in the witness a feeling of special obligation to speak the truth, and also it may impress upon the witness the danger of criminal punishment for perjury, to which the judicial oath or an equivalent solemn affirmation would be a prerequisite condition. Wigmore considers that the objection for want of an oath is incidental and not essential, and suggests that this is demonstrated by the fact that a hearsay statement, even if under oath, is still rejected.[27] But the fact that the oath is not the only requirement to satisfy the rule against hearsay does not prove that it is not an important one. Nor does the fact that the oath may have diminished in significance with the passage of time [28] mean that today it is without significance; no disposition to abolish it (other than to allow affirmation as a substitute) is apparent.[29]

Personal presence at trial. Another objection early asserted and repeated of late is the want of opportunity, in respect to the out-of-court declarant, for observation of his demeanor, with the light that this may shed on his credibility, that would be afforded if he were a witness on the stand.[30]

The solemnity of the occasion and possibility of public disgrace can scarcely fail to impress the witness,[31] and falsehood no doubt becomes more difficult if the person against whom directed is present.

Moreover, personal presence eliminates the danger that in the oral reporting of an out-of-court statement the witness reporting the statement may do so inaccurately. It seems probable that the reporting of words spoken is subject to special dangers of inaccuracy beyond the fallibility common to all reproduction from memory of matters of observation,[32] and this seems a substantial danger in the admission of hearsay. It is true as Wigmore points out [33] that not all hearsay is subject to this danger. Written statements can be produced in court and can be tested with reasonable accuracy for genuineness and freedom from alteration. Moreover, as Morgan has suggested, the reporting in court of spoken words for nonhearsay purposes, as in proving the making of an oral contract or the utterance of a slander,[34] is subject to this same risk of misreporting. Neither argument seems conclusive. The vulnerability of most hearsay, though not all, to errors in re-

26. Bridges v. Wixon, 326 U.S. 135, 153 (1945); Chapman v. Chapman, 2 Conn. 347, 7 Am.Dec. 277 (1817); State v. Saporen, 205 Minn. 358, 285 N.W. 898 (1939); Hawkins, Pleas of the Crown, b. II, c. 46, § 44 (1716), in 5 Wigmore, Evidence, p. 4; Gilbert, Evidence, p. 4 (1760 ed.).

27. 5 Wigmore, Evidence § 1362, p. 7.

28. Morgan, supra n. 24, Selected Writings on Evidence and Trial at 770.

29. See, e. g., F.R.Ev. (R.D.1971) 603.

30. Mattox v. United States, 156 U.S. 237, 242 (1895), quoted with approval, Douglas v. Alabama, 380 U.S. 415 (1965); Universal Camera Corp. v. NLRB, 340 U.S. 474, 495 (1951); People v. Bob, 29 Cal.2d 321, 175 P.2d 12 (1946); Appalachian Stave Co. v. Pickard, 266 Ky. 565, 99 S.W.2d 472 (1937); Sahm, Demeanor Evidence: Elusive and Intangible Imponderables, 47 A.B.A.J. 580 (1961).

31. Strahorn, supra n. 24, Selected Writings at 756.

32. Compare Gardner, The Perception and Memory of Witnesses, 18 Corn.L.Q. 391, 393, 405, n. 107 (1933).

33. 5 Wigmore, Evidence § 1363(1).

34. Where the utterance of the words is an "operative fact," see Morgan, A Suggested Classification of Utterances Admissible as Res Gestae, 31 Yale L.J. 229 (1922). See § 249, infra.

porting tends to support the failure of the existing rule to distinguish between written and spoken hearsay.[35] As to "operative" words, oral contracts, slanders and the like, it is true that the danger is similar to that in oral hearsay but the need for the proof is manifestly greater, and hence it might well be thought that the risk in proving words for this purpose, but not for the other, must be borne.

Cross-examination. It would be generally agreed today that the third factor is the main justification for the exclusion of hearsay. This is the lack of any opportunity for the adversary to cross-examine the absent declarant whose out-of-court statement is reported by the witness. Thus as early as 1668 we find a court rejecting hearsay because "the other party could not cross-examine the party sworn." [36] Judicial expressions stress this as a principal reason for the hearsay rule.[37] Cross-examination, as Bentham pointed out,[38] was a distinctive feature of the English trial system, and the one which most contributed to the prestige of the institution of jury trial. He called it "a security for the correctness and completeness of testimony." The nature of this safeguard which hearsay lacks is indicated by Chancellor Kent: "Hearsay testimony is from the very nature of it attended with . . . doubts and difficulties and it cannot clear them up. 'A per-

son who relates a hearsay is not obliged to enter into any particulars, to answer any questions, to solve any difficulties, to reconcile any contradictions, to explain any obscurities, to remove any ambiguities; he entrenches himself in the simple assertion that he was told so, and leaves the burden entirely on his dead or absent author.' . . . . The plaintiff by means of this species of evidence would be taken by surprise and be precluded from the benefit of a cross-examination of S. as to all those material points which have been suggested as necessary to throw full light on his information."[39] Similarly, a Georgia judge has said that cross-examination "is the most efficacious test which the law has devised for the discovery of truth." [40] Morgan analyzed the protective function of cross-examination and concluded (1) that while the fear of exposure of falsehoods on cross-examination is a stimulus to truth-telling by the witness, actual exposure of wilful falsehood is rarely accomplished in actual practice and (2) that the most important service of cross-examination in present day conditions is in affording the opportunity to expose faults in the perception and memory of the witness.[41]

It is easy, however, to overplay the unreliability of hearsay. Eminent judges have spoken of its "intrinsic weakness." [42] If this were meant to imply that all hearsay of its very nature is unworthy of reliance in a court of law, of course the implication is quite insupportable. The contrary is proved by the

---

35. The English Evidence Act 1938, 1 & 2 Geo. VI, c. 28, accorded a greater admissibility to hearsay evidence in documentary form. The distinction was virtually abandoned when the Civil Evidence Act 1968, c. 64, Pt. I, § 2, greatly broadened the admissibility of hearsay without regard to its form.

36. 2 Rolle's Abr. 679, pl. 9 (1668), cited by Morgan, Jury Trials and the Exclusionary Rules of Evidence, 4 U.Chi.L.Rev. 247, 253 (1937).

37. Pointer v. Texas, 380 U.S. 400, 406 (1965); Novicki v. Department of Finance, 373 Ill. 342, 26 N.E.2d 130 (1940); Sconce v. Jones, 343 Mo. 362, 121 S.W.2d 777 (1938).

38. Rationale of Judicial Evidence, b. II, ch. IX, and b. III, ch. XX, (1827) quoted 5 Wigmore, Evidence § 1367.

39. Coleman v. Southwick, 9 John. 50 (N.Y.1812), in 5 Wigmore, Evidence, § 1362, p. 4.

40. Nisbet, J. in McCleskey v. Leadbetter, 1 Ga. 551, 555 (1846).

41. Hearsay Dangers and the Application of the Hearsay Concept, 62 Harv.L.Rev. 177, 186, 188 (1948), in Selected Writings on Evidence and Trial 764, 770, 772 (Fryer ed. 1957).

42. Marshall, C. J. in Mima Queen v. Hepburn, 7 Cranch 295 (1813) and Story, J. in Ellicott v. Pearl, 10 Pet. 412, 436, 9 L.Ed. 475 (1836), both cited 5 Wigmore, Evidence § 1363.

fact that courts are constantly receiving, as we shall see, hearsay evidence of various kinds under the numerous exceptions to the hearsay rule,[43] and by the doctrine established in most jurisdictions that when hearsay evidence, which would have been excluded if objected to, is let in without objection, it may be taken into consideration if it appears to be reliable in the particular case, as sufficient to sustain a verdict or finding of the fact thus proved.[44] The truth, of course, is that hearsay evidence, ranging as it does from mere thirdhand rumors to sworn affidavits of credible observers, has as wide a scale of reliability, from the highest to the lowest, as we find in testimonial or circumstantial evidence generally, depending as they all do upon the frailties of perception, memory, narration, and veracity of men and women. Indeed, it is the failure of the courts to adjust the rules of admissibility more flexibly and realistically to these variations in the reliability of hearsay that as we shall see has constituted one of the pressing needs for liberalization of evidence law.[45]

246. A Definition of Hearsay.[46]

Too much should not be expected of a definition. It cannot furnish answers to all the complex problems of an extensive field (such as hearsay) in a sentence. The most it can accomplish is to furnish a helpful starting point for discussion of the problems, and a memory aid in recalling some of the solutions. But if the definition is to remain brief and understandable, it will necessarily distort some parts of the picture. Simplification has a measure of falsification.

With these warnings the following definition is proposed: *Hearsay evidence is testimony in court, or written evidence, of a statement made out of court, the statement being offered as an assertion to show the truth of matters asserted therein, and thus resting for its value upon the credibility of the out-of-court asserter.*[47]

---

43. Chs. 25–33, infra; Ladd, The Hearsay We Admit, 5 Okla.L.Rev. 271 (1952).

44. See Annot., 104 A.L.R. 1130, and § 54, supra, where the matter is developed.

45. See § 325 infra. Loevinger, Facts, Evidence and Legal Proof, 9 W.Res.L.Rev. 154, 165 (1958), suggests "that there can be little utility in a class which is so broad as to include the prattling of a child and the mouthings of a drunk, the encyclical of a pope, a learned treatise, an encyclopedia article, a newspaper report, an unverified rumor from anonymous sources, an affidavit by a responsible citizen, a street corner remark, the judgment of a court . . . ."

46. For discussions, see 5 Wigmore, Evidence § 1361, 6 id. § 1766; Maguire, The Hearsay System: Around and Through the Thicket, 14 Vand.L.Rev. 741 (1961); Morgan, The Hearsay Rule, 12 Wash. L.Rev. 1 (1937); A Suggested Classification of Utterances Admissible as Res Gestae, 31 Yale L.J. 229 (1922); Some Suggestions for Defining and Classifying Hearsay, 86 U.Pa.L.Rev. 258 (1938);

Hearsay Dangers and the Application of the Hearsay Concept, 62 Harv.L.Rev. 177 (1948), in Selected Writings on Evidence and Trial 764 (Fryer ed. 1967); Basic Problems of Evidence 243–253 (1962); Strahorn, A Reconsideration of the Hearsay Rule and Admissions, 85 U.Pa.L.Rev. 484 (1937), in Selected Writings, supra, 756; Weinstein, Probative Force of Hearsay, 46 Iowa L.Rev. 331 (1961); Introductory Note: The Hearsay Problem, F.R.Ev. (R.D.1971) p. 94.

For cases discussing and illustrating the nature of hearsay, see Morgan, Evidence 1941–1945, 59 Harv. L.Rev. 481, 541 (1946); Dec.Dig. Crim.Law ☞419, Evidence ☞314–324.

47. Two problems dealt with in later discussion are left ambiguous in the definition, first, the problem of whether acts evincing belief are to be treated as hearsay when offered to prove the fact believed (§ 250, infra) and second, the question whether depositions and former testimony are to be admitted (when the rules do admit them) under an exception to the hearsay rule, or as satisfying the standards safeguarded by the hearsay rule (§ 254, infra).

Compare the following:

Uniform Rule 63: "Evidence of a statement which is made other than by a witness while testifying at the hearing offered to prove the truth of the matter stated is hearsay evidence . . . ."

Id., Rule 62(1): " 'Statement' means not only an oral or written expression but also nonverbal conduct of a person intended by him as a substitute for words in expressing the matter stated."

F.R.Ev. (R.D.1971) 801:

"(a) Statement. A 'statement' is (1) an oral or written assertion or (2) nonverbal conduct of a person, if it is intended by him as an assertion. . . .

What strikes one's attention at once about this definition is that it fixes a stringent condition on the popular notion of hearsay as being merely what a witness says he heard someone else say. In truth, that popular notion is quite inadequate as a definition of what is excluded by the hearsay rule. This employment of a popular term in a nonpopular usage is unfortunate, and is responsible for some confusion in handling hearsay problems in classroom and court, but the introduction of a new technical term for prohibited hearsay would add as many dificulties as it would remove.

Why must the complicated and confusing condition be added, that the out-of-court statement is only hearsay when offered for the truth of the matter asserted? The answer is clear when we revert to the principal reasons for the exclusion of hearsay, namely the want of the normal safeguards of oath, confrontation and cross-examination for the credibility of the out-of-court declarant.[48] W, a witness, reports on the stand that D, a declarant, has stated that X was driving a stolen care 60 miles an hour at a given time and place. If the proponent is trying with this evidence to prove those facts about X's conduct we are vitally interested in the credibility of D, his opportunity and capacity to observe, his powers of memory, the accuracy of his reporting, and his tendency to lie or tell the truth. The want of oath, confrontation and opportunity to cross-examine D may greatly diminish the value of his testimony; the "hearsay dangers" are present. But the same evidence of D's declaration may be offered for quite different purposes, as for ex-

ample, to show that D at the time he spoke, was conscious, or was able to speak English, or as evidence of the utterance by D of defamatory statements in an action for slander brought by X. Where offered for these purposes, the evidence would still be evidence of an out-of-court statement by D, but its value would not at all hinge upon D's credibility. Hence, when the declarations are offered for these purposes, the want of safeguards for his credibility is of no consequence. We are interested only in the question, did D speak these words, and for that we have the testimony of W, on the stand, fully supported by all the safeguards.[49]

In the light of our discussion, then, we can say that the suggested definition, which is supported by many judicial expressions,[50] seeks to limit the term "hearsay" to situations where the out-of-court assertion is offered as equivalent to testimony to the facts so asserted by a witness on the stand. Only then does the want of such safeguards as cross-examination become material.

When the witness reports on the stand that one declarant stated to him that another declarant made a given statement, this may be termed "double hearsay," if both statements are offered to prove the facts asserted. "Multiple hearsay" would include double hearsay and instances where the chain of repeated statements is longer still, as where the witness reports that A told him that B said that C had stated a given fact. And, of course, a similar situation may be presented when documentary hearsay incorporates oth-

---

(c) Hearsay. 'Hearsay' is a statement, other than one made by the declarant while testifying at the trial or hearing, offered in evidence to prove the truth of the matter asserted."

See also the suggested definition in Maguire, The Hearsay System: Around and Through the Thicket, 14 Vand.L.Rev. 741, 768 (1961).

48. See § 245, supra.

49. See § 249, infra.

50. Among the more recent are Pauling v. News Syndicate Co., 335 F.2d 659 (2d Cir. 1964); Petition of Earle, 355 Mich. 596, 95 N.W.2d 833 (1959); Mash v. Missouri Pacific R. Co., 341 S.W.2d 822 (Mo.1961); Ellsworth v. Watkins, 101 N.H. 51, 132 A.2d 136 (1957); Wilson v. Hartford Acc. & Indem. Co., 272 N.C. 183, 158 S.E.2d 1 (1967); Auseth v. Farmers Mut. Auto Ins. Co., 8 Wis.2d 627, 99 N.W.2d 700 (1939).

er hearsay.[51] Multiple hearsay is, of course, even more vulnerable to all the objections which attach to simple hearsay, and it seems that if it is to come in at all, each of the out-of-court statements must satisfy the requirements of some exception to the hearsay rule.[52]

The requirement in the definition of hearsay is that the statement be offered to prove the truth of the matter asserted. What if the immediate purpose is to prove the fact asserted but the ultimate purpose is to draw a circumstantial inference of another fact, not asserted in the statement? Suppose the witness reports that D told him, a week before D's body was found in the bay, that he was planning to go fishing the next day with X in the latter's boat. If offered to show D's intent it is plainly hearsay, and it is no less subject to the hearsay weaknesses simply because a further inference, i. e. that D did go fishing with X, is to be built upon the matter asserted, i. e. D's intent. Accordingly we find the courts treating the statement as hearsay wherever the *first* purpose is to prove the fact asserted in it, even though other secondary inferences are sought to be built upon the first.[53]

Not in presence of party against whom offered. A remarkably persistent bit of court-house folklore is the practice of objecting to out-of-court statements because not made in the presence of the party against whom offered. From the foregoing discussion, the lack of relationship between this objection and the concept of hearsay is apparent.[54] The presence or absence of the party against whom an out-of-court statement is offered has significance only in a few particular situations, e. g., when a statement spoken in his presence is relied upon to charge him with notice,[55] or when failure to deny a statement spoken in his presence is the basis for claiming that he acquiesced in or adopted the statement.[56]

247. Distinction Between Hearsay Rule and Rule Requiring Firsthand Knowledge.

There is a rule, more ancient than the hearsay rule, and having some kinship in policy, which is to be distinguished from it. This is the rule that a witness is qualified to testify to a fact susceptible of observation, only if it appears that he had a reasonable opportunity to observe the fact.[57] Thus, if a witness testifies that on a certain day the westbound train came in to the station at X on time, and from his other evidence it appears that he was not in X at the time in question, and hence could only have spoken from conjecture or report of other persons, the proper objection is not hearsay but want of personal knowledge. Conversely, if the witness testifies that his brother *told* him that he came in on the train and it arrived on time, the objection for want of knowledge of when the train arrived is inappropriate, because the witness purports to speak from his own knowledge only of what his brother said, and as to this he presumably had knowledge. If the testi-

51. See, for example, hearsay statements included as personal history in hospital records, discussed in § 313, infra.

52. See United States v. Grayson, 166 F.2d 863, (2d Cir. 1948); United States v. Bartholomew, 137 F.Supp. 700 (W.D.Ark.1956). See § 310, infra.

Uniform Rule 66: "Multiple Hearsay. A statement within the scope of an exception to Rule 63 shall not be inadmissible on the ground that it includes a statement made by another declarant and is offered to prove the truth of the included statement if such included statement itself meets the requirements of an exception."

See also West's Ann.Cal.Evid.Code, § 1201; F.R. Ev. (R.D.1971) 805.

53. This reasoning is implicit in the cases which discuss the admissibility of declarations of state of mind to prove an act, as a question of the scope of an exception to the hearsay rule. See § 295, infra.

54. Adkins v. Brett, 184 Cal. 252, 193 Pac. 251 (1920); People v. Carpenter, 28 Ill.2d 116, 190 N.E.2d 738 (1963).

55. See § 249, n. 83, infra.

56. See § 250, n. 54, infra.

57. See § 10, supra.

mony in this latter case was offered to show the time of the train's arrival, the appropriate objection is hearsay.[58] The distinction is one of the form of the testimony, whether the witness purports to give the facts directly upon his own credit (though it may appear later that he was speaking only on the faith of reports from others) or whether he purports to give an account of what another has told him and this is offered to evidence the truth of the other's report. However, when it appears, either from the phrasing of his testimony or from other sources, that the witness is testifying on the basis of reports from others, though he does not in terms testify to their statements, the distinction loses much of its significance, and courts may simply apply the label "hearsay." [59]

248. Instances of the Application of the Hearsay Rule.

A few recent and typical examples of the rejection of evidence under the general hearsay rule excluding extra-judicial assertions offered to prove the facts asserted will indicate the scope of its operation. Evidence of the following oral statements has been excluded:

on the issue whether deceased had transferred his insurance to his new automobile, testimony that he said he had made the transfer; [60] to prove that veniremen had read newspaper articles, testimony of deputy sheriff that attorney said that one venireman said that other venireman had read the articles; [61] testimony of deputy sheriff that his investigation disclosed the existence of ill feelings by defendant toward the deceased; [62] to prove that driver was driving with consent of insured owner, testimony that the owner said after the accident that the driver had his permission; [63] testimony of investigator that liquor store manager told him that symbols on bottles had specified meaning.[64]

In criminal cases, the arresting or investigating officer will often explain his going to the scene of the crime or his interview with the defendant, or a search or seizure, by stating that he did so "upon information received" and this of course will not be objectionable as hearsay,[65] but if he becomes more specific by repeating definite complaints of a particular crime by the accused, this is so likely to be misused by the jury as evidence of the fact asserted that it should be excluded as hearsay.[66]

---

58. For discussion of the distinction, see 2 Wigmore, Evidence § 657, 5 id. §§ 1361, 1363(3).

59. See, e. g., First Nat. Bank in Greenwich v. National Airlines, Inc., 288 F.2d 621 (2d Cir. 1961) (testimony of witness who participated in search for bodies of plane crash victims, that "They found some off Petit Bois Island"); Elsberry v. Great Northern R. Co., 265 Minn. 352, 121 N.W.2d 716 (1963) (testimony of witness, offered to prove notice of dangerous condition, that it was common knowledge, though he could give no specific instances of complaints); State v. Conway, 351 Mo. 126, 171 S.W.2d 677 (1943) (testimony of officer as to money in possession of accused when arrested, apparently based on reports of others); Robertson v. Coca Cola Bottling Co. of Walla Walla, Wash., 195 Ore. 668, 247 P.2d 217 (1952) (testimony of bottling plant manager as to strength and thickness of glass in bottle based upon measurements made by third parties). When a hearsay statement is offered as coming within an exception to the hearsay rule, it is usually required that the declarant must meet the knowledge-qualification, see § 10, supra. This is sometimes confused with the hearsay objection.

60. Carantzas v. Iowa Mut. Ins. Co., 235 F.2d 193 (5th Cir. 1956).

61. Lowell v. Daly, 148 Conn. 266, 169 A.2d 888 (1961).

62. Agee v. State, 185 So.2d 671 (Miss.1966).

63. Coureas v. Allstate Ins. Co., 198 Va. 77, 92 S. E.2d 378 (1956). Distinguish the speaking of words of permitting as a verbal act under § 249, n. 78, infra.

64. Boatright v. Commonwealth, 198 Va. 753, 96 S.E.2d 772 (1957).

65. Hemphill v. Commonwealth, 379 S.W.2d 223 (Ky.1964); State v. Barnes, 345 S.W.2d 130 (Mo. 1961); Foster v. Commonwealth, 209 Va. 297, 163 S.E.2d 565 (1968).

66. Smith v. United States, 70 U.S.App.D.C. 255, 105 F.2d 778 (1939); State v. Kimble, 214 La. 58,

Instances of exclusion of written statements as hearsay when offered in court as evidence of their truth are likewise frequent. Thus, the following have recently been determined to be hearsay:

written estimates of damages or cost of repairs, made by an estimator who does not appear as a witness; [67] New York telephone directory listings as proof of listee's absence from California; [68] invoices, bills, and receipts as independent evidence of the making of repairs, payment, and reasonableness of charges; [69] the written statement of an absent witness to an accident; [70] newspaper accounts as proof of matters of fact reported therein; [71] statements in will

that testator's second wife had agreed to devise property to his children, as proof of that agreement; [72] medical report, by a physician who did not testify, to prove that plaintiff had sustained injuries in a subsequent accident; [73] manufacturer's advertising claims as proof of reliability of "Intoximeter." [74]

249. Out-of-Court Utterances Which Are Not Hearsay.[75]

The hearsay rule forbids evidence of out-of-court assertions to prove the facts asserted in them. Manifestly, proof of utterances and writings may be made with an almost infinite variety of other purposes, not resting for their value upon the veracity of the out-of-court declarant and hence falling outside the hearsay classification. A few of the more common types of nonhearsay utterances are discussed in the present section.

Verbal acts.[76] When a suit is brought for breach of a written contract, it would not occur to anyone, when a writing is offered as evidence of the contract sued on, to suggest that it is hearsay. Similarly proof of oral utterances by the parties in a contract suit constituting the offer and acceptance which brought the contract into being, are not evidence of assertions offered testimonially but rather of utterances—verbal conduct—to which the law attaches duties and liabilities.[77] Other obvious instances are ev-

36 So.2d 637 (1948). The cases cited in the preceding footnote state or imply that the rule is so. However, the decisions are by no means uniform. Some allow mention of the nature of the offense or of the identity of the defendant, though seemingly not of both in conjunction. State v. Lopez, 182 Kan. 46, 318 P.2d 662 (1957) (report of theft of men's suits mentioned but without identifying defendant); Platt v. State, 402 S.W.2d 898 (Tex.Cr. App.1966) (officer testified that he received information about defendant but nature of information not disclosed). Some cases sanction complete disclosure, with a limiting instruction. Powell v. State, 231 Ark. 737, 332 S.W.2d 483 (1960); Estes v. State, 224 Ga. 687, 164 S.E.2d 108 (1968). The propriety of this latter practice is questionable, since the need for the evidence is negligible with respect to jury issues and the effectiveness of limiting instructions is doubtful. See Bruton v. United States, 391 U.S. 123 (1968); § 59, supra.

67. Schaefer v. Schaefer, 235 Ark. 870, 362 S.W.2d 444 (1962); Home Mutual Fire Ins. Co. v. Hagar, 242 Ark. 693, 415 S.W.2d 65 (1967); Alliance Mut. Cas. Co. v. Atkins, 316 S.W.2d 783 (Tex.Civ.App. 1958).

68. People v. Crosby, 58 Cal.2d 713, 25 Cal.Rptr. 847, 375 P.2d 839 (1962).

69. Pacific Gas & Elec. Co. v. G. W. Thomas Drayage & R. Co., 69 Cal.2d 33, 69 Cal.Rptr. 561, 442 P.2d 641 (1968). The courts have indicated, however, that the items would be admissible to corroborate testimony. And see People v. Davis, 269 Ill. 256, 110 N.E. 9 (1915); Byalos v. Matheson, 328 Ill. 269, 159 N.E. 242 (1927), as to receipted bills.

70. Izzo v. Crowley, 157 Conn. 561, 254 A.2d 904 (1969).

71. Hickock v. Hand, 190 Kan. 224, 373 P.2d 206 (1962); Marley v. Providence Journal Co., 86 R.I.

229, 134 A.2d 180 (1957); Deramus v. Thornton, 160 Tex. 494, 333 S.W.2d 824 (1960).

72. Colgrove v. Goodyear, 325 Mich. 127, 37 N.W.2d 779, 10 A.L.R.2d 1029 (1949).

73. Potts v. Howser, 274 N.C. 49, 161 S.E.2d 737 (1968).

74. City of Sioux Falls v. Kohler, 80 S.D. 34, 118 N.W.2d 14 (1962).

75. See Morgan, Basic Problems of Evidence 249 (1962); 6 Wigmore, Evidence § 1766.

76. See Morgan, A Suggested Classification of Utterances Admissible as Res Gestae, 31 Yale L.J. 229 (1922); 6 Wigmore, Evidence § 1770.

77. Creaghe v. Iowa Home Mut. Cas. Co., 323 F.2d 981 (10th Cir. 1963); United States Fidelity &

idence of the utterance by the defendant of words relied on as constituting a slander or deceit for which damages are sought. Additional cases illustrating the principle are described in the note.[78]

Verbal parts of acts.[79] The significance of acts taken alone and isolated from surrounding circumstances may be unclear. Thus the bare physical act of handing over money to another person is susceptible of many interpretations. The possibilities include loan, payment of a debt, bribe, bet, gift, and no doubt many other kinds of transactions. Explanatory words which accompany and give character to the transaction are not hearsay.[80] Similar considerations prevail when the character of an establishment is sought to be proved by evidence of statements made in connection with activities taking place on the premises.[81]

Utterances and writings offered to show effect on hearer or reader.[82] When it is proved that D made a statement to X, with the purpose of showing the probable state of mind thereby induced in X, such as being put on notice or having knowledge,[83] or motive,[84] or to show the information which X had as bearing on the reasonableness[85] or

See also the discussion in connection with the nebulous concept *res gestae*, infra § 288.

81. For example, statements and conversations indicative of gambling are admissible under this theory. The evidence may consist of incoming telephone calls from unidentified persons seeking to place bets. State v. Tolisano, 136 Conn. 210, 70 A.2d 118, 13 A.L.R.2d 1405 (1949); State v. Di Vincenti, 232 La. 13, 93 So.2d 676 (1957); Annot., 13 A.L.R.2d 1409, or it may consist of matters heard directly. State v. Rhoten, 174 Kan. 394, 257 P.2d 141 (1953) (witness heard through window "New man shooting" and other gambling "lingo").

82. See 6 Wigmore, Evidence § 1789.

83. Webb v. Fuller Brush Co., 378 F.2d 500 (3d Cir. 1967) (published articles to show notice of dangers of hormone facial cream); Smedra v. Stanek, 187 F.2d 892 (10th Cir. 1951) (statement in operating room that sponge count was off, to show negligence in leaving sponge in plaintiff in course of surgery).

84. Emich Motors Corp. v. General Motors Corp., 181 F.2d 70 (7th Cir. 1950), rev'd on other grounds 340 U.S. 558 (complaining letters from customers, offered to show that cancellation of dealer's franchise was not motivated by dealer's refusal to finance car sales through defendant's affiliate).

85. Crespin v. Albuquerque Gas & Elec. Co., 39 N.M. 473, 50 P.2d 259 (1935) (action against electric power company for injury from shock when plaintiff picked up live wire; plaintiff's evidence that fellow employee told him that current was off, held not hearsay and proper); McAfee v. Travis Gas Corp., 137 Tex. 314, 153 S.W.2d 442 (1941) (plaintiff sues for injury due to gas explosion, when man to whom plaintiff was pointing out leaks in pipeline struck match: on issue of contributory negligence plaintiff's evidence that the man told him he was an employee of the pipeline company, admissible to show information on which plaintiff acted); Moen v. Chestnut, 9 Wash.2d 93, 113 P.2d 1030 (1941) (as bearing on reasonableness

---

Guaranty Co. v. Davis, 3 Ariz.App. 259, 413 P.2d 590 (1966); Gyro Brass Mfg. Corp. v. United Auto. etc. Workers, 147 Conn. 76, 157 A.2d 241 (1959).

78. Hanson v. Johnson, 161 Minn. 229, 201 N.W. 322 (1924) (spoken words constituting a partition of corn crop between landlord and tenant); State v. Sweeney, 180 Minn. 450, 231 N.W. 225, 73 A.L.R. 380 (1930) (defendant prosecuted for accepting bribes as an alderman, in confederation with Maurer, another alderman; held, evidence of conversations of Maurer and third persons in which bribes were arranged for, admissible as "utterances within the issue" and "verbal acts"); Patterson-Stocking, Inc. v. Dunn Bros. Storage Warehouses, Inc., 201 Minn. 308, 276 N.W. 737 (1937) (evidence of instructions given by owner to driver admissible to show whether driver was acting with owner's consent at time of accident; owner's words and conduct were part of fact in issue); Commonwealth v. Wiswesser, 134 Pa.Super. 488, 3 A.2d 983 (1939) (prosecution for corrupt solicitation of a juror; conversations of defendant's agent with juror held admissible and not hearsay).

79. 6 Wigmore, Evidence §§ 1772–1786; C.J.S. Evidence § 256.

80. National Bank of the Metropolis v. Kennedy, 84 U.S. (17 Wall.) 19, 21 L.Ed. 554 (1873) (conversation between parties on issue whether cashier made loan for bank or for himself); Barnett v. Hitching Post Lodge, Inc., 101 Ariz. 488, 421 P.2d 507 (1967) (on issue of validity of mortgage, mortgagor's statements that he wanted the property "plastered" so that his estranged wife could not "get her hooks into it"); In re Cronholm's Estate, 38 Ill.App.2d 141, 186 N.E.2d 534 (1962) (statement of depositor indicating lack of donative intent in establishing joint bank account); Butler v. Butler, 253 Iowa 1084, 114 N.W.2d 595 (1962) (statements showing that conveyance was in trust).

good faith [86] of the subsequent conduct of X, or anxiety,[87] the evidence is not subject to attack as hearsay. The same rationale applies to proof by the defendant, in cases of assault or homicide, of communicated threats made to him by the person whom he is alleged to have killed or assaulted. If offered to show his reasonable apprehension of danger it is not offered for a hearsay purpose; [88] its value for this purpose does not depend on the truth of the statement.

Declarations offered to show circumstantially the feelings or state of mind of the declarant. The substantive rules often make rights and duties depend on the existence of particular states of mind or feeling. The intent to steal or to kill, to have a certain paper take effect as a deed or a will, or the maintenance or transfer of the affections of a wife, are examples of states of mind or emotion which may come into issue in litigation.[89] Moreover, mental or emotional states may become relevant as circumstantial evidence of other facts, as for example when evidence of a plan or design in a man's

mind is received as evidence that he later carried it out by suitable actions.[90]

When in one of these connections an inquiry is afoot into the thoughts, desires, hopes or fears of the person in question, an obvious resort is to evidence of such of his actions as would shed light on the inquiry. His significant conduct, however, will manifestly consist not only of what he did but what he said. When we seek to show his mind or feeling by what he said, we are met with the question: is it hearsay?

Applying the definition earlier suggested [91] we would say that if the utterance would reasonably be understood as an assertion by the declarant of the existence of his state of mind or feelings which it is offered to prove, it would be hearsay. But, actually, direct declarations of thoughts and feelings are much less frequently offered in evidence than are declarations which only impliedly, indirectly, or inferentially indicate the existence of the mental or emotional state they are tendered to prove. Declarations offered for this purpose are not hearsay under the suggested definition.[92] Some examples may illustrate the types of evidence discussed. In a contested will case the proponent might seek to support the validity of testator's bequest to his son Harold against the charge of undue influence by showing that long before the time when the alleged influence was exerted, the testator had shown a special fondness for Harold.

---

of actions of driver of car involved in collision, evidence on her behalf that her companion before action warned her that intersection they were approaching was dangerous, proper and not hearsay).

86. Frank v. United States, 220 F.2d 559 (10th Cir. 1955) (using mails to defraud by selling oil securities by representing that oil could be found by using "doodle bug"; error to exclude statements made to defendant that the device was reliable); People v. Vogel, 46 Cal.2d 798, 299 P.2d 850 (1956) (statement of first wife of defendant charged with bigamy that she was going to get a divorce).

87. Ferrara v. Galluchio, 5 N.Y.2d 16, 176 N.Y.S.2d 996, 152 N.E.2d 249 (1958) (statement to plaintiff by dermatologist that condition might become cancerous, in medical malpractice action for causing X-ray burns).

88. Some courts, however, required that overt acts of hostility by the threatener be shown in order to let in proof of communicated threats. See, e. g., State v. Albright, 144 Mo. 638, 46 S.W. 620 (1898); 2 Wigmore, Evidence § 647; Dec. Dig. Homicide ☞190(8).

89. See § 294, infra.

90. See § 295, infra.

91. See § 246, supra.

92. Admittedly the uncross-examined statement is subject to all the hearsay dangers, except to the extent that deliberate falsification diminishes when a statement is not used to prove anything asserted therein. See Morgan, Basic Problems of Evidence 249 (1962). The same problem exists when the nonassertive conduct is nonverbal. See the discussion in § 250, infra. See also the definition of hearsay in F.R.Ev. (R.D.1971) 801, quoted in § 246, n. 47, supra.

For this purpose evidence might be offered (a) that the testator had paid the expenses of Harold, and for none other of his children, in completing a college course, (b) that the testator said, "Harold is the finest of my sons," and (c) that he said, "I care more for Harold than for any of my other children." When offered to show the testator's feelings toward his son, under the suggested definition item (a) would present no hearsay question,[93] item (b) would be considered a nonhearsay declaration raising a circumstantial inference as to the testator's feelings,[94] and (c) a direct statement offered to prove the fact stated, and hence dependent for its value upon the veracity of the declarant, would be considered hearsay.

Fortunately, a widely recognized exception to the hearsay rule admits declarations of a present state of mind or feelings,[95] and the occasion to make such refined distinctions as the foregoing is limited largely to the realm of theory.[96]

Knowledge.[97] This circumstantial nonassertive use of utterances to show state of mind is perhaps most clearly applicable to declarations evincing knowledge, notice, consciousness, or awareness of some fact, which fact is established by other evidence in the case.

Thus if evidence is given that the operator of a machine stated before the accident sued on, that the brakes were defective, this would be admissible as evidence tending to show circumstantially that he knew of the defective condition, if it was defective.[98] To

---

93. See, however, the discussion of nonverbal conduct as hearsay in § 250, infra.

94. See, e. g., Loetsch v. New York City Omnibus Corp., 291 N.Y. 308, 52 N.E.2d 448 (1943), a suit by a husband for the death of his wife. On the issue of damages, which was measured by the pecuniary value to the husband of his wife's continuance of life, the defendant offered in evidence the will of the wife, containing this statement: "Whereas I have been a faithful, dutiful, and loving wife to my husband, Dean Yankovich, and whereas he reciprocated my tender affections for him with acts of cruelty and indifference, and whereas he has failed to support and maintain me in that station of life which would have been possible and proper for him, I hereby limit my bequest to him to one dollar." On appeal, the exclusion of this statement was held erroneous, and the court (Thacher, J.) said, "Such declarations are evidence of the decedent's state of mind and are probative of a disposition on the part of the declarant which has a very vital bearing upon the reasonable expectancy, or lack of it, of future assistance or support if life continues. . . . No testimonial effect need be given to the declaration, but the fact that such a declaration was made by the decedent, whether true or false, is compelling evidence of her feelings toward, and relations to, her husband. As such it is not excluded under the hearsay rule but is admissible as a verbal act."

95. See § 294, infra.

96. Nuttall v. Reading Co., 235 F.2d 546 (3d Cir. 1956).
". . . [T]here does not seem to be a single practical consequence that may or may not ensue according to whether the evidence is received as original or received by way of exception to the hearsay rule." Cross, Evidence 475 (3rd ed. 1967).
Similar hearsay questions arise with respect to public opinion and other polls. See the thoughtful opinion of Feinberg, J., in Zippo Mfg. Co. v. Rogers Imports, Inc., 216 F.Supp. 670 (S.D.N.Y.1963). Since the question whether responses given by those polled are hearsay does not affect admissibility, the critical issues tend to hinge upon the acceptability of techniques employed, the propriety of the questions used, the selection of the universe to be studied, choice of samples, and so on, all of which lie in the realm of relevancy. Literature on the subject includes: Blum et al., The Art of Opinion Research: A Lawyer's Appraisal of an Emerging Service, 24 U.Chi.L.Rev. 1 (1956); Bonynge, Trademark Surveys and Techniques and Their Use in Litigation, 48 A.B.A.J. 329 (1962); Early, The Use of Survey Evidence in Antitrust Proceedings, 33 Wash.L.Rev. 380 (1958); Sherman, The Use of Public Opinion Polls in Continuance and Venue Hearings, 50 A.B.A.J. 357 (1964); Sprowls, The Admissibility of Sample Data into a Court of Law: A Case History, 4 U.C.L.A.L.Rev. 222 (1957); Zeisel The Uniqueness of Survey Evidence, 45 Cornell L. Q. 322 (1960); Annot., 76 A.L.R.2d 919.

97. See 2 Wigmore, Evidence § 266; C.J.S. Evidence § 257.

98. Borderland Coal Co. v. Kerns, 165 Ky. 487, 177 S.W. 266 (1915) (declarations by foreman before accident as to incompetence of fellow servant received to show foreman's and company's knowledge); McCall's Ferry Power Co. v. Price, 108 Md. 96, 69 A. 832 (1908) (similar to last); Robert A. Pierce Co. v. Sherman Gardens Co., 82 Nev.

show the latter fact, other evidence is relied on. Proof that one talks about a matter demonstrates on its face that he was conscious or aware of it, and his veracity simply does not enter into the situation. Even though the statement is assertive as to the existence of knowledge, "I *know* the brakes are bad," and is offered to show he did know it, it can still rest on the nonhearsay ground that (bad brakes having been otherwise shown) his remark tends to show that if the brakes were bad he was aware of it. The existence of knowledge is apparent without any reliance on his veracity.

Of course, this theory is only available where the inference sought to be drawn is the declarant's knowledge at the very time of the declaration. Thus if the declarant, a week after the accident stated that he knew of the bad brakes before the accident, and this is offered to show his previous knowledge, it is hearsay and can come in only under some exception to the hearsay rule, such as for admissions of parties and their agents.[99]

When the existence of knowledge is sought to be used as the basis for a further inference, caution is required lest the hearsay rule be infringed upon. Thus, in a Wisconsin case [1] evidence was received in a trial for mistreatment of a little girl, that the girl in reporting the incident gave a description of the house and its surroundings and of the room and its furnishings, where the mistreatment occurred. Other evidence showed that this description fitted exactly the house and room where the defendant lived. Morgan suggested that this evidence depended for its value upon "the observation, memory and veracity" of the girl and thus shared the hazards of hearsay.[2] It seems, however, that the testimony had value without regard to her veracity. Other witnesses had described the physical characteristics of the house. Her testimony was not relied on for that, but to show her knowledge as a "trace," as it were, on her mind of her visit at the time of the crime. Significantly the undisputed proof excluded the possibility of other means by which she could have acquired the knowledge, and thus the hearsay dangers were eliminated. However, statements of memory or belief are not generally allowed as proof of the happening of the event remembered or believed, since allowing the evidence would destroy the hearsay rule.[3] For this purpose, knowledge would seem to be indistinguishable from memory and belief, save under unusual circumstances.

Insanity. One of the main sources of proof of mental competency or incompetency is the conduct of the person in question,

---

395, 419 P.2d 781 (1967) (statement showing knowledge as to which construction project payment was applicable); Annot., 141 A.L.R. 704, 713.

99. Kutchera v. Minneapolis St. P. & S. S. M. Ry. Co., 54 N.D. 897, 212 N.W. 51 (1927) (statement of agent of railway made after accident that he knew machine was dangerous held improperly admitted: extensive discussion); Couch v. Hutcherson, 243 Ala. 47, 8 So.2d 580 (1942); Annot., 141 A.L.R. 704. See Chapter 26, infra.

The agent's declaration showing his then knowledge is of course evidence of his knowledge at a later time. Fox v. Manchester, 183 N.Y. 141, 75 N.E. 1116, 2 L.R.A., N.S., 474, 1905 (dictum). A few decisions, admitting "post rem" declarations, suggest by their facts that as to declarations after the crucial event, the circumstances may well show that the knowledge must have been acquired before the happening sued on. Wainwright v. Westborough Country Club, 45 S.W.2d 86 (Mo.App. 1932); Fenner v. American Surety Co. of N. Y., 97 S.W.2d 741 (Tex.Civ.App., 1936). These and other cases are discussed in Annot., 141 A.L.R. 704.

1. Bridges v. State, 247 Wis. 350, 19 N.W.2d 529 (1945); Note, 44 Mich.L.Rev. 480.

For a similar elimination of hearsay dangers by circumstances, see Edwards v. Druien, 235 Ky. 835, 32 S.W.2d 411 (1930) (to show hearing impairment, testimony of physician as to plaintiff's answers during hearing test with watch or tuning fork at various distances while blindfolded). Cf. Shaughnessy v. Holt, 236 Ill. 485, 86 N.E. 256 (1908) (responses to examining physician held hearsay even though plaintiff testified they were true).

2. Morgan, Evidence 1941–1945, 59 Harv.L.Rev. 481, 544 (1946).

3. See § 296, infra.

showing his normal or abnormal response to the circumstances of his environment. By this test, every act of the subject's life, within reasonable limits of time, would be relevant to the inquiry.[4] As to nonverbal conduct no problem of hearsay is involved under the definition of hearsay previously suggested.[5] While it may be argued that, since abnormal conduct can be simulated, the significance of such acts may in some degree be dependent upon the want of deceptive intent,[6] no doubt exists as to the admissibility of the evidence, subject to the practical limitations of relevancy.[7] The same approach is adopted in receiving evidence of verbal conduct, as for example, statements tending to show the existence of hallucinations or insane delusions, which are characteristic symptoms of most forms of mental disorder.[8] These expressions are treated as evidence of irrational conduct, rather than as hearsay statements of belief offered to show that the declarant does entertain the belief which he asserts. Even if the declaration were in the form of an express assertion of belief, "I believe that I am King Henry the Eighth," it seems clear that the courts would admit it on the nonhearsay theory of verbal conduct offered circumstantially,[9] though possibly

the proponent might also succeed on an alternative theory of the use of the statement as hearsay coming in under the exception for declarations of present mental state, namely, belief. But there is obvious common sense in the judicial tendency to treat alike all irrational expressions, regardless of form, offered to show mental incompetence, and to admit them all under the simpler formula of nonhearsay conduct.

Indirect versions of hearsay statements; negative results of inquiries. If the apparent purpose of offered testimony is to use an out-of-court statement to evidence the truth of facts stated therein, the hearsay objection cannot be obviated by eliciting the purport of the statements in indirect form.[10] Thus evidence as to the purport of "information received" by the witness,[11] or a statement of the results of investigation made by other persons,[12] offered as evidence of the facts as-

---

4. 2 Wigmore, Evidence §§ 228, 229; Green, Proof of Mental Incompetency and the Unexpressed Major Premise, 53 Yale L.J. 271, 276 (1944); Dec. Dig. Criminal Law ⊙354, Mental Health ⊙8.

5. See § 246, supra.

6. See the discussion of conduct as hearsay, § 250, infra.

7. People v. Wolfe, 61 Cal.2d 795, 40 Cal.Rptr. 271, 394 P.2d 959 (1964); Ross v. State, 217 Ga. 569, 124 S.E.2d 280 (1962); McGarrh v. State, 249 Miss. 247, 148 So.2d 494, 506 (1963).

8. See Green, op. cit., supra n. 4, at pp. 272, 273. People v. Wolfe, supra n. 7; Young v. Colorado Nat. Bank, 148 Colo. 104, 365 P.2d 701, 710 (1961); Ross v. State, supra n. 7; Sollers v. State, 73 Nev. 248, 316 P.2d 917 (1957).

9. See the discussion of declarations offered as proof of declarant's state of mind in the text at notes 93–96, supra. Compare Hinton, States of Mind and the Hearsay Rule, 1 U.Chi.L.Rev. 394, 397, 398 (1934): "It has sometimes been argued by judges

and writers that, where the issue is the sanity of the testator, and some absurd statement by him is proved, e. g., 'I am the Emperor Napoleon', no hearsay use is involved because we are not seeking to prove that he really was Napoleon, and hence that we are making a purely circumstantial use of his words to prove his irrational belief. The difficulty is that this view ignores the implied assertion of belief. If the statement had taken the form, 'I believe that I am Napoleon', and were offered to prove that the testator so believed, it would be generally conceded that the statement was hearsay, and receivable only because of an exception to the rule. The former assertion is simply a short method of stating the speaker's opinion or belief. Implied assertions seem to fall within the hearsay category as well as express assertions."

10. Falknor, "Indirect" Hearsay, 31 Tul.L.Rev. 3 (1956).

11. Hobart v. Hobart Estate Co., 26 Cal.2d 412, 159 P.2d 958 (1945) (dictum); Dougherty v. City of New York, 267 App.Div. 828, 45 N.Y.S.2d 808 (1944), and see the cases in § 248, notes 62, 65 and 66.

12. Greenland Development Corp. v. Allied Heating Products Co., 184 Va. 588, 35 S.E.2d 801, 164 A.L.R. 1312 (1945) (trial court excluded on grounds of want of knowledge and of hearsay and ruling held correct; as to which rule was applicable, the form of the testimony, not clearly disclosed, would in principle determine, see § 247, supra).

serted out of court, have been held to be hearsay. While in theory this approach may be applicable to such situations as the collective decision of a group of doctors, reached after consultation,[13] the result is either the loss of valuable and reliable data or extreme awkwardness in presenting it.[14] It is suggested that the hearsay ban ought not to apply, either on the theory that cross-examination requirements are satisfied by the availability of one of the participants in the joint decision, or by analogy to the view that expert opinions may be based in part on observed data and in part on reports by others.[15]

Analogous questions arise in respect to testimony by a witness that he has made inquiries among the residents of a given place where a certain person is alleged to live, and that he has been unable to find anyone who knows him or has any information about him. Upon an issue as to whether due diligence has been shown in attempting to locate a missing witness or other person, it is clear that testimony as to results of similar inquiries is not hearsay, but is merely a narration of the acts and efforts claimed to constitute due diligence.[16] However, the inquiries and the inability to secure information, may be offered as evidence of the nonexistence of the person sought to be located, or of the fact that no such person lives at the place in question. Then it can be argued that this is merely an indirect way of placing in evidence the statements of those of whom inquiry was made for the purpose of proving the truth of the fact stated, namely their want of knowledge of such a person. The evidence has occasionally been excluded on this ground.[17] It is true that the residents of whom inquiry was made could be brought in to testify to their want of knowledge of the person,[18] but it would usually be more convenient and equally just to permit the evidence of fruitless inquiries, as most of the cases do,[19] and leave the adversary to bring in direct proof of the existence or residence of the person, which if his claim is true he will most often be easily able to do. An escape from the hearsay objection is furnished by the theory that fruitless inquiries are evidence of inability of the inquirer to find after diligent search and this in turn is circumstantial evidence of the nonexistence or nonresidence of the person in question.[20]

---

13. Carter v. People, 119 Colo. 342, 204 P.2d 147 (1949); Bauman v. People, 130 Colo. 248, 274 P. 2d 591 (1954); Village of Ponca v. Crawford, 18 Neb. 551, 26 N.W. 365 (1886).

14. The collective decision is frequently one reached at a staff meeting. Uneasiness as to the proper handling of the evidence is apparent in at least two states. Compare Grammer v. State, 239 Ala. 633, 196 So. 268 (1940) with Prince v. Lowe, 263 Ala. 410, 82 So.2d 606 (1955); also compare Nail v. State, 231 Ark. 70, 328 S.W.2d 836 (1959) with Downs v. State, 231 Ark. 466, 330 S.W.2d 281 (1959).

15. See § 15, supra.

16. New York Central Ry. Co. v. Pinnell, 112 Ind. App. 116, 40 N.E.2d 988 (1942); Britton v. State, 2 Md.App. 285, 234 A.2d 274 (1967); 5 Wigmore, Evidence § 1414.

17. See, e. g., State v. Rosenthal, 123 Wis. 442, 102 N.W. 49 (1905).

18. As was done in People v. Kosearas, 410 Ill. 456, 102 N.E.2d 534 (1951), and Dunn v. State, 15 Okl.Cr. 245, 176 P. 86, 90 (1918).

19. State v. DePietro, 243 La. 897, 148 So.2d 593 (1963) (as proof that fatal shooting did not occur at time and place claimed by accused, officer testified that his investigation disclosed no one who heard shots); People v. Sharp, 53 Mich. 523, 19 N.W. 168 (1884) (negative results of inquiries, to prove nonexistence of alleged subscribing witness); State v. Wentworth, 37 N.H. 196, 200, 217 (1858) (same as to person in whose company at another place accused claimed to have been at time of crime); Thomas v. State, 54 Okl.Cr. 97, 14 P.2d 953 (1932) (same as to nonexistence of purported drawer of check).

Jardine Estate, Inc. v. Koppel, 24 N.J. 536, 133 A.2d 1 (1957) (recognizes the principle but holds mere check of telephone listings not sufficient).

20. See Note, 46 Harv.L.Rev. 715 (1933); 5 Wigmore, Evidence § 1414(2). The result could also be rationalized as the recognition of a special exception to the hearsay rule. Jendresak v. Chicago & N. W. R. Co., 330 Ill.App. 157, 70 N.E.2d 863 (1946) (dictum). The analogy to public opinion polls is evident. See n. 96, supra.

The demands of practicality seem to outweigh any hesitation based on prohibitions against using

Where as here a choice of reasonable theories is presented, the expediency of the result may properly sway the choice.

Reputation. In the earlier stages of jury trial, when the jurors were expected to seek out the facts by neighborhood inquiries (instead of having the witnesses bring the facts through their testimony in court) community reputation was a frequent source of information for the jurors. When in the late 1600's the general doctrine excluding hearsay began to take form [21] the use of reputation either directly by the jurors or through the testimony of the witnesses, in certain areas of proof, was so well established that exceptions to the hearsay rule for reputation in these ancient uses soon came to be recognized.[22]

Reputation is a composite description of what the people in a community have said and are saying about a matter. A witness who testifies to reputation testifies to his generalized memory of a series of out-of-court statements. Whether reputation is hearsay depends on the same tests we have applied to evidence of other particular out-of-court statements.[23] Accordingly proof of reputation will often not be hearsay at all. Thus, in an action for defamation, where an element of damages is injury to the plaintiff's reputation, and the defendant offers on the issue of damages, evidence that the plaintiff's reputation was bad before the slander,[24] the evidence is not hearsay. Another example is proof of reputation in the community offered as evidence that some person in the community had knowledge of the reputed facts.[25]

Applying again the general definition we may conclude that evidence of reputation is hearsay only when offered to prove the truth of the fact reputed and hence depending for its value on the veracity of the collective asserters.[26] There are moreover, exceptions to the rule against hearsay, for reputation of particular facts, often restricted to certain uses and issues.[27]

Evidence of reputation, not falling within the established exceptions, when offered to prove the fact reputed, is constantly being excluded as hearsay,[28] as for example, when reputation is offered to prove ownership,[29] sanity,[30] or the existence of a partnership.[31]

---

memory or belief to prove the matter remembered or believed. See § 296, infra.

21. See § 244, supra.

22. 5 Wigmore, Evidence § 1580.

23. See § 246, supra.

24. As to the restrictions upon, and the allowability of the evidence under varying circumstances, see 1 Wigmore, Evidence §§ 70–76.

25. Otis Elevator Co. v. McLaney, 406 P.2d 7 (Alas.1965) (knowledge of condition of elevator door); Brennan v. Mayo, Sheriff, 105 Mont. 276, 72 P.2d 463 (1937) (sheriff's knowledge of plaintiff's ownership in action for conversion by him). In these cases, an inference is required from the existence of reputation to the fact of knowledge.

Other cases inject reputation as an element of negligent failure to inquire as to matters which inquiry would have disclosed. Western Stone Co. v. Whalen, 151 Ill. 472, 38 N.E. 241 (1894) (negligence in employing incompetent servant); Monahan v. City of Worcester, 150 Mass. 439, 23 N.E. 228 (1890) (same). The reputation of a third person may be a circumstance bearing upon the reasonableness of conduct in other ways. E. g. Lopez v. Heezen, 69 N.M. 206, 365 P.2d 448 (1961) (on issue whether defendant negligently sold firearm with improperly designed safety device, good reputation of manufacturer of device properly admitted).

In general, see 2 Wigmore, Evidence §§ 249, 251–259.

26. Brown v. Brown, 242 Ala. 630, 7 So.2d 557 (1942); Otis Elevator Co. v. McLaney, supra n. 25; 5 Wigmore, Evidence §§ 1580, 1609; and see § 324, infra.

27. See § 324, infra.

28. See cases collected in Dec.Dig. Evidence ⊝322, 324.

29. Brown v. Brown, 242 Ala. 630, 7 So.2d 557 (1942); Louisville & N. Terminal Co. v. Jacobs, 109 Tenn. 727, 72 S.W. 954 (1903).

30. In re Nelson's Will, 210 N.C. 398, 186 S.E. 480, 105 A.L.R. 1441 (1936) with annotation on this point.

31. Greep v. Bruns, 160 Kan. 48, 159 P.2d 803, 811 (1945); 5 Wigmore, Evidence § 1624.

Admissions of a party-opponent. The question whether an admission of a party-opponent is hearsay but admissible as an exception or is not hearsay at all, is discussed in a subsequent section.[32]

250. Conduct as Hearsay: "Implied Assertions."

Nonverbal conduct: assertive and nonassertive. One intriguing question which stands at the hearsay threshold is whether the hearsay label attaches only to evidence of what someone has previously said or written, or whether it may also include evidence of what he has *done.* We have seen that the hearsay rule has been stated as applying only to evidence of out-of-court statements offered for the purpose of proving that the facts are as asserted in the statement.[33] Evidence of out-of-court statements offered for any other purpose, e. g., to prove the making of a declaration as evidence of the publication of a slander, or to show that the one who uttered or heard it had notice of the facts asserted, is, of course, not hearsay. It is only when the statement is offered as the basis for the inferences, first, that the declarant *believed* it, and, second, that the facts were in accordance with his belief, that the evidence is said to be hearsay. These inferences are believed to be too unreliable to permit the evidence to be thus used by a jury. The declarant, in the first place, may be consciously lying and hence not have believed what he says, and second, even though he believed it, he may have been mistaken because of defects of perception, memory, or narrative powers. These deficiencies would be exposed by cross-examination. All this is the well-worn everyday logic leading to the exclusion of hearsay statements. Does it apply to anything other than statements? More particularly does it apply to evidence of *conduct?*

By way of prelude, it must be observed that the line of cleavage between conduct and statements is one that must be drawn in the light of substance, rather than form. No one would contend, if, in response to a question "Who did it?", one of the auditors held up his hand, that this gesture could be treated as different from an oral or written statement, in the application of the hearsay rule, any more than could the sign-speech of the dumb. Obviously, though described in terms of conduct, the actions are as much a part of the speaker's effort at expression as his words are, and of course in all cases where the gesture or other act is done, so far as appears, solely for the purpose of expression it is on a parity for all present purposes with any purely verbal statement.[34]

At the other extreme are instances of behavior so patently involuntary that they could not by the greatest stretch of imagination be treated as the equivalent of a verbal assertion.[35]

The *"implied assertion" problem.* Between these clear instances of hearsay and nonhearsay lies an area of controversy. If the sanity of X is in question, is it hearsay to prove that Y, who has been shown to have known X well all his life, agreed to marry him, when the evidence is offered to support the inference that Y believed him sane, and hence that

---

32. § 262, infra.

33. See § 246, supra.

34. United States v. Ross, 321 F.2d 61 (2d Cir. 1963) testimony of investigator that employee pointed to list in response to question as to salesman's number, classed as hearsay).

In the most frequently encountered instance, testimony as to the making of a prior out-of-court identification by pointing or similar act, the identifier usually also testifies as a witness, thus raising the question whether prior statements by witnesses are hearsay. See § 251, infra.

35. Cole v. United States, 327 F.2d 360 (9th Cir. 1964) (to establish that robbery was by intimidation, testimony that bank teller was pale and shaking not hearsay); Bagwell & Stewart, Inc. v. Bennett, 214 Ga. 780, 107 S.E.2d 824 (1959) (testimony that members of family became sick and vomited because of odors of defendant's plant not hearsay).

he *was* sane? If the issue is as to which member of a group insulted S, is evidence that B, her brother, who heard the insult, and thereupon attacked D, one of the crowd, hearsay when offered to show that D was the insulter? Other examples, gleaned from opinions of the judges in a celebrated case [36] are: (1) proof that the underwriters have paid the amount of the policy, as evidence of the loss of a ship; (2) proof of payment of a wager, as evidence of the happening of the event which was the subject of the bet; (3) precautions of the family, to show the person involved was a lunatic; (4) as evidence of sanity, the election of the person in question to high office; (5) "the conduct of a physician who permitted a will to be executed by a sick testator;" (6) "the conduct of a deceased captain on a question of seaworthiness, who, after examining every part of the vessel embarked in it with his family."

Moreover, if hearsay is limited to statements offered to prove the existence of facts asserted therein, the same question arises when *words*, even though assertive in form, are offered, not to prove what is asserted, but to prove the belief of the declarant regarding a certain fact and thus to suggest the existence of the fact itself. Of this type was the evidence offered in the leading case above referred to, Wright v. Tatham.[37]

It was a celebrated and hard-fought cause, which wound its way from the common law courts to chancery and back again, and was argued and reargued, and elicited numerous opinions, in the King's Bench, the Exchequer Chamber, and the House of Lords, which fill literally hundreds of pages in the reports. One John Marsden was a country gentleman, seized of certain rich manors in Lancashire, who died at a ripe old age, leaving his estate by will to one Wright, who had risen from a menial station to the position of steward and general man of business for Marsden. Marsden's heir at law, Admiral Tatham, in 1830 instituted litigation, including an action of ejectment for the real estate, to oust the menial intruder from these manors, on the ground, *inter alia*, of Marsden's mental incompetency to make a will. So great was the prejudice supposed to prevail in Lancashire, that one of the branches of the litigation was tried in the York assizes. At the ejectment trial, the ex-steward Wright, the defendant, supporting the will, offered in evidence several letters all written to the deceased by persons no longer living. Among them was one from a relative in America, giving news and expressing affection, and of a tenor such as would be written to one of ordinary understanding and there were likewise three others which related to matters of business which presumably would only be written to one who was believed by the writers to be able to comprehend and act intelligently upon practical affairs.[38] All these letters were admitted by the trial judge as evidence of the testator's competency, and the jury returned a verdict for the defendant sustaining the will, after hearing a mass of other evidence which fills two volumes in the verbatim report.[39] Sir

36. Wright v. Tatham, 7 Adolph. & E. 313, 386, 112 Eng.Rep. 488 (Exch.Ch.1837), and 5 Cl. & F. 670, 739, 47 Rev.Rep. 136 (H.L.1838). The pertinent extracts are quoted in 2 Wigmore, Evidence § 267.

37. Supra n. 36. For further details of the litigation occasioned by "Silly" Marsden's will, see the entertaining and perceptive article, Maguire, The Hearsay System: Around and Through the Thicket, 14 Vand.L.Rev. 741 (1961).

38. The letters are set out in full in 112 Eng.Rep. Repr. 490–494 (1837). One of the letters, from the Vicar of the Parish, strongly urges the testator to have his attorney meet with the attorney of the Parish, for the purpose of agreeing upon a statement of facts about some dispute between the testator and the Parish to be laid before counsel to whose opinions both sides should submit. Another is from a curate appointed by the testator, written on his resignation and expressing his gratitude and respect. Two others invite the testator to come, in company with the steward, to certain meetings to be held apparently for purposes connected with local public business or politics.

39. 112 Eng.Rep.Repr. 492, note (a) (1837).

Frederick Pollock the elder, on behalf of the victorious ex-steward, argued strongly that the letters were properly admitted, as showing "treatment" of the testator as a sane man by those who knew him, but the King's Bench held against him, and the case went down for a new trial, the letters were then excluded, and this time the heir, Admiral Tatham, secured a verdict against the will, and the question of the admissibility of the letters again started up the rounds of the judicial ladder. The case was twice acutely argued in the Exchequer Chamber, and all of the judges who considered the point seemed to have agreed in holding that the letters, in the absence of evidence that Marsden, the addressee, acted upon or at least read them, were inadmissible as being equivalent to hearsay evidence of the opinions of the writers. The holding was perhaps most pithily put by Baron Parke in these words:

"The conclusion at which I have arrived is, that proof of a particular fact which is not of itself a matter in issue, but which is relevant only as implying a statement or opinion of a third person on the matter in issue, is inadmissible in all cases where such a statement or opinion not on oath would be of itself inadmissible; and, therefore, in this case the letters which are offered only to prove the competence of the testator, that is the truth of the implied statements therein contained, were properly rejected, as the mere statement or opinion of the writer would certainly have been inadmissible." [40]

This opinion prevailed with all the other judges who alluded to this question, both in the Exchequer Chamber and on the further appeal to the House of Lords, though the judges of the former court were equally divided upon the question whether the proof sufficiently showed that the testator had read and acted on the letters so as to render them

admissible on that ground. Finally in 1838, the House of Lords ended eight years of strenuous litigation by holding the letters inadmissible.

In subsequent cases, the hearsay issue has often gone unrecognized, especially when the conduct in question was nonverbal.[41] When the hearsay objection has been raised, the rulings have been divided. The older cases tended to favor the objection,[42] but the current trend is in the opposite direction.[43]

To describe the evidence in these cases as "implied assertions," as suggested by Baron Parke,[44] is to prejudge the issue, for it is to extrajudicial assertions that the hearsay rule applies. A satisfactory resolution can be had

---

40. 7 Adolph. & E. at 388, 112 Eng.Rep. at 516.

41. Falknor, The "Hear-Say" Rule as a "See-Do" Rule: Evidence of Conduct, 33 Rocky Mt.L.Rev. 133, 135 (1961).

42. Hanson v. State, 160 Ark. 329, 254 S.W. 691 (1923) (to show failing condition of bank, evidence that other banks demanded payment of collections in cash); People v. Bush, 300 Ill. 532, 133 N.E. 201 (1921) (on issue whether prosecuting witness had venereal disease, evidence that institution in which she was placed did not segregate her, as was done with venereal cases); Powell v. State, 88 Tex.Cr.R. 367, 227 S.W. 188 (1921) (to rebut claim of accused that his grandmother had authorized him to sell her cow, evidence that on her return she demanded back the cow from the purchaser).

Similarly, flight of a third person has been held to be the equivalent of a confession by him and hence inadmissible as hearsay. People v. Mendez, 193 Cal. 39, 223 P. 65 (1924); State v. Menilla, 177 Iowa 283, 158 N.W. 645 (1916). However, note should be taken of the trend to admit third-person confessions under the hearsay exception for declarations against interest. See § 278, infra.

43. State v. Izzo, 94 Ariz. 226, 383 P.2d 116 (1963) (evidence that wife did not return home night before her murder as proof of her fear of accused husband); Taylor v. Centennial Bowl, Inc., 65 Cal.2d 114, 52 Cal.Rptr. 561, 416 P.2d 793 (1966) (evidence of requests for police assistance as proof of prior disturbances on premises); Belvidere Land Co. v. Owen Park Plaza, Inc., 362 Mich. 107, 106 N.W.2d 380 (1960) (evidence of receipt of telephone calls and visitors asking for Owen Park Plaza to show confusion with Owen Park Apartments). See also the discussion of conduct as evidence of marriage, legitimacy, family history, etc., in 2 Wigmore, Evidence §§ 268–272.

44. Supra, text at n. 40.

only by making an evaluation in terms of the dangers which the hearsay rule is designed to guard against, i. e., imperfections of perception, memory, and narration. It is believed that such an analysis can result only in rejecting the view that evidence of conduct, from which may be inferred a belief, from which in turn may be inferred the happening of the event which produced the belief, is the equivalent of an assertion that the event happened and hence hearsay. People do not, prior to raising their umbrellas, say to themselves in soliloquy form, "It is raining," nor does the motorist go forward on the green light only after making an inward assertion, "The light is green." [45] The conduct, offered in the one instance to prove it was raining and in the other that the light was green, involves no intent to communicate the fact sought to be proved, and it was recognized long ago that purposeful deception is less likely in the absence of intent to communicate.[46] True, the threshold question whether communication was in fact intended may on occasion present difficulty,[47] yet the probabilities against intent are so great as to justify imposing the burden of establishing it upon the party urging the hearsay objection.[48]

Even though the risks arising from insincerity may be slight or nonexistent in the absence of intent to communicate, the objection remains that the actor's perception and memory are untested by cross-examination for the possibility of honest mistake. However, in contrast to the risks from insincerity, those arising from the chance of honest mistake seem more sensibly to be factors useful in evaluating weight and credibility rather than grounds for exclusion. Moreover, the kind of situation involved is ordinarily such as either to minimize the likelihood of flaws of perception and memory or to present circumstances lending themselves to their evaluation. While the suggestion has been advanced that conduct evidence ought to be admitted only when the actor's behavior has an element of significant reliance as an assurance of trustworthiness,[49] a sufficient response here too is that the factor is one of evaluation, not a ground for exclusion.[50] Undue complication ought to be avoided in the interest of ease of application. The same can be said with respect to the possibility that the conduct may be ambiguous so that the trier of fact will draw a wrong inference.[51] Finally, a rule attaching the hearsay tag to the kind of conduct under consideration is bound to operate unevenly, since the possibility of a hearsay objection will more often than not simply be overlooked.[52]

The position that hearsay includes neither non-assertive conduct nor assertive state-

---

45. The examples are from Falknor, The "Hear-Say" Rule as a "See-Do" Rule: Evidence of Conduct, 33 Rocky Mt.L.Rev. 133 (1960).

46. Seligman, An Exception to the Hearsay Rule, 26 Harv.L.Rev. 146, 148 (1912).

47. Finman, Impied Assertions as Hearsay: Some Criticism of the Uniform Rules of Evidence, 14 Stan.L.Rev. 682, 695 (1962). See, e. g., Norris v. Detroit United Ry., 185 Mich. 264, 151 N.W. 747 (1915) (testimony of physician that plaintiff flinched when pressure was applied to allegedly injured ankle, held hearsay).

48. Falknor, supra n. 45 at 136; Maguire, The Hearsay System: Around and Through the Thicket, 14 Vand.L.Rev. 741, 765 (1961).

49. Varying versions are found in McCormick, The Borderland of Hearsay, 39 Yale L.J. 489, 504 (1930); Morgan, Hearsay and Non-Hearsay, 48 Harv.L.Rev. 1138, 1159 (1935); Falknor, Silence as Hearsay, 89 U.Pa.L.Rev. 192, 217 (1940). The position was essentially a transitional one, with the element of reliance being advanced as a justification for breaking away from the existing pattern of exclusion, rather than as a requirement. See n. 50, infra.

50. Morgan, Hearsay, 25 Miss.L.J. 1, 8 (1953); Falknor, The "Hear-Say" Rule as a "See-Do" Rule: Evidence of Conduct, 33 Rocky Mt.L.Rev. 133, 137 (1961).

51. Maguire, The Hearsay System: Around and Through the Thicket, 14 Vand.L.Rev. 741, 760 (1961). Cf. Finman, Implied Assertions as Hearsay: Some Criticism of the Uniform Rules of Evidence, 14 Stan.L.Rev. 682, 688 (1962).

52. Falknor, supra n. 50, at 137.

ments not offered to prove what is asserted finds solid adherence in recent and current statutes and rules dealing with the subject.[53]

Silence as hearsay. A specialized and oft-recurring aspect of the conduct-as-hearsay problem is presented by the cases where a failure to speak or act is offered as the basis for an inference that conditions were such as would not evoke speech or action in a reasonable person.[54]

Probably most of these cases fall in the following classes: (a) on an issue as to defects in goods, or unwholesomeness of food served, evidence is offered by the seller that goods or food of the same quality have been sold or served to other customers and that there has been no complaint by the other customers,[55] (b) on the question of the existence of an injury or injurious situation, or the happening of an injurious event, evidence is offered of the absence of complaint by other persons affected,[56] and (c) on the issue of

the happening of some event affecting a member of the family, or a claim to or disposition of property by such member, evidence is offered from other members of the family that he never mentioned such matter.[57] Taking these silence cases as a whole, there had probably been a greater proportion of instances where the evidence is admitted, than in the case of affirmative conduct. The instances where the hearsay problem is recognized or mentioned are even

---

53. Uniform Rule 62(1); West's Ann.Cal.Evid.Code, §§ 225, 1200; Kan.Code Civ.P. § 60–459(a); N.J.R. Ev. 62(1); F.R.Ev. (R.D.1971) 801.

54. Falknor, Silence as Hearsay, 89 U.Pa.L.Rev. 192 (1940), The "Hear-Say" Rule as a "See-Do" Rule, 33 Rocky Mt.L.Rev. 133, 134 (1961); Note, 24 N.C.L.Rev. 274 (1946).

55. Illustrative cases favoring admissibility are Katz v. Delohery Hat Co., 97 Conn. 665, 118 A. 88 (1922) (absence of complaints from other purchasers of fur from same lot); Schuler v. Union News Co., 295 Mass. 350, 4 N.E.2d 465 (1936) (no complaints from other purchasers of turkey sandwiches); St. Louis S.W. Ry. v. Arkansas & T. Grain Co., 42 Tex.Civ.App. 125, 95 S.W. 656 (1906) (absence of complaints from other purchasers of corn).

Contra, Stokely-Van Camp, Inc. v. Ferguson, 271 Ala. 120, 122 So.2d 356 (1960) (absence of complaints not evidence of due care); Siegel, King & Co. v. Penny & Baldwin, 176 Ark. 336, 2 S.W.2d 1082 (1928); (circumstances may have been different; other purchasers may have been damaged without complaining); George W. Saunders Live Stock Com'n Co. v. Kincaid, 168 S.W. 977 (Tex.Civ.App. 1914) (absence of complaints from other purchasers excluded as hearsay).

56. Admissibility was upheld in Cain v. George, 411 F.2d 572 (5th Cir. 1969) (on issue whether gas heater in motel room was defective, absence of complaints from others who had occupied the

room); Zheutlin v. Sperry & Hutchinson Co., 149 Conn. 364, 179 A.2d 829 (1962) (absence of complaints concerning condition of premises); Silver v. N.Y. Central R.R., 329 Mass. 14, 105 N.E.2d 923 (1952) (absence of complaints by other passengers that Pullman car was cold).

Contra, Menard v. Cashman, 94 N.H. 428, 55 A.2d 156 (1947) (if not hearsay, inconclusive silence).

57. Cases upholding admissibility include Latham v. Houston Land & Trust Co., 62 S.W.2d 519 (Tex. Civ.App.1933) (testimony that widow and attorney had never heard alleged settlor mention trust fund held not hearsay and admissible on issue of existence of fund); Sloan v. Sloan, 32 S.W.2d 513 (Tex. Civ.App.1930) (deceased did not state at dinner party that he and plaintiff were married, admitted on issue of marriage); Donovan v. Selinas, 85 Vt. 80, 81 Atl. 235 (1911) (fact that member of household never heard husband claim ownership of property relevant to show wife's ownership). See also State v. Childers, 196 La. 554, 199 So. 640 (1940) (on trial for forging wills where one defendant claimed will drawn by certain lawyer, since deceased, evidence of clerk in such lawyer's office that lawyer never mentioned having drawn alleged will, held, not hearsay; relevant to refute defendant's claim).

Contra, Planters' Chemical & Oil Co. v. Stearnes, 189 Ala. 503, 66 So. 699 (1914) (testimony that signers never heard any of other signers say they signed notes individually inadmissible except as it tends to contradict plaintiff's evidence that they signed as individuals); Sherling v. Continental Trust Co., 175 Ga. 672, 165 S.E. 560 (1932) (testator never said anything to witnesses about alleged oral contract of testator, to prove no contract existed; held irrelevant, immaterial and in nature of hearsay); Lake Drainage Commissioners v. Spencer, 174 N.C. 36, 93 S.E. 435 (1917) (fact that mother, now dead, said nothing to her children about having been served with summons, inadmissible as hearsay when offered to show that it was not served on her); Karlen v. Trebble, 45 S.D. 570, 189 N.W. 519 (1922) (witness living with plaintiff had not heard plaintiff's mother or father or anyone else claim ownership of auto, held incompetent for any purpose).

more infrequent than in the cases of positive conduct, and exclusion is often based on
relevancy grounds. As in the other conduct-
as-hearsay cases, the trend is in the direction
of admitting the evidence as nonhearsay,
which finds support in the recent statutes
and rules.[58]

Silence as an admission by a party-
opponent is treated elsewhere.[59]

251. Prior Statements of Witnesses as Substantive Evidence.[60]

As previously observed,[61] the traditional
view is that a prior statement of a witness
is hearsay if offered to prove the happening
of matters asserted therein. This categori-
zation does not, of course, preclude using the
prior statement for other purposes, e. g., to
impeach the witness by showing a self-
contradiction if the statement is inconsistent
with his testimony[62] or to support his credi-

bility under certain circumstances when the
statement is consistent with his testimony.[63]
But the prior statement is admissible as
proof of matter asserted therein, i. e. as "substantive" evidence, only when falling within
one of the exceptions to the hearsay rule.
This position has increasingly come under
attack in recent years on both logical and
practical grounds.

The logic of the orthodox view is that the
previous statement of the witness is hearsay
since its value rests on the credit of the declarant, who was not (1) under oath, (2)
subject to cross-examination, or (3) in the
presence of the trier, when the statement
was made.[64]

The counter-argument goes as follows: (1)
The oath is no longer a principal safeguard
of the trustworthiness of testimony.[65] Affidavits, though under oath, are not exempted
from the hearsay rule. Moreover, of the
numerous exceptions where evidence is admitted despite its being hearsay, in only one
instance is the out-of-court statement required to have been under oath. And that
instance, namely prior testimony, may argu-

---

58. See n. 53, supra.

59. See the general coverage in § 270, infra, and
the discussion of the particular problems of treating the silence of a criminal defendant as an admission or confession in § 161, supra.

60. 3A Wigmore, Evidence (Chadbourn rev.) § 1018;
4 id. § 1132; Dec.Dig. Witnesses ☞397; Annot.,
133 A.L.R. 1454.

61. § 34, supra, with respect to prior inconsistent
statements. The same view has generally prevailed also with respect to prior consistent statements. Dyer v. Dyer, 141 Neb. 685, 4 N.W.2d
731 (1942) (report of court-appointed investigator
in divorce case, giving statements of parties, who
apparently testified, and others; judge offered both
sides opportunity to cross-examine investigator
and his informants; held error, report was hearsay); Grand Forks Building & Dev. Co. v. Implement Dealers Mut. Fire Ins. Co., 75 N.D. 608, 31
N.W.2d 495 (1948) (error to admit written report
of defendant's investigator, who testified); 4 Wigmore, Evidence § 1132.

62. § 34, supra. The opposite party is, of course,
entitled to a jury instruction as to the limited use
of the evidence. Winchester & Partridge Mfg.
Co. v. Creary, 116 U.S. 161 (1885); Ritter v. People,
130 Ill. 255, 22 N.E. 605 (1889); Medlin v. Board
of Education, 167 N.C. 239, 83 S.E. 483 (1914).
Failure to give the instruction, even though not
requested, has been held plain error. United States
v. Lipscomb, 425 F.2d 226 (6th Cir. 1970).

63. See § 49, supra.

64. State v. Saporen, 205 Minn. 358, 285 N.W. 898
(1939); Ruhala v. Roby, 379 Mich. 102, 150 N.W.2d
146 (1967); Beaver and Biggs, Attending Witnesses' Prior Declarations as Evidence: Theory vs.
Reality, 3 Ind.Leg.Forum 309 (1970). The Supreme Court of California used the same logic
to conclude that a departure from traditional doctrine violated the Sixth Amendment right of confrontation. People v. Johnson, 68 Cal.2d 646, 68
Cal.Rptr. 599, 441 P.2d 111 (1968) cert. denied 393
U.S. 1051, and People v. Green, 70 Cal.2d 654, 75
Cal.Rptr. 782, 451 P.2d 422 (1969). This conclusion was rejected and Green reversed in California
v. Green, 399 U.S. 149 (1970). See also on remand, People v. Green, 3 Cal.3d 981, 92 Cal.Rptr.
494, 479 P.2d 998 (1971).

65. Morgan, Hearsay Dangers and the Application
of the Hearsay Concept, 62 Harv.L.Rev. 177 (1948),
in Selected Writings on Evidence and Trial 764
(Fryer ed. 1957). See 6 Wigmore, Evidence § 1827
for discussions of value of oath and id. § 1831 for
similar references on the efficacy of penalties for
perjury.

ably be regarded as a case of nonhearsay rather than as a hearsay exception.[66]

(2) The principal reliance for achieving credibility is no doubt cross-examination,[67] and this condition is thought to be satisfied. As Wigmore, who originally adhered to the traditional view, expressed it:

"Here, however, by hypothesis the witness is present and subject to cross-examination. There is ample opportunity to test him as to the basis for his former statement. The whole purpose of the hearsay rule has been already satisfied."[68]

The question remains whether cross-examination in order to be effective must take place at the time when the statement is made. The opinion where the orthodox view finds its most vigorous support urges:

"The chief merit of cross-examination is not that at some future time it gives the party opponent the right to dissect adverse testimony. Its principal virtue is the immediate application of the testing process. Its strokes fall while the iron is hot. False testimony is apt to harden and become unyielding to the blows of truth in proportion as the witness has opportunity for reconsideration and influence by the suggestions of others   .   .   ."[69]

Yet the fact in the case was that the witness did change his story very substantially; rather than hardening, his testimony yielded to something between the giving of the statement and the time of testifying.[70] This ap-

pears to be so in a very high proportion of the cases, and the circumstances most frequently suggest that the "something" which caused the change was an improper influence.

(3) With respect to affording the trier of fact the advantage of observing the demeanor of the witness while testifying, the considerations are similar to those respecting cross-examination. As Judge Learned Hand's classic statement puts it:

"If, from all that the jury see of the witness, they conclude that what he says now is not the truth, but what he said before, they are none the less deciding from what they see and hear of that person and in court."[71]

An additional persuasive factor against the orthodox rule is the superior trustworthiness of earlier statements, on the basis that memory hinges on recency. The prior statement is always nearer and usually very much nearer to the event than is the testimony. The fresher the memory, the fuller and more accurate it is.[72] The requirement of the hearsay exception for memoranda of past recollection, that the matter have been recorded while fresh in memory,[73] is based precisely on this principle.

These various considerations led to a substantial movement to abandon the orthodox view completely. Thus the Model Code of Evidence provided:

"Evidence of a hearsay declaration is admissible if the judge finds that the de-

---

66. See § 254, infra.

67. Morgan, op.cit., supra n. 65; 5 Wigmore, Evidence § 1367.

68. 3A Wigmore, Evidence (Chadbourn rev.) § 1018, p. 996. See also Model Code of Evidence, Comment to Rule 503(b), p. 234.

69. State v. Saporen, 205 Minn. 358, 362, 285 N.W. 898, 901 (1939).

70. Both *Saporen*, supra n. 69, and Ruhala v. Roby, 379 Mich. 102, 150 N.W.2d 146 (1967), a more recent vociferous defense of the orthodox view,

reveal a searching disclosure of the inconsistencies between earlier statement and testimony and of the witness' explanation of his change of position.

71. Di Carlo v. United States, 6 F.2d 364, 368 (2d Cir. 1925).

72. See Stewart, Perception, Memory, and Hearsay: A Criticism of Present Law and the Proposed Federal Rules of Evidence, 1970 Utah L.Rev. 1, 8–22, discussing the characteristics of memory and citing numerous psychological authorities.

73. See § 301, infra.

clarant . . . is present and subject to cross-examination." [74]

The same position was taken in the Uniform Rules [75] and substantial support for it began to appear in the decisions.[76]

Nevertheless some uneasiness was manifested lest complete rejection of the orthodox view encourage a practice whereby lawyers would offer in evidence a carefully prepared statement in lieu of testimony, merely tendering the witness to be cross-examined concerning it. Such a practice seems not in fact to have materialized in jurisdictions following the lead of Wigmore and the Model Code, due no doubt to the trial bar's conclusion that testimony of a live witness in the vast majority of cases carries greater conviction than his previously prepared statement. Nevertheless, the abuse of prepared statements was a substantial possibility. The result was an intermediate position, neither rejecting nor admitting prior statements of witnesses *in toto*, but allowing certain ones thought by circumstances to be free of the danger of abuse, namely, statements of identification, inconsistent statements, and consistent statements when admissible to rebut a charge of "recent fabrication."

Statements of identification. When A testifies that on a prior occasion B pointed to the accused and said, "That's the man who robbed me," the testimony is clearly hearsay. If, however, B is present in court and available for cross-examination, a case within the present section is presented. Similarly if B has himself testified to the prior identification. Admissibility of the prior identification in all these situations has the support of substantial authority in the cases, often without recognition of the presence of a hearsay problem.[77] Recent statutes and rules also favor admissibility.[78] Justification is found in the unsatisfactory nature of courtroom identification [79] and the safeguards which now surround staged out-of-court identifications.[80]

Inconsistent statements. Other than the identification cases, the cases of prior statements of witnesses in the vast majority of instances involve inconsistent statements.[81] Here any planned use of statement in place of witness is unlikely. Moreover, the witness who has told one story aforetime and another today has opened the gates to all the vistas of truth which the common law practice of cross-examination and re-examination was invented to explore. The two questioners will lay bare the sources of the change of face, in forgetfulness, carelessness, pity, terror, or greed, and thus cast light on which is the true story and which the false. It is hard to escape the view that evidence of a previous inconsistent statement, when declarant is on the stand to explain it if he can, has in high

74. Model Code of Evidence Rule 503(b).

75. Uniform Rule 63(1); Kan.Code Civ.P. § 60–460 (a).

76. Jett v. Commonwealth, 436 S.W.2d 788 (Ky. 1969); Thomas v. State, 186 Md. 446, 47 A.2d 43 (1946); Letendre v. Hartford Acc. & Indem. Co., 21 N.Y.2d 518, 289 N.Y.S.2d 183, 236 N.E.2d 467 (1968); Vance v. State, 190 Tenn. 521, 230 S.W.2d 987 (1950) cert. denied 339 U.S. 988. See also the discussion in United States v. De Sisto, 329 F.2d 929 (2d Cir. 1964).

77. Annot., 71 A.L.R.2d 449.

United States v. DeSisto, supra n. 76, was actually a case involving the admissibility of extrajudicial statements of identification by a witness, with the added factors that some of the statements were made before the grand jury and some at a former trial of the case.

78. West's Ann.Cal.Evid.Code § 1238; N.J.Ev.Rule 63(1) (c); F.R.Ev. (R.D.1971) 801(d) (1).

79. 4 Wigmore, Evidence § 1130.

80. United States v. Wade, 388 U.S. 218 (1967); Gilbert v. California, 388 U.S. 263 (1967); Stovall v. Denno, 388 U.S. 293 (1967). Although the California Court generally condemned prior statements of witnesses as violating the right of confrontation, n. 64 supra, admissibility of a prior statement of identification was upheld in People v. Gould, 54 Cal.2d 621, 354 P.2d 865, 7 Cal.Rptr. 273 (1960).

81. See cases cited in n. 76, supra.

degree the safeguards of examined testimony. Allowing it as substantive evidence pays an added dividend in avoiding the ritual of a limiting instruction unlikely to be heeded by a jury. Accordingly, jurisdictions which shy away from admitting prior statements of witnesses generally may not hesitate to admit when the statement is inconsistent with already-given testimony.[82]

A subsidiary question is, when is a prior statement inconsistent? On the face of it, a prior statement describing an event may not be inconsistent with testimony that the witness no longer remembers the event.[83] Yet circumstances clearly may be such as to warrant the judge in concluding that the assertion of lack of memory is untrue and in effect a repudiation of the prior statement, thus justifying its admission in evidence.[84]

Prior consistent statements. While prior consistent statements are hearsay by the traditional view and inadmissible as substantive evidence, they have under that view nevertheless been allowed a limited admissibility for the purpose of supporting the credibility of a witness, particularly to show that a witness whose testimony has allegedly been influenced told the same story before the influence was brought to bear.[85] No sound reason is apparent for denying substantive effect when the statement is otherwise admissible. The witness can be cross-examined fully. No abuse of prepared statements is evident. The attack upon the witness has opened the door. The giving of a limiting

instruction is needless and useless. The trend is in accord with these suggestions.[86]

252. Constitutional Problems of Hearsay: Confrontation and Due Process.[87]

A discussion of constitutional limitations upon the use of hearsay might well commence with the observation that their outline is somewhat less than clear.[88] This unclarity may be the result of choosing the Sixth Amendment as the principal vehicle. The Sixth Amendment to the Federal Constitution adopted in 1787 requires "that in all criminal prosecutions, the accused shall enjoy the right . . . to be confronted with the witnesses against him." Nearly every state constitution has a like provision.[89] Prior to 1965, the federal provision was not applicable to the States,[90] but in that year the Supreme

---

82. Hobbs v. State, 359 P.2d 956 (Alas.1961); Gelhaar v. State, 41 Wis.2d 230, 163 N.W.2d 609 (1969); West's Ann.Cal.Evid.Code, § 1235; N.J. Ev.Rule 63(1) (a); F.R.Ev. (R.D.1971) 801(d) (2).

83. People v. Sam, 71 Cal.2d 194, 77 Cal.Rptr. 804, 454 P.2d 700 (1969) (two years between event and trial). See generally § 34, supra.

84. United States v. Insana, 423 F.2d 1165 (2d Cir. 1970); People v. Green, 3 Cal.3d 981, 92 Cal.Rptr. 494, 479 P.2d 998 (1971).

85. See § 49, supra.

86. Cal.Evid.Code §§ 791, 1236; F.R.Ev. (R.D.1971) 801(d) (1).

87. See generally 5 Wigmore, Evidence §§ 1365, 1395–1400; Note, Confrontation, Cross-Examination, and the Right to Prepare a Defense, 56 Geo. L.J. 939 (1968); Note, The Use of Prior Recorded Testimony and the Right of Confrontation, 54 Iowa L.Rev. 360 (1968); Note, Federal Confrontation: A Not Very Clear Say on Hearsay, 13 U.C. L.A.L.Rev. 366 (1966); Note, Confrontation and the Hearsay Rule, 75 Yale L.J. 1434 (1966); Dec.Dig. Criminal Law ☞662; C.J.S. Criminal Law §§ 999–1009; Annot., 23 L.Ed.2d 853.

88. The point is illustrated by the judicial history of West's Ann.Cal.Evid.Code, § 1235 exempting prior inconsistent statements of a witness from the ban of the hearsay rule. All seven members of the Supreme Court of California united in the conclusion that the admission of such testimony was in violation of the right of confrontation guaranteed by the Constitution of the United States. People v. Johnson, 68 Cal.2d 646, 68 Cal. Rptr. 599, 441 P.2d 111 (1968) cert. denied 393 U.S. 1051; People v. Green, 70 Cal.2d 654, 75 Cal.Rptr. 782, 451 P.2d 422 (1969), vacated and remanded 399 U.S. 149. In California v. Green, 399 U.S. 149 (1970), all but one of the justices of the Supreme Court of the United States agreed that the California Court was in error.

89. They are collected and quoted in 5 Wigmore, Evidence § 1397.

90. West v. Louisiana, 194 U.S. 258 (1904). Of course, a State's interpretation of its own confrontation requirements could, and still may, result in exclusion. See, e. g., State v. Storm, 127 Mont. 414, 265 P.2d 971 (1954).

Court ruled that the Fourteenth Amendment made the federal confrontation clause obligatory upon the States.[91] Consequently the emphasis in this discussion is upon the federal decisions.

The Confrontation Clause in terms is applicable only to criminal prosecutions [92] and may be invoked only by the accused. Thus it is unavailable to the prosecution in a criminal proceeding or to either party in civil litigation.[93] So basic, however, are the values served by confrontation that they are found constitutionally extended to others than the accused in a criminal case as an aspect of due process.[94]

Certain characteristics of the right of confrontation, while relevant to the values sought to be protected by the hearsay rule, do not bear directly upon it. Of these characteristics, one is the right of an accused to be present at every stage of his trial.[95] Another, the scope of which is currently difficult to estimate, is a right to such information prior to trial as may be necessary to enable an ultimate confrontation at trial to be meaningful.[96] Certainly the *Jencks* decision and statute [97] are a limited move in that direction, and the right to counsel at a police-staged lineup is a yet more substantial one.[98] In contrast, despite the enormous impact of sentencing upon one convicted of crime, the right of confrontation is not applicable in a proceeding for that purpose.[99]

Turning to examination of the relationship between the hearsay rule and the constitu-

---

91. Pointer v. Texas, 380 U.S. 400 (1965). The decision resulted in a substantial increase in confrontation cases, which previously had been relatively infrequent.

92. An investigative proceeding may be so essentially criminal in nature as to make the clause applicable. Jenkins v. McKeithen, 395 U.S. 411 (1969) (Louisiana Labor-Management Commission charged with exposing violators of criminal laws).

93. The hearsay rule is, of course, not subject to these limitations.

94. Greene v. McElroy, 360 U.S. 474 (1959) (security clearance proceeding); Willner v. Committee on Character and Fitness, 373 U.S. 96 (1963) (denial of admission to bar after passing examination); Rauh, Nonconfrontation in Security Cases: The Greene Decision, 45 Va.L.Rev. 1175 (1959).

95. The earlier view that a trial could never proceed in the absence of the defendant, Lewis v. United States, 146 U.S. 370 (1892), now stands substantially modified. An accused may lose the right to be present by voluntarily absenting himself after the trial has begun, Diaz v. United States, 223 U.S. 442 (1912), or by conducting himself in so disruptive a manner that the trial cannot proceed with him in the courtroom, Illinois v. Allen, 397 U.S. 337 (1970).

Whether the right of confrontation entitles an accused to be present at a view is discussed in § 216, n. 13, supra.

96. Semerjian, The Right of Confrontation, 55 A.B. A.J. 152 (1969), emphasizing the need of advance information in order to cross-examine effectively; Note, Confrontation, Cross-Examination, and the Right to Prepare a Defense, 56 Geo.L.J. 939 (1968), a somewhat broader approach to defense information generally. Cf. United States ex rel. Meadows v. New York, 426 F.2d 1176 (2d Cir. 1970) (Sixth Amendment does not entitle accused to discovery of all evidence in possession of prosecution but only to test trustworthiness of evidence actually presented against him at trial).

The Sixth Amendment does not require the prosecution to call any particular witness. United States v. Polisi, 416 F.2d 573 (2d Cir. 1969); Eberhart v. United States, 262 F.2d 421 (9th Cir. 1958); Curtis v. Rives, 75 U.S.App.D.C. 66, 123 F.2d 936 (1941.)

97. See § 97, supra.

98. United States v. Wade, 388 U.S. 218 (1967).

99. Williams v. People of State of New York, 337 U.S. 241 (1949) (trial judge overrode jury recommendation of life imprisonment and imposed death sentence on basis of pre-sentence report; held, consistent with modern penological philosophy of fitting the punishment to the offender, not readily accomplished through open-court testimony with cross-examination; due process not violated). For critical comment see Note, 81 Harv.L.Rev. 821, 826–829 (1968). Controversy centers in fact, not upon the question of confrontation, but upon whether the report shall be disclosed to the accused. A.B.A. Project on Minimum Standards for Criminal Justice, Standards Relating to Sentencing Alternatives and Procedures §§ 4.3–4.5 and Commentary, pp. 210–228 (1968). In Specht v. Patterson, 386 U.S. 605 (1967), the Court held *Williams* inapplicable to sentencing to an indeterminate life sentence under the Colorado Sex Offenders Act, following a conviction of indecent liberties carrying a maximum of 10 years. The Court pointed out that sentencing under the Act required new findings, thus resembling recidivist statutes, bringing confrontation into play.

tional right of confrontation, the confrontation cases emphasize the importance of (1) personal presence of the witness at the trial,[1] enabling the trier to observe his demeanor as an aid in evaluating his credibility and making false accusation more unlikely because of the presence of the accused and the solemnity of the occasion, and (2) affording opportunity for cross-examination.[2] Yet, as will be seen, neither presence of the witness

nor cross-examination is indispensable in every case. Indeed, on occasion both may be dispensed with.

The similarity to the underpinnings of the hearsay rule is evident.[3] In the late 1700's when confrontation provisions were first included in American bills of rights, the general rule against hearsay had been accepted in England for a hundred years,[4] but it was equally well established that hearsay under certain circumstances might be admitted.[5] A fair appraisal may be that the purpose of the American provisions was to guarantee the maintenance in criminal cases of the hard-won principle of the hearsay rule, without abandoning the accepted exceptions which had not been questioned as to fairness, but forbidding especially the practice of using depositions taken in the absence of the accused.[6] This last had been much complained of,[7] and was later abandoned by the English judges [8] and forbidden by statute.[9] While the Clause, as it appears in the Sixth Amendment, in terms makes no provision for exceptions, in fact it has not so been construed.[10]

---

1. Barber v. Page, 390 U.S. 719 (1968) (at time of trial, witness was incarcerated in federal penitentiary in adjoining state; prosecution made no effort to induce federal authorities to produce him; held error to admit transcript of his testimony given at preliminary hearing, even asuming waiver of right to cross-examine at preliminary hearing. "The right to confrontation is basically a trial right. It includes both the opportunity to cross-examine and the occasion for the jury to weigh the demeanor of the witness." P. 725.) In Mattox v. United States, 156 U.S. 237, 242 (1895) the Court pointed out that the primary purpose of the Confrontation Clause "was to prevent depositions or *ex parte* affidavits . . . in lieu of a personal examination and cross-examination of the witness in which the accused has an opportunity, not only of testing the recollection and sifting the conscience of the witness, but of compelling him to stand face to face with the jury in order that they may look at him, and judge by his demeanor on the stand and the manner in which he gives his testimony whether he is worthy of belief."

2. Pointer v. Texas, 380 U.S. 400 (1965) (error to admit at trial testimony given by now absent witness at preliminary hearing where accused was not represented by counsel. "It cannot seriously be doubted . . . that the right of cross-examination is included in the right of an accused in a criminal case to confront the witnesses against him." P. 404. "Because the transcript" was not taken "at a time and under circumstances affording petitioner through counsel an adequate opportunity to cross-examine" confrontation was denied. P. 407.).

Douglas v. Alabama, 380 U.S. 415 (1965) (prosecutor called accomplice, who refused to testify on grounds of self-incrimination; prosecutor then read his confession, implicating accused, in sections, asking after each whether witness had made that statement and meeting in each instance refusal to answer on grounds of the privilege; held error, since the statement was in fact before the jury and could not be cross-examined upon. "Our cases construing the clause hold that a primary interest secured by it is the right of cross-examination . . . .")

3. See § 245, supra.

4. See § 244, supra.

5. E. g., former testimony, Rex v. Vipont, 2 Burr. 1163, 97 Eng.Repr. 767 (1761); Rex v. Radbourne, 1 Leach C.L. 457 (1787); Rex v. Jolliffe, 4 Term R. 285, 100 Eng.Repr. 1022 (1791), all cited 15 A.L.R. 498, 500; and dying declarations, 5 Wigmore, Evidence § 1430; § 281, supra.

6. "The primary object of the constitutional provision in question was to prevent depositions or *ex parte* affidavits . . . being used against the prisoner in lieu of a personal examination and cross-examination of the witness . . . ." Mattox v. United States, 156 U.S. 237, 242 (1895).

7. 1 Stephen, Hist.Crim.Law of England 225 (1883).

8. 5 Wigmore, Evidence § 1364(8); 9 Holdsworth, Hist.Eng.Law 219 (1926).

9. 11 and 12 Vict. ch. 42 (1848), known as Sir John Jervis's Act; see 1 Stephen, Hist.Crim.Law of England 220 (1883).

10. Situations which have been held not to violate the right of confrontation include dying declarations, Mattox v. United States, 156 U.S. 237 (1895); declarations of a co-conspirator, Delaney v. United States, 263 U.S. 586 (1924), Dutton v. Evans, 400

That departures may be allowable does not, of course, mean that they coincide completely with those of the hearsay rule, a conclusion that becomes more evident when the hearsay aspect is measured by State rules of evidence and the constitutional confrontation standard is federal. In fact the Supreme Court on more than one occasion has expressly rejected the idea that the hearsay rule and the right of confrontation are simply different ways of stating the same thing.[11] Nevertheless, instances in which an item of evidence admissible under traditional hearsay concepts has been held to violate the confrontation right are rare.[12] On the other hand, the clause has not stood as a solid barrier to liberalization of the admissibility of hearsay.[13]

If the word "witness" in the Confrontation Clause is read as including hearsay declarants, the literal result would be the exclusion of all hearsay, since the clause contains no exceptions. As indicated above, this has not been the result. The fact is that some hearsay is constitutionally admissible,[14] some is not.[15] The confrontation clause may be too blunt an instrument for effecting a satisfactory division in view of its uncompromising terms.[16] Perhaps it should be reserved for dealing with the problems discussed earlier in this section,[17] leaving hearsay to be treated under the more flexible concept of due process.[18]

U.S. 74 (1970); former testimony of a now unavailable witness when opportunity for cross-examination was afforded, Mattox v. United States, supra, California v. Green, 399 U.S. 149 (1970); recorded past recollection, United States v. Kelly, 349 F.2d 720 (2d Cir. 1965); public records, especially those of routine character, Reed v. Beto, 343 F.2d 723 (5th Cir. 1965), Note 56 Geo.L.J. 939, 943–944 (1968); and entries in the regular course of business, United States v. Lipscomb, 435 F.2d 795 (5th Cir. 1971), Hanley v. United States, 416 F.2d 1160 (5th Cir. 1969); cf. United States v. Williams, 424 F.2d 344, on rehearing 431 F.2d 1168 (1970), and see Comment, 56 Geo.L.J. 939, 944–945 (1968).

11. Stein v. New York, 346 U.S. 156, 196 (1953), Jackson, J.: "The hearsay-evidence rule, with all its subtleties, anomalies and ramifications, will not be read into the Fourteenth Amendment."

California v. Green, 399 U.S. 149, 155 (1970): "While it may readily be conceded that hearsay rules and the Confrontation Clause are generally designed to protect similar values, it is quite a different thing to suggest that the overlap is complete and that the Confrontation Clause is nothing more or less than a codification of the rules of hearsay and their exceptions as they existed historically at common law."

12. Possible examples are Kirby v. United States, 174 U.S. 47 (1899) (error to convict of possessing stolen postage stamps when only evidence of theft was record of conviction of thieves), with which compare Uniform Rule 63(20); and Barber v. Page, 390 U.S. 719 (1968), expanding the requirement of unavailability beyond what previously had rather widely been thought necessary.

13. California v. Green, 399 U.S. 149 (1970) (broadened admissibility of prior statements of witnesses sustained); Dutton v. Evans, 400 U.S. 74 (1970) (sustained conviction in which judge admitted declaration of co-conspirator on greatly expanded theory, four judges dissenting). In Snyder v. Massachusetts, 291 U.S. 97, 107 (1934), Cardozo, J., the Court said with respect to confrontation exceptions, "The exceptions are not even static, but may be enlarged from time to time if there is no material departure from the reason of the general rule." See also Mattox v. United States, 156 U.S. 237, 243–244 (1895).

14. See n. 10, supra.

15. E. g., Barber v. Page, n. 1, supra, and cases cited in n. 2, supra.

16. Comment, Confrontation, Cross-Examination, and the Right to Prepare a Defense, 56 Geo.L.J. 939 (1968).

17. See Note, Confrontation and the Hearsay Rule, 75 Yale L.J. 1434 (1966) suggesting that the Confrontation Clause be construed as a "standard of prosecutorial behavior."

18. In California v. Green, 399 U.S. 149, 182 (1970), a rather literal reading of the Confrontation Clause led Mr. Justice Harlan, in a concurring opinion, to assert that its effect was to require "the production of a witness when he is available to testify." However, in a concurring opinion in Dutton v. Evans, 400 U.S. 74, 95, 96 (1970), he recognized that his earlier position would result in excluding much that was acceptable (business records, official statements, learned treatises, trade reports). He concluded that the Confrontation Clause was "not well designed for taking into account the numerous factors which must be weighed in passing on the appropriateness of rules of evidence" and that due process was a more suitable standard.

In Note, Preserving the Right to Confrontation—A New Approach to Hearsay Evidence in Criminal Cases, 113 U.Pa.L.Rev. 741 (1965), a rather wholesale rejection of hearsay exceptions is based on an overly literal reading of the clause.

253. Unavailability and the Hearsay Exceptions.[19]

Several exceptions to the hearsay rule [20] involve a requirement that the declarant be shown to be unavailable as a witness at the present trial. Historically the determination of what satisfies the requirement of unavailability has been worked out in connection with each of these particular exceptions, but today this approach has little to commend it. Whether unavailability should be required is, of course, a question to be resolved in connection with each exception,[21] but as uniform as possible a pattern of what constitutes unavailability is desirable and represents the current trend.[22] Differences in the situation of a criminal accused, constitutional or otherwise, may, however, demand or justify differences in treatment.

When unavailability of the declarant is made a condition precedent to admitting his hearsay statement, a rule of preference is in fact being stated. His personal presence in court, under oath and subject to cross-examination, would be preferred. If, however, that cannot be had, then his hearsay statement falling within the particular hearsay exception, although admittedly inferior, is still to be preferred over doing entirely without evidence from that source. Thus the group of hearsay exceptions where unavailability is required are in a sense second class in comparison with the far larger number of exceptions where availability or unavailability is simply not a factor.

In line with the discussion in the preceding section, unavailability as a condition precedent to dispensing with personal presence and cross-examination of a declarant is difficult to reconcile with the Confrontation Clause. Either the accused is "confronted with the witnesses against him" or he is not, and reasons why he is not confronted seem to have no place under the clause. If, however, the situation is approached as a problem of due process, this difficulty seems to disappear. In any event, whether the appropriate formula is due process or a somewhat tortured version of confrontation, the courts have attached substantial importance to the unavailability requirement and to what satisfies it.

Preliminarily it may be observed that while the rather general practice is to speak loosely of unavailability of the witness, the critical factor is actually the unavailability of his testimony.[23] As will be seen, the witness may be physically present in court but his testimony nevertheless unavailable. Of course if the unavailability is by procurement of the party offering the hearsay state-

---

19. See 5 Wigmore, Evidence §§ 1401–1414, 1456; Note, Evidence: The Unavailability Requirement of Declaration Against Interest Hearsay, 55 Iowa L. Rev. 477 (1969); Note, Hearsay Under the Proposed Federal Rules: A Discretionary Approach, 15 Wayne L.Rev. 1079, 1101–1106 (1969); C.J.S. Criminal Law § 892, n. 21; C.J.S. Evidence §§ 391–396; 29 Am.Jur.2d Evidence §§ 618, 750–759; Dec. Dig. Evidence ⚖284, 576, 577, Criminal Law ⚖542, 543.

20. The usual ones are declarations against interest, § 280, infra; dying declarations, § 282, infra; statements of pedigree and family history, § 322, infra; and former testimony, § 255, infra. See the cited sections for further treatment of unavailability with respect to the particular exceptions. After an uneasy history, unavailability has virtually disappeared as a requirement of entries in the regular course of business. See § 311, infra.

The great bulk of the cases have arisen in connection with former testimony, and most of the citations in this section are of that variety.

21. See sections cited in n. 20, supra.

For advocacy of extending the unavailability requirement to additional hearsay exceptions where not now applicable, see Stewart, Perception, Memory, and Hearsay: A Criticism of Present Law and the Proposed Federal Rules of Evidence, 1970 Utah L. Rev. 1, 25–36.

22. See, e. g., the comprehensive definitions in Uniform Rule 62(7), West's Ann.Cal.Evid.Code, § 240, N.J.Ev.R. 62(6), F.R.Ev. (R.D.1971) 804(a).

23. Mason v. United States, 408 F.2d 903 (10th Cir. 1969); Johnson v. People, 152 Colo. 586, 384 P.2d 454 (1963), cert. denied 376 U.S. 922; State v. Stewart, 85 Kan. 404, 116 P. 489 (1911).

ment, the requirement ought not to be regarded as satisfied.[24]

In principle probably anything which constitutes unavailability in fact ought to be considered adequate. However, the rules have grown up around certain recurring fact situations, and the problem is therefore approached in that pattern. Depositions receive special treatment at the end of the section.

(1) *Death*, of course, satisfies the requirement of unavailability and was the form which it originally assumed with respect to most of the exceptions.[25]

(2) *Absence*. If a witness cannot be found, he obviously is unavailable.[26] The degree of effort which must be made to find him is usually described as "due diligence," which is susceptible of requiring greater effort when the hearsay evidence is offered against an accused than in other situations.[27] Absence by procurement of the opposite

party would seem in any event to be a sufficient showing of unavailability.[28]

Permanent or indefinite absence from the state was commonly held to satisfy the unavailability requirement in both civil [29] and criminal cases, but that view, as will be seen, is no longer valid when the hearsay evidence is offered against an accused. In the civil cases, sometimes an additional showing is required that the deposition of the witness could not have been taken,[30] and sometimes one that the witness cannot be induced voluntarily to return and testify.[31] The significance of absence from the jurisdiction lies actually in being immune to process to compel attendance. Therefore, if the reach of a subpoena does not extend throughout the jurisdiction, then absence beyond its reach, even though still within the jurisdiction, should suffice.[32] While temporary absence

---

24. Motes v. United States, 178 U.S. 458 (1900) (chief witness for government disappeared from custody because of extraordinary conduct of officer in charge of case, which Court charitably described as "negligent"); Uniform Rule 62(7); West's Ann.Cal.Evid.Code § 240; N.J.Ev.Rule 62 (6); F.R.Ev. (R.D.1971) 804(a).

25. Mattox v. United States, 156 U.S. 237 (1895) (former testimony).

26. Commonwealth v. Gallo, 275 Mass. 320, 175 N.E. 718 (1931); State v. Ortego, 22 Wash.2d 552, 157 P.2d 320 (1945).

27. Instances of due diligence as against an accused: Commonwealth v. Gallo, supra n. 26 (search at places witness known to frequent and inquiry of numerous persons who knew her); State v. Ortego, supra n. 26 ("diligent search and due inquiry"). Lack of diligence: State v. Carr, 67 S.D. 481, 294 N.W. 174 (1940) (not at home; inquiry of neighbor). See 5 Wigmore, Evidence § 1405; C.J.S. Evidence § 393, n. 94.

Compare the Iowa practice under statute construed to allow testimony at former trial simply on showing witness is not in court, La Sell v. Tri-States Theater Corp., 235 Iowa 492, 17 N.W.2d 89 (1945), but held not applicable to testimony given at preliminary hearing, State v. Washington, 160 N.W.2d 337 (Iowa 1968).

McCormick et al on Evid. 2nd Ed. HB—39

28. Reynolds v. United States, 98 U.S. 145, 158 (1878); Patterson v. Ward, 61 So.2d 595 (La.App. 1952); State v. Brown, 285 S.W. 995 (Mo.1926); State v. Maynard, 184 N.C. 653, 113 S.E. 682 (1922); C.J.S. Evidence § 393, n. 6.

29. Wolski v. National Life & Acc. Ins. Co., 135 Neb. 643, 283 N.W. 381 (1939) (permanent); Healy v. Rennert, 9 N.Y.2d 202, 213 N.Y.S.2d 44, 173 N.E.2d 777 (1961) (permanent); Norton v. State, 148 Tex. Cr.R. 294, 186 S.W.2d 347 (Tex.Cr.1945) (time of return indefinite).

30. Stephens v. Hoffman, 275 Ill. 497, 114 N.E. 142 (1916); A. T. Stearns Lbr. Co. v. Howlett, 239 Mass. 59, 131 N.E. 217 (1921); 31A C.J.S. Evidence § 393, n. 96; and see Uniform Rule 62(7). This added requirement imposes a needless burden, particularly difficult to justify in the case of former testimony with its great similarity to a deposition. Contra, Toledo Traction Co. v. Cameron, 69 C.C.A. 28, 137 F. 48 (1905); Ross-Lewin v. Germania Life Ins. Co., 20 Colo.App. 262, 78 P. 305 (1904); West's Ann.Cal. Evid.Code, § 240; F.R.Ev. (R.D.1971) 804(a).

31. C.J.S. Evidence § 393, n. 97. Contra, Giberson v. Patterson Mills Co., 187 Pa. 513, 41 A. 525 (1898); McGovern v. Smith, 75 Vt. 104, 53 A. 326 (1902).

32. Toledo Traction Co. v. Cameron, 137 F. 48 (6th Cir. 1905); Gaty v. United Rys. Co., 251 S.W. 61 (Mo.1923). That the difference may be substantial is indicated by the federal provisions: 100 miles in civil cases, F.R.Civ.P. 45(e) (1), and throughout the United States in criminal cases, F.R.Crim.P. 17(e) (1).

has been held sufficient,[33] the situation would seem to be one more appropriately dealt with according to principles governing continuances.[34]

In criminal cases the pattern of unavailability by reason of absence was changed substantially from the foregoing by the Supreme Court's decision in Barber v. Page.[35] In an Oklahoma prosecution for armed robbery, one of the defendants testified for the State at the preliminary hearing. At the time of trial this witness was incarcerated in a federal penitentiary in Texas, 225 miles distant from the place of trial. Other than ascertaining this fact, the State made no effort to obtain his presence. The transcript of his preliminary hearing testimony was admitted. The Supreme Court reversed the conviction on grounds of denial of confrontation. Mere absence from the jurisdiction, said the Court, is no longer sufficient to dispense with confrontation. For witnesses not in prison, the Uniform Act To Secure the Attendance of Witnesses from Without a State in Criminal Proceedings [36] generally provides a means for in effect extraditing a witness. And if a witness is in prison, cooperation now being given by governing authorities in this respect no longer makes it impossible to obtain his attendance. In either event a good faith effort must be made to obtain the presence of the witness at the trial, either by proceeding under the Uniform Act [37] or taking appropriate steps to induce the incarcerating authorities to produce him.

(3) *Physical disability* to attend the trial or to testify is a recognized ground.[38] The scarcity of decisions passing upon the degree of permanency required leads to the conclusion that most of the cases involving temporary disability are handled by continuance. However, some authority accepts a temporary disability as sufficient.[39] As in the cases where absence is relied upon to satisfy the requirement, a higher standard may now well be demanded when the hearsay evidence is offered against an accused. A mere temporary disability appears not to conform with the standard established by Barber v. Page.[40]

---

33. Mechanics Bank v. Woodward, 74 Conn. 689, 51 A. 1084 (1902); Minneapolis Mill Co. v. Minneapolis, etc. R. Co., 51 Minn. 304, 53 N.W. 639 (1892). Contra, Williams v. Calloway, 281 Ala. 249, 201 So.2d 506 (1967). See C.J.S. Evidence § 393, n. 2, 3.

34. E. g., Ill.Supreme Ct. Rule 231 (S.H.A. ch. 110A): "Motions for Continuance

"(a) *Absense of Material Evidence.* If either party applies for a continuance of a cause on account of the absence of material evidence, the motion shall be supported by the affidavit of the party so applying or his authorized agent. The affidavit shall show (1) that due diligence has been used to obtain the evidence, or the want of time to obtain it; (2) of what particular fact or facts the evidence consists; (3) if the evidence consists of the testimony of a witness, his place of residence, or if his place of residence is not known, that due diligence has been used to ascertain it; and (4) that if further time is given the evidence can be procured.

"(b) *When Continuance Will Be Denied.* If the court is satisfied that the evidence would not be material, or if the other party will admit the affidavit in evidence as proof only of what the absent witness would testify to if present, the continuance shall be denied unless the court, for the furtherance of justice, shall consider a continuance necessary."

35. 390 U.S. 719 (1968).

36. 9 U.L.A. 50 (1967 supp.).

37. The case did not, of course, actually deal with the question of witnesses not in custody. That problem was, however, passed upon in Berger v. California, 393 U.S. 314 (1969) consistently with the statement in the text. See on remand People v. Berger, 272 Cal.App.2d 584, 77 Cal.Rptr. 617 (1969).

38. Vigoda v. Barton, 348 Mass. 478, 204 N.E.2d 441, 26 A.L.R.3d 482 (1965) (illness must be such as to render witness unable to travel); Norburn v. Mackie, 264 N.Car. 479, 141 S.E.2d 877 (1965) (must be detrimental to health to appear as witness).

39. Chase v. Springvale Mills Co., 75 Me. 156 (1883); People v. Droste, 160 Mich. 66, 125 N.W. 87 (1910); Harris v. Reeves, 421 S.W.2d 689 (Tex.Civ.App. 1967).

40. Supra n. 35.

Compare Peterson v. United States, 344 F.2d 419 (5th Cir. 1965) (pregnancy with complications not sufficient) and People v. King, 269 Cal.App.2d 40, 74 Cal.Rptr. 679 (1969) (unavailability established by testimony that witness was suffering from cerebral

(4) *Mental incapacity.* The decisions, in general terms, recognize insanity as a ground of unavailability.[41] They do not discuss the question whether the derangement must be such that it disqualifies the person from testifying about the matter in question. Of course, not all insanity renders the witness so incompetent. Competency to testify requires only a minimum degree of ability to observe, remember and recount.[42] If the person is proved to have become insane since the hearsay statement was made, it seems that the admission of the statement should depend not on whether the subsequent insanity has rendered the witness incompetent, but whether having in mind the witness's later loss of mental powers the previous statement is probably substantially more reliable than the present testimony of the insane person would be, a question upon which some discretion must be conceded to the trial court.[43]

(5) *Failure of memory.* If the witness has lost his memory of the relevant matters, because of the failure of his faculties due to disease or senility, this is a good ground of unavailability.[44] If the gap in the recollection or fading of memory is due merely to the lapse of time, the effect is the same, namely the inability of the witness to give to the court his former firsthand knowledge of the facts. In common sense it seems that the legal consequence, that is, the use of the former testimony, should likewise be the same.[45] Some courts, however, have jibbed at this point, on the ground that this would open the door to a perjured claim of forgetfulness by a witness who learns that the adversary has discovered facts which give a new handle for cross-examination.[46] The danger of the success of such an attempt, which would expose the witness to cross-examination on his motives and his memory, seems greatly outweighed by the need for the use of the former testimony when the assertion of forgetfulness is true. Forgetfulness by a disinterested witness of facts of no personal moment to him, in the course of a delayed lawsuit, is frequent and familiar enough. The inconvenience of this narrow view, that forgetfulness is not a ground of unavailability, it seems, should be avoided by treating lapse of memory if complete as a ground of unavailability, or if partial as a

---

thrombosis, was confused and unable to speak; that condition was unlikely to clear up for another 8 weeks; that witness could not then be moved to court to testify).

41. United States v. Hughes, 411 F.2d 461 (2d Cir. 1969) (supervening schizophrenia); Marler v. State, 67 Ala. 55, 65, 42 Am.Rep. 95 (1880) ("There is no real or practical difference between the death of the mind and the death of the body." But there is. One is total, the other may be partial, and not disqualifying.); Atwood v. Atwood, 86 Conn. 579, 89 A. 29, Ann.C.1914B 281; Whitaker v. Marsh, 62 N.H. 477 (1883) ("mental condition was such he was incapacitated to testify"); Security Realty & Development Co. v. Bunch, 143 S.W.2d 687 (Tex. Civ.App.1940).

42. See § 62, supra.

43. See People v. Crandall, 43 Cal.App.2d 238, 110 P.2d 682 (1941) where a somewhat comparable problem was presented. See also Tift v. Jones, 74 Ga. 469 (1885) where it was held that the deposition of a witness taken when he was well and strong would be admitted, though the witness testified at the trial, where the latter testimony was hesitating and uncertain due to illness and weakening of memory.

44. United States v. Hughes, 411 F.2d 461 (2d Cir. 1969) (terms schizophrenia and memory failure used interchangeably); State v. New Orleans Waterworks Co., 107 La. 1, 38, 31 So. 395 (1901); Rothrock v. Gallaher, 91 Pa. 108, 112 (1879); 5 Wigmore, Evidence § 1408; Annot., 129 A.L.R. 843, 845.

45. Support for this view is found in the authorities holding that unavailability is established by refusal to testify. See text at n. 50, infra.

46. Rio Grande Southern Ry. Co. v. Campbell, 55 Colo. 493, 136 P. 68, Ann.C.1914C, 573; A. T. Stearns Lumber Co. v. Howlett, 239 Mass. 59, 61, 131 N.E. 217 (1921). See also, to similar effect in rejecting this as a ground of unavailability, Stein v. Swenson, 46 Minn. 360, 49 N.W. 55, 24 Am.St.Rep. 234 (1891); Turner v. Missouri-Kansas-Texas Ry. Co., 346 Mo. 28, 142 S.W.2d 455, 129 A.L.R. 829 (1940); Velott v. Lewis, 102 Pa. 326, 333 (1883); C.J.S. Evidence § 395, n. 14. Contra (sustaining forgetfulness as a ground): Anderson v. Gaither, 120 Fla. 263, 162 So. 877 (1935) and see 5 Wigmore, Evidence § 1408, note 6.

ground for admitting both the former, and the present testimony of the witness.[47] Perhaps a liberalization for former testimony of the requirements for memoranda of past recollection recorded, especially the requirement as to the time of making the memorandum, might be a convenient basis for this extension of the use of former testimony.[48]

(6) *Exercise of privilege.* The exercise of a privilege not to testify renders the witness unavailable to the extent of the scope of the privilege.[49]

(7) *Refusal to testify.* If a witness simply refuses to testify, despite the bringing to bear upon him of all appropriate judicial pressures, the conclusion that as a practical matter he is unavailable can scarcely be avoided, and that is the holding of the great weight of authority.[50]

(8) *Supervening disqualification.*[51] If the witness was competent at the time the former testimony was taken, but later becomes incompetent, as by the death of the adverse party, under the Dead Man's Statutes,[52] or by becoming so insane as to disqualify him to testify,[53] the requirement of unavailability is satisfied.

Depositions.[54] Unavailability may appear as a requirement at two different stages in connection with depositions: (1) the right to take a deposition at all may be subject to certain conditions, of which the most common is unavailability to testify at the trial,[55]

---

47. See Anderson v. Gaither, 120 Fla. 263, 162 So. 877, 879 (1935) ("The admission in evidence of Stuart's deposition taken in 1929, although Stuart was personally in court and called as a witness at the last trial held in 1933, was (at least) within the sound discreion of the court, when it appeared from the circumstances that witness's memory at time of giving the earlier deposition was obviously clearer as to details than his personal testimony given from the witness stand four years later. Both versions together constituted appropriate evidence to be received and considered in connection with each other."—citing authorities).

48. See the discussion of the requirements of that theory, § 301, infra. Instances of cases of the admission of former testimony where it seems that the court may have been influenced by this analogy: People v. McFarlane, 138 Cal. 481, 487, 488, 71 P. 568 (1903); State v. New Orleans Waterworks Co., 107 La. 1, 38, 31 So. 395 (1901).

49. United States v. Elmore, 423 F.2d 775 (4th Cir. 1970); Annot., 45 A.L.R.2d 1354. And see United States v. Mobley, 421 F.2d 345 (5th Cir. 1970) (refusal to testify based on unjustifiable reliance on Fifth Amendment; Mason v. United States, 408 F. 2d 903 (10th Cir. 1969) (same). The privileges invoked commonly are self-incrimination or interspousal.

50. United States v. Mobley, 421 F.2d 345 (1970); Mason, v. United States, 408 F.2d 903 (10th Cir. 1969); Johnson v. People, 152 Colo. 586, 384 P.2d 454 (1963); People v. Pickett, 339 Mich. 294, 63 N.W.2d 681, 45 A.L.R.2d 1341 (1954). Contra, Pleau v. State, 255 Wis. 362, 38 N.W.2d 496 (1949).

51. See Wigmore, Evidence § 1409.

52. Habig v. Bastian, 117 Fla. 864, 158 So. 508 (1935).

53. See § 62, supra.

54. 5 Wigmore, Evidence §§ 1411, 1415, 1416; 23 Am.Jur.2d Depositions §§ 7, 11, 112–120, 311; C.J. S. Depositions §§ 9–16, 92(2).

55. E. g., F.R.Crim.P. 15(a): "When Taken. If it appears that a prospective witness may be unable to attend or prevented from attending a trial or hearing, that his testimony is material and that it is necessary to take his deposition in order to prevent a failure of justice, the court at any time after the filing of an indictment or information may upon motion of a defendant and notice to the parties order that his testimony be taken by deposition and that any designated books, papers, documents or tangible objects, not privileged, be produced at the same time and place. If a witness is committed for failure to give bail to appear to testify at a trial or hearing, the court on written motion of the witness and upon notice to the parties may direct that his deposition be taken. After the deposition has been subscribed the court may discharge the witness."

See 8 Moore's Federal Practice (Cipes) ¶¶ 15.01, 15.03 (1970); Wright, Federal Practice and Procedure: Criminal § 241.

For state statutes and rules containing similar restrictions in both civil and criminal cases, see 5 Wigmore, Evidence § 1411.

Restrictions on the right to take a deposition lose their significance and tend to disappear as emphasis on depositions shifts away from use at trial as a substitute for testimony by the deponent in person to such other uses as discovery and obtaining statements with a view to impeachment or introduction as an admission of a party-opponent. Thus no general restrictions upon the right to take depositions are imposed by the Federal Rules of Civil Procedure and State rules patterned upon

or (2) the right to use a deposition at the trial in place of the personal appearance of the deponent is usually conditioned upon his unavailability.[56] The matter is largely governed by statute or rule, and those in force locally should be consulted.[57]

The use of depositions in criminal cases requires particular consideration in view of the higher standards of confrontation applicable to evidence presented against an accused. Legislation providing for depositions in criminal cases, sometimes by express constitutional sanction, is in effect in a number of jurisdictions.[58] No problems except those of policy are apparent when the deposition is to be taken and used by the accused.[59] When,

however, the deposition is to be used *against* the accused, it seems evident that the unavailability standards of Barber v. Page,[60] previously discussed in this section, are applicable.[61] If these standards are met, there must, of course, be meaningful opportunity to confront and cross-examine, with its concomitant right to counsel, when the deposition is taken.[62]

---

them, although judicial restraints may be imposed in exceptional situations. See F.R.Civ.P. 26(c), 30(d).

56. E. g., F.R.Civ.P. 32(a) (3):

"The deposition of a witness, whether or not a party, may be used by any party for any purpose if the court finds: (A) that the witness is dead; or (B) that the witness is at a greater distance than 100 miles from the place of trial or hearing, or is out of the United States, unless it appears that the absence of the witness was procured by the party offering the deposition; or (C) that the witness is unable to attend or testify because of age, sickness, infirmity, or imprisonment; or (D) that the party offering the deposition has been unable to procure the attendance of the witness by subpoena; or (E) upon application and notice, that such exceptional circumstances exist as to make it desirable, in the interest of justice and with due regard to the importance of presenting the testimony of witnesses orally in open court, to allow the deposition to be used".

The high degree of similarity between the foregoing specifications of what satisfies unavailability and those for hearsay discussed earlier in this section is, of course, evident.

57. See statutes and rules collected in 5 Wigmore, Evidence § 1411.

58. See 5 Wigmore, Evidence §§ 1398, n. 6, 1411.

59. See, e. g., the limited circumstances under which an accused may take a deposition in a federal prosecution. F.R.Crim.P. 15(a), supra n. 55. The provisions for use are more specific, F.R.Crim.P. 15(e):

"(e) Use. At the trial or upon any hearing, a part or all of a deposition, so far as otherwise admissible under the rules of evidence, may be used if it appears: That the witness is dead; or that the

witness is out of the United States, unless it appears that the absence of the witness was procured by the party offering the deposition; or that the witness is unable to attend or testify because of sickness or infirmity; or that the party offering the deposition has been unable to procure the attendance of the witness by subpoena. Any deposition may also be used by any party for the purpose of contradicting or impeaching the testimony of the deponent as a witness. If only a part of a deposition is offered in evidence by a party, an adverse party may require him to offer all of it which is relevant to the part offered and any party may offer other parts."

Whether the right of confrontation carries a broader right of discovery, including taking depositions, has been discussed elsewhere. See § 252 at n. 96, supra.

60. Supra n. 35.

61. While the Federal Criminal Rule allows taking only at the instance of the accused, apparently a deposition thus taken may be admitted at trial at the instance of either party. When the government is the offering party, it seems evident that one ground of unavailability specified in the rule, i. e. inability to procure attendance by subpoena, does not conform to Barber v. Page standards.

62. See § 252 at n. 2, supra.

F.R.Crim.P. 15(c) provides:

"(c) Defendant's Counsel and Payment of Expenses. If a defendant is without counsel the court shall advise him of his right and assign counsel to represent him unless the defendant elects to proceed without counsel or is able to obtain counsel. If it appears that a defendant at whose instance a deposition is to be taken cannot bear the expense thereof, the court may direct that the expenses of travel and subsistence of the defendant's attorney for attendance at the examination shall be paid by the government. In that event the marshal shall make payment accordingly."

Since the rule makes no provision for taking at the instance of the government, the only situation raising cross-examination problems in federal cases would seem to be the rare one of a witness' deposition being taken at his own instance. See F.R. Crim.P. 15(a), supra n. 55. However, some state provisions allow depositions by the prosecution, and there the text statement is fully applicable.

CHAPTER 25

TESTIMONY TAKEN AT A FORMER HEARING
OR IN ANOTHER ACTION [1]

254. Introductory: Is It Hearsay? Scope of Statutes and Rules.

Upon compliance with requirements which are designed to guarantee an adequate opportunity of cross-examination, evidence may be received in the pending case, in the form of a written transcript or an oral report, of a witness's previous testimony. This testimony may have been given by deposition or at a trial, either in a separate case or proceeding, or in a former hearing of the present pending case.[2] Usually called former testimony, this evidence may be classified, depending upon the precise formulation of the rule against hearsay, as an exception to the hearsay prohibition on the one hand, or as a class of evidence where the requirements of the hearsay rule are complied with, on the other. The former view is accepted generally by the courts[3] and textwriters;[4] the latter is espoused by Wigmore.[5] The present work adheres to the former classification by adopting a definition of hearsay which would include all testimony given by deposition or at a previous trial or hearing, in the present or another litigation, provided it is now offered as evidence of the facts testified to.[6]

1. See 5 Wigmore, Evidence §§ 1370, 1371, 1386–1389 (requirements of adequate opportunity to cross-examine); §§ 1402–1415 (unavailability of witness); §§ 1660–1669 (proof by official notes, records, reports, etc.); 7 id. §§ 2098, 2099, 2103 (must entire testimony be proved?); Falknor, Former Testimony and the Uniform Rules: A Comment, 38 N.Y.U.L.Rev. 651 (1963); Hale, The Missouri Law of Former Testimony, 14 St. Louis L.Rev. 375 (1929); Hinton, Changes in Hearsay Exceptions, 29 Ill.L.Rev. 422, 427 (1934); Symposium on the Proposed Federal Rules of Evidence, 15 Wayne L.Rev. 1061, 1201 (1969); Advisory Committee's Note, F.R. Ev. (R.D.1971) pp. 126–128.

See also Dec.Dig. Evidence ⬩575–583, Criminal Law ⬩540–548; C.J.S. Evidence §§ 384–402; Annots., 15 A.L.R. 495, 79 id. 1392, 122 id. 425, 159 id. 1240, 159 id. 119.

2. For opinions stating the rule, see, e. g., Gaines v. Thomas, 241 S.C. 412, 128 S.E.2d 692 (1962); State v. Carr, 67 S.D. 481, 294 N.W. 174 (1940); State v. Ortego, 22 Wash.2d 552, 157 P.2d 320 (1945).

3. George v. Davie, 201 Ark. 470, 145 S.W.2d 729 (1941); Walker v. Walker, 14 Ga. 242, 249 (1853); Gaines v. Thomas, 241 S.C. 412, 128 S.E.2d 692 (1962); Lone Star Gas Co. v. State, 137 Tex. 279, 153 S.W.2d 681 (1941).

4. See, e. g., Cross, Evidence 453 (3d ed. 1967); 1 Greenleaf, Evidence § 163 (3d ed. 1846); 3 Jones, Evidence § 308 (5th ed. 1958); Morgan, Basic Problems of Evidence 255 (1962). See also Uniform Rule 63(3); F.R.Ev. (R.D.1971) 804(b)(1).

5. 5 Wigmore, Evidence § 1370. This view has occasionally been approved by the courts, see, e. g., Habig v. Bastian, 117 Fla. 864, 158 So. 508, 510 (1935); Garner v. Pennsylvania Public Utilities Com'n, 177 Pa.Super. 439, 110 A.2d 907 (1955), and has been adopted by other textwriters, e. g. Chamberlayne, Trial Evidence § 729 (2d ed. by Tompkins, 1936).

6. See § 246, supra.

The reasons for this choice are, first, it follows the usage most familiar to the profession, and second, it probably facilitates the wider admission of former testimony, which is generally of a relatively high degree of trustworthiness, under a liberalized exception. An insistence upon the equivalent of a present opportunity to cross-examine disregards the other elements of special reliability in former testimony such as the oath, the solemnity of the occasion, and in the case of transcribed testimony, the accuracy of reproduction of the words spoken.[7]

Many of the exceptions to the hearsay rule have been developed almost solely through the judicial process; others have been widely regulated by statute, and the present exception is of the latter class. It will be impossible in this brief work to describe the variations in the statutes of the different states. The usual approach, however, is that these statutes on former testimony are "declaratory" of the common law, so far as they go, and not the exclusive test of admissibility. Accordingly, if the evidence meets the common law requirements, it will usually come in even though the permissive provisions of the statute do not mention the particular common law doctrine which the evidence satisfies,[8] and correspondingly when the common law imposes a restriction not mentioned in the statute, the restriction has been said to govern, unless the circumstances show a legislative intention to abrogate it.[9]

It is important to notice at the outset that former testimony may often be given in evidence without meeting the requirements discussed in this chapter such as identity of parties and issues and unavailability of the witness. These requirements are applicable only when admission of the evidence is sought under this particular exception. When the former testimony is offered for some nonhearsay purpose,[10] as to show the commission of the act of perjury,[11] or to show that the witness by testifying adversely to the accused furnished the motive for the murder of the witness,[12] or to refresh recollection, or impeach a witness at the present trial by proving that he testified differently on a former occasion,[13] the restrictions of the hearsay exception do not apply. Likewise, if offered for a hearsay purpose but under some other exception, e. g., as the ad-

9. Illinois Steel Co. v. Muza, 164 Wis. 247, 159 N. W. 908 (1916) (Wis.St.Ann. 325.31 providing for admission of former testimony "where the party against whom it is offered shall have had an opportunity to cross-examine" is declaratory of common law and hence is qualified by condition that the opportunity to cross-examine must be on substantially the same issues).

10. See 5 Wigmore, Evidence § 1387, notes 5–7.

11. See State v. Wykert, 198 Iowa 1219, 199 N.W. 331 (1924) where admissibility for this purpose is assumed, and where proof of former testimony of other witnesses to show the materiality of the perjured testimony is also sanctioned.

12. Suggested by the facts in Nordan v. State, 143 Ala. 13, 39 So. 406 (1905) though the opinion does not quite reach this point.

13. People v. Ferraro, 293 N.Y. 51, 55 N.E.2d 861 (1944). See also People v. Hawley, 111 Calif. 78, 43 P. 404 (1896) (testimony of accused at preliminary hearing admissible to impeach: it seems that it would have been as readily receivable as an admission).

Use of depositions to impeach or contradict the deponent's testimony as a witness is provided under F.R.Civ.P. 26(d) (1) and F.R.Crim.P. 15(e).

7. The restrictions upon the use of former testimony are attributed to the dominance in Anglo-American trials of the adversary or contentious theory of procedure rather than to a consideration of the capacities of the jury to evaluate such evidence. Morgan, The Jury and the Exclusionary Rules of Evidence, 4 U.Chi.L.Rev. 247, 256 (1937).

8. In re White's Will, 2 N.Y.2d 309, 141 N.E.2d 416, 160 N.Y.S.2d 841 (1957), (testimony given in lunacy proceeding held admissible in proceeding to contest lunatic's will, under statute declaring former testimony admissible if subject matter and parties are the same); State v. Ham, 224 N.C. 128, 29 S.E.2d 449 (1944) (statute making testimony on preliminary hearing admissible when subscribed and certified does not limit admission under common law practice where stenographer swears report accurate, though not subscribed or certified). Contra, Tom Reed Gold Mining Co. v. Moore, 40 Ariz. 174, 11 P.2d 347 (1932).

mission of a party-opponent,[14] only the requirements of the exception under which it is offered, and not those of the present exception need be satisfied.

255. The Requirement of Oath and Opportunity for Cross-Examination: Confrontation and Unavailability.

The former testimony, to be admitted under this exception to the hearsay rule, must have been given under the sanction of the oath [15] or such form of affirmation as is accepted as legally sufficient. More important, because more often drawn in question, is the requirement that the party against whom the former testimony is now offered, or a party in like interest, must have had a reasonable opportunity to cross-examine.[16] Actual

cross-examination, of course, is not essential, if the opportunity was afforded and waived.[17] The opportunity must have been such as to render the conduct of the cross-examination or the decision not to cross-examine meaningful in the light of the circumstances which prevail when the former testimony is offered. A change of circumstances may be such as to bar compliance with this requirement.[18] In many of the cases [19] the former testimony was given at a preliminary hearing, and an argument can be made that strategy often dictates little or no cross-examination at that stage, since ample opportunity will be afforded at trial. However, the argument has not been received favorably by the courts.[20] If a right to counsel exists when the former testimony is offered, a denial of counsel when the testimony was taken

---

14. Bogie v. Nolan, 96 Mo. 85, 9 S.W. 14 (1888); Tuttle v. Wyman, 146 Neb. 146, 18 N.W.2d 744 (1945). See 5 Wigmore, Evidence, § 1416(1).

As to depositions, see F.R.Civ.P. 26(d) (2); Cusumano v. Pitzer Trucking Co., 29 Misc.2d 919, 209 N.Y.S. 2d 715 (1961).

15. While it has been held that predicate for admission of former testimony is not laid without an affirmative showing that the witness was sworn, Monahan v. Clemons, 212 Ky. 504, 508, 279 S.W. 974 (1926), the preferable view is that evidence that the witness testified justifies an inference that he was sworn. Poe v. State, 95 Ark. 172, 129 S.W. 292 (1910); Meyers v. State, 112 Neb. 149, 198 N.W. 871 (1924); Keith v. State, 53 Ohio App. 58, 4 N.E.2d 220 (1936).

16. United States v. Jones, 402 F.2d 851 (2d Cir. 1968), and Young v. United States, 132 U.S.App. D.C. 142, 406 F.2d 960 (1968) (testimony given by witnesses before grand jury not admissible against accused); Fender v. Ramsey, 131 Ga. 440, 62 S.E. 527 (1908) (ex parte affidavit used in former trial inadmissible); Edgerley v. Appleyard, 110 Me. 337, 86 A. 244, Ann.Cas.1914D, 474 (testimony taken at coroner's inquest inadmissible for want of opportunity to cross-examine); Citizens' Bank and Trust Co. v. Reid Motor Co., 216 N.C. 432, 5 S.E.2d 318 (1939) (direct examination taken before Workmen's Compensation Commissioner where witness refused to submit to cross-examination not receivable in evidence in judicial proceeding for compensation); and cases cited C.J.S. Evidence § 390; Dec. Dig. Evidence ⊕578, Criminal Law ⊕544. See Stearsman v. State, 237 Ind. 149, 143 N.E.2d 81 (1957) (witness died of a heart attack during cross-examination; that part of his testimony as to which he had been cross-examined admitted).

What constitutes a party "in like interest" is considered in § 256, infra.

17. State v. Logan, 344 Mo. 351, 126 S.W.2d 256, 122 A.L.R. 417 (1939) (murder: witness at former trial not cross-examined by counsel for accused); State v. Roebuck, 75 Wash.2d 67, 448 P.2d 934 (1968); 5 Wigmore, Evidence § 1371.

18. United States v. Franklin, 235 F.Supp. 338 (D.C. Dist.1964) (judge rejected government's offer of former testimony of co-defendant on retrial of accused, pointing out that vigorous cross-examination of co-defendant's testimony on behalf of defense at first trial might have reflected badly on accused.)

The problem is explored with respect to identity of parties and issues, infra §§ 256, 257.

19. Probably due to the prevalence of statutes, e. g., West's Ann.Cal.Pen.Code, § 686(3). See § 257, n. 49, infra. In State v. Carr, 67 S.D. 481, 294 N.W. 174 (1940), testimony given at the preliminary hearing is said to be admissible by "settled rule in practically all the courts."

20. Commonwealth v. Mustone, 353 Mass. 490, 233 N.E.2d 1 (1968) (risk of unavailability of witness at trial and consequent loss of cross-examination is assumed); State v. Crawley, 242 Ore. 601, 410 P.2d 1012 (1966). Cf. Government of Virgin Islands v. Aquino, 378 F.2d 540 (3d Cir. 1967) (rule of admissibility followed with reluctance). In California v. Green, 399 U.S. 149 (1970), the argument was rejected as a ground of constitutional attack. Similarly, many depositions are taken merely for discovery, with slight incentive to cross-examine, but F.R.Civ.P. 26(d) attaches no significance to this fact when the witness becomes unavailable and the deposition is offered in his stead. Wright Root Beer Co. v. Dr. Pepper Co., 414 F.2d 887 (5th Cir. 1969). Compare Ill.Sup.Ct.R. 202, 212.

renders it inadmissible.[21] An improper curtailment of the right to cross-examine has been held to be a denial of an adequate opportunity to cross-examine,[22] but restrictions by the judge upon cross-examination where they fall within the range of the judge's discretionary control would surely not be such a denial.

Is the opportunity for direct and redirect examination the equivalent of the opportunity for cross-examination? If party A (or his predecessor in interest) calls and examines a witness in the first hearing, and this testimony is offered against A in a second trial, may it come in against the objection of want of opportunity to cross-examine? The decisions sensibly hold that it may.[23]

If former testimony is offered under the former testimony exception to the hearsay rule, then it is offered as a substitute for testimony given in person in open court, and the strong policy favoring personal presence requires that unavailability of the witness be shown, before the substitute is acceptable.

This requirement of unavailability and problems of confrontation, common to certain other hearsay exceptions, are discussed elsewhere.[24] If the witness is present in court and testifies, then cognizance should be taken of the possibility that his former testimony may be receivable as a prior statement of a witness.[25] Thus in a jurisdiction allowing the latter, exclusion for reasons having to do with availability will be required only when the witness is absent from court but not unavailable in the necessary degree.[26]

If the former testimony is used as a prior inconsistent statement for impeachment or as an admission of a party-opponent, unavailability is not a prerequisite.[27]

256. "Identity of Parties" as a Supposed Requirement.[28]

The haste and pressure of trials compel lawyers and judges to speak in catchwords or shorthand phrases in talking about evidence rules. Thus "identity of parties" is often spoken of as a requirement for the admission of former testimony.[29] It is a convenient phrase to indicate a situation where the underlying requirement of adequacy of the present opponent's opportunity of cross-examination would usually be satis-

---

21. Pointer v. Texas, 380 U.S. 400 (1965) (error to admit at trial testimony given at preliminary hearing where accuseds were not represented by counsel; Sixth Amendment right of confrontation includes opportunity to cross-examine by counsel in this situation and applies to proceedings in state as well as federal courts).

22. State v. Halsey, 34 N.M. 223, 279 P. 945 (1929); Gill v. State, 148 Tex.Cr.R. 513, 188 S.W.2d 584 (1945) and see the original opinion in the same case, 147 Tex.Cr.R. 392, 181 S.W.2d 276 (1944).

23. Louisville & N. Ry. Co. v. Scott, 232 Ala. 284, 167 So. 572 (1936); People v. Bird, 132 Cal. 261, 64 P. 259 (1901); Dwyer v. State, 154 Me. 179, 145 A.2d 100 (1958); Pratt v. State, 53 Tex.Cr.R. 281, 109 S.W. 138 (1908); West's Ann.Cal.Evid.Code, § 1291; Kan.Code Civ.P. § 60–460(c); N.J.Ev. Rule 63(3); McKinney's N.Y. CPLR 4517; F.R.Ev. (R.D. 1971) 804(b) (1).

In view of the close parallel between depositions and former testimony, it is noteworthy that F.R.Civ.P. 26(d) makes depositions admissible against any party present at, represented at, or with due notice of the taking. See also 5 Wigmore, Evidence § 1389.

Whether testimony previously offered by a party may be treated as an adoptive admission is discussed in § 269, notes 67–70, infra.

24. See §§ 252, 253, supra.

25. See § 251, supra.

26. See California v. Green, 399 U.S. 149 (1970), pointing out, with respect to constitutional requirements of confrontation, that former testimony may be admitted if the witness is unavailable to the requisite degree and that no different result should follow where the witness is actually produced.

27. See § 37 supra (prior inconsistent statements), § 262 (admissions).

28. See generally 5 Wigmore, Evidence § 1386; Falknor, Former Testimony and the Uniform Rules: A Comment, 38 N.Y.U.L.Rev. 651, 652–655 (1963); 20 Am.Jur., Evidence § 690; C.J.S. Evidence §§ 387, 388; Dec.Dig. Evidence ☞580, Criminal Law ☞546; Annot., 142 A.L.R. 673.

29. Unfortunately some statutes and rules are phrased in this way, see e. g., Ariz.R.Civ.P. 43(e); McKinney's N.Y. CPLR 4517.

fied. But a *requirement* of identity of parties—and so we shall see of "identity of issues" [30]—is hardly a useful generalization, because it obscures the end in view, and because it must be hedged with qualifications too many and too wide for the rule to be helpful. Some of these follow.

It is clear, for example, that if the two present adversary parties, proponent of the evidence and his opponent, were parties in the former proceedings in which the testimony was taken, it is immaterial that there are additional parties in either or both proceedings not common to the two suits.[31]

Again, whether we have regard to the present party offering the former testimony, or only to the present party against whom it is offered (which we shall see is the better view) it is sufficient that the present party, though not the same, is a successor in interest to the corresponding party in the former suit.[32] This notion, to which the courtroom

attaches the slogan "privity" is again sometimes spoken of as a requirement, rather than merely as a situation which satisfies the aim of adequate protection of the party-opponent. As a requirement it is indefensibly strict.[33]

Even more important is another inroad upon "identity." This is the recognition, under Wigmore's guidance,[34] by modern judges who place substance before form, that it is only the party *against* whom the former testimony is now offered, whose presence as a party in the previous suit is significant.[35] The older decisions which insisted on "reciprocity" or "mutuality," that is, that the

---

30. See § 257, infra.

31. Philadelphia, W. & B. R. Co. v. Howard, 54 U.S. (13 How.) 307, 14 L.Ed. 157 (1851) (additional co-plaintiff in former suit); Allen v. Chouteau, 102 Mo. 309, 14 S.W. 869, 871 (1890) (additional parties in former suit); Annot., 142 A.L.R. 689.

Likewise if parties have been dropped. Freeby v. Incorporated Town of Sibley, 195 Iowa 200, 186 N.W. 685, 195 Iowa 200, 191 N.W. 867 (1922).

32. See Bryan v. Malloy, 90 N.C. 508, 511 (1883) where the court said "Privity in the sense here used is a privity to the former action. To make one a privy to an action, he must be one who has acquired an interest in the subject-matter of the action, either by inheritance, succession, or purchase from a party to the action subsequent to its institution."

Illustrations of privity in the strict sense are grantor-grantee, Stephens v. Hoffman, 263 Ill. 197, 104 N.E. 1090 (1914), and in ordinary litigation a now deceased party and his administrator, Gibson v. Gagnon, 82 Colo. 108, 257 P. 348 (1927). In wrongful death cases the decisions are divided, some ruling in favor of privity between deceased and his administrator, Kentucky Traction & Terminal Co. v. Downing's Adm'r, 159 Ky. 502, 167 S.W. 683 (1914), and others holding to the contrary on the dubious ground that the wrongful death cause of action is a new one created by statute rather than one which survives, Arsnow v. Red Top Cab Co., 159 Wash. 137, 292 P. 436 (1930). Privity has been

held not to exist between husband and wife, Lord v. Boschert, 47 Ohio App. 54, 189 N.E. 863 (1934), or between passenger and driver, Osburn v. Stickel, 187 So.2d 89 (Fla.App.1966).

33. There is no magic for this purpose in the fact of succession. The question is whether the former party had substantially the same motive to cross-examine about the same matters as the present party would have. So the better later cases look to "identity of interest" rather than to succession. See note 39, infra.

34. 5 Wigmore, Evidence § 1388, p. 103.

35. Insul-Wool Insulation Corp. v. Home Insulation, 176 F.2d 502 (10th Cir. 1949) (depositions taken in prior action for infringement admissible against plaintiff in subsequent action against other defendants for infringement of same patent); Myrick v. Sievers, 104 Ga.App. 95, 121 S.E.2d 185 (1961) (deposition taken by plaintiff in companion action arising out of same occurrence properly admitted against defendant); North River Ins. Co. v. Walker, 161 Ky. 368, 170 S.W. 983 (1914) (suit on fire insurance policy; defense, arson by plaintiff and her deceased husband; held testimony of deceased witness taken at examining trial of plaintiff and husband admissible against plaintiff); Harrell v. Quincy, O. & K. R. Co., 186 S.W. 677 (Mo.1916) (deposition taken in widow's action for wrongful death admissible against same defendant in similar action by children); School District of City of Pontiac v. Sachse, 274 Mich. 345, 264 N.W. 396 (1936) (evidence taken in criminal trial for fraud admitted against same defendant when sued civilly for restitution); Gaines v. Thomas, 241 S.C. 412, 128 S.E. 2d 692 (1962) (testimony of deceased witness given at instance of defendant in action by administrator of driver of other car against owner of truck involved in collision properly admitted in action by injured bystander against administrator; Bryant v. Trinity Universal Ins. Co., 411 S.W.2d 945 (Tex.Civ.App.1967) (facts same as North River Ins. Co. v. Walker, supra).

party *offering* the former testimony in the present suit must also have been a party in the prior proceeding,[36] seem without any supporting basis in fairness or expediency. It is said by the sponsors of the older view that if the party against whom the testimony is offered were seeking to use the same testimony against the offering party he could not do so, because the present proponent was not a party to the former suit. This is true, if identity or privity is insisted on, but the result in that imaginary situation seems to have little bearing on the question of what is fair in respect to the actual situation where former testimony is offered against a party who did have adequate opportunity to cross-examine. The "reciprocity" doctrine can best be explained as proceeding from a mere uneasiness over the extension of the admission of former testimony to the entire area in which the justifying grounds are applicable.[37]

Moreover, under what seems the practical and expedient view, if the party against whom the former testimony is now offered though not a party to the former suit, or in "privity" as a successor in interest of any party therein, yet actually cross-examined the witness (personally or by counsel) about the matters which he would now want to cross-examine about, or was actually accorded a fair opportunity for such cross-examination and had a like motive for such examination, then the former testimony may be received.[38] Finally, the natural next step is to

36. Morgan v. Nicholl, L.R. 2 C.P. 117 (1866) (action in ejectment by father; plaintiff seeks to use testimony of deceased witness taken in former action for the same land brought by son who supposed that his father was dead; excluded on ground that testimony could not have been used by defendants against present plaintiff for want of privity or identity of parties); Metropolitan St. Ry. Co. v. Gumby, 99 F. 192, 198 (2d Cir. 1900) (suit by infant's mother claiming damages for loss of services due to injury, held, testimony of deceased witness taken in former suit brought in infant's behalf against the same defendant for the same injury could not be used by plaintiff, no privity or reciprocity); McInturff v. Insurance Co. of North America, 248 Ill. 92, 93 N.E. 369, 140 Am.St.Rep. 153, 21 Ann.Cas. 176 (1910) (M. was tried on criminal charge for arson; after trial he kills T., witness for state; M. then sues on fire insurance policy; held, insurance company cannot use testimony of T. given at the criminal trial; surely this is a flagrant sacrifice of justice on the altar of technicalism); Concordia Fire Ins. Co. v. Wise, 114 Okl. 254, 246 P. 595, 46 A.L.R. 456 (1926) (suit on fire policy; former testimony in trial of present plaintiff for arson, not admissible against him in present action); Annot., 142 A.L.R. 687, citing additional cases. Referring to some of these cases, the North Carolina court said: "These authorities, in our opinion, sacrifice substance to form, and exclude material evidence which has been subjected to the tests of truth, and in favor of a party who has had an opportunity to cross-examine." Hartis v. Charlotte Elec. Ry. Co., 162 N.C. 236, 237, 78 S.E. 164 (1913).

37. See the court's remarks in the McInturff case in the next preceding note: "If the rule contended for by plaintiff in error were good law, then in an action against a carrier by a passenger for a personal injury the testimony of a witness since deceased would be admissible against the same carrier for an injury sustained in the same accident by another passenger, an employé, a licensee, or a trespasser, simply because the carrier against whom the testimony was offered had on the former trial an opportunity to cross-examine the witness. This rule would carry us too far afield for proof, and we cannot sanction it." (93 N.E. at p. 371). Cf. Wade v. King, 19 Ill. 301 (1857).

38. Tug Raven v. Trexler, 419 F.2d 536 (4th Cir. 1969) (testimony given at Coast Guard inquiry into cause of disaster admissible in wrongful death proceeding against respondent who was represented and allowed to cross-examine; also admissible against others similarly situated who had not appeared); In re Durant, 80 Conn. 140, 67 A. 497, 10 Ann.Cas. 539 (1907) (disbarment proceedings charging that defendant conspired to procure perjured testimony of Mrs. D in a divorce suit; testimony of Mrs. D in that divorce suit now offered against defendant, who had cross-examined as attorney for the wife: held admissible. "The requirement of an identity of parties is only a means to an end. This end was attained when the defendant availed himself of the unrestricted opportunity to cross-examine Mrs. Delkescamp."); Brownlee v. Bunnell, 31 Ky.L. 669, 103 S.W. 284 (1907) (former testimony received against defendants in present suit on ground that though not parties to former suit they employed lawyers who defended the action at their instance); Charlesworth v. Tinker, 18 Wis. 633, 635 (1864) (civil action for assault; testimony given in prior criminal assault prosecution admissible, relying on statute giving power to complainant to control prosecution for assault; ". . . the true test . . . is, did the party who is to be affected by it have the power of cross-examin-

recognize, as progressive courts have done, that neither identity of parties nor privity between parties is essential. These are merely means to an end. Consequently, if it appears that in the former suit a party having a like motive to cross-examine about the same matters as the present party would have, was accorded an adequate opportunity for such examination, the testimony may be received against the present party.[39] Iden-

ing the witness, or at least have an opportunity of doing so?"); Fleury v. Edwards, 14 N.Y.2d 334, 251 N.Y.S.2d 647, 200 N.E.2d 550 (1964) (testimony of one driver, given at license revocation hearing of both drivers, held admissible in death action by his administrator against other driver, who was present and cross-examined; outstanding opinions). Compare Rumford Chemical Works v. Hygienic Chemical Co., 215 U.S. 156 (1909) (testimony in a former suit inadmissible against one who contributed to expense of defending former suit, but had no "right to intermeddle").

Cases disclosing relaxation of strict requirements in disbarment proceedings are collected in Annot., 161 A.L.R. 898.

39. This view finds support in a growing number of decisions. Tug Raven v. Trexler, supra n. 38; Cox v. Selover, 171 Minn. 216, 213 N.W. 902 (1927), (testimony taken in former trial against guarantor, who was officer, stockholder, and attorney for corporate principal maker, which intervened after first trial, admissible against intervenor in later trial); Bartlett v. Kansas City Public Service Co., 349 Mo. 13, 160 S.W.2d 740, 142 A.L.R. 666 (1942) (testimony given for defendant in prior suit by husband for loss of services of injured wife, admissible for defendant in wife's separate action for same injury); Travelers Fire Ins. Co. v. Wright, 322 P.2d 417 (Okl.1958) (action on fire policy by two partners, with defense of arson by one partner; testimony given against one partner in criminal trial for arson admissible); Proulx v. Parrow, 115 Vt. 232, 56 A.2d 623 (1948) (testimony given in previous action against husband for removal of boundary fence admissible against wife in later action for declaration of location of boundary). In cases where privity in the strict sense does not exist between a person suing for injuries and his administrator suing for death caused thereby, identity of interest is advanced as a basis for admitting in the later case testimony given in the former. Hartis v. Charlotte Elec. Ry. Co., 162 N.C. 236, 78 S.E. 164, Ann.Cas.1915A, 811 (1913); St. Louis Southwestern R. R. v. Hengst, 36 Tex.Civ.App. 217, 81 S.W. 832 (1904). See F.R. Ev. (R.D.1971) 804(b)(1) and Advisory Committee's Note.

The case law has not as yet explored the validity of this theory with respect to criminal defendants.

tity of interest in the sense of motive, rather than technical identity of cause of action or title, is the test. The argument that it is unfair to force upon a party another's cross-examination or decision not to cross-examine a witness loses its validity with the realization that other hearsay exceptions involve no cross-examination whatever, and further that the choice is not between perfect and imperfect conditions for the giving of testimony but between imperfect conditions and no testimony at all.[40]

257. Identity of Issues.[41]

Questions as to identity of the issues, or of the facts, involved in the former and present proceedings often arise in association with questions about identity or privity of parties. This is to be expected because any supposed requirement of identity of issues, is like the rule about parties,[42] merely a means of fulfilling the policy of securing an adequate opportunity of cross-examination by the party against whom testimony is now offered or by someone in like interest. It is often said that the issue in the two suits must be the same.[43] But certainly the policy mentioned does not require that all the issues (any more than all the parties) in the two proceedings must be the same, but at most that the issue on which the testimony was offered in the first suit must be the same as the issue upon which it is offered in the second. Additional issues or differences in regard to issues upon which the former testi-

40. Morgan, The Law of Evidence, 1941-1945, 59 Harv.L.Rev. 481, 551 (1946). And see Falknor, Former Testimony and the Uniform Rules: A Comment, 38 N.Y.U.L.Rev. 651, 655 (1963).

41. See 5 Wigmore, Evidence §§ 1386, 1387; C.J.S. Evidence § 389; Dec.Dig. Evidence ☜579, Criminal Law ☜545; Annot., 70 A.L.R.2d 494.

42. See § 256, supra.

43. Statutes occasionally so provide, e. g., New Mexico 1953 Comp. § 21-1-1(43) (a) (1) ("in any subsequent trial or hearing of the same issue between the same parties"); Pennsylvania, 19 P.S. § 582 ("of the same criminal issue").

mony is not offered are of no consequence.[44] Moreover, insistence upon precise identity of issues, which might have some appropriateness if the question were one of res judicata or estoppel by judgment, are out of place with respect to former testimony where the question is not of binding anyone, but merely of the salvaging, for what it may be worth, of the testimony of a witness not now available in person. Accordingly, modern opinions qualify the requirement by demanding only "substantial" identity of issues.[45]

It follows that neither the form of the proceeding, the theory of the case, nor the nature of the relief sought needs be the same. Though there have been occasional holdings imposing such requirements,[46] it is manifest that they have no pertinence to the policy of adequacy of opportunity for cross-examination, and the more convincing opinions reject them.[47] Thus, in criminal cases where the first indictment charges one offense, e. g., robbery, and the second, another distinct offense, such as murder of the person robbed, it is usually considered sufficient that the two indictments arise from the same transaction.[48] Other patterns recur in the cases. One involves introducing at the trial of a criminal case testimony given at the preliminary hearing. In another, testimony given against the accused in an earlier criminal trial is offered against him in a civil case to which he is a party. In both situations admissibility is favored.[49] It seems, then, that the re-

---

44. Bartlett v. Kansas City Public Service Co., 349 Mo. 13, 160 S.W.2d 740, 142 A.L.R. 666 (1942) (immaterial that husband's prior action involved issue of loss of wife's services not present in wife's later personal injury action, since witnesses did not testify on issue of damages); Hartis v. Charlotte Elec. R. Co., 162 N.C. 236, 78 S.E. 164, 1915A, 811 (1913) (similarly as to different measures of damages between personal injury action and later wrongful death action).

45. State v. Brinkley, 354 Mo. 337, 189 S.W.2d 314 (1945) (testimony for defendants in prosecution against police officers for fatally assaulting M admissible for accused in prosecution for perjured testimony before grand jury that police had beaten him and M); In re White's Will, 2 N.Y.2d 309, 160 N.Y.S.2d 841, 141 N.E.2d 416 (1957) (testimony given in lunacy proceeding where issue was capacity to manage affairs admissible in will contest on issue of competency to make a will). Many cases state the rule in terms of "substantial" identity of issues, e. g. School District of City of Pontiac v. Sachse, 274 Mich. 345, 264 N.W. 396 (1936); Proulx v. Parrow, 115 Vt. 232, 56 A.2d 623 (1948). Some statutes likewise specify "substantial" identity of issues as the test. Ga.Code, § 38–314; Wis.Stat. Ann. 325.31.

For examples of failure to meet the test of substantial identity of issues, see State v. Augustine, 252 La. 983, 215 So.2d 634 (1968) (testimony given at hearing on competency to stand trial not admissible on issue of insanity at time of offense); Monahan v. Monahan, 29 App.Div.2d 1246, 289 N.Y.S.2d 812 (1968) (impeachment testimony by female witness for prosecution in unrelated felony trial of D that she had stayed at hotels with D, not admissible to prove adultery in divorce action against D).

46. Tom Reed Gold Mines Co. v. Moore, 40 Ariz. 174, 11 P.2d 347 (1932) (under statute limiting use to "the same action" testimony taken in personal injury action cannot be used in later death action); Hooper v. Southern Ry. Co., 112 Ga. 96, 37 S.E. 165, 168 (1900) (testimony taken in suit for personal injuries to minor brought by father as next friend not admissible in suit by father for his own loss of the child's services, there being different defenses available in the two suits—not substantially the same issue); Seward v. Schmidt, 49 N.E. 2d 696 (Ohio App.1942) (similar to last case).

47. See cases cited in n. 44 and 45 supra.

48. Fox v. State, 102 Ark. 393, 144 S.W. 516 (1912) (first trial of defendant for being accessory to murder, second, for being accessory to robbery, on same occasion); State v. Boyd, 140 Kan. 623, 38 P.2d 665 (1934) (embezzlement, misappropriation by custodian of public funds); State v. Brown, 331 Mo. 556, 56 S.W.2d 405 (1932); State v. Brinkley, 354 Mo. 337, 189 S.W.2d 314 (1945) (first trial manslaughter prosecution against officers who arrested present defendant and his companion, who died after the arrest; second trial, prosecution of defendant for perjury in testifying before grand jury that he and his companion were beaten by officers at time of first arrest); State v. Swiden, 62 S.D. 208, 252 N.W. 628 (1934) (robbery, murder); State v. Dawson, 129 W.Va. 279, 40 S.E.2d 306 (1946) (robbery, murder); cases are collected in Annot., 122 A.L.R. 430.

49. Admissibility of testimony given at the preliminary hearing is provided by statutes in fair number. 5 Wigmore, Evidence § 1375. Ample support also exists in the cases. Id.; Annots., 15 A.L. R. 495, 79 id. 1392, 122 id. 425, 159 id. 1240; see also § 255, supra. In Stearsman v. State, 237 Ind. 149, 143 N.E.2d 81 (1957), the court cited the preliminary hearing cases as support for admitting testimony given at a hearing on motion to suppress.

quirement should be restated, not as a mechanical one of identity or even of substantial identity of issues, but rather as a requirement that the issues in the first proceeding and hence the purpose for which the testimony was there offered, must have been such that the present opponent (or some person in like interest) had an adequate motive for testing on cross-examination the credibility of the testimony now offered.[50]

258. The Character of the Tribunal and of the Proceedings in Which the Former Testimony Was Taken.

If the accepted requirements of the administration of the oath, adequate opportunity to cross-examine on substantially the same issue, and present unavailability of the witness, are satisfied then the character of the tribunal and the form of the proceedings are immaterial, and the former testimony should be received.[51] Accordingly, when these conditions are met, testimony taken before arbitrators,[52] or before a committing magistrate

at a preliminary hearing,[53] or in a sworn examination before the Comptroller by the Corporation Counsel of a person asserting a claim against a city,[54] or at a driver's license revocation hearing,[55] or at a broker's license revocation hearing,[56] has been held admissible. For lack in the particular proceeding of some of these requisites, testimony given in the course of a coroner's inquest,[57] of a legislative committee hearing,[58] and of a general examination before the referee under the Bankruptcy Act,[59] has been excluded. Or a statute may call for exclusion.[60]

The modern decisions likewise support admissibility in the criminal-civil situation. North River Ins. Co. v. Walker, 161 Ky. 368, 170 S.W. 983 (1914) (arson); School District of City of Pontiac v. Sachse, 274 Mich. 345, 264 N.W. 396 (1936) (embezzlement); Bryant v. Trinity Universal Ins. Co., 411 S.W.2d 945 (Tex.Civ.App.1967) (arson).

50. State v. Von Klein, 71 Ore. 159, 142 P. 549 (1914) (testimony as to polygamous marriage given on trial for larceny of jewels of supposed wife, as evidence of scheme, admissible on later trial for polygamy). See also rules and statutes to this effect cited in § 261, n. 98. Cf. Williams v. State, 42 Okl.Cr. 399, 276 P. 515 (1929) (trial for robbery, excluding former testimony in another robbery case to show scheme and disapproving State v. Von Klein).

51. See 6 Wigmore, Evidence §§ 1373–1376; C.J.S. Evidence §§ 385, 386; Dec.Dig. Evidence ☞577½, Criminal Law ☞539(1).

52. Bailey v. Woods, 17 N.H. 365, 372 (1845) ("It does not seem to be an objection to the competency of the evidence of the deceased witness, that it was given at a hearing before arbitrators. We do not understand that the admissibility of such evidence depends so much upon the particular character of the tribunal, as upon other matters. If the testimony be given under oath in a judicial proceeding, in which the adverse litigant was a party, and where he had the power to cross-ex-

amine, and was legally called upon to do so, the great and ordinary tests of truth being no longer wanting, the testimony so given is admitted in any subsequent suit between the parties. Greenl.Ev. 1. It seems to depend rather upon the right to cross-examine, than upon the precise nominal identity of the parties. Id. An arbitration is a judicial proceeding, and the principle of the rule seems to apply as well to cases of this character as to technical suits at law."). The principle was reaffirmed in Orr v. Hadley, 36 N.H. 575, 580 (1858) but the testimony was excluded because of want of opportunity for cross-examination by the present opponent or one in like interest.

53. See § 255, n. 20, and § 257, n. 49, supra; Dec. Dig., Criminal Law ☞539–545.

54. Boschi v. City of New York, 187 Misc. 875, 65 N.Y.S.2d 425 (1946); Rothman v. City of New York, 273 App.Div. 780, 75 N.Y.S.2d 151 (1947).

55. Fleury v. Edwards, 14 N.Y.2d 334, 251 N.Y.S.2d 647, 200 N.E.2d 550 (1964).

56. Wellden v. Roberts, 37 Ala.App. 1, 67 So.2d 69 (1952), aff'd 259 Ala. 517, 67 So.2d 75.

57. Edgerley v. Appleyard, 110 Me. 337, 86 A. 244 (1913) (for want of opportunity of cross-examination—a leading case); Wilson v. Marshall Enterprises, 361 F.2d 887 (4th Cir. 1966); 6 Wigmore, Evidence § 1374. Occasionally it is made competent by statute. Los Angeles County v. Industrial Accident Commission, 123 Cal.App. 12, 11 P.2d 434 (1932) (in workmen's compensation proceedings).

58. Newman v. United States ex rel. Frizzel, 43 App. D.C. 53 (1914) (here said to be incompetent and irrelevant) reversed on other grounds, 238 U.S. 537 (1915); State ex rel. Blankenship v. Freeman, 440 P.2d 744, 759 (Okl.1968).

59. In re National Boat and Engine Co., 216 F. 208 (D.Me.1914) (for want of a defined issue); Todd v. Bradley, 99 Conn. 307, 122 A. 68 (1923) (here the testimony of third person; use of bankrupt's testimony as admission distinguished).

60. State Road Dept. v. Levato, 199 So.2d 714 (Fla. 1967) (provision requiring exclusion at trial of tes-

It has been held that if the court in the former proceeding lacked jurisdiction of the subject matter, the former testimony is inadmissible,[61] but it was determined in a Colorado case,[62] that the fact that it may ultimately be held that the court is without power to grant the relief sought, does not deprive the court of power to compel attendance of witnesses and to administer oaths, and accordingly the former testimony was held admissible.[63] The question it seems is not one of regularity but of reliability. A glaring usurpation of judicial power would call for a different ruling, but where the first court has substantial grounds for believing that it has authority to entertain the proceeding, and the party called upon to cross-examine should consider that the existence of jurisdiction is reasonably arguable, it seems that the guaranties of reliability are present. The question it seems should be viewed, not as one of limits of jurisdiction, but of whether the sworn statements of a witness, now dead or unavailable, about the facts of which he had knowledge, were made under such circumstances of opportunity and motive for cross-examination as to make them sufficiently trustworthy to be used in the effort to ascertain the truth. In like vein, no significance attaches to the circumstance that the earlier trial resulted in a mistrial [64] or a hung jury.[65]

259. Objections and Their Determination.[66]

May objections to the former testimony, or parts thereof, which could have been asserted when it was first given in evidence, be made for the first time when offered at the present trial? There are sweeping statements in some opinions that this may always be done,[67] and in others that it is never allowable.[68] The more widely approved view, however, is that objections which go merely to the form of the testimony, as on the ground of leading questions, unresponsiveness, or opinion, must be made at the original hearing, when they can be corrected,[69] but objections which go to the relevancy or the competency of the evidence may be asserted for the first time when the former testimony is offered at the present trial.[70]

Whether the former testimony meets the requirements of the present exception to the hearsay rule may depend on a question of fact. For example, is the witness unavail-

66. C.J.S. Criminal Law § 892; C.J.S. Evidence § 384, p. 948; Annot., 159 A.L.R. 119.

67. Wellden v. Roberts, 37 Ala.App. 1, 67 So.2d 69 (1962), aff'd 259 Ala. 517, 67 So.2d 75; Calley v. Boston & M. R., 93 N.H. 359, 42 A.2d 329, 159 A.L.R. 115 (1945).

68. Leach v. Nelson, 50 N.D. 538, 196 N.W. 755 (1924), critically noted 8 Minn.L.Rev. 629.

69. Kemp v. Government of Canal Zone, 167 F.2d 938 (5th Cir. 1948); People v. Britt, 62 Cal.App. 674, 217 P. 767 (1923); Sherman Gas & Elec. Co. v. Belden, 103 Tex. 59, 123 S.W. 119, 27 L.R.A.,N.S., 237 (1909); Note, 8 Minn.L.Rev. 629; Annot., 159 A.L.R. 119.

70. Aetna Ins. Co. v. Koonce, 233 Ala. 265, 171 So. 269 (1936) (dictum).

A similar rule with respect to depositions is found in F.R.Civ.P. 32(c). See also C.J.S. Depositions § 101.

With respect to objections to the competency of the witness, compare State v. Pierson, 337 Mo. 475, 85 S.W.2d 48 (1935) (error to refuse to allow accused to go into possible incompetency at time of giving original testimony by witness whose insanity supervened), and Habig v. Bastian, 117 Fla. 864, 158 So. 508 (1935) (testimony given by party at former trial not rendered inadmissible by supervening death of opposite party which rendered witness incompetent).

timony of appraisers at pretrial hearing under "quick take" eminent domain statute).

61. In re Colbert's Estate, 51 Mont. 455, 153 P. 1022 (1915); Deering v. Schreyer, 88 App.Div. 457, 85 N.Y.S. 275 (1903), noted 17 Harv.L.Rev. 422. The court in McAdams' Executors v. Stilwell, 13 Pa.St. 90 (1850) assumes that jurisdiction is essential.

62. Jerome v. Bohn, 21 Colo. 322, 40 P. 570 (1895).

63. The result is consistent with United States v. United Mine Workers, 330 U.S. 258 (1947).

64. People v. Schwarz, 78 Cal.App. 561, 248 P. 990 (1926).

65. People v. Hines, 284 N.Y. 93, 29 N.E.2d 483 (1940).

able? This and other preliminary questions of fact are treated elsewhere.[71]

Impeachment of witnesses whose former testimony is introduced is considered under the topic of impeaching hearsay declarants generally.[72]

260. Method and Scope of Proof.[73]

When only a portion of the former testimony of a witness is introduced by the proponent, the result may be a distorted and inaccurate impression. Hence the adversary is entitled to the introduction of such other parts as fairness requires, and to have them introduced at that time, rather than waiting until the presentation of his own case.[74] He may, however, wait if he chooses.[75]

In proving the former testimony at least four theories of admissibility may be employed.

(1) Any *firsthand* observer of the giving of the former testimony may testify to its purport from his unaided memory.[76] This

and the next method were formerly used much more frequently than in the present era of court stenographers. The witness, to qualify, need not profess to be able to give the exact words of the former witness,[77] but he must, if the evidence is to come in under the present exception, satisfy the court that he is able to give the substance of all that the witness has said, both on direct and cross-examination,[78] about the subject matter relevant to the present suit.[79] By the more convenient practice the proponent need not prove all of the former testimony relevant to the present case, but only such as he desires to use, leaving to the adversary to call for such of the remaining part as he wishes.[80]

(2) A firsthand observer may testify to the purport of the former testimony by using a memorandum, such as the judge's, counsel's, or the stenographer's notes, or the ste-

---

71. See § 53, supra.

72. See § 37 at n. 54–57, supra.

73. See 4 Wigmore, Evidence § 1330, 5 id. §§ 1666–1669, 7 id. §§ 2098, 2099, 2103; Dec.Dig. Criminal Law ⟜547, Evidence ⟜582; C.J.S. Criminal Law § 898; C.J.S. Evidence §§ 397–401; Annot., 11 A.L.R.2d 30.

74. The additional portions will usually, though not necessarily, consist of the original cross-examination. Waller v. State, 102 Ga. 684, 28 S.E. 284 (1897); City of Boulder v. Stewardson, 67 Colo. 582, 189 P. 1 (1920); Randall v. Peerless Motor Car Co., 212 Mass. 352, 99 N.E. 221, 231 (1912).

75. F.R.Civ.P. 32(a) (4) provides: "If only part of a deposition is offered in evidence by a party, an adverse party may require him to introduce any other part which ought in fairness to be considered with the part introduced, and any party may introduce other parts." The important thing is the timing, rather than which party does the introducing.

76. Meyers v. United States, 84 U.S.App.D.C. 101, 171 F.2d 800 (1948) cert. denied 336 U.S. 912; Vander Veen v. Yellow Cab Co., 89 Ill.App.2d 91, 233 N.E.2d 68 (1967); State ex rel. Blankenship v. Freeman, 440 P.2d 744, 760 (Okl.1968); State v. Crawley, 242 Ore. 601, 410 P.2d 1012 (1966); State v. Roebuck, 75 Wash.2d 67, 448 P.2d 934 (1968).

77. Ruch v. Rock Island, 97 U.S. 693 (1878) (precise language not necessary; "if a witness from mere memory, professes to give the exact language, it is a reason for doubting his good faith and veracity"); Vander Veen v. Yellow Cab Co., 89 Ill.App. 2d 91, 233 N.E.2d 68 (1967); 7 Wigmore, Evidence § 2098, note 4.

78. Tibbets v. Flanders, 18 N.H. 284, 292 (1846); Monahan v. Clemons, 212 Ky. 504, 276 S.W. 924 (1926).

79. Bennett v. State, 32 Tex.Cr.R. 216, 22 S.W. 684 (1893) ("If a witness can testify to the substance of all that is said on direct and cross examination upon one subject, it will be admissible, though there may be other portions of said testimony, as to other matters, not remembered by the witness."); Foley v. State, 11 Wyo. 464, 72 P. 627 (1903) (must state "the whole of what was said on the particular subject which he is called to prove"); 7 Wigmore, Evidence, §§ 2098, note 4, 2099(4). But the sensible qualification, that it suffices if the proponent is able to fill the gaps by the testimony of other witnesses has been made in a case where the former testimony was proved, not under the present exception, but to support a charge of perjury. Commonwealth v. Shooshanian, 210 Mass. 123, 96 N.E. 70 (1911).

80. Waller v. State, 102 Ga. 684, 28 S.E. 284 (1897); City of Boulder v. Stewardson, 67 Colo. 582, 189 P. 1 (1920); Randall v. Peerless Motor Car Co., 212 Mass. 352, 99 N.E. 221 (1912).

nographer's transcript, to *refresh the present memory* of the witness.[81]

(3) In most states the magistrate's report of the testimony at a preliminary criminal hearing,[82] and the official stenographer's transcribed notes of the testimony [83] at the trial of a case, civil or criminal, are admitted, when properly authenticated, as evidence of the fact and purport of the former testimony either by statute or under the hearsay exception for *official written statements*.[84] There is generally no rule of preference for these reports, however, and any observer, including the stenographer himself, may be called to prove the former testimony without producing the official report or transcript.[85]

(4) A witness who has made written notes or memoranda of the testimony at the time of the former trial, or while the facts were fresh in his recollection, and who will testify that he knows that they are correct may use the notes as memoranda of *past recollection recorded*.[86]

261. The Need for Improvement in Existing Practice.

The traditional restrictions upon the admission of evidence of former testimony are understandable as the reflections of an earlier era when there were no court reporters,[87] and as logical deductions from the premise that cross-examination is the only substantial safeguard for the reliability of this evidence. But when we view them in comparison with doctrines admitting other types of oral declarations as exceptions to the hearsay rule, such as declarations against interest, declarations of present bodily or mental state, and

81. Ruch v. City of Rock Island, 97 U.S. 693 (1878); Armstrong Furniture Co. v. Nickle, 110 Ga.App. 686, 140 S.E.2d 72 (1964); Commonwealth v. Mustone, 353 Mass. 490, 233 N.E.2d 1 (1968); Travelers Fire Ins. Co. v. Wright, 322 P.2d 417 (Okla.1958). As to refreshing recollection generally, see § 9 supra.

82. Haines v. State, 109 Ga. 526, 35 S.E. 141 (1900); 5 Wigmore, Evidence, § 1667 (citing cases pro and con).

83. See, e. g., Snyder v. Cearfoss, 190 Md. 151, 57 A.2d 786 (1948); Blalock v. Whisnant, 216 N.C. 417, 5 S.E.2d 130 (1939) (transcript contained in case on appeal); Proulx v. Parrow, 115 Vt. 232, 56 A.2d 623 (1948) (certified copy of transcript). Statutes to this effect and F.R.Civ.P. 80 are cited in 5 Wigmore, Evidence § 1669, note 2. See also cases (and statutes cited therein) in Dec.Dig. Evidence ⊂=582(3).
Objections to the use of the common law bill of exceptions based on the manner of its preparation are no longer pertinent in view of modern methods of reporting testimony. See Roth v. Smith, 54 Ill. 431 (1870); 5 Wigmore, Evidence § 1668.

84. For the requirements of this exception see Ch. 32, infra.

85. Napier v. Commonwealth, 306 Ky. 75, 206 S.W. 2d 53 (1947) (county attorney's evidence as to testimony before grand jury); Terry v. State, 132 Tex.Cr. 283, 103 S.W.2d 766 (1937) (stenographer can testify from recollection); 4 Wigmore, Evidence § 1330(2).
Since the matter sought to be proved is the former testimony and not the contents of the transcript, literally the so-called Best Evidence Rule does not apply. § 233 supra. However, the importance of accuracy and the superiority of the transcript in this respect make a powerful argument for the opposite result. Cowart v. State, 44 Ala.App. 201,

205 So.2d 250 (1967); Walker v. Walker, 14 Ga. 242 (1853); State v. Luttrell, 366 S.W.2d 453 (Mo. 1963); and see Prettyman, J., dissenting in Meyers v. United States, 84 U.S.App.D.C. 101, 115, 171 F.2d 800, 814 (D.C.Cir.1948), noted 23 So.Cal.L.Rev. 113.

86. See, e. g., Commonwealth v. Mustone, 353 Mass. 490, 233 N.E.2d 1 (1968) (any witness may qualify his notes as a reliable record of past recollection); State v. Maynard, 184 N.C. 653, 113 S.E. 682 (1922) (proper for stenographer to read his notes of preliminary examination, where he testifies to their correctness, though not subscribed or certified as required for official record); Newton v. State, 150 Tex.Cr. 500, 202 S.W.2d 921 (1947) (stenographer may read from notes, if he swears correct); 3 Wigmore, Evidence (Chadbourn rev.) § 737(1).
For the requirements of this theory of admissibility, see §§ 299–303 herein.
Whether the witness testifies on the basis of present recollection refreshed or past recollection recorded seems to be of little practical importance in proving former testimony, and the cases usually make no point of the matter.

87. "Since an official stenographic report of former testimony, given in the same cause with full privilege of cross examination, is now available in courts of record, the caution sometimes expressed where parol testimony is relied upon to prove the former testimony of the witness is not so essential." Bouldin, J., in Aetna Ins. Co. v. Koonce, 233 Ala. 265, 171 So. 269, 271 (1936).

excited or spontaneous utterances, which seem far less reliable, the restrictions upon declarations in the form of sworn testimony in open court or official hearing, seem fantastically strict. As Morgan said, "Were the same strictness applied to all hearsay, evidence of reported testimony would constitute the only exception to the hearsay rule." [88]

In the light of this broader view, therefore, it seems that the most immediate improvement would come from the wider acceptance among the courts of the attitude that the present scheme of admissibility of former testimony should be applied with a reasonable liberality favoring in case of doubt the admission of this type of evidence.[89]

The standard of unavailability of the witness in former testimony cases should be no more exacting than for depositions, in view of the strong similarity between these forms of evidence.[90] And in some respects the requirement in former testimony cases may be satisfied with less.[91] In criminal cases, the constitutional right of confrontation imposes stricter standards of unavailability.[92]

The present trend toward broader admissibility generally of prior statements of a witness [93] would of course be reflected in a broader admissibility of his former testimony. Thus in case of inconsistency the trier has before it both versions, with the former testimony having the possible advantages of nearness of time and recency of memory.

A persuasive argument can be made for admitting former testimony without regard to opportunity for cross-examination. Other types of admissible hearsay, e. g., declarations against interest and statements of bodily symptoms,[94] involve no cross-examination and are made under circumstances far less conducive to trustworthiness than sworn testimony in open court, and with far greater hazard of fabrication or mistake in the reporting of the declaration of the witness. Following this reasoning, reliance would be upon relevancy as the sole test of admissibility, and efforts to insure opportunity to cross-examine, or its equivalent, would be abandoned. This was substantially the position of the Model Code of Evidence, which in addition virtually abandoned unavailability as a requirement.[95] Professor McCormick believed that this should be the law in civil cases.[96] While this is the effect of the Eng-

---

88. The Law of Evidence, 1941–1945, 59 Harv.L.Rev. 481, 552 (1946).

89. Conspicuous instances of this attitude are Trexler v. Tug Raven, 290 F.Supp. 429 (E.D.Va.1968); In re Durant, 80 Conn. 140, 67 A. 497, 10 Ann.C. 539 (1907); Bartlett v. Kansas City Pub. Service Co., 349 Mo. 13, 160 S.W.2d 740, 142 A.L.R. 666 (1942); State v. Brinkley, 354 Mo. 337, 189 S.W.2d 314 (1945); Fleury v. Edwards, 14 N.Y.2d 334, 251 N.Y.S.2d 647, 200 N.E.2d 550 (1964); and Lyon v. Rhode Island Co., 38 R.I. 252, 94 A. 893 (1915).

90. See the provisions of F.R.Civ.P. 26(d) (3).

91. E. g., claims of privilege or simply obdurate refusal to testify, which arise in former testimony cases but not with respect to depositions. See the general discussion of unavailability of the declarant as a hearsay requirement in § 253, supra.

92. See § 252, supra.

93. See § 251, supra.

94. The failure of existing rules admitting these other types of hearsay declarations to furnish guaranties of trustworthiness comparable to the test of cross-examination is demonstrated in detail in Morgan, Foreword, Model Code of Evidence, pp. 36–49 (1942).

95. See Rule 503: "Evidence of a hearsay declaration is admissible if the judge finds that the declarant

"(a) is unavailable as a witness, or

"(b) is present and subject to cross-examination."

Rule 511: "Evidence of a hearsay statement which consists of testimony given by the declarant as a witness in an action or in a deposition taken according to law for use in an action is admissible for any purpose for which the testimony was admissible in the action in which the testimony was given or for use in which the deposition was taken, unless the judge finds that the declarant is available as a witness and in his discretion rejects the evidence."

See also the Comment appended to Rule 511 explaining the effect of the two rules.

96. McCormick, Evidence 501 (1954).

lish Evidence Act of 1968,[97] no American jurisdiction appears to have gone as far, al-

though substantial relaxation of traditional strict requirements is evident.[98]

97. Civil Evidence Act 1968, c. 64, Part I, § 2(1). The act requires the giving of notice of intended use of the evidence. Id., § 8.

98. See §§ 255–257, supra. The liberalizing trend is found in recent rules and statutes. Uniform Rule 63(3) (b); West's Ann.Cal.Evid.Code, §§ 1290–1292; Kan.Code Civ.P. § 460(c) (2); N.J.Ev.Rule 63(3); F.R.Ev. (R.D.1971) 804(b) (1). All reflect the influence of Uniform Rule 63(3) which admits as an exception to the rule against hearsay, "Subject to the same limitations and objections as though the declarant were testifying in person, (a) testimony in the form of a deposition taken in compliance with the law of this state for use as testimony in the trial of the action in which offered, or (b) if the judge finds that the declarant is unavailable as a witness at the hearing, testimony given as a witness in another action or in a deposition taken in compliance with law for use as testimony in the trial of another action, when (i) the testimony is offered against a party who offered it in his own behalf on the former occasion, or against the successor in interest of such party, or (ii) the issue is such that the adverse party on the former occasion had the right and opportunity for cross examination with an interest and motive similar to that which the adverse party has in the action in which the testimony is offered."

CHAPTER 26

ADMISSIONS OF A PARTY-OPPONENT [1]

262. Nature and Effect.

Admissions are the words or acts of a party-opponent, or of his predecessor or representative, offered as evidence against him. As indicated, they may be classified as *express* admissions, which are statements of the opposing party, or of some person such as an agent or a predecessor in interest, whose words may fairly be used against him, and admissions by *conduct* of the party-opponent or of those representing him. Among the many theories on which the probativeness and admissibility of admissions have been ex-

plained and supported, the following seem most helpful.

Morgan's view [2] is that admissions come in as an exception to the hearsay rule, if hearsay is given the usual definition of declarations made out of court, not subject to cross-examination, and received as evidence of the truth of the matter declared. However, exceptions to the hearsay rule usually are justified on the ground that the evidence meeting the requirements of exception possesses special reliability (greater than hearsay generally), plus perhaps special need because of the unavailability of the declarant by reason of his death, absence or the like. But no objective guaranty of trustworthiness is furnished by the admissions rule. The party is not even required to have had first-hand knowledge of the matter declared, and the declaration may have been self-serving when it was made. As Morgan himself admits, "The admissibility of an admission made by the party himself rests not upon any no-

1. 4 Wigmore, Evidence §§ 1048–1087; Falknor, Vicarious Admissions and the Uniform Rules, 14 Vand.L.Rev. 855 (1961), Hearsay, 1969 Law & Soc. Order 591, 600–605; Hetland, Admissions in the Uniform Rules: Are They Necessary? 46 Iowa L. Rev. 307 (1961); Morgan, The Rationale of Vicarious Admissions, 42 Harv.L.Rev. 461 (1929), Admissions, 12 Wash.L.Rev. 181 (1937); Morris, Admissions and the Negligence Issue, 29 Tex.L.Rev. 407 (1951); Strahorn, A Reconsideration of the Hearsay Rule and Admissions, 85 U.Pa.L.Rev. 484 (1937); Dec.Dig. Evidence ⇐200–265, Criminal Law ⇐405– 415; C.J.S. Evidence §§ 270–383; Uniform Rules 63 (7), 63(8), 63(9); F.R.Ev. (R.D.1971) 801(d) (2); West's Ann.Cal.Evid.Code §§ 1220–1227.

2. Morgan, Basic Problems of Evidence 265 (1962).

tion that the circumstances in which it was made furnish the trier means of evaluating it fairly, but upon the adversary theory of litigation. A party can hardly object that he had no opportunity to cross-examine himself or that he is unworthy of credence save when speaking under sanction of an oath." [3]

Wigmore, after pointing out that the party's declaration has generally the probative value of any other person's assertion, says that it has in addition a special value when offered *against* him, in that he is discredited (like a witness impeached by contradictory statements) by his statements inconsistent with his present claim asserted in his pleadings and in the testimony on which he relies. And it passes the gauntlet of the hearsay rule, which requires that extra-judicial assertions be excluded if there was no opportunity for the opponent to cross-examine, because it is the opponent's own declaration and "he does not need to cross-examine himself." He then adds that "the Hearsay Rule is satisfied" since the party "now as opponent has the full opportunity to put himself on the stand and explain his former assertion." [4]

Strahorn, in a valuable article, suggests an alternative theory which classes all admissions of a party offered against him, whether words or acts, as being *conduct* offered as circumstantial evidence rather than for its assertive, testimonial value. Its circumstantial value is that which Wigmore pointed out, namely, the quality of inconsistency with the party's present claim. "The hearsay rule applies to those statements for which the only justification is their narrative content. It is inapplicable to those which are conduct, i.e., for which the trustworthiness of the utterance is a matter of indifference. So it is with admissions. The writer feels that inas-

much as all admissions, express and otherwise, can be rationalized as the relevant conduct of the speaker, it is unnecessary to predicate their admissibility on the basis of a possible narrative effect not possessed by all of them." [5]

On balance, the most satisfactory justification of the admissibility of admissions is that they are the product of the adversary system, sharing, though on a lower and nonconclusive level, the characteristics of admissions in pleadings or stipulations. This view has the added advantage of avoiding the need to find with respect to admissions the circumstantial guarantees of trustworthiness which traditionally characterize hearsay exceptions; admissions are simply classed as nonhearsay.[6] Nevertheless, the usual practice is to regard admissions as an exception to the hearsay rule, and as a matter of convenience the discussion of them is located at this point in this textbook.[7]

Regardless of the precise theory of admissibility, it is clear today that admissions of a party come in as substantive evidence of the facts admitted,[8] and that no foundation

---

3. Morgan, Basic Problems of Evidence 266 (1962).

4. 4 Wigmore, Evidence § 1048, pp. 2–5, approved in Milton v. U. S., 71 App.D.C. 394, 110 F.2d 556 (1940).

5. Strahorn, The Hearsay Rule and Admissions, 85 U.Pa.L.Rev. 484, 564 at 573, 576 (1937). For a similar judicial discussion of the rationale, see Schloss v. Traunstine, 135 N.J.L. 11, 49 A.2d 677 (1946).

6. F.R.Ev. (R.D.1971) 801(d) (2). And see Cox v. Esso Shipping Co., 247 F.2d 629, 632 (5th Cir. 1957). The various theories are summarized in Hetland, Admissions in the Uniform Rules: Are They Necessary? 46 Iowa L.Rev. 307, 308 (1961).

7. For examples of the conventional treatment see the original edition of this work, Ch. 27; Morgan, Basic Problems of Evidence 265 (1962); Uniform Rules 63(7), (8), (9); West's Ann.Cal.Evid.Code, §§ 1220–1227.

8. Olson v. Hodges, 236 Iowa 612, 19 N.W.2d 676 (1945) (error to instruct the jury that an admission could be considered merely as discrediting the party's testimony); Lambros v. Coolahan, 185 Md. 463, 45 A.2d 96 (1945) (report by witness of party's oral admission, though denied by party, sufficient to take the issue to jury); Litman v. Peper, 214 Minn. 127, 7 N.W.2d 334 (1943) (admission, though making of it denied by party, sufficient to take case to jury on issue of negligence); Greenwood v. Harris, 362 P.2d

or predicate, by examining the party himself, such as may be required for impeaching evidence,[9] is prerequisite for proof of admissions.[10]

When we speak of admissions, without qualifying adjective, we customarily mean evidential admissions, that is, words oral or written, or conduct of a party or his representative offered in evidence against him. These *evidential* admissions are to be distinguished from *judicial* admissions. Judicial admissions are not evidence at all, but are formal admissions in the pleadings in the case, or stipulations, oral or written, by a party or his counsel which have the effect of withdrawing a fact from issue and dispensing wholly with the need for proof of the fact.[11] Thus the judicial admission, unless it should be allowed by the court to be withdrawn, is conclusive, whereas the evidential admission is not conclusive (unless the adversary should fail to meet it with contrary evidence) but is always subject to be contradicted or explained.[12]

Confessions of crime are, of course, but one kind of admission, discussed in the chapter on Confessions.[13]

A type of evidence with which admissions may be confused is evidence of declarations against interest. The latter, coming in under a separate exception to the hearsay rule, to be admissible must have been against the declarant's interest when made.[14] No such requirement applies to admissions. If a party states that a note or deed is forged, and then later buys the note or the land, and sues upon the note or for the land, obviously the previous statement will come in against him as an admission, though he had no interest when he made the statement. Of course, most admissions are actually against interest when made, but there is no such requirement.[15] Hence the common phrase in judi-

---

Minn. 212, 7 N.W.2d 757, 759 (1943) ("Plaintiff's testimony cannot be rejected simply because at the hospital he gave the statement containing a contrary version"); Rosenblatt v. Percy, 313 Mass. 757, 49 N.E.2d 114 (1943) (wrongful death; plaintiffs introduced evidence that defendant in criminal proceeding had pleaded guilty to negligent driving; evidence that defendant did this to save time and expense admitted); 4 Wigmore, Evidence §§ 1058, 1059.

13. Ch. 14, supra.

14. See § 276, infra.

15. One of the clearest expressions to this effect is in State v. Anderson, 10 Ore. 448, 452 (1882). On a charge of murdering his brother, the state gave in evidence defendant's admissions that he had no means before his brother's death. In holding these admissible over the objection that they were not against interest, the court said: "But the admissibility of a party's own previous statements or declarations in respect to the subject in controversy, as evidence against him, does not in any manner depend upon the question whether they were for or against his interest at the time they were made, or afterwards. The opposite party has a right to introduce them if relevant and voluntarily made, no matter how they may stand or have stood in relation to the interest of the party making them." For similar expressions, see Caswell v. Maplewood Garage, 84 N.H. 241, 149 A. 746 (1930). On the same principle rest the cases admitting the party's previous offers to buy or sell, or valuation for tax-purposes at a different value than he now contends for. Erceg v. Fairbanks Exploration Co., 95 F.2d 850 (9th Cir. 1938) (offer to buy); Manning v. Lowell, 173 Mass. 100, 53 N.E. 160 (valuation to

---

85 (Okl.1961), noted 1 Washburn L.J. 614 (defendant's admission sufficient to supply need for expert testimony in medical malpractice action); Peterson v. Richards, 73 Utah 59, 272 P. 229 (1928) (sufficient to support finding of fact); Dec.Dig. Evidence ☞200, 217, 222(1), 265(1); 4 Wigmore, Evidence §§ 1055, 1056. But particular testimony attesting to an oral admission may be insufficient to support a finding. O'Neill v. Claypool, 341 S.W.2d 129 (Mo.1960). Other circumstances such as the want of knowledge of the admitter may deprive it of substantial weight in a particular case. Binewicz v. Haglin, 103 Minn. 297, 115 N.W. 271 (1908).

9. See § 37, supra.

10. Cox v. Esso Shipping Co., 247 F.2d 629, 632 (5th Cir. 1957); Howe v. Messimer, 84 Mont. 304, 275 P. 281 (1929); 4 Wigmore, Evidence § 1051(1).

11. Polk v. Missouri–Kansas–Texas R. Co., 341 Mo. 1213, 111 S.W.2d 138, 114 A.L.R. 873 (1937); Dec. Dig. Evidence ☞265(7); 4 Wigmore, Evidence § 1058, 9 id. §§ 2588–2595. In the same category are admissions in response to requests to admit under F.R.Civ.P. 36. Finman, The Request for Admissions in Federal Civil Procedure, 71 Yale L.J. 371 (1962).

12. Cooper v. Brown, 126 F.2d 874 (3d Cir. 1942); Pierce v. Gruben, 237 Iowa 329, 21 N.W.2d 881 (1946) (contradiction allowed); Aide v. Taylor, 214

cial opinions, "admissions against interest," [16] is an invitation to confuse two separate exceptions to the hearsay rule and to engraft upon admissions a requirement without basis in reason or authority. Other apparent distinctions are that admissions must be the statements of a party to the lawsuit (or his predecessor or representative) and must be offered, not for, but against him, whereas the declaration against interest need not be and usually is not made by a party or his predecessor or representative, but by some third person.[17] Finally, the declaration against interest exception admits the declaration only when the declarant, by death or otherwise, has become unavailable as a witness, whereas obviously no such requirement is applied to admissions of a party.[18]

If there are several parties on one side of the litigation, whether plaintiffs or defendants, the admission of one of these co-parties is admissible only against himself and not against the other parties with whom he is aligned.[19]

263. Testimonial Qualifications: Mental Competency: Personal Knowledge.[20]

The nature of admissions as a general proposition denies any significance to the question whether the party making the admission must meet standards of competency established for witnesses.[21] Thus such disqualifications, if still recognized, as those arising from conviction of crime, the marital relationship, or "Dead Man's" acts lack relevancy in the case of admissions. No reason exists to exclude an otherwise receivable admission because the party making it was a convict or married, or is now dead. The single exception calling for consideration is lack of mental capacity. Some cases involve statements by badly injured persons, possibly also under sedation. While the older decisions tended to mount an inquiry into the capacity of the declarant and to exclude if it was found not to exist,[22] the more modern ones view the question as going to weight rather than admissibility.[23] The latter position represents a preferable allocation of the functions of judge and jury and is consistent with current thinking concerning mental competency as a qualification of witnesses.[24] Other cases involve admissions by children, and a similar approach seems clearly to be indicated,[25] although cases may be found which seem to confuse the matter with substantive liability for torts or capacity to contract.[26]

secure tax reduction). See 4 Wigmore, Evidence § 1048, notes 3 and 4.

16. E. g., in Kellner v. Whaley, 148 Neb. 259, 27 N. W.2d 183, 189 (1947); Hack v. State Farm Mut. Auto. Ins. Co., 37 Wis.2d 1, 154 N.W.2d 320 (1967).

17. Downs v. McCampbell, 203 S.W.2d 302 (Tex.Civ. App.1947). See § 276, infra.

18. The distinctions are fully expounded in Elliotte v. Lavier, 299 Mich. 353, 300 N.W. 116 (1941) and McComb v. Vaughn, 358 Mo. 951, 218 S.W.2d 548 (1949); and see 4 Wigmore, Evidence, §§ 1048, 1049; F.R.Ev. (R.D.1971) 801(d) (2), 804 (b) (4).

19. There may, of course, be an additional relationship, over and above that of being co-parties, which will render the evidence admissible. See §§ 267, 268, infra.

20. See 4 Wigmore, Evidence § 1053.

21. See Ch. 7, supra.

22. Jacobson v. Carlson, 302 Mich. 448, 4 N.W.2d 721 (1942); Ammundson v. Tinholt, 228 Minn. 115, 36 N.W.2d 521 (1949). Oddly, both cases speak of utterances of a party incapable of narrating.

23. Currier v. Grossman's of New Hampshire, Inc., 107 N.H. 159, 219 A.2d 273 (1966); Finnerty v. Darby, 391 Pa. 300, 138 A.2d 117 (1958).

Attention is directed to legislation restricting the admissibility of statements obtained from injured persons within specified periods after the injury was sustained. Mass.Gen.Laws Ann. c. 271; Minn.Stats. Ann. § 602.01; Wis.Stats.Ann. 325.28. Cases involving statutes of this nature are collected in Annot., 22 A.L.R.2d 1269.

24. § 62, supra.

25. Admissions by children under 9 years of age were ruled admissible in Hardman v. Helene Curtis Industries Inc., 48 Ill.App.2d 42, 198 N.E.2d 681 (1964); Atchison, T. & S. F. R. Co. v. Potter, 60 Kan. 808, 58 P. 471 (1899); Rolfe v. Olson, 87 N.J. Super. 242, 208 A.2d 817 (1965). Cases are collected in Annot., 12 A.L.R.3d 1051.

26. See, e. g., Howard v. Hall, 112 Ga.App. 247, 145 S.E.2d 70 (1965).

The requirement that a witness speak from firsthand knowledge would seem to be applicable to hearsay declarations generally[27] and it has sometimes been applied to admissions,[28] but the traditional view and the greater number of decisions hold that it is not.[29] These latter argue that when a man speaks against his own interest it is to be supposed that he has made an adequate investigation.[30] While this self-disserving feature might attach to most admissions, we have seen that admissions are competent evidence though not against interest when made. As to these the argument does not apply, and it seems sufficient to justify the general dispensing with the knowledge qualification to say that admissions which become relevant in litigation usually concern some matter of substantial importance to the declarant upon which he would probably have informed himself so that they possess, even when not based on firsthand observation, greater reliability than the general run of hearsay. Moreover, the possibility is substantial that the declarant may have come into possession of significant information not known to his opponent.

264. Admissions in Opinion Form: Conclusions of Law.

If the want of knowledge of the party does not exclude his admissions, as indicated in the preceding section, it would seem clear that the opinion rule should not. As we have seen, that rule has as its object the regulation of the interrogation of a witness on the stand, so as to elicit his answers in the more concrete form rather than in terms of inference. In its modern form it is a rule of preference for the more concrete answers, if the witness can give them, rather than a rule of exclusion.[31] In any view, this rule, designed to promote the concreteness of answers on the stand, is grotesquely misapplied to out-of-court statements, such as admissions, where the declarant's statements are made without thought of the form of courtroom testimony and where it can only be applied by excluding the statement, whereas in the courtroom if the opinion objection is sustained, counsel may reframe his question in the preferred form. Accordingly, the prevailing view is that admissions in the form of opinions are competent.[32] Most often the

---

27. See e. g., §§ 285, 300, 310, infra.

28. Coca-Cola Bottling Co. v. Munn, 99 F.2d 190, 197 (4th Cir. 1938) (previous admission by plaintiff, now suing for injury due to lye in bottled drink, that it would be impossible for a bottle to have any lye in it after going through defendant's plant, held properly excluded); Paschall v. Gulf, C. & S. F. Ry. Co., 100 S.W.2d 183, 192, 193 (Tex.Civ.App. 1936) (action for death of husband in collision, letter of wife, who was not present, that family was not holding defendant, a friend of deceased, responsible, written before investigating facts, held improperly admitted—a very appealing result on the facts).

29. Smedra v. Stanek, 187 F.2d 892 (10th Cir. 1951) (defendant surgeon said he had been delayed because sponge count, conducted by nurses, did not come out correctly); Janus v. Akstin, 91 N.H. 373, 20 A.2d 552 (1941) (action for attack by defendant's dog, defendant's statement that dog jumped on the decedent held admissible though defendant not present); Reed v. McCord, 160 N.Y. 330, 341, 54 N.E. 737 (1899) (statement by defendant, employer, as to how injury happened, though he was not present); Salvitti v. Throp, 343 Pa. 642, 23 A.2d 445 (1942) (automobile collision; evidence that owner of truck acknowledged that his driver was at fault admitted, though owner not present); Berkowitz v. Simone, 96 R.I. 11, 188 A.2d 665 (1963) (similar to Janus v. Akstin, supra). Additional cases are collected in Annot., 54 A.L.R.2d 1069. See also 4 Wigmore, Evidence § 1053.

This question is often joined with the problem whether repetition of another's statement is an adoptive admission, see Reed v. McCord, supra, and § 269, infra.

30. On occasion it may appear affirmatively that an investigation was in fact conducted. Pekelis v. Transcontinental & Western Air, Inc., 187 F.2d 122 (2d Cir. 1951).

31. See § 18, supra.

32. Cox v. Esso Shipping Co., 247 F.2d 629 (5th Cir. 1957), noted 36 Tex.L.Rev. 514 (master's report that seaman's injury was due in part to own neglect); Pekelis v. Transcontinental & Western Air, Inc., 187 F.2d 122 (2d Cir. 1951) (report by airline investigating board as to cause of accident); Strickland v. Davis, 221 Ala. 247, 128 So. 233 (1930) (defendant after accident said it was his fault; held inadmissible, rejecting the application to admissions

question arises in connection with statements of a participant in an accident that it was his fault, or not the fault of the other participant. Against these and like statements, the additional objection is often urged that they are conclusions of law. But this should be no objection either. While conceivably a party might give an opinion on an abstract question of law, such are not the statements actually offered in evidence. These always include in them an application of a standard to the facts; thus they suggest what the declarant thinks the facts are to which he is applying the standard of "fault," or other legal or moral standard involved in his statement. The factual bearing is not to be ignored merely because the statement may also indicate the party's assumptions as to the law.[33]

265. Admissions in Pleadings:[34] Pleas of Guilty.

The final pleadings upon the which the case is tried state the contentions of each party as to the facts, and by admitting or denying the opponent's pleading, they define the fact issues which are to be tried by the process of proof. Thus, the court must look to the pleadings as part of the record in passing on the relevancy of evidence, and in ascertaining the issues to be submitted to the jury. For these purposes it is not necessary to offer the pleadings in evidence.[35] They are used as judicial and not as evidential admissions, and for these purposes, until withdrawn or amended, are conclusive.[36] But suppose a party desires to use an averment or admission in his adversary's final pleading, as a basis in his argument for the existence of some subordinate fact or as the foundation for some adverse inference. The greater number of states permit the party to do this by quoting or reading the pleading as part of the record,[37] but a substantial minority require that the party, in order to make this use of it, must first have introduced the relevant passage from the opponent's pleading as part of his own evidence during the course of the trial.[38] This requirement affords an opportunity to the pleader to give explanatory evidence, such as that the allegation was

of requirements for testimony on the stand, and the objection that the statement expressed a conclusion of law); Swain v. Oregon Motor Stages, 160 Ore. 1, 82 P.2d 1084, 118 A.L.R. 1225 (1938) (plaintiff, bus passenger suing for injury in collision with automobile, stated in accident report that driver of automobile to blame, admissible; extensive discussion); Wells v. Burton Lines, 228 N.C. 422, 45 S.E.2d 569 (1947) (plaintiff after collision said it was his fault); Grodsky v. Consolidated Bag Co., 324 Mo. 1067, 26 S.W.2d 618 (1930) ("Plaintiff's statement that it was her 'opinion the truck driver was entirely responsible for the accident' was inconsistent with her subsequent action in attempting to place the blame upon other parties. The trial court did not err in admitting the statement."; extensive discussion, but see Wright v. Quattrochi, below); Woods v. Townsend, 144 Tex. 594, 192 S.W. 2d 884 (1946) (will contest for undue influence; admission of proponent, "we got the papers fixed . . . but the old man didn't know what he was doing"); Southern Passenger Motor Lines v. Burke, 187 Va. 53, 46 S.E.2d 26 (1948) (plaintiff's statement that collision not due to fault or negligence of defendant's driver); 4 Wigmore, Evidence § 1053(3); Annot., 118 A.L.R. 1230.

Contra: Wright v. Quattrochi, 330 Mo. 174, 49 S.W. 2d 3 (1932) (defendant said he had talked to driver and it was driver's fault, held incompetent as conclusion of law, distinguishing *Grodsky* case, supra, because admitter was witness in that case, and not in this); Kellner v. Whaley, 148 Neb. 259, 27 N.W. 2d 183 (1947) (dictum that admission to be admissible must not be opinion or conclusion of law); C.J.S. Evidence § 272(b).

33. See decisions cited in 32, supra.

34. 4 Wigmore, Evidence §§ 1064–1067; Dec.Dig. Evidence ☞208, 265(8) (11); C.J.S. Evidence §§ 300–306; Annot., 52 A.L.R.2d 516; Notes 27 Mo.L. Rev. 258 (1962), 106 U.Pa.L.Rev. 98 (1957).

35. Wright v. Lincoln City Lines, Inc., 160 Neb. 714, 71 N.W.2d 182 (1955).

36. Note, 64 Colum.L.Rev. 1121 (1964).

37. Grand Trunk Western Ry. Co. v. Lovejoy, 304 Mich. 35, 7 N.W.2d 212 (1942); Hildreth v. Hudloe, 282 S.W. 747 (Mo.App.1926); Gibson v. Koutsky-Brennan-Vana Co., 143 Neb. 326, 9 N.W.2d 298 (1943); and cases cited in 4 Wigmore Evidence § 1064, note 1.

38. Louisiville & N. R. Co. v. Hull, 113 Ky. 561, 68 S.W. 433 (1902); Gossler v. Wood, 120 N.C. 69, 27 S.E. 33 (1897); Mullen v. Union Cent. L. Ins. Co., 182 Pa. 150, 37 A. 988 (1897) (affidavit of defense).

made through inadvertence or mistake,[39] so far as this may be allowable, and avoids the possibility of a surprise inference from the pleading in closing argument. It may be that these considerations justify the departure from consistency.

Under the systems of pleading as developed at common law and in chancery, there were certain limitations upon the use of the pleadings against the pleader, whether sought to be used as judicial admissions, or offered in evidence as admissions, as the local practice might dictate. For example the practice of pleading inconsistent counts and inconsistent defenses,[40] each unqualified in form, gave rise to the rule that as to each separate issue only the pleadings leading up to that particular issue could be considered against the pleader, and not the other counts or defenses on which other issues were raised.[41] For a time, under the influence of the Field Code of 1848, the view prevailed that in a given case there could exist only one set of facts and that inconsistent statements and defenses were therefore not allowable.[42] Nevertheless, uncertainty persists as to how a case will in fact develop at trial, and some procedure is needed for dealing with problems of variance. The modern equivalent of the common law system is the use of inconsistent, alternative, and hypothetical forms of statement of claims and defenses.[43] It can readily

be appreciated that pleadings of this nature are directed primarily to giving notice and lack the essential character of an admission. To allow them to operate as admissions would render their use ineffective and frustrate their underlying purpose. Hence the decisions with seeming unanimity deny them status as judicial admissions,[44] and generally disallow them as evidential admissions.[45]

Subject to the foregoing exceptions, which result largely from the necessities occasioned by the variance problem, pleadings are ordinarily usable against the pleader. If they are the effective pleadings in the case, they have the standing of judicial admissions, as noted previously.[46] If a pleading, or allegation therein, is amended, withdrawn, or superseded by a substitute pleading, it ceases to be usable as a conclusive judicial admission,[47] but is admissible in evidence in the case in which filed at the instance of the adversary as an evidentiary admission.[48]

---

39. This reason is given in Smith v. Nimocks, 94 N.C. 243 (1886).

40. "Records containing from ten to fifteen special counts or pleas are by no means rare. . . . Of these, the greater proportion and frequently the whole relate to the same substantial cause of action or defence. They are merely different expositions of the same case, and expositions of it often inconsistent with each other." Report of Common Law Procedure Commission, Parlt. Papers 1830, quoted in 9 Holdsworth, Hist.Eng.Law 305, 306 (3d ed. 1944).

41. Harington v. Macmorris, 5 Taunt 228, 128 Eng. Repr. 675 (1813); Herman v. Fine, 314 Mass. 67, 49 N.E.2d 597 (1943).

42. Clark, Code Pleading 460 (2d ed. 1947).

43. James, Civil Procedure 90 (1965).

44. McCormick v. Kopmann, 23 Ill.App.2d 189, 161 N.E.2d 720 (1959) (allegation of decedent's freedom from contributory negligence in count 1 not negated by allegation that his intoxication caused accident in count 4); Aetna Ins. Co. v. Klein, 318 S.W.2d 464 (Tex.Civ.App.1958) rev'd on other grounds 160 Tex. 61, 325 S.W.2d 376 (general denial not negated by contrary statements in special pleas).

45. Macheca v. Fowler, 412 S.W.2d 462 (Mo.1967); Van Sickell v. Margolis, 109 N.J.Super. 14, 262 A.2d 209 (1969), aff'd 55 N.J. 355, 262 A.2d 203; Furlong v. Donhals, Inc., 81 R.I. 46, 137 A.2d 734 (1958). Contra, Tway v. Hartman, 181 Okla. 608, 75 P.2d 893 (1938).

46. Supra, n. 36.

47. Taliaferro v. Reirdon, 197 Okl. 55, 168 P.2d 292 (1946); Kirk v. Head, 137 Tex. 44, 152 S.W.2d 726 (1941).

48. Raulie v. United States, 400 F.2d 487, 526 (10th Cir. 1968); Littell v. Bi-State Transit Development Agency, 423 S.W.2d 34 (Mo.1968); Foster v. Feder, 135 Colo. 585, 316 P.2d 576 (1957). The California view that superseded pleadings ought not to be admitted because in derogation of the policy of allowing amendments to be made liberally, Meyer v. State Board of Equalization, 42 Cal.2d 376, 267 P.2d 257 (1954), has not met with general acceptance. Cf. the treatment of the variance problem, supra, nn. 44, 45.

The question whether a plea of guilty, formally tendered, in a criminal case shall come in evidence as an admission where the accused is later allowed to plead not guilty and is tried on the charge, presents competing considerations of policy. On the one hand, it may be argued, a plea of guilty if freely and understandingly made is so likely to be true that to withhold it from the jury seems to ask them to do justice without knowledge of one of the most significant of the relevant facts. Similar admissions have been received in civil cases, leaving it to the adversary to rebut or explain.[49] But here, liberty or life is at stake, and a decision can scarcely be reached without taking into account the circumstances surrounding the withdrawal. If the leave to withdraw is granted because of denial of assistance of counsel, lack of ratification by the accused, involuntariness, or similar reason,[50] it is evident that a manifest injustice is sought to be corrected. If the withdrawn plea is nevertheless allowed into evidence, the effectiveness of the corrective measure is greatly impaired. Additionally, allowing the evidence virtually compels the accused to explain why he pleaded guilty, with resultant encroachment upon the privilege against self-incrimination and intrusion into sensitive areas of the attorney-client relationship. Under these circumstances the withdrawn plea should be excluded.[51] If, on the contrary, withdrawal may be made without a showing of the kind described above,[52] exclusion would not follow automatically but would depend upon principles governing the admissibility of confessions.[53]

The use of pleadings as evidentiary admissions is by no means confined to the situations discussed above of their employment in the very case in which the pleading was filed. A party's pleading in one case, whether a final one, or one later withdrawn, amended or superseded, is freely usable against him as an evidentiary admission in any other litigation,[54] unless excluded under the limitations described above[55] based on the prevalence of alternative or hypothetical allegations in the traditional systems.[56] Especially frequent is the use of a plea of guilty to a

---

Compare the status of a withdrawn statement made at pretrial conference. In Laird v. Air Carrier Engine Service, Inc., 263 F.2d 948 (5th Cir. 1959), the court held that to admit as an evidential admission would destroy the effectiveness of pretrial proceedings; hence the statement should be excluded.

49. See, e. g., Morrissey v. Powell, 304 Mass. 268, 23 N.E.2d 411, 124 A.L.R. 1522 (1939) (in action for personal injuries defendant's plea of guilty to criminal charge of driving while drunk, though the plea was later withdrawn and upon a trial he was acquitted, held competent); 40 Colum.L.Rev. 915, 8 Duke B.A.J. 134, 26 Va.L.Rev. 514.

50. These are set forth as grounds for withdrawal in A.B.A. Project on Minimum Standards for Criminal Justice, Standards Relating to Pleas of Guilty 53 (Approved Draft, 1968).

51. Kercheval v. United States, 274 U.S. 220 (1927); People v. Spitaleri, 9 N.Y.2d 168, 212 N.Y.S.2d 53, 173 N.E.2d 35 (1961); A.B.A. Project on Minimum Standards for Criminal Justice, Standards Relating to Pleas of Guilty 59 (Approved Draft, 1968). West's Ann.Cal.Evid.Code, § 1153 and F.R.Ev. (R.D. 1971) 410 make the withdrawn plea inadmissible in both civil and criminal proceedings. Cases pro and con are collected in Annot., 86 A.L.R.2d 326.

52. E. g., under Ga.Code, § 27–1404 (1953) making withdrawal a matter of right prior to judgment, or under a local rule making withdrawal discretionary with the judge. A.B.A. Project on Minimum Standards for Criminal Justice, Standards Relating to Pleas of Guilty 58 (Approved Draft, 1968).

53. The same would seem to be true with respect to "pleas of guilty" made, often without formal authorization of law, before committing magistrates. See cases in Annot., 141 A.L.R. 1335.

54. Frank R. Jelleff, Inc. v. Braden, 98 U.S.App.D.C. 180, 233 F.2d 671 (1956); Missouri Pacific R. Co., v. Zolliecoffer, 209 Ark. 559, 191 S.W.2d 587 (1946); Bartalotta v. Calvo, 112 Conn. 385, 152 A. 306 (1930); Himelson v. Galusz, 309 Mich. 512, 15 N.W.2d 727 (1944); Dec.Dig. Evidence ⚖208(2); C.J.S. Evidence § 303.

55. See n. 40–45, supra.

56. In Schusler v. Fletcher, 74 Ill.App.2d 249, 219 N.E.2d 588 (1966), the court extended the principle of excluding alternative inconsistent allegations in the same complaint to encompass separate actions by plaintiff, each claiming a separate cause for his injuries. The cases have not generally followed. Cf. Carlson v. New York Life Ins. Co., 76 Ill.App. 2d 187, 222 N.E.2d 363 (1966).

criminal charge offered as an admission in a later civil suit arising from the same transaction.[57] While a plea of guilty to a traffic offense is in theory no different from a plea of guilty to other offenses,[58] recognition that people plead guilty to traffic charges for reasons of convenience and without much regard to guilt and collateral consequences has led to some tendency to exclude them from evidence.[59] Pleas of *nolo contendere* or *non vult*, in jurisdictions where allowed,[60] are generally regarded as inadmissible,[61] and in fact that attribute is a principal reason for their employment.[62]

How far is it necessary to connect the pleading with the party against whom it is sought to be used in evidence as an admission? Certainly if it be shown to have been sworn to,[63] or signed by the party himself

that would be sufficient.[64] More often, however, the pleading is prepared and signed by counsel, and the older view holds that it is not sufficient to show that the pleading was filed or signed by the party's attorney of record, and that the statements therein will be presumed to be merely "suggestions of counsel" unless other evidence is produced that they were actually sanctioned by the client.[65] The trend today, however, is to the sensible view that pleadings shown to have been prepared or filed by counsel employed by the party, are prima facie regarded as authorized by him and are entitled to be received as his admissions.[66] It is open to the party to give evidence that the pleading was filed upon incorrect information and without his actual knowledge but such a showing goes only to the weight, not the admissibility of the pleading.[67]

266. Testimony by the Party Against Himself.[68]

It happens not infrequently that a party while testifying on the stand or on pretrial examination may admit some fact which if true is fatal, or at least adverse, to his cause of action or defense. If at the end of the trial the party's admission stands unimpeached and uncontradicted, then like unimpeached

---

57. State Farm Mut. Auto. Ins. Co. v. Worthington, 405 F.2d 683 (8th Cir. 1968); Teitelbaum Furs, Inc. v. Dominion Ins. Co., 58 Cal.2d 601, 25 Cal.Rptr. 559, 375 P.2d 439 (1962); Johnson v. Tucker, 383 S.W.2d 325 (Ky.1964); Annot., 18 A.L.R.2d 1287, 1307. The authorities agree that evidence is admissible to explain the guilty plea.

58. Ando v. Woodberry, 8 N.Y.2d 165, 203 N.Y.S.2d 74, 168 N.E.2d 520 (1960), 9 Buffalo L.Rev. 373, 74 Harv.L.Rev. 1452.

59. Hannah v. Ike Topper Structural Steel Co., 120 Ohio App. 44, 201 N.E.2d 63 (1963). Statutory prohibitions against introducing traffic convictions have been construed as applying also to guilty pleas. Jones v. Talbot, 87 Idaho 498, 394 P.2d 316 (1964). See also § 318, n. 23, infra.

60. E. g., F.R.Crim.P. 11.

61. Federal Deposit Ins. Corp. v. Cloonan, 165 Kan. 68, 193 P.2d 656 (1948); State v. La Rose, 71 N.H. 435, 52 A. 943 (1902); F.R.Ev. (R.D.1971) 410. It may be assumed that this is a factor considered by the judge in exercising his discretion to allow or deny the plea.

62. For the use of the plea in antitrust actions, see City of Burbank v. General Electric Co., 329 F.2d 825 (9th Cir. 1964); Seamans et al., Use of Criminal Pleas in Aid of Private Antitrust Actions, 10 Antitrust Bull. 795 (1965).

63. Hall v. Guthrie, 10 Mo. 621 (1847) (sworn bill in chancery); Johnson v. Butte, 41 Mont. 158, 108 P. 1057 (1910) (admission in sworn answer); Dec.Dig. Evidence ⊜208(4).

64. Radclyffe v. Barton, 161 Mass. 327, 37 N.E. 373 (1894); Annot., 14 A.L.R. 26.

65. Fidelity & Deposit Co. v. Redfield, 7 F.2d 800 (9th Cir. 1925); Reichert v. Jerome H. Sheip, Inc., 206 Ala. 648, 91 So. 618 (1921). Cases pro and con are collected in Annots. 14 A.L.R. 22, 23, 90 A.L.R. 1393, 1394, 63 A.L.R.2d 412, 428, 444.

66. Frank R. Jelleff, Inc. v. Braden, 98 U.S.App.D.C. 180, 233 F.2d 671 (1956); Fibreboard Paper Prod. Corp. v. East Bay Union, 227 C.A.2d 675, 39 Cal. Rptr. 64, 83 (1964); Collens v. New Canaan Water Co., 155 Conn. 477, 234 A.2d 825 (1967); Allen v. United States F. & G. Co., 269 Ill. 234, 109 N.E. 1035 (1915); Carlson v. Fredsall, 228 Minn. 461, 37 N.W.2d 744 (1949).

67. Cases cited in n. 66, supra.

68. See 9 Wigmore, Evidence § 2594a; Annot., 169 A.L.R. 798; Notes, 22 Va.L.Rev. 365, 36 Mich.L. Rev. 688, 9 Vand.L.Rev. 879; Dec.Dig. Evidence ⊜265(10); C.J.S. Evidence § 1040(3).

and uncontradicted testimony generally it is conclusive against him. Frequently this situation is what the courts are referring to when they say somewhat misleadingly that a party is "bound" by his own testimony.[69] The controversial question is whether he is bound by his own testimony in the sense that he will not be allowed to contradict it by other testimony, or if contradictory testimony has been received the judge and jury are required to disregard it and to accept as true the party's self-disserving testimony, as a judicial admission.

Three main approaches are reflected in the decisions. They tend to some extent to merge together and do not necessarily lead to different results in particular situations. First, the view that a party's testimony in this respect is like the testimony of any other witness called by the party, that is, the party is free (as far as any rule of law is concerned) to elicit contradictory testimony from the witness himself or to call other witnesses to contradict him.[70] Obviously, however, the problem of persuasion may be a difficult one when the party seeks to explain or contradict his own words, and equally obviously the trial judge would often be justified in saying, on motion for directed verdict, that reasonable minds in the particular state of the proof could only believe that the party's testimony against his interest was true.

Second, the view that the party's testimony is not conclusive against contradiction except when he testifies unequivocally to matters "in his peculiar knowledge." These matters may consist of subjective facts, such as his own knowledge or motivation,[71] or they may consist of objective facts observed by him.[72]

Third, the doctrine that a party's testimony adverse to himself is in general to be treated as a judicial admission, conclusive against him,[73] so that he may not bring other witnesses to contradict it, and if he or his adversary does elicit such conflicting testimony it will be disregarded. Obviously, this general rule demands many qualifications and exceptions. Among these are the following: (1) The party is free to contradict,

---

69. E. g., Flanagan v. John Hancock Mutual Life Ins. Co., 349 Mass. 405, 208 N.E.2d 497 (1965); Bunkers v. Mousel, 83 S.D. 45, 154 N.W.2d 208 (1967).

70. Alamo v. Del Rosario, 69 App.D.C. 47, 98 F.2d 328 (1938) (personal injury from automobile collision; plaintiff testified that defendant, his host, the driver, stopped the car, whereas negligence alleged was that he made an untimely left turn; held, jury entitled to believe other witnesses; masterly exposition of the policy of the doctrine, by Edgerton, J.); Guenther v. Armstrong Rubber Co., 406 F.2d 1315 (3d Cir. 1969) (variance in describing tire which caused injury); Kanopka v. Kanopka, 113 Conn. 30, 154 A. 144, 80 A.L.R. 619 (1931) (collision; plaintiff, foreigner speaking through interpreter, excited at time of accident and trial, not concluded by her testimony; general rule that party's testimony, unless intended as unequivocal concession, not conclusive); Cox v. Jones, 138 Ore. 327, 5 P.2d 102 (1931) (automobile collision at intersection, plaintiff's testimony as to her own speed and as to seeing approaching truck not conclusive); Wiley v. Rutland Ry. Co., 86 Vt. 504, 86 A. 808 (1913) (injury to pedestrian run over by backing train; plaintiff's testimony as to when she looked at track, not a judicial admission); Gale v. Kay, 390 P.2d 596 (Wyo. 1964).

71. Monsanto Chemical Co. v. Payne, 354 F.2d 965 (5th Cir. 1966); Findlay v. Rubin Glass and Mirror Co., 350 Mass. 169, 213 N.E.2d 858 (1966); Peterson v. American Family Mut. Ins. Co., 280 Minn. 482, 160 N.W.2d 541 (1968); Bockman v. Mitchell Bros. Truck Lines, 213 Ore. 88, 320 P.2d 266 (1958).

72. Bell v. Harmon, 284 S.W.2d 812 (Ky.1955) (plaintiff's verson of automobile collision in which he was involved); Verry v. Murphy, 163 N.W.2d 721, 735 (N.D.1969) (plaintiff's version of business transaction).

73. Stearns v. Chicago, R. I. and P. R. Co., 166 Iowa 566, 578, 148 N.W. 128 (1914) (plaintiff's testimony that he did not stop his train as he should have, though contradicated, conclusive on contributory negligence); Taylor v. Williams, 190 So.2d 872 (Miss.1966) (plaintiff passenger's testimony that defendant was not driving, conclusive despite admission in his answer and testimony. "Swore herself out of court"); Massie v. Firmstone, 134 Va. 450, 114 S.E. 652 (1922) (plaintiff real estate broker suing for commission testified that his commission was conditional on sale going through and that it had not; despite contradictory testimony, plaintiff bound by his own evidence).

See also cases in note 72, supra.

and thus correct, his own testimony; only when his own testimony taken as a whole unequivocally affirms the statement does the rule of conclusiveness apply.[74] The rule is inapplicable, moreover, when the party's testimony (2) may be attributable to inadvertence [75] or to a foreigner's mistake as to meaning,[76] or (3) is merely negative in effect,[77] or (4) is avowedly uncertain, or is an estimate or opinion [78] rather than an assertion of concrete fact, or (5) relates to a matter as to which the party could easily have been mistaken, such as the swiftly moving events just preceding a collision in which the party was injured.[79]

Of these three approaches the first, which rejects any restrictive rule and leaves to the judgment of the jurors, the judge, and the appellate court, to evaluate the party's testimony and the conflicting evidence, in the circumstances of the particular case, with only the standard of reason to guide them, seems preferable in policy and most in accord with the tradition of jury trial.

The second theory, binding the party as to facts within his "peculiar knowledge," is based on the assumption that as to such facts the possibility that he may be mistaken sub-

stantially disappears. If the facts are subjective ones (knowledge, motivation), the likelihood of successful contradiction is slight, but even then the assumption may be questioned. "If he is human it does not disappear. Knowledge may be 'special' without being correct. Often we little note nor long remember our 'motives, purposes, or knowledge.' There are few if any subjects on which plaintiffs are infallible." [80]

The third theory is also of doubtful validity. In the first place the party's testimony, uttered by a layman in the stress of examination, cannot with justice be given the conclusiveness of the traditional judicial admission in a pleading or stipulation,[81] deliberately drafted by counsel for the express purpose of limiting and defining the facts in issue.[82] Again, a general rule of conclusiveness necessitates an elaboration of qualifications and exceptions which represent a transfer to the appellate court of some of the traditional control of the jury by the trial judge, or in a nonjury case of the judge's factfinding function. These duties call for an exercise of judgment by the judge who has heard and seen the witnesses. The supervision by appellate judges of this trial process can best be exercised under a flexible standard, rather than a rule of conclusiveness.

---

74. Chaplain v. Dugas, 323 Mass. 91, 80 N.E.2d 9 (1948); Virginia Elec. & Power Co. v. Mabin, 203 Va. 490, 125 S.E.2d 145 (1962).

75. Martin v. Kansas City, 340 S.W.2d 645 (Mo. 1960) (statement immediately corrected); Security National Bank v. Johnson, 195 Okl. 107, 155 P.2d 249, 169 A.L.R. 790 (1944) (where doubtful whether statement of party was a slip of the tongue, and was inconsistent with other parts of his testimony, question is for jury).

76. Krikorian v. Dailey, 171 Va. 16, 197 S.E. 442 (1938).

77. Waller v. Waller, 187 Va. 25, 46 S.E.2d 42, 45 (1948).

78. Taylor v. Williams, 190 So.2d 872 (Miss.1966); Van Buskirk v. Missouri-Kansas-Texas R. Co., 349 S.W.2d 68 (Mo.1961); Petit v. Klinke, 152 Tex. 142, 254 S.W.2d 769 (1953).

79. McCormack v. Haan, 20 Ill.2d 75, 169 N.E.2d 239 (1960); Crew v. Nelson, 188 Va. 108, 49 S.E.2d 326 (1948).

80. Edgerton, J., in Alamo v. Del Rosario, 69 App.D. C. 47, 98 F.2d 328, 332 (1938).

81. As to judicial admissions see § 262 at n. 11, supra, and 9 Wigmore, Evidence §§ 2588–2594.

82. This much, however, should be conceded, even under the liberal view contended for that a party is not generally concluded by his testimony. That is, if a party testifies deliberately to a fact fatal to his case, the judge if his counsel, on inquiry, indicates no intention to seek to elicit contradictory testimony, may give a nonsuit or directed verdict. Under these circumstances, the party and his counsel advisedly manifest an intention to be bound. See Kanopka v. Kanopka, 113 Conn. 30, 154 A. 144, 147 (1931), and the annotator's discussion, 169 A.L.R. 801. Compare Oscanyan v. Arms Co., 103 U.S. 261, 263 (1880) holding it proper to direct a verdict on counsel's opening statement.

Moreover, this rule leads to mechanical solutions, unrelated to the needs of justice and calculated to proliferate appeals, in certain special situations. One is the situation where the opponent by adroit cross-examination has maneuvered the party into an improvident concession.[83] Another is the case of the defendant who is protected by liability insurance and who testifies to facts which will help the plaintiff to win.[84] Yet another is the situation where both parties testify against their respective interests.[85] Here the rule of conclusiveness may be thought to decide the issue against the party who has the burden of proof.[86]

Finally, the moral emphasis is wrong. Early cases where the rule of conclusiveness was first used may have been cases where the judges were outraged by seeming attempts by parties to play fast and loose with the court. But examination of numerous decisions demonstrates that this is far from

being the typical situation of the party testifying to self-disserving facts. Instead of the unscrupulous party, it is the one who can be pushed into an admission by the ingenuity or persistence of adverse counsel,[87] or it is the unusually candid or conscientious party willing to speak the truth to his own hurt, who is penalized by the rule of conclusiveness.[88] It is to be hoped that the courts may revert to the older, simpler, and more flexible practice.

267. Representative Admissions.[89]

When a party to the suit has expressly authorized another person to speak on his behalf, it is an obvious and accepted extension of the admission rule, to admit against the party the statements of such person.[90] In the absence of express authority, how far will the statements of an agent be received as the principal's admission by virtue of the

---

83. See, e. g., Driscoll v. Virginia Elec. & Power Co., 166 Va. 538, 181 S.E. 402 (1935).

84. E. g., Vondrashek v. Dignan, 200 Minn. 530, 274 N.W. 609 (1937) (on question of contributory negligence of plaintiff passenger, defense concluded by defendant's testimony that nobody could tell that he was under the influence). See Note, 36 Mich.L. Rev. 688. Preferable results are to deny conclusiveness to the testimony of defendant-insured, Christie v. Eager, 129 Conn. 62, 26 A.2d 352 (1942), or to allow the introduction of contradicting evidence by the defense. King v. Spencer, 115 Conn. 201, 161 A. 103 (1932), 32 Colum.L.Rev. 1243; contra, Spadaro v. Palmisano, 109 So.2d 418 (Fla. App. 1959). In Horneman v. Brown, 286 Mass. 65, 190 N.E. 735 (1935), in a compulsory liability insurance jurisdiction the defense was allowed to impeach the defendant-insured by a prior inconsistent statement.

85. See, e. g., Sutherland v. Davis, 286 Ky. 743, 151 S.W.2d 1021 (1941) (suit by woman, guest, who had been picked up by defendant, driver of car; plaintiff testified that she knew that defendant was too drunk to drive and that she could have alighted after she knew this; defendant testified that though he had had some drinks, he was sober; held, the admissions by plaintiff precluded recovery, and she was barred from producing any evidence to the contrary).

86. See Chakales v. Djiovanides, 161 Va. 48, 170 S.E. 848 (1933) and Annot., 169 A.L.R. at 815.

87. See, e. g., Gilbert v. Bostona Mines Co., 121 Mont. 397, 195 P.2d 376 (1948); Kipf v. Bitner, 150 Neb. 155, 33 N.W.2d 518 (1948) (admission extracted from plaintiff on taking of deposition, not conclusive).

88. "Since his testimony was adverse to his interests, he is more likely to have been mistaken than lying. The proposed rule actually punishes him for two things, his honesty and his error." Edgerton, J. in Alamo v. Del Rosario, 69 App.D.C. 47, 98 F.2d 328, 331 (1938), and see Burruss v. Suddith, 187 Va. 473, 47 S.E. 546 (1948).

89. Uniform Rule 63(9) admits as an exception to the hearsay rule the following: "*Vicarious Admissions.* As against a party, a statement which would be admissible if made by the declarant at the hearing if (a) the statement concerned a matter within the scope of an agency or employment of the declarant for the party and was made before the termination of such relationship, or (b) the party and the declarant were participating in a plan to commit a crime or a civil wrong and the statement was relevant to the plan or its subject matter and was made while the plan was in existence and before its complete execution or other termination, or (c) one of the issues between the party and the proponent of the evidence of the statement is a legal liability of the declarant, and the statement tends to establish that liability".

Compare West's Ann.Cal.Evid.Code, §§ 1222–1224; F.R.Ev. (R.D.1971) 801(d) (2).

90. Nuttall v. Holman, 110 Utah 375, 173 P.2d 1015 (1946).

employment relationship? The early texts and cases used as analogies the doctrine of the master's substantive responsibility for the acts of the agent, and the notion then prevalent in evidence law that words accompanying a relevant act are admissible as part of the *res gestae*. Thus they formulated the theory that the agent's statements could be received against the principal only when made at the time of, and in relation to, some act then being performed in the scope of the agent's duty.[91] This inadequate[92] theory finds reflection in some current opinions, where the fashion lingers of testing the admissibility of the agent's statements by the test of "res gestae."[93] A theory that gained

wide currency in the later writings[94] and opinions,[95] is that the evidential admissibility of the agent's statements as admissions of the principal is measured by precisely the same tests as the principal's substantive responsibility for the acts and conduct of the agent, that is, the words of the agent will be received in evidence as the admissions of the principal if they were spoken or written within the scope of the authority of the agent to speak or write for the employer. This formula makes it plain that the statements of an agent employed to give information may be received as the employer's admissions, regardless of want of authority to act otherwise, and conversely that authority to act, e. g., the authority of a chauffeur to drive a car, would not carry with it automatically the authority to make statements to others describing what he was doing or

---

91. "The acts of an agent, within the scope of the authority delegated to him, are deemed the acts of the principal. . . . 'But it must be remembered,' says Greenleaf, 'that the admission of the agent cannot always be assimilated to the admission of the principal. The party's own admission, whenever made may be given in evidence against him; but the admission or declaration of his agent binds him only when it is made during the continuance of the agency in regard to a transaction then depending, *et dum fervet opus*. It is because it is a verbal act and part of the *res gestae* that it is admissible at all; and, therefore, it is not necessary to call the agent to prove it; but wherever what he did is admissible in evidence, there it is competent to prove what he said about the act *while he was doing it*.' 1 Greenleaf, § 113." Harlan, J. in Vicksburg & Meridian Railroad v. O'Brien, 119 U.S. 99 (1886). For similar expressions, see Fairlie v. Hastings, 10 Ves.Jr. 123, 127, 32 Eng.Rep. 792 (Ch., 1804).

92. The *res gestae* term had been applied (a) to words of the agent used not for a hearsay purpose but as fixing substantive liability upon the principal as constituting, for example, a deceit or an acceptance of an offer, or (b) to spontaneous exclamations following an exciting event. See §§ 288, 297, infra, and Morgan, A Suggested Classification of Utterances Admissiible as Res Gestae, 31 Yale L.J. 229 (1922). In likening the hearsay use of the agent's admissions to these earlier situations by employing the same term, *res gestae*, the courts were obscuring the simpler notion of representation, and were inviting the application of requirements imposed on the other types of evidence and inappropriate here.

93. Alabama Power Co. v. Sellers, 283 Ala. 137, 214 So.2d 833 (1968); Crawford v. County of Sacramento, 239 C.A.2d 791, 49 Cal.Rptr. 115 (1966);

Gorman v. McCleaf, 369 Mich. 237, 119 N.W.2d 636 (1963); Teague v. Duke Power Co., 258 N.C. 759, 129 S.E.2d 507 (1963).

94. See 4 Wigmore, Evidence § 1078; Morgan, Admissions, 12 Wash.L.Rev. 181, 193 (1937); Notes, 3 Baylor L.Rev. 594 (1951), 43 Harv.L.Rev. 936 (1930), 4 Tex.L.Rev. 506, (1926); Restatement, Second Agency, §§ 284–291, especially § 286: "In an action between the principal and a third person, statements of an agent to a third person are admissible in evidence against the principal to prove the truth of facts asserted in them as though made by the principal, if the agent was authorized to make the statement or was authorized to make, on the principal's behalf, any statements concerning the subject matter.";
§ 288: . . .
"(2) Authority to do an act or to conduct a transaction does not of itself include authority to make statements concerning the act or transaction.
"(3) Authority to make statements of fact does not of itself include authority to make statements admitting liability because of such facts."

95. Griffiths v. Big Bear Stores, Inc., 55 Wash.2d 243, 347 P.2d 532, 535 (1959) (" . . . [D]eclarations and admissions against interest by an agent may not be shown except when they are within the scope of the agency, as established by the evidence in the case;"); Rudzinski v. Warner Theatres, Inc., 16 Wis.2d 241, 114 N.W.2d 466, 468 (1962) ("In order for an agent's statement to be admissible against his principal, it must have been spoken within the scope of the authority of the agent to speak for the principal.").

had done. Examples of cases applying the test are given below.[96]

Probably the most frequent employment of this test is in the exclusion of statements made by employees after an accident, to the injured party, to a police officer, or to some bystander, about the accident not made in furtherance of the employer's interest, but as a "mere narrative." [97] This is the logical application of these tests, but the assumption that the test for the master's responsibility for the agent's *acts* should be the test for using the agent's statements as *evidence* against the master is a shaky one. The rejection of such post-accident statements coupled with the admission of the employee's testimony on the stand is to prefer the weaker to the stronger evidence. The agent is well informed about acts in the course of the business, his statements offered against the employer are normally against the employer's interest, and while the employment continues, the employee is not likely to make the statements unless they are true. Moreover, if the admissibility of admissions is viewed as arising from the adversary system, responsibility for statements of one's employee is a consistent aspect. Accordingly, the trend is in the direction of broader admissibility of admissions by agents, exemplified by the Model Code provision which lets in the agent's statement, if "the declaration concerned a matter within the scope" of the declarant's employment "and was made before the termination of the agency or employment." [98] Cases in increasing number support this wider test.[99] Its acceptance by courts generally seems expedient.

---

96. Admissions of agent received against principal: Pan-American Petroleum & Transport Co. v. United States, 273 U.S. 456 (1927) (statements by president of corporations before Senate Committee investigating Teapot Dome oil leases admissible in suit by government against corporations to cancel leases); Cox v. Esso Shipping Co., 247 F.2d 629 (5th Cir. 1957) (shipmaster's report of accident); Partin v. Great Atlantic & Pacific Tea Co., 102 N.H. 62, 149 A.2d 860 (1959) (store manager's statement indicating plaintiff's fall due to negligence of employees); Arenson v. Skouras Theatres Corp., 131 N.J.L. 303, 36 A.2d 761 (1944) (report of theater employee to manager as to condition causing injury, in presence of plaintiff); Spett v. President Monroe Bldg. & Mfg. Corp., 19 N.Y.2d 203, 278 N.Y.S.2d 826, 225 N.E.2d 527 (1967) (statement by manager of business indicating that skid causing plaintiff's injury was put in place by employees); McDonnell v. Montgomery Ward & Co., 121 Vt. 221, 154 A.2d 469 (1959) (statement by service representative as to condition of appliance); Griffiths v. Big Bear Stores, Inc., 55 Wash.2d 243, 347 P.2d 532 (1959) (statement by store manager indicating fault for fall).

Statements of agent excluded: Bristol Wholesale Gro. Co. v. Municipal Lighting Plant Com'n, 347 Mass. 668, 200 N.E.2d 260 (1964) (statement of plant manager that explosion was defendant's fault); Roush v. Alkire Truck Lines, Inc., 299 S.W.2d 518 (Mo.1957) (truck driver's statement that brakes were defective); Lakeside Hospital v. Kovar, 131 Ohio St. 333, 2 N.E.2d 857 (1936) (statement of managing director of hospital of circumstances of injection of wrong solution into patient); Preston v. Lamb, 20 Utah 2d 260, 436 P.2d 1021 (1968) (statement of waitress that floor on which plaintiff slipped had been waxed excessively); Rudzinski v. Warner Theatres, Inc., 16 Wis.2d 241, 114 N.W.2d 466 (1962) (usher's admonition of janitor for not having mopped wet spots).

It is important to distinguish situations where the declaration of the agent comes in on other theories. Thus, if the agent and the principal are both parties to the suit, the agent's admission is of course received against him, though it may not be admissible against the master. Annot., 27 A.L.R.3d 966. Again, the agent's declaration often comes in as a spontaneous exclamation made under stress of excitement, sometimes referred to as *res gestae* (see § 297, infra).

97. See cases of exclusion, in n. 96, supra.

98. Model Code of Evidence Rule 508(a). This is now embodied in Uniform Rule 63(9) (a), set out in n. 89, above, and is found in the same or substantially the same language in Kan.Code C.P. § 60–460(i); N.J.R.Ev. 63(9); F.R.Ev. (R.D.1971) 801 (d) (2) (iv). No corresponding provision is found in West's Ann.Cal.Evid.Code.

These provisions do not, of course, exclude the conventional authorized statement. See Uniform Rule 63(8); Kan.Code C.P. § 60–460(h); N.J.R.Ev. 63(8); F.R.Ev. (R.D.1971) 801(d) (2) (iii).

99. Grayson v. Williams, 256 F.2d 61 (10th Cir. 1958); KLM Royal Dutch Airlines v. Tuller, 110 U.S.App.D.C. 282, 292 F.2d 775 (1961), cert. denied 368 U.S. 921; Joseph T. Ryerson & Sons, Inc. v. H. A. Crane & Bro., Inc., 417 F.2d 1263 (3d Cir. 1969); Martin v. Savage Truck Line, 121 F.Supp. 417 (D.D.C.1954); state court cases are collected in 4 Wigmore, Evidence § 1078.

Under any of these views, the party offering evidence of the alleged agent's admission must first prove the fact and scope of the agency of the declarant for the adverse party.[1] This he may of course do by the testimony of the asserted agent himself, or by anyone who knows, or by circumstantial evidence. Evidence of the purported agent's past declarations asserting the agency, are inadmissible hearsay when offered to show the relation.[2] If this preliminary fact of the declarant's agency is disputed, the question is one of "conditional relevancy." [3]

The question also arises whether a statement by an agent, in order to qualify as an admission, must be made to an outsider rather than to the principal or to another agent. Typical instances are the railway conductor's report of a wreck or accident, or a letter to the home office from a manager of a branch office of a bank. If the agent's statement

thus offered against the principal as an admission, though plainly made in the scope of authority, was a statement made to the principal himself, many courts refuse to admit it,[4] unless the principal has himself adopted it.[5] An equal number let such a statement come in.[6] The issue is usually assumed to be

Dow, KLM v. Tuller: A New Approach to Admissibility of Prior Statements of a Witness, 41 Neb. L.Rev. 598 (1962); Falknor, Vicarious Admissions and the Uniform Rules, 14 Vand.L.Rev. 855 (1961), Hearsay, 1969 Law & Soc.Order 591, 600; Morgan, The Rationale of Vicarious Admissions, 42 Harv.L. Rev. 461 (1929).

1.   Labor Hall Ass'n v. Danielsen, 24 Wash.2d 75, 163 P.2d 167, 161 A.L.R. 1079 (1945); 4 Wigmore, Evidence § 1078; Dec.Dig. Evidence ⟠258(1).

2.   Neither the fact nor the extent of the agency can be so proved. 4 Wigmore, Evidence § 1078, p. 123; Notes, 36 Ky.L.J. 471 (1948), 23 U.Cinc.L.Rev. 269 (1954), 10 U.Kan.L.Rev. 74 (1961), 18 Wash. & Lee L.Rev. 151 (1961). But the purported agent's declarations if offered to show that the other party dealt with him as an agent would not be hearsay, and would be admitted. Friend Lumber Co. v. Armstrong Bldg. Finish Co., 276 Mass. 361, 177 N.E. 794, 80 A.L.R. 599 (1931), with note on this point. And the asserted agent's declarations may come in to show his intention to act for the principal rather than for himself, either under the hearsay exception for declarations of mental state (see § 268, infra) or as circumstantial evidence of the intention. Mattan v. Hoover, 350 Mo. 506, 166 S.W.2d 557 (1942) (declaration of vacuum cleaner salesman after accident that he was on his way to make a demonstration). The possibility of using the spontaneous declaration of the agent should also be considered. See § 297, infra.

3.   See § 53, supra.

4.   E. g., Swan v. Miller [1919], 1 Ir.R. 151 (C.A.) (reviewing English authorities); Lever Bros. Co. v. Atlas Assur. Co., 131 F.2d 770, 776 (7th Cir. 1942) (report of investigating engineers on explosion); Standard Oil Co. of Calif. v. Moore, 251 F.2d 188, 218 (9th Cir. 1958) (reports of employees), noted 44 Va.L.Rev. 619; Nuttall v. Reading Co., 235 F.2d 546 (3d Cir. 1956) (statements by plaintiff's fellow employees to defendant's agent about accident made in preparation for trial), noted 35 Tex.L.Rev. 437; United States v. United Shoe Machinery Corp., 89 F.Supp. 349 (D.Mass.1950) (intracorporate letters and reports: principle and authorities ably discussed by Wyzanski, D. J., recognizing that they may come in as admissions if adopted by directors); Carroll v. East Tennessee, V. & G. Ry., 82 Ga. 452, 10 S.E. 163, 6 L.R.A. 214 (1889) (written report of accident, made after investigation, by conductor to superintendent); Atchison, T. & S. F. Ry. v. Burks, 78 Kan. 515, 96 Pac. 950, 18 L.R.A. N.S. 231 (1908) (reports of car inspectors as to defective coupler, inadmissible against railway company as admissions, unless adopted by company; extensive review of principles and authorities by Burch, J.); Warner v. Maine Central R. R., 111 Me. 149, 88 Atl. 403, 47 L.R.A.,N.S. 830 (1913) (station agent's report to general manager about fire); Bell v. Milwaukee Electric Ry. & Light Co., 169 Wis. 408, 172 N.W. 791 (1919) (written report of accident made by street-car conductor, at end of his run); Restatement, Second, Agency § 287:

"Statements by an agent to the principal or to another agent of the principal are not admissible against the principal as admissions; such statements may be admissible in evidence under other rules of evidence."

5.   United States v. United Shoe Machinery Corp., supra, n. 4; Pekelis v. Transcontinental and Western Air, Inc., 187 F.2d 122, 23 A.L.R.2d 1349 (2d Cir. 1951) (reports of investigating boards, appointed by airline, admitted as adoptive admissions).

6.   E. g., The Solway, 10 P.D. 137 (1885) (letter by master of ship to owners); Chicago, St. P. M. & O. Ry. Co. v. Kulp, 102 F.2d 352, 133 A.L.R. 1445 (8th Cir. 1939) (conductor's report to employer as to cause of injury to brakeman); Hilbert v. Spokane International Ry., 20 Idaho 54, 116 Pac. 1116 (1911) (section foreman's written report to company about a fire); Lemen v. Kansas City Southern Ry., 151 Mo.App. 511, 515, 132 S.W. 13 (1910) (oral report by conductor to station-agent, "Better send your section gang up the road. I think we set something on fire there."); Metropolitan Life

this: are such reports competent as admissions? Under the former view the question, does the agent speak for the principal in such a report, is answered: the doctrine of *respondeat superior* does not apply to transactions between the agent and the principal.[7] This statement is doubtless intended to suggest that some analogies, not specified, in the rules of substantive liability of principals should be controlling. But why other analogies, such as instances of statements made by a party himself not intended for the outside world, as where he is overheard talking to himself, or where he makes entries in a secret diary, should not be equally available, is not apparent. It seems clear that these latter statements and entries would be received against him as admissions.

The analogies are helpful as makeweight arguments to support a choice already made. But the decision whether reports of this kind should be used as evidence ought to be guided by more practical considerations. First, do they as a class have the degree of trustworthiness required to counterbalance the hazards of hearsay? While slightly less reliable as a class than the agent's authorized statements to outsiders, intra-organization reports are generally made as a basis for some action, and when this is so, they share the reliability of business records.[8] They will only be offered against the principal when they admit some fact disadvantageous to the principal, and this kind of statement

by an agent is likely to be true. No special danger of surprise, confusion, or prejudice from the use of the evidence is apparent. There seems little basis, then, for shaping our rule of competency of admissions to exclude this type of statements.

Attorneys.[9] Borrowing a popular term, how far is a lawyer the "mouthpiece" of the client? If an attorney is employed to manage a party's conduct of a lawsuit he has *prima facie* authority to make relevant judicial admissions by pleadings, by oral or written stipulations, or by formal opening statement, which unless allowed to be withdrawn are conclusive.[10] Such formal and conclusive admissions should be, and are, framed with care and circumspection, and in a leading English case, these admissions are contrasted with an attorney's oral out-of-court statement, and the latter characterized as "merely a loose conversation," [11] and it is often said that the client is not "bound" by the "casual" statements of his attorney out of court.[12] The use of the word "bound" is obviously misleading. The issue is not whether the client is "bound," as he is by a judicial

Ins. Co. v. Moss, 109 S.W.2d 1035 (Tex.Civ.App. 1937) (medical examiner's report to insurance company of state of health of applicant); Supreme Lodge, Knights of Honor v. Rampy, 45 S.W. 422 (Tex.Civ.App.1898, writ of error refused) (report by officers of local lodge to supreme lodge concerning good standing of member).

7. Morgan, The Rationale of Vicarious Admissions, 42 Harv.L.Rev. 461, 463 (1929).

8. This special trustworthiness is pointed out by Professor Morgan in the article referred to in the next preceding note (42 Harv.L.Rev. at 463, n. 4), but he contends that this furnishes no reason for using the representation formula in this situation as a theory of admissibility.

9. 4 Wigmore, Evidence § 1063; Morgan, Admissions, 12 Wash.L.Rev. 181, 188 (1937); Dec.Dig. Evidence ☞246.

10. See the discussion of judicial admissions, supra, § 265.

11. Petch v. Lyon, 9 Q.B. 147, 153, 115 Eng.Rep. 1231, 1233 (1846).

12. E. g., Jackson v. Schine Lexington Corp., 305 Ky. 823, 205 S.W.2d 1013, 1014 (1947) (copy of intended pleading, never filed, sent to plaintiff's attorney by defendant's, containing admission, held inadmissible. "The general rule is that an attorney has no power to prejudice his client by admissions of fact made out of court. Though he may be the agent of his client, such agency does not carry the implication of authority to make binding admissions other than in the actual management of the litigation."); Hogenson v. Service Armament Co., 77 Wash.2d 209, 461 P.2d 311, 314 (1969) (letter from plaintiff's attorney to defendant giving notice of breach of warranty and inaccurate version of circumstances of injury. "The sentence . . . was gratuitous information . . . tentative and casual . . . . It is neither distinct nor formal nor intended to dispense with the formal proof of a fact at trial.").

admission, but whether the attorney's extra-judicial statement is admissible against the client as a mere evidential admission made by an agent on his behalf. A natural if unconscious tendency to protect the client, and perhaps the attorney, against the hazard of evidence of statements by his attorney more strictly than in respect to statements by other types of agents is more manifest in the older cases.[13] The later cases, properly it seems, measure the authority of the attorney to make out-of-court admissions by the same tests of express or implied authority as would be applied to other agents,[14] and when they meet these tests admit as evidentiary admissions the statements of attorneys in letters or oral conversations made in the course of efforts for the collection or resistance of claims, or negotiations for the settlement of suits or controversies, or the management of any other business in behalf of the client.[15]

Partners.[16] A partner is an agent of the partnership for the conduct of the firm business.[17] Accordingly, when the existence and scope of the partnership have been proved,[18] the statement of a partner made in the conduct of the business of the firm comes in evidence as the admission of the partnership.[19] What of statements of a former part-

Possible application of the privilege for offers of compromise should not be overlooked. See § 274, infra.

16. 4 Wigmore, Evidence § 1078, p. 126; Crane and Bromberg, Partnership 320, 459 (3d ed. 1968); Rowley, Partnership § 51.9 (2d ed. 1960); Dec.Dig. Evidence ☞249; Annot., 73 A.L.R. 447.

17. As to the scope of the partner's agency, see Crane and Bromberg, Partnership § 49, p. 275 (3d ed. 1968).

18. This, of course, must be established by evidence other than the out-of-court declarations of the purported partner. Humboldt Livestock Auction, Inc. v. B & H Cattle Co., 155 N.W.2d 478 (Iowa 1967). See notes 1 and 2, supra, for like holdings as to agents.

19. Uniform Partnership Act, § 11: "An admission made by any partner concerning partnership affairs within the scope of his authority as conferred by this act is evidence against the partnership."; Wieder v. Lorenz, 164 Ore. 10, 99 P.2d 38 (1940) (failure by one member of firm to answer letter to him on firm business, admitted against partnership); King v. Wesner, 198 S.C. 289, 16 S.E.2d 289 (1941) statement of partner about accident of employee, made to representative of Industrial Commission who was investigating accident was in course of firm business and admissible against firm).

13. See, e. g., Wagstaff v. Wilson, 4 Barn. & Ad. 339, 110 Eng.Rep. 483 (1832) (trespass for taking a horse: letter offered from defendant's attorney of record stating that defendant had distrained the horse, written in reply to letter from plaintiff's attorney to defendant, excluded for want of proof that it was written with defendant's sanction); Saunders v. McCarthy, 90 Mass. 42, 45 (1864) (oral statements by attorney of relevant facts during conversation with adverse party before suit for the purpose of settling the controversy, held, "mere matters of conversation").

14. "If the admission is clearly within the scope of his agency, express or implied, he has the same authority to bind his client as any other agent." Offutt, J. in Brown v. Hebb, 167 Md. 535, 175 A. 602, 607, 97 A.L.R. 366 (1934).

15. Gerhart v. Henry Disston & Sons, Inc., 290 F.2d 778, 789 (3d Cir. 1961) (statement by lawyer handling business negotiation); Suntken v. Suntken, 223 Iowa 347, 272 N.W. 132 (1937) (admissions of fact in attorney's letter written in course of negotiations for compromise); Brown v. Hebb, 167 Md. 535, 175 A. 602, 97 A.L.R. 366 (1937) (doctor sends bill for $1500, patient's lawyer replies by letter offering $300 "for the services rendered" held admissible as an acknowledgment of a debt for services, tolling limitations); Noel v. Roberts, 449 S.W. 2d 572 (Mo.1970) (letter from plaintiff's attorney stating that employee rather than defendant assaulted plaintiff, on question of punitive damages).

Morgan, Admissions, 12 Wash.L.Rev. 181, 194 (1937) points out the failure of the courts to apply as consistently to statements by partners as in case of admissions by agents, the test of authority to speak. He says: "[In a tort case] a partner admits the existence of a defect in the instrumentality involved. Is this receivable against the other partners? Theoretically no, unless the speaker was authorized to talk about it. And such is the holding in about half of the pertinent cases. In the others, it seems to be assumed that the partner has such authority, for the evidence is received. And in contract actions, the holdings are almost unanimous to that effect. In this respect the language of many of the decisions makes no distinction between the situation where the words would be operative to create legal relations and the situation where they can have no operative effect and are merely narrative and evidential. If they are to be harmonized with the agency cases, it must be on the ground that each partner has authority to talk about any partnership transaction."

ner made after dissolution? The cases are divided,[20] but it seems that since a continuing power is recognized in each former partner to do such acts as are reasonably necessary to wind up and settle the affairs of the firm,[21] he should likewise be regarded as having authority to speak for the former partners in making such statements of fact as are reasonably incident to collecting the claims and property and paying the debts of the firm.[22] Beyond this, it seems that his admissions should be competent only against himself.

Co-conspirators.[23] Analogous to partnerships are conspiracies to commit a crime or an unlawful or tortious act. If A and B are engaged in a conspiracy the acts and declarations of B occurring while the conspiracy is actually in progress and in furtherance of the design are provable against A, because they are acts for which he is criminally or civilly responsible, as a matter of substantive law.[24] But B's declarations may also be proved against A as representative admissions, to prove the truth of the matter declared, and only then are they within our present topic. The courts have seldom discriminated between declarations offered as conduct constituting part of the conspiracy and declarations offered as vicarious admission of the facts declared,[25] and even when offered for the latter purpose, generally have imposed the same test, namely that the declaration must have been made while the conspiracy was continuing, and must have constituted a step in furtherance of the venture.[26]

Literally applied, the "in furtherance" requirement calls for general exclusion of statements possessing evidential value solely as admissions,[27] yet in fact more emphasis seems to be placed upon the "during continuation" aspect and any statement so qualifying in point of time may be admitted in evidence without much regard to whether it in fact furthered the conspiracy.[28] These latter

---

20. They are collected in Annot., 73 A.L.R. 459–473.

21. Crane and Bromberg, Partnership § 80, p. 454 (3d ed. 1968).

22. Crane and Bromberg, Partnership § 80, p. 459 (3d ed. 1968); Rowley, Partnership § 51.9, p. 447 (2d ed. 1960).

23. 4 Wigmore, Evidence § 1079; Klein, Conspiracy —The Prosecutor's Darling, 24 Brooklyn L.Rev. 1 (1957); Levie, Hearsay and Conspiracy, 52 Mich. L.Rev. 1159 (1954); Morgan, Admissions, 12 Wash. L.Rev. 181, 194 (1937), Rationale of Vicarious Admissions, 42 Harv.L.Rev. 461, 464 (1929); Note, 25 U.Chi.L.Rev. 530 (1958); Dec.Dig. Criminal Law ☞423–427, Evidence ☞253.

24. 4 Wigmore, Evidence § 1079.

25. See, e. g., Schine Chain Theatres v. United States, 334 U.S. 110, 117 (1948) (where in a suit for injunction against antitrust law violations the Court said: "It is sufficient at this point to say that since a conspiracy between Schine and each of the named distributors was established by independent evidence, these inter-office letters and memoranda were admissible against all conspirators as declarations of some of the associates so far as they were in furtherance of the unlawful project.").

26. Krulewitch v. United States, 336 U.S. 440 (1949); Wong Sun v. United States, 371 U.S. 471, 490 (1963); Marjason v. State, 225 Ind. 652, 75 N.E.2d 904 (1947); People v. Davis, 56 N.Y. 95, 102 (1874).
The existence of the conspiracy must be proved independently to justify the admission of the declaration. Glasser v. United States, 315 U.S. 60, 75 (1942); 4 Wigmore, Evidence § 1079(a). But in his discretion, the judge may vary the order of proof, and admit the declaration contingent upon the later production of the preliminary proof. United States v. Halpin, 374 F.2d 493 (1967) cert. denied 386 U.S. 1032. The preliminary question is for the judge, and the quantum of proof required is described as satisfying him that it would support a finding, Carbo v. United States, 314 F.2d 718 (9th Cir. 1963), or as a fair preponderance of the evidence, United States v. Geaney, 417 F.2d 1116 (2d Cir. 1969).

27. State v. Podor, 154 Iowa 686, 135 N.W. 421 (1912) (declaration of one co-conspirator that he and another were going to cause girls to become prostitutes not admissible against other).

28. United States v. Annunziato, 293 F.2d 373 (2d Cir. 1961) (statement of employer that he intended to make payments to labor union official, in prosecution for receiving unlawful payment); Salazar v. United States, 405 F.2d 74 (9th Cir. 1968) (statement by co-conspirator to undercover agent, waiting to purchase narcotics, that other co-conspirator was inside making preparations).
Model Code of Evidence Rule 508(b) eliminated any requirement that the statement be in furtherance, and Uniform Rule 63(9) (b) is to the same effect.

decisions may represent a parallel to the cases allowing in evidence against the principal declarations of an agent which relate to the subject of the agency, even though the agent was not authorized to make a statement.[29] Both the "in furtherance" and the "during continuation" requirement call for exclusion of admissions and confessions made after the termination of the conspiracy.[30] Questions arise, of course, as to when termination occurs. Under some circumstances, extending the duration of the conspiracy beyond the commission of the principal crime to include concomitant and closely connected disposition of its fruits or concealment of its traces appears justifiable, as in the case of police officers engaged in writing up a false report to conceal police participation in a burglary[31] or disposal of the body after a murder.[32] However, attempts to expand the so-called "concealment phase" to include all efforts to avoid detection have generally failed, as in Krulewitch v. United States,[33] a Mann Act prosecution, where the Court held it error to admit evidence of a co-conspirator's statement that it would be better for the girls to take the blame than the defendant, because "he couldn't stand it." The statement was made after the round trip travel was finished and the various participants had been arrested.[34]

While statements made after the termination of the conspiracy are inadmissible, subsequent acts which shed light upon the nature of the conspiratorial agreement have been held admissible.[35]

The existence of a conspiracy in fact is sufficient to support admissibility, and a conspiracy count in the indictment is not required.[36] The evidence is similarly admissible in civil cases, where the conspiracy rule applies to tortfeasors acting in concert.[37]

Declarations of principal offered against surety. It is asserted that when two parties are jointly liable as obligors, the declarations of one are receivable as an admission against the other.[38] The element of authorization to speak in furtherance of the common enterprise, as in the case of agency, partnership or conspiracy, can hardly be spelled out from the mere relation of joint obligors, and admissibility of declarations on this basis has been criticised.[39] In fact, almost all the

accused, made more than a year after the commission of the crime, and wholly unrelated to any effort at concealment, immediate or otherwise. The conviction was sustained against constitutional attack in Dutton v. Evans, 400 U.S. 74 (1970). See § 252, supra.

See also State v. Roberts, 95 Kan. 280, 147 Pac. 828 (1915), for an expanded application of the "concealment phase."

35. Lutwak v. United States, 344 U.S. 604 (1953) (subsequent acts of parties admissible to show phony nature of marriages in prosecution for conspiracy to evade immigration laws).

36. Kelley v. United States, 364 F.2d 911 (10th Cir. 1966); People v. Niemoth, 409 Ill. 111, 98 N.E.2d 733 (1951) cert. denied 344 U.S. 858. Contra, United States v. Harrell, 436 F.2d 606 (5th Cir. 1970) (without discussion or citation of authority). The popularity of conspiracy charges among prosecutors, particularly federal prosecutors, may suggest that they largely share the latter view.

37. Nathan v. St. Paul Mut. Ins. Co., 251 Minn. 74, 86 N.W.2d 503 (1957); Greer v. Skyway Broadcasting Co., 256 N.C. 382, 124 S.E.2d 98 (1962).

38. 4 Wigmore, Evidence § 1077; Lowe v. Huckins, 356 Ill. 360, 190 N.E. 683 (1934) (joint makers of note).

39. Morgan, Admissions, 12 Wash.L.Rev. 181, 195 (1937).

See n. 89, supra. However, doubts raised by conspiracy prosecutions in principle and by the tenuous character of the agency concept in this context have led to rejection of this extension of admissibility, and "in furtherance" continues as a requirement in West's Ann.Cal.Evid.Code, § 1223; N.J.R.Ev. 63(9); F.R.Ev. (R.D.1971) 801(d) (2) (v).

29. See nn. 98 and 99, supra.

30. See the many cases in Annot., 4 A.L.R.3d 671.

31. Reed v. People, 156 Colo. 450, 402 P.2d 68 (1965).

32. Dailey v. State, 233 Ala. 384, 171 So. 729 (1937).

33. 336 U.S. 440 (1949). See also Annot., 4 A.L.R. 3d 671.

34. Compare Evans v. State, 222 Ga. 392, 150 S.E. 2d 240 (1960), in which the "concealment phase" was extended to the extraordinary limit of allowing a co-conspirator's statement implicating the

modern cases adduced in support are cases involving the special situation of declarations of a principal offered as admissions against a surety, guarantor, indemnitor or other person secondarily liable.[40] The declarations are usually held admissible,[41] and the practice is sanctioned by a provision in the Model Code of Evidence, Rule 508, subs. (c) as follows: "Evidence of a hearsay declaration is admissible against a party to the action if the judge finds that . . . one of the issues between the party and the proponent of the evidence is a legal liability of the declarant, and the matter declared tends to establish that liability."[42] The facts that the matters admitted are likely to be in the special knowledge of the declarant, and that the admissions will nearly always be against the declarant's interest, again support the trustworthiness of such evidence.

268. Declarations by "Privies in Estate": Joint Tenants and Predecessors in Interest.[43]

The notion that "privity," or identity of interest, as between the declarant and the party against whom the declaration is offered, justifies its introduction against the party as an admission has been generally accepted by the courts. Thus the declaration of one joint tenant or joint owner against another is received,[44] but not that of a tenant in common,[45] a co-legatee or co-devisee,[46] or a co-trustee,[47]—so strictly is the distinction derived from the law of property applied in this context. The more frequent and important application of this property analogy is the use of declarations of a predecessor in title to land or personalty or choses in action,

40. See 4 Wigmore, Evidence § 1077, cases cited n. 91, supra.

41. See, e. g., Scovill Mfg. Co. v. Cassidy, 275 Ill. 462, 114 N.E. 181, 185 (1916) (statement of president of corporation, whose account was guaranteed by defendant, made to plaintiff, to whom guaranty was made, admissible since made as part of the operations of the business which was the subject of the guaranty); Linnell v. London & Lancashire Indemnity Co., 74 N.D. 379, 22 N.W.2d 203 (1946) (suit on fidelity bond of manager of business; books kept by manager or under his supervision with respect to business covered by bond, admissible against surety); United American Fire Ins. Co. v. American Bonding Co., 146 Wis. 573, 131 N.W. 994 (1911) (suit on surety bond of agent of insurance company; agent's statement to secretary of insurance company as to amount collected, made after he had resigned but while he was under duty to account, admissible as "res gestae"). Contra: Atlas Shoes Co. v. Bloom, 209 Mass. 563, 95 N.E. 952 (1911) (admissions of one, whose account was guaranteed by defendant, that he had received goods described in account presented to him, inadmissible against defendant). Stearns, Suretyship 343 (5th ed. 1951). Annots., 60 A.L.R. 1500, 65 A.L.R.2d 632. As with declarations of agents, supra, notes 91 and 92 supra, a *res gestae* requirement is often specified.

42. This is now incorporated in Uniform Rule 63 (9) (c), see n. 89, above. Also West's Ann.Cal.Evid. Code, § 1224, and Kan.Code C.P. § 60-460(i) (3). The provision is not found in N.J.R.Ev. 63(9) or in F.R.Ev. (R.D.1971) 801(d) (2) on the theory that declarations against interest or other hearsay exceptions will take care of cases of necessity. The California provision has been held inapplicable to the statement of an employee whose employer is sought to be held liable under *respondeat superior.* Markley v. Beagle, 66 Cal.2d 951, 59 Cal.Rptr. 809, 429 P.2d 129 (1967).

43. 4 Wigmore, Evidence §§ 1080-1087; Morgan, Rationale of Vicarious Admissions, 42 Harv.L.Rev. 462, 470 (1929), Admissions, 12 Wash.L.Rev. 181, 197 (1937); Falknor, Hearsay, 1969 Law & Soc. Order 591, 603; Model Code of Evidence, Comment on Rule 508; Dec.Dig. Evidence ☞226, 229-236; C.J.S. Evidence §§ 322-341.

44. 4 Wigmore, Evidence § 1081, p. 147; La Furia v. New Jersey Ins. Co., 131 Pa.Super. 413, 200 A. 167 (1938) (in suit against fire insurance company by husband and wife, where property held by entireties, husband's admission receivable against wife). Cf. Pope v. Hogan, 92 Vt. 250, 102 A. 937 (1918) (admission of husband tenant by entireties excluded because his interest not identical with wife's). In Meyer v. Nordmeyer, 332 Ill.App. 165, 74 N.E.2d 716 (1947), tenants in common were described as "joint owners" and admission by one received against all to toll running of statute of limitations on mortgage note.

45. Dan v. Brown, 4 Cow. (N.Y.) 483, 492 (1825). Cf. Meyer v. Nordmeyer, n. 44, supra.

46. Shailer v. Bumstead, 99 Mass. 112, 127 (1868). And in will contests most courts go to the extreme of saying that since it is not admissible against the others, it is not even admissible against the colegatee himself who made the declaration, since there can only be a judgment for or against the will as a whole. See, e. g., Belfield v. Coop, 8 Ill.2d 293, 134 N.E.2d 249, 58 A.L.R.2d 1008 (1956).

47. Davies v. Ridge, 3 Esp. 101, 170 Eng.R.R. 553 (N.P.1800).

against his successor. The successor has been thought of as acquiring his interest burdened with the same liability of having the declarations used against him that his predecessor was subject to.[48] The declarations presumably must relate to the declarant's interest in the property or to his transactions and intentions in reference thereto, and they must have been made while he was the owner of the interest now claimed by the successor party, not before the declarant acquired or after he parted with such interest.[49] Under this theory are received the declarations of grantors, transferors, donors, and mortgagors of land and personalty against the transferees and mortgagees;[50] of decedents against their representatives, heirs and next of kin;[51] by a prior possessor against one who claims prescriptive title relying on such prior possession;[52] and of former holders of notes and other choses in action against their assignees.[53] It should be borne in mind that such substantive concepts as bona fide purchase and holder in due course may make the evidence immaterial and hence inadmissible for that reason.[54]

48. Expressions of judges and writers are quoted in 4 Wigmore, Evidence § 1080, pp. 135, 136.

49. Austin v. Austin, 237 Ark. 127, 372 S.W.2d 231 (1963) (grantor's statement made after delivery of deed not admissible against grantee); Charles R. Allen, Inc. v. Island Co-Op. Assn., 234 S.C. 537, 109 S.E.2d 446 (1959) (assignor's statement made after assignment of draft not admissible against assignee); Dec.Dig. Evidence ☜230(3); C.J.S. Evidence § 323.

50. Kennedy v. Oleson, 251 Iowa 418, 100 N.W.2d 894 (1960) (admission of predecessor that building encroached); Liberty Nat. Bank & Trust Co. v. Merchants' and Manufacturers' Paint Co., 307 Ky. 184, 209 S.W.2d 828 (1948) (statement of predecessor about party-wall); 4 Wigmore, Evidence § 1082; Dec.Dig. Evidence 231–233.

51. Webb v. Martin, 364 F.2d 229 (3d Cir. 1966) (testimony given by decedent in criminal case receivable as admission in action against his administrator); Estate of Fushanis v. Poulos, 85 Ill.App.2d 114, 229 N.E.2d 306 (1967) (writing in files of decedent admissible to establish trust against his estate); Mannix v. Baumgardner, 184 Md. 600, 42 A.2d 124 (1945) (statement in subsequently revoked will admissible on issue of existence of contract to devise); Dec.Dig. Evidence ☜236.

In wrongful death actions by administrators or other representatives, some courts by a hypertechnical concept of privity have said that, since the statute gives a new cause of action at death, the administrator's death claim is not derivative, and statements of the deceased are not receivable against the administrator as admissions. They may, of course, qualify under other hearsay exceptions but with stricter requirements for admissibility. In other aspects of the same case, however, privity undeniably exists, e. g., when liability is asserted *against* the estate or when the administrator joins a claim for conscious suffering, if it survives. The result is a hodgepodge of inconsistencies. See Shamgochian v. Drigotas, 343 Mass. 139, 177 N.E.2d 588 (1961) (decedent's statement of not blaming driver who struck him admissible as admission on count for conscious suffering, but barely gets in on wrongful death count under statute allowing statements of decedents made on personal knowledge); Carpenter v. Davis, 435 S.W. 2d 382 (Mo.1968) (statement by decedent of no fault of defendant barred as admission in wrongful death case by lack of privity, and not qualified as declaration against interest because in opinion form, though opinion aspect would not require exclusion of an admission). The results are indefensible.

52. Barnes v. Young, 238 Ark. 484, 382 S.W.2d 580 (1964); Atlantic Coast Line Ry. Co. v. Gunn, 185 Ga. 108, 194 S.E. 365 (1938).

53. Taylor-Reed Corp. v. Mennen Food Products, Inc., 324 F.2d 108 (7th Cir. 1963) (statement by assignor of patent admissible against assignee); Baptist v. Bankers Indemnity Co., 377 F.2d 211 (2d Cir. 1967) (statement by insured admissible against his judgment creditor in latter's action against liability insurer, on theory that judgment creditor was in effect assignee of insured); Johnson v. Riecken, 185 Neb. 78, 173 N.W.2d 511 (1970) (statement by assignor of claim for medical expenses); Trudeau v. Lussier, 123 Vt. 358, 189 A.2d 529 (1963) (statement by assignor of past due note).

In a suit on a life insurance policy by the beneficiary may the declarations of the insured in his lifetime be offered by the defendant insurance company against the beneficiary, as the admissions of a predecessor in interest? The answer has been made in some cases to turn upon the technical distinction between policies wherein the insured reserves the power to change the beneficiary and those where no such power is reserved. Bernard v. Metropolitan Life Ins. Co., 316 Ill.App. 655, 45 N.E.2d 518 (1942); Rosman v. Travelers' Insurance Co., 127 Md. 689, 96 A. 875, Ann.Cas.1918C, 1047 (1916); 4 Wigmore, Evidence § 1081, n. 6; Annot., 86 A.L.R. 146, 161. The distinction is tenuous.

54. Bradstreet v. Bradstreet, 158 Me. 140, 180 A.2d 459, 463 (1962); 4 Wigmore, Evidence § 1084.

The importation into the evidence field of the niceties of property doctrines of identity of interest and privity of estate has been criticized by Morgan. "The dogma," he says, "of vicarious admissions, as soon as it passes beyond recognized principles of representation, baffles the understanding. Joint ownership, joint obligation, privity of title, each and all furnish no criterion of credibility, no aid in the evaluation of testimony."[55] While Wigmore counters that "the Hearsay rule stands in dire need, not of stopping its violation, but of a vast deal of (let us say) elastic relaxation. And this is one of the places where that relaxation can best be granted, in view of the commonly useful service of this class of evidence. After the heat of a controversy has brought it into court, testimony on the stand is often much less trustworthy than the original statements of the same persons made before controversy."[56] His argument is actually one for expanding the admissibility of contemporaneous statements, with privity a more or less fortuitous aspect. Following Morgan's view, the Model Code omitted any provision for admitting these declarations.[57] In any event, the meritorious cases will in general qualify as declarations against interest or other hearsay exception more soundly based than admissions founded on privity.

269. Admissions by Conduct: (a) Adoptive Admissions.[58]

One may expressly adopt another's statement as his own. That is an explicit admission like any other, is to be classed as an express admission, and calls for no further discussion. In this text the term adoptive admission is applied to evidence of other conduct of a party which manifests circumstantially the party's assent to the truth of a statement made by another person.[59]

The mere fact that the party declares that he has heard that another person has made a given statement is not standing alone sufficient to justify a finding that the party has adopted the third person's statement.[60] The circumstances surrounding the party's declaration must be looked to in order to determine whether the repetition did indicate an approval of the statement.[61]

---

55. Morgan, Admissions, 12 Wash.L.Rev. 181, 202 (1937). If the admissibility of admissions is regarded as the product of the adversary system, rather than as arising from circumstantial guarantees of trustworthiness justifying a hearsay exception, the conclusion is nevertheless the same, since the privity concept goes beyond reasonable standards of party responsibility.

56. 4 Wigmore, Evidence § 1080a, p. 144.

57. See Model Code of Evidence Rules 502, 503, 509. So also Uniform Rule 63(7–9); Kan.Code C.P. § 60–460(g–i); N.J.R.Ev. 63(7–9); F.R.Ev. (R.D. 1971) 801(d) (2). Contra, West's Ann.Cal.Evid. Code, § 1225. Falknor, Hearsay, 1969 Law & Soc. Order 591, 603, suggests that the arguments against privity-based admissions may go too far and undercut the whole concept of representative admissions.

58. 4 Wigmore, Evidence §§ 1069–1075.

59. See Uniform Rule 63(8): "*Authorized and Adoptive Admissions*. As against a party, a statement (b) . . . of which the party with knowledge of the content thereof has, by words or other conduct, manifested his adoption or his belief in its truth". This is an adaptation of Model Code of Evidence R. 507. To the same effect are West's Ann.Cal.Evid.Code, § 1221; Kan.C.C.P. § 60–460 (h); N.J.Ev.R. 63(8); F.R.Ev. (R.D.1971) 801(d) (2) (ii).

In this text, admissions by silence are treated separately. See § 270, infra.

60. Stephens v. Vroman, 16 N.Y. 381 (1857) (stresses the hearsay nature of the statements, without discussing whether repetition is adoption); Reed v. McCord, 160 N.Y. 330, 54 N.E. 737, 740 (1899) (employer's statement as to facts of accident, though he was without personal knowledge, admissible, but distinguishing a statement that "he had heard" that such was the fact, which would be inadmissible).

61. Circumstances show adoption: Pekelis v. Transcontinental & Western Air, Inc., 187 F.2d 122 (2d Cir. 1951) (report of accident investigating board used by defendant as a basis for remedial measures and also filed with CAB); In re Gaines' Estate, 15 Cal.2d 255, 100 P.2d 1055 (1940) (statement by nephew to bank officers, as to what uncle said was his purpose in placing deposit box and bank account in joint tenancy with nephew); Oxley v. Linnton Plywood Assn., 205 Ore. 78, 284 P.2d 766 (1955) (timber cruiser's report filed by defendant in support of SEC registration statement). Insuffi-

The question of adoption often arises in life and accident insurance cases when the defendant insurance company offers statements which the plaintiff beneficiary attached to the proof of death or disability, such as the certificate of the attending physician, or the coroner's report. The fact that the beneficiary has thus tendered it as an exhibit accompanying a formal statement or "proof" presented for the purpose of having the company act upon it by paying the claim, should certainly be enough, standing alone, to secure the admission of the accompanying statements.[62] In actual life, however, the surrounding circumstances often show that an inference of adoption would be most unrealistic. This is clear when the beneficiary expressly disavows the accompanying statement,[63] and it seems that exclusion of the attached statement should likewise follow when the statements of the beneficiary in the proofs are clearly contrary to those in the exhibits.[64] Moreover, when the company's agent prepared the proof for signature and procured the accompanying documents, as he frequently does as a helpful service to the beneficiary, it seems reasonable to hold that the inference of adoption of statements in the exhibits should not be drawn, if the agent has failed to call the beneficiary's attention to inconsistencies between the proof and the exhibits.[65] Again the argument seems strong that if accompanying statements, such as the certificate of the attending physician as to particular facts called for, are required to be furnished under the terms of the policy, the statements are not then attached by the choice or will of the beneficiary, and the sponsorship inferable from a voluntary tendering of another's statement cannot here be inferred.[66]

Does the introduction of evidence by a party constitute an adoption of the statements therein, so that they may be used against him as admissions [67] in a subsequent lawsuit? The answer ought to depend upon whether the particular circumstances warrant the conclusion that adoption in fact occurred, and not upon the discredited notion that a party vouches for his own witnesses. When a party offers in evidence a deposition or an affidavit to prove the matters stated therein, he knows or should know the contents of the

---

cient to show adoption: Cowan v. Allamakee County Benevolent Soc., 232 Iowa 1387, 8 N.W.2d 433 (1943) (insurance beneficiary's statement that the doctors told him that insured had died of cancer).

62. Cases admitting the statements on this theory are numerous, see e. g., Russo v. Metropolitan Life Ins. Co., 125 Conn. 132, 3 A.2d 844 (1939) (but court stressed there was no contractual obligation here to furnish the doctor's certificate filed with the proof); Rudolph v. John Hancock Mut. Life Ins. Co., 251 N.Y. 208, 167 N.E. 223 (1929) (statement in doctor's certificate an adoptive admission, though contrary to beneficiary's own statement in the proof of death, and though attending doctor's statement was required by policy; three judges dissenting); Thornell v. Missouri State Life Ins. Co., 249 S.W. 203 (Tex.Com.App.1923) (rule applied though proofs prepared by agents of company). Contra, Liberty Nat. Life Ins. Co. v. Reid, 276 Ala. 25, 158 So.2d 667 (1963) (claimant not "bound" unless "made at his request or ratified by him"). Decisions are collected in 4 Wigmore, Evidence § 1073, note 10; Dec.Dig. Evidence ☜215(1); Annot., 1 A.L.R.2d 365.

63. Krantz v. John Hancock Mut. Life Ins. Co., 335 Mass. 703, 141 N.E.2d 719 (1957); Goldschmidt v. Mutual Life Ins. Co., 102 N.Y. 486, 7 N.E. 408 (1886). In the absence of disavowal, it is arguable that the case is one of admission by failure to deny. See § 270, infra.

64. See the dissenting opinion in *Rudolph* supra n. 62.

65. New York Life Ins. Co. v. Taylor, 79 U.S.App. D.C. 66, 147 F.2d 297 (1945).

66. This view is supported by the decision in Bebbington v. Calif. Western Life Ins. Co., 15 Cal. 2d 255, 100 P.2d 1055 (1947), 61 Harv.L.Rev. 535; Carson v. Metropolitan Life Ins. Co., 156 Ohio St. 104, 100 N.E.2d 197, 28 A.L.R.2d 344 (1951). The *Rudolph* case, note 62, supra, is opposed.

67. Thus escaping the requirements which would be imposed if it were offered under the hearsay exception for Former Testimony (see Ch. 25, supra) such as identity of parties and issues, and unavailability of the witness.

Whether offering the testimony on direct satisfies the former testimony requirement of cross-examination is discussed in § 255, at note 23, supra.

writing so offered, and presumably he desires that all of the contents be considered on his behalf, since he is at liberty to offer only part, if he desires. Accordingly, it is reasonable to conclude that the writing so introduced may in another suit be used against him as an adoptive admission.[68] In respect to oral testimony, however, the inference of sponsorship of the statements is not always so clear, but here, too, circumstances may justify the conclusion that when the proponent placed the witness on the stand to prove a particular fact, and the witness so testified, this was an adoptive admission of the fact in a later suit. But how is the party offering the testimony in the later suit to show that a given statement of the witness at the former trial was intended to be elicited by the proponent who put him on the stand, or was contrary to or outside that intention? The form and context of the proponent's question would usually, but not always, give the clue. In view of the prevailing custom of interviewing one's witness before putting him on the stand, it would seem that a practical working rule would admit against the proponent the direct testimony of his own witness as presumptively elicited to prove the facts stated, in the absence of counter proof that the testimony came as a surprise to the interrogator, or was repudiated in the course of argument.[69] Testimony elicited on cross-examination may be drawn out to reveal the witness's mendacity and should not be assumed to have been relied on by the examiner as evidence of the facts stated,[70] but reliance must affirmatively appear.

In conformity with the views expressed in the general discussion herein of the respective functions of judge and jury in determining preliminary questions of fact, it is believed that the statement should be admitted upon the introduction of evidence sufficient to support a finding of adoption.[71]

Similar to adoptive admissions are the instances where the party has referred an inquirer to another person whose anticipated statements he approves in advance.[72] These admissions by reference to a third person are perhaps more properly classifiable as representative or vicarious admissions, rather than adoptive.

270. Admissions by Conduct: (b) Silence.[73]

If a statement is made by another person in the presence of a party to the action, con-

---

68. Richards v. Morgan, 10 Jurist N.S. 559, 122 Eng. Rep. 600 (Q.B.1864) (depositions); Hallett v. O'Brien, 1 Ala. 585, 589 (1840) (affidavit or deposition said to be adopted if used in evidence, but not where merely filed); 4 Wigmore, Evidence § 1075, note 2.

69. Bageard v. Consolidated Traction Co., 64 N.J.L. 316, 45 A. 620 (1900) (testimony of witness at former trial which corroborated plaintiff's testimony which is now inconsistent with his present version); Keyser Canning Co. v. Klots Throwing Co., 98 W.Va. 487, 128 S.E. 280 (1925) (testimony as to cause of fire). Contra, British Thomson-Houston Co. v. British, etc., Cables, Ltd. [1924] 2 Ch. 160, 38 Harv.L.Rev. 262 (involving expert testimony, a most unlikely situation for finding nonadoption).

70. In O'Connor v. Bonney, 57 S.D. 134, 231 N.W. 521 (1930) questions and answers on cross-examination by the present defendant of expert witnesses at a previous trial of the present malpractice action, were held inadmissible against the defendant.

71. The situation is one of conditional relevancy, treated in §§ 53, 58, supra.

72. See, e. g., General Finance Co. v. Stratford, 71 App.D.C. 343, 109 F.2d 843 (1940) (plaintiff in garnishment directed by garnishee's agent to go over records with bookkeeper; bookkeeper's statements admissible against garnishee); 4 Wigmore, Evidence § 1070.

73. See 4 Wigmore, Evidence §§ 1071–1073; Heller, Admissions by Acquiescence, 15 U. of Miami L.Rev. 161 (1960); Morgan, Admissions, 12 Wash. L.Rev. 181, 187 (1937); Note, 112 U.Pa.L.Rev. 210 (1960); Annot., 70 A.L.R.2d 1099; Dec.Dig. Evidence ⬅220, Criminal Law ⬅407; C.J.S. Evidence §§ 294–298.

The general question whether silence is hearsay is treated in § 250, notes 54–58, supra, and particular aspects of silence as an admission in criminal cases are discussed in § 161, supra.

Model Code of Evidence Rule 507: "Evidence of a hearsay statement is admissible against a party to the action if the judge finds that . . . (b) the party with knowledge of the content of the

taining assertions of facts which, if untrue, the party would under all the circumstances naturally be expected to deny, his failure to speak has traditionally been receivable against him as an admission.[74] Whether the justification for receiving the evidence is the assumption that the party has intended to express his assent and thus has adopted the statement as his own, or the probable state of belief to be inferred from his conduct is probably unimportant.[75] Since it is the failure to deny that is significant, an equivocal or evasive response may similarly be used against him on either theory,[76] but if his total response adds up to a clear-cut denial, this theory of implied admission is not properly available.[77]

Despite the offhand appeal of this kind of evidence, the courts have often suggested that it be received with caution and have surrounded it with various restrictions and safeguards.[78] These are based upon several considerations. First, the nature of the evidence is an open invitation to manufacture evidence, which must be guarded against.[79] Second, constitutional limitations imposed by *Miranda* serve to circumscribe this type of evidence in criminal cases.[80] Third, while in theory the statement is not offered as proof of its contents but rather to show what the party acquiesced in,[81] the distinction is indeed a subtle one; the statement is ordinarily very damaging, and substantial assurances are required that acquiescence did in fact occur.

These assurances have assumed a variety of forms, of which the following are illustrative. (1) The statement must have been heard by the party claimed to have acquiesced, a proposition scarcely requiring citation. (2) It must have been understood by him.[82] (3)

statement by words or other conduct manifested his adoption or approval of the statement or his belief in its truth." To like effect are Uniform Rule 63(8); West's Ann.Cal.Evid.Code, § 1221; Kan.Code C.P. § 60–460(h); N.J.Ev.R. 63(8); F.R. Ev. (R.D.1971) 801(d) (2) (ii).

74. 4 Wigmore, Evidence § 1071.

75. See the commentary, Model Code of Evidence, Rule 507.

76. Examples of responses held to be equivocal: People v. Tolbert, 70 Cal.2d 790, 76 Cal.Rptr. 445, 452 P.2d 661 (1969) ("Forget about it," in reply to landlady's statement that police had found gun in bathroom and question whether he had put it there); Commonwealth v. Jefferson, 430 Pa. 532, 243 A.2d 412 (1968) ("Glad it was all over," when confronted with a statement implicating him). Not infrequently the equivocal response is the result of trying to outsmart a skilled interrogator who knows the ground rules. E. g., Commonwealth v. McGrath, 351 Mass. 534, 222 N.E.2d 774 (1967). Examples of responses held not to be equivocal: People v. Hanley, 317 Ill. 39, 147 N.E. 400 (1925) ("it will take twelve men to try me."); Boulton v. State, 214 Tenn. 94, 377 S.W.2d 936 (1964) ("Why did you do this to me?," in response to accusation is presence of alleged victim). The lack of a satisfactory dividing line deprives the "equivocal response" theory of much of its validity.

77. Commonwealth v. Locke, 335 Mass. 106, 138 N.E.2d 359 (1956); Commonwealth of Pa. ex rel. Smith v. Rundle, 423 Pa. 93, 223 A.2d 88 (1966).

78. People v. Aughinbaugh, 36 Ill.2d 320, 223 N.E.2d 117 (1967); Boulton v. State, 214 Tenn. 94, 377 S.W.2d 936 (1964).
"If silence is the only response by the defendant, the accusation must have occurred (1) in the defendant's presence and (2) within his hearing; (3) he must have understood it; (4) it ordinarily must have embraced facts within his personal knowledge; (5) he must have been physically able to speak and (6) psychologically at liberty to speak; and (7) the statement and surrounding circumstances must have naturally called for a reply. If, however, the defendant made an ambiguous statement . . . the inquiry is only whether the response affords a permissible inference of guilt." Note, Tacit Criminal Admissions, 112 U.Pa.L.Rev. 210, 213–214 (1963).

79. Particularly in criminal cases when the accused is in custody and hence conveniently at hand to be confronted with a detailed accusatory statement. See, e. g., People v. Bennett, 413 Ill. 601, 110 N.E.2d 175 (1953) (error to admit).
Concern with this aspect is also evident in the concluding portion of this section of text.

80. See § 160, supra.

81. Greenberg v. Stanley, 30 N.J. 485, 153 A.2d 833 (1959).

82. People v. Aughinbaugh, 36 Ill.2d 320, 223 N.E.2d 117 (1967) (error to admit evidence of defendant's failure to respond to identification in lineup in absence of showing that he knew what crime he was charged with).

The subject matter must have been within his knowledge. At first glance, this requirement may appear inconsistent with the general dispensation with firsthand knowledge with respect to admissions,[83] yet the unreasonableness of expecting a person to deny a matter of which he is not aware seems evident;[84] he simply does not have the incentive or the wherewithal to embark upon a dispute. (4) Physical or emotional impediments to responding must not be present.[85] (5) The personal makeup of the speaker, e. g., young child,[86] or his relationship to the party or the event, e. g., bystander,[87] may be such as to make it unreasonable to expect a denial. Other factors will suggest themselves, and the list is by no means an exclusive one. It should be borne in mind that the essential inquiry in each case is whether a reasonable person would have denied under the circumstances, with answers not lending themselves readily to mechanical formulations.

Preliminary questions of admissibility in connection with admissions by acquiescence appear to fall within the category of conditional relevancy. The judge should admit the evidence upon the introduction of foundation proof sufficient to support a finding that the requirements for admissibility have been satisfied.[88]

Failure to reply to a letter or other written communication.[89] If a written statement is handed to a party and read by him, in the presence of others, his failure to deny assertions contained therein, when under the circumstances it would be natural for him to deny them if he did not acquiesce, may be received as an admission, as in case of similar failure to deny an oral statement.[90] Moreover, if a party receives a letter containing several statements, which he would naturally deny if untrue, and he states his position as to some of the statements, but fails to comment on the others, this failure will usually be received as evidence of an admission.[91] More debatable is the question whether the failure to reply at all to a letter or other written communication shall come in as an admission by silence. Certainly such a failure to reply will often be less convincing than silence in the face of an oral charge.[92]

Many of the cases cited in this section would now be decided on *Miranda* grounds. However, they continue to be authority for the handling of non-*Miranda* situations.

83. See § 263, supra.

84. Dierks Lumber & Coal Co. v. Horne, 216 Ark. 155, 224 S.W.2d 540 (1949); Refrigeration Discount Corp. v. Catino, 330 Mass. 230, 112 N.E.2d 790 (1953). Cf. 4 Wigmore, Evidence § 1072.

85. E. g., physical injury of the party or the confusion attending an accident. Klever v. Elliott, 212 Ore. 490, 320 P.2d 263, 70 A.L.R.2d 1094 (1958), Beck v. Dye, 200 Wash. 1, 92 P.2d 1113, 127 A.L.R. 1022 (1939).

86. Robinson v. State, 235 Miss. 100, 108 So.2d 583 (1959) (error to admit evidence of failure to deny statement of two and one-half year old child, "Daddy shot mother dear." Cf. Doherty v. Edwards, 227 Iowa 1264, 290 N.W. 672 (1940) (proper to admit evidence of defendant driver's failure to deny statement by fatally injured passenger, "We were going too fast.")

87. Cases cited note 85, supra.

88. See the general treatment of preliminary questions in §§ 53, 58, supra.

89. See 4 Wigmore, Evidence § 1073, nn. 3 and 4; Note, 4 Vand.L.Rev. 364 (1951); Dec.Dig. Evidence ☞220(8); C.J.S. Evidence § 297(b); Annots., 8 A.L.R. 1163, 34 id. 560, 55 id. 460.

90. See Grier v. Deputy, 15 Del. 152, 40 A. 716 (1894) (item in newspaper read to party).

91. Hellenic Lines, Ltd. v. Gulf Oil Corp., 340 F.2d 398 (2d Cir. 1965); Wieder v. Lorenz, 164 Ore. 10, 99 P.2d 38 (1940).

92. "Men use the tongue much more readily than the pen. Almost all men will reply to and deny or correct a false statement verbally made to them. It is done on the spot and from the first impulse. But when a letter is received making the same statement, the feeling which readily prompts the verbal denial not unfrequently cools before the time and opportunity arrive for writing a letter. Other matters intervene. A want of facility in writing, or an aversion to correspondence, or habits of dilatoriness may be the real causes of the silence. As the omission to reply to letters may be explained by so many causes not applicable to silence when the parties are in personal conversation, we do not think the same weight should be attached to it as evidence." Aldis, J. in Fenno v. Watson, 31 Vt. 345, 352 (1858).

And it is often announced as a "general rule," subject to exceptions, that failure to answer a letter is not receivable as an admission.[93] This negative form of statement seems undesirable as tending toward over-strict rulings excluding evidence of material value.[94] It is believed that the more acceptable view is that the failure to reply to a letter, containing statements which it would be natural under all the circumstances for the addressee to deny if he believed them untrue, is receivable as evidence of an admission by silence.[95] Two factors particularly tend to show that a denial would be naturally forthcoming, first, where the letter was written as part of a mutual correspondence between the parties,[96] and second, where the proof shows that the parties were engaged together in some business or other relationship or transaction which would make it improbable that an untrue communication from one to the other about the transaction or relationship would be ignored.[97] The most common instance of this latter situation is the transmission by one party to such a business relationship to the other of a statement of account or bill rendered. A failure to question such a bill or statement is uniformly received as evidence of an admission of its correctness.[98] On the other hand, if the negotiations have been broken off by one party's taking a final stand, thus indicating his view that further communication would be fruit-

---

93. See, e. g., Fidelity & Casualty Co. v. Beeland Bros. Merc. Co., 242 Ala. 591, 7 So.2d 265, 267 (1942); Levin v. Van Horn, 412 Pa. 322, 194 A.2d 419 (1963); Annot., 8 A.L.R. 1163.

94. See cases described in the second paragraph of n. 97, infra.

95. Megarry Bros., Inc. v. United States, 404 F.2d 479 (8th Cir. 1968); Boerner v. U. S., 117 F.2d 387, 390, 391 (2d Cir. 1941); Mahoney v. Kennedy, 188 Wis. 30, 205 N.W. 407, 411 (1925).

96. The significance of this is always conceded, see, e. g., Boerner v. U. S., 117 F.2d 387, 391 (2d Cir. 1941); Wieder v. Lorenz, 164 Ore. 10, 99 P.2d 38, 44, 45 (1940); Annot., 8 A.L.R. 1163.

97. Willard Helburn, Inc. v. Spiewak, 180 F.2d 480, 482 (2d Cir. 1950) (letter stating terms of previous oral transaction between caller and callee, held, circumstances such as to make an answer natural); E. P. Hinkel & Co. v. Washington Carpet Corp., 212 A.2d 328 (D.C.App.1965) (correspondence arising from six-year course of mutual dealings); Commonwealth Life Ins. Co. v. Elliott, 423 S.W.2d 898 (Ky.1968) (rule applied to retention of premium receipt book by beneficiary who could not read!); Ross v. Reynolds, 112 Me. 223, 91 A. 952 (1914) (failure of seller to reply to letter from buyer, complaining that automobile sold had been misrepresented by seller); Keeling-Easter Co. v. R. B. Dunning, 113 Me. 34, 92 A. 929 (1915) (similar to last); Trainer v. Fort, 310 Pa. 570, 578, 165 A. 232 (1933) (action by real estate broker for commission under oral contract made over the telephone with defendant; letter written by defendant to plaintiff immediately after conversation reciting terms of agreement differently, and unanswered by plaintiff, admissible).

But this factor is often disregarded, and a letter from one with whom the addressee is engaged in business transactions is treated as if it no more called for a reply than would a letter from a stranger, "a bolt from the blue." See, e. g., A. B. Leach & Co. v. Peirson, 275 U.S. 120, 55 A.L.R. 457 (1927) (suit by one who had purchased bonds from defendant investment concern upon alleged oral agreement by defendant's agent that defendant would repurchase bonds at same price on demand. Held, defendant's failure to answer plaintiff's letter asserting such contract, inadmissible. Holmes, J.: "A man cannot make evidence for himself by writing a letter containing the statements that he wishes to prove. He does not make the letter evidence by sending it to the party against whom he wishes to prove the facts. He no more can impose a duty to answer a charge than he can impose a duty to pay by selling goods." But is it not "natural" to answer such a letter from a customer who has bought bonds? Of course, it is the silence, not the letter alone, that is significant, and the question is one not of duty but of probability); Fidelity & Casualty Co. v. Beeland Bros. Merc. Co., 242 Ala. 591, 7 So.2d 265 (1942) (claim by assisting attorneys in suit defended by liability insurance company for attorney's fees against insurance company, which defended on ground plaintiffs were employed by insured; letter written by plaintiffs to defendants, after original suit concluded, setting out their version of the arrangement for their services, and unanswered, excluded.)

This restrictive attitude is especially marked in the seduction, breach of promise, and bastardy cases, where the defendant fails to answer an accusatory letter from the alleged victim. See e. g., Snead v. Commonwealth, 138 Va. 787, 121 S.E. 82, 34 A.L.R. 550 (1924).

98. Megarry Bros., Inc. v. United States, 404 F.2d 479 (8th Cir. 1968); Milliken v. Warwick, 306 Mass. 192, 28 N.E.2d 224 (1940); Bradley v. McDonald, 218 N.Y. 351, 113 N.E. 340 (1916).

less,[99] or if the letter was written after litigation was instituted, these circumstances tend to show that failure to answer is not to be received as an admission.[1]

271. Admissions by Conduct: (c) Flight and Similar Acts.[2]

"The wicked flee when no man pursueth." Many acts of a defendant after the crime seeking to escape the toils of the law are uncritically received as admissions by conduct, constituting circumstantial evidence of consciousness of guilt and hence of the fact of guilt itself. In this class are flight from the scene[3] or from one's usual haunts[4] after the crime, assuming a false name,[5] shaving off a beard,[6] resisting arrest,[7] attempting to bribe arresting officers,[8] forfeiture of bond by failure to appear,[9] escapes or attempted escapes from confinement,[10] and attempts of the accused to take his own life.[11]

If the flight is from the scene of the crime, evidence of it seems to be wholly acceptable as a means of locating the accused at the critical time and place. However, in many situations, the inference of consciousness of guilt of the particular crime is so uncertain and ambiguous and the evidence so prejudicial[12] that one is forced to wonder whether the evidence is not directed to punishing the "wicked" generally rather than resolving the issue of guilt of the offense charged.[13] Particularly troublesome are the cases where defend-

---

99. Kitzke v. Turnidge, 209 Ore. 563, 307 P.2d 522 (1957) (to defendant's letter suggesting settlement the "Bible way" plaintiff responded by filing suit).

1. Canadian Bank of Commerce v. Coumbe, 47 Mich. 358, 11 N.W. 196, 199 (1882).

2. See, for general statements, State v. Owen, 94 Ariz. 404, 385 P.2d 700 (1963), vacated on other grounds 378 U.S. 574, on remand 96 Ariz. 274, 394 P.2d 206; State v. Torphy, 217 Ind. 383, 28 N.E.2d 70, 72 (1940); State v. Barry, 93 N.H. 10, 34 A.2d 661 (1943); State v. Henderson, 182 Ore. 147, 184 P.2d 392, 413 (1947). See also Hutchins and Slesinger, Consciousness of Guilt, 77 U.Pa.L.Rev. 725 (1929); 2 Wigmore, Evidence § 276; Dec.Dig. Criminal Law ⊕351.

3. State v. Townsend, 201 Kan. 122, 439 P.2d 70 (1968); Davis v. State, 171 Neb. 333, 106 N.W.2d 490 (1960). If a "flight" instruction is given, it must be reasonable to infer flight. Compare State v. Bruton, 66 Wash.2d 111, 401 P.2d 340 (1965) (error to instruct that flight might be considered as evidence of guilt when defendants merely walked away from scene of alleged shoplifting), and State v. Owen, 94 Ariz. 404, 385 P.2d 700 (1963) vacated on other grounds 378 U.S. 574, on remand 96 Ariz. 274, 394 P.2d 206 (flight instruction not erroneous when defendants left rape victim in desert and returned to town).

4. Pierce v. State, 256 N.E.2d 557 (Ind.1970). Testimony which merely describes a search of certain areas, without establishing them as customary resorts of the accused, does not qualify. Commonwealth v. Carita, 356 Mass. 132, 249 N.E.2d 5 (1969).

5. People v. Waller, 14 Cal.2d 693, 96 P.2d 344 (1939).

6. People v. Slutts, 259 Cal.App.2d 886, 66 Cal.Rptr. 862 (1968).

7. People v. Sustak, 15 Ill.2d 115, 153 N.E.2d 849 (1958) (details admissible as going to weight; fact that resisting arrest is a separate offense does not require exclusion). Nor is resistance essential in order to admit the circumstances of arrest. Lenzi v. State, 456 S.W.2d 99 (Tex.Cr.App.1970) (possession of pistol at time of arrest).

8. Cortes v. State, 135 Fla. 589, 185 So. 323, 327 (1938); State v. Nelson, 65 N.M. 403, 338 P.2d 301 (1959).

9. Affronti v. U. S., 145 F.2d 3 (8th Cir. 1944) (government could show defendant by failing to appear forfeited bonds in other cases pending against him, as well as this one); Williams v. State, 148 Tex.Cr.R. 427, 187 S.W.2d 667 (1945).

10. State v. Ford, 259 Iowa 744, 145 N.W.2d 638 (1966); State v. Thomas, 63 Wash.2d 59, 385 P.2d 532 (1963).

11. People v. Duncan, 261 Ill. 339, 103 N.E. 1043 (1914); Commonwealth v. Goldenberg, 315 Mass. 26, 51 N.E.2d 762 (1943); State v. Painter, 329 Mo. 314, 44 S.W.2d 79 (1931); State v. Lawrence, 196 N.C. 562, 146 S.E. 395 (1929) (but Brogden, J. dissented on this point); Commonwealth v. Giacobbe, 341 Pa. 187, 19 A.2d 71 (1941); Annot., 22 A.L.R.3d 840.

12. For an example of apparent misuse by the jury, see Fugate v. Commonwealth, 445 S.W.2d 675 (Ky. 1969) (involuntary manslaughter by motor vehicle; evidence of leaving scene insufficient to support guilty verdict).

13. See, e. g., Wong Sun v. United States, 371 U.S. 471, 483, n. 10 (1963) ("[W]e have consistently doubted the probative value in criminal trials of evidence that the accused fled the scene of an actual or supposed crime."); Bailey v. United States, 135 U.S.App.D.C. 95, 416 F.2d 1110, 1115 (1969) (the evidence may be admitted with "cautious application in view of its innate shortcomings.").

ant flees when sought to be arrested for another crime,[14] or is wanted for another crime,[15] or is not shown to know that he is suspected of the particular crime.[16] Is a general sense of guilt to be accepted? [17] Perhaps the chief offenders are the cases of attempted suicide.[18]

While the great bulk of the decisions involve criminal prosecutions, flight also finds recognition in civil actions.[19]

The entire area calls for closer scrutiny of the validity of the suggested inference under the facts and circumstances of each particular case.

272.   Admissions by Conduct: (d) Failure to Call Witnesses or Produce Evidence:[20] Refusal to Submit to a Physical Examination.[21]

When it would be natural under the circumstances for a party to call a particular

witness,[22] or to take the stand himself as a witness,[23] or voluntarily to produce documents or other objects in his possession as evidence,[24] and he fails to do so, tradition has allowed his adversary to use this failure as the basis for invoking an adverse inference. An analogous inference may be drawn if a party unreasonably declines to submit, upon request, to a physical examination.[25]

Most of the controversy arises in respect to the failure to call a witness. It is often stated that when a potential witness is available, and appears to have special information relevant to the case, so that his testimony would not merely be cumulative,[26] and where

---

14. State v. Nelson, 65 N.M. 403, 338 P.2d 301 (1959) (murder; proper to admit evidence of attempt to bribe officer and flight when arrested for reckless driving).

15. People v. Yazum, 13 N.Y.2d 302, 196 N.E.2d 263, 246 N.Y.S.2d 626 (1963) (evidence of flight not excluded in New York trial because accused was also wanted in Ohio).

16. Shorter v. United States, 412 F.2d 428 (9th Cir. 1969) (showing of knowledge is not required). In general the cases simply overlook the problem. However an occasional case specifies knowledge as a requirement. People v. Harris, 23 Ill.2d 270, 178 N.E.2d 291 (1961), and see Embree v. United States, 320 F.2d 666 (9th Cir. 1963), sought to be distinguished in *Shorter,* supra. Circumstantial proof of knowledge may, of course, suffice. Commonwealth v. Osborne, 433 Pa. 297, 249 A.2d 330 (1969).

Cf. 2 Wigmore, Evidence § 276.

17. Martin v. State, 236 Ind. 524, 141 N.E.2d 107, 109 (1957) (resistance to arrest is evidence of guilt, "though not necessarily guilt of the crime charged.").

18. Note 11, supra; Fordham, Note, 7 N.C.L.Rev. 290 (1929).

19. Gaul v. Noiva, 155 Conn. 218, 230 A.2d 591 (1967) (attempt to flee from scene of automobile accident); Jones v. Strelecki, 49 N.J. 513, 231 A.2d 558 (1967) (failure to stop after striking pedestrian, in violation of Motor Vehicle Act).

20. See 2 Wigmore, Evidence §§ 285–291; Note, 17 Okla.L.Rev. 74 (1964); Dec.Dig. Evidence ⊕77, Criminal Law ⊕317; C.J.S. Evidence § 156.

21. 8 Wigmore, Evidence (McNaughton rev.) § 2220, note 19; Dec.Dig. Damages ⊕206(8).

22. Secondino v. New Haven Gas Co., 147 Conn. 672, 165 A.2d 598 (1960).

23. United States v. Fields, 102 F.2d 535, 537 (8th Cir. 1939); Williams v. Ricklemann, 292 S.W.2d 276 (Mo.1956).

A similar inference is available if a party takes the stand but fails to give evidence as to relevant matters within his knowledge. Caminetti v. United States, 242 U.S. 470, 492–495 (1917) (accused as witness: comment by judge but limited to failure to give details of matters about which he had testified); State v. Feinberg, 105 Conn. 115, 134 A. 228 (1926) (similar). See § 132, supra, as to extent to which accused waives privilege against self-incrimination by testifying.

24. Gray v. Callahan, 143 Fla. 673, 197 So. 396, 400 (1940); Martin v. T. L. James & Co., 237 La. 633, 112 So.2d 86 (1959); Welsh v. Gibbons, 211 S.C. 516, 46 S.E.2d 147 (1948).

25. Texas & N. O. Ry. Co. v. Rooks, 292 S.W. 536 (Tex.Com.App.1927) (but request addressed to attorneys insufficient); 8 Wigmore, Evidence (McNaughton rev.) § 2220, n. 19. The significance of the inference in respect to physical examination is greatly diminished by prevailing rules providing for compulsory physical examination and penalties for noncompliance. E. g., F.R.Civ.P. 35, 37(b). See § 3, supra.

26. Gafford v. Trans-Texas Airways, 299 F.2d 60 (6th Cir. 1962) (co-pilot testified; command pilot not called; held merely cumulative). When, however, there is a sharp issue of fact, failure to produce a witness who would corroborate the party's version can scarcely be regarded as "merely cumulative." Geiger v. Schneyer, 398 Pa. 69, 157 A.2d 56 (1960) (defendant driver failed to produce wife-passenger to corroborate his disputed testimony that view was obstructed); State v. Davis, 73 Wash.2d 271, 438 P.2d 185 (1968) (state failed to produce an officer

his relationship with one of the parties is such that the witness would ordinarily be expected to favor him,[27] then if such party does not produce his testimony, the inference arises that it would have been unfavorable.

Despite the plenitude of cases supporting the inference, caution in allowing it is suggested with increasing frequency.[28] This counsel of caution is reinforced by several factors. Possible conjecture or ambiguity of inference is often present.[29] The possibility that the inference may be drawn invites waste of time in calling unnecessary witnesses [30] or in presenting evidence to explain why

they were not called.[31] Anticipating that the inference may be invoked entails substantial possibilities of surprise.[32] And finally, the availability of modern discovery procedures serves to diminish both the justification [33] and the need [34] for the inference.

It is often said that if the witness is "equally available" to both parties, no inference springs from the failure of either to call him.[35] This can hardly be accurate, as the inference is frequently allowed when the witness could easily be called or subpoenaed by either party. What is in fact meant is that when so far as appears the witness would be as likely to be favorable to one party as the other, there will be no inference.[36] But even here, it seems that equality

who was present when disputed waiver of defendant's constitutional rights occurred); Schemenauer v. Travelers Indemnity Co., 34 Wis.2d 299, 149 N.W.2d 644 (1967) (failure of defendant to produce his physician to fortify claim of retrograde amnesia).

27. Secondino v. New Haven Gas Co., 147 Conn. 672, 165 A.2d 598 (1960) (personal injury plaintiff failed to call treating physician); Feldstein v. Harrington, 4 Wis.2d 380, 90 N.W.2d 566 (1958) (defendant failed to call physician who examined plaintiff at defendant's request); Carr v. Amusement, Inc., 47 Wis.2d 368, 177 N.W.2d 388 (1970) (plaintiff failed to call wife, who knew how much alcohol he had consumed); Georgia S. & F. R. Co. v. Perry, 326 F.2d 921 (5th Cir. 1964) (defendant railroad did not call locomotive engineer in grade-crossing case); State v. Davis, 73 Wash.2d 271, 438 P.2d 185 (1968) (state failed to call one of two officers allegedly present at disputed waiver of defendant's constitutional rights). Compare the following cases, in which the inference was said not to be available: United States v. Tant, 412 F.2d 840 (5th Cir. 1969) cert. denied 396 U.S. 876 (government failed to call "special employee," though present in court and sworn); Dawson v. Jost, 35 Wis.2d 644, 151 N.W.2d 717 (1967) (infant plaintiffs failed to call 8-year old sister).
Cases are collected in Annot., 5 A.L.R.2d 893.

28. Wynn v. United States, 130 U.S.App.D.C. 60, 397 F.2d 621 (1967); Jenkins v. Bierschenck, 333 F.2d 421 (8th Cir. 1964); Ballard v. Lumbermens Mut. Cas. Co., 33 Wis.2d 601, 148 N.W.2d 65 (1967).

29. Oliphant v. Snyder, 206 Va. 932, 147 S.E.2d 122, 126 (1966) ("Any presumption that he [10-year old passenger-son of defendant driver] would have testified adversely to his father is pure speculation.").

30. See, e. g., Ballard v. Lumbermens Mut. Cas. Co., 33 Wis.2d 601, 148 N.W.2d 65, 73 (1967) ("A party to a lawsuit does not have the burden, at his peril, of calling every possible witness to a fact, lest his failure to do so will result in an inference against him.").

31. The party is, of course, entitled to explain the nonproduction. Case v. New York Central R. Co., 329 F.2d 936 (2d Cir. 1964).

32. State v. Clawans, 38 N.J. 162, 183 A.2d 77 (1962) (suggesting that proper practice is to require party proposing to invoke the inference give notice at the close of the opponent's case).

33. The important thing is the availability of discovery. If it is not employed, the party ought not to be allowed to resort to the necessarily somewhat speculative inference when discovery would substitute certainty. Jenkins v. Bierschenk, 333 F.2d 421 (8th Cir. 1964). Cf. Cromling v. Pittsburgh & L. E. R. Co., 327 F.2d 142 (3d Cir. 1963). The argument against allowing the inference is even stronger when a deposition has in fact been taken. Atlantic Coast Line R. Co. v. Larisey, 269 Ala. 203, 112 So. 2d 203 (1959); Critzer v. Shegogue, 236 Md. 411, 204 A.2d 180 (1964); Bean v. Riddle, 423 S.W.2d 709 (Mo.1968). And see Rawlings, J., dissenting, State v. Parker, 261 Iowa 88, 151 N.W.2d 505 (1967) (defendant's inability to take deposition of uncalled prosecution witness advanced as reason for allowing inference).

34. Discovery procedures offer a more direct means of compelling the production of evidence. A parallel to the diminished importance of the so-called best evidence rule is evident. Cleary and Strong, The Best Evidence Rule: An Evaluation in Context, 51 Iowa L.Rev. 825 (1966).

35. Atlantic Coast Line R. Co. v. Larisey, 269 Ala. 203, 112 So.2d 203 (1959); Ellerman v. Skelly Oil Co., 227 Minn. 65, 34 N.W.2d 251 (1948), noted 33 Minn.L.Rev. 423.

36. See Deaver v. St. Louis Pub. Service Co., 199 S.W.2d 83, 85 (Mo.App.1947) ("However the availability of a witness is not to be determined from his mere physical presence at the trial or his ac-

of favor is nearly always debatable, and that though the judge thinks the witness would be as likely to favor one party as the other, he should permit either party to argue the inference against the adversary.[37] At least, it would appear in this supposed case of "equal favor," if the witness's knowledge is directed toward a particular issue, then the argument should be available against the party who has the burden of persuasion on that issue.[38]

A party may be at liberty to call a witness, but may have a privilege against the witness's being called by the adversary, as when under the local statute an accused in a criminal case may call his wife, but the state may not. Or it may be clear that all the information that a witness has is subject to a privilege which the party may exert, as in the case where by statute the party is privileged against disclosure by his physician of information learned in consultation or examination. In these situations probably the majority of courts would forbid an adverse inference from a failure to call.[39] Of course, an inference from the failure of the accused himself in a criminal case to take the stand is constitutionally forbidden.[40] The policy considerations in respect to the allowability

of comment upon the exercise of evidential privileges are discussed elsewhere.[41]

The specific procedural effect of the inference from failure to call a witness is seldom discussed, doubtless because local usage is so familiar that other possibilities are not considered.

Some courts say that the party's failure to call the witness or produce the evidence creates a "presumption"[42] that the testimony would have been unfavorable. It is usually phrased in terms, however, of "may" rather than "must" and seemingly could at most be only a "permissive," not a mandatory presumption, i. e. an inference described as a presumption in order to avoid local prohibitions against judges' commenting on the evidence.[43] Moreover, unlike the usual presumption, it is not directed to any specific presumed fact or facts which are required or permitted to be found. One who has the burden of producing evidence of a fact in issue, cannot supply the lack of proof by relying on this "presumption."[44] "The extent of a party's right to invoke his opponent's failure to call an available witness, when such right exists, is to impair the value of the latter's proofs, and to give greater credence to the positive evidence of the former, upon any issue upon which it is shown that such witness might have knowledge."[45]

---

cessibility for the service of a subpoena upon him. On the contrary, his availability may well depend, among other things, upon his relationship to one or the other of the parties, and the nature of the testimony that he might be expected to give in the light of his previous statements or declarations about the facts of the case"); United States v. Beekman, 155 F.2d 580 (2d Cir. 1946) (employees of defendant not called by him; government comment allowed: when likelihood of bias, not "equally available").

37. United States v. Dibrizzi, 393 F.2d 642 (2d Cir. 1968); Dawson v. Davis, 125 Conn. 330, 5 A.2d 703 (1939); Baker v. Salvation Army, Inc., 91 N.H. 1, 12 A.2d 514 (1940); Note, 73 Dick.L.Rev. 337 (1969).

38. General Motors Acceptance Corp. v. Bearden, 114 Ga.App. 392, 151 S.E.2d 517 (1966).

39. See § 80, supra.

40. See § 131, supra.

41. See § 80, supra.

42. See, e. g., Stephenson v. Golden, 279 Mich. 710, 276 N.W. 849 (1938); Robinson v. Haydel, 177 Miss. 233, 171 So. 7 (1937); Wolfe v. Wolfe, 120 W.Va. 389, 198 S.E. 209 (1938).

43. See discussion of these terms in Ch. 36, infra.

44. Maszczenski v. Myers, 212 Md. 346, 129 A.2d 109 (1957); Stimpson v. Hunter, 234 Mass. 61, 125 N.E. 155 (1919); Pacific Finance Corp. v. Rucker, 392 S.W.2d 554 (Tex.Civ.App.1965); 2 Wigmore, Evidence § 290, p. 179. Cf. Morrow v. United States, 408 F.2d 1390 (8th Cir. 1969) (in prosecution for placing life in jeopardy, jury could infer that gun was loaded in absence of introduction of contrary evidence by accused).

45. Snow, J. in Stocker v. Boston & M. R. Co., 84 N.H. 377, 151 A. 457, 70 A.L.R. 1320, 1323, (1930). See Annot., 70 A.L.R. 1326.

A possible practical effect of calling it a presumption is that it might incline some courts adopting this usage to regard its inclusion in the instructions as a matter of right. Most courts customarily speak of the party's conduct as creating an "inference." [46] Doubtless some of these courts would consider that the party has a right to have such inference explained in the instructions, on proper request. Others no doubt would say that the instruction is proper but not required.[47] Still others would condemn it as a comment on the evidence.[48]

Of course, all courts permit counsel to argue the inference where the inference is an allowable one. Most of the courts, moreover, whether or not they customarily include in their instructions a charge on the "presumption" or "inference," assume that they are required to keep a firm rein upon arguments on this inference. In these jurisdictions reversals for arguments thought to be unjustified by the rules as to when the inference is allowable, are fairly frequent.[49]

In jurisdictions where the judge retains his common law power to comment on the evidence, certainly a fair comment on failure to produce witnesses or evidence is traditionally allowable. In other jurisdictions, there is no harm if local practice sanctions a discretion in the judge to include such an instruction. It is submitted, however, that a practice which gives a party a right to such instruction is undesirable.[50] If made a matter of right it is hard to escape the development of elaborate rules of law defining the circumstances when the right exists. To make it a matter of right has the advantage, it is true, of focussing past experience on the problem presented at the trial, but the cost here of complex rules far outweighs the gain.

A similar effect, of spinning a web of rules, flows from the practice of tight control of the argument on the inference. It is wiser to hold that if an argument on failure to produce proof is fallacious, the remedy is the usual one, namely the answering argument and the jury's good sense.[51] Thus the judge would be called on to intervene only when the argument can be said, under the general standard, to be not merely weak or unfounded, but unfair and prejudicial.[52]

---

46. See, e. g., Gross v. Williams, 149 F.2d 84 (8th Cir. 1945); National Life Co. v. Brennecke, 195 Ark. 1088, 115 S.W.2d 855 (1938); Dawson v. Davis, 125 Conn. 330, 5 A.2d 703 (1939).

47. See Knott v. Hawley, 163 Minn. 239, 203 N.W. 785 (1925).

For illustrative instructions, see Cromling v. Pittsburgh & L. E. R. Co., 327 F.2d 142 (3d Cir. 1964); Schemenauer v. Travelers Indemnity Co., 34 Wis. 2d 299, 149 N.W.2d 644 (1967).

48. Hartman v. Hartman, 314 Mo. 305, 284 S.W. 488 (1926).

49. See, e. g., Atlantic Coast Line R. Co. v. Larisey, 269 Ala. 203, 112 So.2d 203 (1959); Ellerman v. Skelly Oil Co., 227 Minn. 65, 34 N.W.2d 251 (1948).

50. "If it commends itself to reason, born of common judgment and experience, the jury will apply it without hint or argument from the Court. The practice of placing this mere argument in instructions violates the plain provisions of Section 1530 of the 1942 Code. Those cases are sound which deny to the inference any quality other than mere argument. Here again a safe and logical test is: if counsel is free to argue it, the Court is not." Alexander, Presumptions: Their Use and Abuse, 17 Miss.L.J. 1, 14 (1945).

51. In United States v. Cotter, 60 F.2d 689, 692 (2d Cir. 1932) the court (L. Hand, J.) in rejecting defendant's complaint of the judge's refusal to instruct the jury to disregard the prosecution's argument based on defendant's failure to call witnesses, said, "A judge is not required to intervene here any more than in any other issue of fact. He must indeed, as he always must, keep the prosecution in a criminal case within bounds; . . . just as he must keep passion out of the debate and hold the parties to the issues. But he is not charged with correcting their non sequiturs; the jury are to find these for themselves. So the judge in the case at bar was not required to correct the argument, that the failure of the defendants to call the four witnesses was a ground for supposing that they would swear against them. He might have done so, but he need not; so far as we know, Sears v. Duling, 79 Vt. 334, 65 A. 990, is the only decision to the contrary and it does not persuade us." See also Alabama Power Co. v. Goodwin, 210 Ala. 657, 99 So. 158 (1924) (trial judge must not pass upon the logical propriety of arguments).

52. In passing on this the trial judge has a substantial measure of discretion. Lebas v. Patriotic Assur. Co., 106 Conn. 119, 137 A. 241 (1927).

273. Admissions by Conduct: (e) Misconduct Constituting Obstruction of Justice.[53]

A party's failure to produce evidence when he is free to produce or withhold, may as we have seen in the preceding section be treated as an admission.   As might be expected, wrongdoing by the party in connection with his case, amounting to an obstruction of justice is also commonly regarded as an admission by conduct.   By resorting to wrongful devices he is said to give ground for believing that he thinks his case is weak and not to be won by fair means.   Accordingly, a party's false statement about the matter in litigation, whether before suit[54] or on the stand,[55] his fabrication of false documents,[56] his undue pressure, by bribery[57] or intimidation[58] or other means, to influence a witness to testify for him or to avoid testifying, his destruction or concealment of relevant documents or objects,[59] his attempt to corrupt the jury,[60] his hiding[61] or transferring[62] property in anticipation of judgment —all these are instances of this type of admission by conduct.   Of course, it is not enough to show that a third person did the acts, such as bribing a witness, charged as obstructive.   They must be fastened to the party himself, or in the case of a corporation to one of its superior officers, by showing that he did the act or authorized it by words or other conduct.[63]   Moreover, the circum-

---

53.   2 Wigmore, Evidence §§ 278, 291; Maguire and Vincent, Admissions Implied from Spoliation, 45 Yale L.J. 226 (1935); Dec.Dig. Criminal Law ⊃351 (8), 351(10), 408, Evidence ⊃78, 79, 110, 219(2); C.J.S. Evidence §§ 151–155, 293.

54.   Wilson v. United States, 162 U.S. 613 (1896) (false explanations of incriminating circumstances in murder case); People v. Showers, 68 Cal.2d 639, 68 Cal.Rptr. 459, 440 P.2d 939 (1968) (false explanation by accused as to why he was searching in patch of ivy where heroin was found); Commonwealth v. Lettrich, 346 Pa. 497, 31 A.2d 155 (1943) (child-murder by custodian, false statements as to child's whereabouts to avert inquiry and suspicion); Note, 5 Willamette L.J. 253 (1969).

55.   Sheehan v. Goriansky, 317 Mass. 10, 56 N.E.2d 883 (1944) (defendant's testimony which from other evidence jury could find to be false); Hall v. Merrimack Mut. Fire Ins. Co., 91 N.H. 6, 13 A.2d 157 (1940) (deliberately false testimony at first trial, acknowledged to be false at the second); Note, 5 Willamette L.J. 253 (1969).

56.   United States v. Wilkins, 385 F.2d 465 (4th Cir. 1967) (letter fabricated to explain failure to report income for tax purposes); Western States Grocery Co. v. Mirt, 190 Okl. 299, 123 P.2d 266 (1942) (falsified witness-statement placed in evidence).

57.   People v. Gambony, 402 Ill. 74, 83 N.E.2d 321 (1949) (indecent liberties with a child: attempts to "buy off" the prosecuting witnesses); Davis v. Commonwealth, 204 Ky. 601, 265 S.W. 10 (1924) (letter offering bribe for favorable testimony); State v. Rolfe, 92 Idaho 467, 444 P.2d 428 (1968) (attempt to bribe witness).

58.   State v. Adair, 106 Ariz. 4, 469 P.2d 823 (1970); State v. Hill, 47 N.J. 490, 221 A.2d 725 (1966); Price v. State, 37 Wis.2d 117, 154 N.W.2d 222 (1967).   And see State v. Nelson, 182 Neb. 31, 152 N.W.2d 10 (1967) (witness assaulted by accused for not having "left the country.").

59.   Jones v. State, 223 Ga. 157, 154 S.E.2d 228 (1967) rev'd on other grounds 389 U.S. 24 (murder; accused buried body); Hubbard v. State, 187 So.2d 885 (Miss.1966) (accused pushed his automobile into 40-foot deep lake after fatal accident); Welborn v. Rigdon, 231 S.W.2d 127 (Mo.1950) (suit by plaintiff for money advanced to improve defendant's property; defendant's conduct in wilfully destroying plaintiff's receipts held "an admission of plaintiff's claim").

60.   People v. Marion, 29 Mich. 31, 39 (1874); McHugh v. McHugh, 186 Pa. 197, 40 A. 410 (1898).

61.   State v. Bruce, 24 Me. 71 (1844) (procuring property by threats; evidence of concealment).

62.   Burdett v. Hipp, 252 Ala. 37, 39 So.2d 389 (1949) (defendant's conveyance of his property to kin after suit filed); Johnson v. O'Brien, 258 Minn. 502, 105 N.W.2d 244, 88 A.L.R.2d 577 (1960) (same); Annot., 80 A.L.R. 1139.

63.   Morgan v. Commonwealth, 283 Ky. 588, 142 S.W.2d 123 (1940) (attempted bribery of witness, error to admit because no showing of defendant's connection with the act); Meacham v. Gjarde, 194 Wash. 526, 76 P.2d 605 (1938) (misconduct of counsel not admissible without proof of authorization by party—a clear holding that implied or general authority is not enough). The suggestion in the text as to corporations is taken from Maguire and Vincent, Admissions Implied from Spoliation, 45 Yale L.J. 226, 251 (1935).   Compare City of Austin v. Howard, 158 S.W.2d 556 (Tex.Civ.App.1942) (attempts by Mayor and City Manager to prevent witness from testifying in suit against City, held admissible though assent of Council not shown.   "Manifestly they were active-

stances of the act must manifest bad faith. Mere negligence is not enough,[64] for it does not sustain the inference of consciousness of a weak case.

A question may well be raised whether the relatively modest probative value of this species of evidence is not often outweighed by its prejudicial aspects.[65] The litigant who would not like to have a stronger case must indeed be a rarity. It may well be that the real underpinning of the rule of admissibility is a desire to impose swift punishment, with a certain poetic justice, rather than concern over niceties of proof.[66] In any event, the evidence is generally admitted.

What is the probative reach of these various kinds of "spoliation" admissions, beyond their great tactical value in darkening the atmosphere of the party's case?[67] They should, it seems, entitle the proponent to an instruction that the adversary's conduct may be considered as tending to corroborate the proponent's case generally, and as tending to discredit the adversary's case generally.[68] This is worthwhile in itself and as carrying with it the corresponding right of the proponent's counsel to argue these inferences. But a crucial and perplexing question remains, namely, does the adverse inference from the party's obstructive conduct supply the want of any evidence of a fact essential to the other party's case? Certainly the primitive impulse is strong, and an analogy has been suggested to the practice under statutes and rules permitting the court to enter a default against a party who refuses to make discovery.[69] Certainly also when the conduct points toward an inference about a particular specific fact, as in the case of bribery of an attesting witness to absent

---

ly interested and participating on behalf of the City in the conduct of the trial as they had a right to do, and their conduct should be deemed, under such circumstances, to be within the general scope of their authority."). But in Nowack v. Metropolitan Street Ry. Co., 166 N.Y. 433, 439, 60 N.E. 32, 34 (1901) evidence of attempted bribery by defendant's mere claim agent was held receivable, not only as the representative admission of defendant corporation, but because it cast doubt upon the other witnesses secured by him.

64. Berthold-Jennings Lumber Co., 80 F.2d 32 (8th Cir. 1935) (action for overcharge; waybills covering shipments had been destroyed by defendant, held, doctrine of spoliation inapplicable; only applies to conduct indicating fraud, whereas destruction here was routine, with no desire to suppress evidence); Gallup v. St. Louis, I. M. and S. Ry. Co., 140 Ark. 347, 215 S.W. 586 (1919) (similar).

65. One of the few decisions discussing the problem, Price v. State, 37 Wis.2d 117, 154 N.W.2d 222 (1967), held that the trial judge did not abuse his discretion in admitting the evidence. See generally § 185, supra.

66. Few opinion writers have been as frank as in Pomeroy v. Benton, 77 Mo. 64, 86 (1882): "It is because of the very fact that the evidence of the plaintiff, the proofs of his claim or the muniments of his title, have been destroyed [by defendant], that the law, in hatred of the spoiler, baffles the destroyer, and thwarts his iniquitous purpose, by indulging a presumption which supplies the lost proof, and thus defeats the wrong-doer by the very means he had so confidently employed to perpetrate the wrong."

67. For an illuminating discussion, see Maguire and Vincent, Admissions Implied from Spoliation, 45 Yale L.J. 226, 235–249 (1935).

68. See Maguire and Vincent, op. cit. at 243–249, and see Prudential Insurance Co. v. Lawnsdail, 235 Iowa 125, 15 N.W.2d 880 (1944) (destruction of record "authorizes an inference which tends to corroborate the evidence" on the other side); Hay v. Peterson, 6 Wyo. 419, 45 P. 1073, 1076–9 (1896) (destruction of records of deceased by plaintiff, defendant entitled to instruction on presumption but one requested by him not properly qualified).

The courts often speak of a "presumption" against the spoliator. Long v. Earle, 277 Mich. 505, 269 N.W. 577 (1936); Dec.Dig. Evidence ⊂⇒78, 79. Most presumptions may stand in lieu of proof of specific facts, see Ch. 36, infra, but this "presumption" against the spoliator is usually given only a general persuasive effect, rather than a probative one. Walker v. Herke, 20 Wash.2d 239, 147 P.2d 255 (1944), as to which see n. 71, infra.

69. As in Rule 37, Federal Rules of Civil Procedure, and compare Feingold v. Walworth Bros. Inc., 238 N.Y. 446, 454, 144 N.E. 675, 678 (1924) applying a statute of similar purport, discussed in Maguire and Vincent, op. cit. at 235. See also Crook v. Schumann, 292 Ky. 750, 167 S.W.2d 836 (1943) (defendant's disobedience to order to produce records on which proof of plaintiff's case depends; court had discretion to enter decree pro confesso but should have given defendant notice before doing so).

himself from the probate hearing, or the destruction of a particular deed or letter, there is likely to be a greater willingness to allow an inference as to the fact,[70] though your only other information is the proponent's claim about it in his pleading. Where the conduct is not directed toward suppression of any particular fact, as in attempts to "buy off" the prosecution, to suborn the jury, or to defeat recovery by conveyance of property, an inference as to the existence of a particular fact not proved seems to be more strained. Without adverting to this distinction most of the decisions have supported the general doctrine that the inference from obstructive conduct by the adversary will not supply a want of proof of a particular fact essential to the proponent's case.[71]

70. See 2 Wigmore, Evidence § 291, wherein the author contends that the failure or refusal to produce, or the destruction of a document, sufficiently identified by the proof, is evidence from which alone its contents can be inferred to be unfavorable to the one chargeable with the obstructive conduct. For an excellent opinion supporting this view see McCleery v. McCleery, 200 Ala. 4, 75 So. 316 (1917, by McClellan, J.).

Compare also the famous case of Armory v. Delamirie, 1 Stra. 505, 93 Eng.Rep. 664 (K.B.1722) where the chimney sweeper's boy found a mounted jewel and took it to a goldsmith's shop to be valued. But the goldsmith's apprentice kept the stone, and gave back only the socket. The boy sued the goldsmith for the conversion of the jewel. After evidence had been given of what a jewel of the finest water that would fit the socket would be worth, the Chief Justice instructed the jury, "that unless the defendant did produce the jewel, and shew it not to be of the finest water, they should presume the strongest against him, and make the value of the best jewels the measure of their damages." It will be noted that in this picturesque landmark case, the limits of the inference were marked out by the evidence of the size of the socket, and of the value of the finest jewel that would fit it.

71. Gage v. Parmelee, 87 Ill. 329, 343 (1877) (bill to set aside for fraud a partnership settlement agreement; proof showed that on being shown a copy of the bill, defendant burned all the bills and papers of the firm. "This culpable act of the destruction of the books justly prejudices the case of the appellee, and we have the inclination to give to it the full legitimate effect against him that may be warranted. But we do not see how, under the proofs in the case, it can be made avail of here, to

the advantage of appellant, unless there be allowed to it the effect of supplying proof. This, we do not think, can rightly be done. Proof must be made of the allegations of the bill. The destruction of the books does not make such proof. The presumption of law does not go to that extent. In the weighing of conflicting testimony, there might be scope for the operation of this presumption against the appellee; or, in the denial to him of any benefit of secondary evidence."); Parsons v. Ryan, 340 Mass. 245, 163 N.E.2d 293 (1960) (defendant's evasive conduct and false statements not enough to prove negligence); Login v. Waisman, 82 N.H. 500, 136 A. 134 (1927) (evidence, though probably not competent, that defendant had bribed an eyewitness to leave the state; held, not sufficient to take plaintiff's case to jury, without other evidence of essential facts of agency and negligence); Patch Mfg. Co. v. Protection Lodge, 77 Vt. 294, 329, 60 A. 74 (1905); (presumption from spoliation does not relieve other party of burden of producing evidence to prove his case so far as he has burden); Walker v. Herke, 20 Wash.2d 239, 147 P.2d 255 (1944) (extensive discussion, citing cases).

Supporting the contrary view, that evidence of spoliation does supply proof of facts alleged by the proponent, are statements in the following opinions, though the holdings may not reach so far: Middleton v. Middleton, 188 Ark. 1022, 68 S.W.2d 1003, 1006 (1934) (son destroyed father's will leaving part of his property to daughters; in suit by daughters to establish as lost will, son cannot rely on statute requiring proof of contents by disinterested witnesses, only proof possible being that of interested witnesses, which was furnished); Pomeroy v. Benton, 77 Mo. 64, 85 (1882) (suit by partner after dissolution agreement to set aside agreement and hold the other partner to account as fraudulent trustee: defendant destroyed records necessary for ascertaining amount of profits made on goods for which he was required to account; held, because of spoliation, amount claimed in plaintiff's complaint, $200,000, would be taken as measure; but on rehearing, some evidence relevant to amount was found in the record, and by reference thereto, recovery was much reduced); Gough v. Gough, 321 Mo. 414, 11 S.W.2d 729 (1928) (similar to last); and see In re Lambie's Estate, 97 Mich. 49, 56 N.W. 223, 225 (1893) (where proponent of earlier will is shown to have destroyed later revoking will, latter is presumed to have been legally executed and its terms may be proved by declarations of testatrix). A sprinkling of decisions has even gone further and has ascribed to spoliation the effect of a conclusive presumption, that the despoiler cannot dispute. Middleton v. Middleton, supra ("where the instrument destroyed is of such nature as to destroy all evidence, there follows a conclusive presumption that if produced it would have established the claim of the adversary"). Or hold that the despoiler cannot dispute the presumption by his own unsupported testimony. Downing v. Plate, 90 Ill. 268, 273 (1878). But more recent cases reject the conclusive presumption theory. Hall v. Merrimack Mut. Fire

274. Admissions by Conduct: (f) Offers to Compromise Disputed Claim.[72]

In general. An offer by the claimant to accept a sum in compromise of a disputed claim may be urged against him as an admission of the weakness of his claim. Or, conversely, an offer by his adversary to pay a sum in compromise may be urged against the adversary as an admission of the weakness of his position. In either case there is general agreement that the offer of compromise is not admissible on the issue of liability, although the reason for exclusion is not always clear.

Two grounds for the rule of inadmissibility may be advanced: lack of relevancy and policy considerations.[73] (1) The relevancy of the offer will vary according to circumstances, with a very small offer of payment to settle a very large claim being much more readily construed as a desire for peace rather than an admission of weakness of position. Relevancy would increase, however, as the amount of the offer approached the amount claimed. (2) The policy aspect is to promote the settling of disputes, which would be discouraged if offers of compromise were admitted in evidence.[74] Resting the rule on this basis has the advantage of avoiding difficult questions of relevancy. On this basis, the rule would be akin to a privilege, rather than a rule of competency. One has the privilege if he has made the offer in question, and is a party to the suit in which the evidence is offered.[75]

To call into play the exclusionary rule, there must be an actual dispute,[76] or at least an apparent difference of view between the parties as to the validity or amount of the claim.[77] An offer to pay an admitted claim is not privileged.[78] There is no policy of encouraging compromises of undisputed claims. They should be paid in full. If the validity of the claim and the amount due are undisputed, an offer to pay a lesser sum in settlement[79] or to pay in installments[80] would accordingly be admissible.

What is excluded? The offer of course,[81] and any suggestions or overtures of settlement.[82] How far do any accompanying statements of fact made by either party during negotiations or correspondence looking to settlement share the privilege? The generally accepted doctrine has been that an admission

Ins. Co., 91 N.H. 6, 13 A.2d 157, 159 (1940); Walker v. Herke, 20 Wash.2d 239, 147 P.2d 255, 261 (1944).

72. 4 Wigmore, Evidence §§ 1061, 1062; Dec.Dig. Evidence ☜213, 214, 219(3), Criminal Law ☜408; C.J.S. Evidence §§ 285–290.

73. See the discussion of theory in Morgan, Basic Problems of Evidence 209 (1962). The cases in general do not display much concern as to the basis of the rule.

74. See § 74, supra.

75. See § 74, supra.

76. Ogden v. George F. Alger Co., 353 Mich. 402, 91 N.W.2d 288 (1958) (substantial offer to plaintiff for surrender of his contract, made before controversy arose).

77. Tindal v. Mills, 265 N.C. 716, 144 S.E.2d 902 (1965).

78. Hunter v. Hyder, 236 S.C. 378, 114 S.E.2d 493 (1960) (defendant admitted cutting timber from plaintiff's land and said he wanted to straighten it out).

79. Person v. Bowe, 79 Minn. 238, 82 N.W. 480 (1900) (plaintiff sued for wages claimed to be due him as a farm laborer, and offered evidence that when he demanded his pay the defendant said that he could not pay then, but would let the plaintiff have $20, and would pay the rest about the middle of November, and if the plaintiff "would throw off five dollars" he would at once pay the claim).

80. Tindal v. Mills, 265 N.C. 716, 144 S.E.2d 902 (1965) (offer to give a series of notes for undisputed claim).

81. Outlook Hotel Co. v. St. John, 287 F. 115 (3d Cir. 1923) (letter offering settlement privileged though not expressly without prejudice).

82. Wood v. Morrissey, 31 F.Supp. 449 (D.C.La. 1940) ("we might discuss compromise, if you care to submit an offer"); Armstrong v. Kline, 64 Cal. App.2d 704, 149 P.2d 445 (1944) ("she asked me what I thought about settling"); North River Ins. Co. v. Walker, 161 Ky. 368, 170 S.W. 983 (1914) ("if you will come to Paducah we will try to make a compromise settlement."). Cf. Shaeffer v. Burton, 151 W.Va. 761, 155 S.E.2d 884 (1967) ("I am sure that if we get together . . . we can settle this problem amicably," admissible).

of fact in the course of negotiations is not privileged [83] unless it is hypothetical [84]—"we admit for the sake of the discussion only"— or unless it is expressly stated to be "without prejudice," [85] or unless it is inseparably connected with the offer,[86] so that it cannot be correctly understood without reading the two together.[87]

This generally accepted doctrine of denying the protection of the exclusionary rule to statements of fact has serious drawbacks, however. It tends to discourage freedom of communication in attempting compromise, and, taken with its exceptions, it involves difficulties of application. As a result the trend is to extend the protection to all statements made in compromise negotiations.[88]

The exclusionary rule is designed to exclude the offer of compromise only when it is tendered as an admission of the weakness of the offering party's claim or defense, not when the purpose is otherwise. Thus, for example, the rule does not call for exclusion when the compromise negotiations are sought to be proved as an explanation of delay in taking action [89] or to explain prior statements [90] or to show the extent of legal services rendered in conducting them.[91] As in other situations where evidence is admissible for one purpose but not for another, an evaluation is required in terms of weighing probative value and need against likelihood of prejudice, with due regard to the probable efficacy of a limiting instruction.[92]

Evidence of present party's compromise with third persons. In an action between P and D a compromise offer or a completed compromise by D with T, a third person, having a claim similar to P's arising from the same transaction may be relevant as showing D's belief in the weakness of his defense in P's present action. Nevertheless, the same consideration of policy which actuates the courts to exclude an offer of compromise made by D to P, namely the danger of discouraging compromises, also applies here. Accordingly the prevailing view is that the compromise offer or payment made by the present defendant is privileged when offered as an implied admission of liability.[93] But,

---

83. State v. Stevens, 248 Minn. 309, 80 N.W.2d 22 (1956) (admission of paternity in effort to compromise paternity claim); Cole v. Harvey, 200 Okl. 564, 198 P.2d 199 (1948) (suit for work done; no error in receiving evidence of statements of amount due, during negotiations for compromise); Dunning v. Northwestern Elec. Co., 186 Ore. 379, 199 P.2d 648 (1948) rev'd on other grounds 186 Ore. 379, 206 P.2d 1177 (reference in letter to injuries sustained "when you ran into fallen pole"). Numerous cases are collected in Annot., 15 A.L.R.3d 13.

84. Jones v. Jernigan, 29 N.M. 399, 223 P. 100 (1924).

85. White v. Old Dominion S. S. Co., 102 N.Y. 660, 6 N.E. 289 (1886) and cases cited, Annot., 15 A.L.R. 3d 13, 33.

86. See cases on "independent" statements, Annot., 15 A.L.R.3d 13, 27.

87. Home Ins. Co. v. Baltimore Warehouse Co., 93 U.S. 527, 548 (1876); Sanford v. John Finnegan Co., 169 S.W. 624 (Tex.Civ.App.1914).

88. West's Ann.Cal.Evid.Code, §§ 1152, 1154; F.R. Ev. (R.D.1971) 408.

89. Waiver of failure to give notice or make proof of loss within required time; Federal Mut. Ins. Co. v. Lewis, 231 Md. 587, 191 A.2d 437 (1963); Travelers Ins. Co. v. Barrett, 366 S.W.2d 692 (Tex.Civ. App.1963); Graham v. San Antonio Machine & Supply Corp., 418 S.W.2d 303 (Tex.Civ.App.1967); Annot., 49 A.L.R.2d 87.

90. Fieve v. Emmeck, 248 Minn. 122, 78 N.W.2d 343 (1956); Malatt v. United Transit Co., 99 R.I. 263, 207 A.2d 39 (1965).

91. Wolf v. Mutual Ben. Health & Acc. Ass'n, 188 Kan. 694, 366 P.2d 219 (1961).

92. See § 59, supra.

93. Hawthorne v. Eckerson Co., 77 F.2d 844 (2d Cir. 1935); Lewis v. Dixie-Portland Flour Mills, Inc., 356 F.2d 54 (6th Cir. 1966); McCallum v. Harris, 379 S.W.2d 438 (Ky.1964); Tregellas v. American Oil Co., 231 Md. 95, 188 A.2d 691 (1963); Annot., 20 A.L.R.2d 304; Uniform Rules 52, 53; West's Ann.Cal.Evid.Code, §§ 1152, 1154; F.R.Ev. (R.D. 1971) 408.
A settlement which is offered as proof of the liability of a third party, arising out of the transaction in suit, is not within the privilege since the evidence will not harm the parties to the compromise. But it may be an offer of conduct-as-hearsay and

though inadmissible for this purpose, it may well come in for another purpose. A defendant for example places on the stand in a personal injury case a witness who was injured in the same collision. Here it seems clear that if the witness has made a claim on his own account against the defendant, inconsistent with his present favorable testimony, this may be proved to impeach the witness. And it further seems reasonable that if the witness has been paid or promised money in compromise of his claim, this may likewise be shown in impeachment, as evidence of bias.[94] The need for evaluating the credibility of the witness may be as insistent as the policy of encouraging compromise. If, however, the witness sought to be impeached by showing the compromise with a third person, is one of the present parties, the question is more debatable. The danger that the evidence will be used substantively as an admission is greater, and as the party's interest is apparent the need for additional evidence on credibility is less. This impeachment of party-witnesses, however, has occasionally been sanctioned.[95]

Compromise-evidence in criminal cases.[96] An offer by the accused to pay money to "buy off" the prosecuting witness and stifle prosecution, though sometimes mistakenly theorized as an offer of compromise and held inadmissible,[97] is not within the policy of encouraging compromises, and hence is not usually regarded as privileged.[98] Indeed, we have seen that it is classed as an implied admission and received in evidence as such.[99] On the other hand, offers by the accused to the state's attorney to plead guilty in return for leniency seem to be within the policy. Effective criminal law administration in many localities would hardly be possible if a large proportion of the charges were not disposed of by such compromises. Accordingly most courts seem to recognize such offers as privileged.[1] If the transaction on which

---

excluded as such. See, e. g., Daly v. Publix Cabs, 128 Neb. 403, 259 N.W. 163 (1935) (suit by passenger against operator of taxicab for injury incurred when another automobile collided with taxicab; evidence offered by taxicab operator that driver of other automobile paid damages to taxicab, excluded as hearsay as to passenger). See § 250, supra.

A compromise may take the form of a consent judgment. Hentschel v. Smith, 278 Minn. 86, 153 N.W. 2d 199 (1967).

94. Dornberg v. St. Paul City Ry. Co., 253 Minn. 52, 91 N.W.2d 178 (1958); Joice v. Missouri-Kansas-Texas R. Co., 354 Mo. 439, 189 S.W.2d 568, 161 A.L.R. 383 (1945); Rynar v. Lincoln Transit Co., 129 N.J.L. 525, 30 A.2d 406 (1945) (Case, J., discusses balance of need for impeachment and danger of improper use; here admissible in judge's discretion); Annot., 161 A.L.R. 395; F.R.Ev. (R.D.1971) 408. Of course, the opponent would be entitled to an instruction limiting the use of the evidence to the question of credibility. Contra, Fenberg v. Rosenthal, 348 Ill.App. 510, 109 N.E.2d 402 (1952). See § 40 at n. 1, supra.

95. Luis v. Cavin, 88 Cal.App.2d 107, 198 P.2d 563 (1948); Burke v. Commercial Standard Ins. Co., 38 So.2d 644 (La.App.1949).

When a payment made by another tortfeasor is relied upon to reduce the liability of the defendant, the preferable practice is for the judge, rather than the jury, to perform the arithmetic, Brooks v. Daley, 242 Md. 185, 218 A.2d 184 (1966); Sheets v. Davenport, 181 Neb. 621, 150 N.W.2d 224 (1967); 9 U.L.A. 242.

96. See Dec.Dig. Criminal Law ⚷408.

97. See, e. g., Richardson v. State, 28 Ala.App. 432, 186 So. 574 (1939).

98. Amburgey v. Commonwealth, 415 S.W.2d 103 (Ky.1967); State v. Givens, 87 S.C. 525, 70 S.E. 162 (1911); Carter v. State, 161 Tenn. 698, 34 S.W.2d 208 (1931); 4 Wigmore, Evidence § 1061 (d) (8).

99. See § 273, supra.

1. State v. Byrd, 203 Kan. 45, 453 P.2d 22 (1969); Bennett v. Commonwealth, 234 Ky. 333, 28 S.W.2d 24 (1930); State v. McGunn, 208 Minn. 349, 294 N.W. 208 (1940); State v. Abel, 320 Mo. 445, 8 S.W.2d 55 (1928); Stafford v. State, 125 Tex.Cr.R. 174, 67 S.W.2d 285 (1934); West's Ann.Cal.Evid. Code, § 1153; F.R.Ev. (R.D.1971) 410. The proposed federal rule also includes statements made during negotiations.

Participation in the current reexamination of plea bargaining is beyond the scope of this work. See President's Commission on Law Enforcement and Administration of Justice, Task Force Report: The Courts 108, 112–114 (1967); A.B.A. Project on Minimum Standards for Criminal Justice: Standards Relating to Pleas of Guilty §§ 1.8, 3.1 (1967); Alschuler, The Prosecutor's Role in Plea Bargaining, 36 U.Chi.L.Rev. 50 (1968).

the prosecution is based gives rise also to a civil right of action, a compromise or offer of compromise of the civil claim if no agreement to stifle the criminal prosecution is involved should seemingly be privileged when offered at the criminal trial.[2]

Effect of acceptance of offer of compromise. If an offer of compromise is accepted and a contract is thus created, the party aggrieved may sue on the contract and obviously may prove the offer and acceptance.[3] Moreover, if after such a contract is made and the offering party repudiates it, the other may elect to sue on the original cause of action and here again it seems the repudiating party may not claim privilege against proof of the compromise.[4] The shield of the privilege does not extend to the protection of those who repudiate the agreements the making of which the privilege is designed to encourage.

275. Admissions by Conduct: (g) Safety Measures After an Accident.[5]

After an accident causing injury, the owner of the premises or of the enterprise will often take remedial measures by repairing a defect, installing a safety device, changing safety rules, or discharging the employee apparently at fault. Are these new safety

2. Ecklund v. United States, 159 F.2d 81 (6th Cir. 1947) (prosecution for selling automobile above ceiling price).

3. Union Trust Co. v. Resisto Mfg. Co., 169 Md. 381, 181 A. 726 (1935); C.J.S. Evidence § 290.

4. Reese v. McVittie, 119 Colo. 29, 200 P.2d 390 (1948).

5. 2 Wigmore, Evidence § 283; Dec.Dig. Negligence ⊕131; Annot., 170 A.L.R. 7, 64 A.L.R.2d 1296.

Uniform Rule 51: "*Subsequent Remedial Conduct.* When after the occurrence of an event remedial or precautionary measures are taken, which, if taken previously would have tended to make the event less likely to occur, evidence of such subsequent measures is not admissible to prove negligence or culpable conduct in connection with the event." See also F.R.Ev. (R.D.1971) 407.

measures, which might have prevented the injury, admissible to prove negligence as an implied acknowledgment by conduct that due care required that these measures should have been taken before the injury? In many instances the evidence, particularly when the remedial measures follow immediately the happening of the injury, may be very persuasive of the actor's belief as to the precautions required by due care before the accident. Nevertheless, the courts on occasion broadly assert that the evidence when offered for this purpose is irrelevant.[6] While, like much circumstantial evidence, it admits of varying explanations,[7] some of them consistent with due care, for this purpose it would often meet the usual standards of relevancy.[8] The predominant reason for excluding such evidence, however, is not lack of probative significance but a policy against discouraging the taking of safety measures.[9] At all events the courts do exclude, when offered as admissions of negligence or fault, evidence of remedial safety measures taken

6. See, e. g., Columbia and P.S.R. Co. v. Hawthorne, 144 U.S. 202 (1892); Terre Haute & I. R. Co. v. Clem, 123 Ind. 15, 23 N.E. 965, 966 (1890); Morse v. Minneapolis & St. Louis R. Co., 30 Minn. 465, 16 N.W. 358, 359 (1883).

Also see Bramwell, B., in Hart v. Lancashire & Yorkshire Ry. Co., 21 L.T.R.N.S. 261, 263 (1869), denying that "because the world gets wiser as it gets older, therefore it was foolish before."

7. See § 185, supra.

8. See § 185, supra.

9. See § 74. Compare the court's statement in Ashland Supply Co. v. Webb, 206 Ky. 184, 266 S.W. 1086 (1925): "There are two reasons why evidence of subsequent repair should not be admitted. One is that, while it may be necessary to subsequently repair the appliance, it does not follow from that that the appliance was defective at the time of the accident. The other reason is that, if such evidence were admitted, it would have a tendency to cause employers to omit making needed repairs for fear that the precaution thus taken by them could be used as evidence against them."

In most of the cases the courts have not felt called upon to state the basis of the rule.

after an injury,[10] such as repairs,[11] changes in construction,[12] installation of new safety devices [13] such as lights, gates, or guards, changes in rules and regulations,[14] changes in the practice of the business,[15] or the discharge of an employee charged with causing the injury.[16]

When the repairs or changes are effected by a third person, the policy ground for exclusion is no longer present, and the tendency is to admit the evidence.[17]

The ingenuity of counsel in suggesting other purposes has made substantial inroads upon the general rule of exclusion.[18] Thus evidence of subsequent repairs or changes has been admitted as evidence of the defendant's ownership or control [19] of the premises or his duty to repair [20] where these are disputed; as evidence of the possibility or feasibility of preventive measures, when properly in issue; [21] as evidence, where the jury has taken a view, or where the defend-

---

10. Annot., 64 A.L.R.2d 896.

An analogous doctrine should be applied when a person concerned in an accident gives or offers aid to the victim or pays or offers to pay his medical expenses. Barber v. Southern Ry. Co., 193 N.C. 691, 138 S.E. 17, 19 (1927); Hughes v. Anchor Enterprises, 245 N.C. 131, 95 S.E.2d 577, 63 A.L.R.2d 685 (1956); Uniform Rule 52; F.R.Ev. (R.D.1971) 409. See cases collected in 2 Wigmore, Evidence § 283a, n. 1, and Annot., 20 A.L.R.2d 291.

11. Kentucky & W. Va. Power Co. v. Stacy, 291 Ky. 325, 164 S.W.2d 537, 170 A.L.R. 1 (1942); Potter v. Dr. W. H. Groves etc. Hospital, 99 Utah 71, 103 P.2d 280 (1940).

12. Limbeck v. Interstate Power Co., 69 F.2d 249 (8th Cir. 1934); Livingston v. Fuel, 245 Ark. 618, 433 S.W.2d 380 (1968).

13. Erickson's Dairy Products Co. v. Northwest etc. Co., 165 Ore. 553, 109 P.2d 53 (1941) (use of asbestos to protect wall against fire).

14. Ware v. Boston & M.R. R., 92 N.H. 373, 31 A.2d 58 (1943). Distinguish rules in effect at the time of the occurrence, which are generally held admissible, though somewhat similar policy considerations are present. Winters, The Evidentiary Value of Defendant's Safety Rules in a Negligence Action, 38 Neb.L.Rev. 906 (1959); Annot., 50 A.L.R.2d 16.

15. Hatfield v. Levy Bros., 18 Cal.App.2d 798, 112 P.2d 277 (1941) (evidence that defendant company stopped waxing floor after accident), reversed on other grounds, 18 Cal.2d 798, 117 P.2d 841 (1941).

16. Armour & Co. v. Skene, 153 F. 241 (1st Cir. 1907) (discharge of driver one year after accident erroneously admitted but not prejudicial); Turner v. Hearst, 115 Cal. 394, 47 P. 129 (1896) (libel; error to permit plaintiff to prove discharge of reporter, "similar to proof of precaution taken after an accident"). See also Rynar v. Lincoln Transit Co., 129 N.J.L. 525, 30 A.2d 406 (1943); Engel v. United Traction Co., 203 N.Y. 321, 96 N.E. 731 (1911).

17. Louisville & Nashville R. Co. v. Williams, 370 F.2d 839 (5th Cir. 1966) (evidence that highway

commission improved crossing after accident, properly admitted); Wallner v. Kitchens of Sara Lee, Inc., 419 F.2d 1028 (7th Cir. 1970) (guards installed on machine by owner after accident, properly admitted against manufacturer); Brown v. Quick Mix Co., 75 Wash.2d 833, 454 P.2d 205 (1969) (same). The relevancy problem, of course, becomes more acute as the theory of an admission is not available. Moreover, a hearsay problem arises if conduct is regarded as hearsay. See § 250, supra.

18. See, e. g., Norwood Clinic Inc. v. Spann, 240 Ala. 427, 199 So. 840, 843 (1941) ("if such evidence has a tendency to prove some other disputed issue," admissible); Annot., 64 A.L.R.2d 1296, 1305.

19. Powers v. J. B. Michael & Co., 329 F.2d 674 (6th Cir. 1964) (defendant contractor subsequently put out warning signs, to show control of that section of highway); Dubonowski v. Howard Savings Institution, 124 N.J.L. 368, 12 A.2d 384 (1941) (control by landlord of stairs); Scudero v. Campbell, 288 N.Y. 328, 43 N.E.2d 66 (1942) (similar).

20. Wallner v. Kitchens of Sara Lee, Inc., 419 F.2d 1028 (7th Cir. 1970) (installation of guard, to show responsibility for repair and maintenance of machine); Karlson v. 305 E. 43rd St. Corp., 370 F.2d 467 (2d Cir. 1967) (installation of safety device to show control of elevator); Carleton v. Rockland, T. & C. St. Ry., 110 Me. 397, 86 A. 334, Ann.C. 1915A 1209 (repairs by street railway of steps leading from platform).

21. Determining when feasibility is properly an issue has proved troublesome. If defendant claims the precaution was not feasible, the evidence is clearly admissible. See note 25, infra. Some cases limit admissibility to this situation. Conry v. Boston & M. R. R., 227 Mass. 411, 116 N.E. 733 (1917); Kansas City M. & O. Ry. Co. v. Meakin, 146 S.W. 1057 (Tex.Civ.App.1912). However, the nature of the accident as proven by plaintiff may raise a doubt whether preventive measures were practicable. See, e. g., Indianapolis, etc., R.R. Co. v. Horst, 93 U.S. 291, 295, 296 (1876); Boeing Airplane Co. v. Brown, 291 F.2d 310 (9th Cir. 1961); Brown v. Quick Mix Co., 75 Wash. 2d 833, 454 P.2d 205 (1969). Or plaintiff may

ant has introduced a photograph of the scene, to explain that the situation at the time of the accident was different; [22] as evidence of what was done later to show that the earlier condition as of the time of the accident was as plaintiff claims, if the defendant disputes this; [23] as evidence that the faulty condition,

later remedied, was the cause of the injury by showing that after the change the injurious effect disappeared; [24] and as evidence contradicting facts testified to by the adversary's witness.[25]

As suggested above, the extrinsic policy of encouraging remedial safety measures is the predominant reason for holding evidence of these measures to be privileged. It is apparent that the free admission of such evidence for purposes other than as admissions of negligence is likely to defeat this paramount policy. It is submitted that before admitting the evidence for any of these other purposes, the court should be satisfied that the issue on which it is offered is of substantial importance and is actually, and not merely formally in dispute, that the plaintiff cannot establish the fact to be inferred conveniently by other proof,[26] and consequently that the

rely on a statute which is construed to make proof of feasibility a part of plaintiff's case. Rich v. Tite-Knot Pine Mill, 245 Ore. 185, 421 P.2d 370 (1966). But even in these latter cases, the plaintiff might well be limited to other types of evidence, such as opinion or customary practices of such businesses, where these are available and sufficient. See Miniea v. St. Louis Cooperage Co., 175 Mo.App. 91, 157 S.W. 1006, 1012 (1913); Blais v. Flanders Hardware Co., 93 N.H. 370, 42 A.2d 332, 335 (1945) ("descriptive testimony could readily be given"). Unrestricted use of feasibility evidence would obviously eliminate the exclusionary rule in its entirety.

22. Lunde v. National Citizens' Bank, 213 Minn. 278, 6 N.W.2d 809 (1942) (view); Achey v. Marion, 126 Iowa 47, 101 N.W. 435 (1904) (to explain photograph introduced by defendant). But the plaintiff may not introduce a photograph of the altered scene merely for the purpose of showing the repairs in the guise of explanation. Gignoux v. St. Louis Pub. Service Co., 180 S.W.2d 784 (Mo.App. 1944); Hadges v. New York Rapid Transit Corp., 259 App.Div. 154, 18 N.Y.S.2d 304 (1940).

23. Spurr v. LaSalle Constr. Co., 385 F.2d 322 (7th Cir. 1967) (defendant claimed that protective chain-barrier was in place when plaintiff fell into pit); Chicago v. Dalle, 115 Ill. 386, 5 N.E. 578 (1885) (injury due to alleged loose plank in sidewalk, evidence that sidewalk repaired at this place to show previous condition); Chicago, B. & Q. R. Co. v. Krayenbuhl, 65 Neb. 889, 91 N.W. 880, 885, 59 L.R.A. 920 (1902) (agent's locking of turntable to show it was unlocked at time of injury to child); Eargle v. Sumpter Lighting Co., 110 S.C. 560, 96 S.E. 909 (1918) (defect in electrical appliances provable, where necessary, by evidence of later repairs). But it is obvious that this doctrine, unless limited to cases where the condition is disputed and the proof by repairs is essential, can serve to rob the principal rule of practical effect. See e. g., City of Montgomery v. Quinn, 246 Ala. 154, 19 So. 2d 529 (1944) (action for death caused by falling of rotten limb of tree; act of city in immediately removing other dead limbs admitted to show condition); Williams v. Milner Hotels Co., 130 Conn. 507, 36 A.2d 20 (1944) (suit by guest for injury by being bitten by rat while in bed in his room; apparently existence of rat holes was formally denied in pleadings but not actually in dispute; plaintiff allowed to introduce photographs showing holes covered with tin, as evidence of previous condition). See critical note on the last case, 92 U.Pa.L.Rev. 456.

24. Kentucky Utilities Co. v. White Star Coal Co., 244 Ky. 759, 52 S.W.2d 705 (1932) (proof that everything went well following a second fire, when a defective transformer was removed, admissible to show cause); Texas & N. O. R. Co. v. Anderson, 61 S.W. 424 (Tex.Civ.App.1901) (evidence of removal of obstruction in ditch and that thereafter flood water ran off plaintiff's land, admitted to show obstruction cause of flooding).

25. American Airlines, Inc. v. United States, 418 F. 2d 180 (5th Cir. 1969) (evidence of change in instrument and in flight practices after accident to rebut claims of adequacy and nonfeasibility); Daggett v. A., T. & S.F.R. Co., 48 Cal.2d 655, 313 P.2d 557, 64 A.L.R.2d 1283 (1957) (evidence that flashing light was installed in place of wigwag signal after crossing accident to impeach testimony that wigwag was safest type); Koskoff v. Goldman, 86 Conn. 415, 85 A. 588 (1912); Reynolds v. Maine Mfg. Co., 81 N.H. 421, 128 A. 329 (1925) (proof of use of chain on wagon to rebut testimony that chain could not be used); Lombardi v. Yulinsky, 98 N.J.L. 332, 119 A. 873 (1923) (where defendant testified that he always put up danger lights at night on pile of bricks on highway, and evidence showed accident resulted from lack of light, proper to ask on cross-examination if he put up light after accident, as bearing on credibility); Jefferson v. City of Raleigh, 194 N.C. 479, 140 S.E. 76 (1927) (proof that defendant furnished goggles after accident to refute testimony that use of goggles was impractical).

26. Schuman v. Bader & Co., 227 Ill.App. 28 (1922) (repairs not admissible to prove prior condition

need for the evidence outweighs the danger of its misuse.[27]   The defendant of course, upon request, will be entitled to an instruction limiting its use to the issue upon which it is admitted.[28]

where plaintiff had proved such condition by other witnesses); Miniea v. St. Louis Cooperage Co., see note 21, supra; Blais v. Flanders Hardware Co., note 21, supra.

27.   Smith v. Twin State Gas & Elec. Co., 83 N.H. 439, 144 A. 57, 61 A.L.R. 1015 (1928) ("Evidence of subsequent repairs not being competent to show negligence, it should not be used for other purposes incidentally in issue unless the reasons therefor are counterbalancing").   Generally, see § 185, supra.

28.   Lunde v. National Citizens' Bank, 213 Minn. 278, 6 N.W.2d 809 (1942); Lombardi v. Yulinsky, 98 N.J.L. 332, 119 A. 873 (1923).

CHAPTER 27

DECLARATIONS AGAINST INTEREST

276. General Requirements: Distinction Between Declarations Against Interest and Parties' Admissions.[1]

To satisfy the instant exception to the hearsay rule in its traditional form, two main requirements must be met: first, the declaration must state facts which are against the pecuniary or proprietary interest of the declarant, or the making of the declaration itself must create evidence which would endanger his pocketbook if the statement were not true;[2] second, the declarant must be unavailable at the time of trial.[3] These two requirements, when satisfied, are believed to furnish respectively the safeguard of special trustworthiness and the requisite of special need for the use of hearsay, which are the traditional justifying elements of most of the exceptions to the hearsay rule. Minor qualifications may be added. The interest involved must not be too indirect or remote.[4]

The declarant, as in the case of hearsay exceptions generally,[5] must, so far as appears, have had the opportunity to observe the facts,[6] as witnesses must have.[7]

of too remote a nature"); Giberson v. Wilson, 322 S.W.2d 466 (Ky.1959) ("the act of an insured in changing the beneficiary of an insurance policy is not against his pecuniary or proprietary interest" although he gives up the right to have proceeds paid to his estate); Tennison v. St. Louis-San Francisco Ry. Co., 228 S.W.2d 718 (Mo.1950) (action for wrongful discharge of brakeman for intoxication: statement of another brakeman that plaintiff was not intoxicated not admissible as against interest on theory that discharge would aid declarant's advancement); In re Estate of Simms, 442 S.W.2d 426 (Tex.Civ.App.1969) (statement of declarant that she had destroyed will and codicil of another, at a time when declarant had no interest in the estate of the maker of the will, was not a declaration against interest). This commonsense requirement is sometimes strained. See In re Forsythe's Estate, 221 Minn. 303, 22 N.W.2d 19 (1946) (declarations of legatee casting doubt on sanity of testatrix before her death admissible as a declaration against interest, without discussion of contingent nature of the interest).

5. See, e. g., §§ 285, 300, 310, infra.

6. The requirement is often more stringently stated by demanding that the facts must have been "within the declarant's peculiar knowledge." See, e. g., Gleadow v. Atkins, 1 C. and M. 410, 149 Eng.Rep. 459 (Exch.1833); Price v. Humble Oil & Ref. Co., 152 S.W.2d 804, 813 (Tex.Civ.App.1941). But doubtless nothing more than the usual knowledge qualification is intended to, or can reasonably, be required. See Aetna Life Ins. Co. v. Strauch, 179 Okl. 617, 67 P.2d 452, 454 (1937) ("must have concerned a fact personally cognizable by declarant"); Windorski v. Doyle, 219 Minn. 402, 18 N.W.2d 142, 146 (1945) ("a matter of which he was personally cognizant"); 9 Wigmore, Evidence § 1471(a); C.J.S. Evidence § 220.

7. See § 10, supra.

---

1. See generally, 5 Wigmore, Evidence §§ 1455–1477; Jefferson, Declarations Against Interest: An Exception to the Hearsay Rule, 58 Harv.L.Rev. 1 (1944) and Morgan, Declarations Against Interest, 5 Vand.L.Rev. 451 (1952); Dec.Dig. Evidence ⊂═272–284, Criminal Law ⊂═417(15); C.J.S. Evidence §§ 217–224.

2. See §§ 277–279, infra.

3. See § 280, infra.

4. See, e. g., Smith v. Blakey, L.R. [1916] 2 Q.B. 326 (letter of clerk advising employer of arrival of "three huge cases" in his charge and stating terms of contract with consignor, held not admissible, "the possibility that this statement might make him liable in case of their being lost is an interest

Some judicial opinions and texts fail to distinguish this exception from the one for parties' admissions.[8] But it is undoubtedly more desirable to accept the traditional distinctions, adopted by Wigmore,[9] and to draw the line clearly between the two exceptions.[10] Under this view, the admissions of a party-opponent come in without satisfying any of the requirements for declarations against interest. The admissions need not have been against interest when made,[11] though it will usually happen that they were. The party making the admission need not be, and seldom is, unavailable.[12] Nor does the party making the admission need to have had personal knowledge of the fact admitted.[13] Accordingly, when the admission of a party, or a party's predecessor in interest, is sought to be introduced, it should be offered as and tested by the requirements for parties' admissions, not those for declarations against interest. On the other hand, when the statements were those of a nonparty declarant, now dead or unavailable and the position of the declarant is found not to meet the requirements of "privity" necessary to class him as a party's predecessor, then the theory of declarations against interest may be a case-saving ticket of admission.[14]

277. Declarations Against Pecuniary or Proprietary Interest: [15] Declarations Affecting Claim or Liability for Damages.

The traditional field for this exception has been that of declarations against proprietary or pecuniary interest. Common instances of the former are acknowledgments that the declarant does not own certain land or personal property,[16] or that he has conveyed or transferred it.[17] Moreover, a statement by one in possession that he holds an interest less than complete ownership has traditionally been regarded as a declaration against interest,[18] though it is obviously ambivalent, and in England has even been received when offered to establish the existence of the interest claimed by the declarant.[19] Similarly, declarations of an owner in possession as to his boundary line have been

8. See Ch. 26, supra.

9. 5 Wigmore, Evidence § 1475; see also 2 Chamberlayne, Evidence § 1235 (1911) (3d ed.); C.J.S. Evidence § 217b.

10. Among opinions emphasizing the distinction are Home Ins. Co. v. Allied Telephone Co., 246 Ark. 1065, 442 S.W.2d 211 (1969); Elliotte v. Lavier, 299 Mich. 353, 300 N.W. 116 (1941) (Butzel, J.); and Roe v. Journegan, 175 N.C. 261, 95 S.E. 495 (1918) (Allen, J.).

11. See § 262 at nn. 14–16, supra; § 277, infra.

12. See § 262 at n. 18, supra.

13. See § 263, supra.

14. See, e. g., Kwiatowski v. John Lowry, Inc., 276 N.Y. 126, 11 N.E.2d 563, 114 A.L.R. 916 (1937) annotated (in death action, statements against interest by decedent come in as declarations against interest); Aetna Life Ins. Co. v. Strauch, 179 Okl. 617, 67 P.2d 452 (1937) (suit by administrator of wife against insurance company on policy on her

life; confession of husband, since electrocuted, of plot to secure policy and kill her, admitted as declaration against interest); Carpenter v. Davis, 435 S.W.2d 382 (Mo.1968); and see C.J.S. Evidence § 219d. For discussion of privity, see § 268, supra.

15. 5 Wigmore, Evidence §§ 1458–1460; C.J.S. Evidence § 219.

16. In re Thompson, 205 Fed. 556, 560 (D.N.J.1913) (statement of bankrupt, in possession of dredge, that another, not himself, was the owner).

17. Dean v. Wilkerson, 126 Ind. 338, 26 N.E. 55 (1890) (declarations of father, offered by the son after father's death, that he had given notes to son); Smith v. Moore, 142 N.C. 277, 55 S.E. 275 (1906) (declaration by deceased life tenant that she had made a deed to her son-in-law and the reason for making the deed); First Nat. Bank v. Holland, 99 Va. 495, 39 S.E. 126, 128 (1890) (husband's declaration of gift to wife).

18. McLeod v. Swain, 87 Ga. 156, 13 S.E. 315 (1891) (plaintiff in ejectment offers her former tenant's declarations that they held land as her tenants); Lamar v. Pearre, 90 Ga. 377, 17 S.E. 92 (1892) (possessor's declarations that land had been bought with trust funds); Dooley v. Baynes, 86 Va. 644, 10 S.E. 974 (1890) (possessor's declarations that he held only a life estate).

19. In Regina v. Overseers of Birmingham, 1 B. & S. 763, 121 Eng.Rep. 897 (K.B.1861) and in Regina v. Governors and Guardians of Exeter, L.R. 4 Q.B. 341 (1869) declarant's assertions of tenancy were admitted, not to prove that he did not have a fee simple, but that he had a tenancy at the stated rental. This use is disapproved in 5 Wigmore, Evidence § 1458.

classed as declarations against interest, though this seems questionable unless he had previously made a wider claim; but the cases present situations where the declarations could have come in without question as admissions of a party's predecessor.[20]

The clearest example of a declaration against pecuniary interest is an acknowledgment that the declarant is indebted.[21] Here the declaration, standing alone, is against interest on the theory that to owe a debt is against one's financial interests. This theory is routinely followed even though it may not be applicable in particular circumstances. Less obviously an acknowledgment of receipt of money in payment of a debt owing to the declarant is also traditionally classed as against interest.[22] Here the fact of payment, looked on at the time it is received and assuming it is then undisputed, is advantageous to the receiver. But looking at the declaration retrospectively as the courts do, they say it is against interest because it is evidence of the reduction or extinguishment of the debt.[23] Of course, a receipt for money

which the receiver is to hold for another is an acknowledgment of a debt.[24] Similarly, a statement that one holds money in trust is against interest.[25]

We have seen that an acknowledgment of indebtedness by the declarant is recognized as against interest. The English cases seem to have been narrowly channeled in the areas of debt and property, but the American cases have properly extended the field of declarations against interest to include acknowledgment of facts which would give rise to a liability for unliquidated damages for tort[26]

---

20. Carr v. Bizzell, 192 N.C. 212, 134 S.E. 462 (1926); Barlow v. Greer, 222 S.W. 301 (Tex.Civ. App.1920); Kay Corporation v. Anderson, 72 Wash. 2d 879, 436 P.2d 459 (1967); see also, Putnam, Coffin and Burr, Inc. v. Halpern, 154 Conn. 507, 227 A.2d 83 (1967) (rule held not to apply on issue of whether easement existed).

21. German Ins. Co. v. Bartlett, 188 Ill. 165, 58 N.E. 1075 (1900) (in suit of deceased husband's creditors against wife to whom he had conveyed property, she was allowed to prove his declarations that he was indebted to her); Truelsch v. Northwestern Mut. Life Ins. Co., 186 Wis. 239, 202 N.W. 352 (1925) (suit by wife on life policy on husband; husband's employer claims lien on policy for money embezzled and used to pay premiums; husband's letter to wife before his suicide acknowledging defalcations admitted as declaration against interest).

22. Palter Cap Co. v. Great Western Life Assur. Co., [1936] 2 D.L.R. 304 (physician's entry in cash book of money received from patient, to show date of consultation); Mentzer v. Burlingame, 85 Kan. 641, 118 Pac. 698 (1911) (declaration of holder that notes were paid).

23. See, e. g., Coffin v. Bucknam, 12 Me. 471, 473 (1835) (entry of part payment on note by deceased former holder admitted for administrator suing

on note, to avoid statute of limitations; "the indorsement was then clearly against his interest, furnishing proof that he had received part of the contents of the note"; Chenango Bridge Co. v. Paige, 83 N.Y. 178 (1880) (treasurer's books showing amount of tolls received admitted "as they charged him with the amount of such tolls"). Cases supporting this theory are cited and analyzed in Jefferson, op. cit., § 276, n. 1, 58 Harv.L. Rev. at 8–17, and Morgan, op. cit. § 276, n. 1, 5 Vand.L.Rev. 454–456. Wigmore, however, without adequate discussion, rejects it. 5 Wigmore, Evidence § 1462.

24. Manning v. Lechmere, 1 Atk. 453, 26 Eng.Rep. 288 (Ch.1737) (L.Ch. Hardwicke: "Where there are old rentals, and bailiffs have admitted money received by them, these rentals are evidence of the payment because no other can be had"); Barry v. Bebbington, 4 Term R. 514, 100 Eng.Rep. 1149 (1792) (steward's receipts); Keesling v. Powell, 149 Ind. 372, 49 N.E. 265 (1898) (statement by tax officer that taxes had been paid in).

25. Gleadow v. Atkin, 1 Cr. & M. 410, 149 Eng.Rep. 459 (Ex., 1833). See also Wilkins v. Enterprise TV, Inc., 231 Ark. 958, 333 S.W.2d 718 (1960) (declarant, ostensibly the president and principal stockholder of the corporation, stated he was only salaried employee).

26. Weber v. Chicago, R. I. & P. Ry. Co., 175 Iowa 358, 151 N.W. 852, 864 (1915) (action by passenger for injury in derailment: declaration of K., who later became insane, that he had unbolted the rails, admitted as against interest as constituting "basis of an action against him for damages"); Halvorsen v. Moon & Kerr Lbr. Co., 87 Minn. 18, 91 N.W. 28 (1902) (plaintiff sues defendant for destruction of his shop from fire on defendant's premises; held, defendant entitled to prove declarations of S., plaintiff's employee, since deceased, that plaintiff's fire due to boiling over of lard kettle, of which S. was in charge, while S. had gone out of the room; the facts furnish the basis of a "pecuniary claim" for negligence); Windorski v. Doyle, 219 Minn. 402, 18 N.W.2d 142 (1945) (action against tavern

or seemingly for breach of contract.[27] A corresponding extension to embrace statements of facts which would constitute a defense to a claim for damages which the declarant would otherwise have, has been recognized in this country.[28]

owner for death of patron struck by another patron; declarations of bartender, since dead, that assault was unprovoked, and that he had warned offending patron against threats, held receivable for plaintiff as declaration against interest; the facts "may reasonably furnish a basis of a pecuniary claim against him as he was in sole charge of the bar-room;" in this case, consciousness of speaking against interest seems unlikely and the real source of reliability seems rather the absence of motive to falsify); Duncan v. Smith, 393 S.W.2d 798 (Tex.1965) (statement of a driver that he passed illegally on the right side of a vehicle and ran into a bridge). But compare Aetna Life Ins. Co. v. Strauch, 179 Okl. 617, 67 P.2d 452 (1937) where the confession of a husband who had insured his wife's life for his own benefit and then murdered her, was received as a declaration against interest, but the court derided the theory that it was against interest as admitting a tort liability and relied on the theory that the facts confessed deprived him of the right to collect the policy.

Remarks were held insufficient to furnish basis for tort liability in Markley v. Beagle, 66 Cal.2d 951, 59 Cal.Rptr. 809, 429 P.2d 129 (1967); Potter v. Finan, 6 Mich.App. 696, 150 N.W.2d 539 (1967) (remark of declarant that he was intoxicated but not too much). Compare driver's more detailed statements concerning intoxication and driving in Frazier v. Burke, 95 Ill.App.2d 51, 238 N.E.2d 78 (1968).

Some cases apply a more liberal rule. See, e. g., Gichner v. Antonio Triano Tile and Marble Co., 133 U.S.App.D.C. 250, 410 F.2d 238 (1968) (it is enough if the statement could reasonably provide an important link in a chain of evidence that is the basis for civil liability; statement that declarant smoked in a building later found burned held sufficiently against interest).

27. Jefferson, op. cit., supra § 276, n. 1 at 30, n. 62, but the cases cited are explainable under the theory of admissions of a party's predecessor.

28. Georgia Railroad & Banking Co. v. Fitzgerald, 108 Ga. 507, 509, 34 S.E. 316 (1899) (action for death of brakeman, in coupling cars; declaration of deceased that injury was caused by his foot striking an obstacle on tracks, held admissible against widow who claimed death due to "flying switch," first because she is "in privity" with deceased, and hence an admission, and second, declaration against interest, but query as to latter, whether he was probably conscious that the fact was against interest); Walker v. Brautner, 59 Kan. 117, 121, 124, 52 Pac. 80 (1898) (action for death of engineer; his declarations after the collision

278. Penal Interest:[29] Interest of Prestige or Self-Esteem.

In 1844 in the Sussex Peerage Case[30] the House of Lords, ignoring precedents, determined that a declaration confessing a crime committed by declarant is not receivable as a declaration against interest. This decision, perhaps more than any other, has been influential in confining the development of this exception to the hearsay rule within narrow materialistic limits. It has been generally followed in this country in criminal cases.[31] In civil cases, the courts, while not repudiating the limitation, have sometimes been able to justify the admission of the third person's confession of crime upon the theory that the particular crime was also a tort and thus the fact declared was against ma-

that he had not kept a lookout received as against interest); Kwiatowski v. John Lowry Inc., 276 N.Y. 126, 11 N.E.2d 563, 114 A.L.R. 916 (1937) (death action; statements by deceased showing no liability admissible both as admissions and as declarations against interest); Jewell v. El Paso Elec. Co., 47 S.W.2d 328 (Tex.Civ.App.1932) (death action; statement of deceased that it was his own fault, admitted as against interest); Annot., 114 A.L.R. 921. But compare Tucker v. Oldbury Urban Dist. Council, [1921] 2 K.B. 317 (Ct.App.) where in death action for alleged injury causing blood poison, declarations of deceased after time of alleged injury that he left work because of a "whitlow," were held properly rejected because he then had made no claim and was not conscious that the statement was against interest.

See also Home Insurance v. Allied Telephone Co., 246 Ark. 1065, 442 S.W.2d 211 (1969) (statement of nonparty driver of automobile, that "it looks like something that could not be helped", held against interest since declarant was potentially liable and declaration absolved another driver in accident of fault).

29. 5 Wigmore, Evidence §§ 1476, 1477, Annot., 162 A.L.R. 446; C.J.S. Criminal Law § 749; Dec.Dig. Criminal Law ⊕417(15).

30. 11 Cl. & F. 85, 8 Eng.Rep. 1034 (1844).

31. Holley v. McDonald, 154 Conn. 228, 224 A.2d 727 (1966) (confession of person other than defendant); Bryant v. State, 197 Ga. 641, 30 S.E.2d 259 (1944); Rushing v. State, 88 Okl.Cr. 82, 199 P.2d 614 (1948); Commonwealth v. Antonini, 165 Pa. Super. 501, 69 A.2d 436 (1949) (offered against the accused), and numerous cases cited in sources in note 29, supra.

terial interest in subjecting the declarant to liability for damages.[32]

Can the practice of excluding third-person confessions in criminal cases be justified? It certainly cannot be justified on the ground that an acknowledgment of facts rendering one liable to criminal punishment is less trustworthy than an acknowledgment of a debt. The motivation for the exclusion is probably a different one, namely, the fear of opening a door to a flood of perjured witnesses falsely testifying to confessions that were never made. This fear seems reflected in the Texas decisions which while receiving such confessions, have hedged their admission with restrictions seeking to limit their use to situations where they are most needed and most reliable.[33]

Wigmore, however, is probably right in believing that the argument of the danger of perjury is a dubious one since the danger is one that attends all human testimony, and in concluding that "any rule which hampers an honest man in exonerating himself is a bad rule, even if it also hampers a villain in falsely passing for an innocent."[34] Under this banner, saluted also by Holmes, J.,[35] in a famous dissent, a few progressive courts have relaxed the rule of exclusion of declarations against penal interest in particular situations[36] or generally.[37] Statements against penal interest have also been made admissible by a few rules or statutes.[38]

Moreover, the restriction to material interests, ignoring as it does other motives just as influential upon the minds and hearts of men, should be more widely relaxed. Declarations against social interests, such as acknowledgments of facts which would subject

---

32. See, e. g., Weber v. Chicago, R. I. & P. Ry. Co., 175 Iowa 358, 151 N.W. 852, 864 (1915) (confession that declarant had unbolted rail, causing derailment of train).

33. Cameron v. State, 153 Tex.Cr. 374, 217 S.W.2d 23 (1949) (admissible when the state is relying solely upon circumstantial evidence, when guilt of declarant is inconsistent with guilt of accused and when facts show that declarant was so situated that he might have committed crime.) See also the several Maryland cases, Brady v. State, 226 Md. 422, 174 A.2d 167 (1961).

34. 5 Wigmore, Evidence § 1477.

35. "The confession of Joe Dick, since deceased, that he committed the murder for which the plaintiff in error was tried, coupled with circumstances pointing to its truth, would have a very strong tendency to make anyone outside of a court of justice believe that Donnelly did not commit the crime. I say this, of course, on the supposition that it should be proved that the confession really was made, and that there was no ground for connecting Donnelly with Dick. The rules of evidence in the main are based on experience, logic, and common sense, less hampered by history than some parts of the substantive law. There is no decision by this court against the admissibility of such a confession; the English cases since the separation of the two countries do not bind us; the exception to the hearsay rule in the case of declarations against interest is well known; no other statement is so much against interest as a confession of murder; it is far more calculated to convince than dying declarations, which would be let in to hang a man (Mattox v. United States, 146 U.S. 140); and when we surround the accused with so many safeguards, some of which seem to me excessive, I think we ought to give him the benefit of a fact that, if proved, commonly would have such weight. The history of the law and the arguments against the English doctrine are so well and fully stated by Mr. Wigmore that there is no need to set them forth at greater length. 2 Wigmore, Ev. §§ 1476, 1477." Holmes, J., dissenting in Donnelly v. United States, 228 U.S. 243 (1913).

36. See, e. g., People v. Lettrich, 413 Ill. 172, 108 N.E.2d 488 (1952), noted 6 Vand.L.Rev. 924; Brady v. State, 226 Md. 422, 174 A.2d 167 (1961) (discussion of previous Maryland cases); Hines v. Commonwealth, 136 Va. 728, 117 S.E. 843, 35 A.L.R. 431 (1923) (murder, with circumstantial evidence pointing both to accused and to third person, since deceased; held, accused entitled to prove third person's confession); Newberry v. Commonwealth, 191 Va. 445, 61 S.E.2d 318 (1950) (defendant charged with murder of his wife; circumstances indicated his brother as possible killer; brother refused to testify on ground of immunity as joint indictee; held, "under facts and circumstances of this case," accused was entitled to introduce brother's confession).

37. People v. Spriggs, 60 Cal.2d 868, 36 Cal.Rptr. 841, 389 P.2d 377 (1964); People v. Brown, 26 N.Y. 2d 88, 308 N.Y.S.2d 825, 257 N.E.2d 16 (1970).

38. West's Ann.Cal.Evid.Code, § 1230; K.S.A. § 60–460(j); N.J.Ev.Rule 63(10). See also Uniform Rule 63(10), quoted in note 39, infra, and F.R.Ev. (R.D. 1971) 804(b) (4).

the declarant to ridicule or disgrace,[39] or facts calculated to arouse in the declarant a sense of shame or remorse,[40] seem adequately buttressed in trustworthiness and should be received under the present principle.

279. Balancing the Interests.[41]

(a) *The Tradition.* The determination in cases of conflicting interests, of what declarations were receivable as against interest, was discussed in the English decisions of the 1700s and early 1800s with what seems to us a rather arid casuistry. It was, however, a casuistry mainly directed toward widening rather than contracting admissibility, by expanding the old, narrow categories such as bailiffs' and receivers' entries, and declarations of possessors claiming a limited interest, under a new principle of declarations against interest. The tendency was to look only to the prima facie aspect of the declaration. If the declaration was disserving from this aspect as of the time it was made it was admitted, though offered to prove a fact that was obviously self-serving.[42] This tendency finds reflection in some later English and American holdings,[43] but the courts today may probably be expected to scrutinize more often the purpose for which the evidence is offered, and limit the use of the declaration only to show facts against the declarant's interest, as of the time of the trial.[44]

Also, when a declaration against interest was shown in the earlier cases, other declarations which formed part of the same statement, were admitted even though these latter

---

39. See State v. Alcorn, 7 Idaho 599, 64 Pac. 1014, 1017 (1901) (homicide by abortion of unmarried girl: victim's declaration that she was pregnant admissible here as res gestae; "the declaration was against the interest of deceased").

See Uniform Rule 63(10), which admits under an exception to the hearsay rule "a statement which the judge finds was at the time of the assertion so far contrary to the declarant's pecuniary or proprietary interest or so far subjected him to civil or criminal liability or so far rendered invalid a claim by him against another or created such risk of making him an object of hatred, ridicule or social disapproval in the community that a reasonable man in his position would not have made the statement unless he believed it to be true." See also statutes and rules cited in n. 38, supra.

40. Probably some cases admitting declarations made before death, that the declarant has shot himself with intent to commit suicide, may best be justified on this ground. See, e. g., Commonwealth Life Ins. Co. v. Clarke, 276 Ky. 151, 123 S.W.2d 811 (1938).

41. 5 Wigmore, Evidence §§ 1463, 1464; Jefferson, Declarations Against Interest: An Exception to the Hearsay Rule, 58 Harv.L.Rev. 1, 43–63 (1944); Morgan, Declarations Against Interest, 5 Vand.L. Rev. 451, 470–473 (1952).

42. See, e. g., Warren v. Greenfield, 2 Strange 1129, 93 Eng.Rep. 1079 (K.B.1740) (to show surrender of a widow's interest in 1699, attorney's book containing a charge for drawing the surrender, and entry of payment therefor, admitted to fortify the presumption from lapse of time); Peaceable d. Uncle v. Watson, 4 Taunt. 16, 128 Eng.Rep. 232 (C.P. 1811) (declaration of tenant that he was tenant of X, to show he was such tenant and hence that X was seized); Higham v. Ridgway, 10 East 109, 103 Eng.Rep. 717 (K.B.1808) (to prove date of birth, midwife's entry showing attendance on birth and charge therefor, coupled with entry of payment of charges six months later, admitted since entry of payment "was in prejudice of the party making it").

43. See, e. g., Queen v. Governors and Guardians of Exeter, L.R. 4 Q.B. 341 (1869) (entry by occupier of house that he was tenant at certain rent, and had paid it, admissible as against interest, to show both facts of tenancy and payment); Taylor v. Witham, 3 Ch.D. 605 (1875) (Taylor paid Witham £ 2000 and after Taylor's death his executor contends this was a loan and Witham asserts it was a gift; entry in Taylor's books of three month's interest, £ 20 paid by Witham, admitted for the executor to show a loan since "the natural meaning of the entry standing alone" was against interest); Knapp v. St. Louis Trust Co., 199 Mo. 640, 98 S.W. 70 (1906) (on issue of testamentary capacity, doctor's entry of charge for attendance for "hyperaemia of brain" and entry of payment on same day admitted, relying on Higham v. Ridgway, supra n. 42); Wilson County Board of Education v. Lamm, 276 N.C. 487, 173 S.E.2d 281 (1970) (defendant, who took position that interest of plaintiff in real property was limited was permitted to introduce statement of deceased prior owner that he furnished land to plaintiff under the limitations claimed by defendant).

44. See, e. g., Allen v. Dillard, 15 Wash.2d 35, 129 P.2d 813 (1942). That was a suit to enforce an alleged contract by J. to leave part of her estate to plaintiff. Plaintiff offered a declaration of T., that he and J. had agreed to leave their property to each other or the other's heirs. The court held in a discriminating opinion by Beals, J., that while the declaration may have been against interest in reciting T.'s obligation under the contract, it was not so in reciting J.'s promise and could not be received to prove such promise.

declarations were neutral as to the declarant's interest or were self-serving.[45] A certain latitude as to contextual statements, neutral as to interest, giving meaning to the declaration against interest, seems defensible, but bringing in self-serving statements contextually seems questionable.

(b) *Disserving Quality Dependent on Outside Facts.* It may often happen that a declaration acknowledging some act, or some relationship, of the declarant may be for his interest or against his interest at the time it was made dependent upon outside facts not disclosed in the declaration. Admissibility then should hinge on these external facts. Thus admissibility of a statement that declarant is a member of a certain partnership should depend upon whether the firm is clearly solvent, or is on the other hand of doubtful solvency or insolvent.[46] A declaration that

one has a contract to purchase a given amount of wheat at a certain price is against, or for interest, depending upon the market value of wheat when the declaration was made.

(c) *Disserving Quality Dependent upon Purpose for Which Declaration Is Offered: The Relativity of Interest.* Most quantitative statements, except the "all" or "nothing" kind, have a double aspect. One who declares, "I hold a 10-year lease on the X building" is declaring, first, that his leasehold is for not less than ten years, and second, that it is for not more than 10 years. The like is obviously true of declarations about the amount of a debt owed to or by the declarant, or of the acreage or boundary of his farm. Thus it seems that if the claim of the 10-year lease is offered to show that declarant had a tenancy of that duration, as against an adverse contention that the tenancy was for only five years, it could be rejected as in favor of interest. If, on the other hand, it were offered to rebut a claim by the adversary that the tenancy was for 15 years it could be received as against interest. Moreover, it could be argued that when so offered it is immaterial that the declaration was *made* by the declarant with the self-assertive purpose of claiming as much as he could. He would still have been conscious that if his lease were actually longer it would be against his interest to claim less.

This type of declaration could be judged self-serving or disserving depending upon whether the declaration is offered to show that the amount is not less than, or not more than, the amount asserted by the declarant.[47]

---

45. The leading case for admitting contextual statements is Higham v. Ridgway, described supra n. 2, where the entry of payment made six months after the entry of charge for the services was held to bring in the latter. "By the reference to the ledger, the entry there is virtually incorporated in the other entry [of payment], of which it is explanatory." See also Smith v. Moore, 142 N.C. 277, 286, 55 S.E. 275, 278 (1906) ("The declaration is admissible as an entirety, including statements therein which were not in themselves against interest, but which are integral or substantial parts of the declaration, the reason why this is so being that the portion which is trustworthy, because against interest, imparts credit to the whole declaration.") Cases to like effect are cited in 5 Wigmore, Evidence § 1465, and in Jefferson, op. cit. supra n. 41, 58 Harv.L.Rev. 57–63, where he criticises the doctrine. See also the Model Code of Evidence, Rule 509(2) (". . . a declaration against interest and such additional parts thereof, including matter incorporated by reference, as the judge finds to be so closely connected with the declaration against interest as to be equally trustworthy.").

46. Compare Humes v. O'Bryan, 74 Ala. 64, 78 (1883). This was a suit against Humes upon an alleged partnership debt contracted by Glover in the operation of a plantation. The court held that a declaration by Glover, made when the plantation business was insolvent, that Humes was not a partner, was a declaration against interest, but otherwise if the business had not been insolvent. See also Flood v. Russell, L.R., Ireland [1891] 29 Ch. 91, 96, involving a wife's declaration that her

husband had made his will leaving her a half-interest in his property, where it appeared that under the terms of a family settlement and under the law of survivorship she would have taken a larger interest if he had died intestate.

47. This is the view of the commentators. The leading case presenting the question held to the contrary. Veach's Adm'r v. Louisville & I. Ry. Co., 190 Ky. 678, 238 S.W. 35 (1921) (death action; to

In effect, this viewpoint stresses the use of the declaration at the trial. There is relatively little case authority for it. The opposing viewpoint, that subsequent use at the trial is irrelevant to the application of the instant exception, appears to be more consistent with the reasons for the exception. The judgment that a declaration is trustworthy because it was against self-interest seems as a matter of logic to require trustworthiness when the declaration was made regardless of its later use at a trial.

(d) *Declarations Containing Self-Serving and Disserving Facts.* When a declaration contains statements of facts in favor of interest, and in addition statements of facts against interest, three methods of handling the evidence under this exception have been advocated. First, admit the entire declaration because part is disserving [48] and hence by a kind of contagion of truthfulness, all will be trustworthy. Second, compare the strength of the self-serving interest and the disserving interest in making the statement as a whole, and admit it all if the disserving interest preponderates, and exclude it all if the self-serving interest is greater.[49] Third, admit the disserving parts of the declaration, and exclude the self-serving parts.[50] The third solution seems the most realistic method of adjusting admissibility to trustworthiness, where the serving and disserving parts can be severed.

A particular statement may have self-serving and disserving aspects. In determining whether such a statement is against interest, the balancing of declarant's self-serving and disserving motives is appropriate.[51] The classic instance is the acknowledgment of receipt of part payment on a note. If the payment is acknowledged as made before the statute of limitations has run, the statement is preponderantly against interest and comes in under the exception.[52] If the payment is acknowledged to be made after the running of the state, in a jurisdiction where such a payment revives the note, it is considered preponderantly in favor of interest.[53]

(e) *Motive to Falsify.*[54] It has traditionally been stated as a requisite to admissibility under this exception that there must have been no motive to falsify the facts.[55] This is too sweeping, and the limitation can probably best be understood merely as a qualification that even though a declaration be against interest in one respect, if it appears that the declarant had some other motive whether of self-interest or otherwise, which

---

show that decedent earned *at least* so much, decedent's income tax return showing an income of $4000 for the year, held inadmissible as "self-serving," whereas it seems that if her income were less she would have been conscious that it was against her interest to report so much), criticised in Note, 30 Yale L.J. 854, 5 Wigmore, Evidence § 1464, n. 2, Morgan, op. cit. supra n. 41, 5 Vand.L.Rev. 471.

48. Higham v. Ridgway, and other authorities cited in n. 45, supra.

49. Massee-Felton Lbr. Co. v. Sirmans, 122 Ga. 297, 50 S.E. 92 (1905) (sheriff's entry showing tax execution, levy on land, sale and charging himself with price paid by bidder and discharging himself by stating that he applied the money to the tax, held, admitted as a whole because, on balance against interest).

50. Allen v. Dillard, 15 Wash.2d 35, 129 P.2d 813 (1942), described n. 44, supra; Jefferson, op. cit.

supra n. 41, 58 Harv.L.Rev. 50; and see Morgan, op. cit. supra n. 41, 5 Vand.L.Rev. 470–473.

51. Demasi v. Whitney Trust & Savings Bank, 176 So. 703, 711 (La.App., 1937) (affidavit by depositor signed in order to get remaining funds in disputed account, stating that challenged withdrawals were with her consent, rejected as a whole because self-interest in getting cash preponderated); 5 Wigmore, Evidence § 1464, note 2.

52. Addams v. Seitzinger, 1 W. & S. 243 (Pa.1841); 5 Wigmore, Evidence § 1466.

53. Small v. Rose, 97 Me. 286, 54 Atl. 726 (1903).

54. 5 Wigmore, Evidence § 1464; Jefferson, op. cit. supra n. 41, at 52–57; C.J.S. Evidence § 221.

55. See, e. g., German Ins. Co. v. Bartlett, 188 Ill. 165, 58 N.E. 1075, 1077 (1900); Halvorsen v. Moon & Kerr Lumber Co., 87 Minn. 18, 91 N.W. 28, 29 (1902).

was likely to lead him to misrepresent the facts, the declaration will be excluded.[56]

280. Unavailability of the Declarant.[57]

There is substantial argument for dispensing with any requirement that the declarant be unavailable as a witness as a prerequisite for receiving his declarations under this exception to the hearsay rule. The reasoning which admits the admissions of a party[58] and spontaneous declarations (such as excited utterances or declarations of present mental or bodily state),[59] without regard to the availability of the party or the declarant —namely that the admission, or the spontaneous declaration, is just as credible as his present testimony would be—seems equally applicable to the declaration against interest.[60] However, the early English cases limited the scope of the exception to decedents'

declarations[61] and the only question in this country generally has been whether other grounds of unavailability would be accepted. Some jurisdictions have required that the declarant be dead.[62] Only in recent decades has insanity been recognized as a ground.[63] Any reason why the declarant cannot be brought in at the trial should suffice, such as physical incapacity,[64] absence of the witness from the jurisdiction[65] or inability of the party to find him,[66] his supervening disqualification as a witness,[67] or his successful claim

---

56.   Demasi v. Whitney Trust & Savings Bank, 176 So. 703 (La.App.1937) (affidavit of depositor that previous withdrawals had been with her consent, excluded because it appeared that affidavit was presented by bank for her signature as prerequisite to her withdrawing balance of account); Roe v. Journegan, 175 N.C. 261, 95 S.W. 495 (1918) (issue as to delivery of deed of 1881 from father to son; son's declaration thereafter that he had no land and that his father had offered him some but he would not accept it, excluded, because son "evidently thought the deed of 1881, conveying to him a life estate was injurious to him" and apparently believed he would get the land in fee by deed or inheritance). But occasionally this kind of countermotive seems to be treated as a mere matter of credibility. See Johnson v. Peterson, 101 Neb. 504, 163 N.W. 869, 871 (1917).

57.   5 Wigmore, Evidence § 1456; Jefferson, Declarations Against Interest: An Exception to the Hearsay Rule, 58 Harv.L.Rev. 1, 6–8 (1944); Morgan, Declarations Against Interest, 5 Vand.L.Rev. 451, 475 (1952); C.J.S. Evidence § 218.

58.   See § 262, supra.

59.   See §§ 294, 297, infra.

60.   Accordingly, Uniform Rule 63(10) dispenses with the requirement of unavailability. In this regard, K.S.A. § 60–460(j), and N.J.Ev.Rule 63(10) are similar. The requirement is, however, preserved in West's Ann.Cal.Evid.Code, § 1230 and F.R.Ev. (R.D.1971) 804(b) (4). As to what satisfies the requirement, see § 253, supra, in addition to authorities in the notes which follow.

61.   Harrison v. Blades, 3 Camp. 457, 170 Eng.Rep. 1444 (N.P.1813) (illness insufficient; "if such a relaxation . . . were permitted there would be very sudden indispositions and recovery"); Stephen v. Gwenap, 1 M. & Rob. 120, 174 Eng.Rep. 41 (Ex. 1831) (absence of witness in America insufficient).

62.   See, e. g., McDonald v. Protestant Episcopal Church, 150 Mont. 332, 435 P.2d 369 (1967).

63.   Weber v. Chicago, R. I. & P. Ry. Co., 175 Iowa 358, 151 N.W. 852, 861 (1915); Jones v. Henry, 84 N.C. 320, 324 (1881) (dictum); New Amsterdam Cas. Co. v. First Nat. Bank, 134 S.W.2d 470 (Tex. Civ.App.1939).

64.   See Griffith v. Sauls, 77 Tex. 630, 14 S.W. 230 (1890) (declarations of bystander as to running of boundary line, which court assumed would be competent if declarant shown unavailable, held, fact that declarant was old and had lost power of speech sufficient; "In what would he be better than a dead man, in so far as the production of his testimony is concerned?"). Compare Harrison v. Blades, n. 61, supra.

65.   Sufficient: Walnut Ridge Merc. Co. v. Cohn, 79 Ark. 338, 96 S.W. 413, 416 (1906) (receipt inadmissible because writer now shown to be "dead or beyond the jurisdiction of the court"); Shearman v. Akins, 21 Mass. 283, 293 (1826); Kay Corporation v. Anderson, 72 Wash.2d 879, 436 P.2d 459 (1967). Contra: Stephen v. Gwenap, supra, n. 61. As to criminal cases, see § 253, n. 48, supra.

66.   Pennsylvania R. Co. v. Rochinski, 81 U.S.App. D.C. 320, 158 F.2d 325 (1946) (defendant's claim agent unable to find declarant at address he gave; sufficient to show unavailability) noted 15 Geo. Wash.L.Rev. 486.

67.   Disqualification for interest, sufficient. Dwight v. Brown, 9 Conn. 83, 93 (1831); Harriman v. Brown, 35 Va. (8 Leigh) 697, 713 (1837). Contra: Tom Love Grocery Co. v. Maryland Casualty Co., 166 Tenn. 275, 61 S.W.2d 672 (1933) (declarant disqualified by conviction for burglary: "The exception should not be extended to include infamy along with insanity and death as another ground of unavailability").

of privilege.[68]   But the holdings are checkered.

68.   Sutter v. Easterly, 354 Mo. 282, 189 S.W.2d 284
      162 A.L.R. 437 (1945) (suit to set aside judgment
      secured by perjured testimony: affidavit of witness
      who participated in conspiracy to secure the judg-
      ment received as declaration against interest,
      ground of unavailability the fact that the affiant re-
      fused in present suit to testify about the conspiracy
      claiming self-incrimination privilege) noted 24 Tex.
L.Rev. 217, but see State v. Gorden, 356 Mo. 1010,
204 S.W.2d 713 (1947) where this ground of unavailability is held insufficient to let in a declaration against the accused in a criminal case, as being
inconsistent with right of confrontation; People v.
Brown, 26 N.Y.2d 88, 308 N.Y.S.2d 825, 257 N.E.2d
16 (1970).
Various other less substantial reasons for unavailability have been disregarded.   See, e. g., Swearinger v. Klinger, 91 Ill.App.2d 251, 234 N.E.2d 60
(1968) (declarant at home caring for child with
measles).

CHAPTER 28

DYING DECLARATIONS

281. Introductory.[1]

Of the doctrines which authorize the admission of special classes of out-of-court statements as exceptions to the hearsay rule, the doctrine relating to dying declarations is the most mystical in its theory and traditionally the most arbitrary in its limitations. The notion of the special likelihood of truthfulness of deathbed statements was widespread, of course, long before the recognition of a general rule against hearsay in the early seventeen hundreds. It is natural enough, then, that about as soon as we find a hearsay rule we also find a recognized exception for dying declarations.[2]

282. Requirements that Declarant Must have been Conscious of Impending Death and that Death Actually Ensue.

The central notions of the popular reverence for deathbed statements are embodied in two of the important rules that limit the dying declaration exception. Unlike the more recent limitations, which will be mentioned later, these two rules are arguably rational, though possibly they have drawn too sharply the lines of restriction.

The first of these rules is the limitation that the declarant must at the time he made his statement have been conscious that death was near and certain.[3] He must have lost all hope of recovery.[4] It is arguable that a belief in the mere probability of impending death would make most men strongly disposed to tell the truth and hence guarantee the needed special reliability. But belief in the certainty of impending death, not its mere likelihood or probability, is the formula insisted on and rigorously applied. Perhaps this limitation reflects some lack of confidence in the reliability of "deathbed" statements generally. Usually this belief in the certainty of impending death is proved by evidence of the declarant's own statements of belief at the time, his expression of his

1. See 5 Wigmore, Evidence §§ 1430–1452; Dec.Dig. Homicide ⚖200–221, Evidence ⚖275½; C.J.S. Homicide §§ 286–306; 40 Am.Jur.2d Homicide §§ 347–394; Quick, Some Reflections on Dying Declarations, 6 How.L.Rev. 109 (1960); Note, 46 Iowa L.Rev. 375 (1961).

2. See the early cases listed in 5 Wigmore, Evidence § 1430, note 1.

3. For statements of the formula, see, e. g., People v. Tilley, 406 Ill. 398, 94 N.E.2d 328, 331 (1950); State v. Dunlap, 268 N.C. 301, 150 S.E.2d 436 (1966) ("full apprehension of danger of death" is necessary); Thomas v. Commonwealth, 183 Va. 501, 32 S.E.2d 711 (1945).

4. Shepard v. United States, 290 U.S. 96 (1933) (leading opinion by Cardozo, J.); Tillman v. State, 44 So.2d 644 (Fla.1950); People v. Allen, 300 N.Y. 222, 90 N.E.2d 48 (1949). But if made under consciousness of doom a later revival of hope will not be ground of exclusion. State v. Reed, 53 Kan. 767, 37 Pac. 174 (1894); Goff v. Commonwealth, 433 S.W.2d 350 (Ky.1968).

"settled hopeless expectation." [5]   That the deceased should have made such a statement is not required,[6] however; and his belief may be shown circumstantially by the apparent fatal quality of the wound,[7] by the statements made to the declarant by the doctor or by others that his condition is hopeless,[8] and by other circumstances.[9]

The method of dealing with the preliminary fact question of consciousness of impending death is discussed in a previous chapter.[10]

The second rule which is related to the popular reverence for deathbed statements is the limitation that the declarant must be dead, when the evidence is offered.[11]   It is not required that the death must have followed at any very short interval after the declaration.   Periods even extending into months have been held not too long.   The test is the declarant's belief in the nearness of death when he made the statement, not the actual swiftness with which death ensued.[12]

283.   Limitation to Use in Prosecutions for Homicide, and Other Arbitrary Limitations.

If the courts in their creation of rules about dying declarations had stopped here, we should have had a narrow, perhaps, but rational and understandable practice.   The requirement of consciousness of impending death arguably tends to guarantee a sufficient degree of special reliability, and the requirement that declarant be dead and thus unavailable as a witness is an ample showing of the necessity for the use of hearsay.   This simple rationale of dying declarations sufficed the courts up to the beginning of the eighteen hundreds, and these declarations were admitted in civil and criminal cases without distinction [13] and seemingly without untoward results.   The subsequent history of the rule is an object lesson in the dangers of the use by the judges of our system of precedents to preserve and fossilize the judicial mistakes of an earlier generation.

A mistake this development seems to have been.   Sergeant East in 1803 in his widely used treatise, Pleas of the Crown, wrote: "Besides the usual evidence of guilt in general cases of felony, there is one kind of evidence more peculiar to the case of homicide, which is the declaration of the deceased, after the mortal blow, as to the fact itself, and the party by whom it is committed.   Evidence of this sort is admissible in this case on the fullest necessity;   for it often happens

5.   See, e. g., Long v. Commonwealth, 262 Ky. 619, 90 S.W.2d 1007 (1936); State v. Eubanks, 277 Minn. 257, 152 N.W.2d 453 (1967); Hawkins v. State, 220 Tenn. 383, 417 S.W.2d 774 (1967).

6.   State v. Mitchell, 209 N.C. 1, 182 S.E. 695 (1935); Commonwealth v. Knable, 369 Pa. 171, 85 A.2d 114 (1952), and see Shepard v. United States, 290 U.S. 96, 100 (1933) ("There is no unyielding ritual of words to be spoken by the dying").

7.   Bland v. State, 210 Ga. 100, 78 S.E.2d 51 (1953); Rouse v. State of Mississippi, 222 So.2d 145 (Miss. 1969); Commonwealth v. Smith, 424 Pa. 9, 225 A.2d 691 (1967).   But the mere fact that the wound was mortal will not alone show consciousness of doom unless its nature were such as to reveal to the declarant its fatal character.   Fulton v. State, 209 Miss. 565, 47 So.2d 883 (1950); State v. McDaniel, 272 N.C. 556, 158 S.E.2d 874 (1968) vacated on other grounds 392 U.S. 665 (showing that declarant was actually at the point of death and in great agony held insufficient).

8.   Sisk v. State, 182 Ga. 448, 185 S.E. 777 (1936) (doctor); State v. Peters, 90 N.H. 438, 10 A.2d 242 (1939) (nurse); Chandler v. State, 7 Md.App. 646, 256 A.2d 695 (1969) (police officer).

9.   See cases collected in 5 Wigmore, Evidence § 1442; Dec.Dig. Homicide ☞203–205.

10.   See § 53, supra.

11.   State v. Carden, 209 N.C. 404, 183 S.E. 898 (1936); 5 Wigmore, Evidence § 1431.

12.   See, e. g., Emmett v. State, 195 Ga. 517, 25 S.E. 2d 9 (1943) (survived 3½ months, admitted); People v. Denton, 312 Mich. 32, 19 N.W.2d 476 (1945) (survived 11 days); 5 Wigmore, Evidence § 1441; Dec.Dig. Homicide ☞204.

13.   See Wright v. Littler, 3 Burr. 1244, 1247, 1255, 97 Eng.Rep. 812 (K.B.1761) (in ejectment, death-bed statement that declarant had forged a will, received) and other cases cited 5 Wigmore, Evidence § 1431, note 1.

that there is no third person present to be an eye-witness to the fact; and the usual witness on occasion of other felonies, namely, the party injured himself, is gotten rid of." [14] This was seized upon for what it was obviously not intended to be, namely, an announcement that the sole justification of the admission of dying declarations is the necessity of punishing murderers, who might otherwise escape for lack of the testimony of the victim. This need may exist, but the proposition that the use of dying declarations should be limited to instances where it exists surely does not follow. Nevertheless this proposition has been elaborated into a series of what may well be classed as arbitrary limiting rules, as contrasted with the two more rational limitations already mentioned.

The first of these is the rule that the use of dying declarations is limited to criminal prosecutions for homicide.[15] Although the English courts in the seventeen hundreds had not hesitated to do so,[16] nearly all courts, building upon the later theory of necessity, now refuse to admit dying declarations in civil cases,[17] whether death actions or other civil cases, or in criminal cases other than those charging homicide as an essential part of the offense. Thus in prosecutions for abortion [18] and rape,[19] though death of the woman may have ensued, the declarations are held inadmissible. Probably this restriction proceeds from a feeling on the part of the judges that dying declarations, despite their supposed guaranty of trustworthiness, are a dangerous kind of testimony, which a jury is likely to handle too emotionally. But is their emotion likely to be less in a murder prosecution than in a civil action for death or in a prosecution for abortion?

The concept of necessity limited to protection of the state against the slayer who might go free because of the death of his victim, spins out into another consequence. This is the further limitation that not only must the charge be homicide, but also, the defendant in the present trial must be charged with the death of the declarant.[20] In a case [21] in which a marauder shot a man and his wife at the same time, and the defendant was put on trial for the murder of the husband only, the dying declaration of the wife identifying the defendant as the assailant was offered by the State. It was excluded under this doctrine. Wigmore's comment is, "Could one's imagination devise a more senseless rule of exclusion, if he had not found it in our law?" [22]

Somewhat less arbitrary, but a source of much controversy, is the third of these corollary limitations, i. e., that the declarations are admissible only insofar as they relate

---

14. East, 1 Pleas of the Crown, 353, 1803, quoted 5 Wigmore, Evidence § 1431.

15. United States v. Sacasas, 381 F.2d 451 (2d Cir. 1967) (bank robbery, etc., excluded); People v. Stison, 140 Mich. 216, 103 N.W. 542 (1905) (incest, excluded); Taylor v. Commonwealth, 122 Va. 886, 94 S.E. 795, 797 (1918) (assault excluded); Dec.Dig. Homicide ☞211.

16. See n. 13, supra.

17. Prudential Ins. Co. v. Keeling's Adm'x, 271 Ky. 558, 112 S.W.2d 994 (1938) (claim for double indemnity for fatal accident, in suit on life policy); Ross v. Cooper, 38 N.D. 173, 164 Pac. 679 (1917) (death injury); Blair v. Rogers, 185 Okl. 63, 89 P. 2d 928 (1939) (death injury); Dec.Dig. Evidence ☞275½. For statutes and rules relaxing this restriction, see § 287, infra.

18. Winfrey v. State, 174 Ark. 729, 296 S.W. 82 (1927); State v. Meyer, 64 N.J.L. 382 (1900) (death not an essential element of the crime, but only affected the punishment). But where the crime charged is homicide by abortion, the declaration is admissible. State v. Yochelman, 107 Conn. 148, 139 Atl. 632 (1927) (manslaughter); Piercy v. State, 138 Neb. 301, 293 N.W. 99 (1940).

19. Frogge v. Commonwealth, 296 Ky. 726, 178 S.W. 2d 405 (1944).

20. People v. Cox, 340 Ill. 111, 172 N.E. 64, 69 A.L.R. 1215 (1930) (annotated); State v. Puett, 210 N.C. 633, 188 S.E. 75 (1936); Dec.Dig. Homicide ☞211.

21. Westberry v. State, 175 Ga. 115, 164 S.E. 905 (1932).

22. 5 Wigmore, Evidence § 1433, note 1.

to the circumstances of the killing and to the events more or less nearly preceding it in time and leading up to it.[23] Under this rule declarations about previous quarrels between the accused and his victim would be excluded, while transactions between them leading up to and shortly before the present attack would be received.[24] The vagueness of the criterion invites reversals.

284. Admissible on Behalf of Accused as Well as for Prosecution.

One might have anticipated that the strict application of the above mentioned concept of necessity would have led the courts to restrict the use of dying declarations to introduction by the prosecution, but the unfairness of such a result was too apparent, and it is well settled that they will be received on behalf of the defendant.[25]

285. Application of Other Evidentiary Rules: Personal Knowledge: Opinion: Rules about Writings.

Other principles of evidence law present recurrent problems in their application to dying declarations. If it appears that the declarant did not have adequate opportunity to observe the facts recounted, the declaration will be rejected for want of the knowledge qualification.[26] This knowledge requirement is sometimes confused with the opinion rule, and in some instances this confusion may have led courts to make the statement that opinions in dying declarations will be excluded.[27] Of course the opinion rule, designed as a regulation of the manner of questioning of witnesses in court, is entirely inappropriate as a restriction upon out-of-court declarations.[28] Accordingly, most courts including some that have professed to apply the opinion rule here, admit declarations such as "He shot me down like a dog," [29] "He shot me without cause," [30] and "He done it a-purpose" [31] and the like,[32] which would ordinarily be excluded as opinions, if spoken by a witness on the stand.

Another problem is the application of the so-called best evidence rule.[33] Often the dying victim, perhaps as different people visit him, will make several oral statements about

23. Lucas v. Commonwealth, 153 Ky. 424, 155 S.W. 721 (1913); Connor v. State, 225 Md. 543, 171 A.2d 699 (1961) (proper for court to exclude reference to residence of defendant, etc., when remaining statement of deceased was complete); Walthall v. State, 144 Tex.Cr.R. 585, 165 S.W.2d 184 (1942); 5 Wigmore, Evidence § 1344; Dec.Dig. Homicide ☞214 (2).

24. Smith v. Commonwealth, 236 Ky. 736, 33 S.W.2d 688 (1930) (that defendant had fired on deceased at previous times); Jones v. State, 236 P.2d 102 (Okl.Cr.1951) (that defendant had threatened to kill deceased the day before the killing); Webb v. State, 133 Tex.Cr.R. 32, 106 S.W.2d 683 (1937) (describing previous quarrel, on same afternoon, which had subsided, excluded).

25. Mattox v. United States, 146 U.S. 140, 151 (1892); State v. Puett, 210 N.C. 633, 188 S.E. 75 (1936).

26. Jones v. State, 52 Ark. 347, 12 S.W. 704 (1889) (where declarant could not see who shot him, declaration that H. shot him properly excluded); Strickland v. State, 167 Ga. 452, 145 S.E. 879, 881 (1928) (requirement satisfied); 5 Wigmore, Evidence § 1445(2). When there is room for doubt as to whether the statement is based on knowledge, the question is for the jury. Bland v. State, 210 Ga. 100, 78 S.E.2d 51 (1953).

27. E. g., Roberts v. Commonwealth, 301 Ky. 294, 191 S.W.2d 242 (1946) (but declarations here held admissible); State v. Wilks, 278 Mo. 481, 213 S.W. 118 (1919); Hollywood v. State, 19 Wyo. 493, 120 Pac. 471 (1912). See also, Miller v. Goodwin, 246 Ark. 552, 439 S.W.2d 308 (1969) (if both matter of fact and of opinion are involved, the judge has discretion to admit subject to request for instruction that matter of opinion not be considered).

28. See Commonwealth v. Plubell, 367 Pa. 452, 80 A.2d 825 (1951), and Pendleton v. Commonwealth, 131 Va. 676, 109 S.E. 201, 209 (1921), following 5 Wigmore, Evidence § 1447. See § 18, supra.

29. State v. Saunders, 14 Ore. 305, 12 Pac. 441 (1886). See Finley v. State, 92 Tex.Cr. 543, 244 S.W. 527 (1922) ("He shot me in cold blood.").

30. State v. Williams, 168 N.C. 191, 83 S.E. 714 (1914).

31. Pippin v. Commonwealth, 117 Va. 919, 86 S.E. 152 (1915).

32. Powell v. State, 238 Miss. 283, 118 So.2d 304 (1960). Decisions are collected in 5 Wigmore, Evidence § 1447; Annots., 25 A.L.R. 1370, 63 A.L.R. 567, 86 A.L.R.2d 905; C.J.S. Homicide § 299; Dec. Dig. Homicide ☞215(4).

33. See Ch. 23, supra.

the facts of the crime; and in addition, he may make a written statement by his own hand; or the person hearing the statement may write it down and procure the declarant to sign it. When is the writing required to be produced or its absence accounted for? As to the separate oral statement, it is clear that this is provable without producing a later writing.[34] It is equally clear, of course, that the terms of a written dying statement cannot be proved as such without producing or accounting for the writing.[35] What if the witness who heard the oral statement, which was taken down and signed, offers to testify to what he heard? Wigmore argues that the execution of the writing does not call into play the parole evidence rule, since that rule is limited to contracts and other "legal acts;"[36] but to a limited extent the courts have held otherwise. They have not excluded evidence of other oral statements on the same occasion, not embraced in the writing,[37] but as to oral declarations taken down and embodied in a writing signed or adopted by the deceased, these have been held not provable by one who heard them, but only by producing the written statement itself if available.[38] Even though it represents a departure from the usual practice of freedom in proving oral statements, and an extension of the doctrine of integration into a new field, the result may be justified by the need here for accuracy in transmitting to the tribunal the exact terms of the declarant's statement.

286. Instructions as to the Weight to be Given to Dying Declarations.[39]

There has been much theorizing in texts and opinions as to the weight to be given to dying declarations, abstractly or in comparison with the testimony of a witness. In consequence the practice has grown up in some states of requiring[40] or permitting[41] the judge to instruct the jury that these declarations are to be received with caution. In other states such instructions are held to be improper.[42] Again one court requires that the jury be told that a dying declaration is not to be regarded as having the same value and weight as sworn testimony.[43] Others consider it proper to direct the jury that they should give the dying declaration the same weight as the testimony of a witness.[44] While there may be merit in a standardized practice of giving cautionary instructions, the direc-

34. Gray v. State, 185 Ark. 515, 48 S.W.2d 224 (1932); Dunn v. People, 172 Ill. 582, 50 N.E. 137 (1898); State v. Sweeney, 203 Iowa 1305, 214 N.W. 735 (1927).

35. See § 233, supra.

36. 5 Wigmore, Evidence § 1450(b).

37. Commonwealth v. Haney, 127 Mass. 455 (1879) (oral declarations of consciousness of impending death on same occasion as the written statement, allowed to be proved).

38. Rex v. Gay, 7 C. & P. 230, 173 Eng.Rep. 101 (N.P.1835); Williams v. State, 26 Ala.App. 531, 163 So. 333 (1935) (rule stated but here not shown to be signed); People v. Glenn, 10 Cal. 32, 37 (1858) (prosecution bound to produce writing but having done so can prove similar oral declarations made at other times); Couch v. State, 93 Tex.Cr. 27, 245 S.W. 692 (1922) (similar to Williams v. State, above). Contra: State v. Whitson, 111 N.C. 695, 16 S.E. 332 (1892) (dictum).

39. Cases are collected in Notes, 32 Neb.L.Rev. 461 (1953), 41 Iowa L.Rev. 375 (1961); Annot., 167 A. L.R. 147; C.J.S. Homicide § 304.

40. Humphreys v. State, 166 Tenn. 523, 64 S.W.2d 5 (1933); State v. Mayo, 42 Wash. 540, 85 Pac. 251 (1906).

41. Dowdell v. State, 194 Ga. 578, 22 S.E.2d 310 (1942); Commonwealth v. Meleskie, 278 Pa. 383, 123 Atl. 310 (1924).

42. Shenkenberger v. State, 154 Ind. 630, 57 N.E. 519 (1900).

43. People v. Mleczko, 298 N.Y. 153, 81 N.E.2d 65 (1948); People v. Bartelini, 285 N.Y. 433, 35 N.E.2d 29 (1941). See also approving such a charge, Mitchell v. Commonwealth, 178 Va. 407, 17 S.E.2d 370 (1941).

44. State v. Johns, 152 Iowa 383, 132 N.W. 832 (1911). See also Hubbard v. State, 208 Ga. 472, 67 S.E.2d 562 (1951) (holding it not erroneous to instruct that dying declarations "stand upon the same plane of solemnity as statements made under oath"); Commonwealth v. Brown, 388 Pa. 613, 131 A.2d 367 (1957) (court approved instruction that declaration can be given "the same effect as though it were made under oath", but added it would seem advisable for judge to omit any comparison).

tion to give the declaration a predetermined fixed weight seems of questionable wisdom. The weight of particular dying declarations depends upon so many factors varying from case to case that no standardized instruction will fit all situations. Certainly in jurisdictions where the judge retains his common law power to comment on the weight of the evidence, the dying declaration is a most appropriate subject for individualized comment. But where he is shorn (as in most American jurisdictions) of this power, it seems wiser to leave the weight of the declaration to the argument of counsel, the arbitrament of the jury, and the consideration of the judge on motion for new trial.

287. Decisional and Statutory Extensions of Common Law Admissibility.

Without benefit of statute or court rule, one court had the statesmanship to break the shackles of those restrictions on the use of dying declarations which have been mentioned above as the more arbitrary and irrational ones. "We are confronted," the court said, "with a restrictive rule of evidence commendable only for its age, its respectability resting solely upon a habit of judicial recognition, formed without reason, and continued without justification." [45] The court conclud-

ed that in an action by the executor of the seller to recover upon a land sale contract the dying statement of the seller of "the truth about the sale" should be admitted. At least three states have taken a short step forward by enacting statutes which admit dying declarations in civil actions for death injuries.[46] Colorado has carried the reform to broader ground by a statute which admits dying declarations "in all civil and criminal trials and other proceedings before Courts, Commissions and other tribunals." [47] To similar effect are statutes in two states [48] and the Uniform Rule, which, without any limitation upon the type of action in which the evidence is offered, admits "a statement by a person unavailable as a witness because of his death if the judge finds that it was made voluntarily and in good faith and while the declarant was conscious of his impending death and believed that there was no hope of his recovery." [49]

---

45. Thurston v. Fritz, 91 Kan. 468, 475, 138 Pac. 625 (1914).

46. Ark.Stats. § 28–712; N.Car.G.S. § 28–173; Ore. Rev.Stats. 41.900(4).

47. Colo.Rev.Stat.1963, 52–1–20.

48. West's Ann.Cal.Evid.Code, § 1242; Kan.Stat. Ann. 60–460(e). N.J.Ev.Rule 63(5) is also similar but is restricted to criminal cases.

49. Uniform Rule 63(5). F.R.Ev. (R.D.1971) 804(b) (4) limits admissibility to statements concerning the cause or circumstances of what declarant believed to be his impending death but contains no limit as to type of case in which offered; unavailability is not confined to death.

CHAPTER 29

SPONTANEOUS DECLARATIONS

288. Res Gestae and the Hearsay Rule.[1]

The term *res gestae* seems to have come into common usage in discussions of admissibility of declarations accompanying material acts or situations in the early 1800's.[2] At this time the understanding of what is and what is not hearsay was not well developed and the various exceptions to the hearsay rule were not clearly defined. In this context, the phrase *res gestae* served as a convenient vehicle for escape from the hearsay rule in two primary situations. In the first, it was used to explain the admissibility of declarations that were not hearsay at all.[3] In the second, it was used to justify the admissibility of declarations which today come within the four exceptions discussed in this chapter: (1) declarations of present bodily condition, (2) declarations of present mental states and emotions, (3) excited utterances, and (4) declarations of present sense impressions. Despite the increased sophistication of the hearsay rule and its exceptions today, however, courts still occasionally speak in terms of *res gestae* rather than in terms of more precise hearsay doctrine.

Initially, the term *res gestae* was employed to denote words which accompanied the principle litigated fact, such as the murder, collision, or trespass, which was the subject of the action. Usage developed, however, to the point where the phrase seemed to embody the notion that evidence of any concededly relevant act or condition might bring in likewise the words which accompanied it. Two main policies or motives are discernable in this recognition of *res gestae* as a password for the admission of otherwise inadmissible evidence. One is a desire to permit each witness to tell his story in a natural way by telling all that happened at the time of the narrated incident, including those details which give life and color to the story. Truth is a seamless web, and the naturalness with which the details fit each other gives confirmation to the witness' entire account.[4] The other

---

1. See generally, 6 Wigmore, Evidence §§ 1745, 1767; Comment, Res Gestae: A Synonym for Confusion, 20 Baylor L.Rev. 229 (1968); 29 Am.Jur.2d Evidence §§ 708–737; C.J.S. Evidence §§ 403–421.

2. 6 Wigmore, Evidence § 1767.

3. See § 289, infra.

4. "[T]he admissibility of the proofs as res gestae has as its justifying principle that truth, like the

policy, emphasized by Wigmore and those following his leadership, is the recognition of spontaneity as the source of special trustworthiness. This quality of spontaneity characterizes to some degree nearly all the types of declarations which have been labeled *res gestae*.

Commentators[5] and, less frequently, courts,[6] have criticized use of the phrase *res gestae*. Its vagueness and imprecision are, of course, apparent. Moreover, traditional limitations on the doctrine, such as the requirement that it be used only in regard to the principal litigated fact and the frequent insistence of concurrence (or at least a close relationship in time) between the words and the act or situation, have restricted its usefulness as a tool for avoiding unjustified application of the hearsay rule. Historically, however, the phrase served its purpose well. Its very vagueness made it easier for courts to broaden it and thus provide for the admissibility of certain declarations in new fields. But it seems clear that the law has now reached a stage at which this desirable policy of widening admissibility will be best served by other means. The ancient phrase

can well be jetisoned, with due acknowledgment that it has served well its era in the evolution of evidence law.

289. Spontaneous Declarations as Nonhearsay: Circumstantial Proof of a Fact in Issue.[7]

The types of spontaneous declarations discussed in this chapter are often treated by courts as hearsay and in that event it is considered that they must come within an exception to the general rule excluding hearsay in order to be admissible. In many cases, however, this maneuver is unnecessary because the declarations are probably not hearsay in the first place. As suggested in an earlier section,[8] hearsay is most appropriately defined as assertive statements or conduct offered to prove what is asserted. But many so-called spontaneous declarations are in fact not assertive statements or, if assertive, are not offered to prove the truth of the assertions made. For example, it is clear that the statements, "I plan to spend the rest of my life here in New York" or "I have lost my affection for my husband" are hearsay, when offered to prove the plan to remain in New York or the loss of affection. On the other hand, statements such as "I have been happier in New York than in any other place," when offered to show the speaker's intent to remain in New York, or "My husband is a detestable wretch", offered to show lack of affection for the husband, will or will not be classed as hearsay, depending upon the position taken with respect to the question whether "implied assertions" are to be classed as hearsay. That question is discussed elsewhere.[9]

If the statement which is offered in evidence is not classed as hearsay, then no fur-

---

Master's robe, is of one piece, without seam, woven from the top throughout, that each fact has its inseparabe attributes and its kindred facts materially affecting its character, and that the reproduction of a scene with its multiple incidents, each created naturally and without artificiality and not too distant in point of time, will by very quality and texture tend to disclose the truth." Robertson v. Hackensack Trust Co., 1 N.J. 304, 63 A.2d 515, 519 (1949) (Case, J.)

5. "The marvelous capacity of a Latin phrase to serve as a substitute for reasoning, and the confusion of thought inevitably accompanying the use of inaccurate terminology, are nowhere better illustrated than in the decisions dealing with the admissibility of evidence as 'res gestae'. It is probable that this troublesome expression owes its existence and persistence in our law of evidence to an inclination of judges and lawyers to avoid the toilsome exertion of exact analysis and precise thinking." Morgan, A Suggested Classification of Utterances Admissible as Res Gestae, 31 Yale L.J. 229 (1922). See also 6 Wigmore, Evidence § 1767.

6. See, e. g., Cox v. State, 64 Ga. 374, 410 (1897) (Bleckley, C. J.).

7. See generally 6 Wigmore, Evidence §§ 1715, 1766–1790.

8. See § 246, supra.

9. See § 250, supra.

ther consideration of the matters developed in this chapter is required. But if it is classed as hearsay, then these matters may become pertinent to the question of admissibility.

290.   "Self-Serving" Aspects of Spontaneous Declarations.[10]

The notion that a party's out-of-court declarations could not be evidence in his favor because of their "self-serving" nature seems to have originated as an accompaniment of the now universally discarded rule forbidding parties to testify.[11]   When this rule of disqualification for interest was abrogated by statute, any sweeping rule of inadmissibility regarding "self-serving" declarations should have been regarded as abolished by implication.   This, however, has not been the case.

The basic rule rendering hearsay declarations inadmissible rests in part upon the danger that such statements may be self-serving and that this characteristic cannot be sufficiently presented to the trier of fact to assure that it will be taken into account in judging the credibility of the declaration.[12]   Thus no specific rule is necessary to cover so-called self-serving out-of-court declarations.[13]   On

the other hand, when declarations with a self-serving aspect fall within exceptions to the hearsay rule, the judgment underlying the exception, that as to those declarations the special need and assurance of trustworthiness outweigh the dangers inherent in hearsay, should be taken as controlling and the declarations admitted despite their self-serving aspects.   Most courts would agree that this is the proper approach when the self-serving declaration falls within one of the well-established exceptions, such as the business records exception, excited utterances, and spontaneous declarations of present bodily feelings or symptoms.   But in regard to less settled exceptions, such as that for declarations of present state of mind or emotion, there is less agreement.   Some courts have applied a purported general rule of exclusion of self-serving statements in this area.[14]   Others have rejected any blanket rule of exclusion, although the self-serving aspects of the declaration have been taken into account in applying a requirement that the declarations have been made under circumstances of apparent sincerity.[15]   Especially in areas where the danger of injustice is high—where, for example, declarations of the accused in homicide and assault cases are offered to prove his peaceful intentions or his fear of the victim [16]—the latter approach seems de-

10.   See generally, 6 Wigmore, Evidence § 1732; Comment, Admissibility of Self-Serving Declarations, 14 Ark.L.Rev. 105 (1959); Comment, 61 Mich. L.Rev. 1306 (1963); 29 Am.Jur.2nd Evidence §§ 621–622; C.J.S. Evidence § 216; Dec.Dig. Evidence ⟨key⟩271, Criminal Law ⟨key⟩413.

11.   See Phipson, Evidence 231 (9th ed. 1952). The rule forbidding parties to testify is discussed at § 65, supra.

12.   See § 245, supra.

13.   See Caplan v. Caplan, 83 N.H. 318, 142 Atl. 121 (1928); Cowan v. T. J. Stewart Lumber Co., 177 Okl. 266, 58 P.2d 573 (1936). Nevertheless, some courts continue to discuss the matter in terms of a rule excluding self-serving statements. E. g., Sebastian v. Commonwealth. 436 S.W.2d 66 (Ky. 1969) (objection to question put to witness was properly sustained "because the question was designed simply to get into evidence a self-serving statement"); Lagrone v. Helman, 233 Miss. 654, 103 So.2d 365 (1958) (statements made by plaintiff after accident to the effect that a nurse had bumped into him "were all self-serving . . . and were therefore incompetent.").

14.   See cases cited in n. 16, infra.

15.   E. g., Lee v. Mitcham, 69 App.D.C. 17, 98 F.2d 298 (1938); United States v. Matot, 146 F.2d 197 (2nd Cir. 1944); Kelly v. Bank of America, 112 Cal.App.2d 388, 246 P.2d 92 (1952); Caplan v. Caplan, 83 N.H. 318, 142 Atl. 121 (1928).

16.   People v. Smith, 8 Cal.2d 502, 104 P.2d 510 (1940) (letters of defendant to his wife not admissible in his prosecution for her murder to prove affection); State v. Barnett, 156 Kan. 746, 137 P. 2d 133 (1943) (statement of defendant tending to show fear not admissible); State v. Brooks, 360 S.W.2d 622 (Mo.1962) (witness not permitted to testify that two months prior to homicide defendant exhibited injuries and told witness that the injuries had been inflicted by the victim); Dominguez v. State, 445 S.W.2d 729 (Tex.Cr.App.1969) (witness not permitted to testify that a month prior to homicide defendant had said the victim had beaten her and had exhibited wounds).

sirable. If made under circumstances of apparent sincerity, they should be admitted and the trier of fact permitted to consider their self-serving characteristics in evaluating their credibility.

291. Declarations of Bodily Feelings, Symptoms, and Condition: (a) In General.[17]

Declarations of the declarant's present bodily condition and symptoms, including pain and other feelings, are admissible to prove the truth of the declarations as an exception to the hearsay rule.[18] Special reliability is considered to be furnished by the spontaneous quality of the declarations, assured by the requirement that the declarations purport to describe a condition presently existing at the time of the declaration.[19] This assurance of reliability is almost certainly not always effective, however, since some statements describing present symptoms or the like are probably not spontaneous but rather calculated misstatements. Nevertheless, a sufficiently large percentage are probably spontaneous to justify the exception. The strong likelihood of spontaneity is also the basis for the special need for receiving the declarations. Being spontaneous, they are considered of greater probative value than the present testimony of the declarant, and consequently are admissible despite the availability of the declarant at the time of trial.[20]

Despite some indication to the contrary,[21] declarations of present bodily condition need not be made to a physician in order to qualify for the present exception. Any person who had the opportunity to hear the declaration may testify to it.[22] The exception is, however, limited to descriptions of present condition, and therefore excludes description of past pain or symptoms[23] as well as ac-

17. See generally, 6 Wigmore, Evidence §§ 1718–1723; McBaine, Admissibility in California of Declarations of Physical or Mental Condition, 19 Calif. L.Rev. 231 (1931); Notes, 51 Mich.L.Rev. 902 (1953), 13 N.C.L.Rev. 228 (1935); Uniform Rule 63 (12); F.R.Ev. (R.D.1971) 803(3); Annot., 64 A.L.R. 557; 29 Am.Jur.2nd Evidence §§ 655–656; C.J.S. Evidence §§ 242–246; Dec.Dig. Evidence ⬅127, 128, 268.

18. E. g., Fidelity Service Ins. Co. v. Jones, 280 Ala. 195, 191 So.2d 20 (1966) (declarant complained of sickness or blackouts); Shover v. Iowa Lutheran Hospital, 252 Iowa 706, 107 N.W.2d 85 (1961) (witness testified, concerning plaintiff, that "She said she hurt."); Indian Oil Tool Co. v. Thompson, 405 P.2d 104 (Okl.1965) (deceased stated that he had a tight feeling in his chest); Claspermeyer v. Florsheim Shoe Co., 313 S.W.2d 198 (Mo.App. 1958) (wife complained to husband that she had a pain in her chest); Fagan v. Newark, 78 N.J. 294, 188 A.2d 427 (1963) (deceased said he felt dizzy and ill).

19. See 6 Wigmore, Evidence § 1714.

20. Kennard v. Burton, 25 Me. 39, 46 (1845): "If other persons could not be permitted to testify to [present declarations of bodily condition] when the person injured might be a witness, there might often be a defect of proof. The person injured might be unable to recollect or state them by reason of the agitation and suffering occasioned by it." See 6 Wigmore, Evidence § 1718.

21. West Chicago St. Ry. Co. v. Kennelly, 170 Ill. 508, 48 N.E. 996 (1897) (although witness could testify that plaintiff "was complaining awful bad" on the morning after the accident, she could not testify as to the specifics of the complaint because she was not a physician); Cross v. Blood, 22 Ill. App.2d 496, 161 N.E.2d 349 (1959) (following Kennelly, and holding it not error to exclude testimony by a "nonexpert" as to whether the plaintiff complained of pain and suffering while at work); Kennedy v. Rochester City and B. R. Co., 130 N.Y. 654, 29 N.E. 141 (1891) (in view of statute making plaintiff competent to testify, evidence that a few hours after the accident plaintiff complained of pain in her side and head was not admissible).

22. Shover v. Iowa Lutheran Hospital, 252 Iowa 706, 107 N.W.2d 85 (1961) (hospital patient's roommate); Caspermeyer v. Florsheim Shoe Store Co., 313 S. W.2d 198 (Mo.App.1958) (wife); Fagan v. Newark, 78 N.J.Super. 294, 188 A.2d 427 (1963) (wife); Plank v. Heirigs, 83 S.D. 173, 156 N.W.2d 193 (1968) (nurse).

23. Lowery v. Jones, 219 Ala. 201, 121 So. 704 (1929); Martin v. P. H. Hanes Knitting Co., 189 N.C. 644, 127 S.E. 688 (1925). See generally, 6 Wigmore, Evidence § 1722(b). Courts have sometimes been relatively lax in classifying symptoms, as "present" symptoms, however. See Hartford Accident & Indemnity Co. v. Baugh, 87 F.2d 240 (5th Cir. 1937), noted in 36 Mich.L.Rev. 142 (1937) ("He came to the office and told me that his sputum was stained with blood" admissible); Bloomberg v. Laventhal, 179 Cal. 616, 178 P. 496 (1919) (testimony that plaintiff complained that he

counts of the events furnishing the cause of the condition.[24]

It is generally stated that in order to come within this exception, a declaration must be a "natural and spontaneous" expression of present bodily condition.[25] It is doubtful, however, that this means that the foundation required for admission consists of more than a showing that the declaration purports to describe a then existing bodily condition of the declarant. The trial judge does, on the other hand, probably have the duty to consider the circumstances under which the declaration was made and the discretionary power to exclude the offered declaration if he finds that it was made with a view to making evidence.[26]

292. Declarations of Bodily Feelings, Symptoms, and condition: (b) Declarations to Physicians Consulted for Treatment.[27]

Statements of a presently existing bodily condition made by a patient to a doctor [28]

consulted for treatment are almost universally admitted as evidence of the facts stated,[29] and even courts greatly limiting the admissibility of declarations of bodily condition generally will admit statements made under these circumstances.[30] Although statements to physicians are not likely to be spontaneous, since they are usually made in response to questions, their reliability is assured by the likelihood that the patient believes that the effectiveness of the treatment he receives may depend largely upon the accuracy of the information he provides the physician.[31]

---

had pains in the head and could not sleep admissible).

24. See 6 Wigmore, Evidence § 1722(a).

25. Rogers v. Detroit, 289 Mich. 86, 286 N.W. 167 (1939) ("The controlling test of the admissibility of exclamations of pain is 'spontaneity.' "); Caspermeyer v. Florsheim Shoe Store Co., 313 S.W.2d 198 (Mo.App.1958); Fagan v. Newark, 78 N.J.Super. 294, 188 A.2d 427 (1963).

26. Appellate courts, affirming trial court decisions to admit such declarations, have often emphasized those circumstances of the declarations which suggest reliability. E. g., Fagan v. Newark, 78 N.J. Super. 294, 188 A.2d 427 (1963) (deceased's declaration that he felt dizzy and ill was made naturally and without apparent premeditation); Indian Oil Tool Co. v. Thompson, 405 P.2d 104 (Okl.1965) (emphasis on fact that deceased's declaration that he had a pain in his chest made while "under shock").

27. See generally, 6 Wigmore, Evidence §§ 1719– 1720; 29 Am.Jur.2nd Evidence §§ 683–686; C.J.S. Evidence § 246(b); Annot., 37 A.L.R.3d 778, 783– 816; Dec.Dig. Evidence ☞128.

28. The cases indicate that psychiatrists will be treated no differently from other physicians for purposes of the rules relating to the admissibility of statements made to them. See Simpson v. Heiderich, 4 Ariz.App. 232, 419 P.2d 362 (1966)

(psychiatrist, consulted for treatment, could testify to statements made by plaintiff, not to prove truth of statements but to explain basis of diagnosis); Miller Mutual Fire Ins. Co. of Texas v. Ochoa, 432 S.W.2d 118 (Tex.Civ.App.1968) (psychiatrist, consulted for treatment, could give opinion as to plaintiff's prognosis based upon history related by plaintiff); Lemmon v. Denver and Rio Grande Western Railroad Co., 9 Utah 2d 195, 341 P.2d 215 (1959) (psychiatrist consulted for treatment can relate conversations with patient, not as proof of truth of patient's statements but to explain his own testimony). The more restrictive rules have also been applied in this context. Gonzales v. Hodson, 91 Idaho 330, 420 P.2d 813 (1966) (exclusion of neuropsychiatrist's report was proper since the consultation had been for purposes of obtaining the physician's testimony in a criminal case); Wilhelm v. Maryland Traffic Safety Commission, 230 Md. 91, 185 A.2d 715 (1962) (psychiatrist not consulted for treatment could not relate history given by plaintiff); Conner v. State, 225 Md. 543, 171 A.2d 699 (1961) (psychiatrist not consulted for treatment could not testify as to history or subjective symptoms related by defendant).

29. E. g., Kometani v. Heath, 50 Hawaii 89, 431 P. 2d 931 (1967). Georgia, however, seems to adhere to a much more limited rule. See, e. g., Paulk v. Thomas, 115 Ga.App. 436, 154 S.E.2d 872 (1967) (testimony regarding plaintiff's complaints to treating physician not admissible unless equivalent to spontaneous or involuntary manifestations of pain and suffering).

30. See § 291, n. 21, supra. The rule applies to a criminal as well as civil litigation. State v. Orsini, 155 Conn. 367, 232 A.2d 907 (1967).

31. "All . . . declarations made by the patient to the examining physician as to his present or past symptoms are known by the patient who is seeking medical assistance to be required for proper diagnosis and treatment and by reason thereof, are viewed as highly reliable and apt to state true facts." Goldstein v. Sklar, 216 A.2d 298, 305 (Me.1966).

This strong assurance of reliability has caused some courts to expand the exception to include statements made by a patient to a physician concerning *past* symptoms.[32] This seems appropriate, as patients are likely to recognize the importance to their treatment of accurate statements as to past as well as present symptoms.[33] Wider acceptance of this expansion might well be expected,[34] although at present more courts would probably admit the testimony for the limited purpose of explaining the basis for the physician's conclusion than would admit it to prove the fact of the prior symptoms.[35]

The exception might be taken one step further to encompass statements made to a physician concerning the cause or the external source of the condition to be treated. In some cases the special assurance of reliability—the patient's belief that accuracy is essential to effective treatment—also applies

to statements concerning the cause, and a physician who views this as related to diagnosis and treatment might reasonably be expected to communicate this to the patient and perhaps take other steps to assure a reliable response. Thus one court has held that a plaintiff's statement to her physician that she had been struck from behind by a two-by-four was admissible, placing emphasis upon the fact that the physician testified that he considered her ability to call what had happened to her as important to his diagnosis.[36] On the other hand, when statements as to causation enter the realm of fixing fault it is unlikely that the patient or the physician regarded them as related to diagnosis or treatment. In such cases, the statements lack any assurance of reliability and would properly be excluded. Thus the same court has reasonably held inadmissible a patient's statement to his physician that the injuries being treated were sustained when another car forced the vehicle in which the patient was riding onto the left hand portion of the road.[37] The greater number of courts probably still adhere to a position requiring the exclusion of any statements related to cause,[38] although the better

---

32. Meaney v. United States, 112 F.2d 538 (2d Cir. 1940) (excellent discussion by L. Hand, J.); Roosa v. Boston Loan Co., 132 Mass. 439 (1882); Peterson v. Richfield Plaza, 252 Minn. 215, 89 N.W.2d 712, 712–22 (1958) (physician permitted to testify as to plaintiff's statements concerning symptoms experienced prior to examination); Kennedy v. Upshaw, 66 Tex. 442, 1 S.W. 308 (1886); Missouri, K. & T. R. Co. v. Dalton, 56 Tex.Civ.App. 82, 120 S.W. 240 (1909).

33. See the discussions in Meaney v. United States, 112 F.2d 538 (2d Cir. 1940) and Peterson v. Richfield Plaza, 252 Minn. 215, 89 N.W.2d 712, 719–22 (1958).

34. Uniform Rule 63(12) would admit, in the absence of a finding of bad faith, a statement as to "previous symptoms, pain or physical sensation, made to a physician consulted for treatment or for diagnosis with a view to treatment, and relevant to an issue of declarant's bodily condition." F.R.Ev. (R.D. 1971) 803(4) would admit "statements made for purposes of medical diagnosis or treatment and describing . . . past . . . symptoms, pain, or sensations . . . ."

35. E. g., Goldstein v. Sklar, 216 A.2d 298 (Me. 1966) (evidence of plaintiff's statements to physician as to past pain and suffering and complaints admissible not to establish the truth of these statements but to show the basis for the physician's opinion). Other courts, of course, would hold such statements inadmissible for any purpose. E. g., Brewer v. Henson, 96 Ga.App. 501, 100 S.E.2d 661 (1957).

36. Cestero v. Ferra, 110 N.J.Super. 264, 265 A.2d 387 (1970).

37. Pinter v. Parsekian, 92 N.J.Super. 392, 223 A.2d 635 (1966).

38. Brewer v. Henson, 96 Ga.App. 501, 100 S.E.2d 661 (1957) (physician's testimony as to what plaintiff said concerning circumstances of automobile collision not admissible); Bauer v. Independent Stave Co., 417 S.W.2d 693 (Mo.App.1967) (surgeon's testimony that plaintiff reported that he did considerable tugging and pulling on a small cart properly disregarded in determining how injury occurred); Mott v. Clark, 88 R.I. 257, 146 A.2d 924 (1958) (statement to physician at time of admission to hospital that injuries were sustained when plaintiff was knocked down by someone opening restaurant door not admissible); Floyd v. Dep't of Labor and Industries, 68 Wash.2d 938, 416 P.2d 355 (1966) (cause of accident not established by physician's testimony as to plaintiff's statements). The declarations may be admissible for the limited purpose of explaining the physician's testimony. See Traveler's Ins. Co. v. Smith,

view would seem to be that statements as to the inception or general nature of the cause should be admissible insofar as they were reasonably pertinent to diagnosis or treatment.[39]

293. Declarations of Bodily Feelings, Symptoms, and Condition: (c) Declarations Made to Physicians Employed Only to Testify.[40]

Many courts draw a sharp line between declarations made to physicians consulted by the declarant for purposes of treatment and those made to physicians consulted solely with the anticipation that the physician will testify in court on the declarant's behalf. The limitations placed on the latter differ among jurisdictions. In order of the increasing strictness, these restrictions are as follows:

1. Probably a majority of courts have held or would hold that descriptive statements of present pain or symptoms made to a physician consulted solely for purposes of

preparing him to testify in the declarant's behalf are not admissible as substantive evidence of the pain or symptom under the general exception to the hearsay rule for statements of bodily condition.[41] This restriction is based on the conclusion that where the declarant does not anticipate that his treatment's effectiveness will depend upon the accuracy of his statements, the underlying rationale for the exception does not exist. Moreover, if the declarant anticipates that enhancement of his symptoms will inure to his benefit in the subsequent litigation, there is also an affirmative motive to falsify or at least exaggerate. On these bases, the general exception has been held inapplicable.

2. If a physician has been consulted for purposes of treatment, some courts that would refuse to admit the physician's testimony of the "history" related by the patient as evidence of the truth of the matters asserted would admit it for the limited purpose of explaining the basis of the physician's conclusions and opinions testified to.[42] When used for this purpose, of course, the testimony is not offered to prove the truth of the out-of-court declarations and is therefore not hearsay.[43] Although most courts would apply the same rule to a physician not

---

448 S.W.2d 541 (Tex.Civ.App.1969) (physician's testimony that deceased told him that he had been manipulating some equipment when he experienced sudden pain admissible to explain the the physician's opinion that the strain of moving the equipment caused damage to deceased's heart but not to prove the fact of moving the equipment). There is some indication that courts may be more willing to admit the declarations when the declarant is presently unavailable, the "cause" is closely related to the "symptoms", and the latter arguably not explainable without reference to the former, and some elements of spontaneity exist. See the discussion in Pinter v. Parsekian, 92 N.J. Super. 392, 223 A.2d 635 (1966). If the requirements for the excited utterance exception are met, the statement may come in under that exception; see § 297, infra.

39. See F.R.Ev. (R.D.1971) 803(4), making admissible "statements made for purpose of medical diagnosis or treatment and describing . . . the inception or general character of the cause or external source thereof insofar as reasonably pertinent to diagnosis or treatment."

40. See generally, Annots., 130 A.L.R. 977, 80 A.L.R. 1527, 67 A.L.R. 10; 29 Am.Jur.2nd Evidence § 684; C.J.S. Evidence § 246(b); Annot., 37 A.L.R.3d 778, 816–26.

41. See, e. g., Gentry v. Watkins-Carolina Trucking Co., 249 S.C. 316, 154 S.E.2d 112 (1967), adopting the "majority" view that a physician consulted as a prospective witness may testify to the plaintiff's statements of present condition and past symptoms; that the testimony is not admissible as proof of the facts stated but, in the absence of fraud or bad faith, as information relied upon by the physician to support his opinion. See also Wilkinson v. Grover, 181 So.2d 591 (Fla.App.1965); Wolfson v. Rumble, 121 Ga.App. 549, 174 S.E.2d 469 (1970) (subjective complaints of pain made to "examining physician" not admissible to prove pain but admissible to explain diagnosis).

42. See § 292 n. 35, supra. See also Commonwealth Division of Forestry v. Farler, 391 S.W.2d 371 (Ky. App.1965); Uberto v. Kaufman, 348 Mass. 171, 202 N.E.2d 822 (1964). See generally Dec.Dig. Evidence ☞555(j).

43. See § 289, supra.

consulted for purposes of treatment, a few have held or indicated that physicians consulted solely for purposes of testimony may not recount what was told them, even for the nonhearsay purpose of explaining their opinions or conclusions.[44]

3. A few courts, emphasizing the self-serving nature of representations made to physicians consulted for purposes of subsequent testimony, have adopted the extreme position that those physicians are confined to giving opinions based solely upon objective facts personally observed by them or upon hypothetical questions. Any opinion or conclusion based even in part upon "subjective" facts, i. e., what the subject has said about the history of his condition or his symptoms, is therefore inadmissible.[45] This, of course, is inconsistent with general medical practice which involves use of this information in forming opinions acted upon in the course of treatment and with the modern rule that medical opinions based in part upon factors not within the personal knowledge of the testifying physician are admissible.[46]

The dubious propriety of these restrictions is probably at least partially responsible for the restrictive view taken by the courts as to what constitutes consultation solely for purposes of obtaining testimony from the physician consulted. The ultimate issue is whether there was any significant treatment motive; if this existed, any additional motive of obtaining testimony is ignored.[47] For example, a physician's testimony is not within these restrictions despite the fact that he was consulted after the declarant retained an attorney [48] or even at the attorney's recommendation.[49] The fact that no treatment was actually given is not controlling,[50] but subsequent reliance upon advice of a treatment nature given by the physician is strong evidence of a treatment motive for the initial consultation.[51]

44. E. g., Korleski v. Needham, 77 Ill.App.2d 328, 222 N.E.2d 334 (1966); Mary Helen Coal Corp. v. Bigelow, 265 S.W.2d 69 (Ky.App.1954); Cruce v. Gulf, Mobil, & Ohio R. Co., 361 Mo. 1138, 238 S.W.2d 674 (1951) (may relate declarations of present symptoms only); Brotherhood of L., F., & E. v. Raney, 101 S.W.2d 863 (Tex.Civ.App.1937).

45. Brown v. Blauvelt, 152 Conn. 272, 205 A.2d 773 (1964); Jensen v. Elgin, Joliet and Eastern Railway Co., 24 Ill.2d 383, 182 N.E.2d 211 (1962) (diagnosis of ruptured disc was based entirely on "subjective symptoms" and therefore erroneously admitted); Rossello v. Griedel, 243 Md. 234, 220 A.2d 537 (1966); Hinds v. Johnson, 55 Wash.2d 325, 347 P.2d 828 (1959). The uncomfortableness of many courts with this position is evident from the development of methods of circumventing it. Thus the opinion may be given in response to a hypothetical question, Crane Co. v. Industrial Com'n, 32 Ill.2d 348, 205 N.E.2d 425 (1965), and receiving the opinion is not error if the physician testifies that his opinion would have been the same even if he had not heard the history, Liberty Mutual Ins. Co. v. Taylor, 376 S.W.2d 406 (Tex.Civ.App.1964), or if the substance of the history has been proved at trial by competent evidence, Di Marzo v. Columbus Transit Co., 100 Ohio App. 521, 137 N.E.2d 766 (1933). Restrictive definitions of "subjective" evidence have been adopted. Dickeson v. Baltimore & Ohio Chicago Term. R. Co., 42 Ill.2d 103, 245 N.E.2d 762 (1969) (I.Q. test results were not "subjective"); Hinds v. Johnson, 55 Wash.2d 325, 347 P.2d 828 (1959) (results of eye examination not "subjective," although it required obtaining answers from subject as to what he saw).

46. See § 15, supra.

47. E. g., Jensen v. Elgin, Joliet and Eastern Railway Co., 24 Ill.2d 383, 182 N.E.2d 211 (1962); Erdman v. Frazin, 39 Wis.2d 1, 158 N.W.2d 281 (1968).

48. Yellow Cab Co. v. Hicks, 224 Md. 563, 168 A.2d 501 (1961); General Motors Corp. v. Altson, 252 Md. 51, 249 A.2d 130 (1969); Plesko v. Milwaukee, 19 Wis.2d 210, 120 N.W.2d 130 (1963).

49. Yellow Cab Co. v. Hicks, 224 Md. 563, 168 A.2d 501 (1961).

50. Fisher Body Division, General Motors Corp. v. Altson, 252 Md. 51, 249 A.2d 130 (1969).

51. Padgett v. Southern Railway Co., 396 F.2d 303, 308 (6th Cir. 1968) (actual reliance by plaintiff upon physician's advice "is sufficient to eliminate the danger of self-serving declarations made to physician merely to qualify him as an expert for trial."); Conway v. Tamborini, 68 Ill.App.2d 190, 215 N.E.2d 303 (1966) (daily performance of exercises prescribed by physician relied upon in sustaining trial court's finding that consultation was not solely for purposes of obtaining testimony).

It is doubtful whether the restrictions placed upon the testimony of physicians consulted with a view to future litigation can stand vigorous analysis. The task of considering declarations only as an explanation of the basis for an opinion and not as proof of the truth of those declarations is probably beyond the ability and inclination of jurors; the first restriction, then, is probably useless. In view of the difficulty of lay evaluation of complex medical testimony, the second restriction seems to avoid contrived evidence at too great a cost. If jurors are to be expected reasonably to decide cases involving medical issues, they must be provided not only with conclusory opinions but with the full explanation for these opinions. Finally, the third restriction seems entirely unjustified. The general reliance upon "subjective" facts by the medical profession and the ability of its members to evaluate the accuracy of assertions made to them seem sufficient protections against contrived symptoms leading to erroneous expert testimony. The best view would seem to be that no distinction whatsoever should be drawn between the testimony of physicians consulted for treatment and those consulted for purposes of obtaining expert testimony during litigation.[52]

---

294. Declarations of Mental State: (a) Declarations of Present Mental or Emotional State to Show a State of Mind or Emotion in Issue.[53]

The substantive law often makes legal rights and liabilities hinge upon the existence of a state of mind in a person involved in the transaction at issue. When this is so and a legal proceeding arises from the transaction, the mental state of the person becomes an ultimate object of search. It is not sought to be proved as circumstantial evidence of the person's earlier or later conduct but as an operative fact upon which a cause of action or defense depends. While such a state of mind may be proved by the person's actions, the declarations of the person whose state of mind is at issue are often a primary source of evidence on this matter. In most cases, the declarations are not assertive of the declarant's present state of mind and are therefore not necessarily within the hearsay exclusionary rule. Courts, however, have tended to lump together declarations asserting the declarant's state of mind with those tending to prove the state of mind circumstantially, and have developed a general exception to the hearsay rule for them without regard to the possibility that many could be treated simply as nonhearsay.[54]

But see Jensen v. Elgin, Joliet and Eastern Railway Co., 24 Ill.2d 383, 182 N.E.2d 211 (1962) (where plaintiff consulted physician at attorney's request and without knowledge of his regular doctor there was nothing to indicate that plaintiff thought his statements would be used as a basis for treatment and the physician was treated as one consulted solely in anticipation of testimony).

52. F.R.Ev. (R.D.1971) 803(4) provides for the admission of statements describing medical history, or past or present symptoms, pain, sensations, or the inception or general character of the cause or external source "made for purposes of medical *diagnosis or* treatment." (Emphasis supplied.) The commentary indicates that the Advisory Committee saw as the only possible alternative a rule permitting the introduction of these statements for the limited purpose of explaining the basis of the opinion. Since the committee regarded the distinction as unlikely to be made by juries, it therefore rejected any distinction between the situations.

53. See generally, 6 Wigmore, Evidence §§ 1714, 1725–1740; Hinton, States of Mind and the Hearsay Rule, 1 U.Chi.L.Rev. 394 (1934); McBaine, Admissibility in California of Declarations of Physical and Mental Condition, 19 Calif.L.Rev. 231 (1931); Morgan, Evidence 1941–1945, 59 Harv.L. Rev. 481 (1946); 29 Am.Jur.2nd Evidence §§ 650– 652, 654; C.J.S. Evidence §§ 255–258; Dec.Dig. Evidence ⚬268, 269, 271(6), Criminal Law ⚬415 (1), (3), (5).

54. E. g., Rosenbloom v. Metromedia, Inc., 289 F. Supp. 737, 748 (E.D.Pa.1968) rev'd on other grounds 415 F.2d 892 (plaintiff's testimony that former customers stated, "You are a racketeer. We won't have anything to do with you." admissible to establish customer's motive for refusing to deal with plaintiff); Beliveau v. Goodrich, 185 Neb. 98, 173 N.W.2d 877 (1970) (agent's declaration after loss of suit that a new petition would be filed was admissible to prove the bona fides of the defense of the

The special assurance of reliability for declarations of present state of mind rests, as in the case with declarations of bodily condition, upon their spontaneity and probable sincerity.[55] This is assured by the requirements that the declarations must purport to relate to a condition of mind or emotion existing at the time of the statement and must have been made under circumstances indicating apparent sincerity.[56] The special need for use of the declarations does not rest on the unavailability of the declarant—this is not required—but upon the ground that if the declarant were called to testify "his own memory of his state of mind at a former time is no more likely to be clear and true

than a bystander's recollection of what he then said." [57]

Common examples of statements used to prove mental state at the time of the declaration include declarations of intent to make a certain place the declarant's home offered to establish domicile,[58] declarations expressive of mental suffering to prove that element of damages,[59] a statement of willingness to allow one the use of the declarant's automobile offered to prove that the car was used with the owner's consent under the terms of an insurance policy,[60] declarations accompanying a transfer of property showing intent, or lack of intent, to defraud creditors,[61] and declarations of ill will to show malice or the required state of mind in criminal cases.[62]

Although it is required that the declaration describe a state of mind or feeling existing at the time of the declaration, the evidentiary effect of the declaration is broadened by the notion of the continuity in time of

first suit); Doern v. Crawford, 36 Wis.2d 470, 153 N.W.2d 581 (1967) (statement of plaintiff that he did not like being away from his wife was admissible to prove his intent that his absence was only temporary where plaintiff's status as an insured under an insurance policy depended upon whether his absence was intended to be permanent). Some courts are drawing the distinction between declarations which are not hearsay and those which, because they are hearsay, must come within an exception. E. g., Betts v. Betts, 3 Wash. App. 53, 473 P.2d 403 (1970), rev. denied, (child's statement, "[Daddy] killed my brother and he'll kill my mommie too" nonhearsay and admissible in custody case to show child's state of mind; excellent discussion to distinction between nonhearsay declarations and those admissible only under state of mind exception); Atlanta Gas Light Co. v. Slaton, 117 Ga.App. 317, 160 So.2d 414 (1968) (testimony that person observed tampering with gas meter had said, "I am trying to see what is the matter with the gas" admissible as circumstantial evidence of the motive of the person who may have caused gas to flow into plaintiff's house). Some courts, however, continue to ignore the distinction (or its legal significance). See, e. g., Fulmer v. State, 445 S.W.2d 546 (Tex.Civ.App.1969) (testimony that juror in barratry case said before trial, "[The defendant] ought to be stopped from practicing law", labeled as circumstantial evidence of state of mind but held admissible under an exception to hearsay rule).

55. See 6 Wigmore, Evidence § 1714.

56. Elmer v. Fessenden, 151 Mass. 359, 24 N.E. 208 (1889) (must be "made with no apparent motive for misstatement"); Hall v. American Friends Service Committee, Inc., 74 Wash.2d 467, 445 P.2d 616 (1968) (must be "circumstantial probability" of trustworthiness). But see Smith v. Smith, 364 Pa. 1, 70 A.2d 530 (1950) (self-serving nature of declaration goes only to weight).

57. Mutual Life Ins. Co. v. Hillmon, 145 U.S. 285, 295 (1892).

58. Matter of Newcomb, 192 N.Y. 238, 84 N.E. 950 (1908) (evidence that testatrix wrote to friends indicating her intention to make New Orleans her permanent home admissible); Smith v. Smith, 364 Pa. 1, 70 A.2d 630 (1950) (statement of intent to live in Florida admissible). See generally, 6 Wigmore, Evidence §§ 1727, 1984; Note, Evidentiary Factors in the Determination of Domicile, 61 Harv. L.Rev. 1232, 1237 (1948).

59. Missouri, K. & T.R. Co. v. Linton, 141 S.W. 129 (Tex.Civ.App.1911) (plaintiff's statement that "She felt like her heart would burst and that she could not live" admissible to prove damages for mental anguish).

60. American Employers Ins. Co. v. Wentworth, 90 N.H. 112, 5 A.2d 265 (1939).

61. Sanger Brothers v. Colbert, 84 Tex. 668, 19 S.W. 863 (1892) (transferor's statement when receiving price that he intended to pay his debts admissible).

62. E. g., Hall v. State, 31 Tex.Cr.R. 565, 21 S.W. 368 (1893) (threats against victim admissible in murder case in which accused introduced evidence of intoxication to disprove malice). See generally, 6 Wigmore, Evidence § 1732; Note, 20 Tex.L.Rev. 487 (1942).

states of mind. For example, if a declarant tells on Tuesday of his then-existing intention to go on a business trip for his employer the next day, this will be evidence not only of his intention at the time of the declaration but also of a similar purpose the next day when he is on the road.[63] Continuity may also look backwards. Thus, when there is evidence that a will has been mutilated by the maker, his subsequent declarations of a purpose inconsistent with the will are received to show his intent to revoke it at the time he mutilated it.[64] Similarly, whether payment of money or a conveyance was intended by the donor as a gift may be shown by his declaration made before, at the time of, or after the act or transfer.[65] Since, however, the duration of states of mind or emotion varies with the particular attitudes or feelings at issue and with the cause, it is reasonable to require as a condition of invoking the continuity notion that the declaration mirror a state of mind which, in light of all the circumstances including proximity in time, has some probability of being the same condition existing at the material time. Where there is room for doubt, the matter should be left to the discretion of the trial judge.

Declarations such as those involved here frequently include assertions other than as to state of mind, as, for example, assertions that the defendant's acts caused the state of mind. The truth of those assertions may coincide with other issues in the case, such as whether the defendant's acts did in fact cause the state of mind. When this is so, the normal practice is to admit the declaration and direct the jury to consider it only in proof of the state of mind and to disregard it as evidence of the other issues.[66] Compliance with these instructions is probably beyond the jury's ability and almost certainly beyond their willingness. Where there is adequate evidence on the other issues, this probably does little harm. But in a case where the mental state is provable by other available evidence and the danger of harm from improper use by the jury of the offered declarations is substantial, the judge's discretion to exclude the declarations has been recognized.[67]

---

63. Lewis v. Lowe & Campbell Athletic Goods Co., 247 S.W.2d 800 (Mo.1952). See also Ickes v. Ickes, 237 Pa. 582, 85 Atl. 885 (1912) (husband's declarations on day before leaving wife admissible to prove his motive on that day and the next when he did leave); In re Goldsberry's Estate, 95 Utah 379, 81 P.2d 1106 (1938) (declarations of testator on day before will executed admissible to show undue influence on that day and on next when will was executed).

64. Crampton v. Osborn, 356 Mo. 125, 201 S.W.2d 336 (1947).

65. Casey v. Casey, 97 Cal.App.2d 875, 218 P.2d 842 (1950) (declarations of decedent after conveyance admissible to show whether it was intended as gift or in trust); O'Neal v. O'Neal, 9 N.J. Super. 36, 74 A.2d 614 (1950) (oral declarations of transferor of land admissible to rebut resulting trust. It has been held that if the donor's words at the time of transfer unequivocally indicate an intent to make a gift, his subsequent declarations to the contrary will not be received. Shaver v. Canfield, 21 Cal.App.2d 734, 70 P.2d 507 (1937); Wilbur v. Grover, 140 Mich. 187, 103 N.W. 583 (1905). But this has been held inapplicable where the issue is whether there was, at the time of transfer, the intent required for delivery and thus for a gift. Williams v. Kidd, 170 Cal. 631, 151 Pac. 1 (1915). See generally, Annot., 105 A.L.R. 399, 402, 410.

66. Greater New York Live Poultry Chamber of Commerce v. United States, 47 F.2d 156 (2d Cir. 1931) (in prosecution for conspiracy to restrain interstate trade in poultry, declarations of receivers as to why they refused to sell to recalcitrant market men admissible to show state of mind of declarants but not to show external facts asserted as the basis for this state of mind, and defendant would have been entitled to such an instruction had he requested it); Adkins v. Brett, 194 Cal. 252, 193 Pac. 251 (1920) (in alienation of affection case, wife's statements concerning relations with defendant admissible to show feelings of wife but not to prove acts and conduct of defendant described in the statements); Johnson v. Richards, 50 Idaho 150, 294 Pac. 507 (1930) (husband's declarations concerning wife, when admissible in suit for alienation of affections, competent only to prove husband's state of mind); Elmer v. Fessenden, 151 Mass. 359, 24 N.E. 208 (1889); Schoot v. Townsend, 106 Tex. 322, 166 S.W. 1138 (1914).

67. See the excellent discussion by Olney, J. in Adkins v. Brett, 184 Cal. 252, 193 Pac. 251, 254

295. Declarations of Mental State: (b) Declarations of Intention Offered to Show Subsequent Acts of Declarant.[68]

In the previous section, it was made clear that declarations of mental state are generally admissible to prove the declarant's state of mind when that state of mind is at issue. But the probative value of a state of mind obviously goes beyond the state of mind itself, as indicated by general acceptance of the proposition that evidence of design or intent is relevant and admissible to show conduct.[69] Where a state of mind would tend to prove subsequent conduct, can the two inferential processes be linked together and the declarations of state of mind be admitted as proof of the conduct? Can, in other words, X's declarations indicating an intent to kill Y be admitted to prove that intent and also that X did in fact subsequently kill Y? The problem at the latter point becomes one of relevancy.

This presents a somewhat more difficult question than the matter of admissibility of declarations to show only the state of mind. The special reliability of the declarations is less in the present situation, since it is sig-

nificantly less likely that a declared intention will be carried out than it is that a declared state of mind is actually held. X's declaration that he intends to kill Y is much stronger proof that at the time of the declaration (or subsequently) X bore Y malice than it is proof that X in fact later killed Y. In addition, it is arguable that there is less special need for the use of declarations of state of mind to prove conduct than there is for use of such declarations to prove state of mind as an end in itself. State of mind is a matter inherently difficult of proof; where it is at issue, the usual absence of other evidence reliably tending to prove it arguably justifies relaxing normal exclusionary rules in order to bring in the declarations of the person best able to know the state of mind. On the other hand, this special difficulty of proof does not exist generally in regard to conduct, so arguably there is less justification for relaxation where it is at issue.

Despite the failure until recently to recognize the potential value of declarations of state of mind to prove subsequent conduct, it is now clear that out-of-court statements which tend to prove a plan, design, or intention of the declarant are admissible, subject to the usual limitations as to remoteness in time and apparent sincerity common to all declarations of mental state, to prove that the plan, design, or intention of the declarant was carried out by the declarant.[70] The lead-

---

(1920), suggesting that the party against whom such evidence "is introduced is entitled to such protection against its misuse as can reasonably be given him without impairing the ability of the other party to prove his case, or depriving him of the use of competent evidence reasonably necessary for that purpose." In some cases, he suggests, the portion of the statement tending to prove the acts can be separated from that tending to prove state of mind, in which event only the latter should be admitted. See § 185, supra, for discussion of balancing probative value against prejudicial effect.

68. See generally, 6 Wigmore, Evidence §§ 1725–26; Hinton, States of Mind and the Hearsay Rule, 1 U.Chi.L.Rev. 394 (1934); Hutchins and Slesinger, Some Observations on the Law of Evidence—State of Mind to Prove an Act, 38 Yale L.J. 283 (1929); J. Maguire, The Hillmon Case—Thirty-three Years After, 38 Harv.L.Rev. 709 (1925); Seligman, An Exception to the Hearsay Rule, 26 Harv.L.Rev. 146 (1912); 29 Am.Jur.2nd Evidence § 653; C.J.S. Evidence § 256, p. 675.

69. See 1 Wigmore, Evidence § 102.

70. E. g., United States v. Annunziato, 293 F.2d 373 (2d Cir. 1961) (testimony that H. Terker said that he had received a phone call from defendant requesting some money and that he had agreed to deliver it admissible to prove delivery); Nuttall v. Reading Co., 235 F.2d 546, 551–52 (3d Cir. 1956) (testimony that deceased asked his employer over the phone, "Why are you forcing me to come to work the way I feel?" and then said, "I guess I will have to come, then," admissible in FELA case to prove that deceased did go to work under compulsion); Smith v. Slifer, 1 Cal.App.3d 748, 81 Cal.Rptr. 871 (1969) (deceased's declarations tending to show that she intended to pay defendant for automobile rides admissible to prove that payments were made); Maryland Paper Products Co. v. Judson, 215 Md. 557, 139 A.2d 219 (1958) (wife's

ing case is Mutual Life Ins. Co. v. Hillmon,[71] arising out of a suit on life insurance policies by the wife of the insured, Hillmon. The principal issue was whether Hillmon had in fact died; a body had been found at Crooked Creek, Kansas, and the parties disputed whether the body was that of Hillmon. Plaintiff's theory was that Hillmon had left Wichita, Kansas, about March 5, 1879, with one Brown and that on the night of March 18, 1879, while Hillmon and Brown were camped at Crooked Creek, Hillmon was killed by the accidental discharge of a gun. The defendants, on the other hand, maintained that one Walters had accompanied Hillmon and that the body found at Crooked Creek was Walters'. Defendants offered testimony that Walters had, on or about March 5, 1879, written to his sister that "I expect to leave Wichita on or about March 5, with a certain Mr. Hillmon." An objection to this and similar evidence was sustained. The United States Supreme Court reversed on the ground that the evidence of the letters should have been admitted:

> "The letters . . . were competent not as narratives of facts communicated to the writer by others, nor yet as proof that he actually went away from Wichita, but as evidence that, shortly before the time when other evidence tended to show that he went away, he had the intention of going, and of going with Hillmon, which made it more probable both that he did go and that he went with Hillmon than if there had been no proof of such intention." [72]

There are two limitations which might be imposed upon the use of declarations for this purpose, although the decisions indicate that courts have been unwilling to impose them. First, since the need for the testimony is arguably greater when the declarant is unavailable as a witness, it might be reasonable to limit this use of the declarations to those cases.[73] Although in most of the cases admitting the declarations for this purpose the declarant has in fact been unavailable, the decisions do not indicate that this is a requirement. Second, the danger of unreliability is greatly increased when the action sought to be proved is not one that the declarant could have performed alone but rather is one that required the cooperation of another person. If completion of a plan or design requires not only the continued inclination and ability of the declarant to complete it but also the inclination and ability of someone else, arguably the likelihood that the design or plan was completed is substantially less. Use of declarations of state of mind to prove subsequent conduct might, then, be limited to proof of conduct that would not have required the substantial cooperation of persons other than the declarant. Despite some objection,[74] however,

73. See the suggestion in Hutchins and Slesinger, Some Observations on the Law of Evidence—State of Mind to Prove an Act, 38 Yale L.J. 283, 289 (1929). Hinton, States of Mind and the Hearsay Rule, 1 U.Chi.L.Rev. 394, 416 (1934) takes the opposite position.

74. Cf. the dissenting opinion by Mr. Justice Traynor in People v. Alcalde, 24 Cal.2d 177, 148 P.2d 627, 633 (1944):

> "It is my opinion that the trial court erred in admitting the testimony that the deceased said . . . that she was going out with 'Frank' [the evening of her murder] . . . . A declaration of intention is admissible to show that the declarant did the intended act. . . . A declaration as to what one person intended to do, however, cannot safely be accepted as evidence of what another probably did. . . . The declaration of the deceased in this case that she was going out with Frank is also a declaration that he was going out with her, and it could not be ad-

testimony that deceased told her that it would be necessary to go to work because he had to stop off on the way to pick up a gear wheel admissible to prove that deceased had in fact picked up the gear wheel).

71. 145 U.S. 285 (1892). The case is discussed in the sources cited in n. 68, supra.

72. 145 U.S. at 295–96.

courts have not imposed the limitation. In *Hillmon* itself, in fact, Walters' successful completion of his plan to leave Wichita depended upon the continued willingness of Hillmon to have Walters as a companion and upon Hillmon's willingness and ability to leave at the time planned. Nevertheless, the Supreme Court failed even to consider this aspect of the case.[75]

A further related problem is raised when the declarant's statements tend to prove co-operative actions on the part of others. If those cooperative actions themselves are at issue, there is a significant danger that the jury will use the declarant's statements as proof not only of the declarant's actions but also of the cooperative actions by a third person. In effect, the declarant's statement will be taken as proof of the other person's intent and as proof that this intent was carried out. For example, in the homicide prosecution of Frank, a witness testifies that on the morning of the killing the victim said, "I am going out with Frank tonight." While this tends to prove the victim's acts, it also tends to prove that Frank went out with the victim, a fact very much in issue. Despite the danger that juries will be neither willing nor able to make the distinction, courts have tended to admit the statements in these cases

with limiting instructions directing the jury to consider them only on the issue of the declarant's actions.[76]

Acceptance of this use of declarations of state of mind and recognition of occasions for its application have differed among types of situations. In will cases, for example, it is now generally established that when the acts of the decedent are at issue, his previous declarations of intention are received as evidence of his later conduct.[77] Such declarations may come in on issues of forgery,[78] alteration,[79] contents of a will,[80] and whether acts of revocation were done by the testa-

---

mitted for the limited purpose of showing that she went out with him at the time in question without necessarily showing that he went with her."

The concern of Mr. Justice Traynor is with the use of the declaration to prove an act on the part of one other than the declarant when that act is itself an important issue in the case. Much the same objection, however, can be raised to using the declaration to prove only the act of the declarant when that act must necessarily have involved cooperative acts by others, even cooperative acts not directly at issue or material.

75. In addition to People v. Alcalde, 24 Cal.2d 177, 148 P.2d 627 (1944), discussed in note 74, supra, see Hunter v. State, 40 N.J.L. 495 (1878) (declaration of murder victim that he was going on a business trip with the accused properly admitted). And State v. Vestal, 278 N.C. 561, 180 S.E.2d 755 (1971) (same).

76. See the cases cited in n. 75, supra. See also, State v. Farnam, 82 Ore. 211, 161 P. 417 (1916) involving a homicide prosecution. Testimony was received that on the day of the killing the victim, when invited to a friend's house, replied that she could not come because she thought the accused was coming. This was affirmed, although the appellate court indicated that the defendant would have been entitled to a limiting instruction had he requested one. An even more difficult feat by the jury may be called for by an instruction limiting the purpose of the evidence to proving opportunity. State v. Phillips, 68 N.D. 113, 277 N.W. 609 (1938), noted 86 U.Pa.L.Rev. 904.

See also State v. Gause, 489 P.2d 830 (Ariz.1971), holding that "when in human experience they have sufficient reliability" expressions of fear by a homicide victim that the defendant would kill him are admissible in the defendant's trial to prove his identity as the killer. Apparently this is not on the theory that fear is evidence of conduct by the defendant justifying the fear (see § 296, infra, note 13), but rather on the theory that the victim's reasonable anticipation that the defendant would kill him is admissible to prove that the defendant fulfilled that expectation.

77. See 6 Wigmore, Evidence § 1735.

78. Atherton v. Gaslin, 194 Ky. 460, 239 S.W. 771 (1922); State v. Ready, 78 N.J.L. 599, 75 Atl. 564 (Ct. of Errors and Appeals, 1909); Johnson v. Brown, 51 Tex. 65, (1879). Contra, Throckmorton v. Holt, 180 U.S. 552 (1901). Such evidence, however, weighs lightly when contradicted by the testimony of expert document examiners. See In re Creger's Estate, 135 Okl. 77, 274 Pac. 30 (1929). See generally, Annot., 119 A.L.R. 1366; Annot., 62 A.L.R. 698.

79. Doe d.Schallcross v. Palmer, 16 Q.B. 747, 117 Eng.Rep. 1067 (1851).

80. Sugden v. Lord St. Leonards, 1 Prob.Div. 154 (Ct.App.1876).

tor.[81] Despite early decisions to the contrary, or decisions greatly restricting their use,[82] declarations of intent to commit suicide have been admitted when offered by the accused in homicide cases to prove that the victim took his own life and in insurance cases to show that the insured took his own life.[83] There has been greater resistance, however, to accepting in criminal cases threats of a third person to commit the act with which the accused is charged as evidence that the act was committed by the third person and therefore not by the accused. Although some opinions suggest an absolute exclusionary rule,[84] others recognize a discretionary power in the trial judge to admit them if he finds sufficient accompanying evidence of motive, overt acts, opportunity, or other circumstances giving substantial significance to the threats.[85]

Homicide and assault cases present another special problem. If the accused claims self-defense, and threats of the victim were known to the accused, these threats are admissible to prove the accused's apprehension of danger and its reasonableness.[86] When used for this purpose, of course, the declarations of the victim are not hearsay. But uncommunicated threats pose a more serious problem. They are admissible, if at all, to show the victim's intention to attack the accused and further that he carried out his intention, thus committing the first act of aggression in the fatal altercation.[87] Fear that juries will abuse the evidence has led some courts [88] to admit proof of uncommuni-

---

81. Stuart v. McWhorter, 238 Ky. 82, 36 S.W.2d 842 (1931). See generally, Annot., 115 A.L.R. 713; Annot., 79 A.L.R. 1403.

82. E. g., Commonwealth v. Felch, 132 Mass. 22 (1882); State v. Punshon, 124 Mo. 448, 27 S.W. 1111 (1894), both overruled by decisions cited in n. 83, infra. See generally, 6 Wigmore, Evidence § 1726 n. 4.

83. Probably the leading homicide case is Commonwealth v. Trefethen, 157 Mass. 180, 31 N.E. 961 (1892), overruling previous case law. See also People v. Salcido, 246 Cal.App.2d 450, 54 Cal.Rptr. 820 (1966); People v. Parriera, 237 Cal.App.2d 275, 46 Cal.Rptr. 835 (1965); Bowie v. State, 185 Ark. 834, 49 S.W.2d 1049 (1932); State v. Ilgenfritz, 215 Mo. 615, 173 S.W. 1041 (1915); Commonwealth v. Santos, 275 Pa. 515, 119 A. 596 (1932). In regard to insurance cases, see Browner v. Royal Indemnity Co., 246 F. 637 (5th Cir. 1917); Smith v. National Beneficial Society, 123 N.Y. 85, 25 N.E. 197 (1890); Klein v. Knights and Ladies of Security, 87 Wash. 179, 151 P. 241 (1915). See generally, Annot., 86 A.L.R. 146, 157; Dec.Dig. Homicide ⟨⟩177. Cf. Annot., 93 A.L.R. 413, 426 (admissibility of declarations of insured to negative defense of suicide).

84. People v. King, 276 Ill. 138, 114 N.E. 601 (1916); Buel v. State, 104 Wis. 132, 80 N.W. 78 (1899). See generally, 1 Wigmore, Evidence § 140.

85. Alexander v. United States, 138 U.S. 353 (1891); Marrone v. State, 359 P.2d 969, 984–85 (Alas. 1961); People v. Perkins, 59 P.2d 1069, 1074–75 (Cal.App.) aff'd 8 Cal.2d 502, 66 P.2d 631 (1937); Dubose v. State, 10 Tex.App. 230 (1881). The re-

stricted admissibility of the evidence has been justified as follows:

"[T]his rule . . . rests fundamentally upon the same considerations which led to the early adoption of the elementary rules that evidence to be admissible must be both relevant and material. It rests upon the necessity that trials of cases must be both orderly and expeditious . . . . To this end it is necessary that the scope of inquiry into collateral and unimportant issues must be severely limited. It is quite apparent that if evidence of motive alone upon the part of other persons were admissible, that in a case involving the killing of a man who had led an active and aggressive life it might be possible for the defendant to produce evidence tending to show that hundreds of other persons had some motive or animus against the deceased; that a great many trial days might be consumed in the pursuit of inquiries which could not be expected to lead to any satisfactory conclusion." People v. Mendez, 193 Cal. 39, 223 P. 65, 70 (1924).

86. State v. Jackson, 94 Ariz. 117, 383 P.2d 229 (1963); Decker v. State, 234 Ark. 518, 353 S.W.2d 168 (1962); State v. Mitchell, 144 Me. 320, 68 A.2d 387 (1949). See generally, 2 Wigmore, Evidence § 249; Dec.Dig. Homicide ⟨⟩190(8).

87. See the discussion in Commonwealth v. Rubin, 318 Mass. 587, 63 N.E.2d 344 (1945). Communicated threats are also admissible for this purpose, of course, but this use is usually ignored because of their stronger significance as proof of reasonable apprehension by the accused. See generally 18 U.Chi.L.Rev. 337 (1951); Annot., 98 A.L.R.2d 9 (homicide cases); Annot., 98 A.L.R.2d 195 (assault cases); Dec.Dig. Homicide ⟨⟩190(7).

88. Some courts have held the evidence admissible without mention of qualification. Carnes v. Commonwealth, 453 S.W.2d 595 (Ky.App.1970). Others have held it inadmissible without mention of any

cated threats only under qualification. Some of them require only that there be some additional evidence that the victim was the aggressor; testimony by the accused will ordinarily be sufficient.[89] Others require that proof other than the accused's own testimony must admit of some doubt that the accused was the aggressor.[90] Still others hold that the other evidence must itself be sufficient to present a jury question on the issue of which participant was the initial aggressor.[91]

The matter of the admissibility of declarations of state of mind to prove subsequent conduct is a far different question from that of the sufficiency of these declarations, standing alone, to support a finding that the conduct occurred.[92] It has reasonably been said that the declarations are themselves insufficient to support the finding and there-

fore that declarations of intention are admitted in corroboration of other evidence to show the acts.[93]

296. Declarations of Mental State: (c) Declarations of State of Mind to Show Memory or Belief as Proof of Previous Happenings.[94]

The holding of Mutual Life Ins. Co. v. Hillmon[95] that declarations of state of mind tending to show a plan or intent to perform an act are admissible as proof that the act was performed[96] has been criticised on the ground that its logical consequence would be to require that declarations of state of mind also be received to prove memory and belief that the declarant has performed an act in the past as proof of the performance of that act. Taken one step further, declarations of present memory might be admitted to prove that the declarant observed the matter remembered and therefore that it existed or occurred. Either, it has been urged, would amount to allowing the exception for declarations of mental state to swallow substantially the entire hearsay rule.[97]

Forty years after *Hillmon,* the Supreme Court of the United States specifically declined so to extend the rule of that case. In Shepard v. United States,[98] a murder prosecution, the trial court had admitted testimony that the victim, the wife of the physi-

---

circumstances in which it might be properly admitted. Burgess v. State, 226 Ga. 529, 175 S.E.2d 829 (1970).

89. Rowell v. State, 105 So.2d 877 (Ala.App.1958) (must be a "showing" of self-defense); Harris v. State, 400 P.2d 64 (Okl.Cr.1965) (some other evidence to support a plea of self-defense).

90. Sanders v. State, 245 Ark. 321, 432 S.W.2d 467 (1968) (must be doubt as to who was aggressor); Decker v. State, 234 Ark. 518, 353 S.W.2d 168 (1962); Bowyer v. State, 2 Md.App. 454, 235 A.2d 317 (1967) (must be some evidence of self-defense and some question as to who was aggressor); State v. Debo, 8 Ohio App.2d 325, 222 N.E.2d 656 (1966) (evidence must leave it doubtful who was aggressor).

91. State v. Murdle, 5 N.C.App. 610, 169 S.E.2d 17 (1969) (requiring "testimony *ultra* sufficient to carry the case to the jury tending to show that the killing may have been done from a principle of self preservation"). Some courts would apparently require that the proof amount to a showing of some specific overt act on the part of the victim. State v. Mitchell, 144 Me. 320, 68 A.2d 387 (1949) (must be evidence of some act on the part of the victim that might constitute an attack justifying self-defense); Shinall v. State, 199 So.2d 251 (Miss.1967) cert. denied 389 U.S. 1014 (other proof must show some overt act at the time of the homicide that would cause the slayer to believe that his life was in imminent danger).

92. See Atherton v. Gaslin, 194 Ky. 460, 239 S.W. 771 (1922).

93. E. g., Prichard v. Harvey, 272 Ky. 58, 113 S.W.2d 865 (1938) (declarations alone insufficient to rebut presumption of revocation of lost will).

94. See generally, Hinton, States of Mind and the Hearsay Rule, 1 U.Chi.L.Rev. 394, 403–23 (1934); Hutchins and Slesinger, Some Observations on the Law of Evidence—State of Mind to Prove an Act, 38 Yale L.J. 283, 289–98 (1929); J. Maguire, The Hillmon Case—Thirty-three Years After, 38 Harv.L. Rev. 709, 719–31 (1925); Seligman, An Exception to the Hearsay Rule, 26 Harv.L.Rev. 146 (1912).

95. 145 U.S. 285 (1891).

96. See § 295 at n. 71, supra.

97. Seligman, An Exception to the Hearsay Rule, 26 Harv.L.Rev. 146, 157 (1912).

98. 290 U.S. 96 (1933).

cian-defendant, had stated to a nurse, "Dr. Shepard has poisoned me." Reversing, the Supreme Court rejected the argument that the statement was admissible as a declaration of state of mind:

> "[Mutual Life Ins. Co. v. Hillmon] marks the high water line beyond which courts have been unwilling to do. It has developed a substantial body of criticism and commentary. Declarations of intention, casting light upon the future, have been sharply distinguished from declarations of memory, pointing backwards to the past. There would be an end, or nearly that, to the rule against hearsay if the distinction were ignored.

> "The testimony now questioned faced backwards and not forward. This at least it did in its most obvious implications. What is even more important, it spoke of a past act by someone not the speaker.[99] "

Since *Shepard*, the basis for the hearsay rule has come under increasing scrutiny, with the result that blanket exclusion of statements of memory or belief to prove past events has been increasingly questioned. In the case law, however, the exclusion has generally survived except in will cases. By the preponderance of recent decisions, a testator's declarations made after the alleged event are received to show that he has or has not made a will, or that he has made a will of a particular purport, or that he has or has not revoked a will.[1] Some courts reach

this result by adopting a special exception to the hearsay rule for retrospective declarations in will cases.[2] This can be defended on the ground that special need exists by virtue of the fact that the testator, usually the one who best knew the facts and often the only one with such knowledge, is unavailable. Special reliability is strongly suggested by firsthand knowledge and the lack of selfish interest,[3] although there is often the possibility that the testator may have wanted to deceive his relatives.[4] Other courts have regarded these declarations as statements of belief or memory raising the circumstantial inference that the belief must have been prompted by facts, and therefore within the

---

99. Id. at 105–06.

1. Loy v. Loy, 246 S.W.2d 578 (Ky.App.1952) (declarations of testator competent to corroborate other evidence of execution); Lewis v. Lewis, 241 Miss. 83, 129 So.2d 353 (1961) (testimony that deceased had said, "I have got [my will] right here in my pocket" admissible to show existence of will when authorship of offered holographic will in doubt); In re Roeder's Estate, 44 N.M. 429, 103 P.2d 631 (1940) (declarations admissible to corroborate other evidence of changes in will); In re Karras' Estate, 109 Ohio App. 403, 166 N.E.2d 781 (1959) (declara-

tions of deceased in regard to execution of will admissible where execution was at issue). Contra, Barger v. Barger, 221 Ind. 530, 48 N.E.2d 813 (1943) (post-testamentary declarations inadmissible as evidence of contents of will); Hursh v. Crook, 292 S.W.2d 305 (Mo.1956) (where genuineness of signature at issue, deceased's statement that "Katie wrote my name and I saw her do it" inadmissible). Such declarations, if admissible, are probably not enough to sustain a finding. Loy v. Loy, 246 S.W. 2d 578 (Ky.App.1952) (declarations of deceased alone not enough to sustain a finding of execution of a lost will). See generally 6 Wigmore, Evidence § 1736; Annot., 28 A.L.R.3d 994 (admissibility of declarations of testator on issue of revocation by mutilation, alteration or cancellation); Annot., 5 A.L.R.3d 360 (admissibility of declaration of testator on mistake of fact); Annot., 68 A.L.R.2d 855 (admissibility of declarations of testator on genuineness of purported will); Annot., 41 A.L.R.2d 393, 399–400 (admissibility of declarations of testator to prove due execution of lost will): Annots., 148 A.L.R. 1225, 79 A.L.R. 1447 (1932) (admissibility of testator's declaration on undue influence); Dec. Dig. Wills ☞297.

See also West's Ann.Cal.Evid.Code, § 1260; F.R.Ev. (R.D.1971) 803(3).

2. Loy v. Loy, 246 S.W.2d 578 (Ky.App.1952); In re Roeder's Estate, 44 N.M. 429, 103 P.2d 631 (1940).

3. See the argument of Jessell, M.R. in Sugden v. Lord St. Leonards, L.R. [1876] 1 Prob.Div. 154, 241 (Ct.App.).

4. Boylan v. Meeker, 28 N.J.L. 274, 283 (1860):

"A devisor . . . . may, to secure his own peace and comfort during life, to relieve himself from unpleasant importunities of expectant heirs, conceal the nature of his testamentary dispositions, and make statements calculated and intended to deceive those with whom he is conversing."

present exception.[5] In the alternative, the declarations may be regarded not as statements offered to prove the truth of assertions contained therein, but as conduct circumstantially evincing a belief and thus not falling within a restrictive definition of hearsay.[6]

Commentators and legislatures have shown somewhat more willingness than courts to expand the law in this area. Legislation in some states, for example, allows receipt of declarations of a deceased person made in good faith and upon personal knowledge before the commencement of the action.[7] The Model Code of Evidence provided broadly for the admission of any hearsay declaration of an unavailable declarant.[8] The Uniform Rules of Evidence would require, in addition to the unavailability of the declarant, that the statement describe or explain an event or condition recently perceived by the declarant while his recollection was clear and that it have been made in good faith prior to the commencement of the action in which it is offered.[9] The commentary to the Uniform Rule indicates that the draftsmen were aware of "an attitude of reluctance" regarding this type of evidence and that they intended to require "most careful scrutiny" before its admission.[10] The Proposed Rules of Evidence for the Federal Courts go somewhat further in limiting the admissibility of such evidence. "A statement . . . . which narrates, describes, or explains an event or condition" is admissible only if (a) the declarant is unavailable, (b) the condition or event was recently perceived by the declarant, (c) the declarant's recollection was clear at the time of the statement, (d) the statement was made in good faith, (e) the statement was made not in contemplation of pending or anticipated litigation in which the declarant was interested, and (f) the statement was not in response to the instigation of a person engaged in investigating, litigating, or settling a claim.[11]

The commentators are clearly in advance of the courts,[12] although there is some evi-

5.   Keen v. Keen, L.R. 1873, 3 P. & D. 105; 6 Wigmore, Evidence § 1736, p. 115.

6.   Sugden v. Lord St. Leonards, L.R. [1876] 1 Prob. Div. 154, 202.

7.   Mass.Gen.Laws Ann. c. 233, § 65; R.I.Gen.Laws 1956, § 9–19–11.

8.   Model Code of Evidence Rule 503(a).

9.   Uniform Rule 63(4) (c). Uniform Rule 63(12) specifically excludes evidence of "memory or belief to prove the fact remembered or believed." See also West's Ann.Cal.Evid.Code, § 1250; F.R.Ev. (R.D. 1971) 803(3).

10.   Uniform Rules, Comment to Rule 63(4) (c).

11.   F.R.Ev. (R.D.1971) 804(b) (2). The final requirement was imposed to meet criticism that the broad language of the Uniform Rules permitted the use of the statements carefully prepared under the direction of lawyers, claim adjusters, or investigators. Id., Advisory Committee's Note.

12.   Most courts still indicate a reluctance to admit this kind of testimony in most cases. See United States v. Murray, 297 F.2d 812, 816 (2d Cir. 1962) cert. denied 369 U.S. 828 (objection properly sustained to question as to whether given individual ever indicated that he had lent Ed Murray money because this would tend primarily to show whether or not such a loan had been made); Pope v. United States, 296 F.Supp. 17, 19–20 (S.D.Cal.1968) (testimony of decedent stated she had earlier bargained for transfer of trust remainder to children in 1936 not admissible to prove what was bargained for in 1936); State v. Vestal, 278 N.C. 561, 180 S.E.2d 755 (1971) (error to admit note written by homicide victim which would tend to prove victim's assertion that facts existed which would give defendant motive to kill victim, although victim's statements of intent to go on trip with victim were admissible). Where, however, strong need exists and indications of reliability are present, some courts have admitted it. Lee v. Mitcham, 69 App.D.C. 17, 98 F.2d 298 (1938) (notes jotted by deceased on note to the effect that it had not been paid but only transferred to him admitted); Yarborough v. Prudential Insurance Co., 99 F.2d 874, on rehearing, 100 F.2d 547 (5th Cir. 1939) (widow-beneficiary permitted to testify that her husband had handed her insurance policy and said it was paid for); Quayle v. Mackert, 92 Idaho 563, 447 P.2d 679 (1968) (in action for constructive trust, conveyance of title and quieting title to realty held by deceased based on theory that deceased had made an oral contract to devise land to plaintiff after death, testimony of neighbors and businessmen that deceased said he would leave land to plaintiff admitted to prove oral contract, with heavy reliance by analogy on will cases). See also Lloyd v. Powell Duffryn Steam Coal Co. Ltd., L.R. [1914] App.C. 733 (House of

dence of an increased judicial willingness to admit evidence of memory or belief to prove the fact remembered or believed when this is closely related to declarations tending to prove intent or plan.[13] A more liberal view than has traditionally been taken by most courts may be appropriate.[14]

297. Excited Utterances.[15]

Although some still discuss the matter under the terminology of *res gestae*,[16] all courts

Lords) (in action by alleged illegitimate child under Workmen's Compensation Act, declarations of deceased that he knew of pregnancy of child's mother and that he intended to marry her admitted to prove paternity and probability that he would have supported the child).

13. United States v. Annunziato, 293 F.2d 373 (2d Cir. 1961) cert. denied 368 U.S. 919 (Friendly, J.). A witness had testified that his father had told him that he (the father) had received a call from Annunziato requesting some money for a specific project and that he had agreed to send it. This was held admissible to prove the fact of the phone call as well as the subsequent delivery of the money.

See also People v. Merkouris, 52 Cal.2d 672, 344 P.2d 1 (1959) holding homicide victims' statements that defendant had threatened them admissible, not to prove "directly" that threats had been made but to prove victims' fear. Such fear was relevant "because it is some evidence that they had reason to fear him." Overruled by West's Ann.Cal.Evid.Code § 1250(b); see Comment—Assembly Committee on Judiciary.

14. In the absence of additional foundation, this would not mean that the declaration offered in Shepard v. United States (see text at note 98, supra) would be admissible. There was in that case no indication that the declarant had any opportunity to know that her husband had in fact poisoned her.

15. See generally, 6 Wigmore, Evidence §§ 1745–64; Hutchins and Slesinger, Spontaneous Exclamations, 28 Colum.L.Rev. 432 (1928); Slough, Spontaneous Statements and State of Mind, 46 Iowa L.Rev. 224 (1961); Notes, 45 Cornell L.Q. 810 (1960), 29 La.L. Rev. 661 (1969), 54 Mich.L.Rev. 133 (1955), 22 Minn. L.Rev. 391 (1938); Annot., 13 A.L.R.3rd 1114 (statements relating to cause of fires); Annot., 4 A.L.R. 3rd 149 (accusatory statements by homicide victims); Annot., 78 A.L.R.2d 300 (statements by bystanders at time of arrest); Annot., 53 A.L.R 2d 1245 (statements relating to cause of motor vehicle accidents); Annot., 163 A.L.R. 15 (in actions founded on accidents); 29 Am.Jur.2nd Evidence §§ 708–737; C.J.S. Evidence §§ 403–421; Dec.Dig. Evidence ⚮118–128½, Criminal Law, ⚮363, 366, 368.

16. E. g., Carroll v. Guffey, 20 Ill.App.2d 470, 156 N.E.2d 267 (1959).

today recognize an exception to the hearsay rule for certain statements made under the influence of a startling event. Formulations of the exception differ, but all agree on two basic requirements. First, there must be some occurrence or event sufficiently startling to render normal reflective thought processes of an observer inoperative. Second, the statement of the declarant must have been a spontaneous reaction to the occurrence or event and not the result of reflective thought. Although some courts have imposed additional requirements, which will be discussed subsequently, these two elements are undeniably the essence of the exception.

The rationale for the exception lies in the special reliability which is regarded as furnished by the excitement suspending the declarant's powers of reflection and fabrication.[17] This factor also serves to justify dispensing with any requirement that the declarant be unavailable, because it suggests that his testimony on the stand, given at a time when his powers of reflection and fabrication are operative, is less reliable than his out-of-court declaration.[18] The entire basis for the exception is, of course, subject to question. While psychologists would probably concede that excitement minimizes the possibility of reflective self-interest influencing the declarant's statements, they would likely question whether this might be outweighed by the distorting effect of shock and excitement upon the declarant's observation and judgment.[19] Despite this doubt concern-

17. See generally, 6 Wigmore, Evidence § 1747.

18. See Mobile & Montgomery R. Co. v. Ashcraft, 48 Ala. 15, 31 (1872): "We regard these declarations as . . . more convincing . . . than the testimony to that effect of the persons themselves some time after the occurrence."

19. "One need not be a psychologist to distrust an observation made under emotional stress; everybody accepts such statements with mental reservation. M. Gorphe cites the case of an excited witness to a horrible accident who erroneously declared that the coachman deliberately and vindictively ran down a helpless woman. Fiore tells of

ing its justification, however, the exception is well established.

The sufficiency of the event or occurrence itself to qualify under this exception—as contrasted with its effect upon the declarant— is seldom questioned. An automobile accident,[20] pain or an injury,[21] an attack by a dog,[22] or a fight,[23] all may qualify. The courts seem to look primarily to the effect upon the declarant and, if satisfied that the event was such as to cause adequate excitement, the inquiry is ended. A somewhat more serious issue is raised by the potential need in a few cases to prove the exciting event by some proof other than the declaration. Under generally prevailing practice, the declaration itself is taken as sufficient proof of the exciting event and therefore the declaration is admissible despite absence of other proof that an exciting event occurred.[24] The Texas courts, however, have recently taken

the position that an excited utterance is admissible only if other proof is presented which supports a finding of fact that the exciting event did occur.[25]

The question most frequently raised when a purported excited utterance is offered involves the second requirement. In all cases the ultimate question is whether the statement was the result of reflective thought or whether it was rather a spontaneous reaction to the exciting event. Initially, of course, it is necessary that the declarant be affected by the exciting event. It is generally not required that he be actually involved in the event; an excited utterance by a bystander is admissible.[26] Nor is it necessary that he have actually observed the event (unless he could not have perceived what he asserted to be true unless he had observed it). Most courts, however, would probably be extremely skeptical regarding whether one merely informed of an event could become so excited upon hearing of it as to lose the power of reflective thought.[27]

---

an emotionally upset man who testified that hundreds were killed in an accident; that he had seen their heads rolling from their bodies. In reality only one man was killed, and five others injured. Another excited gentlemen took a pipe for a pistol. Besides these stories from real life, there are psychological experiments which point to the same conclusion. After a battle in a classroom, prearranged by the experimenter but a surprise to the students, each one was asked to write an account of the incident. The testimony of the most upset students was practically worthless, while those who were only slightly stimulated emotionally scored better than those left cold by the accident." Hutchins and Slesinger, Spontaneous Exclamations, 28 Colum. L.Rev. 432, 437 (1928) (footnote references omitted). See also, Stewart, Perception, Memory, and Hearsay: A Criticism of Present Law and the Proposed Federal Rules of Evidence, 1970 Utah L.Rev. 1, 27.

20. McCurdy v. Greyhound Corp., 346 F.2d 224 (3d Cir. 1965).

21. Arkansas Louisiana Gas Co. v. Evans, 397 P.2d 505 (Okl.1964) (pain in chest running into arms).

22. Johnston v. Ohls, 76 Wash.2d 398, 457 P.2d 194 (1969).

23. Martin v. Estrella, 266 A.2d 41 (R.I.1970).

24. See, e. g., Stewart v. Baltimore & Ohio R. Co., 137 F.2d 527 (2d Cir. 1943); Industrial Commission v. Diveley, 88 Colo. 190, 294 P. 532 (1930); Johnston v. W. S. Nott Co., 183 Minn. 309, 236 N.W. 466 (1931); Collins v. Equitable Life Ins. Co., 122 W.Va. 171, 8 S.E.2d 825 (1940), noted in 47 W.Va.L.Q. 340 (1941). See § 53, n. 91, supra.

25. The leading case is Truck Ins. Exchange v. Michling, 364 S.W.2d 172 (Tex.1963), reversing 358 S.W.2d 697 (Tex.Civ.App.1962), a workmen's compensation case. The deceased had returned home, pale, batting his eyes, and stumbling. He reported to his wife that he had struck his head when the bulldozer he had been driving had slipped off a hill. This statement was held inadmissible as there was no evidence of the exciting event other than the assertion in the statement itself. See also Hartford Accident and Indemnity Co. v. Hale, 400 S.W. 2d 310 (Tex.1966). In Travelers Ins. Co. v. Smith, 448 S.W.2d 541 (Tex.Civ.App.1969) a statement of the deceased was offered to the effect that he had experienced pain while manipulating some heavy equipment. It was argued that evidence that the deceased had left at 9:00 a. m. to go on his regular run, which involved lifting cans and containers, and returned at 10:00 a. m. was sufficient proof of an exciting event. This was rejected on the grounds that at most it established that an exciting event could have occurred, while *Michling* required proof to sustain a finding of fact that such an event did in fact occur. A critical dissent was entered by Preslar, J.

26. E. g., Watts v. Smith, 226 A.2d 160 (D.C.App. 1967); Martin v. Estrella, 266 A.2d 41 (R.I.1970).

27. See Zukowsky v. Brown, 1 Wash.App. 94, 459 P.2d 964 (1969) (statement by one who did not wit-

Probably the most important of the many factors entering into this determination is the time factor.[28] If the statement occurs while the exciting event is still in progress, courts have little difficulty finding that the excitement prompted the statement.[29] But as the time between the event and the statement increases, so does the reluctance to find the statement an excited utterance. Although one court has held a statement made fourteen hours after a physical beating to be the product of the excitement caused by the beating,[30] other courts have held statements made within minutes of the event not admissible.[31] Perhaps an accurate rule of thumb might be that where the time interval between the event and the statement is long enough to permit reflective thought, the statement will be excluded in the absence of some proof that the declarant did not in fact engage in a reflective thought process.[32] Testimony that the declarant still appeared "ner-

vous" or "distraught" and that there was a reasonable basis for continuing emotional upset will often suffice.[33] The nature of the exciting event and the declarant's concern with it are relevant, of course. Thus a statement made by the victim's wife one hour after a traffic accident was held admissible where the husband was still in the emergency room and she was obviously still concerned about his condition.[34] Other factors may indicate the opposite conclusion. Evidence that the statement was self-serving [35] or made in response to an inquiry,[36] while not justification for automatic exclusion, is an indication that the statement was the result of reflective thought, and where the time interval permitted such thought these factors might swing the balance in favor of exclusion. Proof that between the event and the statement the declarant performed tasks requiring relatively careful thought, of course, is strong evidence that the effect of the exciting event had subsided.[37] Because of the wide variety

ness collapse of seat and injury to plaintiff but was told about it five minutes later that he was not surprised because it happened twice before inadmissible because declarant not sufficiently concerned with exciting event).

28. See Annot., 56 A.L.R.2d 372 (spontaneity as question for court or jury).

29. E. g., Schwam v. Reece, 213 Ark. 431, 210 S.W.2d 903 (1948) (bus driver's exclamation, "I have no brakes" just before collision admissible); New York, C. & St. L. Ry. Co. v. Kovatch, 120 Ohio St. 532, 166 N.E. 682 (1929) (exclamation that train had run over child made while train was still passing crossing held admissible).

30. State v. Stafford, 237 Iowa 780, 23 N.W.2d 832 (1946).

31. Alabama Power Co. v. Ray, 249 Ala. 568, 32 So. 2d 219 (1947) (five minutes); Swearinger v. Klinger, 91 Ill.App.2d 251, 234 N.E.2d 60 (1968) (five to 15 minutes).

32. E. g., Taft v. Western World Ins. Co., 220 So.2d 226 (La.App.1969) (error to admit statements concerning accident by another patient in nursing home made 30 minutes after patient had fallen); Fontenot v. Pan American Fire & Casualty Co., 209 So.2d 105 (La.App.1968) (statement by driver made 40 minutes after accident inadmissible); Marshall v. Thomason, 241 S.C. 84, 127 S.E.2d 177 (1962) (statements to police officer 30 minutes after accident inadmissible).

33. E. g., McCurdy v. Greyhound Corp., 346 F.2d 224 (3d Cir. 1965) (statement to police officer 15 minutes after accident admissible; testimony that declarant was still "nervous" and "shooken up" when police arrived); May v. Wright, 62 Wash.2d 69, 381 P.2d 601 (1963) (statement by witness to accident involving an automobile running over a child made 20 minutes after accident admissible; officer testified declarant "seemed upset").

34. Gibbs v. Wilmeth, 261 Iowa 1015, 157 N.W.2d 93 (1968).

35. Micheli v. Toye Brothers Yellow Cab Co., 174 So.2d 168 (La.App.1965) (self-serving statement made to employer's investigator 15 minutes after automobile accident properly excluded).

36. Gibbs v. Wilmeth, 261 Iowa 1015, 157 N.W.2d 93 (1968): ("[A] statement in answer to a question does not necessarily violate the res gestae rule. The important consideration is the spontaneity of the statement, however elicited."); Bosin v. Oak Lodge Sanitary District No. 1, 251 Ore. 554, 447 P.2d 285 (1968) (fact that statement was in response to question is "not conclusive against admissibility" but a factor for consideration).

37. Compare Hamilton v. Missouri Petroleum Products Co., 438 S.W.2d 197 (Mo.1969) (where evidence showed that after accident declarant put out flares to warn traffic, went to the aid of an injured party, and advised injured party not to move, statements made 25 minutes after accident inadmis-

of factual situations, appellate courts have recognized wide discretion in trial courts to determine whether in fact a declarant was at the time of an offered statement still under the influence of an exciting event.[38]

Some courts, in stating the requirements for excited utterances, require in addition to the two primary characteristics discussed above that the substance of the assertion relate to the exciting event,[39] and a few courts have excluded excited utterances on the ground that they fail to meet this test.[40] The matter usually arises when an excited utterance by an agent following an accident is offered to prove either the existence or scope of the agency. The purported requirement that the declaration elucidate the exciting event seems to have been taken from the verbal act doctrine without adequate analysis.[41] While it is arguable that the probabilities are somewhat higher that a statement relating to an excited event itself is a spontaneous reaction to that event than is the case where the statement relates to something else, it is unlikely that the difference in probabilities is high enough to justify drawing a line at this point. In a leading case, the United States Court of Appeals for the District of Columbia reasonably concluded that this alleged requirement was a

"spurious element" of the exception.[42] The extent to which the utterance related to the event, the court emphasized, must be taken into account in determining whether the declaration was really a spontaneous utterance:

"[A]s soon as the excited utterance goes beyond description of the exciting event and deals with past facts or with the future it may tend to take on a reflective quality and must be more carefully scrutinized with respect to the second element, that of true spontaneity. In other words, the very fact that the utterance is not descriptive of the exciting event is one of the factors which the trial court must take into account in the evaluation of whether the statement is truly a spontaneous, impulsive expression excited by the event. [43] "

Must the declarant meet the tests of competency for a witness? In a modified manner the requirement that a witness have had an opportunity to observe that to which he testifies [44] is applied. Direct proof is not necessary; if the circumstances appear consistent with opportunity by the declarant, this is sufficient.[45] If there is doubt the question is for the jury.[46] Especially in cases where the declaration is of low probative value, however, it is usually held inadmissible if there

---

sible) with McCurdy v. Greyhound Corp., 346 F.2d 224 (3d Cir. 1965) (where proof showed that after accident declarant first muttered incomprehensibly and then walked around aimlessly and was still nervous when police arrived, statement made 15 minutes after accident admissible).

38. See, e. g., Swearinger v. Klinger, 91 Ill.App.2d 251, 234 N.E.2d 60 (1968); Johnston v. Ohls, 76 Wash.2d 398, 457 P.2d 194 (1969).

39. See 6 Wigmore, Evidence §§ 1752, 1754.

40. Cook v. Hall, 308 Ky. 500, 214 S.W.2d 1017 (1948) (statement by son of automobile's owners after accident that he had permission to drive the car inadmissible); Bagwell v. McLellan Stores Co., 216 S.C. 207, 57 S.E.2d 257 (1949) (bystander's statement, after observing fall, that the floor had just been oiled inadmissible).

41. See 6 Wigmore, Evidence § 1752.

42. Murphy Auto Parts Co. v. Ball, 102 U.S.App.D.C. 416, 249 F.2d 508 (1957) cert. denied 355 U.S. 932.

43. Murphy Auto Parts Co. v. Ball, 102 U.S.App.D.C. 416, 249 F.2d 508, 511 (1957) cert. denied 355 U.S. 932 (1958). *Murphy* was applied in Felder v. Pinckney, 244 A.2d 481 (D.C.App.1968) (statement of one who observed co-employee fall that Mr. Pinckney hired him admissible); Sawyer v. Miseli, 156 A.2d 141 (D.C.App.1959) (statement of driver after accident that owner had given him permission to drive car admissible).

44. See § 10, supra.

45. See § 10, supra. E. g., Powers v. Temple, 250 S.C. 149, 156 S.E.2d 759 (1967) (admission of statements made by unidentified person to witness some minutes after accident not abuse of discretion). Cf. Garrett v. Howden, 73 N.M. 307, 387 P.2d 874 (1963). See also n. 47, infra.

46. See §§ 53, 58, supra.

is no reasonable suggestion that the declarant had an opportunity to observe.[47]

On the theory that there is a countervailing assurance of reliability—the requirement of excitement—the other aspects of competency are not applied. Thus an excited utterance is admissible despite the fact that the declarant was a child and would have been incompetent as a witness for that reason,[48] or the declarant was incompetent by virtue of mental illness [49] or a prior felony conviction,[50] or the declarant was a spouse of the defendant in the criminal case in which the declaration was offered.[51]

It is sometimes stated that an excited utterance must not be an opinion.[52] Such a blanket limitation seems unjustified, in view of the nature of the opinion rule.[53] Where the declarant is an in-court witness, it is probably appropriate to require him to testify in concrete terms rather than conclusory generalizations. But in everyday life people often talk in conclusory terms and when these statements are later offered in court there is no opportunity to require the declarant to substitute more specific language. Here, as elsewhere, the opinion rule should be applied sparingly, if at all, to out-of-court speech. Nevertheless, courts have sometimes excluded excited utterances on the grounds that they violate the opinion rule, especially in situations in which the declarant's statement places blame upon himself or another.[54] Despite possible danger that these opinions may be given exaggerated weight by a jury, the need for knowledge of the facts usually outweighs this danger and the better view admits excited statements of opinion.[55]

47. Warfield v. Shell Oil Co., 106 Ariz. 181, 472 P. 2d 50 (1970) (offer of statement of bystander failed to show that speaker had witnessed event); Ungefug v. D'Ambrosa, 250 Cal.App.2d 61, 58 Cal. Rptr. 223 (1967) (where ambulance driver merely reported that someone had said the victim had been hit by a car that had not stopped, there was insufficient proof of an opportunity to observe; although direct proof that declarant witnessed the event is not necessary, "the fact that the declarant was a percipient witness should not be purely a matter of speculation or conjecture"); Clements v. Peyton, 398 S.W.2d 477 (Ky.App.1965) (testimony that "some guys sitting in the bar" said there had been another wreck at the corner inadmissible because there was no showing of their reasonable opportunity to observe facts on which to base this conclusion). Cf. Annot., 7 A.L.R.2d 1324 (inability of declarant to recollect and narrate facts as to which statement relates as affecting admissibility of excited utterance).

48. New York C. & St. L. Ry. Co. v. Kovatch, 120 Ohio St. 532, 166 N.E. 682 (1929) (five year old girl); Houston v. Quinones, 142 Tex. 282, 177 S.W. 2d 259 (1944) (three year old girl); Johnston v. Ohls, 76 Wash.2d 398, 457 P.2d 194 (1969) (four year old girl "presumably not competent to testify directly" told officer that dog which had attacked her had jumped out at motorcycle on which she had been riding with her father). See generally Annot., 83 A.L.R.2d 1368 (declarant's age as affecting admissibility of excited utterance).

49. Wilson v. State, 49 Tex.Cr.R. 50, 90 S.W. 312 (1905). But cf. Gough v. General Box Co., 302 S. W.2d 884 (Mo.1957) (excited utterance inadmissible because declarant was unconscious at the time of the declaration).

50. Blocker v. State, 118 Tex.Cr.R. 202, 40 S.W.2d 803 (1931).

51. Robbins v. State, 73 Tex.Cr.R. 367, 166 S.W. 528 (1914) (declaration of murder defendant's wife, "Poor man! He lost his life trying to protect me." admissible).

52. E. g., Johnston v. Ohls, 76 Wash.2d 398, 457 P.2d 194 (1969).

53. See § 18, supra.

54. Whitney v. Sioux City, 172 Iowa 336, 154 N.W. 497 (1915) (declaration by passenger in automobile, "We were going too fast" inadmissible); Gray v. Boston Elev. R. Co., 215 Mass. 143, 102 N.E. 71 (1913) (declaration by spectator to sudden start of train "It was his own fault," inadmissible); Bowers v. Kugler, 140 Neb. 684, 1 N.W.2d 299 (1941) (declaration by driver of one vehicle in accident, "Oh, my God! It might have been my fault." inadmissible); Neisner Bros. v. Schaefer, 124 Ohio St. 311, 178 N.E. 269 (1931) (store clerk's declaration, "I am sorry I caused it; I should not have dropped the paper on the floor," inadmissible).

55. Cross Lake Logging Co. v. Joyce, 83 Fed. 989 (8th Cir. 1897) (statement "I wouldn't have lost my leg if you had done as you agreed to and put another man in his place," admissible); Atlantic Coast Line Ry. Co. v. Crosby, 53 Fla. 400, 43 So. 318 (1907) (declaration of mother of injured child, "It was all my fault," admissible); State v. Sloan, 47 Mo. 604 (1871) (declaration of shooting victim to the effect that defendant had not been at fault because victim had drawn on the difficulty by attacking the defendant, admissible).

In rape cases,[56] and increasingly in cases of sex offenses generally,[57] evidence is admissible that the victim made complaint. The only time requirement is that the complaint have been made without a delay which is unexplained or is inconsistent with the occurrence of the offense, in general a much less demanding time aspect than with the typical excited utterance situation.[58] In its origin, the theory of admissibility was to repel any inference that because the victim did not complain no outrage had in fact transpired. Accordingly, if the victim did not testify, evidence of complaint was not admissible.[59] While admissible evidence under traditional doctrine included only the fact that complaint was made,[60] the trend is to allow details of the offense and the identity of the offender, a result which appears wholly justifiable.[61] It is, of course, possible to go beyond the theory of mere corroboration and to admit independently if excited utterance requirements are met.

298. Unexcited Declarations of Present Sense Impressions.[62]

Although Dean Wigmore's creative work has done much to clarify the murky concept of *res gestae*, his analysis of spontaneous declarations may have led to one unfortunate restricting development of this exception. Professor Thayer, reviewing the *res gestae* cases in 1881,[63] concluded that this was an exception based on the contemporaneousness of statements. He read the law as creating an exception for "statements . . . made by those present when a thing took place, made about it and importing what is present at the very time . . . ."[64] Wigmore, however, saw as the basis for the spontaneous exclamation exception to the hearsay rule not the contemporaneousness of the exclamations but rather the nervous excitement produced by the exposure of the declarant to an exciting event.[65] As a result, the American law of spontaneous statements shifted emphasis from what Thayer had observed to a requirement of an exciting event and a resulting stilling of the declarant's reflective faculties.[66] This, as Professor Morgan has pointed out, was unfortunate.[67] Given the danger of unreliability caused by the very emotional excitement required for excited utterances, it makes little sense to admit them while excluding other out-of-court declarations which may have the same assurances of reliability and lack the inherent defects of excited utterances.[68]

Under Morgan's leadership strong arguments have been made for another exception

---

56. 4 Wigmore, Evidence §§ 1134–1140; 6 id. §§ 1760, 1761.

57. People v. Burton, 55 Cal.2d 328, 11 Cal.Rptr. 65, 359 P.2d 433 (1961) (indecent liberties with child); People v. Bonneau, 323 Mich. 237, 35 N.W. 2d 161 (1948) (same). Contra, People v. Romano, 306 Ill. 502, 138 N.E. 169 (1923).

58. See the careful explication of the distinctions between excited utterances and complaint of rape by Underwood, J., in People v. Damen, 28 Ill.2d 464, 193 N.E.2d 25 (1963). See also Annot., 19 A. L.R.2d 579.

59. People v. Lewis, 252 Ill. 281, 96 N.E. 1005 (1911) (victim died before trial); 4 Wigmore, Evidence § 1136.

60. 6 Wigmore, Evidence § 1760.

61. Cases cited in 6 Wigmore, Evidence § 1761, n. 2.

62. See generally, Hutchins and Slesinger, Some Observation on the Law of Evidence, 28 Colum.L. Rev. 432, 439–40 (1928); Morgan, Res Gestae, 12 Wash.L.Rev. 91 (1937); Morgan, A Suggested Classification of Utterances Admissible as Res Gestae,

31 Yale L.J. 229, 236–38 (1922); Note, Spontaneous Exclamations in the Absence of a Startling Event, 46 Colum.L.Rev. 430 (1946). Cf. Annot., 140 A.L.R. 874 (admissibility of statements regarding conduct of driver of car subsequently involved in a collision).

63. Thayer, Bedingfield's Case—Declarations as a Part of the Res Gestae, 15 Am.L.Rev. 1 (1881).

64. Id. at 83.

65. Morgan, Res Gestae, 12 Wash.L.Rev. 91, 98 (1937).

66. Id. at 96.

67. Id.

68. Morgan, A Suggested Classification of Utterances Admissible as Res Gestae, 31 Yale L.J. 229, 236 (1922).

to the hearsay rule for declarations concerning nonexciting events which the declarant is observing at the time he makes the declarations. Although these declarations lack whatever assurance of reliability there is in the effect of an exciting event, other factors may provide adequate safeguards. First, since the report concerns observations being made at the time of the declaration it is safe from any error caused by a defect of the declarant's memory. Second, a requirement that the declaration be made contemporaneously with the observation means that there will be little or no time for calculated misstatement and thus provides protection analogous to that provided by the impact of an exciting event. Third, the statement will usually have been made to a third person (the witness who subsequently testifies to it) who, being present at the time and scene of the observation, will usually have an opportunity to observe the situation himself and thus provide a check on the accuracy of the declarant's statement. Moreover, since the declarant himself will usually be available for cross-examination, his credibility will be subject to substantial verification before the trier of fact.[69]

Despite the reasonableness of Professor Morgan's views, only the Texas courts have specifically rejected the Wigmore position that an exciting event is necessary and adopted an additional exception to the hearsay rule for unexcited declarations of present sense impressions. Some courts, however, have admitted evidence of this sort under general *res gestae* language, although others have rejected it.[70] In addition, both the Model Code [71] and the Proposed Rules of Evidence

---

69. The case most commonly cited is Houston Oxygen Co., Inc. v. Davis, 139 Tex. 1, 161 S.W.2d 474 (1942). Defendant had offered the testimony of a Mrs. Cooper that when the plaintiff's car passed her about four miles before the accident at issue she had said that "they must have been drunk, that we would find them somewhere on the road wrecked if they kept that rate of speed up." Objection to the testimony concerning the remark was sustained, and the Texas Supreme Court reversed. "[The statement] is sufficiently spontaneous to save it from the suspicion of being manufactured evidence. There was no time for a calculated statement." 161 S.W.2d at 476. See also Anderson v. State, 454 S.W.2d 740 (Tex.Cr.App. 1970) (witness' testimony that a neighbor had said, "Seems like there is a car being stripped down the street there" admissible); Claybrook v. Acreman, 373 S.W.2d 287 (Tex.Civ.App.1963) (statements of bystanders such as "They won't last long at that rate of speed" improperly excluded). It is, of course, arguable that an exciting event was in fact present in each of these cases.

70. Kelly v. Hanwick, 228 Ala. 336, 153 S. 269 (1934) (bystander's statement when he saw automobile coming that at the speed at which it was traveling it could not make the curve held admissible); Moreno v. Hawbaker, 157 Cal.App.2d 627, 321 P.2d 538 (1958) (testimony of witness that when he saw two motorcycles proceeding at a high rate of speed and without lights he said, "Look at those fools go" admissible as a spontaneous utterance); Tampa Elec. Co. v. Getrost, 151 Fla. 558, 10 So.2d 83 (1942) (statement of lineman that circuit was open held admissible); McCaskill v. State, 227 So. 2d 847 (Miss.1969) (testimony that victim had called witness and said she was at the doctor's getting something done about her pregnancy admissible, but suggestion that rule is limited to abortion prosecutions); Sellers v. Montana-Dakota Power Co., 99 Mont. 39, 41 P.2d 44 (1935) (statements by persons in burning building that the smell of the smoke indicated that the fire came from gas held admissible); Hornschurch v. Southern Pacific Co., 101 Ore. 280, 203 Pac. 886 (1921) (testimony that bystander called to those in automobile to stop held admissible); Marks v. I. M. Pearlstine & Sons, 203 S.C. 318, 26 S.E.2d 835 (1943) (statement by one watching trucks racing by that the "trucks are going to kill someone" held admissible). Contra, Wrange v. King, 114 Kan. 539, 220 Pac. 259 (1923) (statement of bystander, "See that fellow jump in front of that automobile," excluded because of absence of shock or excitement); Ideal Cement Co. v. Killingsworth, 198 So.2d 248 (Miss.1967) (bystander's statement concerning passing vehicle, "Damn, he's in a helluva hurry" properly excluded); Shadowski v. Pittsburg Rys. Co., 226 Pa. 537, 75 Atl. 730 (1910) (bystander's statement, "Look at that damn fool; he will run over that little girl up there," inadmissible because it did not emanate from the litigated act, the accident itself); Barnett v. Bull, 141 Wash. 139, 250 Pac. 955 (1926) (statement of bystanders that party was driving in a careless manner inadmissible). See generally Note, Spontaneous Statements in the Absence of a Startling Event, 46 Colum.L.Rev. 430 (1946).

71. Model Code of Evidence Rule 512(a).

for the Federal Courts [72] provide for the admission of a statement describing an event or condition made while the declarant was perceiving the event or condition, or immediately thereafter. This somewhat expands Morgan's proposal by discarding the requirement of strict contemporaneousness and permitting use of a statement made soon after the observation. If "immediately thereafter" is interpreted to mean a time within which, under the conditions, it is unlikely that the declarant had an opportunity to form a purpose to misstate his observations, this is a desirable expansion.

72. F.R.Ev. (R.D.1971) 803(2).

CHAPTER 30

RECORDS OF PAST RECOLLECTION

299. History and Theoretical Basis of the Exception.[1]

By the middle 1600s it had become customary to permit a witness to refresh his memory by looking at a written memorandum and to testify from his then-revived memory.[2] It often happened, however, that, although examining the writing did not bring the facts recorded back to the witness' memory, he was able to recognize the writing as one prepared by him and was willing to testify on the basis of the writing that the facts recited in it were true. By the 1700s this also was accepted as proper,[3] although the theoretical difficulty of justifying the result was often swept under the rug by referring to it by the old term of "refreshing recollection," which clearly did not fit it.[4] Beginning with the early 1800s, the courts came to distinguish between the two situations, and to recognize that the use of past recollection recorded was a far different matter from permitting the witness to testify from a memory refreshed by examining a writing.[5]

As the rule permitting the introduction of past recollection recorded developed, it required that four elements be met: (1) the witness must have had firsthand knowledge of the event, (2) the written statement must be an original memorandum made at or near the time of the event and while the witness had a clear and accurate memory of it, (3) the witness must lack a present recollection of the event, and (4) the witness must vouch for the accuracy of the written memorandum.[6]

There has been some dispute as to the nature of the doctrine of past recollection recorded. A few courts have suggested that the writing is not itself admissible in evidence,[7] although the majority hold that the

1. See generally 3 Wigmore, Evidence (Chadbourn rev.) §§ 735–755; Morgan, The Relation Between Hearsay and Preserved Memory, 40 Harv.L.Rev. 712 (1927); Note, Past Recollection Recorded, 28 Iowa L.Rev. 530 (1943); Notes, 12 Okla.L.Rev. 165 (1959), 15 Wash.L.Rev. 257 (1940), 63 W.Va.L.Rev. 73 (1960); Annots., 82 A.L.R.2d 473, 125 A.L.R. 19, 80–187; 29 Am.Jur.2d Evidence § 877; C.J.S. Evidence § 696; Dec.Dig. Evidence ☞355, 356, 377, Criminal Law ☞435, Witnesses ☞253–260; West's Ann. Cal.Evid.Code, § 1237; N.J.Ev.Rule 63(1) (b); F.R. Ev. (R.D.1971) 803(5).

2. 3 Wigmore, Evidence (Chadbourn rev.) § 735. See § 9, supra.

3. Id.

4. Id.

5. See, e. g., Acklen's Executor v. Hickman, 63 Ala. 494 (1879); State v. Easter, 185 Iowa 476, 170 N.W. 748 (1919); State v. Legg, 59 W.Va. 315, 53 S.E. 545 (1906).

6. See United States v. Kelly, 349 F.2d 720, 770–71 (2d Cir. 1965); Kinsey v. State, 49 Ariz. 201, 65 P.2d 1141 (1937); Mathis v. Stricklind, 201 Kan. 655, 443 P.2d 673 (1968).

7. Bendett v. Bendett, 315 Mass. 59, 52 N.E.2d 2 (1943); Hoffman v. Chicago M. & St. P. Ry. Co., 40 Minn. 60, 41 N.W. 301 (1889) (dictum).

effect of successfully invoking the doctrine is to make the writing itself admissible to prove the truth of facts asserted in it as true.[8] It has also been argued that since the reliability of the assertions rests upon the veracity of a witness who is available and testifying that the writing is not hearsay and therefore the doctrine of past recollection recorded is not properly regarded as an exception to the hearsay rule.[9] The requirements for admissibility seem not in practical effect to have been influenced by adherence to or rejection of this argument. Classification as a hearsay exception does, however, make for convenience in treatment due to the limited and peculiar nature of the unavailability which is required, i. e. a less than total lack of memory.

300. The Requirement of Firsthand Knowledge.

The usual requirement for witnesses[10] and also for hearsay declarants[11] that they must have had firsthand knowledge of the facts is also enforced in regard to past recollection recorded. Thus, where an inventory was offered and the witness produced to lay the necessary foundation testified that it had been made only partly from his own inspection and partly from information provided by his assistant, the inventory was inadmissible.[12] If, however, each person with personal knowledge had been produced, it is likely that an adequate foundation would have been established and the inventory admissible.[13]

301. The Requirement of an Original Written Statement Made at or near the Event While the Witness' Memory was Clear.

Despite some cases suggesting the contrary,[14] the exception as generally stated requires that there be a written formulation of the memory.[15] Moreover, the original memorandum must be produced unless it is unavailable, in which case a copy may be used.[16] This writing need not, however, have been prepared by the witness himself if the

8. E. g., Fisher v. Swartz, 333 Mass. 265, 130 N.E.2d 575 (1955), overruling Bendett v. Bendett, supra n. 7. West's Ann.Cal.Evid.Code § 1237(d) prohibits the introduction of the physical document itself unless offered by an adverse party. People v. Davis, 265 Cal.App.2d 341, 71 Cal.Rptr. 242, 248 (1968). The purpose of this rule is apparently to prevent the physical document from going to the jury because of the danger that this will result in its being given undue weight. F.R.Ev. (R.D.1971) 803(5) adopts this position.

9. See Kinsey v. State, 49 Ariz. 201, 65 P.2d 1141, 1149 (1937), arguing that past recollection recorded was hearsay only if offered by someone other than the person who made it or at whose direction it had been made. Compare Morgan, The Relation Between Hearsay and Preserved Memory, 40 Harv. L.Rev. 712, 719 (1927). See also Curtis v. Bradley, 65 Conn. 99, 31 Atl. 591, 595 (1894) for a discussion of the theoretical issue.

10. See § 10, supra.

11. See § 247, n. 59, supra.

12. Town of Norwalk ex rel. Fawcett v. Ireland, 68 Conn. 1, 35 Atl. 804 (1896). See also United States v. Keppler, 1 F.2d 315 (3d Cir. 1924) (memorandum not admissible where witness had never known facts recorded); People v. Zalimas, 319 Ill. 186, 149 N.E. 759 (1925) (druggist's memorandum of sale of arsenic to a given person not admissible to prove sale to that person because druggist did not have firsthand knowledge of purchaser's identity).

13. See §§ 303, 308, infra.

14. Shear v. Van Dyke, 17 N.Y.S.Ct.Rep. 528, 10 Hun. 528 (1877) (to prove amount of hay loaded, plaintiff offered R's testimony to the effect that he could not now recall but that he had known and had told the plaintiff, who then testified that he had been told by R that fourteen loads had been loaded); Hart v. Atlantic Coast Line Ry. Co., 144 N.C. 91, 56 S.E. 559 (1907).

15. See 3 Wigmore, Evidence (Chadbourn rev.) § 744.

16. General Accident Fire & Life Assur. Corp. v. Camp, 348 S.W.2d 782 (Tex.Civ.App.1961) (copy of doctor's report concerning examination of X rays not admissible where no attempt made to explain nonproduction of original). Compare Cohen v. Berry, 188 A.2d 302 (D.C.App.1963) (not error to admit sheets containing entries taken from notebook regarding hours worked; original is required if available "but if lost or otherwise unavailable, and there is no indication that it has been discarded for fraudulent purposes, the witness may testify from a memorandum made of the original records").

witness read it and acknowledged its correctness.[17]

The writing must have been prepared or recognized as correct at a time close to the event.[18] Some opinions use the older strict formulation that requires the writing to have been made or recognized as correct "at or near the time" of the events recorded.[19] This finds some support in psychological research suggesting that a rapid rate of forgetting occurs within the first two or three days following the observation of the event.[20] But the tendency seems to be towards acceptance of the formulation favored by Wigmore [21] which would require only that the writing be made or recognized at a time when the events were fairly fresh in the mind of the witness. No precise formula can be applied to determine whether this test has been met; perhaps the best rule of thumb is that the requirement is not met if the time lapse is such, under the circumstances, as to suggest that the writing is not likely to be accurate.[22]

302.   The Requirement of No Present Recollection.[23]

The traditional formulation of the rule, still adhered to by most courts, requires that before a past recollection recorded could be received in evidence the witness who made or recognized it as correct must testify that he lacks present memory of the events and therefore is unable to testify concerning them.[24] If examining the writing refreshes

---

17. Washington v. Washington, Virginia & Maryland Coach Co., 250 F.Supp. 888, 890 (D.D.C.1966) (accident report by bus driver admissible where driver's supervisor, who had been along on trip, testified that he had no present recollection of accident but he had read the accident report and if it had failed to correctly state the facts he would have caused it to be corrected); Jordan v. People, 151 Colo. 133, 376 P.2d 699 (1962), cert. denied 373 U.S. 944 (typewritten version of officer's interview with suspect admitted although officer did not prepare it himself). But see Bennefield v. State, 281 Ala. 283, 202 So.2d 55 (1967) (only stenographer who took down confession could authenticate it, and detective's affirmance of its correctness "merely compounded its hearsay character").

18. Maxwell's Executors v. Wilkinson, 113 U.S. 656 (1885); 3 Wigmore, Evidence (Chadbourn rev.) § 745.

19. E. g., Gigliotti v. United Illuminating Co., 151 Conn. 114, 193 A.2d 718, 723 (1963) (written statement must be excluded if it was not made "at or about the time of the events recorded in it"). See also Mercer v. Department of Labor and Industries, 74 Wash.2d 96, 442 P.2d 1000 (1968) (letter regarding pension claim written by supervisor of claims department not admissible because it had not been written "contemporaneously with the events described therein").

20. See Hutchins and Slesinger, Some Observations on the Law of Evidence—Memory, 41 Harv.L.Rev. 860 (1928); Gardner, The Perception and Memory of Witnesses, 18 Corn.L.Q. 391, 393 (1933); Stewart, Perception, Memory, and Hearsay: A Criticism of Present Law and the Proposed Federal Rules of Evidence, 1970 Utah L.Rev. 1.

21. 3 Wigmore, Evidence (Chadbourn rev.) § 745.

22. United States v. FMC Corp., 306 F.Supp. 1106, 1135–37 (E.D.Pa.1969) supplemented 317 F.Supp. 443 (no inflexible criterion for determining remoteness, but grand jury testimony inadmissible because of remoteness; heavy reliance on witness' inability to recall material aspects of transactions at time of appearance before grand jury); Gigliotti v. United Illuminating Co., 151 Conn. 114, 193 A.2d 718, 723 (1963) (written statement made six weeks after events properly excluded); General Accident Fire & Life Assur. Corp. v. Camp, 348 S.W.2d 782, 785 (Tex.Civ.App.1961) (written copy of report of doctor's examination of X ray dated 1959 not admissible where X rays were taken in 1951 and date of examination and original report not shown).

23. See generally, 3 Wigmore, Evidence (Chadbourn rev.) § 738.

24. Railway Express Agency, Inc. v. Epperson, 240 F.2d 189, 193–94 (8th Cir. 1957) (accident report by witnesses who testified from present memory as to same facts "probably not admissible"); Bennefield v. State, 281 Ala. 283, 202 So.2d 55 (1967) (written transcript of confession not admissible where witness did not testify to lack of present memory); Cohen v. Berry, 188 A.2d 302 (D.C.App. 1963); Noumoff v. Rotkvich, 88 Ill.App.2d 116, 232 N.E.2d 107 (1967) (police report erroneously admitted where offering party failed to establish clearly on record that officer did not have an independent recollection of the facts and that reviewing the report did not refresh his recollection); Gray v. Nathan, 221 So.2d 859, 867 (La.App.1969) (written statement which witness testified was "a true picture of how the accident transpired" not admissible although witness testified that he "could not remember accident very clearly" and his testimony from present memory was "inconclusive and very indecisive"); Rogalsky v. Plymouth Homes,

the recollection of the witness, under this approach the writing is thus rendered inadmissible and the witness must testify from his newly refreshed recollection.

Some courts have rejected this requirement, especially in circumstances suggesting that although the witness may have sufficient present recollection to cause the offer not to meet the traditional requirement nevertheless the circumstances of the case suggest that the prior recorded statement would be more complete and more reliable than testimony based upon the present memory of the witness.[25] In many cases, perhaps most,

it is undoubtedly true that present recollection, clouded by the passage of time, is much less satisfactory than a statement made at a time when recollection was fresh and clear. But complete abandonment of this requirement might permit the use of statements prepared for purposes of the litigation under the supervision of claims adjusters or attorneys or under other circumstances casting significant doubt upon the reliability of the statement.[26] An accommodation of these various aspects may be found in phrasing the requirement as a lack of sufficient present recollection to enable the witness to testify fully and accurately, a standard which is gaining increasing adherents.[27]

303. The Requirement that a Witness Vouch for the Accuracy of the Written Statement [28]: Multi-Party Situations.

As a final assurance of reliability, it has traditionally been required that the witnesses laying the foundation for the written

---

Inc., 100 N.J.Super. 501, 242 A.2d 655 (1968) (prejudicial error to admit police accident report where officer "had sufficient recollection to testify and did testify fully as to everything in the report"); State v. Contreras, 253 A.2d 612 (R.I.1969) (written statement not admissible despite witness' testimony that events were fresher in his mind when statement was prepared than during testimony); Maryland Casualty Co. v. Heald, 125 Vt. 116, 211 A.2d 177 (1965) (written statement of testifying witness erroneously admitted because it was not admissible to corroborate testimony and it was not the "best testimony" of what the witness knew).

If it is apparent from the face of the statement that a reasonable person could not presently recall the facts, failure to establish lack of present knowledge by direct testimony will not cause the admission of the statement to become error. Cohen v. Berry, 188 A.2d 302 (D.C.App.1963) (despite lack of record on present knowledge, admission of record of exact days and hours worked over an eight month period not error because it is "inconceivable" that witness could have recalled figures); Shea v. Fridley, 123 A.2d 358, 362 (D.C.Mun.App. 1956) (list of 200 items admissible despite lack of clear record on present knowledge, since it is inconceivable that average witness could remember this many items).

25. The leading case seems to be Jordan v. People, 151 Colo. 133, 376 P.2d 699 (1962), cert. denied 373 U.S. 944 (1963) (transcript of a police officer's interview with the defendant not rendered inadmissible by the failure to seek and obtain the officer's statement that he lacked present recollection). Accuracy would be better served in this case, the court held, by relying upon the recorded memory, in view of police officers' difficulty of remembering the details of specific cases. But compare Larson v. Chaussee, 168 Colo. 437, 452 P.2d 30 (1969) (written memorandum containing alleged terms of agreement not admissible because its accuracy was disputed, it was not made in the presence of the adverse party, and it was merely cumu-

lative of what the witness had testified). For other cases dispensing with the requirement of lack of present recollection, see Hall v. State, 223 Md. 158, 162 A.2d 751 (1960) (where detective testified that he could testify with considerably greater accuracy as to defendant's confession from his notes than from his recollection, it was not error to permit him to read the notes); State v. Bindhammer, 44 N.J. 372, 209 A.2d 124, 132 (1965) ("Since the judicial search is for truth and accuracy it would indeed be self-defeating for a court to compel a reporter to testify from memory rather than from his notes or transcription; and this would be so regardless of the extent of the reporter's present recollection."); State v. Sutton, 253 Ore. 24, 450 P.2d 748 (1969) (checklist used by police officer in administering breath analysis machine admissible despite officer's apparently refreshed recollection, because it was likely to be more trustworthy).

26. See F.R.Ev. (R.D.1971) 803(5), Advisory Committee's Note.

27. Vicksburg & Meridian R. R. v. O'Brien, 119 U.S. 99 (1886); Ahern v. Webb, 268 F.2d 45 (10th Cir. 1959); NLRB v. Federal Dairy Co., 297 F.2d 487 (1st Cir. 1962); West's Ann.Cal.Evid.Code § 1237; N.J.Ev. Rule 63(1) (b); F.R.Ev. (R.D.1971) 803(5). In most of the cases cited in n. 25, supra, the witness could be said to have met this criterion.

28. See generally, 3 Wigmore, Evidence (Chadbourn rev.) § 747.

statement not only establish firsthand knowledge, preparation of the statement at a time sufficiently close to the event, and at least some inability presently to recall the event, but in addition that either the person who prepared the writing or one who read it at a time close to the event testify to its accuracy.[29] This may be accomplished by a statement that he presently remembers that he correctly recorded the fact or that he recognized the writing as accurate at the time he read it.[30] But if his present memory is less effective, it is sufficient if he testifies that he knows it is correct because it was his habit or practice to record such matters accurately or to check them for accuracy.[31] At the extreme, it is even sufficient if he testifies that he recognizes the signature on the statement as his and he believes it correct because he would not have signed it if he had not believed it true at the time.[32]

If an adequate foundation has been laid, it is not grounds for exclusion that the witness' testimony as to the accuracy of the statement is contradicted by other testimony.[33]

The traditional past recollection recorded was a one-man affair. The verifying witness was also the person who made the original observation and the person who recorded it. When the verifying witness has not prepared the report but merely examined it and found it accurate, the matter involves what might be called a cooperative report. But in this situation, only the person who read and verified the report need be called. A somewhat similar type of cooperative report exists when a person (R) reports orally facts known to him to another person (W), who writes them down. A salesman or timekeeper, for example, may report sales or time to a bookkeeper. In this type of situation, courts have held the written statement admissible if R swears to the correctness of his oral report (although he may not remember the detailed facts) and W testifies that he faithfully transcribed R's oral report.[34]

29. E. g., Dickinson Supply, Inc. v. Montana-Dakota Utilities Co., 423 F.2d 106 (8th Cir. 1970); Williams v. Stroh Plumbing & Electric, Inc., 250 Iowa 599, 94 N.W.2d 750 (1959).

30. E. g., Stanton v. Pennsylvania R. Co., 32 Ill. App.2d 406, 178 N.E.2d 121 (1961) (patient-slips from doctor's office admissible where nurse testified that she had made entries and that they were accurate when made); Mathis v. Stricklind, 201 Kan. 655, 443 P.2d 673 (1968) (inventory of safe deposit boxes admissible when those making examination testified that notes were correct when taken).

31. Hancock v. Kelly, 81 Ala. 368, 2 So. 281, 286 (1887).

32. Washington v. Washington, Virginia & Maryland Coach Co., 250 F.Supp. 888, 890 (D.D.C.1966) (accident report admissible where supervisor of driver who prepared it testified that he had read

it and if it had failed to correctly state the facts he would have caused it to be corrected); Walker v. Larson, 284 Minn. 99, 169 N.W.2d 737 (1969) (it is adequate if one with knowledge recognizes the signature as his and testifies that he would not have signed it without reading it and determining it to be accurate, and suggestions in Hodas v. Davis, 203 App.Div. 297, 196 N.Y.S. 801 (1922) to the contrary disapproved).

33. Asaro v. Parisi, 297 F.2d 859, 863 (1st Cir. 1962) cert. denied 370 U.S. 904.

34. See Curtis v. Bradley, 65 Conn. 99, 31 Atl. 591 (1894); Rathbun v. Brancatella, 93 N.J.L. 222, 107 Atl. 279 (1919).

CHAPTER 31

REGULARLY KEPT RECORDS

304. Admissibility of Regularly Kept Records.

Entries in business books and other regularly kept records may be offered in evidence in many different situations, although in almost all the entry is offered as evidence of the truth of its terms. In such cases the evidence is clearly hearsay and some exception to the hearsay rule must be invoked if the entries are to be admitted. Often no specific exception is needed, however, as the entries come within the terms of other exceptions. For example, if the entries were made by a party to the suit they are admissible against him as admissions.[1] If the entrant is produced as a witness, the entries may be used to refresh his memory[2] or may come in as records of past recollection.[3] Sometimes entries may be admissible as declarations against interest.[4] The present chapter is concerned only with those situations in which none of these alternative theories of admissibility is available and a specific exception to the hearsay rule for regularly kept records must be invoked.

305. The Origin of the Regularly Kept Records Exception and the Shopbook Vestige.[5]

By the 1600's in England a custom emerged in the common law courts of receiving the

---

1. Stein v. C. I. R., 322 F.2d 78, 82 (5th Cir. 1963) ("It was not error for the Tax Court to accept the entries in Stein's notebooks that showed daily net gambling winnings and fail to give credence to the entries in said notebooks that showed daily net losses. The entries showing daily net gambling winnings were in the nature of declarations against interest while the entries showing daily net losses were in the nature of self serving declarations."); Vickers v. Ripley, 226 Ark. 802, 295 S.W.2d 309 (1956); Parker v. Priestley, 39 So.2d 210, 215 (Fla. 1949) (party's account books admitted against him as admission despite statute providing such books shall be admissible in his favor); Wentz v. Guaranteed Sand & Gravel Co., 205 Minn. 611, 287 N.W.

113 (1939); Utilities Ins. Co. v. Stuart, 134 Neb. 413, 278 N.W. 827 (1938). See generally § 239, supra; Dec.Dig. Evidence ☞354(18).

2. E. g., Cohen v. Berry, 188 A.2d 302 (D.C.Ct.App. 1963). See generally § 9, supra; Dec.Dig. Witnesses ☞255(7)–(8).

3. Ettelson v. Metropolitan Life Ins. Co., 164 F.2d 660 (2d Cir. 1947). See generally Ch. 30, supra; Dec.Dig. Evidence ☞355(5)–(6).

4. See generally, Ch. 27, supra; Dec.Dig. Evidence ☞354(24).

5. See generally, 5 Wigmore, Evidence § 1518; Radtke v. Taylor, 105 Ore. 559, 210 Pac. 863 (1922) (Harris, J.); 30 Am.Jur.2d Evidence §§ 918–926.

"shop books" of tradesmen and craftsmen as evidence of debts for goods sold or services rendered on open accounts. This practice seems to have been based largely on necessity and convenience, because the party himself was disqualified as a witness. Since most tradesmen were their own bookkeepers, the rule permitted a reasonable means of avoiding the harsh common law rule preventing a party from appearing as a witness in his own behalf. Nevertheless, theoretical objections to the self-serving nature of this evidence, apparently coupled with abuse of it in practice, led to statutory limitation upon the use of shopbooks of a party in 1609.[6] Specifically, the statute limited the use of shopbooks to a period of one year after the debt was created except where a bill of debt was given or where the transaction was between merchants and tradesmen. The higher courts refused to recognize the books at all after the year had elapsed, although in practice such evidence was received in the lower courts with small claims jurisdiction.

During the 1700's a broader doctrine began to develop in the English common law courts. At first, this permitted only the use of regular entries in the books of a party by a deceased clerk, but this was expanded to cover books regularly kept by third persons who had since died. By 1832 the doctrine was firmly grounded and its scope was held to include all entries made by a person, since deceased, in the ordinary course of his business.

The development of the doctrine in America was less satisfactory, however. In the colonies limited exceptions for the books of a party based on the English statute of 1609 and Dutch practice were in force. In addition to requiring that the entries be regularly made at or about the time of the transaction and as a part of the routine of the business, other restrictions were often imposed.

These included requirements that (1) the party using the book not have had a clerk, (2) the party file a "supplemental oath" to the justness of the account, (3) the books bear an honest appearance, (4) each transaction not exceed a certain limited value, (5) witnesses testify from their experience in dealing with the party that the books are honest, (6) the books be used only to prove open accounts for goods and services furnished the defendant (thus making them unavailable for proof of loans, and goods and services furnished under special contract or furnished to third persons on defendant's credit), and (7) other proof be made of the actual delivery of some of the goods.[7]

Not until the early 1800's did the American equivalent of the English general exception for regular business entries by deceased persons emerge. As the doctrine gained acceptance, however, often no provision was made for the "shop books" of a party, whose admissibility continued to be controlled by the restrictive statutes. This made little sense, especially in view of the fact that abolition of the party's disqualification as a witness [8] removed the justification for treating the books of a party as a special problem. Most courts today take the reasonable position that if shop book statutes remain, they

---

6. 7 Jac. I, ch. 12 (1609).

7. See sources cited in n. 5, supra.

8. See § 65, supra. The retention of a vestige of the old common law disqualification of a party in the "dead man's statutes" adopted by many jurisdictions created a special problem. These statutes prohibited a party from testifying in an action brought by or against a decedent's estate regarding transactions with the deceased; see § 65, supra. It has generally been held, however, that use of the shop books (and the supplemental oath necessary for their use) was not "testimony" within the meaning of the dead man's statutes, Roth v. Headlee, 238 Iowa 1340, 29 N.W.2d 923 (1947), or that for some other reason the dead man's statutes did not prohibit the use of shop books in actions within the scope of the dead man's statute, Fidelity & Columbia Trust Co. v. Lyons, 302 Ky. 839, 196 S.W.2d 605 (1946). Contra, Tipps v. Landers, 182 Cal. 771, 190 Pac. 173 (1920). See generally, 5 Wigmore, Evidence § 1554; Annot., 6 A.L.R. 756.

are to be regarded as an alternative ground of admissibility. A party's books offered in his own behalf, then, may be admissible even if they do not meet the shop book act requirements, if they meet the tests for regularly kept records generally.

306. The Regularly Kept Records Exception In General.[9]

The admissibility of regularly kept records is now largely a matter of statute because of widespread adoption of the Commonwealth Fund Act [10] (which is codified in the federal statute [11]) and the Uniform Business Records as Evidence Act.[12] Several other versions of

---

9. See generally, 5 Wigmore, Evidence §§ 1517–1561; Morgan, et al., The Law of Evidence, Some Proposals for Its Reform, ch. 5 (1927); Lauer, Business Records as Evidence in Missouri, 1964 Wash. U.L.Q. 24; Laughlin, Business Entries and the Like, 46 Iowa L.Rev. 276 (1961); Note, Business Records Rule: Repeated Target of Legal Reform, 36 Brooklyn L.Rev. 241 (1970); Note, Revised Business Entry Statutes: Theory and Practice, 48 Colum.L.Rev. 920 (1948); Comment, Business Records in Louisiana as an Exception to the Hearsay Rule, 21 La.L.Rev. 449 (1961); Comment, Hearsay and Business Entries: The Uncertain Path of Maine Law, 17 Maine L.Rev. 205 (1965); Annot., 13 A.L.R.3d 284 (admissibility of party's books to prove loans or payment by that party); 30 Am.Jur.2d Evidence §§ 927–961; C.J.S. Evidence §§ 682–695; Dec.Dig. Evidence ⟳350, 354, 361, 376, 383(8), Criminal Law ⟳434.

10. "Any writing or record, whether in the form of an entry in a book or otherwise, made as a memorandum or record of any act, transaction, occurrence or event shall be admissible in evidence in proof of said act, transaction, occurrence or event, if the trial judge shall find that it was made in the regular course of any business, and that it was the regular course of such business to make such memorandum or record at the time of such act, transaction, occurrence or event or within a reasonable time thereafter. All other circumstances of the making of such writing or record, including lack of personal knowledge by the entrant or maker, may be shown to affect its weight, but they shall not affect its admissibility. The term business shall include business, profession, occupation and calling of every kind." Morgan et al., The Law of Evidence, Some Proposals for Its Reform 63 (1927).

11. 28 U.S.C.A. § 1732.

12. "§ 1. Definition. The term 'business' shall include every kind of business, profession, occupation, calling or operation of institutions, whether carried on for profit or not.

the exception have been offered, one by Professor Roy R. Ray [13] (which was adopted by the Texas Legislature) [14] and another in the Uniform Rules of Evidence.[15] Recently an-

---

"§ 2. Business Record. A record of an act, condition or event, shall, in so far as relevant, be competent evidence if the custodian or other qualified witness testifies to its identity and the mode of its preparation, and if it was made in the regular course of business, at or near the time of the act, condition or event, and if, in the opinion of the court, the sources of information, method and time of preparation were such as to justify its admission." 9A U.L.A. 506 (1965).

13. See Ray, Business Records—A Proposed Rule of Admissibility, 5 Sw.L.J. 33 (1951).

14. "Section 1. A memorandum or record of an act, event or condition shall, in so far as relevant, be competent evidence of the occurrence of the act or event or the existence of the condition if the judge finds that:

"(a) It was made in the regular course of business;

"(b) It was the regular course of that business for an employee or representative of such business with personal knowledge of such act, event or condition to make such memorandum or record or to transmit information thereof to be included in such memorandum or record;

"(c) It was made at or near the time of the act, event or condition or reasonably soon thereafter.

"Sec. 2. The identity and mode of preparation of the memorandum or record in accordance with the provisions of paragraph one (1) may be proved by the testimony of the entrant, custodian or other qualified witness even though he may not have personal knowledge as to the various items or contents of such memorandum or record. Such lack of personal knowledge may be shown to affect the weight and credibility of the memorandum or record but shall not affect its admissibility.

"Sec. 3. Evidence to the effect that the records of a business do not contain any memorandum or record of an alleged act, event or condition shall be competent to prove the non-occurrence of the act or event or the non-existence of the condition in that business if the judge finds that it was the regular course of that business to make such memoranda or records of all such acts, events or conditions at the time or within reasonable time thereafter and to preserve them.

"Sec. 4. 'Business' as used in this Act includes any and every kind of regular organized activity whether conducted for profit or not." Vernon's Ann.Tex. Civ.St. art. 3737e.

15. Uniform Rule 63(13) provides for the admission of:

"(13) *Business Entries and the Like.* Writings offered as memoranda or records of acts, conditions or events to prove the facts stated therein, if the judge finds that they were made in the regular course of

other version has been offered by the Committee on Rules of Practice and Procedure of the Judicial Conference of the United States.[16] Even in those states in which there is no statute comparable to any of these model formulations, however, it is likely that the development of the common law exception will follow closely interpretations of the model formulations.[17] These formulations, to varying degrees, represent primarily the codification and modernization of a preexisting common law exception.

The common law exception had four elements: (a) the entries must be original entries made in the routine of a business, (b) the entries must have been made upon the personal knowledge of the recorder or of someone reporting to him, (c) the entries must have been made at or near the time of the transaction recorded, and (d) the recorder and his informant must be shown to be unavailable. If these conditions were met, the business entry was admissible to prove the facts recited in it.

The exception is justified on grounds analogous to those underlying other exceptions to the hearsay rule. Unusual reliability is regarded as furnished by the fact that in practice regular entries have a comparatively high degree of accuracy (as compared to other memoranda) because such books and records are customarily checked as to correctness by systematic balance-striking, because the very regularity and continuity of the records is calculated to train the record-keeper in habits of precision, and because in actual experience the entire business of the nation and many other activities constantly function in reliance upon entries of this kind. The necessity for resort to these hearsay statements was manifested at common law by the requirement that the entries be used only upon a showing that the person or persons who made the entry and upon whose knowledge it was based were unavailable as witnesses because of death, insanity, disappearance or other reason. Today, the inconvenience of calling those with firsthand knowledge and the unlikelihood of their remembering accurately the details of specific transactions convincingly demonstrate the need for recourse to their written records, without regard to physical unavailability.

307. Types of Entries [18]: Opinions: Absence of Entry.

The usual statement of the rule as requiring a "record" suggests that oral reports are not within it, even if the other requirements for admissibility are met. The Uniform Rules speak specifically of a "writing," [19] although the federal statute refers to "any writing or record." [20] The policy underlying the rule suggests that only reports preserved in some relatively permanent manner will have those characteristics relied upon to establish accuracy. Nevertheless, the English position is that oral reports may

---

a business at or about the time of the act, condition or event recorded, and that the sources of information from which they were made and the methods and circumstances of their preparation were such as to indicate their trustworthiness."

16. F.R.Ev. (R.D.1971) 803(6):

"**Records of Regularly Conducted Activity.** A memorandum, report, record, or data compilation, in any form, of acts, events, conditions, opinions, or diagnoses, made at or near the time by, or from information transmitted by, a person with knowledge, all in the course of a regularly conducted activity, as shown by the testimony of the custodian or other qualified witness, unless the sources of information or other circumstances indicate lack of trustworthiness."

17. See Laughlin, Business Entries and the Like, 46 Iowa L.Rev. 276, 305 (1961).

18. See generally, 5 Wigmore, Evidence § 1528. See also Annot., 8 A.L.R.Fed. 919 (personal checkbook or account as business record under federal statute); Annot., 83 A.L.R. 806 (admissibility of loose leaf systems of account); Annot., 68 A.L.R. 692 (check stubs).

19. Uniform Rule 63(13). However, the term writing is defined with extraordinary breadth. Id. 1(13).

20. 28 U.S.C.A. § 1732.

qualify under the exception[21] and some American courts have admitted oral reports on the basis of a partial analogy to business records.[22]

Under the common law exception, the entries were required to be "original" entries and not mere transcribed records or copies.[23] This was based on the assumption that the original entries were more likely to be accurate than subsequent copies or transcriptions. In business practice, however, it is customary for daily transactions such as sales or services rendered to be noted upon slips, memorandum books or the like by the person most directly concerned, and for someone else to collect these memoranda and from them make entries into a permanent book such as a journal or ledger. In these cases, the entries in the permanent record sufficiently comply with the requirement of originality.[24] They would certainly be admissible if the slips or memoranda disappeared, and should, it seems, be admissible as the original permanent entry without proof as to the unavailability of the tentative memoranda. This also serves the interest of convenience, since it is much easier to use a ledger or similar source than slips or temporary memoranda when the inquiry is into the whole state of an account. Of course, the slips or memoranda would also be admissible if they should be offered.

It has been suggested that entries in the form of opinions are not admissible if the declarant was not an expert making a statement concerning a matter within his expertise and as to which he would be competent to express an opinion if testifying in person.[25] In general, the opinion rule should be restricted to governing the manner of presenting courtroom testimony and should have

21. 5 Wigmore, Evidence § 1528, citing Sussex Peerage Case, 11 Cl. & F. 113 (1844). See also Cross, Evidence 406 (3d ed. 1967). Wigmore suggests that the English requirement that the person making the report have a duty to do so (see § 308, infra) provides a sufficient additional assurance of reliability to justify expanding the exception to include oral reports.

22. Williams v. Walton & Whann Co., 9 Houst. (Del.) 322, 32 Atl. 726 (1892) (oral reports admissible if made regularly); Geralds v. Champlin, 93 N.H. 157, 37 A.2d 155 (1944) (oral reports of deceased foreman to superintendent regarding employee's complaints of trouble with his leg, made as part of checkup system admissible). See Notes, 8 U.Det. L.J. 42 (1944), 93 U.Pa.L.Rev. 101 (1944).

23. See generally, 5 Wigmore, Evidence §§ 1532, 1558; Annot., 17 A.L.R.2d 235; 30 Am.Jur.2d Evidence §§ 941–945. In a typical double-entry bookkeeping system, the journal or daybook in which transactions are entered in chronological order is the first permanent record. A strict literal interpretation of "book of original entry" under this system would be limited to the journal. The ledger, to which items are transferred according to classification and which furnishes the "controls" of the business, however, obviously serves up information in far more usable form, and its accuracy is equally assured by its being a part of the entire system. Accordingly, while insistence is sometimes found that the journal be used, the case has generally been otherwise. Statutes containing the expression "book of original entry" offer occasional difficulty.

The requirement of original entry is not to be confused with the rule preferring the original of a document. See § 230, supra.

McCormick et al on Evid. 2nd Ed. HB—46

24. E. g., Graves v. Garvin, 272 F.2d 924 (4th Cir. 1959) (day books in which bookkeeper made entries from receipts admissible as books of original entry); Vickers v. Ripley, 226 Ark. 802, 295 S.W.2d 309 (1956) (ledger account made up from sales tickets or invoices admissible); Tull v. Turek, 38 Del.Ch. 182, 147 A.2d 658 (1958) (ledger in which entries were made once each year from data supplied by plaintiffs admissible); Cascade Lumber Terminal, Inc. v. Cvitanovich, 215 Ore. 111, 332 P.2d 1061 (1958) (looseleaf subsidiary ledger in which bookkeeper made entries from log scalers' sheets on which number of logs delivered was initially entered admissible); Tri-Motor Sales, Inc. v. Travelers Indemnity, 19 Wis.2d 99, 119 N.W.2d 327 (1963) (account books made from purchase invoices and hard copies of sales slips, and not the invoices and slips themselves, were "original entries").

25. Standard Oil Co. v. Moore, 251 F.2d 188, 214 (9th Cir. 1957):

"A good many of the exhibits . . . contain expressions of opinion, or conclusions, concerning the reason why another oil company or a noncustomer service station operator took, or failed to take, certain action, or concerning the probable course such companies would follow in the future. Expressions of opinion or conclusions on such matters do not call for professional or scientific knowledge or skill. It follows that exhibits containing such recitals were not admissible [under the federal statute]."

little if any application to the admissibility of out-of-court statements.[26] It would, however, be appropriate to recognize a discretionary power in the trial judge to exclude an entry if the form in which it was made renders it so vague or speculative as to cause its probative value to be outweighed by the danger that it would mislead or confuse the jury.[27]

Occasionally the absence of an entry relating to a particular transaction is offered as proof that no such transaction took place.[28] In a recent case, for example, proof was offered that a car rental agency's records showed no lease or rental activity in regard to a certain vehicle, as tending to show that the defendant in whose possession it was found had stolen it.[29] The majority of courts admit the evidence for this purpose,[30] and both the Uniform Rule[31] and the Proposed Rules of Evidence for the Federal Courts[32] specifically so provide.

308. The Requirement that the Entries be Made in the Routine of a "Business."[33]

The early cases construed the requirement of a "business" literally, and accordingly excluded, as not concerned with "business", records of temperature kept daily as an avocation[34] and even private records kept in connection with an individual's financial affairs.[35] The Commonwealth Fund Act defines "business" as including "business, profession, occupation and calling of any kind"[36]; both the Uniform Rules[37] and the Uniform Act[38] have added "operation of institution" and specifically dispensed with any requirement that the activity be carried on for profit. Thus in current practice records kept by nonprofit organizations, such as churches, are admissible,[39] and even private financial records are probably within the exception.[40] Where the activity is purely personal, as in the case of a personal diary, the cases are still split.[41]

---

26. See § 18, supra.

27. This is certainly possible under statutes and rules requiring that the sources of information and method of preparation justify the record's admission. See further, § 313, n. 5, infra (hospital records).

28. See generally, 5 Wigmore, Evidence § 1531; 30 Am.Jur.2d Evidence § 959; C.J.S. Evidence § 687.

29. United States v. De Georgia, 420 F.2d 889 (9th Cir. 1969).

30. See the excellent discussion in United States v. De Georgia, 420 F.2d 889, 891–94 (9th Cir. 1969). For cases holding the evidence admissible, see McCanahan v. United States, 292 F.2d 630, 636–37 (5th Cir. 1961); Zurich v. Wehr, 163 F.2d 791 (3d Cir. 1947); People v. Torres, 201 Cal.App.2d 290, 20 Cal.Rptr. 315 (1962) (citing extensively from the case law). For cases holding or suggesting that the evidence is inadmissible, see Shreve v. United States, 77 F.2d 2, 7 (9th Cir. 1935), overruled by United States v. De Georgia, 420 F.2d 889 (9th Cir. 1969); Riley v. Boehm, 167 Mass. 183, 45 N.E. 84 (1896) (alternative ground); Gravel Products Division of Buffalo Crushed Stone Corp. v. Sunnydale Acres, Inc., 10 Misc.2d 323, 171 N.Y.S.2d 519 (1958).

31. Uniform Rule 63(14).

32. F.R.Ev. (R.D.1971) 803(7). Statutes in a number of states specifically provide for admissibility. See United States v. De Georgia, 420 F.2d 889, 892 n. 9 (9th Cir. 1969).

33. See generally, 30 Am.Jur.2d Evidence §§ 937, 939; C.J.S. Evidence § 685(1).

34. Arnold v. Hussey, 111 Me. 224, 88 Atl. 724 (1913).

35. In re Cummings' Estate, 226 Iowa 1207, 286 N.W. 409 (1939) (plaintiff's memorandum book of loans made by him inadmissible because he was not in the loan business). See Annot., 68 A.L.R. 692.

36. See § 306, n. 10, supra.

37. Uniform Rule 63(12).

38. Uniform Business Records as Evidence Act § 2. See § 306, n. 12, supra.

39. Ford v. State, 82 Tex.Cr.R. 639, 200 S.W. 841 (1918) (church's register of birth and baptism held admissible); Leach v. State, 80 Tex.Cr.R. 376, 189 S.W. 733 (1916) (Sunday School's attendance record admissible to prove alibi).

40. McCary v. McMorris, 265 Ala. 493, 92 So.2d 319 (1957) (passbook admissible); In re Tracy's Estate, 299 S.W. 884 (Iowa 1941) (check stubs kept by private individual admissible). See generally, 5 Wigmore, Evidence § 1523.

41. Compare Buckley v. Altheimer, 152 F.2d 502 (7th Cir. 1945) (rejecting a diary under the Model Act) with Carozza v. Williams, 190 Md. 143, 57 A.2d 782 (1948) (admitting a diary under the Model Act). The restrictions which seem to inhere in use of the term "business," however broadly defined, are sought to be avoided by substituting "regularly

Under the English and Canadian rules, both the matter or event recorded and the recording of it must have been performed pursuant to a duty to a third person.[42] This is not the case under the American law.[43]

More serious problems are raised by the relationship between the report and the business being conducted. The leading case is Palmer v. Hoffman,[44] a suit against railroad trustees for injuries and death arising out of an accident at a railroad crossing. The engineer of the train involved was interviewed two days after the accident by a representative of the railroad and a representative of the state Public Utilities Commission. He signed a statement concerning his version of the incident. The engineer died before trial, and the statement was offered. The proponents of its admissibility offered to prove that the railroad obtained such statements in the regular course of its business. Affirming the trial court's exclusion of the report, the Supreme Court of the United States stated:

> "[The report] is not a record made for the systematic conduct of the business as a business. An accident report may affect that business in the sense that it affords information on which the management may act. It is not, however, typical of entries made systematically or as a matter of routine to record events or occurrences, to reflect transactions with others, or to provide internal controls. . . . Unlike payrolls, accounts receivable, accounts payable, bills of lading and the like, these reports are calculated for use essentially in the court, not in the busi-

ness. Their primary use is in litigating, not in railroading." [45]

Consequently, the report was held not to have been made "in the regular course" of the business within the meaning of the federal statute providing for the admissibility of business records.[46]

It has been urged that *Palmer* violated the letter of the statute,[47] and the lower courts have not dealt with it uniformly. The most reasonable reading of it, however, is that it does not create a blanket rule of exclusion for "self-serving" accident reports or similar records kept by businesses. Rather, it recognizes a discretionary power in the trial court to exclude evidence which meets the letter of the business records exception but which, under the circumstances, appears to lack the reliability which business records are assumed to ordinarily have.[48] The existence of

45. Id. at 113–14.

46. Id. at 111.

47. Laughlin, Business Entries and the Like, 46 Iowa L.Rev. 276, 289 (1961). Contra, Comment, 43 Colum.L.Rev. 392 (1943).

48. Among the cases holding reports of this kind inadmissible in reliance upon *Palmer*, see Colorificio Italiano Max Meyer S. P. A. v. S/S Hellenic Wave, 419 F.2d 223 (5th Cir. 1969) (survey report inadmissible in admiralty case, because intended use is in litigation); Picker X-Ray Corp. v. Freker, 405 F.2d 916 (8th Cir. 1969) (hospital "incident report" concerning accident, written by business manager shown to have been aware at the time of the possibility of litigation, inadmissible); Hussein v. Isthmian Lines, Inc., 405 F.2d 946 (5th Cir. 1968) (forms used by ship's officers to cause agents in foreign ports to obtain medical attention for crew members inadmissible, because they were essentially reports by physicians to an employer regarding employees' physical condition); Brewer v. Hawkins, 248 Ark. 1325, 455 S.W.2d 864 (1970) (daily and weekly reports of state troopers regarding arrests and dispositions offered to prove cash bonds received by sheriff not admissible, because testimony showed no motive for accuracy and some deliberate falsification). For cases ruling in favor of admissibility, see Mitchell v. American Export Isbrandtsen Lines, Inc., 430 F.2d 1023 (2d Cir. 1970) (report of illness by ship's physician admissible, because it was not made for purposes of litigation and the maker was available for examination at trial); Caldecott v. Long Island Lighting Co., 417 F.2d 994 (2d Cir. 1969) (medical examiner's

conducted activity" in the Proposed Federal Rules of Evidence. F.R.Ev. (R.D.1971) 803(6).

42. Cross, Evidence 407 (3d ed. 1967).

43. Hutchins v. Berry, 75 N.H. 416, 75 Atl. 650 (1910); Lebrun v. Boston & M. R. Co., 83 N.H. 293, 142 Atl. 128 (1928) (dictum). See generally, 5 Wigmore, Evidence, § 1524.

44. 318 U.S. 109 (1943).

a motive and opportunity to falsify the record, especially in the absence of any counterveiling factors weighing against such action should be primary factors considered.[49] The Proposed Federal Rules of Evidence would incorporate this reading of *Palmer* by providing for the admission of reports meeting the requirements of business records "unless the sources of information or other circumstances indicate lack of trustworthiness." [50]

309. The Requirement that the Entries have been Made at or near the Time of the Transaction Recorded.[51]

A substantial factor in the reliability of any system of records is the promptness with which transactions are recorded. According-

ly, all formulations of the exception for regularly kept records require that the entry be made either at the time of the transaction or within a reasonable time thereafter. Whether an entry made subsequent to the transaction has been made within a sufficient time to render it within the exception depends upon whether the time span between the transaction and the entry was so great as to suggest a danger of inaccuracy by lapse of memory. Only if such a danger appears from the circumstances of the case should the entry be held to have been made beyond the time limitation.[52]

report properly admitted, because there was no incentive to falsify); Gaussen v. United Fruit Co., 412 F.2d 72 (2d Cir. 1969) (suggestion—but no holding —that letter from ship's captain to employer regarding accident investigation on ship revealing that injured employee was intoxicated would be admissible; strong disagreement by Kaufman, J.); Vaccaro v. Alcoa Steamship Co., 405 F.2d 1133 (2d Cir. 1968) (report made by army employee should have been admitted since he had no motive to falsify). Where the party offering the report was not the party with the opportunity to falsify it, the report has been held admissible on the ground that no prejudice to the complaining party is possible. Korte v. New York, N. H. & H. R. Co., 191 F.2d 86 (2d Cir. 1951) cert. denied 342 U.S. 868, noted 37 Corn.L.Q. 290, 5 Vand.L.Rev. 651 (plaintiff offers report of physical examination made by physician employed by defendant); Yates v. Bair Transport, Inc., 249 F.Supp. 681 (S.D.N.Y.1965) (same). See also Leon v. Penn Central Co., 428 F.2d 528 (7th Cir. 1970) (plaintiff offers accident report made by defendant's employee).

49. Thus where the only function that the report serves is to assist in litigation or its preparation, many of the normal checks upon the accuracy of business records are not operative. Reliance upon the reports' accuracy in the day-to-day operation of the business is significant.

50. F.R.Ev. (R.D.1971) 803(6). A similar result is accomplished in the Uniform Business Records as Evidence Act by providing for admissibility "if, in the opinion of the court, the sources of information, method and time of preparation were such as to justify its admission." Uniform Business Records as Evidence Act § 2, 9A U.L.A. 506 (1965).

51. See generally, 5 Wigmore, Evidence §§ 1526, 1550; 30 Am.Jur.2d Evidence § 938; C.J.S. Evidence § 690; Dec.Dig. Evidence ☞354(12).

52. See Standard Oil Co. of Cal. v. Moore, 251 F.2d 188, 223 (9th Cir. 1957) cert. denied 356 U.S. 975 (not error to admit entries in ledger, even though some were not made until several months after transaction, where "there was no evidence to show that this lag introduced inaccuracies or uncertainties as to the reliability of the ledger"); Metropolitan Protection Service, Inc. v. Tanner, 182 Neb. 507, 155 N.W.2d 803, 805 (1968) ("Circumstances affecting admissibility [under the contemporaneous requirement] are complexity of the information in the record, training and skill of the recorder, and reasonableness of the elapsed time generally."). See also Henderson v. Zubik, 390 Pa. 521, 136 A.2d 124 (1957) (not error to admit book entries showing purchaser, sale price and cost of material although all entries were made at the time of sale and figures as to initial cost were based on memory, especially in view of proof of established market price for material). For cases excluding offered records for failure to comply with the requirement, see Kemp v. Pinal County, 8 Ariz.App. 41, 442 P.2d 864 (1968) (entry in record book offered to prove numerical result of blood alcohol test inadmissible where entry was made 59 days after test, 100 tests per month may have been performed, and the entry consisted of a figure "which could easily be transposed or otherwise confused"); E.Z.E., Inc. v. Jackson, 235 So.2d 337 (Fla.App.1970) (ledger offered to prove payments made to offeror erroneously admitted because entries were made a week or 10 days after completion of jobs and were made from memory; ledger characterized as "merely a collection of personal notations made . . . at various intervals after the transaction involved"); Yates v. Helms, 154 So.2d 731 (Fla.App.1963) (written memorandum of bookkeeper, made from statements of employees, properly excluded); In re Robinson's Estate, 253 Iowa 82, 11 N.W.2d 275 (1961) (books of account not admissible under shopbook rule where entries were summaries entered "long" after the fact); Adams v. New Jersey State Fair, 71 N.J.Super. 528, 177 A.2d 486 (1962) (error to admit 1955 balance entry on 1956 ledger because

310. The Requirement that Entries have been Made upon the Personal Knowledge of the Recorder or of Someone Reporting to Him.[53]

The common law exception for business records required that the entries have been made by one with personal knowledge of the matter entered or upon reports to him by one with personal knowledge.[54] If the entrant himself lacked personal knowledge, the foundation for the records required the testimony of all those giving information to their personal knowledge or proof of their unavailability. Rathborne v. Hatch[55] provides an illustration of the difficulties of laying such a foundation. Books of a stockbroker were offered to prove the price at which shares of stock had been purchased. Although the broker's floor member testified that he had knowledge of prices and reported these accurately to telephone boys, the books were held inadmissible because the telephone boys were not called to testify that they accurately relayed this information and their unavailability was not established. As one commentator has observed,[56] enforcement of such a requirement would make the exception virtually useless in the modern world.

The status of the common law requirement concerning personal knowledge has not always been clear in the reform legislation. The Commonwealth Fund Act provides that "all . . . circumstances of the making of such writing or record [other than having been made in the regular course of business], including lack of personal knowledge by the entrant or maker, may be shown to affect its weight but shall not affect its admissibility."[57] The Uniform Act does not address itself to the matter directly, but does provide for admissibility only if, "in the opinion of the court, the sources of information . . . were such as to justify its admission."[58] The Proposed Federal Rules of Evidence, however, require that the entry have been made "by, or from information transmitted by, a person with knowledge, all in the course of a regularly conducted activity," with the qualification that the record may be held inadmissible if the source of information indicates lack of trustworthiness.[59] The Texas statute requires a finding of entry by one with personal knowledge or the transmission to the recorder of one with such knowledge.[60]

The problem is, of course, essentially one of "double hearsay."[61] While the business records exception may serve to justify admitting the out-of-court declarations of the maker of the record as to what he said from his own personal knowledge, it does not follow that this justifies admitting the declaration of someone else simply because the maker of the record testifies to it. It has reasonably been suggested that this should be treated no differently from other double hearsay problems.[62] Thus a business record containing an assertion by someone other than the maker should be admitted to prove the truth of that assertion only if the assertion itself

that entry was merely carried forward from book of prior year and thus was not made at or near time of event).

53. See generally, 5 Wigmore, Evidence §§ 1530, 1530a, 1555; 30 Am.Jur.2d Evidence §§ 951–53; C.J.S. Evidence §§ 692–93; Dec.Dig. Evidence ☞354(11).

54. E. g., Lord v. Moore, 37 Me. 208, 220 (1854).

55. 80 App.Div. 115, 80 N.Y.Supp. 347 (1903).

56. Comment, Hearsay and Business Entries: The Uncertain Path of Maine Law, 17 Me.L.Rev. 205, 213 (1965).

The only advance beyond the hearsay exception for recorded recollection would be in allowing use of the record when the person was unavailable.

57. § 306, n. 10 supra.

58. § 306, n. 12 supra.

59. § 306, n. 16 supra.

60. § 306, n. 14 supra.

61. See generally, Laughlin, Business Entries and the Like, 46 Iowa L.Rev. 276, 296–99 (1961). For discussion with specific reference to hospital records, see § 313, notes 95–99 and 1–3, infra.

62. Laughlin, op. cit., n. 61, supra, at 298.

comes within an exception to the hearsay rule. In most cases this involves essentially a double application of the business records exception. First, the entry is admissible to prove the truth of what the maker knew of his own knowledge, i. e., that he was told something of an informant, if the entry was made in the course of business by the maker. Second, the entry is admissible to prove the truth of what the informant told the maker only if the informant's action in reporting this was within the regular course of business, i. e., if the informant was a part of the business organization with a duty to make such reports. If, however, the informant's statement comes within another exception, this double application of the business entry exception is unnecessary. For example, a police report of an accident might contain an assertion made by one driver soon after the accident. The driver's statement might be an excited utterance, and the police report a business record. The police report would therefore be admissible to prove the truth of the driver's spontaneous utterance, despite the fact that the driver had no business duty to make the statement.

This is probably the approach that most courts would take under the various formulations of the business records exception. The Texas statute requires not only that the entry be based upon the personal knowledge of someone, but in addition that the person with the personal knowledge have a duty in the regular course of the business to transmit this information to the maker of the record. The Proposed Federal Rules, by requiring that the transmittal from the person with personal knowledge to the person making entry be "in the course of a regularly conducted activity," impose a similar requirement. This requirement—that the entry be based on information from one with personal knowledge and a business duty to obtain and transmit this knowledge—would prob-

ably be applied by almost all courts today.[63] Both the Commonwealth Fund Act and the Uniform Act could be read as eliminating a strict requirement of firsthand knowledge. The language of the Commonwealth Fund Act permits a reading to the effect that lack of personal knowledge may not serve as the basis for exclusion, and must be regarded as affecting only weight. The Uniform Act, on the other hand, if it dispenses with an absolute requirement of personal knowledge, seems clearly to permit exclusion on the basis that the lack of personal knowledge in some situations at least justifies a finding that the sources of information do not justify the admission of the record. It is unlikely, however, that any court would interpret either statute to dispense with the requirement of firsthand knowledge. But it is less clear that the statutes require the imposition of the business duty criterion. From a policy point of view, however, the requirement of a business duty to transmit the information seems a reasonable means of assuring reliability, and it is likely that most courts would read the Commonwealth Fund Act or the Uniform Act as requiring that the entry be based upon information transmitted to the recorder by one with firsthand knowledge and a business duty to know and report the information.[64]

63. Probably the leading case is Johnson v. Lutz, 253 N.Y. 124, 170 N.E. 517 (1930), holding a police officer's report inadmissible under New York's version of the Commonwealth Fund Act insofar as it was not based upon his personal knowledge but rather upon information provided by a bystander. Wigmore is bitterly critical of this decision, 5 Wigmore, Evidence § 1530a, n. 1, and would apparently require only that the recorder obtain, in the regular course of his business, the information from one with personal knowledge. See 5 Wigmore, Evidence § 1530, p. 379.

64. Under the federal statutory codification of the Commonwealth Fund Act, it is clear that the lack of personal knowledge on the part of the maker of the entry goes to weight and not admissibility. Southern Glass and Builders Supply Co. v. United States, 398 F.2d 109 (5th Cir. 1968); United States v. Re, 336 F.2d 306, 313 (2d Cir. 1964) cert. denied 379 U.S. 904. There is significant support for the

Direct proof of actual knowledge may be difficult, and it may even be impossible to prove specifically the identity of the informant with actual knowledge. Evidence that it was someone's business duty in the organization's routine to observe the matter will be prima facie sufficient to establish actual knowledge. This does not dispense with the need for personal knowledge, but permits it to be proved by evidence of prac-

proposition that the individual with personal knowledge must have a business duty to have such knowledge and report it. United States v. Graham, 391 F.2d 439 (6th Cir. 1968) (police report not admissible under federal statute to prove truth of matter asserted by third party because no business duty on third party's part to know facts); Standard Oil Co. of Cal. v. Moore, 251 F.2d 188, 215–15 (9th Cir. 1957) cert. denied 356 U.S. 975 (records inadmissible under federal statute because it was self-evident that person supplying information had no relationship with company which could give rise to a duty to report). The position has been taken that the problem is one of double hearsay, and the record is admissible if some exception justifies each step. Juaire v. Nardin, 395 F.2d 373, 379 (2d Cir. 1968); Yates v. Bair Transport, Inc., 249 F. Supp. 681 (S.D.N.Y.1965). But see Pekelis v. Transcontinental & Western Air, Inc., 187 F.2d 122 (2d Cir. 1951) (reports of organization of boards to investigate airline crashes not inadmissible because conclusions were arguably derived from information from persons under no business duty to report, because under the statute this goes to weight rather than admissibility); United States v. Wolosyn, 411 F.2d 550 (9th Cir. 1969) (police report admissible to prove date of theft).

There is strong support for a similar interpretation of the Uniform Business Records as Evidence Act. Taylor v. Centennial Bowl, Inc., 65 Cal.2d 114, 52 Cal.Rptr. 561, 416 P.2d 793 (1966) (police report would be admissible only if contents were based upon observations of police officer himself or other officials whose job it was to know the facts recorded); Fagen v. Newark, 78 N.J.Super. 294, 188 A.2d 427, 440–41 (1962) (where maker has no personal knowledge of facts recorded, informant must have a duty to make a truthful account or his statement must come within some other exception to the hearsay rule); Fauceglia v. Harry, 409 Pa. 155, 185 A.2d 598 (1962) (business record admissible if "someone in the organization has personally observed the event recorded"). Cf. Schmitt v. Doehler Die Casting Co., 143 Ohio St. 421, 55 N.E. 2d 644 (1944) (where nurse who wrote notation regarding accident on card testified that her information came from the injured party himself five days after the accident, the "sources of information, method and time of preparation of report" were not such as to justify their admission).

tice and a reasonable assumption that general practice was followed in regard to a particular matter. But if the proof shows that a particular report was not in fact based upon information from one with personal knowledge, the report is rendered inadmissible.

Perhaps the area where the personal knowledge requirement has the most impact concerns police reports and similar reports of investigations.[65] In such cases there is little doubt that the report of the investigating officer was made in the regular course of a business. The reports often, however, contain information obtained by the investigating officer from witnesses and similar sources. When applied to such cases, the requirement of firsthand knowledge of one with a business duty to transmit the knowledge means, of course, that insofar as the reports are offered to prove the truth of assertions made by witnesses to the investigating officer they are inadmissible, because almost none of these witnesses could be said to have a duty in the regular course of police business to transmit this information. It is not altogether clear that this is an appropriate result. Arguably a skilled and experienced investigator can be assumed to include an assertion in his report only if, after adequate checking, he determines its accuracy. This might provide a sufficient basis for finding reliability, and the language of both the Uniform Act and the Commonwealth Fund Act would permit such a result. On the other hand, it is arguable that this assurance of reliability is inadequate, especially in the absence of proof of the skill of the particular investigator and his basis for crediting a particular out-of-court statement.[66]

65. See the cases cited in notes 63 and 64, supra. See generally, Annot., 69 A.L.R.2d 1148 (police or other official reports as proof regarding accidents).

66. Reports of this kind may be admissible as official written statements; see § 317, infra.

311.   Unavailability as a Requirement.[67]

The judicial opinions and the commentaries tend unfortunately to confuse the requirement that some of or all those involved in the preparation of a record be shown to be unavailable and the manner by which one who offers proof under the regularly kept record exception must establish the foundation for the admissibility of his proof. Although the two are related, they are separable issues; the matter of the required foundation is discussed in the next section.

The common law rule required that before business records were received as evidence of their truth under this exception the entrant or, in the case of a cooperative entry based upon information given to the entrant by someone else, both the entrant and the informants who reported the facts recited in the record must be proved to be unavailable for production as witnesses.[68] Illness,[69] death,[70] disqualifying insanity,[71] and absence from the jurisdiction[72] constituted unavailability. In addition, however, it seems clear that if an informant or entrant was shown not to recollect the facts sought to be proved, he was unavailable for purposes of this requirement.[73] And Wigmore's suggestion that mercantile inconvenience satisfied the requirement[74] has probably been almost universally accepted. Thus a showing that under the circumstances it would be unreasonably inconvenient for the offering party to produce some or all of those concerned in the production of the record should have sufficed to excuse their nonproduction.

Failure to establish unavailability, of course, did not render the record completely useless. If the record was made upon the personal knowledge of the entrant and he was produced, the record could be used to refresh his memory. If he was unable to recall the facts, the record was usable as a record of past recollection as well as a business record if his lack of recollection was equivalent to unavailability.[75] The same alternatives would be available if preparation of the record had involved an informant as well as an entrant. Insofar as the record reflected the past knowledge and former statement of the absent participant, it was admissible as a business record. If it reflected the past knowledge of a witness without present memory of the transactions, it might be used as either a business record or a past recollection recorded.

The Commonwealth Fund Act, the Uniform Business Records as Evidence Act, and the Texas statute do not expressly address themselves to the unavailability requirement. This silence seems intended to dispense with the requirement. The Proposed Rules of Evidence for the Federal Court specifically make the availability of the makers and entrant immaterial. It appears, therefore, that under any statutory formulation or under present common law doctrines of admissibility the requirement of unavailability has for

---

67. See generally, 5 Wigmore, Evidence § 1521; Dec. Dig. Evidence ⊙⇒354(22)–(22½).

68. 5 Wigmore, Evidence § 1521.

69. Griffin v. Boston & M. R. Co., 87 Vt. 278, 89 A. 220 (1913).

70. Cf. Robinson v. Puls, 28 Cal.2d 664, 171 P.2d 430 (1946).

71. Town of Bridgewater v. Town of Roxbury, 54 Conn. 213, 6 Atl. 415 (1886).

72. Gus Dattilo Fruit Co. v. Louisville & N. R. Co., 238 Ky. 322, 37 S.W.2d 856 (1931).

73. See the language of L. Hand, J., in Massachusetts Bonding & Ins. Co. v. Norwich Pharmacal Co., 18 F.2d 934, 938 (2d Cir. 1927): "It ought to appear that . . . . the missing entrants, if called, would in the nature of things have no recollection of the events recorded and could do no more than corroborate the existing testimony as to the course of business in which they had a part . . . . ."

74. 5 Wigmore, Evidence § 1521(3).

75. Wigmore believes that if the entrant were available, the record was not admissible as a business record but only as a record of past recollection recorded. 5 Wigmore, Evidence § 1521(5). Thayer seems to believe that the record was admissible as a business record even if the entrant testified. Thayer, Cases on Evidence 575 (2d ed. 1900).

all practical purposes been abandoned.[76] Apparent acceptance of inability to recall as satisfying the requirement, together with the commonsense recognition that in any of the situations likely to give rise to a business record the persons involved are unlikely to recall the details of specific transactions, means that proof that a record was made in the regular course of a routine activity constitutes a sufficient showing that calling the participants would be either unduly inconvenient or of no value.[77] This resolution, however, does not address itself to the question how the offeror must establish that the record meets the other requirements which is the subject of the next section.

312. The Matter of Proof: Who Must be Called to Establish Admissibility.[78]

Implementing the common law exception, courts have traditionally required that one offering proof under the regularly kept records exception either call as witnesses all links in the organizational chain by which the entry was made, i. e., all entrants, informants, and intermediaries, or establish their unavailability.[79] This was not part of the requirement of unavailability. To the contrary, it assumed that availability did not render the proof inadmissible, apparently on the reasonable anticipation that the participants would not remember the particular transaction at issue. The requirement was one as to the manner of proving that the offered record met the other requirements of the exception.

In light of present business practices, the common law requirement is clearly unreasonable. The complex nature of modern business organizations is such that all participants in the preparation of a record can most often not be identified or, if they can be pinpointed, could not reasonably be expected to have any helpful recollection concerning the specific transactions at issue. Moreover, production of the large numbers of participants that would be required would be a substantial burden on the offering party, a burden not likely to be justified by the benefits to be derived from requiring production of all participants. The revisions of the exception have dealt with this problem in various manners. The Commonwealth Fund Act did not deal with the matter expressly, although it seems clear that it was proposed principally to alleviate the burdensome method of proof required by some courts under the common law rule.[80] The same is true of the Model Code of Evidence [81] and the Uniform Rules of Evidence.[82] On the other hand, the Uniform Act,[83] the Texas statute,[84] and the Proposed Federal Rules [85] specifically provide that the foundation may be laid by "the custodian or other qualified witness," thus expressly rejecting the requirement that all participants be called.

---

76. See Green, The Model and Uniform Statutes Relating to Business Entries as Evidence, 31 Tulane L.Rev. 49, 55 (1956).

77. See Rossemanno v. Laclede Cab Co., 328 S.W.2d 677 (Mo.1959), holding that a medical report was admissible under the Uniform Act although the doctor who made the report was in the city and apparently available. After suggesting that there was no requirement of unavailability, the court added, "Moreover, it is inconceivable that a busy medical practitioner would have an independent recollection of each entry made in his business records and be able to testify from personal recollection as to when and by whom all entries were made." Id. at 681–82.

78. See generally, 5 Wigmore, Evidence § 1530; Laughlin, Business Entries and the Like, 46 Iowa L. Rev. 276, 294–96 (1961); 30 Am.Jur.2d Evidence §§ 947–453; C.J.S. Evidence §§ 682(3), 693; Annot., 21 A.L.R.2d 773.

79. 5 Wigmore, Evidence § 1530. For an example, see Rathborne v. Hatch, 80 App.Div. 115, 80 N.Y.S. 347 (1903), discussed in § 310 at n. 55, supra.

80. See § 305, supra.

81. Model Code of Evidence rule 514.

82. See § 306, n. 15, supra.

83. See § 306, n. 12, supra.

84. See § 306, n. 14, supra.

85. See § 306, n. 16, supra.

It is likely that today few if any courts would enforce the old requirement that all participants be produced or their unavailability established. At most, they would recognize a discretionary power in the trial judge either to enforce the traditional requirement or, in his discretion, to permit the offered record to be verified by a supervising officer who can testify that the records have been regularly kept. This discretionary power to dispense with the production of the entrants and informants should be exercised when it appears that the inconvenience of producing the participants, in light of their number and probable lack of present knowledge, outweighs the value of producing them for examination and cross examination.[86]

313. Special Problems: (a) Hospital Records.[87]

In some jurisdictions, specific statutory authority for the admission of hospital records exists.[88] Although some courts in other jurisdictions initially hesitated to expand the business record exception to non-commercial establishments such as hospitals,[89] all would concede today that hospital records are admissible upon the same basis as other regularly kept records. This result is appropriate, for the safeguards of trustworthiness of the records of the modern hospital are at least as substantial as the guarantees of reliability of the records of business establishments.[90] Progress in medical skills has been accompanied by improvements and standardization of the practice of recording facts concerning the patient, and these recorded facts are routinely used to make decision upon which the health and life of the patient depend. The application of the exception to this subject area raises no new problems, but hospital records are sufficiently different from traditional business records to justify a brief discussion of several problems which arise when the regularly kept records exception is applied to them.

Preliminary proof. As in the case of commercial records, a foundation for hospital records must be established by proof of a practice to make such records accurately and promptly and of the making of the specific record in the course of this hospital routine.[91] Although the common law requirement that each entrant and informant be produced has been enforced,[92] courts have modified this requirement in its application to hospital

---

86. The leading opinion is that by L. Hand, J. in Massachusetts Bonding & Ins. Co. v. Norwich Pharmacal Co., 18 F.2d 934 (2d Cir. 1927). See also Jennings v. United States, 73 F.2d 470 (5th Cir. 1934) (work record vouched for by employment manager in charge of records admissible—"It was not necessary to produce or account for the person or persons who had made the notations in the absence of some proof throwing suspicion upon the genuineness of the record itself."); Continental Nat. Bank v. First Nat. Bank, 108 Tenn. 374, 68 S.W. 497 (1912); Heid Bros., Inc. v. Commercial Nat. Bank, 240 S.W. 908, 24 A.L.R. 904 (Tex.Com.App. 1922); French v. Virginia Ry. Co., 121 Va. 383, 93 S.E. 585 (1917); Willett v. Davis, 30 Wash.2d 622, 193 P.2d 321 (1948); State v. Larue, 98 W.Va. 677, 128 S.E. 116 (1925).

87. See generally, 6 Wigmore, Evidence § 1707; Hale, Hospital Records as Evidence, 14 So.Cal.L. Rev. 99 (1941); Braham, Case Records of Hospitals and Doctors Under Business Records Act, 21 Temple L.Q. 113 (1948); Laughlin, Business Entries and the Like, 46 Iowa L.Rev. 276, 299–305 (1961); Comment, Admissibility of Hospital Records as Evidence in Missouri, 24 Mo.L.Rev. 51 (1959); Annot., 75 A.L.R. 378; Annot., 120 A.L.R. 1124.

88. These are compiled in 6 Wigmore, Evidence § 1707, n. 1.

89. See Mutual Ben. Health & Acc. Ass'n v. Bell, 49 Ga.App. 640, 176 S.E. 124 (1934); Levy v. J. L. Mott Iron Works, 143 App.Div. 7, 127 N.Y.S. 506 (1911).

90. See Globe Indemnity Co. v. Reinhart, 152 Md. 439, 446, 137 A. 43, 46 (1927); Schmidt v. Reimenschneider, 196 Minn. 612, 265 N.W. 816, 817 (1936).

91. State v. Guaraneri, 59 R.I. 173, 194 Atl. 589 (1937); State v. Weeks, 70 Wash.2d 951, 425 P.2d 885 (1967).

92. Wright v. Upson, 303 Ill. 120, 135 N.E. 209 (1922) (hospital record inadmissible because one of two nurses who participated in entries was not accounted for); Clayton v. Metropolitan Life Ins. Co., 96 Utah 331, 85 P.2d 819 (1938) (record inadmissible because nurse who made entry neither produced nor accounted for).

records as well as with other business records.[93]

History. Under standard practice, a trained attendant at hospitals enters upon the record a "personal history,"[94] including an identification of the patient and an account of the present injury or illness and the events and symptoms leading up to it. This information, which may be obtained from the patient himself or someone accompanying him, is sought for its bearing upon diagnosis and treatment of the patient's injury or disease. Is this history admissible to prove assertions of facts it may contain? This, of course, is the "double hearsay" problem.[95] The first issue is whether the hospital record is admissible to prove that the statement was made. This is a matter of application of the regularly kept records rule, and the primary issue is whether or not the specific entry involved was an entry made in the regular course of the hospital's business. If the subject matter falls within those things which under hospital practice are regarded as relevant to diagnosis or treatment, it is within the regular course of business.[96] If, on the other hand, the subject matter does not relate to diagnosis or treatment, the making of the

entry was not within the regular course of the hospital's business and thus it is not admissible even for the limited purpose of proving that the statement was made.[97]

More difficult problems are often raised by the application of the second step of the "double hearsay" problem analysis. Assuming that the hospital record is admissible to prove that the statement contained in the history was made, is this statement admissible to prove the truth of assertions made in it? In accordance with the general rule, it seems clear that the business record exception cannot support use of the history because the declarant's action in relating the history was not part of a business routine of which he was a regular participant. Here as elsewhere, however, if the history comes within one of the other exceptions to the hearsay rule it is admissible. For example, insofar as the history was given to a physician consulted for treatment and is reasonably related to diagnosis and treatment, it may be admissible under the exception for such spontaneous statements.[98] The statements might also constitute admissions of a party opponent when offered against the patient,[99] dying declarations,[1] declarations against interest,[2] and excited utterances.[3]

---

93. E. g., Harris v. Smith, 372 F.2d 806, 816–17 (8th Cir. 1967) (adequate foundation was laid under federal statute when attending physician identified hospital record as photostatic copy of hospital record concerning patient; not fatal that no witness specifically stated that in the hospital doctors routinely made reports, since court can rely upon "ordinary habits and customs"); State v. Anderson, 384 S.W.2d 591 (Mo.1964) (testimony by custodian that record was from hospital medical records library which was kept in the usual and ordinary course of the business of the hospital was adequate foundation under the Uniform Act). See § 312, supra.

94. See Hale, Hospital Records as Evidence, 14 So. Cal.L.Rev. 90, 113–14 (1941).

95. See § 310, supra.

96. See Watts v. Delaware Coach Co., 5 Del.Super. 283, 58 A.2d 689 (1948), holding that the patient's statement that he twisted his ankle while walking along a street was sufficiently related to diagnosis and treatment.

97. See Green v. Cleveland, 150 Ohio St. 441, 83 N.E.2d 63 (1948) (statement of patient that she fell off a street car and caught her heel not incident to treatment); Commonwealth v. Harris, 351 Pa. 325, 41 A.2d 688 (1945) (patient's statement that had been shot by a white man not related to treatment, since race of man who shot him not material to treatment).

98. See § 292, supra.

99. Watts v. Delaware Coach Co., 5 Del.Super. 283, 58 A.2d 689 (1948).

1. See Ch. 28, supra.

2. See Ch. 27, supra.

3. See § 297, supra. If none of these can be successfully invoked, the record is not admissible. See A. H. Angerstein, Inc. v. Jankowski, 55 Del. 304, 187 A.2d 81 (1962) (statement in medical record by unidentified person who called physician at hospital could not be used to prove that patient had received electrical shock); Baugh v. Life & Casualty Ins. Co. of Tenn., 307 S.W.2d 660 (Mo.

Diagnostic statements. Professional standards for hospital records contemplate that entries will be made of diagnostic findings at various stages.[4] These entries are clearly in the regular course of the operations of the hospital. The problem which they pose is one of the admissibility of "opinions."[5] In the hospital records area, the opinion is usually one of an expert who would unquestionably be permitted to give it if personally testifying. While the requirement of qualification does not disappear, if it is shown that the record is from a reputable institution, in the absence of any indication to the contrary it may be inferred that regular entries were made by qualified personnel.[6]

When an expert opinion is offered by a witness personally testifying, the expert is available for cross-examination on that opinion. If the opinion is offered by means of a hospital record, no cross-examination is possible. Consequently, there is a tendency somewhat to limit those opinions which can be introduced by this method. The admissibility of ordinary diagnostic findings customarily based on objective data and not usually presenting more than average difficulty of interpretation is usually conceded.[7]

On the other end of the continuium, diagnostic opinions which on their face are speculative are reasonably excluded.[8] In the absence of the availability of the declarant for explanation and cross-examination, the probative value of this evidence is outweighed by the danger that it will be abused or mislead the jury. In regard to those cases in between, primarily those containing opinions based on subjective symptoms or involving difficulty of interpretation, such as psychiatric diagnoses, most courts will nevertheless permit the introduction of the record.[9] Especially under the Uniform Act, it would not be unreasonable in borderline cases to permit introduction of the record only if the declarant were produced for cross-examination. Even if he lacked present recollection regarding the entry, it is arguable that the information he could provide by testimony as to his general practices would be

1957) (statement in record that patient related that at age seven he had been told by a doctor that he had a leaky heart was not admissible to prove existence of congenital heart disease).

4. See Hale, Hospital Records as Evidence, 14 So. Cal.L.Rev. 90, 113–14 (1941).

5. See § 307, n. 25, supra.

6. Allen v. St. Louis Public Service Co., 285 S.W.2d 663 (Mo.1956) (qualifications of physician will be "presumed" from testimony that he was a resident at a hospital); Webber v. McCormick, 63 N.J. Super. 409, 164 A.2d 813 (1960) (X-ray report prepared by hospital technician and entered in hospital record admissible without proof of technician's qualifications, since it would be presumed from making of report in course of hospital business). But see Dunn v. Ove Skou Rederi A/S, 45 F.R.D. 18 (E.D.Pa.1968) (lack of proof that an authorized intern or physician employed by hospital made entry rendered entry inadmissible).

7. In re Estate of Morton, 428 P.2d 725 (Wyo.1967) (nurses' reports on patient's behavior and opinion

such as "lethargic" admissible to prove testamentary capacity); Travis Life Ins. Co. v. Rodriguez, 326 S.W.2d 256 (Tex.Civ.App.1959) error ref. n. r. e., noted in 14 Sw.L.J. 115 (1960) (Texas statute permits introduction of hospital record to prove diagnosis of leukemia). See also Reed v. Order of United Commercial Travelers, 123 F.2d 252 (2d Cir. 1941) (diagnosis of "well under the influence of alcohol" admissible); Ulm v. Moore-McCormick Lines, 117 F.2d 222 (2d Cir. 1941); Wickman v. Bohle, 173 Md. 694, 196 Atl. 326 (1938). See 38 Mich.L.Rev. 219 (1939); 27 Temple L.Q. 223 (1953); 54 Yale L.J. 868 (1945).

8. Boland v. Jundo, 395 S.W.2d 206 (Mo.1965) (interpretation of X ray as, it "could be a small chip fracture" could have been excluded as based upon speculation); La Mantia v. Bobmeyer, 382 S.W.2d 455 (Mo.App.1964) (statement in record by physician that "I have a hunch [the patient] will have further difficulty from time to time . . ." not admissible because it was based on speculation and conjecture).

9. See, e. g., Rivers v. Union Carbide Corp., 426 F.2d 633, 637–38 (3d Cir. 1970); Thomas v. Hogan, 308 F.2d 355, 360–61 (4th Cir. 1962). But see New York Life Ins. Co. v. Taylor, 147 F.2d 297 (D.C.Cir. 1945), holding that the trial judge properly excluded a hospital record showing a diagnosis of "psychoneurosis, hysteria, conversion type" by a psychiatrist. A strong dissent was entered by Edgerton, J. The case is noted in 33 Geo.L.J. 349 (1945), 23 Tex.L.Rev. 178 (1945), 94 U.Pa.L.Rev. 112 (1945), 54 Yale L.J. 868 (1945).

sufficient to tip the scales in favor of admissibility.

Privilege. In most states, patients have been afforded a privilege against disclosure by physicians of information acquired in attending the patient and necessary for diagnosis and treatment.[10] It is possible to interpret the privilege broadly as including any information obtained by hospital personnel related to treatment. While it seems fairly clear that hospital records are privileged to the extent that they incorporate statements made by the patient to the physician and the physician's diagnostic findings,[11] application of the privilege to information obtained by nurses or attendants presents a greater problem. On one hand, it is arguable that privilege statutes should be strictly construed and most do not mention nurses or attendants.[12] On the other hand, information is usually gathered and recorded by them as agents for the physician and for the purpose of aiding the physician in treatment and diagnosis.[13] The problem is one of interpreting

the underlying privilege. If it would bar the direct testimony of the nurses or attendants, it should also bar use of their hearsay statements under this exception; if it would not, the statements in the hospital records should not be held privileged.

314. Special Problems: (b) Computer Print-Outs.[14]

Perhaps the most interesting recent expansion of the regularly kept records exception has been its use to obtain the admission of computer print-outs. In a recent federal case,[15] for example, a computer print-out was the primary evidence corroborating the defendant's confession in a prosecution for transporting a stolen vehicle across state lines. Documentary proof was produced to establish that the vehicle was owned by a car rental agency and that it had been returned to the agency at a New York airport on June 30, 1968. The rental agency's security manager then testified that he had consulted the company's master computer control office, into which all rental and lease information is routinely fed, and that the computer indicated no subsequent rental or lease agreement. This, he testified, indicated that the vehicle had been stolen.

Several potential problems arise in the application of the regular records exception to the computer print-out. The first has to do with the foundation necessary for introduction of the print-out. In general terms, this

---

10. See Ch. 11, supra.

11. The language in most cases suggests that hospital records are privileged only to the extent that they contain communications from physicians that would be privileged were the physician testifying in person. Ferguson v. Quaker City Life Ins. Co., 129 A.2d 189 (D.C.Ct.App.1957); Newman v. Blom, 249 Iowa 836, 89 N.W.2d 349 (1958); State ex rel. Benoit v. Randall, 431 S.W.2d 107 (Mo.1968); Unick v. Kessler Memorial Hospital, 107 N.J.Super. 121, 257 A.2d 134 (1969); Sims v. Charlotte Liberty Mutual Ins. Co., 256 N.C. 32, 125 S.E.2d 326 (1962).

12. A few statutes do specifically mention nurses. See 8 Wigmore, Evidence (McNaughton rev.) § 2380 n. 5.

13. The general approach seems to be that a nurse or other member of a hospital staff comes within the privilege only if acting under the direction of a specific physician. See Sims v. Charlotte Liberty Mutual Ins. Co., 256 N.C. 32, 125 S.E.2d 326 (1962) (dictum) (entries by nurses, technicians or others in hospital records not privileged unless assisting or acting under the direction of a physician). See also Collins v. Howard, 156 F.Supp. 322 (S.D.Ga. 1957) (dictum) (nurse taking blood test was agent of hospital rather than physician and therefore privilege would not include her); State v. Burchett, 302 S.W.2d 9 (Mo.1957) (nurse who was on duty as hospital employee and helped patient into hos-

pital before physician arrived was not acting as agent of physician and therefore not within privilege). The privilege has been held applicable to an intern. Franklin Life Ins. Co. v. William J. Champion and Co., 353 F.2d 919 (6th Cir. 1965).

14. See generally, Comment, Computer Print-Outs of Business Records and Their Admissibility in New York, 31 Albany L.Rev. 61 (1967); Note, Admissibility of Computer-Kept Business Records, 55 Cornell L.Rev. 1033 (1970); 41 Miss.L.J. 604 (1970); Note, Evidence: The Admissibility of Computer Print-Outs in Kansas, 8 Washburn L.J. 330 (1969); Annot., 11 A.L.R.3d 1377.

15. United States v. De Georgia, 420 F.2d 889 (9th Cir. 1969).

foundation does not differ from that required for other business records.[16] But in view of the complex nature of the operation of computers and general lay unfamiliarity with their operation, this raises special problems. It appears, therefore, that when computer print-outs are offered, the trial court should take special care to be certain that the foundation is sufficient to warrant a finding of trustworthiness and that the opposing party has full opportunity to inquire into the process by which information is fed into the computer.[17]

The second major problem involves the process by which information is obtained from computers for use in specific litigation. There is seldom if ever any doubt that the information stored in a computer is assembled and used in the routine of the business in which the computer is being used. But it is possible that the specific print-out (or other reading) offered in a litigated case has been obtained from the computer specifically for use in the litigation. This raises possible questions as to whether, under Palmer v. Hoffman, the specific record offered was prepared "in the regular course of business."[18] There seems no reason why the courts should not take the same approach in regard to computer print-outs that they have taken with other records—if the manner of preparation is such, considering the circumstances under which it was prepared, that there is substantial doubt raised as to its reliability, it may be excluded. Mere preparation of a print-out in anticipation of its use in evidence would be insufficient justification for excluding it; nevertheless, if other factors suggested that the computer had been operated in a manner casting doubt upon the reliability of this particular print-out, exclusion would be proper.

Despite the new problems raised, courts have relatively freely approved use of computer print-outs as regular records. This result has been reached under the federal statute [19] (embodying the Commonwealth Fund Act), the Uniform Act,[20] and the common law exception.[21]

16. See § 312, supra.

In contrast to the views here expressed, the English Civil Evidence Act 1968 provides a painstakingly detailed scheme of dealing with computer evidence. St.1968, ch. 64, Part I, § 5. Commentators have observed that "the section is a morass of drafting, and on principle it should not be necessary to legislate specially for them. The problem with computer evidence is not the accuracy of the calculation but the reliability of the data fed in and the transcription and interpretation of the 'print-out' data produced." Newark and Samuels, Civil Evidence Act 1968, 31 Mod.L.Rev. 668, 670 (1968).

17. See United States v. De Georgia, 420 F.2d 889, 893 n. 11 (9th Cir. 1969). "Garbage in, garbage out." Proxmire, Out with the Garbage, 7 Trial No. 2, p. 18 (1971).

18. See § 308, n. 44, supra.

19. United States v. De Georgia, 420 F.2d 889 (9th Cir. 1969).

20. Merrick v. United States Rubber Co., 7 Ariz. App. 314, 440 P.2d 314 (1968); Transport Indemnity Co. v. Seib, 178 Neb. 253, 132 N.W.2d 871 (1965).

21. King v. State ex rel. Murdock Acceptance Corp., 222 So.2d 393 (Miss.1969).

CHAPTER 32

OFFICIAL WRITTEN STATEMENTS AND CERTIFICATES

315. The Exception for Official Written Statements: (a) In General.[1]

A common law exception to the hearsay rule exists for written statements of public officials made by officials with a duty to make them, made upon firsthand knowledge of the facts.[2] These statements are admissible as evidence of the facts recited in them. Their admissibility is now, however, largely governed by statutes which minutely and variously regulate the admissibility of various kinds of records and documents,[3] and reference must almost always be had to the specific statute governing a particular situation rather than to the common law exception.

The special trustworthiness of official written statements is found in the declarant's official duty and the high probability that the duty to make an accurate report has been performed.[4] The possibility that public inspection of some official records will reveal any inaccuracies and cause them to be corrected (or will deter the official from making them in the first place) has been emphasized by the English courts, which have imposed a corresponding requirement that the official

---

1. See generally, 5 Wigmore, Evidence §§ 1630–1684; Wallace, Official Written Statements, 46 Iowa L. Rev. 256 (1961); Dutton, The Official Records Exception to the Hearsay Rule in California, 6 Santa Clara Law. 1 (1965); Note, 30 Mont.L.Rev. 227 (1969); F.R.Ev. (R.D.1971) 803(8)–(10); Model Code of Evidence Rules 515–522; Uniform Rules 63(15)–(22), 64; Dec.Dig. Evidence ⊜333–349, 383(3), (4), Criminal Law ⊜429, 430.

2. E. g., Edwards v. Firemen's Retirement System of St. Louis, 410 S.W.2d 560, 568 (Mo.App.1966) (reports of medical examiners of retirement system's board of trustees are public records and "admissible without the aid of any statute saying that they should be admitted").

3. E. g., 28 U.S.C.A. § 1733(a):
"Books or records of account or minutes of proceedings of any department or agency of the United States shall be admissible to prove the act, transaction or occurrence as a memorandum of which the same were made or kept."

4. See 5 Wigmore, Evidence § 1631. The duty requirement is still sometimes used to explain the inadmissibility of some statements, although it is likely that the result could also have been put on other grounds. See Knox Lime Co. v. Maine State Highway Commission, 230 A.2d 814 (Me.1967) (Special Mineral Economic Report prepared by state Department of Economic Development not admissible because there was "no express statutory authority to compile it and it was not essential to any express statutory duty"); Beamer v. Beamer, 17 Ohio App.2d 89, 244 N.E.2d 775 (1969) (report of investigator, made under authority of court in divorce proceedings where custody of children is in issue to order investigation made, not admissible in proceeding on motion to change custody order because "no particular official is designated [by statute] to make the investigation and report"); State ex rel. Blankenship v. Freeman, 440 P.2d 744, 759 (Okl.1968) (report and transcript of state legislative investigating committee inadmissible because it was not within class of records required to be kept or filed in public office; legislature required only to keep a journal of its proceedings).

statement be one kept for the use and information of the public.[5] This limitation has been criticised and the American courts reasonably have not adopted it.[6] Although public inspection may provide some assurance of reliability, requiring public access to the record would mean that many classes of statements would be rendered inadmissible although they seem to be sufficiently reliable to justify admission.[7]

A special need for this category of hearsay is found in the inconvenience of requiring public officials to appear in court and testify concerning the subject matter of their statements.[8] Not only would this disrupt the administration of public affairs, but it almost certainly would create a class of official witnesses. Moreover, given the volume of business in public officers, the official written statement will usually be more reliable than the official's present memory. For these same reasons, there is no requirement that the declarant be shown to be unavailable as a witness.

316. The Exception for Official Written Statements: (b) Relaxation of the Requirement of Official Duty for Reports Regarding Vital Statistics.

If the requirement that the out-of-court declarant have an official duty to make the report were strictly enforced, such matters as a clergyman's return upon a marriage license indicating his performance of the ceremony and the report of an attending physician as to the fact and date of birth or death would be inadmissible. Consequently this requirement has been somewhat relaxed in regard to matters involving various general statistics. Where the report was made to a public agency by one with a professional— although not necessarily "public"—duty to make the report, such as a minister or a physician, the law has generally admitted the record to prove the truth of the reporter's statement.[9] But if the required report is one which by its nature is subject to suspicion— such as the reports motorists involved in accidents may be required to file—the reports are held inadmissible despite the statutory duty to file them.[10] The Proposed Federal Rules of Evidence reasonably take a liberal position, providing for the admissibility of "records or data compilation, in any form, of births, fetal deaths, deaths, or marriages, if the report thereof was made to a public office pursuant to requirements of law." [11] This abandons the "official" and "professional" duty requirements, but only in a limited category of cases in which the need for the proof, the firsthand knowledge of the reporter, and the disinterestedness of the reporter furnish a sufficient basis for admissibility.

317. The Exception for Official Written Statements: (c) Relaxation of the Firsthand Knowledge Requirement for Reports of Official Investigations.[12]

Expansion of the official written statements exception to the hearsay rule has been most severely limited by vigorous enforcement, even under statutory formulations, of

5. See Lilley v. Pettit, [1946] K.B. 401, [1946] 1 All. E.R. 593, holding the regimental records of a soldier inadmissible because they were not kept for the use and information of the public. See generally, Cross, Evidence 429–30 (3d ed. 1967).

6. 5 Wigmore, Evidence § 1632. See also Cross, Evidence 429 (3d ed. 1967).

7. 5 Wigmore, Evidence § 1632.

8. 5 Wigmore, Evidence § 1631.

9. 5 Wigmore, Evidence § 1633a.

10. E. g., Ezzo v. Geremiah, 107 Conn. 670, 142 Atl. 461 (1928).

11. F.R.Ev. (R.D.1971) 803(9).

12. See generally, McCormick, Can the Courts Make Wider Use of Official Investigations? 42 Iowa L.Rev. 363 (1957); 27 N.Y.U.L.Rev. 158 (1952); Comment, Evaluative Reports By Public Officials—Admissible as Official Statements? 30 Tex. L.Rev. 112 (1951).

the requirement of firsthand knowledge and a version of the opinion rule. For example, an attending physician's certificate regarding the time and cause of death is generally admissible to prove those facts. But it has been held that the certification is not admissible to prove the time of origin of the fatal ailment where the illness began before the physician had been consulted and of which he consequently lacked firsthand knowledge.[13] Under statutes making such a certificate *prima facie* evidence of the "facts" stated, statements as to cause of death (as by suicide) are not infrequently held inadmissible to prove that death was so caused, on the ground that this statement was not one of fact but rather of inference or merely recounting a hearsay statement of another declarant.[14]

13. Williams v. Metropolitan Life Ins. Co., 116 S.C. 277, 108 S.E. 110 (1921). Contra, Meth v. United Benefit Life Ins. Co., 198 F.2d 446 (4th Cir. 1952) (statement of attending physician admissible to prove time of onset of illness as well as time and cause of death, although onset of illness occurred before physician was called into case).

14. See Charleston National Bank v. Hennessy, 404 F.2d 539 (5th Cir. 1968) (statement of coroner in death certificate that "deceased jumped out of a motor vehicle, during argument" and that death was "probably accident" inadmissible because from coroner it constitutes hearsay); Backstrom v. New York Life Ins. Co., 183 Minn. 384, 236 N.W. 708 (1931), noted in 16 Minn.L.Rev. 209 (1932); Carson v. Metropolitan Life Ins. Co., 156 Ohio St. 104, 100 N.E.2d 197 (1951). But see Biro v. Prudential Ins. Co., 110 N.J.Super. 391, 265 A.2d 830 (1970) rev'd 57 N.J. 204, 271 A.2d 1 (concluding after extensive discussion, that a death certificate is admissible as *prima facie* proof of suicide as cause of death under statute providing that report is prima facie evidence of the "official determinations contained therein."); Branford Trust Co. v. Prudential Ins. Co., 102 Conn. 481, 129 Atl. 379 (1929). See generally, Morgan, The Law of Evidence 1941–1945, 59 Harv.L.Rev. 481, 560–61 (1946).

Compare California State Life Ins. Co. v. Fuqua, 40 Ariz. 148, 10 P.2d 958 (1932) (in action of life policy, error to exclude death certificate describing cause of death as "gunshot wounds inflicted by officers . . . in the performance of their duties") and State v. Barker, 94 Ariz. 383, 385 P.2d 516 (1963) (proper in murder prosecution to exclude death certificate stating "justifiable homicide;" civil rule not applicable in criminal cases.)

Many writings that would otherwise meet the requirements of official written statements consist in part of conclusions or summaries of the investigating official or agency. Police reports, for example, routinely contain not only statements based upon the reporting officer's own observations but conclusions based upon what he was told by others and his own inferential processes. Vigorous application of the requirement of firsthand knowledge has generally resulted in the limitation of the use of these reports to the proof of those things which the reporting official himself observed.[15] Is this appropriate? To

15. E. g., Emmet v. American Ins. Co., 265 A.2d 602 (D.C.Ct.App.1970) (official report of fire investigator not admissible to prove his opinion as to cause of fire); Dale v. Trent, 256 N.E.2d 402 (Ind. App.1970) ("facts" contained in police report admissible but opinions not admissible because they invade province of court or jury); Middlesex Supply, Inc. v. Martin & Sons, Inc., 354 Mass. 373, 237 N.E.2d 692 (1968) (report of assistant fire chief not admissible to prove truth of statement, "Probable cause, carelessly discarded cigarette"); Hall v. Boykin, 207 So.2d 645 (Miss.1968) (admission of highway patrolman's accident report showing positions of vehicles before and after accident error because officer had not witnessed accident); Phillips v. Erie Lackawanna Railroad Co., 107 N.J.Super. 590, 259 A.2d 719 (1969) (report of Board of Public Utility's hearing examiner, based on hearings, concerning accident held inadmissible after full discussion of law); State ex rel. Blankenship v. Freeman, 440 P.2d 744, 759 (Okla.1968) (report and transcript of state legislative investigative committee not admissible); Knoff v. United States Fidelity and Guarantee Co., 447 S.W.2d 497, 503 (Tex.Civ. App.1969) (report by Fire Marshall's investigator consisting largely of hearsay statements to investigator not admissible); Wilder v. Classified Risk Ins. Co., 47 Wis.2d 286, 177 N.W.2d 109 (1970) (police traffic accident report inadmissible to prove statements attributed to witnesses or to prove conclusions of investigating officer).

If the assertion is one of "fact," the report is admissible as proof of it. E. g., Finchum v. Lyons, 247 Ore. 255, 428 P.2d 890 (1967) (finding in report of state plant pathologist that potatoes were infected with bacterial ring rot is finding of fact, involving exercise of no discretion, and report is admissible to prove it). If the challenged aspect would come under one of the other exceptions to the hearsay rule, of course, the problem is overcome. See Corey v. Wilson, 93 Idaho 54, 454 P.2d 951 (1969) (statement in death certificate that "infraction ileum" was a contributing factor to death was admissible in medical malpractice action be-

some extent, the conclusions of a professional investigator making inquiries required by his professional and public duty contain assurances of reliability analogous to those relied upon as assuring accuracy of his statements of fact from firsthand knowledge. A skilled investigator can be presumed to report as accurate or to rely upon a hearsay statement only after inquiry into its accuracy. Often such an inquiry, by one professionally equipped to make it well and on the scene at a time when events are fresh and inquiry is most likely to be fruitful, could be relied upon to assure the reliability of those hearsay statements upon which he relies. Much the same could be said of his conclusions. In both cases, it is clear that the report and its conclusions are recognized by all concerned to lay the foundation for future official action, which is likely to stimulate the same habitual accuracy in reporting facts known that underlies the exception for official records generally.[16]

The Uniform Rules adopt an extremely broad rule of admissibility by providing for the admission of "written reports or findings of fact" of a public official if the making of it was within his duty and his duty also included the investigation of the facts concerning the act, condition or event involved and the

making of findings or the drawing of conclusions based upon such investigation.[17] A more moderate position is embodied in the Proposed Federal Rules of Evidence, which provide for the admission of "factual findings" in a public record or statement which result from an investigation made pursuant to authority granted by law.[18] Two limitations, however, are imposed: First, because of the potential conflict with a defendant's right of confrontation this provision is applicable only to civil litigation and to offers made against the government in criminal cases. Second, the trial judge is expressly granted the authority to exclude such a report if "the sources of information or the method or circumstances of the investigation indicate lack of trustworthiness." The more limited expansion of the traditional position as suggested by the Proposed Federal Rules is probably most appropriate.[19]

318. The Exception for Official Written Statements: (d) Judgments in Previous Cases, Especially Criminal Convictions Offered in Subsequent Civil Cases.[20]

Insofar as reports of official investigations are admissible under the official written statement exception, it would seem that the judgment of a court, made after the full investigation of a trial, would also be admissible in subsequent litigation to prove the truth of

---

cause it was a statement of a party-opponent and defendant physician, as an expert, could have testified to his conclusion if on the stand).

Not infrequently vehicle accident reports are specifically rendered inadmissible by statute. E. g., Leebove v. Rovin, 363 Mich. 569, 111 N.W.2d 104 (1961) (enforcing statutory provisions of Indiana and Michigan rendering police accident report inadmissible). See Krizak v. Brooks & Sons, Inc., 320 F.2d 37, 44 (4th Cir. 1963), suggesting that the Virginia statute requiring accident reports from drivers and making them inadmissible means only that the written report is inadmissible and therefore a testifying driver could be cross-examined regarding prior inconsistent statement in the report if it was not disclosed to the jury that the prior statements were contained in such a report.

16. See State v. Stone, 104 Ariz. 339, 452 P.2d 513 (1969) (in wrongful death action against State, proper to admit police report that accident was caused by faulty highway markings).

17. Uniform Rule 63(15).

18. F.R.Ev. (R.D.1971) 803(8).

19. See Franklin v. Skelly Oil Co., 141 F.2d 568, (10th Cir. 1944), suggesting that admissibility of fire marshall's report to prove opinion of investigator that cause of fire was installation of improper piping for butane gas was a matter of trial judge's discretion.

20. See generally, 4 Wigmore, Evidence § 1346a; 5 id. § 1671a; Cowen, The Admissibility of Criminal Convictions in Subsequent Civil Proceedings, 40 Calif.L.Rev. 225 (1952); Hinton, Judgment of Conviction—Effect on a Civil Case as Res Judicata or as Evidence, 27 Ill.L.Rev. 195 (1932); Note, Admissibility and Weight of a Criminal Conviction in a Subsequent Civil Action, 39 Va.L.Rev. 995 (1953); Annot., 18 A.L.R.2d 1287; Annot., 31 A.L.R. 261; Dec.Dig. Judgments ⚬648.

those things necessarily determined in the first action. Guilty pleas and statements made in the course of litigation may constitute declarations against interest [21] or admissions of a party-opponent [22] and be admissible on those grounds.[23] Where the doctrines of res judicata or collateral estoppel make the determinations in the first case binding in the second, of course, the judgment in the first case is not only admissible in the second, but it is as a matter of substantive law conclusive evidence against the party. If neither res judicata nor collateral estoppel apply, however, the courts have traditionally been unwilling to admit judgments in previous cases.[24]

A variety of reasons have been advanced for this rule. Civil cases often involve numerous issues and it may be difficult to determine what issues a judgment in fact determined. This, however, argues only for a requirement that one offering a judgment establish as a prerequisite for its admissibility that it did in fact determine an issue relevant to the instant litigation. It is also argued that the party against whom the judgment is offered may not have had an opportunity to be present and to participate in the first action. This misses the point, however as the appropriate question in deciding whether the hearsay objection should be sustained in this context is not the party's opportunity to have been present at the official investigation but rather whether that investigation provided adequate assurance of reliability. In many cases the party will in fact have been present and have had not only an opportunity but a strong motive to defend. This argument against admissibility does, nevertheless, have merit in regard to judgments of any sort against anyone other than the defendant and perhaps even judgments in civil cases against the defendant, offered in subsequent criminal litigation. Accepting the former judgments would certainly violate the defendant's constitutional right of confrontation,[25] and perhaps the latter. Other arguments against admissibility of prior judgments relate to the danger of undue prejudice, and orderly administration. It is sometimes asserted that juries are unlikely to grasp the distinction between a prior judgment offered as mere evidence and one offered under circumstances making the judgment conclusive; thus even if there is no substantive law making the judgment conclusive, juries are likely to give it that effect. In addition, it is argued that there is a danger that if such judgments are admissible parties offering them will tend to rely heavily upon them and not introduce significant amounts of other evidence, with the result that the evidence available in the second case will not be adequate upon which to reach a reliable decision.

These arguments have caused many courts to exclude a prior civil judgment offered in a subsequent civil case. There is, however, a growing tendency to admit a prior conviction for a serious criminal offense in a subsequent civil action. In these situations, the party against whom the judgment is offered was generally the defendant in the criminal case and therefore had not only the opportunity but also the motive to defend fully. In addition, because of the high burden of proof in criminal cases, a judgment in such a situation

---

21. See Ch. 27, supra.

22. See Ch. 26, supra.

23. E. g., Weiss v. Wasserman, 91 N.H. 164, 15 A.2d 861 (1940) (plea of guilty to speeding admissible). But see Kirkendall v. Korseberg, 247 Ore. 75, 427 P.2d 418 (1967) holding inadmissible in a personal injury action proof of forfeiture of bail on a traffic citation, because "this means of disposing of a traffic citation is used too frequently as a matter of convenience only to treat it as a plea of guilty." See § 265, notes 57–59, supra.

24. 5 Wigmore, Evidence § 1671a.

25. Kirby v. United States, 174 U.S. 47 (1899) (error to convict for possession of stolen postage stamps where only evidence that stamps were stolen was the record of thieves' conviction). Distinguish situations where conviction is an element of an offense, e. g., selling firearms to a convicted felon.

represents significantly more reliable evidence than a judgment in a civil case. The tendency is most noticeable when the judgment is offered in a subsequent civil case in which the convicted defendant seeks affirmatively to benefit from his criminal offense. The strong desire to prevent this result undoubtedly has influenced courts to permit the introduction of the judgment of conviction,[26] and some courts also hold that the judgment is conclusive proof that the party committed the relevant acts with the state of mind required for criminal liability.[27] It is a short step, and one which a number of courts have taken, from this position to the admissibility of a prior criminal conviction generally in a civil action against the criminal defendant.[28]

26. The leading case is Schindler v. Royal Ins. Co., 258 N.Y. 310, 179 N.E. 711 (1932) (in suit by plaintiff on insurance policy, defended by insurer on ground that plaintiff's fraudulent claim voided policy, insurer could introduce plaintiff's conviction for presenting false and fraudulent proof of loss, although this would only be prima facie proof of facts). See also Hudson v. Otero, 80 N.M. 668, 459 P.2d 830 (1969) (in suit by plaintiff for damages based on injuries administered by defendants, defended on theory that plaintiff was engaged in crime at the time, defendants could introduce plaintiff's conviction for burglary but it would only be prima facie proof that the crime was committed).

27. The leading case is Eagle, Star and British Dominions Ins. Co. v. Heller, 149 Va. 82, 140 S.E. 314 (1927) (in suit by plaintiff on insurance policy, defended by insurer on theory that loss was not accidental but rather fraudulently caused by insured, plaintiff's conviction for willfully burning goods with intent to injure insurer was not only admissible but also determinative and could only be attacked upon grounds of fraud, perjury, collusion or some similar theory). See also In re Estate of Laspy, 409 S.W.2d 725 (Mo.App.1966) (wife's conviction for murder of husband admissible and conclusive in her suit based upon claim to husband's estate); Travelers Ins. Co. v. Thompson, 281 Minn. 547, 163 N.W.2d 289 (1968) appeal dismissed 395 U.S. 161 (in husband's suit as beneficiary upon insurance policy upon wife's life, defended on theory that husband killed wife, husband's conviction of first degree murder for wife's death held to collaterally estop husband; good discussion of cases and theory).

28. E. g., Asato v. Furtado, 474 P.2d 288, 293 (Haw. 1970):
"While there is a divergence of authority on this point, we think the better reasoned rule is that . . . the prior judgment should be admissible

A number of courts have limited this rule to convictions for serious offenses, reasoning that convictions for misdemeanors do not represent sufficiently reliable determinations to justify dispensing with the hearsay objections.[29] Judgments of acquittal, however, are

as evidence where the following factors are present. (1) It must be shown that the issue on which the judgment is offered was necessarily decided in the prior trial. (2) A judgment on the merits must have been rendered. (3) It must appear that the party against whom the judgment is offered had a full and fair opportunity to litigate the claim, and especially to contest the specific issue on which the judgment is offered. In other words, it must appear that the party against whom the judgment is offered had a full and complete 'day in court' on that issue, with the opportunity to call and cross examine witnesses and to be presented by counsel."

The majority of courts admitting the conviction do not hold it conclusive. Asato v. Furtado, supra; Weichhand v. Garlinger, 447 S.W.2d 606 (Ky.1969) (defendant's conviction for negligent homicide admissible but not conclusive on issue of negligence in personal injury action); Markowitz v. Fein, 54 Misc.2d 507, 282 N.Y.S.2d 1016 (1967) (in plaintiff's wrongful death action against defendant on basis of defendant's allegedly having killed plaintiff's husband, defendant's conviction for willful killing of husband admissible but does not estop defendant from relitigating issue as to whether he in fact killed husband, relying on Schindler v. Royal Ins. Co., 258 N.Y. 310, 179 N.E. 711 (1932)). But see United States Fidelity & Guaranty Co. v. Moore, 306 F.Supp. 1088, 1094–95 (N.D.Miss.1969) (defendant's criminal conviction for bank robbery probably conclusive in suit by insurer against alleged robbers for civil damages).

A number of courts apparently still adhere to the traditional position that these judgments are not admissible, at least if the convicted criminal is not affirmatively attempting to take financial advantage of his crime. E. g., Brooks v. Daley, 242 Md. 185, 218 A.2d 184 (1966) (criminal conviction is not competent proof of negligence); Bolen v. Buyze, 16 Mich.App. 252, 167 N.W.2d 808 (1969) (defendant's conviction for reckless driving not admissible in personal injury action); Gray v. Grayson, 76 N.M. 255, 414 P.2d 228 (1966) (defendant's conviction for careless driving not admissible in tort suit because it "has no probative force to show negligence").

29. Haynes v. Rollins, 434 P.2d 234 (Okl.1967); Kirkendall v. Korseberg, 247 Ore. 75, 427 P.2d 418 (1967); Loughner v. Schmelzer, 421 Pa. 283, 218 A.2d 768 (1966) (evidence of defendant's conviction for failure to drive on the right side of the highway not admissible in personal injury action, although felony conviction would be); Annot., 18 A.L.R.2d 1287, 1295; Notes, 50 Colum.L.Rev. 529, 35 Cornell L.Q. 872.

still inadmissible in large part, of course, because they may not present a determination of innocence but rather only a decision that the prosecution has not met its heavy burden of proof beyond a reasonable doubt.[30]

The trend in this area is towards broader admissibility. The Model Code of Evidence provides for the admissibility of a judgment "adjudging a person guilty of a crime or a misdemeanor" to prove the facts recited therein "and every fact essential to sustain the judgment."[31] The Uniform Rules adopt this view with the important limitation to convictions for a felony.[32] The most detailed formulation is that of the Proposed Federal Rules of Evidence which contain the following significant limitations: (1) a judgment entered upon a plea of *nolo contendere* is not admissible, (2) the offense must be one punishable by death or imprisonment for more than one year, (3) judgments against persons other than the accused are not admissible when offered by the government in a criminal prosecution.[33]

319. The Exception for Official Certificates: (a) In General.

An official record often involves a "return" by an official with a public duty to make a return—the written document is officially given into the custody of an official custodian. This must be distinguished from what strictly speaking is a certification procedure.[34] In the latter, the person certifying does not transfer his written statement to an official custodian but rather gives it to the applicant and it is then preserved by him. The distinction is perhaps clearest in the alternative methods of documenting a marriage. If the license issued is returned by the celebrant to an official custodian and a copy given to the parties, the return to the custodian becomes a public record. If, however, the celebrant merely issues a certification that he has performed the marriage and gives this to the parties, this document is clearly not a public record. If it is to be admissible, it must be under another exception to the hearsay rule.

Wigmore states that at common law a certificate was admissible to prove the facts stated in it only if the person certifying to the facts had done so under express statutory duty.[35] As a result, the certificate of the celebrant of a marriage appears to have been inadmissible at early common law.[36] This is a matter now largely covered by statutes, which often not only create a statutory duty to make certifications but also expressly provide for the admissibility of the certificates.[37]

320. The Exception for Official Certificates: (b) Certified Copies or Summaries of Official Records.

A special, and most frequently encountered, aspect of the certification problem is presented when what purports to be a copy of an official written statement is offered with only a written statement on its face that purports to be the certification of the official custodian to the effect that this is a true and accurate copy of an official record in his custody. Though the official written statements exception may serve to justify admitting the

---

30. Mew Sun Leong v. Honolulu Rapid Transit Co., 472 P.2d 505 (Haw.1970) (acquittal of driver on criminal charges arising out of accident not admissible in civil action, "nor should it be mentioned by counsel to the jury); Massey v. Meurer, 25 A.D. 2d 729, 268 N.Y.S.2d 735 (1966) (error to admit defendant's acquittal for driving while intoxicated in personal injury action).

31. Model Code of Evidence Rule 521.

32. Uniform Rule 63(20).

33. F.R.Ev. (R.D.1971) 803(22).

34. See generally, 5 Wigmore, Evidence § 1674.

35. 5 Wigmore, Evidence § 1674(1).

36. 5 Wigmore, Evidence § 1645.

37. The statutes are collected in 5 Wigmore, Evidence § 1674 n. 7. See also F.R.Ev. (R.D.1971) 803 (12), providing for the admissibility of certificates of marriage, baptism and similar matters made by a person authorized to perform the ceremony and issued within a reasonable time thereafter.

statement as proof of assertions made therein, if the statement is an assertive one, this does not solve the initial problem of justifying acceptance of the custodian's hearsay assertion that what is offered is in fact an accurate copy of what that official record contains. The latter requires invoking the exception for certifications.[38]

At early common law the requirement of an express statutory duty was applied. This unwillingness to rely on a duty implied from the official position greatly impeded the effectiveness of the written official statements exception.[39] The United States Supreme Court early rejected this position, however, and it can be said that American common law is to the effect that a custodian has by virtue of his office the implied duty and authority to certify to the accuracy of a copy of a record in his official possession.[40] Thus the usual requirement for the production of the original document[41] is not applied to public records.[42] In view of the many statutory provisions for admission of a copy,[43] however, it is seldom necessary to invoke this general authority. Certified copies of this sort have become the most usual and convenient means of proving the purport of records of official

acts and private documents recorded in public offices, such as deeds and security agreements.

No common law authority exists, however, for the admissibility of a paraphrase or summary of records by the custodian. In the absence of specific statutory authority, a certification by the custodian or official written statements that "our records show X" is not admissible to prove X.[44]

For similar reasons, the common law rule did not permit the introduction of the certification of the custodian as to the absence of an official written statement or of the absence of an entry in such a statement to prove the lack of statement or entry. Only the custodian himself could testify as to due search and inability to find the relevant document.[45] Wigmore refers to this rule as "one of the stupid instances of legal pedantry in our annals,"[46] and it has been modified by statute or court rule in many jurisdictions.[47]

---

38. See § 319, supra.

39. 5 Wigmore, Evidence § 1677.

40. See United States v. Percheman, 32 U.S. (7 Pet.) 51 (1883); Church v. Hubbart, 6 U.S. (2 Cranch) 187 (1804).

41. See § 230, supra.

42. E. g., Havas v. 105 Casino Corp., 82 Nev. 282, 417 P.2d 239 (1966) (proper foundation laid by production of certification by public official with custody of original that copy was true, full, and correct copy of original). Compare Interstate Life & Accident Ins. Co. v. Byrd, 277 Ala. 299, 169 So.2d 321 (1964) (purported copy of coroner's certificate with printed words, "Coroner's Certified Copy, Certificate of Death, Charleston County, S. C." not admissible because the certification contained no statement that the copy was a true and correct copy of any record kept in any public office). See § 240, supra.

43. See 5 Wigmore, Evidence § 1680; F.R.Ev. (R.D. 1971) 902(1)–(4).

44. E. g., In re Kostohris' Estate, 96 Mont. 226, 29 P.2d 829 (1934) (custodian's certificate that records show certain listed payments to veteran inadmissible to prove the payments). See also Steeves v. Irwin, 233 A.2d 126, 129–30 (Me.1967), holding inadmissible an attorney's affidavit stating the contents of the proceeding of an Industrial Accident Commission:

"A mere certification or affidavit of a magistrate, clerk, recording or certifying officer, or other witness knowledgeable of the record, stating the existence of the record and what it purports to show is never receivable as evidence, unless made so by statute. What the record itself factually declares must be made known to the Court by a duly authenticated copy. The Court, before which it is produced, should be in the position to inspect the record and decide what it contains and proves. The construction of the record and its import must be left to the Court and not entrusted to the certifying officer or witness." See generally, 5 Wigmore, Evidence § 1678(6), criticizing the rule. The numerous statutory provisions for certificates of the effect or substance of documents in the possession of the custodian are collected in 5 Wigmore, Evidence § 1678(6), n. 2.

45. 5 Wigmore, Evidence § 1678(7).

46. Id.

47. Id. at n. 4; F.R.Ev. (R.D.1971) 804(10).

CHAPTER 33

VARIOUS OTHER EXCEPTIONS TO THE HEARSAY RULE

321. Treatises and Other Professional Literature.[1]

Books, treatises, and other professional literature regarding specialized areas of knowledge or skills are, when offered to prove the truth of matters asserted in them, clearly hearsay. Nevertheless, Wigmore has argued strongly for an exception for such material.[2] In practice, he asserts, much of the testimony of experts testifying in person consists of information they have obtained from such sources. Permitting the sources to be proved directly would not be as great a change as might at first be supposed and would greatly improve the quality of information presented to trial courts in litigated cases. Moreover, he suggests there are sufficient assurances of trustworthiness to justify equating a learned treatise with a personally-testifying expert. Not only does the author of the treatise have no bias in any particular case, but it is also likely that he was motivated in writing the treatise by a strong desire to state accurately the full truth. The authors are also aware that their material will be read and evaluated by others in their field, and there is therefore additional strong pressure to be accurate.

Virtually all courts do, to some extent, permit the use of learned materials in the cross-examination of an expert witness.[3] Most courts would permit this use where the expert has relied upon the specific material in forming the opinion to which he testified on direct;[4] some of these courts would extend the rule to situations in which the witness admits to having relied upon some general authorities although not that particular material sought to be used to impeach him.[5] Other courts would require only that the witness himself acknowledge that the material sought to be used to impeach him is a recognized authority in his field; if he does so, the material may be used although the witness himself may not have relied upon it.[6] Finally, some courts would permit this use without regard to the witness' having relied upon or acknowledged the authority of the source if the cross-examiner establishes the general authority of the material by any proof or by judicial notice.[7] Traditionally, however, the

---

1. See generally, 6 Wigmore, Evidence §§ 1690–1708; Note, Learned Treatises, 46 Iowa L.Rev. 463 (1961); Note, Medical Treatises as Evidence—Helpful But Too Strictly Limited, 29 U.Cinn.L.Rev. 255 (1960); 66 Mich.L.Rev. 183 (1967); 29 Am.Jur.2d Evidence §§ 888–893; C.J.S. Evidence §§ 717–722; Annots., 84 A.L.R.2d 1338, 65 A.L.R. 1102 (medical treatises as evidence); Annot., 75 A.L.R.2d 778 (admissibility of safety codes on the issue of negligence); Dec. Dig. Evidence ☞318(6), 360–365, 381.

2. 6 Wigmore, Evidence §§ 1690–1692.

3. See generally, Annot., 60 A.L.R.2d 77 (use of treatises in the cross-examination of expert witnesses).

4. See cases cited in Annot., 60 A.L.R.2d 77, 81–87.

5. See cases cited in Annot., 60 A.L.R.2d 77, 87–93.

6. See cases cited in Annot., 60 A.L.R.2d 77, 94–98.

7. See cases cited in Annot., 60 A.L.R.2d 77, 98–104; Darling v. Charleston Community Memorial Hospital, 33 Ill.2d 326, 211 N.E.2d 253 (1965).

material may be considered only as going to the witness' competency or the accuracy of his conclusions, and may not be regarded as substantive evidence on the issues of the case.[8]

In a few limited situations the traditional-minded courts have gone further and held that certain books and reports of narrow scope are admissible as substantive evidence of the truth of assertions they contain. Market reports of current prices in journals used by the trade,[9] recognized business registers and city directories,[10] and mortality and annuity tables used by life insurance companies[11] are within this group.

In general, however, most courts have been unwilling to adopt a broad exception to the hearsay rule for treatises and other professional literature.[12] Wigmore suggests a number of arguments in support of this position, none of which he feels justifies the refusal to recognize the exception: (a) professional skills and knowledge shift rapidly, so printed material is likely to be out of date; (b) a trier of fact is likely to be confused by being exposed to material designed for the professionally-trained reader; (c) the opportunity to take sections of material out of context creates a danger of unfair use; (d) most matters of expertise are really matters of skill rather than academic knowledge of the sort that can or is put on written pages, and therefore personally-appearing witnesses are likely to be better sources of evidence than written material. The only meritorious objection, Wigmore concludes, is the basic hearsay objection that the author is not available for cross-examination. This, he feels, is outweighed by the need for the evidence and the other assurances of its accuracy.[13]

Only two courts have judicially adopted a broad exception of this nature,[14] although

---

8. E. g., Goodnight v. Phillips, 458 S.W.2d 196 (Tex. Civ.App. 1970) (if witness acknowledged medical book as a standard authority, it would be usable only to discredit his testimony or to test its weight "and could not be taken as sustaining the issues in the case"). See also Brown v. United States, 419 F.2d 337, 341 (8th Cir. 1969) (statement in "noted medical textbook" that dyspnea as a symptom of a heart attack should not be confused with a mere cough, properly excluded where testifying physician had neither expressed an opinion on the matter nor indicated that he was confused on it).

9. E. g., Virginia v. West Virginia, 238 U.S. 202, 212 (1915) ("It is unquestioned that, in proving the fact or market value, accredited price-current lists and market reports, including those published in trade journals or newspapers which are accepted as trustworthy, are admissible in evidence."). See generally, 6 Wigmore, Evidence § 1704; 29 Am.Jur. 2d Evidence § 892; C.J.S. Evidence §§ 724–25.

10. Williams v. Campbell Soup Co., 80 F.Supp. 865 (W.D.Mo.1948), noted in 2 Baylor L.Rev. 104 (1949) (city directory); Louisville & N. R. Co. v. Kice, 109 Ky. 786, 60 S.W. 705 (1901) (American stud books admissible to prove pedigree of horse); State ex rel. Keefe v. McInerney, 63 Wyo. 280, 182 P.2d 28 (1947) (telephone and city directories admissible to show whether signers of petition were residents of city). See generally, 6 Wigmore, Evidence § 1706.

11. Kershaw v. Sterling Drug, Inc., 415 F.2d 1009 (5th Cir. 1969) (mortality tables admissible even though plaintiff, whose life expectancy was at issue, was not in good health); Sherman v. Springfield, 111 Ill.App.2d 391, 250 N.E.2d 537 (1969). See generally, 6 Wigmore, Evidence § 1698; 29 Am.Jur. 2d Evidence §§ 894–898; C.J.S. Evidence § 719; Dec.Dig. Evidence ⇐364.

12. E. g., Brown v. United States, 419 F.2d 337 (8th Cir. 1969) ("noted medical textbook" not admissible); Brown v. Collins, 223 So.2d 453 (La.App. 1969) (chart from American Jurisprudence showing percent of alcohol necessary to produce various degrees of intoxication not admissible); Superior Ice & Coal Co. v. Belger Cartage Service, Inc., 337 S.W.2d 897 (Mo.1960) (fire chief properly not permitted to read portions of Handbook of Fire Protection regarding use of acetylene torches); Catholic Diocese of Natchez-Jackson v. Jaquith, 224 So.2d 216 (Miss.1969) (pamphlets describing safety precautions for gymnasium issued by governmental agency not admissible); Swank v. Halivopoulos, 108 N.J.Super. 120, 260 A.2d 240 (1969) (Standards and Recommendations of the American Academy of Pediatrics not admissible to prove standard of care required in administration of oxygen to premature infant); Podio v. American Colloid Co., 83 S.D. 528, 162 N.W.2d 385 (1968) (statements in a medical treatise could not be considered in workman's compensation case).

13. 6 Wigmore, Evidence § 1690.

14. One is Alabama, see City of Dothan v. Hardy, 237 Ala. 603, 188 So. 264 (1939), and in Lewandowski v. Preferred Risk Mutual Ins. Co., 33 Wis.2d 69, 146 N.W.2d 505 (1966), noted in 66 Mich.L.Rev. 183 (1967), the Wisconsin Supreme Court prospectively

statutes in a number of jurisdictions have to some extent permitted the use of the material.[15] Other courts, by permitting the use of published professional standards in tort cases as tending to prove the standard of care seem to be making inroads upon the traditional position.[16] The commentators have favored a broad exception. The Uniform Rules of Evidence [17] provide for the admissibility of any "published treatise, periodical or pamphlet on a subject of history, science or art" to prove the truth of matters therein stated, if the item is a reliable authority on the subject; the item's authority may be established by judicial notice or by testimony by an expert in the subject. The Proposed Rules of Evidence for the Federal Courts [18] propose a somewhat more limited exception for "published treatises, periodicals, or pamphlets on a subject of history, medicine, or other science or art" established as a "reliable authority" by judicial notice or testimony. The items are admissible only if relied upon by an expert witness during direct examination or called to his attention during cross-examination. This limitation is designed to minimize the dangers of confusing the finders of fact and of abuse by limiting the admissibility of professional literature to situations in which one qualified in the area is available and on the witness stand to assist in the interpretation of the literature.

322. Statements and Reputation as to Pedigree and Family History.[19]

One of the oldest exceptions to the hearsay rule encompasses, under certain conditions, statements concerning family history, such as the date and place of births and deaths of members of the family and facts about marriage, descent, and relationship. Under the traditional rule, declarations of the person whose family situation is at issue are admissible,[20] as are declarations by other members of the family [21] and even, under a liberal view adopted by some courts, declarations by nonfamily members with a close relationship to the family.[22] These statements are ad-

---

held that treatises recognized by the medical profession as authoritative could be admitted as independent evidence. See also Halldin v. Peterson, 39 Wis.2d 668, 159 N.W.2d 738 (1968) (dictum) (standard of care and violation in malpractice suit could be established by use of medical textbooks).

15. The statutes are collected in 6 Wigmore, Evidence § 1693 n. 2. See also 66 Mich.L.Rev. 183, 184 n. 4 (1967); Annot., 84 A.L.R.2d 1338, 1347–1350. Because the statutory language often used is seemingly appropriate to the exception for reputation, see § 324, notes 65–68, infra, the statutes have sometimes been interpreted as referring only to matters admissible under that exception or other existing exceptions. See 6 Wigmore, Evidence § 1693.

16. See Grudt v. Los Angeles, 2 Cal.3d 575, 86 Cal. Rptr. 465, 468 P.2d 825 (1970) (police tactical manual pertaining to use of firearms admissible to prove standard of care required of police officer in use of weapon); Nordstrom v. White Metal Rolling & Stamping Corp., 75 Wash.2d 629, 453 P.2d 619 (1969) (American Standard Safety Code for Portable Metal Ladders, held admissible, after extensive discussion).

17. Uniform Rule 63(31), adapted from Model Code of Evidence Rule 529.

18. F.R.Ev. (R.D.1971) 803(18). In addition, F.R.Ev. (R.D.1971) 803(17) provides for a hearsay exception for "market quotations, tabulations, lists, directories, or other published compilations, generally used or relied upon by the public or by persons in particular occupations"; see text at notes 9 and 10, supra.

19. See generally, 5 Wigmore, Evidence §§ 1480–1503, 1601–1606; Hale, Proof of Facts of Family History, 2 Hastings L.J. 1 (1950); Comment, Admissibility of Hearsay Evidence on Matters of Family History, 5 Ark.L.Rev. 58 (1951); Note, 32 Iowa L. Rev. 779 (1947); 29 Am.Jur.2d Evidence §§ 508–522; C.J.S. Evidence §§ 225–231; Annot., 15 A.L.R.2d 1412 (declarations of persons other than family member as to pedigree); Annot., 29 A.L.R. 372 (entries in family Bible as evidence); Dec.Dig. Evidence ⊝285–297.

20. E. g., Balazinski v. Lebid, 65 N.J.Super. 483, 168 A.2d 209 (1961) (declarant's statement as to his own marriage).

21. E. g., Minor Child v. Michigan State Health Com'r, 16 Mich.App. 128, 167 N.W.2d 880 (1969) (mother's statement as to identity of son's father).

22. For the "liberal" (and minority) view, see Minor Child v. Michigan State Health Commissioner, 16 Mich.App. 128, 167 N.W.2d 880 (1969) (statements of "family and close acquaintances" regarding child's paternity admissible); In re Lewis' Estate, 121 Utah 385, 242 P.2d 565 (1952) (declaration as

missible, however, only upon a showing that the declarant is unavailable,[23] that the statement was made before the origin of the controversy giving rise to the litigation in which the statement is offered (i. e., *ante litem motam*) [24] and that there was no apparent motive for the declarant to misrepresent the facts.[25] The firsthand knowledge requirement is not enforced; it is unnecessary to show that the declarant had personal knowledge of the facts of birth, death, kinship, or the like.[26] Special need for this type of evidence is found in the general difficulty of ob-

taining other evidence of family matters, reflected in the unavailability requirement.[27] Special assurances of reliability are found in the probability that in the absence of any motive for lying, the discussions of relatives (and others intimately related to them) as to family members will be accurate.[28]

The traditional exception goes beyond oral declarations and permits the use of contemporary records of family history, such as entries in a family Bible [29] or on a tombstone,[30] even though the author may not be identifiable. Further, evidence of the traditional reputation in the family as to such facts is admissible,[31] and some courts have extended this to the reputation in the community of matters of family history.[32]

Both the Uniform Rules of Evidence [33] and the Proposed Federal Rules of Evidence [34] adopt liberal positions, abandoning the requirement that declarations have been made *ante litem motam* and providing for the admission of statements of a nonfamily member

to paternity of child by woman who had made arrangements for birth and who was present at birth admissible, although she was not related to family whose pedigree was questioned; "the likelihood of her declarations being true are very great"). Compare O'Neill v. Lauderdale, 80 Okl. 170, 195 P. 121 (1921) (declarations of woman who had raised child that mother was dead and child was an orphan inadmissible). See generally, 5 Wigmore, Evidence § 1487 (criticizing the requirement of family membership); Annot., 15 A.L.R.2d 1412. Because a nonfamily member often offers to testify not simply as to the conclusory fact but rather to the community or neighborhood reputation as to that fact, the issue may be intertwined with the admissibility of reputation.

23. E. g., In re Stone's Estate, 78 Idaho 632, 308 P.2d 597 (1957).

24. This requirement means that the statement must have been made not only prior to the litigation but also prior to the development of the controversy that subsequently ended in litigation. Hartford Nat. Bank & Trust v. Prince, 28 Conn.Super. 348, 261 A.2d 287 (1968) (declarations of deceased amounting to a denial of paternity inadmissible in litigation concerning trust income payable to declarant's children because the statements were made after divorce litigation had begun; support of children is potential issue in every divorce proceeding); In re Estate of Cunha, 49 Haw. 273, 414 P.2d 925 (1966) (declarations in sworn pleadings filed in divorce case amounting to a denial of paternity not admissible in litigation to determine whether child would take under will because although litigation was different the same matter was involved). See generally, 5 Wigmore, Evidence § 1483.

25. See Hartford Nat. Bank & Trust v. Prince, 28 Conn.Super. 348, 261 A.2d 287 (1968), holding denials of paternity inadmissible because they were made at a time when the declarant was interested in another woman and therefore had some motive to misrepresent his relationship to his estranged wife by denying sexual relationships with her.

26. See generally, 5 Wigmore, Evidence § 1486.

27. 5 Wigmore, Evidence § 1481.

28. 5 Wigmore, Evidence § 1482.

29. See generally, 29 Am.Jur.2d Evidence §§ 873–874; Annot., 29 A.L.R. 372.

30. Conn v. Boylan, 224 N.Y.S.2d 823 (Sup.Ct.1962).

31. Kelly's Heirs v. McGuire, 15 Ark. 555 (1885) ("general repute in the family" admissible); Geisler v. Geisler, 160 Minn. 463, 200 N.W. 742 (1924).

32. Wigmore states that community reputation is always admissible to prove that persons living together were married. 5 Wigmore, Evidence § 1602. See, e. g., Daniels v. Johnson, 216 Ark. 374, 226 S.W.2d 571 (1950). Some courts have gone further. See In re Wulf's Estate, 242 Iowa 1012, 48 N.W.2d 890 (1951) (testimony that it was "common talk or general report" that X was Y's father admissible). But see Young Ah Chor v. Dulles, 270 F.2d 338 (9th Cir. 1959) (testimony that "the common knowledge in the village" was that X was Y's father was not admissible where witness was not a member of X's family; exception is limited to reputation in the family).

33. Uniform Rule 63(23)–(27).

34. F.R.Ev. (R.D.1971) 803(19) (reputation concerning personal or family history); id., 803(13) (family records); id., 804(b) (5) (statements of personal or family history, requiring a showing of unavailability of declarant).

if the declarant was so intimately associated with the family as to be likely to have accurate information concerning the subject of the statement.

323. Recitals in Ancient Writings and Documents Affecting an Interest in Property.[35]

As discussed in a preceding section,[36] a writing is usually regarded as sufficiently authenticated if the offering party proves that it is at least 30 years old, the trial judge finds that it is unsuspicious in appearance, and the party proves that it was produced from a place of custody natural for such a writing. This "ancient documents" rule, however, traditionally relates only to authentication. American courts have nevertheless sometimes held that if a writing meets these requirements it is admissible to prove the truth of statements made in it.[37] Thus what originated as an exception to general requirements of authentication has become in some jurisdictions also an exception to the hearsay rule.

Is the exception justified? The age requirement probably assures that there will be a special need for dispensing with the hearsay rule, for the same reasons which give rise to the special authentication rule. After passage of such a period of time, witnesses are unlikely to be available or, if available, to recall reliably the events at issue. But it is more doubtful whether there are sufficient assurances of special trustworthiness to justify admissibility. The mere age of the writing it may be contended, offers little assurance of truth; it is unlikely that lying was less common 30 years ago. Advocates of the exception [38] argue, however, that given the special need for the evidence sufficient assurances of reliability exist. First, the dangers of mistransmission are minimized since the rule applies only to written statements. Second, the age requirement virtually assures that the assertion will have been made long before the beginning of the present controversy. Consequently, it is unlikely that the declarant had a motive to falsify, and, in any case, the statements are almost certainly uninfluenced by partisanship. Finally, some additional assurance of reliability is provided by insistence, insofar as practicable, that the usual qualifications for witnesses and out-of-court declarants be met. Thus the writing would be inadmissible if the declarant lacked the opportunity to know firsthand the facts asserted.[39]

---

35. See generally, Wickes, Ancient Documents and Hearsay, 8 Tex.L.Rev. 451 (1930); Note, The Use of Ancient Documents in Evidence, 26 Harv.L.Rev. 544 (1913); Note, The Effect of the Ancient Document Rule on the Hearsay Rule, 83 U.Pa.L.Rev. 247 (1934); Comment, Ancient Documents as an Exception to the Hearsay Rule, 33 Yale L.J. 412 (1924); 29 Am.Jur.2d Evidence §§ 856, 861–865; C.J.S. Evidence §§ 743–752 (especially § 745); Annot., 46 A.L.R.2d 1318 (admissibility of maps, plats, field notes, surveys and tracings under the ancient documents rule); Annot., 6 A.L.R. 1437 (admissibility of recital in ancient deed as evidence of the facts recited); Dec.Dig. Evidence ☞372. Cf. Annot., 29 A.L.R. 630 (dispensing with proof of proper custody as a condition of invoking the ancient documents rule). Wigmore at one point takes the position that the ancient documents rule relates only to authentication. 7 Wigmore, Evidence § 2145a. But see 5 Wigmore, Evidence §§ 1573–1574 (hearsay exception for ancient deed recitals offered to prove a lost deed, boundary, pedigree or destroyed record).

36. See § 223, supra.

37. E. g., Kirkpatrick v. Tapo Oil Co., 301 P.2d 274, 144 Cal.App.2d 404 (1956); State of Nebraska, Dept. of Public Roads v. Parks, 185 Neb. 794, 178 N.W.2d 788 (1970); Muehrcke v. Behrens, 43 Wis.2d 1, 169 N.W.2d 86 (1969). See generally, Wickes, Ancient Documents and Hearsay, 8 Tex.L.Rev. 451 (1930). For decisions contra, see n. 41, infra.

38. Wickes, Ancient Documents and Hearsay, 8 Tex.L.Rev. 451 (1930).

39. Russell v. Emerson, 108 N.H. 518, 240 A.2d 52 (1968) (map dated 1888 not admissible under ancient documents rule because there was no evidence as to who prepared it); Budlong v. Budlong, 48 R.I. 144, 136 Atl. 308 (1927) (book found in desk of office of poor farm not admissible to prove truth of entry suggesting birth of child to specific individual, because there was not proof of the qualifications of the writer to testify to this, and in fact no proof of writer's identity at all).
The requirement that the writing not be suspicious on its face has also been enforced. See Muehrcke

Nearly all courts will apply an exception to the hearsay rule when the matter involves ancient deed recitals. Thus deed recitals of the contents and execution of an earlier instrument, of heirship, and of consideration are nearly everywhere received to prove those facts.[40] It is arguable that, especially where possession has been taken under the deed, these cases involve unusual assurances of reliability and the rule should be limited to them.[41] A number of courts, however, have applied the exception to other types of documents.[42] Both Wigmore and the Uniform

Rules do not recognize any exception to the hearsay rule for ancient documents as such, but do recognize an exception for recitals in deeds without regard to the age of the deed.[43] The Uniform Rules would extend this to recitals in wills and other documents purporting to transfer land or personal property, but would require that the judge find that the matter stated would be relevant upon an issue as to an interest in the property and that dealings with the property since the statement was made have not been inconsistent with the truth of the statement. The Proposed Federal Rules of Evidence provide a similar exception for statements affecting an interest in property,[44] and also would recognize a specific exception for ancient documents with the common law age requirement reduced from 30 to 20 years.[45]

324. Reputation.[46]

Traditionally the common law jury was not restricted in its considerations to information presented by the parties during trial, and the jurors' right to consider common repute or knowledge which they brought with them was well established.[47] Obviously, logic also required that the parties be permitted to prove general repute or knowledge. As the law began to restrict juries' consideration to proof produced in court and, by means of the hearsay rule, to limit the proof that might be produced, the older practice became an exception to the developing rule excluding hearsay. During the 1700's, as the hearsay

---

v. Behrens, 43 Wis.2d 1, 169 N.W.2d 86 (1969), in which a 1932 town record book was offered to prove that the town board had regarded certain land as a public highway. In the description of the land, the number "160" had been superimposed over "80" rods. The court held that where the instrument shows alterations on its face, the offering party has the burden of explaining the alteration; the book was found properly admitted, however, since other evidence established that the approximate length of the land was 160 rods.

40. See 5 Wigmore, Evidence §§ 1573–1574; Annot., 6 A.L.R. 630. The age requirement is insisted upon. Caranta v. Pioneer Home Improvements, Inc., 81 N.M. 393, 467 P.2d 719 (1970) (recital in deed that grantor was sole heir of X not admissible to prove heirship because deed was only 12 years old).

41. See Town of Ninety Six v. Southern Railway Co., 267 F.2d 579 (4th Cir. 1959), involving the admissibility of a letter written in 1872 (and recorded in 1905) by a predecessor in title purporting to claim a lesser right of way for a railroad than was specified in the legislative charter. After examining the various positions, the court held the letter inadmissible on the basis that the ancient documents rule related only to authentication and that the hearsay exception was limited to wills, deeds, and other documents purporting to transfer land or personal property. See also Robinson v. Peterson, 200 Va. 186, 104 S.E.2d 788 (1958) (private plat, made in 1901 by surveyor, not admissible because ancient documents rule deals only with authentication).

42. E. g., State for Use of Common Schools v. Taylor, 135 Ark. 232, 205 S.W. 104 (1918) (recital of sale of land in "plat book" of state land office); Kirkpatrick v. Tapo Oil Co., 144 Cal.App.2d 404, 301 P.2d 274 (1956) (account book); Whitman v. Shaw, 166 Mass. 451, 44 N.E. 333 (1896) (map to show boundaries); Department of Public Roads v. Parks, 185 Neb. 794, 178 N.W.2d 788 (1970) (consent petition, filed to make land a public road); Wiener v. Zweib, 128 S.W. 699 (Tex.Civ.App.1910), aff'd 105 Tex. 262, 141 S.W. 771 (1911), 147 S.W. 867 (1912) (entries in minutes of lodge to show fact

and time of member's death); Muehrcke v. Behrens, 43 Wis.2d 1, 169 N.W.2d 86 (1969) (town record book).

43. 5 Wigmore, Evidence §§ 1573–1574; Uniform Rule 63(29).

44. F.R.Ev. (R.D.1971) 803(15).

45. F.R.Ev. (R.D.1971) 803(16).

46. See generally, 5 Wigmore, Evidence §§ 1580–1626; 29 Am.Jur.2d Evidence §§ 503–507; C.J.S. Evidence §§ 422–453; Dec.Dig. Evidence ☞322, 324.

47. See 5 Wigmore, Evidence § 1580.

rule and its exceptions came to be developed with greater specificity, the use of reputation was limited to several specific situations.[48] In general, these are situations in which an exception to the hearsay rule is demanded by necessity and justified by special assurances of reliability.[49] A general lack of other reliable sources of information provides the necessity. A high probability of reliability is provided by restricting the use of reputation to those subjects in regard to which persons with personal knowledge are likely to have disclosed facts which have been the subject of general inquiry; thus the community's conclusion is likely to be accurate.

Two of the areas in which reputation is admissible despite the hearsay rule have been discussed elsewhere. Where personal character is at issue, reputation is admissible to prove it;[50] thus the character of a witness for veracity[51] or the character of a criminal accused for the trait involved in the crime of which he is accused may be proved by reputation.[52] In addition, facts of family history may be proved by reputation in the family and, under one view, by reputation in the community.[53] Reputation is admitted as proof of the reputed facts in two other situations.

When the location of boundaries of land is at issue, reputation is admitted to prove that location.[54] Traditionally, the reputation had not only to antedate the beginning of the present controversy but also be "ancient," i. e., go back to a past generation.[55] The recent cases suggest that the requirement is only that the monuments or markers of the original survey must have disappeared.[56] The Uniform Rules[57] and the Proposed Rules of Evidence for the Federal Courts,[58] would dispense completely with a requirement that the reputation be ancient or that the passage of time have rendered other evidence of the boundaries unavailable.

Reputation is also admissible to prove a variety of facts which can best be described as matters of general history.[59] Wigmore

---

48. Reputation, or the existence of a belief of a large group of persons as to a particular fact may, of course, be material for reasons other than to prove the truth of the fact believed. In those cases, use of proof of the reputation is not hearsay. This situation arises most often when reputation is shown as proof that someone in the range of the reputation had knowledge of the reputed fact. See Fake v. Addicks, 45 Minn. 37, 47 N.W. 450 (1890) (reputation of dog as vicious admitted to prove owner's knowledge of dog's viciousness); Guedon v. Rooney, 160 Ore. 621, 87 P.2d 209 (1939) (driver's reputation for recklessness admitted to prove car owner's awareness of driver's incompetence); Alexander v. Ritchie, 132 W.Va. 865, 53 S.E.2d 735 (1949).

49. See 5 Wigmore, Evidence § 1580.

50. See § 186, supra.

51. See § 44, supra.

52. See § 191, supra.

53. See § 322, supra.

54. E. g., Eagan v. Colwell, 86 Idaho 525, 388 P.2d 999 (1964); Burrow v. Brown, 190 So.2d 855 (Miss. 1966); Kardell v. Crouch, 326 S.W.2d 869, 879 (Tex.Civ.App.1959). See generally, 5 Wigmore, Evidence §§ 1582–1595; 12 Am.Jur.2d Boundaries § 106–110; C.J.S. Evidence § 234(b); Dec.Dig. Boundaries ⚬35(2). In England the use of the evidence is limited to public boundaries or other public rights. Nichols v. Parker, 14 East. 331n., 104 Eng.Rep. 629 (N.P.1805). But in this country (except in a few states) it extends also to private boundaries. Hail v. Haynes, 312 Ky. 357, 227 S.W. 2d 918 (1950); Hemphill v. Hemphill, 138 N.C. 504, 51 S.E. 42 (1905). See 5 Wigmore, Evidence § 1587. Some cases have expanded the exception beyond evidence of reputation and admitted hearsay statements of specific individuals. E. g., Kay Corp. v. Anderson, 72 Wash.2d 879, 436 P.2d 459 (1967) (statement of out-of-court declarant as to location of boundary admitted under rule).

55. 5 Wigmore, Evidence § 1582.

56. Johnstone v. Nause, 233 Miss. 584, 102 So.2d 889 (1958) (where monuments of a survey have disappeared, evidence of common reputation is admissible as to location of boundaries and corners); Kardell v. Crouch, 326 S.W.2d 869, 879 (Tex.Civ. App.1959) (admissible after destruction of markers and a "long lapse of time"). Cf. Blain v. Woods, 145 W.Va. 297, 115 S.E.2d 88 (1960) (where monuments of survey not lost, proper to exclude testimony of grantor's children as to boundary).

57. Uniform Rule 63(27) (a).

58. F.R.Ev. (R.D.1971) 803(20).

59. See generally, 5 Wigmore, Evidence §§ 1597–1599; 29 Am.Jur.2d Evidence §§ 506–507, 887;

suggests that the matter must be an ancient one "or one as to which it would be unlikely that living witnesses could be obtained." [60] Neither the Uniform Rules [61] nor the Proposed Rules of Evidence for the Federal Courts [62] requires this, although by use of the term "history" some requirement of age is no doubt imposed. In addition, the matter must be one of general interest, so that it can accurately be said that there is a high probability that the matter underwent general scrutiny as the community reputation was formed.[63] Thus when the navigable nature of a certain river was at issue, newspaper accounts and histories describing the use made of it during the nineteenth century were admissible to prove its general reputation for navigability at that time.[64]

In addition to these well-developed exceptions, reputation evidence is sometimes admitted under statute or local law to prove a variety of other miscellaneous matters,[65] such as ownership of property,[66] financial standing,[67] and maintenance of a house as an establishment for liquor-selling or prostitution.[68]

C.J.S. Evidence §§ 233–237; Annot., 58 A.L.R.2d 615. See also, Morris v. Harmer's Heirs' Lessee, 32 U.S. (7 Pet.) 554, 558 (1833): "Historical facts of general and public notoriety may indeed be proved by reputation, and that reputation may be established by historical works of known character and accuracy."

The kinship to judicial notice is apparent. See § 330, infra.

60. 5 Wigmore, Evidence § 1597.

61. Uniform Rule 63(27) (b).

62. F.R.Ev. (R.D.1971) 803(20).

63. 5 Wigmore, Evidence § 1598; Annot., 58 A.L.R. 2d 615, 619–626.

64. Montana Power Co. v. FPC, 87 U.S.App.D.C. 316, 185 F.2d 491, 497–498 (1950), cert. denied 340 U.S. 947. See also United States v. Louisiana, 225 F. Supp. 353, 375 (E.D.La.1963) aff'd 380 U.S. 145 (newspaper accounts of proceedings of state constitutional convention's committee on Sufferage and Elections admissible to prove legislative history of constitution).

65. See 5 Wigmore, Evidence §§ 1620–1626.

66. Chicago & Eastern Ill. R. Co. v. Schmitz, 211 Ill. 446, 71 N.E. 1050 (1904) (reputation that particular railway owned tracks sufficient evidence of ownership in personal injury action). See 5 Wigmore, Evidence § 1626(4).

67. Lucas v. Swan, 67 F.2d 106, 110 (4th Cir. 1933) (reputation of endorsers for insolvency). Contra, Coleman v. Lewis, 183 Mass. 485, 67 N.E. 603 (1903). See generally, 5 Wigmore, Evidence § 1623.

68. Elder v. Stark, 200 Ga. 452, 37 S.E.2d 598 (1946) (reputation as "blind tiger"); State v. Mauch, 236 Iowa 217, 17 N.W.2d 536 (1945) (reputation of premises and defendant as to keeping house of ill fame). See 5 Wigmore, Evidence § 1620; Dec.Dig. Disorderly House ⊕16.

In the latter situation, common usage has absorbed the rule of evidence into the terms "house of ill fame" and "house of ill repute."

CHAPTER 34

THE PRESENT AND FUTURE OF RULES ABOUT HEARSAY

325. Evaluation of the Present Rules.

Before laying down his pen as he concluded his work on evidence in 1842, Professor Greenleaf wrote:

"The student will not fail to observe the symmetry and beauty of this branch of the law . . . and will rise from the study of its principles convinced, with Lord Erskine, that 'they are founded in the charities of religion,—in the philosophy of nature,—in the truths of history,—and in the experience of common life.' " [1]

Few readers today of the foregoing several chapters on the subject of hearsay would arrive at a similar evaluation of the treatment of hearsay as developed at the common law. Did the common law tradition go overboard in its insistence on the best? Certainly, picking a quarrel with insistence upon high quality in judicial factfinding would be difficult to justify in the abstract, and yet more than a suspicion is raised that the rules have not always yielded the quality sought and have exacted too high a price. Criticism centers upon the complexity of the pattern of the rules and upon doubts whether in reality they achieve their purpose of screening the good from the bad.

First, with respect to the complexity of the rule against hearsay and its exceptions, the number of exceptions naturally depends upon the minuteness of the classification. The Uniform Rules,[2] for example, contain 31 paragraphs of exceptions, with some treating more than a single exception. Wigmore requires over a thousand pages to cover hearsay, and its treatment preempted 25% of the original edition of the present work. Most of the complication of course arises in connection with the exceptions, leading readily to the conclusion that a general rule so riddled with exceptions is "farcical." [3] The conclusion may not, however, be totally warranted. Probably less than 10, and possibly no more than a half dozen, of the exceptions are encountered with any frequency in the trial of cases, and to require mastery of them, plus an awareness of the others and a working knowledge of what is and is not hearsay, would seem not unduly to tax the intellectual resources of a learned profession.

The second complaint, that the rule against hearsay and its exceptions fail to screen reliable from unreliable hearsay on a realistic basis, is of more serious proportion. The trustworthiness of hearsay ranges from the highest reliability to utter worthlessness. Among the kinds of hearsay, i. e., uncross-examined statements offered to prove the facts stated in them, are the following: history books, newspapers, business records, official records and certificates, affidavits, letters and other written statements, simple oral hearsay (A reports B said), multiple

---

1. Greenleaf, Evidence § 584 (1st ed. 1842).
2. Uniform Rule 63. The Proposed Federal Rules of Evidence list 30 exceptions, including two "catch-all" provisions. F.R.Ev. (R.D.1971) 803, 804. Compare Cross, who counted 20. Cross, The Scope of the Rule Against Hearsay, 72 L.Q.Rev. 91 (1956).
3. Nokes, The English Jury and the Law of Evidence, 31 Tulane L.Rev. 153, 167 (1956).

hearsay (A reports that B said that C said, and so on), reputation, and gossip or rumors.[4] Whether these varying, plastic situations can ever be completely and satisfactorily captured in a set of rules may well be doubted. Yet similar doubts pervade most other areas of the law and are not generally regarded as cause for despair. If the heart of the problem is that the exceptions are unacceptable in detail, a perusal of the preceding chapters dealing with hearsay indicates that much has been done in recent years to rationalize the rules and to improve their practical workability, more along evolutionary lines than revolutionary. But if the basic difficulty is simply that no hearsay system based on classes of exceptions can truly succeed, a totally different approach would be required.

326. Basic Shifts in the Contemporary Pattern.

Prompted by a suggestion from James Bradley Thayer, the Massachusetts Hearsay Statute of 1898 was enacted as follows: "A declaration of a deceased person shall not be inadmissible in evidence as hearsay if the Court finds that it was made in good faith before the commencement of the action and upon the personal knowledge of the declarant."[5] It has since been amended by striking out the requirement that the declaration must have been made before the commencement of the action, and in other minor particulars, but the elements of the original reform remain in effect.[6]

After a quarter century of experience under the Act a questionnaire was addressed by a responsible committee to the lawyers and judges of the state, to ascertain their views as to the merits of the Act, and 638 answers were received. Of those having experience with the operation of the Act, 71 percent thought that its effects were wholesome and only 19 percent were of the opposite opinion.[7] Thus the extensive available evidence indicates that the Act has worked well.[8] The American Bar Association in 1938 recommended a liberalized version of the Act for adoption by the states.[9]

The English Evidence Act of 1938 [10] allowed the introduction of written statements, made on the personal knowledge of the maker or in the regular course of business, if the maker was called as a witness or was unavailable. Even though the maker was neither called nor unavailable, the judge might admit the statement if satisfied that undue delay or expense would otherwise be involved. Statements made by interested persons when proceedings were pending or instituted were excluded from the act.

---

4. McCormick, Tomorrow's Law of Evidence, 24 A.B. A.J. 507, 512 (1938); Morgan, Foreword, Model Code of Evidence 46 (1942). See § 245, n. 45, supra.

5. Mass. Acts 1898, ch. 535. Rhode Island has a similar statute. R.I.Gen.Laws 1956, § 9–19–11.

6. The present version of the Act is as follows: "In any action or other civil judicial proceeding, a declaration of a deceased person shall not be inadmissible in evidence as hearsay or as private conversation between husband and wife, as the case may be, if the court finds that it was made in good faith and upon the personal knowledge of the de-

clarant." Mass.G.L.Ann. c. 233, § 65, as amended 1941 and 1943.

7. Morgan et al. (constituting the Commonwealth Fund Committee), The Law of Evidence: Some Proposals for Its Reform 39–49 (1927).

8. For other approving expressions, see Vanderbilt, C. J. in Robertson v. Hackensack Trust Co., 1 N.J. 304, 318, 63 A.2d 515, 522 (1949) ("This sensible statute"); Maguire, Evidence, Common Sense and Common Law 153–155 (1947); Terwilliger and Effland, Legislative Comment, 1938 Wis.L.Rev. 587, 592; 5 Wigmore, Evidence § 1576.

9. "That declarations of a deceased or insane person should be received in evidence if the trial judge shall find (1) that the person is dead or insane, (2) that the declaration was made and (3) that it was made in good faith before the commencement of the action and upon the personal knowledge of the declarant." Vanderbilt, Minimum Standards of Judicial Administration 321, 338 (1949).

10. St.1938, c. 28, Evidence. See Maugham, Observations on the Law of Evidence, 17 Can.Bar Rev. 469 (1939); Cowen and Carter, The Interpretation of the Evidence Act, 1938, 12 Mod.L.Rev. 145 (1949); Comment, 34 Ill.L.Rev. 974 (1940).

These limitations were loosened and new ones added in 1968.[11] Hearsay statements, whether written or oral, are made admissible to the extent that testimony of the declarant would be admissible, regardless of whether he is called as a witness,[12] though it is contemplated that ordinarily prior statements would not be admitted at the behest of the proponent if the declarant is called.[13] Notice is required of intent to offer a hearsay statement under the act, and the opposite party is given the right to require production of declarant as a witness, if available.[14] The act is far more complex than the foregoing résumé would indicate. Like its predecessor of 1938 and the Massachusetts statute, it applies only in civil cases.

The drafters of the Model Code of Evidence of the American Law Institute took a bold course about hearsay. They drafted a sweeping new exception to the hearsay rule as follows:

"Evidence of a hearsay declaration is admissible if the judge finds that the declarant

"(a) is unavailable as a witness, or

"(b) is present and subject to cross-examination." [15]

This rule, however, was qualified and safeguarded by other rules which (1) limited its application to declarations by persons with personal knowledge and excluded hearsay upon hearsay,[16] and (2) empowered the trial judge to exclude such hearsay whenever its probative value was outweighed by the likelihood of waste of time, prejudice, confusion or unfair surprise.[17] The traditional exceptions, in addition to the new sweeping one, were retained in general.[18]

The liberalizing of the use of hearsay was a chief ground of opposition to the Model Code in professional discussion and no doubt substantially accounted for the failure of the Code to be adopted in any jurisdiction.[19]

Nevertheless, the controversy over the Model Code awakened a new interest in many enlightened lawyers in the improvement of evidence law. Accordingly, the Commissioners on Uniform State Laws, in cooperation with the American Law Institute and building on the foundation of the Model Code, drafted and adopted a more modestly reformative code, styled the Uniform Rules of Evidence.[20] The American Bar Association approved this action.[21]

Instead of admitting, as the Model Code does, virtually all firsthand hearsay when the declarant is unavailable, the drafters of the Uniform Rules hedged the extension with careful safeguarding restrictions. The relevant provisions are the following:

"Rule 63. Evidence of a statement which is made other than by a witness while testifying at the hearing offered to prove the truth of the matter stated is hearsay evidence and inadmissible except:

"(1) A statement previously made by a person who is present at the hearing and available for cross examination with respect to the statement and its subject matter, provided the statement would be

---

11. St.1968, c. 64, Civil Evidence. Comment, Newark and Samuels, 31 Mod.L.Rev. 668 (1968).

12. Id., Part I, § 2(1).

13. Id., Part II, § 2(2).

14. Id., Part I, § 8(2).

15. Model Code of Evidence Rule 503.

16. Id., Rule 501(3).

McCormick et al on Evid. 2nd Ed. HB—48

17. Id., Rule 303.

18. Id., Rules 504–529.

19. Despite its failure to achieve adoption, the influence of the Code upon decisions and writings in the field of evidence has been enormous.

20. 9A U.A.L.

21. 39 A.B.A.J. 1029 (1953).

admissible if made by declarant while testifying as a witness; [22]

. . .

"(4) . . . (c) if the declarant is unavailable as a witness, a statement narrating, describing or explaining an event or condition which the judge finds was made by the declarant at a time when the matter had been recently perceived by him and while his recollection was clear, and was made in good faith prior to the commencement of the action; "

As in the Model Code the other traditional exceptions are retained and liberalized,[23] and the judge may exclude hearsay (as other evidence) when its value is outweighed by the danger of prejudice, confusion, surprise and waste of time.[24] The significant restrictive provision is sub. 4(c), which instead of letting in all declarations on personal knowledge of unavailable declarants requires the judge's finding (1) that the statement was made within a brief period after the matter was perceived ("recently"), (2) while memory was clear, (3) in good faith, and (4) before the commencement of the action.[25] All this includes the safeguard that the judge, if he does not believe that the

statement was made at all, cannot make the necessary findings for admission and will exclude it.[26]

This treatment of hearsay, while it opens the door more narrowly than the Model Code, nevertheless empowers judges to admit much needed and highly reliable evidence, particularly in the cases of fatal accidents to solitary workmen and in many cases involving transactions with persons since deceased, which would now have to be excluded.

From the foregoing analysis, it will be seen that the pattern of a general rule of exclusion of hearsay, subject to numerous exceptions ticketed in advance by class, has persisted. Even the English Act of 1968 specifically preserved some of the old landmark exceptions (admissions, published works dealing with matters of a public nature, public documents, records, and reputation as proof of various matters and exempted them from the notice provisions of the act.[27] Presumably, as in the American enumerations of exceptions where unavailability is not a factor, the hearsay evidence is considered as good as or better than testimony by the declarant on the witness stand.

The individual exceptions have, in recent years, been markedly improved by decision, rule, or statute in almost every instance, and

---

22. See the discussion of prior statements of a witness, supra, § 251.

23. Uniform Rule 63, subsecs. 1–31.

24. Uniform Rule 45.

25. Despite these safeguards, Rule 63(4) (c) was excluded from the New Jersey Rules of Evidence and the California Evidence Code, although the latter does include a provision that a decedent's statement is admissible in actions against his estate. West's Ann.Cal.Evid.Code, § 1261. One of the objections to the Uniform Rule was its failure to guard against the use of statements prepared by lawyers or investigators with a view to litigation. Quick, Excitement, Necessity and the Uniform Rules: A Reappraisal of Rule 63(4), 6 Wayne L.Rev. 204, 219–224 (1960). Accordingly, the proposed federal rule excludes such statements and those by persons interested in pending or anticipated litigation, though otherwise the Uniform Rule is followed. F.R.Ev. (R.D.1971) 804(b) (2).

26. The original edition of this work suggested that the judge, if he did not believe the statement was made at all, could not make the requisite findings and would exclude it. McCormick, Evidence 633 (1954). However, the procedure of excluding evidence because the judge does not believe it has been described as "altogether atypical, extraordinary." Chadbourn, Bentham and the Hearsay Rule— A Benthamic View of Rule 63(4) (c) of the Uniform Rules of Evidence, 75 Harv.L.Rev. 932, 947 (1962). A more appropriate treatment would be found in the allocation of functions between judge and jury in cases where secondary evidence of contents of a document is offered and there is dispute whether the original ever in fact existed. The judge admits upon a prima facie showing of existence of the original. See Uniform Rule 70(2); F.R.Ev. (R.D.1971) 1008, § 237, supra.

27. St.1968, c. 64, Part I, § 9.

problems presented by the unavailable declarant, whose statement does not qualify under one of the just-as-good exceptions, are dealt with more adequately.

A significant further development, designed to dissipate contentions that the hearsay exceptions are a closed system, is found in the revised version of the Proposed Federal Rules of Evidence, following the enumeration of various exceptions:

> "A statement not specifically covered by any of the foregoing exceptions but having comparable circumstantial guarantee of trustworthiness." [28]

327. The Future of Hearsay.

Regardless of whether the hearsay rule was, as a matter of history, the child of the jury system,[29] there seems to be little doubt that the felt need for controlling the use of hearsay is more pronounced in jury cases than in nonjury cases. In part this attitude may be a product of the close association between the right to a jury and the right of confrontation in criminal cases. The English developments in the direction of relaxing limitations on hearsay[30] seem obviously to have been inspired by the virtual disappearance in that country of jury trial in civil cases. Corresponding changes have not transpired with respect to criminal cases, where the jury remains.

In the United States, the right of confrontation and jury trial, both constitutionally based, combine to make unlikely any unprecedented wholesale opening of the gates to hearsay. One may, however, speculate that the civil jury is entering upon a period of attrition, commencing with a trend to reduce its size following the recent decision of the Supreme Court of the United States

that the jury contemplated in the right to jury trial may consist of less than 12 members,[31] and some effect on the rules of evidence may be expected. Cognizance has been taken in an earlier section[32] of the generally more relaxed attitude in administering the exclusionary rules of evidence in nonjury cases. This attitude of course encompasses the rule against hearsay. Perhaps no more than an acceleration of this process is involved in the vigorous advocacy of eliminating the hearsay rule entirely in nonjury civil cases which is encountered in some quarters.[33]

In somewhat different vein is the suggestion that admissibility of hearsay in civil cases, jury or nonjury, be based upon the judge's *ad hoc* evaluation of its probative force, with certain procedural safeguards.[34] Obviously a substantially greater measure of discretion in the judge is contemplated, with a corresponding decrease in the impact of precedent and predictability.[35] Moreover, the judge is thrust squarely into the area of credibility, traditionally reserved to juries. Suggested procedural safeguards are notice, judge's comment on evidence, greater control by judges over juries, and greater control

---

28. F.R.Ev. (R.D.1971) 803(24) (availability of declarant immaterial, 804(b) (6) (declarant unavailable).

29. See § 244, supra.

30. See § 326, notes 9–13, supra.

31. Williams v. Florida, 399 U.S. 78 (1970).

32. § 60, supra.

33. E. g., Davis, Hearsay in Nonjury Cases, 83 Harv. L.Rev. 1362 (1970) (hearsay should be admitted in nonjury civil cases without ruling on its admissibility).

34. See Weinstein, Probative Force of Hearsay, 46 Iowa L.Rev. 331 (1961), collecting the literature and making an impressive case in its own right.

35. "It is tempting to meet such variability by giving trial judges some range of discretion as to admissibility. But it is uncomfortable to go to trial without knowing whether important evidence will be let in or excluded." Maguire, The Hearsay System: Around and Through the Thicket, 14 Vand.L.Rev. 741, 776 (1961).

"The suitor must feel that success is dependent upon the truth of his contentions and not upon the personality of the judge . . . who determines what evidence he will receive or submit to the consideration of the jury." Lehman, Technical Rules of Evidence, 26 Colum.L.Rev. 509, 512 (1926).

by appellate courts over trial courts. A notice requirement has the disadvantage of adding a further complication to an already overcrowded array of pretrial procedures and is contrary to modern theories of general pleading implemented by discovery.[36] And the controls envisioned, as with admissibility in the first instance, find their roots in discretionary judicial evaluation of the evidence. These objections are, however, by no means conclusive and may be thought less objectionable than the deficiencies of the existing system.

In projecting changes of the kinds suggested above, a further factor to be considered is the impact of having more than one set of rules for dealing with hearsay. Confrontation plus jury trial seem to stake out certain limits in criminal cases, and waiver of a jury seems unlikely to affect that result. It may well be that, as with the English, we are headed for different rules in civil and criminal cases, but there are disadvantages:

complication of the rules overall, a possibly inferior quality of factfinding in civil cases, frustration of the effort to involve the trial bar in criminal cases. In any event, setting up different rules for civil jury and nonjury cases may well be calculated to induce shopping for admissibility via demand for or waiver of jury trial. While this may be a possibility at present, the encouragement of the practice seems unwise.

In the long run the process of liberalizing the admissibility of hearsay in civil cases, will no doubt continue. Whether it is accelerated may well depend upon the fate of the civil jury.[37] Whether companion developments occur in the criminal field will depend on the nature of the civil changes and the effect given the Confrontation Clause.

---

36. The emphasis on notice in the English statute probably derives at least in part from the virtual nonexistence of discovery in the English practice. See § 326, n. 13, supra.

37. In any event, it seems likely that as rules of admissibility become more liberal, principles which formerly governed admission and exclusion will become guidelines for evaluation and thus reduce the chaos which otherwise might result from free admissibility. Ladd, The Relationship of the Principles of Exclusionary Rules of Evidence to the Problem of Proof, 18 Minn.L.Rev. 506 (1934). A parallel may be found in the conversion of common law grounds of disqualification of witnesses into grounds of impeachment. See On Lee v. United States, 343 U.S. 747, 757 (1952); § 61, supra.

TITLE 11

JUDICIAL NOTICE

CHAPTER 35

JUDICIAL NOTICE

328. The Need for and the Effect of Judicial Notice.[1]

The traditional notion that trials are bifurcated proceedings involving both a judge and a panel of twelve jurors has obviously had a profound impact on the overall development of common law doctrine pertaining to evidence. The very existence of the jury, after all, helped create the demand for the rigorous guarantees of accuracy which typify the law of evidence, witness the insistence upon proof by witnesses having firsthand knowledge, the mistrust of hearsay, and the insistence upon original documents and their authentication by witnesses. Thus it is that the facts in dispute are commonly established by the jury after the carefully controlled introduction of formal evidence, which ordinarily consists of the testimony of witnesses. In light of the role of the jury, therefore, it is easy enough to conclude that, whereas questions concerning the tenor of the law to be applied to a case fall within the province of the judge, the determination of questions pertaining to propositions of fact is uniquely the function of the jury. The life of the law has never been quite so elementary, however, because judges on numerous occasions take charge of questions of fact and excuse the party having the burden of establishing a fact from the necessity of producing formal proof. These hybrid questions of fact, dealt with by judges as if they were questions pertaining to law, are the raw materials out of which the doctrine of judicial notice has been constructed.[2]

1. See generally, 9 Wigmore, Evidence §§ 2565–2583; Thayer, Preliminary Treatise on the Law of Evidence, c. 7 (1898); J. Maguire, Evidence—Common Sense and Common Law 166–175 (1947); Davis, Official Notice, 62 Harv.L.Rev. 537 (1949), Judicial Notice, 55 Colum.L.Rev. 945 (1955); Keeffe, Landis and Shaad, Sense and Nonsense about Judicial Notice, 2 Stan.L.Rev. 664 (1950); McNaughton, Judicial Notice—Excerpts Relating to the Morgan-Wigmore Controversy, 14 Vand.L.Rev. 779 (1961); Morgan, Judicial Notice, 57 Harv.L.Rev. 269 (1944); Roberts, Preliminary Notes Toward a Study of Judicial Notice, 52 Cornell L.Q. 210 (1967); Comment, The Presently Expanding Concept of Judicial Notice, 13 Vill.L.Rev. 528 (1968); Dec.Dig. Evidence ⊕1–52; C.J.S. Evidence §§ 6–102; 29 Am.Jur.2d Evidence §§ 14–122.

2. Harper v. Killion, 345 S.W.2d 309, 311 (Tex.Civ. App.1961) ("The doctrine of judicial notice is one of common sense. The theory is that, where a fact is well-known by all reasonably intelligent people in the community, or its existence is so easily determinable with certainty from unimpeachable sources, it would not be good sense to require formal proof."). See also Porter v. Sunshine Packing Corp., 81 F.Supp. 566, 575 (W.D.Pa.1948), rev'd in part 181 F.2d 348; Williams v. Commonwealth, 190 Va. 280, 291–292, 56 S.E.2d 537, 542–543 (1949).

With what manner of questions pertaining to facts do judges concern themselves? [3] Whether a well known street was in fact within a local business district as alleged by a litigant, in which case a certain speed limit obtained, may be dealt with by the judge during the trial of a negligence case.[4] That is to say, the judge may instruct the jury that the street in question was within a business district, dispensing thereby with the need to introduce evidence to this effect.[5] Then again, questions of fact arise about which reasonably intelligent people might not have in mind the information in question, but where they would agree that the facts are verifiable with certainty by consulting authoritative reference sources. At a time when Sunday contracts were taboo, for example, the question arose during the trial of a warranty action whether the relevant sales instrument, dated June 3, 1906, had been executed on a Sunday. In this instance the trial judge was reversed for leaving the question to the jury to deliberate upon as a question of fact.[6] Experience reveals, therefore, that two categories of facts clearly fall within the perimeters of judicial notice, these being facts generally known with certainty by all the reasonably intelligent people in the community and facts capable of accurate and ready determination by resort to sources of indisputable accuracy.

In both of the examples enumerated thus far it should be carefully noted that the facts of which judicial notice was taken were "adjudicative" facts. They were facts about the particular event which gave rise to the lawsuit and, like all adjudicative facts, they helped explain who did what, when, where, how, and with what motive and intent.[7] Further, either because they were facts so

---

3. Compare with the classification in the text Uniform Rule 9: "*Facts which Must or May be Judicially Noticed.*

"(1) Judicial notice shall be taken without request by a party, of the common law, constitutions and public statutes in force in every state, territory and jurisdiction of the United States, and of such specific facts and propositions of generalized knowledge as are so universally known that they cannot reasonably be the subject of dispute.

"(2) Judicial notice may be taken without request by a party, of (a) private acts and resolutions of the Congress of the United States and of the legislature of this state, and duly enacted ordinances and duly published regulations of governmental subdivisions or agencies of this state, and (b) the laws of foreign countries, and (c) such facts as are so generally known or of such common notoriety within the territorial jurisdiction of the court that they cannot reasonably be the subject of dispute, and (d) specific facts and propositions of generalized knowledge which are capable of immediate and accurate determination by resort to easily accessible sources of indisputable accuracy.

"(3) Judicial notice shall be taken of each matter specified in paragraph (2) of this rule if a party requests it and (a) furnishes the judge sufficient information to enable him properly to comply with the request and (b) has given each adverse party such notice as the judge may require to enable the adverse party to prepare to meet the request."

Compare with this rule and with the classification in the text F.R.Ev. (R.D.1971) 201:

"Judicial Notice of Adjudicative Facts.

"(a) Scope of Rule. This rule governs only judicial notice of adjudicative facts.

"(b) Kinds of Facts. A judicially noticed fact must be one not subject to reasonable dispute in that it is either (1) generally known within the territorial jurisdiction of the trial court or (2) capable of accurate and ready determination by resort to sources whose accuracy cannot reasonably be questioned.

"(c) When Discretionary. A judge or court may take judicial notice, whether requested or not.

"(d) When Mandatory. A judge or court shall take judicial notice if requested by a party and supplied with the necessary information.

"(e) Opportunity To Be Heard. A party is entitled upon timely request to an opportunity to be heard as to the propriety of taking judicial notice and the tenor of the matter noticed. In the absence of prior notification, the request may be made after judicial notice has been taken.

"(f) Time of Taking Notice. Judicial notice may be be taken at any stage of the proceeding.

"(g) Instructing Jury. The judge shall instruct the jury to accept as established any facts judicially noticed."

4. Varcoe v. Lee, 180 Cal. 338, 181 P. 223 (1919).

5. Id. at 344, 181 P. at 226 ("Judicial notice is a judicial short cut, a doing away . . . with the formal necessity of evidence because there is no real necessity for it.").

6. Beardsley v. Irving, 81 Conn. 489, 71 Atl. 580 (1909).

7. Davis, Judicial Notice, 55 Colum.L.Rev. 945, 952 (1955).

commonly known in the jurisdiction or so manifestly capable of accurate verification, they were facts reasonably informed people in the community would regard as propositions not reasonably subject to dispute.

Another species of facts figures prominently in discussions of judicial notice which, to continue to employ the terminology coined by Professor K. C. Davis,[8] are denominated "legislative" facts. Judicial notice of these facts occurs when a judge is faced with the task of creating law, by deciding upon the constitutional validity of a statute,[9] or the interpretation of a statute,[10] or the extension or restriction of a common law rule,[11] upon grounds of policy, and the policy is thought to hinge upon social, economic, political or scientific facts. Illustrative of this phenomenon was Hawkins v. United States [12] in which the Court refused to discard the common law rule that one spouse could not testify against the other, saying, "Adverse testimony given in criminal proceedings would, we think, be likely to destroy almost any marriage." This conclusion rests upon a certain view of the facts about marriage but, needless to say, the facts taken to be true in this instance were hardly indisputable. Observe, moreover, that these facts were not part and parcel of the disputed event being litigated but bore instead upon the court's own thinking about the tenor of the law to be invoked in deciding that dispute.

It is axiomatic, of course, that the judge decides whether a given set of facts constitutes an actionable wrong or a certain line of cross-examination is relevant. A judge, unless he is to be reversed on appeal, is bound to know the common and statutory law of his own jurisdiction. Commonly enough even this truism has been incorporated into the law of evidence by saying that judges must judicially notice the law of their own forum.[13] This manner of speaking has served to interpolate into the field of judicial notice the procedural mechanisms by which the applicable law is fed into the judicial process.[14] Foreign law, of course, was once more germane to the topic of judicial notice because that body of law was (for convenience) treated as fact, so much so that the law of a jurisdiction other than the forum had to be pleaded and proved just like any other question of fact, but a peculiar one which only the judge came to decide, and hence its inclusion within the topic of judicial notice.[15] Indeed, lumped along with foreign law as a proper subject for treatment under the caption of judicial notice has been the forum's own administrative law and local municipal ordinances, together with a hotchpot of internal judicial administrative details concerning the courts themselves, such as their own personnel, records, organization and jurisdictional boundaries.[16] The recognition appears to be growing, however, that the manner in which the law is insinuated into the judicial process is not so much a problem of evidence as it is a con-

8. Davis, An Approach to Problems of Evidence in the Administrative Process, 55 Harv.L.Rev. 364 (1942).

9. Perez v. Lippold, 32 Cal.2d 711, 198 P.2d 17 (1948).

10. Potts v. Coe, 78 U.S.App.D.C. 297, 140 F.2d 470 (1944).

11. Southern Cotton Oil Co. v. Anderson, 80 Fla. 441, 86 So. 629 (1920). Although the term judicial notice is not actually invoked, an excellent illustration of this phenomenon is inherent in Gillespie v. Dew, 1 Stew. 229, 230 (Ala.1827).

12. 358 U.S. 74, 78 (1958).

13. Hoyt v. Russell, 117 U.S. 401 (1886).

14. Cross, Evidence 130–131 (3d ed. 1967) ("It is sometimes said that the judges take judicial notice of the Common Law, but there is no need to deal separately with this aspect of the subject.").

15. Keeffe, Landis and Shaad, Sense and Nonsense About Judicial Notice, 2 Stan.L.Rev. 664, 673–675 (1950).

16. See § 335, infra.

cern better handled within the context of the rules pertaining to procedure.[17]

The courts' willingness to resort to judicial notice is apparently influenced by a number of less specifically definable circumstances. A court is more willing to notice a general than a specific fact, as for example, the approximate time of the normal period of human gestation, but not the precise maximum and minimum limits.[18] A court may be more willing to notice a fact if it is not an ultimate fact, that is, a fact which would be determinative of a case.[19] Suppose, for example, that a plaintiff in a vehicular negligence action specifically alleged that the defendant was driving too fast in a business district and the testimony, if believed, would indicate that the automobile in question caused a long skid mark on the highway surface. The trial judge might be less willing to notice that the street in question was within the business district than he would to notice that any properly equipped automobile travelling at the maximum speed appropriate in such a district could be stopped within x feet of the braking point. In the first example, the trial judge would appear to be invading the province of the jury to determine the facts pertinent to what had happened, whereas in the second he would be merely establishing rather

quickly a piece of data which would aid the jury during their deliberations on the ultimate issue of negligence.[20]

Judges have been prone to emphasize the need for caution in applying the doctrine of judicial notice.[21] The great writers of evidence, on the other hand, having perhaps a wider view of the needs of judicial administration, advocate a more extensive use of the doctrine. Thus Thayer suggests: "Courts may judicially notice much that they cannot be required to notice. That is well worth emphasizing; for it points to a great possible usefulness in this doctrine, in helping to shorten and simplify trials. . . . The failure to exercise it tends daily to smother trials with technicality and monstrously lengthens them out." [22] And Wigmore says, "The principle is an instrument of usefulness hitherto unimagined by judges." [23]

329. Matters of Common Knowledge.

The oldest and plainest ground for judicial notice is that the fact is so commonly known in the community as to make it unprofitable to require proof, and so certainly known as to make it indisputable among reasonable men.[24] Though this basis for notice

---

17. See, e. g., F.R.Ev. (R.D.1971) 201; F.R.Civ.P. 44.1, 28 U.S.C.A.

18 Compare Equitable Trust Co. v. McComb, 19 Del.Ch. 387, 168 A. 203 (1933), with Commonwealth v. Kitchen, 299 Mass. 7, 11 N.E.2d 482 (1937).

19. This idea was suggested in Thayer, Preliminary Treatise on the Law of Evidence 306 (1898) and was repeated in McCormick, Evidence § 323 (1954), and Comment, The Presently Expanding Concept of Judicial Notice, 13 Vill.L.Rev. 528, 533–534 (1968). Illustrative of a case involving the judicial notice of an ultimate fact is State v. Lawrence, 120 Utah 323, 234 P.2d 600 (1951), where the lower court took judicial notice of the fact that the value of the car allegedly stolen by the defendant was worth in excess of $50.00, the amount required for a larceny conviction, but on appeal was reversed. Note that F.R.Ev. (R.D.1971) 201 would apply to "adjudicative facts."

20. However, in Varcoe v. Lee, supra, n. 4, judicial notice was taken that the street was in a business district, and in Hughes v. Vestal, 264 N.C. 500, 142 S.E.2d 361 (1965) the trial judge was reversed for instructing the jury from a table of stopping distances. See § 332, n. 14, infra.

21. See, e. g., Varcoe v. Lee, 180 Cal. 338, 345, 181 P. 223, 226 (1919); State v. Clousing, 205 Minn. 296, 285 N.W. 711, 123 A.L.R. 465, 470 (1939).

22. Thayer, Preliminary Treatise on Evidence 309 (1898).

23. 9 Wigmore, Evidence § 2583, p. 585.

24. Varcoe v. Lee, 180 Cal. 338, 346–347, 181 P. 223, 227 (1919). ("The test, therefore, in any particular case where it is sought to avoid or excuse the production of evidence because the fact to be proven is one of general knowledge and notoriety, is: (1) Is the fact one of common, everyday knowledge in that jurisdiction, which everyone of average intelligence and knowledge of things about him can be presumed to know? and (2) is it certain and indisputable? If it is, it is a proper case for

is sometimes loosely described as universal knowledge, manifestly this could not be taken literally [25] and the more reflective opinions speak in terms of the knowledge of "most men," [26] or of "what well-informed persons generally know," [27] or "the knowledge that every intelligent person has." [28] Observe that these phrases tend progressively to widen the circle of facts within "common knowledge." Moreover, though usually facts of "common knowledge" will be generally known throughout the country, it is sufficient as a basis for judicial notice that they be known in the local community where the trial court sits. [29]

What a judge knows and what facts a judge may judicially notice are not identical data banks. A famous colloquy in the Year Books shows that a clear difference has long been taken between what judges may notice judicially and the facts that the particular judge happens personally to know. [30] It is not a distinction easy for a judge to follow in application, but the doctrine is accepted that actual private knowledge by the judge is no sufficient ground for taking judicial notice of a fact as a basis for a finding or a final judgment, [31] though it may still be a

dispensing with evidence, for its production cannot add or aid.").

25. The late Dean F. McDermott of Suffolk Law School aptly exposed the absurdity of this approach by succinctly translating it into the rule that "Judicial notice may only be taken of those facts every damn fool knows." See, however, Layne v. Tribune Co., 108 Fla. 177, 183, 146 So. 234, 237 (1933) ("What everybody knows the courts are assumed to know, and of such matters may take judicial cognizance."); In re Buszta's Estate, 18 Misc.2d 716, 717, 186 N.Y.S.2d 192, 193 (Surr.Ct.1959) ("Generally speaking, a court may take judicial notice of facts which are universally known and recognized.").

26. Rives v. Atlanta Newspapers, Inc., 110 Ga.App. 184, 190, 138 S.E.2d 100, 104 (1964), rev'd on other grounds 220 Ga. 485, 139 S.E.2d 395 ("Consequently, courts will take judicial notice of that which is within the knowledge of most men").

27. Brandon v. Lozier-Broderick & Gordon, 160 Kan. 506, 511, 163 P.2d 384, 387 (1945).

28. Strain v. Isaacs, 59 Ohio App. 495, 514, 18 N.E. 2d 816, 825 (1938).

29. Varcoe v. Lee, 180 Cal. 338, 346, 181 P. 223, 226 (1919) ("It would be wholly unreasonable to require proof, if the fact became material, as to the general location in the city of San Francisco of its city hall before a judge and jury made up of residents of that city and actually sitting in the building. But before a judge and jury in another county, proof should be made. The difference lies in the fact being one of common knowledge in one jurisdiction and not in the other."); Morgan, Judicial Notice, 57 Harv.L.Rev. 269, 277 (1944) ("Even in the federal court sitting in San Francisco the trial judge and jury might be ignorant of the fact, and the judge might well without a further showing . . . let the jury determine the fact according to the weight of the evidence.").

But "night club gossip and stories appearing in newspapers" . . . . while their content may be common knowledge, are not a source indisputable facts pertaining to "wealth or . . . any other necessary fact." Berry v. Chaplin, 74 Cal.App.2d 669, 675–676, 169 P.2d 453, 458 (1946) (Los Angeles trial court could not take judicial notice of extent of wealth of Charles Chaplin based upon his public image as presented in the press).

There are intimations that local customs may not be noticed. See, e. g., First National Bank v. Commercial Bank & Trust Co., 137 Wash. 335, 242 P. 356 (1926). But, under the present principle, if generally and certainly known in the community, they should be.

30. Anon., Y.B. 7 Hen. IV, f. 41, pl. 5 (1406), from which the following is an excerpt: "Tirwhit: Sir, let us put the case that a man kills another in your presence and sight, and another who is not guilty is indicted before you and is found guilty of the same death, you ought to respite the judgment against him, for you know the contrary, and report the matter to the King to pardon him. No more ought you to give judgment in this case . . . Gascoigne, C. J. One time the King himself asked me about this very case which you have put, and asked me what was the law, and I told him just as you say, and he was well pleased that the law was so."

31. Gibson v. Von Glahn Hotel Co., 185 N.Y.S. 154, 155 (Sup.Ct.1920) (where the issue of absolute liability as an innkeeper turned on the question whether defendant's establishment was a hotel, the trial judge volunteered: "I know the Von Glahn Hotel as well as the witness does himself; I will give you a ruling now it is a hotel." Held, reversed). Accord: Darnell v. Barker, 179 Va. 86, 18 S.E.2d 271 (1942); Shafer v. Eau Claire, 105 Wis. 239, 81 N.W. 409 (1900).

It is believed that only rarely today would one encounter a trial judge who felt free to use his personal knowledge of facts. Morgan, Judicial Notice, 57 Harv.L.Rev. 269, 274 n. 7 (1944). But see: Beychok v. St. Paul Mercury Indemnity Co., 119 F.Supp. 52 (W.D.La.1954) (trial judge took ju-

ground, it is believed, for exercising certain discretionary powers, such as granting a motion for new trial to avoid an injustice,[32] or in sentencing.[33]

Similarly, what a jury member knows in common with every other human being and what facts are appropriately circumscribed by the doctrine of judicial notice are not the same thing. Traditionally those facts so generally known within the community as not to be reasonably subject to dispute have been included within the perimeters of judicial notice under the caption of common knowledge. At the same time, however, it is often loosely said that the jury may consider, as if proven, facts within the common knowledge of the community.[34] Thus it is

very easy to confound into one common denominator facts to which the evidentiary discipline of judicial notice applies and the residual data the jury members bring along with them as rational human beings. Whereas in the typical vehicular accident case the well-known character of a street can be dealt with informally as background information which helps everyone visualize the scene, the question becomes a formal one to be dealt with as part of the doctrine of judicial notice if the precise character of the street becomes an adjudicative fact in the case being tried.[35] Again, while the meaning of words is normally left to the informal common sense of the jury, the precise meaning of a word in a contract case which may be outcome determinative should be dealt with formally as a problem of judicial notice.[36]

The cases in which judicial notice is taken of indisputable facts commonly known in the community where the facts noticed are actually adjudicative ones appear to be relatively rare. In most instances, notwithstanding the invocation of the language of judicial notice, the facts either involve background information helpful in assaying the evidence relevant to the adjudicative facts [37] or involve facts relevant to the proc-

---

dicial notice that the luncheonette stool from which plaintiff fell "had been in the same condition for at least fifteen years before plaintiff's unfortunate accident occurred, without any incidents having taken place, so far as we know, to have indicated that it was a source of danger." The judge, however, treated this datum as a matter of "common knowledge.").

32. It is clear that trial judges have a great deal of discretion in ruling upon motions for new trials. Osborne v. United States, 351 F.2d 111 (8th Cir. 1965); Commonwealth v. Brown, 192 Pa. Super. 498, 162 A.2d 13 (1960). Given this wide discretion it has been suggested that not only can courts use judicial notice quite freely, but that "perhaps" they should. Comment, The Presently Expanding Concept of Judicial Notice, 13 Vill.L. Rev. 528, 540 (1968).

33. Williams v. New York, 337 U.S. 241 (1949).

34. Marshall v. State, 54 Fla. 66, 44 So. 742, 743 (1907) (Instruction, "You will bring to bear in consideration of the evidence . . . in addition, all that common knowledge of men and affairs, which you as reasonable men have and exercise in the everyday affairs of life," approved); Note, 16 Tex.L.Rev. 403 (1938); Annot., 144 A.L.R. 932. In principle of course the knowledge of a juror about the facts of the particular case should not be considered. He should testify. Cf. § 68, supra. Perhaps, in strictness, expertness of particular jurors about values, skills, or occupational knowledge should not be used by the jury, not being common to the jurors and shared by the community. Some courts have held that instructions on jury-knowledge which fail to make this clear are ground for reversal. Downing v. Farmers' Mutual Fire Ins. Co., 158 Iowa 1, 138 N.W. 917 (1912). But there is much force to the contrary

view that this restriction sacrifices one of the chief values of jury trial, and is a restriction which jurors cannot and will not obey. Solberg v. Robbins Lumber Co., 147 Wis. 259, 133 N.W. 28 (1911) (instruction permitting jurors to pool their individual knowledge, approved).

35. See, e. g., Davis, A System of Judicial Notice Based on Fairness and Convenience, in Perspectives on Law 69, 73–74 (Pound ed. 1964).

36. See, e. g., Palestroni v. Jacobs, 8 N.J. 438, 73 A.2d 89, rev'd 10 N.J.Super. 266, 77 A.2d 183 (1953). Compare Tennessee Gas Transmission Co. v. Hall, 277 S.W.2d 733 (Tex.Civ.App.1955) (jurors took into account the chance that a deep "chisel" plow could cut into an underground pipe). Technical words, having been compiled in dictionaries, may differ from facts known only to farmers familiar with their own technology.

37. See, e. g., Pacific Gas & Electric Co. v. W. H. Hunt Estate Co., 49 Cal.2d 565, 319 P.2d 1044

ess of formulating the tenor of the law to be applied to the resolution of the controversy.[38] Indeed, there is a growing recognition that the common knowledge variety of fact plays only a very minor role on the judicial notice scene.[39]

330. Facts Capable of Certain Verification.

The earlier and probably still the most familiar basis for judicial notice is "common knowledge," but a second and distinct principle has come to be recognized as an even more significant ground for the invocation of the doctrine. This extension of judicial notice was first disguised by a polite fiction so that when asked to notice a fact not generally known, but which obviously could easily be ascertained by consulting materials in common use, such as the day of the week on which January 1 fell ten years ago, the judges resorted to calendars but purported to be "refreshing memory" as to a matter of common knowledge.[40] Eventually it was recognized that involved here was an important extension of judicial notice to the new field of facts "capable of accurate and

ready demonstration," [41] "capable of such instant and unquestionable demonstration, if desired, that no party would think of imposing a falsity on the tribunal in the face of an intelligent adversary," [42] or "capable of immediate and accurate demonstration by resort to easily accessible sources of indisputable accuracy." [43] It is under this caption, for example, that courts have taken judicial notice of the scientific principles which, while verifiable but not likely commonly known, justify the evidentiary use of radar,[44] blood tests for intoxication [45] and nonpaternity,[46] handwriting [47] and typewriter identification,[48] and ballistics.[49]

Attempts to formulate inventories of verifiable facts of which courts will take judicial notice have begun to fall into disrepute because the principle involved can better be illustrated by way of example.[50] Thus in

---

(1957) (water pipes sometimes break from accidental causes); Portee v. Kronzek, 194 Pa.Super. 193, 166 A.2d 328 (1960) (people visit taverns to meet friends). Compare: Hughes v. Vestal, 264 N.C. 500, 142 S.E.2d 361 (1965); Ennis v. Dupree, 262 N.C. 224, 136 S.E.2d 702 (1964).

38. Hawkins v. United States, 358 U.S. 74 (1958); Perez v. Lippold, 32 Cal.2d 711, 198 P.2d 17 (1948).

39. Comment, The Presently Expanding Concept of Judicial Notice, 13 Vill.L.Rev. 528, 532 (1968) ("[T]he traditional test [is] whether the fact to be noticed is within the common knowledge of the community. However, there has been a modern trend away from this test and towards one which provides that a fact may be noticed if it is verifiably certain by reference to competent, authoritative sources.").

40. See, e. g., Friend v. Burnham & Morrill Co., 55 F.2d 150, 151 (1st Cir. 1932) ("The District Court in this case was warranted, therefore, in taking judicial notice of any common or general knowledge relating to canning cooked foods, and to refresh his recollection by reference to standard publications.").

41. Note, 47 Colum.L.Rev. 151 (1947).

42. 9 Wigmore, Evidence § 2571, p. 548.

43. Uniform Rule 9(2) (d) quoted § 328, n. 3, supra.

44. State v. Graham, 322 S.W.2d 188 (Mo.1959). For a discussion of the limits to which counsel may go in arguing scientific facts before a jury, see Levin and Levy, Persuading the Jury with Facts Not in Evidence: The Fiction-Science Spectrum, 105 U.Pa. L.Rev. 139 (1956).

45. State v. Miller, 64 N.J.Super. 262, 165 A.2d 829 (1960). There has recently developed a tendency to make scientific evidence admissible by legislative enactment, e. g., Uniform Chemical Test for Intoxication Act, 9 U.L.A. 61 (1967 supp.).

46. Jordan v. Mace, 144 Me. 351, 69 A.2d 670 (1949); Houghton v. Houghton, 179 Neb. 275, 137 N.W.2d 861 (1965). See also, Uniform Act on Blood Tests to Determine Paternity, 9 U.L.A. 110.

47. Adams v. Ristine, 138 Va. 273, 122 S.E. 126 (1924); Fenelon v. State, 195 Wis. 416, 217 N.W. 711 (1928). See generally, Note, Evolving Methods of Scientific Proof, 13 N.Y.L.For. 677 (1968).

48. United States v. Hiss, 107 F.Supp. 128 (S.D.N.Y. 1952); People v. Risley, 214 N.Y. 75, 108 N.E. 200 (1915).

49. People v. Fisher, 340 Ill. 216, 172 N.E. 743 (1930).

50. See, e. g., Keeffe, Landis and Shaad, Sense and Nonsense About Judicial Notice, 2 Stan.L.Rev. 664, 667 (1950) ("General rules describing particular facts that can be judicially noticed are worthless.").

State v. Damm [51] defendant was on trial for rape after one of his stepdaughters gave birth to a child. The defense sought a court order authorizing blood tests by which it was hoped to prove his innocence by way of negative results. Even if the tests produced a negative result, however, the testimony recounting the tests would be relevant to the question of guilt or innocence only if it was true that properly administered blood tests evidencing a negative result excluded the possibility of paternity. To leave this preliminary question pertaining to the then present state of scientific knowledge to the jury to decide as best they could on the basis of possibly conflicting testimony would appear absurd.[52] There being only one right answer to the question whether the principle was accepted in the appropriate scientific circles, the question fell within the province of judicial notice. Even so, the trial judge in this particular case was held not to have erred in refusing the request because, given the time and place, the defense was not able to produce the data necessary to illustrate to him that the principle was an accepted one within the scientific community. Presumably, of course, an opposite result would obtain today.[53]

Thus it is that while the various propositions of science are a suitable topic of judicial notice, the content of what will actually be noticed is subject to change as the tenets of science evolve.[54] It is manifest,

moreover, that the principle involved need not be commonly known in order to be judicially noticed; it suffices if the principle is accepted as a valid one in the appropriate scientific community. In determining the intellectual viability of the proposition, of course, the judge is free to consult any sources that he thinks are reliable,[55] but the extent to which judges are willing to take the initiative in looking up the authoritative sources will usually be limited. By and large, therefore, it is the task of counsel to find and to present in argument and briefs such references, excerpts and explanations as will convince the judge that the fact is certain and demonstrable. Puzzling enough in this regard, it was recently noted that "nowhere can there be found a definition of what constitutes competent or authoritative sources

---

51. 64 S.D. 309, 266 N.W. 667 (1936).

52. Keeffe, Landis and Shaad, op. cit. n. 50, supra, at 670. ("It brings discredit upon the legal profession and it makes a mockery of a court of justice to permit a jury to accept or reject in accordance with their prejudices a fact capable of exact scientific determination.").

53. See n. 46, supra.

54. State v. Damm, 64 S.D. 309, 266 N.W. 667 (1936) was decided five years after the trial, by which time the principle behind blood tests to determine paternity had become well established. While conceding as much, the appellate court did not reverse

the trial judge's earlier decision to exclude the test results because, when made, that decision had not been an erroneous one.

Thus far the results of lie detector tests have not been judicially noticed as reliable because the results depend more upon the expertise of the operator than upon the inherent reliability of the mechanism itself. Frye v. United States, 54 App. D.C. 46, 293 Fed. 1013 (1923); State v. Brown, 177 So.2d 532 (Fla.1965). Even so, polygraph results have sometimes been admitted when the litigants themselves have agreed upon a stipulation of admissibility. People v. Houser, 85 Cal.App.2d 686, 193 P.2d 937 (1948). Narco analysis and hypnotism have not yet received any judicial recognition of reliability in any degree. Orange v. Commonwealth, 191 Va. 423, 61 S.E.2d 267 (1950) (refusal to admit the results of narco-interrogation even under stipulation); People v. McNichol, 100 Cal.App. 2d 554, 224 P.2d 21 (1950) (rejection as hearsay and self-serving statements of defendant while under hypnosis). But see State v. Nebb, No. 39, 540 (Ohio C.P. May 28, 1962); Teitelbaum, Admissibility of Hypnotically Adduced Evidence and the Arthur Nebb Case, 8 St.Louis L.J. 205 (1963).

55. Brown v. Piper, 91 U.S. 37, 42 (1875) ("any means . . . which he may deem safe and proper"); People v. Mayes, 113 Cal. 618, 626, 45 P. 860, 862 (1896) ("any source of information which he may deem authentic, either by inquiry of others, or by the examination of books, or by receiving the testimony of witnesses"); Fringer v. Venema, 26 Wis.2d 366, 372–73, 132 N.W.2d 565, 569 (1965) ("can be verified to a certainty by reference to competent authoritative sources"); 9 Wigmore, Evidence § 2568a, at pp. 537–538.

for purposes of verifying judicially noticed facts." [56]

Illustrative as they are, scientific principles hardly exhaust the verifiable facts of which courts take judicial notice.[57] Historical facts fall within the doctrine, such as the dates upon which wars began and terminated.[58] Geographical facts [59] are involved, particularly with reference to the boundaries of the state in which the court is sitting [60] and of the counties,[61] districts [62] and townships [63] thereof, as well as the location of the capital of the state and the location and identity of the county seats.[64] Whether common knowledge or not, courts notice the identity of the principal officers of the national govern-ment [65] and the incumbents of principal state offices.[66] Similarly, while obviously not necessarily a matter of common knowledge, judges take notice of the identity of the officers of their courts, such as the other judges,[67] the sheriffs,[68] clerks,[69] and attorneys; [70] of the duration of terms and sessions,[71] and of the rules of court.[72]

It would seem obvious that the judge of a court would take notice of all of the records

---

56. Comment, The Presently Expanding Concept of Judicial Notice, 13 Vill.L.Rev. 528, 545 (1968).

57. In the past, after rendering articulate the notion that both matters of common knowledge and facts capable of accurate verification constitute the raw materials of judicial notice, traditional textbooks have then passed into a detailed treatment of specific topics which have proved amenable to judicial notice, e. g., historical facts, geographic facts, etc. 9 Wigmore, Evidence §§ 2574–82, pp. 562–580; 29 Am.Jur.2d Evidence §§ 62–122. See also West's Ann.Cal.Evid.Code, §§ 451–52. Because all these data are verifiable from sources of indisputable accuracy, there seems to be no real need to continue this practice.

58. Unity Co. v. Gulf Oil Corp., 141 Me. 148, 40 A.2d 4, 156 A.L.R. 297 (1944) (dates of declaration of World War II and beginning of rationing); Miller v. Fowler, 200 Miss. 776, 28 So.2d 837 (1947) (that acts of warfare between Japan and the United States had not entirely ceased on Aug. 14, 1945); 29 Am.Jur.2d Evidence §§ 73–76.

59. See, e. g., Swarzwald v. Cooley, 39 Cal.App.2d 306, 103 P.2d 580 (1940) (meaning of phrase, "ordinary hightide," in the vicinity of Laguna Beach).

60. Watson v. Western Union Tel. Co., 178 N.C. 471, 101 S.E. 81 (1919); 29 Am.Jur.2d Evidence § 63.

61. State ex Inf. Gentry v. Armstrong, 315 Mo. 298, 286 S.W. 705 (1926) (location of city and county of St. Louis); Elmore County v. Tallapoosa County, 221 Ala. 182, 128 So. 158 (1930) (area and boundaries); 29 Am.Jur.2d Evidence § 64.

62. Board of Education v. State, 222 Ala. 70, 131 So. 239 (1930) (school district).

63. Nelson v. Thomas, 103 Cal.App. 108, 283 P. 982 (1930).

64. Bunten v. Rock Springs Grazing Ass'n, 29 Wyo. 461, 215 P. 244 (1923).

65. United States ex rel. Petach v. Phelps, 40 F.2d 500 (2d Cir. 1930) (assistants to the Secretary of Labor); Lyman Flood Prevention Ass'n v. City of Topeka, 152 Kan. 484, 106 P.2d 117 (1940) (time of retirement of Woodring as Secretary of War).

66. See, e. g., Picking v. Pennsylvania R. Co., 151 F.2d 240 (3d Cir. 1945) (that named defendants were officials of Pennsylvania and New York); Patten v. Miller, 190 Ga. 123, 8 S.E.2d 757 (1940) (chairman, State Highway Board).

67. Payne v. Williams, 47 Ariz. 396, 56 P.2d 186 (1936) (Supreme Court notices names of superior court judges, their counties and terms); Alexander v. Gladden, 205 Ore. 375, 288 P.2d 219 (1955) (Supreme Court notices the organization of its own court and lower courts under its supervision).

68. Sowers-Taylor Co. v. Collins, 14 S.W.2d 692 (Mo. App.1929) (names of officers authorized to serve process).

69. Favre v. Louisville & N. R. Co., 180 Miss. 843, 178 So. 327 (1938).

70. Squire v. Bates, 132 Ohio St. 161, 5 N.E.2d 690 (1936) (persons who have been admitted and dates of their admission).

71. Vance v. Harkey, 186 Ark. 730, 55 S.W.2d 785 (1933) (Supreme Court knows that term at which decree entered has elapsed).

72. A trial court, of course, knows its own rules without formal proof. Wallace v. Martin, 166 So. 874 (La.App.1936). And on general principles an appellate court knows judicially what the trial court judicially knew. See § 333, n. 32, infra. Nevertheless, many appellate courts have refused to notice trial court rules, unless embodied in the bill of exceptions. See e. g., Scovill Mfg. Co. v. Cassidy, 275 Ill. 462, 114 N.E. 181 (1916) (where municipal court rules not in bill of exceptions, appellate court erred in ordering the rules certified to them and considering them when certified); and cases cited C.J.S. Evidence § 49. This inconvenient formalism has been repudiated by statute in Illinois, see Boettcher v. Howard Engraving Co., 389 Ill. 75, 58 N.E.2d 866 (1945) (applying S.H.A. ch. 51, § 48b). And elsewhere by decision, see e. g., Hudson v. Hoster, 47 N.E.2d 637 (Ct.App.Ohio, 1942) (Court of Appeals will notice rules and customary practices of the Common Pleas Court).

of the institution over which he presides, but the courts have been slow to give the principle of judicial notice its full reach of logic and expediency. It is settled, of course, that the courts, trial and appellate, take notice of their own respective records in the present litigation, both as to matters occurring in the immediate trial,[73] and in previous trials or hearings.[74] The principle seemingly is equally applicable to matters of record in the proceedings in other cases in the same court, and some decisions have recognized this,[75] but many courts still adhere to the needless requirement of formal proof, rather than informal presentation, of recorded proceedings in other suits in the same court.[76] Matters of record in other courts are usually denied notice even though it would appear manifest that these public documents are logically subject to judicial notice as readily verifiable facts.[77]

In the increasingly important practice of judicial notice of scientific and technological facts, some of the possibilities of error are,

first, that the courts may fail to employ the doctrine of judicial notice in this field to the full measure of its usefulness; second, that they may mistakenly accept as authoritative scientific theories that are outmoded or are not yet received by the specialists as completely verified; and third, that in taking judicial notice of accepted scientific facts, the courts, in particular cases may misconceive the conclusions or applications which are supposed to flow from them. Of these, it seems that the first has thus far been the most frequent shortcoming.

331. Social and Economic Data Used in Judicial Law-Making: "Legislative" Facts.[78]

It is conventional wisdom today to observe that judges not only are charged to find what the law is, but must regularly make new law when deciding upon the constitutional validity of a statute,[79] interpreting a statute,[80] or extending or restricting a common law rule.[81] The very nature of the judicial process necessitates that judges be guided, as legislators are, by considerations of expediency and public policy.[82] They must, in the nature of things, act either upon knowledge already possessed or upon assumptions,[83] or

---

73. Nichols v. Nichols, 126 Conn. 614, 13 A.2d 591 (1940) (superseded pleading, claimed to constitute admission, will be noticed but must be called to trial court's attention); 29 Am.Jur.2d Evidence § 57.

74. Collins v. Leahy, 347 Mo. 133, 146 S.W.2d 609 (1940) (where city map was part of record of prior appeal to Supreme Court, court would take notice of it on subsequent appeal though not introduced in evidence at later trial); 29 Am.Jur.2d Evidence § 57.

75. Willson v. Security-First Nat. Bank, 21 Cal.2d 705, 134 P.2d 800 (1943); South Shore Land Co. v. Petersen, 226 Cal.App.2d 725, 38 Cal.Rptr. 392 (1964); Johnson v. Marsh, 146 Neb. 257, 19 N.W. 2d 366 (1945); Meck v. Allen Properties, Inc., 206 Misc. 251, 132 N.Y.S.2d 674 (1954).

76. Guam Invest. Co. v. Central Bldg., Inc., 288 F.2d 19 (9th Cir. 1961); Murphy v. Citizens' Bank, 82 Ark. 131, 100 S.W. 894 (1907); Fleming v. Anderson, 187 Va. 788, 48 S.E.2d 269 (1948); 29 Am.Jur. 2d Evidence § 58.

77. But see Zahn v. Transamerica Corp., 162 F.2d 36, 48 n. 20 (3d Cir. 1947). See also Funk v. Commissioner, 163 F.2d 796 (3d Cir. 1947). It has been suggested, moreover, that in practice trial judges do look at related court files. Maguire, Weinstein, Chadbourn and Mansfield, Cases and Materials on Evidence 21 (5th ed. 1965).

78. See Davis, Administrative Law Treatise, Ch. 15 (1958, supp. 1965), an unusually original and enlightening discussion; Davis, An Approach to Problems of Evidence in the Administrative Process, 55 Harv.L.Rev. 364, 402 (1942); Davis, Judicial Notice, 55 Colum.L.Rev. 945, 952 (1955); Note, Social and Economic Facts—Appraisal of Suggested Techniques for Presenting Them to the Courts, 61 Harv.L.Rev. 692 (1948).

79. Perez v. Lippold, 32 Cal.2d 711, 198 P.2d 17 (1948) (statute outlawing interracial marriage).

80. Potts v. Coe, 78 U.S.App.D.C. 297, 140 F.2d 470 (1944) (interpretation of patent law).

81. Southern Cotton Oil Co. v. Anderson, 80 Fla. 441, 86 So. 629 (1920) (whether on basis of fatality statistics the automobile is a "dangerous instrumentality").

82. Cardozo, The Nature of the Judicial Process 113–125 (1921); Frank, Law and the Modern Mind, ch. 4 (1930).

83. See, e. g., Village of Euclid v. Ambler Realty Company, 272 U.S. 365 (1926) (proper exercise of

upon investigation of the pertinent general facts, social,[84] economic,[85] political,[86] or scientific.[87] An older tradition once prescribed that judges should rationalize their result solely in terms of analogy to old doctrines leaving the considerations of expediency unstated. Contemporary practice indicates that judges in their opinions should render explicit their policy-judgments and the factual grounds therefor. These latter have been helpfully classed as "legislative facts," as contrasted with the "adjudicative facts" which are historical facts pertaining to the incident which give rise to lawsuits.[88]

Constitutional cases argued in terms of due process typically involve reliance upon legislative facts for their proper resolution. Whether a statute enacted pursuant to the police power is valid, after all, involves a twofold analysis. First, it must be determined that the enactment is designed to achieve an appropriate objective of the police

power; that is, it must be designed to protect the public health, morals, safety, or general welfare.[89] The second question is whether, in light of the data on hand, a legislature still beholden to reason could have adopted the means they did to achieve the aim of their exercise of the police power.[90] In Burns Baking Co., v. Bryan,[91] for example, the question was whether, concerned about consumers being misled by confusing sizes of bread, the Nebraska legislature could decree not only that the bakers bake bread according to distinctively different weights but that they wrap their product in wax paper lest any post-oven expansion of some loaves undo these distinctions. A majority of the court held the enactment unconstitutional because, in their opinion, the wrapping requirement was unreasonable. Mr. Justice Brandeis, correctly anticipating the decline of substantive due process, dissented, pointing out that the only question was whether the measure was a reasonable legislative response in light of the facts available to the legislators themselves.[92] Then, in a marvellous illustration of the Brandeis-brief technique, he recited page after page of data illustrating how widespread was the problem of shortweight and how, in light of nationwide experience, the statute appeared to be a reasonable response to the environmental situation.[93]

---

police power to exclude apartment houses from residential districts because they tend to be mere parasites and come near to being nuisances); Potts v. Coe, 78 U.S.App.D.C. 297, 140 F.2d 470 (1944) (incentive to invent supplied by patent law will not work in organized research because it destroys teamwork).

84. Brown v. Board of Education, 347 U.S. 483 (1954), supplemented 349 U.S. 294, (racially segregated schools can never be equal notwithstanding their equality of teachers or equipment because the very act of segregation brands the segregated minority with a feeling of inferiority).

85. SEC v. Capital Gains Research Bureau, Inc., 300 F.2d 745 (2d Cir. 1961), rev'd 375 U.S. 180, (judicial notice taken that advice tendered by small advisory service could not influence stock market generally); same case, 375 U.S. 180 (1963) (judicial notice taken that the advice tendered could influence the market price).

86. Baker v. Carr, 369 U.S. 186 (1962) (contemporary notions of justice require that equal apportionment of voting districts be made a legal and perforce largely mathematical question rather than a purely political one).

87. Durham v. United States, 94 U.S.App.D.C. 228, 214 F.2d 862 (1954) (psychiatric learning pertinent to the scientific soundness of the right-and-wrong test of criminal insanity).

88. Davis, Administrative Law Treatise § 15.03 (1958).

89. Bilbar Construction Co. v. Board of Adjustment, 393 Pa. 62, 141 A.2d 851 (1958).

90. See the discussion running throughout the several opinions in Griswold v. Connecticut, 381 U.S. 479 (1965).

91. 264 U.S. 504 (1924).

92. Accord: West Coast Hotel Co. v. Parrish, 300 U.S. 379 (1937); Olsen v. Nebraska ex. rel. Western Reference & Bond Ass'n, 313 U.S. 236, 133 A.L.R. 1500 (1941). See also Lochner v. New York, 198 U.S. 45 (1905) (Holmes, J. dissenting.)

93. The opponents of a statute can resort to extra-record legislative facts to support their argument that it is invalid. In Burns Baking Co. v. Bryan, 264 U.S. 504 (1924), the statute regulating bread sizes was struck down because it was "contrary to common experience and unreasonable to assume there could be any danger of . . . deception." See also Defiance Milk Products Co. v. DuMond,

Given the bent to test due process according to the information available to the legislature, the truth-content of this data is not directly relevant. The question is whether sufficient data exists which could influence a reasonable legislature to act, not whether ultimately this data is true.[94] This is not the same case as when a court proceeds to interpret a constitutional norm and, while they still rely upon data, the judges *qua* legislators themselves proceed to act as if the data were true. In Brown v. Board of Education,[95] for example, the Court faced the issue whether segregated schools, equal facility and teacher-wise, could any longer be tolerated under the equal protection clause. The question was not any longer whether a reasonable legislator could believe these schools could never be equal, but whether the *judges* believed that the very act of segregating branded certain children with a feeling of inferiority so deleterious that it would be impossible for them to obtain an equal education no matter how equal the facilities and teachers. Thus the intellectual legitimacy of this kind of decision turns upon the actual truth-content of the legislative facts taken into account by the judges who propound the decision. While not necessarily indisputably true, it would appear that these legislative facts must at least appear to be more likely than not true if the opinion is going to have the requisite intellectual legitimacy upon which the authority of judge-made rules is ultimately founded.[96]

When making new common law, judges must, like legislators, do the best they can assaying the data available to them and make the best decision they can of which course wisdom dictates they follow. Should they, for example, continue to invoke the common law rule of *caveat emptor* in the field of real property, or should they invoke a notion of implied warranty in the instance of the sale of new houses? [97] Should they require landlords of residential units to warrant their habitability and fitness for the use intended? [98] While sociological, economic, political and moral doctrine may abound about questions like this, none of this data is likely indisputable.[99]

---

96. See. e. g., the reaction to Durham v. United States, 94 U.S.App.D.C. 228, 214 F.2d 862 (1954), wherein on the basis of psychiatric data the court formulated a new test for criminal insanity. Some psychiatrists accepted the result: Roche, Criminality and Mental Illness—Two Faces of the Same Coin, 22 U.Chi.L.Rev. 320 (1955). The American Law Institute rejected it. Model Penal Code, Tentative Draft No. 4, 159–60 (1955). See also Brown v. Board of Education, 347 U.S. 483 (1954), supplemented 349 U.S. 294, wherein for the psychological impact of segregation the court relied upon, inter alia, the work of Dr. Kenneth B. Clark. Dr. Clark felt compelled thereafter publicly to respond to critics of his work. Clark, The Desegregation Cases: Criticism of the Social Scientists Role, 5 Vill.L.Rev. 224, 236–40 (1960). But see Van den Haag, Social Science Testimony in the Desegregation Cases—A Reply to Professor Kenneth Clark, 6 Vill.L.Rev. 69 (1960).

97. Schipper v. Levitt & Sons, Inc., 44 N.J. 70, 207 A.2d 314 (1965) (mass developer of homes who assembled final product out of component parts treated as a manufacturer and implied warranty imposed).

98. Lemle v. Breeden, 51 Haw. 426, 462 P.2d 470 (1969) (application of implied warranty recognizes changes in history of leasing transactions and takes into account contemporary housing realities).

99. See particularly Davis, A System of Judicial Notice Based on Fairness and Convenience, in Perspectives of Law, 69, 82 (Pound ed. 1964) ("judge-

---

30 N.Y. 537, 132 N.E.2d 829 (1956) (statute requiring inordinately large size cans for retail sale of evaporated skimmed milk held invalid because judicial notice was taken that it would be incredible to believe consumers needed protection against deception practiced with regard to the nature of this product).

94. In theory, at least, the Uniform Rules of Evidence would not allow the judges to take judicial notice of any of the data with which the cases in this section are concerned since none of it is "indisputably" true. See the text of these rules reproduced in § 328, note 3, supra. Given the practice of courts to notice less than indisputably true facts within a legislative context, the Uniform Rules might be interpreted to apply only to adjudicative facts. But see Davis, A System of Judicial Notice Based on Fairness and Convenience, in Perspectives of Law 69, 82 (Pound ed. 1964). Note that F.R.Ev. (R.D.1971) 201 deals only with adjudicative facts. See n. 3, § 328, supra.

95. 347 U.S. 483 (1954), supplemented 349 U.S. 294.

Thus it is that, in practice, the legislative facts upon which judges rely when performing their lawmaking function are not indisputable. At the same time, cognizant of the fact that his decision as lawmaker can affect the public at large, in contradistinction to most rulings at trials which affect only the parties themselves, a judge is not likely to rely for his data only upon what opposing counsel tender him. Obviously enough, therefore, legislative facts tend to be the most elusive facts when it comes to propounding a codified system of judicial notice.[1]

332. The Parameters of Judicial Notice.[2]

Agreement is not to be had whether the perimeters of the doctrine of judicial notice enclose only facts which are indisputably true or encompass also facts more than likely true.[3] If, on the one hand, the function of the jury is to resolve disputed questions of fact, an argument can be made that judges should not purport to make decisions about facts unless they are indisputable facts. If this argument is accepted, it follows that once

a fact has been judicially noticed, evidence contradicting the truth of the fact is inadmissible because by its very nature, a fact capable of being judicially noticed is an indisputable fact which the jury must be instructed to accept as true.[4] If, on the other hand, the function of judicial notice is to expedite the trial of cases, an argument can be made that judges should dispense with the need for time-consuming formal evidence when the fact in question is likely true. If this argument is accepted, it follows that evidence contradicting the judicially noticed fact is admissible and that the jury are ultimately free to accept or reject the truth of the fact posited by judicial notice.[5]

made law would stop growing if judges, in thinking about questions of law and policy, were forbidden to take into account the facts they believe, as distinguished from facts which are 'clearly . . . within the domain of the indisputable.' ") If the data available on appeal are conflicting, however, a court can remand the case to trial so these data can be more effectively explored by introducing them there in the form of evidence subject to cross-examination. See, e. g., Borden's Farm Products Co. v. Baldwin, 293 U.S. 194 (1934).

1. Note that F.R.Ev. (R.D.1971) 201, reproduced at § 328, n. 3, supra, does not purport to regulate the notice of legislative facts.

2. See Thayer, Preliminary Treatise on the Law of Evidence 308–309 (1898); 9 Wigmore, Evidence § 2567; Davis, A System of Judicial Notice Based on Fairness and Convenience, in Perspectives of Law 69 (Pound ed. 1964); Morgan, Judicial Notice, 57 Harv.L.Rev. 269 (1941); McNaughton, Judicial Notice—Excerpts Relating to the Morgan-Wigmore Controversy, 14 Vand.L.Rev. 779 (1961); Roberts, Preliminary Notes Toward a Study of Judicial Notice, 52 Cornell L.Q. 210 (1967).

3. See e. g. McNaughton, Judicial Notice—Excerpts Relating to the Morgan-Wigmore Controversy, 14 Vand.L.Rev. 779 (1961).

McCormick et al on Evid. 2nd Ed. HB—49

4. Most convincingly expounded by Morgan, Judicial Notice, 57 Harv.L.Rev. 269 (1944), and by the same author in The Law of Evidence 1941–1945, 59 Harv.L.Rev. 481, 482–487 (1946). In agreement are Maguire, Evidence—Common Sense and Common Law, 174 (1947) ("the judge's decision to take judicial notice should be final"); Keeffe, Landis, and Shaad, Sense and Nonsense About Judicial Notice, 2 Stan.L.Rev. 664, 668 (1950) ("The better view would seem to be that a fact, once judicially noticed, is not open to evidence disputing it"); McCormick, Judicial Notice, 5 Vand.L.Rev. 296, 321–322 (1952) ("the weight of reason and the prevailing authority support the view that a ruling that a fact will be judicially noticed precludes contradictory evidence and requires that the judge instruct the jury that they must accept the fact as true"); McNaughton, Judicial Notice—Excerpts Relating to the Morgan-Wigmore Controversy, 14 Vand.L.Rev. 779, 780 (1961) ("the impregnability of Morgan's position"). In accord also are Uniform Rule 11 and F.R.Ev. (R.D.1971) 201, supra, § 328, n. 3.

Judicial authority includes Phelps Dodge Corp. v. Ford, 68 Ariz. 190, 196, 203 P.2d 633, 638 (1949) ("A fact of which a court may take judicial notice must be indisputable. This being true it follows that evidence may not be received to dispute it"); Nicketta v. National Tea Co., 338 Ill.App. 159, 87 N.E.2d 30 (1949) (trial court properly took notice on pleadings that trichinosis cannot be contracted from eating properly cooked pork, and dismissed complaint; evidence thereon unnecessary); Commonwealth v. Marzynski, 149 Mass. 68, 21 N.E. 228 (1889) (court will take notice that tobacco and cigars are not medicine and exclude testimony to the contrary); Soyland v. Farmers Mut. Fire Ins. Co., 71 S.D. 522, 528, 26 N.W.2d 696, 699 (1947) ("it is not permissible for a court to take judicial knowledge of a fact that may be disputed by competent evidence.").

5. Most convincingly expounded by Wigmore in 9 Wigmore, Evidence § 2567a ("That a matter is

A facile resolution of this conflict suggests itself readily enough. That is, the controversy might be exposed as a misunderstanding caused by a failure to take into account the distinction between "adjudicative" and "legislative" facts.[6] This would be true if the instances where judicial notice was restricted to indisputable facts involved only adjudicative facts whereas potentially disputable facts were only noticed within a legislative context. Whether the decided cases sustain this symmetry is itself a matter of dispute because authority exists which illustrates that some courts are not loathe judicially to notice a potentially disputable fact within what is at least arguably an adjudicative context.[7]

The most recent efforts to deal with judicial notice have exhibited a trend away from extrapolating an all-inclusive definition of a doctrine in favor of promulgating modest guidelines which would regularize what are perceived to be the essential applications of judicial notice. One approach would restrict formalized judicial notice regulation to those situations in which only adjudicative facts are involved.[8] Another would narrow the range of judicial notice by de-escalating the significance of the conflict between questions peculiarly the province of juries and questions of fact handled by judges.[9] Judges have, for example, always dealt with preliminary questions of fact even in jury trials.[10] Thus, while the admissibility of the results of blood tests raises a question of fact pertaining to the reliability of such tests, the judges deal with this question as a preliminary step in ruling on relevancy, a function that is itself peculiarly a judicial one.[11] Indeed, if trials are examined functionally, it can be demonstrated that judges have always had to decide questions pertaining to facts without any apparent infringement of the jury's domain, whether this be in ruling on demurrers,[12] during pretrial hearings,[13] on motions for nonsuit or to set aside verdicts,[14]

---

judicially noticed means merely that it is taken as true without the offering of evidence by the party who should ordinarily have done so. This is because the Court assumes that the matter is so notorious that it will not be disputed. But the opponent is not prevented from disputing the matter by evidence, if he believes it disputable"). In agreement are Thayer, A Preliminary Treatise on Evidence at the Common Law 308 (1898) ("taking judicial notice does not import that the matter is indisputable"); Davis, A System of Judicial Notice Based on Fairness and Convenience, in Perspectives of Law 69, 94 (Pound ed. 1964) ("the ultimate principle is that extra-record facts should be assumed whenever it is convenient to assume them"); Davis, Judicial Notice, 1969 L. & Soc. Order 513, 515–516 ("the practical course is to take notice and allow challenge later whenever the court believes that challenge is unlikely").

Makos v. Prince, 64 So.2d 670, 673 (Fla.1953) (judicial notice "does not prevent an opponent's disputing the matter"); Macht v. Hecht Co., 191 Md. 98, 102, 59 A.2d 754, 756 (1948) ("judicial notice . . . does not . . . prevent the presentation of contrary evidence"); Timson v. Manufacturers Coal & Coke Co., 220 Mo. 580, 598, 119 S.W. 565, 569 (1909) ("Judicial notice . . . does not preclude the opposite party from rebutting such prima facie case"). See also, State v. Duranleau, 99 N.H. 30, 104 A.2d 519 (1954); State v. Kincaid, 133 Ore. 95, 285 P. 1105 (1930).

6. See §§ 328, 330, supra.

7. See, e. g., Securities and Exchange Com'n v. Capital Gains Research Bureau, Inc., 375 U.S. 180 (1963); Daniel v. Paul, 395 U.S. 298 (1969). Compare Davis, Judicial Notice, 1969 L. & Soc. Order 515, 521–523, and Cleary, Foreword to Symposium on Federal Rules of Evidence, 1969 L. & Soc. Order 509, 510.

8. F.R.Ev. (R.D.1971) 201, Advisory Committee's Note, Subdivision (a). "This is the only evidence rule on the subject of judicial notice. It deals only with judicial notice of 'adjudicative' facts."

9. See particularly Comment, The Presently Expanding Concept of Judicial Notice, 13 Vill.L.Rev. 528 (1968).

10. Maguire and Epstein, Preliminary Questions of Fact in Determining the Admissibility of Evidence, 40 Harv.L.Rev. 392 (1927).

11. Gorton v. Hadsell, 63 Mass. (9 Cush.) 508, 511 (1852) ("But it is the province of the judge, who presides at trial, to decide all questions on the admissibility of evidence.").

12. Nicketta v. National Tea Co., 338 Ill.App. 159, 87 N.E.2d 30 (1949).

13. Stafford v. Ware, 187 Cal.App.2d 227, 9 Cal.Rptr. 706 (1960).

14. Clayton v. Rimmer, 262 N.C. 302, 136 S.E.2d 562 (1964) (reviewing court took judicial notice of

or at sentencing.[15] This may indicate, after all, that the scope of judicial notice varies according to the function the judge is performing when judicial notice is taken.

It may be the case that there is no easy rule-of-thumb technique adequate unto the day to serve as an easy capsulation of the judicial notice phenomenon. Protagonists of the indisputable-only definition of judicial notice concede that in criminal cases the jury must be left free in the ultimate analysis to determine the truth or falsity of any adjudicative fact.[16] Protagonists of the disputability thesis might be expected to resolve the controversy by suggesting that, whereas in jury cases there is some merit in the notion that judicial notice should be restricted to indisputable facts in order not to infringe on the role of the jury,[17] the disputable theory works quite efficiently within the context of the jury-waived cases, which probably means that it applies in most cases which come to trial.[18] The fact of the matter

is that this solution has not received as much notoriety as might be expected.[19]

The very fact that the trend of these recent investigations has been calculated to resolve the problems associated with judicial notice by narrowing the dimensions of that concept has, however, raised a new problem which must be dealt with in the future. If judicial notice is restricted to instances where judges deal with facts in an adjudicative context, the instances where judges deal with legislative facts is left unregulated insofar as procedural guide-lines are concerned. The significance of this problem can be best illustrated within the context of the next section.

333. Procedural Incidents.

An elementary sense of fairness might indicate that a judge before making a final ruling that judicial notice will be taken should notify the parties of his intention to do so and afford them an opportunity to present information which might bear upon the propriety of noticing the fact, or upon the truth of the matter to be noticed.[20] Although the Uniform Rules of Evidence require it,[21] only a rare case insists that a judge

table of stopping distances of automobiles in reversing denial of motion for nonsuit). Compare Hughes v. Vestal, 264 N.C. 500, 142 S.E.2d 361 (1965) (error to instruct jury as to stopping distance at given speed, taken from same table).

15. Williams v. New York, 337 U.S. 241 (1949).

16. State v. Main, 94 R.I. 338, 180 A.2d 814 (1962); State v. Lawrence, 120 Utah 323, 234 P.2d 600 (1951).

17. In large measure the Morgan rationale limiting judicial notice to indisputable facts assumes a jury trial context, see particularly Morgan, Judicial Notice, 57 Harv.L.Rev. 269, particularly 269 (1944). Nonjury tried cases may be more analogous to administrative practice in which case it is suggested that judges "should assume facts freely, stating them whenever a party may possibly want to challenge them." Davis, A System of Judicial Notice Based on Fairness and Convenience, in Perspectives of Law 69, 80 (Pound ed. 1964).

18. See particularly, Davis, A System of Judicial Notice Based on Fairness and Convenience, in Perspectives of Law 69, 69–73 (Pound ed. 1964).

Note should be taken that the indisputable theory does not foreclose consideration of countervailing data but merely fixes the time of consideration at the preliminary determination whether judicial notice should be taken. In nonjury cases the difference may be without practical significance. See § 333, infra.

19. A possible explanation may be found in the close, if not complete, coincidence between a disputable judicially noticed fact and a rebuttable presumption. This relationship has largely passed undetected and without comment. One of the few cases sensing the relationship is Fringer v. Venema, 26 Wis.2d 366, 132 N.W.2d 565, reh. denied 26 Wis.2d 366, 133 N.W.2d 809 (1965) (action under statute imposing absolute liability on owner of bull over six months old; absent proof of age of defendant's bull which escaped and serviced plaintiff's heifers, court refused to take judicial notice that bull with such capacity was six months old but raised a rebuttable presumption to that effect). See § 334, n. 42, infra; § 343, infra.

20. Model Code of Evidence Rule 804 (1942).

21. Uniform Rule 10(1) provides: "The judge shall afford each party reasonable opportunity to present to him information relevant to the propriety of taking judicial notice of a matter or the tenor of the matter to be noticed." Compare F.R.Ev. (R.D. 1971) 201(e), quoted at § 328, n. 3, supra, providing for a hearing on request.

must notify the parties before taking judicial notice of a fact on his own motion,[22] and some authorities suggest that such a requirement is needless.[23] It may very well be the case that a trial judge need only consider notifying the parties if on his own motion he intends to take judicial notice of a less than obviously true fact.[24] In every other instance, after all, the request by one party asking the judge to take judicial notice will serve to apprise the opposing party of the question at hand. While there may, nevertheless, exist in practice a rough consensus with regard to procedural niceties when trial judges take judicial notice of adjudicative facts, this is not the end of the matter. The cases universally assume the nonexistence of any need for a structured adversary-style ancillary hearing with regard to legislative facts.[25] Indeed, even with regard to adjudi-

cative facts, the practices of appellate courts tend to support the argument that there exists no real felt need to formalize the practice of taking judicial notice.[26]

Legislative facts, of course, have not fitted easily into any effort to propound a formalized set of rules applicable to judicial notice. These facts, after all, tend to be less than indisputable ones and hence beyond the pale of judicial notice according to a literal reading of the Uniform Rules of Evidence.[27] What then of the requirement that, before judicial notice is taken, the parties be afforded a reasonable opportunity to present information relative to the propriety of taking judicial notice and the tenor of the matter to be noticed?[28] By and large the parties have this opportunity during arguments over motions as to the appropriate law to be applied to the controversy, by exchanging briefs, and by employing the technique exemplified by the Brandeis brief. It appears, therefore, that there exists no felt need to formalize the procedures pertaining to the opportunity to be heard with reference to legislative facts.[29] Even so, there are cases where the legislative facts which form the basis of an appellate opinion first appear in the decision itself and counsel never have the opportunity to re-

22. Compare Fringer v. Venema, 26 Wis.2d 366, 373, 132 N.W.2d 565, 570, reh. denied 26 Wis.2d 366, 133 N.W.2d 809 (1965) ("However, before judicial notice of such fact can be taken, adequate notice must be given to the parties to enable them to be heard on the question of verifiable certainty.") with Varcoe v. Lee, 180 Cal. 338, 343, 181 P. 223, (1919) ("It would have been much better if counsel for the plaintiff or the trial judge himself had inquired of defendants' counsel . . . whether there was any dispute").

23. Davis, A System of Judicial Notice Based on Fairness and Convenience, in Perspectives of Law 69, 75 (Pound ed. 1964) ("In ninety-nine instances of judicial notice out of a hundred, a notification of the parties of intent to take judicial notice is inconvenient and serves no good purpose.") The fact probably is that most instances of judicial notice pass without detection, and that most of those which are detected are not questioned. Hence an inclusive requirement of advance notice would result only in confusion and controversy where none existed before. See § 334, n. 47, infra.

24. Comment, The Presently Expanding Concept of Judicial Notice, 13 Vill.L.Rev. 528, 543–44 (1968) (suggesting that it would be a waste of time to notify the parties when the fact to be noticed is "a truly indisputable" one but warning that, should a trial judge notice a debatable adjudicative fact without notice to the parties, there might occur a denial of the right to trial by jury).

25. See, e. g., Judge Jerome Frank's concurring opinion in U. S. v. Roth, 237 F.2d 796, 814 (2d Cir. 1956) (in case involving allegedly obscene publications, appellate judge relied in part upon letter

written to him by a sociologist in response to his own inquiry); G. Currie, Appellate Courts Use of Facts Outside the Record by Resort to Judicial Notice and Independent Investigation, 1960 Wis.L. Rev. 39.

26. See, e. g., Mills v. Denver Tramway Corp., 155 F.2d 808 (10th Cir. 1946).

27. Uniform Rule 9, quoted above at § 328, n. 3, draws no distinction between adjudicative and legislative facts, requiring all facts to be indisputable before they can be judicially noticed.

28. Uniform Rule 10(1).

29. See, e. g., F.R.Ev. (R.D.1971) 201 Advisory Committee Note at p. 17 (denying need for "any formal requirements of notice other than those already inherent in affording opportunity to hear and be heard and exchanging briefs.") But see Davis, Judicial Notice, 1969 Law & Soc. Order 513, 526 (suggesting that procedural rules are needed to assure adequate opportunity to be heard when legislative facts are noticed).

spond to them.[30] Presumably current practice relies upon the sound discretion of judges to maintain discipline in this regard by presupposing a peer-group style general insistence among the judges on a fundamental notion of elementary fairness.[31]

With regard to the treatment of adjudicative facts by appellate courts, the common starting point is the axiom that these tribunals can take judicial notice to the same extent as can trial courts.[32] At the very least, this rule suggests the obvious fact that appellate courts can review the propriety of the judicial notice taken by the court below [33] and can even take judicial notice on their own initiative of facts not noticed below.[34] Nonetheless the recitation of these principles fails to portray the full flavor of the actual practice of appellate courts in taking judicial notice on their own initiative of what would appear to be adjudicative facts.

In this regard the case of Mills v. Denver Tramway Corp.,[35] may be instructive. Plaintiff had alighted from a trolley car, walked behind it and crossed the parallel set of tracks, where he was struck by a car going in the opposite direction. Plaintiff appeared to be manifestly guilty of contributory negligence, a sound enough conclusion plaintiff next attempted to overcome by invoking the doctrine of the last-clear-chance. That is, at the penultimate moment of the trial, plaintiff requested a jury instruction to the effect that, if the motorman had had a chance to sound the trolley bell, the harm might still have been avoided, in which case plaintiff was entitled to prevail. The trial judge refused the instruction because no evidence was ever introduced to indicate that the trolley had a bell.[36] The appellate tribunal reversed, giving plaintiff a new trial, reciting the fact that "streetcars have bells." If all trolley cars had bells, a fact the trial court could have taken judicial notice of had it ever been requested to do so, it would be quite appropriate for the appellate court to take notice of the very same fact. But was it an indisputable fact that *all* streetcars had bells? Arguably most did, in which case the appellate court was taking judicial notice, not of an indisputable fact, but only of a more-than-likely-true fact. More plausibly, the court reasoned that, in all likelihood, the trolley had a bell, in which instance plaintiff should have, as part of his case, proceeded to introduce evidence to substantiate a plausible claim on the last-clear-chance theory. Alternatively, had no bell existed, plaintiff

30. United States v. Roth, 237 F.2d 796, 814 (2d Cir. 1956) (see note 25 above). When the same case was on appeal to the Supreme Court, the Solicitor General sent that court a carton of "hard-core pornography" for their perusal. Lockhart and McClure, Censorship of Obscenity: The Developing Constitutional Standards, 45 Minn.L.Rev. 5, 26 (1960). See also People v. Finkelstein, 11 N.Y.2d 300, 229 N.Y.S.2d 367, 183 N.E.2d 661 (1961) cert. denied 371 U.S. 863.

31. Durham v. United States, 94 U.S.App.D.C. 228, 214 F.2d 862 (1954) (court relied upon the articles by many medico-legal writers in establishing a new test for criminal responsibility, all of which may not have been debated by counsel as to their respective merits).

32. Varcoe v. Lee, 180 Cal. 338, 181 P. 223 (1919); Uniform Rule 12(3) ("The reviewing court in its discretion may take judicial notice of any matter specified in Rule 9 whether or not judicially noticed by the judge."); Note, 42 Mich.L.Rev. 509 (1943) (collection of cases.)

33. In re Bowling Green Milling Co., 132 F.2d 279 (6th Cir. 1942); Verner v. Redman, 77 Ariz. 310, 271 P.2d 468 (1954); Fringer v. Venema, 26 Wis.2d 366, 132 N.W.2d 565 (1965). Uniform Rule 12(2) ("The rulings of the judge . . . are subject to review.")

34. Hunter v. New York, O. & W. R. R., 116 N.Y. 615, 23 N.E. 9 (1889) (took judicial notice of height of typical man to reverse judgment based upon notion that claimant was seated when box car entered railway tunnel).

35. 155 F.2d 808 (10th Cir. 1946).

36. Interestingly enough, Professor Davis might suggest in this instance that the trial judge would have been right not to take judicial notice. Davis, A System of Judicial Notice Based on Fairness and Convenience, in Perspectives of Law 94 (Pound ed. 1964), ("Nothing short of bringing facts into the record, so that an opportunity is allowed for cross-examination and for presentation of rebuttal evidence and argument, will suffice for disputed adjudicative facts at the center of the controversy.")

should have made that omission the basis of his claim. In either event, a sense of justice cried out for a trial of the case with all the facts fully developed. If, however, this was the sense of justice which moved the appellate tribunal, their invocation of the statement that "all streetcars have bells," a disputable proposition, sheds no real light either on the question whether judicial notice extends to disputable adjudicative facts or whether the parties must be afforded a hearing before judicial notice is taken. Given the need for appellate courts on occasion to reverse results below on a factual basis, judicial notice serves as a convenient device by which to give the practice the appearance of legal propriety. This being true, it would appear that the chances of adequately formalizing judicial notice even of adjudicative facts at the appellate level may be a slim one indeed.[37]

334. Trends in the Development of Judicial Notice of Facts.

It appears that, by and large, agreement can be reached within the none too distant future on the parameters of judicial notice as applied to adjudicative facts at the trial level.[38] A workable procedural schemata which would appear to guarantee fairness already exists in the event that judicial notice is restricted to indisputable facts.[39] The only question remaining is whether, in order to expedite the trial of cases, judges should be allowed to excuse the proponent of a fact likely true of the necessity of producing formal evidence thereof, leaving it to the jury to accept or reject the judicially noticed fact, and of course, allowing the opponent to introduce evidence contradicting it.[40] Indeed, the present controversy might be put in a

new light by limiting judicial notice to indisputable facts [41] and then raising the question, whether, as part of the law associated with the burden of proof and presumptions, a judge can properly expedite trials by himself ruling that very likely true facts are presumptively true unless the jury care to find otherwise.[42]

Whatever the ultimate doctrinal synthesis of judicial notice of adjudicative facts comes to be, a viable formulation of rules laying down a similarly rigid procedural etiquette with regard to legislative facts has not proved feasible.[43] Given the current recognition that nonadjudicative facts are inextricably part and parcel of the law formulation process in a policy-oriented jurisprudence, there may be no need to formulate a

---

37. See *seriatim* the decisions in Securities and Exchange Com'n v. Capital Gains Research Bureau, Inc., 191 F.Supp. 897 (S.D.N.Y.1961), 300 F.2d 745 (2d Cir. 1961), 375 U.S. 180 (1963).

38. See § 333, supra.

39. See § 333, supra.

40. See § 332, supra.

41. See, e. g., F.R.Ev. (R.D.1971) 201, reproduced at § 328, n. 3, supra.

42. This obviously is a compromise. Some authorities limit judicial notice to indisputable facts in every instance, whether the facts be either adjudicative or legislative ones. Uniform Rule 9; Morgan, Judicial Notice, 57 Harv.L.Rev. 269 (1944). Others seem to suggest that all judicially noticed facts are assumptions capable of being rebutted by proof. Thayer, A Preliminary Treatise on Evidence at the Common Law 309 (1898); 9 Wigmore, Evidence § 2567. It has been the peculiar genius of Professor K. C. Davis to perceive the difference between adjudicative and legislative facts. Davis, Official Notice, 62 Harv.L.Rev. 537 (1949). Even so, recent efforts to codify judicial notice have insisted upon the indisputability concept with respect to adjudicative facts only. F.R.Ev. (R.D.1971) 201. Professor Davis remains adamant that adjudicative facts can be disputable ones. Davis, Judicial Notice, 1969 Law & Soc. Order 513. The Thayer-Wigmore-Davis argument is that efficiency cries out for a mechanism by which formal evidence can be dispensed with when a fact appears to be fairly incontestable. Thayer appears to have perceived that this kind of fact was a variant of the law of procedure. See, e. g., Morgan, Judicial Notice, 57 Harv.L.Rev. 269, 285–286 (1944) ("Both [Wigmore's] and Mr. Thayer's statements of the proper effect of taking judicial notice are startlingly like their statements of the effect of presumptions.") See also Fringer v. Venema, 26 Wis.2d 366, 132 N.W.2d 565 (1965); § 332, n. 19, supra; § 343, infra.

It will be observed that the Proposed Federal Rules of Evidence make no effort to set forth a catalog of presumptions. F.R.Ev. (R.D.1971) 301. Cf. West's Ann.Cal.Evid.Code, §§ 630–668.

43. See § 333, supra.

distinctly judicial notice-captioned procedure with regard to nonadjudicative facts. This data is fed into the judicial process now whenever rules of law are brought to the attention of judges in motions, memoranda and briefs. Thus, whatever rules govern the submission of law in the litigation process have already preempted the nonadjudicative field and made unnecessary separate treatment thereof within the context of judicial notice.[44]

There has been an increasing awareness, moreover, that, quite apart from judicial notice, the trial process assumes that the participants therein bring with them a vast amount of everyday knowledge of facts in general.[45] To think after all, presupposes some data about which to think. In an automobile accident case, for example, both the judge and the jury constantly draw on their own experiences as drivers, as observers of traffic, and as live human beings, and these experiences are reduced in their minds to propositions of fact which, since they have survived themselves, are probably fairly accurate. This substratum of data the participants bring into the courthouse has, however, tended to confuse the judicial notice scene. On the one hand, this subliminal-like data is sometimes confused with the "common knowledge"-style of adjudicative facts with which formal judicial notice is concerned. On the other hand, judges constantly invoke references to these same everyday facts when they write opinions because, when formally articulated, it is impossible "to think" without reference to them.[46] It may

very well be the case that judges have tended, when extrapolating the obvious, to invoke the words, "I take judicial notice of" to explain the presence of these facts in their minds, thereby unnecessarily glutting the encyclopedias with trivia which are, when formally collected, highly misleading indices of the true scope of judicial notice as such.[47]

All of which would appear to indicate that the doctrine of judicial notice may ultimately be reduced to a workable consensus. Current trends would indicate that this consensus will, if it comes to fruition, involve reducing judicial notice to narrow confines within an adjudicative context. Controversy and intellectual excitement will not end there, however, because the phenomena excluded from the domain of judicial notice will then have to be collected and rationalized within the perimeters of a new concept, perhaps oriented around the study of thinking-about-facts techniques involved within the judicial process.[48]

---

liable under a statute making it a crime to doctor meat, judge concluded they both were because "the hamburger has become one of the most popular menu items in the United States.")

47. Often enough these propositions of generalized knowledge are not picked up as illustrations of judicial notice, which after all proves the point. See, e. g., Village of Euclid v. Ambler Realty Co., 272 U.S. 365 (1926) (apartment houses come near to being nuisances in single-family residential areas); Escola v. Coca Cola Bottling Co., 24 Cal. 2d 453, 150 P.2d 436 (1944) (concurring opinion) (manufacturers are best situated to underwrite losses attributable to defective products); Webster v. Blue Ship Tea Room, Inc., 347 Mass. 421, 198 N.E.2d 309 (1964) (in considering whether restaurant impliedly warranted fish chowder to be free of all miniscule bones court reflected that "Chowder is an ancient dish preëxisting even 'the appetities of our seamen and fishermen' ").

48. This would, in fact, represent a return to Thayer. See, e. g., Preliminary Treatise on Evidence at the Common Law 278–279 (1898) ("Whereabout in the law does the doctrine of judicial notice belong? Wherever the process of reasoning has a place, and that is everywhere. Not peculiarly in the law of evidence. . . . The subject of judicial notice, then, belongs to the general topic of legal or judicial reasoning.")

---

44. See, e. g., F.R.Ev. (R.D.1971) 201, reproduced at § 328 n. 3, supra.

45. See § 329, supra.

46. See, e. g., People v. Enders, 38 Misc.2d 746, 237 N.Y.S.2d 879 (N.Y.C.Crim.Ct.1963) (in deciding which, if either, between an absentee store proprietor and his butcher to whom he gave orders, was

335. The Judge's Task as Law-Finder: Judicial Notice of Law.

It would appear to be self-evident that it is peculiarly the function of the judge to find and interpret the law applicable to the issues in a trial, and in a jury case, to announce his findings of law to the jury for their guidance. The heavy-footed common law system of proof by witnesses and authenticated documents is too slow and cumbrous for the judge's task of finding what the applicable law is. Usually this law is familiar lore and if not he relies on the respective counsel to bring before him the statutes, reports, and source books, and these everyday companions of judge and counsel are read from informally in discussion or cited and quoted in trial and appellate briefs. Occasionally the judge will go beyond the cited authorities to make his own investigation. In the ordinary process of finding the applicable law, the normal method then is by informal investigation of any sources satisfactory to the judge. Thus this process has been traditionally described in terms of the judge taking judicial notice of the law applicable to the case at hand. Indeed, when the source-material was not easily accessible to the judge, as in the case of "foreign law" or city ordinances, law has been treated as a peculiar species of fact, requiring formal proof. We shall see, however, that as these materials become more accessible, the tendency is toward permitting the judges to do what perhaps they should have done in the beginning, that is, to rely on the diligence of counsel to provide the necessary materials, and accordingly to take judicial notice of *all* law. This seems to be the goal toward which the practice is marching.

Domestic Law. As to domestic law generally, the judge is not merely permitted to take judicial notice but required to do so,[49] at least if requested, although in a particular case a party may be precluded on appeal from complaining of the judge's failure to notice a statute where his counsel has failed to call it to the judge's attention.[50] This general rule that judicial notice will be taken of domestic law means that state trial courts will notice Federal law,[51] which is controlling in every state, and has been held to mean that in a Federal trial court the laws of the states, not merely of the state where it is sitting, are domestic and will be noticed.[52] Similarly all statewide or nationwide

49. Strain v. Isaacs, 59 Ohio App. 495, 514, 18 N.E. 2d 816, 825 (Ohio App.1938) (dictum); Randall v. Comm., 183 Va. 182, 186, 31 S.E.2d 571, 572 (1944) (dictum); 29 Am.Jur.2d Evidence § 27; Uniform Rule 9(2) quoted § 328, n. 3, supra. Some states provide by statute for judicial notice of local public statutes; e. g., West's Ann.Cal.Code, Civ. Proc. § 1875; McKinney's N.Y. CPLR 4511(a).

50. Great American Ins. Co. v. Glenwood Irr. Co., 265 F. 594 (10th Cir. 1920) (in action for damage from fire trial court's failure to charge that, under Colorado statute, leaving fire unextinguished would impose liability regardless of negligence, could not be complained of because plaintiff failed to call statute to judge's attention). See, however, an illuminating comment, Overlooking Statutes, 30 Yale L.J. 855 (1921), which suggests that errors arising from ignorance of a statute should be corrected on appeal except in cases where the public interest is not involved and counsel's failure to cite the statute can be construed as a waiver.
A judge, of course, may undertake an independent investigation of the applicable law, but ordinarily judges rely on opposing counsel to bring to their attention the appropriate sources of law. Matthews v. McVay, 241 Mo.App. 998, 1006, 234 S.W.2d 983, 988–989 (1950).

51. Peters v. Double Cola Bottling Co., 224 S.C. 437, 79 S.E.2d 710 (1954). Some states by statute provide for judicial notice of the Federal Constitution and statutes, e. g., West's Ann.Cal. Code Civ.Proc. § 1875; McKinney's N.Y. CPLR 4511(a).

52. In a federal court exercising original jurisdiction, its local law is the law of all the states. Hanley v. Donoghue, 116 U.S. 1 (1885); Lane v. Sargent, 217 F. 237 (1st Cir. 1914); Gediman v. Anheuser Busch, 299 F.2d 537 (2d Cir. 1962); Gallup v. Caldwell, 120 F.2d 90 (3d Cir. 1941). This rule of judicial notice being a matter of procedure rather than substantive law, it seems that the controlling force of state substantive law, under Erie R. Co. v. Tompkins, 304 U.S. 64 (1938), is inapplicable. But see Keeffe, Landis and Shaad, Sense and Nonsense about Judicial Notice, 2 Stan. L.Rev. 664, 686 (1950).
On appeal, however, from a state court, the Federal Supreme Court will not notice the law of another

executive orders and proclamations, which are legally effective, will be noticed.[53] Under this same principle, even the laws of antecedent governments will be noticed.[54]

State and national administrative regulations having the force of law will also be noticed, at least if they are published so as to be readily available.[55] When such documents are published in the Federal Register it is provided that their contents shall be judicially noticed.[56] Private laws [57] and municipal ordinances,[58] however, are not commonly included within the doctrine of judicial notice and these must be pleaded and proved. To the extent that these items become readily available in compilations, it may be expected that they will become subject to judicial notice; [59] whereas, in the meantime, it would appear appropriate for judges to take judicial notice of both private laws and municipal ordinances if counsel furnish a certified copy thereof.

The law of sister states. It is easy to see how the difference of languages and inaccessibility of source books should have led the English courts to develop the common law rule that the laws of foreign nations would not be noticed but must be pleaded and proved as facts.[60] The assumption in the earlier cases in this country [61] that the courts of one state must treat the laws of another state as foreign for this purpose is less understandable and to the after-view seems a deplorable instance of mechanical jurisprudence. Yet it remains today, in nearly every one of the increasingly few states which have not yet adopted a reformatory statute, the common law rule that notice will

state unless the state court below would have done so. Hanley v. Donoghue, 116 U.S. 1 (1885).

53. Dennis v. United States, 339 U.S. 162 (1949) (executive order of the President providing standards for discharge of government employees on loyalty grounds); Heyward v. Long, 178 S.C. 351, 183 S.E. 145, 114 A.L.R. 1130 (1936) (Governor's proclamation declaring highway department in state of insurrection); 29 Am.Jur.2d Evidence § 40; Dec.Dig. Evidence ☞46.

54. Ponce v. Roman Catholic Church, 210 U.S. 296 (1908) (Spanish laws in Puerto Rico); South Shore Land Co. v. Petersen, 226 Cal.App.2d 725, 38 Cal. Rptr. 392 (1964) (Mexican laws in California).

55. Case authority illustrates that some courts will take judicial notice of administrative regulations. Southwestern Bell Tel. Co. v. Bateman, 223 Ark. 432, 266 S.W.2d 289 (1954); Groendyke Trans. Inc. v. State, 208 Okl. 602, 258 P.2d 670 (1953); Smith v. Highway Board, 117 Vt. 343, 91 A.2d 805 (1952). Contra: Atlanta Gas Light Co. v. Newman, 88 Ga.App. 252, 76 S.E.2d 536 (1953); Finlay v. Eastern Racing Ass'n. Inc., 308 Mass. 20, 30 N.E.2d 859 (1941). Several states provide by statute for judicial notice of administrative regulations, e. g., West's Ann.Cal.Code Civ.Proc. § 1875; McKinney's N.Y. CPLR 4511. Other states provide by statute for judicial notice of published compilations of administrative regulations, e. g., Alas. Stats. 44.62.110 (1962); Wis.Stats.Ann. 328.-021.

56. 44 U.S.C.A. § 307. While some state courts take judicial notice of federal administrative regulations, Hough v. Rapidair, Inc., 298 S.W.2d 378 (Mo.1957); Dallas General Drivers v. Jax Beer Co., 276 S.W.2d 384 (Tex.Civ.App.1955), others will not. Gladieux v. Parney, 93 Ohio App. 117, 106 N.E.2d 317 (1951); Buice v. Scruggs Equip. Co., 37 Tenn. App. 556, 267 S.W.2d 119 (1953). It would appear that the Federal Register Act should bind state courts. Mastrullo v. Ryan, 328 Mass. 621, 622, 105 N.E.2d 469, 470 (1952).

57. Chambers v. Atchison, T. & S. F. Ry. Co., 32 Ariz. 102, 255 P. 1092 (1927); Bolick v. City of Charlotte, 191 N.C. 677, 132 S.E. 660 (1926).

58. Reid & Sibell, Inc. v. Gilmore & Edwards Co., 134 Cal.App.2d 60, 285 P.2d 364 (1955); Rinn v. City of Boulder, 131 Colo. 243, 280 P.2d 1111 (1955); Perrine v. Hokser, 158 Neb. 190, 62 N.W.2d 677 (1954). A municipal court may be required to take judicial notice of the local municipal ordinances. Tipp v. District of Columbia, 69 App. D.C. 400, 102 F.2d 264 (1939); Wis.Stats.Ann. 328.02.

59. 29 Am.Jur.2d Evidence § 35. Judicial notice of municipal ordinances is sometimes provided for by statute, e. g., Mich.Comp.Laws Ann. § 89.7 (1948); McKinney's N.Y. CPLR 4511; Purdon's Pa. Stat.Ann. tit. 28 § 301.

60. See, e. g., Fremoult v. Dedire, 1 P.Wms. 429, 24 Eng.Rep. 458 (1718); Mostyn v. Fabrigas, 1 Cowp. 161, 98 Eng.Rep. 1021 (1774). For the history of this rule see Sass, Foreign Law in Civil Litigation: A Comparative Survey, 16 Am.J.Comp.L. 332, 335–339 (1968).

61. See, e. g., Brackett v. Norton, 4 Conn. 517, 520 (1823).

not be given to the laws of sister states.[62] This is probably the most inconvenient of all the limitations upon the practice of judicial notice. Notice here could certainly be justified on the principle of certainty and verifiability,[63] and the burden on the judge could be minimized by casting the responsibility upon counsel either to agree upon a stipulation as to the law or to produce on each side for the benefit of the court all materials necessary for ascertaining the law in question.

Under the present practice when a required pleading and proof of the foreign law has been overlooked, or has been unsuccessfully attempted, the resulting danger of injustice is somewhat mitigated by the presumption that the law of the sister state is the same as that of the forum,[64] or more simply the practice of applying local law if the law of the other state is not invoked and proven.[65] But this presumption-tool is too rough for the job in hand, particularly when the materials for ascertaining the laws of sister states are today almost as readily accessible as those for local law, and in any event counsel as officers of the court are available to find and present those materials to the judge in just the same informal and convenient fashion as if they were arguing a question of local law.[66]

In 1936 the Conference of Commissioners on Uniform Laws drafted the Uniform Judicial Notice of Foreign Law Act [67] which has since been adopted in substance by more than half the states.[68] This legislation provides that every court within the adopting state shall take judicial notice of the common law and statutes of every other state. While the Act removes the necessity to prove the law of another state, most courts do not feel obliged by it to notice the law of another

---

modern day with easy access to many law libraries with copies of the state statutes and the state and national reporter systems, and the obvious fact that the states are not 'foreign' to each other, the reason for the common law rule no longer exists.").

67. Its substantive provisions follow:
"Section 1. (Judicial Notice.) Every court of this state shall take judicial notice of the common law and statutes of every state, territory and other jurisdiction of the United States. Section 2. (Information of the Court.) The court may inform itself of such laws in such manner as it may deem proper, and the court may call upon counsel to aid it in obtaining such information. Section 3. (Ruling Reviewable.) The determination of such laws shall be made by the court and not by the jury, and shall be reviewable. Section 4. (Evidence as to Laws of other Jurisdiction.) Any party may also present to the trial court any admissible evidence of such laws, but, to enable a party to offer evidence of the law in another jurisdiction or to ask that judicial notice be taken thereof, reasonable notice shall be given to the adverse parties either in the pleadings or otherwise. Section 5. (Foreign Country.) The law of a jurisdiction other than those referred to in Section 1 shall be an issue for the court, but shall not be subject to the foregoing provisions concerning judicial notice." 1936 Handbook Nat'l. Conference of Commissioners on Unif. State Laws 355–359; 1945 id. 124; 9A Uniform Laws Ann. 553 (1965).

68. 9A Uniform Laws Ann. 550 (1965); Am.Jur.2d Desk Book, Document 129. Listed therein are Delaware, Florida, Hawaii, Illinois, Indiana, Kansas, Kentucky, Louisiana, Maine, Maryland, Minnesota, Missouri, Montana, Nebraska, New Jersey, North Dakota, Ohio, Oklahoma, Pennsylvania, Rhode Island, South Carolina, South Dakota, Tennessee, Washington, Wisconsin and Wyoming.

Some states have enacted their own legislation providing for judicial notice of law of sister states, e. g., Ark.Stats. § 28–109 (1947); West's Ann.Cal. Code Civ.Proc. § 1875; N.M.1953 Comp. § 21–1–1 (44); McKinney's N.Y. CPLR 4511.

---

62. Southern Exp. Co. v. Owens, 146 Ala. 412, 41 So. 752 (1906); Gapsch v. Gapsch, 76 Idaho 44, 277 P.2d 278, 54 A.L.R.2d 416 (1954); Brown v. Perry, 104 Vt. 66, 156 A. 910 (1931). But see Prudential Insurance Co. of America v. O'Grady, 97 Ariz. 9, 12–13, 396 P.2d 246, 248 (1964).

This rule is modified somewhat even in some of these states because, if the statute is properly pleaded, it need not be proved if the Uniform Proof of Statutes Act is in effect. See, e. g., Idaho Code §§ 9–304—9–306; Barthel v. Johnston, 92 Idaho 94, 437 P.2d 366 (1968).

63. See § 330, supra.

64. Scott v. Scott, 153 Neb. 906, 46 N.W.2d 627, 23 A.L.R.2d 1431 (1951).

65. Haggard v. First Nat. Bank, 72 N.D. 434, 8 N.W.2d 5 (1942).

66. Prudential Ins. Co. of America v. O'Grady, 97 Ariz. 9, 12, 396 P.2d 246, 248 (1964) ("In this

state on their own initiative.[69] Indeed, in order to invoke the benefits of the Act a litigant must give reasonable notice in the pleadings or otherwise to the adverse party of his intention to do so,[70] failing which the courts are apt to refuse to take judicial notice or admit evidence as to the sister-state law relied on, invoking once again the presumption that it is the same as the law of the forum.[71]

In light of the uncertainties which becloud state-by-state practice with regard to taking judicial notice of each others' law, it has been suggested with much persuasiveness that Congress should, under the authority conferred by the Full Faith and Credit clause of the Constitution, prescribe this practice for the courts of all states.[72]

The law of foreign countries.[73] At common law, foreign law was treated as a matter of fact: pleading and proof were required, and the jury decided what the foreign law was.[74] When no statute authorizing judicial notice is applicable, proof of foreign-country law is still required today, and this situation still obtains in the overwhelming majority of American jurisdictions.[75] Interestingly enough the Uniform Judicial Notice of Foreign Law Act, adverted to in the preceding section, contains no provision for notice of the law of other nations.[76] Accordingly in most jurisdictions the burden of strict proof must be undertaken. When the foreign law is in the form of a statute or decree, it is generally held at least in the earlier cases in this country that an authenticated copy must be produced.[77] This would require, in strictness, a sworn or officially certified copy but as in respect to the laws of sister states,[78] this has been ameliorated by statutes or decisions permitting the use of a copy in a book purporting to be printed by authority of the foreign state or proved to be commonly recognized in its courts.[79] Ordinarily the written text must be interpreted in the light of the applicable decisions, treatises and commentaries, and this under common law proof must be accomplished by taking the testi-

---

69. Kingston v. Quimby, 80 So.2d 455 (Fla.1955) ("a party invoking . . . the Act is required to have the record reveal that fact and to have the record show the authorities which will be relied upon with reference to the foreign law."); Strout v. Burgess, 144 Me. 263, 68 A.2d 241, 12 A.L.R.2d 939 (1949).

70. Boswell v. Rio De Oro Uranium Mines, Inc., 68 N.M. 457, 362 P.2d 991 (1961) (cases construing Act generally hold that the judicial notice requirement merely relieves party of formal proof but was not designed to remove necessity of at least informing court of the content of foreign law to be noticed).

71. Scott v. Scott, 153 Neb. 906, 46 N.W.2d 627, 23 A.L.R.2d 1431 (1951).

72. Hartwig, Congressional Enactment of Judicial Notice Act, 40 Mich.L.Rev. 174 (1941).

73. For valuable discussions, see—Nussbaum, The Problem of Proving Foreign Law, 50 Yale L.J. 1018 (1941), Proving the Law of Foreign Countries, 3 Am.J.Comp.L. 60 (1954), Proof of Foreign Law in New York: A Proposed Amendment, 57 Colum. L.Rev. 348 (1957).

74. See generally, 9 Wigmore, Evidence § 2573; Graveson, The Conflict of Laws 397–401 (4th ed. 1960).

75. 29 Am.Jur.2d Evidence § 49. See, e. g., Chicago Pneumatic Tool Co. v. Ziegler, 151 F.2d 784 (3d Cir. 1945) (the state of foreign law is a matter of fact and requires proof.) It should be kept in mind that, unlike the law of a sister state, the sources on the law of foreign nations are not easily accessible even in urban centers. See Report of the Committee on Foreign and Comparative Law of the Assoc. of the Bar of the City of New York, 22 The Record (Supplement—Committee Reports 1966–67) 31 (1967). See also Telesphore Couture v. Watkins, 162 F.Supp. 727, 730–731 (E.D.N.Y.1958).

76. See the text of that act produced at note 67, supra. Section 5 does make the tenor of the foreign law a question for the court and not the jury, even though that law is not otherwise subject to judicial notice under the act.

According to Uniform Rule 9, a court in New York would have to take judicial notice of the law of Puerto Rico, a Territory, whereas the relatively similar law of Ontario would be "foreign law." See § 328, n. 3, supra.

77. See, e. g., Pierce v. Indseth, 106 U.S. 546 (1882).

78. See n. 62, supra.

79. See Uniform Proof of Statutes Act, 9B Uniform Laws Ann. 628 (1966).

mony in person or by deposition of an expert in the foreign law.[80] The adversary of course is free to take the testimony of other experts if he can find them on his side, and the cross-examination of conflicting experts is likely to accentuate the disagreements.[81] This method of proof seems to maximize expense and delay [82] and hardly seems best calculated to ensure a correct decision by our judges on questions of foreign law. It could be vastly improved by pre-trial conferences in which agreements as to undisputed aspects of the foreign law could be secured, and by the appointment by the court of one or more experts on foreign law as referees or as court-chosen experts to report their findings to the court.[83]

Following the lead of several states which by statute have provided that the court must take judicial notice [84] or permit the court to do so in its discretion,[85] the practice obtaining in the federal courts has been codified to make the tenor of foreign law a question of law for the court.[86] Thus it is that a party who intends to raise an issue of foreign-nation law must give notice of his intention to do so, either in his pleadings or by any other reasonable method of written notice.[87] Once the issue of foreign law is raised, the court need not, in its effort to determine the tenor of that law, rely upon the testimony and other materials proffered by the litigant, but may engage in its own research and consider any relevant material thus found.

The unwillingness of the courts to notice the laws of other countries creates difficulties where the party whose case or defense depends, under conflicts rules, upon foreign law and he fails to prove that law as a fact. There are several solutions. First, the court may decide the issue against him for failure of proof.[88] This is often a harsh and arbitrary result. Second, the court may simply apply the law of the forum on the ground

---

80. A case illustrating this practice is In re Nielsen's Estate, 118 Mont. 304, 165 P.2d 792 (1946) (deposition of legal counselor of Danish Legation discussing legal treatises and giving opinion as to inheritance rights of aliens under Danish law). See also, Application of Chase Manhattan Bank, 191 F.Supp. 206 (D.C.N.Y.1961) (a mere translation of foreign statute without the background, context, or area of internal application is insufficient to establish the precise tenor of what foreign law is).

81. "It is the writer's impression that under the present practice of the courts, skillful advocates may succeed in developing confusing divergencies between experts on purely verbal matters in situations where coherent and well-substantiated written opinions would eliminate all difficulties." Nussbaum, op. cit. supra at n. 73, 50 Yale L.J. 1018, 1029.

82. Professor Nussbaum cites an example where a court would not be satisfied unless plaintiffs brought an Argentine lawyer to New York City. Nussbaum, Proving the Law of Foreign Countries, 3 Am.J.Comp.L. 60, 63–64 (1954).

83. The parties can stipulate the tenor of the foreign law. Harris v. American Int. Fuel & Petrol. Co., 124 F.Supp. 878 (W.D.Pa.1954). See also Model Expert Testimony Act, 9A Uniform Laws Ann. 536 (1965).

84. See, e. g., Mass.Gen.Laws Ann. c. 233, § 70 ("The court shall take judicial notice of the law . . . of any state . . . or of a foreign country whenever the same shall be material.") The attention of the court must be drawn to the foreign law

before this statute becomes mandatory. Commercial Credit Corp. v. Stan Cross Buick, 343 Mass. 622, 180 N.E.2d 88 (1962).

85. See, e. g., McKinney's N.Y. CPLR 4511(b).

86. F.R.Civ.Proc. 44.1: "A party who intends to raise an issue concerning the law of a foreign country shall give notice in his pleadings or other reasonable written notice. The court, in determining foreign law, may consider any relevant material or source, including testimony, whether or not submitted by a party or admissible under Rule 43. The court's determination shall be treated as a ruling on a question of law."

Rule 26.1 of the Federal Rules of Criminal Procedure is substantially the same.

87. Ruff v. St. Paul Mercury Ins. Co., 393 F.2d 500 (2d Cir. 1968) (court would not take judicial notice of Liberian law when plaintiff never gave written notice of intent to rely upon foreign law).

88. Walton v. Arabian American Oil Co., 233 F.2d 541 (2d Cir. 1956) cert. denied 352 U.S. 872 (Arkansas plaintiff sued Delaware corporation in federal court in New York for injuries sustained in Saudi Arabia, did not allege or offer to prove foreign law; case dismissed because plaintiff failed to introduce evidence of foreign law upon which issue burden of proof was his). See also Cuba Railroad v. Crosby, 222 U.S. 473 (1912).

that no other law is before it,[89] especially if the parties have tried the case as if local law were applicable.[90]　Third, the court may presume that the law of the other country is the same as that of the forum,[91] thus reaching the same result as under the second theory but raising intellectual difficulties because the presumption is so frequently contrary to fact.　When the doctrine involved is one of common law, but the other nation is not a common law country, some courts will decline to apply the presumption.[92]　On the other hand, when the common law rule invoked is a part of the common fund of all civilized systems, such as the binding force of ordinary commercial agreements, the presumption is applied though the foreign country is not a common law country.[93]　Moreover, by what is probably the prevailing and more convenient view, if the question would be governed locally by a statute, a like statute in the foreign country may be presumed.[94]

International and Maritime Law.　The rules, principles and traditions of "international law," or "the law of nations," will be noticed in Federal and state courts.[95]　Maritime law is similarly subject to judicial notice but only insofar as these rules have become part of the general maritime law.[96]　Less widely recognized maritime rules of foreign countries are treated like foreign law generally and are required to be proved,[97] unless they have been published here by government authority as the authentic foreign law,[98] or they have been embodied in a widely adopted international convention.[99]　Peculiarly enough, the presumption of identity of foreign law with the local law, which would seem to be unusually convenient and realistic in the maritime field, has been narrowly restricted.[1]

89.　Leary v. Gledhill, 8 N.J. 260, 84 A.2d 725 (1951) (in suit arising out of transaction executed in France wherein plaintiff did not prove foreign law, court applied domestic law); Note, 37 Cornell L.Q. 748 (1952).

90.　Watford v. Alabama & Florida Lumber Co., 152 Ala. 178, 44 So. 567 (1907).

91.　See generally, the illuminating discussion in Nussbaum, op. cit. supra at n. 73, 50 Yale L.J. 1018, 1035 et seq. (1941); Medina Fernandez v. Hartman, 260 F.2d 569 (9th Cir. 1958) (absent a showing to the contrary it is a familiar principle that foreign law is presumed same as domestic); Leary v. Gledhill, 8 N.J. 260, 84 A.2d 725 (1951).

92.　Cuba R. Co. v. Crosby, 222 U.S. 473 (1912) (law of Cuba as to responsibility of employer for injury to employee); Philp v. Macri, 261 F.2d 945 (9th Cir. 1958) (law of defamation of Peru cannot be presumed same as that of State of Washington). But see Louknitsky v. Louknitsky, 123 Cal.App.2d 406, 266 P.2d 910 (1954) (law of China presumed to be identical with community property law of California).

93.　Cuba R. Co. v. Crosby, 222 U.S. 473 (1912) (dictum); Parrot v. Mexican Central R. Co., 207 Mass. 184, 93 N.E. 590 (1941) (presumption that defendant would be liable in Mexico on agreement made there by its general passenger agent, under "universally recognized fundamental principles of right and wrong").

94.　Wickersham v. Johnson, 104 Cal. 407, 38 P. 89 (1894) (sale of note by English executors, powers of executors presumed to be limited as under California statute); Murphy v. Murphy, 145 Cal. 482, 78 P. 1053 (1904) (California statutory rate of interest presumed to prevail as to amount due on English judgment).　Contra: Parrot v. Mexican Cent. R. Co., 207 Mass. 184, 93 N.E. 590 (1911) (dictum).

95.　The Paquete Habana, 175 U.S. 677, 700 (1899) ("International law is part of our law and must be ascertained and administered by the courts of justice.　.　.　."); Skiriotes v. Florida, 313 U.S. 69, 73 (1941) (international law is "a part of our law and as such is the law of all States of the Union").

96.　The New York, 175 U.S. 187 (1899); Boyd v. Conklin, 54 Mich. 583, 20 N.W. 595 (1884).

97.　Black Diamond S. S. Corp. v. Robert Stewart & Sons, Ltd., 336 U.S. 386 (1949).

98.　The New York, 175 U.S. 187 (1899).

99.　Black Diamond S. S. Corp. v. Robert Stewart & Sons, Ltd. 336 U.S. 386 (1949).

1.　Ozanic v. United States, 165 F.2d 738 (2d Cir. 1948) (in libel for damage to Yugoslavian vessel on high seas libellant has burden to prove Yugoslav law as fact. "However it might be in respect to British maritime law, we cannot assume that the law of Yugoslavia, a civil law country and not even a great maritime power, is the same in respect

The future of judicial notice of law. When a judge presiding in the presence of a jury decides a question of fact, a sufficiently unique event occurs to merit special treatment because the jury is thought to perform the factfinding role in common law countries. This appears to explain why judicial notice of facts has been a topic of evidence law ever since Thayer authored his pioneering treatise. There is nothing very remarkable about a judge ruling on the tenor of the law to be applied to the resolution of the controversy, however, because by definition this is the very function judges are supposed to perform. When the sources of law were dubious at best, the job of sorting out the applicable law was shifted to the jury, witness how foreign law and municipal ordinances were treated as questions of fact. When next judges began to rule on the tenor of this law, even though it was still "fact" to be developed by the parties, there may have been some justification for describing this process as judicial notice. As all law has become increasingly accessible and judges have tended to assume the duty to rule on the tenor of all law, the notion that this process is part of judicial notice has become increasingly an anachronism. Evidence, after all, involves the proof of facts. How the law is fed into the judicial machine is more appropriately an aspect of the law pertaining to procedure.[2]

to the measure of damages as that of the United States."); Sonnesen v. Panama Transport Co., 298 N.Y. 262, 82 N.E.2d 569 (1948) (court would not notice Panamanian law as to seaman's right of maintenance and cure, nor would it assume Panamanian maritime law same as ours).

2. Note on Judicial Notice of Law, F.R.Ev. (R.D. 1971) 201, p. 21.

TITLE 12

BURDEN OF PROOF AND PRESUMPTIONS

CHAPTER 36

THE BURDENS OF PROOF AND PRESUMPTIONS [1]

336. The Burdens of Proof: The Burden of Producing Evidence and the Burden of Persuasion.

"Proof" is an ambiguous word. We sometimes use it to mean evidence, such as testimony or documents. Sometimes, when we say a thing is "proved" we mean that we are convinced by the data submitted that the alleged fact is true. Thus, "proof" is the end result of conviction or persuasion produced by the evidence. Naturally, the term "burden of proof" shares this ambivalence. The term encompasses two separate burdens of proof.[2] One burden is that of producing evidence, satisfactory to the judge, of a particular fact in issue.[3] The second is the bur-

1. See 9 Wigmore, Evidence §§ 2483–2498 (general theory), 2499–2550 (burdens and presumptions in specific instances); Morgan, Basic Problems of Evidence, chs. 2, 3 (1962), Some Problems of Proof under the Anglo-American System of Litigation 70–86 (1956); James, Civil Procedure §§ 7.5–7.11 (1965); Model Code of Evidence Rules 1(2, 3), 701–704; Uniform Rules 1(4), 13–16; F.R.Ev. 301–303 (R.D. 1971); Ball, The Moment of Truth: Probability Theory and Standards of Proof, 14 Vand.L.Rev. 807 (1961); Christie and Pye, Presumptions and Assumptions in the Criminal Law: Another View, 1970 Duke L.J. 919; Cleary, Presuming and Pleading: An Essay on Juristic Immaturity, 12 Stan.L.Rev. 5 (1959); Gausewitz, Presumptions in a One-Rule World, 5 Vand.L.Rev. 324 (1952); Laughlin, In Support of the Thayer Theory of Presumptions, 52 Mich.L.Rev. 195 (1953); McCormick, Charges on Presumptions, 5 N.C.L.Rev. 291 (1927), What Shall the Trial Judge Tell the Jury about Presumptions?, 13 Wash.L.Rev. 185 (1938); McNaughton, Burden of Production of Evidence: A Function of a Burden of Persuasion, 68 Harv.L.Rev. 1382 (1955). Decisions are collected in C.J.S. Evidence §§ 103–157; 29 Am.Jur.2d Evidence §§ 159–248, 1163–1178; Dec.Dig. Evidence ⊙53–98, Trial ⊙ 205, 234(7), 237, Criminal Law ⊙305–336, 778, 789.

2. The two meanings of "burden of proof" were pointed out by certain nineteenth century judges, e. g., Shaw, C. J. in Powers v. Russell, 30 Mass. (13 Pick.) 69, 76 (1832), and Brett, M. R., in Abrath v. N. E. Ry. Co., 11 Q.B.D. 440, 452 (1883), but the distinction and its consequences were first emphasized and elaborated by James Bradley Thayer in his Preliminary Treatise on Evidence ch. 9 (1898). Modern cases making the distinction are collected in Dec.Dig. Evidence ⊙90.

3. The burden of producing evidence is sometimes termed the "burden of evidence" (C.J.S. Evidence § 103) or "the duty of going forward." Thayer, supra n. 2, at 355.

den of persuading the trier of fact that the alleged fact is true.[4]

The burden of producing evidence on an issue means the liability to an adverse ruling (generally a finding or directed verdict) if evidence on the issue has not been produced. It is usually cast first upon the party who has pleaded the existence of the fact, but as we shall see, the burden may shift to the adversary when the pleader has discharged his initial duty.[5] The burden of producing evidence is a critical mechanism in a jury trial, as it empowers the judge to decide the case without jury consideration when a party fails to sustain the burden.

The burden of persuasion becomes a crucial factor only if the parties have sustained their burdens of producing evidence and only when all of the evidence has been introduced. It does not shift from party to party during the course of the trial simply because it need not be allocated until it is time for a decision. When the time for a decision comes, the jury, if there is one, must be instructed how to decide the issue if their minds are left in doubt. The jury must be told that if the party having the burden of persuasion has failed to satisfy that burden, the issue is to be decided against him. If there is no jury and the judge finds himself in doubt, he too must decide the issue against the party having the burden of persuasion.

The significance of the burden of persuasion, particularly as compared to the burden of producing evidence, has been questioned.[6]

Clearly, the principal significance of the burden of persuasion is limited to those cases in which the trier of fact is actually in doubt. Possibly, even in those cases, juries disregard their instructions on this question and judges, trying cases without juries, pay only lip service to it, trusting that the appellate courts will not disturb their findings of fact. Yet, even if an empirical study were conclusively to demonstrate both a regular disregard for jury instructions and a propensity on the part of judges to decide issues of fact without regard to their express statements concerning the allocation of the burden of persuasion, rules allocating and describing that burden could not be discarded by a rational legal system. A risk of nonpersuasion naturally exists anytime one person attempts to persuade another to act or not to act. If the other does not change his course of action or nonaction, the person desiring change has, of course, failed.[7] If no burden of persuasion were acknowledged by the law, one possible result would be that the trier of fact would purport to reach no decision at all. The impact of nondecision would then fall by its own weight upon the party, usually the plaintiff, who sought a change in the status quo. Although this is generally where the law would place the burden anyhow, important policy considerations may dictate that the risk should fall on the opposing party.[8]

Another possibility would be that the trier of fact would itself assign a burden of persuasion, describing that burden as it saw fit by substituting its own notions of policy for

4. Wigmore terms this "the risk of nonpersuasion." 9 Evidence § 2485. Thayer, supra, n. 2 at 353, noting one meaning of "burden of proof", said: ". . . It marks . . . [t]he peculiar duty of him who has the risk of any given proposition on which parties are at issue,—who will lose the case if he does not make this proposition out, when all has been said and done." Se-Ling Hosiery v. Margulies, 364 Pa. 45, 70 A.2d 854, 856 (1950).

5. See § 338, infra.

6. In the first edition of this text, Dean McCormick stated:
"In the writer's view [the burden of producing evidence] has far more influence upon the final out-

come of cases than does the burden of persuasion, which has become very largely a matter of the technique of the wording of instructions to juries. This wording may be chosen in the particular case as a handle for reversal, but will seldom have been a factor in the jury's decision." § 307, at 634 n. 2.

7. For a comparison of the burden of persuasion in litigated and in nonlitigated situations see 9 Wigmore, Evidence § 2485.

8. See § 337, infra.

those now made available to it as a matter of law. Such a result would be most undesirable. Considerations of policy that are sufficient to suggest that in some instances the burden of persuasion be assigned to the party desiring a maintenance of the status quo are strong enough to dictate the need for a consistent, rather than a case by case determination of the question. Other policy considerations, such as those that have led the law to require that the prosecution in a criminal case prove the defendant guilty beyond a reasonable doubt,[9] are sufficient to require that the jury be explicitly and clearly instructed as to the measure of the burden as well as its allocation. Although judges and juries may act contrary to the law despite the best attempts to persuade them to do otherwise, we can at least give them the benefit of thoughtful guidance on the questions of who should bear the burden of persuasion and what the nature of that burden should be. In jury trials, perhaps the problem has not been in the concept of a burden of persuasion, but rather in the confusing jury instructions that abound on this point of law. In nonjury trials, if judges are not in fact following rules of law allocating the burden, the fault may lie not in the concept but with thoughtless judicial and legislative allocations and descriptions of the burden.

337. Allocating the Burdens of Proof.[10]

In most cases, the party who has the burden of pleading a fact will have the burdens of producing evidence and of persuading the jury of its existence as well.[11] The pleadings therefore provide the common guide for apportioning the burdens of proof. For example, in a typical negligence case the plaintiff will have the burdens of (1) pleading the defendant's negligence (2) producing evidence of that negligence and (3) persuading the trier of fact of its existence. The defendant will usually have the same three burdens with regard to the contributory negligence of the plaintiff.[12]

However, looking for the burden of pleading is not a foolproof guide to the allocation of the burdens of proof. The latter burdens do not invariably follow the pleadings. In a federal court, for example, a defendant may be required to plead contributory negligence

---

9. See § 341, infra.

10. James, Civil Procedure § 7.8 (1965); 9 Wigmore, Evidence § 2486; Cleary, Presuming and Pleading: An Essay on Juristic Immaturity, 12 Stan.L.Rev. 5 (1959); C.J.S. Evidence §§ 103–110, 112–113; Dec.Dig. Evidence ☞90–97.

11. Reliance Life Ins. Co. v. Burgess, 112 F.2d 234 (8th Cir. 1940) cert. denied 311 U.S. 699; Buda v. Fulton, 261 Iowa 981, 157 N.W.2d 336 (1968); In re Ewing's Estate, 234 Iowa 950, 14 N.W.2d 633 (1944); Dec.Dig. Evidence ☞91.

McCormick et al on Evid. 2nd Ed. HB—50

12. The relationship of the burden of pleading to the burdens of proof raises the question of the consequences of a party mistakenly pleading a fact upon an issue which his adversary had the burden of raising by an affirmative pleading. In the relatively few cases dealing with the question, the prevailing view is that a mistake in pleading will not generally affect the allocation of the burdens of proof. For example, the courts have held that plaintiff's unnecessary allegation that he was in the exercise of due care, does not affect the defendant's burdens with regard to contributory negligence. Fitchburg Ry. Co. v. Nichols, 85 Fed. 945 (1st Cir. 1898); Bevis v. Vanceburg Tel. Co., 132 Ky. 385, 113 S.W. 811 (1908); Wintrobe v. Hart, 178 Md. 289, 13 A.2d 365 (1940). However, if a trial judge erroneously assigns the burdens of proof to a party who has mistakenly pleaded an issue, a few courts have held that this party has invited the error and has no ground of complaint. Vycas v. St. George Guard Society, 97 Conn. 509, 117 A. 692, 693 (1922) ("A defendant who unnecessarily elaborates a general denial by alleging facts inconsistent with the allegations denied is in no position to complain, in case the court takes him at his word and erroneously instructs the jury as to the burden of proof."); Hatch v. Merigold, 119 Conn. 339, 176 A. 266, 96 A.L.R. 1114, 1116 (1935) (plaintiff by pleading lack of contributory negligence waived benefit of statute placing burden of persuasion on defendant on this issue); Boswell v. Pannell, 107 Tex. 433, 180 S.W. 593, 596 (1915) (defendant by pleading affirmatively voluntarily assumed burden of persuasion and cannot complain when assigned to him). Probably the greater number of cases would reject this qualification. See e. g., Schmitz v. Mathews, 133 Wash. 335, 336, 233 P. 660, 661 (1925) ("not an invitation . . . to commit error . . . merely an opportunity"). See Comment, Effect of Unnecessary Affirmative Pleading upon the Burden of Proof, 39 Yale L.J. 117 (1929).

as an affirmative defense and yet, where jurisdiction is based upon diversity of citizenship, the applicable substantive law may place the burdens of producing evidence and persuasion with regard to that issue on the plaintiff.[13] More significantly, reference to which party has pleaded a fact is no help at all when the rationale behind the allocation is questioned or in a case of first impression where there are no established pleading rules.

The burdens of pleading and proof with regard to most facts have been and should be assigned to the plaintiff who generally seeks to change the present state of affairs and who therefore naturally should be expected to bear the risk of failure of proof or persuasion. The rules which assign certain facts material to the enforcibility of a claim to the defendant owe their development partly to traditional happen-so and partly to considerations of policy.[14]

The determination of appropriate guidelines for the allocation of the burdens has been somewhat hindered by the judicial repetition of two doctrines, one erroneous and the other meaningless. Statements are found primarily in older cases to the effect that even though a party is required to plead a fact, he is not required to prove that fact if his averment is negative rather than affirmative in form.[15] Such a rule would place

an entirely undue emphasis on what is ordinarily purely a matter of choice of forms. Moreover, these statements were probably to be understood as properly applying only to the denial by a party of an opponent's previous pleading, and now one who has the burden of pleading a negative fact as part of his cause of action generally has the accompanying burdens of producing evidence and persuasion.[16] The second misleading doctrine is that the party to whose case the element is essential has the burdens of proof. Such a rule simply restates the question.[17]

The actual reasons for the allocation of the burdens may be no more complex than the misleading statements just discussed. The policy of handicapping a disfavored contention [18] probably accounts for the require-

---

13. See Palmer v. Hoffman, 318 U.S. 109 (1943); Sampson v. Channell, 110 F.2d 754 (1st Cir. 1940) cert. denied 310 U.S. 650; James, supra n. 10, § 3.6 at 106–07; 2A Moore, Federal Practice ¶8.27[2] at 1849 (2d Ed. 1968).

14. Although the following discussion generally relates to all cases, civil and criminal, there are additional problems in criminal cases, particularly with regard to the allocation of the burden of persuasion. See § 341, infra.

15. See e. g., Walker v. Carpenter, 144 N.C. 674, 676, 57 S.E. 461 (1907) ("The first rule laid down in the books on evidence is to the effect that the issue must be proved by the party who states an affirmative, not by the party who states a negative.") Similar statements can be found in more recent cases, see, e. g., Levine v. Pascal, 94 Ill.App. 2d 43, 236 N.E.2d 425 (1968).

16. Chase Manhattan Bank v. O'Connor, 82 N.J. Super. 382, 197 A.2d 706, 709 (1964) (party alleging nondelivery of stock certificates had the burden of proving that issue); Saari v. George C. Dates and Associates, 311 Mich. 624, 19 N.W.2d 121 (1945) (wrongful discharge: defendant pleaded plaintiff's failure to perform, burden on defendant); Johnson v. Johnson, 229 N.C. 541, 50 S.E.2d 569 (1948) (plaintiff alleging in reply that deed was forged had burden of establishing nonexecution by purported grantor). It is sometimes said that the party pleading a negative need not prove it when the facts are peculiarly within the knowledge of the other party. E. g., Allstate Finance Corp. v. Zimmerman, 330 F.2d 740, 744 (5th Cir. 1964). Or more mildly that as to the party pleading a negative the law will be satisfied with a lesser quantum of proof, particularly when the facts are within the knowledge of the adverse party. In re Chicago Rys. Co., 175 F.2d 282, 290 (7th Cir. 1949), cert. denied 338 U.S. 850. The important consideration in these cases, however, is not which party has the negative, but which party has the knowledge of the facts. See Wiles v. Mullinax, 275 N.C. 473, 168 S.E.2d 366 (1969), (plaintiff had the burden of proving the defendant's failure to procure insurance coverage, notwithstanding negative form of the issue; Sharp, J. arguing in dissent that the burden should be placed upon the defendant, not only because of its negative form but also because the defendant had "peculiar knowledge of the fact in issue and therefore the better means of proving it.") See text accompanying n. 18, infra. See also C.J.S. Evidence §§ 105, 112; Dec.Dig. Evidence ⊂⇒92, 93.

17. See Cleary, supra n. 10, at 11.

18. The phrase is borrowed from Clark, Code Pleading § 96 at 610 (2d ed. 1947) where these consider-

ment that the defendant generally has all three burdens with regard to such matters as contributory negligence, statute of limitations, and truth in defamation. Convenience in following the natural order of storytelling may account for calling on the defendant to plead and prove those matters which arise after a cause of action has matured, such as payment, release, and accord and satisfaction.

A doctrine often repeated by the courts is that where the facts with regard to an issue lie peculiarly in the knowledge of a party, that party has the burden of proving the issue. Examples are the burdens commonly placed upon the defendant to prove payment, discharge in bankruptcy, and license.[19] This consideration should not be overemphasized. Very often one must plead and prove matters as to which his adversary has superior access to the proof. Nearly all required allegations of the plaintiff in actions for tort or breach of contract relating to the defendant's acts or omissions describe matters peculiarly in the defendant's knowledge. Correspondingly, when the defendant is required to plead contributory negligence, he pleads facts specially known to the plaintiff.

Perhaps a more frequently significant consideration in the fixing of the burdens of proof is the judicial estimate of the probabilities of the situation. The risk of failure of proof may be placed upon the party who contends that the more unusual event has

occurred.[20] For example, where a business relationship exists, it is unlikely that services will be performed gratuitously. The burden of proving a gift is therefore placed upon the one who claims it. Where services are performed for a member of the family, a gift is much more likely and the burden of proof is placed on the party claiming the right to be paid.[21]

In allocating the burdens, courts consistently attempt to distinguish between the constituent elements of a promise or of a statutory command, which must be proved by the party who relies on the contract or statute, and matters of exception, which must be proved by his adversary.[22] Often

20. See Cleary, supra n. 10 at 12–13, observing that in assigning the burdens sometimes the courts will consider the probabilities of the situation generally and sometimes will consider the probabilities with reference to litigated cases. "No reason for the shift is apparent, and it may be unconscious. The litigated cases would seem to furnish the more appropriate basis for estimating probabilities."

In Ball, The Moment of Truth: Probability Theory and Standards of Proof, 14 Vand.L.Rev. 807, 817–818 (1961) the author questions the use of probabilities to allocate the burden of persuasion. He suggests that if the burden is assigned to the party whose case depends upon the happening of the least likely event the probabilities are really counted against him twice—once in the jury's own initial assessment of the probabilities which is likely to be similar to that made by the courts and once in the assignment of the burden of persuasion. A similar point is made with regard to the use of presumptions having their basis in probability in Laughlin, In Support of the Thayer Theory of Presumptions, 52 Mich.L.Rev. 195, 212 (1953).

21. See James, supra n. 10, at 257.

22. With regard to contracts, see Corbin, Contracts § 751 (1960); 5 Williston, Contracts § 674 (1961). With regard to statutes, see Annot. 130 A.L.R. 440. On the question generally see, Cleary, supra note 10, at 8–10; Stone, Burden of Proof and the Judicial Process, 60 L.Q.Rev. 262 (1944).

The operation of the distinction in insurance contracts may be illustrated as follows: In an action on a life insurance policy with an exception for death by suicide the defendant has all of the burdens on the issue of suicide. But in a suit on an accident policy, or on the double indemnity provision of a life policy, since suicide is not an accident, the plaintiff must plead accident and, at least tentatively, will have both burdens of proof on the issue. See, e. g., New York Life Ins. Co. v. Pre-

ations and the relation of the pleading rules to the burden of proof are lucidly discussed.

19. See, e. g., F.R.Civ.P. 8(c); Cleary, supra n. 10 at 12. Expanded pretrial discovery would seem to have diminished greatly whatever importance this factor had in allocating the burdens. However, there has been no rush by the courts to reassess allocations between the parties in the light of expanded discovery, perhaps attesting to the fact that exclusive knowledge in one party has seldom been the controlling reason for assigning the burdens of proof.

the result of this approach is an arbitrary allocation of the burdens, as the statutory language may be due to a mere casual choice of form by the draftsman. However, the distinction may be a valid one in some instances, particularly when the exceptions to a statute or promise are numerous. If that is the case, fairness usually requires that the adversary give notice of the particular exception upon which he relies and therefore that he bear the burden of pleading. The burdens of proof will not always follow the burden of pleading in these cases.[23] However, exceptions generally point to exceptional situations. If proof of the facts is inaccessible or not persuasive, it is usually fairer to act as if the exceptional situation did not exist and therefore to place the burden of proof and persuasion on the party claiming its existence.[24]

As has been stated, the burdens of producing evidence and of persuasion with regard to any given issue are both generally allocated to the same party. Usually each is assigned but once in the course of the litigation and a safe prediction of that assignment can be made at the pleading stage. However, the initial allocation of the burden of producing evidence may not always be final. The shifting nature of that burden may cause both parties to have the burden with regard to the same issue at different points in the trial.[25] Similarly, although the burden of persuasion is assigned only once—when it is time for a decision—a prediction of the allocation of that burden, based upon the pleadings, may have to be revised when evidence is introduced at trial.[26] Policy considerations similar to those that govern the initial allocation of the burden of producing evidence and tentatively fix the burden of persuasion govern the ultimate assignment of those burdens as well.[27]

In summary, there is no key principle governing the apportionment of the burdens of proof. Their allocation, either initially or ultimately, will depend upon the weight that is given to any one or more of several factors, including: (1) the natural tendency to place the burdens on the party desiring

---

jean, 149 F.2d 114 (5th Cir. 1945) (double indemnity provision); Blythe v. Kanawha Ins. Co., 279 F.Supp. 8 (W.D.N.C.1968) (same). See also, Note, Burden of Proof of Excepted Clauses in Insurance Policies, 46 Colum.L.Rev. 802, 810 (1946). The allocation of the burdens of proof to the plaintiff in an accident policy or double indemnity provision case may be only tentative due to the operation of a presumption against suicide. See §§ 343, 345, infra.

23. An illustration of a divergence between the burdens of pleading and proof in an analogous situation is the treatment of conditions precedent in contracts, particularly in insurance contracts, by most courts. For example, in a federal court the defendant will be required to plead the non-occurrence of a particular condition precedent [F.R. Civ.P. 9(c)] but he may not have the burdens of proof with regard to that issue. See 2A Moore, Federal Practice ¶ 9.04 at 1945 (2d ed. 1968); 5 Williston, Contracts § 674 at 181 (1961).

24. This consideration, of course, is simply a specific application of the use of an estimate of the probabilities to fix the burdens. In Stone, supra, n. 22, the learned writer examines the opinions in Joseph Constantine Steamship Ltd. v. Imperial Smelting Corp., Ltd., [1942] A.C. 154 (H.L.) which determined the novel question whether upon the plea of frustration in an action on a contract, the defendant or the plaintiff has the burdens of producing evidence and of persuasion on the issue whether the frustration was contributed to by the fault of the defendant. The opinions in placing the burdens upon the plaintiff stress the formal distinction between an essential element of the

defense and an exception to its operation, and purport to reach their conclusions mainly upon definitions, logic and analogy. The author urges that as to this new question, the judges might more fruitfully have grounded their decision upon considerations of justice and policy, such as the following: "Let it be assumed then that in the great majority of frustration cases no fault of the parties was operative; and let it be assumed that in these cases the impossibility of proof mentioned by the lords is present. A rule requiring the defendant pleading frustration to negative fault will then *ex hypothesi* do injustice to the great majority of defendants. While on the other hand, a rule requiring the plaintiff to prove fault will *ex hypothesi* do injustice to only a small minority of plaintiffs." (p. 278).

25. See § 338, infra.

26. See § 345, infra.

27. See § 343, infra.

change, (2) special policy considerations such as those disfavoring certain defenses, (3) convenience, (4) fairness, and (5) the judicial estimate of the probabilities.[28]

28. Declaratory judgment actions provide an excellent example of the problems of allocating the burdens of proof. Where the plaintiff seeks a declaratory judgment as a basis for some further affirmative claim against the defendant, there is no special problem; the burdens will be allocated as usual, with the major share going to the plaintiff. See, e. g., Jerry Vogel Music Co. v. Forster Music Publisher, 147 F.2d 614 (2d Cir. 1945), cert. denied 325 U.S. 880 (suit for declaration that plaintiff was owner of copyrighted song; plaintiff had burden to establish ownership and defendant to establish defense of joint ownership); McNally v. Moser, 210 Md.App. 127, 122 A.2d 555 (1956) (defendant landlord claiming illegal use of leased premises had both the burden of producing evidence and the burden of persuasion on the question). But when the traditional positions of plaintiff and defendant are transposed, the courts have had considerable difficulty in determining the allocation of the burdens. In these cases, the competing policies discussed in this section clearly emerge. For example, some courts have held that when an insurance company sues for a declaration of nonliability the defendant insured should have the burden on the issues on which he would bear the burden had he sued to establish his rights under the policy. The leading case is Travelers Ins. Co. v. Greenough, 88 N.H. 391, 190 A. 129 (1937) where the court stated that a contrary conclusion "would place the plaintiff in a position of undue disadvantage." See also Preferred Accident Ins. Co. v. Grasso, 186 F.2d 987 (2d Cir. 1951) (opinion by Clark, J.) Other courts have seen no such disadvantage and hold that the burdens should rest on the party bringing the suit. See, e. g., Reliance Life Ins. Co. v. Burgess, 112 F.2d 234 (1940) cert. denied 311 U.S. 699 (Sanborn, J. dissenting on this question); First National Bank of Ore. v. Malady, 242 Ore. 353, 408 P.2d 724 (1965) (strong dissent on this question by Perry, J.). The competing policies are also reflected in Professor Moore's discussion of this problem, 6A Moore, Federal Practice ¶ 57.31[2] at 3155 (2d ed. 1966). He argues that the doctrine of the *Greenough* case is "unwise in its own context," in that it is "reasonable and fair" for the plaintiff insurer to bear the burdens in such a case. He takes a different view, however, of the burdens in an action by an alleged infringer for a declaration of noninfringement or invalidity of defendant's patent, copyright or trademark. Professor Moore bases his argument on the very relevant considerations that it may be very difficult for the accused infringer to prove that his activities have in no way infringed the defendant's rights and that in the vast majority of such cases, the basis for the declaratory action is an extrajudicial charge of infringement "which the defendant has made and nobody knows better

338. Satisfying the Burden of Producing Evidence.

Let us suppose that the plaintiff, claiming an estate in land for John Smith's life, had the burden of pleading, and has pleaded, that John Smith was alive at the time the action was brought. He seeks to fulfill the burden of producing evidence of this fact.

To do this he may offer *direct* evidence, e. g., of witness Jones, who saw Smith alive in the clerk's office when the complaint in the action was filed. From this the inference of the truth of the fact to be proved depends only upon the truthfulness of Jones. Or, he may offer *circumstantial* evidence, which requires a weighing of probabilities as to matters other than merely the truthfulness of the witness. For example, he may secure the testimony of Jones that Jones received a letter in the mail which was signed "John Smith" one month before the action was brought and that he recognized the signature as Smith's. Patently in this latter case, the tribunal may be satisfied that Jones is speaking the truth, and yet the tribunal may decline to infer the fact of Smith's being alive when the action began.

How strongly persuasive must the offered evidence be to satisfy the burden? A "scintilla" of evidence will not suffice.[29] The evidence must be such that a reasonable man could draw from it the inference of the existence of the particular fact to be proved

than he what lies behind his charge." Id. at 3158. See generally on these questions, Annot., 23 A.L.R. 2d 1243; Dec.Dig. Declaratory Judgment ⊕342, 343.

29. See James, Civil Procedure § 7.11 at 272 (1965) where the author refers to the "judicial legend" that there once was a "scintilla rule" under which an adverse verdict could be directed only when there was literally no evidence and states that "if there ever was such a notion all that remains of it today is its well nigh universal repudiation." See also Dec.Dig. Trial ⊕139(1). The above cited section of the James text contains a full discussion of the question of the sufficiency of evidence to withstand a motion for directed verdict. See also 9 Wigmore, Evidence § 2494.

or, as put conversely by one federal court, "if there is substantial evidence opposed to the [motion for directed verdict], that is evidence of such quality and weight that reasonable and fair-minded men in the exercise of impartial judgment might reach different conclusions, the [motion] should be denied." [30]

One problem that has troubled the courts is whether the test for the granting of a directed verdict should vary, depending upon the required measure of persuasion if the case goes to the jury. For example in a criminal case where the prosecution must persuade the jury beyond a reasonable doubt,[31] should the test for a directed verdict be whether the evidence could satisfy reasonable men beyond a reasonable doubt? Some courts have said no, perhaps believing with Judge Learned Hand that, although the gravity of the consequences often makes judges more exacting in criminal cases, the line between proof that should satisfy reasonable men and the evidence that should satisfy reasonable men beyond a reasonable doubt is, in the long run, "too thin for day to day use." [32] However, many other courts,

including many of the United States Courts of Appeal apply the stricter test.[33] Logical arguments have been made that the gauge for the burden of producing evidence must necessarily reflect the measure of persuasion that will ultimately be required.[34]

Generally no difficulty occurs where the evidence is direct. Except in rare cases,[35] it is sufficient, though given by one witness only, however negligible a human being he may be. But if the evidence is circumstantial, forensic disputes often arise as to its sufficiency to warrant a jury to draw the desired inference. In fact, in few areas of the law have so many words been spoken by the courts with so little conviction. One test frequently expounded in criminal cases is that where the prosecution relies upon circumstantial evidence, the evidence must be so conclusive as to exclude any other reasonable inference inconsistent therewith.[36]

---

30. Boeing Co. v. Shipman, 411 F.2d 365, 374 (5th Cir. 1969). The above quoted statement refers also to motions for judgment notwithstanding the verdict. The tests are usually the same. See 5 Moore, Federal Practice ¶ 50.07(2) (1967).

Because the ruling that a party has not satisfied his burden of producing evidence precludes a jury determination of the merits of the case, some courts, particularly federal courts, have been plagued by constitutional worries in formulating tests for the granting of directed verdicts. For an excellent discussion of the directed verdict in the federal courts, see Cooper, Directions for Directed Verdicts: A Compass for Federal Courts, 55 Minn.L.Rev. 903 (1971).

31. See § 341, infra.

32. United States v. Feinberg, 140 F.2d 592, 594 (2d Cir. 1944) cert. denied 322 U.S. 726. See also Hays v. United States, 231 F. 106 (8th Cir. 1916); State v. Nutley, 24 Wis.2d 527, 129 N.W.2d 155, 163 (1964), cert. denied 380 U.S. 918. This approach, of course, leaves the beyond-a-reasonable-doubt standard as a test to be applied by the jury.

33. E. g., Riggs v. United States, 280 F.2d 949 (5th Cir. 1960); Curley v. United States, 81 U.S.App. D.C. 389, 160 F.2d 229 (D.C. Cir. 1947), cert. denied 331 U.S. 837; State v. Rocker, 475 P.2d 684 (Haw. 1970). See also F.R.Ev. (R.D.1971) 303, Advisory Committee's Note. In an interesting footnote to a recent case, the Supreme Court stated, by way of dictum: " . . . a court should always set aside a jury verdict of guilt when there is not evidence from which a jury could find a defendant guilty beyond a reasonable doubt." United States v. Vuitch, 402 U.S. 62, 72, n. 7 (1971). The significance of this offhand remark may be increased in light of the Court's holding in In re Winship, 397 U.S. 358 (1970) that due process requires proof beyond a reasonable doubt for conviction. See § 341, n. 89 and accompanying text, infra.

34. See McNaughton, Burden of Production of Evidence: A Function of a Burden of Persuasion, 68 Harv.L.Rev. 1382 (1955).

35. In extreme circumstances, such as where a witness's testimony is flatly contradicted by indisputable physical facts or laws of nature, his testimony may be disregarded. See, e. g., Scott v. Hansen, 228 Iowa 37, 289 N.W. 710 (1940). In a few other instances, such as where a defendant is charged with perjury, the law imposes an artificial requirement of corroboration. See James, supra n. 29 at 273–274.

36. E. g., State v. Love, 106 Ariz. 215, 474 P.2d 806 (1970); People v. Branion, 47 Ill.2d 70, 265 N.E.2d 1 (1970); Dec.Dig. Criminal Law ⚮552(3).

The test is accurate enough in criminal cases, but adds little at least to the stricter test for criminal cases discussed above. A similar formula is sometimes expounded in civil cases [37] but seems misplaced in civil litigation. It leaves little for the jury and far exceeds what is needed to prevent verdicts based upon speculation and conjecture. Courts rejecting the formula in civil cases have stated that the burden of producing evidence is satisfied, even by circumstantial evidence, if "there be sufficient facts for the jury to say reasonably that the preponderance favors liability." [38]

Other tests and other phrasings of the tests discussed here are myriad,[39] but irrespective of the test articulated, in the last analysis the judge's ruling must necessarily rest on his individual opinion, formed in the light of his own common sense and experience, as to the limits of reasonable inference from the facts proven. However, certain situations recur and give rise repeatedly to litigation, and a given judge, in his desire for consistency and the consequent saving of time and mental travail, will rule alike whenever the same situation is proved and its sufficiency to warrant a certain inference is questioned. Other judges follow suit and a standardized practice, ripening into a rule of law results. Most of these rules are positive rather than negative. They announce that certain types of fact-groups are sufficient to enable the person who has the first duty to go forward with evidence to fulfill that burden, i. e., they enable him to rest after proving them without being subject to the penalty of an adverse ruling.

Suppose the one who had the initial burden of offering evidence in support of the alleged fact, on pain of an adverse ruling, does produce evidence barely sufficient to satisfy that burden, so that the judge can just say, "A reasonable jury *could* infer that the fact is as alleged, from the circumstances proved." If the proponent then rests, what is the situation? Has the duty of going forward shifted to the adversary? Not if we define that duty as the liability to a peremptory adverse ruling on failing to give evidence, for if at this juncture the original proponent rests and the adversary offers no proof, the proponent will not be entitled to the direction of a verdict in his favor on the issue, but rather the court will leave the issue to the decision of the jury. But it is frequently said that in this situation the duty of going forward has shifted to the adversary,[40] and this is unobjectionable [41] if we bear in mind that the penalty for silence is very different here from that which was

In Holland v. United States, 348 U.S. 121 (1954), the Court held that the trial court did not err in refusing to instruct the jury in these terms. Although this holding would not seem to compel the rejection of this language as a directed verdict test, most federal circuits have so held. E. g., United States v. Thomas, 303 F.2d 561 (6th Cir. 1962); United States v. Hamrick, 293 F.2d 468 (4th Cir. 1961). Contra, Battles v. United States, 388 F.2d 799 (5th Cir. 1968).

37. E. g., Bowers v. Maire, 179 Neb. 239, 137 N.W. 2d 796 (1965); Schmidt v. Pioneer United Dairies, 60 Wash.2d 271, 373 P.2d 764 (1962). See also Burns, Weighing Circumstantial Evidence, 2 S. Dak.L.Rev. 36 (1957).

38. Smith v. Bell Telephone Co., 397 Pa. 134, 153 A.2d 477 (1959). See also Rumsey v. Great Atlantic & Pacific Tea Co., 408 F.2d 89 (3d Cir. 1969); Comment, 12 Vill.L.Rev. 326 (1967).

39. A frequently stated corollary to the rules concerning the sufficiency of circumstantial evidence is that one circumstantial inference may not be based upon another. See cases collected at Annot., 5 A.L.R.3d 100. Despite its frequent repetition by some courts, such a rule can actually amount to nothing more than a makeweight argument to be used when a court believes that the inferences sought to be drawn are too remote or speculative. See Shutt v. State, 233 Ind. 169, 117 N.E.2d 892 (1954). Any other interpretation of the rule would severely impede the ordinary and valid uses of circumstantial evidence. See generally 1 Wigmore, Evidence § 41.

40. See, e. g., Speas v. Merchants Bank & Trust Co., 188 N.C. 524, 530, 125 S.E. 398, 401 (1924); C.J.S. Evidence § 110 at 187.

41. But see Stansbury, North Carolina Evidence § 203 (1963) at 526 n. 27 where the author refers to such a characterization as "misleading at least."

applied to the original proponent. If he had remained silent at the outset he would irrevocably have lost the case on this issue, but the only penalty now applied to his adversary is the risk, if he remains silent, of the jury's finding against him, though it may find for him. Theoretically he may have this risk still, even after he has offered evidence in rebuttal. It is simpler to limit "duty of going forward" to the liability, on resting, to an adverse ruling, and to regard the stage just discussed (where the situation is that if both parties rest, the issue will be left to the jury) as one in which neither party has any duty of going forward.

In the situation just discussed, the party who first had the duty, i. e., the necessity, of giving proof, has produced evidence which requires the judge to permit the jury to infer, as it chooses, that the fact alleged is or is not true. It is a permitted, but not a compulsory, inference. Is it possible for the original proponent of evidence to carry his proof to the stage where if he rests, he will be entitled to a directed verdict, or its equivalent, on the issue? Undoubtedly, with a qualification to be noted, this is possible, and when it occurs there is a shifting to the adversary of the duty of going forward with the evidence, in the strictest sense. Such a ruling means that in the judge's view the proponent has not merely offered evidence from which reasonable men could draw the inference of the truth of the fact alleged, but evidence from which (in the absence of evidence from the adversary) reasonable men could not help but draw this inference. Thus, as long ago as 1770, Lord Mansfield told the jury that upon the issue of whether defendant had published a libel, proof of a sale of the book in defendant's shop was, being unrebutted, "conclusive." [42] In the case first supposed at the beginning of this sec-

tion, if the plaintiff brought forward the *direct* evidence of Jones that Smith was alive when the complaint was filed, and there is no contrary evidence at all, or if he brings forward circumstantial evidence (that is, evidence that Smith was seen alive in perfect health 10 minutes before the complaint was filed) which is, in the absence of contrary circumstances, irresistibly convincing, the jury should no more be left to refuse at will to draw the only rational inference, than they should be permitted to draw an inference from insufficient data, where the proponent has failed to sustain his initial duty of producing evidence enough to support the inference desired. Here again the ruling, from repeated occurrence of similar facts, may become a standardized one. However, the statement that one who has the duty of going forward can go forward far enough not merely to escape an adverse peremptory ruling himself, but to subject his opponent to one if the latter declines to take up the gage by producing evidence, has the following qualification. Obviously if the testimony were conflicting as to the truth of the facts from which the inference of the fact in issue is desired to be drawn, and the judge believes the inference (conceding the truth of the premise) is irresistible to rational minds, he can only make a conditional peremptory ruling. He directs the jury, if you believe the evidence that fact A is so then you must find fact B, the fact in issue. And in some jurisdictions, if the party seeking the ruling has the burden of persuasion on the issue, as assigned on the basis of the pleadings, he can only get such a conditional ruling, though his witnesses are undisputed and unimpeached.[43] But, in either event, if the infer-

---

42. Rex v. Almon, 5 Burr. 2686, 98 Eng.Rep. 411 (K.B.1770).

43. E. g., Alexander v. Tingle, 181 Md. 464, 30 A.2d 737 (1943); Hoerath v. Sloan's Moving & Storage Co., 305 S.W.2d 418 (Mo.1957). Contra, Colthurst v. Lake View State Bank of Chicago, 18 F.2d 875 (1927). See generally cases cited in Annot., 62 A.L.R.2d 1191.

ence is overwhelming, the jury is instructed not to cogitate over that, but only over the truthfulness of those who testify to the basic data.

We have seen something of the mechanics of the process of "proceeding" or "going forward" with evidence, viewed from the point of view of the *first* party who is stimulated to produce proof under threat of a ruling foreclosing a finding in his favor. He may in respect to a particular issue pass through three states of judicial hospitality: (a) where if he stops he will be thrown out of court; (b) where if he stops and his adversary does nothing, his reception will be left to the jury; and (c) where if he stops and his adversary does nothing, his victory (so far as it depends on having the inference he desires drawn) is at once proclaimed. Whenever the first producer has presented evidence sufficient to get him to the third stage and the burden of producing evidence can truly be said to have shifted, his adversary may in turn pass through the same three stages. His evidence again may be (a) insufficient to warrant a finding in his favor, (b) sufficient to warrant a finding, or (c) irresistible, if unrebutted.

339.   Satisfying the Burden of Persuasion: (a) The Measure of Persuasion in Civil Cases Generally.[44]

According to the customary formulas a party who has the burden of persuasion of a fact must prove it in criminal prosecutions "beyond a reasonable doubt,"[45] in certain exceptional controversies in civil cases, "by

clear, strong and convincing evidence,"[46] but on the general run of issues in civil cases "by a preponderance of evidence."[47] The "reasonable doubt" formula points to what we are really concerned with, the state of the jury's mind, whereas the other two divert attention to the evidence, which is a step removed, being the instrument by which the jury's mind is influenced.[48] These latter phrases, consequently, are awkward vehicles for expressing the degree of the jury's belief.[49]

What is the most acceptable meaning of the phrase, proof by a preponderance, or greater weight, of the evidence? Certainly the phrase does not mean simple volume of evidence or number of witnesses.[50] One definition is that evidence preponderates when it is more convincing to the trier than the opposing evidence. This is a simple commonsense explanation which will be un-

44. 9 Wigmore, Evidence § 2498; Morgan, Basic Problems of Evidence 21–26 (1962); Morgan, Some Problems of Proof 81–86 (1956); Ball, The Moment of Truth: Probability Theory and Standards of Proof, 14 Vand.L.Rev. 807 (1961); McBaine, Burden of Proof: Degrees of Belief, 32 Calif.L.Rev. 242 (1944); Winter, The Jury and the Risk of Nonpersuasion, 5 Law & Society Rev. 335 (1971); Annot., 93 A.L.R. 155; C.J.S. Evidence §§ 1021, 1022; Dec.Dig. Evidence ☞598, Trial ☞237.

45. See § 341, infra.

46. See § 340, infra.

47. In McBaine, supra n. 44 at 246, Prof. McBaine cogently suggests that these formulas are equivalent to statements that the trier must find that the fact is (a) almost certainly true, (b) highly probably true, and (c) probably true.

48. See Morgan, Basic Problems of Evidence, supra n. 44, at 23.

49. This may be evidenced by a recent study which showed that the jurors responding to a questionnaire asking them to express their beliefs in terms of numerical probabilities had a significantly different understanding of the phrase "by a preponderance of evidence" than did judges responding to the same questionnaire. The jurors thought the requirement called for a far greater showing of probability than did the judges. Simon, Quantifying Burdens of Proof, 5 Law & Society Rev. 319, 325 (1971). Similarly, in 1937, 843 jurors responded to a questionnaire asking the question, "What propositions of law were most difficult to understand?" Highest on the list was "preponderance of the evidence," named by 232 jurors. "Proximate cause" was second with 203. Trial by Jury (report of a conference), 11 U.Cin.L.Rev. 119, 192 n. 18 (1937).

50. Courts often specifically inform the jury that the number of witnesses is not conclusive. See e. g., Illinois Pattern Jury Instruction (Civil) 2.07 (1961); South Dakota Pattern Jury Instruction (Civil) 2.07 (1968); Livingston v. Schreckengost, 255 Iowa 1102, 125 N.W.2d 126, 131 (1963).

derstood by jurors and could hardly be misleading in the ordinary case. It may be objected, however, that it is misleading in a situation where, though one side's evidence is more convincing than the other's, the jury is still left in doubt as to the truth of the matter.[51] Compelling a decision in favor of a party who has introduced evidence that is simply better than that of his adversary would not be objectionable if we hypothesize jurors who bring none of their own experience to the trial and who thus view the evidence in a vacuum. Of course, no such case could exist.[52] We expect and encourage jurors to use their own experience to help them reach a decision, particularly in judging the credibility of witnesses.[53] That experience may tell them, for example, that although the plaintiff has introduced evidence and the defendant has offered nothing in opposition, it is still unlikely that the events occurred as contended by the plaintiff. Thus, it is entirely consistent for a court to hold that a party's evidence is sufficient to withstand a motion for directed verdict and yet to uphold a verdict for his adversary.[54]

The most acceptable meaning to be given to the expression, proof by a preponderance,

seems to be proof which leads the jury to find that the existence of the contested fact is more probable than its nonexistence.[55] Thus the preponderance of evidence becomes the trier's belief in the preponderance of probability. Some courts have boldly accepted this view.[56]

Other courts have been shocked at the suggestion that a verdict, a truth-finding, should be based on nothing stronger than an estimate of probabilities. They require that the trier must have an "actual belief"

51. See discussion by Wolfe, J., in McDonald v. Union Pac. R. Co., 109 Utah 493, 167 P.2d 685, 689 (1946) (". . . I can conceive of a case where the jury might be more convinced that the evidence of one side is nearer the truth than that of the other side and yet not feel that the evidence satisfied them as to the right to recover.") See also McBaine, supra n. 44 at 248; Trickett, Preponderance of Evidence and Reasonable Doubt, 10 The Forum, Dickinson School of Law 75, 77 (1906) quoted 9 Wigmore, Evidence § 2498 at 326.

52. See Winter, supra n. 44 at 339.

53. See, e. g., Illinois Pattern Jury Instructions (Civil) 1.04, 2.01 (1961). See also Ball, supra n. 44, at 829, where the author suggests that "instructions which tell the jury that they shall use what they know in common as men, should be juxtaposed with the direction to find 'from the evidence.'"

54. See Morgan, Basic Problems of Evidence, supra n. 44, at 22.

55. See Model Code of Evidence Rule 1(3): "'Burden of persuasion of a fact' means the burden which is discharged when the tribunal which is to determine the existence or non-existence of the fact is persuaded by sufficient evidence to find that the fact exists."; 1(5): "'Finding a fact' means determining that its existence is more probable than its non-existence . . ." See also Morgan, Some Problems of Proof, supra n. 44, at 84–85.

56. E. g., Murphy v. Waterhouse, 113 Cal. 467, 45 Pac. 866 (1896) (error to charge that jury must be "convinced"; "preponderance of probability" is sufficient); Norton v. Futrell, 149 Cal.App.2d 586, 308 P.2d 887, 891 (1957) ("The term 'probability' denotes an element of doubt or uncertainty and recognizes that where there are two choices, it is not necessary that the jury be absolutely certain or doubtless, but that it is sufficient if the choice selected is more probable than the choice rejected."); Beckwith v. Town of Stratford, 129 Conn. 506, 29 A.2d 775 (1942) (standard in civil cases is proof which produces a reasonable belief of probability of the existence of the material facts); Moffie v. Slawsby, 77 N.H. 555, 94 A. 193 (1915) (a finding that the transferee probably knew that the note was usurious is a finding that the party having the burden had satisfied the trier of fact); Livanovitch v. Livanovitch, 99 Vt. 327, 328, 131 A. 799 (1926) ("If . . . you are more inclined to believe from the evidence that he did so deliver the bonds . . . even though your belief is only the slightest degree greater than that he did not, your verdict should be for the plaintiff," approved; "a bare preponderance is sufficient though the scales drop but a feather's weight"); Washington Pattern Jury Instructions (Civil) 21.01 (1967) ("When it is said that a party has the burden of proof on any proposition . . . it means that you must be persuaded, considering all the evidence in the case, that the proposition on which he has the burden of proof is more probably true than not true.") See also discussion by Judge Maris in Burch v. Reading Co., 240 F.2d 574 (3d Cir. 1957) cert. denied 353 U.S. 965; C.J.S. Evidence § 1021 at 652, n. 99.

in, or be "convinced of" the truth of the fact by this "preponderance of evidence."[57] Does this mean that they must believe that it is certainly true? Hardly, since it is apparent that an investigation by fallible men based upon the testimony of other men, with all their defects of veracity, memory, and communication, cannot yield certainty. Does it mean a kind of mystical "hunch" that the fact must be true? This would hardly be a rational requirement. What it would most naturally be understood to mean by the jury (in the unlikely event that it should carry analysis so far) is that it must be persuaded that the truth of the fact is not merely more probable than not, but highly probable. This is more stringent than our tradition or the needs of justice warrant, and seems equivalent to the standard of "clear, strong and convincing proof," hitherto thought to be appropriate only in exceptional cases.[58]

Much of the time spent in the appellate courts over the metaphysics of "preponderance" has been wasted because of the courts' insistence upon the cabalistic word. This bemusement with word-magic is particularly apparent in the decisions dealing with the use of the word "satisfaction" or its derivatives in referring to the effect of the evidence on the jury's mind.[59] Some courts, with more logic than realism, have condemned its use as equivalent to proof beyond a reasonable doubt unless qualified by the word "reasonable".[60] Other courts have pragmatically, although perhaps reluctantly permitted its use, even without the qualification.[61] Although certainly juries should be clearly and accurately instructed with regard to the question of the measure of persuasion in civil cases, it is hard to believe that variations in language such as those involved in the courts' difficulties with the use of the word "satisfaction" lead to any differences in jurors' attitudes.[62] Thoughtfully

---

57. See the remarks of Lummus, J. in Sargent v. Massachusetts Accident Co., 307 Mass. 246, 29 N.E.2d 825, 827 (1940) ("It has been held not enough that mathematically the chances somewhat favor a proposition to be proved; for example, the fact that colored automobiles made in the current year outnumbered black ones would not warrant a finding that an undescribed automobile of the current year is colored and not black, nor would the fact that only a minority of men die of cancer warrant a finding that a particular man did not die of cancer. . . . After the evidence has been weighed, that proposition is proved by a preponderance of the evidence if it is made to appear more likely or probable in the sense that actual belief in its truth, derived from the evidence, exists in the mind or minds of the tribunal notwithstanding any doubts that may still linger there.") See also Lampe v. Franklin American, 339 Mo. 361, 96 S.W.2d 710, 723, 107 A.L.R. 465 (1936) (no error to refuse charge, "If you find and believe that it is more probable," etc., since a verdict must be based on "what the jury finds to be facts rather than what they find to be 'more probable'"); Anderson v. Chicago Brass Co., 127 Wis. 273, 106 N.W. 1077, 1079 (1906) (not only must charge require that party with burden produce evidence of greater convincing power but that "it must be such as to satisfy or convince . . . the jury of the truth of his contention.")

58. See § 340, infra.

59. See the unbelievable number of decisions on this question in Annot., 147 A.L.R. 380. The volume of cases dealing with the issue has, however, decreased considerably in more recent years. See Dec.Dig. Trial ⟳237(6).

60. Torrey v. Burney, 113 Ala. 496, 21 So. 348, 351 (1897) ("Before it can be said that the mind is 'satisfied' of the truth of a proposition, it must be relieved of all doubt or uncertainty, and this degree of conviction is not required even in criminal cases."); Nelson v. Belcher Lumber Co., 232 Ala. 116, 166 So. 808 (1936) (usual statement, "reasonably satisfies the jury by the evidence"); Rasp v. Baumbach, 223 S.W.2d 472 (Mo.1949) (the word "reasonable" essential).

61. E. g., Netzer v. Northern Pac. Ry. Co., 238 Minn. 416, 57 N.W.2d 247 (1953) cert. denied 346 U.S. 831 (not misleading when use is in conjunction with a detailed and correct instruction of fair preponderance of the evidence); McDonald v. Union Pac. Ry. Co., 109 Utah 493, 167 P.2d 685 (1946) (use permitted); Burks v. Webb, 199 Va. 296, 99 S.E.2d 629, 639 (1957) (use was harmless error but phrase "preponderance of the evidence" preferable).

62. Difficulties of language have led some courts to hold that the phrase "preponderance of evidence" is one of common knowledge and that it is not necessary to define it. See, e. g., Brunton v. Stapleton, 65 Colo. 576, 179 P. 815 (1919); Hardee

drafted pattern jury instructions should prove helpful in reducing unnecessarily spent appellate court time on these questions.[63] Where no pattern of instruction is available, however, trial judges would be wise to search for the locally accepted phraseology and to adhere to it religiously.

340. Satisfying the Burden of Persuasion: (b) Requirement of Clear and Convincing Proof.[64]

While we have seen that the traditional measure of persuasion in civil cases is by a preponderance of evidence,[65] there is a limited range of claims and contentions which the party is required to establish by a more exacting measure of persuasion. The formula varies from state to state, but among the phrases used are the following: "by clear and convincing evidence," [66] "clear, convincing and satisfactory," [67] "clear, cogent and convincing," [68] and "clear, unequivocal, satisfactory and convincing." [69] The phrasing within most jurisdictions has not become as standardized as is the "pre-

ponderance" formula, but even here the courts sometimes are surprisingly intolerant of slight variations from the approved expression.[70] No high degree of precision can be attained by these groups of adjectives. It has been persuasively suggested that they could be more simply and intelligibly translated to the jury if they were instructed that they must be persuaded that the truth of the contention is "highly probable." [71]

The requirement of proof more than usually convincing for certain types of contentions seems to have had its origins in the standards prescribed for themselves by the chancellors in determining questions of fact in equity cases,[72] but it has now been extended to certain types of actions tried before

---

v. York, 262 N.C. 237, 136 S.E.2d 582 (1964) (in the absence of a prayer for special instructions); Annot., 93 A.L.R. 155, 156.

63. See, e. g., Illinois Pattern Jury Instruction (Civil) 21.01 (1961); South Dakota Pattern Jury Instruction (Civil) 21.01 (1968); Washington Pattern Jury Instruction (Civil) 21.01 (1967). Not all pattern jury instructions on this question are helpful to the jury even though they may withstand appeal. See, e. g., Florida Standard Jury Instruction 3.9 (1967): " 'Greater weight of the evidence' means the more persuasive and convincing force and effect of the entire evidence in the case."

64. 9 Wigmore, Evidence § 2498, pp. 329–334; C.J.S. Evidence § 1023; 30 Am.Jur.2d Evidence §§ 1166, 1167; Dec.Dig. Trial ☞237(3).

65. See § 339, supra.

66. E. g., Murillo v. Hernandez, 79 Ariz. 1, 281 P.2d 786, 791 (1955) (oral trust).

67. In re Williams' Will, 256 Wis. 338, 41 N.W. 2d 191 (1950) (mental incapacity and undue influence).

68. Frazier v. Loftin, 200 Ark. 4, 137 S.W.2d 750, 752 (1940) (claim of fraud inducing signing of contract, leases and deed).

69. Capps v. Capps, 110 Utah 468, 175 P.2d 470, 473 (1946) (oral trust).

70. See, e. g., Molyneux v. Twin Falls Canal Co., 54 Idaho 619, 35 P.2d 651, 94 A.L.R. 1264 (1934) ("clear, positive, and unequivocal" imposes too heavy a burden as opposed to "clear and satisfactory" or "clear and convincing"). See also Williams v. Blue Ridge Building & Loan Ass'n, 207 N.C. 362, 177 S.E. 176 (1934) where the court, with perhaps more justification, held that the trial judge had erred in telling the jury that the words "clear, strong and convincing" proof meant that the plaintiffs "must . . . satisfy you to a moral certainty."

71. McBaine, Burden of Proof: Degrees of Belief, 32 Calif.L.Rev. 242, 246, 253–254 (1944).

72. See Henkle v. Royal Exchange Assurance Co., 1 Ves.Sen. 317, 319, 27 Eng.Rep. 1055, 1056 (Ch. 1749) (suit to reform insurance policy: relief denied for insufficiency of proofs; Lord Ch. Hardwicke: "There ought to be the strongest proof possible"); Marquis Townshend v. Stangroom, 6 Ves.Jun. 328, 333, 31 Eng.Rep. 1076 (Ch. 1801) (similar); Carpenter v. Providence Washington Ins. Co., 45 U.S. (4 How.) 185, 224 (1846) (suit in equity to require the defendant insurance company to indorse an acknowledgment of notice on the policy; held, claim of fraud fails because such a charge should be strengthened "by very satisfactory auxiliaries though not perhaps by so strong evidence as is necessary in reforming contracts.") American equity cases on the degree of proof necessary in reforming contracts are collected in 3 Pomeroy Equity Jurisprudence § 859a (5th ed., Symons, 1941). In Iowa the requirement of "clear, satisfactory and convincing" proof is limited to cases in equity. Provident Mutual Life Ins. Co. v. Bennett, 58 F.Supp. 72 (N.D.Iowa, 1944); Jamison v. Jamison, 113 Iowa 720, 84 N.W. 705 (1900).

juries, and the chancellors' cautionary maxims are now conveyed to the jury in the form of instructions on the burden of persuasion.[73]

Among the classes of cases to which this special standard of persuasion has been applied are the following: (1) charges of fraud [74] and undue influence,[75] (2) suits on oral contracts to make a will,[76] and suits to establish the terms of a lost will,[77] (3) suits for the specific performance of an oral contract,[78] (4) proceedings to set aside, reform or modify written transactions [79] or official acts [80] on grounds of fraud, mistake or incompleteness, and (5) miscellaneous types of claims and defenses,[81] varying from state

---

73. See, e. g., Minton v. Farmville-Woodward Lumber Co., 210 N.C. 422, 187 S.E. 568 (1936) (suit to establish oral trust; facts tried to jury in North Carolina); Ziegler v. Hustisford Farmers' Mut. Ins. Co., 238 Wis. 238, 298 N.W. 610 (1941) (defense of arson in action on fire insurance policy); Washington Pattern Jury Instructions (Civil) 160.02, 160.03 (1967); Dec.Dig. Trial ☞237(3). In Texas, however, where, as in North Carolina, the facts in equity as well as law issues are tried to a jury, the "clear and convincing" standard may not be prescribed in the instructions. The trial judge, moreover, may not direct a verdict if he considers the evidence not "clear and convincing," but he may use the test, in appropriate cases, to set aside a verdict. Sanders v. Harder, 148 Tex. 593, 227 S.W. 2d 206 (1950), critically noted, 28 Tex.L.Rev. 988 (1950). See also Boenker v. Boenker, 405 S.W.2d 843 (Tex.Civ.App.1966).

74. E. g., Holley Coal Co. v. Globe Ind. Co., 186 F.2d 291 (4th Cir. 1950) (suit on employees' fidelity bond, defense that plaintiff's officers colluded with embezzlers); Buzard v. Griffin, 89 Ariz. 42, 358 P.2d 155 (1961) (election fraud); Dec.Dig. Fraud ☞58(1). In some instances the policy of placing such a special burden on one who claims to be the victim of fraud is debatable. See Rice-Stix Dry Goods Co. v. Montgomery, 164 Ark. 161, 261 S.W. 325, 329 (1924) where the court said: "While fraud at law, as well as in equity, is never to be presumed and must be proved, yet in actions at law one who has the burden of proof to establish fraud meets the requirements of the rule when he proves the fraud only by a preponderance of the evidence. The same rule likewise prevails in equity, except in those cases where the rescission, cancellation, or reformation of a writing for fraud of one party and mistake of the other, or mutual mistake, is the relief sought, in which latter case, as we have stated, the proof of fraud or mistake must be clear, unequivocal, and decisive." See also Household Finance Corp. v. Altenberg, 5 Ohio St.2d 190, 214 N.E.2d 667 (1966) (no special standard in action to recover money, even where fraud is alleged).

75. E. g., In re Mazanec's Estate, 204 Minn. 406, 283 N.W. 745, 748 (1939).

76. E. g., Lindley v. Lindley, 67 N.M. 439, 356 P. 2d 455 (1960). And so of an oral gift asserted after the donor's death. Wyatt v. Moran, 81 R.I.

399, 103 A.2d 801 (1954). Apparently even stronger proof is needed of such claims in Missouri. See St. Louis Union Trust Co. v. Busch, 346 Mo. 1237, 145 S.W.2d 426 (1940) (claim of oral gift; forceful, clear and conclusive testimony which convinces the court beyond a reasonable doubt of its truthfulness).

77. E. g., In re Ainscow's Will, 42 Del. 3, 27 A.2d 363, 365 (1942). See also 7 Wigmore, Evidence § 2106.

78. E. g., Hyder v. Newcomb, 236 Ark. 231, 365 S.W.2d 271, 274 (1963) (evidence of parol contract to convey land must be clear, satisfactory and convincing); Steketee v. Steketee, 317 Mich. 100, 26 N.W.2d 724, 726 (1947) (terms of agreement must be established by convincing proof).

79. E. g., Philippine Sugar Estates Development Co. v. Government of Philippine Islands, 247 U.S. 385 (1918) (reformation of written contract for mutual mistake); Newmister v. Carmichael, 29 Wis.2d 573, 139 N.W.2d 572 (1966) (same); Carlisle v. Carlisle, 225 N.C. 462, 35 S.E.2d 418, 421 (1945) (to establish an oral trust in land taken by deed absolute); Gillock v. Holdaway, 379 Ill. 467, 41 N.E.2d 504 (1942) (to show that deed was intended as mortgage); Dec.Dig. Mortgages ☞38(2). But see, Ward v. Lyman, 108 Vt. 464, 188 A. 892, 893 (1937) ("The jurisdiction of a court of equity to reform a written instrument will be exercised only when the mistake is established by evidence so strong and conclusive as to place it beyond reasonable doubt.")

80. E. g., Bernstein v. Bernstein, 398 Ill. 52, 74 N.E. 2d 785 (1947) (proof to impeach the correctness of a notary's certificate of acknowledgment of a deed); Nichols v. Sauls' Estate, 250 Miss. 307, 165 So.2d 352 (1964) (same as to acknowledgment of power of attorney).

81. E. g., Krisher v. Duff, 331 Mich. 699, 50 N.W. 2d 332 (1951) (statutory presumption that member of owner's family was driving it with his consent can be overcome only by testimony that is clear, positive and credible and plaintiff entitled to have jury instructed to that effect: see discussion § 345, infra); In re Berge's Estate, 234 Minn. 31, 47 N.W.2d 428 (1951) (to establish oral contract to adopt); Vaux v. Hamilton, 103 N.W.2d 291 (N.D. 1960) (negligence action; where agency is denied must be proved by clear, convincing and satisfactory evidence); Marcum v. Zaring, 406 P.2d 970 (Okl.1965) (invalidity of marriage); Stevenson v. Stein, 412 Pa. 478, 195 A.2d 268 (1963) (to prove

to state, where there is thought to be special danger of deception, or where the court considers that the particular type of claim should be disfavored on policy grounds.

The appellate court, under the classical equity practice, tried the facts *de novo,* upon the deposition testimony in the record, and thus it was called on to apply anew the standard of clear and convincing proof in its study of the evidence. But in the modern system there are usually restrictions upon appellate review of a judge's findings of fact, even in equity issues. Thus, in the federal courts under Rule 52(a) his findings will only be reversed when "clearly erroneous." And in jury-tried cases the verdict will be reviewed only to the extent of determining whether there was evidence from which reasonable men could have found the verdict. Will the appellate court, then, today, if there was substantial evidence from which the judge or jury could have made the findings it did, consider the question whether the evidence met the "clear and convincing" standard, in a case where it applies? On the one side is the argument that the judge or jury, seeing the witnesses, had superior opportunities to assess their convincingness, [82] and on the other the view that rules

should be so shaped as to free the courts of last resort to employ most effectively their wisdom and sense of justice.[83]

341. Satisfying the Burden of Persuasion: (c) Proof Beyond a Reasonable Doubt.[84]

As we have seen with reference to civil cases, a lawsuit is essentially a search for probabilities. A margin of error must be anticipated in any such search. Mistakes will be made and in a civil case a mistaken judgment for the plaintiff is no worse than a mistaken judgment for the defendant. However, this is not the case in a criminal action. Society has judged that it is significantly worse for an innocent man to be found guilty of a crime than for a guilty man to go free. The consequences to the life, liberty and good name of the accused from an erroneous conviction of a crime are usually more serious than the effects of an erroneous judgment in a civil case. Therefore, as stated by the Supreme Court in recognizing the inevitability of error even in criminal cases, "[w]here one party has at stake an interest of transcending value—as a criminal defend-

---

Valley Ranches, Inc. v. Small, 90 Idaho 354, 411 P.2d 943 (1966). See also Dec.Dig. Appeal and Error ⬚1009(4).

83. See dissenting opinion of Judge Traynor in Beeler v. American Trust Co., supra n. 82; Note, Appellate Review in Federal Courts of Findings Requiring More than a Preponderance, 60 Harv.L. Rev. 111, 118 (1946). Examples of cases where the appellate courts have imposed their own measure of "clear and convincing proof" to reverse the finding below include: Equitable Life Assur. Soc. v. Aaron, 108 F.2d 777 (6th Cir. 1940) (reformation of policy); Langford v. Sigmon, 292 Ky. 650, 167 S.W.2d 820 (1943) (oral trust in land conveyed); Hurst v. Stowers, 399 P.2d 477 (Okl. 1965) (adverse possession). The problem discussed in the text is quite similar to the question of the relationship of the measure of proof to the burden of producing evidence, discussed above, § 338, text accompanying nn. 35–38. See also, Morgan, Basic Problems of Evidence 24–26 (1962).

84. 9 Wigmore, Evidence § 2497; Morgan, Some Problems of Proof 85 (1956); McBaine, Burden of Proof: Degrees of Belief, 32 Calif.L.Rev. 242, 255 (1944); C.J.S. Criminal Law §§ 566–578, §§ 1267–1284; Dec.Dig. Criminal Law ⬚326–336, 789.

---

adverse possession; "credible, clear and definitive proof"); Wilson v. Wilson, 145 Tex. 607, 201 S.W. 2d 226 (1947) (presumption that property acquired during marriage is community property can only be overcome by clear and satisfactory evidence); King v. Prudential Ins. Co., 13 Wash.2d 414, 125 P.2d 282 (1942) (services by daughter in father's shop presumed gratuitous and presumption could not be overcome except by clear and convincing evidence).

82. See, e. g., Beeler v. American Trust Co., 24 Cal.2d 1, 147 P.2d 583 (1944) (review of judge's findings); Davis v. Pursel, 55 Colo. 287, 134 P. 107 (1913) (review of findings of judge and jury). In both these cases the lower court found that deeds were intended as mortgages and on appeal it was held that, there being substantial evidence, it was for the trial court alone to decide whether the evidence was clear and convincing. Examples of more recent, similar cases are: Buck v. Jewett, 170 Cal.App.2d 115, 338 P.2d 507 (1959); Gem-

ant his liberty—this margin of error is reduced as to him by the process of placing on the other party the burden . . . of persuading the factfinder at the conclusion of the trial of his guilt beyond a reasonable doubt." [85] In so doing, the courts have undoubtedly increased the total number of mistaken decisions in criminal cases, but with the worthy goal of decreasing the number of one kind of mistake—conviction of the innocent.[86]

The demand for a higher degree of persuasion in criminal cases was recurrently expressed from ancient times,[87] but its crystallization into the formula "beyond a reasonable doubt" seems to have occurred as late as 1798.[88] It is now accepted in common law jurisdictions as the measure of persuasion by which the prosecution must convince the trier of all the essential elements of guilt. In 1970, the Supreme Court explicitly held that the due process clause "protects the accused against conviction except upon proof beyond a reasonable doubt of every fact necessary to constitute the crime with which he is charged."[89]

A simple instruction that the jury will acquit if they have a reasonable doubt of the defendant's guilt of the crime charged in the indictment is ordinarily sufficient.[90] Courts, however, frequently paint the lily by giving the jury a definition of "reasonable doubt." A famous early instance was the oft-echoed statement of Chief Justice Shaw in the trial of Prof. Webster for the murder of Dr. Parkman: "It is that state of the case, which, after the entire comparison and consideration of all the evidence, leaves the minds of jurors in that condition that they cannot say they feel an abiding conviction, to a moral certainty, of the truth of the charge." [91] It is an ancient maxim that all definitions are dangerous and this one has been caustically criticized as raising more questions than it answers.[92] Other definitions, often more carefully balanced to warn against the overstressing of merely possible or imaginary doubts, have become customary in some jurisdictions.[93] Reasonable

---

85. Speiser v. Randall, 357 U.S. 513, 525–526 (1958). See also In re Winship, 397 U.S. 358, 369–372 (1970) (concurring opinion by Harlan, J.).

86. See Ball, The Moment of Truth: Probability Theory and Standards of Proof, 14 Vand.L.Rev. 807, 816 (1961). See also Kaplan, Decision Theory and the Factfinding Process, 20 Stan.L.Rev. 1065, 1073–1077 (1968); Winter, The Jury and the Risk of Nonpersuasion, 5 Law & Society Rev. 335, 339–343 (1971).

87. Thayer, Preliminary Treatise on Evidence 558, 559 (1898) quotes passages in Corpus Juris, dating from the fourth century, and from Coke's 3d Institute, to this effect.

88. "Its first appearance, so far as we have been able to determine, was in the high-treason cases tried in Dublin in 1798, as reported by MacNally [Rules of Evidence on Pleas of the Crown; Dublin, 1802], who was himself counsel for the defense. 'It may also,' he says, 'at this day, be considered a rule of law, that, if the jury entertain a reasonable doubt upon the truth of the testimony of witnesses given upon the issue they are sworn well and truly to try, they are bound' to acquit." May, Reasonable Doubt in Civil and Criminal Cases, 10 Am.L.Rev. 642, 656 (1876) quoted in Note, 69 U.S.L.Rev. 169, 172 (1935).

89. In re Winship, supra n. 85, at 364. In that case, the Court held that proof beyond a reasonable doubt is among the essentials of due process and fair treatment required during the adjudicatory stage when a juvenile is charged with an act which would constitute a crime if committed by an adult.

The jury is not required to believe each fact in an aggregate of circumstantial evidence beyond a reasonable doubt. People v. Klinkenberg, 90 Cal.App. 2d 608, 204 P.2d 47, 62 (1949); State v. Raine, 93 Idaho 862, 477 P.2d 104 (1970); State v. Barry, 93 N.H. 10, 34 A.2d 661, 663 (1943) (not essential that each fact bearing on identity be established beyond reasonable doubt). Or facts unrelated to guilt, such as venue. Barragan v. State, 141 Tex.Cr.R. 12, 147 S.W.2d 254, 256 (1941).

90. See, e. g., State v. Lafferty, 416 S.W.2d 157 (Mo. 1967); Illinois Pattern Jury Instructions (Criminal) 2.03, 2.05 (1968).

91. Commonwealth v. Webster, 59 Mass. (5 Cush.) 295, 320 (1850).

92. Trickett, Preponderance and Reasonable Doubt, 10 The Forum, Dickinson School of Law, 76 (1906) quoted, 9 Wigmore, Evidence § 2497 at 322.

93. They are set out by the hundreds in Dec.Dig. Criminal Law ☞789 and in 36 Words and Phrases 483–544 (Perm. Ed. 1962).

doubt is a term in common use almost as familiar to jurors as to lawyers. As one judge has said, it needs a skillful definer to make it plainer by multiplication of words,[94] and as another has expressed it, the explanations themselves often need more explanation than the term explained.[95] A definition in terms locally approved is proper, but if not requested by accused is not required.[96] Whether if so requested it is the judge's duty to define the term, is a matter of dispute,[97]

but the wiser view seems to be that it lies in his discretion,[98] which should ordinarily be exercised by declining to define, unless the jury itself asks for a fuller explanation.[99]

There are certain excuses or justifications allowed to the defendant, which although provable for the most part under the plea of not guilty, are spoken of for some purposes as "affirmative defenses." [1] Among these are self-defense,[2] duress,[3] insanity,[4] intoxication [5] and claims that the accused is within an exception or proviso in the statute defining the crime.[6] The older decisions and treatises [7] placed the "burden of proof" upon matters of justification or excuse upon the accused, without discrimination between the two meanings, of producing evidence and of persuading, and many statutes still retain

94. Newman, J. in Hoffman v. State, 97 Wis. 571, 73 N.W. 51, 52 (1897).

95. Mitchell, J. in State v. Sauer, 38 Minn. 438, 38 N.W. 355 (1888) referring to the definition, "a doubt for which you can give a reason," said, "Like many other definitions of the term which have been given, it does not define, but itself requires definition. The most serious objection to it is that it is liable to be understood as meaning a doubt for which a juror could express or state a reason in words. A juror may, after a consideration and comparison of all the evidence, feel a reasonable doubt as to the guilt of a defendant, and yet find it difficult to state the reason for the doubt. The term 'reasonable doubt' is almost incapable of any definition which will add much to what the words themselves imply. In fact it is easier to state what it is not than what it is; and it may be doubted whether any attempt to define it will not be more likely to confuse than to enlighten a jury. A man is the best judge of his own feelings, and he knows for himself whether he doubts better than any one else can tell him. Where any explanation of what is meant by a reasonable doubt is required, it is safer to adopt some definition which has already received the general approval of the authorities, especially those in our own state."

96. See, e. g., State v. Hall, 267 N.C. 90, 147 S.E. 2d 548 (1966) and cases cited C.J.S. Criminal Law § 1268 at 657, n. 63. See also People v. Cagle, 41 Ill.2d 528, 244 N.E.2d 200, 204 (1969) ("This court has repeatedly held that the legal concept of 'reasonable doubt' needs no definition, and that where an involved instruction on that concept is given it may be deemed prejudicial error [citing cases].").

97. Recognizing a duty are Mundy v. United States, 85 U.S.App.D.C. 120, 176 F.2d 32 (1949) (here waived by failure to request); Blatt v. United States, 60 F.2d 481 (3d Cir. 1932) (reversal for refusal to define); Friedman v. United States, 381 F.2d 155 (8th Cir. 1967) (duty recognized; given charge approved).

No duty: Jackson v. State, 225 Ga. 553, 170 S.E.2d 281 (1969); State v. Velsir, 61 Wyo. 476, 159 P.2d 371 (1945). For cases pro and con, see Dec.Dig. Criminal Law ⊂⇒789(3).

98. E. g., State v. Broome, 268 N.C. 298, 150 S.E.2d 416 (1966).

99. Pattern jury instructions defining reasonable doubt include California Jury Instruction (Criminal) 21 (1958); North Carolina Pattern Instructions (Criminal) 101.10 (1971).

1. 9 Wigmore, Evidence §§ 2501, 2512, 2514; 22A C.J.S. Criminal Law §§ 572–577; Dec.Dig. Criminal Law ⊂⇒329–333.

2. E. g., Brown v. State, 48 Del. 427, 105 A.2d 646 (1954); see also cases collected C.J.S Homicide § 195.

3. E. g., State v. Sappienza, 84 Ohio St. 63, 95 N.E. 381 (1911).

4. E. g., State v. Finn, 257 Minn. 138, 100 N.W.2d 508 (1960).

5. E. g., State v. Church, 169 N.W.2d 889 (Iowa 1969).

6. E. g., State v. Tonnisen, 92 N.J.Super. 452, 224 A.2d 21 (1966) (separate proviso clause).

7. See, e. g., Rex v. Greenacre, 8 Car. & P. 35, 42, 173 Eng.Rep. 338 (1837) ("where it appears that one person's death has been occasioned by the hand of another, it behooves that other to show from evidence, or by inference from the circumstances of the case, that the offence is of a mitigated character, and does not amount to the crime of murder"); Foster, Crown Law 255 (1762) ("In every charge of murder, the fact of killing being first proved, all the circumstances of accident, necessity, or infirmity are to be satisfactorily proved by the prisoner, unless they arise out of the evidence produced against him; for the law presumeth the fact to have been founded in malice, until the contrary appeareth.")

this form of expression.[8] A few states place both the burden of first producing evidence and the burden of persuasion upon the defendant as to some of the defenses.[9] This practice is most prevalent in respect to the defense of insanity, a plea which many courts evidently feel is to be disfavored on policy grounds.[10] Although most states assigning this burden to the defendant require proof only by a preponderance of the evidence,[11] the Supreme Court has held constitutional the allocation of the burden of persuasion to the defendant even in a case in which the defendant was required to establish his insanity beyond a reasonable doubt.[12] Attempts to assign the burden of persuasion to the defendant to prove an alibi have not had the same reception. One United States Court of Appeals has struck down such a state court practice as violative of due process[13] and the Supreme Court has at least suggested its approval of that opinion.[14] Certainly there is at least a superficial difference between the defense of insanity and the claim of alibi. Alibi, although sometimes characterized as an affirmative defense,[15] is not really a defense in the same sense as, for example, insanity or duress—a justification for admitted conduct. Rather, an alibi is better characterized as a mere form of denial of participation in the criminal act.[16]

The above distinction between an alibi and a claim of insanity is presently sufficient for the purpose of testing the constitutionality of a state procedure. However, it is not persuasive as a reason for assigning the burden of persuasion with regard to even the traditionally labeled affirmative defenses to the

---

8. See, e. g., West's Ann.Cal.Pen.Code, § 1105 (1970): "Upon a trial for murder, the commission of the homicide being proved, the burden of proving circumstances of mitigation, or that justify or excuse it devolves upon him . . . "; Vernon's Tex.Ann. P.C. art. 46 (1952): "When the facts have been proved which constitute the offense, it devolves upon the accused to establish the facts or circumstances on which he relies to excuse or justify the prohibited act or omission."

9. The cases cited in notes 2–6, supra, so hold.

10. See generally cases cited in Annot., 17 A.L.R.3d 146, 195–221. The practice stems from the classic McNaghten's Case, 10 Cl. & Fin. 200, 8 Eng.Rep. 718 (1843) ("the jurors ought to be told that every man is presumed to be sane and to possess a sufficient degree of reason to be responsible for his crime until the contrary be proved to their satisfaction").

11. E. g., State v. Park, 159 Me. 328, 193 A.2d 1 (1963); State v. McCauley, 130 W.Va. 401, 43 S.E. 2d 454 (1947).

12. Leland v. Oregon, 343 U.S. 790 (1952). For interesting recent discussions of the *Leland* case with reference to the constitutional limitations upon the creation and effect of affirmative defenses, see Ashford and Risinger, Presumptions, Assumptions, and Due Process in Criminal Cases: A Theoretical Overview, 79 Yale L.J. 165, 186–193, 202–203 (1969); Christie and Pye, Presumptions and Assumptions in the Criminal Law: Another View, 1970 Duke L.J. 919, 933–938. See also Working Papers of the National Commission on Reform of Federal Criminal Laws, Volume 1, 18–19 (1970) (issued in connection with the Study Draft of a New Federal Criminal Code). Questions with regard to the constitutionality of affirmative defenses, particularly as compared to presumptions, are further discussed in § 346, notes 92–95 and accompanying text, infra. Cf. Speiser v. Randall, 357 U.S. 513 (1958) where

the Court held that a California statute denying a tax exemption to persons advocating the overthrow of the government, etc., violated due process by placing on the taxpayer the burdens of proving that he was not a person falling within the group denied the exemption.

13. Stump v. Bennett, 398 F.2d 111 (8th Cir. 1968) cert. denied 393 U.S. 1001, striking down an Iowa practice. Iowa has discontinued the practice. State v. Galloway, 167 N.W.2d 89 (Iowa 1969).

14. In Johnson v. Bennett, 393 U.S. 253 (1968), a case involving the same Iowa practice was vacated and remanded to the Eighth Circuit for consideration in light of Stump v. Bennett, supra, n. 13. The Eighth Circuit then applied its holding in the *Stump* case to the *Johnson* case. 414 F.2d 50 (8th Cir. 1969).

Despite the rulings in the *Stump* and *Johnson* cases, the Georgia courts have refused to hold that the practice of requiring the defendant to establish his alibi to the "reasonable satisfaction" of the jury violates due process. See, e. g., Thornton v. State, 226 Ga. 837, 178 S.E.2d 193 (1970). The United States District Courts in Georgia have, however, taken a different view. See Smith v. Smith, 321 F.Supp. 482 (N.D.Ga.1970).

15. See, e. g., People v. Silvia, 389 Ill. 346, 59 N.E. 2d 821 (1945).

16. See Stump v. Bennett, supra n. 13, at 116.

defendant. As to all these claims for exoneration, their truth goes in final analysis to the guilt, to the rightness of punishing, the accused. Thus it seems inconsistent to demand as to some elements of guilt, such as an act of killing, that the jury be convinced beyond a reasonable doubt, and as to others, such as duress or capacity to know right from wrong, the jury may convict though they have such doubt. Accordingly, the recent trend is to treat these so-called matters of defense as situations wherein the accused will usually have the first burden of producing evidence in order that the issue be raised and submitted to the jury, but at the close of the evidence the jury must be told that if they have a reasonable doubt of the element thus raised they must acquit.[17]

Despite occasional statements to the contrary,[18] the reasonable doubt standard generally has been held inapplicable in civil cases, regardless of the nature of the issue involved.[19] For example, when a charge of crime is at issue in a civil action, the threatened consequences of sustaining the accusation, though often uncommonly harmful to purse or prestige, are not generally as serious as in a prosecution for the crime. Accordingly the modern American cases have come around to the view that in the interest of justice and simplicity a reasonable doubt measure of persuasion will not be imposed.[20] Most courts have said that a preponderance of the evidence is sufficient,[21] although some have increased the standard to "clear and convincing."[22]

342. Presumptions: In General.[23]

One ventures the assertion that "presumption" is the slipperiest member of the family

---

17. In the case of insanity, some courts have stated that the prosecution's initial burden of producing evidence is satisfied by a "presumption of sanity." (See § 342, n. 43; § 346 notes 90–91 and accompanying text, infra.). The burden of producing evidence to rebut that presumption is then shifted to the defendant. Once the defendant's burden of going forward is satisfied, the prosecution is assigned the burden of proving legal sanity beyond a reasonable doubt. See, e. g., Hartford v. United States, 362 F.2d 63, 64 (9th Cir. 1966) cert. denied 385 U.S. 883 (1966); State v. Martin, 102 Ariz. 142, 426 P.2d 639 (1967). The same results have been achieved with regard to other defenses without reference to a presumption, see, e. g., State v. Currie, 267 Minn. 294, 126 N.W.2d 389 (1964) (withdrawal from a scheme); Jenkins v. State, 80 Okl. Cr. 328, 161 P.2d 90, 162 P.2d 336 (1945) (self-defense). See also Illinois Pattern Jury Instructions (Criminal), Chapter 24 (1968). See also Christie and Pye, supra n. 12 at 934, 936.

Proposed New Federal Criminal Code § 103 divides what have been here referred to generally as affirmative defenses into (1) defenses, which need not be negated by the prosecution unless "the issue is in the case as a result of evidence sufficient to raise a reasonable doubt on the issue," and (2) affirmative defenses, which must be proved by the defendant by a preponderance of evidence. See Final Report of the National Commission on Reform of Federal Criminal Laws 3 (1971).

18. See, e. g., St. Louis Union Trust Co. v. Busch, 346 Mo. 1237, 145 S.W.2d 426, 430 (1940) ("It is a general rule that a gift, inter vivos, sought to be established after the alleged donor's death, must

be proven by forceful, clear and conclusive testimony which convinces the court beyond a reasonable doubt of its truthfulness.")

19. See 9 Wigmore, Evidence § 2498.

20. See, e. g., Sundquist v. Hardware Mut. Fire Ins. Co., 371 Ill. 360, 21 N.E.2d 297, 124 A.L.R. 1375 (1939) (suit on fire policy, defense of false statement by assured; abandons earlier rule in Illinois, and reviews similar shift of decisions elsewhere); Sivley v. American National Ins. Co., 454 S.W.2d 799 (Tex.Civ.App.1970) (drunk driving). See also cases cited in Annot., 124 A.L.R. 1378; Dec.Dig. Evidence ☞596(2).

21. See cases cited n. 20, supra.

22. See, e. g., Ziegler v. Hustisford Farmers' Mut. Ins. Co., 238 Wis. 238, 298 N.W. 610 (1941) (suit on fire policy, defense, arson by insured; court correctly placed burden on defendant by "clear and satisfactory evidence.")

There are varying views on the necessary measure of persuasion in civil actions with criminal overtones, such as disbarment proceedings. In disbarment proceedings, most courts seem to reject the reasonable doubt standard as the measure of proof, but are divided upon whether "preponderance" or "clear and convincing" is the measure. Compare, In re Trask, 46 Haw. 404, 380 P.2d 751 (1963) (preponderance) with In re Farris, 229 Ore. 209, 367 P.2d 387 (1961) (clear and convincing). See also cases cited at C.J.S. Attorney and Client § 33(3).

23. 9 Wigmore, Evidence §§ 2490–2492; Morgan, Basic Problems of Evidence 31–32 (1962); Thayer, Preliminary Treatise on Evidence, ch. 8 (1898);

of legal terms, except its first cousin, "burden of proof." One author has listed no less than eight senses in which the term has been used by the courts.[24] Agreement can probably be secured to this extent, however: a presumption is a standardized practice, under which certain facts are held to call for uniform treatment with respect to their effect as proof of other facts.

Returning for a moment to the discussion of satisfying the burden of producing evidence,[25] assume that a party having the burden of producing evidence of fact A, introduces proof of fact B. The judge, using ordinary reasoning, may determine that fact A might reasonably be inferred from fact B, and therefore that the party has satisfied his burden, or as sometimes put by the courts, has made out a "prima facie" case.[26] The judge has not used a presumption in the sense of a standardized practice, but rather has simply relied upon a rational inference. However, in ruling on a motion for directed verdict the judge may go beyond his own mental processes and experience and find that prior decisions or existing statutes have established that proof of fact B is sufficient to permit the jury to infer the existence of fact A. He has thus used a standardized practice but has he necessarily used a presumption? Although some courts have described such a standardized inference as a presumption,[27] most legal scholars have disagreed.[28] They have saved the term to describe a significantly different sort of a rule, one that dictates not only that the establishment of fact B is sufficient to satisfy a party's burden of producing evidence with regard to fact A, but also at least compels the shifting of the burden of producing evidence on the question to his adversary. Under this view, if proof of fact B is introduced and a presumption exists to the effect that fact A can be inferred from fact B, the party denying the existence of fact A must then introduce proof of its nonexistence or risk having a verdict directed against him. Further, many authorities state that a true presumption should not only shift the burden of producing evidence, but also require that the party denying the existence of the presumed fact assume the burden of persuasion on the issue as well. The question of whether the only effect of a presumption should be to shift the burden of producing evidence or whether it also should operate to allocate the burden of persuasion will be discussed below.[29]

Certainly the description of a presumption as a rule that, at a minimum, shifts the burden of producing evidence is to be preferred, at least in civil cases.[30] Inferences that a trial judge decides may reasonably be drawn from the evidence need no other

---

Gausewitz, Presumptions in a One-Rule World, 5 Vand.L.Rev. 324 (1952); C.J.S. Evidence §§ 114–118; Dec.Dig. Evidence ⊙—53–89.

24. Laughlin, In Support of the Thayer Theory of Presumptions, 52 Mich.L.Rev. 195, 196–207 (1953).

25. See § 338, supra.

26. The term "prima facie case" is often used in two senses and is therefore an ambiguous and often misleading term. It may mean evidence that is simply sufficient to get to the jury, or it may mean evidence that is sufficient to shift the burden of producing evidence. See 9 Wigmore, Evidence § 2494. The term is used here in its former sense —evidence that is simply sufficient to withstand a motion for directed verdict. This is the meaning also used in § 103(5) of the proposed Federal Criminal Code. Final Report, National Commission on Reform of Federal Criminal Laws (1971).

27. E. g., Hunt v. Eure, 189 N.C. 482, 127 S.E. 593, 597 (1925): "A presumption of negligence, when establishing a prima facie case, is still only evidence of negligence for the consideration of the jury, and the burden of the issue remains on the plaintiff."

28. E. g., Thayer, supra n. 23, at 317, 321, 326; 9 Wigmore, Evidence § 2490. See also Morgan, supra n. 23, at 32.

29. See § 345, infra.

30. See, e. g., Uniform Rule 13: "A presumption is an assumption of fact resulting from a rule of law which requires such fact to be assumed from another fact or group of facts found or otherwise established in the action." See also F.R.Ev. 301 (R.D. 1971); West's Ann.Cal.Evid.Code, § 600(a).

description, even though the judge relies upon precedent or a statute rather than his own experience in reaching his decision. In most instances, the application of any other label to an inference will only cause confusion.[31] In criminal cases, however, there are rules that traditionally have been labeled presumptions, even though they do not operate to shift even the burden of producing evidence. A true shifting of the burden of producing evidence to the defendant in a criminal case would mean that the court would be compelled to direct the jury to find against him with regard to the presumed fact if he fails to introduce sufficient proof on the issue. As will be discussed below, a directed verdict or a peremptory ruling against the accused in a criminal case, even as to a single element of the crime, is abhorrent to the criminal law. Therefore, modern draftsmen, while retaining the term presumption for criminal cases, have reduced the effect of presumptions in those cases to that of a standardized inference. The jury is permitted but not required to accept the existence of the presumed fact even in the absence of contrary evidence.[32] The term presumption will be used in this text in the preferred sense discussed above in referring to civil cases, but with the qualification suggested in referring to criminal cases.

There are rules of law that are often incorrectly called presumptions that should be specifically distinguished from presumptions at this point:

Conclusive presumptions. The term presumption as used above always denotes a rebuttable presumption, i. e., the party against whom the presumption operates can always introduce proof in contradiction. In the case of what is commonly called a conclusive or irrebuttable presumption, when fact B is proven, fact A must be taken as true, and the adversary is not allowed to dispute this at all. For example, if it is proven that a child is under seven years of age, the courts have stated that it is conclusively presumed that he could not have committed a felony. In so doing, the courts are not stating a presumption at all, but simply expressing the rule of law that someone under seven years old cannot legally be convicted of a felony.[33]

Res ipsa loquitur. Briefly and perhaps oversimply stated, res ipsa loquitur is a rule that provides that a plaintiff may satisfy his burden of producing evidence of a defendant's negligence by proving that he has been injured by a casualty of a sort that normally would not have occurred in the absence of the defendant's negligence.[34] Although a few jurisdictions have given the doctrine the effect of a true presumption even to the extent of using it to assign the burden of persuasion,[35] most courts agree that it simply

---

31. In the first edition of this text, Dean McCormick used the term "permissive presumption" to describe a rule of law that held that a fact was sufficient to warrant, but not require, a desired inference. Some cases use the term "presumption of fact" to describe the same sort of rule. See, e. g., Bradley v. S. L. Savidge, Inc., 13 Wash.2d 28, 123 P.2d 780 (1942). For the reasons set forth in the text, both of these labels are here rejected. Certainly, standardized inferences are valuable to the law and there are times when courts will specifically want to bring their existence to the attention of the jury. However, their value will remain intact and the jury may still be informed of their existence when it is beneficial to do so, without the need to refer to them by a label that implies that they have a greater procedural effect than the one with which they are naturally endowed. See discussion with regard to res ipsa loquitur, this section, below.

32. See § 346, notes 96–2 and accompanying text, infra.

33. See Morgan, supra n. 23, at 31; 9 Wigmore, Evidence § 2492.

34. See Prosser, Torts §§ 39, 40 (4th ed. 1971); 2 Harper and James, Law of Torts §§ 19.5–19.12 (1956); James, Proof of the Breach in Negligence Cases, 37 Va.L.Rev. 179, 194–228 (1951); Prosser, Res Ipsa Loquitur in California, 37 Calif.L.Rev. 183 (1949); 9 Wigmore, Evidence § 2509.

35. See, e. g., Weiss v. Axler, 137 Colo. 544, 328 P. 2d 88 (1958); Prosser, Torts, supra n. 34, at 230–231. Prosser states that the burden of persuasion

describes an inference of negligence.[36] Prosser calls it a "simple matter of circumstantial evidence." [37] Most frequently, the inference called for by the doctrine is one that a court would properly have held to be reasonable even in the absence of a special rule. Where this is so, res ipsa loquitur certainly need be viewed no differently from any other inference.[38] Moreover, even where the doctrine is artificial—where it is imposed for reasons of policy rather than logic [39]—it nevertheless remains only an inference, permitting but not requiring, the jury to find negligence. The only difference is that where res ipsa loquitur is artificially imposed, there is better reason for informing the jury of the permissibility of the inference than there is in the case where the doctrine simply describes a ra-

tional inference. Although theoretically a jury instruction of this kind might be viewed as violating a state rule prohibiting comment on the evidence, the courts have had little difficulty with the problem and have consistently approved and required, where requested, instructions that tell the jury that a finding of negligence is permissible.[40] Obviously these instructions can and should be given without the use of the misnomer "presumption".

The presumption of innocence. Assignments of the burdens of proof prior to trial are not based on presumptions. Before trial no evidence has been introduced from which other facts are to be inferred. The assignment is made on the basis of a rule of substantive law providing that one party or the other ought to have one or both of the burdens with regard to an issue.[41] In some instances, however, these substantive rules are incorrectly referred to as presumptions. The most glaring example of this mislabeling is the "presumption of innocence" as the phrase is used in criminal cases.[42] The

may properly be shifted to the defendant for reasons of policy in certain res ipsa loquitur cases such as those in which the defendant (e. g., a carrier) owed a special responsibility to plaintiff. He adds, however, that for these same policy reasons, the burden of persuasion "should rest upon [the defendant] even when the plaintiff offers the direct testimony of eyewitnesses; and such a policy does not seem properly to be connected with res ipsa loquitur at all."

36. E. g., Sweeney v. Erving, 228 U.S. 233, 240 (1913) (injury to patient from X-ray machine; held, no error to refuse charge that placed burden of persuasion on defendant; "res ipsa loquitur means that the facts of the occurrence warrant the inference, not that they compel such an inference.") See also Gardner v. Coca Cola Bottling Co., 267 Minn. 505, 127 N.W.2d 557 (1964).

37. Prosser, Torts, supra n. 34, at 231.

38. As in the case of any inference, on occasion res ipsa loquitur may have such rational force as to compel a shifting of the burden of producing evidence and a directed verdict for the plaintiff if defendant does not satisfy the shifted burden. See, e. g., Alabama & V. R. Co. v. Groome, 97 Miss. 201, 52 So. 703 (1910); Whitley v. Hix, 207 Tenn. 683, 343 S.W.2d 851 (1961). Such a shift is not artificial in the sense that it is imposed for policy reasons. It occurs simply as a result of the logical strength of plaintiff's case. See discussion § 338, supra.

39. See, e. g., Ybarra v. Spangard, 25 Cal.2d 486, 154 P.2d 687 (1944) (unconscious patient permitted to have benefit of res ipsa loquitur against all the doctors and hospital employees involved despite fact that not all could reasonably have been held responsible).

40. See, e. g., Powell v. Moore, 228 Ore. 255, 364 P.2d 1094 (1961) (instruction on res ipsa loquitur permissible). See also Centennial Mills, Inc. v. Benson, 234 Ore. 512, 383 P.2d 103 (1963) where the court recognized the rule of the *Powell* case as an exception to the general rule prohibiting instructions on inferences. For other cases permitting or requiring an instruction that an inference of negligence is warranted in a res ipsa loquitur case see Annot., 173 A.L.R. 880. For an example of the form of such an instruction see Illinois Pattern Jury Instructions (Civil) 22.01 (1961).

41. See § 337, supra.

42. The above discussion refers only to the common use of the term in reference to the accused in criminal cases. Although there may be a true presumption of innocence with regard to charges of misconduct or crime in civil cases or in criminal cases with regard to alleged crimes collaterally involved, most courts using the phrase in these cases are probably only talking about an inference of innocence. The language is usually ambiguous; e. g., TRW, Inc. v. NLRB, 393 F.2d 771, 774 (6th Cir. 1968) (". . . it must be presumed in the absence of evidence, that one who chooses to exercise a right conferred by law intends to exercise that right in a legal manner."); Moroni v. Brawders, 317 Mass. 48, 57 N.E.2d

phrase is probably better called the "assumption of innocence" in that it describes our assumption that, in the absence of contrary facts, it is to be assumed that any person's conduct upon a given occasion was lawful.[43] In criminal cases, the "presumption of innocence" has been adopted by judges as a convenient introduction to the statement of the burdens upon the prosecution, first of producing evidence of the guilt of the accused and, second, of finally persuading the jury or judge of his guilt beyond a reasonable doubt. Most courts insist on the inclusion of the phrase in the charge to the jury,[44] despite the fact that at that point it consists of nothing more than an amplification of the prosecution's burden of persuasion. Although the phrase is technically inaccurate and perhaps even misleading in the sense that it suggests that there is some inherent probability that the defendant is in-

nocent, it should not be discarded.[45] Like the requirement of proof beyond a reasonable doubt, it at least indicates to the jury that if a mistake is to be made it should be made in favor of the accused, or as Wigmore stated, "the term does convey a special and perhaps useful hint . . . in that it cautions the jury to put away from their minds all the suspicion that arises from the arrest, the indictment, and the arraignment, and to reach their conclusion solely from the legal evidence adduced." [46]

343. Reasons for the Creation of Presumptions: Illustrative Presumptions.[47]

A presumption shifts the burden of producing evidence, and as we shall see, under the preferable view operates to assign the burden of persuasion as well. Therefore naturally, the reasons for creating particular presumptions are similar to the considerations, which have already been discussed,[48] that bear upon the initial or tentative assignment of those burdens.[49] Thus, just as the burdens of proof are sometimes allocated for reasons of fairness, some presumptions are created to correct an imbalance resulting from one party's superior ac-

---

14, 18 (1944) ("[The presumption of innocence] is not only a technical presumption, one 'of law', but is also . . . a presumption 'of fact,' which means that an inference that conduct is of that sort is warranted even when not required."); Immerman v. Ostertag, 83 N.J.Super. 364, 199 A.2d 869, 874 (1964) ("Ordinarily there is a reasonable presumption that individuals would not commit a crime as serious as perjury or false swearing. However, that presumption loses its force where, as here, the evidence shows that the persons in question lack respect for the truth.")

43. "In the first place, the so-called presumption of innocence is not, strictly speaking, a presumption in the sense of an inference deduced from a given premise. It is more accurately an assumption which has for its purpose the placing of the burden of proof upon anyone who asserts any deviation from the socially desirable ideal of good moral conduct." Alexander, J., in Carr v. State, 192 Miss. 152, 4 So.2d 887, 888 (1941). See also Ashford and Risinger, Presumptions, Assumptions and Due Process in Criminal Cases, A Theoretical Overview, 79 Yale L.J. 165, 173 (1969).

44. A leading case is Commonwealth v. Madeiros, 255 Mass. 304, 151 N.E. 297 (1926) (refusal to instruct on presumption reversible error though judge instructed that indictment and custody were not to be taken against him and that they should not decide on suspicion). See also McDonald v. United States, 109 U.S.App.D.C. 98, 284 F.2d 232 (1960) and cases collected in C.J.S. Criminal Law § 1221; Dec. Dig. Criminal Law ☞778(3).

45. In the first edition of this text, Dean McCormick stated: "It seems, however, that the standard instruction on the state's burden of proving the crime beyond a reasonable doubt amply covers these points. If not they should be covered specifically, and not by a phrase which can only suggest to a juror that there is some inherent probability that a person tried for a crime is innocent. The instruction on "presumption of innocence" should, it seems, be regarded merely as a traditional but unnecessary amplification of the instructions on the prosecution's burdens of evidence and of persuasion beyond a reasonable doubt." (p. 649).

46. Wigmore, Evidence § 2511 at 407.

47. Particular presumptions are listed in 9 Wigmore, Evidence §§ 2499–2540; C.J.S. Evidence §§ 120–157; Dec.Dig. Evidence ☞55–83.

48. See § 337, supra.

49. For other discussions of the bases of presumptions see Watkins v. Prudential Ins. Co., 315 Pa. 497, 173 Atl. 644, 648 (1934); Morgan, Basic Problems of Evidence 32–34 (1962).

cess to the proof. An example of such a presumption is the rule that as between connecting carriers, the damage occurred on the line of the last carrier.[50] Similarly, notions, usually implicit rather than expressed, of social and economic policy incline the courts to favor one contention by giving it the benefit of a presumption, and correspondingly to handicap the disfavored adversary. A classic instance is the presumption of ownership from possession, which tends to favor the prior possessor and to make for the stability of estates.[51] A presumption may also be created to avoid an impasse, to reach some result, even though it is an arbitrary one. For example, presumptions dealing with the survivorship of persons who died in a common disaster are necessary in order that other rules of law may operate, even though there is actually no factual basis upon which to believe that one party or the other was likely to have died first.[52] Generally, however, the most important consideration in the creation of presumptions is probability. Most presumptions have come into existence primarily because the judges have believed that proof of fact B renders the inference of the existence of fact A so probable that it is sensible and time-saving to assume the truth of fact A until the adversary disproves it.[53]

Obviously, most presumptions are based not on any one of these grounds alone, but have been created for a combination of reasons. Usually, for example, a presumption is based not only upon the judicial estimate of the probabilities but also upon the difficulties inherent in proving that the more probable event in fact occurred.[54]

Although it would be inappropriate to attempt to list the hundreds of recognized presumptions,[55] following is a brief discussion of a few illustrative presumptions and the reasons for their creation:

Official actions by public officers, including judicial proceedings, are presumed to have been regularly and legally performed.[56] Reason: probability and the difficulty of proving that the officer conducted himself in a manner that was in all ways regular and legal.

A letter properly addressed, stamped and mailed is presumed to have been duly deliv-

---

trouble of proving sanity in the great number of cases where the question will not be raised." Undoubtedly, procedural convenience is a reason for this rule. However, as has previously been noted, the so-called presumption of sanity is simply a description of the initial assignment of the burden of producing evidence to the defendant and is not actually a presumption. See § 342, n. 43; § 341 n. 17.

54. See § 337, supra, nn. 20, 24.

55. For lists of some traditional common law presumptions, see West's Ann.Cal.Evid.Code, §§ 600 et seq., and Ore.Rev.Stat. § 41.360 (1969).

56. Thompson v. Consol. Gas Utilities Corp., 300 U.S. 55 (1937) (regulations of administrative board, purporting to be made under delegated authority, presumed to be supported by justifying facts); S. S. Kresge Co. v. Davis, 277 N.C. 654, 178 S.E. 2d 382 (1971) (good faith administration of the law by law enforcement officers and city officials is presumed); State ex rel. Lawrence v. Burke, 253 Wis. 240, 33 N.W.2d 242 (1948) (habeas corpus after judgment of conviction; judge presumed to have informed accused of right to counsel); West's Ann.Cal.Evid.Code, § 664; 9 Wigmore, Evidence § 2534; Dec.Dig. Evidence ☞82, 83. See also Hammond v. Brown, 323 F.Supp. 326, 355 (N.D.Ohio 1971) where, in an action to enjoin criminal prosecutions arising out of the Kent State rioting, the court presumed that the petit jurors who would hear the case would act impartially.

---

50. When the shipper proves that he delivered the goods to the first carrier in good condition and received them from the last in bad condition, the damage is presumed to have occurred on the line of the last carrier. Chicago & N. W. Ry. Co. v. C. C. Whitnack Prod. Co., 258 U.S. 369 (1922) (the rule is not changed by the Carmack Amendment making initial carrier liable); C.J.S. Carriers § 440 n. 35.

51. Oklahoma R. Co. v. Guthrie, 175 Okl. 40, 52 P.2d 18, 23 (1935) (railway premises); Guyer v. Snyder, 133 Md. 19, 104 Atl. 116 (1918) (personal property); Ore.Rev.Stat. 41.360(11) (1969); 9 Wigmore, Evidence § 2515.

52. See Morgan, supra n. 49, at 33.

53. In the first edition of this text, Dean McCormick stated that another ground for the creation of presumptions is "procedural convenience" and cited the example of the presumption of sanity as it operates in criminal cases to save "the state the fruitless

ered to the addressee.[57] Reason: probability and the difficulty of proving delivery in any other way.

When the plaintiff has been injured by the negligent operation of a vehicle, then upon proof of further facts he may have the benefit of presumptions in moving against the nondriving defendant. If the plaintiff seeks to prove agency, he may secure the advantage of the presumption that the person driving the vehicle was doing so in the scope of his employment and in the course of the business of the defendant, merely by proving that the defendant was the owner.[58] In a number of states the plaintiff must not only prove ownership to gain the benefit of the presumption of agency, but also that the driver is regularly employed by the defend-

ant.[59] If the plaintiff seeks to prove liability in a state having a statute making the owner liable for acts of one driving with the owner's consent, the plaintiff may secure the advantage of the presumption that the person driving was doing so with the owner's consent merely by showing ownership.[60] In some states the plaintiff must not only prove ownership to gain the benefit of the presumption but also that a special relationship existed between the driver and the defendant.[61] Reasons behind these presumptions: probability, fairness in the light of defendant's superior access to the evidence, and the social policy of promoting safety by widening the responsibility in borderline cases of owners for injuries caused by their vehicles.

When a bailor proves delivery of the property to the bailee in good condition and return in a damaged state, or a failure to return after due demand, a presumption arises that the damage or loss was due to the negligence or fault of the bailee.[62] Reason:

---

57. Franklin Life Ins. Co. v. Brantley, 231 Ala. 554, 165 So. 834 (1936); Employer's Nat. Life Ins. Co. v. Willits, 436 S.W.2d 918 (Tex.Civ.App.1968); 9 Wigmore, Evidence § 2519; Dec.Dig. Evidence ⊕71.

58. 9 Wigmore, Evidence § 2510a. See, e. g., Malone v. Hanna, 275 Ala. 534, 156 So.2d 626 (1963); Van Court v. Lodge Cab Co., 198 Wash. 530, 89 P.2d 206, 211 (1939); Hollen v. Reynolds, 123 W.Va. 360, 15 S.E.2d 163 (1941); and see decisions collected Dec.Dig. Automobiles ⊕242(5), 242(6); Annots., 42 A.L.R. 898, 900, 74 A.L.R. 951, 96 A.L.R. 634; Note, 1953 U.Ill.L.F. 121. Proof, in turn, that a business vehicle bore defendant's name raises a "presumption" of ownership, and hence of agency and scope of employment, under this view. Brill v. Davajon, 51 Ill.App.2d 445, 201 N.E.2d 253 (1964); Cappello v. Aero Mayflower Transit Co., 116 Vt. 64, 68 A.2d 913 (1949). So also as to proof that the car bore a license number issued to defendant. Frew v. Barto, 345 Pa. 217, 26 A.2d 905 (1942).

In some states, there is an inference of agency from ownership rather than a presumption. See, e. g., Chappell v. Dean, 258 N.C. 412, 128 S.E.2d 830 (1963) (interpreting North Carolina statute); Breeding v. Johnson, 208 Va. 652, 159 S.E.2d 836 (1968). See also Walker v. Johnston, 236 S.W.2d 534 (Tex.Civ.App.1951) ("inference" of ownership from identification on vehicle); Rodgers v. Jackson Brewing Co., 289 S.W.2d 307 (Tex.Civ.App.1956) ("rebuttable presumption" of ownership from identification on vehicle): Kimbell Milling Co. v. Marcet, 449 S.W.2d 100 (Tex.Civ.App.1969) (citing both the *Walker* and the *Rodgers* case but finding it unnecessary to determine whether the rule describes an inference or a presumption).

59. Manion v. Waybright, 59 Idaho 643, 86 P.2d 181 (1938) ("operated by one in the general employ of defendant"); Galloway Motor Co. v. Huffman's Adm'r, 281 Ky. 841, 137 S.W.2d 379 (1940); Collins v. Leahy, 347 Mo. 133, 146 S.W.2d 609 (1941); Howell v. Olson, 452 P.2d 768 (Okl.1969); Dec.Dig. Automobiles ⊕242(6); Annots., 42 A.L.R. 915, 74 A.L.R. 962, 96 A.L.R. 641.

60. Young v. Masci, 289 U.S. 253 (1933); McKirchy v. Ness, 256 Iowa 744, 128 N.W.2d 910 (1964); West's Ann.Cal. Vehicle Code, § 17150; Iowa Code Ann. § 321.493 (West's); McKinney's N.Y.Vehicle and Traffic Law § 388(1).

61. O'Dea v. Amodeo, 118 Conn. 58, 170 A. 486 (1934); Christiansen v. Hilber, 282 Mich. 403, 276 N.W. 495 (1937); Conn.Gen.St.Ann. § 52–182 (West's) (making presumption of consent applicable to the family car or boat); Mich.Comp. Laws Ann. § 257.401. See also § 345, infra, nn. 46–50 and accompanying text.

62. See, e. g., Bowman v. Vandiver, 243 Ky. 139, 47 S.W.2d 947, 948 (1932); Gray v. E. J. Longyear Co., 78 N.M. 161, 429 P.2d 359 (1967); Trammell v. Whitlock, 150 Tex. 500, 242 S.W.2d 157 (1951); 9 Wigmore, Evidence § 2508; Comment, 4 Baylor L. Rev. 327 (1952); C.J.S. Bailments § 50; Dec.Dig. Bailments ⊕31(1). The presumption casts the burden on the bailee of proceeding with evidence of the cause of the loss, e. g., fire, theft, damage from collision. Some cases hold that, if the facts thus

fairness in the light of the superior access of the bailee to the evidence of the facts surrounding the loss; probability.

Proof that a person has disappeared from his home and has absented himself therefrom for at least seven years and that during this time those who would be expected to hear from him have received no tidings from him and after diligent inquiry have been unable to find his whereabouts, raises a presumption that he died at some time during the seven year period.[63] The rule, though

not very ancient,[64] is already antiquated in that the seven year period is undoubtedly

C.J.S. Death § 6; Dec.Dig. Death ☞2. The presumption has been enacted into statute in somewhat more than half the states. See Jalet, supra at 198.

A few jurisdictions dispense with the requirement of search and inquiry. See, e. g., Banks v. Metropolitan Life Ins. Co., 142 Neb. 823, 8 N.W.2d 185 (1943). See also cases collected in Annot., 99 A.L.R.2d 307.

It is often stated that it is one of the required facts of the presumption that the absence be "unexplained." E. g., Butler v. Mutual Life Ins. Co., 225 N.Y. 197, 121 N.E. 758 (1919). See cases collected at C.J.S. Death § 6 n. 39. It is believed, however, that this is misleading. The more reasonable view, it seems, is not that the proponent of the presumption must show that the absence is "unexplained," but that explanatory circumstances (e. g., that the person was a fugitive from justice), whether brought out by the proponent or the opponent, are to be considered by the jury in rebuttal of the presumption. See, e. g., Shaw v. Prudential Ins. Co. of America, 158 Wash. 43, 290 Pac. 694 (1930); see also Ewing v. Metropolitan Life Ins. Co., 191 Wis. 299, 210 N.W. 819 (1926).

Under the majority view, there is no presumption as to the time of death within the seven years. E. g., Peak v. United States, 353 U.S. 43 (1957) (construing federal statute); Ferril v. Kansas City Life Ins. Co., 345 Mo. 777, 137 S.W.2d 577 (1940). But a minority, in aid of the settlement of controversies over succession, recognize a presumption that the death occurred at the end of the seven years. In re Chicago & N. W. Ry. Co., 138 F.2d 753 (7th Cir. 1943) (Illinois law) (presumption of continuance of life controls for period up to the end of seven years, when person is first accounted dead); Edwards v. Equitable Life Assur. Soc. of United States, 296 Ky. 448, 177 S.W.2d 574 (1944). But under either view the circumstances of the disappearance may be sufficient evidence that the death occurred at or about the time of disappearance. See Edwards v. Equitable Life Assur. Soc., supra; Ferril v. Kansas City Life Ins. Co., supra. See also Hefford v. Metropolitan Life Ins. Co., 173 Ore. 353, 363, 144 P.2d 695 (1944).

disclosed are consistent with due care, e. g., a fire of unknown origin, the bailee has satisfied the burden. Exporters' & Traders Compress & Warehouse Co. v. Schulze, 265 S.W. 133 (Tex.Com.App. 1924) (fire); Chaloupka v. Cyr, 63 Wash.2d 463, 387 P.2d 740 (1963) (fire). But other cases, more soundly it seems, require the bailee to go further and give evidence of facts from which the jury could reasonably find that the loss was not caused by the bailee's negligence. Downey v. Martin Aircraft Service, Inc., 96 Cal.App.2d 94, 214 P.2d 581 (1950) (fire); Gen. Exch. Ins. Corp. v. Service Parking Grounds, Inc., 254 Mich. 1, 235 N.W. 898 (1931) (damage to car while stolen).

Section 7–403(1) (b) of the Uniform Commercial Code provides that a bailee may excuse his failure to deliver goods to the party holding a document of title by establishing "damage to or delay, loss or destruction of the goods for which the bailee is not liable [, but the burden of establishing negligence in such cases is on the person entitled under the document]." The bracketed language is optional. Most jurisdictions have omitted it (37 out of 51 adopting the code). See Uniform Commercial Code Reporting Service, Current Materials (1971). In most jurisdictions in which the section has been adopted without the optional language the question is still open as to whether the bailee has the burden of persuasion as well as the burden of producing evidence on the question of negligence. See Bigham, Presumptions, Burden of Proof and the Uniform Commercial Code, 21 Vand.L.Rev. 177, 191 (1968). However, at least one recent case has held that the bailor still has the burden of persuasion on the question. Canty v. Wyatt Storage Corp., 208 Va. 161, 156 S.E.2d 582 (1967).

63. E. g., Green v. Royal Neighbors of America, 146 Kan. 571, 73 P.2d 1 (1937); Magers v. Western & Southern Life Ins. Co., 335 S.W.2d 355 (Mo.App. 1960); Donea v. Massachusetts Mut. Life Ins. Co., 220 Minn. 204, 19 N.W.2d 377 (1945). See the exhaustive treatment of this presumption in Jalet, Mysterious Disappearance: The Presumption of Death and the Administration of the Estates of Missing Persons or Absentees, 54 Iowa L.Rev. 177 (1968). See also 9 Wigmore, Evidence § 2531a;

64. Thayer traces it to an English case of 1804. Doe d. George v. Jesson, 6 East 80, 102 Eng.Rep. 1217. But the period of seven years seems to derive from the Bigamy Act of 1604 and from a statute of 1667 which provided "in the case of estates and leases depending upon the life of a person who should go beyond the seas, or otherwise absent himself within the kingdom for seven years, that where the lessor or reversioner should bring an action to recover the estate, the person thus absenting himself should 'be accounted as naturally dead,' if there should be no 'sufficient and evident proof of the life,' and that the judge should 'direct the jury to give their verdict as if the person . . . were

too long considering modern communications and transportation.[65] Reasons: probability and the social policy of enforcing family security provisions such as life insurance, and of settling estates.[66]

In the tracing of titles to land there is a useful presumption of identity from name. Thus, when the same name appears in the chain of title first as grantee or heir and then as grantor, it will be presumed that it was the same person in each case.[67] Reasons: the convenience of enabling the court and the parties to rely upon the regularity of the apparent chain of title, until this is challenged by evidence contesting identity; the social policy of quieting claims based on the face of the record; and probability.

Proof that a child was born to a woman during the time when she was married creates the presumption that the offspring is the legitimate child of the husband.[68] De-

spite the controversy over whether presumptions generally shift the burden of persuasion upon the opponent,[69] it is universally agreed that in the case of this presumption, the adversary contending for illegitimacy does have the burden.[70] This burden, moreover, is usually measured not by the normal standard for civil cases of preponderance of the evidence, but rather by the requirement of clear, convincing, and satisfactory proof, as most courts say,[71] or even by the criminal formula, beyond a reasonable doubt.[72] In addition, as pointed out elsewhere in this work, the contender for illegitimacy is fur-

---

dead.' " Preliminary Treatise on Evidence 319–324 (1898).

65. See 9 Wigmore, Evidence § 2531b. Wigmore advocated the adoption of the Uniform Absence as Evidence of Death and Absentees' Property Act which provides no set period for a presumption of death but left the matter of death to be determined in each case as a question of fact. 9 U.L.A. § 1 (1957). The act was adopted in three states, Maryland, Tennessee and Wisconsin in 1941, but has not been adopted since.

66. See Robb v. Horsey, 169 Md. 227, 181 Atl. 348, 351 (1935). See also Jalet, supra, n. 63 at 181–182.

67. E. g., Edelstein v. Pon, 183 Cal.App.2d 795, 7 Cal.Rptr. 65 (1960); Huston v. Graves, 213 S.W. 77 (Mo.1919). See also Breznik v. Braun, 11 Ill.2d 564, 144 N.E.2d 586 (1957). See general discussion of inferences or presumptions from identical names in 9 Wigmore, Evidence § 2529 and cases collected in Dec.Dig. Evidence ⟜55, Names ⟜14.

68. In re Findlay, 253 N.Y. 1, 170 N.E. 471, 473 (1930) (opinion by Cardozo, C. J., tracing the history and limits of the presumption); Bernheimer v. First Nat. Bank, 359 Mo. 1119, 225 S.W.2d 745 (1949) ("presumption of legitimacy is the strongest known to law"); 9 Wigmore, Evidence § 2527; Notes, 33 Harv.L.Rev. 306 (1920), 35 Mo.L.Rev. 449 (1970); C.J.S. Bastards § 3; 10 Am.Jur.2d Bastards §§ 10–44; Dec.Dig. Bastards ⟜2–4. The presumption applies even when the child was conceived before, and born after, marriage. State v. E. A. H., 246 Minn. 299, 75 N.W.2d 195 (1956). See cases

collected Annot., 57 A.L.R.2d 729. Interesting problems of presumptions arise when a child is conceived while the wife is married to husband number one and is born after she married number two. See cases collected in Annot., 57 A.L.R.2d 729, 778. Presumptions have often developed into rules of substantive law. Here, however, the course of evolution has been from a rule of substantive law into a rebuttable presumption. But the strictness of an older day when if the husband was not beyond the four seas, the child was conclusively assumed to be his, lingers in modified form. Thus, for example, West's Ann.Cal.Evid.Code, § 621 provides that "the issue of a wife cohabiting with her husband, who is not impotent, is conclusively presumed to be legitimate." Somewhat more moderately, the court in Haugen v. Swanson, 219 Minn. 123, 16 N.W.2d 900, 902 (1944) held that a husband's paternity could be excluded "by proof of miscegenation, or of his impotency, or of the negative results of reliable blood tests by impartial physicians." For the use of blood tests to exclude paternity see § 211, supra.

69. See § 345, infra.

70. See the opinion of Sturdevant, J., in In re Jones' Estate, 110 Vt. 438, 8 A.2d 631, 128 A.L.R. 704 (1939) recognizing this allocation of the burden of persuasion, but characterizing this apportionment of the burden as a "rule of substantive law"—an analysis that may be questioned, see § 345, infra. Cases are collected in Annot., 128 A.L.R. 713.

71. The variations in phraseology are wide. In re Davis' Estate, 169 Okl. 133, 36 P.2d 471 (1934) ("strong, satisfactory and conclusive"); State ex rel. Walker v. Clark, 144 Ohio St. 305, 58 N.E.2d 773 (1945) ("clear and convincing"); In re Thorn's Estate, 353 Pa. 603, 606, 46 A.2d 258, 260 (1946) ("clear, direct, satisfactory and irrefragable"); Annot., 128 A.L.R. supra n. 70 at 718–722.

72. E. g., In re Jones' Estate, 110 Vt. 438, 8 A.2d 631, 128 A.L.R. 704 (1939); Annot., 128 A.L.R. supra n. 69 at 717; Wis.Stat.Ann. § 328.39(1)(a) (West's).

ther handicapped by a rule rendering incompetent the testimony or declarations of the spouses offered to show nonaccess, when the purpose is to bastardize the child.[73] Reasons: social policy, to avoid the visitation upon the child of the sins of the parents caused by the social stigma of bastardy and the common law rules (now generally alleviated by statutes) as to the incapacities of the *filius nullius,* the child of no one; probability.

When violent death is shown to have occurred and the evidence is not controlling as to whether it was due to suicide or accident, there is a presumption against suicide.[74] Reasons: the general probability in case of a death unexplained, which flows from the human revulsion against suicide, and, probably, a social policy which inclines in case of doubt toward the fruition rather than the frustration of plans for family protection through insurance.

344. Constitutional Limitations upon the Creation and Effect of Presumptions.[75]

Because of its relationship to the burdens of proof, the impact of a presumption upon the parties in the litigation is potentially great. In civil cases, where the presumption at least shifts the burden of producing evidence, its operation may totally preclude jury consideration of the issue. In criminal cases, even though its effect may be no more than that of a permissible inference, a presumption may be sufficient to take an otherwise defective prosecution case to the jury and ultimately result in a conviction that otherwise could not have occurred. Furthermore, the existence of the presumption as to a particular element of the crime may force the defendant to introduce proof in rebuttal, including his own testimony, and thus force him to waive his constitutional right to remain silent. A recognition of the impact of these procedural consequences has caused the courts to review the creation and use of presumptions in the light of the due process clauses of the Fifth and Fourteenth Amendments to the Constitution of the United States. Although theoretically due process problems may arise with regard to any presumption regardless of whether it has been created by the courts or by the legislatures, vigorous constitutional attacks upon presumptions have been limited to statutory presumptions. The common law presumptions are now well entrenched, and, in any event, most operate in civil cases where, as we shall see, the due process questions are not as difficult. However, how far the legislature, state or national, can go in creating presumptions is a troublesome question, particularly in criminal cases. The urge for simplifying the task of the prosecutor in certain cases is balanced by the very real fear that going too far in this direction may result in substituting an inquisitorial procedure for our traditional accusatorial system.

---

73. See § 67, supra.

74. See, e. g., Dick v. New York Life Insurance Co., 359 U.S. 437 (1959) (North Dakota law); Life & Casualty Ins. Co. v. Daniel, 209 Va. 332, 163 S.E.2d 577 (1968); C.J.S. Evidence § 1356; Dec.Dig. Evidence ☜59. See also cases collected Annot., 85 A.L.R.2d 722. In some states an inference rather than a presumption against suicide is recognized. See, e. g., Watkins v. Prudential Ins. Co. of America, 315 Pa. 497, 173 A. 644 (1934); C.J.S. § 1355b nn. 29, 30.

75. Among the more significant recent discussions of the questions raised in this section are: Abrams, Statutory Presumptions and the Federal Criminal Law: A Suggested Analysis, 22 Vand.L.Rev. 1135 (1969); Ashford and Risinger, Presumptions, Assumptions and Due Process in Criminal Cases: A Theoretical Overview, 79 Yale L.J. 165 (1969); Christie and Pye, Presumptions and Assumptions in the Criminal Law: Another View, 1970 Duke L.J. 919; Soules, Presumptions in Criminal Cases, 20 Baylor L.Rev. 277 (1968) (Texas law); Note, The Unconstitutionality of Statutory Criminal Presump-

tions, 22 Stan.L.Rev. 341 (1970); Note, Abrogation of Criminal Statutory Presumptions, 5 Suffolk L. Rev. 161 (1970). See also Dec.Dig. Constitutional Law ☜266.

Because the problems are essentially different, any treatment of the constitutional limitations on the creation and use of presumptions must be divided into separate discussions of criminal and civil cases.

Criminal cases. The Supreme Court has substantially defined the constitutional limitations on the use of presumptions in criminal cases in a relatively recent series of opinions, culminating in the 1970 decision in Turner v. United States.[76]

The first of these cases was Tot v. United States,[77] decided in 1943. In the *Tot* case, the defendants were convicted under a provision of the Federal Firearm's Act making it "unlawful for any person who has been convicted of a crime of violence to receive any firearm . . . which has been shipped . . . in interstate . . . commerce" and further providing that "the possession of a firearm . . . by any such person shall be presumptive evidence that such firearm was . . . received by such person in violation of this Act." In holding that the presumption violated due process, the Court stated that "a statutory presumption cannot be sustained if there be no rational connection between the fact proved and the ultimate fact presumed, if the inference of the one from proof of the other is arbitrary because of lack of connection between the two in common experience."[78] The court noted that although state laws might make acquisition difficult, it did not follow from proof of mere possession that the firearms must have been received by the defendants in interstate commerce subsequent to the adoption of the federal act. The firearm might have been acquired intrastate in violation of state law, or, since manufactured years earlier, acquired

prior to the adoption of either the state regulation or the federal statute in question.

Perhaps as significant as the Court's adoption of a "rational connection" test for presumptions in criminal cases, was its treatment of two other tests suggested by the government. In addition to advancing rationality as a test, the government had argued that the validity of the presumption could alternatively be tested by the "comparative convenience of producing evidence of the ultimate fact."[79] The Court answered that argument by stating that "comparative convenience" was simply a "corollary" to the controlling rational connection test and that "[t]he argument from convenience is admissible only where the inference is a permissible one . . . ."[80]

The government had also argued that Congress' *greater power* to enact a statute to prohibit the possession of all firearms by persons convicted of violent crimes, necessarily *included the lesser power* to create the presumption in question.[81] The court

76. 396 U.S. 398 (1970).

77. 319 U.S. 463 (1943).

78. Id. at 467.

79. The government's argument was apparently based upon a statement by Cardozo, J., in Morrison v. California, 291 U.S. 82, 91 (1934) to the effect that, even if there is no "sinister significance" in the evidence presented there "must be in any event a manifest disparity in convenience of proof and opportunity for knowledge." The *Morrison* case, however, dealt not with presumptions but rather with rules creating affirmative defenses. See discussion infra, § 346, n. 94 and accompanying text.

80. 319 U.S. at 467–470.

81. The government's argument was based upon Ferry v. Ramsey, 277 U.S. 88 (1928), a civil action in which the Court, through Holmes, J., upheld a Kansas statute imposing liability upon bank directors who, knowing of their bank's insolvency, assented to the reception of deposits, and further providing that proof of the bank's insolvency should be prima facie evidence of the directors' knowledge and assent. Mr. Justice Holmes noted: "It is said that the liability is founded by the statute upon the directors' assent to the deposit and that when this is the ground the assent cannot be proved by artificial presumptions that have no warrant from experience. But the short answer is that the statute might have made the directors personally liable to depositors in every case, if it had been so minded, and that if it had purported to do so, whoever ac-

rejected the argument, stating first that the government's contention could not sustain the presumption of acquisition after the effective date of the act, and second that "it is plain that Congress, for whatever reason, did not seek to pronounce general prohibition of possession . . . in order to protect interstate commerce, but dealt only with their future acquisition in interstate commerce." [82]

Additional enlightenment with regard to constitutional limits on the creation of presumptions came in two 1965 cases dealing with presumptions enacted to aid the government in prosecuting liquor cases. In United States v. Gainey,[83] the Court considered the validity of a statute which provided that presence at the site is sufficient to convict a defendant of the offense of carrying on the business of distilling without giving bond, "unless the defendant explains such presence to the satisfaction of the jury." The Court applied the rational connection test of *Tot,* but this time sustained the validity of the presumption. However, in United States v. Romano,[84] the court struck down as violative of the principle of *Tot,* an identical presumption with regard to the companion offense of possession of an illegal still.

The Court's reasoning in distinguishing the two presumptions is not difficult to follow. The crime of *carrying on* an illegal dis-

tilling business, involved in the *Gainey* case, was an extremely broad one, which, viewed in the light of the aiding and abetting statute, covered almost every conceivable act connected with the operation of a still. A person's unexplained presence at the still made it highly likely that he had something to do with the operation. Yet, as the Court noted, prior to the enactment of the statutory presumption, the courts had differed in assessing the natural inference that might be derived from such facts. The Court in *Gainey* concluded:

"Congress was undoubtedly aware that manufacturers of illegal liquors are notorious for the deftness with which they locate arcane spots for plying their trade. Legislative recognition of the implications of seclusion only confirms what the folklore teaches—that strangers to the illegal business rarely penetrate the curtain of secrecy. . . ." [85]

It is fair to interpret *Gainey* as simply sustaining Congress' power to standardize a natural inference. However, no such natural inference existed with regard to the presumption of *possession* from unexplained presence in the statute involved in *Romano.* As to that presumption, the Court stated:

"Presence tells us only that the defendant was there and very likely played a part in the illicit scheme. But presence tells us nothing about what the defendant's specific function was and carries no legitimate, rational or reasonable inference that he was engaged in one of the specialized functions connected with possession, rather than in one of the supply, delivery or operational activities having nothing to do with possession. Presence is relevant and admissible evidence in a trial on a possession charge; but absent some showing of the defendant's function at the still, its connection with possession is too tenuous to permit a rea-

---

cepted the office would assume the risk. The statute in short imposed a liability that was less than might have been imposed, and that being so, the thing to be considered is the result reached, not the possibly inartificial or clumsy way of reaching it. . . ."

Although this reasoning was properly rejected by the Court in the *Tot* case as inapplicable to a criminal prosecution, there is no good reason why Justice Holmes' points are not still valid in a civil case. See n. 20 and accompanying text, infra.

82.   319 U.S. at 472.

83.   380 U.S. 63 (1965).

84.   382 U.S. 136 (1965).

85.   380 U.S. at 67.

sonable inference of guilt—'the inference of the one from proof of the other is arbitrary . . . .' " [86]

In *Romano,* the court also rejected the "greater includes the lesser argument" urged in the *Tot* case, this time somewhat more clearly:

". . . It may be, of course, that Congress has the power to make presence at an illegal still a punishable crime, but we find no clear indication that it intended to so exercise this power. The crime remains possession, not presence, and, with all due deference to the judgment of Congress, the former may not constitutionally be inferred from the latter." [87]

Tot, Gainey and *Romano* left important questions unanswered. First, the "rational connection" test was vague. Was it a test of relevancy or a test of probative sufficiency? If it was a test of relevancy, a presumption would be valid if the proved fact tended to prove the presumed fact. If it was a test of sufficiency, the existence of the presumed fact would have to be shown to be more likely than not to exist or perhaps even have to be shown to exist beyond a reasonable doubt. Second, the presumption approved in *Gainey* enacted into statute an inference that might fairly have been drawn even without the statute. Would the Court sustain a presumption not based upon a natural inference but upon Congressional review of empirical data which was not to be submitted to the jury in each individual case? [88] Third, would Mr. Justice Black's

dissent in *Gainey* eventually attract a majority of the Court? In that dissent,[89] joined in part by Mr. Justice Douglas,[90] Mr. Justice Black stated that the use of the presumption in question unconstitutionally impaired the defendant's "right to have a jury weigh the facts of his case without any congressional interference through predetermination of what evidence would be sufficient to prove the facts necessary to convict in a particular case." [91] He further condemned the presumption as depriving the defendant of his right to remain silent by forcing him to rebut the presumed facts.[92] An adoption of the Black view would necessarily mean the abrogation of all statutory presumptions operating against the defendant in a criminal case.

In 1969, the Court partially answered the first of these questions and at least suggested answers to the other two. In Leary v. United States [93] it considered a presumption providing that possession of marihuana was sufficient evidence to authorize conviction of transporting and concealing the drug *with knowledge of its illegal importation* unless the defendant explained his possession to the satisfaction of the jury. In reviewing the prior holdings on the question, the court stated:

"The upshot of *Tot, Gainey* and *Romano* is, we think, that a criminal statutory presumption must be regarded as 'irrational' or 'arbitrary,' and hence unconstitutional, un-

---

86. 382 U.S. at 141.

87. Id. at 144.

88. The Court in *Gainey* perhaps suggested the answer to this question, stating: "The process of making the determination of rationality is, by its nature, highly empirical, and in matters not within specialized judicial competence or completely commonplace, significant weight should be accorded the capacity of Congress to amass the stuff of actual experience and cull conclusions from it. . . ." 380 U.S. at 67.

89. Id. at 74–88.

90. Mr. Justice Douglas approved the statute as providing a mere "rule of evidence" that the jury was free to accept or reject as it saw fit. Id. at 72. He believed, however, that the judge's charge to the jury that the inference could be drawn "unless the defendant by the evidence in the case and by proven facts and circumstances explains such presence to the satisfaction of the jury" was an improper comment on the defendant's silence. Id. at 74.

91. Id. at 81.

92. Id. at 87–88.

93. 395 U.S. 6 (1969) (opinion by Harlan, J.).

less it can at least be said with substantial assurance that the presumed fact is more likely than not to flow from the proved fact on which it is made to depend. And in the judicial assessment the congressional determination favoring the particular presumption must, of course weigh heavily." [94]

The Court then went on to hold that the presumption, insofar as it dealt with the defendant's knowledge that the drug was illegally imported, was unconstitutional under this standard. It did not purport to consider the validity of the other presumed fact under the statute—the actual illegal importation. To support its conclusion, the Court conducted an extensive examination of both the legislative history of the statute, which it found to be inadequate standing alone to support the presumption, and other, governmental and nongovernmental, reports and books, published before and after the enactment of the statute in 1956. From this examination, the Court concluded that, although most domestically consumed marihuana comes from abroad, "it would be no more than speculation were we to say that even as much as a majority of possessors 'knew' the source of their marihuana." [95] This conclusion was, the Court found, sufficient to render the "knowledge" portion of the presumption invalid.

The Court in *Leary* did not merely hold that the proved fact must rationally tend to prove the presumed fact. It held, as its careful examination of the available literature clearly indicates, that the presumed fact must actually be more likely than not to exist if the proved fact exists.[96] In a footnote to its above quoted statement of the "more likely than not" rule, the Court added

that because of its finding that the presumption was unconstitutional under this standard, it would not reach the question "whether a criminal presumption which passes muster when so judged must also satisfy the criminal 'reasonable doubt' standard if proof of the crime charged or an essential element thereof depends upon its use." [97]

Moreover, the Court's extensive reference to data outside the record as well as failure to incorporate into its opinion the objections raised by Mr. Justice Black in his dissent in *Gainey*,[98] suggested that the other two questions raised above would, in the future, be answered in favor of the statutory presumption. This suggestion was borne out in 1970 in *Turner v. United States*.[99]

In *Turner,* the Court dealt with two presumptions. One was identical with the presumption struck down in *Leary,* except that the drugs involved in *Turner* were heroin and cocaine rather than marihuana. The other provided that the absence of appropriate tax paid stamps from narcotic drugs found in the defendant's possession would be "prima facie evidence" that he purchased or distributed the drugs from other than the original stamped package. Again the Court conducted an extensive review both of the legislative records with regard to these statutes and of other pertinent literature in the field. In addition, it surveyed the records of other narcotics cases for evidence to support or rebut the inferences called for by the statutes. It concluded that the "overwhelming evidence" was that the heroin consumed in

---

94. Id. at 36.

95. Id. at 53.

96. See the analysis of this aspect of the *Leary* case in Note, The Unconstitutionality of Statutory Criminal Presumptions, 22 Stan.L.Rev. 341, 346 (1970).

97. 395 U.S. at 36 n. 64.

98. Mr. Justice Black wrote a concurring opinion in *Leary* holding the presumption invalid essentially for the reasons stated in his *Gainey* dissent. Id. at 55–56.

99. 396 U.S. 398 (1970). For discussions of the *Turner* case see Christie and Pye, Presumptions and Assumptions in the Criminal Law: Another View, 1970 Duke L.J. 919; Note, 2 St. Mary's L.J. 115 (1970); Note, 24 Sw.L.J. 551 (1970); Note, The Unconstitutionality of Statutory Criminal Presumptions, 22 Stan.L.Rev. 341 (1970).

the United States is illegally imported and that Turner therefore must have known this fact.[1] Based upon this conclusion, the presumption as to illegal importation of heroin was upheld. In contrast, the Court struck down the same presumption with regard to the illegal importation of cocaine, finding that it could not be "sufficiently sure either that the cocaine that Turner possessed came from abroad or that Turner must have known that it did." [2] Similarly, the Court sustained the "stamped package" presumption as to heroin and struck it down as to cocaine, finding that "there can be no reasonable doubt" that one who possessed heroin did not purchase it from a stamped package [3] but that because of the availability of cocaine from legal channels there was "a reasonable possibility" that Turner had in fact obtained the cocaine from a legally stamped package.[4]

In *Turner,* the Court again found it unnecessary specifically to adopt a test that would require that the presumed fact be shown to exist beyond a reasonable doubt. However, the Court's frequent reference to that standard in *Turner,*[5] coupled with its decision in In re Winship [6] recognizing that such a measure of proof is constitutionally required in criminal cases, makes it likely that the reasonable doubt standard will be applied to test the validity of presumptions in the future.[7]

The *Turner* case is undoubtedly even more significant because of the answer it gives to the second question posed above: the legislatures will be permitted to create presumptions based, not only upon inferences that might naturally be derived from the facts, but also upon information that will never be given to the jury. The Court in *Turner,* in order to sustain the heroin presumptions, was willing to use its power to notice legislative facts [8] to review information far beyond the record before it. Perhaps the prime example of the Court's flexibility in this regard is its reference to the fact that "thousands of defendants" have had an opportunity to rebut the inference of illegal importation, but in no case has "substantial evidence showing domestic production of heroin . . come to light." [9] Moreover, the Court did not merely use the information it collected to support the presumption of illegal importation, but also used it to support the inference of the defendant's knowledge, as to which it had no actual data. Once the absence of domestic heroin is proved beyond a reasonable doubt, defendant's knowledge becomes a natural inference from the facts.[10]

---

1. Id. at 415–416.

2. Id. at 419.

3. Id. at 422.

4. Id. at 423–424.

5. For example, the Court stated:
". . . To possess heroin *is* to possess imported heroin. Whether judged by the more-likely-than-not standard applied in Leary v. United States, supra, or by the more exacting reasonable-doubt standard normally applicable in criminal cases, § 174 is valid insofar as it permits a jury to infer that heroin possessed in this country is a smuggled drug. . . ." Id. at 416.

6. 397 U.S. 358 (1970). See § 341, supra, at n. 89.

7. See Christie and Pye, supra n. 99, at 923 n. 24. In its apparent adoption of the reasonable doubt

standard, the Court did not recognize the argument put forth by some writers that in order for a presumption to be valid, not only must there be a high probability of correlation between the fact proved and the fact presumed, but there must also be a high probability that the accused can rebut the presumption. See Ashford and Risinger, Presumptions, Assumptions and Due Process in Criminal Cases: A Theoretical Overview, 79 Yale L.J. 165 (1969); Note, Statutory Criminal Presumptions: Judicial Sleight of Hand, 53 Va.L.Rev. 702, 735 (1967). For a criticism of this approach see Christie and Pye, supra, at 926–933. See also Abrams, Statutory Presumptions and the Federal Criminal Law: A Suggested Analysis, 22 Vand.L.Rev. 1135, 1145–46 (1969).

8. See § 331, supra, dealing with judicial notice of "legislative facts."

9. 396 U.S. at 409.

10. In this regard, the Court stated: " 'Common sense' . . . tells us that those who traffic in heroin will inevitably become aware that the product they deal in is smuggled, unless they practice a studied ignorance to which they are not entitled." Id. at 417.

Therefore, contrary to the suggestion of some writers,[11] the Court's apparent adoption of a beyond-a-reasonable-doubt standard for statutory presumptions, does not necessarily spell the death of the statutory presumption in criminal cases. If the legislative record is substantial in terms of empirical data or if the prosecution, where the presumption is challenged, can support the existence of the presumed fact with evidence from either inside or outside the record in the case, the presumption will survive and prosecutors will be relieved of the need to present such proof in every case in which it is used.[12]

Mr. Justice Black's objections to the use of statutory presumptions remain. In *Turner,* he dissented again, this time even more vigorously and this time with the full support of Mr. Justice Douglas.[13] His arguments were much the same as in *Gainey* although this time he stated that the presumption deprived the defendant of most of the incidents of procedural due process. Additionally, he commented adversely on the important question of the majority's use of facts outside the record and noted: ". . . [P]etitioner was never given an opportunity to confront before the jury the many expert witnesses now arrayed against him in the footnotes of the Court's opinion. Nor does it apparently matter to the Court that the fact-finding

role it undertakes today is constitutionally vested not in this Court but in the jury."[14]

Although the logic and wisdom of Justice Black's positions, both with regard to the tremendous impact that the presumption has on the defendant in a criminal case and with regard to the Court's use of data outside the record, may be compelling to many, his view seems unlikely to persuade a majority of the Court in the forseeable future.

The *Turner* case does not fully bring to a close the controversy over statutory presumptions in criminal cases. All the cases discussed above bear two things in common. All were federal prosecutions, and all involved instances in which the jury was clearly instructed that they were permitted, but not required, to find the presumed fact. With regard to the first aspect, it would seem unlikely that the Court would apply a different test for the validity of presumptions under the Fourteenth Amendment from that applied under the Fifth and therefore that state presumptions would be treated differently from federal presumptions.[15] With regard to the second aspect, it is unlikely that the Court would approve the use of a presumption in a criminal case other than as a permissible inference. The point is fully explained below.[16]

Civil cases. The stringent tests that govern the validity of statutory presumptions in criminal cases are simply inapplicable in civil litigation. In civil cases there is no reason either to limit the creation of presumptions to instances in which there is a rational connection between the proved fact and the pre-

---

11. See Note, The Unconstitutionality of Statutory Criminal Presumptions, 22 Stan.L.Rev. 341, 354; Note, Abrogation of Criminal Statutory Presumptions, 5 Suffolk L.Rev. 161, 185–186 (1970). Christie and Pye, supra n. 99, at 925, state: "The high standards of proof with which the Court has surrounded presumptions, together with the expanded notions of the reach of congressional power, have considerably reduced whatever importance the use of presumptions might formerly have played in criminal prosecutions in the federal courts."

12. For an interesting discussion of the potentials of "empirical data presumptions" see Abrams, supra n. 7, at 1149–1153.

13. 396 U.S. at 425–434.

14. Id. at 433.

15. For a good collection of state court opinions considering the constitutionality of statutory presumptions in criminal cases see, Note, 2 St. Mary's L.J. 115, 117–119 (1970). See also Soules, Presumptions in Criminal Cases, 20 Baylor L.Rev. 277 (1968) (presumptions in Texas).

16. Infra § 346, nn. 96–2 and accompanying text. See also Abrams, supra n. 7 at 1147.

sumed fact or to limit the effect that a presumption may have upon the burdens of proof.

In a criminal case, the scales are deliberately overbalanced in favor of the defendant through the requirement that the prosecution prove each element of the offense, as it is alleged in the indictment or information, beyond a reasonable doubt.[17] Any rule that has even the appearance of lightening the state's burden is viewed with the most extreme caution. However, there is no need for this special protection for any one party to a civil action. The burdens of proof are fixed at the pleading stage, not for constitutional reasons, but for reasons of probability, social policy and convenience.[18] There is no reason why the same policy considerations, as reflected in the operation of a presumption, should not be permitted further to effect an allocation of the burdens of proof during the course of the trial. To impose a "rational connection" limitation upon the creation or operation of presumptions in civil cases would mean that only presumptions based on probability would be permissible. Such a limitation would ignore other, equally valid, reasons for the creation of the rules. Thus, although there is undoubtedly some outer limit on the creation of a presumption in a civil case, great latitude is and should be given. Considerations which have now been explicitly rejected in criminal cases, such as the comparative knowledge of the parties with regard to the facts [19] and the power of the legislature to do away with a claim or a defense entirely,[20] should remain

significant in determining the validity of a civil presumption.[21]

Perhaps the only question open to argument with regard to civil presumptions is whether a presumption may operate to assign the burden of persuasion. The question arises from the contrast between two Supreme Court cases considering the validity of presumptions of negligence operating against railroads. In the first, Mobile, J. & K. C. R. R. v. Turnipseed,[22] decided in 1910, the Court considered a Mississippi statutory presumption of negligence operating against a railroad in an action for death of an employee in a derailment. The statute provided that proof of injury inflicted by the running of railroad cars would be "*prima facie* evidence of the want of reasonable skill and care" on the part of the railroad. Noting that the only effect of the statute was to impose on the railroad the duty of producing some evidence to the contrary, the court held that the rational connection between the fact proved and the fact presumed was sufficient to sustain the presumption.

However, in 1929, in Western & Atlantic R. R. v. Henderson,[23] the Court struck down a Georgia statute making railroads liable for damage done by trains, unless the railroad made it appear that reasonable care had been used, "the presumption in all cases being against the company." In the *Henderson* case, the plaintiff alleged that her husband had been killed in a grade crossing collision. The jury was instructed that negligence was presumed from the fact of injury and that the burden was therefore on the railroad to

---

17. See § 341, supra, with regard to the nature of the prosecution's burden; see § 346, infra, with regard to the constitutional limits on the effect that a presumption may have upon that burden.

18. See § 337, supra.

19. See, Morrison v. California, 291 U.S. 82, 91 (1934), discussed in n. 79, supra, and in § 346, n. 94, infra.

20. See Ferry v. Ramsey, 277 U.S. 88 (1928), discussed in n. 81, supra.

21. See F.R.Ev. (R.D.1971) 301, Advisory Committee's Note. Even Justice Black, dissenting in *Gainey*, 380 U.S. at 78, carefully distinguished between civil and criminal cases noting that the "validity of each presumption must be determined in the light of the particular consequences that flow from its use." See also Note 55 Colum.L.Rev. 527, 538–39 (1955).

22. 219 U.S. 35 (1910).

23. 279 U.S. 639 (1929).

show that it exercised ordinary care. The Court held that the mere fact of a collision between a train and a vehicle at a crossing furnished no basis for any inference as to negligence and that therefore the presumption was invalid. The *Turnipseed* case was distinguished on the ground that the Mississippi presumption raised "merely a temporary inference of fact" while the Georgia statute created "an inference that is given effect of evidence to be weighed against opposing testimony and is to prevail unless such testimony is found by the jury to preponderate." [24]

Although perhaps a grade crossing collision differs from a derailment and therefore *Turnipseed* and *Henderson* can be distinguished on their facts, it is nevertheless fair to read *Henderson* as imposing constitutional limitations on the effect of at least some presumptions. However, as has been cogently pointed out,[25] *Henderson* may simply no longer be valid law. The case assumed the necessity of a showing of negligence. But the concept of negligence has lost most of its sanctity since 1929.[26] Although there is considerable doubt as to what the Court would have done in that year, there is little doubt today that a legislature would be permitted at least to relegate lack of negligence to the status of an affirmative defense. If negligence could be so reduced, a presumption which assigned the burden of persuasion could logically be treated no differently.[27]

Since *Henderson,* the Court has, on at least one occasion, approved a state presumption that operated to fix the burden of persuasion on the party controverting the presumed fact. In that case, Dick v. New York Life Ins. Co.,[28] the Court approved a North Dakota common law rule that imposed on the defendant insurance company, defending against the operation of an accidental death clause, the burden of persuading the jury that the death of the insured was due to suicide.

The questionable status of the *Henderson* case in light of recent developments in tort law, the holding of the Court in the *Dick* case, and the illogic of treating presumptions differently from other rules of law allocating the burden of persuasion, all make it extremely unlikely that there are now serious constitutional limits on the effect that may be given to presumptions in civil cases.[29]

345. The Effect of Presumptions in Civil Cases.[30]

A presumption may have significance in a civil jury trial at two stages: (1) when one party or the other moves for a directed verdict and (2) when the time comes for the judges to instruct the jury.[31]

24. Id. at 643–644.

25. F.R.Ev. (R.D.1971) 301, Advisory Committee's Note. See also Fornoff, Presumptions—The Proposed Federal Rules of Evidence, 24 Ark.L.Rev. 401, 412–413 (1971).

26. See Prosser, Torts 494–496 (4th ed. 1971).

27. F.R.Ev., supra n. 25.

28. 359 U.S. 437 (1959).

29. The possibility of constitutional limitations on the effect of presumptions caused the draftsmen of the Uniform Rules of Evidence to distinguish between presumptions having probative value, as to which the burden of persuasion is upon the party against whom the presumption operates, and presumptions without probative value, which disappear where contrary proof is introduced. Uniform Rule 14. See Morgan, Presumptions, 10 Rutgers L.Rev. 512, 513 (1956). This distinction now seems completely unnecessary. See the excellent discussion of this question in Note, 53 Calif.L. Rev. 1439, 1467–71 (1965). See also § 345, infra.

30. Morgan, Basic Problems of Evidence 34–44 (1962), Some Problems of Proof 74–81 (1956); 9 Wigmore, Evidence §§ 2490–2493; James, Civil Procedure § 7.9 (1965); Bohlen, The Effect of Rebuttable Presumptions of Law upon the Burden of Proof, 68 U.Pa.L.Rev. 307 (1920); Cleary, Presuming and Pleading: An Essay on Juristic Immaturity, 12 Stan.L.Rev. 5 (1959); Fornoff, Presumptions—The Proposed Federal Rules of Evidence, 24 Ark.L.Rev. 401 (1971); Gausewitz, Presumptions in a One-Rule World, 5 Vand.L.Rev. 324 (1952); Laughlin, In Support of the Thayer Theory of Presumptions, 52 Mich.L.Rev. 195 (1953); Annot., 5 A.L.R.3d 19; C.J.S. Evidence §§ 117, 119; Dec.Dig. Evidence 🔑85–89, Trial 🔑205.

31. A presumption may be similarly significant in a case tried without a jury. In such a case, the

Sometimes the effect of a presumption, at either stage, is easy to discern; it follows naturally from the definition of the term. Thus, where a party proves the basic facts giving rise to a presumption,[32] he will have satisfied his burden of producing evidence with regard to the presumed fact and therefore his adversary's motion for directed verdict will be denied. If his adversary rests at that point, or if the adversary offers evidence going only to the existence of the basic facts giving rise to the presumption and not to the presumed fact, the jury will be instructed that if they find the existence of the basic facts, they must also find the presumed fact.[33] To illustrate, suppose plaintiff proves that a letter was mailed, that it was properly addressed, that it bore a return address, and that it was never returned. Such evidence is generally held to raise a presumption that the addressee received the letter.[34] Defendant's motion for a directed verdict, based upon nonreceipt of the letter, will be denied. Furthermore, if the defendant offers no proof on this question (or if he attempts only to show that the letter was not mailed and offers no proof that the letter was not in fact received) the jury will be instructed that if they find the existence of the facts as contended by plaintiff, they must find that the letter was received.

But the problem is far more difficult where the defendant does not rest and does not confine his proof to contradiction of the basic facts, but instead introduces proof tending to show the nonexistence of the presumed fact itself. For example, what is the effect of the presumption in the illustration given above, if the defendant takes the stand and testifies that he did not in fact receive the letter? If the plaintiff offers no additional proof, is the defendant now entitled to the directed verdict he was denied at the close of the plaintiff's case? If not, what effect, if any, should the presumption have upon the judge's charge to the jury? The problem of the effect of a presumption when

---

judge must consider what effect, if any, the presumption has, both when he decides whether a party having the burden of producing evidence has satisfied that burden and when he decides the case based upon all of the evidence. However, most of the problems concerning the effect to be given presumptions have centered around the question of what if anything, a jury is to be told about them. This section is therefore primarily directed to the jury trial. Nevertheless, it should be remembered throughout the discussion that many of the problems raised, particularly with regard to the effect of a presumption upon the burden of persuasion, exist whether or not the case is tried to a jury.

32. The test for whether evidence is sufficient to support a finding of the existence of the basic facts of a presumption should be the same as that used to assess the sufficiency of any proof introduced for the purpose of satisfying a party's burden of producing evidence. The problem in general is discussed in § 338, supra. Theoretically, there is no reason why the basic facts of a presumption cannot be proved by circumstantial rather than direct evidence, or even by the use of another presumption, the basic facts of which are established by sufficient evidence. See, e. g., Savarese v. State Farm Mutual Automobile Ins. Co., 150 Cal.App.2d 518, 310 P.2d 142 (1957) (proof of a regular business practice of mailing of a cancellation notice held to be sufficient to give rise to a presumption of receipt of that notice). A problem may arise, however, from the fact that a presumption is, by definition, a standardized inference. Therefore, a party seeking to establish the basic facts of a presumption through the use of circumstantial evidence may run head-on into the dogma that an inference may not be based upon another inference. See cases collected at 5 A.L.R.3d 100 (1966). The answer to the dilemma is that the "rule" against basing an inference on an inference or a presumption on a presumption should not be viewed as a rule at all but rather only as a warning against the use of inferences that are too remote or speculative. See § 338, n. 39. Such a warning ought to be heeded in the case of the basic facts of presumptions but should not be elevated to the status of an inflexible rule.

33. Whether a party who has relied on a presumption and who has introduced undisputed and unimpeached evidence with regard to the basic facts of that presumption may have a verdict directed in his favor on the issue, instead of the conditional peremptory ruling suggested in the text, will depend upon whether there is a prohibition in the jurisdiction against directing a verdict in favor of the party to whom the burden of persuasion is tentatively assigned on the basis of the pleadings. See § 338, n. 43 and accompanying text, supra.

34. See § 343 n. 57 and accompanying text, supra.

met by proof rebutting the presumed fact has literally plagued the courts and legal scholars. The balance of this section is devoted to that problem.

(A) The "Bursting Bubble" Theory and Deviations from It.

The Theory. The most widely followed theory of presumptions in American law has been that they are "like bats of the law flitting in the twilight, but disappearing in the sunshine of actual facts." [35] Put less poetically, under what has become known as the Thayer or "bursting bubble" theory, the only effect of a presumption is to shift the burden of producing evidence with regard to the presumed fact. If that evidence is produced by the adversary, the presumption is spent and disappears. In practical terms, the theory means that, although a presumption is available to permit the party relying upon it to survive a motion for directed verdict at the close of his own case, it has no other value in the trial. The view is derived from Thayer,[36] sanctioned by Wigmore,[37] and adopted in the Model Code of Evidence.[38]

It has been adopted, at least verbally, in countless modern decisions.[39]

The theory is simple to state, and if religiously followed, not at all difficult to apply. The trial judge need only determine that the evidence introduced in rebuttal is sufficient to support a finding contrary to the presumed fact.[40] If that determination is made, certainly there is no need to instruct the jury with regard to the presumption.[41] The opponent of the presumption may still not be entitled to a directed verdict, but if his motion is denied, the ruling will have nothing to do with the existence of a presumption. As has been discussed, presumptions are frequently created in instances in which the basic facts raise a natural inference of the presumed fact. This natural inference may be sufficient to take the case to the jury, despite the existence of contrary evidence and despite the resultant destruction of the presumption. For example, in the case of the presumption of receipt of a letter, referred to above, the defendant may destroy the presumption by denying receipt. Nevertheless, a jury question is presented, not because of the presumption, but because of the natural inference flowing from the plaintiff's showing that he had mailed a properly addressed letter that was not returned.[42]

35. Lamm. J. in Mockowik v. Kansas City, St. J. & C. B. R. Co., 196 Mo. 550, 571, 94 S.W. 256, 262 (1906), quoted in 9 Wigmore, Evidence § 2491. See also Bohlen, supra n. 30 at 314, where presumptions are described: "Like Maeterlinck's male bee, having functioned they disappear."

36. Thayer, Preliminary Treatise on Evidence, ch. 8, *passim*, and especially at 314, 336 (1898). Thayer, however, seems not to have had in mind a rule of law as inflexible as the doctrine that bears his name. He at least recognized the possibility of different rules for different presumptions. See Gausewitz, Presumptions, 40 Minn.L.Rev. 391, 406–408 (1956) where the "Thayer" doctrine, but not Thayer's scholarship, is criticized.

37. 9 Wigmore, Evidence § 2491(2). See, however, the apparent modification of his views as expressed later in the same volume, § 2498a, sub-sec. 21.

38. Model Code of Evidence Rule 704(2) (1942): ". . . when the basic fact . . . has been established . . . and evidence has been introduced which would support a finding of the non-existence of the presumed fact . . . the existence or non-existence of the presumed fact is to be determined exactly as if no presumption had ever been applicable . . . ," and Comment, "A

presumption, to be an efficient legal tool must . . . (2) be so administered that the jury never hear the word presumption used since it carries unpredictable connotations to different minds. . . ."

39. See cases collected at Annot., 5 A.L.R.3d 19; Dec.Dig. Evidence ⬤85–86, 89.

40. The evidence must be "credible." See Hildebrand v. Chicago, B. & Q. R. R., 45 Wyo. 175, 17 P.2d 651 (1933); Cleary, supra n. 30 at 18. See also Gausewitz, supra n. 30 at 327–328.

41. See, e. g., Orient Ins. Co. v. Cox, 218 Ark. 804, 238 S.W.2d 757 (1951); Ammundson v. Tinholt, 228 Minn. 115, 36 N.W.2d 521 (1949).

42. Rosenthal v. Walker, 111 U.S. 185 (1884); American Surety Co. v. Blake, 54 Idaho 1, 27 P.2d 972, 91 A.L.R. 153 (1933); Winkfield v. American Continental Ins. Co., 110 Ill.App.2d 156, 249 N.E. 2d 174, 176 (1969) ("If the addressee denies the receipt of the letter then the presumption is rebutted

Deviations from the theory—in general.
The "bursting bubble" theory has been soundly criticized as giving to presumptions an effect that is too "slight and evanescent" when viewed in the light of the reasons for the creation of the rules.[43] Presumptions, as we have seen, have been created for policy reasons that are similar to and just as strong as those that govern the allocation of the burdens of proof prior to the introduction of evidence.[44] These policy considerations generally persist despite the existence of proof rebutting the presumed fact. They may be completely frustrated by the Thayer rule when the basic facts of the presumption do not give rise to an inference that is naturally sufficient to take the case to the jury. Similarly, even if the natural inference is sufficient to present a jury question, it may be so weak that the jury is unlikely to consider it in its decision unless specifically told to do so. If the policy behind the presumption is not to be thwarted, some instruction to the jury is needed despite any theoretical prohibition against a charge of this kind.

These considerations have not gone unrecognized by the courts. Thus, courts, even

though unwilling to reject the dogma entirely, often find ways to deviate from it in their treatment of at least some presumptions, generally those which are based upon particularly strong and visible policies. Perhaps the best example is the presumption of legitimacy arising from proof that a child was born during the course of a marriage. The strong policies behind the presumption are so apparent that the courts have universally agreed that the party contending that the child is illegitimate not only has the burden of producing evidence in support of his contention, but also has a heavy burden of persuasion on the issue as well.[45]

Another example of special treatment for certain presumptions is the effect given by some courts to the presumption of agency or of consent arising from ownership of an automobile.[46] The classic theory would dictate that the presumption is destroyed once the defendant or the driver testifies to facts sufficient to support a finding of nonagency or an absence of consent. Some courts have so held.[47] However, other courts have recognized that the policies behind the presumption, i. e., the defendant's superior access to the evidence and the social policy of widening the responsibility for owners of motor vehicles, may not die with the introduction of evidence on the question from the defendant, particularly when that evidence comes in the form of his own or his servant's testimony. These courts have been unwilling to rely solely upon the natural inferences that might arise from plaintiff's proof,[48] and in-

---

and receipt becomes a question to be resolved by the trier of fact."); Stacey v. Sankovich, 19 Mich. App. 688, 173 N.W.2d 225 (1969) ("[The] presumption may be rebutted by evidence, but whether it was is a question for the trier of fact."); Southland Life Ins. Co. v. Greenwade, 138 Tex. 450, 159 S.W.2d 854, 857 (1942) ("We agree . . . that a presumption as such is not evidence and that it vanished as such in view of the opposing evidence; but we do not agree that the evidentiary facts upon which it was established, could no longer be considered by the trier of facts."). Cf. Grade v. Mariposa County, 132 Cal. 75, 64 Pac. 117 (1901); Tremayne v. American SMW Corp., 125 Cal.App.2d 852, 271 P.2d 229 (1954) (nonjury cases in which court affirmed finding of nonreceipt based upon simple denial despite evidence that the correspondence was duly mailed).

43. Morgan and Maguire, Looking Backward and Forward at Evidence, 50 Harv.L.Rev. 909, 913 (1937). See also, Morgan, Some Problems of Proof 74–81 (1956). Other writers are in accord, see, e. g., Cleary, supra n. 30 at 18; Gausewitz, supra n. 30 at 342. Contra, Laughlin, supra n. 30.

44. See § 343, supra.

45. See § 343, nn. 68–73 and accompanying text, supra.

46. See § 343, nn. 58–61 and accompanying text, supra.

47. E. g., Peoples v. Seamon, 249 Ala. 284, 31 So.2d 88 (1947); McIver v. Schwartz, 50 R.I. 68, 145 Atl. 101 (1929). See additional cases collected at Annot., 5 A.L.R.3d 19, 66–69.

48. Where the presumption is held to be destroyed, the natural inference arising from plaintiff's proof of ownership may or may not be sufficient to send

stead require more from the defendant in rebuttal, such as, that his evidence be "uncontradicted, clear, convincing and unimpeached." [49] Moreover, many courts also hold that the special policies behind the presumption require that the jury be informed of its existence.[50]

Deviations from the theory—conflicting presumptions. Frequent deviations from the rigid dictates of the "bursting bubble" theory occur in the treatment of conflicting presumptions. A conflict between presumptions may arise as follows: W, asserting that she is the widow of H, claims her share of his property, and proves that on a certain day she and H were married. The adversary then proves that three or four years before her marriage to H, the alleged widow married another man. W's proof gives her the benefit of the presumption of the validity of a marriage. The adversary's proof gives rise to the general presumption of the continuance of a status or condition once proved to exist, and a specific presumption of the continuance of a marriage relationship. The

presumed facts of the claimant's presumption and those of the adversary's are contradictory.[51] How resolve the conflict? Thayer's solution would be to consider that the presumptions in this situation have disappeared and the facts upon which the respective presumptions were based shall simply be weighed as circumstances with all the other facts that may be relevant, giving no effect to the presumptions.[52] Perhaps when the conflicting presumptions involved are based upon probability or upon procedural convenience, the solution is a fairly practical one.[53]

The particular presumptions involved in the case given as an example, however, were not of that description. On the one hand, the presumption of the validity of a marriage is founded not only in probability, but in the strongest social policy favoring legitimacy and the stability of family inheritances and expectations.[54] On the other hand, the

---

the case to the jury, depending both upon the court's view of the inference and the nature of the rebutting proof. Compare, e. g., Peoples v. Seamon, supra n. 47 (question for the jury), with Kavanaugh v. Wheeling, 175 Va. 105, 7 S.E.2d 125 (1940) (inference insufficient to prove car used in owner's business; verdict for plaintiff set aside).

49. Bradley v. S. L. Savidge, Inc., 13 Wash.2d 28, 123 P.2d 780, 791 (1942) (defendant's evidence held to meet test). See also Standard Coffee Co. v. Trippet, 108 F.2d 161 (5th Cir. 1939) (Texas law); Krisher v. Duff, 331 Mich. 699, 50 N.W.2d 332, 337 (1951) ("Generally speaking, the evidence to make this presumption disappear should be positive, unequivocal, strong and credible. The presumption is given more weight because of the dangerous instrumentality involved and the danger of permitting incompetent driving on the highway; and because the proof or disproof of consent or permission usually rests almost entirely with the defendants.").

50. See, e. g., Grier v. Rosenberg, 213 Md. 248, 131 A.2d 737 (1957) (citing first edition of this text); Krisher v. Duff, supra n. 49 (no need to mention statute, but jury should be told that defendant must come forward with evidence of a clear, positive and credible nature to refute the presumptions of knowledge or consent).

51. For an exhaustive collection of cases discussing these presumptions and the conflict between them see Annot., 14 A.L.R.2d 7. Recent cases include Yarbrough v. United States, 341 F.2d 621 (Court of Claims 1965); Ventura v. Ventura, 53 Misc.2d 881, 280 N.Y.S.2d 5 (1967); DeRyder v. Metropolitan Life Ins. Co., 206 Va. 602, 145 S.E.2d 177 (1965).

52. See Thayer, Preliminary Treatise on Evidence 346 (1898) followed in 9 Wigmore, Evidence § 2493; Model Code of Evidence Rules 701(3), 704 (2). For a convincing exposition of the contrary view that as between conflicting presumptions the one founded on the stronger policy should prevail, see Morgan, Some Observations Concerning Presumptions, 44 Harv.L.Rev. 906, 932 n. 41 (1931).

53. See City of Montpelier v. Town of Calais, 114 Vt. 5, 39 A.2d 350 (1944) where each side invoked the presumption of official regularity in respect of the acts of its own officers, and the court held that the case would be determined without regard to the presumptions.

54. State v. Rocker, 130 Iowa 239, 106 N.W. 645, 649 (1906) ("where necessary to sustain the legitimacy of children or in making disposition of property interests. . . ."). See Nixon v. Wichita Land & Cattle Co., 84 Tex. 408, 19 S.W. 560, 561 (1892), where Gaines, J. quotes the following from 1 Bishop, Marriage and Divorce § 457 (6th Ed. 1881): "It being for the highest good of the parties, of the children, and of the community that all intercourse between the sexes in form matrimonial should be such in fact, the law, when administered by enlightened judges, seizes upon all probabilities, and

presumptions of continuance of lives and marriage relationships are based chiefly on probability and trial convenience, and the probability, of course, varies in accordance with the length of time for which the continuance is to be presumed in the particular case. This special situation of the questioned validity of a second marriage has been the principal area in which the problem of conflicting presumptions has been discussed by the courts. They have not been willing here to follow Thayer's suggestion of disregarding both rival presumptions and leaving the issue to the indifferent arbitrament of a weighing of circumstantial inferences. They have often preferred to formulate the issue in terms of a conflict of presumptions and to hold that the presumption of the validity of marriage is "stronger" and should prevail.[55] This doctrine that the weightier presumption prevails should probably be available in any situation which may reasonably be theorized as one of conflicting presumptions, and where one of the presumptions is grounded in a predominant social policy.

Another and perhaps even better approach to the problem is to sidestep the conflict entirely and create a new presumption. Such a presumption has evolved in cases involving conflicting marriages. Under this rule, where a person has been shown to have been married successively to different spouses, there is a presumption that the earlier marriage was dissolved by death or divorce before the later one was contracted.[56] While of course the presumption is rebuttable, as in the case of the presumption of legitimacy, many courts place a special burden of persuasion upon the party attacking the validity of the second marriage by declaring that the presumption can only be overcome by clear, cogent and convincing evidence.[57]

Deviations from the theory—instructions to the jury. Because of the strength of the natural inferences that generally arise from the basic facts of a presumption, judges are seldom faced with the prospect of directing a verdict against the party relying upon a presumption. Similarly, conflicting presumptions are relatively rare. However, far more frequently, courts have justifiably held that the policies behind presumptions necessitate an instruction that in some way calls the existence of the rule to the attention of the jury despite the Thayerian proscription against the practice. The digests give abundant evidence of the widespread and unquestioning acceptance of the practice of informing the jury of the rule despite the fact that countervailing evidence has been adduced upon the disputed inference.[58]

---

presses into its service all things else, which can help it in each particular case to sustain the marriage, and repel the conclusion of unlawful commerce."

55. See, e. g., Smiley v. Smiley, 247 Ark. 933, 448 S.W.2d 642 (1970); Apelbaum v. Apelbaum, 7 App. Div.2d 911, 183 N.Y.S.2d 54 (1959); Meade v. State Compensation Com'r, 147 W.Va. 72, 125 S.E.2d 771 (1962); Greensborough v. Underhill, 12 Vt. 604, 607 (1839); cases collected in Annot., 14 A.L.R.2d, supra n. 51, at 37–44; Dec.Dig. Marriage ☞40(9). See also Uniform Rule 15: "If two presumptions arise which are conflicting with each other the judge shall apply the presumption which is founded on the weightier considerations of policy and logic. If there is no such preponderance both presumptions shall be disregarded."

56. E. g., J. J. Cater Furn. Co. v. Banks, 152 Fla. 377, 11 So.2d 776 (1943); Nicholas v. Idaho Power Co., 63 Idaho 675, 125 P.2d 321 (1942); Brown v. Brown, 51 Misc.2d 839, 274 N.Y.S.2d 484 (1966); cases collected in 9 Wigmore, Evidence § 2506, Annot., 14 A.L.R.2d at 20–29, 55 C.J.S. Marriage § 43(3) (1948), Dec.Dig. Marriage, ☞40(5, 6). Since the policy reasons are absent, the presumption is held inapplicable in prosecutions for bigamy. Fletcher v. State, 169 Ind. 77, 81 N.E. 1083 (1907); Wright v. State, 198 Md. 163, 81 A.2d 602 (1951).

57. Kolombatovich v. Magma Copper Co., 43 Ariz. 314, 30 P.2d 832 (1934); In re Jubala's Estate, 40 N.M. 312, 59 P.2d 356 (1936); Marcum v. Zaring, 406 P.2d 970 (Okla.1965); Annot., 14 A.L.R.2d at 45–47; Dec.Dig. Marriage ☞40(10, 11).

58. Dec.Dig. Trial ☞205, 234(7). See also Devitt and Blackmar, Federal Jury Practice and Instructions, ch. 71 (2d ed.); Nevada Pattern Civil Jury Instructions 2.41; Washington Pattern Jury Instructions (Civil) 24.00 (1967).

Given the frequency of the deviation, however, the manner in which the jury is to be informed has been a matter of considerable dispute and confusion. The baffling nature of the presumption as a tool for the art of thinking bewilders one who searches for a form of phrasing with which to present the notion to a jury. Most of the forms have been predictably bewildering. For example, judges have occasionaly contented themselves with a statement in the instructions of the terms of the presumption, without more. This leaves the jury in the air, or implies too much.[59] The jury, unless a further explanation is made, may suppose that the presumption is a conclusive one, especially if the judge uses the expression, "the law presumes."

Another solution, formerly more popular than now, is to instruct the jury that the presumption is "evidence," to be weighed and considered with the testimony in the case.[60] This avoids the danger that the jury may infer that the presumption is conclusive, but it probably means little to the jury, and certainly runs counter to accepted theories of the nature of evidence.

More attractive theoretically, is the suggestion that the judge instruct the jury that the presumption is to stand accepted, unless they find that the facts upon which the presumed inference rests are met by evidence of equal weight, or in other words, unless the contrary evidence leaves their minds in equipoise, in which event they should decide against the party having the burden of persuasion upon the issue.[61] It is hard to phrase such an instruction without conveying the impression that the presumption itself is "evidence" which must be "met" or "balanced."[62] The overriding objection, however, is the impression of futility that it conveys. It prescribes a difficult metaphysical task for the jury, and, in actual use, may mystify rather than help the average juror.[63]

One possible solution, perhaps better than those already mentioned, would be for the trial judge simply to mention the basic facts

---

59. See the criticism of such a charge in Garrettson v. Pegg, 64 Ill. 111 (1872). See also Kettlewell v. Prudential Ins. Co. of America, 6 Ill.App.2d 434, 128 N.E.2d 652 (1955). But an instruction merely directing the jury to consider the presumption against suicide without explaining its effect was thought sufficient in Radius v. Travelers Ins. Co., 87 F.2d 412 (9th Cir. 1937).

60. For example, prior to 1965, the California courts held that a presumption is evidence to be weighed along with all other evidence in the case and that the jury should be so instructed. See, e. g., Smellie v. Southern Pac. Co., 212 Cal. 540, 299 Pac. 529 (1931) (setting forth the doctrine); Gigliotti v. Nunes, 45 Cal.2d 85, 286 P.2d 809, 815 (1955) (setting forth a typical instruction). In 1965, however, the state adopted a new evidence code which classified the procedural effect of presumptions according to the policies behind their creation and which specifically rejected the notion that a presumption is evidence. West's Ann.Cal.Evid.Code, § 600. See thorough discussion of this shift in Note, 53 Calif.L.Rev. 1439, 1480–87 (1965). See also notes 78–80 and accompanying text, infra.

For a collection of cases holding that a presumption is evidence see Annot., 5 A.L.R.3d 19, 35–39. For criticisms of the "presumption is evidence" rule see McBaine, Presumptions; Are They Evidence? 26 Calif.L.Rev. 519 (1938); Gausewitz, Presumptions in a One-Rule World, 5 Vand.L.Rev. 324, 333–34 (1952).

61. See, e. g., Klunk v. Hocking Valley R. Co., 74 Ohio St. 125, 77 N.E. 752 (1906); Tresise v. Ashdown, 118 Ohio St. 307, 160 N.E. 898 (1928). Although the general rule in Ohio now seems to be that a presumption disappears when met by contrary proof, see, e. g., Ayers v. Woodward, 166 Ohio St. 138, 140 N.E.2d 401 (1957), 1 Ohio Jury Instructions § 5.13 (1968), a standard instruction has been issued in that state in substantially the form suggested in the text with regard to an inference of contributory negligence arising from the plaintiff's own proof, 1 Ohio Jury Instructions § 9.11 (1968) and in somewhat similar form with regard to the presumption of agency arising from the owner's presence in an automobile. 1 Id. § 15.31 (1968).

62. Such an instruction was disapproved on this ground in Bollenbach v. Bloomenthal, 341 Ill. 539, 173 N.E. 670, 673 (1930). But see Hildebrand v. Chicago, B. & Q. R. R., 45 Wyo. 175, 17 P.2d 651 (1933).

63. Similar problems exist with regard to instructions that inform the jury that they should find for the proponent of the instruction unless they believe evidence which reasonably tends to rebut the presumed fact in which case the presumption should be disregarded and the case decided from all of the evidence. See, e. g., Washington Pattern Jury Instructions 24.03 (1967).

of the presumption and to point out the general probability of the circumstantial inference as one of the factors to be considered by the jury.[64] By this technique, however, a true presumption would be converted into nothing more than a permissible inference. Moreover, the solution is simply not a feasible one in many jurisdictions without at least a new interpretation of another aspect of the law. The trial judge in most states must tread warily to avoid an expression of opinion on the facts. Although instructions on certain standardized inferences such as *res ipsa loquitur* are permitted,[65] the practice, wisely or not, may frown on any explanation of the allowable circumstantial inferences from particular facts as "invading the province of the jury." [66]

Undoubtedly the best solution is the approach consistently used with regard to the presumption of legitimacy and frankly adopted by some courts with regard to other presumptions. In these cases, the courts hold that the presumption operates to fix the burden of persuasion upon the adversary.[67] In

terms of instructions to the jury, this means that, regardless of whether the word "presumption" is ever mentioned to the jury, it is told that the opponent must prove the nonexistence of the presumed fact by a preponderance of the evidence. In effect, the courts in these cases hold that the policies giving rise to the presumptions are stronger than the policies that fixed the burden of persuasion prior to the introduction of evidence. As will be more thoroughly discussed below, the decision is almost always a sound one.

(B) The Possibility of a Single Rule Governing the Effect of Presumptions.

Perhaps the greatest difficulty with the "bursting bubble" approach is that, despite its apparent simplicity, the conflicting desires of the courts to adopt it in theory and yet to avoid its overly-rigid dictates have turned it into a judicial nightmare of confusion and inconsistency. Is there a single better theory for all presumptions or must we simply continue to meet the problem on a presumption by presumption basis?

Many legal scholars have now come to the view that there is a single better rule: anything worthy of the name "presumption" has the effect of fixing the burden of persuasion on the party contesting the existence of the presumed fact.[68] The principal objection to

64. A suggestion of the propriety of such a charge was made in Jefferson Standard Life Ins. Co. v. Clemmer, 79 F.2d 724 (4th Cir. 1935). In federal court, however, the trial judge retains his common law powers to explain allowable inferences from circumstantial evidence.

65. See § 342 n. 40 and accompanying text, supra.

66. See, e. g., Pridmore v. Chicago, R. I. & P. R. Co., 275 Ill. 386, 114 N.E. 176 (1916); Kennedy v. Phillips, 319 Mo. 573, 5 S.W.2d 33 (1928).

67. E. g., Dick v. New York Life Ins. Co., 359 U.S. 437 (1959) (North Dakota rule re presumption of accidental death); Lewis v. New York Life Ins. Co., 113 Mont. 151, 124 P.2d 579 (1942) (presumption of accidental death); In re Swan's Estate, 4 Utah 2d 277, 293 P.2d 682 (1956) (presumption of fraud and undue influence in will contest). See also O'Dea v. Amodeo, 118 Conn. 58, 170 Atl. 486, 488 (1934) (statutory presumption that car driven by member of owner's family was being operated as a family car; ". . . the presumption shall avail the plaintiff until such time as the trier finds proven the circumstances of the situation with reference to the use made of the car and the authority of the person operating it to drive it, leaving the burden then upon the plaintiff to establish, in view of the facts so found, that the car was

being operated at the time as a family car."); Krisher v. Duff, 331 Mich. 699, 50 N.W.2d 332, 339 (1951) (under statutory presumption that member of family using car is doing so with owner's consent, error to refuse to charge the jury that the adversary must come forward with evidence of a "clear, positive and credible nature" to refute the presumption).

68. See, e. g., F.R.Ev. (R.D.1971) 301, Advisory Committee's Note; Morgan, Some Problems of Proof 74–81 (1956); Cleary, supra n. 30 at 20; Gausewitz, supra n. 30 at 342. The rule that a presumption operates to fix the burden of persuasion has been called the Pennsylvania rule. However, if the rule ever had general application in that state, it certainly no longer does. See, e. g., Allison v. Snelling & Snelling, Inc., 425 Pa. 519, 229 A.2d 861 (1967); Waters v. New Amsterdam Cas. Co., 393

such a rule has been that it requires a "shift" in the burden of persuasion, something that is, by definition of the burden, impossible.[69] The argument, however, assumes that the burden of persuasion is fixed at the commencement of the action. This is simply not the case. As we have seen,[70] the burden of persuasion need not finally be assigned until the case is ready to go to the jury. Thus, using a presumption to fix that burden would not cause it to shift, but merely cause it to be assigned on the basis of policy considerations arising from the evidence introduced at trial rather than those thought to exist on the basis of the pleadings.[71] Certainly there is no reason why policy factors thought to be controlling at the pleading stage should outweigh factors bearing upon the same policies that arise from the evidence. Just the reverse should be true.

As has been discussed, many courts do view at least certain presumptions as fixing the burden of persuasion. Why should all presumptions do so? Perhaps the best answer to that question is the one given by the late Professor Edmund Morgan:

"Just as the courts have come to recognize that there is no a priori formula for fixing the burden of persuasion, so they should recognize that if there is a good reason for putting on one party or the other the burden of going forward with evidence —if it might not as well have been determined by chance—it ought to be good enough to control a finding when the mind of the trier is in equilibrium." [72]

Although Professor Morgan served as a reporter for the Model Code of Evidence, he was unable to persuade the draftsmen of that code to incorporate into it a provision embracing his view of the effect of presumptions.[73] The Model Code instead takes a rigid Thayerian position.[74] However, Morgan also was active in the drafting of the Uniform Rules of Evidence, where considerably more success in inducing an adoption of his theory was encountered. The Uniform Rules provide that where the facts upon which the presumption is based have "probative value" the burden of persuasion is assigned to the adversary; where there is no such probative value, the presumption has only a Thayerian effect and dies when met by contrary proof.[75] This rule, although certainly a step forward from the Model Code, is obviously still not a comprehensive and dependable guide to the treatment of presumptions.[76] Different courts may give different answers to the question of whether a particular presumption has probative value. The possibilities of inconsistency and confusion, although reduced by the rule, are still present. Further, the distinction made is a thin one that disregards the existence of strong social policies behind some presumptions that lack probative value. Certainly if a presumption is not based on probability but rather is based solely upon social policy there is more, and not less, reason to preserve it in the face of contrary proof. A presumption based on a natural inference can stand on its own weight, either when met by a motion for directed verdict or in the jury's deliberations. A presumption based on social policy may need an extra boost in order to insure that that policy is not overlooked.

Pa. 247, 144 A.2d 354 (1958). See also Levin, Pennsylvania and the Uniform Rules of Evidence: Presumptions and Dead Man Statutes, 103 U.Pa. L.Rev. 1 (1954).

69. See, e. g., Laughlin, supra n. 30 at 211.

70. See § 336, supra.

71. The policies behind the allocation of the burden of persuasion generally are discussed in § 337, supra. The policies behind the creation of presumptions are discussed in § 343, supra.

72. Some Problems of Proof, supra n. 68 at 81.

73. See Morgan, Foreword to Model Code of Evidence at 54–65 (1942).

74. Rule 704.

75. Rule 14.

76. See the criticism of the rule in Cleary, supra n. 30 at 28; Gausewitz, Presumptions, 40 Minn.L. Rev. 391, 401–410 (1956).

Morgan apparently recognized the weakness of the distinction made by the rule and seemed to have agreed to it only to allay fears that a provision giving to all presumptions the effect of fixing the burden of persuasion might be unconstitutional.[77] As has been previously discussed, these fears are no longer warranted.

An approach almost directly opposite to the one taken in the Uniform Rules is taken in California's Code of Evidence, adopted in 1965. Under the California code, presumptions based upon "public policy" operate to fix the burden of persuasion;[78] presumptions that are established "to implement no public policy other than to facilitate the determination of the particular action" are given a Thayerian effect.[79] The California approach is an improvement over the Uniform Rules but is still not completely satisfactory. Except to the extent that presumptions are specifically covered in the code, the California courts will still have to determine the policy behind each individual presumption. The line between presumptions based on public policy and those which are not may not be easy to draw.[80] Furthermore, although the California distinction is more sound than that made in the Uniform Rules, it is not completely convincing. The fact that the policy giving rise to a presumption is one that is concerned with the resolution of a particular dispute rather than the implementation of broader social goals, does not necessarily mean that the policy is satisfied by a shifting of the burden of producing evidence and that it disappears when contrary proof is introduced. The California code asks the wrong question about the policies behind presumptions. The inquiry should not be directed to the breadth of the policy but rather to the question whether the policy considerations behind the presumptions are sufficient to override the policies that tentatively fixed the burdens of proof at the pleading stage. Generally, such a question must be answered in favor of the policies behind the presumption. To paraphrase Professor Morgan, if a reason is good enough to shift the burden of going forward, it ought to be good enough to control a finding when the jury is in doubt.

A comprehensive approach to the problem has finally been taken by, what are at this writing, the proposed Federal Rules of Evidence. Proposed Rule 301 provides:

"In all cases not otherwise provided for by Act of Congress or by these rules a presumption imposes on the party against whom it is directed the burden of proving that the nonexistence of the presumed fact is more probable than its existence."

Unfortunately, despite the apparent breadth of this rule, it will have a somewhat limited impact even in the federal courts. Under the *Erie* doctrine, the effect of a presumption, particularly with respect to a fact which is an element of a claim or defense, will often be governed by state law.[81] The proposed rule will affect only presumptions in matters governed by federal law and presumptions in cases governed by state law where less than an element of a claim or defense is involved.[82] However, as in the case of the Federal Rules of Civil Procedure, the Federal Rules of Evidence may provide a model for state adoption.[83]

77. Morgan, Presumptions, 10 Rutgers L.Rev. 512, 513 (1956).

78. West's Ann.Cal.Evid.Code, §§ 605–606.

79. Id. §§ 603–604.

80. See Note, 53 Calif.L.Rev. 1439, 1445–50 (1965).

81. See F.R.Ev. (R.D.1971) 302, Advisory Committee's Note.

82. It has been suggested that the proper use of presumptions is only with regard to facts not constituting an element of the case. Where a presumption has been used with regard to an element of a claim or defense, the result that it achieves can be more easily and directly achieved through the normal processes of pleading. Cleary, supra n. 30 at 21–27.

83. See Fornoff, supra n. 30 at 416; Comments, 37 Tenn.L.Rev. 556 (1970), 1970 Wis.L.Rev. 1173.

The approach taken by the proposed federal rules leaves at least one question open with regard to the effect of presumptions—whether the existence of the presumptions should be specifically mentioned to the jury. The question is perhaps particularly significant where a presumption operates to allocate the burden of persuasion to a party who already has that burden.[84] Presumably a federal judge will retain his powers to comment on the evidence and could, in his discretion, mention the presumption. But should he? If a rule such as that contained in the proposed federal rules is adopted in a jurisdiction in which the trial judge has more limited powers, should the rule provide for the presumption to be mentioned to the jury? The best answer to both of these questions is probably no. The policies behind a presumption are usually fully satisfied by placing the burden of persuasion upon the adversary. If the courts feel that more is needed, the measure of persuasion can be increased as is now done in the case of the presumption of legitimacy.[85] There is no more need to tell the jury why one party or the other has the burden of persuasion where that burden is fixed by a presumption than there is where the burden is fixed on the basis of policies apparent from the pleadings. If the policy considerations existing at the pleading stage and those arising from the evidence both place the burden of persuasion on the same party, we can be fairly certain that the burden is in the right place. However, unless we are willing to increase the measure of persuasion nothing can be gained by informing the jury of the coincidence.[86] The word

"presumption" would only tend to confuse the issue.[87]

346. The Effect of Presumptions in Criminal Cases.

As has been earlier pointed out, the courts and the legislatures do not always use the term presumption in the sense either that the term is used in this text or by the same courts and legislatures on other occasions.[88] The use of loose terminology is perhaps even more prevalent in dealing with presumptions operating in criminal cases than in civil cases. The best example is one that has already been given. The "presumption of innocence" is not a presumption at all, but simply another way of stating the rule that the prosecution has the burden of proving the

---

84. See discussion in Levin, supra n. 68 at 27.

85. The proposed federal rules contain no provision for an increased measure of persuasion. See F.R. Ev. (R.D.1971) 301. See also Fornoff, supra n. 30 at 409.

86. The problem of instructing the jury with regard to a presumption operating against the party having the burden of persuasion is most likely to oc-

cur in the case of the presumption of due care. See State of Maryland for the Use of Geils v. Baltimore Transit Co., 329 F.2d 738 (4th Cir. 1964) cert. denied 379 U.S. 842, particularly the thoughtful dissent by Haynsworth, J., 329 F.2d at 742–748.

87. See also James, Civil Procedure 266 (1965). Dean McCormick, in the first edition of this text, disagreed with this position stating (p. 672): "As I have indicated earlier in this paper, I am inclined to think that it is a more natural practice, especially under the American tied-judge system, to mention the presumption, so that the jury may appreciate the legal recognition of a slant of policy or probability as the reason for placing on the party this particular burden. If this is true when the presumption operates (as it usually would) in favor of the plaintiff, who has the general burden of proof, so that the presumption would result in an issue being singled out and the burden thereon placed on the defendant, much more is it true when the presumption operates in favor of the defendant. In such case under the orthodox view the presumption would be swallowed up in the larger instruction that the plaintiff has the burden on everything that he has pleaded. This smothers any hint of the recognized policy or probabilities behind the particular presumption."

88. See § 342, n. 24 and accompanying text, supra. The converse of the proposition stated in the text is also true: rules that are treated as presumptions are not always called by that name. For an illustration of the use and misuse of terminology in this area of the law see the list of statutes "that provide that proof of specified facts has a procedural effect" contained in the Working Papers of the National Commission on Reform of Federal Criminal Laws, Volume 1, at 27–31 (1970).

guilt of the accused beyond a reasonable doubt.[89]

Similarly, the term presumption has been used in connection with rules that define the elements of, and create affirmative defenses to, a crime. These rules define the crime as consisting, for example, of the elements A and B and provide that the defendant may not be guilty if he proves C. They may specify that the defendant simply has the burden of producing evidence with regard to C or may also fix the burden of persuasion on the defendant as well. They do not operate with regard to inferences drawn from the evidence, but rather operate as principles of substantive law governing the entire proceeding. An example of such a rule of law mislabeled a presumption is the "presumption of sanity," as it operates against the defendant in a criminal case.[90] The so-called "presumption" is simply a rule stating that the defendant has the burden of producing evidence (or of proving) his insanity at the time of the offense. The use of the term presumption is only confusing.[91]

Although there are constitutional limitations upon the creation of affirmative defenses,[92] the limitations are different from those imposed upon presumptions. Principally, there would seem to be no need for a rational connection between the elements of the offense and the affirmative defense, as there must be between an element and the presumption used to establish its existence.[93] In the case of a presumption, the legislature has chosen to include the element established through the presumption in its description of the offense. In such a case, it is no argument to say that the legislature could have deleted the element from the definition. The point is that it did not do so. The included element must therefore be established either by facts in evidence proving its existence beyond a reasonable doubt or by a presumed fact that may be inferred beyond a reasonable doubt from the facts proved. But in the case of the affirmative defense, the legislature defines the offense as including certain elements, A and B, and gives notice that proof beyond a reasonable doubt of these elements will subject the violator to punishment. The existence of an affirmative defense, C, does not detract from the given notice, but rather adds another factor to the case which, if proved, may exonerate

89. See § 342, supra.

90. See § 341, n. 17; above; § 342, n. 43, supra.

91. Another instance of a rule of substantive law mislabeled a presumption is the rule existing, for example, in North Carolina to the effect that two elements of murder, that the act was unlawful and that it was done with malice, are "presumed" when the state establishes that the defendant intentionally killed the deceased by using a deadly weapon. When the "presumption" goes into effect, the defense has the burden of proving to the satisfaction of the jury "the legal provocation that will rob the crime of malice and thus reduce it to manslaughter, or that will excuse it altogether upon the ground of self-defense." See, e. g., State v. Boyd, 278 N.C. 682, 180 S.E.2d 794 (1971); State v. Barrow, 276 N.C. 381, 172 S.E.2d 512 (1970). The rule resembles a presumption more than either the presumption of innocence or the presumption of sanity discussed in the text, because it arises only after the production of some evidence. However, it is better described as a rule of substantive law, providing that provocation and self-defense are affirmative defenses in a specific type of murder case. The rule is so deeply ingrained in the common law of the state that the defendant is necessarily put on notice that, where he has intentionally

used a deadly weapon, unlawfulness or malice are not elements of the state's case and that he may be excused only if he proves that his acts were justified or excused. The effect of the rule is identical to that of a rule fixing the burdens of proof with regard to an affirmative defense prior to the introduction of any evidence and the rule should therefore be treated identically.

The distinction between presumptions and affirmative defenses is clearly maintained in both the Model Penal Code, § 1.12 (Proposed Official Draft 1962) and the Proposed New Federal Criminal Code § 103, Final Report of the National Commission on Reform of Federal Criminal Laws (1971).

92. See § 341, nn. 12–16 and accompanying text, supra.

93. See the discussion of the constitutionality of presumptions § 344, supra. See also Christie and Pye, Presumptions and Assumptions in the Criminal Law: Another View, 1970 Duke L.J. 919, 936.

the accused. There is no point in requiring a rational connection between A and B and the nonexistence of C.[94] As has been perceptively stated, to impose such a requirement may leave "the defendant materially worse off" in that the legislature might refuse to recognize any defense at all.[95]

Once things that are not presumptions have been weeded out, the question of the permissible effect of a true presumption remains. Through the operation of an affirmative defense, the accused may have both the burden of producing evidence and the burden of persuasion with regard to an issue. Can either of these burdens ever be allocated to him as the result of the operation of a presumption? The answer to this question would appear to be no. Presumptions upheld in cases such as United States v. Gainey[96] and Turner v. United States[97] had only the effect of a permissible inference. The jury was told that it could but was not required to find the existence of the presumed fact. In the *Gainey* case, the Court particularly emphasized the permissive nature of the presumption.[98] Both the right of the defendant to trial by jury and his right to have the prosecution prove each element of the offense beyond a reasonable doubt are constitutionally protected. A rule that shifted the burden of producing evidence with regard to an element of the offense so as to require the jury to find against the defendant in the absence of rebutting evidence or that required that the defendant persuade the jury of the nonexistence of such an element would violate both these rights.[99] Mr. Justice Black's arguments in his dissents in *Gainey*[1] and *Turner*[2] would apply with greater and certainly compelling force to such a rule.

Given the constitutional limitations upon the effect of presumptions in criminal cases, other questions remain. When is it proper to submit an issue involving a presumed fact to the jury? If the issue is submitted to the jury, what, if anything, should the jury be told about the presumption?

Different answers to the first question have been given in recent attempts to codify the law. The Model Penal Code[3] and the

---

94. Christie and Pye, supra n. 93. Contra, Ashford and Risinger, Presumptions, Assumptions and Due Process in Criminal Cases: A Theoretical Overview, 79 Yale L.J. 165 (1969). Perhaps the controlling considerations in determining the constitutional validity of an affirmative defense, as opposed to a presumption, are still those stated by Mr. Justice Cardozo in Morrison v. California, 291 U.S. 82, 91 (1934):

"For a transfer of the burden, experience must teach that the evidence held to be inculpatory has at least a sinister significance . . . , or if this at times be lacking, there must be in any event a manifest disparity in convenience of proof and opportunity for knowledge, as, for instance, where a general prohibition is applicable to every one who is unable to bring himself within the range of an exception. . . . The list is not exhaustive. Other instances may have arisen or may develop in the future where the balance of convenience can be redressed without oppression to the defendant through the same procedural expedient. The decisive considerations are too variable, too much distinctions of degree, too dependent in last analysis upon a common sense estimate of fairness or of facilities of proof, to be crowded into a formula. One can do no more than adumbrate them; sharper definition must await the specific case as it arises." (Footnote omitted).

95. Christie and Pye, supra n. 93 at 937.

96. 380 U.S. 63 (1954). See discussion § 344, supra.

97. 396 U.S. 398 (1970). See discussion § 344, supra.

98. 380 U.S. at 70.

99. See also F.R.Ev. (R.D.1971) 303, Advisory Committee's Note. Soules, Presumptions in Criminal Cases, 20 Baylor L.Rev. 277, 283 (1968) (Texas law). The states have generally recognized the limitation expressed in the text without the need of a Supreme Court ruling specifically on the point. See Note, 2 St. Mary's L.J. 115, 118 (1970), where the author lists state court cases involving rulings on the validity of presumptions. In no case was the presumption given more than a permissive effect.

1. 380 U.S. at 74–88.

2. 396 U.S. at 425–434.

3. § 1.12(5) (a) (Proposed Official Draft 1962). See also Tentative Draft No. 4, Comments § 1.13 at 114–118 (1955).

Proposed New Federal Criminal Code [4] provide that the issue of the existence of the presumed fact must be submitted to the jury unless the court is satisfied that the evidence as a whole clearly negatives the presumed fact.   On the other hand, the proposed Federal Rules of Evidence distinguish between presumptions that operate with regard to an element of offense or that negative a defense and those having a lesser effect, and provide a different rule for each:

"When the presumed fact establishes guilt or is an element of the offense or negatives a defense, the judge may submit the question of guilt or of the existence of the presumed fact to the jury, if, but only if a reasonable juror on the evidence as a whole, including the evidence of the basic facts, could find guilt or the presumed fact beyond a reasonable doubt.   When the presumed fact has a lesser effect, its existence may be submitted to the jury if the basic facts are supported by substantial evidence, or are otherwise established, unless the evidence as a whole negatives the existence of the presumed fact." [5]

The test used by most of the United States Courts of Appeal for determining the sufficiency of the prosecution's evidence is whether reasonable men could find the existence of each element of the offense beyond a reasonable doubt.[6]   As has been stated, the test is a logical one and one that may be constitutionally required.[7]   There would seem to be no reason to permit a less stringent test to be applied to the evidence when a presumption is involved.

Similarly, different approaches have been taken with regard to the question of instructing the jury once the trial judge decides to submit the issue to it.   The Proposed New Federal Criminal Code provides that the jury should be told that "although the evidence as a whole must establish the presumed fact beyond a reasonable doubt, the jury may arrive at that judgment on the basis of the presumption alone, since the law regards the facts giving rise to the presumption as strong evidence of the fact presumed." [8]   The Model Penal Code [9] and the proposed Federal Rules of Evidence [10] also provide for an instruction to the effect that, although the presumed fact must be found beyond a reasonable doubt, it may be so found on the basis of the evidence presented. However, there is no added provision for telling the jury that the facts giving rise to the presumptions are "strong evidence of the fact presumed."   The additional language required by the Proposed New Federal Criminal Code is based upon the theory that unless the jury is told of the value of the basic facts they may acquit when conviction is justified because the value of the basic facts may not be readily apparent to them.[11]   Whether the added statement goes too far, is a question which must await resolution by the Court.   The prosecution has already received substantial benefit from the presumption.   The presumption may have taken an otherwise insufficient case to the jury.   The additional benefit of a charge telling the jury that the evidence that has been presented is sufficient to support a finding of guilt is probably adequate to ef-

---

4.   § 103(4) (a) See also Working Papers, National Commission on Reform of Federal Criminal Laws, vol. 1 at 19–24 (1970).

5.   Rule 303(b).

6.   See F.R.Ev. (R.D.1971) 303, Advisory Committee's Note.

7.   See § 338, nn. 33, 34 and accompanying text, supra.

8.   § 103(4) (b).

9.   § 1.12(5) (b).

10.   Rule 303(c).

11.   See Working Papers, National Commission on Reform of Federal Criminal Laws, vol. 1 at 21 (1970).
"This portion of the charge departs from existing law only in the use of the words' strong evidence" . . . . Id. at 24.

fectuate fully the policies behind the presumption. The added statement that the facts presented are "strong evidence" may unduly weigh the scales against the accused.

347. Choice of Law Problems.[12]

The significance of the burdens of proof and of the effect of presumptions upon those burdens has already been discussed. Certainly the outcome of litigation may be altered depending upon which party has the burden of persuasion.[13] Where there is little evidence available on an issue, the burden of producing evidence may also control the outcome.[14] Recognizing the impact of these rules upon outcome, the federal courts, applying the doctrine of Erie Railroad Co., v. Tompkins,[15] have consistently held that where an issue is to be decided under state law, that law controls both the burdens of proof and presumptions with regard to that issue.[16] The proposed Federal Rules of Evidence limit the operation of this rule with respect to presumptions to cases in which the presumption operates "respecting a fact which is an element of a claim or defense as to which state law supplies the rule of decision."[17] "Tactical presumptions," those

that operate as to a lesser aspect of the case, will be governed by the federal rule.[18] While no court has specifically made the distinction contemplated in the proposed rules, the reasoning is sound. Although tactical presumptions may in some instances influence the outcome of a case, their effect is no greater than that of a rule governing the admission or exclusion of a single item of evidence. As in the case of those rules, the desirability of providing a uniform procedure for federal trials through a fixed rule governing tactical presumptions outweighs any preference for increased certainty of identity of result in state and federal courts.

Of course *Erie* problems are not the only choice of law problems. The question remains, even for federal courts having resolved to apply state rather than federal law:[19] what state's law is applicable? Unlike the federal courts applying the *Erie* rule, the state courts generally have not considered the impact of the burdens of proof and presumptions on the outcome of the lawsuit to be controlling. The general rule expressed is that both the burdens of proof and presumptions are "procedural" in the sense that the law of the forum governs rather than the law of the state whose substantive rules are

---

12. Morgan, Choice of Law Governing Proof, 58 Harv.L.Rev. 153, 180–194 (1944); Sedler, The Erie Outcome Test as a Guide to Substance and Procedure in the Conflicts of Laws, 37 N.Y.U.L.Rev. 813, 855–865 (1962); Restatement, Second, Conflict of Laws §§ 133, 134 (1971); Annot., 35 A.L.R.3d 289; C.J.S. Conflict of Laws § 22(9); Dec.Dig. Actions ⊂⟶66.

13. See § 336, supra.

14. See § 338, supra. See also §§ 342 and 345, supra, as to the operation of presumptions with regard to both the burden of producing evidence and the burden of persuasion.

15. 304 U.S. 64 (1938).

16. See, e. g., Dick v. New York Life Ins. Co., 359 U.S. 437 (1959); Palmer v. Hoffman, 318 U.S. 109 (1943); Cities Service Oil Co. v. Dunlap, 308 U.S. 208 (1939). See also, 5 Moore Federal Practice ¶ 43.08 (1969).

17. F.R.Ev. (R.D.1971) 302.

18. Id., Advisory Committee's Note. The following example of a tactical presumption is taken from Cleary, Presuming and Pleading: An Essay on Juristic Immaturity, 12 Stan.L.Rev. 5, 26 (1959): "In an action upon an account, plaintiff, desiring to prove defendant's failure to deny as an admission of liability, may prove the mailing of a statement of account to defendant and rely upon the presumption that it was received by him in due course of the mails. The presumed fact of delivery is much smaller than an element in the case. . . ."

19. In determining which state law to apply, the federal courts are bound by the conflict of laws rule of the state in which they are sitting. Klaxon v. Stentor Electric Mfg. Co., 313 U.S. 487 (1941). See generally cases collected in Annot., 21 A.L.R. 2d 247, 257. For a recent example of the approach taken by a federal court in a situation where a choice between the laws of two states with regard to presumptions had to be made, see Maryland Casualty Co. v. Williams, 377 F.2d 389 (5th Cir. 1967).

otherwise applicable.[20]   However, as in the case of most general rules with regard to the subject matter of this chapter, instances in which an exception to this general rule has been held applicable are perhaps as numerous as instances in which the rule has been applied.   The principal exception to the basic dogma has been variously phrased but its gist is that the forum will apply the rule of a foreign jurisdiction with respect to the burdens of proof or presumptions where that rule is inseparably connected to the substantive right created by the foreign state.[21]

The general rule and its principal exception[22] have proved difficult to apply.   The plethora of conflicting decisions under the test amply illustrates the problems inherent in attempting to distinguish between rules that are inseparably connected with substantive law and those that are not.[23]   The distinction is indeed a hollow one.   Regardless of the nature of the claim or defense, rules with respect to the burdens of proof always have the same potential effect upon the decision in the case.   If insufficient evidence is available, the party having the burden of producing evidence will lose the decision.   If the jury is in doubt, the party having the burden of persuasion will lose.   As has been observed, cases in which the burden of proof is so closely interwoven with the substantive right as to make a separation of the two improper constitute either all or none of the litigated cases.[24]

A somewhat better approach to the problem is taken by the Second Restatement of Conflict of Laws which states that the forum will apply its own local law in determining which party has the burdens of proof "unless the primary purpose of the relevant rule of the otherwise applicable law is to affect decision of the issue rather than to regulate the conduct of the trial."[25]   The rule sounds

20.   See, e. g., Broderick v. McGuire, 119 Conn. 83, 174 Atl. 314 (1934) (New York presumption arising from certificate of superintendent of banks not applicable); Davis Cabs Inc. v. Evans, 42 Ohio App. 493, 182 N.E. 327 (1932) (Kentucky presumption of negligence where speed limit exceeded not applicable).   See cases collected in Annot., 35 A.L.R.3d 289, 299.

21.   See, e. g., Pilot Life Ins. Co. v. Boone, 236 F.2d 457, 462 (5th Cir. 1956) ("The effect of this presumption against suicide is so inseparably connected with the substantive right to defend under the applicable policy exception, that we think that the law of South Carolina [which was held to govern the substantive issues] should be given effect in preference to the contrary rule prevailing in Alabama [the state in which the district court was sitting]."); Buhler v. Maddison, 109 Utah 267, 176 P.2d 118, 123 (1947) ("Where a substantive right based upon foreign law is so inseparably connected with matters procedural in nature, that such procedural matters must be enforced in order to preserve the integrity of the substantive right, the court will apply the foreign law in determination of such matters even though procedural in nature."); Precourt v. Driscoll, 85 N.H. 280, 157 Atl. 525, 527 (1931) (setting forth an exception to the general rule calling for the application of the local law "when the foreign remedy is so inseparable from the cause of action that it must be enforced to preserve the integrity and character of the cause and when such remedy is practically available;" the court noted that the exception should apply "when no local policy is adversely affected.").

22.   Another frequently stated exception is that the law of the foreign jurisdiction governs "conclusive presumptions."   See, e. g., Maryland Casualty Co. v. Williams, supra n. 19 at 394–95.   However, as discussed earlier in this chapter, § 342, n. 33 and accompanying text, these "presumptions" are better viewed as rules of substantive law and are therefore clearly not within the purview of the general rule.

23.   See generally cases collected in Annot., supra n. 20, at 303 et seq.   The courts are perhaps most divided on this issue where the forum's rule with regard to the burden of proving contributory negligence differs from that of the foreign state whose law is otherwise applicable.   Compare Foley v. Pittsburgh-Des Moines Co., 363 Pa. 1, 68 A.2d 517 (1949) and Weir v. New York, N. H. & H. R. Co., 340 Mass. 66, 162 N.E.2d 793 (1959) (law of the forum controls) with Gordon's Transports, Inc. v. Bailey, 41 Tenn.App. 365, 294 S.W.2d 313 (1956); Valleroy v. Southern R. Co., 403 S.W.2d 553 (Mo. 1966) (foreign law controls.)   See Restatement, Second, Conflict of Laws § 133, Reporter's Note at 369 (1971).   See also cases collected at Annot., supra n. 20, at 318–327.

24.   Morgan, supra n. 12, at 185.

25.   §§ 133, 134 (1971).   Section 595 of the first Restatement stated that the law of the forum governs both "proof" and "presumptions."   The comment to

very much like the test applied in *Erie* cases. However, the comments and illustrations to the applicable sections of the Restatement indicate that the Restatement is to be interpreted in much the same way as the more traditional statements just discussed; the assumption is that the rule is one concerned with "trial administration", not the decision of the issue.[26] The assumption seems wrong. The burdens of proof are almost always allocated for the primary purpose of affecting the decision in the case where there is no evidence or where the jury is in doubt. To say that these rules merely govern the conduct of the trial, as in the case of rules concerning the admission and exclusion of evidence, gives far too much emphasis to form over substance.[27]

A better approach to the choice of law problem would be to adopt the federal rule used in *Erie* cases as a rule of general application. Such a rule would provide that the law of the state or states supplying the substantive rules of law otherwise applicable should govern questions concerning the burdens of proof as well as presumptions operating with regard to a fact constituting an element of a claim or defense.[28]

that section (p. 710) noted that the foreign law might be applied if "the remedial and substantive portions of the foreign law are so bound together that the application of the usual procedural rule of the forum would seriously alter the effect of the operative facts under the law of the appropriate foreign state."

26. Id., § 133, Comment at 366–68, § 134, Comment at 370–72.

27. Where the evidence is plentiful, of course, the allocation of the burden of producing evidence cannot have a significant effect upon the decision in the case. In such a case, the rule assigning the burden is simply a rule affecting the order of proof —a matter that logically should be governed by the law of the forum. However, providing differ-

ent rules to be applied where there is sufficient evidence to satisfy the burden of producing evidence and where there is not, would require a full review of the evidence before a decision as to choice of law could be made, a procedure at best wasteful of precious judicial time.

As long as the allocation of the burden of producing evidence has a potentially significant impact on the decision in the case, as it must have in every situation, a single rule, calling for the allocation of the burden of producing evidence as part of the substantive law to be applied in the case, should be followed. For a discussion suggesting the possibility of a different rule where there is plentiful evidence see Sedler, supra n. 12, at 865.

28. For a similar view, see Sedler, supra note 12.

In the first edition of this text, Dean McCormick took the position that the burden of persuasion has a relatively insignificant effect upon the outcome of the litigation (see discussion of this question in § 336, supra) and that the allocation of that burden should therefore be viewed as a matter of "procedure." (p. 686). Professor Morgan took an opposite approach, recognizing the impact of the burden of persuasion upon the outcome, but relegating the burden of producing evidence to the status of procedure. Morgan, supra n. 12, at 191–194.

TITLE 13

ADMINISTRATIVE EVIDENCE

CHAPTER 37

ADMINISTRATIVE EVIDENCE

348. Introduction to Administrative Adjudication.[1]

As the problems facing federal and state governments have multiplied in number and complexity, these governments have created administrative agencies to devise and enforce new policies. Administrative trials far exceed the number of judicial trials. For example, in fiscal 1963—the most recent figures available—almost 70,000 administrative trials involving oral testimony and verbatim transcripts were heard by the more than 100 agencies of the federal government.[2] In comparison the federal district courts heard fewer than 11,000 civil and criminal cases that year, and not even 6,000 of these were jury trials.[3] Administrative hearings extend from relatively insubstantial workmen's compensation claims to precedent-setting antitrust merger rulings involving millions of dollars and affecting thousands of employees.

At first glance many, and perhaps most, administrative adjudications appear to be merely carbon copies of judicial trials. Their hearings are usually public, and the majority are conducted in an orderly and dignified manner, although not necessarily with the formality of a judicial trial.

Closer analysis reveals many differences.[4] Agency hearings tend to produce evidence

---

1. See generally 1 Davis, Administrative Law Treatise, ch. 1 (1958, 1970 Supp.) (hereinafter "Davis"); 1 Cooper, State Administrative Law, chs. 1–3 (1965) (hereinafter "Cooper").

2. Subcommittee on Administrative Practice and Procedure, Senate Comm. on the Judiciary, 88th Cong., 2d Sess., Statistical Data Related to Administrative Proceedings, 82 (Comm. Print 1964) (Part II of the "Statistical Greenbook").

3. Annual report of the Director of the Administrative Office of the United States Courts 1969, in Reports of the Proceedings of the Judicial Conference of the United States 134 (1970).

4. See Benjamin, Administrative Adjudication in the State of New York 174–75 (1942) (hereinafter "Benjamin") (footnotes omitted):
"The law of evidence as it now exists, however useful it may be in practical operation in the courts, is unsystematized, difficult to understand in detail, and difficult to apply. Its successful application requires trained and experienced judges . . . . Its successful application requires also trained and experienced counsel. The law of evidence as applied in judicial proceedings is not self-executing.
. . . .
"It is a frequent characteristic of [state] quasi-judicial proceedings that the hearing officer is not a trained

of general conditions as distinguished from facts relating solely to the respondent. Administrative agencies more consciously formulate policy by adjudicating—as well as by rulemaking—than do courts. Consequently, administrative hearings require that the hearing officer consider the impact of his decision upon the public interest as well as upon the particular respondent. Testimonial evidence and cross-examination play less important roles in many administrative hearings.[5]

Even more important is the fact that an administrative hearing is tried to the *trial examiner* and never to a *jury*. Since many of the rules governing the admission of proof in judicial trials are designed to protect the jury from unreliable and possibly confusing evidence,[6] the rules need not be applied with the same vigor in proceedings solely before a judge or trial examiner.[7] The trial exam-

iner decides both the facts and the law to be applied. Usually a lawyer, he is often an expert on the very question he must decide. Consequently, the technical common law rules barring the *admissibility* of evidence have generally been abandoned by administrative agencies.[8]

Courts accept whatever cases the parties present; their familiarity with the subject matter is accidental. Agencies, on the other hand, usually handle selected cases; trial examiners and agency chiefs are either experts or have at least a substantial familiarity with the subject matter since their jurisdictions tend to be restricted. In addition, an agency usually is staffed by experts whose reports, commonly relating to matters adjudicated before the agency, are made available to examiners and commissioners alike. While this development of agency experience and expertise is commonly offered as a justification for administrative agencies,[9] it also creates a basic conflict between assuring fairness to the respondent on the one hand and promoting efficient use of reliable information on the other. The respondent, for example, wants an opportunity to rebut or explain all the "evidence" which the examiner or agency relies upon in making its decision. Yet the agency wishes to avoid the burden of having to prove once again previously established "facts."

349. Law Governing Administrative Evidence.

The legal framework governing the conduct of administrative adjudications is not

---

lawyer; nor would mere legal training of hearing officers assure expertness in the field of evidence. It is another frequent characteristic of quasi-judicial proceedings that the parties are not represented by counsel. The essential conditions of the successful application of the rules of evidence are therefore lacking, in many instances. For those instances at least, administrative adjudication must be able (as in my judgment it is) to operate satisfactorily without a legal requirement that the exclusionary rules of evidence be applied."
Since the time of the "Benjamin Report" many states have improved the status and the stature of their hearing examiners. See 1 Cooper 331–38, W. Gellhorn and Byse, Administrative Law 885 n. 4 (5th ed. 1970).

5. For some penetrating insights on whether such evidence can be dispensed with in deciding questions of policy, see Robinson, The Making of Administrative Policy: Another Look at Rulemaking and Adjudication and Administrative Procedure Reform, 118 U.Pa.L.Rev. 485, 521–22 (1970).

6. "[The law of evidence is] a piece of illogical, but by no means irrational, patchwork; not at all to be admired, nor easily to be found intelligible, except as a product of the jury system . . . where ordinary untrained citizens are acting as judges of fact." Thayer, Preliminary Treatise on Evidence at the Common Law 509 (1898).

7. Regardless of whether the hearsay and best evidence rules are products of the jury system, see 2 Davis § 14.03 (collecting authorities), in fact neither rule is applied with the same strictness in

cases tried to a judge and not the jury. See § 60 and Ch. 34, supra.

8. See §§ 350, 351, infra.

9. The significance of this experience and expertness has also been questioned. See, e. g., Jaffe, Judicial Control of Administrative Action 25 (1965); W. Gellhorn, Federal Administrative Proceedings 28 (1941); Schwartz, Legal Restriction of Competition in the Regulated Industries: An Abdication of Judicial Responsibility, 67 Harv.L.Rev. 436, 471–75 (1954).

complex and can probably be best understood by first examining the law which determines the kind of proof an agency can receive into evidence.

(a) *Federal law.* Until the passage of the Administrative Procedure Act of 1946,[10] the receipt of evidence in federal administrative proceedings was limited only by general constitutional requirements of fairness and privilege together with the vague directions implicit in the standard for judicial review developed by appellate courts or written into agency enabling acts. The requirement of fairness generally means only that the respondent

> "shall have an opportunity to be heard and cross-examine the witnesses against him and shall have time and opportunity at a convenient place, after the evidence against him is produced and known to him, to produce evidence and witnesses to refute the charges . . .".[11]

The test for judicial review typically provides that "[t]he finding of the Commission as to the facts, if supported by substantial evidence, shall be conclusive." [12] Either standard could be read as a command that administrative agencies must rely upon common law rules of evidence barring hearsay and other secondary evidence, since the respondent could neither confront nor cross-examine upon the evidence or since the evidence was not competent and therefore not substantial. Neither the agencies nor the courts have ac-

cepted these contentions.[13] The exclusionary rules of evidence were originally designed to assure that evidence admitted would be relevant and reliable. But the opportunity for confrontation and cross-examination is not the sole measure of reliability. As early as the turn of this century, the Supreme Court ruled that the Interstate Commerce Commission—the first regulatory agency to conduct formal adjudicatory hearings—was not bound by the exclusionary rules:

> "The [ICC's] inquiry should not be too narrowly constrained by technical rules as to the admissibility of proof. Its function is largely one of investigation, and it should not be hampered in making inquiry pertaining to interstate commerce by those narrow rules which prevail in trials at common law . . .".[14]

Occasionally federal authority has held that the admission of legally incompetent evidence is reversible error. But these decisions are exceptional and erroneous unless other grounds can be established for rejecting the evidence.[15] Thus, by 1941 the Supreme Court could confidently note that "it has long been settled that the technical rules for the exclusion of evidence applicable in jury trials do not apply to proceedings before federal administrative agencies in the absence of a

---

10. 5 U.S.C.A. §§ 551–559, 701–706, 3105, 3344, 5362, 7521.

11. NLRB v. Prettyman, 117 F.2d 786, 790 (6th Cir. 1941). See also Morgan v. United States, 304 U.S. 1, 18–19 (1938); Hornsby v. Allen, 326 F.2d 605, 608 (5th Cir. 1964).

12. Developments in the Law—Remedies Against the United States and its Officials, 70 Harv.L.Rev. 827, 904–05 (1957) (a distillation of the most typical provisions of the statutes providing for judicial review).

13. See Davis, Administrative Law Text 271–273 (2d ed.).

14. ICC v. Baird, 194 U.S. 25, 44 (1904). In response to a challenge to an ICC order based partly on hearsay, the Court observed that "[e]ven in a court of law, if evidence of this kind is admitted without objection, it is to be considered, and accorded its natural probative effect . . . ." Spiller v. Atchison, Topeka & S. F. Ry., 253 U.S. 117, 130 (1920).

15. Compare Tri-State Broadcasting Co. v. FCC, 68 App.D.C. 292, 96 F.2d 564 (1938), with FTC v. Cement Institute, 333 U.S. 683, 705–06 (1948). In response to the *Tri-State* ruling that the admission of all hearsay is improper since it deprives the respondent of its right to cross-examine, Dean Wigmore commented acidly: "No wonder the administrative agencies chafe under such unpractical control." 1 Wigmore, Evidence § 4b, p. 34.

statutory requirement that such rules are to be observed." [16]

With the adoption of the Administrative Procedure Act (APA), Congress codified this case law by providing that "[a]ny oral or documentary evidence may be received" in an administrative hearing.[17] Specific statutes may, however, override the application of the APA to agency hearings. In a few instances Congress has either exempted an agency's hearings from the APA or has specified that other procedures shall govern certain administrative hearings.[18]

Sometimes the congressional objective is not clear.[19] Of more concern is a recent

Court of Appeals decision which held that the general provisions of the Social Security Act override the APA's hearing provisions. In Cohen v. Perales,[20] the Fifth Circuit ruled that since the Social Security Act permits the Secretary of Health, Education and Welfare to adopt rules of evidence, procedures established under this power are not subject to the provisions of the APA, a decision perhaps calculated to encourage other agencies unnecessarily to restrict rules of evidence in administrative hearings. In reversing this decision on the ground that the procedure followed did in fact conform to both statutes, the Supreme Court ruled that the question need not be decided.[21]

(b) *State law.* The constitutional limitations applied to federal agencies also impose restraints upon state hearings. The states in turn have freed their administrative agencies from the "rules of evidence," but not always for the same reasons. Most state agencies were created as political-administrative bodies rather than as quasi-judicial commissions.

"Fifty years ago, the typical state agencies would include, perhaps, rural township supervisors who as members of local boards of assessors would estimate the value of their neighbors' farms, and statehouse politicians who as a railroad commission would bargain with railroad attorneys concerning the granting of franchises and the fixing of rates, and insurance commission-

16. Opp Cotton Mills, Inc. v. Administrator, Dep't of Labor, 312 U.S. 126, 155 (1941).

17. 5 U.S.C.A. § 556(d).

18. See S.Doc. 248, 79th Cong., 2d Sess. 216 (1946); cf. 8 U.S.C.A. § 1252(b) (1964), applied in Marcello v. Bonds, 349 U.S. 302 (1955).

19. For example, the Taft-Hartley Act amended the National Labor Relations Act to provide that the Board's adjudications, "shall, so far as practicable, be conducted in accordance with the rules of evidence applicable in the district courts of the United States under the rules of civil procedure for the district courts of the United States. . . ." Labor-Management Relations Act § 10(b), 61 Stat. 146 (1947), 29 U.S.C.A. § 160(b). Section 10(b) of the 1935 Act, which Taft-Hartley modified, provided that "rules of evidence prevailing in courts of law or equity shall not be controlling." 49 Stat. 454 (1935). Although it seems doubtful that this amendment had the intention of imposing jury trial rules on Board hearings, at least one court has held that "hearsay evidence must [now] be excluded from consideration by the Board and by [the reviewing court]." NLRB v. Amalgamated Meat Cutters, 202 F.2d 671, 673 (9th Cir. 1953); accord, 1 Cooper 384. But see NLRB v. International Union of Oper. Engrs., Local 12, 413 F.2d 705, 707 (9th Cir. 1969). Fortunately, however, most reviewing courts have taken the sensible stand that the mere admission of hearsay is not within the purview of the Taft-Hartley amendment. E. g., NLRB v. Philadelphia Iron Works, Inc., 211 F.2d 937, 942–43 (3d Cir. 1954); NLRB v. Carpet, Linoleum & Resilient Tile Layers Local 419, 213 F.2d 49, 53 (10th Cir. 1954). See generally Archer, Query: Should Administrative Agencies Tailor Exclusionary Evidence Rules Specifically for Their Own Proceedings? An Illustrative Study of the N. L. R. B., 3 Ind.Leg.F. 339 (1970).

20. 412 F.2d 44, rehearing denied 416 F.2d 1250 (5th Cir. 1969) noted 1970 Duke L.J. 146.

21. Richardson v. Perales, 402 U.S. 389 (1971). The particular ruling was that physicians' reports adduced by the agency were admissible and satisfied the requirement of "substantial evidence," though opposed by live expert testimony on behalf of claimant. Considerable emphasis was placed on claimant's failure to subpoena the authors of the reports, though entitled to do so. However, the significance of this aspect is difficult to estimate in view of emphasis also placed on the routine character of the reports, suggesting at least overtones of entries in the regular course of business.

ers who would watch with a wary eye the premiums charged by fire insurance companies . . . , and—in the more progressive states—'committees of arbitration' who would informally arbitrate compensation claims of workers injured in industrial accidents under the newfangled workmen's compensation laws." [22]

Neither these state agencies nor the parties appearing before them could have followed judicial rules of evidence. As the agencies became more sophisticated, and their hearings more formal, the presentation of evidence was formalized. Now, as with federal agencies, their hearings are often indistinguishable from nonjury civil trials. Nevertheless, the original approach that state agencies are not restricted by common law rules in the admission of evidence has continued.[23] One leading observer has contended that this liberal approach has outrun its reasons.[24] Attributing its continuance to legislative lethargy, to arbitrary agency desire to operate with a free hand, and to the judicial trend toward relaxation of exclusionary rules in court cases, he decries this laxity concerning the application of common law rules and suggests that state agencies should be "required to follow the rules of evidence to about the same extent and in about the same way as

judges do when trying cases without juries."[25] His argument fails to recognize, however, that this standard is more indefinite than might be thought.[26] The Revised Model State Act furthers this suggestion by proposing that the rules of evidence applicable in nonjury civil cases should be followed in state agency adjudication. Only six states have adopted this provision.[27]

Thus, the trend in state agencies, both by statute and court rule, continues to be away —rather than toward—the technical rules of admissibility.

350. Admissibility of Evidence.

Administrative agencies generally are not restricted in the kind of evidence they can admit. The mere admission of proof that would be excluded as irrelevant, immaterial, incompetent, or redundant under the rules of evidence adopted in a jury trial will not restrict enforcement of an agency's decision.[28]

---

22. 1 Cooper 379 (footnotes omitted).

23. Many state statutes explicitly provide that the common law rules of evidence applicable to jury trials shall not govern agency hearings. E. g., Mass.Gen.Laws Ann. c. 30A, § 11(2) (1966); West's Ann.Cal.Labor Code, § 5709 (1971). Several practical reasons have been offered for not following rigid common law rules of evidence in state hearings: agency hearings are often held at one or a few central locations distant from the scene of events, making it difficult for eyewitness participants to testify; hearings may be held shortly after the complaint is filed, making the advance preparation and the marshalling of the best witnesses and documentary evidence difficult; and the heavy case-load volume, much of which is routine and involves only matters of small consequence, renders formal requirements of proof inappropriate. See Benjamin 175–76.

24. 1 Cooper 380–81.

25. Id.

26. 2 Davis § 14.04.
See § 60, supra, for discussion of the application of the exclusionary rules in nonjury trials.

27. Revised Model State Administrative Procedure Act § 10(1) (1961), criticized in Davis, Administrative Law 584 (1965). The three state statutes following the 1961 Revised Model Act are: Ga.Code, § 3A–101 et seq. (1970); R.I.Gen.Laws § 42–35–1 et seq. (1969); W.Va.Code, § 29A–1–1 et seq. (1969). Three other states have similar provisions: Colo. Rev.Stat. § 3–16–4(7) (1969); Mich.Comp.Laws Ann. § 24.275 (1970); N.D.Cent.Code § 28–32–06 (1969). While continuing this suggestion, the 1970 version of the state APA makes the helpful addition that "[w]hen necessary to ascertain facts not reasonably susceptible of proof under these rules, evidence not admissible thereunder may be admitted (except where precluded by statute) if it is the type commonly relied upon by prudent men in the conduct of their affairs." Revised Model State Administrative Procedure Act § 10(1) (1970). See also § 351 infra.

28. Opp Cotton Mills, Inc. v. Administrator, Dep't of Labor, 312 U.S. 126, 155 (1941). On the other hand, several states have followed the lead of the Revised Model Act that "[i]rrelevant, immaterial, or unduly repetitious evidence *shall* be excluded." Alaska Stat. § 44.62.460(d) (1967); West's Ann.Cal. Gov.Code, § 11513(c) (1966); Ga.Code, § 3A–116 (a) (1969); Mo.Rev.Stat. § 536.070(8) (1970); R.I.

The APA confirms this practice in section 7 (c) by providing that "[a]ny oral or documentary evidence may be received, but the agency as a matter of policy shall provide for the exclusion of irrelevant, immaterial, or unduly repetitious evidence." [29] Note that the APA opens the door to *any* evidence which the examiner admits and only *suggests* that insignificant and redundant evidence should be rejected, giving the agencies broad discretion. Moreover, the APA pointedly omits hearsay or other "incompetent" evidence from the list of evidence which should not be received.[30] Thus, the exclusion of otherwise legally inadmissible evidence from an administrative hearing may be error.[31] Fur-

thermore, it is clear that the exclusion of relevant, material, and competent evidence by the trial examiner will be grounds for reversal if that refusal is prejudicial.[32]

The courts have pressed the agencies to abide by the spirit of these rules. The leading example of such pressure—which in fact antedates the APA—is found in Samuel H. Moss, Inc. v. FTC,[33] where a distinguished panel of the Second Circuit admonished a hearing examiner for rigidly following the rules of evidence:

"[I]f the case was to be tried with strictness, the examiner was right . . .. Why either he or the [Federal Trade] Commission's attorney should have thought it desirable to be so formal about the admission of evidence, we cannot understand. Even in criminal trials to a jury it is better, nine times out of ten, to admit, than to exclude, evidence and in such proceedings as these the only conceivable interest that can suffer by admitting any evidence is the time lost, which is seldom as much as that inevitably lost by idle bickering about irrelevancy or incompetence. In the case at bar it chances that no injustice was done, but we take this occasion to point out the danger always involved in conducting such a proceeding in such a spirit, and the absence of any advantage in depriving either the Commission or ourselves of *all evidence which can conceivably throw any light upon the controversy.*" [34]

Many reasons support the open admission of hearsay and other legally incompetent evi-

---

Gen.Laws Ann. § 42–35–10(a) (1969); W.Va.Code, § 29A–5–2(a) (1966); Wis.Stat.Ann. § 227.10(1) (1967). There is, however, a paucity of case authority interpreting and applying these statutes, although courts have occasionally expressed their disapproval of the admission of such evidence. See Bunting Bristol Transfer, Inc. v. Pennsylvania Pub. Util. Com'n, 418 Pa. 286, 292, 210 A.2d 281, 284 (1965); D. F. Bast, Inc. v. Pennsylvania Pub. Util. Com'n, 397 Pa. 246, 251, 154 A.2d 505, 508 (1959). Several cases suggest that state courts have been critical of agency receipt of hearsay evidence, essentially on grounds that the particular evidence lacked probative force. E. g., Gomez v. Industrial Com'n, 72 Ariz. 265, 233 P.2d 827 (1951); Zawisza v. Quality Name Plate, Inc., 149 Conn. 115, 176 A. 2d 578 (1961). But only occasional—and usually earlier—state decisions have reversed agency rulings merely on the grounds of the receipt of hearsay evidence. See, e. g., In re Trustees of Village of Westminster, 108 Vt. 352, 187 Atl. 519 (1936).

29. 5 U.S.C.A. § 556(d). Not only the Act's words but also the legislative history make clear that the exclusionary rules do not govern the admissibility of evidence in administrative hearings and that the provision for exclusion applies only to "irrelevant, immaterial, or unduly repetitious evidence" and not to legally incompetent evidence. United State ex rel. Dong Wing Ott v. Shaughnessy, 116 F.Supp. 745, 750 (S.D.N.Y.1953) aff'd on other grounds 220 F.2d 537 (2d Cir.) cert. denied 350 U.S. 847 (1955); see 2 Davis § 14.05. See also Richardson v. Perales, 402 U.S. 389 (1971).

30. See the authorities cited in n. 29, supra. In this context, the definition of hearsay, is secondhand information which would not come within any of the exceptions to the "hearsay rule."

31. See, e. g., Brotherhood of R. R. Trainmen v. Illinois Cent. R. R., 26 Ad.L.2d 216 (E.D.Ill.1969); 2 Davis § 14.09.

32. NLRB v. Burns, 207 F.2d 434 (8th Cir. 1953); Prince v. Industrial Com'n, 89 Ariz. 314, 361 P.2d 929 (1961); People ex rel. Hirschberg v. Board of Supervisors, 251 N.Y. 156, 167 N.E. 204 (1929); see 1 Cooper 367–71 (collecting authorities). But see note 19, § 349 supra.

33. 148 F.2d 378 (2d Cir. 1945) (per curiam decision by Clark, A. Hand and L. Hand, JJ.) cert. denied 326 U.S. 734.

34. Id. 380 (emphasis added).

dence in administrative hearings.[35] Foremost among them is the fact that the exclusionary rules do not determine the probative value of the proffered evidence. Professor Davis, the leading proponent that hearing officers should make no distinction between hearsay and nonhearsay evidence, makes the point this way:

> "[T]he reliability of hearsay ranges from the least to the most reliable. The reliability of non-hearsay also ranges from the least to the most reliable. Therefore the guide should be a judgment about the reliability of particular evidence in a particular record in particular circumstances, not the technical hearsay rule with all its complex exceptions."[36]

To require that a trial examiner refuse to admit hearsay makes no sense where there is no jury to protect and the trier of fact is equally exposed to the evidence whether he admits or excludes it.[37] Admission without a ruling—as long as the evidence has some element of reliability—does no harm and can prove more efficient than the requiring of a ruling which may later be held erroneous. Discarding the exclusionary rules of admission eliminates the need for the parties to interpose protective objections—the objections being preserved by their briefs to the examiner or agency—and relieves the ex-

aminer of making difficult rulings before all the evidence is available. It assures a complete, yet not necessarily an unduly long, record and might well avoid the need to reopen the record. Hearsay, of course, is not subject to current, in-court cross-examination, but that limitation affects the weight the evidence carries, not its admissibility.[38]

The fact that administrative hearings need not follow the exclusionary rules and the fact that the admission of remote or repetitious evidence is not reversible error does not suggest that "anything goes" or that all proffered evidence, whatever its relevance or trustworthiness, should be admitted. Wholesale admission would only add to delay and further expand records which are already too long. Nor can an efficient adjudicatory system decide anew each time the question is presented whether some particular evidence should be admitted. Regrettably, most agencies have not fully developed regulations governing the extent to which the exclusionary rules should not be applied.[39] In general, the admissibility of evidence in administrative hearings depends more upon the *importance* of the evidence in relation to the ultimate issues rather than upon the legal standards of relevance and materiality.[40]

However, several significant and useful deviations from the judicial pattern appear in administrative hearings. The first, of course, involves the relatively free receipt of hearsay evidence. Equally important is the man-

---

35. Patterson, Hearsay and the Substantial Evidence Rule in the Federal Administrative Process, 13 Mercer L.Rev. 294, 304–06 (1962); cf. Builders Steel Co. v. Commissioner, 179 F.2d 377, 379 (8th Cir. 1950); Davis, Hearsay in Nonjury Cases, 83 Harv.L.Rev. 1362, 1366 (1970).

36. Davis, Hearsay in Administrative Hearings, 32 Geo.Wash.L.Rev. 689 (1964). One commentator has asserted that nine-tenths of the problems involved in applying the exclusionary rules in administrative hearings—or, at least, those that come to reviewing courts—involve hearsay. Note, Exclusionary Rules of Evidence in Non-Jury Proceedings, 46 Ill. L.Rev. 915, 919 n. 23 (1952).

37. Donnelly Garment Co. v. NLRB, 123 F.2d 215, 224 (8th Cir. 1942). But cf. Note, Improper Evidence in Nonjury Trials: Basis for Reversal? 79 Harv.L.Rev. 407, 409–11 (1965).

38. See Peters v. United States, 187 Ct.Cl. 63, 408 F. 2d 719, 724 (1969); W. Gellhorn and Byse, Administrative Law 713–14, 772 (5th ed. 1970).

39. 2 Davis § 14.07.

40. The basic point made earlier should not be ignored—namely, that administrative hearings generally follow the time-tested judicial pattern of receiving evidence. Cf. W. Gellhorn, Federal Administrative Proceedings 75–82 (1941). It is also clear that agencies have not adequately explored methods to streamline the process of obtaining reliable evidence. See Selected Reports of the Administrative Conference of the United States 1961–1962, S.Doc.No.24, 88th Cong., 1st Sess. 90–91 (1963).

ner in which oral testimony is received. Witnesses in agency hearings are frequently permitted freedom to testify in a simple, natural and direct fashion, without unnecessary interruptions from either the attorney who is directing the questioning or his adversary.[41] Only when the witness strays far afield, or the question is remote will an objection be sustained. A third departure permitted from judicial practice occurs when the examiner is uncertain whether to exclude the evidence on the grounds of incompetency, irrelevancy or immateriality. In administrative hearings the tendency is to admit the evidence. Other techniques, principally the use of written presentations and shortened hearings are discussed below.[42]

Since administrative hearings differ so widely in scope and significance, it is impossible to suggest a single standard to govern the admission of all evidence. It is probably still true, however, as one keen observer noted almost 30 years ago, that the more closely administrative proceedings approach judicial proceedings in formality and in the nature of the issues to be tried, the greater the degree to which the exclusionary rules will be applied.[43] Nor has improvement been made to the standard suggested by the Attorney General's Committee on Administrative Procedure in 1941: "The ultimate test of admissibility must be whether the proffered evidence is reliable, probative and relevant. The question in each case must be whether the probability of error justifies the burden of stricter methods of proof."[44]

351. Evaluation of Evidence.

In contrast to the effect of a trial court's decision to receive hearsay evidence in a jury trial, a hearing officer's decision to receive hearsay in an administrative adjudication is only the first step in determining its impact upon the tribunal's decision. The admission of evidence in a jury trial is often considered the last effective legal control because of the assumption that the jury will rely upon or be swayed by it regardless of whether its reliability has been established. In an administrative hearing, on the other hand, as in the case of nonjury trials, it is assumed that the trial examiner will not rely upon untrustworthy evidence in reaching his decision. Thus if there is "competent" or trustworthy evidence to support the decision, the reviewing court presumes that the examiner or trial judge relied on that evidence in reaching his decision.[45]

Nevertheless, the more difficult—and often crucial—question for the hearing officer is the determination of whether he should rely upon hearsay evidence in reaching his decision. The examiner's concern is with the reliability or probative worth of the evidence.[46] Jury trial rules of evidence exclude hearsay on the theory that it is untrustworthy unless within an exception.[47] The party against whom the evidence is admitted can neither confront nor cross-examine the out-of-court declarant to test its probative worth. But on the other side of the ledger is the fact that each of us constantly relies upon hearsay evidence in making important decisions. Without hearsay, commerce would stop, government would cease to function,

41. See W. Gellhorn and Lauer, Administration of the New York Workmen's Compensation Law II, 37 N.Y.U.L.Rev. 204, 209 (1962).

42. See § 356 infra.

43. Benjamin 178; see Davis, An Approach to Problems of Evidence in the Administrative Process, 55 Harv.L.Rev. 364, 386–90 (1942).

44. Final Report of Attorney General's Committee on Administrative Procedure, S.Doc.No.8, 77th Cong., 1st Sess. 71 (1941).

45. See generally Note, Improper Evidence in Nonjury Trials: Basis for Reversal? 79 Harv.L.Rev. 407 (1965); § 60, supra.

46. The same weighing process is often involved in the examiner's decision whether to receive the evidence. If it is unlikely to be probative, he will not receive it regardless of the inapplicability of the hearsay rule. See § 350 infra.

47. See § 245, supra.

and education would be reduced to each teacher's personal experience (and even the latter would often be based upon hearsay). It is not surprising, then, that no legal system outside the Anglo-American realm has adopted so restrictive a rule of evidence. Scholars have rejected its across-the-board application and the courts are increasingly rejecting its application, even in jury cases.[48]

On the other hand, the fact that some hearsay may prove reliable is no guarantee that all hearsay is reliable. Nor is it responsive to observe that the rules of evidence already admit much that is worthless. Why, it could be asked, should more that is worthless be admitted in order to find some that is trustworthy, particularly when there is no assurance that the factfinder wil rely on the latter and disregard the former? It could also be contended that unless probative evidence could be distilled or some alternative protection devised, the admission of hearsay would not promote justice. The administrative regulations governing the receipt and evaluation of evidence indicate that the agencies themselves have not adequately wrestled with this issue.[49]

The courts have provided only scant guidance in upholding administrative reliance on some hearsay evidence. Judge Learned Hand has offered the classic formulation:

"[The examiner] did indeed admit much that would have been excluded at common law, but the act specifically so provides . . . [N]o doubt, that does not mean mere rumor will serve to 'support' a finding, but hearsay may do so, at least if more is not conveniently available, and if in the end the finding is supported by *the kind of evidence on*

which responsible persons are accustomed to rely in serious affairs."[50]

Hearing officers and agencies have adhered to this commonsense standard instinctively.[51] At the same time, several criteria applied in evaluating the reliability of hearsay can be discerned.[52]

The following are the most significant:

(a) What is the "nature" of the hearsay evidence? If the hearsay is likely to be reliable, it usually becomes an exception to the hearsay rule. Moreover, if the evidence is intrinsically trustworthy, agencies have taken the next logical step and relied, if necessary, upon this evidence in deciding cases, even though it technically constitutes hearsay and does not fall within any of the recognized exceptions. One example of intrinsically reliable hearsay, intra- and inter-corporate documents not shown to be within the business records exception, was the subject of a celebrated opinion by Judge Wyzanski in a nonjury trial not dissimilar from an administrative hearing.[53] An even

---

48. See, e. g., Weinstein, Probative Force of Hearsay, 46 Iowa L.Rev. 331 (1961). See also F.R.Ev. (R.D.1971) 803(24), 804(b)(6); ch. 34, supra.

49. See 2 Davis § 14.07.

50. NLRB v. Remington Rand, 94 F.2d 862, 873 (2d Cir. 1938) cert. denied 304 U.S. 576 (emphasis added), rev'd on other grounds 110 F.2d 148 (2d Cir. 1940). See also International Ass'n of Machinists, etc. v. NLRB, 71 App.D.C. 175, 110 F.2d 29, 35 (1939) aff'd 311 U.S. 72; John Bene & Sons, Inc. v. FTC, 299 Fed. 468, 471 (2d Cir. 1924). Several states—both by judicial decree and by statute—have adopted this test to permit agency departures from the exclusionary rules where compliance is impracticable and where the evidence is "of a type commonly relied upon by reasonably prudent men in the conduct of their affairs." See, e. g., Ring v. Smith, 5 Cal.App.3d 197, 204, 85 Cal. Rptr. 227, 232 (1970); Ga.Code, § 3A–116(a) (1969); Mich.Comp.Laws Ann. § 24.275; N.D.Cent.Code, § 28–32–06 (1969); R.I.Gen.Laws § 42–35–10 (1969); W.Va.Code, § 29A–5–2(a) (1964).

51. Sigmon, Rules of Evidence Before the I.C.C., 31 Geo.Wash.L.Rev. 258 (1962); Note, Evidence Problems in NLRB Hearings and the Applicability of the Proposed Code of Evidence, 55 Harv.L.Rev. 820, 827–33 (1942).

52. 2 Davis § 14.10, pp. 296–303.

53. United States v. United Shoe Mach. Corp., 89 F.Supp. 349, 355–56 (D.Mass.1950), noted in 60 Yale L.J. 363 (1951).

clearer example of the reliability criteria is newspaper reports.[54] Stories of significant news events are likely to be reliable. Newspapers normally do not report accidents which did not occur. On the other hand, newspaper summaries of public comments are commonly inaccurate—at least if one may believe those who claim to be misquoted—because of the difficulty of hearing and then summarizing another's views. Even so-called verbatim transcripts commonly suffer from significant errors as a result of the pressure of time deadlines. Note that the hearsay quality of each report is identical. Yet the accident report will be treated as solid support for an administrative decision and the speech summary, unless corroborated, will not.[55]

(b) Is better evidence available? The necessary substantiation for the reliability of hearsay evidence may arise from the failure of respondent to controvert the hearsay when the necessary proof is readily available to him, even though there is no testimonial or documentary exhibit of such available "support." The leading example of this position is United States ex rel. Vajtauer v. Commissioner,[56] where the Supreme Court upheld a deportation order based on a finding that the alien had advocated the overthrow of the government by force. The alien gave his name as Emanuel Vajtauer, a "Doctor of Psychology" and editor of the "Spravedlvost." In making his finding the director relied upon two items of hearsay: a pamphlet bearing the name of Dr. E. M. Vajtauer as author; and a newspaper report of a speech by a Dr. Vajtauer, editor of the

"Spravedlvost," supporting revolution. Both items became convincing evidence when "the appellant, confronted by this record, stood mute. . . . His silence without explanation other than that he would not testify until the entire evidence was presented, was in itself evidence that he was the author." [57]

(c) How important or unimportant is the subject matter in relation to the cost of acquiring "better" evidence? Many examples are available. If the out-of-hearing declarant is readily available and the question involves the respondent's livelihood or security—as is often the case in loyalty and deportation matters—hearsay by itself carries little weight.[58] If, however, the matter is but one of thou-

---

54. See Davis, An Approach to Problems of Evidence in the Administrative Process, 55 Harv.L.Rev. 364, 390 (1942); cf. Dallas County v. Commercial Union Assur. Co., 286 F.2d 388 (5th Cir. 1961).

55. See Montana Power Co. v. FPC, 87 U.S.App. D.C. 316, 185 F.2d 491, 498 (1950) cert. denied 340 U.S. 947 (1951); United States ex rel. Vajtauer v. Com'r, 273 U.S. 103 (1927).

56. Note 55, supra.

57. Id. at 111. But cf. Griffin v. California, 380 U.S. 609 (1965). Workmen's compensation cases furnish a further illustration. In one typical case, the testimony revealed that the workman went home, told his wife that he was hurt while at work, repeated the same story to a doctor, and then died. No one saw the accident. No better evidence was available. Placing special reliance on the statute's remedial purpose, the agency relied upon this hearsay evidence even though it fell outside the spontaneous exclamation exception. Greenfarb v. Arre, 62 N.J.Super. 420, 163 A.2d 173 (1960); see John W. McGrath Corp. v. Hughes, 264 F.2d 314 (2d Cir. 1959); Associated Gen. Contractors of America, Inc., v. Cardillo, 70 App.D.C. 303, 106 F.2d 327, 329 (1939); cf. G. & C. Merriam Co. v. Syndicate Pub. Co., 207 Fed. 515, 518 (2d Cir. 1913) (quoting trial court opinion by L. Hand, J.). See generally, Larson, The Law of Workmen's Compensation § 79 (1952) and 2 id. (Supp.1970). On the other hand, if credible firsthand witnesses were to have told another story—for example, that the accident happened elsewhere—the hearing officer would likely have rejected the hearsay testimony, especially if the eyewitness testimony is corroborated by convincing circumstantial evidence. Jacobowitz v. United States, 191 Ct.Cl. 444, 424 F.2d 555 (1970); In re Rath Packing Co., 14 N.L. R.B. 805, 817 (1939); see Glaros v. Immigration & Naturalization Service, 416 F.2d 441 (5th Cir. 1969) (hearsay corroborated by other evidence); NLRB v. Operating Engineers, Local 12, 25 Ad.L.2d 832 (9th Cir. 1969) (no objection raised to admission of hearsay).

58. E. g., Young v. Board of Pharmacy, 81 N.M. 5, 462 P.2d 139 (1969); Outagamie County v. Town of Brooklyn, 18 Wis.2d 303, 118 N.W.2d 201 (1962); see Reilly v. Pinkus, 338 U.S. 269 (1949). Contra, Peters v. United States, 187 Ct.Cl. 63, 408 F.2d 719 (Ct.Cl.1969), criticized in Note, Hearsay and Confrontation in Administrative Hearings, 48 N.C.L. Rev. 608 (1970).

sands of compensation claims—as in social security and workmen's compensation cases —and the declarant's appearance would be relatively costly or time-consuming, hearsay alternatives such as letters or other written evidence might prove decisive.[59] It has likewise been held that in the granting of a license an agency may rely upon evidence which would not be adequate in revoking the same license.[60]

(d) How precise does the agency's factfinding need to be? The ICC's reliance on "typical evidence" and the FTC's use of survey evidence are examples of agency dependence on statistical averages to determine facts in particular cases where legal or policy decisions are not dependent upon exact determinations. For instance, survey evidence of consumer understanding indicating that from 9 to 100 percent of the public were misled by respondent's advertising will support a finding that it constitutes an unfair or deceptive act.[61] Still another example is the fixing of a rate for commodities transported by one carrier on the basis of costs incurred by similarly situated carriers.[62]

(e) What is the administrative policy behind the statute being enforced? The range of necessary reliability is affected by the type of policy which the administrative hearing is designed to promote. For example, the social security and workmen's compensation programs are intended to provide benefits quickly at low cost. The refusal to rely upon reports in such hearings would run counter to the purposes for which the statutes are designed.[63]

When focusing on these criteria, it is essential to consider the central point that evaluation of hearsay and other technically incompetent evidence cannot be accomplished in the abstract; the evidence must be examined in the light of the particular record. This includes, at a minimum, an examination of the quality and quantity of the evidence on each side, as well as the circumstantial setting of the case.[64]

352. The Substantial Evidence Rule.

Once the agency has determined that legally incompetent evidence can be admitted and relied upon in making an administrative decision, it might appear that the subject of hearsay evidence in administrative hearings has been exhausted. While the agency's admission and use of legally incompetent evidence is subject to judicial review, this review of administrative determinations of fact should be confined to determining whether the decision is supported by the evidence in the record. Judicial review of ad-

59. Richardson v. Perales, 402 U.S. 389 (1971), supra § 349, n. 21; Marmon v. Railroad Retirement Board, 218 F.2d 716 (3d Cir. 1955); Ellers v. Railroad Retirement Board, 132 F.2d 636 (2d Cir. 1943). For an interesting reverse application of this principle, see Staskel v. Gardner, 274 F.Supp. 861, 863 (E.D. Pa.1967) (hearsay not sufficient evidence to deny claim); Rios v. Hackney, 294 F.Supp. 885 (N.D. Tex.1967).

60. Davis, Hearsay in Administrative Hearings, 32 Geo.Wash.L.Rev. 689, 699 (1964); see FTC v. Cement Institute, 333 U.S. 683, 705–06 (1948).

61. E. g., Arrow Metal Prods. Corp., 53 F.T.C. 721, 727, 733–34, aff'd per curiam, 249 F.2d 83 (3d Cir. 1957); Rhodes Pharmacal Co., 49 F.T.C. 263 (1952), aff'd 208 F.2d 382, 386–87 (7th Cir. 1953), rev'd on other grounds 348 U.S. 940 (1955).

62. Atchison, Topeka & S. F. R. R. v. United States, 225 F.Supp. 584 (D.Colo.1964); New England Division Case, 261 U.S. 184, 197–98 (1923); see 2 Sharfman, The Interstate Commerce Com'n 376–80 (1931). See also Skelly Oil Co. v. FPC, 375 F.2d 6 (10th Cir. 1967), modified sub. nom. Permian Basin Area Rate Cases, 390 U.S. 747.

63. Richardson v. Perales, 402 U.S. 389 (1971), supra § 349, n. 21. Several states have also adopted specific statutes governing the use of copies of documentary evidence. See Ga.Code, § 3A–116(b) (1970); Hawaii Rev.Stat. § 91–10(1)–(2) (1968); Md.Code, art. 41, § 252(b) (1965); Mass. Gen.Laws Ann. c. 30A, § 11(4) (1966); Mich.Comp. Laws Ann. § 24.276 (1970); Minn.Stat.Ann. § 15.-0419(2) (1967); Neb.Rev.Stat. § 84–914(3) (1966); 75 Okl.Stat.Ann. § 310(2) (1965); Ore.Rev.Stat. § 183.450(1) (1964); R.I.Gen.Laws § 42–35–10(b) (1969); Wash. RCWA § 34.04.100(2) (1965).

64. For a review of the cases, see Jacobowitz v. United States, 191 Ct.Cl. 444, 424 F.2d 555 (1970).

ministrative evidence has not been so limited, however. As a substitute for rules of admissibility, courts apply the so-called "substantial evidence" rule to judicial review of agency action in seeking to assure fairness to the parties.

As applied to administrative findings, the substantial evidence rule possesses two branches, one of which is sound, and the other unsound. The first consists of an overall standard of review of the findings of fact. In essence, it does not differ materially from the "sufficiency" standard applied in judicial review of jury verdicts.[65] In this sense, substantial evidence is evidence

> "affording a substantial basis of fact from which the fact in issue can be reasonably inferred. . . . [I]t must be enough to justify, if the trial were to a jury, a refusal to direct a verdict when the conclusion sought to be drawn from it is one of fact for the jury." [66]

This standard measures both the quantitative and qualitative sufficiency of the evidence.[67] Its proper application takes into account the rationale of the exclusionary rules of evidence, the reliability of the hearsay evidence—including the opportunity for cross-examination, the availability of better evidence, and the appearance of corroborating evidence—and the needs of administrative economy. According to the leading opinion of Universal Camera Corp. v. NLRB,[68] this judicially evolved standard of review of administrative factfinding is incorporated into the Administrative Procedure Act, except that the Act broadens judicial review to assure that the reviewing court takes "into account whatever in the record fairly detracts from its weight."[69] In other words, the reviewing court should review the whole record to determine whether there is a rational basis in it for the findings of fact supporting the agency's decision.[70]

In reviewing administrative decisions, some appellate courts—primarily state—added a second branch to the substantial evidence test, warping the test into a rigid rule for denying credibility to uncorroborated hearsay evidence. Known as the "legal residuum rule" because it requires that an administrative finding be supported by some evidence admissible in a jury trial—that is, by a residuum of legal evidence—it has been severely criticized by scholars, and its application has strained judicial reasoning.[71]

---

65. E. g., Wilkerson v. McCarthy, 336 U.S. 53, 57 (1949); § 339, supra.

66. NLRB v. Columbian Enameling & Stamping Co., 306 U.S. 292, 299–300 (1939); see Consolo v. FMC, 383 U.S. 607, 618–621 (1966); Richardson v. Perales, 402 U.S. 389 (1971), supra § 349, n. 21. The substantial evidence test applied to jury verdicts and administrative findings is in contrast to appellate review of a court's fact determinations in a nonjury case where findings are measured by the "clearly erroneous" test. See United States v. United States Gypsum Co., 333 U.S. 364, 395 (1948); NLRB v. Southland Mfg. Co., 201 F.2d 244, 246 (4th Cir. 1952); Wright, Federal Courts 429–32 (2d ed. 1970).

67. See Benjamin 192; 1 Cooper 404–05.

68. 340 U.S. 474 (1951).

69. Id. at 488.

70. The intricacies and problems which arise in applying this standard are not within our concern here. See generally 4 Davis ch. 29. For a review of state authority which also is extremely critical of the substantial evidence standard, see 2 Cooper 722–55.

71. 2 Davis § 14.10; Benjamin 189–92; 1 Wigmore, Evidence, § 4b, p. 39. But see 1 Cooper 410–12.
The earliest case applying this rule illustrates its weakness. In Carroll v. Knickerbocker Ice Co., 218 N.Y. 435, 113 N.E. 507 (1916), the New York Court of Appeals reversed a workmen's compensation award in a death case where the commission's finding of accidental injury was based wholly on hearsay testimony of statements by the deceased workman. The workman, who developed delirium tremens and died within six days, had told his wife, a neighbor, and his family and hospital physicians that a 300-pound cake of ice had fallen upon his abdomen. Each party related this story to the commission. However, the case record also contained substantial contradictory evidence. The workman's helper on the ice truck, along with two cooks working in the saloon where the ice was delivered also testified that they were present at the

The residuum rule is both logically unsound and administratively impractical. In a trial before a lay jury hearsay evidence admitted without objection is given its natural, probative effect and may be the sole support for a verdict. But under the residuum rule hearsay cannot support a decision by an expert administrator. The rule ignores the reliability of technically incompetent evidence, rendering all such evidence ineffective unless corroborated. However, if corroborated, regardless of how slight the legal evidence, the same hearsay evidence will provide the substantial evidence needed to support the administrative finding.

This rule may also become a trap for the unwary, particularly where the hearing officer is not expert in the rules of evidence or where the parties are not represented by counsel. In fact it encourages trial examiners to apply the hearsay rule and exclude probative evidence in order to avoid possible error. In its instinctive protection of fairness in administrative hearings, through assuring that the decision is supported by evidence subject to confrontation and cross-examination, the residuum rule seems unassailable. What it fails to consider, however, is that much "legal" evidence within the hearsay exceptions is equally untested. Yet the latter is accepted even in jury trials because of its probable reliability. Consequently the residuum rule's mechanical prohibition against uncorroborated hearsay is unsound. Its sound objectives can be secured through the sensitivity of the hearing officers and the wise application of the substantial evidence test which measures the quantity and quality of the supporting evidence regardless of its category or label.

As others have recounted at substantial length, the residuum rule generally lacks acceptance in federal courts.[72] The states are still undecided over its validity.[73]

353. Opinion Evidence and Expert Testimony.[74]

The presentation of expert and nonexpert opinions is increasingly common in administrative hearings. Medical issues arising in workmen's compensation claims are often complex, technical and beyond the knowledge of either the hearing officer or the agency. An administrative decision to license a hydroelectric plant, to locate a public housing project, to discontinue a bus line, or to grant a liquor license frequently evokes strong community concern.[75] The public views advanced are likely to be expressed in terms of opinions and to include reference to the views of others. To deny the public an opportunity to testify is to invite public rejection of the agency decision.

time and place where the accident presumably occurred but they neither saw nor heard the incident. In addition, the hospital physicians found no bruises, discolorations, or abrasions on the workman's body. In light of the lack of testimonial or physical corroboration of the workman's story which probably would have been available if the hearsay statement had been trustworthy, the obvious self-interest in the deceased's statement, and the possibility of the workman's being inebriated when he made his statement, the court reasonably could have ruled that credence could not be placed in the supporting hearsay evidence and that it did not, therefore, constitute substantial evidence. Instead, after noting that the commission could "accept any evidence that is offered" under the New York Workman's Compensation Act, the court laid down the rule that "still in the end there must be a residuum of legal evidence to support the claim before an award can be made." Id. at 441, 113 N.E. at 509. It therefore held that when substantial evidence is required, "hearsay testimony is no evidence." Id.

72. 2 Davis § 14.11, and see Richardson v. Perales, 402 U.S. 389 (1971), supra § 349, n. 21.

73. See Tauber v. County Board of Appeals, 257 Md. 202, 262 A.2d 513, 518 (Md.Ct.App.1970); Neuman v. City of Baltimore, 251 Md. 92, 246 A.2d 583 (1968); 1 Cooper 406–10; 2 Davis § 14.12.

74. See generally 2 Davis § 14.13.

75. Cf. Scenic Hudson Preservation Conference v. FPC, 354 F.2d 608 (2d Cir. 1965) cert. denied 384 U.S. 941 (1966); Citizens for Allegan County, Inc. v. FPC, 134 U.S.App.D.C. 229, 414 F.2d 1125 (1969); Office of Communication of United Church of Christ v. FCC, 123 U.S.App.D.C. 328, 359 F. 2d 994 (1966); Norwalk CORE v. Norwalk Redevelopment Agency, 395 F.2d 920 (2d Cir. 1968).

The general admissibility of expert and nonexpert testimony in administrative hearings is no longer open to question, but doubt still exists regarding the weight an expert's views should be given.[76] For a time agencies and reviewing courts followed early judicial reasoning and refused to hear expert testimony on the very question that the agency was created to decide.[77] Other courts took the position that it would be unfair for an agency to rely on its own expertise or the expert testimony of its staff when their opinions were contradicted by outside experts.[78] In rejecting these contradictory appeals to ignorance, courts now recognize legislative intention to establish expert agencies. Therefore, agency decisions which rely on the agency's own expertness are upheld when the respondent offers no contrary expert testimony or when expert testimony offered by staff members and outside experts conflicts.[79] Some courts have gone even

further and given excessive deference to the knowledge of the administrative agency by upholding its decision in the face of uncontradicted expert testimony to the contrary.[80] However, the demands of fairness are now generally accepted, and an agency seeking to rely on its expertise must present expert testimony subject to cross-examination on the record or give the respondent fair notification that official notice will be taken of such "facts." [81]

354. Privilege in Administrative Proceedings.

Witnesses in administrative hearings have the same general duty incumbent on all citizens in judicial trials to give testimony; "the public has a right to every man's testimony." [82] Because the demand comes from

---

76. See Davis & Randall, Inc. v. United States, 219 F.Supp. 673, 679 (W.D.N.Y.1963); Keller v. FTC, 132 F.2d 59, 61 (7th Cir. 1942); Gloyd v. Commissioner, 63 F.2d 649, 650 (8th Cir. 1933) cert. denied 290 U.S. 633.

77. Cf. § 12, supra; Corn v. State Bar, 68 Cal.2d 461, 67 Cal.Rptr. 401, 439 P.2d 313 (1968). The courts have generally discarded the former view that agency opinions need supporting expert testimony, and agencies are now free to use their own judgment. Compare, e. g., Boggs & Buhl v. Commissioner, 34 F.2d 859 (3d Cir. 1929), with Kline v. Commissioner, 130 F.2d 742 (3d Cir. 1942) cert. denied 317 U.S. 697.

78. E. g., Brennan v. State Board of Medical Examiners, 101 Cal.App.2d 193, 225 P.2d 11 (1950).

79. E. g., Pacific Power & Light Co. v. FPC, 141 F.2d 602 (9th Cir. 1944); Contractors v. Pillsbury, 150 F.2d 310, 313 (9th Cir. 1945); see McCarthy v. Sawyer-Goodman Co., 194 Wis. 198, 215 N.W. 824 (1927).

This is an exceedingly brief summary of what can be a complex issue. For an excellent analysis and attempt to balance the right of respondent to a decision based on "record" evidence with the administrative need to avoid unproductive hearings, see Davis & Randall, Inc. v. United States, supra n. 76, where Judge Friendly applied the following test:

"Without wishing to be held to the letter, we suggest that a rejection of unopposed testimony by a

qualified and disinterested expert on a matter susceptible of reasonably precise measurement, without the agency's developing its objections at a hearing, ought to be upheld only when the agency's uncommunicated criticisms appear to the reviewing court to be both so compelling and so deeply held that the court can be fairly sure the agency would not have been affected by anything the witness could have said had he known of them, *and* the court would have been bound to affirm, despite the expert's hypothetical rebuttal, out of deference for the agency's judgment on so technical a matter." Id. at 679.

80. See, e. g., Gaddy v. State Bd. of Registration for Healing Arts, 397 S.W.2d 347, 355 (Mo.1965); Arc Realty Co. v. Commissioner, 295 F.2d 98, 103 (8th Cir. 1961). But cf. Jaffe, Judicial Control of Administrative Action 607–10 (1965). Judicial approval of agency reliance upon its own expertise is inappropriate, of course, where the expert opinion is patently fallacious or "intrinsically nonpersuasive." See Davis & Randall, Inc. v. United States, supra n. 76, at 678; Sternberger v. United States, 185 Ct.Cl. 528, 401 F.2d 1012, 1016 (1968). Approval is equally inappropriate where the opinion is based on inferences from facts in the record. Interstate Power Co. v. FPC, 236 F.2d 372, 385 (8th Cir. 1956) cert. denied 352 U.S. 967; see Market St. Ry. Co. v. Railroad Com'n, 324 U.S. 548, 559–60 (1945).

81. E. g., Moschogianis v. Concrete Material & Mfg. Co., 179 Minn. 177, 228 N.W. 607 (1930); see § 357 infra.

82. 12 Cobbett's Parliamentary History 675, 693 (1812), quoted in 4 Wigmore, Evidence 2965–66 (1st ed. 1905).

the community as a whole, rather than from the parties, and because the obligation is essential to any search for justice, "all privileges of exemption from this duty are exceptional." [83] Read literally, the APA's provision in section 7(c) that "[a]ny oral or documentary evidence may be received," [84] authorizes the receipt of privileged evidence in administrative hearings. [85] Nevertheless, administrative hearings have generally followed the judicial lead in recognizing numerout exceptions to the obligation to testify. The exceptions are of two kinds. A few, such as the exclusion of illegally obtained evidence and the assertion of the right against self-incrimination, are constitutional commands. Others, such as the privileges protecting attorney-client and marital communications, are founded upon the need to protect interests without constitutional dimension yet these relationships have sufficient social importance to warrant the sacrifice of full factual disclosure.

Even though administrative agencies do not as a rule impose criminal penalties, their adjudicative procedures are not exempt from constitutional limitations, and the chapters of this text which deal with the various constitutional privileges should be consulted. In Camara v. Municipal Court, [86] and See v. Seattle, [87] the Supreme Court applied the Fourth Amendment's strictures against unreasonable searches and seizure of property to administrative health and fire inspections, [88] albeit in somewhat qualified form. While these cases involved direct challenges to administrative inspections, it is also clear that the constitutional objection is available at the hearing even though no objection is asserted at the time the inspection is made. [89] And, in Knoll Associates, Inc. v. FTC, [90] the Court of Appeals of the Seventh Circuit set aside an FTC order on the ground that the Commission's acceptance and use of corporate documents, known to be stolen on behalf of the government, violated the Fourth Amendment. Many cases uphold the Fifth Amendment privilege against self-incrimina-

---

83. 8 Wigmore, Evidence (McNaughton rev.) § 2192, p. 73.

84. 5 U.S.C.A. § 556(d).

85. Professor Davis has made the provocative suggestion that § 7(c) authorizes agency rejection of unsound or questionable privileges. 2 Davis § 14.08, at 287. It seems doubtful, however, that this provision can reasonably be interpreted as addressing itself to the question of testimonial privilege; rather, the legislative history suggests that its purpose is to avoid binding administrative agencies to technical rules of evidence. 92 Cong.Rec. 2157, 5653 (1946); see Attorney General's Manual on Administrative Procedure Act 76 (1947). Legislative omission, moreover, is seldom convincing support for deviation from common law practices. See CAB v. Air Transp. Ass'n, 201 F.Supp. 318 (D.D.C.1961).

Privileges under state law are generally governed by statutes sufficiently broad in terms to apply to administrative proceedings. The same generalization cannot be made in the federal area, although it is possible that measures will be taken to make the Proposed Federal Rules of Evidence, if adopted, applicable to agencies as well as courts.

86. 387 U.S. 523 (1967).

87. 387 U.S. 541 (1967).

88. See generally Note, Enforcement of Municipal Housing Codes, 78 Harv.L.Rev. 801 (1965); Note, The Fourteenth Amendment and Housing Inspections, 77 Yale L.J. 521 (1968).

Compare Wyman v. James, 400 U.S. 309 (1971), declining to apply the Fourth Amendment's proscription to visit by caseworker to welfare recipient's home under compulsion of loss of benefits.

Search and seizure is treated in Ch. 15, supra.

89. See Finn's Liquor Shop, Inc. v. State Liquor Authority, 24 N.Y.2d 647, 249 N.E.2d 440, 301 N.Y.S.2d 584 (1969) cert. denied 396 U.S. 840; LeograndeV. State Liquor Authority, 25 App.Div.2d 225, 268 N.Y.S.2d 433 (1966) rev'd on other grounds 19 N.Y.2d 418, 227 N.E.2d 302, 280 N.Y.2d 381 (1967); Pennsylvania Liquor Control Board v. Leonardziak, 210 Pa.Super. 511, 233 A.2d 606 (1967); cf. Parrish v. Civil Service Com'n, 66 Cal.2d 260, 57 Cal.Rptr. 623, 425 P.2d 223 (1967). Compare Elder v. Board of Medical Examiners, 241 Cal.App.2d 246, 50 Cal.Rptr. 304 (1966) (dictum), with Pierce v. Board of Nursing Ed. & Nurse Registration, 255 Cal.App.2d 463, 63 Cal.Rptr. 107 (1967) (dictum). Contra, NLRB v. South Bay Daily Breeze, 415 F.2d 360, 364 (9th Cir. 1969) (alternative holding) cert. denied 397 U.S. 915; Solomon v. Liquor Control Com'n, 4 Ohio St.2d 31, 212 N.E.2d 595 (1966) cert. denied 384 U.S. 928.

90. 397 F.2d 530 (7th Cir. 1968).

tion in administrative proceedings.[91] However, the self-incrimination privilege has been limited. First, it applies only to natural persons and therefore does not protect corporations and other legal entities.[92] Second, it can be circumvented by the grant of immunity from criminal prosecution.[93] Federal agencies commonly have been authorized to grant immunity and compel a witness to testify even if the evidence implicates him.[94] Third, the privilege against self-incrimination is also avoided if the information is sought from records "required to be kept."[95] However, this avoidance of the self-incrimination exception has been narrowed by recent Supreme Court rulings.[96] The courts have also given some exploratory consideration to the application of other Fifth and Sixth Amendment exclusionary rules to administrative proceedings, but few definitive determinations have been issued. Some agencies have taken action to protect constitutional rights, at least where criminal sanctions are possible. For example, Internal Revenue Service agents must now provide *Miranda*[97] warnings that an accused has a right to remain silent and seek counsel in order to protect the admissibility of a taxpayer's statements or of evidence discovered as a result of the investigation.[98] Agency

---

91. E. g., Murphy v. Waterfront Com'n, 378 U.S. 52 (1964); Smith v. United States, 337 U.S. 137 (1949). In this situation, the respondent fears the potential administrative order less than the subsequent use of his testimony in a criminal proceeding.
See generally Ch. 13, supra.

92. See § 128, supra.

93. See Compulsory Testimony Act of 1893, 27 Stat. 443 (1893), 49 U.S.C.A. § 46:
"No person shall be excused from . . . testifying . . . on the ground . . . that the testimony or evidence . . . may tend to criminate him . . . . But no person shall be prosecuted or subjected to any penalty of forfeiture for or on account of any transaction, matter or thing, concerning which he may testify, or produce evidence, documentary or otherwise, before said Commission, or in obedience to its subpoena . . . ."
See also Ullmann v. United States, 350 U.S. 422 (1956); Brown v. Walker, 161 U.S. 591 (1896); Note, The Federal Witness Immunity Acts in Theory and Practice: Treading the Constitutional Tightrope, 72 Yale L.J. 1568 (1963) (noting 44 federal witness immunity acts). Most of these statutes were repealed and incorporated with substantial modification into the Organized Crime Control Act of 1970, 18 U.S.C.A. § 6004. Immunity may still be granted to witnesses appearing before administrative agencies, but approval of the Attorney General is first required.
See general discussion in § 143, supra.

94. See Shapiro v. United States, 335 U.S. 1, 6 (1948) (citing 26 federal statutes). Similar state statutes are common. E. g., Ill.Rev.Stat.1969, c. 120 § 453.10a. See Halpin v. Scotti, 415 Ill. 104, 112 N.E.2d 91 (1953). However, application of the immunity provision does not preclude an agency from issuing an order against persons so testifying, even though the order is based upon such testimony. Drath v. FTC, 99 U.S.App.D.C. 289, 239 F.2d 452 (1956) cert. denied 353 U.S. 917.

95. Shapiro v. United States, n. 94 supra. See § 142, supra.

96. In Marchetti v. United States, 390 U.S. 39 (1968), and Grosso v. United States, 390 U.S. 62 (1968), the Court upheld assertion of the privilege against self-incrimination as a defense to criminal prosecutions for violations of both the registration and taxing provisions of the federal wagering tax statutes. The obligation to pay taxes could not be separated from the information and incriminatory purposes of the statutes. The required records exception was not applicable, the Court concluded, because the three premises of that doctrine had not been met. They are:
"first, the purposes of the United States' inquiry must be essentially regulatory; second, information is to be obtained by requiring the preservation of records of a kind which the regulated party has customarily kept; and third, the records themselves must have assumed 'public aspects' which render them at least analogous to public documents." Id. 67–68.
Accord, Leary v. United States, 395 U.S. 6 (1969); Haynes v. United States, 390 U.S. 85 (1968) (invalidating registration provisions of the National Firearms Act). But see United States v. Knox, 396 U.S. 77 (1969).

97. Miranda v. Arizona, 384 U.S. 436 (1966).
See § 152, supra.

98. United States v. Dickerson, 413 F.2d 1111, 1117 & n. 13 (7th Cir. 1969); Mathis v. United States, 391 U.S. 1 (1969). See generally Andrews, The Right to Counsel in Criminal Tax Investigations under Escobedo and Miranda: "The Critical Stage," 53 Iowa L.Rev. 1074 (1968). On the other hand, *Miranda* warnings have not generally been extended to other administrative investigations because they are not criminal in nature and do not involve the "custodial" feature so critical to *Miranda*. See,

adjudications have in general only skirted these issues and there remain many unanswered questions.[99]

On the federal level, neither the Congress nor the agencies have focused on whether administrative agencies must recognize testimonial privileges not constitutionally required. In a leading case concerning the enforcement of an SEC subpoena, Judge Learned Hand expressly assumed that agency proceedings are "subject to the same testimonial privileges as judicial proceedings."[1] Except for the Ninth Circuit, other federal courts have either made the same assumption or considered the matter a question of federal law.[2] At any rate, agencies have generally accorded privileged treatment to communications between attorney and client, physician

and patient and husband and wife.[3] But they have not been anxious to extend such privileges. For example, the accountant-client privilege recognized by a few states has not been accepted by federal agencies.[4] Business secrets have been protected grudgingly, although agencies have become more sophisticated in recent years in protecting both the witness and the adjudicative process by *in camera* receipt of sensitive data.[5]

Claims of privilege for government secrets are particularly important in administrative hearings. Any attempt to probe the government's case by discovery, subpoena of agency witnesses, or cross-examination is quickly met by claims that the information sought is privileged. Actually, the government secrets privilege is asserted as an umbrella for three types of information: state secrets involving military or diplomatic information; requests that executive officers testify; and official government information which may range from the identity of informers and internal management materials to staff studies unrelated to any litigation.[6] Only the third, omnibus exception has special significance for administrative adjudications; the judicial rules applicable to state secrets and executive officer testimony are followed in agency hearings. An exploration of all the twists and turns given agency applications of the omnibus exception is beyond

e. g., Harris v. Smith, 418 F.2d 899 (2d Cir. 1969); F. J. Buckner Corp. v. NLRB, 401 F.2d 910 (9th Cir. 1968) cert. denied 393 U.S. 1084; Wilber J. Allingham, 164 NLRB 230 (1967); In re A——, 19 Ad.L.2d 372 (Bd.Imm.App.1966); Mumford v. Department of Alcoholic Bev. Cont., 258 Cal.App. 2d 49, 65 Cal.Rptr. 495 (1968). See generally Note, Extending Miranda to Administrative Investigations, 56 Va.L.Rev. 690 (1970). But see United States v. Casias, 306 F.Supp. 166 (D.Colo.1969) (draft board).

99. For example, contentions for the appointment of counsel for an indigent respondent in administrative proceedings have met with only minimal success. Compare In re American Chinchilla Corp., 26 Ad.L.2d 284 (F.T.C. Dec. 23, 1969), noted 1970 Duke L.J. 112; 84 Harv.L.Rev. 1026 (1971), with Nees v. SEC, 414 F.2d 211, 221 (9th Cir. 1969), and Boruski v. SEC, 340 F.2d 991, 992 (2d Cir.) cert. denied 381 U.S. 943.

1. McMann v. SEC, 87 F.2d 377, 378 (2d Cir. 1937) cert. denied 301 U.S. 684.

2. E. g., Colton v. United States, 306 F.2d 633 (2d Cir. 1962) cert. denied 371 U.S. 951 (1963); Falsone v. United States, 205 F.2d 734 (5th Cir. 1953) cert. denied 346 U.S. 864; United States v. Threlkeld, 241 F.Supp. 324 (W.D.Tenn.1965); In re Kearney, 227 F.Supp. 174 (S.D.N.Y.1964). Contra, Baird v. Koerner, 279 F.2d 623 (9th Cir. 1960); In re Bretto, 231 F.Supp. 529, 531 (D.Minn.1964) (*Baird* applied pursuant to stipulation of the parties). For a perceptive student comment questioning the accuracy of this assessment of the choice of law problem, see Comment, Privileged Communications Before Federal Administrative Agencies: The Law Applied in the District Courts, 31 U.Chi.L.Rev. 395 (1964).

3. E. g., Colton v. United States, n. 2 supra; CAB v. Air Transp. Ass'n of America, 201 F.Supp. 318 (D. D.C.1961); Viviano Macaroni Co., [1965–67 Transfer Binder] Trade Reg.Rep. ¶ 17,467 (F.T.C.1966). Contra, Air Transp. Ass'n, [1960–64 Transfer Binder] Av.L.Rep. ¶ 21,355 (1963); cf. Petersen, Attorney-Client Privileges in Internal Revenue Service Investigations, 54 Minn.L.Rev. 67 (1969).

4. See, e. g., FTC v. St. Regis Paper Co., 304 F.2d 731 (7th Cir. 1962); Falsone v. United States, n. 2 supra.

5. See generally E. Gellhorn, Business Secrets in Administrative Agency Adjudication, 22 Ad.L.Rev. 515 (1970).

6. See Ch. 12, supra.

the scope of this chapter.[7] In any event, exculpatory information in an agency's possession or file data which may aid respondent's preparation or presentation of his case must be disclosed by the agency.[8] The alternative is to drop the prosecution against the respondent.[9] Anything less would violate the commands of procedural due process which every adjudication must observe.[10]

Almost half the states provide that rules of privilege applicable in court proceedings must apply in administrative hearings.[11] Courts and agencies in other states have reached the same position as a matter of policy.[12] The scope of the statutory recognition of privileged communications in the states tends to exceed the testimonial exception recognized by federal courts.[13] On the other hand, where agency proceedings are ex-

cepted or where no statutory mandate exists, state agencies have relaxed or avoided testimonial privileges where the rationale for the privilege is weak or not particularly appropriate. For example, several states have held that the physician-patient privilege cannot bar a workmen's compensation commission's search for the truth.[14]

In summary, the trend appears to be toward narrowing testimonial privileges in administrative hearings and, where practical, toward resort to alternative protections against unnecessary public disclosure.

355. Presentation of Case: Burden of Proof and Presumptions.

The customary common law rule that the moving party has the burden of proof—including not only the burden of going forward but also the burden of persuasion—is generally observed in administrative hearings. Section 7(c) of the APA, for example, provides: "Except as otherwise provided by statute, the proponent of a rule or order has the burden of proof." [15] State courts have reached the same result in connection with state administrative proceedings.[16] In most hearings the burden of persuasion is met by the usual civil case standard of "a preponderance of evidence." However, where grave issues of personal security are at stake in an administrative hearing, as in a deportation proceeding, the Supreme Court has imposed the standard that the government establish its alle-

7. For an explanation of one agency's approach, see E. Gellhorn, The Treatment of Confidential Information by the Federal Trade Commission: The Hearing, 116 U.Pa.L.Rev. 401, 423–27 (1968); E. Gellhorn, The Treatment of Confidential Information by the Federal Trade Commission: Pretrial Practices, 36 U.Chi.L.Rev. 113, 157–77 (1968); cf. Moore-McCormack Lines, Inc., v. U. S., 188 Ct.Cl. 644, 413 F.2d 568 (1969). The Freedom of Information Act of 1966 which amended § 3 of the APA, 5 U.S.C.A. § 552, has eased access to some agency files for the public, but it has had little effect on agency adjudication. See § 108, supra.

8. E. g., Sperandeo v. Dairy Employees Local 537, 334 F.2d 381 (10th Cir. 1964); NLRB v. Capitol Fish Co., 294 F.2d 868 (5th Cir. 1961); Union Bag-Camp Paper Corp. v. FTC, 233 F.Supp. 660, 666 (S.D.N.Y.1964); Sperry & Hutchinson Co. v. FTC, 256 F.Supp. 136 (S.D.N.Y.1966); cf. Miller v. Pate, 386 U.S. 1 (1967); Giles v. Maryland, 386 U.S. 66 (1967); Brady v. Maryland, 373 U.S. 83, 87–88 (1963); United States v. Bryant, 439 F.2d 642 (D.C.Cir. 1971).

9. See Sperandeo v. Dairy Employees Local 537, n. 26 supra; cf. United States v. Andolschek, 142 F.2d 503 (2d Cir. 1944); Berger and Krash, Government Immunity from Discovery, 59 Yale L.J. 1451, 1453 (1950).

10. E. g., FCC v. Pottsville Broadcasting Co., 309 U.S. 134, 143–44 (1940).

11. 1 Cooper 396–97 (collecting authorities.)

12. E. g., New York City Council v. Goldwater, 284 N.Y. 296, 31 N.E.2d 31 (1940); Benjamin 171.

13. E. g., 75 Okl.Stat.Ann. § 310(1) (1965).

14. See, e. g., Cooper's Inc. v. Long, 224 So.2d 866 (Miss.1969); Danussi v. Easy Wash, Inc., 270 Minn. 465, 134 N.W.2d 138 (1965).

15. 5 U.S.C.A. § 556(d).

16. E. g., State ex rel. Utilities Com'n v. Carolina Power & Light Co., 250 N.C. 421, 109 S.E.2d 253 (1959); Pennsylvania Labor Relations Bd. v. Sansom House Enterprises, Inc., 378 Pa. 385, 106 A.2d 404 (1954); Crossroads Recreation, Inc. v. Broz, 4 N.Y.2d 39, 172 N.Y.S.2d 129, 149 N.E.2d 65 (1958); International Minerals & Chem. Corp. v. New Mexico Pub. Serv. Com'n, 81 N.M. 280, 466 P.2d 557 (1970).

gations by "clear, unequivocal, and convincing evidence." [17]

Increasingly, the courts are also employing the substantial evidence standard to impose a special burden of proof on administrative agencies distributing compensation benefits. A series of cases involving social security and workmen's compensation proceedings have required that the agency accept the claimant's uncontroverted evidence even though the claimant has the burden of proof.[18] Nor can these cases be explained away on the grounds of judicial acceptance of uncontradicted medical testimony in support of the claim, since the agencies are also dealing with malingering and false claims. On the other hand, reviewing courts are more concerned with the remedial, risk-spreading purposes of the statutes and the comparative inability of the claimant to present additional proof.[19] Similar tendencies occasionally appear in such diverse areas as police suspen-

sion matters [20] and draft exemption cases [21] where the courts have given increasing scrutiny to the overall fairness of administrative adjudications. It would seem safe to predict the spread of this tendency to less formalized adjudications [22] where the agency deals with individual liberties or claims.

These cases can also be viewed as establishing a presumption in certain administrative adjudications since they affect the burden of proof. The history of workmen's compensation illustrates this alternative analysis. Although many state acts have created a presumption in favor of the claimant, several state courts formerly gave these provisions no effect.[23] In interpreting a federal compensation act in Del Vecchio v. Bowers,[24] the Supreme Court held that this "benefit" presumption was sufficient to carry claimant's burden of persuasion in the absence of opposing evidence. However, once rebuttal evidence is introduced, the statutory presumption is overcome and the agency must decide the case solely on the evidence in the record.[25] Similar analysis supports the presumption of the correctness of official administrative action.[26]

17. Woodby v. Immigration & Naturalization Service, 385 U.S. 276 (1966); see Jaffe, Administrative Law: Burden of Proof and Scope of Review, 79 Harv.L.Rev. 914 (1966).

18. E. g., Kerner v. Flemming, 283 F.2d 916 (2d Cir. 1960); Young & Co. v. Shea, 397 F.2d 185 (5th Cir. 1968), rehearing en banc denied 404 F.2d 1059, cert. denied 395 U.S. 920; Stanley v. Moan, 71 Ariz. 359, 227 P.2d 389 (1951); Dole v. Industrial Com'n, 115 Utah 311, 204 P.2d 462 (1949). The recent social security cases from just one federal circuit, the Sixth, include: York v. Gardner, 397 F.2d 209 (6th Cir. 1968); Nelms v. Gardner, 386 F.2d 971 (6th Cir. 1967); Colwell v. Gardner, 386 F.2d 56 (6th Cir. 1967); Branham v. Gardner, 383 F.2d 614 (6th Cir. 1967); Sayers v. Gardner, 380 F.2d 940, 942–43 (6th Cir. 1967) (noting "the repeated necessity of reversing the Secretary [of HEW] in these cases"); Erickson v. Ribicoff, 305 F.2d 638 (6th Cir. 1962); Hall v. Flemming, 289 F.2d 290 (6th Cir. 1961); King v. Flemming, 289 F.2d 808 (6th Cir. 1961). See generally Jaffe, Judicial Control of Administrative Action 608 (1965).

19. However, where the evidence is likely to be available only to respondent, the burden of persuasion or of going forward may be imposed on him. See, e. g., Day v. National Transp. Safety Bd., 414 F.2d 950 (5th Cir. 1969); Smyth v. United States Civil Serv. Com'n, 291 F.Supp. 568, 573 (E.D. Wis.1968).

20. E. g., Kelly v. Murphy, 20 N.Y.2d 205, 282 N.Y.S.2d 254, 229 N.E.2d 40 (1967).

21. Dickinson v. United States, 346 U.S. 389, 396 (1953); cf. Mulloy v. United States, 398 U.S. 410 (1970). But see Dickinson v. United States, supra at 399 (dissenting opinion).

22. See generally Davis, Discretionary Justice (1969).

23. E. g., Joseph v. United Kimono Co., 194 App. Div. 568, 185 N.Y.S. 700 (1921).

24. 296 U.S. 280 (1935).

25. Id. at 286. This view now prevails in some state courts. E. g., Cellurale's Case, 333 Mass. 37, 127 N.E.2d 787 (1955); 2 Larson, The Law of Workmen's Compensation § 80.33 (1952). This also illustrates that problems of burden of proof are, in essence, often questions of substantive law. 2 Davis, § 14.14, at 328; see Republic Aviation Corp. v. NLRB, 324 U.S. 793 (1945); 2 Davis § 15.04, at 372–73.

26. E. g., Cupples Hesse Corp. v. State Tax Com'n, 329 S.W.2d 696 (Mo.1959); Goldfarb v. Department of Revenue, 411 Ill. 573, 104 N.E.2d 606 (1952).

On the other hand, precisely the opposite trend is beginning to surface in administrative adjudications where the activities of business respondents are tested. For example, an advertiser may have the burden of establishing any advertising claim, and if it is the type of claim whose truth can be determined only by scientific tests—for example, a claim that respondent's tires will stop a car 25 percent more quickly than other tires —the advertiser's fully-documented proof must *antedate* the representation; the prosecuting agency need only show that the claim was made.[27] As increasing weight is given to the public interest in fair dealing and in a healthier environment, we can expect further developments either imposing strict liability on certain business activities [28] or requiring that the business establish by substantial evidence that its practices should not be prohibited.

356. Presentation of Case: Written Evidence and Cross-Examination.

Perhaps the most distinctive feature of many administrative hearings, particularly in contrast to nonjury trials, is the substitution of written evidence for oral testimony. This written evidence takes several forms. In its simplest and least productive aspect, some witnesses appear, if at all, simply for cross-examination, with the written questions and answers read into the record in lieu of the usual oral question-answer format. This "canned dialogue" has been savagely and justly criticized as an abomination leading to the withholding of the true facts from the hearing examiner and assuring that the case will be decided on grounds other than the evidence in the record.[29] But if applied more sensitively, written evidence can expedite and simplify formal administrative proceedings through reducing the controversy to verified written statements which are then exchanged by the parties for the purpose of rebuttal.[30] Federal administrative agencies have frequently relied upon this technique; the ICC for almost half a century.[31] With cooperation of the parties, this procedure can result in greater precision than where the facts are presented orally.

The ICC's written procedures are probably the most sophisticated of all agencies. In time, the Commission's "modified" procedure has been streamlined into an extraordinary

---

27. The Federal Trade Commission's theory in recent complaints is that an advertiser making performance claims without substantiating proof in hand shows a reckless disregard for the rights of the public. The conduct is therefore illegal whether or not the claim is ultimately established. See, e. g., Firestone Tire & Rubber Co., [1967–70 Transfer Binder] Trade Reg.Rep. ¶ 19,011 (FTC 1970); Chas. Pfizer & Co., [1967–70 Transfer Binder] Trade Reg.Rep. ¶ 19,209 (FTC 1970); id. 3 Trade Reg.Rep. ¶ 19,370. See also Heinz W. Kirchner, 63 F.T.C. 1282, 1294–95 (1963).

28. See 18 C.F.R. § 250.43 (Interior 1970) (imposing strict liability on off-shore oil well lessees for pollution damage).

29. As one leading administrative practitioner describes the impact of canned testimony:
"I don't believe that I am wholly unique in being put immediately to sleep when it is read. That tedium is eliminated when the written testimony is used, without reading, as direct examination subject to oral cross. I have not, however, yet seen an examiner who has really mastered the unspoken direct testimony. The 25% that is really strong won't be touched in cross-examination and cannot easily be brought out in redirect, so in most cases the examiner proceeds until briefing time, at the best, and forever at the worst, in amiable ignorance of the heart of the testimony. The few hours of direct examination that are saved by written direct testimony come at too high a price." Gardner, Shrinking the Big Case, 16 Ad.L.Rev. 5, 12–13 (1963).

30. See W. Gellhorn, Federal Administrative Proceedings 100–15 (1941); Selected Reports of the Administrative Conference of the United States 1961–1962, S.Doc. No. 24, 88th Cong., 1st Sess. 92 (1963); Woll, Administrative Law 37–48 (1963); Final Report of Attorney General's Committee on Administrative Procedure, S.Doc. No. 8, 77th Cong., 1st Sess. 69–70 (1941); Brown, Public Service Commission Procedure—A Problem and a Suggestion, 87 U.Pa.L.Rev. 139 (1938).

31. State agencies have also made extensive use of written evidence. See letter from member of State Corporation Commission of Virginia, 38 J.Am.Jud. Soc. 61 (1954).

administrative version of summary judgment.[32] Under rule 45 of the ICC's current procedure, any party may request use of the modified procedure by filing a verified statement setting forth the facts, argument, and exhibits on which he relies.[33] The opposing party must either admit or deny each material allegation, explaining each exception he takes to the facts and argument of his adversary. Unless there are material facts in dispute or the objecting party explains why he cannot properly present his case by affidavits, a decision will then be rendered on the written case. Note that this rule exceeds the concept of summary judgment currently applied under Rule 56 of the Federal Rules of Civil Procedure by placing the burden on the parties to prove that an oral hearing is necessary.[34] An oral hearing is not presumed to be the proper method for hearing a case.

Written evidence has been relied upon most successfully in rate or price control proceedings, where economic and expert analysis rather than sensorily-perceived phenomena provide the bulk of the evidence.[35] Credibility based upon conflicting stories relating what each witness observed is seldom involved. Often the advance preparation of written evidence is limited to the contentions of the party having the burden of proof; in others the opposing party's evidence is included. The elimination of surprise cannot be objected to since surprise has no proper place in the hearing when credibility is not in issue. Cross-examination is not used to establish a party's case. Its major purpose here is "not to reduce . . . [the expert] witness to a shattered hulk by the admission of error, but to explore all of the considerations entering into what must remain a matter of judgment." [36]

As explained by the Second Interim Administrative Conference, the benefits of written evidence are manifold:

"(1) [the] exchange of written evidence facilitates settlement techniques in situations in which there is staff participation; (2) the hearing examiner, after studying the direct evidence of the parties prior to hearing, can participate in the case in an intelligent fashion, leading to more effective use of conference techniques and more informed rulings at the hearing; (3) in a substantial number of cases, particularly those of less moment, the parties may be satisfied with their written presentations, and an oral hearing becomes unnecessary; and (4) the efforts of the parties at the oral hearing, if one

---

32. Early in the 1920's, the ICC abbreviated the usual oral hearing before a commissioner or examiner through the use of a "shortened" procedure. Upon consent of the parties, oral testimony was dispensed with, and a decision was rendered upon stipulated, sworn statements of fact. Despite encomiums from administrative law experts, this procedure did not prove particularly successful, since the parties could avoid the shortened procedure at any time by requesting a formal hearing. Consequently, in 1942 the ICC substituted what it called a "modified" procedure whereby each party submitted his case in writing for the purpose of obtaining agreement on as many facts as possible. The parties then confined their oral testimony to the remaining points in dispute. While more successful than the "shortened" procedure, this modified procedure did not eliminate a formal hearing when the parties could not agree on the facts. See Woll, The Development of Shortened Procedure in American Administrative Law, 45 Cornell L.Q. 56, 62–66 (1959); Hosmer, Some Notes on a Perennial Procedural Problem, 5 I.C.C.Prac.J. 275 (1938); Mohundro, Improvements in Procedure Before the Commission, 20 I.C.C.Prac.J. 75, 79–81 (1952); Three Letters on Procedure Before the I. C. C., id. 196.

33. 49 C.F.R. § 1100.45 (ICC 1970); see id. §§ 1100.49, 1100.50, 1100.53.

34. See E. Gellhorn and Robinson, Summary Judgment in Administrative Adjudication, 84 Harv.L. Rev. 612 (1970). The ICC's procedure has withstood attacks upon due process grounds. E. g., Allied Van Lines Co. v. United States, 303 F.Supp. 742 (C.D.Cal.1969).

35. See Selected Reports of the Administrative Conference of the United States 1961–1962, S.Doc. No. 24, 88th Cong., 1st Sess. 92 (1963).

36. Id.

is necessary, are confined to clarifying the major issues through informed cross-examination. Properly handled, written procedures should result in a more adequate record being produced in a shorter space of time." [37]

Section 7(c) of the APA recognizes the propriety of written presentations with only limited cross-examination: "In rule making or determining claims for money or benefits or applications for initial licenses any agency may, when a party will not be prejudiced thereby, adopt procedures for the submission of all or part of the evidence in written form." [38] While denying the broad application of their recommendation to all adjudications, some commentators have suggested the use of written presentations by any agency in a type of proceeding where the interest of any party is not prejudiced.[39] Existing case authority on the point supports this conclusion.[40]

Where cross-examination is necessary for protection against untrustworthy evidence, it cannot be avoided. Section 7(c) of the APA specifically preserves the right of cross-examination in agency adjudications: "A party is entitled . . . to conduct such cros-examination as may be required for a full and true disclosure of the facts." [41] State law is identical.[42] Through this provision the APA recognizes one of the fundamentals of a fair hearing—namely a reasonable opportunity to test and controvert adverse evidence whether or not such evidence is a statement of opinion, observation, or con-

sideration of the witness. Cross-examination has several potential uses: to bring out matters left untouched by direct examination; to test the accuracy of a witness' preception as well as his ability to observe; to probe his truthfulness; to question his memory and narration; and to expose the basis of any opinions he has expressed. In other words, "cross-examination is a means of getting at the truth; it is not truth itself." [43] Yet unless credibility is directly in issue—and then only on occasion—cross-examination usually does no more than demonstrate forensic talent or score trial points irrelevant to the final decision.[44] As an experienced agency practitioner, now an eminent federal judge, has observed: "Only rarely . . . can you accomplish something devastating on cross-examining an expert. . . . [M]ore often it is love's labor lost." [45]

Perception of this point is the key to a reconciliation of the right of cross-examination with the seemingly inconsistent administrative practice of relying on hearsay testimony and written evidence whether or not the declarant is unavailable. The legislative history of the APA makes clear that Congress was seeking to draw a line between an unlimited right of unnecessary cross-examination and a reasonable opportunity to test opposing evidence.[46] The test, stated abstractly, is that cross-examination must be allowed when it is required for determining the truth. If witness veracity and demeanor are not critical, there is no requirement for cross-examination so long as sufficient opportunity for rebuttal exists; if credibility

37. Id. 93.

38. 5 U.S.C.A. § 556(d).

39. See 2 Davis § 14.16; Attorney General's Manual on the Administrative Procedure Act 77–78 (1947).

40. See Yakus v. United States, 321 U.S. 414 (1944). See also 2 Davis § 14.16.

41. 5 U.S.C.A. § 556(d).

42. See Hyson v. Montgomery County Council, 242 Md. 55, 67–68 & n. 1, 217 A.2d 578, 585–86 & n. 1 (1966); 1 Cooper 371–79 (collecting cases).

43. W. Gellhorn and Byse, Administrative Law 713 (5th ed. 1970).

44. See § 30, supra.

45. Leventhal, Cues and Compasses for Administrative Lawyers, 20 Ad.L.Rev. 237, 246 (1968); accord, Prettyman, Trying an Administrative Dispute, 45 Va.L.Rev. 179, 190–91 (1959).

46. Sen.Doc. No. 248, 79th Cong.2d Sess. 208–09, 271 (1946); Attorney General's Manual on the Administrative Procedure Act 77–78 (1947).

is a key factor, and the objecting party can show that the absence of cross-examination of the witness may have prejudiced his case, the denial of cross-examination could be fatal to an agency decision.[47] Statistical compilations and surveys are admissible only if the person responsible for—and having full knowledge of the preparation of—the exhibit is available. In addition, the raw data upon which the exhibit is based should be available to the opposing party.[48] One administrative lawyer has proposed that the right to cross-examine be reduced to a privilege "to be granted only in the virtually unlimited discretion of the hearing officer" as part of a restructuring of the administrative hearing into a conference proceeding where almost all the evidence would be submitted in written form.[49] This proposal may prove to be the path of the future in resolving economic disputes and sophisticated problems arising in industry regulation.

Finally, administrative agencies are required to apply the "*Jencks* rule"—namely, that after a government witness has testified, the prosecution must disclose prior statements by the witness relating to his testimony.[50] Ap-

plication of this rule in agency hearings has been riddled with controversy.[51] The Administrative Conference has offered this sensible solution—that prior statements be made available to the respondent at the prehearing conference. If this view is adopted the question is no longer one of evidence but rather one of discovery.[52]

357. Official Notice.[53]

Official notice, like its judicial notice counterpart, involves reliance by the presid-

States v. SACB, 102 U.S.App.D.C. 395, 254 F.2d 314 (1958) and NLRB v. Adhesive Prods. Corp., 258 F. 2d 403 (2d Cir. 1958); see Selected Reports of the Administrative Conference of the United States 1961–1962, S.Doc. No. 24, 88th Cong., 1st Sess. 132 (1963). See generally § 97, supra, for discussion of the rule in its present statutory form.

51. FTC: Papercraft Corp. 25 Ad.L.2d 1063 (FTC 1969); Allied Chemical Corp., 24 Ad.L.2d 1122 (FTC 1969); Star Office Supply Co., 24 Ad.L.2d 472 (FTC 1968); enforced by order [1967–1970 Transfer Binder] Trade Reg.Rep. ¶ 19,228 (FTC 1970); Inter-State Builders, Inc., 19 Ad.L.2d 7 (FTC 1966), 21 Ad.L.2d 1078 (FTC 1967); L. G. Balfour Co., 19 Ad.L.2d 35 (FTC 1966); Viviano Macaroni Co., 19 Ad.L.2d 69 (FTC 1966); see E. Gellhorn, The Treatment of Confidential Information by the Federal Trade Commission: The Hearing, 116 U.Pa.L.Rev. 401, 428–33 (1968). NLRB: NLRB v. Borden Co., 392 F.2d 412 (5th Cir. 1968); see Alleyne, The "Jencks Rule" in NLRB Proceedings, 9 B.C.Ind. & Comm.L.Rev. 891 (1968). Department of Labor: Wirtz v. Rosenthal, 388 F.2d 290 (9th Cir. 1967); Wirtz v. B.A.C. Steel Prods., Inc., 312 F.2d 14 (4th Cir. 1962); Mitchell v. Roma, 265 F.2d 633 (3d Cir. 1959). Selective Service: Rogers v. United States, 263 F.2d 283 (9th Cir.) cert. denied 359 U.S. 967; Bouziden v. United States, 251 F.2d 728 (10th Cir.) cert. denied 356 U.S. 927.

52. Recommendation No. 21—Discovery in Agency Adjudication (adopted June 3, 1970); see Tomlinson, Discovery in Agency Adjudication, 1971 Duke L.J. 89.

53. See generally, 2 Davis, ch. 15, at 383–434; 1 Cooper 412–20; Final Report of the Attorney General's Committee on Administrative Procedure, S. Doc. No. 8, 77th Cong., 1st Sess. 71–73 (1941); Benjamin 206–21; W. Gellhorn, Federal Administrative Proceedings 82–99 (1941); W. Gellhorn, Official Notice in Administrative Adjudication, 20 Tex. L.Rev. 131 (1941); Jaffe, Administrative Procedure Re-Examined: The Benjamin Report, 56 Harv.L. Rev. 704, 717–19 (1943).

The term "official notice" is probably unfortunate in suggesting too much of a parallel to judicial notice. Much that is done and advocated to be done in the

47. E. g., In re Chapman Radio & Television Co., 6 F.C.C.2d 768 (1967); see Peters v. United States, 187 Ct.Cl. 63, 408 F.2d 719 (1969); Brown v. Macy, 222 F.Supp. 639 (E.D.La.1963) aff'd 340 F.2d 115 (5th Cir. 1965).

48. Wirtz v. Baldor Elec. Co., 119 U.S.App.D.C. 122, 337 F.2d 518 (1964); see Carter-Wallace, Inc. v. Gardner, 417 F.2d 1086, 1095–96 (4th Cir. 1969) (party not entitled to cross-examination if alternative method of investigating accuracy available); Zeisel, The Uniqueness of Survey Evidence, 45 Cornell L.Q. 322, 345–46 (1960). See generally § 249, supra.

49. Westwood, Administrative Proceedings: Techniques of Presiding, 50 A.B.A.J. 659, 660 (1964). See also Recommendation No. 19, Selected Reports of the Administrative Conference of the United States 1961–62, S.Doc. No. 24, 88th Cong. 1st Sess. 51, 96–97 (1963); Cramton, Some Modest Suggestions for Improving Public Utility Rate Proceedings, 51 Iowa L.Rev. 267, 276–78 (1966).

50. Jencks v. United States, 353 U.S. 657 (1957). The "*Jencks* rule" was initially applied to administrative agencies in Communist Party of the United

ing officer—in this case the hearing examiner—on extra-record information. That is, the examiner in making a decision relies upon facts and opinions not supported by evidence "on the record." Official notice, however, is distinguishable from judicial notice in several ways. First, a specific procedure has been established to receive extra-record facts, with the parties receiving notice and an opportunity to rebut the "noticed" facts.[54] Second, extra-record facts usually have first been developed by the agency's expert staff or accumulated from previous agency decisions. But official notice is not limited to information in agency files. In fact, it is often taken at the initiation of one of the parties. Third, agency recognition of extra-record facts is clearly not limited to either "indisputable" or "disputable" facts. Rather, official notice may extend to almost any information useful in deciding the adjudication as long as elemental fairness is observed.[55]

On the other hand, in administrative adjudication, official notice is frequently confused with the process of decision-making. In reaching a conclusion, the examiner or agency may rely on its special skills, whether they include particular expertise in engineering, economics, medicine or electricity, just as a judge may freely use his legal skills in reading statutes and applying decided cases in the preparation of his opinion. But such evaluations are not within the concept of official notice. Official notice is concerned with the *process of proof,* not with the *evaluation of evidence.* The difference between an administrative tribunal's use of nonrecord information included in its expert knowledge, as a substitute for evidence or notice, and its application of its background in evaluating and drawing conclusions from the evidence that is in the record, is, however, primarily a difference of degree rather than of kind. In principle, reliance upon the examiner's knowledge in the process of proof is permissible only within the confines of official notice, whereas the examiner's use of his experience in the evaluating "proof" is not only unavoidable but, indeed, desirable.[56] The troublesome problem, as with most questions of law, is that a fine line cannot be drawn with precision. Benjamin illustrates the point:

"When the State Liquor Authority concludes, from evidence in the record as to the size of food bills and gas bills paid (in relation to the volume of liquor business), that the holder of a restaurant liquor license is not conducting a *bona fide* restaurant, is the Authority using its experience and knowledge to evaluate and draw conclusions from the evidence, or is it using its experience and knowledge as a substitute for further evidence as to the normal relation of the size of food and gas bills to the volume of food business? . . . My own view is that . . . the procedure described is permissible [evaluation]; but until the courts have decided specific questions of this character, it is impos-

---

name of official notice might with less violence to the language be catalogued under presumptions. The latter affinity is noted elsewhere. See § 332, supra.

54. APA § 7(d), 5 U.S.C.A. § 556(d). See § 333, supra.

55. At least one observer has suggested that agencies should apply the doctrine of judicial notice to broad, general facts of common knowledge which are of an undisputed nature, thus avoiding the notice and rebuttal requirements of official notice, and limit official notice—with its procedural requirements—to disputable facts. Muir, The Utilization of Both Judicial and Official Notice by Administrative Agencies, 16 Ad.L.Rev. 333 (1964); see Davis § 15.09 (1970 Supp.). The agencies, however, have not explicitly adopted this suggestion. The kinds of facts noticeable in judicial proceedings are discussed in §§ 329–332, supra.

56. See, e. g., ICC v. Louisville & Nashville R. R., 227 U.S. 88, 98 (1913); Feinstein v. N. Y. Central R. R., 159 F.Supp. 460, 464 (S.D.N.Y.1958) (L. Hand, J.).

sible to anticipate with any certainty what their decision would be." [57]

Beyond this or other examples, little guidance can be offered.

The primary thrust behind official notice is to simplify or ease the process of proof. Where facts are known or can be safely assumed, the process of proving what is already known is both time consuming and unduly formal. When facts have been proven before, further proof becomes tiresome, redundant, and lacking in common sense. At times even the obvious could be difficult or time-consuming to prove, without affecting the final result, which was never in doubt. Moreover, administrative agencies were often created to become repositories of knowledge and experience. It would defeat their existence to require adherence to traditional methods of proof when alternative and equally fair methods are readily available. On the other hand, in developing an alternative method, it is necessary to safeguard the elements of a fair trial preserved by the traditional forms of proof. The Attorney General's Committee accurately summarized the need:

> "The parties, then, are entitled to be apprised of the data upon which the agency is acting. They are entitled not only to refute but, what in this situation is usually more important, to supplement, explain, and give different perspective to the facts upon which the agency relies. In addition, upon judicial review, the court must be informed of what facts the agency has utilized in order that the existence of supporting evidence may be ascertained." [58]

Congress sought to recognize and reconcile these concerns by a single sentence in section 7(d) of the APA: "When an agency decision rests on official notice of a material fact not appearing in the evidence in the record, a party is entitled, on timely request, to an opportunity to show the contrary." [59]

The procedure is simple. Official notice is a means by which an agency can avoid hearing further evidence on a material fact in the case if it notifies the parties that unless they prove to the contrary the agency's findings will include that particular fact and allows the parties an opportunity to present contrary evidence. Federal Trade Commission cases illustrate the practice. After hearing dozens of cases indicating that consumers preferred American to foreign-made goods— and holding, therefore, that a failure to disclose the foreign origin of these goods was a false and deceptive act [60]—the Commission advised respondents in Manco Watch Strap Co.[61] that it would not hear evidence on this issue in the future. Then, in subsequent cases where the FTC took official notice and the respondents could not prove that American consumers preferred their foreign goods or that the consumers had no particular preference, the Commission upheld orders barring sales of goods not bearing the requisite disclosures.[62] On the other hand, if respond-

---

57. Benjamin 212.

58. Final Report of the Attorney General's Committee on Administrative Procedure, supra n. 53, at 72; see Ohio Bell Tel. Co. v. Public Util. Com'n, 301 U.S. 292, 303–04 (1937).

59. 5 U.S.C.A. § 556(e).

60. E. g., American Merchandise Co., 28 F.T.C. 1465 (1939) (gloves and thumbtacks); Vulcan Lamp Works, Inc., 32 F.T.C. 7 (1940) (flashlight bulbs); The Bolta Co., 44 F.T.C. 17 (1947) (sunglass lenses); L. Heller & Son, Inc., 47 F.T.C. 34 (1950), aff'd, 191 F.2d 954 (7th Cir. 1951) (imitation pearls); Atomic Prods., Inc., 48 F.T.C. 289 (1951) (mechanical pencils); Rene D. Lyon Co., 48 F.T.C. 313, 787 (1951) (watch bands); Royal Sewing Mach. Corp., 49 F.T.C. 1351 (1953) (sewing machine parts); William Adams, Inc., 53 F.T.C. 1164 (1957) (cutlery handles); Utica Cutlery Co., 56 F.T.C. 1186 (1960) (stainless steel hardware); Oxwall Tool Co., 59 F.T.C. 1408 (1961) (hand tools). This listing is also further testimony to the FTC's historic concentration on trivia.

61. 60 F.T.C. 495 (1962).

62. Savoy Watch Co., 63 F.T.C. 473 (1963) (watch cases); Baldwin Bracelet Corp., 61 F.T.C. 1345

ents could show that consumers preferred French over American perfumes, for example, the "noticed finding" would not apply.[63]

Practically, then, the primary effect of taking official notice is to transfer the burden of proof on that material fact—usually from the agency to the respondent. The significance of this tactic varies in proportion to the difficulty of the proponent in establishing that fact originally, and of the cost and effort of the opponent in disproving it. In most instances where agencies have taken official notice, the costs have been slight since the result has seemed obvious. Where the fact is less obvious, however, that cost could prove substantial.[64]

The academic controversy over official notice has centered upon attempts to categorize the types of facts which can be officially noticed. The APA's guidance is slender; it merely sets forth the procedure which must be followed for taking notice of "material facts." By omission it apears to suggest that facts which are not material can be noticed in the manner of a judge at a judicial trial, but it does not tell how to determine which facts are material and can therefore be noticed. In any event, the term "material" seems not to be used in its classic sense.

The Attorney General's Committee on Administrative Procedure suggested a distinction between "litigation" and "non-litigation" facts:

> "If information has come to an agency's attention in the course of investigation of the pending case, it should be adduced only by the ordinary process. . . . But if the information has been developed in the usual course of business of the agency, if it has emerged from numerous cases, if it has become part of the factual equipment of the administrators, it seems undesirable for the agencies to remain oblivious of their own experience [and, they should take notice of such facts]." [65]

Professor Davis, on the other hand, rejects the notion that significance could be attached to the time when the factual data was collected. His criticism of the Committee's distinction stems from his conclusion that it would "encourage guesswork" and "discourage extra-record research of the kind that is especially needed for creation of law or policy. It would mean . . . [for example, that] an agency could notice only those statutes that it has previously encountered!" [66] This criticism seems somewhat unfair since the Committee's basic point defining reliable facts—those previously established by the agency—is sound. Davis is right, however, when he points out that the Committee rule is too narrow. As an alternative, he offers a different standard

---

(1962) aff'd 117 U.S.App.D.C. 85, 325 F.2d 1012 (1963) (watch cases); Brite Mfg. Co., 65 F.T.C. 1067 (1964) aff'd 120 U.S.App.D.C. 383, 347 F.2d 477 (1965) (watch bands).

63. In its pursuit of the Grail, the FTC has in fact held that consumers prefer French perfumes and that it therefore is deceptive not to disclose the domestic origin of perfume. See, e. g., Fioret Sales Co., 26 F.T.C. 806, aff'd, 100 F.2d 358 (2d Cir. 1938); Etablissements Rigaud, Inc., 29 F.T.C. 1032 (1939) modified 125 F.2d 590 (2d Cir. 1942); Harsam Distrib., Inc., 54 F.T.C. 1212 (1958) aff'd 263 F.2d 396 (2d Cir. 1959).

64. In the unusual event that the evidence is split with the moving party having the burden of establishing that material fact by a preponderance of the evidence, official notice may be the difference between winning and losing the case. In assessing the place of official notice, one should also take into account (a) the cost of establishing a general negative—which is, in part, the reason for assigning the burden of proof to the moving party, see § 337, n. 16, supra; (b) the desirability of cross-examination; and (c) the impact of denying confrontation—all of which are intimately connected with the decision as to whether official notice is appropriate. The relevance of presumption theory is evident. See §§ 342, 343, supra.

65. Final Report of the Attorney General's Committee on Administrative Procedure, supra n. 53, at 72.

66. 2 Davis § 15.03, at 363–64 n. 43.

for deciding whether an administrator may use extra-record facts:

> "When a court or an agency finds facts concerning the immediate parties—who did what, where, when, how, and with what motive or intent—[it] is performing an adjudicative function, and the facts are conveniently called adjudicative facts. When a court or an agency develops law or policy, it is acting legislatively; the courts have created the common law through judicial legislation, and the facts which inform the tribunal's legislative judgment are called legislative facts. . . . Legislative facts are ordinarily general and do not concern the immediate parties." [67]

On this basis, he asserts that legislative facts usually need not be brought into the record by official notice; where critical, a party should be able to challenge them by brief and argument. He contends that adjudicative facts, on the other hand, must be brought into the record—unless they are indisputable—either through direct proof or by official notice. Nothing less will meet the cardinal principles of a fair hearing—notice and an opportunity to test and rebut opposing evidence. Whether adjudicative facts can be officially noticed or must be established by direct proof depends, he says, on three variables: how close the facts are to the center of the controversy; the extent to which the facts are adjudicative or legislative; and the degree to which the facts are certain. As the adjudicative facts move closer to the basic issues of the hearing, relate to the parties, and are disputed, the usual methods of proof must be observed; as they move in the opposite direction, official notice is permissible.[68]

67. 2 Davis § 15.03, at 353.

68. Id. § 15.10.

Professor Jaffe has entered the fray briefly to point out that in his opinion, Professor Davis has succumbed to the lure of labels.

> "[W]here the facts bear closely and crucially on the issue, and are prima facie debatable, they should be developed in evidentiary fashion—by which is meant simply that they should be referred to in such a manner as to enable the opponent to offer rebuttal. Such facts will not necessarily be 'adjudicative'. . . ." [69]

As Davis readily concedes, the categories he defines do not in themselves resolve which facts can be noticed in particular cases. He is certainly correct when he points out that the central problem is to reconcile procedural fairness with convenience and the use of agency knowledge. The difficulty with his analysis lies not in his categories which are original and helpful, but rather that many cases fall outside his definitions. A sampling of cases illustrates this point. The existence of the Great Depression is a "legislative" fact which an agency can include in its findings without notice to the parties, but a specific price trend, also a general legislative fact, cannot be used to update the figures in the record without notice to the parties.[70] Since a specific price trend can be readily verified, taking notice is appropriate; the burden of proving any substantial error is not likely to be significant. Similarly, the courts have upheld agencies' official notice of scientific data,

69. Jaffe, Administrative Procedure Re-Examined: The Benjamin Report, 56 Harv.L.Rev. 704, 719 (1943); cf. Wyzanski, A Trial Judge's Freedom and Responsibility, 65 Harv.L.Rev. 1281, 1295–96 (1952). The Davis labels of "adjudicative" and "legislative" facts are commonly recited by agencies and courts to justify official notice decisions.

70. Ohio Bell Tel. Co. v. Public Util. Com'n, 301 U.S. 292 (1937); West Ohio Gas Co. v. Public Util. Com'n, 294 U.S. 63, 68 (1935); cf. United States v. Baltimore & Ohio S. W. R. R., 226 U.S. 14, 20 (1912).

technical facts, and articles in academic journals,[71] although many courts contend that this places too great a burden on the opponent to refute the "noticed evidence." [72]

Of greater consequence is the fact that reliance upon Davis' categories distracts from the central question of fairness—that is, is it fair in the particular hearing to take official notice and *transfer the burden of proof* to the opposing party? Two cases involving the use of the record of a related hearing, each of which reaches an opposite result, are perhaps the clearest examples of this suggested "fairness of the transfer of the burden of proof" analysis. In United States v. Pierce Auto Freight Lines, Inc.,[73] the ICC held two separate hearings on competing applications for truck service between San Francisco and Portland. Each applicant intervened in the other hearing, but the cases were not consolidated. In reaching its decision, the Commission relied on evidence appearing in only one record. This procedure was upheld because both applicants were parties to both proceedings and both had ample opportunity to present evidence, to cross-examine witnesses, and otherwise to protect their interests.

In the second case, Dayco Corp. v. FTC,[74] the FTC sought to take official notice of the distribution system and practices used by the respondent, a manufacturer of auto replacement parts, since the system had been the subject of a prior proceeding. That prior proceeding, in which respondent was only a witness, was brought against his customers. The court ruled that the FTC's attempt to take official notice of these "adjudicative" facts from the first proceeding was improper because the manufacturer was not a party, but only a witness to the prior proceeding. To allow official notice in this circumstance, the court reasoned, would have eliminated the Commission's entire burden of proof. The agency had asserted that its reliance on prior knowledge merely shifted the burden of going forward to respondent and this burden (of correcting any FTC errors in describing respondent's distribution system) was minimal when compared with the cost of proving these same facts again. The FTC's argument is not persuasive. If the agency merely sought to shift the burden of going forward, it could have introduced the prior record as reliable hearsay evidence subject to rebuttal or as written evidence with an offer to make the witnesses available for cross-examination. If handled in this manner—rather than under the official notice rubric—the fact-trier would still have to determine whether the prior record accurately portrayed respondent's distribution system. The court may also have perceived that there was no compelling need to approve the Commission's proposal since the FTC could (and should) have avoided the burden of re-proof by joining the respondent as a party in the first proceeding. Official notice, in other words, is not properly a procedural device to avoid the requirement of section 7(c) of the APA that the moving party has the burden of proof. If that burden is to be placed on re-

---

71. E. g., McDaniel v. Celebrezze, 331 F.2d 426 (4th Cir. 1964); Alabama-Tennessee Natural Gas Co. v. FPC, 359 F.2d 318 (5th Cir. 1966) cert. denied 385 U.S. 847; see 46 C.F.R. § 502.226 (FMC 1970). The CAB's rules note 43 separate reports and other resource materials of which it automatically takes official notice in economic proceedings. 14 C.F.R. § 302.24(m) (1) (CAB 1970).

72. See, e. g., Sayers v. Gardner, 380 F.2d 940, 952–55 (6th Cir. 1967); Ross v. Gardner, 365 F.2d 554, 558–59 (6th Cir. 1966); Sosna v. Celebrezze, 234 F.Supp. 289 (E.D.Pa.1964); Cook v. Celebrezze, 217 F.Supp. 366 (W.D.Mo.1963).

73. 327 U.S. 515 (1946); see Safeway Stores, Inc. v. FTC, 366 F.2d 795, 803 (9th Cir. 1966) cert. denied 386 U.S. 932; cf. Zimmerman v. Board of Regents, 31 App.Div.2d 560, 294 N.Y.S.2d 435 (1968).

74. 362 F.2d 180 (6th Cir. 1966). The judicial reception is more hospitable where the fact being noticed is of a less personal (i. e., adjudicative) nature. See, e. g., Dombrovskis v. Esperdy, 321 F.2d 463, 467 (2d Cir. 1963).

spondent as a condition of doing business, it should be accomplished openly through a shift in substantive policy rather than covertly by manipulation of procedural devices.

When the issue of official notice is viewed in this manner, the Davis criteria and the Attorney General's Committee's distinctions are helpful, but not dispositive.

TABLE OF CASES

References are to Pages

H

M

References are to Pages

Y

INDEX

References are to Pages

OBSERVATION
See Firsthand Knowledge

OBSTRUCTION OF JUSTICE
Admission by attempt, 660
Inference from, 662

OFFER OF PROOF
Cross-examination, 110
Exhibits, 109
Method of making, 110
Necessity of, 110
Procedure, 110
"Protecting the record," 109

OFFICIAL NOTICE
See Administrative Adjudication; Judicial Notice

OFFICIAL WRITTEN STATEMENTS
Generally, 735
Certificates, 741
Certified copies, 557, 741
Investigations, reports of, 736
Judgments,
    Civil, 738
    Criminal, 738
Original writing rule, 574
Police reports, 736
Statutory provisions, 735, 736

OPENING AND CLOSING
Right of, 5

"OPENING THE DOOR"
Inadmissible evidence admitted, 131
Re-direct examination, 65

OPINIONS
    See, also, Expert Witnesses; Prior Inconsistent
        Statements
    Generally, 22
Administrative proceedings, 848
Admission by party-opponent, 632
Character, 443
Dying declarations, 683
Handwriting, 499, 547
Hearsay statements containing, 41
Hospital records, 732
Legal conclusions, 28
Regularly kept records, 720
Relativity of, 26
Relaxation of rule against, 24
Rule against, 23
Ultimate issue, 26
Veracity of witness, 90

ORDER OF PRESENTATION
    See, also, Burden of Proof; Presumptions
Administrative proceedings, 853
"Connecting up," 133
Cross-examination, 5
Defendant, 5
Direct examination, 5
Plaintiff, 5
Re-direct examination, 6

ORIGINAL WRITING RULE
Generally, 559
Accounting for nonproduction, 570
Admission by party to prove terms, 577
Appellate review, 577
"Best evidence," 559
Carbons, 568
Collateral writings, 565
Confessions, 565
Copies, 567
Degrees of secondary evidence, 575
Duplicates, 567
Dying declarations, 683
Existence denied, 124
Harmless error, 577
Inscriptions, 562
Nonproduction, accounting for, 570
Notice to produce, 572
Objects, 562
Original, what is, 566
Photographs, 563
Preference in secondary proof, 575
Public records, 574
Reasons for rule, 561
Reproductions, 568
Secondary evidence, degrees of, 575
Sound recordings, 562
Terms, what constitutes proving, 563
X rays, 563

OTHER CRIMES
Relevance, 447

OWN TESTIMONY
"Binding" effect, 636

OWN WITNESS
See Cross-Examination; Impeachment

PART OF WRITING OR CONVERSATION
Effect of introduction, 130

PARTNERS
Statements by, 644

PATERNITY
Blood tests, 518
Exhibiting child, 526

PEDIGREE
Hearsay exception, 745

PHOTOGRAPHS
Demonstrative evidence, 530
Original required, 563
Posed, 532

PHYSICAL EXAMINATION
Compulsory, 3
Order for, 3
Refusal to submit to, 656

PHYSICIAN-PATIENT PRIVILEGE
Generally, 212
Confidentiality,
    Nurses, 216
    Presence of other persons, 216
    Public records, 217
Consultation, purpose of, 213